ANNOTATED LAWS
MASSACHUSETTS

Containing all the Laws of Massachusetts of

a general and permanent nature

completely annotated

By the Editorial Staff of the Publishers

2001

GENERAL INDEX
P to Z

Table of Statutes by Popular Name

LEXIS Publishing™

LEXIS-NEXIS® · MARTINDALE-HUBBELL®
MATTHEW BENDER® · MICHIE™ · SHEPARD'S®

P.O. Box 7587, Charlottesville, VA 22906-7587

4309012

ISBN 0-327-13198-5

www.lexis.com

Customer Service: 800/833-9844

LEGAL ANALYSTS
Sharon Wright, J.D.
Stephen J. White, J.D.

COORDINATING EDITOR
Andrea L. Greene

iii

CONTENTS

Preface

This three-volume replacement index has been revised and updated to include treatment of legislation enacted through the end of the 2000 General Court session (Chapter 428 of the 2000 Session Laws). The new General Index provides detailed coverage of all general laws, court rules, selected special laws and the United States and Massachusetts Constitutions.

The general index is a topical index. Main headings were derived from the language of the Annotated Laws of Massachusetts and the rules of court, from terminology commonly used in the legal profession, and frequently used nonlegal terms. To reduce the amount of repetition of treatment under different headings and to keep the size of the index manageable, cross references have been employed.

Quick Index: At the front of the first General Index volume is a Quick Index which provides researchers with an alternative/-and faster/-way to find the chapters of the General Laws which deal with their issues.

Popular Names Table: The third General Index volume includes a Table of Statutes by Popular Name. This is an alphabetical listing of selected Massachusetts laws which are commonly referred to by a popular name or statutory short title. The Table affords an effective and practical method of finding Massachusetts laws when the researcher knows only the names of the laws provided by frequent popular usage or as designated by the General Court.

Each volume also includes a **Table of Titles and Chapters.**

We solicit your help in keeping this index as usable as possible and ask that you inform us of any popular names that may have eluded us, errors we may have made or improvements you think we should make. LEXIS Law Publishing also maintains a **toll-free Index hotline (1-800-897-7922)** for use by those needing immediate help in locating a particular section or by those desiring to make comments or suggestions. Additionally, you may reach the Indexers by **fax (1-804-972-7686)** or by **Internet E-mail (llpindexinglexis-nexis.com).** All suggestions, questions or comments receive serious consideration. For non-index questions and comments or to place orders, Customer Service may be reached by the **toll-free Customer Service number (1-800-833-9844)** or by **toll-free fax (1-800-643-1280).**

A few basic suggestions for using this index are:

(1) *Begin your search with WORDS AND PHRASES*. WORDS AND PHRASES is a collection of entries for terms defined in the text of the Annotated Laws of Massachusetts. Starting a search in this heading exposes the index user to a diverse sampling of statutory terminology which could suggest to the user other headings to consult.

(2) *Use descriptive words or phrases to aid in your search, including commonly used phrases or terms of art*. Examples would be LEMON LAW, INCOME TAX and RAFFLES AND BAZAARS.

(3) *Consult the principal subject and not the secondary subject. Thus, for motor vehicle rentals look under MOTOR VEHICLE RENTAL and not under MOTOR VEHICLES; for attorneys' fees look under ATTORNEYS' FEES and not FEES; and for accident and sickness insurance look under ACCIDENT AND SICKNESS INSURANCE and not under INSURANCE.*

LEXIS·NEXIS·· MARTINDALE-HUBBELL·
MATTHEW BENDER·· MICHIE·· SHEPARD'S·

TABLE OF TITLES AND CHAPTERS
ANNOTATED LAWS OF MASSACHUSETTS

PART I

ADMINISTRATION OF THE GOVERNMENT

TITLE I

JURISDICTION AND EMBLEMS OF THE COMMONWEALTH, THE GENERAL COURT, STATUTES AND PUBLIC DOCUMENTS

CHAPTER 1.   Jurisdiction of the Commonwealth and of the United States.
CHAPTER 2.   Arms, Great Seal and Other Emblems of the Commonwealth.
CHAPTER 3.   The General Court.
CHAPTER 4.   Statutes.
CHAPTER 5.   Printing and Distribution of Laws and Public Documents.

TITLE II

EXECUTIVE AND ADMINISTRATIVE OFFICERS OF THE COMMONWEALTH

CHAPTER 6.   The Governor, Lieutenant Governor and Council, Certain Officers Under the Governor and Council, and State Library.
CHAPTER 6A.   Executive Offices.
CHAPTER 6B.   Acute Hospital Finance. [Repealed.]
CHAPTER 7.   Executive Office for Administration and Finance.
CHAPTER 7A.   Office of the Comptroller.
CHAPTER 7B.   Asset Management Board.
CHAPTER 8.   State Superintendent of Buildings, and State House.
CHAPTER 9.   Department of the State Secretary.
CHAPTER 9A.   Address Confidentiality Program.
CHAPTER 10.   Department of the State Treasurer.
CHAPTER 11.   Department of the State Auditor.
CHAPTER 12.   Department of the Attorney General and the District Attorneys.
CHAPTER 12A. Office of Inspector General.
CHAPTER 12B. State Gambling Advisory Commission.
CHAPTER 13.   Division and Boards of Registration.
CHAPTER 14.   Department of Revenue.
CHAPTER 15.   Department of Education.
CHAPTER 15A. Public Education.
CHAPTER 15B. The New England Educational Loan Marketing Corporation Act. [Repealed.]
CHAPTER 15C. Massachusetts College Student Loan Authority.
CHAPTER 16.   Department of Highways.
CHAPTER 17.   Department of Public Health.
CHAPTER 18.   Department of Transitional Assistance.
CHAPTER 18A. Department of Youth Services.
CHAPTER 18B. Department of Social Services.

CHAPTER 19.   Department of Mental Health.
CHAPTER 19A.   Department of Elder Affairs.
CHAPTER 19B.   Department of Mental Retardation.
CHAPTER 19B.   Disabled Persons Protection Commission. [Repealed.]
CHAPTER 19C.   Disabled Persons Protection Commission.
CHAPTER 19D.   Assisted Living.
CHAPTER 20.   Department of Food and Agriculture.
CHAPTER 21.   Department of Environmental Management.
CHAPTER 21A.   Executive Office of Environmental Affairs.
CHAPTER 21B.   Mining Regulation and Reclamation.
CHAPTER 21C.   Massachusetts Hazardous Waste Management Act.
CHAPTER 21D.   Massachusetts Hazardous Waste Facility Siting Act.
CHAPTER 21E.   Massachusetts Oil and Hazardous Material Release Prevention and Response Act.
CHAPTER 21F.   Coastal Facilities Improvement.
CHAPTER 21G.   Massachusetts Water Management Act.
CHAPTER 21H.   Solid Waste Facilities.
CHAPTER 21I.   Massachusetts Toxics Use Reduction Act.
CHAPTER 21J.   Underground Storage Tank Petroleum Product Cleanup Fund.
CHAPTER 21K.   Mitigation of Hazardous Materials.
CHAPTER 22.   Department of Public Safety.
CHAPTER 22A.   Central Register for Missing Children.
CHAPTER 22B.   Capitol Police. [Repealed.]
CHAPTER 22C.   The Department of State Police.
CHAPTER 22D.   Department of Fire Services.
CHAPTER 22E.   State DNA Database.
CHAPTER 23.   Department of Labor and Workforce Development.
CHAPTER 23A.   Department of Economic Development.
CHAPTER 23B.   Department of Housing and Community Development.
CHAPTER 23C.   Board of Conciliation and Arbitration.
CHAPTER 23D.   Massachusetts Industrial Service Program.
CHAPTER 23E.   Division of Industrial Accidents.
CHAPTER 23F.   The Economic Diversification Program.
CHAPTER 23G.   The Massachusetts Development Finance Agency.
CHAPTER 24.   Department of Industrial Accidents. [Repealed.]
CHAPTER 24A.   Office of Consumer Affairs and Business Regulation.
CHAPTER 25.   Department of Public Utilities.
CHAPTER 25A.   Division of Energy Resources.
CHAPTER 25B.   Massachusetts Appliance Efficiency Standards Act.
CHAPTER 26.   Department of Banking and Insurance.
CHAPTER 27.   Department of Correction.
CHAPTER 28.   Metropolitan District Commission.
CHAPTER 28A.   Office of Child Care Services.

TITLE III

LAWS RELATING TO STATE OFFICERS

CHAPTER 29.   State Finance.
CHAPTER 29A.   Financing of the Judicial System.
CHAPTER 29B.   State Revenue Growth Control [Repealed.]
CHAPTER 29C.   Water Pollution Abatement Revolving Loan Program.
CHAPTER 29D.   The Health Care Security Trust.
CHAPTER 30.   General Provisions Relative to State Departments, Commissions, Officers and Employees.
CHAPTER 30A.   State Administrative Procedure.
CHAPTER 30B.   Uniform Procurement Act.

TITLE IV

CIVIL SERVICE, RETIREMENT AND PENSIONS

CHAPTER 31.   Civil Service.
CHAPTER 31A.   Municipal Personnel Systems.
CHAPTER 32.   Retirement Systems and Pensions.
CHAPTER 32A.   Contributory Group General or Blanket Insurance for Persons in the Service of the Commonwealth.
CHAPTER 32B.   Contributory Group General or Blanket Insurance for Persons in the Service of Counties, Cities, Towns and Districts, and Their Dependents.

TITLE V

MILITIA

CHAPTER 33.   Militia.

TITLE VI

COUNTIES AND COUNTY OFFICERS

CHAPTER 34.   Counties and County Commissioners.
CHAPTER 34A.   County Charter Procedures.
CHAPTER 34B.   Abolition of County Government.
CHAPTER 35.   County Treasurers, State Supervision of County Accounts and County Finances.
CHAPTER 36.   Registers of Deeds.
CHAPTER 37.   Sheriffs.
CHAPTER 38.   Medical Examiners and Inquests.

TITLE VII

CITIES, TOWNS AND DISTRICTS

CHAPTER 39.   Municipal Government.
CHAPTER 40.   Powers and Duties of Cities and Towns.
CHAPTER 40A.   Zoning.
CHAPTER 40B.   Regional Planning.
CHAPTER 40C.   Historic Districts.
CHAPTER 40D.   Industrial Development of Cities and Towns.
CHAPTER 40E.   Massachusetts Industrial Development Auth.
CHAPTER 40F.   The Massachusetts Community Development Finance Corporation.
CHAPTER 40G.   Massachusetts Technology Development Corporation.
CHAPTER 40H.   Community Economic Development Assistance Corporation.
CHAPTER 40I.   The Bay State Skills Corporation Act. [Repealed.]
CHAPTER 40J.   Massachusetts Technology Park Corporation.
CHAPTER 40K.   Massachusetts Product Development Corporation. [Repealed.]
CHAPTER 40L.   Agricultural Incentive Areas.
CHAPTER 40M.   Governmental Units Pooled Insurance.
CHAPTER 40N.   Model Water and Sewer Commission.
CHAPTER 40O.   Business Improvement Districts.
CHAPTER 40O.   The Massachusetts Rent Control Prohibition Act. [Repealed.]
CHAPTER 40P.   The Massachusetts Rent Control Prohibition Act.
CHAPTER 41.   Officers and Employees of Cities, Towns and Districts.
CHAPTER 42.   Boundaries of Cities and Towns.
CHAPTER 43.   City Charters.
CHAPTER 43A.   Standard Form of Representative Town Meeting Government.
CHAPTER 43B.   Home Rule Procedures.

CHAPTER 43C.   Optional Forms of Municipal Administration Act.
CHAPTER 44.   Municipal Finance.
CHAPTER 44A.   Qualified Bond Act.
CHAPTER 44B.   Community Preservation.
CHAPTER 45.   Public Parks, Playgrounds and the Public Domain.
CHAPTER 46.   Return and Registry of Births, Marriages and Deaths.
CHAPTER 47.   Infirmaries.
CHAPTER 48.   Fires, Fire Departments and Fire Districts.
CHAPTER 49.   Fences, Fence Viewers, Pounds and Field Drivers.
CHAPTER 49A.   Use of Certain Animals for Scientific Investigation, Experiment or Instruction. [Repealed.]

TITLE VIII

ELECTIONS

CHAPTER 50.   General Provisions Relative to Primaries, Caucuses and Elections.
CHAPTER 51.   Voters.
CHAPTER 52.   Political Committees.
CHAPTER 53.   Nominations, Questions to Be Submitted to the Voters, Primaries and Caucuses.
CHAPTER 54.   Elections.
CHAPTER 54A.   Election of Certain City and Town Officers by Proportional Representation or Preferential Voting. [Repealed.]
CHAPTER 55.   Disclosure and Regulation of Campaign Expenditures and Contributions.
CHAPTER 55A.   The Massachusetts Clean Elections Law.
CHAPTER 55B.   The State Ballot Law Commission.
CHAPTER 56.   Violations of Election Laws.
CHAPTER 57.   Congressional, Councillor and Senatorial Districts, and Apportionment of Representatives.

TITLE IX

TAXATION

CHAPTER 58.   General Provisions Relative to Taxation.
CHAPTER 58A.   Appellate Tax Board.
CHAPTER 59.   Assessment of Local Taxes.
CHAPTER 59A.   Classification of Real Property. [Repealed.]
CHAPTER 60.   Collection of Local Taxes.
CHAPTER 60A.   Excise Tax on Registered Motor Vehicles in Lieu of Local Tax.
CHAPTER 60B.   Excise on Boats, Ships and Vessels in Lieu of Local Property Tax.
CHAPTER 61.   Classification and Taxation of Forest Lands and Forest Products.
CHAPTER 61A.   Assessment and Taxation of Agricultural and Horticultural Land.
CHAPTER 61B.   Classification and Taxation of Recreational Land.
CHAPTER 62.   Taxation of Incomes.
CHAPTER 62A.   Simplified Method of Computing Individual Income Taxes. [Repealed.]
CHAPTER 62B.   Withholding of Taxes on Wages and Declaration of Estimated Income Tax.
CHAPTER 62C.   Administrative Provisions Relative to State Taxation.
CHAPTER 62D.   Set-Off Debt Collection.
CHAPTER 62E.   Wage Reporting System.
CHAPTER 62F.   Limitation on the Growth of State Tax Revenues.
CHAPTER 63.   Taxation of Corporations.
CHAPTER 63A.   Taxation of Certain Corporations, Associations and Organizations Engaged in the Sale of Alcoholic Beverages.
CHAPTER 63B.   Declaration of Estimated Tax by Corporations.
CHAPTER 63C.   Taxation of Income of Certain Corporations. [Repealed.]
CHAPTER 64.   Taxation of Stock Transfers. [Repealed.]
CHAPTER 64A.   Taxation of Sales of Gasoline.
CHAPTER 64B.   Excise Upon Charges for Meals Served to the Public. [Repealed.]

CHAPTER 64C.   Cigarette Excise.
CHAPTER 64D.   Excise on Deeds, Instruments and Writings.
CHAPTER 64E.   Taxation of Special Fuels Used in the Propulsion of Motor Vehicles.
CHAPTER 64F.   Taxation of Fuel and Special Fuels Acquired Outside and Used Within the Commonwealth.
CHAPTER 64G.   Room Occupancy Excise.
CHAPTER 64H.   Tax on Retail Sales of Certain Tangible Personal Property.
CHAPTER 64I.   Tax on the Storage, Use or Other Consumption of Certain Tangible Personal Property.
CHAPTER 64J.   Taxation of Fuels Used in the Propulsion of Aircraft.
CHAPTER 64K.   Controlled Substances Tax.
CHAPTER 65.   Taxation of Legacies and Successions.
CHAPTER 65A.   Taxation of Transfers of Certain Estates.
CHAPTER 65B.   Settlement of Disputes Respecting the Domicile of Decedents for Death Tax Purposes.
CHAPTER 65C.   Massachusetts Estate Tax.

TITLE X

PUBLIC RECORDS

CHAPTER 66.   Public Records.
CHAPTER 66A.   Fair Information Practices.

TITLE XI

CERTAIN RELIGIOUS AND CHARITABLE MATTERS

CHAPTER 67.   Parishes and Religious Societies.
CHAPTER 68.   Donations and Conveyances for Pious and Charitable Uses.
CHAPTER 68A.   Limitations Upon the Conduct of Certain Trusts and Corporations Having Charitable Interests.

TITLE XII

EDUCATION

CHAPTER 69.   Powers and Duties of the Department of Education.
CHAPTER 70.   School Funds and State Aid for Public Schools.
CHAPTER 70A.   Equal Educational Opportunity Grants. [Repealed.]
CHAPTER 70B.   School Building Assistance Program.
CHAPTER 71.   Public Schools.
CHAPTER 71A.   Transitional Bilingual Education.
CHAPTER 71B.   Children with Special Needs.
CHAPTER 72.   School Registers and Returns.
CHAPTER 73.   State Colleges.
CHAPTER 74.   Vocational Education.
CHAPTER 74A.   Independent Agricultural and Technical Schools.
CHAPTER 75.   University of Massachusetts.
CHAPTER 75A.   University of Lowell. [Repealed.]
CHAPTER 75B.   Southeastern Massachusetts University. [Repealed.]
CHAPTER 75C.   Private Correspondence Schools.
CHAPTER 75D.   Private Business Schools.
CHAPTER 76.   School Attendance.
CHAPTER 77.   School Offenders and County Training Schools. [Repealed.]
CHAPTER 78.   Libraries.
CHAPTER 78A.   Youth Conservation and Service Corps.

TITLE XIII

EMINENT DOMAIN AND BETTERMENTS

Chapter 79.   Eminent Domain.
Chapter 79A.   Relocation Assistance.
Chapter 80.   Betterments.
Chapter 80A.   Eminent Domain Takings and Betterment Assessments by Judicial Proceedings.

TITLE XIV

PUBLIC WAYS AND WORKS

Chapter 81.   State Highways.
Chapter 81A.   The Massachusetts Turnpike Authority and the Metropolitan Highway System.
Chapter 82.   The Laying Out, Alteration, Relocation and Discontinuance of Public Ways and Specific Repairs Thereon.
Chapter 83.   Sewers, Drains and Sidewalks.
Chapter 84.   Repair of Ways and Bridges.
Chapter 85.   Regulations and By-Laws Relative to Ways and Bridges.
Chapter 86.   Boundaries of Highways and Other Public Places, and Encroachments Thereon.
Chapter 87.   Shade Trees.
Chapter 88.   Ferries, Canals and Public Landings.
Chapter 89.   Law of the Road.
Chapter 90.   Motor Vehicles and Aircraft.
Chapter 90A.   The Highway Safety Act.
Chapter 90B.   Motorboats, Other Vessels and Recreational Vehicles.
Chapter 90C.   Procedure for Motor Vehicle Offenses.
Chapter 90D.   Motor Vehicle Certificates of Title.
Chapter 90E.   Bikeways.
Chapter 90F.   Uniform Operation of Commercial Motor Vehicles Act.
Chapter 90G.   Civil Infractions. [Repealed.]
Chapter 90H.   Gateway Roads Program.
Chapter 91.   Waterways.
Chapter 91A.   Port of Boston Commission. [Repealed.]
Chapter 92.   Metropolitan Sewers, Water and Parks.
Chapter 92A.   Commonwealth Zoological Corporation. [Repealed.]
Chapter 92B.   Commonwealth Zoological Corporation.

TITLE XV

REGULATION OF TRADE

Chapter 93.   Regulation of Trade and Certain Enterprises.
Chapter 93A.   Regulation of Business Practices for Consumers Protection.
Chapter 93B.   Regulation of Business Practices Between Motor Vehicle Manufacturers, Distributors and Dealers.
Chapter 93C.   Protection of Consumers Against Careless and Erroneous Billings. [Repealed.]
Chapter 93D.   Control of Outdoor Advertising Adjacent to the Interstate and Primary Highway Systems.
Chapter 93E.   Regulation of Dealers' Agreements for the Sale of Gasoline.
Chapter 93F.   Regulation of Certain Business Practices Between Motion Picture Distributors and Exhibitors.
Chapter 93G.   Equipment Dealers.
Chapter 94.   Inspection and Sale of Food, Drugs and Various Articles.
Chapter 94A.   Milk Control.
Chapter 94B.   Hazardous Substances.
Chapter 94C.   Controlled Substances Act.
Chapter 94D.   Controlled Substances Therapeutic Research Act.
Chapter 94E.   Provisions Concerning Certain Tobacco Manufacturers.
Chapter 95.   Measuring of Leather.

Chapter 96.   Measurement of Lumber.
Chapter 97.   Surveying of Land.
Chapter 98.   Weights and Measures.
Chapter 99.   The Metric System of Weights and Measures.
Chapter 100.   Auctioneers.
Chapter 100A.   Motor Vehicle Damage Repair Shops.
Chapter 101.   Transient Vendors, Hawkers and Pedlers.
Chapter 102.   Shipping and Seamen, Harbors and Harbor Masters.
Chapter 103.   Pilots.
Chapter 104.   Agents, Consignees and Factors.
Chapter 104A.   Consignment of Fine Art.
Chapter 105.   Public Warehouses.
Chapter 105A.   Self-Service Storage Facilities.
Chapter 106.   Uniform Commercial Code. [Repealed.]
Chapter 106.   Uniform Commercial Code.
Chapter 107.   Money and Registration, Issuance and Redemption of Bonds and Other Securities, Facsimile Signatures.
Chapter 107A.   Assignments of Accounts Receivable. [Repealed.]
Chapter 108.   Criminal Offences Relative to Bills of Lading.
Chapter 108A.   Partnerships.
Chapter 109.   Limited Partnership.
Chapter 109A.   Uniform Fraudulent Transfer Act.
Chapter 110.   Labels, Trade Marks, Names and Registration Thereof.
Chapter 110A.   Uniform Securities Act.
Chapter 110B.   Registration and Protection of Trademarks.
Chapter 110C.   Regulation of Take-Over Bids in the Acquisition of Corporations.
Chapter 110D.   Regulation of Control Share Acquisitions.
Chapter 110E.   Regulation of Control Share Acquisitions of Foreign Corporations.
Chapter 110F.   Business Combinations With Interested Shareholders.

TITLE XVI

PUBLIC HEALTH

Chapter 111.   Public Health.
Chapter 111A.   Drug Addiction Rehabilitation. [Repealed.]
Chapter 111B.   Alcoholism.
Chapter 111C.   Emergency Medical Care.
Chapter 111D.   Clinical Laboratories.
Chapter 111E.   Drug Rehabilitation.
Chapter 111F.   Hazardous Substances Disclosure by Employers.
Chapter 111G.   Early Childhood Intervention Services.
Chapter 111H.   Massachusetts Low-level Radioactive Waste Management Act.
Chapter 111I.   Women's, Infants and Children Program.
Chapter 111J.   Alcohol and Drug Counselors.
Chapter 111K.   Catastrophic Illness in Children Relief Fund Commission.
Chapter 112.   Registration of Certain Professions and Occupations.
Chapter 113.   Promotion of Anatomical Science.
Chapter 114.   Cemeteries and Burials.

TITLE XVII

PUBLIC WELFARE

Chapter 115.   Veterans' Benefits.
Chapter 115A.   Soldiers' Homes.
Chapter 116.   Settlement. [Repealed.]
Chapter 117.   Support by the Commonwealth. [Repealed.]
Chapter 117A.   Support by the Commonwealth.

CHAPTER 118.   Aid to Families With Dependent Children.

CHAPTER 118A.   Assistance to the Aged and Disabled.

CHAPTER 118B.   The Merit System in the Administration of Aid to Families With Dependent Children and Old Age Assistance. [Repealed.]

CHAPTER 118C.   Coverage of Certain Employees Under the Federal Social Security Act.

CHAPTER 118D.   Assistance to Persons Who are Disabled. [Repealed.]

CHAPTER 118E.   Division of Medical Assistance.

CHAPTER 118F.   Department of Medical Security. [Repealed.]

CHAPTER 118G.   Health Care Finance and Policy.

CHAPTER 119.   Protection and Care of Children, and Proceedings Against Them.

CHAPTER 119A.   Child Support Enforcement.

CHAPTER 120.   Department of Youth Services and Massachusetts Training Schools.

CHAPTER 121.   Powers and Duties of the Department of Public Welfare, and the Massachusetts Hospital School. [Repealed.]

CHAPTER 121A.   Urban Redevelopment Corporations.

CHAPTER 121B.   Housing and Urban Renewal.

CHAPTER 121C.   Economic Development and Industrial Corporations.

CHAPTER 121D.   Affordable Housing Trust Fund.

CHAPTER 122.   Tewksbury Hospital.

CHAPTER 123.   Mental Health.

CHAPTER 123A.   Care, Treatment and Rehabilitation of Sexually Dangerous Persons.

CHAPTER 123B.   Mental Retardation.

TITLE XVIII

PRISONS, IMPRISONMENT, PAROLES AND PARDONS

CHAPTER 124.   Powers and Duties of the Department of Correction.

CHAPTER 125.   Correctional Institutions of the Commonwealth.

CHAPTER 126.   Jails, Houses of Correction and Reformation, and County Industrial Farms.

CHAPTER 127.   Officers and Inmates of Penal and Reformatory Institutions. Paroles and Pardons.

TITLE XIX

AGRICULTURE AND CONSERVATION

CHAPTER 128.   Agriculture.

CHAPTER 128A.   Horse and Dog Racing Meetings.

CHAPTER 128B.   Conservation of Soil and Soil Resources and Prevention and Control of Erosion. [Repealed.]

CHAPTER 128C.   Simulcast Wagering of Horse and Dog Racing.

CHAPTER 129.   Livestock Disease Control.

CHAPTER 129A.   Marine Fish and Fisheries, Inland Fish and Fisheries, Birds and Mammals; General Provisions. [Repealed.]

CHAPTER 130.   Marine Fish and Fisheries.

CHAPTER 131.   Inland Fisheries and Game and Other Natural Resources.

CHAPTER 131A.   Massachusetts Endangered Species Act.

CHAPTER 132.   Forestry.

CHAPTER 132A.   State Recreation Areas Outside of the Metropolitan Parks District.

CHAPTER 132B.   Massachusetts Pesticide Control Act.

TITLE XX

PUBLIC SAFETY AND GOOD ORDER

CHAPTER 133.   Disposition of Old and Infirm Animals.

CHAPTER 134.   Lost Goods and Stray Beasts.

CHAPTER 135.   Unclaimed and Abandoned Property.

CHAPTER 136.   Observance of a Common Day of Rest and Legal Holidays.

CHAPTER 137. Gaming.
CHAPTER 138. Alcoholic Liquors.
CHAPTER 139. Common Nuisances.
CHAPTER 140. Licenses.
CHAPTER 140A. Regulation of Certain Credit Transactions. [Repealed.]
CHAPTER 140B. Control of Certain Junkyards.
CHAPTER 140C. Consumer Credit Cost Disclosure. [Repealed.]
CHAPTER 140D. Consumer Credit Cost Disclosure.
CHAPTER 140E. Consumer Account Disclosure.
CHAPTER 141. Supervision of Electricians.
CHAPTER 142. Supervision of Plumbing.
CHAPTER 142A. Regulation of Home Improvement Contractors.
CHAPTER 143. Inspection and Regulation of, and Licenses for, Buildings, Elevators and Cinematographs.
CHAPTER 144. Tenement Houses in Cities.
CHAPTER 145. Tenement Houses in Towns.
CHAPTER 146. Inspection of Boilers, Air Tanks, etc; Licenses of Engineers, Firemen and Operators of Hoisting Machinery.
CHAPTER 147. State and Other Police, and Certain Powers and Duties of the Department of Public Safety.
CHAPTER 148. Fire Prevention.

TITLE XXI

LABOR AND INDUSTRIES

CHAPTER 149. Labor and Industries.
CHAPTER 150. Conciliation and Arbitration of Industrial Disputes.
CHAPTER 150A. Labor Relations.
CHAPTER 150B. Peaceful Settlement of Industrial Disputes Dangerous to Public Health and Safety.
CHAPTER 150C. Collective Bargaining Agreements to Arbitrate.
CHAPTER 150D. Registration of Labor Replacements or Strike Breakers. [Repealed.]
CHAPTER 150E. Labor Relations: Public Employees.
CHAPTER 151. Minimum Fair Wages.
CHAPTER 151A. Employment and Training.
CHAPTER 151B. Unlawful Discrimination Because of Race, Color, Religious Creed, National Origin, Ancestry or Sex.
CHAPTER 151C. Fair Educational Practices.
CHAPTER 151D. Health, Welfare and Retirement Funds.
CHAPTER 151E. Prohibition of Certain Discrimination by Businesses.
CHAPTER 152. Workers' Compensation.
CHAPTER 153. Liability of Employers to Employees for Injuries Not Resulting in Death.
CHAPTER 154. Assignment of Wages.

TITLE XXII

CORPORATIONS

CHAPTER 155. General Provisions Relative to Corporations.
CHAPTER 156. Business Corporations.
CHAPTER 156A. Professional Corporations.
CHAPTER 156B. Certain Business Corporations.
CHAPTER 156C. Limited Liability Company Act.
CHAPTER 157. Co-operative Corporations.
CHAPTER 157A. Employee Cooperative Corporations.
CHAPTER 157B. Cooperative Housing Corporations.
CHAPTER 158. Certain Miscellaneous Corporations.
CHAPTER 159. Common Carriers.
CHAPTER 159A. Common Carriers of Passengers by Motor Vehicle.

CHAPTER 159B. Carriers of Property by Motor Vehicle.
CHAPTER 160. Railroads.
CHAPTER 161. Street Railways.
CHAPTER 161A. Massachusetts Bay Transportation Authority.
CHAPTER 161B. Transportation Facilities, Highway Systems and Urban Development Plans.
CHAPTER 161C. Rail Transportation in the Commonwealth.
CHAPTER 161D. The Massachusetts Intercity Bus Capital Assistance Program.
CHAPTER 162. Electric Railroads.
CHAPTER 163. Trackless Trolley Companies.
CHAPTER 164. Manufacture and Sale of Gas and Electricity.
CHAPTER 164A. New England Power Pool.
CHAPTER 165. Water and Aqueduct Companies.
CHAPTER 166. Telephone and Telegraph Companies and Lines for the Transmission of Electricity.
CHAPTER 166A. Community Antenna Television Systems.
CHAPTER 167. Supervision of Banks.
CHAPTER 167A. Bank Holding Companies.
CHAPTER 167B. Electronic Branches and Electronic Fund Transfers.
CHAPTER 167C. Bank Locations.
CHAPTER 167D. Deposits and Accounts.
CHAPTER 167E. Mortgages and Loans.
CHAPTER 167F. Investments and Other Powers.
CHAPTER 167G. Trust Department.
CHAPTER 167H. Mutual Holding Companies.
CHAPTER 168. Savings Banks.
CHAPTER 169. Deposits with Others than Banks. [Repealed.]
CHAPTER 169. Receipts of Deposits for Transmittal to Foreign Countries.
CHAPTER 169A. Licensing of Check Cashers.
CHAPTER 170. Co-operative Banks.
CHAPTER 171. Credit Unions.
CHAPTER 172. Trust Companies.
CHAPTER 172A. Banking Companies.
CHAPTER 173. Mortgage Loan Investment Companies. [Repealed.]
CHAPTER 174. Bond and Investment Companies. [Repealed.]
CHAPTER 174A. Regulation of Rates for Fire, Marine and Inland Marine Insurance, and Rating Organizations.
CHAPTER 174B. Regulation of Automobile Clubs.
CHAPTER 175. Insurance.
CHAPTER 175A. Regulation of Rates for Certain Casualty Insurance, Including Fidelity, Surety and Guaranty Bonds, and for All Other Forms of Motor Vehicle Insurance, and Regulation of Rating Organizations.
CHAPTER 175B. Unauthorized Insurer's Process Act.
CHAPTER 175C. Urban Area Insurance Placement Facility.
CHAPTER 175D. Massachusetts Insurers Insolvency Fund.
CHAPTER 175E. Regulation of Rates for Motor Vehicle Insurance.
CHAPTER 175F. Medical Malpractice Self-Insurance Trust Funds.
CHAPTER 175G. The Pollution Liability Reinsurance Corporation.
CHAPTER 175H. False Health Care Claims.
CHAPTER 175I. Insurance Information and Privacy Protection.
CHAPTER 175J. Administrative Supervision and Hazardous Financial Conditions of Insurities.
CHAPTER 176. Fraternal Benefit Societies.
CHAPTER 176A. Non-Profit Hospital Service Corporations.
CHAPTER 176B. Medical Service Corporations.
CHAPTER 176C. Non-Profit Medical Service Plans.
CHAPTER 176D. Unfair Methods of Competition and Unfair and Deceptive Acts and Practices in the Business of Insurance.
CHAPTER 176E. Dental Service Corporations.
CHAPTER 176F. Optometric Service Corporations.

Chapter 176G. Health Maintenance Organizations.
Chapter 176H. Legal Services Plans.
Chapter 176I. Preferred Provider Arrangements.
Chapter 176J. Small Group Health Insurance.
Chapter 176K. Medicare Supplement Insurance Plans.
Chapter 176L. Risk Retention and Risk Purchasing Groups.
Chapter 176M. Nongroup Health Insurance.
Chapter 176N. Portability of Health Insurance.
Chapter 176O. Health Insurance Consumer Protections.
Chapter 176P. Limited Societies.
Chapter 177. Assessment Insurance. [Repealed.]
Chapter 178. Savings Bank Life Insurance. [Repealed.]
Chapter 178A. Savings Bank Life Insurance.
Chapter 179. Proprietors of Wharves, Real Estate Lying in Common, and General Fields.
Chapter 180. Corporations for Charitable and Certain Other Purposes.
Chapter 180A. Management of Institutional Funds.
Chapter 181. Foreign Corporations.
Chapter 182. Voluntary Associations and Certain Trusts.

PART II

REAL AND PERSONAL PROPERTY AND DOMESTIC RELATIONS

TITLE I

TITLE TO REAL PROPERTY

Chapter 183. Alienation of Land.
Chapter 183A. Condominiums.
Chapter 183B. Real Estate Time-Shares.
Chapter 184. General Provisions Relative to Real Property.
Chapter 184A. Statutory Rule Against Perpetuities.
Chapter 184B. Short Form Terms for Wills and Trusts.
Chapter 185. The Land Court and Registration of Title to Land.
Chapter 185A. Housing Court of the City of Boston. [Repealed.]
Chapter 185B. Housing Court of the County of Hampden. [Repealed.]
Chapter 185C. Housing Court Department.
Chapter 186. Estates for Years and at Will.
Chapter 187. Easements.
Chapter 188. Homesteads.
Chapter 189. Dower and Curtesy.

TITLE II

DESCENT AND DISTRIBUTION, WILLS, ESTATES OF DECEASED PERSONS AND ABSENTEES, GUARDIANSHIP, CONSERVATORSHIP AND TRUSTS

Chapter 190. Descent and Distribution of Real and Personal Property.
Chapter 190A. Effect of Apparently Simultaneous Deaths Upon Devolution and Disposition of Property, Including Proceeds of Insurance.
Chapter 191. Wills.
Chapter 191A. Disclaimer of Certain Property Interest Act.
Chapter 191B. Uniform Statutory Will Act.
Chapter 192. Probate of Wills and Appointment of Executors.
Chapter 193. Appointment of Administrators.
Chapter 194. Public Administrators.
Chapter 195. General Provisions Relative to Executors and Administrators.
Chapter 196. Allowances to Widows and Children, and Advancements.

CHAPTER 197.   Payment of Debts, Legacies and Distributive Shares.
CHAPTER 198.   Insolvent Estates of Deceased Persons.
CHAPTER 199.   Settlement of Estates of Deceased Non-Residents.
CHAPTER 199A. General Provisions Regarding Certain Foreign Fiduciaries.
CHAPTER 200.   Settlement of Estates of Absentees.
CHAPTER 200A. Abandoned Property.
CHAPTER 201.   Guardians and Conservators.
CHAPTER 201A. Uniform Transfers to Minors Act.
CHAPTER 201B. Uniform Durable Power of Attorney Act.
CHAPTER 201C. Statutory Custodianship Trusts.
CHAPTER 201D. Health Care Proxies.
CHAPTER 201E. Uniform Transfer on Death Security Registration Act.
CHAPTER 202.   Sales, Mortgages and Leases of Real Estate by Executors, Administrators, Guardians and Conservators.
CHAPTER 203.   Trusts.
CHAPTER 203A. Uniform Common Trust Fund Act.
CHAPTER 203B. Uniform Custodial Trust Act.
CHAPTER 203C. Prudent Investment.
CHAPTER 204.   General Provisions Relative to Sales, Mortgages, Releases, Compromises, Etc., by Executors, Etc.
CHAPTER 205.   Bonds of Executors, Administrators, Guardians, Conservators, Trustees, and Receivers.
CHAPTER 206.   Accounts and Settlements of Executors, Administrators, Guardians, Conservators, Trustees and Receivers.

TITLE III

DOMESTIC RELATIONS

CHAPTER 207.   Marriage.
CHAPTER 208.   Divorce.
CHAPTER 209.   Husband and Wife.
CHAPTER 209A. Abuse Prevention.
CHAPTER 209B. Massachusetts Child Custody Jurisdiction Act.
CHAPTER 209C. Children Born Out of Wedlock.
CHAPTER 209D. Uniform Interstate Family Support Act.
CHAPTER 210.   Adoption of Children and Change of Names.

PART III

COURTS, JUDICIAL OFFICERS AND PROCEEDINGS IN CIVIL CASES

TITLE I

COURTS AND JUDICIAL OFFICERS

CHAPTER 211.   The Supreme Judicial Court.
CHAPTER 211A. Appeals Court.
CHAPTER 211B. Trial Court of the Commonwealth.
CHAPTER 211C. Commission on Judicial Conduct.
CHAPTER 211D. Committee for Public Counsel Services.
CHAPTER 211E. Massachusetts Sentencing Commission.
CHAPTER 211F. Office of Community Corrections.
CHAPTER 212.   The Superior Court.
CHAPTER 213.   Provisions Common to the Supreme Judicial and Superior Courts.
CHAPTER 214.   Equity Jurisdiction.
CHAPTER 215.   Probate Courts.
CHAPTER 216.   Courts of Insolvency. [Repealed.]
CHAPTER 217.   Judges and Registers of Probate and Insolvency.
CHAPTER 218.   District Courts.

CHAPTER 219. Trial Justices. [Repealed.]
CHAPTER 220. Courts and Naturalization.
CHAPTER 221. Clerks, Attorneys and Other Officers of Judicial Courts.
CHAPTER 221A. The Massachusetts Legal Assistance Corporation Act.
CHAPTER 221B. Child Support Hearing Officers.
CHAPTER 221C. Court Interpreters for the Trial Court.
CHAPTER 222. Justices of the Peace, Notaries Public and Commissioners.

TITLE II

ACTIONS AND PROCEEDINGS THEREIN

CHAPTER 223. Commencement of Actions, Service of Process.
CHAPTER 223A. Jurisdiction of Courts of the Commonwealth over Persons in Other States and Countries.
CHAPTER 224. Arrest on Mesne Process and Supplementary Proceedings in Civil Actions.
CHAPTER 225. Process after Judgment for Necessaries or Labor. [Repealed.]
CHAPTER 226. Bail. [Repealed.]
CHAPTER 227. Proceedings against Absent Defendants and upon Insufficient Service.
CHAPTER 228. Survival of Actions and Death and Disabilities of Parties.
CHAPTER 229. Actions for Death and Injuries Resulting in Death.
CHAPTER 230. Actions by and against Executors and Administrators.
CHAPTER 231. Pleading and Practice.
CHAPTER 231A. Procedure for Declaratory Judgments.
CHAPTER 231B. Contribution Among Joint Tortfeasors.
CHAPTER 231C. Structured Settlement Contracts.
CHAPTER 232. Set-Off and Tender. [Repealed.]
CHAPTER 232A. Tender.
CHAPTER 233. Witnesses and Evidence.
CHAPTER 234. Juries.
CHAPTER 234A. Office of Jury Commissioner for the Commonwealth.
CHAPTER 235. Judgment and Execution.
CHAPTER 236. Levy of Executions on Land.

TITLE III

REMEDIES RELATING TO REAL PROPERTY

CHAPTER 237. Writs of Entry.
CHAPTER 238. Writs of Dower. [Repealed.]
CHAPTER 239. Summary Process for Possession of Land.
CHAPTER 240. Proceedings for Settlement of Title to Land.
CHAPTER 241. Partition of Land.
CHAPTER 242. Waste and Trespass.
CHAPTER 243. Actions for Private Nuisances.
CHAPTER 244. Foreclosure and Redemption of Mortgages.
CHAPTER 245. Information by the Commonwealth.

TITLE IV

CERTAIN WRITS AND PROCEEDINGS IN SPECIAL CASES

CHAPTER 246. Trustee Process.
CHAPTER 247. Replevin.
CHAPTER 248. Habeas Corpus and Personal Liability.
CHAPTER 249. Audita Querela, Certiorari, Mandamus and Quo Warranto.
CHAPTER 250. Writs of Error, Vacating Judgment, Writs of Review.
CHAPTER 251. Uniform Arbitration Act for Commercial Disputes.

CHAPTER 252.   Improvement of Low Land and Swamps.
CHAPTER 253.   Mills, Dams and Reservoirs.
CHAPTER 254.   Liens on Buildings and Land.
CHAPTER 255.   Mortgages, Conditional Sales and Pledges of Personal Property, and Liens Thereon.
CHAPTER 255A.   Trust Receipts and Pledges without Possession in the Pledgee. [Repealed.]
CHAPTER 255B.   Retail Installment Sales of Motor Vehicles.
CHAPTER 255C.   Insurance Premium Finance Agencies.
CHAPTER 255D.   Retail Installment Sales and Services.
CHAPTER 255E.   Licensing of Certain Mortgage Lenders and Brokers.
CHAPTER 256.   Recognizances for Debts.
CHAPTER 257.   Seizure and Libelling of Forfeited Property.
CHAPTER 258.   Claims and Indemnity Procedure for the Commonwealth, its Municipalities, Counties and Districts and the Officers and Employees Thereof.
CHAPTER 258A.   Compensation of Victims of Violent Crimes.
CHAPTER 258B.   Rights of Victims and Witnesses of Crime.
CHAPTER 258C.   Compensation of Victims of Violent Crimes.

TITLE V

STATUTES OF FRAUDS AND LIMITATIONS

CHAPTER 259.   Prevention of Frauds and Perjuries.
CHAPTER 260.   Limitations of Actions.

TITLE VI

COSTS AND FEES

CHAPTER 261.   Costs in Civil Actions.
CHAPTER 262.   Fees of Certain Officers.

PART IV

CRIMES, PUNISHMENTS AND PROCEEDINGS IN CRIMINAL CASES

TITLE I

CRIMES AND PUNISHMENTS

CHAPTER 263.   Rights of Persons Accused of Crime.
CHAPTER 264.   Crimes against Governments.
CHAPTER 265.   Crimes against the Person.
CHAPTER 266.   Crimes against Property.
CHAPTER 267.   Forgery and Crimes against the Currency.
CHAPTER 268.   Crimes against Public Justice.
CHAPTER 268A.   Conduct of Public Officials and Employees.
CHAPTER 268B.   Financial Disclosure by Certain Public Officials and Employees.
CHAPTER 269.   Crimes against Public Peace.
CHAPTER 270.   Crimes against Public Health.
CHAPTER 271.   Crimes against Public Policy.
CHAPTER 272.   Crimes against Chastity, Morality, Decency and Good Order.
CHAPTER 273.   Desertion, Non-Support and Illegitimacy.
CHAPTER 273A.   Uniform Reciprocal Enforcement of Support. [Repealed.]
CHAPTER 274.   Felonies, Accessories and Attempts to Commit Crimes.

TITLE II

PROCEEDINGS IN CRIMINAL CASES

CHAPTER 275. Proceedings to Prevent Crimes.
CHAPTER 276. Search Warrants, Rewards, Fugitives from Justice, Arrest, Examination, Commitment and Bail; Probation Officers and Board of Probation.
CHAPTER 276A. District Court Pretrial Diversion of Selected Offenders.
CHAPTER 277. Indictments and Proceedings before Trial.
CHAPTER 278. Trials and Proceedings before Judgment.
CHAPTER 279. Judgment and Execution.
CHAPTER 280. Fines and Forfeitures.

PART V

THE GENERAL LAWS, AND EXPRESS REPEAL OF CERTAIN ACTS AND RESOLVES

CHAPTER 281. The General Laws and Their Effect.
CHAPTER 282. Express Repeal of Certain Acts and Resolves. [Repealed.]

Annotated Laws of Massachusetts General Index

P

PACIFIC COAST STOCK EXCHANGE.
Uniform Securities Act, exemptions, **110A:402.**

PACKAGES.
See CONTAINERS OR PACKAGES.

PACKING MATERIAL.
Fire hazards, ordering removal, **148:5.**

PADLOCKING ACT, 139:16A.

PAGES OF GENERAL COURT, 3:18 et seq.
See GENERAL COURT.

PAID HOLIDAYS.
See SUNDAYS AND HOLIDAYS.

PAID-UP LIFE INSURANCE, 175:144.
Dividends, purchase, **175:140.**
Group insurance, nonforfeiture, **175:136.**

PAID-UP SHARES.
Co-operative banks.
Shares and accounts.
See COOPERATIVE BANKS.

PAIN AND SUFFERING.
Impounded dogs, prohibition of painful killing, **140:151A, 140:153.**
Motor vehicle accidents, restriction on right to claim damages for pain and suffering resulting, **231:6D.**
Recovery of damages for conscious suffering in death action, **229:6, 229:6C.**

PAINLESS DENTISTRY.
Advertising, **112:52A.**

PAINT, 94:291-94:295.
Alcohol.
Licenses to paint dealers for sale, **138:76.**
Tax on alcohol as inapplicable to paint dealers, **138:21.**
Art.
See ART AND ARTISTS.
Buildings.
Structural painting, regulation, **149:6, 149:13.**

PAINT —Cont'd
Deceptive labeling or marking prohibited, **94:291.**
Defined, **94:1.**
Enforcement of statutory requirements, **94:293, 94:294.**
Fires and fire prevention.
Automatic sprinklers, **148:26.**
Use as paint shop of building used for habitation, **148:24.**
Hours for meals, paint works as exempt from regulations, **149:101.**
Inspection, **94:293, 94:294.**
Lead poisoning, **111:189A et seq.**
See LEAD POISONING.
Manufacture and sale, regulation of, **94:291-94:295.**
Possession of article violating requirements as prima facie evidence of violation, **94:292.**
Public buildings and works.
Contract bids, specifications' categories, **149:44F.**
Prevailing wage law as applicable to painting, **149:27D, 149:44F.**
Sales, **94:291-94:295.**
Lead-based paints and glazes, **111:196.**
Licenses to paint dealers for sale of alcohol, **138:76.**
Structural painting, regulation, **149:6, 149:13.**
Public buildings and works. See within this heading, "Public buildings and works."

PAJAMAS.
Flammable children's sleepwear, manufacture or sale, **111:186B.**

PALMER.
Congressional district, **57:1.**
District court, **218:1.**
Medical examiner district, **38:1.**
Senatorial district, **57:3.**

PALMER RIVER.
Shad, **130:100C.**

PAMPHLETS, CIRCULARS, OR BULLETINS.
Civil service promotional bulletins, **31:29, 31:36.**
Cosmetics, notice as to adulterated article, **94:194.**

PAMPHLETS, CIRCULARS, OR BULLETINS —Cont'd
Credit unions, advertisements, **171:55.**
Development and industrial commission, **40:8A.**
Elections.
See ELECTIONS.
Injuring or detaining pamphlets in libraries, **266:99A, 266:100.**
Legislative committee hearings, **5:12.**
Manuals.
See MANUALS.
Ordinances, publication, **40:32A.**
Publication, defined for purposes of depository library for Massachusetts state publications, **6:39.**
Religious literature, requirement of license to sell, **101:17.**
Secretary of state.
Laws, publication of pamphlet edition, **5:4.**
Legislative committee hearings, sale of bulletins, **5:12.**
Session laws, distribution of copies, **5:4.**
Telephone services.
Consumer information booklets provided by local exchange carriers, **93:111.**
Uniform Securities Act, provision for filing of sales and advertising literature, **110A:403.**
Veterans' rights, copies of booklets showing, **115:13.**

PANAMANIAN INTERVENTION FORCE VETERAN.
Defined, **4:7.**

PANELS OF JUSTICES OF APPEALS COURT, 211A:3.
Review and revision by majority of justices of appeals court, **211A:11.**

PANHANDLING.
See BEGGING.

PAPER AND PAPER PRODUCTS.
Arsenic, sale of paper containing, **270:11, 270:12.**
Cartons, sale of viscous or semi-solid commodities, **98:22.**

1

PAPER AND PAPER PRODUCTS —Cont'd

Fires.
See FIRES AND FIRE PREVENTION.
Lien on account of labor and materials furnished in processing, **255:31A, 255:31B.**
Mass transportation facilities and service payments, powers of state tax commission as to determination, **58:25B.**
Milk containers, **98:16, 98:17.**
Mills, hours for meals, exemption from regulations, **149:101.**
Minors under sixteen not to work on certain machines, **149:61.**
Parchment, engrossment of constitutional amendments and legislative bills, **3:23, 3:24.**
Public records, quality, **66:3.**
Recycled paper products, purchase, **7:22.**
Reformatory, state purchasing agent to furnish paper to state, **7:27.**
Weighting bale with foreign substance as offense, **94:305.**

PAPER BALLOTS.

Arrangement of names and questions on voting machines, **54:33.**
Regulations of state secretary, approved methods of voting, **54:37.**
Type of paper used for ballots, **54:44.**

PAPERLACE MACHINES.

Minors under sixteen not to work on certain machines, **149:61.**

PAP TESTS.

Hospitals required to offer and perform, **111:53A.**

PARADES.

Children allowed in body of pick-up truck, **90:13.**
Flag used as receptacle for collecting money, etc., **264:5.**
Militia.
Armories, air installations and drill grounds.
See MILITIA.
Drills and parades.
See MILITIA.
Overtime pay for policemen on duty, **41:111H.**
Sunday, activities permitted, **136:6.**

PARADISE, GRAINS.

Adulteration of beverages, **270:1.**

PARAFFIN.

Frozen dessert or frozen dessert mix containing, sale or possession, **94:65L.**

PARALYZED VETERANS OF AMERICA.

Public charities division, exemption from requirement of filing copy of charter, **12:8E.**

PARAMEDICS.

Emergency medical services system, **111C:1 to 111C:24.**
See EMERGENCY MEDICAL SERVICES SYSTEM.
Emergency responders memorial day, **6:15RRR.**

PARAPLEGIC PERSONS.

Civil service employment in police and fire departments, **31:63.**
Fish.
See FISH AND GAME.
Recreation and snow vehicles, carrying of firearms by paraplegics, **90B:26.**
Veterans, **115:6A-115:6C.**
See VETERANS AND VETERANS' ORGANIZATIONS.

PARAPSYCHOLOGICAL PHENOMENON.

Real estate transactions.
Disclosures.
Not deemed material fact required to be disclosed, **93:114.**

PARASITES.

Veterinarians examined on subject, **112:56.**

PARCELS.

Containers.
See CONTAINERS OR PACKAGES.

PARCHMENT.

Engrossment of constitutional amendments and legislative bills, **3:23, 3:24.**

PARDONS, 127:152 to 127:169; MA Const Part 2 Ch 2 Sec 1 Art 8.

Advisory board of pardons, **127:152-127:154.**
Annual list to general court, **127:152.**
Applicants for, statements of persons representing, **127:167.**

PARDONS —Cont'd

Attorney General and District Attorney notice, **127:153.**
Clemency procedures.
Penalty for violation of regulations governing, **127:168.**
Regulations, **127:166, 127:168.**
Statement of applicant's representative, **127:167.**
Statutes as part of petition, **127:169.**
Conditions, violation of.
Violation of terms and conditions. See within this heading, "Violation of terms and conditions."
Confinement of violator for unexpired term of sentence, **127:156.**
Constitution of the United States.
See CONSTITUTION OF THE UNITED STATES.
Corrections department.
Duties with respect to pardons, **127:152-127:154.**
Furnishing information, **127:135, 127:136.**
Defined, **127:152.**
District attorneys, duties, **127:152-127:154.**
Divorce, pardon as eliminating ground, **208:2.**
Governor and council may grant, **127:152.**
Habitual criminal status as affected, **279:25.**
Hearing on petition, **127:152, 127:154.**
Impeachment, President may not pardon, **US Const Art 2 Sec 2 cl 1.**
Infants, **127:152.**
List of pardons, transmittal to general court, **127:152.**
Payment or receipt of money, **127:166-127:169.**
Petitions, **127:152-127:154, 127:169.**
Presidential power, **US Const Art 2 Sec 2 cl 1.**
Procedure.
Clemency procedure. See within this heading, "Clemency procedures."
Public officer pardoned, effect on right to hold office, **279:30.**
Rearrest of pardoned prisoner for violation of conditions, **127:155.**
Recommendations and reports, **127:154.**

PARDONS —Cont'd
Records, reports, and returns.
  List of pardons, **127:152.**
    Sealing of records after pardon,
      127:152.
    Warrant, return, **127:157.**
  Revocation, **127:152.**
  Sealing of records after pardon,
    127:152.
Statements to be filed by persons
  representing applicants,
  127:167.
State prison, petition for pardon of
  prisoner, **127:153.**
Terms, violations of.
  Violation of terms and
    conditions. See within this
    heading, "Violation of terms
    and conditions."
Violation of terms and conditions.
  Confinement for unexpired term
    of sentence, **127:156.**
  Rearrest in case, **127:155.**
Violent crimes, admissibility of
  records sealed after pardon,
  127:152.
Vote by executive council, **127:152.**
Warrant of pardon, **127:152.**
  Execution and return, **127:157.**
  Revocation of pardon, execution
    of warrant, **127:152.**
Witnesses before advisory board,
  127:154.

PARENS PATRIAE.
Restraints of trade, **93:9, 93:12.**

PARENTAL LEAVE.
Municipal employees, continuation
  of insurance while on leave,
  32A:10E.

PARENT AND CHILD.
Children.
  See CHILDREN AND MINORS.
Schools and education.
  Parental involvement.
    Curriculum accommodation
      plans, **71:38Q1/2.**
Special education.
  Workshop on rights of students
    and parents, **70B:19.**
    Curriculum, **71B:9A.**
Termination of parental rights.
  Abused and neglected children,
    119:26.
  Adoption of children, **210:3.**

PAREVE.
Kosher food, **94:156.**

**PARIMUTUEL RACING AND
  WAGERING.
See HORSE AND DOG RACING
  MEETINGS.**

**PARK COMMISSIONERS, 45:2
  et seq.**
Acquisition of property, **45:3.**
Annual report, **45:9.**
Appointment.
  Cities, appointment, **45:2.**
  Employees, appointment and
    control over, **45:5.**
    Playground employees, **45:14.**
Authority, **45:5.**
Building lines, establishment,
  45:11.
Connection of parks with other
  parts of city or town, **45:4.**
Election in town, **45:2.**
Eligibility, **45:2.**
Eminent domain, powers, **45:3.**
Employees, appointment and
  control over, **45:5.**
  Playground employees, **45:14.**
Height of buildings on parkways,
  regulation, **45:11.**
Planning board of town may serve,
  41:72, 41:81C.
Playgrounds, control, **45:14.**
Police, appointment and control,
  45:5.
Powers, **45:5.**
Public works board of town as
  successor, **41:69D.**
Public works department
  members, **45:2.**
Removal from office, **45:2.**
Reports, annual, **45:9.**
Rescission of vote authorizing
  selectmen to act, **41:23.**
Road commissioners, **45:2.**
Selectmen, **41:21, 41:23, 45:7.**
Streets or ways leading to parks,
  powers, **45:4.**
Structures in parks, duties as to
  erection, **45:7.**
Temporary playground in
  tenement districts, **45:17.**
Term of office, **45:2.**
Town selectmen acting as park
  commissioners, **45:2.**
Vacancies in cities, filling, **45:2.**

**PARKING AND PARKING
  STATIONS.**
Abandoned motor vehicles, duties
  of parking clerk, **90:22B.**
Aldermen and selectmen, adoption
  of parking regulations by
  board of selectmen, **90:20A,
  90:20A½.**
Appropriations by cities and towns
  for parking places, **40:5.**
Architectural barriers in off-street
  parking facilities, **40:22B.**

**PARKING AND PARKING
  STATIONS** —Cont'd
Authority.
  See PARKING AUTHORITY.
Beach districts, **40:12C, 40:12G.**
Bicycles, **85:11B.**
  Off-street areas, **40:22B,
    40:22C.**
  Purchase and installation of
    equipment for parking,
    40:22A, 40:22C.
Boston.
  Traffic and parking commission.
    See BOSTON.
Bradford Durfee College of
  Technology, vehicles on
  campus, **74:42Q.**
Brookline, violations, **90:20A.**
Burden of proof.
  Presumptions and burden of
    proof. See within this
    heading, "Presumptions and
    burden of proof."
Coin-operated locking devices for
  bicycle parking,
  40:22A-40:22C.
Colleges.
  Motor vehicles and parking.
    See COLLEGES AND
    UNIVERSITIES.
County facilities.
  Abolition of county governments.
    Right, title and interest to
      property owned by county
      transferred to
      Commonwealth, **34B:6.**
Crimes and offenses.
  Violations. See within this
    heading, "Violations of
    parking laws."
Disabled persons, **22:13A.**
  Fines for parking in space
    reserved, **40:21, 40:22A.**
  International Symbol of Access
    license plates, **90:2.**
  Pick-up truck, license plates and
    special parking
    identification plates, **90:2.**
  Regulation of parking, **40:21,
    40:22A, 40:22B, 40:22D.**
  Special parking identification
    plates, **40:21, 40:22, 40:22A,
    40:22D, 90:2, 90:33.**
  Veterans, parking, **40:21-40:22A.**
Disclaimer of liability by owner or
  operator on sign, ticket, or
  receipt, effect, **231:85M.**
District courts.
  Violations of parking laws. See
    within this heading,
    "Violations of parking laws."

**PARKING AND PARKING
STATIONS** —Cont'd
Drive-it-yourself system owners,
provisions for avoidance of
liability for parking violations,
90:20E.
Driver's license, suspension for
failure to appear, **90:20A.**
Dwelling house, parking in front,
40:21.
Evidence of violations, **90:20A,
90:20A½, 90:20C, 266:120A.**
Facsimile signatures may be used
in complaints for violations,
218:14.
Financing by municipality, **44:7.**
Fines, **90:20A, 90:21, 90:22A.**
Fire hydrant, fine for parking
near, **90:20A½.**
Fires and fire prevention.
Open-air parking spaces,
licensing, **148:56.**
Parking at or near fire, **89:7A.**
Fire apparatus, regulation of
parking vehicle on private
way so as to obstruct
access, **40:21.**
Handicapped persons.
Disabled persons. See within
this heading, "Disabled
persons."
Housing projects, parking for
tenants, **121B:32A.**
Illegal parking.
Violations. See within this
heading, "Violations of
parking laws."
Inspection of parking devices, fees,
143:62A.
Insurance coverage of parked
vehicle, **90:34O.**
International Symbol of Access
license plates for disabled
persons, **90:2.**
Landlord and tenant.
Housing project tenants,
parking, **121B:32A.**
Massachusetts Bay
Transportation Authority,
lease of land, **40:3.**
Public land, lease for parking
facility, **40:22B, 81:7H.**
Lights required on parked
vehicles, **85:15, 90:7.**
Local regulation of private ways
and parking areas, **90:18.**
Locking parked vehicles, **90:13.**
Mail, adjudication or challenge of
violations, **90:20A, 90:20A½.**
Massachusetts Bay transportation
authority, **161A:46.**
Off-street parking facilities,
40:3.

**PARKING AND PARKING
STATIONS** —Cont'd
Massachusetts Parking Authority.
See PARKING AUTHORITY.
Meters.
See PARKING METERS.
Mobile homes.
See MANUFACTURED HOMES
AND MANUFACTURED
HOUSING
COMMUNITIES.
Motorcycles.
Local ordinances allowing two
motorcycles per parking
space, **40:22A.**
Motor to be stopped, **90:13.**
New Bedford Institute of
Technology, vehicles on
campus, **74:42Q.**
Notice.
Handicapped persons, reserved
spaces, **22:13A.**
Lease of public land, **81:7H.**
Violations, **90:20A, 90:20E.**
Off-street parking areas or
facilities.
Architectural barriers in
off-street parking facilities,
40:22B.
Cities and towns, **44:7.**
Commercial area
revitalization district. See
within this subheading,
"Commercial area
revitalization district."
Debt limits, **44:7.**
Commercial area revitalization
district, **Spec L 21:1-Spec
L 21:4.**
Administrative secretary.
Financial assistance for
municipal parking,
programs, **Spec L 21:2.**
State bonds, request for
issuance, **Spec L 21:4.**
Authorization of off-street
parking projects, **Spec L
21:1.**
Board of selectmen,
authorization of off-street
parking projects, **Spec L
21:1.**
Bonds and notes for municipal
parking projects, **Spec L
21:4.**
City manager, authorization of
off-street parking projects,
Spec L 21:1.
Contracts, powers or parking
agencies, **Spec L 21:1.**
Debt limits, **Spec L 21:1,
21:3, 44:, 44:7.**

**PARKING AND PARKING
STATIONS** —Cont'd
Off-street parking areas or
facilities —Cont'd
Commercial area revitalization
district —Cont'd
Eminent domain, powers of
parking agencies, **Spec L
21:1.**
Governor, state bonds
authorized, **Spec L 21:4.**
Indebtedness authorized,
Spec L 21:3, 44:7.
Interest on state bonds for
municipal parking, **Spec
L 21:4.**
Leases, powers of parking
agencies, **Spec L 21:1.**
Maintenance, **40:22B, 40:22C,
Spec L 21:1 et seq.**
Mayor, authorization of
off-street parking projects,
Spec L 21:1.
Parking agencies,
implementation of
municipal parking
projects, **Spec L 21:1.**
State treasurer, state bonds
issued, **Spec L 21:4.**
Town council, authorization of
off-street parking projects,
Spec L 21:1.
Indebtedness authorized, **44:7.**
Installation of meters, **40:22B,
40:22C.**
Insurance, **40:22C.**
Meters, **40:22B, 40:22C.**
Regional transportation
authority, establishment of
off-street parking facilities,
40:3, 161B:6.
On-campus parking.
Motor vehicles and parking.
See COLLEGES AND
UNIVERSITIES.
Open-air parking spaces.
Licensing, **148:56.**
Operation by Massachusetts Bay
Transportation Authority,
148:56.
Owners and operators of motor
vehicles, liability, **90:20E.**
Police.
See POLICE.
Presumptions and burden of proof.
Notice to parking offender,
presumption, **90:20C.**
Private way, burden of proof as
to trespass by parking
motor vehicle, **266:120A.**
Private ways.
Removal of parked cars,
266:120D.

PARKING AND PARKING STATIONS —Cont'd

Private ways —Cont'd
Town regulation of parking of unattended vehicles, **40:21.**
Trespass by parking, **266:120A, 266:120D.**
Public works and departments.
Lease of land for public parking facility, **81:7H.**
Municipal off-street parking, **44:7.**
Real estate time-shares, termination of contract or lease, **183B:23.**
Records to be kept by parking lots, **90:32.**
Regional transportation authority, establishment of off-street parking facilities, **161B:6.**
Registrar of motor vehicles, inspection of records, **90:32.**
Rental cars, liability for parking violations, **90:20E.**
Safety precautions, **90:13.**
Sale of motor vehicles placed for storage and not claimed, **255:39A.**
Schools.
Colleges.
Motor vehicles and parking.
See COLLEGES AND UNIVERSITIES.
Regional school districts, authorization to incur debts, **71:16.**
Snow removal, moving parked vehicles interfering, **85:2A.**
Special regulations, enactment, **90:18.**
Speed in parking areas, **90:18.**
Sprinkler systems in parking structures, **148:26G.**
State highways, **85:2C.**
State-owned vehicles, as exempted from provision for towing of illegally parked vehicles, **40:22D.**
State parks, charges for parking, **132A:7.**
Superintendent of buildings, care and operation for buildings of state, **8:9.**
Taxicab owners, provisions for avoidance of liability by cab drivers, **90:20E.**
Towing.
See TOWING.
Trespass regarding, **266:120A.**
Unclaimed vehicles, sale, **255:39A.**

PARKING AND PARKING STATIONS —Cont'd

Universities.
See COLLEGES AND UNIVERSITIES.
Veterans, parking for disabled, **40:21-40:22B, 40:22D.**
Violations of parking laws, **90:20A.**
Brookline, **90:20A.**
Disabled or handicapped person, exemption from penalty imposed for violations, **40:22, 40:22A.**
District courts, **90:20C, 218:14.**
Enforcement of violations, **90:20A.**
Drive-it-yourself system owners, liability, **90:20E.**
Facsimile signatures may be used in complaints for parking violations, **218:14.**
Fines for parking violations, **90:20A, 90:20A½.**
Fire hydrant, proximity, **90:20A½.**
Lessors of vehicles, liability, **90:20E.**
Noncriminal disposition, **90:20A, 90:20C.**
Tags, penalty for removal, **90:20D.**
Taxicab owners, liability, **90:20E.**
Towing.
See TOWING.
Zoning, parking around public buildings, **40A:3.**

PARKING AUTHORITY, Spec L 71:1-Spec L 71:25.
Abandoned property auction, **Spec L 71:14A.**
Agreements, trust, **Spec L 71:9.**
Annual reports, **Spec L 71:14.**
Auctioning off unclaimed property, **Spec L 71:14A.**
Audit of books, **Spec L 71:14.**
Bonds and notes.
Common garage revenue bonds, **Spec L 71:8.**
Investment, eligibility, **Spec L 71:13.**
Refunding bonds, **Spec L 71:17.**
Remedies of bondholders, **Spec L 71:12.**
Cities.
Municipalities. See within this heading, "Municipalities."
Common garage revenue bonds, **Spec L 71:8, 71:17.**
Commonwealth, credit of not pledged, **Spec L 71:4.**

PARKING AUTHORITY —Cont'd

Constitutional construction, **Spec L 71:21.**
Construction of Act, **Spec L 71:20, 71:21.**
Construction of common garage, **Spec L 71:14.**
Credit of Commonwealth or political subdivision not pledged, **Spec L 71:4.**
Declaration of necessity, **Spec L 71:1.**
Definitions, **Spec L 71:2.**
Design of projects, assistance to Authority, **Spec L 71:14.**
Effective date, **Spec L 71:25.**
Exemption from taxation, **Spec L 71:16.**
Expenses, preliminary, **Spec L 71:18.**
Fees, penalty for failure to pay, **Spec L 71:14.**
Garage revenue bonds, **Spec L 71:8, 71:17.**
Governing law, **Spec L 71:23.**
Group insurance for employees and their dependents, **32A:2, 32A:8.**
Immunity waiver, **Spec L 71:14.**
Investment, bonds eligible, **Spec L 71:13.**
Labor relations policy, **Spec L 71:22.**
Liability in tort, **Spec L 71:14.**
Lien for payment of fee, **Spec L 71:14.**
Mandamus to enforce bondholders' rights, **Spec L 71:12.**
Massachusetts Parking Authority, **Spec L 71:3.**
Municipalities.
Conveyance of necessary interest in common, **Spec L 71:7.**
Conveyance of real property to Massachusetts Parking Authority, **Spec L 71:14.**
Credit not pledged, **Spec L 71:4.**
Transfer of project, **Spec L 71:15.**
Necessity, declaration, **Spec L 71:1.**
Notes and bonds.
Bonds and notes. See within this heading, "Bonds and notes."
Operation of projects, assistance to Authority, **Spec L 71:14.**
Penalties, failure to pay prescribed fee, **Spec L 71:14.**
Pledge of credit by Commonwealth or political subdivision, **Spec L 71:4.**

PARKING AUTHORITY
—Cont'd

Police, protection of Authority garage project, **Spec L 71:14.**

Political subdivisions.
Municipalities. See within this heading, "Municipalities."

Powers, **Spec L 71:5, 71:6.**

Preliminary expenses of Authority, **Spec L 71:18.**

Public buildings, structures defined, **22:13A.**

Real property, conveyance to Authority, **Spec L 71:14.**

Refunding bonds, **Spec L 71:17.**

Remedies of bondholders, **Spec L 71:12.**

Rental of real property to Authority by municipality, **Spec L 71:14.**

Repair of garages by Massachusetts Parking Authority, **Spec L 71:14.**

Repeal of other statutes, **Spec L 71:23.**

Retirement systems and pensions affecting employees, **32:1, 32:2.**

Revenue bonds.
Bonds and notes. See within this heading, "Bonds and notes."

Revenues, **Spec L 71:10.**

Taxation, exemption, **Spec L 71:16.**

Tort liability, **Spec L 71:14.**

Transfer of project to city, **Spec L 71:15.**

Trust agreements, **Spec L 71:9.**

Trust funds, **Spec L 71:11.**

Tunnels, construction as obligatory, **Spec L 71:19.**

Unclaimed property, auctioning, **Spec L 71:14A.**

Waiver of immunity, **Spec L 71:14.**

Words and phrases, **Spec L 71:2.**

Wrongful death, liability, **Spec L 71:14.**

PARKING METERS,
40:22A-40:22C.

Advertising forbidden, **40:22A.**

Disabled person, no fee or penalty imposed, **40:22, 40:22A.**

Municipal powers as to, **4:22A-4:22C.**

Off-street parking areas, **40:22B, 40:22C.**

Public works department, control, **85:2.**

Receipts from, **40:22B.**

PARKING METERS —Cont'd

Supervisors.
Civil service, status, **31:48, 31:51-31:53.**
Police officers in Boston, supervisors, **90:20C.**

PARKS AND RESERVATIONS,
45:1 et seq.

Actions for purpose of protecting natural resources and environment, **214:7A.**

Aldermen.
See ALDERMEN AND SELECTMEN.

Appearances before clerks of district court, **21:6F.**

Apportionment of expense among cities and towns, **92:54.**

Appropriations by towns, **40:5.**

Architects, exemption of park planners and supervisors from law, **112:60L.**

Armed forces.
Military affairs. See within this heading, "Military affairs."

Ball park sales by restaurant liquor licensee, **138:12.**

Beach property, acquisition by towns, **45:23A-45:23C.**

Bequests and devises, **45:3.**

Bets, penalty for registering, **271:10, 271:17.**

Betterments, application, **45:6.**

Bicycle paths, construction, **90E:3.**

Bonds for conveyance to city or town, **45:3.**

Borrowing for acquisition, **44:7.**

Boulevards, funds available to meet cost and maintenance, **90:34.**

Boundary markers, fences and buildings, **86:2.**

Boxing and boxing matches.
Age regulations, **147:39.**
Sponsoring of matches, **147:50, 147:50A.**

Buildings, **45:7, 45:11, 45:14, 45:17.**
Boundary markers, **86:2.**
Building line, **45:11.**

Bureau of recreation, **21:4E.**

Cambridge.
Metropolitan parks.
See CAMBRIDGE.

Care of public grounds by improvement associations, **45:12.**

Changing names, **85:3.**

Clerks of cities.
See CITY AND TOWN CLERKS.

PARKS AND RESERVATIONS
—Cont'd

Coastal reservations.
Shore reservations in towns. See within this heading, "Shore reservations in towns."

Commissioners of parks, **45:2 et seq.**
See PARK COMMISSIONERS.

Commons.
Public squares and commons. See within this heading, "Public squares and commons."

Concessions, **21:4A.**
Construction of stands, **45:7.**
Leasing, **45:5A.**

Condemnation.
Eminent domain. See within this heading, "Eminent domain."

Connections with other parks of city or town, **45:4.**

Conservation of soil, water and related resources.
Duties of committee, **21:20.**
Restrictions for purposes of achieving, public recreational land use as subject, **184:31.**

County superintendent, discharge, **35:51.**

Crimes and offenses.
Complaints by park rangers, **132A:7A.**
Fines and penalties. See within this heading, "Fines and penalties."

Damaging or injuring, **45:13.**

Devises and bequests, **45:3.**

Director of division of parks, advice regarding care and maintenance of parks or reservations, **132A:8.**

Disabled persons, facilities, **22:13A, 92:41.**

Districts, **92:33-92:59.**
See METROPOLITAN DISTRICTS.

Drinking fountains, town appropriations, **40:5.**

Driving animals, **45:13.**

Drug free parks and playgrounds, **94C:32J.**

Economic development department, promotion and financial assistance, **23A:14.**

Economic development supplement, **41:81D.**

Electric companies.
See GAS AND ELECTRIC COMPANIES.

PARKS AND RESERVATIONS
—Cont'd
Eminent domain, **92:79, 92:80.**
Acquiring land for parks, **45:3.**
Electric company not to take
right of way or easement,
164:72.
Energy companies prohibited,
164:69S.
Natural gas pipeline companies
not to take right of way or
easement, **164:75C.**
Shore reservations in towns,
eminent domain by county
commissioners, **45:23C.**
State parks, reservations, and
recreation areas, acquisition
of land, **132A:2A, 132A:3,
132A:3A.**
Tax on recreational land, effect,
61B:7.
Way, acquiring park, **79:5.**
Engineers and surveyors,
exemption from law, **112:81R.**
Environmental affairs executive
office, duties and functions,
21A:2.
Environmental management
board, management plans,
21:2F.
Environmental protection division
in office of attorney general,
authority, **12:11D.**
Federal government.
Installations and reservations.
See FEDERAL
GOVERNMENT AND
STATUTES.
Fines and penalties.
Bets, penalty for registering,
271:10, 271:17.
Damaging or injuring, **45:13.**
Metropolitan park district
regulations, violation, **92:37,
92:39.**
Picnics and picnic groves. See
within this heading, "Picnics
and picnic groves."
Rules and regulations, violation
of, **45:24.**
Throwing glass in or near parks,
265:32.
Trees, shrubs or plants,
damaging or injuring, **87:12.**
Trespass on public grounds,
45:13.
Wildflowers, pulling or digging
up, **266:116A.**
Fisheries department.
See FISHERIES, WILDLIFE,
AND RECREATIONAL
VEHICLES DEPARTMENT.

PARKS AND RESERVATIONS
—Cont'd
Forests.
See FORESTS AND PARKS
DIVISION.
Gas.
See GAS AND ELECTRIC
COMPANIES.
Gifts, grants, and gratuities, **45:3.**
Metropolitan districts, **92:34,
92:40.**
Shore reservations in towns,
acceptance of gifts, **45:23C.**
Governor.
State parks, reservations, and
recreation areas.
See GOVERNOR.
Great Ponds, public access, **131:45.**
Handicapped persons, facilities,
22:13A, 92:41.
Height of buildings on ways,
regulation, **45:11.**
Highways.
Ways. See within this heading,
"Ways."
Housing and community
development department,
powers and duties, **23B:3.**
Hunting, **131:59.**
Improvement associations, care of
public grounds, **45:12.**
Indebtedness of city or town, **44:7.**
Injunction against erection of
buildings, **45:7.**
Insurance, amusement parks,
140:205A.
Interest on money.
Excess payment on tax on
recreation land, **61B:4.**
Roll-back taxes, **61B:8.**
Special or betterment
assessments, **61B:13.**
Landowner's liability, **21:17C.**
Laying out and improvement, **45:5.**
Leasing of certain park
concessions, **45:5A.**
Local parks, **45:2-45:11.**
Master plan, **41:81D.**
Metropolitan district commission.
See METROPOLITAN
DISTRICT COMMISSION.
Metropolitan district police.
See METROPOLITAN
DISTRICT COMMISSION.
Military affairs.
Metropolitan park district's
boating and bathing
facilities, admission of
disabled veterans, **92:41.**
Permission required for use for
military exercises and
evolutions, **45:8.**

PARKS AND RESERVATIONS
—Cont'd
Mobile homes.
See MANUFACTURED HOMES
AND MANUFACTURED
HOUSING
COMMUNITIES.
Motor vehicles.
Ways. See within this heading,
"Ways."
Mount Greylock state reservation.
See MOUNT GREYLOCK
STATE RESERVATION.
Municipal finance.
Recreational facilities and
programs.
See MUNICIPAL FINANCE.
Notice.
Posting. See within this heading,
"Posting."
Open to public, **45:11.**
Outdoor recreation facilities,
extension of in anticipation of
federal funds, **21:1.**
Outside city or town limits, **45:14.**
Peddling near picnic grove,
140:190.
Penalties.
Fines and penalties. See within
this heading, "Fines and
penalties."
Picnics and picnic groves.
Fines and penalties.
Operation without license,
140:189.
Peddling near picnic grove,
140:190.
Licenses and permits, **140:188,
140:189.**
Operation without license,
140:189.
Peace officers, entry, **140:201.**
Peddling near picnic grove
penalized, **140:190.**
State parks, recreation areas,
and reservations, part of
planning, **132A:2D.**
Pipelines, right of way, **30:44B,
164:75C.**
Planning boards.
Ways and parks.
See ZONING AND
PLANNING.
Playgrounds, **45:14-45:18.**
See PLAYGROUNDS.
Police.
Appointment and control, **45:5.**
Metropolitan district police.
See METROPOLITAN
DISTRICT
COMMISSION.

PARKS AND RESERVATIONS
—Cont'd
Police —Cont'd
Picnic groves, entry, **140:201.**
Retirement systems and
pensions, **32:3, 32:85B,
32:94.**
Posting.
Forest and parks division,
regulations, **21:4A, 132A:7.**
Mobile homes and mobile home
parks, **140:32D.**
Premises liability, **21:17C.**
Programs and activities at places
other than public parks, **45:5.**
Public access board and fund,
enforcement and management,
21:17A.
Public squares and commons.
Buildings on, erection, **45:7.**
Driving animals, **45:13.**
Improvement associations, care
of public grounds, **35:12.**
Marketplaces, **40:10.**
Park defined, **45:1.**
Town appropriations or wells,
etc., **40:5.**
Trespass on public grounds,
penalty, **45:13.**
Purchase of lands, **45:3.**
Railroad not to enter public parks,
160:240.
Recreation bureau, transfer of
powers and duties, **21:4E.**
Refreshment structures, erection,
45:7.
Regional planning district
commission's plans and
recommendations to include,
40B:5.
Retirement systems and pensions,
32:3, 32:85B, 32:94.
Rules and regulations.
Forests and parks division,
21:4A.
Penalty for violation of.
Fines and penalties. See
within this heading,
"Fines and penalties."
Sales of park land, disposition of
proceeds, **44:63.**
Second Century Fund for fee
increases in parks and forests,
29:2EE.
Selectmen.
See ALDERMEN AND
SELECTMEN.
Self-supporting service revolving
funds, cities and towns to
establish recreation and park,
44:53D.

PARKS AND RESERVATIONS
—Cont'd
Self-supporting service revolving
funds, cities or towns revoking
acceptance of, **44:53D.**
Shade trees, **45:12.**
Function of tree warden
concerning, **87:2.**
Shelters, erection, **45:7.**
Shore reservations in towns,
45:23A-45:23C.
Duties of county commissioners
with respect to petitions,
45:23B.
Eminent domain by county
commissioners, **45:23C.**
Establishment, **45:23A.**
Petition, **45:23A.**
Size of buildings in, limitation,
45:7.
Soil conservation.
Conservation of soil, water and
related resources. See
within this heading,
"Conservation of soil, water
and related resources."
Squares.
Public squares and commons.
See within this heading,
"Public squares and
commons."
State finance.
Metropolitan parks.
See STATE FINANCE.
State treasurer's annual
financial statement as to
park districts, **10:11.**
State recreation areas.
See STATE RECREATION
AREAS.
Streets.
Ways. See within this heading,
"Ways."
Subdivisions and plats,
requirement, **41:81U.**
Superintendents, powers, **21:4A.**
Tax exemption, **59:5.**
Throwing glass in or near parks,
265:32.
Trailer coach parks.
See MANUFACTURED HOMES
AND MANUFACTURED
HOUSING
COMMUNITIES.
Trees or shrubs.
Damaging or injuring, **87:12.**
Shade trees. See within this
heading, "Shade trees."
Trespass on public grounds,
penalty, **45:13.**
Trusts, city or town may take and
hold trust for purpose of parks
and reservations, **45:3.**

PARKS AND RESERVATIONS
—Cont'd
Veterans, disabled, admission to
public bathing and boating
facilities, **92:41.**
Violation of rules and regulations,
penalty for.
Fines and penalties. See within
this heading, "Fines and
penalties."
Water conservation.
Conservation of soil, water and
related resources. See
within this heading,
"Conservation of soil, water
and related resources."
Ways.
Boston may incur indebtedness,
44:7.
Boulevards, funds available to
meet cost and maintenance,
90:34.
Buildings lines, regulation,
45:11.
Closing streets for use as
playgrounds, **45:17A.**
Connection with other sections
of city or town, **45:4.**
Exclusion of vehicles, **90:18.**
Federal aid highway projects,
replacement of land used in
connection, **81:7M.**
Forest and parks division
powers, **21:4A.**
Height of buildings, regulation,
45:11.
Number plates of vehicles used
by park board, **90:2.**
Planning for state parks,
132A:2D.
Registration fee, park vehicles
as exempt, **90:33.**
Rules and regulations, penalty
for violating, **45:24.**
Wildflowers, pulling or digging up,
offense, **266:116A.**
Youth conservation and service
corps, **78A:3.**
Zoning.
Ways and parks.
See ZONING AND
PLANNING.

PARLIAMENTARY LAW.
Secret ballot at town meetings,
39:15.

**PARLIAMENTARY LAW
MONTH.**
Annual observance, **6:15QQ.**

PARLOR CARS.
Drinking water, exception from
requirement, **160:174.**

PARLOR CARS —Cont'd
Wages of employees of parlor car
corporation, payment other
than weekly, **149:148.**

PAROCHIAL SCHOOLS.
See PRIVATE SCHOOLS.

PAROL CONVEYANCE.
Estate at will, effect of parol
conveyance, **183:3.**

PAROLE ACT, 127:128 et seq.
See PROBATION AND
PAROLE.

PAROLEE SUPERVISION ACT.
Interstate, **127:151A et seq.**

PAROL EVIDENCE.
Lease contracts under Commercial
Code, **106:2A-202.**
Negotiable instruments.
Other agreements affecting
instrument, **106:3-117.**
"Or return" term of sales contract,
106:2-326.
Regional medical panels, **32:6.**
Restraints of trade and
monopolies, **93:8.**
Sales contract.
Admissibility to vary terms,
106:2-202.
"Or return" term of sales
contract, **106:2-326.**

PARSONAGES.
Local assessment of parsonages
held in irrevocable trust for
religious corporations, **59:5.**
Minister may take parsonage land,
68:5.
Property tax exemption, eligibility
and application for abatement,
59:5.

PARTIAL BALLOT, 54:45, 54:76.

PARTIAL DELIVERY.
Cancellation or notation of
document of title, **106:7-403.**

PARTIAL DISTRIBUTION.
Executors.
Distribution of estates.
See EXECUTORS AND
ADMINISTRATORS.

PARTIAL INCAPACITY.
Workers' compensation,
152:35-152:36A, 152:73A.

PARTIALITY.
See PREJUDICE OR BIAS.

PARTIAL REDEMPTION.
Tax sale, **60:76A.**

PARTIAL REJECTION.
Goods, partial rejection, **106:2-601.**

PARTIAL REVOCATION.
Acceptance of nonconforming
goods, revocation, **106:2-608.**

PARTIAL SALE.
Executors.
Real property.
See EXECUTORS AND
ADMINISTRATORS.

PARTIAL SERVICE OUTSIDE
STATE.
Employment security provisions,
151A:3.

PARTIAL UNEMPLOYMENT.
Amount of benefits, **151A:29.**
Defined, **151A:1.**
Waiting period, **151A:23.**

PARTICULARS, BILLS OF.
See BILLS OF PARTICULARS.

PARTIES POLITICAL.
See POLITICAL PARTIES.

PARTIES TO ACTIONS.
Abatement.
See ABATEMENT, SURVIVAL,
AND REVIVAL.
Absent defendants,
223A:1-223A:11, 227:1-227:17.
See ABSENT DEFENDANTS.
Absentee's estate, state treasurer
as party to proceedings, **200:1.**
Alcoholic liquors, parties to
proceedings after seizure.
Costs paid by party failing to
sustain claim, **138:54.**
Interest in seized beverages,
138:50.
Amendments, **231:51.**
Ancient mortgage, proceedings for
discharge, **240:15.**
Anti-trust laws.
Restraints of trade and
monopolies. See within this
heading, "Restraints of
trade and monopolies."
Appeal.
See APPEAL AND REVIEW.
Arbitration and compromise of
wills, **204:15.**
Assignee, **231:6.**
Attorney general.
Party to action, attorney general
as state's representative.
See ATTORNEY GENERAL.
Business trusts, **182:6.**
Carriers, joinder of affiliated
companies in proceedings
involving, **159:34A.**

PARTIES TO ACTIONS —Cont'd
Certiorari proceedings, joinder of
party respondent, **249:4.**
Child born out of wedlock,
determining paternity,
support, visitation, or custody,
209C:5.
Chose in action, action by
assignee, **231:6.**
Cities, **40:2.**
Class actions, unfair trade
practices or methods of
competition, **93A:9, 93A:11.**
Clerk of court to keep alphabetical
list of parties, **221:23.**
Conservators, representation of
wards, **201:37, 228:13.**
Consumer protection action
involving multiple defendants,
93A:4.
Contested elections of presidential
electors, **54:120.**
Conveyance of estate subject to
future interests, proceedings,
183:50.
Corporations.
See CORPORATIONS.
Costs of actions.
See COSTS OF ACTION.
County treasurer as party to
actions against county, **35:20.**
Deaf parties, appointment of
interpreters, **221:92A.**
Death of party.
Abatement.
See ABATEMENT,
SURVIVAL, AND
REVIVAL.
Judgment in writ of entry, death
after, **237:36, 237:37.**
Declaratory judgment proceedings,
231A:8.
Dismissal.
See DISMISSAL AND
NONSUIT.
Distribution of estate, proceedings
for sale of realty for purpose,
202:19.
Documents in suit, right to copies,
231:68.
Domicile or residence, effect of
parties' domicile or residence
on venue of transitory action,
223:2.
Electors, contested elections of
presidential electors, **54:120.**
Employee trust fund, intervention
in action for depletion,
151D:3.
Equal rights to be, **93:102.**
Equity petition to enjoin false
advertising, **266:91B.**

9

PARTIES TO ACTIONS —Cont'd

Ethics commission, enforcement of financial disclosure and interest provisions, **268A:9, 268B:4.**

Executors.
  See EXECUTORS AND ADMINISTRATORS.

False advertising, bill in equity to enjoin, **266:91B.**

Fines, apportionment, **280:2.**

Flats, parties in proceedings to determine boundaries, **240:24.**

Foreign corporations, liability to be sued and have property attached, **181:15.**

Foreign states, factors affecting recognition of judgment rendered, **235:23A.**

Fraternal benefit societies.
  Attorney general, actions society, **176:33, 176:37.**
  Beneficiary as party to action on certificate, **176:31.**
  Deposits of foreign or alien societies, actions, **175:185.**

Frauds, statute of.
  Admissions by parties.
    See STATUTE OF FRAUDS.
  Consent orders, **231:72.**

Gas and electric companies, joinder of affiliated companies in proceedings involving, **164:76A.**

Group health insurance policies for old persons, unincorporated association issuing, **175:110C.**

Guardians, representation of wards, **201:37, 228:13.**

Hazardous waste insolvency fund, **21C:19, 21C:21.**

Health care services, definition, plaintiff personal injury listing, **93:95.**

Impleader.
  See IMPLEADER.

Inquest as to cause of death, interested persons as entitled to attend, **38:8.**

Insurance.
  See INSURANCE.

Interpleader.
  See INTERPLEADER.

Interpreters for deaf parties, **221:92A.**

Intoxicating liquor.
  Alcoholic liquors. See within this heading, "Alcoholic liquors, parties to proceedings after seizure."

PARTIES TO ACTIONS —Cont'd

Joinder of offenses.
  Indictments, informations, and complaints.
    See JOINDER OF OFFENSES AND OFFENDERS.

Joinder of parties.
  See JOINDER OF PARTIES.

Limitation of action as affecting dismissal for failure to join parties defendant, **260:17.**

Management of own suits by parties, **221:48.**

Married women, **209:6.**

Massachusetts Centers of Excellence Corporation, capacity to sue and be sued, **40J:12.**

Massachusetts child custody jurisdiction act, **209B:4.**

Mechanics' lien foreclosure suit, **254:5.**

Medical service corporations, parties to actions against for enforcement of laws, **176B:17.**

Mental condition of parties, determination, **123:4, 123:15, 123:17, 123:19.**

Mesne process, arrest on, definitions, **224:1.**

Mill dam, action for damages caused, **253:30.**

Monopolies.
  Restraints of trade and monopolies. See within this heading, "Restraints of trade and monopolies."

Mortgages.
  Ancient mortgage, proceedings for discharge, **240:15.**
  Foreclosure action, **244:8, 244:13.**

Municipal corporation, **40:2.**

Negotiable instruments.
  Defined, **106:3-103.**

New parties, bringing, **231:51.**

Next friend.
  See NEXT FRIEND.

Nonresidents, indorsement of writ or bill by responsible inhabitant in actions by or against, **231:42 et seq.**

Nonsuit.
  See DISMISSAL AND NONSUIT.

Owner of place of prostitution as party to action for abatement, **139:7.**

Partition.
  See PARTITION.

Pleading, **231:6B-231:6D.**

PARTIES TO ACTIONS —Cont'd

Presence of defendant, **223A:1-223A:11, 227:1-227:17.**
  See ABSENT DEFENDANTS.

Presidential electors, contested elections, **54:120.**

Principal on probate bond, **205:27, 205:28.**

Proprietors of wharves and real estate lying in common, actions, **179:6.**

Prostitution, owner of place where permitted as party to action for abatement, **139:7.**

Quieting title.
  See QUIETING TITLE.

Registration of land titles.
  See REGISTRATION OF LAND TITLES.

Residence.
  Domicile or residence, **223:2.**

Restraints of trade and monopolies.
  Final judgment or decree under Massachusetts Antitrust Act as estoppel between parties, **93:11.**
  Jurisdiction, burden of establishing, **93:3.**
  Standing to sue, **93:12.**

Revenue commissioner as party to proceedings by foreign fiduciary to receive and dispose of personal property, **204:3.**

Seizure of alcoholic liquors, parties to proceedings after.
  Alcoholic liquors. See within this heading, "Alcoholic liquors, parties to proceedings after seizure."

Service on defendants, **223:31, 223:34, 223:35, 223:37-223:40.**
  See PROCESS AND SERVICE OF PROCESS AND PAPERS.

Statute of frauds.
  Admissions by parties.
    See STATUTE OF FRAUDS.
  Consent orders, **231:72.**

Stenographer, defendant's right to employ, **221:91B.**

Substitution of parties.
  See SUBSTITUTION OF PARTIES.

Survival of action.
  See ABATEMENT, SURVIVAL, AND REVIVAL.

Tax foreclosures, **60:66.**

Third party practice.
  Impleader.
    See IMPLEADER.

PARTIES TO ACTIONS —Cont'd
Third party practice —Cont'd
Interpleader.
  See INTERPLEADER.
Third persons.
  See THIRD PERSONS.
Towns, **40:2.**
Transitory actions, domicile or
  residence of parties as
  affecting venue, **223:2.**
Trusts, proceedings for transfer,
  203:30, 203:31.
Uniform rules of adjudicatory
  procedure, **30A:10.**
Unknown persons.
  See UNKNOWN PERSONS.
Welfare and social services,
  children born out of wedlock,
  209C:5.
Wharves, actions by proprietors,
  179:6.
Wills.
  Arbitration of controversies,
    actions concerning, **204:15.**
  Attorney general as party to
    certain probate proceedings,
    192:1A.
  Creditors of decedent, actions,
    197:32.
Witnesses.
  See WITNESSES.
Zoning.
  Appeals to superior court,
    40A:17.
  Definition of "parties in
    interest," **40A:11.**
  Standing to appeal to permit
    granting authority, **40A:8.**

PARTITION, 241:1-241:37.
Accounts and accounting.
  Federal savings and loans
    associations share accounts,
    investment of unclaimed
    proceeds, **241:34.**
  Parties, accounting between,
    241:25.
Additional property, inclusion,
  241:4.
Ad litem guardian.
  Guardian ad litem. See within
    this heading, "Guardian ad
    litem."
Administrator or executor, land
  held on execution or mortgage,
  206:13.
Advancements, consideration,
  196:8.
Adverse claimant.
  Cotenant of party, **241:20.**
  Entire property, **241:21.**
  Time for bringing action, **241:19.**

PARTITION —Cont'd
Adverse claimant —Cont'd
  Undivided interests, **241:19.**
Advertisement, notice, **241:8.**
Affidavit.
  Registry of deeds, affidavit of
    filing notice, **241:7.**
  Service of process, **241:8.**
Amendment.
  Commissioners, amendment of
    return, **241:16.**
  Petition, court's power to require
    amendment, **241:17.**
Assessments, division of special or
  local assessment upon sale of
  property, **80:15.**
Attachment of property.
  Decree, effect of, as to
    attachment of share of
    cotenant, **241:28.**
  Parties to partition, attachment
    creditors not necessary,
    241:6.
Attorneys' fees, **241:22.**
Auction, sale of property, **241:31.**
Availability of remedy, **241:1.**
Bond or undertaking.
  Receivers, **241:25.**
  Trustee, **241:35.**
Building improvements.
  Improvements. See within this
    heading, "Improvements on
    property, compensation."
Certificate of oath of
  commissioners, **241:12.**
Change.
  Amendment. See within this
    heading, "Amendment."
Citations, issuance and service,
  241:8.
Commissioners, **241:12.**
  Amendment of return, **241:16.**
  Confirmation or setting aside of
    report, **241:16.**
  Equalizing differences, **241:14.**
  Fees, **241:22.**
  Land in different counties,
    241:13.
  Notice of proceedings, **241:12,
    241:32.**
  Report, **241:12, 241:16.**
  Sale of property, **241:31, 241:32.**
  Warrant, **241:12, 241:13, 241:35.**
  Water rights, apportionment,
    241:36.
Complaint.
  Petition. See within this
    heading, "Petition."
Condominiums.
  Common areas and facilities,
    183A:5.

PARTITION —Cont'd
Condominiums —Cont'd
  Failure of unit owners to agree
    to restoration, **183A:17,
    183A:18.**
Conservators.
  Guardians. See within this
    heading, "Guardians,
    conservators, and
    committees."
Contribution.
  Costs and expenses, **241:22.**
  Execution, **241:22.**
  Tax or encumbrance paid by
    party, **241:10.**
Costs and expenses, **241:22.**
Death of party to proceedings,
  241:26.
Decree, **241:16.**
  Conclusiveness, **241:18.**
  Fees, serving execution upon
    judgment, **262:8.**
  Interlocutory decree. See within
    this heading, "Interlocutory
    decree."
  Persons and rights not affected,
    241:19-241:21.
  Registered land, **185:86, 185:87,
    185:91 et seq.**
  Setting off improved portion to
    party making
    improvements, **241:23.**
Description of property, power of
  court to investigate, **241:17.**
Disability of spouse, partition or
  transfer of property in
  circumstances, **209:14-209:24.**
Dispute as to ownership of share,
  241:11.
Division of property, **241:5.**
Dower interests, **189:12.**
Effect, **241:18.**
Electric companies' property held
  in common, agreements,
  164:99A.
Encumbrances.
  Mortgages and liens. See within
    this heading, "Mortgages
    and liens."
Equity jurisdiction of probate
  court, **241:25.**
Estates for years, **241:1, 241:6,
  241:35.**
Eviction by paramount title from
  properties set off.
  Compensation for improvements,
    241:29.
  New partition, **241:27.**
Examination of title.
  Title examination. See within
    this heading, "Title
    examination, court may
    order."

PARTITION —Cont'd

Execution for contribution and costs, **241:22.**

Executor, land held on execution or mortgage, **206:13.**

Federal savings and loan association share accounts, investment of unclaimed proceeds, **241:34.**

Fees, **241:22.**
  Entry of petition, **262:40.**
  Land court, **262:39.**
  Serving execution upon judgment, **262:8.**

Fee simple estates, **241:1.**

Fiduciary, share held by, effect, **241:30.**

General fields, **179:38, 179:39.**

Guardian ad litem, **241:9.**
  Adverse interests of guardian or conservator, appointment in event, **201:39.**
  Fees, **241:22.**

Guardians, conservators, and committees, **201:39, 209:17.**
  Guardian ad litem. See within this heading, "Guardian ad litem."

Husband and wife, partition or transfer of property when either spouse is under disability, **209:14-209:24.**

Identification of property, investigation, **241:17.**

Improvements on property, compensation, **241:23, 241:24.**
  On eviction by paramount title, **241:29.**

Incidental relief in connection, **241:25.**

Incorporeal hereditaments, **241:36.**

Index of records of instruments, **36:27.**

Indivisible property, **241:14, 241:15.**

Interlocutory decree, **241:10.**
  Registry of deeds, necessity of filing notice, **241:7.**

Investment of unclaimed proceeds, **241:34.**

Judgment.
  Decree. See within this heading, "Decree."

Jurisdiction.
  Equity jurisdiction, exercise, **241:25.**
  Exclusive in probate courts, **241:2.**
  Land in two or more counties, **241:3.**

Landlord and tenant, **241:1.**
  Electric companies, **164:99A.**

PARTITION —Cont'd

Landlord and tenant —Cont'd
  Eviction.
    See LANDLORD AND TENANT.
  Partition proceedings, **241:1.**

Liens.
  Mortgages and liens. See within this heading, "Mortgages and liens."

Life estates, **241:1, 241:6, 241:35.**

Lis pendens, **241:7.**

Local property tax, apportionment, **59:78A.**

Mental illness or other disability of spouse, **209:14-209:24.**

Mill privileges, **241:36, 241:37.**

Money payments to equalize shares, **241:14, 241:15.**
  Security for payment, **241:15.**

Mortgages and liens.
  Conclusiveness of decree, **241:28.**
  Distribution by commissioners without notice of claims, effect, **241:32.**
  Effect of payment, **241:10.**
  Intervention, **241:6.**
  Notice, **241:6, 241:17, 241:32.**
  Party accepting share without disclosing rights, penalty, **241:33.**
  Rights of lienholders, **241:28.**
  Tax liens. See within this heading, "Tax liens."

Municipal tax title on part of land, **60:61A.**

New England Power Pool property owned in common, waiver of right of partition, **164A:5.**

Nonnavigable stream, partition of waters, **241:37.**

Notice.
  Citation, service, **241:8.**
  Lienholders, **241:6, 241:17, 241:32.**
  Proceedings, **241:6-241:8.**
  Recording, **241:7.**
  Sale of property, **241:31.**
  Time and place for making partition, **241:12.**

Oath.
  Affidavit. See within this heading, "Affidavit."
  Commissioners' oath, certificate, **241:12.**

Order of sale, **241:31.**

Owelty, payment, **241:14, 241:15.**
  Security for payment, **241:15.**

Paid-up shares of cooperative banks, investment of unclaimed proceeds, **241:34.**

PARTITION —Cont'd

Paramount title.
  Eviction by paramount title. See within this heading, "Eviction by paramount title from properties set off."

Partial redemption from tax sale, **60:76A.**

Parties to proceedings, **241:1, 241:6.**
  Accounting between, **241:25.**
  Adverse claimant. See within this heading, "Adverse claimant."
  Conclusiveness of partition, **241:18.**
  Death of, effect, **241:26.**
  Decree, setting off improved portion to party making improvements, **241:23.**
  Lienholder's rights, **241:28.**
  New parties, **241:17.**
  Omitted parties, rights, **241:19, 241:20.**
  Successive interests, trustee, **241:35.**
  Unknown and incompetent parties, **241:9.**

Petition, **241:6.**
  Amendment of petition, court's power to require, **241:17.**
  Fees, entry of petition, **262:40.**

Petitioner, setting off portion, **241:5.**

Plan, court may order making, **241:17.**
  Cost, **241:22.**

Portion of common property, partition, **241:4.**

Postponement of determination of rights, **241:11.**

Private or public sale of property, **241:31.**

Probate Court.
  Jurisdiction, **241:2.**
  Revocation of warrant or commission, **215:35.**

Proceeds of sale.
  Disposition of unclaimed shares, **241:34.**
  Distribution by commissioners without notice of claims, **241:32.**
  Lienholders' rights, **241:28.**
  Penalty for accepting share without disclosing lien rights, **241:33.**
  Third person claiming share, **241:19, 241:20.**

Process and service of process and papers, **241:8.**

PARTITION —Cont'd
Proof of service of citations, **241:8.**
Proprietors of wharves and real estate lying in common, **179:14.**
Publication, notice, **241:8.**
Real estate time-shares, **183B:14.**
Receivers, appointment, **241:25.**
Recording of instruments, **241:16.**
Notice of proceedings, **241:7.**
Redemption.
Estate in land subject to redemption, **241:1.**
Partial redemption from tax sale, **60:76A.**
Registers.
See REGISTERS AND REGISTRIES OF DEEDS.
Registration of land titles, **185:86 et seq.**
See REGISTRATION OF LAND TITLES.
Rents and profits, collection and distribution, **241:25.**
Sale of property, **241:31.**
Assessments, division of special or local assessment upon sale of property, **80:15.**
Notice, **241:31.**
Partial redemption from tax sale, **60:76A.**
Proceeds of sale. See within this heading, "Proceeds of sale."
Water rights and other incorporeal hereditaments, **241:36.**
Savings and loan association share accounts, investment of unclaimed proceeds, **241:34.**
Security for award of money to equalize shares, **241:15.**
Service of notices and citations, **241:8.**
Successive interests, trustees, **241:35.**
Tax liens.
Apportionment of taxes on real estate subsequently divided, effect, **59:78A.**
Municipal tax title on part of land, effect, **60:61A.**
Term for years, **241:1.**
Title examination, court may order, **241:17.**
Costs, **241:22.**
Trust companies, deposit of unclaimed funds, **241:34.**
Trustee.
Bond, **241:35.**
Share held by, effect, **241:30.**
Successive interests, trustees, **241:35.**

PARTITION —Cont'd
Undertaking.
Bond or undertaking. See within this heading, "Bond or undertaking."
Venue, **241:2.**
Waiver of right to partition property.
Electric companies' property held as tenants in common, **164:99A.**
New England power pool, **164A:5.**
Warrant of commissioners, **241:12, 241:13, 241:35.**
Waste during pendency of action, **242:4.**
Water rights, **241:36, 241:37.**
Wharves, proprietors, **179:14.**

PARTNERSHIPS, 108A:1 et seq.
Accident and sickness insurance, blanket policy, **175:110.**
Accountants.
See ACCOUNTANTS.
Accounting by partners, **108A:20-108A:22.**
Benefits received, duty, **108A:21.**
Dissolution, accounting, **108A:40.**
Individual partners as entitled, **108A:22.**
Surviving partners, accounting, **108A:21, 108A:43.**
Transferee of interest of partner, rights, **108A:27.**
Acquisition of assets by partner as fraud on creditors, **109A:2.**
Actions by all partners, **108A:9.**
Acts of partner as binding, **108A:9.**
Additional partner.
New partner. See within this heading, "New partner."
Adjusters, insurance, partnerships, **175:173.**
Administrators.
Executors and administrators. See within this heading, "Executors and administrators."
Admissions by partner, firm as bound, **108A:11.**
Agreement of partnership.
Continuation after expiration, **108A:23.**
Damages for breach, **108A:38.**
Limited partnerships, **109:17, 109:18.**
Rescission for fraud, **108A:39.**
Alcoholic liquors.
See ALCOHOLIC LIQUORS.

PARTNERSHIPS —Cont'd
Arbitration, authority of partner to agree, **108A:9.**
Architecture.
"Landscape architect," use of title, **112:101.**
Practice, **112:60L.**
Articles of partnership.
Agreement of partnership. See within this heading, "Agreement of partnership."
Assignment for benefit of creditors.
Authority of partner to make assignment for firm, **108A:9.**
Liability of partner to contribute to payment of firm debts as enforceable by trustee, **108A:40.**
Assignment of partner's interest.
Transfer of partner's interest. See within this heading, "Transfer of partner's interest."
Assumption of liabilities.
Dissolved partnership, **108A:36.**
New member, **108A:17.**
Attachment of property.
Foreign limited partnerships, **109:55.**
Interest of partner in partnership property, **108A:25.**
Judgment, attachment after, **223:86A.**
Trustee process, **246:7.**
Authority of partners, **108A:9.**
Automobiles.
Motor vehicles. See within this heading, "Motor vehicles."
Bank commissioner, annual reports and examinations by or, **168:20, 170:19, 172:18.**
Bankruptcy.
Insolvency and bankruptcy. See within this heading, "Insolvency and bankruptcy."
Banks and banking.
Credit unions.
See CREDIT UNIONS.
Loan to insolvent partnership, penalty, **266:53A.**
Benefits received by partner, accounting, **108A:21.**
Binding effect of instruments affecting interest in real property, **108A:48.**
Books and records.
Records, reports, and returns. See within this heading, "Records, reports, and returns."

PARTNERSHIPS —Cont'd
Breach of partnership agreement, damages, **108A:38.**
Business, defined, **108A:2.**
Carrier's license or certificate, transfer to remaining or surviving partners, **159A:7, 159B:11.**
Certificates and certification.
  Assumed or fictitious name, certificate, **110:5, 110:6.**
  Licenses and permits. See within this heading, "Licenses and permits."
  Limited partnerships.
    See LIMITED PARTNERSHIPS.
Children's allowance, partnership property as not subject, **108A:25.**
Cigarette tax law violations, liability of partner aiding, **64C:21.**
Citation of Uniform Act, **108A:1.**
Common law superseded by Uniform Act, **108A:4.**
Compensation.
  Members of partnership, **108A:18.**
  Workers' compensation. See within this heading, "Workers' compensation."
Conduct of partner warranting dissolution, **108A:32.**
Confessing judgment, authority of partner, **108A:9.**
Construction of Uniform Act, **108A:4.**
Continuation of business.
  Death of partner, **108A:41, 108A:42.**
  Dissolution, **108A:23, 108A:38, 108A:41.**
  Expiration of agreed term, **108A:23.**
Contracts and agreements.
  Agreement of partnership. See within this heading, "Agreement of partnership."
  Allocation of profit or loss, **108A:18.**
  Arbitration agreement, **108A:9.**
  Dissolution by agreement, **108A:31.**
  Group annuity contracts, **175:132A.**
  Public works contracts, **149:179A.**
  Water pollution control division, **21:38.**
Contribution by partners, **108A:18.**
  Liabilities incurred after dissolution, **108A:34.**

PARTNERSHIPS —Cont'd
Contribution by partners —Cont'd
  Limited partnerships.
    Financing of limited partnership.
      See LIMITED PARTNERSHIPS.
  Where assets insufficient to pay debts, **108A:40.**
Conveyances, **108A:8, 108A:10.**
  Assignment for benefit of creditors. See within this heading, "Assignment for benefit of creditors."
  Defined, **108A:2.**
  Fraudulent conveyances or sales. See within this heading, "Fraudulent conveyances or sales."
  Transfer of partner's interest. See within this heading, "Transfer of partner's interest."
Co-operative nominee partnerships for retirement systems of public employees, establishment, **32:23.**
Co-operative, use of word in firm name, **157:8.**
Corporations.
  Authority to act as partner, **156B:9A.**
  Use of word in firm name, **110:4A.**
Creditors.
  Acquisition of assets by partner as fraud, **109A:2.**
  Assignment for benefit of. See within this heading, "Assignment for benefit of creditors."
  Business of partnership not to be enjoined or restrained during creditor's action, **214:3.**
  Death of partner, property of decedent as subject to partnership debts, **108A:36, 108A:40.**
  Dissolution, rights on.
    Creditors' rights on dissolution. See within this heading, "Creditors' rights on dissolution."
  Insolvency and bankruptcy. See within this heading, "Insolvency and bankruptcy."
  Limited partnerships.
    Debtors and creditors.
      See LIMITED PARTNERSHIPS.

PARTNERSHIPS —Cont'd
Creditors —Cont'd
  Special jurisdiction of supreme judicial and superior courts in creditor's actions to reach partnership property, **214:3.**
  Creditors' rights on dissolution, **108A:40, 108A:41.**
    Application of assets to debts, **108A:38.**
    Individual partners, remedies of creditors, **108A:28.**
    Not advised of dissolution, **108A:35.**
    Suits to subject partnership interest to debts, **108A:44.**
Credit unions.
  See CREDIT UNIONS.
Curtesy, partner's interest not subject, **108A:25.**
Death of partner.
  Annuity paid widow as indication of partnership, **108A:7.**
  Claims against insolvent estate, **198:21.**
  Devolution of decedent's interest, **108A:25.**
  Dissolution, **108A:31, 108A:34.**
  Interest of partner paid, **108A:42.**
  Limited partnership, **109:43.**
  Property of decedent as subject to partnership debts, **108A:36, 108A:40.**
  Surviving partners. See within this heading, "Surviving partners."
Debtor and creditor.
  Creditor. See within this heading, "Creditors."
Deceit.
  Fraud and deceit. See within this heading, "Fraud and deceit."
Deeds.
  Conveyances. See within this heading, "Conveyances."
Definitions, **108A:2.**
  Dissolution, **108A:29.**
  Interest of partner, **108A:26.**
  Limited partnerships, **109:1.**
  Notice, **108A:3.**
  Partnership, **108A:6.**
  Partnership property, **108A:8.**
Detention of money by employees as larceny, **266:38.**
Disability or capacity.
  Incompetency. See within this heading, "Incompetency of partner."

PARTNERSHIPS —Cont'd
Dissolution and liquidation,
  108A:29-108A:43.
Accounting by last surviving
  partner, **108A:21.**
Agreement, dissolution,
  108A:31.
Application of assets to debts,
  108A:38.
Assets, what are, **108A:40.**
Authority of partners, effect,
  108A:33.
Circumstances causing,
  108A:31.
Continuing business after,
  108A:23, 108A:38, 108A:41.
Creditors' rights on dissolution.
  See within this heading,
  "Creditors' rights on
  dissolution."
Death, **108A:31, 108A:34.**
Defined, **108A:29.**
Effect where caused by act,
  death, or bankruptcy of
  partner, **108A:34.**
Expiration of term. See within
  this heading, "Expiration of
  term."
Incompetency of partner as
  ground for dissolution. See
  within this heading,
  "Incompetency of partner."
Interest of partner. See within
  this heading, "Interest of
  partner."
Judicial dissolution, **108A:32.**
Knowledge or notice, **108A:35.**
Liability of partners as affected,
  108A:36.
Limited partnerships.
  See LIMITED
  PARTNERSHIPS.
Order in which debts to be paid,
  108A:40.
Partnership as terminated,
  108A:30.
Partners' rights, **108A:38.**
Power of partner to require,
  108A:31.
Proceedings against partner's
  interest as causing,
  108A:28.
Sale of partner's interest as
  causing, **108A:27.**
Settlement of accounts, **108A:40.**
Transferee of partner's interest,
  rights, **108A:27.**
Distinguished from other
  relationships, **108A:6, 108A:7.**
Dower, partner's interest not
  subject, **108A:25.**

PARTNERSHIPS —Cont'd
Dwellings.
  Posting of information
    concerning owner, **143:3S.**
  Tenement houses in cities,
    meaning of "person" in
    statute relating to service of
    process, **145:60C.**
Embalming business, conduct,
  112:87.
Embezzlement by partner, liability
  of firm, **108A:14.**
Employment security, services of
  employees outside United
  States as included, **151A:4A.**
Engineers, practice, **112:81R.**
Entireties, tenancy by,
  distinguished, **108A:7.**
Estates.
  Tenancy in partnership. See
    within this heading,
    "Tenancy in partnership."
Estoppel and waiver.
  Applicability of law, **108A:4.**
  Partnership, estoppel to deny,
    108A:16.
Evidence.
  Admissions or representations
    by partner, **108A:11.**
  Continuing business beyond
    time fixed for termination,
    108A:23.
  Existence of partnership,
    108A:7.
Execution against partner's
  interest, **108A:25, 108A:28.**
Executors and administrators.
  Affairs of partnership, right of
    surviving partners to wind
    up, **108A:37.**
  Allowance to widows and
    children, partnership
    property not subject,
    108A:25.
  Debts, decedent's property as
    subject, **108A:36.**
Exemptions.
  Attachment or execution,
    partner's interest as exempt,
    108A:25.
  Dower or curtesy, exemption,
    108A:25.
  Income tax, shares subject, **59:5.**
  Partners, exemption rights,
    108A:28.
Expenditures by partner,
  reimbursement and
  contribution, **108A:18.**
Expiration of term.
  Continuation of business after,
    108A:23.

PARTNERSHIPS —Cont'd
Expiration of term —Cont'd
  Dissolution, **108A:31, 108A:32.**
Fair employment practices law,
  applicability, **151B:1.**
Financial condition, false
  statement, **266:92.**
Fines and penalties.
  Cigarette tax law violations,
    liability of partner aiding,
    64C:21.
  Detention of money by
    employees as larceny,
    266:38.
  Embezzlement by partner,
    liability of firm, **108A:14.**
  False statements as to condition
    of partnership, **266:92.**
  Foreign limited partnerships,
    109:55.
  Late filing of tax return, **62C:34.**
  Loan by bank to insolvent
    partnership, **266:53A.**
  Partnership liability for
    penalties, **108A:13.**
Fire adjuster, acting, **175:173.**
Firm name.
  Name. See within this heading,
    "Name of firm."
Foreign state or country.
  Employment security, services of
    employees outside United
    States as included,
    151A:4A.
  Exemption of motor vehicles of
    foreign partnership, **60A:1.**
  Limited liability partnerships,
    108A:47.
Fraud and deceit.
  Acquisition of assets by partner
    as fraud on creditors,
    109A:2.
  Conveyances and sales.
    Fraudulent conveyances or
      sales. See within this
      heading, "Fraudulent
      conveyances or sales."
  Financial condition, false
    statement, **266:92.**
  Partnership agreement induced,
    108A:39.
  Status as partner, false
    assertion, **108A:16.**
Fraudulent conveyances or sales,
  109A:2.
  When partnership deemed
    insolvent, **109A:3.**
Funeral directing, engaging in
  business, **112:87.**
Gain.
  Profit or loss. See within this
    heading, "Profit or loss."

PARTNERSHIPS —Cont'd
Garnishment, service of district
    court trustee process, **246:7.**
Gas fitting, **142:3B.**
Good will.
    Individual partners' authority to
      dispose, **108A:9.**
    Partnership not shown by
      receipt of share of profits as
      consideration for sale,
      108A:7.
Gross returns, sharing, **108A:7.**
Group annuity contracts,
    175:132A.
Holding one out as partner, effect,
    108A:16.
Horse and dog racing meetings,
    registration, **128A:9A.**
Income tax.
    See INCOME TAX.
Incompetency of partner.
    Dissolution, ground, **108A:32.**
    Limited partnerships, rights of
      incompetent partner,
      109:43.
"Incorporated," use of word in firm
    name, **110:4A.**
Indemnity and indemnification.
    Against other partners, **108A:18.**
    Contribution by partners. See
      within this heading,
      "Contribution by partners."
    Person induced by fraud to
      become partner, **108A:39.**
Insanity.
    Incompetency of partner. See
      within this heading,
      "Incompetency of partner."
Insolvency and bankruptcy.
    Acts of remaining partner,
      108A:34, 108A:37.
    Assignment for benefit of
      creditors. See within this
      heading, "Assignment for
      benefit of creditors."
    Bank loan to insolvent
      partnership, penalty,
      266:53A.
    Contributions by partners,
      108A:40.
    Definitions, **108A:2.**
    Dissolution and liquidation. See
      within this heading,
      "Dissolution and
      liquidation."
    Estate of deceased partner,
      claims against, **198:21.**
    Fraud on creditors, **109A:3.**
    Priorities, **108A:40.**
    Receivership, **108A:28.**
    Winding up affairs, **108A:37.**

PARTNERSHIPS —Cont'd
Insurance.
    Accident and sickness insurance,
      blanket policy, **175:110.**
    Advisers, licensing of
      partnership, **175:177B.**
    Agents and brokers.
      See INSURANCE AGENTS
        AND BROKERS.
    Commissioner.
      Insurance commissioner. See
        within this heading,
        "Insurance commissioner."
    Group annuity contracts,
      175:132A.
    Limited liability partnerships,
      amount of insurance,
      108A:45.
    Rating organization, acting,
      152:52C.
Insurance commissioner.
    Adjusters, partnerships,
      175:173.
    Licensing as insurance advisers,
      175:177B.
Interest of partner.
    Attachment or execution,
      exempt, **108A:25.**
    Defined, **108A:26.**
    Devolution on death, **108A:25.**
    Dissolution.
      Creditors' rights on
        dissolution, suits to
        subject partnership
        interests to debts,
        108A:44.
      Effect, **108A:38.**
    Dower or curtesy, not subject,
      108A:25.
    Exemption rights, **108A:28.**
    Nature as personal property,
      108A:26.
    Payment for, on death or
      retirement, **108A:42.**
    Receiverships for partnership
      interest, **108A:28.**
    Redemption from judicial
      proceedings, **108A:28.**
    Specific property, interest,
      108A:25.
    Surviving partner, buying out
      other partner's interest,
      108A:42.
    Transfer of. See within this
      heading, "Transfer of
      partner's interest."
Interest on money, partner's
    advances to firm, **108A:18.**
Interpretation of Uniform Act.
    Construction of Uniform Act,
      108A:4.

PARTNERSHIPS —Cont'd
Joint and several liability of
    partners, **108A:15.**
Knowledge.
    Notice and knowledge. See
      within this heading, "Notice
      and knowledge."
"Landscape architect,"
    partnership's use of title,
    112:101.
Land surveyors, practice, **112:81R.**
Law merchant, applicability,
    108A:5.
Liberal construction of Uniform
    Act, **108A:4.**
Licenses and permits.
    Horse and dog racing meetings,
      registration, **128A:9A.**
    Insurance advisers, licensing of
      partnership, **175:177B.**
    Limited liability partnerships,
      registration of, **108A:45 et
      seq.**
    Lobster permit authorized to be
      held by partnership,
      130:38B.
    Milk, sale, **94:40.**
    Motor carrier's license or
      certificate, transfer to
      remaining or surviving
      partner, **159A:7, 159B:11.**
    Professional fund-raising counsel
      or professional solicitor,
      registration, **68:23.**
    Real estate brokers' or
      salesmen's license, **112:87,
      112:87TT, 112:87UU.**
    Revocation or suspension.
      Motor vehicle certificate of
        registration, **90:22A.**
      Motor vehicle finance license,
        partners' acts as ground
        for revocation, **255B:7.**
      Sales finance companies,
        255D:7.
    Vending machines, application of
      license for sale of food
      through, **94:309.**
    Workers' compensation rating
      organization, license for
      partnership to work,
      152:52C.
Limited liability partnerships.
    Binding effect of instruments
      affecting interest in real
      property, **108A:48.**
    Fees, payment of, **108A:49.**
    Foreign partnerships, **108A:47.**
    Registration, **108A:45, 108A:45
      et seq.**
    Words to follow name of
      partnership, **108A:46.**

PARTNERSHIPS —Cont'd
Limited partnerships, **109:1 et seq.**
  See LIMITED PARTNERSHIPS.
Liquidation.
  Dissolution and liquidation. See within this heading, "Dissolution and liquidation."
Loans, penalty for bank loan to insolvent partnership, **266:53A.**
Lobster permit authorized to be held, **130:38B.**
Loss.
  Profit or loss. See within this heading, "Profit or loss."
Majority decisions, **108A:18.**
Management of business.
  Accounting to partner excluded, **108A:22.**
  Continuation of business. See within this heading, "Continuation of business."
  Equality of rights, **108A:18, 108A:24.**
  Transferee not entitled to share, **108A:27.**
Medical service plan provisions, term medical organization as including partnerships for purpose, **176C:1.**
Mental illness.
  Incompetency of partner. See within this heading, "Incompetency of partner."
Milk, license to sell, **94:40.**
Misapplication of funds by partner, liability of firm, **108A:14.**
Misrepresentation.
  Fraud and deceit. See within this heading, "Fraud and deceit."
Motor vehicles.
  Carrier's license, transfer to surviving partners, **159A:7, 159B:11.**
  Certificate of registration, suspension, **90:22A.**
  Driver schools, operation, **90:32G.**
  Financing license, act of partners as ground for revocation, **255B:7.**
Name of firm.
  Assumed or fictitious name, certificate, **110:5, 110:6.**
  Co-operative, use of word in firm name, **157:8.**
  "Corporation" or "incorporated" prohibited, **110:4A.**

PARTNERSHIPS —Cont'd
Name of firm —Cont'd
  Limited liability partnerships, **108A:46.**
  Limited partnerships, **109:2, 109:3, 109:5.**
    Foreign limited partnership, **109:51.**
  True surname of partner, exemption from requirement of filing certificate in case of operation, **110:6.**
  Use after retirement of partner, **110:4.**
Negligence of partner, liability of firm for, **108A:13.**
New partner.
  Consent to taking, **108A:18.**
  Liability, **108A:17.**
  Limited partnerships.
    See LIMITED PARTNERSHIPS.
  Rights of creditors, **108A:41.**
Notice and knowledge.
  Defined, **108A:3.**
  Dissolution, **108A:35.**
  Dwelling, posting of information as to owner, **143:35.**
  Effect of notice to partner, **108A:12.**
  Lack of authority, effect of knowledge, **108A:9.**
  Limited partnership, filing certificate of as notice, **109:15.**
  Partner's knowledge as imputed to firm, **108A:12.**
"Organization" as including, **106:1-201.**
Penalties.
  Fines and penalties. See within this heading, "Fines and penalties."
Permits.
  Licenses and permits. See within this heading, "Licenses and permits."
Personal property.
  Property. See within this heading, "Property of partnership."
"Person," defined, **4:7, 223A:1.**
Physical therapy referrals by physician, disclosure of financial interest, **112:12AA, 112:23P½.**
Plumbing partnerships, **142:3B.**
Posting of information as to owner of dwelling, **143:35.**
Profit or loss.
  Accounting for profits, **108A:21.**

PARTNERSHIPS —Cont'd
Profit or loss —Cont'd
  Allocation in absence of agreement, **108A:18.**
  Dissolution, loss as ground, **108A:32.**
  Limited partnerships.
    See LIMITED PARTNERSHIPS.
  Participation in profit or loss, as evidence of partnership, **108A:7.**
Property of partnership, **108A:24-108A:28.**
  Assignment of interest in specific property, **108A:25.**
  Attachment of property. See within this heading, "Attachment of property."
  Binding effect of instruments affecting interest in real property, **108A:48.**
  Conveyance of, **108A:10.**
  Creditors. See within this heading, "Creditors."
  Defined, **108A:8.**
  Dissolution, disposition, **108A:38.**
  Fraudulent conveyance, **109A:2.**
  Interest of partner. See within this heading, "Interest of partner."
  Personal property tax, **59:18.**
  Priorities against, **108A:40.**
  Real property defined, **108A:2.**
  Tenancy in partnership. See within this heading, "Tenancy in partnership."
Psychologists employed by, penal provisions as applicable, **112:123.**
Public employees and their partners, restrictions on activities.
  County employees, **268A:12.**
  Municipal employees, **268A:18, 268A:19.**
  State employees, **268A:5, 268A:6, 268A:12.**
Public works contracts, preference to partnerships composed of citizens in awarding, **149:179A.**
Purchase of partner's interest.
  Transfer of partner's interest. See within this heading, "Transfer of partner's interest."
Real estate brokers' or salesmen's license, **112:87, 112:87TT, 112:87UU.**

PARTNERSHIPS —Cont'd
Real property.
  Property of partnership. See
    within this heading,
    "Property of partnership."
Receiverships for partnership
  interest, **108A:28.**
Records, reports, and returns.
  Assignee of partner, inspection,
    108A:27.
  Limited partnerships.
    See LIMITED
      PARTNERSHIPS.
  Tax returns, penalty for late
    filing, **62C:34.**
Registration.
  Licenses and permits. See
    within this heading,
    "Licenses and permits."
Remaining partners.
  Surviving partners. See within
    this heading, "Surviving
    partners."
Reports.
  Records, reports, and returns.
    See within this heading,
    "Records, reports, and
    returns."
Representations.
  False representations.
    Fraud and deceit. See within
      this heading, "Fraud and
      deceit."
  Membership in firm, **108A:16.**
  Partner, firm as bound by
    representations, **108A:11.**
Retirement.
  Interest of partner paid,
    108A:42.
  Name of firm, use after
    retirement of partner, **110:4.**
  State employees and teachers,
    establishment of
    co-operative nominee
    partnerships for retirement
    systems, **32:23.**
Revocation or suspension of
  license.
  Licenses and permits. See
    within this heading,
    "Licenses and permits."
Salaries of members, **108A:18.**
Sale.
  Assets, authority of partner to
    sell, **108A:9.**
  Fraudulent conveyances and
    sales. See within this
    heading, "Fraudulent
    conveyances or sales."
  Good will, partnership not
    shown by receipt of share of
    profits as consideration for
    sale, **108A:7.**

PARTNERSHIPS —Cont'd
Sale —Cont'd
  Transfer of partner's interest.
    See within this heading,
    "Transfer of partner's
    interest."
  Vending machines, application of
    license for sale of food
    through, **94:309.**
Sales finance companies,
  suspension or revocation of
  licenses, **255D:7.**
School-community partnerships,
  71:59D.
Sealed instruments, unsealed
  instruments given effect, **4:9A.**
Service of district court trustee
  process, **246:7.**
Services of employees outside
  United States as included
  under employment security,
  151A:4A.
Settlement of accounts on
  dissolution, **108A:40.**
Several liability of partners,
  108A:15.
Special jurisdiction of supreme
  judicial and superior courts in
  creditors' actions to reach
  partnership property, **214:3.**
State treasurer authorized to
  establish co-operative nominee
  partnerships for benefit of
  state retirement systems,
  32:23.
Superior courts.
  Limited partnership, dissolution
    by decree, **109:45.**
  Property as reachable in
    creditor's action, **214:3.**
Surviving partners.
  Accounting, **108A:21, 108A:43.**
  Acts of, as binding firm,
    108A:34.
  Buying out other partner's
    interest, **108A:42.**
  Continuation of business,
    108A:41, 108A:42.
  Motor carrier's license or
    certificate, transfer to
    remaining or surviving
    partner, **159A:7, 159B:11.**
  Taking over of business,
    108A:25.
  Winding up, **108A:37.**
Suspension of license.
  Licenses and permits. See
    within this heading,
    "Licenses and permits."
Taxation.
  Cigarette tax law violations,
    liability of partner aiding,
    64C:21.

PARTNERSHIPS —Cont'd
Taxation —Cont'd
  Income tax, **62:17.**
    See INCOME TAX.
  Individuals liable for tax on
    corporation or partnership,
    62C:31A.
  Personal property tax, **59:18.**
  Shares subject to income tax,
    exemption, **59:5.**
  Ships or vessels, assessment,
    59:8, 59:18.
Telecommunications and energy
  department's examination of
  firm connected with public
  utility company, **182:8.**
Tenancy in partnership, **108A:25.**
  Co-tenancies distinguished,
    108A:7.
Tenement houses in cities,
  meaning of "person" in statute
  relating to service of process,
  145:60C.
Termination.
  Dissolution and liquidation. See
    within this heading,
    "Dissolution and
    liquidation."
Title acquired by conveyance of
  property, **108A:10.**
Tort of partner, liability, **108A:13.**
Trade name.
  Name of firm. See within this
    heading, "Name of firm."
Transferable shares, partnerships
  having.
  See BUSINESS TRUSTS.
Transfer of partner's interest,
  108A:27.
  Creditors, rights, **108A:41.**
  Limited partnerships.
    See LIMITED
      PARTNERSHIPS.
  Motor carrier's license or
    certificate, transfer to
    remaining or surviving
    partners, **159A:7, 159B:11.**
  Purchaser, dissolution, **108A:32.**
  Specific property, **108A:25.**
Traps for catching game, use by
  partnership, **131:80.**
Trustee process of district court,
  service, **246:7.**
Trusts and trustees.
  Assignment for benefit of
    creditors, liability of partner
    to contribute to payment of
    form debts as enforceable by
    trustee, **108A:40.**
  Partners, **108A:21.**
Unanimous action, when required,
  108A:9.

PARTNERSHIPS —Cont'd
Unemployment compensation, **151A:4A.**
Uniform laws, **108A:1 et seq.**
Unusual transactions, authority of partner, **108A:9.**
Urban renewal projects, partnership engaging, **121A:18C.**
Wages, etc.
   Compensation. See within this heading, "Compensation."
Waiver.
   Estoppel and waiver. See within this heading, "Estoppel and waiver."
Water pollution control division, contracts, **21:38.**
"Whoever" as including, **4:7.**
Widow's allowance, partnership property not subject, **108A:25.**
Winding up.
   Dissolution and liquidation. See within this heading, "Dissolution and liquidation."
Withdrawal of partner.
   Certificate as to assumed or fictitious name, **110:5.**
   Continuing business after, **108A:38, 108A:41.**
   Firm name, continued use, **110:4.**
   Limited partnerships.
     Distributions and withdrawal. See LIMITED PARTNERSHIPS.
   Payment for interest of withdrawing partner, **108A:42.**
Workers' compensation.
   Employer, partnership, **152:1.**
   License for partnership to work as workmen's compensation rating organization, **152:52C.**
Wrongful act of partner, liability, **108A:13.**

PART-TIME EMPLOYMENT.
See LABOR AND WORKFORCE DEVELOPMENT.

PART-TIME STUDENT.
Definition, **15A:7B.**
Grant program, **15A:7, 15A:16.**
Higher education coordinating council, part-time student grant program, **15A:16.**

PART-TIME VETERANS' AGENT.
Definition, **115:1.**

PARTY LINES.
See TELEPHONE AND TELEGRAPH COMPANIES.

PAR VALUE.
Corporate stocks, **155:16.**
   See CORPORATIONS.
Insurance.
   See INSURANCE.
Railroads.
   See RAILROADS.

PASSBOOKS.
Banks.
   See BANKS AND BANKING.
Credit unions.
   See CREDIT UNIONS.

PASSENGERS.
Bicycles, passengers carried, **85:11B.**
Carriers, 159A:1 to 159A:16.
   See CARRIERS.
Motorcycles.
   Learner's permit holder carrying passenger, **90:8B.**
   Protective headgear required, **90:7.**
   Safety provisions, **90:7, 90:13.**
Motor vehicles.
   Commercial carriers of passengers.
     CARRIERS.
   Guest passengers.
     See MOTOR VEHICLES.
   Motorcycles.
     See MOTORCYCLES.
Railroads.
   See RAILROADS.

PASSES.
Forgery.
   Tickets and passes.
     See FORGERY AND COUNTERFEITING.
Highways.
   See HIGHWAYS AND STREETS.
Railroads.
   Tickets.
     See RAILROADS.
Restrictions as to free carrier passes, **159:15.**
Street railways passes, **161:107.**
   School pupils, **161:108.**
   Stolen or counterfeited employee transportation pass, **161:113A.**

PASSING.
Traffic regulations.
   See TRAFFIC REGULATIONS AND RULES OF THE ROAD.

PASSOVER.
Kosher food, **94:156.**

PASSPORT.
Employment permit, evidence of age, **149:87.**
Marriage, proof of age for purpose, **207:33A.**

PASSWORDS.
Illegally obtaining.
   Identity fraud, **266:37E.**

PASTEURIZED MILK.
See MILK AND MILK PRODUCTS.

PASTORAL COUNSELING FOR PRISONERS.
Correctional institutions, **127:36B.**

PASTURES.
Forest cutting regulations inapplicable to maintenance cutting, **132:44.**
General fields.
   See GENERAL FIELDS.
Horses.
   Liens for keeping or pasturing.
     See HORSES.
Lien for pasturing domestic animals, **255:24, 255:26 et seq.**
   Dissolution, **255:32, 255:33.**
Public ways, local regulation as to pasturing animals, **85:10.**

PATENT MEDICINES.
Formulary of generic or chemical names of drugs, exclusions, **17:13.**
Guarantee by supplier of correctness of labeling as exonerating dealer, **94:184A.**
Inspection of places selling, **13:25.**
Labeling packages of medicine containing alcohol or certain drugs, **94:184A, 94:187.**

PATENTS.
Ballot box vendors or lessors to give indemnifying bond against infringement, **54:39.**
Bradford Durfee College of Technology research foundation, powers, **74:46B.**
Counterfeit marks, **266:147.**
Energy conservation patents, income tax deductions, **62:2.**
Exclusive rights of inventors, **US Const Art 1 Sec 8 cl 8.**
Voting machine vendors or lessors to give indemnifying bond against infringement, **54:39.**

PATERNITY PROCEEDINGS,
209C:1, 209C:2, 273:15 et
seq.
Adjudication of paternity.
  Conclusiveness as to support
    obligation, **273:15.**
  Vacation, **273:17.**
Authenticated copy of judgment,
  paternity established, **190:7.**
Bail and recognizance, recoveries,
  273:18.
Birth records of illegitimate
  children.
  See BIRTHS.
Child support enforcement.
  Genetic marker test to establish,
    119A:3A.
Default judgment, **209C:8.**
Dismissal, allowance and effect,
  273:17.
Exclusion of public from trial,
  209C:12.
Forfeited bail may be used for
  support, **273:18.**
Full faith and credit, **209C:2.**
Guardians, conservators, and
  committees, **209C:5.**
Intermarriage of parents after
  adjudication of paternity,
  209C:23.
Interstate Family Support Act,
  determination of parentage,
  209D:7-701.
Joinder of husband or former
  husband in support
  proceeding, **209C:6.**
Maintenance, dismissal of case on
  provision, **273:17.**
Penalties and procedures, **273:16.**
Pregnancy, action to establish
  paternity may be instituted
  during, **209C:14.**
Presumptions and burden of proof,
  209C:6, 209C:7.
Special rules, **209C:3, 209C:24,**
  215:4, 218:19.
Support of children, **46:3C.**
Trial of proceedings, exclusion of
  public, **278:16A.**

PATHOLOGY AND
PATHOLOGISTS.
Autopsy, employment of
  pathologist, **38:6.**
Medical examiners.
  See MEDICAL EXAMINERS
    AND INQUESTS.
Medicolegal investigations
  committee, membership,
  6:184.
Physical therapists, subject of
  examination for registration,
  112:23E.

PATHOLOGY AND
PATHOLOGISTS —Cont'd
Subjects covered in examination
  for registration as physician or
  surgeon, **112:3.**
Veterinarians, subjects for
  examination, **112:56.**

PATIENT LIFTS.
Sales tax exemptions, **64H:6.**

PATIENT PROTECTION,
OFFICE OF.
Established with department of
  public health, authority,
  111:217.
Oversight, managed care oversight
  board, **6A:16D.**

PATIENTS' BILL OF RIGHTS,
111:70E.

PATIO INSTALLATIONS.
Home improvement contractors,
  142A:14.

PATRICK CARR.
Commemoration of death, **6:12D.**

PATRIOTIC SONG.
"Massachusetts (Because of You
  Our Land is Free)" designated
  as patriotic song of the
  Commonwealth, **2:31.**

PATRIOTS' DAY.
Annual observance, **6:12J.**
Firemen working on, additional
  time off or pay, **48:57A,**
  48:57D, 48:57E.
Legal holiday, **4:7.**
Police, day off or extra pay,
  147:17A.
State employees required to work
  on, additional day off or extra
  pay, **30:24A.**
Sunday laws, applicability, **136:13.**

PATROLS.
Fire patrol.
  See FOREST FIRES.
Police.
  See POLICE.
School safety patrols, **71:48A.**

PAUPERS.
See POOR PERSONS.

PAVEMENT.
Highways.
  See HIGHWAYS AND
    STREETS.

PAWNBROKERS, 140:70-140:85,
140:202-140:205.
Abandonment of property,
  presumption, **200A:3.**

PAWNBROKERS —Cont'd
Aldermen.
  Selectmen. See within this
    heading, "Selectmen."
Auction of unredeemed articles,
  140:71.
Bonds and obligations, loans,
  140:76.
Bonds and undertakings,
  pawnbrokers' license as
  requiring, **140:77.**
Books.
  Record books. See within this
    heading, "Record books."
Chief of police.
  Premises, entry and inspection,
    140:73.
  Record books, inspection, **140:81,**
    140:87.
Clothing.
  Wearing apparel. See within this
    heading, "Wearing apparel,
    license for loans."
Commercial Code definition of
  buyer in ordinary course of
  business, **106:1-201.**
Contract, disposition of property as
  affected, **140:71.**
Contractor's tools, loans, **140:83,**
  140:84.
Entry of premises by authorities,
  140:73, 140:74.
Examination and inspection.
  Books, **140:81, 140:87.**
  Premises and articles, **140:73,**
    140:74.
Exceptions regarding retention of
  articles, **140:71.**
Fees for licenses, **140:77, 140:202.**
Fines and penalties, **140:82.**
  Acting without license, **140:75.**
  Interest rates, violations,
    140:72.
  Obstructing entry of authorities,
    140:74.
  Tools, violations as to loans,
    140:84.
Inspection.
  Examination and inspection. See
    within this heading,
    "Examination and
    inspection."
Interest on money, **140:78, 140:91.**
  Penalty for violations, **140:72,**
    140:82.
  Rate limited, **140:72.**
Jewelry, license for loans, **140:76.**
Licenses and permits, **140:70,**
  140:202-140:205.
  Authorities empowered to grant,
    140:70.

PAWNBROKERS —Cont'd
Licenses and permits —Cont'd
Bond, **140:77.**
Fees, **140:77, 140:202.**
Personal property loans,
regulations, **140:76.**
Revocation, **140:70, 140:84,
140:205.**
Unlicensed operation of
business, penalty, **140:75.**
Wearing apparel, license to
make loans on. See within
this heading, "Wearing
apparel, license for loans."
Mechanics' tools, loans, **140:83,
140:84.**
Memorandum to pledgor, **140:80.**
Money.
Interest on money. See within
this heading, "Interest on
money."
Notice of sale to owner of
unredeemed articles, **140:71.**
One thousand dollars,
inapplicability of provisions
concerning loans, **140:95.**
Ornaments, license for loans,
140:76.
Penalties.
Fines and penalties. See within
this heading, "Fines and
penalties."
Perishable property, disposition,
140:71.
Permits.
Licenses and permits. See
within this heading,
"Licenses and permits."
Personal property, license for
loans, **140:76.**
Photographs of persons pawning
articles, **140:79.**
Pledgors, memorandums, **140:80.**
Police officers.
Chief of police. See within this
heading, "Chief of police."
State police. See within this
heading, "State police."
Presumption of abandonment of
property left after 5 years,
200A:3.
Rate of interest limited, **140:72.**
Record books, **140:79.**
Amount loaned on tools, **140:83.**
Inspection, **140:81, 140:87.**
Tools, loans, **140:83, 140:84.**
Registered mail, notice to owner of
unredeemed articles, **140:71.**
Regulations, establishment,
140:78.
Retention of pledged property,
140:71.

PAWNBROKERS —Cont'd
Revocation of licenses, **140:70,
140:84, 140:205.**
Selectmen.
Entry of premises for inspection,
140:73.
Licensing power, **140:70.**
Small loan act inapplicable,
140:85.
State police.
Entry on premises, **140:73,
140:74.**
Inspection of books, **140:81.**
Statutes regulating loans
inapplicable, **140:85.**
Stolen articles accepted in pawn,
liability of pawnbroker,
140:82A.
Suspension of licenses, **140:70,
140:84, 140:205.**
Tickets to be provided to
borrowers, requirements,
140:86.
Time articles must be retained,
140:71.
Tools, loans, **140:83, 140:84.**
Unlicensed pawnbrokers,
penalties, **140:75.**
Unredeemed articles, sale, **140:71.**
Watches, loans, **140:86.**
Wearing apparel, license for loans,
140:76.
Disposal of pawned articles,
140:71.

PAXTON.
Congressional district, **57:1.**
District court, **218:1.**
Medical examiner district, **38:1.**
Senatorial district, **57:3.**

PAXTON SOIL SERIES.
Official soil of Commonwealth,
designation, **2:33.**

**PAYMENT BY BENEFICIARY'S
BANK TO BENEFICIARY.**
Words and phrases, **106:4A-405.**

**PAYMENT BY ORIGINATOR
TO BENEFICIARY.**
Words and phrases, **106:4A-406.**

**PAYMENT BY SENDER TO
RECEIVING BANK.**
Words and phrases, **106:4A-403.**

PAYMENT DATE.
Words and phrases, **106:4A-401.**

PAYMENT INTO COURT.
Deposits in court.
See DEPOSITS IN COURT.

**PAYMENTS IN LIEU OF
TAXES.**
See TAXATION.

PAYOR BANK.
See BANKS AND BANKING.

PAY PHONES.
Convalescent or nursing homes,
111:72D.
Fraud, **266:75, 266:75B.**
Limited-access ways, **85:2D.**

**PAYROLL AND PAYROLL
DEDUCTIONS.**
Accident or sickness insurance,
premiums on blanket policies,
175:110.
Aldermen.
See ALDERMEN AND
SELECTMEN.
Annuity contracts, deductions,
154:8.
Apprentice training programs,
149:148.
Assignment of wages, **154:8,
208:36, 209:32E.**
Auditors of cities and towns,
approval, **41:52.**
Banks.
See BANKS AND BANKING.
Bonds, government, deductions for
purchase, **154:8.**
Centralized weekly payroll system,
29:31.
Charitable contributions, **154:8,
180:17B.**
Checks.
See CHECKS.
Children or minors.
Child support assistance by
agency, withholding of
income, **119A:7.**
Stoppage of machinery, penalties
for violations as to
deductions from wages,
149:58.
Cities or towns, **41:41-41:43.**
Aldermen.
See ALDERMEN AND
SELECTMEN.
Auditors, approval, **41:52.**
Collective bargaining
organization's service fees,
180:17G.
Contents of payroll, **41:42.**
Council.
City council. See within this
heading, "City council."
Credit unions, deduction from
wages for payment,
149:178B.
Examination or inspection,
41:52.
Lighting plant payroll, approval,
164:56.

PAYROLL AND PAYROLL DEDUCTIONS —Cont'd

Cities or towns —Cont'd

Mayor, approval of delivery of payroll checks to department heads, **41:41A.**

Oath required, **41:41.**

Penalties, **41:43.**

Relief associations of municipal departments, dues payable, **180:17A.**

Treasurer.

City or town treasurer. See within this heading, "City or town treasurer."

City council.

Deductions for municipal employees, acceptance of statute, **180:17A, 180:17B.**

Requirements as to payrolls, **41:41-41:43.**

City or town treasurer, **44:41-44:43.**

Acceptance of statute, **180:17A, 180:17B.**

Checks, delivery to department heads, **41:41A.**

Credit unions or savings banks, payroll deductions, **149:178B.**

Employees' collective bargaining organization's service fees, deduction, **180:17G.**

Insurance premiums of school teachers, deduction and transmittal, **180:17D.**

Teachers.

See TEACHERS.

Civil service.

Centralized weekly payroll system, **29:31.**

Examination by administrator, **31:5.**

Community Chest, **180:17B.**

Construction contracts, **149:148.**

Public contractor to advise employees, **149:150A.**

Contributions, **180:17B, 180:17F.**

Authorized depository for credit union deductions from pay of public employees, **149:178B.**

Deduction deposits, **154:8.**

Direct deposit of wages, **41:41B.**

Co-operative banks.

See COOPERATIVE BANKS.

Counties.

Certification of payroll records, **35:19.**

Classification titles, **35:52.**

Notification as to payroll deductions of officers and employees, **35:19.**

PAYROLL AND PAYROLL DEDUCTIONS —Cont'd

Counties —Cont'd

Teachers' association of county, payroll deductions for dues, **180:17C.**

United fund, deduction for contributions of county employees, **180:17B.**

Credit unions.

See CREDIT UNIONS.

District employees, deduction from wages for payment to credit unions, **149:178B.**

Dues.

County teachers' association, payroll deductions, **180:17C.**

Massachusetts Nurses Association, dues payable, **180:17A.**

Pay slip requirements, **149:150A.**

School nurses, payroll deductions on account of dues to associations of public school teachers, **180:17E.**

State employees' association, **180:17A.**

Teachers' association dues, **180:17C.**

Union.

See LABOR RELATIONS AND DISPUTES.

Employment security.

Deductions from wages, notice, **149:150A.**

Definition, **151A:1.**

Examination, inspection, or investigation, **31:5, 41:52, 149:27B.**

Farm laborers, wage statements issued by farm labor contractors, requirements for contents, **149:168A.**

Federal income tax, withholding, **58:28A, 58:28B.**

Fines.

Penalties. See within this heading, "Penalties."

Garnishment.

Trustee process. See within this heading, "Trustee process."

Hospital service corporations, deductions for premiums, **154:8, 176A:27.**

Income tax, withholding of, **62B:1-62B:12.**

See WITHHOLDING OF TAX.

Insurance.

Accident or sickness insurance, premiums on blanket policies, **175:110.**

PAYROLL AND PAYROLL DEDUCTIONS —Cont'd

Insurance —Cont'd

Hospital service corporations, **154:8, 176A:27.**

Medical service corporations. See within this heading, "Medical service corporations, deductions."

Medical service plans, **176B:16A, 176C:16A.**

Premiums, deductions for, **154:8, 175:110, 180:17D, 180:17J.**

School teachers, **180:17D.**

Labor relations.

Dues and assessments.

See LABOR RELATIONS AND DISPUTES.

Lottery ticket purchases, **10:27.**

Mandatory retirement age, deductions from salaries of employees working past, **32:90G, 32:95A.**

Mayor, approval of delivery of checks to department heads, **41:41A.**

Medical service corporations, deductions, **176B:16A, 176C:16A.**

Wage assignment laws inapplicable, **154:8.**

Medical service plans, **176B:16A, 176C:16A.**

Municipalities.

Cities or towns. See within this heading, "Cities or towns."

New employees, **149:150A.**

Notice of wage deductions, **35:19, 149:150A.**

Nurses, dues, **180:17A, 180:17E.**

Oath to municipal payroll, persons authorized or designated to make, **41:41.**

Parking fees.

State employees.

Payroll deductions for near-site parking, **180:17K.**

Pay slip requirements, **149:148, 149:150A.**

Penalties.

Children or minors, deductions from wages for stoppage of machinery, **149:58.**

Neglect or refusal as to municipal payroll requirements, **41:43.**

Subscriptions to stock, penalty for failure to remit, **154:8.**

Tardiness, docking pay, **149:152.**

PAYROLL AND PAYROLL DEDUCTIONS —Cont'd

Pensions.
Retirement systems and pensions. See within this heading, "Retirement systems and pensions."
Postponement of pay increases of state employees, **30:46.**
Public works and departments.
Contracts, detailed records of payroll to be kept by contractor, **149:27B.**
Inspection of records, obtaining authorization, **149:27B.**
Qualified state tuition program, **180:17L.**
Regional school districts.
Bargaining association charges, **180:17G.**
Nurses, deductions on account of teachers' association dues, **180:17E.**
Relief associations of municipal departments, dues payable, **180:17A.**
Resignation of public employee prior to separation from payroll, **30:46.**
Retirement systems and pensions, **32:19, 32:19A, 32:22, 32:92.**
Mandatory retirement age, deductions from salaries of employees working past, **32:90G, 32:95A.**
Pay slip requirements, **149:150A.**
Savings banks.
Deposits, **154:8.**
Public employees, **149:178B.**
School teachers.
See TEACHERS.
State employees.
Dues for employees' association, **180:17A.**
Group insurance for state employees, **32A:8, 32A:10A-32A:10C, 175:138A.**
Massachusetts independent health agencies, deduction of contributions, **180:17F.**
Parking fees.
Payroll deductions for near-site parking, **180:17K.**
Postponement of pay increases, **30:46.**
United fund, deduction of contributions, **180:17B.**
Stock purchase plans, deductions, **154:8.**

PAYROLL AND PAYROLL DEDUCTIONS —Cont'd

Stopping of machinery, deductions from wages of women and children on account, **149:158.**
Subscriptions to stock, **154:8.**
Support of persons, wage assignment, **208:36, 209:32E.**
Tardiness to work, deductions, **149:152.**
Teachers.
See TEACHERS.
Time for payment over after deduction, **71:37B, 149:178B, 154:8.**
Towns.
Cities or towns. See within this heading, "Cities or towns."
Trust companies, deductions for deposit, **149:178B, 154:8.**
Trustee process.
Assignment, payroll deductions as valid, **154:8.**
Deposit, effect of wage deductions, **149:178B, 154:8.**
Exemption of payroll accounts from attachment, **246:20.**
Tuition.
Qualified state tuition program, **180:17L.**
Unemployment compensation.
Employment security. See within this heading, "Employment security."
Union.
Dues and assessments.
See LABOR RELATIONS AND DISPUTES.
United fund, deduction for contributions of state, county or town employees, **180:17B.**
Vacation, **149:150A.**
Withdrawal of authorization of deductions for contributions for Community Chest or United Fund, **180:17B.**
Withholding of tax, **62B:1-62B:12.**
See WITHHOLDING OF TAX.
Women, deductions from wages for stoppage of machinery, penalties for violations, **149:58.**

PCB.
Penalties for use, **94C:31.**

PEABODY.
Congressional district, **57:1.**
District court, **218:1.**
Medical examiner district, **38:1.**
Metropolitan air pollution control district, membership, **111:142B.**

PEABODY —Cont'd
Senatorial district, **57:3.**

PEABODY SCHOOL FOR GIRLS.
"Net maintenance sum," how determined, **74:1.**

PEACE BOND.
See THREATS.

PEACEFUL PERSUASION.
Procedure legalized, **149:24.**

PEACE OFFICERS.
Constables.
See CONSTABLES.
Justices of the peace.
See JUSTICES OF THE PEACE.
Police.
See POLICE.
Sheriffs.
See SHERIFFS AND DEPUTIES.

PEARL HARBOR DAY.
Observance, **6:12DD.**

PEAS.
Seed package label requirements, **128:87.**

PEA SHOOTERS.
Manufacture or sale, penalty, **269:12.**

PEDACYCLE.
Motor vehicles, attaching to outside of prohibited, **90:13.**

PEDDLERS, 101:1-101:30.
See TRANSIENT VENDORS.

PEDESTRIANS.
Traffic regulations.
See TRAFFIC REGULATIONS AND RULES OF THE ROAD.

PEDIATRICS.
AIDS advisory board, representation, **111:2F.**
Physical therapists, subject of examination for registration, **112:23E.**

PEDIGREE.
False pedigree of animals, **266:93.**

PEER REVIEW COMMITTEE.
Malpractice, **111:203, 111:204.**
Medical care and assistance, **111:1.**

PEEWEE EGGS.
Standard sizes in connection with sale and distribution of eggs, **94:90B.**

PELHAM.
Congressional district, **57:1.**
Medical examiner district, **38:1.**

PELHAM —Cont'd
Senatorial district, **57:3.**

PELLET GUN.
Children and minors, possession, **269:12B.**

PEMBROKE.
Congressional district, **57:1.**
District court, **218:1.**
Medical examiner district, **38:1.**
Senatorial district, **57:3.**

PENAL INSTITUTIONS, 125:1 et seq., 126:1 et seq., 127:1 et seq.
See CORRECTIONAL INSTITUTIONS.

PENAL SUM.
See PROBATE BONDS.

PENALTIES.
See FINES AND PENALTIES.

PENDING ACTIONS.
Abuse, pendente lite protection, **209A:4.**
Adoption of charter by city as affecting, **43:24.**
Alimony pendente lite, **208:17.**
Attachment of property.
 Insurance during pendency of delinquency proceeding, **175:180F.**
 Waste during pendency of action, jurisdiction to stay, **242:9.**
Consolidation of cross actions or actions arising out of same accident, event or transaction pending in district courts, **223:2A.**
Credit unions, consolidating credit unions, **171:78.**
Criminal cases.
 Extradition as affected by pending action, **276:20G, 276:20K.**
 Repeal of statute, effect, **281:6.**
Death.
 Executor or administrator death or removal from office during pendency of action, **230:11.**
 Fire district's action for penalties, effect of death of chief engineer, **48:78.**
Executors.
 See EXECUTORS AND ADMINISTRATORS.
Extradition.
 In state action pending, effect, **276:20G.**

PENDING ACTIONS —Cont'd
Extradition —Cont'd
 Out of state action pending, effect, **276:20K.**
Fire district's action for penalties, effect of death of chief engineer, **48:78.**
Lis pendens.
 See LIS PENDENS.
Registration of land titles.
 See REGISTRATION OF LAND TITLES.
Repeal of statute as affecting, **4:6, 281:6.**
Transfer to superior court where cross actions or actions arising out of same accident, event or transaction are pending in both superior and district courts, **223:2B.**
Trustee process.
 See TRUSTEE PROCESS.
Uniform Securities Act, registration of broker-dealers and agents as affected, **110A:204.**
Waste of property, **242:6.**
 Partition, waste during petition, **242:4.**
 Stay of waste during pending action, **242:9.**

PEN GUNS.
Sales, **140:131N.**

PENICILLIN.
State health department to furnish drugs for treatment of certain rheumatic fever patients, **111:14A.**

PENNSYLVANIA.
First Congress, representation in, **US Const Art 1 Sec 2 cl 3.**

PENSIONGENS, 32:1 et seq.

PENSION RESERVE FUND.
See RETIREMENT SYSTEMS AND PENSIONS.

PENSIONS.
Firemen, **32:80 et seq.**
Generally.
 See RETIREMENT SYSTEMS AND PENSIONS.
Laborers, **32:77 et seq.**
Policemen, **32:83 et seq.**

PEPPERELL.
Congressional district, **57:1.**
District court, **218:1.**
Medical examiner district, **38:1.**
Senatorial district, **57:3.**
Squannacook and Nissitissit Rivers Sanctuary established, **132A:17.**

PEPPER SPRAY.
Firearms identification card valid for purchasing and possessing, **140:129B.**
Firearms licenses and permits valid for purchasing and possessing, **140:131.**

PERCH, 131:22.

PEREMPTORY CHALLENGES.
See JURY AND JURY TRIAL.

PERFECTION OF SECURITY INTEREST.
See SECURED TRANSACTIONS.

PERFORMANCE BONDS, 30:39A-30:39E, 30:40, 43:29, 149:28, 149:29.
See CONSTRUCTION CONTRACTS AND WORK.

PERFORMANCE EVALUATIONS.
Appellate tax board, **58A:1.**
Banks.
 Examination of banks.
 See BANKS AND BANKING.
Civil service.
 See CIVIL SERVICE.
Teachers, **71:38.**

PERFUSIONISTS, 112:211 to 112:220.
Addresses.
 Residence and place of business, **112:220.**
Appeals.
 Complaint for review.
 Disciplinary proceedings, **112:215A.**
Applications for licenses, **112:213.**
Board of registration, **13:11E.**
 Defined, **112:211.**
 Duties, **112:212.**
 Powers, **112:212.**
 Record of proceedings, **112:219.**
 Roster of licensees, **112:219.**
 Rules and regulations, **112:219.**
Change of address, **112:220.**
Complaint for review.
 Disciplinary proceedings, **112:215A.**
Defined terms, **112:211.**
Disciplinary proceedings.
 Complaint for review, **112:215A.**
 Grounds, **112:215.**
Examinations, **112:214.**
False personation, **112:216.**
Fees.
 Applications for licenses, **112:213.**

PERFUSIONISTS —Cont'd

Licensing.

    Examinations, **112:214.**

    Exceptions to licensing
        provisions, **112:216.**

    Reciprocity, **112:217.**

    Requirements, **112:213.**

    Unlicensed practice, **112:216.**

Limitations on practice, **112:218.**

Practicing medicine.

    Limitations on practice, **112:218.**

Roster of licensees, **112:219.**

Unlicensed practice, **112:216.**

PERIODICALS.

**See MAGAZINES AND
    PERIODICALS.**

**PERIODIC WATERSHED
    MANAGEMENT PLANS.**

Adoption, **92:116.**

PERIOD IN GROSS, 184A:3.

Perpetuities, **184A:3.**

PERISHABLE PROPERTY.

Absentee's estate, sale of property,
    200:9.

Attached perishable property,
    appraisal and sale, **223:88,
    223:89, 223:92.**

Bradford Durfee College of
    Technology, purchases,
    74:42N.

Carriers, sale, **135:5.**

Forfeiture proceedings, sale,
    257:15.

Metropolitan district commission's
    sale of lost property, **92:92.**

Military stores, disposition,
    33:113.

New Bedford Institute of
    Technology, purchases,
    74:42N.

Pawnbrokers, sales, **140:71.**

Police custody, sale of property,
    135:9.

State colleges, purchases, **73:15.**

Sunday sale of foods, **136:6.**

Unfair Sales Act as applicable to
    sales, **93:14G.**

PERJURY, 268:1-268:6.

Accessory after fact, admissibility
    of perjury record to impeach
    credibility, **274:4.**

Accounts and accounting.

    Claim against city or town, false
        oath as to account, **41:52.**

    Constables, filing of accounting
        of fees received from service
        of civil process, **262:8A.**

Acupuncture, false oaths and
    representations, **112:159.**

PERJURY —Cont'd

Aid to families with dependent
    children, **118:2B, 118:3.**

Arrest on presumption, **268:4.**

Assessors' valuation lists,
    statements, **59:52.**

Asset management and
    maintenance, disclosure
    statements filed with
    commissioner, **7:40J.**

Associations, reports by, to be
    signed under penalty of
    perjury, **182:12.**

Bail bonds, statements by sureties,
    276:61.

Books necessary to prosecution,
    detention, **268:5.**

Campaign expenditures and
    contributions, false affidavit,
    55:18.

Capital cases, perjury, **268:1.**

Certificates and certification.

    County payroll records,
        certification of under
        penalty of perjury, **35:19.**

    Public work plans or
        specifications, certificates
        authorizing deviations,
        30:39H.

Charitable corporations, officer,
    180:26A.

Civil service.

    Annual list by appointing
        officers, **31:67.**

    Applicants for examination,
        statements required, **31:20.**

    Examinations, **31:16.**

Claim against municipality, **41:52.**

Commission on Judicial Conduct,
    failure to sign complaint as
    perjury, **211C:2.**

Commitment on presumption,
    268:4.

Constables, filing of accounting of
    fees received from service of
    civil process, **262:8A.**

Contracts and agreements,
    Commonwealth, disclosure
    statements in contracts, **7A:6.**

County payroll records,
    certification of under penalty
    of perjury, **35:19.**

Criminal offense, **268:1, 268:2.**

Death of terminally ill patient,
    pronouncement by registered
    nurses, **46:9.**

Deputy sheriffs, filing of
    accounting of fees received for
    service of civil process,
    262:8A.

Disclosure statements.

    Contracts with Commonwealth,
        7A:6.

PERJURY —Cont'd

Disclosure statements —Cont'd

    Financial disclosure by public
        officers and employees. See
        within this heading,
        "Financial disclosure by
        public officers and
        employees."

Divorce suits, perjury, **208:41.**

Documents necessary to
    prosecution, detention, **268:5.**

Drugs.

    Fraud or false statements.

        See DRUGS AND
            NARCOTICS.

Election offenses.

    Innholder's or lodginghouse
        keeper's report, **51:10A.**

    Registration of voters. See
        within this heading,
        "Registration of voters."

Elections.

    Clean elections law.

        Reports filed subject to
            penalty of perjury,
            55A:15.

Employment agency registers,
    entries, **140:46J.**

Employment security, perjury in
    testifying, **151A:43.**

Engineer's registration, false
    swearing to obtain, **112:81T.**

Financial disclosure by public
    officers and employees.

    Penalties, **268B:7.**

    Statement of financial interest
        signed under penalty of
        perjury, **268B:5.**

    Sworn complaint, **268B:4.**

Fire insurance, false oath as to
    subscriptions to mutual
    company as perjury, **175:73.**

Fires, investigation, **148:3.**

General Court.

    Committees, oath administered
        by members, **3:27, 3:63.**

    Testimony before general court
        or committees, **3:28.**

Hospice program patient,
    pronouncement of death by
    registered nurses, **46:9.**

Immunity granted to witness as
    affecting prosecution,
    233:20D, 233:20G.

Indictment, **277:43.**

    Form, **277:79.**

    Subornation, **277:44.**

Insurance.

    See INSURANCE.

Judicial conduct commission,
    failure to sign complaint as
    perjury, **211C:2.**

PERJURY —Cont'd

Judicial proceedings, **268:1.**

Labor relations commission, witnesses before, **150A:7.**

Land surveyor's registration, false swearing to obtain, **112:81T.**

Licenses and permits, **140:32B.**

Life insurance, false statement as perjury, **175:127.**

Materiality requirement, **268:1.**

Medical assistance program vouchers, signature, **6:131G, 118E:20.**

Motor vehicle theft and fraudulent insurance claims, procedures concerning, **266:29.**

Municipal lighting plants, claim against, **164:56.**

Narcotics.

See DRUGS AND NARCOTICS.

Nurses' pronouncement of death of terminally ill patient, **46:9.**

Papers necessary to prosecution, detention, **268:5.**

Pensions.

Retirement systems and pensions. See within this heading, "Retirement systems and pensions, statements."

Presumption of perjury, commitment, **268:4.**

Public assistance.

See WELFARE AND SOCIAL SERVICES.

Public officers and employees.

Civil service. See within this heading, "Civil service."

Financial disclosure by public officers and employees. See within this heading, "Financial disclosure by public officers and employees."

Testimony, **268A:4, 268A:11, 268A:17.**

Quaker or Friend as subject to penalties of perjury when serving as witness by affirmation, **233:17.**

Rebates, perjury in prosecution for giving, **175:183.**

Recognizances, statements by sureties, **276:61.**

Registrar of motor vehicles, perjury in proceedings on appeal, **90:28.**

Registration of voters, **56:1, 56:6, 56:7.**

Penalty, **56:6, 56:7.**

Revision and correction of registers, qualification of voters, **51:38.**

PERJURY —Cont'd

Registration of voters —Cont'd

Subsequent examination of registrants for cause, **51:47B.**

Reports under oath, false statements, **268:6.**

Retention of documents where perjury suspected, **268:5.**

Retirement systems and pensions, statements, **32:18.**

Natural guardian's account of accidental death benefit, **32:9.**

Subornation of perjury, **268:2, 268:3.**

Attempt, **268:3.**

Grand jury investigation, immunity of witness appearing during, **233:20D.**

Indictment, **277:44.**

Punishment, **268:2.**

Sureties on bail bonds and recognizances, **276:61.**

Terminally ill patient, pronouncement of death by registered nurses, **46:9.**

Unemployment compensation, **151A:43.**

Verification of instruments, **268:1A.**

Veterinarian's statement that dog has been spayed, **140:139.**

Welfare.

See WELFARE AND SOCIAL SERVICES.

Written affirmation or oath, **268:1A.**

PERKINS SCHOOL FOR THE BLIND.

Fund raising activities for benefit of the blind, provisions as to inapplicable, **6:142.**

PERMANENT INCAPACITY.

Workers' compensation, **152:34, 152:34A.**

See WORKERS' COMPENSATION.

PERMITS.

See LICENSES AND PERMITS.

PERPETUAL CARE.

Cemeteries.

See CEMETERIES.

PERPETUAL SUCCESSION.

Business corporations, perpetual succession to corporate name, **156:4, 156B:9.**

PERPETUATION OF TESTIMONY.

Depositions, **233:46-233:63.**

See DEPOSITIONS.

PERPETUITIES, RULE AGAINST, 184A:1 et seq.

Age contingency, when reduced, **184A:2.**

Benefit plans for employees, trust forming, **184A:4.**

Class gift, validity, **184A:3.**

Conditional fee, when to become fee simple absolute, **184A:3.**

Construction of chapter, **184A:5.**

Contingent remainders as subject, **184A:3.**

Contract to make or not to revoke will or trust, **184A:4.**

Determinable fee, when to become fee simple absolute, **184A:3, 184A:5.**

Divorce or separation settlements, **184A:4.**

Easements, **184A:5.**

Electric companies' property held in common, restraints on alienation, **164:99A.**

Employees, exemption of pension and profit-sharing plans, **203:3A.**

Fee simple determination, **184A:3, 184A:5.**

Fiduciaries, power to appoint, **184A:4.**

"Heirs" or "next of kin," determination of class in limitation of property to class described, **184:6A.**

Legal and equitable interest, chapter applicable, **184A:4.**

Life estate defined, **184A:1.**

Power of appointment created, **184A:2.**

Preemptive rights regarding interest in land or minerals, **184A:5.**

Premarital or postmarital agreements, **184A:4.**

Right of entry for condition broken, fee simple subject to, when to become fee simple absolute, **184A:3.**

Severability of provisions of chapter, **184A:6.**

PER PROCHEIN AMI PLAINTIFFS.

See NEXT FRIEND.

PERRY ACT, 30:59.

Suspension of employee, **30:59.**

PERSIAN GULF VETERAN.

Defined, **4:7.**

U.S. Massachusetts Honor Roll for citizens who died in Persian Gulf **6:124A.**

PERSONAL DATA OR INFORMATION.
Checks, personal identification information, **93:105.**
Credit cards, personal identification information, **93:105.**
Fair information practices.
See FAIR INFORMATION PRACTICES.
Words and phrases, personal information, **175I:2.**

PERSONAL INJURIES.
Abused.
See ABUSED AND NEGLECTED CHILDREN.
Advance payments to party claiming or suing for damages, effect, **231:140B.**
Aqueducts, **165:27.**
Attorneys at law.
Furnishing copies of written statement as to injuries, **233:23A.**
Hospital employees prohibited from furnishing information to attorneys concerning, **221:44A, 221:44B.**
Automobile insurance.
See AUTOMOBILE INSURANCE.
Bills for medical, dental, or hospital services in personal injury actions, admissibility, **233:79G, 233:79H.**
Blasting, liability for resulting damages without proof of negligence, **148:20C.**
Building code of state, liability of owner or occupant of building for injuries from violations, **143:51.**
Burns.
See BURNS.
Cause of injury.
See CAUSE OF INJURY OR ACCIDENT.
Civil service.
Injuries.
See CIVIL SERVICE.
Coal mine to carry insurance against, **21B:5.**
Contribution among joint tortfeasors.
See CONTRIBUTION AMONG JOINT TORTFEASORS.
Contributory negligence, amount of damages as affected, **231:85.**
Dalkon Shield Claimants Trust, limitation of actions for claims, **260:2E.**

PERSONAL INJURIES —Cont'd
Damages.
See DAMAGES.
Death, actions for injuries resulting in.
See WRONGFUL DEATH.
Defective sewer cover, complaint of motorist for injuries, **Spec L 17:3 Form 1.**
Dental service corporations, liability, **176E:14.**
Dogs.
See DOGS.
Evidence.
Bills for medical, dental, or hospital services, admissibility, **233:79G, 233:79H.**
Justifiable injury of persons unlawfully in dwelling, **231:85T.**
Written statements, **233:23A, 271:44.**
Executors.
Highway or street defects.
See EXECUTORS AND ADMINISTRATORS.
Judgments and decrees.
See EXECUTORS AND ADMINISTRATORS.
Explosives, damages from illegal use, storage, and transportation, **148:22.**
Firemen absent from duty on legal holidays because of personal injuries, **48:57D.**
First aid.
See EMERGENCIES.
Fraudulent claims board, investigative powers, **26:8B.**
Grand jury investigations concerning fraudulent personal injury claims, immunity of witnesses during, **233:20D.**
Hazardous waste insolvency fund, definition of covered claim, **21C:15.**
Health care providers, actions against, availability of information, personal injury listings, **93:95-93:100.**
Highways.
Defects.
See HIGHWAYS AND STREETS.
Hospitals.
See HOSPITALS AND HEALTH CARE FACILITIES.
Ice.
Injury.
See SNOW AND ICE.

PERSONAL INJURIES —Cont'd
Interest on damages awarded, **231:6B.**
Jurors, **268:13B.**
Juvenile delinquent, restitution, **119:62.**
Labor and employment, **153:1-153:9.**
See LABOR AND WORKFORCE DEVELOPMENT.
Limitation of actions, **260:2A-260:4, 260:4B.**
Limitation of consequential damages caused to buyer, **106:2-719.**
Listings.
See MEDICAL CARE AND ASSISTANCE.
Maiming.
See MAIMING.
Malicious mischief.
See MALICIOUS MISCHIEF OR INJURY.
Medical records, **233:79G, 233:79H.**
Medical service corporation, charges and fees for services, **176B:7.**
Mentally ill patient, restraint, **123:21.**
Motor vehicles.
Accidents.
See MOTOR VEHICLES.
Optometric service corporations, liability, **176F:14.**
Parents' liability for injuries caused by willful acts of minor children, **231:85G.**
Personal jurisdiction based upon causing tortuous injury in Commonwealth, **223A:3.**
Physical exercise training programs, willful, wanton or reckless causing of serious bodily injury in, **265:40.**
Physicians, liability of doctors rendering emergency treatment, **112:12B.**
Police.
Injury or death.
See POLICE.
Public aid, assignment of certain funds by persons requiring, **118:11.**
Public construction, validity of indemnification provision, **149:29C.**
Public ways, defects, **84:15-84:27A.**
Railroads.
Accidents.
See RAILROADS.

PERSONAL INJURIES —Cont'd

Recording instruments, admissibility in personal injury action of statements taken, **233:23A.**

Ski patrol members providing emergency care, treatment, or transportation, liability, **231:85I.**

Snow.
See SNOW AND ICE.

Streets.
Defects.
See HIGHWAYS AND STREETS.

Students, exemption from liability for emergency first aid or transportation rendered to injured students, **71:55A.**

Sunday law as defense to action, **136:11.**

Survival of action, **228:1.**

Trials or other criminal proceedings, injuries to jurors or witnesses, **268:13B.**

Underground storage tank petroleum product cleanup fund, **21J:4, 21J:9.**

Uninsured motorist causing personal injuries, compulsory insurance coverage against, **175:113L.**

Unsafe condition in rented or leased property, landlord's liability in damages for personal injuries after failure to correct after notice, **186:19.**

Venue of action, **223:7.**

Welfare recipients' assignment of receipts, **118:11.**

Witnesses, injuries, **268:13B.**

Workers' compensation.
See WORKERS' COMPENSATION.

Written statements of injured persons, **233:23A, 271:44.**

Wrongful death.
See WRONGFUL DEATH.

PERSONAL JURISDICTION.
See JURISDICTION.

PERSONAL LEAVE.
Justices, **211B:4.**

PERSONAL LIBERTY.

Divorce, protection of personal liberty of wife during pendency, **208:18.**

Guaranty of, **US Const 5th Amend, 14th Amend.**

Proceedings to obtain, **248:1 et seq.**
See HABEAS CORPUS.

PERSONAL LIBERTY —Cont'd

Separate maintenance proceedings, protection, **209:32.**

PERSONAL NEEDS.

Public assistance recipients, retention of income, **118E:10 note, 177:8 note.**

PERSONAL PROPERTY.

Abandoned property.
See ABANDONED, LOST, AND UNCLAIMED PROPERTY.

Abandoned spouse of either sex authorized to sell, convey or receive certain property, **209:30.**

Accountant, working papers as property, **112:87E.**

Acts against persons and properties, prohibition, **265:39, 266:127A, 266:127B.**

Advancements, **196:3.**

After-acquired property.
See AFTER-ACQUIRED PROPERTY.

Antitrust laws, **93:2.**

Appropriations to reimburse certain employees for certain personal property loss or damage, cities and towns authorized to make, **40:5.**

Aqueduct companies, conveyance of property in payment for capital stock, **165:14.**

Arrest on mesne process.
Property of defendant.
See ARREST ON MESNE PROCESS AND SUPPLEMENTARY PROCEEDINGS.

Asset management board.
See ASSET MANAGEMENT BOARD.

Attachment of property.
See ATTACHMENT OF PROPERTY.

Auctions.
See AUCTIONS AND AUCTIONEERS.

Bailments.
See BAILMENTS.

Banks.
Property.
See BANKS AND BANKING.

Bradford Durfee College of Technology, powers of trustees, **74:42L, 74:42M.**

Burning as criminal offense, **266:2, 266:5, 266:10.**

Charitable organizations.
Authority to hold personal property, **180:6.**

PERSONAL PROPERTY
—Cont'd

Charitable organizations —Cont'd
Taxation of personal property, **59:5.**

Cheating, offense of obtaining property, **266:75, 266:76.**

Checking rooms.
See CHECKING ROOMS.

Churches.
Religion and religious societies.
See within this heading, "Religion and religious societies."

Cities and towns.
Insurance, **40:5.**
Power to hold and dispose of personal property, **40:3, 40:21.**

Community economic development assistance corporation, powers, **40H:4.**

Concealed property.
See CONCEALMENT.

Condemnation.
Eminent domain. See within this heading, "Eminent domain."

Constables.
Limitation of actions against constable for seizure or conversion, **260:4.**
Service of notice of termination of lease, **231:85H.**

Conversion of funds.
See CONVERSION OF FUNDS OR PROPERTY.

Corporations.
See CORPORATIONS.

Correctional institutions.
Property and funds of prisoners.
See CORRECTIONAL INSTITUTIONS.

Cushing Hospital, personal property of patients or residents, **111:64K.**

Custody.
See CUSTODY AND CUSTODIANS OF PROPERTY.

Dead body, delivery of property found, **38:15.**

Default involving security covering real and personal property, **106:9-501.**

Definition, **150A:1.**

Descent and distribution, **190:2.**
See DESCENT AND DISTRIBUTION.

Destruction of property.
See DESTRUCTION OF PROPERTY.

PERSONAL PROPERTY
—Cont'd
Disclaimer, interest in property defined for purpose, **191A:1.**
Electric companies.
Property.
See GAS AND ELECTRIC COMPANIES.
Eminent domain.
Damages for injury to or taking of personal property, **79:10.**
Removal from property taken, **79:1, 79:13, 79:14, 81:22.**
Executions, **235:28 et seq.**
Bonds, personal property attached in award of execution in action, **223:97.**
Keeper of property taken on execution, appointment, **223:48.**
Trustee process.
See TRUSTEE PROCESS.
Executors.
See EXECUTORS AND ADMINISTRATORS.
Exemption from claims of creditors.
See EXEMPTION FROM CLAIMS OF CREDITORS.
Federal liens, uniform procedure for recording or filing, **36:24, 185:46, 185:78, 185:80.**
Fees.
Entry of petition for sale of real or personal estate, **262:40.**
Filing attachment of bulky personal property, **262:34.**
Recording fees, **262:34.**
Services of officer on judicial sale, **262:8.**
Fraudulent pledge by consignee or factor, offense, **266:88.**
Garnishment.
See TRUSTEE PROCESS.
Gas.
Property.
See GAS AND ELECTRIC COMPANIES.
Goods.
See GOODS OR COMMODITIES.
Guardians.
See GUARDIANS, CONSERVATORS, AND COMMITTEES.
Historical commission, **9:26, 40:8D.**
Holidays, motor transport of goods in commerce, **136:14.**
Hotels.
See HOTELS, MOTELS, AND ROOMINGHOUSES.

PERSONAL PROPERTY
—Cont'd
Household furniture and effects, exemption from personal property tax, **59:5.**
Identity.
See IDENTIFICATION.
Industrial development facilities, municipal transfer of property, **40D:19.**
Insurance.
See INSURANCE.
Judicial sales, **235:36-235:45.**
See JUDICIAL SALES.
Leased property.
See BAILMENTS.
Licenses for sale of property, information contained, **65C:14.**
Liens.
See LIENS AND ENCUMBRANCES.
Limited partnership interest, **109:39.**
Lost property.
See ABANDONED, LOST, AND UNCLAIMED PROPERTY.
Malicious mischief.
Wanton or willful injuries to, **266:127.**
Marine resources, trust funds for purpose of protection, **130:17.**
Medical care and assistance applicant, effect of transfer of personal property, **118E:13.**
Militia, **33:98-33:116.**
See MILITIA.
Morris plan banks.
See MORRIS PLAN BANKS.
Municipal conservation commissions' authority to acquire, **40:8C.**
Municipal historical commissions, powers, **40:8D.**
Municipalities.
Cities and towns. See within this heading, "Cities and towns."
New Bedford Institute of Technology powers of trustees, **74:42L, 74:42M.**
Nuncupative will disposing, **191:6.**
Obtaining goods under pretense of carrying on business, **266:73.**
Partnerships.
See PARTNERSHIPS.
Pawnbroker's loans, **140:76.**
Perishable property.
See PERISHABLE PROPERTY.
Prisoners.
See CORRECTIONAL INSTITUTIONS.

PERSONAL PROPERTY
—Cont'd
Probate decrees relating to sale of property, information contained, **202:37.**
Professional corporation's right to own, **156A:4.**
Recreation and snow vehicles as personal property for tax purposes, **90B:31.**
Religion and religious societies.
Pews, **67:38.**
Proprietors of meeting houses may hold personalty, **67:25.**
Society may hold personal property, **67:21.**
Removal of property.
See REMOVAL OF PROPERTY.
Restraints of trade and monopolies, **93:2.**
Return of property.
See RETURN OF PROPERTY.
Savings bank, sale or liquidation, **167:24, 167:25.**
Spouses of certain deceased persons, disposition of property, **196:1, 196:2, 200:1, 200:10.**
State colleges, gifts, **73:14.**
State hospitals.
See STATE HOSPITALS.
Stolen property.
See LARCENY AND THEFT.
Street railways.
Increase of capital stock or issue of bonds for acquiring personal property, **161:25.**
Lease, purchase, or sale, departmental approval, **159:54.**
Power to hold personalty, **161:41.**
Tangible personal property defined, **64H:1, 64I:1.**
Taxation.
See TAXATION.
Technology development corporation, powers, **40G:3.**
Tewksbury hospital.
See TEWKSBURY HOSPITAL.
Title.
See TITLE AND OWNERSHIP.
Towns.
Cities and towns. See within this heading, "Cities and towns."
Trackless trolley companies may hold, **163:11.**
Trustee process.
See TRUSTEE PROCESS.
Trusts.
See TRUSTS AND TRUSTEES.

PERSONAL PROPERTY
—Cont'd
Tuberculosis institutions, conveyance of property to Commonwealth, **111:83.**
Use tax.
See USE, CONSUMPTION, OR STORAGE TAX.
Worthier title to property doctrine, abolition, **184:33A, 184:33B.**

PERSONAL PROTECTION INSURANCE LAW, 90:34M.

PERSONAL RECOGNIZANCE.
Appeal of refusal to grant, **276:58.**
Conditions, **276:65.**
Release without surety, procedure, **276:58.**

PERSONAL REPRESENTATIVES.
See FIDUCIARIES.

PERSONAL RESPONSIBILITY AND WORK OPPORTUNITY, FEDERAL ACT.
Benefits to aliens or citizens within meaning of provisions, **6A:16C.**

PERSONAL SERVICE OF PROCESS.
See PROCESS AND SERVICE OF PROCESS AND PAPERS.

PERSONAL SERVICES.
Abandonment of property deposited to secure payment or performance, **200A:4.**
Contracts, termination, **255:13K.**
Day of rest and Sunday laws inapplicable to persons engaged, **149:50.**
Degree-granting institutions as exempt from contract cancellation provisions, **255:13K.**
Notice to beneficiary of right to terminate personal services contract, **255:13K.**
Owner-operator of motor carrier equipment, separate payment for services and for hire of equipment, **159B:6A.**
Seller's place of business, cancellation of contracts for personal services not entered into, **93:48.**
Speedy trial of actions, **231:59A.**

PERSONATION.
False personation.
See FALSE PERSONATION.

PERSONNEL ADMINISTRATOR.
Civil service.
Occupational injuries.
Development and maintenance of information regarding, **30:46I.**
Civil service commission, **7:28, 30:49, 30:57.**
Firefighters and police officers, physical fitness, **31:61A, 32:5.**
Occupational injuries.
Developing and maintaining information, **30:46I.**

PERSONNEL AND STANDARDIZATION BUREAU.
See ADMINISTRATION AND FINANCE EXECUTIVE OFFICE.

PERSONNEL APPEALS BOARD, 30:53, 30:57.
Classification of office or position of state employees, appeals, **30:49.**
Decisions, **30:57.**
Director of personnel and standardization, duties, **30:57.**
Executive office for administration and finance, agencies within, **7:4G.**
Jurisdiction, **30:53.**

PERSONNEL BOARDS OR DIVISIONS.
Administrative division.
See ADMINISTRATION AND FINANCE EXECUTIVE OFFICE.
Appeals board.
See PERSONNEL APPEALS BOARD.
County officers and employees, **35:48 et seq.**
See COUNTY OFFICERS AND EMPLOYEES.

PERSONNEL RECORDS BUREAU.
Human resources division, bureau within, **7:4J.**

PERSONNEL SYSTEMS.
Municipal personnel systems, **31A:1 et seq.**

PERSUASION.
Peaceful persuasion legalized, **149:24.**

PERTUSSIS.
School children, immunization, **76:15.**

PERU.
District court held, **218:1.**
Medical examiner district, **38:1.**
Senatorial district, **57:3.**

PERVERSION.
Obscenity and lewdness, **272:16, 272:28-272:32, 272:53, 272:61, 277:45, 277:79.**
See OBSCENITY AND LEWDNESS.

PESTICIDES, 132B:1 et seq.
Actions for purpose of protecting natural resources and environment, **214:7A.**
Active ingredient, defined, **132B:2.**
Adjudicatory hearings, **132B:13.**
Adulterated food, raw agricultural commodity containing pesticide, **94:186.**
Adulterated pesticides, defined, **132B:2.**
Advisory council, **132B:2.**
Stakeholder work group, **132B:7A.**
Agencies.
Defined, **132B:2.**
Use reporting system, **132B:7A.**
Agricultural commodity, defined, **132B:2.**
Agriculture Department.
Food and Agriculture Department. See within this heading, "Food and Agriculture Department."
Alternative methods.
Promotion, **132B:5A.**
Animal, defined, **132B:2.**
Anti-microbial pesticides.
Defined, **132B:2.**
Review.
Schools and day care centers, applicability, **132B:6K.**
Applications.
Experimental use permits, **132B:8.**
Licensed pesticide dealers, **132B:9.**
Registration of pesticides, **132B:7.**
Reporting system, use, **132B:7A.**
Arsenic, **270:12.**
Beneficial insects, defined, **132B:2.**
Biological controls.
Alternative methods, promotion, **132B:5A.**
Board of pesticides, **132B:3, 132B:5.**
Lands and Natural Resources Office, licensing, **41:69G.**
Brands and labels.
Alteration, etc., **132B:6.**
Defined, **132B:2.**

PESTICIDES —Cont'd
Brands and labels —Cont'd
Misbranding, **132B:2.**
Certification to use pesticides, **132B:10.**
Certified applicator, defined, **132B:2.**
Cities and towns, state furnishing with supplies of pesticides, **132:16.**
Civil service status of director of programs, **132B:4.**
Commercial applicator.
Defined, **132B:2.**
Pesticide control board, member, **132B:3.**
Compensation of board of pesticide control, **132B:3.**
Contracts with governmental agencies, **132B:5.**
Control of, **132B:1 et seq.**
Cooperative agreements with governmental agencies, **132B:5.**
Day care centers.
Anti-microbial pesticides.
Review for applicability, **132B:6K.**
Application restrictions, **132B:6C.**
Compliance with application requirements, **28A:10C.**
Defined, **132B:2.**
Emergency applications, **132B:6H.**
Indoor use, products eligible, **132B:6F.**
Integrated pest management plans, **132B:6E.**
Notice of application, **132B:6C.**
Outdoor use, products eligible, **132B:6G.**
Records of applications, **132B:6I.**
Rules and regulations, enforcement, **132B:14A.**
Training programs exempted, **132B:6J.**
Dealers.
Distribution of pesticides. See within this heading, "Distribution of pesticides."
Death of holder of license to use pesticides, **132B:10.**
Definitions, **132B:2, 132B:3.**
Defoliant, defined, **132B:2.**
Desiccant, defined, **132B:2.**
Devise, defined, **132B:2.**
Director.
Program director. See within this heading, "Program director."

PESTICIDES —Cont'd
Disposal of pesticides, **132B:11.**
Distribution of pesticides, **132B:1 et seq.**
Defined, **132B:2.**
Licensed pesticide dealers. See within this heading, "Licensed pesticide dealers."
Penalties for violation, **132B:14.**
Prohibition as to certain pesticides, **132B:6.**
Enforcement of chapter, **132B:14A.**
Environmental affairs executive office, duties, **21A:2, 21A:8.**
Environment, defined, **132B:2.**
Examinations relating to certifications and licenses to use pesticides, **132B:10.**
Experimental use permits, **132B:8.**
Issuance, **132B:3A.**
Federally registered pesticide, defined, **132B:2.**
Federal standards, **132B:2.**
Fees.
Certifications and licenses to use pesticides, **132B:10.**
Experimental use permits, **132B:8.**
Licensed pesticide dealers, **132B:9.**
Registration of pesticides, **132B:7.**
FIFRA, defined, **132B:2.**
Fines, **132B:14A.**
Food and Agriculture Department, **132B:5.**
Commissioner as member of pesticide control board, **132B:3.**
Promulgation of forms for control, **132B:5.**
Funds.
Children and families protection fund, **132B:16.**
Fungi, defined, **132B:2.**
General use, classification, **132B:7.**
Governmental bodies.
Reporting system, use, **132B:7A.**
Hearings, adjudicatory hearings, **132B:13.**
Imminent hazard.
Defined, **132B:2.**
Determinations provisionally effective, **132B:13.**
Orders requiring production of samples and records, **132B:12.**
Inert ingredient, defined, **132B:2.**
Insect, defined, **132B:2.**
Integrated pest management.
Alternative methods, promotion, **132B:5A.**

PESTICIDES —Cont'd
Integrated pest management —Cont'd
Defined, **132B:2.**
Registration requirements, **132B:10.**
Integrated pest management plans.
Schools and day care centers, **132B:6E.**
Labels.
Brands and labels. See within this heading, "Brands and labels."
Land, defined, **132B:2.**
Lands and Natural Resources Office, **41:69G.**
Licensed pesticide dealers.
Applications, **132B:8.**
Defined, **132B:2.**
Possession of currently valid license, **132B:6.**
Licenses and permits.
Registration or licensing. See within this heading, "Registration or licensing."
Licensing of Lands and Natural Resources Office, **41:69G.**
Membership of Board of Pesticide Control, **132B:3, 132B:3A.**
Misbranding, **132B:2.**
Negligence in placement of rat poison, **270:3A.**
Nematode, defined, **132B:2.**
Notice.
Application near schools or day care centers, **132B:6C, 132B:6D.**
Assessment of penalty, **132B:14A.**
Orders requiring production of samples and records, **132B:12.**
Packaging, **132B:11.**
Penalties for violation, **132B:14.**
Pest, defined, **132B:2.**
Pesticide, defined, **132B:2.**
Plant regulator, defined, **132B:2.**
Pollution by pesticides, **12:11D, 21A:2, 21A:8, 214:7A.**
Private applicator, defined, **132B:2.**
Produced, defined, **132B:2.**
Program director, **132B:4.**
Secretary of Pesticide Board, **132B:3.**
Protect health and the environment, defined, **132B:2.**
Quorum, board of pesticide control, **132B:3.**
Rat poison, careless placement, **270:3A.**

PESTICIDES —Cont'd

Raw agricultural commodity containing, **94:186.**

Reciprocity relating to certifications and licenses to use pesticides, **132B:10.**

Registrant, defined, **132B:2.**

Registration or licensing, **132B:7, 132B:10.**

Experimental use permits. See within this heading, "Experimental use permits."

Judicial review, **132B:13.**

Lands and Natural Resources Office, **41:69G.**

Licensed pesticide dealers. See within this heading, "Licensed pesticide dealers."

Registrant, defined, **132B:2.**

Renewals. See within this heading, "Renewals."

Revocation or suspension. See within this heading, "Revocation or suspension of registration."

Removal, programs director, **132B:4.**

Renewals.

Certifications and licenses to use pesticides, **132B:10.**

Licensed pesticide dealers, **132B:9.**

Reporting system, use, **132B:7A.**

Restricted use, classification, **132B:7.**

Revocation or suspension of registration.

Experimental use permits, **132B:8.**

Licensed pesticide dealers, **132B:9.**

Registration of pesticides, **132B:7.**

Use pesticides, certifications and licenses, **132B:10.**

Rules and regulations.

Schools and day care centers, enforcement, **132B:14A.**

Salaries and compensation of board of pesticide control, **132B:3.**

Sale or transfer of property, **64H:6.**

Sales tax, **64H:6.**

Schools.

Anti-microbial pesticides. Review for applicability, **132B:6K.**

Application restrictions, **132B:6C.**

Compliance with application requirements, **71:68.**

PESTICIDES —Cont'd

Schools —Cont'd

Defined, **132B:2.**

Emergency applications, **132B:6H.**

Indoor use, products eligible, **132B:6F.**

Integrated pest management plans, **132B:6E.**

Notice of application, **132B:6C.**

Outdoor use, products eligible, **132B:6G.**

Records of applications, **132B:6I.**

Rules and regulations, enforcement, **132B:14A.**

Training programs exempted, **132B:6J.**

Scientific experimental use, pesticide law's applicability to substances intended, **132B:3A.**

Search and seizure, **132B:15.**

Secretary of Board of Pesticide Control, programs director, **132B:3.**

Short title, **132B:1.**

Stakeholder work group, **132B:7A.**

Standards, power of food and agriculture department relating, **132B:5.**

State furnishing municipalities with supply, **132:16.**

Storage, **132B:11.**

Subcommittee of Pesticide Board, **132B:3A.**

Superior court jurisdiction relating to violations, **132B:14.**

Suspension of license.

Revocation or suspension. See within this heading, "Revocation or suspension of registration."

Sustainable agriculture.

Alternative methods, promotion, **132B:5A.**

Terms of office.

Board of Pesticide Control, **132B:3.**

Programs director, pesticide, **132B:4.**

Tort liability for discharges into water, **91:59A.**

Under the direct supervision of a certified applicator, defined, **132B:2.**

Use of pesticides consistent with regulations, **132B:6A.**

Violations, penalties, **132B:14.**

Votes and voting, board of pesticide control, **132B:3.**

Weed, defined, **132B:2.**

Wildlife, defined, **132B:2.**

PESTILENCE.

Removal of prisoners in case, **126:26.**

PETER FRANCISCO DAY.

Holiday, **4:7.**

Observance, **6:12S.**

PETERSHAM.

Congressional district, **57:1.**

District court, **218:1.**

Medical examiner district, **38:1.**

Senatorial district, **57:3.**

PETITIONS.

Abatement of taxes on certain abandoned real property, expedited procedure, **58:8.**

Adoption of children.

See ADOPTION OF CHILDREN.

Alcoholic liquors.

See ALCOHOLIC LIQUORS.

Antitrust laws, **93:8.**

Appellate tax board, **58A:7.**

Attorneys at law.

Examinations for admission to bar.

See ATTORNEYS AT LAW.

Removal of attorney, petition, **221:40.**

Banks, petition for review of commissioner's findings regarding unfair or deceitful consumer transaction practices, **167:2D-167:2F.**

Building code of state, amendments, **143:97.**

Buildings, petition to restrain illegal construction or alteration, **143:57.**

Change of name.

Petitions for change, **210:12.**

General court, petition, **3:5.**

Charities.

See CHARITIES AND CHARITABLE CONTRIBUTIONS.

Cities.

See CITIES AND TOWNS.

Civil service.

See CIVIL SERVICE.

Complaint.

See COMPLAINT.

Conservators.

See GUARDIANS, CONSERVATORS, AND COMMITTEES.

Constitution of Massachusetts.

Initiative and referendum.

See CONSTITUTION OF MASSACHUSETTS.

PETITIONS —Cont'd
County charter procedures act,
**34A:3, 34A:4, 34A:11,
34A:13-34A:16.**
County commissioners, fee for
filing of petition, **262:4A.**
Credit unions, reduction of
account, **171:52.**
Dams.
Damages.
See DAMS AND
RESERVOIRS.
Easements.
Action to try rights, petition to
require, **240:1.**
Land court, fee for examination
of title on petition to
register easements, **262:39.**
Educational institution's power to
grant degrees, revocation or
suspension, **69:30A.**
Employment security.
Assignment of error against
petition for judgment for
delinquent contributions,
151A:15.
Reassessment, hearing on
petition, **151A:15.**
Review, petition, **151A:42.**
Energy facilities siting.
Certificate of environmental
impact and public need,
petition to council, **164:69K.**
Eminent domain power, right to
petition for exercise,
164:69R, 164:69S.
National pollutant discharge
elimination system permit,
petition, **164:69H.**
Executors.
See EXECUTORS AND
ADMINISTRATORS.
Fees.
See FEES.
Fiduciaries.
Forms.
See FIDUCIARIES.
Fisheries, petition for control and
regulation, **130:94.**
Fluoridation of public water
supply, petition for election,
111:8C.
Gas.
See GAS AND ELECTRIC
COMPANIES.
General court.
See GENERAL COURT.
Guardians.
See GUARDIANS,
CONSERVATORS, AND
COMMITTEES.

PETITIONS —Cont'd
Habeas corpus.
See HABEAS CORPUS.
Highways.
See HIGHWAYS AND
STREETS.
Home rule petitions, **43B:3,
43B:10, 43B:15.**
Hospital service corporations.
Enforcement of laws as to
hospital service
corporations, petitions,
176A:6.
Proposed contracts or rates of
payment, appeal from
commissioner's decision
disapproving, **176A:5.**
Incorporation of city or town and
annexation of municipalities,
petition to general court, **3:5.**
Initiative.
See INITIATIVE AND
REFERENDUM.
Insanity.
Mentally ill and retarded
persons. See within this
heading, "Mentally ill and
retarded persons."
Labor commission authorized to
investigate decertification
petitions, **150A:5.**
Labor relations.
See LABOR RELATIONS AND
DISPUTES.
Legacy and succession taxes.
Abatement of taxes, **65:27,
65:27A.**
Accounting as to estate of
nonresident by official of
state of domicile, **65:24C.**
Enforcement of lien, **65:31.**
Local option statute, revocation of
acceptance, **4:4B.**
Lowlands and swamps.
Construction of roads to swamp,
fee for recording, **252:22.**
Improvement of swamps and
lowlands, **252:15 et seq.**
Low-level radioactive waste,
111:24.
Mentally ill and retarded persons,
123:5 et seq.
Administration of estate,
123B:13.
Municipalities.
See CITIES AND TOWNS.
Municipal lighting and heating
plants, **164:58F, 164:69.**
Optional Forms Municipal
Administration Act, adoption
of optional forms by cities and
towns, petition to vote, **43C:4,
43C:5, 43C:11-43C:13.**

PETITIONS —Cont'd
Partition.
See PARTITION.
Private ways.
Registration of title of land
bounding on private way,
185:29.
Probate.
See PROBATE AND FAMILY
COURT.
Public administrator, petition for
administration, **192:1.**
Quieting title.
Action to try title, petition to
require.
See QUIETING TITLE.
Discharge of mortgages, petition
to land court for.
See QUIETING TITLE.
Railroad crossings.
See RAILROAD CROSSINGS.
Railroads.
See RAILROADS.
Registration of land titles.
See REGISTRATION OF LAND
TITLES.
Registration of voters.
See REGISTRATION OF
VOTERS.
Reservoirs.
See DAMS AND RESERVOIRS.
Restraints of trade and
monopolies, **93:8.**
Retarded persons.
Mentally ill and retarded
persons. See within this
heading, "Mentally ill and
retarded persons."
Road construction, **252:15 et seq.**
Secretary of state.
See SECRETARY OF STATE.
Sexual offenses.
See SEXUAL OFFENSES AND
OFFENDERS.
Special assessments.
See SPECIAL ASSESSMENTS.
State police.
See STATE POLICE.
Statutes accepted by local option,
revocation of approval, **4:4B.**
Street railways.
See STREET RAILWAYS.
Succession taxes.
Legacy and succession taxes. See
within this heading, "Legacy
and succession taxes."
Swamps.
Lowlands and swamps. See
within this heading,
"Lowlands and swamps."

PETITIONS —Cont'd
Tax deeds and titles.
  Foreclosure of rights of
    redemption, petition, **60:65,
    60:75.**
  Low value lands sold by
    municipality, petition to
    establish title, **60:80B.**
Taxpayer's petition to authorize
  schoolhouse fire escape
  expenditure, **143:32.**
Telecommunications and energy
  department.
  Appeals petitions to be filed with
    secretary of commission,
    25:5.
  Corporate matters, petitions to
    general court, **3:5.**
  Interstate commerce law,
    petition for relief from
    violations, **159:41.**
Towns.
  See CITIES AND TOWNS.
Unemployment compensation.
  Employment security. See within
    this heading, "Employment
    security."
Voter registration.
  Initiative and referendum
    petitions.
    See REGISTRATION OF
      VOTERS.
  Voter registration sessions,
    approval of petitions,
    51:42B.
Zoning, special permits, **40A:11.**

PETIT TREASON.
Murder, prosecution and
  punishment, **265:1.**

PETROLEUM.
Fuel.
  See FUEL.
Gas and oil.
  See GAS AND OIL.

PETS.
See ANIMALS.

PEYOTE.
Controlled dangerous substance,
  94C:31.

**PHARMACISTS AND
  PHARMACIES,
  112:24-112:42A.**
Abuse of patients or residents in
  long term care facilities,
  reports, **111:72G.**
Advertising regulated, **112:38.**
Alcoholic liquors.
  See ALCOHOLIC LIQUORS.

**PHARMACISTS AND
  PHARMACIES** —Cont'd
Assistants.
  Registration, **112:24, 112:24A.**
  Sale of drugs and medicines,
    112:30.
Board of registration, **13:22-13:25.**
  Agents, **13:25.**
  Alcoholic liquors.
    See ALCOHOLIC LIQUORS.
  Annual report, **112:25.**
  Approval of schools and courses
    in pharmacy, **112:24B.**
  Certificate of conviction of
    pharmacists sent, **112:34.**
  Civil service status of secretary,
    13:23.
  Complaints. See within this
    heading, "Complaints
    against."
  Consultation relative to certain
    registration of persons who
    may possess controlled
    substances, **94C:7, 112:80E.**
  Drug business, regulation,
    112:37-112:42A.
  Expenditures authorized,
    112:42.
  Investigation of complaints,
    112:32, 112:36C.
  Meetings, **13:23.**
  Membership, **13:22.**
  Notice of expiration of
    registration, **112:24A.**
  Organization, **13:22 et seq.**
  Pharmacy technicians, **112:24C.**
    Investigation of complaints,
      112:24D.
  Public or lay members, **13:22.**
  Record of registered pharmacists
    and assistants, **112:24A,
    112:25.**
  Reports, **13:25, 112:25, 112:32,
    112:34, 112:36C.**
  Reregistration, hearing with
    respect, **112:24A.**
  Revocation or suspension of
    registration or permit,
    112:24B, 112:40, 112:42A.
  Rules and regulations, **112:42A.**
    General provisions, **112:88.**
  Salaries and expenses, **13:24.**
  Secretary, **13:23, 13:24.**
  Standards for schools and
    courses in pharmacy,
    112:24B.
  Striking from register, **112:24A.**
  Violations of law, report, **13:25,
    112:32, 112:34, 112:36C.**
Brands and labels.
  Labels. See within this heading,
    "Labels."

**PHARMACISTS AND
  PHARMACIES** —Cont'd
Certificate of conviction of
  pharmacists sent to board of
  registration, **112:34.**
Certificates of registration, **112:24.**
  Assistants in pharmacy, **112:24,
    112:24A.**
  Citizenship required, **112:24.**
  Drugs, suspension for improper
    use, **112:29.**
  Duplicate certificate, **112:88.**
  Exhibit, **112:26.**
  General provisions as to
    furnishing, **112:88.**
  Intoxicants, suspension for
    improper use, **112:29.**
  Reciprocity, **112:24.**
  Renewal, **112:24A.**
  Revocation or suspension of
    certificate. See within this
    heading, "Revocation or
    suspension of certificate or
    permit."
  Without examination, **112:24.**
Chain pharmacist.
  Defined, **13:22.**
Civil service status of secretary of
  pharmacy registration board,
  13:23.
Colleges, standards, **112:24B.**
Complaints against.
  Access to documents of board,
    112:33.
  Complaints resulting from
    conviction, time for making,
    board of registration,
    112:27.
  Decision upon, **112:28.**
  Hearings, **112:27, 112:61,
    112:62.**
  Investigation by board, **112:32,
    112:36C.**
  Notice of hearing, **112:27,
    112:62.**
  Pendency of criminal action as
    affecting, **112:63.**
  Pharmacy board agents, filing,
    13:25.
  Reconsideration by board,
    112:28.
  Time for filing, **112:27.**
  Witnesses in hearings, **112:27,
    112:62.**
Conduct of retail drug business
  regulated, **112:38, 112:39.**
Continuance of business of
  deceased or incapacitated
  pharmacist, **112:36.**
Continuing education requirement,
  112:24A.

PHARMACISTS AND PHARMACIES —Cont'd

Contraceptives, furnishing of upon doctor's prescription, **272:21A.**

Controlled dangerous substances, registration fee for dealing, **94C:7.**

Counseling of persons presenting new prescriptions, **94C:21A.**

Crimes.
Violations of law. See within this heading, "Violations of law."

Day of rest laws, **136:6, 149:50.**

Deceased pharmacist, continuance of business, **112:36.**

Deceit.
Fraud and deceit. See within this heading, "Fraud and deceit."

Display of certificate of registration and permit, **112:26, 112:38.**

Drug business defined, **94C:1, 112:37.**

Elderly persons, print size on prescription labels, **94C:21.**

False representation.
Fraud and deceit. See within this heading, "Fraud and deceit."

Fees.
Registration and permits. See within this heading, "Registration and permits."
Wholesaler's license, **112:36B.**

Fines and penalties.
Improper use of drugs, **112:29.**
Practicing after revocation or suspension of certificate, **112:65.**
Retail drug business, unlawful transaction, **112:41.**
Schools and courses of pharmacy, violations concerning, **112:24B.**
Unlawful sale of drugs and medicines, **112:30.**
Weights and measures, use of untested, **98:48.**
Wholesale druggists, violations, **112:36D.**

Food store pharmacy, retail, regulation, **112:38, 112:39.**

Formulary commission, membership, **17:13.**

Fraud and deceit.
False representations to evade or violate laws, **94:187D.**
Revocation or suspension of certificate, **112:61.**

Gratuitous prescriptions by, law relating to physicians and surgeons inapplicable, **112:7.**

PHARMACISTS AND PHARMACIES —Cont'd

Gross misconduct, revocation or suspension of certificate, **112:61.**

Hospitals and clinics, dispensing of medicines or drugs to certain persons by pharmacists employed, **112:42A.**

Improper use of drugs, penalty, **112:29.**

Incapacitated pharmacists, continuance of business, **112:36.**

Independent from other business, **112:39.**

Independent pharmacist.
Defined, **13:22.**

Insanity, revocation or suspension of certificate, **112:61.**

Inspectors to report violations, **13:25.**

Insurance policy, discrimination in reimbursement or payment, **175:193K.**

Interactions of drugs, prospective drug review for prevention of, **94C:21A.**

Intoxicating liquors, sale, **112:27, 112:29, 112:40.**

Labels.
Affixing of required, **94C:21.**
Misbranded drugs, health department to furnish list, **94:187.**
Print size on prescription labels, **94C:21.**

Licenses.
Registration and permits. See within this heading, "Registration and permits."
Wholesale druggists. See within this heading, "Wholesale druggists."

Limitations and restrictions.
Restricted pharmacies. See within this heading, "Restricted pharmacies."

Malpractice, revocation or suspension of certificate, **112:61.**

Medical assistance division to create pharmacy assistance pilot program, **118E:16B.**

Misbranded drugs, health department to furnish list, **94:187.**

Name.
Trademarks and trade names. See within this heading, "Trademarks and trade names."

PHARMACISTS AND PHARMACIES —Cont'd

Name —Cont'd
Use of term "drugs, **112:38.**
Wholesale druggist, use of term, **112:36C, 112:36D.**

Nonintoxicating beverage regulations inapplicable, **140:21D.**

Notice and knowledge.
Complaints, notice of hearing, **112:27, 112:62.**
Registration, expiration, **112:24A.**
Revocation or suspension of permit, notice and hearing, **112:40, 112:42A.**

Nuclear pharmacy.
See DRUGS AND NARCOTICS.

Nurses, exemption from law, **112:80B.**

Nursing and rest homes, obtaining of medicine for old age assistance recipients, **118A:1.**

Offenses.
Violations of law. See within this heading, "Violations of law."

Old age assistance patients in nursing and rest homes, obtaining of medicine, **118A:1.**

Penalties.
Fines and penalties. See within this heading, "Fines and penalties."

Permits.
Registration and permits. See within this heading, "Registration and permits."

Pharmacy assistance pilot program, **118E:16B.**

Pharmacy technicians.
Change of address.
Notice, **112:24F.**
Investigation of complaints, **112:24D.**
Registration, **112:24C.**
Unregistered practice, **112:24E.**

Physicians and surgeons, inapplicability of law, **112:7.**

Pregnancy kits which are self-administered, instructional brochures required, **94:192A.**

Prescription drugs.
See DRUGS AND NARCOTICS.

Prescription labels, print size, **94C:21.**

Prospective drug review prior to dispensing new prescription, **94C:21A.**

Records and reports.
Reports. See within this heading, "Reports."

PHARMACISTS AND PHARMACIES —Cont'd

Refilling prescriptions originally filled by another HMO clinic pharmacy, **94C:23.**
Registration and permits, **94C:7, 94C:31, 112:24-112:42A.**
  Assistant pharmacists, **112:24, 112:24A.**
  Biennial expiration, **112:24A.**
  Board of registration. See within this heading, "Board of registration."
  Certificates of registration. See within this heading, "Certificates of registration."
  Consultation with board of pharmacy, **94C:7, 112:80E.**
  Continuing education, **112:24A.**
  Controlled dangerous substances, registration fee for dealing, **94C:7.**
  Corporations, **112:39.**
  Courses in pharmacy, standards, **112:24B.**
  Display, **112:38.**
  Examinations, **112:24.**
  Expiration, **112:24A.**
  Fees, **94C:7, 112:39.**
    Controlled dangerous substances, fee for dealing, **94C:7.**
    Examination fee, **112:24.**
    General provisions, **112:88.**
    Re-examination, **112:24.**
    Renewal of registration, **112:24A.**
    Re-registrations, **112:24A.**
  Issuance, **94C:12, 112:39.**
  Notice of expiration, **112:24A.**
  Permission to operate unregistered store, in town or voting precinct, **112:38.**
  Pharmacy technicians, **112:24C.**
  Public interest, determination before issuance of registration, **94C:12.**
  Required, **112:38.**
  Re-registration, **112:24A.**
  Retirees, pharmacies restricted, **112:39A, 112:40.**
  Revocation or suspension. See within this heading, "Revocation or suspension of certificate or permit."
  Striking from register, **112:24A.**
  Veterans, **112:24.**
  Wholesale druggists. See within this heading, "Wholesale druggists."
Reports.
  Board of registration, **13:25, 112:25.**

PHARMACISTS AND PHARMACIES —Cont'd

Reports —Cont'd
  Public health department, **111:72G.**
Restricted pharmacies.
  Retirees, registration of pharmacies restricted, **112:39A.**
  Revocation of registration, **112:40.**
Retail drug business, **94C:1.**
Retail food store pharmacy, **112:38, 112:39.**
Revocation or suspension of certificate or permit.
  Controlled substances violations, **94C:13, 94C:14.**
  Drug stores, **112:24B, 112:40, 112:42A.**
  Penalty for practicing after, **112:65.**
  Powers of board, **112:61.**
  Revision or reversal by supreme judicial court, **112:64.**
  Use of intoxicants or drugs, **112:29.**
  Violations of law, **112:28.**
Rules and regulations.
  Board of registration. See within this heading, "Board of registration."
Sale of drugs and medicines.
  Certificate of conviction of violation, **112:34.**
  Penalty for unlawful sale, **112:30.**
  Unlawful sale, **112:29, 112:30.**
  Wholesale druggists. See within this heading, "Wholesale druggists."
Sales tax, exemption of prescription drugs, **64H:6.**
Schools and education.
  Continuing education requirement, **112:24A.**
  Standards for schools, **112:24B.**
Suspension.
  Revocation or suspension. See within this heading, "Revocation or suspension of certificate or permit."
Trademarks and trade names.
  Apothecaries' measures, trademarks, **98:47.**
  "Drugstore," etc., use of terms, **112:38.**
  "Wholesale druggists," use of terms, **112:36C, 112:36D.**
Unregistered copartner or stockholder, provision as to sale of drugs inapplicable, **112:30.**

PHARMACISTS AND PHARMACIES —Cont'd

Unused medication, return and redistribution, **111:25H.**
Veterinarians.
  See VETERINARIANS.
Violations of law.
  Complaints. See within this heading, "Complaints against."
  False representation to evade or violate laws, **94:187D.**
  Fines and penalties. See within this heading, "Fines and penalties."
  Reports to board of registration, **13:25, 112:32, 112:34, 112:36C.**
  Revocation or suspension of certificate, **112:28.**
Visually-impaired or elderly persons, print size on prescription labels, **94C:21.**
Weights.
  See WEIGHTS AND MEASURES.
Wholesale druggists, **112:36A-112:36D.**
  False representation, **94:187D.**
  Guarantee of wholesaler as protection under Pure Food and Drug Act, **94:193, 94:194.**
  Inspection, **112:36B.**
  Issuance of registration, determination of public interest, **94C:12.**
  License, **112:36A.**
    Fees, **112:36B.**
    For each location, **112:36B.**
    Renewals, **112:36B.**
  Penalties for violation of law, **112:36D.**
  Possession of hypodermic syringe or needle, **94C:27, 94C:38.**
  Registration or permit, **94C:7, 94C:12.**
  Report of violations of law, **112:36C.**
  Revocation and suspension of registration, **94C:13.**
  Sale or delivery of hypodermic syringe or needle, **94C:27, 94C:38.**
  Sale without license, prohibited, **112:36A.**
  Use of term, restricted, **112:36C.**
Widow's continuance of business, **112:36.**

PHARMACISTS AND PHARMACIES —Cont'd
Witnesses.
  Hearings on complaints before board of registration, **112:27, 112:62.**
  Revocation or suspension of registration or permit, proceedings, **112:40, 112:42A.**

PHARMACOPOEIA OF UNITED STATES, 94:186, 94C:1.

PHARMACY TECHNICIANS.
Change of address.
  Notice, **112:24F.**
Investigation of complaints, **112:24D.**
Registration, **112:24C.**
Unregistered practice, **112:24E.**

PHEASANT.
Commercial shooting preserves, taking, **131:31.**
Damage to agricultural property, killing, **131:37.**
Field trials and training of dogs, **131:20.**
Liberation of, regulated, **131:19A.**

PHENYLKETONURIA.
Newborn children to be subjected to tests, **111:110A.**
Program to combat, **111:4E.**

PHILIPPINE INSURRECTION.
Benefits to veterans, **115:1-115:15.**

PHILLIPS-COX ACT, 214:6.
Labor injunction, **214:6.**
Labor relations and disputes, **214:6.**

PHILLIPSTON.
Congressional district, **57:1.**
District court, **218:1.**
Medical examiner district, **38:1.**
Senatorial district, **57:3.**

PHONES.
See TELEPHONE AND TELEGRAPH COMPANIES.

PHONOGRAPH RECORDS.
Unauthorized reproduction and transfer, **266:143-266:143E.**
  Conviction of crime, **266:143E.**
  Definitions, **266:143.**
  Fines and penalties, **266:143D.**
  Live performance, **266:143B.**

PHOSPHORUS.
Household cleaning products containing phosphorus, regulation of, **111:5R.**

PHOTOGRAPHIC COPIES OF BUSINESS AND PUBLIC RECORDS AS EVIDENCE, 233:79E.

PHOTOGRAPHS.
See PICTURES OR PHOTOGRAPHS.

PHOTOMETER.
Inspection of gas, **164:109.**

PHOTOSTATIC COPIES.
Admission in evidence, **151A:44, 233:79, 233:79A, 233:79D, 233:79E, 261:25A.**
Births outside Commonwealth, evidence, **46:1B.**
Credit unions, negotiable withdrawal order accounts, **171:31.**
Deaths outside Commonwealth, evidence, **46:1C.**
Federal securities and exchange commission documents, copies of as evidence, **233:76A.**
Legacy and succession tax computation sheet, copy, **65:35A.**
Marriage outside Commonwealth, evidence, **207:36.**
Microphotography.
  See MICROPHOTOGRAPHY.
Minor's employment permit, **149:87.**
Register of deeds, fees, **262:38.**
Reproduction of certain destroyed business and public records, admissibility in evidence, **233:79E.**
Secretary of state, authority to destroy original records previously reproduced, **9:19.**
Veterans' benefits, copies of discharge papers for purpose, **115:3A.**

PHOTOTHERAPY DEVICE.
See TANNING FACILITIES.

PHOTOVOLTAICS CENTER.
Centers of Excellence, establishment, **40J:12.**

PHYSICAL DISABILITY.
See DISABLED OR HANDICAPPED PERSONS.

PHYSICAL EDUCATION AND FITNESS.
Adult physical education or fitness programs, **71:71B, 71:71E.**
Appointment and duties of director, **69:1A.**
Athletics.
  See ATHLETICS.

PHYSICAL EDUCATION AND FITNESS —Cont'd
Department of education, appointment of physical director, **69:1A.**
Gymnastics.
  See GYMNASTICS.
Police officers and firefighters, **31:61A, 32:5.**
Public employees, **31:61A.**
Public schools, physical education, **71:1, 71:3, 71:47.**
School gymnasiums, use for adult programs, **71:71B.**
Training school inmates, **120:6A.**

PHYSICAL EXAMINATION.
See MEDICAL AND PHYSICAL EXAMINATION.

PHYSICAL EXERCISE PROGRAMS.
Willful, wanton or reckless injury to participants, **265:40.**

PHYSICAL INJURY.
See PERSONAL INJURIES.

PHYSICAL PUNISHMENT.
Schools, prohibition against corporal punishment, **71:37G.**

PHYSICAL RESTRAINT.
Schools and education.
  Use on students, **71:37G.**

PHYSICAL THERAPISTS, 112:23A-112:23Q.
Abbreviations indicating practice, **112:23L.**
Abuse of patients or residents in long-term care facilities, reports, **111:72G.**
Acupuncture licensing and registration, exemptions, **112:162.**
Aliens, registration, **112:23C, 112:23F.**
Allied health professions.
  See ALLIED HEALTH PROFESSIONS.
American Medical Association, approval of schools or courses for physical therapists, **112:23C.**
Board of registration in medicine.
  Board defined, **112:23A.**
  Functions, **112:23A-112:23K.**
  Record of proceedings, **112:23J.**
  Rules, **112:23J.**
    General provisions, **112:88.**
Chiropractor, **112:23A.**
  Unauthorized practice, **112:23N.**
Corporations, professional services within professional corporations law, **156A:2.**

PHYSICAL THERAPISTS
—Cont'd
Crimes.
Violations and offenses. See within this heading, "Violations and offenses."
Definitions, **112:23A.**
Diagnosis as included in definition of physical therapy, **112:23A.**
Disclosure of physician's financial interest, referrals to physical therapists, **112:12AA, 112:23P½.**
Drugs and narcotics.
Prescription required, **112:23A, 112:23H, 112:23I, 112:23N.**
Registration, revocation, **112:23I.**
Early intervention services, dependent coverage, **175:47C, 176A:8B, 176B:4C, 176G:4.**
Educational requirements, **112:23C.**
Enforcement of law, **112:23K.**
English language, requirement of proficiency, **112:23C.**
Evidence.
See EVIDENCE.
Examinations for registration, **112:23C, 112:23E.**
Discretion of board of registration and discipline in medicine as to number of times applicant may take, **112:23E.**
Dispensing, **112:23F.**
Fees, **112:23E.**
Other states, physical therapists from, without examination, **112:23D.**
Practice pending, **112:23H.**
Subjects covered, **112:23E.**
Fees.
Registration. See within this heading, "Registration."
Financial interest of physician, disclosure upon referrals to physical therapists, **112:12AA, 112:23P½.**
Fines and penalties.
Violations. See within this heading, "Violations and offenses."
Foreign state or territory, registration without examination of physical therapist registered or licensed, **112:23D.**
Gross negligence as ground for suspension of certificate of registration, **112:23I.**

PHYSICAL THERAPISTS
—Cont'd
Imprisonment for violations, **112:23M.**
Insurance policy, discrimination in reimbursement or payment for services legally performed under provisions, **175:193K.**
Law enforcement agency, reporting of violations, **112:23K.**
List of registered physical therapists, **112:23J.**
Medical care and assistance, furnishing of, **118E:6.**
Medical malpractice claims, physical therapists as providers of health care for purposes, **231:60B.**
Names indicating practice, **112:23L.**
Narcotics.
Drugs and narcotics. See within this heading, "Drugs and narcotics."
Nurses and nursing services, **112:80B.**
Soldiers' Home in Holyoke, nurses employed, **112:23O.**
Offenses.
Violations and offenses. See within this heading, "Violations and offenses."
Osteopathy, unauthorized practice by physical therapist, **112:23N.**
Physicians and surgeons.
Prescription or supervision of, practice, **112:23A, 112:23H, 112:23I, 112:23N.**
Referral of physician. See within this heading, "Referral of physician."
Unauthorized practice of medicine by physical therapist, **112:23N.**
Prescription of licensed physician required, **112:23A, 112:23H, 112:23I, 112:23N.**
Professional services within professional corporations law, **156A:2.**
Radium, use unauthorized, **112:23A.**
Records.
Board, records, **112:23J.**
Evidence in civil actions, **233:79G.**
Referral of physician.
Disclosure of financial interest, **112:12AA, 112:12P½.**
Necessity, **112:23N.**

PHYSICAL THERAPISTS
—Cont'd
Referral of physician —Cont'd
Suspension of certificate for practicing physical therapy without, **112:23I.**
Registered Physical Therapists Law, citation of law, **112:23Q.**
Registration, **112:23A-112:23Q.**
Aliens, **112:23F.**
Applications, **112:23B, 112:23D.**
Board of registration in medicine. See within this heading, "Board of registration in medicine."
Educational prerequisites, **112:23C.**
Eligibility and qualifications, **112:23C.**
Examinations. See within this heading, "Examinations for registration."
Fees, **112:23B, 112:23D, 112:23G.**
Examination fees, **112:23E.**
General provisions, **112:88.**
Foreign state or territory, registration without examination of physical therapist registered or licensed, **112:23D.**
Fraud in obtaining etc., **112:23I, 112:23L, 112:23M.**
Issuance of certificate of registration, **112:23F.**
General provisions, **112:88.**
Lapse of, for failure to renew, **112:23G.**
List of registered physical therapists, **112:23J.**
Other state, registration of physical therapists from, without examination, **112:23D.**
Partial invalidity of law, saving clause, **112:23P.**
Refusal to register or renew, grounds, **112:23I.**
Renewal, **112:23G.**
Revival or extension of lapsed registration, **112:23G.**
Revocation or suspension. See within this heading, "Revocation or suspension of registration."
Violations, fraud in obtaining or attempting to obtain registration, **112:23I, 112:23L, 112:23M.**
Retirement benefits, rehabilitation facilities, **32:21.**

PHYSICAL THERAPISTS
—Cont'd
Revocation or suspension of
registration.
Grounds, **112:23I.**
Unauthorized use of words
indicating person as
physical therapist after,
112:23L.
Roster of registered physical
therapists, maintenance,
112:23J.
Schools for, American Medical
Association's approval,
112:23C.
Soldiers' Home in Holyoke, nurses
employed, **112:23O.**
Supervision or direction of licensed
physician, practice, **112:23A,
112:23H, 112:23I, 112:23N.**
Suspension of registration.
Revocation or suspension of
registration. See within this
heading, "Revocation or
suspension of registration."
United States, employees,
112:23O.
Unregistered person representing
himself or practicing as
physical therapist, **112:23L,
112:23O.**
Violations and offenses,
112:23K-112:23O.
Imprisonment, **112:23M.**
Investigation and prosecution,
112:23K.
Particular offenses, **112:23A,
112:23L-112:23N.**
Registration, fraud in obtaining
or attempting to obtain,
112:23I, 112:23L, 112:23M.
Reports, **112:23K.**
X-ray, use unauthorized, **112:23A.**

**PHYSICIAN ASSISTANTS,
94C:1, 94C:7, 94C:9, 112:9A,
112:9C-112:9H, 112:80B.**
Abuse or neglect of patients in
long-term care facilities.
Reporting requirements,
111:72G.
Board of approval and
certification, **13:10B, 13:11C,
112:9C et seq.**
Approval of programs for
education and training,
112:9G.
Establishment, membership,
duties, etc., **112:9F.**
Notification of employment,
112:9G.
Powers and duties, **112:9G.**

PHYSICIAN ASSISTANTS
—Cont'd
Board of approval and certification
—Cont'd
Records, **112:9G, 112:9H.**
Certificates of registration.
Registration. See within this
heading, "Registration."
Chiropractic practice, prohibition
from engaging, **112:9D.**
Definitions, **112:9C.**
Duties, **112:9E.**
Educational requirements for
registration, **112:9I, 112:9K.**
Elder abuse, reporting of, **19A:15.**
Emergency medical care or
treatment, immunity from
liability, **112:12B.**
Employment.
Legal responsibility of
supervising person or
agency, **112:9E.**
Regulation of employment of
physician assistants,
112:9G.
Services and duties. See within
this heading, "Services and
duties performed."
Expenses, reimbursement of
members of board of approval
and certification, **112:9F.**
Fees, **112:9G.**
Fraudulent practices, **112:9H,
112:9J.**
Hearings relating to complaints,
112:9H.
Labor.
Employment. See within this
heading, "Employment."
Legal responsibility for actions or
omission, **112:9E.**
Limited practice, **112:9A.**
Qualifications, **112:9A.**
Records of board, **112:9G, 112:9H.**
Registration, **13:11C, 112:9A,
112:9F, 112:9G.**
Board of approval and
certification. See within this
heading, "Board of approval
and certification."
Time, **112:9I.**
Reports, **112:9G.**
Elder abuse, reporting of,
19A:15.
Reyes syndrome, reports by
persons examining or treating
disease, **111:110B.**
Services and duties performed,
112:9E.
Prohibited services, **112:9D.**
Supervision, **112:9E.**

PHYSICIAN ASSISTANTS
—Cont'd
Tests in hospitals and laboratories,
employment of assistants,
112:3.
Time for registration with board,
112:9I.
Title of "physician assistant,"
unauthorized use, **112:9H.**
Trainees, services performed,
112:9E.
Unapproved person, penalties for
practice, **112:9H.**

**PHYSICIANS AND SURGEONS,
112:2-112:12A.**
Abortion performed, **112:12I,
112:12M, 112:12R.**
Abused and neglected children.
Custody of physician, child may
be kept, **119:51C.**
Reports to be made by
physician, **119:51A.**
Abuse of patients or residents in
long-term care facilities,
reports, **111:72G.**
Accident.
See ACCIDENT AND
SICKNESS INSURANCE.
Acupuncture practice, **112:162.**
Acute care hospitals.
Physician ownership or
investment, regulations,
112:5M.
Addiction to drugs as ground for
discipline, **112:5.**
Aiding and abetting, **112:2, 265:10.**
AIDS testing, **111:2F, 111:70F.**
Air pollution emergencies advisory
council, membership, **111:2B.**
Alcoholic liquors.
Abuse of.
Alcoholism and intoxication.
See within this heading,
"Alcoholism and
intoxication."
Excise tax on sales to
physicians, **138:21.**
Furnishing alcoholic liquors
under direction of
physicians, **268:26, 268:29.**
Impairment of ability to
practice, discipline, **112:5.**
License, **138:76.**
Prescription for alcohol, **138:29.**
Alcoholism and intoxication.
Blood test to determine
intoxication of motor vehicle
operator, **90:24.**
Cancellation of registration for
gross use of alcoholic
beverages, **112:2.**

PHYSICIANS AND SURGEONS
—Cont'd
Alcoholism and intoxication
—Cont'd
Compliance with alcohol
program, exemption of
reporting requirements of
health care providers, **112:5.**
Court ordered examinations
regarding commitment,
123:35.
Discipline, drunkenness as
ground, **112:5.**
Treatment and rehabilitation
facilities, right of patient to
retain private physician,
111B:11.
Aliens.
Foreign state or country. See
within this heading,
"Foreign state or country."
Ambulances attendants,
physician's liability for advice
given, **111C:13.**
American College of Surgeons,
non-profit medical service
plans provided by medical
organizations composed of
members of staff of hospital
approved, **176C:1, 176C:5.**
American medical association.
See AMERICAN MEDICAL
ASSOCIATION.
Amphetamines, discipline of doctor
dependent, **112:5.**
Anatomy as covered subject in
examination for registration,
112:3.
Anesthesia.
See ANESTHESIA AND
ANESTHETICS.
Applications for registration as,
informing change in law,
112:2.
Appointment of physicians for
hospitals and health care
facilities, **17:6, 111:87.**
Arbitration.
Medical malpractice.
See ARBITRATION.
Report of arbitration award
against, board of
registration, **112:5E.**
Assistants, **112:9A,
112:9C-112:9H.**
See PHYSICIAN ASSISTANTS.
Assumed name, practice, **112:6.**
Attorneys' fees.
Medical malpractice, services
rendered on behalf of
claimant or defendant,
231:60I.

PHYSICIANS AND SURGEONS
—Cont'd
Attorneys' fees —Cont'd
Report to board, **112:5F.**
Automobile liability insurance.
Coverage for medical expenses,
90:34A, 90:34M.
"No-fault" coverage, effect of
physician's notification to
insurer as to patient's
disability, **90:34M.**
Barbiturates, discipline of doctor
addicted, **112:5.**
Barnstable county hospital chief of
medical staff and
administrator, procedure for
dismissal, **35:51.**
Bills for medical services.
Division of medical assistance,
bills to be submitted within
90 days after service
rendered, **118E:20.**
Motor vehicle insurer,
submission of medical bills
for review, **90:34M.**
Personal injury actions,
admissibility of bills,
233:79G.
Biology as covered subject in
examination for registration,
112:3.
Births.
See BIRTHS.
Blindness.
Report of examination
establishing, **6:136.**
Study of problems relating,
6:145.
Blood test to determine
intoxication of motor vehicle
operator, **90:24.**
Board of registration, **13:10, 13:11.**
Agencies and executive offices,
reports, **112:5C.**
Annual report or summary,
111:53B, 112:5J.
Certificates of registration. See
within this heading,
"Certificates of registration."
Compensation of members,
112:2.
Control over physical therapists.
See PHYSICAL
THERAPISTS.
Data repository, establishment,
112:5.
Data required of hospitals,
physicians, health
maintenance organizations
and other medical service
providers, **112:5I.**

PHYSICIANS AND SURGEONS
—Cont'd
Board of registration —Cont'd
Discipline of physicians and
surgeons for violating
regulations, **112:2, 112:5,
112:5A, 112:61.**
Drug violations reported to,
certain interchangeable,
112:12D.
Exception of board of
registration in medicine to
supervision by director of
registration, **112:1.**
Finding by tribunal, clerk of
court to send copy to board,
231:60B.
Hospital and laboratory tests,
employment of assistants,
112:3.
Imposition of fines, and other
sanctions in disciplinary
cases, **112:5.**
Insurance, **112:2, 112:5C.**
Investigation of complaints,
112:5.
Malpractice liability insurance
or bond, **112:2.**
Members, **112:2, 112:2B.**
Physical therapy referrals by
physicians, disclosure of
financial information,
112:12AA.
Records, **112:4.**
Registration of physicians,
112:2.
Renewal of certificates of
registration, requirement,
112:2.
Reports, **111:53B, 112:5A,
112:5C.**
Annual, **112:4.**
Violation of law, **112:5.**
Reprimand or censure of doctor,
112:5.
Restrictions on license
prohibiting certain
procedures, **112:5A.**
Revocation or suspension of
registration, powers of
board, **112:2, 112:5, 112:61.**
Risk management unit, **112:5,
112:5C.**
Rules and regulations, **112:2.**
Practice of medicine, **112:5.**
Prioritization of investigation
complaint and reports,
rules and regulations
relative, **112:5K.**
Superior court, examination on
order of board, **112:5H.**

PHYSICIANS AND SURGEONS
—Cont'd
Boxing.
  See BOXING AND BOXING
    MATCHES.
Breast implantation warnings,
  111:70E.
Building inspectors, examination,
  32:90F.
Bullet wounds, report, **112:12A.**
Canadian medical school
  graduates, licensing, **112:2.**
Capital punishment, persons
  present at execution, **279:65.**
Cardiopulmonary resuscitation,
  exempting certain individuals
  from civil liability for
  emergency, **112:12V.**
Cardiopulmonary resuscitation,
  exempting certain individuals
  from civil liability for
  emergencies.
  Public access defibrillation
    program, **112:12V½.**
Cerebral palsy reports, duties,
  111:111A.
Certificates of registration.
  Applications for certificate to be
    provided by registration
    board, **112:2.**
  Assistants, programs of training
    and qualification, **112:9G.**
  Duplicate certificate, **112:88.**
  False certificate or certified
    statement, recording, **112:8.**
  Fees.
    Duplicate certificate, **112:88.**
    Recording, **112:8, 262:34.**
  General provisions, **112:88.**
  In lieu of examination, **112:2A.**
  Issuance, **112:2.**
  Limited registration, certificate,
    112:2, 112:9, 112:9A.
  Lost certificate, procedure in
    case, **112:8.**
  Recording before practice, **112:8.**
  Revocation or suspension. See
    within this heading,
    "Revocation or suspension of
    registration."
  Unlawful practice with respect,
    112:8.
Chemicals and chemistry.
  Autopsy, employment of chemist,
    38:6.
  Distribution of formulary of
    chemical names of drugs,
    17:13.
  Required subject for registration
    of physician, **112:3.**
Children.
  See CHILDREN AND MINORS.

PHYSICIANS AND SURGEONS
—Cont'd
Chiropodists, **112:13-112:22.**
  See PODIATRY AND
    PODIATRISTS.
Chiropractic.
  See CHIROPRACTIC AND
    CHIROPRACTORS.
Citizenship.
  Foreign state or country. See
    within this heading,
    "Foreign state or country."
City.
  See CITY AND TOWN
    PHYSICIANS.
Civil immunity.
  Immunity from liability. See
    within this heading,
    "Immunity from liability."
Civil service exemption, **31:48.**
Clinical laboratories, **111D:4,
  111D:7, 111E:8.**
Clinics, exception as to licensing,
  111:52.
Colleges for.
  See MEDICAL SCHOOLS.
Colonel in militia, term of office,
  33:26.
Commissioner of public health,
  appointment of physician and
  employees for institutions
  under jurisdiction of public
  health department, **17:6.**
Commitment by physician of
  person to mental institution,
  123:12.
Committee members.
  Lead poisoning prevention
    program advisory
    committee, membership,
    111:190.
  Medicolegal investigations
    committee, membership,
    6:184.
  Professional society, immunity
    from liability of committee
    member, **231:85N.**
Communication skills, programs
  designed to improve, **112:5.**
Compensation.
  Wages, salaries, and
    compensation. See within
    this heading, "Wages,
    salaries, and compensation."
Complaints and charges against.
  Hearings, **112:61, 112:62.**
  Investigation of, by board, **112:5.**
  Notice of hearings, **112:62.**
  Pendency of criminal action as
    affecting, **112:63.**
  Witnesses on hearings, **112:62.**

PHYSICIANS AND SURGEONS
—Cont'd
Compromise and settlement,
  112:5C, 112:5E, 231:60E.
Confidential information.
  See PRIVILEGED AND
    CONFIDENTIAL
    MATTERS.
Consent to treatment.
  Abortion, **112:12P, 112:12Q.**
  Minor's ability to give, reliance,
    112:12F.
  Sterilization procedures, consent
    in writing before
    performing, **112:12W.**
Contagious.
  See CONTAGIOUS AND
    INFECTIOUS DISEASES.
Contraceptives, prescription and
  furnishing, **272:21A.**
Conviction of crime.
  Cancellation of registration,
    112:2.
  Clerks to report convictions of
    registered physicians or of
    unregistered practitioners,
    221:26.
  False name, practicing, **112:6.**
Cornea transplants, authorization,
  113:14.
Corporations, **156A:2.**
  See PROFESSIONAL
    CORPORATIONS AND
    ASSOCIATIONS.
Correction commissioner,
  appointment of physician,
  27:2.
Council on juvenile behavior,
  psychiatrist as member, **6:159.**
County tuberculosis institutions,
  appointment of physicians to
  staff, **111:87.**
Covenants, **112:12X.**
Crimes and offenses, **112:5,
  112:5E.**
  Conviction of crime. See within
    this heading, "Conviction of
    crime."
  Fines and penalties. See within
    this heading, "Fines and
    penalties."
Cross-examination, **233:79G.**
Damages.
  Abortion or sterilization
    procedures, effect of
    physician's refusal to
    perform on moral or
    religious grounds, **112:12I.**
  Ambulance operators and
    attendants, liability of
    physicians, hospitals, and
    nurses for advice given,
    111C:13.

41

PHYSICIANS AND SURGEONS
—Cont'd

Damages —Cont'd

Deceased physicians, admissibility in actions for damages of medical reports, **233:79H.**

Immunity from liability. See within this heading, "Immunity from liability."

Data, availability to physician where medical or psychiatric emergency arises, **66A:2.**

Deafness.

See OTOLARYNGOLOGISTS.

Death.

Certificate, physicians and hospital officers to give, **46:9, 46:9B, 46:10.**

Death sentence, persons present at execution, **279:65.**

Medical examiners.

See MEDICAL EXAMINERS AND INQUESTS.

Public employees, medical board to determine cause of death, **32:89, 32:89A, 32:89B.**

Reports of deceased physicians as to medical findings or treatment of wrongful death victim, admissibility in evidence, **233:79H.**

Terminally ill patient, pronouncement of death by registered nurses, **46:9.**

Veteran, death certificate to state cause of death, **46:10.**

Death sentence, persons present at execution, **279:65.**

Deceit.

Fraud and deceit. See within this heading, "Fraud and deceit."

Defibrillators.

Good Samaritan law, **112:12V.**

Public access defibrillation program, **112:12V½.**

Definitions, **94D:1, 113:7.**

Dentists, **112:43-112:53.**

See DENTISTS.

Dependency on alcohol or drugs as ground for discipline, **112:5.**

Deposition of medical witness, **233:24A.**

Disabled and handicapped persons.

Blindness. See within this heading, "Blindness."

Physician's ability to practice impaired by physical disability, **112:5.**

PHYSICIANS AND SURGEONS
—Cont'd

Disabled and handicapped persons —Cont'd

Rehabilitation. See within this heading, "Rehabilitation."

Review, disability benefits, **32:8.**

Disciplinary actions, financial interest disclosure in physical therapy referrals, **112:12AA, 112:23P½.**

Disclosures.

Financial interest, disclosure of, referrals to physical therapists, **112:12AA, 112:23P½.**

Health care applicants, effect of disclosures concerning patients who are, **112:12G.**

Privileged.

See PRIVILEGED AND CONFIDENTIAL MATTERS.

Psychotherapists, disclosures of mental or nervous condition, **233:20B.**

Treatment by physician, patients right to information prior, **112:124, 176B:3.**

Venereal disease, disclosure by physician or surgeon, **112:12.**

Discrimination in reimbursement or payment for services legally performed under provisions of insurance policy, **175:193K.**

Dismissal of charges against, **112:5.**

Dispensary staff privileges, report of termination, **111:53B.**

Dispensing opticians.

See OPTICIANS.

Disqualification.

Qualification and disqualification. See within this heading, "Qualification and disqualification."

Dog bites, reporting required, **112:12Z.**

Drugs.

See DRUGS AND NARCOTICS.

Drunkenness.

Alcoholism and intoxication. See within this heading, "Alcoholism and intoxication."

Education.

Medical schools.

See MEDICAL SCHOOLS.

School and education.

See SCHOOLS AND EDUCATION.

PHYSICIANS AND SURGEONS
—Cont'd

Electrologists.

Member of board, physician, **13:58.**

Registration law, exemption of physician, **112:87FFF.**

Emergencies.

Air pollution emergencies advisory council, membership, **111:2B.**

Attendance at football games by physicians or persons trained in emergency medical care, **71:54A.**

Data, availability to physicians where medical or psychiatric emergency arises, **66A:2.**

Inapplicability of regulatory laws in case of emergency, **112:7.**

Liability for rendering emergency treatment, **112:12A, 112:12B, 112:12F.**

Retired physicians, emergency employment by public and mental health departments, **32:91.**

Emergency medical services system.

Immunity from liability for advice or orders, **111C:20.**

Employment security for interns, **151A:6.**

Examinations by.

See MEDICAL AND PHYSICAL EXAMINATION.

Examinations for registrations.

Registration. See within this heading, "Registration."

Examinations of specimens by clinical laboratories, requests, **111D:8.**

Examiners, **38:1-38:19.**

See MEDICAL EXAMINERS AND INQUESTS.

Exemptions and exceptions.

Board of registration, **112:1.**

Civil service exemption, **31:48.**

Electrologist's registration law, **112:87FFF.**

Jury service, exemption, **234:1.**

Nonresident physicians, exemption from liability for giving aid, **112:12B.**

Nurses, physicians and surgeons as exempt from law, **112:80B.**

Tattooing, exception in law prohibiting, **265:34.**

PHYSICIANS AND SURGEONS
—Cont'd

Expenses and expenditures.
Attendance at football games by physicians or persons trained in emergency medical care, **71:54A.**
Fees. See within this heading, "Fees."
Medical care.
See MEDICAL CARE AND ASSISTANCE.
Physician assistant programs, reimbursement of board members, **112:9F.**
Eyes of baby, duties, **111:109A, 111:110, 111:111.**
False.
Fraud and deceit. See within this heading, "Fraud and deceit."
Family planning services, dispensation of controlled substances by physicians, **94C:9.**
Fees.
Automobile insurance protection against medical and surgical fees, **90:34A, 90:34M.**
Medical service corporation, services, **176B:7.**
Physician assistant program, fees in connection, **112:9G.**
Registration. See within this heading, "Registration."
Treatment, examination, or consultation, fees for.
Wages, salaries, and compensation. See within this heading, "Wages, salaries, and compensation."
Workers' compensation.
See WORKERS' COMPENSATION.
Fetal death certificates, **46:9.**
Financial interest disclosure, physical therapy referrals, **112:12AA, 112:23P½.**
Fines and penalties.
Assistants, penalty for practice by unapproved person, **112:9H.**
Board of registration, imposition of fines, **112:5.**
Damages claim or action, physician failing to comply with reporting requirement, **112:5E.**
Death certificate, falsifying or failure to furnish, **46:9B.**

PHYSICIANS AND SURGEONS
—Cont'd

Fines and penalties —Cont'd
Death sentence, **279:65.**
False name, practicing, **112:6.**
Gross misconduct, revocation or suspension of certificate, **112:61.**
Impersonating other physicians, penalty, **112:6.**
Technologist or technician schools, violations, **112:2B, 112:2C.**
Unlawful practice, **112:6.**
After revocation or suspension of certificate, **112:65.**
Fluoroscopic shoe-fitting machines, operation, **111:186A.**
Football games, attendance by physician or persons trained in emergency medical care, **71:54A.**
Foreign state or country.
Canadian graduates, **112:2.**
Controlled substances prescribed by out-of-state physicians, **94C:18.**
Education council for foreign medical graduates, **112:2, 112:9.**
Extension of service in mental health care facilities for foreign medical graduates, **112:9.**
Interns, **112:9.**
Liability for giving aid, exemption, **112:12B.**
Limited application of law, **112:7.**
Prescription by nonresident physician for controlled substances, **94C:18.**
Registration of licensees from other states or countries, **112:2, 112:9B.**
Fraud and deceit.
Certificate of registration, false, **112:58.**
Discipline, **112:5.**
Drugs, fraud and deceit for purpose of evading or violating regulations, **94:187D.**
Examinations for registration, penalty for fraud, **112:6.**
Practicing under false name, **112:6.**
Registration, **112:2, 112:8.**
Suspension of physician, **112:61.**
Unlicensed persons, discipline of physicians permitting medical practice, **112:5.**

PHYSICIANS AND SURGEONS
—Cont'd

Gas and electricity not to be shut off, where physician certifies to serious illness, **164:124A.**
Generic names of drugs, preparation and distribution of formulary, **17:13.**
Gift of human body, physician or surgeon as donee, **113:9.**
Good Samaritans.
See GOOD SAMARITANS.
Gross incompetence, misconduct, or negligence as ground for discipline, **112:5, 112:61.**
Grounds for revocation or suspension of certificate, **112:5, 112:61, 112:65.**
Guardian appointed for mentally ill person, **201:6.**
Gunshot wounds, report, **112:12A.**
Gynecologists.
See OBSTETRICS AND GYNECOLOGY.
Habitual drunkenness or drug use as ground for discipline, **112:5.**
Hallucinogens, discipline of doctor addicted to or dependent, **112:5.**
Hazardous and toxic substances.
Community resident's physician to be given MSDS, **111F:20.**
Employee's physician to be given MSDS, **111F:12.**
Lead poisoning. See within this heading, "Lead poisoning."
Revealing information as to formulation, **94B:3.**
Health board or department appointments, **17:6, 32:91, 111:26, 111:27.**
Health care applicants, effect of disclosures concerning patients who are, **112:12G.**
Health council membership, **17:3.**
Health maintenance organizations.
Physician ownership or investment, regulations, **112:5M.**
Hearing aids.
See HEARING AIDS.
Hospice programs, registered nurses' pronouncement of death of terminally ill patient, **46:9.**
HTLV-III, testing for antibodies or antigens, **111:70F.**
Hygiene as covered subject in examination for registration, **112:3.**
Hypodermic instruments, suspension of certificate for violations, **112:2.**

PHYSICIANS AND SURGEONS
—Cont'd
Immunity from liability.
  Accident victims, emergency aid
    rendered, **112:12B.**
  Emergency medical services
    system.
    Advice or orders given to EMS
      personnel, **111C:20.**
  Medical staff of licensed
    hospital, **231:85N.**
  Mentally ill persons, civil
    immunity for commitment,
    123:22.
  Public health programs,
    112:12C.
  Utilization review activities,
    118E:26.
Impersonating other physicians,
  penalty, **112:6.**
Industrial accident board,
  introduction in evidence of
  medical reports of
  incapacitated, disabled, or
  deceased physicians who
  attended or examined
  plaintiff, **152:20B.**
Industrial schools, **120:3.**
Infectious diseases.
  See CONTAGIOUS AND
    INFECTIOUS DISEASES.
Insanity.
  See MENTALLY ILL AND
    RETARDED PERSONS.
Insurance.
  Accident.
    See ACCIDENT AND
      SICKNESS INSURANCE.
  Automobile liability insurance.
    See within this heading,
    "Automobile liability
    insurance."
  Board of registration, **112:2,**
    112:5C.
  Discrimination in
    reimbursement or payment
    for services legally
    performed under provisions
    of insurance policy,
    175:193K.
  Hospital service corporations.
    See HOSPITAL SERVICE
      CORPORATIONS.
  Liability insurance may include
    medical expenses, **90:34A,**
    90:34M, 175:111C.
  Malpractice.
    See MALPRACTICE.
  Medical service corporations.
    See MEDICAL SERVICE
      CORPORATIONS.

PHYSICIANS AND SURGEONS
—Cont'd
Insurance —Cont'd
  Medical service plans.
    See MEDICAL SERVICE
      PLANS.
  Psychiatric clinical specialists,
    reimbursement, **175:47B,**
    176A:8A, 176B:4A.
  Report concerning actions or
    claims against physician,
    112:5C.
  Tuberculosis, indemnity
    insurance, **111:83A.**
Intensive care unit for mentally ill
  women.
  Civil immunity of physician,
    123:22.
  Psychosurgery not to be
    performed in unit, **123:23.**
Interchangeable drug products,
  prescription, **112:12D.**
Interns.
  See INTERNS.
Intoxicating liquors.
  Alcoholic liquors. See within this
    heading, "Alcoholic liquors."
Isolation hospitals, regulation of
  physicians within limits,
  111:93.
Jury service, exemption, **234:1,**
  234A:4.
Juvenile behavior, council, **6:159.**
Labor.
  See LABOR AND WORKFORCE
    DEVELOPMENT.
Laboratories.
  See LABORATORIES.
Lead poisoning.
  Membership on lead poisoning
    prevention program
    advisory committee,
    111:190.
  Reports, **111:191.**
  Screening of patients, **112:12BB.**
Lens requirements, eyeglasses
  prescribed by physicians,
  270:1A.
Libel and slander in connection
  with physician's disclosure to
  fiancee of person infected with
  venereal disease, **112:12.**
Licensed practical nurse week,
  observance, **6:15LL.**
Licenses.
  Registration. See within this
    heading, "Registration."
Limitation of actions.
  Medical malpractice actions,
    260:4.
  Minors, claims, **231:60D.**
Limited application of laws, **112:7.**

PHYSICIANS AND SURGEONS
—Cont'd
Limited registration.
  Registration. See within this
    heading, "Registration."
Malpractice.
  See MALPRACTICE.
Mammography, qualifications,
  standards, and criteria
  applicable to physicians who
  read and interpret, **112:5L.**
Mandatory retirement age,
  examination by physician to
  permit employees to continue
  working and retire as veterans
  after reaching, **32:90G.**
Medicaid payments, submission of
  bills, **118E:20.**
Medical.
  See MEDICAL AND PHYSICAL
    EXAMINATION.
Medical advisory board, creation,
  90:8C.
Medical care and assistance,
  118E:1 et seq.
  See MEDICAL CARE AND
    ASSISTANCE.
Medical corporations and
  associations.
  See MEDICAL
    CORPORATIONS AND
    ASSOCIATIONS.
Medical examiners, **38:1-38:19.**
  See MEDICAL EXAMINERS
    AND INQUESTS.
Medical milk commission,
  180:20-180:25.
Medical reports of deceased
  physicians, admissibility in
  evidence, **233:79H.**
Medical schools.
  See MEDICAL SCHOOLS.
Medical service corporations,
  176B:1-176B:17.
  See MEDICAL SERVICE
    CORPORATIONS.
Medical Society of Massachusetts,
  111C:7, 112:2C.
Medicolegal investigations
  committee, membership,
  6:184.
Mentally ill.
  See MENTALLY ILL AND
    RETARDED PERSONS.
Military medical officers,
  physicians' registration laws
  as applicable, **112:2, 112:7.**
Militia.
  Eligibility of medical officer,
    33:21.
  State surgeon as adviser, **33:15.**

PHYSICIANS AND SURGEONS
—Cont'd
Militia —Cont'd
Term of office of colonel in
militia, **33:26.**
Misbranded drugs, health
department to furnish list,
94:187.
Misrepresentation.
Fraud and deceit. See within
this heading, "Fraud and
deceit."
Municipal officers.
See CITY AND TOWN
PHYSICIANS.
Narcotic drugs.
See DRUGS AND NARCOTICS.
Neglected children.
Abused or neglected children.
See within this heading,
"Abused and neglected
children."
Negligence on repeated occasions
as ground for discipline, **112:5.**
"No-fault" automobile liability
insurance, effect of physician's
notification of patient's
disability to insurer, **90:34M.**
Nonresident physician.
Foreign state or country. See
within this heading,
"Foreign state or country."
Nurses.
Generally.
Physicians and surgeons as
exempt from law as to
nurses, **112:80B.**
Hospice programs, registered
nurses' pronouncement of
death of patient, **46:9.**
Physicians and surgeons as
exempt from law, **112:80B.**
Nursing homes, reporting and
suspension requirement
exemptions, **111:203.**
Obstetrics.
See OBSTETRICS AND
GYNECOLOGY.
Ophthalmologists.
See OPHTHALMOLOGISTS
AND OPHTHALMOLOGY.
Optometrists, practice by
physicians and surgeons,
112:73.
Osteopaths.
See OSTEOPATHS.
Otolaryngologists.
See OTOLARYNGOLOGISTS.
Party line telephone calls,
166:15C.
Pathology.
See PATHOLOGY AND
PATHOLOGISTS.

PHYSICIANS AND SURGEONS
—Cont'd
Patients' rights, **111:70E.**
Information prior to treatment
by physicians, **112:12Y,
176B:3.**
Pediatrics.
See PEDIATRICS.
Peer review committee, **111:1,
111:203, 111:204.**
Penalties.
Fines and penalties. See within
this heading, "Fines and
penalties."
Pensions.
See RETIREMENT SYSTEMS
AND PENSIONS.
Phenylketonuria test for newborn
children, duties, **111:110A.**
Phototherapy device, **111:213.**
Physical disability, discipline of
doctor who practices while
suffering, **112:5.**
Physically present and actively
treating the patient,
governmental units will pay
physicians only if, **118E:20.**
Physical therapists.
See PHYSICAL THERAPISTS.
Physics as covered subject in
examination for registration,
112:3.
Physiology as covered subject in
examination for registration,
112:3.
Podiatrists, **112:13-112:22.**
See PODIATRY AND
PODIATRISTS.
Premature birth, reports, **111:67A.**
Prescriptions.
See DRUGS AND NARCOTICS.
Prisoners' hospitalization,
certification of necessity,
127:117.
Privileged.
See PRIVILEGED AND
CONFIDENTIAL
MATTERS.
Prize fighting.
See BOXING AND BOXING
MATCHES.
Professional corporations, **156A:2.**
Physical therapists within
definition of professional
services, **156A:2.**
See PROFESSIONAL
CORPORATIONS AND
ASSOCIATIONS.
Provider of health care defined for
purposes of medical
malpractice claims, **231:60B.**

PHYSICIANS AND SURGEONS
—Cont'd
Psychiatry.
See PSYCHIATRY.
Psychologists.
See PSYCHOLOGY.
Public access defibrillation
program, **112:12V½.**
Public employees, board to
determine cause of death,
32:89, 32:89A, 32:89B.
Public employment, physicians.
Extension of limited registration
of certain physicians
employed in state
institutions, **112:2.**
Mental health department,
employment by.
See MENTALLY ILL AND
RETARDED PERSONS.
Retired physicians, emergency
employment by health
department, **32:91.**
State, physicians employed by.
See within this heading,
"State, physicians
employed."
Public health officers, designation,
17:7A, 30:46C.
Public health programs, immunity
from civil liability in
connection, **112:12C.**
Puerto Rican medical school
graduates, registration
without examination, **112:2.**
Qualification and disqualification.
Definition of "qualified"
physician, **123:1.**
Mammography, qualifications,
standards, and criteria
applicable to physicians who
read and interpret, **112:5L.**
Medical service plans,
physicians participating,
176C:5.
Public health department,
physicians appointed, **17:4,
17:6.**
Registration, **112:2.**
Radiation protection advisory
council, doctor as member,
111:4F.
Rape, reporting requirements of
physicians attending victims,
112:12A½.
Records, reports, and returns.
Abused and neglected children
under 16, **119:51A.**
Abuse or neglect of patients in
long-term care facilities,
111:72G.

45

PHYSICIANS AND SURGEONS
—Cont'd
Records, reports, and returns
—Cont'd
Assistant programs, reports
regarding, **112:9G.**
Births, **46:3B, 46:4, 46:8,**
111:24B.
Blindness, report of examination
establishing, **6:136.**
Board of registration. See within
this heading, "Board of
registration."
Bullet wounds, failure to report,
112:72A.
Cerebral palsy, reports, duties,
111:111A.
Certificates of registration,
recording before practice,
112:8.
Convictions of registered
physicians or of
unregistered practitioners,
report, **221:26.**
Dog bites, **112:12Z.**
Hospital, reports by physician
attending birth after which
mother and child not
admitted, **46:3B.**
Injured persons, reports,
175:111F.
Lead poisoning, reports, **111:191.**
Medical examiner, reports of
certain deaths, **38:6.**
Minor's health records,
physician-patient privilege,
112:12F.
Premature birth, reports,
111:67A.
Rape, reporting requirements of
physicians attending
victims, **112:12A½.**
Risk management organization
concerning actions or claims
against physician, **112:5C.**
Sexual crime victims, attending
physician's reporting
requirements, **112:12A½.**
Violent crimes, reports
concerning victims,
112:12A½.
Wounds by guns or knives,
112:12A.
Wrongful death victim, reports
of deceased physicians as to
medical findings or
treatment, admissibility in
evidence, **233:79H.**
Regional medical panels, **32:6.**
Registration, **112:2-112:12A.**
Aliens, **112:2.**
Applications, **112:2.**

PHYSICIANS AND SURGEONS
—Cont'd
Registration —Cont'd
Assistants in medicine, **112:9A,**
112:9G.
Board of registration. See within
this heading, "Board of
registration."
Canadian medical school
graduates, licensing, **112:2.**
Cancellation.
Revocation or suspension. See
within this heading,
"Revocation or suspension
of registration."
Certificates of registration. See
within this heading,
"Certificates of registration."
Certified statement, recording,
112:8.
City and town clerks,
registration, **112:8.**
Complaints and charges. See
within this heading,
"Complaints and charges
against."
Diplomats of specialty boards,
112:2.
Education council for foreign
medical graduates.
See EDUCATION COUNCIL
FOR FOREIGN
MEDICAL GRADUATES.
Electrologists' registration law,
exemption of physicians,
112:87FFF.
Examinations, **112:2.**
Certificate of registration in
lieu, **112:2A.**
Chiropractic.
See CHIROPRACTIC AND
CHIROPRACTORS.
Fees, **112:2.**
Fraud in, penalty, **112:6.**
Hospital and laboratory tests,
employment of assistants,
112:3.
Re-examinations, **112:2.**
Subjects, **112:3.**
Family remedies, law
inapplicable to domestic
administration, **112:7.**
Fees.
Certificates of registration.
See within this heading,
"Certificates of
registration."
Examination fees, **112:2.**
General provisions, **112:88.**
Interns, **112:9.**
Physician assistants, **112:9G.**

PHYSICIANS AND SURGEONS
—Cont'd
Registration —Cont'd
Fees —Cont'd
Recording of certificate, **112:8,**
262:34.
Re-examinations, **112:2.**
Registration without
examination, **112:2A.**
Temporary registration,
112:9B.
Foreign medical school
graduates, **112:2.**
Fraud in securing, **112:2, 112:8.**
Insanity as ground for revoking
registration, **112:61.**
Interns, limited application of
laws, **112:7.**
Limited registration.
Alien physician, **112:2.**
Extension of limited
registration of certain
physicians, **112:2.**
Interns, **112:9.**
Medical students, **112:9A.**
Podiatrists, **112:16A, 112:16C.**
Practice of medicine under
authority, **112:9.**
Medical assistant, qualifications
for registration, **112:9A.**
Military medical officers,
physicians' registration laws
applicable, **112:2, 112:7.**
National board of examiners,
acceptance of certificate,
112:2A.
Osteopaths.
See OSTEOPATHS.
Other states, licensees, **112:2.**
Penalties, **112:6.**
Qualifications, **112:2.**
Renewal, **112:2.**
Revocation or suspension. See
within this heading,
"Revocation or suspension of
registration."
Temporary registration of
certain qualified physicians,
112:9B.
Without examination, **112:2,**
112:2A.
Rehabilitation.
Commission on rehabilitation,
employment, **6:79.**
Facilities for, right of patient to
retain private physician,
111B:11.
Reports.
Records. See within this
heading, "Records, reports,
and returns."

PHYSICIANS AND SURGEONS
—Cont'd

Residents in medical specialties, establishment of program for hospital training, **17:6A.**

Resignation, acceptance of, report to board of registration in medicine, **111:53B.**

Restrictive covenants unenforceable against, **112:12X.**

Retarded persons.
  See MENTALLY ILL AND RETARDED PERSONS.

Retirement systems.
  See RETIREMENT SYSTEMS AND PENSIONS.

Revocation or suspension of registration.
  Complaints and charges, **112:5, 112:61 to 112:63.**
  Grounds, **112:2, 112:5, 112:61, 112:65.**
  Interns, **112:9.**
  Medical students, **112:9A.**
  Penalty for practicing after, **112:65.**
  Powers of board, **112:2, 112:61.**
  Reissuance after, **112:2.**
  Revision or reversal by supreme judicial court, **112:64.**

Reyes syndrome, reports by persons examining or treating disease, **111:110B.**

Rules and regulations.
  Board of registration. See within this heading, "Board of registration."
  General provisions, **112:88.**

Salaries.
  Wages, salaries, and compensation. See within this heading, "Wages, salaries, and compensation."

Schools.
  Generally.
    See SCHOOLS AND EDUCATION.
  Medical schools.
    See MEDICAL SCHOOLS.

Sexual offenses and offenders, reporting requirements of physicians attending victims, **112:12A½.**

Sexual sterilization procedures.
  Sterilization procedures. See within this heading, "Sterilization procedures."

Shoe-fitting machines, operation, **111:186A.**

Smallpox regulations, **111:93.**

PHYSICIANS AND SURGEONS
—Cont'd

Social Security Act Title XVIII health insurance, registration contingent on agreement, **112:2.**

Social services department physicians, appointment and removal, **18:9.**

Soldiers' Home in Holyoke, medical staff, **6:71.**

Specialty boards, mental retardation department, **19B:8.**

Spiritual healers, inapplicability of laws as to physicians, **112:7.**

Stabbings, report as to treatment, **112:12A.**

State, physicians employed.
  American Medical Association, certification of physicians prior to appointment or employment in state department or institution, **17:4, 17:6.**
  Contributory retirement appeal board of state physicians, **32:16.**
  Lien for services furnished in hospitals, **111:70A.**
  Office buildings of state, appointment and duties of physician, **7:6E.**
  Recruitment of physicians in service, **30:46.**

State hospitals.
  See MENTALLY ILL AND RETARDED PERSONS.

State surgeon.
  See STATE SURGEON.

Sterilization procedures.
  Refusal to perform on moral or religious grounds, **112:12I.**
  Written consent necessary before performing, **112:12W.**

Students, practice of medicine, **112:9A.**

Subpoenas, **112:5.**

Surgery.
  Osteopaths not to engage, **112:11.**
  Subject covered in examination for registration, **112:3.**
  Training grants for fellows, **115A:10.**

Surgical devices, **94:1, 94:189-94:194.**
  See SURGICAL DEVICES.

Suspension of registration.
  Revocation or suspension of registration. See within this heading, "Revocation or suspension of registration."

PHYSICIANS AND SURGEONS
—Cont'd

Tattooing, exception in law prohibiting, **265:34.**

Teachers examined by school physician, **71:54, 71:55B.**

Teaching physician, temporary registration, **112:9B.**

Telephone calls on party lines, **166:15C.**

Temporary registration, **112:9B.**

Therapists.
  See PHYSICAL THERAPISTS.

Town physicians.
  See CITY AND TOWN PHYSICIANS.

Toxic substances.
  Hazardous and toxic substances. See within this heading, "Hazardous and toxic substances."

Transcripts, recording of testimony, **112:5.**

Tribunal for hearing of medical malpractice claims, composition and establishment, **231:60B.**

Tuberculosis.
  Appointment, **17:6, 111:87.**
  Indemnity insurance, **111:83A.**

Unemployment compensation for interns, **151A:6.**

United States, medical officers, **112:2, 112:7.**

University of Massachusetts, **75:36C.**

Unlawful practice.
  Aiding and abetting, **112:2, 112:5, 265:10.**
  Certificate of registration or certified statement, recording of false, **112:8.**
  Compensation, unlawful practice as precluding recovery, **112:6.**
  Osteopaths, **112:11.**
  Penalties for.
    Fines and penalties. See within this heading, "Fines and penalties."
  Revocation or suspension of registration on ground, **112:2, 112:61, 112:65.**

Venereal diseases, **112:12.**

Veteran, physician furnishing death certificate to state causes of death, **46:10.**

Veterinarians, **112:54-112:60.**
  See VETERINARIANS.

Violation of laws, rules, or regulations pertaining to practice of medicine as grounds for discipline, **112:5.**

PHYSICIANS AND SURGEONS
—Cont'd

Violent crimes, required reports concerning victims, **112:12A½.**

Visiting physicians.
Good Samaritan law, temporary licensees as entitled to protection, **112:12B, 112:12C.**
Temporary registration, **112:9B.**

Visual services, reimbursement for performance, **151D:4, 175:108, 175:110.**

Voter, certifying as to physical disability, **54:86.**

Wages, salaries, and compensation.
Board of registration and discipline in medicine, **112:2.**

Discrimination in reimbursement or payment for services legally performed under provisions of insurance policy, **175:193K.**

Fees. See within this heading, "Fees."

Hospital treatment charges, liability of physician hospitalizing injured person, **112:12B.**

Medical examiners.
See MEDICAL EXAMINERS AND INQUESTS.

State house physician, **7:6B.**

State office building physician, **7:6E.**

Unlawful practices as precluding recovery, **112:6.**

Visual services, reimbursement for performance, **151D:4, 175:108, 175:110.**

Workers' compensation.
See WORKERS' COMPENSATION.

Workers' compensation.
See WORKERS' COMPENSATION.

Written consent necessary before performing sterilization procedures, **112:12W.**

X-Rays.
Malpractice, instructions to jury, **231:60J.**
Membership on radiation protection advisory council, **111:4F.**
Shoe-fitting machines, supervision of operation, **111:186A.**

Youth services department, **120:2, 120:3.**

PHYSICIAN'S REGISTRATION ACT, 112:2 et seq.

PHYSICS.

Physical therapists, subject of examination for registration, **112:23E.**

Physician or surgeon, subjects covered in examination for registration, **112:3.**

PHYSIOLOGY.

Optometrists, subject of examination for registration, **112:68.**

Physical therapists, subject of examination for registration, **112:23E.**

Physicians, required subject of examination for registration, **112:3.**

Schools, required to be taught, **71:18.**

Veterinarians, subject of examination for registration, **112:56.**

PICK CLOCKS.
Testing, **98:41.**

PICKEREL.
Sale prohibited, **131:22.**

PICKER MACHINES.
Minors under sixteen working, **149:61.**

PICKETING.
Courts, jurors, and witnesses, **268:13A.**

Labor relations.
See LABOR RELATIONS AND DISPUTES.

Medical facilities, **266:120E.**

Obstruction of justice, **268:13A.**

Private detectives interfering, **147:30.**

PICKPOCKETS.
Discharge on recognizance, **272:57.**
Vagabonds, pickpockets as within meaning, **272:68.**

PICNIC AREAS.
Parks.
See PARKS AND RESERVATIONS.

PICTURES OR PHOTOGRAPHS.
Arrest.
Fingerprinting and photographing.
See ARREST.

Cemeteries, consent for taking of commercial photographs, **114:42B.**

PICTURES OR PHOTOGRAPHS —Cont'd

Child pornography, **272:29A-272:31.**
See CHILD PORNOGRAPHY.

Commercial driver license, **90F:7, 90F:8.**

Controlled Substances Act, effect of felony charge, **94C:45.**

Copies.
See PHOTOSTATIC COPIES.

Costs in civil action as including expense, **261:25A.**

Dentists, illegal advertising, **112:52A.**

Felony.
Controlled Substances Act, effect of felony charge, **94C:45.**
Photographing of persons arrested for commission, **263:1A.**

Gas and electric company employees' badges to display, **164:116.**

Horse and dog racing meetings, licensed persons required to wear photographic identification, **128A:9A.**

Hospital records, admissibility of photographic or microphotographic records, **233:79.**

Liability of photographer for unauthorized use, **214:3A.**

Library books, defacement, **266:99.**

License photographs, **90:8, 90F:7, 90F:8.**

Liens for work performed, **255:31F.**

Mentally ill and retarded persons, commercial exploitation of patient, **19:19, 19B:15.**

Microphotography.
See MICROPHOTOGRAPHY.

Motion pictures.
See MOTION PICTURES.

Motor vehicle operator's license, photograph of licensee to appear, **90:8.**

Pawning of articles, photographing of persons involved, **140:79.**

Photostatic copies.
See PHOTOSTATIC COPIES.

Police.
Commissioner of public safety, fingerprints and photographs of persons arrested for commission of felony to be forwarded, **263:1A.**
Compensation for assignment to photographic work, **41:108I.**

PICTURES OR
PHOTOGRAPHS —Cont'd
Police —Cont'd
Riot or similar disturbance,
photographing and
fingerprinting of persons
arrested in connection,
41:98.
Portraits.
See PORTRAITS.
Probate court orders and decrees
to be recorded by means of
photographic process, **215:36.**
Public records as including, **4:7.**
Reproduction of destroyed business
and public records,
admissibility in evidence,
233:79E.
Riots and similar disturbances,
photographing of persons
arrested during, **41:98.**
Sales tax exemptions, photography
studios or services, **64H:1.**
Secretary of state, authority to
destroy certain original
records previously reproduced,
9:19.
Service defined for tax purposes,
64H:1, 64I:1.
State house.
Former governors, portraits,
8:19, 8:19A.
Portraits and art objects,
availability of photographs,
9:28.
Subversive organizations.
Pictures and other papers used,
264:11.
Search warrant for pictures and
other papers used, **276:1A.**
Sunday, sale or processing of
photographic films, **136:6.**
Trademark, registration of portrait
of living person, **110B:3.**
Trial.
Admission in evidence of
photographic copies,
151A:44, 233:79, 233:79A,
233:79D, 233:79E.
Expense of photographs used,
261:25A.
Unauthorized use, liability of
photographer, **214:3A.**
Water company, district employees'
badges to display, **165:11D.**

PIECEWORK.
See LABOR AND WORKFORCE
DEVELOPMENT.

PIERS, 88:14-88:19.
See WHARVES, PIERS, AND
DOCKS.

PIGEONS.
Killing or frightening, penalty,
266:132.
Protection of homing pigeons,
131:84.
Shooting for target practice,
272:87.

PIGS.
See SWINE.

PIKE PERCH.
Sale, regulated, **131:22.**

PILES.
Commonwealth land, driving,
91:22.
Licensing, **91:14-91:18.**
Tidewaters, driving, **91:20, 91:22.**

PILFERAGE.
See LARCENY AND THEFT.

PILGRIM TERCENTENARY
COMMISSION.
Property in Plymouth acquired by,
powers, **91:2A.**

PILLOW.
Defined under law regulating
inspection of bedding, **94:270.**

PILLS.
Distribution of medicines, penalty,
270:3.

PILOT LIGHTS.
Appliances, prohibition, **148:25E.**

PILOTS OF AIRPLANES.
See AIRCRAFT AND
AVIATION.

PILOTS OF VESSELS,
103:1-103:35.
Acceptance.
Offers of pilotage. See within
this heading, "Offer of
pilotage."
Accounts to be rendered to
commissioners, **103:5.**
Anchoring of vessel.
Harbor master's regulations,
anchoring in accordance,
102:21.
Immigration or quarantine
inspection, failure to anchor
vessel, **103:33.**
Arbitration of controversies
between, **103:34.**
Bond, **103:6.**
Discharge of surety, **103:15.**
New bond, **103:15, 103:16.**
Boston harbor, pilot district, **103:1.**
Pilotage rates, **103:31.**
Secretary to commissioners of
district, **103:4.**

PILOTS OF VESSELS —Cont'd
Boston marine society,
appointment and
compensation of
commissioners, **103:2, 103:5.**
Commissioners and deputy
commissioners, **103:2.**
Compensation, **103:5.**
Powers and duties, **103:3.**
Secretary, first district, **103:4.**
Commissions, **103:3.**
Exhibitions to shipmasters,
103:19.
Rates paid by district one pilots,
103:5.
Revocation or suspension of. See
within this heading,
"Revocation or suspension of
commission."
Unlicensed person acting as
pilot, **103:35.**
Compulsory pilotage.
Exemptions, **103:28.**
Vessel refusing to take pilot
liable for fees, **103:21.**
Deputy commissioners.
Commissioners and deputy
commissioners. See within
this heading,
"Commissioners and deputy
commissioners."
Discrimination in taking vessels,
prohibited, **103:21.**
District one percentage paid to
commissioners, **103:5.**
Districts.
Boston harbor, pilot district. See
within this heading, "Boston
harbor, pilot district."
Exhibition of commission to
shipmaster, **103:19.**
Fees, **103:31.**
Establishment by
commissioners, **103:3.**
Lien for pilot's, **103:17.**
Percentage to be paid to
commissioners, **103:5.**
Port of Boston, **103:31.**
Rates. See within this heading,
"Rates."
Refusal of pilotage, **103:21.**
Fines and penalties.
Acting without license, **103:35.**
False return as to fees, **103:5.**
Humane society property, pilots
to make complaint against
persons injuring, **266:133.**
First vessel signaling, duty to
take, **103:21.**
Humane society, complaint against
persons injuring property,
266:133.

PILOTS OF VESSELS —Cont'd
Lien for fees, **103:17.**
Negligence, liability, **103:18.**
Offer of pilotage.
  Refusal of, payment of fees,
    103:21.
Penalties.
  Fines and penalties. See within
    this heading, "Fines and
    penalties."
Quarantine.
  Penalty for failure to anchor
    vessel under quarantine at
    proper place, **103:33.**
Rates.
  Boston harbor pilot districts
    rates for pilotage, **103:31.**
  District one, rates paid to
    commission by pilots, **103:5.**
Revocation or suspension of
  commission, **103:3.**
  Failure to anchor for
    immigration or quarantine
    inspection, **103:33.**
  Taking vessel of deeper draft
    than authorized, **103:20.**
Salaries and compensation.
  Fees. See within this heading,
    "Fees."
Surety on bond, discharge, **103:15.**

PILOT STUDIES.
Administration and finance
  executive office, duties, **7:9.**

PIMPING.
Criminal offense, **272:7, 272:8.**

PINBALL MACHINES.
See AUTOMATIC AMUSEMENT
  DEVICES.

PINE LOOPERS.
Suppression, **132:11.**
Transportation, **266:119.**

PIONEER VALLEY TRANSIT
  AUTHORITY.
Authorization, **161B:2.**

PIPED-IN MUSIC.
Sales tax exemption, **64H:1.**

PIPEFITTERS AND
  REFRIGERATION
  TECHNICIANS, 146:81 et
  seq.
Apprentice pipefitter, defined,
  146:81.
Bureau.
  Defined, **146:81.**
  Membership, **22:10A.**
Definitions, **146:81.**
Examination and licensing,
  146:83.
  Applicability of law to certain
    workers, **146:87, 146:88.**

PIPEFITTERS AND
REFRIGERATION
TECHNICIANS —Cont'd
Examination and licensing
  —Cont'd
  Application, filing, **146:85.**
  Classification of licenses, **146:86.**
  Examiners, **146:83.**
  Exceptions as to licensing
    requirements, **146:87,**
    146:88.
  Fees, **146:85.**
  Inapplicability of law to certain
    workers, **146:87, 146:88.**
  Limitations in license based on
    size of refrigeration system,
    146:86.
  Refrigeration systems,
    limitations in license based
    on size, **146:86.**
  Rules and regulations, **146:82.**
  Unlicensed work, **146:84.**
  Violation of provisions, penalty,
    146:89.
Fire sprinkler system contractors
  and fitters, defined, **146:81.**
Inspection of refrigeration
  systems, **146:45A.**
Journeyman pipefitter, defined,
  146:81.
Licenses and permits.
  Examination and licensing. See
    within this heading,
    "Examination and
    licensing."
Master pipefitter, defined, **146:81.**
Pipefitting, defined, **146:81.**
Refrigeration.
  Contractor, **146:81.**
  Defined, **146:81.**
  Technician, defined, **146:81.**
  Trainee, defined, **146:81.**

PIPES AND PIPELINES,
  164:75B-164:75E.
Atomic energy installations, duties
  of board of boiler rules as
  piping used, **146:2.**
Cities.
  See CITIES AND TOWNS.
Coal mining licenses, contents of
  application, **21B:5.**
Construction and maintenance,
  164:75C.
Easements.
  Parks, **30:44B, 164:75C.**
  State highways, **81:7D.**
  State lands, **30:44B.**
Eminent domain for location,
  164:69S.
Franchise tax, pipeline companies,
  63:52A.

PIPES AND PIPELINES
  —Cont'd
Gas.
  See GAS AND ELECTRIC
    COMPANIES.
Highways and streets, pipelines
  along or under, **40:42-40:43A.**
  See HIGHWAYS AND
    STREETS.
Metropolitan districts.
  Boulevards and reservations,
    granting right of way for
    pipelines, **30:44B.**
Municipal finance.
  See MUNICIPAL FINANCE.
Natural gas pipeline companies.
  See NATURAL GAS PIPELINE
    COMPANIES.
Oil.
  See GAS AND OIL.
Parks and reservations, right of
  way, **30:44B, 164:75C.**
Pipefitters.
  See PIPEFITTERS AND
    REFRIGERATION
    TECHNICIANS.
Plastic pipe, grounding of
  electrical systems upon
  installation, **165:1C.**
Public lands.
  State lands. See within this
    heading, "State lands."
Public works and departments.
  Construction or repairs,
    approval of, pipeline
    company's proposed,
    164:75C.
  Easements in state highways,
    81:7D.
  Taxation, **59:3C.**
  Water mains and aqueducts,
    borrowing outside debt limit
    for reconstructing, etc., **44:8.**
Railroad grade crossing, removal
  or relocation upon abolition,
    159:74, 159:75.
Right of way.
  Easements. See within this
    heading, "Easements."
State lands.
  Easements, **30:44B.**
  Forest lands, granting right of
    way for gas lines over,
    132:34A.
Taxation, **40:43, 59:3C, 59:18.**
  Assessors, **59:3C, 59:38, 59:38A.**
  Franchise tax for pipeline
    companies, **63:52A.**
  Generally.
    See TAXATION.
  Valuation, **59:38A.**

PIPES AND PIPELINES
—Cont'd
Towns.
See CITIES AND TOWNS.
Valuation, appeal from
commissioner's determination,
telephone and telegraph
companies, **59:38A, 59:41,
59:42.**
Waters.
See WATERS AND
WATERWAYS.
Waterworks.
See WATERWORKS AND
WATER SUPPLY.

**PIPE SMOKING.
See TOBACCO.**

PIPETTES.
Testing of milk.
See MILK AND MILK
PRODUCTS.

PISTOL CANE.
Manufacture and sale of, penalty,
269:12.

PITTSFIELD.
Alcoholic beverage licenses,
hearing on appeals to
commission, **138:67.**
County commissioners, meeting,
34:9.
District court held, **218:1.**
Medical examiner district, **38:1.**
Motor carriers of property,
hearings upon certificates of
public convenience and
necessity, **159B:3.**
Nurses' examinations for
registration, places for
holding, **112:74.**
Probate court sessions for
Berkshire county to be held,
215:62.
Senatorial district, **57:3.**
Superior court sittings, **212:14.**

**PITTSFIELD OFFICE
BUILDING.**
Commissioner's duties regarding
use of space, **7:40F.**
Superintendent of buildings, care
and operation for buildings of
state, **8:9.**

PIVOT GUN.
Use in taking of birds forbidden,
131:68.

PLACARDS.
Lottery prosecution, prima facie
evidence, **271:21.**
Malicious injury to, penalty,
266:125.

PLACARDS —Cont'd
Prima facie evidence of keeping
firearms for purpose of sale,
140:126.

**PLACEMENT OF CHILDREN.
See CHILDREN AND MINORS.**

PLAGUE.
Removal of prisoners in case,
126:26.

PLAIN ENGLISH LAW.
Credit unions, real estate loans,
171:65.
Insurance policies as governed,
175:2B.

PLAINFIELD.
Congressional district, **57:1.**
Medical examiner district, **38:1.**
Senatorial district, **57:3.**

**PLAINTIFF.
See PARTIES TO ACTIONS.**

PLAINVILLE.
Congressional district, **57:1.**
District court, **218:1.**
Medical examiner district, **38:1.**
Senatorial district, **57:3.**

**PLAN A FORM OF CITY
GOVERNMENT, 43:46-43:55.
See CITY CHARTERS.**

**PLAN B FORM OF CITY
GOVERNMENT, 43:56-43:63.
See CITY CHARTERS.**

**PLAN C FORM OF CITY
GOVERNMENT, 43:64 et
seq.
See CITY CHARTERS.**

**PLAN D FORM OF CITY
GOVERNMENT, 43:79-92A.
See CITY CHARTERS.**

**PLAN E FORM OF CITY
GOVERNMENT,
43:93-43:116.
See CITY CHARTERS.**

**PLAN F FORM OF CITY
GOVERNMENT,
43:117-43:127.
See CITY CHARTERS.**

**PLANE RECTANGULAR
CO-ORDINATES SYSTEM.**
Maps, plats, and surveys,
97:8-97:17.

PLANETARIUMS.
Discrimination because of race,
color, etc., **272:92A, 272:98.**

PLANING BUSINESS.
Dust removal provisions for emery
wheels inapplicable to planing
mills, **149:121.**

PLANING BUSINESS —Cont'd
Minors under sixteen not to work
on planers, **149:61.**

PLANNED PARENTHOOD.
Contraceptives.
See CONTRACEPTIVES.
Social services department,
administration of programs,
18B:2.

PLANNING ACT, 41:70 et seq.
Cities, **41:70 et seq.**
Zoning and planning.
See ZONING AND PLANNING.

**PLANNING AND RESEARCH
BUREAU.**
Human resources division, **7:4J.**

**PLANNING ASSISTANCE
BUREAU.**
Housing and community
development department,
statutory references as
meaning or referring, **23B:10.**

**PLANNING BOARDS.
See ZONING AND PLANNING.**

**PLANNING ECONOMIC
DEVELOPMENT.
See ECONOMIC
DEVELOPMENT
DEPARTMENT.**

**PLANS AND
SPECIFICATIONS.**
Aircraft to be designed to meet
federal standards, **90:48.**
Airport plan, preparation and
revision, **90:39A.**
Architects.
See ARCHITECTS AND
ARCHITECTURE.
Architectural Barriers Board to
receive copies, **22:13A.**
Assisted living residences,
operating plan, **19D:4.**
Boston harbor, planning, **91:9,
91:9A.**
Boundaries of flats, plan of
commissioners establishing,
240:20, 240:21.
Bridges.
See BRIDGES.
Building projects prepared for
agency subject to division of
capital operations, plans,
studies, programs, and
designs, **7:41B.**
Buildings and structures, **143:62.**
Capital projects, plans and
specifications for bidding,
149:44B, 149:44F.

PLANS AND SPECIFICATIONS
—Cont'd
Cemeteries at or near water
supply, approval of plan,
114:35.
Cities.
See CITIES AND TOWNS.
Civil service director's approval
and supplementation of job
specifications, **31:5.**
Coal mines.
Abandonment, **21B:12.**
Comprehensive reclamation plan
for coal mining licenses,
21B:5.
Commission of public works,
powers, **16:5.**
Common victualler's or innholder's
license, requirements, **140:6.**
Compliance, **30:39I.**
Comprehensive programs.
See COMPREHENSIVE
PROGRAMS OR PLANS.
Condominium, certification of
copies of plans required to
accompany deeds, **183A:8,
183A:9.**
Conservation district supervisors,
powers and duties, **21:24.**
Copies.
See COPIES.
Costs in civil actions as including
expense, **261:25A.**
Dams.
Approval of plans.
See DAMS AND
RESERVOIRS.
Deeds.
Condominium, certification of
copies of plans required to
accompany deeds, **183A:8,
183A:9.**
Registers.
See REGISTERS AND
REGISTRIES OF DEEDS.
Unregistered land conveyed by
deed, requirements as to
identification of property for
recording, **183:6A.**
Deviation, **30:39I.**
Districts' authority to borrow
money for preparation, **44:7.**
Drains.
See SEWERS AND DRAINS.
Energy supply shortage
contingency plans and energy
emergencies, **25A:8.**
Engineers.
See ENGINEERS AND
SURVEYORS.
Environmental affairs executive
office, duties and functions,
21A:2.

PLANS AND SPECIFICATIONS
—Cont'd
Evidence.
Expense of preparation, plans,
drawings, photographs and
certified copies, **261:25A.**
Subdivision control law,
endorsements or certificates
on plan, **41:81K.**
Eyeglass and sunglass lenses,
specifications, **270:1A.**
Federal standards, aircraft plans
and specifications to meet,
90:48.
Forest cutting operations, **132:42.**
Grade crossings, abolition, **159:70,
161:129.**
Handicapped persons, design of
public facilities, **143:3W.**
Hazardous waste insolvency fund,
21C:15, 21C:23.
Hazardous waste management act,
license requirements, **21C:7.**
Health council, duties, **111:3.**
Housing.
See HOUSING AND URBAN
RENEWAL.
Housing and community
development department.
See HOUSING AND
COMMUNITY
DEVELOPMENT
DEPARTMENT.
Improvements to real property,
limitations on actions for
damages arising out of,
260:2B.
Insurance rates.
Casualty insurance.
See INSURANCE RATES
AND RATING
ORGANIZATIONS.
Fire, etc.
See INSURANCE RATES
AND RATING
ORGANIZATIONS.
Land court fees for filing, **262:39.**
Land plans, recording of certain,
41:81X.
Landscape architects' seals,
112:100.
Land titles.
See REGISTRATION OF LAND
TITLES.
Manufactured homes and
manufactured housing
communities, plan showing
set-up of premises, **140:32H.**
Maps.
See MAPS, PLATS, AND
SURVEYS.

PLANS AND SPECIFICATIONS
—Cont'd
Mass transportation facilities and
services, duties of
transportation planning and
development bureau, **16:3A.**
Master plan.
See MASTER PLAN.
Materials, **30:39M.**
Mines.
Coal mines. See within this
heading, "Coal mines."
Morris plan banks.
See MORRIS PLAN BANKS.
Municipalities.
See CITIES AND TOWNS.
Overhead wires and poles, plans
for progressive removal,
166:22D.
Partition.
Cost of plan, **241:22.**
Court as ordering plan, **241:17.**
Physically handicapped, design of
public buildings to facilitate
use, **143:3W.**
Planning boards.
See ZONING AND PLANNING.
Playgrounds, master plan, **41:81D.**
Public construction materials,
specification, **30:39M.**
Public works, **16:5, 149:44B,
149:44F.**
Registration seal of architect or
engineer, when required,
143:54A.
Railroads.
See RAILROADS.
Reclamation plan for coal mining
licenses, **21B:5.**
Records and recording.
Boundaries of flats, recording of
report and plan
establishing, **240:20, 240:21.**
Land plans, recording of certain,
41:81X.
Municipal planning boards,
master plan, **41:81D.**
Registers of deeds, filing of
plans, **36:13A, 36:13B,
262:38.**
Term "record" as including plans
and specifications, **66:3.**
Regional refuse disposal districts.
See REGIONAL REFUSE
DISPOSAL DISTRICTS.
Registers.
See REGISTERS AND
REGISTRIES OF DEEDS.
Registration of land titles.
See REGISTRATION OF LAND
TITLES.

PLANS AND SPECIFICATIONS
—Cont'd

Sample as superseded by specifications in considering inconsistent warranties, **106:2-317.**

School buildings, notice of change in plans for construction or alteration, **43:34.**

Seal of architect or engineer, when required on building plans and specifications, **143:54A.**

Sewers.
See SEWERS AND DRAINS.

Shore reservations in towns, establishment, **45:23B.**

Signature of engineer or land surveyor on, requirement, **112:81M.**

State airport plan, preparation and revision, **90:39A.**

Street railways.
Abolition of grade crossings, approval of plans by aldermen or selectmen, **161:129.**
Application for authority to purchase or lease land, plan, **161:55.**
Bridges, construction plans to be submitted to department, **159:83.**

Subdivision control law.
See ZONING AND PLANNING.

Surveys.
See MAPS, PLATS, AND SURVEYS.

Tidal bounds of streams, fixing, **131:4.**

Transportation and construction executive office.
See TRANSPORTATION AND CONSTRUCTION EXECUTIVE OFFICE.

Wage rates in textile factories, failure to post specifications, **149:156.**

Warranties.
Compliance with specifications, seller's warranty as affected, **106:2-312.**
Sample or description as superseded by specifications in considering inconsistent warranties, **106:2-317.**

Water pollution.
See WATER POLLUTION.

Zoning and planning, **40A:1-40A:22, 41:70-41:72.**
See ZONING AND PLANNING.

PLANTATIONS.
Records, **66:5, 66:7.**

PLANT CLOSING.
Definition, **151A:71A.**
Report, **151A:71B.**

PLANT PEST CONTROL ACT, **128:16 et seq.**

PLANT REGULATOR.
Defined, pest control, **132B:3.**

PLANTS AND PLANT DISEASES AND PESTS.

Actions against owners, **128:24.**

Agriculture, commissioner.
Appeals, **128:25, 128:26.**
Enforcement of laws, **128:2.**
Prosecutions instituted and directed, **128:30.**

Appeals from action of director, **128:25, 128:26.**

Berry-bearing shrubbery, compensation for destruction, **128:23.**

Browntail moth.
See BROWNTAIL MOTH.

Bureau of insect pest control, entry on land in discharge of duties by agents, **132:8.**

Certificate of inspection.
Out-of-state shipments, **128:20.**
Required for sale or shipment, **128:19.**

Cities and towns.
County aid for suppression, **132:26D.**
Expenditures by Commonwealth, **132:14, 132:16.**
Foliage-destroying pests, suppression, **132:25.**
Limitation on expenditures, **132:16.**
Notice to cities and towns as to financial liability, **132:14.**
Reimbursement by Commonwealth, **132:14.**
State aid, **132:14, 132:16.**

Commissioner of Agriculture.
Agriculture, commissioner of.
See within this heading, "Agriculture, commissioner."

Commonwealth land, suppression of moths and other insect pests, **132:12A.**

Compensation of owner with respect to suppression of white pine blister rust, **128:23.**

Cutting or carrying away plants as criminal offense, **266:113.**

Definitions, **132B:3.**

Department of food and agriculture, enforcement of laws by, **20:6, 128:2.**

PLANTS AND PLANT DISEASES AND PESTS
—Cont'd

Destruction of property.
Dutch elm disease, **132:26A, 132:26E to 132:26G.**
Proceedings after appeal, **128:26.**
San Jose scale, **128:24.**
White pine blister rust, compensation, **128:23.**

Digging up plants of certain wildflowers as criminal offense, **266:116A.**

Director, **128:16-128:31A.**
Appeals from actions, **128:25, 128:26.**
Certificate to nurseries, **128:17, 128:20.**
Entry on public or private grounds, **128:16.**
Examination and inspections.
Nurseries, **128:17.**
Orchards, fields, etc., **128:24.**
Fruit imported into state, duties, **128:21.**
Office placed under civil service, **128:1.**
Publication of information, **128:27.**
Reciprocal agreements with other states as to nursery stock, **128:27.**
Revocation of nursery agent's license, **128:18.**
Rules and regulations, **128:27.**

Director of office of lands and natural resources to assume duties of local superintendents of insect pest control, **41:69G.**

District moth supervisors, entry on land in discharge of duties, **132:8.**

Dutch elm disease, **132:11, 132:26A-132:26D.**
Certified itemized statements of expenditures, **132:15.**
County aid to municipalities, **132:26D.**
Diagnosis, procedure following notice, **132:26E-132:26G.**
Entry into land and premises, **132:8.**
Local superintendents of insect pest control, **132:13.**
Reimbursement of cities and towns by Commonwealth, **132:14.**
Removal and destruction of infected trees, **132:26A, 132:26E-132:26G.**

PLANTS AND PLANT DISEASES AND PESTS
—Cont'd
Dutch elm disease —Cont'd
State aid to municipalities, **132:14, 132:16.**
Elm leaf beetles, **132:11-132:27.**
Endangered species act.
See ENDANGERED SPECIES ACT.
Enforcement by department of agriculture, **128:2.**
Environmental management department, **132:11, 132:13, 132:14.**
European corn borer.
See EUROPEAN CORN BORER.
Examination and inspection.
Certificate of inspection, **128:19, 128:20.**
Director. See within this heading, "Director."
Fees, **128:27.**
Gardens, **128:24.**
Nurseries, **128:17.**
Orchards, **128:24.**
Out-of-state nursery stock and plants, **128:21.**
San Jose scale, plants infested, **128:24.**
Trees and shrubs, **128:24.**
Fines.
See FINES AND PENALTIES.
Flowers.
See FLOWERS AND FLORICULTURE.
Foliage-destroying pests in cities or towns, jurisdiction over suppression, **132:25.**
Food.
See FOOD AND AGRICULTURE DEPARTMENT.
Forest and shade tree pests and diseases, suppression, **132:11.**
Forest warden, duties, **132:37.**
Fruits imported from out of state, **128:21.**
Gardens, inspection, **128:24.**
Gypsy moth.
See GYPSY MOTH.
Hawkers and peddlers, sale of flowering plants, **101:17.**
Highways.
Inspection, **128:24.**
Hindrance of officers, penalty, **128:29.**
Importation of insect pests as criminal offense, **266:119.**
Importation of plants.
Certificate of inspection required, **128:20.**

PLANTS AND PLANT DISEASES AND PESTS
—Cont'd
Importation of plants —Cont'd
Destruction or treatment of infested plants, **128:21.**
European corn borer, importation of plant infested, **128:31.**
Inspection, **128:21.**
Notice to director of division of plant pest control, **128:21.**
Nursery stock, **128:20, 128:21.**
Prohibition, **128:27.**
Insects, **132:1 et seq.**
Inspection.
Examination and inspection. See within this heading, "Examination and inspection."
Local moth superintendents, town public works board as successor, **41:69D.**
Local superintendents of insect pest control.
Accounts, **132:15.**
Appointment, **132:13.**
Director of office of lands and natural resources to assume duties, **41:69G.**
Duties and powers, **132:13.**
Foliage-destroying pests, jurisdiction over suppression, **132:25.**
Interfering with work of, penalty, **132:12.**
Itemized statements of expenditures, **132:15.**
License, **132:13.**
Notice of appointment to commissioner, **132:13.**
Private work performed in cities and towns, voucher, **132:15.**
Marine plants, taking by mechanical means, **130:102.**
Moths.
See MOTHS.
Motor vehicle junkyards, plantings to screen, **140B:3.**
Municipalities.
Cities and towns. See within this heading, "Cities and towns."
Notice and knowledge.
Cities and towns, financial liability for suppression of moths, etc., **132:14.**
Dutch elm disease, procedure following notice of positive diagnosis, **132:26E.**
Imported plants, **128:21.**

PLANTS AND PLANT DISEASES AND PESTS
—Cont'd
Notice and knowledge —Cont'd
Nursery stock shipped from out of state, **128:20, 128:21.**
Posting of signs designating infested trees, **132:8.**
Proceedings after appeal involving plant pests or diseases, **128:26.**
Publication of orders for control, **128:31.**
Nuisances, **128:24, 132:1A, 132:16.**
Nurseries.
See NURSERIES AND NURSERY STOCK.
Orchards, inspection, **128:24.**
Oriental hag moth.
Suppression, **132:11-132:27.**
Transportation, **266:119.**
Penalties.
See FINES AND PENALTIES.
Pesticides, **132B:1 et seq.**
See PESTICIDES.
Pine loopers.
Suppression, **132:1.**
Transportation, **266:119.**
Plant regulation, defined, **132B:3.**
Posting of signs designating infested trees, **132:8.**
Private land, trees infected by Dutch elm disease, **132:26F.**
Prosecutions for violations of law, **128:30.**
Publication of orders for suppression, **128:31.**
Public nuisance, moths, **132:1A.**
Quarantine, **128:27.**
Publication of orders for suppression, **128:31.**
Reciprocal agreements with other states as to nursery stock, **128:27.**
Records of moth superintendent's expenditures, **132:1A.**
Report to commissioner of natural resources, **132:1A.**
Roadside plants, inspection, **128:24.**
Sales tax, exemptions, **64H:6.**
San Jose scale, regulations for protection against, **128:24.**
Seeds.
See SEEDS.
Shade trees, **40:5, 87:7.**
Shrubs.
See SHRUBS AND SHRUBBERY.
Soil, water and related resources committee, powers and duties, **21:20.**

PLANTS AND PLANT DISEASES AND PESTS
—Cont'd

State aid to cities or towns, **132:14, 132:16.**

Sunday, sales of plants, **136:6.**

Superintendents.
Local superintendents of insect pest control. See within this heading, "Local superintendents of insect pest control."

Suppression of moths and other insect pests, **132:11-132:16, 132:25, 132:26A, 132:26D-132:26G.**

Tent caterpillars, suppression, **132:11-132:27.**

Towns.
Cities and towns. See within this heading, "Cities and towns."

Transportation of insect pests as offense, **266:119.**

Trapa natans, spread, **128:20A.**

Treatment of infested plants, **128:24.**
Out-of-state shipments, **128:21.**
San Jose scale, plants infested, **128:24.**

Tree trimming or cutting regulations as affecting control, **87:5.**

Tree wardens.
Assisting in suppression of moths and insect pests, **132:13.**
Foliage-destroying pests, duties, **132:25.**

University of Massachusetts, experiments and investigations on diseases, **75:17, 132:26A.**

Water chestnut, spread, **128:20A.**

White pine blister rust.
See WHITE PINE BLISTER RUST.

PLAQUES.
Historic homestead plaque awarded if site over 100 years old, **9:27D.**

PLASMA.
Banks.
See BLOOD BANKS OR RESERVOIRS.

PLASTER.
Lead poisoning.
See LEAD POISONING.

PLASTIC GUNS.
Sales of guns designed to elude x-ray machines and metal detectors, **140:131N.**

PLASTICS.
Bags and film, **111:5D.**

Bottles and containers, labeling, **94:323A.**
Definitions, **94:321.**
Exemptions, **94:326.**

Caps for toy pistols, provisions, **148:39.**

Containers.
Bottles and containers. See within this heading, "Bottles and containers, labeling."

Eyeglass and sunglass lenses, testing, **270:1A.**

Health department's regulation of plastic bags and film, **111:5D.**

Lien on account of labor and materials furnished in processing, **255:31A, 255:31B.**

PLATED ITEMS.
Local tax exemption, **59:5.**

PLATE GLASS INSURANCE.
Authorized business, **175:47.**

Combination with other classes, **175:48, 175:48A, 175:51, 175:54.**

Foreign insurance companies, **175:151.**

Mutual companies, **175:48A, 175:54, 175:90, 175:93A.**

Number of risks in force, effect on authority of insurance companies to do business, **175:93A.**

Rates and rating organizations applied to plate glass insurance, **175A:4.**

Stock companies, **175:48, 175:51.**

PLATES.
Carriers.
See CARRIERS.

Libraries, defacement of plates, **266:99.**

Making or having tools for counterfeiting, **267:13.**

Motor vehicles.
Number plates.
See MOTOR VEHICLES.

PLATFORMS.
Insurance against loss or damage caused by falling, **175:47.**

Public transportation facility, throwing filth or rubbish on platforms, **161:94A.**

Railroads.
See RAILROADS.

Street railways.
Station or platform.
See STREET RAILWAYS.

PLATFORM SCALES.
Hay and coal scales, testing, **98:49.**

PLATINUM.
Record of purchase or sale, **266:142A.**

PLATOON SYSTEM.
Fire departments, adoption, **48:59.**

PLATS, 97:1 et seq.
See MAPS, PLATS, AND SURVEYS.

PLAYGROUNDS, 45:14-45:18.
Acceptance of playground act by towns, **45:16.**

Acquisition of land and buildings, **45:14.**

Adult use, **45:18.**

Aldermen.
Parks and playgrounds.
See ALDERMEN AND SELECTMEN.

Appropriations by city or town, **45:14.**

Awards, appropriations, **40:5.**

Buildings.
Acquisition, **45:14.**
Construction and lease, **45:14, 45:17.**

Charging admission, **45:14.**

Closing streets or public ways for use, **45:17A.**

Concessions, lease, **45:5A.**

Drug sales, **94C:32J.**

Duty of municipalities to provide, **45:15.**

Employees, appointment, **45:14.**

Equipment or apparatus, willful destruction, **266:98A.**

Establishment and maintenance by municipalities, **45:14.**

Fines and penalties.
Equipment, willful destruction, **266:98A.**
Playgrounds, violations relating, **45:24.**

Governing body, **45:14.**

Highways and streets, closing streets for use as playgrounds, **45:17A.**

Housing and urban renewal projects, municipal construction of playgrounds in aid, **121B:23.**

Indebtedness of city or town, **44:7.**

Laying out, **45:14.**

Leases.
Concessions, **45:5A.**
Land and buildings, **45:14, 45:17.**

Master plan of municipal planning boards, **41:81D.**

PLAYGROUNDS —Cont'd

Municipal finance, **45:14.**
  Awards, appropriations, **40:5.**
  Borrowing, **44:7.**
Number to be provided by cities
  and towns, **45:15.**
Obligation of city or town to
  provide, **45:15.**
Outside city or town limits,
  authority to construct, **45:14.**
Park commissioners, control,
  45:14.
Penalties.
  Fines and penalties. See within
    this heading, "Fines and
    penalties."
Recreational camps for children,
  111:127A.
Regional school districts,
  authorization to incur debts,
  71:16.
Rules and regulations, penalty for
  violation, **45:24.**
School teachers, appointment for
  playground, **45:14.**
Special age groups, use by
  children, **45:18.**
Subdivision plans to provide,
  41:81U.
Temporary playgrounds, **45:17.**
Tenement houses in cities and
  towns, temporary playgrounds
  in neighborhood, **45:17.**
Token awards in contests or
  competitions, town
  appropriation, **40:5.**
Town as including cities, **45:1.**
Transfer of land no longer needed,
  40:15A.
Urban redevelopment corporations
  may contract with
  municipality for construction,
  121A:14.
Use and control, **45:14.**
Zoning and planning, acquisition
  of playgrounds, **45:14.**

PLAYS.

Children under fifteen
  participating, **149:104,
  149:105.**
Legal holidays, activities
  permitted, **136:14.**
Sunday, amusements, **136:3,
  136:4.**

PLAZAS.
See SHOPPING CENTERS.

PLEADING.

Abatement, plea in.
  See ABATEMENT, SURVIVAL,
    AND REVIVAL.

PLEADING —Cont'd

Absentee trust beneficiaries,
  pleadings in proceedings to
  transfer estates, **203:30,
  203:31.**
Administrative proceedings,
  standard rules, **30A:9.**
Admissions by parties.
  See ADMISSIONS BY PARTIES.
Affidavits of indigency, filing and
  request for waiver of court
  costs, **261:27B.**
Agreements as to amendment,
  231:72.
Alimony.
  Divorce and alimony. See within
    this heading, "Divorce and
    alimony."
Amendments, **231:51-231:55.**
  Demurrer, amendment after,
    231:52.
  Divorce, **208:11.**
  Final judgment, amendment
    prior, **231:51.**
  Notice, necessity, **231:138.**
  Orders permitting amendment
    before trial, **231:71.**
Answers.
  See PLEAS AND ANSWERS.
Appeal and review.
  District court appellate
    divisions, **231:108.**
  Zoning appeals, **40A:17.**
Assignee, joinder of parties, **231:6.**
Attachment of property.
  See ATTACHMENT OF
    PROPERTY.
Attorneys at law, soliciting
  employment in claims for
  damages, complaint alleging,
  221:43.
Banks, unfair or deceitful practices
  in consumer transactions,
  167:2C to 167:2F.
Bills of particulars.
  See BILLS OF PARTICULARS.
Binding effect of allegations,
  231:87.
Certiorari proceedings, right of
  party respondent after joinder,
  249:4.
Change.
  Amendment. See within this
    heading, "Amendments."
Civil rights.
  Complaint.
    See CIVIL RIGHTS AND
      DISCRIMINATION.
Civil service, complaints as to
  discharge, suspension of
  employees, **31:42, 31:43.**

PLEADING —Cont'd

Complaint.
  See COMPLAINT.
Condominiums.
  Complaint.
    See CONDOMINIUMS.
Consolidation of causes.
  Trial courts, **223:2A.**
Corporations.
  See CORPORATIONS.
Costs of action.
  See COSTS OF ACTION.
Counterclaims.
  See SETOFF AND
    COUNTERCLAIM.
Deceit.
  Fraud and deceit. See within
    this heading, "Fraud and
    deceit."
Declaration.
  See COMPLAINT.
Declaratory judgment, application
  for further relief based,
  231A:5.
Decree.
  Judgments, orders, and decrees.
    See within this heading,
    "Judgments, orders, and
    decrees."
Defenses.
  See DEFENSES.
Demurrer.
  See DEMURRER.
Discovery stayed on filing special
  motion to dismiss, **231:59H.**
Discrimination.
  Complaint.
    See CIVIL RIGHTS AND
      DISCRIMINATION.
Dismissal, special motions,
  231:59H.
Divorce and alimony.
  Amendment to pleadings to
    name co-respondent, **208:11.**
  Petition for alimony after
    divorce, **208:34.**
Election contest, **54:120.**
Eminent domain proceedings,
  79:22.
Entry, writs of, **237:9-237:11.**
  See ENTRY, WRITS.
Equity, **231:31.**
  Avoidance of defenses, **231:35.**
  Equitable defenses, **231:31.**
Estoppel.
  Waiver. See within this heading,
    "Waiver."
Evidence, pleadings, **231:87.**
Fair employment practices.
  Complaints.
    See FAIR EMPLOYMENT
      PRACTICES.

PLEADING —Cont'd
Fees.
Land court, fees for entry of
petition, **262:39.**
Registers of probate and
insolvency, **262:40.**
Forfeiture of property, proceedings
to enforce, **257:6.**
Fraud and deceit.
Attachment, pleadings in prior
action as affecting
proceedings for dissolution,
223:109.
Banks, unfair or deceitful
practices in consumer
transactions, **167:2C to
167:2F.**
Frauds, statute of, admissions in
pleadings, **106-2:201.**
Guardians.
See GUARDIANS,
CONSERVATORS, AND
COMMITTEES.
Impleader.
See IMPLEADER.
Indictments, informations.
See INDICTMENTS,
INFORMATIONS AND
COMPLAINTS.
Indigency, filing affidavit of and
request for waiver of court
costs, **261:27B.**
Insurance.
See INSURANCE.
Interest on judgment, **231:6B,
231:6C, 231:6I.**
Interpleader.
See INTERPLEADER.
Issues.
General issue, plea, **231:22.**
When formed, **231:39.**
Joinder of actions.
See JOINDER OF ACTIONS OR
ISSUES.
Joinder of parties.
See JOINDER OF PARTIES.
Judgments, orders, and decrees.
Abatement.
See ABATEMENT,
SURVIVAL, AND
REVIVAL.
Declaratory judgment,
application for further relief
based, **231A:5.**
Demurrer, time for amendment
of pleading after, **231:52.**
Final judgment, amendments
prior, **231:51.**
Interest on judgment, **231:6I.**
Jurisdictional amount increased in
certain courts, **231:102C,
231:104.**

PLEADING —Cont'd
Land court, **185:22.**
Fees for entry of petition,
262:39.
Libel to commence action.
See COMPLAINT.
Limitation of actions.
See LIMITATION OF ACTIONS.
Medical malpractice claims,
prohibition of ad damnum
clauses, **231:60C.**
Motions.
See MOTIONS.
Nonresidents' pleadings,
endorsement, **231:42, 231:43.**
Obscene publication proceedings,
272:28C-272:28G.
Orders.
Judgments, orders, and decrees.
See within this heading,
"Judgments, orders, and
decrees."
Pain and suffering, **231:6D.**
Particulars.
See BILLS OF PARTICULARS.
Parties, **231:6B-231:6D.**
Payment, pleading of, pleas and
answers, **232A:1.**
Petitions.
See PETITIONS.
Pleas.
See PLEAS AND ANSWERS.
Probate.
See PROBATE AND FAMILY
COURT.
Process.
See PROCESS AND SERVICE
OF PROCESS AND
PAPERS.
Redemption of tax title, suit to
foreclose, **60:65-60:76.**
Registration of land titles.
See REGISTRATION OF LAND
TITLES.
Replication, **231:35.**
Review.
Appeal and review. See within
this heading, "Appeal and
review."
Savings banks employees
retirement association,
powers, **168:39.**
Service of process.
See PROCESS AND SERVICE
OF PROCESS AND
PAPERS.
Setoff.
See SETOFF AND
COUNTERCLAIM.
Signatures.
Corporation, **231:139.**

PLEADING —Cont'd
Signatures —Cont'd
Pleas.
See PLEAS AND ANSWERS.
Special motion to dismiss,
231:59H.
Statute of frauds, **106-2:201.**
Statute of limitations.
See LIMITATION OF ACTIONS.
Stipulations as to amendments,
231:72.
Strategic litigation, limitations on,
231:59H.
Uniform rules of adjudicatory
procedure, **30A:10.**
Usury, voiding of transactions
involving criminal usury,
271:49.
Verification by corporate officer or
agent, **231:139.**
Waiver.
Indictment, application for
waiver, **263:4A.**
Indigency, filing affidavit of and
request for waiver of court
costs, **261:27B.**
Wills.
See WILLS.
Zoning appeals, **40A:17.**

PLEA IN ABATEMENT, 231:21.
**See ABATEMENT, SURVIVAL,
AND REVIVAL.**

PLEAS AND ANSWERS.
Abatement, plea in.
See ABATEMENT, SURVIVAL,
AND REVIVAL.
Absentee trust beneficiary,
proceedings to transfer estate,
203:30, 203:31.
Administrative proceedings,
standard rules, **30A:9.**
Admissions by parties.
See ADMISSIONS BY PARTIES.
Amendments.
Civil rights and discrimination,
151B:5.
Conditioning on payment of
costs, **261:18.**
Certiorari proceedings, right of
party respondent after joinder,
249:4.
Civil rights and discrimination,
151B:5.
Amendments, **151B:5.**
Condemnation of property.
Eminent domain. See within
this heading, "Eminent
domain."
Consolidation.
See JOINDER OF ACTIONS OR
ISSUES.

PLEAS AND ANSWERS —Cont'd

Corporations.

Order of notice to corporation to appear and answer, **223:37.**

Trustee process against corporation, answer, **246:15, 246:19.**

Costs, items, **261:2, 261:8, 261:18, 261:23, 261:26, 262:34.**

Date.

Time or date. See within this heading, "Time or date."

Demurrer.

See DEMURRER.

Dilatory pleas.

See DILATORY PLEAS AND TACTICS.

Discrimination.

Civil rights and discrimination, **151B:5.**

District courts.

See DISTRICT COURTS.

Eminent domain.

Damages, answer to petition in superior court, **79:22.**

Judicial procedure, alternative method of taking property, **80A:5.**

Special assessments, **80A:5.**

Equity.

See EQUITY.

Evidence.

Admissions by parties.

See ADMISSIONS BY PARTIES.

Executor or administrator, defense, **231:6.**

Fair educational practice proceedings, **151C:3.**

Fair employment practices, **151B:5.**

Forfeited property, answer in proceedings, **257:6.**

Frauds, statute of.

See STATUTE OF FRAUDS.

Garnishment.

See TRUSTEE PROCESS.

General issue, **231:22.**

Guilty plea.

See GUILTY PLEA.

Insolvency, costs when defendant alleges, **261:2.**

Interrogatories, **231:62 et seq.**

See INTERROGATORIES.

Issue, action deemed to be at issue when plea filed, **231:39.**

Joinder of actions.

See JOINDER OF ACTIONS OR ISSUES.

Knowledge.

Notice and knowledge. See within this heading, "Notice and knowledge."

PLEAS AND ANSWERS —Cont'd

Libel and slander, **231:93.**

Merits, plea to, when required, **231:21.**

Motor vehicle, operation without consent of owner as affirmative defense, **231:85A, 231:85B.**

Nolo contendere.

See NOLO CONTENDERE.

Not guilty plea.

See NOT GUILTY PLEA.

Notice and knowledge.

Corporation, order of notice to appear and answer, **223:37.**

Interrogatories, notice as to entry of judgment for failure to answer, **231:64.**

Payment, pleading, **232A:1.**

Personal actions, answers, **231:22.**

Records, reports, and returns, action deemed at issue when plea is filed, **231:39.**

Redemption of tax title, suit to foreclose, **60:67-60:70.**

Replication, **231:35.**

Sentence.

See SENTENCE AND PUNISHMENT.

Slander, **231:93.**

Special assessments.

Abatement, **80:9.**

Eminent domain, **80A:5.**

Statute of frauds.

See STATUTE OF FRAUDS.

Statute of limitations.

See LIMITATION OF ACTIONS.

Subversive organization, proceeding for adjudication, **264:18.**

Superior Court, eminent domain, answer to petition in superior court for damages, **79:22.**

Tax title, suit to foreclose redemption, **60:67-60:70.**

Tender, effect of pleading, **232A:1.**

Time or date.

Dilatory pleas.

See DILATORY PLEAS AND TACTICS.

Interrogatories, answers to.

See INTERROGATORIES.

Trustee process.

See TRUSTEE PROCESS.

Unfair labor practice proceedings, **150A:6.**

Uniform rules of adjudicatory procedure, **30A:10.**

Withdrawal of guilty plea, prior to sentence, **278:29B.**

Writ of entry, pleading, **237:10.**

PLEDGE, 106:9-102, 140:87 to 140:89.

Pawnbrokers, generally, **140:70 et seq., 140:202-140:205.**

See PAWNBROKERS.

Secured transactions.

See SECURED TRANSACTIONS.

Statutory definition, **4:7.**

PLUMBERS AND GAS FITTERS, 13:37, 13:38, 142:1 et seq.

Additional inspectors, appointment, **142:12.**

Advertising to contain license number, **142:3.**

Annual reports of proceedings of building inspectors and health board, **142:15.**

Apprentices.

Application of laws, **142:14.**

Defined, **142:1, 142:3A.**

Fees, licensing and examination, **142:5.**

License, **142:3, 142:3A, 142:4, 142:5.**

Penalties for violations, **142:16.**

Performance of work for municipalities, corporations, or institutions, **142:4A.**

Probationary license, **142:4.**

Violations of laws, **142:16.**

Assignment of licenses, regulation, **142:6.**

Bakeries, sanitary requirements, **94:9G.**

Barnstable county, regulations as to towns, **142:13.**

Bay Transportation Authority, **142:21.**

Bids on public contracts, **149:44F.**

Board of examiners, **13:37, 13:38.**

Defined, **142:1.**

Examinations of plumbers, rules and regulations, **142:4.**

Regulations, promulgation, **142:13.**

State buildings, rules in respect, **142:21.**

Violation of statutes, notice, **142:7.**

Boston, permit to engage in gas fitting, **143:3N.**

Building authority, **142:21.**

Building code as applicable, **143:3N.**

Building inspectors.

Appointment, **142:11.**

Notice of violations to examiners, **142:7.**

PLUMBERS AND GAS FITTERS —Cont'd

Buildings, regulations as to, **142:13, 142:21.**
Certificates and certification.
Defined, **142:1.**
Gas fitting corporation or partnership, **142:1, 142:3B.**
Plumbing corporations or partnerships, **142:1, 142:3B.**
Cities and towns.
Application of laws, **142:2, 142:13.**
Civil service, exemption of certain town inspectors, **142:11.**
Inspector of gas piping and appliances, appointment, **143:3O.**
Notice by person intending to engage in business, **143:3N.**
Regularly employed plumbers, work, **142:4A.**
Civil service, inspectors, **31:48, 31:52, 142:11.**
Code of regulations, **142:13.**
Commonwealth.
Board of examiners. See within this heading, "Board of examiners."
Buildings, regulation as to plumbing and gas fitting work, **142:21.**
Forfeiture by city or towns, **142:16.**
Conduits for gas, fittings, **142:3B.**
Corporations, **142:3B.**
Correctional institutions and jails, health department's authority as to plumbing facilities, **111:21.**
Defined, **142:1.**
Drain layers, **111:127, 142:3.**
Drains.
Sewers and drains. See within this heading, "Sewers and drains."
Engineers and surveyors, exemption from laws, **112:81R.**
Examinations and examiners.
Board of examiners. See within this heading, "Board of examiners."
Fees, **142:5.**
Inspection and inspectors. See within this heading, "Inspections and inspectors."
Veterans' preference, **142:4.**
Fees.
Deferred renewal of license, **142:6.**

PLUMBERS AND GAS FITTERS —Cont'd

Fees —Cont'd
Examinations, **142:5.**
Licenses, **142:5.**
Fines, penalties, and forfeitures.
Apprentice regulations, violation, **142:16.**
City's or town's forfeiture to Commonwealth for violations of regulations, **142:16.**
Hot water tanks, violations as to regulations, **142:22.**
Unlicensed plumbing and gas fitting work or business, **142:16.**
Violation of building regulations, **143:3N.**
Fire sprinkler system contractors and fitters, journeymen, **146:81-146:84.**
Forfeitures.
Fines, penalties, and forfeitures. See within this heading, "Fines, penalties, and forfeitures."
Gas fitting corporation, gas company, **142:3B.**
Government center commission, **142:21.**
Health boards, departments, and officers.
Annual reports of proceedings, **142:15.**
Fixtures and labor, approval, **142:13.**
Inspection districts, expenses, **142:10.**
Inspectors of plumbing and gas fitting, appointment, **142:11.**
Registration of licenses, **142:6.**
Rules and regulations relating to plumbing and gas fitting, approval, **142:13.**
State buildings, approval of plumbing and gas fitting, **142:21.**
Inspections and inspectors, **142:10-142:12.**
Appointment, **142:11, 142:11A, 143:3O, 143:12.**
Building inspectors. See within this heading, "Building inspectors."
Cities and towns fail to appoint inspector, **143:3O.**
Civil service, **31:48, 31:52, 142:11.**
Continuing education, **142:11B.**
Districts, creation, **142:10.**

PLUMBERS AND GAS FITTERS —Cont'd

Inspections and inspectors —Cont'd
Duties, **143:3O.**
Failure to appoint city or town inspector, **143:3O.**
Municipal regulations, **142:13.**
Permits for installation of liquefied petroleum gas, **143:3O.**
Qualifications, **143:3O.**
Undiluted liquefied petroleum gas installer, **143:3O.**
Insurance required, **142:21A.**
Journeymen.
Application of laws, **142:14.**
Defined, **142:1.**
Fees for licenses and examinations, **142:5.**
Fire sprinkler system contractors and fitters, **146:81-146:84.**
License, **142:3.**
Penalty for violations, **142:16.**
Performance of work for municipalities, corporations, or institutions, **142:4A.**
Refrigeration technician, fire sprinkler system contractors and fitters, **146:81-146:85.**
Knowledge.
Notice and knowledge. See within this heading, "Notice and knowledge."
Liability insurance required, **142:21A.**
Licenses and permits, **142:3.**
Advertising or signs to contain number, **142:3.**
Apprentices, **142:3, 142:3A, 142:4, 142:5.**
Assignment, **142:6.**
Boston, engaging in gas fitting, **143:3N.**
Corporations, plumbing and gas fitting, **142:3B.**
Deferred renewal, **142:6.**
Drain layers, **142:3.**
Exhibition, **142:3.**
Installation of liquefied petroleum gas, **143:3O.**
Insurance, **142:21A.**
Partnerships, plumbing and gas fitting, **142:3B.**
Registration, **142:6.**
Renewal, **142:6.**
Revocation, **142:6.**
Term, **142:6.**
Transfer, **142:6.**
Unlicensed work, penalty, **142:16.**

PLUMBERS AND GAS FITTERS —Cont'd

Licenses and permits —Cont'd
Valid throughout Commonwealth, **142:6.**
Limited undiluted liquefied petroleum gas installer, defined, **142:1.**
Master.
Defined, **142:1.**
Display of license, **142:3.**
Fees for licenses and examinations, **142:5.**
License, **142:3.**
Penalty for violations, **142:16.**
Performance of work for municipalities, corporations, or institutions, **142:4A.**
Metropolitan district commission, **142:21.**
Military service.
Veterans. See within this heading, "Veterans."
Municipalities.
Cities and towns. See within this heading, "Cities and towns."
Notice and knowledge.
Examinations, **142:4.**
Violations of law, notice to examiners, **142:7.**
Partnerships, **142:3B.**
Penalties.
Fines, penalties, and forfeitures. See within this heading, "Fines, penalties, and forfeitures."
Permits.
Licenses and permits. See within this heading, "Licenses and permits."
Pipes and fittings on hot water tanks, regulations, **142:19.**
Plumber to have knowledge of gasfitting, **142:4.**
Plumbing code.
Applicability to all cities and towns, **142:2, 142:13.**
State building code, incorporation of specialized construction codes, **143:96.**
Port Authority, **142:21.**
Practical plumber, defined, **142:1.**
Probationary license for apprentice, **142:4.**
Professional engineers and land surveyors, exemption from laws, **112:81R.**
Public contract bids, **149:44F.**
Range boilers sold as junk, exceptions, **142:20.**

PLUMBERS AND GAS FITTERS —Cont'd

Refrigeration technician, fire sprinkler system contractors and fitters, journeymen, **146:81-146:85.**
Register, defined, **142:1.**
Registration board, **13:37, 13:38.**
Registration of licenses, **142:6.**
Reports and returns.
Building inspectors, proceedings, **142:15.**
Health boards, proceedings, **142:15.**
Revocation and suspension of licenses, **142:6.**
Safety devices required on hot water tanks, **142:19.**
Sewers and drains.
Drain layers, **111:127, 142:3.**
Exemption from drainage regulations, **111:127.**
Regulations, **142:13.**
Separate systems for sewage and storm waters, **83:5.**
Special assessments, granting tax abatements for improvements to real estate, **59:38.**
State.
Commonwealth. See within this heading, "Commonwealth."
Surveyors and professional engineers, exemptions, **112:81R.**
Suspension of license, **142:6.**
Thermostatic controls on hot water tanks, regulations, **142:19.**
Towns.
Cities and towns. See within this heading, "Cities and towns."
Transfer of licenses, regulations, **142:6.**
Turnpike authority, **142:21.**
Undiluted liquefied petroleum gas installer, defined, **142:1.**
Vacuum in hot water tank, safety device to prevent, **142:19.**
Veterans.
Credit on examination, **142:4.**
Preferences, **142:4.**
Time of service counted as experience for purposes of appointment of inspector, **142:11.**
Violation of statutes, notice to examiners, **142:7.**
Vocational schools, establishment of job training program in plumbing, **142:3A.**

PLUMBING CODE, 142:1 et seq.

Applicability, **142:2, 142:13.**

PLUMBING CODE —Cont'd

Incorporation in state building code, **143:96.**

PLURALITY VOTE.

Constitutional requirement of plurality vote in election, **MA Const Amend Art 14.**
Defined under election law, **50:1.**
Elections.
See ELECTIONS.
Results of elections, **50:2.**

PLURAL NUMBER.

Singular in statutes as including, **4:6.**

PLYMOUTH.

Congressional district, **57:1.**
Councillor district, **57:2.**
County.
See PLYMOUTH COUNTY.
Medical examiner district, **38:1.**
Pilgrim tercentenary, jurisdiction and control over structures erected in connection, **91:2A.**
Senatorial district, **57:3.**

PLYMOUTH CORRECTIONAL INSTITUTION.

State prison camp at Plymouth designated, **125:1.**

PLYMOUTH COUNTY.

Additional judges for probate and insolvency, **217:2.**
Administration of criminal law and defense of civil actions, district, **12:13.**
Clerks of courts.
Additional assistants, **218:10, 221:4, 221:5.**
Appointment of fourth assistant clerk of courts, **221:5.**
Assistant clerks, **221:4, 221:5, 221:6I, 221:6J.**
Criminal proceedings, assistant clerks, **221:6J.**
Designation of assistant clerk to perform duties of clerk in equity proceedings of superior court, **221:6I.**
Equity proceedings, assistant clerks, **221:6I.**
Fourth district court, salary of clerk, **218:79.**
In equity proceedings in superior court, **221:6I.**
Number of assistant clerks, **221:5.**
Provision for assistant clerk in Fourth District Court, **218:10.**
Salary, **218:79, 221:94.**

PLYMOUTH COUNTY —Cont'd

Clerks of courts —Cont'd

Third district court, provision for assistant clerk, **218:10.**

Councillor, district, **57:2.**

Court officers for, **217:30.**

Development council.

See PLYMOUTH COUNTY DEVELOPMENT COUNCIL.

District court, **218:1.**

Clerks of courts. See within this heading, "Clerks of courts."

Justices of District Court within Plymouth County, **231:108.**

Marine boundaries of Commonwealth, **1:3.**

Misdemeanors.

Trial by jury of 6, **218:26.**

Place of holding, **218:1.**

Territorial jurisdiction, **218:1.**

Wareham, fourth district court to be held, **218:1.**

Embalmers' and funeral directors' registration board, representation, **13:29.**

Equity proceedings, designation of clerk, **221:6I.**

General court, representatives, **57:4.**

Grand jurors, **277:2D.**

Justices of District Courts within, **231:108.**

Juvenile court jurisdiction, **218:57 et seq.**

Masters in chancery, **221:53.**

Medical examiner district, **38:1.**

Meeting of county commissioners, **34:9.**

Probate court.

Judges, number, **217:2.**

Officers of court, **217:30.**

Registers of probate.

See REGISTERS OF PROBATE AND INSOLVENCY.

Sessions, **215:62.**

Registers of probate.

See REGISTERS OF PROBATE AND INSOLVENCY.

Representatives in general court, **57:4.**

Salaries.

Clerks of court, **218:79, 221:94.**

Registers of probate and insolvency, **217:35A.**

Senatorial district of Norfolk and Bristol, inclusion of Plymouth, **57:3.**

Sessions of court, **215:62.**

Six-man jury trial of criminal cases, right, **218:27A.**

PLYMOUTH COUNTY —Cont'd

Superior Court.

Clerk for equity proceedings, **221:61.**

Institution of proceedings as to civil and criminal matters within marine boundaries of Commonwealth, **1:3.**

Sittings at Plymouth county, **212:14.**

Surveys in co-ordinate system, **97:8.**

Wareham, fourth district court to be held, **218:1.**

PLYMOUTH COUNTY DEVELOPMENT COUNCIL.

Financial assistance and promotion services from economic development department, **23A:14.**

PLYMOUTH ROCK.

Historical rock of the Commonwealth, **2:23.**

PLYMPTON.

Congressional district, **57:1.**

District court, **218:1.**

Medical examiner district, **38:1.**

Senatorial district, **57:3.**

PNEUMATIC PRESSURE.

Corporations furnishing, **158:3, 158:12-158:14.**

PODIATRY AND PODIATRISTS, 112:13-112:22.

Abused and neglected children, reporting requirements, **119:51A.**

Abuse of patients or residents in long-term care facilities, reports, **111:72G.**

Accident and sickness insurance coverage, **175:110.**

Admissibility in evidence of bills, **233:79G.**

Alcohol, unprofessional conduct in connection, **112:18, 112:19.**

Board of registration.

Appointment, **13:12A.**

Approval of podiatry schools, **112:16.**

Compensation and expenses, **13:12C.**

Examinations, **112:15, 112:16.**

Investigation of complaints, **112:17A.**

Limited or temporary registration, **112:16A, 112:16C.**

PODIATRY AND PODIATRISTS —Cont'd

Board of registration —Cont'd

Meetings and organization, **13:12B.**

Persons assisting board, liability, **112:17B.**

Public or lay member, provision, **13:12A.**

Records, **112:17A.**

Reports, **112:17A.**

Rules and regulations, **112:17A.**

General provisions, **112:88.**

Students, facilities, **112:16B.**

Certificates of registration.

Duplicate certificate, **112:88.**

Expiration date, **112:16.**

Fees for recording, **262:34.**

General provisions as to furnishing, **112:88.**

Issuance, **112:16.**

Recording, **112:21, 262:34.**

Refusal to issue, **112:18.**

Renewal, **112:16.**

Revocation, **112:18, 112:61.**

Suspension, **112:20, 112:61.**

Clinical laboratories, requests for examination of specimens, **111D:8.**

Colleges and schools for, approval, **112:16.**

Continuing education requirements, renewal of registration certificate as affected, **112:16.**

Controlled substances.

Narcotics. See within this heading, "Narcotics."

Conviction of crime, revocation of certificate, **112:18.**

Deceit.

Fraud. See within this heading, "Fraud."

Definition, **112:13, 112:19.**

Discrimination by hospitals as to application for staff membership, **111:51C.**

Education.

Schools and education. See within this heading, "Schools and education."

Evidence, admissibility of podiatrists' bills, **233:79G.**

Examinations for registration.

Registration. See within this heading, "Registration."

False.

Fraud. See within this heading, "Fraud."

Fees.

Registration. See within this heading, "Registration."

PODIATRY AND PODIATRISTS
—Cont'd

Fluoroscopic shoe-fitting machines, operation, **111:186A.**

Fraud.
  False representation, **94:187D.**
  Revocation of certificate, **112:18, 112:19.**

Hospitals.
  Discrimination as to application for staff membership, **111:51C.**
  Limited or temporary registration, **112:16A, 112:16C.**

Insurance coverage for services rendered, **175:110.**

Licenses.
  Registration of. See within this heading, "Registration."

Limited or temporary registration, **112:16A, 112:16C.**

Local registration, **112:21.**

Medical care and assistance, furnishing, **118E:6.**

Medical malpractice claims, podiatrists as providers of health care for purposes, **231:60B.**

Medical service corporations, payment for services, **176B:4.**

Medical students, limited registration, **112:16A, 112:16B.**

Moral turpitude, revocation of certificate, **112:18.**

Narcotics.
  Addiction, disqualification for podiatrist's certificate, **112:18.**
  Hypodermic syringe or needle, possession or sale, **94C:27.**
  Unprofessional conduct by unlawfully selling or giving, **112:19.**
  Use by podiatrist, refusal or revocation of certificate on ground, **112:18.**

Nondiscriminatory basis, provision of health services, **176G:1, 176G:6.**

Penalties for violation of registration laws, **112:22.**

Physician assistants prohibited from practicing, **112:9D.**

Physicians, podiatrists' registration law inapplicable, **112:13.**

Police officers and firefighters, indemnification for certain podiatry expenses, **41:100, 41:100B.**

PODIATRY AND PODIATRISTS
—Cont'd

Prescriptions.
  Hospital and clinic prescription blanks, requirements as to use, **112:21A.**

Professional services within professional corporations law, **156A:2.**

Records and recording.
  Board of registration to keep records, **112:17A.**
  Certificate, recording, **112:21, 262:34.**

Refusal to issue certificate, grounds, **112:18.**

Registration, **112:13-112:22.**
  Applications, **112:16.**
  Board of registration. See within this heading, "Board of registration."
  Certificates of registration. See within this heading, "Certificates of registration."
  Colleges, approval, **112:16.**
  Examinations.
    Duties of board, **112:15.**
    Fees, **112:16.**
    Passing score, **112:16.**
    Subjects, **112:17.**
  Expiration date, **112:16.**
  Fees.
    Certificate of registration, recording, **262:34.**
    Examinations, **112:16.**
    Local registration, **112:21.**
    Reexamination, **112:16.**
    Registration without examinations, **112:16.**
    Temporary registration, **112:16A, 112:16C.**
  General provisions, **112:88.**
  Local registration, **112:21.**
  Penalties for violations, **112:22.**
  Prohibited acts in absence, **112:14.**
  Qualifications, **112:16.**
  Records and recording. See within this heading, "Records and recording."
  Re-examinations, **112:16.**
  Renewals, **112:16.**
  Required, **112:14.**
  Without examination, when, **112:16.**

Revocation of certificate, **112:18, 112:61.**

Schools and education.
  Approval of colleges and schools for podiatrists, **112:16.**
  Facilities for students, **112:16B.**

PODIATRY AND PODIATRISTS
—Cont'd

Schools and education —Cont'd
  Pupils, examination of feet, **71:57.**

Suspension of certificate, **112:20, 112:61.**

Unprofessional conduct.
  Definition, **112:19.**
  Fraud. See within this heading, "Fraud."
  Revocation of certificate, **112:18.**

POD SECURITY REGISTRATION, 201E:101 to 201E:402.

See TRANSFER ON DEATH SECURITY REGISTRATION.

POEMS.

"Blue Hills of Massachusetts" as official Commonwealth poem, **2:21.**

POINTS.

Mortgages, fees and points charged, **183:63.**

POISON IVY.

Suppression, **132:11.**
  Appropriations by towns, **40:5.**

Transportation of, as criminal offense, **266:119.**

POISONS.

Analyses.
  Prima facie proof of contents, analyses by governmental agencies, **111:13.**
  University of Massachusetts Medical School, analysis, **75:36B, 111:13.**

Animals, poisoning, **266:112, 272:85A.**
  Dog poisoning, **266:47.**
  Rat poison, placing where domestic animal may be injured, **270:3A.**

Arsenic.
  See ARSENIC.

Atmospheric pollution by toxic substances, regulation and control by local health boards, etc., **111:31C.**

Attempt to murder, **265:16.**

Benzol, marking containers, **149:142A-149:142G.**

Carbon tetrachloride, marking containers, **149:142A-149:142G.**

Cattle and horses, poisoning, **266:112.**

Certificate of result of analysis, furnishing, **111:13.**

POISONS —Cont'd
Childhood lead poisoning
prevention program.
See CHILDHOOD LEAD
POISONING PREVENTION
PROGRAM.
Children and minors.
Lead poisoning.
See CHILDHOOD LEAD
POISONING
PREVENTION
PROGRAM.
Sale of substances capable of
releasing toxic vapors,
270:19.
Coal mining regulation and
reclamation.
Insurance against toxic
chemicals, **21B:5.**
Rules and regulations as to
control of toxic chemicals,
21B:11.
Coastal waters, pollution, **130:23.**
Commercial feed, finding of
adulteration, **128:54.**
Containers.
Benzol, marking containers,
149:142A-149:142G.
Carbon tetrachloride, marking
containers,
149:142A-149:142G.
Comprising materials from
which containers made,
94:186, 111:8A.
Discard or disposal of
containers, violations,
111:8A.
Seed package labeled to indicate
poisonous contents, **128:85.**
Wood alcohol containers,
warning notice, **94:303C.**
Conviction of pharmacist for
violation as to sale of, effect,
112:34.
Criminal offense, poisoning as,
265:28.
Discard or disposal of containers,
violation, **111:8A.**
Dog poisoning, **266:47.**
Fish.
See FISH AND GAME.
Glue or cement capable of
releasing toxic vapors, sales to
minors, **270:19.**
Health department.
Analysis, **111:12, 111:13.**
Atmospheric pollution by toxic
substances, regulation and
control by local health
boards, **111:31C.**

POISONS —Cont'd
Health department —Cont'd
Poison information and control
center, establishment in
public health department,
17:4A.
Industrial homework, unlawful,
149:144, 149:147G.
Information and control center as
to poison, establishment in
public health department,
17:4A.
Lead poisoning, **111:189A et seq.**
See LEAD POISONING.
Medical examiners, notice of death
due to poison, **38:3.**
Medicine, poisoning, **265:28.**
Minors.
Children and minors. See within
this heading, "Children and
minors."
Murder attempt, **265:16.**
Pesticides.
See PESTICIDES.
Physicians, reports of acute
poisoning, **94C:24.**
Rat poison, placing where person
or domestic animal may be
injured, **270:3A.**
Sales.
Arsenic, articles containing,
114:51, 270:10-270:12.
Toxic vapors, use, possession, or
sale of substances releasing,
270:18, 270:19.
Seed package labeled to indicate
poisonous contents, **128:85.**
"Toxic," defined, **94B:1.**
University of Massachusetts
Medical School, analysis,
75:36B, 111:13.
Vapors, sale, use, or possess of
substances releasing toxic
vapors, **270:18, 270:19.**
Veteran paralyzed by, annuity,
115:6A-115:6C.
Wells, **265:16.**
Wood alcohol containers, warning
notice, **94:303C.**

POLAND.
Veterans of armed forces of,
entitled to hospital benefits,
115A:4.

POLEAX.
Inhumane method of slaughter of
livestock, **94:139E.**

POLE DICKEY OR DOLLY.
Trailer under motor vehicle
regulation act, **90:1.**

POLES AND WIRES.
See TRANSMISSION LINES
AND EQUIPMENT.

POLICE, 41:96-41:101.
Abandoned motor vehicles, duties
of police, **90:22B.**
Abandoned property.
See ABANDONED, LOST, AND
UNCLAIMED PROPERTY.
Absence, leave of.
Leave of absence. See within
this heading, "Leave of
absence."
Abuse prevention.
Abused.
See ABUSED AND
NEGLECTED
CHILDREN.
Authority of officer to prevent
abuse to family or household
member, **209A:6.**
Patients or residents in
long-term care facilities,
reports of abuse, **111:72G.**
State police, arrest forms
providing space to indicate
offenses involving, **22C:49.**
Abutting owners, notice and bond
required of one entering land
of another without permission,
266:120B.
Accident and sickness insurance,
group or blanket policies for
police, **32B:11D, 175:110.**
Accidents, police duties in
connection.
Gas and electricity, report of
accidents caused, **164:95.**
Motor vehicle accidents.
Reports of.
See TRAFFIC
REGULATIONS AND
RULES OF THE ROAD.
Vehicles removed from scene
of accident by
metropolitan district
police, storage, **255:39A.**
Administration and finance
executive office, **7:4H.**
Age.
See AGE.
Agricultural and horticultural
societies, assignment to
exhibitions, **128:46.**
Aiding.
Bystander, **263:3, 268:24.**
Calling for assistance, duty to
aid, **268:24.**
Escape from police, **268:16,**
268:17.

POLICE —Cont'd
Aiding —Cont'd
Indemnification for damage,
injury or death to assistants
and third persons, **41:100.**
Lists of persons between 3 and
21 years of age, assistance
of police department in
making, **51:14A.**
Mutual aid programs, **40:5,
40:8G.**
Other city or town, assisting
police force of upon proper
request, **41:99.**
Payments to dependents of
persons dying while aiding
police officers, **32:88.**
Refusal or neglect to aid,
penalty, **268:24, 269:2.**
Air pollution emergency orders,
enforcement, **111:2B.**
Air rifle, permit to minor,
269:12B.
Alarms or signal systems of,
interference, **268:32.**
Alcoholic liquors.
See ALCOHOLIC LIQUORS.
Alcoholism.
See ALCOHOLISM AND
INTOXICATION.
Aldermen.
Selectmen and aldermen. See
within this heading,
"Selectmen and aldermen."
Ammunition, licensing sale,
140:122B.
Animals.
See ANIMALS.
Annuities to dependents of
policeman dying in
performance of duty, **32:89,
32:89A-32:89D, 32:95A,
32:100.**
Appeal.
See APPEAL AND REVIEW.
Appearances before clerks of
district court, **21:6F.**
Appointment, **41:96.**
Capital police, **8:4.**
Chief of police. See within this
heading, "Chief of police."
Conviction of crime as barring
appointment as police
officer, **41:96A.**
Express company, appointment
on petition of company,
159:92-159:95.
New Bedford Institute of
Technology, appointment of
police officers, **74:42Q.**
Parks and reservations,
appointment and control,
45:5.

POLICE —Cont'd
Appointment —Cont'd
Probationary period, duration of,
41:133.
Selectmen and aldermen. See
within this heading,
"Selectmen and aldermen."
Sheriffs.
See SHERIFFS AND
DEPUTIES.
Special constables to enforce
motor vehicle laws,
appointment, **90:29.**
State police, **41:87A.**
Arbitration.
Committee to oversee, **150E:9.**
Petitioning by police officers,
150E:9.
Armories used for meeting to raise
funds for policemen's benefit
association, **33:122.**
Arrest, power of, **41:98, 41:98A.**
See ARREST.
Arson squads, **148:32.**
Assassination of police officer,
reward for information
concerning, **276:10.**
Assault.
See ASSAULT AND BATTERY.
Assault weapons, seizure, **269:10.**
Assignment to duty in another
community, **41:99.**
Assistance.
Aiding. See within this heading,
"Aiding."
Association.
See POLICE ASSOCIATION.
Attempt to extort money by threat,
265:25.
Attorney general, conferences,
12:6A.
Augmentation of police force from
another city or town, **41:99.**
Automobile insurance.
Exemption of police vehicles
from certificate as to
compulsory insurance,
90:1A.
Notice provision in insurance
policy covering motor
vehicles, **175:191A.**
Theft claims, notice, **175:113O,
266:29.**
Uninsured motor vehicles,
90:34J, 90:34P.
Automobiles.
Motor vehicles. See within this
heading, "Motor vehicles."
Auxiliary police.
See CIVIL DEFENSE.
Badges, **159:92.**
Boston terminal corporation
police, **159:92.**

POLICE —Cont'd
Badges —Cont'd
Capitol police, **8:4.**
County police, inscriptions on
badges, **147:8.**
Display by arresting officer,
90:21.
Express company police, **159:92.**
Imitation and misuse, **268:35.**
Issuance and exhibition, **41:98C,
41:98D, 90:21.**
Name not required, **41:98C.**
Officers of law enforcement
division, **21:6C.**
Steamboat police, **159:92.**
Street railway police, **159:92.**
Ballot boxes, key, **54:66.**
Battery.
See ASSAULT AND BATTERY.
BB guns, possession by minor,
269:12B.
Benefit association fundraising
activities, use of armories,
33:122.
Bicycle violations, duties in
connection, **85:11A-85:11C.**
Billiard and poolroom
establishments, entry,
140:201.
Blood test.
See DRIVING WHILE UNDER
INFLUENCE OF
ALCOHOL OR DRUGS.
Bond or undertaking of one
entering land of another
without permission, **266:120B.**
Borrowing money for
communication installations,
44:7.
Boston.
See BOSTON.
Boston municipal court, **262:53A,
262:53C.**
Boston terminal corporation.
See BOSTON TERMINAL
CORPORATION.
Boxing matches not licensed,
injunction against, **147:45.**
Bradford Durfee College of
Technology, appointment of
police officers, **74:42Q.**
Breach of peace.
See BREACH OF PEACE AND
DISORDERLY CONDUCT.
Breath tests.
See DRIVING WHILE UNDER
INFLUENCE OF
ALCOHOL OR DRUGS.
Bribery of persons connected with
horse race, **271:39.**
Burial expenses of those killed in
line of duty, payment,
41:100G.

POLICE —Cont'd
Bylaws of towns with respect to police, **40:21.**
Cable television company's duty to provide cable drop to police stations, **166A:5.**
Cadets, appointment, qualifications, and duties, **147:21A.**
Call box, penalty for damage to or interference, **268:32.**
Calling for assistance, duty to aid, **268:24.**
Capitol police.
  Additional hours of duty, **8:4, 149:30A, 149:30B.**
  Appointment and promotion, **8:4.**
  Authority as to dispersion and suppression of unlawful assemblies, **269:1.**
  Badges, **8:4.**
  Career incentive pay program, **41:108L.**
  Civil service, **31:64, 31:65.**
  Hours of labor, **8:4, 149:30A, 149:30B.**
  Indemnification, **258:9A.**
  In-service and supervisory training, **41:96B.**
  Overtime, **8:4, 149:30A, 149:30B.**
  Retirement systems and pensions, **32:3.**
  Riots and mobs, **269:7, 269:8.**
  Salaries and compensation, **8:4, 30:46.**
    Overtime, **8:4.**
    Reallocation of job groups in general schedule, **30:46 note.**
  Smoking regulations, **31:64.**
  Unlawful assemblies, suppression, **269:1.**
Cardiopulmonary resuscitation, required training, **111:201.**
Career incentive pay program, **41:108L.**
Carriers, status of investigators and examiners employed by motor carriers of property, **159B:14.**
Cat, report of death or injury by motor vehicle, **272:80H.**
Certificates and certification.
  Gross vehicle weight rating certificate, inspection by police, **90:19D.**
  Hawkers and peddlers license, certification by police chief of good reputation of applicant, **101:22.**

POLICE —Cont'd
Certificates and certification —Cont'd
  Police motor vehicles, exemption from certificates as to compulsory insurance, **90:1A.**
  State police officer's certification of witness fees and travel expenses, **262:53B.**
  Travel expenses of police officer in criminal case, **262:53A, 262:53B.**
Chaplain of municipal police department, blue flashing lights used, **90:7E.**
Charities and charitable contributions.
  Armories used for meetings to raise funds for police benefit association, **33:122.**
  Investigations as to charitable corporations proposing to change locations, **180:5.**
  Permission to solicit on public ways, **85:17A.**
  Police organizations, **41:98E, 68:20.**
Charter cities.
  See CITY CHARTERS.
Chief hearing officer of administration and finance executive office to conduct appeals as to punishment duty, **7:4H.**
Chief of police.
  Ammunition, licensing sale, **140:122B.**
  Appointment.
    By selectmen and aldermen, election authorizing, **41:21, 41:23, 41:97, 41:97A, 41:101.**
    In towns accepting certain statutory provisions, **41:97, 41:97A.**
    Notification to public safety commissioner, **147:31.**
  Arrested persons, report of physical examination, **276:33.**
  Association, **111C:7.**
  Authority in certain towns having departments established by selectmen, **41:97, 41:97A.**
  Capitol police. See within this heading, "Capitol police."
  Civil service, **31:48.**
  Commissioner of public safety, **41:101.**

POLICE —Cont'd
Chief of police —Cont'd
  Common nuisances, abatement, **139:16A.**
  Conventions, attendance, **41:97E.**
  Criminal history systems board, members, **6:168.**
  Criminal justice committee, **6:156, 6:156A.**
  Criminal Justice Training Council, membership, **6:116.**
  Dead bodies, removal, **38:6.**
  Employment contracts, **41:108O.**
  Hawkers and peddlers license, certification by police chief of good reputation of applicant, **101:22.**
  Hearings before removal, **41:21A.**
  Holidays.
    Additional day's pay for duty, **147:17F.**
    Issuance of permits for work, **136:14, 136:15.**
  Medicolegal investigations committee, membership, **6:184.**
  Monthly reports of arrests, **124:9.**
  Motor vehicles stored and not claimed, notice of sale, **255:39A.**
  Nonprofit organizations, permit to solicit on public ways, **85:17A.**
  Notice.
    Motor vehicles stored and not claimed, notice of sale, **255:39A.**
    Pardons, notice to and duties of local chief with respect, **127:152-127:154.**
    Parole of prisoner serving life sentence, notice of hearing, **127:133A.**
  Other city or town, requisition for police, **41:99.**
  Pardons, notice to and duties of local chief with respect, **127:152-127:154.**
  Parole of prisoner serving life sentence, notice of hearing, **127:133A.**
  Pawnbrokers.
    Premises, entry and inspection, **140:73.**
    Record books, inspection, **140:81, 140:87.**
  Payment of police officers for off-duty work details, **44:53C.**

POLICE —Cont'd

Chief of police —Cont'd

Powers and duties, **41:97, 41:97A, 41:98.**

Proposal review board of criminal justice committee, **6:156A.**

Public records, **6:172.**

Rate of compensation, **48:57G.**

Record books, inspection, **140:81, 140:87.**

Removal from office, **41:21A.**

Rescission of selectmen's power to appoint, **41:23.**

Secondhand motor vehicles, inspection of premises for sale, **140:66.**

Solicitation on public ways, permit for nonprofit organizations, **85:17A.**

Sunday work, permits, **136:7.**

Trespasses against town, prosecutions, **41:36.**

Children.

Juvenile offenders and delinquents. See within this heading, "Juvenile offenders and delinquents."

Minors. See within this heading, "Minors."

Chiropody, indemnification of police officers for charges incurred as a result of injuries in line of duty, **41:100, 41:100B.**

Chiropractic services, indemnification for expense, **41:100, 41:100B.**

Cigarette tax.

Appointment of special police officers, **64C:26.**

Enforcement of provisions, **64C:8, 64C:10, 64C:26.**

Cities and towns, **41:96 et seq.**

City charters.

See CITY CHARTERS.

City council.

See CITY COUNCIL.

City marshals.

See CITY MARSHALS.

Civil defense.

See CIVIL DEFENSE.

Civil service.

See CIVIL SERVICE.

Clothing.

Uniforms. See within this heading, "Uniforms."

Collective bargaining.

See LABOR RELATIONS AND DISPUTES.

Colleges.

See COLLEGES AND UNIVERSITIES.

POLICE —Cont'd

Commercial vehicles.

Motor vehicles. See within this heading, "Motor vehicles."

Commissioner of police.

Charitable corporations, investigation of proposed, **180:5.**

Designation of police station for detention and confinement of females, **147:18.**

Dog kennels inspected by police commissioner, **140:137C.**

Records. See within this heading, "Records."

Witnesses before, **233:8.**

Commissioner of public safety.

Annual report, **147:1.**

Duties, **147:1 et seq.**

Fingerprints and photographs of persons arrested for commission of felony to be forwarded, **263:1A.**

Fixing compensation of police, **41:101.**

List of police sent, **147:31.**

Special officers. See within this heading, "Special officers."

State police.

See STATE POLICE.

Towns to send police list, **147:31.**

Committee to oversee police arbitration and collective bargaining proceedings, **150E:9.**

Common nuisance, abatement, **139:16A.**

Commonwealth zoological corporation, police protection, **92B:5.**

Communication installations.

Alarms or signal systems of police, interference, **268:32.**

Cable television company's duty to provide cable drop to police stations, **166A:5.**

Cities may borrow, **44:7.**

Utility poles, removal, **166:22J.**

Compensation.

Salaries and compensation. See within this heading, "Salaries and compensation."

Computer terminals under control of registrar of motor vehicles, **90:30A.**

Constables.

See CONSTABLES.

Contracts and agreements.

Employment contracts for police chiefs, **41:108O.**

POLICE —Cont'd

Contracts and agreements —Cont'd

Mutual aid programs of police departments, authority for cities or towns to enter into agreements, **40:5, 40:8G.**

Public contracts, **149:34B, 152:1.**

Reserve or special officers employed by public contractors, **149:34B, 152:1.**

State college, police officer attending, agreement to remain as police officer after completion of work, **73:20.**

Controlled substances.

See DRUGS AND NARCOTICS.

Conventions, attendance, **41:97E, 147:17, 147:17D.**

Convicts ineligible for appointment, **41:96A.**

Copper wire or scrap dealers, inspection of books and records, **266:142.**

Correctional institutions.

See CORRECTIONAL INSTITUTIONS.

Counterfeit.

Bills and coins, seizure, **267:30.**

Transportation passes, **161:113A.**

County commissioners.

See COUNTY COMMISSIONERS.

County officers and employees, **147:8.**

Accidental death insurance for police and firefighters killed on duty, **32B:11D.**

Sheriffs.

See SHERIFFS AND DEPUTIES.

Course of study, removal of officer for failure to complete, **41:96B.**

Court officers, performance of police duties and powers, **221:70A.**

Court order for temporary protection of persons suffering abuse, enforcement, **208:34C.**

Credit card offenders, arrest without warrant of certain, **266:37B, 266:37C.**

Crimes and offenses.

Alarms or signal systems of police, interference, **268:32.**

Badges of officers, unauthorized use, **268:35.**

Conviction of crime as barring appointment as police officer, **41:96A.**

POLICE —Cont'd
Crimes and offenses —Cont'd
False claim as to identity,
268:33.
Fines and penalties. See within
this heading, "Fines and
penalties."
Motor vehicle offenses, citations,
90C:2.
Police vehicles, obstruction,
89:7A.
Vehicles, sale without removing
distinctive markings,
266:92A.
Criminal case, compensatory time
off to attend, **262:53C.**
Criminal history systems board,
membership, **6:168.**
Criminal identification bureau,
147:14 et seq.
Accumulation of days off,
147:17.
Approval of five-day week,
147:16C.
Attendance at Massachusetts
Police Association
Convention, **147:17,
147:17D.**
Compensation, **147:14 et seq.**
Overtime, time off,
147:17A-147:17C.
Public emergency as preventing
days off, **147:17.**
Saturday holiday, day off falling,
147:17A.
State police, **22C:36.**
Criminal justice committees,
membership, **6:156, 6:156A.**
Criminal justice training council,
membership, **6:116.**
Criminal offender record
information system,
continuing educational
program in use and control,
6:171.
Criminal procedure.
See CRIMINAL PROCEDURE.
Criminal records furnished by
clerks of court without charge,
262:5.
Cruelty to animals, prosecution or
prevention, **272:84, 272:88,
272:89.**
Daily log, **41:98F.**
Damages or injury to property
seized or used by police or fire
department, appropriations to
pay, **40:5.**
Days off.
Holidays and Sundays. See
within this heading,
"Holidays and Sundays."

POLICE —Cont'd
Dead bodies, report of person
exposed to infectious disease
through attending, assisting
or transporting deceased
person, **111:111C.**
Death.
Injury or death. See within this
heading, "Injury or death."
Defacing library contents,
ascertaining the identity of
offender upon warrantless
arrest, **266:100.**
Defenses of actions against,
41:100.
Delay in serving warrants,
penalty, **268:22.**
Dependents.
Minors. See within this heading,
"Minors."
Persons dying while aiding
police officers, payments to
dependents, **32:88.**
Policemen killed in line of duty,
annuities or compensation
for dependents, **32:89,
32:89A-32:89D, 32:95A,
32:100.**
Deputy chiefs, commissioner of
public safety may appoint,
41:101.
Detectives.
See DETECTIVES.
Discharge and release, exception
to inadmissibility, **271:44.**
Disqualification.
Qualification and
disqualification. See within
this heading, "Qualification
and disqualification."
District attorneys, reports of
deaths, **38:6.**
District courts.
See DISTRICT COURTS.
District for employing and paying,
town may establish, **40:44.**
Dogs.
Exemption from quarantine,
129:22A.
Horse and dog race meetings,
compensation of police
assigned, **128A:8.**
Indemnification for damages
caused, **41:100H, 140:155A.**
Kennels inspected by police
commissioner, **140:137C.**
Unmuzzled dogs, duties,
140:167.
Willfully injuring, penalty,
272:77A.
Domestic violence, training of law
enforcement personnel,
6:116A.

POLICE —Cont'd
Domicile and residence.
Fees and expenses of police
officers attending court as
witnesses outside, **262:53A,
262:53B.**
Nonresidents. See within this
heading, "Nonresidents."
Place of residence, **41:99A.**
Special police officers,
appointment, **149:176.**
Tax exemption for real property
of surviving spouses of
policemen, **59:5.**
Drugs.
See DRUGS AND NARCOTICS.
Drunk driver.
See DRIVING WHILE UNDER
INFLUENCE OF
ALCOHOL OR DRUGS.
Drunks.
See ALCOHOLISM AND
INTOXICATION.
Duties, **41:98, 269:1-269:6.**
Education.
Colleges.
See COLLEGES AND
UNIVERSITIES.
Compensation while in
attendance at school,
41:96B, 41:108M.
Increased compensation for
continuing, **41:108L.**
Missing children, notice, **22A:9.**
Scholarships for children of
certain officers, award,
15A:7.
Training schools or courses. See
within this heading,
"Training schools or
courses."
Elections.
Acceptance of statute with
respect to police
departments of certain
towns, **41:97A.**
Accidental death insurance for
town policemen and firemen,
acceptance, **32B:11D.**
Ballot boxes, key, **54:66.**
Chief of police appointed by
selectmen, election
authorizing, **41:21.**
Duties during, **54:71-54:75.**
Initiative and referendum. See
within this heading,
"Initiative and referendum."
Listing of persons 17 years of
age or over, assistance in
making, **51:14A.**
Minimum annual compensation,
election, **41:108E, 41:108G.**

POLICE —Cont'd
Elections —Cont'd
Offenses, power of arrest without warrant, **56:57.**
Officers of election, police protection, **54:72.**
Overtime pay on election day, **41:111H.**
Polls and polling places, police details, **54:72-54:75.**
Duty to act under directions of presiding officer, **54:71.**
Regional police districts, elections as to establishment, **41:99D.**
Town meeting. See within this heading, "Town meeting."
Electricity.
Gas and electricity. See within this heading, "Gas and electricity."
Emergencies.
See EMERGENCIES.
Entry into land.
See ENTRY INTO LAND AND PREMISES.
Environmental officials, **21:6B.**
Escape.
See ESCAPE.
Examination, inspection, and investigation.
Arrested persons, physical examination, **276:33.**
Blood test.
See DRIVING WHILE UNDER INFLUENCE OF ALCOHOL OR DRUGS.
Commercial driver license.
See UNIFORM OPERATION OF COMMERCIAL MOTOR VEHICLES.
Copper and scrap dealers, police inspection of books and records, **266:142.**
Detectives.
See DETECTIVES.
Driving while under influence of alcohol.
See DRIVING WHILE UNDER INFLUENCE OF ALCOHOL OR DRUGS.
Federal bureau of investigation.
See FEDERAL BUREAU OF INVESTIGATION.
Garages and parking stations, inspection of records, **90:32.**
Lie detector tests, use by employers, **149:19B.**
Lodging houses, **140:25.**
Massage establishments, **140:52.**
Medicolegal investigations. See within this heading, "Medicolegal investigations."

POLICE —Cont'd
Examination, inspection, and investigation —Cont'd
Motor carriers of property, status of investigators and examiners, **159B:14.**
Private detectives.
See PRIVATE DETECTIVES AND INVESTIGATORS.
Prospective jurors, investigation, **234:4.**
Sanitary conditions of police stations, **40:36B, 111:20-111:22.**
Searches.
See SEARCHES AND SEIZURES.
State police.
See STATE POLICE.
Suspicious persons, examination, **41:98.**
Used car lots, **140:66.**
Exemptions.
Police dog quarantine, **129:22A.**
Police motor vehicles.
Compulsory insurance, exemption from certificate, **90:1A.**
Marked police vehicle from other state, exemption from registration, **90:9B.**
Registration fee, exemption, **90:33.**
Safety precautions, **90:13.**
Ships and other watercraft exempt from excise taxes, **60B:3.**
Surviving spouse or minor children of deceased policeman, exemption, **59:5.**
Expenses.
F.B.I training schools, appropriations for expenses of local police attending, **40:5.**
Fees. See within this heading, "Fees."
Funeral and burial expenses of policemen killed in line of duty, **41:100G.**
Medical care and expenses. See within this heading, "Medical care or expenses."
Paid by Commonwealth, **262:50.**
Service in other cities and towns, **41:99.**
State police.
See STATE POLICE.
Training schools for local police officers and certain employees, **40:5.**

POLICE —Cont'd
Expenses —Cont'd
Traveling expenses. See within this heading, "Traveling expenses."
Express companies.
See EXPRESS COMPANIES.
Extortion attempted by threats, punishment, **265:25.**
Extra-jurisdictional right of arrest on fresh and continued pursuit, **41:98A.**
Failure of person to report crime, penalty, **268:40.**
False crime report, filing, **269:13A.**
False personation.
See FALSE PERSONATION.
FBI.
See FEDERAL BUREAU OF INVESTIGATION.
Fees.
Criminal records furnished by clerks of court without charge, **262:5.**
Juvenile offenders, attendance at prosecution, **262:27.**
Leave of absence, attendance in criminal cases, **262:53B, 262:53C.**
Mileage fees, **262:53B.**
Railroad police, fees and expenses, **262:55.**
Salaries and allowances as exclusive, **262:50, 262:53A.**
Service of subpoena on witness, **262:53.**
State police officer's witness fees and travel expenses, **262:53B.**
Witness fees, **262:50-262:53C, 262:55, 262:56.**
Female.
Compensation of police officers, equality, **41:108K.**
Detention and confinement, designation of places, **147:18.**
Intensive care unit for mentally ill women. See within this heading, "Intensive care unit for mentally ill women."
Matrons. See within this heading, "Matrons."
Fines and penalties.
Arrest, penalty for refusal, **268:23.**
Badge, unlawful use, **268:35.**
Cars, violation of provisions as to sale, **266:92A.**
Extortion attempted by threats, punishment, **265:25.**

POLICE —Cont'd

Fines and penalties —Cont'd

Horses or dogs used by police, penalty for willfully injuring, **272:77A.**

Leaving prisoners at large, penalty, **268:21.**

Police list, failure to send to commissioner, **147:31.**

Refusal or neglect to aid, penalty, **268:24, 269:2.**

Right-of-way of police vehicle, obstruction, **89:7.**

Signal systems, penalty for tampering, **268:32.**

Warrants, penalty for delay in serving, **268:22.**

Fingerprints.

See FINGERPRINTS.

Fire alarm operators, children of police officers killed in the line of duty, eligibility for appointment, **31:26.**

Firearms and other weapons.

Air rifle, permit to minor, **269:12B.**

Ammunition, licensing of sale, **140:122B.**

Assault weapons, seizure, **269:10.**

BB guns, possession by minor, **269:12B.**

Carrying by police of, **41:98, 147:2, 147:8A.**

Discharge, **269:12E.**

License requirements, **140:122B, 140:129C, 140:131G.**

Permissible possession, **140:129C.**

Reports by unlicensed residents selling not more than four firearms within calendar year, **140:128A.**

Search of person suspected of possessing, **41:98.**

Silencers, use or ownership, **269:10A.**

Sporting weapons, police deemed to have license required, **140:131G.**

Fire escapes, seizure of articles obstructing, **143:22.**

Firefighters and police officers, performing other's duties, **41:97F, 48:88.**

Fire hazards, duties as to abatement, **148:5.**

Fish.

See FISH AND GAME.

Five day week, **147:16B, 147:16C, 147:17B.**

POLICE —Cont'd

Foot patrol, certain cities and towns to provide, **41:98B.**

Foreign states.

See FOREIGN STATES OR COUNTRIES.

Forest employees, **132A:7.**

Forfeited property, seizure, **257:1.**

Forgery.

Counterfeit. See within this heading, "Counterfeit."

Forty-hour week, **147:17B.**

Free or reduced rates service on railroads, **159:15.**

Fugitives from justice and out-of-state criminals, apprehension, **276:20A to 276:20C.**

Funeral and burial expenses of policeman killed in line of duty, **41:100G.**

Gaming and gaming houses.

Arrest without warrant for gaming, **271:2, 271:6, 271:10, 271:10A.**

Obstruction of access, **271:25, 271:26.**

Searches, **271:23.**

Telephones used in gambling, approval of reinstallation, **271:47.**

Garages and parking stations, inspection of records, **90:32.**

Garbage and refuse, enforcement of provisions as to unlawful disposal, **270:16, 270:16A.**

Gas and electricity.

Entry upon premises to disconnect services in event of fire or explosion, **164:116A.**

Report of accidents caused, **164:95.**

Utility poles, removal of communication equipment, **166:22J.**

General court.

See GENERAL COURT.

Glue or cement sold to minors, inspection of register of names of minors, **270:19.**

Governor.

See GOVERNOR.

Grades of service, **31:64.**

Graves of police dying in performance of duty, town appropriation with respect, **40:5.**

Gross motor vehicle weight certificate to be made available for inspection by police officer, **90:19D.**

POLICE —Cont'd

Group insurance, surviving spouse's privileges, **32B:9E, 32B:9G.**

Harbor police, powers and duties as to motorboat offenses, **90B:12, 90B:13, 90B:17.**

Hawkers and peddlers, police chief's certification of good character of applicants for licenses, **101:22.**

Hazardous waste, seizure and forfeiture of property, **21C:14.**

Health.

Dead bodies, report of person exposed to infectious disease through attending, assisting or transporting deceased person, **111:111C.**

Health department. See within this heading, "Health department."

Health department.

Plans for station houses and lockups, approval by state health department, **111:22.**

Rules and regulations regarding station houses, lockups, and the like, **111:21.**

Stations, lockups, houses of detention, jails, houses of correction, prisons and reformatories, inspection and general sanitary condition, **40:36B, 111:20-111:22.**

Wellness programs, **31:61A.**

Hearings prior to discharge, right, **41:21A, 41:96, 41:97.**

Holidays and Sundays, **147:17 et seq.**

Chief of police. See within this heading, "Chief of police."

Criminal identification bureau, **147:17 et seq.**

Injured or on vacation on holiday, **147:17A.**

Issuance of permits for work, **136:7, 136:14, 136:15.**

Memorial day.

See MEMORIAL DAY.

Parades by police associations on Sunday, **136:6.**

Pay for holiday as regular compensation, **32:1.**

Time off or additional pay for officers working, **147:17A.**

Veterans Day as holiday for veterans, **30:9H.**

Honor rolls for, town appropriation, **40:5.**

POLICE —Cont'd

Horse.

See HORSE AND DOG RACING MEETINGS.

Horses.

See HORSES.

Hospitals and health care facilities, expenses, **40:5, 41:100, 41:100B.**

Hotels, motels, and roominghouses.

Access for purposes of inspecting, **140:37, 140:38.**

Licensing of houses, **140:34.**

Hours of labor, **149:33A, 149:33B.**

Capitol police, **8:4.**

Criminal identification bureau. See within this heading, "Criminal identification bureau."

Holidays and Sundays. See within this heading, "Holidays and Sundays."

Initiative and referendum. See within this heading, "Initiative and referendum."

Night duty. See within this heading, "Night duty."

Overtime pay, **8:4, 41:111H, 147:17A-147:17C, 147:17F, 147:17G.**

State police.

See STATE POLICE.

House of prostitution, court authorizing entry, **272:9.**

Housing authority police, **121B:7.**

Hunter's or sportsman's weapon, report of personal injury or death, **131:60.**

Husband and wife.

Surviving spouse. See within this heading, "Surviving spouse."

Identity and identification.

Badges. See within this heading, "Badges."

Criminal identification bureau. See within this heading, "Criminal identification bureau."

Fingerprints.

See FINGERPRINTS.

Photography. See within this heading, "Photography."

Immunity from civil or criminal liability.

Emergency care or treatment, **111C:14.**

Mental health, **123:22.**

Indemnity and indemnification.

Complaint, **258:9A Form 1.**

POLICE —Cont'd

Indemnity and indemnification —Cont'd

Of persons responsible for injuries to police, **41:100, 41:111F.**

Of police, **40:5, 41:100, 41:100B, 41:100H, 140:155A, 258:9A.**

Capitol police, **258:9A.**

Infected articles or goods, executing warrant for removal, **111:101.**

Infectious disease, report of person exposed through attending, assisting or transporting infected individual or deceased person, **111:111C.**

Initiative and referendum.

Distribution by police of literature for referendum pertaining to hours of labor or compensation, **54:65.**

Five day work week for police, **147:16C.**

Injury or death.

Accident and sickness insurance, group or blanket policies, **32B:11D, 175:110.**

Annuities or compensation to dependents, **32:88, 32:89, 32:89A to 32:89D, 32:95A, 32:100.**

Assassination of police officer, reward for information concerning, **276:10.**

Assistants and third persons, indemnification, **41:100.**

Burial expenses, **41:100G.**

Capitol police. See within this heading, "Capitol police."

Compensation due to deceased officer, payment without administration, **41:111I.**

Fire alarm operators, children of officer killed in line of duty, **31:26.**

Funeral or burial expenses of policemen killed in line of duty, **40:5, 41:100G.**

Indemnification or reimbursement for hospital, medical and other expenses, **40:5, 41:100, 41:100B, 41:100H.**

Leave without loss of pay for certain incapacitated policemen, **41:111F.**

Line of duty, additional time off or pay for absences caused by injuries sustained, **147:17A.**

POLICE —Cont'd

Injury or death —Cont'd

Municipal park police, death benefits, **32:94.**

Overtime compensation due, payment, **147:17E.**

Report to police of injury or death caused by hunter's or sportsman's weapon, **131:60.**

In-service and supervisory training, **41:96B.**

Inspection.

Examination, inspection, and investigation. See within this heading, "Examination, inspection, and investigation."

Installment sales of motor vehicles.

Motor vehicle retail installment sales. See within this heading, "Motor vehicle retail installment sales."

Insurance.

Against accidents or illness, **32B:11D, 175:110.**

Automobile insurance. See within this heading, "Automobile insurance."

Intensive care unit for mentally ill women.

Civil immunity, **123:22.**

Notification of absence of patient or resident, **123:30.**

Intermittent force appointments to regular force from, computation of full-time service of permanent-intermittent officers, **32:4.**

Interns employed in police departments, **40:5.**

Investigation.

Examination, inspection, and investigation. See within this heading, "Examination, inspection, and investigation."

Jurors, investigation of prospective jurors, **234:4.**

Justices of the peace, summonses for motor vehicle violations, **90:27.**

Juvenile offenders and delinquents.

Compensatory time off to officers in attendance in criminal cases, **262:53C.**

Detention in police stations, **119:66, 119:67.**

Fee for attendance at prosecution, **262:27.**

POLICE —Cont'd

Juvenile offenders and delinquents
—Cont'd

Filing petition for children in
need of services, **119:39E.**

Patrol wagon, transporting child,
119:34.

Service of summons in
proceedings involving,
119:55.

Labor relations.

See LABOR RELATIONS AND
DISPUTES.

Larceny.

Stolen property. See within this
heading, "Stolen property."

Law officers defined, **209A:1.**

Laws enacted, attorney general to
give notice, **12:6A.**

Leave of absence.

Attendance in criminal cases,
fees and compensatory time
off, **262:53B, 262:53C.**

Leave without loss of pay,
41:111F.

Sick leave, **41:111F.**

Witness fees and travel
allowance for state police
officers, **262:53B.**

Leaving prisoners at large,
penalty, **268:21.**

Library contents, ascertaining
identity of offender upon
warrantless arrest for
defacing, **266:100.**

License for firearms, police as
subject to requirements of,
140:129C, 140:131G.

Licenses provided to special police
officers, **22C:53, 22C:59,
22C:60 et seq.**

Lie detector test, exception in
prohibition as to giving,
149:19B.

Lists or schedules, **22C:11, 147:31.**

Assistance of police department
in making lists of persons
between 3 and 21 years of
age, **51:14A.**

Towns to send to commissioner
of public safety list of police,
147:31.

Livestock disease control director,
assistance, **129:6.**

Loans, holding stolen articles
pledged, **140:88.**

Lockups.

See LOCKUPS.

Loitering or trespassing on public
transportation facility
premises, power of arrest,
161:94A, 161:95.

POLICE —Cont'd

Lost property.

See ABANDONED, LOST, AND
UNCLAIMED PROPERTY.

Lowell.

Superintendent, additional day's
pay for duty on certain
holidays, **147:17F.**

Marine fisheries laws,
enforcement, **130:8A.**

Marshals.

See MARSHALS.

Massachusetts Bay transportation
authority.

See MASSACHUSETTS BAY
TRANSPORTATION
AUTHORITY.

Massachusetts Chiefs of Police
Association, **111C:7.**

Massachusetts civil rights act,
enforcement of court orders,
12:11J.

Massage establishments,
inspection, **140:52.**

Matrons, **147:18-147:21.**

Appointment, **147:18.**

Compensation, **147:19.**

Duties, **147:19, 147:20.**

Tenure of office, **147:19.**

Mayors.

See MAYORS.

Medical and physical fitness
examinations, **31:61A, 32:5.**

Medical care or expenses, **40:5,
41:100, 41:100B.**

Chiropody, charges incurred as
result of injuries in line of
duty, **41:100, 41:100B.**

Chiropractic services,
indemnification for expense,
41:100, 41:100B.

Municipal appropriations, **40:5.**

Medical examiners.

See MEDICAL EXAMINERS
AND INQUESTS.

Medical or physical examination of
arrestee, **276:33.**

Medicolegal investigations.

Committee, membership, **6:184.**

Investigation office, co-operation,
38:2.

Memorial day.

See MEMORIAL DAY.

Memorials to those dying in line of
duty, town appropriations,
40:5.

Mentally ill.

See MENTALLY ILL AND
RETARDED PERSONS.

Metropolitan District Commission.

See METROPOLITAN
DISTRICT COMMISSION.

POLICE —Cont'd

Mileage fees, **262:53B.**

Militia.

See MILITIA.

Minimum annual compensation,
41:108E, 41:108G.

Minors.

Abuse of, penalty for failure to
report, **119:51A.**

Air rifle, permits to minors,
269:12B.

BB guns, possession by minor,
269:12B.

Exemption for minor children of
deceased policeman, **59:5.**

Filing petition for children in
need of services, **119:39E.**

Fire alarm operators, children of
police officers killed in line
of duty, **31:26.**

Glue or cement sold to minors,
270:19.

Juvenile offenders and
delinquents. See within this
heading, "Juvenile offenders
and delinquents."

Missing persons. See within this
heading, "Missing persons."

Nonresident students operating
motor vehicles, **90:3.**

Notice.

Intoxicated child, parents to
receive notice of police
custody, **111B:8.**

Missing persons. See within
this heading, "Missing
persons."

Parents to receive notice of
police custody of intoxicated
child or minor, **111B:8.**

Patrol wagons, children not to
be transported, **119:34.**

Protective custody of intoxicated
child or minor, **111B:10.**

Rights of children of policemen,
**32:89, 32:89A, 32:89B,
32:100.**

Runaway child, probable cause
for arrest, **119:39H.**

Scholarships for children of
certain officers, award,
15A:7.

Street trades, enforcement of
laws as to minors, **149:77.**

Sudden unexpected death of,
reporting, **38:3.**

Missing persons.

Entering information into
central register for missing
children, **22A:4.**

Environmental police searchers,
132A:7A.

POLICE —Cont'd
Missing persons —Cont'd
Law enforcement division,
notification, **21:6A.**
Schools, notice of missing
children, **22A:9.**
Mobs.
Riots and mobs. See within this
heading, "Riots and mobs."
Monthly reports of arrests, **124:9.**
Motels.
Hotels, motels, and
roominghouses. See within
this heading, "Hotels,
motels, and roominghouses."
Motorboat laws, enforcement,
90B:12, 90B:13, 90B:17.
Motor carriers of property, status
of investigators and
examiners, **159B:14.**
Motorcycles lessors, duties,
90:32H.
Motor vehicle retail installment
sales.
Creditor's report of repossession,
255B:20C.
Enforcement of law, **255B:6.**
Motor vehicles.
Abandoned vehicles, duties of
police, **90:22B.**
Accidents. See within this
heading, "Accidents, police
duties in connection."
Animal, report of injury or death
by motor vehicle, **272:80H.**
Citations for offenses, **90C:2.**
Commercial driver license.
See UNIFORM OPERATION
OF COMMERCIAL
MOTOR VEHICLES.
Commercial vehicle division,
powers of employees,
25:12F.
Definitions of police officer in
motor vehicle act, **90:1.**
Drivers' licenses.
Commercial driver license.
See UNIFORM
OPERATION OF
COMMERCIAL
MOTOR VEHICLES.
Production, **90:21, 90:25.**
Driving while under influence of
alcohol.
See DRIVING WHILE
UNDER INFLUENCE OF
ALCOHOL OR DRUGS.
Emergency vehicles, approach,
89:7A.
Exemptions. See within this
heading, "Exemptions."

POLICE —Cont'd
Motor vehicles —Cont'd
Gross vehicle weight rating
certificate inspection by
police, **90:19D.**
Installment sales.
Motor vehicle retail
installment sales. See
within this heading,
"Motor vehicle retail
installment sales."
Insurance.
Automobile insurance. See
within this heading,
"Automobile insurance."
Junkyard act, enforcement,
140B:8.
Justices of the peace,
summonses for motor
vehicle violations, **90:27.**
Lessors of motorcycles, duties of
police, **90:32H.**
Loss prevention central
organization, reports filed,
175:1130.
Marked police vehicles from
other states, temporary
exemption from registration,
90:9B.
Marking of vehicles, **147:29.**
Metropolitan district
commission.
See METROPOLITAN
DISTRICT
COMMISSION.
Nighttime operator to give
officer name and address
when requested during,
85:16.
Nonresident students operating
motor vehicles, **90:3.**
Obedience, failure of operator to
give to officer, **90:25.**
Operation by police, **89:7-89:7B.**
Blue lights on front of vehicle,
90:7.
Compulsory insurance,
exemption from
certificate, **90:1A.**
Exemptions. See within this
heading, "Exemptions."
Number plates, **90:2.**
Obstruction of police vehicles,
89:7A.
Registration.
Exemptions. See within this
heading, "Exemptions."
Special rights and privileges,
89:6A, 89:7B.
Other states, fire apparatus and
marked police vehicles,
90:9B.

POLICE —Cont'd
Motor vehicles —Cont'd
Parking. See within this
heading, "Parking."
Patrol wagons. See within this
heading, "Patrol wagons."
Public transportation facility
premises. See within this
heading, "Public
transportation facility
premises."
Registrar of motor vehicles, use
of computer terminals under
control, **90:30A.**
Registration.
Computer terminals, **90:30A.**
Exemptions. See within this
heading, "Exemptions."
Revocation or suspension of
private owner's
registration, police to pick
up certificate after, **90:29.**
Removal of motor vehicle from
private property, notice
requirement, **266:120D.**
Repossession, creditor's report
as to, **255:13J, 255B:20C.**
Sales.
Retail installment sales.
Motor vehicle retail
installment sales. See
within this heading,
"Motor vehicle retail
installment sales."
Secondhand vehicles.
Inspection by police, **140:66.**
Sale of vehicle used as police
car, **266:92A.**
Sheriffs.
See SHERIFFS AND
DEPUTIES.
Signature, refusal to comply
with officer's request, **90:25.**
Snow traveling and recreation
vehicles, enforcement of
laws and regulations,
90B:32.
Special constables to enforce
motor vehicle law, **90:29.**
State police.
See STATE POLICE.
Supervisors, inspectors, police
powers, **90:29.**
Suspension of revocation of
registration, police officers
to pick up certificate after,
90:29.
Towing away ordered by police,
establishment of maximum
charges, **40:22D, 92:35A,
159B:6B.**

POLICE —Cont'd

Motor vehicles —Cont'd

Traffic regulations.

See TRAFFIC
REGULATIONS AND
RULES OF THE ROAD.

Uniform operation of commercial
motor vehicles.

See UNIFORM OPERATION
OF COMMERCIAL
MOTOR VEHICLES.

Uniforms of police officers, effect
on motorists, **90:25.**

Uninsured motor vehicles,
notice, **90:34J, 90:34P.**

Violations, arrest without
warrant, **90C:3.**

Municipal park police.

See PARKS AND
RESERVATIONS.

Mutual aid programs of police
departments, authority for
cities or towns to enter into
agreements as to and
appropriate moneys for
implementation, **40:5, 40:8G.**

Names.

Driver of vehicle at night,
disclosure of name to police,
85:16.

Identification badge, name not
required to appear, **41:98C.**

Pedestrians required to give
name, **90:18A.**

Providing false name or Social
Security number to law
enforcement officer,
268:34A.

Narcotics.

See DRUGS AND NARCOTICS.

Neglect.

Refusal or neglect to aid, **268:24,
269:2.**

Suppression of unlawful
assemblies, neglect, **269:3.**

New Bedford Institute of
Technology, appointment of
police officers, **74:42Q.**

Next of kin, payment of
compensation due to deceased
police officer, **41:111I.**

Night duty.

Compensatory time off to officers
attending daytime criminal
proceedings, **262:53C.**

Persons abroad during
nighttime, examination,
41:98.

Witness fees and travel
allowances of night duty
officers, **262:53-262:53B.**

POLICE —Cont'd

Nonprofit organizations,
permission to solicit on public
ways, **85:17A.**

Nonresidents.

Protection of property,
appointment and conduct of
nonresidents hired as
special police, **149:176,
149:177.**

Students as nonresidents
operating motor vehicles to
make report, **90:3.**

Notice. .

Abutting owners, notice and
bond required of one
entering land of another
without permission,
266:120B.

Attorney general to give notice
of laws enacted, **12:6A.**

Automobile insurance, notice
provision in policy covering
motor vehicles, **175:191A.**

Chief of police. See within this
heading, "Chief of police."

Intensive care unit for mentally
ill women, notification of
absence of patient or
resident, **123:30.**

Intoxicated child, parents to
receive notice of police
custody, **111B:8.**

Missing persons. See within this
heading, "Missing persons."

Removal of motor vehicle from
private property, notice
requirement, **266:120D.**

Sex offenders, notice or
information, **123A:9.**

State police.

See STATE POLICE.

Uninsured motor vehicles,
90:34J, 90:34P.

Nuisances, abatement, **139:16A.**

Obstructing entry to amusements,
140:201.

Off-duty work details, municipal
receipt and disbursement of
monies received, **44:53C.**

Offenses.

Crimes and offenses. See within
this heading, "Crimes and
offenses."

Other city or town, requisition for
service, **41:99.**

Overtime pay, **8:4, 41:111H,
147:17A-147:17C, 147:17F,
147:17G.**

Paint, turpentine and linseed oil
regulations, duty to enforce,
94:290-94:293.

POLICE —Cont'd

Parades, not to interfere, **33:50.**

Pardons, notice to and duties of
local police chief with respect,
127:152.

Parking.

Control officers, appointment
and authority, **147:10F.**

Meter supervisors as police
officers, **90:20C.**

Removal of illegally parked
vehicle from private
property, notice to police,
266:120D.

Violations, handling, **90:20A.**

Parks.

See PARKS AND
RESERVATIONS.

Parole.

See PROBATION AND
PAROLE.

Patrol wagons.

Children not to be transported,
119:34.

Number plates, **90:2.**

Right-of-way, **89:7.**

Pawnbrokers.

See PAWNBROKERS.

Pedestrians violating rules, duties,
90:18A.

Penalties.

Fines and penalties. See within
this heading, "Fines and
penalties."

Pensions.

See RETIREMENT SYSTEMS
AND PENSIONS.

Personal injury.

Injury or death. See within this
heading, "Injury or death."

Photography.

Commissioner of public safety,
fingerprints and
photographs of persons
arrested for commission of
felony to be forwarded,
263:1A.

Compensation for assignment to
photographic work, **41:108I.**

Riot or similar disturbance,
photographing and
fingerprinting of persons
arrested in connection,
41:98.

Physical fitness standards, **31:61A,
32:5.**

Pictures.

Photography. See within this
heading, "Photography."

Plans for station houses and
lockups, approval by state
health department, **111:22.**

POLICE —Cont'd
Podiatry, indemnification of officers for expenses incurred in line of duty, **41:100, 41:100B.**
Police officer's week, observance, **6:15N.**
Polls and polling places, police details at.
Elections. See within this heading, "Elections."
Port authority.
See PORT AUTHORITY.
Powers and duties, **41:98, 269:1-269:6.**
Precious metals, record of purchase or sale, **266:142A.**
Presumptions.
See PRESUMPTIONS AND BURDEN OF PROOF.
Private detectives.
See PRIVATE DETECTIVES AND INVESTIGATORS.
Probate and Family Court.
Guardian ad litem, assistance, **215:56A, 215:56B.**
Service of capias, **215:34A.**
Probation.
See PROBATION AND PAROLE.
Probationary period for full-time officers, duration of, **41:133.**
Probation officers.
See PROBATION OFFICERS.
Process.
See PROCESS AND SERVICE OF PROCESS AND PAPERS.
Promotion, **31:20.**
Proposal review board of criminal justice committee, membership, **6:156A.**
Prospective jurors, investigation, **234:4.**
Protection of property, assistance by nonresidents, **149:176, 149:177.**
Province land regulations, enforcement, **91:27.**
Public emergency as preventing taking day off, **147:17.**
Public Safety Department.
Badges of special police officers, **159:92.**
Commissioner of public safety.
See within this heading, "Commissioner of public safety."
Officers and inspectors of department, powers and duties, **147:2.**
Private detectives.
See PRIVATE DETECTIVES AND INVESTIGATORS.

POLICE —Cont'd
Public Safety Department —Cont'd
State police.
See STATE POLICE.
Public safety secretary.
Capitol police. See within this heading, "Capitol police."
Public transportation facility premises.
Arrest of persons placing filth or rubbish, **161:94A.**
Loitering or trespassing on, power of arrest, **161:94A, 161:95.**
Punishment duty, chief hearing officer of administration and finance executive office to hear appeals, **7:4H.**
Qualification and disqualification.
Conviction of crime as rendering person ineligible for appointment, **41:96A.**
Physical fitness standards, **31:61A, 32:5.**
State police officers and inspectors, **22:6.**
Training for qualification.
Training schools or courses.
See within this heading, "Training schools or courses."
Racing events.
Bribery of persons connected with horse race, **271:39.**
Overtime pay for police officers, **41:111H.**
Raffles and bazaars, authority as to conduct, **271:7A.**
Railroads, **159:92-159:95.**
See RAILROADS.
Rape.
See RAPE.
Records.
Commissioner of police.
Pawnbrokers, inspection of record books, **140:81, 140:87.**
Public records, **6:172.**
Examination, inspection, and investigation. See within this heading, "Examination, inspection, and investigation."
Precious metals, record of purchase or sale, **266:142A.**
Reports. See within this heading, "Reports."
Refuse and rubbish, enforcement of provisions against unlawful disposal, **270:16, 270:16A.**

POLICE —Cont'd
Regional police districts, **41:99B-41:99K.**
See REGIONAL POLICE DISTRICTS.
Registrars.
Of motor vehicles, use of computer terminals under control, **90:30A.**
Of voters, presence at meeting, **51:53.**
Registration and licensing of vehicles.
Motor vehicles. See within this heading, "Motor vehicles."
Removal, **41:21A, 41:96, 41:96B, 41:97, 41:97A.**
Removal of motor vehicle from private property, notice, **266:120D.**
Reports.
Abused and neglected children under 16, **119:51A.**
Abuse of patients, **111:72G.**
Accident reports.
See TRAFFIC REGULATIONS AND RULES OF THE ROAD.
Alcohol and drug testing of commercial drivers, report of results or refusals, **90F:11.**
Arrests, monthly reports, **124:9.**
Dead bodies, report of person exposed to infectious disease through attending, assisting or transporting deceased person, **111:111C.**
District attorneys, reports of deaths, **38:6.**
Failure to report crime, penalty, **268:40.**
False crime report, filing, **269:13A.**
Firearms sales, **140:128A.**
Motor vehicle loss prevention central organization, reports filed, **175:113O.**
Requisition for service in other city or town, **41:99.**
Reservations.
See PARKS AND RESERVATIONS.
Reserve forces, **147:11 et seq.**
Boston authorized to maintain, **147:11.**
Cities, particularly, **147:11-147:13, 147:13B.**
Civil service, appointment subject, **31:60, 147:11, 147:13B, 147:13C.**

POLICE —Cont'd

Reserve forces —Cont'd

Compensation, **147:13, 147:13A.**

Duties, **147:13, 147:13A.**

Full-time service of reserve or permanent-intermittent officers, computation, **32:4.**

Number of members in cities, **147:12.**

Physical fitness standards, reserve officers, **31:61A.**

Powers, **147:13, 147:13A.**

Public contractor, employment, **149:34B, 152:1.**

Retirement systems.

See RETIREMENT SYSTEMS AND PENSIONS.

Training courses, requirement, **41:96B.**

Workers' compensation for reserve or special police employed by contractors in public contracts, **152:1.**

Residence.

Domicile and residence. See within this heading, "Domicile and residence."

Resignation.

Matron, appointment of successor on resignation, **147:19.**

Officer, payment of overtime compensation, **147:17E.**

Sheriffs.

See SHERIFFS AND DEPUTIES.

Retail installment sales and service law, enforcement, **255D:6.**

Retail installment sales of motor vehicles.

Motor vehicle retail installment sales. See within this heading, "Motor vehicle retail installment sales."

Retirement, **32:80-32:90.**

See RETIREMENT SYSTEMS AND PENSIONS.

Reward for information concerning assassination of police officer, **276:10.**

Right of way for patrol wagons, **89:7.**

Riots and mobs, **41:98, 269:1-269:6.**

Capitol police, **269:7, 269:8.**

Emergency police officers, **149:176.**

Sheriffs.

See SHERIFFS AND DEPUTIES.

POLICE —Cont'd

Roominghouses.

Hotels, motels, and roominghouses. See within this heading, "Hotels, motels, and roominghouses."

Runaway child, probable cause for arrest, **119:39H.**

Salaries and compensation.

Alternate schedule of compensation, **41:108G.**

Attendance at school, compensation while, **41:96B, 41:108M.**

Attendance in criminal cases, compensatory time off, **262:53C.**

Boston terminal company police, **159:95.**

Cadets, **147:21A.**

Capitol police. See within this heading, "Capitol police."

Career incentive pay program, **41:108L.**

Certain towns, departments established by selectmen, **41:97, 41:97A.**

Chief of police, **48:57G.**

Clothing allowances, **40:6B.**

Colleges or universities, compensation while attending certain courses of study, **41:108M.**

Commissioner of public safety, fixing, **41:101.**

Days off, **147:14 et seq.**

Express company police, **159:95.**

Fees, as exclusive, **262:50, 262:53A.**

Female officers, equality of compensation, **41:108K.**

Fingerprint identification, compensation for assignment to do, **41:108I.**

Holiday pay as regular, **32:1.**

Horse and dog race meetings, police officers assigned, **128A:8.**

Injury or death. See within this heading, "Injury or death."

Metropolitan district commission.

See METROPOLITAN DISTRICT COMMISSION.

Minimum annual compensation, **41:108E, 41:108G.**

Next of kin, payment of compensation due to deceased police officer, **41:111I.**

POLICE —Cont'd

Salaries and compensation —Cont'd

Off-duty work details, payment of police officers, **44:53C.**

Overtime, **8:4, 41:111H, 147:17A-147:17C, 147:17F, 147:17G.**

Payment, **147:17E.**

Deceased officer, amounts owed, **41:111L.**

Photographic work, compensation for assignment, **41:108I.**

Police Association, time spent in meetings, **41:100G½.**

Police matrons, **147:19.**

Prisoners, reimbursement for transportation expenses, **262:21.**

Public Safety Department, commissioner fixing compensation of police, **41:101.**

Railroad or street railway police, **159:95.**

Referendum as to compensation or hours of labor for police, distribution of literature, **54:65.**

Reserve police forces in cities and towns, **147:13, 147:13A.**

Sheriffs and deputies.

See SHERIFFS AND DEPUTIES.

Skin divers, **40:5.**

Special duty, leave without loss of pay for police injured, **41:111F.**

State college, police officer attending, **73:20.**

State police.

See STATE POLICE.

Steamboat police, **159:95.**

Training school, compensation while attending, **41:96B.**

Vacations and vacation pay. See within this heading, "Vacations and vacation pay."

Veterans' Retirement Act, allowances, **32:58C.**

Witness in criminal case, **262:53A, 262:53C.**

Schedules.

Lists or schedules. See within this heading, "Lists or schedules."

Schools.

Education. See within this heading, "Education."

POLICE —Cont'd
Search warrants, duties as to.
See SEARCHES AND
SEIZURES.
Secondhand vehicles.
Motor vehicles. See within this
heading, "Motor vehicles."
Selectmen and aldermen.
Appointment of police
department personnel,
**41:21, 41:23, 41:96, 41:97,
41:97A, 41:101.**
Rescission of power to appoint,
41:23.
Chiefs of police, appointment,
**41:21, 41:23, 41:97, 41:97A,
41:101.**
Regulation of police departments
of certain towns, **41:97,
41:97A.**
Removal of police officers, **41:97,
41:97A.**
Salaries and compensation
established by selectmen in
certain towns, **41:97,
41:97A.**
Service of officers in other places
on requisition, **41:99.**
Service of process.
See PROCESS AND SERVICE
OF PROCESS AND
PAPERS.
Sex offenders, notice or
information, **22C:37, 123A:9.**
Shellfish constables, **130:98.**
Sheriffs and deputies, **37:1 et seq.**
See SHERIFFS AND
DEPUTIES.
Ships and other watercraft.
Excise taxes, law enforcement
vessels exempt, **60B:3.**
Steamboat police, **159:92-159:95.**
See STEAMBOATS AND
STEAMBOAT
COMPANIES.
Shoes and clothing, **40:6B.**
Sick leave, **41:111F.**
Signal boxes and systems,
damaging or tampering,
268:32.
Silencers, use or ownership of
weapons, **269:10A.**
Skin divers, payment for services
rendered, **40:5.**
Smoking regulations.
See TOBACCO.
Snow traveling and recreation
vehicles, enforcement of law
and regulations, **90B:32.**

POLICE —Cont'd
Social security numbers.
Providing false name or Social
Security number to law
enforcement officer,
268:34A.
Solicitation.
Charities and charitable
contributions. See within
this heading, "Charities and
charitable contributions."
Special constables to enforce motor
vehicle law, appointment,
90:29.
Special duty.
Indemnification of regular officer
assigned, **41:100.**
Leave without loss of pay for
police injured, **41:111F.**
Other community assignments
to special duty, **41:99.**
Special officers.
Abused and neglected children,
special police societies for
prevention, **22C:56.**
Appointment, **37:4, 64C:26,
149:176.**
Badges, **159:92.**
Civil defense, appointment of
defense agency employees as
special police officers,
22C:64.
Licenses and permits, **22C:53,
22C:59 et seq.**
Lottery of state, **22C:67.**
Nonresidents, appointment,
149:176.
Parole board employees,
127:127.
State police.
See STATE POLICE.
Speed restrictions, right to violate,
89:7B.
Sporting weapons, police deemed
to have license required,
140:131G.
Stabbings, report, **112:12A.**
State colleges.
See COLLEGES AND
UNIVERSITIES.
State highways, jurisdiction over,
81:19.
State House.
Capitol police. See within this
heading, "Capitol police."
State parks and forests, powers
and duties when employed,
132A:7.
State police.
See STATE POLICE.
State superintendent of buildings.
Capitol police. See within this
heading, "Capitol police."

POLICE —Cont'd
State treasurer.
Appointment of special state
police officers, **10:5.**
Authority of treasurer as to
regional police districts,
41:99H.
Stations.
Cable television company's duty
to provide cable drop to
police stations, **166A:5.**
Defined, **147:21.**
Detention of children, **119:66,
119:67.**
Females, designation of stations
for detention, **147:18.**
Health department rules and
regulations regarding
station houses, **40:36B,
111:20-111:22.**
Matrons. See within this
heading, "Matrons."
Statutes and honor rolls for, town
appropriation, **40:5.**
Steamboat police, **159:92-159:95.**
See STEAMBOATS AND
STEAMBOAT COMPANIES.
Stolen property.
Inventory of property upon
arrest of person, **266:48.**
Transportation passes, arrest of
persons using stolen or
counterfeited, **161:113A.**
"Stop and frisk" authority, **41:98.**
Street railways, **159:92-159:95.**
Subpoena, fee for service of upon
witnesses, **262:53.**
Suicide prevention training,
40:36C.
Sundays.
Holidays. See within this
heading, "Holidays and
Sundays."
Superintendent of buildings.
Capitol police. See within this
heading, "Capitol police."
Superior courts.
See SUPERIOR COURTS.
Supervision services, **262:21.**
Surviving spouse.
Group insurance privileges,
32B:9E, 32B:9G.
Payment of compensation owed,
41:111I.
Pensions for widows of police
officers killed in
performance of duty, **32:100.**
Tax exemption, **59:5.**
Suspicious person, search, **41:98.**
Tabulation center, transportation,
54:105A.

POLICE —Cont'd
Taxation.
Cigarette tax. See within this
heading, "Cigarette tax."
Exemption for surviving spouse
or minor children of
deceased policeman, **59:5.**
Telephones.
Gambling, approval of
reinstallation of telephones
used, **271:47.**
Persons held by police telephone
calls, **276:33A.**
Utility poles, removal of
communication equipment,
166:22J.
Television, duty of cable television
company to provide cable drop
to police stations, **166A:5.**
Tenure of office, **41:96, 41:97A.**
Testimonial dinners for public
officers and employees,
268:9A.
Toll roads or bridges, reports of
accidents, **90:29.**
Towing of motor vehicles, **40:22D,
92:35A, 159B:6B.**
Town meeting.
Acceptance of statute as to
police departments in
certain towns, **41:97A.**
Accidental death insurance for
policemen, acceptance,
32B:11D.
Minimum annual compensation
for, vote, **41:108E, 41:108G.**
Overtime pay for police, vote,
41:111H.
Police association convention,
vote as to time off for police
attending, **147:17D.**
Police cadets, appointment,
147:21A.
Time off for police attending
police association convention
vote, **147:17D.**
Traffic regulations.
See TRAFFIC REGULATIONS
AND RULES OF THE
ROAD.
Training schools or courses, **40:5,
41:96B.**
Appropriations for attendance,
40:5.
Attendance, **41:96B.**
Capitol police, in-service and
supervisory training,
41:96B.
Cardiopulmonary resuscitation,
required training, **111:201.**
Compensation while attending,
41:96B.

POLICE —Cont'd
Training schools or courses
—Cont'd
Criminal justice training council,
6:116-6:119.
See CRIMINAL JUSTICE
TRAINING COUNCIL.
Criminal offender record
information center, **6:171.**
Expenses of policemen
attending, **40:5.**
Federal Bureau of Investigation,
40:5.
In-service and supervisory
training, **41:96B.**
Instructions, qualification, **6:118.**
Municipal training school, **6:118.**
Narcotic and harmful drug laws,
training programs, **12:11C.**
Police training council, **6:17,
41:96B, 125:9.**
Police Training Officers
Association, nomination of
members of criminal justice
training council, **6:116.**
Removal of officer for failure to
complete, **41:96B.**
Reserve officers, courses
required, **41:96B.**
Transportation of prisoners, police
supervision services, **262:21.**
Traveling expenses.
Attendance as witness, **262:53A,
262:53B.**
Service in other places on
requisition, **41:99.**
Sheriffs and deputies.
See SHERIFFS AND
DEPUTIES.
State police officers, **262:53B.**
Trespassing and trespassers.
Arrest, **266:120, 266:131.**
Public transportation facility
premises, power of arrest for
loitering or trespassing,
161:94A, 161:95.
Towns, prosecutions of
trespasses against, **41:36.**
Tuberculosis patients, assisting in
detention or transportation,
111:94A, 111:94B.
Uniform operation of commercial
motor vehicles.
See UNIFORM OPERATION OF
COMMERCIAL MOTOR
VEHICLES.
Uniforms.
Clothing allowance, **40:6B.**
Law enforcement division,
officers, **21:6C.**
Motorists, effect on powers with
respect, **90:25.**

POLICE —Cont'd
Uniforms —Cont'd
Municipal appropriations, **40:6B.**
Uninsured motor vehicles, notice,
90:34J, 90:34P.
University.
See COLLEGES AND
UNIVERSITIES.
University of Lowell.
See UNIVERSITY OF LOWELL.
University of Massachusetts,
22C:50.
Unlawful assemblies.
Riots and mobs. See within this
heading, "Riots and mobs."
Unmuzzled dogs, duties, **140:167.**
Urine tests.
See DRIVING WHILE UNDER
INFLUENCE OF
ALCOHOL OR DRUGS.
Utility poles, removal of police
communication installations,
166:22J.
Vacations and vacation pay,
**41:111A, 41:111D, 41:111E,
41:111G, 41:111G½, 41:111L.**
Additional day off when vacation
day falls on legal holiday,
147:17, 147:17A.
Vapor bath establishments,
inspection, **140:52.**
Vessels.
Ships and other watercraft. See
within this heading, "Ships
and other watercraft."
Veterans.
Memorial Day as holiday for
veterans, **149:44.**
State police.
See STATE POLICE.
Veterans' Retirement Act,
allowances, **32:58C.**
Wages.
Salaries and compensation. See
within this heading,
"Salaries and
compensation."
Warrants.
Infected articles of goods,
executing warrant for
removal, **111:101.**
Motor vehicle violations, arrest
without warrant, **90C:3.**
Penalty for delay in service of
warrant, **268:22.**
Search warrants, duties as to,
276:2.
See SEARCHES AND
SEIZURES.
Special state police officer for
service of warrants,
127:127.

POLICE —Cont'd

Waterworks and water supply.
Arrest of person found in act of corrupting or bathing in water supply, **111:171.**
Indemnification by water districts, **41:100, 41:111F.**
Territorial jurisdiction of police employed by water boards or districts, **111:173A.**

Weapons.
Firearms and other weapons. See within this heading, "Firearms and other weapons."

Wearing apparel.
Uniforms. See within this heading, "Uniforms."

Weights.
See WEIGHTS AND MEASURES.

Widow.
Surviving spouse. See within this heading, "Surviving spouse."

Witnesses.
See WITNESSES.

Workers' compensation.
See WORKERS' COMPENSATION.

Written petition for order of commitment, mental health, **123:35.**

Youth services department, furnishing information, **119:69A.**

POLICE ASSOCIATION.

Chiefs of police, **111C:7.**
Criminal Justice Training Council, nomination of members, **6:116.**
Meetings, compensation for time spent, **41:100G½.**
Time off for officers to attend convention, **147:17, 147:17D.**

POLICE COURTS.
See DISTRICT COURTS.

POLICE DOGS.
See POLICE.

POLICE MEMORIAL DAY.
Annual observance, **6:15JJJ.**

POLICEMEN'S RETIREMENT AND PENSION ACT, 32:83 et seq.

POLICE SURGEONS, 38:1-38:19.
See MEDICAL EXAMINERS AND INQUESTS.

POLICE TRAINING COUNCIL.
Change of name, **6:17, 41:96B.**

POLICE TRAINING COUNCIL —Cont'd

Employment dislocations and assistance in reemployment of dislocated workers, **6:17.**
Establishment of municipal police training council and schools, **125:9.**
Governor, supervision, **6:17.**
Municipal police training council, change of name, **6:17, 41:96B.**

POLICE TRAINING OFFICERS ASSOCIATION, INC.

Criminal Justice Training Council, nominations of members, **6:116.**

POLICY GAME.
See LOTTERIES.

POLICYHOLDERS.
See INSURANCE.

POLIOMYELITIS.

Admission to Lakeview sanatorium of persons crippled, **111:65A.**
School children, immunization, **76:15.**
Other community, assignment to special duty, **41:99.**

POLISH-AMERICAN HERITAGE MONTH.

October designated as, **6:15WWW.**

POLISH-AMERICAN VETERANS.

Benefits, **115A:4.**
Insignia, unlawful use, **266:70.**
Municipal appropriations for proper observances of certain patriotic holidays, **40:5.**
Patriotic holiday observances, municipal appropriations, **40:5.**
Proceedings, printing and distribution, **5:9.**
State house, rooms, **8:17.**
Uniform, unlawful use, **264:10A.**

POLISH ARMY VETERANS.

Admissions to soldiers' homes, **115A:4.**

POLISH CONSTITUTION DAY.
Observance, **6:12R.**

POLISHING TEETH.

Dental hygienists as qualified to perform, **112:51.**

POLITICAL ADVERTISING.

Definition, **164:33A.**
Gas or electric company, recovery from ratepayer of direct or indirect expenditure for promotional or political advertising, **164:33A.**

POLITICAL COMMITTEES, 52:1-52:10.

Advertising, use of party name, **56:40.**
Alteration.
Change. See within this heading, "Change."
Arrangement of candidates' names on ballots, **53:34.**
Associate members, appointment, **52:4.**
Ballots.
Arrangement of candidates' names, **53:34.**
Marking of, primary ballots for candidates for committees, **53:35.**
Board of election commissioners, vacancies on board, **51:16A.**
Campaign financing, **55:1 et seq.**
See CAMPAIGN EXPENDITURES AND CONTRIBUTIONS.
Canvass of returns and declaration of results at presidential primaries, **53:70F.**
Caucuses.
See CAUCUSES.
Challenger of voters, appointment, **54:85A.**
Change.
Enrollment change or cancellation, **53:38.**
Residence, effect, **52:2, 52:6.**
City, ward, and town committees, **52:2-52:10.**
Composition of city committees, **52:3.**
Contributions, limitation, **55:6, 55:7.**
Conventions.
See POLITICAL CONVENTIONS.
Death, withdrawal, or ineligibility of candidate, filling vacancy in case, **53:70G.**
Declaration of result of election at presidential primaries, **53:70F.**
Definitions, **50:1.**
Delegates.
Caucuses or primaries, **53:2.**
City, ward, and town committees.
Final date to notify state committee of number of delegates, **52:9.**
Nomination of delegates, **53:70D.**
Election of delegates to 1972 state convention, **52:4.**
Final date to notify state committee of number, **52:9.**

POLITICAL COMMITTEES
—Cont'd
Delegates —Cont'd
Method of election, **53:2, 53:70B.**
Misconduct as to opening ballot, **56:12.**
Nomination of delegates. See within this heading, "Nomination of delegates."
Nonpartisan election, **53:2, 53:117-53:120.**
Number, **53:70B.**
Presidential primaries.
See PRESIDENTIAL PRIMARIES.
Rules for selecting delegates to national convention, **53:70B.**
State committees. See within this heading, "State committees."
Depository candidates, purchase of goods and services from political committee of their party, **55:1.**
Disposition of funds upon redivision of city into wards, **52:7.**
Disqualification of committeemen for accepting more than one nomination, **53:45.**
Election officers, lists submitted for appointment.
Cities, **54:11B.**
Towns divided into voting precincts, **54:12.**
Ward committees, **54:11B.**
Existing committees, organization, **52:8.**
Failure to elect or organize, procedure, **52:4.**
Filing of lists of officers and members, **52:1, 52:5.**
Indorsement for nomination of members by state committee, **53:17A, 53:70D.**
Intention to participate in city and town primaries, notice, **53:57.**
Lists of officers and members.
Election officers. See within this heading, "Election officers, lists submitted for appointment."
Filing, **52:5.**
Marking of primary ballots of candidates, **53:35.**
Members at large, election, **52:1.**
Modification.
Change. See within this heading, "Change."
Naturalization fees, penalty for payment, **56:45.**

POLITICAL COMMITTEES
—Cont'd
Nomination of delegates, **53:45, 53:70B, 53:70D, 53:70E.**
Disqualification of committeemen by accepting more than one nomination, **53:45.**
Nomination papers.
Candidates for election to state, ward, and town committees, **53:46, 53:70D.**
Delegates to national conventions, **53:70D.**
Official ballots, filing of nomination papers in caucuses using, **53:99.**
State committees. See within this heading, "State committees."
Nonelected political committees, campaign contributions, **55:7.**
Non-partisan selection of members, **53:2, 53:117-53:120.**
Notice.
Intent to participate in municipal primaries, **53:57.**
Number of members of municipal, etc., committees, time for giving notice, **52:9.**
Precincts, holding caucuses, **53:73.**
Recount of ballots for statewide office, notice to state political committees, **54:135.**
Number of delegates to national convention, **53:70B.**
Number of members, **52:9.**
Officers, selection, **52:4.**
Organization.
City, ward, and town committees, **52:4.**
Existing committees, **52:8.**
State committees, **52:1.**
Precincts, notice of holding caucuses, **53:73.**
Presidential primary.
Declaration of results of election, **53:70F.**
Election of members, **52:1, 52:2, 53:70B.**
System of state committee for selection of delegates and alternate delegates to national conventions, **53:1, 53:70B.**
Vacancies, **53:70G.**
Primary elections.
See PRIMARY ELECTIONS.
Redistricting of wards and voting precincts of members of political committees, **52:2.**

POLITICAL COMMITTEES
—Cont'd
Redivision of city into wards, disposition of funds, **52:7.**
Residence requirement for election to state committee, **52:1.**
Rules and regulations, making, **52:10.**
Secretary of state.
Local committees, filing list, **52:5.**
Number of members to be elected to city or town committees, notice, **52:9.**
Number of votes in elections to state committees, report, **54:133.**
State committees, filing list, **52:1.**
State committees, **52:1.**
Advertising, consent to use of party name, **56:40.**
Canvass of returns and declaration of results at presidential primaries, **53:70F.**
Challenger of voters, appointment, **54:85A.**
Change or cancellation of enrollment, **53:38.**
Death, withdrawal, or ineligibility of candidate, filling vacancy in case, **53:70G.**
Delegates.
Final date for city, ward, and town committees to notify state committee of number of delegates, **52:9.**
Nominated by state committee, appearance of names on primary ballots, **53:70E.**
Election at presidential primaries and state conventions, **52:1, 53:70B.**
Filing list of officers and members with secretary of state, **52:1.**
Indorsement for nomination of members, **53:17A, 53:70D.**
Members at large, election, **52:1.**
National convention rules for selecting delegates, **53:70B.**
Nomination of members by convention, **53:17A.**
Nomination papers of candidate.
Candidates for election to state, ward, and town committees, **53:46.**
Reelection, **53:70D.**

POLITICAL COMMITTEES
—Cont'd
State committees —Cont'd
Number of delegates to
conventions, **53:70B.**
Number of votes in elections to,
state secretary's report,
54:133.
Organization, **52:1.**
Presidential primaries, election,
52:1, 53:70B.
Primary ballots of candidates
for, arrangement and form,
53:34.
Redistricting of wards and
voting precincts of members
of political committees, **52:2.**
Residence requirement for
election, **52:1.**
Rules and regulations for calling
conventions, **52:10.**
Secretary of state, filing list of
members and officers, **52:1.**
Successful candidates in state
primaries, city and town
clerks to certify names,
53:52.
Terms of office, **52:1.**
Tie vote among candidates for,
filling vacancy caused,
53:53, 53:70G.
Vacancies, filling, **52:1, 53:70G.**
Among candidates for
nomination, nominations
in case, **53:49.**
Voting lists, obtaining free copy,
51:57.
Ward, city and town committees,
organization, **52:4.**
Street lists, availability of listings
to city and town committee
chairman, **51:7.**
Successful candidate in state
primaries, city and town
clerks to certify names, **53:52.**
Termination of membership, **52:2.**
Term of office, **52:1, 52:2.**
Tie vote, filling vacancy caused by.
City or town primary, **53:62.**
State committee, tie vote, **53:53,
53:70G.**
State primary, **53:53.**
Town committees, **52:3-52:10.**
Treasurer.
See CAMPAIGN
EXPENDITURES AND
CONTRIBUTIONS.
Unenrolled candidates,
designation, **53:6, 53:8, 53:38,
53:48, 53:72, 54:41, 54:52.**
Vacancy, filling, **52:6, 53:14.**
Board of election commissioners,
vacancies, **51:16A.**

POLITICAL COMMITTEES
—Cont'd
Vacancy, filling —Cont'd
Presidential primaries, **53:70G.**
State committees. See within
this heading, "State
committees."
Tie vote, filling vacancy caused
by. See within this heading,
"Tie vote, filling vacancy
caused by."
Voting lists, obtaining copy, **51:55.**
Primaries, certified copies of
lists, **53:37.**
State committee, **51:57.**
Street lists, **51:6.**
Ward committees, number of
members, **52:9.**

POLITICAL CONTRIBUTIONS,
55:1 et seq.
**See CAMPAIGN
EXPENDITURES AND
CONTRIBUTIONS.**

POLITICAL CONVENTIONS.
Calling and holding for nomination
of candidates, **53:4.**
Certificates of nomination.
Contents, **53:8.**
Vacancies, statements as to
filling of certain, **53:8.**
Defined, **50:1.**
Delegates.
See POLITICAL COMMITTEES.
Municipal appropriations for
entertainment, **40:5.**
Nomination of candidates.
Calling and holding, **53:4.**
Certificates of nomination by,
53:8.
Parties eligible to make
nominations, **53:1.**
Time for holding, **53:4.**
Nomination papers, party
delegates for presidential
convention, **53:70D.**
Nonpolitical parties, **53:2.**
Pre-primary conventions,
designations of districts on
nomination papers, **53:61.**
Presidential primaries.
See PRESIDENTIAL
PRIMARIES.
Primary ballots, arrangement of
candidates' names, **53:34.**
Time.
Nomination of candidates for
presidential conventions,
time for holding, **53:4.**
Number of delegates to national
presidential conventions,
time for giving notice,
53:70B.

POLITICAL CONVENTIONS
—Cont'd
Vacancies.
Nominations, filling of vacancy,
53:14.
Statements as to filling of
certain vacancies, **53:8.**

**POLITICAL INFLUENCE OR
OPINIONS.**
City or town employees, **43:92,
43:92A.**
Civil service, **7:4I, 31:75.**
Horse or dog racing meetings,
influencing employment,
271:40.
Public service companies,
employment, **271:40, 271:41.**
School teachers, inquiries of
candidates for position
forbidden, **71:39.**

POLITICAL PARTIES.
Absent registration, representation
with respect, **51:22A.**
Advertising, **56:39.**
Committees, **56:40.**
Educational television executive
committee sponsoring TV
programs etc., **71:13I.**
Outdoor advertising board
members, **16:14.**
Use of party name, **56:40.**
Aeronautics commission,
membership, **6:57.**
Alcoholic beverages commission
membership, limitations, **6:43.**
Alcoholic liquor licensing boards,
appointment, **138:4.**
Alteration.
Change of enrollment. See
within this heading,
"Change of enrollment."
Appointment to board,
commission, or other body,
party enrollment, **4:12.**
Armories used for meetings or
rallies, **33:122.**
Ballots.
Committees, **53:34, 53:35.**
Election officers, ballot clerks,
54:17.
Municipal parties, party
enrollment as affecting right
to ballot, **53:38.**
Party enrollment as prerequisite
to candidate's name
appearing on ballot for
primary election, **53:38,
53:48, 53:61.**
State ballot law commission
membership as affected by
membership in political
party, **55B:1, 55B:2.**

POLITICAL PARTIES —Cont'd

Biennial count of voters, **53:38A.**

Bipartisan boards, effective date of establishment, cancellation or change of enrollment in cases affecting membership, **4:12.**

Boards of election commissioners, two members always to represent each one of the two leading political parties, **51:16A.**

Campaign financing, **55:1 et seq.**
See CAMPAIGN EXPENDITURES AND CONTRIBUTIONS.

Campaign literature to show party designation, **56:44.**

Candidates.
Ballots, placement of candidates for political committees, **53:70E.**
Choice of political designation where nominated by more than one party, **54:41.**
Committee candidates, nomination papers, **53:70D.**
Independent candidate, status as affected by membership in political party, **53:6, 53:48.**
Nomination of candidates. See within this heading, "Nomination of candidates."
Nomination papers. See within this heading, "Nomination papers."
Party designation, list of candidates not bearing, **56:44.**
Party enrollment as prerequisite to candidate's name appearing on ballot for primary election, **53:38, 53:48, 53:61.**
Roll call vote for president, **53:70I.**
State primaries, requirements as to enrollment of candidates, **53:48.**
Vacancies, filling, **53:70G.**

Caucuses, **53:71-53:121.**
See CAUCUSES.

Certificates and certification.
Ballots, certificate as to party enrollment, **53:48.**
Erroneous enrollment, certificate of error, **53:38.**
Party designation on certificates of nomination, **53:8.**
Registrars of voters, certificates of enrollment, **53:37, 53:38, 53:48.**

POLITICAL PARTIES —Cont'd

Challenge of votes.
Appointment of challengers by party permitted, **54:85A.**
Credentials and rights of party challengers, **54:85A.**
Party caucuses, challenge, **53:76, 53:109.**

Change of enrollment, **53:37, 53:38, 53:48.**
Bipartisan boards, cancellation or change of enrollment in cases affecting membership, **4:12.**
Effect, **53:38, 53:48.**
Primary elections.
See PRIMARY ELECTIONS.
Terminating membership on ward or town committee, **52:2.**

Cities.
Towns and cities. See within this heading, "Towns and cities."

Civil service.
Commission, limitation on membership, **7:4I.**
Rights of civil servants, **31:75.**

Committees of political parties, **52:1-52:10.**
See POLITICAL COMMITTEES.

Communist party.
See COMMUNISM AND COMMUNIST PARTY.

Contributions, **55:1 et seq.**
See CAMPAIGN EXPENDITURES AND CONTRIBUTIONS.

Conventions.
See POLITICAL CONVENTIONS.

Corrupt practices.
See CORRUPT PRACTICES.

Defined under election law, **50:1.**

Delegates.
See POLITICAL COMMITTEES.

Depository candidates, purchase of goods and services from political committee of their party, **55:1.**

Designation.
Campaign literature to show party designation, **56:44.**
Certificates of nomination and nomination papers, designation, **53:8.**
Choice of political designation where nominated by more than one party, **54:41.**
Posters and stickers, political designation, forbidden, **54:65.**

POLITICAL PARTIES —Cont'd

Educational television executive committee sponsoring TV programs etc., **71:13I.**

Effective date of enrollment in party in cases affecting membership of bipartisan boards or bodies, **4:12.**

Election commissioners, representation on board, **51:16A.**

Election officers.
Ballot clerks, **54:17.**
Committees.
See POLITICAL COMMITTEES.
Depository candidates, purchase of goods and services from political committee of their party, **55:1.**
Party representation, **54:13, 54:67.**
Procedure for appointment, **54:11B.**
Vacancies, filling, **54:14.**

Eligibility to make nominations, **53:1.**

Employment security division, director, appointees and employees, **23:9K.**

Enrollment.
Age, **51:42.**
Appointment to board, commission, or other body, party enrollment, **4:12.**
Ballots, certificate as to party enrollment, **53:48.**
Change of enrollment. See within this heading, "Change of enrollment."
Effective date of enrollment in cases affecting membership of bipartisan boards or bodies, **4:12.**
Erroneous enrollment, certificate of error, **53:38.**
Forms, change in enrollment, **53:38.**
General court.
See GENERAL COURT.
List of voters, preparation and furnishing, **53:37.**
Party enrollment as prerequisite to candidate's name appearing on ballot for primary election, **53:38, 53:48, 53:61.**
Primary elections.
See PRIMARY ELECTIONS.
Registrars of voters. See within this heading, "Registrars of voters."

POLITICAL PARTIES —Cont'd

Ethics Commission, members, **268B:2.**

Finance, **55:1 et seq.**
See CAMPAIGN EXPENDITURES AND CONTRIBUTIONS.

Floor leaders of major parties, additional compensation, **3:9.**

General court.
See GENERAL COURT.

Horse or dog racing commission, **6:48, 271:40.**

House majority second assistant floor leader, compensation, **3:9.**

Incorporation, **55:5.**

Independent candidates' status as affected by membership, **53:6, 53:48.**

Lists and listing.
Candidates not bearing party designation, distribution of lists, **56:44.**
Street lists, availability of listings to city and town committee chairman, **51:7.**
Voters, preparation and furnishing list, **53:37.**

Lottery commission members, political affiliation, **10:23.**

Mobile homes commission, affiliation of members, **6:108.**

Municipal parties.
Defined under election law, **50:1.**
Party enrollment as affecting right to ballot, **53:38.**
Town caucus as affecting caucuses, **53:121.**

Nomination of candidates, **53:1, 53:2.**
Caucuses, **53:2, 53:71.**
Certificates of nomination, party designation, **53:8.**
Choice of political designation where nominated by more than one party, **54:41.**
Conventions.
See POLITICAL CONVENTIONS.
Vacancies in nomination, procedure for filling, **53:14.**

Nomination papers.
Change of party enrollment by candidate, effect, **53:38, 53:48.**
Committees.
See POLITICAL COMMITTEES.

Party designation, **53:8.**

Presidential convention, **53:70D.**

POLITICAL PARTIES —Cont'd

Nonpartisan caucuses, **53:117-53:121.**
See CAUCUSES.

Nonpartisan city elections, **43:49.**

Notice of intention as to participation in city and town primaries, **53:57.**

Officers of elections.
Election officers. See within this heading, "Election officers."

Outdoor advertising board members, **16:14.**

Posters and stickers, political designations, forbidden, **54:65.**

Presidential conventions, party delegates, **53:70D.**

Primaries, **53:1, 53:37, 53:37A, 53:38.**
See PRIMARY ELECTIONS.

Public service companies, employment, **271:40, 271:41.**

Public utilities commission, political affiliations of members, **25:2.**

Public works commission, membership, **16:1.**

Racing commission, **6:48, 271:40.**

Registrars of voters, **51:52, 53:37, 53:38, 53:42, 53:48.**
Absent registration, representation with respect, **51:22A.**
Affiliation, **51:18, 51:19.**
Assistant registrars in cities and towns, **51:22.**
Change of enrollment, **53:38, 53:48.**
Enrollment of voters in political parties, **53:38.**
Removal of member to preserve equal political representation, **51:19.**
Temporary registrars filling vacancies, **51:20.**
Annual register, party enrollment of voter entered, **53:37.**
Certificate of enrollment, **53:38, 53:48.**
Count of voters of each political party, board of registrars, **53:38A.**
Enrollment of voters in political parties, **53:38.**
Annual register, **53:37, 53:38.**
Certificate of enrollment, **53:37, 53:38, 53:48.**
Establishing or changing of enrollment in political parties, **53:38.**

POLITICAL PARTIES —Cont'd

Revenue Department, policy against political influence and partiality, **14:1.**

Roll call vote for president, voting by delegates subject to candidates' approval, **53:70I.**

Separate voting machines for candidates of each political party, **54:33.**

State ballot law commission membership as affected by membership, **55B:1, 55B:2.**

State committees.
See POLITICAL COMMITTEES.

State lottery commission, political affiliation of members, **10:23.**

Street lists, availability of listings to city and town committee chairman, **51:7.**

Teachers, activities, **71:39.**

Television programs in aid of political parties, sponsorship by educational television executive committee, **71:13I.**

Tie vote.
Committees.
See POLITICAL COMMITTEES.
Selection of state committee members in event, **53:53, 53:70G.**

Time for filing, **53:48.**

Towns and cities.
Assistant registrars in cities and towns, affiliation, **51:22.**
Cancellation or change of enrollment as terminating membership on ward or town committee, **52:2.**
Caucus by political party, town caucus, **53:121.**
Committees in cities, wards, and towns, **52:2-52:10.**
See POLITICAL COMMITTEES.
Definition under election law, **50:1.**
Enrollment as affecting right to ballot, **53:38.**
Municipal parties. See within this heading, "Municipal parties."
Officers of cities and towns, political activity, **43:92, 43:92A.**
Participation in city and town primaries, notice of intention, **53:57.**
Street lists, **51:7.**

Two leading political parties.
Defined, **50:1.**

POLITICAL PARTIES —Cont'd

Two leading political parties
—Cont'd

Election commissioners,
representation on board,
51:16A.

Election officers, filling vacancies
in number, **54:14.**

Legislative research council
membership divided
between, **3:56.**

Unauthorized use of name in
advertisements, etc., **56:40.**

Vacancies.

Candidacies of various
committees, filling, **53:70G.**

Conventions.

See POLITICAL
CONVENTIONS.

Election officers, filling vacancies
in number, **54:14.**

Temporary registrars filling
vacancies, **51:20.**

POLITICAL SUBDIVISIONS.

Advisory commission on local
government, **3:62.**

Air pollution control, **111:142E.**

Carriers, exemption from charges,
159B:19A.

Cigarettes sold below cost, **64C:15.**

Cities and towns.

See CITIES AND TOWNS.

Civil defense volunteers,
indemnification, **40:5.**

Commercial Code, organization
within, **106:1-201.**

Correspondence school, operation,
75C:1.

Counties.

See COUNTIES.

False claims against
Commonwealth or political
subdivisions, **12:5A to 12:5O.**

See FALSE CLAIMS AGAINST
COMMONWEALTH.

Fire insurance companies,
members, **175:76.**

Gas or electricity supplied after
expiration of contract,
164:125A.

Health, welfare and retirement
funds law, applicability,
151D:7.

Joint enterprises, **40:4A.**

Limitation of action based on right
of entry for condition broken,
260:31A.

Mechanics' liens against, **254:6,
254:31.**

Purchasing agent, liability, **7:22B.**

POLITICAL SUBDIVISIONS
—Cont'd

Radio and television technicians
registration law, applicability,
112:87QQQ.

Regional planning, exchange of
information, **40B:19.**

Retirement systems.

See RETIREMENT SYSTEMS
AND PENSIONS.

POLKA.

Official polka of Commonwealth,
2:44.

**POLLS AND POLLING
PLACES.**

See ELECTIONS.

POLL TAKER.

Employment security law,
exclusion, **151A:6.**

POLL TAX.

Constitution of Massachusetts,
veterans not disqualified to
vote by reason of nonpayment
of poll tax, **MA Const Amend
Art 28.**

Constitution of the United States,
**US Const Art 1 Cl 1; 4th
Amend, 24th Amend.**

POLLUTION.

Air pollution, **111:142A-111:142C.**

See AIR POLLUTION.

Amherst economic development
and industrial corporation
financing, **Spec L 23:5.**

County finance, water pollution,
21:37, 21H:3.

Liability insurance.

See POLLUTION LIABILITY
REINSURANCE
CORPORATION.

Municipal finance, pollution
abatement, **21H:3, 44:28C.**

Water pollution, **21:26 et seq.**

See WATER POLLUTION.

**POLLUTION LIABILITY
REINSURANCE
CORPORATION,
175G:1-175G:7.**

Environmental protection
department.

Definitions, **175G:1.**

Ex-officio non-voting member of
board, commissioner,
175G:2.

Establishment, **175G:2.**

POLO.

Bribery, **271:39A.**

POLYGAMY.

Children of polygamous marriage.

Care and custody, **207:18.**

Legitimacy, **207:17.**

Crime, **272:15.**

Indictment, **277:79.**

Voidness of polygamous marriage,
207:4.

Death or divorce removing
impediment, **207:6.**

POLYMER SCIENCE CENTER.

Centers of Excellence,
establishment, **40J:12.**

PONDS.

Actions for purpose of protecting
natural resources and
environment, **214:7A.**

Algae, weeds and aquatic
nuisances, control, **40:5,
111:5F.**

Artificial ponds of coastal waters,
plans, **130:28.**

Cemetery at or near, **114:35.**

Draining of, regulated, **131:40,
131:48.**

Enclosure, regulation, **131:47.**

Environmental protection
department.

See ENVIRONMENTAL
PROTECTION
DEPARTMENT.

Fires and fire prevention, surface
impoundment ponds not
defined as underground
storage tanks for purposes,
148:38B.

Fish.

Drainage affecting, regulation,
131:48.

Great ponds, regulation, **131:45.**

Marine fish and fisheries. See
within this heading,
"Marine fish and fisheries."

Measuring, **131:46.**

Stocking of ponds, **131:5.**

Great Ponds.

See LAKES.

Ice ponds.

See ICE PONDS.

Lakes.

See LAKES.

Marine fish and fisheries.

Herring fisheries, **130:93.**

Occupancy for propagation and
distribution of fish
frequenting coastal waters,
130:17.

Riparian owners, **130:28.**

Measuring, **131:46.**

Metropolitan parks district,
regulation of spaces along or
near, **92:33.**

PONDS —Cont'd
Mills.
See MILLS AND MILLPONDS.
Notice and knowledge.
Great ponds, notice of fish and
game director's occupation,
131:4.
Intention to drain, notice,
131:40, 131:48.
Other state, situated partly in,
fishing, **131:49.**
Pollution abatement equipment or
devices exempt from taxation,
59:5.
Public works.
Artificial ponds of coastal
waters, plans, **130:28.**
Great ponds.
See LAKES.
Measuring of ponds, **131:46.**
Riparian owners of ponds formed
from coastal waters, exclusive
fishery, **130:28.**
Roads, etc., **252:15-252:23.**
Watershed management division,
responsibilities, **92:106.**

PONDVILLE HOSPITAL,
111:69E-111:69I.
Admissions, **111:69E.**
Needy person, notice of
admission, **111:69F,**
111:69G.
Charges for support, **111:69H,**
111:69I.
Commissioner of public health,
supervision and control,
111:69E.
Discharges, **111:69E.**
Eligibility for admission as needy
person, determination,
111:69G.
Evidence in proceedings to collect
charges, **111:69I.**
Out-patient department, **111:69E.**

PONIES.
Prizes for and exhibits, **128:2.**

PONKAPOAG RECREATIONAL
FUND, 29:2U.

POOLED INCOME FUND.
Taxation of income, **62:11A,**
62:11B.

POOLED INSURANCE.
See INSURANCE.

POOLING OF DEBTS.
Practice of law, services for debtor
in connection with debt
pooling plan, **221:46C.**

POOLING OF RISKS.
Automobile insurance.
See AUTOMOBILE
INSURANCE.

POOLING OF RISKS —Cont'd
Fire insurance.
See FIRE INSURANCE.
Foreign insurance companies.
See FOREIGN INSURANCE
COMPANIES.
Workers' compensation.
See WORKERS'
COMPENSATION.

POOL ROOMS.
See BILLIARD AND
POOLROOMS.

POOLS.
Swimming pools, **140:206.**

POOL SELLING, 137:1.
See GAMING AND GAMES OF
CHANCE.

POOR ACT, 117A:1 et seq.

POOR PERSONS, 18:1 et seq.,
18B:1 et seq.
Abatement of taxes against, **59:71.**
Affidavit of poverty.
See COSTS OF ACTION.
Aged.
See AGED AND DISABLED,
ASSISTANCE.
Alcoholic liquors, prohibition as to
sales or deliveries, **138:69.**
Appeals, **18:16, 261:27B-261:27D.**
Payment of rent after waiver of
appeal bond, **239:5.**
Appropriations by cities and
towns, **40:5.**
Armed forces.
Military personnel. See within
this heading, "Military
personnel."
Assignment of counsel.
See ASSIGNMENT OF
COUNSEL.
Assignments.
See ASSIGNMENTS.
Attorneys' fees.
See ATTORNEYS' FEES.
Banks.
See BANKS AND BANKING.
Begging.
See BEGGING.
Bonds and undertakings, **239:5,**
261:27A.
Breakfast programs for needy
school children, **15:1G.**
Burial of poor person, **118:2,**
119:23.
Children, payment by social
services department for
burial, **119:23.**
Expenses of burial, paying,
119:23.

POOR PERSONS —Cont'd
Burial of poor person —Cont'd
Giving body to medical school,
113:1-113:5.
Town welfare board, burial of
unclaimed or unidentified
bodies, **38:15.**
Veterans, burial expenses, **115:7,**
115:8.
Children.
See CHILDREN AND MINORS.
Civil service appointments for
disadvantaged persons
completing work-training
program, **31:47A.**
Commonwealth, support by, **18:1**
et seq., 18B:1 et seq.
See WELFARE AND SOCIAL
SERVICES.
Correctional institutions.
See CORRECTIONAL
INSTITUTIONS.
Costs of action.
See COSTS OF ACTION.
Criminal procedure.
See CRIMINAL PROCEDURE.
Death.
Burial. See within this heading,
"Burial of poor person."
Informal administration of
estates of public support
recipients, **195:16.**
Debtors, imprisonment of, **127:22,**
127:145, 127:146.
Decrees.
Judgments, orders, and decrees.
See within this heading,
"Judgments, orders, and
decrees."
Definition of court costs, law
governing, **261:27A.**
Delinquent children.
Juvenile courts and delinquent
children. See within this
heading, "Juvenile courts
and delinquent children."
Department of transitional
assistance, **18:1 et seq., 18B:1**
et seq.
Department renamed
department of transitional
assistance, **18:1.**
Welfare and social services.
See WELFARE AND SOCIAL
SERVICES.
Disabled persons.
See AGED AND DISABLED,
ASSISTANCE.
District courts.
See DISTRICT COURTS.
Drugs and medicines to be
furnished free, **123:31.**

POOR PERSONS —Cont'd

Economic assistance coordinating council, **23A:3A, 23A:3D.**

Emergency fuel assistance program for certain low income household, **118:2.**

Estate of deceased recipient of public support, **195:16.**

Estoppel.

Waiver and estoppel. See within this heading, "Waiver and estoppel."

Eviction, bond or security required of indigent tenant, **239:5.**

Eyeglasses for school children of, town appropriation, **40:5.**

Family duty to support, **122:14, 122:16.**

See FAMILY AND RELATIVES.

Findings as to indigency, written report by court, **261:27B, 261:27C.**

Food services.

See FOOD SERVICES AND FREE LUNCH PROGRAMS.

Forma pauperis, **261:27A-261:27G.**

See COSTS OF ACTION.

Fraudulent motor vehicle insurance claims, restitution, **266:27A, 266:111B.**

Fuel assistance program for certain low income households, emergency, **118:2.**

Funerals.

Burial of poor person. See within this heading, "Burial of poor person."

Handicapped persons, aid to.

See AGED AND DISABLED, ASSISTANCE.

Health.

See HEALTH AND HEALTH DEPARTMENTS.

Hearing aids for school children of, municipal appropriations, **40:5.**

Hospitals.

See HOSPITALS AND HEALTH CARE FACILITIES.

Housing.

See HOUSING AND URBAN RENEWAL.

Housing and community development department.

See HOUSING AND COMMUNITY DEVELOPMENT DEPARTMENT.

POOR PERSONS —Cont'd

Housing court.

Appeals from denial of relief from court costs by in matters arising in housing court, **261:27D.**

Filing affidavit of and request for waiver of cost of action, **261:27B.**

Payment of fees, **185C:19.**

Income tax exemption for individuals of modest means, **62:5.**

Infirmaries, erection and maintenance for treatment of poor persons, **47:1.**

Insane persons.

Mentally ill and retarded persons. See within this heading, "Mentally ill and retarded persons."

Judgments, orders, and decrees.

Amount of recovery by as affecting obligation to repay waived court costs, **261:27E.**

Cost of obtaining order, **261:27A.**

Vacation of judgment, filing affidavit of indigency and request for waiver of costs in petition to, **261:27B.**

Juvenile courts and delinquent children.

Appeals from denial of relief from court costs in matters arising in juvenile court, **261:27D.**

Filing affidavit of and request for waiver of cost of action, **261:27B.**

Kindred, duty to support, **122:14, 122:16.**

See FAMILY AND RELATIVES.

Land court.

Appeals from denial of relief from court costs by in matters arising in land court, **261:27D.**

Filing affidavit of and request for waiver of cost of action, **261:27B.**

Legal aid.

See ATTORNEYS AT LAW.

Marginally indigent defendants.

Assignment of counsel.

See ASSIGNMENT OF COUNSEL.

Attorneys' fees.

See ATTORNEYS' FEES.

Medical care.

See MEDICAL CARE AND ASSISTANCE.

POOR PERSONS —Cont'd

Medical malpractice claims, bond requirements as to poor persons bringing, **231:60B.**

Mentally ill and retarded persons, **221:34E.**

Appointment of counsel for indigent patient, **123:17.**

Drugs and medicines furnished, **123:31.**

Military personnel.

Municipal appropriations for relief, **40:5.**

Dependents in need, **115:1.**

Veterans. See within this heading, "Veterans."

Minors.

See CHILDREN AND MINORS.

Names, disclosure of, forbidden, **18:11, 40:51, 66:17A, 271:43.**

Notice and knowledge.

Affidavit of indigency, serving on opposing parties, **261:27B.**

Costs of actions, limits of indigency for waiver, **261:27C.**

State sanatorium or hospital, notice of admission of needy person, **111:69F, 111:69G.**

Older persons.

Assistance.

See AGED AND DISABLED, ASSISTANCE.

Low income, elderly persons of, defined, **20:13.**

Orders.

Judgments, orders, and decrees. See within this heading, "Judgments, orders, and decrees."

Pensioned or retired public employee becoming public charge, effect, **32:92.**

Pregnant women, assistance, **118:2.**

Prematurely born infants, liability and assessment of expense of care, **111:67C.**

Prisoners.

See CORRECTIONAL INSTITUTIONS.

Probate.

See PROBATE AND FAMILY COURT.

Probation, temporary support of persons, **276:95.**

Process.

See PROCESS AND SERVICE OF PROCESS AND PAPERS.

Public counsel services committee.

See PUBLIC COUNSEL SERVICES COMMITTEE.

POOR PERSONS —Cont'd
Registration, registers, and
registrars.
Filing affidavit of and request
for waiver of court costs,
261:27B.
Public posting of by register of
court indigency limits,
261:27C.
Reimbursement.
Assignment of funds, **118:11.**
Excess payments,
reimbursement of
department, **18:18.**
Welfare.
See WELFARE AND SOCIAL
SERVICES.
Workers' compensation benefits,
118:11.
Relatives, duty to support, **122:14,
122:16.**
See FAMILY AND RELATIVES.
Rent.
See LANDLORD AND TENANT.
Retarded persons.
Mentally ill and retarded
persons. See within this
heading, "Mentally ill and
retarded persons."
Retired public employee becoming
public charge, effect, **32:92.**
Rheumatic fever patients, drugs
for treatment, **111:14A.**
Room occupancy tax, exemption of
certain institutions, **64G:2.**
Service of process.
See PROCESS AND SERVICE
OF PROCESS AND
PAPERS.
Settlement, removal to place of,
122:12.
Social services, **18:1 et seq., 18B:1
et seq.**
See WELFARE AND SOCIAL
SERVICES.
State hospital or sanatorium,
notice of admission of needy
person, **111:69F.**
Summary process to recover land.
Affidavit of indigency and
request for waiver of court
costs, filing, **261:27B.**
Payment of rent after waiver of
appeal bond, **239:5.**
Superior courts.
Appeals from denial of relief
from court costs by
indigents in matters arising
in superior court, **261:27D.**
Filing affidavit of indigency and
request for waiver of cost of
action arising in superior
court, **261:27B.**

POOR PERSONS —Cont'd
Support of poor persons, **18:1 et
seq., 18B:1 et seq.**
Cities and towns.
Appropriations, **40:5.**
Medical and hospital care,
40:4, 40:5.
Family, **122:14, 122:16.**
See FAMILY AND
RELATIVES.
Mesne process or execution,
support in jail of person
arrested, **224:12.**
Probation, temporary support of
persons, **276:95.**
Welfare and social services.
See WELFARE AND SOCIAL
SERVICES.
Taxation.
See TAXATION.
Trust companies, financial
information requested, **18:15.**
Tuberculosis and tuberculin.
Legal settlement, **111:94E,
111:121.**
Payment for care and treatment,
111:78-111:80, 111:94E.
Public institutions, treatment of
persons, **111:121.**
Unfair Sales Act as inapplicable to
sales to relief agencies,
93:14G.
Veterans.
Burial expenses, **115:7, 115:8.**
Domicile and residence.
Admission to soldiers' home,
requirements, **115A:3.**
Commissioner of veterans'
services to determine
residence, **115:2.**
Eligibility for benefits and
services, **115:5.**
Waiver and estoppel.
Abuse prevention, waiver of
assessment of fines,
209A:10.
Appeal bond, payment of rent
after waiver, **239:5.**
Filing affidavit of indigency and
request for waiver of court
costs, **261:27B.**
Limits of indigency for waiver of
costs of action, **261:27C.**
Welfare.
See WELFARE AND SOCIAL
SERVICES.
Welfare and social services
department, **18:1 et seq.,
18B:1 et seq.**
See WELFARE AND SOCIAL
SERVICES.

POOR PERSONS —Cont'd
Witnesses.
Fees as extra court cost,
261:27A.
Travel expenses for witnesses
paid by Commonwealth for
indigent defendant, **262:29.**
Workers' compensation benefits,
effect of, **118:11.**

POPPY STRAW.
See DRUGS AND NARCOTICS.

POPULATION.
Alcoholic liquor licenses based,
138:17.
Census.
See CENSUS.
General statutory construction,
4:7.
Weights and measures, annual
tests of devices in towns of
certain population, **98:33A.**
Zoning and planning, special
permit for population increase,
40A:9.

PORCUPINE.
Possession without permit,
authorized, **131:5.**
Removal from hole in ground,
131:76.

PORK.
See SWINE.

**PORNOGRAPHY, 272:16,
272:28-272:32, 272:53, 272:61,
277:45, 277:79.**
**See OBSCENITY AND
LEWDNESS.**

PORTABLE SAW MILLS.
Spark arresters, **48:21, 48:22.**

**PORT AUTHORITY, Spec L
73:1-Spec L 73:34.**
Acquisition of property, **Spec L
73:4.**
Action to enforce bondholders'
rights, **Spec L 73:16.**
Agreement of trust, bonds, **Spec L
73:12.**
Agreements with Authority to
further purposes of Act, **Spec
L 73:4C.**
Air National Guard facilities,
Spec L 73:23.
Airport payments, application,
Spec L 73:7.
Airport properties, **Spec L 73:5,
73:32.**
Smokers as ineligible to work in
certain positions at Logan
International Airport, **Spec
L 73:3A.**

PORT AUTHORITY —Cont'd

Annual reports, **Spec L 73:21.**

Appropriations, **Spec L 73:26.**

Assistance in projects by other agencies and departments, **Spec L 73:23.**

Bank investment trusts, deferred compensation plans funding, **Spec L 73:22A.**

Bonds and notes.
Additional revenue bonds, **Spec L 73:9.**
Investments, bonds eligible, **Spec L 73:18.**
Issuance, **Spec L 73:8.**
Provisions application to all bonds, **Spec L 73:10.**
Revenue refunding bonds, **Spec L 73:19.**

Borrowed money, provisions applicable, **Spec L 73:10A.**

Boston, port commission of. See PORT OF BOSTON COMMISSION.

Bridges.
Mystic River Bridge, vesting of title in Authority, **Spec L 73:34.**
Operation, **Spec L 73:13.**

Buildings, structures defined as public buildings, **22:13A.**

Center for trade and transportation, **Spec L 73:4A.**

Chairman as member of metropolitan area planning council, **40B:24.**

Charts, transfer to Port Authority, **Spec L 73:23.**

Cities, credit not pledged, **Spec L 73:11.**

Commonwealth.
Credit of not pledged, **Spec L 73:11.**
Transfer of projects, **Spec L 73:25.**

Commonwealth pier, lease, **Spec L 73:3 note.**

Conflicts of interest, **Spec L 73:23.**

Constitutional construction, **Spec L 73:28.**

Construction and interpretation of Act, **Spec L 73:27, 73:28.**

Counties, credit not pledged, **Spec L 73:11.**

Credit of Commonwealth not pledged, **Spec L 73:11.**

Definitions, **Spec L 73:1.**

Employees.
Deferred compensation contracts, **Spec L 73:22A, 73:22B.**

PORT AUTHORITY —Cont'd

Employees —Cont'd
Labor relations policy, **Spec L 73:24.**
Retirement systems. See within this heading, "Retirement systems."
Transfer, **Spec L 73:22.**

Equity action to enforce bondholders' rights, **Spec L 73:16.**

Exemption from taxation, **Spec L 73:17.**

Expenditures prohibited, **Spec L 73:23.**

Financing of project, **Spec L 73:4B.**

Flight patterns, regulation, **Spec L 73:3A.**

Funds in trust, **Spec L 73:15.**

Governing law, **Spec L 73:29.**

Hearings on airport flight patterns, **Spec L 73:3A.**

Inconsistent laws, applicability, **Spec L 73:29.**

Individual retirement accounts for employees, funding, **Spec L 73:22B.**

Interest in subject matter, **Spec L 73:23.**

Investment, bonds eligible, **Spec L 73:18.**

Labor relations policy, **Spec L 73:24.**

Liability in tort, **Spec L 73:23.**

Liberal construction of Act, **Spec L 73:27.**

Life insurance contracts, funding, **Spec L 73:22A.**

Mandamus to enforce bondholders' rights, **Spec L 73:16.**

Maps, transfer to Port Authority, **Spec L 73:23.**

Massachusetts Port Authority, **Spec 73:2.**
Retirement allowances, increase, **32:90A to 32:90E.**

Metropolitan area planning council, port authority chairman as member, **40B:24.**

Municipalities, credit not pledged, **Spec L 73:11.**

Mutual funds, deferred compensation plan funding, **Spec L 73:22A.**

Mystic River Bridge, vesting of title in Authority, **Spec L 73:34.**

National Guard facilities, **Spec L 73:23.**

Negligence, liability, **Spec L 73:23.**

PORT AUTHORITY —Cont'd

Operation of bridges, **Spec L 73:13.**

Patterns of flight, regulation, **Spec L 73:3A.**

Payments, application of, **Spec L 73:7.**

Penalties.
Conflict of interest, **Spec L 73:23.**
Failure to pay toll, **Spec L 73:23.**

Pensions.
Retirement systems. See within this heading, "Retirement systems."

Pier 5, lease, **Spec L 73:3 note.**

Planning council, chairman as member of metropolitan area planning council, **40B:24.**

Plans, transfer to Port Authority, **Spec L 73:23.**

Pledge of credit by Commonwealth, **Spec L 73:11.**

Plumbers and gas fitters, **142:21.**

Police.
Pensions for widows, **32:100.**
Protection of Port Authority projects, **Spec L 73:23.**

Political subdivisions, credit not pledged, **Spec L 73:11.**

Port of Boston Commission. See PORT OF BOSTON COMMISSION.

Powers of Authority, **Spec L 73:3, 73:6.**

Privation contracts, definition, **7:53.**

Properties.
Acquisition, **Spec L 73:4.**
Airport properties. See within this heading, "Airport properties."
Port properties, **Spec L 73:6, 73:33.**
Title. See within this heading, "Title."

Publication of actions, **Spec L 73:23.**

Public buildings, structures defined, **22:13A.**

Records.
Reports and records. See within this heading, "Reports and records."

Refunding bonds, **Spec L 73:19.**

Reimbursement.
Retirement systems. See within this heading, "Retirement systems."

Remedies of bondholders, **Spec L 73:16.**

PORT AUTHORITY —Cont'd
Repair of projects by Port
  Authority, **Spec L 73:23.**
Reports and records.
  Annual report, **Spec L 73:21.**
  Retirement systems, **32:20,**
    32:21.
  Transfer to Port Authority, **Spec
    L 73:23.**
Residential sound insulation
  program, **268A:7, Spec L
  573:23.**
Retirement systems.
  Actuary to determine amount to
    be paid for pension fund,
    32:22.
  Administration, **32:20.**
  Commissioner of insurance,
    violations of contributory
    retirement laws, notice to
    authority, **32:24.**
  Cost-of-living adjustments in
    pensions, **32:102.**
  Dereliction of duty by members,
    initiation of proceedings,
    32:15.
  Description of system, **32:2.**
  Employee, defined, **32:1.**
  Group classification, **32:3.**
  Guarantees of allowances by
    governmental unit, **32:100.**
  Insurance commissioner,
    violations of contributory
    retirement laws, notice to
    authority, **32:24.**
  Legal counsel of authority,
    32:20.
  Member, defined, **32:1.**
  Members of retirement board,
    32:20.
  Notice of violations, Public
    Employee Retirement
    Commissioner, **32:24.**
  Payment of checks, **32:11.**
  Political subdivision, defined,
    32:1.
  Public safety employees assigned
    to port authority, **Spec L
    73:34A.**
  Reimbursement.
    Commonwealth, **32:21.**
    Members of board, expenses,
      32:20.
  Reports, **32:20, 32:21.**
  Secretary-treasurer, **32:23.**
  System, defined, **32:1.**
  Violations of contributory
    retirement laws,
    commissioner of insurance
    to give notice, **32:24.**
  Widows of deceased fire fighters,
    police officers or corrections
    officers, pensions, **32:100.**

PORT AUTHORITY —Cont'd
Retirement systems —Cont'd
  Workers' compensation benefits,
    effect, **32:14.**
Revenue bonds.
  Bonds and notes. See within this
    heading, "Bonds and notes."
Revenues, **Spec L 73:14.**
Smokers as ineligible to work in
  certain positions at Logan
  International Airport, **Spec L
  73:3A.**
Sound insulation program, **268A:7,
  Spec L 573:23.**
Suit to enforce bondholders' rights,
  Spec L 73:16.
Taxation, exemption, **59:2B, Spec
  L 73:17.**
Title.
  Airport properties, certain laws
    inoperative upon vesting,
    Spec L 73:32.
  Mystic River Bridge in
    Authority, certain laws
    inoperative, **Spec L 73:34.**
  Port properties, vesting in
    authority, certain laws
    inoperative, **Spec L 73:33.**
  Transfer to Commonwealth,
    Spec L 73:25.
  Vesting of title. See within this
    heading, "Vesting of title."
Tolls, failure to pay, **Spec L 73:23.**
Tort liability of Port Authority,
  Spec L 73:23.
Towns, credit not pledged, **Spec L
  73:11.**
Trade and transportation center,
  Spec L 73:4A.
Transfer of employees, **Spec L
  73:22.**
Transfer of projects to
  Commonwealth, **Spec L
  73:25.**
Transportation and construction
  executive office, agencies
  within, **6A:19.**
Transportation center, **Spec L
  73:4A.**
Trusts and trust funds.
  Bonds, trust agreements, **Spec
    L 73:12.**
  Deferred compensation plans
    funding bank investment
    trusts, **Spec L 73:22A.**
  Revenues of Authority held in
    trust, **Spec L 73:15.**
Vesting of title.
  Airport properties, **Spec L
    73:32.**
  Mystic River Bridge, **Spec L
    73:34.**

PORT AUTHORITY —Cont'd
Vesting of title —Cont'd
  Port properties, **Spec L 73:33.**
  Words and phrases, **Spec L 73:1.**

**PORT OF BOSTON, 91:1 et seq.
See BOSTON HARBOR.**

**PORT OF BOSTON
  COMMISSION, 6:56.**
Contracts as to harbor facilities,
  making, **91:9A.**
Control of harbor and facilities,
  91:3.
Employees.
  Dislocations and assistance in
    reemployment of dislocated
    workers, **6:17.**
  Retirement system group
    classification, **32:3.**
Fund, **91:6, 91:24, 91:52.**
Governor and council's powers,
  6:17.
Harbor, **91:1-91:9A.**
  See BOSTON HARBOR.
Labor and employment.
  Employees. See within this
    heading, "Employees."
Leasing of facilities, **91:9A.**
Reemployment of dislocated
  workers, assistance, **6:17.**
Retirement system group
  classification of employees,
  32:3.
Supervision by governor and
  council, **6:17.**

PORTRAITS.
Former governors, portraits, **8:19,
  8:19A.**
General Court members and other
  state officers, **5:18.**
Remedy for unauthorized use,
  214:3A.
Reports of sales of books
  containing portraits of
  members of general court,
  5:18.
Secretary of state.
  Photographs of portraits and art
    objects in state house,
    availability, **9:28.**
  Sale of books containing
    portraits and biographical
    sketches of members of
    general court, **5:18.**
State house.
  Art objects and portraits,
    photographs, **9:28.**
  Former governors, portraits,
    8:19, 8:19A.
Trademarks, **110B:3.**

PORTS AND HARBORS,
102:17-102:28.
Abandoning vessels.
See SHIPWRECKS.
Access to, state licenses as
affecting right, **91:17.**
Bilge water, discharging into,
91:59.
Borrowing by cities and towns for
improvement, **44:7.**
Boston.
Commission.
See PORT OF BOSTON
COMMISSION.
Harbor, **91:1-91:9A.**
See BOSTON HARBOR.
Boundaries.
Boston harbor.
See BOSTON HARBOR.
Burning refuse within marine
boundaries prohibited,
270:20.
Certain harbors, boundaries,
102:4.
Establishment of harbor lines,
91:34.
Licenses as affected by harbor
line established by general
court, **91:17.**
Burning of refuse within marine
boundaries or near shoreline
prohibited, **270:20.**
Cables and conduits, restrictions,
91:14.
Cities and towns.
Funds for improvement or
maintenance. See within
this heading, "Funds for
improvement or
maintenance."
Coastal facilities, improvement,
21F:1 et seq.
Adherence to rules, regulations
and procedures, **21F:6.**
Application for assistance,
21F:2, 21F:4.
Assistance, qualifications, **21F:5.**
Coastal city or town, definition
and designation, **21F:3.**
Definitions, **21F:2, 21F:3.**
Designated port area defined,
21F:2.
Harbor or waterfront
improvement, **21F:4.**
Promulgation of rules and
regulations, **21F:7.**
Purpose, **21F:1.**
Contracts and agreements.
Facilities, contracts relating,
91:9A.
Improvement and preservation
of harbors, **91:31.**

PORTS AND HARBORS
—Cont'd
Docks.
See WHARVES, PIERS, AND
DOCKS.
Dredging and cleaning of,
91:52-91:56.
Dumping, **91:52 et seq., 102:17.**
Environmental affairs executive
office, duties and functions,
21A:2, 21A:10.
Environmental protection
department.
Coastal facilities improvement,
designated port area
defined, **21F:2.**
Harbor lines established, **91:34.**
Powers and duties, **91:10.**
Federal aid, application, **91:36.**
Fines and penalties.
Bilge water, discharge, **91:59.**
Burning, **270:20.**
Dumping in ports and harbors,
98:52 et seq., 102:17.
Injuries to harbor, **91:30.**
Masters, penalties for violation
of orders, **102:28.**
Motorboat regulations and
offenses, **90B:12, 90B:13,
90B:17.**
Obstruction of ports and
harbors, **102:17, 102:18.**
Oil discharged into ports and
harbors, **91:59.**
Stones, illegal deposit of into
ports and harbors, **102:17.**
Violations, fines and penalties,
102:17, 102:28.
Funds for improvement or
maintenance.
Appropriations by cities, **91:29.**
Borrowing by cities, **44:7.**
Boston, port, **91:6, 91:24, 91:52.**
Environmental officers executive
office, **21A:10.**
Gasoline and motor fuel tax
receipts, distribution,
64A:13.
Municipal establishment of
waterways improvement
and maintenance fund, **40:5.**
State costs and expenses for
removal of wharves, piers,
or docks, credit to
maintenance fund, **91:49B.**
Garbage and refuse.
Burning within marine
boundaries, **270:20.**
Dumping in ports and harbors,
91:52 et seq., 102:17.
Gasoline and motor fuel tax
receipts, distribution, **64A:13.**

PORTS AND HARBORS
—Cont'd
Governor's approval of certain
contracts, **91:31.**
Gravel, removal, **91:30.**
Grounding vessels within, **91:49.**
Harbor masters, **102:19-102:28.**
See HARBOR MASTERS.
Harbor plan, definition, **21F:2.**
Health nuisances in, examinations,
regulations, etc., **111:122.**
Improvements and repairs, **21F:1
et seq., 84:12, 84:14, 91:31.**
Acquisition of property, **91:5,
91:31.**
Federal aid, application, **91:36.**
Funds for improvement or
maintenance. See within
this heading, "Funds for
improvement or
maintenance."
Governor's approval of certain
contracts, **91:31.**
Public works department, **91:9A,
91:11.**
Licenses and permits.
Access, state licenses as
affecting right, **91:17.**
Dredging and cleaning of ports
and harbors, licensing and
supervision, **91:52-91:56.**
Harbor masters.
See HARBOR MASTERS.
Lines, effect of establishment of
harbor lines, **91:17.**
Lumber, permit to unload,
102:22.
Marina, license to operate,
91:59B.
Structures and encroachments
in watercourses, **91:15.**
Structures in harbors, records as
to licenses, **91:18.**
Limits of certain, **102:4.**
Logs and timber.
Illegal deposit in ports, **102:17.**
Permit for unloading lumber,
102:22.
Maintenance.
Funds for. See within this
heading, "Funds for
improvement or
maintenance."
Marinas.
See MARINAS.
Masters, **102:19-102:28.**
See HARBOR MASTERS.
Motorboat regulations and
offenses, **90B:12, 90B:13,
90B:17.**

PORTS AND HARBORS
—Cont'd
Municipal finance for
improvements.
Funds for improvement or
maintenance. See within
this heading, "Funds for
improvement or
maintenance."
New Bedford harbor.
See NEW BEDFORD HARBOR.
Obstruction, **102:17, 102:18.**
Notice to remove, **91:40.**
Oil discharged into, **91:59.**
Passing line across channel
forbidden, **102:18.**
Penalties.
Fines and penalties. See within
this heading, "Fines and
penalties."
Permits.
Licenses and permits. See
within this heading,
"Licenses and permits."
Piers.
See WHARVES, PIERS, AND
DOCKS.
Pipe lines, restrictions, **91:14.**
Planning, **91:9A.**
Police, enforcement of motorboat
regulations, **90B:12, 90B:13,
90B:17.**
Port authority.
See PORT AUTHORITY.
Preference, clearing regulation as
to, **US Const Art 1 Sec 9 cl
6.**
Preservation of harbors, contracts
and agreements, **91:31.**
Public works department.
See PUBLIC WORKS.
Railroads.
See RAILROADS.
Records, reports, and returns.
Boston Harbor, records of
property and improvements,
91:3.
Licenses for structures in
harbors, **91:18.**
Refuse.
Garbage and refuse. See within
this heading, "Garbage and
refuse."
Repairs.
Improvements and repairs. See
within this heading,
"Improvements and repairs."
Salem harbor.
See SALEM HARBOR.
Stones, illegal deposit, **102:17.**
Structures in watercourses, **91:15.**

PORTS AND HARBORS
—Cont'd
Surveys, **91:10, 91:11, 91:31-91:34.**
Timber.
Logs and timber. See within this
heading, "Logs and timber."
United States government surveys
of, governor and council to
cooperate, **6:9.**
Wharves.
See WHARVES, PIERS, AND
DOCKS.
Wrecked.
See SHIPWRECKS.

**PORTUGUESE-AMERICAN
MONTH, 6:15GGGG.**

**PORTUGUESE WAR
VETERANS.**
**See AMERICAN PORTUGUESE
WAR VETERANS
ASSOCIATION.**

POSSE.
Refusal to aid sheriff, **268:24.**
Sheriff may call for aid, **37:13.**

POSSESSION.
Adverse possession.
See ADVERSE POSSESSION.
Ammunition.
Gunpowder, possession with
intent to injure, **266:102.**
Persons exempt from prohibition
against, **140:122B,
140:129C.**
Antique dealers and collectors,
possession of firearms,
140:128A.
Cigarette tax.
See CIGARETTE TAX.
Criminal prosecution, proof in,
278:9.
Drugs.
See DRUGS AND NARCOTICS.
Executions.
See EXECUTIONS.
Fee for service of writ of
possession, **262:8.**
Firearms.
See FIREARMS AND
WEAPONS.
Fish and game.
Fish, birds, mammals or carcass,
possession contrary to
regulations, **131:5.**
Legal when, **131:1.**
Smelt, **130:34, 130:35.**
Forgery.
See FORGERY AND
COUNTERFEITING.
Indictments, informations, and
complaints.
Cigarettes, illegal transportation
or possession, **64C:8.**

POSSESSION —Cont'd
Indictments, informations, and
complaints —Cont'd
Dangerous weapons, **277:79.**
Hypodermic instruments, form
for indictment, **277:79.**
Infernal machines, possession,
266:102A.
Hoax device, **266:102a½.**
Lotteries.
Evidence of tickets use, **271:20.**
Tickets or shares, possession,
271:9.
Mortgage foreclosure.
See MORTGAGE
FORECLOSURE.
Mortgages.
See MORTGAGES AND DEEDS
OF TRUST.
Process of papers.
Writ of possession. See within
this heading, "Writ of
possession."
Secured transactions.
See SECURED
TRANSACTIONS.
Shotguns.
See SHOTGUNS.
Tenant's right to recover
possession of residential
property from which he was
unlawfully removed or
excluded, **186:15F.**
United States, possessions of.
See TERRITORIES AND
DEPENDENCIES OF
UNITED STATES.
Writ of possession, **235:15.**
Fee for service, **262:8.**

POSSIBILITY OF REVERTER.
Limitation of action based,
260:31A.

POSTAL CARD.
Absent voting ballot application,
form, **54:87.**
Voting list, warning that failure to
respond to mailing may result,
51:4.

POSTAL CARRIERS.
See MAILMEN.

**POSTAL INSURANCE
COMPANIES.**
Process Act, actions under as to
postal insurance companies,
175B:1-175B:6.

POSTAL SERVICES.
See MAIL AND MAILING.

POSTDATING.
Invoice for shipment of goods,
postdating, **106:2-310.**

POSTERS.
Advertising.
  See ADVERTISING AND
    ADVERTISEMENTS.
Election offenses.
  See ELECTION OFFENSES.
Elections.
  See ELECTIONS.
Malicious injury to, penalized,
  266:125.
Placards.
  See PLACARDS.
Theft and mutilation of library
  materials, **266:99A, 266:100.**

POST EXCHANGE.
Prepackaged poultry, weighing at
  time of retail sale, **98:56B.**
Use of term in business
  designation restricted, **110:4B.**

POSTHUMOUS CHILDREN.
Fiduciary's account, representation
  in proceedings for allowance,
  206:24.
Guardian ad litem in probate
  proceedings, **192:1C.**
Inheritance rights, **190:8.**
Treated as living at parent's death,
  190:8.
Wills, rights, **191:20, 191:25,
  191:28, 191:29.**
Workers' compensation law,
  dependents, **152:32, 152:35A.**

POSTING.
Absentee's estate, notices,
  200:2-200:4.
Absentee voting.
  See ELECTIONS.
Agreements.
  Contracts and agreements. See
    within this heading,
    "Contracts and agreements."
Agricultural shows and fairs, rules
  and regulations, **128:48.**
Agriculture laws, preparation and
  distribution of extracts, **128:7.**
Alcoholic liquors.
  See ALCOHOLIC LIQUORS.
Animals.
  See ANIMALS.
Anti-discrimination laws.
  Civil rights and discrimination.
    See within this heading,
    "Civil rights and
    discrimination."
Aqueduct companies, notice of sale
  of shares for failure to pay
  assessments, **165:18.**
Assessors' warrants, notice, **60:88.**
Beach district regulations, posting,
  40:12C.

POSTING —Cont'd
Blind persons, posting of license to
  conduct fund raising activities
  for benefit, **6:139.**
Boating and bathing, statutes
  affecting, **140:195.**
Boilers, posting of certificate of
  inspection or license, **146:8,
  146:27, 146:51.**
Bylaws of town, **40:32.**
Camps, rules and regulations,
  140:32D.
Candidates for elections, list,
  54:49, 54:52.
Carriers, notice of hearing on
  certificate of public
  convenience and necessity for
  motor carrier of property,
  159B:3.
Carrying concealed weapons,
  posters, **269:11.**
Caucuses.
  Nonpartisan caucuses, **53:118.**
  Official ballot, caucuses without,
    53:83.
Cigarette sales to minors, **270:7.**
Cities.
  See CITIES AND TOWNS.
Civil rights and discrimination.
  Notices of anti-discrimination
    laws, **151B:1, 151B:5,
    151B:7.**
  Orders of commission against
    discrimination, **151B:5.**
  Prohibition of notice of
    discrimination because of
    race or creed, **272:92A.**
Civil service.
  See CIVIL SERVICE.
Commercial shooting preserves,
  131:31.
Contracts and agreements.
  Copy of section requiring
    security for labor and
    materials, **149:29.**
  Schedule of wages during life of
    contract, **149:27.**
Credit unions.
  See CREDIT UNIONS.
Curfew, imposition, **40:37A.**
Dancing and roller skating,
  posting of laws regarding,
  140:199.
Decree for permanent injunction or
  abatement of nuisance,
  139:16A.
Deed registers, **36:13A.**
Defacing or destroying posted
  notice, **48:26, 266:122,
  266:124, 266:125.**

POSTING —Cont'd
Discrimination.
  Civil rights and discrimination.
    See within this heading,
    "Civil rights and
    discrimination."
District meetings, notice, **41:119.**
Dwellings, posting name, address,
  and telephone number of
  owner or agent, **143:3S.**
Easement, prevention, **187:3,
  187:4.**
Election offenses.
  See ELECTION OFFENSES.
Elections.
  See ELECTIONS.
Elevator inspection, certificate,
  143:65.
Employment agencies and
  bureaus.
  Copies of laws, **140:46P.**
  License, **140:46B.**
  Name of applicant for license,
    140:46D.
Execution sale, posting of notice,
  236:28.
Fair employment practice laws
  and regulations, **151B:1,
  151B:7.**
Farm labor camps, certificate of
  occupancy, **111:128G.**
Fees.
  See FEES.
Fiduciary's sale of real estate,
  202:15, 202:17.
Firearms, clerk of city or town
  posting notices regarding,
  269:11, 269:11A.
Fire district meetings, **48:66.**
Fishways, protection, **130:19,
  130:36.**
Forest and parks division
  regulations, **21:4A.**
Forest cutting practices, rules and
  regulations, **132:41.**
Forest fires, **48:25.**
  Destruction of posted notices,
    48:26.
Forfeiture of property.
  Notice of libel to enforce, **257:5.**
  Seized property, notice, **276:5.**
Fund-raising activities for benefit
  of the blind, posting of license,
  6:139.
Gasoline.
  See GASOLINE AND MOTOR
    FUELS.
Hospital employees prohibited
  from furnishing information
  about personal injury cases to
  attorneys or their
  representatives, posting of
  statute regarding, **221:44B.**

POSTING —Cont'd

Hotels.

    See HOTELS, MOTELS, AND ROOMINGHOUSES.

Hot water heating boiler certificate of inspection, posting, **146:79, 146:80.**

Indigency limits, public posting, **261:27C.**

Infested trees, **132:8.**

Jeweler's lien, **255:31C.**

Labor.

    See LABOR AND WORKFORCE DEVELOPMENT.

Land.

    Fiduciary's sale, **202:15, 202:17.**

    Fish.

        See FISH AND GAME.

    Prescriptive easement, notice for prevention, **187:3, 187:4.**

    Registration of land title, notice of proceedings, **185:39.**

    Restrictions running with, notice by posting in action to enforce, **240:10B.**

    Trespassers, penalty for defacement or removal of notices against, **266:122.**

Land courts, process issued, **262:16.**

Lead poisoning, posting of notices on dwellings found to be possible sources, **111:194.**

Lists.

    Candidates for elections, **43:44D, 54:49, 54:52.**

    Impediments to marriage, **207:37.**

    Primaries, **50:5.**

    Schedules. See within this heading, "Schedules."

Longshore and waterfront employees, rules and regulations, **149:18G.**

Lost property, notice of finding, **134:1.**

Malicious injury to posted notice, **266:122, 266:124, 266:125.**

Manufactured homes, **140:32D.**

Marine fish and fisheries.

    Fishways for spawning salt water fish, **130:19.**

    Shellfish contamination areas, **130:74.**

    Smelt, spawning areas, **130:36.**

Marriage, posting list of impediments, **207:37.**

Master plumber, display of license or certificate, **142:3.**

Maternity leave, statutory provisions concerning required to be posted, **149:105D.**

POSTING —Cont'd

Meetings.

    Annual district meetings, notice, **41:119.**

    Caucuses. See within this heading, "Caucuses."

    Public bodies, meetings, **34:9F.**

Minimum wages, **151:10, 151:16.**

    Domestic service in employer's home, exception, **151:16.**

Mobile homes and mobile home parks, **140:32D.**

Motor carriers of property, notice of hearing upon certificates of public convenience and necessity, **159B:3.**

Municipal employees' compensation plan, notice of public hearing on rules or regulations, **41:108A.**

New voting precincts, **54:5, 54:8.**

Nonpartisan caucuses, **53:118.**

No smoking signs, regulation of posting, **270:21.**

Nuisance injurious to public health, notice of abatement, **111:124, 139:16A.**

Parks.

    Forest and parks division, regulation, **21:4A, 132A:7.**

    Mobile homes and mobile home parks, **140:32D.**

Placards.

    See PLACARDS.

Polling places, designation and location, **54:24.**

Pounds.

    Impounding, **49:34.**

    Sale of impounded beasts, **49:37.**

Preliminary elections in charter plan cities, posting list of candidates for nomination, **43:44D.**

Prescriptive easement, notice for prevention, **187:3, 187:4.**

Prices.

    See GASOLINE AND MOTOR FUELS.

Primary elections.

    Lists and notices, **50:5.**

    Specimen and sample ballots, **53:36.**

Public transportation facility, notices concerning prohibited acts, **161:94A, 161:95.**

Public works and departments.

    Schedule of wages, **149:27.**

    Section requiring security for labor and materials, **149:29.**

Quieting title, posting of notice of action, **240:7.**

POSTING —Cont'd

Railroads.

    See RAILROADS.

Real property.

    Land. See within this heading, "Land."

Registers of deeds, **36:13A.**

Registration of land title, notice of proceedings, **185:39.**

Registration of voters.

    See REGISTRATION OF VOTERS.

Restrictions running with land, notice by posting in action to enforce, **240:10B.**

Roller skating, laws regarding, **140:199.**

Sales.

    Aqueduct companies, notice of sale of shares of for failure to pay assessments, **165:18.**

    Cigarette sales to minors, **270:7.**

    Execution sale, posting notice, **236:28.**

    Fiduciary's sale of real estate, **202:15, 202:17.**

    Sales finance company, posting license, **255D:2.**

    Sheriffs, deputy sheriffs, and constables, fees for posting notices of sale, **262:8.**

    Tax sales, **60:42.**

Schedules.

    Admission prices for traveling circuses, carnivals, or other entertainment, **140:181B.**

    Fees, schedules, **262:34, 262:46.**

    Wages during life of contract, schedule, **149:27.**

Seized property, forfeiture, **276:5.**

Self-storage facilities, advertisement of sale of property, **105A:4.**

Sessions of registrars of voters, notice, **51:32.**

Shellfish contamination areas, **130:74.**

Sheriffs fees, **262:8.**

Small loan business license, **140:101.**

Spawning areas, **130:19, 130:36.**

Specimen ballots at primary elections, **53:36.**

State boards and commissions, notice of meetings, **30A:11A.**

State parks, rules and regulations, **21:4A, 132A:7.**

Steamboat licenses, **140:192.**

Stray beasts, notice of finding, **134:2.**

Street railways, posting notices of change of service, **161:111.**

POSTING —Cont'd

Taxation.

    Lists, tax lists, **59:29, 60:88.**

    Sales, tax sales, **60:42.**

    Titles, sale of land held under tax titles, **60:79.**

Trailers.

    Mobile homes and mobile home parks, **140:32D.**

Trespassers, penalty for defacement or removal of notices against, **266:122.**

Voting lists, **50:5, 51:57.**

    See ELECTIONS.

Voting precincts, **43A:3, 54:5, 54:8.**

Wages.

    Minimum wages. See within this heading, "Minimum wages."

    Schedule of wages during life of contract, **149:27.**

Weapons, posters on carrying concealed weapons, **269:11.**

Wildlife sanctuary, establishment, **131:9.**

Zoning and planning, notice of hearing on adoption or change of ordinance or bylaw, **40A:5.**

POSTMASTER GENERAL.

Railroads, transportation of mail upon request of postmaster general, **160:201-160:203.**

POST MORTEM EXAMINATION.

See AUTOPSY.

POST OFFICES.

Mail.

    See MAIL AND MAILING.

POSTPARTUM CARE.

Blanket, general, accident or sickness policy, benefits to be provided, **175:47F.**

Childbirth, hospital stays after in-patient deliveries, **32A:17C, 118E:10A, 175:47F, 176A:8H, 176B:4H, 176G:4I.**

Hospital service plan, benefits to be provided, **176A:8H.**

POSTPONEMENT OF PROCEEDING.

See CONTINUANCE OR ADJOURNMENT.

POSTS.

Boundary markers.

    See BOUNDARIES AND MARKERS.

Football goal posts, injuring or removing, **266:104A.**

Guide posts.

    See GUIDE POSTS.

POTASH.

Defined, commercial fertilizers, **128:64.**

POTATOES, 94:117G-94:117L.

Containers, **94:117B, 94:117H.**

Definitions, **94:117G, 128:84.**

Enforcement of law by commissioner, **94:117J.**

Frozen blanched potatoes, marking of containers, **94:117H.**

Grades and grading, **94:117H.**

    Advertisements to state grades, **94:117H.**

    Fine or penalty for violations, **94:117K, 94:117L.**

    Grade or grades defined, **94:117G.**

    Official grades established by commissioner, **94:117I.**

Hearings and notice, **94:117I, 94:117K.**

Inspection, **94:117J.**

Marking of container, **94:117H.**

Rules and regulations, **94:117J.**

Seeds.

    Definition, **128:84.**

    Sales, **128:101.**

Standards or grades.

    Grades and grading. See within this heading, "Grades and grading."

POTENTIAL EARNINGS.

Retirement allowance modification, **32:8.**

POTS.

Violations and penalties, **94:117K, 94:117L.**

Weirs, nets, seines, trawls and traps, **130:29-130:32, 130:38, 130:38A.**

    See MARINE FISH AND FISHERIES.

POULTRY AND POULTRY PRODUCTS.

Action on bond of person engaged in business, **94:152D.**

Adulterated food, what constitutes, **94:186.**

Agricultural experiment station of University of Massachusetts.

    University of Massachusetts. See within this heading, "University of Massachusetts, investigations and experiments."

Agriculture department.

    Food and agriculture department. See within this heading, "Food and agriculture department."

POULTRY AND POULTRY PRODUCTS —Cont'd

Artificial coloring, **272:80D.**

Baby chicks, **129:26B, 272:80D.**

Bakeries, exclusion, **94:9I.**

Bill of sale required for transportation, **94:152B.**

Birds endangering poultry, permits for trapping, **131:38.**

Bond required of dealer, **94:152A-94:152G.**

Breaking and entering place where poultry kept, **266:22.**

Breeding of, corporations to promote, **180:2.**

    Annual return of corporation, **180:26A.**

    Incorporation for breeding of poultry, **180:1-180:11.**

Claims of producers, satisfaction, **94:152D.**

Commissioner of agriculture, powers and duties, **94:152A, 94:152D-94:152G.**

Contracts for raising and delivery of poultry, **94:152E.**

Crimes and offenses.

    Breaking and entering place where poultry kept, **266:22.**

    Buying and transporting, violations, **94:152C.**

    Dyeing or sale of live chicks, ducklings, etc., **272:80D.**

    Fines and penalties. See within this heading, "Fines and penalties."

    Itinerant buyer requirements, **94:152C.**

    Officers to prosecute violations, **272:84.**

    Sale at retail other than by weight, **94:92B.**

Dealers.

    Itinerant dealers. See within this heading, "Itinerant dealers."

Definitions, **94:152A, 128:1A, 128:2, 129:1.**

Detention of persons unlawfully entering places where poultry is kept, **266:22.**

Diseases.

    Baby chicks, **129:26B.**

    Control of disease in purchase, sale of live poultry, **129:26B.**

    Defined as domestic animal, **129:1.**

Dogs, "Fowl" defined for purpose of laws relating, **128:2.**

Dressed poultry slaughtered outside state, **94:139B.**

POULTRY AND POULTRY PRODUCTS —Cont'd

Dressing for sale, removal of crop and entrails, **94:153.**

Ducklings, restrictions on sale, **272:80D.**

Dyeing or coloring chicks, ducklings, etc., **272:80D.**

Eggs.
  See EGGS.

Examination.
  Inspection. See within this heading, "Inspection."

Exhibits and prizes awarded by food and agriculture department, **128:2.**

Federal agency, inspection, **94:139B.**

Fees.
  Buyer's license, fee, **94:152A.**
  University of Massachusetts, fee for testing poultry, **75:21.**

Fighting birds.
  See FIGHTING BIRDS AND ANIMALS.

Fines and penalties.
  Breaking and entering places where poultry kept, **266:22.**
  Crop and entrails, failure to remove, **94:153.**
  Eggs.
    See EGGS.
  Improperly dressed poultry, penalty for sale, **94:153.**
  Sale or transportation, violation of law, **94:92B, 94:152C.**

Food and agriculture department.
  Enforcement of bond of itinerant dealer, **94:152D.**
  Exhibits and prizes awarded by department, **128:2.**
  "Native" use of word in sale or packaging of turkeys, enforcement, **94:107.**

Hawkers, peddlers, and transient vendors.
  Itinerant dealers. See within this heading, "Itinerant dealers."

Humane slaughter of livestock, exclusion from definition of livestock for purpose of statute regulating, **94:139C.**

Incorporation for breeding of poultry, **180:1-180:11.**

Inspection, **94:124, 94:147A, 94:153.**
  Federal agency, inspection, **94:139B.**
  Poultry inspection section, establishment in public health department, **17:4.**

POULTRY AND POULTRY PRODUCTS —Cont'd

Inspection —Cont'd
  University of Massachusetts. See within this heading, "University of Massachusetts, investigations and experiments."

Itinerant dealers.
  Crimes and offenses, **94:152C.**
  License and bond, **94:152A, 94:152D.**

Kosher food, **94:156.**

Licenses.
  Buyers and dealers, **94:152A-94:152C.**
  Fees, **94:152A.**
  Itinerant dealers, **94:152A, 94:152D.**

Trapping of birds endangering poultry, permits, **131:38.**

Merchant, defined under food inspection law, **94:152A.**

Misbranding of food, what constitutes, **94:187.**

"Native," use of term in connection with sale, packaging or advertising of turkeys, **94:99B, 94:107.**

Offenses.
  Crimes and offenses. See within this heading, "Crimes and offenses."

Other state, dressed poultry slaughtered, **94:139B.**

Penalties.
  Fines and penalties. See within this heading, "Fines and penalties."

Prepackaged poultry, weighing at time of retail sale, **98:56B.**

Price of retail sale to be marked on package, **94:181.**

Prizes awarded by food and agriculture department, **128:2.**

Producers.
  Claims of, satisfaction, **94:152D.**
  Defined, **94:152A.**
  Protection of producers by dealers, **94:152D.**

Sale and transportation, **94:152A-94:152G, 94:153.**
  Bill of sale or memorandum, **94:152B.**
  Bond of buyers and sellers, **94:152A, 94:152D.**
  Control of animal disease in purchase, sale of live poultry, **129:26B.**
  Dressing of poultry for sale, **94:153.**

POULTRY AND POULTRY PRODUCTS —Cont'd

Sale and transportation —Cont'd
  Eggs, grading, **94:90C-94:90E.**
  Fines and penalties for violation of law, **94:92B, 94:152C.**
  License of dealers, **94:152A, 94:152D.**
  Live baby chicks, ducklings, etc., **272:80D.**
  "Native," use of term in connection with sale of turkeys, **94:99B.**
  Officers to prosecute violations, **272:84.**
  Proof of ownership to be in possession of person transporting, **94:152B.**
  Retail price to be marked on package, **94:181.**
  Statements required of licensees, **94:152D.**
  Sunday, sale, **136:6.**
  Weight.
    Retail sale only, **94:92B.**
    Time of retail sale, weighing of prepackaged poultry, **98:56B.**

Sales tax, exemptions, **64H:6.**

Satisfaction of producers' claims, **94:152D.**

Sausage and sausage meat, inclusion of poultry products, **94:1.**

Schools for instructions in raising, **74:15-74:17.**

Slaughterhouses.
  See SLAUGHTERHOUSES.

Statements required of licensee, **94:152D.**

Sunday sales, **136:6.**

Taxes.
  Excise tax on domestic fowl, **59:8A.**
  Exemption, **59:5, 64H:6.**
  Sales tax, exemptions, **64H:6.**

Terms "agriculture" and "farming" as including raising, **128:1A.**

Transportation.
  Sale and transportation. See within this heading, "Sale and transportation."

Trespass.
  By fowl, **266:118.**
  Where poultry kept, **266:22.**

University of Massachusetts, investigations and experiments, **75:17.**
  Fee, **75:21.**

Weight.
  Sale. See within this heading, "Sale and transportation."

POUNDAGE.
Personal property attached, replevied, or taken on execution, **262:8.**

POUNDS, 49:22 et seq.
Animals running at large.
　Dogs, **140:151A, 140:153, 140:164.**
　Field drivers taken up, **49:24.**
　Impounding, **49:25.**
　Sunday, impounding, **49:24, 49:25.**
　Third persons taking up, fees, **49:24.**
Cities and towns.
　Municipal officers and employees. See within this heading, "Municipal officers and employees."
Claims of impounder.
　Determination of disputed amount, **49:35.**
　Sale of beast for nonpayment, **49:37.**
　Statement, **49:31.**
Damage, taking or impounding of beasts doing, **49:30.**
　Amount of damages, determination, **49:35, 49:36.**
　Distraint, **49:29.**
　Escaped beast may be retaken, **49:39.**
　Fence, effect of sufficiency or insufficiency, **49:41.**
　Impounding, **49:30.**
　Legality of distraint, how tried, **49:41.**
　No delivery until cost paid, **49:32.**
　Replevin as remedy of owner, **49:41.**
　Rescue, **49:39, 49:40.**
　Sale upon nonpayment of damages, etc., **49:37.**
　Disposition of proceeds, **49:38.**
　Statement of person distraining as to demands, **49:31.**
　Warrant for damage by impounded beast, fee, **262:34.**
Destruction of property.
　Damage, taking or impounding of beasts doing. See within this heading, "Damage, taking or impounding of beasts doing."
Distraint.
　Animals doing damage, distraint, **49:29.**
　Legality of distraint, how tried, **49:41.**

POUNDS —Cont'd
Distraint —Cont'd
　Rescue of distrained or impounded beast, **49:39, 49:40.**
　Sale upon nonpayment of damages, statement of person distraining as to demands, **49:31.**
Escaped beast may be retaken, **49:39.**
Establishment and maintenance, **49:22.**
　Expenses of impounding, payment by owner, **49:27.**
Fees.
　Claims of impounder, determination of disputed amount, **49:35.**
　Damages, costs and expenses with respect to impounded beast, determination, **49:36.**
　Field driver and pound keeper, **49:26.**
　Payment by owner, **49:27.**
　Third person taking up animals at large, **49:24.**
　Warrant for damages by impounded animals, fee, **262:34.**
Field drivers.
　Appointment, **49:22.**
　Beasts at large, taking up, **49:24.**
　Fees, **49:26.**
　General fields, selection by proprietors, **179:21.**
　Pound keeper, treated, **49:28.**
　Powers and duties, **49:24-49:28, 49:39.**
　Premises as pounds, **49:28.**
Fines and penalties.
　Dog, penalty for not confining, **140:164.**
　Injury to pound, **49:23.**
　Rescue of distrained or impounded beast, **49:40.**
General fields, selection of field drivers by proprietors, **179:21.**
Health inspector, appointment of full-time, **41:102B.**
Injuring pounds, penalty, **49:23.**
Keeper.
　Appointment, **49:22.**
　Fees, **49:26.**
　Field driver, **49:28.**
　Notice. See within this heading, "Notice to owner or keeper."
Labor and employment.
　Municipal officers and employees. See within this heading, "Municipal officers and employees."

POUNDS —Cont'd
Mules, **49:24, 49:25.**
Municipal officers and employees.
　Field drivers. See within this heading, "Field drivers."
　Keeper. See within this heading, "Keeper."
Notice to owner or keeper, **49:33.**
　Demand of distrainer of animal doing damage, **49:31.**
　Sale of impounded beasts, **49:37.**
　Unknown owner, notice, **49:34.**
Penalties.
　Fines and penalties. See within this heading, "Fines and penalties."
Posting or publication of notice.
　Impounding, **49:34.**
　Sale of impounded beasts, **49:37.**
Repairs and maintenance.
　Establishment and maintenance. See within this heading, "Establishment and maintenance."
Replevin.
　See REPLEVIN.
Rescue of distrained or impounded beast, **49:39, 49:40.**
Sale of impounded beasts, **49:37.**
　Damage, taking or impounding of beasts doing. See within this heading, "Damage, taking or impounding of beasts doing."
　Disposition of proceeds, **49:38.**
Sunday, taking up and impounding animals at large, **49:24, 49:25.**
Unknown owners, notice, **49:34.**
Warrant for damage by impounded animals, fee, **262:34.**

POVERTY.
See POOR PERSONS.

POWDERS.
Distribution of injurious medicines, penalty, **270:3.**
Incapacitating powders, commission of crime using, **269:10C.**

POWER AND POWER PLANTS.
Atomic energy.
　See ATOMIC ENERGY.
Energy facilities siting.
　See ENERGY FACILITIES SITING.
Gas.
　See GAS AND ELECTRIC COMPANIES.
New England power pool.
　See NEW ENGLAND POWER POOL.

POWER CORPORATIONS.
Petition to general court, **3:5.**

POWER OF ATTORNEY.
Health care proxies, **201D:16.**

POWER PUNCHES.
Minors under sixteen not to work
on certain machines, **149:61.**

**POWERS OF APPOINTMENT
AND DISPOSAL.**
Acknowledgment of release of
powers, **204:28.**
Confirmation of land title without
registration, petition, **185:26A.**
Conveyances subject,
183:49-183:51.
Discharge and release.
Release and disclaimers. See
within this heading,
"Releases and disclaimers."
Disclaimers.
Releases and disclaimers. See
within this heading,
"Releases and disclaimers."
Divorce or annulment of marriage
as revoking, **191:9.**
Eminent domain, taking of
property subject to power,
79:24-79:26.
Estate taxes.
Inclusion in taxable estate,
65C:2.
Liability for taxes by person in
possession, **65C:14.**
Foreign fiduciaries, powers as
affecting payments, **199A:2.**
Gifts to minors, transfer by
exercise of power of
appointment, **201A:4.**
Intent of creator, fulfillment,
191:1B.
Liberal construction of statutes
pertaining to release of
powers, **204:33.**
Marriage as not revoking will
exercising, **191:9.**
Mentally ill or retarded person,
power vested in, may be
exercised by guardian, **201:45.**
Mortgage of property subject,
183:49-183:51.
Perpetuities, rule against,
184A:1-184A:4, 184A:6.
Probate and Family Court.
Record of release, **204:28.**
Sale subject to power,
183:49-183:61.
Registration of title, holder may
petition, **185:26.**
Releases and disclaimers,
204:27-204:36.
Acknowledgment, **204:28.**

**POWERS OF APPOINTMENT
AND DISPOSAL** —Cont'd
Releases and disclaimers —Cont'd
Effect of releases or provisions
pertaining to releases,
204:29, 204:35.
Execution, **204:28.**
Extinguishment of power,
191A:7.
Form, **204:28.**
Instruments included in word
"release," **204:31.**
Interests acquired by exercise or
nonexercise of powers,
disclaimer, **191A:2.**
Liberal construction of statute
concerning releases, **204:33.**
Manner, **204:28.**
Notice, **204:28.**
Partial release, **204:28, 204:30.**
Powers subject, **204:27.**
Real property interests, powers
of appointment, etc., as for
purposes of disclaimer,
191A:1.
Recording, **204:28.**
Restraint of alienation or
anticipation, effect of
provisions with respect to
releases, **204:32.**
Separability of statutory
provisions concerning
releases, **204:36.**
Two or more persons, release
powers exercisable, **204:30.**
Restraint of alienation or
anticipation, effect of
provisions, involving, **204:32.**
Sale.
See POWERS OF SALE.
Separability of statutory
provisions concerning release
of powers of appointment,
204:36.
Taxes.
Estate taxes. See within this
heading, "Estate taxes."
Wills.
Exercise of powers, **191:1A,
191:9.**
General bequest exercising
power, **191:1A.**
Marriage of testator, will
exercising not revoked,
191:9.

POWERS OF ATTORNEY.
Assignment of wages, execution by
attorney not permissible,
154:3.
Automobiles.
Motor vehicles. See within this
heading, "Motor vehicles."

POWERS OF ATTORNEY
—Cont'd
Compulsory motor vehicle liability
insurance, cancellation,
90:34K.
Durable power of attorney act,
201B:1-201B:7.
Evidence of delivery, record, **183:5.**
Express company, appointment of
general agent for foreign
company, **159:5-159:7.**
Fees.
Recording, **262:34.**
Registration by land court,
262:39.
Forgery, **267:1, 267:5.**
Indexing of record, **36:27.**
Insurance agents and brokers,
Managing General Agents Act,
175:177G.
Motor vehicles.
Appointment of registrar as
attorney, motor vehicle
operation by nonresident,
90:3A.
Compulsory motor vehicle
liability insurance,
cancellation, **90:34K.**
Sales contract, invalidity,
255B:20.
Nonresidents.
Motor vehicle operation as
appointment of registrar as
attorney, **90:3A.**
Service of process, appointment
of agents, **227:5.**
Premium finance agreement,
provisions prohibited,
255C:16.
Process and service of process.
Service of process. See within
this heading, "Service of
process."
Real estate brokers' and
salesmen's registration law
not applicable, **112:87QQ.**
Real property, execution of
statement as to breach of
condition, **184:19.**
Reciprocal insurance exchanges.
See RECIPROCAL INSURANCE
EXCHANGES.
Registered land.
Dealing, **185:110.**
Fees for registration by land
court, **262:39.**
Rent, tender to attorney for
landlord, **186:11.**
Retail installment sales
agreement, provisions
prohibited, **255D:10.**

POWERS OF ATTORNEY
—Cont'd
Service of process, **223:39B.**
Foreign corporation's power of attorney to receive, **181:3, 181:4.**
Nonresidents, appointment of agents for service of process, **227:5.**
Taxpayer's right to representation in in-person interviews with revenue department employees, **62C:80.**
Uniform Durable Power of Attorney Act, adoption, **201B:1-201B:7.**
Uttering forged power of attorney, **267:5.**
Veterans' services, commissioner, **115:2.**

POWERS OF SALE, 183:49-183:51.
Fiduciaries, determination of right to exercise power of sale, **240:27, 240:28.**
Mortgage foreclosure.
See MORTGAGE FORECLOSURE.
Registration of land titles.
Assurance fund not liable for improper exercise, **185:107.**
Trust with power of sale, notation, **185:73.**

POWS/MIA DAY.
Governor proclamation, **6:15BBB.**

PRACTICAL ART CLASSES.
Definition of vocational education and schools, **74:1.**
Federal funds for vocational education and schools, **74:14A.**
Towns may establish and maintain vocational education and schools, **74:14.**

PRACTICAL CONSTRUCTION.
Sales contract, **106:2-208.**

PRACTICAL NURSES.
See NURSES AND NURSING SERVICES.

PRACTICAL NURSING EDUCATION WEEK.
Annual observance of practical nursing education week, **6:15UU.**

PRACTICE ACT, 231:1 et seq.

PRACTICE OF DENTISTRY.
See DENTISTS.

PRACTICE OF LAW, 221:37-221:52.
See ATTORNEYS AT LAW.

PRACTICE OF MEDICINE, 112:2-112:12A.
See PHYSICIANS AND SURGEONS.

PRACTICE SCHOOLS.
State colleges, maintenance in connection, **73:3.**

PRAYERS.
Schools, **71:1A, 71:1B.**

PRECEDING SECTION.
Statutory reference, **4:7.**

PRECEPTS.
Criminal case.
Fees for service of process, **262:8, 262:21.**
Magistrate or court in criminal cases, return, **279:39.**
Return of expense of officer of under oath, **262:47.**
Fees.
Service, **262:8, 262:21.**
Return to magistrate or court in criminal cases, **279:39.**
Sheriffs and their deputies to serve, **37:11.**

PRECINCTS.
Elections.
See ELECTIONS.

PRECIOUS METALS.
Sales tax exemption for certain metals, **64H:6.**

PREDATING.
See ANTEDATING.

PREFERENCES AND PRIORITIES.
Absentee persons, appointment of receiver, **200:5.**
Agricultural incentive areas, priorities upon purchase of land, **40L:8.**
AIDS research and treatment, funding priorities, **111:2E.**
Appeal.
See APPEAL AND REVIEW.
Arbors, priority in allotment of vacant lands, **20:15.**
Attachment of property.
See ATTACHMENT OF PROPERTY.
Bailee and conditional vendor, priority between, **255:35.**
Bankruptcy.
See INSOLVENCY AND BANKRUPTCY.
Child support, priority of order of income assignment, **119A:12.**
Civil service.
See CIVIL SERVICE.

PREFERENCES AND PRIORITIES —Cont'd
Claims in settlement of estates by receivers, **206:31.**
Condominium common expense liens, priority of, **183A:6.**
Contracts.
See CONTRACTS AND AGREEMENTS.
Cotenant's lien for taxes paid, **60:86, 60:98.**
Creditor under later attachment, remedies, **236:31.**
Credit unions.
See CREDIT UNIONS.
Domicile and residence.
Free employment offices, preferences as to residents of Commonwealth, **149:164.**
Hiring for public works projects, preference for residents.
See PUBLIC WORKS.
Elderly persons, acceleration of speedy trial, **231:59F.**
Electricians and plumbers and gas fitters exam, preference for veterans, **141:2A, 142:4.**
Employment security.
See EMPLOYMENT SECURITY.
Executors.
See EXECUTORS AND ADMINISTRATORS.
Exhaustion of estate assets, preferred claims, payments as bar to others, **197:5.**
Free employment offices, preference to residents, **149:164.**
Hiring by school committees, **112:23E.**
Homestead as affecting liens or mortgages, **188:1, 188:5, 188:6.**
Insolvency.
See INSOLVENCY AND BANKRUPTCY.
Insurance.
See INSURANCE.
Labor.
See LABOR AND WORKFORCE DEVELOPMENT.
Liens.
See LIENS AND ENCUMBRANCES.
Mechanics' liens.
See MECHANICS' LIENS.
Medical expenses, preferences in case of insolvency, **198:1.**
Mortgages.
See MORTGAGES AND DEEDS OF TRUST.

**PREFERENCES AND
PRIORITIES** —Cont'd
Open-end credit plan secured by
mortgages of residential real
estate, **183:28B.**
Public works.
See PUBLIC WORKS.
Rate for such year, defined,
121A:10.
Real property, priority of open-end
credit plans secured by
mortgages of residential
property, **183:28B.**
Residence.
Domicile and residence. See
within this heading,
"Domicile and residence."
School committees, priorities in
hiring, **112:23E.**
Secured transactions.
See SECURED
TRANSACTIONS.
Set-off debt collection, **62D:13.**
Speedy trial.
See SPEEDY TRIAL.
State purchase of supplies and
equipment, **7:22, 7:23A.**
Superior court, precedence of
certain prosecutions, **212:24.**
Telephone.
See TELEPHONE AND
TELEGRAPH COMPANIES.
Unemployment compensation.
See EMPLOYMENT
SECURITY.
Urban redevelopment plans,
actions for judicial review of
disapproval, **121A:6C.**
Veterans.
See VETERANS AND
VETERANS'
ORGANIZATIONS.
Water pollution control priority
list, **21:26A.**
Workers' compensation, claims,
152:52B, 175:46A.
Zoning actions, judicial review,
40A:17.

**PREFERRED PROVIDER
ARRANGEMENTS, 176I:1 et
seq.**
Accreditation, consumer
protection, **176O:1 to
176O:17.**
See HEALTH INSURANCE
CONSUMER
PROTECTION.
Annual reports, **176I:7.**
Application, **176I:10.**
Assessments, **176I:11.**
Bond of surety, **176I:6.**

**PREFERRED PROVIDER
ARRANGEMENTS** —Cont'd
Commissioner, defined, **176I:1.**
Consumer protection, **176O:1 to
176O:17.**
See HEALTH INSURANCE
CONSUMER
PROTECTION.
Covered person, defined, **176I:1.**
Covered services, defined, **176I:1.**
Definitions, **176I:1.**
Discrimination, **176I:4.**
Genetic information and testing,
176I:4A.
Emergency care, defined, **176I:1.**
Financial and utilization records,
176I:5.
Guarantees that obligations will
be performed, **176I:6.**
Health benefit plan, defined,
176I:1.
Health care provider, defined,
176I:1.
Health care services, defined,
176I:1.
Minimum requirements, **176I:3.**
Organization, defined, **176I:1.**
Payment of assessments, **176I:11.**
Payment of provider, arrangement
provisions, **176I:2.**
Powers of commissioner, **176I:8.**
Preferred provider arrangement,
defined, **176I:1.**
Preferred provider, defined, **176I:1.**
Records, **176I:5.**
Rights of insureds.
Health insurance consumer
protection, **176O:1 to
176O:17.**
See HEALTH INSURANCE
CONSUMER
PROTECTION.
Standardized insurance claim
forms to be produced, **176I:8.**
Standards, **176I:2.**
Utilization and financial records,
176I:5.

**PREFERRED STOCK.
See CORPORATIONS.**

PREGNANCY.
Abortion.
See ABORTION.
Accident and sickness insurance,
175:47E, 175:47F.
Advertising means of preventing,
272:20, 272:21.
Assistance, **118:2.**
Birth control.
See BIRTH CONTROL.
Births.
See BIRTHS.

PREGNANCY —Cont'd
Blanket, general, accident or
sickness policy, benefits for
care, **175:47E, 175:47F.**
Childbirth, hospital stays after
in-patient deliveries, **32A:17C,
118E:10A, 175:47F, 176A:8H,
176B:4H, 176G:4I.**
Contraceptives.
See CONTRACEPTIVES.
Correctional institutions.
See CORRECTIONAL
INSTITUTIONS.
Death sentence, effect of
pregnancy, **279:61, 279:62.**
Fetal deaths.
See FETAL DEATH.
Health maintenance organizations,
176G:4.
Hospitals and health care
facilities, **175:47F, 176A:8H.**
Hospital service plan, benefits to
be provided, **175:47F,
176A:8H.**
Illegitimate children, action to
establish paternity may be
instituted during pregnancy,
209C:14.
Insurance for medical care,
175:47D.
Kits, instructional brochures,
requirements, **94:192A.**
Maintenance services,
establishment, **111:51B.**
Maternity leave, provisions,
149:105D, 149:180.
Medical assistance division,
118E:10.
Medical care and assistance
programs, establishment,
111:24D.
Medical certificate for marriage,
207:28A.
Medical corporations and
associations, **176B:4H.**
Medical service corporations,
benefits for treatment of
pregnant women, **175:47C,
176A:8B, 176B:4C, 176B:4F,
176B:4H, 176G:4.**
Midwives.
See NURSES AND NURSING
SERVICES.
Non-profit hospital service
corporations, **176A:8G.**
Nurse-midwifery, practice,
112:80C, 112:80D.
Obstetrics.
See OBSTETRICS AND
GYNECOLOGY.
Postpartum care.
See POSTPARTUM CARE.

PREGNANCY —Cont'd
Prenatal, childbirth, and postpartum care, **32A:17C, 118E:10A, 176A:8H, 176B:4H, 176G:4I.**
Public health department, assistance programs, **111:24C.**
Public school students' pregnancy as ground for expulsion or other disciplinary action, **71:84.**
Tanning facilities, **111:209.**
Unwed mothers, **119:23A, 119:23B.**
See UNWED MOTHERS.
Wasserman test for pregnant women, **111:121A.**
X-rays, safety precautions in using, **111:5J.**

PREJUDICE OR BIAS.
Appeal.
See APPEAL AND REVIEW.
Change of venue, **223:13.**
Eminent domain proceedings, acceptance of payment as prejudice to right to claim larger sum, **79:7G.**
Hate crimes.
See HATE CRIMES.
Jurors, examination, **234:28.**
Vacation of arbitration award in labor dispute on ground of arbitrator's partiality, **150C:11.**

PRELIMINARY ELECTIONS.
See ELECTIONS.

PRELIMINARY ENGINEERING REPORTS.
Massachusetts Water Resources Authority, **21:33B.**

PRELIMINARY INJUNCTIONS.
See INJUNCTIONS.

PRELIMINARY PROJECT IMPACT REPORTS.
Hazardous waste.
See HAZARDOUS WASTE FACILITIES SITING.

PREMATURELY BORN CHILDREN, 111:67A, 111:67C, 111:67E.
See BIRTHS.

PREMEDITATION.
Murder, element, **265:1.**

PREMIUM FINANCE AGENCIES, 255C:11-255C:13.
See INSURANCE PREMIUM FINANCE AGENCIES.

PREMIUMS.
Bonds.
See BONDS AND UNDERTAKINGS.
Industrial finance agency.
See INDUSTRIAL FINANCE AGENCY.
Insurance.
See INSURANCE.
Trading stamps.
See TRADING STAMPS.
Workers' compensation.
See WORKERS' COMPENSATION.

PRENATAL CARE.
See PREGNANCY.

PREPACKAGED COMMODITIES.
Brands and labels, **94:117, 94:181.**
Weights and measures.
Label to show weight, **94:181.**
Meat, poultry or fish, **98:56B.**

PREPAYMENT.
See ADVANCES.

PRESCRIPTION DRUGS, CATASTROPHIC INSURANCE PROGRAM, 19A:39, 19A:40.

PRESCRIPTIONS.
See PHARMACISTS AND PHARMACIES.

PRESCRIPTIVE TITLE.
Adverse possession.
See ADVERSE POSSESSION.
Easements.
See EASEMENTS.

PRESENCE.
See ABSENCE OR PRESENCE.

PRESENTENCE INVESTIGATION.
See SENTENCE AND PUNISHMENT.

PRESENTMENT, DISHONOR, AND PROTEST.
Check, notice of dishonor of, **266:37.**
Checks.
Dishonored check fees.
Credit unions, **171:41A.**
Fees for dishonored checks, **167D:3.**
Negotiable instruments. See within this heading, "Negotiable instruments."
Documentary drafts.
Bank deposits and collections.
Duty to send for presentment, **106:4-501.**

PRESENTMENT, DISHONOR, AND PROTEST —Cont'd
Documentary drafts —Cont'd
Bank deposits and collections —Cont'd
On arrival drafts, **106:4-502.**
Document of title, dishonor of as affecting tender of delivery, **106:2-503.**
Evidence.
Notaries public, certificate as prima facie evidence of protest and notice, **107:13.**
Fees for notice of protest, **262:41.**
Filing fee for notice of protest, **262:41.**
Forms.
Protest, **106:3-106, 106:3-505, 106:3-508, 106:4-210, 106:4-501, 106:4-504, 106:4-509.**
Fraudulent checks, notice of dishonor, **266:37.**
Leases under Commercial Code, dishonor of check after delivery, **106:2A-304, 106:2A-305.**
Letters of credit, **106:5-108 to 106:5-111.**
Negotiable instruments.
Defined, **106:3-501.**
Evidence, **106:3-105.**
Excused presentment, **106:3-504.**
Notice of dishonor, **106:3-504.**
Notice.
Evidence, **106:3-105.**
Excuse.
Presentment, **106:3-404.**
Procedure, **106:3-503.**
Protest defined, **106:3-505.**
Rules governing, **106:3-502.**
Presumption, **106:3-505.**
Protest defined, **106:3-505.**
Rules governing, **106:3-501, 106:3-502.**
Special provisions, **106:3-502.**
Warranties, **106:3-407.**
Notaries public.
Certificate as prima facie evidence of protest and notice, **107:13.**
Fee for notice of protest for nonpayment, **262:41.**
Notice and knowledge.
Fraudulent checks, notice of dishonor, **266:37.**
Negotiable instruments. See within this heading, "Negotiable instruments."
Registration of land titles.
See REGISTRATION OF LAND TITLES.

PRESENTMENT, DISHONOR, AND PROTEST —Cont'd

Sales, effect of dishonor on check, **106:2-511.**

Tender of delivery, dishonor of document of title as affecting, **106:2-503.**

Tender of delivery of goods, dishonor of document of title as affecting, **106:2-503.**

Title.

Document of title, dishonor as affecting tender of delivery, **106:2-503.**

Transferability of title obtained in exchange for check later dishonored, **106:2-403.**

Transferability of title obtained in exchange for check later dishonored, **106:2-403.**

PRESERVATIVES.

Frozen desserts or dessert mix, **94:650.**

Misbranding, **94:187.**

PRESERVES AND SANCTUARIES.
See FISH AND GAME.

PRESIDENTIAL ELECTORS.

Absence from meeting of, filling vacancy in case, **54:138.**

Acceptance in writing, **53:8.**

Appointment.

Election officers, **54:11, 54:12, 54:16.**

Of electors, **US Const Art 2 Sec 1 cl 2.**

Supervisors of elections, appointment, **54:23.**

Ballots, **US Const Amend 12.**

Contents, **54:42.**

Electors, names on ballots, **54:41.**

Form, **54:42.**

Marking, **54:78.**

Matter to appear, **53:8, 54:43.**

Names of presidential and vice-presidential candidates whose names do not appear on official printed ballot, voting for electors pledged, **54:78A.**

New residents, **54:41, 54:42, 54:66, 54:107.**

Order of appearance of names of candidates, **54:43A.**

Write-in votes for electors, **54:42.**

Biennial state election, chosen, **54:151.**

PRESIDENTIAL ELECTORS —Cont'd

Canvassing of vote for president of the United States, **US Const Amend 12.**

Certification, **54:118.**

Clerks of cities and towns, certification of list of write-in candidates, **54:78A.**

Illegally or improperly certified voter, **51:48, 51:49.**

New residents. See within this heading, "New residents, voting."

Nomination by state convention, contents of certificate, **53:8.**

Omission or error, issuance of certificate in event, **51:59.**

Qualified voters, certification, **54:132.**

Challenged new resident voter, administration of oath, **54:85.**

Compensation, **54:149.**

Congress may appoint time of choosing electors, **US Const Art 2 Sec 1 cl 4.**

Constitution of the United States. See CONSTITUTION OF THE UNITED STATES.

Contesting, **54:119, 54:120.**

Copies.

New residents, posting of copies of law prescribing penalties, **51:12.**

Summons to person illegally qualified as voter, **51:48.**

Death, procedure in case, **54:138.**

Domicile and residence.

New residents. See within this heading, "New residents, voting."

Requirements to vote for presidential electors, **51:1F.**

Electoral college, **US Const Art 2 Sec 1.**

Envelopes and containers, self-incrimination in election contest, **54:120.**

Examination and certification of returns of votes, **54:118.**

Examination of applicants and witnesses, **51:33, 51:49.**

Examination of voters, **51:33, 51:44.**

Illegally or improperly certified voter, **51:49.**

Complaint, **51:48.**

New residents. See within this heading, "New residents, voting."

General court, when to be chosen, **54:138.**

PRESIDENTIAL ELECTORS —Cont'd

House of representatives of US, member cannot be elector, **US Const Art 2 Sec 1 cl 2.**

Journal of proceedings, **54:148.**

Lists.

Candidates, requirement as to posting lists, **54:49.**

Voting lists, **51:60.**

Write-in votes for electors, lists of candidates, **54:78A.**

Majority vote as necessary to elect President or Vice-President, **US Const Amend 12.**

Marking of ballots, **54:78.**

Meetings, **54:148.**

Mileage allowance, **54:149.**

Mistake, omission, or error, issuance of certificate in event, **51:59.**

New residents, voting.

Affidavits of registration, **51:36, 51:42.**

Annual register, applicability of law, **51:37.**

Ballot boxes, **54:66.**

Ballots, **54:41, 54:42.**

Business hours, receiving applications during, **51:33.**

Candidates, requirement as to posting lists, **54:49.**

Certificates and certification.

Ballots cast at polling place, certification, **54:107.**

Error or omission, issuance of certificate in case, **51:59.**

Governor to issue certificate of election, **54:118.**

Illegal or improper certification of voter, **51:48, 51:49.**

Number of qualified voters, **51:61.**

Qualified voters, certificate, **54:132.**

Challenged voter, administration of oath, **54:85.**

Clerical errors, proceedings, **51:59.**

Close of registration, acceptance of applications after, **51:34.**

Count of voters and ballots cast, **54:105.**

Election officers.

Appointment, **54:11, 54:12, 54:16.**

Place of registration and voting, application of law, **51:3.**

Supervisors of election, appointment, **54:23.**

PRESIDENTIAL ELECTORS
—Cont'd
New residents, voting —Cont'd
Election officers —Cont'd
Terms, **54:13.**
Vacancies, filling, **54:16.**
Examination of voters.
Complaint, **51:48.**
Oath or affirmation, **51:33,
51:44.**
Personal appearance required of
applicant, **51:42.**
Place of registration and voting,
application of law, **51:3.**
Posting of copies of law
prescribing penalties, **51:12.**
Revision and correction of
registers, **51:38.**
Seals for polling places, use and
custody, **54:30.**
Striking name from register,
51:49.
Time or date.
Applications to qualify, **51:26.**
Applications to vote, **51:32.**
Polling places, preparation,
54:24.
Sessions for registration, time
for holding, **51:26, 51:28.**
Total vote sheet, entries, **54:105.**
Voting machines, **54:34.**
Nomination by state convention,
contents of certificate, **53:8.**
Nomination papers, time for filing,
53:10.
Nominees, pledge of party
regularity required, **53:8.**
Notice and hearing in contest,
54:119.
Number.
Qualified voters, number, **51:61.**
To be elected, **54:151.**
Oath or affirmation.
Voting. See within this heading,
"Voting for electors."
Office holders under United States
cannot be electors, **US Const
Art 2 Sec 1 cl 2.**
Place of registration and voting,
51:3.
Poll or other tax, payment not to
be prerequisite to voting for
electors, **US Const Amend
24.**
Primaries.
See PRESIDENTIAL
PRIMARIES.
Proclamation of result, **54:118,
54:119.**
Qualifications.
Electors, **US Const Art 2 Sec 1
cl 2; Amend 14 Sec 3.**

PRESIDENTIAL ELECTORS
—Cont'd
Qualifications —Cont'd
Voters to vote for electors, **51:26,
51:28, 54:132.**
Records.
Examination and Certification,
54:118, 54:119.
Proceedings of presidential
electors, **54:148.**
Voting for electors. See within
this heading, "Voting for
electors."
Registration.
Applications accepted after close
of registration, **51:34.**
New residents, **51:36, 51:38,
51:42.**
Place, **51:3.**
Revision and correction, **51:28.**
Sessions, **51:26, 51:28.**
Residence.
Domicile and residence. See
within this heading,
"Domicile and residence."
Results as to, proclamation,
54:118.
Secretary of State.
Contents and filing of lists of
electors, **54:78A.**
Meeting of electors, duties with
respect, **54:148.**
Self-incrimination, election
contest, **54:120.**
Senator of United States cannot be
elector, **US Const Art 2 Sec 1
cl 2.**
Supervisors of elections,
appointment, **54:23.**
Time.
Congress may appoint time of
choosing electors, **US Const
Art 2 Sec 1 cl 4.**
Electing, time, **54:151.**
New residents, voting by. See
within this heading, "New
residents, voting."
Nomination papers, time for
filing, **53:10.**
Transmission of record of votes,
54:112.
Vacancies, how filled, **54:16,
54:138.**
Voting by electors, how given and
transmitted, **US Const
Amend 12.**
Voting for electors.
Candidates for president and
vice president whose names
do not appear on official
printing ballot, voting for
electors pledged, **54:78A.**

PRESIDENTIAL ELECTORS
—Cont'd
Voting for electors —Cont'd
Domicile and residence,
requirements, **51:1F.**
List of candidates, posting,
54:49.
Manner of voting, **54:78, 54:151.**
Names.
Ballots, **54:41.**
Certification of persons
qualified to vote, **54:132.**
Count of names after polls
close, **54:105.**
Issuance of certificate in case
of omission or error,
51:59.
Striking name from register,
51:49.
Transmission of voting lists,
51:60.
New residents, count of voters
and ballots cast, **54:105.**
Oath or affirmation.
Challenged voter, **54:85.**
Examination of applicants,
51:33, 51:44.
Posting of copies of laws
prescribing penalties,
51:12.
Poll or other tax, payment not to
be prerequisite to vote for
electors, **US Const Amend
24.**
Posting copies of laws
prescribing penalties, **51:12.**
Records.
General register, applicability
of law requiring records to
be kept, **51:36.**
Total vote sheet, entry of
separate records, **54:105.**
Transmission of records,
54:112.
Use of voting machines, **54:34.**
Write-in votes for electors. See
within this heading,
"Write-in votes for electors."
Voting machines, **54:34.**
Wards and voting precincts,
improperly or illegally
certified votes for presidential
electors, **51:49.**
Witnesses.
Contest of election of
presidential electors, **54:120.**
Examination of applicants and
witnesses, **51:33, 51:49.**
Write-in votes for electors.
Ballots to contain blank space
for use in voting, **54:42.**

PRESIDENTIAL ELECTORS
—Cont'd
Write-in votes for electors —Cont'd
Lists of candidates for electors,
contents, filing, **54:78A.**
Voting for, effect, **54:78.**

**PRESIDENTIAL PRIMARIES,
53:70A-53:70H.**
Absentee ballots, **53:34, 54:86.**
Ballot boxes, preparation,
54:135A.
Ballots.
Absentee ballots, **53:34, 54:86.**
Arrangement of names of
candidates, **53:70E.**
Boxes, preparation of ballot
boxes, **54:135A.**
Delegates for president,
preference, **53:70E.**
Manner of placing candidates'
names, **53:70E.**
Names of candidates, **53:70B,
53:70E, 53:70F.**
Nondelivery, provision in case,
53:32.
Political committees, names of
candidates, **53:70E.**
Preparation, **53:32, 53:70E.**
Primary ballots, placing of
names, **53:70B, 53:70E.**
Secretary of state, duties,
53:70E.
State ballot law commission. See
within this heading, "State
ballot law commission."
Voters' preference, **53:70E.**
What candidates' names to
appear, **53:70E.**
Candidates.
Ballots, arrangement of
candidates' names, **53:70E.**
Certificates, **53:70F.**
Preferred candidate, **53:70E,
53:70I.**
Signatures for candidates,
review, **55B:6.**
Time for submission of lists,
53:70E.
"Veteran," candidate using
designation in nomination
papers, **53:70D.**
Canvass of returns, **53:70F.**
Voters' preference, **53:70E.**
Certificates and certification.
Nomination papers, certification,
53:7, 55B:5.
Objections to certification of
nomination, **55B:5.**
Registrars' meeting dates for
certification of candidate,
53:46.

PRESIDENTIAL PRIMARIES
—Cont'd
Certificates and certification
—Cont'd
Successful candidates,
certificates, **53:70F.**
Change or cancellation of party
enrollment, **53:38.**
Counting of preferential votes,
53:70E.
District-wide recounts, **54:135.**
Date.
Time and date. See within this
heading, "Time and date."
Delegates.
At large delegates, voting,
53:70I.
Names of candidates for
delegate at large and
alternate to appear on
ballot, **53:70E.**
National conventions, delegates
to, **53:70B-53:70H, 57:1.**
Nomination of candidates for
delegate at large, **53:70D.**
Nonpolitical parties, selection,
53:117-53:120.
Presidential preference of
delegates to appear on
ballots, **53:70E.**
Selection, **53:1, 53:70B.**
Direct plurality vote, **53:70B.**
District delegates, nomination of
candidates, **53:70D.**
Elections.
Declaration of result of
presidential primaries,
53:70F.
Nomination papers, number of
signatures required on
presidential primaries,
53:70D.
Primary ballot, placing of
names, **53:70B, 53:70E.**
Selectman or town moderator
ineligible to act as election
officer, **54:15.**
First roll call vote, how to vote,
53:70I.
Laws applicable, **53:70H.**
Lists of voters, **51:55.**
Misspelling or inaccuracy, voter's
presidential preference,
53:70E.
Names of candidates to appear on
ballot, **53:70B, 53:70E,
53:70F.**
National convention, delegates to.
Delegates. See within this
heading, "Delegates."
Nomination for president, canvass
and certification of votes cast,
53:70F.

PRESIDENTIAL PRIMARIES
—Cont'd
Nomination papers, **53:70D.**
Certification, **53:7, 55B:5.**
Elimination of restriction as to
number of signatures from
one county, **53:70D, 53:70E.**
Last day for filing, **53:48.**
Laws applicable, **53:70H.**
Statement on nomination papers
of candidate for reelection to
state committee, **53:70D.**
Time for submission, **53:7,
53:46.**
Veteran, candidate using
designation in nomination
papers. See within this
heading, "Veteran, candidate
using designation in
nomination papers."
Nonpolitical parties, selection of
delegates, **53:117-53:120.**
Notice.
Secretary of state.
Wards and precincts, notice of
holding of presidential
primary, **53:70C.**
To successful candidates, **53:70F.**
Number of delegates, **53:70B.**
Objections to certification of
nomination, **55B:5.**
Political committees.
See POLITICAL COMMITTEES.
Precincts.
Wards, voting precincts, and
town political committees.
See within this heading,
"Wards, voting precincts,
and town political
committees."
Preferential votes, counting of.
Counting of preferential votes.
See within this heading,
"Counting of preferential
votes."
Preferred candidate, **53:70E,
53:70I.**
Recounts, **54:135.**
Registration.
Dates of meetings for
certification of candidates,
53:46.
Sessions, **51:26-51:28.**
Removal, time for affidavit,
53:70E.
Requirements for voting, **53:70I.**
Results, **53:70F.**
Canvass of returns. See within
this heading, "Canvass of
returns."
Secretary of state.
Ballots, duties, **53:70E.**
Canvass of returns, **53:70F.**

PRESIDENTIAL PRIMARIES
—Cont'd
Secretary of state —Cont'd
Declaration of results, **53:70F.**
Delegates to national presidential conventions, time for giving notice as to number, **53:70B.**
Nomination papers, furnishing, **53:70D.**
Wards and precincts, notice of holding of presidential primary, **53:70C.**
Selection of delegates, **53:1, 53:70B.**
Signatures.
Nomination papers, number of signatures, **53:70D, 53:70E.**
Review, **55B:6.**
Speedy trial of actions under election laws, **231:59D.**
State ballot law commission, **55B:4.**
Decisions as to primaries, **55B:10.**
Signatures for candidates, review, **55B:6.**
State committeemen, election, **52:1.**
Time and date.
Candidates, time for submission of lists, **53:70E.**
Nomination papers, **53:7, 53:46, 53:48.**
Place of holding, **53:28, 53:70C.**
Town elections.
Authorization to change date, **53:28.**
Rescheduling in event of conflict with presidential primary, **39:9A, 39:10.**
Town political committees.
Wards, voting precincts, and town political committees. See within this heading, "Wards, voting precincts, and town political committees."
Vacancy, filling, **53:70G.**
Veteran, candidate using designation in nomination papers, **53:70D.**
Lists for voting, **51:55.**
Voting machines, preparation, **54:135A.**
Wards, voting precincts, and town political committees.
Election of committees, **52:2.**
Holding of primary by wards and precincts, **53:28, 53:70C.**

PRESIDENTIAL PRIMARIES
—Cont'd
Wards, voting precincts, and town political committees —Cont'd
Notice, **53:70C.**

PRESIDENT OF SENATE.
Massachusetts.
See GENERAL COURT.
United States.
See SENATE OF UNITED STATES.

PRESIDENT OF UNITED STATES.
Appointments by, **US Const Art 2 Sec 2 cl 2.**
Recess vacancies, filling of, **US Const Art 2 Sec 2 cl 3.**
Approval.
Consent. See within this heading, "Consent."
Ballots.
Electors.
See PRESIDENTIAL ELECTORS.
House of Representatives to choose President by, when, **US Const Amend 12.**
Primary.
See PRESIDENTIAL PRIMARIES.
Bills passed by Congress to be presented to, **US Const Art 1 Sec 7 cl 2.**
Canvassing of vote for, **US Const Amend 12.**
Commander in chief, **US Const Art 2 Sec 2 cl 1.**
Compensation not to be altered during term of office, **US Const Art 2 Sec 1 cl 7.**
Congress of United States.
See CONGRESS OF UNITED STATES.
Consent.
Bills passed by Congress, **US Const Art 1 Sec 7 cl 2.**
Orders, resolutions of Congress, **US Const Art 1 Sec 7 cl 3.**
Death, **US Const Art 2 Sec 1 cl 6; 20th Amend, 25th Amend.**
Disability of President, person to act in case of, **US Const Art 2 Sec 1 cl 6; Amend 25.**
Election.
Canvassing of vote for, **US Const Amend 12.**
Certification of nomination, objections, **55B:5.**
Electors.
See PRESIDENTIAL ELECTORS.

PRESIDENT OF UNITED STATES —Cont'd
Election —Cont'd
House of Representatives, election by, **US Const Amend 12.**
More than once, **US Const Amend 22.**
Nomination of candidates, president's power to make, **US Const Art 2 Sec 2 cl 2.**
Primaries.
See PRESIDENTIAL PRIMARIES.
Signatures, review, **55B:6.**
Electors.
See PRESIDENTIAL ELECTORS.
Eligibility.
Qualifications. See within this heading, "Qualifications."
Emoluments not to be received by, **US Const Art 2 Sec 1 cl 7.**
Entertainment expenses, allowance to governor, **6:8.**
Executive powers vested in, **US Const Art 2 Sec 1 cl 1.**
House of representatives.
Election of president by house of representatives, **US Const Amend 12.**
Electoral college, United States representative not to be member of, **US Const Art 2 Sec 1 cl 2.**
Impeachment, power of, **US Const Art 1 Sec 2 cl 5.**
Succession to office of President, powers as to, **US Const Amend 20 Sec 4.**
Impeachment.
Chief Justice to preside at trial, **US Const Art 1 Sec 3 cl 6.**
Pardon may not be granted, **US Const Art 2 Sec 2 cl 1.**
Removal, **US Const Art 2 Sec 4.**
Joint resolutions of Congress to be presented to, **US Const Art 1 Sec 7 cl 2.**
Message to Congress, **US Const Art 2 Sec 3.**
Nominations, power to make, **US Const Art 2 Sec 2 cl 2.**
Oath of office, **US Const Art 2 Sec 1 cl 8.**
Pardoning power, **US Const Art 2 Sec 2 cl 1.**
Presidents Day, annual observance, **6:15VV.**
Primaries.
See PRESIDENTIAL PRIMARIES.

PRESIDENT OF UNITED STATES —Cont'd

Qualifications.

Age, **US Const Art 2 Sec 1 cl 5.**

Citizenship, **US Const Art 2 Sec 1 cl 5.**

Electors.

See PRESIDENTIAL ELECTORS.

Residence, **US Const Art 2 Sec 1 cl 5.**

Removal on conviction on impeachment, **US Const Art 2 Sec 4.**

Reprieves, power to grant, **US Const Art 2 Sec 2 cl 1.**

Senate, advice and consent of, when necessary, **US Const Art 2 Sec 2 cl 2.**

Succession to Presidency, **US Const Art 2 Sec 1 cl 6 and Amend 20 and Amend 25.**

Term of office, **US Const Art 2 Sec 2 cl 1.**

Beginning and ending of, **US Const Amend 20 Sec 1.**

Compensation not to be altered during, **US Const Art 2 Sec 1 cl 7.**

More than two terms, forbidden, **US Const Amend 22.**

Treaties, power to make, **US Const Art 2 Sec 2 cl 2.**

Vacancy in office.

Electors, **54:16, 54:138.**

Recess vacancies, power to fill, **US Const Art 2 Sec 2 cl 3.**

Succession to presidency in case of, **US Const Art 2 Sec 1 cl 6; 20th Amend, 25th Amend.**

Veto.

See VETO.

Vice-president of United States.

Acting as, circumstances requiring, **US Const Art 2 Sec 1 cl 6; 20th Amend, 25th Amend Sec 3.**

Succession to Presidency, **US Const Art 2 Sec 1 cl 6; 20th Amend, 25th Amend.**

PRESIDENT PRO TEMPORE.

Senate, **US Const Art 1 Sec 3 cl 5.**

PRESIDENTS DAY.

Proclamation of annual observance, **6:15VV.**

PRESS.

Freedom of press.

See SPEECH, FREEDOM OF.

PRESS —Cont'd

Newspapers.

See NEWSPAPERS.

PRESSES.

Counterfeiting, penalty for possession of press, **267:13, 267:20.**

Hours of labor, women and children, **149:56, 149:57, 149:66-149:68, 149:78.**

Industrial purposes, building used, **149:1.**

Minors under sixteen not to work, **149:61.**

Sanitary cloths for cleaning printing presses, **149:142, 149:180.**

PRESSURE TANKS.

Compressed air tanks, **146:34-146:41.**

See AIR, COMPRESSED.

Steam boilers.

See STEAM BOILERS AND ENGINES.

PRESSURE VESSELS, 146:1 et seq.

See STEAM BOILERS AND ENGINES.

PRESUMPTIONS AND BURDEN OF PROOF.

Abandoned, lost.

See ABANDONED, LOST, AND UNCLAIMED PROPERTY.

Abuse.

Evidence of present or past abuse as factor in child custody decision.

Presumption of unfitness, **208:31A, 209:38.**

Out of court statements by child abuse victims, unavailability, **233:81, 233:82.**

Acceptance of goods as placing burden on buyer to establish breach, **106:2-607.**

Administrators.

Executors and administrators.

See within this heading, "Executors and administrators."

Air pollution regulations, presumption of compliance with statute by filing, **111:142A.**

Antitrust laws, **93:3.**

Bad checks, **266:37.**

Banks and banking.

Deposits and collections.

Abandonment of deposit, presumption, **200A:3, 200A:5.**

PRESUMPTIONS AND BURDEN OF PROOF —Cont'd

Banks and banking —Cont'd

Fraud or embezzlement by bank officials, **266:53.**

Negotiable instruments.

Notice of dishonor, **106:3-505, 106:3-510.**

Board measure, presumed rule, **96:11A.**

Boats.

Ships and vessels. See within this heading, "Ships and vessels."

Bottles, unauthorized use of registered, **110:19.**

Breach of contract, acceptance of goods as placing burden on buyer to prove, **106:2-607.**

Building license, presumption as to acting without, **143:60.**

Carriers.

Affiliates and carriers, burden of proof as to reasonableness of dealings between, **159:34A.**

Increase in schedule of rates, carriers seeking, **159:20.**

Charitable gifts of land, enforceability of restrictions, **184:30.**

Charitable purposes, enforceability of restrictions on gifts of land, **184:30.**

Checks.

Bad checks, **266:37.**

Child custody.

Evidence of present or past abuse as factor in custody decision.

Presumption of unfitness, **208:31A, 209:38.**

Coal, presumption of excessiveness of noncombustible residue, **94:249E½.**

Commercial Code definitions, **106:1-201.**

Commitment of party or witness on presumption of perjury, **268:4.**

Common carriers.

Carriers. See within this heading, "Carriers."

Common disaster, presumption of survivorship as to deaths, **190A:1 et seq.**

Comparative negligence, burden of proof, **231:85.**

Competency to stand trial, **123:15.**

Consent.

Insured's consent to operation of vehicle by another, **231:85A, 231:85B, 231:85C.**

**PRESUMPTIONS AND
BURDEN OF PROOF**
—Cont'd

Consent —Cont'd

Unlawful taking of boats, vehicle or animal with presumed consent of owner, **266:63.**

Consumers' protection act, burden of proving exemptions, **93A:3.**

Consumption tax.

Use, consumption, or storage tax. See within this heading, "Use, consumption, or storage tax."

Contributory negligence, **231:85.**

Controlled substances law, allegations, presumptions, and proof in prosecutions as to violation, **277:38.**

Conveyances.

Deeds and conveyances. See within this heading, "Deeds and conveyances."

Corporation taxes, presumptions in determination, **63:38, 63:39A.**

Courts martial, presumption of jurisdiction, **33:80.**

Credit card offenses, **266:37B, 266:37C.**

Credit insurance combination policies, proof of loss provision, **175:117B.**

Credit, presumption as to signing of revolving credit agreement, **255D:1.**

Death, **200:13.**

Generally.

See DEATH.

Wrongful death, **231:85.**

Deeds and conveyances.

Delivery, **183:5.**

Fee simple, **183:13.**

Spouse, conveyance, **184:7.**

Delivery.

Life insurance policy, presumption from delivery, **175:186A.**

Recording, presumption of delivery, **183:5.**

Divorce action as defeated by prior filing of other actions, **208:22.**

Dog-bite actions, burden of proof, **140:155.**

Driving while intoxicated or under influence of liquor, percentage of alcohol in blood as proof, **90:24.**

Drugs, presumptions and proof under controlled substances law, **277:38.**

**PRESUMPTIONS AND
BURDEN OF PROOF**
—Cont'd

Due care by victim, presumption, **231:85.**

Elections, presumptions in criminal prosecutions, **50:8.**

Electric companies, reasonableness of arrangements with affiliated company, **164:94C.**

Entirety, tenancy by highest obtainable price in case of sale by fiduciary, **202:38.**

Environmental Protection Department licensee ownership of land, **183A:2.**

Executors and administrators.

Abandonment of bequests, **200A:2.**

Highest possible price obtainable for realty, **202:38.**

False claims against Commonwealth.

Preponderance of the evidence, **12:5L.**

Fee simple.

Conveyance or reservation, **183:13.**

Devise as giving, **191:18.**

Firearms and weapons.

Numbers defaced or altered, **269:11C.**

Police officers, presumption of licenses for firearms carried, **140:131G.**

Firemen and policemen.

Death or disability resulting from disease as suffered in line of duty, **32:94A.**

Licenses for firearms carried by police officers, **140:131G.**

Medical examination, effect of certain fire and police officers passing subsequent to employment, **32:94.**

Pensions for widows of fire fighters or police officers killed in performance of duty, applicability of statutory presumptions, **32:100.**

Gas and electric companies, reasonableness of arrangement with affiliated company, **164:94C.**

Harbor, burden of proving permit to ground or abandon vessels, **91:49.**

Hazardous waste management act, presumptions, **21C:10.**

Health care proxies.

See HEALTH CARE PROXIES.

**PRESUMPTIONS AND
BURDEN OF PROOF**
—Cont'd

Heirs, public administration of estate, burden of proof as to existence, **194:16.**

Highways and streets.

Trees as presumptively within highway boundary, **87:1.**

Trespass by parking vehicle on private way, burden of proof, **266:120A.**

Housing court department, presumption in favor of proceedings before, **185C:2.**

Husband and wife.

Conveyance or devise to husband and wife, **184:7.**

Joint ownership of motor vehicle, **90D:15A.**

Work and labor by married woman on own account, **209:4.**

Illegitimate children, proceedings to establish paternity, **209C:6, 209C:7.**

Indecent assault and battery, consent by child or minor, **265:13B.**

Indictment, presumptions not required to be alleged, **277:33.**

Inquests as to cause of death, persons deemed interested persons for purposes of attending, **38:8.**

Insurance.

Conditions precedent to attaching of policy or contract, presumption of performance, **175:186A.**

Credit insurance combination policies, proof of loss provision, **175:117B.**

Endowment insurance proceeds, presumption of abandonment, **200A:5A.**

Life insurance. See within this heading, "Life insurance."

International log rule, contracts for purchase and sale of logs presumed made on basis, **96:11A.**

Interstate Family Support Act, **209D:3-316.**

Investment securities under Commercial Code, establishing effectiveness of signature, **106:8-114.**

Issue, presumption as to death without, **184:6.**

Joint grantees, presumption from conveyance or devise, **184:7.**

**PRESUMPTIONS AND
BURDEN OF PROOF**
—Cont'd

Joint tenants and tenants in
common, **90D:15A, 184:7.**
Judgment, presumption of
satisfaction after 20 years,
260:20.
Judicial notice.
See JUDICIAL NOTICE.
Jury and jury trial, examination of
prospective jurors as to
burden of proof, **234:28.**
Landlord and tenant.
Condition of premises, landlord's
knowledge, **239:8A.**
Reprisal by landlord, **186:18.**
Leases under UCC.
See LEASES UNDER
COMMERCIAL CODE.
Legacy or succession tax,
discharge of lien, **65:9.**
Letters of credit.
Damages, **106:5-111.**
Licenses.
See LICENSES AND PERMITS.
Life insurance.
Abandoned or unclaimed life
insurance funds, **175:149A,
175:186A, 200A:5A.**
Common disaster, presumption
of survivorship in death,
190A:4, 190A:5.
Delivery of policy, presumptions,
175:186A.
Marriage as provable by evidence
of facts creating inference,
207:47.
Married women.
Husband and wife. See within
this heading, "Husband and
wife."
Massachusetts register, judicial
notice, **30A:6.**
Medical examination, effect of
certain fire and police officers
passing examination
subsequent to employment,
32:94.
Medical malpractice claims, offers
of proof, **231:60B.**
Meetings of governmental bodies,
public records, burden of
respondent, **66:17C.**
Mental competence, **123:15.**
Minimum wages, conclusive
presumption as to oppressive
and unreasonable wage, **151:1.**
Motorboats, proof in prosecution as
to numbering, **90B:2.**
Motor vehicles.
See MOTOR VEHICLES.
Narcotics offenses, **277:38.**

**PRESUMPTIONS AND
BURDEN OF PROOF**
—Cont'd

Negligence, **231:85.**
Negotiable instruments.
Notice of dishonor, **106:3-505.**
Obscene books and matter,
proceedings against, **272:28H.**
Oppressive and unreasonable
wage, presumption, **151:1.**
Option to accelerate, lack of good
faith in exercise, **106:1-208.**
Parking and parking stations.
Notice to parking offender,
presumption, **90:20C.**
Private way, burden of proof as
to trespass by parking
motor vehicle, **266:120A.**
Paternity, **209C:6, 209C:7.**
Pensions.
See RETIREMENT SYSTEMS
AND PENSIONS.
Perjury, commitment of party or
witness on presumption,
268:4.
Permits.
See LICENSES AND PERMITS.
Personal property, presumption
after failure to return after
notice of termination of lease,
231:85H.
Police.
Firemen and policemen. See
within this heading,
"Firemen and policemen."
Premises, landlord's knowledge of
condition, **239:8A.**
Prima facie evidence.
See PRIMA FACIE EVIDENCE.
Private way, burden of proof as to
trespass by parking motor
vehicle, **266:120A.**
Protective orders issued by public
utilities, **25:5D.**
Public inspection, records open to,
presumption that record is
public, **66:10.**
Public records.
Burden of proof as to exemption
from inspection, **66:10.**
Delivery, presumption from
recording, **183:5.**
Meetings of governmental
bodies, burden of
respondent, **66:17C.**
Presumption that record is
public, **66:10.**
Public utilities commission, burden
of proof on appeals from
rulings, **25:5.**
Public way, existence, **233:79F.**

**PRESUMPTIONS AND
BURDEN OF PROOF**
—Cont'd

Records.
Public records. See within this
heading, "Public records."
Restraints of trade and
monopolies, **93:3.**
Restrictions on land imposed as
part of common scheme,
presumption as to
enforceability, **184:26.**
Retirement systems.
See RETIREMENT SYSTEMS
AND PENSIONS.
Revolving credit agreement
deemed signed, **255D:1.**
Roads.
Highways and streets. See
within this heading,
"Highways and streets."
Sales contract.
Burden of proving breach with
respect to accepted goods,
106:2-607.
Fiduciary's sale of realty,
presumption of highest
obtainable price, **202:38.**
International log rule, contracts
for purchase and sale of logs
presumed made on basis,
96:11A.
Sales taxes.
Gross receipts from sale of
tangible personal property
as sales subject to tax,
64H:8.
Sanitary code presumptions,
reprisal against tenant
reporting violations, **186:18.**
Satisfaction of judgment 20 years
old, **260:20.**
Securities act.
Civil liabilities, **110A:410.**
Exemption or exception from
definitions, **110A:402.**
Shade trees as presumptively
within highway boundary,
87:1.
Ships and vessels.
Chemical analysis of blood or
breath, **90B:8.**
Grounding, burden of proof of
permit, **91:49.**
Motorboats, burden of proof in
prosecution as to
numbering, **90B:2.**
Shoplifter, presumption of guilt by
concealment of goods,
231:94B.
Simultaneous death law, **190A:1
et seq.**

PRESUMPTIONS AND BURDEN OF PROOF
—Cont'd

Skiers and ski areas, assumption of risk, **143:71O.**

Social worker and client communications, refusing disclosure, **112:135B.**

Special education.

Existence of special needs for requirement of special education, presumption against, **71B:3.**

Regular education, presumption of child's assignment, **71B:3.**

Spouse.

Husband and wife. See within this heading, "Husband and wife."

Steam boilers and engines, prima facie evidence of operation by unlicensed person, **146:47.**

Storage tax.

Use, consumption, or storage tax. See within this heading, "Use, consumption, or storage tax."

Streets.

Highways and streets. See within this heading, "Highways and streets."

Summary process to recover land, reprisal against tenant, **239:2A.**

Taxation.

See TAXATION.

Tenant.

Landlord and tenant. See within this heading, "Landlord and tenant."

Trademarks and trade names, effect of registration or renewal, **110B:4.**

Treason, proof, **264:4.**

Trees as presumptively within highway boundary, **87:1.**

Trespass by parking on private way, **266:120A.**

Trust beneficiary or distributions.

Abandonment of securities unclaimed, **200A:5, 200A:5B, 200A:5C.**

Death of absentee beneficiary, **203:32.**

Two or more persons, presumption from conveyances or devises, **184:7.**

Unfair or deceptive trade practices, locus of such act or practice, **93A:11.**

PRESUMPTIONS AND BURDEN OF PROOF
—Cont'd

Use, consumption, or storage tax.

Motor vehicles or trailers, presumption that transfers of registration are for storage, use, or other consumption in Commonwealth, **64I:26.**

Tax liability, **64I:8.**

Vessels.

Ships and vessels. See within this heading, "Ships and vessels."

Wages, conclusive presumption as to oppressive and unreasonable wage, **151:1.**

Weapons.

Firearms and weapons. See within this heading, "Firearms and weapons."

Wife.

Husband and wife. See within this heading, "Husband and wife."

Wills.

See WILLS.

Workers' compensation.

See WORKERS' COMPENSATION.

Wrongful death.

Due care on part of decedent, **231:85.**

Negligence by agent or custodian of injured person, **231:85.**

Zoning, acquiescence presumed in granting of special permit, **40A:11.**

PRESUMPTION STATUTE (COMPENSATION), 152:7A.

PRETENSES.

False pretenses, **266:30 et seq.**

See FRAUD AND DECEIT.

PRETERMITTED CHILD, 191:20.

Appointment of guardian ad litem in probate proceedings, **192:1C.**

Contribution, rights and liabilities, **191:25, 191:28, 191:29.**

PRETRIAL CONFERENCE.
See PRETRIAL PROCEEDINGS.

PRETRIAL DIVERSION OF SELECTED OFFENDERS, 276A:1-276A:9.

Advisory board, establishment, membership and functions, **276A:9.**

PRETRIAL DIVERSION OF SELECTED OFFENDERS
—Cont'd

Arrests, effect of subsequent arrests, **276A:6.**

Assessment.

Continuance, **276A:3.**

Defined, **276A:1.**

Program director's report and assessment, **276A:5.**

Boston municipal court jurisdiction, **276A:2.**

Commissioner, defined, **276A:1.**

Commissioner of probation, powers and duties, **276A:8.**

Continuance for assessment, **276A:3.**

Definitions, **276A:1.**

Director, defined, **276A:1.**

District court jurisdiction, **276A:2.**

Eligibility and qualifications for diversion, **276A:2.**

Continuance for assessment, **276A:3.**

Determination, **276A:5.**

Limitations on eligibility, **276A:4.**

Probation officers investigation, **276A:3.**

Employment and training division in labor and workforce department, **276A:9.**

First offenders, **279:6A, 279:11.**

Jurisdiction, **276A:2.**

Official designee, defined, **276A:1.**

Periodic progress reports, **276A:6.**

Plan of service, defined, **276A:1.**

Probation officer's duties, **276A:1 et seq.**

Inspection and investigation, **276A:3.**

Program, defined, **276A:1.**

Program director's report and assessment, **276A:5.**

Qualifications.

Eligibility and qualifications for diversion. See within this heading, "Eligibility and qualifications for diversion."

Reports.

Periodic progress reports, **276A:6.**

Program director's report and assessment, **276A:5.**

Sentence and punishment.

Remission of fine or imprisonment of first offenders, **279:11.**

Special sentences of imprisonment for first offenders, **279:6A.**

PRETRIAL DIVERSION OF SELECTED OFFENDERS —Cont'd

Stay of proceedings, **276A:5.**

Extension, **276A:7.**

Successful completion of program, effect, **276A:7.**

Violation of program conditions, effect, **276A:6.**

PRETRIAL PROCEEDINGS.

Bail.

See BAIL AND RECOGNIZANCE.

Criminal offender record information system, **6:167 et seq.**

Discovery.

See DISCOVERY AND DISCLOSURE.

Diversions, **276A:1-276A:9.**

See PRETRIAL DIVERSION OF SELECTED OFFENDERS.

Joinder of actions or issues, pretrial motions, **223:2A.**

Motions, **277:47A.**

Joinder of actions or issues, pretrial motions, **223:2A.**

PREVAILING WAGE LAW.

Minimum wages.

See MINIMUM WAGES.

Public works and contracts, **5:1, 7:22, 149:26 to 149:27D.**

PREVENTION OF ABUSE.
See ABUSE PREVENTION.

PREVENTION OF FIRES.
See FIRES AND FIRE PREVENTION.

PRICING PRACTICES.

Adjustment of public works contract price for difference in site conditions from those specified in plans or contract, **30:39N.**

Cigarettes, regulation of price, **64C:14-64C:20.**

Consumer products, price regulation practices, **6:184B-6:184E.**

Dentists or dental hygienists, illegal advertising of fixed prices, **112:52A.**

Fair trade law, **93:14E-93:14K.**

See UNFAIR SALES ACT.

Fixing of prices generally, **93:6.**

Food, price to be marked, **94:181, 94:184B-94:184E, 98:56D.**

Fraud and deceit.

Advertising, **266:91A, 266:91B.**

Alcoholic liquors, affirmation of price paid, **138:25D.**

PRICING PRACTICES —Cont'd

Fraud and deceit —Cont'd

Penalty for misrepresentation as to price of commodity or service sold by weight or measure, **94:177.**

Grocery stores, price marking, **94:184B-94:184E, 98:56D.**

Hairdressers, beauty shops, regulating prices, **112:87CC.**

Indictments, description, **277:24.**

Labels, retail price, **94:181.**

Mobile homes, certain charges included in advertising, **93B:5A.**

Monopolies.

See RESTRAINTS OF TRADE AND MONOPOLIES.

Motor vehicles.

Manufacturers, distributors, and dealers, unfair trade practices as between, **93B:4.**

Warranty provisions of used motor vehicles, definition of purchase price, **90:7N¼.**

Optometrists, regulations, **112:73A.**

Parens patriae action as to price fixing, **93:9.**

Podiatrists, unprofessional conduct in connection with advertising fixed prices, **112:19.**

Restraints of trade.

See RESTRAINTS OF TRADE AND MONOPOLIES.

Tickets.

Penalty for failure to have price printed on face, **140:182A.**

Resale price regulated, **140:185D.**

Street railways, free tickets, **161:107.**

PRIESTS.
See RELIGION AND RELIGIOUS SOCIETIES.

PRIMA FACIE EVIDENCE.

Alcohol in blood, **90:24.**

Antitrust laws, **93:11.**

Architect's certificate, **112:60I.**

Auditors, findings and reports, **221:57.**

Bedding, prima facie evidence of labeling violations, **94:272.**

Bottles, prima facie evidence of unauthorized use of registered bottles, **110:19.**

Bucket shop transactions, **137:6, 271:38.**

Certificates.

Alcohol in blood, **90:24.**

Architect's certificate, **112:60I.**

PRIMA FACIE EVIDENCE —Cont'd

Certificates —Cont'd

Ballistics expert, certificate as prima facie evidence, **140:121A.**

Commercial code, **106:1-202.**

Commercial feed, certificates of analysis, **128:61.**

County, district, or town notes, **35:39F.**

Director of division of forests and parks, certificate, **21:4A.**

Drug analysis certificate, **111:13.**

Farm products, **94:117D.**

Minor, failure to exhibit employment certificate as evidence of illegal employment, **149:94.**

Motor vehicle certificate of title as prima facie evidence, **90D:10.**

Physical therapists certificate, **112:23F.**

Rules and regulations of public bodies, admissibility of as affected by certification, **233:75.**

Third-party documents under Commercial Code, **106:1-202.**

Commercial Code third-party documents, **106:1-202.**

Commercial feed, certificate of analysis as prima facie evidence, **128:61.**

Credit unions, affidavit setting forth contents of safe deposit box, **171:75.**

Desertion from militia, prima facie evidence, **33:56.**

Drawing or uttering fraudulent check with intent to defraud, **266:37.**

Drug analysis by public safety department chemist, certificate as prima facie evidence, **111:13.**

Engineers' registration, prima facie evidence, **112:81H, 112:81M.**

Evidence generally.

See EVIDENCE.

Execution and return, effect of recording, **236:22.**

Farm products, **94:117D.**

Firearm with defaced or obliterated serial number, possession, **269:11C.**

Forests and parks director, certificate, **21:4A.**

PRIMA FACIE EVIDENCE
—Cont'd
Fuel oils, possession of preprinted delivery ticket as prima facie evidence of intent to violate law, **94:303F.**
Gaming and games of chance, **271:19-271:21, 271:27.**
Insurance.
Policy or certificate, **106:1-202.**
Theft of vehicle, **233:79I.**
Lobsters, sale of undersized, **130:44.**
Machine or device with defaced serial number, possession, **266:139A.**
Milk and milk products.
Rules and regulations under Milk Control Law, adoption, **94A:19.**
Unlawful use of milk cans, etc., **110:22.**
Minor, failure to exhibit employment certificate as evidence of illegal employment, **149:94.**
Motor vehicles.
See MOTOR VEHICLES.
Notes of county, district or town, **35:39F.**
Percentage of alcohol in blood, chemist's certificate as prima facie evidence, **90:24.**
Physical therapists, certificates, **112:23F.**
Primary elections, testimony of city and town clerk as prima facie evidence of regularity of proceedings, **50:8.**
Recreation areas, rules and regulations, **132A:7.**
Registered owner of motor vehicle, **266:120A.**
Restraints of trade and monopolies, final judgment or decree as prima facie evidence in subsequent action, **93:11.**
Rules and regulations of public bodies, **233:75.**
Safe deposit box, statements in books as to opening for unpaid rent, as prima facie evidence of facts stated, **158:17.**
"Short sales," intent as to delivery, **137:6.**
Small claims action, finding for plaintiff in action removed, **218:23.**
Smelt, unlawful possession or sale, **130:34, 130:35.**

PRIMA FACIE EVIDENCE
—Cont'd
Speedometer or odometer, tampering with intent to misrepresent mileage, **266:141, 266:141A.**
Statutes and ordinance, **233:75.**
Steam boilers and engines, operation by unlicensed person, **146:47.**
Substandard article, prima facie character of possession, **94:292.**
Third-party documents under Commercial Code, **106:1-202.**
Tramp, prima facie evidence of being, **272:63.**
Trespasser giving notice of court order, **266:120.**
Upholstered furniture, labeling violations, **94:272.**

PRIMARY ELECTIONS, 53:23 to 53:40A.
Absent voters.
City and town primaries, **54:103A, 54:103P.**
Other political party, enrolled voter not entitled to ballot, **53:38.**
Party enrollment, **53:37A, 53:38.**
Preparation of ballots by secretary of state, **53:34A.**
State and presidential primaries, voting, **53:34, 54:86.**
Acceptance of candidates, **50:3A.**
City and town primaries. See within this heading, "City and town primaries."
State primaries, acceptance written on nomination papers, **53:45.**
Withdrawal of acceptance of nomination. See within this heading, "Withdrawal of acceptance of nomination."
Writing in name, **53:3, 53:35B.**
Advertising, use of party name, **56:40.**
Aiding or abetting illegal voting, **56:28.**
Alcoholic liquor sales during polling hours, **138:33.**
All primaries, statutory provisions applicable, **53:23-53:40A.**
Armories used, **33:122.**
Ballot boxes.
Delivery to polls, **53:36.**
Presidential primary, preparation for use, **54:135A.**

PRIMARY ELECTIONS —Cont'd
Ballot clerk's duties as to party enrollment, **53:37.**
Ballots, **53:32.**
Absent voters. See within this heading, "Absent voters."
Alphabetical listing of names of candidates, **53:34.**
Arrangement and form, **53:34.**
Attorney general's office, **54:43A.**
Blank spaces for writing in names, **53:34.**
Boxes. See within this heading, "Ballot boxes."
Candidates' names, **53:17A, 53:34, 53:48, 54:43A.**
City and town primaries. See within this heading, "City and town primaries."
Colors for different parties, **53:33.**
Contents, **53:34, 53:35.**
Counting, **53:39, 53:51.**
Delivery at polls, **53:36.**
Error in party enrollment, effect, **53:38.**
Lost or stolen, provision in case, **53:32.**
Marking, **53:35.**
Misconduct of election officers, **56:12.**
Name of candidate, **53:17A, 53:34, 53:48, 54:43A.**
Nondelivery, provision in case, **53:32.**
Number of persons to be voted for stated, **53:34.**
Official state ballot, form and arrangement in accordance, **53:34.**
Order of names of candidates, **53:34, 54:43A.**
Order of questions, **54:43A.**
Other political party, enrolled voter not entitled to ballot, **53:38.**
Party enrollment.
Absent voters, **53:37, 53:38.**
Prerequisite to candidate's name appearing on ballot, **53:48.**
Pasters, **53:35A, 53:40.**
Posting of specimen and sample ballots, **53:36.**
Preparation and number, **53:32.**
Presidential primaries.
See PRESIDENTIAL PRIMARIES.
Printed in establishment owned or managed by city of Boston, forbidden, **53:32.**

PRIMARY ELECTIONS —Cont'd
Ballots —Cont'd
Specimen ballots at polling places, **53:33.**
State ballot law commission.
See STATE BALLOT LAW COMMISSION.
Statements relating to candidate permissible, **53:34.**
Stickers, **53:35A, 53:40.**
Voting machine sample ballots, **53:33.**
Writing in name, **53:3, 53:34.**
Biennial count of voters, **53:38A.**
Booths, posting specimen ballots, **53:36.**
Campaign expenditures.
See CAMPAIGN EXPENDITURES AND CONTRIBUTIONS.
Cancellation of party enrollment, **53:37, 53:38, 53:48.**
Candidates, selection of, **53:2.**
Canvassing and counting of votes, **53:39, 53:51, 53:52, 53:64.**
Apparatus for canvassing, delivery at polling places, **53:36.**
Biennial count of voters, **53:38A.**
Clerks of cities and towns. See within this heading, "Clerks of cities and towns."
Marking of ballot as affecting, **53:35.**
Presidential primaries, **53:70E, 53:70F.**
Recount of votes. See within this heading, "Recount of votes."
State primaries, **53:51, 53:52.**
Certificates and certification.
Nomination papers.
City and town primaries. See within this heading, "City and town primaries."
Generally. See within this heading, "Nomination papers."
Party enrollment, **53:38, 53:48.**
Voting lists, certificate in case of omission of error, **51:59.**
Voting machines, certificate of necessity for release for use in ensuing primary, **54:135A.**
Challenge of registrations of voters, **51:48, 51:49.**
Change of party enrollment of voters, **53:37, 53:38, 53:48.**
Charter cities.
See CITY CHARTERS.
City and town primaries, **53:55-53:64.**
Absent voting, **54:103A.**

PRIMARY ELECTIONS —Cont'd
City and town primaries —Cont'd
Acceptance of candidates, **53:59.**
Withdrawal, **53:25, 53:55, 53:59, 53:62.**
Write in nominee, **53:35B.**
Application of laws relating particularly to city or town, **50:6.**
Ballots.
Clerks, **30:32.**
Order of names, **53:34.**
Party enrollment, **53:38.**
Candidates for nomination.
Enrolled member of political party, candidate for nomination required to be, **53:48.**
Notice to successful candidates, **53:64.**
Vacancies among candidates, filling, **53:55, 53:59, 53:62.**
Withdrawals of candidates, **53:25, 53:55, 53:59, 53:62.**
Canvass of returns of votes, **53:64.**
Certification of names on nomination papers, **53:56.**
Change or cancellation of enrollment, **53:38.**
Charter cities.
See CITY CHARTERS.
Clerks of cities and towns. See within this heading, "Clerks of cities and towns."
Enrolled member of political party, candidate for nomination required to be, **53:48.**
Nomination papers, **53:9A, 53:56, 53:58-53:62.**
Acceptance of candidates, **53:59.**
Blank forms, **53:58.**
Certification, **53:56, 53:61.**
Contents, **53:59.**
Death of candidate, filling vacancy in case, **53:62.**
Filing, **53:10, 53:61.**
Furnishing, **53:17, 53:58.**
Ineligibility of candidate, filling vacancy caused, **53:62.**
Number of candidates, **53:59, 53:60.**
Party enrollment of candidate, **53:61.**
Signatures, **53:56, 53:59.**
Vacancies, filling, **53:62.**
Withdrawal of candidate, showing vacancy caused, **53:62.**

PRIMARY ELECTIONS —Cont'd
City and town primaries —Cont'd
Notices.
Clerks of cities and towns. See within this heading, "Clerks of cities and towns."
Holding of primaries, result of election, **53:56.**
Intention to participate in primaries, **53:57.**
Successful candidates, notice, **53:64.**
Objections to nominations, **53:55.**
Party enrollment of candidate.
See within this heading, "Party enrollment of candidate."
Political parties.
Candidates, **53:55.**
Defined, **50:1.**
Intention to participate in primaries, notice, **53:57.**
Party enrollment as affecting, **53:38, 53:48.**
Polls, opening and closing, **53:63.**
Preparation and number, **53:32.**
Presidential primaries.
See PRESIDENTIAL PRIMARIES.
Registration of voters.
See REGISTRATION OF VOTERS.
Submission of question of holding, to voters, **53:56.**
Time and place of holding, **53:28.**
Unenrolled candidate, **53:6.**
Vacancies, filling, **53:55, 53:58, 53:59, 53:62.**
Voting machines, discontinuance of use, **54:34.**
Wards and precincts. See within this heading, "Wards and precincts."
Clerks of cities and towns.
Authority to regulate primaries, **50:7.**
Ballots, furnishing, **53:32.**
Blank nomination papers in city or town primaries, furnishing, **53:58.**
Canvass of returns.
City and town primaries, **53:64.**
Presidential primaries, **53:70F.**
State primaries, **53:52.**
Certificates of nomination filed, **53:9.**

PRIMARY ELECTIONS —Cont'd
Clerks of cities and towns —Cont'd
Delivery of ballots to polling
places, **53:36.**
Inspectors and tellers,
designation, **53:29, 53:30.**
Nomination papers in city and
town primaries, **53:58,
53:61.**
Notice.
Holding of primaries, notice to
state secretary as to
result of election, **53:56.**
Intention to participate in city
and town primaries filed
with clerks, **53:57.**
Successful candidates in
presidential primaries,
notice, **53:70F.**
Write-in primary nominee,
notice as to acceptance,
53:35B.
Number of voting machines in
each polling place at state
primary, **54:33.**
Objections to nominations filed,
53:55.
Officers to serve at primaries,
designation, **53:29-53:31.**
Paraphernalia, delivery, **53:36.**
Presidential primaries, duties
with respect, **39:9A, 39:10,
53:70F.**
Testimony of, as prima facie
evidence of regularity of
proceedings, **50:8.**
Voting lists, duties, **53:37.**
Withdrawal of candidate filed,
53:55.
Closing.
Polls and polling places. See
within this heading, "Polls
and polling places."
Commissioners.
Election commissioners. See
within this heading,
"Election commissioners."
Committees.
Political committees. See within
this heading, "Political
committees."
Computation of time in election
law, **50:4.**
Conduct of, **53:24.**
Corrupt practices, **53:24, 55:34.**
Counting of votes.
Canvassing and counting of
votes. See within this
heading, "Canvassing and
counting of votes."

PRIMARY ELECTIONS —Cont'd
Crimes and offenses.
Offenses and penalties. See
within this heading,
"Offenses and penalties."
Date.
Time or date. See within this
heading, "Time or date."
Death of candidates, filling
vacancies in case, **53:14.**
City and town primaries, **53:58,
53:62.**
Nomination to fill vacancy in
case, **53:49.**
State primaries, **53:49, 53:50.**
State, ward, or town committee,
53:70G.
Defined, **50:1.**
Delegates to national conventions,
selection of, **53:70B.**
Direct plurality vote, nominations
and elections, **53:2.**
Disabled or handicapped persons,
voting, **54:86.**
Disclosing vote by voter, **56:25.**
Election commissioners.
Establishment of duties of
board, **51:16A.**
Number of voting machines in
polling place for state
primary, **54:33.**
Powers, rights, privileges,
liabilities, and duties
relating to primaries,
51:16A.
Election laws as applicable, **50:6,
53:24.**
Enrollment of voters.
Party enrollment of voters. See
within this heading, "Party
enrollment of voters."
Equipment and apparatus.
Ballot boxes. See within this
heading, "Ballot boxes."
Canvassing equipment, delivery
at polling places, **53:36.**
Voting machines. See within this
heading, "Voting machines."
False answers or statements,
53:45, 56:25.
Federal service personnel.
Registration, **51:50.**
Fines and penalties.
Offenses and penalties. See
within this heading,
"Offenses and penalties."
General court.
Ballots, arrangement of
candidates' names, **53:34.**
Number of signatures required
for candidates, **53:44.**

PRIMARY ELECTIONS —Cont'd
General court —Cont'd
Party enrollment of candidate in
state primaries, certificate,
53:48.
General election provisions as
applicable, **53:24.**
Governor.
Ballots, arrangement of
candidates' names, **53:34.**
Number of signatures required
for candidates, **53:44.**
Handicapped persons, voting,
54:86.
Holiday, effect of election day
falling, **50:4.**
Illegal voting, **56:25, 56:26.**
Incumbents elected or appointed,
order of placing names on
ballots, **53:34.**
Independent candidates, certificate
as to party enrollment, **53:48.**
Inspectors, appointment, **53:29.**
Instructions for voters, penalty for
defacing or removing, **56:24.**
Interference with voting,
56:28-56:31.
Lieutenant governor.
See LIEUTENANT
GOVERNOR.
Limitations, candidate's limitation
to one office, **53:46.**
Lists and listing.
Ballots, alphabetical listing of
candidates, **53:34.**
Defacing or removing list of
candidates, penalty, **56:24.**
Distribution of lists of
candidates, **56:44A.**
Offenses and penalties. See
within this heading,
"Offenses and penalties."
Voting lists. See within this
heading, "Voting list used."
Machines for voting. See within
this heading, "Voting
machines."
Marking ballots, **53:35.**
Nomination of candidates, **53:2,
53:41.**
Nomination papers, **53:44-53:48,
53:50, 53:53A, 53:70D.**
Acceptance of candidates. See
within this heading,
"Acceptance of candidates."
Certificates and certification.
Cities and towns, **53:56, 53:61.**
Filing, **53:9, 53:10, 53:48.**
State primaries, certification
of names, **53:46.**
Change or cancellation of
enrollment, **53:38, 53:48.**

PRIMARY ELECTIONS —Cont'd
Nomination papers —Cont'd
City and town primaries. See
within this heading, "City
and town primaries."
Contents, **53:5.**
Designation of districts, **53:45,
53:46.**
Disqualification of candidates for
office of ward or town
committeeman, **53:45.**
False statements, punishment,
53:45.
Furnished by state secretary,
53:47.
Last day for filing, **53:48.**
Name of candidate, **53:45, 53:46.**
Number of candidates, **53:45.**
Number of signatures required,
53:44, 53:70D.
One office, limitation, **53:46.**
Political party whose nomination
is sought, nomination paper
to state, **53:45.**
Public offices which candidates
holds or has held,
statement, **53:45.**
Renomination.
Ballot, **53:34.**
Statement, **53:45.**
Residence of candidates placed,
50:3A, 53:45.
Secretary of state.
Certificate acknowledging time
and date of filing of
papers, issuance, **53:48.**
Preparation and furnishing
nomination papers, **53:47.**
Signatures, **53:44.**
City and town primaries,
53:59, 53:60.
Placing signature and address
on one of group of papers,
50:3A.
Presidential primaries,
53:70D.
Time for filing, **50:4, 53:5, 53:10,
53:48.**
Ward or town committeeman,
disqualification of
candidates for office, **53:45.**
Notices.
City and town primaries. See
within this heading, "City
and town primaries."
Clerks of cities and towns. See
within this heading, "Clerks
of cities and towns."
Establishment, change, or
cancellation of voter's
enrollment in party, **53:38.**

PRIMARY ELECTIONS —Cont'd
Notices —Cont'd
National conventions, notice of
number of delegates,
53:70B.
Pasters or write-ins, notice,
53:35B, 53:52.
Penalty for defacing or
removing, **56:23.**
Place for posting, **50:5.**
Posting, **50:5, 53:36.**
Voting machines. See within this
heading, "Voting machines."
Wards and precincts, notice of
holding, **53:42.**
Objections to nominations.
City and town primaries, **53:55.**
State primaries, **53:50, 53:53A.**
Offenses and penalties.
Ballots, misconduct of election
officers, **56:12.**
False answers or statements,
53:45, 56:25.
Illegal voting, **56:25, 56:26,
56:28.**
Interference with voting,
56:28-56:31.
List of candidates.
Defacing or removing, **56:24.**
Distribution of lists, **56:44A.**
Notices, penalty for defacing or
removing, **56:23.**
Officer serving, **53:29-53:31.**
Ballots, misconduct of election
officers a, **56:12.**
Eligibility, **53:31, 54:15.**
Overtime pay for police,
41:111H.
Withdrawal of candidate,
nominations after, **53:50.**
Opening and closing.
Polls and polling places. See
within this heading, "Polls
and polling places."
Overtime pay for policemen on
primary day, **41:111H.**
Party enrollment of candidate.
City and town primaries, **53:61.**
Unenrolled candidate, **53:6.**
Party enrollment of voters, **53:37,
53:37A, 53:38.**
Age, **51:42.**
Ballots. See within this heading,
"Ballots."
Certificate, **53:38, 53:48.**
Change or cancellation, **53:37,
53:38, 53:48.**
Effective date in cases affecting
membership of bipartisan
bodies, **4:12.**
Municipal party, right to ballot,
53:38.

PRIMARY ELECTIONS —Cont'd
Party enrollment of voters
—Cont'd
Other political party, not to
receive ballot, **53:38.**
Processing of absentee ballot
shall establish, **53:38.**
Registered voter, petitions for
recount to be signed by
registered voters enrolled on
or before last day to
register, **53:40A.**
State primary, **53:38, 53:46,
53:48.**
Time for filing, **51:42, 53:38.**
Voting lists to contain, **51:44,
53:37, 53:38.**
Pasters or write-ins.
Acceptance by candidate
nominated, **53:3, 53:35B.**
Blank spaces on ballot for
writing in names, **53:34.**
Notice, **53:35B, 53:52.**
Use, **53:35A, 53:40.**
Penalties.
Offenses and penalties. See
within this heading,
"Offenses and penalties."
Physically disabled voters, absent
voting, **54:86.**
Place of voting, **51:3, 53:28.**
Polls and polling places. See
within this heading, "Polls
and polling places."
Political calendar for 1974, **53:28
note.**
Political committees.
Ballots, contents and form,
53:34, 53:35.
Intent to participate, **53:57.**
Ward or town committeemen.
See within this heading,
"Ward or town
committeemen."
Political parties, **53:1, 53:37,
53:37A, 53:38.**
Polls and polling places, **51:3,
51:28.**
Apparatus, ballots, delivery,
53:36.
Cities and towns, **53:63.**
Opening and closing, **53:43.**
Ballots not to be counted until
close of polls, **53:51.**
City and town primaries,
53:63.
Specimen ballots, **53:33.**
Voting machines number, **54:33.**
Posting.
Lists and notices, **50:5.**
Specimen and sample ballots,
53:36.

PRIMARY ELECTIONS —Cont'd

Preliminary elections in charter cities.
See CITY CHARTERS.

Presidential convention, delegates, **53:70D.**

Presidential primaries, **53:70A-53:70H.**
See PRESIDENTIAL PRIMARIES.

Presumption of regularity in criminal prosecutions, **50:8.**

Recount of votes, **54:135.**
Change or cancellation of enrollment, **53:38.**
Time for copying lists used in primaries, **53:37.**
Uniform petition, **54:135.**
Who may sign petition, **53:40A.**

Registration of voters.
See REGISTRATION OF VOTERS.

Renomination, **53:34, 53:45.**

Residence of candidates placed on nomination papers, **50:3A, 53:45.**

Result of election.
Canvassing and counting of votes. See within this heading, "Canvassing and counting of votes."
City and town primaries, adoption of law, **53:56.**
Determination, **50:2, 53:2, 53:52.**
Presidential primaries, declaration of result, **53:70F.**
State primaries, **53:52.**

Return of votes, **53:52, 53:64.**
Presidential primaries, **53:70F.**

Secretary of state.
Absentee ballots, preparation, **53:34A.**
Certificate of candidate as to party enrollment, filing, **53:48.**
Holding of city and town primaries, notice of result of election, **53:56.**
National conventions, notice of number of delegates, **53:70B.**
Nomination papers. See within this heading, "Nomination papers."
Number of signatures required for candidates, **53:44.**
Presidential primaries.
See PRESIDENTIAL PRIMARIES.
Recounts, **54:135.**
Returns of votes in state primaries, **53:52.**

PRIMARY ELECTIONS —Cont'd

Secretary of state —Cont'd
State primary.
Declaration of results, **53:52.**
Nomination papers, **53:47, 53:48.**
Notice of number of voting machines in polling place, **54:33.**
Time for giving notice of number of delegates to national presidential conventions, **53:70B.**
Vacancies caused by withdrawal, filling, **53:50.**
Withdrawal of nominee filed, **53:53A.**

Signature.
Nomination papers. See within this heading, "Nomination papers."
Number of signatures required for candidates, **53:44.**
Registered voter, petitions for recount to be signed only by registered votes on or before last day to register, **53:40A.**

Special primaries.
Absentee ballots, **54:86.**
Certification of names on nomination papers, **53:46.**
Change or cancellation of enrollment, **53:38.**
Filing of nomination papers, **53:48.**
Meetings of registrars, **53:46.**
Notice of holding by wards or precincts, **53:42.**
Time for holding, **53:28.**

Specimen ballots, **53:33, 53:36.**

Speedy trial of actions under election laws, **231:59D.**

State ballot law commission.
See STATE BALLOT LAW COMMISSION.

State primaries, **53:41-53:53A.**

State ward committees, selection of, **53:70B.**

Stickers.
Pasters or write-ins. See within this heading, "Pasters or write-ins."

Sunday, effect of election day falling, **50:4.**

Supplies, **53:36.**

Tellers, **53:29.**

Tie vote, vacancy in case.
City and town primaries, **53:62.**
State primaries, **53:53.**
State, ward, or town committees, **53:70G.**

PRIMARY ELECTIONS —Cont'd

Time or date, **53:28.**
Certificates of nomination papers, time for filing, **53:10.**
Cities and towns, **53:28, 53:61.**
Computation of time, **50:4.**
Copies of voting lists used in primaries, time for obtaining, **53:37.**
Enrollment in party, effective date, **4:12.**
Hours that polling places to be kept open. See within this heading, "Polls and polling places."
Nomination papers, **50:4, 53:5, 53:10, 53:48.**
Party enrollment, time for filing, **51:42, 53:38.**
Presidential conventions, time for giving notice of number of delegates, **53:70B.**
Registered voter petitions for recounts to be signed only by registered voters on or before last day to register, **53:40A.**

Town primaries.
City and town primaries. See within this heading, "City and town primaries."

Vacancies, filling.
City and town primaries, **53:55, 53:58, 53:59, 53:62.**
Death of candidates, filling vacancies in case. See within this heading, "Death of candidates, filling vacancies in case."
State primaries, **53:49, 53:50, 53:53.**
State, ward, or town committees, **53:70G.**
Tie vote, vacancy in case. See within this heading, "Tie vote, vacancy in case."

Voting lists, time to obtain copies, **53:37.**

Voting list used, **51:44, 51:55, 53:37, 53:38.**
Candidate entitled to copy, **53:37.**
Certificate in case of omission or error, **51:59.**
Delivery, **53:36.**
Party enrollment of voters appearing, **51:44, 53:37, 53:38.**
Political committee entitled to copy, **53:37.**

PRIMARY ELECTIONS —Cont'd

Voting list used —Cont'd
Posting, **50:5.**
Preparation, **51:55.**
Voting machines.
Delivery, **53:36.**
Discontinuance of use by cities and towns, **54:34.**
Labels, precedence of offices, **54:43A.**
Locked and sealed voting machines, release for use in ensuing primaries, **54:135A.**
Notice.
Discontinuance of use of voting machines, **54:34.**
Number of machines in polling places, **54:33.**
Number of machines in polling place, **54:33.**
Order of names and questions, **54:43A.**
Sample ballots, **53:33.**
Use, **54:35B.**
Ward or town committeemen.
Death of candidates, filing vacancies in case, **53:70G.**
Disqualification of candidates for office, **53:45.**
Selection of, **53:70B.**
Wards and precincts, **53:28.**
Presidential primaries, **53:70C.**
State primaries, **53:42.**
Willfully obstructing voting, penalty, **56:30.**
Withdrawal of acceptance of nomination.
City and town primaries, **53:25, 53:55, 53:59, 53:62.**
State, ward, or town committees, **53:70G.**
Write-in candidate, **53:3.**
Withdrawal of candidates, **53:29, 53:49, 53:50, 53:53A, 53:70E.**
City or town preliminary election, **43:44F.**
Write-ins.
Pasters or write-ins. See within this heading, "Pasters or write-ins."

PRIMITIVE FIREARM-ARCHERY STAMP, 131:11.

PRINCETON.
Congressional district, **57:1.**
District court, **218:1.**
Leominster district court, inclusion, **6:172.**
Medical examiner district, **38:1.**
Senatorial district, **57:3.**

**PRINCIPAL AND AGENT.
See AGENTS AND AGENCY.**

PRINCIPAL AND INCOME.
Guardians.
See GUARDIANS, CONSERVATORS, AND COMMITTEES.
Life estates.
See LIFE ESTATES, REMAINDERS, AND REVERSIONS.
Trusts.
See TRUSTS AND TRUSTEES.

**PRINCIPAL AND SURETY.
See SURETIES AND SURETY COMPANIES.**

**PRINCIPAL OF SCHOOL.
See SCHOOLS AND EDUCATION.**

PRINTERS AND PRINTING.
Accident and sickness insurance policies, **175:108.**
Annual town report, authority for printing, **40:49.**
Appeals court.
Expenditures, **221A:7.**
Reporter of decisions, publication, **211A:9.**
Rules not required for printing of records and briefs, **211A:13.**
Apples, printed sales statements, **94:103, 94:108.**
Ballots.
See ELECTIONS.
Bank bills, retaining with intent to pass, **266:43.**
Bradford Durfee College of Technology, purchases, **74:42N.**
"Building used for industrial purposes," print shop, **149:1.**
Cities and towns.
Annual report, **40:49.**
Budget, **44:32.**
Municipal finance.
See MUNICIPAL FINANCE.
Records, power to appropriate money for printing, **40:5.**
Cloth, lien, **255:31A, 255:31B.**
Copyright.
See COPYRIGHT.
Counterfeiting, penalty for possession of press, **267:13, 267:20.**
Elections.
See ELECTIONS.
Engraving.
See ENGRAVING.

PRINTERS AND PRINTING
—Cont'd

False advertising, **266:91, 266:91B.**
Fees.
Clerks of court for copies of records and documents to be printed, **262:5.**
Land court, fee for printing notice, **262:39.**
Fire insurance policies, **175:99.**
International trade office, costs and fees for printing lists, **23A:24.**
Jeweler's lien, **255:31C.**
Judicial decisions of Supreme Judicial and Appeals Courts, **221:64A.**
Junk collector regulations not applicable to prints, **140:55.**
Jury list, **40:49, 234:5.**
Labor statute definitions, **149:1.**
Land court, fee for printing notice, **262:39.**
Lettershops, hours of labor for women and children, **149:56, 149:57, 149:66-149:68, 149:78.**
Life insurance companies' annual statements, disbursements listed, **175:25.**
Lottery tickets, **271:18.**
Use as evidence, **271:19.**
Meal hours, **149:101.**
Mental retardation, printing and distribution of documents, **5:11.**
Metropolitan districts, financial statement of state treasurer, **10:11.**
Motor vehicle sales contracts, **255B:9, 255B:10.**
Municipalities.
Cities and towns. See within this heading, "Cities and towns."
New Bedford Institute of Technology, purchases, **74:42N.**
Personal service contracts, termination notice, **255:13K.**
Polish-American Veterans of Massachusetts, distribution of copies of proceedings, **5:9.**
Presses.
See PRESSES.
Probate Court proceedings, printing requirements as to service of summons by publication, **215:3.**
Publication, defined for purposes of depository library for Massachusetts state publications, **6:39.**

PRINTERS AND PRINTING
—Cont'd

Public notices regarding firearms, payment, **269:11.**

Purchasing agent of state.
See STATE PURCHASING AGENT.

Real estate brokers and salesmen, publication containing lists, **112:87.**

Register of probate and insolvency to print names of persons signing filed instruments, **217:15A.**

Residential repair or remodeling contracts, printing of exculpatory provisions, **143:90.**

Retail installment sales agreement, **255B:9, 255D:9, 255D:26.**

Sales and use tax.
Exemption, **64H:6.**
Furnishing printed information as subject, **64H:1.**

School committee reports, **40:49.**

State ballot law commission, **55B:4, 55B:7.**

State colleges, purchases, **73:15.**

State printing.
See STATE PRINTING.

Street lists of voters, **51:6.**

Superior courts.
Copies of rules, **213:3A.**
Trial lists, **213:3.**

Supreme judicial court rules, **213:3A.**

Towns.
Cities and towns. See within this heading, "Cities and towns."

Trial list, **213:3.**

Use tax.
Sales and use tax. See within this heading, "Sales and use tax."

Veterans and veterans' organizations.
Copies of printed matter showing veterans' rights, **115:13.**
Proceedings, **5:9.**

Voting lists, **51:6, 51:55.**

"Written" and "in writing" used in statutes to include printing, **4:7.**

PRINTERS' INK ACT, 266:91.
False advertising, **266:91.**

PRIOR ENCUMBRANCES.
Mortgages.
See MORTGAGES AND DEEDS OF TRUST.

PRIORITIES.
See PREFERENCES AND PRIORITIES.

PRIORITY DISPOSAL SITE.
Oil and hazardous material release prevention and response act, **21E:2, 21E:3A.**

PRIOR JEOPARDY, 263:7 to 263:8A, 265:5; US Const Amend 5.

PRIOR OFFENSE.
Conviction.
See CONVICTION OF CRIME.

PRIOR SERVICE.
Retirement.
See RETIREMENT SYSTEMS AND PENSIONS.

PRISONERS CAGES.
Courtroom use, **34:3.**

PRISONERS OF WAR.
Commemoration of POW/MIA Day, **6:15BBB.**

Conservator, appointment for estate, **201:16A.**

License plates for motor vehicles, **60A:1, 90:2, 90:33.**

Motor vehicles, distinctive registration plates for surviving spouse of deceased prisoner of war, **60A:1, 90:2.**

PRISONS.
Abandoned property or money of former prisoners, disposition, **127:96A, 127:96B, 200A:14.**

Absent voting by inmates, **54:86, 54:89, 54:100, 54:103B.**

Abstract of mittimus upon commitment of female to jail, **126:21.**

Accounts and accounting.
Aid to discharged prisoners, **127:161, 127:163.**
Annual reports, **127:10.**
Bills for supplies, **125:21, 127:72.**
County prisons.
See COUNTY PRISONS.
Inmate savings accounts, **127:3, 127:48A.**
Receipts from labor of prisoners, **127:71.**
Treasurer's duties as, **125:6.**

Acting superintendents, **125:5.**

Administrator, **125:1.**

Agents and agency.
Aid to discharged prisoners, duties regarding, **127:158.**
Selling agents for prison-made goods, **127:68.**

PRISONS —Cont'd
Agents and agency —Cont'd
State purchasing agent. See within this heading, "State purchasing agent."

Agricultural labor by prisoners, **127:83, 127:84.**

Aiding escape of prisoner, **268:15, 268:17.**

Aid to discharged prisoners, **127:158-127:165.**

Account of expenditures by agents, **127:161.**

Annual report of agents, **127:163.**

Board and lodging, furnishing to prisoner upon discharge, **127:161, 127:165.**

County commissioners, aid by, **127:164.**

Disabled prisoner, care, **127:151.**

Duties of agents, **127:158.**

House of correction, payment by superintendent or keeper, **127:165.**

Jail, payment by superintendent or keeper, **127:165.**

Monetary aid upon discharge, **127:165.**

Parole board's duty as, **27:5, 127:160.**

Alcoholic liquors.
Alcoholism and intoxication. See within this heading, "Alcoholism and intoxication."
Prisoners, furnishing liquor, **268:26, 268:27, 268:29.**
State form sentence for drunkenness, **279:36.**
Use to excess as ground for removal of employee, **127:12, 127:14.**

Alcoholism and intoxication.
Bridgewater correctional institution.
See BRIDGEWATER CORRECTIONAL INSTITUTION.
Framingham correctional institution.
See FRAMINGHAM CORRECTIONAL INSTITUTION.
Removal of employee, ground, **127:12, 127:14.**
State farm, sentence, **279:36.**
Treatment and rehabilitation centers established in correctional institutions, **111B:4.**

PRISONS —Cont'd

Annual reports of officers, **127:10.**

Any county, sentence, **279:15.**

Appeal and review.

Child in need of services, appeal after arrest and detention, **119:39H, 119:39I.**

Commitment pending appeal, **278:18.**

Dismissal of prisoner's appeal, notice, **278:28C.**

Jailer's fees upon withdrawal, **278:26.**

Superior court appellate division sitting in correctional institution, **278:28A.**

Approval of plans for, by State Health Department, **111:22.**

Arbitration and award.

Contract of correctional institution, dispute over, **125:20, 127:73.**

Prison goods for public offices and institutions, **127:55, 127:58, 127:73.**

Arrest.

See ARREST.

Arrest on mesne process.

See ARREST ON MESNE PROCESS AND SUPPLEMENTARY PROCEEDINGS.

Arson, **266:2.**

Assault by prisoner on guard or employee, **127:38A, 127:38B, 265:13D.**

Athletics.

Recreation. See within this heading, "Recreation."

Attorneys.

Conferences with and visits by, **127:36A.**

District.

See DISTRICT AND PROSECUTING ATTORNEYS.

Inmates charged with offenses, assignment of counsel, **278:16.**

Visitation rights, **127:36A.**

Bail.

See BAIL AND RECOGNIZANCE.

Bedding, **94:273, 111:21.**

Accounts as to bedding furnished, **126:33, 127:8.**

Sterilization of bedding before reuse, **94:273.**

Bertillon measurements.

Identification measurements of prisoners. See within this heading, "Identification measurements of prisoners."

PRISONS —Cont'd

Bills for supplies, **125:21.**

Births to inmates.

Custody and care of newborn, **119:23A.**

Notice, **46:6, 46:8.**

Blood donations, reduction in sentence of prisoners making, **127:133.**

Board and lodging for prisoners, furnishing upon discharge, **127:161, 127:165.**

Bond of superintendents, deputies, and officers, **125:2, 125:5, 125:6, 126:16, 126:24.**

Boston penal institutions commissioner.

See BOSTON.

Bridgewater correctional institution.

See BRIDGEWATER CORRECTIONAL INSTITUTION.

Buildings, superintendent's control over, **125:14.**

Cages for prisoners, use in courtroom abolished, **34:3.**

Calendars and dockets.

Record of prisoners, **127:5.**

Return at opening of court session, **126:7.**

Camps.

Civil service status of directors, **127:83D.**

Group classification of officers for contributory retirement program, **32:3.**

Prisoners prior to parole, camp, **127:83E.**

Reduction of sentence for good conduct, **127:129C.**

Reforestation camp. See within this heading, "Reforestation camp."

Removal of certain prisoners, **127:83A, 127:83B.**

Capital cases.

See CAPITAL CASES.

Cedar Junction, **31:48, 125:1, 127:49B.**

Certificates and certification.

Discharge certificate for prisoner on service of reduced sentence, **127:129C.**

Employment in correctional institutions, certificate of eligibility, **125:4, 125:9.**

Hospitalization of prisoners, **127:117, 127:117A.**

Pregnant prisoners, **127:118.**

Change of name, **125:1.**

PRISONS —Cont'd

Change of venue, custody, **277:54.**

Chapels and chaplains, **125:13.**

Advisory committee on chaplains, **6:166B.**

Constitution of Massachusetts, penal and reformatory institution inmates entitled to freedom of religion, **MA Const Amend Art 18.**

Pastoral counseling for prisoners, **127:36B.**

Religious services, **127:88-127:90.**

Children and minors, **120:1 et seq.**

Births to inmates. See within this heading, "Births to inmates."

Detention pending trial, **119:25-119:27, 119:66-119:68.**

Funeral or last illness of child or close relative, prisoner's attendance at, **127:90A.**

Interstate Corrections Compact, **Spec L 138:1.**

Labor of prisoners, child labor laws as applicable, **149:85.**

Segregation, **119:68, 127:22.**

Youth services department.

See YOUTH SERVICES DEPARTMENT AND MASSACHUSETTS TRAINING SCHOOLS.

Cigarette excise tax stamps, **64C:38.**

City or town prisons, **40:34-40:37.**

Civil service.

Business manager and adjutant, **31:49.**

Camp directors, **127:83D.**

Certification of eligible persons, **125:4, 125:9.**

Educational requirement, **31:21, 31:64.**

Eligibility for appointment, **31:50, 125:4, 125:9.**

Height requirements for correction officers, **31:21, 31:58, 31:64.**

Holiday, working, **30:24A.**

Nurses, exclusion or exemption, **31:48.**

Officers and employees.

Applicability, **31:48.**

Eligibility qualifications of certain, **31:50, 125:4.**

Opportunities for convicts, **31:5.**

Practical nurses excluded from, **31:48.**

PRISONS —Cont'd
Civil service —Cont'd
Removal, restrictions as, **30:9B.**
Retirement, **32:3.**
Superintendent substituted for master, **32:3.**
Teacher, tenure, **30:9D.**
Classification of prisoners, **127:20-127:22.**
Deputy commissioner for classification, **27:2, 124:2, 127:20.**
Female prisoners. See within this heading, "Female prisoners."
Periodic classification board, **127:20A.**
Segregated units, **127:39.**
Closing of county correctional facility for noncompliance with standards, **127:1B.**
Clothes.
Wearing apparel. See within this heading, "Wearing apparel."
Commissioner of corrections, **27:1 et seq., 124:1 et seq.**
Commitment warrant.
Mittimus. See within this heading, "Mittimus."
Committed offender, **125:1.**
Committees for determination of inmate's fitness to participate in outside programs, **127:49A.**
Common night walkers, discharge, **127:143.**
Commonwealth service corps, purpose of creation, **6:121.**
Communication with prisoners, penalty, **268:30.**
Compensation and salaries.
Educational programs, participants, **127:48, 127:49.**
Identification measurements of criminals, no compensation with regard, **127:30.**
Payment of salaries and wages, **127:72.**
Prison labor, **127:48A.**
Trial, compensation for prisoners acquitted or discharged without, **277:73.**
Work release programs, **127:86F.**
Comptroller of state.
List of articles made in institutions, **127:57.**
Unclaimed money of former prisoners, duties as, **127:96A.**
Concord correctional institution.
See CONCORD CORRECTIONAL INSTITUTION.

PRISONS —Cont'd
Conferences with attorneys, **127:36A.**
Constitution of Massachusetts, penal and reformatory institution inmates entitled to freedom of religion, **MA Const Amend Art 18.**
Contagious diseases.
Diseases. See within this heading, "Diseases."
Contracts, **124:1, 125:20, 127:73.**
Interest on money of prisoners, expenditure, **127:3.**
Interstate compacts.
See INTERSTATE COMPACTS AND AGREEMENTS.
Labor of prisoners, **127:51, 127:73.**
Purchase of tools and materials, **127:66, 127:66A.**
Conversion of public health hospitals for use as, **30:64.**
Conveyance of articles to and from, forbidden, **268:26-268:29, 268:31.**
Convict labor.
Labor of prisoners. See within this heading, "Labor of prisoners."
Convicts as correction officers, **125:9.**
Correctional employment fund, **127:71.**
Correction officers.
Officers and employees. See within this heading, "Officers and employees."
Corrections department.
See CORRECTIONS DEPARTMENT.
Correspondence of prisoners, regulated, **127:87.**
Costs.
Expenses. See within this heading, "Expenses and expenditures."
Costs of action.
Indigent persons' court costs.
Statement of inmate's account, **261:29.**
Counsel.
Attorneys. See within this heading, "Attorneys."
County commissioners.
See COUNTY COMMISSIONERS.
County correction fund, **64D:13.**
County industrial farms, **126:35 et seq.**

PRISONS —Cont'd
County prisons.
See COUNTY PRISONS.
County treasurers.
See COUNTY TREASURERS.
Court orders.
Orders of court. See within this heading, "Orders of court."
Courts-martial, confinement after sentence, **33:78.**
Credits.
Prisoner committed for nonpayment of fine, **127:144.**
Prison labor, credit to prisoners, **127:48A.**
Trial, imprisonment pending, **127:129B, 279:33A.**
Crime or offense committed.
Assault by prisoner, **127:38A, 127:38B, 265:13D.**
Assignment of counsel, **278:16.**
Communication with prisoner, **268:30.**
Disturbing of institution, **268:30.**
Furnishing liquor or other articles to prisoners, **268:26-268:29, 268:31.**
Hostages, holding, **127:38A.**
Injury to property of institution, **266:129, 266:130.**
Report, **127:38C.**
Sexual relations between prisoner and officer, **268:21A.**
Trespass on land of institution, **266:123.**
Criminal offender record information systems, **127:2, 127:28, 127:29.**
Damage to property, **266:97, 266:129, 266:130.**
Dangerous weapons, emergency release of persons convicted of carrying, **269:10.**
Dead bodies, disposition, **111:111C, 125:17, 126:22.**
Death.
Benefits for hypertension or heart disease, **32:94.**
Notice to town clerk of inmate's death, **46:6, 46:8.**
Death sentence, hospitalization at Norfolk, **127:117.**
Debtors imprisoned.
Discharge, **127:145, 127:146.**
Segregation, **127:22.**
Deduction of sentence for good conduct while confined at, **127:129C.**
Deeds excise fund, **64D:11, 64D:12.**

PRISONS —Cont'd

Deer Island, sentences, **218:48.**

Defacement of county buildings, reimbursement of total damages by persons convicted, **266:97.**

Defined, **123:1, 125:1.**

Department of correction.
See CORRECTIONS DEPARTMENT.

Deposits of money, superintendent substituted for master, **35:22, 35:22A.**

Deputies.
Master, keeper, deputy, or jailer. See within this heading, "Master, keeper, deputy, or jailer."

Destruction of property of correctional institution as offense, **266:97, 266:129, 266:130.**

Detainers outstanding against prisoners.
See INTERSTATE COMPACTS AND AGREEMENTS.

Dipsomaniacs.
Alcoholism and intoxication. See within this heading, "Alcoholism and intoxication."

Director of account to examine shops, **35:45.**

Discharge or release of prisoners.
Aid to discharged prisoners. See within this heading, "Aid to discharged prisoners."

Bail.
See BAIL AND RECOGNIZANCE.

Certificate of discharge, **127:129C.**

Common nightwalkers, **127:143.**

Costs or fees, liability, **278:14, 280:6.**

Debtors imprisoned for failure to pay, **127:145, 127:146.**

Disability existing at time of discharge, care and support during, **127:151.**

Earnings from prison labor paid upon, **127:48A.**

Federal correctional institution, effect of transfer of state prisoner, **127:97A.**

Firearms offenses, temporary release of persons convicted, **269:10.**

PRISONS —Cont'd

Discharge or release of prisoners —Cont'd

Habeas corpus.
Subsequent imprisonment for some cause, **248:24.**
When required, **248:23.**

Indictments, informations, and complaints.
After indictment, **277:47.**
Arson, notice to state fire marshal of discharge of one indicted or convicted, **127:162A.**
Not indicted, **277:15.**

Juvenile courts.
See JUVENILE COURTS AND DELINQUENT CHILDREN.

Mentally ill person confined during course of criminal proceeding, **123:17.**

Mesne process, discharge from imprisonment, **224:12, 224:21.**

Nonpayment of fine, discharge of prisoner committed, **127:144-127:146.**

Not indicted, discharge or release of prisoner as, **277:15.**

Penalty for leaving prisoner at large, **268:21.**

Poor prisoners, **127:144-127:146.**

Pregnant female prisoners, **127:142.**

Reforestation camps, prisoners, **127:83B.**

Rehabilitation facilities and programs. See within this heading, "Rehabilitation and rehabilitation programs."

Sunday, where time ends, **127:150.**

Temporary release of prisoners, **127:90A, 268:16.**

Venereal disease or tuberculosis, **111:121.**

Wearing apparel, **127:161, 127:162, 127:165.**

Work release programs. See within this heading, "Work release programs."

Discontinuance by commissioner, **124:1.**

Diseases.
County prisons, removal of prisoners from, **126:26.**
Examination of prisoners, **127:16-127:18.**

PRISONS —Cont'd

Diseases —Cont'd

Exposure to infectious disease through attending, assisting or transporting infected individual or deceased person, reporting requirements, **111:111C.**

Isolation and treatment, **111:108.**
Venereal disease or tuberculosis, **111:121.**

Jails and houses of correction, **111:108.**

Places caring for persons with, **111:92.**

Tuberculosis.
Discharge, care and treatment of prisoners, **127:151.**
Examination of prisoners, **127:16-127:18.**
Isolation and treatment, **111:121.**

Vaccination against, **111:182.**

Venereal disease, **111:121, 127:16-127:18.**

Dismissal of appeal of prisoner, notice, **278:28C.**

District.
See DISTRICT AND PROSECUTING ATTORNEYS.

Disturbing, as criminal offense, **268:30.**

Divorce for confinement, **208:2.**

Dockets.
Calendars and dockets. See within this heading, "Calendars and dockets."

Domicile and residence.
Jailer or keeper provided with dwelling house, sheriff not to receive rent from, **126:17.**
Superintendents and deputies, **125:15.**
Temporary release to obtain residence upon discharge, **127:90A.**

Drill for prisoners, **127:19.**

Drugs and narcotics.
Good conduct deductions for drug offenders before serving minimum mandatory sentence, prohibition, **94C:32H.**

PRISONS —Cont'd
Drugs and narcotics —Cont'd
Penalty for bringing contraband
into prison upon return
from furlough or work
program, **268:31.**
Prison book record as to
medicine furnished to
prisoners, **127:8.**
Unauthorized delivery to
prisoners, **268:28.**
Drunkards.
Alcoholism and intoxication. See
within this heading,
"Alcoholism and
intoxication."
Educational programs.
See SCHOOLS AND
EDUCATION.
Elections.
Absent voting by inmates, **54:86,
54:89, 54:100.**
Voting precincts, division of
cities and towns, **54:2, 54:6.**
Emergency release of persons
convicted of carrying
dangerous weapons, **269:10.**
Employment.
Fund, **127:71.**
Gainful employment defined
under corrections law,
125:1.
Hours of labor. See within this
heading, "Hours of labor."
Labor of prisoners. See within
this heading, "Labor of
prisoners."
Officers and employees. See
within this heading,
"Officers and employees."
Programs for inmates, **127:48 et
seq.**
Temporary release of inmate to
obtain upon discharge,
127:90A.
Escape, **268:15-268:24.**
Examination.
Inspection. See within this
heading, "Inspection."
Medical and physical
examination. See within this
heading, "Medical and
physical examination."
Exchange of prisoners, foreign
countries, **127:97B.**
Expenses and expenditures.
Annual reports, **127:10.**
Commissioner of correction,
powers, **124:1.**
Commitment or removal,
expense, **127:123, 262:21,
262:50.**

PRISONS —Cont'd
Expenses and expenditures
—Cont'd
County prisons, **126:28-126:34.**
Employment fund, **127:71.**
Fees. See within this heading,
"Fees."
Health services, inmates as
exempt from paying cost,
7:3B.
Hospitalization of prisoners. See
within this heading,
"Hospitalization of
prisoners."
Inmate earnings, payment of
personal, family, or legal
expenses, **127:48A.**
Maintenance of federal
prisoners, **125:11.**
Officer training, **125:9.**
Prison-made goods, meetings in
connection with, **127:54.**
Rearrangement or enlargement
of shops, **127:48A.**
Receipts from prison industries
applied, **127:71.**
Temporary release of inmate,
127:90A.
Travel expenses.
See TRAVELING EXPENSES.
Extension of limits of confinement,
127:90A.
Extradition.
See EXTRADITION.
Falsely assuming to be official of
bureau of special
investigations, **268:33.**
Federal penitentiary.
Commitment.
See FEDERAL COURTS.
Divorce for confinement in
federal penitentiary, **208:2.**
Forfeiture of state office after
sentence, **279:30.**
Maintenance of federal prisoner,
125:11.
Transfer of state prisoner to,
effect, **127:97A.**
Federal service personnel defined
for absentee voting purposes,
54:103B.
Fees.
Appeal, jailer's fees in event of
withdrawal, **278:26.**
Discharge or release of prisoner,
278:14, 280:6.
Mittimus. See within this
heading, "Mittimus."
Supplementary proceedings for
commitment of defendant,
262:14.

PRISONS —Cont'd
Fees —Cont'd
Transportation of prisoners,
262:21, 262:48.
Witnesses held in jail, **262:30.**
Female prisoners.
Abstract of mittimus upon
commitment to jail, **126:21.**
Births to inmates. See within
this heading, "Births to
inmates."
Care and custody of infants,
119:23A.
Classification of, **127:20, 127:21,
127:22.**
Commissioner, designation of
facilities by, **125:16.**
County prisons.
Abstract of mittimus
committing female to be
sent to Commissioner of
correction, **126:21.**
Separation and classification,
127:21, 127:22.
Framingham correctional
institution.
See FRAMINGHAM
CORRECTIONAL
INSTITUTION.
Good conduct deductions for
drug offenders before
serving minimum
mandatory sentence,
prohibition, **94C:32H.**
Keeping together prisoners of
different sexes, **268:29.**
Place of imprisonment,
279:16-279:20.
Pregnancy.
Births to inmates. See within
this heading, "Births to
inmates."
Discharge, **127:142.**
Hospitalization, **127:118.**
Removal or transfer of females
held for trial, **125:16.**
Segregation, **127:22.**
Transportation, **276:53.**
Financial aid.
Aid to discharged prisoners. See
within this heading, "Aid to
discharged prisoners."
Fines and penalties.
Accounts, **280:8.**
Assault and battery by prisoner,
127:38B.
Commitment in lieu of payment
of fine, **279:1, 279:1A,
279:10.**
Communication with prisoners,
268:30.

PRISONS —Cont'd
Fines and penalties —Cont'd
Credits of prisoner committed for nonpayment, **127:144.**
Defacement of prison, **266:97, 266:129, 266:130.**
Disturbing correctional institutions, **268:30.**
Furlough.
Bringing contraband into prison upon return, **268:31.**
Failure to return from, **268:16.**
Illicit conveyance of articles, **268:31.**
Leaving prisoner at large, penalty, **268:21.**
Nonpayment of, discharge of prisoner committed, **127:144-127:146.**
Payment, **280:8, 280:14, 280:15.**
Quarterly returns, **280:10.**
Segregation of prisoners, lack, **268:29.**
Sentence for nonpayment, **279:7, 279:9, 279:10.**
Superintendent, payment, **280:8, 280:14, 280:15.**
Firearms offenses, temporary release of persons convicted, **269:10.**
Fitness of inmate's participation in outside education, training and employment programs, determination, **127:49A.**
Food and meals.
Commissioner of correction, duties, **124:1.**
Isolation units, **127:40, 127:41.**
Jail or house of correction, **126:34.**
Segregated units, **127:39.**
Foreign countries, prisoner exchanges, **127:97B.**
Framingham correctional institution.
See FRAMINGHAM CORRECTIONAL INSTITUTION.
Frivolous claims or proceedings. Deduction from good conduct credits, **231:6F.**
Funds of prisoners.
Property and funds of prisoners. See within this heading, "Property and funds of prisoners."
Funeral of relative, temporary release of inmate, **127:90A.**
Furlough, **127:90A, 268:16, 268:31.**

PRISONS —Cont'd
Furniture.
Bedding. See within this heading, "Bedding."
Charge and custody of furniture, **125:14.**
Isolation units, furniture, **127:40, 127:41.**
Supplying furniture, **126:33.**
Further sentences of court, **279:28.**
Gag, **127:38.**
Gainful employment defined under correction, **125:1.**
Games.
Recreation. See within this heading, "Recreation."
G.E.D. tests, certain inmates may be permitted to take, **127:92A.**
Giving articles to prisoners without permission, **268:28.**
Good conduct deductions from sentence, provisions as, **94C:32H.**
Frivolous claims or proceedings. Deduction from good conduct credits, **231:6F.**
Governor, appointments by, **27:1.**
Governor's council.
Advisory committee, appointment, **27:1.**
Classification of prisoners, **127:20.**
Commissioner's reports, **124:5.**
Corrections department.
See CORRECTIONS DEPARTMENT.
Right to visit, **127:36.**
Rules and regulations for, approval, **124:1.**
Habeas corpus.
See HABEAS CORPUS.
Hard labor, women sentenced, **279:20.**
Health conditions and regulations, **40:36B, 111:20-111:22.**
Clinics for chronic alcoholics, fixing standards, **125:16, 125:19.**
Diseases. See within this heading, "Diseases."
Expiration of sentence, care of disabled prisoner after, **127:151.**
Hospitalization of prisoners. See within this heading, "Hospitalization of prisoners."
Inspection and report as to, **40:36B, 111:20-111:22.**
Isolation units, **127:40, 127:41.**
Medical care. See within this heading, "Medical care."

PRISONS —Cont'd
Health conditions and regulations —Cont'd
Nurses, civil service, **31:48.**
Physical examination.
See MEDICAL AND PHYSICAL EXAMINATION.
Physicians, **27:2.**
Plans for institution, approval by health department, **111:22.**
Regulations by state health department, **111:20, 111:21.**
Vaccination of prisoners, **111:182.**
Venereal disease, examination of prisoners, **127:16-127:18.**
High school equivalency certificate, reduction of sentence for prisoners receiving, **127:129D.**
Holidays.
Sundays and holidays. See within this heading, "Sundays and holidays."
Hospitalization of prisoners, **127:117, 127:117A.**
Births to inmates. See within this heading, "Births to inmates."
Capital crimes, **127:117.**
Certificates and certification. See within this heading, "Certificates and certification."
Disability at time of expiration of sentence, **127:151.**
Expenses and expenditures.
Payment, **127:123.**
Prisoner removed to Bridgewater Correctional Institution, **127:126.**
Mental illness, transfer of prisoners in need of hospitalization by reason, **123:18.**
Pregnant females, **127:118.**
Removal of prisoner, **127:117.**
Sentence, time as part, **127:119.**
Temporary release pursuant, **127:90A.**
Transfer of prisoners in need of hospitalization for mental illness, **123:18.**
Hospitals and health care facilities.
Conversion of hospital for use as correctional institution, **30:64.**
Employment security law, exemption for prisoner labor in hospitals, **151A:6.**

PRISONS —Cont'd

Hospitals and health care facilities
—Cont'd

Exemptions, **7:3B, 151A:6.**

Hospitalization of prisoners. See
within this heading,
"Hospitalization of
prisoners."

Hostages, holding of, penalty,
127:38A.

Hours of labor.

Officers and employees,
149:30A, 149:30B, 149:39.

Prisoners, **127:49.**

Husband and wife.

Divorce for confinement, **208:2.**

Funeral or deathbed of spouse,
temporary release, **127:90A.**

Pensions for widows of
correction officers, **32:100.**

Visit by spouse, statement of
relationship upon, **127:36.**

Identification measurements of
prisoners, **127:23-127:30.**

Commissioner of public safety,
transmission of
measurements, **127:23,
127:25, 127:29.**

District attorney to furnish case
history, **127:27.**

Fugitives from justice, in aid of
apprehension, **127:25.**

No compensation to officers
taking, **127:30.**

Publication regulated, **127:29.**

Record, **127:28.**

Illness of relative, temporary
release of inmate in case,
127:90A.

Indictments.

Discharge or release of
prisoners. See within this
heading, "Discharge or
release of prisoners."

Transmission of indictment to
correctional institution,
279:35.

Indigent persons' court costs.

Costs of action.

Statement of inmate's account,
261:29.

Industries at.

Labor of prisoners. See within
this heading, "Labor of
prisoners."

Inebriates.

Alcoholism and intoxication. See
within this heading,
"Alcoholism and
intoxication."

PRISONS —Cont'd

Infants.

Children and minors. See within
this heading, "Children and
minors."

Infectious diseases.

Diseases. See within this
heading, "Diseases."

Injury to employee, compensation
and benefits, **32:94, 152:74.**

Injury to property at correctional
and penal institutes, **266:97,
266:129, 266:130.**

Inmates defined, **125:1.**

Insane and mentally ill prisoners.

Corrections department, **27:2A,
123:18.**

Crimes punishable by
imprisonment, **19:10, 19:19,
19B:10, 19B:15.**

Duties, **123:18.**

Employment at facilities of
department, **127:49B.**

Examination, **127:39.**

Psychological or psychiatric
treatment, release of
inmate, **127:90A.**

Release of mentally ill person
confined during course of
criminal prosecution,
123:17.

Segregated units, psychiatric
treatment, **127:39.**

State prison, imprisonment,
19B:10.

Transfer of prisoners in need of
hospitalization, **123:18.**

Inspection, **111:20.**

County prisons.

See COUNTY PRISONS.

Health conditions and
regulations. See within this
heading, "Health conditions
and regulations."

Institution defined under
corrections law, **125:1.**

Insurrection, suppression, **127:33.**

Interest on prisoner's money,
127:3, 127:48A.

Interstate supervision of
probationers and parolees,
127:151A-127:151K.

Intoxicating liquor.

Alcoholic liquors. See within this
heading, "Alcoholic liquors."

Investigation of grievances and
misconduct, **124:1.**

Investigative and fugitive
apprehension unit, **127:127.**

Isolation and isolation units,
127:40, 127:41.

Diseases. See within this
heading, "Diseases."

PRISONS —Cont'd

Isolation and isolation units
—Cont'd

Records, **127:4.**

Segregated units, **127:39.**

Tuberculosis patients, **111:121.**

Venereal disease, **111:121.**

Jails.

County prisons.

See COUNTY PRISONS.

Lockups, **40:34-40:37.**

See LOCKUPS.

Judgments.

See JUDGMENTS, ORDERS,
AND DECREES.

Jury service, exemption of officers
and employees from, **234:1.**

Juvenile courts.

See JUVENILE COURTS AND
DELINQUENT CHILDREN.

Keeper.

Master, keeper, deputy, or jailer.
See within this heading,
"Master, keeper, deputy, or
jailer."

Labor of prisoners, **127:48-127:76.**

Accounting for receipts from,
127:71.

Arbitration of controversies as,
127:55, 127:58, 127:73.

Child labor laws as applicable,
149:85.

Compensation of prisoners,
127:48A.

Contracts, **127:51, 127:73.**

Corrections officers, convicts as,
125:9.

Cultivation of lands, **127:83,
127:84.**

Director of accounts to examine,
35:45.

Disposition.

Manufactured goods, **127:67,
127:68.**

Prisoner's earnings, **127:48A.**

Receipts from prison labor,
127:71.

Employment security law,
exclusion from, **151A:6.**

Escapes while working on public
lands or buildings, **127:49.**

Hard labor, women sentenced,
279:20.

Hours of labor, **127:49.**

Industries, **127:51, 127:61.**

Accounting for receipts from,
127:71.

Establishment and
maintenance, **127:51.**

Expenses of, use of receipts
from labor, **127:71.**

PRISONS —Cont'd
Labor of prisoners —Cont'd
Lists of prison-made articles,
   127:55, 127:57.
Manufactured goods.
   Agents for sale, **127:68.**
   Places for sale, **127:67.**
   Prices for sale, **127:58.**
Outdoor labor, **127:83-127:84.**
Outside programs, **127:49,
   127:49A.**
Premises, labor, **127:49.**
Prices of articles made, **127:58.**
Private persons, labor, **127:51,
   127:84.**
Public land and buildings,
   127:49, 127:49B.
Public officers and institutions,
   manufacture of goods,
   127:53-127:60.
Public works department,
   employment by, **127:84.**
Purchase of personal articles out
   of earnings from, **127:48A.**
Receipts from, accounting and
   disposition, **127:71.**
Reclamation of wastelands,
   127:83-127:84.
Reforestation employment,
   127:84, 132:7.
Report or record, **124:6, 126:12,
   127:8, 127:69, 127:158.**
Sentence, work deductions
   credited, **127:48A,
   127:129D.**
Sex offenders, **127:49.**
Sheriffs report, **126:12.**
State forests, labor,
   **127:83A-127:83E, 127:84,
   132:7.**
Styles, designs, etc., **127:54.**
Tools and materials.
   Payment of bills, **127:72.**
   Purchase, **127:66, 127:66A.**
   Superintendent's control over,
      125:14.
Wastelands, improvement,
   127:84.
Workers' compensation, **152:74.**
Work release programs. See
   within this heading, "Work
   release programs."
Land court.
   Hampden County, appeals to
      land court department,
      40A:17.
   Punishment for contempt,
      185:25A.
Length of sentence, **279:33.**
Liberty permits.
   See LIBERTY PERMITS.

PRISONS —Cont'd
Life imprisonment.
   See LIFE IMPRISONMENT.
Limitation of actions.
   Actions by prisoners, **260:7.**
   Escaping inmates of
      Massachusetts training
      schools, claims for damage
      by, **120:13A.**
   Support, actions to recover,
      260:1.
Liquor.
   Alcoholic liquors. See within this
      heading, "Alcoholic liquors."
Lists of prison-made articles,
   127:55, 127:57.
Lockups, **40:34-40:37.**
Lottery ticket sales to prisoners,
   10:27.
Maintenance.
   Order, obedience, etc., **127:33.**
   Repairs or maintenance, **34:14,
      125:11.**
Malicious injury to property at,
   266:129, 266:130.
Manufacture.
   Labor of prisoners. See within
      this heading, "Labor of
      prisoners."
Marriage of inmates, notice,
   207:20.
Master, keeper, deputy, or jailer.
   Appeal, fees on withdrawal,
      278:26.
   Bond, **37:2.**
   Deputy commissioner for
      classification, **27:2, 124:2,
      127:20.**
   Fines, payment to jailer,
      **280:7-280:10, 280:14,
      280:15.**
   Hypertension or heart disease,
      death or disability benefits,
      32:94.
   Pensions and retirement
      benefits, **32:46-32:48.**
   Precept to be left with, **279:39.**
   Statutes distributed, **5:3.**
   Superintendents. See within this
      heading, "Superintendents."
   Surplus funds in hands, **35:22.**
Meals.
   Food and meals. See within this
      heading, "Food and meals."
Measurements of prisoners.
   Identification measurements.
      See within this heading,
      "Identification
      measurements of prisoners."
Medical and physical examination.
   Inmates, **127:16-127:18.**
   Segregated units, **127:39.**

PRISONS —Cont'd
Medical care.
   Cost of health services, prisoners
      exempt from paying, **7:3B.**
   Hospitalization of prisoners. See
      within this heading,
      "Hospitalization of
      prisoners."
   Hospitals and health care
      facilities. See within this
      heading, "Hospitals and
      health care facilities."
   Nurses, civil service, **31:48.**
   Records.
      Medical records. See within
         this heading, "Medical
         records."
   Removal or transfer of inmates,
      **111:108, 127:117, 127:117A,
      127:118.**
   Tuberculosis or venereal disease,
      isolation and treatment,
      111:121.
Medical examiner, reporting
   deaths to, **38:3.**
Medical records, **127:8, 127:17.**
   Parole board, reports, **127:135,
      127:136.**
   Prison book, **127:8.**
Mental illness.
   Insane and mentally ill
      prisoners. See within this
      heading, "Insane and
      mentally ill prisoners."
Mesne process, discharge from
   imprisonment, **224:12, 224:21.**
Minimum standards for care and
   custody of persons committed
   to county correctional
   facilities, **127:1A.**
Minors.
   Children and minors. See within
      this heading, "Children and
      minors."
Misdemeanor, service of sentence
   for to be in jail, **279:5.**
Mittimus.
   Abstract of, upon female's
      commitment to jail, **126:21.**
   Expense for commitment of
      prisoners, **262:21, 262:50.**
   Extra-county powers of officers
      in execution, **279:38.**
   Federal penitentiary,
      commitment to.
      See FEDERAL COURTS.
   Fees for execution, **127:7,
      279:39.**
      Aid in serving writ, **262:47.**
      Conveying several prisoners at
         one time, **262:48.**

PRISONS —Cont'd
Mittimus —Cont'd
Fees for execution —Cont'd
Joint conviction and sentence, **262:49.**
Juvenile offender cases, **262:27.**
General laws, statement as to laws on which conviction founded to accompany mittimus, when, **279:35.**
Housing court department, service by, **185C:15.**
Indictment transmitted with, **279:35.**
Juvenile offenders, fees and expenses of officers in cases against, **262:27.**
Name of crime to be stated, **279:37.**
New mittimus of further sentence, **279:40.**
Removal of prisoner, mittimus accompanying, **127:120.**
Safekeeping of writ, **127:7.**
Service of new writ on convict, **279:40.**
Monetary aid upon discharge, **127:165.**
Monroe correctional institution, **125:1.**
Narcotics.
Drugs and narcotics. See within this heading, "Drugs and narcotics."
Noncompliance with standards for county correctional facilities, effect, **127:1B.**
Norfolk.
See NORFOLK.
Notice.
Dismissal of prisoner's appeal, **278:28C.**
Marriage of inmates, **207:20.**
Transfer of prisoners, **127:38D.**
Violations of standards for county correctional facilities, **127:1B.**
Nurses, civil service, **31:48.**
Oath of officers, **125:10.**
Obedience, maintenance, **127:33.**
Offense.
Crime or offense committed. See within this heading, "Crime or offense committed."
Officers and employees, **27:2, 127:1 et seq.**
Additional officers, **125:13.**
Age qualifications, **125:4.**
Alcoholic beverages furnished to prisoners, **268:26, 268:27, 268:29.**

PRISONS —Cont'd
Officers and employees —Cont'd
Annual reports, **127:10.**
Appointment of officers and employees, **125:2-125:5.**
Assault by prisoner, **127:38A, 127:38B, 265:13D.**
Certification of names of persons eligible for appointment, **125:4.**
Civil service. See within this heading, "Civil service."
Confinement or conviction of felony as disqualification for employment, **125:9.**
Continued employment on temporary basis, **125:9.**
Convicts as officer or employee, **125:9.**
Department of corrections.
See CORRECTIONS DEPARTMENT.
Deputies.
Master, keeper, deputy, or jailer. See within this heading, "Master, keeper, deputy, or jailer."
Drunkards, removal of employees for being, **127:12, 127:14.**
Eligibility for employment, **125:4.**
Execution of orders of removal, **127:121.**
Federal penitentiary, forfeiture of state office after sentence, **279:30.**
Felony, employment of person convicted, **125:9.**
Forfeiture of state office after imprisonment, **279:30.**
Former prisoners, prohibited from employing, **125:9.**
Fugitive apprehension unit, **127:127.**
Group classification in contributory retirement system, **32:3.**
Hearing officers recommendations as to parole, **27:5.**
Heart disease or hypertension, death or disability benefits, **32:94.**
Holidays falling on Saturday, **30:24A.**
Horse or dog race meeting employees, exception in act as, **271:41.**
Hostages, holding of officers and employees by prisoners, **127:38A.**

PRISONS —Cont'd
Officers and employees —Cont'd
Hours of work of certain officials and employees, **149:30A, 149:30B, 149:39.**
Hypertension or heart disease causing death or disability, **32:94.**
Infectious disease, report of persons exposed through attending, assisting or transporting infected individual or deceased person, **111:111C.**
Instructors and supervisors in prison industries, **127:52.**
Intoxicating liquors.
Alcoholism and intoxication. See within this heading, "Alcoholism and intoxication."
Investigative and fugitive apprehension unit, **127:127.**
Jury service, exemption from, **234:1.**
Maintenance of order, obedience, etc., **127:33.**
Master, keeper, deputy, or jailer. See within this heading, "Master, keeper, deputy, or jailer."
Nurses, **31:48.**
Oath of officers, **125:10.**
Officers authorized, **125:13.**
Overtime pay laws, exception from, **149:30B.**
Pensions.
Retirement benefits and pensions for employees. See within this heading, "Retirement benefits and pensions for employees."
Permitting escape or improper liberties, **268:18-268:21.**
Physical examination of prisoners, neglect of duties as, **127:18.**
Physicians, **27:2.**
Prison camps, directors and officers, **127:83D.**
Probationary period for officer trainees, **125:9.**
Public service corporation employees, exception in act as, **271:41.**
Purchase of prison made goods, **127:60.**
Refusal to take charge of prisoner, **268:20.**
Removal of officers and employees, **127:12, 127:14.**

PRISONS —Cont'd
Officers and employees —Cont'd
Reports of penal institution
officers, **127:10.**
Retirement benefits and
pensions for employees. See
within this heading,
"Retirement benefits and
pensions for employees."
Salaries.
Compensation and salaries.
See within this heading,
"Compensation and
salaries."
Sales agent for prison made
goods, **127:68.**
Sexual relations between
prisoner and officer,
268:21A.
Sheriffs. See within this
heading, "Sheriffs."
Smoking regulations, **27:2.**
State purchasing agent. See
within this heading, "State
purchasing agent."
Superintendents. See within this
heading, "Superintendents."
Suppression of insurrection,
127:33.
Teachers, tenure, **30:9D.**
Temporary employees, **125:9.**
Term of office, **125:2, 125:3.**
Trainees, status, **125:9.**
Treasurers, **125:6.**
Treatment of prisoners, **127:32.**
Uniforms, **125:8, 126:9A.**
Vaccination, **111:182.**
Wages.
Compensation and salaries.
See within this heading,
"Compensation and
salaries."
Weekly payment of salaries and
wages, **149:148.**
Witnesses in custody, ill
treatment, **276:54.**
Workers' compensation, **152:74.**
Order, maintenance, **127:33.**
Orders of court.
Prisoners to be held in
accordance with, **125:12.**
Record of prisoner disclosed,
127:29.
Outdoor labor of prisoners,
127:83-127:84.
Outside education, training and
employment programs for
inmates, **127:49, 127:49A.**
Parole, **127:128 et seq.**
Pastoral counseling for prisoners,
127:36B.

PRISONS —Cont'd
Penal institution defined under
corrections law, **125:1.**
Penalties.
Fines and penalties. See within
this heading, "Fines and
penalties."
Pensions.
Retirement benefits and
pensions for employees. See
within this heading,
"Retirement benefits and
pensions for employees."
Periodic classification of prisoners,
establishment of board for,
127:20A.
Permits for visits, **127:36, 127:37.**
Personal property.
Property and funds of prisoners.
See within this heading,
"Property and funds of
prisoners."
Persons held for trial, removal
between jails and correctional
institutions, **276:52A.**
Physical examination of prisoners.
Medical and physical
examination. See within this
heading, "Medical and
physical examination."
Physical training of prisoners,
127:19.
Physicians, **27:2.**
Plans for, approval, **34:14, 111:22.**
Plymouth correctional institution,
125:1.
Police.
Information from or, **127:158.**
Leaving prisoners at large,
penalty, **268:21.**
Refusal to receive prisoners,
268:20.
Sheriffs. See within this
heading, "Sheriffs."
Special state police officer,
appointment and powers,
127:127.
Poor persons.
Debtors imprisoned for failure to
pay. See within this
heading, "Debtors
imprisoned."
Practical nurses as excluded from
civil service, **31:48.**
Precept, filing copy, **279:39.**
Pregnancy.
Births to inmates. See within
this heading, "Births to
inmates."
Prices of prison-made articles,
127:58.

PRISONS —Cont'd
Printing contract, purchasing
agent to furnish paper, **7:27.**
Prisoners, **125:1, 127:16 et seq.**
Prison-made goods, purchase by
state, **7:22.**
Prisons, defined, **125:1.**
Privileges.
Correspondence, **127:87.**
Funerals of spouse or relatives,
attendance at, **127:90A.**
Religious services,
127:88-127:90.
Visits and visitation. See within
this heading, "Visits and
visitation."
Process and papers.
Filing, **127:7.**
Mittimus. See within this
heading, "Mittimus."
Removal of prisoner, papers,
127:120.
Service of process on inmates,
127:6.
Warrants. See within this
heading, "Warrants."
Procurements.
See UNIFORM
PROCUREMENT ACT.
Programs outside facilities,
regulation of participation of
inmates, **127:49, 127:49A.**
Property and funds of prisoners.
Compensation from labor,
disposition, **127:48A.**
Correctional employment fund,
prisoner employment
receipts deposited, **127:71.**
Interest, **127:3, 127:48A.**
Marking, **125:12.**
Records, **127:3.**
Safekeeping and delivery, **127:3.**
Unclaimed money or property of
former prisoners,
disposition, **127:96A,
127:96B.**
Property, injury or destruction,
266:97, 266:129, 266:130.
Property of institution,
superintendent's control over,
125:14.
Psychological or psychiatric
treatment, release of inmate,
127:90A.
Psychologist or psychiatric social
worker, qualifications as,
27:2A.
Public buildings and grounds,
supervised work, **127:49,
127:49B.**
Public gathering outside facility,
address by inmate, **127:86H,
127:86I.**

PRISONS —Cont'd
Public health department,
regulations by, **111:21.**
Public officers.
Officers and employees. See
within this heading,
"Officers and employees."
Public works and contracts, **34:3,
126:7, 127:84.**
Purchasing agent.
State purchasing agent. See
within this heading, "State
purchasing agent."
Racing information, punishment
for transmission, **271:31A.**
Receiving prisoners, reception
center, **127:20.**
Reclamation of wastelands,
127:83-127:84.
Records and reports.
Accounts and accounting. See
within this heading,
"Accounts and accounting."
Calendars and dockets, record of
prisoners, **127:5.**
Commissioner of correction,
reports to.
See CORRECTIONS
DEPARTMENT.
County correctional facilities,
127:1A.
Criminal offender record
information system, **127:2,
127:28, 127:29.**
Disclosure of records of prisoner
on order of court, **127:29.**
Fines, quarterly returns of
superintendent of house of
corrections as, **280:15.**
Identification measurements of
prisoners, **127:28.**
Infectious disease, report of
persons exposed through
attending, assisting or
transporting infected
individual or deceased
person, **111:111C.**
Information to be furnished to
parole board, **127:135.**
Inmates, **124:1.**
Inspection, **111:20, 127:1B.**
Labor of prisoners, **124:6,
126:12, 127:8, 127:69,
127:158.**
Medical records. See within this
heading, "Medical records."
Physical examination of
prisoners, **127:17, 127:18.**
Prisoners, record, **127:2, 127:8,
127:17, 127:135.**
Process and papers. See within
this heading, "Process and
papers."

PRISONS —Cont'd
Records and reports —Cont'd
Property of prisoners, **127:3.**
Solitary imprisonment, **127:4.**
Superintendent's duties, **127:2.**
Treasurer's duties as, **125:6.**
Unclaimed property of former
prisoners, disposition,
127:96B.
Visitors, **127:37.**
Warrants, etc., **127:7.**
Recreation.
Duties of deputy commissioner
for classification and
treatment, **124:2.**
Organized athletic sports for
prisoners, **127:19.**
Segregated units to have limited
recreational facilities,
127:39.
Reduction of sentence, **94C:32H,
127:129D, 127:133.**
Reforestation camp,
127:83A-127:83E, 132:7.
Escape from, **127:83C.**
Established by youth services
division, **120:11.**
Male prisoners, **132:7.**
Reduction or deduction of
sentence of prisoner,
127:83B.
Reformatories, **18A:1 et seq.,
120:1 et seq.**
Refusal of jailer or officer to
receive prisoner, **268:20.**
Rehabilitation and rehabilitation
programs, **124:1, 124:2.**
Camps for male prisoners prior
to discharge on parole,
127:83E.
Commissioner of corrections,
duties, **124:1.**
Deputy commissioner of
corrections, duties, **124:2.**
Sabbath school, **127:89.**
Studies as to rehabilitation of
criminals, **124:1.**
Release.
Discharge or release of
prisoners. See within this
heading, "Discharge or
release of prisoners."
Religious matters.
Chapels and chaplains. See
within this heading,
"Chapels and chaplains."
Removal or transfer,
127:97-127:127.
Change of venue, **277:54.**
Correctional institution to jail,
127:97, 127:97A.

PRISONS —Cont'd
Removal or transfer —Cont'd
Dead bodies, **111:111C.**
Defective delinquents, **127:111A.**
Expense, **127:123.**
Federally maintained
correctional institutions,
127:97A.
Federal prisoners, **127:113.**
Females held for trial, transfer
to Framingham Correctional
Institution, **125:16.**
Mittimus accompanying,
127:120.
Notice, **127:38D.**
Officers qualified to execute
orders, **127:121.**
Order, **127:120.**
Persons held for trial, **125:16,
276:52A.**
Sentence as affected by, **127:116.**
Sheriff's powers, **127:97,
127:115.**
Sick prisoners, **111:108,
111:111C, 127:117,
127:117A, 127:118.**
Special state police officer,
appointment and powers,
127:127.
Support of transferred prisoners,
expense, **127:124-127:126.**
Terms of original sentence to
apply, **127:116.**
Repairs or maintenance, **34:14,
125:11.**
Reports.
Records and reports. See within
this heading, "Records and
reports."
Rescuing prisoners, **268:15.**
Residence.
Domicile and residence. See
within this heading,
"Domicile and residence."
Retirement benefits and pensions
for employees, **32:46-32:48.**
Camps, group classification for
contributory retirement
program of officers, **32:3.**
Instructors or supervisors,
classification, **32:3.**
Length of service, **32:47.**
Payment to incarcerated
members, **32:6, 32:7.**
Trainees' benefits, **125:9.**
Widows of corrections officers,
pensions, **32:100.**
Review.
Appeal and review. See within
this heading, "Appeal and
review."

PRISONS —Cont'd
Riots.
  Crimes and offenses committed.
    See within this heading,
    "Crime or offense
    committed."
  Suppression, **127:33.**
Rules and regulations, **124:1.**
Sabbath school, **127:89.**
Salaries.
  Compensation and salaries. See
    within this heading,
    "Compensation and
    salaries."
Sale of county owned facilities,
  34:14.
Sanitary conditions.
  Health conditions and
    regulations. See within this
    heading, "Health conditions
    and regulations."
Saturdays, exception as to time off
  for state employees where
  holiday falls, **30:24A.**
Security measures, **124:1.**
Segregation.
  Debtors imprisoned for failure to
    pay, **127:22.**
  Isolation and isolation units. See
    within this heading,
    "Isolation and isolation
    units."
  Minors, **119:68, 127:22.**
  Penalties for failure to segregate
    prisoners, **268:29.**
  Transportation of prisoners,
    segregation of sexes, **276:53.**
  Units for segregation, **127:39.**
Selection of sites for new facilities,
  124:10.
Service of process and papers.
  Process and papers. See within
    this heading, "Process and
    papers."
Several sentences, commitment,
  279:8, 279:8A, 279:9.
Sexual offenses.
  See SEXUAL OFFENSES AND
    OFFENDERS.
Sexual relations between prisoner
  and officer, **268:21A.**
Sheriffs.
  Alcoholic beverages, furnishing
    prisoners with, disability or
    disqualification, **268:29.**
  Bond of, default of jailer, **37:2.**
  Change of venue, transfer of
    custody in case, **277:54.**
  Conveying articles to and from
    penal institutions, offense,
    268:31.

PRISONS —Cont'd
Sheriffs —Cont'd
  County prisons.
    See COUNTY PRISONS.
  Labor of prisoners, report as,
    126:12.
  Living quarters and subsistence,
    37:17.
  Lockups accessible, **40:37.**
  Penalty for failure to segregate
    prisoners, **268:29.**
  Report as to labor of prisoners,
    126:12.
  Transportation of prisoner. See
    within this heading,
    "Transportation of prisoner."
Shops.
  Labor of prisoners. See within
    this heading, "Labor of
    prisoners."
Sick prisoners.
  Medical care. See within this
    heading, "Medical care."
Single fees for conveyance of
  several prisoners at one time,
  262:48.
Smoking regulations, prison
  employees, **27:2.**
Smuggling articles into or out,
  268:26-268:29, 268:31.
Social services.
  Care of prisoner disabled at time
    of discharge, **127:151.**
  Centers located in prisons,
    18B:17.
  Temporary release of inmate to
    obtain, **127:90A.**
Solitary confinement.
  Isolation and isolation units. See
    within this heading,
    "Isolation and isolation
    units."
Special state police officer,
  appointment and powers,
  127:127.
Sports and games.
  Recreation. See within this
    heading, "Recreation."
Standards for, establishment and
  enforcement, **124:1.**
State comptroller.
  Comptroller of state. See within
    this heading, "Comptroller
    of state."
State correctional facility, defined,
  125:1.
State forests, prisoner labor,
  127:83A-127:83E, 127:84,
  132:7.
State health department, health
  regulations by, **111:21.**

PRISONS —Cont'd
State lottery ticket sales to prison
  and jail inmates, **10:27.**
State printing contract, purchasing
  agent to furnish papers, **7:27.**
State prisons, **125:1 et seq.**
State purchase of goods and
  services of inmates, **7:22.**
State purchasing agent.
  Contracts on account, **125:20.**
  Prison-made articles, purchase,
    127:57, 127:60, 127:127.
  Purchase of tools and materials,
    127:66, 127:66A.
Statutes distributed to
  superintendents, master, or
  keepers, **5:3.**
Suffolk county.
  See SUFFOLK COUNTY.
Suggestions for alterations in rules
  and regulations, **125:7.**
Sundays and holidays.
  Discharge of prisoner whose
    term ends on holiday,
    127:150.
  School for inmates on Sabbath,
    127:89.
  State employees, exception from
    rule of time off when
    holiday falls on Saturday,
    30:24A.
Superintendents, **124:2,**
  127:2-127:14.
  Acting superintendent, **125:5.**
  Advisory committee on chaplains
    in state institutions,
    membership, **6:166B.**
  Appointment, **125:2.**
  Bond, **125:2, 125:5.**
  Certification of persons eligible
    for appointment, **125:4.**
  County industrial farms, **126:36,**
    126:37.
  Creation of offices, **125:13.**
  Defined under corrections law,
    125:1.
  Escapes, prevention, **127:33.**
  Fines paid, **280:8, 280:14,**
    280:15.
  Funds extended for welfare of
    prisoners upon release,
    127:162.
  Maintenance of order, obedience,
    etc., **127:33.**
  Master, superintendent
    substituted, **32:3, 35:22,**
    35:22A.
  Oath of officers, **125:10.**
  Report of labor of prisoners,
    127:69.
  Residing within institution,
    125:15.

PRISONS —Cont'd
Superintendents —Cont'd
Service of process on inmates, **127:6.**
Statutes distributed, **5:3.**
Suggestions for alterations in rules, **125:7.**
Treatment of prisoners, **127:32.**
Uniforms, **126:9A.**
Superior courts.
Appellate division sitting in correctional institution, **278:28A.**
Cages in courtroom abolished, **34:3.**
Closing of county facility for noncompliance with standards, **127:1B.**
Record of prisoner disclosed on order, **127:29.**
Sheriff reporting as to prisoners in house of correction, **126:12.**
Support, determination of amount, **127:25.**
Supplies and materials.
Bills, **125:21, 127:72.**
County prisons.
See COUNTY PRISONS.
Labor. See within this heading, "Labor of prisoners."
Purchase, **127:66, 127:66A.**
Support in prison.
County prisons, **126:28-126:34, 127:124-127:126.**
Defendant arrested on mesne process or on execution, **224:12.**
Determination of amount of support, **127:25.**
Disability of prisoner after expiration of sentence, **127:151.**
Federal prisoners, expense of maintaining, **125:11.**
Food and meals. See within this heading, "Food and meals."
Transferred prisoners, **127:124-127:126.**
Suspension of commitment to reformatory, **279:2.**
Teacher employed by, tenure, **30:9D.**
Telephone, prisoner's right to use, **276:33A.**
Temporary employees, **125:9.**
Temporary release of prisoners, **127:90A, 268:16, 268:31.**
Tewksbury hospital.
See TEWKSBURY HOSPITAL.

PRISONS —Cont'd
Tools.
Labor of prisoners. See within this heading, "Labor of prisoners."
Training programs.
See SCHOOLS AND EDUCATION.
Training schools, **120:1 et seq.**
Transfer.
Removal or transfer. See within this heading, "Removal or transfer."
Transportation of prisoner.
Allowances, **262:21, 262:48.**
Change of venue, **277:54.**
Expenses, **127:30.**
Removal or transfer. See within this heading, "Removal or transfer."
Segregation of sexes, **276:53.**
Sheriffs, **37:21, 37:24, 37:25.**
Through another county, **276:43.**
Upon discharge, **127:161, 127:165.**
Traveling expenses of prisoner, **262:21, 262:48.**
Treasurer of county.
See COUNTY TREASURERS.
Treasurers of institution, **125:6.**
Treatment of prisoners, **127:32.**
Trespass.
Confinement of trespassers, **266:120, 266:131.**
Upon land of institution, **266:123, 266:132.**
Tuberculosis.
Diseases. See within this heading, "Diseases."
Unclaimed property or money of former prisoners, disposition, **127:96A, 127:96B, 200A:14.**
Uniforms for officers and employees, **125:8, 126:9A.**
Vaccination of prisoners and employees, **111:182.**
Venereal diseases, examination and treatment of prisoners, **111:121, 127:16-127:18.**
Ventilation, **111:21.**
Visits and visitation, **123:1, 127:36, 127:36A, 127:37.**
Attorneys, **127:36A.**
Clergyman, **127:88.**
Commissioner of correction, **127:36.**
Prisoner visit to dying spouse or relative, **127:90A.**
Voting.
Elections. See within this heading, "Elections."

PRISONS —Cont'd
Wages.
Compensation and salaries. See within this heading, "Compensation and salaries."
Walpole correctional institution.
See WALPOLE CORRECTIONAL INSTITUTION.
Warrants.
Filing, **127:7.**
Mittimus. See within this heading, "Mittimus."
Wastelands, prisoner labor for improvement or reclamation, **127:84.**
Weapons, penalty for bringing contraband into prison upon return from furlough or work program, **268:31.**
Wearing apparel.
Discharge, **127:161, 127:162, 127:165.**
Furnishing, **126:33.**
Officers and employees, **125:8, 126:9A.**
Prison book, statements, **127:8.**
Welfare.
Social services. See within this heading, "Social services."
Widows of corrections officers, pensions, **32:100.**
Wife.
Husband and wife. See within this heading, "Husband and wife."
Witnesses, duty of commissioner of corrections, **276:52.**
Women.
Female prisoners. See within this heading, "Female prisoners."
Work release programs, **127:86F.**
Compensation, **127:86F.**
Credit, **127:48A.**
Good conduct, **127:129D.**
Penalty for bringing contraband into prison upon return, **268:31.**
Sex offenders ineligible, **127:49.**
Suffolk County house of correction, **127:86G.**
Youth services, **120:2 et seq.**

PRIT (PENSION RESERVES INVESTMENT TRUST) FUND, 32:1, 32:22, 32:22B, 40:5D.

PRIVACY.
Fair information practices, **66A:1 to 66A:3.**

PRIVACY —Cont'd
Invasion.
  See INVASION OF PRIVACY.

**PRIVATE BUSINESS
  SCHOOLS, 75D:1-75D:14.**
Accounting, schools teaching
  included in definition, **75D:1.**
Accrediting agencies, **75D:9.**
Advertising, **75D:5, 75D:14.**
Advisory committees, **75D:2.**
Allied health related occupational
  skills, schools teaching
  included in definition, **75D:1.**
Approval by commissioner,
  75D:10.
Bond, **75D:14.**
Business administration, schools
  teaching included in
  definition, **75D:1.**
Civil service examinations, schools
  teaching preparation for
  included in definition, **75D:1.**
Computer operation, schools
  teaching included in
  definition, **75D:1.**
Damages, liability for treble
  damages for
  misrepresentations, **75D:14.**
Data processing, schools teaching
  included in definition, **75D:1.**
Defined, **75D:1.**
Duration of licensing of schools
  and representatives, **75D:5,
  75D:7.**
Enforceability of agreement with
  unlicensed school or
  representative, **75D:12.**
Fair educational practices, **151C:1
  et seq.**
False advertising by.
  See ADVERTISING AND
    ADVERTISEMENTS.
Fees for licensing, **75D:2.**
Financial statements submitted to
  state auditor, **75D:3.**
Fine for operating private school
  without license, **75D:3.**
Health occupational skills, schools
  teaching included in
  definition, **75D:1.**
Liability for misrepresentation,
  75D:14.
Licensing of schools and
  representatives,
  75D:2-75D:14.
  Advisory committee, **75D:2.**
  Approval of separate courses
    and course changes, **75D:4.**
  Bond required, **75D:14.**
  Content of application, **75D:4,
    75D:7.**

**PRIVATE BUSINESS
  SCHOOLS** —Cont'd
Licensing of schools and
  representatives —Cont'd
  Duration, **75D:5, 75D:7.**
  Enforceability of agreements
    with unlicensed schools and
    representatives, **75D:12.**
  Exemptions, **75D:2.**
  Fees, **75D:2.**
  Financial statements submitted
    to state auditor, **75D:3.**
  Issuance of license, **75D:4,
    75D:7.**
  List of licensed schools and
    representatives, **75D:13.**
  Operation without license,
    penalty, **75D:11.**
  Revocation or suspension,
    75D:5, 75D:7.
Limitation of consumer protection
  actions involving, **260:5A.**
Misrepresentation, liability,
  75D:14.
Operation of school or acting as
  representative without license,
  75D:11.
Other regulation, schools regulated
  otherwise not governed by this
  chapter, **75D:1.**
Regulations, **75D:8.**
Representatives, licensing of.
  Licensing of schools and
    representatives. See within
    this heading, "Licensing of
    schools and
    representatives."
Revocation or suspension of
  license, **75D:5.**
Sales techniques, schools teaching
  included in definition, **75D:1.**
Secretarial skills, schools teaching
  included in definition, **75D:1.**
Social skills, habits, or customs,
  schools teaching included in
  definition, **75D:1.**
Student health insurance
  programs, exceptions, **15A:7B.**
Tractor-trailer operating skills,
  schools teaching included
  within definition, **75D:1.**

**PRIVATE CARRIER.
See CARRIERS.**

**PRIVATE DETECTIVES AND
  INVESTIGATORS, 147:22 et
  seq.**
Agents, assistants, or employees.
  Employment, **147:28.**
  Filing of statement by employee,
    147:28.

**PRIVATE DETECTIVES AND
  INVESTIGATORS** —Cont'd
Agents, assistants, or employees
  —Cont'd
  Former licensee whose license
    has been revoked, **147:28.**
  Licensing, **147:23 et seq.**
  Person convicted of felony,
    147:28.
Age requirement, **147:24.**
Armed guards, records required of
  agencies employing, **147:29A.**
Assistants.
  Agents, assistants, or employees.
    See within this heading,
    "Agents, assistants, or
    employees."
Badge, inscription on badge worn
  by guard or watchman in
  uniform, **147:29.**
Bonds and sureties.
  Investigator of applicants for
    indemnity bond not required
    to be licensed as private
    detective or investigator,
    147:23.
  Licensees, **147:26.**
Business, defined, **147:22.**
Commissioner of administration,
  determination of license fees,
  147:26.
Communications orally or by wire,
  illegal interception, **147:25.**
Conviction.
  Felony conviction. See within
    this heading, "Felony
    conviction."
Crimes and offenses.
  Felony conviction. See within
    this heading, "Felony
    conviction."
Definitions, **147:22.**
Employees.
  Agents, assistants, or employees.
    See within this heading,
    "Agents, assistants, or
    employees."
Entering place of employment to
  organize employees,
  prohibited, **147:27.**
False reports, **147:28.**
Fees, for renewal of license issued
  under prior law, **147:26.**
Felony conviction.
  Eligibility for employment by
    licensee after, **147:28.**
  License eligibility after, **147:25.**
Fines, penalties, and forfeitures.
  Acting without license, **147:23.**
  Badges, violations, **147:29.**
  False reports and statements,
    147:28.

PRIVATE DETECTIVES AND INVESTIGATORS —Cont'd

Fines, penalties, and forfeitures —Cont'd

Labor dispute or strike, activities in connection, **147:30.**

Wrongfully divulging information, **147:28.**

Genealogist exempt from provisions, **147:23.**

Identification card, **147:29.**

Labor relations.

Entering place of employment to organize employees, prohibited, **147:27.**

Interference with employees' selection of union, prohibited, **147:30.**

Right of action by labor union on licensee's bond, **147:26, 147:27.**

Licenses and permits, **147:23 et seq.**

Agents, assistants, and employees, **147:23 et seq.**

Application, **147:24.**

Certificate of reputation, **147:24.**

Contents, **147:24, 147:25.**

Exceptions from licensing requirement, **147:23.**

Fee, **147:26.**

Genealogist exempt from requirements, **147:23.**

Minimum age removed, **147:24.**

Qualifications, **147:24, 147:25.**

Renewal, **147:25.**

Requirement, **147:24.**

Revocation or suspension.

Entering place of employment to organize employees, **147:27.**

Failure to post license, **147:25.**

False statement by licensee as to persons in his employ, **147:28.**

Good cause, **147:25.**

Illegal eavesdropping as ground, **147:25.**

Term, **147:25.**

Unlicensed operation, penalty, **147:23.**

Validity of license issued under prior law, **147:23.**

Minimum age removed, **147:24.**

Minors, employment as investigators or guards, **147:28.**

Names used by, approval, **147:25.**

PRIVATE DETECTIVES AND INVESTIGATORS —Cont'd

Penalties.

Fines, penalties, and forfeitures. See within this heading, "Fines, penalties, and forfeitures."

Permits.

Licenses and permits. See within this heading, "Licenses and permits."

Police.

Regulations inapplicable, **147:23.**

Vehicles, marking, **147:29.**

Public Safety Commissioner.

Licensing, **147:23-147:26.**

Names, approval, **147:25.**

Weapons and equipment, approval, **147:29.**

Regulations inapplicable, **147:23.**

Revocation and suspension.

Licenses and permits. See within this heading, "Licenses and permits."

State employee not required to be licensed, **147:23.**

Strike or labor dispute, prohibited activities in connection, **147:30.**

Sureties.

Bonds and sureties. See within this heading, "Bonds and sureties."

Unlicensed person acting, **147:23.**

Vehicles, marking, **147:29.**

Weapons and equipment which may be carried by, approval, **147:29.**

PRIVATE FOUNDATIONS.

Attorney General, rights and powers unaffected by act, **68A:7.**

Charitable trusts, annual distributions required, **68A:2.**

Corporate private foundations.

Articles of organization.

Distributions for purposes, **68A:5.**

Exception in accordance with terms, **68A:6.**

Exceptions to prohibited acts, **68A:6.**

Prohibited acts, **68A:4, 68A:6.**

Courts, rights and powers unaffected by act, **68A:7.**

Distributions, **68A:2, 68A:5.**

Income Tax.

Internal revenue code. See within this heading, "Internal revenue code."

PRIVATE FOUNDATIONS —Cont'd

Internal revenue code.

Application of certain provisions, **68A:1, 68A:2, 68A:4, 68A:5.**

Future amendments, inclusion of references, **68A:8.**

Prohibited acts.

Corporate private foundations, **68A:4, 68A:6.**

Exceptions, **68A:3, 68A:6.**

In administration, **68A:1.**

Split-interest trust, prohibited acts in administration, **68A:1.**

Trusts, **68A:3.**

PRIVATE PENSION ASSOCIATIONS.

Taxation, **32:41, 59:5.**

PRIVATE SCHOOLS.

Academies.

See ACADEMIES.

Alcoholic liquor license for premises near, **138:16C.**

Approval by school committees, **76:1.**

Business schools, **75D:1-75D:14.**

See PRIVATE BUSINESS SCHOOLS.

Civil rights.

Discrimination. See within this heading, "Discrimination."

Compulsory attendance law, compliance, **76:1.**

Constitution of Massachusetts, grants-in-aid to private higher educational institutions, students, or parents, **MA Const Amend Art 18.**

Discrimination.

Loan of public school texts, **71:48.**

Public health services for students as affected, **71:57.**

Educational collaboratives, payment of private school tuition, **71:71D.**

Fair educational practices, **151C:1 et seq.**

Fines and penalties.

Private business or correspondence schools, operation without license, **75C:1A, 75D:3.**

Private trade schools, violations of regulations, **93:21B.**

Fraternal benefit societies, maintenance, **176:14.**

Injury to building used for religious instruction, **266:98.**

Juvenile court, furnishing information, **119:69.**

PRIVATE SCHOOLS —Cont'd

Loan of public school texts as affected by discrimination, **71:48.**

Medical and physical examination, **71:57.**

Overtime pay, **151:1A.**

Penalties.

Fines and penalties. See within this heading, "Fines and penalties."

Physical examinations of pupils, **71:57.**

Public school committees, approval, **76:1.**

Public school texts, discrimination as affecting loan, **71:48.**

Records of private school students, transfer, **71:34G.**

Religious instruction.

Compulsory attendance law, effect on compliance, **76:1.**

Injury to building used, **266:98.**

School buses.

Transportation. See within this heading, "Transportation of pupils."

School committees.

Approval, **76:1.**

Number of pupils enrolled for full-time attendance in nonpublic schools, ascertainment, **72:2.**

Special education.

Agreement for provision, **71B:4.**

Referral to private schools, **71B:10, 71B:12.**

Teachers.

Academies, **71:30.**

Jury service, instructors as exempt, **234:1.**

Appropriations for support, **67:17, 67:27.**

Conviction of crime, ineligibility for employment, **264:20.**

Text books of public schools, discrimination as affecting loan, **71:48.**

Trade schools, **93:21 et seq.** See TRADE SCHOOLS.

Transitional assistance department placing certain children, **119:32.**

Transportation of pupils, **40:5.**

Public expense, **76:1.**

Street or elevated railways, special rates, **161:108.**

PRIVATE WAYS.

Abandonment of motor vehicle. Penalty, **90:22B.**

PRIVATE WAYS —Cont'd

Abandonment of motor vehicle —Cont'd

Removal of abandoned vehicles, **90:22C.**

Abandonment or discontinuance.

Bond upon application to county commissioners, **82:31.**

County commissioners, **82:30, 82:31, 82:32A.**

Damages to property caused by, recovery, **82:24.**

Persons applying for, to indemnify town for damages and charges, **82:24.**

Powers of city and town officers, **82:21.**

Public ways to be private upon abandonment by county commissioners, **82:32A.**

Abutting owners.

Conveyances, **183:58.**

Registration, **185:29, 185:46.**

Agent for service of process, **90:3A, 90:3B.**

Alteration.

Laying out, alteration, or relocation. See within this heading, "Laying out, alteration, or relocation."

Assessments in connection, **84:14.**

Automobiles.

Motor vehicles. See within this heading, "Motor vehicles."

Bond upon application to county commissioners for laying out, alteration, etc., **82:31.**

Boundaries, fences fronting on private way taken, **86:2.**

Bridges.

Repair and maintenance, **84:12-84:14.**

Speed, regulation, **85:22.**

Certificate of land title as affected, **185:46.**

Cities and towns.

Acquisition of land for laying out, alteration, or relocation of ways, **82:24.**

Construction contracts and work, **41:77.**

Laying out, alteration, or relocation, **82:21, 82:23, 82:24, 82:29, 83:1.**

Leaving vehicles in private ways, town bylaws, **40:21.**

Master plan of municipal planning boards, **41:81D.**

Officers.

Powers, **82:21.**

Procedure by officers, **82:21-82:25.**

PRIVATE WAYS —Cont'd

Cities and towns —Cont'd

Plans for private ways, filing, **41:74.**

Proprietors of private ways and bridges, calling of meetings, **84:12.**

Repair and maintenance. See within this heading, "Repairs and maintenance."

Snow and ice removal, appropriations by cities and towns, **40:6C, 40:6D.**

Survey boards, **41:74, 41:77.**

Collection of expense assessments in connection, **84:14.**

Complaint.

Petition, **185:29.**

Completion by county commissioners, **82:28.**

Condemnation.

Eminent domain. See within this heading, "Eminent domain."

Construction contracts and work, **84:14.**

Municipalities, **41:77.**

Sewers and drains, construction in accordance with plans affecting municipal authority to lay, **41:77.**

County commissioners.

Abandonment or discontinuance, **82:30, 82:31, 82:32A.**

Bond required upon application for laying out, alteration, etc., **82:31.**

Boundaries, determination, **82:36.**

Completion, **82:28.**

Laying out, relocation, or alteration, **82:28, 82:29.**

Procedure, **82:28-82:32B.**

Damages or compensation for laying out, alteration, or relocation, **82:7, 82:12, 82:24.**

Dedicated ways, liability for injuries from defects, **84:23-84:25.**

Discontinuance.

Abandonment or discontinuance. See within this heading, "Abandonment or discontinuance."

Drains.

Sewers and drains. See within this heading, "Sewers and drains."

Easements.

See EASEMENTS.

PRIVATE WAYS —Cont'd

Electric companies.
Gas and electric companies. See within this heading, "Gas and electric companies."
Electricians' laws inapplicable to lighting, **141:7.**
Eminent domain, **82:24.**
Repairs, **252:20.**
Fences.
Boundaries unknown, **86:2.**
Obstructions, removal, **86:5.**
Financing of repairs in connection, **84:14.**
Gas and electric companies.
Electricity service lines, constructed on easements, **187:5.**
Gas mains and appurtenances constructed in private ways, **187:5.**
Gates, bars, and other obstructions, right to remove, **86:5.**
Intention, notice of, laying out or relocation, **82:22.**
Interested persons, agreements between, **84:12.**
Laying out, alteration, or relocation.
Abandonment or discontinuance. See within this heading, "Abandonment or discontinuance."
Acquisition of land by town for purpose, **82:24.**
Applicant, to indemnify town for damages and charges, **82:24.**
Bond upon application to county commissioners, **82:31.**
Cities and towns, **82:21, 82:23, 82:24, 82:29, 83:1.**
Completion by county commissioners, **82:28.**
Construction contracts and work. See within this heading, "Construction contracts and work."
County commissioners, powers, **82:28, 82:29.**
Damages to property caused by, recovery, **82:7, 82:12, 82:24.**
Eminent domain, taking land, **82:24.**
Notice of intention, **82:22.**
Record conclusive, **82:32.**
Restrictions, **82:30.**
Sewers and drains, **41:77, 83:1.**
Towns, **82:21, 82:23, 82:24, 82:29.**
Leaving vehicles in, town bylaws, **40:21.**

PRIVATE WAYS —Cont'd

Left turn into or from private way, crossing center line during, **89:1.**
Limitation of liability, removal of vehicles, **266:120D.**
Limited access ways.
See LIMITED ACCESS WAYS.
Local regulation, **90:18.**
Maintenance.
Repairs and maintenance. See within this heading, "Repairs and maintenance."
Master plan of municipal planning boards, **41:81D.**
Motor vehicles.
Abandonment of motor vehicle. See within this heading, "Abandonment of motor vehicle."
Parking and parking stations. See within this heading, "Parking and parking stations."
Traffic regulations.
See TRAFFIC REGULATIONS AND RULES OF THE ROAD.
Municipalities.
Cities and towns. See within this heading, "Cities and towns."
Narcotics, driving on way while under influence, **90:24.**
Neglect or refusal to repair, liability, **84:13.**
Notice.
Injury or damage due to defective condition, **84:21.**
Intention to lay out, relocate, or alter, **82:22.**
Organization of proprietors and election of officers, **84:12-84:14.**
Parking and parking stations.
Removal of parked cars, **266:120D.**
Town regulation of parking of unattended vehicles, **40:21.**
Trespass by parking, **266:120A, 266:120D.**
Petition, registration of title of land bounding on private way, **185:29.**
Process and service of process, **90:3A, 90:3B.**
Proprietors of private ways and bridges, **84:12-84:14, 85:22.**
Registrar as agent for service, **90:3A, 90:3B.**

PRIVATE WAYS —Cont'd

Registration of title to land abutting.
Effect, **185:46.**
Petition, **185:29.**
Relocation.
Laying out, alteration, or relocation. See within this heading, "Laying out, alteration, or relocation."
Removal of vehicles, **266:120D.**
Repairs and maintenance, **84:12, 84:14.**
Bridges, **84:12-84:14.**
Cities or towns, **40:5, 40:6N.**
Temporary minor repairs, **40:6N.**
Condemnation, repairs of ways acquired, **252:20.**
Construction contracts and work. See within this heading, "Construction contracts and work."
Penalty for failure or neglect of duty, **84:13.**
Sewers and drains, **83:3A.**
Right of way, obtaining for isolated property, **252:15-252:23.**
Service of process, **90:3A, 90:3B.**
Sewers and drains.
Laying out in private ways, **83:1.**
Plans, effect on municipal authority to lay sewers of construction not in accordance, **41:77.**
Repair of sewers, **83:3A.**
Snow and ice removal, appropriations by cities or towns, **40:6C, 40:6D.**
Survey boards, **41:74, 41:77.**
Telephone service lines, construction on private ways, **187:5.**
Towns.
Cities and towns. See within this heading, "Cities and towns."
Traffic regulations.
See TRAFFIC REGULATIONS AND RULES OF THE ROAD.
Urban redevelopment corporations contracting with municipality, **121A:14.**
Vehicles.
Motor vehicles. See within this heading, "Motor vehicles."

PRIVATION CONTRACTS.
State services, purchase of, **7:52 et seq.**

PRIVIES.
See TOILETS.

PRIVILEGED AND CONFIDENTIAL MATTERS.
Abortions, informed consent of pregnant woman prior, **112:12S.**
Abused and neglected children, **119:51B.**
Disclosure of confidential information to aid in investigation, **119:51B.**
Out of court statements by victims, **233:81, 233:82.**
Reports, confidentiality, **119:51E, 119:51F.**
Abuse of disabled persons, investigation of, **19:5.**
Abuse of elderly persons, reports, **19A:15, 19A:23.**
Abuse or neglect of patients in long-term care facilities.
Invocation in response to report prohibited, **111:72G.**
Adoption of children, **112:135, 233:20B.**
Air pollution emergency orders, disclosures during investigation of violations, **111:2B.**
Alcoholism treatment and rehabilitation facilities, records of patients, **111B:11.**
Antitrust laws, **93:2, 93:8.**
Banks, compliance review proceedings, **167:51.**
Bidders on public contracts, statements furnished, **29:8B.**
Birth certificate, evidence upon which new certificate made and original certificate to be kept confidential, **46:13.**
Births, information furnished commissioner of public health, **111:24B.**
Cancer reports to public health department, **111:111B.**
Care and protection proceedings, **119:51A.**
Children and minors.
Abused and neglected children. See within this heading, "Abused and neglected children."
Custody of children. See within this heading, "Custody of children."
Drug treatment for children in need, **111E:13A.**
Health records, **112:12F.**

PRIVILEGED AND CONFIDENTIAL MATTERS
—Cont'd
Children and minors —Cont'd
Paternity, **209C:13, 209C:16.**
Support, **62D:10, 119A:12.**
Child support, **62D:10, 119A:12.**
Enforcement.
Personal data collected and maintained by IV-D agencies, **119A:5A.**
Petition to disclose privileged information, **119A:5B.**
Civil service.
Disclosure of questions and answers on examinations, **31:70.**
Employees, confidential, **30:7, 31:48, 31:49.**
Examinations, **31:70, 31:74.**
Secrets furnished to person taking examination, **31:74.**
Clergy, communications, **233:20A.**
Commission on judicial conduct, proceedings, **211C:6.**
Commonwealth, confidentiality of contracts, **30:39R.**
Confession.
See CONFESSION.
Congress.
Publishing proceedings of, **US Const Art 1 Sec 5 cl 3.**
Speeches in congress as privileged, **US Const Art 1 Sec 6 cl 1.**
Controlled Dangerous Substances, reports to commissioner of mental health, **94C:24.**
Court records of examinations and commitments, privacy, **123:36A.**
Criminal files, access by militia, **6:172.**
Criminal justice agency employees, confidentiality of addresses and phone numbers of, **66:10.**
Criminal offender record information system, accessibility and dissemination of information, **6:172, 6:177.**
Custody of children.
Psychotherapist and patient, **233:20B.**
Social workers, **112:135, 119:51A.**
Definition of confidential communication, **233:20J.**
DNA database.
Records, **22E:9 to 22E:15.**
Drugs and narcotics.
Children in need, drug treatment, **111E:13A.**

PRIVILEGED AND CONFIDENTIAL MATTERS
—Cont'd
Drugs and narcotics —Cont'd
Mental health commissioner, research projects and drug treatment reports, **94C:24.**
Dying declarations, **233:65.**
Employment agencies, labor and workforce development commissioner's information concerning, **140:46R.**
Employment security records and reports, **151A:46, 151A:64, 151A:64A.**
Energy Resources Department, records and reports, **25A:7.**
Environmental management department, confidentiality of records, **21D:6.**
Ethics commission.
Records relating to preliminary investigation as confidential, **268B:4.**
Request for advisory opinions, **268B:3.**
Fair information practice, **66A:1-66A:3.**
Income tax, confidentiality of personal data, **62C:21, 62C:22, 62C:74.**
Family abuse prevention, **209A:8.**
Family and marital therapy patients, **112:135, 233:20B.**
Financial matters.
Investigations, **268B:4.**
Penalty for violations, **268A:7.**
Public officers and employees, **268B:5.**
Trade secrets and commercial and financial information corporation, **40J:12.**
Fines and penalties.
Abused and neglected children, release of information, **119:51E, 119:51F.**
Aid and assistance, persons receiving, **40:51, 271:43.**
Financial disclosure by public officers and employees, penalty for violations of confidentiality, **268A:7.**
Venereal disease records, **111:119.**
Vocational rehabilitation, disclosure of applicants, **6:84.**
Wage reporting system, **62E:8.**
Fire insurance company records obtained in course of fire loss investigation, **148:32.**

**PRIVILEGED AND
  CONFIDENTIAL MATTERS**
  —Cont'd

Fires and fire prevention,
  underground storage tanks,
  148:38I.

Hazardous waste management act.
  Records, **21C:12.**
  Trade secrets, protection under
  act, **21C:4, 21C:12.**

Health department, cancer reports
  received, **111:111B.**

Health maintenance organizations,
  confidentiality of records and
  reports, **176G:10.**

Hospitals.
  See HOSPITALS AND HEALTH
  CARE FACILITIES.

Husband-wife privilege, **233:20,
  273:7.**

Illegitimate children, **209C:13,
  209C:16.**

Industrial accident board and
  accident reviewing board,
  removal of member, **23E:8.**

Inspector general, confidentiality
  of records, **12A:13.**

Insurance.
  Commissioner of insurance,
  175:4.
  Landlord, disclosure of
  insurance information,
  186:21.
  Medical malpractice insurance,
  experience review committee
  information, **175A:5C.**
  Mental health care, disclosure of
  insured's condition,
  175:108E.
  Premium finance agencies,
  reports as to investigations,
  255C:6.
  Urban area insurance placement
  facility reports and
  communications, **175C:6.**

Interception of wire or oral
  communications, secrecy of
  papers and recordings made
  pursuant to warrant
  authorizing, **272:99.**

Invasion of privacy.
  See INVASION OF PRIVACY.

Judicial conduct commission,
  proceedings, **211C:6.**

Jury commissioner for
  Commonwealth.
  See JURY COMMISSIONER
  FOR COMMONWEALTH.

Landlord requesting insurance
  information, disclosure,
  186:21.

**PRIVILEGED AND
  CONFIDENTIAL MATTERS**
  —Cont'd

Legislative research bureau,
  delivery of information
  deemed confidential, **3:60.**

Library records, personal
  information, **4:7.**

Low-level radioactive waste,
  111H:7.

Massachusetts water management
  act, confidentiality of records,
  21G:13.

Mediation of disputes, **150:10A,
  150E:9, 233:23C.**

Medical assistance division,
  118E:49.

Medical malpractice insurance,
  information furnished to
  experience review committee,
  175A:5C.

Medical peer review committee,
  confidentiality of information
  obtained, **111:1, 111:204,
  111:205, 112:5.**

Medical service corporations,
  patient information, **176B:12.**

Meetings and records of public
  body, **30A:11A, 34:9G.**

Mentally ill.
  See MENTALLY ILL AND
  RETARDED PERSONS.

Milk and milk products.
  Hearings, **94A:18.**
  Information obtained under Milk
  Control Law, **94A:13.**

Minors.
  Children and minors. See within
  this heading, "Children and
  minors."

Motor vehicle loss prevention
  central organization, reports
  to, **175:113O.**

Neglected children.
  Abused and neglected children.
  See within this heading,
  "Abused and neglected
  children."

Nursing or rest homes.
  Criminal background checks on
  applicants for employment,
  6:172E.

Parole board records, **127:130.**

Paternity, **209C:13, 209C:16.**

Patients' rights, **111:70E.**

Physician assistants, records of
  complaints, **112:9H.**

Physicians and surgeons.
  Conduct of physician,
  information, **112:5G.**
  Disclosure of venereal disease,
  112:12.

**PRIVILEGED AND
  CONFIDENTIAL MATTERS**
  —Cont'd

Physicians and surgeons —Cont'd
  Minor's health record, **112:12F.**

Peer review committee
  information, **111:204.**

Podiatrist, **112:19.**

Psychiatrist and patient,
  privileged communications
  between, **233:20B, 233:23B.**

Seizure of property, prohibition,
  276:1.

Podiatrist, **112:19.**

Poultry, status of information
  obtained by investigation of
  persons licensed to sell and
  transport, **94:152G.**

Priest-penitent privilege, **233:20A.**

Professional corporations, **156A:6.**

Psychiatrist-patient privilege,
  233:20B, 233:23B.

Psychotherapists.
  Communication with patients,
  233:20B.
  Practice partners, **112:129A.**

Public assistance, disclosure of
  names of recipients, **18:11.**

Public charities, investigations
  concerning, **12:8H.**

Public officer or employee,
  acceptance of employment or
  engagement in business or
  professional activity requiring
  disclosure, **268A:23.**

Public records, exceptions as to
  disclosures of, **4:7.**

Public safety employees,
  confidentiality of addresses
  and phone numbers of, **66:10.**

Rape and sexual assaults.
  Reports and investigations,
  41:97D.
  Victim and counselors, **233:20J.**

Rehabilitation commission,
  information and records, **6:84.**

Religion and religious societies,
  communications to clergy,
  67:1-67:3, 233:20A.

Restraints of trade and
  monopolies, **93:2, 93:8.**

Reyes syndrome, records and
  reports concerning, **111:110B.**

Scientific studies to reduce
  morbidity and mortality,
  111:24A.

Search and seizure, confidential
  relationships having custody
  of property, search and seizure
  prohibited, **276:1.**

Securities Act, **110A:406.**

PRIVILEGED AND CONFIDENTIAL MATTERS —Cont'd

Self-incrimination.
  See SELF-INCRIMINATION.
Sexual offender registration and community notification.
  Authority to examine information to confirm registration, **6:178F.**
Social services department, client data and information, **18B:7.**
Social worker and client communications, privilege of refusal to disclose, **112:135B.**
Social workers, **18:21, 112:135-112:135B, 119:51A.**
State employees, **30:7.**
State ethics commission.
  Ethics commission. See within this heading, "Ethics commission."
Surgeons.
  Physicians and surgeons. See within this heading, "Physicians and surgeons."
Tax information, **62C:21, 62C:74.**
Toxic use reduction, trade secret protection, **21I:20.**
Trade secrets.
  See TRADE SECRETS.
Treason conviction on confession in open court, **US Const Art 3 Sec 3 cl 1.**
Unemployment security records, **151A:46, 151A:64.**
Uniform Securities Act, **110A:406.**
Urban area insurance placement facility reports and communications, **175C:6.**
Vocational rehabilitations, disclosure of applicants, **6:84.**
Voter, disclosure of vote, **56:25.**
Wage reporting system, fines and penalties, **62E:8.**
Water management act, confidentiality of records, **21G:13.**
Water pollution control division director as having access, **21:40.**
Wiretapping, **272:99.**
Work products of mediators, factfinders and arbitrators, confidentiality, **150:10A, 150E:9.**

PRIVILEGE TAXES.
See LICENSES AND PERMITS.

PRIVITY OF CONTRACT.
Warranty, breach, **106:2-318.**

PRIZEFIGHTING.
See BOXING AND BOXING MATCHES.

PRIZES AND AWARDS.
Agricultural exhibitions, **128:2.**
Animals prohibited from being offered, **272:80F.**
Assignment of state lottery prizes, **10:28.**
Auction sales, prohibited, **100:9.**
Beano, prizes awarded per day, **10:38.**
Breeding ponies, **128:2.**
Child support, **10:28A.**
Forfeiture of lottery prizes, **271:14.**
Gasoline dealers' agreements as to premiums, **93E:3A.**
Gasoline station's offering of, prohibition, **271:6C.**
Homestead plaque awarded if site over 100 years old, **9:27D.**
Horse and dog racing meetings, Massachusetts bred greyhounds, **128:2.**
Lotteries.
  See LOTTERIES.
Marathons or walkathons, awarding prizes, **272:103.**
Medals.
  See MEDALS.
Militia, prizes for competitions within, **33:68.**
Municipal employees, cash awards for suggestions, **40:5.**
Playground or recreation commission, appropriation for token awards, **40:5.**
Public service corporation employees, request for appointment or discharge, **271:40.**
Real estate time-shares, **183B:52.**
School pupils, awards for meritorious performance in certain fields, **71:47.**
State employees, prizes for suggestions, **7:31A.**
Thoroughbred race horses, **128:2.**

PROBABLE CAUSE.
Alcoholic beverages.
  Search warrant for alcoholic beverages, contents, **138:44.**
  Testing of commercial driver licensee, for alcohol concentration level, **90F:11.**
Divorce action, probable cause of arrest of person violating protection orders, **276:28.**
Drugs and narcotics.
  Administrative inspection warrant, **94C:30.**

PROBABLE CAUSE —Cont'd
Drugs and narcotics —Cont'd
  Arrest without warrant, **94C:41.**
  Electronic surveillance warrant, **272:99.**
  Employment discrimination, **151B:5.**
  False arrest or imprisonment, **231:94A, 231:94C.**
    Driving while intoxicated, police officer's liability for arrest on suspension, **90:24.**
    Shoplifting, arrest, **231:94B.**
Fish and game violations, noncriminal disposition, **21:6F.**
Forfeiture of property proceedings on seizure without cause, damages, **257:9.**
Narcotics.
  Drugs and narcotics. See within this heading, "Drugs and narcotics."
Review of finding of no probable cause to support complaint of employment discrimination, **151B:5.**
Search and seizure, **MA Const Part 1 Art 14; US Const 4th Amend.**
  See SEARCHES AND SEIZURES.

PROBATE AND FAMILY COURT, 215:1 et seq.
Abatement, survival and revival of actions, **228:5, 228:5A.**
Absentee trust beneficiaries, judgments involving transfer of trust estates, **203:30, 203:32, 203:38.**
Abuse prevention, **209A:1 et seq.**
  See ABUSE PREVENTION.
Accounts and accounting.
  Common trust fund accounts, filing, **203A:3.**
  Executors.
    See EXECUTORS AND ADMINISTRATORS.
  Guardians.
    See GUARDIANS, CONSERVATORS, AND COMMITTEES.
  Trusts and trustees.
    Annual account of common trust fund, **203:3.**
    Co-operative bank trust accounts subject to probate jurisdiction, effect of deposit, **170:16.**
    Filing of common trust fund accounts, **203A:3.**

PROBATE AND FAMILY COURT —Cont'd

Accounts and accounting —Cont'd
Veterans' Administration representing persons in allowance of account, **206:24.**
Act appealed from, effect of appeal, **215:22-215:26.**
Adjournment, **215:59.**
Administrative justices.
See ADMINISTRATIVE JUSTICES.
Administrators, **192:1 et seq., 193:1 et seq.**
See EXECUTORS AND ADMINISTRATORS.
Adoption of children, **210:1-210:11A.**
See ADOPTION OF CHILDREN.
Affidavits.
Indigency, filing affidavit, **261:27B.**
Removal of causes, affidavit in connection, **215:6.**
Wills.
See WILLS.
Affirmance of decree, **215:28, 262:40.**
Aggrieved person's appeal to supreme judicial court, **215:9.**
Alphabetical index of orders, decrees and cases, **215:36, 215:37.**
Annuities, sale of land subject to payment, **183:52.**
Annulment actions, **215:3, 262:40.**
See ANNULMENT OF MARRIAGE.
Appeal and review, **215:9-215:28.**
Appeals court. See within this heading, "Appeals court."
Award of fees after receiving rescript, **215:39B.**
Consolidation of appeals, **215:19, 215:20.**
Contempt proceedings, **215:34B.**
Court of appeals.
Appeals court. See within this heading, "Appeals court."
Domestic relations procedure, effect of appeal, **215:24.**
Effect of appeal upon act appealed, **215:22-215:26.**
Fees, appeal of award, **231:6G.**
Fiduciaries, validity of acts pending appeal, **215:9A.**
Full court, appeal to be heard, **215:10.**
Further report on appeals from probate court, **231:125A.**

PROBATE AND FAMILY COURT —Cont'd

Appeal and review —Cont'd
Indigency, appeal from denial of relief from court costs in matters arising in probate court, **261:27D.**
Insolvent estates, **215:17.**
Interlocutory decrees on appeal, **215:14, 215:22, 231:118.**
Jurisdiction of probate court, appeals from, **MA Const Part 2 Ch 3 Art 5.**
Jury issues, **215:22.**
Modification of decree appealed, **215:27.**
Reports, **215:11, 231:125A.**
Reservation and report of case to appeals court, **215:13.**
Reversal or affirmance of decree appealed, **215:28.**
Revision of interlocutory decrees on appeal, **215:14.**
Stay of proceedings pending appeal, **215:22.**
Stenographer, appointment, **215:18.**
Supreme Judicial Court, appeal, **215:9, 215:45.**
Validity of acts of certain fiduciaries pending appeal from decree of appointment, **215:9A.**
Appeals court.
Fees, award upon receipt of rescript from appeals court, **215:39B.**
Judge's reservation and report of case, **215:13.**
Review of decisions, **211A:10.**
Appearances, **215:42.**
Appointments.
Additional justices, **211B:2.**
Auditors, masters, and referees, **221:58, 221:61.**
Executors.
See EXECUTORS AND ADMINISTRATORS.
Fiduciaries. See within this heading, "Fiduciaries."
Power of appointment. See within this heading, "Power of appointment."
Trustees, **203:5.**
Appraisals and appraisers.
Appointment of appraisers, **217:22.**
Determination of amount due for services as appraiser, **215:39.**
Executors and administrators, failure to file inventory in appraisal, **217:16.**

PROBATE AND FAMILY COURT —Cont'd

Appraisals and appraisers —Cont'd
Revocation of warrant or commission for appraisal, **215:35.**
Arbitration of claims by fiduciary, authority, **204:13-204:18.**
Assessors, compensation paid for by state, **221:55.**
Assignment.
Dower, **215:35.**
Judge, **215:62.**
License of probate court for sale or assignment of debt or claim by executor or administrator, **231:6.**
Assignment of justices, **215:62.**
Attachments, **215:6A.**
Deceased person's property, attachment as requiring permission of probate court, **230:7.**
Principal on probate bond, surety's attachment of property, **205:28.**
Attorneys at law.
Appearances entered, **215:42.**
Fees.
See ATTORNEYS' FEES.
Registers to give notice of decrees and orders, **215:36.**
Auditor, master, or referee, **221:57.**
Appointment, **221:58, 221:61.**
Compensation, **32:91, 221:55, 221:61.**
Hearings, **221:58.**
Incapacity or death before filing final report, **221:62A.**
Pensioner appointed as, payment for services, **32:91.**
Report, filing, **221:62, 221:62A.**
Travel expenses, award and payment, **221:61.**
Authentication of documents used for legacy and succession taxes, **65:25.**
Bankruptcy.
See INSOLVENCY AND BANKRUPTCY.
Banks.
Investments in, **215:41.**
Savings deposits in name of probate judge, **241:34.**
Barnstable, sessions of court, **215:62.**
Berkshire, court, **215:62.**
Birth registrations, ordering, **46:13A.**
Bold type, when names of estates and parties to proceedings shall be printed, **215:3.**

PROBATE AND FAMILY COURT —Cont'd

Bonds and undertakings, **205:1 et seq.**
  See PROBATE BONDS.
Books and papers.
  Records, reports, and returns.
    See within this heading, "Records, reports, and returns."
Bristol county.
  See BRISTOL COUNTY.
Calendar.
  Docket and index. See within this heading, "Docket and index."
Cancellation of instruments, proceedings, **204:1.**
Capias.
  Service of citation and capias. See within this heading, "Service of citation and capias."
Certificates and certification.
  Justice of supreme judicial court, certification of additional facilities for probate court, **215:54.**
Change of name, proceedings, **210:12-210:14.**
Change of venue, **215:8A.**
Change or modification.
  Decree appealed, modification, **215:27.**
  Interlocutory decrees or appeal, revision, **215:14.**
  Name change, jurisdiction, **215:3.**
  Places of holding courts, **210:12-210:14.**
  Venue, **215:8A.**
Charges for payment of money, sale of lands subject, **183:52.**
Charities, filing of financial reports, **12:8F.**
Chief judge of probate court.
  See PROBATE AND INSOLVENCY JUDGES.
Chief justice for administration and management, approval of assignment of justices by, **215:62.**
Children and minors.
  Abuse.
    Evidence of present or past abuse as factor in custody decision, **208:31A, 209:38.**
  Adoption of children.
    See ADOPTION OF CHILDREN.
  Appointment of guardian ad litem, **215:56A, 217:17.**

PROBATE AND FAMILY COURT —Cont'd

Children and minors —Cont'd
  Contempt proceedings for violation of decrees involving custody, **215:56B.**
  Custody of minors. See within this heading, "Custody of minors."
  Education and support of children over 21 years old, **208:28, 209:37.**
  Guardians.
    See GUARDIANS, CONSERVATORS, AND COMMITTEES.
  Illegitimate children, **209C:3, 209C:24, 215:4, 218:19.**
  Information as to placement of, power to compel, **119:35.**
  Punishment for violation of support order, **215:34, 215:34A.**
  Small funds currently held by executor or administrator and to which minor is entitled, delivery to parent, **215:41A.**
  Support proceedings. See within this heading, "Support proceedings."
  Transitional assistance department authorized to seek and accept custody, **119:23.**
  Visitation of child by parent, guardian, or next of kin, power to compel transitional assistance department to permit, **119:35.**
Citations.
  Contempt citations in support and child custody proceedings, **215:34A.**
  Publication, requirements in connection with citation, **215:3.**
  Service of citation and capias. See within this heading, "Service of citation and capias."
Civil Procedure Rules.
  See CIVIL PROCEDURE RULES.
Collective investment funds, investment of funds by fiduciary, **167G:3.**
Commissioners.
  County commissioners. See within this heading, "County commissioners."

PROBATE AND FAMILY COURT —Cont'd

Commissioners —Cont'd
  Fiduciaries. See within this heading, "Fiduciaries."
Commissions, revocation, **215:35.**
Common trust funds.
  Trusts and trustees. See within this heading, "Trusts and trustees."
Commonwealth.
  Designation of judges of probate to sit in other counties, payment of expenses by Commonwealth, **217:6B.**
  Guardian ad litem instituting contempt proceedings, payment of compensation, **215:56B.**
  Investigations, payment of compensation, **215:56A.**
  Preservation of dockets, Commonwealth to pay expense, **215:55.**
  Recording probate proceedings in Suffolk county, expenses paid by Commonwealth, **215:56.**
  Registers, payment of salaries, **217:35A.**
  Stenographer, payment of compensation and expenses, **215:18.**
  Suffolk County recording expenses, payment, **215:56.**
  Treasurer, notice of forfeiture of bond of register, **217:11.**
Communist countries, payment of legacies or distributive shares of residents, **206:27B.**
Compensation.
  Wages, salaries, and compensation. See within this heading, "Wages, salaries, and compensation."
Competency adjudications in cases involving treatment with antipsychotic medications, **201:6, 201:6A, 201:14.**
Complaints.
  Petitions and complaints. See within this heading, "Petitions and complaints."
Compromise of claims by fiduciaries, authority, **204:13-204:18.**
Concealing property, examination under oath of person suspected, **215:44.**
Concurrent jurisdiction, **185C:3, 204:1, 209C:3, 218:19.**

PROBATE AND FAMILY COURT —Cont'd

Conditional limitations, sale subject, **183:49-183:51.**

Confirmation of doubtful acts of fiduciary, **204:24.**

Conservators or committees, **201:1 et seq.**

See GUARDIANS, CONSERVATORS, AND COMMITTEES.

Consolidation of appeals, **215:19, 215:20.**

Constitution of Massachusetts.

See CONSTITUTION OF MASSACHUSETTS.

Contempt.

Attorney's fees, **215:34A.**

Burden of proof, **215:34.**

Child custody, **215:56B.**

Citations for, in support proceedings, **215:34A.**

Domestic relations judgments, rules governing actions for contempt, **215:34, 215:34A.**

Guardian ad litem to institute proceedings, **215:56B.**

Punishing, **215:34-215:34B, 215:57.**

Review of underlying judgment before confining person to jail in contempt, **215:34B.**

Contracts, specific performance, **204:1.**

Corporate stock, jurisdiction of attachment, **215:6A.**

Costs of actions, **215:45.**

Accounts and accounting. See within this heading, "Accounts and accounting."

Attorneys' fees.

See ATTORNEYS' FEES.

Fees. See within this heading, "Fees."

Indigency. See within this heading, "Indigency."

Libel for divorce, filing, **262:40.**

Service of citation and capias, **215:34A.**

Waiver for indigents, **261:27B.**

Counsel.

Attorneys at law. See within this heading, "Attorneys at law."

County commissioners.

Courtrooms and rooms for record, county commissioners to provide, **215:53.**

Preservation of dockets, **215:55.**

Court officers, **217:39.**

Courtrooms, **215:53, 215:54.**

PROBATE AND FAMILY COURT —Cont'd

Courts always open, **215:58.**

Courts of record, **215:1.**

Curtesy.

Dower and curtesy, **215:35.**

Custody of minors.

Abuse.

Evidence of present or past abuse as factor in custody decision, **208:31A, 209:38.**

Contempt proceedings for failure to obey decrees, **215:56B.**

Decrees, **215:56B.**

Effect of appeal upon act appealed from in custody case, **215:24.**

Jurisdiction of court, **209:32, 215:4.**

Separated spouses, children, **209:32.**

Service of citation and capias in custody contempt cases, **215:34A.**

Welfare department, custody on order of probate court, **119:23.**

Declaration of trust filed in registry of probate, **203A:1.**

Declaratory judgments, **231A:1.**

Decrees, **215:34.**

Deed, decree in equity operating, **183:43.**

Definition of probate court, **4:7.**

Delivery of property by executor or trustee, enforcement, **215:40, 215:41A.**

Demurrer, amendment of pleadings after, **231:52.**

Depositions, **233:24.**

Deposits.

Banks. See within this heading, "Banks."

Fiduciary deposits for benefit of others, **206:27.**

Judges.

See PROBATE AND INSOLVENCY JUDGES.

Trust companies, **241:34.**

Unclaimed funds, **206:25-206:28.**

Desertion and nonsupport, **209:32 et seq.**

Review of probate court judgment before confining to jail for contempt, **215:34B.**

Discharge.

Release, **183:43.**

Discovery procedures, **215:44.**

Discretion of court in payment of legacy or distributive share of resident of communist country, **206:27B.**

PROBATE AND FAMILY COURT —Cont'd

Discrimination, jurisdiction of actions, **151B:9.**

Divorce.

See DIVORCE AND ALIMONY.

Docket and index, **215:36, 215:37.**

Preservation of dockets, **215:55.**

Domestic relations rules, **215:1 et seq.**

Dower and curtesy, revocation of warrant or commission for assignment, **215:35.**

Drugs and narcotics, probate court adjudications of competency in cases involving treatment with antipsychotic medications, **201:6, 201:6A, 201:14.**

Dukes county.

Appointment of deputy assistant register and clerk, **217:29A.**

Judges, **217:6B.**

Sessions of court, **215:62.**

Time for holding, **215:62.**

Traveling expenses, payment by Commonwealth, **217:42.**

Education and support of children over 21 years old, orders, **208:28, 209:37.**

Election days, no courts, **215:60.**

Eminent domain, appointment of trustee, **79:26, 79:30.**

Entry fee for removal of cause, **215:6.**

Equity.

Attachments, **215:6A.**

Deed, decree in equity operating, **183:43.**

Divorce actions, **215:6.**

Effect of appeal upon act appealed, **215:23.**

Injunctions. See within this heading, "Injunctions."

Jurisdiction, **215:6, 215:6A, 215:25, 241:25.**

Pleading defenses, **231:35.**

Removal or transfer of equity actions, **215:6.**

Essex county.

See ESSEX COUNTY.

Estate administration process.

Information provided to interested parties, **215:30B.**

Estate taxes.

See ESTATE TAXES.

Evidence.

Depositions, **233:24.**

Registers of probate.

See REGISTERS OF PROBATE AND INSOLVENCY.

PROBATE AND FAMILY COURT —Cont'd

Examination, inspection, and investigation.

Claims against insolvent estates, revocation of warrant or commission for examining, **215:35.**

Compensation for investigations, payment by Commonwealth, **215:56A.**

Concealing property, examination under oath of person suspected, **215:44.**

Health, welfare, and retirement funds, investigation, **151D:3.**

Police, guardian ad litem assisting investigation, **215:56A.**

Public inspection of docketed index of cases, right, **215:37.**

Execution.

Attachments. See within this heading, "Attachments."

Costs, issuance of, execution, **215:45.**

Executors and administrators, **192:1 et seq., 193:1 et seq.**

See EXECUTORS AND ADMINISTRATORS.

Executory devises, sale subject, **183:49-183:51.**

Ex parte matters, **215:33.**

Expenses.

Administrative committee of probate court, **215:38.**

Chief judge, payment of certain expenses, **217:8A.**

Commonwealth. See within this heading, "Commonwealth."

Costs of actions. See within this heading, "Costs of actions."

Fees. See within this heading, "Fees."

Suffolk, recording probate proceedings, **215:56.**

Facts, report, **215:11.**

Family relations proceedings, **215:1 et seq.**

Fees.

Amount, **262:40.**

Appeal of award, **231:6G.**

Appeals court, award upon receipt of rescript, **215:39B.**

Attorneys' fees.

See ATTORNEYS' FEES.

Entry fee for removal of cause, **215:6.**

Indigents, normal fees and costs, **261:27A.**

PROBATE AND FAMILY COURT —Cont'd

Fees —Cont'd

Injunction, fee, **262:40.**

Interest in or benefit by fees or emoluments arising from matter pending in probate court, **217:6B.**

Judges, fees in addition to compensation prohibited, **217:43.**

Registers' fees, **262:40.**

Rescript from appeals court, award of fees receipt, **215:39B.**

Sheriff's fees for service of writs, precepts or process, **262:8.**

Will probate, **262:40.**

Fiduciaries.

Arbitration of claims, **204:13-204:18.**

Attorneys' fees, allowance to fiduciaries, **206:16.**

Bonds of.

See PROBATE BONDS.

Court-appointed fiduciaries.

Arbitration and compromises, **204:13, 204:14.**

Bonds.

See PROBATE BONDS.

Compensation of commissioners paid by state, **221:55.**

Failure of proof of notice of appointment, **204:26.**

Irregularity in appointment, effect, **204:25.**

Ratification of doubtful acts, **204:24.**

Resignation by guardian or conservator of fiduciary, **204:37.**

Trustees, **203:5.**

Void or voidable acts, **204:23.**

Deposit for benefit of others, **206:27.**

Executors and administrators, **192:1 et seq., 193:1 et seq.**

See EXECUTORS AND ADMINISTRATORS.

Foreign fiduciaries. See within this heading, "Foreign fiduciaries."

Guardians, conservators, and committees, **201:1 et seq.**

See GUARDIANS, CONSERVATORS, AND COMMITTEES.

Ratification of doubtful acts, **204:23, 204:24.**

Receivers. See within this heading, "Receivers."

PROBATE AND FAMILY COURT —Cont'd

Fiduciaries —Cont'd

Trusts and trustees. See within this heading, "Trusts and trustees."

Fines and penalties.

Contempt, **215:34, 215:34A, 215:57.**

Violation of support order, **215:34, 215:34A.**

Fireproof rooms, providing, **215:53, 215:54.**

First court taking jurisdiction to retain it, **215:7.**

First justice of probate and insolvency, appointment of, **217:2.**

Foreclosure, jurisdiction of action to enjoin, **215:6.**

Foreign fiduciaries.

Personal property transferred, **204:3, 204:3A.**

Sale by foreign executors, **204:7.**

Trustees, **203:10, 204:7.**

Foreign support judgments, jurisdiction to grant equitable relief to enforce, **215:6.**

Foreign wills, **192:9-192:11.**

See WILLS.

Forma pauperis.

Indigency. See within this heading, "Indigency."

Forms.

Adoption.

Affidavit of petitioner for adoption, **210:6 (Form 2).**

Citation.

Decree, adoption and change of name, **10:6 (Form), 210:6 (Form).**

Parental consent, **210:3 (Form).**

Decree of adoption, **210:6 (Form 3).**

Parental consent to.

Decree to dispense with, **210:3 (Form 2).**

Petition to dispense with, **210:3 (Form 1).**

Petition for, **210:6 (Form 1).**

Annulment, complaint for, **207:14 (Form), Form 1A.**

Appointment of counsel, **Form 14.**

Attachment, **Forms 19-23.**

Capias, **Form 27.**

Citation.

Temporary shelter or foster care, **119:23 (Form 3).**

Complaint, **Forms 1-4.**

PROBATE AND FAMILY COURT —Cont'd

Forms —Cont'd

Conservatorship.
Medical certificate, **Form 33.**
Mentally retarded person, clinical team report, **201:6A (Form), 201:16B (Form).**
Permanent decree of, **201:16 (Form 2), Form 35.**
Petition, **201:16 (Form 1), Form 32.**
Temporary decree of, **201:16 (Form), Form 34.**
Contempt, **Forms 3, 8, 18, 28.**
Counsel, waiver or appointment, **Forms 13, 14.**
Custody.
Decree of, **119:23 (Form 2).**
Petition for, **119:23 (Form 1).**
Divorce, complaint, **Form 1.**
Divorce nisi, judgment, **Form 17.**
Estate administration process.
Information provided to interested parties, **215:30B.**
Execution, **Forms 29, 30.**
Ex parte order on approval of attachment, **Forms 20, 22.**
Financial statement, **Form 12.**
Guardianship.
Clinical team report, **Form 40.**
Medical certificate, **201:6 (Form 2), Form 37.**
Mentally retarded person, clinical team report, **201:6A (Form), 201:16B (Form).**
Permanent decree of, **201:6 (Form 3), Form 39.**
Petition, **201:6 (Form 1), Form 36.**
Temporary decree of, **201:14 (Form), Form 38.**
Judgments, **Forms 16-18, 24.**
Marriage without delay, **Form 26.**
Medical assistance, affidavit of, Probate and Family Court, **Form 31.**
Minors, marriage without delay, **Form 26.**
Mittimus for contempt, **Form 28.**
Modification of support, **Form 4.**
Motion, **Form 14A.**
Notice restraining order, **Form 11.**

PROBATE AND FAMILY COURT —Cont'd

Forms —Cont'd

Preliminary injunction, **Form 25.**
Restraining order, **Forms 11, 25.**
Rights of beneficiaries.
Information provided to interested parties, **215:30B.**
Separate support, **Forms 2, 16.**
Service by publication, order, **Form 6.**
Summons, **Forms 5-11.**
Temporary orders, **Forms 15, 25.**
Temporary restraining order, **Form 25.**
Trustee process, attachment on, **Forms 21, 22.**
Trustee, summons to, **Form 10.**
Visitation, grandparent's, **119:39D (Form), Form 4A.**
Waiver of counsel, **Form 13.**
Writ of attachment, **Form 23.**
Franklin county, sessions of court, **215:62.**
Fraudulent concealment of property, examination of persons suspected, **215:44.**
French spoliation awards, **215:5.**
Full court, appeal to be heard, **215:10.**
Further report on appeals, **231:125A.**
Gifts to minors.
Uniform transfers to minors act, **201A:1 to 201A:24.**
See TRANSFERS TO MINORS.
Grandparents, visitation rights, **119:39D.**
Guardian ad litem.
See GUARDIAN AD LITEM.
Guardians and conservators, **201:1 et seq.**
See GUARDIANS, CONSERVATORS, AND COMMITTEES.
Habeas corpus, proceedings in nature, **248:36-248:40.**
Hampden county, sessions of court, **215:62.**
Hampshire county.
See HAMPSHIRE COUNTY.
Health, welfare, and retirement funds, investigation, **151D:3.**
Hearings.
Appeal to be heard by full court, **215:10.**

PROBATE AND FAMILY COURT —Cont'd

Hearings —Cont'd

Auditors, masters, or referees, **221:58.**
Failure of proof of notice of appointment or sale of real estate, remedy in case, **204:26.**
Land contracts, specific performance, **204:1.**
Notice, **215:31.**
Holidays.
Sundays and holidays. See within this heading, "Sundays and holidays."
Housing court department, concurrent jurisdiction, **185C:3.**
Husband and wife.
Marriage. See within this heading, "Marriage."
Illegitimate children, **209C:3, 209C:24, 215:4, 218:19.**
Index and docket.
Docket and index. See within this heading, "Docket and index."
Indictments, informations, and complaints, children born out of wedlock, forms of complaints, **209C:24.**
Indigency.
Affidavit and request for waiver of costs, **261:27B.**
Appeals from denial of relief from court costs in matters arising in probate court, **261:27D.**
Fees, **261:27A.**
Infants.
Children and minors. See within this heading, "Children and minors."
Injunctions.
Attachment made, **215:6A.**
Discrimination, jurisdiction of actions for damages and injunctive relief on account, **151B:9.**
Fees, **262:40.**
Foreclosure, jurisdiction of action to enjoin, **215:6.**
Jurisdiction, **215:6.**
Insolvency.
See INSOLVENCY AND BANKRUPTCY.
Inspection.
Examination, inspection, and investigation. See within this heading, "Examination, inspection, and investigation."

PROBATE AND FAMILY COURT —Cont'd

Interest in or benefit by fees or emoluments arising from matter pending in probate court, **217:6B.**

Interlocutory decrees and orders, **231:43, 231:118.**

Effect of appeal, **215:22.**

Revision on appeal, **215:14.**

Interrogatories, **215:43, 215:56A.**

Inventory information as to real property, recording, **217:15B, 217:16.**

Investigation.

Examination, inspection, and investigation. See within this heading, "Examination, inspection, and investigation."

Investments, **215:41.**

Collective investment funds, **167G:3.**

First judge of court, investments to be in name, **217:2.**

Remainders, investment of proceeds of sale of property subject, **183:51.**

Unclaimed funds, **206:25-206:28.**

Judges of probate, **215:1, 217:1 et seq.; MA Const Part 2 Ch 6 Art 2.**

See PROBATE AND INSOLVENCY JUDGES.

Judgments, decrees, and orders, **215:34.**

Judicial council, composition, **221:34A.**

Jurisdiction, **204:1, 208:36A, 209:32, 215:1 et seq., 241:2; MA Const Part 2 Art 5 Ch 3.**

Jury issues, effect of appeal from order granting or refusing, **215:22.**

Justice of the peace, administration of oaths, **215:38.**

Knowledge.

Notice and knowledge. See within this heading, "Notice and knowledge."

Land contracts, specific performance, **204:1.**

Legacy.

See LEGACY AND SUCCESSION TAXES.

Legal holiday as affecting summons, **215:60.**

Libel for divorce, **215:3, 262:40.**

License of probate court for sale or assignment of property, **231:6.**

PROBATE AND FAMILY COURT —Cont'd

Local property assessment, persons liable for tax, **59:12B.**

Long-arm jurisdiction, **208:36A.**

Mail, service of citation by registered mail, **215:46.**

Maintenance of order, **215:57.**

Marriage.

Annulment actions, **215:3, 262:40.**

See ANNULMENT OF MARRIAGE.

Divorce.

See DIVORCE AND ALIMONY.

Dower, **215:35.**

Judge's wife as defendant in action on bond, **205:25.**

Marital home, court's authority to order either spouse to vacate, **208:34B.**

Registers of probate and insolvency.

Libel for divorce or for affirmance or annulment of marriage, fee, **262:40.**

Records, reproduction, **46:19A.**

Separated spouses, jurisdiction of proceedings involving, **209:32.**

Separate estate of married women, **215:4.**

Master.

Auditor, master, or referee. See within this heading, "Auditor, master, or referee."

Mentally ill persons.

See GUARDIANS, CONSERVATORS, AND COMMITTEES.

Middlesex county.

See MIDDLESEX COUNTY.

Minors.

Children and minors. See within this heading, "Children and minors."

Mortgages.

Foreclosure by trustee, **203:24A, 203:24B.**

Judgments, decrees, and orders.

Realty mortgaged by fiduciary, **202:30.**

Trust estate, authority for mortgage, **203:24.**

Registration of land titles, effect on mortgages by fiduciaries, **185:98.**

Trust estate, **203:24.**

Motions for framing jury issues, fees for filing, **262:40.**

PROBATE AND FAMILY COURT —Cont'd

Name.

Change of name, **210:12-210:14.**

Investments to be in name of first judge of court, **217:2.**

Jurisdiction of changes, **215:3.**

Spouses, use of names of both on documents and communications, **217:22A.**

Trust companies, deposits in name of probate judge, **241:34.**

Nantucket county.

See NANTUCKET COUNTY.

Newspapers for notices, selection, **215:49.**

Nonresidents, endorsement of writ or bill by responsible inhabitant in actions by or against, **231:42.**

Nonsupport.

Desertion and nonsupport. See within this heading, "Desertion and nonsupport."

Norfolk County, Probate and Family Court, **215:62, 217:1, 217:30.**

Notary public, administration of oaths, **215:38.**

Notice and knowledge, **215:36.**

Application for counsel fees, **215:39A.**

Appointment or sale of real estate, remedy in case of failure of proof of notice, **204:26.**

Hearings, **215:31.**

Judges of probate and insolvency.

Forfeiture of bond of register, notice to state treasurer, **217:11.**

Teste of first judge of court, notices to bear, **217:2.**

Land contracts, specific performance, **204:1.**

Perpetuation of evidence of notice of sale, **202:16.**

Publication, requirements in connection with notice, **215:3, 215:49.**

Ratification of doubtful acts of fiduciaries due to defect, **204:24.**

Registers of probate.

See REGISTERS OF PROBATE AND INSOLVENCY.

Remainders, notice of sale of property subject, **183:50.**

PROBATE AND FAMILY COURT —Cont'd

Notice and knowledge —Cont'd

Removal of cause, filing of notice, **215:6.**

Selection of newspapers, **215:49.**

Waiver of notice, **215:47.**

Wills.

See WILLS.

Oaths, **215:38.**

Affidavits. See within this heading, "Affidavits."

Concealing property, examination under oath of person suspected, **215:44.**

Judges of probate and insolvency.

Administration of oaths, **215:38.**

Oath of judge, **217:5.**

Registers of probate and insolvency.

Administration of oaths by register, **215:38.**

Judge's oath to be filed with register, **217:5.**

Oath of register, **217:5A.**

Open courts, **215:58.**

Order, maintenance, **215:57.**

Orders, **215:34.**

Original will may be taken from registry, **215:52.**

Out of court business, transaction, **215:32, 215:33.**

Partition.

Jurisdiction, **241:2.**

Revocation of warrant or commission, **215:35.**

Paternity actions, **209C:3, 209C:24, 215:4, 218:19.**

Patients' funds, procedure for establishment of claims, **111:65D.**

Penalties.

Fines and penalties. See within this heading, "Fines and penalties."

Pensions.

Retirement and pension systems. See within this heading, "Retirement and pension systems."

Petitions and complaints.

Adoption of children, jurisdiction of petitions, **215:3.**

Children born out of wedlock, forms of complaints, **209C:24.**

Public administrator, petition by, copy of death certificate, **192:1.**

PROBATE AND FAMILY COURT —Cont'd

Petitions and complaints —Cont'd

Sale of land, sufficiency of decree upon petition, **202:37.**

Sufficiency of decree upon petition to sell real or personal property, **202:37.**

Wills.

See WILLS.

Place of holding court, **215:62; MA Const Part 2 Ch 3 Art 4.**

Pleading.

Petitions and complaints. See within this heading, "Petitions and complaints."

Plymouth county.

See PLYMOUTH COUNTY.

Police.

Guardian ad litem, assistance, **215:56A, 215:56B.**

Service of capias, **215:34A.**

Poor persons.

Indigency. See within this heading, "Indigency."

Power of appointment.

Record of release, **204:28.**

Sale subject, **183:49-183:61.**

Preservation of dockets, **215:55.**

Presumption in favor of proceedings of probate courts, **215:2.**

Probate court rules.

Abandoned appeals.

Dismissal of abandoned appeals, **Rule 30.**

Depositions.

Applicable provisions, **Rule 27A.**

Discovery.

Applicable provisions, **Rule 27A.**

Dismissal of abandoned appeals, **Rule 30.**

Evidence.

Applicable provisions, **Rule 27A.**

Interrogatories.

Applicable provisions, **Rule 27A.**

Summary judgments.

Applicable provisions, **Rule 27B.**

Process.

Service. See within this heading, "Service of citation and capias."

Publication, names of estates and parties to be printed in bold type in case of service, **215:3.**

Public charities, filing of financial reports, **12:8F.**

PROBATE AND FAMILY COURT —Cont'd

Public inspection of docketed index of cases, right, **215:37.**

Public service corporation employees, request for appointment or discharge, **271:40.**

Ratification of acts of fiduciaries, **204:23, 204:24.**

Real property.

Sale of property. See within this heading, "Sale of property."

Receipts.

Recording of receipts to executors, **215:50.**

Registers of probate.

See REGISTERS OF PROBATE AND INSOLVENCY.

Receivers.

Consolidation of appeals settling different accounts, **215:19.**

Determination of amount due for services, **215:39.**

Effect of appeal upon act appealed from in case of removal, **215:25.**

Enforcement of delivery of property by resigning receivers, **215:40.**

Receipts, recording, **215:50.**

Reconveyance, proceedings, **204:1.**

Record, courts, **215:1.**

Records, reports, and returns.

Adoption records, inspection, **210:5C.**

Another county, filing of records of real property interests located, **217:15C.**

Appeals, **215:13, 231:125A.**

County commissioners to provide record books, **215:53.**

Decrees, **215:36.**

Facts, report, **215:11.**

Further report on appeals from probate court, **231:125A.**

Indexes, **215:36.**

Indigency, filing affidavit, **261:27B.**

Inventory information as to real property, recording, **217:15B.**

Judges.

See PROBATE AND INSOLVENCY JUDGES.

Judgment directing conveyance, recording if not complied, **183:43.**

Pleadings in proceedings removed to superior court, filing, **215:6.**

PROBATE AND FAMILY COURT —Cont'd

Records, reports, and returns —Cont'd

Providing of rooms, **215:53, 215:54.**

Public charities, filing of financial reports, **12:8F.**

Receipts to executors or trustees, **215:50.**

Registers of probate.

See REGISTERS OF PROBATE AND INSOLVENCY.

Release of power of appointment, **204:28.**

Removal of cause, filing of notice, **215:6.**

Reservation and report of case to appeals court, **215:13.**

Restrictions on land contained in will, **184:16, 184:19.**

Sale of realty, **202:16.**

Suffolk County, expense of recording probate proceedings, **215:56.**

Referees.

Auditor, master, or referee. See within this heading, "Auditor, master, or referee."

Registered mail, service of citation, **215:46.**

Registers, **215:1, 217:1-217:43.**

See REGISTERS OF PROBATE AND INSOLVENCY.

Registration of land titles as affecting sales or mortgages by fiduciaries, **185:98.**

Release, decree operating, **183:43.**

Remainders, sale subject, **183:49-183:51.**

Removal from office.

Executor, effect of appeal upon act appealed from in case of removal, **215:25.**

Public service corporation employees, **271:40.**

Register, **211:4.**

Trustee, **68:14.**

Removal of causes.

Transfer of cases. See within this heading, "Transfer of cases to or from."

Repeals as affecting, **281:4.**

Reports.

Records, reports, and returns. See within this heading, "Records, reports, and returns."

Rescript from appeals court, award of fees after receipt, **215:39B.**

PROBATE AND FAMILY COURT —Cont'd

Reservation and report of case to appeals court, **215:13.**

Resigning executors, enforcement of delivery of property, **215:40.**

Restrictions on land contained in will, recording, **184:16, 184:19, 184:29.**

Retention of jurisdiction by court first taking it, **215:7.**

Retirement and pension systems.

Auditor or master, payment for services of pensions appointed, **32:91.**

Health, welfare, and retirement funds, investigation, **151D:3.**

Judges, pensions, **32:65A-32:65D.**

Registers of probate included in retirement systems of counties, **32:2.**

Reversal or affirmance of decree appealed, **215:28.**

Reversions, sale subject, **183:49-183:51.**

Revocation of warrants and commissions, **215:35.**

Rights of beneficiaries.

Information provided to interested parties, **215:30B.**

Rooms for records, **215:53, 215:54.**

Rules and forms, **215:30.**

Information provided to interested persons of estate, **215:30B.**

Rules of court, **215:30.**

Salaries.

Wages, salaries, and compensation. See within this heading, "Wages, salaries, and compensation."

Sale of property.

Annuities or charges, sale subject, **183:52.**

Appraisals and appraisers. See within this heading, "Appraisals and appraisers."

Confirmation or ratification of void or doubtful sales, **204:23, 204:24.**

Consent of deceased person, **204:2.**

Decree upon petition to sell, sufficiency, **202:37.**

Deed, decree operating, **183:43.**

Dower or curtesy, sale free, **202:3.**

Examination of persons licensed to sell land, **204:11.**

PROBATE AND FAMILY COURT —Cont'd

Sale of property —Cont'd

Executors.

See EXECUTORS AND ADMINISTRATORS.

Failure of proof of notice, remedy in case, **204:26.**

Land contracts of decedents, conveyances, **204:1.**

License of probate court for sale, **231:6.**

Registration of title as affecting, **185:98.**

Remainders, conveyance subject, **183:49-183:51.**

Timber, proceedings for sale during life estate, **184:14.**

Title acquired from sale as affected by adjudication of debts, **204:21.**

Venue, **202:6.**

Foreign executors, proceeds for sale, **204:7.**

Saturdays, sessions, **215:58.**

School tuition to be reimbursed by state, determination, **76:11.**

Securities and securities regulation, **196:9, 215:41.**

Security, **205:1 et seq.**

See PROBATE BONDS.

Selection of newspapers for notices, **215:49.**

Separate estate of married women, **215:4.**

Service of citation and capias, **215:34A.**

Registered mail, **215:46.**

Removal to superior court, **215:6.**

Sheriff's fees, **262:8.**

Summons. See within this heading, "Summons."

Sessions of courts, **215:57-215:62.**

Small sums to which minor is entitled, authority to have executor or administrator deliver to minor's parents, **215:41A.**

Soldiers' homes, trusts as to funds of former patients, **115A:6, 115A:7.**

Special masters, compensation paid for by state, **221:55.**

Specific performance, **204:21.**

State.

Commonwealth. See within this heading, "Commonwealth."

State police to assist guardian ad litem, **215:56A, 215:56B.**

Stay of proceedings, **215:22, 215:23.**

**PROBATE AND FAMILY
COURT** —Cont'd

Stenographer, appointment and
compensation, **215:18, 215:28.**

Suffolk county.
Additional judges, **217:2.**
Appointment of official
stenographer for probate
court, **215:18.**
Clerk for probate and
insolvency, **217:28.**
Deputy assistant register,
appointment, **217:28.**
Expense of recording probate
proceedings, **215:56.**
Guardian ad litem, appointment,
217:27A.
Official stenographer, **215:18.**
Sessions of court, **215:62.**

Summons.
Legal holiday and election day
as affecting, **215:60.**
Printing requirements as to
service by publication,
215:3.
Service by mail, **215:46.**

Sundays and holidays.
Sessions of court, **215:58,
215:60.**
Summons, legal holiday as
affecting, **215:60.**

Superior court, removal of causes,
215:6.
Superior jurisdiction, **215:2.**
Supplemental rules of probate
court, **Rules 101 et seq.**
Domestic relations rules, **215:1
et seq.**

Support proceedings.
Children, orders for support,
**208:28, 208:36A, 209:37,
209C:3, 218:19, 221B:3.**
Concurrent jurisdiction to order
parent or spouse to support
dependent child, **209:32F.**
Contempt for violation of
support orders, **215:34,
215:34A.**
Desertion and nonsupport. See
within this heading,
"Desertion and nonsupport."
Jail sentence of husband or
father for failure to obey
orders, **215:34.**
Jurisdiction to enforce support
judgments, **208:36A, 215:6.**
Punishment for violation of
order, **215:34, 215:34A.**
Review of underlying judgment
before confining to prison for
contempt, **215:34B.**

**PROBATE AND FAMILY
COURT** —Cont'd

Support proceedings —Cont'd
Separation of spouses, support
in event of.
See SEPARATE
MAINTENANCE OR
SUPPORT.
Service of citation and capias,
215:34A.
Transfer of case from district
court or Boston municipal
court, **209C:3.**

Supreme judicial court.
See SUPREME JUDICIAL
COURT.
Sureties, **205:1 et seq.**
See PROBATE BONDS.

Taxation.
Abatement proceedings,
jurisdiction of appeals,
62C:39.
Local property assessment,
persons liable for tax,
59:12B.

Temporary investments, **215:41.**
Temporary service by retired
judges, **32:65E.**
Terminable interest property, rules
of construction, **191:1A.**
Testamentary trustees, **203:4.**
Tewksbury Hospital, disposition of
unclaimed patients' funds,
122:7.
Timber, proceedings for sale
during life estate, **184:14.**

Title and ownership.
Registration of land titles as
affecting sales or mortgages
by fiduciaries, **185:98.**
Title acquired from sale affected
by adjudication, **204:21.**
Transaction of business out of
court, **215:32, 215:33.**
Transfer of cases to or from,
211:4A.
Equity proceedings, **215:6.**
Superior court, procedure as to
transfers, **215:6.**
Transfers to minors act, **201A:1 to
201A:24.**
See TRANSFERS TO MINORS.
Traveling expenses, payment by
Commonwealth, **217:42.**

Trial or hearing.
Hearings. See within this
heading, "Hearings."
Trust companies, deposits in name
of probate judge, **241:34.**
Trusts and trustees, **203:1 et seq.**
Accounts and accounting. See
within this heading,
"Accounts and accounting."

**PROBATE AND FAMILY
COURT** —Cont'd

Trusts and trustees —Cont'd
Annual account of common trust
fund, filing, **203A:3.**
Appointment of trustees, **203:5.**

Bonds.
See PROBATE BONDS.

Common trust funds.
Declaration of trust filed in
registry of probate,
203A:1.
Filing of annual account,
203A:3.
Compensation of trustee,
determination, **215:39.**
Consolidation of appeals settling
different accounts of trustee,
215:19.
Counsel fees in connection with
construction of trust,
215:39B.
Determination of amount due for
services, **215:39.**
Dower or curtesy, sale of
decedent's realty free, **202:3.**
Effect of appeal upon act
appealed from in case of
removal of trustee, **215:25.**
Eminent domain, appointment of
trustee, **79:26, 79:30.**
Enforcement of delivery of
property by trustee, **215:40.**

Estate administration process.
Information provided to
interested parties,
215:30B.
Foreclosure of mortgage by
trustee, disposition of
process, **203:24A, 203:24B.**
Foreign trustee, **203:10.**
Judge of probate and insolvency
appointed as trustee, **217:7.**
Jurisdiction in connection with
trusts, **215:6, 215:8.**
Mortgage of trust estate, **203:24.**
Receipts, recording, **215:50.**
Removal, **68:14.**

Rights of beneficiaries.
Information provided to
interested parties,
215:30B.
Soldiers' homes, trusts as to
former patients, **115A:6,
115A:7.**
Testamentary trustees, **203:4.**
Vacancies, filling, **203:5, 203:10,
203:12.**
Validity of acts of trustees
pending appeal from decree
of appointment, **215:9A.**

PROBATE AND FAMILY COURT —Cont'd

Trusts and trustees —Cont'd
Venue of proceedings for sales by
foreign trustees, **204:7.**
Twenty-one years of age, orders for
education and support of
children beyond, **208:28,
209:37.**
Unclaimed funds.
Deposit and disposition of,
206:25-206:28.
Tewksbury Hospital, disposition
of unclaimed patients' funds,
122:7.
Uniform transfers to minors act,
201A:1 to 201A:24.
See TRANSFERS TO MINORS.
Vacancies in trusts, filling, **203:5,
203:10, 203:12.**
Venue.
Change, **215:8A.**
Sale of property, **202:6, 204:7.**
Veterans' administration to
represent persons in allowance
of probate accounts, when,
206:24.
Wages, salaries, and compensation.
Assessors, referees, masters,
commissioners, and
arbitrators, **221:55.**
Auditor, master, or referee,
32:91, 221:55, 221:61.
Commonwealth. See within this
heading, "Commonwealth."
Court officers, **217:39.**
Fees. See within this heading,
"Fees."
Guardian ad litem, **215:56A,
215:56B.**
Judges.
See PROBATE AND
INSOLVENCY JUDGES.
Messengers, **217:39.**
Registers for recording receipts,
215:50.
Registers of probate.
See REGISTERS OF
PROBATE AND
INSOLVENCY.
Retirement and pension
systems. See within this
heading, "Retirement and
pension systems."
Schedule, **217:35A, 217:35B.**
Stenographer, **215:18.**
Traveling expenses, **217:42.**
Trustees, determination, **215:39.**
Waiver.
Bond, **205:4.**
Court's power to require bond
affected by waiver, **205:5.**

PROBATE AND FAMILY COURT —Cont'd

Waiver —Cont'd
Indigents, waiver of costs and
fees, **261:27B.**
Notice, **215:47.**
Warrants.
Revocation, **215:35.**
Service of citation and capias.
See within this heading,
"Service of citation and
capias."
Welfare department.
Custody of child on order of
probate court, **119:23.**
Subrogation rights, proceedings
to enforce, **18:21.**
Visitation of child by parent,
guardian, or next of kin,
power to compel transitional
assistance department to
permit, **119:35.**
Wharves, piers and docks,
enforcement of
Commonwealth's lien for cost
of removal when unsafe,
91:49B.
Wills, **192:1 et seq., 215:1 et seq.**
See WILLS.
Witnesses.
Depositions, **233:24.**
Fees, **262:29.**
Worcester county.
See WORCESTER COUNTY.
Written decrees, necessity, **215:36.**

PROBATE AND FAMILY COURT RULES.

Abandoned appeals.
Dismissal of abandoned appeals,
Rule 30.
Accounts and accounting.
Inclusions, **Rule 29A.**
Schedule, recording, **Rule 25.**
Trusts and trustees, valuation of
assets, **Rule 29A.**
Affidavits.
Notice, **Rules 3, 29, 29B.**
Public auction sales, **Rule 25.**
Amendments to pleadings, **Rule 7.**
Answer, **Rule 4.**
Appointments.
Docket, **Rule 13.**
Stenographers, **Rule 18.**
Auction sales, affidavits for. **Rule
25.**
Auditor, master, or referee,
findings of fact, **Rules 22, 23.**
Civil Procedure Rules.
See CIVIL PROCEDURE
RULES.

PROBATE AND FAMILY COURT RULES —Cont'd

Commissions, depositions,
commissions to take, **Rule 9.**
Contracts and agreements,
recording agreement for
compromise of will, **Rule 25.**
Copies of pleadings given to
adverse parties, **Rule 4.**
Custodian to record decree, **Rule
25.**
Custody of exhibits, Register of
court, **Rule 26.**
Depositions, **Rule 9.**
Applicable provisions, **Rule 27A.**
Commissions, **Rule 9.**
Filing and use, **Rule 11.**
Manner of taking, **Rule 10.**
Subscribing witnesses, **Rule 12.**
Disability or incapacity to act,
Rule 5.
Discharge or release, dower,
recording release of, **Rule 25.**
Discovery.
Applicable provisions, **Rule 27A.**
Dismissal of abandoned appeals,
Rule 30.
Divorce and alimony, judgments,
recording, **Rule 25.**
Docket and index, appointments,
Rule 13.
Documents, copies of, **Rule 4.**
Domestic relations.
See DOMESTIC RELATIONS
RULES OF PROCEDURE.
Domestic relations special rules.
See DOMESTIC RELATIONS
SPECIAL RULES.
Dower and courtesy, recording
assignment or release, **Rule
25.**
Evidence.
Applicable provisions, **Rule 27A.**
Exhibits, custody by register of,
Rule 26.
Registers of probate and
insolvency, custody of
exhibits, **Rule 26.**
Report, **Rule 19.**
Execution order, recording of,
Rule 25.
Exhibits, custody of, **Rule 26.**
Fees, auditors and masters, **Rule
20.**
Findings of fact.
Auditors, **Rules 22, 23.**
Jury issues, **Rule 16.**
Foreign law, **Rule 17.**
Forms.
Abuse, **Forms 62-64.**
Address impoundment, **Form
65.**

PROBATE AND FAMILY COURT RULES —Cont'd

Forms —Cont'd

Adoption, **210:6.**

Affidavit of medical assistance, **Form 52.**

Annulment.
Complaint, **Form 2.**

Appointment of counsel, **Form 23.**

Attachment.
Writ of, **Form 39.**

Birth record correction, **Form 17.**

Capias, **Form 45.**

Child court guidelines.
Findings, **Form 25.**
Worksheet, **Form 24.**

Complaints, **Forms 1 to 11.**
Protection from abuse, **Form 62.**

Conservatorship, **Forms 53-56.**

Contempt.
Complaint, **Form 5.**
Judgments, **Form 31.**
Mittimus for contempt, **Form 46.**
Summons, **Form 15.**

Counsel.
Appointment of, **Form 23.**
Waiver of, **Form 22.**

Custody, **119:23.**

Divorce.
Certificate of absolute divorce, **Forms 32, 33.**
Complaint, **Form 1.**
Complaint for separate court, **Form 4.**
Joint petition for, **Form 3.**
Judgment of divorce nisi, **Form 29, 30.**
Judgment of separate court, **Form 28.**

Domestic relations.
Summons, **Form 12.**

Executions, **Forms 47, 48.**

Financial statement, **Form 21.**

Guardianship, **Forms 57-61.**

Injunctions.
Preliminary injunction, **Form 41.**

Judgments, **Form 40.**
Contempt, **Form 31.**
Divorce nisi, **Form 29, 30.**
Paternity, **Form 16.**
Separate court, **Form 28.**

Marriage.
Without delay, **Form 44.**

Minors.
Marriage without delay, **Form 44.**

PROBATE AND FAMILY COURT RULES —Cont'd

Forms —Cont'd

Mittimus for contempt, **Form 46.**

Modification.
Complaint for, **Form 6.**

Motion, **Form 26.**

Orders, **Forms 34, 49-51.**
Defendant information form in restraining order cases, **Form 66.**
Domestic relations protective order, **Form 42, 43.**
Finding and order for approval of attachment, **Form 35.**
Finding and order of approval of attachment on trustee process, **Form 37.**
Findings and ex parte order for approval of attachment, **Form 36.**
Findings and ex parte order for approval of attachment on trustee process, **Form 38.**
Order of notice, **Form 20.**
Restraining order, **Form 20.**
Service by publication, **Form 13.**
Temporary order, **Form 27.**

Paternity.
Complaint, **Forms 8, 9, 11.**
Judgment of paternity, **Form 16.**
Voluntary acknowledgment, **Form 10.**
Stipulation, **Form 51A.**

Publication.
Order for service by, **Form 13.**
Summons with publication, **Form 14.**

Summons, **Form 18, 20.**
Contempt, **Form 15.**
Domestic relations, **Form 12.**
Trustee, **Form 19.**
With publication, **Form 14.**

Temporary order, **Form 27.**

Temporary restraining orders, **Form 41.**
Defendant information form **Form 66.**

Trustee process.
Findings and order of attachment, **Forms 37, 38.**
Summons, **Form 19.**

Visitation.
Complaint for grandparents, **Form 7.**

Voluntary acknowledgment of parentage, **Form 10.**

PROBATE AND FAMILY COURT RULES —Cont'd

Forms —Cont'd

Waiver of counsel, **Form 22.**

Writ of attachment, **Form 39.**

Fraud and deceit.
Guardians, conservators, and committees.
Accounts and accounting, valuation of assets, **Rule 29A.**
Temporary guardians and conservators, **Rule 29B.**

Guardians, conservators, and committees.
Mentally ill and retarded persons, **Rule 5.**
Notice and knowledge, temporary guardianship, **Rule 29B.**

Hearings, interlocutory decrees and orders, **Rule 15.**

Interlocutory decrees and orders, hearings on, **Rule 15.**

Interrogatories.
Applicable provisions, **Rule 27A.**

Jury issues, **Rule 16.**

Military affidavits regarding probate of will, **Rule 28.**

Motions, **Rules 15, 29.**
Hearings, **Rule 15.**

Name, change of, records and recording.
Pleadings, amendment of, **Rule 7.**
Recording of papers, **Rule 25.**

Notice and knowledge.
Additional notice, **Rule 8.**
Affidavits, **Rules 3, 29, 29B.**
Service, **Rule 3.**
Temporary conservatorship, motion for, **Rule 29B.**

Objections, will contest, **Rule 2A.**

Partition.
Recording of instruments, warrant, **Rule 25.**
Warrant of commissioners, recording of, **Rule 25.**

Pleadings, **Rule 4.**

Protection writ, **Rule 14.**

Records, reports, and returns.
Depositions, filing and use of, **Rule 11.**
Dower, recording assignment or release of, **Rule 25.**
Evidence, report of, **Rule 19.**
Execution order, **Rule 25.**
Filing, **Rule 25.**
Inter vivos trusts, **Rule 25.**
License to sell real property, **Rule 25.**

PROBATE AND FAMILY COURT RULES —Cont'd

Records, reports, and returns —Cont'd

Wills, rules as to recording, **Rule 25.**

Registers of probate and insolvency, evidence, custody of exhibits, **Rule 26.**

Release of dower, recording of, **Rule 25.**

Return days, **Rule 6.**

Sale of property, auction sale, affidavits, **Rule 25.**

Separate maintenance or support, recording and notice of decree, **Rule 25.**

Service of process and papers.

Citation and capias, service of, return days, **Rule 6.**

Notice, service of, **Rule 3.**

Signatures on pleadings, **Rule 28.**

Standing orders.

Assignment of cases to Middlesex satellite sessions at Concord and Marlborough, **Standing Order 1-89.**

Individual calendar sessions, **Standing Order 2-83.**

Middlesex satellite sessions, assignment of cases, **Standing Order 1-89.**

Pretrial conferences, **Standing Order 2-88.**

Service by facsimile or other electronic telephonic transmittal, **Standing Order 2-97.**

Time standards, **Standing Order 1-88.**

Subscribing witnesses, deposition of, **Rule 12.**

Summary judgments.

Applicable provisions, **Rule 27B.**

Supplemental rules of probate court.

Affidavits, writ of protection, **Rule 103.**

Appointment of stenographers, **Rule 202.**

Attachments, **Rule 101.**

Court stenographers, **Rule 202.**

Custody of exhibits, register of court, **Rule 203.**

Divorce and alimony, support pending judgment, **Rule 101.**

Electronic recording of courtroom proceedings, **Rule 201.**

PROBATE AND FAMILY COURT RULES —Cont'd

Supplemental rules of probate court —Cont'd

Evidence, custody of exhibits, **Rule 203.**

Exhibits, custody of, **Rule 203.**

Forms, printing of, **Rule 204.**

Hearings.

Interlocutory decrees and orders, **Rule 101.**

Motions and interlocutory matters, **Rule 101.**

Interlocutory decrees and orders, hearings on, **Rule 101.**

Motions, hearings, **Rule 101.**

Notice and knowledge.

Additional notice, **Rule 102.**

Temporary support, motion for, **Rule 101.**

Practice before court, **Rules 101 et seq.**

Protection writ, **Rule 103.**

Recording of court proceedings, **Rule 201.**

Registers of probate and insolvency, custody of exhibits, **Rule 203.**

Separate maintenance or support, judgments, support pending, **Rule 101.**

Support proceedings.

Divorce, support of children pending judgment of, **Rule 101.**

Temporary support, **Rule 101.**

Witnesses, writ of protection, **Rule 103.**

Writ of protection, **Rule 103.**

Temporary guardians or conservators, **Rule 29B.**

Trusts and trustees, recording of inter vivos trusts, **Rule 25.**

Uniform practices of probate courts.

Accounts.

Compliance with statute and rules, **Rule XV.**

Numbering of items, **Rule XV.**

Time for allowance of, **Rule XVII.**

Adoption.

Plan of adoption required in petitions to establish consent, **Rule X.**

Tracking system, **Rule Xa.**

Agents, certification of securities held by, **Rule I.**

Annulment of marriage.

Corroborating witness, **Rule II.**

PROBATE AND FAMILY COURT RULES —Cont'd

Uniform practices of probate courts —Cont'd

Annulment of marriage —Cont'd

Notice, **Rule XII.**

Petition, **Rule XVIII.**

Appeal and review, dismissal, notice, **Rule XIX.**

Arrearages, contempt hearings, **Rule IV.**

Auditor, master, or referee, periodic report by, **Rule XXVIII.**

Certificates and certification.

Physician, **Rule XXII.**

Securities held by corporate fiduciary, custodian, or agent, certification of, **Rule I.**

Change or modification, temporary orders, **Rule XXIII.**

Charitable interests, notice to Attorney General, **Rule XXXIV.**

Clinical team report, **Rule XXII.**

Complaint, acceptance of service of, **Rule XIII.**

Computer generated forms, standards for, **Rule XXXIII.**

Contempt.

Arrearages, contempt hearings, **Rule IV.**

Summons, **Rule XXVII.**

Corporate fiduciary, certification of securities held by, **Rule I.**

Corroborating witness in uncontested divorce and annulment matters, **Rule II.**

Court stenographers, **Rule IX.**

Custodians, certification of securities held by corporate custodian, **Rule I.**

Deeds and conveyances, separate maintenance proceedings, conveyance of real estate, **Rule XIV.**

Delinquent payments, **Rule IV.**

Dismissal of notice, **Rule XIX.**

Divorce and alimony.

Corroborative witness, **Rule II.**

Financial statements, filing of, **Rule XXX.**

Injunctions, temporary restraining order, **Rule IV.**

Judgments, notice of decree, **Rule XII.**

PROBATE AND FAMILY COURT RULES —Cont'd
Uniform practices of probate courts —Cont'd
Divorce and alimony —Cont'd
Notice of decree, **Rule XII.**
Service of process, **Rule XIII.**
Temporary restraining order, **Rule IV.**
Equity, temporary restraining orders, **Rule V.**
Executors and administrators.
Limitations on appointment of administrators, **Rule XXIX.**
Fees, **Rule VIII.**
Fiduciaries.
Certification of Securities held by, **Rule I.**
Court-appointed fiduciaries, special administrators, limitations on appointment of, **Rule XXIX.**
Financial statement, divorce or separate support, **Rule XXX.**
Forms, computer generated, standards for, **Rule XXXIII.**
Guardians ad litem.
Certification of securities held by corporate fiduciary, custodian, or agent, **Rule I.**
Compensation of, limitation on hours, **Rule XXXII.**
Guardians, conservators, and committees.
Clinical team report, **Rule XXII.**
Corporate stock, certification of securities held by guardian, **Rule I.**
Heirs, will probate, **Rule XXVI.**
Mentally ill and retarded persons, **Rule XXVI.**
Notice and knowledge, temporary guardianship, **Rule III.**
Physical and mental examinations, **Rule XXII.**
Temporary guardians and conservators, **Rule III.**
Hearings, assignment of trial date, **Rule XI.**
Heir, incompetency of, **Rule XXVI.**
Inclusions, **Rule XV.**
Injunctions, temporary restraining orders, **Rules V, VI.**

PROBATE AND FAMILY COURT RULES —Cont'd
Uniform practices of probate courts —Cont'd
Limitation on appointments of special administrators, **Rule XXIX.**
Medical or physical examination, **Rule XXII.**
Military affidavits regarding probate of will, **Rule XXV.**
Motions.
Lists, **Rule XXI.**
Temporary conservatorship, notice of motion for, **Rule 29B.**
Notice and knowledge.
Assessment of arrearage, **Rule IV.**
Charitable interests, **Rule XXXIV.**
Dismissal, **Rule XIX.**
Divorce, notice of decree of, **Rule XII.**
Modification of temporary orders, **Rule XXIII.**
Sale or transfer of real property, **Rule XIV.**
Trial date, **Rule XI.**
Physician's certificate, **Rule XXII.**
Power of appointment waiver of guardian ad litem, **Rule XVI.**
Records, reports, and returns.
Clinical team report, **Rule XXII.**
Financial statements, **Rule XXX.**
Master's periodic reports, **Rule XXVIII.**
Sale of property, **Rule XIV.**
Securities held by corporate fiduciary, custodian, or agent, certification of, **Rule I.**
Separate maintenance or support.
Deeds and conveyances, **Rule XIV.**
Filing of financial statement, **Rule XXX.**
Recording and notice of decree, **Rule XII.**
Temporary restraining orders, **Rule VI.**
Special administrators, limitation on appointments, **Rule XXIX.**
Summons for contempt, **Rule XXVII.**

PROBATE AND FAMILY COURT RULES —Cont'd
Uniform practices of probate courts —Cont'd
Support proceedings.
Financial statement, **Rule XXX.**
Orders for support, generally, **Rules VI.**
Separate maintenance or support. See within this heading, "Separate maintenance or support."
Temporary guardians or conservators, **Rule III.**
Temporary restraining orders, **Rules V, VI.**
Tracking system.
Social services department or other child welfare agency, petitions filed by, **Rule Xb.**
Termination petitions, **Rule Xa.**
Wills.
Mentally incompetent person, probate of will of, **Rule XXVI.**
Military affidavits regarding probate of will, **Rule XXV.**
Witnesses, corroborating witness in divorce and annulment actions, **Rule II.**
Valuation of trust assets, **Rule 29A.**
Waiver, recording of wills, **Rule 25.**
Wills.
Agreement to compromise, recording, **Rule 25.**
Deposition of witness, **Rule 12.**
Recording of will, **Rule 25.**
Subscribing witnesses, deposition of, **Rule 12.**
Waiver of provisions, recording, **Rule 25.**
Witnesses.
Subscribing witnesses, wills, depositions, **Rule 12.**
Writ of protection, **Rule 14.**

PROBATE AND INSOLVENCY JUDGES, 215:1, 217:1 et seq.; MA Const Part 2 Ch 6 Art 2.
Acting judge, bonds, **217:10.**
Additional judges in certain counties, **217:2.**
Adjournment of court, **215:59.**
Administration of oaths, **215:38.**
Administrative justices.
See ADMINISTRATIVE JUSTICES.

PROBATE AND INSOLVENCY JUDGES —Cont'd

Adoption proceedings, hearing in chambers, **210:6.**

Advisory committee on personnel standards, administrative justice as member, **211B:8.**

Appointment.

Guardian, **217:7.**

Guardian ad litem, **215:56A.**

Officers, appointment, **217:30.**

Stenographer, **215:18.**

Approval of probate bonds, **205:10, 217:9.**

Assignment to other counties, **217:8.**

Barnstable probate court, **217:29C.**

Berkshire probate court, **217:29D.**

Birth registration, authority, **46:13A.**

Board of election examiners, judges as members, **54:122.**

Bonds and undertakings, **205:1 et seq.**

See PROBATE BONDS.

Bristol county.

Deputy assistant registers, **217:29G.**

Chief judge, **217:8, 217:8A.**

Administrative staff, **217:8A.**

Continuing education of judges and court personnel, agreements concerning programs, **7:28A.**

Executive clerk to chief judge, **217:8A.**

Expenses, payment of certain, **217:8A.**

Powers and duties, **217:8.**

Traveling expenses of judges sitting in other counties under direction, **217:42.**

Child custody or maintenance decrees, appointment of guardian ad litem to institute contempt proceedings for enforcement, **215:56B.**

Citations to bear teste of first judge of court, **217:2.**

Compensation.

Salaries. See within this heading, "Salaries."

Conflicts of interest, special judge, **217:6B.**

Contempt.

See PROBATE AND FAMILY COURT.

Counties, designation of judges for, **217:2, 217:3B, 217:7.**

Court officers, appointment, **217:30.**

PROBATE AND INSOLVENCY JUDGES —Cont'd

Decree out of county, **217:9.**

Deposits.

For burial expenses of wards in name of judge, **201:48A.**

To be in name of first judge of court, **217:2.**

Disinterest of judge as requirement, special judge, **217:6B.**

Dukes county judge, other counties, sitting in upon designation, **217:6B.**

Election examiners, member of board, **54:122.**

Executive clerk to chief judge, **217:8A.**

Executors or administrators, restrictions on appointment as, **192:7, 217:6B, 217:7.**

Fees in addition to compensation prohibited, **217:43.**

First judge, senior judge, **217:2.**

Foreign county.

Out of county. See within this heading, "Out of county."

Foreign state, jurisdiction to require filing of proof of marriage, **207:36.**

Governor, traveling expenses, approval, **217:8.**

Guardian ad litem, **215:56A, 215:56B, 217:27A.**

Guardian or conservator, restrictions on appointment, **217:7.**

Hampshire County, **217:3B, 217:7.**

Husband and wife, defendants on probate bond, **205:25.**

Impartiality, **217:6B.**

Inspection of records, **217:11.**

Investments to be in name of first judge of court, **217:2.**

Marriage in another state, jurisdiction to require filing of proof, **207:36.**

Nantucket county, **217:6B.**

Probate bonds, judge as obligor in actions, **205:24, 205:25.**

Traveling expenses, **217:42.**

Notices.

Forfeiture of bond of register, notice to state treasurer, **217:11.**

Teste of first judge of court, notices to bear, **217:2.**

Number of justices, **211B:2.**

Oath, **217:5.**

Administration of oaths, **215:38.**

Orders to bear teste of first judge of court, **217:2.**

PROBATE AND INSOLVENCY JUDGES —Cont'd

Out of county.

Decree, **217:9.**

Expenses of judge sitting in other counties, **217:6B, 217:42.**

Payment of bond to present incumbent, **205:7A.**

Pensions, **32:65A-32:65C.**

Plymouth county.

Deputy assistant registers, **217:29I.**

Number of judges, **217:2.**

Powers and duties, **217:2.**

Railroads passes to, prohibited, **160:199.**

Records.

Chief judge's requiring keeping, **217:8.**

Inspection, **217:11.**

Registers of probate.

See REGISTERS OF PROBATE AND INSOLVENCY.

Regulation of practice, **215:30.**

Reservation and report of case to appeals court, **215:13.**

Retired judges, temporary service, **32:65F.**

Retirement benefits, **32:65A-32:65D.**

Salaries, **211B:4, 217:35A.**

Fees in addition to compensation prohibited, **217:43.**

Permanent officer to act as guardian ad litem in Suffolk County, compensation, **217:27A.**

State, compensation payable, **217:39, 217:42.**

Senior judge, **217:2.**

Special judge, **217:6B.**

Pensions, **32:65B.**

Suffolk County, **217:2.**

Temporary service by retired judges, **32:65F.**

Traveling expenses, **217:6B, 217:8, 217:42.**

Trust companies.

See TRUST COMPANIES.

Trusts.

See TRUSTS AND TRUSTEES.

Uniforms to be worn by court officers, **217:30.**

Wages.

Salaries. See within this heading, "Salaries."

Widows of certain judges, benefits, **32:65C.**

PROBATE BONDS, **205:1 et seq.**

Absentees, estates of.

See ABSENTEES' ESTATES.

PROBATE BONDS —Cont'd

Accounting.
  Action on bond for neglect, **206:18.**
  Condition as to accounting, bond, **205:1.**
Acting judge, bond given, **217:10.**
Actions on bonds, **205:20 et seq.**
  Adding principal as party, **205:27, 205:28.**
  Claims accruing after one year, bond to secure, **197:15-197:17.**
  Commissioner's bond, **205:29.**
  Conservator's bond, **205:29.**
  Costs, **205:26.**
  Creditor's action, **205:20, 205:21, 205:23.**
  Endorsement for costs, **205:26.**
  Execution award, **205:31-205:34.**
  Insolvent decedent's estate, creditors, **205:21.**
  Judge as obligor, **205:24, 205:25.**
  Judgment against principal, **205:28.**
  Limitation of actions on bond of guardian or conservator, **205:35.**
  Maladministration of decedent's estate, action by persons aggrieved, **205:23.**
  Neglect of executor or administrator to account, **206:18.**
  Next of kin, actions, **205:22.**
  Principal summonable, when, **205:27, 205:28.**
  Receiver's bond, **205:29.**
  Sales of real estate, negligence or misconduct, **204:11.**
  Trusts and trustees. See within this heading, "Trusts and trustees."
  Unmatured obligations, bond to secure, **197:15-197:17.**
  Venue, **205:30.**
  Wife of probate judge as defendant, **205:25.**
Additional bond on sale or mortgage of real estate by fiduciary, **205:13.**
Administrator with will annexed.
  Cum testamento annexo administrator. See within this heading, "Cum testamento annexo administrator."
Amount, reduction, **205:18.**
Appointment of trustee by court, **203:6.**
Approval by judge or register, **205:10, 217:9.**

PROBATE BONDS —Cont'd

Arrest of principal by surety, **205:28.**
Attachment of goods of principal by surety, **205:28.**
Commissioner's bond, **205:29.**
  Form, **205:7A.**
Conditions, **205:1-205:3, 205:7A.**
  Breach, **205:31-205:34.**
  Payment of debts and legacies, bond conditioned, **202:13, 205:3.**
Consent to serving without bond, **205:4.**
Conservator's bond, action, **205:29.**
Continuing liability for discharged surety, **205:17.**
Corporate sureties.
  Eligibility, **205:9.**
  Foreign surety company, acceptability as surety on probate bond, **175:105.**
  Reduction of penal sum in case, **205:18.**
Costs and expenses, **205:26.**
  Fiduciary's bond cost chargeable to estate, **206:17.**
Court officer's duty to give bond, **217:11, 217:30.**
Creditors' actions on bonds, **205:20, 205:21, 205:23.**
Cum testamento annexo administrator.
  Exemptions, **205:4, 205:4A.**
  Form and conditions, **205:1.**
  Residuary legatee, administrator named, **205:3.**
Debts and legacies.
  Payment of, bond conditioned, **202:13, 205:3.**
  Rents, effect of giving of bond upon debts paid, **202:4A.**
Declination of trust or resignation by failure to give bond, **205:4, 205:8.**
Discharge of sureties, **205:15.**
  Continuing of liability until approval of new bond, **205:17.**
  Final account and discharge of principal, **206:22.**
  Manner of obtaining, **205:15.**
  Marriage of female fiduciary as ground, **205:19.**
  New bond, **205:15.**
Distribution of estates.
  Conditions as to bond, **205:1.**
  Distributee's right of action on bond, **205:22.**
  Power to require bond from distributee, **197:21.**

PROBATE BONDS —Cont'd

Equity, enforcement, **205:7A.**
Execution on bond, **205:31-205:34.**
Executors and administrators, **192:4, 196:2.**
  Action on bond of executor, **205:21.**
  Cum testamento annexo administrator. See within this heading, "Cum testamento annexo administrator."
  Indemnification for tax on legacy required to be paid within one year, **197:21.**
  Inventory, **195:5.**
  Letters testamentary granted to other executors for failure to pay bond, **192:5.**
  Minor named as executor, **192:6.**
  Necessity, **192:4.**
  Payment prior to issuance of letters of administration with will annexed, **193:7.**
  Public administrator. See within this heading, "Public administrator."
  Refusal to pay, effect, **192:5.**
  Temporary executors and administrators. See within this heading, "Temporary executors and administrators."
  Time within which personal injury or death actions may be brought, **197:9A.**
Exemptions.
  Administrator with will annexed, **205:4, 205:4A.**
  National banks, **205:6A.**
  Sureties on trustee's bond, **205:5.**
  Temporary fiduciaries, **205:4A.**
Expenses.
  Costs and expenses. See within this heading, "Costs and expenses."
Failure to give, effect, **205:4, 205:8, 205:12.**
Final account and discharge of principal, discharge of surety on bond after, **206:22.**
Foreign fiduciaries.
  Filing of copy of bond, **199A:5.**
  Sale of real estate, **202:34.**
Foreign surety company, acceptability as surety on probate bond, **175:105.**
Form, **205:1-205:3, 205:7A.**
French spoliation cases, **205:2.**
Gifts to Minors Act, bond of custodian, **201A:15, 201A:18.**

PROBATE BONDS —Cont'd
Guaranty and suretyship.
  Sureties. See within this
    heading, "Sureties."
Husband and wife, judge's wife as
  defendant in action on bond,
  205:25.
Inhabitants of state, sureties to be,
  205:9.
Insufficiency, new bond in case,
  205:14.
Joint and several obligations,
  205:7A.
Joint fiduciaries and sureties,
  205:11, 205:12.
  Agreements for joint control,
    205:19A.
Judge as obligor in action on bond,
  205:24, 205:25.
Judgment against principal,
  205:28.
Labor and employment.
  Temporary executors and
    administrators. See within
    this heading, "Temporary
    executors and
    administrators."
Legacies.
  Debts and legacies. See within
    this heading, "Debts and
    legacies."
Limitation of actions on bond,
  205:35, 260:11.
Limitations and restrictions on
  bonds.
  Conditions. See within this
    heading, "Conditions."
Loans.
  Debts and legacies. See within
    this heading, "Debts and
    legacies."
Maladministration, liability,
  205:23.
Marriage of female fiduciary,
  effect, **205:19.**
Mortgage of real estate.
  Trusts and trustees. See within
    this heading, "Trusts and
    trustees."
National banks serving as
  fiduciaries, **205:6A.**
Necessity of giving bond, **205:1,
  205:7.**
Neglect.
  Accounting, action on bond for
    neglect, **206:18.**
  Resignation or declination of
    trust, neglect in giving bond,
    205:4, 205:8.
  Sale, action on bond for neglect,
    204:11.

PROBATE BONDS —Cont'd
New bond.
  Discharge of sureties, new bond,
    205:15.
  Insufficiency of sureties or penal
    sum, **205:14.**
  Liability of sureties on prior
    bond until approval, **205:17.**
  Marriage of female fiduciary,
    205:19.
  Removal for failure to give,
    205:16.
Next of kin, action on bond,
  205:22.
Nonpayment of claims, breach of
  condition, **197:16.**
Penal sum.
  New bond in case of
    insufficiency, **205:14.**
  Reduction, **205:18.**
Premiums on bonds.
  Charging to estate, **206:17.**
  Deductions in determining tax
    on income for trust estates,
    62:10.
Principal added as party in action
  on bond, **205:27, 205:28.**
Public administrator, **194:2.**
  Action for deposit due state
    treasurer, **194:11.**
  Sale of real and personal
    property, **194:9.**
  Substitution, **194:8.**
Real estate, sale of.
  Sale of real estate. See within
    this heading, "Sale of real
    estate."
Receivers.
  See RECEIVERS AND
    RECEIVERSHIPS.
Reduction of bond, **205:18.**
Register's bond, **217:11, 217:12.**
  See REGISTERS OF PROBATE
    AND INSOLVENCY.
Release of sureties.
  Discharge of sureties. See within
    this heading, "Discharge of
    sureties."
Remainders, sale of real estate
  subject, **183:51.**
Removal of fiduciary for failure to
  give bond, **205:4, 205:8,
  205:16.**
Residuary legatee, administrator
  or executor also designated,
  205:3.
Resignation or declination of trust
  by neglect to give bond, **205:4,
  205:8.**
Sale of real estate.
  Additional bond, **205:13.**

PROBATE BONDS —Cont'd
Sale of real estate —Cont'd
  Foreign guardian selling
    property, **202:34.**
  Neglect or misconduct in, action
    on bond, **204:11.**
  Public administrator, **194:9.**
  Remainders, property subject,
    183:51.
  Trusts and trustees. See within
    this heading, "Trusts and
    trustees."
Statutory forms, **205:7A.**
Substitution of public
  administrator, **194:8.**
Successor trustee, **203:6.**
Summons of principals by sureties,
  205:27, 205:28.
Sureties, **205:1 et seq.**
  Amount for services, **215:39.**
  Arrest of principal, **205:28.**
  Attachment of goods of principal,
    205:28.
  Contingent claims against
    estates of decedents,
    198:28-198:30.
  Continuing liability on prior
    bond until approval of new
    bond, **205:17.**
  Corporate sureties. See within
    this heading, "Corporate
    sureties."
  Discharge of sureties. See within
    this heading, "Discharge of
    sureties."
  Exemption from giving sureties,
    205:4-205:6A, 205:7A.
  Expenses of procuring as
    chargeable against estate,
    206:17.
  Final account and discharge of
    fiduciary as exoneration,
    206:22.
  Foreign surety company,
    acceptability as surety on
    probate bond, **175:105.**
  Inhabitants of state, sureties to
    be, **205:9.**
  Insolvent estate of deceased
    person, surety's claim
    against, **198:28-198:30.**
  Insufficiency, new bond in case,
    205:14.
  Joint fiduciaries and sureties.
    See within this heading,
    "Joint fiduciaries and
    sureties."
  Limitation of actions on bond of
    guardian or conservator,
    205:35.
  National banks, exempt, **205:6A.**

PROBATE BONDS —Cont'd

Sureties —Cont'd

Principals summonable, **205:27, 205:28.**

Statutory form of bond, **205:7A.**

Trustee's bond, exemption from surety requirement, **205:5.**

Temporary executors and administrators, **205:1.**

Exemption from bonding, **205:4A.**

Trusts and trustees.

Accounting, condition, **205:1.**

Action, **205:29.**

Sales of real estate, neglect or misconduct, **204:11.**

Court appointee, **203:6.**

Deductions of trustee bond premium when determining tax on income for trust estates, **62:10.**

Exemption from giving sureties on bond, **205:5.**

Form and conditions of bond, **205:1, 205:7A.**

Joint trustees, **205:11.**

National banks exempt from giving sureties, **205:6A.**

Necessity, **205:7.**

Resignation or declination of trust, failure to give bond, **205:4, 205:8.**

Sale or mortgage of real estate.

Additional bond in case, **205:13.**

Neglect or misconduct in sale, action on bond, **204:11.**

Successor trustee, **203:6.**

Waiver, power of court to require notwithstanding trustee's bond, **205:5.**

Uniform Gifts to Minors Act, bond of custodian, **201A:15, 201A:18.**

United States veterans' bureau cases, sureties, **205:9.**

Venue of actions, **205:30.**

Waiver of bond, **205:4.**

Court's power to require bond affected, **205:5.**

Wife of probate judge as defendant in action on bond, **205:25.**

Will annexed, bond of administrator with.

Cum testamento annexo administrator. See within this heading, "Cum testamento annexo administrator."

PROBATION AND PAROLE, 127:128-127:151K, 276:83 et seq.

Accessibility of information in reports, **276:100.**

Accounts of probation officers. See ACCOUNTS AND ACCOUNTING.

Administrative justices. See ADMINISTRATIVE JUSTICES.

Administrative Procedures Act, board of parole subject, **30A:1C.**

Aid or assistance to prisoners on parole, **127:158-127:165.** See CORRECTIONAL INSTITUTIONS.

Alcoholic beverage law violations by certain young adults, rehabilitative programs and community service work, **276:87A.**

Annual report to general court, **276:101.**

Applications.

Petitions. See within this heading, "Petitions."

Armed offenses.

Augmenting penalties, **265:18B.**

Burglary being armed, **266:14.**

Carrying dangerous weapon, **269:10.**

Dwelling houses, armed assaults, **265:18A.**

Arrest for violation, **127:131, 127:149, 279:3.**

Arson, persons convicted, **127:133.**

Assault and battery, **127:133.**

Armed assaults in dwelling houses, eligibility for parole of person convicted, **265:18A.**

Collecting loan, eligibility upon second offense for assault and battery for purpose, **265:13C.**

Community parole supervision for life, **265:45, 275:18.**

Family trouble cases, **276:42A.**

Indecent assault on mentally retarded person, eligibility upon conviction, **265:13F.**

Parole officer, assault and battery, **265:13D.**

Associate commissioner of probation, appointment and qualifications, **276:98.**

Attorney's services to obtain, regulated, **127:166-127:169.**

PROBATION AND PAROLE —Cont'd

Battery.

Assault and battery. See within this heading, "Assault and battery."

Blood donations, eligibility for parole of prisoners making, **127:133.**

Board of parole, **27:4 et seq.**

Administrative Procedures Act, subject, **30A:1C.**

Advisory board of pardons, **127:152, 127:154.**

Aiding discharged prisoners, **27:5, 127:160.**

Chairman.

Criminal history systems board, member, **6:168.**

Criminal justice committee, member, **6:156.**

Criminal justice training council, member, **6:116.**

Rehabilitation commission advisory board, chairman as member, **6:76.**

Weapon, carrying, **147:8A.**

Compensation of members, **27:4.**

Crime victim's impact statement, inclusion in board's records on perpetrator, **258B:3.**

Criminal justice committee proposal review board, **6:156A.**

Defined, **127:1.**

Governor's council, **27:4, 127:127.**

Grant of parole permits, **127:133, 127:133A, 127:134.**

Health and human services executive office, parole board as agency, **6A:16.**

Hearing before, **127:134, 127:136.**

Information to be furnished, **127:135, 127:136.**

Qualifications of members, **27:4.**

Recommendations of hearing officer, appointment of single member to hear, **27:5.**

Records.

Meetings and decisions, **6:172, 127:130.**

Prisoners, records, **127:135, 127:136.**

Rehabilitation commission advisory council, chairman as member, **6:76.**

Release of prisoner, votes required, **127:133.**

PROBATION AND PAROLE
—Cont'd

Board of parole —Cont'd

Seeing inmates before granting permits, **127:134.**

Temporary appointments, **27:7.**

Training required for employees, **41:96B.**

Unavailability, **127:133A.**

Victim and witness assistance program funds, **258B:9.**

Visiting institutions, right, **127:36.**

Weapon, carrying of by parole board chairman or officer, **147:8A.**

Burglary, probation after second conviction for armed, **266:14.**

Camps for prisoners prior, **127:83E.**

Certificates and certification.

Termination of sentence, issuance of certificate, **127:130A.**

Terms and conditions, **127:130.**

Chairman of parole board.

Board of parole. See within this heading, "Board of parole."

Change of name, reports, **210:13, 210:14.**

Charges.

Fees and charges. See within this heading, "Fees and charges."

Chief administrative justice.

See CHIEF ADMINISTRATIVE JUSTICE.

Child.

Bail, **119:68.**

Delinquent children.

See JUVENILE COURTS AND DELINQUENT CHILDREN.

Desertion of child, **273:2.**

Probation officers.

See PROBATION OFFICERS.

Restrictions on parole, **127:29, 276:87.**

Civil service status of probation commissioner employees, **30:45.**

Commissioner of correction, duties of, **127:135, 127:136.**

Commissioner of probation, **30:45, 276:98, 276:99.**

Accommodations, **276:98.**

Administrative assistant, **276:98.**

Annual report to general court, **276:101.**

Appointment, **276:98.**

PROBATION AND PAROLE
—Cont'd

Commissioner of probation
—Cont'd

Change of name, reports, **210:13, 210:14.**

Compensation, **276:98.**

Criminal history systems board, member, **6:168.**

Criminal justice committee, probation commissioner as member, **6:156.**

Criminal justice committee proposal review board, membership, **6:156A.**

Criminal justice training council, membership, **6:116.**

Department of youth services to supply information, **276:100.**

Deputy commissioners, **276:98.**

Disciplinary action against probation officers, **276:99.**

District offices, powers, **276:88.**

Employees, **276:98.**

Classification, **30:45.**

Probation officers.

See PROBATION OFFICERS.

Expenses, **276:98.**

Forms of blanks and records, uniform, **276:101A.**

Inspection of records, **276:100.**

Juvenile courts.

See JUVENILE COURTS AND DELINQUENT CHILDREN.

Member of youth services advisory committee, **18A:9.**

Notice of appointment, removal, retirement, resignation, death, or leave of absence of probation officers, **276:103.**

Powers and duties, **276:99.**

Pretrial diversion of selected offenders, duties, **276A:8.**

Qualifications of probation officers, fixing, **276:99.**

Rehabilitation commission advisory council, commissioner as member, **6:76.**

Reports, **276:100, 276:101.**

Salary, **276:98.**

Supervisors of court probation services, **276:98.**

Temporary probation officers, powers, **276:89.**

Term of office, **276:98.**

Training and orientation programs for probation officers, **276:99.**

PROBATION AND PAROLE
—Cont'd

Commissioner of probation
—Cont'd

Uniform blanks and forms, establishment, **276:101A.**

Youth services coordinating council, membership, **120:10.**

Community parole supervision for life.

Sexual offenses and offenders, **265:45, 275:18.**

Compensation.

Wages, salaries, and compensation. See within this heading, "Wages, salaries, and compensation."

Complaint.

Petitions. See within this heading, "Petitions."

Conditions and terms, **127:130, 127:131, 127:133A, 127:133B, 276:87.**

Conduct.

Good conduct. See within this heading, "Good conduct."

Conferences, **276:99.**

Controlled Substances Act, first conviction of offense, **94C:34.**

Conviction.

Arson, parole eligibility of person convicted, **127:133.**

Courts may place defendants on probation either prior to or after verdict of guilty, **276:87.**

New crime while free on parole, **272:61.**

Sealing criminal records in probation commissioner's office, **94C:34, 276:100A-276:100C.**

Copy of terms and conditions given to parolee, **127:131.**

Costs of prosecution, payment as condition to probation, **280:6.**

Costs of returning violators under interstate compact, **127:151I.**

County industrial farms, prisoners, **126:37.**

Criminal offender record information system, **276:100.**

Probation Department to advise as to information to public, **279:1.**

Provisions as to sealing certain records, **276:100A-276:100C.**

Death, notice, **276:103.**

Deceased victims.

Family members appearing at hearing, **127:133C.**

PROBATION AND PAROLE
—Cont'd

Department of youth services.
See YOUTH SERVICES
DEPARTMENT AND
MASSACHUSETTS
TRAINING SCHOOLS.
Deputy commissioner, **276:98.**
District courts, **276:83, 276:83A,
276:89.**
See DISTRICT COURTS.
District offices, **276:88.**
Driving under influence of alcohol,
probation of person charged,
90:24D.
Drugs and narcotics, **94C:34.**
Eligibility for parole, **127:83E,
127:128, 127:133, 127:133A,
127:133B.**
Employees.
Officers and employees. See
within this heading,
"Officers and employees."
Employment and training division
in labor and workforce
department, confidential
information, **151A:46.**
Employment, assistance in
obtaining, **127:158.**
Employment security information,
151A:46.
Expenses, **276:98.**
Extradition, interstate supervision
of parolees,
127:151A-127:151K.
Violators of parole, **276:12,
276:20K, 276:20L.**
Family members of victim at
hearing, **127:133C.**
Family trouble cases, additional
terms of probation, **276:42A.**
Federal correctional institutions,
transfer of state prisoner,
127:97A.
Fees and charges.
Assessment of fees, **276:87A.**
Search of probation reports,
276:100.
Female prisoners, pregnancy as
factor, **127:142.**
Firearms.
Offenses.
Armed offenses. See within
this heading, "Armed
offenses."
Weapons. See within this
heading, "Weapons."
First degree murder, eligibility for
parole, **265:2.**
Fish and game violations,
disposition, **21:6F.**

PROBATION AND PAROLE
—Cont'd

Foreign states.
Authority to conduct hearings,
127:134.
Extradition. See within this
heading, "Extradition,
interstate supervision of
parolees."
Permitting parolee to reside,
127:151C.
Prisoners serving Massachusetts
sentence, **127:134, 127:136.**
Supervision of parolees and
probationers,
127:151A-127:151K.
Franklin and Hampshire counties,
probation officers, **276:83.**
Good conduct.
Deduction from sentence,
127:129C.
Reasons for granting parole
permit, **127:130.**
Reduction of sentence for good
conduct while confined in
prison camp, **127:129C.**
Governor's council.
Board employees, appointment
as special state police
officers, **127:127.**
Board members, appointment,
27:4.
Sites for camps for male
prisoners prior to release on
approval of parole, **127:83E.**
Guilty verdict, probation of person
prior to or after, **276:87.**
Habitual criminals, eligibility,
127:133B.
Health and human services
executive office, parole board
as agency within, **6A:16.**
Hearing officers.
Designation, **127:134.**
Not board members, **127:134,
127:136.**
Recommendations of,
appointment of single
member of parole board to
hear, **27:5.**
Hearings.
Before board, **127:134, 127:136.**
Other jurisdiction, inmate
serving Massachusetts
sentence, **127:134.**
Victims of crime, appearance at
parole hearings, **127:1,
127:133A.**
Family members of deceased
victim, **127:133C.**
Houses of correction and jails,
127:134, 127:136.

PROBATION AND PAROLE
—Cont'd

Indecent assault and battery on a
child under fourteen.
Community parole supervision
for life, **265:45, 275:18.**
Indecent assault and battery on
mentally retarded person,
eligibility upon conviction,
265:13F.
Initiative of parole board, release
to be solely, **127:136.**
Inspection of records, **276:90,
276:100.**
Interstate compacts and
agreements,
**127:151A-127:151K, 276:12,
276:20K, 276:20L.**
Interstate supervision of parolees
and probationers,
127:151A-127:151K.
Jails and houses of correction,
127:134, 127:136.
Jurisdiction and powers of courts,
276:87, 279:1, 279:1A.
Juvenile delinquents, **119:58.**
See JUVENILE COURTS AND
DELINQUENT CHILDREN.
Liberty permits.
See LIBERTY PERMITS.
Life sentences, prisoners serving,
127:133A.
Maintenance.
Support and maintenance. See
within this heading,
"Support and maintenance."
Medical records of prisoner, report
to parole board, **127:135,
127:136.**
Mentally ill persons.
Assault, **265:13F.**
Computation of period of
incompetency to stand trial,
123:16.
Minimum term, service, **127:133.**
Minors.
Child. See within this heading,
"Child."
Monetary aid upon discharge,
127:165.
Municipal courts.
See MUNICIPAL COURTS.
Murder as affecting parole
eligibility, **265:2.**
Name, report of change, **210:13,
210:14.**
Notice.
Parole permit and terms thereof,
notice to police, **127:131A.**

PROBATION AND PAROLE
—Cont'd
Notice —Cont'd
Probation officers, notice to
commissioner of
appointment, removal,
retirement, resignation,
death or leave of absence,
276:103.
Violent felonies, release of
probationers convicted of,
127:151L.
Officers and employees.
Assault and battery on parole
officer, **265:13D.**
Chairman of parole board.
Board of parole. See within
this heading, "Board of
parole."
Civil service status of probation
commissioner employees,
30:45.
Commissioner of probation. See
within this heading,
"Commissioner of
probation."
Correctional institutions, officers
and employees.
Duties of agents, **127:158.**
Visitation of institutions,
127:36.
Employment and training
division in labor and
workforce department,
confidential information,
151A:46.
Hearing officers. See within this
heading, "Hearing officers."
Police. See within this heading,
"Police."
Probation officers,
276:83-276:97.
See PROBATION OFFICERS.
Weapon, carrying of by parole
board chairman or officer,
147:8A.
Order permitting probationer to
reside in another state,
127:151B.
Out of state supervision, **127:151A
et seq.**
Pardons.
See PARDONS.
Parole, **127:128-127:151K.**
Parole board.
Board of parole. See within this
heading, "Board of parole."
Payment or receipt of money,
127:166-127:169.
Permits.
Hearings in other states,
127:134.

PROBATION AND PAROLE
—Cont'd
Permits —Cont'd
Minimum term of sentence to be
served, **127:133.**
Petitions.
Forbidden, **127:136.**
Printing statutes on form,
127:169.
Statement to be filed by
representative, **127:167.**
Temporary custody, grounds and
procedure for taking parolee
into, **127:149A.**
Violation of parole, arrest,
**127:149, 127:149A,
127:151J.**
Pimps or purveyors,
imprisonment, **272:7.**
Police.
Cooperation with probation
officers, **276:100.**
Duty to report information to
probation commissioner,
276:100.
Inspection of probation records,
276:90, 276:100.
Notice of hearing for parole of
prisoner serving life
sentence, **127:133A.**
Powers of, probation officer
invested, **276:90.**
Probation officers.
See PROBATION OFFICERS.
Pregnant female prisoners,
127:142.
Preparation for parole in state
camps, **127:83E.**
Pretrial diversion, **276A:1-276A:9.**
See PRETRIAL DIVERSION OF
SELECTED OFFENDERS.
Prison camps, eligibility for parole
of prisoners confined, **127:133.**
Prisons and prisoners, **127:134,
127:136.**
Probation officers, **276:83-276:97.**
See PROBATION OFFICERS.
Public officers and employees.
Officers and employees. See
within this heading,
"Officers and employees."
Rape.
Community parole supervision
for life, **265:45, 275:18.**
Eligibility for furlough or release
after crime, **265:22.**
Records, reports, and returns,
6:168A, 276:100.
Accessibility of information,
276:100.
Accessibility of information in,
6:168A.

PROBATION AND PAROLE
—Cont'd
Records, reports, and returns
—Cont'd
Annual reports, **127:10.**
Board to be furnished records of
prisoners, **127:135, 127:136.**
Change of name, **210:13, 210:14.**
Charges for search, **276:100.**
Commissioner of probation,
276:100, 276:101.
Criminal justice management
information system, **6:168A.**
Criminal offender record system,
use of. See within this
heading, "Criminal offender
record information system."
Hearings in other states,
127:134.
Information to be furnished to
parole board, **127:136.**
Inspection, **276:90, 276:100.**
Juvenile delinquency records,
sealing, **276:100B.**
Medical records of prisoner,
report to parole board,
127:135, 127:136.
Officers, **276:85, 276:90,
276:100.**
See PROBATION OFFICERS.
Reasons for granting permit,
127:134.
Sealing criminal records in
probation commissioner's
office, **94C:34,
276:100A-276:100C.**
Reduction in prisoner's minimum
term of service before eligible,
127:133.
Reforestation camp, prisoners,
127:83B.
Release from probation, **276:85.**
Reports.
Records, reports, and returns.
See within this heading,
"Records, reports, and
returns."
Research director and assistants,
276:98.
Residence in another state,
supervision and terms,
127:151A-127:151K.
Restitution, **276:92.**
Return of escapees to
Commonwealth, account of
agent for paid by
Commonwealth, **276:20M.**
Revocation or suspension.
Arrest and return to prison,
127:149, 279:3.
Interstate compact, retaking,
127:151J.

PROBATION AND PAROLE
—Cont'd

Revocation or suspension —Cont'd
Liberty permits.
See LIBERTY PERMITS.
Sentence. See within this
heading, "Sentence."
Sexual offenders, revocation of
parole for failure to register
with police, **6:178E.**
Term of sentence as affected,
127:149.
Salaries.
Wages, salaries, and
compensation. See within
this heading, "Wages,
salaries, and compensation."
Second offenders, **265:13C, 266:14,
276:87.**
Sentence.
Certificate of termination of
sentence issued to parolee,
127:130A.
Restitution, **276:92.**
Second sentence, release on
parole as commencement,
279:8A.
Serving portion of, before parole,
127:133-127:133B.
Suspension of sentence.
Probation during, **279:1,
279:1A.**
Second conviction for armed
robbery, **266:14.**
Term of sentence as affected by
revocation or suspension of
parole, **127:149.**
Violation of parole, term of
sentence after, **127:149.**
Serving portion of sentence before
parole, **276:87.**
Sexually dangerous persons,
123A:9.
Conditional release, **123A:9.**
Parole, **123A:9.**
Revocation of parole for failure
to register with police,
6:178E.
Sexual offenders.
Community parole supervision
for life, **265:45, 275:18.**
Jurisdiction of parole board,
127:133D.
Special police officers, appointment
of employees of parole board,
127:127.
Stalking, eligibility for probation
or parole for persons convicted
of, **265:43.**
Statistics, preparation, **276:98.**
Superior courts.
Assistant supervisor of
probation, **276:80.**

PROBATION AND PAROLE
—Cont'd

Superior courts —Cont'd
Guilty verdict, probation prior or
subsequent, **276:87.**
Officers.
See PROBATION OFFICERS.
Support and maintenance, **273:6,
273:18A.**
Nonsupport of spouse or
children, criminal
proceedings on charges,
276:42A.
Probation officers.
Illegitimacy proceedings,
forfeited bail used for
support of child, **273:18.**
Support of probationers,
276:95.
Suspension.
Revocation or suspension. See
within this heading,
"Revocation or suspension."
Temporary custody of parolee,
length, **127:149A.**
Temporary release of prisoner
prior, **127:90A.**
Termination of sentence, issuance
of certificates, **127:130A.**
Term of sentence after parole
violation, **127:149.**
Terms and conditions, **127:130,
127:131, 127:133A, 127:133B,
276:87.**
Time, **127:133-127:133B.**
Training, employees, **41:96B,
151A:46.**
Trial.
Hearings. See within this
heading, "Hearings."
Unemployment compensation,
151A:46.
Victims and witness assistance
programs, funds, **258B:9.**
Victims of crime, appearance at
parole hearings, **127:1,
127:133A.**
Family members of deceased
victim, **127:133C.**
Violation of parole or probation.
Arrest, **127:131, 127:149, 279:3.**
Conviction while free on parole,
272:61.
Extradition on ground, **276:12,
276:20K, 276:20L.**
Habitual criminals, **127:133B.**
Interstate compact, **127:151I,
127:151J.**
Life imprisonment, **127:133A.**
Parole board, members, **27:4.**
Prompt disposition of cases
pending against violators of
probation, **279:3.**

PROBATION AND PAROLE
—Cont'd

Violation of parole or probation
—Cont'd
Reimprisonment, **127:131.**
Temporary custody in detention,
127:149A.
Term of sentence after parole
violation, **127:149.**
Violent felonies, notice
requirements for release of
probationers, **127:151L.**
Wages, salaries, and compensation.
Commissioner and deputy
commissioners of probation,
276:98.
Parole board members, **27:4.**
Probation officers.
See PROBATION OFFICERS.
Warrants.
Retaking of parolee under
interstate compact,
127:151J.
Temporary custody of parolee
arrested on parole officer's
warrant, length, **127:149A.**
Weapons.
Armed offenses. See within this
heading, "Armed offenses."
Parole board chairman or officer,
carrying of weapon, **147:8A.**
Withdrawal, warrant for
temporary custody, **127:149A.**
Witnesses.
Parole board authorized to
summon, **233:8.**
Victim and witness assistance
program funds, **258B:9.**
Work record, no parole granted,
127:130.
Work release program, effect on
eligibility for parole, **127:86F.**
Youth services department.
See YOUTH SERVICES
DEPARTMENT AND
MASSACHUSETTS
TRAINING SCHOOLS.

PROBATIONARY
EMPLOYMENT.

Civil service.
See CIVIL SERVICE.
Classification of probationary
employees, **30:45.**
Women and children, employment
without compensation,
prohibited, **149:158A.**

PROBATIONER AND
PAROLEE SUPERVISION
ACT.

Interstate, **127:151A et seq.**

PROBATION OFFICERS,
276:83-276:97.

Accounts and accounting.
Examination of accounts, 35:45.
Expenses, accounting, 276:94,
276:95.
Fines and penalties, failure to
account for funds or
co-operate with director of
accounts, 35:47.
Administrative assistant, duties
and salary, 276:83.
Appeal from disapproval of
appointment, 276:99.
Appointment and removal, 276:83,
276:83A, 276:85A, 276:85B,
276:98.
Appeal from disapproval of
appointment, 276:99.
Authorities empowered to
appoint or remove, 276:83,
276:83A, 276:89.
Chief administrative justice,
review and approval of
appointments and removal,
276:83, 276:99.
Notice to probation
commissioner, 276:103.
Qualification for appointment,
276:99.
Superior courts, 276:83, 276:89,
276:89A.
Temporary probation officers,
276:89.
Arrest of person on probation,
279:3.
Assistant chief probation officers,
276:80, 276:83, 276:83A.
Authorities empowered to appoint
or remove, 276:83, 276:83A,
276:89.
Bail and recognizance.
Child held for trial, probation
officer with custody as
having powers of surety on
recognizance, 119:68.
Illegitimacy proceedings,
forfeited bail used for
support of child, 273:18.
Professional bondsmen, excluded
from provisions, 276:61B.
Boston juvenile court.
Appointment, 276:83.
Deputy probation officers,
276:86.
Service of process by probation
officers, 276:91.
Bristol County Juvenile Court,
powers, 276:83, 276:94,
276:95.
Chief administrative justice,
review of appointments and
demotions, 276:83, 276:99.

PROBATION OFFICERS
—Cont'd
Chief justice for administration
and management, 276:83,
276:89A, 276:98, 276:99.
Chief probation officers.
Appointment, 276:83.
Assistant chief probation
officers, 276:80, 276:83,
276:83A.
Public employee bargaining
units, inclusion, 150E:3.
Support and transportation of
probationers, 276:95.
Children.
Bail and recognizance, 119:68.
Delinquent children, 276:83,
276:86.
See JUVENILE COURTS
AND DELINQUENT
CHILDREN.
Parents deserting children,
supervision, 273:2.
Clerical assistants, 276:88.
Collective bargaining units for
public employees, inclusion of
chief probation officers,
150E:3.
Commitment of persons, 276:87.
Compensation, 276:83, 276:83A,
276:99B.
Administrative assistant,
276:83.
Clerical assistants, 276:88.
Deputy probation officers,
276:89A.
Expenses, 276:94, 276:95.
Retirement systems and
pensions. See within this
heading, "Retirement
systems and pensions."
Salary schedule, 276:99B.
Temporary officers, 276:89.
Conditional release of sexually
dangerous person under
jurisdiction, 123A:9.
Conferences, traveling expenses in
attending, 276:94, 276:99.
Convicted persons placed in care
of, 276:87.
Correction commissioner,
furnishing information,
127:17.
County treasurers.
Payment of expenses of
probation officers, 276:94.
Unclaimed money collected by
probation officers, 276:93.
Death, notice, 276:103.
Defined, 119:52.
Demotion, 276:83.

PROBATION OFFICERS
—Cont'd
Department of youth services.
See YOUTH SERVICES
DEPARTMENT AND
MASSACHUSETTS
TRAINING SCHOOLS.
Deputy probation officers, 276:83,
276:86, 276:89A.
Disciplinary action against,
276:99.
District courts, 276:83, 276:83A,
276:89.
See DISTRICT COURTS.
Divorce cases, investigation,
208:16.
Driving records, access, 90C:4.
Duties, 276:85 et seq., 276A:1 et
seq.
Education requirements, 276:83.
Employment security information
as available to probation
officer in performance of
official duties, 151A:46.
Examination, inspection, and
investigation, 276:85.
Accounts, examination, 35:45.
Pretrial diversion of selected
offenders, 276A:3.
Records of probation officer,
276:90, 276:100.
What to include in
investigations, 119:57.
Expenses, 276:89A, 276:94,
276:95, 276:99.
False personation, 268:33.
Financing of judicial system,
29A:1.
Fines and penalties.
Failure to account for funds or
co-operate with director of
accounts, 35:47.
Neglect of duties, 276:96.
Payment to probation officer,
279:1, 279:1A.
Receipts for fines paid, 279:1,
279:1A.
First assistant chief probation
officer, 276:83.
Group classification for
compensation purposes,
276:99B.
Indexing of records of, clerical
assistance for purpose, 276:88.
Inspection.
Examination, inspection, and
investigation. See within
this heading, "Examination,
inspection, and
investigation."
Interference with department of
youth services, 276:97.

PROBATION OFFICERS
—Cont'd

Interstate supervision of parolees or probationers, deputizing probation officer of other state, **127:151H.**

Investigations.
Examination, inspection and investigation. See within this heading, "Examination, inspection, and investigation."

Jurisdiction to act in any part of state, **276:90.**

Juvenile courts and delinquent children, **276:83, 276:86.**
See JUVENILE COURTS AND DELINQUENT CHILDREN.

Labor relations, inclusion of chief probation officers in bargaining units, **150E:3.**

Leave of absence, notice, **276:103.**

Length of service necessary for permanent employment, **276:83.**

Limitation on expenditures for support of probationers, **276:95.**

Maintenance and support.
Support and maintenance. See within this heading, "Support and maintenance."

Minors.
Children. See within this heading, "Children."

Motor vehicle parking violations, report by offenders, **90:20C.**

Municipal courts, pensions of probation officers, **32:75-32:76A.**

Neglect of duties, penalty, **276:96.**

Notice of appointment, removal, retirement, resignation, death, or leave of absence, **276:103.**

Orientation and in-service training, **276:85.**

Parents deserting children, supervision, **273:2.**

Parole board, furnishing information for use, **127:135.**

Payment.
County treasurers, payment of expenses of probation officers, **276:94.**
Probation officer, payment, **276:92, 276:94, 279:1, 279:1A.**
Restitution to injured persons, **276:92.**

Pedestrians violating rules not required to report, **90:18A.**

PROBATION OFFICERS
—Cont'd

Penalties.
Fines and penalties. See within this heading, "Fines and penalties."

Pensions.
Retirement systems and pensions. See within this heading, "Retirement systems and pensions."

Permanent employee, length of service for status, **276:83.**

Placing persons in care, **276:87.**

Police officers.
Inspection of records of probation officers, **276:90.**
Powers of, probation officer invested, **276:90.**
To co-operate with probation officers, **276:100.**

Pretrial diversion of selected offenders, **276A:1 et seq.**

Probationers, support, **276:95.**

Professional bondsmen, excluded from provisions, **276:61B.**

Public service corporation employees, **271:41.**

Qualifications, **276:83, 276:99.**

Receipts.
For fines paid, **279:1, 279:1A.**
For restitution made, **276:92.**

Recommendations to place convicted persons on probation, **276:85.**

Records and reports, **276:85, 276:90, 276:100.**
Blanks and forms, **276:101A, 276:102.**
Fines and penalties paid, **279:1, 279:1A.**
Indexing, **276:88.**
Inspection, **276:90, 276:100.**
Motor vehicle parking violations, report by offenders, **90:20C.**
Payments received, **276:92, 279:1, 279:1A.**
Pedestrians violating rules not required to report to probation officer, **90:18A.**
Prior conviction of defendant, **276:85.**

Release from probation, written statement as to terms and conditions, **276:85.**

Removal.
Appointment and removal. See within this heading, "Appointment and removal."

Reports.
Records and reports. See within this heading, "Records and reports."

PROBATION OFFICERS
—Cont'd

Resignation, notice, **276:103.**

Restitution payments, handling, **276:92.**

Retirement systems and pensions, **32:3, 32:75-32:76A.**
Boston, **32:75-32:76A, 276:86.**
Juvenile courts.
See JUVENILE COURTS AND DELINQUENT CHILDREN.
Notice of retirement, **276:103.**

Salary.
Compensation. See within this heading, "Compensation."

Separate maintenance proceedings, investigations, **209:32.**

Service of process by officers of Boston juvenile court, **276:91.**

Sexually dangerous person, conditional release under jurisdiction of probation officer, **123A:9.**

Superior courts.
Administrative assistant, duties and salary, **276:83.**
Appointment and compensation, **276:83, 276:89, 276:89A.**
Assistant chief probation officer, designation, **276:80, 276:83.**
Demotion, **276:83.**
Deputy probation officers, **276:89A.**
Expenses, **276:94.**
Placing certain persons in care, **276:87.**
Temporary probation officers, **276:89.**

Support and maintenance.
Illegitimacy proceedings, forfeited bail used for support of child, **273:18.**
Nonsupport of spouse or children, criminal proceedings on charges, **276:42A.**
Probationers, support, **276:95.**

Surplus funds in hands of, deposit, **35:22.**

Suspended sentence, payment of fines during, **279:1, 279:1A.**

Temporary probation officers, appointment and salaries, **276:89.**

Temporary support or transportation of probationers, **276:95.**

Training programs, **276:85, 276:99.**

PROBATION OFFICERS
—Cont'd

Transportation of probationers, expenditures, **276:95.**

Travel expenses, **276:94, 276:99.**

Unclaimed funds in hands, **276:93.**

Violators of probation, arrest without warrant, **279:3.**

Visiting institutions, right, **127:36.**

Vouchers for expenses, **276:94, 276:95.**

Wages.
Compensation. See within this heading, "Compensation."

Youth services department.
See YOUTH SERVICES DEPARTMENT AND MASSACHUSETTS TRAINING SCHOOLS.

PROCEDURE.
See PRACTICE AND PROCEDURE.

PROCEEDS.

Abandoned property.
See ABANDONED, LOST, AND UNCLAIMED PROPERTY.

Attachment of property.
See ATTACHMENT OF PROPERTY.

Attorney's lien for fees and expenses upon proceeds derived from suit, **221:50.**

Districts.
See DISTRICTS.

Guardians.
See GUARDIANS, CONSERVATORS, AND COMMITTEES.

Judicial sales.
See JUDICIAL SALES.

Municipal finance.
See MUNICIPAL FINANCE.

Partition.
See PARTITION.

Secured transactions.
See SECURED TRANSACTIONS.

PROCESS AND SERVICE OF PROCESS AND PAPERS, 223:31, 223:34, 223:35, 223:37-223:40.

Absent defendants, **223A:1-223A:11, 227:1.**

Agents for service, **227:5, 227:5A.**

Clerk of city or town appointed as agent for service of process, **227:5A.**

Dismissal of action, when authorized, **227:6.**

PROCESS AND SERVICE OF PROCESS AND PAPERS
—Cont'd

Absent defendants —Cont'd
Further notice to absent defendant, **223:34.**
Long-arm statute.
Nonresidents. See within this heading, "Nonresidents."
Nonresidents. See within this heading, "Nonresidents."
Several defendants, prosecution of action against those served, **227:15.**
Spouse, jurisdiction of absent, **223A:3.**
State secretary, service, **64I:33, 227:5.**

Absentee's estate, notice, **200:2.**

Absentee trust beneficiaries, proceedings for transfer of estate, **203:28, 203:29.**

Abuse prevention orders, **209A:7.**

Accounting for fees received by deputy sheriffs, **262:8A.**

Adjudicatory hearings, service of notice of claims, **30:39Q.**

Administrative procedure, **30A:9, 30A:12, 30A:14.**

Administrators.
See EXECUTORS AND ADMINISTRATORS.

Adoption of children.
Notice of motion to extend time for conducting adoption inquiry, **210:5A.**
Personal service required, **210:4.**

Affidavits.
See AFFIDAVITS.

Agent for service, **156B:12, 156B:49, 223:37, 227:5A.**
Absent defendants, **227:5, 227:5A.**
Administrators, **195:8-195:10.**
Appointment of agents, **227:5, 227:5A.**
Auctioneer licenses, applications, **100:3.**
Corporations, **156B:12, 156B:109, 181:3, 223:37, 227:5A.**
See CORPORATIONS.
Guardians and conservators, nonresident, **201:49.**
Insurance.
See INSURANCE.
Leaving summons with agent, service, **223:31.**
Long-arm statute.
Nonresidents. See within this heading, "Nonresidents."

PROCESS AND SERVICE OF PROCESS AND PAPERS
—Cont'd

Agent for service —Cont'd
Partnerships, **227:5.**
Real estate time-shares, cancellation notice, **183B:41.**
Small loan companies, **140:104.**
State secretary as agent for absent defendant, **64I:33, 227:5.**
Tenement houses, **145:60.**
Title registration proceeding, **185:35.**
Voter registration complaints, **51:48.**

Aircraft.
See AIRCRAFT AND AVIATION.

Air pollution control regulations, order to cease and desist from violating, **111:142E.**

Alcoholic liquors.
See ALCOHOLIC LIQUORS.

Alcoholics and drunkards, arrest upon failure to appear in court when summoned, **123:35.**

Aldermen of city, service, **223:37.**

Amendments or alterations, **231:51-231:55.**
Fictitious name, writ issued, **223:19.**
Summons, **233:1.**

Animals.
See ANIMALS.

Antitrust laws, **93:8.**

Appeal.
See APPEAL AND REVIEW.

Appellate tax board, **58A:9.**
Petitions, **58A:7.**

Arbitration.
See ARBITRATION.

Arrest.
See ARREST.

Arrest on mesne process, **224:1-224:30.**
See ARREST ON MESNE PROCESS AND SUPPLEMENTARY PROCEEDINGS.

Assessments, special, proceedings for abatement, **80:9.**

Assessors.
See TAX ASSESSORS.

Associations.
Voluntary associations. See within this heading, "Voluntary associations."

Attachment of property.
See ATTACHMENT OF PROPERTY.

**PROCESS AND SERVICE OF
PROCESS AND PAPERS**
—Cont'd
Attorney in fact.
  Powers of attorney. See within
    this heading, "Powers of
    attorney."
Attorneys at law.
  See ATTORNEYS AT LAW.
Audita querela, transfer of causes
  between supreme judicial
  court and other courts,
  211:4A.
Automobile insurance.
  See AUTOMOBILE
    INSURANCE.
Banks.
  See BANKS AND BANKING.
Bond or undertaking.
  Constable required to give,
    41:92.
  Executor's bond, indorsement of
    writ in action, **205:26.**
Boston juvenile court, service by
  probation officers, **276:91.**
Building code of state, notice of
  violation, **143:51.**
Building regulations, proof of
  service of notice of violation on
  nonresident, **143:11.**
Burden of proof.
  Proof of service. See within this
    heading, "Proof of service of
    process or papers."
Business trusts, service, **182:6.**
Capias.
  See CAPIAS.
Carriers, **159:37.**
  Commercial motor vehicle
    division, service by
    employees, **159B:14.**
  Express companies. See within
    this heading, "Express
    companies."
  Railroads. See within this
    heading, "Railroads."
  Telecommunications and energy
    department, service of
    orders, **159:37.**
Certificates and certification,
  262:10, 262:19.
  Engineer, revocation of
    certificate, **112:81P.**
  Return of process, **262:63.**
  Surveyor's certificate, revocation,
    112:81P.
Certiorari, **249:4, 249:4A.**
  See CERTIORARI.
Change.
  Amendments or alterations. See
    within this heading,
    "Amendments or
    alterations."

**PROCESS AND SERVICE OF
PROCESS AND PAPERS**
—Cont'd
Charities and charitable
  contributions, **12:8G, 68:30,
  68:31.**
  Foreign corporations or
    organizations, **68:29.**
  Soliciting contributions from
    public, **68:29.**
Children and minors.
  Adoption of children. See within
    this heading, "Adoption of
    children."
  Custody of child, **215:34A.**
  Labor law violations, **149:84.**
  Paternity, **209C:4.**
  Support, **209:32F.**
Cigarette tax, service of process in
  forfeiture proceedings, **64C:8.**
City or town, service, **223:37.**
  Clerk of city or town. See within
    this heading, "Clerk of city
    or town, service."
  Constables. See within this
    heading, "Constables."
Civil arrest.
  See ARREST ON MESNE
    PROCESS AND
    SUPPLEMENTARY
    PROCEEDINGS.
Civil rights proceedings, **151B:5.**
Claims and indemnity procedure
  as to public bodies and
  officers.
  Abuse of process, applicability of
    claims and indemnity
    provisions as to claims
    arising out, **258:10.**
  Public attorney or executive
    officer of public employer,
    service, **258:6.**
Clerk of city or town, service,
  223:37.
  Absent defendant, clerks of city
    or town appointed as agent
    for process, **227:5A.**
  Tenement house law, **145:60B.**
Clerks of court.
  See CLERKS OF COURT.
Collection notices imitating
  process, **272:97A.**
Collective bargaining agreements
  to arbitrate, **150C:5, 150C:7,
  150C:14.**
Commercial motor vehicle division,
  service by employees,
  159B:14.
Condemnation.
  Eminent domain proceedings.
    See within this heading,
    "Eminent domain
    proceedings."

**PROCESS AND SERVICE OF
PROCESS AND PAPERS**
—Cont'd
Constables, **41:92, 220:7.**
  Arrest on mesne process.
    See CONSTABLES.
  Attachment, **223:47.**
  Auction sales, services of
    constable as auctioneer, fees,
    262:8.
  Bond required, **41:92.**
  Civil process, service, **41:92,
    41:94.**
  Criminal process, service, **41:94,
    262:8, 262:21, 262:48.**
  Delinquent children, **119:55.**
  Duties, **41:94.**
  Ejectment, fees for service of
    execution, **262:17.**
  Election precepts, fees for
    service, **262:13.**
  Fees for service, **262:8-262:21.**
  Furnaces for iron melting or
    glass making, service of
    order as to alterations,
    140:116.
  Indorsement on writ, **262:19.**
  Jurisdiction outside town limits,
    41:95.
  Land court process, fees for
    service, **262:16.**
  Lease of personal property,
    termination, **231:85H.**
  Leaving copy of writ, fees,
    262:11.
  Reciprocal Enforcement of
    Support Act, fees for service
    of process, **262:8.**
  Replevin, **41:92.**
  Return of process, **262:9.**
  Steam engines, service of order
    as to alterations, **140:116.**
  Warrants.
    See CONSTABLES.
Constitution of Massachusetts,
  provisions respecting writs,
  MA Const Part 2 Ch 6 Art 5.
Consumer transaction practices.
  See BANKS AND BANKING.
Contempt, service of process in
  connection with commitment,
  215:34A, 220:14.
Contracts and agreements.
  Collective bargaining
    agreements to arbitrate,
    150C:5, 150C:7, 150C:14.
  Waiver in contract action,
    231:13A.
Copies, fees, **262:8, 262:11, 262:15,
  262:16.**
Corporations.
  See CORPORATIONS.

**PROCESS AND SERVICE OF
PROCESS AND PAPERS**
—Cont'd
Correctional institutions.
See CORRECTIONAL
INSTITUTIONS.
Correspondence schools, service,
75C:11.
Counsel.
See ATTORNEYS AT LAW.
County commissioners, service,
223:37.
County, service, **223:37.**
Court costs of indigent persons,
261:27A.
Courts-martial, **33:77.**
Credit insurance combination
policies, contents, **175:117B.**
Credit unions.
See CREDIT UNIONS.
Custody of child, service of citation
and capias in contempt
proceedings, **215:34A.**
Declaratory judgments, necessity,
231A:1.
Decrees.
See JUDGMENTS, ORDERS,
AND DECREES.
Deeds, proceedings for proof of
unacknowledged deed, **183:36.**
Defects.
Notice of injury from defects,
84:19, 84:21.
Time for new suit on abatement
because of defective service,
260:32.
Defendant, service on, **223:31,
223:34, 223:35, 223:37-223:40.**
Delay in service of warrant,
penalty, **268:22.**
Delinquent children.
See JUVENILE COURTS AND
DELINQUENT CHILDREN.
Demands not requiring service by
officer, sheriff may serve,
37:12.
Depositions.
See DEPOSITIONS.
Deposits.
See BANKS AND BANKING.
Deposits, adverse claims, **167D:31.**
Desertion, nonsupport, and child
custody contempt proceedings,
service of citation and capias,
215:34A.
Disclaimers, **191A:5.**
Dismissal of action.
Absence of defendant when
authorized, **227:6.**
Endorsement of writs, dismissal
for failure to procure
endorser, **231:47.**

**PROCESS AND SERVICE OF
PROCESS AND PAPERS**
—Cont'd
Dismissal of action —Cont'd
Insufficient service, dismissal,
223:84.
Nonresidents, stay or dismissal
on ground that action
should be heard in another
forum, **223A:5.**
District.
See DISTRICT AND
PROSECUTING
ATTORNEYS.
District courts, **223:31, 223:34,
223:35, 223:37-223:40.**
See DISTRICT COURTS.
Divorce.
See DIVORCE AND ALIMONY.
Documents imitating court process
as prohibited, **272:97A.**
Dogs required to be muzzled or
restrained, service of notice
regarding, **140:168.**
Domicile and residence.
Correspondence schools, service,
75C:11.
Leaving, service by. See within
this heading, "Leaving,
service."
Nonresidents. See within this
heading, "Nonresidents."
Resident agent.
Agent for service. See within
this heading, "Agent for
service."
Summons served on witness,
233:2.
Dower.
See DOWER AND CURTESY.
Easement prevented by notice,
187:3, 187:4.
Elections.
See ELECTIONS.
Emergency medical care, actions to
enforce provisions regarding,
111C:11.
Eminent domain proceedings.
Notice of taking, **79:7C.**
Petition for damages, **79:22.**
Employment agencies, service of
process, **140:46G.**
Endorsement of writs,
231:42-231:48.
After entry, **231:43.**
Before entry, **231:42.**
Dismissal for failure to procure
endorser, **231:47.**
Fees, **262:19.**
New endorser, when may be
required, **231:45.**

**PROCESS AND SERVICE OF
PROCESS AND PAPERS**
—Cont'd
Endorsement of writs —Cont'd
Removal of endorser, effect,
231:45.
Removal of plaintiff, indorser,
231:44.
Return of process, endorsement
of fees on writs of process,
262:19.
Substitute endorser, **231:48.**
Engineer, revocation of certificate,
112:81P.
Entry, writs of, **237:1 et seq.**
See ENTRY, WRITS.
Equity, issuance of process in
action, **214:4, 240:7.**
Evidence of service.
Proof of service of process or
papers. See within this
heading, "Proof of service of
process or papers."
Executions.
See EXECUTIONS.
Executors.
See EXECUTORS AND
ADMINISTRATORS.
Exemption of witness from another
state in criminal proceeding,
233:13C.
Express companies.
Return of process by express,
mileage, **262:9.**
Service, **159:5-159:7.**
Extradited fugitive, immunity,
276:20N.
Fair educational practices
proceedings, **151C:3, 151C:4.**
False arrest or imprisonment,
102:3, 102:4.
False statements regarding
service, penalties, **268:6B.**
Fees, **90:3C, 90:3D, 262:8-262:21.**
Clerks of courts, **262:4B.**
Constables' fees, **262:8-262:21.**
Copies, **262:8, 262:11, 262:15,
262:16.**
Endorsement of writ, **262:19.**
Inquests, **262:26.**
Justices of the peace, **262:1.**
Land court, **262:16.**
Mittimus, no fee for serving
more than one, **262:49.**
Reciprocal Enforcement of
Support Act, proceedings,
262:8.
Return of process.
See RETURN OF PROCESS.
Revenue commissioner as agent
for foreign corporation,
181:3.

**PROCESS AND SERVICE OF
PROCESS AND PAPERS**
—Cont'd
Fees —Cont'd
Scire facias, **262:8.**
Service of writs, **262:8.**
Sheriffs, deputies and
constables, **262:8, 262:8A.**
Single fees only for service of
process at same time,
262:48.
Special justices, **262:3.**
Subpoena, service, **262:53.**
Summons.
See SUMMONS.
Supplementary proceedings,
262:14.
Traveling expenses. See within
this heading, "Traveling
expenses."
Use of conveyance, allowance,
262:10.
Venire, service, **262:8.**
Fictitious name, writ issued,
223:19.
Fines and penalties.
Delay of service of warrant,
268:22.
False statements regarding
service, **268:6B.**
Forfeiture of property seized
under search warrant,
notice, **276:5.**
Fires and fire prevention.
Order for removal of combustible
materials, **148:5.**
Violation of rules or orders,
notice, **148:30.**
Fish, birds, mammals, reptiles, or
amphibians afflicted with a
contagious or infectious
disease or parasite, notice or
order of quarantine, **129:22,
131:25A.**
Flats, service in proceeding to
determine boundaries, **240:20.**
Foreign corporations, **156B:12,
156B:49, 181:3, 181:4, 181:8,
223:37, 223:38, 227:5A.**
See FOREIGN
CORPORATIONS.
Foreign fiduciaries, **199A:11,
201:49.**
Foreign insurance companies.
See FOREIGN INSURANCE
COMPANIES.
Foreign state, country or entity.
Nonresidents. See within this
heading, "Nonresidents."
Forest and parks division, powers
of officers, **21:4A.**

**PROCESS AND SERVICE OF
PROCESS AND PAPERS**
—Cont'd
Forfeiture.
Cigarette tax, **64C:8.**
Search warrant, property seized,
276:5.
Fraternal benefit societies.
See FRATERNAL BENEFIT
SOCIETIES.
Furnaces, orders as to alterations,
140:116.
Garnishment, **246:5-246:8, 246:32.**
See TRUSTEE PROCESS.
General Court, service by officers,
3:17.
General fields, service on
proprietors, **223:37.**
Governmental units pooled
insurance, certificate of
approval, **40M:4.**
Grade crossings, order for
abolition, **159:70.**
Group health insurance policies for
old persons, unincorporated
association issuing, **175:110C.**
Guardian, service, **201:49.**
Habeas corpus, **248:6.**
See HABEAS CORPUS.
Hairdressers' registration,
proceedings for suspension,
112:87EE.
Health, welfare, and retirement
funds, service of process on
trustees or plan
administrators, **151D:3.**
Highways and streets.
Defects, notice of injury, **84:19,
84:21.**
Foreign corporation constructing
or repairing, attorney for
service, **181:3.**
Housing court.
See HOUSING COURT.
Husband and wife, **209:32F,
223A:3.**
Illegitimate children, **209C:4.**
Immunity of extradited fugitive
from justice, **276:20N.**
Income tax return, writ of
mandamus to compel filing,
62C:9.
Indemnity of public entities.
Claims and indemnity procedure
as to public bodies and
officers. See within this
heading, "Claims and
indemnity procedure as to
public bodies and officers."
Indictment, **263:4A, 277:65,
277:67.**

**PROCESS AND SERVICE OF
PROCESS AND PAPERS**
—Cont'd
Indigents.
Affidavit to be served on
opposing parties, **261:27B.**
Alternative means of providing
substitute or replacement
for service in cases, **261:27F.**
Service of process as normal
court cost, **261:27A.**
Indorsement of writs.
Endorsement of writs. See
within this heading,
"Endorsement of writs."
Inhabitant of political subdivision,
service, **223:37.**
Inquest, fees and expenses for
service of process relative,
262:26.
Inspector general.
See INSPECTOR GENERAL.
Insurance.
See INSURANCE.
Insurance commissioner.
See INSURANCE
COMMISSIONER.
Interception of wire or oral
communications, service of
warrant authorizing, **272:99.**
Jeweler's lien, notice to owner,
255:31C.
Judgments.
See JUDGMENTS, ORDERS,
AND DECREES.
Judicial Conduct Commission,
subpoena of witnesses and
documents, **211C:5.**
Jurisdiction.
Nonresidents. See within this
heading, "Nonresidents."
Jurors, summoning of,
234:24-234:24B.
See JURY AND JURY TRIAL.
Justices of the peace.
See JUSTICES OF THE
PEACE.
Juvenile courts.
See JUVENILE COURTS AND
DELINQUENT CHILDREN.
Labor relations.
See LABOR RELATIONS AND
DISPUTES.
Land court.
See LAND COURT.
Landlord and tenant.
Attachment, **262:8.**
Leaving summons with tenant,
223:31.
Tenement house service on
owners' attorneys, **145:60A.**

PROCESS AND SERVICE OF PROCESS AND PAPERS
—Cont'd

Larceny of writs and process, **266:30.**

Law enforcement division officers, powers, **21:6B.**

Leased or rented personalty, demand for return, **231:85H, 266:87.**

Lease of real property.
Landlord and tenant. See within this heading, "Landlord and tenant."

Leaving, service, **276:25.**
Fees, giving or leaving copy of writ, **262:11.**
Return to state place of leaving, **223:35.**
Summons, **223:31, 223:35.**

Letter rogatory, issuance outside of Commonwealth, **223A:6, 223A:10.**

Levy on real estate, **236:44.**

Limitation of time, defective service as tolling time for new action, **260:32.**

Limited liability companies, resident agents to accept service for, **156C:5, 156C:54.**

Limited partnerships, **109:4, 109:52.**

Litter laws, notice to appear for violation, **270:16A.**

Livestock.
Animals. See within this heading, "Animals."

Long-arm statute.
Nonresidents. See within this heading, "Nonresidents."

Low value tax land, proceedings to establish title, **60:80B.**

Mail.
See MAIL AND MAILING.

Mandamus.
See MANDAMUS.

Massachusetts trusts, service, **182:6.**

Mileage allowance.
Traveling expenses. See within this heading, "Traveling expenses."

Milk control proceedings, **94A:17-94A:19.**

Minors.
Children and minors. See within this heading, "Children and minors."

Mittimus.
See CORRECTIONAL INSTITUTIONS.

PROCESS AND SERVICE OF PROCESS AND PAPERS
—Cont'd

Modifications.
Amendments or alterations. See within this heading, "Amendments or alterations."

Money judgments rendered in foreign states, factors affecting recognition, **235:23A.**

Motor vehicles.
See MOTOR VEHICLES.

Municipalities.
City or town. See within this heading, "City or town, service."

Mutual insurance assessments, notice, **175:83.**

Name of defendant unknown, proceedings in event, **223:19.**

Negotiable instruments.
Trustee process to reach obligations evidenced by negotiable instruments, **246:32.**

Waiver of process clauses, validity, **231:13A.**

New process allowed upon motion to dismiss for insufficient service, **223:84.**

Nonresidents, **90:3A et seq., 223A:1-223A:11.**
Acts or conduct within Commonwealth, personal jurisdiction based, **223A:3.**

Administrator, nonresident's agent for service of process, **195:8-195:10.**

Agent for service. See within this heading, "Agent for service."

Anti-litter laws, service on nonresidents violating, **270:16A.**

Building regulations, proof of service of notice of violation on nonresident, **143:11.**

Commission, issuance, **223A:10.**

Compelling production of evidence to be used in proceeding in tribunal outside of Commonwealth, **223A:11.**

Continuing contact with Commonwealth, personal jurisdiction based, **223A:2.**

Corporations, **156B:12, 181:4, 181:8, 223:37, 227:5A.**
See FOREIGN CORPORATIONS.

PROCESS AND SERVICE OF PROCESS AND PAPERS
—Cont'd

Nonresidents —Cont'd
Definition of person under long arm statute, **223A:1.**

Depositions taken outside of Commonwealth to obtain evidence in action pending in Commonwealth, **223A:10.**

Exemption from witness from another state in criminal proceeding, **233:13C.**

Fiduciaries.
See FOREIGN FIDUCIARIES.

Guardian or conservator's agent, service, **201:49.**

Health, welfare, and retirement fund nonresident trustee or plan administrator, service of process, **151D:3.**

Husband and wife, long-arm jurisdiction of absentee spouse, **223A:3.**

Individuals who may make service outside of Commonwealth, **223A:7.**

Informations for recovery of land, publication, **245:4.**

Insurance companies.
See FOREIGN INSURANCE COMPANIES.

Judgment rendered in foreign state, jurisdiction over person as affecting conclusiveness, **235:23A.**

Letter rogatory, issuance, **223A:6, 223A:10.**

Long-arm statute, **90:3A et seq., 223A:1 et seq.**

Manner and proof of service outside of Commonwealth, **223A:6.**

Motor vehicles, **90:3A et seq.**
See MOTOR VEHICLES.

Probate court, long-arm jurisdiction to enforce support orders, **208:36A.**

Real estate broker or salesman, service on agents, **112:87WW.**

Real property's nonresident owner charged with discriminatory practices, service, **151B:5.**

Sales tax enforcement, **64H:32, 64I:33.**

Service within Commonwealth in aid of tribunals and litigants outside of Commonwealth, **223A:9.**

PROCESS AND SERVICE OF PROCESS AND PAPERS
—Cont'd

Nonresidents —Cont'd

Small loan companies, agent for service, **140:104.**

Stay or dismissal on ground that action should be heard in another forum, **223A:5.**

Trusts and trustees, **203:15.**

Where law of Commonwealth requires one or more designated individuals to be served, **223A:8.**

Nuisances.

See NUISANCES.

Officer, allowance, **262:10.**

Old and infirm animals, proceedings involving destruction, **133:1.**

Orders.

See JUDGMENTS, ORDERS, AND DECREES.

Outside Commonwealth.

Nonresidents. See within this heading, "Nonresidents."

Overdue taxes, imprisonment, **60:29.**

Parish, service, **223:37.**

Partition proceedings, citation, **241:8.**

Paternity, **209C:4.**

Penalties.

Fines and penalties. See within this heading, "Fines and penalties."

Perjury, **268:6B.**

Police, service, **41:98, 41:99.**

Constables. See within this heading, "Constables."

Fees, **262:53.**

Fire hazards, service of order for abatement, **148:5.**

Motor vehicle violations, **90:27.**

Sheriffs and deputies.

See SHERIFFS AND DEPUTIES.

Poor persons.

Indigents. See within this heading, "Indigents."

Possession, **235:15, 262:8.**

Postal insurance companies, process act, **175B:1-175B:6.**

Powers of attorney.

Foreign corporation's power of attorney to receive service, **181:3, 181:4.**

Nonresidents, appointment of agents for service of process, **227:5.**

Reciprocal insurance exchanges, **223:39B.**

PROCESS AND SERVICE OF PROCESS AND PAPERS
—Cont'd

Precepts.

See PRECEPTS.

Probate.

See PROBATE AND FAMILY COURT.

Probate bond, summoning principal, **205:28.**

Probation officers of Boston juvenile court, **276:91.**

Proof of service of process or papers.

Accident and sickness insurance, premium notices, **175:110B.**

Affidavit, **233:20E.**

Appeals from decisions of telecommunications and energy department, service of process by mail, **25:5.**

Automobile insurance, notice of cancellation, **175:113A.**

Banks, notice and other process related to hearings to investigate consumer transactions, **167:2C.**

Building regulation violations, proof of service of notice on nonresident, **143:11.**

Foreign insurance company, notice of revocation of authority, **175:5.**

Insurance, **175:5, 175:110B, 175:113A.**

Outside Commonwealth, **223A:6.**

Proprietors of real estate lying in common, **223:37.**

Public accountants not subject to subpoena, **112:87E½.**

Public health nuisances, proceedings for abatement, **111:123, 111:124.**

Public records, judicial enforcement of procedures, **66:17C.**

Public utilities.

Public utilities department. See

TELECOMMUNICATIONS AND ENERGY DEPARTMENT.

Quarantine of infected animals, notice, **129:22, 131:25A.**

Quieting title, **240:1.**

Determination of validity of encumbrances, service in proceedings, **240:12, 240:13.**

Equity suit to quiet title, service, **240:7.**

Restrictions running with land, service of notice in action to enforce, **240:10B.**

PROCESS AND SERVICE OF PROCESS AND PAPERS
—Cont'd

Quo warranto, **249:6-249:13.**

See QUO WARRANTO.

Railroads.

Nonresidents engaged in construction or repair, agent for service of process, **227:5.**

Orders for abolition of grade crossings, **159:70.**

Petition upon appeal from decision in certain matters as to crossings, **160:112.**

Rating organizations for insurance, **174A:8, 175A:8.**

See INSURANCE RATES AND RATING ORGANIZATIONS.

Real estate time-shares.

See REAL ESTATE TIME-SHARES.

Reciprocal enforcement of support act.

Fees, **262:8.**

Reciprocal insurance exchanges.

See RECIPROCAL INSURANCE EXCHANGES.

Records and reports.

Accounting for fees, **262:8A.**

Constable's report, **262:8A.**

Deputy's report, **262:8A.**

Sunshine law, **39:23C, 66:17C.**

Recovery of land held by state pursuant to judgment, service of process in subsequent action, **245:10.**

Registered mail, **231:13A.**

Probate court citation, **215:46.**

Registration of land titles, **185:61, 185:116.**

Nonresident petitioner for registration, agent for service, **185:35.**

Petition, notice, **185:38, 185:39.**

Registration of voters, complaints, **51:48.**

Religious society, service, **223:37.**

Relocation assistance payments, exemption from attachment or execution, **79:6A.**

Replevin.

See REPLEVIN.

Reports.

Records and reports. See within this heading, "Records and reports."

Residence.

Domicile and residence. See within this heading, "Domicile and residence."

PROCESS AND SERVICE OF PROCESS AND PAPERS
—Cont'd

Resident agent for service of process.

Agent for service. See within this heading, "Agent for service."

Restraints of trade and monopolies, **93:8.**

Return of process.

See RETURN OF PROCESS.

Revenue commissioner, service of summonses issued, **58:25B.**

Roads.

Highways and streets. See within this heading, "Highways and streets."

Sailors or seamen, prosecution for unlawful arrest or holding baggage, **102:3, 102:4.**

Sales and use tax laws, service of nonresidents in judicial proceedings, **64I:33.**

Scire facias.

See SCIRE FACIAS.

Searches.

See SEARCHES AND SEIZURES.

Secretary of state.

Foreign corporations.

See FOREIGN CORPORATIONS.

Service on state secretary as agent of absent defendant, **64I:33, 227:5.**

Security interest in airplane, place of business of debtor for purposes of service of process, **106:9-103.**

Seisin.

See ENTRY, WRITS.

Selectmen of town, service, **223:37.**

Several defendants, prosecution of action against those served, **227:15.**

Sheriffs and deputies.

See SHERIFFS AND DEPUTIES.

Signature, **223:20.**

Endorsement of writs. See within this heading, "Endorsement of writs."

Simultaneous service, fees as affected, **262:48.**

Small claims procedure, **218:21, 218:22, 218:25.**

Small loan company, agent for service, **140:104.**

Snow and ice, service of notice of injuries caused, **84:19, 84:21.**

PROCESS AND SERVICE OF PROCESS AND PAPERS
—Cont'd

Social services.

See WELFARE AND SOCIAL SERVICES.

Special assessments, abatement, **80:9.**

Standing committees, service, **223:37.**

State.

Board of trustees of state college, powers of policemen appointed, **73:18.**

Building code of state, **143:51.**

Certiorari, service when defendant is board or commission, **249:4A.**

Claims against, **258:6.**

Secretary of state. See within this heading, "Secretary of state."

Steam engines, service of order as to alterations, **140:116.**

Streets.

Highways and streets. See within this heading, "Highways and streets."

Subpoenas.

See SUBPOENAS.

Subscription.

Signature. See within this heading, "Signature."

Substituted service.

Agent for service. See within this heading, "Agent for service."

Substitute or replacement for service, **181:4.**

Alternatives for indigents unable to pay normal fee, **261:27F.**

Subversive organizations, actions against, **264:18.**

Suffolk County, officer for service of venires and processes of supreme judicial court, **221:78.**

Summary process for possession of land, **239:1-239:13.**

See SUMMARY PROCESS TO RECOVER LAND.

Summons.

See SUMMONS.

Sundays, prohibition as to service, **136:8.**

Superior court.

Any county, **213:2.**

Fictitious name, writ designating defendant, **223:19.**

Issuance of writs in, **223:20.**

Replevin writ returnable in superior court, bond in event, **247:8.**

PROCESS AND SERVICE OF PROCESS AND PAPERS
—Cont'd

Superior court —Cont'd

Sheriff's fees, **262:8.**

Venire facias writs, issuance, **212:20A.**

Zoning and planning, notice of superior court appeal, **40A:17.**

Supplementary proceedings.

See ARREST ON MESNE PROCESS AND SUPPLEMENTARY PROCEEDINGS.

Supplementary process, **223:84-223:86A.**

See ATTACHMENT OF PROPERTY.

Supreme judicial court.

See SUPREME JUDICIAL COURT.

Surveyor's certificate, revocation, **112:81P.**

Taxation.

See TAXATION.

Tenant.

Landlord and tenant. See within this heading, "Landlord and tenant."

Tender offer accepted as affecting costs incurred for subsequent service, **232A:2.**

Tenement houses.

Agents, service, **145:60.**

Notices, **145:60.**

Owner, **145:60, 145:60A-145:60C.**

Teste.

See TESTE.

Time of service.

Adoption of children, notice of motion to extend time for conducting inquiry, **210:5A.**

Delay in service of warrant, penalty, **268:22.**

Limitation of time, **260:32.**

Time to respond, foreign fiduciaries, **199A:11.**

Tolling of limitations by defective service, **260:32.**

Town, service on.

City or town, service on. See within this heading, "City or town, service."

Transient vendors, service, **101:6A.**

Transmission of writ or process on appeal, **231:101.**

Traveling expenses, **262:8, 262:10, 262:16, 262:48.**

Criminal cases, **262:14, 262:19, 262:21.**

PROCESS AND SERVICE OF PROCESS AND PAPERS
—Cont'd
Traveling expenses —Cont'd
Habeas corpus.
See HABEAS CORPUS.
Return by mail or express, **262:9.**
Treasurer of political subdivision, service, **223:37.**
Tribunals outside of Commonwealth, **223A:9, 223A:11.**
Trustee process, **246:5-246:8, 246:32.**
See TRUSTEE PROCESS.
Trusts and trustees, **223:40.**
Absentee beneficiaries, proceedings for transfer of estate, **203:28, 203:29.**
Attachment of property in divorce proceedings, **208:13.**
Business trusts, **182:6.**
Citation to seek domestic appointment, **203:11.**
Health, welfare and retirement funds, **151D:3.**
Massachusetts trusts, **182:6.**
Nonresident trustee, **203:15.**
State college board of trustees, powers of policemen appointed, **73:18.**
Subpoena served on trustee of trust with absentee beneficiaries, **203:28.**
Unacknowledged deed, proceedings for proof of execution, **183:36.**
Unauthorized insurers, service, **175B:1-175B:6.**
Undertaking.
Bond or undertaking. See within this heading, "Bond or undertaking."
Unfair insurance practices, hearing, **176D:6.**
Unfair trade practices against consumers, proceedings, **93A:6.**
Uniform rules of adjudicatory procedure, **30A:10.**
Uniform securities act.
See SECURITIES ACT.
United States property, service within limits, **1:7.**
Unknown defendant, **223:19.**
Vacancy in sheriff's office as affecting return of process, **37:14.**
Venire facias, **212:20A, 234:10, 234:32.**
Venires, service of.
See JURY AND JURY TRIAL.

PROCESS AND SERVICE OF PROCESS AND PAPERS
—Cont'd
Voluntary associations, **182:6, 223:40.**
Voters.
See ELECTIONS.
Waiver.
Contract action, **231:13A.**
Indictment, service of complaint upon waiver, **263:4A.**
Written instrument, waiver, **231:13A.**
Warrants.
See WARRANTS.
Welfare.
See WELFARE AND SOCIAL SERVICES.
Wharves, service on proprietors, **223:37.**
Witnesses.
See WITNESSES.
Workers' compensation, **152:25G.**
Costs paid out of trust fund, **152:65.**
Insurance commissioner, service, **152:25G.**
Notice of claim, **152:43.**
Zoning, notice of superior court appeal, **40A:17.**

PROCESSING DIVISION.
Department of Revenue, inclusion, **14:1.**

PROCESSING OF FILM.
Sunday, processing of photographic films, **136:6.**

PROCLAMATIONS.
Candle safety day, **6:12XX.**
Curfew, imposition, **40:37A.**
Fees for dispersing, **262:8.**
Governor.
See GOVERNOR.
Homicide victims.
Survivors of homicide victims awareness month, **6:15HHHH.**
Irish-American heritage month, **6:15FFFF.**
Italian-American heritage month, **6:15EEEE.**
Leif Erickson Day, **6:15YY.**
Pearl Harbor Day, **6:12DD.**
Portuguese-American month, **6:15GGGG.**
Public health month, **6:15IIII.**
Survivors of homicide victims awareness month, **6:15HHHH.**

PROCUREMENT AND GENERAL SERVICES DEPARTMENT.
Administration and finance executive office including, **7:4A.**

PRODUCT DEVELOPMENT CORPORATION.
Economic diversification program, **23F:4.**

PRODUCTION OF BOOKS AND PAPERS, 231:68.
Administration and finance executive office, powers of commissioner, **7:4E.**
Administration commissioner, powers, **7:4, 7:11.**
Alcoholic liquors, books of manufacturers, **138:21.**
Antitrust laws, **93:8.**
Appellate tax board, **58A:11.**
Arbitration and award.
Compelling in arbitration proceedings, **251:7.**
Labor disputes before board of conciliation and arbitration, **150:8.**
Audits and auditors.
Municipal accounts, powers of director of accounts with respect, **44:45.**
State auditor, powers, **11:12.**
Automobile insurance.
Motor vehicles. See within this heading, "Motor vehicles."
Ballot law commission.
State ballot law commission. See within this heading, "State ballot law commission."
Banks and banking, investigative hearing on consumer transactions, **167:2C.**
Barbers' board of registration, power, **112:87M.**
Bribery, production of books and papers used in prosecution, **271:39.**
Building regulations and standards board, powers and duties, **143:94.**
Business records, compliance with subpoena duces tecum, **233:79J.**
Carriers, telecommunications and energy department's power, **159:34, 159B:16A.**
Consumer transaction practices, investigative hearing, **167:2C.**
Contest of elections of presidential electors, **54:120.**

PRODUCTION OF BOOKS AND PAPERS —Cont'd

Controlled substances tax, **74K:13.**

Depositions, court order as to production of books and paper in connection, **233:42.**

Discrimination, powers of commission against, **151B:3.**

Drug business, proceedings for revocation or suspension of license, **112:40, 112:42A.**

Employment agencies, powers of labor and workforce development commissioner in connection, **140:46D, 140:46Q.**

Employment security.
Division's confidential records, **151A:46.**
Officials of division, powers, **151A:43.**

Energy Resources Department, records and reports, **25A:7.**

Financial disclosure by public officers and employees, production of books, papers and records for investigation, **268B:4.**

Fires and fire prevention, underground storage tanks, **148:38G, 148:38I.**

Foreign organizations soliciting contributions from public, service of subpoena duces tecum, **68:29.**

Foreign state, use of evidence, **223A:11.**

General Court, penalty for refusal of witness to produce papers before, **3:28A.**

Grand jury investigation, witnesses granted immunity, **233:20C et seq.**

Hairdressers' board of registration, powers, **112:87EE.**

Hazardous waste management act, enforcement, **21C:9.**

Industrial homework, investigations, **149:147F.**

Inspection, **231:68.**

Insurance.
Commissioner, **175:8A, 176D:6.**
Unfair practices, **176D:6.**
Motor vehicles. See within this heading, "Motor vehicles."
Premium finance agencies, production during investigation, **255C:6.**
Rebates on insurance, self-incrimination, **175:183.**
Unfair insurance practice proceedings, **176D:6.**

PRODUCTION OF BOOKS AND PAPERS —Cont'd

Labor and workforce development commissioner, powers as to employment agencies, **140:46D, 140:46Q.**

Labor disputes before board of conciliation and arbitration, **150:8.**

Marine fisheries division, powers of director, **130:21.**

Medical care and assistance, conduct of hearing on appeal by aggrieved person, **118E:22.**

Mental health department, powers of trustees of public institutions under control, **19:14.**

Militia courts-martial, power, **33:77.**

Milk control law hearing, **94A:18.**

Motor carriers of property, powers of telecommunications and energy department, **159B:16A.**

Motor vehicles.
Financing investigations, **255B:4, 255B:6.**
Insurance rating bureau, inspections, **26:8E.**
Liability policies and bonds, powers of board of appeal, **26:8A.**
Loss prevention central organization, subpoena duces tecum for reports filed, **175:113O.**
Registrar of motor vehicles, appeals, **90:28.**
Telecommunications and energy department's powers as to motor carriers, **159B:16A.**

Public works department, hearing examiner's power, **16:5.**

Rebates on insurance, self-incrimination, **175:183.**

Registrar of motor vehicles, appeals, **90:28.**

Restraints of trade and monopolies, **93:8.**

Retail installment sales and services.
Investigation of person other than licensee, **255D:6.**
Sales finance company, requirement, **255D:3 et seq.**

Revenue commissioner's authority to require, **58:25B.**

Sealing up portions of books and documents, **231:67.**

State administrative procedure, **30A:12.**

PRODUCTION OF BOOKS AND PAPERS —Cont'd

State auditor, powers, **11:12.**

State ballot law commission.
Power to require production, **55B:4.**
Registrars' power to compel production, **55B:7.**

State tax commissions' authority to require, **58:25B.**

Subdivision control law, powers of chairman of appeals board, **41:81AA.**

Taxation.
Appellate tax board, **58A:11.**

Telecommunications and energy department, powers, **159:34, 159B:16A.**

Tribunal outside of Commonwealth, compelling production of evidence to be used in proceeding, **223A:11.**

Unemployment compensation.
Employment security. See within this heading, "Employment security."

Unfair insurance practice proceedings, **176D:6.**

Unfair trade practices against consumers, examination of books and records of persons suspected, **93A:6.**

Wage reporting system, special investigations bureau, **62E:6A.**

Will, production for probate, **191:12-191:14.**

Workers' compensation cases, **152:5.**

PRODUCTS LIABILITY.

Firearms and weapons.
Sale without functioning safety lock, **140:131K.**

Insurance, risk retention and risk purchasing groups, **176L:1.**

PROFANITY.
See ABUSIVE OR OFFENSIVE LANGUAGE.

PROFESSIONAL ATHLETES.
See ATHLETICS.

PROFESSIONAL CONDUCT, RULES OF.

Clerks of courts.
See COMMITTEE ON PROFESSIONAL RESPONSIBILITY FOR CLERKS OF COURTS RULES.

Supreme judicial court, **Rule 3:07.**

PROFESSIONAL CORPORATIONS AND ASSOCIATIONS, 156A:1 et seq.

Accountants.
 See ACCOUNTANTS.
Agents.
 Directors, officers, and agents. See within this heading, "Directors, officers, and agents."
Annual certificate, **156A:5.**
Annual report, **156A:18.**
Articles of organization.
 Contents, **156A:7.**
 Purchase of shares on death or disqualification of shareholder, provision, **156A:12.**
Attorneys at law.
 Application of law, **221:46.**
 Within definition of professional services, **156A:2.**
Bonds, investment, **156A:4.**
Certificates and certification.
 Annual certificate, **156A:5.**
 License to practice of incorporators, directors, officers, and shareholders, certificate, **156A:7.**
Chiropractors within definition of professional service, **156A:2.**
Clerk or assistant, **156A:5.**
Death of shareholder, purchase or redemption of shares, **156A:12.**
Definitions, **156A:2.**
Dentists.
 Law requiring dental office to be operated under name of owner as inapplicable, **112:49.**
 Penalty for unlicensed practice of dentistry, **112:52.**
 Professional services within professional corporations law, definition as to dentists, **156A:2.**
Directors, officers, and agents.
 License to practice, certificate, **156A:7.**
 Majority of directors and officers to be licensed, **156A:9.**
 Method of rendering professional services by corporation, **156A:5.**
Disclosure of lists of present and prospective licensees, **66A:2.**
Dissolution by state secretary, **156A:15.**
Electrologists within definition of professional service, **156A:2.**

PROFESSIONAL CORPORATIONS AND ASSOCIATIONS —Cont'd

Engineers within definition of professional service, **156A:2.**
Foreign professional corporations, registration, **156A:17.**
General business provisions, applicability, **156A:4.**
Investment of funds, **156A:4.**
Land surveyors, regulation of professional societies, **231:85N.**
Licenses.
 Certification that incorporators, officers, directors, and shareholders are licensed, **156A:7.**
 Dentistry, penalty for unlicensed practice, **112:52.**
 Disclosure of lists of present and prospective licensees, **66A:2.**
 Officers, employees, and agents, **156A:5.**
 Majority of directors and officers to be licensed, **156A:9.**
Merger or consolidation, **156A:14, 156A:16.**
Mortgages, investment, **156A:4.**
Name, **112:49, 156A:8.**
Nonregistered performance of professional services, **156A:5.**
Officers.
 Directors, officers, and agents. See within this heading, "Directors, officers, and agents."
Optometrists within definition of professional services, **156A:2.**
Organization, **156A:3, 156A:7.**
 Articles of organization. See within this heading, "Articles of organization."
Ownership of property, **156A:4.**
Personal property ownership, **156A:4.**
Physical therapists within definition of professional services, **156A:2.**
Physicians within definition of professional service, **156A:2.**
Podiatrists within definition of professional service, **156A:2.**
Practice of law.
 Attorneys at law. See within this heading, "Attorneys at law."
Privileged or confidential communications, **156A:6.**
Property, right to own, **156A:4.**
Proxies, **156A:11.**
Psychologists within definition of professional services, **156A:2.**

PROFESSIONAL CORPORATIONS AND ASSOCIATIONS —Cont'd

Real property ownership, **156A:4.**
Redemption of shares, **156A:12, 156A:13.**
Regulating boards, defined, **156A:1.**
Regulation of professional corporations, **156A:19.**
Reports and reporting, **156A:18.**
Secretary of state.
 Dissolution, **156A:15.**
 Organization, **156A:7.**
Short title, **156A:1.**
Sole shareholder, redemption or transfer in case, **156A:13.**
Specific type of professional service, limitation to rendering, **156A:4.**
Stock and stockholders.
 Investment, **156A:4.**
 Issuance and transfer, **156A:10.**
 Liability, **156A:6.**
 License to practice, certificate, **156A:2, 156A:15.**
 Proxies and voting trusts, **156A:11.**
 Purchase or redemption of shares on death or disqualification of shareholder, **156A:12.**
 Redemption, **156A:12, 156A:13.**
 Restrictions on issuance and transfer of shares, **156A:10.**
Surgeons within definition of professional service, **156A:2.**
Taxation, **63:30.**
Teachers.
 See TEACHERS.
Uniform Securities Act, exemptions, **110A:402.**
Veterinarians within definition of professional services, **156A:2.**
Voting trusts, **156A:11.**

PROFESSIONAL DEVELOPMENT SCHOOLS GRANT PROGRAM, 15A:20, 15A:21.

PROFESSIONAL DRIVER EDUCATION ASSOCIATION OF MASSACHUSETTS.
Governor's Highway Safety Committee, members, **90A:1.**

PROFESSIONAL ENGINEERS, 112:81D et seq.
See ENGINEERS AND SURVEYORS.

PROFESSIONAL FIRE FIGHTERS OF MASSACHUSETTS.

Attendance by delegates at conventions without loss of pay, **48:57B.**

Leave with pay, organizational work, **48:57I.**

PROFESSIONAL PERSONNEL.

Civil service, **31:16, 31:48.**

Defined, **150E:1.**

Educational measurement audit council, **15:55A.**

Education department, **15:1E, 15:1F.**

Licenses.
See LICENSES AND PERMITS.

Minimum wage law, applicability, **151:2.**

Overtime pay, **151:1A.**

Standards of conduct.
Revenue Department employees, **14:1.**

State offices, recruitment, **30:46.**

PROFESSIONAL SCHOOLS.

See COLLEGES AND UNIVERSITIES.

PROFESSIONAL SOLICITORS.

See CHARITIES AND CHARITABLE CONTRIBUTIONS.

PROFESSIONS, 112:1 et seq.
See TRADES, OCCUPATIONS, AND PROFESSIONS.

PROFESSORS.

See COLLEGES AND UNIVERSITIES.

PROFIT AND LOSS.

Accountability of seller for profit on resale of goods, **106:2-706.**

Charitable corporations, effect of distribution of profits to stockholders on tax exemption, **59:5.**

Collateral security, secured party as entitled to hold profits, **106:9-207.**

Condominiums, distribution of common profits, **183A:6.**

Decedent's debts, profits from management of real estate used for payment, **202:4A.**

Income tax.
See INCOME TAX.

Insurance.
See INSURANCE.

Limited liability companies, **156C:29.**

PROFIT AND LOSS —Cont'd

Limited partnerships, **109:25, 109:29.**

Morris plan banks.
Certificate funds limited by undivided profits, **172A:5.**
Dividends, net profit as limiting, **172A:11.**
Surplus fund to be established out of net profits, **172A:11.**

Partnerships.
See PARTNERSHIPS.

Pension funds, amortization of losses sustained on sale or maturity of investments, **32:22.**

Rents.
See RENTS AND PROFITS.

Secured transactions.
See SECURED TRANSACTIONS.

Sharing of profits.
See PROFIT SHARING.

Street railways, losses included in cost of service, **161:116.**

Trusts.
See TRUSTS AND TRUSTEES.

PROFIT SHARING.

Annuity contracts under profit sharing plan, **175:132F.**

Beneficiary, designation, **167D:30.**

Credit unions.
See CREDIT UNIONS.

Divorce and alimony, profit sharing as marital property, **208:34.**

Income tax.
Plans, Part B adjusted gross income as affected by employer contributions, **62:2.**
Trusts, exemption from tax, **62:5.**

Life insurance under profit sharing plan, **175:132F.**

Physical therapy referrals by physicians, disclosure of financial information, **112:12AA, 112:23P½.**

Rules against perpetuities, employer trusts created as part of plan as exempt from operation, **203:3A.**

Uniform Securities Act, exemptions, **110A:402.**

PROGRAMMING OFFICE, 7:41A, 7:41B.

Long range capital facilities agencies, submission, **29:7D.**

PRO HAC VICE.

Court approval, **221:46A.**

PROHIBITION.

Amendment.
See CONSTITUTION OF THE UNITED STATES.

Supreme judicial court, transfer of causes to and from other courts, **211:4A.**

Suspension of final judgment pending appeal from order, **231:117.**

PROJECT DEVELOPMENT BUREAU.

Housing and community development department, statutory references as meaning or referring, **23B:10.**

PROJECTION.

Buildings, **40:23, 85:9.**

PROJECTION BOOTH.

Motion pictures.
See MOTION PICTURES.

PROJECT MANAGEMENT OFFICE.

Change orders, provisions, **7:42E-7:42I.**

Contract modifications, provisions, **7:42E-7:42I.**

Cost estimate, project assistance, **7:42J.**

Director.
Acceptance of federal aid, **7:42K.**
Appointment, **7:42A.**
Powers and duties, **7:42B.**
Removal, **7:42C.**

Establishment, **7:42A.**

Federal aid, acceptance, **7:42K.**

Project manager, appointment and duties, **7:42D, 7:42E.**

Resident engineer, project assistance, **7:42J.**

PRO-LIFE MONTH.

Observance, **6:15FF.**

PROMISE.

Breach of promise to marry, abolition of right of action, **207:47A.**

Employment certificate for union, **149:87.**

Negotiable instruments.
See NEGOTIABLE INSTRUMENTS.

New promise as affecting limitation of actions, **260:13, 260:15, 260:16.**

Warranty as to goods created, **106:2-313.**

Written promises, when required, **259:1, 260:13.**

PROMISSORY NOTES.
See NEGOTIABLE
INSTRUMENTS.

PROMOTION.
Advertising.
See ADVERTISING AND
ADVERTISEMENTS.
Apples.
See APPLES.
Civil service.
See CIVIL SERVICE.
Military affairs.
See MILITARY AFFAIRS.
Municipal personnel.
See MUNICIPAL PERSONNEL
SYSTEMS.
Retirement systems and pensions.
Laborers, promotion to
supervisory position as
affecting, **32:77C.**
School janitor or custodian
promotions as affecting
retirement, **32:45B.**
Sales taxes.
See SALES TAXES.
School teachers, provisions as to
promotion, **32:45B, 71:38.**
State department, **30:45, 30:46.**
State police.
See STATE POLICE.
Veteran's status as affecting,
31:26.

PROMOTIONAL
ADVERTISING.
Definition, **164:33A.**

PROOF, 231:85 et seq.
Evidence.
See EVIDENCE.

PROPAGATION OF WILDLIFE.
Marine fish.
See MARINE FISH AND
FISHERIES.

PROPANE GAS.
Contracts between subsequent
home purchasers and gas
dealers, binding effect, **93:94.**
Dealers, binding effect of contracts
with subsequent home
purchasers, **93:94.**
Definition, **164:69G.**
Delivery ticket issued for delivery
of more than 20 gallons,
94:303F.
Homeowners and gas dealers,
agreements, **93:94.**
Subsequent home purchasers and
gas dealers, binding effect of
agreements, **93:94.**

PROPANE GAS —Cont'd
Vendor and purchaser, binding
effect of contracts between
subsequent home purchasers
and gas dealers, **93:94.**

PROPERTY.
Personal.
See PERSONAL PROPERTY.
Real.
See REAL PROPERTY.

PROPERTY MANAGEMENT
SERVICES BUREAU.
Housing and community
development department,
statutory references as
meaning or referring, **23B:10.**

PROPERTY OFFICER.
State property officer, **33:15.**

PROPHYLAXIS.
Dental hygienists as qualified to
make applications to teeth for
prophylactic purposes, **112:51.**

PROPOSITION 2½, 59:21C.
See TAX AND BUDGET LIMITS
FOR LOCAL
GOVERNMENT.

PROPRIETARY MEDICINES.
See PATENT MEDICINES.

PROPRIETORS OF WHARVES
AND REAL ESTATE LYING
IN COMMON, 179:1-179:17.
Actions by and against, **179:6.**
Application for incorporation,
179:1.
Aqueducts.
See AQUEDUCTS AND
AQUEDUCT COMPANIES.
Assessments, levying and
collection, **179:11-179:13.**
Assets, sale of entire estate,
179:14.
Bylaws, **179:7.**
Certificate of organization, **179:3.**
Clerk, **179:4.**
Collectors, **179:3.**
Committees, **179:3.**
Copies of records, **66:5, 179:15,**
262:34.
Dissolution, **179:16, 179:17.**
Fees for deposits or for copies of
records, **179:15, 262:34.**
Incorporation, **179:1-179:3.**
Meetings, **179:9.**
After division of property,
179:17.
First meeting, **179:1-179:3.**
Notice of meeting. See within
this heading, "Notice of
meeting."

PROPRIETORS OF WHARVES
AND REAL ESTATE LYING
IN COMMON —Cont'd
Moderator of meeting, **179:8.**
Notice of meeting.
Agenda to be set forth, **179:9.**
First meeting, **179:2.**
Officers, **179:3.**
Organization, **179:3.**
Proxies, **179:10.**
Records.
Copies, **66:5, 179:15, 262:34.**
Disposition, **179:15.**
Fees for deposits or for copies,
179:15, 262:34.
Redemption of shares sold to pay
assessment, **179:13.**
Sale of all assets, **179:14.**
Service of process, **223:37.**
Treasurer, **179:3, 179:5.**
Voting, **179:10.**

PRORATION.
See APPORTIONMENT.

PROSECUTING ATTORNEYS,
12:1 et seq.
See DISTRICT AND
PROSECUTING
ATTORNEYS.

PROSECUTIONS.
Criminal procedure, **275:1 et seq.**
See CRIMINAL PROCEDURE.

PROSPECTIVE JURORS.
Lists, **234A:14-234A:16.**
Summoning for examination,
234:4.

PROSPECTIVE OPERATION
OR EFFECT.
See RETROACTIVE OR
PROSPECTIVE
OPERATION.

PROSPECTUS.
False statements in, as criminal
offense, **266:92.**
Securities act.
See SECURITIES ACT.

PROSTHETIC APPLIANCES.
Dentures.
See DENTURES.
Medical care and assistance
program, services for which
financial assistance provided,
118E:6.
Medical malpractice, instructions
to jury, **231:60J.**
Motor vehicle insurance protection
against costs, **90:34A.**
National guardsmen's prosthetic
devices damaged or destroyed
while on active duty,
replacement, **33:88.**

PROSTHETIC APPLIANCES
—Cont'd

Retired police officers and firefighters, indemnification for cost of certain prosthetic devices, **41:100B.**

Sales tax, exemptions, **64H:6.**

Workers' compensation to include, **152:30.**

PROSTITUTION, 272:53, 277:79.

Abduction, **272:2.**

Abused and neglected children.
Child prostitution. See within this heading, "Child prostitution."

Aiding and abetting, enticing person to engage in prostitution, **272:12.**

Alcoholic liquors.
Detaining person through use, **272:13.**
Solicitation in licensed premises, **272:26, 272:27.**

Arrest, **272:9, 272:10, 272:54.**

Bail and recognizance.
Admission to bail, **272:57.**
Discharge, **272:57.**
Repetition of offense as breach of recognizance, **272:56.**

Child prostitution.
Child abuse, investigation and notification to district attorney, **119:51B.**
Earnings, support, **272:4B.**
Houses of prostitution, **149:64, 149:78.**
Penalty for inducing minor to solicit, **272:4A, 272:4B.**

Common nightwalkers.
Criminal offense, **272:53, 277:79.**
Discharge from house of correction, **127:143.**
Indictment, **277:79.**
Recognizance, discharge, **272:56, 272:57.**
Repetition as breach of recognizance, **272:56.**
Second or subsequent conviction, **272:56, 272:61.**
Sentence and punishment, **272:53, 272:61, 272:62.**
Third conviction, **272:62.**

Corroboration, necessity, **272:11.**

Criminal offense, **272:53.**

Deriving support from earnings of prostitute, **272:7.**

Discharge, **127:143, 272:57.**

Disorderly houses.
See DISORDERLY HOUSES.

PROSTITUTION —Cont'd

Employment agency sending person to house, **140:46K, 272:12.**

Enticing.
Person to practice, **272:12.**
Woman from home, **272:2.**

Fines and penalties.
Sentence and punishment. See within this heading, "Sentence and punishment."

Form of indictment or complaint, **277:79.**

House of ill fame.
See DISORDERLY HOUSES.

Immoral solicitation, **272:26.**

Innholder permitting solicitation, penalty, **140:26.**

Intoxicating liquors.
Alcoholic liquors. See within this heading, "Alcoholic liquors."

Limitation of time to prosecute, **272:11.**

Liquors.
Alcoholic liquors. See within this heading, "Alcoholic liquors."

Nightwalkers.
Common nightwalkers. See within this heading, "Common nightwalkers."

Nuisances.
See NUISANCES.

Owner of premises permitting use, **272:6.**

Pandering and pimping, **140:26, 272:7, 272:8.**

Procuring of prostitutes, **272:12.**

Punishment.
Sentence and punishment. See within this heading, "Sentence and punishment."

Resorting to restaurant or cafe for immoral purposes, **272:26, 272:27.**

Second and subsequent offenses, **272:56, 272:61.**

Sentence and punishment.
Child prostitution, **272:4A, 272:4B.**
Common nightwalkers, **272:53, 272:61, 272:62.**
Employment agency sending person to house of ill fame, **272:12.**
Engaging in sexual conduct for fee, **272:53A.**
House of prostitution, **149:78, 272:6, 272:24.**
Pimping, **272:7, 272:8.**
Restaurants, solicitation, **272:26, 272:27.**

PROSTITUTION —Cont'd

Sentence and punishment —Cont'd
Second offenses, **272:56, 272:61.**
Sharing in earnings of prostitute, **272:7.**
Soliciting business for prostitute, **140:26, 272:8, 272:26, 272:27.**

PROTECTED SPECIES.
See FISH AND GAME.

PROTECTION, LOSS.

Wrongful death, damages for loss of protection, **229:2.**

PROTECTION OF CHILDREN.
See CHILDREN AND MINORS.

PROTECTION OF CONSUMERS.
See CONSUMERS AND CONSUMER PROTECTION.

PROTECTIVE CUSTODY.

Children and minors.
Alcoholism and intoxication, **111B:10.**
Controlled substances, **94C:36.**

Custody of person.
See CUSTODY OF PERSON.

Intoxicated persons, detention, **111B:8, 111B:10.**

PROTECTIVE DEVICES.
See SAFETY AND SAFETY DEVICES.

PROTECTIVE ORDERS.
See JUDGMENTS, ORDERS, AND DECREES.

PROTECTIVE SERVICES.

Elderly persons, abuse reports, **19A:14, 19A:15, 19A:16, 19A:18, 19A:20, 19A:23, 112:135.**

Social services department, administration of programs, **18B:2.**

PROTEST.

Corporate or trade name, protest against other corporation's use, **155:9.**

False protest by master of vessel, **266:111.**

Fees for notice of protest of negotiable instruments, **262:41.**

Negotiable instruments.
See PRESENTMENT, DISHONOR, AND PROTEST.

Taxes, protest as condition to recover back, **60:98.**

PROTESTANT EPISCOPAL SOCIETY.
Organization as religious society, **67:39.**

PROTOCOLS.
Drugs.
  See DRUGS AND NARCOTICS.

PROVIDERS.
Medical care.
  See MEDICAL CARE AND ASSISTANCE.

PROVINCE LANDS, 45:19-45:23.
See PUBLIC LANDS.

PROVINCETOWN.
District court held, **218:1.**
Harbor, taxation of certain state lands privately occupied, **59:5.**
Medical examiner district, **38:1.**

PROVINCIAL STATE HOUSE.
Care and maintenance, **8:20.**

PROVISIONAL REMEDIES.
Delinquent taxes, period which goods may be held for collection, **60:25.**
Injunctions.
  See INJUNCTIONS.
Receivers.
  See RECEIVERS AND RECEIVERSHIPS.

PROVISOS.
Criminal statutes, effect of proviso, **277:37.**

PROXIES.
Co-operative banks, **170:8.**
Corporations.
  See CORPORATIONS.
Credit unions, **171:11.**
Emergency guardianship proxies.
  See GUARDIANS, CONSERVATORS, AND COMMITTEES.
Fraternal benefit societies, **176:3.**
Health care proxies.
  See HEALTH CARE PROXIES.
Insurance.
  See INSURANCE.
Mutual insurance companies, reorganization.
  Votes of members of reorganized company, **175:19K.**
Proprietors of wharves and real estate lying in common, **179:10.**
Reclamation districts, proxy voting at meetings, **252:6.**
Street railways, voting by proxy, **161:17.**

PROXIMATE CAUSE.
Operation of unregistered or improperly equipped motor vehicle, effect, **90:9.**

PRUDENTIAL COMMITTEES.
Church, committee, **67:49.**
Corrective change in law, **44:35, 44:40.**
Districts.
  See DISTRICTS.
Fire districts.
  See FIRE DISTRICTS.
Reclamation districts, **252:6, 252:14A.**
Town improvement districts, **40:44.**
Town meeting, chairman as acting moderator, **39:14.**

PRUDENT INVESTOR ACT, 203C:1 to 203C:11.
See TRUSTS AND TRUSTEES.

PRUDENT MAN RULE.
Income or principal, distributions to trustees, **203:21A.**
Prudent investor act, **203C:1 to 203C:11.**
  See TRUSTS AND TRUSTEES.

PSYCHIATRY.
Admissibility of statements of defendant made while undergoing psychiatric examination, **233:23B.**
Alcoholism and intoxication.
  Court ordered examinations regarding commitment, **123:35.**
  Services provided under Alcoholism Treatment and Rehabilitation, **111B:4.**
Certificates and certification, psychiatric clinical specialists, insurance reimbursement, **175:47B, 175:47E, 176A:8A, 176B:4A.**
Children and minors.
  Abuse, reporting requirements, **119:51A.**
  Children in need of psychiatry, **119:39E, 119:39G.**
  Juvenile behavior council, membership, **6:159.**
  Sexually abused children, out of court statements, **233:81, 233:82.**
Civil service status of trainees and program for doctors, **19:10.**
Clinical specialists, **175:47B, 175:47E, 176A:8A, 176B:4A.**
Committee member of professional society, immunity from liability, **231:85N.**

PSYCHIATRY —Cont'd
Confidential information of patients in family or marital therapy, **112:135, 233:20B.**
Data available to physician where psychiatric emergency arises, **66A:2.**
Death sentence, examination of person, **279:58.**
Definitions, **112:118.**
Emergency release of persons convicted of carrying dangerous weapons, **269:10.**
Examination by.
  See MENTALLY ILL AND RETARDED PERSONS.
Health.
  Mental health department. See within this heading, "Mental health department."
Insurance reimbursement, clinical specialists, **175:47B, 175:47E, 176A:8A, 176B:4A.**
Juvenile behavior council, membership, **6:159.**
Mental health department.
  Civil service status, **19:2, 19:10.**
  Deputy commissioner, psychiatric training, **19:3, 19:4.**
  Nursing, qualifications of chief supervisor, **19:10.**
  Social worker, qualifications of head, **19:10.**
  Training program for residents in psychiatric services, **19:6, 19:10.**
Mental retardation department, **19B:2.**
Minors.
  Children and minors. See within this heading, "Children and minors."
Physical therapists, psychiatry as subject of examination for registration, **112:23E.**
Physicians and surgeons, psychiatry as subject of examination for registration, **112:3.**
Privileged communications with patient, **233:20B.**
Psychiatric nurse mental health clinical specialists prescribing and dispensing controlled substances, **94C:7, 94C:9.**
Sexual offenses.
  See SEXUAL OFFENSES AND OFFENDERS.
State training grants to residents in psychiatry and related subjects, **19:6, 19:10.**

PSYCHIATRY —Cont'd

Violence by patients, duty to take precautions against, **112:129A, 123:1, 123:36B, 233:20B.**

Witnesses.
Admissibility of defendant's statements made while undergoing psychiatric examination, **233:23B.**
Privileged communications between psychotherapist and patient, **233:20B.**

Youth services division, employment of psychiatrists, **120:2.**

PSYCHOLOGICAL ASSOCIATION.

Health and welfare commission, membership, **6:125.**

PSYCHOLOGICAL RESEARCH OR SERVICES DIRECTOR.

Qualifications, **19:10.**

PSYCHOLOGISTS' REGISTRATION ACT, 112:118 et seq.

PSYCHOLOGY.

Bridgewater state hospital, **123:15, 123:18, 123:22.**

Certificates, granting or denial, **71:38G.**

Children and minors.
Abuse or neglect of child, mandated reports, **119:51A.**
Psychological services, children in need, **119:39E, 119:39G.**
Sexually abused children, out of court statements, **233:81, 233:82.**

Civil immunity for commitment of mentally ill persons, **123:22.**

Commitment of mentally ill person, examination, **123:12.**

Competency to stand trial, evaluations, **123:15, 123:17-123:19.**

Corrections department, qualifications of applicants for positions, **27:2A.**

Disclosures by psychotherapists, mental or nervous condition, benefits, **233:20B.**

Disqualification.
Qualification or disqualification. See within this heading, "Qualification or disqualification."

Education.
Schools and education. See within this heading, "Schools and education."

PSYCHOLOGY —Cont'd

Educational psychologists. See EDUCATIONAL PSYCHOLOGISTS.

Guardianship evaluations, performance, **201:6.**

Involuntary admissions to mental hospitals, performance of evaluations, **123:12.**

Licensing.
Registration and licensing. See within this heading, "Registration and licensing."

Medical malpractice claims, psychologists as providers of health care for purposes, **231:60B.**

Minors.
Children and minors. See within this heading, "Children and minors."

Physical therapists, psychology as subject of examination for registration, **112:23E.**

Professional services within professional corporations law, **156A:2.**

Qualification or disqualification, **19:10, 112:119.**
Board of registration, members, **13:76.**
Corrections department, **27:2A.**
Definition of "qualified psychologist" under mental health law, **123:1.**
Research and services director, **19:10.**

Qualified psychologist, defined, **123:1.**

Records of patients, nondisclosure to patients, **112:12CC.**

Registration and licensing, **112:118-112:129.**
Applicant previously licensed in another jurisdiction, **112:121.**
Applications for licensing, **112:119.**
Board for.
Registration board. See within this heading, "Registration board."
Definitions, **112:118.**
Educational psychologists, **13:88-13:90.**
Enforcement of order of revocation or suspension of license, **112:128.**
Examinations, **112:120.**
Excluded activities, **112:125.**
Exclusion from penalty provisions, **112:123.**

PSYCHOLOGY —Cont'd

Registration and licensing —Cont'd
Fees, **112:126.**
Hearing on revocation or suspension of license, **112:128.**
Nonresident practicing within state, **112:124.**
Notice of contemplated revocation or suspension of license, **112:128.**
Penalties, **13:76-13:79, 112:118-112:129A.**
Practice of psychology defined, **112:118.**
Professions and occupations excluded from regulation, **112:125.**
Psychologist defined, **112:118.**
Qualifications for licensing, **112:119.**
Recognized educational institution, defined, **112:118.**
Reinstatement of license, **112:129.**
Renewal of license, **112:127.**
Revocation or suspension of license, **112:128.**
Temporary licenses, **112:124.**
Violations, **112:122.**

Registration board.
Appointment of successor, **13:77.**
Hearing for removal from office, **13:78.**
Meetings, **13:79.**
Membership qualifications, **13:76.**
Officers, **13:79.**
Penalties, licensing requirements, **13:76-13:79, 112:118-112:129A.**
Powers and duties, **13:79.**
Removal from office, **13:78.**
Term of office, **13:77.**

Research.
Employment of psychologists by research facilities, penal provisions as applicable, **112:123.**
Mental health department, psychological research director, **19:10.**

Schools and education, **112:119.**
Adjustment counselors, psychology-related professions excluded from regulations, **112:125.**
City school system, tenure of psychologist, **71:38P.**
Licensing of educational psychologists, **13:88-13:90.**

PSYCHOLOGY —Cont'd
Schools and education —Cont'd
Penal provisions as applicable to psychologists employed by schools, **112:123.**
Tenure, **71:41.**
Youth services department, employment of psychologists, **120:2.**

PSYCHOPATHIC PERSONALITY ACT, 123A:1 et seq.
See MENTALLY ILL AND RETARDED PERSONS.

PSYCHOSURGERY.
Intensive care unit for women, psychosurgery not to be performed, **123:23.**

PSYCHOTHERAPISTS.
Defined, **233:20B.**

PSYCHOTROPIC DRUGS.
Public schools, **71:54B.**

PSYCHROMETERS.
Textile factories, **149:109.**

PT VETERANS ASSOCIATION.
Insignia, unlawful use, **266:70.**
Uniform, unlawful use, **264:10A.**

PUB BREWERIES.
Defined, **138:1.**
Employment of minors, **138:34.**
Hours for sale, **138:12.**
Licenses, **138:19D.**
On-premises consumption, **138:12s.**

PUBLIC ACCESS BOARD AND FUND, 21:17A.
Environmental affairs executive office, funds, **21A:10.**
Fisheries, **21:17A, 21A:8, 64A:13.**
Gasoline and motor fuel taxes, distribution of receipts, **64A:13.**
Marine fish and fisheries.
Costs and expenses chargeable, **21:17A.**
Crediting of receipts from gasoline taxes, **64A:13.**
Snow traveling and recreation vehicle fees, allocation, **90B:35.**
Wildlife and recreational vehicles department, functions and duties, **21A:8.**

PUBLIC ACCOMMODATIONS ACT.
Civil rights, **272:98.**

PUBLIC ACCOUNTANTS.
See ACCOUNTANTS.

PUBLIC ADDRESS SYSTEM, CREDIT UNIONS.
Advertisements, **171:55.**

PUBLIC ADMINISTRATORS, 194:1 et seq.
See EXECUTORS AND ADMINISTRATORS.

PUBLIC ASSISTANCE.
See WELFARE AND SOCIAL SERVICES.

PUBLICATION.
Abandoned property, state treasurer to publish notice, **200A:8.**
Absence of newspaper in city or town, requirements in case, **4:6.**
Administration and finance commissioner, annual report, **7A:12.**
Adulterated commercial feed, **128:62.**
Adulterated or misbranded cosmetic or surgical device, notice, **94:194.**
Advertising.
See ADVERTISING AND ADVERTISEMENTS.
Age discrimination, name of employer guilty, **149:24G.**
Agriculture, commissioner, **128:2, 128:3, 128:5, 128:6.**
Air carriers, tariffs, **159:14A.**
Alcoholic liquors.
See ALCOHOLIC LIQUORS.
Alcoholism treatment and rehabilitation facilities, publication of list, **111B:5.**
Annual reports of state officers, **5:6-5:8, 35:27.**
Anti-discrimination commission, duties, **151B:3.**
Appeal from purchasing agent's publication of state documents and reports, **7:29.**
Appeals court.
See APPEALS COURT.
Appellate tax board.
Publication, sale and distribution of reports and opinions, **58A:3.**
Aqueduct companies, sale of shares for failure to pay assessments, **165:18.**
Arbitration of labor dispute, reasons for party's not submitting, **150B:3.**
Archivist of Commonwealth, duties, **9:2.**
Assault weapon rosters, **269:10.**

PUBLICATION —Cont'd
Automobiles.
See MOTOR VEHICLES.
Bids.
See BIDS AND BIDDING.
Bills and resolves.
Legislative bills and resolves.
See within this heading, "Legislative bills and resolves."
Blind persons, restrictions on publication of lists of names, **6:149.**
Bradford Durfee College of Technology, rules, **74:42F.**
Business corporations.
See CORPORATIONS.
Bylaws.
Ordinances and bylaws. See within this heading, "Ordinances and bylaws."
Candidates and questions to be submitted at election, lists, **54:52.**
Charter cities, publication of ordinances, etc., **40:23, 40:32A.**
Children involved in court proceedings, names, **119:38.**
Chiropractors, publication of lists of registered, **112:96.**
Cities.
See CITIES AND TOWNS.
Civil service.
See CIVIL SERVICE.
Coal mining operations, notice, **21B:5.**
Conservation districts, notice of proceedings, **21:21, 21:22, 21:24.**
Constitution of Massachusetts and amendments, publication, **5:2; MA Const Part 2 Ch 6 Art 11.**
Conviction, facts concerning, **94:152.**
Corporations.
See CORPORATIONS.
Cosmetics, notice of adulteration or misbranding, **94:194.**
Counties.
See COUNTIES.
Credit cards and telecommunication services, fraudulent disclosure or publication of numbering or coding systems, **266:37D.**
Credit unions.
See CREDIT UNIONS.
Curfew, imposition, **40:37A.**

PUBLICATION —Cont'd

Decisions of Supreme Judicial Court.
  See REPORTER OF DECISIONS.

Defined, **6:39.**

Dogs running at large, fish and game director's order restraining, **131:82.**

Elder affairs department, summaries of research and evaluations, **19A:12.**

Elections.
  See ELECTIONS.

Electrical wiring in buildings, regulations, **143:3L.**

Electric companies.
  See GAS AND ELECTRIC COMPANIES.

Electric railroads.
  Agreement of association, **162:6.**
  Auction sale of new shares, **159:50.**
  Routes, notice of hearing, **162:8.**

Employment security laws, rules, and reports, **151A:63.**

Escheats, **245:4.**

Examiner's report from land recorder, notice of filing, **185:38.**

Execution sale, publication of notice, **236:28.**

Explosives, notice of hearing upon licenses, **148:13.**

False advertising, **266:91.**

Federal monies, publication of receipts and disbursements of, **US Const Art 1 Sec 9 cl 7.**

Fertilizers.
  Nitrogen, as contents, **128:73.**
  Sales data, **128:80.**

Fire district, bylaws and regulations, **48:77.**

Fire prevention regulations, notice of hearing on proposed changes, **148:10.**

Fish and wildlife sanctuaries, publication of order establishing, **131:9.**

Fluoridation of public water supply, order directing, **111:8C.**

Food.
  Conviction for selling or exposing for sale of unwholesome food, publication, **94:152.**
  Injurious properties, publicizing, **94:194.**
  State health department, publication of analyses, **111:13, 111:25.**

PUBLICATION —Cont'd

Foreign insurance companies.
  See FOREIGN INSURANCE COMPANIES.

Forfeiture, notice of libel to enforce, **257:4, 257:5.**

Fraternal benefit societies.
  See FRATERNAL BENEFIT SOCIETIES.

Gas.
  See GAS AND ELECTRIC COMPANIES.

General court.
  See GENERAL COURT.

Hazardous waste management act, duties of environmental Protection Department, **21C:4.**

Health, **111:24.**
  See HEALTH AND HEALTH DEPARTMENTS.

Historical commission, powers of secretary of state, **9:26.**

Hospital service corporations, assets and liabilities, **176A:12.**

Identification measurements of criminals, records, **127:29.**

Industrial development financing authority, publication of financial statement, **40D:18.**

Insurance.
  See INSURANCE.

International trade office, publication of lists, **23A:24.**

Jury list, **234:9.**

Labor.
  See LABOR AND WORKFORCE DEVELOPMENT.

Labor relations and disputes.
  Notice of hearing on question of normal operation of business, **150:4.**
  Reasons for refusal of party to dispute to submit to arbitration, **150B:3.**
  Rules and regulations of labor relations commission, **23:9R.**

Lack of newspaper in city or town, requirements in case, **4:6.**

Land court, fees for notices, **262:39.**

Land recorder, notice of filing of examiner's report, **185:38.**

Landscape architects, publication of announcements of examinations of applicants for registration, **112:102.**

Legislative bills and resolves, **3:23, 5:2.**
  Mailing to subscribers, **5:13.**
  Pamphlet edition, **5:4.**

PUBLICATION —Cont'd

Legislative committee hearings, notice, **3:33-3:35.**

Libel, publication of retraction, **231:93.**

Libraries.
  See LIBRARIES AND LIBRARIANS.

Livestock disease control director, publication of orders and regulations, **129:5.**

Lost property, notice of finding, **134:1.**

Mechanics' liens, sale of real estate to satisfy, **254:5A.**

Metropolitan districts, financial statements of secretary of state concerning, **10:11.**

Military service, prohibition against publishing names of persons receiving aid during, **40:51.**

Militia regulations, **33:5.**

Minimum wages, publication of names of employers violating wage rates and regulations, **151:11.**

Morris plan banks, return of condition, **172A:4.**

Motor vehicles.
  See MOTOR VEHICLES.

Municipalities.
  See CITIES AND TOWNS.

Municipal lighting and heating plants, **164:56D, 164:58.**

Mutual insurance companies, reorganization.
  Public hearing on plan of reorganization, **175:19H.**

Names.
  Age discrimination, name of employer guilty, **149:24G.**
  Blind persons, restrictions on publication of lists of names, **6:149.**
  Children involved in court proceedings, names, **119:38.**
  Military service, prohibition against publishing names of persons receiving aid during, **40:51.**
  Public assistance, publication of names of recipients, **18:11, 40:51.**

New Bedford Institute of Technology rules, **74:42F.**

Newspapers.
  See NEWSPAPERS.

New voting precincts, maps, **54:5.**

Obscene books and literature, notice of orders, **272:28C.**

PUBLICATION —Cont'd

Ordinances and bylaws, **40:32, 40:32A, 43:23.**
  Fire districts, **48:77.**
  Zoning ordinances or bylaws, **40A:6.**
Partition, publication of notices of petitions, **241:8.**
Pedestrian rules, **90:18A.**
Perpetuation of testimony, publication in newspaper as to proceedings on application for taking, **233:60, 233:61.**
Plant pest control, **128:27, 128:31.**
Posting.
  See POSTING.
Potatoes, uniform rules for marking and grading, **94:117J.**
Pounds.
  See POUNDS.
Printers.
  See PRINTERS AND PRINTING.
Public money, receipts and expenditures to be published, **US Const Art 1 Sec 9 cl 7.**
Purchasing agent.
  See STATE PURCHASING AGENT.
Quieting title, publication of notice of action, **240:7.**
Railroads.
  See RAILROADS.
Real estate brokers and salesmen, publication containing lists, **112:87.**
Real property inventory, **7:40K.**
Registration of land title, notice of petition, **185:38, 185:39.**
Rented garments and towels, registration, **110:25A.**
Reporter of decisions.
  See REPORTER OF DECISIONS.
Resolves of General Court, **3:23, 5:2.**
Restrictions running with land, notice by publication in action to enforce, **240:10B.**
Rifles, order prohibiting possession or use of in certain areas, **131:4.**
Savings bank life insurance, notice of hearing, **178A:6.**
School district proposed annual budgets, publication of notice of public hearing, **71:38N.**
Secretary of state.
  See SECRETARY OF STATE.
Self-storage facilities, advertisement of sale of property, **105A:4.**

PUBLICATION —Cont'd

Sewers, publication of regulations, **83:10.**
Sexual orientation, publication of results of investigations regarding discrimination on basis, **151B:3.**
Special legislation, notice of application, **3:5.**
Spinners' liens, publication of notice of sale to enforce, **255:31B.**
State agencies, regulations, **30A:6.**
State college board of trustees, rules and regulations, **73:1.**
State officers, annual reports, **5:6-5:8.**
State printing, **5:1-5:18, 29:28, 30:31.**
  See STATE PRINTING.
State purchasing agent.
  See STATE PURCHASING AGENT.
Statutes, **5:2.**
  City or town, absence of newspaper, **4:6.**
Street railways.
  See STREET RAILWAYS.
Subversive organization, adjudication, **264:18.**
Supreme Judicial Court decisions.
  See REPORTER OF DECISIONS.
Taxation.
  Appellate tax board.
    Publication, sale and distribution of reports and opinions, **58A:3.**
Tax titles, advertising sale of low value land held by municipality, **60:79.**
Telecommunication services, fraudulent avoidance of payment, **266:37D.**
Telephone and telegraph companies, notice of sale of new stock, **166:8.**
Towns.
  See CITIES AND TOWNS.
Trading stamps, notice of default in redemption, **93:14Q.**
Trust companies.
  See TRUST COMPANIES.
Unemployment compensation, **151A:63.**
Uniform rules of adjudicatory procedure, **30A:10.**
University of Massachusetts.
  Annual reports, **75:15.**
  Rules and regulations, **75:3.**
Urban renewal or redevelopment projects, notice to landowners of hearing, **121B:47.**

PUBLICATION —Cont'd

Voting lists, posting of, **50:5.**
  See ELECTIONS.
Watershed system, posting and publication of rules and regulations, **92:108.**
Welfare, publishing names of persons receiving, **18:11, 40:51.**
Wildlife sanctuary, order establishing, **131:9.**
Zoning.
  See ZONING AND PLANNING.

PUBLIC BEQUEST COMMISSION.
Employment dislocations and assistance in reemployment of dislocated workers, **6:17.**
Governor, supervision, **6:17.**

PUBLIC BONDS.
See BONDS AND DEBENTURES.

PUBLIC BUILDING ACT (CONSTRUCTION AND REPAIR), 149:29.

PUBLIC BUILDINGS.
See BUILDINGS AND STRUCTURES.

PUBLIC CELEBRATIONS.
Incorporation or settlement of cities and towns, special fund for, **44:53I.**
Municipal appropriations, **40:5, 40:9.**
Overtime pay for policemen, **41:111H.**

PUBLIC CHARITIES, 68:1-68:16, 180:1 et seq.
See CHARITIES AND CHARITABLE CONTRIBUTIONS.

PUBLIC CHARITIES DIVISION.
See ATTORNEY GENERAL.

PUBLIC CONTRACTS.
See CONTRACTS AND AGREEMENTS.

PUBLIC CONVENIENCE.
Certificates of public convenience.
  See CERTIFICATES OF PUBLIC CONVENIENCE AND NECESSITY.
Credit unions, **171:3.**
Ocean sanctuaries, activities permitted, **132A:16.**
Polling places, designation in adjacent precincts, **54:24.**

PUBLIC CORPORATION.
Control share acquisitions,
**110D:1-110D:8,
110E:1-110E:7.**
Foreign corporations, regulation of
control share acquisitions,
110E:1-110E:7.

**PUBLIC COUNSEL SERVICES
COMMITTEE, 211D:1 et
seq.**
Aggrieved counsel, remedy,
211D:12.
Annual report, **211D:4.**
Appeals and post-conviction
proceedings, **211D:14.**
Appointment or assignment of
counsel, **211D:5.**
Children and family law program,
211D:6A.
Claims, certification, **211D:12.**
Client complaint resolution,
211D:10.
Compensation rates, establishment
and review, **211D:11.**
Concurrent felonies,
representation of persons
charged, **211D:7.**
Conflicts of interest, **211D:1.**
Contractual agreements, **211D:6.**
Fees, **211D:2A.**
Gifts, grants and contributions,
211D:3.
Indigency, definition, **211D:2.**
Membership of committee, **211D:1.**
Monitoring and evaluating
counsel, **211D:10.**
Murder, representation of persons
accused, **211D:8.**
Nonlegal staff, **211D:13.**
Private counsel division, **211D:6.**
Reimbursement of committee
members, **211D:1.**
Roxbury community advisory
board, consultation, **211D:15.**
Rules and regulations, **211D:4.**
Sex offense registry.
Indigent services, provision,
211D:16.
Standards.
Development and establishment,
211D:2, 211D:9.
Justices to submit comments on
standard of performance,
211D:10.
Training of counsel, **211D:4.**
Use of public counsel division,
211D:6.
Waiver of fee, **211D:2A.**

PUBLIC DEBT.
Constitution of the United States.
See CONSTITUTION OF THE
UNITED STATES.

PUBLIC DOMAIN, 45:19-45:23.
See PUBLIC LANDS.

PUBLIC EMPLOYEES.
See PUBLIC OFFICERS AND
EMPLOYEES.

**PUBLIC EMPLOYEES
APPRECIATION DAY.**
Annual observance, **6:15TT.**

**PUBLIC EMPLOYEES
RETIREMENT ACT, 32:1 et
seq.**

**PUBLIC EMPLOYMENT
OFFICES.**
See EMPLOYMENT
SECURITY.

PUBLIC FUNDS.
See FINANCES AND FUNDS.

PUBLIC HALLS, 143:35.
Definitions, **144:2, 145:2.**
Discrimination in use, **272:98.**
Meetings.
See MEETINGS.
Violation of regulations, **143:35,
143:51.**

PUBLIC HEALTH.
See HEALTH AND HEALTH
DEPARTMENTS.

**PUBLIC HEALTH
COMMISSIONER, HEALTH
CARE PROXIES.**
Special proceedings, **201D:17.**

PUBLIC HEARINGS.
See TRIAL OR HEARINGS.

PUBLIC HOLDING COMPANY.
Uniform Securities Act,
exemptions, **110A:402.**

PUBLIC IMPROVEMENTS.
See IMPROVEMENTS.

PUBLIC INDEBTEDNESS.
Bonds.
See BONDS AND
DEBENTURES.
Defined, **6:134.**

PUBLIC INTEREST.
See PUBLIC POLICY OR
INTEREST.

PUBLIC LANDS, 45:19-45:23.
Appropriations, **45:19, 45:23.**
Beaches.
See BEACHES.
Buildings and structures, **45:22.**
Removal of buildings, **91:37.**
Driving animals on, penalty,
45:13.
Eminent domain, **45:20.**

PUBLIC LANDS —Cont'd
Establishment by city or town,
45:19.
Exceeding appropriations, **45:23.**
Executive session of governmental
body to discuss purchase,
exchange, lease, or value of
real property, **30A:11A½,
34:9G, 39:23B.**
Federal grants, provisions as to
organizations utilizing, **29:2C.**
Flats.
See TIDE LANDS AND
WATERS.
Garbage and rubbish, unlawful
disposal on public property,
270:16.
Gifts, **45:19.**
Government land bank.
See GOVERNMENT LAND
BANK.
Highways and streets.
Limited access ways, disposal of
unnecessary land acquired,
81:7E.
Sale or transfer of state lands
for highway purposes,
30:44A.
Hunting on state lands, **131:59.**
Improvement association, **45:12.**
Indebtedness of city or town, **44:7.**
Indictments.
See INDICTMENTS,
INFORMATIONS, AND
COMPLAINTS.
Itemized accounts of sales of
property by state institutions,
30:41.
Judgment, recovery of lands held
pursuant, **245:9, 245:10.**
Leases.
See LANDLORD AND TENANT.
Licenses and permits with respect
to shore lands and submerged
or overflow land, **91:12-91:18.**
Life estates, remainders, and
reversions, **184:27, 184:28.**
Limitation of actions based on
possibility of reverter,
260:31A.
United States, reverter of state
lands acquired, **1:6, 1:7.**
Writ of entry to recover, actions
against Commonwealth,
237:2.
Limitation of actions by
Commonwealth for recovery,
260:31.
Limited access ways, disposal of
unnecessary land acquired,
81:7E.

PUBLIC LANDS —Cont'd
Littoral property.
See TIDE LANDS AND
WATERS.
Militia.
See MILITIA.
Nuisances.
See NUISANCES.
Parks and reservations, **45:1 et
seq.**
See PARKS AND
RESERVATIONS.
Penalties, **45:24.**
Petroleum pipe lines, right of way,
30:44B.
Pipes and pipelines.
Easements, **30:44B.**
Forest lands, right of way for
gas lines, **132:34A.**
Playgrounds, **45:14 et seq.**
See PLAYGROUNDS.
Prison labor, **127:49, 127:49B,
127:49C.**
Public access board and fund,
enforcement and management,
21:17A.
Public water supply, **45:19, 45:21.**
Regional community colleges,
transfers, **43:30.**
Remainders and reversions.
Life estates, remainders, and
reversions. See within this
heading, "Life estates,
remainders, and reversions."
Removal of soil from town lands,
40:21.
Restrictions, removal of buildings
pursuant, **91:37.**
Reversions.
Life estates, remainders, and
reversions. See within this
heading, "Life estates,
remainders, and reversions."
Rules and regulations, penalty for
violation, **45:24.**
Shore.
See TIDE LANDS AND
WATERS.
Special forest committee, **45:21.**
State boundary markers, malicious
injury, **1:5.**
State treasurer as custodian of
deeds, **29:41.**
Streets.
Highways and streets. See
within this heading,
"Highways and streets."
Submerged lands.
Licenses and permits with
respect, **91:12-91:18.**
Public works department,
duties, **91:2, 91:11.**

PUBLIC LANDS —Cont'd
Taxation.
See TAXATION.
Tidelands.
See TIDE LANDS AND
WATERS.
Title research by department of
public works, **91:2.**
Title to lands, **45:19.**
Trespass, **12:7, 41:36, 45:13, 91:2,
245:1, 245:2, 245:9, 266:123.**
See TRESPASS.
Uses, **45:19.**
Vacant public land, defined, **20:13.**
Waterways, **91:1-91:59.**
Willful acts of children, parents'
civil liability, **231:85G.**

PUBLIC MARKETS.
Municipal markets, **40:10.**

**PUBLIC MEETINGS.
See MEETINGS.**

**PUBLIC MONEYS.
See FINANCES AND FUNDS.**

**PUBLIC NUISANCES.
See NUISANCES.**

PUBLIC OFFERING.
Real estate time-shares,
183B:36-183B:39.

**PUBLIC OFFICERS AND
EMPLOYEES, 149:25-149:44.**
Abatement, survival, and revival
of action by or against, **228:2.**
Judgment for or against
executor or administrator,
228:3.
Removal, death, or resignation
of public officers, **228:14.**
Accountants, applicability of
restrictions as to use of
designation, **112:87D.**
Accounts.
See ACCOUNTS AND
ACCOUNTING.
Accumulated allowances upon
death or separation from
service, payment, **29:31A.**
Acknowledgments, officers
authorized to take, **183:30.**
Commissioners to qualify public
officers, **222:6.**
Addicted state employees,
assistance program, **7:28B.**
Advances, **29:23-29:25.**
Retirement systems and
pensions, **32:98.**
Salaries, **29:31, 44:66.**
Affirmative action officer in
counties, designation and
appointment, **35:53A.**

**PUBLIC OFFICERS AND
EMPLOYEES** —Cont'd
Age limit for service of employees,
32:3.
Agency, **268A:4 et seq.**
Conflict with discharge of duties,
public officer or employee to
avoid acting as agent in
case, **268A:4.**
Fines and penalties, acting as
agent or attorney on sale of
land to Commonwealth,
30:44.
Alcoholic liquors.
See ALCOHOLIC LIQUORS.
Aldermen.
See ALDERMEN AND
SELECTMEN.
Alternate appeal procedure under
civil service law, **31:41A.**
Annuities.
See ANNUITIES AND
ANNUITY CONTRACTS.
Antitrust laws, **93:8.**
Appointments.
See APPOINTMENTS.
Appreciation day, annual
observance, **6:15TT.**
Arbitration.
See LABOR RELATIONS AND
DISPUTES.
Assassination or violence toward,
advocating, **264:11.**
Assault and battery committed
against public employee in
performance of official duties,
264:11, 265:13D.
Attempt to extort money by threat,
265:25.
Attorney general.
See ATTORNEY GENERAL.
Attorneys.
Acting as attorney, **268A:4 et
seq.**
Legal representation of public
employees, **32:6, 258:2,
258:9A.**
Ballot boxes, violations by public
officer, **54:131.**
Banks.
See BANKS AND BANKING.
Boarding and lodging, freedom,
149:25, 149:180.
Bonds.
See BONDS AND
UNDERTAKINGS.
Books.
Accounts.
See ACCOUNTS AND
ACCOUNTING.
Records.
See RECORDS, REPORTS,
AND RETURNS.

PUBLIC OFFICERS AND EMPLOYEES —Cont'd

Bribery.
See BRIBERY.
Campaign expenditures.
See CAMPAIGN EXPENDITURES AND CONTRIBUTIONS.
Candidates for elective offices, right of employees to become, **150E:6.**
Cities and towns.
See CITIES AND TOWNS.
Civil actions, **12:3E.**
Civil defense.
See CIVIL DEFENSE.
Civil service.
See CIVIL SERVICE.
Claims against Commonwealth.
See CLAIMS AGAINST COMMONWEALTH.
Classification of officers.
See CIVIL SERVICE.
Commissioners to qualify public officers, **30:11, 30:13, 222:3.**
Commission to office.
See COMMISSION TO OFFICE.
Compensation.
See WAGES, SALARIES, AND COMPENSATION.
Conduct of public officials and employees, **268A:1-268A:24.**
See CONDUCT OF PUBLIC OFFICIALS AND EMPLOYEES.
Confidential information not to be disclosed or used, **268A:4, 268A:23.**
Conflict of interest.
See CONDUCT OF PUBLIC OFFICIALS AND EMPLOYEES.
Constitution of Massachusetts.
See CONSTITUTION OF MASSACHUSETTS.
Constitution of the United States.
See CONSTITUTION OF THE UNITED STATES.
Consultants.
See CONSULTANTS.
Contract negotiations, executive sessions of governmental bodies, **39:23B.**
Conviction of crime, effect, **31:20, 31:50, 264:20, 279:30.**
Co-operative banks.
See COOPERATIVE BANKS.
Copies.
Fees precluded to public employees, **30:43.**
Rules and regulations of state departments, officers filing attested copies, **30:37.**

PUBLIC OFFICERS AND EMPLOYEES —Cont'd

Counterclaim.
See SETOFF AND COUNTERCLAIM.
Counties.
See COUNTY OFFICERS AND EMPLOYEES.
Crimes, **268A:1 et seq., 268B:1 et seq.**
Criminal record sealed, effect on public employment, **276:100A-276:100C.**
Cushing Hospital, staff members as employees of Commonwealth, **111:64I.**
Data processing professionals, employment, **30:45, 30:46.**
Day care facilities for state employees, provision, **7:40F.**
Death, survival of action against officer following, **228:14.**
Deferred compensation programs.
See DEFERRED COMPENSATION PROGRAMS.
Delay by, as offense, **268:22.**
Deposits.
See DEPOSITS AND DEPOSITORIES.
Deputies.
See DEPUTIES.
Disability, **31:39.**
Massachusetts office, **6:185.**
Disadvantaged persons completing work-training program, civil service appointments based, **31:47A.**
Discharge.
See REMOVAL FROM OFFICE OR EMPLOYMENT.
Discipline or discharge of, **30:9B.**
Discovery and disclosure.
Financial disclosure by public officers.
See FINANCIAL DISCLOSURE BY PUBLIC OFFICERS AND EMPLOYEES.
Improper influence or favor, written disclosure to avoid appearance, **268A:23.**
Public employment service program, **23:9L.**
Discrimination on ground of race, religion, etc., **149:43, 151B:1-151B:10.**
Distribution of laws, **5:3.**
District.
See DISTRICT AND PROSECUTING ATTORNEYS.

PUBLIC OFFICERS AND EMPLOYEES —Cont'd

Districts.
See DISTRICTS.
Dog officers, records to be maintained, **140:151A.**
Drugs and narcotics.
Addicted state employees, assistance program, **7:28B.**
Registration, exemptions, **94C:7.**
Educational collaborative, public employer as including, **258:1.**
Election offenses.
See ELECTION OFFENSES.
Elections, **54:11-54:23.**
See ELECTIONS.
Electric companies, reimbursement in full for expenses incurred by employees sent to aid similar governmental units or, **152:74A.**
Embezzlement, **266:50, 266:51.**
Pension and retirement, **32:15, 151D:6.**
Emergency medical technician incapacitated during performance of duty, **41:111M.**
Eminent domain.
See EMINENT DOMAIN.
Employment security.
See EMPLOYMENT SECURITY.
Engineers.
See ENGINEERS AND SURVEYORS.
Equal opportunity, **149:43, 151B:1-151B:10.**
Equity.
Compelling delivery of public record, **66:13.**
Financial disclosure by public officers and employees, definition, **268B:1.**
Executions.
See EXECUTIONS.
Executive or administrative officers, employment contract, **41:108N.**
Extortion, **265:25.**
Fair employment practices law, applicability, **151B:1.**
False imprisonment, scope of action, **263:3.**
False personation, **268:33-268:35.**
False reports, **268:6A.**
Federal income tax, withholding, **58:28A, 58:28B.**
Fees, **262:1-262:64.**
See FEES.
Filing requirements for regulations adopted by departments, **30:37.**

PUBLIC OFFICERS AND EMPLOYEES —Cont'd

Financial disclosure by public officers.
See FINANCIAL DISCLOSURE BY PUBLIC OFFICERS AND EMPLOYEES.

Fines and penalties.
Assault and battery committed against public employee performing official duty, **264:11, 265:13D.**

Conduct of public officials.
See CONDUCT OF PUBLIC OFFICIALS AND EMPLOYEES.

Foreign powers, emoluments or presents not to be accepted from, without consent of Congress, **US Const Art 1 Sec 9 cl 8.**

Forfeiture of office by sentence to Federal or state prison, **279:30.**

Forgery.
See FORGERY AND COUNTERFEITING.

Fraternal benefit societies limiting membership, **176:45.**

Fraud and deceit.
Cities.
See CITIES AND TOWNS.
Claims against public bodies and officers, **258:5, 258:10.**
False personation, **268:33-268:35.**
False reports, **268:6A, 268:33.**

Freedom of contract, **149:25, 149:180.**

Garnishment, **246:32.**

General court.
See GENERAL COURT.

Governmental units pooled insurance, authorization of public employer self-insurance group, **40M:1.**

Governor.
See GOVERNOR.

Governor's council.
See GOVERNOR'S COUNCIL.

Grade, classification of.
See CIVIL SERVICE.

Grievances, hearing.
See LABOR RELATIONS AND DISPUTES.

Group insurance.
Municipal employees, **32B:1-32B:14.**
Notification of claims to governmental unit, **32B:3.**

PUBLIC OFFICERS AND EMPLOYEES —Cont'd

Group insurance —Cont'd
State employees, **32A:1 et seq.**
See GROUP INSURANCE FOR STATE EMPLOYEES.

Half holidays, **41:110, 92:65, 149:33, 149:41.**

Handicapped persons, placement of, by rehabilitation commission, **6:81.**

Health.
See HEALTH AND HEALTH DEPARTMENTS.

Health coverage, health maintenance organization, **32A:2, 32A:14.**

Highways.
See HIGHWAYS AND STREETS.

Holidays for.
See SUNDAYS AND HOLIDAYS.

Horse and dog racing meetings, seeking to influence employment, **271:40, 271:41.**

Hotels.
See HOTELS, MOTELS, AND ROOMINGHOUSES.

Hours of labor.
See HOURS OF LABOR OR SERVICES.

House of representatives of United States.
See HOUSE OF REPRESENTATIVES OF UNITED STATES.

Housing and community development department.
See HOUSING AND COMMUNITY DEVELOPMENT DEPARTMENT.

Housing authorities, employment of elected municipal officials, **39:6A, 268A:20.**

Income tax.
See INCOME TAX.

Incompatible offices.
See INCOMPATIBLE OFFICES.

Indemnity.
See INDEMNITY AND INDEMNIFICATION.

Indictment, suspension while, **30:59.**

Institutional employees, protection against removal after six months' service, **30:9B.**

Insurance.
See INSURANCE.

PUBLIC OFFICERS AND EMPLOYEES —Cont'd

Job group, classification according, **149:27.**

Joint authority under statute, construction, **4:6.**

Jury duty, **234:1, 234:1B.**

Laborers, **149:38.**

Labor relations and disputes, **150E:1 et seq.**
See LABOR RELATIONS AND DISPUTES.

Labor relations commission.
See LABOR RELATIONS COMMISSION.

Land court.
See LAND COURT.

Leave of absence.
See LEAVE OF ABSENCE.

Legislative bills.
See LEGISLATIVE BILLS AND RESOLVES.

Libraries and librarians.
Bonds of officers, **78:10.**
Employment contracts, **78:34.**
Salaries, **78:14.**

Life insurance.
See LIFE INSURANCE.

Lists, **7:30, 149:27.**

Lodging.
See HOTELS, MOTELS, AND ROOMINGHOUSES.

Lottery ticket sales agents, not to act, **10:27.**

Lowlands.
See LOWLANDS AND SWAMPS.

Loyalty oath.
See LOYALTY OATH.

Massachusetts Centers of Excellence Corporation, powers, **40J:12.**

Massachusetts office on disability, **6:185.**

Mayors.
See MAYORS.

Memorial day.
See MEMORIAL DAY.

Mentally ill.
See MENTALLY ILL AND RETARDED PERSONS.

Merit certificates for suggestions, **7:31A.**

Metropolitan district commission.
See METROPOLITAN DISTRICT COMMISSION.

Metropolitan districts.
See METROPOLITAN DISTRICTS.

Military affairs.
See MILITARY AFFAIRS.

**PUBLIC OFFICERS AND
EMPLOYEES** —Cont'd

Militia.
  See MILITIA.
Misconduct, **268A:1-268A:24.**
  See CONDUCT OF PUBLIC
    OFFICIALS AND
    EMPLOYEES.
Model water and sewer
  commission board members
  as, **40N:4.**
Morris plan banks.
  Credit union deductions from
    pay, authorized depository,
    149:178B.
  Direct deposit of wages, etc.,
    41:41B.
Mortgage review board members,
  167:14A.
Multiple elective offices, **268A:20.**
Municipal officers and employees.
  See CITIES AND TOWNS.
Names of both spouses to be used
  on documents and
  communications, **41:34B,**
  41:38A.
Narcotics.
  Drugs and narcotics. See within
    this heading, "Drugs and
    narcotics."
Natural resources.
  See NATURAL RESOURCES.
Notice.
  Claim against public bodies and
    officers, notice, **258:4.**
  Financial disclosure by public
    officers and employees,
    268B:2-268B:4.
  Financial interest, **268A:6A.**
  Impending retirement of elected
    officer, notice, **50:6A.**
  License or consent of officer in
    charge, notices or
    advertisements on public
    property as requiring,
    266:126.
  Vacancies in office.
    Assistant clerk of court, notice
      to secretary of state of
      vacancy, **221:13.**
    Certain offices, **54:146.**
    Town boards, notice of
      vacancy, **41:11.**
Oath or affirmation, **4:7, 30:11,**
  30:12, 268A:4, 268A:11.
Official bonds.
  See BONDS AND
    UNDERTAKINGS.
Open meeting law, reinstatement
  of employee discharged at
  meeting held in violation,
  39:23B.

**PUBLIC OFFICERS AND
EMPLOYEES** —Cont'd

Other business or employment,
  engaging, **30:23.**
Overtime pay, **149:30B, 151:1A.**
Pardon as affecting forfeiture of
  office, **279:30.**
Partnerships.
  County employees, **268A:12.**
  Municipal employees, **268A:18,**
    268A:19.
  State employees, **268A:5,**
    268A:6, 268A:12.
Payroll.
  See PAYROLL AND PAYROLL
    DEDUCTIONS.
Pensions.
  See RETIREMENT SYSTEMS
    AND PENSIONS.
Performance evaluation system.
  See CIVIL SERVICE.
Perjury.
  See PERJURY.
Physical fitness standards, **31:61A.**
Physicians.
  See PHYSICIANS AND
    SURGEONS.
Police.
  See POLICE.
Preferences, **149:26.**
Probation.
  See PROBATION AND
    PAROLE.
Professional personnel.
  See PROFESSIONAL
    PERSONNEL.
Professional standards and
  conduct, Revenue Department
  employees, **14:1.**
Promotion.
  See PROMOTION.
Provisional appointments.
  See CIVIL SERVICE.
Public employees week, **6:12CC.**
Public safety department.
  See PUBLIC SAFETY
    DEPARTMENT.
Public safety employees,
  confidentiality of addresses
  and phone numbers of, **66:10.**
Public service companies, seeking
  to influence employment,
  271:40, 271:41.
Public transportation employees,
  assault and battery, **265:13D.**
Public utilities.
  Public utilities department.
    See
      TELECOMMUNICATIONS
      AND ENERGY
      DEPARTMENT.

**PUBLIC OFFICERS AND
EMPLOYEES** —Cont'd

Qualification, **30:11-30:13, 222:3.**
Quo warranto to determine right
  to hold office, **249:9.**
Racial discrimination in public
  employment, **149:43,**
  151B:1-151B:10.
Real estate brokers and salesmen
  registration law not applicable
  to public employees,
  112:87QQ.
Records.
  See RECORDS, REPORTS, AND
    RETURNS.
Registration of voters.
  See REGISTRATION OF
    VOTERS.
Removal from office.
  See REMOVAL FROM OFFICE
    OR EMPLOYMENT.
Reports.
  See RECORDS, REPORTS, AND
    RETURNS.
Representation of public employee
  by public attorney, **258:2.**
Residents of county, town, or
  district, preference, **149:26.**
Resignation.
  See RESIGNATION.
Restitution, offers or payment,
  149:27, 149:27C.
Restraints of trade and
  monopolies, **93:8.**
Retirement systems.
  See RETIREMENT SYSTEMS
    AND PENSIONS.
Retraining programs, disabled
  employees returning to work,
  31:39.
Revenue department.
  See REVENUE DEPARTMENT
    AND COMMISSIONER.
Revival of action.
  Abatement, survival, and revival
    of action. See within this
    heading, "Abatement,
    survival, and revival of
    action by or against."
Safety Department.
  See PUBLIC SAFETY
    DEPARTMENT.
Salaries.
  See WAGES, SALARIES, AND
    COMPENSATION.
Saturdays.
  Half holiday, **41:110, 92:65,**
    149:33, 149:41.
  Legal holiday falling on
    Saturday, **30:24A.**
  Office hours, **30:24.**

PUBLIC OFFICERS AND EMPLOYEES —Cont'd

Schools.
See SCHOOLS AND EDUCATION.
Sealed criminal records, effect on public employment, **276:100A-276:100C.**
Seals and sealed instruments, **4:9A, 4:9B.**
Selectman.
See ALDERMEN AND SELECTMEN.
Septic tanks installed by members of board of health, **111:26G.**
Setoff.
See SETOFF AND COUNTERCLAIM.
Sick leave.
See SICK LEAVE.
Small business loan review boards, **167:14C.**
Social security, **118C:1-118C:10.**
See SOCIAL SECURITY.
Social services department employees, protection from assault and battery, **265:13D.**
State, **30:1 et seq.**
Statutes distributed, **5:3.**
Street railways.
See STREET RAILWAYS.
Streets.
See HIGHWAYS AND STREETS.
Subversives barred from public service, **264:20.**
Suggestions, increase in awards, **40:5.**
Sundays.
See SUNDAYS AND HOLIDAYS.
Survival of actions.
Abatement, survival, and revival of action. See within this heading, "Abatement, survival, and revival of action by or against."
Surviving spouse.
Accident and sickness insurance, state employee's premiums paid for surviving spouse, **32A:11, 32B:1.**
Payment of earnings without administration, **29:31D.**
Taxation.
See TAXATION.
Tenure.
See TENURE AND SENIORITY.
Term of office.
See TERM OF OFFICE.
Testimonial dinners for, prohibition, **268:9A.**

PUBLIC OFFICERS AND EMPLOYEES —Cont'd

Tewksbury hospital.
See TEWKSBURY HOSPITAL.
Time.
See TIME OR DATE.
Towns.
Cities and towns. See within this heading, "Cities and towns."
Trade, freedom, **149:25, 149:180.**
Trades, occupations, and professions, public official or employee engaging in professional activity requiring disclosure of confidential information, **268A:23.**
Traveling expenses.
See TRAVELING EXPENSES.
Trust companies.
Depository for credit union deductions from pay, **149:178B.**
Direct deposit of wages and salaries, **41:41B.**
Trustee process against, **246:32.**
Trusts and trustees, **268A:4 et seq.**
Deferred compensation, investment, **29:64, 35:57, 44:67.**
Unemployment compensation.
See EMPLOYMENT SECURITY.
Union dues, payroll deduction, **180:17A.**
Utilities.
Public utilities department.
See TELECOMMUNICATIONS AND ENERGY DEPARTMENT.
Veterans.
See VETERANS AND VETERANS' ORGANIZATIONS.
Wages, salaries.
See WAGES, SALARIES, AND COMPENSATION.
Widows and widowers.
Surviving spouse. See within this heading, "Surviving spouse."
Witnesses.
See WITNESSES.
Worcester County, group insurance coverage for employees, **32A:2, 32A:8, 32B:1 et seq.**
Workers' compensation.
See WORKERS' COMPENSATION.

PUBLIC OFFICERS AND EMPLOYEES —Cont'd

Youth services department.
See YOUTH SERVICES DEPARTMENT AND MASSACHUSETTS TRAINING SCHOOLS.

PUBLIC OPINION LAW, **53:18-53:22.**

Transmission of record of votes, **54:112.**

PUBLIC PARKS ACT, **45:2 et seq.**

PUBLIC PARTICIPATION COORDINATOR.

Low-level radioactive waste management board, **111H:6.**

PUBLIC PEACE.

Breach of peace and disorderly conduct, **269:1 et seq., 272:38 et seq.**
See BREACH OF PEACE AND DISORDERLY CONDUCT.

PUBLIC POLICY OR INTEREST.

Anti-discrimination laws, formulation of policies to effectuate, **151B:2.**
Civil rights and discrimination.
Age discrimination in employment, **149:24A.**
Anti-discrimination laws, formulation of policies to effectuate, **151B:2.**
Schools, policy concerning racial imbalance, **71:37.**
Controlled dangerous substances, determination of public interest in issuance of registration, **94C:12.**
Crimes.
See CRIMES AND OFFENSES.
Discrimination.
Civil rights and discrimination.
See within this heading, "Civil rights and discrimination."
Dwellings unfit for human habitation, effect of tenant's waiver of benefits provided, **111:127K.**
Elections.
See ELECTIONS.
Foreign states, factors affecting recognition of judgment rendered, **235:23A.**
Income tax.
See INCOME TAX.

PUBLIC POLICY OR
INTEREST —Cont'd
Labor relations and disputes,
150A:1.
Peaceful settlement of industrial
disputes dangerous to public
safety and health, **150B:1.**
Leases.
See LANDLORD AND TENANT.
Minimum wages, **151:1.**
Motor carriers of property, **159B:1.**
Parking facility owner's or
operator's disclaimer of
liability on sign, ticket, or
receipt, as void against public
policy, **231:85M.**
State ballot law commission
having no jurisdiction over,
55B:4.
Summary process to recover land,
validity of lease provision
waiving right to obtain stay of
proceedings, **239:12.**
Underground storage tank
petroleum product cleanup
fund administrative review
board, **21J:8.**
Waiver of interest provisions as
against public policy, **140:90.**

PUBLIC PRINTING.
See PRINTERS AND
PRINTING.

PUBLIC RECORDS.
See RECORDS, REPORTS,
AND RETURNS.

PUBLIC SAFETY
DEPARTMENT, 22:1 et seq.
Advice and advisory bodies,
111:4F.
Air conditioning and refrigeration
systems, inspection, **146:45A.**
Air rifles or BB guns, duties,
269:12B.
Alcoholic liquors, disposition of
forfeited beverages and
containers, **138:51.**
Aldermen and selectmen.
Acting as commission, **41:21,**
41:23.
Appointment of commissioner,
41:101.
Amusements, exhibitions, sports,
and games.
Boxing. See within this heading,
"Boxing."
Sunday, licensing, **136:4.**
Animals fighting, exhibition of,
duties of commissioner,
272:88, 272:89.

PUBLIC SAFETY
DEPARTMENT —Cont'd
Architectural Barriers Board,
22:13A.
Arming of officers and inspectors,
147:2.
Badges of special police officers,
159:92.
Blasting operations, examination
and certification of competency
of persons conducting,
148:20B.
Blood analysis to determine
percentage of alcohol,
chemist's certificate as prima
facie evidence, **90:24.**
Boiler Rules Board, **22:10,**
146:2-146:4.
See STEAM BOILERS AND
ENGINES.
Boxing.
Commissioner as member of
boxers' fund board, **6:99.**
State Boxing Commission, **22:5,**
22:12.
Boxing, amateur boxing and
sparring matches, **147:35A.**
Buildings and structures.
Building code of state.
See BUILDING CODE OF
STATE.
"Department" defined under
building inspection law,
143:1.
Enforcement of laws and
regulations, **143:59.**
Inspectors, **22:6.**
Interference with commissioner,
143:50.
Petition to restrain illegal
construction or alteration,
143:57.
Public buildings, **22:4A.**
State house, means of egress
and fire protection, **143:2B.**
Bungee jumping, regulation of,
22:11B, 149:129D.
Bureau of Pipefitters and
Refrigeration Technicians,
22:10A.
Central register for missing
children.
See CENTRAL REGISTER FOR
MISSING CHILDREN.
Certificate of inspection of
hospitals, institutions for
unwed mothers or clinics,
111:51.
Charitable homes for the aged,
duties of commissioner,
111:71.

PUBLIC SAFETY
DEPARTMENT —Cont'd
Chemical analysis.
See ANALYSIS AND
ANALYSTS.
Chief of inspections.
Board of Boiler Rules, member,
22:10.
Board of Elevator Regulations,
member, **22:11.**
Civil service, **22:4A.**
Compensation, **22:4A.**
State board of building
regulations and standards,
members, **143:93.**
Civil service.
See CIVIL SERVICE.
Commissioner, **22:1, 41:101.**
Compensation.
Salaries and compensation. See
within this heading,
"Salaries and
compensation."
Compressed air tanks, inspection,
146:34, 146:36, 146:38.
Confiscated weapons, disposition,
269:10, 269:11B, 269:11C,
269:12B.
Criminal conviction of felony as
bar to appointment, **22:6A.**
Criminal history systems board,
commissioner as member,
6:168.
Criminal identification, powers
and duties, **127:23, 127:25,**
127:29.
Criminal justice committee,
commissioner as member,
6:156.
Criminal justice training council,
commissioner's membership,
6:116.
Death benefits.
Employees, **22:7B.**
Officers killed in line of duty,
32:100A.
Deputy commissioner, **22:5.**
Detectives.
Private detectives and
investigators. See within
this heading, "Private
detectives and
investigators."
Discharge from office of inspector,
147:3.
District engineering inspectors,
22:6.
Divisions, **22:3.**
Elevator Appeals Board,
appointment of persons,
22:11A.

PUBLIC SAFETY DEPARTMENT —Cont'd

Elevator operators, licenses, **143:71G.**

Elevator Regulations Board, membership and duties, **22:11.**

Emergency commission relating to necessaries of life, commissioner as member, **23:9H.**

Emergency medical care advisory board, membership of commissioner, **111C:7.**

Employees.
  Officers and employees. See within this heading, "Officers and employees."

Engineers and firemen, regulation of examination procedure, **146:64.**

Establishment, **22:1.**

Ethics commission, **268B:2.**

Examination, inspection, or investigation, **22:4A, 147:1 et seq.**
  Air conditioning and refrigeration systems, **146:45A.**
  Blasting operations, **148:20B.**
  Boilers and pressure vessels, **146:6.**
  Buildings and structures. See within this heading, "Buildings and structures."
  Chief of inspections. See within this heading, "Chief of inspections".
  Compressed air tanks, **146:34, 146:36, 146:38.**
  Districts, **22:4A.**
  Engineers and firemen, regulation of examination procedures, **146:64.**
  Inspection division. See within this heading, "Inspection division."
  Inspectors. See within this heading, "Inspectors."
  Labor disputes, investigation, **150B:3.**
  Lighting of factories and workshops investigation, **149:116.**
  Loans, record books, **140:87.**
  Mechanical amusement devices, **140:205A.**
  Medicolegal investigations committee, commissioner as member, **6:184.**
  Oil burner technicians, **146:67A.**

PUBLIC SAFETY DEPARTMENT —Cont'd

Examination, inspection, or investigation —Cont'd
  Private detectives and investigators. See within this heading, "Private detectives and investigators."
  Secondhand motor vehicles, inspection of premises for sale, **140:66.**

Executive office.
  Agencies within, **6A:18.**
  Architectural Barriers Board, membership, **22:13A.**
  Building Code Appeals Board, **143:100.**
  Committee on criminal justice, membership of secretary, **6:156.**
  Establishment, **6A:2.**
  Fire service commissions established, **6:165B.**
  Mentally retarded persons, reports and plans on evaluation of residential facilities, **19:19.**
  Secretary, **6A:3 et seq.**
  State board of building regulations and standards, **143:93-143:95.**
    See BUILDING REGULATIONS AND STANDARDS, STATE BOARD.

Expenses and expenditures, **22:7, 22:7A.**

Explosions.
  See EXPLOSIONS AND EXPLOSIVES.

Eye protective devices worn while attending classes in public schools, requirements, **71:55C.**

Felony, fingerprints and photographs of persons accused of to be forwarded to commissioner, **263:1A.**

Fingerprinting of persons arrested for commission of felony, **263:1A.**

Firearms.
  See FIREARMS AND WEAPONS.

Fire departments.
  See FIRE DEPARTMENTS.

Fires.
  See FIRES AND FIRE PREVENTION.

Fire services department.
  See FIRE SERVICES DEPARTMENT.

PUBLIC SAFETY DEPARTMENT —Cont'd

Fraud and deceit, **22C:68.**

Fraudulent claims board, member, **26:8B.**

Fuel.
  See UNDERGROUND STORAGE TANK PETROLEUM PRODUCT CLEANUP FUND.

Governor and council, approval of personnel, **22:6.**

Governor's highway safety committee, membership of commissioner, **90A:1.**

Highways and streets, **22:7B.**

Holidays and Sundays, permit for activities, **136:4, 136:14.**

Hospitals, institutions for unwed mothers, or clinics, certificate of inspection, **111:57.**

Infernal machine, notice of seizure, **266:102A.**

Inflammables.
  Expert assistance, employment to aid in enforcement of laws, **148:11.**
  Laboratory maintained to aid in enforcement of laws, **148:11.**
  Regulations, **148:9, 148:23.**
  Reports to public safety department, **148:9, 148:16.**

Inspection.
  Examination, inspection, or investigation. See within this heading, "Examination, inspection, or investigation."

Inspection division, **22:4A.**
  Board of boiler rules, membership, **22:10.**
  Chief of inspections. See within this heading, "Chief of inspections."
  Classification of state offices and positions, **30:50.**
  Duties of commissioner, **147:1.**
  Inspector general. See within this heading, "Inspector general."
  Inspectors. See within this heading, "Inspectors."

Inspector general.
  Elective offices, right to hold, **12A:4.**
  Membership of inspector general council, **12A:3.**
  Witnesses, compelling testimony, **12A:7.**

Inspectors, **22:4A, 22:8, 22:11, 147:2.**
  Arming, **147:2.**

PUBLIC SAFETY
    DEPARTMENT —Cont'd
Inspectors —Cont'd
  Chief of inspections. See within
    this heading, "Chief of
    inspections."
  Discharge from office, **147:3.**
  Expenses, **22:7, 22:7A.**
  Inspector general. See within
    this heading, "Inspector
    general."
  Qualifications, **22:6.**
  Review of actions, **22:4A.**
  Rewards received by inspectors,
    penalty, **147:3.**
Insurance companies, prosecution
  for violations, **175:3A.**
Investigation.
  Examination, inspection, or
    investigation. See within
    this heading, "Examination,
    inspection, or investigation."
Investigators.
  Private detectives and
    investigators. See within
    this heading, "Private
    detectives and
    investigators."
Killed in the line of duty, benefits,
  32:100A.
Labor disputes, investigation,
  150B:3.
Licenses and permits.
  Elevator licenses, **143:71G.**
  Exhibitions, permits for special,
    143:82.
  Hospitals, institutions for unwed
    mothers or clinics, duties in
    connection with licensing,
    111:51.
  Motion pictures, special licenses
    and permits, **143:82, 143:85.**
  Private detectives and
    investigators,
    147:23-147:26.
  Sundays and holidays, activities,
    136:4, 136:14.
  Warehousemen, **105:1, 105:2A,**
    105:6.
Lighting of factories and
  workshops, investigation,
  149:116.
Line of duty death benefits,
  32:100A.
Loans, inspection of record books,
  140:87.
Mechanical amusement devices
  such as Ferris wheels,
  carousels, etc., certificate of
  examination and insurance by
  liability carrier furnished,
  140:205A.

PUBLIC SAFETY
    DEPARTMENT —Cont'd
Medical expenses of officers and
  inspectors, **22:7A.**
Medicolegal investigations
  committee, commissioner as
  member, **6:184.**
Metropolitan area planning
  council, membership of
  commissioner, **40B:24.**
Motion pictures.
  Exhibitions, permits for special,
    143:82.
  Regulations and rules, **143:73.**
  Special licenses, **143:85.**
Motorcycle lessors, duties of
  commissioner, **90:32H.**
Motor transportation of
  merchandise on holidays,
  permit, **136:14.**
Motor vehicles.
  Auto theft strike force,
    175A:10A.
  Inspection of premises for sale of
    secondhand, **140:66.**
Nursing or rest homes,
  regulations, **143:3Q.**
Oaths, **22:7, 22:8.**
  Officers and inspectors, oath of
    office, **22:8.**
  Witnesses, summoning and
    administration of oath,
    233:8.
Officers and employees, **22:6,**
  147:2.
  Chief of inspection. See within
    this heading, "Chief of
    inspections."
  Confidentiality of addresses and
    phone numbers of, **66:10.**
  Discharge or removal from office,
    147:3.
  Inspector general. See within
    this heading, "Inspector
    general."
  Inspectors. See within this
    heading, "Inspectors."
  Killed in the line of duty
    benefits, **32:100A.**
  Powers and duties, **147:2.**
  Revolvers and clubs, authority
    for carrying, **147:2.**
  Rewards, penalty for receiving,
    147:3.
  State police.
    See STATE POLICE.
Oil burner technicians,
  examination for certification,
  146:67A.
Pensions.
  See RETIREMENT SYSTEMS
    AND PENSIONS.

PUBLIC SAFETY
    DEPARTMENT —Cont'd
Permits.
  Licenses and permits. See
    within this heading,
    "Licenses and permits."
Physical fitness standards, public
  employees, **31:61A.**
Pipefitters' and refrigeration
  technicians' bureau, **22:10A.**
Pipelines, regulations, **40:43A.**
Plumbing, specifications, of hot
  water tanks used, **142:17.**
Police.
  See POLICE.
Power lawnmowers, establishment
  of specifications and
  requirements for safety
  devices, **147:56.**
Pressure vessels and boilers,
  inspection, **146:6.**
Private detectives and
  investigators.
  Licensing, **147:23-147:26.**
  Names, approval, **147:25.**
  Weapons and equipment,
    approval, **147:29.**
Public buildings, restrictions on
  authority of commissioner,
  22:4A.
Public officers and employees.
  Officers and employees. See
    within this heading,
    "Officers and employees."
Qualifications of personnel, **22:6.**
Radiation protection advisory
  council, membership of
  commissioner, **111:4F.**
Raffles and bazaars, authority as
  to conduct, **271:7A.**
Recreational tramway board,
  members, **143:71H.**
Refrigeration systems, inspection,
  146:45A.
Reports.
  Division of Subversive Activities,
    reports, **22:3.**
  Duties, **147:1.**
  Mentally retarded persons,
    reports and plans on
    evaluation of residential
    facilities, **19:19.**
  Stabbings, treatment, **112:12A.**
  Underground storage tank
    petroleum product cleanup
    fund, **21J:2.**
Retirement systems.
  See RETIREMENT SYSTEMS
    AND PENSIONS.
Review of actions of inspectors by
  commissioner, **22:4A.**

PUBLIC SAFETY
  DEPARTMENT —Cont'd
Salaries and compensation.
  Chief of inspections, **22:4A.**
  Commissioner, **22:2.**
  Death or injury, compensation,
    22:7B.
  Officers and inspectors, **22:7.**
  Skin divers, **22:6.**
Search and seizure.
  Disposition by commissioner of
    property seized under
    search warrant, **276:3.**
  Infernal machine, notice of
    seizure, **266:102A.**
Secondhand motor vehicles,
  inspection of premises for sale,
  140:66.
Secretary.
  Boxing commission, duties,
    22:12.
  Capitol police.
    See POLICE.
  Criminal history systems board,
    member, **6:168.**
  Deputy commissioner to serve,
    22:5.
  Duties of, **22:5.**
  Fire training council and
    firefighting academy,
    6:164-6:165A.
Selectmen.
  Aldermen and selectmen. See
    within this heading,
    "Aldermen and selectmen."
Skin divers, employment and
  compensation, **22:6.**
State Boxing Commission, **22:12.**
State building code.
  See BUILDING CODE OF
    STATE.
State Ethics Commission,
  personnel and other assistants
  made available, **268B:2.**
State house, means of egress and
  fire protection, **143:2B.**
State police.
  See STATE POLICE.
Steam boilers, boiler rules board
  for, **22:10, 146:2-146:4.**
  See STEAM BOILERS AND
    ENGINES.
Subversive Activities Division,
  duties, **22:3.**
Sundays and holidays, licensing of
  activities, **136:4, 136:14.**
Survivors of officers or inspectors,
  compensation, **22:7B.**
Term of office of commissioner,
  22:2.

PUBLIC SAFETY
  DEPARTMENT —Cont'd
Underground storage tank
  petroleum product cleanup
  fund.
  See UNDERGROUND
    STORAGE TANK
    PETROLEUM PRODUCT
    CLEANUP FUND.
Vessels dismantled, duties,
  91:46-91:49.
Veterans status as affecting
  promotions, **31:26.**
Wages.
  Salaries and compensation. See
    within this heading,
    "Salaries and
    compensation."
Warehousemen, licensing by
  department of public safety,
  105:1, 105:2A, 105:6.
Weapons.
  See FIREARMS AND
    WEAPONS.
Witnesses.
  Inspector general, compelling
    testimony, **12A:7.**
  Summoning and administration
    of oath, **233:8.**

PUBLIC SALE.
Auctions.
  See AUCTIONS AND
    AUCTIONEERS.
Executors.
  See EXECUTORS AND
    ADMINISTRATORS.
Judicial sales.
  See JUDICIAL SALES.
Self-storage facilities, enforcement
  of operator's lien, **105A:4.**

PUBLIC SCHOOLS.
Schools.
  See SCHOOLS AND
    EDUCATION.

PUBLIC SECURITIES.
See BONDS AND
  DEBENTURES.

PUBLIC SERVICE
  COMPANIES.
See TELECOMMUNICATIONS
  AND ENERGY
  DEPARTMENT.

PUBLIC SERVICE
  CONTRACTS.
Governmental units, authority,
  40:4A.

PUBLIC SERVICE
  SCHOLARSHIP
  PROGRAM, 15A:7.

PUBLIC SQUARES.
See PARKS AND
  RESERVATIONS.
PUBLIC TELEPHONES.
See TELEPHONE AND
  TELEGRAPH COMPANIES.
PUBLIC TELEVISION.
See EDUCATIONAL
  TELEVISION.
PUBLIC TRANSPORTATION.
See TRANSPORTATION.
PUBLIC TRIAL.
See TRIAL OR HEARINGS.
PUBLIC UTILITIES
  DEPARTMENT.
Energy facilities siting division
  transferred to
  telecommunications and
  energy department, **25:12N,**
  164:69H.
Generally.
  See TELECOMMUNICATIONS
    AND ENERGY
    DEPARTMENT.
Inquests in cases of accidental
  death upon conveyance
  regulated by, **38:8, 38:9.**
PUBLIC UTILITIES SEIZURE
  ACT, 150B:1 et seq.
PUBLIC WATER SUPPLY,
  40:38-40:42, 165:1-165:11C.
See WATERWORKS AND
  WATER SUPPLY.
PUBLIC WAYS.
Defined, **4:7.**
Highways and streets.
  See HIGHWAYS AND
    STREETS.
PUBLIC WELFARE
  ADMINISTRATORS'
  ASSOCIATION OF
  MASSACHUSETTS.
Health and welfare commission
  advisory committee,
  membership, **6:127.**
PUBLIC WELFARE AND
  WELFARE DEPARTMENT,
  18:1 et seq., 18B:1 et seq.
Department renamed department
  of transitional assistance,
  18:1.
Welfare and social services.
  See WELFARE AND SOCIAL
    SERVICES.
PUBLIC WORKS, 16:1 et seq.,
  81:1 et seq., 149:25 et seq.,
  149:44A et seq.
Abandonment or discontinuance of
  state highways, **81:5.**
County commissioners' consent
  required, **81:8.**

PUBLIC WORKS —Cont'd

Abandonment or discontinuance of state highways —Cont'd
Land or rights taken, **81:12.**
Acceptance of gifts of easements for landscaping of state highways, **81:13A.**
Actions for labor performed, **149:28.**
Contractors' bonds, **149:29.**
Limitation of actions.
See LIMITATION OF ACTIONS.
Additions, included in term construction, **149:27D.**
Administration commissioner, reports, **16:5.**
Administrative services division, **16:2.**
Advancement for work on non-state owned lands, **81:7I.**
Advertising.
Outdoor advertising. See within this heading, "Outdoor advertising."
State highway construction proposals, advertisements, **81:8.**
Advice to local officers as to public ways, **81:1.**
Air rights over highways, provisions as to leasing, **81:7L.**
Aldermen.
See ALDERMEN AND SELECTMEN.
Annual report of commission, **16:5.**
Appeal.
See APPEAL AND REVIEW.
Appointments.
See APPOINTMENTS.
Apportionment of construction of state highways among counties, **81:8.**
Apprentices, employment, **149:26, 149:27.**
Aquatic nuisances, exemption from requirement of license to apply chemicals for control, **111:5E.**
Architects.
Life cycle cost estimates for, filing, **149:44M.**
Selection of designers, **7:38A½.**
Artificial ponds of coastal waters, plans, **130:28.**
Atomic energy, studies and recommendations, **6:91.**
Attorneys at law.
Chief counsel, **16:4.**
Commission, appointment of hearing examiner, **16:5.**

PUBLIC WORKS —Cont'd

Beaches.
Control and supervision, **21:4, 91:11.**
Transfer of control and operating funds to division of forests and parks, **132A:10.**
Bids.
See BIDS AND BIDDING.
Bikeways program, **90E:1 to 90E:3.**
Billboards and other outdoor advertising, authority to discontinue flashing lights, **85:9A.**
Board of contract appeals, commission, **16:5.**
Boat trailers, exemption from permit, **90:19.**
Bonds and undertakings.
Bids.
See BIDS AND BIDDING.
Commission, **16:1.**
Contractor's bond, **30:39A-30:39E, 30:40, 43:29, 149:28, 149:29.**
See CONSTRUCTION CONTRACTS AND WORK.
Foreign surety company, resident agent, **175:157.**
Town superintendent of public works, **41:69E.**
Transportation charges. See within this heading, "Transportation charges."
Borrowing by cities or towns for useful public works projects, limitation, **44:1.**
Boston.
Harbor.
See BOSTON HARBOR.
Meetings, **16:5.**
Metropolitan area planning council, commissioner as member, **40B:24.**
Boundaries.
State boundaries. See within this heading, "State boundaries."
Town boundaries, duties, **42:7-42:9.**
Bridges.
Appointment of bridge engineer, **16:4.**
Highways, powers concerning bridges, **85:35.**
Licensing of bridges crossing pond or outlet, **91:13.**
Brush and shrubbery, clearance, **81:13.**

PUBLIC WORKS —Cont'd

Buildings.
Construction contracts.
See CONSTRUCTION CONTRACTS AND WORK.
Bureaus, sections and officers, establishment, **16:3.**
Capital projects, bidding procedure for, **149:44A-149:44J.**
See BIDS AND BIDDING.
Carriers.
Dump truck operations, bond, **30:39A-30:39E.**
Notice of hearing upon certificate of public convenience and necessity, **159B:3.**
Powers, **90:31A, 159A:13, 159B:20.**
Cattle passes, granting easements in state highways, **81:7D.**
Certificates and certification.
Applications for certification, **149:44D.**
Certificate of eligibility and update statement accompanying bids, **149:44D.**
Civil service, certification of persons for positions, **31:66.**
Laying out of state highway, **81:5, 81:13.**
Notice of hearing upon certificate of public convenience and necessity, **159B:3.**
Public way, effect of certificate of particular way as being, **233:79F.**
Change orders, **7:42E-7:42I.**
Chauffeurs, employment, **149:26, 149:27.**
Chemicals for control of aquatic nuisances, exemption from requirement of license to apply, **111:5E.**
Chief counsel, **16:4.**
Chief engineer and deputies, **16:4.**
Cities and towns.
Actions against, **149:28.**
Advancements by public works department for work on property of state highways, **81:7I.**
Advice to local officers on public ways, **81:1.**
Application of sums paid by Commonwealth as contribution towards costs of project, **44:53B.**

PUBLIC WORKS —Cont'd
Cities and towns —Cont'd
Apportionment of monies among certain cities and towns, authority, **44:7.**
Board of public works, **41:69C-41:69F.**
Selectmen acting, **41:21, 41:23.**
Borrowing within debt limits for public works projects, **44:1, 44:7, 44:8.**
Boundaries of towns, duties, **42:7-42:9.**
Clerks.
City and town clerks. See within this heading, "City and town clerks."
Contracts for construction, reconstruction, alteration, remodeling, or repair, or for purchase of material, **30:39M.**
Contracts with state for construction of public works, **40:4D.**
Debt limitations, **44:1, 44:7, 44:8.**
Eminent domain for streets in cities and towns, **81:29A.**
Great ponds, approval of municipal regulations, **131:45.**
Information to state department, **81:2.**
Joint enterprises between, **40:4A.**
Laying out, alteration, or relocation of highways, reimbursement of cities and towns, **44:6, 44:6A.**
Meetings of public works board, **16:5, 41:69C, 41:69F.**
Notice to local officers to make repairs to ways, **81:25.**
Parking, approval of specifications for municipal off-street parking areas, **44:7.**
Pavement markings, installation by cities and towns, **89:1, 89:4.**
Payment to state, **40:4D, 44:7, 44:8.**
Reimbursement for services to other governmental units, **40:4A.**
Reports to department by local officials, **81:2.**
Small towns, determination of contributions for repairs to highways, **81:29.**

PUBLIC WORKS —Cont'd
Cities and towns —Cont'd
Superintendent of public works, **41:69E.**
Superintendent of streets, approval of appointment for two or more towns, **41:67.**
Taxes on public land, reimbursement of cities and towns for loss, **58:13.**
Town meetings of public works board, **16:5, 41:69C, 41:69F.**
Transportation charges on public works projects, contractor's bond to secure, **30:39A-30:39E.**
Citizens' preferences for employment, **149:26, 149:179A.**
City and town clerks.
Filing statement of amount due for labor, **149:28.**
Transportation charges for materials used in public construction, **149:29.**
Civil service, **16:1, 16:4, 31:66.**
Exemption of employees, **31:48.**
Classification of jobs by commissioner of labor and workforce development, **149:27.**
Appeal, **149:27A.**
Coastal waters, **130:28, 130:105.**
Collective bargaining as affecting minimum wage rates, **149:26.**
Commission, **16:1.**
Annual report, **16:5.**
Appointment of hearing examiner, **16:5.**
Board of contract appeals, **16:5.**
Contracts, approval, **16:5.**
Meetings, **16:5.**
Members' qualifications, **16:1.**
Powers and duties, **16:5.**
Rules and regulations, **16:5.**
Secretary, **16:5.**
Commissioner of administration, reports, **16:5.**
Commissioner of public works.
Appointment of employees, **16:4.**
Approval or disapproval of excess motor vehicle weight permits, **85:30A.**
Bikeways, powers and duties, **90E:2.**
Board of contract appeals, commissioner, **16:5.**
Bureaus and offices, establishment, **16:3.**
Concurrence of associate commissioners, **16:5.**

PUBLIC WORKS —Cont'd
Commissioner of public works —Cont'd
Description of organization, preparation, **16:3.**
Employees, appointment and removal, **16:4.**
Highway fund, duties, **58:18B, 81:31, 81:32.**
Highway safety committee, members, **90A:1.**
Metropolitan area planning council, member, **40B:24.**
Outdoor advertising board, member, **16:14.**
Powers and duties, **16:2-16:4.**
Revocation of motor vehicle weight permit, **90:19D.**
Compensation.
Salaries. See within this heading, "Salaries."
Condemnation.
Eminent domain. See within this heading, "Eminent domain."
Conduct of public officials.
See CONDUCT OF PUBLIC OFFICIALS AND EMPLOYEES.
Conduits, granting easements in state highways, **81:7D.**
Conflict of interest of public officials.
See CONDUCT OF PUBLIC OFFICIALS AND EMPLOYEES.
Connecticut River, control over, **91:10.**
Consent.
See CONSENT.
Construction contracts.
See CONSTRUCTION CONTRACTS AND WORK.
Contribution toward costs of useful projects, **44:53B, 81:29.**
Conveyances.
Deeds and conveyances. See within this heading, "Deeds and conveyances."
Co-operative engineering students' program, **16:4B.**
Counties.
Apportionment of state highway construction among, **81:8.**
Consent of commissioners to discontinuance of state highway, **81:12.**
Construction contracts.
See CONSTRUCTION CONTRACTS AND WORK.

PUBLIC WORKS —Cont'd
Counties —Cont'd
Contracts for construction, reconstruction, alteration, remodeling, or repair, or for purchase of material, **30:39M.**
Custody of records, **16:1.**
Dams.
See DAMS AND RESERVOIRS.
Deaths in which motor vehicles involved, notice, **38:8.**
Debarment, public construction, **7:38H.**
Decrees.
Judgments, orders, and decrees. See within this heading, "Judgments, orders, and decrees."
Deeds and conveyances.
Certain lands, **81:7E, 91:2.**
Executed by department, **81:7E.**
Registry of deeds, filing plan of land taken for state highways abandoned, **81:12.**
United States, land conveyed, **1:6.**
Definitions under state departments and employees law, **30:39R.**
Demolition work.
Contractor, prompt payment, **30:39K.**
Prevailing wages, payment, **149:27D.**
Subcontractors, payments, **30:39F.**
Departments, **16:1 et seq., 81:1 et seq.**
Deputy chief engineers, **16:4.**
Description of organization, duties of commissioner, **16:3.**
Design services, contracts, **7:30A½ et seq.**
Destruction of property.
Demolition work. See within this heading, "Demolition work."
Digging up state highways, regulation, **82:21.**
Discontinuance of state highway.
Abandonment or discontinuance. See within this heading, "Abandonment or discontinuance of state highways."
Discounts.
Rebate. See within this heading, "Rebate."
Discretion in expenditure of funds appropriated for particular way, **81:24.**

PUBLIC WORKS —Cont'd
Discrimination in employment, **272:98B.**
Dispensation of state aid to keep highways open in winter, **84:11.**
District highway engineer, appointment, **16:4.**
Divisions of departments, **16:2.**
Drainage of highways, **83:4.**
Drawbridges, regulation of passage of vessels through, **85:26.**
Dredged material, transportation and dumping in tidewater, supervision, **91:52-91:56.**
Driveways opening on state highways, permit for location or alteration, **81:21.**
Dumping or placing materials upon state highways, regulation, **81:21.**
Dump truck operations, bond to secure charges, **30:39A-30:39E.**
Easements.
Acceptance of gifts of, for landscaping on state highways, **81:13A.**
Limited access ways, taking easements, **81:7C.**
Outside of location of state highways, taking, **81:7A-81:7B.**
Public utilities companies, acquisition for relocating facilities, **81:7G.**
Slope easement, taking of by eminent domain, **81:7B.**
State highways, granting for certain purposes, **81:7D.**
Wires, taking easement for by eminent domain, **81:7D.**
Eminent domain.
Entry on land, damages, **1:9.**
Federal Uniform Relocation Assistance and Real Property Acquisition Policies Act, public works department to comply, **81:7J.**
Harbor improvements, **91:5.**
Relocation payments to persons displaced by proceedings, **81:7J.**
Road materials, land taken, **81:11.**
State highways, **81:7C, 81:7D.**
Abandonment of land or rights taken, **81:12.**
Cities and towns, taking land for streets, **81:29A.**

PUBLIC WORKS —Cont'd
Eminent domain —Cont'd
State highways —Cont'd
Connecting ways, alteration or relocation, **81:7A.**
Damages for taking, **81:7A, 81:11.**
Road materials, supply, **81:11.**
Employees and officers of department.
Appointment and removal, **16:3, 16:4.**
Chauffeurs, **149:26, 149:27.**
Citizens, preference for employment, **149:26.**
Civil service. See within this heading, "Civil service."
Commissioner. See within this heading, "Commissioner of public works."
Engineers. See within this heading, "Engineers."
Entry on land by. See within this heading, "Entry on land by officers, agents, or employees."
Mechanics, **81:3.**
Retirement systems.
See RETIREMENT SYSTEMS AND PENSIONS.
Salaries. See within this heading, "Salaries."
Secretary, **16:5.**
Transfer to department, **16:1.**
Veterans, preference for in employment, **149:26.**
Workers' compensation for police employed by contractor on Department project **152:1.**
Employment on public work projects, **149:25 et seq.**
Employment security, supplementary unemployment benefit fund payments to be included in established wage rate on public construction projects, **149:26, 149:27, 149:29.**
Encroachments upon state highway, removal, **81:22.**
Energy resources executive office.
See ENERGY RESOURCES EXECUTIVE OFFICE.
Engineers.
See ENGINEERS AND SURVEYORS.
Entry on land by officers, agents, or employees, **1:8, 1:9, 81:7F.**
Junkyards, public works commissioner's authority to enter, **140B:5, 140B:6.**

PUBLIC WORKS —Cont'd

Environmental management department.

See ENVIRONMENTAL MANAGEMENT DEPARTMENT.

Environmental Protection Department's powers, **40:4, 44:7, 44:8.**

Equity action to assert claim for labor and materials, **149:29.**

Ethics commission, employees' duty to file, **268A:14.**

Evidence.

Department hearing examiner's power to take testimony under oath, **16:5.**

Statement of claim under contractors' bond, **149:29.**

Substantial evidence rule, **30:39J.**

Examination, inspection, and investigation.

Applications for certification and evaluations as public records, **149:44D.**

Atomic energy, studies and recommendations, **6:91.**

Books, documents, papers, or records of contractor or subcontractors, examination by commissioner of asset management and maintenance, **30:39R.**

Deaths involving motor vehicles, **38:8.**

Hearings. See within this heading, "Hearings."

Public ways, investigations, **81:1.**

Records and statements kept or filed as public records, **30:39R.**

State boundaries, **1:4.**

Excavations.

Public ways, permits, **81:21.**

Shoring and bracing, **149:129A.**

Exclusion of persons or vehicles from state highways, power, **90:18.**

Expenditures.

Funds appropriated for particular way, **81:24.**

Injunction against unlawful expenditures, **29:63.**

Limitation on expenditures for land for road materials, **81:11.**

Outdoor recreation projects, **21:1.**

PUBLIC WORKS —Cont'd

Fair competition in bidding on public works contracts, **149:44A-149:44J.**

See BIDS AND BIDDING.

False entries concerning, **266:67C.**

False reports to, penalty, **268:6.**

Federal Uniform Relocation Assistance and Real Property Acquisition Policies Act, compliance, **81:7J.**

Fee for filing of claim for labor and materials, **262:34.**

Fines and penalties.

Accepting rebate, refund, or gratuity from wages, **149:27.**

Bidding procedure violation, **149:44J.**

Classification of employees, violation, **149:27, 149:27C.**

Construction contracts.

See CONSTRUCTION CONTRACTS AND WORK.

Discrimination in employment, **272:98B.**

False entries, **266:67C.**

Preferences in employment, violations, **149:27, 149:27C.**

Transportation charges on public works, taking rebate or refund, **30:39E.**

Wages, violations, **149:27, 149:27C, 149:27F.**

Flood plains and seacoasts, orders, for protection, **131:40.**

Floors, prevailing wage law as applicable to installation, **149:27D.**

Foreign corporations, work, **30:39L.**

General court, reports and recommendations, **16:5.**

Geoscience data of the Commonwealth, duties, **81:1.**

Gifts of easements for landscaping on state highways, acceptance, **81:13A.**

Governor.

See GOVERNOR.

Governor's council.

Bonds, discharge or substitution, **30:40.**

Department, approval of purchase of land, **81:3.**

Grading of state highways, contracts, **81:8.**

Gravel or fill, transportation of to or from public works projects as included in list of public works jobs, **149:27.**

PUBLIC WORKS —Cont'd

Great ponds.

Lakes. See within this heading, "Lakes."

Harbors, **91:10.**

Agreements with soil conservation service for improvement, **91:11.**

Boston harbor.

See BOSTON HARBOR.

Development and establishment of harbor plans, **91:9A.**

Improvements, **91:5, 91:9A, 91:11.**

Report of violations by harbormaster, **102:27.**

Health and welfare plans, wages as affected, **149:26, 149:27, 149:27H.**

Hearings.

Examiner, **16:5.**

State highway, hearing upon laying out, **81:5.**

Witnesses. See within this heading, "Witnesses."

Heavy vehicles and those likely to injure highways, regulated, **85:30, 85:30A, 90:19D.**

High-accident locations, duties as to assistance to eliminate, **90:33B.**

Highway fund, duties of public works commissioner with regard, **58:18B, 81:31, 81:32.**

Highways.

See HIGHWAYS AND STREETS.

Historic sites and scenery adjacent to federal-aid highways, preservation, **81:13B.**

Horse trailers, exemption from permit, **90:19.**

Hours of labor.

See HOURS OF LABOR OR SERVICES.

Ice.

Snow and ice. See within this heading, "Snow and ice."

Illumination of state highways, **81:20A.**

Industrial development financing authority, powers, **40D:7.**

Injunctions against unlawful contracts or expenditures, **29:63, 40:53.**

Inland wetlands, notice of hearings on and effect of orders regulating, **131:40A.**

Inquests into deaths involving motor vehicles, notice, **38:8.**

PUBLIC WORKS —Cont'd
Inspection or investigation.
    Examination. See within this
        heading, "Examination,
        inspection, and
        investigation."
Interest of public officers.
    See CONDUCT OF PUBLIC
        OFFICIALS AND
        EMPLOYEES.
Interest on sums due contractors,
    rate, **30:39G.**
Investigation.
    Examination, inspection, and
        investigation. See within
        this heading, "Examination,
        inspection, and
        investigation."
Islands, control over, **91:2.**
Joint enterprises between cities,
    towns, and districts, **40:4A.**
Judgments, orders, and decrees.
    Change orders, **7:42E-7:42I.**
    Subcontractor's claim or security
        for payment of labor,
        judgment in equity action to
        enforce, **149:29.**
Junkyards, entry, **140B:5, 140B:6.**
Labor.
    Employees and officers. See
        within this heading,
        "Employees and officers of
        department."
Labor and workforce development
    department.
    Wage determinations.
        Trucks and other equipment
            for use on public works,
            determination of
            operators' wages, **149:27F.**
Lakes.
    Approval of municipal
        regulations as to great
        ponds, **131:45.**
    Bridges crossing pond or outlet
        to be licensed, **91:13.**
    Islands in great ponds, power to
        convey or lease, **91:2.**
    Jurisdiction over ponds, **91:11.**
Landlord and tenant.
    Leasing. See within this
        heading, "Leasing."
Landscaping of state highways,
    81:13A.
Laying out, alteration, or
    relocation of highways.
    Certificate, **81:5, 81:13.**
    Driveways opening on state
        highways, **81:21.**
    Federal aid, **81:29A, 81:30.**
    Generally.
        See HIGHWAYS AND
            STREETS.

PUBLIC WORKS —Cont'd
Laying out, alteration, or
    relocation of highways
    —Cont'd
    Hearing, **81:5.**
    Petition to Commonwealth, **81:4.**
    Reimbursement of cities and
        towns, **44:6, 44:6A.**
    State highway, **81:6, 81:8.**
    Ways connected to state
        highway, alteration, **81:7A.**
    Zoning.
        See ZONING AND
            PLANNING.
Leasing.
    Air rights, **81:7L.**
    Certain lands, **81:7E, 91:2.**
    Harbor facilities, Boston, **91:6.**
    Islands in great ponds, **91:2.**
    Public parking facility, land for
        use, **81:7H.**
Licenses and permits.
    Aquatic nuisances, control,
        111:5E.
    Certain operations on state
        highways, **81:21.**
    Excavations, **81:21.**
    Trailers, **90:8, 90:19, 90:19A,
        90:30.**
    Water, notice of department
        license for structures in or
        over, **91:18.**
    Weight of motor vehicles, **85:30,
        85:30A, 90:19D.**
Life cycle cost estimates, filing,
    149:44M.
Lighting of highways and streets,
    81:20A, 85:2.
Limitation of actions.
    See LIMITATION OF ACTIONS.
Limited access ways.
    See LIMITED ACCESS WAYS.
List or schedule.
    Jobs, list, **149:27.**
    Wages, schedule, **149:27.**
Loss of taxes on public land,
    reimbursement of cities and
    towns, **58:13.**
Lowlands.
    See LOWLANDS AND
        SWAMPS.
Machinery, management and
    maintenance, **81:3.**
Maintenance.
    Repairs and maintenance. See
        within this heading,
        "Repairs and maintenance."
Majority action by commissioners,
    16:5.
Manufacture and purchase of road
    machinery, **81:3.**

PUBLIC WORKS —Cont'd
Maps, plats, and surveys.
    Preparation and sale of maps,
        81:1.
    Topographical survey, authority,
        91:33.
Markers, lights, traffic signals,
    etc., on highways, **85:2 et seq.**
Materials and supplies.
    Bond of contractor.
        See CONSTRUCTION
            CONTRACTS AND
            WORK.
    Fee for filing of claim for labor
        and materials, **262:34.**
    Purchase, **7:23A, 81:3, 81:11.**
    Road materials, taking of land,
        81:11.
    Transportation charges for
        materials used in
        construction, claim, **149:29.**
Mechanics' liens prohibited, **254:6,
    254:31.**
Mechanics, power to employ, **81:3.**
Meeting.
    Public meeting to be held
        annually, **81:1.**
    Public works commission,
        meetings, **16:5, 41:69C,
        41:69F.**
Mental health department
    facilities, construction and
    maintenance of roads on
    grounds, **19:1, 19B:1.**
Merrimack River, control over,
    91:10.
Metropolitan area planning
    council, membership, **40B:24.**
Mineral resources, exploration for
    and extraction of from coastal
    waters for public purposes,
    21:54.
Minimum wage rates,
    149:26-149:27D.
Mosquito control and other
    projects, effect of actions by
    environmental management
    department regarding scenic
    and recreational rivers and
    streams, **21:17B.**
Motor carriers.
    Carriers. See within this
        heading, "Carriers."
Motor vehicles.
    See MOTOR VEHICLES.
Municipalities.
    Cities and towns. See within
        this heading, "Cities and
        towns."
Notice.
    Annual public meeting, **81:1.**

PUBLIC WORKS —Cont'd
Notice —Cont'd
Bids and bidding on public works, notice of invitation to bid, **149:44D.**
Certificate of public convenience and necessity, notice of hearing, **159B:3.**
Commission, notice as to meetings, **16:5.**
Deaths caused by motor vehicles, **38:8.**
Injury by defect in state highway, **81:18.**
License for structures in or over water, notice of department, **91:18.**
Local officers to make repairs to ways, notice, **81:25.**
Posting. See within this heading, "Posting."
Oath.
Hearing examiner, **16:5.**
Statement of amount due for labor, **149:28.**
Obstruction of state highways, removal, **81:14, 81:21.**
Ocean sanctuaries, activities permitted, **132A:16.**
Officers.
Employees and officers of department. See within this heading, "Employees and officers of department."
Orders.
Judgments, orders, and decrees. See within this heading, "Judgments, orders, and decrees."
Outdoor advertising.
Employee of department as member of outdoor advertising board, **16:14.**
Flashing lights on billboards and other outdoor advertising, **85:9A.**
Regulation and control of billboards, signs, and other advertising devices, **16:13.**
Outdoor recreation projects.
Beaches. See within this heading, "Beaches."
Expenditures for extension or enlargement, **21:1.**
Paint.
See PAINT.
Parking.
Lease of land for public parking facility, **81:7H.**
Municipal off-street parking, **44:7.**

PUBLIC WORKS —Cont'd
Pavement markings, installation by cities and towns, **89:1, 89:4.**
Payment, **7:42C, 30:39G.**
Cities' and towns' payment to state for construction, **40:4D, 44:7, 44:8.**
Supplementary unemployment benefit fund payments, inclusion in wage rate on public construction projects, **149:29.**
Payroll records.
Contracts, detailed records of payroll to be kept by contractor, **149:27B.**
Inspection of records, obtaining authorization, **149:27B.**
Pedestrians using ways, rules, **85:2, 90:18A.**
Penalties.
Fines and penalties. See within this heading, "Fines and penalties."
Pension.
See RETIREMENT SYSTEMS AND PENSIONS.
Permits.
Licenses and permits. See within this heading, "Licenses and permits."
Personnel director, appointment, **16:4.**
Petition requesting Commonwealth to lay out and take charge of public way, **81:4.**
Pipes.
See PIPES AND PIPELINES.
Plans.
See PLANS AND SPECIFICATIONS.
Planting trees upon state highways, regulation, **81:13, 81:13A, 81:21.**
Poles, granting easements in state highways, **81:7D.**
Ponds.
Artificial ponds of coastal waters, plans, **130:28.**
Great ponds.
Lakes. See within this heading, "Lakes."
Measuring of ponds, **131:46.**
Ports.
Harbors. See within this heading, "Harbors."
Posting.
Schedule of wages, **149:27.**
Section requiring security for labor and materials, **149:29.**

PUBLIC WORKS —Cont'd
Preference in employment.
Citizens, **149:26.**
Discrimination because of race, color, or religion prohibited, **272:98B.**
Residents.
County, town, or district, **149:26.**
Highway district, **149:27E.**
Veterans, **149:26, 149:27C.**
Preliminary work, "Construction" as including, **149:27D.**
Prevailing wage law as to public works and contracts, **5:1, 7:22, 149:26-149:27D.**
Prisoners, work, **127:49B, 127:84.**
Private property, entry upon for purpose of making surveys, soundings, and drillings, **81:7F.**
Proposals for construction of state highways, duties, **81:8.**
Province lands, powers and duties, **91:25-91:27.**
Public information, appointment of director, **16:4.**
Public utilities companies, acquisition of land or easements for relocating facilities, **81:7G.**
Qualifications of commission members, **16:1.**
Railroads.
See RAILROADS.
Rates.
See RATES AND CHARGES.
Rebate.
Transportation charges on public works projects, rebates forbidden, **30:39C, 30:39E.**
Wages, forbidden, **149:27.**
Records, reports, and returns, **16:1, 16:5.**
Annual report of commission, **16:5.**
Award of contract without public opening of bids in extreme emergency, **149:44A.**
Description of organization, filing, **16:3.**
Employment records, **149:27B.**
Examination of books, documents, papers, or records of contractor or subcontractors by commissioner of asset management and maintenance, **30:39R.**
Fee for filing of claim for material and labor, **262:34.**

PUBLIC WORKS —Cont'd
Records, reports, and returns —Cont'd
General court, reports, **16:5.**
Harbormaster to report violations, **102:27.**
Labor, filing statement of amount due, **149:28.**
Life cycle cost estimates, **149:44M.**
Local officials, information to department, **81:2.**
Marine boundary reports, **1:3.**
Payroll records. See within this heading, "Payroll records."
Recreation projects.
Outdoor recreation projects. See within this heading, "Outdoor recreation projects."
Refunds.
Rebates. See within this heading, "Rebate."
Registry of deeds, filing of plan of land taken for state highways abandoned, **81:12.**
Reimbursement for services for other governmental units, **40:4A, 44:6, 44:6A, 58:13.**
Relocation of highways.
Laying out, alteration, or relocation of highways. See within this heading, "Laying out, alteration, or relocation of highways."
Relocation payments to persons displaced by public acquisition of property, **81:7J.**
Reorganization of department, effect on action or suit, **16:1.**
Repairs and maintenance.
Boundaries of state, **1:4.**
Contracts for repair, **30:39M.**
Contributions by small towns for highway repairs, **81:29.**
Highways.
See HIGHWAYS AND STREETS.
Machinery, **81:3.**
Notice to local officers to make, **81:25.**
Pipeline company's, **164:75C.**
Ports and harbors, **91:9A, 91:11.**
State highways, **81:13-81:22.**
Ways improved by state funds, **81:25.**
Reports.
Records, reports, and returns. See within this heading, "Records, reports, and returns."

PUBLIC WORKS —Cont'd
Residents.
Preference. See within this heading, "Preference in employment."
Retention deducted from payment, **30:39G.**
Retirement systems.
See RETIREMENT SYSTEMS AND PENSIONS.
Right-of-way bureau, appointment of director, **16:4.**
Right to bid, **268A:1.**
Rules and regulations.
Effect of reorganization of department, **16:1.**
Pedestrians, rules, **90:18A.**
Powers and duties of public works commission, **16:5.**
State highways, regulations excluding persons, **85:2E.**
Salaries.
Classification of jobs, **149:27, 149:27A.**
Commissioner and associate commissioners, **16:1.**
Employees, **16:4.**
Hearing examiner, **16:5.**
Laborers employed by department, **149:26.**
Minimum wage rates, **149:26-149:27D.**
Municipal agent, **41:103.**
Overtime pay for purchasing agent, **151:1A.**
Payroll records. See within this heading, "Payroll records."
Posting schedule of wages, **149:27.**
Prevailing wage law, **5:1, 7:22, 149:26-149:27D.**
Secretary, **16:5.**
State agent, **7:4A.**
Supplementary unemployment benefit fund payments, inclusion in wage rate on public construction projects, **149:29.**
Welfare plans, effect, **149:26, 149:27.**
Schedule.
List or schedule. See within this heading, "List or schedule."
Schools.
Co-operative engineering students' program, **16:4B.**
Crossings, specifications and standards for objects erected, **85:21A.**
Speed of motor vehicles in school zones, **90:17.**

PUBLIC WORKS —Cont'd
Secretary to commission, **16:5.**
Semi-trailers.
Trailers and semi-trailers. See within this heading, "Trailers and semi-trailers."
Sentence and punishment.
Fines and penalties. See within this heading, "Fines and penalties."
Sewers and drains, public works board as successor to office of sewer commissioners, **41:69D.**
Shade trees.
Trees. See within this heading, "Trees."
Ships and vessels, regulation of passage through drawbridges, **85:26.**
Shrubbery and brush, removal, **81:13, 81:14.**
Sidewalks along state highways, construction and maintenance, **81:20.**
Signs, duties, **85:2, 85:2D.**
Slope easement for state highways, power to take, **81:7B.**
Snow and ice.
Civil service status of snow removal employees, **31:48.**
Duty to keep state highways clear, **81:19.**
Storage and use of snow removal chemicals, regulations, **85:7A.**
Soil conservation service, agreements with for improvement of harbors, **91:11.**
Soil explorations, "Construction" as including, **149:27D.**
Solar energy utilization estimates for state construction, **149:44M.**
Solid waste disposal.
See GARBAGE AND RUBBISH.
Specifications.
See PLANS AND SPECIFICATIONS.
State boundaries.
Inspection and repair, **1:4.**
Permission for removal of boundary marks, **1:5.**
State ethics commission, employees' duty to file, **268A:14.**
State geologist, appointment and duties, **16:4.**
State highways, **81:1 et seq., 90:18.**

PUBLIC WORKS —Cont'd

Statements required from contractors, **30:39R.**

State parks, reservations, and recreation areas, co-operation in development, **132A:2C.**

Station wagons, restrictions on authority of department to regulate operation, **85:2, 90:18.**

Statistics relative to public ways, compilation, **81:1.**

Statute of limitations.
See LIMITATION OF ACTIONS.

Storage of road machinery, acquiring real estate, **81:3.**

Stream improvements, **91:5, 91:11.**

Street railways.
See STREET RAILWAYS.

Subcontractors.
See CONSTRUCTION CONTRACTS AND WORK.

Subdivision control law, alternate security for construction of ways and municipal services, **41:81U.**

Substantial completion, payment of contractor upon, **30:39G.**

Substantial evidence rule, **30:39J.**

Superintendent of public works, **41:69E.**

Superintendent of streets, approval of appointment for two or more towns, **41:67.**

Supplementary unemployment benefit fund payments to be included in established wage rate on public construction projects, **149:26, 149:27, 149:29.**

Supplies.
Materials and supplies. See within this heading, "Materials and supplies."

Sureties.
Bonds and undertakings. See within this heading, "Bonds and undertakings."

Surveys.
Maps, plats, and surveys. See within this heading, "Maps, plats, and surveys."

Taxes on public land, reimbursement of cities and towns for loss, **58:13.**

Test borings, "Construction" as including, **149:27D.**

Through ways, designation, **89:9.**

Tidal bounds, establishing, **131:4.**

Tidelands.
See TIDE LANDS AND WATERS.

PUBLIC WORKS —Cont'd

Time.
Award of contract, **149:44A.**
Limitation of actions.
See LIMITATION OF ACTIONS.

Topographical survey, authority, **91:33.**

Towns.
Cities and towns. See within this heading, "Cities and towns."

Trade, workmen's freedom, **149:25.**

Traffic regulations, powers, **85:2, 85:30, 89:1, 89:4, 89:9, 90:18, 90:18A.**

Trailers and semi-trailers.
Exemption from special permit requirements, **90:19A.**
Permits, **90:8, 90:19, 90:19A, 90:30.**

Transportation and construction executive office, agencies within, **6A:19.**

Transportation charges, **30:39A-30:39E, 149:29.**
Dump truck operations, bond for transportation charges, **30:39A-30:39E.**
Security for payment, **149:29.**

Transportation planning and development bureau, **16:3A.**

Trees.
Obstructing view upon state highway, removal, **81:14.**
Planting or removing upon state highways, regulation, **81:13, 81:13A, 81:21.**

Trial or hearing.
Hearings. See within this heading, "Hearings."

Trucks.
Bond for dump truck operations charges, **30:39A-30:39E.**
Operators of trucks and other rented equipment, **149:27F.**
Trailers, permits, **90:8, 90:19, 90:19A, 90:30.**

Unemployment compensation, **149:26, 149:27, 149:29.**

United States, conveyance of Commonwealth lands, **1:6.**

Urban redevelopment corporations, **121A:6, 121A:14.**

Veterans' preferences, **149:26, 149:27C.**

Wages.
Salaries. See within this heading, "Salaries."

Walk signals for pedestrians on public ways prohibited, **85:2.**

PUBLIC WORKS —Cont'd

Warehouses.
See WAREHOUSES.

Water resources commission, works of improvement under direction of, **21:9, 21:14, 21:15.**
See WATER RESOURCES DIVISION AND COMMISSION.

Waters.
See WATERS AND WATERWAYS.

Weight permits for motor vehicles, commissioner's powers and duties, **85:30, 85:30A, 90:19D.**

Width of state highway, **81:5.**

Wind energy utilization estimates for state construction, **149:44M.**

Winter, state aid to keep highways open, **84:11.**

Wires, granting easements in state highways, **81:7D.**

Witnesses.
Powers of hearing examiner, **16:5.**
Summoning of witnesses on appeal from decision of registrar of motor vehicles as to public works department, **90:28.**

Workers' compensation for police employed by contractor constructing project **152:1.**

Zoning.
See ZONING AND PLANNING.

PUBLIC WORKS BUILDING POLICE.
Smoking regulations, **31:64.**

PUBLIC WORKS DEPARTMENT ACT, 16:1 et seq.

PUERTO RICO.
Aircraft financial responsibility law, applicability, **90:49O.**

Insurance.
Fire or marine insurance company agents' balances, **175:25.**
Real property in Puerto Rico, insurance company loans, **175:63, 175:65-175:66B.**
Rehabilitation or liquidation of certain insurers, applicability of law, **175:180A.**

Medical school graduates, registration without examination, **112:2.**

PUERTO RICO —Cont'd
Registration without examination of physical therapist licensed or registered, **112:23D.**
Taxation, deductions for capital stock taxes imposed by as disallowed, **63:1.**

PULASKI.
Observance of anniversary of death of General Pulaski, **6:12B.**

PULLETS.
Standard sizes of eggs, **94:90B.**

PULLTABS.
Soft drink and malt beverage containers, **94:319.**

PUMPS.
Gasoline pumps.
  Brand or trademark marked, **94:295F.**
  Penalty for certain acts with respect to quantity and price indicators on meter face, **94:295E.**
  Price of fuel dispensed to be displayed, **94:295C.**
Insurance against damage by or, **175:47.**
  Combination policies, **175:117A.**
  Mutual insurance, **175:48A, 175:93A, 175:93C, 175:117A.**
Municipal indebtedness for pumping stations, **44:8.**

PUNCHCARD VOTING SYSTEMS.
Loans for replacement of systems, **9:30, 29:2PP.**

PUNCHES.
Counterfeiting punches, possession.
  Compensation of prosecutors, etc., **267:31.**
  Penalty, **267:20.**
Minors under sixteen not to work on power punches, **149:61.**
Presses.
  See PRESSES.

PUNISHMENT, 279:1-279:55.
Fines and penalties, **264:1 et seq., 280:1-280:16.**
  See FINES AND PENALTIES.
Sentence and punishment.
  See SENTENCE AND PUNISHMENT.

PUNITIVE DAMAGES.
See DAMAGES.

PUPILS.
See SCHOOLS AND EDUCATION.

PURCHASE.
See SALE OR TRANSFER OF PROPERTY.

PURCHASED SERVICES OFFICE.
Establishment and provisions, **6A:16 note, 7:4A note.**

PURCHASE MONEY MORTGAGE.
See MORTGAGES AND DEEDS OF TRUST.

PURCHASE MONEY SECURITY INTEREST.
See SECURED TRANSACTIONS.

PURCHASE OPTION.
See OPTION TO PURCHASE.

PURCHASER IN GOOD FAITH.
See BONA FIDE PURCHASERS.

PURCHASING AGENTS.
Bribery or improper influencing, **271:39.**
Cities and towns, **41:103, 41:104.**
  Prison-made goods, **127:57, 127:60.**
  Unemployment in cities and towns, preference by state purchasing agent, **7:22.**
Correctional institutions.
  See CORRECTIONAL INSTITUTIONS.
Metropolitan district commission, agent, **28:4.**
Political subdivisions serving as purchasing agents, liability, **7:22B.**
State purchasing agent.
  See STATE PURCHASING AGENT.
Wages, salaries, and compensation.
  Municipal agent, **41:103.**
  Overtime pay for purchasing agent, **151:1A.**
  State agent, **7:4A.**

PURE FOOD, DRUG, AND COSMETIC ACT, 94:186 to 94:195.
Enforcement of pure food and drug provisions, **94:192.**
Evidence of violation of pure food and drug provisions, **94:188, 94:189.**
Fine or penalty for violations, **94:190, 94:305A.**

PURE FOOD, DRUG, AND COSMETIC ACT —Cont'd
Grand jury investigations, **233:20D.**
Guarantee of wholesaler, jobber, or manufacturer as protecting dealer under Pure Food and Drug Act, **94:193, 94:194.**
Sampling and analysis, Pure Food Law provisions, **94:188, 94:189.**

PURE SEED.
See SEEDS.

PURGE OF RECORDS.
Criminal information system.
  See CRIMINAL OFFENDER RECORD INFORMATION SYSTEM.

PURIFICATION PLANTS.
Shellfish.
  See SHELLFISH.

PURITY OF GAS, 164:109.
See GAS AND ELECTRIC COMPANIES.

PURITY OF WATER SUPPLY.
See WATERWORKS AND WATER SUPPLY.

PURPLE HEART.
Military order.
  See MILITARY ORDER OF THE PURPLE HEART.
Observance of Purple Heart Day, **6:12T.**

PURSE NETS.
Inland waters, **131:54.**

PURSUIT.
Arrest.
  See ARREST.
Escape.
  See ESCAPE.
Extra-jurisdictional arrest on fresh and continued pursuit, **41:98A, 276:10A-276:10D.**
Marine fishing laws violations, **130:15A.**

PYRAMID PLANS.
Distribution companies.
  See MULTI-LEVEL DISTRIBUTION COMPANIES.

PYROTECHNICS.
See FIREWORKS.

Q

QUABBIN FISHERMEN'S ASSOCIATION.
Quabbin watershed advisory committee, members, **92:114.**

QUABBIN RESERVOIR.
"Watershed system," definition for purposes of provision creating watershed management division, 92:104.

QUABBIN WATERSHED.
Quabbin watershed advisory committee.
See QUABBIN WATERSHED ADVISORY COMMITTEE.
"Watershed system," definition for purposes of provision creating watershed management division, 92:104.

QUABBIN WATERSHED ADVISORY COMMITTEE.
Creation, purpose, and meetings, 92:114.
Defined, for purposes of provisions establishing watershed management division, 92:104.
Periodic watershed management plans, participation of committee, 92:116.

QUAHAUGS.
Clams.
See CLAMS AND CLAM BAIT.
Defined under marine fish and fisheries law, 130:1.
Fisheries, conservation and management, 130:52.
Minimum size regulations, 130:60.
Sale by weight, 94:88B.

QUAIL.
Commercial shooting preserves, taking, 131:31.
Field trials and training of dogs, 131:20.
Regulation, 131:19A.

QUAKERS.
See FRIENDS, SOCIETY OF.

QUALIFIED BONDS, 44A:1 et seq.
See MUNICIPAL FINANCE.

QUALIFIED HOSPITALIZATION.
Words and phrases, 62C:81.

QUALIFYING HEALTH PLAN.
Words and phrases, 176J:1.

QUALIFYING INCOME INTEREST FOR LIFE.
Estate taxes, 65A:5, 65A:5A.

QUARANTINE.
Animal diseases.
See ANIMAL DISEASES.
Barber shop, 112:87K.

QUARANTINE —Cont'd
Fines and penalties for violation of quarantine orders or regulations, 111:101-111:113, 131:25C, 266:119.
Health board, powers, 111:95.
Hospitals.
See HOSPITALS AND HEALTH CARE FACILITIES.
Insect pests, quarantines, 132:1A, 266:119.
Isolation hospitals.
See HOSPITALS AND HEALTH CARE FACILITIES.
Local health board's authority, 111:95.
Notice.
Fish, birds, mammals or reptiles, 131:25A.
Livestock disease control, 129:21, 129:22, 129:24.
Penalty for removal or defacing, 111:104.
Pilots of vessels.
Penalty for failure to anchor vessel under quarantine at proper place, 103:33.
Plants and plant diseases and pests, 128:27.
Publication of orders for suppression, 128:31.
Residence of persons suffering from infectious disease, 111:95.
Surviving spouse's quarantine, 196:1.
Town appropriations for quarantine ground, 40:5.
Travelers, 111:106.
Vessels.
Pilots of vessels.
Penalty for failure to anchor vessel under quarantine at proper place, 103:33.
Veterinarian medicine, board of registration, 112:54.
Wage earner quarantined, compensation for time lost, 111:95.

QUARE CLAUSUM FREGIT.
See TRESPASS.

QUARRIES.
Drainage and rights of way for development, 252:15-252:23.
Roads to, fee for recording petition and order, 262:34.

QUARTERLY WAGE.
Employment security law, meaning, 151A:1.

QUARTERMASTER, 6:18, 33:15.
See MILITIA.

QUARTZ-HALOGEN HEADLAMPS.
Motor vehicles, prohibition from sale or installation of headlamps, 90:7.

QUASHING.
See SETTING ASIDE.

QUEMOY.
Tax exemption for surviving spouses of deceased combat veterans, 59:5.

QUESTIONS OF LAW AND FACT.
Commercial Code, "Conspicuous" character of term or clause, 106:1-201.
Criminal prosecutions, questions for jury, 278:2.
Jury, 278:2.
Kidnapping, jury determination of consent of victim as defense to charge, 265:27.
Land court to determine question of fact, when, 185:15.
Obscene matters, determinations, 272:28D.
Superior court.
See SUPERIOR COURTS.
Supreme judicial court.
See SUPREME JUDICIAL COURT.
Trustee process proceedings, trial of fact questions, 246:17.
Usage of trade embodied in writing, 106:1-205.
Workers' compensation, effect of certification of questions of law, 152:11.

QUESTIONS SUBMITTED TO VOTERS.
Elections, 53:18-53:22.
See ELECTIONS.

QUIETING TITLE, 240:1-240:29.
Absent defendants in equity suit to quiet title, 240:6.
Action to try title, petition to require, 240:1-240:5.
Appearances and answers, 240:3.
Bond, power to require, 240:2.
Commonwealth not affected, 240:5.
Conveyances and releases, power to order, 240:2.
Costs, 240:3.
Decree, 240:3.
Default decree, 240:2.

QUIETING TITLE —Cont'd

Action to try title, petition to require —Cont'd

Description of parties, **240:1.**

Disclaimer to avoid costs, **240:3.**

Easements, **240:1.**

Equity suit. See within this heading, "Equity suit to quiet title."

Form and contents, **240:1.**

Notice of proceedings, **240:2, 240:4.**

Parties, **240:1.**

Proceedings upon petition, **240:2.**

Rights barred without actual notice, remedy, **240:4.**

Service, **240:1.**

Adverse claims.

Action to try title. See within this heading, "Action to try title, petition to require."

Encumbrances, determination of validity. See within this heading, "Encumbrances, determination of validity."

Equity suits to quiet title, **240:6.**

Affidavits as to title, use as evidence, **183:5A.**

Ancient conditions, restrictions, and encumbrances.

Encumbrances, determination of validity. See within this heading, "Encumbrances, determination of validity."

Appeals from decree registering land free from restrictions, **240:18.**

Commonwealth, applicability of provisions to interest, **240:5.**

Complaint.

Action to enforce restrictions running with land, **240:10A.**

Petition.

Action to try title, petition to require. See within this heading, "Action to try title, petition to require."

Conditions.

Encumbrances, determination of validity. See within this heading, "Encumbrances, determination of validity."

Constructive service on parties in equity suit to quiet title, **240:7.**

Costs.

Action to try title, on petition to require, **240:3.**

Boundaries of flats and overflowed lands, proceedings to determine, **240:22.**

QUIETING TITLE —Cont'd

Costs —Cont'd

Determining validity of encumbrances, proceedings, **240:14.**

Guardian ad litem and next friend, expenses, **240:9.**

Covenantor's right to compel supposed claimant to try title, **240:1.**

Covenants running with land.

Restrictions running with land. See within this heading, "Restrictions running with land, civil action to enforce."

Damages.

Action to enforce restrictions running with land, **240:10C.**

Assessment on freeing land from restrictions, **240:17.**

Decree.

Action to try title, on petition to require, **240:3.**

Appeals, **240:18.**

Confirmation and registration of land title, effect of decree, **185:45.**

Default decree on petition to require action to try title, **240:2.**

Determination of validity of encumbrances, **240:14.**

Equity suits to quiet title, **240:10.**

Release of realty, decree in action to quiet title as operating, **240:10.**

Remedy of party against whom decree rendered without actual notice, **240:4.**

Defects in deed, limitation of action based, **184:24.**

Depositions to perpetuate testimony, **233:63.**

Description of parties.

Action to try title, petition to require, **240:1.**

Restrictions running with land, action to enforce, **240:10A.**

Unknown or unidentified defendants in equity suits, **240:6.**

Validity of encumbrances, action for determining, **240:12.**

Description of property in action to enforce restrictions running with land, **240:10A.**

Discharge of mortgages, petitions to land court, **240:15.**

Jurisdiction of court, **185:1.**

QUIETING TITLE —Cont'd

Discharge or release of real property, effect of decree in action for quieting title, **240:10.**

Easement, petition to require action to try title, **240:1.**

Encumbrances, determination of validity, **240:11-240:14A.**

Class of persons, description of respondents, **240:12.**

Costs, **240:14.**

Decree, **240:14.**

Joinder in proceedings, **240:11.**

Nature of encumbrances, **240:11.**

Notice of proceedings, **240:13.**

Parties. See within this heading, "Parties."

Registered land, restrictions, **240:16-240:18.**

Unknown respondents, description, **240:12.**

Who may petition, **240:11.**

Zoning laws, **240:14A.**

Equity suit to quiet title, **240:6-240:10C.**

Adverse claims, **240:6.**

Compensation of guardian ad litem, chargeable to plaintiff, **240:9.**

Constructive service by publication of notice, **240:7.**

Decree, **240:10.**

Description of parties, **240:6.**

Guardian ad litem or next friend, **240:8, 240:9.**

In personam jurisdiction, exercise, **240:10.**

In rem, nature of proceeding, **240:10.**

Notice of proceedings, **240:7.**

Parties. See within this heading, "Parties."

Release or conveyance of rights, effect of decree, **240:10.**

Restrictions running with land, action to enforce, **240:10A-240:10C.**

Supreme judicial, superior or land courts, actions in, **240:6.**

Unknown or unidentified defendants, **240:6.**

Evidence, affidavit as to title, **183:5A.**

Flats, determination of boundaries of.

See TIDE LANDS AND WATERS.

Guardian ad litem, appointment for nonappearing defendants in equity suits, **240:8, 240:9.**

QUIETING TITLE —Cont'd
Identity or description.
Description of parties. See
within this heading,
"Description of parties."
Indefinite references in recorded
instruments, protection of
land titles against effects,
184:25.
In personam jurisdiction, exercise,
240:10.
In rem proceedings, **240:10.**
Restrictions running with land,
action to enforce, **240:10C.**
Joinder of parties, **240:1.**
Determination of validity of
encumbrances, **240:11.**
Discharge of mortgages,
proceedings, **240:15.**
Equity suits to quiet title,
plaintiffs, **240:6.**
Judgment.
Decree. See within this heading,
"Decree."
Jurisdiction.
In personam jurisdiction,
exercise, **240:10.**
Land court. See within this
heading, "Land court."
Restrictions running with land,
jurisdiction of action to
enforce, **240:10A.**
Land court, **240:1 et seq.**
Boundaries of flats,
determination, **185:1.**
Discharge of mortgages. See
within this heading,
"Discharge of mortgages,
petitions to land court."
Equity suit to quiet title,
240:6-240:10C.
Miscellaneous cases, jurisdiction
to quiet title, **185:1.**
Petition for determination of
validity of encumbrances,
240:11.
Procedure, **240:29.**
Registration of land free from
restrictions, **185:1.**
Restrictions on registered land,
determining validity,
240:16-240:18.
Restrictions running with land,
jurisdiction of action to
enforce, **240:10A.**
Settlement of land titles, **185:1,**
240:29.
Validity of encumbrances,
determination, **185:1.**
Zoning ordinance, petition for
judicial determination of
validity, **240:14A.**

QUIETING TITLE —Cont'd
Liens.
Encumbrances, determination of
validity. See within this
heading, "Encumbrances,
determination of validity."
Limitation of action based on
defects in deed, **184:24.**
Limitations and restrictions.
Restrictions on property, validity
as to registered land,
240:16-240:18.
Lis pendens, recording notice,
184:15.
Low value land, determining
validity of tax title, **60:80B.**
Mortgages.
Discharge of mortgages. See
within this heading,
"Discharge of mortgages,
petitions to land court."
Next friend, appointment for
nonappearing defendants in
equity suits, **240:8, 240:9.**
Notice.
Action to try title, proceedings to
require, **240:2, 240:4.**
Determination of validity of
encumbrances, **240:13.**
Equity suit to quiet title, **240:7.**
Lis pendens, recording notice,
184:15.
Restrictions running with land,
notice of action to enforce,
240:10A.
Parties.
Action to try title, petitioner,
240:1.
Description of parties. See
within this heading,
"Description of parties."
Discharge of mortgages, joinder
in proceedings, **240:15.**
Encumbrances, determining
validity, **240:11.**
Agent for unknown
respondents, **240:13.**
Unknown respondents,
description, **240:12.**
Equity suits to quiet title, **240:6.**
Guardian ad litem or next
friend for unknown
defendants, **240:8, 240:9.**
Joinder of parties. See within
this heading, "Joinder of
parties."
Proceedings, parties bound,
240:2, 240:4.
Restrictions running with land,
parties in action to enforce,
240:10A, 240:10B.

QUIETING TITLE —Cont'd
Petition.
Action to try title, petition to
require. See within this
heading, "Action to try title,
petition to require."
Discharge of mortgages, petition
to land court for. See within
this heading, "Discharge of
mortgages, petitions to land
court."
Procedure in land court, provisions
governing, **240:29.**
Process and service.
Service. See within this heading,
"Service."
Registration of land title, effect of
decree of confirmation and
registration, **185:45.**
Release, decree in action to quiet
title as operating to release
realty, **240:10.**
Restrictions on property, validity
as to registered land,
240:16-240:18.
Restrictions running with land,
civil action to enforce.
Complaint, contents, **240:10A.**
Damages, enforcement by
award, **240:10C.**
In rem nature of determination,
240:10C.
Judicial determination or
declaration, nature and
effect, **240:10C.**
Jurisdiction, **240:10A.**
Notice and service of notice,
240:10B.
Parties, **240:10A, 240:10B.**
Representative of interested
persons, appointment,
240:10B.
Service, **240:1.**
Determination of validity of
encumbrances, service in
proceedings, **240:12, 240:13.**
Equity suit to quiet title, service,
240:7.
Restrictions running with land,
service of notice in action to
enforce, **240:10B.**
Superior court.
Damages in proceedings to free
property from restrictions,
assessment, **240:17.**
Equity suit to quiet title,
240:6-240:10C.
Restrictions running with land,
jurisdiction of action to
enforce, **240:10A.**

QUIETING TITLE —Cont'd
Supreme judicial court.
  Appeal from decree registering
    land free from restriction,
    240:18.
  Equity suit to quiet title,
    240:6-240:10C.
Tax title to low value land,
  determining validity, **60:80B.**
Unknown or unidentified
  defendants, description in
  equity suits, **240:6.**
Zoning laws, determination of
  validity, **240:14A.**

QUINCY.
Congressional district, **57:1.**
District court, **218:1.**
Medical examiner district, **38:1.**
Metropolitan air pollution control
  district, membership,
  111:142B.
Metropolitan area planning
  district, membership, **40B:26.**
Parks, provision by metropolitan
  commission, **92:33.**
Pilotage rates, **103:31.**
Refuse disposal, **92:9A.**
Senatorial district, **57:3.**

QUINTAL.
Fish, quintal weight, **94:84.**

QUITCLAIM DEED.
See DEEDS AND
  CONVEYANCES.

QUORUM.
Accountants, quorum of board,
  13:34.
Alcoholic liquor licensing boards,
  138:6.
Appeals court, **211A:3.**
Appellate division justices,
  quorum, **231:108.**
Architects.
  Architects' registration board,
    13:44B.
  Landscape architects'
    registration board, **13:68.**
Banks.
  Savings banks.
    See SAVINGS BANKS.
  Trust companies, assignment
    and transfer of shares,
    172:11.
Building regulations and
  standards, state board,
  143:93.
Charter cities, city councils, **43:18,**
  43:85, 43:99.
Committee for conservation of soil,
  water and related resources,
  21:19.

QUORUM —Cont'd
Community economic development
  assistance corporation,
  quorum of board directors,
  40:3.
Congress, **US Const Art 1 Sec 5**
  cl 1 and Art 12 and 12th
  Amend.
Conservation of soil, water and
  related resources, commission,
  21:19.
Constitution of Massachusetts,
  quorum of general court, **MA**
  Const Amend Art 33.
Constitution of the United States.
  See CONSTITUTION OF THE
    UNITED STATES.
Corporations.
  See CORPORATIONS.
County commissioners, **34:12.**
County governmental body, **34:9F,**
  34:9G.
Credit unions.
  See CREDIT UNIONS.
Criminal justice committee,
  meetings, **6:156.**
Dental examiners board, quorum,
  112:43.
Discrimination, state commission
  against, **6:56.**
Elevators.
  Appeals board, **22:11A.**
  Regulations board, **22:11.**
Energy Advisory Board, **25A:10.**
Fisheries and wildlife board,
  21:7E.
Industrial accidents division,
  23E:15.
Insurance directors, **175:57,**
  175:77, 175:88, 175:90.
  National emergency, **175:180O.**
Labor relations commission,
  23:9O.
Landscape architects, quorum of
  board registration, **13:68.**
Massachusetts Centers of
  Excellence Corporation, Board
  of Directors, **40J:12.**
Medicolegal investigations
  committee, meetings, **6:184.**
Municipal boards, **39:23A.**
Municipal industrial development
  financing authorities, quorum
  of directors, **40D:5.**
Mutual insurance companies,
  meetings of directors, **175:77,**
  175:88, 175:90.
National emergency, insurance
  company board of directors
  during, **175:180O.**
Plan D charter cities, city councils,
  43:85.

QUORUM —Cont'd
Plan E charter cities, city councils,
  43:99.
President, quorum of House of
  Representatives for election of,
  US Const 12th Amend.
Professional engineers and land
  surveyors, board of
  registration, **13:46.**
Public accountants, quorum of
  board, **13:34.**
Public works commission, **16:5.**
Radio and television technicians
  registration board, **13:62.**
Railroads.
  Stockholders' meetings, **160:33.**
  Street railways.
    See STREET RAILWAYS.
Real estate brokers and salesmen,
  board of registration, **13:55.**
Representative town meetings,
  43A:5.
Savings banks.
  Corporators, annual meeting,
    168:9A.
  Trustees, meetings, **168:11.**
School committee budget hearings,
  71:38N.
Senate, **US Const Art 1 Sec 5 cl**
  1 and Art 12 and 12th
  Amend.
State Ethics Commission, **268B:2.**
State governmental body,
  30A:11A½, 39:23A.
Statutes concerning, construction,
  4:6.
Street railways.
  See STREET RAILWAYS.
Supreme judicial court, quorum,
  211:2.
Technology development
  corporation, quorum of board,
  40G:2.
Thrift Institutions Fund for
  Economic Development, Board
  of Directors, **63:1 (note).**
Town governmental body, private
  meetings by quorum, **39:23B.**
Town meetings, **39:13, 43A:5.**
Trust company, **172:11.**
Turnpike authority, **81A:2.**
Underground storage tank
  petroleum product cleanup
  fund administrative review
  board, **21J:8.**
Veterinary medicine registration
  board, quorum, **112:54.**
Vice President, quorum of Senate
  for election of, **US Const 12th**
  Amend.
Water commissioners, town board,
  41:69A.

QUORUM —Cont'd

Workers' compensation advisory council, meetings, **23E:15.**

QUOTATION.

Market price.

See MARKET PRICE OR QUOTATION.

QUOTAX.

Licenses for sale of alcoholic liquors, quotas, **138:17.**

Revenue department, production goals or quotas for individual employees prohibited, **14:7.**

Sales, allocation of production and deliveries by quota, **106:2-615, 106:2-616.**

QUO WARRANTO, 249:6-249:13.

Attorney general.

Duties as to quo warranto proceedings, effect of statutes, **249:13.**

Fine or forfeiture, demand of judgment, **249:7.**

Intervention, **249:7.**

Service of complaint, **249:6.**

Availability of remedy, **249:6.**

Corporation, exercise of franchise or privilege not conferred by law, **249:6.**

Costs, **249:8.**

Duties of attorney general not affected by provisions authorizing, **249:13.**

Injunction, issuance, **249:6.**

Judgment, **249:8.**

Jurisdiction of actions against persons holding public office, **249:9.**

Public office, right or title, **249:9.**

Superior court, **249:6, 249:9.**

Supreme judicial court, **249:6, 249:9.**

Venue, **249:6.**

R

RABBIS.

Jury service, exemption, **234:1.**

Marriage.

Clergymen.

See MARRIAGE.

Residences exempt from taxation, **59:5.**

Wholesaler's and importer's license to sell wine, **138:18.**

RABBITS.

See HARES.

RABIES.

Cats, certification of inoculation for, **140:145B.**

RABIES —Cont'd

Cities or town to furnish vaccine, **140:145A.**

Description of symptoms on dog license, **140:145.**

Dog licenses, certificate of inoculation, **140:145B.**

Dogs and cats, rabies vaccination required, **140:145B.**

Examination to detect, **111:15.**

Prevention Week, **6:15EEE.**

Veterinarians to notify city and town clerks of vaccinations of dogs, **140:145B.**

RACEMETHORPHAN.

Controlled dangerous substance, **94C:31.**

RACEMORAMIDE.

Controlled dangerous substance, **94C:31.**

RACEMORPHAN.

Controlled dangerous substance, **94C:31.**

RACES AND RACING.

Bicycle races, regulation, **85:11B.**

Bribery of persons connected with horse race, **271:39.**

Commission.

See RACING COMMISSION.

Criminal offense of registering bets on speed contests, **271:17.**

Second offense, **271:10.**

Gaming.

See GAMING AND GAMES OF CHANCE.

Horse and dog race meetings, **128A:1 et seq.**

See HORSE AND DOG RACING MEETINGS.

Mayors.

Horse or dog racing meeting employees, request for appointment or discharge, **271:40.**

Place as race grounds, authorization, **271:33.**

Motorboats.

See MOTORBOATS.

Motorcycle racing on Sunday, **136:4.**

Motor vehicles.

See MOTOR VEHICLES.

Police.

See POLICE.

Records and reports.

Financial report of racing corporations, **180:26A.**

General court, report of commission, **6:48.**

RACES AND RACING —Cont'd

Records and reports —Cont'd

Horse.

See HORSE AND DOG RACING MEETINGS.

Restaurant liquor licensee, sales at more than one location, **138:12.**

State racing commission established, **6:48.**

Traffic regulations and rules of the road, **90:24.**

Speed.

See TRAFFIC REGULATIONS AND RULES OF THE ROAD.

RACIAL DISCRIMINATION, 151B:1 et seq.

See CIVIL RIGHTS AND DISCRIMINATION.

RACIAL IMBALANCE LAW, 15:1I et seq., 71:37C, 71:37D.

RACIAL ISOLATION AREAS.

Transportation expenses of non-white and minority pupils, **15:1I.**

RACING ACT, 128A:1 et seq.

RACING COMMISSION.

Appointment of exempt positions, **6:48.**

Civil service status of employees of racing commission, **6:48.**

Employment dislocations and assistance in reemployment of dislocated workers, **6:17.**

Horse.

See HORSE AND DOG RACING MEETINGS.

Police.

Bribery of persons connected with horse race, **271:39.**

Overtime pay, **41:111H.**

Trust funds, **128A:3, 128A:5 notes.**

Veterinarians as employees, **6:48.**

Wagered money, division of between parties, **128A:5 (note).**

RADIATION AND RADIOACTIVE WASTE.

Advisory council on radiation protection, **111:4F.**

Atmospheric pollution, regulation and control by local health boards, etc., **111:31C.**

Control agency, designation of Public Health Department, **111:5N.**

RADIATION AND RADIOACTIVE WASTE
—Cont'd

Definition of radioactive substance, **94B:1.**

Dentists, member of radiation protection advisory council, **111:4F.**

Environmental affairs office, authority to license and control ionizing radiation, **111:5E.**

Fines and penalties.
Low-level radioactive waste, **111H:8, 111H:9.**
Occupational diseases caused by ionizing radiation, violation of regulations for prevention, **149:6.**
Radiation control, **111:5O, 111:5P, 111H:8.**
Shoe-fitting machines, using fluoroscopic x-ray or radiation principles, **111:186A.**

Fire insurance.
Combination fire insurance policies covering contamination risks, **175:102C, 175:111A.**
Mutual insurance policy covering property used for working on special nuclear material, **175:80.**
Nuclear reaction, policy as covering loss due to radiation, **175:99A, 175:102C.**

Food subjected, **94:186.**

Health.
Atomic energy.
See HEALTH AND HEALTH DEPARTMENTS.
Interstate compacts.
See INTERSTATE COMPACTS AND AGREEMENTS.
Ionizing radiation.
Fines and penalties. See within this heading, "Fines and penalties."
Labor and workforce development. See within this heading, "Labor and workforce development."
Occupational diseases caused by, penalty for violation of regulations for prevention, **149:6.**

RADIATION AND RADIOACTIVE WASTE
—Cont'd

Labor and workforce development.
Membership of labor and workforce development commissioner on radiation protection advisory council, **111:4F.**
Penalty for violations of ionizing radiation regulations, **149:6.**

Low-level radioactive waste.
See LOW-LEVEL RADIOACTIVE WASTE.

Nuclear power.
See NUCLEAR POWER AND WASTE DISPOSAL VOTER APPROVAL AND LEGISLATIVE CERTIFICATION ACT.

Occupational diseases caused by ionizing radiation, penalty for violation of regulations for prevention, **149:6.**

Penalties.
Fines and penalties. See within this heading, "Fines and penalties."

Physical therapists not authorized to use, **112:23A.**

Radiologists and radiology, membership of radiology section of Massachusetts Medical Society authority approving schools for training medical x-ray technicians, **112:2C.**

Roentgen rays.
See X-RAYS.

Shielding devices required in therapeutic use, **111:5J.**

Shoe-fitting machine using radiation principles, regulation of use, **111:186A.**

Tanning facilities.
See TANNING FACILITIES.

Waters, pollution, **21:27, 21:38.**

X-rays.
See X-RAYS.

RADIATION CONTROL AGENCY.
Designation, **111:5N.**

RADIATORS.
Insurance against loss or damages caused by leakage, **175:47, 175:93A-175:93C, 175:117A.**

RADIO AND TELEVISION.
Advertising.
Credit unions, **171:55.**
Technicians, inclusion of license number in advertising of television technicians, **112:87RRR.**
Technician's services, contents of signs, **112:87RRR.**

Amateur radio operator's motor vehicle number plates, fees, **90:33.**

Ambulance attendants, liability of physicians and nurses for emergency medical advice communicated, **111C:13.**

Automobiles.
Motor vehicles. See within this heading, "Motor vehicles."

Board of higher education, Massachusetts corporation for educational telecommunication, **15A:3A.**

Board of registration of radio and television technicians, **13:61 et seq., 112:87PPP.**
Administrator, appointment and duties, **13:62.**
Members, appointment, **13:61.**
Rules and regulations, **112:87RRR.**
Wages, salaries, and compensation, **13:62, 13:63.**

Boxing matches, payment to Commonwealth of proceeds from broadcasting, **147:40.**

Building regulations, definitions for purpose, **143:1.**

Business sign of television technician, what to contain, **112:87RRR.**

Cable television, **166A:1-166A:20.**
See COMMUNITY ANTENNA TELEVISION SYSTEMS.

Campaign expenditures and contributions, restrictions on radio and television expenses, **55:32.**

Cellular telephones, radio utility rates, **159:12C.**

Children, employment, **149:60, 149:78, 149:86.**

Cities and towns.
Community antenna television systems.
See COMMUNITY ANTENNA TELEVISION SYSTEMS.

Educational television, **71:13F, 71:13I.**

RADIO AND TELEVISION
—Cont'd
Civil service status of
administrator of technicians
registration board, **13:62.**
Community antenna television
systems, **166A:1-166A:20.**
See COMMUNITY ANTENNA
TELEVISION SYSTEMS.
Compensation.
Wages, salaries, and
compensation.
Technicians' registration
board, **13:62, 13:63.**
Consent.
Community antenna television
systems.
See COMMUNITY ANTENNA
TELEVISION SYSTEMS.
Owner, affixing television lines
and structures to property
without consent, **166:35.**
Contracts and agreements.
Cable TV operator's agreement,
166A:22.
Educational TV contracts,
71:13I.
Noncompete clauses.
Void for broadcast industry
employees, **149:186.**
Credit unions, advertisements,
171:55.
Crimes and offenses, radios or
boom boxes used without
earphones, **265:42.**
Curfew, announcement of
imposition, **40:37A.**
Damages.
Exemption of radio station from
liability for damages for
defamatory matter uttered
by certain persons, **231:91A.**
Television lines, damage to
abutting owners, **166:29.**
Defamatory matter uttered by
certain persons, station as
exempt from liability for
damages, **231:91A.**
Dental business, advertising,
112:52C.
Disqualification.
Radio and television technicians,
board of registration,
members, **13:61.**
Education.
Applicability of law to certain
government agencies,
schools, etc., **112:87QQQ.**
Educational TV, **71:13F et seq.**
See EDUCATIONAL
TELEVISION.

RADIO AND TELEVISION
—Cont'd
Elections.
Campaign expenditures,
restrictions, **55:32.**
Names of voters at polling
places, broadcasting, **54:76.**
Employment contracts.
Noncompete clauses.
Void for broadcast industry
employees, **149:186.**
Examination, inspection, or
investigation.
Cable television commission,
166:17, 166A:2A.
Technician's license
examinations, **112:87SSS.**
Exemptions and exceptions.
Defamatory matter uttered by
certain persons, exemption
of radio station from
liability for damages,
231:91A.
Racing information, exception as
to transmission, **271:31A.**
Registration requirements,
exemption, **112:87QQQ.**
Tax exemption. See within this
heading, "Tax exemption of
radio and television sets."
Unauthorized sound
reproduction, exception,
266:143.
Federal Communications
Commission.
License for Massachusetts
Educational
Communications
Commission, **6:158.**
Operators of radio transmitting
equipment, registration and
licensing requirements,
112:87QQQ.
Fines and penalties.
Community antenna television
systems, violations,
166A:18.
Lines and structures, violations,
166:35, 166:36.
Technician engaging in business
without license, **112:87VVV.**
Firearms, possession during course
of television program,
**140:129C, 140:131F½,
269:10.**
Governor.
Technicians board of
registration, appointment of
members, **13:61.**
Hazardous waste, distribution of
list of suggested sites, **21D:9.**

RADIO AND TELEVISION
—Cont'd
Imported radio and television sets,
sale, **94:277B.**
Inspection.
Examination, inspection, or
investigation. See within
this heading, "Examination,
inspection, or investigation."
Learners' permits for technicians,
112:87RRR.
Licenses.
Community antenna television
systems.
See COMMUNITY ANTENNA
TELEVISION SYSTEMS.
Firearms, carrying, **140:129C,
140:131F½, 269:10.**
Technicians.
Registration of radio and
television technicians. See
within this heading,
"Registration of radio and
television technicians."
Lines and structures.
Affixing lines to property
without permission, **166:35.**
Construction of lines, **166:21,
166:29, 166:35.**
Damages caused by construction
or alteration, **166:29.**
Municipal regulation, **166:25.**
Name of corporation to be
affixed to pole or structure,
166:36.
Penalties for violations, **166:35,
166:36.**
Mobile radio telephone utility
companies, **159:12A to
159:12E.**
See MOBILE RADIO
TELEPHONE UTILITY
COMPANIES.
Motor vehicles.
Amateur radio operator's
number plates, fee, **90:33.**
Mobile radio telephone utility
companies.
See MOBILE RADIO
TELEPHONE UTILITY
COMPANIES.
Television sets, **90:13.**
Municipalities.
Cities and towns. See within
this heading, "Cities and
towns."
Noncompete clauses.
Void for broadcast industry
employees, **149:186.**

RADIO AND TELEVISION
—Cont'd

Penalties.

Fines and penalties. See within this heading, "Fines and penalties."

Physicians' and nurses' liability for emergency medical advice radioed to ambulance attendants, **111C:13.**

Qualification and disqualification.

Radio and television technicians board of registration, members, **13:61.**

Racing information, exception as to transmission, **271:31A.**

Registration of radio and television technicians, **112:87PPP et seq.**

Advertising of television technicians, inclusion of license number, **112:87RRR.**

Board of registration. See within this heading, "Board of registration of radio and television technicians."

Business sign of technicians, contents, **112:87RRR.**

Civil service status of director of registration board, **13:62.**

Definitions, **112:87PPP.**

Federally licensed operators of radio transmitting equipment, **112:87QQQ.**

Law inapplicable to certain persons, governmental agencies, schools, etc., **112:87QQQ.**

Licenses, **112:87RRR.**

Advertising of television technicians, inclusion of license number, **112:87RRR.**

Examination, issuance without, **112:87SSS.**

Expiration date, **112:87SSS.**

Federal licenses, **112:87QQQ.**

Fees, **112:87UUU.**

Learners' permits, **112:87RRR.**

Penalty for engaging in business without, **112:87VVV.**

Renewal license, fee, **112:87UUU.**

Requirements for issuance, **112:87RRR, 112:87SSS, 112:87TTT.**

Restrictions on political campaign expenditures, **55:32.**

RADIO AND TELEVISION
—Cont'd

Salaries.

Wages, salaries, and compensation.

Technicians' registration board, **13:62, 13:63.**

Sales.

Imported radio and television sets, **94:277B.**

Tax exemptions.

Information services used by broadcasters, **64H:1.**

Transmission and broadcasting equipment, **64H:1, 64H:6.**

Schools and education.

Applicability of law to certain government agencies, schools, etc., **112:87QQQ.**

Board of higher education, Massachusetts corporation for educational telecommunication, **15A:3A.**

Educational TV, **71:13F et seq.**

See EDUCATIONAL TELEVISION.

Signs advertising technicians, contents, **112:87RRR.**

Sunday, **134:4, 134:6.**

Tax exemption of radio and television sets, **59:5.**

Sales tax, exemptions from, **64H:1, 64H:6.**

Theft of cable television service equipment, **166:42A, 166:42B.**

Towns.

Cities and towns. See within this heading, "Cities and towns."

Unauthorized sound reproduction, exceptions, **266:143.**

University of Massachusetts, establishment and maintenance of television center, **75:37.**

Video taping.

Board of higher education, Massachusetts corporation for educational telecommunication, **15A:3A.**

Children and minors, videotaped testimony, **278:16D.**

Clothing store dressing rooms, video cameras, **93:89.**

Disclosure of records of video rental business, **93:106.**

Film.

See FILM AND VIDEO DEVELOPMENT OFFICE.

RADIO AND TELEVISION
—Cont'd

Video taping —Cont'd

Home video rental business, Sunday operation, **136:6.**

Meetings of governmental bodies, **39:23B.**

Unauthorized reproduction and transfer of sound recordings, **266:143-266:143E.**

Witnesses.

See WITNESSES.

Voting.

Elections. See within this heading, "Elections."

Wages, salaries, and compensation.

Technicians' registration board, **13:62, 13:63.**

RADIOLOGIC TECHNOLOGISTS.

Licenses and permits, **111:5Lql.**

RADIOLOGISTS.

Membership of radiology section of Massachusetts Medical Society on authority approving schools for training medical X-ray technicians, **112:2C.**

RADIOPHARMACEUTICAL DRUGS.

See DRUGS AND NARCOTICS.

RADIO TELEPHONES.

See MOBILE RADIO TELEPHONE UTILITY COMPANIES.

RAFFLES AND BAZAARS.

Beano licensees conducting, **10:39A.**

Records, reports, and returns, **10:39A, 271:7A.**

Taxation, **62C:2, 62C:18, 271:7A.**

RAFTS.

Buoy, penalty for mooring raft, **266:135.**

Railroad drawbridges, penalty for obstructing passage to or through draw, **160:127.**

Temporary mooring, **91:10A.**

RAGS.

Fires.

See FIRES AND FIRE PREVENTION.

Weighting bale with foreign substance as offense, **94:305.**

RAGWEED.

Municipal appropriation for eradication, **40:5.**

RAILERS AND BRAWLERS.

Criminal offense, **272:53.**

RAILERS AND BRAWLERS
—Cont'd
Discharge on recognizance, **272:56, 272:57.**
Second or subsequent offense, **272:56, 272:61.**

RAILINGS.
Highways.
Guardrails and barriers.
See HIGHWAYS AND STREETS.
Tanning facilities, handrails, **111:207.**

RAILROAD CAR COMPANIES.
Railroads authorized to hold stock, **160:65A.**

RAILROAD CROSSINGS,
159:57 et seq., 160:95 et seq.
Abolition of grade crossings, **159:65-159:82.**
Accounts of expense, **159:78.**
Action by Commonwealth to recover expenses of removal or relocation of tracks, conduits, pipes, wires, or poles, **159:74.**
Agreement, **159:80.**
Aldermen, petition, **159:65.**
Alteration of crossings, inapplicability of laws, **159:82.**
Apportionment of costs, **159:61, 159:70, 159:80.**
Interest on expense apportioned to county, city, or town, **159:78.**
Maintenance and repair after abolition, **159:77.**
Audit of accounts of expense, **159:78.**
Barred claim for damages, settlement, **159:76.**
Board for apportionment of costs, **159:70.**
Budget estimate of public works department to include sums, **159:70.**
Buildings and structures, removal or relocation, **159:74.**
Change of locations, **159:74.**
Commissioners to apportion costs, **159:70.**
Commonwealth. See within this heading, "Commonwealth."
Conduits, removal or relocation, **159:74.**
Consent of telecommunications and energy department to orders of public works department, **159:70.**

RAILROAD CROSSINGS
—Cont'd
Abolition of grade crossings
—Cont'd
Construction of highways, **159:72.**
Costs, **159:78.**
Attorney general as member of board to determine, **159:70.**
Estimates, **159:70.**
Sewers, drains, and pipes, relocating or changing, **159:74, 159:75.**
Streams and watercourses, relocating or changing, **159:75.**
Structures on private land, removal or relocation, **159:74.**
Counties.
Agreement, county may join, **159:80.**
Construction of county ways, **159:79.**
Petition by county commissioners, **159:65.**
Damages, **159:75, 159:76, 159:78.**
Directors of railroad, petition, **159:65.**
Disputes as to account of expense, determination, **159:78.**
Drains, expenses of changing or relocating, **159:75.**
Eminent domain, taking land, **159:74-159:76, 159:80.**
Enforcement of law, **159:79.**
Estimates of cost, public works department may require, **159:70.**
Federal moneys excluded in apportionment of costs, **159:70.**
Filing and recording.
Agreement, **159:80.**
Lists of crossings to be abolished, **159:65.**
Orders of public works department, **159:70.**
Program order of telecommunications and energy department, **159:65.**
Hearings, **159:65, 159:70.**
Interest on expense apportioned to county, city, or town, **159:78.**
Joinder of department of public works in agreement, **159:80.**

RAILROAD CROSSINGS
—Cont'd
Abolition of grade crossings
—Cont'd
Limitation as to settlement of barred claims, **159:76.**
Limits determined by order of public works department, **159:70.**
Locations, change, **159:74.**
Maintenance and repair.
Agreement, **159:80.**
Expense, **159:77.**
Manner and limits of making.
Agreement, **159:80.**
Determined by order of public works department, **159:70.**
Notice.
Agreement, **159:80.**
Hearings, **159:65, 159:70.**
Petition, **159:65.**
Payment of apportioned expense, **159:78.**
Petitions, **159:65.**
Party aggrieved by apportionment of costs, **159:70.**
Pipes, removal or relocation, **159:74, 159:75.**
Plans and specifications, **159:70, 161:129.**
Poles, removal or relocation, **159:74.**
Program designated by order of telecommunications and energy department, **159:65.**
Public works department.
Agreement, joinder, **159:80.**
Audit of accounts of expense, **159:78.**
Board for apportionment of costs, membership, **159:70.**
Budget estimate to include sums for abolition, **159:70.**
Construction of state highway or county way, requirement as to view may be dispensed, **159:72.**
Eminent domain, taking land, **159:74-159:76, 159:80.**
Estimates, **159:70.**
Expenses, **159:80.**
Estimates, **159:70.**
Orders for payment, **159:78.**
Hearings, **159:65, 159:70.**
Investigations, **159:65.**
Damages, amounts presented for allowances, **159:75, 159:78.**

RAILROAD CROSSINGS
—Cont'd
Abolition of grade crossings
—Cont'd
Public works department
—Cont'd
Limits determined, **159:70.**
Lists of grade crossings to be
abolished, **159:65.**
Manner of abolition
determined, **159:70.**
Orders for payment of
expenses, **159:78.**
Orders to be filed, **159:70,
159:74.**
Payments of apportioned
expense by city, county, or
town determined, **159:78.**
Petitions for abolition of
crossings received, **159:65.**
Plans, specifications, and
estimates of cost may be
required, **159:70.**
Program order filed, **159:65.**
Removal or relocation of
tracks, conduits, pipes,
wires or poles, **159:74.**
Service of orders, **159:70.**
Structures upon private land,
removal and relocation,
159:74.
Supervision of work, **159:70.**
Regulated, **159:65.**
Report to state comptroller of
accounts of expense, **159:78.**
Review of departmental orders,
159:79.
Selectmen, petition, **159:65.**
Service of orders of public works
department, **159:70.**
Settlement of barred claim,
159:76.
Sewers, expenses of relocating or
changing, **159:75.**
State.
Commonwealth. See within
this heading,
"Commonwealth."
Streams and watercourses,
expenses of relocating or
changing, payment, **159:75.**
Street railways.
See STREET RAILWAYS.
Structures upon private lands,
removal and relocation,
159:74.
Superior court, enforcement of
law, **159:79.**
Supervision of work by public
works department, **159:70.**

RAILROAD CROSSINGS
—Cont'd
Abolition of grade crossings
—Cont'd
Supreme judicial court.
Petition by person aggrieved
by apportionment of costs,
159:70.
Review of departmental
orders, **159:79.**
Telecommunications and energy
department.
Agreement, approval, **159:80.**
Board for apportionment of
costs, membership,
159:70.
Carrier entitled to hearing
before department
consents to orders of
public works department,
159:70.
Disputes as to account of
expense, determination,
159:78.
Lists of crossings to be
abolished, **159:65.**
Orders, **159:65, 159:70,
159:79.**
Program, order designating,
159:65.
Public works department,
consent to orders, **159:70.**
Supreme judicial court, review
of orders, **159:79.**
Wires, removal or relocation,
159:74.
Access.
Land, crossing where owner cut
off from access, **160:110.**
Littoral proprietor's action for
cutting off access to sea,
160:96.
Actions.
Alterations, action for share of
expense, **159:64.**
Failure to comply with order for
crossing, recovery of
forfeiture, **160:110.**
Littoral proprietor's action for
cutting off access to sea,
160:96.
Removal of conduits, tracks, and
poles on abolition of grade
crossing, recovery of
expense, **159:74.**
Repairs, action for failure of
railroad to make, **160:107.**
Signs, recovery of penalty for
failure to erect, **160:145.**
Adverse possession.
Crossings acquired, **160:114.**
Lend acquired, **160:88.**

RAILROAD CROSSINGS
—Cont'd
Agreements.
Contracts and agreements. See
within this heading,
"Contracts and agreements."
Aldermen or selectmen.
Abolition of grade crossings,
petition, **159:65.**
Alteration of crossings. See
within this heading,
"Alteration of crossings."
Authorization of crossings,
application, **160:102,
160:104.**
Obstruction of highways by
crossings, applications and
decrees, **160:106.**
Signboards at grade crossings,
160:141.
Alteration of crossings,
159:59-159:64.
Abolition of grade crossings,
provisions inapplicable,
159:82.
Agreements, **159:61, 159:64,
159:80.**
Aldermen or selectmen.
Agreements by, proceedings,
159:80.
Application, **159:59.**
Appointment of commission to
determine who shall make
and pay for alterations,
application, **159:62.**
Apportionment of costs and
expenses. See within this
heading, "Apportionment of
costs and expenses."
Commission to determine
questions, **159:61-159:63.**
County commissioners. See
within this heading,
"County commissioners."
County may join in agreements,
159:80.
Damages, **159:60-159:64.**
Directors of railroads, agreement
as to alteration deemed
necessary by, **159:80.**
Eminent domain, taking land,
159:60, 159:80.
Expenses and charges, payment,
159:61-159:64.
Apportionment of costs and
expenses. See within this
heading, "Apportionment
of costs and expenses."
Filing agreements, **159:80.**
Hearings, **159:59, 159:80.**
Highway purchases inapplicable,
82:20.

RAILROAD CROSSINGS
  —Cont'd
Alteration of crossings —Cont'd
  Jury trial as to decision of
    commission, **159:63.**
  Location of crossing, charge,
    159:74.
  Maintenance and repair,
    agreement, **159:80.**
  Manner and limits of making,
    agreement, **159:80.**
  Notice, **159:59.**
    Agreements, **159:80.**
    Appointment of commission to
      determine who shall make
      and pay for alterations,
      159:62.
    Hearing before commission to
      determine who shall make
      and pay for alterations,
      159:62.
    Hearings, **159:59, 159:80.**
    Jury trial for revision of
      award by commission,
      159:63.
    Person designated to make
      failing to do so, any party
      may make, **159:64.**
    Public works department,
      **159:59, 159:62,
      160:111-160:113.**
      Agreement to have effect of
        order, **159:80.**
      Decision of public works
        department upon
        alteration of crossings.
      County commissioners. See
        within this heading,
        "County
        commissioners."
    Recovery of proportioned
      expenses by party making,
      159:64.
    Revision of award by
      commission to determine
      who shall make and pay,
      159:63.
    Street railway may join in
      agreement, **159:80.**
    Telecommunications and energy
      department. See within this
      heading,
      "Telecommunications and
      energy department."
    Vote of town authorizing
      agreement, **159:80.**
  Alteration of highways, **160:100,
    160:101, 160:103.**
    Notice and hearing, **159:61,
      159:62, 160:101.**
    Procedures for highways
      inapplicable to crossings,
      82:20.

RAILROAD CROSSINGS
  —Cont'd
Appeal.
  County commissioners, appeals
    from decision,
    160:111-160:113.
  Matters, **159:59, 159:79.**
  Telecommunications and energy
    department, powers upon
    appeals from certain
    decisions of county
    commissioner, **160:113.**
Apportionment of costs and
  expenses.
  Abolition of grade crossings. See
    within this heading,
    "Abolition of grade
    crossings."
  Alteration of crossings, **159:61.**
    Agreements, **159:80.**
    Recovery of proportioned
      expense by party making,
      159:64.
  Cities and towns. See within
    this heading, "Cities and
    towns."
  Commission for, powers and
    duties, **160:106.**
    Interlocking signals, **160:137.**
    Protection at crossings, **160:147.**
    Repairs at crossings, **160:106.**
  Separating grade crossings
    between two or more
    railroads by agreement,
    160:95.
Attorney general.
  Member of board for
    apportionment of cost of
    abolition of grade crossings,
    159:70.
  Recovery of penalties for failure
    to erect signs at crossings,
    160:145.
Authorization of grade crossings.
  Telecommunications and energy
    department. See within this
    heading,
    "Telecommunications and
    energy department."
Automobiles.
  Motor vehicles. See within this
    heading, "Motor vehicles."
Bonds and notes.
  Highway fund as available for
    payment of interest, **90:34.**
Bonds or undertakings.
  Alteration of highways and
    construction of crossings,
    160:100, 160:101.
  Obstructions at or repairs to
    crossings, security for
    performance of decree,
    160:106.

RAILROAD CROSSINGS
  —Cont'd
Boston.
  Legislative authority required
    for crossing over Boston
    harbor, **160:96.**
Boulevards crossing railroads,
  92:49-92:52.
Bridges.
  Alteration of crossing,
    applicability of proceedings,
    159:59.
  Construction expense, **160:107.**
  Overhead crossings and
    underpasses. See within this
    heading, "Overhead
    crossings and underpasses."
  Railroad bridges.
    See RAILROADS.
  Repairs, **159:77, 159:84,
    160:106, 160:107.**
  Space under, regulated, **160:98.**
Buildings and structures, removal
  or relocation upon abolition of
  grade crossings, **159:74.**
Canals, repair of crossings over,
  160:107.
Change.
  Alteration. See within this
    heading, "Alteration of
    crossings."
Cities and towns.
  Agreements.
    Alteration of crossing, **159:80.**
    Protection at crossings,
      agreements to share
      expense, **160:147.**
  Aldermen or selectmen. See
    within this heading,
    "Aldermen or selectmen."
  Appeals in certain matters,
    160:111.
  Apportionment of cost.
    Of alteration, **159:61.**
    Of repairs, **160:106.**
  Boston. See within this heading,
    "Boston."
  Expenses.
    Prior railroad, expense of
      crossing of public way
      across, **160:107.**
    Protection at crossings,
      160:47.
  Failure of railroad to repair
    crossings, recovery of
    damages, **160:107.**
  Indemnification, **160:100,
    160:101, 160:106.**
  Laying out highway across
    railroad, **160:104.**
  Recovery over against railroad
    for injury by defect in
    highway, **160:229.**

RAILROAD CROSSINGS
—Cont'd
Cities and towns —Cont'd
Security to indemnify city in
alteration of highway for
crossings, **160:100, 160:101.**
Signs at crossings, erection,
160:142-160:145.
Taking of land for alteration of
highways upon crossings,
indemnification of town,
160:101.
Collisions at, liability for damages,
160:232.
Commonwealth.
Action for removal of conduits,
tracks, and poles on
abolition of crossing, **159:74.**
Apportionment of cost of
protecting, or altering grade
crossing, **159:61, 160:147.**
Comptroller's duties as to
abolition of grade crossings,
159:78.
Elimination of grade crossing,
159:76.
Settlement of barred claim for
grade crossing elimination,
159:6.
Condemnation.
Eminent domain. See within
this heading, "Eminent
domain, taking of property."
Contracts and agreements.
Abolition of crossings, **159:80.**
Alteration of crossings, **159:61,
159:64, 159:80.**
Apportionment of cost of repairs,
160:106.
Cities and towns. See within
this heading, "Cities and
towns."
Public works department,
contributions to expense of
protection at crossings,
160:147.
Two or more railroads,
agreements between,
160:95, 160:96.
Waiver of appeal from decision
of commissioners in certain
matters as to crossings,
160:112.
Costs and expenses.
Abolition of grade crossings. See
within this heading,
"Abolition of grade
crossings."
Alteration of crossings. See
within this heading,
"Alteration of crossings."

RAILROAD CROSSINGS
—Cont'd
Costs and expenses —Cont'd
Apportionment. See within this
heading, "Apportionment of
costs and expenses."
Bridges, expense of construction,
160:107.
Cities and towns. See within
this heading, "Cities and
towns."
Counties.
Abolition of grade crossings. See
within this heading,
"Abolition of grade
crossings."
Alterations, apportionment of
cost, **159:61.**
Commissioners.
County commissioners. See
within this heading,
"County commissioners."
Expense of crossing of public
way over prior railroad
borne, **160:107.**
Protecting crossings,
apportioning cost, **160:147.**
Repairs, apportionment of cost,
160:106.
Signs, erection,
160:142-160:145.
County commissioners.
Abolition of crossings, petition,
159:65.
Alteration of crossings, **159:59,
159:61.**
Alteration of highways, **160:100,
160:101, 160:103.**
Appeal from decision as to
alteration of crossings,
160:111-160:113.
Application for commission to
determine who shall make
and pay for alterations of
crossings, **159:62.**
Authorization of grade crossings
between highway and
railroad, **160:97, 160:102.**
Bridges, application to
department to compel
repair, **159:84.**
Certification of decision as to
alteration of crossings,
159:59.
Costs of application for
alteration of crossings,
payment, **159:61.**
Decision of public works
department upon alteration
of crossings.
Appeal, **160:111-160:113.**
Filing, **159:59.**

RAILROAD CROSSINGS
—Cont'd
County commissioners —Cont'd
Laying out highway across
railroad, **160:104.**
Level crossings, authorization,
160:102.
Manner of crossing highways
determined, **160:75.**
Obstruction of highways by
crossings, powers and
duties, **160:97, 160:106,
160:108.**
Obstructions of crossings,
decree, **160:106.**
Rails at highway crossings at
grade, decree for protection,
160:103.
Raising or lowering highway
under direction, **160:100.**
Removal of standing wood at
crossings, **160:150.**
Repairs at crossings, decree,
160:106.
Safeguards at crossings,
requirement, **160:103.**
Crossing signs.
Signals and signs. See within
this heading, "Signals and
signs."
Damages.
Alteration of railroad crossings,
159:60-159:64.
Collisions at crossings, liability
for damages, **160:232.**
Elimination of grade crossings,
159:75, 159:76, 159:78.
Injury by highway defect, city or
town recovery over against
railroad, **160:229.**
Repair of crossings, recovery of
damages for railroad's
failure to make, **160:107.**
Decisions.
County commissioners. See
within this heading,
"County commissioners."
Eminent domain, taking of
property.
Abolition of grade crossings,
159:74-159:76, 159:80.
Alteration of crossings, **159:60.**
Alteration of highways, **160:101.**
Laying out highway across
railroad, **160:104.**
Separation of grade crossings
between two or more
railroads, **160:95.**
Engineers.
Penalty for failing to stop train
at crossing between
railroads, **160:135.**

RAILROAD CROSSINGS
—Cont'd
Engineers —Cont'd
Report, crossings to be shown,
160:18.
Examination or investigation.
Abolition of grade crossings. See
within this heading,
"Abolition of grade
crossings."
Expenses.
Costs and expenses. See within
this heading, "Costs and
expenses."
Filing and recording.
Abolition of grade crossings. See
within this heading,
"Abolition of grade
crossings."
Alteration of crossings,
agreements and decisions,
159:59, 159:61.
Appeal on certain matters
concerning crossings, notice
and petition, **160:111,
160:112.**
Inquest as to person killed at,
inspector to attend, **159:29.**
Laying out highway across
railroad, proceedings,
160:104.
Waiver of appeal in certain
matters, **160:112.**
Fines and penalties.
Access to land, noncompliance
with order to provide
crossings for owner cut off,
160:110.
Engineer failing to stop train at
grade crossing between
railroads, **160:135.**
Gates at private crossings,
neglect to close, **160:224.**
Motorist failing to take required
precautions, **90:15.**
Obstructing public highways,
160:151.
Protection required, failure to
provide, **160:148.**
Signs, violations, **160:145,
160:146, 160:148.**
Flagmen, requirement, **160:147,
160:148.**
Freight trains, regulation of use,
160:152.
Gates.
Department's requirement,
160:147, 160:148.
Luminous paint to be used,
160:147A.
Neglect to close at private
crossing, **160:224.**

RAILROAD CROSSINGS
—Cont'd
Grade of highway, change,
160:100.
Hearing.
Notice and hearing. See within
this heading, "Notice and
hearing."
Inflammable fluids carriers to stop
at railroad crossing, **90:15.**
Injunction.
Running of trains on railroad
failing to observe crossing
regulations, **160:136.**
Use of crossing until fencing
laws complied, **160:93.**
Investigations by public works
department.
Abolition of grade crossings. See
within this heading,
"Abolition of grade
crossings."
Jury trial as to which party to
make and pay for alterations,
159:63.
Laying out highway across
railroad, **160:104.**
Liability for damages in collision
cases, **160:232.**
Littoral proprietors, obstruction of
access to sea by crossings,
160:96.
Lowering highways, **160:100.**
Luminous paint on signs, gates
and other devices at crossings,
rule, **160:147A.**
Maintenance and repair.
Repairs and maintenance. See
within this heading,
"Repairs and maintenance."
Manner and limits of making.
Abolition of grade crossings. See
within this heading,
"Abolition of grade
crossings."
Purchase or taking of land,
manner of crossing
highways to be established
prior, **160:75.**
Massachusetts Bay transportation
authority, protection of
crossings of railroads operated
under contract, **160:147.**
Metropolitan district boulevards,
92:49-92:52.
Motor vehicles.
Occupying crossing, **160:152.**
Required precautions at
crossings, **90:15.**
Municipalities.
Cities and towns. See within
this heading, "Cities and
towns."

RAILROAD CROSSINGS
—Cont'd
Navigable waters, consent of
public works department
required to crossing over,
160:96.
Notes.
Bonds and notes. See within this
heading, "Bonds and notes."
Notice and hearing.
Abolition of grade crossings. See
within this heading,
"Abolition of grade
crossings."
Alteration of crossings. See
within this heading,
"Alteration of crossings."
Alteration of highways, **159:61,
159:62, 160:101.**
Appeal from decisions of county
commissioners, **160:113.**
Authorization of highway
crossings at grade,
application, **160:102.**
Commission to determine who
shall make and pay for
alterations to crossings,
159:61, 159:62.
Flagmen, order, **160:147.**
Flashing light signals,
requirement, **160:147.**
Freight trains, use of crossings,
160:152.
Gates, requirement, **160:147.**
Grade crossings, applications for
authorization, **160:102.**
Laying out highway across
railroad, **160:104.**
Manner of crossing highways,
determination, **160:75.**
Metropolitan boulevards
crossing railroads, proposed
action with respect, **92:50.**
Obstructions.
Cars occupying crossing,
160:152.
Construction of crossing as
obstruction of highway,
160:97, 160:106, 160:108.
County commissioners'
jurisdiction, **160:108.**
Penalty against railroad for
obstructing crossing,
160:151.
Reflector devices on signs,
160:142.
Removal of, **160:106, 160:108.**
Repairs to crossings, **160:106.**
Signboards, **160:141, 160:142.**
Standing wood, removal,
160:150.

RAILROAD CROSSINGS
—Cont'd
Overhead crossings and
underpasses.
Agreement with cities and towns
as to wearing surfaces,
160:99.
Construction, **160:98.**
Lowering highway, **160:100.**
Maintenance and repair, **159:77,**
160:106, 160:107.
Raising highway, **160:100.**
Required, **160:97.**
Signals at overhead crossings,
160:149.
Space, regulated, **160:98.**
Penalties.
Fines and penalties. See within
this heading, "Fines and
penalties."
Petition.
Abolition of grade crossings. See
within this heading,
"Abolition of grade
crossings."
Appeal from county
commissioners, **160:112.**
Injunction against running
trains on railroad failing to
observe crossing regulations,
160:136.
Laying out highway across
railroad, **160:104.**
Standing wood, removal,
160:150.
Pipes, removal or relocation upon
abolition of grade crossings,
159:74, 159:75.
Poles and wires, removal or
relocation, **159:74, 160:104A.**
Prescriptive rights, **160:114.**
Private railroads, **160:245,**
160:246.
Protective devices, installation,
160:147.
Public works department.
Abolition of grade crossings. See
within this heading,
"Abolition of grade
crossings."
Agreement to share expense of
protection at crossings,
160:147.
Alteration of crossings. See
within this heading,
"Alteration of crossings."
Grade crossings, authorization,
160:102.
Laying out highway across
railroad, **160:104.**
Navigable or tide waters,
consent to crossing, **160:96.**

RAILROAD CROSSINGS
—Cont'd
Public works department —Cont'd
Signs at crossings, erection,
160:142-160:145.
Supreme judicial court, review of
orders, **159:79.**
Rails to be protected at grade
crossings, **160:103.**
Raising highways, **160:100.**
Recording.
Filing and recording. See within
this heading, "Filing and
recording."
Reflector devices on signs,
160:142.
Regulations by
telecommunications and
energy department, **160:136.**
Repairs and maintenance,
160:106, 160:107.
Abolition of grade crossings. See
within this heading,
"Abolition of grade
crossings."
Highway procedures,
inapplicability to crossings,
82:20.
Report of engineer to show number
and manner, **160:18.**
School bus safety precautions at
crossings, **90:15.**
Security.
Bonds or undertakings. See
within this heading, "Bonds
or undertakings."
Selectmen.
Aldermen or selectmen. See
within this heading,
"Aldermen or selectmen."
Severance of private land, crossing
in case, **160:109.**
Signals and signs,
160:135-160:152.
Aldermen or selectmen, **160:141.**
Bell, ringing, **160:138.**
Collision caused by neglect to
give, liability for damages,
160:232.
Erection of, **160:142-160:145.**
Failure to erect, **160:145.**
Fines and penalties, **160:145,**
160:146, 160:148.
Flashing light signals,
department may order,
160:147, 160:148.
Form and size, **160:140.**
Furnished by railroads, **160:143.**
Luminous paint to be used,
160:147A.
Manual warning signals at some
crossings, **160:138A.**

RAILROAD CROSSINGS
—Cont'd
Signals and signs —Cont'd
Overhead crossings, **160:149.**
Placement, **160:142.**
Reflector buttons or devices,
160:142.
Release from requirement of,
when impracticable,
160:144.
Tampering, **160:146.**
Whistle, sounding, **160:138,**
160:139.
Standards for luminous paint to be
used on crossing signs, gates,
and other devices, **160:147A.**
Standing wood, removal, **160:150.**
State.
Commonwealth. See within this
heading, "Commonwealth."
Street railways.
See STREET RAILWAYS.
Supreme judicial court.
Abolition of grade crossings. See
within this heading,
"Abolition of grade
crossings."
Enforcement of laws as to
crossings, **160:136.**
Restraining use of crossings
until fencing laws complied,
160:93.
Review of orders, **159:79.**
Telecommunications and energy
department.
Abolition of grade crossings. See
within this heading,
"Abolition of grade
crossings."
Alteration of crossings, **159:59,**
159:61, 159:62.
Approval of agreements,
159:80.
Appeal.
County commissioners, appeal,
160:111-160:113.
Order for alteration of
crossing, appeal, **159:59.**
Appointment of commission to
determine who shall make
and pay for alterations,
159:62.
Authorization of grade crossings,
160:97, 160:102, 160:104.
Condition precedent to taking
or purchase of land,
160:75.
Costs of application for
alteration of crossings,
payment, **159:61.**
Flagmen, requirement, **160:147,**
160:148.

RAILROAD CROSSINGS
—Cont'd

Telecommunications and energy
department —Cont'd
Flashing light signals, order,
160:147, 160:148.
Freight trains, use of crossings,
160:152.
Gates, requirement, **160:147,
160:148.**
Laying out highway across
railroad at grade, consent,
160:104.
Member of department to be
member of commission to
determine who shall make
and pay for alterations,
159:62.
Reflector devices on signs,
160:142.
Release of railroad, county, city,
or town from sign
requirements, where
impracticable, **160:144.**
Rules and regulations, **160:136.**
Signals at overhead crossings
may be required, **160:149.**
Signboards at grade crossings,
application to require
erection, **160:141.**
Signs at crossings, approval of
form and size, **160:140.**
Two railroads, consent to
crossings between, **160:96.**
Waiver of appeal from county
commissioners, **160:112.**
Tidewaters, consent of public
works department required for
crossing over, **160:96.**
Towns.
Cities and towns. See within
this heading, "Cities and
towns."
Traffic regulations.
Motor vehicles. See within this
heading, "Motor vehicles."
Trial or hearing.
Notice and hearing. See within
this heading, "Notice and
hearing."
Tunnels.
Overhead crossings and
underpasses. See within this
heading, "Overhead
crossings and underpasses."
Turnpike authority, **81A:4.**
Underpasses.
Overhead crossings and
underpasses. See within this
heading, "Overhead
crossings and underpasses."

RAILROAD CROSSINGS
—Cont'd

Warning signs or devices.
Signals and signs. See within
this heading, "Signals and
signs."
Waters and watercourses, **159:75,
160:96.**
Whistles sounding at crossing,
160:138, 160:139.
Wires, disconnection or removal
for certain purposes, **159:74,
160:104A.**
Woodlands, removal of standing
wood, **160:150.**

RAILROAD EQUIPMENT
COMPANIES.
Railroads authorized to hold stock,
160:65A.

RAILROAD FULL CREW ACT,
160:185.

RAILROAD POLICE,
159:92-159:95.
See RAILROADS.

RAILROAD RETIREMENT ACT
OR BOARD.
Deduction of taxes paid pursuant
to Federal Railroad
Retirement Act, **62:3.**
Employment security.
Federal agencies and programs.
See EMPLOYMENT
SECURITY.

RAILROADS, 160:1-160:252.
Abandonment.
Electric railroads, abandonment
of route, **162:9.**
Location, abandonment, **160:86.**
Passenger stations,
abandonment, **160:128,
160:128A.**
Purchaser of abandoned rights
of way, liability of
municipality, **40:54A.**
Rights of way, municipalities'
liability to purchasers of
abandoned, **40:54A.**
Sale of unclaimed goods, **135:6.**
Service, abandonment, **159:16A,
160:128, 160:128A.**
Youth conservation and service
corps, **78A:3.**
Abolition of crossings,
159:65-159:82.
See RAILROAD CROSSINGS.
Access to land, owner cut off,
160:110.
Access to sea, obstruction of by
crossings, **160:96.**

RAILROADS —Cont'd
Accidents, **160:229-160:233.**
Annual return to contain
statement, **160:242.**
Assumption of risk by
employees, **153:4.**
Collisions at grade crossings,
liability for damages,
160:232.
Contributory negligence as
defense to action for
collision, **160:232.**
Death, accidents causing. See
within this heading,
"Death."
Debris caused by derailments,
removal, **160:241.**
Employees' liability, **153:1,
153:4.**
Expressmen.
Railroads not liable for acts,
160:233.
Season ticket, injuries while
riding, **160:193.**
Facsimile signature of resident
agent on policy of accident
insurance, **175:157.**
Highway defect within location
of railroad, liability of
railroad to city or town,
160:229.
Investigation, **159:29.**
Municipal liability for failure to
place warning signs at
crossing, **160:145.**
Negligence. See within this
heading, "Negligence."
Notice, **38:8, 159:28.**
Penalty for negligence of
engineer, fireman, or other
agent causing personal
injury, **160:231.**
Removal of wreckage and debris
caused by derailments,
160:241.
Telecommunications and energy
department. See within this
heading,
"Telecommunications and
energy department."
Accommodations.
Equal facilities. See within this
heading, "Equal facilities
and accommodations."
Passengers' accommodations
must be reasonable,
160:172.
Stations. See within this
heading, "Stations and
depots."
Street railroads.
See STREET RAILWAYS.

RAILROADS —Cont'd
Accounts and accounting.
Abolition of grade crossings, accounts of expense reported to state comptroller, **159:78.**
Audit of accounts of expense upon abolition of grade crossings, **159:78.**
Corporation operating railroad under contract with trustees, **160:51.**
Examination, **159:35, 160:242.**
Forms prescribed by telecommunications and energy department, **159:31.**
Motor vehicle, reports relating to transportation, **160:70A.**
Supervision by public utilities commission, **25:7.**
Telecommunications and energy department. See within this heading, "Telecommunications and energy department."
Actions or suits.
Assessment upon shares of stock, collection, **160:40.**
Change of name of corporation not to defeat, **160:217.**
Costs of actions. See within this heading, "Costs of actions."
Crossings.
See RAILROAD CROSSINGS.
District attorney, actions to recover penalties. See within this heading, "District attorney, actions to recover penalties."
District court. See within this heading, "District court."
Embankments, culverts, walls, or fences ordered, double damages for failure of railroad to construct, **160:91, 160:92.**
Equipment on cars and trains, recovery of penalty for violations, **160:160.**
Fencing, recovery of costs, **160:94.**
Filing and recording. See within this heading, "Filing and recording."
Fire.
Grass or forest land, recovery of expenses incurred in extinguishment of, fire, **160:241.**
Insurance policy upon property destroyed by fire caused by locomotive, **160:234.**

RAILROADS —Cont'd
Actions or suits —Cont'd
Freight, recovery of forfeitures for violations, **160:209.**
Labor and material, actions against railroads, **159:96-159:100.**
City and town clerks, filing, **159:98, 159:99.**
Construction contractor not to have, **149:27C, 159:97.**
Contract with person other than railroad corporation, **159:96.**
Fences, labor lien for construction, **160:94.**
Filing and recording. See within this heading, "Filing and recording."
Limitation of actions, **159:100.**
Notice of intention to claim right of action for materials, **159:98, 262:34.**
Statement of amount due for labor, **159:99, 262:34.**
Waiver of appeal from certain decisions, **160:112.**
Limitation of actions. See within this heading, "Limitation of actions."
Platform gates, recovery of penalty for violations, **160:167.**
Revival, petition, **3:5.**
Superior court. See within this heading, "Superior court."
Supreme judicial court. See within this heading, "Supreme judicial court."
Trial or hearing. See within this heading, "Trial or hearing."
Adverse possession.
Crossing may not be acquired, **160:114.**
Land of railroad may not be obtained, **160:88.**
Advertising, exemption of rolling stock from outdoor advertising requirements, **93:32.**
Advice of department, effect on duties and liabilities, **159:38.**
Affidavit of clerk as to serving of notice of first meeting, **160:29.**
After-acquired property, power to pledge or mortgage, **160:47.**
Agents.
Employees, officers, and agents. See within this heading, "Employees, officers, and agents."
Agreement of association.
Assumed name to be stated, **160:14, 160:248.**

RAILROADS —Cont'd
Agreement of association —Cont'd
Certificates.
Annexed certificates to agreement, **160:23, 160:24.**
Publication and posting, certificate of clerk as conclusive evidence, **160:16.**
Void unless certificate of incorporation issued within one year, **160:26.**
Cities and counties in which located to be named in agreement of association, **160:14.**
Contents, **160:14.**
Filing and recording. See within this heading, "Filing and recording."
Foreign countries, corporations to construct and operate railroads and telegraphs, **160:248, 160:249.**
Increase of bonds or capital stock beyond amounts fixed, **160:41.**
Intent to be stated in agreement of association. See within this heading, "Intent to be stated in agreement of association."
Liability of subscriber to take shares, **160:14.**
Making, **160:13.**
Par value, agreement to show, **160:14.**
Posting, **160:16.**
Presented for inspection of department, **160:23.**
Publication, **160:16.**
Subscription, **160:14.**
Termini to be stated in agreement of association. See within this heading, "Termini to be stated in agreement of association."
Void unless certificate of incorporation issued within one year, **160:26.**
Agreements.
Contracts and agreements. See within this heading, "Contracts and agreements."
Aid.
See AID AND ASSISTANCE.
Air conditioning systems, exception as to inspection, **146:45A.**
Aircraft.
See AIRCRAFT AND AVIATION.

RAILROADS —Cont'd

Air gun, discharging across right-of-way, **269:12B.**

Alcoholic liquors.
Excise tax on sales, **138:21.**
Licensing, **138:13.**
Transportation and delivery, **138:22.**

Aldermen or selectmen.
Agreement with directors fixing route, **160:20.**
Altering highway unlawfully, petition to enjoin, **160:100.**
Complaints and petitions.
By selectmen, **159:24.**
Consent to location of railroad, **160:77.**

Crossings.
See RAILROAD CROSSINGS.

Description of location, copy filed with board, **160:80.**

Establishment of through routes, notice of hearing, **159:21.**

Fixing route by department, notice, **160:21.**

Highways and streets.
Petition.
Altering highway unlawfully, petition to enjoin, **160:100.**
Laying out highway across railroad, **160:104.**
Private railroads, consent to use of public way, **160:245.**
Spurs and branches, consent to laying in public way, **160:22.**

Maintenance and repair of bridges, application to department to compel, **159:84.**

Map of route submitted, **160:19.**

Private railroads, consent to use of public way, **160:245.**

Relocation of stations and depots, approval, **160:129.**

Report of engineers submitted, **160:19.**

Spurs and branches, consent to laying in public way, **160:22.**

State house, consent to location within three miles, **160:77.**

Street railways.
See STREET RAILWAYS.

Variation of direction, consent, **160:86.**

Alteration or amendment.
Change or modification. See within this heading, "Change or modification."

RAILROADS —Cont'd

Animals.
Barriers against, duty to erect, **160:93.**
Damages for animals injured on tracks, **160:222, 160:223.**
Horses. See within this heading, "Horses."
Offenses and penalties. See within this heading, "Offenses and penalties."
Rest and feeding during transportation, **272:81.**
Seeing eye dogs accompanying blind persons, **272:98A.**

Annual meeting.
Bondholders or creditors. See within this heading, "Bondholders or creditors."
Stockholders, **160:33.**
Trustees for benefit of creditors, annual meeting for bondholders and creditors, **160:52, 160:53.**

Annual return.
Connecting railroads, statements of facts concerning contracts and leases, **160:62.**
Contents and form.
Forms. See within this heading, "Forms."
Express companies, **159:33.**
Leases. See within this heading, "Leases."

Appeals.
Crossings, **159:59, 159:79, 160:111-160:113.**
See RAILROAD CROSSINGS.
Telecommunications and energy department. See within this heading, "Telecommunications and energy department."
Waiver of appeal in certain cases, **160:112.**

Appropriations, **161C:4.**
Street railways, **40:5, 161:161.**

Approval of issue of bonds, notes, etc., **160:48.**

Arrest.
See ARREST.

Arson, insured property, **160:234.**

Assaulting or interfering with employees, **159:104.**

Assessments.
Sale of stock for failure to pay assessments, **160:39.**
Street railways.
See STREET RAILWAYS.

RAILROADS —Cont'd

Assignment for benefit of creditors.
Trustees for benefit of creditors.
See within this heading, "Trustees for benefit of creditors."

Assignment to railroad of fire insurance on property which it was held liable for burning, **160:234.**

Associates' authority as to incorporation, **160:15.**

Assumption of risk by employees, **153:4.**

Attachment of property.
Cars and engines, attachment, **223:43.**
Employees' relief associations, funds, **159:88.**

Attorney general.
Crossings.
Member of board for apportionment of cost of abolition of grade crossings, **159:70.**
Recovery of penalties for failure to erect signs at crossings, **160:145.**
Petition for enforcement of laws, **160:252.**
Recovery of penalties.
Cars and equipment, violations, **160:160.**
Failure to erect signs at crossings, **160:145.**
Freight, violations, **160:209.**
Platform gates, violations, **160:167.**

Auction.
Assessments, sale of stock for failure to pay, **160:39.**
New shares upon increase of capital stock, **159:51.**
Street railways.
Assessment, sale for failure to pay, **161:21, 161:22.**
Notice of auction, sale of new shares, **159:51.**

Audit of accounts of expense upon abolition of grade crossings, **159:78.**

Automatic couplers on cars, **160:156, 160:157, 160:160, 160:161.**

Automatic signals at crossings between two or more railroads, **160:136, 160:137.**

Auxiliary services, **160:70A.**

Badges for employees, **159:92, 160:177.**
Forged railroad badges, uttering, **267:6.**

RAILROADS —Cont'd
Baggage.
  Bicycles, transportation as
    baggage, **160:196.**
  Cars.
    Baggage cars. See within this
      heading, "Baggage cars."
  Checks, **160:194.**
  Electric railroads as carriers,
    162:14.
  Storage upon weekends,
    160:195.
  Street railways as carriers,
    161:53.
Baggage cars.
  Heating, **160:165.**
  Platform gates, **160:167.**
Bailments.
  Leases. See within this heading,
    "Leases."
Barriers.
  Gates and barriers. See within
    this heading, "Gates and
    barriers."
Bars, fences to have, **160:93.**
BB gun, discharging across
  right-of-way, **269:12B.**
Bell, ringing, **160:138.**
Bicycles.
  See BICYCLES.
Blind persons.
  Examination of employees for
    sight defects, **160:178.**
  Free or reduced rate
    transportation, **159:15.**
  Seeing eye dogs, blind persons
    accompanied, **272:98A.**
Board for apportionment of costs
  of abolition of grade crossings,
  159:70.
Boilers of locomotives, testing,
  160:168.
Bondholders or creditors.
  Annual meeting, **160:52.**
  Election of trustees, **160:53.**
  Consent to contract by trustees
    for benefit of creditors,
    meeting to grant, **160:51.**
  Examination of books and
    financial condition upon
    request of bondholders,
    159:35.
  Notice of meetings, **160:51,**
    160:52.
  Trustees for benefit of creditors.
    See within this heading,
    "Trustees for benefit of
    creditors."
Bonds and undertakings.
  Application to commissioners on
    severance of private land,
    160:109.

RAILROADS —Cont'd
Bonds and undertakings —Cont'd
  Crossings.
    See RAILROAD CROSSINGS.
  Employees, security not to be
    required, **159:4.**
  Indemnity bond, employees not
    to be required to give, **159:4.**
  Street railways.
    Railway company, **161:12,**
      161:13.
    Transportation area, **161:148.**
  Treasurer, bond, **160:32.**
Bonds, notes, etc.
  Approval of issue, **160:48.**
  Bondholders or creditors. See
    within this heading,
    "Bondholders or creditors."
  Branches and extension, taking
    bonds and notes to aid in
    construction, **160:69.**
  Computing amount of capital
    stock as basis for issue,
    159:53.
  Connecting railroads, taking or
    guaranteeing securities,
    160:68, 160:69.
  Coupon bonds, exchange for
    registered bonds, **160:49.**
  Crossings.
    Highway fund as available for
      payment of interest on
      bonds, **90:34.**
  Holders.
    Bondholders or creditors. See
      within this heading,
      "Bondholders or
      creditors."
  Increase of, purpose for which
    allowed, **160:41.**
  Issue, **159:53, 160:47, 160:48.**
  Leased railroad, taking or
    guaranteeing bonds, **160:68.**
  Negotiation at less than par,
    validity, **160:50.**
  Other corporations, taking or
    guaranteeing securities of,
    160:64-160:70.
  Proceeds from issue, **160:48.**
  Registered bonds, **160:49.**
  Sale at less than par, validity,
    160:50.
  State funds, investment in
    certain railroad obligations,
    29:38.
  Stock. See within this heading,
    "Stock and stockholders."
  Telecommunications and energy
    department's duties as to
    issuance, **25:7, 160:48.**
  Uniform securities act,
    exemptions, **110A:402.**

RAILROADS —Cont'd
Bonds, notes, etc —Cont'd
  Validity where sold at less than
    par, **160:50.**
Books and records.
  Records, reports, and returns.
    See within this heading,
    "Records, reports, and
    returns."
Boston.
  Alteration of crossings,
    application to
    telecommunications and
    energy department, **159:59.**
  Auction sales in, increase in
    capital stock, **159:51.**
  Commutation tickets in area,
    160:190.
  Crossings.
    See RAILROAD CROSSINGS.
  Duties imposed upon county
    commissioners devolve upon
    city council and
    telecommunications and
    energy department, **160:2.**
  Elevated railways.
    See ELEVATED RAILWAYS.
  Freight differential against,
    160:210.
  Harbor.
    Boston harbor. See within this
      heading, "Boston harbor."
  Lease or contract between
    connecting carriers not
    authorized, **160:62.**
  Morning and evening trains,
    160:197.
  Notice of meetings of
    bondholders or creditors,
    publication, **160:51, 160:52.**
  Result of examination of books
    and financial condition in,
    publication, **159:35.**
  Stock, sale of new stock, **159:51.**
  Street railways.
    See STREET RAILWAYS.
  Terminal corporation.
    See BOSTON TERMINAL
      CORPORATION.
  Workingmen's trains, **160:198.**
Boston harbor.
  Crossings over, **160:96.**
  Freight differential against,
    160:210.
  Piers and wharves, connections,
    91:4.
Boston terminal corporation.
  See BOSTON TERMINAL
    CORPORATION.
Boundaries of state, intersection,
  1:4.

RAILROADS —Cont'd

Brakemen.
Assaulting or interfering,
159:104.
Conductors must have
experience,
160:180-160:183.
Number required, **160:154.**
Street railways.
Assaulting or interfering with
brakemen, **159:104.**
Hours of labor, **161:103.**
Brakes.
Cars, **160:154.**
Locomotives, **160:155, 160:160,
160:161, 160:169, 160:170.**
Mufflers on vacuum brakes,
160:169, 160:171.
Periodic testing, **160:155.**
Trains, **160:155, 160:160,
160:161.**
Branches and extensions.
Changes in construction to
prevent improper use of
crossings by freight trains,
160:152.
Construction of, **160:115.**
Department may order extension
of lines, **159:16.**
Fixing route, **160:22.**
Opening for public use, **160:118,
160:119.**
Stocks, notes, or bonds of, to aid
in construction, **160:69.**
Street railways, stopping at
branch crossings, **161:92.**
Unauthorized extension by
consolidated corporation,
160:42.
Bridges, **159:83-159:85.**
Canals, bridges over, **160:107.**
Construction of, plans to be
submitted to department,
159:83.
Crossings.
See RAILROAD CROSSINGS.
Drawbridges. See within this
heading, "Drawbridges."
Engineer's report as to kind and
amount of bridging, **160:18.**
Examination, **159:83.**
Guards, **160:134.**
Minimum clearance, **160:98.**
Repair and maintenance,
159:84.
Enforcement, **159:85.**
Street railways, liability for
defects, **161:89, 161:90.**
Telecommunications and energy
department. See within this
heading,
"Telecommunications and
energy department."

RAILROADS —Cont'd

Bridging, kind and amount to be
shown in engineer's report,
160:18.
Brush.
Grass lands. See within this
heading, "Grass lands."
Buffet car.
Alcoholic liquor license to
railroad corporation, **138:13.**
Drinking water, **160:174.**
Buildings and structures.
Abolition of grade crossings,
removal and relocation,
159:74.
Clearance of track in yards,
160:134A.
Platforms. See within this
heading, "Platforms."
Right of way, permit to build
structure, **40:54A.**
Stations and depots. See within
this heading, "Stations and
depots."
Business corporations.
Applicability of law, **156:2,
156B:3, 158:1.**
Foreign countries. See within
this heading, "Foreign
countries or states."
Limitation on holding of capital
stock of domestic
corporations, **156B:15.**
Bylaws, **160:30-160:33.**
Annual meeting governed,
160:33.
Appointment of officers and
agents, manner prescribed
by bylaws, **160:32.**
Bond of treasurer prescribed,
160:32.
First meeting, adoption, **160:30.**
Officers and agents may be
authorized, **160:31, 160:32.**
Quorum of stockholders
provided, **160:33.**
Relief corporations. See within
this heading, "Relief
corporations."
Vacancies, manner of filing
prescribed in bylaws,
160:32.
Caboose.
Sanitary facilities, **160:172A.**
Unlawful riding, **160:220.**
Canals.
Alteration of course, **160:105.**
Bridges over, **160:107.**
Expenses of repairs to crossings
over, **160:107.**
Canopies on track motor cars,
160:163A.

RAILROADS —Cont'd

Cap, uniform cap for employees,
160:177.
Car and equipment companies,
holding stock, **160:65A.**
Car houses, acquisition of land,
160:78, 160:83.
Cars and rolling stock.
Alcohol, license to sell on car,
138:13, 138:14.
Attachment of cars and engines,
223:43.
Baggage cars. See within this
heading, "Baggage cars."
Blind person accompanied by
seeing eye dog, carriage,
272:98A.
Brakes and brakemen, **160:154.**
Breaking and entering, **266:19.**
Buffet car. See within this
heading, "Buffet car."
Burning of, as arson, **266:2.**
Canopy on track motor car,
160:163A.
Crimes and offenses.
Arson, **266:2.**
Breaking and entering,
266:19.
Disorderly conduct, **272:43.**
Endangering safety of persons,
160:226.
Equipment, offenses in
connection, **160:160,
160:228.**
Expectoration, **270:14, 270:15.**
Gambling, **271:2.**
Obstructing passage, **160:226.**
Racial discrimination,
272:92A, 272:98.
Riding unlawfully, **160:220.**
Smoking, **272:43A.**
Spitting, **270:14, 270:15.**
Stealing, **266:20.**
Tampering, **159:103, 160:228.**
Dining cars. See within this
heading, "Dining cars."
Disorderly conduct, **272:43.**
Drawbridges, stopping, **160:125,
160:126.**
Drinking water and cups,
160:174, 160:175.
Endangering safety of persons,
160:226.
Equipment.
Brakes. See within this
heading, "Brakes."
Mufflers. See within this
heading, "Mufflers."
Recovery of penalty for
violations in connection,
160:160.

RAILROADS —Cont'd
Cars and rolling stock —Cont'd
Equipment —Cont'd
Safety appliances or devices.
See within this heading,
"Safety appliances and
devices."
Express cars, platform gates,
160:167.
Freight cars. See within this
heading, "Freight cars."
Gambling, **271:2.**
Grab irons, **160:158, 160:160,
160:161.**
Heating, **160:165.**
Houses, acquisition of land for
car houses, **160:78, 160:83.**
Installation of safety windows
and doors, **160:163.**
License to sell alcohol on car,
138:13, 138:14.
Lighting, explosive oils or fluids
not to be used, **160:166.**
Locomotives. See within this
heading, "Locomotives."
Mail cars. See within this
heading, "Mail cars."
Obstructing passage, **160:226.**
Operation on through routes,
159:21.
Outdoor advertising
requirements, exempt,
93:32.
Parlor cars, **149:148, 160:174.**
Platform gates, **160:167.**
Protective appliances, **160:163,
160:176.**
Racial discrimination, **272:92A,
272:98.**
Reasonable accommodations
must be furnished for
passengers, **160:172.**
Recommendations of department
for additions, **159:23.**
Recovery of penalties in
connection, **160:160.**
Safety switches on tracks used,
160:132.
Secured transactions.
Application of article to rolling
stock, **106:9-103.**
Equipment trust covering
rolling stock, exclusion,
106:9-104.
Multistate transactions,
perfection of security
interest, **106:9-103.**
Smoking, **272:43A.**
Women and children not to be
required to ride in
smoking cars, **160:173.**

RAILROADS —Cont'd
Cars and rolling stock —Cont'd
Spitting, **270:14, 270:15.**
Stealing, **266:20.**
Stock in car and equipment
companies, **160:65A.**
Street railways.
See STREET RAILWAYS.
Tampering, **159:103, 160:228.**
Telecommunications and energy
department. See within this
heading,
"Telecommunications and
energy department."
Testing of, promulgation of
regulations, **160:168.**
Throwing or shooting at train,
bus, etc., **159:104.**
Arrest and jurisdiction,
159:93, 159:94, 159:104.
Tools.
Equipment, **160:163.**
Tampering, **160:228.**
Unlawful riding, **160:220.**
Cemetery, making roadway
through, **272:76.**
Certificates and certification.
Agreement of association. See
within this heading,
"Agreement of association."
Approval of transfer, lease,
purchase, or sale of
franchise and property,
159:54.
Capital stock, increase or
reduction, **160:15, 160:25.**
Clerks. See within this heading,
"Clerks."
Compliance with provisions,
160:24, 160:76.
Construction and location. See
within this heading,
"Construction and location."
Decision upon application for
alteration of crossings,
159:59.
Directors. See within this
heading, "Directors."
Electric railroads.
See ELECTRIC RAILROADS.
Evidence. See within this
heading, "Evidence."
Examination of employees for
color blindness or sight
defects, **160:178.**
Facsimile signature or seal, use
on certificates, **160:38.**
Fees. See within this heading,
"Fees."
Foreign corporations exempt
from filing annual certificate
of condition, **181:12.**

RAILROADS —Cont'd
Certificates and certification
—Cont'd
Foreign countries. See within
this heading, "Foreign
countries or states."
Gauge, change, **160:25.**
Incorporation, certificate,
160:24.
Fees. See within this heading,
"Fees."
First meeting upon issuance,
160:29.
Forms. See within this
heading, "Forms."
Time for construction after
issuance, **160:27.**
Time within which must be
issued, **160:26.**
Location.
Construction and location. See
within this heading,
"Construction and
location."
Maps and statements filed upon
opening of road for public
use, **160:119.**
Name of corporation, certificates
upon change, **160:216.**
Offer to purchase facilities to be
sent by registered mail,
161C:7.
Publication or posting of
agreement of association,
certificate as conclusive
evidence, **160:16.**
Public convenience and
necessity.
Application for certificate,
160:17.
Branches and extensions,
construction, **160:115.**
Electric railroads.
See ELECTRIC
RAILROADS.
Notice to railroads of hearing
upon motor carriers' of
property certificate,
159B:3.
Street railways.
See STREET RAILWAYS.
Route, fixing, **160:21.**
Stock certificates, **160:38.**
Street railways.
See STREET RAILWAYS.
Certified mail, offer to purchase
railroad facilities to be sent,
161C:7.
Change or modification.
Canals, alteration of course,
160:105.

RAILROADS —Cont'd
Change or modification —Cont'd
Charter, petition to general
court for amendment, **3:5.**
Crossings, alteration of,
159:59-159:64.
See RAILROAD CROSSINGS.
Eminent domain, taking
property by. See within this
heading, "Eminent domain,
taking property."
Freight trains, change in
manner of making up,
160:139.
Gauge, change, **160:15, 160:25.**
Highways, **160:100, 160:101,
160:103.**
Notice and hearing, **159:61,
159:62, 160:101.**
Procedures for highways
inapplicable to crossings,
82:20.
Location, change, **160:81,
160:85, 160:86, 160:95.**
River or stream location
changed on abolition of
grade crossing, **159:75.**
Telecommunications and
energy department. See
within this heading,
"Telecommunications and
energy department."
Name, change, **160:215-160:217.**
Petitions. See within this
heading, "Petitions and
complaints."
Rules and regulations
concerning motor carriers of
passengers, petition for
alteration, **159A:12.**
Street railways.
See STREET RAILWAYS.
Charges, **159B:6, 159B:6A,
159B:7, 160:208-160:211.**
See RATES AND CHARGES.
Charter.
Amendment of, petition to
general court, **3:5.**
Bylaws. See within this heading,
"Bylaws."
Concurrent legislation with
other states, railroad
corporations chartered,
160:4.
Extension, petition to general
court, **3:5.**
Foreign corporation, **160:4.**
Increase of stocks or bonds
beyond amounts fixed,
160:41.
Special charters. See within this
heading, "Special charters."

RAILROADS —Cont'd
Charter —Cont'd
Street railways.
See STREET RAILWAYS.
Unauthorized acts by
consolidated corporation
which may cause forfeiture,
160:42.
Children or minors.
Employment, **149:62, 149:78.**
Reduced rates, **159:18.**
Smoking cars, children not to be
required to ride, **160:173.**
Street railways.
See STREET RAILWAYS.
Cigarette tax, determination of
amount payable to mass
transportation facilities and
services from revenues,
58:25B.
Cities and towns.
Abandoned rights of way or
other property, duties
regarding, **40:54A.**
Agreement of association, city in
which located to be named,
160:14.
Aldermen or selectmen. See
within this heading,
"Aldermen or selectmen."
Alterations of highways, notice,
160:101.
Auction sales of new shares of
capital stock, places for
holding prescribed by
department, **159:51.**
Borrowing outside debt limit in
connection with street
railways, **44:8.**
Boston. See within this heading,
"Boston."
Clerks.
City and town clerks. See
within this heading, "City
and town clerks, filing."
Contracts and agreements. See
within this heading,
"Contracts and agreements."
Crossings.
See RAILROAD CROSSINGS.
Electric railroads.
See ELECTRIC RAILROADS.
Fire extinguishment, liability of
railroad for expense,
160:241.
Laying out highway across
railroad, **160:104, 160:107.**
Master plan of municipal
planning boards, **41:81D.**
Prior railroad, expense of
crossing of public way across
borne by cities and towns,
160:107.

RAILROADS —Cont'd
Cities and towns —Cont'd
Recovery over against railroad
for injury by defect in
highway, **160:229.**
Street railways.
See STREET RAILWAYS.
Tax levy for interest on debt for
railroad aid, **44:57.**
Through routes, notice of
hearing upon establishment,
159:21.
Water supply systems of towns,
effect on railroads, **40:39C.**
City and town clerks, filing.
Electric railroads, city clerk's
mailing notice of hearing as
to routes, **162:8.**
Labor, filing notice of claim,
159:99.
Materials, filing notice of claim,
159:98.
City council of Boston, duties of
county commissioners devolve,
160:2.
Civil rights.
Discrimination. See within this
heading, "Discrimination."
Cleaning requirements for freight
depots, **149:113.**
Clerks.
Affidavit of service of notice of
first meeting, **160:29.**
Appointment by directors prior
to organization, **160:15.**
Certificate.
Annexation to agreement of
association by clerk,
160:23.
Publication and posting of
agreement of association
conclusive evidence,
160:16.
City and town clerks. See within
this heading, "City and town
clerks, filing."
Election, **160:32.**
Oath, **160:32.**
Record of proceedings at first
meeting, **160:30.**
Required, **160:31.**
Stockholders' meetings, notice,
160:33, 160:34.
Town clerks.
City and town clerks. See
within this heading, "City
and town clerks, filing."
Trustees, filing decree
confirming election of with
clerk of court, **160:53.**
Votes, keeping record, **160:32.**

RAILROADS —Cont'd
Collection of stock assessment, **160:40.**
Color blindness, examination of employees, **160:178.**
Color, discrimination because, **272:92A, 272:98.**
Commonwealth.
  State. See within this heading, "State."
Commutation tickets, **159:18, 160:190.**
Compensation.
  Wages and compensation. See within this heading, "Wages and compensation."
Complaints.
  Civil complaints.
    Petitions. See within this heading, "Petitions and complaints."
  Criminal complaints.
    See INDICTMENTS, INFORMATIONS, AND COMPLAINTS.
Compressed air tanks used, **146:34.**
Concurrent legislation with other states, railroad corporations chartered, **160:4.**
Condemnation.
  Eminent domain. See within this heading, "Eminent domain, taking property."
Conductors.
  Certificate for extra fare for ticket bought upon train, **160:188.**
  Experience required, **160:180-160:183.**
  Fires, duty upon discovery, **160:237.**
  Street railways.
    See STREET RAILWAYS.
Conduits, removal or relocation upon abolition of grade crossings, **159:74.**
Confirmation of election of trustees, **160:53.**
Connecting railroads, **160:58-160:63.**
  Apportionment of expenses and income, **160:60.**
  Compensation for drawing cars of other corporation, **160:59, 160:60.**
  Consent to use of road by another railroad, **160:58.**
  Contract that one shall perform all transportation for the other, **160:62.**

RAILROADS —Cont'd
Connecting railroads —Cont'd
  Drawing cars of other railroad, **160:59, 160:60.**
  Foreign corporations to have privileges relative, **160:61.**
  Freight, forwarding, **160:207.**
  Freight of other carriers, duties, **160:59.**
  Guaranty of each other's bonds, **160:68.**
  Lease of one to the other, **160:62, 160:63.**
  Passengers of other carriers, duties, **160:59.**
  Station accommodations for passengers and merchandise of other corporation, **160:59.**
  Taking securities of other corporation, **160:68, 160:69.**
  Telecommunications and energy department. See within this heading, "Telecommunications and energy department."
  Use of each other's roads, **160:58.**
Connections.
  Switches and switch connections. See within this heading, "Switches and switch connections."
Conservation.
  Environmental advantages. See within this heading, "Environmental advantages."
Consolidation, **160:71-160:74.**
  Agreement of companies, **160:72.**
  Application to department, **160:72.**
  Approval of department, **159:54.**
  Capital stock not to be increased, **160:73.**
  Consent by stockholders, **160:72.**
  Facilities not to be diminished, **160:73.**
  Hearing, **160:72.**
  Indebtedness not to be increased, **160:73.**
  Rates not to be increased, **160:73.**
  Restrained, **160:71, 160:74.**
  Stock and stockholders. See within this heading, "Stock and stockholders."
  Unauthorized acts by consolidated corporation, **160:42, 160:74.**
Violations, **160:42, 160:74.**

RAILROADS —Cont'd
Constables may arrest without warrant persons unlawfully riding trains, **160:220, 160:221.**
Construction and location, **160:75-160:114.**
  Abandonment of location by change, **160:86.**
  Agreement fixing location, **160:80.**
  Agreement of association, counties and cities in which located to be named, **160:14.**
  Bridges, plans to be submitted to department, **159:83.**
  Capital stock.
    Auction sales of new shares, places for holding prescribed by department, **159:51.**
    Subscription requirements prerequisite to taking of land, **160:76.**
  Certificates.
    Change in location, **160:81.**
    Fixing locations, **160:80.**
    Route, **160:21.**
    Subscription to capital stock, certificate a prerequisite to taking land, **160:76.**
  Change of direction or location.
    Change or modification. See within this heading, "Change or modification."
  Conditions precedent, **160:75-160:77.**
  Consent to location, requirements, **160:77.**
  Cost estimate prerequisite to taking land, **160:76.**
  Crossing warning signs, location, **160:42.**
  Crossties, piling or keeping on location or right of way, **160:235.**
  Culverts, construction, **160:91, 160:92.**
  Description of location, **160:80.**
    Certification by clerk of department required, **160:89.**
    Forms prescribed by department, **160:89.**
  Direction, change, **160:86.**
  Electric railroads, **162:8-162:10.**
  Embankments, construction, **160:91, 160:92.**
  Engineer's report, manner of construction to be shown, **160:18.**

RAILROADS —Cont'd

Construction and location —Cont'd

Executive office of transportation and construction. See within this heading, "Executive office of transportation and construction."

Fencing of land taken for construction, **160:90.**

Fixing location, **160:80.**

Foreign countries. See within this heading, "Foreign countries or states."

Freight depots, relocation, **160:129.**

Grievous damage, change of location to avoid, **160:81.**

Location, change, **160:81, 160:85, 160:86, 160:95.**

Map to be prepared by directors, **160:18.**

Metropolitan district commission's grant of location, recording fees, **262:34.**

Nonresidents engaged in construction, agents for service of process, **227:5.**

Order of department fixing location, **160:80.**

Petitions.

Change in location, **160:81, 160:85.**

Fixing location, **160:80.**

Variation of direction, **160:86.**

Prerequisites to taking of land, **160:76.**

Purchase of land, **160:78, 160:79.**

Description of land purchased to be filed with county commissioners, **160:79.**

Fencing land purchased before construction, **160:90.**

Manner of crossing highways to be established prior, **160:75.**

Other railroad or public service corporation, purchasing land, **160:84.**

Purposes for which land may be purchased, **160:78.**

What land may be purchased, **160:78, 160:84.**

Report of competent engineer to be procured by directors, **160:18.**

Routes.

Fixing, **160:20-160:22.**

Certificate of incorporation must be issued within one year after, **160:26.**

RAILROADS —Cont'd

Construction and location —Cont'd

Routes —Cont'd

Fixing —Cont'd

Publication and posting of agreement of association prior, **160:16.**

Location outside of routes fixed, **160:86.**

Map, **160:18, 160:19.**

Purchase of land, **160:78.**

Special charter, corporations established, **160:10-160:12.**

Variations from first proposed route to be made upon map, **160:21.**

Safety devices on cars, location, **160:163.**

Special charter, railroads established, **160:12.**

State house, location within three miles of, prohibited, **160:77.**

Stations and depots, relocation, **160:129.**

Street railways.

See STREET RAILWAYS.

Switch connection locations, granting, **159:21.**

Taxability of land outside of location, **160:87.**

Telecommunications and energy department. See within this heading, "Telecommunications and energy department."

Time for construction, **160:27.**

Trackless trolley companies, **163:2, 163:6, 163:8.**

Walls, construction, **160:91, 160:92.**

Contracts and agreements.

Alteration of crossings, **159:61, 159:64, 159:80.**

Annual return to set forth copies, **159:33.**

Association.

Agreement of association. See within this heading, "Agreement of association."

Cities and towns, agreements.

Bridges, agreement as to wearing surfaces, **160:99.**

Protection at crossings, agreement as to contributing to expense, **160:147.**

Reimbursement for deficits, **161:152A.**

RAILROADS —Cont'd

Contracts and agreements —Cont'd

Connecting railroads, contracts and agreements between, **160:58-160:63.**

Consolidation, **160:72.**

Construction work and contracts.

Construction and location. See within this heading, "Construction and location."

Conveyance of passengers at reduced rates, **160:187.**

Crossings.

See RAILROAD CROSSINGS.

Financial assistance, **161C:5.**

Fixing route, **160:20.**

Grade crossings between two or more railroads, separation by agreement, **160:95.**

Labor and materials furnished under contract, **149:27C, 159:96, 159:97.**

Local express business, person engaged in to indemnify railroad for loss and damage to goods, **160:206.**

Location, **81:7I, 160:77, 160:80.**

Materials used in railroad or railway construction, fee for filing notice of intent to claim right of action, **159:98, 262:34.**

Public works department, **161C:5, 161C:6.**

Expense of protection at crossings, agreement to contribute, **160:147.**

Relocation or other work, contracts, **81:7I.**

Recovery of costs of fencing, **160:94.**

Repairs at crossings, apportionment of cost, **160:106.**

Route, agreement fixing, **160:20.**

Secretary of executive office of transportation and construction authorized to enter, on behalf of executive office of transportation and construction, **161C:6.**

Telecommunications and energy department, transportation upon road of one company to be performed by another, contracts subject to approval, **159:54.**

RAILROADS —Cont'd
Contracts and agreements
—Cont'd
Trustees for benefit of creditors
may contract with
corporation for operation,
160:51.
Waiver of appeal from decision
of commissioners in certain
matters as to crossings,
160:112.
Contributory negligence in
collision at grade crossing,
160:232.
Corporations, **160:3-160:5.**
Agreement of association to
show par value of stock,
160:14.
Business corporations. See
within this heading,
"Business corporations."
Sale of bonds and notes below
par, **160:50.**
Street railways.
See STREET RAILWAYS.
Costs of actions.
Application concerning
obstructions or repairs to
crossings, **160:106.**
Location, petition to fix, **160:80.**
Route, petition for fixing,
160:21.
Costs or expense.
Expenses. See within this
heading, "Expenses and
expenditures."
Council, free passes to members
prohibited, **160:199.**
Counterfeiting tickets, passes,
stamps, etc., **267:2,**
267:4-267:6.
Counties.
Agreement of association,
counties in which located to
be named, **160:14, 161:4.**
Commissioners.
County commissioners. See
within this heading,
"County commissioners."
Crossings.
See RAILROAD CROSSINGS.
Medical examiner, notice of fatal
accident, **159:28.**
Sheriff or constable, arrest for
unlawful riding, **160:220,**
160:221.
County commissioners.
Application to department to
compel maintenance and
repair of bridges, **159:84.**

RAILROADS —Cont'd
County commissioners —Cont'd
Boston, duties of commissioners
devolve upon civil council
and telecommunications and
energy department, **160:2.**
Crossings.
See RAILROAD CROSSINGS.
Decree prescribing alterations of
highways, **160:100, 160:101.**
Embankments, culverts, walls,
or fences, orders for
construction, **160:91,**
160:92.
Free passes prohibited, **160:199.**
Land purchased, description
filed with commissioners,
160:79.
Laying out highway across
railroad, **160:104.**
Manner of crossing highways
determined, **160:75.**
Petitions to, **34:19.**
Proceedings of public works
department in laying out
highway across railroad,
filing of copy, **160:104.**
Repair of bridges, application to
department to compel,
159:84.
Service of petition upon appeal
from decisions, **160:112.**
Severance of private land,
application to
commissioners, **160:109.**
Taking of land for alteration of
highways, **160:101.**
Waiver of appeal from certain
decisions, filing, **160:112.**
Couplers on cars, **160:156,**
160:157, 160:160, 160:161.
Coupons to be detached from
mileage tickets, **160:189.**
Creditors.
Bondholders or creditors. See
within this heading,
"Bondholders or creditors."
Credit unions investing in, **171:67.**
Credit unions, shares, deposits,
and investments, **171:67.**
Crews, number of men forming
train crews, **160:185.**
Crimes and offenses.
Offenses and penalties. See
within this heading,
"Offenses and penalties."
Crossings, **159:57 et seq., 160:95**
et seq.
See RAILROAD CROSSINGS.
Cross-ties, piling or keeping on
location or right-of-way,
160:235.

RAILROADS —Cont'd
Culverts, county commissioners
may order construction,
160:91, 160:92.
Cups for drinking water for
passengers, **160:174, 160:175.**
Curvature tables to be filed with
map upon opening for public
use, **160:119.**
Cuttings, acquisition of land,
160:78, 160:83.
Damages.
Abolition of grade crossings,
159:75, 159:76, 159:78.
Alteration of crossings,
159:60-159:64.
Animals injured on tracks,
160:222, 160:223.
Collisions at grade crossings,
160:232.
Crossings.
See RAILROAD CROSSINGS.
Defect in highway, personal
injury due, **160:229.**
Double damages upon failure to
construct embankments,
culverts, walls, or fences
ordered, **160:91, 160:92.**
Eminent domain. See within
this heading, "Eminent
domain, taking property."
Endangering safety of persons
upon trains, **160:226.**
Failure to repair crossings,
160:107.
Freight, violations, **160:209.**
Gates and barriers at private
crossing, neglect to close,
160:224.
Littoral proprietor, damages for
cutting off access to sea,
160:96.
Loss by fire caused by
locomotive, **160:234.**
Malicious injury, treble damages,
160:225.
Obstructing engine or car,
160:226.
Relief corporation benefits
considered in mitigation,
153:8.
Removal of standing wood at
crossings, **160:150.**
Street railways.
Passenger riding upon
platform, recovery,
161:106.
Trackless trolley companies to
give security for damages,
163:12.
Transportation area leases to
provide, **161:157.**

RAILROADS —Cont'd

Damages —Cont'd

Treble damages. See within this heading, "Treble damages."

Days of rest for certain employees, **160:184.**

Death.

Accident causing.

Investigation, **159:29.**

Liability for wrongful death, **153:1, 229:2.**

Notice of accident, **38:8, 159:28.**

Employee's death employer's liability, **153:1.**

Inquest, expense of evidence taken, **38:11.**

Street railways.

Investigation of accident, **159:29.**

Notice of accident, **38:8, 159:28.**

Wrongful death, liability, **229:2.**

Debris caused by derailments, removal, **160:241A.**

Debts and obligations.

Advice or request of department as affecting liabilities of railroad, **159:38.**

Agreement of association to take shares, liability of subscriber, **160:14.**

Aid by city or town, tax levied to pay interest or indebtedness, **44:57.**

Increased by consolidation, lease, or sale, **160:73.**

Incurring for unauthorized purpose, **160:48.**

Relief corporation funds not liable, **159:88.**

Decrees.

Judgments and decrees. See within this heading, "Judgments and decrees."

Defects.

Complaints by employees, **159:30.**

Highway defects, **160:229.**

Street railways.

Bridges, liability for defects, **161:89, 161:90.**

Complaints by employees, **159:30.**

Definitions, **160:1, 161C:2.**

Depots.

Stations and depots. See within this heading, "Stations and depots."

Deputy sheriff, warrantless arrest of person unlawfully riding train, **160:220.**

RAILROADS —Cont'd

Derailments, removal of wreckage and debris caused, **160:241A.**

Description of location.

Construction and location. See within this heading, "Construction and location."

Development companies, holding stock, **160:65B.**

Devise of lands, secretary of executive office of transportation and construction authorized to receive, **161C:6.**

Dining cars.

Alcohol, license to sell, **138:13, 138:14.**

Drinking water for passengers, **160:174.**

Direction, change, **160:86.**

Directors.

Agreement of association and certificates filed, **160:24.**

Alteration of crossings.

See RAILROAD CROSSINGS.

Annual return, **160:242.**

Assessments upon stock, **160:39.**

Auction sale of new shares upon increase of capital stock, **159:51.**

Certificate of public convenience and necessity, application, **160:17.**

Certificate of vote for change of name signed and sworn, **160:216.**

Certificates annexed to agreement of association, **160:23.**

Clerk, appointment and election, **160:15, 160:32.**

Consolidation, application, **160:72.**

Corporation may associate itself with relief corporation upon vote, **159:88.**

Debt or liability, incurring for unlawful purpose, **160:48.**

Election, **160:30, 160:32.**

Establishment of fares, **160:186.**

Examination of books and financial condition upon request, **159:35.**

First meeting, calling, **160:29.**

Foreign countries. See within this heading, "Foreign countries or states."

Grade crossings, petition for abolition, **159:65.**

Lease of connecting railroads, agreement, **160:62.**

RAILROADS —Cont'd

Directors —Cont'd

Location, petition for fixing, **160:80.**

Maintenance and repair of bridges, application to department to compel, **159:84.**

Maps. See within this heading, "Maps."

Meetings, **160:37.**

Must be stockholders, **160:32.**

Notice to stockholders of increase in capital stock, **159:50.**

Number required, **160:31.**

Persons to act as named in agreement of association, **160:14.**

President, election, **160:32.**

Publication of agreement of association, **160:16.**

Report of competent engineer to be obtained, **160:18.**

Route, fixing, **160:20, 160:21.**

Stock and stockholders. See within this heading, "Stock and stockholders."

Submission to aldermen or selectmen, **160:19.**

Transfer of stock for failure to pay assessments, **160:39.**

Treasurer, appointment and election, **160:15, 160:32.**

Unlawful issue of stock or scrip, liability, **160:48, 160:57.**

Use of railroad, power to regulate, **160:186.**

Vacancies, filling before organization, **160:15.**

Variation of direction, petition to department, **160:86.**

Discharge or release.

Release. See within this heading, "Release."

Discrimination, **160:205, 160:206, 272:92A, 272:98.**

Equal facilities and accommodations. See within this heading, "Equal facilities and accommodations."

Freight, discrimination forbidden, **160:211.**

Milk, transportation, **160:212-160:214.**

Disorderly or annoying conduct, **159:93, 159:94, 272:43, 272:43A.**

Dispatcher, days of rest, **160:184.**

RAILROADS —Cont'd
District attorney, actions to recover
    penalties.
    Care and equipment violations,
        160:160.
    Failure to erect crossing signs,
        160:145.
    Freight violations, **160:209.**
    Platform gate violations,
        160:167.
District court.
    Free passes to justices
        prohibited, **160:199.**
    Jurisdiction of persons arrested
        by police, **159:94.**
Dividend in stock or scrip.
    Stock and stockholders. See
        within this heading, "Stock
        and stockholders."
Division of railroad track
    inspection, **25:7.**
Docks.
    Acquisition of land, **160:78,**
        160:83.
    Maintenance and operation,
        160:70A.
    Wharves and piers, charges for
        use, **91:2A, 91:6, 91:7.**
Dogs, seeing eye dogs
    accompanying blind persons,
    272:98A.
Double damages for failure to
    construct embankments,
    culverts, walls, or fences
    ordered, **160:91, 160:92.**
Drains.
    See SEWERS AND DRAINS.
Drawbars on freight cars, standard
    height, **160:159 to 160:161.**
Drawbridges, **160:120-160:127A.**
    Engineer to ascertain that draw
        is closed before crossing,
        160:125, 160:126.
    Exemption of bridges not opened
        for five years, **160:127A.**
    Gates, **160:124.**
    Master of vessel passing
        through, duties, **160:122.**
    Passage of vessels, how
        regulated, **160:122.**
    Penalties for violations, **160:126,**
        160:127.
    Regulations, **160:120.**
    Signals required, **160:123,**
        160:126.
    Stopping passenger trains before
        crossing, **160:125, 160:126.**
    Tender, **160:120, 160:121.**
        Penalties for violations,
            160:126.
    Time allowed trains for crossing,
        160:122.

RAILROADS —Cont'd
Drawbridges —Cont'd
    To be kept closed, **160:121.**
Drawing cars of connecting
    railroad, **160:59, 160:60.**
Drinking water for passengers,
    160:174, 160:175.
Easements.
    Rights of way. See within this
        heading, "Rights of way."
Ejection of passenger for failure to
    pay fare, **159:101.**
Election.
    Voters and voting. See within
        this heading, "Voters and
        voting."
Electric companies.
    See GAS AND ELECTRIC
        COMPANIES.
Electricians and electricity.
    Electric railroads.
        See ELECTRIC RAILROADS.
    Exclusion of railroad work from
        laws as to electricians,
        141:7.
    Order to change to electric
        power, **159:16.**
Electric railroads.
    See ELECTRIC RAILROADS.
Electrification of railroads, **159:16,**
    160:153.
Elevated railways, **159:50 et seq.**
    See ELEVATED RAILWAYS.
Embankments.
    Acquisition of land, **160:83.**
    County commissioners may
        order construction, **160:91,**
        160:92.
    Double damages for failure to
        construct, **160:91, 160:92.**
Emergency exit in passenger
    trains, **160:163B.**
Eminent domain, taking property,
    160:80-160:84.
    Abolition of grade crossings,
        159:74-159:76, 159:80.
    Canals, alteration of course,
        160:105.
    Certificates of compliance with
        provisions prerequisite,
        160:76.
    Change.
        Crossings, alteration, **159:60.**
        Highways, alteration of for
            crossing purposes,
            160:101.
        Location, **160:81, 160:85.**
    Commonwealth, taking, **160:7.**
    Cost of construction estimated
        as prerequisite, **160:76.**
    County commissioners, award of
        damages for injury by
        railroad, **79:7, 79:10.**

RAILROADS —Cont'd
Eminent domain, taking property
    —Cont'd
    Crossings.
        See RAILROAD CROSSINGS.
    Damages.
        Award, **79:7, 79:10.**
        Change in location to avoid
            grievous damages, **160:81.**
    Elimination of grade crossings,
        159:74-159:76, 159:80.
    Fencing land taken before
        construction, **160:90.**
    Highway, taking land, **160:101,**
        160:104.
    Manner of crossing to be
        established prior, **160:75.**
    Location of railroad, taking,
        160:82.
    Manner of crossing highways to
        be established prior, **160:75.**
    New location, land, **159:74,**
        159:86, 160:85, 160:86.
    Notice to railroads, requirement,
        160:7.
    Other railroads or public service
        corporations, taking land,
        160:84.
    Prerequisites, **160:75, 160:76,**
        160:81, 160:86.
    Proceedings preliminary to
        taking for location, **160:80,**
        160:81.
    Public use, land already, **79:5.**
    Purposes for which land may be
        taken, **160:82-160:84.**
    Secretary of executive office of
        transportation and
        construction, powers,
        161C:6.
    Separation of grade crossings
        between two or more
        railroads, **160:95.**
    State institutions, land, **79:5.**
    Street railways.
        See STREET RAILWAYS.
    What land may be taken, **79:5,**
        160:82-160:84.
Employees, officers, and agents,
    160:31, 160:32.
    Action for labor.
        Actions or suits. See within
            this heading, "Actions or
            suits."
    Appointment, **160:32.**
    Assaulting or interfering,
        159:104.
    Assumption of risk of injuries,
        153:4.
    Badges. See within this heading,
        "Badges for employees."

RAILROADS —Cont'd
Employees, officers, and agents —Cont'd
Bond or security not to be required, **159:4.**
Brakemen. See within this heading, "Brakemen."
Bylaws may authorize, **160:31.**
Certificate of freedom from color blindness or other sight defect, **160:178.**
Chief accounting officers, annual returns sworn, **160:242.**
Color blindness, examination, **160:178.**
Complaint of defects, **159:30.**
Conductors. See within this heading, "Conductors."
Crews, number of men, **160:185.**
Days of rest, **160:184.**
Debt or liability, incurring for unlawful purpose, **160:48.**
Definitions, **149:133, 153:1.**
Directors. See within this heading, "Directors."
Drawbridge tender.
Drawbridges. See within this heading, "Drawbridges."
Election, **160:30-160:33.**
Majority of stockholders must be present, **160:33.**
Engineers. See within this heading, "Engineers."
Expressmen. See within this heading, "Expressmen."
Eyes, examination, **160:178.**
Facsimile signature of resident agent on policy of accident insurance, **175:157.**
Fellow servants, employer's liability for injuries, **153:4.**
Firemen. See within this heading, "Firemen."
Fires.
Duty upon discovery, **160:237, 160:238.**
Instructions concerning, **160:239.**
Free passes to former employees, **160:200.**
Funds of employees' relief associations, **159:88.**
Gross negligence in management of trains, penalty, **160:231.**
Hostlers, excepted from engineer experience requirements, **160:182.**
Hours of labor.
See HOURS OF LABOR OR SERVICES.
Indemnity not to be required, **159:4.**

RAILROADS —Cont'd
Employees, officers, and agents —Cont'd
Influencing appointment or discharge, **271:40, 271:41.**
Injuries to or death of, liability of employer, **153:1.**
Instructions concerning fires and fire prevention, **160:239.**
Lockers for clothes, **149:139.**
Longshoremen and waterfront employees, signs and signals to protect, **149:18H.**
Means to fight fires to be provided, **160:239.**
Minors, employment, **149:62, 149:78.**
Negligence causing personal injury, penalty, **160:231.**
Nonresidents, agents for service of process, **227:5.**
Overtime pay, **151:1A.**
Passes, **160:200, 161:113A.**
Police. See within this heading, "Police officers."
President. See within this heading, "President."
"Railroad establishment" meaning in statute, as to toilet facilities, **149:133.**
Railway labor act.
See RAILWAY LABOR ACT.
Sectionmen. See within this heading, "Sectionmen."
Service of process on nonresidents, agents, **227:5.**
Sight defects, examination, **160:178.**
State officers, free passes, **160:199.**
Stolen passes, **161:113A.**
Switches to be blocked for protection, **160:133.**
Term of office, **160:32.**
Toilet facility, **149:133-149:138, 149:180.**
Uniform caps, **160:177.**
Unlawful issue of stock or bonds, or use of proceeds therefrom, penalty, **160:48.**
Wages and compensation. See within this heading, "Wages and compensation."
Workers' compensation law, applicability, **152:25A.**
Employment security.
Federal agencies and programs. See EMPLOYMENT SECURITY.
Encumbrances.
Liens and encumbrances. See within this heading, "Liens and encumbrances."

RAILROADS —Cont'd
Endangering persons on trains, **160:226.**
Enforcement.
Laws, **160:252.**
Lien for labor and materials in constructing fences, **160:94.**
Order for construction of embankments, culverts or fences, **160:92.**
Engineers.
Bridges, examination, **159:83.**
Certification of maps and statements filed upon opening of road for public use, **160:119.**
Excavation, report, **160:18.**
Intersections of railroads. See within this heading, "Intersections of railroads."
Locomotive engineers.
Drawbridges, duty in crossing, **160:125, 160:126.**
Experience required, **160:179, 160:181-160:183.**
Fires, duty upon discovery, **160:237.**
Grade crossings, duties, **160:135-160:137.**
Negligence causing personal injury, penalty, **160:231, 265:30.**
Penalty for negligence causing personal injury, **160:231, 265:30.**
Report, **160:18.**
Deposited with department, **160:23.**
Directors to procure, **160:18.**
Special charter, to accompany petition, **160:8.**
Submission to aldermen or selectmen, **160:19.**
Surveys. See within this heading, "Surveys."
Entry on land or property by railroad for purpose of survey, **160:75, 160:76, 266:120C.**
Environmental advantages, **161C:1.**
Purchase for rail transportation in Commonwealth, **161C:4.**
Environmental management department, posting of signs, **160:235A.**
Equal facilities and accommodations, **160:205, 160:206.**
Criminal offense of denying because of race, etc., **272:92A, 272:98.**

RAILROADS —Cont'd

Equipment companies, holding stock, **160:65A.**

Equipment securities, insurance companies may invest, **175:63.**

Establishment and maintenance of railroads by executive office of transportation and construction, **161C:3.**

Evasion of payment of fare, **159:101.**

Evening and morning trains, **160:197.**

Evidence.

Badge as evidence that police officer is lawfully on duty, **159:92.**

Certificate as conclusive evidence of publication and posting of agreement of association, **160:16.**

Certificate of incorporation or copy as conclusive evidence of existence, **160:24.**

Certificate of judge as conclusive evidence of responsibility of subscriber, **160:76.**

Electric railroads.

Certificate of city or town clerk, conclusive evidence of mailing of notice, **162:8.**

Certificate of clerk of corporation, conclusive evidence of publication of agreement of association, **162:6.**

Inquest, liability for expense of evidence taken, **38:11.**

Police officers. See within this heading, "Police officers."

Responsibility of subscriber of capital stock, **160:76.**

Street railways.

See STREET RAILWAYS.

Witnesses. See within this heading, "Witnesses."

Examination.

Inspection, examination, and investigation. See within this heading, "Inspection, examination, and investigation."

Excavation, kind and amount to be shown in engineer's report, **160:18.**

Exceptions.

Exemptions and exceptions. See within this heading, "Exemptions and exceptions."

Executive committee of corporation to operate in foreign country, **160:250.**

RAILROADS —Cont'd

Executive council, free passes to members prohibited, **160:199.**

Executive office of administration and finance to enter contracts for financial assistance, **161C:5.**

Executive office of transportation and construction.

Authorization to spend money, **161C:4.**

Definition, **161C:2.**

Establishment of rail systems, **161C:3.**

First refusal as to purchase of railroad facilities, **161C:7.**

Permit to build structure in railroad right of way, consent prior to issuance, **40:54A.**

Secretary of executive office of transportation and construction. See within this heading, "Secretary of executive office of transportation and construction."

Exemptions and exceptions.

Cars and equipment, exemption from certain requirements, **160:162.**

Certain miscellaneous corporations, exception of railroads from law, **158:1.**

Drawbridges not opened for five years, exemption, **160:127A.**

Fencing requirements, **160:93.**

Foreign corporation exempt from filing annual certificate of condition, **181:12.**

Four wheel cars excepted from certain provisions, **160:161.**

Inspection, examination, and investigation. See within this heading, "Inspection, examination, and investigation."

Locomotives. See within this heading, "Locomotives."

Outdoor advertising requirements, exemption of rolling stock, **93:32.**

Sales tax exemption, **64H:6.**

Taxation, limited exemption of railroad property, **160:87.**

Transmitting, receiving, and delivering messages, railroads excepted from liability, **166:19.**

Uniform Securities Act, exemptions, **110A:402.**

RAILROADS —Cont'd

Expectoration in cars, stations, etc., **270:14, 270:15.**

Expenses and expenditures.

Actions.

Costs of actions. See within this heading, "Costs of actions."

Annual return to show, **160:242.**

Connecting railroads, apportionment of expenses and income, **160:60.**

Crossings.

See RAILROAD CROSSINGS.

Fees. See within this heading, "Fees."

Fences, lien for cost of.

Liens and encumbrances. See within this heading, "Liens and encumbrances."

Fires, expense of extinguishing, **160:241.**

Inquest, liability for expense of evidence taken, **38:11.**

River or stream relocation on abolition of grade crossing, expenses, **159:75.**

Street railways, inclusion of interest expenses in cost of services, **161:116, 161:118.**

Taking of land, cost estimate as prerequisite, **160:76.**

Explosions.

See EXPLOSIONS AND EXPLOSIVES.

Express cars, platform gates, **160:167.**

Express companies.

See EXPRESS COMPANIES.

Expressmen.

Accidents. See within this heading, "Accidents."

Equal facilities and accommodations to local expressmen, **160:206.**

Railroads not liable for acts, **160:233.**

Season tickets, **160:193.**

Express trains.

MBTA.

See MASSACHUSETTS BAY TRANSPORTATION AUTHORITY.

Street railways.

See STREET RAILWAYS.

Extension of charter, petition to general court, **3:5.**

Extensions.

Branches and extensions. See within this heading, "Branches and extensions."

RAILROADS —Cont'd

Extinguishing fires.
 Fires and fire prevention. See
  within this heading, "Fires
  and fire prevention."
Eye examination of employees,
 160:178.
Facility companies, holding stock,
 160:65B.
Facsimile signature or seal, stock
 certificates, **160:38.**
Fares.
 See RATES AND CHARGES.
Federal law as affecting
 Commonwealth's right of first
 refusal, **161C:7.**
Federal moneys excluded in
 apportionment of costs of
 abolition of grade crossings,
 159:70.
Federal railroad retirement board.
 Federal agencies and programs.
 See EMPLOYMENT
  SECURITY.
Federal railroad unemployment
 insurance act.
 Federal agencies and programs.
 See EMPLOYMENT
  SECURITY.
Federal railway labor act.
 See RAILWAY LABOR ACT.
Fees.
 Branches and extensions, filing
  certificate for construction,
  160:115.
 Certificate of compliance with
  provisions prerequisite to
  taking of land, filing,
  160:76.
 Certificate of incorporation,
  160:24.
 Foreign countries,
  corporations to operate,
  160:249.
 Labor, filing of statement of
  amount due, **159:99, 262:34.**
 Materials, fee for notice of intent
  to claim right of action,
  262:34.
 Notice of claim for materials,
  filing, **159:98, 262:34.**
 Public utility department filing
  fees, **25:10B.**
 Rates and charges, **159B:6,
  159B:6A, 159B:7,
  160:208-160:211.**
  See RATES AND CHARGES.
 Recording metropolitan district
  commission's grant of
  location, **262:34.**

RAILROADS —Cont'd

Fees —Cont'd
 Sheriff or constable arresting
  person for unlawful riding of
  train, payment of fees,
  160:221.
 Street railways.
  See STREET RAILWAYS.
 Witness for Commonwealth,
  railroad police attending,
  262:55.
Fellow servant, liability of
 employer for injury, **153:4.**
Fences, **160:90-160:94.**
 Costs, lien for.
  Liens and encumbrances. See
   within this heading,
   "Liens and
   encumbrances."
 County commissioners may
  order construction, **160:91,
  160:92.**
 Double damages for failure to
  construct, **160:91, 160:92.**
 Duty of railroad to erect and
  maintain, **160:93.**
 Land taken for construction,
  fencing, **160:90.**
 Liens and encumbrances. See
  within this heading, "Liens
  and encumbrances."
 Mechanics' liens, **185:84.**
 Openings, duty of railroad to
  erect fences, **160:96.**
 Orders for construction, **160:92.**
 Proceeding for exemptions of
  requirements, **160:93.**
 Provisions as to construction,
  160:93A.
Ferries, operation, **160:70A.**
Filing and recording.
 Actions for labor and materials.
  Notice of claim for materials,
   159:98, 262:34.
  Statement of amount due for
   labor, **159:99, 262:34.**
 Agreement of association and
  annexed certificates, **160:24.**
 Foreign countries,
  corporations to operate,
  160:249.
 Branches and extensions,
  certificate for construction,
  160:115.
 Capital stock, certificate of
  increase or reduction,
  160:25.
 Change of name, vote and
  authorization, **160:216.**
 City and town clerks, filing with.
  See within this heading,
  "City and town clerks,
  filing."

RAILROADS —Cont'd

Filing and recording —Cont'd
 Compliance, certificate, **160:24.**
 Connecting carriers, awards
  concerning, **160:60.**
 Crossings.
  See RAILROAD CROSSINGS.
 Electric railroads.
  See ELECTRIC RAILROADS.
 Fees. See within this heading,
  "Fees."
 First meeting, copy of notice of
  to be recorded in books and
  records, **160:29.**
 Foreign corporation exempt from
  filing annual certificate of
  condition, **181:12.**
 Foreign countries. See within
  this heading, "Foreign
  countries or states."
 Gauge, certificate of change,
  160:25.
 Joint occupation of station,
  railroad, or grounds, award
  of compensation, **160:131.**
 Land purchased, description,
  160:79.
 Location, description, **160:80.**
 Map and profile when road is
  opened for public use,
  160:119.
 Materials used in construction,
  fee for filing notice of intent
  to claim right of action,
  262:34.
 Preferred stock, vote creating
  and order approving,
  160:44.
 Proceedings of public works
  department in laying out
  highway across railroad,
  160:104.
 Public utility department, fees
  for filing, **25:10B.**
 Taking of land, certificate of
  compliance with provisions
  prerequisite, **160:76.**
 Terminal facilities, order
  granting authority to
  operate, **160:131A.**
 Transfer, lease, purchase, or sale
  of franchise and property,
  certificate of approval,
  159:54.
 Trustees, decree confirming
  election, **160:53.**
 Waiver of appeal from decision
  of commissioners in certain
  matters as to crossings,
  160:112.
Filling, kind and amount to be
 shown in engineer's reports,
 160:18.

RAILROADS —Cont'd
Financial assistance.
City or town, aid, **44:57.**
Contracts, **161C:5.**
Secretary of executive office of
transportation and
construction authorized to
apply, **161C:6.**
Financial condition.
Examination, **159:35.**
Statement of, exemption of
foreign corporations from
requirement of annual
filing, **181:12.**
Street railways.
See STREET RAILWAYS.
Fines and penalties.
Offenses and penalties. See
within this heading,
"Offenses and penalties."
Fire insurance on property along
route which railroad may be
held liable for burning,
160:234.
Firemen.
Engineers must have experience,
160:179, 160:181-160:183.
Free or reduced rate service,
159:15.
Negligence causing personal
injury, penalty, **160:231.**
Fires and fire prevention,
160:234-160:241.
Actions. See within this heading,
"Actions or suits."
Clearing land adjoining location,
160:235, 160:235A, 160:236.
Employees. See within this
heading, "Employees,
officers, and agents."
Extinguishing fires.
Duty of sectionmen and other
employees, **160:238.**
Liability to city or town for
expense, **160:241.**
Firemen. See within this
heading, "Firemen."
Forest lands, liability of railroad
for expenses of
extinguishing fires, **160:241.**
Forest warden, land adjoining
tracks cleared subject to
direction, **160:236.**
Grass lands, liability of railroad
for expenses of
extinguishing fires, **160:241.**
Inflammables. See within this
heading, "Inflammables."
Instructions to employees of
duties, **160:239.**
Insurance upon property along
route, **160:234.**

RAILROADS —Cont'd
Fires and fire prevention —Cont'd
Locomotives causing fires,
liability of railroad, **160:234.**
Means of fighting to be provided
employees, **160:239.**
Notice of fires to sectionmen and
telegraph station, **160:237.**
Passenger cars, lighting with
explosive oils, **160:166.**
Posting notices and warnings,
160:235.
Public parks or reservations,
entry for fire prevention not
authorized, **160:240.**
Signals upon discovery of fire,
160:237.
Spark arresters required,
160:235.
Fireworks or pyrotechnic signals,
148:39, 148:44.
First meeting of corporation,
160:29, 160:30.
Fixing routes.
Construction and location. See
within this heading,
"Construction and location."
Flagmen at crossings, **160:147,
160:148.**
Flashing light signals at crossings,
160:147, 160:148.
Foreclosure of mortgage, rights
and duties of purchaser,
160:55.
Foreign countries or states,
160:247-160:252.
Agents for service of process on
residents of foreign states,
227:5.
Authority to form, **160:247.**
Capital stock.
Increase or reduction,
160:250.
Statements in agreement of
association, **160:248.**
Certificates.
Capital stock, increase or
decrease, **160:250.**
Compliance with
requirements, **160:249.**
Incorporation, **160:249.**
Corporations chartered by
foreign states.
Foreign railroad corporations.
See within this heading,
"Foreign railroad
corporations."
Directors.
Agreement of association and
certificate to be filed,
160:249.

RAILROADS —Cont'd
Foreign countries or states
—Cont'd
Directors —Cont'd
Classification, **160:250.**
Designation in agreement of
association, **160:248.**
Election at annual meeting,
160:250.
Term of office, **160:250.**
Executive committee, **160:250.**
Fee for certificate of
incorporation, **160:249.**
Filing.
Agreement of association and
certificate of compliance,
160:249.
Capital stock, certificate of
increase or decrease,
160:250.
Form of certificate of
incorporation, **160:249.**
Intent to be stated in agreement
of association, **160:248.**
Laws governing, **160:251.**
Lease of property, **160:250.**
Name, **160:248.**
Other corporations, purchase or
lease, **160:250.**
Purchase of other corporations
or property, **160:250.**
State secretary.
Agreement of association and
certificate of compliance,
filing, **160:249.**
Certificate of incorporation,
issuance, **160:249.**
Certificate of increase or
decrease of capital stock,
filing, **160:250.**
Steamship company associated
with, power to purchase or
lease company or property,
160:250.
Taking securities of other
corporations, **160:250.**
Telecommunications and energy
department, clerk to issue
certificate of compliance
with requirements, **160:249.**
Termini designated in articles of
agreement, **160:248.**
Foreign railroad corporations.
Concurrent legislation with
other states, corporations
chartered, **160:4.**
Connecting railroads, privileges,
160:61.
Exemption from filing annual
certificates of condition,
181:12.

RAILROADS —Cont'd
Foreign railroad corporations
   —Cont'd
   Street railways.
      See STREET RAILWAYS.
Foreign states.
   Foreign countries or states. See
      within this heading,
      "Foreign countries or
      states."
Forests and woodlands.
   Crossing, removal of standing
      wood, **160:150.**
   Expense of extinguishing fires
      in, liability, **160:241.**
   Slash, clearing and disposal,
      48:16, 48:18-48:20.
   Warden, land adjoining tracks
      cleared subject to direction,
      160:236.
Forgery of tickets, passes, stamps,
   etc., **267:2, 267:4-267:6.**
Forms.
   Accounts, records, etc., **159:31.**
   Annual return, contents and
      form, **160:242.**
   Express companies, **159:33.**
   Certificate of incorporation,
      160:24.
      Foreign countries,
         corporations to operate,
         160:249.
   Description of location, **160:89.**
   Motor vehicle, reports as to
      transportation, **160:70A.**
   Street railways.
      See STREET RAILWAYS.
Four-wheel cars excepted from
   certain provisions, **160:161.**
Franchise.
   Lease, purchase or sale, **159:54.**
   Power to mortgage or pledge,
      160:47.
   Sale, **159:38, 159:54.**
   Street railways, approval of
      lease, purchase, or sale of
      franchise, **159:54.**
   Unauthorized acts of
      consolidated corporation
      which may cause forfeiture,
      160:42.
Fraudulent evasion of payment of
   fare, **159:101.**
Free.
   Gifts. See within this heading,
      "Gifts."
Freight, **160:204-160:211.**
   Baggage. See within this
      heading, "Baggage."
   Boston, freight differential
      against, **160:210.**

RAILROADS —Cont'd
Freight —Cont'd
   Cars.
      Freight cars. See within this
         heading, "Freight cars."
   Connecting railroads. See within
      this heading, "Connecting
      railroads."
   Depots.
      Freight depots and houses.
         See within this heading,
         "Freight depots and
         houses."
   Discrimination forbidden,
      160:211.
   Electric railroads as carriers,
      162:14.
   Equal facilities, **160:205,
      160:206.**
   Forwarding, **160:207.**
   Motor carriers of property. See
      within this heading, "Motor
      carriers of property."
   Penalties for violations, **160:209.**
   Rates and charges,
      160:208-160:211.
      See RATES AND CHARGES.
   Receipt to shippers, **160:204.**
   Street railways.
      See STREET RAILWAYS.
Freight cars.
   Automatic couplers, **160:156,
      160:157.**
   Brakes and brakemen, **160:154.**
   Drawbars, standard height,
      160:159-160:161.
   Grab irons or hand holds,
      160:158, 160:160, 160:161.
   Safety couplers, **160:156.**
   Tools, equipment, **160:163.**
   Unlawful riding, **160:220.**
Freight depots and houses.
   Acquisition of land, **160:78,
      160:83.**
   Lights, ventilation, cleaning,
      149:113.
   Relocation, **160:129.**
Freight trains.
   Cars.
      Freight cars. See within this
         heading, "Freight cars."
   Making up and shifting,
      manner, **160:139.**
   Telecommunications and energy
      department. See within this
      heading,
      "Telecommunications and
      energy department."
   Tramps, persons riding without
      permission, **272:63.**
   Use of crossings by, regulation,
      160:152.

RAILROADS —Cont'd
Fuel.
   Gas and oil. See within this
      heading, "Gas and oil."
   Sales tax exemption, **64H:6.**
Full crew act, **160:185.**
Funds.
   Aid by city or town, **44:57.**
   Appropriations. See within this
      heading, "Appropriations."
   Employees' relief associations,
      funds, **159:88.**
   Expenditure, **161C:4.**
   Financial assistance. See within
      this heading, "Financial
      assistance."
Furnaces, cars not to be heated,
   160:165.
Gambling in cars or trains, **271:2.**
Gas and oil.
   Gas and electric companies.
      See GAS AND ELECTRIC
         COMPANIES.
   Lighting passenger cars with
      explosive oils, **160:166.**
   Sales tax exemption, **64H:6.**
Gates and barriers.
   Bridge guards, **160:134.**
   Cattle, barriers against, **160:93.**
   Crossings.
      See RAILROAD CROSSINGS.
   Drawbridges, **160:124.**
   Fences to have gates, **160:93.**
   Platform gates on certain cars,
      160:167.
   Street railway gateman.
      Hours of labor, **161:103.**
Gauge.
   Change, **160:15, 160:25.**
   Electric railroads, **162:5.**
   Narrow gauge railroads. See
      within this heading,
      "Narrow gauge railroads."
   Statement in agreement of
      association, **160:14.**
   Street railways, **161:4.**
General court.
   Books and records to be
      submitted for inspection,
      160:72, 160:242.
   Boston harbor, consent to
      crossing, **160:96.**
   Consolidation, **160:72.**
   Free passes to members
      prohibited, **160:199.**
   Petition, **3:5, 160:8.**
   Revision of fares, **3:5, 160:8,
      160:186.**
   Street railways.
      See STREET RAILWAYS.
Gifts.
   Free passes, **159:15, 160:199,
      160:200.**

RAILROADS —Cont'd
Gifts —Cont'd
Secretary of executive office of transportation and construction authorized to accept gift of land, **161C:6.**
State house, land around, **8:16.**
Governor.
Free passes to prohibited, **160:199.**
Street railways rendering service at cost, appointment of directors, **161:124.**
Grab irons on cars, **160:158, 160:160, 160:161.**
Grade.
Crossings, **159:57 et seq.**
See RAILROAD CROSSINGS.
Report of engineer to show, **160:18.**
Street railways, grades of fares.
See STREET RAILWAYS.
Tables of to be filed on opening of road for public use, **160:119.**
Grain elevators.
See GRAIN AND MEAL.
Grants.
Gifts. See within this heading, "Gifts."
Grass lands.
Clearance and disposal of brush, **48:16, 48:18-48:20.**
Fires in, liability for extinguishing, **160:241.**
Gravel, acquisition of land, **160:78, 160:83.**
Gross negligence.
Grade crossing accident, gross negligence of injured person as defense, **160:232.**
Passengers, gross negligence in carriage of, offense and penalty, **160:231, 265:30.**
Guards.
Bridges, **160:134.**
Crossings, **160:147, 160:148.**
Gates and barriers. See within this heading, "Gates and barriers."
Harbors.
Boston harbor. See within this heading, "Boston harbor."
Terminal facilities, acquisition of property, **91:5.**
Hats, uniform hats for employees, **160:177.**
Hazardous materials, safety standard for rail transport, **25:5C.**
Headlights for track motor cars, **160:176A.**

RAILROADS —Cont'd
Hearings.
Trial or hearing. See within this heading, "Trial or hearing."
Heating of cars, **160:165.**
Height.
Drawbars for freight cars, standard height, **160:159-160:161.**
Proper clearance of track in railroad yards, **160:134A.**
Street railways, overhead structures above railroad track, **161:130.**
Highways and streets.
Aldermen or selectmen. See within this heading, "Aldermen or selectmen."
Alteration, **160:100, 160:101.**
Change or modification. See within this heading, "Change or modification."
Crossing, **159:57 et seq., 160:95 et seq.**
See RAILROAD CROSSINGS.
Defect in highway within location of railroad, liability for personal injuries, **160:229.**
Electric railroads.
Boulevards, **92:43-92:47.**
Location of railroad in highway, **162:10.**
Eminent domain. See within this heading, "Eminent domain, taking property."
Laying across railroad, **160:104.**
Obstruction, **160:151.**
Private railroads, **160:245.**
Spurs and branches, **160:22.**
Street railways.
See STREET RAILWAYS.
Horses.
Negligently permitting horse to go on railroad, penalized, **160:223.**
Riding, driving, or leading on railroad, **160:222.**
Hostlers excepted from experience requirements of engineers, **160:182.**
Hours of labor.
See HOURS OF LABOR OR SERVICES.
Housing and urban renewal operating agencies, reimbursement of relocation costs, **121B:13.**
Identity or description.
Construction and location. See within this heading, "Construction and location."

RAILROADS —Cont'd
Improvements, **161C:4.**
Incorporation under general laws, **160:13-160:28.**
Increase of stock.
Stock and stockholders. See within this heading, "Stock and stockholders."
Indemnity from employees not to be required, **159:4.**
Indictments.
See INDICTMENTS, INFORMATIONS, AND COMPLAINTS.
Industrial development and facilities companies, holding stock, **160:65B.**
Inflammables.
Crossings, motor vehicles carrying inflammable liquids to stop, **90:15.**
Lighting passenger cars, **160:166.**
Injunctions.
Alteration of highway, **160:100.**
Crossings.
Running of trains on railroad failing to observe crossing regulations, **160:136.**
Use of crossing until fencing laws complied, **160:93.**
Petitions, **160:100, 160:136.**
Street railways, injunction to enforce laws, **161:142.**
Violation of laws, **160:252.**
Injuries.
Accidents. See within this heading, "Accidents."
Inspection, examination, and investigation.
Accident investigations, **159:29.**
Air conditioning systems, exception, **146:45A.**
Books and financial condition, **159:35, 160:242.**
Bridges, **159:83.**
Crossings.
See RAILROAD CROSSINGS.
Director, stockholder, or bondholder, examination of books and records on request, **159:35.**
Division of railroad track inspection, **25:7.**
Evidence taken at inquest, expense, **38:11.**
Exemptions and exceptions to inspection requirements.
Air conditioning and refrigeration systems, **146:45A.**

RAILROADS —Cont'd
Inspection, examination, and
investigation —Cont'd
Exemptions and exceptions to
inspection requirements
—Cont'd
Locomotives, **146:7.**
Financial condition, **159:35.**
Incorporation, documents
submitted to department for
inspection, **160:23.**
Locomotives, exemption from
annual inspection, **146:7.**
Notice of examination by
department upon complaint,
159:24.
Quarterly returns, **160:243.**
Refrigeration systems, exception,
146:45A.
Relief corporations, books and
records, **159:87.**
Street railways.
See STREET RAILWAYS.
Tracks, **159:83.**
Witnesses. See within this
heading, "Witnesses."
Insurance.
See INSURANCE.
Intent to be stated in agreement of
association, **160:14.**
Foreign countries, corporations
operating, **160:248.**
New company upon sale by
receivers, **161:136.**
Interest.
Crossings, highway fund as
available for payment of
interest on bonds, **90:34.**
Person making alterations to
crossings may recover
interest on expense of other
party, **159:64.**
Street railways, inclusion in cost
of service, **161:116, 161:118.**
Tax levied to pay indebtedness
or interest for aid by city or
town, **44:57.**
Interference.
Obstruction or interference. See
within this heading,
"Obstruction or
interference."
Interlocking signals at crossings
between two or more
railroads, **160:136, 160:137.**
Intersections of highways, **159:57
et seq., 160:95 et seq.**
See RAILROAD CROSSINGS.
Intersections of railroads.
Apportionment of expenses of
separating, **160:95.**

RAILROADS —Cont'd
Intersections of railroads —Cont'd
Branches and extensions. See
within this heading,
"Branches and extensions."
Change of highways upon
separation, **160:95.**
Consent of department required,
160:96.
Duties of engineer, **160:135.**
Exemption upon establishing
system of interlocking or
automatic signals,
160:136, 160:137.
Expense of system of
interlocking or automatic
signals, **160:137.**
Hearing upon application for
system of interlocking or
automatic signals, **160:137.**
Interlocking or automatic
signals, **160:136, 160:137.**
Operation of trains,
160:135-160:137.
Separation by agreement,
160:95.
Intoxicating liquor.
Alcoholic liquors. See within this
heading, "Alcoholic liquors."
Investigations.
Inspection, examination, and
investigation. See within
this heading, "Inspection,
examination, and
investigation."
Investments.
Credit unions, **171:67.**
Increase in stock for purpose,
160:41.
Insurance companies,
investments, **175:63.**
Other corporations, taking or
guaranteeing securities of,
160:64-160:70.
Stock. See within this heading,
"Stock and stockholders."
Street railways.
See STREET RAILWAYS.
Uniform Securities Act,
exemptions, **110A:402.**
Joint occupation of station,
railroad, or grounds,
compensation, **160:131.**
Judges.
Certificate as conclusive
evidence of responsibility of
subscriber, **160:76.**
Free passes, **160:199.**
Judgments and decrees.
Alteration of crossings,
determination of which
party to make and pay,
159:63.

RAILROADS —Cont'd
Judgments and decrees —Cont'd
Confirming election of trustees,
160:53.
Obstructions at or repairs to
crossings, **160:106.**
Jurisdiction.
District court, **159:94.**
Mortgages, questions arising,
160:54.
Street railways.
District court, jurisdiction of
persons arrested by
railway police, **159:94.**
Local jurisdiction laws
inapplicable to grade
crossings, **82:20.**
Telecommunications and
energy department,
159:12.
Telecommunications and energy
department, **159:12.**
Throwing or shooting at train,
arrest and jurisdiction,
159:93, 159:94, 159:104.
Labor.
Employees. See within this
heading, "Employees,
officers, and agents."
Ladder tracks, clearance in yards,
160:134A.
Landlord and tenant.
Leases. See within this heading,
"Leases."
Larceny and theft.
Car, stealing, **266:20.**
Transportation pass for
employees, stolen or
counterfeited, **161:113A.**
Lead tracks, clearance in yards,
160:134A.
Leases.
Annual return.
Connecting railroads,
statement of facts
concerning contracts and
leases, **160:62.**
Copies of, annual return to set
forth, **160:242.**
Lessee of railroads, making of
returns, **160:244.**
Bonds of leased railroads, taking
or guaranteeing, **160:68.**
Capital stock not to be
increased, **160:73.**
Connecting railroads, lease of
one to the other, **160:62.**
Facilities not to be diminished,
160:73.
Fees, applications to lease state
property, **161C:4.**

RAILROADS —Cont'd
Leases —Cont'd
Foreign countries, corporations to operate, **160:250.**
Franchise and property leases subject to approval by department, **159:54.**
Indebtedness not to be increased, **160:73.**
Rates not to be increased, **160:73.**
Returns for leased railroad, who to make, **160:244.**
Secretary of executive office of transportation and construction, lease of land, **161C:6.**
Street railways.
See STREET RAILWAYS.
Term, **160:63.**
Legislation concurrent with that of other states, corporations chartered, **160:4.**
Length of road to be stated in agreement of association, **160:14.**
Levermen, days of rest, **160:184.**
Licenses and permits.
Alcoholic liquors, licensing, **138:13.**
Fees, application to license state property, **161C:4.**
Locomotives, exception from requirement of license for operation of steam boiler or engine, **146:46.**
Public warehouse, railroad licensed, **105:1.**
Right of way, permit to build structure, **40:54A.**
Street railways.
Authority for carrying of freight, baggage, express, and newspapers, **161:53.**
Opening public ways and bridges, **161:89.**
Liens and encumbrances.
Fences.
Labor and materials, lien, **160:94.**
Registered land, enforcement of liens on, for cost of erecting fences, **185:84.**
Mechanics' liens. See within this heading, "Mechanics' liens."
Mortgages. See within this heading, "Mortgages."
Pledge of property and equipment, **160:47, 160:48.**
Lieutenant governor, free passes to prohibited, **160:199.**

RAILROADS —Cont'd
Lights.
Freight depots, **149:113.**
Passenger cars, explosive oils or fluids not to be used, **160:166.**
Police department of railroad, display of blue light by vehicles, **90:7.**
Switch stands, **160:133A.**
Track motor cars, **160:176A.**
Limitation of actions.
Grade crossing elimination, settlement of barred claim, **159:76.**
Labor and material, **159:100.**
Recovery of forfeiture for violations as to freight, **160:209.**
Street railways.
See STREET RAILWAYS.
Limitations on contracts for financial assistance, **161C:5.**
Limits to be specified in special charter, **160:11.**
Lines.
Routes or lines. See within this heading, "Routes or lines."
Liquors.
Alcoholic liquors. See within this heading, "Alcoholic liquors."
List of stockholders, department to have access, **159:31.**
Littoral proprietors, obstruction of access to sea by crossings, **160:96.**
Livestock.
Animals. See within this heading, "Animals."
Loans, secretary of executive office of transportation and construction authorized to make application, **161C:6.**
Local express business, equal facilities and accommodations, **160:206.**
Location.
Construction and location. See within this heading, "Construction and location."
Locomotives.
Boilers, testing, **160:168.**
Brakes, **160:155, 160:160, 160:161, 160:169, 160:170.**
Compressed air tanks, **146:34.**
Endangering safety of persons, **160:226.**
Engineers. See within this heading, "Engineers."
Exemptions and exceptions.
Annual inspection, exemption, **146:7.**

RAILROADS —Cont'd
Locomotives —Cont'd
Exemptions and exceptions —Cont'd
License to operate steam boiler or engine, exception from, requirement, **146:46.**
Fires caused, **160:234.**
Liability of employer for negligence of employee in charge, **153:1.**
Mufflers, use on vacuum brakes or safety valves, **160:169, 160:170.**
Obstructing passage, **160:226.**
Power which may be used, **159:16, 160:153.**
Sanitary conditions, **160:172A.**
Spark arresters required, **160:235.**
Throwing missiles at, penalty, **159:104.**
Unlawful riding, **160:220.**
Loitering, **161:95.**
Stations, **160:219, 272:68.**
Street railways, **161:94A, 161:95.**
Longshore and waterfront employees, signs and signals to protect, **149:18H.**
Lowlands and swamps, **252:15-252:23.**
See LOWLANDS AND SWAMPS.
Luggage.
Baggage. See within this heading, "Baggage."
Mail.
Free tickets or special rates for mail carriers, **159:15, 161:107.**
Purchase of facilities, offer to be sent by certified mail, **161C:7.**
Transportation of, **160:165, 160:167, 160:201-160:203, 161:52.**
Mail cars.
Heating, **160:165.**
Platform gates, **160:167.**
Maintenance and repairs.
Repairs and maintenance. See within this heading, "Repairs and maintenance."
Malicious injuries to, civil and criminal liability, **160:225, 266:94.**
Maps.
Filing upon opening for public use, **160:119.**

RAILROADS —Cont'd
Maps —Cont'd
Petition for special charter,
maps to accompany, **160:8.**
Route map to be prepared by
directors, **160:18.**
Deposited with department,
160:23.
Submission to aldermen and
selectmen, **160:19.**
Variations from proposed
route to be made, **160:21.**
Surveys. See within this
heading, "Surveys."
Waters, electric railroad map,
plan, or certificate to show
navigable waters, **162:7.**
Masonry, kind and amount to be
shown in engineer's report,
160:18.
Massachusetts Bay transportation
authority, **161A:1 to 161A:47.**
See MASSACHUSETTS BAY
TRANSPORTATION
AUTHORITY.
Master in chancery, certificate of
conclusive evidence of
responsibility of subscriber,
160:76.
Master plan of municipal planning
boards, **41:81D.**
Materials.
Actions or suits. See within this
heading, "Actions or suits."
Fences, lien for materials used
in constructing, **160:94.**
Mayor.
Agreement as to alteration of
crossings signed, **159:80.**
Complaint, **159:24.**
Street railways.
See STREET RAILWAYS.
Veto powers, **160:1.**
Mechanics' liens.
Erection of fence, **160:94,**
185:84.
Limitation of actions, **159:100.**
Medical examiner, notice of
accidents, **38:8, 159:28.**
Meetings.
Annual meeting. See within this
heading, "Annual meeting."
Directors, meetings, **160:37.**
Stockholders' meetings. See
within this heading,
"Stockholders' meetings."
Trustees for benefit of creditors.
See within this heading,
"Trustees for benefit of
creditors."
Merger.
Consolidation. See within this
heading, "Consolidation."

RAILROADS —Cont'd
Metropolitan district commission.
Crossings, location of boulevards
with respect, **92:49-92:52.**
Street railways.
See STREET RAILWAYS.
Mileage books and tickets,
160:189.
Forging, **267:4.**
Milk, transportation,
160:212-160:214.
Minors.
Children or minors. See within
this heading, "Children or
minors."
Missiles, throwing or shooting at
cars or trains, **159:104.**
Modification.
Change or modification. See
within this heading,
"Change or modification."
Morning and evening trains,
160:197.
Mortgages.
After-acquired property, power
to pledge or mortgage,
160:47.
Equipment and personal
property, **160:47, 160:48.**
Exchange of registered bonds for
coupons, mortgages not
affected, **160:49.**
Purchaser upon foreclosure,
rights and duties, **160:55.**
Supreme judicial court to have
jurisdiction of questions
arising, **160:54.**
Motive power used, **160:153.**
Order for change to electricity,
159:16.
Motor carriers of passengers.
Operation, **160:70A.**
Petition for alteration or
revocation of rules and
regulations concerning,
159A:12.
Subsidiary companies for
operation of, taking stock,
160:70.
Tampering with motor bus,
159:103.
Motor carriers of property.
Notice to railroads of hearing
upon certificate of public
convenience and necessity,
159B:3.
Operation, **160:70A.**
Taking stock of subsidiary
companies by railroads,
160:70.

RAILROADS —Cont'd
Motor cars.
Track motor cars. See within
this heading, "Track motor
cars."
Mufflers.
Safety valves, **160:170.**
Vacuum brakes, **160:169,**
160:171.
Multiple damages for failure to
construct embankments,
culverts, walls, or fences
ordered, **160:91, 160:92.**
Municipal finance.
Cities and towns. See within
this heading, "Cities and
towns."
Name.
Assumed name to be stated in
agreement of association,
160:14, 160:248.
Change, **160:215-160:217.**
Foreign corporation, **160:248.**
Stations, signs to indicate,
160:130.
Naphtha not to be used for
lighting passenger cars,
160:166.
Narrow gauge railroads.
Change of gauge, **160:15,**
160:25.
Paid-up capital stock must equal
one-half cost before
operation, **160:28.**
Statement of gauge in
agreement of association,
160:14.
Natural gas pipelines,
construction, **164:75C.**
Navigable waters, crossings over,
160:96.
Negligence.
Animal on railroad, penalty for
negligently permitting,
160:223.
Contributory negligence as
defense to action for
collision at grade crossing,
160:232.
Defect in highway within
location of railroad, liability
for personal injuries,
160:229.
Employer's liability for
negligence of employee,
153:1, 153:4, 160:231.
Gross negligence. See within
this heading, "Gross
negligence."
Operation of trains, **265:30.**
Passenger trains, penalty for
negligent operation of,
160:231.

RAILROADS —Cont'd

Nonresidents engaged in construction and repair of railroads to appoint agents for service of process, **227:5.**

Notice.

Abandoning or diminishing accommodations of station, hearing, **160:128, 160:128A.**

Accidents, **38:8, 159:28.**

Alteration of highways, **160:101.**

Annual meeting of creditors or bondholders, **160:52.**

Assessments, sale of stock for failure to pay, **160:39.**

Auction sale of new shares on increase of capital stock, **159:51.**

Change of location, hearing, **160:85.**

Change of name, **160:215, 160:216.**

Clearing of land adjoining tracks, **160:236.**

Compensation for joint occupation, hearing, **160:131.**

Confirmation of election of trustees, hearing, **160:53.**

Connecting carriers, hearing upon questions arising between, **160:72.**

Consent to contract for operation of railroad, meeting of bondholders or creditors to give, **160:51.**

Consolidation, hearing, **160:72.**

Contract that all transportation upon road of one company be performed by another, **159:54.**

Crossings.

See RAILROAD CROSSINGS.

Cutting off of owner from access to land, hearing, **160:110.**

Directors' meetings, **160:37.**

Electric railroads.

See ELECTRIC RAILROADS.

Elevated railways.

Auction sale of new shares on increase of capital stock, **159:51.**

Increase in capital stock, **159:50.**

Eminent domain, requirement of notice to railroads, **160:7.**

Establishment of through routes, hearing, **159:21.**

Examination by department upon complaint of mayor, selectmen, or voters, **159:24.**

RAILROADS —Cont'd

Notice —Cont'd

Exemptions from fencing requirements, proceedings, **160:93.**

Fire notices, **160:235, 160:237.**

First meeting, **160:29.**

Fixing location, hearing, **160:80.**

Fixing route, **160:21.**

Freight trains or cars, hearing upon petition for changes in manner of making up or shifting, **160:139.**

Increase in capital stock, **159:50.**

Intention to claim right of action for materials furnished, **159:98.**

Local express business, hearing prior to recommendation for person to engage, **160:206.**

Mail, unwillingness to transport, **160:202.**

Maintenance and repair of bridges, hearing upon application, **159:84.**

Maps and engineer's report submitted by directors, hearing, **160:19.**

Materials used in railroad construction, notice of intent to claim right of action, **159:98, 262:34.**

Metropolitan boulevards crossing railroads, notice of proposed action with respect, **92:50.**

Milk transportation, hearing upon fixing of rates, **160:215.**

Motor carriers of property, notice to railroads of hearing upon certificate of public convenience and necessity, **159B:3.**

Posting. See within this heading, "Posting."

Publication. See within this heading, "Publication."

Severance of private land, hearing upon application to commissioners, **160:109.**

Special charter, petition, **160:10.**

Stockholders' meetings, **160:33, 160:34.**

Street railways.

See STREET RAILWAYS.

Taking of railroad by eminent domain, **160:7.**

Terminal facilities, hearing upon petition for authority to operate, **160:131A.**

RAILROADS —Cont'd

Notice —Cont'd

Through routes, notice of hearing on establishment, **159:21.**

Transfer, lease, purchase, or sale of franchise and property, **159:54.**

Waiver. See within this heading, "Waiver."

Whistles, hearing upon petition for changes in manner of sounding, **160:139.**

Number.

Brakemen, **160:154.**

Crews, men, **160:185.**

Incorporators, **160:13.**

Oaths.

Annual return, **160:242.**

Certificate of vote for change of name, **160:216.**

Clerk, **160:32.**

Return of express company, **159:33.**

Statement of amount due for labor, **159:99.**

Obligations.

Debts and obligations. See within this heading, "Debts and obligations."

Obstruction or interference.

Crossings.

See RAILROAD CROSSINGS.

Employees, interference, **159:104.**

Passage of train, obstructing, **160:226.**

Public highways, obstruction, **160:151.**

Street railways.

Public ways, **161:96.**

Tracks, **161:94.**

Transit authority, penalty for obstruction of tracks under control, **161:94.**

Offenses and penalties.

Access to land, noncompliance with order to provide for owner, **160:110.**

Accidents, failure to give notice, **159:28.**

Accounts, failure to keep in method prescribed by department, **159:31.**

Animals.

Negligently permitting upon tracks, **160:223.**

Riding, driving, or leading upon tracks, **160:222.**

Annual return, neglect to make, **160:242.**

RAILROADS —Cont'd
Offenses and penalties —Cont'd
Arrests without warrant, **159:93, 159:94, 159:104, 160:220.**
Arson, **266:2.**
Assaulting or interfering with employees, **159:104.**
Attorney general. See within this heading, "Attorney general."
Automatic couplers, violations, **160:160.**
Badges for employees, violations, **160:177.**
Baggage checks, violations, **160:194.**
BB gun or air gun, discharge across right of way, **269:12B.**
Books, refusal to submit for examination by department, **159:31.**
Boston terminal corporation.
Loitering in station, **160:219.**
Passenger, arrest for failure to pay fare, **159:93, 159:94.**
Unlawful riding, **160:220.**
Brakemen, violations, **160:154.**
Brakes, violations, **160:154, 160:160.**
Breaking and entering, **266:19.**
Bus, tampering, **159:103.**
Caboose, unlawful riding, **160:220.**
Cars, offenses in.
Cars. See within this heading, "Cars and rolling stock."
Charter or franchise of consolidated corporation, acts which may cause forfeiture, **160:42.**
Consolidation, violations, **160:42, 160:74.**
Counterfeiting tickets, passes, etc., **267:2, 267:4 et seq.**
Crossings.
See RAILROAD CROSSINGS.
Day of rest requirements, violation, **160:184.**
Debt or liability, incurring for unauthorized purpose, **160:48.**
Director's liability for unlawful issue of stock or scrip, **160:57.**
Disorderly or annoying conduct, **159:93, 159:94, 272:43, 272:43A.**
District attorney, actions to recover penalties. See within this heading, "District attorney, actions to recover penalties."

RAILROADS —Cont'd
Offenses and penalties —Cont'd
Drawbars for freight cars, violations as to height, **160:160.**
Drawbridges, violations, **160:126, 160:127.**
Drinking water, failure to furnish, **160:175.**
Electric railroads, walking on tracks, **162:18.**
Endangering persons in trains, **160:226.**
Equipment, recovery of penalty for violations, **160:160.**
Examinations for color blindness of employees, violations, **160:178.**
Expectoration in cars, stations, etc., **270:14, 270:15.**
Experience requirements for engineers and conductors, violations, **160:183.**
Explosive oils or fluids, use to light passenger cars, **160:166.**
Extra fare regulations, violation of, on mileage tickets, **160:189.**
Failing to stop train at grade crossing between railroads, engineer, **160:135.**
Fences, failure to maintain and erect, **160:93.**
Firemen's negligence causing personal injury, **160:231.**
Forging tickets, **267:2, 267:4 et seq.**
Fraudulent evasion of payment of fare, **159:101.**
Freight, violations, **160:209.**
Gambling in cars, **271:2.**
Gates of private crossings, neglect to close, **160:224.**
Grab irons on cars, violations, **160:160.**
Gross negligence in carriage of passengers, **160:231, 265:30.**
Heating of cars, violations, **160:165.**
Indemnity, requiring from employees, **159:4.**
Influencing appointment or discharge of employees, **271:40, 271:41.**
Larceny and theft. See within this heading, "Larceny and theft."
Locomotive with untested boiler, **160:168.**
Loitering in stations, **160:219.**

RAILROADS —Cont'd
Offenses and penalties —Cont'd
Malicious injuries, **160:225, 266:94.**
Milk transportation, violations, **160:214.**
Missiles, throwing or shooting at car or train, **159:104.**
Mufflers, violations, **160:171.**
Negligent operation of trains, **160:231, 265:30.**
Obstructing engines or cars, **160:226.**
Obstructing public highways, **160:151.**
Passes, violations, **160:199.**
Platform gates, violations, **160:167.**
Protection required at crossings, failure to provide, **160:148.**
Quarterly returns, failure to make, **160:243.**
Reasonable accommodations for passengers, failure to furnish, **160:172.**
Receipts for freight, failure to give, **160:204.**
Recovery of penalties.
Attorney general. See within this heading, "Attorney general."
District attorney. See within this heading, "District attorney, actions to recover penalties."
Relief corporations, failure to allow examination of books and papers, **159:87.**
Safety switches, failure to use, **160:132.**
Sale of tickets, violations, **160:198A, 160:198B.**
Scalping tickets, **160:198B.**
Shooting at car or train, **159:104.**
Signals, injury, **159:102.**
Signs at crossings, violations, **160:145, 160:146, 160:148.**
Smoking cars, requiring women or children to ride, **160:173.**
Spitting in cars, **270:14, 270:15.**
Station name, failure to indicate by signs, **160:130.**
Stealing from cars, **266:20.**
Stocks or bonds, unlawful issue or disposition of proceeds, **160:48.**
Stopping trains, **160:227.**
Street railways.
See STREET RAILWAYS.
Switches, failure to block, **160:133.**

231

RAILROADS —Cont'd
Offenses and penalties —Cont'd
Switch stands, violations,
160:133A.
Tampering.
Signals or equipment,
159:103.
Tools on cars, **160:228.**
Throwing missiles at car or
train.
Cars. See within this heading,
"Cars and rolling stock."
Tools.
Failure to equip trains and
cars, **160:163.**
Tampering, **160:228.**
Torpedoes, failure to mark,
159:102.
Tracks, tampering, **159:103.**
Treble damages. See within this
heading, "Treble damages."
Trespass, **90:15, 159:93,**
160:218, 160:220.
Uniform caps or hats, violations,
160:177.
Unlawful riding upon locomotive
or car, **160:220.**
Walking on track, **160:218.**
Windshield or canopy, operating
track motor car without,
160:163A.
Offer to purchase railroad facilities
for rail transportation in
Commonwealth, **161C:7.**
Officers.
Employees, officers, and agents.
See within this heading,
"Employees, officers, and
agents."
Oil.
Gas and oil. See within this
heading, "Gas and oil."
Opening for public use, **160:118,**
160:119.
Openings, duty of railroad to erect
fences, **160:93.**
Operating corporation of other
railroads, **160:5.**
Organization in general, **160:29,**
160:30.
Outdoor advertising regulations,
applicability, **93:32.**
Overhead crossings.
See RAILROAD CROSSINGS.
Overtime pay for employees,
151:1A.
Par.
Agreement of association to
show par value of stock,
160:14.
Sale of bonds and notes below
par, **160:50.**

RAILROADS —Cont'd
Par —Cont'd
Street railways.
See STREET RAILWAYS.
Parlor cars, **149:148, 160:174.**
Passenger cars.
Cars. See within this heading,
"Cars and rolling stock."
Passenger service, abandonment,
160:128, 160:128A.
Passes.
Tickets. See within this heading,
"Tickets."
Penalties.
Offenses and penalties. See
within this heading,
"Offenses and penalties."
Permits.
Licenses and permits. See
within this heading,
"Licenses and permits."
Personal injuries.
Accidents. See within this
heading, "Accidents."
Personal property, power to
mortgage or pledge, **160:47.**
Petitions and complaints.
Abolition of grade crossings,
159:65, 159:70.
Aldermen or selectmen. See
within this heading,
"Aldermen or selectmen."
Appeal from decision of county
commissioners as to
crossings, **160:112.**
Change.
Charter, **3:5.**
Direction, **160:86.**
Location, **160:81, 160:85.**
Compensation for joint
occupation of station,
railroad, or grounds,
160:131.
Connecting carriers,
determination of questions
arising between, **160:60.**
Construction and location. See
within this heading,
"Construction and location."
County commissioners, petitions
to, **34:19.**
Crossings.
See RAILROAD CROSSINGS.
Defects, employees' complaints,
159:30.
Enforcement of laws, **160:252.**
Enjoining railroads from
altering highways
unlawfully, **160:100.**
Enjoining running of trains upon
railroad failing to observe
crossing regulations,
160:136.

RAILROADS —Cont'd
Petitions and complaints —Cont'd
Freight trains or cars, manner of
makeup and shifting,
160:139.
General court, petitions, **3:5,**
160:8.
Laying out highway across
railroad, **160:104.**
Location, fixing, **160:80.**
Mayor, complaint, **159:24.**
Motor carriers of passengers,
petition for alteration or
revocation of rules and
regulations concerning,
159A:12.
Notice of examination by
department upon complaint,
159:24.
Price of transportation of mail,
160:202, 160:203.
Release from obligation to erect
signs where impracticable,
160:144.
Removal of standing wood at
crossings, **160:150.**
Route, fixing, **160:21.**
Special charter, **160:8.**
State police, railroad commission
petitioning for special police,
22C:51, 22C:52.
Street railways.
See STREET RAILWAYS.
Switch connections,
establishment, **160:117.**
Whistles, changes in manner of
sounding, **160:139.**
Workingmen's trains, **160:198.**
Pipes and conduits, removal or
relocation upon abolition of
grade crossings, **159:74,**
159:75.
Place or location.
Construction and location. See
within this heading,
"Construction and location."
Plans and planning.
Bridges, **159:83.**
Commonwealth, rail
transportation, **161C:6.**
Grade crossings, plans for
abolition, **159:65, 159:70.**
Master plan of municipal
planning boards, **41:81D.**
Platforms.
Clearance of tracks in yards,
160:134A.
Expectoration, **270:14, 270:15.**
Gate on platforms of certain
cars, **160:167.**
Street railways.
See STREET RAILWAYS.

RAILROADS —Cont'd

Pledge or mortgage of property and equipment, **160:47, 160:48.**

Poles, removal or relocation upon abolition of grade crossings, **159:74.**

Police officers, **159:92-159:95.**
Arrests, **159:93, 159:94, 160:220, 161:94A.**
Badges, **159:92.**
Blue light, display by motor vehicle of railroad police, **90:7.**
Compensation, **159:95.**
Complaint against persons arrested, **159:94.**
District court jurisdiction of persons arrested, **159:94.**
Duties, **159:94.**
Evidence.
Badge as evidence that officer lawfully upon duty, **159:92.**
Fees and expenses for attendance as witnesses, **262:55.**
Filing and recording. See within this heading, "Filing and recording."
Free or reduced rate service, **159:15.**
Liability for misconduct, **159:95.**
Powers of, **159:93, 159:104, 161:95.**
Street railways.
See STREET RAILWAYS.
Telecommunications and energy department. See within this heading, "Telecommunications and energy department."
Warrant, arrests without, **159:93, 159:94, 160:220.**
Witnesses, fees and expenses, **262:55.**

Policy and purpose of providing rail transportation in Commonwealth, **161C:1.**

Ports.
Harbors. See within this heading, "Harbors."

Possession.
Adverse possession. See within this heading, "Adverse possession."

Posting.
Agreement of association, **160:16.**
Duties, **160:235A.**
Fire notices and warnings, **160:235.**

RAILROADS —Cont'd

Posting —Cont'd
Maps and engineer's reports submitted by directors, notice of hearing, **160:19.**

Power which may be used, **159:16, 160:153.**

Preferred stock.
Certificates of stock, preferences to be, **160:44.**
Designation, **160:44.**
Issue and increase, **160:43.**
Limitation on amount, **160:45.**
Offered to common stockholders first, **160:46.**
Sale, **160:46.**
Subsequent classes to be subordinate to previously created classes, **160:45.**
Voting power, **160:45.**

President.
Agreement as to alterations of crossings, **159:80.**
Certificate of vote for change of name, signed and sworn, **160:216.**
Certification of map and statements filed upon opening of road for public use, **160:119.**
Consolidation, application, **160:72.**
Election, **160:32.**
Grain elevator corporation, president to represent railroad at meetings, **160:67.**
Required, **160:31.**
Signature to certificate of increase or decrease of capital stock of corporation to operate in foreign country, **160:250.**
Stock certificate signed, **160:38.**
Stockholders' meetings called, **160:33.**

Prisoners to be transported from institution, allowance of expenses, **262:21, 262:48.**

Private railroads.
Inquest in case of death, **38:8-38:12.**
Street railways stopped at private railroad crossings, **161:92.**

Private side tracks, switch connections, **159:21.**

Probate judges, free passes to prohibited, **160:199.**

Process.
Service of process. See within this heading, "Service of process."

RAILROADS —Cont'd

Protective appliances for passenger cars, **160:176.**

Proxy, voting, **160:36, 160:251.**

Publication.
Agreement of association, **160:16, 160:23.**
Auction sale of new shares of capital stock, notice, **159:51.**
Certificates annexed to agreement of association, **160:23.**
Clearing land adjoining tracks, notice, **160:236.**
Electric railroads.
See ELECTRIC RAILROADS.
Examination of books and financial condition, result, **159:35.**
Exemptions from fencing requirements, notice, **160:93.**
Maps and engineer's reports submitted by directors, notice of hearing, **160:19.**
Meetings of bondholders or creditors, **160:51, 160:52.**
Method of crossing highways, notice of hearing, **160:75.**
Posting. See within this heading, "Posting."
Special charter, notice of petition, **160:10.**
Street railways.
See STREET RAILWAYS.
Terminal facilities, notice of hearing upon petition for authority to operate, **160:131A.**

Public body, petitions for enforcement of laws, **160:252.**

Public convenience and necessity.
Certificates. See within this heading, "Certificates and certification."

Public health department, drinking water and cups for passengers subject to approval, **160:174, 160:175.**

Public parks or reservations, railroads not to enter, **160:240.**

Public use, opening, **160:118, 160:119.**

Public warehouses.
Warehouses. See within this heading, "Warehouses."

Public works department.
Authorized to spend money, **161C:4.**
Contracts and agreements. See within this heading, "Contracts and agreements."

RAILROADS —Cont'd
Public works department —Cont'd
Crossings.
  See RAILROAD CROSSINGS.
  Financial assistance, contracts,
    161C:5.
  Laying out highway across
    railroad, **160:104.**
  Navigable or tide waters,
    consent to crossing, **160:96.**
  Powers of department, **161C:6.**
  Private railroad, consent to use
    of public way, **160:245.**
  Street railways.
    See STREET RAILWAYS.
Purchases.
  Sales. See within this heading,
    "Sales."
Pyrotechnic signals, **148:39,
  148:44.**
Quarterly returns, **160:243.**
Quorum.
  Stockholders' meetings, **160:33.**
  Street railways.
    See STREET RAILWAYS.
Racial discrimination, **272:92A,
  272:98.**
Railroad crossings, **159:57 et seq.,
  160:95 et seq.**
  See RAILROAD CROSSINGS.
Rates and charges, **159B:6,
  159B:6A, 159B:7,
  160:208-160:211.**
  See RATES AND CHARGES.
Real estate companies, holding
  stock, **160:65B.**
Real property, **160:76 et seq.**
Reasonable accommodations must
  be furnished for passengers,
  160:172.
Receipts.
  Annual return to contain
    statement, **160:242.**
  Shippers of freight, **160:204.**
Records, reports, and returns.
  Accident investigations, **159:29.**
  Accounts and accounting. See
    within this heading,
    "Accounts and accounting."
  Agreement fixing location,
    160:80.
  Annual meeting of bondholders
    or creditors, **160:52.**
  Annual return. See within this
    heading, "Annual return."
  Bondholders or creditors,
    examination, **159:35.**
  Bridges, examination, **159:83.**
  Consolidation, report by
    department to general court,
    160:72.

RAILROADS —Cont'd
Records, reports, and returns
  —Cont'd
  Electric railroads.
    See ELECTRIC RAILROADS.
  Engineers. See within this
    heading, "Engineers."
  Express companies, **159:33.**
  Filing and recording. See within
    this heading, "Filing and
    recording."
  First meeting, recording, **160:29.**
  Forms prescribed, **159:31,
    160:70A.**
  General court, submission for
    inspection, **160:72, 160:242.**
  Grade crossings, expenses of
    abolition, **159:78.**
  Labor, statement of amount due,
    159:99.
  Lessee to make, **160:244.**
  Mileage books and tickets. See
    within this heading,
    "Mileage books and tickets."
  Motor vehicles, transportation,
    160:70A.
  Opening for public use,
    statements made in
    connection, **160:119.**
  Petition for special charter to be
    accompanied, **160:8.**
  Quarterly returns, **160:243.**
  Receipts. See within this
    heading, "Receipts."
  Relief corporations, **159:87.**
  Stock and stockholders.
    List of stockholders to
      department, **159:31.**
    Reports by public utilities
      commission, **25:7.**
  Street railways.
    See STREET RAILWAYS.
  Track inspection division, duties,
    25:7.
Reflector devices on signs at
  crossings, **160:142.**
Registered bonds, **160:49.**
Related facilities or equipment
  defined, **161C:2.**
Release.
  Expressman's release from
    liability for personal injury
    upon issuance of season
    ticket, **160:193.**
  Impracticability of signs, release
    from obligation to erect,
    160:144.
Relief corporations, **159:86-159:88.**
  Benefits from considered in
    mitigation of damages for
    injury, **153:8.**

RAILROADS —Cont'd
Relief corporations —Cont'd
  Bylaws, **159:87.**
  Provisions for representation
    of railroad corporation,
    159:88.
  Employees may form, **159:86,
    159:88.**
  Examination of books and
    papers by department,
    159:87.
  Financial transaction statements
    to department, **159:87.**
  Funds, not liable to attachment,
    159:88.
  Membership statement to
    department, **159:87.**
  Purposes for which formed,
    159:86.
  Railroad corporation may
    associate with employees in
    forming, **159:88.**
  Returns, **159:87.**
  Street railways.
    See STREET RAILWAYS.
Removal.
  Brush and sage, **48:18-48:20.**
  Wires at crossings, **160:104A.**
  Wreckage and debris caused by
    derailments, **160:241A.**
Repairs and maintenance.
  Bridges. See within this
    heading, "Bridges."
  Complaint by employees as to
    defects, **159:30.**
  Crossings.
    See RAILROAD CROSSINGS.
  Executive office of transportation
    and construction,
    maintenance of facilities,
    161C:3.
  Freight depots, **149:113.**
  Nonresident engaged in, agents
    for service of process, **227:5.**
  Other corporation, maintenance,
    160:5.
  Recommendations by
    department, **159:23.**
  Street railways.
    See STREET RAILWAYS.
Reports.
  Records, reports and returns.
    See within this heading,
    "Records, reports, and
    returns."
Request of department, effect on
  duties and liabilities of
  railroad, **159:38.**
Reserved rights of Commonwealth,
  160:6, 160:7.
Rest.
  Animals, rest and feeding during
    transportation, **272:81.**

RAILROADS —Cont'd
Rest —Cont'd
Employees, rest days, **160:184.**
Retirement Act or board.
Employment security.
See EMPLOYMENT SECURITY.
Tax deductions, **62:3.**
Retirement system funds invested in securities, **32:23.**
Returns.
Records, reports, and returns. See within this heading, "Records, reports, and returns."
Revenue commissioner, filing of stock classification, **160:44.**
Review.
Appeals. See within this heading, "Appeals."
Revision of award by commission to determine which party to make and pay for alterations of crossings, **159:63.**
Revival, petition to general court, **3:5.**
Revocation or suspension.
Street railways.
See STREET RAILWAYS.
Right of first refusal as to purchase of railroad facilities, **161C:7.**
Rights of way.
Abandoned rights or way, duties of cities and towns, regarding, **40:54A.**
Air gun or BB gun, discharging across right of way, **269:12B.**
Contracts for financial assistance, **161C:5.**
Cross-ties, piling or keeping on right of way, **160:235.**
Defined, **161C:2.**
Fees for applications to lease or license, **161C:4.**
Permit to build structure, **40:54A.**
Purchase, **161C:4.**
Sale or disposal, **161C:7.**
Wires over crossings, disconnection or removal for certain purposes, **159:74, 160:104A.**
Youth conservation and service corps, **78A:3.**
Rights reserved by Commonwealth, **160:6, 160:7.**
Rivers and streams, expenses of relocating or changing on abolition of grade crossings, **159:75.**

RAILROADS —Cont'd
Roadbed, examination, **159:83.**
Rolling stock.
Cars and rolling stock. See within this heading, "Cars and rolling stock."
Roundhouses, acquisition of land, **160:78, 160:83.**
Routes or lines.
Construction and location. See within this heading, "Construction and location."
Electric railroads.
See ELECTRIC RAILROADS.
Fire insurance for property along, **160:234.**
Maps. See within this heading, "Maps."
Special charter, routes of corporation established, **160:10-160:12.**
Street railways.
See STREET RAILWAYS.
Through routes, establishment, **159:21.**
Safety appliances and devices.
Emergency exits for passengers, **160:163B.**
Freight cars, safety couplers, **160:156.**
Location of safety devices on cars, **160:163.**
Mufflers on safety valves, **160:170, 160:171.**
Passenger cars, safety or protective appliances, **160:132, 160:163, 160:176.**
Safety switches, **160:132.**
Street cars or railways, requirement, **161:98.**
Tracks, erection of fences where necessary for public safety, **160:93A.**
Whistles. See within this heading, "Whistles."
Salary.
Wages and compensation. See within this heading, "Wages and compensation."
Sales.
Auction. See within this heading, "Auction."
Bonds and notes, validity where sold at less than par, **160:50.**
Capital stock not to be increased, **160:73.**
Commonwealth, right to acquire property, **160:6.**

RAILROADS —Cont'd
Sales —Cont'd
Construction and location, purchase of land for.
Construction and location. See within this heading, "Construction and location."
Description of land purchased, filing with county commissioners, **160:79.**
Equipment, purchase, **161C:4.**
Facilities.
First refusal to purchase, **161C:7.**
Not to be diminished by sales, **160:73.**
Offer to purchase to be sent by certified mail, **161C:7.**
First refusal as to purchase of railroad facilities, Commonwealth to have right, **161C:7.**
Foreclosure, rights and duties of purchaser, **160:55.**
Foreign countries, purchasing other corporations, **160:250.**
Franchise and property, approval by department, **159:38, 159:54.**
Indebtedness not to be increased, **160:73.**
Mortgage foreclosure sale, right of purchaser, **160:55.**
Other corporations or property by corporations to operate in foreign countries, **160:250.**
Rates not to be increased, **160:73.**
Right of Commonwealth, **160:6, 161C:7.**
Rights of way, **161C:7.**
Secretary of executive office of transportation and construction, purchase of land, **161C:6.**
Telecommunications and energy department, sale of franchise and property subject to approval, **159:38, 159:54.**
Ticket sales regulated, **160:198A, 160:198B.**
Trackless trolleys, purchase of property, **163:11.**
Unclaimed goods, **135:6.**
Sales tax exemption, **64H:6.**
Savings bank may invest in obligations, **168:44.**
Scalping of tickets, **160:198B.**

RAILROADS —Cont'd
Scrip or stock dividends.
  Stock and stockholders. See
    within this heading, "Stock
    and stockholders."
Seals.
  Stock certificate to bear seal,
    160:38.
  Street railways.
    See STREET RAILWAYS.
Season tickets.
  Tickets. See within this heading,
    "Tickets."
Secretary of executive office of
  transportation and
  construction.
  Defined, **161C:2.**
  Planning of rail facilities,
    161C:6.
  Powers and duties, **161C:6.**
Secretary of state.
  State secretary. See within this
    heading, "State secretary."
Sectionmen.
  Extinguishing fires, duty,
    160:238.
  To be notified of discovery of fire,
    160:237.
Secured transactions.
  Cars and rolling stock. See
    within this heading, "Cars
    and rolling stock."
  Liens and encumbrances. See
    within this heading, "Liens
    and encumbrances."
Security.
  Bonds and undertakings. See
    within this heading, "Bonds
    and undertakings."
Seeing eye dog, carriage of blind
  person accompanied, **272:98A.**
Selectmen.
  Aldermen or selectmen. See
    within this heading,
    "Aldermen or selectmen."
Service of process.
  Nonresidents engaged in
    construction and repair,
    agent for service of process,
    227:5.
  Orders for abolition of grade
    crossings, **159:70.**
  Petition upon appeal from
    decision in certain matters
    as to crossings, **160:112.**
Severance of private land,
  160:109.
Sewers.
  See SEWERS AND DRAINS.
Sheriff, arrest without warrant of
  person unlawfully riding,
  160:220, 160:221.

RAILROADS —Cont'd
Shooting, **159:93, 159:94, 159:104.**
Side tracks.
  Switches and switch
    connections. See within this
    heading, "Switches and
    switch connections."
Sight defects, examination of
  employees, **160:178.**
Signalmen, days of rest, **160:184.**
Signals.
  Crossings, **160:135-160:152.**
    See RAILROAD CROSSINGS.
  Drawbridges, **160:123, 160:126.**
  Electric railroads, **162:16.**
  Fire signal, **160:237.**
  Highway crossings.
    See RAILROAD CROSSINGS.
  Injury, **159:103.**
  Liability for negligence of
    employee in charge of
    marking torpedoes, **159:102.**
  Longshoremen and waterfront
    employees, signs and signals
    to protect, **149:18H.**
  Negligence of employee in
    charge of signals, liability,
    153:1.
  Pyrotechnic signals, **148:39,**
    148:44.
  Street railways.
    Department may require
      signals, **159:22.**
    Injury to or tampering with
      signals, **159:102, 159:103.**
  Telecommunications and energy
    department. See within this
    heading,
    "Telecommunications and
    energy department."
  Two or more railroads,
    automatic signals at
    crossings between, **160:136,**
    160:137.
  Whistles, **160:138, 160:139,**
    162:16.
  Yards, clearance of tracks,
    160:134A.
Signal towers, days of rest for
  certain employees, **160:184.**
Signature, facsimile or
  reproduction of stock
  certificates, **160:38.**
Signs.
  Crossings.
    See RAILROAD CROSSINGS.
  Fire placards, **160:235.**
  Longshoremen and waterfront
    employees, signs and signals
    to protect, **149:18H.**
  Outdoor advertising regulations,
    applicability, **93:32.**

RAILROADS —Cont'd
Signs —Cont'd
  Release from obligation to erect
    where impracticable,
    160:144.
  Signals. See within this heading,
    "Signals."
  Station names, **160:130.**
Slash, clearing and disposal,
  48:16, 48:18-48:20.
Smoking in public places,
  regulation, **270:21.**
  Cars, smoking in.
    Cars. See within this heading,
    "Cars and rolling stock."
Spark arresters on locomotives,
  160:235.
Special charters, **160:8-160:12.**
  Construction and location of
    railroads established,
    160:12.
  Engineer's report to accompany
    petition, **160:8.**
  Hearings upon petition, **160:9.**
  Limits to be specified, **160:11.**
  Maps to accompany petition,
    160:8.
  Notice of petition, **160:10.**
  Petition to general court, **160:8.**
  Plans upon petition, **160:9.**
  Routes of corporations
    established, **160:10-160:12.**
Special law, increase of stock or
  bonds beyond allowance fixed
  in, when allowed, **160:41.**
Special meetings of stockholders,
  160:34.
Special police, railroad commission
  petitioning, **22C:51, 22C:52.**
Specific performance of order for
  construction of embankments,
  culverts, walls, or fences,
  160:92.
Spitting in cars, stations, etc.,
  270:14, 270:15.
Spurs and sidings.
  Switches and switch
    connections. See within this
    heading, "Switches and
    switch connections."
Stamping railroad ticket with
  forged stamp, penalty,
  267:4-267:6.
Standing wood at crossings,
  removal, **160:150.**
State.
  Appropriations, Commonwealth's
    share for alteration of
    crossings paid from
    maintenance and repair of
    state highways, **159:61.**

RAILROADS —Cont'd
State —Cont'd
Crossings.
See RAILROAD CROSSINGS.
Eminent domain, property taken by Commonwealth, **160:7.**
Environmental advantages, purchase for rail transportation in Commonwealth, **161C:4.**
Federal law as affecting state's right of first refusal, **161C:7.**
Fees, applications to lease, license, or use property of state, **161C:4.**
Foreign state. See within this heading, "Foreign countries or states."
Free passes to state officers, **160:199.**
Intersection of state boundaries, **1:4.**
Investment of funds in railroad obligations, **29:38.**
Plans upon petition for special charter deposited in state library, **160:9.**
Policy and purpose of providing rail transportation, **161C:1.**
Purchase of facilities, **160:G, 161C:7.**
Rail transportation in, **161:1-161:7.**
Reimbursement of deficits in operation of street railroads, **161:152A.**
Reserved rights of Commonwealth, **160:6, 160:7.**
Secretary of state.
State secretary. See within this heading, "State secretary."
Settlement of barred claim for grade crossing elimination, **159:76.**
Street railways.
See STREET RAILWAYS.
State house, location on land around, **8:16, 160:77.**
State police, railroad commission petitioning for special police, **22C:51, 22C:52.**
State secretary.
Approval of transfer, lease, purchase, or sale of franchise and property, filing certificate, **159:54.**
Capital stock, filing certificate of increase or reduction, **160:25.**

RAILROADS —Cont'd
State secretary —Cont'd
Certificate of incorporation issued, **160:24.**
Foreign countries. See within this heading, "Foreign countries or states."
Gauge, filing certificate of change, **160:25.**
Map and profile filed with, upon opening for public use, **160:119.**
Name of railroad, certificates upon change, **160:216.**
Street railways.
See STREET RAILWAYS.
Taking of land, filing of certificate of compliance with provisions, **160:76.**
Terminal facilities, filing of order granting authority to operate, **160:131A.**
Stations and depots, **160:128-160:131A.**
Abandonment, **160:128, 160:128A.**
Accommodations.
Connecting railroads, **160:59.**
Diminishing, **160:128, 160:128A.**
Acquisition of land, **91:5, 160:78, 160:83.**
Business corporations may own and operate terminal facilities, **160:131A.**
Days of rest for certain employees, **160:184.**
Equal facilities. See within this heading, "Equal facilities and accommodations."
Expectoration, **270:14, 270:15.**
Freight depots. See within this heading, "Freight depots and houses."
Harbor terminal facilities, **91:5.**
Intermodal transportation terminals, authority to construct, **121B:46.**
Joint occupation, compensation, **160:131.**
Loitering prohibited, **160:219, 272:68.**
Name to be indicated by signs, **160:130.**
Posting notices, **160:235A.**
Racial discrimination, **272:92A, 272:98.**
Regulation of advertising signs, **93:32.**
Relocation, **160:129.**
Street railways.
See STREET RAILWAYS.

RAILROADS —Cont'd
Stations and depots —Cont'd
Telecommunications and energy department. See within this heading, "Telecommunications and energy department."
Statute of limitations.
Limitation of actions. See within this heading, "Limitation of actions."
Stay on appeal in certain matters as to crossings, **160:111.**
Stealing.
Larceny. See within this heading, "Larceny and theft."
Steamboats.
See STEAMBOATS AND STEAMBOAT COMPANIES.
Stock and stockholders, **160:38-160:46.**
Additional subscription in connection with construction of branches and extensions, **160:115.**
Agreement of association, statements, **160:14, 160:16.**
Air carriers, taking stock of subsidiary companies by railroad, **160:70.**
Assessments upon shares, **160:39, 160:40.**
Bonds and notes, limited, **160:47.**
Branches and extensions, taking stocks to aid in construction, **160:69.**
Business corporations other than railroads holding stock in railroad company, **156:5.**
Car and equipment companies, holding stock, **160:65A.**
Cash must be paid before issue of stock, **160:56, 160:57.**
Certificates, **160:38.**
Collection of assessment, **160:40.**
Common stock, when offered to preferred stockholders, **160:46.**
Computing amount as basis for issue, **159:53.**
Computing amount of, as basis for bond issue, **159:53.**
Connecting railroads, approval by stockholders of lease, **160:62.**
Consolidation.
Application and consent by stockholders, **160:72.**
Increase after, **160:73.**

RAILROADS —Cont'd
Stock and stockholders —Cont'd
Construction and location. See
within this heading,
"Construction and location."
Department to have access to
list of stockholders, **159:31.**
Development companies, holding
stock, **160:65B.**
Directors.
Elected by stockholders,
160:32.
Must be stockholders, **160:32.**
Dividends in stock or scrip,
160:56, 160:57.
Street railways, **161:36,
161:37.**
Preferred stock dividends
included in cost of
service, **161:116.**
Proceeds of sale, use for
dividends, **161:68.**
Unauthorized stock dividend
by consolidated
corporation, **160:42.**
Domestic railroads, taking stock
of, restrained, **160:71,
160:74.**
Equipment companies, capital
stock as limiting
stockholdings, **160:65A.**
Examination of books and
financial condition upon
request of stockholders,
159:35.
Foreign countries. See within
this heading, "Foreign
countries or states."
Forfeiture for failure to pay
assessments, **160:39.**
Increase, **160:15, 160:25.**
Amount determined by
department, based upon
price fixed by
stockholders, **159:52.**
Charter, increase beyond
amount fixed, **160:41.**
Disposition of new shares,
159:50, 159:51.
Maximum, **160:56, 160:57.**
Notice to stockholders, **159:50.**
Not to be increased by
consolidation, lease, or
sale, **160:73.**
Price of new shares
established by
stockholders, **159:50.**
Determination of amount by
department based,
159:21.
Purposes for which allowed,
160:41.

RAILROADS —Cont'd
Stock and stockholders —Cont'd
Industrial companies, holding
stock, **160:65B.**
Issue, **160:47, 160:48.**
Judge's certificate as conclusive
evidence of responsibility of
subscriber, **160:76.**
Liability of subscriber for unpaid
assessments, interest, and
charges of sale, **160:39.**
Limitation on holding of capital
stock of domestic
corporations, **156B:15.**
Location.
Construction and location. See
within this heading,
"Construction and
location."
Meetings.
Stockholders' meetings. See
within this heading,
"Stockholders' meetings."
Motor carriers of property
companies, taking stock of
subsidiaries, **160:70.**
Narrow gauge railroads, paid up
capital stock must equal one
half cost before operation,
160:28.
Par value to be stated in
agreement of association,
160:14.
Preferred stock. See within this
heading, "Preferred stock."
Proceeds from issue, **160:48,
160:56, 160:57.**
Real estate companies, holding
stock, **160:65B.**
Records, reports, and returns.
See within this heading,
"Records, reports, and
returns."
Reduction, **160:15, 160:25.**
Sale for failure to pay
assessments, **160:39.**
Seals, certificates to bear,
160:38.
Special meeting, holders of one
tenth of capital stock may
apply, **160:34.**
Subscription.
Certificate submitted to
department, **160:23.**
New shares, **159:50, 159:51,
160:46.**
Requirements prerequisite to
taking of land, **160:76.**
Telecommunications and energy
department. See within this
heading,
"Telecommunications and
energy department."

RAILROADS —Cont'd
Stock and stockholders —Cont'd
Transfer for failure to pay
assessments, **160:39.**
Warehouse companies, holding
stock, **160:65B.**
Stockholders' meetings, **160:33,
160:34.**
Annual meeting, **160:33.**
Bonds and notes must be
authorized, **160:47.**
Change of name, meeting to
authorize, **160:215.**
Connecting railroads, approval
of lease, **160:62.**
First meeting, **160:29, 160:30.**
Quorum, **160:33.**
Special meetings, **160:34.**
Waiver of notice, **160:29, 160:33.**
Stone, acquisition of land for
procuring, **160:78, 160:83.**
Stoves, passenger, mail, or
baggage cars not to be heated,
160:165.
Streams and watercourses,
expenses of relocating or
changing upon abolition of
grade crossings, **159:75.**
Street railways.
See STREET RAILWAYS.
Streets.
Highways and streets. See
within this heading,
"Highways and streets."
Structures.
Buildings and structures. See
within this heading,
"Buildings and structures."
Subscription to agreement of
association, **160:14.**
Subscription to stock.
Stock. See within this heading,
"Stock and stockholders."
Suits.
Actions or suits. See within this
heading, "Actions or suits."
Sunday, activities permitted,
136:6.
Superior court.
Actions to recover expense of
extinguishing fires in grass
or forest lands, **160:241.**
Appointment of commission to
determine who shall make
and pay for alterations to
crossings, **159:62.**
Enforcement of laws, **160:252.**
Free passes to justices
prohibited, **160:199.**
Grade crossings, enforcement of
laws as to abolition, **159:79.**

RAILROADS —Cont'd

Superior court —Cont'd

Maintenance and repair of bridges, enforcement, **159:85.**

Street railways.

See STREET RAILWAYS.

Supplies.

Materials.

Actions or suits. See within this heading, "Actions or suits."

Fences, lien for materials used in constructing, **160:94.**

Supreme judicial court.

Appointment of commissioners to fix price to be paid for transportation of mails, **160:202, 160:203.**

Compensation for joint occupation, jurisdiction to revise award, **160:131.**

Confirmation of election of trustees, **160:53.**

Connecting carriers, awards concerning, **160:60.**

Crossings.

See RAILROAD CROSSINGS.

Enforcement of laws, **160:252.**

Enjoining unlawful alteration of highway, **160:100.**

Free passes to justices prohibited, **160:199.**

Mortgages and trustees, jurisdiction of questions, **160:54.**

Order for construction of embankments, culverts, walls, or fences, enforcement, **160:92.**

Removal of trustees, **160:54.**

Street railways.

See STREET RAILWAYS.

Surveys.

Entry on property by railroad for purpose, **160:75, 160:76, 266:120C.**

Route, survey in connection, **160:18.**

Suspension.

Revocation or suspension.

Police officers, revocation of appointment, **22:9N.**

Switches and switch connections.

Aldermen or selectmen, consent to laying in public way, **160:22.**

Blocking switches, **160:133.**

Highways, spurs and branches, **160:22.**

Negligence of employee in charge of liability of employer, **153:1.**

RAILROADS —Cont'd

Switches and switch connections —Cont'd

Private side track, requiring switch connection, **159:21, 160:116.**

Safety switches on tracks used by passenger or mixed trains, **160:132.**

Shipper, ordering upon application, **160:116, 160:117.**

Stands.

Switch stands. See within this heading, "Switch stands."

Street railways.

See STREET RAILWAYS.

Telecommunications and energy department. See within this heading, "Telecommunications and energy department."

Through route, creation by switch connection, **159:21.**

Yards, clearance of tracks, **160:134A.**

Switch stands.

Clearance of tracks, **160:134A.**

Regulation, **160:133A.**

Tampering.

Offenses and penalties. See within this heading, "Offenses and penalties."

Taxation.

Bonds, **59:4.**

Exemptions, **64H:6, 160:87.**

Fuel used, sales tax exemption, **64H:6.**

Generally.

See TAXATION.

Levy by city or town to pay interest on debts incurred in aid, **44:57, 59:24.**

Subscription indebtedness, assessment for interest, **59:24.**

Utility company franchise tax, **63:52A.**

Telecommunications and energy department.

Accidents.

Investigation, **159:29.**

Notice, **159:28.**

Accounts and accounting.

Forms prescribed, **159:31.**

Supervision by public utilities commission, **25:7.**

Agreement of association and attached certificates submitted, **160:23.**

Annual return submitted, **160:242.**

RAILROADS —Cont'd

Telecommunications and energy department —Cont'd

Appeals from certain decisions of county commissioner, powers, **160:113.**

Approval of contracts for transportation on road of one company by another, **159:54.**

Auction sales of new shares of capital stock, place, **159:51.**

Blocking of switches, approval of method, **160:133.**

Boilers of locomotives, testing, **160:168.**

Bond issues, duties, **25:7, 160:48.**

Books, examination on request of director, stockholder, or bondholder, **159:35.**

Boston, duties of county commissioners devolve upon department, **160:2.**

Boulevard, right to cross and manner of crossing railroad, **92:50.**

Branches and extensions, filing of certificate for construction, **160:115.**

Bridges.

Distance above track, **160:98.**

Examination, **159:83.**

Guards, approval, **160:134.**

Maintenance and repair, **159:84.**

Plans for new bridges, **159:83.**

Capital stock issues, approval, **160:48.**

Cars and other equipment, **160:162.**

Promulgation of regulations for testing, **160:168.**

Recommendations for addition, **159:23.**

Certificate of compliance by foreign countries, **160:249.**

Change in location, **160:85.**

Taking by eminent domain, **160:81.**

Change of name of corporation, authorization, **160:215.**

Commissioners forbidden to have interest in railroads, **25:3.**

Commutation tickets, approval, **160:190.**

Condition and operation, examination into upon complaint by mayor, selectmen, or voters, **159:24.**

RAILROADS —Cont'd
Telecommunications and energy
department —Cont'd
Connecting railroads.
Consent to use of each others'
roads, **160:58.**
Copies of contracts and leases
deposited with
department, **160:62.**
Determination of questions
arising between, **160:60.**
Consolidation, **160:72.**
Contract that one company
perform all transportation
upon road of another subject
to approval, **159:54.**
Cost of construction, estimate
submitted for approval of
department, **160:76.**
Crossings between two railroads,
consent, **160:96.**
Crossings with highways.
See RAILROAD CROSSINGS.
Defects, complaints by
employees to department,
159:30.
Description of land purchased,
160:79.
Drawbridges not opened for five
years, exemption, **160:127A.**
Duties and liabilities of railroad,
effect of advice or request of
department, **159:38.**
Duties upon appeal from certain
decisions of commissioners,
160:113.
Electric power, order for change,
159:16.
Electric railroads.
See ELECTRIC RAILROADS.
Elevated railways.
See ELEVATED RAILWAYS.
Extension of lines, **159:16.**
Fees for filing applications or
documents, **25:10B.**
Fencing requirements, granting
exemptions, **160:93.**
Financial condition, examination
on request of director,
stockholder, or bondholder,
159:35.
Franchise, transfer, lease,
purchase, or sale of, subject
to approval by department,
159:54.
Free transportation for
employees, **159:15.**
Freight trains and cars.
Recommendations as to
manner of making up and
shifting, **160:139.**

RAILROADS —Cont'd
Telecommunications and energy
department —Cont'd
Freight trains and cars —Cont'd
Regulation of use of crossings,
160:152.
Heating of cars, approval of
methods, **160:165.**
Incorporation, relative
provisions, **160:24.**
Inspector to investigate
accidents, **159:29.**
Joint occupation of station,
railroad, or grounds, award
of compensation, **160:131.**
Jurisdiction, **159:12.**
Lease of franchise and property
subject to approval, **159:54.**
Limitations on voting power of
preferred stock approved,
160:45.
List of stockholders, access,
159:31.
Local express business,
recommendation to engage,
160:206.
Location.
Description, **160:80, 160:89.**
Fixing, **160:80.**
State house, consent to
location within three
miles, **160:77.**
Switch connections, **159:21.**
Map prepared by directors
deposited, **160:23.**
Milk transportation, fixing rates,
160:213.
Mufflers for vacuum brakes,
approval, **160:169.**
Opening road for public use,
160:118.
Operation of railroads,
recommendations for
changes, **159:23.**
Orders of department, appeal,
159:16.
Orders, submission of evidence
of compliance, **159:16.**
Owner cut off from access to
land, crossing may be
ordered by department,
160:110.
Park boulevard, right to cross
and manner of crossing
railroad, **92:50.**
Platform gates, approval of
pattern, **160:167.**
Power used by railroads to be
approved, **160:153.**
Preferred stock, approval of
issue and increase, **160:43,
160:44, 160:46.**

RAILROADS —Cont'd
Telecommunications and energy
department —Cont'd
Private railroads, regulation,
160:246.
Private sidings, establishment of
switch connections, **159:21.**
Property, transfer, lease,
purchase, or sale of, subject
to approval by department,
159:54.
Protective appliances for
passenger cars,
requirement, **160:176.**
Public convenience and
necessity, application for
certificate, **160:17.**
Purchase of franchise and
property subject to approval,
159:54.
Quarterly returns, **160:243.**
Rates on through routes,
division between railroads,
159:21.
Relief corporations, approval and
examination, **159:87.**
Repairs recommendations,
159:23.
Route, fixing, **160:21.**
Safety switches, approval,
160:132.
Sale of franchise and property
subject to approval, **159:54.**
Service, abandonment, **159:16A.**
Signal may be required, **159:22.**
Recommendations for
additions to or changes,
159:23.
Signal systems, approval,
160:136, 160:137.
Spark arresters, approval,
160:235.
Stations and depots.
Abandonment or diminishing
accommodations, **160:128,
160:128A.**
Joint occupation, award of
compensation, **160:131.**
Relocation, approval, **160:129.**
Stock.
Access to stockholders' list,
159:31.
Amount determined by
department upon basis of
price fixed by
stockholders, **159:52.**
Auction sales, place, **159:51.**
Reports by public utilities
commission, **25:7.**
Street railways.
See STREET RAILWAYS.

RAILROADS —Cont'd
Telecommunications and energy
department —Cont'd
Subscription to capital stock,
approval prerequisite to
taking land, **160:76.**
Switch connections.
Construction and
maintenance, **160:117.**
Private sidings, connections,
159:21.
Switch stands, exemptions from
requirements, **160:133A.**
Taking of land, provisions
relative, **160:76.**
Terminal facilities, application
for authority to own and
operate, **160:131A.**
Through routes, establishment,
159:21.
Tools, orders that trains and
cars be equipped, **160:163.**
Track inspection division,
establishment and duties,
25:7.
Tracks, roadbeds, and tunnels,
examination, **159:83.**
Train crews, changes in number
of men forming, **160:185.**
Transfer of franchise and
property subject to approval,
159:54.
Variation of direction, consent,
160:86.
Vote creating preferred stock
filed, **160:44.**
Whistles, regulation, **160:139.**
Workingmen's trains, order,
160:198.
Telegraphs and telephones.
Days of rest for employees,
160:184.
Liability in transmitting,
receiving, delivering
messages, railroads
excepted, **166:19.**
Station to be notified of
discovery of fire, **160:237.**
Taking stock, **160:65.**
Tender.
Drawbridges. See within this
heading, "Drawbridges."
Unlawful riding, **160:220.**
Terminal companies.
Boston terminal corporation.
See BOSTON TERMINAL
CORPORATION.
Taking stock and securities,
160:70.
Terminal facilities.
Stations. See within this
heading, "Stations and
depots."

RAILROADS —Cont'd
Termini to be stated in agreement
of association, **160:14.**
Foreign countries, corporations
to operate, **160:248.**
Testing equipment, **160:168.**
Brakes, **160:155.**
Theft.
Larceny. See within this
heading, "Larceny and
theft."
Through routes, establishment,
159:21.
Throwing at train, bus, etc.
Cars. See within this heading,
"Cars and rolling stock."
Tickets.
Bicycles, transportation of for
holder of ticket, **160:196.**
Commutation tickets, **159:18,
160:190.**
Forgery or counterfeiting, **267:2,
267:4-267:6.**
Mail carriers, free tickets or
special rates, **159:15,
161:107.**
Mileage books and tickets. See
within this heading,
"Mileage books and tickets."
Sale regulated, **160:198A,
160:198B.**
Scalping prohibited, **160:198B.**
Season tickets, **160:191-160:193,
160:197, 160:198.**
Deposit, **160:191.**
Express messengers, **160:193.**
Morning and evening trains,
160:197.
Reimbursement of holder for
fare paid, **160:192.**
Workingmen's trains, **160:198.**
Sold outside of ticket offices,
160:188.
Street railways.
Free tickets, **161:107.**
School pupils, **161:108.**
Stolen or counterfeited
employee transportation
pass, **161:113A.**
Types which may be issued,
159:18.
Uttering forged railroad tickets,
267:6.
Tidewaters, crossings over, **160:96.**
Time.
Branches and extensions, time
within which construction
must be commenced and
completed, **160:115.**
Certificate of incorporation.
Certificates. See within this
heading, "Certificates and
certification."

RAILROADS —Cont'd
Time —Cont'd
Construction time limited,
160:27.
Drawbridges, time allowed
trains for crossing, **160:122.**
Electric railroads.
See ELECTRIC RAILROADS.
Street railways.
See STREET RAILWAYS.
Tobacco.
Cars, smoking in. See within
this heading, "Cars and
rolling stock."
Smoking in public places,
regulation, **270:21.**
Toilet facilities for employees,
**149:133-149:138, 149:180,
160:172A.**
Tools.
Cars. See within this heading,
"Cars and rolling stock."
Offenses and penalties. See
within this heading,
"Offenses and penalties."
Tampering, **160:228.**
Trains and cars to be equipped,
160:163.
Tops on track motor cars,
160:163A.
Torpedoes, marking, **159:102.**
Towermen, days of rest, **160:184.**
Towns.
Cities and towns. See within
this heading, "Cities and
towns."
Track motor cars.
Canopies or tops, **160:163A.**
Lights, **160:176A.**
Street railways, acquisition and
use of motor cars, **161:44.**
Windshields, **160:163A.**
Tracks.
Animals injured, **160:222,
160:223.**
Clearance in yards, **160:134A.**
Division of track inspection,
25:7.
Examination, **159:83.**
Switches and switch
connections. See within this
heading, "Switches and
switch connections."
Tampering, **159:103.**
Tramps, persons riding freight
trains without permission,
272:63.
Transfers of property.
Sales. See within this heading,
"Sales."

RAILROADS —Cont'd

Transportation and construction executive office.

Executive office of transportation and construction. See within this heading, "Executive office of transportation and construction."

Treasurer.

Annual return sworn, **160:242.**

Appointment by directors prior to organization, **160:15.**

Assessments on stock paid, **160:39.**

Bond required, **160:32.**

Certificate annexed to agreement of association, **160:23.**

Certificate of vote for change of name signed and sworn, **160:216.**

Debt or liability, incurring for unauthorized purpose, **160:48.**

Election, **160:32.**

Notice of assessments upon shares, **160:39.**

Required, **160:31.**

Sale of stock for failure to pay assessments, **160:39.**

Stock certificate signed, **160:38.**

Street railways.

See STREET RAILWAYS.

Unlawful issue of stocks or bonds or use of proceeds therefrom, penalty, **160:48.**

Treble damages.

Endangering safety of persons upon trains, **160:226.**

Malicious injury, **160:225.**

Obstructing engine or car, **160:226.**

Trees.

Forests and woodlands. See within this heading, "Forests and woodlands."

Trespass.

Clearing land adjoining tracks, **160:236.**

Death of trespassers on railroad property, liability, **229:2.**

Penalty, **90:15, 159:93, 160:218, 160:220.**

Trial or hearing.

Abandonment of passenger service, public hearing as prerequisite, **160:128, 160:128A.**

Compensation for joint occupation of station, railroad, or grounds, **160:131.**

RAILROADS —Cont'd

Trial or hearing —Cont'd

Connecting carriers, questions arising between, **160:60.**

Consolidation, **160:72.**

Crossings.

See RAILROAD CROSSINGS.

Election of trustees, confirmation, **160:53.**

Electric railroads.

See ELECTRIC RAILROADS.

Exemptions from certain requirements as to cars and equipment, **160:162.**

Extension of lines, **159:16.**

Fixing route, **160:21.**

Freight cars and trains, changes in manner of making up and shifting, **160:139.**

Local express business, recommendation for person to engage, **160:206.**

Location, **160:80, 160:85.**

Mail transportation, fixing price, **160:202, 160:203.**

Maintenance and repair of bridges, **159:84.**

Maps and engineer's reports submitted by directors, **160:19.**

Milk transportation, fixing rates, **160:213.**

Motor carriers of property, notice to railroads of hearing upon certificate of public convenience and necessity, **159B:3.**

Motor vehicles, operation by railroads, **160:70A.**

Name of corporation, change, **160:215.**

Owner cut off from access to land, **160:110.**

Special charter, petition, **160:9.**

Stations, abandoning or diminishing accommodations, **160:128, 160:128A.**

Street railways.

See STREET RAILWAYS.

Switch connections, petition for establishment, **160:117.**

Terminal facilities, authority to operate, **160:131A.**

Through routes, establishment, **159:21.**

Train crew, changes in number of men forming, **160:185.**

Transfer, lease, purchase, or sale of franchise and property, **159:54.**

RAILROADS —Cont'd

Trial or hearing —Cont'd

Whistles, changes in manner of sounding, **160:139.**

Trustees for benefit of creditors, **160:51-160:54.**

Accounting by corporation operating, **160:51.**

Contract with corporation to operate, **160:51.**

Election, **160:53.**

Meetings.

Annual meeting of bondholders and creditors, **160:52, 160:53.**

Contract, meeting to grant consent, **160:51.**

Removal, **160:54.**

Trusts and trustees.

Benefit of creditors, trustees for.

Trustees for benefit of creditors. See within this heading, "Trustees for benefit of creditors."

Equipment trust covering rolling stock, applicability of secured transactions article, **106:9-104.**

Other corporations, trustees operating railroads, **160:5.**

Street railways.

See STREET RAILWAYS.

Tunnels, examination, **159:83.**

Undertakings.

Bonds and undertakings. See within this heading, "Bonds and undertakings."

Unemployment Insurance Act.

Federal agencies and programs. See EMPLOYMENT SECURITY.

Uniform caps or hats for employees, **160:177.**

Uniform Securities Act, exemptions, **110A:402.**

Uttering forged railroad badges and tickets, **267:6.**

Vacuum brakes, mufflers, **160:169, 160:171.**

Ventilation of freight depots, **149:113.**

Voters and voting.

Complaints by voters, **159:24.**

Corporation's voting rights upon its own stock, **160:35.**

Officers and agents, election of.

Employees, officers and agents. See within this heading, "Employees, officers, and agents."

Preferred stock, voting rights, **160:45.**

RAILROADS —Cont'd
Voters and voting —Cont'd
Proxy voting, **160:36, 160:251.**
Stockholders' voting rights,
160:36.
Street railways.
See STREET RAILWAYS.
Town vote authorizing
agreement as to alterations
of crossings, **159:80.**
Trustees for benefit of creditors,
election, **160:53.**
Wages and compensation.
Connecting railroad, driving
cars, **160:59, 160:60.**
Fees. See within this heading,
"Fees."
Joint operation, **160:131.**
Overtime pay, **151:1A.**
Police of railroad, **159:95.**
Statements for employees,
149:148.
Streets railways.
Overtime for employees,
151:1A.
Police, **159:95.**
Transportation area trustees,
161:146.
Weekly payment, **149:148.**
Workers' compensation, **152:25A.**
Waiver.
Appeal from decision of county
commissioners in certain
matters as to crossings,
160:112.
Director's meetings, notice,
160:37.
Stockholders' meetings, notice,
160:29, 160:33.
Street railways.
Directors' meetings, waiver of
notice, **161:18.**
First meeting of incorporators,
waiver of notice, **161:10.**
Stockholders' meetings, waiver
of notice, **161:14.**
Walking on tracks, penalty,
160:218.
Walls.
County commissioners may
order construction, **160:91,
160:92.**
Double damages for failure to
construct, **160:91, 160:92.**
Warehouses.
Holding stock in warehouse
companies, **160:65B.**
Licensed as public
warehouseman need not
receive property, **105:1.**
Warrant, arrests without, **159:93,
159:94, 159:104, 160:220.**

RAILROADS —Cont'd
Water and cups for drinking to be
supplied to passengers,
160:174, 160:175.
Water for drinking, locomotives
and cabooses, **160:172A.**
Waters and watercourses.
Canals. See within this heading,
"Canals."
Crossings, **159:75, 160:96.**
Electric railroad, showing
navigable waters in map,
plan, or certificate, **162:7.**
Harbors. See within this
heading, "Harbors."
Obstruction of littoral owner's
access to sea, **160:96.**
Pollution, **21:27.**
Relocating or changing on
abolition of grade crossing,
159:75.
Tidewaters, crossings over,
160:96.
Water supply system of towns as
affecting, **40:39C.**
Wharves, piers, and docks.
Docks. See within this heading,
"Docks."
Whistles.
Crossings, sounding, **160:138,
160:139.**
Electric railroads, **162:16.**
Windshields on track motor cars,
160:163A.
Wires over crossings, removal or
relocation, **159:74, 160:104A.**
Witnesses.
Accident causing death,
inspector may summon to
inquest, **159:29.**
Fees for police attending,
262:55.
Women not to be required to ride
in smoking cars, **160:173.**
Woodlands.
Forests and woodlands. See
within this heading,
"Forests and woodlands."
Workers' compensation law,
applicability, **152:25A.**
Workingmen's trains, **160:198.**
Wreckage caused by derailments,
removal, **160:241A.**
Wrongful death.
Death. See within this heading,
"Death."
Yards.
Acquisition of land, **160:78,
160:83.**
Clearance of tracks, **160:134A.**
Street railway freight yards,
161:54.

RAILROADS —Cont'd
Yards —Cont'd
Switch stands, **160:133A.**
Youth conservation and service
corps, **78A:3.**

RAILWAY LABOR ACT.
Industrial disputes dangerous to
public health and safety,
federal provisions for
peaceable settlement, **150B:7.**
Labor contracts, effect on successor
employers, **149:179C.**
State labor relations law as
inapplicable to employees
subject to federal act,
150A:10.

RAIN.
See WEATHER.

RAINBOW TROUT, 131:51.

RANDOLPH.
Congressional district, **57:1.**
District court, **218:1.**
Medical examiner district, **38:1.**
Senatorial district, **57:3.**

RANGE BOILERS.
Junk, sale, **142:20.**

RANGE LIGHTS.
Conveyance of land to United
States, **1:6, 1:7.**

RANGES.
Militia.
Armories, air installations, and
drill grounds.
See MILITIA.

RAPE, 265:22 et seq.
Abuse of child under 16, **265:22A,
265:23.**
Address confidentiality of domestic
violence victims, **9A:1 to 9A:7.**
See ADDRESS
CONFIDENTIALITY OF
DOMESTIC VIOLENCE
VICTIMS.
Adoption of child, effect, **210:6.**
Aggravated rape, **277:39.**
Assault with intent to commit
rape.
Child, **265:24B.**
Graduated penalties, **265:24.**
Sex-neutral terms, definition,
265:24, 277:79.
Child, rape, **265:22A, 265:23.**
Adoption, effect, **210:6.**
Assault with intent to commit,
265:24B.
Investigation and notification of
district attorney, **119:51B.**

RAPE —Cont'd
Child, rape —Cont'd
Release of sex offenders and
youth offenders committing
crimes against children,
120:12.
Statute of limitations, **277:63.**
Confidentiality.
See PRIVILEGED AND
CONFIDENTIAL
MATTERS.
Correctional facilities.
Sexual relations between
prisoner and officer,
268:21A.
Criminal offense, **265:22 et seq.**
Crisis center, defined, **233:20J.**
Defined, **265:24, 277:39, 277:79.**
Drug-induced, **272:3.**
Evidence.
Preservation of evidence,
41:97B.
Reputation of victim, **233:21B.**
Victim's sexual reputation,
233:21B.
Fines and penalties.
Sentence and punishment. See
within this heading,
"Sentence and punishment."
Graduated penalties, **265:22.**
Indictment, meaning of term,
277:39.
Interviews by special police units
with rape victims, **41:97B.**
Mandatory imprisonment,
265:22A.
Medical treatment.
Mental health coverage
required.
Accident and sickness
insurance, **175:47B.**
Group insurance for state
employees, **32A:22.**
Health maintenance
organizations, **176G:4M.**
Hospital service corporations,
176A:8A.
Medical service corporations,
176B:4A.
Murder connected with, jury's
recommendation against death
penalty, **265:2.**
Name of victim withheld from
public inspection, **265:24C.**
Parole of persons convicted,
127:133.
Penalty.
Sentence and punishment. See
within this heading,
"Sentence and punishment."
Physicians attending victims,
reporting requirements,
112:12A½.

RAPE —Cont'd
Police special units and services,
6:156, 41:97B, 41:97C.
Preservation of evidence, **41:97B.**
Prevention and prosecution.
Duties of criminal justice
committee regarding, **6:156.**
Special police units and services,
6:156, 41:97B, 41:97C.
Prisons.
Sexual relations between
prisoner and officer,
268:21A.
Probation and parole.
Community parole supervision
for life, **265:45, 275:18.**
Punishment for.
Sentence and punishment. See
within this heading,
"Sentence and punishment."
Records, reports, and returns,
112:12A½, 265:24C.
Physicians attending victims,
reporting requirements,
112:12A½.
Reporting and prosecution unit,
establishment, membership,
functions, **41:97B.**
Release of sex offenders and youth
offenders committing crimes
against children, **120:12.**
Reports.
Records, reports, and returns.
See within this heading,
"Records, reports, and
returns."
Reputation of victim, admissibility
of sexual, **233:21B.**
School bus operators' licenses as
affected by conviction, **90:8A.**
Second offense, **265:22, 265:23.**
Sentence and punishment, **265:22
et seq.**
Child or minor, rape, **265:22A,
265:23.**
Parole and discharge, **127:133.**
Second and subsequent offense,
265:22, 265:23.
Sexual assault counselor.
See SEXUAL ASSAULT
COUNSELOR.
Sexually dangerous persons,
123A:1 et seq.
Statutory rape.
Sexual relations between
prisoner and officer,
268:21A.
Statutory rape, punishment for
second offense, **265:23.**
Time or date, preservation of
evidence of rape, **41:97B.**

RAPE —Cont'd
Venue, **265:24A.**
Victims.
Communications with
counselors, privilege,
233:20J.
Counseling, **41:97B, 233:20J.**
Physicians attending victims,
reporting requirements,
112:12A½.
Police interviews, **41:97B.**
Sexual reputation, admissibility,
233:21B.

RAPE CRISIS CENTER.
Definition, **233:20J.**

**RAPID ECONOMIC
RESPONSE TEAM.**
Economic development
department, **23A:2.**

RAPTORS.
Defined, fish and game division,
131:1.

RASPBERRIES.
Containers in which sold, **94:98.**

RATE BASIS TYPE.
Words and phrases, **176J:1.**

RATE REGULATION ACT.
Casualty and surety insurance,
175A:1 et seq.

RATE REGULATORY ACT.
Fire, marine, and inland marine
insurance, **174A:1 et seq.**

RATES AND CHARGES.
Accident insurance.
Premiums.
See ACCIDENT AND
SICKNESS INSURANCE.
Accountants.
Motor vehicle insurance rating
bureau, employment, **26:8E.**
Aid to families with dependent
children, payment of overdue
utility bills for families
receiving, **118:2.**
Aircraft.
See AIRCRAFT AND AVIATION.
Airports, charges, **90:51H.**
Aldermen.
See ALDERMEN AND
SELECTMEN.
Alteration.
Changes in rates. See within
this heading, "Changes in
rates."
Ambulance service, authority of
municipalities to charge, **40:5.**
Annual percentage rates.
Finance charges.
See TRUTH IN LENDING.

RATES AND CHARGES
—Cont'd
Arrest of passenger for failure to pay fare, **159:93, 159:94.**
Attorney general.
Gas and electric rates to be filed, **164:94.**
Intervention in legal proceedings concerning utility rates and tariffs, **12:11E.**
Auto club service fees as excluded from insurance premiums, **175:113Q.**
Automobile insurance.
See AUTOMOBILE INSURANCE.
Aviation.
See AIRCRAFT AND AVIATION.
Baggage, **160:96, 160:195.**
Banks.
See BANKS AND BANKING.
Bathhouses, public, **40:12.**
Bicycles, transportation as baggage, **160:96.**
Bills or invoices, statement of service charges on, **149:152A.**
Blind person, free or reduced rate carriage, **159:15.**
Boats.
Ships and shipping. See within this heading, "Ships and shipping."
Boston harbor, pilotage rates, **103:31.**
Boston, rate differential against as prohibited, **160:210.**
Business trust, public service company owned or controlled, **182:11.**
Canals, tolls, **88:9, 88:11.**
Carriers.
Railroads and carriers. See within this heading, "Railroads and carriers."
Changes in rates.
Gas and electric rates, changes in schedule, **164:94.**
Insurance rates.
See INSURANCE RATES AND RATING ORGANIZATIONS.
Railroads and carriers. See within this heading, "Railroads and carriers."
Telegraph or telephone rates, **159:24.**
Children, free or reduced rate passage on railroads, **159:18.**
Cities and towns.
Local tax collectors, waiver of charges, **60:15.**

RATES AND CHARGES
—Cont'd
Cities and towns —Cont'd
Lockups, charges for detention and support of persons committed, **40:36.**
Mayor. See within this heading, "Mayor."
Necessities supplied by towns in time of distress, **40:20.**
Reduced rates for telephone and telegraph service, **159:15.**
Selectmen.
See ALDERMEN AND SELECTMEN.
User charges by cities and towns for amounts required by water pollution abatement districts, **21:36.**
Civil rights and discrimination.
Discriminatory rates. See within this heading, "Discriminatory rates."
Classes and classification.
Insurance rates.
See INSURANCE RATES AND RATING ORGANIZATIONS.
Railroads and carriers. See within this heading, "Railroads and carriers."
Commissioner of asset management and maintenance, establishment of rules and regulations for acquisition, utilization, and disposition of real property, **7:40L.**
Commonwealth, reduced rates by telephone and telegraph companies, **159:15.**
Community antenna television systems, regulation, **166A:15.**
Complaints.
Discriminatory rates of carriers, **159:14, 159:14A.**
Telephone and telegraph companies, public hearing on complaint, **159:24.**
Condominiums, **183A:14.**
Gas and electric rates, **164:94H.**
Mortgages, late charges, **183:59.**
Consumer reporting agencies, charges to consumer for certain disclosures and reports, **93:59.**
Contracts.
See CONTRACTS AND AGREEMENTS.
Convalescent, nursing or rest homes, charges for publicly aided patients, **111:82.**

RATES AND CHARGES
—Cont'd
Conversion of oil to coal by electric generating facilities, **164:94G½.**
Cooperative banks.
See COOPERATIVE BANKS.
Corporation taxes.
See CORPORATION TAXES.
Credit insurance.
Applicability of law, **175A:4.**
Limitation on premiums, **255:12G.**
Provisions as to charges, **175:134, 255D:26.**
Credit unions.
Service charges.
See CREDIT UNIONS.
Dental service corporations, subscribers' rates, **176E:4.**
Directory assistance, prohibition of charge, **159:19.**
Discounts.
See DISCOUNTS AND REBATES.
Discriminatory rates.
Air carriers, **159:14A.**
Complaint to department, **159:14, 159:14A.**
Examination or investigation, **159:14.**
Freight rates, **160:211.**
Insurance rates, **151B:4, 174:3-174:18, 175:120, 175:122, 176D:4.**
See INSURANCE RATES AND RATING ORGANIZATIONS.
Medical service corporations, **176B:4.**
Milk, carriage, **160:212-160:214.**
Motor carriers of property, **159B:6A, 159B:7, 159B:19.**
Reparation to person paying, **159:14.**
District reserve fund, establishment, **40:5C.**
Dogs.
See DOGS.
Dormant bank accounts, prohibition of service charges, **200A:15C.**
Dump trucks.
Contractor's bond required to secure transportation charges on public works projects, **30:39A-30:39E.**
Violation of requirements as to payment of charges, **159B:19A.**
Ejection for nonpayment of fare, **159:101.**

RATES AND CHARGES
—Cont'd
Electricity.
See GAS AND ELECTRIC COMPANIES.
Elevated railways, tickets for school pupils, **161:108.**
Employment agencies.
See EMPLOYMENT AGENCIES AND BUREAUS.
Employment security.
See EMPLOYMENT SECURITY.
Estoppel.
Waiver and estoppel. See within this heading, "Waiver and estoppel."
Evasion of payment of fare.
Railroads and carriers. See within this heading, "Railroads and carriers."
Evidence.
Hospitals, proceedings to collect charges, **111:69I.**
Rates of carriers and filed schedule as evidence of reasonableness of charges, **159:17.**
Schedule rates, burden of proof for increase, **159:20.**
Examination, inspection, or investigation.
Carriers.
Changes in schedule rates, **159:20.**
Discriminatory rates, **159:14.**
Rates, **159:13.**
Air carriers, **159:14A.**
Schedules, inspection, **159:19.**
Air carriers, **159:14A.**
Street railways, investigation of service at cost companies, **161:125.**
Gas and electric rates, **164:94, 164:94F.**
Insurance rates.
See INSURANCE RATES AND RATING ORGANIZATIONS.
Facilities for disposal of privy, cesspool, and septic tank contents, establishment of charges for use, **111:31D.**
Fees.
See FEES.
Ferries, fares or tolls, **88:2.**
FHA loans, reimbursement of charges on anticipatory repayment, **183:56.**
Finance charges.
See FINANCE CHARGES.

RATES AND CHARGES
—Cont'd
Foreign insurance companies.
See FOREIGN INSURANCE COMPANIES.
Fraternal benefit societies.
Premiums or contributions.
See FRATERNAL BENEFIT SOCIETIES.
Fraud and deceit.
Railroads and carriers. See within this heading, "Railroads and carriers."
Free or reduced rate service, **159:15, 159:18.**
Railroads, **160:187-160:200.**
Street railways, **161:107, 161:108, 161:115-161:128.**
Telephone and telegraph service for state, cities, and towns, **159:15.**
Freight.
Railroads and carriers. See within this heading, "Railroads and carriers."
Garbage.
See GARBAGE AND RUBBISH.
Gas.
See GAS AND ELECTRIC COMPANIES.
General court, alteration or revision of carrier's rates, **160:186.**
Gifts.
Free or reduced rate service. See within this heading, "Free or reduced rate service."
Health care finance.
See HEALTH CARE FINANCE AND POLICY.
Health maintenance organization, reasonableness requirement of rates, **176G:17.**
Hearings.
Changes in rates of common carriers, **25:4A, 159:20.**
Insurance rates.
See INSURANCE RATES AND RATING ORGANIZATIONS.
Telephone or telegraph companies, notice as to public hearing on complaint, **159:24.**
Horse, refusal to pay for use of, as criminal offense, **266:64.**
Hospitals.
Charges for treatment and services.
See HOSPITALS AND HEALTH CARE FACILITIES.

RATES AND CHARGES
—Cont'd
Hospital service corporations.
Group hospital service plans, **176A:10.**
Payments to hospitals, **176A:5.**
Subscribers' contracts, **176A:6.**
Income tax.
See INCOME TAX.
Infirmaries, rate for persons able to pay, **47:10.**
Inspection.
Examination, inspection, or investigation. See within this heading, "Examination, inspection, or investigation."
Insurance, **174A:1 et seq., 175A:1 et seq.**
See INSURANCE RATES AND RATING ORGANIZATIONS.
Interest on money.
See INTEREST ON MONEY.
Interstate commerce act, applicability of free or reduced rate service provisions, **94:65L, 159:15.**
Interstate commerce commission schedules of carriers subject, **159:19.**
Investigations and inquiries.
Examination, inspection, or investigation. See within this heading, "Examination, inspection, or investigation."
Invoices, statement of service charges, **149:152A.**
Judgments and decrees.
Orders.
Fire insurance.
See INSURANCE RATES AND RATING ORGANIZATIONS.
Public utilities.
See TELECOMMUNICATIONS AND ENERGY DEPARTMENT.
Late charges.
See LATE CHARGES.
Lease, rates of carriers not to be increased by reason, **160:73.**
Levy of execution, fees and charges added to debt, **236:45.**
Life insurance.
Premiums.
See LIFE INSURANCE.
Lists.
Schedules and tariffs. See within this heading, "Schedules and tariffs."

RATES AND CHARGES
—Cont'd

Massachusetts water management
act, rate determination as
considering fee schedule,
21G:19.

Mayor.
Street railway fares, notice of
changes, **161:112.**
Telecommunications and energy
department hearings as to
change in rates or reduction
of service, notice, **25:4A.**
Telegraph or telephone
companies, public hearing
on complaint, **159:24.**

Medex.
See MEDEX.

Medical assistance division,
**118E:13, 118E:13A, 118E:14,
118E:42.**

Medical service corporations,
176B:4.

Mental health, charges for care
of patients, **123:22.**

Metropolitan districts.
See METROPOLITAN
DISTRICTS.

Mileage rates for carriers
furnishing special service
or school service,
159A:11A.

Mileage tickets, **159:18, 160:189.**

Milk, transportation,
160:212-160:214.

Minimum charge or cover charge,
prohibition as to requiring
payments by persons under
13 years of age,
140:183D.

Morris plan banks, charges on
loans, **172A:9.**

Motor carriers.
Railroads and carriers. See
within this heading,
"Railroads and carriers."

Motor vehicle retail installment
sales.
See MOTOR VEHICLE RETAIL
INSTALMENT SALES.

Motor vehicles.
See MOTOR VEHICLES.

Municipal historical commissions,
powers and duties,
40:8D.

Municipalities.
Cities and towns. See within
this heading, "Cities and
towns."

RATES AND CHARGES
—Cont'd

Municipal lighting.
See MUNICIPAL LIGHTING
AND HEATING PLANTS.

Necessities supplied by towns in
time of distress, **40:20.**

Nonprofit hospital service
corporation, approval of
contracts or rates, **176A:6.**

Nursing.
See NURSING OR REST
HOMES.

Optometric service corporations,
subscribers' rates, **176F:4.**

Orders.
Fire insurance.
See INSURANCE RATES
AND RATING
ORGANIZATIONS.
Public utilities.
See
TELECOMMUNICATIONS
AND ENERGY
DEPARTMENT.

Other governmental entities,
assessment of costs on
municipalities, **59:20A.**

Overhead wires.
See GAS AND ELECTRIC
COMPANIES.

Passes.
Free or reduced rate service. See
within this heading, "Free
or reduced rate service."

Patients' rights, **111:70E.**

Pilots of vessels.
Boston harbor pilot districts
rates, **103:31.**
District one, rates paid to
commission by pilots,
103:5.

Police, free or reduced rate service,
159:15, 161:107.

Property taxes.
See TAXATION.

Publication of tariffs by air
carriers, **159:14A.**

Public contracts as to
transportation charges,
30:39A-30:39E, 149:29.

Public emergency, free or reduced
rate service by carriers,
159:15.

Public utilities.
See TELECOMMUNICATIONS
AND ENERGY
DEPARTMENT.

RATES AND CHARGES
—Cont'd

Public works and departments,
30:39A-30:39E.

Dump truck operations, bond for
transportation charges,
30:39A-30:39E.

Security for payments, **149:29.**

Railroads and carriers, **159B:6,
159B:6A, 159B:7,
160:208-160:211.**

Agricultural carrier by motor
vehicle, filing of schedule,
159B:15A.

Air carriers.
Aircraft and aviation.
See AIRCRAFT AND
AVIATION.

Arrest of passenger for failure to
pay fare, **159:93, 159:94.**

Baggage, storage on weekends,
160:195.

Bicycles, transportation as
baggage, **160:196.**

Blind persons, free or reduced
rate service, **159:15.**

Boston, freight differential
against prohibited, **160:210.**

Brokers' tariffs, filing, **159B:5.**

Burden of proof on carrier
seeking increase in schedule
rates, **159:20.**

Business trust owning or
controlling, **182:11.**

Certificate of conductor for extra
fare for ticket bought on
train, **160:188.**

Changes in rates, **159:19,
159:20.**

Discriminatory rates, **159:14,
159:14A.**

General court, alteration or
revision, **160:186.**

Recommendations by
department, **159:23.**

Regional transportation
authorities fares, **161B:8.**

Selectmen to be notified as to
time and place of hearing,
25:4A.

Street railways.
See STREET RAILWAYS.

Charities, free or reduced rate
service, **159:15.**

Children, reduced rates, **159:18,
161:107, 161:108.**

Classes of rates.
Interstate commerce act, free
or reduced rate carriage of
classes provided, **94:65L,
159:15.**

Power of carriers to make,
159:18.

RATES AND CHARGES
—Cont'd
Railroads and carriers —Cont'd
Classes of rates —Cont'd
Schedule to show, **159:19.**
Common carriers, **159B:6,
159B:6A.**
Commutation tickets, **159:18,
160:190.**
Conductor's certificate for extra
fare for ticket bought upon
train, **160:188.**
Connecting carriers,
compensation for drawing
cars of other carriers,
160:59, 160:60.
Consolidation, rates not to be
increased, **160:73.**
Contract carriers, **159B:7.**
Determination of just and
reasonable rates by
telecommunications and
energy department, **159:14.**
Differential against Boston
forbidden, **160:210.**
Different rate from filed
schedule not to be charged,
159:19.
Directors may establish fares,
160:186.
Discounts and rebates, **159B:6A,
159B:7, 159B:19.**
Discriminatory rates. See within
this heading,
"Discriminatory rates."
Division of rates on through
routes, **159:21.**
Dump trucks. See within this
heading, "Dump trucks."
Ejection of passenger for
nonpayment of fare,
159:101.
Employees, free or reduced rate
service, **159:15.**
Establishment of fares, **160:186.**
Evening and morning trains,
season tickets, **160:197.**
Evidence, schedules or tariffs as
evidence of reasonableness,
159:17.
Examination, inspection, or
investigation. See within
this heading, "Examination,
inspection, or investigation."
Excursion tickets, **159:18.**
Extra fares for tickets sold
elsewhere than at ticket
offices, **160:188.**
Failure by irregular route
carrier to file rates, **159B:3.**

RATES AND CHARGES
—Cont'd
Railroads and carriers —Cont'd
Filing and recording of rates.
Schedules and tariffs. See
within this heading,
"Schedules and tariffs."
Fines and penalties.
Boston Terminal Corporation,
arrest of passenger for
failure to pay fare, **159:93,
159:94.**
Nonpayment of fares, **159:101.**
Firemen, free or reduced rate
service, **159:15, 161:107.**
Fixing of rates subject to
approval of department,
159:18.
Fraudulent evasion of payment
of fare, **159:101, 159A:16.**
Arrest, **159:93, 159:94.**
Fraudulently obtaining
transportation for less than
scheduled rate, **159B:19.**
Free or reduced rate service. See
within this heading, "Free
or reduced rate service."
Freight, **160:208-160:211.**
General court, alteration or
revision of charges and
fares, **160:186.**
Hearings upon changes in rates,
25:4A, 159:20.
Investigation, **159:13.**
Joint interchangeable mileage
tickets, **159:18.**
Joint rates, **159:21.**
Lease, rates not to be increased,
160:73.
Lien of carrier for transportation
charges, **106:7-307.**
Mailmen, free or reduced rate
service, **159:15, 161:107.**
Mail, transportation, **160:202,
160:203.**
Mileage rates for carriers
furnishing special service or
school service, **159A:11A.**
Mileage tickets, **159:18, 160:189.**
Milk, transportation,
160:212-160:214.
Minimum rate may be
prescribed by department,
159:20.
Minors, reduced rates, **159:18,
161:107, 161:108.**
Morning and evening trains,
season tickets, **160:197.**
Payment of transportation
charges to, requirements,
159B:19A.

RATES AND CHARGES
—Cont'd
Railroads and carriers —Cont'd
Policemen, free or reduced rate
service, **159:15, 161:107.**
Public emergency, free or
reduced rate service, **159:15.**
Public works, definition of
transportation charges,
30:39B.
Regional transit authorities,
changes in rates and fares,
161B:8.
Regulation, **159:14, 159:17.**
Reimbursement of fares paid,
160:192.
Reparation to person paying
discriminatory rate, **159:14.**
Revocation or suspension. See
within this heading,
"Revocation or suspension."
Sale, rates not to be increased,
160:73.
Schedules and tariffs. See within
this heading, "Schedules
and tariffs."
School buses. See within this
heading, "School buses and
transportation of pupils."
Ships and shipping. See within
this heading, "Ships and
shipping."
Street railways.
See STREET RAILWAYS.
Telecommunications and energy
department personnel, free
transportation, **159:15.**
Through routes, division of
rates, **159:21.**
Tickets. See within this heading,
"Tickets."
Workingmen's tickets, **159:18,
160:198, 161:107.**
Rebates.
See DISCOUNTS AND
REBATES.
Reduced rates.
Free or reduced rate service. See
within this heading, "Free
or reduced rate service."
Regional transportation authority's
fares, changes, **161B:8.**
Reimbursement for rail fares paid,
160:192.
Retail installment sales.
See RETAIL INSTALLMENT
SALES AND SERVICES.
Revocation or suspension.
Charges in schedule rates of
carriers, order suspending
taking effect, **159:20.**

RATES AND CHARGES
—Cont'd

Revocation or suspension —Cont'd
Tariffs of air carriers, **159:14A.**
Sale of carrier, rates not to be
increased by reason, **160:73.**
Schedules and tariffs.
Accident and sickness insurance,
table of rates to be filed
with commissioner of
insurance, **175:108.**
Air carriers, **159:14A.**
Carriers, **159B:6, 159B:6A.**
Agricultural carriers,
159B:15A.
Brokers, **159B:5.**
Classes of rates, schedules to
show, **159:19.**
Contract carriers, **159B:7.**
Different rate from filed
schedule not to be
charged, **159:19.**
Evidence, filed schedules of
carriers as evidence of
reasonableness, **159:17.**
Fraudulently obtaining
transportation for less
than scheduled rate,
159B:19.
Irregular route carrier's
failure to file, **159B:3.**
Changes in rates. See within
this heading, "Changes in
rates."
Gas.
See GAS AND ELECTRIC
COMPANIES.
Inspection.
Examination, inspection, or
investigation. See within
this heading,
"Examination, inspection,
or investigation."
Milk, department to fix tariff,
160:213.
Presumption of lawfulness of
rates filed, **159:17.**
Public utilities.
See
TELECOMMUNICATIONS
AND ENERGY
DEPARTMENT.
Street railways.
See STREET RAILWAYS.
Water companies, **164:94, 165:2.**
Water districts, **165:2A.**
School buses and transportation of
pupils.
Elevated railways, tickets for
pupils, **161:108.**
Mileage rates for carriers
furnishing special service or
school service, **159A:11A.**

RATES AND CHARGES
—Cont'd

School buses and transportation of
pupils —Cont'd
Special rates by carriers, **159:18,
161:107, 161:108.**
Selectmen.
See ALDERMEN AND
SELECTMEN.
Senior citizens' nonpayment of
utility bills, regulation of
shutting off gas and electric
service, **164:124E.**
Service charges.
Books or accounts, service
charges on, **175:177,
175:184, 200A:15C.**
Credit unions.
See CREDIT UNIONS.
Disclosure of information to
public regarding financial
institutions, accounts, and
services, **167D:34.**
Employees, payment, **149:152A.**
Sewers.
See SEWERS AND DRAINS.
Ships and shipping.
Arrest of steamboat passenger
for failure to pay fare,
159:93, 159:94.
Pilots of vessels. See within this
heading, "Pilots of vessels."
Street railways.
See STREET RAILWAYS.
Sunday, payment and collection of
tolls, **136:6.**
Supreme judicial court, transfer of
cases to and, **211:4A.**
Surcharges.
See SURCHARGES.
Suspension.
Revocation or suspension. See
within this heading,
"Revocation or suspension."
Tariffs.
Schedules and tariffs. See within
this heading, "Schedules
and tariffs."
Taxation.
See TAXATION.
Telephone.
See TELEPHONE AND
TELEGRAPH COMPANIES.
Through routes of carriers,
division of rates, **159:21.**
Tickets.
Commutation tickets, **159:18,
160:190.**
Excursion tickets, **159:18.**
Extra fares for tickets sold
elsewhere than at ticket
offices, **160:188.**

RATES AND CHARGES
—Cont'd

Tickets —Cont'd
Free or reduced rate
transportation, passes,
159:15.
Mileage tickets, **159:18, 160:189.**
Scalping of tickets, **140:185D,
160:198B.**
School children, tickets, **159:18,
161:107, 161:108.**
Season tickets, **159:18,
160:191-160:193, 160:197,
160:198.**
Street or elevated railways, free
or reduced rate tickets,
161:107, 161:108.
Types which may be issued by
carriers, **159:18.**
Workingmen's tickets, **159:18,
160:198, 161:107.**
Tolls.
See TOLLS.
Towing charges, **40:22D, 159B:6B,
266:120D.**
Towns.
Cities and towns. See within
this heading, "Cities and
towns."
Transportation.
Railroads and carriers. See
within this heading,
"Railroads and carriers."
Trial.
Hearings. See within this
heading, "Hearings."
Tuberculosis and tuberculin.
Fixing of charges, **111:78,
111:78A, 111:79, 111:82,
111:88, 111:91C.**
Isolation hospitals, **111:116.**
Payment, **111:78, 111:79, 111:80,
111:94E, 111:121.**
Unjust charges by carriers
unlawful, **159:17.**
Use tax.
See USE, CONSUMPTION, OR
STORAGE TAX.
Utility rates.
See TELECOMMUNICATIONS
AND ENERGY
DEPARTMENT.
Veterans attending school under
GI bill of rights, special
streetcar rates, **161:107.**
Waiver and estoppel.
Insurance rating organizations,
waiver of hearing on
application for deviation,
174A:9, 175A:9.
Local tax collector, waiver of
charges, **60:15.**

RATES AND CHARGES
—Cont'd
Water pollution abatement
districts, user charges by cities
and towns for amounts
required, **21:36.**
Waterworks.
See WATERWORKS AND
WATER SUPPLY.
Wharves and piers, charges for
use, **91:2A, 91:6, 91:7.**
Workers' compensation.
See WORKERS'
COMPENSATION.
Workingmen's tickets may be
issued by carriers, **159:18,
160:198, 161:107.**

RATIFICATION.
Agricultural and horticultural
co-operative corporations,
ratification of choice of
directors, **157:12.**
Constitution of the United States.
Amendments to Constitution,
US Const Art 5.
Effectiveness of Federal
Constitution, ratification as
necessary for, **US Const
Art 7.**
Corporation, ratification of acts of
officers and stockholders on
revival, **155:56.**
Executors.
See EXECUTORS AND
ADMINISTRATORS.
General law, effect of repeal on
ratified acts, **281:4.**
Guardians.
See GUARDIANS,
CONSERVATORS, AND
COMMITTEES.
Municipal lighting plants, effect of
election as to acquisition,
164:35.
Trusts.
See TRUSTS AND TRUSTEES.
Wrongful acceptance of goods,
ratification, **106:2-606.**

RATING BUREAU
PERSONNEL.
Assessments, **26:8E.**

RATS AND MICE.
Destruction or control, **128:8A,
131:43.**
Permit for use of poison, **131:43.**
Poison for destruction, **131:43,
270:3A.**
Refuse treatment and disposal
facilities as nuisance,
111:150A.

RATTAN GOODS.
Automatic sprinklers in buildings
for manufacturing, etc.,
148:26.

RAYNHAM.
Congressional district, **57:1.**
District court held, **218:1.**
Medical examiner district, **38:1.**
Senatorial district, **57:3.**

RAZORHEADS.
Children, penalties for sale,
269:16.

RCRA.
Resource Conservation Recovery
Act, Federal, **21C:2 et seq.**

REACH PROGRAM.
Schools, **15:55.**

REACTORS.
Atomic energy.
See ATOMIC ENERGY.

READING.
Constitution of Massachusetts,
reading as qualification for
voters and office holders, **MA
Const Amend Art 20.**
Real estate time-shares, illiteracy,
183B:5.
Schools.
See SCHOOLS AND
EDUCATION.

READING ROOMS.
Agriculture department to
encourage establishment,
128:15.
Annual return of corporations
maintaining, **180:26A.**
Boxing matches, forfeiture of
charter for violations, **180:28.**
Change of location, **180:26.**
Entertainments, local regulation,
180:29.
Gaming laws, forfeiture of charter
for violation, **180:27.**
Incorporation for establishing,
180:1 et seq.
Liquor laws, forfeiture of charter
for violation, **180:27.**
Municipal corporations may
establish, **40:3.**

READING, TOWN OF.
Appellate division of district court,
claim for review to be reduced
to writing, **231:108.**
Congressional district, **57:1.**
District court, **218:1.**
Medical examiner district, **38:1.**
Senatorial district, **57:3.**

READJUSTMENT OF
CONTRACT.
Sales contract, **106:2-201 to
106:2-210.**

REAL ESTATE, 184:1 et seq.
Real property.
See REAL PROPERTY.
Words and phrases, **112:173.**

REAL ESTATE APPRAISERS.
See APPRAISERS AND
APPRAISALS.

REAL ESTATE BROKERS AND
SALESPERSONS, 112:87PP
to 112:87DDD.
Action or suit.
Appeal from decisions of board
of registration, **112:87BBB,
112:87RR.**
Bond of broker, action,
112:87TT.
Unlicensed person, action for
fees or commission,
112:87RR.
Address.
Change of business address,
notice to board of. See
within this heading,
"Change of business
address, notice to board."
Adjustment of license fee in
proportion to term of license,
112:87ZZ.
Appeal from decisions of board of
registration, **112:87BBB,
112:87RR.**
Application for license or renewal,
112:87, 112:87TT.
Associations, licensing, **112:87TT,
112:87UU.**
Attorneys.
Licensing of attorney as broker,
112:87SS.
Registration law not applicable
to attorneys, **112:87QQ,
112:87SS.**
Revocation or refusal of license,
right to attorney at
hearings, **112:87BBB.**
Auctions and auctioneers,
registration law inapplicable,
112:87QQ.
Blind person exempt from
payment of fees, **112:87ZZ.**
Blockbusting, **112:87AAA, 151B:3,
151B:4.**
Board of registration, **13:54 et
seq.**
Appeal from decisions,
112:87BBB, 112:87RR.

REAL ESTATE BROKERS AND SALESPERSONS —Cont'd

Board of registration —Cont'd

Change of business address, notice to board of. See within this heading, "Change of business address, notice to board."

Civil service status of employees of registration board, **13:57.**

Compensation of members, **13:57.**

Defined, **112:87PP.**

Enforcement of law, powers and duties, **112:87BBB.**

Fees for licenses. See within this heading, "Fees for licenses."

General provisions as to medical registration boards, not applicable, **112:87DDD.**

Qualification of members, **13:54.**

Record of licensed brokers and salesmen, **112:87.**

Renewal of license. See within this heading, "Renewal of license."

Revocation or suspension of license. See within this heading, "Revocation or suspension of license."

Rules, regulations and bylaws, **112:87SS.**

General provisions, **13:56, 112:88.**

Salaries and compensation, **13:57.**

Service of process on nonresident, chairman of board as agent, **112:87WW.**

Bond of broker, **112:87TT.**

Bylaws.

Board of registration. See within this heading, "Board of registration."

Change of business address, notice to board.

Brokers, **112:87YY.**

Revocation or suspension of license. See within this heading, "Revocation or suspension of license."

Salesmen, **112:87VV.**

Civil service status of employees of registration board, **13:57.**

Compensation and fees.

Board of real estate brokers and salesmen, **13:57.**

Independent testing service's examination of brokers, fees, **112:87ZZ.**

License as prerequisite to recovery, **112:87RR.**

REAL ESTATE BROKERS AND SALESPERSONS —Cont'd

Compensation and fees —Cont'd

License fees.

Fees for licenses. See within this heading, "Fees for licenses."

Revocation or suspension of license for improper acts, **112:87AAA.**

Salesmen not to accept from third person, **112:87VV.**

Small home mortgages, including brokerage fees in computation of interest, **140:90A.**

Tenants, fee for locating dwelling, **112:87DDD½.**

Trust corpus, chargeable, **203:22.**

Complaints against, **112:87AAA.**

Costs on appeal from decisions of board of registration, **112:87BBB.**

Death of broker, **112:87QQ, 112:87TT, 112:87UU.**

Decisions of board of registration, appeal, **112:87BBB, 112:87RR.**

Definitions, **112:87PP.**

Dentists, laws as to registration of, not applicable, **112:87DDD.**

Discrimination in sale of certain real estate, **112:87AAA, 151B:1 to 151B:6.**

Display of license, **112:87YY.**

Disqualification.

Qualification or disqualification. See within this heading, "Qualification or disqualification."

Domicile or residence.

Change of business address, notice to board. See within this heading, "Change of business address, notice to board."

Nonresidents. See within this heading, "Nonresidents."

Publication containing list, **112:87.**

Requirement for licensing of brokers, **112:87PP, 112:87SS.**

Education courses required for renewal of licenses, **112:87XX½.**

Employment security law, exclusion from coverage, **151A:6.**

REAL ESTATE BROKERS AND SALESPERSONS —Cont'd

Examination, inspection or investigation.

Boards of real estate brokers and salespersons, records, **13:55.**

Independent testing service. See within this heading, "Independent testing service."

Investigations involving brokers and agents, **112:87AAA, 112:87BBB.**

License examination.

Registration and licensing. See within this heading, "Registration and licensing."

Executors.

See EXECUTORS AND ADMINISTRATORS.

Fees for licenses.

Broker's license, **112:87ZZ.**

Corporations, **112:87UU.**

Examination fee, **112:87ZZ.**

Exemptions, **112:87ZZ.**

Monthly adjustment, **112:87ZZ.**

Return when license not issued, **112:87TT.**

Salesperson's license, **112:87ZZ.**

Veterans and blind persons exempted from payment, **112:87ZZ.**

Fees for services.

Compensation and fees. See within this heading, "Compensation and fees."

Fines.

Penalties. See within this heading, "Penalties."

Good moral character of applicant for license, **112:87TT.**

Hearings before board of registration, **112:87BBB.**

Home inspectors.

Notice to buyers as to home inspection process, **112:87YY½.**

Independent testing service.

Examination of applicants, **112:87SS.**

Fee for examination of license applicants, **112:87ZZ.**

Inspection.

Examination, inspection or investigation. See within this heading, "Examination, inspection or investigation."

Notice to consumers about home inspection process, **112:87YY½.**

REAL ESTATE BROKERS AND SALESPERSONS —Cont'd

Interest on small home mortgages, including brokerage fees in computation, **140:90A.**

Investigations.
Examination, inspection or investigation. See within this heading, "Examination, inspection or investigation."

Lead poisoning, notice to prospective purchasers, **111:197A.**

Licenses.
Registration and licensing. See within this heading, "Registration and licensing."

Net listings prohibited, **112:87AAA.**

Nonresidents.
Defined, **112:87PP.**
Licensing, **112:87WW.**
Service of process, **112:87WW.**

Notice.
Change of business address, notice of. See within this heading, "Change of business address, notice."
Suspension of license on notice of violation of antidiscrimination order, **112:87AAA.**

Number of license applicants who may be examined, **112:87SS.**

Other broker, salespersons not to be affiliated, **112:87RR, 112:87VV.**

Other states, regulation of sale of land located, **112:87AAA.**

Own business or property, registration laws inapplicable, **112:87QQ.**

Partnerships, licensing, **112:87TT, 112:87UU, 112:87XX.**

Penalties.
Acting without license, penalty, **112:87CCC.**
Revocation or suspension of license, other punishment not affected, **112:87AAA.**

Pharmacy registration board, laws as to, not applicable, **112:87DDD.**

Physicians, laws as to registration of, not applicable, **112:87DDD.**

Publication containing lists, **112:87XX.**

Qualification or disqualification, **112:87SS to 112:87UU.**
Members of board of registration, **13:54.**

REAL ESTATE BROKERS AND SALESPERSONS —Cont'd

Racial discrimination, **112:87AAA, 151B:1, 151B:4, 151B:5, 151B:6.**

Real estate broker defined under registration of professions law, **112:87PP.**

Real estate defined under registration of professions law, **112:87PP.**

Real estate salesman defined under registration of professions law, **112:87PP.**

Reciprocity in licensing, **112:87WW.**

Records of board of registration, **13:55, 13:56, 112:87XX.**

Registration and licensing, **13:54 et seq., 112:87PP to 112:87DDD.**
Appeals, **112:87BBB.**
Application for license or renewal, **112:87TT, 112:87XX.**
Board of registration. See within this heading, "Board of registration."
Bond for broker's license, **112:87TT.**
Corporations, associations, or partnerships, licensing, **112:87TT, 112:87UU, 112:87XX.**
Definitions, **112:87PP.**
Display of license, **112:87YY.**
Duplicate license, **112:88.**
Examination for license, **112:87SS.**
Dispensing, **112:87RR.**
Fee, **112:87ZZ.**
Independent testing service. See within this heading, "Independent testing service."
Law school course as qualification, **112:87SS.**
Exemption from requirement, **112:87QQ, 112:87SS.**
Fees for licenses. See within this heading, "Fees for licenses."
Form of license, **112:87XX.**
General provisions, **112:88.**
General provisions as to medical registration boards, not applicable, **112:87DDD.**
Issuance of license, **112:87TT to 112:87XX.**
Law school course as qualification for examination for license, **112:87SS.**

REAL ESTATE BROKERS AND SALESPERSONS —Cont'd

Registration and licensing —Cont'd
Nonresidents, **112:87WW.**
Penalties. See within this heading, "Penalties."
Postponement of requirement, **112:87RR.**
Renewal of license. See within this heading, "Renewal of license."
Requirements for issuance of license, **112:87PP, 112:87SS to 112:87UU.**
Revocation or suspension of license. See within this heading, "Revocation or suspension of license."
Stay pending appeal, **112:87BBB.**
Temporary license on death of broker, **112:87TT, 112:87UU.**
Term of license, **112:87XX, 112:87ZZ.**
Time for examination of license applicants, **112:87SS.**
Unlicensed persons. See within this heading, "Unlicensed persons."

Renewal of license, **112:87XX.**
Fee, **112:87XX, 112:87ZZ.**
Further training courses required, **112:87XX½.**
Refusal, **112:87AAA.**

Representative of broker, salespersons must be, **112:87RR.**

Residence.
Domicile or residence. See within this heading, "Domicile or residence."

Revocation or suspension of license, **112:87AAA.**
Alien failing to become naturalized, **112:87TT.**
Change of business address, revocation for failure to give notice.
Broker's license, **112:87YY.**
Salesman's license, **112:87VV.**
Failure to comply with order of commission against discrimination, **112:87AAA.**
Grounds, **112:87AAA.**
Hearing as to, right to attorney, **112:87BBB.**
Other punishment not affected, **112:87AAA.**
Reinstatement, **112:87AAA.**

REAL ESTATE BROKERS AND SALESPERSONS —Cont'd

Rules and regulations.
Board of registration. See within this heading, "Board of registration."
Salaries.
Compensation and fees. See within this heading, "Compensation and fees."
Service of process on nonresident agent or broker, **112:87WW.**
Small home mortgages, including brokerage fees in computation of interest, **140:90A.**
Societies, licensing, **112:87TT, 112:87UU, 112:87XX.**
Suit.
Action or suit. See within this heading, "Action or suit."
Sunday, sales or rentals, **136:5, 136:6.**
Suspension of license.
Revocation or suspension. See within this heading, "Revocation or suspension of license."
Temporary license on death of broker, **112:87TT, 112:87UU.**
Tenants, fee for locating dwelling, **112:87DDD½.**
Time for examining license applicants, **112:87SS.**
Trusts and trustees.
Commission, apportionment, **203:22.**
Registration law not applicable to sales by trustees, **112:87QQ.**
Unemployment compensation, **151A:6.**
Unlicensed persons.
Broker not to engage unlicensed salesmen, **112:87VV.**
Doing business without license, prohibited, **112:87RR.**
Penalty, **112:87CCC.**
Usual place of business, requirement of maintaining, **112:87YY.**
Nonresident brokers, **112:87WW.**
Veterans exempted from payment of fees, **112:87ZZ.**
Veterinarians' registration, laws not applicable, **112:87DDD.**
Wages.
Compensation and fees. See within this heading, "Compensation and fees."
Workers' compensation law, employment exclusion, **152:1.**

REAL ESTATE CORPORATION.

Duration, **156:7.**
Life insurance companies, investments, **175:66D.**
Railroad may hold stock, **160:65B.**

REAL ESTATE TIME-SHARES, 183B:1-183B:55.

Actions and remedies.
Association, **183B:20.**
Breach of contract, **183B:25.**
Developer, tort action, **183B:25.**
Owner of time-share, suit by or against, **183B:25.**
Statute of limitations, warranties, **183B:48.**
Tort action, **183B:25.**
Advertisements, prizes or inducements, **183B:52.**
Affiliate of developer, exchange company, **183B:53.**
Agency, law applicable, **183B:8.**
Agent for service of process, cancellation notice, **183B:41.**
Agents and employees, **183B:20.**
Alteration of votes and expense liabilities, **183B:13.**
Appraisers, termination of shares, **183B:15.**
Attorneys' fees, liens for assessments, **183B:29.**
Bankruptcy, special developer right, **183B:22.**
Broker, sales and offers to made, **183B:55.**
Budgets, **183B:20.**
Bylaws, **183B:20.**
Cancellation of purchase contract, **183B:41.**
Capacity to contract, **183B:8.**
Class action, recreational or parking areas, termination of contract, **183B:23.**
Coercion or duress, **183B:8.**
Conflict with other statutes, **183B:9.**
Construction of provisions, unified coverage, **183B:10.**
Contracts.
Breach of contract action, **183B:25.**
Power of association to make, **183B:20.**
Substantial performance, **183B:8.**
Unconscionable contract or clause, **183B:5.**
Corporations, law, **183B:8.**
Courts, enforcement, **183B:5, 183B:7.**

REAL ESTATE TIME-SHARES —Cont'd

Creditors, termination of shares, **183B:15.**
Damages, **183B:7.**
Deed, time-share estate to be evidenced, **183B:18.**
Definitions, **183B:1.**
Developer, duties, **183B:21.**
Discharge of manager, **183B:35.**
Disclaimer of implied warranties of quality, **183B:47.**
Eminent domain, law applicable, **183B:8.**
Encumbrances.
Liens and encumbrances. See within this heading, "Liens and encumbrances."
Equity, principles, **183B:8.**
Estate for years, **183B:3, 183B:18.**
Estoppel.
Waiver and estoppel. See within this heading, "Waiver and estoppel."
Exchange program, participation, **183B:53.**
Expense assessments, **183B:28.**
Express warranties, **183B:45.**
Fees.
Attorneys' fees, liens for assessments, **183B:29.**
Exchange program, participation, **183B:53.**
Fee simple estate, **183B:3.**
Financial records, assessments for expenses, **183B:30.**
Fire insurance, **183B:26.**
Foreclosure, **183B:15.**
Special developer right, **183B:22.**
Fraud, **183B:8, 183B:49.**
Freehold estate, time-share estate coupled, **183B:18.**
Good faith requirement, **183B:6.**
Illiteracy, unconscionable contract or clause, **183B:5.**
Implied warranties of quality, **183B:47.**
Improvements, **183B:20.**
Completion, **183B:50, 183B:51.**
Indemnification of directors and officers, **183B:20.**
Inducements, **183B:52.**
Inspection of records of addresses of time-share owners, **183B:32.**
Insurance, **183B:26.**
Insurance trustee, designation method, recording, **183B:12.**
Judgments.
Assessments to pay, **183B:28.**

REAL ESTATE TIME-SHARES
—Cont'd
Judgments —Cont'd
Association, judgment against,
 183B:25.
Judicial sales, special developer
 right, **183B:22.**
Lapse of membership, exchange
 program, **183B:53.**
Leases.
 Association's power to impose
  rental charges, **183B:20.**
 Notice of time-share lease,
  183B:18.
 Recreational or parking areas,
  termination of contract or
  lease, **183B:23.**
Liberal administration of
 remedies, **183B:7.**
Licenses, **183B:15.**
 Notice of time-share license,
  183B:18.
Liens and encumbrances.
 Assessments or fines, **183B:29.**
 Enforcement, **254:5.**
 Form, **254:5A.**
 Judgment for money against
  association, **183B:25.**
 Managing entity, court
  appointment, **183B:19.**
 Public offering, **183B:38.**
 Recording, **183B:3, 183B:44.**
 Releases of liens, recording,
  183B:44.
Maintenance.
 Repairs and maintenance. See
  within this heading,
  "Repairs and maintenance."
Management offices, **183B:16.**
Managing agents, **183B:20.**
Managing entity, **183B:19.**
 Maintenance, repair, and
  replacement, **183B:24.**
Mistake, **183B:8.**
Models, **183B:16.**
Mortgagees, approval of actions of
 units owners, **183B:17.**
Multi-location developer,
 information to purchaser,
 183B:54.
"Need not be built," promotional
 materials, **183B:50.**
Notice.
 Cancellation of contract to
  purchase, **183B:41,**
  183B:43.
 Insurance, unavailability,
  183B:26.
 Taxes and assessments, notices,
  183B:3.
Out-of-state sales, real estate
 brokers and salesmen, **183B:9.**

REAL ESTATE TIME-SHARES
—Cont'd
Parking areas, termination of
 contract or lease, **183B:23.**
Partition, **183B:14.**
Personal liability of time share
 owner, **183B:24, 183B:25.**
Petitions to managing entity,
 voting, **183B:33.**
Prizes or inducements, **183B:52.**
Public offering, **183B:36-183B:41.**
 Prospective purchaser,
  documents to be provided,
  183B:41.
 Securities and Exchange
  Commission, registration,
  183B:40.
Punitive damages, **183B:7.**
Receivership, **183B:8, 183B:22.**
Recording, **183B:3, 183B:12.**
 Judgment for money against
  association, **183B:25.**
 Liens and encumbrances,
  assessments or fines,
  183B:29.
 Releases of liens, **183B:44.**
Recreational or parking areas,
 termination of contract or
 lease, **183B:23.**
Referendum, **183B:34.**
Repairs and maintenance,
 183B:20.
 Insurance, **183B:26.**
 Managing entity, **183B:24.**
Rules and regulations, **183B:20,**
 183B:39A.
Sales offices, **183B:16.**
Securities and Exchange
 Commission, registration,
 183B:40.
Service of process.
 Agent for service, cancellation
  notice, **183B:41.**
 Liens to be foreclosed or
  enforced, **183B:44.**
Special damages, **183B:7.**
Special developer right, **183B:22.**
Statute of limitations, warranties,
 183B:48.
Subdivision control law, **183B:9.**
Subrogation, insurance, **183B:26.**
Substantial performance, **183B:8.**
Successor to special developer
 right, **183B:22.**
Surplus funds, **183B:27.**
Taxes and assessments.
 Liens for assessments, **183B:29.**
 One parcel for purpose, **183B:3.**
Termination of contract or lease,
 recreational or parking areas,
 183B:23.

REAL ESTATE TIME-SHARES
—Cont'd
Termination of shares, **183B:15.**
Trustee.
 Insurance trustee, recording
  designation method,
  183B:12.
 Termination of shares, trustee to
  effect sale, **183B:15.**
 Third person dealing, **183B:31.**
Unconscionable contract or clause,
 183B:5.
Unfair or deceptive act or practice,
 183B:49.
Unincorporated associations, law,
 183B:8.
Value of interest, termination of
 shares, **183B:15.**
Violations, list of, public offering,
 183B:39.
Voting, **183B:11, 183B:13,**
 183B:32-183B:35.
Waiver and estoppel.
 Principles of estoppel, **183B:8.**
 Provisions, waiver, **183B:4.**
 Voting, **183B:32, 183B:33.**
Warranties, **183B:22,**
 183B:45-183B:48.

REAL PROPERTY, 184:1 et seq.
Abandoned property.
 See ABANDONED, LOST, AND
  UNCLAIMED PROPERTY.
Abandoned spouse of either sex
 authorized to receive certain
 property, **209:30.**
Abatement, survival, and revival,
 184:20.
Absent defendants.
 See ABSENT DEFENDANTS.
Adjoining.
 See ADJOINING OR
  ADJACENT PROPERTY.
Administrators.
 See EXECUTORS AND
  ADMINISTRATORS.
Advancements.
 See ADVANCEMENTS.
Adverse possession.
 See ADVERSE POSSESSION.
Affidavits concerning title.
 See TITLE AND OWNERSHIP.
Agents and agency.
 Brokers and agents, **112:87PP**
  to 112:87DDD.
 See REAL ESTATE
  BROKERS AND
  SALESPERSONS.
 Managing agent of real property,
  real estate brokers' and
  salesmen's registration law
  as inapplicable, **112:87QQ.**

REAL PROPERTY —Cont'd
Agents and agency —Cont'd
Notice of restriction on real
property signed by attorney
or agent, **184:29.**
Agriculture.
See AGRICULTURE.
Airports.
See AIRPORTS AND LANDING
FIELDS.
Alienation of land.
Deeds, **183:1 et seq.**
See DEEDS AND
CONVEYANCES.
Sale or transfer of property.
See SALE OR TRANSFER OF
PROPERTY.
Aliens, holding, **184:1.**
Alimony judgment as conveyance,
208:34A.
Another county, filing of records of
real property interests located,
217:15C.
Antitrust laws, **93:2.**
Appraisers.
See APPRAISERS AND
APPRAISALS.
Aqueducts and aqueduct
companies.
Authority to hold in excess of
limit, **165:28.**
Payment of capital stock by
conveyance of real estate,
165:14.
Proprietors to hold real estate in
common upon dissolution,
165:23.
Arrest on mesne process.
Property of defendant.
See ARREST ON MESNE
PROCESS AND
SUPPLEMENTARY
PROCEEDINGS.
Assessment of land.
See TAXATION.
Asset management board.
See ASSET MANAGEMENT
BOARD.
Attachment of property,
223:62-223:70.
See ATTACHMENT OF
PROPERTY.
Attorney general.
See ATTORNEY GENERAL.
Attorneys at law.
Execution of statement as to
breach of condition, **184:19.**
Licensing of attorney as broker
for real estate, **112:87SS.**
Notice of restriction signed by
attorney or agent, **184:29.**

REAL PROPERTY —Cont'd
Attorneys at law —Cont'd
Residential mortgages,
responsibility and fees of
attorneys employed in
connection, **184:17B.**
Trust instruments for land to be
signed by attorney, **203:1.**
Banks.
See BANKS AND BANKING.
Blockbusting, **112:87AAA, 151B:3,
151B:4.**
Boundaries.
See BOUNDARIES AND
MARKERS.
Bradford Durfee College of
Technology.
Research foundation, powers,
74:46B.
Trustees, management, **74:42L,
74:42M.**
Breach of condition, entry for.
See ENTRY INTO LAND AND
PREMISES.
Brokers and salespersons,
112:87PP to 112:87DDD.
See REAL ESTATE BROKERS
AND SALESPERSONS.
Building loans, misuse, **266:38A.**
Building restrictions, limitations
on proceedings relating,
184:23A.
Business trusts for investment in
or management of real estate,
182:1-182:14.
Cemeteries, **114:1-114:50, 272:71
et seq.**
See CEMETERIES.
Charges on property.
See CHARGES ON PROPERTY.
Charities.
See CHARITIES AND
CHARITABLE
CONTRIBUTIONS.
Children.
Real estate.
See CHILDREN AND
MINORS.
Cities.
See CITIES AND TOWNS.
City council.
See CITY COUNCIL.
Civil rights.
See CIVIL RIGHTS AND
DISCRIMINATION.
Closing costs, relocation assistance
payments, **79A:7.**
Commercial shooting preserves,
131:31.
Common property.
See COMMON PROPERTY OR
AREAS.

REAL PROPERTY —Cont'd
Common scheme.
Conditions and restrictions. See
within this heading,
"Conditions and
restrictions."
Commonwealth of property of.
See PUBLIC LANDS.
Complaint.
Confirmation of land title
without registration,
petition, **185:26A.**
More than one county, land,
218:12.
Nonresident owners charged
with discriminatory
practices, **151B:5.**
Restrictions running with land,
complaint in action to
enforce, **240:10A.**
Summary process for possession
of land, form of writ, **239:2.**
Condemnation, **79:1-79:45.**
See EMINENT DOMAIN.
Conditions and restrictions.
Affordable housing, **184:26,
184:31-184:33.**
Attorney or agent, signing of
notice of restriction, **184:29.**
Breach of condition, execution of
statement, **184:19.**
Building restrictions, limitation
of actions and proceedings
relating, **184:23A.**
Certificates of title, when notice
or extension of restriction to
be noted, **184:29.**
Common scheme.
Grounds for refusing
enforcement of restrictions
other than award of
money damages, **184:30.**
Presumption as to
enforceability of
restriction imposed as
part, **184:26.**
Time for enforcement of
restriction, **184:27.**
Conservation restrictions,
184:31-184:33.
Covenants.
See COVENANTS.
Damages, **184:30, 240:10C,
240:17.**
Deeds.
See DEEDS AND
CONVEYANCES.
Definitions under real property
law, **184:26.**
Description of land, **184:26,
240:10A.**

REAL PROPERTY —Cont'd
Conditions and restrictions
—Cont'd
Disability, signing of notice of
restriction on behalf of
person, **184:29.**
Enforcement, **184:26-184:30,
240:10A-240:10C.**
Grounds for refusing
enforcement other than
award of money damages,
184:30.
Entry for breach of condition.
See ENTRY INTO LAND AND
PREMISES.
Equitable restrictions,
determination by land court,
185:1, 240:16-240:18.
Grounds for refusing
enforcement of restrictions
other than award of money
damages, **184:30.**
Indexing of records of notice or
extension of restrictions,
184:29.
Injunction, power of court to
issue temporary injunction,
184:30.
Joinder of owners of parcels in
giving notice of restriction,
184:29.
Land court, determinations by,
**185:1, 240:11-240:14,
240:16-240:18.**
See LAND COURT.
Limitation of restrictions or
conditions, **184:23, 184:23A.**
Limiting conveyance or
occupancy on basis of race,
color, etc., **151B:4A,
184:23B.**
Mortgaging or conveying
property subject,
183:49-183:51.
Multiple restrictions, notice of
restrictions applicable,
184:29.
Notice of restriction.
Attorney or agent, signature,
184:29.
Certificates of title, when
notice or extension of
restriction to be noted,
184:29.
Extending period of
enforceability.
Restrictions imposed after
December 31, 1961,
184:27.
Restrictions imposed before
January 1, 1962,
184:28.

REAL PROPERTY —Cont'd
Conditions and restrictions
—Cont'd
Notice of restriction —Cont'd
Joinder of owners of parcels in
giving notice, **184:29.**
When effective, **184:29.**
Parties.
Enforcement of restrictions
imposed after December
31, 1961, parties entitled,
184:27.
Notice of restriction, parties
entitled, **184:29.**
Preservation restrictions,
recording, **184:33.**
Presumption as to enforceability
of restriction imposed as
part of common scheme,
184:26.
Probate court, recording
restrictions on land
contained in will, **184:16,
184:19, 184:29.**
Protection of land titles from
uncertain and obsolete
restrictions, **184:26 et seq.**
Race discrimination, **184:23B.**
Records and recording.
Conservation or preservation
restrictions, **184:33.**
Notice of restriction, **184:27,
184:28.**
Sufficiency of description of
land, **184:26.**
Wills, recordation of
restrictions contained,
184:16, 184:19, 184:29.
Registered land, decree of
registration as agreement
running with land, **185:52.**
State lands provisions as to
property owned and
conveyed by Commonwealth,
184:27, 184:28.
Time for enforcement.
Restrictions imposed after
December 31, 1961,
184:27.
Restrictions imposed before
January 1, 1962, **184:28.**
Uncertain and obsolete
restrictions, protection of
land titles, **184:26-184:30.**
Validity of determination in land
court, **185:1, 240:11-240:14.**
Wills, recordation of restrictions
contained, **184:16, 184:19,
184:29.**
Condominiums, **183A:1-183A:19.**
See CONDOMINIUMS.

REAL PROPERTY —Cont'd
Confirmation without registration.
See REGISTRATION OF LAND
TITLES.
Congress to have power over land
owned by United States, **US
Const Art 1 Sec 8 cl 17.**
Conservation.
See CONSERVATION.
Conservators.
See GUARDIANS,
CONSERVATORS, AND
COMMITTEES.
Consideration.
Deeds and conveyances.
See CONSIDERATION.
Fair consideration, **109A:3.**
Constitution of Massachusetts.
See CONSTITUTION OF
MASSACHUSETTS.
Constitution of the United States.
See CONSTITUTION OF THE
UNITED STATES.
Construction loans, misuse,
266:38A.
Controlled substances, disposition,
94C:47.
Conveyances.
Deeds, **183:1 et seq.**
See DEEDS AND
CONVEYANCES.
Sale or transfer of property.
See SALE OR TRANSFER OF
PROPERTY.
Cooperative banks.
Mortgages.
See COOPERATIVE BANKS.
Co-operative corporations and
associations.
Pledge or mortgage, **157:11.**
Power to determine rights of
members, **157:13.**
Corporations.
See CORPORATIONS.
Corporation taxes, amount of
credit against excise for
corporation operating eligible
business facility, **63:38E.**
Counties.
See COUNTIES.
Covenants.
See COVENANTS.
Credit unions.
Real estate loans.
See CREDIT UNIONS.
Crematory corporations, **114:8.**
Criminal offenses.
Fines and penalties. See within
this heading, "Fines and
penalties."
Curtesy, **189:1 et seq.**
See DOWER AND CURTESY.

REAL PROPERTY —Cont'd

Damages.
  See LAND DAMAGES.
Damage to real property.
  See DESTRUCTION OF
    PROPERTY.
Decedents' estates.
  See DECEDENTS' ESTATES.
Dedication.
  See DEDICATION.
Deeds, **183:1 et seq.**
  See DEEDS AND
    CONVEYANCES.
Deeds of trust.
  See MORTGAGES AND DEEDS
    OF TRUST.
Defacement of, punishment,
  266:126.
Definitions, **4:7.**
  Real estate, **112:173.**
  Real estate appraisal trainee,
    112:173.
Delegation of authority.
  See DELEGATION OF
    AUTHORITY OR POWER.
Delivery of instruments, record as
  evidence, **183:5.**
Dental service corporations,
  acquisition, **176E:10.**
Descent and distribution, **190:3 et
  seq.**
  See DESCENT AND
    DISTRIBUTION.
Descriptions or identification.
  Coordinate system zone to be
    designated, **97:9.**
  Eminent domain, land taken,
    79:1, 79:4.
  Executions, land levied, **236:11.**
  Massachusetts coordinate
    system, **97:13.**
  Meaning of X or Y coordinates,
    97:10.
  Partition, investigation of
    description by court, **241:17.**
Quieting title.
  See QUIETING TITLE.
Restrictions running with land,
  184:26, 240:10A.
Security agreement, description
  of realty, **106:9-203.**
Summary process to recover
  land, **239:2.**
Unregistered land, requirements
  as to identification as
  condition for recording of
  instrument conveying,
  183:6A.
Devises.
  See WILLS.

REAL PROPERTY —Cont'd

Discharge or release.
  Decree in equity as operating to
    release realty, **183:43,
    183:44.**
  Deeds.
    See DEEDS AND
      CONVEYANCES.
  Estate tax lien, license or decree
    to state discharge, **65C:14.**
  Land court.
    See LAND COURT.
  Mortgages.
    See MORTGAGES AND
      DEEDS OF TRUST.
  Quieting title, effect of decree in
    action, **240:10.**
  Registration of land titles.
    See REGISTRATION OF
      LAND TITLES.
  Subdivision lots, release from
    covenant, **41:81U.**
  Tax deeds.
    See TAX DEEDS AND
      TITLES.
Discovery and disclosure.
  Financial disclosure of public
    officers and employees,
    268B:5.
Discrimination.
  See CIVIL RIGHTS AND
    DISCRIMINATION.
Dismissal.
  See DISMISSAL AND
    NONSUIT.
Disposal by sureties, **276:61A.**
Divorce action, assignment or
  conveyance of encumbered
  real estate, **208:34A.**
Dower, **189:1 et seq.**
  See DOWER AND CURTESY.
Due process of law, to be taken
  only by, **14 Sec 1, US Const
  Amend 5.**
Dwelling houses.
  See DWELLING HOUSES.
Easements, **187:1 et seq.**
  See EASEMENTS.
Economic development and
  industrial corporations.
  Attachment, levy and execution,
    121C:8.
  Taxation, **59:5, 121C:9.**
Ejectment.
  See EJECTMENT.
Electric companies.
  See GAS AND ELECTRIC
    COMPANIES.
Eminent domain, **79:1-79:45.**
  See EMINENT DOMAIN.
Encumbrances.
  See LIENS AND
    ENCUMBRANCES.

REAL PROPERTY —Cont'd

Entirety, estates by, **209:1.**
  See ESTATES BY ENTIRETY.
Entry into land.
  See ENTRY INTO LAND AND
    PREMISES.
Entry, writs of.
  See ENTRY, WRITS.
Equitable restrictions,
    determination by land court,
    185:1, 240:16-240:18.
Estates.
  See ESTATES.
Eviction.
  See LANDLORD AND TENANT.
Evidence of title.
  See TITLE AND OWNERSHIP.
Executions.
  See EXECUTIONS.
Executors and administrators,
  sales by, **202:1 et seq.,
  240:27, 240:28.**
  See EXECUTORS AND
    ADMINISTRATORS.
Exemptions from taxation,
  veterans and veterans'
  organizations, **59:5.**
Extension of land contracts,
  recording, **184:17A.**
Federal government.
  See FEDERAL GOVERNMENT
    AND STATUTES.
Federal liens, uniform procedure
  for recording or filing, **36:24,
  185:46, 185:78, 185:80.**
Fee simple.
  See FEE SIMPLE.
Fee tail.
  See ESTATES TAIL.
Fences.
  See FENCES AND FENCE
    VIEWERS.
Fiduciaries.
  See FIDUCIARIES.
Financial disclosure of public
  officers and employees,
  268B:5.
Fines and penalties.
  Covenant or condition as void,
    151B:4A.
  Deeds.
    See DEEDS AND
      CONVEYANCES.
  Defacement of property,
    266:126.
  Discrimination in housing or
    real estate, **151B:4A,
    151B:5.**
  Grantee of real estate, failure to
    furnish owner's name and
    address to tax assessor,
    184:8A.

REAL PROPERTY —Cont'd

Fines and penalties —Cont'd

Information, owner or lessee of real property failing to submit, **59:38D.**

Larceny and theft. See within this heading, "Larceny and theft."

Sureties on bail disposing of property, **276:61A.**

Fitness of dwelling houses for human habitation.

See DWELLING HOUSES.

Fixtures.

See FIXTURES.

Flats.

See TIDE LANDS AND WATERS.

Forcible entries forbidden, **184:18.**

Foreclosure of mortgage.

See MORTGAGE FORECLOSURE.

Foreign corporations, **181:9.**

Insurance.

Foreign insurance companies. See within this heading, "Foreign insurance companies."

Officers' authority to convey lands, **155:8.**

Foreign fiduciaries.

See FOREIGN FIDUCIARIES.

Foreign insurance companies.

Schedule, **175:25.**

Valuation, **175:11.**

Forests.

See FORESTS AND FORESTRY.

Forms, **183:1, 183:8-183:17, 184:23.**

Fraternal benefit societies.

Consolidation or merger, effect, **176:7.**

Home office building, **176:40.**

Taxes, **176:49.**

Fraud.

See FRAUD AND DECEIT.

Frauds, statute of.

See STATUTE OF FRAUDS.

Gas.

See GAS AND ELECTRIC COMPANIES.

General fields.

See GENERAL FIELDS.

Government land bank.

See GOVERNMENT LAND BANK.

Government, land formerly owned, **59:2C.**

Grand jury investigation of fraudulent property damage claims, grant of immunity to witnesses during, **233:20D.**

REAL PROPERTY —Cont'd

Guardians.

See GUARDIANS, CONSERVATORS, AND COMMITTEES.

"Heirs" or "next of kin," determination of class in limitation of property to class described, **184:6A.**

Historical commission.

See HISTORICAL COMMISSION.

Historic districts.

See HISTORIC DISTRICTS AND SITES.

Homesteads, **188:1 et seq.**

See HOMESTEADS.

Hospital school and hospital for state minor wards, joint use, **111:62R.**

Hospital service corporations.

Authority as to purchase, use, and occupancy, **176A:16, 176B:10.**

Investments, **176A:16.**

Housing.

See HOUSING AND URBAN RENEWAL.

Husband.

Sale or transfer of real property. See HUSBAND AND WIFE.

Identity.

Description. See within this heading, "Descriptions or identification."

Incompetent's land contract, specific performance, **204:1.**

Indictments.

See INDICTMENTS, INFORMATIONS, AND COMPLAINTS.

Injunction as to conditions or restrictions, temporary, **184:30.**

Inland wetland, notice of public hearing of order affecting, **131:40A.**

Instruments concerning.

Deeds.

See DEEDS AND CONVEYANCES.

Registration of land titles.

See REGISTRATION OF LAND TITLES.

Wills.

See WILLS.

Insurance.

See INSURANCE.

Intestate succession to land.

See DESCENT AND DISTRIBUTION.

REAL PROPERTY —Cont'd

Inventory.

See INVENTORY.

Issue, defined for purposes of statutory construction, **4:7.**

Joint tenants.

See JOINT TENANTS AND TENANTS IN COMMON.

Judicial power of United States as extending to controversies over land claimed under grants by different states, **US Const Art 3 Sec 2 cl 1.**

Judicial sales, **236:26-236:30.**

See JUDICIAL SALES.

Jurisdiction of courts over person having interest in, using, or possessing real property in Commonwealth, **223A:3.**

Land court, **60:64-60:75, 185:1-185:25A.**

See LAND COURT.

Land damages.

See LAND DAMAGES.

Landlord and tenant, **111:127A et seq., 186:13 et seq.**

See LANDLORD AND TENANT.

Larceny and theft, **266:30.**

Form of indictment for larceny, **277:79.**

Married woman, stealing, **266:30.**

Lead-based substances in dangerous levels, duties of owners of premises where detected, **111:197.**

Leases, **111:127A et seq., 186:13 et seq.**

See LANDLORD AND TENANT.

Legacy.

See LEGACY AND SUCCESSION TAXES.

Licenses to sell, **231:6.**

Liens.

See LIENS AND ENCUMBRANCES.

Life estates.

See LIFE ESTATES, REMAINDERS, AND REVERSIONS.

Life insurance.

See LIFE INSURANCE.

Limitation of actions, **260:21 et seq.**

See LIMITATION OF ACTIONS.

Limitations.

Conditions and restrictions. See within this heading, "Conditions and restrictions."

Lis pendens.

See LIS PENDENS.

REAL PROPERTY —Cont'd

Low-level radioactive waste management board, **58:13, 111H:4.**

Low value lands acquired under tax liens without foreclosure by municipalities, sale, **60:79.**

Managing agent of, real estate brokers' and salesmen's registration law not applicable, **112:87QQ.**

Maps.
See MAPS, PLATS, AND SURVEYS.

Marine resources, acquisition and control of land and improvements for purpose of protecting and improving, **130:17.**

Marriage.
See MARRIAGE.

Medical care and assistance, effect of transfer of property upon eligibility, **18:5D, 118E:13.**

Medical service corporations.
Authority to purchase and use property, **176B:10.**
Investment, **176B:10.**

Memoranda.
See MEMORANDA.

Mentally ill or incompetent person, specific performance of land contract, **204:1.**

Metropolitan district commission, entry upon private land, **92:103.**

Militia, **33:98-33:116.**
See MILITIA.

Morris plan banks.
See MORRIS PLAN BANKS.

Mortgages.
See MORTGAGES AND DEEDS OF TRUST.

Municipal conservation commissions' authority to acquire, **40:8C.**

Municipal finance.
See MUNICIPAL FINANCE.

Municipal historical commissions, powers, **40:8D.**

Municipal industrial development financing authorities, powers with respect to property, **40D:7.**

Municipalities.
See CITIES AND TOWNS.

Municipal light charges as lien, **60:23, 164:58B.**

New Bedford Institute of Technology, management of property, **74:42L, 74:42M.**

REAL PROPERTY —Cont'd

Nondomiciliaries, personal jurisdiction based on ownership of real property, **223A:3.**

Nonpayment of taxes, taking of land for, **60:53-60:56.**
See TAX LIENS.

Nonsuit.
See DISMISSAL AND NONSUIT.

Notice.
See NOTICE AND KNOWLEDGE.

Optometric service corporation's authority to acquire, **176F:10.**

Ownership.
See TITLE AND OWNERSHIP.

Paramount title, effect of irregularities in fiduciary sales claimed by claimant, **204:20.**

Parks.
See PARKS AND RESERVATIONS.

Partition, **241:1-241:37.**
See PARTITION.

Partnerships.
See PARTNERSHIPS.

Penalties.
Fines and penalties. See within this heading, "Fines and penalties."

Perpetuities, rule against, **184A:1 et seq.**
See PERPETUITIES, RULE AGAINST.

Personal jurisdiction over person having interest in, using or possessing real property in Commonwealth, **223A:3.**

Pest control law, land defined, **132B:3.**

Plans.
See PLANS AND SPECIFICATIONS.

Possession.
See POSSESSION.

Posting.
See POSTING.

Preservation restrictions, recording, **184:33.**

Presumption as to enforceability of restriction imposed as part of common scheme, **184:26.**

Priority of open-end credit plans secured by mortgages of residential property, **183:28B.**

Private ways.
See PRIVATE WAYS.

Probate.
See PROBATE AND FAMILY COURT.

REAL PROPERTY —Cont'd

Professional corporation's right to own, **156A:4.**

Proprietors of wharves and real estate lying in common, **179:1-179:17.**
See PROPRIETORS OF WHARVES AND REAL ESTATE LYING IN COMMON.

Psychologically impacted property. Not deemed material fact required to be disclosed in real estate transactions, **93:114.**

Public housing projects, sale, **121B:34.**

Public lands.
See PUBLIC LANDS.

Public recreation purposes, liability of landowner permitting use without charge, **21:17C.**

Purchasers.
Deeds, **183:1 et seq.**
See DEEDS AND CONVEYANCES.
Sale or transfer of property.
See SALE OR TRANSFER OF PROPERTY.

Qualification.
See REAL ESTATE BROKERS AND SALESPERSONS.

Quieting title, **240:1-240:29.**
See QUIETING TITLE.

Railroads, **160:76 et seq.**
See RAILROADS.

Receivers and receivership, applicability of real estate brokers' and salesmen's registration law, **112:87QQ.**

Records.
See RECORDS, REPORTS, AND RETURNS.

Recovery of land or tenements.
Ejectment.
See EJECTMENT.
Entry into land.
See ENTRY INTO LAND AND PREMISES.
Mortgage foreclosure.
See MORTGAGE FORECLOSURE.
Remedies limited, **184:18.**
Summary process to recover land.
See SUMMARY PROCESS TO RECOVER LAND.
Survival of actions for recovery of land, **184:20.**

Redevelopment and housing authorities, tax status of real estate owned, **121B:16.**

REAL PROPERTY —Cont'd

Regional refuse disposal districts.
Leases.
See REGIONAL REFUSE
DISPOSAL DISTRICTS.
Power to acquire, **71:16.**
School buildings.
See REGIONAL SCHOOL
DISTRICTS.
Regional school districts.
See REGIONAL SCHOOL
DISTRICTS.
Regional transit authorities.
Power to hold property, **161B:2.**
Sales of real estate, **161B:8.**
Registers.
See REGISTERS AND
REGISTRIES OF DEEDS.
Registration of land titles.
See REGISTRATION OF LAND
TITLES.
Release.
Discharge or release. See within
this heading, "Discharge or
release."
Religion.
See RELIGION AND
RELIGIOUS SOCIETIES.
Remainders.
See LIFE ESTATES,
REMAINDERS, AND
REVERSIONS.
Removal of property.
See REMOVAL OF PROPERTY.
Reservation from sale of land
containing items of
archeological interest, **9:26A.**
Residential property.
Appeal from denial of residential
exemption, **59:5C.**
Attorney's responsibility and
fees in connection with
mortgages on residential
property, **184:17B.**
Conservation of energy in,
service to promote, **Spec L
61:1-10.**
See RESIDENTIAL
CONSERVATION
SERVICE.
Deeds.
See DEEDS AND
CONVEYANCES.
Discrimination in sale or lease,
151B:4, 151B:4A, 151B:5.
Dwelling houses.
See DWELLING HOUSES.
Landlord.
See LANDLORD AND
TENANT.

REAL PROPERTY —Cont'd

Residential property —Cont'd
Lead-based substances in
dangerous levels, duties of
owner of premises where
detected, **111:197.**
Mortgages.
See MORTGAGES AND
DEEDS OF TRUST.
Tenement houses.
See TENEMENT HOUSES.
Veterans, discrimination against,
151B:5.
Restraints of trade and
monopolies, **93:2.**
Restrictions.
Conditions and restrictions. See
within this heading,
"Conditions and
restrictions."
Retail installment sales and
services for repair,
requirement, **255D:9A.**
Reversions.
See LIFE ESTATES,
REMAINDERS, AND
REVERSIONS.
Revival of actions.
See ABATEMENT, SURVIVAL,
AND REVIVAL.
Sale.
See SALE OR TRANSFER OF
PROPERTY.
Salespersons, **112:87PP to
112:87DDD.**
See REAL ESTATE BROKERS
AND SALESPERSONS.
Savings banks.
Investments, **167F:2.**
Mortgages.
See SAVINGS BANKS.
Schools and education, **40:3, 40:14,
71:16, 128:45.**
See SCHOOLS AND
EDUCATION.
Seal on instrument affecting
interest in land, **183:1A.**
Secured transactions.
See SECURED
TRANSACTIONS.
Sentence and punishment.
Fines and penalties. See within
this heading, "Fines and
penalties."
Settlement of land titles.
See QUIETING TITLE.
Shores, municipal appropriations
for construction of structures
along, **91:29A.**
Smoke detectors installed upon
sale or transfer, **148:26F.**

REAL PROPERTY —Cont'd

Solar energy systems, protection of
access to sunlight, **184:23C.**
Specific performance.
See SPECIFIC
PERFORMANCE.
State colleges, management of
grants or devises, **73:14.**
State highway, rights of owners of
land abutting, **81:22.**
State, lands of.
See PUBLIC LANDS.
State treasurer.
See STATE TREASURER.
Statute of frauds.
See STATUTE OF FRAUDS.
Stealing.
Larceny. See within this
heading, "Larceny and
theft."
Street railways.
See STREET RAILWAYS.
Strike or lockout, employer may
hire personnel to protect
property, **149:22A.**
Sufferance, estates by.
See ESTATES BY
SUFFERANCE.
Summary process to recover,
239:1-239:13.
See SUMMARY PROCESS TO
RECOVER LAND.
Superior courts.
See SUPERIOR COURTS.
Survival of actions.
See ABATEMENT, SURVIVAL,
AND REVIVAL.
Taxation, **59:2 et seq., 60:1 et
seq.**
See TAXATION.
Technology development
corporation, powers, **40G:3.**
Tenants, **111:127A et seq., 186:13
et seq.**
See LANDLORD AND TENANT.
Tenants in common.
See JOINT TENANTS AND
TENANTS IN COMMON.
Theft.
Larceny. See within this
heading, "Larceny and
theft."
Third persons as bound by
proceedings affecting title,
184:15.
Tidelands.
See TIDE LANDS AND
WATERS.
Time or date.
Broker's or salesperson's license,
112:87SS.

REAL PROPERTY —Cont'd
Time or date —Cont'd
Duration of real estate
corporation, **156:7.**
Enforcement of restriction, time
for.
Conditions and restrictions.
See within this heading,
"Conditions and
restrictions."
Time-shares, **183B:1-183B:55.**
Title.
See TITLE AND OWNERSHIP.
Tolling limitation, sufficiency of
entry, **260:28.**
Towns.
See CITIES AND TOWNS.
Trackless trolley companies may
hold, **163:11.**
Transfers.
Deeds, **183:1 et seq.**
See DEEDS AND
CONVEYANCES.
Sale or transfer of property.
See SALE OR TRANSFER OF
PROPERTY.
Trespass.
See TRESPASS.
Trials or other criminal
proceedings, damage to
property of jurors or
witnesses, **268:13B.**
Tuberculosis and tuberculin.
Acquisition of property, **111:86.**
Conveyance to Commonwealth,
111:83.
Reimbursement of cities and
towns for tax loss,
58:13-58:17A.
Turnpike authority, **81A:4.**
United States.
See FEDERAL GOVERNMENT
AND STATUTES.
University of Massachusetts.
See UNIVERSITY OF
MASSACHUSETTS.
Unknown persons, assessment of
taxes upon property, **59:11.**
Unlawful entry, informations by
Commonwealth, **245:1-245:12.**
Urban redevelopment corporations.
See URBAN
REDEVELOPMENT
CORPORATIONS.
Value and valuation.
Opinion as to real property
value by mortgagee in
processing mortgage
application, **184:17C.**
Real estate taxes, **59:5.**

REAL PROPERTY —Cont'd
Vendor and purchaser.
Deeds, **183:1 et seq.**
See DEEDS AND
CONVEYANCES.
Sale or transfer of property.
See SALE OR TRANSFER OF
PROPERTY.
Venue, **223:1-223:15.**
See VENUE.
Veterans.
See VETERANS AND
VETERANS'
ORGANIZATIONS.
Waste of property.
See WASTE OF PROPERTY.
Water impoundment sites,
acquisition by water resources
commission, **21:9A.**
Water resources development, cost
of land acquired, **44:8.**
Will, estates at, **186:1 et seq.**
See ESTATES AT WILL.
Wills.
See WILLS.
Words and phrases.
Definitions. See within this
heading, "Definitions."
Worthier title to property doctrine,
abolition, **184:33A, 184:33B.**
Years, estates for, **186:1 et seq.**
See ESTATES AT WILL.

REALTY TRUSTS, 182:1-182:14.
See BUSINESS TRUSTS.

REAPPEARANCE.
Absent person, reappearance,
200:12, 200:13.

REAPPORTIONMENT.
Elections.
See ELECTIONS.

REAR-END COLLISION.
Motor vehicle property protection
insurance, coverage, **90:34O.**

REAR LIGHTS.
See TAIL LIGHTS.

REAR VISION MIRRORS.
Motor vehicles to be equipped,
90:7.

REASONABLE TIME.
Firm offers, period of
irrevocability, **106:2-205.**
Sales under commercial code.
See SALES UNDER
COMMERCIAL CODE.

REASSESSMENT OF TAXES,
59:76-59:78.
See TAXATION.

REBATES.
See DISCOUNTS AND
REBATES.

REBELLION.
Constitution of the United States.
See CONSTITUTION OF THE
UNITED STATES.
Debts incurred in aid of, not to be
assumed, **US Const 14th**
Amend Sec 4.
Habeas corpus may be suspended
in case of, where public safety
requires, **US Const Art 1 Sec**
9 cl 2.
Participation in, disqualification
from holding office by, **US**
Const Amend 14 Sec 3.

REBUILDING.
See RECONSTRUCTION.

RECALL.
Motor vehicles, emission of
contaminants, **90:2, 111:142K.**

RECALL TO EMPLOYMENT.
Employment security as affected
by failing to return to work
after, **151A:38.**
Industrial accident board and
industrial accident reviewing
board, recall of former
members, **23E:7.**

RECAPPED TIRE.
Defined under motor vehicles law,
90:1.

RECAPTURE.
See ESCAPE.

RECEIPT OF GOODS.
Defined under Commercial Code,
106:2-103.

RECEIPTS.
Appeal bond, deposit in lieu,
231:99.
Appropriations offset by estimated
receipts from fees, **44:53,**
44:53E.
Architect registration board's
expenditures as limited,
13:44D.
Assessors of taxes.
Tax assessors. See within this
heading, "Tax assessors."
Automobiles.
Motor vehicles. See within this
heading, "Motor vehicles."
Barber registration board's
expenditures as limited, **13:41.**
Check cashers, licensing of,
169A:7.
C.I.F. sales, **106:2-320.**

261

RECEIPTS —Cont'd

Costs of actions for indigent persons, bills and vouchers covering, **261:27G.**

County treasurers.
See COUNTY TREASURERS.

Credit unions, credit cards, **171:59A.**

Defined under Commercial Code, **106:2-103.**

Deposits and depositories.
Appeal bond, deposit in lieu, **231:99.**
Foreign states or countries, receipts for money deposits in foreign banks, **169:8.**
Security deposits, **186:15B.**

Engineers and surveyors, expenditures of registration board as limited by receipts, **13:47.**

Estate taxes.
Discharge of executor, **65C:7.**
Tax paid, copy of receipt, **65C:24.**

F.A.S. terms, **106:2-319.**

Foreign states or countries, receipts for money deposits in foreign banks, **169:8.**

Forgery of receipt for money, **267:1, 267:5.**

Fraternal benefit societies, receipts or expenditures, **176:13.**

Gasoline.
See GASOLINE AND MOTOR FUEL TAXES.

Gifts to minors, receipt for custodial property, **201A:8.**

Gross receipts.
See GROSS RECEIPTS OR INCOME.

Hairdressers registration board, expenditures as limited by receipts, **13:44.**

Indigent persons, bills and vouchers covering court costs, **261:27G.**

Jewelers, giving receipt as affecting lien, **255:31C.**

Legacy.
See LEGACY AND SUCCESSION TAXES.

Money.
Foreign states or countries, receipts for money deposits in foreign banks, **169:8.**
Forgery of receipt, **267:1, 267:5.**

Motor vehicles.
Buyer's right to receipt, **255B:19.**
Operator's license, receipt for licensing fee, **90:8.**

RECEIPTS —Cont'd

Municipal finance.
See MUNICIPAL FINANCE.

Pledge receipts given to borrowers or depositors, **140:86.**

Probate and Family Court.
Recording of receipts to executors, **215:50.**
Registers of probate.
See REGISTERS OF PROBATE AND INSOLVENCY.

Probation officers.
Fines paid, receipt, **279:1, 279:1A.**
Restitution made, receipt, **276:92.**

Professional engineers and land surveyors registration board, expenditures as limited by receipts, **13:47.**

Proof of service by mail outside of Commonwealth, **223A:6.**

Publication of statements of, **US Const Art 1 Sec 9 cl 7.**

Railroads.
Annual return to contain statement of receipts, **160:242.**
Shippers of freight, **160:204.**

Registers of probate.
See REGISTERS OF PROBATE AND INSOLVENCY.

Reimbursement for tax paid on special fuel, receipts to accompany application, **64E:5.**

Sales under commercial code.
See SALES UNDER COMMERCIAL CODE.

Secured transactions.
Pledges, receipts to borrowers, **140:86.**
Trust receipts.
See SECURED TRANSACTIONS.
Warehouse receipts.
See SECURED TRANSACTIONS.

Small home mortgage, payments, **140:90C.**

Small loan, receipt for part payment, **140:109.**

Tax assessors.
Annual notice, **41:54A.**
Setting annual tax rate, receipts used by assessors, **59:23.**

Trustee's receipt of property delivered to him, **203:20.**

Turnpike tolls, **81A:4.**

University of Massachusetts.
Accounting of receipts and expenditures, **75:6.**

RECEIPTS —Cont'd

University of Massachusetts —Cont'd
Students activities, **75:11.**

Use tax.
See USE, CONSUMPTION, OR STORAGE TAX.

Vehicles.
Motor vehicles. See within this heading, "Motor vehicles."

Vouchers.
See VOUCHERS.

Warehouse receipts, **106:7-101 to 106:7-210, 106:7-401 to 106:7-603.**
See WAREHOUSE RECEIPTS.

RECEIVER GENERAL.

Constitution of Massachusetts.
State treasurer and receiver general.
See CONSTITUTION OF MASSACHUSETTS.

RECEIVERS AND RECEIVERSHIPS.

Absentees, estate of.
See ABSENTEES' ESTATES.

Accounts and accounting.
Appearance of absentee or his personal representative, accounts and settlements, **200:12.**
Examination under oath as to accounts, **206:3.**
Insurance commissioner examining accounts, **175:78, 175:180.**
Mental retardation department, **206:7, 206:24.**

Alcoholic liquors, sale, storage, and transportation, **138:2, 138:23, 138:25.**

Anti-discrimination laws, applicability, **151B:1.**

Appeal on appointment of receivers, interlocutory orders pending, **231:117.**

Attachment, dissolution by appointment of receiver, **223:130, 223:131.**

Banks and banking.
Co-operative banks, investment of funds, **205:19A.**
Embezzlement by bank receivers, **266:55.**

Bond, **205:29, 214:17.**
Absentees, estates of.
See ABSENTEES' ESTATES.
Partition, **241:25.**

Carriers.
Certificate, transfer, **159A:7, 159B:11.**

**RECEIVERS AND
 RECEIVERSHIPS** —Cont'd
Carriers —Cont'd
 Conditional transfer of
 certificate, license, or
 permit, **159B:11.**
 Failure to submit accounts and
 records for inspection,
 159B:17.
Compromise and settlement.
 Absentees' estates, powers and
 duties, **200:9.**
 Priority of claims in settlement
 of estates by receivers,
 206:31.
Co-operative banks, investment of
 funds by receivers in paid-up
 shares and accounts, **205:19A.**
Corporations.
 See CORPORATIONS.
Creditors, status, **106:1-201.**
Deceit.
 Fraud and deceit. See within
 this heading, "Fraud and
 deceit."
Dental service corporations,
 176E:13.
Discrimination, applicability of
 laws prohibiting, **151B:1.**
Dissolution of attachment by
 appointment, **223:130,
 223:131.**
District Courts' equity jurisdiction
 to enforce sanitary code,
 218:19C.
Dividends by, trustee process to
 reach, **246:23.**
Dwelling houses unfit for
 occupation, receivers for.
 Fitness for human habitation.
 See DWELLING HOUSES.
Embezzlement or defalcation by
 receivers, **266:55.**
Enforcement of judgment in action
 for appointment, stay order,
 231:116.
Federal savings and loan
 associations, investment of
 funds, **205:19A.**
Fees of registers for entry of
 petition for appointment of
 administrator, conservator,
 trustee or receiver of
 absentee's estate, **262:40.**
Fire insurance reference
 proceedings, effect, **175:101G.**
Foreign insurance companies.
 See FOREIGN INSURANCE
 COMPANIES.
Fraternal benefit societies, **176:33.**
Fraud and deceit.
 Final discharge as affected,
 206:22.

**RECEIVERS AND
 RECEIVERSHIPS** —Cont'd
Fraud and deceit —Cont'd
 Property fraudulently conveyed,
 receivers, **109A:8.**
Garnishment against, **246:23.**
Hazardous waste insolvency fund,
 definition of impaired licensee,
 21C:15.
Hospital service corporations,
 176A:23.
Income tax.
 Application of provisions to
 trustees, **62:13.**
 Personal liability, **62:13.**
 Returns, **62C:6.**
Insurance, **175:178-175:180.**
 See INSURANCE.
Interlocutory orders pending
 appeal on appointment,
 231:117.
Joint control of estate with
 sureties, agreements, **205:19A.**
Labor contracts, effect on successor
 employers, **149:179C.**
Land contracts, specific
 performance, **204:1, 204:36.**
Long term care facilities,
 appointment of receiver,
 111:72M to 111:72U.
Married woman, **209:5.**
Massachusetts life and health
 insurance guaranty
 association law, **175:147.**
Mechanics' liens of subcontractors
 and suppliers upon
 receivership, **254:31.**
Medical service corporations,
 176B:13.
Medical service plans, **176C:13.**
Mental retardation department,
 accounts and settlements,
 206:7, 206:24.
Milk.
 See MILK AND MILK
 PRODUCTS.
Motor carriers.
 Carriers. See within this
 heading, "Carriers."
Motor vehicle dealers, exclusions
 from definition in motor
 vehicle practices law, **93B:1.**
Numerical order, corporation's
 issuance of obligations
 redeemable in, as ground for
 appointment, **107:8.**
Optometric service corporations,
 176F:13.
Partition proceedings,
 appointment, **241:25.**
Partnerships, **108A:28.**

**RECEIVERS AND
 RECEIVERSHIPS** —Cont'd
Priority of claims in settlement of
 estates held by receivers,
 206:31.
Probate.
 See PROBATE AND FAMILY
 COURT.
Probate bonds.
 Bond. See within this heading,
 "Bond."
Real estate brokers' and
 salesmen's registration law
 not applicable, **112:87QQ.**
Real estate time-shares, **183B:8,
 183B:22.**
Registers of probate and
 insolvency, fee for entry of
 petition for appointment of
 receiver of absentee's estate,
 262:40.
Savings and loan associations,
 investment of funds, **205:19A.**
Settlement.
 Compromise and settlement. See
 within this heading,
 "Compromise and
 settlement."
Stay order as to enforcement of
 judgment in action for
 appointment, **231:116.**
Street railways, **161:135-161:137.**
 See STREET RAILWAYS.
Subcontractors and suppliers,
 mechanics liens upon
 receivership, **254:31.**
Taxation.
 Income tax. See within this
 heading, "Income tax."
Transient vendors, applicability of
 restrictions on sales, **101:7.**
Trustee process against, **246:23.**
Uniform Securities Act,
 exemptions, **110A:402.**
Workers' compensation.
 Deposit with state treasurer,
 duties of receivers, **152:60.**
 Priority of claims, **175:46A.**
 Receivers as employers, **152:1.**

RECEIVING BANK.
Words and phrases, **106:4A-103.**

**RECEIVING STOLEN
 PROPERTY, 266:60.**
Bailed property, **266:86.**
Common receivers of stolen goods,
 266:62.
Criminal offense, **266:60.**
Fines and penalties.
 Sentence and punishment. See
 within this heading,
 "Sentence and punishment."

RECEIVING STOLEN PROPERTY —Cont'd

First offense, penalty, **266:60.**

Grand jury investigation, immunity of witness appearing during, **233:20D.**

Indictment, **277:42.**
Form, **277:79.**

Motor vehicles, **266:28, 277:58A.**

Pawnbrokers, penalty for accepting stolen property, **140:82A.**

Restitution as mitigating punishment, **266:61.**

Sentence and punishment.
Common receiver of stolen goods, **266:62.**
Motor vehicles, **266:28.**
Trade secrets, **266:60A, 266:61.**
Value of property as affecting, **266:60.**

Successive offenses, **266:62.**

Trade secrets, **266:60A.**

Trailers, **266:28, 277:58A.**

Venue, **277:58A.**

RECEPTION CENTER.

Classification of prisoners, reception centers, **127:20.**

Clinical services bureau of youth services department to operate, **18A:5.**

Concord, convicts sentenced to state prison, removal to reception center, **279:28.**

RECESS.

General court.
See GENERAL COURT.

RECESS COMMISSION.

General Court, **3:32.**

Public meetings and records, inapplicability of law, **30A:11A.**

RECIPROCAL ENFORCEMENT OF SUPPORT ACT.

Constables, fees for service of process, **262:8.**

Interstate family support act.
See INTERSTATE FAMILY SUPPORT ACT.

Service of process, fees, **262:8.**

Wage information sharing, **62D:10A, 62E:11, 62E:12.**

RECIPROCAL INSURANCE EXCHANGES, **175:94A-175:94M.**

Accounts and accounting, adoption of system as prerequisite to doing business, **175:94D.**

RECIPROCAL INSURANCE EXCHANGES —Cont'd

Advisory committee, **175:94K.**

Alteration or modification of standard form fire insurance policy, **175:99.**

Annual statements, **175:94I.**
Attorney in fact, **175:94I.**
Form, **175:25.**

Assets, maintenance, **175:94H.**

Attorney in fact.
Annual statements, **175:94I.**
Form, **175:25.**
Assets, maintenance, **175:94H.**
Commission on premiums authorized, **175:94J.**
Contracts, execution, **175:94B.**
Defined, **175:94A.**
Failure to file annual statements, **175:94I.**
Form of power of attorney, **175:94D.**
License as agent not necessary, **175:94J.**
Premiums.
Commission premiums authorized, **175:94J.**
Premium deposit return controlled by power of attorney, **175:94M.**
Principal office, **175:94B.**
Qualifications, **175:94D.**
Subscribers.
Copy of power of attorney, subscribers to receive, **175:94L.**
Information as to, when required, **175:94I.**
Service on attorney in fact, **223:39B.**

Audit by insurance commissioner, **175:94I.**

Automobile insurance business, prerequisites, **175:94D, 175:94E.**

Boiler insurance, requirements prior to doing business, **175:94D, 175:94E.**

Certificates and certification.
Authority to do business, **175:94C, 175:94D.**
Foreign exchange, compliance with laws of home state before doing business, **175:94E.**
Subscriptions, solicitation, **175:94C.**

Claim manager, employment of, prior to doing business, **175:94D.**

Classes of business, foreign exchange restricted, **175:94E.**

RECIPROCAL INSURANCE EXCHANGES —Cont'd

Classifications, regulation, **175:94M.**

Commissioner of insurance.
Insurance commissioner. See within this heading, "Insurance commissioner."

Contingent liability of subscribers, **175:94G.**

Contracts authorized, **175:94B.**
Execution, **175:94B.**
Form, **175:94D, 175:99.**
Inter-insurance contracts, **175:94B.**
Nonassessable policies, issue, **175:94E, 175:94G.**
Terms, **175:94G.**

Conversion of domestic exchanges into domestic mutual insurance company, **175:94N.**

Corporations authorized to participate as subscribers in exchange of insurance contracts, **155:12B.**

Definitions, **175:94A, 176D:2.**

Deposits of premium.
Premium deposits. See within this heading, "Premium deposits."

Deposits with treasurer of state.
Automobile insurance business, condition of doing, **175:94D.**
Nonassessable policies, prerequisite for issue, **175:94G.**
Premium deposits. See within this heading, "Premium deposits."

Designation or name of exchange, **175:94D.**

Dividends, **175:94M.**

Domestic exchanges.
Authority to do business, application, **175:94D.**
Defined, **175:94A.**
Nonassessable policies, issue, **175:94G.**
Organization, **175:94C, 175:94D.**
Surplus, investment, **175:94H.**

Employers' liability insurance, requisites for doing business, **175:94D, 175:94E.**

Examination by commissioner of insurance, **175:94I.**

Financial statement, foreign exchange to file before doing business, **175:94E.**

Fines and penalties.
Exceeding limitation of single risk, **175:94J.**

RECIPROCAL INSURANCE EXCHANGES —Cont'd

Fines and penalties —Cont'd
Failure to file annual statements, **175:94I.**
Fire insurance, modification of standard form of policy, **175:99.**
Foreign exchanges.
Application for license to do business, **175:94E.**
Defined, **175:94A.**
Licenses, **175:94E, 175:94F.**
Nonassessable policies, **175:94E, 175:94G.**
Forms.
Annual statement, **175:25.**
Contract or policy, **175:94D, 175:99.**
Power of attorney, **175:94D.**
Guaranty fund, **175:94A.**
Insurance commissioner.
Domestic exchanges, organization, **175:94C, 175:94D.**
Examination of insurance, **175:94I.**
Licenses, **175:94F.**
Insurance in force, amount required prior to doing business.
Domestic exchanges, **175:94D.**
Foreign exchanges, **175:94E.**
Inter-insurance contracts.
Contracts authorized. See within this heading, "Contracts authorized."
Investment of surplus, **175:94H.**
Laws applicable, **175:94M.**
Liability of subscribers, **175:94B, 175:94G.**
License.
See LICENSES AND PERMITS.
License as insurance agent not required for attorney in fact, **175:94J.**
Limitation of amount, single risk, **175:94J.**
Location of office, **175:94B, 175:94D.**
Name or designation of exchange, **175:94D.**
Nonassessable policies, issue, **175:94E, 175:94G.**
Number of risks, minimum prior to doing business.
Domestic exchanges, **175:94D.**
Foreign exchanges, **175:94E.**
Organization of domestic exchanges, **175:94C, 175:94D.**
Participation of corporations, **155:12B.**

RECIPROCAL INSURANCE EXCHANGES —Cont'd

Penalties.
Fines and penalties. See within this heading, "Fines and penalties."
Policies.
Contracts authorized. See within this heading, "Contracts authorized."
Power of attorney.
Attorney in fact. See within this heading, "Attorney in fact."
Premium deposits.
Disposition, **175:94M.**
Payment of, prior to doing business, **175:94D.**
Surplus in premium reserve, deposits to maintain, **175:94H.**
Premiums.
Automobile insurance business, amount of premiums prior to doing, **175:94D, 175:94E.**
Calculation of premium reserve, **175:94H.**
Deposits of.
Premium deposits. See within this heading, "Premium deposits."
Power of attorney.
Attorney in fact. See within this heading, "Attorney in fact."
Principal office, **175:94B, 175:94D.**
Process.
Service of process and papers. See within this heading, "Service of process."
Public supervision, **175:94I.**
Rebates, regulation, **175:94M.**
Reciprocal contract.
Contracts authorized. See within this heading, "Contracts authorized."
Records, reports and returns.
Statements. See within this heading, "Statements."
Reinsurance.
Applicability of laws, **175:94J.**
Domestic exchanges, **175:94D.**
Requirement of, prior to doing business, **175:94D.**
With companies not authorized to do business in Commonwealth, **175:94J.**
Representatives, laws as to agents applicable, **175:94J.**
Reserve liability, calculation, **175:94H.**
Return, rate of, regulation, **175:94M.**

RECIPROCAL INSURANCE EXCHANGES —Cont'd

Rules applicable, **175:94J.**
Service of process.
Attorney in fact, service, **223:39B.**
Insurance commissioner as attorney, **175:94D.**
Statements.
Annual statements, **175:94I.**
Form, **175:25.**
Financial statement, foreign exchange to file before doing business, **175:94E.**
State treasurer.
Deposits with treasurer of state. See within this heading, "Deposits with treasurer of state."
Statutes applicable, **175:94J.**
Subscribers.
Attorney in fact. See within this heading, "Attorney in fact."
Authority to participate, **155:12B.**
Contingent liability, **175:94G.**
Copy of power of attorney to be furnished, **175:94L.**
Defined, **175:94A.**
Deposits to maintain surplus, **175:94H.**
Disposition of moneys collected, **175:94C.**
Liability, **175:94B, 175:94G.**
Names and addresses to be furnished, when, **175:94I.**
Service of process. See within this heading, "Service of process."
Unused or unabsorbed portions of premium deposits returned or credited to subscribers, **175:94M.**
Venue of actions by or against, **223:8A.**
Subscriptions, solicitation and disposition, **175:94C.**
Surplus.
Disposition, **175:94M.**
Establishing prior to doing business.
Domestic exchanges, **175:94D.**
Foreign exchanges, **175:94E.**
Maintenance, **175:94H.**
Suspension of license for failure to file annual statement, **175:94I.**
Treasurer of state, deposits with.
Deposits with treasurer of state. See within this heading, "Deposits with treasurer of state."

RECIPROCAL INSURANCE EXCHANGES —Cont'd

Trustee, maintenance of assets and surplus, **175:94H.**

Underwriter, employment of, prior to doing business, **175:94D.**

Venue of actions by or against subscribers, **223:8A.**

Workers' compensation.

Insurer defined, **152:1.**

Laws applicable, **175:94J, 175:94M.**

Prerequisites to doing business, **175:94D, 175:94E.**

Writ and process.

Process. See within this heading, "Service of process."

RECIPROCITY.

Abandoned property loss, reciprocal enforcement, **200A:11.**

Acupuncture, licensing, **112:153.**

Aircraft, suspension of operating privilege, **90:49H.**

Appraisers and appraisals, reciprocal certification with other states, **112:182, 112:183.**

Automobiles.

See MOTOR VEHICLES.

Charitable solicitation, reciprocal agreements between states for exchange of information, **68:27.**

Chiropractors, registration, **112:92.**

Criminals, furnishing information, **127:29.**

Dependent children, reciprocal agreements with other states as to aid, **118:4A.**

Dieticians and nutritionists.

Licensure, **112:208.**

Dispensing opticians, registration, **112:73E.**

Electricians, licensing, **141:2B.**

Electrologists, registration, **112:87OOO.**

Embalmers and funeral directors, **112:85A.**

Employment security reciprocal agreements with other states and countries, **151A:66, 151A:66A.**

Engineers and land surveyors licensed by other states, **112:81J.**

Exchanges for reciprocal insurance, **175:94A-175:94M.**

See RECIPROCAL INSURANCE EXCHANGES.

Extraterritorial arrest on fresh pursuit, **276:10A-276:10D.**

RECIPROCITY —Cont'd

Farm vehicles, registration, **90:5.**

Foreign insurance companies.

Liquidation proceedings begun in reciprocal state, **175:180I.**

Obligations and prohibitions, **175:159.**

Gasoline and motor fuel taxes, **64F:4, 64F:5.**

Hairdressers, registration, **112:87Z.**

Hearing instrument specialists, **112:197A.**

Hospital service corporations in other jurisdictions, agreements, **176A:5.**

Income tax.

Disclosure of tax information, **62C:22.**

Federal authorities, reciprocal authorization of inspection of returns, **62C:23.**

Pensions of retired employees of other states, **62:3.**

Insurance.

See INSURANCE.

Judgment rendered in foreign state, factors for recognition, **235:23A.**

Landscape architects, registration, **112:104.**

Land surveyors and engineers licensed by other states, registration, **112:81J.**

Manicurists, registration, **112:87Z.**

Milk shipments, interstate, **94:16C.**

Motor vehicles.

See MOTOR VEHICLES.

Nurses and practical nurses, registration, **112:76, 112:76B.**

Perfusionists.

Licensing, **112:217.**

Pharmacists, registration, **112:24.**

Physical therapists, registration, **112:23D.**

Police and fire vehicles from certain other states, exemption from registration, **90:9B.**

Real estate brokers and salesmen, licensing, **112:87WW.**

Recreation and snow vehicle operators, reciprocal agreements with other states, **90B:30.**

Sanitarians, registration, **112:87NN.**

Snow traveling and recreational vehicles, reciprocal agreements as to registration, **90B:30.**

RECIPROCITY —Cont'd

Social workers, licensing, **112:132.**

Solicitation of charitable contributions from public, exchange of information between states, **68:26.**

Taxation.

See TAXATION.

Transitional assistance department, reciprocal agreements with other states, **18:14.**

Unemployment compensation, **151A:66, 151A:66A.**

Vocational rehabilitation, **6:79.**

Welfare department, reciprocal agreements with other states, **18:14.**

Witnesses in criminal cases, **233:12-233:13D.**

RECKLESS CONDUCT.

Charitable organizations, tort liability of individual trustees, directors, officers or agents limited, **231:85K.**

Death resulting, **229:2.**

Driving recklessly, **85:11, 90:24, 90B:8.**

Motorboats, **90B:8.**

RECLAMATION.

Coal mining regulation and reclamation, **21B:1-21B:15.**

See COAL MINING REGULATION AND RECLAMATION.

Dams.

Coal mining regulation and reclamation.

See DAMS AND RESERVOIRS.

Construction of temporary dam on land of nonparty, **252:13.**

Power of commissioners to lower water in dam for purpose, **252:13.**

Lowlands, **252:4A et seq.**

See LOWLANDS AND SWAMPS.

State reclamation and mosquito control board, **252:2.**

RECODIFICATION COUNSEL.
See GENERAL COURT.

RECOGNIZANCES.

Bail.

See BAIL AND RECOGNIZANCE.

Bail and recognizance rules.

See BAIL AND RECOGNIZANCE RULES.

RECOGNIZANCES —Cont'd
Cigarette tax.
Bond or recognizance.
Appeal bonds, forfeiture
proceedings, **64C:8.**
Payment of tax, bond, **64C:30.**
County commissioners.
See COUNTY
COMMISSIONERS.
Executions.
See EXECUTIONS.

RECOMMENDATIONS.
Administration and finance
commission, recommendations,
7:7, 7:8.
Agricultural incentive areas,
procedure for adopting area
plans, **40L:4.**
Art commission, reports to
governor, **6:20.**
Carriers, recommendations of
telecommunications and
energy department, **159:11,
159A:11.**
Civil rights and discrimination.
Advisory agency
recommendations as to
discrimination, **151B:3.**
Commission on discrimination,
recommendations to officials
and political subdivisions,
151B:2.
Civil service.
See CIVIL SERVICE.
Classification or allocation of state
office, **30:45.**
Credit unions.
See CREDIT UNIONS.
Discrimination.
Civil rights and discrimination.
See within this heading,
"Civil rights and
discrimination."
Economic diversification program,
23F:1, 23F:6.
Fraternal benefit societies, reading
of recommendations of
insurance commissioner,
176:44.
General court.
See GENERAL COURT.
Governor.
See GOVERNOR.
Governor's council.
See GOVERNOR'S COUNCIL.
Health and welfare commission,
coordination of services with
other departments, **6:126.**
Legislative bills and resolves,
30:33, 30:33A.
See LEGISLATIVE BILLS AND
RESOLVES.

RECOMMENDATIONS —Cont'd
Massachusetts water management
act, **21G:10.**
Municipal problems commission,
recommendations, **3:62.**
Nutrition board, recommendations,
6:182.
Obscene literature control
commission, recommendations
to attorney general, **6:101.**
Public construction projects,
recommendations of designers,
7:38A½.
Recodification counsel,
recommendations, **3:55A.**
Senate art committee, **3:65.**
Social services.
Welfare and social services. See
within this heading,
"Welfare and social
services."
State budget, **29:6, 30:45.**
Water pollution.
Public health commissioner,
recommendations for
prevention of water
pollution, **111:23.**
Water resources commission,
duty to make
recommendations, **21:41.**
Welfare and social services.
Health and welfare commission
for coordination of services,
6:126.
Improving quality of social
services, recommendations,
18B:3.

**RECONSIDERATION OF
LEGISLATION.**
Bills objected to by President, **US
Const Art 1 Sec 7 cl 2.**
Joint resolutions objected to by
President, **US Const Art 1
Sec 7 cl 1.**
Zoning and planning,
reconsideration of proposed
change after unfavorable
action, **40A:5, 40A:8, 40A:16.**

RECONSIGNMENT.
Bills of lading, **106:7-303.**
See BILLS OF LADING.

RECONSTRUCTION.
Architectural barriers board,
22:13A.
Condominiums.
See CONDOMINIUMS.
Fire insurance company,
rebuilding of premises, **175:99.**
Exception from limitation as to
value, **175:96A.**

RECONSTRUCTION —Cont'd
International Bank for
Reconstruction and
Development, **175:63.**
Motor vehicles, reassembling
vehicle from other vehicles,
90D:20F.
Municipal lighting and heating
plants, **164:41.**
Appropriations, **164:57.**
Debts, **44:8, 164:40.**
Nonconforming use under zoning
regulations as affected by
rebuilding, **40A:5.**

RECORDING.
**See RECORDS, REPORTS,
AND RETURNS.**
Tape recording, generally.
See ELECTRONIC
RECORDING DEVICES
AND EQUIPMENT.

RECORD ON APPEAL.
See APPEAL AND REVIEW.

**RECORDS CONSERVATION
BOARD.**
Members, **30:42.**
Powers and duties, **30:42, 66:8.**
Preservation and destruction of,
provisions, **66:8.**
State secretary, agencies within
department, **9:29.**

**RECORDS, REPORTS, AND
RETURNS, 66:1 et seq.**
Abandoned children, increase in
age limitation as to reports
and care concerning, **119:23.**
Abandoned property.
See ABANDONED, LOST, AND
UNCLAIMED PROPERTY.
Abatement of taxes, **59:60.**
See TAXATION.
Abstract copies of birth, death, and
marriage records, **262:34.**
Abused and neglected children.
See ABUSED AND
NEGLECTED CHILDREN.
Abuse or neglect of patients in
long-term care facilities,
111:72G.
Acceptance or rejection of statute
by city or town, **4:5.**
Access, **30:42.**
Commissioner of
administration's right of
access to records, books of
state agencies, **7:4E.**
Comptroller's access, **7A:9.**
Governor's cabinet, secretaries of
executive offices to have
access to reports, **6A:5.**

RECORDS, REPORTS, AND RETURNS —Cont'd

Access —Cont'd

Higher education faculty, **149:52C.**

Inspector General, **12A:9.**

Public inspection.

See EXAMINATION, INSPECTION, OR INVESTIGATION.

Remedy regarding denial, **1:7.**

Restrictions as to access to public documents, **30:42.**

Accident reports, **85:11B, 90:26, 90:29, 90B:9, 90B:27.**

Accountants.

See ACCOUNTANTS.

Accounts.

See ACCOUNTS AND ACCOUNTING.

Acknowledgment of satisfaction of execution by mortgagor, recording, **244:7.**

Actual notice of unrecorded conveyances, effect, **183:4.**

Acupuncture, record of proceedings, **112:150.**

Adjudicatory proceedings of state administrative bodies, subpoena of books and records, **30A:12.**

Administration and finance executive office, **7:4, 7:7-7:10.**

See ADMINISTRATION AND FINANCE EXECUTIVE OFFICE.

Administration of small estate, **195:16.**

Administrative procedure, **30A:9, 30A:10.**

Admissibility as evidence.

See EVIDENCE.

Adoption of children.

See ADOPTION OF CHILDREN.

Advertising, reports of outdoor advertising board, **16:14.**

Advisory board of pardons, **127:154.**

Affidavits.

Indigents, filing of affidavits, **261:27B.**

Real property recording of affidavits, **183:5A, 183:5B.**

Registrars of voters, preservation of affidavits, **51:41.**

Aging, reports to municipal councils, **40:8B.**

Agricultural and technical institutes.

Enrollment report, **74A:8.**

RECORDS, REPORTS, AND RETURNS —Cont'd

Agricultural lands preservation committee, **132A:11C.**

Agriculture department, **128:5, 129:38.**

Aid.

See AID AND ASSISTANCE.

Air conditioning systems, report of inspection, **146:45A.**

Aircraft.

See AIRCRAFT AND AVIATION.

Alcoholic beverages commission, **6:44.**

Alcoholic liquors.

See ALCOHOLIC LIQUORS.

Alcoholism.

See ALCOHOLISM AND INTOXICATION.

Aldermen.

See ALDERMEN AND SELECTMEN.

Alteration of public records, penalty, **66:15.**

American Legion, printing and distribution of proceedings, **5:9.**

American made papers, preference, **66:3.**

AMVETS, printing and distribution of proceedings, **5:9.**

Ancient records, custody, **66:7.**

Animal diseases.

See ANIMAL DISEASES.

Animal inspectors, records, **129:3, 129:25.**

Annual reports.

See ANNUAL REPORTS OR STATEMENTS.

Answers.

Pleas and answers, **231:39.**

Anti-freeze solutions, reports of analyses, **94:303K.**

Antitrust laws.

See RESTRAINTS OF TRADE AND MONOPOLIES.

Apiary inspectors, records and reports, **128:36A.**

Appeal.

See APPEAL AND REVIEW.

Appeals court.

See APPEALS COURT.

Appellate tax board.

Annual report of recommendations and matters handled, **58A:4.**

Assessment/value ratios, **58:10C.**

Open to public, **58A:13.**

Publication, sale and distribution, **58A:3.**

RECORDS, REPORTS, AND RETURNS —Cont'd

Appellate tax board —Cont'd

Recordation of proceedings, **58A:10.**

Time for delivery, **58A:13.**

Appliances, approval by supervisor of public records, **66:4.**

Apprentice agreements, recording, **23:11G.**

Appropriations, report of state officers as to exceeding, **29:26.**

Aquaculture licenses, reports of shellfish planted, **130:65.**

Aqueduct companies, **165:15.**

See AQUEDUCTS AND AQUEDUCT COMPANIES.

Archaeologist of state to submit reports of investigations of historic sites, **9:27C.**

Architects' registration board, annual report, **13:44C.**

Archivist of Commonwealth, duties, **9:2.**

Armed guards, records required of agencies employing, **147:29A.**

Arrangement of public records for reference, **66:12.**

Arrest.

See ARREST.

Assessment of taxes.

See TAX ASSESSORS.

Asset management and maintenance, records and reports on projects by commissioner, **7:40B.**

Assignment for benefit of creditors, **203:41.**

Assignments.

See ASSIGNMENTS.

Associations.

See ASSOCIATIONS AND SOCIETIES.

Assumed business names, **110:5.**

Atomic energy commission, report, **6:88.**

Attachment of property.

See ATTACHMENT OF PROPERTY.

Attestation.

See ATTESTATION AND ATTESTING WITNESSES.

Attorney general.

See ATTORNEY GENERAL.

Attorneys at law.

See ATTORNEYS AT LAW.

Auctions and auctioneers, **100:7, 100:8.**

Auditor of state, **11:6A, 11:12.**

See STATE AUDITOR.

Audits.

See AUDITS AND AUDITORS.

RECORDS, REPORTS, AND RETURNS —Cont'd

Automobile insurance.
See AUTOMOBILE INSURANCE.
Automobile rental agencies, records, **90:32D.**
Automobiles.
See MOTOR VEHICLES.
Autopsy by medical examiner, **38:6, 38:7.**
Aviation.
See AIRCRAFT AND AVIATION.
Bail.
See BAIL AND RECOGNIZANCE.
Ballot law commission, **55B:3, 55B:12.**
Bank commissioner.
See BANK COMMISSIONER.
Bankruptcy.
See INSOLVENCY AND BANKRUPTCY.
Banks.
See BANKS AND BANKING.
Barbers.
Law violations, barber investigator's reports, **13:40.**
Registration board, **112:87G.**
Bazaars, **10:39A, 271:7A.**
Beano, **10:38.**
Raffles conducted by Beano licensees, reports required, **10:39A.**
Benzol, report to labor and workforce development commissioner as to manufacture or use, **149:142E-149:142G.**
Bicycle accidents, reporting, **85:11B.**
Biennial count of voters, **53:38A.**
Binding of public records, **66:9.**
Birth records, **46:1 et seq.**
See BIRTHS.
Blasting operations, filing bond to cover risk of damages, **262:34.**
Blind persons.
See BLIND PERSONS.
Board of higher education, **15A:33.**
Boats.
See MOTORBOATS.
Bond paper sized with animal glue or gelatin to be used for public records, **66:3.**
Boston harbor, **91:3.**
Port of Boston commission, **91A:1.**
Boston terminal corporation.
See BOSTON TERMINAL CORPORATION.

RECORDS, REPORTS, AND RETURNS —Cont'd

Bottler deposit transaction fund, reports, **94:323B.**
Boundaries, monuments, and markers.
Changes in markers, **1:5.**
Secretary of state, preservation of records concerning town lines, **42:10.**
Boxing and boxing matches.
Commission's report to general court, **147:46.**
Number of tickets sold, **147:40.**
Boxing Commission, records of proceedings, **22:12.**
Bradford Durfee College of Technology, financial reports, **74:42H, 74:42I, 74:42K.**
Budgets.
City budget, time for submission, **44:32.**
State finance.
See STATE FINANCE.
University of Massachusetts, **75:14.**
Building Code Appeals Board, decisions and votes, **143:100.**
Building construction.
See CONSTRUCTION CONTRACTS AND WORK.
Bulk milk tanks, inspection and calibration, **98:46A.**
Bulletins of legislative committee hearings, **5:12.**
Burials, **114:47.**
Bodies brought into state, **114:46.**
Burn injuries.
Public safety commissioner, reporting of treatment of burns, **112:12A.**
Business improvement districts, annual audit, **40O:8.**
Business records, evidence, **233:77 et seq.**
See EVIDENCE.
Business trusts.
See BUSINESS TRUSTS.
Cable television.
See COMMUNITY ANTENNA TELEVISION SYSTEMS.
Campaign expenditures and contributions, **55:18-55:31.**
See CAMPAIGN EXPENDITURES AND CONTRIBUTIONS.
Cancer.
See CANCER.
Capital cases, reports to Attorney General, **12:11.**

RECORDS, REPORTS, AND RETURNS —Cont'd

Capital facility progress report, submission, **7:40D.**
Capital repair and maintenance projects completed, in process, or scheduled, **7:40D.**
Carbon paper for public records, forbidden, **66:4.**
Carbon tetrachloride, report to labor and workforce development commissioner as to manufacture or use, **149:142E-149:142G.**
Carriers.
See CARRIERS.
Case books, publication and distribution, **5:8.**
Catholic charity, information as to public assistance may be disclosed, **66:17A.**
Cats or dogs, motor vehicle killing or injuring, **272:80H.**
Caucuses.
Direct nominations, records of caucuses at which made, **53:80.**
Official ballots, results in caucuses using, **53:110.**
Cemeteries.
See CEMETERIES.
Centers of Excellence, **40J:12.**
Central register for missing children, **22A:1-22A:7.**
See CENTRAL REGISTER FOR MISSING CHILDREN.
Cerebral palsy case reports as public records, **111:111A.**
Certified copies.
See CERTIFIED COPIES.
Certified public accountants.
See ACCOUNTANTS.
Change of name.
See CHANGE OF NAME.
Charities and charitable contributions, **12:8F, 12:8L, 12:8M, 180:11C.**
See CHARITIES AND CHARITABLE CONTRIBUTIONS.
Charter cities.
See CITY CHARTERS.
Check cashers, licensing of, **169A:10, 169A:11.**
Checks and money orders, **167F:4.**
Children.
See CHILDREN AND MINORS.
Chiropractors, records of board of registration, **112:90.**
Churches.
See RELIGION AND RELIGIOUS SOCIETIES.

RECORDS, REPORTS, AND RETURNS —Cont'd

Cigarette tax.
See CIGARETTE TAX.

Cities and towns, **40:48-40:51.**
See CITIES AND TOWNS.

City and town accountants.
See CITY AND TOWN ACCOUNTANTS.

Civil engineers, reports, **253:45.**

Civil rights.
See CIVIL RIGHTS AND DISCRIMINATION.

Civil service.
See CIVIL SERVICE.

Clerks of cities.
See CITY AND TOWN CLERKS.

Clerks of court.
See CLERKS OF COURT.

Closing out or liquidation sales, regulation, **93:28A.**

Coal mining regulation.
See COAL MINING REGULATION AND RECLAMATION.

Collateral security loans, record books, **140:86-140:89.**

Collection agencies and agents.
Bonds, records concerning, **93:27.**
Investigation of licensee's records, **93:24C.**

Collectors of taxes, **60:6-60:12.**
See TAX COLLECTORS.

Colleges.
See COLLEGES AND UNIVERSITIES.

Commerce.
See ECONOMIC DEVELOPMENT DEPARTMENT.

Commercial code, unauthorized or erroneously executed payment orders, **106:4A:204, 106:4A-304.**

Commercial fertilizer data, **128:80.**

Commercial motor vehicle division, duties of director, **25:12F.**

Commercial shooting preserves, holder of permit, **131:31.**

Commissioner of asset management and maintenance.
Establishment of rules and regulations for acquisition, utilization, and disposition of real property, **7:40L.**
Report, submission of, **29:7J.**

Commissioner of executive offices, right of access to records, books of state agencies, **7:4E.**

RECORDS, REPORTS, AND RETURNS —Cont'd

Commissioner of insurance, reports of, **175:4.**
See INSURANCE COMMISSIONER.

Commission on Judicial Conduct, report, **211C:4.**

Commission plan cities, **43:77.**

Common victualler's licenses, **140:2.**

Commonwealth.
See STATE AND STATE DEPARTMENTS.

Community antenna television systems.
See COMMUNITY ANTENNA TELEVISION SYSTEMS.

Community corrections office, **211F:5.**

Community economic development assistance corporation secretary to keep record of proceedings, **40H:3.**

Community preservation committees, **44B:13.**

Compass variations, **97:2.**

Compelling delivery of record to public officer, **66:13.**

Completing incomplete public records, **66:9.**

Compressed air tanks, inspections by insurance companies, **146:38.**

Comptroller of state.
See COMPTROLLER OF STATE.

Compulsory automobile insurance.
See AUTOMOBILE INSURANCE.

Concealment of records of Commonwealth or political subdivision, **231:94C, 266:145.**

Condition of premises, statements furnished by lessor, **186:15B.**

Condominiums.
See CONDOMINIUMS.

Conference report.
See PRETRIAL PROCEEDINGS.

Confidentiality.
Addresses and phone numbers of public safety employees, **66:10.**
Patients' records, **19:16.**

Confirmation of land title without registration, decree, **185:1.**

Conflict of interest law, record of opinion as to violation, **268A:22.**

RECORDS, REPORTS, AND RETURNS —Cont'd

Congress of United States.
Each house as judge of returns of own members, **US Const Art 1 Sec 5 cl 1.**
Election records, **54:140.**
Proof of public records in other state, power to prescribe manner and effect of, **US Const Art 4 Sec 1.**

Conservation.
See CONSERVATION.

Conservation board, **30:42, 66:8.**
See RECORDS CONSERVATION BOARD.

Constables, report of process fees received, **262:8A.**

Constitution of Massachusetts.
See CONSTITUTION OF MASSACHUSETTS.

Construction contracts.
See CONSTRUCTION CONTRACTS AND WORK.

Consumers.
See CONSUMERS AND CONSUMER PROTECTION.

Contagious and infectious diseases, **111:7, 111:113.**
See CONTAGIOUS AND INFECTIOUS DISEASES.

Contracting opportunities and proposed transactions, report by public agencies or authorities and political subdivisions, **9:20A.**

Contractors for public buildings, statements required, **30:39R.**

Controlled substances.
See DRUGS AND NARCOTICS.

Conversion of federal savings and loan association or federal savings bank to state-chartered savings bank, filing copies of minutes of meeting to vote, **168:38.**

Conveyances, records of.
Deeds and conveyances, **36:1 et seq., 183:4.**
See REGISTERS AND REGISTRIES OF DEEDS.

Conviction of crime.
See CONVICTION OF CRIME.

Cooperative banks.
See COOPERATIVE BANKS.

Co-operative corporations, filing fees, **157:7, 157:9, 157:18.**

Coordinator of flexible hours, reports, **7:6F.**

Copies of public records, **9:11, 66:9-66:11, 233:79E.**

RECORDS, REPORTS, AND RETURNS —Cont'd

Copper wire scrap purchasers, records required, **266:142.**

Corporations.
See CORPORATIONS.

Corporation taxes.
See CORPORATION TAXES.

Correctional institutions.
See CORRECTIONAL INSTITUTIONS.

Corrections department.
See CORRECTIONS DEPARTMENT.

Counsel.
See ATTORNEYS AT LAW.

Counterfeiting of records, **267:1, 267:3, 267:5.**

Counties.
See COUNTIES.

County commissioners.
See COUNTY COMMISSIONERS.

County finance.
See COUNTY FINANCE.

County officers.
See COUNTY OFFICERS AND EMPLOYEES.

County prisons.
See COUNTY PRISONS.

County treasurers.
See COUNTY TREASURERS.

Courts.
See COURTS.

Credit bureaus.
See CREDIT BUREAUS.

Creditor under later attachment, request for recording, **236:31.**

Credit reports, disclosure of data to subject, **93:49A.**

Credit unions.
See CREDIT UNIONS.

Crimes and offenses.
Court records, sealing, **276:100C.**
Criminal offender record information system, **6:167 et seq.**
See CRIMINAL OFFENDER RECORD INFORMATION SYSTEM.
Criminal procedure.
See CRIMINAL PROCEDURE.
Failure to report, **268:40.**
False report, **269:13A.**
Files, access to by militia, **6:172.**
Leased or rented motor vehicle, theft, **266:87A.**

Criminal history systems board, reporting requirements, **6:168C.**

RECORDS, REPORTS, AND RETURNS —Cont'd

Criminal justice committee, reports, **6:156, 6:156B.**

Criminal offender record information system, **6:167 et seq.**
See CRIMINAL OFFENDER RECORD INFORMATION SYSTEM.

Criminal procedure.
See CRIMINAL PROCEDURE.

Crop mortgages, **255:7D.**

Curtesy.
Dower and curtesy, **189:6.**

Custodian of property, detaining person for concealment of record, **231:94C, 266:145.**

Custody of children as affecting right of access, **208:31.**

Custody of public records, **66:17.**
Ancient records, **66:7.**
Board or commission records, **66:6.**
City or town records, **40:48, 66:6, 66:7, 66:17.**
Clerks of court, duty regarding custody of records, books and papers, **221:14.**
Commonwealth records, **66:7.**
County records, **66:6, 66:7, 66:17.**
Maps, **34:2.**
Delivery to custodian, **66:13.**
Departmental records, **66:6.**
Designation of custodians of papers and records, **221:27A.**
Education and health records, **208:31.**
General court journals and files, **3:22.**
Penalties for violations, **66:15, 66:17.**
Person entitled to, to demand, **66:13.**
Public office records, **66:6.**
Reproductions of documents held in custodial capacity, admissibility in evidence, **233:79E.**
Wire or oral communications, custody of papers and recordings made pursuant to authorizing interception, **272:99.**
Worn books, **66:9.**

Daily log to be kept by police, **41:98F.**

Dairy farms, inspection reports, **94:16C.**

RECORDS, REPORTS, AND RETURNS —Cont'd

Dams and reservoirs, records and reports regarding, **253:45.**

Dangerous buildings and structures.
Examining board, **143:8.**
Unsafe conditions, **143:6.**

Dangerous diseases, reports of, **111:7, 111:113.**
See CONTAGIOUS AND INFECTIOUS DISEASES.

Day care.
Pesticides.
Records of applications, **132B:6I.**

Dead bodies brought into state, record, **114:46.**

Dealers, records of.
See GASOLINE AND MOTOR FUELS.

Death records.
See DEATH.

Debt, recognizance, **256:2.**

Deceit.
See FRAUD AND DECEIT.

Declaration of estimated income tax, **62B:13.**

Decrees.
See JUDGMENTS, ORDERS, AND DECREES.

Deeds and conveyances, **36:1 et seq., 183:4.**
See REGISTERS AND REGISTRIES OF DEEDS.

Defacing public records, penalty, **66:15.**

Default in recognizance, **276:36, 276:71.**

Definition of terms, **4:7, 6:172, 66:3.**

Delivery.
Charges on delivery, **5:17.**
Compelling delivery to public officer, **66:10, 66:13.**
Injunctions, compelling delivery, **66:13.**
Presumptions, **183:5.**

Dental examiners, board, **112:43.**

Dental service corporations, books and records of, **176E:2, 176E:7-176E:9.**
See DENTAL SERVICE CORPORATIONS.

Dentistry board of registration, liability of persons making reports or furnishing information, **112:52G.**

Dentists.
See DENTISTS.

Dependent children, aid to, reports of department of transitional assistance, **118:5.**

271

RECORDS, REPORTS, AND RETURNS —Cont'd

Deposit insurance fund.
Member banks, **168 Appx (1934):18.**
Depositions, testimony taken by recording device, **233:30.**
Depositors insurance fund.
Savings bank investment fund.
Financial report, **168 Appx (1945):9.**
Semi-annual report, **168 Appx (1932):8.**
Deposits.
See DEPOSITS AND DEPOSITORIES.
Deputy sheriffs to account for fees received for service of civil process, **262:8A.**
Designer selection board, records and reports, **7:38L, 7:38M.**
Designers of public construction projects, recommendations, **7:38A½.**
Destruction of records and papers.
Disposal of records. See within this heading, "Disposal of records."
Lost or destroyed records.
See LOST OR DESTROYED INSTRUMENTS.
Disabled and handicapped persons.
Annual reports.
See ANNUAL REPORTS OR STATEMENTS.
Blind persons.
See BLIND PERSONS.
Disabled persons protection commission.
See DISABLED PERSONS PROTECTION COMMISSION.
Employment of people with disabilities, annual report of commission, **6:107.**
Massachusetts office on disability, annual report to governor, **6:187.**
Printing and distribution of proceedings of Disabled American Veterans of the World War, **5:9.**
Protection commission.
See DISABLED PERSONS PROTECTION COMMISSION.
Disclaimer.
See DISCLAIMER.
Disclosure.
See DISCOVERY AND DISCLOSURE.

RECORDS, REPORTS, AND RETURNS —Cont'd

Discrimination.
See CIVIL RIGHTS AND DISCRIMINATION.
Dispensaries or clinics, **111:70.**
See DISPENSARIES OR CLINICS.
Dispensary staff privileges, report of termination, **111:53B.**
Disposal of records.
City clerks, destruction of certain records, **66:8A.**
Conservation board, **30:42.**
Criminal complaints, **218:35.**
Exception to requirements of preservation, books which supervisor of public records determines may be destroyed, **66:8.**
Fish and game director, **131:4.**
Hospital and clinic records, **111:70.**
Marine fisheries division, destruction of records by director, **130:17.**
Notice as to destruction of obsolete and useless papers and records, **30:42, 221:27A.**
Penalty for destroying public records, **66:15.**
Public assistance records, **66:17A.**
Public records, **30:42, 66:15.**
Register of deeds, destruction, **66:8.**
Registry or record, books of, exception to requirement of preservation, **66:8.**
Secretary of state, destruction or sale of records, **9:19.**
Subversive organizations, destruction of books, **264:21.**
Supervisor of public records, approval, **66:8.**
Time requirements regarding destruction of obsolete papers and records, **221:27A.**
Dissolution of injunction against municipal treasurers, certificate, **41:43A.**
Distribution, **5:7, 5:8.**
District.
See DISTRICT AND PROSECUTING ATTORNEYS.
District courts.
See DISTRICT COURTS.
Districts.
See DISTRICTS.

RECORDS, REPORTS, AND RETURNS —Cont'd

Divorce statistics and records, **111:2, 208:46.**
DNA database, **22E:9 to 22E:15.**
Dog bites, reports, **112:5F.**
Dog officers, records to be maintained, **140:151A.**
Dog racing meetings.
Horse and dog racing meetings. See within this heading, "Horse and dog racing meetings."
Domicile of decedent, determination of arbitration board, **65B:4.**
Dormant bank accounts, prohibition of service charges, **200A:15C.**
Dower and curtesy, dower barred after ten years from recording of conveyance, **189:6.**
Drafts of legislation accompanying annual reports, **30:33.**
Drains.
See SEWERS AND DRAINS.
Dredging and reclamation of land, liens, **254:30.**
Drinking water supply facilities certification board to keep records, **13:66B.**
Driving while under influence of alcohol.
See DRIVING WHILE UNDER INFLUENCE OF ALCOHOL OR DRUGS.
Drug addiction rehabilitation.
See DRUG ADDICTION REHABILITATION.
Druggists and pharmacists.
Board of registration, reports, **13:25, 112:25.**
Public health department, reports, **111:72G.**
Drugs and narcotics, **94C:15.**
See DRUGS AND NARCOTICS.
Drunkards.
See ALCOHOLISM AND INTOXICATION.
Drunken driving.
See DRIVING WHILE UNDER INFLUENCE OF ALCOHOL OR DRUGS.
Duces tecum subpoena.
See PRODUCTION OF BOOKS AND PAPERS.
Dwellings unfit for human habitation, report of inspection, **239:8A.**
Easements.
Abandonment of easement by city or town, **40:15.**

RECORDS, REPORTS, AND RETURNS —Cont'd

Easements —Cont'd

Land titles, indefinite references in recorded instruments, **184:25.**

Eavesdropping and wiretapping.

Annual reports to general court of interceptions of oral and wire communications, **272:99.**

Custody of papers and recordings made pursuant to authorization for interception, **272:99.**

Returns on warrants authorizing interception of communications, **272:99.**

Economic diversification program, **23F:6, 23F:8.**

Economic stabilization trust, **23D:14.**

Education department.

See EDUCATION DEPARTMENT.

Elder affairs department, annual report, **19A:12.**

Election offenses.

See ELECTION OFFENSES.

Elections, **54:110 et seq.**

See ELECTIONS.

Electric company.

See GAS AND ELECTRIC COMPANIES.

Electricians, state examiners, **141:2, 141:3.**

Electric railroads.

Estimate of cost of construction, **162:7.**

Maps and profiles, **162:7-162:9.**

Electrologist, license, **112:87HHH.**

Electronic recording devices.

See ELECTRONIC RECORDING DEVICES AND EQUIPMENT.

Elevators.

See ELEVATORS.

Embalmers and funeral directors, **46:11.**

Board of registration, **112:85.**

Burials, duty as to records, **114:46, 114:47.**

Physician to give death certificate, **46:9, 46:11.**

Emergency medical care advisory board, reports, **111C:7.**

Emergency medical technician's report regarding refusal to allow parent to accompany sick child in emergency vehicle, **111C:10A.**

RECORDS, REPORTS, AND RETURNS —Cont'd

Eminent domain.

See EMINENT DOMAIN.

Employee assistance program, report of coordinator, **7:28B.**

Employment.

See LABOR AND WORKFORCE DEVELOPMENT.

Employment agencies.

See EMPLOYMENT AGENCIES AND BUREAUS.

Employment security, **151A:38, 151A:44-151A:46.**

See EMPLOYMENT SECURITY.

Energy facilities siting.

See ENERGY FACILITIES SITING.

Energy resources executive office, **25A:2, 25A:5-25A:7, 25A:12.**

Engineers, project reports, **7:42J.**

Entries in books and records as evidence, **233:77 et seq.**

See EVIDENCE.

Entry books.

Fees of clerks of courts for entering actions or suits, **262:2, 262:4, 262:4A.**

Forgery, **267:1.**

Entry into land.

See ENTRY INTO LAND AND PREMISES.

Entry, writs.

Execution for possession, **237:42.**

Memorandum relating to writ or other proceeding affecting title to land, **184:15.**

Environmental affairs executive office.

See ENVIRONMENTAL AFFAIRS EXECUTIVE OFFICE.

Environmental impact reports, **30:62, 30:62A et seq.**

See ENVIRONMENTAL IMPACT REPORTS.

Environmental management department.

See ENVIRONMENTAL MANAGEMENT DEPARTMENT.

Environmental protection department.

See ENVIRONMENTAL PROTECTION DEPARTMENT.

Environment, attorney general to maintain records of complaints relating to damage, **12:11D.**

RECORDS, REPORTS, AND RETURNS —Cont'd

Equalized valuations for cities and towns, furnishing of information for determining, **58:10.**

Equine infectious anemia, **129:44A.**

Equipment dealers, examination of records to verify repurchase, **93G:4.**

Erasures, notation, **36:15.**

Estate taxes, returns for, **62C:17, 65C:8.**

See ESTATE TAXES.

Ethics Commission, **268B:3.**

See ETHICS COMMISSION OF STATE.

Evidence.

See EVIDENCE.

Examination, inspection.

See EXAMINATION, INSPECTION, OR INVESTIGATION.

Excise tax on deeds, instruments, and writings, Commonwealth as exempt **64D:1.**

Executions, return of, **235:23, 236:21-236:23.**

See EXECUTIONS.

Ex parte hearings, evidence not to be part of official court record, **208:11.**

Explosions.

See EXPLOSIONS AND EXPLOSIVES.

Express companies.

See EXPRESS COMPANIES.

Extension of mortgages, **36:20, 36:21.**

Extradition.

See EXTRADITION.

Fair educational practices proceedings, reports, **151C:3.**

Fair employment practices, **149:24D, 151:15, 151B:4, 151B:6.**

Fair wage records, place of keeping, **151:15.**

False arrest or imprisonment, **231:94C.**

False crime report, penalty for filing, **269:13A.**

False records, reports.

See FRAUD AND DECEIT.

Family abuse prevention, **209A:1 et seq.**

Farmers' clubs, reports to agriculture commissioner, **128:47.**

Federal aid or funds.

Comptroller's report of federal grants, **7A:4.**

RECORDS, REPORTS, AND RETURNS —Cont'd

Federal aid or funds —Cont'd

Public assistance by federal government, records, **66:17A.**

State agencies, **29:2C.**

Federal documentary stamps, notation, **36:15.**

Federal requirements for records regarding race, color or national origin, employers to observe, **151B:4.**

Federal succession tax receipts, **36:16.**

Federal tax lien notices, **36:24.**

Fees, **262:34.**

Fences and fence viewers.

Fence shares, assignment, **49:6.**

Partition fence, assignment of fees by fence viewers on determination of dispute, **262:34.**

Fertilizers, reports on analysis, **128:58.**

Fetal death.

See FETAL DEATH.

Fictitious business names, **110:5.**

Filing.

Financial statement or condition, filing of. See within this heading, "Financial statement or condition, filing."

Financial disclosure by public officers.

See FINANCIAL DISCLOSURE BY PUBLIC OFFICERS AND EMPLOYEES.

Financial statement or condition, filing.

Elder affairs department, **19A:30.**

Governmental units pooled insurance, **40M:10.**

Railroads, exemption of foreign corporations from requirement of annual filing of statement, **181:12.**

Securities act, filing by registered broker-dealer, **110A:203.**

Financing of judicial system, records as property of Commonwealth for purpose, **29A:2.**

Fines and penalties.

Alteration, removal or destruction of public records, penalty, **66:15.**

Bullet wounds, failure to report, **112:12A.**

RECORDS, REPORTS, AND RETURNS —Cont'd

Fines and penalties —Cont'd

Clerk of court, penalty for failure to report criminal cases, **124:8.**

Consultant services to Commonwealth, filing of statement, **7A:5.**

Copying records or other services, charging fee, **30:43.**

Crime report.

Failure to report crime, **268:40.**

False report, **269:13A.**

Dry cleaners, violations as to filing identification markings, **93:18A.**

Energy resources department, reporting requirements, **25A:7.**

Fees for service, false statement in endorsement on writ of process, **262:19.**

Governmental departments, false reports, **268:6.**

Legislative research bureau, turning over by committees of records and reports, **3:60.**

Petroleum fuel reporting act, penalties for violation, **94:295BB.**

Physician failing to comply with reporting requirement, claim or actions for damages, **112:5E.**

Public officers, violations of duties as to public records, **66:15.**

Quarterly returns of jailer and superintendent of house of correction as to fines collected, **280:15.**

Raffles and bazaars, false information on application or report concerning, **271:7A.**

Retail installment sales, fines for failure to file, **255B:3.**

Sales finance companies, penalty for failure to make report, **255D:3.**

Scrap copper wire purchasers, failure to keep records, **266:142.**

Service of process, false statements regarding, **268:6B.**

State library, reports deposited, **6:39A.**

Tax return, penalty for late filing, **62C:34.**

RECORDS, REPORTS, AND RETURNS —Cont'd

Fines and penalties —Cont'd

Tax stamps, penalty for failure to affix prior to leaving instrument for recording, **64D:6A.**

Venereal disease records, disclosing information, **111:119.**

Wage reporting system.

See WAGE REPORTING SYSTEM.

Firearms.

See FIREARMS AND WEAPONS.

Fire department chiefs, reports, **48:42.**

Fire insurance investigation of fire losses, duty of insurance company to provide records, **148:32.**

Fire marshals.

See FIRE MARSHALS.

Fireproof vaults for public records, **66:11, 66:12.**

Fires.

See FIRES AND FIRE PREVENTION.

Fire training council, annual reports, **6:164.**

Fireworks.

See FIREWORKS.

Fish.

See FISH AND GAME.

Flags, records, **8:17A.**

Flats, recording of report and plan establishing boundaries, **240:20, 240:21.**

Flexible hours coordinator, report, **7:6F.**

Foreign banks.

See BANKS AND BANKING.

Foreign corporations.

See FOREIGN CORPORATIONS.

Foreign fiduciaries, filing copies of appointment and official bond, **199A:5.**

Foreign insurance companies.

See FOREIGN INSURANCE COMPANIES.

Foreign states.

See FOREIGN STATES OR COUNTRIES.

Foreign utilities belonging to New England Power Pool, reports, **164A:10.**

Foreign wills, **192:10.**

Foresters and forest wardens.

Division, reports, **48:28.**

Fires, report, **48:28.**

RECORDS, REPORTS, AND RETURNS —Cont'd

Foresters and forest wardens —Cont'd

Right of way granted, **132:34A.**

State forester, **48:25, 132:4.**

Forests.

See FORESTS AND FORESTRY.

Forgery of records, **267:1, 267:3, 267:5.**

Fraternal benefit societies.

See FRATERNAL BENEFIT SOCIETIES.

Fraud reports of public officers, **268:6A.**

Fraudulent claims board, reports to and, **26:8B.**

Fuel.

See FUEL.

Full faith and credit to be given official records, **US Const Art 4 Sec 1.**

Funeral directors.

Embalmers and funeral directors. See within this heading, "Embalmers and funeral directors."

Furnaces, licenses, **140:115.**

Garbage.

See GARBAGE AND RUBBISH.

Gas.

See GAS AND ELECTRIC COMPANIES.

Gas fitters.

Plumbers and gas fitters, **142:15.**

Gasoline and motor fuel taxes, **64A:3, 64E:3.**

See GASOLINE AND MOTOR FUEL TAXES.

Gateway roads programs, improvement reports, **90H:3.**

General court.

See GENERAL COURT.

Governmental units pooled insurance, **40M:4, 40M:10.**

Governor.

See GOVERNOR.

Governor's cabinet, secretaries of executive offices to have access to reports, **6:163, 6A:5.**

Governor's council.

See GOVERNOR'S COUNCIL.

Grade crossings, expenses of abolition, **159:78.**

Grand Army of the Republic, printing and distribution of proceedings, **5:9.**

Grand jury.

See GRAND JURY.

RECORDS, REPORTS, AND RETURNS —Cont'd

Group insurance.

Municipal employees, group insurance, **32B:3.**

State employees, group insurance for, annual report of commission, **32A:9A.**

Guardian appointed for mentally ill person, **201:6.**

Gulls or terns, prevention of defilement of waters, **111:174A.**

Gunshot wounds, **112:12.**

Handicapped.

Disabled and handicapped. See within this heading, "Disabled and handicapped persons."

Handwriting, public records, **66:3.**

Harbor masters, reports, **102:27.**

Harbors.

See PORTS AND HARBORS.

Hazardous materials mitigation. Confidential records, **21K:9.**

Hazardous waste insolvency fund, **21C:25-21C:27.**

Examination of licensee's books and records, **21O:25.**

Hazardous waste management.

See HAZARDOUS WASTE MANAGEMENT.

Hazardous waste site cleanup professionals, inspection of records by, **21A:19E.**

Hazards.

See HAZARDS AND HAZARDOUS OR TOXIC SUBSTANCES.

Health.

See HEALTH AND HEALTH DEPARTMENTS.

Health and welfare commission, **6:127, 6:128.**

Health care facilities.

See HOSPITALS AND HEALTH CARE FACILITIES.

Health care finance and policy division.

See HEALTH CARE FINANCE AND POLICY DIVISION.

Health care security trust.

Board of trustees, **29D:4.**

Transactions, **29D:2.**

Health code.

Sanitary code. See within this heading, "Sanitary codes."

Hearing aid sellers, records, **93:74.**

Herd register, obtaining by false pretense, **266:93.**

RECORDS, REPORTS, AND RETURNS —Cont'd

Higher education assistance corporation.

See HIGHER EDUCATION ASSISTANCE CORPORATION.

Highways.

See HIGHWAYS AND STREETS.

Historic districts.

See HISTORIC DISTRICTS AND SITES.

Home improvement contractors, **142A:13.**

Homesteads.

Declaration of homestead, **188:2.**

Occupancy by spouse or minor children, order, **188:3.**

Release of recording, **188:7.**

Horse and dog racing meetings.

Annual report, horse racing authority, **128A:25.**

Criminal offender records, access by Commission, **128A:9A.**

License for holding of meeting, recording, **128A:3.**

State secretary receiving reports of results of elections, **128A:14D.**

Wagers at meetings, records, **128A:6.**

Hospitals.

See HOSPITALS AND HEALTH CARE FACILITIES.

Hospital school, reports in connection, **111:62N.**

Hospital service corporations.

See HOSPITAL SERVICE CORPORATIONS.

Hotels, motels, and roominghouses.

Conviction of innholder, record to be sent to specified authorities regarding, **140:32, 140:183C.**

License of innholder, **140:2.**

Hot water heating boilers, inspection reports, **146:77.**

Hours of labor or services.

Employers, **151:15.**

Industrial safety division may inspect records, **149:17.**

Public works, record of hours worked by employees, **149:27B.**

Housing accommodations, prohibited practices as to discrimination in connection, **151B:4.**

Housing and community development department, **23B:3-23B:6.**

RECORDS, REPORTS, AND RETURNS —Cont'd

Housing court department, **185C:14, 185C:18, 185C:21.**

Housing Court of Hampden County, **231:111.**

Human resources division records, **7:30.**

Hunting and fishing licenses issued, **131:18.**

Husband and wife.

Antenuptial marriage contract affecting property, **209:26.**

Conveyances between, **209:3.**

Dower and curtesy, **189:6.**

Fee for filing entry of petition for authority to convey land, **262:40.**

Final orders or decrees in proceedings involving spouse under disability, **209:24.**

Identification measurements of prisoners, **127:23-127:30.**

Illegible signatures, printing name in case, **36:18A.**

Illegitimate children, written authorization of mother regarding transfer of birth records, **46:12.**

Impeachment of witnesses.

See WITNESSES.

"In books," defined for statutory construction purposes, **4:7.**

Incinerators, keeping records, **92:9A.**

Income tax, **62C:4-62C:20.**

See INCOME TAX.

Indexes.

See INDEXES.

Indian affairs commission, annual report of, **6A:8A.**

Indistinct records, rerecording, **36:17.**

Industrial accidents division.

See WORKERS' COMPENSATION.

Industrial development revenue bonds, recording of trust agreement, **40D:14.**

Industrial service programs.

See INDUSTRIAL SERVICE PROGRAMS.

Infectious diseases, **111:7, 111:113.**

See CONTAGIOUS AND INFECTIOUS DISEASES.

Infirmaries.

Admission, records, **47:8.**

Destruction of records, **111:70.**

Inflammable fluids and compounds, certificates and licenses, **148:13.**

RECORDS, REPORTS, AND RETURNS —Cont'd

Information to be recorded in public records, **66:5A.**

Initiative and referendum.

Arguments filed with secretary of state, **54:54.**

Constitution of Massachusetts, **MA Const Amend Art 48 Init Part 2 Sec 3; Amend Art 48 Ref Part 3 Sec 3.**

Time, **53:22A.**

Injunctions.

Compelling delivery of records, **66:13.**

Municipal treasurers, certificate for dissolution of injunction against, **41:43A.**

Nuisances, injunction against, **139:16A.**

Ink, standard and use, **66:4.**

Inland wetlands, recordings of orders and other instruments affecting, **131:40A.**

Inquests, **38:11, 38:12.**

Insolvency.

See INSOLVENCY AND BANKRUPTCY.

Inspection.

See EXAMINATION, INSPECTION, OR INVESTIGATION.

Inspector general.

See INSPECTOR GENERAL.

Institutional abuse or neglect, **28A:10, 119:51B.**

Insurance.

See INSURANCE.

Insurance rates.

See INSURANCE RATES AND RATING ORGANIZATIONS.

Intelligence test scores, purging students' records, **71:87.**

Intensive care unit for mentally ill women, **123:36.**

Inmate deaths, reports to district attorney, **123:28.**

Interceptions of oral and wire communications.

Eavesdropping and wiretapping, **272:99.**

Interlineations, notation, **36:15.**

Interrogatories, **231:61, 231:63.**

Interstate co-operation commission, reports, **9:24.**

Inventory.

See INVENTORY.

Investment securities under commercial code.

See INVESTMENT SECURITIES UNDER COMMERCIAL CODE.

RECORDS, REPORTS, AND RETURNS —Cont'd

Italian American War Veterans of United States, printing and distribution of proceedings, **5:9.**

Jewish kosher food, labeling, **94:156.**

Jewish philanthropy, information as to public assistance may be disclosed, **66:17A.**

Jewish War Veterans of the United States, printing and distribution of proceedings, **5:9.**

Joint committee on banks and banking, report of proposed changes in consumer transactions regulations, **167:2A.**

Joint committee on energy, regarding regulations of Energy Resources Executive Office, **25A:12.**

Journals of general court, printing and distribution, **5:10.**

Judgments.

See JUDGMENTS, ORDERS, AND DECREES.

Judicial conduct commission's report, **211C:4.**

Judicial council, annual report, **221:34B.**

Jury commissioner, office, **234A:72.**

Jury trial, waiver, **263:6.**

Juvenile behavior, reports of state council, **6:161.**

Juvenile courts.

See JUVENILE COURTS AND DELINQUENT CHILDREN.

Kosher food, labeling, **94:156.**

Labor.

See LABOR AND WORKFORCE DEVELOPMENT.

Labor relations.

See LABOR RELATIONS AND DISPUTES.

Labor relations commission.

See LABOR RELATIONS COMMISSION.

Land court.

See LAND COURT.

Landing places, plan and description, **88:14.**

Landlord.

See LANDLORD AND TENANT.

Landscape architects' reports, use of seal, **112:100.**

Land title registration, **185:56, 185:63.**

See REGISTRATION OF LAND TITLES.

RECORDS, REPORTS, AND RETURNS —Cont'd

Larceny of public records, **266:30.**

Law reports, decisions of Supreme Judicial Court, **5:14, 5:15, 221:63-221:68.**

Lead poisoning.
See LEAD POISONING.

Leases for registered lands, registration in lieu of recording, **185:71.**

Legacy.
See LEGACY AND SUCCESSION TAXES.

Legislative agents, late filing of itemized statement of expenditures, penalty, **3:43, 3:44, 3:47.**

Legislative and constitutional officers' compensation advisory board, report, **6:162.**

Legislative documents to be mailed to subscribers, **5:13.**

Legislative post audit and oversight bureau, report of state auditor and legislative auditor, **3:63.**

Legislative research bureau.
See GENERAL COURT.

Lessor to furnish statements as to condition of premises, **186:15B.**

Libraries.
See LIBRARIES AND LIBRARIANS.

Licensing examination as public record, **4:7.**

Liens.
See LIENS AND ENCUMBRANCES.

Lieutenant governor, **54:112.**

Life estates, remainders, and reversions.
Conveyance of life estate, **183:4.**

Life insurance.
See LIFE INSURANCE.

Limitation of actions.
See LIMITATION OF ACTIONS.

Limitation upon application of laws as to public records, **66:18.**

Limited liability companies.
See LIMITED LIABILITY COMPANIES.

Limited partnerships.
See LIMITED PARTNERSHIPS.

Lis pendens, **184:15.**

Livestock disease control director's activities, **129:38.**

Loans.
Collateral security loans, **140:86-140:89.**

RECORDS, REPORTS, AND RETURNS —Cont'd

Loans —Cont'd
Failure to make reports, **255D:3.**
Pawnbrokers.
See PAWNBROKERS.
Small loans. See within this heading, "Small loans."

Lobbying.
See LOBBYING.

Local health boards, reports, **111:28, 111:29.**

Local property assessment, records, **58:1, 58:4-58:4B.**

Location.
Place. See within this heading, "Place."

Lockup facilities.
Cell checks, **40:36B.**
Suicide or self-injury by detainee, **40:36A.**

Loose-leaf records as books, **4:7.**

Lost.
See LOST OR DESTROYED INSTRUMENTS.

Lost property.
See ABANDONED, LOST, AND UNCLAIMED PROPERTY.

Lottery commission of state, reports, **10:24.**

Lowlands.
See LOWLANDS AND SWAMPS.

Low-level radioactive waste, **111H:7, 111H:16, 111H:44, 111H:47.**

Machine guns.
See MACHINE GUNS.

Magistrates, report of inquest, **38:8, 38:11, 38:12.**

Maine lands, custody of books relating, **9:12.**

Malicious mischief or injury, **66:15.**
Fraternal benefit societies, records, **176:1.**

Management engineering task force, reports, **6:163.**

Manner of recording instruments, **36:15.**

Manual of general court, preparation and distribution, **5:11.**

Maps.
See MAPS, PLATS, AND SURVEYS.

Marine Corps League, printing and distribution of proceedings, **5:9.**

Marine fish.
See MARINE FISH AND FISHERIES.

RECORDS, REPORTS, AND RETURNS —Cont'd

Marriage, records, **46:1, 207:39, 207:40.**
See MARRIAGE.

Massachusetts Centers of Excellence Corporation, powers, **40J:12.**

Massachusetts commission for deaf and hard of hearing, **6:199.**

Massachusetts Educational Financial Authority, recordkeeping requirements, **15C:5A, 15C:5B.**

Massachusetts industrial activity board, reports, **6:190.**

Massachusetts Technology Park Corporation, annual report, **40J:8.**

Massachusetts water management act, confidentiality of records, **21G:13.**

Mass transportation and services payments, powers of revenue commissioner as to determination, **58:25B.**

Master plan of municipal planning boards, **41:81D.**

Masters, reports, **221:61, 221:62.**

Materials used in public records, approval, **66:3.**

Meat or meat products contract of employer selling to state, records, **7:22.**

Mechanics' liens, **254:30.**
See MECHANICS' LIENS.

Medical care.
See MEDICAL CARE AND ASSISTANCE.

Medical examiners, **38:7.**
See MEDICAL EXAMINERS AND INQUESTS.

Medical institutions.
See HOSPITALS AND HEALTH CARE FACILITIES.

Medical malpractice insurance, **175A:5C, 175F:6.**

Medical peer review committee, **111:203, 111:204.**

Medical service corporations, **176B:8, 176C:9.**

Meetings, public, **30A:11A, 39:23C, 66:5A, 66:17C.**

Memoranda.
See MEMORANDA.

Mentally ill.
See MENTALLY ILL AND RETARDED PERSONS.

Merit rating plans for automobile insurance, use of records of registry of motor vehicles, **175:113B.**

RECORDS, REPORTS, AND RETURNS —Cont'd

Mesne process, date of execution as affecting time for deposit, **236:4.**

Metropolitan area planning council, duties, **40B:25.**

Metropolitan district commission. See METROPOLITAN DISTRICT COMMISSION.

Metropolitan districts.
Local assessments, **30:35A.**
State treasury, **10:11.**

Microphotography. See MICROPHOTOGRAPHY.

Militia. See MILITIA.

Milk. See MILK AND MILK PRODUCTS.

Mineral resources division, inspection of records, **21:54.**

Minimum wages. See MINIMUM WAGES.

Minority business assistance. See MINORITY BUSINESS ASSISTANCE.

Minors. See CHILDREN AND MINORS.

Mobile homes commission, reports, **6:108.**

Morris plan banks. See MORRIS PLAN BANKS.

Mortgage foreclosure. See MORTGAGE FORECLOSURE.

Mortgages. See MORTGAGES AND DEEDS OF TRUST.

Motels.
Hotels, motels, and roominghouses. See within this heading, "Hotels, motels, and roominghouses."

Moth superintendent's records and reports, **132:1A.**

Motorboats. See MOTORBOATS.

Motor carriers. See CARRIERS.

Motorcycle lessors, duties, **90:32H.**

Motor vehicles. See MOTOR VEHICLES.

Municipal courts, time for filing request for records and reports, **231:108.**

Municipal finance. See MUNICIPAL FINANCE.

Municipalities. See CITIES AND TOWNS.

Municipal lighting. See MUNICIPAL LIGHTING AND HEATING PLANTS.

RECORDS, REPORTS, AND RETURNS —Cont'd

Mutilated records, rerecording, **36:17.**

Mutual holding companies, **167H:8.**

Name.
Person transacting business, filing and renewal of certificates stating, **110:5.**
Rape victims, withholding names, **265:24C.**

Natural heritage program data base, records, **66:17D.**

Neglected children. See ABUSED AND NEGLECTED CHILDREN.

New Bedford Institute of Technology, financial reports, **74:42K.**

New evidence. See EVIDENCE.

New projects involving assessment of cities and towns in metropolitan districts, **30:35A.**

Nomination papers. See ELECTIONS.

Noncompliance with law, remedy in case, **39:23C.**

Northeast Interstate Dairy Compact, **Spec L 139:15.**

Nuisance, injunction against, **139:16A.**

Nurses. See NURSES AND NURSING SERVICES.

Nursing home administrator board of registration, duties, **112:114.**

Nursing homes, filing of statements as to ownership, **111:71.**

Oath. See OATH OR AFFIRMATION.

Obsolete or surplus records and papers, disposal of.
Disposal. See within this heading, "Disposal of records."

Office of child care services, **28A:4, 28A:8.**

Official correspondence as public record, **4:7.**

Official records, **66:1 et seq.**

Official textbooks, publication and distribution, **5:8.**

Oil and hazardous material release prevention and response act, administrative record established, **21E:5A.**

Optometric service corporations. See OPTOMETRIC SERVICE CORPORATIONS.

RECORDS, REPORTS, AND RETURNS —Cont'd

Optometrists. See OPTOMETRISTS AND OPTOMETRY.

Organization of departments, etc., **30:4.**

Organ transplant fund, annual report as to contributions, **62:6E.**

Other counties or districts, recording copy of instrument as to land, **36:13.**

Outdoor advertising board, reports, **16:14.**

Owners of real estate, tax assessors to maintain record of names and addresses, **184:8A.**

Paper, quality, **66:3.**

Pardon.
List of pardons, **127:152.**
Sealing of records after, **127:152.**
Warrant, **127:157.**

Park commissioners, annual reports, **45:9.**

Parole board, records of meetings and decisions, **6:172, 127:130.**

Partition, **241:16.**
Notice of proceedings, **241:7.**

Partnerships. See PARTNERSHIPS.

Passbooks. See BANKS AND BANKING.

Pawnbrokers. See PAWNBROKERS.

Payroll. See PAYROLL AND PAYROLL DEDUCTIONS.

Pedestrians violating rules, **90:18A.**

Penal institutions. See CORRECTIONAL INSTITUTIONS.

Penalties.
Fines and penalties. See within this heading, "Fines and penalties."

Pensions. See RETIREMENT SYSTEMS AND PENSIONS.

Perfusionists' board of registration. Record of proceedings, **112:219.**

Perjury prosecutions, detention of books necessary, **268:5.**

Permit for construction or alteration of dam, recording, **253:45.**

Personal injury or death, report, **131:60, 175:113J, 233:23A.**

RECORDS, REPORTS, AND RETURNS —Cont'd

Pharmacists.

Druggists and pharmacists. See within this heading, "Druggists and pharmacists."

Phonograph records, unauthorized reproduction and transfer, **266:143 et seq.**

Photostatic copies.

See PHOTOSTATIC COPIES.

Physical therapists.

See PHYSICAL THERAPISTS.

Physician assistants.

See PHYSICIAN ASSISTANTS.

Physician assistants, board to keep records relating, **112:9G, 112:9H.**

Physicians.

See PHYSICIANS AND SURGEONS.

Place, **36:12, 36:14.**

Explosives, false report as to location, **277:59A.**

Gas company, fee for recording order granting locations, **262:34.**

Planning boards.

See ZONING AND PLANNING.

Plans.

See PLANS AND SPECIFICATIONS.

Plats.

See MAPS, PLATS, AND SURVEYS.

Pleas and answers, action deemed at issue when plea filed, **231:39.**

Plumbers and gas fitters.

Building inspectors, proceedings, **142:15.**

Health boards, proceedings, **142:15.**

Podiatry and podiatrists.

Board of registration to keep records, **112:17A.**

Certificate, recording, **112:21, 262:34.**

Police.

See POLICE.

Polish-American Veterans of Massachusetts, printing and distribution of proceedings, **5:9.**

Political purposes, reports by treasurer of town or city to campaign and political finance office, **55:22A.**

Pollution liability reinsurance corporation, **175G:6.**

RECORDS, REPORTS, AND RETURNS —Cont'd

Pollution of waters.

See WATER POLLUTION.

Port authority, retirement systems, **32:20, 32:21.**

Portraits of members of general court, reports of sales of books containing, **5:18.**

Ports.

See PORTS AND HARBORS.

Postage on free copies, prepayment, **5:17.**

Powers of attorney.

See POWERS OF ATTORNEY.

Precept in criminal case, return to magistrate or court, **279:39.**

Preferred provider arrangements, **176I:5.**

Preliminary project impact reports.

See HAZARDOUS WASTE FACILITIES SITING.

Preservation of records, **30:42, 66:1, 66:8, 66:9.**

Gasoline and motor fuel taxes, preservation by licensees of records of purchases, sales and use of special fuels, **64E:3.**

Nomination papers and certificates, **53:16.**

Secretary of state, preservation of records concerning town lines, **42:10.**

State Ethics Commission to preserve statements and records filed, **268B:3.**

Presidential electors.

See PRESIDENTIAL ELECTORS.

Presidential primaries, canvass of returns, **53:70E, 53:70F.**

Presumptions.

See PRESUMPTIONS AND BURDEN OF PROOF.

Pretrial diversion of selected offenders.

Periodic progress reports, **276A:6.**

Program director's report and assessment, **276A:5.**

Primary elections, return of votes, **53:52, 53:64.**

See PRIMARY ELECTIONS.

Printing.

See STATE PRINTING.

Prior criminal prosecutions, inspection of record by defendant and counsel prior to sentence, **276:85.**

Prisons.

See CORRECTIONAL INSTITUTIONS.

RECORDS, REPORTS, AND RETURNS —Cont'd

Private pension associations, annual reporting date, **32:40.**

Privileged matters.

Confidentiality. See within this heading, "Confidentiality."

Probate.

Generally.

See PROBATE AND FAMILY COURT.

Registers of probate and insolvency.

See REGISTERS OF PROBATE AND INSOLVENCY.

Probate and insolvency judges.

Chief judge's requiring keeping of records, **217:8.**

Inspection, **217:11.**

Probation.

See PROBATION AND PAROLE.

Process.

See PROCESS AND SERVICE OF PROCESS AND PAPERS.

Procurement contracts, recordkeeping requirements, **30B:3.**

Production of books and papers, **231:68.**

See PRODUCTION OF BOOKS AND PAPERS.

Professional corporations, **156A:18.**

Program review boards of program affairs executive office, **21A:5.**

Proof of official records.

See EVIDENCE.

Property of state and public, public records, **30:42.**

Proprietors of wharves and real estate lying in common.

Copies, **66:5, 179:15, 262:34.**

Disposition, **179:15.**

Fees for deposits or for copies, **179:15, 262:34.**

Public assistance.

See WELFARE AND SOCIAL SERVICES.

Publication, defined for purposes of depository library for Massachusetts state publications, **6:39.**

Public authorities' reports, deposit of in state library, **6:39, 6:39A.**

Public counsel services committee, **211D:4.**

Public employees dispute impasse proceedings, fact-finder's report, **150:9.**

RECORDS, REPORTS, AND RETURNS —Cont'd

Public health.
See HEALTH AND HEALTH DEPARTMENTS.
Public inspection of records.
See EXAMINATION, INSPECTION, OR INVESTIGATION.
Public libraries.
See LIBRARIES AND LIBRARIANS.
Public meetings, **30A:11A, 39:23C, 66:5A, 66:17C.**
Public records, **4:7, 66:1 et seq.**
Public safety department.
See PUBLIC SAFETY DEPARTMENT.
Public utilities.
See TELECOMMUNICATIONS AND ENERGY DEPARTMENT.
Public welfare.
See WELFARE AND SOCIAL SERVICES.
Purchasing agent of state.
See STATE PURCHASING AGENT.
Purchasing departments of cities and towns, **41:103.**
Racing.
Annual financial reports of racing corporations, **180:26A.**
Annual report to general court of racing commission of state, **6:48.**
Horse and dog racing meetings.
See within this heading, "Horse and dog racing meetings."
Raffles and bazaars, **10:39A, 271:7A.**
Railroad crossings.
See RAILROAD CROSSINGS.
Railroads.
See RAILROADS.
Rape.
See RAPE.
Real estate brokers and salespersons, board of registration records, **13:55, 13:56, 112:87.**
Reallocation of state employee positions, **30:49.**
Real property, **36:1-36:39, 183:4.**
Acquisition, utilization, and disposition, **7:40D, 7:40L.**
Estate, recording of inventory information as to real property held, **217:15B.**

RECORDS, REPORTS, AND RETURNS —Cont'd

Real property —Cont'd
Inventory, **7:40K, 7:43A.**
Registers and registries of deeds.
See REGISTERS AND REGISTRIES OF DEEDS.
Rebinding of books, **66:9.**
Reclamation of lowlands.
See LOWLANDS AND SWAMPS.
Recognizance.
See BAIL AND RECOGNIZANCE.
Recommendations.
See RECOMMENDATIONS.
Recount of votes, examination of records, **54:135.**
Recreational vehicles.
Accident reports, **90B:27.**
Offenses, reports, **90B:32.**
Reference, arrangement, **66:12.**
Referendum.
Initiative and referendum. See within this heading, "Initiative and referendum."
Refrigeration and air conditioning systems, reports as to inspection, **146:45A.**
Refunding bonds, report of state treasurer after sale, **29:53A.**
Refuse treatment.
See GARBAGE AND RUBBISH.
Regional planning district, **40B:5.**
Regional police district commissions, report of audit of accounts, **41:99H.**
Regional refuse disposal districts.
Annual report submitted by district, **40:44F.**
Director of accounts in department of corporations and taxation, reports, **40:44I.**
Planning board, reports, **40:44D.**
Regional school districts.
See REGIONAL SCHOOL DISTRICTS.
Regional transit authorities.
See REGIONAL TRANSIT AUTHORITIES.
Registers and registries of deeds, **36:1-36:39, 183:4.**
See REGISTERS AND REGISTRIES OF DEEDS.
Registers of probate.
See REGISTERS OF PROBATE AND INSOLVENCY.
Registration of land titles, **185:56, 185:63.**
Generally.
See REGISTRATION OF LAND TITLES.

RECORDS, REPORTS, AND RETURNS —Cont'd

Registration of professions and occupations, **13:40, 112:1, 112:21.**
Registration of voters.
See REGISTRATION OF VOTERS.
Regulations of state agencies, **30A:6, 30A:6B.**
Rehabilitation.
Drug addiction rehabilitation.
See DRUG ADDICTION REHABILITATION.
Rehabilitation commission of Massachusetts.
See REHABILITATION COMMISSION OF MASSACHUSETTS.
Rejection of statute by city or town, **4:5.**
Release or acknowledgment of payment or satisfaction of debt, **183:54B.**
Religious societies and corporations, **66:16.**
See RELIGION AND RELIGIOUS SOCIETIES.
Relocation assistance payments for recording fees resulting from move, **79A:7.**
Remainders and reversions.
Life estates, remainders, and reversions.
Conveyance of life estate, **183:4.**
Removal of public records, penalty, **66:15.**
Renewal of certificates stating real name of person transacting business, **110:5.**
Renovation and repair of books, **66:9.**
Reporter of decisions.
See REPORTER OF DECISIONS.
Repossession of financed automobile, creditor's notice to police, **255B:20C.**
Reprisal against tenant for reporting violations of law as defense to action for summary process to recover land, **239:2A.**
Reproductions.
See COPIES.
Restraint of mentally ill patient, **123:21.**
Restraints of trade.
See RESTRAINTS OF TRADE AND MONOPOLIES.

RECORDS, REPORTS, AND RETURNS —Cont'd

Restrictions as to access to public documents, **30:42.**

Retail installment sales and services.
Fines for failure to file, **255B:3.**
Sales finance company, reports by, **255D:3.**

Retarded persons.
See MENTALLY ILL AND RETARDED PERSONS.

Retirement systems.
See RETIREMENT SYSTEMS AND PENSIONS.

Retrocession, notice, **1:7A.**

Revenue department.
See REVENUE DEPARTMENT AND COMMISSIONER.

Revenue stamp, notation and cancellation, **36:15.**

Review.
See APPEAL AND REVIEW.

Reyes syndrome, reports by persons examining or treating disease, **111:110B.**

Roominghouses.
Hotels, motels, and roominghouses. See within this heading, "Hotels, motels, and roominghouses."

Rubbish.
See GARBAGE AND RUBBISH.

Safekeeping, fireproof vaults, **66:11, 66:12.**

Salaries.
See WAGES, SALARIES, AND COMPENSATION.

Sale or transfer of property, **5:6, 9:19, 30:42.**

Sales taxes.
See SALES TAXES.

Sales under Commercial Code, recording contract, **106:2-107.**

Sanitary codes.
Central file for sanitary codes of cities and towns, **21A:8, 111:31.**
Investigations or inspections for violations, reports, **111:16, 111:127B.**

Savings bank life insurance, **30A:11A.**

Savings banks.
See SAVINGS BANKS.

Scenic and recreational river or stream, recording of plan and list of abutting owners, **21:17B.**

Schools.
See SCHOOLS AND EDUCATION.

RECORDS, REPORTS, AND RETURNS —Cont'd

Scientific studies to reduce morbidity and mortality, use of data procured in connection, **111:24A.**

Seals.
See SEALS AND SEALED INSTRUMENTS.

Searches.
See SEARCHES AND SEIZURES.

Seasonal employees, quarterly report of wages, **151A:24A.**

Secretary of environmental affairs, annual report, **21A:3.**

Secretary of state, **4:5, 9:2A, 9:2B, 9:4, 9:17, 9:19, 54:54.**
See SECRETARY OF STATE.

Secured transactions.
See SECURED TRANSACTIONS.

Securities act.
See SECURITIES ACT.

Security deposits, lessor's records, **186:15B.**

Semi-trailers.
Trailers and semi-trailers. See within this heading, "Trailers and semi-trailers."

Senate of U.S.
Elections, transmission of records, **54:112.**
List of votes for president and vice president seat to president of senate, **US Const Amend 12.**
Members returns, senate as judge of, **US Const Art 1 Sec 5 cl 1.**

Service of process.
See PROCESS AND SERVICE OF PROCESS AND PAPERS.

Several counties, land, **36:13.**

Sewers.
See SEWERS AND DRAINS.

Sex offenders, reports pertaining, **123A:9.**

Sexually dangerous persons.
Juvenile offenders.
Reports of treatment, **123A:16.**

Sharecropping contracts, **255:7D.**

Shellfish.
Contaminated areas, **130:74A.**
Director of marine fisheries, reports, **130:76.**
Planting, **130:65.**

Sheriffs.
See SHERIFFS AND DEPUTIES.

RECORDS, REPORTS, AND RETURNS —Cont'd

Ships.
See SHIPS AND OTHER WATERCRAFT.

Shotguns, **140:128A.**
Purchasers or donees, **140:128B.**

Signatures.
See SIGNATURES.

Slaughterhouses.
See SLAUGHTERHOUSES.

Small business assistance division of economic development department, reports concerning activities, **23A:23.**

Small loans.
Business making small loans, records, **140:97.**
Commissioner of banks, reports, **140:98.**
Fees charged to borrower, **140:100.**
Pawnbrokers.
See PAWNBROKERS.

Snow removal chemicals, reports as to locations and quantities used, **85:7A.**

Snow vehicles, accident reports, **90B:27.**

Social services.
See WELFARE AND SOCIAL SERVICES.

Social workers.
See SOCIAL WORKERS.

Solemnization of marriages, **46:1, 207:40.**

Solicitation of charitable contributions from public.
See CHARITIES AND CHARITABLE CONTRIBUTIONS.

Solid waste disposal, Environmental Protection Department to keep records, **16:24.**

Southeastern regional planning.
See SOUTHEASTERN REGIONAL PLANNING AND ECONOMIC DEVELOPMENT DISTRICT.

Special assessments.
See SPECIAL ASSESSMENTS.

Special commissions, reports, **4:2A.**

Special education.
See SPECIAL EDUCATION.

Special legislation, recommendations for avoidance, **30:33A.**

Spendthrift, effect of recording petition for appointment of guardian, **201:10.**

RECORDS, REPORTS, AND RETURNS —Cont'd

Stabbings, treatment, **112:12A.**

Standardbred agricultural fair and breeding fund committee, meetings, **20:10.**

Standards of materials used for recording, enforcement, **66:4.**

State.
See STATE AND STATE DEPARTMENTS.

State auditor, **11:6A, 11:12.**
Civil service reports of state officers, **31:69.**

State ballot law commission.
See STATE BALLOT LAW COMMISSION.

State colleges.
See COLLEGES AND UNIVERSITIES.

State finance.
See STATE FINANCE.

State forest, grant of right of way through, **132:34A.**

State library.
See STATE LIBRARY.

Statement of amount of debt due person for labor performed, fee for filing, **262:34.**

State parks, report of commissioner, **132A:9.**

State police.
See STATE POLICE.

State printing.
See STATE PRINTING.

State purchasing agent.
See STATE PURCHASING AGENT.

State sanitoria, annual report as to condition, **111:64.**

State superintendent of buildings, report, **8:17A.**

State treasurer.
See STATE TREASURER.

Statistics.
See STATISTICS.

Statute, acceptance or rejection by city, **4:5.**

Statute of limitations.
Limitation of actions.
See LIMITATION OF ACTIONS.

Statutory recordkeeping requirements, **66:5A.**

Steamboats.
See STEAMBOATS AND STEAMBOAT COMPANIES.

Steam boilers.
See STEAM BOILERS AND ENGINES.

Stolen leased or rental motor vehicle, reporting, **266:87A.**

RECORDS, REPORTS, AND RETURNS —Cont'd

Storage.
See STORAGE.

Stray beasts, report of taking, **134:2.**

Streams, licenses for structures, **91:18.**

Street railways.
See STREET RAILWAYS.

Streets.
See HIGHWAYS AND STREETS.

Student records.
See SCHOOLS AND EDUCATION.

Subdivision control law.
See ZONING AND PLANNING.

Submission to state purchasing agent prior to publication, **7:29.**

Subpoena of records.
See PRODUCTION OF BOOKS AND PAPERS.

Subversive Activities Division, duties, **22:3.**

Subversive organizations.
Destruction or concealment of books, **264:21.**
Search warrants, **276:1A.**

Succession taxes.
See LEGACY AND SUCCESSION TAXES.

Successor in office, surrender of public records, **66:14.**

Suffolk county.
See SUFFOLK COUNTY.

Suicide attempts or threats by persons in police custody, **40:36A.**

Superintendent of state office buildings, report to include account of flags, **8:17A.**

Superior courts.
See SUPERIOR COURTS.

Supervisor of public records, **9:4, 9:5, 66:1.**
Appliances, approval, **66:4.**
Destruction of records, approval, **66:8.**
Ink, standards established and approved by supervisor, **66:4.**
Materials, approval, **66:3.**
Orders compelling delivery of copies, **66:10.**
Petition to obtain compliance with provisions prohibiting use of certain appliances, **66:4.**
Worn books, custody, **66:9.**

RECORDS, REPORTS, AND RETURNS —Cont'd

Supreme judicial court.
See SUPREME JUDICIAL COURT.

Surplus state property, disposition, **7:40F, 7:40F½.**

Surrender of public records to successor in office, **66:14.**

Survey board, plans approved, **41:78.**

Surveys.
See MAPS, PLATS, AND SURVEYS.

Swamps.
See LOWLANDS AND SWAMPS.

Swine, feeding garbage, **129:14B.**

Tanning facilities, **111:212.**

Tape recordings.
See ELECTRONIC RECORDING DEVICES AND EQUIPMENT.

Taxation.
See TAXATION.

Technical colleges or institutes, annual report, **74:44.**

Technical reports, publication and distribution, **5:8.**

Technology development corporation.
Annual report, **40G:6.**
Donation or grant, details in annual report, **40G:3.**
Secretary to keep board records, **40G:2.**

Telecommunications division, duties of director, **25:12E½.**

Telephone.
See TELEPHONE AND TELEGRAPH COMPANIES.

Tenant.
See LANDLORD AND TENANT.

Tewksbury birth and death records, transfer to town clerk, **46:20.**

Tewksbury hospital, disposition of unclaimed patients' valuables, **122:8.**

Theft of public record as larceny, **266:30.**

Thrift Institutions Fund for Economic Development, **63:1 (note).**

Tidal bounds of streams, filing plan, **131:4.**

Time of record, **36:12, 36:14.**
Certification on instrument, **36:23.**
Disclaimer, time for filing, **191A:3.**

RECORDS, REPORTS, AND RETURNS —Cont'd

Time of record —Cont'd

Dower barred after ten years from recording of conveyance, **189:6.**

Initiative and referendum petition, time for filing, **53:22A.**

Limitation of actions.
  See LIMITATION OF ACTIONS.

Obsolete papers and records, time requirements regarding destruction, **221:27A.**

Toll roads or bridges, reports of accidents, **90:29.**

Towns or cities, **40:48-40:51.**
  See CITIES AND TOWNS.

Toxics use reduction act.
  See TOXICS USE REDUCTION ACT.

Trackless trolleys, filing reports and information, **163:8.**

Trademarks.
  See TRADEMARKS AND TRADE NAMES.

Trade secrets, protection, **21C:4.**

Traffic regulations.
  See TRAFFIC REGULATIONS AND RULES OF THE ROAD.

Trailers and semi-trailers.

Garages and open air parking spaces, records required, **90:32.**

Registered owner, report of change in name or address, **90:26A.**

Rental records, **90:32C, 90:32D.**

Training schools.
  See YOUTH SERVICES DEPARTMENT AND MASSACHUSETTS TRAINING SCHOOLS.

Tramway inspectors, reports, **143:71K.**

Transcripts.
  See TRANSCRIPTS.

Transfer of public records, **30:42.**

Transient vendor's licenses, **101:4.**

Transportation charges, filing of claim, **149:29.**

Traps, registration, **131:80.**

Treasurer of county.
  See COUNTY TREASURERS.

Treasurer of state.
  See STATE TREASURER.

Trial court of the Commonwealth; chief administrative justice to report concerning operations, **211B:9.**

RECORDS, REPORTS, AND RETURNS —Cont'd

Trust companies.
  See TRUST COMPANIES.

Trusts.
  See TRUSTS AND TRUSTEES.

Turnpike authority, **81A:17, 81A:20.**

Two or more counties, instruments as to land, **36:13.**

Typewriting, use in public records, **66:3.**

Underground storage tank petroleum product cleanup fund.
  See UNDERGROUND STORAGE TANK PETROLEUM PRODUCT CLEANUP FUND.

Underground tanks.
  See UNDERGROUND TANKS.

Undertakers.

Embalmers and funeral directors. See within this heading, "Embalmers and funeral directors."

Underwater archeological resources, report, **6:180.**

Unemployment compensation, **151A:38, 151A:44-151A:46.**
  See EMPLOYMENT SECURITY.

Uniform operation of commercial motor vehicles.
  See UNIFORM OPERATION OF COMMERCIAL MOTOR VEHICLES.

Uniform rules of adjudicatory procedure, **30A:10.**

Uniform Securities Act.
  See SECURITIES ACT.

Uniform state laws, reports of commissioners, **6:27, 6:28.**

United Spanish War Veterans, printing and distribution of proceedings, **5:9.**

United States attorney, inspector general's reports, **12A:10.**

University of Massachusetts.
  See UNIVERSITY OF MASSACHUSETTS.

Unknown parties, indexing, **36:27.**

Unlawful possession of public records, penalty, **66:15.**

Unrecorded deeds or leases, effect, **183:4, 183:6A.**

Unwed mothers.

Audit of unwed mothers, **111:54.**

Maintenance on transfer of ownership of institution, **111:70.**

RECORDS, REPORTS, AND RETURNS —Cont'd

Unwed mothers —Cont'd

Requirement as to keeping records, **111:53.**

Urban area insurance placement facility.

Insurability of property, liability for statement in reports concerning, **175C:6.**

Urban renewal agencies, reports, **121B:52.**

Use, consumption, or storage tax.

Records, amount of tax collected by vendor to be shown separately from sales price, **64I:6.**

Reporting of gross receipts of rental property, **64I:8.**

Returns, **62C:16, 64I:11.**

Used car sales.

Record books, **140:62.**

Reports by licensees, **140:57.**

Use tax.
  See USE, CONSUMPTION, OR STORAGE TAX.

Uttering forged records, **267:5.**

Vacancy in office of assistant clerk, report, **221:13.**

Variances or special permits under zoning laws, recording requirements, **40A:11.**

Vaults for public records, **66:11, 66:12.**

Vending machine sales of food, reports as to food processed in other states, **94:312.**

Venereal disease records, **111:119.**

Verdict.
  See VERDICT.

Veterans and veterans' organizations, **5:9, 8:18.**
  See VETERANS AND VETERANS' ORGANIZATIONS.

Veterinarians.

Board of registration of veterinary medicine, **112:57.**

Institutional licenses for veterinarian schools, **112:56D.**

Video rental business, disclosure of records of, **93:106.**

Visitors to correctional institutions, **127:37.**

Vital statistics.
  See VITAL STATISTICS.

Vocational education and rehabilitation.

Annual report of superintendent of school district with special fund for culinary arts program, **74:14B.**

RECORDS, REPORTS, AND RETURNS —Cont'd

Vocational education and rehabilitation —Cont'd

Full-time pupils, **72:2A.**

Persons eligible for vocational rehabilitation, records, **6:79.**

Workers' compensation, reporting of cases, **152:30F.**

Voluntary administration of small estates where executor named in will, **195:16A.**

Voluntary imprisonment, **127:3.**

Vote at town meetings, recording, **39:15.**

Wages.
See WAGES, SALARIES, AND COMPENSATION.

Warehouses.
See WAREHOUSES.

Warrant of pardon, execution, **127:157.**

War records commissioner, adjutant general to serve under governor, **6:16.**

Waste storage, notice relative to treatment or disposal, **21C:7, 111:150A, 111:150B.**

Water pollution.
See WATER POLLUTION.

Water resources division and commissioner.

Annual report, **21:11.**

Digging or drilling of wells, **21:16.**

Waterworks.
See WATERWORKS AND WATER SUPPLY.

Weapons.
See FIREARMS AND WEAPONS.

Wearing apparel, wage and hour records required by state of contractors for purchase, **7:22.**

Weights.
See WEIGHTS AND MEASURES.

Welfare.
See WELFARE AND SOCIAL SERVICES.

Well diggers or drillers, **21:16.**

Wharves.

Proprietors of wharves and real estate lying in common. See within this heading, "Proprietors of wharves and real estate lying in common."

Wife.

Husband and wife. See within this heading, "Husband and wife."

RECORDS, REPORTS, AND RETURNS —Cont'd

Wiretapping.

Eavesdropping and wiretapping, **272:99.**

Withholding of tax, **62B:5, 62C:10.**

Returns, **62B:5, 62B:7, 62C:10.**

Wage reporting system, **62B:2, 62E:1 et seq.**
See WAGE REPORTING SYSTEM.

Witnesses of crime, rights, **258B:2.**

Workers' compensation.
See WORKERS' COMPENSATION.

Working papers as property of accountant, **112:87E.**

Worn records.

Preservation and copying, **66:9.**

Rerecording, **36:17.**

Writ of entry.

Entry, writs of. See within this heading, "Entry, writs."

Youth conservation and service corps, **78A:7.**

Youth services department and Massachusetts training schools, **120:1, 120:5.**
See YOUTH SERVICES DEPARTMENT AND MASSACHUSETTS TRAINING SCHOOLS.

Zoning.
See ZONING AND PLANNING.

RECOUNT OF VOTES, 54:134 et seq.
See ELECTIONS.

RECOUPMENT.

"Action" as including, **106:1-201.**

Assistance to the aged and disabled, recoupment of overpayments, **118A:3.**

Credit unions, **171:48.**

Insurers insolvency fund, recoupment of assessments paid, **175D:13.**

Setoff.
See SETOFF AND COUNTERCLAIM.

Wage reporting system, **62E:6.**

Workers' compensation, recoupment of benefits by employer, **152:11D.**

RECREATION.

Accident and sickness insurance, blanket policies authorized for recreational organizations, **175:110.**

Aged persons, town appropriations for recreation programs, **40:5.**

RECREATION —Cont'd

Amusements and exhibitions, **140:181 et seq.**
See AMUSEMENTS AND EXHIBITIONS.

Application for tax treatment as recreational land, notice, **61B:6.**

Athletics.
See ATHLETICS.

Beaches.
See BEACHES.

Boxing and boxing matches, **147:32-147:51.**
See BOXING AND BOXING MATCHES.

Bungee jumping, **22:11B, 149:129D.**

Camps.
See CAMPS.

Certificates and certification.

Information provided by land owner, **61B:3.**

Payment of tax on land, **61B:14, 61B:15.**

Charges or fees, private property owner permitting use without, **21:17C.**

Conservation of soil, water and related resources, powers and duties of commission, **21:20.**

Conservation restrictions, public recreational use of land subject, **184:31.**

Correctional institutions.

Duties of deputy commissioner for classification and treatment, **124:2.**

Organized athletic sports for prisoners, **127:19.**

Segregated units to have limited recreational facilities, **127:39.**

Environmental affairs executive office, funds of as including state recreational areas fund, **21A:10.**

Establishment of centers, **45:14.**

Funds for recreation, **21A:10, 64A:13, 90B:35.**

Gasoline tax receipts, crediting to recreational boating fund, **64A:13.**

Governor.
See GOVERNOR.

Growth and development policy committees, cities and towns, recreational land, **40:4I.**

Highways.
See HIGHWAYS AND STREETS.

RECREATION —Cont'd

Intent to sell or change use of recreational land, notice, **61B:9.**

Interest on money.

Excess payment of tax on recreational land, **61B:4.**

Roll-back taxes, **61B:8.**

Special or betterment assessments on land, **61B:13.**

Liens.

See LIENS AND ENCUMBRANCES.

Metropolitan districts.

See METROPOLITAN DISTRICTS.

Migrant farm workers, recreational opportunities, **111:128H.**

Municipal finance.

See MUNICIPAL FINANCE.

Old persons, leisure time activities allowance, **118A:1.**

Parks and reservations, **45:1 et seq.**

See PARKS AND RESERVATIONS.

Playgrounds, **45:14-45:18.**

See PLAYGROUNDS.

Prisons and prisoners.

Correctional institutions. See within this heading, "Correctional institutions."

Private property, owner's liability for permitting use without charge, **21:17C.**

Public assistance recipients, retention of income, **118E:10 (note), 177:8 (note).**

Public water supply, use of certain lands not needed, **40:15B.**

Public works and departments.

Beaches.

See BEACHES.

Expenditures for extension or enlargement of outdoor recreation facilities, **21:1.**

Quabbin watershed advisory committee, advice regarding fishing, boating, and other recreational activities, **92:114.**

Real estate time-shares, recreational areas, termination of contract or lease, **183B:23.**

Regional school districts, authorization to incur debts, **71:16.**

Registers and registries of deeds.

Change in use, **61B:9.**

Change of ownership, **61B:6.**

RECREATION —Cont'd

Registers and registries of deeds —Cont'd

Recording certificate of tax payment, **61B:15.**

Reimbursement of towns for loss of tax on land used, **58:13-58:17A.**

School department transportation in towns, availability to recreation groups, **159A:32.**

Security deposit regulations inapplicable to short-term rental, **186:15B.**

Service defined for tax purposes, **64H:1, 64I:1.**

Skiing.

See SKIING.

Soil Conservation Service of United States, co-operative agreements, **91:11.**

Special age groups, use of centers, **45:18.**

State areas, **132A:1 et seq.**

See STATE RECREATION AREAS.

Subdivision control, necessity for plan to show parks for recreation purposes, **41:81U.**

Taxation of recreational land, **61B:1-61B:18.**

Token awards in contests, town appropriation, **40:5.**

Tramways.

See RECREATIONAL TRAMWAYS.

Vehicles, **90B:1 et seq.**

See RECREATIONAL VEHICLES.

Watershed management plans, adoption, **92:116.**

Watershed system advisory committee, advice regarding fishing boating, and recreational activities, **92:115.**

RECREATIONAL TRAMWAYS, 143:71H-143:71S.

Appeals from orders of board, **143:71M.**

Board membership and duties, **143:71H, 143:71J.**

Definitions, **143:71I.**

Licensing and fees, **143:71L.**

Skiers, conduct, responsibilities, and duties, **143:71O.**

Ski lift, **143:71H-143:71S.**

RECREATIONAL VEHICLES, 90B:1 et seq.

Accidents, reports, **90B:27.**

Advisory board, membership, **21A:8-21A:11.**

RECREATIONAL VEHICLES —Cont'd

Animals.

Fish and game. See within this heading, "Fish and game."

Appointment and removal of director, **21A:8.**

Bicycles.

See BICYCLES.

Boating and recreational vehicle safety board, **21A:11.**

Certificate of registration and registration numbers, provisions, **90B:22.**

Civil infractions, procedure, **90C:1.**

Credit unions, loans, **171:62.**

Crimes.

Offenses and penalties. See within this heading, "Offenses and penalties."

Dealer's registration, **90B:22.**

Vehicle trailers, **90:5.**

Death, penalty for violation of recreational provisions resulting, **90B:14.**

Definitions under motor vehicle laws, **90B:20.**

Division of marine and recreational vehicles, **21:17A, 21A:8-21A:11, 90B:1 et seq.**

Environmental affairs executive office, enforcement powers, **90B:32.**

Equipment, **90B:24.**

Exemption of publicly owned vehicles from registration requirements, **90B:22.**

Existing laws, ordinances, etc., not superseded, **90B:33.**

Fees.

Allocation, **90B:35.**

Registration fees, **90B:22.**

Finances and funds.

Fund. See within this heading, "Fund."

Fines.

Offenses and penalties. See within this heading, "Offenses and penalties."

Fish and game.

Deer or other wildlife, harassment, **90B:26.**

Department, **21A:7, 21A:8.**

See FISHERIES, WILDLIFE, AND RECREATIONAL VEHICLES DEPARTMENT.

Wardens, enforcement of law and regulations, **90B:32.**

Fund.

Environmental affairs executive office, **21A:10.**

RECREATIONAL VEHICLES
—Cont'd

Fund —Cont'd

Fees collected under provisions regarding snow and recreation vehicles, application, **90B:35.**

Gasoline and motor fuel tax receipts, distribution, **64A:13.**

Public access board and fund, regulation and acquisition, **21:17A.**

Highways and streets.
Public ways, **90B:25.**

Hunting with aid or use of snowmobiles, **131:65.**

Insurance, motor vehicles registrar as member of board of appeal on motor vehicle liability policies and bonds, **26:8A.**

Jet skis, surf jets, and wetbikes, regulation, **90B:1, 90B:11.**

Land of another, operating, **90B:33.**

Law and regulations.
Rules and regulations. See within this heading, "Rules and regulations."

Licenses.
Registration. See within this heading, "Registration."

Manufacturer's registration, **90B:22.**

Marine and recreational vehicles.
Advisory board, membership, **21A:8-21A:11.**

Governor.
See GOVERNOR.

Motorboats, **90B:1 et seq.**
See MOTORBOATS.

Motorcycles.
See MOTORCYCLES.

Mufflers, vehicles to be equipped, **90B:24.**

Name and address on registration certificate, notice of change, **90B:22.**

Noise.
Approval of meters for measuring, **90B:24.**
Unusual or excessive prohibited, **90B:24.**

Nonresidents.
Operation, **90B:30.**
Registration fees charged, **90B:22.**

Notice.
Name and address appearing on registration certificate, notice of change, **90B:22.**

RECREATIONAL VEHICLES
—Cont'd

Notice —Cont'd
Transfer of ownership of vehicle, notice, **90B:23.**

Obnoxious fumes prohibited, **90B:24.**

Offenses and penalties, **90B:32, 90B:34.**

Civil infractions, procedure, **90C:1.**

Death, penalty for violation of recreational vehicle provisions resulting, **90B:14.**

Trespass on private land, penalty, **266:121A.**

Unregistered vehicles, operation, **90B:21.**

Owners' registration. See within this heading, "Registration."

Paraplegics in vehicles, carrying of firearms, **90B:26.**

Penalties.
Offenses and penalties. See within this heading, "Offenses and penalties."

Privately owned property.
Snow vehicles, use on, **90B:26.**

Protective headgear of occupants, **90B:26.**

Public access board, **21:17A.**

Publicly owned vehicles, exemption from registration requirements, **90B:22.**

Public records, division's records, **90B:3.**

Public ways.
Operation on, across, or adjacent, **90B:25.**
Use during public emergency, **90B:25.**

Records.
Reports. See within this heading, "Reports."

Reflectors, **90B:24.**

Refuse and rubbish, unlawful disposal, **270:16, 270:16A.**

Registration, **90B:22.**
Dealer's registration. See within this heading, "Dealer's registration."
Emergency use of vehicles on public ways, authority of motor vehicles registrar to permit, **90B:25.**
Fees, **90B:22.**
Insurance, motor vehicles registrar as member of board of appeal on motor vehicle liability policies and bonds, **26:8A.**

RECREATIONAL VEHICLES
—Cont'd

Registration —Cont'd
Lists, transmittal to local assessors for tax purposes, **90B:11.**

Manufacturer's registration, **90B:22.**

Nonresidents, registration fees charged, **90B:22.**

Operation of unregistered vehicle, **90B:21.**

Other states, reciprocal usage agreements, **90B:30.**

Protective head gear of operators and passengers, establishment by motor vehicles registrar of standards, **90B:26.**

Publicly owned vehicles, exemption from registration requirements, **90B:22.**

Reciprocity, **90B:30.**

Suspension or revocation, **90B:28.**

Trailer dealers, registration, **90:5.**

Transfer of ownership, procedure, **90B:23.**

Regulations.
Rules and regulations. See within this heading, "Rules and regulations."

Reports.
Accident reports, **90B:27.**
Offenses, reports, **90B:32.**

Rules and regulations.
Alteration, amendment, or rescission, **90B:29.**
Enforcement, **90B:32.**
Jet skis, surf jets, and wetbikes, **90B:1, 90B:11.**
Public access board and fund, regulation and acquisition, **21:17A.**

Safety and operating requirements, **90B:24, 90B:26.**

Sales tax.
Calculation with trade-ins, **64H:26.**

Sleds.
See SLEDS.

Snow traveling, **90B:20 et seq.**

Taxation, assessment for purposes, **90B:11, 90B:31.**

Trailers.
See TRAILERS AND SEMI-TRAILERS.

Trails for snowmobiles, construction, **132:38A.**

Trespass on private land, **90B:33, 266:121A.**

RECREATIONAL VEHICLES
—Cont'd
Unregistered vehicles, operation,
90B:21.
Use, consumption or storage tax.
Calculation with trade-ins,
64I:27.
Wardens, enforcement of law and
regulations, **90B:32.**

RECRIMINATION.
Divorce libels, abolition of defense
of recrimination, **208:1.**

RECRUITMENT.
Mentally ill and retarded persons,
recruitment and selection of
area director, **19:15.**
Schools and education,
recruitment for armed forces
on campus, **71:88.**

**RECYCLING, 21H:7, 40:8H,
64H:6, 94:321-94:327.**
Generally.
See GARBAGE AND RUBBISH.

RED ACRE FARM, INC.
Horses owned by cities or towns,
disposition, **133:4.**

RED CROSS.
See AMERICAN RED CROSS.

REDEMPTION.
Administrators.
Executors and administrators.
See within this heading,
"Executors and
administrators."
Bonds.
See BONDS AND
DEBENTURES.
Certificates and certification,
236:34, 266:75C.
Cigarette excise tax stamps,
64C:31.
Collateral, redemption of.
Secured transactions. See within
this heading, "Secured
transactions."
Consumer goods, debtor's right
after repossession, **255:13I,
255:13J.**
Co-operative banks, redemption
from taking or sale of property
for repayment of taxes,
60:76A.
Credit slips, time limitation on
redemption, **93:14S.**
Executions, **236:33-236:42, 236:54.**
See EXECUTIONS.
Executors and administrators.
Land taken on execution,
236:54.

REDEMPTION —Cont'd
Executors and administrators
—Cont'd
Mortgage, land subject, **244:33.**
Gift certificates, **266:75C.**
Heirs.
See HEIRS OR NEXT OF KIN.
Installment sales agreement, right
of buyer, **255D:21, 255D:22.**
Insurance.
Guaranty capital of life, liability
and casualty companies,
175:93E.
Scrip certificates of marine
companies, **175:86.**
Interest of money.
Mortgage redemption,
allowability of interest,
244:28.
Tax sales, rate of interest to
redeem, **51:52, 60:62, 60:63,
60:68.**
Land court.
Fee for entry of decree, **262:39.**
Housing and community
development department,
proceedings to foreclose all
rights of redemption in
abandoned property,
60:81A.
Tax sale, redemption, **60:76,
60:76A.**
Limitation of actions.
Execution, property taken or
sold, **236:39.**
Mortgage foreclosure.
See MORTGAGE
FORECLOSURE.
Mechanics' lien law, sales, **254:20.**
Mortgage foreclosure,
244:18-244:35, 244:39, 244:40.
See MORTGAGE
FORECLOSURE.
Motor vehicle sales finance law,
right of buyer, **255B:20B.**
Municipal bonds and notes,
redemption and refunding,
44:21, 44:21A.
Partition.
Estate in land subject to
redemption, **241:1.**
Partial redemption from tax
sale, **60:76A.**
Pawnbroker's sale of unredeemed
articles, **140:71.**
Professional corporation shares,
156A:12, 156A:13.
Refunding bonds, **29:53A.**
Registers and registries of deeds,
recording certificate of
redemption from the deeds
and titles, **60:62, 60:63.**

REDEMPTION —Cont'd
Secured transactions.
Consumer goods, **255:13J.**
Debtor's right, **106:9-506.**
Mortgage foreclosure.
See MORTGAGE
FORECLOSURE.
Owner of collateral other than
debtor as entitled to
redemption, **106:9-112.**
State bonds and obligations.
Issuance and sale of bonds
subject to call for
redemption, **29:49.**
Payment of lost or destroyed
bond after redemption date,
29:59.
Statute of limitations.
Limitation of actions. See within
this heading, "Limitation of
actions."
Superior courts.
Mortgages held by state, action,
244:40.
Obligations issued or redeemed
in numerical order,
penalties, **107:8.**
Real estate, actions,
236:39-236:41.
Supplementary proceedings,
redemption of property
transferred, **224:17.**
Supreme judicial court,
236:39-236:41.
Mortgages held by state, action
for redemption, **244:40.**
Tax sales, **60:54, 60:62, 60:63,
60:68, 60:76, 60:76A, 62C:57,
62C:58.**
See TAX SALES.
Tax titles, **60:63-60:75.**
See TAX DEEDS AND TITLES.
Trading stamps.
Cash, redemption, **93:14M.**
Default in redemption, **93:14Q.**
Notice of cessation of business,
93:14P.
Water rates, redemption from sale
for nonpayment, **40:42D.**

REDEVELOPMENT.
Housing.
See HOUSING AND URBAN
RENEWAL.

RED FLAG.
Motor vehicles or trailers, display,
90:7, 90:19.

REDISCOUNT.
Credit unions, shares, deposits,
and investments, **171:67.**

RED LIGHTS.
Agricultural vehicles equipped, **90:7.**
Fire departments, regulations as to red lights on certain vehicles, **90:7, 90:7E.**
Motorboats, display, **90B:5.**
Motor vehicles.
See MOTOR VEHICLES.
Traffic regulations.
See TRAFFIC REGULATIONS AND RULES OF THE ROAD.

REDLINING.
Location of property, denial of mortgage on basis, **183:64.**

RED SQUIRREL.
Possession without permit, **131:5.**
Removal from hole in ground, **131:76.**

RED TAG.
Bedding or upholstered furniture, violation of law, **94:276.**

REDUCING SALON.
Hours of labor for women or minors employed, **149:56, 149:57, 149:66, 149:67, 149:78.**

REDUCTION.
Capital.
See CAPITAL AND CAPITAL STOCK.
Civil service.
See CIVIL SERVICE.
Commercial motor vehicle license, reduction of lifetime disqualification, **90F:9.**
Corporation taxes.
See CORPORATION TAXES.
Costs, reduction, where two or more cases tried together, **261:8.**
Credit unions.
See CREDIT UNIONS.
Damages reduced on basis of contributory negligence, **231:85.**
Gas.
See GAS AND ELECTRIC COMPANIES.
Group insurance, rate reductions to be applied for sole benefit of insured, **149:178E.**
Income tax.
See INCOME TAX.
Insurance.
See INSURANCE.
Rank.
See CIVIL SERVICE.

REDUCTION —Cont'd
Schools.
See SCHOOLS AND EDUCATION.
Sentence.
See SENTENCE AND PUNISHMENT.
Taxation.
Corporate taxation, reduction of taxes on account of excess as affected by minimum tax rate, **63:31B.**
Income tax.
See INCOME TAX.
State finance reduction fund, **29:2I.**
Victims and witness assistance programs, reduction of assessment due to financial hardship, **258B:8.**

REENLISTMENT OF OFFICERS.
State police, **22C:10.**

REFEREES, 221:57 et seq.
See AUDITORS, MASTERS, AND REFEREES.

REFEREES, BOXING.
Licensing, **147:35.**
Powers and duties, **147:36.**

REFERENCE TO OTHER TRANSACTION OR INSTRUMENT.
Incorporation by reference.
See INCORPORATION BY REFERENCE.
Marginal references to statute, **4:11.**

REFERENDUM.
See INITIATIVE AND REFERENDUM.

REFERRAL AND PLACEMENT OF CHILD.
Special education, moving to other school district, reevaluation of needs, **71B:5.**

REFINANCING.
Bonds.
See REFUNDING BONDS.
Consumer notes, refinancing charges as affected by violation of law, **255:12C.**
County treasurers' temporary notes, refunding, **35:37B.**
Credit union board of directors, loans made on behalf of credit union, **171:73.**
Finance advisory board to submit recommendations, **6:98.**

REFINANCING —Cont'd
Motor vehicle financing, collection of refinance charge by holder of installment contract, **255B:17.**
Retail installment sales refinancing agreements, **255D:16, 255D:17.**

REFINED.
Lard container, penalty for use of word, **94:61.**

REFINERY TERMINALS.
Cleanup fund.
See UNDERGROUND STORAGE TANK PETROLEUM PRODUCT CLEANUP FUND.

REFLECTORS.
Bicycles, equipment, **85:11B.**
Motor vehicles, **90:7, 90:7A.**
Number plates reflectorized, **90:2.**
Recreation and snow vehicles, **90B:24.**
Recreation and snow vehicles to be equipped, **90B:24.**

REFLEX SYMPATHETIC DYSTROPHY AWARENESS MONTH.
Observance, **6:15OOO.**

REFORESTATION.
See FORESTS AND FORESTRY.

REFORMATORIES, 18A:1 et seq., 120:1 et seq.
See YOUTH SERVICES DEPARTMENT AND MASSACHUSETTS TRAINING SCHOOLS.

REFORMED EPISCOPAL CHURCH.
Organization as religious society, **67:39.**

REFRIGERATION AND REFRIGERATORS.
Administration.
See ADMINISTRATION AND FINANCE EXECUTIVE OFFICE.
Apprentice, fire sprinkler system contractors and fitters, **146:81-146:85.**
Cold storage, **94:66-94:73A.**
See COLD STORAGE.
Corporations, digging up highways and streets, **158:12-158:14.**
Definitions, **25B:2, 146:81.**

REFRIGERATION AND REFRIGERATORS —Cont'd
Door of discarded refrigerator, penalty for failure to remove, **271:46.**
Fees.
  Inspection, **146:45A.**
  Technicians and pipefitters, examination and licensing, **146:85.**
Fines and penalties for violation of regulations, **146:45A.**
Ice skating rink, appropriation, **40:5.**
Kitchen facilities in lodging houses, **140:22A.**
Labeling of electric appliances, **94:314-94:318.**
Landlord's failure to furnish refrigerator service, tenant's waiver, **186:14.**
Malt beverages, special seasonal permits for storage, **138:20.**
Pipefitters.
  See PIPEFITTERS AND REFRIGERATION TECHNICIANS.
Professional engineers, exemption from laws, **112:81R.**
Tax exemption of personal property used, **59:5.**
Testing, certification and efficiency standards, **25B:3-25B:7.**

REFUGEES AND IMMIGRANTS, OFFICE FOR.
Director, **6:206.**
Establishment, **6:205.**
Governor's advisory council, **6:208.**
Powers, **6:207.**

REFUNDING BONDS.
Cities and towns.
  First payment, **44:21A.**
  Issuance, **44:21.**
  School projects, **44:21A.**
County finance.
  See COUNTY FINANCE.
Electric company owning hydro-electric plant, securing refunding mortgage bonds, **164:9.**
First payment, **44:21A.**
Highway infrastructure fund, **29:2O.**
Municipal industrial development revenue bonds, **40D:17.**
State treasurer to issue and sell, **29:53A, 29:60A.**
Street railways, purposes for increasing capital stock or issuance of bonds, **161:25.**

REFUNDING BONDS —Cont'd
Water pollution abatement trust, **29C:9.**
Water resources authority, **67:13, 67:16, Spec L 67:12.**

REFUNDS.
Alcoholic liquors.
  See ALCOHOLIC LIQUORS.
Automobile insurance.
  See AUTOMOBILE INSURANCE.
Bail and recognizance.
  Reversal of judgment, **276:78.**
  Surrender of principal, **276:68, 276:81.**
Banks and banking.
  Cooperative banks.
    See COOPERATIVE BANKS.
Carriers, refund of discriminatory rates, **159:14.**
Cigarette tax.
  See CIGARETTE TAX.
Cities and towns, borrowing of money in anticipation of grants or reimbursements from Commonwealth, **44:6A.**
Commercial code, refund of funds transfer payment, **106:4A-204.**
Condemnation.
  Eminent domain. See within this heading, "Eminent domain."
Contracts for sale or lease of goods or procurement of services, refunds on cancellation of certain, **93:48.**
Cooperative banks.
  See COOPERATIVE BANKS.
County finance.
  See COUNTY FINANCE.
Deed and document tax, **64D:4.**
Dental service corporations, **176E:4.**
Disability retirement benefits, refund in case of excess earnings, **32:91A.**
Discounts.
  See DISCOUNTS AND REBATES.
Discriminatory rates by carriers, refund, **159:14.**
Electric companies.
  Gas and electric companies. See within this heading, "Gas and electric companies."
Eminent domain.
  Condemnee after payment pro tanto, refunds, **79:8A.**
  Petitioner, refunds, **79:7G.**
Employment agency fees, refunds, **140:46O.**

REFUNDS —Cont'd
Employment security.
  See EMPLOYMENT SECURITY.
Federal estate tax, **65A:2, 65A:4.**
  See ESTATE TAXES.
Gas and electric companies.
  Electric companies, **164:122.**
  Gas companies, **164:94F.**
  Incorrect meter, **164:122.**
Gasoline.
  See GASOLINE AND MOTOR FUEL TAXES.
Governmental units pooled insurance, refund of excess moneys, **40M:12.**
Group insurance for municipal employees, **32B:8.**
  See GROUP INSURANCE FOR MUNICIPAL EMPLOYEES.
Health spa contracts, cancellation, **93:82.**
Home improvement contractors, refund of registration fee, **142A:11.**
Horse and dog racing license fees, **128A:4.**
Income tax.
  See INCOME TAX.
Insurance premium finance agencies.
  See INSURANCE PREMIUM FINANCE AGENCIES.
Legacy and succession taxes, **65:20.**
  See LEGACY AND SUCCESSION TAXES.
Life insurance.
  Death of or cancellation by insured, **175:119B, 175:187H.**
  Unearned premiums, credit life insurance, **255B:10.**
Massachusetts life and health insurance guaranty association law, **175:147.**
Motor vehicle retail installment sales.
  Buyer entitled to refund upon seller's failure to deliver copy of contract, **255B:13.**
  Payment before maturity, **255B:16.**
  Unearned premium for credit life, accident and health insurance, **255B:10.**
Motor vehicles, used, warranty provisions, **90:7N½.**
Oil burner technicians, refund of fees to applicant for certification, **148:10D.**

REFUNDS —Cont'd

Pensions.
    See RETIREMENT SYSTEMS
        AND PENSIONS.
Retail installment sales.
    See RETAIL INSTALLMENT
        SALES AND SERVICES.
Retirement systems.
    See RETIREMENT SYSTEMS
        AND PENSIONS.
School bus operator accepting less
    than prescribed wages,
    penalty, **71:7A.**
State treasurer, **62C:39, 62C:40,
    64C:31, 65:27.**
Taxation.
    See TAXATION.
Teachers.
    See TEACHERS.
Transportation charges on public
    works projects, forbidden,
    30:39C, 30:39E.
Truth in lending.
    Credit balance, refund, **140D:22.**
Unemployment compensation.
    See EMPLOYMENT
        SECURITY.
Warranty provisions of used motor
    vehicles, **90:7N¼.**
Water companies, refunds to
    customers, **165:10.**
Workers' compensation.
    Injured state employee having
        sick leave credits, **30:58.**
    Self-insurance groups, **152:25P.**

REFUSE.
See GARBAGE AND RUBBISH.

REFUSE BANK FIRES.
Coal mines, emergency entry,
    21B:10.

REGATTAS.
Motorboats, reckless or negligent
    operation, applicability, **90B:8.**

**REGENTS OF HIGHER
    EDUCATION, BOARD.**
Board of higher education
    generally.
    See BOARD OF HIGHER
        EDUCATION.

**REGIONAL BOARDS,
    AGENCIES, AND
    DISTRICTS.**
Audits.
    See AUDITS AND AUDITORS.
Blind veterans associations, rooms
    in state house, **8:17.**
Community colleges.
    See REGIONAL COMMUNITY
        COLLEGES.

**REGIONAL BOARDS,
    AGENCIES, AND
    DISTRICTS** —Cont'd
Health and welfare commission
    may establish facilities, **6:128.**
Health district, **111:27A-111:27C.**
    Group insurance for employees,
        acceptance, **32B:7A,
        32B:9E, 32B:10.**
    Surviving spouse of insured
        employee contribution
        toward health insurance
        premiums, **32B:9D.**
Housing and community
    development department,
    powers and duties, **23B:3.**
Housing authorities, **121B:3A.**
Library services, **78:19C, 78:19D.**
Mentally ill.
    See MENTALLY ILL AND
        RETARDED PERSONS.
Planning districts, **40B:1 et seq.**
    See REGIONAL PLANNING
        DISTRICTS.
Police districts, **41:99B-41:99K.**
    See REGIONAL POLICE
        DISTRICTS.
Refuse disposal, **16:21, 16:22,
    40:44A-40:44K.**
    See REGIONAL REFUSE
        DISPOSAL DISTRICTS.
Schools, **71:14-71:20.**
    See REGIONAL SCHOOL
        DISTRICTS.
Solid waste disposal districts,
    16:21.
Special education.
    See SPECIAL EDUCATION.
State building code, **143:3A.**
Transit authorities,
    161B:1-161B:25.
    See REGIONAL TRANSIT
        AUTHORITIES.
Welfare.
    See WELFARE AND SOCIAL
        SERVICES.
Zoning.
    See ZONING AND PLANNING.

**REGIONAL COMMUNITY
    COLLEGES.**
Accreditation, accepted applicants
    for admission to be given
    notice, **69:31C.**
Activity fees, **40:8H.**
Annuity contracts for employees of
    board, **15:18A.**
Board of regional community
    colleges, group annuity
    contracts for employees of
    boards, **15:18A.**

**REGIONAL COMMUNITY
    COLLEGES** —Cont'd
City or town, acquisition and
    conveyance of land for use of
    regional community college,
    40:14, 43:30.
Contracts and agreements,
    annuity contracts for
    employees, **15:18A.**
Curricula, establishment, **74:37A.**
Education programs,
    establishment of curricula,
    74:37A.
Fees, **40:8H.**
Group annuities for board
    employees, **15:18A.**
Labor and workforce development.
    Community college workforce
        training incentive grants,
        15A:15F.
Municipalities' authority to acquire
    and convey land for use,
    40:14, 43:30.
Notice, accepted applicants for
    admission to be given notice of
    accreditation, **69:31C.**
President of Massachusetts
    regional community colleges,
    custody of student activity
    fees, **40:8H.**
Secondary school level, courses of
    study beyond, **74:37A.**
State colleges' board of trustees,
    73:1C.
Workforce training incentive
    grants, **15A:15F.**

REGIONAL MEDICAL PANEL.
Retirement and disability, **32:6,
    32:8.**

**REGIONAL PLANNING
    COMPACT.**
Interstate.
    See INTERSTATE COMPACTS
        AND AGREEMENTS.

**REGIONAL PLANNING
    DISTRICTS, 40B:1 et seq.**
Aldermen and selectmen,
    membership on district
    planning commission, **40B:4.**
Alternate delegates to district
    commissions, provision, **40B:4.**
Annual estimates of costs for
    municipalities newly admitted
    to existing districts, **40B:7.**
Application for and admission to
    previously established district,
    40B:3.
Assessments, limit which may be
    charged against member
    communities, **40B:7.**

REGIONAL PLANNING DISTRICTS —Cont'd

Assistant treasurer to give bond, **40B:4.**

Authority of district commissions to act as economic development regional commissions, **40B:5B.**

Bonds, notes, and certificates, applicability of municipal finance provisions, **44:28B.**

Borrowing in anticipation of revenues, **40B:8.**

City council.
Planning commissions, appointment of designee, **40B:4.**
Southeastern regional planning and economic development district, termination of city's membership, **40B:10.**
Vote to establish, **40B:3.**

Commissioner of community affairs as member of district commission, **40B:4.**

Consent of municipality to inclusion, **40B:2A.**

Consultation with district commission, **40B:6.**

Contracts and agreements.
District planning commissions, **40B:5A, 40B:7, 40B:17.**
Federal government and certain municipalities, contracts, **40B:7.**
Public service contracts, authority to enter into, **40:4A.**
Water favorability studies, agreements for conducting, **40B:5A.**

Costs and expenses, estimate, **40B:7.**

Disbursement of funds of district commissions, **40B:7.**

District planning commissions, **40B:4-40B:7.**
Contract for planning studies and service by regional planning commissions, **40B:5A, 40B:7, 40B:17.**

Economic development department planning division, powers and duties, **40B:3.**

Employees of district planning commissions, **40B:4.**

Environmental impact reports to be delivered to commissions, **30:62B.**

Establishment, **40B:3, 40B:4.**

Executive committee, organization, membership, etc., **40B:4A.**

REGIONAL PLANNING DISTRICTS —Cont'd

Federal grants, acceptance, **40B:7.**

Federal installations within planning districts, commanding officers as members of district planning commission, **40B:4C.**

Gifts, **40B:7.**

Grants, **40B:7.**

Information to be furnished district planning commissions, **40B:6.**

Meetings, **40B:4.**

Officers of district planning commissions, **40B:4.**

Payments to district treasurer, **40B:7.**

Planning board, to assist, **40B:5.**

Powers and duties of district planning commissions, **40B:5.**

Public service contracts, authority to enter into, **40:4A.**

Purchase or sale of land for public building, notice, **7:40I.**

Purpose, **40B:2.**

Regional plans, authority as to preparation and adoption, **40B:5.**

Reports, **30:62B, 40B:5.**

Southeastern regional planning and economic development district, **40B:9-40B:19.**
See SOUTHEASTERN REGIONAL PLANNING AND ECONOMIC DEVELOPMENT DISTRICT.

State grants, acceptance, **40B:7.**

Studies and services, contracts or agreements, **40B:5A, 40B:7.**

Time or date of preparation of annual estimates, **40B:7.**

Title of act, **40B:1.**

Treasurer.
Bond of treasurer or assistant treasurer, **40B:4.**
Payments to treasurer, **40B:7.**
Southeastern Regional Planning and Economic Development District, treasury, **40B:15.**

Vote required to establish, **40B:3.**

Water favorability studies, agreements, **40B:5A.**

REGIONAL PLANNING LAW, 40B:1 et seq.

REGIONAL POLICE DISTRICTS, 41:99B-41:99K.

Aldermen and selectmen, **41:99H.**

Applicability of Act to police forces established under other provisions, **41:99B.**

REGIONAL POLICE DISTRICTS —Cont'd

Apportionment of costs among towns.
District commissions, **41:99G.**
Formula, **41:99I.**

Costs of operating.
Operating costs. See within this heading, "Operating costs."

District commission.
Operating costs, determination and apportionment, **41:99G.**
Organization, membership, **41:99F.**

District police departments, organization, powers, **41:99J.**

Establishment, **41:99C.**
Election, **41:99D.**

Expense of operating.
Operating costs. See within this heading, "Operating costs."

Jurisdiction, **41:99C.**

Operating costs.
Apportionment. See within this heading, "Apportionment of costs among towns."
Assessment of local taxes to pay, **41:99H.**
Certification of amounts and payment, **41:99G.**

Police departments of districts, organization, powers, **41:99J.**

Powers and duties, **41:99E.**

Purpose of Act establishing, **41:99B.**

Revocation of acceptance of law, procedure, **41:99K.**

Selectmen and aldermen, **41:99H.**

State treasurer's authority, **41:99H.**

Town treasurers, certification of amount and payment of operating costs, **41:99G.**

Treasurers, **41:99G, 41:99H.**

REGIONAL POSITION.
Definition, public libraries, **78:19C.**

REGIONAL PUBLIC LIBRARIES.
See LIBRARIES AND LIBRARIANS.

REGIONAL REFUSE DISPOSAL DISTRICTS, 16:21, 16:22, 40:44A-40:44K.
Advisory committees, **16:21.**
Agreements.
Contracts and agreements. See within this heading, "Contracts and agreements."

REGIONAL REFUSE DISPOSAL DISTRICTS
—Cont'd

Aldermen.
See ALDERMEN AND SELECTMEN.
Apportionment.
Costs and expenses. See within this heading, "Costs and expenses."
Appropriations for planning boards, **40:44B.**
Assessment limitations, **59:20A, 59:20B.**
Assessment of operating costs, **16:22.**
Audit of accounts, **40:44I.**
Bonds, notes, and obligations.
Applicability of municipal finance laws, **40:44K.**
Facsimile seals, **40:44F.**
Facsimile signatures, **40:44F.**
Tax exemption, **59:5.**
Borrowing money for construction of regional incinerators, municipal authority, **44:8.**
Budget.
Adoption of annual operating budget by district, **40:44F.**
Proposed agreement to make provisions, **40:44C.**
City council.
Creation of planning committee, **40:44A.**
Establishment of district by vote, **40:44E.**
Complaint.
Assignment of place for facility, complaint by person aggrieved, **111:150A.**
Hazardous waste management act, enforcement, **21C:10.**
Condemnation.
Eminent domain. See within this heading, "Eminent domain."
Contracts and agreements.
For sale or lease of property to district, **40:44J.**
Non-member municipalities and other governmental units, contracts, **40:44F.**
Proposed agreement for formation of district. See within this heading, "Proposed agreement for formation of district."
Costs and expenses.
Apportionment.
Annual maintenance and operation costs, **40:44H.**

REGIONAL REFUSE DISPOSAL DISTRICTS
—Cont'd

Costs and expenses —Cont'd
Apportionment —Cont'd
Of audit, **40:44I.**
Assessment, **16:22.**
Federal aid, expenditure, **40:44B.**
Proposed agreement to provide for construction and operation costs, **40:44C.**
Debt, **40:44C, 40:44F, 40:44H, 44:8.**
Designation of districts, **16:21.**
District committee.
Appointment of officers, **40:44G.**
Audit of accounts, **40:44I.**
Financial responsibilities, **40:44H.**
Membership, **40:44C.**
To exercise powers and perform duties of district, **40:44G.**
Duties, **40:44F.**
Eminent domain, **16:19, 92:9A.**
Regional refuse disposal districts, **40:44F.**
Establishment, **40:44E.**
Executive director and other employees, power as to employment, **40:44F.**
Expenses.
Costs and expenses. See within this heading, "Costs and expenses."
Expert assistance, employment, **40:44B.**
Federal aid, acceptance and expenditure, **40:44B.**
Hazardous waste management act's enforcement, complaint, **21C:10.**
Land.
Real property. See within this heading, "Real property."
Lease by member municipalities of property, **40:44J.**
Legal counsel, engagement, **40:44F.**
Limitation on municipal debt, apportionment of amounts pursuant to agreement with district as affecting, **40:44H.**
Mayors.
Appointment of members to planning committee, **40:44A.**
Audit report to be submitted, **40:44I.**
Duties in connection with establishment of district, **40:44E.**

REGIONAL REFUSE DISPOSAL DISTRICTS
—Cont'd

Notes.
Bonds, notes, and obligations.
See within this heading, "Bonds, notes, and obligations."
Notice as to incurring debt, **40:44F.**
Officers, appointment, duties and compensation, **40:44G.**
Payment by cities and towns, **40:44H.**
Planning boards.
Duties and formation, **40:44B.**
Proposed agreement for formation of district, preparation, **40:44C.**
Reports and recommendations, **40:44D.**
Planning committee.
Creation, **40:44A, 111:150A.**
Duty where member city or town disapproves the incurring of indebtedness, **40:44F.**
Formation of planning board, **40:44B.**
Plans for facilities, **40:44C.**
Powers, **40:44F.**
Proposed agreement for formation of district.
Copy to accompany planning board's report, when, **40:44D.**
Provisions, **40:44C.**
Public health department to approve plans, **40:44C.**
Real property.
Acquisition of land, **40:44F.**
Contracts for sale or lease of property to district, **40:44J.**
Records and reports.
Director of accounts in department of corporations and taxation, reports, **40:44I.**
Planning board, reports, **40:44D.**
Submission of annual report by district, **40:44F.**
Reports.
Records and reports. See within this heading, "Records and reports."
Sale of property, **40:44F, 40:44J.**
Secretary, appointment, **40:44G.**
Selectmen.
See ALDERMEN AND SELECTMEN.
Tax exemption for obligations, **59:5.**

**REGIONAL REFUSE
DISPOSAL DISTRICTS**
—Cont'd
Time.
For disapproving incurring of
indebtedness by district,
40:44F.
Terms of payment for sale or
lease of property, **40:44J.**
Town meetings.
Determination of question of
establishment of district,
40:44E.
Planning committee, creation,
40:44A.
Treasurer.
Appointment, duties and
compensation, **40:44G.**
General law provisions
applicable, **40:44G.**

**REGIONAL SCHOOL
DISTRICTS, 71:14 et seq.**
Acceptance.
Gifts and grants, **71:37A.**
Proposed agreement, acceptance,
71:14B, 71:15.
Accounts and accounting.
Audit of accounts, **44:35, 44:40.**
Cost of audit, apportionment,
71:16E.
Installation of accounting
system, **44:35.**
Nonresident and other students,
separate accounts for
tuition, **71:16D½.**
Actions.
Apportioned amount,
proceedings against town
failing to pay, **71:16B.**
Power to sue and be sued, **71:16.**
Agreements.
Contracts and agreements. See
within this heading,
"Contracts and agreements."
Aid.
Committee. See within this
heading, "Committee."
Gifts or grants. See within this
heading, "Gifts or grants."
Local aid.
See COMPACT FUND.
State aid. See within this
heading, "State aid or
reimbursement."
Annual report.
Duty to render to member
towns, **71:16.**
Planning board, report, **71:14A.**
Anticipation of revenue, incurring
of temporary debt, **71:16.**

**REGIONAL SCHOOL
DISTRICTS** —Cont'd
Apportionment of costs among
towns, **71:14B, 71:16B,
71:16E.**
Appropriations.
See APPROPRIATIONS.
Asbestos removal, limitation of
actions involving, **260:2D.**
Assessment of member cities and
towns, authority for, **71:16.**
To cover expense of audit of
committee's accounts,
71:16E.
Attendance, duty of temporary
secretary, **71:16A.**
Attorneys at law.
Collective bargaining, limit on
attorneys' fees, **71:16,
71:37E.**
Employment of attorney, **71:16.**
Indemnification of members of
committee, defense or
settlement by attorney,
71:16.
Attorneys' fee expended during
collective bargaining,
limitation, **71:16, 71:37E.**
Audit of accounts of.
Accounts and accounting. See
within this heading,
"Accounts and accounting."
Ballot, form of question, **71:15.**
Blue Hills regional vocational
school, retirement systems for
employees, **32:1 et seq.**
Bonds, notes, and certificates of
indebtedness.
Facsimile seals and signatures,
71:16.
Investments of proceeds, **44:55.**
Municipal finance provisions
relating to, applicability,
44:28A.
Power to issue, **71:16.**
Qualified bonds, **44A:1 et seq.**
Rebates to federal government,
44:53H.
Tax exemption, **59:5.**
Borrowing.
Indebtedness. See within this
heading, "Indebtedness to be
incurred by district."
Budget.
Committee, preparation, **71:16B.**
Determination, approval, action
upon non-approval, **71:16B,
71:16B½.**
Duty to adopt, **71:16.**
Public hearings on proposed
annual, **71:38N.**

**REGIONAL SCHOOL
DISTRICTS** —Cont'd
Buildings.
Construction of schools. See
within this heading,
"Construction of schools."
Lease, **71:14C, 71:16, 71:16D.**
Repairs or remodeling, **71:16,
71:16A.**
Sale, **71:14C.**
Certificates of indebtedness.
Bonds, notes, and certificates of
indebtedness. See within
this heading, "Bonds, notes,
and certificates of
indebtedness."
Certified personnel, rights and
benefits, **71:42B.**
Cities and towns.
Acceptance of proposed
agreement, **71:14B, 71:15.**
Annual report to member towns,
71:16.
Apportionment of costs and
expenses among member
towns, **71:14B, 71:16B,
71:16E.**
Appropriations for districts,
71:16B.
Assessment of member cities
and towns, authority for.
See within this heading,
"Assessment of member
cities and towns, authority
for."
Collective bargaining, prior
approval of regional school
district's expenditures,
71:16.
Compact fund.
See COMPACT FUND.
Compilation of tax rate as
affected by state aid to
regional school districts,
71:16D.
Equalized valuation for purposes
of computing regional
valuation percentage for
state aid to regional school
districts, **71:16D.**
Limitation of liability for
expenses, **71:16G.**
Meetings.
Town meeting. See within this
heading, "Town meeting."
Qualified bonds, **44A:1 et seq.**
Revocation of statute as to
membership in district,
4:4A.
Simultaneous membership in
vocational school district
and other type of regional
school district, **71:14B.**

REGIONAL SCHOOL
  DISTRICTS —Cont'd
Cities and towns —Cont'd
  State aid or reimbursement. See
    within this heading, "State
    aid or reimbursement."
  Submission of proposed
    agreement for acceptance,
    71:14B.
  Vote concerning budgets,
    notification of regional
    schools, 71:16B.
Civil service, positions placed,
  41:112.
Collaborative educational
  programs.
  Authority to enter into, 40:4E.
  Prepayment of tuition for school
    committee participating,
    41:56, 71:71D.
Collective bargaining.
  Attorneys' fees, limitation, 71:16,
    71:37E.
  Payroll deductions for
    bargaining association
    charges. See within this
    heading, "Payroll deductions
    for bargaining association
    charges."
  Prior approval of regional school
    district's expenditures,
    71:16.
Committee, 71:16A et seq.
  Acceptance and disbursement of
    gifts or grants, 71:37A.
  Apportionment of amounts
    required, 71:16B.
  Audit of accounts, 44:40,
    71:16E.
  Budget, preparation, 71:16B.
  Building committee, 71:16,
    71:16A.
  Chairman, election, 71:16A.
  Community programs, deposit or
    expenditures of funds
    received in connection,
    71:71C.
  Deductions.
    Maintenance and operating
      funds, deduction of aid
      district is to receive,
      71:16B, 71:16D.
    Regional reimbursable
      expenditures, deducting
      receipts, investments,
      grants, and gifts, 71:16D.
  Determination of amount needed
    annually, 71:16B.
  Failure of town to pay amount
    apportioned, proceedings,
    71:16B.

REGIONAL SCHOOL
  DISTRICTS —Cont'd
Committee —Cont'd
  Fiscal year, authority to amend
    agreements to conform to
    change in dates, 71:16B.
  Group insurance for employees,
    authority to pay subsidiary
    or additional rate, 32B:7A,
    32B:9E.
  Indemnification of members of
    committee, defense or
    settlement of claims, 71:16.
  Local option statute, revocation
    of acceptance, 4:4B.
  Magnet school facilities,
    application for grants,
    71:37I.
  Maintenance funds, 71:16D.
  Member, indemnification, 71:16.
  Model education programs,
    agreements, 40:4E.
  Notice of meetings, 39:23A,
    39:23B.
  Operating funds, 71:16B.
  Preference to veterans in
    appointing persons in labor
    service of schools, 41:112.
  Racial imbalance, elimination,
    15:1I, 15:1J, 71:37D.
  School building committee,
    appointment, powers and
    duties, 71:16, 71:16A.
  Secretary. See within this
    heading, "Secretary."
  Statement to be filed with city
    or town clerk, 55:24.
  Student advisory committee,
    meetings, 71:38M.
  Temporary secretary, 71:16A.
  Tenure of teachers, 71:42B.
  Treasurer. See within this
    heading, "Treasurer."
  Vice chairman, 71:16A.
  Vocational school committee,
    71:16A.
Community school programs,
  deposit and expenditure of
  money received by committee
  in connection, 71:71C.
Compact fund.
  See COMPACT FUND.
Compensation.
  Wages, salaries, and
    compensation. See within
    this heading, "Wages,
    salaries, and compensation."
Construction of schools.
  Building committee, 71:16,
    71:16A.
  Power as to, 71:16.

REGIONAL SCHOOL
  DISTRICTS —Cont'd
Construction of schools —Cont'd
  State aid, 71:16D.
Contracts and agreements.
  Collective bargaining. See within
    this heading, "Collective
    bargaining."
  Fiscal year, authority to amend
    agreements to conform to
    change in dates, 71:16B.
  Model education, agreements,
    40:4E.
  Power to enter into, 71:16.
  Proposed agreement.
    Planning board. See within
      this heading, "Planning
      board."
  Public services, power to
    contract for performance,
    40:4A.
  State aid, date of award of
    contract for construction,
    71:16D.
Contributory retirement system,
  71:16F.
Debt.
  Indebtedness to be incurred by
    district. See within this
    heading, "Indebtedness to be
    incurred by district."
Deductions.
  Committee. See within this
    heading, "Committee."
  Payroll deductions for
    bargaining association
    charges. See within this
    heading, "Payroll deductions
    for bargaining association
    charges."
Deeds executed by, validation,
  40:3A.
Defect or omission in creation of,
  effect, 71:15.
Deposit or investment of funds,
  44:55, 44:55A, 71:71C.
Determination of funds acquired
  for operation and
  maintenance, and
  apportionment of total
  among towns of district,
  71:16B.
Director of accounts, audit of
  accounts, 44:35, 44:40.
Discontinuance of certain
  regional school districts,
  71:42B.
Distance of residence of pupil as
  affecting transportation,
  71:16C.

REGIONAL SCHOOL DISTRICTS —Cont'd

Distributive occupations.
  Independent distributive occupations. See within this heading, "Independent distributive occupations schools."
Duties, **71:16.**
Education department, proposed agreement to be submitted, **71:14B.**
Elections.
  See ELECTIONS.
Emergency finance board, powers and duties, **71:14 et seq.**
Employees.
  Collective bargaining. See within this heading, "Collective bargaining."
  Former employee of school committee, employment, **71:42B.**
  Group insurance for employees, authority to pay subsidiary or additional rate, **32B:7A, 32B:9E.**
  Indemnification of insurance, **71:16.**
  Legal counsel, power to engage, **71:16.**
  Lobbying law exemption, **3:50.**
  Retirement systems.
    Generally.
      See RETIREMENT SYSTEMS AND PENSIONS.
  Secretary. See within this heading, "Secretary."
  Superintendent of schools. See within this heading, "Superintendent of schools."
  Surviving spouse of insured employee, contribution toward health insurance premiums, **32B:9D, 32B:9D½.**
  Suspension of officer or employee under indictment, filing notice with district secretary, **268A:25.**
  Teachers and other professional employees. See within this heading, "Teachers and other professional employees."
  Veterans to be given preference in labor service of schools, **41:112.**

REGIONAL SCHOOL DISTRICTS —Cont'd

Employees —Cont'd
  Vocational education personnel superseded by establishment and operation of regional school district, rights, **71:42B.**
  Wages, salaries, and compensation. See within this heading, "Wages, salaries, and compensation."
  Workers' compensation, **152:69.**
Equalized valuation in cities and towns for purpose of computing regional valuation percentage for state aid, **71:16D.**
Equipment.
  Building committees, powers and duties, **71:16A.**
  Community school programs, deposit and expenditure of money received by school committee in connection, **71:71C.**
  Debt, power to incur for purchase of departmental equipment, **71:16.**
  Lease or lease with option to purchase equipment for educational purposes, **71:16.**
Establishment, **71:15.**
  Recommendations of planning boards, **71:14B.**
Excess and deficiency fund, application to reduce assessments, **71:16B½.**
Expenses and expenditures, **71:14 et seq.**
Facsimile seals and signatures on bonds and notes, **71:16.**
Farmers Home Administration, authorization to incur debt financed, **44:8.**
Former employee of town school committee, employment, **71:42B.**
Form of question upon ballot, **71:15.**
Gifts or grants.
  Compensation to teachers or professional employees granted leave of absence, **71:41A.**
  Expenditure of gifts of funds, **44:53A, 71:16D, 71:37A.**
  Magnet school facilities, application for grants, **71:37I.**
  Power to receive and disburse, **71:16, 71:37A.**

REGIONAL SCHOOL DISTRICTS —Cont'd

Group insurance for employees, **32B:19.**
  Authority to pay subsidiary or additional rate, **32B:7A, 32B:9E.**
Health insurance premiums of surviving spouse of municipal employees, **32B:9D½, 32B:9D¾.**
Hearings on proposed annual budget, **71:38N.**
Household arts school, form of proposed agreement, **71:14B.**
Illegal appropriations by, restraint, **40:53.**
Income tax proceeds used, **71:16C.**
Indebtedness to be incurred by district.
  Approval by voters in member towns, **71:14D, 71:16.**
  Bonds, notes, and certificates of indebtedness. See within this heading, "Bonds, notes, and certificates of indebtedness."
  Elections, provisions, **71:16.**
  Equipment, power to incur debt for purchase, **71:16.**
  Farmers Home Administration, financing, **44:8.**
  Repairs or remodeling of buildings, **71:16, 71:16A.**
  Temporary debt, power to incur in anticipation of revenue, **71:16.**
  Vocational regional school districts, **71:16.**
Indemnification insurance, **71:16.**
Independent distributive occupations schools.
  Establishment and maintenance of schools, **74:5A.**
  Form of proposed agreement, **71:14B.**
Indicted officer or employee, filing notice of suspension with district secretary, **268A:25.**
Industrial arts schools.
  Establishment and maintenance, **74:5A.**
  Form of proposed agreement, **71:14B.**
Interest in depository of regional school district funds by treasurer, **44:55.**
Investment of funds, limitation, **44:55.**
Labor and employment.
  Employees. See within this heading, "Employees."

REGIONAL SCHOOL DISTRICTS —Cont'd

Labor relations and disputes.
  Collective bargaining. See within this heading, "Collective bargaining."
Land.
  Real property. See within this heading, "Real property."
Leases, **71:14C.**
  Land, buildings, or equipment, **71:16, 71:16D.**
Legal counsel.
  Attorneys at law. See within this heading, "Attorneys at law."
Limitation of towns liability for expenses, **71:16G.**
Limitation on deposit or investment of funds, **44:55.**
Liquidation of depository of public funds, public officer's liability, **44:55A.**
Lobbying laws, exemptions regarding employees and agents of regional school districts, **3:50.**
Local aid.
  See COMPACT FUND.
Local option statutes, revocation of acceptance, **4:4B.**
Machinery and equipment.
  Equipment. See within this heading, "Equipment."
Magnet school facilities, application for grants, **71:37I.**
Maintenance and operating funds, deduction of aid district is to receive, **71:16B, 71:16D.**
Meetings.
  Governmental bodies, filing notice of meetings, **39:23B.**
  Town meeting. See within this heading, "Town meeting."
Model education, agreements, **40:4E.**
Municipal corporations.
  Cities and towns. See within this heading, "Cities and towns."
Name, power to adopt, **71:16.**
Notice and knowledge.
  Committee meetings, notice, **39:23A, 39:23B.**
  Officer or employee under indictment, filing notice of suspension with district secretary, **268A:25.**
  Proposed borrowing, notice, **71:16.**
  Racial imbalance, existence, **71:37D.**

REGIONAL SCHOOL DISTRICTS —Cont'd

Nurses, payroll deductions on account of dues to associations of public school teachers, **180:17E.**
Occupational guidance and placement directors, **71:38D.**
Operating funds, **71:16B.**
Payroll deductions for bargaining association charges, **180:17G.**
  Nurses, deductions on account of teachers' association dues, **180:17E.**
Pensions.
  See RETIREMENT SYSTEMS AND PENSIONS.
Planning board, **71:14 et seq.**
  Appropriations for expenses, **71:14.**
  Contents of proposed agreement, **71:14B.**
  Creation, **71:14.**
  Duties, **71:14A.**
  Form of proposed agreement, **71:14B.**
  Members, **71:14.**
  Planning committees from two or more towns forming, **71:14.**
  Proposed agreement.
    Acceptance, **71:15.**
    Form and contents, submission, **71:14B.**
  Report, **71:14A.**
Posting of notices as to committee meetings, **39:23B.**
Practical art classes, maintenance, **74:14.**
Preference to veterans in employment in nonprofessional positions, **41:112.**
Prepayment of tuition for collaborative educational program, **41:56.**
Publication of audit of accounts, **44:40.**
Public employer as including educational collaborative, **258:1.**
Public services, authority to contract relative to performance, **40:4A.**
Pupils.
  Students. See within this heading, "Students."
Qualified bonds, **44A:1 et seq.**
Racial imbalance, elimination, **15:1I, 15:1J, 71:37D.**
Real property.
  Leases. See within this heading, "Leases."

REGIONAL SCHOOL DISTRICTS —Cont'd

Real property —Cont'd
  Power to acquire, **71:16.**
  School buildings.
    Buildings. See within this heading, "Buildings."
Records and reports.
  Annual report. See within this heading, "Annual report."
  Filing.
    Secretary. See within this heading, "Secretary."
Registration of voters in regional high schools, **51:42D.**
Reimbursement.
  State aid or reimbursement. See within this heading, "State aid or reimbursement."
Repairs or remodeling of school buildings, power to incur debt for purpose, **71:16, 71:16A.**
Reports.
  Records and reports.
    Annual report. See within this heading, "Annual report."
Retirement systems.
  See RETIREMENT SYSTEMS AND PENSIONS.
Revocation of statute involving membership in regional school district by town, **4:4A.**
Salaries.
  Wages, salaries, and compensation. See within this heading, "Wages, salaries, and compensation."
Sale of school buildings, **71:14C.**
School buildings.
  Buildings. See within this heading, "Buildings."
School buses and transportation of pupils, **71:16C, 71:16D.**
School committee.
  Committee. See within this heading, "Committee."
Seal, power to adopt corporate seal, **71:16.**
Secretary.
  Appointment by committee, **71:16A.**
  Certificates of appointment or election of filing, **41:19A.**
  Suspension of officer or employee under indictment, filing notice with secretary, **268A:25.**
  Temporary secretary, appointment, **71:16A.**
Severability of provisions upon question of constitutionality, **71:16I.**

REGIONAL SCHOOL DISTRICTS —Cont'd

Sewerage systems, acquisition of, **71:16.**

Sex education committees to be established, **71:38O.**

Special education.
See SPECIAL EDUCATION.

Special laws, districts established.
State aid for construction of regional schools, **71:16D.**

Temporary debt, power to incur in anticipation of revenue, **71:16.**

State aid or reimbursement, **71:14B, 71:16B et seq.**
Amount of reimbursement to certain towns etc., **70:4.**

Assessment of taxes for expenses of district, **71:16E.**

Compact fund.
See COMPACT FUND.

Compilation of tax rates of cities and towns as affected, **71:16D.**

Construction of regional schools, **71:16D.**

Equalized valuation in cities and towns for purpose of computing regional valuation percentage, **71:16D.**

Expenditures, **71:16D.**

Local aid fund.
See COMPACT FUND.

Special laws, state aid for construction in districts established, **71:16D.**

Town forming districts, **70:14A.**

Transportation of pupils, **71:16C, 71:16D.**

State treasurer, payments, **71:16C.**

Students.
Advisory committee, election, **71:38M.**

Annual report as to number, **72:2A.**

Subcommittee for purpose of signing payroll warrants, establishment, **71:16A.**

Superintendent of schools.
Power to employ, **71:16.**

Salary, **71:64.**

Union superintendents of schools, salary and expenses, **71:64.**

Surviving spouse of insured employee, contribution toward health insurance premiums, **32B:9D.**

Taxation.
Income tax proceeds used, **71:16C.**

REGIONAL SCHOOL DISTRICTS —Cont'd

Taxation —Cont'd
Reduction in local taxes, **71:16B, 71:16B½.**

State aid or reimbursement. See within this heading, "State aid or reimbursement."

Teachers and other professional employees.
Appropriations for salaries, **71:16, 71:42B.**

Leave of absence, compensation during, **71:41A.**

Occupational guidance and placement directors, **71:38D.**

Retirement systems.
See RETIREMENT SYSTEMS AND PENSIONS.

School nurse, payroll deductions on account of dues to public school teachers' association, **180:17E.**

Tenure, **71:42B.**

Wages, salaries, and compensation, **71:40, 71:42B.**

Town meeting.
Appropriation for district, **71:16B.**

Holding, **71:15.**

Planning board, creation, **71:14.**

Submission of question as to district, **71:15.**

Towns.
Cities and towns. See within this heading, "Cities and towns."

Transportation of pupils, **71:16C, 71:16D.**

Treasurer.
Application of certain laws, **71:16A.**

Appointment, **71:16A.**

Assistant treasurer, **71:16A.**

Certification to towns of amount apportioned to each, **71:16B.**

Compensation, **71:16A.**

Duties, **71:16A.**

Interest in depository of regional school district funds, **44:55.**

Prepayment of tuition for collaborative educational programs, **41:56.**

Removal, **41:39B.**

Transportation costs, reimbursement, **71:16C.**

Tuition.
Collaborative education, prepayment of tuition, **41:56.**

REGIONAL SCHOOL DISTRICTS —Cont'd

Tuition —Cont'd
Separate accounts for nonresident and other students, **71:16D½.**

Vocational education, tuition to be charged pupils residing outside district, **74:7C.**

Unconstitutionality of provision, effect, **71:16I.**

Union superintendents of schools, salary and expenses, **71:64.**

Veterans.
Preference in labor service of schools, **41:112.**

Retirement law for veterans, acceptance, **32:60.**

Vocational education.
Agricultural arts schools maintained by regional school districts, **71:14B, 74:5A.**

Application of chapter to personnel, **71:42B.**

Blue Hills regional vocational school, retirement system for employees, **32:1 et seq.**

Boards of regional school district trustees, **74:5A.**

Committees, compensation of treasurer and assistant treasurer, **71:16A.**

Debts, power to incur, **71:16.**

Personnel superseded by establishment and operation of regional school district, rights, **71:42B.**

Planning committees and boards of, contents of proposed agreement, **71:14B.**

Town simultaneously member of district, and other type of regional school district, **71:14B.**

Tuition to be charged pupils residing outside district, **74:7C.**

Voter registration in regional high schools, **51:42D.**

Wages, salaries, and compensation.
Appropriations, **71:16.**

Payroll deductions for bargaining association charges. See within this heading, "Payroll deductions for bargaining association charges."

Teachers, **71:42B.**

Workers' compensation for employees, **152:69.**

REGIONAL SCHOOL
    DISTRICTS —Cont'd
Zoning.
    Planning board. See within this
      heading, "Planning board."

REGIONAL TRANSIT
    AUTHORITIES,
    161B:1-161B:25.
Accountants, employment,
    161B:12.
Action or suit, protection of the
    rights of bondholders,
    161B:20.
Additional powers of authority,
    161B:6.
Administration and finance
    executive office.
    Contracts to provide 50 percent
      of net cost of service,
      161B:23.
    Rules and regulations pertaining
      to assistance by private
      carriers from bond proceeds,
      161B:17.
    Subsidies of authorities,
      161B:23.
Administrator.
    Additional powers to be
      exercised, **161B:6.**
    Appointment as chief executive
      officer of authority, **161B:4.**
Advisory boards.
    Executive committee, authority
      to appoint, **161B:5.**
    Finance Advisory Board, **6:98.**
    Meetings to establish authority,
      161B:14.
    Membership, voting rights,
      161B:5.
    Reports to be submitted, **161B:8.**
Agreements.
    Contracts or agreements. See
      within this heading,
      "Contracts or agreements."
Annual audit of authority,
    161B:12.
Applicability of certain general
    laws, **161B:24.**
Assessment of net cost of service
    or deficits, **161B:9.**
Assistants, employment, **161B:12.**
Audit of authority, **161B:12.**
    Bond of treasurer or assistant
      treasurer, **40B:4.**
Authorized regional transit
    authorities, **161B:2.**
Bonds and securities.
    Capital costs, bonds for
      payment, **161B:17.**
    Court order for payment to
      bondholders, **161B:11.**

REGIONAL TRANSIT
    AUTHORITIES —Cont'd
Bonds and securities —Cont'd
    Current expenses, payments to
      meet, **161B:11.**
    Debt service on bonds, maturity,
      161B:23.
    Default, methods of payment in
      event, **161B:11.**
    Enforcement, **161B:20.**
    Interest and interest rates. See
      within this heading,
      "Interest and interest rates."
    Issuance of bonds or notes,
      161B:6, 161B:10, 161B:17,
      161B:18, 161B:21.
    Legal investments, bonds,
      161B:19.
    Power to issue bonds, **161B:7.**
    Protection of rights, **161B:20.**
    Rights of bondholders, **161B:11.**
    Trust agreement to secure bonds
      and notes, **161B:18,**
      161B:21.
Borrowing to make payments to
    meet current expenses,
    161B:10.
Budget, **161B:8.**
Bylaws, establishment, **161B:6.**
Capital costs, issuance of bonds for
    payment, **161B:17.**
Cities or towns.
    Municipalities. See within this
      heading, "Municipalities."
Compensation or salary.
    Administrator, **161B:4.**
    Employees, **161B:6.**
Conditions imposed on authority,
    161B:8.
Contiguous municipalities and
    authorities, **161B:3, 161B:8.**
Contracts or agreements, **161B:8.**
    Commonwealth, contract
      assistance may be provided,
      161B:23.
    Power of authority, **161B:6,**
      161B:8.
    Public service contracts, **40:4A.**
    Trust agreement to secure bonds
      and notes, **161B:18,**
      161B:21.
Corporate seal, power to adopt and
    use, **161B:6.**
Costs and expenses.
    Borrowing to make payments,
      161B:10.
    Capital costs, issuance of bonds,
      161B:17.
    Current expenses, payments to
      bondholders to meet,
      161B:11.

REGIONAL TRANSIT
    AUTHORITIES —Cont'd
Costs and expenses —Cont'd
    Deficits, payment by
      Commonwealth and
      assessment against affected
      municipalities, **161B:9.**
    Net cost of service. See within
      this heading, "Net cost of
      service."
    Reimbursement of
      Commonwealth for cost of
      audit, **161B:12.**
Court order for payments to
    bondholders, **161B:11.**
Definitions, **161B:1.**
Designation and ability to form,
    161B:2.
Direct operation of mass
    transportation service by
    authority not authorized by
    chapter, **161B:25.**
Disposition of funds, **29:2O,**
    161B:10.
Easements, acquisition, **161B:7.**
Election.
    Advisory board members, voting
      rights, **161B:5.**
    Organization of transportation
      authority, **161B:15.**
    Termination of membership in
      transit authority, **161B:15.**
Elective office, employees
    prohibited from holding,
    161B:4, 161B:6.
Excess revenues, disposition,
    161B:10.
Executors and administrators.
    Administrator. See within this
      heading, "Administrator."
Exemption from taxation,
    161B:13.
Expenses.
    Costs and expenses. See within
      this heading, "Costs and
      expenses."
Facilities, establishment, **161B:6,**
    161B:7.
Fares charged by transportation
    companies, changes, **161B:8.**
Federal assistance, securing,
    161B:22.
Finance Advisory Board, **6:98.**
Formation of transit authority,
    161B:3.
General court, reports of annual
    audit of authority, **161B:12.**
Gifts and grants, acceptance,
    161B:6.
Governor.
    Establishment, notice, **161B:3.**

REGIONAL TRANSIT AUTHORITIES —Cont'd

Governor —Cont'd

Notice of meeting to establish authority, **161B:14.**

Reports of annual audits of authority, **161B:12.**

Reports on operation to be submitted, **161B:8.**

Interest and interest rates.

Bonds and notes, interest payments, **161B:11, 161B:21.**

Capital improvements, interest on bonds issued, **161B:17.**

Joining of contiguous or noncontiguous authority, **161B:3.**

Landlord and tenant.

Leases. See within this heading, "Leases."

Leases.

Entering into lease arrangements, **161B:7.**

Property belonging to Regional Transit Authorities, lease, **161B:8.**

Legal investments, bonds, **161B:19.**

Limitations, conditions, obligations, and duties of authorities, **161B:8.**

Mandamus, protection of bondholders by action, **161B:20.**

Massachusetts bay transportation authority, effect on, **161A:48.**

Maturity of debt service on bonds, **161B:23.**

Meetings to establish authority, **161B:14.**

Municipalities.

Assessment of net cost of service against, **161B:9.**

Contiguous municipalities outside authority's area, provisions for service, **161B:8.**

Notice of meetings to establish authority, **161B:14.**

Termination of membership in transit authority, **161B:15.**

Net cost of service.

Assessment of cost against municipality, **161B:9.**

Notification to and actions by state treasurer, **161B:10.**

REGIONAL TRANSIT AUTHORITIES —Cont'd

Notes or bonds.

Bonds or securities. See within this heading, "Bonds and securities."

Notice.

Change of service, notice, **161B:8.**

Meetings to establish authority, notice, **161B:14.**

Net cost of service, **161B:10.**

Sales of real property, **161B:8.**

Off-street parking facilities, establishment, **161B:6.**

Other laws, application, **161B:24.**

Parking facilities, establishment, **161B:6.**

Powers, **161B:2.**

Additional powers, **161B:6.**

Principal office or place of business, establishment, **161B:6.**

Private carriers.

Assistance from bond proceeds, procedure for applying, **161B:17.**

Continuation of service by, private transportation companies, **161B:8.**

Programs for mass transportation, **161B:8.**

Protection of rights of bondholders, **161B:20.**

Protective arrangements for private carriers, **161B:8.**

Public service contracts, **40:4A.**

Rates and fares, changes, **161B:8.**

Real property.

Power to hold property, **161B:2.**

Sales of real estate, **161B:8.**

Records and reports.

General court, reports of annual audit of authority, **161B:12.**

Governor. See within this heading, "Governor."

Operations, submission of report, **161B:8.**

Research, conducting, **161B:6.**

Reserve fund, establishment, **161B:10.**

REGIONAL TRANSIT AUTHORITIES —Cont'd

Retirement, pension, and civil service laws, inapplicability to authority employees, **32:1-32:102.**

Salary.

Compensation or salary. See within this heading, "Compensation or salary."

Secretary of executive office of transportation and construction.

Transportation and construction executive office. See within this heading, "Transportation and construction executive office."

Secretary of executive offices for administration and finance, rules and regulations pertaining to assistance by private carriers from bond proceeds, **161B:17.**

Securities.

Bonds and securities. See within this heading, "Bonds and securities."

Separate units of mass transportation facilities, authority to establish, **161B:7.**

Special or local assessments, exemption, **161B:13.**

State.

Contract assistance, Commonwealth may provide, **161B:23.**

Cost of audit, reimbursement of Commonwealth, **161B:12.**

Deficits, payment by Commonwealth and assessment against affected municipalities, **161B:9.**

Disposition of funds, **29:2O.**

Treasurer.

State treasurer. See within this heading, "State treasurer."

State auditor, annual audit of authorities, **161B:12.**

State treasurer.

Borrowing by state treasurer to make payments, **161B:10.**

Certification of payments to meet current expenses, **161B:11.**

Net cost of service, ratification to and actions by state treasurer, **161B:10.**

Taxation, exemption, **161B:13.**

**REGIONAL TRANSIT
AUTHORITIES** —Cont'd

Telecommunications and energy
department to resolve
disputes, **161B:16.**

Termination of membership in
transit authority, election,
161B:15.

Time when transit authority
deemed established, **161B:14.**

Towns.

Municipalities. See within this
heading, "Municipalities."

Transportation and construction
executive office.

Agencies within, **6A:19.**

Bond issues to be approved by
secretary, **161B:17.**

Reports to be submitted to
secretary, **161B:8.**

Treasurer of state.

State treasurer. See within this
heading, "State treasurer."

Trust agreement to secure bonds
and notes, **161B:18, 161B:21.**

Uniform Commercial Code, bonds
as negotiable instruments,
161B:17.

Urban Mass Transportation Act of
1964, assistance to private
carriers, **161B:8.**

Wages.

Compensation or salary. See
within this heading,
"Compensation or salary."

When transit authority deemed
established, **161B:14.**

**REGIONAL
TRANSPORTATION
AUTHORITY ACT, 161B:1
et seq.**

**REGIONAL
TRANSPORTATION
SYSTEMS.**

Growth and development policy
committees, cities and towns,
40:4I.

**REGIONAL WATER
DISTRICTS.**
**See WATERWORKS AND
WATER SUPPLY.**

REGISTERED MAIL.

Defined or construed, **4:7, 41:81L.**

Guardian appointed for mentally
ill person, **201:6.**

Hazardous waste, seizure and
forfeiture of property, **21C:14.**

Mortgage (note), copy to be
forwarded by mail, **140:90B.**

REGISTERED MAIL —Cont'd

Petition to general court, **3:5.**

Service of process, **231:13A.**

Banks, hearings to investigate
consumer transactions,
167:2C.

Probate court citation, **215:46.**

State ballot law commission.

See STATE BALLOT LAW
COMMISSION.

Warehouseman's lien, notice of
enforcement, **106:7-210.**

**REGISTERED PHYSICAL
THERAPISTS LAW, 112:23A
et seq.**

**REGISTER OF
COMMONWEALTH OF
MASSACHUSETTS.**

Distribution, **30A:6.**

Gasoline.

See GASOLINE AND MOTOR
FUELS.

REGISTER OF COURT.

Auditors filing reports in office,
221:62.

Forgery or counterfeiting of court
register's certificate, **267:1,
267:5.**

Indigency limits, public posting of
by register of court, **261:27C.**

Probate and insolvency register,
215:1, 217:1-217:43.

See REGISTERS OF PROBATE
AND INSOLVENCY.

**REGISTERS AND REGISTRIES
OF DEEDS, 36:1 et seq.,
183:4.**

Abandonment of land or
easements by city or town,
record, **40:15.**

Abolition of county governments.

Employees of Commonwealth
upon transfer, **34B:10.**

Powers and duties transferred to
Commonwealth, **34B:4.**

Rights of employees after
transfer, **34B:11.**

Abstract cards for tax assessors,
36:24B.

Accounts, **36:39.**

Examination by director of
accounts, **35:45.**

Stamp tax on deeds and
documents, examination of
books of taxpayers, **64D:6.**

Acknowledgment.

Filing copy of unacknowledged
deed, **183:38.**

Prerequisite to filing, **183:29.**

**REGISTERS AND REGISTRIES
OF DEEDS** —Cont'd

Address.

Grantee, effect of failure to
comply with requirements
as to address and name,
183:6, 185:61.

Inclusion of street address of
property in records, **183:6B,
185:61A.**

Affidavits, **183:5A, 183:5B.**

Invalid tax title, recording
affidavit of notice to holder,
60:83.

Partition, affidavit of filing
notice in registry of deeds,
241:7.

Sale of low value land held
under tax title by city or
town, recording affidavit in
connection, **60:79.**

Tax collector's affidavit filed in
registry as evidence, **60:57.**

Agreements.

Contracts and agreements. See
within this heading,
"Contracts and agreements."

Airport approach regulations,
recording, **90:40A.**

Another county, filing of records of
real property interests located,
217:15C.

Antenuptial marriage contract
affecting property, recording,
209:26.

Apportionment of tax on partition
property, **59:78A.**

Assessments.

See SPECIAL ASSESSMENTS.

Assessors of taxes, abstract cards
or copies of records, **36:24B,
262:38.**

Assignment of rents or profits,
recording, **183:4.**

Assistant recorder of land court,
register, **185:10, 185:11.**

Fees for duties, **262:39.**

Assistant registers, **36:4 et seq.**

Middlesex County. See within
this heading, "Middlesex
County."

Removal or discharge from
employment, **35:51.**

When to act, **36:8.**

Attachment of property.

See ATTACHMENT OF
PROPERTY.

Attestation of records, **36:18,
36:19.**

Bonds and undertakings, **36:3.**

Assistant recorder of Land
Court, **185:11.**

REGISTERS AND REGISTRIES OF DEEDS —Cont'd

Bonds and undertakings —Cont'd
Deed and document stamp tax, **64D:3.**
Reimbursement of county for premiums on bond, **64D:3B.**
Boundaries of flats, recording of report and plan establishing, **240:20, 240:21.**
Business corporations, filing certificate of consolidation or merger, **156B:78, 156B:79.**
Candidate for register of deeds, certificate of party enrollment, **53:48.**
Certificates and certification.
Candidate for register of deeds, certificate of party enrollment, **53:48.**
Consolidation or merger of corporations, filing certificates, **156B:78, 156B:79.**
Copies. See within this heading, "Copies."
Cotenant's lien for paying tax, recording certificate, **60:86.**
Date and place of record, **36:23.**
Elections, certification of record of vote, **54:121.**
Final disposition of proceedings affecting title to realty, **184:16.**
Judgment or decree affecting land, recording certified copy, **184:17.**
Municipal lighting plant, certificate of acceptance filed, **164:58B.**
Recreational land, recording certificate of tax payment, **61B:15.**
Tax collector's certificate of taxes and assessments on real estate, recording, **60:23.**
Tax titles, recording certificate of redemption, **60:62, 60:63.**
Charitable trusts, notice to transitional assistance department as to recording, **36:32.**
Chief clerk, Worcester district, **36:7.**
Cities and towns.
Abandonment of land or easement, record, **40:15.**
Conveyance of low value land, defects in notice or procedure, **60:80C.**

REGISTERS AND REGISTRIES OF DEEDS —Cont'd

Cities and towns —Cont'd
Liens of, recording of certificate, **60:23.**
Lighting plant, certificate of acceptance filed, **164:58B.**
Tax deeds and titles. See within this heading, "Tax deeds and titles."
Clerks.
Allowance for clerical assistance, **36:38.**
Worcester district, chief clerk, **36:7.**
Coastal wetlands regulations to be recorded, **130:105.**
Common nuisance, record of injunction against, **139:16A.**
Community preservation.
Surcharge on recording fees, **44B:8.**
Compensation.
Salary or compensation. See within this heading, "Salary or compensation."
Condominiums, recording of statement as to unpaid common expenses, **183A:6.**
Connecticut River, filing survey, **91:32.**
Conservation and preservation restrictions, filing and recording, **184:33.**
Consideration, acceptance for recording of deed failing to show full consideration, **183:6.**
Consolidation or merger of corporations, **156:46A, 156:46B, 156:46D, 156B:78, 156B:79.**
Constitution of Massachusetts, plurality of offices regulated, **MA Const Part 2 Ch 6 Art 2; Amend Art 8.**
Contracts and agreements, **184:17A.**
Betterment assessments, recordation of deferral and recovery agreements pertaining, **80:13B.**
Purchase and sale of realty, recording agreements, **184:17A.**
Sharecropping agreement, recording, **255:7D.**
Copies.
Birth, marriage, and death records, **46:19A.**
Impossibility of duplication as affecting authority to refuse recording, **36:12A.**

REGISTERS AND REGISTRIES OF DEEDS —Cont'd

Copies —Cont'd
Indexes, **36:28, 36:29.**
Judgment or decree affecting land, recording of certified copy, **184:17.**
Microphotographic copies of books, **36:15.**
Plans, fees for filing copies, **36:13B, 262:38.**
Several counties, recording of certified copies of instruments relating, **36:13.**
Tax assessors, furnishing copies of records, **262:38.**
Unacknowledged deed, recording copy, **183:38.**
Worn, mutilated, or indistinct records, duplication, **36:17.**
Corporations.
Articles of consolidation or merger, filing, **156:46A, 156:46B, 156:46D, 156B:79.**
Certificate of consolidation or merger, filing, **156B:78, 156B:79.**
Cotenant's lien for paying taxes on land, recording certificate, **60:86.**
Counties.
Another county, filing of records of real property interests located, **217:15C.**
Assistant registers in certain counties, **36:5, 36:6.**
Deed and document stamp tax, reimbursement of county for premiums on bond, **64D:3B.**
Districts in certain counties. See within this heading, "Districts in certain counties."
Personnel review board of county, register of deeds as member, **35:51B.**
Salary paid, **36:33.**
Several counties, certified copies of instruments relating to land lying, **36:13.**
Dams and reservoirs, recording of permits regarding, **253:45.**
Date of record, certificate on instrument, **36:23.**
Death before beginning term of office, effect, **54:145.**
Decrees.
Judgments and decrees. See within this heading, "Judgments and decrees."
Deed stamp tax.
Stamp tax. See within this heading, "Stamp tax."

REGISTERS AND REGISTRIES OF DEEDS —Cont'd

Defeasance, recording instruments, **183:53.**

Defective deeds, protection of certain titles against, **184:24.**

Delivery of deed, presumption from recording, **183:5.**

Deposition to perpetuate testimony, recording, **233:50 et seq.**

Deposit of surplus funds, **35:22.**

Disability, temporary register in case, **36:8, 54:143.**

Disclaimer of interest in real property, **191A:5.**

Discriminatory practices, recording of order enjoining other disposition of property of nonresident charged, **151B:5.**

Districts in certain counties, **36:1.**
As place of record, **36:12.**

Document stamp tax.
Bonds and undertakings. See within this heading, "Bonds and undertakings."

Dower barred ten years after recording, **189:16.**

Dredging and reclamation of land, recording liens, **254:30.**

Duplicates.
Copies. See within this heading, "Copies."

Easements.
Notice, prevention of prescription easements, **187:3.**
Record of abandonment by city or town, **40:15.**

Election, **36:2, 54:157.**
Death before beginning term, effect, **54:145.**
Examination and certification of record of vote, **54:121.**
Failure to elect, procedure, **54:143.**
Nomination papers, number of signatures, **53:44.**
Party enrollment of candidate, certificate, **53:48.**
Transmission of record of votes, **54:112.**
Vacancy in office, election to fill, **54:143.**

Eminent domain.
See EMINENT DOMAIN.

Employment security, recording lien of overdue contributions, **151A:16.**

Entry, writs of.
Writs of entry. See within this heading, "Writs of entry."

REGISTERS AND REGISTRIES OF DEEDS —Cont'd

Estate inventory information as to real property, recording, **217:15B.**

Evidence.
Delivery of deed, presumption from recording, **183:5.**
Execution of deed, recording pending proof, **183:38.**
Tax collector's affidavit filed in registry as evidence, **60:57.**

Examination, inspection or investigation.
Accounts. See within this heading, "Accounts."
Elections, examination of record of votes, **54:121.**

Excise on deeds, instruments and writings, **64D:3.**

Executions.
See EXECUTIONS.

Facsimile attestation of records, **36:19.**

Federal government.
Condemnation order for property taken by federal government, record, **79:44.**
Notation as to federal tax stamp, **36:15.**
Succession tax receipts, recording, **36:16.**
Tax liens and discharges thereof, filing, **36:24.**
United States courts, duties as to papers in actions affecting title to land, **223:69.**

Fees, **262:38.**
Accounting, **36:39.**
Community preservation.
Surcharge on recording fees, **44B:8.**
Copying worn, mutilated, or indistinct records, **36:17.**
Federal tax liens, filing, **36:24.**
Land court, fees for duties as assistant recorder, **262:39.**
List of fees to be posted in public offices, **262:46.**
Marginal references, additional, **262:38.**
Plans, filing copies, **36:13B, 262:38.**
Salary or compensation. See within this heading, "Salary or compensation."

Final disposition of proceedings affecting title to realty, recording certificate, **184:16.**

Fire hazard, recording lien for expenses of record, **148:5.**

REGISTERS AND REGISTRIES OF DEEDS —Cont'd

Forms.
Indexes, **36:25.**
Record books, **36:14.**

Grantor-grantee index.
Indexes. See within this heading, "Indexes."

Guardian of spendthrift, effect of record of petition for appointment, **201:10.**

Highways and streets.
Filing order changing name of highway, **85:3B.**
Inclusion of street address of property in records, **183:6B, 185:61A.**

Historic districts and sites.
Landmarks, recording of notice, **9:27, 36:14A.**
Preservation restrictions, filing and recording, **184:33.**

Homestead.
Declaration or order as to recording, **188:2, 188:3.**
Release of recording, **188:7.**

Husband and wife, **189:16.**
Antenuptial marriage contract affecting property, recording, **209:26.**
Conveyances between, **209:3.**
Dower and curtesy, **189:16.**
Fee for filing entry of petition for authority to convey land, **262:40.**
Final orders or decrees in proceedings involving spouse under disability, recording, **209:24.**

Identification of lands conveyed, requirements, **183:6A.**

Illegible signatures on instruments, authority to print or type name, **36:18A.**

Impossibility of duplication or proper recording as affecting authority to refuse recording, **36:12A.**

Incompatibility of offices, **MA Const Part 2 Ch 6 Art 2; Amend Art 8.**

Indefinite references in recorded instruments, protection of land titles against effects, **184:25.**

Indexes, **36:25 et seq.**
Classified copies, annual preparation, **36:28.**
Entries in, **36:24, 36:26, 36:27.**
Expenses, estimate and payment, **36:30.**

REGISTERS AND REGISTRIES OF DEEDS —Cont'd

Indexes —Cont'd
Federal tax liens, indexing, **36:24.**
Form, **36:25.**
Grantor-grantee index, **36:25 et seq.**
New indexes, **36:29.**
Printing and sale, **36:29.**
Suffolk County, index commissioners, **36:28.**
Indistinct records, duplication, **36:17.**
Injunction against nuisances, record, **139:16A.**
Inland wetlands, filing and recording of orders and other instruments affecting, **131:40A.**
Inspection.
Examination, inspection or investigation. See within this heading, "Examination, inspection or investigation."
Invalid tax deed, surrender and discharge, **60:46.**
Invalid tax title, recording affidavit of notice to holder, **60:83.**
Inventory information as to real property, recording, **217:15B.**
Judgments and decrees.
Certified copy of judgment or decree affecting land, recording, **184:17.**
Final disposition of proceedings affecting title to realty, certificate, **184:16.**
Nonresident charged with discriminatory practices, recording order enjoining other disposition of property, **151B:5.**
Ordering conveyance or release of realty, recording of court decree, **183:44.**
Transcription of decree in registry of deeds, **185:1, 185:47.**
Transmission of decrees to register of deeds, **185:23.**
Jury service, register as exempt, **234:1.**
Land court.
See LAND COURT.
Landing places, recording plan and description, **88:14.**
Leases.
Notice of lease for more than seven years, recording, **183:4.**

REGISTERS AND REGISTRIES OF DEEDS —Cont'd

Leases —Cont'd
Reversion of lease for long term treated as fee simple, recording of claim, **184:19.**
Licenses and permits.
Dams and reservoirs, recording of permits regarding, **253:45.**
Waterways, recording of, licenses in connection with structures, **91:18.**
Liens.
Cities and towns, recording of certificate of liens, **60:23.**
Cotenant's liens for paying tax, recording certificate, **60:86.**
Dredging and reclamation of land, recording liens, **254:30.**
Employment security, recording lien of overdue contributions, **151A:15, 151A:16.**
Federal tax liens and discharges thereof, filing, **36:24.**
Mechanics' liens.
See MECHANICS' LIENS.
Mortgages and deeds of trust.
See within this heading, "Mortgages and deeds of trust."
Tax liens. See within this heading, "Tax liens."
Wharves, piers and docks, recording of Commonwealth's lien for removing unsafe, **91:49B.**
Limitation of actions.
Defects, actions based on, as limited to ten years after recording, **184:24.**
Right of entry for condition broken or possibility of reverter as affected by recording of claim, **260:31A.**
Location or place.
Place. See within this heading, "Place."
Lowlands and swamps.
Coastal wetland regulations to be recorded, **130:105.**
Inland wetlands, orders and instruments affecting, **131:40A.**
Papers recorded in connection with improvement project, **252:7.**
Low value lands held by city or town under tax title, recording deed upon sale, **60:79.**

REGISTERS AND REGISTRIES OF DEEDS —Cont'd

Manner of recording instruments, **36:15.**
Marginal notation.
Dower, claim, **189:16.**
Duplicate records of worn, mutilated, or indistinct records, **36:17.**
Fee for entering additional marginal references, **262:38.**
Mortgage records, **36:20, 36:21.**
Tax deeds, instruments affecting, **36:22.**
Marriage contract affecting property, recording, **209:26.**
Mechanics' liens.
See MECHANICS' LIENS.
Memorandum of proceedings affecting title to realty, recording, **184:15.**
Microphotographic copies of books, **36:15.**
Middlesex County.
Assistant registers of deeds for southern district.
Designation, **36:5.**
Salaries or compensation, **36:33.**
Mobile homes.
See MANUFACTURED HOMES AND MANUFACTURED HOUSING COMMUNITIES.
Mortgages and deeds of trust.
Discharge or release, **36:20, 36:21.**
Extension, **36:20.**
Marginal notations, **36:20, 36:21.**
Utility company mortgages including estates less than fee simple, registration and cancellation, **185:59.**
Motels, **140:27, 140:29.**
Motor vehicles, registrar of.
See USED CAR SALES.
Municipal lighting plant, certificate of acceptance filed, **164:58B.**
Mutilated records, duplication, **36:17.**
Names.
Failure to comply with requirements as to grantee's name and address, effect, **183:6.**
Highway, filing order changing name, **85:3B.**
Parties to instruments, indexing names, **36:24, 36:26, 36:27.**

REGISTERS AND REGISTRIES OF DEEDS —Cont'd

Names —Cont'd

Signatures. See within this heading, "Signatures."

Nantucket County, election to fill vacancy, **54:143, 54:143A.**

New indexes, **36:29.**

New records of worn, mutilated, or indistinct instruments, **36:17.**

Nomination papers, number of signatures, **53:44.**

Nonresident charged with discriminatory practices, recording of order enjoining other disposition of property, **151B:5.**

Norfolk County.

Second assistant register, provision, **36:5A.**

Tax assessors, abstract cards, **36:24B.**

Notice.

Absentee's estate, **200:3.**

Charitable trusts, notice of recording, **36:32.**

Historic landmarks, recording of notice, **9:27, 36:14A.**

Invalid tax title, recording affidavit of notice to holder, **60:83.**

Lease for more than seven years, recording of notice, **183:4.**

List of fees to be posted in public offices, **262:46.**

Marginal notation. See within this heading, "Marginal notation."

Partition, affidavit of filing notice in registry of deeds, **241:7.**

Redemption from tax title, notice of filing and disposition of petition for foreclosure of right, **60:75.**

Restrictions running with land, recording notice, **184:29.**

Revenue department, notice as to recording of trust instruments, **36:31A.**

Rules as to size of plans, **36:13A.**

Vacancy in office, **54:146.**

Oath of office, **36:3.**

Assistant recorder of land court, **185:11.**

Office or place of business.

Hours, **36:11.**

Location, **36:1.**

REGISTERS AND REGISTRIES OF DEEDS —Cont'd

Official bond.

Bonds and undertakings. See within this heading, "Bonds and undertakings."

Partition of property.

Affidavit of filing notice in registry of deeds, **241:7.**

Apportionment of tax, **59:78A.**

Party enrollment of candidate for register of deeds, certificate, **53:48.**

Permits.

Licenses and permits. See within this heading, "Licenses and permits."

Place.

Office or place of business. See within this heading, "Office or place of business."

Record, certificate on instruments as to place, **36:23.**

Planning boards.

See ZONING AND PLANNING.

Plans and specifications.

Filing copies, **36:13A, 36:13B, 262:38.**

Landing places, recording plan and description, **88:14.**

Scenic areas, plans to be recorded, **21:17B.**

Tidal bounds of streams, plan, **131:4.**

Plymouth county tax assessors, abstract cards, **36:24B.**

Posting in public offices of lists of fees, **262:46.**

Preservation and conservation restrictions, recording, **184:33.**

Printing of indexes, **36:29.**

Proof.

Evidence. See within this heading, "Evidence."

Public utility company mortgages including estates less than fee simple, registration and cancellation, **185:59.**

Purchase of realty, recording agreements, **184:17A.**

Real estate time-shares.

See REAL ESTATE TIME-SHARES.

Receipt of papers, records, **36:14.**

Reclamation of land by dredging, recording liens, **254:30.**

"Recorded," definition, **4:7.**

Recreational land.

Change in use, **61B:9.**

Change of ownership, **61B:6.**

REGISTERS AND REGISTRIES OF DEEDS —Cont'd

Recreational land —Cont'd

Recording certificate of tax payment, **61B:15.**

Redemption.

Tax deeds and titles. See within this heading, "Tax deeds and titles."

Removal of register of deeds from office, **36:9.**

Assistant registers, **35:51.**

Rents and profits, recording assignment, **183:4.**

Reproductions.

Copies. See within this heading, "Copies."

Restrictions running with land, recording notice or extension of restrictions, **184:29.**

Revenue department or commissioner, **36:24B, 36:31A.**

Revenue stamps.

Stamp tax. See within this heading, "Stamp tax."

Reversion of long term lease treated as fee simple, recording claim, **184:19.**

Right of way.

Easements. See within this heading, "Easements."

Roads.

Highways and streets. See within this heading, "Highways and streets."

Salary or compensation, **36:33, 217:35A, 217:35B.**

Indexes, persons assisting in preparation, **36:30.**

Middlesex County, assistant register, **36:33.**

Title work, no compensation, **36:37.**

Sale of indexes, **36:29.**

Scenic and recreational river or stream, plan of and list of abutting owners to be recorded, **21:17B.**

Secured transactions.

See SECURED TRANSACTIONS.

Sharecropping agreement, recording, **255:7D.**

Signatures.

Illegible signatures on instruments, authority to print or type name, **36:18A.**

Nomination papers, number of signatures, **53:44.**

REGISTERS AND REGISTRIES OF DEEDS —Cont'd

Special assessments.
Deferral and recovery agreements pertaining to betterment assessments, recording, **80:13B.**
Dissolution of lien, filing, **80:12.**
Drains, sewers, and sidewalks, recordation of assessment statements, **83:27.**
Eminent domain proceedings, **80A:10, 80A:11.**
Order, recording of estimate and plan, **80:2.**
Specifications.
Plans and specifications. See within this heading, "Plans and specifications."
Spendthrift, effect of record of petition for appointment of guardian, **201:10.**
Spouses.
Husband and wife. See within this heading, "Husband and wife."
Stallions, **140:176.**
Stamp tax.
Deed and document stamp tax, **64D:3, 64D:3B.**
Federal tax stamp, notation, **36:15.**
Statute of limitations.
Limitation of actions. See within this heading, "Limitation of actions."
Statutes distributed, **5:3.**
Streets.
Highways and streets. See within this heading, "Highways and streets."
Subdivision control law.
See ZONING AND PLANNING.
Successors in office, completion of unfinished business, **36:10.**
Suffolk County.
Assistant registers, **36:5, 36:33.**
Filling vacancy in office of register, **54:143, 54:143A.**
Index commissioners, **36:28.**
Removal by superior court, **36:9.**
Salary, **36:33.**
Superior court, removal, **36:9.**
Surplus funds, deposit, **35:22.**
Surrender of tax deeds for irregularities, **60:46.**
Survey boards, plans not to be recorded unless approved, **41:78.**
Swamps.
Lowlands and swamps. See within this heading, "Lowlands and swamps."

REGISTERS AND REGISTRIES OF DEEDS —Cont'd

Taxation.
Assessors, furnishing abstract cards or copies of records, **36:24B, 262:38.**
Certificates and certification.
Cotenant's lien for paying tax, recording certificate, **60:86.**
Recreational land, recording certificate of tax payment, **61B:15.**
Tax collector's certificate of taxes and assessments on real estate, recording, **60:23.**
Tax titles, recording certificate of redemption, **60:62, 60:63.**
Collectors, **60:23, 60:37A, 60:57.**
Deficiency, liens, **59:12F.**
Federal government. See within this heading, "Federal government.
Liens.
Tax liens. See within this heading, "Tax liens."
Partition property, apportionment, **59:78A.**
Recreational land, recording certificate of tax payment, **61B:16.**
Stamp tax, **36:15, 64D:3, 64D:3B.**
Tax deeds and titles. See within this heading, "Tax deeds and titles."
Tax collectors.
Affidavit of tax collector filed in registry as evidence, **60:57.**
Certificate of taxes and assessments on real estate, recording, **60:23.**
Statement by tax collector as to impossibility of sale for liens, **60:37A.**
Tax deeds and titles.
Affidavits, **60:57, 60:83.**
Certificate of redemption from, recording, **60:62, 60:63.**
Conveyances of tax titles held by city, record, **60:77A.**
Foreclosure of right of redemption from, recording notice of filing and disposition of petition, **60:75.**
Invalid deed or title, **60:46, 60:83.**
Low value lands held by city or town under, recording in connection with sale, **60:79.**

REGISTERS AND REGISTRIES OF DEEDS —Cont'd

Tax deeds and titles —Cont'd
Marginal notation, instruments affecting tax deeds, **36:22.**
Notice to holder of invalid tax title, recording affidavit, **60:83.**
Record of tax deed from city, **60:79.**
Statement of residence to be filed by owner, **60:47.**
Surrender and discharge of invalid tax deed, **60:46.**
Warranties in deeds, recording of statement releasing town from liability, **60:82.**
Tax liens.
Certificates of liens on real estate, recording or registering, **60:23.**
Deficiency, liens, **59:12F.**
Federal tax liens and discharges thereof, filing, **36:24.**
Tax collector's statement as to impossibility of sale for liens, **60:37A.**
Technical assistants, employment, **185:10A.**
Technology purchases, **36:40.**
Temporary registers, **36:8, 54:143.**
Ten years following recording, protection against certain defects after, **184:24.**
Term of office, **36:2, 54:145, 54:157.**
Tidal bounds of streams, filing plan, **131:4.**
Time or date, certificate on instrument as to date of record, **36:23.**
Towns.
Cities and towns. See within this heading, "Cities and towns."
Transitional assistance department, notice of recording of charitable trust, **36:32.**
Trusts.
Charitable trusts, notice to transitional assistance department as to recording, **36:32.**
Effect of recording trust concerning land, **203:2.**
Revenue department, notice as to recording of trust instruments, **36:31A.**
Unacknowledged deed, filing copy, **183:38.**

REGISTERS AND REGISTRIES OF DEEDS —Cont'd

Unemployment compensation, lien of overdue contributions, **151A:16.**

Unfinished business completed by successors in office, **36:10.**

United States.
Federal government. See within this heading, "Federal government."

Unregistered land, requirements for recording of instrument conveying, **183:6A.**

Vacancy in office of register.
Election to fill, **54:143, 54:143A.**
Notice, **54:146.**
Temporary appointment to fill, **36:8, 54:143, 54:143A.**

Veterans, recording of liens on real estate, **115:5A.**

Wages.
Salary or compensation. See within this heading, "Salary or compensation."

Warranties on tax deeds, recording of statement releasing town from liability, **60:82.**

Waters and watercourses.
Connecticut River, filing survey, **91:32.**
Licenses and plans in connection with structures in waterways, recording, **91:18.**
Lowlands and swamps. See within this heading, "Lowlands and swamps."
Scenic and recreational river or stream, plan and list of abutting owners to be recorded, **21:17B.**
Tidal bounds of streams, filing plan, **131:4.**

Welfare department notice of recording of charitable trusts, **36:32.**

Wharves, piers and docks, recording of Commonwealth's lien for removing when unsafe, **91:49B.**

Wife.
Husband and wife. See within this heading, "Husband and wife."

Witnesses, recording of deposition to perpetuate testimony, **233:50 et seq.**

Worcester district, chief clerk, **36:7.**

Worn records, duplication, **36:17.**

REGISTERS AND REGISTRIES OF DEEDS —Cont'd

Writs of entry.
Execution for possession to be recorded in registry of deeds, **237:42.**
Memorandum relating to writ or other proceeding affecting title to land, recording, **184:15.**

Zoning.
See ZONING AND PLANNING.

REGISTERS OF PROBATE AND INSOLVENCY, 215:1, 217:1-217:43.

Absence of register, appointment of temporary register, **217:13.**

Absentee's estate, register's fee for entry of petition for probate, **262:40.**

Accounting, **217:20.**
Examination of accounts by director of accounts, **35:45.**
Penalty for neglect by register, **35:47.**

Adjournment of court, **215:59.**

Ad litem guardian in Suffolk county, appointment of permanent officer to act, **217:27A.**

Administration of oaths, **215:38.**

Administrative deputy assistants, **217:23B.**
Salaries, **217:35, 217:35C.**

Administrative justice.
Advisory committee on personnel standards, membership, **211B:8.**
Annual report, **217:8.**
Chief justice as administrative head of Probate and Family Court Department, **217:8.**
Chief justice for administration and management, **217:35B.**

Administrators.
Executors and administrators. See within this heading, "Executors and administrators."

Adoption of children.
Certificates of adoption, **210:6A.**
Name changes, reports, **210:14.**
Segregation and inspection of papers concerning adoption, **210:5C.**

Affidavit of subscribing witness to will taken before register, evidentiary effect, **192:2.**

Affirmance or annulment of marriage, fee for libel to obtain, **262:40.**

REGISTERS OF PROBATE AND INSOLVENCY —Cont'd

Agency for nonresident executor or administrator, **195:8, 195:9.**

Alimony.
Divorce and alimony. See within this heading, "Divorce and alimony."

Allowance, **217:33.**

Amount of assistance, certification by registers, **217:14.**

Annual report of administrative justice, **217:8.**

Annulment of marriage, fee for libel to obtain, **262:40.**

Appointment.
Agent for nonresident executor or administrator, appointment of new, **195:9.**
Appraisers, appointment, **217:22.**
Guardian ad litem in Suffolk county, appointment of permanent officer to act, **217:27A.**
Guardian of minor child, appointment, **217:7.**
Temporary register, **217:13.**

Appraisals and appraisers.
Appointment of appraisers, **217:22.**
Executors and administrators, failure to file inventory in appraisal, **217:16.**

Assistant registers, **215:1, 217:1, 217:23 et seq.**
Bond.
Liability, **217:11.**
Required, **217:23.**
Deputy assistant registers.
Dukes county, **217:29A.**
Middlesex county, **217:29.**
Nantucket county, **217:29B.**
Suffolk county, **217:28.**
Disinterest of, required, **217:6B.**
Duties of assistant register, **217:27.**
Essex county, assistant register, **217:30.**
Fees, payment, **217:27.**
Hampshire county, **217:23A.**
Liability on bonds, **217:11.**
Official signature of assistant register, **217:26.**
Salaries, **217:35B.**
Paid by Commonwealth, **217:35.**
Vacancy in office, register to report, **217:17.**

Attachments, issuance, **217:22.**

Attorney general, register to send notices of charitable trust, **217:19.**

**REGISTERS OF PROBATE
AND INSOLVENCY** —Cont'd

Attorneys at law.
Notice of orders and decrees to
be given to attorneys,
215:36.
Restrictions on practice of law
by register, **217:6B.**
Authentication of documents used
for legacy and succession tax
purposes, **65:25.**
Barnstable probate court, **217:29C.**
Berkshire probate court, **217:29D.**
Birth records, **46:19A.**
Bonds and undertakings, **217:11,
217:12.**
Approval of probate bonds,
205:10.
Assistant registers. See within
this heading, "Assistant
registers."
Failure to furnish inventories to
commissioner of
corporations and taxation as
constituting breach of
official bond, **217:16.**
Forfeiture of bond for failure to
keep accurate records,
217:11.
Receiver's bond, **200:6.**
State treasurer. See within this
heading, "State treasurer."
Books.
Records, reports, and returns.
See within this heading,
"Records, reports, and
returns."
Certificates and certification.
Adoption certificate, **210:6A.**
Amount of assistance,
certification by registers,
217:14.
Candidate for office, certificate of
party enrollment, **53:48.**
Election of register, certificate,
54:116.
Entry fee payable upon removal
for cause, **215:6.**
Expense of recording probate
proceedings in Suffolk
county, certification, **215:56.**
Fees, **262:40.**
Temporary register, certification,
217:13.
Charitable trusts, registers duty to
send notices to division of
public charities, **217:19.**
Chief justice as administrative
head of Probate and Family
Court Department, **217:8.**
Chief justice for administration
and management, **217:35B.**

**REGISTERS OF PROBATE
AND INSOLVENCY** —Cont'd

Children and minors.
Adoption of children. See within
this heading, "Adoption of
children."
Appointment as guardian, **217:7.**
Pretermitted child's share in
testator's real property,
filing of claim, **191:20.**
Citations, issuance, **215:34A,
217:21.**
Compensation.
Administrative deputy
assistants, **217:35, 217:35C.**
Allowance, **217:33.**
Assistant registers. See within
this heading, "Assistant
registers."
Barnstable probate court,
217:29C.
Berkshire probate court,
217:29D.
Essex county, **35:49.**
Fees. See within this heading,
"Fees."
Recording receipts,
compensation, **215:50.**
Registers and assistant
registers, **217:35, 217:35A,
217:35B.**
Temporary registers, **217:43.**
Constitution of Massachusetts.
Election of registers of probate,
**MA Const Amend Arts 14,
19.**
Plurality of offices regulated,
**MA Const Part 2 Ch 6 Art
2; Amend Art 8.**
Contempt citation, issuance,
215:34A.
Copies, register to make and
furnish, **217:16-217:18.**
Birth, marriage, and death
records, **46:19A.**
Fees, **217:18, 262:40.**
Wills, **217:15C.**
Court examination of creditor
claims and allowance or
disallowance thereof, **198:4.**
Creditors.
Court examination of creditor
claims and allowance or
disallowance thereof, **198:4.**
Insolvent estates, judgments
surrendered against, **198:33.**
Limitation of creditors' actions,
197:9.
Custody of exhibits or records,
217:15.
Death of register.
Appointment of temporary
register, **217:13.**

**REGISTERS OF PROBATE
AND INSOLVENCY** —Cont'd

Death of register —Cont'd
Election, death before beginning
of term of office, **54:145.**
Death records, reproduction of by
register, **46:19A.**
Debts.
Creditors. See within this
heading, "Creditors."
Decrees.
Judgments, decrees, and orders.
See within this heading,
"Judgments, decrees, and
orders."
Deposits of surplus funds in
hands, **35:22.**
Deputy assistant registers.
Assistant registers. See within
this heading, "Assistant
registers."
Disinterest of assistant or special
register, **217:6B.**
Divorce and alimony.
Fees in conjunction with divorce
proceedings, **262:40.**
Return of divorce statistics,
208:46.
Dockets of all cases to be kept,
215:37.
Dower, filing of election to take,
189:1.
Dukes county.
Deputy assistance registers,
217:29A.
Salary of register, **217:35A.**
Duties, **217:15.**
Elections.
Candidate for office, certificate of
party enrollment, **53:48.**
Member of board of examiners,
54:122.
Nomination papers, number of
signatures, **53:44.**
Registers, election, **54:156,
217:4.**
Certificate, **54:116.**
Constitution of Massachusetts,
**MA Const Amend Arts
14, 19.**
Death before beginning term
of office, **54:145.**
Term of office, **217:4.**
Transmission of votes for
registers, record, **54:112.**
Vacancy or failure to elect,
special election in case,
54:142.
Election to take dower, filing,
189:1.
Essex county.
Assistant registers, **217:30.**
Salaries, establishment, **35:49.**

**REGISTERS OF PROBATE
AND INSOLVENCY** —Cont'd

Estimate of department
maintenance and revenues,
211B:13.

Evidence.
See EVIDENCE.

Executors and administrators.
Inventory and appraisal, failure
to file, **217:16.**
Medical assistance division,
118E:32.
Nonresident executors or
administrators, agent for
service of process, **195:8,
195:9.**
Public administrators, duty to
report neglect of duty,
194:16.
Register qualified to act, when,
192:7.

Facsimile signature of register,
validity, **217:22.**

Fees, **262:40.**
Absentee, register's fee for entry
of petition for estate upon
presumption of death,
262:40.
Assistant registers, **217:27.**
Certificates and certification,
262:40.
Copies of records, fees for
furnishing, **217:18, 262:40.**
Decedents' estates, fees in
connection, **262:40.**
Divorce proceedings, fees in
conjunction, **262:40.**
Guardian and ward, matters
concerning, **262:40.**
Injunction or restraining order,
issuance by register of
probate and insolvency,
262:40.
Jury issues, fees for filing
motion for framing, **262:40.**
Prohibition of fees in addition to
compensation, **217:43.**

Files and filing.
Records, reports, and returns.
See within this heading,
"Records, reports, and
returns."

First assistant registers,
appointment, **217:23.**

First justice of probate and
insolvency, **217:2, 217:23 et
seq.**

Forfeiture of bond of register for
failure to keep accurate
records, **217:11.**

**REGISTERS OF PROBATE
AND INSOLVENCY** —Cont'd

Guardian ad litem in Suffolk
county, appointment of
permanent officer to act,
217:27A.

Guardian and ward, fees in
matters concerning, **262:40.**

Guardian of minor child,
appointment, **217:7.**

Hampden probate court's
designation of deputy
assistant registers of probate,
217:29E.

Hampshire county.
Assistant register, appointment,
217:23A.
Salaries, **217:35A.**
Special judge of probate and
insolvency, **217:3B.**

Indexes of records, duty to keep,
217:15.

Informal administration of small
estates, procedure, **195:16.**

Inventories, duty of register to
send, to commissioner of
corporation and department,
taxation, **217:16.**

Issuance of citations and
attachments, **215:34A, 217:21,
217:22.**

Judges of probate and insolvency,
217:2 et seq., 217:5, 217:11.

Judgments, decrees, and orders.
Insolvent estates, judgments
surrendered against, **198:33.**
Notice, **215:36.**

Jury and jury trial.
Exempt from service, **234:1.**
Fees for filing motion for
framing jury issues, **262:40.**

Legacy and succession taxes.
Authentication of documents
used for legacy and
succession taxes, **65:25.**
Enforce tax lien, filing of notice
of action, **65:9.**
Official of state of domicile of
nonresident, notice, **65:24C.**

Limitation of actions by creditors,
197:9.

List of surety companies to be
furnished to each register,
175:105.

Mailing copies of inventories to
revenue department, **217:16.**

Marriage.
Divorce and alimony. See within
this heading, "Divorce and
alimony."

Records, reproduction, **46:19A.**

**REGISTERS OF PROBATE
AND INSOLVENCY** —Cont'd

Medical assistance division,
118E:32.

Middlesex county.
Court officers, **217:30.**
Deputy assistant registers and
clerk, **217:29.**
Salaries, **217:35A.**

Minors.
Children and minors. See within
this heading, "Children and
minors."

More than one county or district,
recording copy of instrument
as to land, **36:13.**

Nantucket county.
See NANTUCKET COUNTY.

Newspapers for publication of
notices, selection, **215:49.**

Nomination papers for candidate
for office, number of
signatures, **53:44.**

Norfolk county, court officers,
217:30.

Notice.
Attorneys to be given notice of
orders and decrees, **215:36.**
Division of public charities,
register to send notices of
charitable trusts, **217:19.**
Medical assistance division,
118E:32.
Official of state of domicile of
nonresident, notice, **65:24C.**
Revenue department register to
send notices, **217:16.**
Sale of real estate, perpetuation
of evidence by giving notice,
202:16.
Selection of newspapers for
notice, **215:49.**
Tax lien, notice of action to
enforce, **65:9.**

Oaths.
Administration of oaths by
register, **215:38.**
Judge's oath to be filed with
register, **217:5.**
Register, oath, **217:5A.**

Official signature of assistant
register, **217:26.**

Orders.
Judgments, decrees, and orders.
See within this heading,
"Judgments, decrees, and
orders."

Original will may be taken,
215:52.

Petitions, register may receive,
217:21.

REGISTERS OF PROBATE AND INSOLVENCY —Cont'd

Plymouth county.
  Court officers, **217:30.**
  Salaries, **217:35A.**
Political party enrollment of candidate for public office, certificate, **53:48.**
Powers of appointment, filing of release, **204:28.**
Practice of law, restrictions, **217:6B.**
Pretermitted child's share in testator's real property, filing of claim, **191:20.**
Printing names of persons signing filed instruments, duty of register, **217:15A.**
Probation commissioner, reports to commissioner of change of name, **210:13, 210:14.**
Public administrators, breaches in duty, **194:16.**
Receipts.
  Petitions, receipt, **217:21.**
  Recording, **215:50.**
Receiver's bond, **200:6.**
Records, reports, and returns.
  Administrative justice, annual report, **217:8.**
  Custody, **217:15.**
  Divorce statistics, **208:46.**
  Dockets of all cases to be kept, **215:37.**
  Expense of recording probate proceedings in Suffolk county, certification, **215:56.**
  Forfeiture of bond of register for failure to keep accurate records, **217:11.**
  Indexes of records, **217:15.**
  Interrogatories, filing, **215:43.**
  Judge's inspection, **217:11.**
  Jury service, exemption, **234:1.**
  List of surety companies to be furnished to each register, **175:105.**
  Names of persons signing filed instruments, register to print, **217:15A.**
  Oath of judge to be filed with register, **217:5.**
  Orders and decrees, recording, **215:36.**
  Receipts, recording, **215:50.**
  Revenue commissioner, furnishing of records, **217:16.**
  Supreme judicial court, reports to be filed with chief judge and executive secretary, **217:8.**

REGISTERS OF PROBATE AND INSOLVENCY —Cont'd

Records, reports, and returns —Cont'd
  Vacancy in office of assistant, duty of register to report, **217:17.**
  Voluntary administration of small estates, **195:16A.**
Removal of register.
  Appointment of temporary register, **217:13.**
  Supreme judicial court, removal, **211:4.**
Reports.
  Records, reports, and returns. See within this heading, "Records, reports, and returns."
Reproduction of records.
  Copies. See within this heading, "Copies, register to make and furnish."
Resignation of register, appointment of temporary register, **217:13.**
Retirement system of county, inclusion, **32:2.**
Returns.
  Records, reports, and returns. See within this heading, "Records, reports, and returns."
Revenue department, register to send notices, **217:16.**
Salaries.
  Compensation. See within this heading, "Compensation."
Sale of real estate by fiduciary, perpetuation of evidence of giving notice, **202:16.**
Secretary of state, report of vacancy in assistant register's office, **217:17.**
Selection of newspapers for notice, **215:49.**
Signatures.
  Assistant register, signature, **217:26.**
  Facsimile signature, validity, **217:22.**
  Nomination papers, number of signatures, **53:44.**
  Persons signing filed instruments, register to print names, **217:15A.**
Small estates, procedure for informal administration, **195:16, 195:16A.**
Special judge of probate and insolvency for Hampshire county, **217:3B.**

REGISTERS OF PROBATE AND INSOLVENCY —Cont'd

Special register, disinterest, **217:6B.**
State secretary, duty of register to report vacancies in office of assistant register, **217:17.**
State treasurer.
  Accounting, **217:20.**
  Bond to be filed, **217:12.**
  Forfeiture of bond for failure to keep records, **217:11.**
  Payment of salaries and traveling expenses by state, **217:35A, 217:42.**
Statistics on divorces, returns, **208:46.**
Succession taxes.
  Legacy and succession taxes. See within this heading, "Legacy and succession taxes."
Suffolk county.
  Appointment of permanent officer to act as guardian ad litem, **217:27A.**
  Court officers, **217:30.**
  Deputy assistant registers and clerk, **217:28.**
  Expense of recording probate proceedings in, certification, **215:56.**
Supreme judicial court.
  Chief judge and executive secretary, reports to be filed, **217:8.**
  Removal of registers, **211:4.**
Surety companies, list to be furnished to each register, **175:105.**
Surplus funds in hands of, deposit, **35:22.**
Temporary register, **217:13.**
  Compensation, **217:43.**
Term of office, **217:4, 217:23.**
Transfer of personnel between departments, consent required, **211B:9.**
Transfer or removal of case, entry fee payable, **215:6.**
Traveling expenses, **217:42.**
Trusts, common trust funds, **203A:1, 203A:3.**
Vacancy in office.
  Assistant, duty of register to report vacancy in office, **217:17.**
  Election to fill, **54:142.**
  Voluntary administration of small estates, filing of records, **195:16A.**
Wages.
  Compensation. See within this heading, "Compensation."

309

**REGISTERS OF PROBATE
AND INSOLVENCY** —Cont'd
Welfare department, register to
send notice of charitable trust,
217:19.
Wills.
See WILLS.
Worcester county.
Court officers, **217:30.**
Probate court's designation of
deputy assistant registers,
217:29F.
Salary of register, **217:35A.**
REGISTRANT.
Defined, **142A:1.**
REGISTRATION.
Abused and neglected children,
119:51F.
Filing reports, **119:51B.**
Abuse of children, frivolous reports
not to be placed in central
registry, **119:51B, 119:51F.**
Age.
See REGISTRATION OF
VOTERS.
Aircraft financial responsibility
act.
See AIRCRAFT FINANCIAL
RESPONSIBILITY ACT.
Air pollution sources, registration,
111:142B.
Alcoholic liquors.
See ALCOHOLIC LIQUORS.
Ambulances.
See AMBULANCES.
Animal feed.
Feed and feeding of animals. See
within this heading, "Feed
and feeding of animals."
Appeals from denial of release
from court costs, filing of with
clerk, **261:27D.**
Automobile insurance.
See AUTOMOBILE
INSURANCE.
Automobiles, **16:5, 16:9, 90:2.**
See MOTOR VEHICLES.
Banks and banking, **167A:5,
167D:23.**
Births.
See BIRTHS.
Bonds.
See BONDS AND
DEBENTURES.
Books, forgery or counterfeiting,
267:1, 267:5.
Bottles, **110:17-110:20.**
Brands of animal feed, **128:53.**
Cancer.
Contributions, reports
concerning registry, **55:12,
55:18, 55:25.**

REGISTRATION —Cont'd
Cancer —Cont'd
Public health department,
establishment of registry,
111:111B.
Cans for milk or ice cream,
110:21-110:25.
Carriers.
See CARRIERS.
Central personnel register for
state employees, **30:38.**
Charities.
See CHARITIES AND
CHARITABLE
CONTRIBUTIONS.
Checks.
See CHECKS.
Civil service.
See CIVIL SERVICE.
Commercial driver license,
national driver registry,
90F:8.
Competitive bidding, notice
requirement, **149:44J.**
Computer terminals, control by
registrar of motor vehicles,
90:30A.
Constitution of Massachusetts,
register of resolutions and
advice of executive council,
**MA Const Part 2 Ch 2 Sec 3
Art 5.**
Corporations.
See CORPORATIONS.
Cosmetologists registration board,
112:87T.
Court register.
See REGISTER OF COURT.
Credit unions.
See CREDIT UNIONS.
Dairies.
See MILK AND MILK
PRODUCTS.
Death.
See DEATH.
Deeds, **36:1-36:39, 183:4.**
See REGISTERS AND
REGISTRIES OF DEEDS.
Destruction of records, **66:8.**
Domestic violence, registry of
offenses regarding, **208:34D,
209:32, 209A:3A, 209A:7,
209C:15.**
Driver education.
See DRIVER EDUCATION.
Driving while under influence of
alcohol or drugs.
Court to report investigation
findings to registrar,
90:24D.

REGISTRATION —Cont'd
Driving while under influence of
alcohol or drugs —Cont'd
Rehabilitation program, report
as to entries on driving
record as prerequisite to
placement, **90:24E.**
Drugs.
See DRUGS AND NARCOTICS.
Education.
Schools and education. See
within this heading,
"Schools and education."
Elections, registration to vote in,
51:15-51:54.
See REGISTRATION OF
VOTERS.
Emergency vehicle.
See AMBULANCES.
Employment agencies.
See EMPLOYMENT AGENCIES
AND BUREAUS.
Employment and training division
in labor and workforce
department, taxation fair
information practices, **62C:21.**
Employment security.
See EMPLOYMENT
SECURITY.
Excise tax on motor vehicles.
See MOTOR VEHICLES.
Executive recruiting firms,
140:46B.
Family Support Act.
See INTERSTATE FAMILY
SUPPORT ACT.
Feed and feeding of animals,
94:126, 128:52.
Brands and labels, **128:53.**
Fees, **262:39.**
Acupuncture, **112:151.**
Ambulances, fee not required,
90:33.
Certificates of registration,
62C:67, 62C:68.
Charities and charitable
organizations, **68:19.**
Deeds, fees for registration of,
262:38.
See REGISTERS AND
REGISTRIES OF DEEDS.
Fertilizers, **128:68.**
Indigency. See within this
heading, "Indigency."
Interstate commerce, **85:30A,
90:19A.**
Massachusetts water
management act,
registration and permit
application fees, **21G:18,
21G:19.**

REGISTRATION —Cont'd
Fees —Cont'd
Mobile home and mobile home
parks, **90:33.**
Probate and insolvency
registers, **262:40.**
See REGISTERS OF
PROBATE AND
INSOLVENCY.
Vendors, fee for registration,
64H:7, 64I:9.
Waived court costs and fees,
procedure for repayment,
261:27E.
Fertilizers, **128:66.**
Fees, **128:68.**
Foreign professional corporations,
156A:17.
Forgery or counterfeiting of court
register's certificate, **267:1,
267:5.**
Frozen dessert containers.
See FROZEN DESSERTS.
Gambling bets.
See GAMING AND GAMES OF
CHANCE.
Garments and towels,
110:25A-110:25C.
Gifts to minors.
Uniform transfers to minors act,
201A:1 to 201A:24.
See TRANSFERS TO
MINORS.
Glue or cement, register of name
and address of minor
purchasers, **270:19.**
Governor.
Publication of executive orders
in Massachusetts register,
30A:6.
State secretary to report
agencies failing to comply
with laws governing
Massachusetts register,
30A:6C.
Historic places, state register,
9:26C, 9:26D.
Holding companies, banks, **167A:5.**
Home improvement contractors,
registration of contractor with
bureau of building regulations
and standards,
142A:9-142A:15.
Horses.
See HORSES.
Hospitals.
See HOSPITALS AND HEALTH
CARE FACILITIES.
Hotels.
See HOTELS, MOTELS, AND
ROOMINGHOUSES.

REGISTRATION —Cont'd
Indigency.
Filing affidavit of and request
for waiver of court costs,
261:27B.
Public posting of court indigency
limits, **261:27C.**
Insecticides.
See PESTICIDES.
Insolvency and probate, **215:1,
217:1-217:43.**
See REGISTERS OF PROBATE
AND INSOLVENCY.
Insurance holding companies,
175:206C.
Interstate Family Support Act.
See INTERSTATE FAMILY
SUPPORT ACT.
Investment securities.
See INVESTMENT
SECURITIES UNDER
COMMERCIAL CODE.
Justices of the peace.
Annual listing of justices of the
peace to be provided by
secretary of state to town
clerks and registrars, **9:16.**
Voters, registrar or assistant
registrar of voters as
permitted to hold office,
51:25.
Labels, **128:53, 128:90.**
Labor.
See LABOR AND WORKFORCE
DEVELOPMENT.
Land titles, **185:26 et seq.**
See REGISTRATION OF LAND
TITLES.
Laser equipment, health
department's authority to
require registration, **111:5I.**
Legacy.
See LEGACY AND
SUCCESSION TAXES.
Legislative agents and lobbyists,
3:41.
Licenses.
See LICENSES AND PERMITS.
Linens, **110:25A-110:25C.**
Lis pendens.
See LIS PENDENS.
Mail.
See REGISTERED MAIL.
Manufactured homes.
Mobile homes and mobile home
parks. See within this
heading, "Mobile homes and
mobile home parks."
Marriages, registry of, **46:1-46:29.**
See MARRIAGE.
Massachusetts Register.
Governor. See within this
heading, "Governor."

REGISTRATION —Cont'd
Massachusetts water management
act, **21G:5, 21G:6,
21G:17-21G:19.**
Medicine Trust Fund, Board of
Registration in, **10:35M.**
Mental health department
facilities, regulating
fiduciaries who control funds
belonging to inpatients or
residents, **123:27.**
Milk.
See MILK AND MILK
PRODUCTS.
Missing children, **22A:1-22A:7.**
See CENTRAL REGISTER FOR
MISSING CHILDREN.
Mobile homes and mobile home
parks, **140:27, 140:32I.**
Fees, **90:33.**
Penalty for false entries, **140:29.**
Motorboats.
See MOTORBOATS.
Motor carriers of passengers.
See CARRIERS.
Motor vehicles, **16:5, 16:9, 90:2.**
See MOTOR VEHICLES.
Mutual holding companies,
167H:8.
Nurses.
See NURSES AND NURSING
SERVICES.
Nursing.
See NURSING OR REST
HOMES.
Occupations, **112:1 et seq.**
See REGISTRATION OF
PROFESSIONS AND
OCCUPATIONS.
Pesticides.
See PESTICIDES.
Physician assistants, registration
requirements, **13:10B,
112:9C-112:9K.**
Police.
See POLICE.
Political parties, count of voters of
each political party by
registrar of voters, **53:38A.**
Poor persons.
Indigency. See within this
heading, "Indigency."
Presidential electors.
See PRESIDENTIAL
ELECTORS.
Presidential primaries.
See PRESIDENTIAL
PRIMARIES.
Probate and insolvency registers,
215:1, 217:1-217:43.
See REGISTERS OF PROBATE
AND INSOLVENCY.

REGISTRATION —Cont'd

Professions, **112:1 et seq.**

  See REGISTRATION OF
    PROFESSIONS AND
    OCCUPATIONS.

Promoters of shows, requirement
  of certificate, **62C:67A.**

Public assistance applicants to
  register for employment,
  117A:3.

Public charity, **12:8E.**

Racing commissions, appointment
  of exempt positions, **6:48.**

Recreational vehicles.

  See RECREATIONAL
    VEHICLES.

Redemption from tax title,
  recording certificate, **60:61,
  60:61A.**

Rehabilitation of veterans, lease of
  facilities of United States for
  purpose, **74:41.**

Rest homes.

  See NURSING OR REST
    HOMES.

Retirement systems and pensions.

  See RETIREMENT SYSTEMS
    AND PENSIONS.

Sale.

  See SALE OR TRANSFER OF
    PROPERTY.

Sales taxes.

  See SALES TAXES.

School buses, **90:1A, 90:2, 90:5,
  90:9.**

  See SCHOOL BUSES AND
    TRANSPORTATION OF
    PUPILS.

Schools and education.

  Driver education.

    See DRIVER EDUCATION.

  Education council for foreign
    medical graduates.

    See EDUCATION COUNCIL
      FOR FOREIGN
      MEDICAL GRADUATES.

  Employment and training
    division in labor and
    workforce department,
    taxation fair information
    practices, **62C:21.**

Securities.

  See SECURITIES AND
    SECURITIES
    REGULATIONS.

Seeds.

  Defined, **128:84.**

  Sale of seeds, false labels,
    128:90.

Sinking fund commissioners,
  bonds held, **44:52, 44:61.**

REGISTRATION —Cont'd

Snow traveling and recreation
  vehicles.

  See RECREATIONAL
    VEHICLES.

Social workers.

  See SOCIAL WORKERS.

State bonds, **29:58.**

Tenement houses, fee for
  registration of owner's or
  lessee's name, **145:59, 262:34.**

Title to land, **185:26 et seq.**

  See REGISTRATION OF LAND
    TITLES.

Trademarks and trade names,
  110:1 et seq., 110B:1 et seq.

  See TRADEMARKS AND
    TRADE NAMES.

Traffic regulations.

  See TRAFFIC REGULATIONS
    AND RULES OF THE
    ROAD.

Trailer parks.

  Mobile homes and mobile home
    parks. See within this
    heading, "Mobile homes and
    mobile home parks."

Trailers and semi-trailers, **90:1A,
  90:2.**

  See TRAILERS AND
    SEMI-TRAILERS.

Transfer of property.

  See SALE OR TRANSFER OF
    PROPERTY.

Transfers to minors, **201A:1 to
  201A:24.**

  See TRANSFERS TO MINORS.

Traps, **131:80.**

Unemployment compensation.

  See EMPLOYMENT
    SECURITY.

Uniform operation of commercial
  motor vehicles, national driver
  registry, **90F:8.**

Uniform transfers to minors act,
  201A:1 to 201A:24.

  See TRANSFERS TO MINORS.

Used cars.

  See USED CAR SALES.

Use tax.

  See USE, CONSUMPTION, OR
    STORAGE TAX.

Use tax law, registration of
  vendors, **64I:9.**

Vendors, **62C:67, 64H:7, 64I:9.**

Veterans.

  Lease of facilities to United
    States for purpose of
    rehabilitation, **74:41.**

  Rosters of veterans, **33:15.**

Voters, **51:15-51:54.**

  See REGISTRATION OF
    VOTERS.

REGISTRATION —Cont'd

Waived court costs and fees,
  procedure for repayment,
  261:27E.

Welfare.

  See SOCIAL WORKERS.

**REGISTRATION OF LAND
  TITLES, 185:26 et seq.**

Abutting landowners.

  Effect of registration, **185:46.**

  Parcels adjacent, **185:31.**

  Petition for registration, **185:29.**

Actions.

  Assurance fund, actions against,
    185:101-185:109.

  Parties to action. See within this
    heading, "Parties to action."

  Pending actions, notice, **185:86
    et seq.**

  Real actions, registration of
    judgment, **185:88.**

Address of grantee, statement,
  185:61.

Adjacent parcels.

  Abutting landowners. See within
    this heading, "Abutting
    landowners."

Administration expenses, use of
  assurance fund income,
  185:106.

Administrators.

  Executors and administrators.
    See within this heading,
    "Executors and
    administrators."

Affidavits.

  Partition, filing of notice, **241:7.**

  Relevancy of affidavit as to title
    certificate, **183:5B.**

Agreement running with land,
  decree of registration, **185:52.**

Alimony.

  Divorce and alimony. See within
    this heading, "Divorce and
    alimony."

Amendment or alteration.

  Certificates of title, **185:114.**

  Fees of register of probate and
    insolvency for amendment of
    record, **262:40.**

  Form, amendments permitting
    change, **231:51.**

  Parties to actions, amendment,
    185:32, 185:44, 231:51.

  Petition for registration, **185:31,
    185:32.**

Answers to petition, **185:41.**

Appeal.

  See APPEAL AND REVIEW.

Assessments.

  Assessed valuation as
    controlling for purposes of
    assurance fund, **185:109.**

REGISTRATION OF LAND TITLES —Cont'd

Assessments —Cont'd
Betterments as affected, **185:46.**
Assignments.
Insolvency.
Bankruptcy and insolvency. See within this heading, "Bankruptcy and insolvency."
Mortgages, assignment, **185:67.**
Assistant recorder.
Register of deeds as assistant recorder of Land Court, **185:10.**
Assurance fund, **185:99-185:109.**
Actions for compensation, **185:101-185:109.**
Administration expenses, use of fund income, **185:106.**
Assessed valuation as controlling for purposes, **185:109.**
Breach of trust, **185:107.**
Confirmation without registration, inapplicable, **185:56A.**
Creation, **185:99.**
Custody, **185:100.**
Defendants in actions against, **185:102, 185:103.**
Elimination upon death of owner of registered land, **185:99.**
Fraudulent conveyances, actions for compensation, **185:101 et seq.**
Income from, application, **185:106.**
Insufficiency of, proceedings in case, **185:104.**
Investment, **185:100, 185:106.**
Judgments against, **185:103, 185:104.**
Limitation of actions against, **185:108.**
Payments, **185:99.**
Restrictions on liability, **185:107.**
State treasurer as defendant, **185:102, 185:103.**
Subrogation of Commonwealth to plaintiff's rights, **185:105.**
Survival of actions against, **185:108.**
Tort actions as affected by actions against, **185:101.**
Value of property, assessed valuation as controlling, **185:109.**
Attachment of property.
See ATTACHMENT OF PROPERTY.

REGISTRATION OF LAND TITLES —Cont'd

Attorney in fact.
Powers of attorney. See within this heading, "Powers of attorney."
Auditors and referees, **185:24, 185:37, 185:43, 185:60.**
Bankruptcy and insolvency, **185:94, 185:95.**
Adjudication of bankruptcy, **262:39.**
Amendment of record, fees of register of probate and insolvency, **262:40.**
Discharge of debtor, registration, **185:95.**
Effect on preference rights, **185:77.**
Trustee in bankruptcy certificate of title, **185:94, 185:95.**
Vacation of proceedings, registered land as affected, **185:95.**
Bill of review as affecting, **185:86.**
Bona fide purchasers protected, **185:45, 185:46.**
Book of registration, **185:56, 185:63.**
Amendments or alteration, **185:114.**
Boundaries of flats and overflowed lands, determination, **185:1, 240:25.**
Breach of trust, assurance fund not liable, **185:107.**
Cancellation.
Fee simple, interests less than, **185:59.**
Certificate of title.
Adverse claims, statement, **185:66.**
Affidavits concerning land titles, relevancy, **183:5B.**
Agreement running with land, certificate, **185:52.**
Amendment or alteration, **185:114.**
Assignee in insolvency, **185:94, 185:95.**
Confirmation of title, issuance of certificate, **185:1.**
Conservators, sale or mortgage, **185:98.**
Decree of confirmation and registration, issuance, **185:1.**
Descent or devise, transfers, **185:97.**
Divorce, amendment of certificate of title, **185:114.**
Easements, **185:59.**

REGISTRATION OF LAND TITLES —Cont'd

Certificate of title —Cont'd
Effective date, **185:49.**
Encumbrances, statement, **185:66.**
Estates less than fee simple, **185:59.**
Execution creditors, rights, **185:85.**
Executors and administrators, sales or mortgages, **185:98.**
Extension of restriction, notation of notice on certificate, **184:29.**
Fiduciaries, sales or mortgages, **185:98.**
Force and effect, **185:46.**
Forms, **185:56.**
Grantee's name, address, and marital status, statement, **185:61.**
Guardians, sales or mortgages, **185:98.**
Judgments and decrees as affecting, **185:86 et seq.**
Judicial sale, obtaining after, **185:85.**
New certificate, issuance, **79:4, 185:66.**
Notation of notice of extension of restriction on certificate, **184:29.**
Original, **185:49.**
Owner's duplicate certificate.
Interest less than fee simple, memorandum, **185:59.**
Partition proceedings, issuance after, **185:92.**
Pending suit as affecting, **185:86 et seq.**
Purchasers, new certificate to purchaser at execution sale, **185:85.**
Restrictions, certificate to show, **184:29.**
Reverter, new certificate, **185:96.**
State, issuance of certificate of title to real property title to which is registered in name of state agency, **7:40E.**
Tenure of holder, **185:46.**
Transcription of decree, **185:47.**
Transfer certificates, **185:49.**
Trustee in bankruptcy, **185:94, 185:95.**
Certificates.
Final disposition of proceedings affecting title, certificate, **184:16.**
Judgment, certificate, **185:86 et seq.**

REGISTRATION OF LAND TITLES —Cont'd

Certificates —Cont'd
Title..
Certificate of title. See within this heading, "Certificate of title."
Certified copies.
Decree, filing copy, **185:1.**
Instruments filed and registered, **185:63.**
Mortgage or lease, filing copy, **185:30.**
Trust in registered land, filing copy, **185:72.**
Change.
Amendment or alteration. See within this heading, "Amendment or alteration."
Children.
Minors. See within this heading, "Minors."
Common, tenants in.
Joint tenants and tenants in common. See within this heading, "Joint tenants and tenants in common."
Condominiums, submission of property to law, **183A:16.**
Confirmation and registration.
Certificate of title, issuance, **185:1.**
Effect of decree, **185:45.**
Summary process to recover possession from adverse occupant after decree, **239:1.**
Without registration.
Confirmation without registration. See within this heading, "Confirmation without registration."
Confirmation without registration, **185:11, 185:56A.**
Petition, **185:26, 185:26A, 185:56A.**
Recording decree, **185:1.**
Consents required, **185:26.**
Conservation and preservation restrictions, recording with plans, **184:33.**
Conservators, sales or mortgages, **185:98.**
Constructive trust, **185:75.**
Contiguous parcels, **185:31.**
Continuance of attachments, **185:80.**
Conveyances, **185:66.**
Assistant recorder of Land Court, register of deeds, **185:10.**

REGISTRATION OF LAND TITLES —Cont'd

Conveyances —Cont'd
Assurance fund, payments, **185:99.**
Conservators, sale or mortgage of certificate of title, **185:98.**
Contract between parties, operation, **185:57.**
Decree as conveyance or release, **183:44.**
Duplicates and certified copies, **185:63.**
Effect of registration, **185:57, 185:58.**
Entry book, entry, **185:63.**
Estate less than fee simple, **185:59.**
Execution sale, new certificate to purchaser, **185:85.**
Fee, conveyances, **185:66.**
Fiduciary, sale, **185:98.**
Filing of deeds, **185:58.**
Form and contents, **185:57, 185:61.**
Fraudulent conveyances. See within this heading, "Fraudulent conveyances."
Good faith purchaser protected, **185:45, 185:46.**
Grantee's name, address, and marital status, statement, **185:61.**
Interest less than fee simple, transfer, **185:59.**
Judicial sale, **185:85.**
Liens and encumbrances.
Conveyance without notice of, penalty, **185:118.**
Statement, **185:66.**
Minors, appointment of trustee under decree for conveyance of registered land, **185:91.**
Mortgages and deeds of trust. See within this heading, "Mortgages and deeds of trust."
Necessity of registration, **185:57.**
New certificate, issuance, **185:66.**
Numbering and indexing, **185:63.**
Owner's duplicate, production, **185:62.**
Pending registration, **185:36.**
Power of sale. See within this heading, "Power of sale."
Powers of attorney, **185:110.**
Purchasers. See within this heading, "Purchasers."
Reconveyance to insolvent debtor or bankrupt, **185:95.**

REGISTRATION OF LAND TITLES —Cont'd

Conveyances —Cont'd
Registers.
See REGISTERS AND REGISTRIES OF DEEDS.
Right of way by necessity, no implication, **185:53.**
Transfers pending petition, record, **185:36.**
Transmission of decrees to register of deeds, **185:23.**
Unregistered conveyance, effect, **185:57.**
Copies.
Duplicates. See within this heading, "Duplicates."
Corporations, petitions, **185:26, 185:26A.**
Correction of errors, **185:114.**
Costs and expenses.
Administration expenses, **185:106.**
Reference, **185:43.**
Survey, **185:33.**
Cotenants.
Joint tenants and tenants in common. See within this heading, "Joint tenants and tenants in common."
Decrees.
Agreement running with land, effect, **185:52.**
Assurance fund, judgments against, **185:103, 185:104.**
Bankruptcy or insolvency, **185:94, 185:95, 262:39.**
Certificate of judgment, registration, **185:86 et seq.**
Conclusiveness, **185:45.**
Confirmation, decree, **185:1, 185:11, 185:45, 185:56A.**
Contents, **185:47.**
Conveyance or release, decree, **183:43, 183:44, 185:91.**
Default decrees. See within this heading, "Default decrees."
Demandant, registration of judgment, **185:88.**
Dismissal of petition, **185:44.**
Dower, judgment in writ, **185:90.**
Effect of entry, **185:36.**
Filing and recording, **185:1, 185:49, 185:86 et seq.**
Fraudulent decree, **185:45.**
Indexes, **185:56.**
More than one district, land lying, **185:1.**
Notice, **185:86.**
Opening or vacating, **185:45.**
Partition, **185:86, 185:87, 185:91, 185:92, 241:16.**

REGISTRATION OF LAND TITLES —Cont'd

Decrees —Cont'd
Register of deeds, transmission of decrees, **185:23.**
Registration of decrees, effect, **185:58.**
Remedies of persons aggrieved, **185:45.**
Summary process to recover possession from adverse occupant after confirmation, **239:1.**
Transcription of decree, **185:47.**
Waste, judgment in writ, **185:90.**
Deeds.
Conveyances. See within this heading, "Conveyances."
Default decrees, **185:42, 185:43.**
Appeal, **185:16.**
Defendants in actions against assurance fund, **185:102, 185:103.**
Demandant.
Parties to action. See within this heading, "Parties to action."
Descent or devise, **185:97, 185:98.**
Assurance fund, payments, **185:99.**
Effect on laws of descent, **185:77.**
Issuance of certificate of title, **185:97.**
Devise.
Descent or devise. See within this heading, "Descent or devise."
Discharge or release.
Attachments, **185:80, 185:83.**
Decree operating, **185:43, 185:44.**
Insolvency or bankruptcy, **185:95.**
Liens, **185:78.**
Mortgages, **185:67, 185:69.**
Dismissal or discontinuance, **185:32, 185:37, 185:44.**
Disposition.
Certificate of final disposition of proceedings affecting, **184:16.**
Of case, memorandum, **185:36.**
Divorce and alimony.
Amendment of certificate of title on divorce, **185:114.**
Contents of petition as to divorce, **185:28.**
Doubts or disputes as to, reference to Land Court, **185:60.**
Dower, judgment in writ, **185:90.**
Duplicates, **185:63.**
Certified copies. See within this heading, "Certified copies."

REGISTRATION OF LAND TITLES —Cont'd

Duplicates —Cont'd
Owner's duplicate.
Interest less than fee simple, memorandum, **185:59.**
Easements.
See EASEMENTS.
Effective date of registration, **185:49.**
Effect of registration, **185:58.**
Election to withdraw or proceed with petition, **185:37, 185:44.**
Eminent domain, **185:77.**
See EMINENT DOMAIN.
Encumbrances.
Liens and encumbrances. See within this heading, "Liens and encumbrances."
Entry, writs, **185:86 et seq.**
See ENTRY, WRITS.
Error.
Mistake. See within this heading, "Mistake."
Estates.
Descent or devise. See within this heading, "Descent or devise."
Executors and administrators. See within this heading, "Executors and administrators."
Less than fee simple, **185:59.**
Reversions and reversioners. See within this heading, "Reversion and reversioners."
Years, petitions by holders of estates, **185:26.**
Evidence, certificate of title, **185:33.**
Examiners of title.
See LAND COURT.
Executions.
See EXECUTIONS.
Executors and administrators.
Actions against assurance fund, **185:108.**
Sale or mortgage of registered land, **185:98.**
Use of income from assurance fund with respect to registered land, **185:106.**
Expenses.
Costs and expenses. See within this heading, "Costs and expenses."
Extension of restrictions, notation of notice on title certificate, **184:29.**
Extension of time.
Liens, **185:80.**
Mortgages, **185:67.**

REGISTRATION OF LAND TITLES —Cont'd

Federal tax lien.
See TAX LIENS.
Fees, **262:39.**
Mechanics' liens, fees, **262:39.**
Register of probate and insolvency for amendment of records, fees, **262:40.**
Fiduciaries.
Executors and administrators. See within this heading, "Executors and administrators."
Guardians. See within this heading, "Guardians."
Sales or mortgages, **185:98.**
Foreclosure of mortgages, **185:70.**
Forgery.
Records, offense of forgery, **267:1, 267:3, 267:5.**
Forms.
Adoption and use, **185:56, 185:57, 185:61.**
Certificate of title, **185:56.**
Notice of petition, **185:38.**
Petition, **185:28.**
Fraudulent conveyances, **185:118.**
Assurance fund, actions for compensation, **185:101 et seq.**
Penalty, **185:118.**
Fraudulent decree, review, **185:45.**
General default, **185:42.**
Grantee's name, address, and marital status, statement, **185:61.**
Guardians.
Confirmation of land title without registration, guardian's petition, **185:26, 185:26A.**
Petitions, **185:26, 185:26A.**
Sales or mortgages, **185:98.**
Hearings, **185:43.**
Highways and streets.
Abutting land owners. See within this heading, "Abutting landowners."
Private ways. See within this heading, "Private ways."
Way by necessity not implied as to registered land, **185:53.**
Husband and wife.
Marriage. See within this heading, "Marriage."
Implied trusts, **185:75.**
Incompetents.
Mentally ill and retarded persons. See within this heading, "Mentally ill and retarded persons."

REGISTRATION OF LAND TITLES —Cont'd

Indexes, **185:22, 185:27, 185:56.**
Conveyance, numbering and indexing, **185:63.**
Infants.
Minors. See within this heading, "Minors."
In rem, nature of proceedings, **185:1.**
Insane persons.
Mentally ill and retarded persons. See within this heading, "Mentally ill and retarded persons."
Insolvency.
Bankruptcy and insolvency. See within this heading, "Bankruptcy and insolvency."
Instruments of registration.
Certificate of title. See within this heading, "Certificate of title."
Insurance.
Assurance fund. See within this heading, "Assurance fund."
Interest less than fee simple, transfer, **185:59.**
Joinder of parties, **185:31, 185:32.**
Joint tenants and tenants in common.
Confirmation of title without registration, **185:26A, 185:56A.**
Partition, right, **185:77.**
Registration, petition, **185:26.**
Judgments and decrees.
Decrees. See within this heading, "Decrees."
Land court, **60:64-60:75, 185:1 et seq.**
Landlord and tenant.
Leases. See within this heading, "Leases."
Leases, **185:26, 185:30.**
Cancellation, **185:59.**
Effect, **185:46.**
Form and contents, **185:57, 185:61.**
Long term lease treated as fee simple, recording claim of reversion, **184:19.**
Registration of notices of leases, **185:71.**
Tenants for years, petitions, **185:26.**
Legal incidents, **185:77.**
Liens and encumbrances, **185:78-185:85.**
Confirmation without registration, **185:56A.**

REGISTRATION OF LAND TITLES —Cont'd

Liens and encumbrances —Cont'd
Conveyances. See within this heading, "Conveyances."
Discharge or release, **185:78.**
Effect, **185:46, 185:47.**
Enforcement, **185:84, 185:85.**
Extension, **185:80.**
Mechanics' liens. See within this heading, "Mechanics' liens."
Mortgages and deeds of trust. See within this heading, "Mortgages and deeds of trust."
New certificate, statement, **185:66.**
Notice. See within this heading, "Notice."
Records and recording, **185:58, 185:78-185:85.**
Reduction, **185:80.**
Registration, **185:58.**
Tax liens.
See TAX LIENS.
Life estates.
Reversion and reversioners. See within this heading, "Reversion and reversioners."
Limitation of actions, against assurance fund, **185:108.**
Limitations and restrictions.
Restrictions. See within this heading, "Restrictions."
Lis pendens, **185:27, 185:86 et seq.**
Land court, fee for registration or notice, **262:39.**
Long term lease treated as fee simple, recording claim of reversion, **184:19.**
Lost duplicate certificates of title, proceedings in case, **185:11.**
Maps.
Plans. See within this heading, "Plans."
Marriage, **185:26, 185:28, 185:47, 185:61.**
Amendment of certificate of title on marriage or termination of marriage, **185:114.**
Divorce and alimony. See within this heading, "Divorce and alimony."
Name of grantee's spouse, showing, **185:61.**
Petitions by married women, **185:26.**
Rights of spouse, **185:77.**
Statement of marital status of grantee, **185:61.**

REGISTRATION OF LAND TITLES —Cont'd

Married women.
Marriage. See within this heading, "Marriage."
Mechanics' liens.
Enforcement, **185:84.**
Fees, **262:39.**
Memorandum.
Disposition of case, **185:36.**
Filing of petition, **185:27.**
Trusts and trustees, memorandum, **185:72.**
Mentally ill and retarded persons.
Appointment of trustee under decree for conveyance, **185:91.**
Petitions by incompetents, **185:26, 185:26A.**
Minors, **185:26.**
Appointment of trustee under decree for conveyance of registered land, **185:91.**
Guardians. See within this heading, "Guardians."
Land title, confirmation of, without registration, **185:26A.**
Mistake.
Assurance fund, actions for compensation, **185:101-185:109.**
Correction, **185:114.**
Modification.
Amendment or alteration. See within this heading, "Amendment or alteration."
More than one registration district, land lying, **185:1.**
Mortgages and deeds of trust, **185:57.**
Assignment, **185:67.**
Conservators, sale or mortgage of certificate of title, **185:98.**
Discharge or release, **185:67, 185:69.**
Executors and administrators, mortgages, **185:98.**
Extension, **185:67.**
Filing copy, **185:30.**
Foreclosure, **185:70.**
Guardians or conservators, mortgages, **185:98.**
Land Court, reference of doubtful questions, **185:60.**
Power of sale, assurance fund, not liable for improper exercise, **185:107.**
Records and recordings, **185:30, 185:67-185:70.**
Registration.
Land subject to mortgage, **185:26, 185:30, 185:46.**

REGISTRATION OF LAND TITLES —Cont'd

Mortgages and deeds of trust —Cont'd

Trust with power of sale, notation, **185:73.**

Motions affecting registered land, filing, **185:115.**

Muniments of title, filing and withdrawal, **185:33.**

Name of grantee, statement, **185:61.**

Nonresident, petitioning by agent, **185:35.**

Notice.

Examiner's report, filing, **185:38.**

Instruments, registration as notice, **185:58.**

Leases, registration of notices of leases, **185:71.**

Liens and encumbrances.

Conveyance without notice of, penalty, **185:118.**

Partition, **185:86, 241:7.**

Pending suits, notice, **185:86 et seq.**

Petition, **185:38, 185:39.**

After registration, **185:61, 185:116.**

Persons bound, **185:42.**

Return day, **185:39.**

Proceedings affecting land, **185:61, 185:116.**

Publication, **185:38.**

Restrictions, notice of extension on title certificate, **184:29.**

Service of notices and processes. See within this heading, "Service of notices and processes."

Order of general default, **185:42.**

Original certificate of title, **185:49.**

Owner's duplicate certificate of title.

Interest less than fee simple, memorandum, **185:59.**

Parties to action.

All the world as defendants, **185:42.**

Amendment, **185:32, 185:44.**

Assurance fund, actions against, **185:102.**

Joinder, **185:31, 185:32.**

Judgment, registration for defendant, **185:88.**

Partition, **185:86 et seq.**

Affidavit of filing of notice in registry of deeds, **241:7.**

Certificate of judgment, registration, **185:87.**

Certificate of title, issuance, **185:92.**

REGISTRATION OF LAND TITLES —Cont'd

Partition —Cont'd

Cotenants, rights, **185:77.**

Judgments or decrees, registration or recording, **185:86, 185:87, 185:91, 185:92, 241:16.**

Notice, **185:86, 241:7.**

Payments to assurance fund, **185:99.**

Pending.

Conveyances, pending registration, **185:36.**

Lis pendens. See within this heading, "Lis pendens."

Suits, notice, **185:86 et seq.**

Petitions affecting registered land, **185:115.**

Confirmation without registration, **185:26A, 185:56A.**

Notice. See within this heading, "Notice."

Petitions for registration, **185:26.**

Additional facts may be required, **185:31, 185:32, 185:34, 185:44.**

Agent for nonresident petitioner, **185:35.**

All the world as defendants, **185:42.**

Amendments, **185:31, 185:32.**

Answers, **185:41.**

Confessed on default, **185:42, 185:43.**

Confirmation of land title without registration, guardian's petition, **185:26, 185:26A.**

Contents and form, **185:28.**

Dismissal, **185:32, 185:37, 185:44.**

Filing, **185:27.**

Form and contents, **185:28.**

Guardians, petitions, **185:26, 185:26A.**

Indexes, **185:22, 185:27, 185:56.**

Memorandum of filing, **185:27.**

Notice. See within this heading, "Notice."

Objections, **185:41.**

Plans and muniments of title, filing, **185:33.**

Private or public way, land bounding, **185:29.**

Recording memorandum, **185:27.**

Reference to title examiner, **185:24, 185:37, 185:43.**

Reversioners, petitions, **185:26.**

Several parcels, **185:31.**

REGISTRATION OF LAND TITLES —Cont'd

Petitions for registration —Cont'd

Transfers pending registration, **185:36.**

Trustee, petition, **185:76.**

Withdrawal, **185:37, 185:44.**

Plans.

Conservation and preservation restrictions, recording, **184:33.**

Filing with petition, **185:33.**

Preparation of plans of registered lands, **185:117.**

Sectional plans, preparation, **185:117.**

Plats.

Plans. See within this heading, "Plans."

Pleadings.

Additional papers, filing, **185:34.**

Answer to petition, **185:41.**

Confirmation without registration, petition, **185:26A, 185:56A.**

Petitions for registration. See within this heading, "Petitions for registration."

Posting notice of petition on property, **185:39.**

Power of appointment and disposal, petition by donee, **185:26, 185:26A.**

Power of sale.

Assurance fund not liable for improper exercise, **185:107.**

Trust with power of sale, notation, **185:73.**

Powers of attorney.

Dealing with registered land, **185:110.**

Fees for registration by land court, **262:39.**

Prescription ineffective against registered land, **185:53.**

Preservation or conservation restrictions, recording with plan, **184:33.**

Private ways.

Effect of registration, **185:46.**

Petition for registration, **185:29.**

Process, service of.

Service of notices and processes. See within this heading, "Service of notices and processes."

Publication of notice of petition or examiner's report, **185:38.**

Public entities permitted to withdraw registered land upon acquisition, **185:52.**

REGISTRATION OF LAND TITLES —Cont'd

Public ways.
Highways and streets. See within this heading, "Highways and streets."
Purchasers.
Execution sale, new certificate to purchaser, **185:85.**
Good faith purchaser as protected, **185:45, 185:46.**
Real action, registration of judgment, **185:88.**
Reconveyance to insolvent debtor or bankrupt, **185:95.**
Recorder of Land Court.
See LAND COURT.
Records and recording, **185:56, 185:63.**
Reduction of liens and encumbrances, **185:80.**
Reference, **185:24, 185:37, 185:43, 185:60.**
Register of probate and insolvency, fees for amendment of records, **262:40.**
Registers.
See REGISTERS AND REGISTRIES OF DEEDS.
Release.
Discharge or release. See within this heading, "Discharge or release."
Report of title examiner, publication of notice of filing, **185:38.**
Residence of grantee, statement, **185:61.**
Restrictions.
Assurance fund, restrictions on liability, **185:107.**
Certificate of title to show, **184:29.**
Conservation and preservation restrictions, recording with plans, **184:33.**
Freeing property, **185:1, 240:16-240:18.**
Validity of restrictions on registered land, determination, **185:1, 240:16-240:18.**
Retarded persons.
Mentally ill and retarded persons. See within this heading, "Mentally ill and retarded persons."
Return day of notice of petition, **185:39.**
Reversion and reversioners.
Long-term lease treated as fee simple, recording claim of reversion, **184:19.**

REGISTRATION OF LAND TITLES —Cont'd

Reversion and reversioners —Cont'd
Petitions, **185:26.**
Reverter, new certificate, **185:96.**
Review.
See APPEAL AND REVIEW, **185:53.**
Sale.
Conveyances. See within this heading, "Conveyances."
Satisfaction of judgment against assurance fund, **185:103, 185:104.**
Sectional plans, preparation, **185:117.**
Service of notices and processes, **185:61, 185:116.**
Nonresident petitioner for registration, agent for service, **185:35.**
Petition, notice, **185:38, 185:39.**
Several parcels.
Joinder by owners, **185:31.**
Special assessments as affected, **185:46.**
Spouse.
Marriage. See within this heading, "Marriage."
State.
Issuance of certificate of title to real property title to which is registered in name of state agency, **7:40E.**
Subrogation in action against assurance fund, **185:105.**
Treasurer as defendant in action against assurance fund, **185:102, 185:103.**
Withdrawal of registered land, **185:52.**
Stipulations on withdrawal of petition, **185:37, 185:44.**
Streets and highways.
Highways and streets. See within this heading, "Highways and streets."
Substitutes and substitutions.
Parties, substitution, **185:32, 185:44.**
Summary process to recover possession from adverse occupant after decree of confirmation, **239:1.**
Survey, court may require, **185:33.**
Survival of actions against assurance fund, **185:108.**
Tax assessors.
See TAX ASSESSORS.
Taxation of registered land.
See TAXATION.

REGISTRATION OF LAND TITLES —Cont'd

Tax liens.
See TAX LIENS.
Tenants in common.
Joint tenants and tenants in common. See within this heading, "Joint tenants and tenants in common."
Time.
Extension of time. See within this heading, "Extension of time."
Title examiners.
See LAND COURT.
Tort action as affected by action against assurance fund, **185:101.**
Transcription of decree in registry of deeds, **185:1, 185:47.**
Transfers.
Conveyances. See within this heading, "Conveyances."
Trusts and trustees, **185:72-185:76.**
Appointment of new trustee, proceedings, **185:74, 185:91.**
Assurance fund not liable for breach of trust, **185:107.**
Certificate of title, trustee in bankruptcy, **185:94, 185:95.**
Constructive trusts, **185:75.**
Filing copy of trust in registered land, **185:72.**
Implied trusts, **185:75.**
Memorandum, **185:72.**
Mortgages and deeds of trust. See within this heading, "Mortgages and deeds of trust."
Powers of sale, trust, **185:73.**
Records and recording of trusts, **185:72-185:76.**
Registration by trustee, **185:76.**
Sales or mortgages by fiduciaries, **185:98.**
Undivided interest.
Joint tenants and tenants in common. See within this heading, "Joint tenants and tenants in common."
Vacation of insolvency or bankruptcy proceedings, **185:95.**
Valuation for assurance fund purposes, **185:109.**
Voluntary dealings with, **185:57-185:63.**
Waste, judgment in writ, **185:90.**
Ways.
Highways and streets. See within this heading, "Highways and streets."

REGISTRATION OF LAND TITLES —Cont'd

Who may apply, **185:26.**

Wife.

  Marriage. See within this heading, "Marriage."

Wills.

  Descent or devise. See within this heading, "Descent or devise."

Withdrawal of petition, **185:37, 185:44.**

Withdrawal of registered land by governmental entities, **185:52.**

Years, petitions by tenants, **185:26.**

REGISTRATION OF MOTOR VEHICLE.

See MOTOR VEHICLES.

REGISTRATION OF PROFESSIONS AND OCCUPATIONS, 112:1-112:129.

Accountants, **112:87A et seq.**

  See ACCOUNTANTS.

Acupuncture.

  See ACUPUNCTURE.

Allied health professions.

  See ALLIED HEALTH PROFESSIONS.

Architects, **112:60A et seq.**

  See ARCHITECTS AND ARCHITECTURE.

Barbers, **112:87F et seq.**

  See BARBERS.

Beauticians, **112:87T et seq.**

  See HAIRDRESSERS AND COSMETOLOGISTS.

Boards of Professional licensure, **112:88.**

  Certified statements, issuance, **112:88.**

  Division of registration of professions and occupations, **13:9B.**

  Education loan defaulters denied issuance or renewal of licenses, **30A:13, 112:61.**

  Hearings on complaints and charges. See within this heading, "Hearings on complaints and charges."

  Offices for various boards, **13:9.**

  Powers of boards, **112:61.**

  Revocation or suspension of certificate of registration. See within this heading, "Revocation or suspension of certificate of registration."

Certified public accountants, **112:87A et seq.**

  See ACCOUNTANTS.

REGISTRATION OF PROFESSIONS AND OCCUPATIONS —Cont'd

Child abuse, obligation of licensed business to report, **112:1A.**

Chiropodists, **112:13 et seq.**

  See PODIATRY AND PODIATRISTS.

Chiropractors, **112:89 et seq.**

  See CHIROPRACTIC AND CHIROPRACTORS.

Civil service.

  See CIVIL SERVICE.

Cosmetologists registration board.

  See COSMETOLOGISTS.

Criminal proceedings, disciplinary action as affected by pendency, **112:63.**

Deceit, revocation or suspension, **112:61.**

Dental hygienists, **112:51, 112:52.**

  Revocation or suspension of registration, **112:52B.**

Dentists, **112:43 et seq.**

  See DENTISTS.

Dieticians and nutritionists, **13:11D.**

Director of professional licensure, **13:8, 112:1.**

Dispensing opticians, **112:73D, 112:73E et seq.**

  See OPTICIANS.

Division of professional licensure, **13:8 et seq.**

  Boards of, **13:9B.**

  Director of professional licensure, **13:8.**

  Examinations, rules and regulations, **13:9A.**

  Offices for various boards, **13:9.**

Drinking water supply operators, **112:87CCCC, 112:87DDDD.**

Drugs.

  See DRUGS AND NARCOTICS.

Education loan defaulters denied issuance or renewal of licenses, **30A:13, 112:61.**

Electricians, **141:1.**

Electrologists, **112:87EEE et seq.**

  See ELECTROLOGISTS.

Embalmers, **112:82.**

  See EMBALMERS AND FUNERAL DIRECTORS.

Engineers.

  See ENGINEERS AND SURVEYORS.

Farmer-breweries, **138:19C.**

Fraud and deceit, revocation or suspension of registration, **112:18, 112:19, 112:59, 112:61, 112:71, 140:46Q, 255D:7.**

REGISTRATION OF PROFESSIONS AND OCCUPATIONS —Cont'd

Funeral directors, **112:82 et seq.**

  See EMBALMERS AND FUNERAL DIRECTORS.

Gas fitters, **142:6.**

Governor.

  See GOVERNOR.

Gross misconduct, revocation or suspension, **112:61.**

Hairdresser, **112:87T et seq.**

  See HAIRDRESSERS AND COSMETOLOGISTS.

Hazardous waste site cleanup professionals, board of registration of, **21A:19A.**

Health and health departments, **112:1 et seq.**

Health maintenance organizations as subject to professional licensing laws, **176G:12.**

Health officers, **112:87WWW to 112:87ZZZ.**

Hearings on complaints and charges, **112:62.**

  Notice, **112:62.**

  Pendency of criminal actions, effect, **112:63.**

  Rules and regulations, **112:61.**

  Witnesses, **112:62.**

Home improvement contractors, **142A:9-142A:15.**

Home inspectors, **13:96, 13:97, 112:221 to 112:226.**

  See HOME INSPECTORS.

Hygienists.

  Dental hygienists. See within this heading, "Dental hygienists."

Insanity, revocation or suspension, **112:61.**

Insurance agents and brokers, **175:177E.**

Interns, **112:7.**

  Limited registration, **112:9.**

  Revocation or suspension, **112:9.**

Landscape architects, **112:98 et seq.**

  See LANDSCAPE ARCHITECTS AND LANDSCAPING.

Lists of current and prospective licensees, professional associations to receive, **66A:2.**

Malpractice, revocation or suspension, **112:61.**

Nurses.

  See NURSES AND NURSING SERVICES.

Nursing home administrators, **112:108 et seq.**

  See NURSING HOME ADMINISTRATORS.

REGISTRATION OF PROFESSIONS AND OCCUPATIONS —Cont'd

Opticians, 112:73D, 112:73E.
See OPTICIANS.
Optometrists, 112:66 et seq.
See OPTOMETRISTS AND OPTOMETRY.
Perfusionists, 13:11E.
Pharmacists.
See PHARMACISTS AND PHARMACIES.
Pharmacists and pharmacies.
See PHARMACISTS AND PHARMACIES.
Physical therapists, 112:23A et seq.
See PHYSICAL THERAPISTS.
Physician assistants.
See PHYSICIAN ASSISTANTS.
Physician assistants, board of professional licensure, 13:11C.
Physicians and surgeons, 112:2 et seq.
See PHYSICIANS AND SURGEONS.
Plumbers, 142:6.
Podiatrists, 112:13 et seq.
See PODIATRY AND PODIATRISTS.
Professional corporation incorporators, officers, directors, and shareholders to be certified as licensed to practice, 156A:7.
Psychologists, 112:118 et seq.
See PSYCHOLOGY.
Radio and television technicians, 112:87PPP et seq.
See RADIO AND TELEVISION.
Real estate salespersons, 13:54 et seq., 112:87PP et seq.
See REAL ESTATE BROKERS AND SALESPERSONS.
Reciprocity.
See RECIPROCITY.
Respiratory care, 112:23U.
Retirees, pharmacies restricted, 112:39A, 112:40.
Revocation or suspension of certificate of registration.
Education loan defaulters, 30A:13, 112:61.
Fraud and deceit, 112:18, 112:19, 112:59, 112:61, 112:71, 140:46Q, 255D:7.
Grounds, 112:61.
Penalty for practicing after, 112:65.
Powers of boards, 112:61.
Revision or reversal by supreme judicial court, 112:64.

REGISTRATION OF PROFESSIONS AND OCCUPATIONS —Cont'd

Rules and regulations.
Examinations, 13:9A.
General provisions, 112:88.
Hearings on complaints and charges, 112:61.
Sanitarians.
See SANITARIANS.
Speech-language pathology and audiology, 13:85 to 13:87, 112:138 to 112:147.
Supervision by director of registration, 112:1.
Surveyors.
See ENGINEERS AND SURVEYORS.
Suspension of certificate.
Revocation or suspension of certificate of registration. See within this heading, "Revocation or suspension of certificate of registration."
Television technicians, 112:87PPP et seq.
See RADIO AND TELEVISION.
Trial.
Hearings on complaints and charges. See within this heading, "Hearings on complaints and charges."
Vendors, tax registration, 64I:9.
Veterinarians, 112:54 et seq.
See VETERINARIANS.

REGISTRATION OF VEHICLES.

See MOTOR VEHICLES.

REGISTRATION OF VOTERS, 51:15-51:54.

Absence of registrar, 51:20, 51:22A, 51:23.
Absentee voting.
Delivery, 54:91B.
Qualification, 54:91A.
Absent voting.
Appointment of officers for registration of voters, 51:22A.
Certification of applications, 54:89, 54:91.
Federal service personnel. See within this heading, "Federal service personnel."
Officers for registration. See within this heading, "Officers for registration."
Physically disabled persons, 51:22A, 51:42A.
Processing of absentee ballots received on election day, 54:95.

REGISTRATION OF VOTERS —Cont'd

Acceptance of other office as causing vacancy, 51:25.
Affidavits of registration, 51:33, 51:36, 51:42, 51:44.
Absentee voters, 51:42E.
Applicant to submit, 56:2.
Bilingual affidavits, availability, 51:36.
Delivery, 51:42H.
False oath or affidavit. See within this heading, "False oath or affidavit."
From other city or town, striking names absent receipt, 51:38.
Military service, persons, 51:42A.
Minors, 51:47A.
Nonresidents, form of affidavit, 51:42F.
Notice of opportunity to register, 51:32.
Preparation and form, 51:36.
Records, 51:36, 51:41, 51:42.
Registrars.
Examination, 51:33.
Preservation, 51:41.
Residents of another city or town, 51:42F.
Transmission of copy to Secretary of State, 51:46A.
Age.
Annual register.
Listing of persons 17 years of age or over, 51:35, 51:37.
Requirements, 51:33, 51:47A.
True names, age at which persons required to give to registrar, 56:4, 56:5.
Aiding or abetting.
False oath as to registration, 56:7.
Illegal voting, 56:28.
Aldermen.
See ALDERMEN AND SELECTMEN.
Announcement of names of applicants before entry on general register, 51:40.
Annual register, 51:37, 51:42.
Duties with respect, 51:37.
Election commissioners in certain cities, duties, 51:41A.
Entry of names during registration hours, 51:34.
Listing of persons 17 years of age or over, 51:35, 51:37.
Notice of omission of names, 51:35, 51:37.

REGISTRATION OF VOTERS
—Cont'd

Annual register —Cont'd

Omitted listings compared with annual registers, **51:35.**

Party enrollment of voters, **53:37, 53:38.**

Presidential or vice presidential electors, revision and correction of annual register, **51:38.**

Revision and correction, **51:38.**

Voting lists, **51:55.**

Application for registration.

Absent voting, certification of applications, **54:89, 54:91.**

Affidavits of registration, submission, **56:2.**

Examinations. See within this heading, "Examinations by registrars."

Male and female applicants, **51:26.**

Preliminary, primary, or election, effect of, application for registration during prohibited period prior, **51:26.**

Preservation, **51:41.**

Rejection of, notice, **51:47.**

Appointments, **51:15, 51:17.**

Election officers in cities, examinations, **54:11B.**

In certain cities, **51:17.**

Other offices not to be held, **51:25.**

Political affiliation as affecting, **51:18, 51:19.**

Temporary registrars, **51:14, 51:20.**

Vacancy or expiration, appointment, **51:15.**

Assistance with registration, **51:42G.**

Assistant registrars, **51:22.**

Affidavits of registration from absentee voters, **51:42E.**

Duties, **51:24.**

High schools and vocational schools, assistant registrar of voters, **51:42E.**

Holding other office, prohibited, **51:25.**

Misconduct or neglect, **56:2, 56:3.**

Oath of office, **51:23.**

Residence, **51:25.**

Supervision by registrars, **51:24.**

Temporary, **51:22.**

Biennial count of voters, **53:38A.**

Bilingual English-Spanish voter registration affidavits, availability, **51:36.**

REGISTRATION OF VOTERS
—Cont'd

Boarding.

See HOTELS, MOTELS, AND ROOMINGHOUSES.

Board of registrars.

City and town clerks. See within this heading, "City and town clerks."

Clerk of board of registrars, **41:19, 51:15, 51:17, 51:23.**

Count of voters of each political party, **53:38A.**

Violations, enforcement by state secretary, **56:60.**

Voter certificates as requiring signatures of majority, **53:46, 53:48.**

Boards of election commissioners to have all powers, rights, duties, and liabilities, **51:16A, 51:41A.**

Boston.

See BOSTON.

Calling out names of applicants, **51:40.**

Cancellation of party enrollment, **53:37, 53:38.**

Candidates.

Independent candidates, **53:9.**

Nomination papers, **53:9A.**

Presidential primaries, meeting dates for certification of candidates, **53:46.**

State primaries, certificate as to party enrollment of candidates, **53:48.**

Town meetings, registrars as candidates, **51:25.**

Certain cities, appointment and term, **51:17.**

Certificates and certification.

Absent voting, certification of applications, **54:89, 54:91.**

Authorization for person to vote, issuance of certificate of, **55B:5.**

Change of party enrollment less than 1 year to prior to last day for filing nomination papers, **53:48.**

Confidential registration certificates, **51:51A.**

Form of registration of voters, **55B:5.**

Independent candidates, furnishing certificate of registration, **53:9.**

Initiative and referendum petitions, **53:22A.**

REGISTRATION OF VOTERS
—Cont'd

Certificates and certification —Cont'd

Majority of board of registrars, voter certificates as requiring signature, **53:46, 53:48.**

Meeting dates for certification of candidates in presidential primaries, **53:46.**

Nomination papers, **53:10.**

Change of party enrollment, **53:48.**

City and town primary nomination papers, **53:56, 53:58-53:61.**

Form of signatures, **53:7.**

State, **53:46.**

Time for certification of names, **53:7.**

Number of registered voters, **51:61.**

Officers of elections, duties as to certificate of supplementary registration, **51:51.**

Omission or error in voting list, certificate in case, **51:59.**

Party enrollment, **53:37, 53:38, 53:48.**

Presentation of certificate authorizing person to vote, **54:67.**

Preservation of certificates, **51:41.**

Signatures of majority of board of registrars, voter certificates as requiring, **53:46, 53:48.**

Special elections, registrars' meeting before, **53:46.**

Cessation, **51:34.**

Challenge of registrations, **51:48, 51:49.**

Change of name of voter, registration, **51:2.**

Change of residence, **51:1, 51:3.**

Changes and corrections in register, **51:38.**

Changing party enrollment, **53:37, 53:38, 53:48.**

Charter cities.

Cities and towns. See within this heading, "Cities and towns."

Cities and towns.

Affidavits of registration, striking names absent receipt of from other city or town, **51:38.**

Aldermen.

See ALDERMEN AND SELECTMEN.

REGISTRATION OF VOTERS
—Cont'd

Cities and towns —Cont'd

Annual register, election commissioners' duties regarding, **51:41A.**

Appointment of registrars, **51:16A, 51:17.**

Candidate for town meeting, registrar, **51:25.**

Certification of nomination papers in city and town primaries, **53:56, 53:61.**

Change of address, **51:3.**

Charter cities.

Definition for purpose of provisions as to registration, **43:80, 43:94.**

Initiative and referendum petitions, duties of registrars, **43:38.**

City council, acceptance of statute in certain cities, **51:17.**

Clerks.

City and town clerks. See within this heading, "City and town clerks."

Examinations by city election officers, **54:11B.**

Home rule for cities and towns. See within this heading, "Home rule for cities and towns."

Initiative and referendum petitions, registrars' duties as to in charter cities, **43:38.**

Listing of eligible voters, **51:4-51:14B.**

Map of new precincts, furnishing registrar with copy, **54:5, 54:8.**

Optional provision as to registration, cities may adopt, **51:17.**

Primary elections. See within this heading, "Primary elections."

Return of registered voters prior to city or town elections, **51:61.**

Street lists. See within this heading, "Street lists."

Wards and voting precincts. See within this heading, "Wards and voting precincts."

Citizens and aliens.

Affidavit from nonresident, **51:42F.**

Nationality, registrars to list, **51:4.**

REGISTRATION OF VOTERS
—Cont'd

Citizens and aliens —Cont'd

Naturalized citizens, production of records, **51:45A.**

New citizens, **51:50.**

City and town clerks, **51:15, 51:23.**

Bilingual registration forms, furnishing, **51:36.**

Board of registrars.

Additional compensation for serving, **41:19G, 41:19H, 41:19J.**

Clerk of board, city or town clerk, **41:19.**

Member of board, clerk of city or town, **51:15.**

Removal of member, **51:19.**

Certification of number of registered voters, **51:61.**

Change of residence, **51:3.**

Death of voter, clerk to report to registrar, **51:14.**

Clerk of board of registrars, **41:19, 51:15, 51:17, 51:23.**

Close of registration as affecting entry of names on registers, **51:34.**

Colleges and universities, registration sessions in, **51:42E.**

Compensation.

Salaries and compensation. See within this heading, "Salaries and compensation."

Complaints and investigations, **51:48, 51:49.**

Conduct.

Misconduct, **56:2, 56:3, 56:9.**

Confidential registration certificates, **51:51A.**

Copies.

Affidavits of registration, transmission of copy to Secretary of State, **51:46A.**

Map of new precincts, **54:5, 54:8.**

Newly registered voters, lists, **51:58.**

Penal law copies to be posted at registration places, **51:12.**

Correction and revision.

Nomination papers.

Appeals from reviews and corrections of local registrars, **58:6.**

Correction of district designation, **53:46, 53:61.**

Party enrollment erroneous, **53:38.**

Registers, **51:38.**

REGISTRATION OF VOTERS
—Cont'd

Crimes.

See ELECTION OFFENSES.

Death.

Appointment of temporary registrar in event of registrar's death, **51:14.**

Clerks of cities and towns to report deaths to registrar of voters, **51:14.**

Notice to registrar, **51:14.**

Removal from voting registers or lists upon death of voter, **51:38.**

Defacing or removing notices relating, **56:10.**

Definitions, **50:1.**

Disorderly conduct, **56:9.**

District designation on nomination papers, correction, **53:46, 53:61.**

District officers, election of, commissioner as registrar of voters, **41:115.**

Documents, preservation, **51:41.**

Domicile.

Residents. See within this heading, "Residents."

Dormitories, residents listed for voter registration, **51:10A.**

Duplicates.

Copies. See within this heading, "Copies."

Duties, **43B:3, 43B:5, 51:22A, 51:24, 51:41A.**

Education.

Schools and education. See within this heading, "Schools and education."

Election commissioners, powers and duties of boards, **51:16A, 51:41A.**

Election offenses.

See ELECTION OFFENSES.

Election officers.

Appointment lists, notice of time to file, **54:11B.**

Examinations, **54:11B.**

Processing absentee ballots in offices, **54:95.**

Supplementary registration, duties as to certificate, **51:51.**

Errors.

Mistaken, incorrect, or illegal registration. See within this heading, "Mistaken, incorrect, or illegal registration."

REGISTRATION OF VOTERS
—Cont'd
Examinations by registrars.
  Applicants, **51:33.**
    Challenged persons, **51:48,
      51:49.**
    Hours, **51:33.**
    Physically disabled persons,
      51:42A.
    Single registrar may examine,
      51:33.
  Election officers in cities,
    appointments, **54:11B.**
  Illegal or incorrect registration,
    proceedings, **51:47B, 51:48,
    51:49, 56:8.**
  Investigations by registrars,
    51:37, 51:38.
Facts to be noted in records, **51:36.**
False listing by, penalty, **56:1,
  56:5.**
False oath or affidavit, **56:1.**
  Penalty, **56:6, 56:7.**
  Revision and correction of
    registers, qualification of
    voters, **51:38.**
  Subsequent examination of
    registrants for cause,
    51:47B.
False registration by individual,
  penalty for, **56:8.**
False registration by registrar,
  penalty, **56:2.**
Federal service personnel.
  Supplementary registration to
    vote, **51:50.**
  Certificate, **51:51.**
Final day, **51:31.**
Fines.
  See ELECTION OFFENSES.
Forms.
  Affidavits, **51:36.**
  Certificate, form, **55B:5.**
  Nomination papers, form of
    signatures, **53:7.**
Fraternity houses and dormitories
  as lodging houses for voter
  registration purposes, **51:10A.**
General court, state secretary's
  report, **54:133.**
Hearings concerning legality of
  registration, **51:49.**
High schools, registration sessions,
  51:42C-51:42E.
Holding of office by registrars of
  voters, **51:25.**
Holiday, effect of final day falling,
  51:31.
Home rule for cities and towns.
  Charter commission, registrar
    and assistance registrar
    may serve as members,
    51:25.

REGISTRATION OF VOTERS
—Cont'd
Home rule for cities and towns
  —Cont'd
  Documents, when deemed filed
    or submitted, **43B:16.**
  Duties of voters, **43B:3, 43B:5.**
Hospitals.
  Absentee voting, **54:91B.**
  Restoration to lists of names of
    voters in hospitals and
    nursing homes, **51:38.**
Hotel, motel, and roominghouse
  residents, **51:37.**
  Fraternity houses and
    dormitories, applicability,
    51:10A.
  Innholders to report, **51:10A.**
  Penalty for failure or refusal
    to give information, **56:4.**
Hours for registration, **51:26.**
  Annual register, entry of names
    during registration hours,
    51:34.
  Examinations by applicants,
    hours, **51:33.**
  Persons in line when
    registration closes, **51:34.**
How conducted, **51:40.**
Illegal or incorrect registration,
  51:48, 51:49, 56:8.
Inability to act, **51:20.**
Incompatible offices, **51:25.**
Independent candidates,
  furnishing of certificate of
  registration, **53:9.**
Initiative and referendum
  petitions.
  Certification of names, **53:22A.**
  Charter cities, registrars' duties
    as to petitions, **43:38.**
  Notice, **54:53.**
  Time of filing, petitions to state,
    53:22A.
Innholders.
  Hotel, motel, and roominghouse
    residents. See within this
    heading, "Hotel, motel, and
    roominghouse residents."
Interference with supervisors of
  registration, penalty, **51:54.**
Interrupting or disturbing, **56:9.**
Jury list to be prepared by
  registrars, **234:4.**
Justice of the peace, registrar of
  voters or assistant may hold
  office, **51:25.**
Labor.
  Election officers. See within this
    heading, "Election officers."
  Federal service personnel. See
    within this heading,
    "Federal service personnel."

REGISTRATION OF VOTERS
—Cont'd
Labor —Cont'd
  Officers for registration. See
    within this heading,
    "Officers for registration."
  Temporary registrars. See within
    this heading, "Temporary
    registrars."
Last day, registration sessions,
  51:28.
Later election although ineligible
  for earlier election,
  registration, **51:26.**
Lists or listings.
  Elections.
    See ELECTIONS.
  Inactive voters list, **51:37A.**
  Omissions from lists. See within
    this heading, "Omissions
    from lists."
  Street lists. See within this
    heading, "Street lists."
Location.
  Place. See within this heading,
    "Place."
Lodging houses keepers.
  Hotel, motel, and roominghouse
    residents. See within this
    heading, "Hotel, motel, and
    roominghouse residents."
Male and female applicants, same,
  51:26.
Manner, **51:42-51:47.**
Map of new precincts, furnishing
  registrar with copy, **54:5, 54:8.**
Marriage as affecting name used
  for registration, **51:36, 151B:4.**
Meeting dates for certification of
  candidates in primaries by
  registrars of voters, **53:46.**
Military.
  Federal service personnel. See
    within this heading,
    "Federal service personnel."
  Militia officer, registrar of voters
    or assistant may hold office,
    51:25.
Minors, **51:47A.**
Misconduct at, penalty, **56:2, 56:9.**
  Assistant registrars, misconduct
    or neglect, **56:2, 56:3.**
Mistaken, incorrect, or illegal
  registration, **51:48, 51:49,
  56:8.**
  Correction and revision. See
    within this heading,
    "Correction and revision."
Motel.
  Hotel, and roominghouse
    residents. See within this
    heading, "Hotel, motel, and
    roominghouse residents."

REGISTRATION OF VOTERS
—Cont'd

Motor vehicle registry, **90:8L.**

Moving from one ward or precinct to another in same city or town, **51:3.**

Multi-unit dwelling owners, furnishing information, **51:10A.**

Municipalities.
Cities and towns. See within this heading, "Cities and towns."

Names.
Affidavits of registration, striking names absent receipt, **51:38.**

Annual register, entry of names, **51:34.**

Appearance by persons whose names are not on annual register, requirement, **51:42.**

Initiative and referendum petitions, certification of names, **53:22A.**

Marriage as affecting name used for registration, **51:36.**

Multi-unit dwelling owners furnishing information to registrar, **51:10A.**

New name, **51:2.**

Nomination papers, time for certification of names, **53:7.**

Omitted voters, **51:35, 51:37.**

Public announcement of names of registrants, **51:40.**

Records, persons not previously listed, **51:8, 51:11, 51:12.**

Registrar of voters, age at which persons required to give true names, **56:4, 56:5.**

Signature, requirement, **51:44.**

State primaries or elections, certification of names on nomination papers, **53:46.**

Striking names from register, **51:38, 51:49.**

Naturalized citizens, production of papers and naturalization, **51:45A.**

Neglect of duty.
Assistant registrars, misconduct or neglect, **56:2, 56:3.**

Registrar or listing board member, penalty, **56:3.**

New divisions of wards and voting precincts, furnishing voting lists for purpose, **51:63.**

New precincts, furnishing registrar with map or description, **54:5, 54:8.**

REGISTRATION OF VOTERS
—Cont'd

New residents.
New citizens, **51:50.**
Penalties as to registration of, posting notice, **51:12.**

Nominating papers.
Appeals from reviews and corrections of local registrars, **58:6.**

Certificates and certification. See within this heading, "Certificates and certification."

Correction and revision. See within this heading, "Correction and revision."

Duties, **53:7, 53:7A.**

Objections to nomination papers. See within this heading, "Objections."

State primaries or elections, certification of names, **53:46.**

Time for certification of names, **53:7.**

Time for obtaining by candidates for city or town office, **53:9A.**

Nonresidents.
Residents. See within this heading, "Residents."

Notary public, registrar or assistant may hold office, **51:25.**

Notice.
Affidavits of registration, **51:32.**
Death, notice to registrar, **51:14.**
Defacing or removing notices, **56:10.**

Initiative and referendum petitions, **54:53.**

Intention to strike names from register, **51:38.**

Nonentry of name on annual register, to voters, **51:35, 51:37.**

Omission of names from annual register, **51:35, 51:37.**

Posting notice. See within this heading, "Posting notice."

Rejection of applicant for registration, **51:47.**

Removal of voter to other community, notice in case, **51:38.**

Sessions for registration, **51:32.**

State primaries or elections, notice of recounts to secretary of state, **54:135.**

Time and place, **51:32.**

Voting lists, posting, **51:57.**

REGISTRATION OF VOTERS
—Cont'd

Numbers and numbering.
Certification of number of registered voters, **51:61.**

Count of voters of each political party, board of registrars, **53:38A.**

Nursing or rest homes.
Annual street listings compiled by registrars, **51:10A.**

Restoration to voting lists of names of persons, **51:38.**

Oath.
Affidavits of registration. See within this heading, "Affidavits of registration."

Aiding or abetting as to false oath, **56:7.**

False oath or affidavit. See within this heading, "False oath or affidavit."

Of office, **51:23.**

Witnesses, summoning and administration of oath, **233:8.**

Objections.
Nomination papers.
Illegality of registration, **56:8.**
In caucuses using official ballots, consideration, **53:104.**

Misconduct or neglect of registrars of voters, **56:2, 56:3.**

Procedure and powers with respect, **51:11, 51:12, 51:14.**

Removing notices or lists, **56:10.**

Registrations, objections, **51:48, 51:49.**

Offenses.
See ELECTION OFFENSES.

Officers for election.
Election officers. See within this heading, "Election officers."

Officers for registration.
Absent voters.
Appointment of officers, **51:22A.**

Compensation, **51:23.**
Oath of officer, **51:23.**
Physically disabled persons, examination, **51:42A.**

Holding of office by registrars of voters, **51:25.**

Public offices not to be held, **51:25.**

Officers of militia, registrar of voters or assistant may hold office, **51:25.**

REGISTRATION OF VOTERS
—Cont'd
Omissions from lists.
Certificate for voter omitted
from voting list, **51:59.**
Compared with annual registers,
51:35.
Notice, **51:35, 51:37.**
Open sessions required, **51:40.**
Optional provision with respect to,
cities may adopt, **51:17.**
Order, authority to maintain,
51:52.
Other offices not to be held, **51:25.**
Penalties.
See ELECTION OFFENSES.
Perjury.
False oath or affidavit. See
within this heading, "False
oath or affidavit."
Personal appearance, **51:42.**
Persons waiting in line when
registration closes, **51:34.**
Petitions.
Initiative and referendum
petitions. See within this
heading, "Initiative and
referendum petitions."
Physically disabled persons,
51:22A, 51:42A.
Place, **51:3.**
Sessions for registration, **51:26.**
Plan D charter cities, definition for
purpose, **43:80.**
Plan E cities, definition for
purpose of provisions, **43:94.**
Political parties.
See POLITICAL PARTIES.
Posting notice.
New residents, penalties as to
registration, **51:12.**
Register of voters, omissions,
51:37.
Statutory penalties, **51:12.**
Voting lists, posting, **51:57.**
Powers, **51:22A, 51:24.**
Precincts.
Wards and voting precincts. See
within this heading, "Wards
and voting precincts."
Preservation.
Documents with respect, **51:41.**
Equal political representation,
51:19.
Presidential electors.
See PRESIDENTIAL
ELECTORS.
Presidential primaries.
See PRESIDENTIAL
PRIMARIES.
Presumption of validity in criminal
prosecution, **50:8.**

REGISTRATION OF VOTERS
—Cont'd
Primary elections.
Candidates in certificate as to
party enrollment, **53:48.**
Challenge of registrations of
voters, **51:48, 51:49.**
City and town primaries,
registration session before.
Nomination papers,
51:58-51:61.
Federal service personnel, **51:50.**
Nomination papers, certification,
53:46, 53:56, 53:58-53:61.
Notice of recounts in state
primaries to state secretary,
54:135.
Petitions for recounts to be
signed only by registered
voters enrolled on or before
last day to register, **53:40A.**
Place of registration and voting,
51:3, 53:28.
Presidential primaries.
See PRESIDENTIAL
PRIMARIES.
Sessions for registration before.
Presidential primaries,
51:26-51:28.
Special primaries.
Meetings of registrars, **53:46.**
Production of naturalization
papers, **51:45A.**
Prudential committee of district
acting, **41:115.**
Public officers and employees.
Labor. See within this heading,
"Labor."
Public offices not to be held, **51:25.**
Qualification, **51:1, 51:3, 51:25,
54:91A.**
Records, reports, and returns,
51:40.
Affidavits of registration, **51:36,
51:41, 51:42.**
Facts to be noted, **51:36.**
General court, state secretary's
report, **54:133.**
Home rule for cities and towns,
filing of documents, **43B:16.**
Hotels, motels, and
roominghouses, report of
residents, **51:10A.**
Jury list to be prepared by
registrar of voters, **234:4.**
Name changes, **51:2.**
Omissions from poll tax list,
51:8.
Open to public inspection, **51:40.**
Persons not previously listed,
names, **51:8, 51:11, 51:12.**

REGISTRATION OF VOTERS
—Cont'd
Records, reports, and returns
—Cont'd
Preservation, **51:41.**
Proceedings of registrar, **51:23.**
Registered voters, returns,
51:61.
Retention, **51:41.**
Recount of votes, duties in
connection, **54:135, 54:135A.**
Referendum petitions.
Initiative and referendum
petitions. See within this
heading, "Initiative and
referendum petitions."
Registrars of voters, **51:15-51:25.**
Removal of registrars, **51:19.**
Assistant registrar, **51:22.**
Equal political representation,
preservation, **51:19.**
Removal of voter to other
community, notice in case,
51:38.
Reports.
Records, reports, and returns.
See within this heading,
"Records, reports, and
returns."
Residents.
Cities and towns, lists of
residents, **51:4, 51:14A.**
Dormitories, listing of residents
for purposes of voter
registration, **51:10A.**
Hotel, motel, and roominghouse
residents. See within this
heading, "Hotel, motel, and
roominghouse residents."
New residents. See within this
heading, "New residents."
Registrars and assistant
registrars, nonresidents,
51:25.
Rest homes.
Nursing or rest homes. See
within this heading,
"Nursing or rest homes."
Revision and correction.
Correction and revision. See
within this heading,
"Correction and revision."
Roominghouses.
Hotel, motel, and roominghouse
residents. See within this
heading, "Hotel, motel, and
roominghouse residents."
Rooms, **51:23.**
Salaries and compensation, **51:23.**
City or town clerk serving on
board of registrars,
additional compensation,
41:19G, 41:19H, 41:19J.

REGISTRATION OF VOTERS
—Cont'd

Saturday.
Sessions for registration. See within this heading, "Sessions for registration."
Schools and education.
Dormitories, listing of residents for purposes of voter registration, **51:10A.**
School committee, board of registrars of voters to transmit lists of persons up to 21 years of age, **51:4, 51:14A.**
Sessions in schools, **51:42C-51:42E.**
Voter education and voluntary registration sessions held by registrars, **51:42C.**
Secretary of state.
See SECRETARY OF STATE.
Selectmen.
See ALDERMEN AND SELECTMEN.
Sessions for registration, **51:26, 51:32.**
Final day for registration, **51:28, 51:31.**
High schools, registration sessions, **51:42C, 51:42D.**
Hours for registration. See within this heading, "Hours for registration."
Maintenance of order and regularity, **51:52, 51:53.**
Notices, **51:32.**
On last day, **51:28.**
Open sessions, **51:40.**
Places for holding, **51:26.**
Police officers, **51:53.**
Presidential electors, voters eligible to qualify for voting, **51:28.**
Presidential primaries, time for hearing application for voting, **51:26-51:28.**
Primary elections. See within this heading, "Primary elections."
Saturday sessions, **51:28.**
Final day for registration, session on Saturday preceding, **51:31.**
Schools, sessions, **51:42C, 51:42D.**
Supervisors of registration, attendance, **51:54.**
Time for holding, **51:26, 51:33.**
Time for receiving applications to vote for presidential electors, **51:26, 51:32.**

REGISTRATION OF VOTERS
—Cont'd

Sessions for registration —Cont'd
Vocational schools, sessions, **51:24C.**
Sex or marital status as affecting surname used on voter registration, **51:36, 151B:4.**
Signing name, requirement, **51:44.**
Single registrar may take registrations, **51:33.**
Soldiers and sailors.
Federal service personnel. See within this heading, "Federal service personnel."
Solicitation of votes or distribution of campaign literature in offices where voter registration is conducted, penalty, **51:52A.**
Special elections.
Certification meeting prior, **53:46.**
Special primaries.
Primary elections. See within this heading, "Primary elections."
State ballot law commission.
See STATE BALLOT LAW COMMISSION.
State secretary, violations, enforcement, **56:60.**
Statutory penalties, posting notice, **51:12.**
Street lists.
Designation of registered voters in list, **51:7.**
Nursing or rest home residents, inclusion, **51:10A.**
Preparation, **51:6.**
Striking names from register, **51:38, 51:49.**
Subsequent examination of registrants for cause, **51:47B.**
Sunday, effect of final day falling, **51:31.**
Supervisors of registration, appointment and duties, **51:54.**
Supplementary registration to vote.
Federal service personnel. See within this heading, "Federal service personnel."
Surname retained after marriage, voter registration, **51:36.**
Temporary registrars.
Appointment, **51:20.**
Assistant registrars, temporary, **51:22.**
Term of office of registrars, **51:15, 51:17, 51:21.**
Assistant registrars, **51:22.**

REGISTRATION OF VOTERS
—Cont'd

Time or date.
Certification in presidential primaries, meeting dates, **53:46.**
Challenge of registrations, time, **51:48.**
Final day for registration of voters, **51:28, 51:31.**
Holding registration sessions, time for, **51:26.**
Hours. See within this heading, "Hours for registration."
Initiative and referendum petitions to state time for filing, **53:22A.**
Nominating papers, **53:7, 53:9A.**
Notice, time and place, **51:32.**
Presidential electors, time for receiving applications to vote, **51:26, 51:32.**
Sessions for registration. See within this heading, "Sessions for registration."
Town clerks.
City and town clerks. See within this heading, "City and town clerks."
Town meetings.
See TOWN MEETINGS.
Towns.
Cities and towns. See within this heading, "Cities and towns."
Unequal political representation on board, procedure, **51:19.**
Vacancies.
Appointment, **51:15.**
Assistant registrar, **51:22.**
Filling, **51:20.**
Holding other office as ground, **51:25.**
Vocational schools, registration sessions, **51:42C-51:42E.**
Voting list at elections.
See ELECTIONS.
Wages.
Salaries and compensation. See within this heading, "Salaries and compensation."
Wards and voting precincts.
Map of new precinct, furnishing registrar with copy, **54:5, 54:8.**
Moving from one ward or precinct to another in same city or town, **51:3.**
New divisions of wards and voting precincts, furnishing voting lists for purposes, **51:63.**

REGISTRATION OF VOTERS
—Cont'd
Wards and voting precincts
—Cont'd
Returns of registered voters,
51:61.
Witnesses, summoning and
administration of oath, **233:8.**

**REGULATION OF BUSINESS
PRACTICE AND
CONSUMER PROTECTION
ACT, 93A:1 et seq.**

**REGULATORY AND
RECLAMATION ACT.**
Coal mining, **21B:1 et seq.**

REHABILITATION.
Abatement of taxes on certain
abandoned real property,
expedited procedure, **58:8.**
Alcoholism.
See ALCOHOLISM AND
INTOXICATION.
Blind persons.
See BLIND PERSONS.
Building regulations and
standards board, rules and
regulations, **143:94.**
Chiropractors, services rendered,
112:97.
Civil service.
Employees of rehabilitation
commission, status, **6:75.**
Released prisoners, development
of programs, **31:5.**
Clinic, institutions within
definition, **111:52.**
Coal mining regulations and
reclamation, rehabilitation of
land to prior use, **21B:3,
21B:5.**
Commission, **6:74-6:84.**
See REHABILITATION
COMMISSION OF
MASSACHUSETTS.
Correctional institutions, **124:1,
124:2.**
See CORRECTIONAL
INSTITUTIONS.
Disability benefits, **32:8.**
Drug addiction rehabilitation.
See DRUG ADDICTION
REHABILITATION.
Economic development and
industrial corporation, power,
121C:5.
Epileptics, health department to
establish program for
rehabilitation, **111:4G.**
Families of handicapped persons,
service to as vocational
rehabilitation services, **6:77,
6:78.**

REHABILITATION —Cont'd
Foreign insurance companies.
See FOREIGN INSURANCE
COMPANIES.
Hazardous waste insolvency fund.
See HAZARDOUS WASTE
INSOLVENCY FUND.
Hospital service corporations,
176A:23.
Housing.
See HOUSING AND URBAN
RENEWAL.
Industrial accident division
rehabilitation board.
See WORKERS'
COMPENSATION.
Insurance companies, **175:6,
175:180A-175:180L.**
See INSURANCE.
Libraries, rehabilitation of
property, funding and grant
programs, **78:19A-78:19C,
78:19E, 78:19G-78:19K,
78:25.**
Massachusetts life and health
insurance guaranty
association law, **175:147.**
Mentally ill.
See MENTALLY ILL AND
RETARDED PERSONS.
Minimum wage law, applicability
to rehabilitation programs of
religious or charitable
institutions, **151:2.**
Nursing rehabilitation program,
committees, membership,
duties and responsibilities,
112:74, 112:80F.
Old age and survivors disability
benefits, vocational
rehabilitation for recipients,
6:78.
Physical therapists,
112:23A-112:23Q.
See PHYSICAL THERAPISTS.
Physicians and surgeons.
Commission on rehabilitation,
employment, **6:79.**
Right of patient to retain private
physician, **111B:11.**
Program, defined, **276A:1.**
Psychology-related professions or
occupations excluded from
regulations, **112:125.**
Retirement and disability data
system, **32:21.**
Social security.
Commissions relation to federal
social security programs,
6:80.
Determination of disability by
rehabilitation commission,
6:80.

REHABILITATION —Cont'd
Social security —Cont'd
Old age and survivors disability
benefits, vocational
rehabilitation services for
persons receiving, **6:78.**
Solid waste management, proper
disposal of debris from
renovation before issuance of
permit, **40:54.**
State and state departments,
vocational rehabilitation
services.
Agreements with
Commonwealth affecting
eligibility, **6:78.**
Inspection of records of
applicants, **6:84.**
State finance, contracts,
organizations providing social,
rehabilitative, health, or
special education services,
29:29B.
Tewksbury Hospital, **122:1.**
Transitional assistance
department, services, **18:2.**
University of Massachusetts,
rehabilitation facilities,
75:36C.
Veterans, **74:22D.**
Institutional on-farm
agricultural schools, **74:54.**
Lease of state property to
federal government for
rehabilitation, **74:41.**
Workers' compensation.
See WORKERS'
COMPENSATION.

**REHABILITATION AND
TREATMENT ACT.**
Alcoholism, **111B:1 et seq.**

**REHABILITATION
COMMISSION OF
MASSACHUSETTS,
6:74-6:84.**
Advisory council, **6:74-6:76.**
Agreements.
Contracts and agreements. See
within this heading,
"Contracts and agreements."
Applications, **6:78.**
Bureau of public employment
offices to cooperate, **23:9L.**
Commissioner of rehabilitation,
6:75.
Advisory council, advice, **6:76.**
Compensation, **6:75.**
Health and welfare commission,
membership, **6:125.**
Medical assistance advisory
council, membership, **6:75.**

REHABILITATION COMMISSION OF MASSACHUSETTS —Cont'd

Commissioner of rehabilitation —Cont'd
Officers and employees, appointment, **6:75.**
Term of office, **6:75.**
Commonwealth Service Corps, duties, **6:121.**
Confidential nature of commission's records, **6:84.**
Contracts and agreements, **6:78, 6:78A, 6:79, 6:80, 6:81.**
Disclosure of information concerning, **6:84.**
Nonprofit organizations, contracts, **6:78A.**
Sheltered workshop program, **6:78A.**
Vocational rehabilitation services, **6:79, 6:81, 152:30E, 152:30H.**
Definitions, **6:77.**
Duties and powers of, **6:79.**
Education, appointment of supervisor, **6:79.**
Eligibility for services, **6:78.**
Employment and training division in labor and workforce department, cooperation, **6:81.**
Employment dislocations and assistance in reemployment of dislocated workers, **6:17.**
Epileptics, vocational rehabilitation program, **6:79.**
Establishment, **6:74.**
Extended sheltered employment for handicapped persons, **6:78, 6:78A.**
Facilities, **6:79.**
Families of handicapped persons, services to as vocational rehabilitation services, **6:77, 6:78.**
Federal aid, **6:74, 6:80, 6:82.**
Fire training council, duties, **6:165.**
Gifts, acceptance and use, **6:83.**
Governor and council, serving, **6:17.**
Head Injury Treatment Services Trust Fund, **10:59.**
Health and human services executive office, agencies within, **6A:16.**
Health department to cooperate, **6:81, 111:2A.**
Incompetents.
Mentally ill and retarded persons. See within this heading, "Mentally ill and retarded persons."

REHABILITATION COMMISSION OF MASSACHUSETTS —Cont'd

Industrial Accidents Division, cooperation, **6:81.**
Information or records, confidential nature, **6:84.**
Mentally ill and retarded persons, **6:181, 123:4.**
Co-operation by commission, **6:81.**
Membership on advisory council of commission, **6:76.**
Old age and survivors disability insurance benefits, services to persons receiving, **6:78.**
Other departments, cooperation with, **6:74, 6:80, 6:81.**
Personnel, **6:74, 6:75.**
Persons receiving old age and survivors disability insurance benefits services, **6:78.**
Powers of, **6:79.**
Public agencies, cooperation, **6:81.**
Public employment offices bureau to co-operate, in placement of handicapped persons, **23:9L.**
Public health departments, cooperation by and, **6:81.**
Qualification.
Eligibility, **6:78.**
Reciprocity with other states, **6:79.**
Recommendations of health and welfare commission for coordination of services, **6:126.**
Records.
Confidential nature of records, **6:84.**
Persons eligible for vocational rehabilitation under, records, **6:79.**
Register of facilities for sheltered workshop program, **6:78A.**
Regional directors of rehabilitation services, appointment by rehabilitation commissioner, **6:75.**
Report to general court, **6:79.**
Retarded persons.
Mentally ill and retarded persons. See within this heading, "Mentally ill and retarded persons."
Salary and compensation of rehabilitation commissioner, **6:75.**
Sheltered workshop program for handicapped persons, **6:78A.**
Social Services Department, **6:74-6:84.**
Advisory council, member, **6:76.**

REHABILITATION COMMISSION OF MASSACHUSETTS —Cont'd

Social Services Department —Cont'd
Cooperation with rehabilitation commission, **6:81.**
State plan, **6:80.**
State treasurer, supervision of funds, **6:82.**
Transfer of functions, **6:74.**
United States Secretary of Health, Education, and Welfare, co-operation and agreement, **6:74, 6:80.**
Vocational rehabilitation services, **6:77-6:81, 6:84, 152:30E, 152:30H.**
Wages, commissioner's salary, **6:75.**
Welfare department.
Social services department. See within this heading, "Social Services Department."

REHABILITATION COUNSELORS.
Licensing, **112:163-112:165.**

REHOBOTH.
Congressional district, **57:1.**
District court held, **218:1.**
Medical examiner district, **38:1.**
Senatorial district, **57:3.**

REINCORPORATION.
Insurance.
See INSURANCE.

REINSURANCE, 175:20, 175:54B.
Accident and sickness insurance, **176J:8.**
Agents.
Insurance agents and brokers. See within this heading, "Insurance agents and brokers."
Authority to reinsure risks, **175:54B, 175:92, 175:93.**
Boiler insurance, **175:92.**
Brokers.
Insurance agents and brokers. See within this heading, "Insurance agents and brokers."
Claims, clauses as to handling in event of insolvency, **175:20.**
Commissioner of insurance.
Insurance commissioner. See within this heading, "Insurance commissioner."
Contracts, **175:2A.**

REINSURANCE —Cont'd
Credit, **175:20A.**
Definition, **175G:1.**
Distinction from original risk, **175:2A.**
Domestic companies may reinsure risks, **175:54B.**
Domestic exchanges, reinsurance contracts entered into, **175:94D.**
Fire insurance, **175:54B, 175:80.**
Rates.
See INSURANCE RATES AND RATING ORGANIZATIONS.
Foreign insurance companies, **175:20.**
See FOREIGN INSURANCE COMPANIES.
Form of policy, exemption from laws, **175:2A.**
Group insurance.
Municipal employees, **32B:3.**
State employees, **32A:4.**
Hazard of, deemed distinct from original risk, **175:2A.**
Hazardous waste insolvency fund, **21C:18.**
Hospital service corporations, **176A:1D.**
Insolvency, clauses as to handling claims in event, **175:20.**
Insurance agents and brokers.
Employer assigned to particular insurer or reinsurance pool, compensation of agent selected, **152:65O.**
Penalty for unauthorized reinsurance, **175:20.**
Insurance commissioner.
Credit, **175:20A.**
Life insurers, regulation of reinsurance, **175:54G.**
Powers and duties as to reinsurance, **175:20.**
Joint reinsurance.
See INSURANCE RATES AND RATING ORGANIZATIONS.
Letters of credit, **175:20A.**
Liability insurance, **175:54B, 175:93.**
Life insurance, **175:20.**
See LIFE INSURANCE.
Limit of single risk, effect, **175:21.**
Medical service corporations, **176B:3A.**
Name of insurance company, inclusion of word, **175:49.**
Obligations of company withdrawing from insurance business, **175:44.**

REINSURANCE —Cont'd
Penalties, **175:20.**
Policy or contract, **175:2A.**
Pollution liability reinsurance corporation, **175G:1-175G:7.**
Pools for reinsurance, **152:65C, 152:65O.**
Reciprocal insurance exchanges.
Applicability of laws as to reinsurance, **175:94J.**
Companies not authorized to do business in Commonwealth, reinsurance, **175:94J.**
Requirement of reinsurance prior to doing business, **175:94D.**
Reserve for, companies other than life, **175:10.**
Savings bank life insurance.
Municipal employees, group insurance, **32B:3.**
State employees, group insurance, **32A:4.**
Unauthorized reinsurance, **175:20.**
Unearned premium liability, reinsurance as affecting, **175:20.**
Withdrawal of company from insurance business, reinsurance of obligations of company, **175:44.**
Workers' compensation.
Minimum amount, **152:25A.**
Pools for rejected risk policies, **152:65C, 152:65H, 152:65O.**
Self-insurers, **152:25A.**

REINSURANCE INTERMEDIARY ACT, 175:177M et seq.

REJECTION.
Goods.
See SALES UNDER COMMERCIAL CODE.
Insurance.
See INSURANCE.
Public construction, **7:42C.**
Sales under commercial code.
See SALES UNDER COMMERCIAL CODE.
Workers' compensation, **152:65A to 152:65M.**
See WORKERS' COMPENSATION.

RELATIVES.
See FAMILY AND RELATIVES.

RELEASE.
See DISCHARGE OR RELEASE.

RELIEF CORPORATIONS AND ASSOCIATIONS.
Cigarette sales below cost to relief agencies, **64C:15.**
Corporate contributions, **155:12A.**
Employer may show benefits to injured employee in mitigation of damages, **153:8.**
Insurance companies, authority to make contributions for purposes, **175:37A.**
Payroll deductions of dues payable to relief associations of municipal departments, **180:17A.**
Railroads.
See RAILROADS.
Steamboats and steamboat companies, **159:86-159:88.**
See STEAMBOATS AND STEAMBOAT COMPANIES.
Street railways, **159:86-159:88.**
See STREET RAILWAYS.

RELIEF VALVES.
Hot water tanks, safety devices required, **142:19.**

RELIGION AND RELIGIOUS SOCIETIES, 67:1 et seq.
Abortion or sterilization procedures, physician's refusal to perform on religious grounds, **112:12I.**
Absentee ballots permissible if unable to cast vote for reasons of religious beliefs, **54:86.**
Accounts of officers, committee for settlement, **68:8.**
Actions, committee to prosecute actions against church officers, **68:8.**
Adoption proceedings, consideration of religious designation of child, **210:5B.**
Affidavit of posting of notice of sale of pews for nonpayment of taxes, **67:31, 67:32.**
African Methodist Episcopal Church societies, allowable annual income of trust property, **67:41.**
Agents.
Officers and agents. See within this heading, "Officers and agents."
Alcoholic liquors.
See ALCOHOLIC LIQUORS.
Alteration or rebuilding of meeting houses.
Pews, taking or selling, **67:19, 67:33, 67:34.**

**RELIGION AND RELIGIOUS
SOCIETIES** —Cont'd

Alteration or rebuilding of meeting
houses —Cont'd
Power to make, **67:27.**
Annual meeting, **67:7.**
Annual reports of certain trustees
etc., **68:13, 68:14.**
Application of law to parishes,
67:20.
Appraisers.
See APPRAISERS AND
APPRAISALS.
Appropriations, **67:17, 67:27.**
Arson as to meeting houses, **266:2.**
Assessments on pews, **67:30,
67:35, 67:36.**
Power to impose, **67:18.**
Assessors or standing committee,
67:7.
Election, **67:8.**
Presiding officer, member may
act, **67:15.**
Term of office, **67:10.**
Auction sale of pews, **67:30-67:33.**
Automatic sprinklers, exemption of
houses of religious worship,
148:26A½.
Baptismal records, **66:5.**
Beano, may conduct game, **10:38.**
Bible.
See BIBLE.
Birth records, **66:5.**
Blasphemy as criminal offense,
272:36.
Blockbusting, penalty, **112:87AAA.**
Bond required of fireworks
manufacturer located within
specified distance from house
of worship, **148:40.**
Boxing match, forfeiture of charter
for illegal match, **180:28.**
Breach of peace and disorderly
conduct, **272:38, 272:39.**
Camp meetings, improper
conduct at or near, **272:39.**
Penalty for disorderly behavior
at meeting, **67:9.**
Buddhist priest or minister,
solemnization of marriage,
207:38.
Buildings.
Chapels.
See CHAPELS.
Meeting houses. See within this
heading, "Meeting houses."
Parsonages. See within this
heading, "Parsonages."
Property tax exemption,
eligibility and application
for abatement, **59:5.**

**RELIGION AND RELIGIOUS
SOCIETIES** —Cont'd

Burial grounds.
See CEMETERIES.
Business corporations.
Discrimination on basis of
religion prohibited, **151E:2.**
Powers to make donations,
156B:9.
Bylaws.
Authority to make, **67:4.**
Corporations to promote
religious purposes, **180:7.**
Incorporation, **67:50.**
Camp meetings, improper conduct
at or near, **272:39.**
Card games for religious purposes,
271:22A.
Catholic churches.
Roman Catholic churches. See
within this heading, "Roman
Catholic churches."
Cemeteries.
See CEMETERIES.
Certificate of incorporation, **67:22.**
Roman Catholic churches, **67:44.**
Certified copies of records or
registers, fee, **66:16, 262:34.**
Change of name or purposes of
corporations to promote
religious purposes, **180:10,
180:11.**
Chapels.
See CHAPELS.
Chaplains.
See CHAPLAINS.
Charities and charitable
contributions, **68:1-68:16,
180:2.**
Cities and towns, trustees of
religious gifts, **68:13, 68:14.**
Corporations. See within this
heading, "Corporations."
Friends or Quakers, **68:10.**
Fundraisers, exception as to
regulation, **68:33.**
Legacy and succession taxes,
exemption, **65:1.**
Management of funds, **180A:1 et
seq.**
See INSTITUTIONAL FUND
MANAGEMENT.
Officers as body corporate for
receiving, **68:1, 68:2.**
Pious and charitable uses,
68:1-68:16.
Trusts and trustees, **68:4.**
Unincorporated societies, **68:12.**
Vestry as body corporate for
purpose of receiving gifts,
68:2.

**RELIGION AND RELIGIOUS
SOCIETIES** —Cont'd

Children.
See CHILDREN AND MINORS.
Christian science.
See CHRISTIAN SCIENCE.
Cities and towns.
Clerk of city or town, delivery of
records, **66:16.**
Trustees of religious gifts, **68:13,
68:14.**
Civil rights, **151B:1 et seq.**
See CIVIL RIGHTS AND
DISCRIMINATION.
Clergy.
Appropriations by religious
societies for support, **67:17,
67:27.**
Body corporate receiving gifts,
members, **68:2.**
Chaplains.
See CHAPLAINS.
Conveyance of church lands,
68:7.
Correctional institutions, **125:13,
127:88.**
Deacons. See within this
heading, "Deacons."
Death penalty, persons present
at execution, **279:65.**
Employment security law,
election by nonprofit
institutions to provide
coverage for employees,
151A:6.
Fund-raisers, exception as to
regulation, **68:33.**
Jury service, exemption, **234:1.**
Marriage.
See MARRIAGE.
Mentally ill person's right to
visit, **123:23.**
Parsonage land, power to take,
68:5.
Privileged communications,
233:20A.
Psychology-related professions or
occupations excluded from
regulations, **112:25.**
Rabbis.
See RABBIS.
State institutions, advisory
committee on chaplains,
6:166B.
Wholesaler's and importer's
license to sell wine, **138:18.**
Clerk.
Certificate of incorporation,
duties, **67:22.**
Delivery of records to city or
town clerk, **66:16.**

RELIGION AND RELIGIOUS SOCIETIES —Cont'd

Clerk —Cont'd
Election, **67:8.**
Presiding officer, may act, **67:15.**
Collections.
See COLLECTIONS AND COLLECTORS.
Columbaria, construction within churches, **114:43D.**
Committees.
Accounts of officers, for settlement, **68:8.**
Assessors or standing committee. See within this heading, "Assessors or standing committee."
Chaplains in state institutions advisory committee, membership and duties, **6:166B.**
Compensation for pews taken upon rebuilding or alteration of meeting house, **67:33, 67:34.**
Conscientious objectors.
See CONSCIENTIOUS OBJECTORS.
Consent to membership required, **67:5.**
Constitution of Massachusetts.
See CONSTITUTION OF MASSACHUSETTS.
Constitution of the United States.
See CONSTITUTION OF THE UNITED STATES.
Contracts of, liability of former member, **67:5.**
Conveyance of land.
Sale of property. See within this heading, "Sale of property."
Corporations, **67:1 et seq., 180:2, 180:7.**
Business corporations. See within this heading, "Business corporations."
Bylaws. See within this heading, "Bylaws."
Change of corporate name for promotion of religious purposes, **180:11.**
Donations, power of business corporations to make, **156B:9.**
Incorporation. See within this heading, "Incorporation."
Life insurance company, religious corporation, **175:118.**
Members, who are, **67:52, 68:2.**
Names, **155:9.**
Officers and agents. See within this heading, "Officers and agents."

RELIGION AND RELIGIOUS SOCIETIES —Cont'd

Corporations —Cont'd
Promotion of religious purposes, corporations, **180:7, 180:10, 180:11.**
Purposes, change of purposes of corporation to promote religious, **180:10, 180:11.**
Records, reports, and returns, **66:16.**
Vestry as body corporate for purpose of receiving gifts, **68:2.**
Correctional institutions.
See CORRECTIONAL INSTITUTIONS.
Damaging church property, **266:2, 266:98, 266:127A.**
Deacons.
Committees to settle accounts, **68:8.**
Conveyance of property.
By church, **68:6.**
To church, **67:53.**
Deemed members of body corporate for purpose of receiving gifts, **68:1, 68:2.**
Marriage solemnization by ordained deacons, **207:38.**
United Methodist church.
See UNITED METHODIST CHURCH.
Death penalty, persons present at execution, **279:65.**
Death records, **66:5.**
Debts of, liability of members, **67:18.**
Deeds and conveyances.
Sale of property. See within this heading, "Sale of property."
Discrimination, **151B:1 et seq.**
See CIVIL RIGHTS AND DISCRIMINATION.
Disorderly conduct.
Breach of peace and disorderly conduct. See within this heading, "Breach of peace and disorderly conduct."
Dissolution of membership, **67:5.**
Disturbances at religious worship, **272:38, 272:39.**
Dwelling houses.
Parsonages. See within this heading, "Parsonages."
Elections.
Absentee voter ballots permissible if unable to cast vote in person for reasons of religious beliefs, **54:86.**
Officers of religious society, election, **67:8, 67:49.**

RELIGION AND RELIGIOUS SOCIETIES —Cont'd

Employment.
Exception as to discrimination on account of religion, **151B:1.**
Fair employment practices law, applicability, **151B:1, 151B:4.**
Minimum wage law as applicable to rehabilitation and training programs, **151:2.**
Psychology-related professions or occupations excluded from regulations, **112:125.**
Sunday labor prohibition, exception for religious sects observing Sabbath on Saturday, **136:6.**
Employment security law, applicability, **151A:6.**
Establishment of religion prohibited, **US Const Amend 1.**
Evidence of incorporation, certification and recording, **67:22.**
Examination or inspection of premises of monastery for fire prevention purposes, **148:4.**
Expectoration in services, **270:14, 270:15.**
Fair educational practices.
See FAIR EDUCATIONAL PRACTICES.
Fair employment practices law, applicability, **151B:1, 151B:4.**
Fees.
Certified copies of records, **66:16, 262:34.**
Incorporation, **67:51.**
Junk collector's or dealer's license, exemption from fee, **140:54.**
Motor bus transporting persons to and from services, registration fee, **90:33.**
Fiduciary's sale of church pews, **204:12.**
Filing and recording.
Records, reports, and returns. See within this heading, "Records, reports, and returns."
Finances and funds.
Charities and charitable contributions. See within this heading, "Charities and charitable contributions."
Fines and penalties.
Damaging property, **266:127A.**

RELIGION AND RELIGIOUS SOCIETIES —Cont'd

Fines and penalties —Cont'd
Death sentence, persons present at execution, **279:65.**
Disorderly behavior, **67:9.**

Fire prevention.
Automatic sprinklers, **148:26A½.**
Inspection of monastery premises, **148:4.**

Fireworks manufacturers located within specified distance of houses of worship, bonds required, **148:40.**

First meeting, **67:22, 67:23.**

Food.
Jury and jury trial, religious requirements, **234A:56A.**
Kosher food. See within this heading, "Kosher food."
Meals. See within this heading, "Meals."

Freedom.
Constitution of Massachusetts. See CONSTITUTION OF MASSACHUSETTS.
Constitution of the United States. See CONSTITUTION OF THE UNITED STATES.

Friends, society of. See FRIENDS, SOCIETY OF.

Gaming and games of chance.
Beano, may conduct game, **10:38.**
Card games for religious purposes, **271:22A.**
Forfeiture of charter for violation of gaming laws, **180:27.**
Raffles and bazaars, conduct, **271:7A.**

Gifts.
Charities and charitable contributions. See within this heading, "Charities and charitable contributions."

Group insurance, **175:133, 175:134.**

Guardian, duty to protect freedom of religion and religious practice, **201:51.**

Health care proxies, **201D:5, 201D:14.**

Houses of worship.
Buildings. See within this heading, "Buildings."

Importer's and wholesaler's license to sell wine, **138:18.**

Inactive or defunct congregations, disposition of property, **214:3.**

RELIGION AND RELIGIOUS SOCIETIES —Cont'd

Incorporation, **67:21-67:23, 67:47-67:55, 180:2.**
By-laws, **67:50.**
Certificate of incorporation. See within this heading, "Certificate of incorporation."
Dissolution or liquidation of churches, **67:5.**
Fees, **67:51.**
Filing record of organization, **67:51.**
Membership in corporation, **67:52.**
Notice of meeting, **67:48.**
Officers, election, **67:49.**
Property, conveyance to church by officers or religious societies, **67:53, 67:54.**
Proprietors of meeting houses, **67:24, 67:26.**
Records as evidence, **67:22.**
Roman Catholic churches, **67:44.**
Special act, powers of society incorporated, **67:28.**
United Methodist Church or African Methodist Episcopal Church, **67:40.**

Institutional fund management, **180A:1 et seq.** See INSTITUTIONAL FUND MANAGEMENT.

Instruction, injury to buildings used, **266:98.**

Judicatory executives, effect of advisory committee on chaplains in state institutions on responsibilities, **6:166B.**

Junk collector or dealer's license, exemption from fee, **140:54.**

Jury service, exemption of clergy, **234:1, 234A:56A.**

Justice of the peace.
First meeting, duties, **67:22, 67:23.**
Meetings, calling, **67:12, 67:22, 67:23.**
Oath of officers, administration, **67:15.**

Kosher food.
Misrepresenting food, **94:156.**
Sunday sale, **136:6.**

Labor.
Employment. See within this heading, "Employment."

Legacy and succession taxes, exemption of property, **65:1.**

Licenses.
Entertainments by religious societies not required to have, **140:182.**

RELIGION AND RELIGIOUS SOCIETIES —Cont'd

Licenses —Cont'd
Food and beverages, license for dispensing, **140:21E, 140:21F.**
Junk collector or dealer's license, exemption from fee, **140:54.**
Motion pictures, special license for showing, **143:85.**
Religious publications, license not required for sale, **101:17.**
Wholesaler's and importer's license to sell wine to clergy, **138:18.**

Life insurance companies, religious corporations, **175:118.**

Limitation of actions, discrimination, **260:5B.**

Management of institutional funds, **180A:1 et seq.** See INSTITUTIONAL FUND MANAGEMENT.

Marriage. See MARRIAGE.

Meals.
Exemption from taxation, **64H:6.**
Licenses for dispensing, **140:21E, 140:21F.**

Meeting houses.
Alteration or rebuilding of meeting houses. See within this heading, "Alteration or rebuilding of meeting houses."
Appropriations, **67:17.**
Arson, **266:2.**
Power to sell, **67:19.**
Property tax exemption, eligibility and application for abatement, **59:5.**
Proprietors of meeting houses. See within this heading, "Proprietors of meeting houses."

Meetings.
Annual meeting, **67:7.**
Certified copies of monthly meetings, fees for recording copies, **262:34.**
Cessation of, disposition of records in case, **66:16.**
Disorderly behavior at, penalty, **67:9.**
First meeting, **67:22, 67:23.**
Justice of the peace may call, when, **67:12, 67:22, 67:23.**
Meeting houses. See within this heading, "Meeting houses."
Notice. See within this heading, "Notice."

RELIGION AND RELIGIOUS SOCIETIES —Cont'd

Meetings —Cont'd
  Presiding officer, **67:15.**
  Proprietors of meeting houses, calling meeting, **67:29.**
  Warning, **67:13.**
  Warrant, **67:14, 67:22, 67:23.**
Members and membership, **67:5, 67:6, 67:18, 67:52.**
  Body corporate receiving gifts, members, **68:2.**
  Liability for debts of parish, **67:18.**
  Minimum number for incorporation, **67:21, 67:23.**
  Officers, members eligible to elect, **67:49.**
Mentally ill and retarded persons, **19:11, 123:23.**
Methodist church, **59:5, 67:40-67:43, 207:38.**
  See UNITED METHODIST CHURCH.
Minimum wage law as applicable to rehabilitation and training programs, **151:2.**
Ministers.
  Clergy. See within this heading, "Clergy."
Minors.
  See CHILDREN AND MINORS.
Moderator.
  Certificate of incorporation, duties, **67:22.**
  Election, **67:8.**
  Powers, **67:9.**
Monastery, inspection of premises for fire prevention purposes, **148:4.**
Motion pictures, special license for showing, **143:85.**
Motor bus transporting persons to and from services, registration fee, **90:33.**
Municipalities.
  Cities and towns. See within this heading, "Cities and towns."
Name of religious corporation, **155:9.**
  Change of corporation's name, **59:5, 67:40, 68:1, 68:6, 180:11, 207:38.**
Nonresidents eligible to membership, **67:6.**
Notice.
  Certification of necessity of marriage, preliminary notice unnecessary, **207:30.**
  Incorporation of churches, meetings, **67:48.**

RELIGION AND RELIGIOUS SOCIETIES —Cont'd

Notice —Cont'd
  Sale of pews for nonpayment of taxes, **67:31, 67:32.**
  Warning of meetings, **67:13.**
  Warrant for meetings, **67:14, 67:22, 67:23.**
"Nursing" as including services incidental to practice of religious tenets, **112:80B.**
Nursing home administrators certified by certain religious denominations, applicability of regulations, **112:108.**
Oath of officers, **67:15.**
Obscene literature control commission, representation of various religious faiths, **6:101.**
Officers and agents.
  Assessors or standing committee, **67:7.**
  Clergy. See within this heading, "Clergy."
  Collectors, **67:7.**
  Committee to settle accounts, **68:8.**
  Conveyance of land, **68:6.**
  Deemed body corporate for accepting gifts, **68:1.**
  Election, **67:8, 67:49.**
  Members eligible to elect, **67:49.**
  Oath, **67:15.**
  Presiding officer in choice of moderator, **67:15.**
  Residence requirements to be deemed bodies corporate, **68:1.**
  Terms of office, **67:7, 67:10.**
  Treasurer, **67:7, 68:8.**
  Vacancies, filling, **67:7.**
  Vestry. See within this heading, "Vestry."
  Wardens. See within this heading, "Wardens."
Orthodox churches and organizations, incorporation, **67:55.**
Parishes.
  Application of law, **67:20.**
  Appropriations for charges, **67:17.**
  Service of process, **223:37.**
  Territorial parish, nonresidents eligible to membership, **67:6.**
Parsonages.
  Local assessment of parsonages held in irrevocable trust for religious corporations, **59:5.**
  Minister may take parsonage land, **68:5.**

RELIGION AND RELIGIOUS SOCIETIES —Cont'd

Personal property.
  Pews, **67:38.**
  Proprietors of meeting houses may hold, **67:25.**
  Society may hold, **67:21.**
Persons and properties, prohibition of acts against, **265:39, 266:127A, 266:127B.**
Pews.
  Appraisers.
    See APPRAISERS AND APPRAISALS.
  Assessments on pews. See within this heading, "Assessments on pews."
  Auction sale, **67:30-67:33.**
  Compensation upon taking for alteration or rebuilding of meeting house, **67:33, 67:34.**
  Fiduciary's sale or transfer, **204:12.**
  Personal property, pews, **67:38.**
  Property tax exemption, eligibility and application for abatement, **59:5.**
  Purchase by society, **67:37.**
  Taking down, **67:19, 67:33.**
  Unpaid taxes, sale, **67:30-67:33.**
Phenylketonuria test for newborn children, objections, **111:110A.**
Physicians and surgeons, refusal on moral or religious grounds to perform abortion or sterilization, **112:12I.**
Powers, **67:1, 67:2.**
Presiding officer in choice of moderator, **67:15.**
Priests.
  Clergy. See within this heading, "Clergy."
Private schools.
  Compulsory attendance law, effect on compliance, **76:1.**
  Injury to building used for religious instruction, **266:98.**
Privileges, **67:1-67:3.**
  Communications to clergy, **233:20A.**
Proprietors of meeting houses.
  Appropriations, powers to make, **67:27.**
  Building new house, powers, **67:27.**
  Income, disposition, **67:25.**
  Incorporation, **67:24, 67:26.**
  Meeting, calling, **67:29.**
  Personal property, power to hold, **67:25.**
  Real estate, power to hold, **67:25.**

RELIGION AND RELIGIOUS SOCIETIES —Cont'd

Proprietors of meeting houses —Cont'd

Record of proceedings of organization, filing, **67:26.**

Sale of pews for nonpayment of taxes, **67:30-67:33.**

Protestant Episcopal societies, **67:39.**

Psychology-related professions or occupations excluded from regulations, **112:125.**

Punishment.

Sentence and punishment. See within this heading, "Sentence and punishment."

Quakers.

See FRIENDS, SOCIETY OF.

Qualification for office, religious test not to be required for, **US Const Art 6 cl 3.**

Rabbis.

See RABBIS.

Raffles and bazaars, conduct, **271:7A.**

Real property.

Damaging church property, **266:2, 266:98.**

Incorporated society may hold, **67:21.**

Limitation on basis of religion of property held by religious organization or institution, **67:46, 184:23B.**

Parsonages. See within this heading, "Parsonages."

Proprietors of meeting houses, power to hold, **67:25.**

Roman Catholic churches, limitation upon property, **67:46.**

Sale of property. See within this heading, "Sale of property."

Zoning and planning restrictions as to use of property, **40A:3.**

Rebuilding of meeting houses.

Alteration or rebuilding of meeting houses. See within this heading, "Alteration or rebuilding of meeting houses."

Records, reports, and returns, **66:16.**

Annual reports of certain trustees etc., **68:13, 68:14.**

Births, baptisms, marriages, and deaths, **66:5.**

Certificate of incorporation, filing, **67:22.**

Certified copies of records, fee, **66:16, 262:34.**

RELIGION AND RELIGIOUS SOCIETIES —Cont'd

Records, reports, and returns —Cont'd

Cessation of meetings, delivery of records in case, **66:16.**

Church records or registers, fees for certified copies, **262:34.**

Copies of records, **66:5.**

Delivery in case of cessation of meetings, **66:16.**

Evidence of incorporation, **67:22.**

Fees for certified copies, **66:16.**

Keeping and preservation of records, **66:1.**

Marriage, records as to solemnization, **66:5, 207:40.**

Methodist Episcopal churches, filing record of organization, **67:43.**

Organization of churches, **67:51.**

Organization of proprietors of meeting house, filing record, **67:26.**

Prison book, **127:8.**

Roman Catholic churches, filing certificate of incorporation, **67:44.**

Supervisor of public records, duties of, **66:1.**

Reformed Episcopal societies, **67:39.**

Reports.

Records, reports, and returns. See within this heading, "Records, reports, and returns."

Roman Catholic churches, **67:44-67:46.**

Deacons authorized to perform marriages, **207:38.**

Incorporation, **67:44.**

Limitation upon property, **67:46.**

Trustees, **67:44-67:46.**

Room occupancy tax, exemptions, **64G:2.**

Sacred music, appropriations, **67:17, 67:27.**

Sale of property, **67:53, 68:6, 68:7.**

Churches, conveyance, **67:54.**

Clergymen, conveyance, **68:7.**

Deacons. See within this heading, "Deacons."

Friends or Quakers, by trustees, **68:11.**

Inactive religious bodies, property, **214:3.**

Licenses. See within this heading, "Licenses."

Meeting house, **67:19.**

Pews, **67:30-67:33.**

RELIGION AND RELIGIOUS SOCIETIES —Cont'd

Sale of property —Cont'd

Trust, church property held, **204:12, 214:3.**

Sales tax, exemptions, **64H:6.**

Saturday as Sabbath, exemption from Sunday labor prohibitions for sects observing, **136:6.**

Schools.

See SCHOOLS AND EDUCATION.

Search and seizure of property in custody of confidential relationship prohibited, **276:1.**

Sentence and punishment.

Blasphemy, **272:36.**

Worship, disturbance, **272:38, 272:39.**

Service of process, **223:37.**

Services sold at retail, sales tax exemptions, **64H:6.**

Sexual orientation, discrimination in employment matters on basis, **151B:4.**

Slaughtering livestock according to ritual requirements of religious faith, **94:139C-94:139G.**

Soldiers' homes, patients in, right of worship, **115A:8.**

Special act, powers of society incorporated, **67:28.**

Special jurisdiction of supreme judicial and superior courts in actions involving inactive religious societies, **214:3.**

Special or local assessment of parsonages held in irrevocable trust for religious corporations, **59:5.**

Spiritual healers, **112:108.**

Stables in vicinity of place of worship, **111:156.**

Standing committee.

Assessors or standing committee. See within this heading, "Assessors or standing committee."

Sunday.

Kosher food, Sunday sale, **136:6.**

Labor restrictions, exemption for Sabbatarians, **136:6.**

Parades, **136:6.**

Supreme judicial court, sales and transfers of property of religious societies, **204:12, 214:3.**

Taxation.

Affidavit as to posting notice of sale of pews for nonpayment of taxes, **67:32.**

RELIGION AND RELIGIOUS SOCIETIES —Cont'd

Taxation —Cont'd

Eligibility for property tax exemption and application for abatement, **59:5.**

Land assessed where and to whom, **59:11.**

Legacy and succession taxes, exemption, **65:1.**

Meals, tax exemption, **64H:6.**

Ministerial fund, real estate held, **59:11.**

Property as exempt from local taxes, **59:5.**

Room occupancy tax, exemption, **64G:2.**

Sales tax, exemption, **64H:6.**

Services sold at retail, sales tax exemptions, **64H:6.**

Teachers.

Candidates for teaching positions, inquiries as to religion forbidden, **71:39.**

Prayer or meditation, announcing period of silence, **71:1A.**

Support of teachers, religious societies and parishes may appropriate money, **67:17, 67:27.**

Television programs in aid of, sponsorship by executive committee for educational television, **71:13I.**

Territorial parish, nonresidents eligible to membership, **67:6.**

Threats to damage place of worship, **266:127A.**

Towns.

Cities and towns. See within this heading, "Cities and towns."

Treasurer, **67:7, 67:8.**

Trusts and trustees.

Annual reports of certain trustees etc., **68:13, 68:14.**

Appointment to hold trust funds, **68:3.**

Body corporate for purpose of receiving gifts, **68:4.**

Cities and towns, trustees of religious gifts, **68:13, 68:14.**

Friends or Quakers, **68:10, 68:11.**

Methodist church.

See METHODIST CHURCH.

Parsonages held in irrevocable trust for religious corporations, local assessment, **59:5.**

RELIGION AND RELIGIOUS SOCIETIES —Cont'd

Trusts and trustees —Cont'd

Reports and returns, annual reports of trustees for religious purposes, **68:13, 68:14.**

Roman Catholic churches, **67:44-67:46.**

Sale of church property held in trust, **204:12, 214:3.**

Unincorporated societies may elect, **68:12.**

Unemployment compensation, **151A:6.**

Uniform Securities Act, exemptions, **110A:402.**

Unincorporated societies, powers, **68:12.**

United Methodist Church, **59:5, 67:40-67:43, 207:38.**

See UNITED METHODIST CHURCH.

Vacancies in offices, filling, **67:7.**

Vestry.

Deacons. See within this heading, "Deacons."

Deemed body corporate for receiving gifts, **68:2.**

Protestant Episcopal societies, power, **67:39.**

Reformed Episcopal societies, powers, **67:39.**

Wardens.

Deacons. See within this heading, "Deacons."

Deemed members of body corporate for purpose of receiving gifts, **68:1, 68:2.**

Vestry. See within this heading, "Vestry."

Warrant for meeting, **67:14, 67:22, 67:23.**

Wells, injury, **266:98.**

Wholesaler's and importer's license to sell wine, **138:18.**

Witnesses, credibility, **233:19.**

Women eligible to membership, **67:6.**

Written consent to membership required, **67:5.**

Zoning and planning restrictions as to use of property, **40A:3.**

RELIGIOUS FREEDOM ACT, 119:33.

RELIGIOUS PROTECTION ACT.

Adoption, **210:5B.**

RELOCATION.

Assistance in relocation, **79A:1-79A:15.**

See RELOCATION ASSISTANCE.

RELOCATION —Cont'd

Change of address.

See CHANGE OF ADDRESS.

College dormitories, exemption from fire insurance requirements, **175:99.**

Highways.

See HIGHWAYS AND STREETS.

Housing and community development department, powers and duties, **23B:3, 23B:10.**

Motor vehicle sales finance company, investigation fee for relocation of office, **255B:2.**

Private ways.

See PRIVATE WAYS.

RELOCATION ASSISTANCE, 79A:1-79A:15.

Agencies.

Advisory agency, **79A:2.**

Displacing agency, payment of moving costs and expenses, **79A:4.**

Provision of relocation assistance required, **79A:3.**

Agriculture.

See AGRICULTURE.

Appeals, **79A:7.**

Businesses.

Aid, **79A:6.**

Moving expenses, **79A:7.**

Costs and expenses.

Moving costs and expenses. See within this heading, "Moving costs and expenses."

Definitions, **79A:1.**

Emergency acquisition of property, effect, **79A:10.**

Eminent domain, **79A:1 et seq.**

Expenses.

Moving costs and expenses. See within this heading, "Moving costs and expenses."

Farms.

See AGRICULTURE.

Federal aid or funds, **79A:7.**

Effect, **79A:5.**

Waiver of statutory provisions barring federal reimbursement, **79A:12.**

Federal Uniform Relocation Assistance and Real Property Acquisition Policies Act, public works department to comply, **81:7J.**

Homeowners, additional payments, **79A:7.**

RELOCATION ASSISTANCE
—Cont'd
Housing.
  See HOUSING AND URBAN
    RENEWAL.
Interest costs, payments for
  mortgage interest increase
  resulting from move, **79A:7.**
Land acquisition funds,
  expenditure for relocation
  purposes, **79A:11.**
Manufactured homes and
  manufactured housing
  communities, **140:32L.**
Massachusetts Bay Transportation
  Authority.
Housing and urban renewal
  operating agencies,
  reimbursement of relocation
  costs, **121B:13.**
Mortgages.
  Financed mortgage issued,
    insured, or subsidized by
    public agency, moving
    expenses of person utilizing,
    79A:14.
  Interest costs, payments for
    mortgage interest increase
    resulting from move, **79A:7.**
Motor vehicle junkyards,
  relocation, **140B:4.**
Moving costs and expenses, **79A:7.**
  Appeals, **79A:7.**
  Attachment or execution,
    exemption, **79:6A.**
  Closing costs, payment of costs
    arising from move, **79A:7.**
  Payment by displacing agency,
    79A:4.
  State sanitary code, moving
    expense incurred in
    enforcement, **79A:13.**
Payments to persons displaced by
  public acquisition of property,
  79A:4, 79A:7, 81:7J.
Personal property, payments for
  losses sustained in moving,
  79A:7.
Plan for relocation, **79A:4.**
Program.
  Approval, **79A:6.**
  Changes after approval, **79A:8.**
  Contents, **79A:6.**
  Review, **79A:5.**
  Suspension, **79A:9.**
Public benefits, exclusion of
  payments in determining
  eligibility of recipient for
  certain, **79A:7.**

RELOCATION ASSISTANCE
—Cont'd
Public works department to
  comply with provisions of
  federal uniform relocation
  assistance and real property
  acquisition policies act, **81:7J.**
Real estate closing costs, payment
  of costs and fees arising from
  move, **79A:7.**
Regulations.
  Rules and regulations. See
    within this heading, "Rules
    and regulations."
Rent, reimbursement of increase
  attributable to relocation,
  79A:7.
Replacement housing, aid in
  securing, **79A:6.**
Rules and regulations.
  Changes after approval, **79A:8.**
  Relocation bureau, regulations,
    79A:12.
  Review, **79A:5.**
  Suspension, **79A:9.**
School superintendents, **71:16,**
  71:41, 71:63.
State sanitary code, moving
  expenses incurred in
  enforcement, **79A:13.**
Tangible personal property,
  payments for losses sustained
  in moving, **79A:7.**
Tenants, additional payments,
  79A:7.
Title examination, payment for
  fees sustained in move, **79A:7.**
Trustee process or execution,
  exemption of payments, **79:6A,**
  79A:7.
Waiver of statutory provisions,
  79A:12.

REMAINDERS AND
  REVERSIONS.
See LIFE ESTATES,
  REMAINDERS, AND
  REVERSIONS.

REMAND.
Appeal.
  See APPEAL AND REVIEW.
District court, **231:102C.**
Habeas corpus, **248:22.**
  See HABEAS CORPUS.

REMARRIAGE.
Annuity to surviving spouse or
  children of certain public
  officials or employees as
  affected, **32:95A.**
Divorce, remarriage after, **208:24.**
  Certificate of divorce to show
    restrictions, **208:24A.**

REMARRIAGE —Cont'd
Divorce, remarriage after —Cont'd
  Limitation of time, **208:24.**
Former marriage, validity of
  marriage during existence,
  207:6.
Judges, widows, **32:65C.**
Polygamy.
  See POLYGAMY.
Restrictions upon remarriage,
  208:24A.
Time limitation as to remarriage
  after divorce, **208:24.**

REMISSION.
Bail, court may remit penalty after
  default of principal, **276:69.**
Fine or imprisonment, remission,
  279:11.

REMODELING.
Buildings.
  See BUILDINGS AND
    STRUCTURES.

REMOVAL FROM OFFICE OR
  EMPLOYMENT.
Abatement survival, and revival of
  actions, effect of removal of
  public officer or trustee under
  statute, **228:14.**
Administration and finance
  executive office.
  Hearings, **7:23, 7:23A.**
Administrative secretary to
  governor, removal, **6:6A.**
Aeronautics director, **6:58.**
Age discrimination, **149:24A,**
  149:24F, 151B:4.
Alcoholic beverages commission,
  members, **6:43.**
Alcoholic liquors.
  Sheriffs furnishing prisoners,
    268:29.
Alcoholic liquors, member of
  licensing board, **138:5,**
  138:10B, 138:23.
Aldermen.
  See ALDERMEN AND
    SELECTMEN.
Appeal and Review.
  Civil service.
    See CIVIL SERVICE.
Municipal lighting and heating
  plants, removal of light
  board or commission
  member, **164:56E.**
School librarians, appeal from
  dismissal, **71:38H.**
Arbitrary removal of certain
  officers and employees,
  protection against, **30:9B.**

REMOVAL FROM OFFICE OR EMPLOYMENT —Cont'd

Architectural Barriers Board, members, **22:13A.**

Art commissioners, **41:83.**

Assessors.

Tax assessors. See within this heading, "Tax assessors."

Attachment of property after removal from office of first attaching officer, **223:55, 223:56.**

Attorneys at law.

See ATTORNEYS AT LAW.

Audits and auditors.

Banks.

See BANKS AND BANKING.

Discharge by court, **221:59.**

State auditor, deputies, **11:5.**

Bar examiners, **221:35.**

Bond, removal for insufficiency, **30:18, 30:19.**

Building regulations and standards, state board, **143:93.**

Bureau of wildlife research and management, superintendent, **21:7H.**

Chief of accidents claims investigations, **26:8B.**

Chief of inspections, **22:4A.**

Chief of police, **41:21A.**

Children.

Minors. See within this heading, "Minors."

City.

See CITY AND TOWN CLERKS.

City council, officers appointed or elected, **39:8A, 121B:6.**

Civil rights.

Discrimination. See within this heading, "Discrimination."

Civil service, **31:39-31:45, 39:8A.**

See CIVIL SERVICE.

Clerks of court.

Assistant clerks, removal, **218:10, 221:1, 221:4, 221:5.**

Duties of assistant clerk upon removal of clerk, **221:33.**

Supreme judicial court, removal of clerk and assistant clerk, **221:1.**

Collective bargaining agreement, discharge of public employee for exercise of rights, **150E:10.**

Collectors of taxes, **41:39B, 60:96.**

See TAX COLLECTORS.

Colleges.

See COLLEGES AND UNIVERSITIES.

Commonwealth Service Corps, employees, **6:121.**

REMOVAL FROM OFFICE OR EMPLOYMENT —Cont'd

Community economic development assistance corporation, removal of member of board, **40H:3.**

Compensation.

See WAGES, SALARIES, AND COMPENSATION.

Congress, removal of public officer in case of disability to hold office, **US Const Amend 14 Sec 3.**

Conservation services director, removal, **21:18.**

Constables in cities, **41:91.**

Conviction of crime as ground, **279:30.**

Corporate directors, **156B:50A.**

County officers and employees, **35:51.**

Indictment, suspension of officers, **268A:25.**

Treasurer, **211:4.**

Court officers, **211:4, 221:1, 221:70, 221:72.**

Clerks of court. See within this heading, "Clerks of court."

Credit unions, officers, **171:13.**

Crime victim or witness who testifies, protection, **258B:3, 268:14B.**

Criminal justice committee, executive director, **6:156B.**

Deed registers.

See REGISTERS AND REGISTRIES OF DEEDS.

Development and industrial commission members, **40:8A.**

Disability commissions, city and town, **40:8J.**

Disbarment of attorneys.

See ATTORNEYS AT LAW.

Discrimination.

Age discrimination, **149:24F, 151B:4.**

Civil rights and liberties division, employees, **12:11A.**

Members of state commission against, **6:56.**

Opposing unfair practices, **151B:4.**

District and prosecuting attorneys.

Supreme judicial court, removal from office, **211:4.**

District courts.

See DISTRICT COURTS.

Economic development department, **23A:9.**

Members, **23A:3, 23A:5.**

Education department.

Commissioner, **15:1F.**

Maintenance employees, **30:9B.**

REMOVAL FROM OFFICE OR EMPLOYMENT —Cont'd

Education department —Cont'd

Treasurers of districts, **41:39B.**

Elder affairs department, **19A:8.**

Unclassified employees, **19A:10.**

Election officers.

See ELECTIONS.

Employment security eligibility as affected by discharge for misconduct, **151A:25.**

Energy Advisory Board, chairman, **25A:10.**

Environmental affairs executive office.

Conservation services, director, **21:18.**

Departmental commissioners, **21A:7.**

Environmental management department.

Board members, **21:2B, 21:2C.**

Directors of divisions, **21:3.**

Ethics Commission, members, **268B:2.**

Execution, procedure in event of removal of officer before completing service and return, **235:50.**

Executors.

See EXECUTORS AND ADMINISTRATORS.

Fees of register of probate and insolvency for entry of petitions for removal of fiduciaries, **262:40.**

Fiduciaries.

See FIDUCIARIES.

Fire chiefs, **48:42, 48:58.**

Fisheries and wildlife board members, **21:7B, 21:7E.**

Food and Agriculture Department, members, **20:4, 20:6.**

Franklin and Hampshire Counties, probation officers, **276:83.**

Gifts to minors, custodian, **201A:18.**

Governor, removal by, **30:9.**

See GOVERNOR.

Governor's council.

Officers appointed by, **7:23, 7:23A, 30:9.**

Sheriff, **37:7.**

Guardians.

See GUARDIANS, CONSERVATORS, AND COMMITTEES.

Health district formed by two or more towns, officers and employees, **111:27A.**

Hearings, **7:23, 7:23A.**

REMOVAL FROM OFFICE OR EMPLOYMENT —Cont'd

Historical commission members, **40:8D.**

Housing and community development department.
Directors or administrators, **23B:4.**
Experts and other personnel employees, **23B:8.**

Human resources division, directors of bureaus, **7:4J.**

Impeachment of officer.
See IMPEACHMENT OF OFFICER.

Indictment, officers, **268A:25.**

Industrial accident board and accident reviewing board, removal of member, **23E:8.**

Institutional employees, **30:9B.**

Insurance.
See INSURANCE.

Interference, **43:92, 43:107.**

Jury service, discharge of employee by reason, **268:14A, 268:14B.**

Labor practices.
Unfair or unlawful labor practices. See within this heading, "Unfair or unlawful labor practices."

Labor relations commission, members, **23:9O.**

Land court, recorder and deputy recorders, **185:6.**

Law enforcement, director, **21:6.**

Librarians in schools, appeal from dismissal, **71:38H.**

Loan agencies, supervisor, **26:4.**

Marine fisheries, director of division, **21A:8.**

Massachusetts Centers of Excellence Corporation, Board of Directors, **40J:12.**

Mayors, **43:59A.**

Mentally ill.
See MENTALLY ILL AND RETARDED PERSONS.

Minors.
Abuse or neglect of child under 16, **119:51A.**
Continuation school, employer's penalty for failure to discharge minor failing to attend, **149:91.**
Report of discharge of minors under sixteen for illegal employment, **149:76.**

Misconduct, employment security eligibility as affected by discharge, **151A:25.**

REMOVAL FROM OFFICE OR EMPLOYMENT —Cont'd

Motor vehicles of Commonwealth, removal from office for failure to comply with marking regulations, **30:36.**

Municipal art commissioners, **41:83.**

Municipal industrial development authority directors, removal, **40D:4.**

Municipal light board or commission member, **164:56E.**

New bond, removal of principal not giving bond when required, **30:19.**

Norfolk county court officers, **221:72.**

Notice, when required, **149:159.**

Opposing unfair practices, **151B:4.**

Outdoor advertising board members, **16:14.**

Pension rights as affected by.
See RETIREMENT SYSTEMS AND PENSIONS.

Physicians and officers of state hospitals or schools, removal, **19:14.**

Plan A cities, removal of officers by mayor, **43:54.**

Plan B cities, removal of officers by mayor, **43:61.**

Plan D cities, removal of officers and employees, **43:90, 43:91.**

Plan E cities, removal of officers and employees, **43:104, 43:105.**

Plan F cities, removal of officers by mayor, **43:124.**

Planning boards.
Zoning and planning. See within this heading, "Zoning and planning."

Police, **41:96, 41:96B, 41:97, 41:97A.**
Civil service, **41:96, 41:96B, 41:97, 41:97A.**

Preference stipulation in public contracts, removal for failure to insert, **7:23A.**

Probate.
See PROBATE AND FAMILY COURT.

Probate bond, failure to give, **205:4, 205:8, 205:16.**

Probate registers.
Registers of probate and insolvency. See within this heading, "Registers of probate and insolvency."

Probation officers.
See PROBATION OFFICERS.

REMOVAL FROM OFFICE OR EMPLOYMENT —Cont'd

Prosecuting attorneys.
District and prosecuting attorneys. See within this heading, "District and prosecuting attorneys."

Protection against arbitrary removal of state officers and employees, **30:9B.**

Public accountancy board members, **13:33.**

Public charities division, employees, **12:8D.**

Public safety, deputy commissioner, **22:5.**

Public works commissioner, powers, **16:4.**

Purchasing, non-compliance with rules regarding state purchasing by public officials, **7:23, 7:23A.**

Qualification, lack of on part of public officer or employee, **30:45.**

Racing commission members, **6:48.**

Registers.
See REGISTERS AND REGISTRIES OF DEEDS.

Registers of probate and insolvency.
Appointment of temporary register, **217:13.**
Supreme judicial court, removal, **211:4.**

Registrar of voters, **51:19.**
Assistant registrar, **51:22.**
Equal political representation, preservation, **51:19.**

Resignation.
See RESIGNATION.

Retirement systems and pensions, **32:10.**
See RETIREMENT SYSTEMS AND PENSIONS.

Revenue department and commissioner, treasurer of municipality, district or regional school district, **41:39B.**

Salaries.
See WAGES, SALARIES, AND COMPENSATION.

Schools.
See SCHOOLS AND EDUCATION.

Selectmen.
See ALDERMEN AND SELECTMEN.

Sergeant at arms, employees, **3:21.**

Severance pay.
See WAGES, SALARIES, AND COMPENSATION.

REMOVAL FROM OFFICE OR EMPLOYMENT —Cont'd

Sheriffs.
  See SHERIFFS AND DEPUTIES.
Sheriffs and deputies.
  Alcoholic beverages, furnishing prisoners with, **268:29.**
Social services.
  Welfare and social services. See within this heading, "Welfare and social services."
Soldiers home in Holyoke, superintendent, **6:71.**
State auditor, deputies, **11:5.**
State treasurer, **10:4.**
Superintendent of schools, notice of intent to remove, **71:63.**
Superintendent of soldiers' home in Holyoke, removal and procedure, **6:71.**
Superior courts.
  See SUPERIOR COURTS.
Supervisors.
  Credit unions, supervisor, **26:4.**
  Public records, supervisor, **9:4.**
Supply purchase regulations, failure to comply, **7:23, 7:23A.**
Supreme judicial court.
  Attorneys at law, removal, **221:40.**
  Certain officers, **211:4, 221:1.**
Survival of action against public officer or trustee appointed under statute, **228:14.**
Tax assessors.
  Appointees of selectmen, **41:25.**
  Assistant assessors, **41:25A.**
  City charters, exemption form removal of assessor by mayor, **43:54.**
Tax collectors, **41:39B, 60:96.**
  See TAX COLLECTORS.
Teachers, **71:42, 71:42D.**
  See TEACHERS.
Town meetings.
  See TOWN MEETINGS.
Town treasurers as collectors, **41:39B.**
Transitional assistance department.
  Welfare and social services. See within this heading, "Welfare and social services."
Transportation.
  Areas trustees, powers, **161:147.**
  Planning and development director, **16:3A.**

REMOVAL FROM OFFICE OR EMPLOYMENT —Cont'd

Treasurers.
  Districts and regional school districts treasurers, removal, **41:39B.**
  State treasurer, **10:4.**
  Town treasurer as collector, **41:39B.**
Trustee process.
  See TRUSTEE PROCESS.
Trustees.
  See TRUSTS AND TRUSTEES.
Unemployment compensation, **151A:25.**
Unfair or unlawful labor practices, **149:24F, 150A:4, 151B:4.**
  Jury service, discharge of employee by reason, **268:14A.**
  Opposition, **151B:4.**
  Subpoena to testify, discharge of employee by reason, **268:14B.**
Uniform Gifts to Minors Act, custodian, **201A:18.**
Uniform state laws, commissioner, **6:26.**
University of Massachusetts, officers and employees, **75:14.**
Vacations of school teachers and superintendents, effect of discharge, **71:42.**
Veterans and veterans' organizations, **30:9A, 30:41.**
  Superintendent of soldiers' home in Holyoke, **6:71.**
  Unclassified offices or positions, veterans holding, **30:9A.**
Veterans' service commissioner, **7:4O.**
Volunteer firefighters responding to emergencies, **149:177B.**
Wages.
  See WAGES, SALARIES, AND COMPENSATION.
Welfare and social services.
  Deputy commissioner of social services, **18B:8.**
  Protection against arbitrary removal, **30:9B.**
  Superintendents of transitional assistance department institutions, **18:9.**
Wildlife research and management bureau, superintendent, **21:7H.**
Zoning and planning, **41:81A.**
  Appeals board members, **40A:12, 41:70, 41:81A, 41:81Z.**
  Mayor's power, **41:70, 41:81A.**

REMOVAL OF ACTIONS.
See TRANSFER OF CASES.

REMOVAL OF PROPERTY.
Abandoned motor vehicles.
  See MOTOR VEHICLES.
Alcoholic liquors.
  See ALCOHOLIC LIQUORS.
Animal on land of another, removal, **131:76.**
Apples, penalty for removing brands or labels, **94:108.**
Art, removal from buildings, **231:85S.**
Attachment of property.
  See ATTACHMENT OF PROPERTY.
Automobile insurance.
  See AUTOMOBILE INSURANCE.
Ballots.
  See ELECTIONS.
Buildings.
  See BUILDINGS AND STRUCTURES.
Cemeteries.
  See CEMETERIES.
Collar of licensed dog, penalty for removal, **266:47.**
Dangerous buildings.
  See DANGEROUS BUILDINGS AND STRUCTURES.
Dead bodies.
  See DEAD BODIES.
Decedent's assets, removal from state to evade taxes, **193:3.**
Derailment of train, removal of wreckage and debris, **160:241A.**
Eminent domain, **79:13, 79:42, 81:22.**
Federal property, penalty for removing, **1:10.**
Fire insurance as affected by removal of property, owner, etc., **175:99.**
Gravestones, removal for purpose of repair or reproduction, **272:73A.**
Hazardous substances label, **94B:3.**
Junkyards, removal, **140B:4.**
Motor vehicles.
  See MOTOR VEHICLES.
Moving of buildings.
  See MOVING OF BUILDINGS.
Nuisances, duty of owner or agent, **139:3A.**
Poles.
  See GAS AND ELECTRIC COMPANIES.

REMOVAL OF PROPERTY
—Cont'd
Public records, penalty for
removal, **66:15.**
Railroads.
Brush and sage, **48:18-48:20.**
Wires at crossings, **160:104A.**
Wreckage and debris caused by
derailments, **160:241A.**
Research animals, unauthorized
removal of, **266:104B.**
Seatbelts, removal, **90:7.**
Snow.
See SNOW AND ICE.
State boundary markers, penalty
for removing, **1:5.**
Steam boilers and engines.
Inspection number or tag,
146:24, 146:33.
Safety appliances, **146:12,
146:33.**
Street railways, removal upon
revocation of location, **161:77.**
Wires at railroad crossings,
160:104A.

**REMOVAL SALE,
93:28A-93:28D.**
See CLOSING OUT SALES.

**RENAL DISEASES.
See KIDNEYS AND KIDNEY
DISEASES.**

**RENDERING PLANTS.
See SLAUGHTERHOUSES.**

RENDITION.
Extradition.
See EXTRADITION.
Interstate compacts.
See INTERSTATE COMPACTS
AND AGREEMENTS.
Witnesses in criminal cases,
233:13A-233:13D.

**RENEWABLE ENERGY
SOURCE PROPERTY.**
Definition, **62:6.**

RENOVATED BUTTER.
Sale regulated, **94:59.**

RENOVATION.
Rehabilitation.
See REHABILITATION.
Repairs.
See REPAIRS AND
MAINTENANCE.

RENTAL.
Bailments.
See BAILMENTS.
Cars.
See MOTOR VEHICLE
RENTAL.

RENTAL —Cont'd
Real property.
See LANDLORD AND TENANT.

**RENTAL ASSISTANCE ACT,
121B:42 et seq.**

**RENTAL HOUSING
DEVELOPMENT ACTION
LOAN PROGRAM.**
Restrictions, **184:31.**

**RENT CONTROL
PROHIBITION, 40P:1 to
40P:5.**
Conflict of laws, **40P:5.**
Definition of rent control, **40P:3.**
Exception, **40P:4.**
Generally, **40P:4.**
Purpose, **40P:2.**
Title, **40P:1.**

RENTS AND PROFITS.
Amherst economic development
and industrial corporation,
Spec L 23:7.
Assignment of rents or profits from
estate or lease, recording,
183:4.
Boston public health commission,
fees collected for services,
programs and other activities
provided under, **Spec L 70:8.**
Commonwealth, liability on
informations, **245:6, 245:11.**
Credit unions.
See CREDIT UNIONS.
Dower.
See DOWER AND CURTESY.
Entry, writs of.
See ENTRY, WRITS.
Exclusion from secured
transactions article,
106:9-104.
Executions.
See EXECUTIONS.
Executors.
See EXECUTORS AND
ADMINISTRATORS.
Industrial development of cities.
See INDUSTRIAL
DEVELOPMENT OF
CITIES AND TOWNS.
Mill repairs, lien, **253:56, 253:58.**
Mortgages and deeds of trust.
Right of mortgagor, **183:26.**
Rights of mortgagee.
See MORTGAGE
FORECLOSURE.
Partition proceedings, **241:25.**
Subsidy program, conflict of
interest, municipal employees,
exceptions, **268A:20.**

RENTS AND PROFITS —Cont'd
Summary process to recover land.
See SUMMARY PROCESS TO
RECOVER LAND.
Trusts and trustees.
Apportionment, **197:27.**
Payable from death of testator,
197:26.

RENUNCIATION.
Contracts.
See CONTRACTS AND
AGREEMENTS.
Gifts to minors, resignation, death,
or removal of custodian,
201A:18.

REORGANIZATION.
Civil service personnel, **30:1 et
seq.**
Constitution of Massachusetts.
Executive department,
reorganization plan
procedure for, **MA Const
Amend Art 87 Secs 1, 2.**
General court, requirement
regarding plan presented to
general court by the
governor under constitution
of Commonwealth, **4:1A.**
Corporations.
See CORPORATIONS.
District courts, **218:6 et seq.**
See DISTRICT COURTS.
Fisheries, wildlife and
environmental law
enforcement, department, **2:7,
21:5 et seq.**
Mutual holding companies.
See MUTUAL HOLDING
COMPANIES.

**REPAIRS AND
MAINTENANCE.**
Abutting owners, entry of one
upon land of another to repair
his buildings, **266:120B.**
Aircraft and aviation, **255:31E.**
Automobile insurance.
See AUTOMOBILE
INSURANCE.
Award of public contracts, **30:39M.**
Bedding and upholstered
furniture.
Definition of repairer, **94:270.**
Label requirements, **94:272.**
Sterilization requirements,
94:273.
Boilers, daily record of repairs,
146:51, 146:55.
Boundaries of state, **1:4.**
Bradford Durfee College of
Technology, purchases,
74:42N.

REPAIRS AND MAINTENANCE
—Cont'd

Bridges.
See BRIDGES.
Building maintenance, defined, **64H:1.**
Building regulations and standards board, rules and regulations, **143:94.**
Buildings and structures, **143:1 et seq.**
Cities.
See CITIES AND TOWNS.
Colleges.
See COLLEGES AND UNIVERSITIES.
Commuter passenger service vessels, sales tax exemption, **64H:6.**
Comptroller of state, unexpended appropriations for ordinary maintenance, **29:13.**
Computer maintenance and repair, service defined for tax purposes, **64H:1, 64I:1.**
Condemnation, private roads acquired, **252:20.**
Condominiums.
See CONDOMINIUMS.
Correctional institutions.
See CORRECTIONAL INSTITUTIONS.
Counties.
See COUNTIES.
County tuberculosis hospitals, **111:85, 111:85A.**
Credit unions.
See CREDIT UNIONS.
Dams and reservoirs, **253:48, 253:51-253:62.**
See DAMS AND RESERVOIRS.
Dangerous buildings.
See DANGEROUS BUILDINGS AND STRUCTURES.
Definitions, **64H:1, 94:270, 143:1.**
Drains.
See SEWERS AND DRAINS.
Economic diversification program, **23F:1.**
Election apparatus and equipment, **54:24, 54:28, 54:30, 54:30A.**
Electrical transmission lines, **166:22.**
Elevators.
See ELEVATORS.
Engineers, exemptions from laws to professional engineers, **112:81R.**
Entry into land and premises.
Abutting owner's entry to repair building, **266:120B.**

REPAIRS AND MAINTENANCE
—Cont'd

Entry into land and premises —Cont'd
Highway drains, **83:4.**
Sewer systems, **83:1.**
Exculpatory provisions in contracts for residential buildings, **143:90.**
Execution creditor, reimbursement on redemption of real estate from levy, **236:33.**
Fences and fence viewers, **49:4-49:10.**
Assignment of shores for repair and maintenance, **49:6, 49:9, 49:10, 49:13, 49:15.**
Waters and waterways, duty as to repair and rebuilding, **49:17.**
Fire insurance, **175:99.**
Exception from limitations as to value, **175:96A.**
Fishways, repair, **130:19.**
Furniture.
Bedding and upholstered furniture. See within this heading, "Bedding and upholstered furniture."
General fields.
See GENERAL FIELDS.
Gravestones, removal for purpose of repair, **272:73A.**
Handicapped persons, regulations to facilitate, **22:13A.**
Harbors, **84:12, 84:14, 91:31.**
See PORTS AND HARBORS.
Hazardous waste management.
Environmental Protection Department, duties, **21C:4.**
License requirements, **21C:7.**
Highways and streets, **81:13-81:22, 82:1 et seq., 84:1-84:27.**
See HIGHWAYS AND STREETS.
Historic districts, property, **40C:9.**
Home improvement loans.
See HOME IMPROVEMENT LOANS.
Hours of labor laws inapplicable to contracts for repair of highways, **149:34, 149:34C, 149:35.**
Income tax exemption for renovating abandoned buildings, **62:3, 63:38O.**
Label requirements of bedding and upholstered furniture, **94:272.**
Landlord and tenant.
Reimbursement of tenant for repairs necessary to cure violations, **111:127L.**

REPAIRS AND MAINTENANCE
—Cont'd

Landlord and tenant —Cont'd
Security deposit forfeiture, tenant damage, **186:15B.**
Libraries, funding and grant programs, renovation and rehabilitation, **78:19A-78:19C, 78:19E, 78:19G-78:19K, 78:25.**
Life insurance companies' annual statements, disbursements listed, **175:25.**
Longshore and waterfront employment, shutting down machinery for repairs, **149:18C.**
Massachusetts Bay Transportation Authority, notice to concerning repairs of roads and highways, **84:7A.**
Mechanics' liens.
See MECHANICS' LIENS.
Mentally ill and retarded persons, maintenance of roads on state mental health facility grounds, **19:1, 19B:1.**
Metropolitan districts.
See METROPOLITAN DISTRICTS.
Militia.
See MILITIA.
Model water and sewer commission, maintenance and repair of systems, **40N:6.**
Mortgages.
See MORTGAGES AND DEEDS OF TRUST.
Motor vehicles.
See MOTOR VEHICLES.
Municipal industrial development authorities, powers, **40D:7.**
Municipal lighting plants, expenditures necessary to service new consumers, **164:41.**
Natural gas pipeline companies, duty to restore properties, **164:75F.**
New Bedford Institute of Technology, purchases, **74:42N.**
Nonconforming use, **40A:5.**
Nonresidents engaged in repair work to appoint agents for service of process, **227:5.**
Nursing or rest homes, **111:71, 143:3Q.**
Outdoor advertising department, control and regulation of billboards, signs, and other advertising devices, **16:13.**

REPAIRS AND MAINTENANCE —Cont'd

Ports and harbors, **84:12, 84:14, 91:31.**
See PORTS AND HARBORS.
Pounds.
See POUNDS.
Private ways, **84:12, 84:14.**
See PRIVATE WAYS.
Public buildings.
Contracts for cleaning and maintenance, prescribed rates of wages, **149:27H.**
Regulations to facilitate physically handicapped persons' use, **22:13A.**
Public ways.
See HIGHWAYS AND STREETS.
Radio.
See RADIO AND TELEVISION.
Railroads.
See RAILROADS.
Real estate time-shares.
See REAL ESTATE TIME-SHARES.
Regional school districts building committee, powers and duties, **71:16A.**
Residential buildings, exculpatory provisions in contracts, **143:90.**
Retail installment sales and services for repairs, requirement, **255D:9A.**
Sales tax on services, **64H:1, 64H:6.**
Sanitary Code, repair of structures failing to comply with requirements, **111:5.**
Schools.
See SCHOOLS AND EDUCATION.
Services, taxing, **64H:1, 64H:6, 64I:1.**
Sewers.
See SEWERS AND DRAINS.
Ships and other watercraft, **255:14-255:22.**
See SHIPS AND OTHER WATERCRAFT.
Special assessments, granting tax abatements for repairs improving real estate, **59:38.**
State boundaries, **1:4.**
State buildings, **7:40D, 8:9, 29:20A, 30:39A.**
State colleges, purchases, **73:15.**
State house, **8:6, 8:7, 8:9, 8:20.**
Steam boilers, record of repairs, **146:51, 146:55.**

REPAIRS AND MAINTENANCE —Cont'd

Sterilization of bedding, **94:273.**
Street railways.
See STREET RAILWAYS.
Streets.
See HIGHWAYS AND STREETS.
Sunday regulation of repair work, **136:6.**
Superintendent of buildings, care and operation for buildings of state, **8:9.**
Superintendent of maintenance as employee of General Court, **3:18.**
Taxation.
Income tax exemption for renovating abandoned buildings, **62:3, 63:38O.**
Motor vehicles.
See MOTOR VEHICLES.
Private ways or bridges, financing of repairs, **84:14.**
Services, taxing, **64H:1, 64H:6, 64I:1.**
Tenants.
Landlord and tenant. See within this heading, "Landlord and tenant."
Town public works board, repairs and maintenance, **41:69D.**
Underground storage tank petroleum product cleanup fund, **21J:4, 21J:9.**
Universities.
See COLLEGES AND UNIVERSITIES.
Upholstered furniture.
Bedding and upholstered furniture. See within this heading, "Bedding and upholstered furniture."
Voting machines, **54:28, 54:30A.**

REPEAL.

Banks consumer transaction regulations, **167:2A.**
Bylaws.
Ordinances and bylaws. See within this heading, "Ordinances and bylaws."
City ordinance, **43:21.**
Co-operative corporations.
See COOPERATIVE CORPORATIONS AND ASSOCIATIONS.
Corporations.
See CORPORATIONS.
Ordinances and bylaws.
City ordinance, **43:21.**

REPEAL —Cont'd

Ordinances and bylaws —Cont'd
Corporation, bylaws, **156:13, 156B:17.**
Zoning and planning ordinances and bylaws, **40A:5.**
Statutes.
See STATUTES.
Zoning ordinances and bylaws, **40A:5.**

REPLEVIN, 247:1-247:22.

Abatement, survival and revival, **228:1, 228:2.**
Animals, replevin of, **49:41, 247:1-247:6.**
See ANIMALS.
Appraisers.
See APPRAISERS AND APPRAISALS.
Attachment of property, **247:7.**
See ATTACHMENT OF PROPERTY.
Availability of remedy, **247:7.**
Bailments.
See BAILMENTS.
Bond of plaintiff, **247:8.**
Approval, **247:14, 247:15.**
Defects in, not cause for dismissal, **247:17.**
Distrained animals, **247:2, 247:3.**
Fee for approval, **247:16.**
Lien claimant, replevin from. See within this heading, "Lien claimant, replevin from."
New bond if original defective, **247:17.**
Notice and hearing as to sureties, **247:15.**
Officer serving writ, responsibility for sufficiency, **247:14.**
Recovery by levying officer on bond, disposition of proceeds, **247:11.**
Sureties. See within this heading, "Sureties on bond, approval."
Time to sue, **247:18.**
Buyer's right to replevy goods identified in sales contract, **106:2-716.**
Certificate of appraisal of replevied animals to be included in return of writ, **247:4.**
Commencement of action, **246:1.**
Constables, service of process, **41:92.**
Contract for sale, buyer's right to replevy goods identified, **106:2-716.**

REPLEVIN —Cont'd

Costs and fees.

Action in superior court, **261:4.**

Bond of plaintiff. See within this heading, "Bond of plaintiff."

Defendant, judgment, **247:9.**

Distrained animals, **247:5, 247:6.**

Lien claimant action, **255:39.**

Recovery by plaintiff, **247:13.**

Right of prevailing party, **261:4, 261:6.**

Service, fees, **262:8.**

Sheriff's fees, **262:8.**

Sureties on bond, fees, **247:16, 262:8.**

Damages.

Assessment, **247:19.**

Defendant, on judgment, **247:9.**

Distrained animals, judgment in connection, **247:5, 247:6.**

Plaintiff, on judgment, **247:13.**

Wrongful replevin of goods attached or levied, **247:10.**

Delaying attachment or levy by wrongful replevin, penalty, **247:10.**

Dismissal for defective bond, **247:17.**

Distrained animals, **49:41, 247:1-247:6.**

See ANIMALS.

District Court jurisdiction of actions, **218:54.**

Executions.

See EXECUTIONS.

Fees.

Costs and fees. See within this heading, "Costs and fees."

Garnishment, **246:1.**

Impounded or distrained animals, **49:1, 247:1-247:6.**

See ANIMALS.

Judgment.

Defendant, judgment for costs, **247:9.**

Distrained animals, **247:5, 247:6.**

Plaintiff, judgment, **247:13.**

Return of goods, effect on attachment or execution, **247:20.**

Wrongful replevin, disposition of amount recovered, **247:11, 247:12.**

Leases under Commercial Code, **106:2A-521.**

Lien claimant, replevin from, **255:36.**

Bond, **255:37.**

Limitation of action, **247:18.**

Costs, **255:39.**

REPLEVIN —Cont'd

Lien claimant, replevin from —Cont'd

Trial, **255:38.**

Limitation of actions, **247:18, 260:2A.**

Mesne process, replevin of goods attached, **247:7.**

Moneys recovered by levying officer on bond, disposition, **247:11.**

New bond to replace defective bond, **247:17.**

Other person than defendant, action, **247:7.**

Prevailing party, right to costs and fees, **261:4, 261:6.**

Process.

Service of process. See within this heading, "Service of process."

Return.

Bond and writ as to distrained animals, **247:2-247:4.**

Execution or attachment, effect of return of goods, **247:20.**

Personal property, writ, **247:8.**

Writ of return, form and effect, **247:21, 247:22.**

Sales contract under Commercial Code, buyer's right to replevy goods identified, **106:2-716.**

Service of process.

Constable's power, **41:92.**

Fees, **262:8.**

Return. See within this heading, "Return."

Sufficiency of service, officer's responsibility, **247:14.**

Sheriff's fees, **262:8.**

Superior court.

Bond where replevin writ returnable, **247:8.**

Costs of action, **261:4.**

Special jurisdiction, **214:3.**

Supreme judicial court, special jurisdiction in actions to compel redelivery, **214:3.**

Sureties on bond, approval, **247:14, 247:15.**

Fees, **247:16, 262:8.**

Notice and hearing, **247:15.**

Trial, action against lien claimant, **255:38.**

Trustee process, commencement of action, **246:1.**

Value of goods must exceed twenty dollars, **247:7.**

Venue of action, **223:4.**

Writs.

Service of process. See within this heading, "Service of process."

REPLEVIN —Cont'd

Wrongful replevin, **247:10-247:12.**

REPORT CARDS.

Request for copy by non-custodial or custodial parent, **71:34H.**

REPORTER OF DECISIONS, 221:63-221:68.

Appeals court, duties of reporter of decisions, **211A:9.**

Appointment, **221:63.**

Clerical expenses, **221:68.**

Compensation of reporter, **221:68.**

Deputy reporter, **221:67.**

Discretion as to cases to be reported, **221:64.**

General court manual delivered, **5:11.**

Head notes, preparation, **221:64.**

Indexes, preparation, **221:64.**

Preparation of reports, **221:64.**

Preservation of opinions until publication, **221:66.**

Regulation of sale and distribution of judicial decisions, **221:64A.**

Safekeeping written court opinions, Commonwealth to provide, **221:66.**

Statutes distributed, **5:3.**

Style of reports, **221:65.**

Supreme Judicial Court, **221:63 et seq.**

Tables of cases, preparation, **221:64.**

REPORTERS OF COURT, 221:82-221:91C.

See COURT STENOGRAPHERS.

REPORTS.

See RECORDS, REPORTS, AND RETURNS.

REPOSSESSION.

Replevin.

See REPLEVIN.

Secured transactions.

See SECURED TRANSACTIONS.

REPRESENTATIVE DISTRICTS.

Candidates for office in redistricted territory, **53:34, 54:41, 54:42, 57:4.**

Congressional districts, **57:1.**

Constitution of Massachusetts, determination of representative districts, **MA Const Amend Arts 16, 101.**

Division of Commonwealth into, **53:34, 53:47, 54:41, 54:42, 57:4.**

REPRESENTATIVE DISTRICTS —Cont'd

Establishment, **57:4.**

Instruction of representatives by submission of questions of public policy to voters, **53:19-53:22.**

Jurisdiction of court relative to division of county into, **56:59.**

Mandamus for division of county into, **56:59.**

Nomination of candidates for office, **53:34.**

Petition for division of county into, **57:4.**

Revision of town precincts, **54:9A.**

Senatorial districts.
See SENATORIAL DISTRICTS.

Supreme Judicial Court, **56:59, 57:4.**

Town precincts used in formation, **54:9A.**

REPRESENTATIVE OR REPRESENTATION.

Class actions, unfair trade practices or methods of competition, **93A:9, 93A:11.**

Commercial Code, definition of representative, **106:1-201.**

Congress of United States.
See CONGRESS OF UNITED STATES.

Constitution of Massachusetts.
See CONSTITUTION OF MASSACHUSETTS.

Executors.
See EXECUTORS AND ADMINISTRATORS.

Fiduciaries.
See FIDUCIARIES.

General court, representative districts, **57:4.**

Guardians.
See GUARDIANS, CONSERVATORS, AND COMMITTEES.

House of representatives of United States.
See HOUSE OF REPRESENTATIVES OF UNITED STATES.

Inheritance, right, **190:3, 190:8, 191:22.**

Receivers.
See RECEIVERS AND RECEIVERSHIPS.

Restrictions running with land, appointment of representative of interested persons in action to enforce, **240:10B.**

REPRESENTATIVE OR REPRESENTATION —Cont'd

Retirement systems and pensions, **32:28K.**

Town meeting act, **43A:1 et seq.**
See TOWN MEETINGS.

Trusts.
See TRUSTS AND TRUSTEES.

Vocational education and schools.
Licensing of representatives, **93:21G.**
Regulations by representatives, **93:21E.**

REPRESENTATIVE TOWN MEETING ACT, 43A:1 et seq.

REPRESENTED PRICE.

Defined, **6:184B.**

RE-PRESENTMENT.

See PRESENTMENT, DISHONOR, AND PROTEST.

REPRIEVES.

President may grant, **US Const Art 2 Sec 2 cl 1.**

REPRISALS AND RETALIATION.

Abuse or neglect of patients in long-term care facilities.
Retaliation against persons reporting, **111:72G.**

Condominiums, **183A:6.**

Conscientious employees, protection of, **149:185.**
Health care workers, **149:187.**

Letters of marque.
See LETTERS OF MARQUE AND REPRISAL.

Manufactured homes and manufactured housing communities, **140:32N.**

Nursing or rest homes.
Abuse or neglect of patients in long-term care facilities.
Retaliation against persons reporting, **111:72G.**

Summary process to recover land, reprisal against tenant for certain activities as defense, **239:2A.**

Taxes, retaliatory.
See CORPORATION TAXES.

Wage and hour law.
Retaliation by employer against employee seeking rights under wage and hour law, **149:148A.**

REPRODUCTIONS.
See COPIES.

REPRODUCTIVE HEALTH FACILITIES.

Obstruction of access, **266:120E1/2.**

REPTILES.

Protection, **131:5.**

Research, **131:4.**

Sale or purchase, **131:22.**

Seasons for taking, **131:5.**

Transporting into or out of state, **131:85.**

REPUDIATION.

Anticipatory repudiation.
See ANTICIPATORY REPUDIATION.

Contracts.
See CONTRACTS AND AGREEMENTS.

REPURCHASE.
See SALE OR TRANSFER OF PROPERTY.

REPUTATION.
See CHARACTER AND REPUTATION.

REQUEST.
See DEMAND.

REQUISITION.

Civil service.
See CIVIL SERVICE.

Employment security, requisitions on unemployment compensation fund, **151A:51, 151A:57.**

Extradition.
See EXTRADITION.

Police officers serving in other cities and towns, **41:99.**

Prison-made articles, requisition, **127:57.**

State superintendent of buildings, requisitions, **8:6.**

Town appropriation for property requisition by police or fire departments, **40:5.**

RESALE.
See SALE OR TRANSFER OF PROPERTY.

RESALE OF TICKETS ACT, 140:185A et seq.

RESALE PRICE MAINTENANCE ACT, 93:14E et seq.

RESCISSION.

Abatement orders as to places of prostitution, **139:11.**

Abatement trust, water pollution, **29C:16.**

RESCISSION —Cont'd
Accident and sickness insurance.
Divorced persons, notice of cancellation and right to reinstatement, **175:110I.**
Notice of cancellation at age sixty-five, **175:110H.**
Auctioneer license, **100:6.**
Automobile insurance, **90:34K, 175:113, 175:113A, 175:176A.**
See AUTOMOBILE INSURANCE.
Bonds and obligations.
Sinking fund bonds. See within this heading, "Sinking fund bonds."
Buyer's right to cancel, **93:48.**
Camping, cancellation of membership contract, **93:48A.**
Cease.
See CEASE AND DESIST ORDERS.
Certification of purchaser of alcoholic liquors, **138:30D.**
Charities and charitable organizations, registration, **68:32.**
Cities and towns.
Caucus, rescission of vote, **53:121.**
Laws, procedure for rescission, **4:4B.**
Primaries, vote as to continuance or discontinuance, **53:56.**
Sinking fund bonds, **44:48, 44:49.**
Statutes, petition for rescission, **4:4B.**
Subdivision plats, rescission of approval, **41:81N.**
Collection agency, cancellation of bond, **93:26.**
Commercial code, cancellation of payment order, **106:4A-211.**
Commercial driver license.
See UNIFORM OPERATION OF COMMERCIAL MOTOR VEHICLES.
Consumers.
See CONSUMERS AND CONSUMER PROTECTION.
Conversion of oil to coal by electric generating facilities, **164:94G½.**
Corporations.
See CORPORATIONS.
Correspondence school bonds, **75C:4.**
Credit services organizations, notice of cancellation, **93:68D.**

RESCISSION —Cont'd
Credit unions.
See CREDIT UNIONS.
Custodianship, **201A:20.**
Dealers.
Gasoline, cancellation by supplier of agreement for sale, **93E:5.**
Uniform Securities Act, registration of broker-dealers and agents, **110A:204.**
Deed and document stamp, **64D:2.**
Definition, termination, **151A:71A.**
Degree-granting institutions as exempt from contract cancellation provisions, **255:13K.**
Dental service corporations.
Membership, **176E:5.**
Subscription certificate, **176E:5.**
Document of title canceled upon delivery of goods, **106:7-403.**
Drivers' licenses.
See MOTOR VEHICLES.
Elections.
See ELECTIONS.
Employer closing facility, report, **151A:71B.**
Fire insurance.
See FIRE INSURANCE.
Form of notice, **93:48, 255D:9.**
Governmental units pooled insurance, **40M:5, 40M:8.**
Group insurance for state employees, notice of cancellation and right to reinstatement, **32A:11A, 32B:9H.**
Guardians.
See GUARDIANS, CONSERVATORS, AND COMMITTEES.
Health spa contracts, **93:81-93:83.**
Horse racing due to weather, substitution of wagering on televised races, **128A:5.**
Hospital service corporations, **176A:8, 176A:8F.**
Disputes, **176A:17.**
Strike of insurance agents, cancellation of contracts during, **175:187F.**
Installment payment agreement with taxpayer, **62C:37B.**
Instrument, **204:1.**
Insurance, **175:11A, 175:112, 175:187B-175:187D.**
See INSURANCE.
Insurance agents.
See INSURANCE AGENTS AND BROKERS.

RESCISSION —Cont'd
Landlord.
See LANDLORD AND TENANT.
Limited partnerships.
See LIMITED PARTNERSHIPS.
Marriage, cancellation of notice of intention, **207:26.**
Membership camping contract, **93:48A.**
Model water and sewer commission, termination or dissolution of, **40N:21.**
Motor vehicle dealer's franchise, unfair competition or practice in connection, **93B:4, 93B:9.**
Multilevel distribution companies, provisions as to cancellation of contracts by participants, **93:69.**
Municipalities.
Cities and towns. See within this heading, "Cities and towns."
Negotiable instruments.
Credit unions.
See CREDIT UNIONS.
Nonprofit hospital service corporation, qualifications for subscriber, **176A:1A.**
Notice.
Contracts not consummated at seller's place of business, notice of cancellation, **93:48.**
Employer failing to withhold taxes, cancellation, **62B:7.**
Form, **93:48, 255D:9.**
Health, welfare and retirement funds, **151D:14.**
Hospital service corporations, notice of cancellation and reinstatement rights, **176A:8F.**
Insurance, **175:187C.**
See INSURANCE.
Sales under commercial code.
See SALES UNDER COMMERCIAL CODE.
Workers' compensation, notice of cancellation, **149:34A.**
Nursing home administrator's license, **112:112.**
Personal service contracts, **255:13K.**
Place of seller's business, contracts signed at other than, **93:48, 255D:9.**
Political party enrollment, **53:37, 53:38.**
Bipartisan boards, change or cancellation of enrollment in cases affecting membership, **4:12.**

RESCISSION —Cont'd
Political party enrollment —Cont'd
Recording cancellation, **53:37.**
Terminating membership on ward or town committee, **52:2.**
Principal and sales representative, agreement between, **104:9.**
Provision of Chapter 31.
See MUNICIPAL PERSONNEL SYSTEMS.
Public officers and employees, actions influenced by misconduct, **268A:9, 268A:15, 268A:21.**
Public works department employees, termination of service in unclassified positions, **16:4.**
Real estate time-shares, purchase contract, **183B:41.**
Registration.
Charities and charitable organizations, **68:32.**
Land titles.
See REGISTRATION OF LAND TITLES.
Trademarks and trade names, cancellation of registration, **110B:8.**
Uniform Securities Act, registration of broker dealers and agents, **110A:204.**
Voters, cancellation of party enrollment, **53:37, 53:38.**
Retail installment sales and services, **255D:27.**
See RETAIL INSTALLMENT SALES AND SERVICES.
Retirement funds, **151D:14.**
Sale or transfer of property.
Commercial code provisions.
See SALES UNDER COMMERCIAL CODE.
Retail installment sales agreements, cancellation prior to delivery of copy, **255D:14.**
Seller's place of business, cancellation of contracts not executed, **93:48.**
Sales representative and principal, termination of agreement between, **104:9.**
Sales under commercial code.
See SALES UNDER COMMERCIAL CODE.
Secured transactions.
See SECURED TRANSACTIONS.

RESCISSION —Cont'd
Seller's place of business, cancellation of contracts not executed, **93:48.**
Sinking fund bonds.
Coupons, cancellation upon payment, **44:48.**
Substituted by new bonds, **44:49.**
Statutes, petitions of cities and towns for rescission, **4:4B.**
Steam boilers.
See STEAM BOILERS AND ENGINES.
Subdivision plats, rescission of planning board's approval, **41:81N.**
Support, termination of public assistance due to excess, **18:21.**
Take-over bids for corporations, damages in action for rescission, **110C:9.**
Taxes, installment payment agreement, **62C:37B.**
Three business day cancellation period, **93:48, 255D:9.**
Towns.
Cities and towns. See within this heading, "Cities and towns."
Trademarks and trade names, cancellation of registration, **110B:8.**
Trusts.
See TRUSTS AND TRUSTEES.
Truth in lending, **140D:10.**
Retail installment sales agreements, **255D:9.**
Uniform operation of commercial motor vehicles.
See UNIFORM OPERATION OF COMMERCIAL MOTOR VEHICLES.
Uniform Securities Act, registration of broker-dealers and agents, **110A:204.**
Warehouses.
Option to terminate storage, **106:7-206.**
Receipt, cancellation upon delivery of goods, **106:7-403.**
Water pollution abatement trust, **29C:16.**
Welfare funds, **151D:14.**
Will, revocation by cancellation, **191:8.**
Workers' compensation.
See WORKERS' COMPENSATION.

RESCRIPT.
Clerk of court, notice of rescript, **221:20.**

RESCRIPT —Cont'd
Supreme Judicial Court.
See SUPREME JUDICIAL COURT.

RESCUE.
Air tanks used by rescue workers, exception, **146:34.**
Animals.
See ANIMALS.
Anti-choking devices in restaurants, liability of persons using, **94:305D.**
Good Samaritan law.
Search and rescue volunteers, **231:85AA.**
Impounded or distrained beast, rescue, **49:39, 49:40.**
Joint rescue services, authorization of agreements between governmental units, **40:4A.**
Search and rescue volunteers.
Immunity from civil liability for rendering assistance, **231:85AA.**
Sheriff or deputy may call for aid in case, **37:13.**
Ski patrol members providing emergency care, treatment, or transportation, liability, **231:85I.**

RESCUE SQUADS.
Emergency medical services system, **111C:1 to 111C:24.**
See EMERGENCY MEDICAL SERVICES SYSTEM.

RESEARCH.
Aids.
See AIDS.
Alcoholic liquors delivered to state departments or agencies for scientific purposes, **138:51.**
Animals.
See ANIMALS.
Biology.
See BIOLOGY.
Blind persons, **6:146.**
Bradford Durfee College of Technology Research Foundation, **74:46B.**
Conservation, **21:7H, 21:24.**
Bureau of wildlife research and management, duties of superintendent, **21:7H.**
Environmental affairs executive office. See within this heading, "Environmental affairs executive office."
Supervisors of conservation districts, powers and duties, **21:24.**

RESEARCH —Cont'd

Corporation tax, **63:38C.**

  See CORPORATION TAXES.

Criminal history systems board, monitoring of research programs, **6:173.**

Development and industrial commission in cities and towns, **40:8A.**

Dogs and cats, use of in scientific investigation, experiment or instruction, **140:174D.**

Drugs.

  See DRUGS AND NARCOTICS.

Economic diversification program, defense-related commercial activity, **23F:1.**

Education department.

  See EDUCATION DEPARTMENT.

Elder affairs department, evaluative research, **19A:12.**

Environmental affairs executive office.

  Duties and functions, **21A:2.**

  Hazardous waste management act, duties of environmental Protection Department, **21C:4.**

Epilepsy, health department to research causes, **111:4G.**

Growth and development policy committees, cities and towns, **40:4I.**

Hazardous waste management act, duties of environmental Protection Department, **21C:4.**

Health and health departments.

  Commission, duties, **6:126.**

  Epilepsy, health department to research causes, **111:4G.**

Health care facilities, notice of expenditure or change in service, **111:25C.**

Human resources division, departmental research by director, **7:28.**

Inland waters of Commonwealth, surveys, **131:2.**

Insurance division, employment of research analyst, **26:7.**

Laboratories.

  See LABORATORIES.

Leaves of absence for teachers, principals or supervisors, **71:41A.**

Legislative research council, **3:56 et seq.**

Legislative Research Program.

  See GENERAL COURT.

Libraries as regional reference and research centers, **78:19C.**

RESEARCH —Cont'd

Marine fish.

  See MARINE FISH AND FISHERIES.

Mass transportation facilities and services, functions of transportation planning and development bureau, **16:3A.**

Medicolegal investigation office, **38:2.**

Mentally ill.

  See MENTALLY ILL AND RETARDED PERSONS.

Municipal historical commissions, powers, **40:8D.**

Ocean sanctuaries, activities permitted, **132A:16.**

Patients' rights, **111:70E.**

Pesticide control, experimental use permits, **132B:3A, 132B:8.**

Professional engineers, exemption from law, **112:81R.**

Psychologists, employment, **112:123.**

Regional transportation authorities, conducting of research, **161B:6.**

Reptiles and amphibians, research, **131:4.**

Research institution defined for purposes of provisions establishing Massachusetts Centers of Excellence Corporation, **40J:12.**

Reyes syndrome, records of reports of, release by public health department to persons authorized to conduct research studies, **111:110B.**

Sales tax exemption, research animals, **64H:6.**

School professional personnel, leave of absence for research, **71:41A.**

Schooner Ernestina Commission, powers and duties, **6:182B.**

Shellfish propagation, **130:20.**

Solid waste facilities and management, **16:20, 21H:5.**

State college board of trustees, powers, **74:14.**

Teachers, leave of absence for research, **71:41A.**

Unfair discriminatory practices, **151B:3.**

University of Massachusetts.

  See UNIVERSITY OF MASSACHUSETTS.

Water pollution control research projects, **21:27, 21:38.**

Wildlife research and management bureau, duties of superintendent, **21:7H.**

RESEARCH —Cont'd

Zoning and planning, special permits for scientific research and development, **40A:9.**

RESEARCH INSTITUTION.

Defined for purposes of provisions establishing Massachusetts Centers of Excellence Corporation, **40J:12.**

RESERVATION OF QUESTIONS.

Superior courts, **213:1B, 231:104.**

  See SUPERIOR COURTS.

Supreme Judicial Court, **211:6.**

  See SUPREME JUDICIAL COURT.

RESERVATION OF RIGHTS.

Auction sales with or without reserve, **106:2-328.**

Corporate names, reservation, **155:9, 155:9A, 156B:11.**

Fee simple, words required for reservation, **183:13.**

Performance or acceptance under reservation, **106:1-207.**

Shipment of goods, **106:2-310.**

States, reserved powers and rights of, **US Const Amend 10.**

Title, reservation of.

  See RESERVATION OF TITLE.

RESERVATION OF TITLE.

Sales contract, reservation for security, **106:2-401.**

Security interest, **106:1-201.**

RESERVATIONS.

Buildings.

  See BUILDINGS AND STRUCTURES.

Greylock reservation commission.

  See GREYLOCK RESERVATION COMMISSION.

Parks and reservations.

  See PARKS AND RESERVATIONS.

Playgrounds.

  See PLAYGROUNDS.

RESERVE BANKS.

Federal reserve.

  See FEDERAL RESERVE BANKS.

RESERVE FORCES.

Fire departments, **48:59B-48:59E.**

  See FIRE DEPARTMENTS.

Leave of absence, **32A:8, 32B:9I, 33:59A.**

Militia, **33:1-33:135.**

  See MILITIA.

RESERVE FORCES —Cont'd
Police.
  See POLICE.

RESERVE FUNDS.
City or town auditor, transfer,
  40:5A, 40:6.
Co-operative banks, reserve
  balances, **170:22, 170:23.**
Co-operative corporations.
  See COOPERATIVE
    CORPORATIONS AND
    ASSOCIATIONS.
Credit unions.
  See CREDIT UNIONS.
Dental service corporations,
  reserves required, **176E:2.**
Employment security, reserve
  percentage, **151A:14.**
Foreign insurance companies.
  See FOREIGN INSURANCE
    COMPANIES.
Fraternal benefit societies.
  See FRATERNAL BENEFIT
    SOCIETIES.
Hospital service corporations,
  contingent reserves, **176A:24.**
Insurance.
  See INSURANCE.
Life insurance.
  See LIFE INSURANCE.
Morris plan banks, **172A:10.**
  Certificate funds as limited by
    unallocated reserves,
    172A:5.
Municipal finance, **40:5A, 40:5C,
  40:6.**
  Fiscal year, establishment,
    40:5A, 40:5C, 40:6.
  Overlay account balance
    transferred to reserve funds,
    59:25.
  Transfer of reserve funds, **40:5A,
    40:6.**
Optometric service corporations,
  reserves required, **176F:2.**
Regional transit authority,
  establishment of reserve fund,
    161B:10.
Retirement systems.
  See RETIREMENT SYSTEMS
    AND PENSIONS.
Savings banks, **168:27A.**
Street railways.
  See STREET RAILWAYS.
Subsidization of rental units,
  condominium profits used,
    121A:18D.
Trust companies.
  See TRUST COMPANIES.
Urban redevelopment corporations,
  operation and maintenance
    charges, **121A:15.**

RESERVE FUNDS —Cont'd
Workers' compensation.
  See WORKERS'
    COMPENSATION.

**RESERVE OFFICERS
ASSOCIATION OF THE
UNITED STATES.**
State house, assignment of
  quarters, **8:17.**

RESERVE PERCENTAGE.
Defined or construed in
  employment security law,
  151A:14.

**RESERVE VALUATION
METHOD.**
Defined or construed under
  insurance law, **175:9.**

**RESERVOIRS, 253:1-253:62.
See DAMS AND RESERVOIRS.**

**RESIDENCE.
See DOMICILE AND
RESIDENCE.**

**RESIDENCE HALLS.
See DORMITORIES.**

RESIDENT.
Definition for income tax purposes,
  62:1.

RESIDENT AGENT.
Foreign insurance companies.
  See FOREIGN INSURANCE
    COMPANIES.
Insurance rates.
  See INSURANCE RATES AND
    RATING ORGANIZATIONS.
Service of process, agent for,
  223:37.
  See PROCESS AND SERVICE
    OF PROCESS AND
    PAPERS.

**RESIDENT ENGINEER.
See ENGINEERS AND
SURVEYORS.**

RESIDENTIAL BUILDINGS.
Dwelling houses generally.
  See DWELLING HOUSES.
Home inspectors generally, **13:96,
  13:97, 112:221 to 112:226.**
  See HOME INSPECTORS.

**RESIDENTIAL CARE AND
FACILITIES.**
Alcohol treatment program, **90:24.**
Architectural Barriers Board,
  powers, **22:13A.**
Mentally ill.
  See MENTALLY ILL AND
    RETARDED PERSONS.

**RESIDENTIAL CARE AND
FACILITIES** —Cont'd
Nursing.
  See NURSING OR REST
    HOMES.
Social services department,
  administration of programs,
    18B:2.
Tuberculosis and tuberculin.
  Definition of "resident" under
    public health law, **111:80.**
  Hospital care and treatment for
    residents, **111:77.**

**RESIDENTIAL
CONSERVATION SERVICE.**
Accounting methods of public
  utilities, approval, **Spec L
    61:7.**
Administrative review of budgets
  of public utilities, **Spec L
    61:7.**
Advertisements of residential
  conservation services, **Spec L
    61:3.**
Appeal of energy resource
  secretary's orders, **Spec L
    61:8.**
Assessments of public utilities for
  residential conservation
    program, **Spec L 61:7.**
Audits.
  Energy audits. See within this
    heading, "Energy audits."
Banks as members of public
  advisory committee, **Spec L
    61:3.**
Budgets, submission by public
  utilities, **Spec L 61:7.**
Cease and desist orders of
  telecommunications and
    energy department, **Spec L
    61:8.**
Charges for energy audits and
  other energy services, **Spec L
    61:7.**
Clerk of house of representatives,
  submission of annual report of
    public advisory committee,
    Spec L 61:3.
Community project directors
  association, membership on
    public advisory committee,
    Spec L 61:3.
Complaints of violations of state
  plan, **Spec L 61:8.**
Conciliation conference upon
  petition for relief, **Spec L
    61:8.**
Consumer price index, charges for
  energy audits determined,
    Spec L 61:7.

RESIDENTIAL CONSERVATION SERVICE
—Cont'd

Contracts by energy resources secretary, **Spec L 61:7.**

Costs and expenses.
Public advisory committee, reimbursement, **Spec L 61:3.**
State plan, distribution of costs of compliance, **Spec L 61:7.**

Definitions, **Spec L 61:1.**

Department of public utilities.
Telecommunications and energy department. See within this heading, "Telecommunications and energy department."

Energy auditors.
Energy resources executive office, removal from list, **Spec L 61:8.**
Registration and training, **Spec L 61:3, Spec L 61:9.**

Energy audits.
Public utilities, charges, **Spec L 61:7.**
Reports, **61:4, Spec L 61:3.**

Energy department, federal, submission of implementation plans, **Spec L 61:6.**

Energy inspectors.
Energy resources executive office, removal from list, **Spec L 61:8.**
Registration and training, **Spec L 61:3.**

Energy installers.
Energy resources executive office, removal from list, **Spec L 61:8.**
Registration and training, **Spec L 61:3.**

Energy lenders.
Energy resources executive office, removal from list, **Spec L 61:3.**
Registration and training, **Spec L 61:3.**

Energy resource executive office.
Energy auditors registration board, creation, **Spec L 61:9.**
Public utilities, assessments charged, **Spec L 61:7.**
State claim, lists with respect, **Spec L 61:8.**

Energy resources secretary.
Contracts, **Spec L 61:7.**
Home suppliers.
Expenses, apportionment, **Spec L 61:7.**

RESIDENTIAL CONSERVATION SERVICE
—Cont'd

Energy resources secretary
—Cont'd
Home suppliers —Cont'd
Participation in state plans, **Spec L 61:4.**
Implementation plans, submission, **Spec L 61:6.**
Petitions for relief, duties with respect, **Spec L 61:8.**
State plan, preparation, **Spec L 61:3.**

Energy suppliers.
Energy resources executive office, removal from list, **Spec L 61:8.**
Home heating suppliers. See within this heading, "Home heating suppliers."
Registration and training, **Spec L 61:3.**

Engineers as members of public advisory committee, **Spec L 61:3.**

Executive office.
Energy resource executive office. See within this heading, "Energy resource executive office."

Federal government.
United States. See within this heading, "United States."

Federal residential conservation service.
Defined, **Spec L 61:1.**
Public utilities, accounting methods, **Spec L 61:7.**
Weatherization program, approval, **Spec L 61:6.**

Fines for violation of state plan, **Spec L 61:8.**

Hearings.
Petition for relief, hearings, **Spec L 61:8.**
Public utilities, review of budgets, **Spec L 61:7.**

Home heating suppliers.
Petition for relief from activities, **Spec L 61:8.**
Residential conservation programs, requirement, **Spec L 61:5.**
Implementation plans by public utilities, submission, **Spec L 61:6.**

Inspectors.
Energy inspectors. See within this heading, "Energy inspectors."

RESIDENTIAL CONSERVATION SERVICE
—Cont'd

Installers.
Energy installers. See within this heading, "Energy installers."

Joint ventures, approval, **Spec L 61:6.**

Labor Department, federal, charges for energy audits, **Spec L 61:7.**

Landlord and tenant, residential conservation program requirement, **Spec L 61:5.**

Legislative findings, **Spec L 61:2.**

Lenders.
Energy lenders. See within this heading, "Energy lenders."

Notice of review of budgets of public utilities, **Spec L 61:7.**

Orders of energy resource secretary, **Spec L 61:8.**

Plans.
State plan. See within this heading, "State plan."

Public advisory committee, establishment and responsibilities, **Spec L 61:3.**

Public utilities.
Accounting by and assessments, **Spec L 61:7.**
Advertisements of conservation programs, **Spec L 61:3.**
Implementation plan, submission, **Spec L 61:6.**
Petition for relief from activities, **Spec L 61:8.**
Residential conservation program requirements, **Spec L 61:5.**

Radio and television, advertising of residential conservation programs, **Spec L 61:3.**

Records and reports.
Energy audit reports, **61:4, Spec L 61:3.**
Public advisory committee, annual report, **Spec L 61:3.**
State plan, records of public utilities, **Spec L 61:7.**

Secretary.
Energy resources secretary. See within this heading, "Energy resources secretary."

Severability of provisions, **Spec L 61:10.**

State plan.
Budgets of public utilities, submission, **Spec L 61:7.**

RESIDENTIAL
CONSERVATION SERVICE
—Cont'd
State plan —Cont'd
Defined, **Spec L 61:1.**
Energy resources executive
office, lists, **Spec L 61:8.**
Energy resources secretary,
preparation, **Spec L 61:3.**
Home heating suppliers,
participation, **Spec L 61:4.**
Implementation plans by public
utilities submission, **Spec L
61:6.**
Suffolk County Superior court,
appeal of orders of energy
resources secretary, **Spec L
61:8.**
Suppliers.
Energy suppliers. See within
this heading, "Energy
suppliers."
Telecommunications and energy
department.
Budgets of public utilities,
submission, **Spec L 61:7.**
Defined, **Spec L 61:1.**
Petition for release, filing, **Spec
L 61:8.**
Public advisory committee,
membership, **Spec L 61:3.**
United States.
Department of Energy, duties
with respect to
implementation plan, **Spec
L 61:6.**
Department of Labor, charges
for energy audits, **Spec L
61:7.**
Federal residential conservation
service, defined, **Spec L
61:1.**
Utilities.
Defined, **Spec L 61:1.**
Public utilities. See within this
heading, "Public utilities."
Weatherization program, inclusion
in implementation plans,
Spec L 61:6.

RESIDUAL WASTE
TREATMENT FACILITY.
Garbage and rubbish.
See GARBAGE AND RUBBISH.
Water pollution.
See WATER POLLUTION.

RESIDUARY LEGATEES.
See WILLS.

RESIGNATION.
Abatement, survival, and revival
of actions, effect of resignation
of public officer or trustee
under statute, **228:14.**

RESIGNATION —Cont'd
Appellate justice, appellate review
as affected by resignation,
231:108.
Boards of selectmen, filling
vacancies caused by
resignations, **41:10.**
Cities and towns.
Mayors. See within this heading,
"Mayors."
Officers, **41:109.**
Representatives in town meeting
government, **43A:5.**
Undated resignation of
prospective city or town
appointees, demand,
268A:21B.
Vacation pay upon resignation's,
41:111E.
Civil service.
Defined, **31:1.**
Eligible lists, persons who have
resigned, **31:25.**
Report of resignation, **31:68.**
Clerk of court, duties of assistant
clerk upon resignation,
221:33.
Conservators.
Guardians, conservators, and
committees. See within this
heading, "Guardians,
conservators, and
committees."
Corporate director, **156B:50A.**
Executors.
See EXECUTORS AND
ADMINISTRATORS.
Fire insurance referee, filling
vacancy on resignation,
175:100A.
Foreign corporations, **181:4A.**
General Court, compensation and
expenses of member resigning,
3:10.
Guardians, conservators, and
committees, **201:18, 201:33.**
Duration of license to sell, **204:8.**
Examination of fiduciary with
respect to resignation,
204:11.
Fiduciary, resignation by
guardian or conservator,
204:37.
Mayors, **43:59A.**
Acting mayor in case of
resignation, **39:5.**
Demand by mayor for undated
resignation from prospective
city appointees, **268A:21B.**
Motor vehicle registrar or deputy,
validity of signature or
facsimile after resignation
from office, **90:33A.**

RESIGNATION —Cont'd
Municipalities.
Cities and towns. See within
this heading, "Cities and
towns."
Pensions.
Retirement systems and
pensions. See within this
heading, "Retirement
systems and pensions."
Physicians and surgeons, report to
board of registration, **111:53B.**
Police.
Matron, appointment of
successor on resignation,
147:19.
Officer, payment of overtime
compensation, **147:17E.**
Sheriffs and deputies. See
within this heading,
"Sheriffs and deputies."
Probation officers, notice as to
resignation, **276:103.**
Representatives in town meeting
government, **43A:5.**
Retirement systems and pensions,
31:10.
Deferral of allowance due on
resignation, etc., **32:10.**
Superannuation retirements,
resignation as affecting,
32:10.
Separation from payroll,
resignation of public
employees prior, **30:46.**
Sheriffs and deputies.
Prisoner to be delivered to
successor on resignation,
126:23.
Warrants, official papers to be
delivered to successor,
127:7.
Survival of action against public
officer or trustee appointed
under statute, **228:14.**
Towns.
Cities and towns. See within
this heading, "Cities and
towns."
Trustees.
See TRUSTS AND TRUSTEES.
Undated resignation, demand for,
from prospective city or town
appointees, **268A:21B.**
Uniform Gifts to Minors Act,
custodian, **201A:18.**
Unpaid salary of resigning state
employee, payment, **29:31.**
Vacation pay of employees as
affected, **41:111E.**

RES JUDICATA.
Appeal.
See APPEAL AND REVIEW.

RES JUDICATA —Cont'd

Apprentice agreements, effect of proceedings and appeals regarding, **23:11K.**

Attachment of property.
See ATTACHMENT OF PROPERTY.

Children born out of wedlock, **209C:11, 209C:22.**

Common trust funds, conclusiveness of allowance of annual of count, **203A:3.**

Fraudulent attachment, effect of judgment in action for dissolution, **223:113.**

Guardian ad litem, persons represented, **201:34.**

Illegitimate children, **209C:22.**

Next friend, persons represented, **201:34.**

Probate decrees, **192:3.**

Restraints of trade and monopolies, **93:9.**

Small claims actions and procedures, **218:23.**

Soldiers' Home in Holyoke, effect of court decision on removal of superintendent, **6:71.**

Vocational rehabilitation services, finality of determination, **152:30H.**

Will, probate as conclusive regarding due execution, **191:7.**

Workers' compensation.
Board orders, **152:16.**
Incapacity, finding, **152:12.**

RESOLUTIONS, 3:51 et seq.

City charters.
See CITY CHARTERS.

Legislative bills and resolves.
See LEGISLATIVE BILLS AND RESOLVES.

RESOURCE CONSERVATION AND RECOVERY ACT.

Fires and fire prevention, **148:38B.**

Underground storage tank petroleum product cleanup fund, **21J:9.**

RESOURCE RECOVERY FACILITIES.

Taxation, **16:24A (note).**

RESPIRATORY CARE.

Cardiopulmonary resuscitation.
See CARDIOPULMONARY RESUSCITATION.

Certificates and certification, **112:23U.**

Defined, **112:23R.**

RESPIRATORY CARE —Cont'd

Licensing practitioners, **13:11B, 112:23R et seq.**

National Board for Respiratory Care, certified respiratory therapy technician, **112:23U.**

Registration, registers, and registrars, **112:23U.**

RESPIRATORY DISEASE.

Fireman's death or disability as suffered in line of duty, **32:94A.**

RESPIRATORY EQUIPMENT.

Asbestos, rules and regulations, **149:6C.**

Longshore and waterfront employees, protection, **149:18A, 149:18B.**
Exhaust from engines, **149:18G.**

RESPIRATORY THERAPIST.

Defined, **112:23R.**

RESPITE.

Capital cases.
See CAPITAL CASES.

RESPONDEAT SUPERIOR.

Electricians, liability of master for work of employees, **141:6.**

RESPONDENTIA BONDS.

Insurance on money loaned, **175:47.**

RESPONDING TO AN EMERGENCY.

Definition, **149:177B.**

RESPONSE ACTION CONTRACTOR.

Hazardous waste insolvency fund, effectiveness extended, strict liability, **21C:15, 21C:19, 21E:2, 21E:16-21E:18.**

REST AREAS.

Advertising at safety rest areas, **93D:1, 93D:6.**

Federal-aid highways, acquisition and use of lands adjacent, **81:13D.**

RESTATEMENT OF ARTICLES OF ORGANIZATION.
See CORPORATIONS.

RESTAURANTS.

Alcoholic liquors, offenses, **272:25-272:27.**

Anti-choking devices as required, **94:305D.**

Architectural barriers against handicapped persons, **22:13A.**

Bed and breakfast establishments, taxation on meals served, **64H:6.**

RESTAURANTS —Cont'd

Booths, enclosing, **272:25, 272:27.**

Cafes.
Enclosing booths, **272:25, 272:26.**
Immoral solicitation in cafes, etc., **272:26, 272:27.**

Choking, restaurants to maintain devices for preventing, **94:305D.**

Common victuallers.
See COMMON VICTUALLERS.

Cover charge, prohibition as to persons under 13 years of age, **140:183D.**

Crimes and offenses, **94:305A, 272:25-272:27, 272:92A, 272:98.**
Licensing authority, convictions of certain offenses to be reported, **272:27.**

Discrimination by reason of race, color or creed, **272:92A, 272:98.**

Disease carriers, employment of, prohibited, **94:305B.**

Fine for violating provisions as to anti-choking devices, **94:305D.**

Frozen desserts, making own, permit not required, **94:65H.**

Gaming equipment, **271:3.**

Horse meat, serving, **94:151A.**

Hotels and motels, regulation as to food for travelers, **140:4.**

Immoral solicitation, **272:25-272:27.**

Licenses for common victuallers, **140:2 et seq.**
See COMMON VICTUALLERS.

Limited access ways, location, **81:7C.**

Lunch counters.
See LUNCH COUNTERS.

Medical examination of persons handling or serving food, **94:305B.**

National Anthem, playing, **264:9.**

Offenses.
Crimes and offenses. See within this heading, "Crimes and offenses."

Oleomargarine or butter substitutes, serving, notice required, **94:58.**

Overtime pay for employees, **151:1A.**

Registered garments and towels, permitting use, **110:25B.**

Stalls, enclosing, **272:25, 272:27.**

Sunday or holiday, sale of meals, **136:6.**

RESTAURANTS —Cont'd

Taverns.

  See TAVERNS.

Tax returns, **62C:16.**

Unsafe or inadequate water supply, **111:122A.**

Unsanitary conditions, general penal provisions, **94:305A.**

Women employees, hours of labor, **149:56.**

REST CAMPS.

State trails or paths, provision for rest camps, **132:38.**

REST HOMES.

See NURSING OR REST HOMES.

RESTITUTION.

Abuse prevention, **209A:10.**

County buildings, defacing, **266:97.**

Credit card offenses.

  Identity fraud, **266:37E.**

Delinquent child, restitution, **119:62.**

Employer accepting or retaining employee's tips, restitution required, **149:152A.**

Fines and penalties, offers or payment of restitution, **149:27, 149:27C.**

Fire, liability for damages caused by negligence in case, **266:8, 266:9.**

Forfeited property, restitution on libelant's failure to maintain action, **257:7.**

Fraud or deceit.

  Identity fraud, **266:37-e.**

Health care claims, false, **175H:7.**

Hearing instrument specialists, **112:200.**

Hospital's lien, payment in disregard, **111:70C.**

Identity fraud, **266:37E.**

Indemnity.

  See INDEMNITY AND INDEMNIFICATION.

Labor and workforce development, effect of restitution offers on punishment, **149:27, 149:27C.**

Letters of credit.

  Issuer's right to restitution, **106:5-108.**

Lost property and strayed beasts, **134:3.**

Malicious destruction of historical monument or building of the Commonwealth, restitution to the Commonwealth, **266:95-266:97.**

RESTITUTION —Cont'd

Monument or marker, malicious destruction, **266:94.**

Motor vehicle theft or fraudulent insurance, conviction, **266:27A, 266:29, 266:111B, 276:92A.**

Probation officer, restitution made through, **276:92.**

Sentence and punishment.

  Probation officer, payments through, **276:92.**

  Receiving stolen property, restitution as mitigating punishment, **266:61.**

Ships or vessels, penalty for destruction, **266:108.**

Stolen property bought, effect of restitution, **266:61.**

Unfair trade practices against consumers, restitution by person engaged, **93A:5.**

Victims of violent crime, **258C:10.**

RESTORATION.

Civil service.

  See CIVIL SERVICE.

Condominiums.

  See CONDOMINIUMS.

Fire insurance company, restoration of property by.

  See FIRE INSURANCE.

Public construction contracts for restoration of essential services, award without competitive bidding, **30:39M.**

RESTRAINING ORDERS.

See INJUNCTIONS.

RESTRAINT OF PERSON.

Children and minors, **123:21, 123B:8.**

Mentally ill and retarded persons, **19:21, 19B:18, 123:1, 123:21.**

RESTRAINTS OF TRADE AND MONOPOLIES, 93:1-93:14A.

Admission, final judgment or decree, **93:11.**

Advertising.

  Goods below cost, **93:14F.**

  Trade or commerce, **93:2.**

Affirmations, investigations by Attorney General, **93:8.**

Agreements in restraint of trade as unlawful, **93:4, 93:6, 93:10.**

Allowances for mileage, investigation, **93:8.**

Alterations by witnesses in transcript of investigation by Attorney General, **93:8.**

Appeal of court order as to investigative demands of Attorney General, **93:8.**

RESTRAINTS OF TRADE AND MONOPOLIES —Cont'd

Applicability of antitrust act, **93:3.**

Attorney general.

  Actions by, **93:9.**

  Appointment of assistants to enforce laws against restraints of trade, **12:10.**

  Definitions, **93:2.**

  Duties in connection with monopolistic practices, **12:10.**

  Enforcement fund, **93:14.**

  Investigations, **93:8.**

  Motor vehicle insurance, action to enjoin monopolistic, etc., practices as to rates for optional, **175E:6.**

  Penalty actions for contracts or combinations in restraint of trade or monopolies, **93:10.**

Attorneys at law.

  Fees.

    Attorneys' fees, **93:9, 93:12.**

  Investigations by Attorney General, right to counsel during, **93:8.**

Attorneys' fees, **93:12.**

  Parens patriae action, **93:9.**

Automobile insurance, monopolies and restraints of trade by providers of optional coverage, **175E:6.**

Boston harbor permits and licenses, when deemed in restraint of trade, **91:16.**

Burden of proof as to jurisdiction, **93:3.**

Cause of action, **93:12.**

  Parens patriae action, **93:9.**

Changes by witness in transcript of Attorney General's investigation, **93:8.**

Cigarettes, sale at price intended to destroy competition prohibited, **64C:12-64C:21.**

Combinations as unlawful when in restraint of trade, **93:4.**

Commerce, defined, **93:2.**

Commercial information, **93:2.**

Compromise, judgment or decree under Massachusetts Antitrust Act as not being prima facie evidence, **93:11.**

Confidentiality of Attorney General's investigations, **93:8.**

Consent judgments and decrees.

  Parens patriae action, **93:9.**

  Prima facie evidence, consent judgments as not being, **93:11.**

RESTRAINTS OF TRADE AND MONOPOLIES —Cont'd

Conspiracy to restrain or destroy trade, **93:4, 93:5.**

Attorney general's duty to investigate, **12:10, 93:8.**

Construction of state law as compatible with that of federal Antitrust statutes, **93:1.**

Contempt of court, disobedience of court order as to investigative demands by Attorney General, **93:8.**

Contracts in restraint of trade as unlawful, **93:4, 93:6, 93:10.**

Corporations.
Defined, **93:2.**
Penalties, **93:10.**
Unlawfulness of contracts in restraint of trade, **93:4, 93:6.**

Counsel, investigation by Attorney General as entitling one to right, **93:8.**

Criminal prosecution, information obtained by Attorney General in investigations, as exempt from use, **93:8.**

Damages.
Treble damages. See within this heading, "Treble damages."

Decrees.
Judgments, orders, and decrees. See within this heading, "Judgments, orders, and decrees."

Definitions, **93:2.**

Demand, defined, **93:2.**

Description of documentary material demanded by Attorney General, **93:8.**

Discounts, **93:6.**

Discovery, investigations by Attorney General, **93:8.**

Domicile and residence, investigation involving oral examination conducted in county of residence of witness, **93:8.**

Enforcement fund, **93:14.**

Enforcement of investigative demand by Attorney General, **93:8.**

Equity, injunctive relief, **93:12.**

Estoppel, final judgment or decree under Massachusetts Antitrust Act, **93:11.**

Evidence.
Final judgment or decree under Massachusetts Antitrust Act as prima facie evidence, **93:11.**

RESTRAINTS OF TRADE AND MONOPOLIES —Cont'd

Evidence —Cont'd
Jurisdiction, burden of establishing, **93:3.**
Witnesses. See within this heading, "Witnesses."

Examination of witnesses, investigations by Attorney General, **93:8.**

Exemption from disclosure of Attorney General's investigations, **93:8.**

Federal antitrust statutes, construction as compatible, **93:1.**

Federal officials, disclosure of Attorney General's investigative materials, **93:8.**

Federal Trade Commission.
Jurisdiction, **93:3.**
State act as inapplicable to activities exempt under federal law, **93:7.**

Fees.
Attorneys' fees. See within this heading, "Attorneys' fees."
Witness fees in Attorney General's investigations, **93:8.**

Fines and forfeitures.
Penalties. See within this heading, "Penalties."

Funds, Antitrust Enforcement Fund, **93:14.**

General Fund, Antitrust Enforcement Fund's excess deposited, **93:14.**

Identification of documentary material demanded by Attorney General, **93:8.**

Imprisonment, contracts or agreements in restraint of trade or monopolies, **93:10.**

Injunctions, **93:12.**
Motor vehicle insurance, action to enjoin monopolistic practice in setting rate, **175E:6.**
Trade secret, misappropriation, **93:42A.**

Insurance, **176D:4.**
See INSURANCE.

Interpretation of law, **93:1.**

Interstate commerce, exemptions under federal antitrust laws as exempt under state law, **93:7.**

Judgments, orders, and decrees.
Consent judgments and decrees. See within this heading, "Consent judgments and decrees."

RESTRAINTS OF TRADE AND MONOPOLIES —Cont'd

Judgments, orders, and decrees —Cont'd
Contempt of court by disobedience of court order as to attorney general's investigation, **93:8.**
Final judgment or decree under Massachusetts Antitrust Act as admission, **93:11.**
Parens patriae action, **93:9.**
Jurisdiction, **93:3, 93:12.**
Parens patriae action, **93:9.**
Penalty actions for contracts or combinations in restraint of trade or monopolies, **93:10.**
Superior court jurisdiction over investigative demands of Attorney General, **93:8.**

Limitation of actions, **93:13.**

Location of Attorneys General's investigations, **93:8.**

Management information, **93:2.**

Merchandising information, **93:2.**

Mileage allowances, investigations by Attorney General, **93:8.**

Milk dealers and dairies, violations of Milk Control Act, **94A:6.**

Motor vehicle insurance, monopolies and restraints of trade by providers of optional coverage, **175E:6.**

Natural person, defined, **93:2.**

New England, defined, **93:2.**

Oaths and affirmations, investigations by Attorney General, **93:8.**

Orders.
Judgments, orders, and decrees. See within this heading, "Judgments, orders, and decrees."

Parens patriae actions, **93:9.**
Stay or other civil actions, **93:12.**

Parties.
Final judgment or decree under Massachusetts Antitrust Act as estoppel between parties, **93:11.**
Jurisdiction, burden of establishing, **93:3.**
Standing to sue, **93:12.**

Penalties.
Contracts or combinations in restraint of trade, **93:10.**
Parens patriae action, **93:9.**

Personal property, offering for sale, rent, etc., as trade or commerce, **93:2.**

**RESTRAINTS OF TRADE AND
MONOPOLIES** —Cont'd

Person, defined, **93:2.**

Petitions, enforcement of
investigative demands by
Attorney General, **93:8.**

Place of investigations by Attorney
General, **93:8.**

Presumptions and burden of proof
as to jurisdiction, **93:3.**

Price.
Cigarettes, prohibition of sale at
price intended to destroy
competition, **64C:12-64C:21.**
Cutting of price, **93:14E-93:14K.**
Fixing of prices.
Price fixing. See within this
heading, "Price fixing."

Price fixing, **93:6.**
Parens patriae action, **93:9.**

Prima facie evidence, final
judgment or decree under
Massachusetts Antitrust Act,
93:11.

Privileged and confidential
matters, investigations by
Attorney General, **93:8.**

Process and service of process and
papers, investigation by
Attorney General, **93:8.**

Production information, **93:2.**

Production of documents, Attorney
General's demand, **93:8.**

Professions, board rules for
registration of certain
professions to preserve
competition, **112:61.**

Protective order in investigation
by Attorney General, **93:8.**

Purpose of law, **93:1.**

Real property, conveyance,
transfer, or use excluded from
"trade or commerce," **93:2.**

Rebates, **93:6.**

Records and recording.
Public record, investigations by
Attorney General as exempt,
93:8.
Sound recording of Attorney
General's investigations,
93:8.

Registration of certain professions,
board rules to preserve
competition, **112:61.**

Residence, investigation involving
oral examination of witness to
be conducted in county, **93:8.**

Res judicata, parens patriae
action, **93:9.**

Sales below cost to injure
competition, **93:14E-93:14K.**

**RESTRAINTS OF TRADE AND
MONOPOLIES** —Cont'd

Scientific information as trade
secret, **93:2.**

Self-incrimination, investigation by
Attorney General, **93:8.**

Serial numbers, defacing of, to
hinder competition, **266:139A.**

Service of process and papers,
Attorney General's
investigations, **93:8.**

Settlement, judgment under
Massachusetts Antitrust Act
as not being admission, **93:11.**

Sound recording of investigations
by Attorney General, **93:8.**

Standing to sue.
Parties. See within this heading,
"Parties."

State officials, disclosure of
Attorney General's
investigative materials, **93:8.**

State Treasurer, enforcement fund,
93:14.

Stay of action, parens patriae
action as staying other civil
actions, **93:12.**

Stenographer, transcription of
testimony of investigations by
Attorney General, **93:8.**

Stipulations, protective orders,
93:8.

Superior court.
Investigations by Attorney
General, petition for
protective order, **93:8.**
Jurisdiction of actions, **93:12.**
Parens patriae action,
jurisdiction over, **93:9.**
Penalty actions for contracts or
combinations in restraint of
trade or monopolies, **93:10.**

Technical information as trade
secret, **93:2.**

Title of Act, **93:1.**

Trade or commerce, defined, **93:2.**

Trade secret, defined, **93:2.**

Transcripts of investigations by
Attorney General,
examination by witness or
counsel, **93:8.**

Treble damages, **93:12.**
Parens patriae action, **93:9.**

United States Department of
Justice, jurisdiction, **93:3.**

Venue, **93:12.**
Parens patriae action, **93:9.**
Penalty actions for contracts or
combinations in restraint of
trade or monopolies, **93:10.**

Waiver, final judgment under
Massachusetts Antitrust Act,
93:11.

**RESTRAINTS OF TRADE AND
MONOPOLIES** —Cont'd

Witnesses.
Examination of witnesses,
investigation by Attorney
General, **93:8.**
Fees in Attorney General's
investigation, **93:8.**
Transcript of investigation by
Attorney General, changes
by witnesses, **93:8.**

Witness fees, investigations by
Attorney General, **93:8.**

Written interrogatories,
investigation by Attorney
General, **93:8.**

**RESTRAINTS ON
ALIENATION.**

Electric companies' property held
as tenants in common, rights,
164:99A.

New England power pool,
restraints on alienation of
property owned in common,
164A:5.

Perpetuities, rule against, **184A:1
et seq.**
See PERPETUITIES, RULE
AGAINST.

Quieting title.
See QUIETING TITLE.

**RESTRICTED LANDING
AREA.**
**See AIRPORTS AND LANDING
FIELDS.**

RESTRICTIVE COVENANTS.
See COVENANTS.

REST ROOMS.
See TOILETS.

RESULTING TRUSTS.
Property subject to execution,
236:1.

RESUMPTION OF BUSINESS.
Insurance.
See INSURANCE.

RESUSCITATION.
**See CARDIOPULMONARY
RESUSCITATION.**

RESUSCITATORS.
Sales tax exemptions, **64H:6.**

RETAIL.
Definitions for tax purposes,
64H:1, 64I:1.
Sales taxes.
See SALES TAXES.
Stores and merchants.
See STORES AND
MERCHANTS.

RETAIL —Cont'd
Use tax.
See USE, CONSUMPTION, OR
STORAGE TAX.

RETAIL CUSTOMER.
Definitions, **164:94G.**

**RETAIL FOOD STORE
PHARMACY.**
Regulation, **112:38, 112:39.**

**RETAIL INSTALLMENT SALES
AND SERVICES,
255D:1-255D:32.**
Account, furnishing statements,
255D:19.
Add-on purchases, consolidation of
agreements, **255D:18.**
Advancements.
See ADVANCEMENTS.
Advances.
See ADVANCES.
Appeals.
Licensing. See within this
heading, "Licensing of sales
finance companies."
Application.
License for sales finance
company, **255D:2.**
Misstatement as basis for
suspension or revocation of
license, **255D:7.**
Assignment or transfer of
agreement.
Motor vehicle retail installment
sales.
Contract, **255B:18.**
Wage assignment in
agreement as invalid,
255B:20.
Purchase and assignment of
installment sales
agreement, **255D:12.**
Time, **255D:9.**
Wage assignment, **255B:20,
255D:10.**
Automobiles.
See MOTOR VEHICLE RETAIL
INSTALLMENT SALES.
Bank commissioner, duties of,
255D:2 et seq.
Billing period, statement furnished
to buyer, **255D:27.**
Blanks in agreements, **255D:10.**
Cancellation or rescission,
255D:27.
Buyer's rights, **255D:9.**
Delivery of copy of agreement,
cancellation prior, **255D:14.**
Disclosure of rights, **255D:9.**
Notice, **255D:9, 255D:14,
255D:27.**

**RETAIL INSTALLMENT SALES
AND SERVICES** —Cont'd
Cancellation or rescission —Cont'd
Refund, **93:48, 255D:14.**
Return of merchandise, parties'
rights and obligations,
255D:14.
Seller's obligations upon notice,
255D:9, 255D:14, 255D:27.
Work commenced within three
business day cancellation
period, responsibility, **93:48,
255D:9.**
Cash buyers, discrimination
against prohibited, **255D:10A.**
Cash register total, concealment
from customer, **98:56C.**
Certificates or coupons.
Completion certificate, when
required, **255D:9A.**
Coupons, defined, **255D:1.**
Merchandise certificate or
coupons. See within this
heading, "Merchandise
certificate or coupons."
Required statement as to right
of return, **255D:11A,
255D:11B.**
Charges.
Collection charges on default,
255D:20.
Extension agreement, inclusion
of statement of charges,
255D:16.
Fees. See within this heading,
"Fees."
Finance charges. See within this
heading, "Finance charges."
Insurance, charges to buyer,
255D:26.
Violations as barring collection,
255D:29.
Collateral, taking possession of,
after default, **255D:22.**
Commercial Code provisions,
106:2-612, 106:9-201.
Completion certificate, when
required, **255D:9A.**
Concealment of cash register total
from customer, **98:56C.**
Confession of judgment provision
prohibited from inclusion in
agreement, **255D:10.**
Consolidation agreements.
Extensions, provisions, **255D:16.**
Provisions, **255D:17, 255D:18.**
Security interests, effect,
255D:15.
Consumers.
See CONSUMERS AND
CONSUMER
PROTECTION.

**RETAIL INSTALLMENT SALES
AND SERVICES** —Cont'd
Contracts, **106:2-612.**
Assignment or transfer of
agreement. See within this
heading, "Assignment or
transfer of agreement."
Consolidation agreements. See
within this heading,
"Consolidation agreements."
Installment sales agreement.
See within this heading,
"Installment sales
agreements."
Limitation of consumer
protection actions involving,
260:5A.
Revolving credit agreement. See
within this heading,
"Revolving credit
agreement."
Coupons.
Certificates or coupons. See
within this heading,
"Certificates or coupons."
Courts.
Avoidance of installment
agreements, **255D:29.**
Superior courts. See within this
heading, "Superior court."
Default.
Delinquency and collection
charges, **255D:20.**
Notice, **255D:21.**
Redemption by buyer after
repossession by seller,
255D:22.
Repossession of goods subject to
security interest, **255D:21.**
Defenses of creditors, sales finance
companies subject, **255:12F.**
Deficiency judgment against buyer,
255D:21, 255D:22.
Definitions, **255D:1.**
Delinquency and collection charges
on default, **255D:20.**
Delivery of agreements,
cancellation prior, **255D:14.**
Deposits, refund, **255D:14.**
Description or identification of
security interest stated in
agreement, **255D:9.**
Disclosure, **255D:9, 255D:18A,
255D:27.**
Discovery.
See DISCOVERY AND
DISCLOSURE.
Downpayment, defined, **255D:1.**
Energy conservation equipment,
purchase by cities and towns,
40:4.

RETAIL INSTALLMENT SALES AND SERVICES —Cont'd

Enforcement of law, **255D:6.**

Entry on premises of buyer for purpose of repossession, **255D:10.**

Examination or investigation.
Sales finance companies. See within this heading, "Sales finance companies."

Extension agreements, terms and conditions, **255D:16.**

Extension of credit on sales agreements, notice to buyer, **255D:18A.**

Fees.
Licensing of sales finance company, **255D:2, 255D:3.**
Motor vehicle retail installment sales.
See MOTOR VEHICLE RETAIL INSTALLMENT SALES.
Official fees, **255D:1, 255D:11.**
Relocation investigation fee, **255D:2.**

Finance charges, **255D:1, 255D:11.**
Computation, **255D:11, 255D:18A.**
Consumer note obtained in violation of law as affecting recovery, **255:12C.**
Disclosure statements, **255D:18A.**
Form of retail installment sales agreements, **255D:9.**
Open-end credit accounts, computation of finance charges in connection, **140:114B.**
Refinancing agreements, **255D:16, 255D:17.**
Refund, **255D:13.**
Revolving credit agreement, assessment of charge, **255D:27.**
Violations as barring recovery, **255D:29.**

Finance corporations.
Sales finance companies. See within this heading, "Sales finance companies."

Fines and penalties.
Installment sales agreements, violations as barring recovery of certain charges, **255D:29.**
Motor vehicle retail installment sales, **255B:21.**
Failure to file reports, **255B:3.**
Obstructing investigations, **255B:4.**

RETAIL INSTALLMENT SALES AND SERVICES —Cont'd

Fines and penalties —Cont'd
Reports by sales finance company, failure to make, **255B:3, 255D:3.**
Sales finance companies. See within this heading, "Sales finance companies."
Violation of provisions of chapter, punishment, **255D:30.**

Forms, **255D:9, 255D:10.**
Disclosure as to extension or modification of credit, **255D:18A.**
Notice of cancellation, **255D:9.**

Fraud in application for license as basis for suspension or revocation, **255D:7.**

Gift certificate, defined, **255D:1.**

Goods and commodities, defined, **255D:1.**

Hearing for suspension or revocation of sales finance company license, **255D:8.**

Holder.
As subject to buyer's defenses against seller, **255D:25A.**
As subject to chapter, **255D:25, 255D:25A.**
Definition, **255D:1.**

Husband and wife, limitation on execution of agreements, **255D:11.**

Installment buyer, defined, **255D:1.**

Installment sales agreements.
Assignment, **255B:18, 255D:12.**
Cancellation for other than seller's breach, **255D:14.**
Courts, avoidance, **255D:29.**
Definition, **255D:1.**
Delivery of copy to buyer, **255D:9.**
Express warranty, provisions limiting, excluding or modifying, **255D:10.**
Extension of credit, notice to buyer, **255D:18A.**
Extensions, provisions, **255D:16.**
Finance charges, **255D:11.**
Form and content, **255D:9, 255D:10.**
Holder of, as subject to provisions of chapter, **255D:25, 255D:25A.**
Limitation of number executed by same parties at same time, **255D:11.**

RETAIL INSTALLMENT SALES AND SERVICES —Cont'd

Installment sales agreements —Cont'd
Limitations and restrictions. See within this heading, "Limitations and restrictions as to installment sales agreements."
Notice, **255D:12, 255D:18A.**
Payment. See within this heading, "Payment."
Purchase and assignment, **255D:12.**
Statements of account, **255D:19.**
Violations as barring recovery of certain charges, **255D:29.**
Waiver of protection afforded to buyer.
Prohibited provisions, **255D:10.**
Statement in agreement, **255D:24.**

Installment seller, defined, **255D:1.**

Insurance.
Additional costs resulting from extension agreements, **255D:16.**
Charges to buyer, **255D:26.**
Credit insurance.
See CREDIT INSURANCE.
Goods sold, **255D:26.**
Life insurance. See within this heading, "Life insurance."
Motor vehicle installment sales credit insurance, refunds, **255B:10.**
Premium finance agency, exemption from provisions as to licensing, **255C:2.**
Refunds in connection, **255D:26.**

Interest on money.
Finance charges. See within this heading, "Finance charges."

Investigations.
Sales finance companies. See within this heading, "Sales finance companies."

Licensing of sales finance companies, **255D:2.**
Appeals.
From orders suspending or revoking license, **255D:8.**
From refusals to license, **255D:5.**
Banking institutions, **255B:2, 255D:2.**
Fees, **255D:2, 255D:3.**
Insurance premium finance agency, exemption from provisions as to licensing, **255C:2.**

RETAIL INSTALLMENT SALES AND SERVICES —Cont'd

Licensing of sales finance companies —Cont'd

Refusal to license, provisions, **255D:2, 255D:5.**

Rules and regulations concerning, **255D:3.**

Suspension and revocation of license. See within this heading, "Suspension and revocation of sales finance company license."

Life insurance.

Coverage on buyer, **255D:26.**

Credit insurance.

See CREDIT INSURANCE.

Sales finance companies, life insurance companies authorized to invest, **175:63.**

Limitation of consumer protection actions involving, **260:5A.**

Limitations and restrictions as to installment sales agreements.

Express warranty, **255D:10.**

Husband and wife, limitation on execution of agreements, **255D:11.**

Modification of agreements, **255D:18A.**

Number of agreements executed by same parties at same time, **255D:11.**

Loan transactions by seller in connection with sale of goods or services, **255D:22A.**

Mailing of notice as sufficient requirement for delivery, **255D:32.**

Merchandise certificate or coupons.

Buyer's right to return for credit, **255D:11A, 255D:11B.**

Defined, **255D:1.**

Modification of sales agreement, **255D:18A.**

Motor vehicle retail installment sales, **255B:1 et seq.**

See MOTOR VEHICLE RETAIL INSTALMENT SALES.

Nonresident buyers as protected, **255D:1.**

Notice.

Assignment of installment sales agreement, **255D:12.**

Cancellation of installment sales agreement, **255D:9, 255D:14, 255D:27.**

Extension of credit, notice to buyer, **255D:18A.**

Hearings for suspension or revocation of licenses, **255D:8.**

RETAIL INSTALLMENT SALES AND SERVICES —Cont'd

Notice —Cont'd

Motor vehicle retail installment sales.

Financing law as applicable, **255B:5, 255B:8.**

Repossession after default, **255B:20A.**

Redemption of repossessed goods by buyer, requisites, **255D:22.**

Refusal of license, **255D:5.**

Repossession of goods subject to security interest, **255D:21.**

Revolving credit agreement, required contents, **255D:27.**

Sale or other disposition of security, **255D:21.**

When deemed delivered, **255D:32.**

Open-end credit accounts, computation of finance charges in connection, **140:114B.**

Payment.

Assignment of installment agreement without notice to buyer, effect, **255D:12.**

Downpayment, defined, **255D:1.**

Motor vehicle retail installment sales.

See MOTOR VEHICLE RETAIL INSTALMENT SALES.

Receipts, **255D:12.**

Release of security in collateral upon payment of obligations, **255D:28.**

Repossession of goods upon default, **255D:21.**

Penalties.

Fines and penalties. See within this heading, "Fines and penalties."

Power of attorney provision prohibited from inclusion in agreement, **255D:10.**

Prepaid finance charges statement included in agreement, **255D:13.**

Production of books and papers.

By sales finance company, requirement, **255D:3 et seq.**

Investigation of person other than licensee, **255D:6.**

Punishment.

Fines and penalties. See within this heading, "Fines and penalties."

Rates.

Charges. See within this heading, "Charges."

RETAIL INSTALLMENT SALES AND SERVICES —Cont'd

Records.

Reports. See within this heading, "Reports."

Redemption by buyer after repossession by seller, **255D:21, 255D:22.**

Refinancing agreements, provisions, **255D:16, 255D:17.**

Refunds.

Credit for prepayment, **255D:13.**

Effect of cancellation of retail installment sales agreements, **93:48, 255D:14.**

In connection with insurance coverage, **255D:26.**

Motor vehicle retail installment sales.

See MOTOR VEHICLE RETAIL INSTALMENT SALES.

Release of security in collateral, furnishing to buyer on payment of obligations, **255D:28.**

Relocation of sales finance company office, investigation fee, **255D:2.**

Repair or improvement transactions, **255D:9A.**

Reporting agencies, private detective licensing provisions inapplicable, **147:23.**

Reports.

Fines for failure to file, **255B:3, 255D:3.**

Sales finance company, reports by, **255D:3.**

Repossession of goods, **255D:21.**

Entry on premises of buyer for purposes, **255D:10.**

Installment sales agreements, prohibited provisions, **255D:10.**

Notice. See within this heading, "Notice."

Redemption of repossessed goods, **255D:21, 255D:22.**

Retention of goods, time, **255D:22.**

Sale of repossessed goods, **255D:21.**

Violations of law as affecting right, **255D:29.**

Rescission.

Cancellation or rescission. See within this heading, "Cancellation or rescission."

RETAIL INSTALLMENT SALES AND SERVICES —Cont'd

Restrictions.
Limitations and restrictions. See within this heading, "Limitations and restrictions as to installment sales agreements."
Return of property.
Merchandise certificate or coupons, buyer's right to return for credit, **255D:11A, 255D:11B.**
Merchandise returned upon cancellation of, parties' rights and obligations, **255D:14.**
Revocation.
Suspension and revocation. See within this heading, "Suspension and revocation of sales finance company license."
Revolving credit agreement, **255D:27.**
Credit life insurance, **255D:26.**
Definition, **255D:1.**
Finance charge, assessment, **255D:27.**
Interest rate, how stated, **255D:27.**
Repossession of goods on default in payment, **255D:21.**
Signed, **255D:1.**
Statement of account, **255D:19.**
Time for notice of change in terms, **255D:27.**
Violations as barring recovery of certain charges, **255D:29.**
Waiver of protection afforded to buyer, statement in agreement, **255D:24.**
Sales agreements.
Installment sales agreements. See within this heading, "Installment sales agreements."
Sales finance companies.
Annual report, failure to submit, **255D:3.**
Banking institutions, **255B:2, 255D:2.**
Books and records required, **255D:3 et seq.**
Creditors' defenses, sales finance companies as subject, **255:12F.**
Definition, **255D:1.**
Examination fees, **255D:3.**
Fines and penalties GEN, **255D:4.**

RETAIL INSTALLMENT SALES AND SERVICES —Cont'd

Sales finance companies —Cont'd
Investigations.
Fee for relocating office, **255B:2, 255D:2.**
Of licensees, **255D:4.**
Of persons other than licensees, **255D:6.**
Licensing. See within this heading, "Licensing of sales finance companies."
Life insurance companies as authorized to invest, **175:63.**
Motor vehicles.
See MOTOR VEHICLE RETAIL INSTALMENT SALES.
Savings and loan associations, **255D:2.**
Suspension and revocation of license. See within this heading, "Suspension and revocation of sales finance company license."
Security interest.
Creation, **255D:15.**
Default, **255D:21.**
Definition, **255D:1.**
Effect of laws governing, **106:9-203.**
Release of security in collateral upon payment of obligations, **255D:28.**
Statutory regulation, effect of Uniform Commercial Code, **106:9-201.**
Seller's obligations upon cancellation, **255D:9, 255D:14.**
Services, definition, **255D:1.**
Shipped goods, cancellation of agreement as affecting ownership, **255D:14.**
Statutory regulation of, effect of Uniform Commercial Code, **106:9-201.**
Superior court.
Installment sales agreements, avoidance, **255D:29.**
Licensing of sales finance companies, appeals, **255D:5, 255D:8.**
Suspension and revocation of sales finance company license.
Grounds, **255D:7.**
Hearing, **255D:8.**
Transfer of agreement.
Assignment or transfer of agreement. See within this heading, "Assignment or transfer of agreement."

RETAIL INSTALLMENT SALES AND SERVICES —Cont'd

Truth in lending.
See TRUTH IN LENDING.
Waiver.
Installment sales agreements, **255D:10, 255D:24.**
Protection afforded by law, **255D:24.**
Work commenced within three business day cancellation period, responsibility, **93:48, 255D:9.**

RETAINED REVENUE.
Defined, **29:1.**
Teachers' retirement system, monthly withholdings from pensions, annuities, or retirement allowance, **32:19B.**
Subject to child support enforcement, **32:19C.**
Withholdings, monthly pensions, annuities, or retirement allowances of teachers, **32:19B.**
Child support enforcement. Withholdings subject to child support liens, **32:19C.**

RETALIATION.
See REPRISALS AND RETALIATION.

RETARDED PERSONS, 19:1 et seq.
See MENTALLY ILL AND RETARDED PERSONS.

RETIREMENT SYSTEMS AND PENSIONS, 32:1 et seq.
Abandonment of employee benefit trust distributions, presumption, **200A:5C.**
Abolition of county governments.
Benefits for employees of abolished counties, **34B:18.**
County retirement systems, continuance, **34B:19.**
Abolition of office or position as affecting amount of pension, **32:10, 32:91A.**
Absence.
Creditable service, **32:4.**
Leave of absence. See within this heading, "Leave of absence, effect."
Retirement in absence of pension system, **32:84.**
Superannuation retirement allowance, **32:5.**
Acceptance of act by cities, towns, and districts, **32:28, 32:54, 32:55.**
Funding schedules, establishment, **32:22D.**

RETIREMENT SYSTEMS AND PENSIONS —Cont'd

Acceptance of act by cities, towns, and districts —Cont'd

Policemen and firemen, acceptance of statute as to retirement, **32:57B.**

Revocation of acceptance, **40:4A.**

Veterans, acceptance of statutes in connection, **32:56, 32:60.**

Accidental death benefits, **32:9.**

Additional pension for dependents, **32:7, 32:9.**

Allowances to beneficiaries pending determination of claims, **32:12A.**

Amount of allowance, **32:7, 32:9.**

Armed forces of Commonwealth, compensation to dependents upon death of member, **33:8.**

Conditions for allowance, **32:7, 32:9.**

Court officers, **32:66.**

Dependents.

Additional pension, **32:7, 32:9.**

Natural guardian of minor dependent, report, **32:9.**

Payments, **32:7, 32:9.**

Policemen and firemen, **32:89 et seq.**

Determination of dependency, **32:9.**

Disability.

Physical or mental incapacity. See within this heading, "Physical or mental incapacity."

Eligibility of member upon recovery from disability, **32:3.**

Guardian or conservator. See within this heading, "Guardian or conservator."

Hearing, **32:16.**

Increase in certain, **32:7, 32:9, 32:81B, 32:83A, 32:85E, 32:90A.**

Involuntary retirement, **32:16.**

Loaned employee injured while aiding other governmental unit, **32:7.**

Medical examination. See within this heading, "Medical examination."

Municipal systems and pensions, death benefits, **32:89A.**

Natural guardian of minor dependent, report, **32:9.**

Notice of death or injury, **32:7, 32:9.**

Policemen and firemen. See within this heading, "Policemen and firemen."

RETIREMENT SYSTEMS AND PENSIONS —Cont'd

Accidental death benefits —Cont'd

Proration for injury sustained in other governmental unit, **32:7.**

Public health commissioner to aid in determination, **32:6.**

Reduction, suspension, or revocation upon reexamination, **32:8.**

Reexamination of retired members, **32:8.**

Restoration of members to active service, **32:8.**

Revocation on amount, **32:9.**

Scrub women in state house, **32:74.**

State police, **32:26.**

Survivor allowance, **32:9.**

Accidental disability retirement, **32:7, 32:8.**

Armed forces of Commonwealth, **33:8.**

Call firemen, retirement of injured, **32:85H.**

Loaned employee injured while aiding other governmental unit, **32:7.**

Metropolitan police, **32:90A.**

Police or firemen, **32:7, 32:94, 32:94A, 32:100.**

Return to service.

Evaluation of ability to perform, **32:26.**

State police.

Reinstatement after disability retirement, **22C:24A.**

State policemen, retirement of injured, **32:26.**

Accountants.

Review of plan, **151D:3A.**

Town accountant, compensation, **32:20.**

Accounts.

See ACCOUNTS AND ACCOUNTING.

Accrued death benefits, firemen's relief as affected by death annuities, **48:83.**

"Accrued portion of normal retirement benefit" defined, **151D:1.**

Accrued rights when chapter 350.

General acts of 1919, became effective, **32:93.**

Accumulated additional deductions.

Defined, **32:1.**

Survival benefits as affected, **32:12B.**

RETIREMENT SYSTEMS AND PENSIONS —Cont'd

Accumulated additional deductions —Cont'd

Time of application for withdrawal, **32:22.**

Accumulated regular deductions, defined, **32:1.**

Accumulated total deductions.

Defined, **32:1.**

Return of. See within this heading, "Return of accumulated total deductions."

Survival benefits as affected, **32:12B.**

Transfer to annuity reserve fund on retirement, **32:22.**

Accumulated vacation allowances upon separation from service, payment, **29:31A.**

Accumulation of assets, credits, **138:21.**

Actions.

Contributory retirement systems.

Beneficiaries, actions on behalf, **151D:3.**

Recovery of contributions, actions, **151D:11.**

Trust fund, action for depletion, **151D:3.**

Depletion of funds, actions, **151D:3.**

Excess earnings of pensioner employed in public service, action to recover, **32:91.**

Incompetents or minors, actions on behalf, **32:17.**

Reimbursement of pension fund.

Loaned employee injured while aiding other governmental unit, **32:7.**

Transferred employee, **32:3.**

Actuarial equivalent, defined, **32:1.**

Actuary.

Assets and liabilities, actual valuation, **32:21.**

Defined, **32:1.**

Duties, **32:21.**

Appropriations, duties, **32:22.**

Information, **32:22.**

Reports, actuarial valuation, **32:21.**

Additional contributions.

Creditable service allowance, **32:4.**

For additional retirement allowance, **32:3.**

RETIREMENT SYSTEMS AND PENSIONS —Cont'd

Additional deductions.

Accumulated additional deductions. See within this heading, "Accumulated additional deductions."

Defined, **32:1.**

For additional annuity, **32:22.**

Additional retirement allowances, makeup payments, **32:3.**

Administration and finance executive office.

Retirement law commission as agency within, **7:4G.**

Teachers' retirement board as agency within, **7:4G.**

Administration by board, **15:16, 32:20.**

Administration expenses.

Expenses of administration and operation. See within this heading, "Expenses of administration and operation."

Administrator of retirement, employment of by state treasurer, **10:5.**

Administrator or executor of deceased member, payments, **32:11.**

Administrators of plan.

Bonds, **151D:12.**

Compliance with other laws of Commonwealth, **151D:10.**

Defined, **151D:1.**

Depletion of fund by or failure to pay beneficiaries, provisions, **151D:3.**

Embezzlement of funds or false reports, penalty, **151D:6.**

Investment of funds, **151D:16.**

Nonresident trustee or plan administrator, appointment of resident agent, **151D:3.**

Restrictions, **151D:3.**

Termination of plan, allocation of benefits in event, **151D:14.**

Adopted children, allowances, **32:12B.**

Adoption of general act or system as affecting existing system, **32:2, 32:28.**

Advance payments.

City, town, or county employees, **32:99.**

State employees, **32:98.**

Advice and advisory bodies.

Banks, advice on investment of funds, **32:23.**

RETIREMENT SYSTEMS AND PENSIONS —Cont'd

Advice and advisory bodies —Cont'd

Custodian, duties, **32:23.**

Investment advisory unit, **7:50.**

Pension matters, advisory committee, **7:50.**

Retirement boards as advisers, **32:23.**

Waiver of vested benefits provisions, copies of request for to be given to advisory committee, **151D:9.**

After retirement employment.

Employment after retirement. See within this heading, "Employment after retirement."

Age for retirement, **32:3, 32:5.**

Capability of continuing to perform, **32:90H, 32:90I.**

City firemen, **32:80, 32:81A.**

City policemen, **32:83, 32:83A.**

Deductions from salaries of employees working past mandatory retirement age, **32:90G, 32:95A.**

Elevator inspectors, **32:90F.**

Judges, **32:65A, 32:65B, 32:90F; MA Const Amend Art 98.**

Laborers, pensions, **32:77, 32:78.**

Maximum age. See within this heading, "Maximum age."

Municipal pensions for teachers, **32:43.**

Permit for certain employees to continue working after reaching mandatory retirement age, **32:90F.**

Prison employees, **32:46.**

Probation officers, **32:75.**

Public employees working beyond mandatory retirement age, **32:3, 32:90F, 32:90G, 32:90G½, 32:90G¾, 32:90J.**

State police officers and inspectors, **32:26.**

Superannuation retirement. See within this heading, "Superannuation retirements."

Town policemen and firemen, **32:85E.**

Agents.

Contributory retirement system for agents and agency employees, **175:36A.**

Nonresident trustee or plan administrator to appoint resident agent, **151D:3.**

RETIREMENT SYSTEMS AND PENSIONS —Cont'd

Agricultural and technical institutes.

Independent agricultural and technical schools.

Employees, **74A:18.**

Airports.

Logan International Airport. See within this heading, "Logan International Airport."

Alcoholic beverage tax, crediting of receipts, **138:21.**

Aldermen.

Selectmen or aldermen. See within this heading, "Selectmen or aldermen."

Alimony.

See DIVORCE AND ALIMONY.

Allocation of benefits in absence of acceptable method of plan termination, **151D:14.**

Allowances.

Accidental death benefits, allowances pending determination of claims, **32:12A.**

Additional allowances, **32:3, 32:56.**

Adopted children, allowances, **32:12B.**

Amount of allowances and pensions. See within this heading, "Amount of allowances and pensions."

Approval of increase in allowance, **32:97.**

Assignment of funds and allowance. See within this heading, "Assignments of funds and allowance."

Bankruptcy laws inapplicable to funds and allowances, **32:19, 32:41.**

Call firemen, **32:7.**

Computation of amount, **32:5.**

Conditions for allowance, **32:6, 32:7, 32:9, 32:13.**

County officers and employees, advance payment of allowances, **32:99.**

Deference of receipt of allowance due or resignation, removal, etc., **32:10.**

Exemption from attachment, execution, taxation, etc., **32:19.**

Guaranty, **32:25.**

Insolvency laws inapplicable to funds and allowances, **32:19, 32:41.**

RETIREMENT SYSTEMS AND PENSIONS —Cont'd

Allowances —Cont'd

Joint and last survivor allowance, option, **32:12.**

Lump sum settlement of small allowances, **32:13.**

Minimum guaranteed allowance, **32:25.**

Mortgage of, invalidity, **32:92.**

Other state's allowance to teachers, effect, **32:3.**

Payment of allowances and funds. See within this heading, "Payment of allowances and funds."

Pledge, **32:92.**

Sales of interest, **32:92.**

Survivor allowance. See within this heading, "Survivor allowance."

Termination retirement allowance. See within this heading, "Termination retirement allowance."

Transfer of rights or interest, invalid, **32:92.**

Veterans' Retirement Act, retirement allowances for employees covered, **32:58C, 32:58D.**

Waiver of part, **32:90B.**

Alteration.

Amendments, modifications, or alterations of plans. See within this heading, "Amendments, modifications, or alterations of plans."

Alternative superannuation retirement benefit program. Teachers, **32:104.**

Ambulance attendants in fire departments, classification, **32:3.**

Amendment of laws as to, effect, **32:25.**

Amendments, modifications, or alterations of plans.

Filing of with board, **151D:3.**

Reports of amendments to board, **151D:3.**

Summary of amendments to be given to employees, **151D:3.**

Amortization of losses sustained at sale or maturity of investments, **32:22.**

Amount of allowances and pensions, **32:5.**

Abolition of office or position as affecting, **32:10, 32:91A.**

RETIREMENT SYSTEMS AND PENSIONS —Cont'd

Amount of allowances and pensions —Cont'd

Accidental death benefits, **32:7, 32:9.**

Accidental disability retirement, **32:7.**

Aiding police or firemen, payments to dependents of persons dying while, **32:88.**

Amendment or repeal of statutes not to change, **32:25.**

Beneficiaries of deceased members, amounts due, **32:11.**

Call firemen suffering injury, pension, **32:85H.**

City fire departments, **32:81, 32:81B.**

City policemen, **32:83, 32:83A.**

Computation, **32:5, 32:13.**

Court officers, **32:66, 32:67.**

Death of public employees in performance of duty, annuities to dependents in case, **32:89 et seq.**

Disability benefits, **32:6, 32:7.**

Failure of reappointment or reelection, effect, **32:10.**

Firemen, **32:80 et seq.**

Group 1 or 2 classification, employees, **32:52.**

Guaranty, **32:25.**

Increase, **32:22, 32:80, 32:90A, 32:96, 32:97.**

Injured call firemen and special police officers, pension, **32:85H.**

Injury in line of duty causing retirement, **32:7, 32:8.**

Judges, **32:65A, 32:65B.**

Widows, **32:65C.**

Length of service as affecting, **32:56, 32:96, 32:97.**

Limitation of annual allowance to survivors under contributory retirement law, **32:12B.**

Mandatory retirement age, employment after, **32:90G¾.**

Municipal laborers, workmen, and the like, **32:77.**

Optional provisions as to pensions for policemen and firemen in towns, **32:81A, 32:81B, 32:83A, 32:85E, 32:85J.**

Policemen, **32:80 et seq.**

Prison employees, **32:48.**

RETIREMENT SYSTEMS AND PENSIONS —Cont'd

Amount of allowances and pensions —Cont'd

Probation officers, **32:76, 32:76A.**

Public safety department officers and inspectors, **32:26.**

Removal or discharge, effect, **32:10.**

Resignation, effect, **32:10.**

School janitors under municipal pension, **32:44, 32:45A, 32:45C.**

Scrubwomen in state house, pension, **32:74.**

Spanish and World War I veterans, **32:56, 32:57.**

Special police officers suffering injury, pension, **32:85H.**

State police officers and inspectors.

Retired for physical or mental incapacity, **32:26.**

Superannuation retirements, **32:5, 32:10.**

Surviving spouse of deceased public official or employee, maximum pension, **32:95B.**

Teachers, municipal pensions, **32:42, 32:43.**

Termination retirement allowances, amount, **32:10.**

Town firemen and policemen, retirement of, **32:85A, 32:85E.**

Two or more systems, membership, **32:3.**

Veterans, **32:10, 32:90G¾.**

Workers' compensation as affecting, **32:14.**

Annual allowance to survivors under contributory retirement law, limitation, **32:12B.**

Annual physical examination.

Medical examination. See within this heading, "Medical examination."

Annual statement or report, **151D:3.**

Board, reports, **32:20.**

Certain small funds, exemption from reporting requirements, **151D:3.**

Copies of annual reports, **32:22D, 151D:3.**

Data system, **32:21.**

Date for filing, **32:20, 32:23.**

Fee for filing, **151D:5.**

Financial condition of system, **32:16, 32:18.**

RETIREMENT SYSTEMS AND PENSIONS —Cont'd
Annual statement or report —Cont'd
Insurance carrier or service, annual report to show, **151D:3.**
Members of retirement system, statement furnished by board, **32:20, 32:22D.**
Private pension associations, **32:40.**
Retirement law commission, **10:35I.**
Summary, **151D:3.**
Annual valuation of assets by actuary, **32:21.**
Annuities and annuity contracts, **32:12, 175:132F.**
Aiding town police or firemen, payments to dependent of persons dying while, **32:88.**
Assignment, **32:19.**
Call firemen, annuities to dependents, **32:89, 32:89A, 32:89B.**
Child support enforcement.
Withholdings subject to child support liens, **32:19C.**
Colleges and universities, **15:18A.**
County systems.
Transmission of deductions to annuity funds, **32:22.**
Death of public employees in performance of duty, annuities to dependents in case, **32:89 et seq.**
Deferred income, use for purchase, **35:57.**
Deficit in annuity reserve fund, **32:22.**
Defined, **32:1.**
Employees of education department and public educational institutions, purchase of annuities, **15:18A.**
Excess of annuity reserve fund transferred to pension fund, **32:22.**
Exemption from attachment, execution, taxation, etc., **32:19.**
Firemen.
Dying in performance of duty, annuities to dependents, **32:89, 32:89A, 32:89B.**
Relief as affected, **48:83.**
Forest warden, annuity to dependents of, for death in line of duty, **32:89.**

RETIREMENT SYSTEMS AND PENSIONS —Cont'd
Annuities and annuity contracts —Cont'd
Funding agreements with holders of pension contracts, **175:132F.**
Group annuities.
Group annuity contract defined, **175:132A.**
Payment of premiums as regular compensation, **32:1.**
Retirement or pension plan contracts, **175:132F.**
Increase.
After retirement, **32:96, 32:97.**
Dependents of certain retired officers, annuities, **32:90A, 32:96, 32:97.**
Length of service, annuities to certain officials not entitled to pensions, etc., **32:95.**
Metropolitan policemen, annuities to dependents, **32:71.**
Mortgage of, invalidity, **32:92.**
Municipal hospital employees, purchase of annuities, **40:55.**
Officials not entitled to pensions, **32:95.**
Options with respect, **32:12.**
Payment of premiums as regular compensation, **32:1.**
Pledge of annuities, **32:92.**
Public charge, effect of annuitant becoming, **32:92.**
Reserve fund.
Annuity reserve fund. See within this heading, "Annuity reserve fund."
Retirement law commission, **10:35I.**
Sales of interest, **32:92.**
Savings fund.
Annuity saving fund. See within this heading, "Annuity saving fund."
Separate investment account, assignment of certain annuity contracts, **175:132F.**
Transfer of rights or interest, invalid, **32:92.**
Widow or children of county, city or town officer or employee, **32:89, 32:89A, 32:89C, 32:89D, 32:95, 32:95A, 32:100.**
Officials or employees not entitled to pensions, **32:95.**

RETIREMENT SYSTEMS AND PENSIONS —Cont'd
Annuities and annuity contracts —Cont'd
Withholdings from teachers' allowances, **32:19B.**
Annuity reserve fund, **32:22.**
Deficiency appropriation for annual reserve fund, **32:22.**
Defined, **32:1.**
Disposition of funds as of Jan 1, 1946, **32:27.**
Examination by actuary, **32:21.**
Regular interest, **32:22.**
Transfer of funds, **32:22.**
Annuity saving fund, **32:22.**
Additional deductions for additional annuity, **32:22.**
Deductions of members, **32:22.**
Defined, **32:1.**
Disposition of funds as of Jan. 1, 1946, **32:27.**
Industrial accident, payments for period interrupted, **32:14.**
Interest, regular, **32:22.**
Intrastate service credit in governmental units where no system existed, payments, **32:3.**
Library employees, duties of treasurer in connection with annuity saving fund, **32:22.**
Make-up payments, **32:3, 32:22.**
Method of financing, **32:22.**
Minimum wage law as affecting deductions, **32:22.**
Noncash maintenance allowance, computation of deductions in case, **32:22.**
Officers charged with withholding of deductions, **32:22.**
Out-of-state teacher's service, payments as to credit, **32:3.**
Reduction of deductions, **32:22.**
Regular interest, **32:22.**
Reinstatement or reentry into active service, make-up payments with respect, **32:3.**
Restoration after disability retirement, effect, **32:22.**
Suspension or termination of deductions, **32:22.**
Transfer.
Accumulated total deductions to annuity reserve fund upon retirement, **32:22.**
Amount credited on account of industrial accident leave to pension fund, **32:14.**

RETIREMENT SYSTEMS AND PENSIONS —Cont'd

Annuity saving fund —Cont'd
Transfer —Cont'd
Deductions transferred, **32:22.**
Make-up payments in case of transfer of reestablishment of membership, **32:3.**
Withdrawal of deductions paid into, **32:22.**
Workers' compensation, effect of receiving, **32:14.**
Appeal.
Contributory retirement appeal board, **32:16, 32:20, 32:21.**
Spanish and World War I veterans retired for incapacity, right, **32:57A.**
Court.
Appeals court. See within this heading, "Appeals court."
Dereliction of duty by members, judicial review, **32:16.**
From involuntary retirement, **32:16.**
Time for passing, **32:16.**
Appeals court.
Associate justice or chief, calculation of pension, **32:65A.**
Judges retiring on or after January 2, 1975, **32:65D.**
Temporary service as affecting pension, **32:65F, 211A:16.**
Applicability to state system of health, welfare and retirement fund law, **151D:7.**
Application.
Accidental disability retirement, application, **32:7.**
Advance payments pending application for retirement, **32:98, 32:99.**
Employee in active service, application for membership, **32:3.**
Ordinary disability retirement, application, **32:6.**
Appointive officials.
Failure to be reelected or reappointed. See within this heading, "Failure to be reelected or reappointed."
Membership in state system, eligibility of appointive officers, **32:3.**
Previous retirement as affecting right to become member of contributory retirement system, **32:5.**

RETIREMENT SYSTEMS AND PENSIONS —Cont'd

Appropriations, **32:22, 32:22C.**
Commonwealth pension liability fund, **32:22C.**
County systems, **32:22.**
Deficiency appropriation for annual reserve fund, **32:22.**
Establishment of retirement funds by cities and towns, **40:5D.**
Financing, method of, **32:22.**
Health and welfare trust fund agreements, appropriations, **32B:15.**
Hospital districts, appropriations allocated, **32:22.**
Metropolitan police pensions and annuities, **32:72.**
Military service credits appropriations for special fund, **32:22.**
Pension funds, **32:22.**
Special law, effect of acceptance of general contributory system on appropriations provided, **32:28.**
Teachers' pensions, municipal appropriations, **32:22, 32:42, 32:43.**
Use of military service fund in reduction, **32:22.**
Approval of plans, **151D:2.**
Refusal of board to approve plan, petition in equity by trustees in probate court to compel approval in event, **151D:2.**
Armed forces.
Military service. See within this heading, "Military service."
Assessment of expenses of supervision, **32:21.**
Assets and liabilities.
Annual valuation by actuary, **32:21.**
Boards to keep data relating, **32:20.**
Crediting of assets to specific fund, **32:22.**
Investments, valuation, **32:22.**
Pension liability fund. See within this heading, "Pension liability fund."
Assignments of funds and allowance, **32:19, 32:19A, 32:39 et seq., 32:92, 32A:10.**
Investment income account, assignment of certain pension contracts to separate, **175:132F.**

RETIREMENT SYSTEMS AND PENSIONS —Cont'd

Associations, private, **32:39 et seq., 151D:1 et seq.**
Assumed name, fee for filing statement of retirement from business conducted, **262:34.**
Athletic program teachers, included, **32:1.**
Attachment or execution.
Exemption from attachment, execution, taxation. See within this heading, "Exemption from attachment, execution, or taxation."
Attainment of maximum group age, retirement, **32:3.**
Attorney general's authority to restrain violations, **151D:15.**
Attorneys at law, employment of private attorney by retirement board, **32:20.**
Auditors.
City auditor, compensation for administration, **32:20.**
Contributory retirement systems, audits by public accountants, **32:21.**
Payment of pensioner for services rendered, **32:91.**
Automobiles.
Motor vehicles. See within this heading, "Motor vehicles."
Bankruptcy laws inapplicable to funds and allowances, **32:19, 32:41.**
Banks.
Advice on investment of funds, **32:23.**
Check cashing limits of pensioners, **167:46.**
Cooperative banks.
See COOPERATIVE BANKS.
Credit unions.
See CREDIT UNIONS.
Custodian of securities held by retirement system, **32:23.**
Deposits and depositories. See within this heading, "Deposits and depositories."
Honoring and cashing checks of pensioners and retirees, **167:46.**
Investments, **32:23, 167F:2.**
Liquidation, creditable service of state employee serving, **32:4.**
Powers of banks, **167F:2.**
Savings banks.
See SAVINGS BANKS.

RETIREMENT SYSTEMS AND PENSIONS —Cont'd

Banks —Cont'd

Trust companies.
See TRUST COMPANIES.

Beach employees of cities and towns, retention of rights, **40:12F.**

Beneficiary defined, **32:1, 151D:1.**

Benefits.

Child support enforcement.
Deductions for arrearages for issuance of benefits, **32:11.**

Blue Hills regional vocational school, retirement systems for employees, **32:1 et seq.**

Board of health, welfare and retirement trust funds, **151D:1 et seq.**

Amendments, modifications, or alterations of plans, filing, **151D:3.**

Examination of books and investigation of administration of trust, **151D:3.**

Refusal to approve plan or trust, petition by trustees in equity to compel approval, **151D:2.**

Board of higher education, **15A:40.**

Boards of retirement, **10:18 et seq., 32:20.**

Advisory council to county retirement board, **32:20.**

Appropriations, duties with respect, **32:22.**

Assets and liabilities, board to keep data relating, **32:20.**

Books and records, examination, **32:16, 32:20.**

Cities and towns, systems for, **32:20.**

Clerical assistants to boards, **10:20, 15:18.**

Compensation of retirement board members, **32:20.**

Continuation of orders and regulations under prior law, **32:2.**

Contributory Retirement Appeal Board, **32:16.**

Correctional institution employees, authority of state boards as to pensioning, **32:46.**

County retirement systems, **32:20.**

RETIREMENT SYSTEMS AND PENSIONS —Cont'd

Boards of retirement —Cont'd

County treasurer as member, **32:20.**

Creditable service, duties in connection, **32:4.**

Defined, **32:1.**

Deputy state treasurer, investments for board, **10:5C.**

Early intervention plans established, **32:5B.**

Eligibility of retired employees as members, **10:18, 32:20.**

Employees' records to be kept, **32:20.**

Employment.

Custodians for securities, **32:23.**

Investment advisers, **32:23.**

Evidence before, **32:16, 32:20.**

Expenses, **32:20.**

Financial reports, **32:23.**

General powers and duties, **32:20.**

Indemnification of members, **32:20A.**

Investment of funds by county and municipal boards, **32:23.**

Involuntary retirement, hearing, **32:16.**

Laborers, authority as to pensions, **32:77.**

Leaves of absence, **32:3.**

Members and membership. See within this heading, "Members and membership."

Municipal boards, **32:20.**

Options, notice, **32:12.**

Part-time, etc., employees, rules and regulations as to superannuation retirement allowance, **32:5.**

Policemen and firemen, authority as to pensions, **32:80, 32:81A, 32:83, 32:85.**

Optional provisions as to pensions, **32:81A, 32:85E.**

Park boards of cities and towns, retirement of police forces, **32:85B.**

Widows of fire fighters or police officers killed in performance of duty, administration of pensions, **32:100.**

Prior service certificates, issuance, **32:4.**

RETIREMENT SYSTEMS AND PENSIONS —Cont'd

Boards of retirement —Cont'd

Private attorney, employment, **32:20.**

Private systems, board for supervision of.

Board of Health, welfare and retirement trust funds.
See within this heading, "Board of health, welfare and retirement trust funds."

Probation officers, pensions, **32:75.**

Removal or discharge of members, hearing, **32:16.**

Retirement certificates, issuance, **32:4.**

Rules and regulations of boards, **32:20, 32:21, 32:24.**

School janitors, municipal pensions, **32:44 et seq.**

Special act, acceptance of general act by city or town as affecting board, **32:28.**

State board, **10:18, 32:20.**

Appointment of member by insurance commissioner, **10:18.**

"Appropriate public authority," defined, **32:89, 32:89A.**

Clerical staff, appointed by state treasurer, **10:20.**

Commonwealth checks, payment, **29:32.**

Correctional institution officers, retirement, **32:46.**

Insurance commissioner to appoint member, **10:18.**

Powers and duties, **32:20.**

Reimbursement.

By districts for pensions or allowances made to retired employees of district, **32:28.**

Loss of salary for members, reimbursement for expenses, **10:19.**

Report, **32:20.**

"Retiring authority of Commonwealth," defined, **32:59.**

State treasurer as chairman, **10:18.**

Teachers' retirement system. See within this heading, "Teachers' retirement system."

RETIREMENT SYSTEMS AND PENSIONS —Cont'd

Boards of retirement —Cont'd
Vacancy in municipal retirement board, notice, **32:20.**
Witnesses before, **32:16, 32:20.**
Bonds, surety.
Failure to file certification, **151D:12.**
Teachers' retirement system, bond for secretary of board, **15:18.**
Trustee, plan administrator, or other officer, bond, **151D:2, 151D:12.**
Books.
Records. See within this heading, "Records."
Boston.
Judges in courts of, pensions, **32:65A, 32:65B.**
Juvenile court.
See BOSTON JUVENILE COURT.
Municipal court.
Municipal court of Boston. See within this heading, "Municipal court of Boston."
Probation officers, pensioning, **32:75 et seq.**
School janitors' municipal pensions as applicable, **32:44 et seq.**
Teachers' retirement system. See within this heading, "Teachers' retirement system."
Boston Arena Authority, employees of, included in state employees' retirement system, **32:1, 32:2.**
Bradford Durfee College of Technology, privileges of officers and employees, **74:42O.**
Brothers and sisters as beneficiaries, **32:12.**
Budget estimate to include contributions by Commonwealth, **29:9A.**
Business corporation, powers, **156B:9.**
Bylaws.
Employment security, **170:31.**
Private pension associations, **32:40.**
Cadet engineers in municipal light or gas plants, **164:69E.**
Call firemen, **32:82, 32:85A, 32:85D.**
Amount of accidental disability allowance, **32:7.**

RETIREMENT SYSTEMS AND PENSIONS —Cont'd

Call firemen —Cont'd
Computation of full-time service, **32:7.**
Credit for service, **32:57B, 32:85G.**
Death in performance of duty, annuities to dependents in case, **32:89, 32:89A, 32:89B.**
Injured firemen, retirement, **32:85H.**
Cancer, death or disability in line of duty, **32:94B.**
Capitol police, group classification, **32:3.**
Cash refund annuity, option, **32:12.**
Cause of death of policemen or firemen, board to determine, **32:89, 32:89A, 32:89B.**
Certificates and certification.
Bonds, failure to file certification, **151D:12.**
County officers and employees, payment of pensions without certified orders of commissioners, **35:11.**
Creditable prior service, certificates, **32:4.**
Issuance of certificate of right to receive pension, **32:4.**
Pensioner employed in public service, certification, **32:91.**
Change in grade or nature of employment, **32:3.**
Change of beneficiary, **32:11.**
Chapter 350 of General Acts of 1919, effect on accrued rights prior to passage, **32:93.**
Checks for benefits.
Commonwealth checks, payment, **29:32.**
Honoring and cashing, **167:46.**
Time for presentation, **32:11.**
Children.
Incompetents or minors. See within this heading, "Incompetents or minors."
Child support enforcement.
Attachment of benefits, **119A:6A.**
Checking for arrearages before issuing benefits, **32:11.**
Filing required reports, **32:20.**
Teachers' retirement system.
Withholdings subject to child support liens, **32:19C.**
Cities.
Municipal systems and pensions. See within this heading, "Municipal systems and pensions."

RETIREMENT SYSTEMS AND PENSIONS —Cont'd

City and town clerks, **41:19B.**
Duties in connection with establishment of retirement system, **32:28.**
City and town treasurers.
Municipal systems and pensions. See within this heading, "Municipal systems and pensions."
City auditor, compensation for administration, **32:20.**
City charters.
See CITY CHARTERS.
City council.
Elderly retired governmental employees, acceptance of law, **32B:11B.**
Nonsalaried services of counselors as creditable service for retirement purposes, **32:4.**
City manager, effect of retired employee's appointment, **32:91.**
Civil service.
See CIVIL SERVICE.
Classification of groups, **32:3, 32:26.**
Coastal wardens, group classification, **32:3.**
Collective bargaining agreement, penalty for employer's failure to provide fringe benefits, **149:181.**
Colleges and universities.
Annuity contracts, **15:18A.**
Lowell Technological Institute building authority. See within this heading, "Lowell Technological Institute building authority."
New Bedford Institute of Technology, **71:16F, 74:42O.**
Optional retirement program, **15A:40.**
Reemployment of retired teachers as consultants or substitute teachers, **32:91.**
State colleges. See within this heading, "State colleges."
"Combination plan" or "split-funded plan," defined, **151D:1.**
Combined investment funds, establishment, **32:23.**
Commissioner of insurance.
Insurance commissioner. See within this heading, "Insurance commissioner."

RETIREMENT SYSTEMS AND PENSIONS —Cont'd

Commission on retirement law.
Retirement Law Commission.
See within this heading,
"Retirement Law
Commission."

Commonwealth, **32:1 et seq.**

Compensation.
City and town treasurers,
compensation as custodian
of funds, **32:20, 32:23,
32:42.**
City auditors, compensation for
services, **32:20.**
City counselors nonsalaried
services as creditable service
for retirement purposes,
32:4.
Classification of employees paid
by United States, **32:3.**
Custodian of system and funds,
32:20, 32:23, 32:42.
Deferred compensation program
established, **29:64, 29:64D.**
Emergency employment. See
within this heading,
"Emergency employment."
General court, payment of
compensation to retired
public employees rendering
services, **32:91.**
Group annuities, payment of
premiums as regular
compensation, **32:1.**
Leave of absence without pay,
32:3.
Minimum wage law. See within
this heading, "Minimum
wage law as affected by
payments."
Other states or federal
government, classification of
military department
employees whose
compensation is paid, **32:3.**
Payment of salary unpaid upon
retirement, **29:31.**
Payroll deductions from
compensation of members.
See within this heading,
"Payroll deductions from
compensation of members."
Pensioners rendering service to
city, **32:91.**
Periodic experience
investigation, salary
increases, **32:21.**
Policemen and firemen, holiday
pay as regular
compensation, **32:1.**

RETIREMENT SYSTEMS AND PENSIONS —Cont'd

Compensation —Cont'd
Retirement board members,
32:20.
Retirement law commission,
10:35I.
Services in departments,
pensioners' right to
payment, **32:91.**
Teacher, effect of compensation
as substitute on pension,
32:9.
Temporary compensation before
retirement, **32:85H.**
Town accountants, compensation
for services, **32:20.**
Vacation pay. See within this
heading, "Vacation pay."
Withholding deductions, from
compensation of members,
32:22.

Compulsory retirement, **151B:4.**

Conditions on payment of
allowances, **32:13.**

Conservation officers, group
classification, **32:3.**

Conservator.
Guardian or conservator. See
within this heading,
"Guardian or conservator."

Constitutional officers.
Defined, **32:1.**
Prior service before existence of
system, credit, **32:3.**

Constitution of Massachusetts.
Certain public officers not
allowed to draw pension,
**MA Const Part 2 Ch 6 Art
2.**
Judicial officers, retirement of,
**MA Const Part 2 Ch 3 Art
1.**

Consultants not employee for
retirement purposes, **32:1.**

Consumer price index,
cost-of-living adjustments in
pensions based, **32:102.**
Establishment of adjustment,
32:103.

Continuation of prior law, **32:2.**

Continued employment after age
seventy, **32:1, 32:3, 32:91.**

Contractual nature of rights,
32:25.

Contributions, **29:9A, 32:8, 32:21,
32:22.**

Contributory retirement systems,
32:1 et seq.

Conviction of crime, pension not
exempt from attachment or
execution in case, **235:34A.**

RETIREMENT SYSTEMS AND PENSIONS —Cont'd

Cooperative banks.
See COOPERATIVE BANKS.

Co-operative nominee partnerships
for benefit of state employees'
retirement funds, **32:23.**

Copies.
Amendment to plan, issuance to
employees, **151D:3.**
Annual reports, publication of
copies of by board, **151D:3.**
Waiver of vested benefits
provisions, copies of request
for to be given to advisory
committee, **151D:9.**

Corporations.
See CORPORATIONS.

Correctional institutions.
See CORRECTIONAL
INSTITUTIONS.

Corrections department.
Classification of employees,
32:28M.
Group classification of employees
in contributory system, **32:3.**

Cost-of-living adjustments, **32:102,
32:103.**

Credit union employees, **171:82.**

Costs of administration and
operation.
Expenses of administration and
operation. See within this
heading, "Expenses of
administration and
operation."

County commissioners.
Certified orders from county
commissioner, payment of
pensions without, **35:11.**
Continuing to work after
retirement age, **32:91.**

County systems, **32:20, 32:22.**
Advance payment to employees
eligible for retirement,
32:99.
Annual report of board, **32:20.**
Annuities. See within this
heading, "Annuities and
annuity contracts."
Appropriations, **32:22.**
Approval of increase in
allowances, **32:97.**
Assessment of supervision
expenses, **32:21.**
Boards of retirement. See within
this heading, "Boards of
retirement."
Certified orders of
commissioners, payment of
pensions without, **35:11.**

RETIREMENT SYSTEMS AND PENSIONS —Cont'd

County systems —Cont'd

Commissioners.

County commissioners. See within this heading, "County commissioners."

Credit unions, direct deposit of retirement income, **35:19C.**

Deductions from pension and retirement allowances, **35:19C.**

Defined, **32:1.**

Description, **32:2.**

Direct deposit of benefits, **35:19C.**

Elected officers, eligibility, **32:3.**

Group insurance premiums of retirees, **32B:9A.**

Guaranty of allowances by county, **32:25.**

Hospital district employee, **32:2, 32:20.**

Housing authorities, acceptance of general act, **32:28.**

Increase of allowances after retirement, **32:96, 32:97.**

Indictment for misconduct, effect on retirement benefits of suspension after, **268A:25.**

Insurance premiums of retired employees, contributing to cost, **32B:9A.**

Interest on money owing, **35:24.**

Investment of funds, **32:23.**

Nantucket, provision for establishment of system, **32:28.**

Noncontributory pensions, payment, **35:11.**

Payment of noncontributory pensions, **35:11.**

Powers and duties of board, **32:20.**

Regional health district offices and positions to be placed, **111:27B.**

Register of probate included, **32:2.**

Special funds for retirement purposes, establishment, **32:22.**

Suffolk County. See within this heading, "Suffolk County."

Superannuation retirement, alternate method of computing allowance, **32:5.**

Suspension of officer or employee after indictment for misconduct, effect upon retirement benefits, **268A:25.**

RETIREMENT SYSTEMS AND PENSIONS —Cont'd

County systems —Cont'd

Town employees included in, when, **32:28.**

Transmission of deductions to annuity fund, **32:22.**

Treasurers.

County treasurers. See within this heading, "County treasurers."

Withholdings, **32:22.**

County treasurers.

Advance payment of retirement allowance to employees, **32:99.**

Board, member, **32:20.**

Deductions from pension and retirement allowances, **35:19C.**

Interest on money owing to county system, **35:24.**

Notice to debtor of system, treasurer to give, **35:24.**

Payment of noncontributory pensions, **35:11.**

Treasurer-custodian of system, **32:23.**

Court officers, **32:66, 32:67.**

Court review.

Appeal. See within this heading, "Appeal."

"Covered service" defined, **151D:1.**

Creditable service, **32:4.**

Absence as affecting, **32:4.**

Active duty, members of armed forces reserve units called, **32:58A.**

Additional contributions, credit, **32:4.**

Banks, creditable service of state employees serving in liquidation, **32:4.**

Boards of retirement, duties in connection, **32:4.**

Call firemen, **32:57B, 32:85G.**

Certificates, **32:4.**

Constitutional officer, credit for service before existence of system, **32:3.**

Contributions as precondition to receiving, **32:8.**

Defined, **32:1, 32:20.**

Dual membership, effect, **32:3, 32:4.**

Elective officials, **32:4.**

Employment and training division in labor and workforce department, **32:4.**

Federal government, creditable service in state system for teacher formerly employed, **32:4.**

RETIREMENT SYSTEMS AND PENSIONS —Cont'd

Creditable service —Cont'd

Filing and verification of statements of service, **32:4.**

General court members, **32:3.**

Injuries, period of absence due, **32:4.**

Intermittent police officer, **32:4.**

Intrastate service in governmental unit where no system existed, **32:3, 32:4.**

Involuntary retirement, creditable service during leave of absence for service in United States Department of State, **32:4.**

Judges, **32:4.**

Leave of absence, effect, **32:3, 32:4.**

Length of service. See within this heading, "Length of service."

Make-up payments as entitling late membership, **32:3.**

Mandatory retirement age, employment after, **32:90G½, 32:90G¾.**

Membership certificates, **32:4.**

Military or naval service, period, **32:4, 32:5, 32:58A.**

Nonsalaried services, credit for certain, **32:4.**

Out-of-state service of teachers, **32:3, 32:4.**

Part-time employees, **32:4.**

Permanent intermittent police officer, service, **32:4.**

Policemen and firemen, **32:85G, 32:85I.**

Intermittent police officer, **32:4.**

Reserve policemen or call firemen, **32:57B, 32:85G 32:4 4.**

Qualifications, **32:4.**

Reinstatement or reentry to active service, **32:3, 32:8.**

Veteran, **32:4, 32:5, 32:58A.**

Reserve policemen, **32:57B, 32:85G.**

Restoration to active service after disability, effect, **32:8.**

Retirement certificates, issuance, **32:4.**

School teachers formerly employed in state education department, **32:4.**

Spanish War veterans, **32:58A.**

Teachers' retirement system, **32:3, 32:4.**

RETIREMENT SYSTEMS AND PENSIONS —Cont'd

Creditable service —Cont'd

Transfer or reestablishment of membership, effect, **32:3.**

United States Department of State, creditable service during leave of absence for service, **32:4.**

Verification of statements, **32:4.**

Vesting of accrued retirement benefits after 10 years, **32:10.**

Veterans, **32:4, 32:5, 32:58A, 32:59A.**

Workers' compensation, during period of receiving, **32:14.**

World War I veterans, **32:58A.**

Credit unions.

See CREDIT UNIONS.

Criminal offenses, **32:15, 32:24, 151D:5, 151D:6, 151D:10.**

Felony convictions, payment to incarcerated members, **32:6, 32:7.**

Fines and penalties. See within this heading, "Fines and penalties."

Perjury. See within this heading, "Perjury as to statements in regard."

Cushing hospital employees as public employees, **32:3.**

Custodian of school, municipal pension, **32:44 et seq.**

Custodian of system and funds, **32:23.**

Administrators of plan. See within this heading, "Administrators of plan."

Banks as custodian of securities held by retirement system, **32:23.**

Boards of retirement employed, **32:23.**

Compensation for services, **32:20, 32:20 4, 32:23.**

Deposits and depositories. See within this heading, "Deposits and depositories."

List of securities held by system, duties of custodian, **32:23.**

State treasurer, **32:23.**

Data system, **32:21.**

Date.

Time or date. See within this heading, "Time or date."

Death and death benefits.

Accidental death benefits. See within this heading, "Accidental death benefits."

RETIREMENT SYSTEMS AND PENSIONS —Cont'd

Death and death benefits —Cont'd

Administrator or executor of deceased member, payments, **32:11.**

Aiding police or firemen, payments to dependents of person while, **32:88.**

Amounts due beneficiaries, payment, **32:11.**

Call firemen, annuities to dependents, **32:89, 32:89A, 32:89B.**

Crash crewmen or crash boatmen, Logan International Airport, **32:94B.**

Disposition of account of deceased member, **32:11, 32:12.**

Evidence as to fireman's death resulting from disease as suffered in line of duty, **32:94A.**

Group insurance coverage for surviving spouse and dependents, **32B:9B.**

Hypertension, death, **32:94.**

Judges, benefits for widows, **32:65C.**

Metropolitan police, **32:71.**

Military service credit fund, effect, **32:22.**

Options on retirement, death without naming beneficiary effect, **32:12.**

Pension fund rights in case of death prior to retirement, **32:11.**

Policemen or firemen, **32:89 et seq., 48:83.**

Survivor allowance. See within this heading, "Survivor allowance."

Debtor of county retirement system, treasurer to give notice, **35:24.**

Debts incurred in payment of, not to be questioned, **US Const Amend 14 Sec 4.**

Deceit.

Fraud. See within this heading, "Fraud."

Deductions of members.

Accumulated additional deductions. See within this heading, "Accumulated additional deductions."

Accumulated regular deductions defined, **32:1.**

RETIREMENT SYSTEMS AND PENSIONS —Cont'd

Deductions of members —Cont'd

Accumulated total deductions. See within this heading, "Accumulated total deductions."

Additional deductions. See within this heading, "Additional deductions."

Annuity savings fund, **32:22.**

Notices. See within this heading, "Notices."

Payroll deductions. See within this heading, "Payroll deductions from compensation of members."

Regular deductions, defined, **32:1.**

Return of. See within this heading, "Return of accumulated total deductions."

Withholding deductions, from compensation of members, **32:22.**

Defective delinquents, classification of state employees having custody, **32:3.**

Deferred compensation.

Allowance due on resignation, removal, etc., **32:10.**

Program established, **29:64, 29:64D.**

Use for purchase of life insurance or annuity contract, **35:37.**

Deficit.

Annuity reserve fund, **32:22.**

Investment income account, **32:22.**

Prior to appropriation, payment from treasury funds, **32:22.**

Definitions, **32:1, 32:59, 151D:1, 175:132A.**

Dental assistants in municipalities, retirement, **32:44C.**

Dental interns in municipal hospitals electing to join retirement system, **32:3.**

Dependents.

Accidental death benefits. See within this heading, "Accidental death benefits."

Accidental disability benefits, **32:7.**

Aiding town police or firemen, payments to dependents of person dying while, **32:88.**

RETIREMENT SYSTEMS AND PENSIONS —Cont'd

Dependents —Cont'd

Annuities, increase, **32:90A, 32:96, 32:97.**

Call firemen, annuities to dependents, **32:89, 32:89A, 32:89B.**

Death benefits.

Death. See within this heading, "Death and death benefits."

Determination, **32:9.**

Firemen's relief as affected by annuities, **48:83.**

Forest warden, annuity to dependent of, for death in line of duty, **32:89.**

Group insurance coverage, **32B:9B.**

Metropolitan policemen, annuities to dependents, **32:71.**

Minors.

Incompetents or minors. See within this heading, "Incompetents or minors."

Public charge, effect of annuitant becoming, **32:92.**

Public employees dying in performance of duty, annuities in case, **32:89 et seq.**

State policeman retired for illness or injury incurred in performance of duty, dependents, **32:26.**

Survivor allowance. See within this heading, "Survivor allowance."

Depletion of funds, action, **151D:3.**

Deposits and depositories, **32:23, 167D:29, 167D:30.**

Direct deposit or credit of retirement income or benefits, **29:31, 35:19C, 41:41C.**

Mandatory retirement age, deposits by members working beyond, **32:90G½, 32:90G¾.**

Public employees, pension and retirement funds, **32:23.**

Turnpike authority employee's retirement allowance, deposit in credit union, **32:20.**

Dereliction of duty by members, **32:15.**

Assignments for restitution, validity, **32:19.**

RETIREMENT SYSTEMS AND PENSIONS —Cont'd

Dereliction of duty by members —Cont'd

Judicial review, **32:16.**

Description of systems, **32:2.**

Direct deposit or credit of retirement income or benefits, **29:31, 35:19C, 41:41C.**

Directors of company, powers as to pensions, **175:36.**

Disability.

Physical or mental incapacity. See within this heading, "Physical or mental incapacity."

Disability retirement, **32:6 et seq.**

Accidental disability retirement. See within this heading, "Accidental disability retirement."

Amount of allowances and pensions. See within this heading, "Amount of allowances and pensions."

Amount of permissible income for veterans retired from public service, **32:56.**

Application, **32:6.**

Conditions for allowance, **32:6.**

Data system, **32:21.**

Eligibility, **32:3, 32:6.**

Hearing, **32:16.**

Hypertension disability, **32:94.**

Insurance commissioner, determination of total incapacitation or disability, **32:21.**

Insurance company officers and employees, **175:36, 175:36A, 175:36B.**

Involuntary retirement, **32:16.**

Line of duty, disability resulting from disease as suffered, **32:94A et seq.**

Medical examination. See within this heading, "Medical examination."

Municipal systems and pensions, authority to increase allowance of retired employees, **32:90D.**

Option available to public employee retired, **32:12.**

Physical fitness standards for police officers and firefighters, distinctions, **32:5.**

Policemen and firemen, **32:3, 32:6, 32:81B, 32:85E.**

RETIREMENT SYSTEMS AND PENSIONS —Cont'd

Disability retirement —Cont'd

Public health commissioner to aid in determination, **32:6.**

Reevaluation, **32:8.**

Reexamination of retired members, **32:8.**

Refund of disability benefits in case of excess earnings, **32:91A.**

Reinstatement or reentry into active service, **32:3, 32:8.**

State police, **32:3, 32:6.**

Reinstatement after disability retirement, **22C:24A.**

Survivor allowance, widows of public employees retired for disability, **32:101.**

Veterans, amount of permissible income, **32:56.**

Discharge.

Removal or discharge. See within this heading, "Removal or discharge from office or employment."

Discontinuance of benefits.

Suspension or discontinuance of benefits. See within this heading, "Suspension or discontinuance of benefits."

Discrimination, observance of terms of bona fide employee benefit plan, **151B:4.**

Disposition.

Child support enforcement. Checking for arrearages before issuing benefits, **32:11.**

Deceased member, disposition of account, **32:11, 32:12.**

Funds as of Jan 1, 1946, disposition, **32:27.**

Military service deductions of members, disposition, **32:12B, 32:22.**

District courts.

Involuntary retirement, judicial review, **32:16.**

Justices of, pensions and retirement benefits, **32:65A et seq.**

Reports as to removal or retirement of justices, **218:43, 231:108.**

Probation officers in, pensions, **32:75 et seq.**

Special justices, computation of pensions, **32:65B, 32:65C.**

Widows of certain judges, pension benefits, **32:65C.**

RETIREMENT SYSTEMS AND PENSIONS —Cont'd

Districts.

Acceptance of act by cities, towns, and districts. See within this heading, "Acceptance of act by cities, towns, and districts."

County system, regional health district offices and positions to be placed, **111:27B.**

Establishment of funds for retirement purposes, **40:5D.**

Expense fund, time for payment, **32:22.**

Fire district laborers, pensions, **32:78, 32:78A, 32:79.**

Fire wardens, classification, **32:3.**

Hospital districts. See within this heading, "Hospital districts."

Inclusion, **32:1.**

Increase of benefits in certain cases, **32:96, 32:97.**

Metropolitan districts. See within this heading, "Metropolitan districts."

Policemen and firemen. See within this heading, "Policemen and firemen."

Prudential committee, approval of increase of retirement allowances, pensions, etc., **32:97.**

Sewer district laborers, pensions, **32:78, 32:78A.**

Special funds for retirement purposes, establishment, **40:5D.**

State system, employees' right to membership, **32:2, 32:28.**

Superannuated employees, provision for approval of additional retirement benefits, **32:90C.**

Water district laborers, pensions, **32:78, 32:78A, 32:79.**

Dividends, duties of custodian of system, **32:23.**

Divorce.

See DIVORCE AND ALIMONY.

Dual membership, **32:3.**

Amount of allowances and pensions, **32:3.**

Creditable service in case, **32:3, 32:4.**

Existing systems, effect, **32:3.**

Military service credit fund, effect, **32:22.**

Suffolk County, provisions applicable to persons employed, **32:3.**

RETIREMENT SYSTEMS AND PENSIONS —Cont'd

Early intervention plans to be established, **32:5B.**

Earnings action to recover for excess earnings of pensioner employed in public service, **32:91.**

Economic development department, rights of employees, **23A:1.**

"Economic hardship" defined, **151D:1.**

Education.

Schools and education. See within this heading, "Schools and education."

Education department and commissioner.

Teachers' retirement system. See within this heading, "Teachers' retirement system."

Elder affairs department, unclassified positions within, **19A:10.**

Election or option.

Mandatory retirement age, employment after, **32:90G¾.**

Membership in plan, election, **32:3.**

Options on retirement. See within this heading, "Options on retirement."

Retired employees, election to contribute to insurance premiums, **32B:9A.**

Turnpike Authority employees' retirement and pensions, election between compensation and pension, **152:73.**

Veterans, optional benefits of surviving spouse, **32:58B.**

Widow and children, options and other rights, **32:12, 32:12B, 32:12C, 32:17.**

Elections.

Adoption by towns, cities, and districts, **32:28.**

Exemption of election officers from provision prohibiting payment of compensation to former public employees receiving pension or retirement allowance, **32:91.**

Failure to be reelected or reappointed. See within this heading, "Failure to be reelected or reappointed."

RETIREMENT SYSTEMS AND PENSIONS —Cont'd

Elections —Cont'd

Officers of elections, retired pensioners as entitled to payments for service, **32:91.**

Officials chosen by.

Elective officials. See within this heading, "Elective officials."

School janitor's municipal pension, acceptance of statute providing, **32:45.**

Towns, acceptance of contributory retirement act, **32:28.**

Elective officials.

Creditable service, **32:4.**

Failure to be reelected or reappointed. See within this heading, "Failure to be reelected or reappointed."

Impending retirement, elections in event, **50:6A.**

Membership in system, eligibility, **32:3, 32:5.**

Previous retirement by official public employee as affecting right to become member of contributory retirement system, **32:5.**

Superannuation retirement allowances, **32:5.**

Vacancy caused by, filling, **50:6A.**

Electricians, classification, **32:3.**

Electric plant owned by municipality.

Municipal lighting and heating plants. See within this heading, "Municipal lighting and heating plants."

Elevators.

Age of retirement for state elevator inspectors, **32:90F.**

Classification for retirement purposes of public employees employed as maintenance men, **32:3.**

Eligibility.

Advance payments to eligible employees, **32:99.**

Beneficiaries other than spouse, **32:58B.**

Restrictions under certain options, **32:12.**

Credit for service, **32:4.**

Disability, eligibility upon recovery, **32:3.**

Election to retirement board, eligibility of retired employees, **10:18, 32:20.**

RETIREMENT SYSTEMS AND PENSIONS —Cont'd

Eligibility —Cont'd

Females receiving public employment retirement benefits as eligible for additional allowances, **32:101.**

Membership, eligibility, **32:3, 32:5.**

Ordinary disability retirement, **32:3, 32:6.**

Owner-operator of motor carrier equipment, qualification for health, welfare, and pension benefit as employee as lessee, **159B:6A.**

Part-time employees, **32:3.**

Policemen and firemen, **32:85C.**

Reemployed persons, **32:3.**

State retirement system, employees with salaries derived from federal grants as eligible for membership, **32:3.**

Termination retirement allowance, **32:3.**

Embezzlement, **32:15, 151D:6.**

Emergency employment.

Retired physicians and nurses by public and mental health departments, **32:91.**

Temporary service by pensioners, compensation, **32:91.**

Police and firemen, **32:83A, 32:85B.**

Emergency medical technicians, **111C:15.**

"Employee" defined, **32:1.**

"Employee or labor organization" defined, **151D:1.**

Employee Retirement Income Security Act.

See INDIVIDUAL RETIREMENT ACCOUNT.

Employees health and welfare funds, **175:110.**

Employment after retirement.

Age seventy exceeded, **32:3, 32:91.**

City manager, effect of retired employee's appointment, **32:91.**

Emergency employment. See within this heading, "Emergency employment."

Excess earnings of pensioner employed in public service, action to recover, **32:91.**

Mental health department employees, **32:91.**

RETIREMENT SYSTEMS AND PENSIONS —Cont'd

Employment after retirement —Cont'd

Payment for services by retired employee, **32:91.**

Public service, pensioners employed, **32:91.**

Employment and training division in labor and workforce department, creditable service, **32:4.**

Employment security, **151A:25, 151A:28, 151A:29.**

See EMPLOYMENT SECURITY.

Endowment associations, private, **32:39 et seq.**

Energy Resources Executive Office, rights and status of officers and employees, **25A:4.**

Enforcement of contributory retirement laws, **32:24.**

Engineers in municipal light or gas plants, **164:69E.**

Environmental affairs executive office.

Experts and other assistants appointed in office, retirement status, **21A:6.**

Fire wardens as members of office's retirement system, **32:3.**

Environmental management department coastal wardens, group classification, **32:3.**

ERISA.

See INDIVIDUAL RETIREMENT ACCOUNT.

Essex agricultural and technical institute.

Benefits for employees of abolished counties, exception, **34B:18.**

Establishment of system.

City or town, **32:28.**

Employment security, **170:30.**

Turnpike Authority, **32:20.**

Estate tax.

Legacy and succession taxes. See within this heading, "Legacy and succession taxes, exemption."

Estimate of administration and operating costs, **32:20.**

Estoppel.

Waiver. See within this heading, "Waiver."

Evaluation of ability to perform. Return to service, **32:26.**

RETIREMENT SYSTEMS AND PENSIONS —Cont'd

Evidence.

Fireman's death or disability resulting from disease as suffered in line of duty, **32:94A.**

Presumptions. See within this heading, "Presumptions."

Retirement boards, evidence before, **32:16, 32:20.**

Witnesses. See within this heading, "Witnesses."

Examination, inspection, or investigation.

Annual physical examination for state inspectors, **32:90I.**

Auditors. See within this heading, "Auditors."

Books and records.

Health, welfare and retirement funds board, **151D:3.**

Private pension association, **32:40.**

Retirement boards, examination, **32:16, 32:20.**

Health, welfare, and retirement funds, **151D:3.**

Insurance commissioner, **32:21.**

Mandatory retirement age, annual physical and mental examination of members working beyond, **32:90G½.**

Medical examination. See within this heading, "Medical examination."

Mortality experience, investigation, **32:21.**

Motor vehicles registry investigator, dependents, **32:89.**

Retirement age of inspectors, **32:90F.**

Retirement law commission, **10:35I.**

System, examination, **32:21.**

Witnesses at investigation of health, welfare, and retirement funds, **151D:3.**

Exceptions and exemptions from law, **32:39, 151D:7, 175:29.**

Excess earnings of pensioner employed in public service, action to recover, **32:91.**

Excess of annuity reserve fund transferred to pension fund, **32:22.**

Executor or administrator of deceased member, payments, **32:11.**

RETIREMENT SYSTEMS AND PENSIONS —Cont'd

Exemption from attachment, execution, or taxation, **32:19, 32:41, 59:5, 246:28.**

Child support, interest in pension not protected in case, **235:34A.**

Conviction of crime, interest in pension not protected in case, **235:34A.**

Divorce, interest in pension not protected in case, **235:34A.**

Insurance of officers and employees, not subject, **175:36A, 175:36B.**

Legacy and succession taxes. See within this heading, "Legacy and succession taxes, exemption."

Private pension associations, **32:41.**

Public officers and employees, funds and benefits, **32:19, 32:23, 62:8.**

Railroads, **62:3.**

Separate maintenance, interest in pension not protected in case, **235:34A.**

Statement of exemptions in writ of trustee process, **246:28.**

Existing systems, effect, **32:2, 32:28.**

Disposition of funds, **32:27.**

Dual membership, **32:3.**

Guaranty of minimum allowances, **32:25.**

Laborers' pensions, **32:79.**

Expense fund, **32:22.**

Annual physical and mental examination for members working beyond mandatory retirement age, payment of fees and expenses, **32:90J.**

Appropriations, **32:22.**

Boards of retirement, payment of expenses, **32:20.**

Defined, **32:1.**

Disability examination expenses, **32:6.**

Disposition of funds as of Jan. 1, 1946, **32:27.**

Fees of medical panel, **32:6.**

Time for payment by towns and districts, **32:22.**

Expenses of administration and operation.

Fund for.

Expense fund. See within this heading, "Expense fund."

State board of retirement, **10:19.**

RETIREMENT SYSTEMS AND PENSIONS —Cont'd

Expenses of administration and operation —Cont'd

Teachers' retirement board, **15:17.**

Warrant to assess tax to defray, **32:21.**

Experience deficiency.

Defined, **151D:1.**

Special payments in cases, **151D:13.**

Failure or refusal to pay benefits, actions, **151D:3, 151D:10, 151D:11.**

Failure to be reelected or reappointed, **32:10.**

Hearing, **32:16.**

Superannuation retirement, right, **32:10.**

Termination retirement allowance. See within this heading, "Termination retirement allowance."

Failure to register fund, fine, **151D:2.**

False reports or statements.

Disability retirement, statement as to earnings after, **32:91A.**

Employee trust funds, filing false statements, **155D:6.**

Health, welfare, and retirement funds, **151D:6.**

Penalty for defrauding system by means of false statements, **32:18, 32:24.**

Perjury. See within this heading, "Perjury as to statements in regard."

Federal matters.

Other states or federal government. See within this heading, "Other states or federal government."

Fees.

Annual physical and mental examination for members working beyond mandatory retirement age, fees and expenses, **32:90J.**

Custodian of system and funds, **32:20, 32:23.**

Expense fund. See within this heading, "Expense fund."

Filing fees, **151D:5, 262:34.**

Witnesses.

Contributory retirement appeal board, **32:16, 32:20.**

Retirement boards, **32:20.**

Felony convictions, payment to incarcerated members, **32:6, 32:7.**

RETIREMENT SYSTEMS AND PENSIONS —Cont'd

Female members, survivorship benefits to children, **32:12B.**

Fiduciary standards established, **32:1, 32:2.**

Filing.

Amendments, modifications, or alterations of plans, filing of with board, **151D:3.**

Annual statements, date for filing, **32:20, 32:23.**

Assumed name, fee for filing statement of retirement from business conducted, **262:34.**

Fees, **151D:5, 262:34.**

Fines and penalties. See within this heading, "Fines and penalties."

Members' records, filing, **32:18.**

Physical or mental incapacity, **151D:3.**

Registration, filing fees, **151D:5.**

Service, statement, **32:4.**

Financial statements by boards or associations, **32:20, 32:23, 32:40.**

Fines and penalties.

Attachment and execution, pension not exempt in case of conviction of crime, **235:34A.**

Bond, failure to file certification, **151D:12.**

Contributions or benefits, failure to pay, **151D:11.**

Criminal offenses, **32:24, 151D:5, 151D:10.**

Embezzlement or misappropriation of trust funds, **32:15, 151D:6.**

Employer's failure to make contributions to pension fund, **149:181.**

Failure to file report, **151D:3.**

Failure to register, **151D:2.**

False statements, penalty for defrauding system by means, **32:18, 32:24.**

Imprisonment for violation of laws, **32:24.**

Misappropriation of property or funds by member, **32:15, 151D:6.**

Misconduct, forfeiture of benefits, **32:15.**

Private pension association, violation by custodian of books and papers, **32:40.**

Public employees' retirement or pension systems, violations relating, **32:24.**

RETIREMENT SYSTEMS AND PENSIONS —Cont'd

Fines and penalties —Cont'd

Rebate in connection with pension plan payments, **149:27.**

Refusal or failure of employer to make contributions or pay benefits, **151D:11.**

Transfer of rights in allowances, **32:92.**

Violations of retirement laws, **32:24.**

Fire districts.

Classification of fire wardens, **32:3.**

Laborers' pensions, **32:78, 32:78A, 32:79.**

Veterans' retirement act, effect, **32:58C.**

Firemen.

Policemen and firemen. See within this heading, "Policemen and firemen."

Fire wardens as members of retirement system of environmental affairs executive office, **32:3.**

Fiscal year changes, conforming, **32:22.**

Foreign state or country.

Other states or federal government. See within this heading, "Other states or federal government."

Forest warden, annuity to dependent of, for death in line of duty, **32:89.**

Forfeitures.

Fines and penalties. See within this heading, "Fines and penalties."

Former spouse as beneficiary under contributory retirement systems, **32:12.**

Former systems.

Existing systems. See within this heading, "Existing systems, effect."

IV-D agency.

Defined, **32:1.**

Fraternal benefit societies, employees, **176:56.**

Fraud.

Criminal liability, **151D:6.**

False reports or statements. See within this heading, "False reports or statements."

Filed statements, protection against fraud with respect, **32:18.**

RETIREMENT SYSTEMS AND PENSIONS —Cont'd

Funding agreements with holders of pension contracts, **175:132F.**

Funding schedule, definitions, **32:1.**

"Fund" or "funding" defined, **32:1, 151D:1.**

Garnishment.

Exemption from attachment. See within this heading, "Exemption from attachment, execution, or taxation."

Gas or electric plant owned by municipality.

Municipal lighting and heating plants. See within this heading, "Municipal lighting and heating plants."

General contributory systems, **32:1 et seq.**

General court.

Cost-of-living adjustments, **32:102.**

Creditable prior service, **32:3.**

Employees of, included, **32:1.**

Payment of compensation to retired public employee rendering service, **32:91.**

Governmental unit, defined, **32:1.**

Government land bank, emerging technology fund, **Spec L 9:8C.**

Governor.

Appointment of retired employee, effect, **32:91.**

Council.

Governor's council. See within this heading, "Governor's council."

Members of teachers' retirement board appointed, **15:16.**

Retirement Law Commission, supervision by governor, **6:17.**

State board of retirement, governor appoints member, **10:18.**

Governor's council.

Commission on retirement law, supervision and appointment, **6:17.**

Service in executive department, pensioner's right to payment, **32:91.**

Greater Lawrence Sanitary District, retirement systems for employees, **32:1 et seq.**

Group insurance.

Defined, **175:133.**

RETIREMENT SYSTEMS AND PENSIONS —Cont'd

Group insurance —Cont'd

Hospice care services, **32A:17B, 176B:4C.**

Inclusion of retired employee, **175:134.**

Payroll deductions, **32:19, 32:19A, 32:92.**

Rules and regulations as to group insurance for elderly retired government employees, **32A:10B.**

State treasurer, **32A:10B.**

Surviving spouse and dependents, group insurance coverage, **32B:9B.**

Teachers, procedures for termination of group health and life insurance for retired teachers, **32B:11E.**

Groups, classification as to, **32:3, 32:26.**

Guarantees of allowances, **32:25.**

Guardian or conservator.

Accidental death benefits.

Minor dependent, report of natural guardian, **32:9.**

Payment of allowances to certain beneficiaries pending determination of claims under retirement law, **32:12A.**

Action on behalf of incompetent members of retirement systems, **32:17.**

Payments, **32:11, 32:12, 32:100.**

Haverhill, conservation officers, membership, **32:3.**

Health department.

Commissioner to assist board in disability and death cases, **32:6.**

Emergency employment of retired physicians and registered nurses, **32:91.**

Withholding of retirement deductions of employees not subject to civil service, **32:22.**

Health, welfare, and retirement trust funds.

Board of health, welfare and retirement trust funds. See within this heading, "Board of health, welfare and retirement trust funds."

Hearings.

Accidental death benefits, hearing, **32:16.**

Contributory retirement appeal board, hearings, **32:16, 32:20.**

RETIREMENT SYSTEMS AND PENSIONS —Cont'd

Hearings —Cont'd
Failure to be reelected or reappointed, hearing, **32:16.**
Involuntary retirement, hearing, **32:16.**
Heart disease, death or disability, **32:94.**
Honorable discharge, creditable service for purpose of retirement system member receiving, **32:4, 32:22.**
Hospital districts.
Appropriations allocated, **32:22.**
Board's administration of systems, **32:20.**
Defined, **32:1.**
Description of systems, **32:2.**
Hospital expenses.
Indemnification of policemen and firemen, **41:100, 41:100B.**
Soldiers' homes, payments, **175:22.**
Hospital operated or owned by municipality.
Annuities, purchase for employees of municipal hospital, **40:55.**
Dentists or physicians interning in, election to join contributory retirement system, **32:3.**
Technicians temporarily reemployed without make-up payments or credit in retirement system, **32:3.**
Housing authorities.
Acceptance of act, **32:28.**
Benefits increased for employees, **32:96.**
Insurance commissioner, duties in connection with acceptance of general act, **32:28.**
Time for acceptance of Veteran's Retirement Law, **32:60.**
Veterans employed, **32:56 et seq.**
Workers' compensation benefits, effect of payment, **32:28.**
Housing court.
Chief justice, judge or justice deemed appointed to trial court for purpose of retirement, **32:65A, 32:65D.**
Clerk of court, **185C:9.**
Housing specialists, **185C:16.**
Housing finance agency.
See HOUSING FINANCE AGENCY.

RETIREMENT SYSTEMS AND PENSIONS —Cont'd

Husband and wife.
Annuity to surviving spouse, **32:95, 32:95A.**
Contributory retirement system, former spouse as beneficiary, **32:12.**
Divorce.
See DIVORCE AND ALIMONY.
Fireman, rights of widow, **32:85J, 32:89 et seq., 32:100.**
Incompetent member, exercise of rights or options, **32:17.**
Judges, benefits for widows, **32:65C.**
Policeman, rights of widow, **32:85J, 32:89 et seq., 32:100.**
Superannuation retirement allowance in case, **32:5.**
Survivor allowance. See within this heading, "Survivor allowance."
Veteran, option in favor of wife, **32:58B.**
Hypertension, death or disability, **32:94.**
Imprisonment for violation of laws, **32:24.**
Inactive members, superannuation retirements, **32:3, 32:5.**
Income tax.
Individual retirement account, **62:2, 62:5.**
Internal Revenue Code, receipt of unemployment compensation, **151A:29.**
Pension plan income.
Deductible from gross income, **62:2, 62:3.**
Exemption from tax, **32:19, 62:3, 62:5.**
Federal government pensions, **62:3.**
Massachusetts gross income, **62:2.**
Other states, taxation of retirement pensions, **62:3.**
Part B adjusted gross income as affected by employer contributions, **62:2.**
Withholding by retiree or annuitant of sums assigned for payment of income taxes, **32:19, 32:19A.**
Incompetents or minors.
Actions on behalf, **32:17.**

RETIREMENT SYSTEMS AND PENSIONS —Cont'd

Incompetents or minors —Cont'd
Adopted children, allowances, **32:12B.**
Annuities and annuity contracts. See within this heading, "Annuities and annuity contracts."
Child support enforcement.
Attachment of benefits, **119A:6A.**
Checking for arrearages before issuing benefits, **32:11.**
Dependents.
Dependents. See within this heading, "Dependents."
Female members, survivorship benefits to children, **32:12B.**
Full-time students, contributory retirement law benefits, **32:7, 32:9.**
Group classification of state employees having custody of insane persons, **32:3.**
Guardian or conservator. See within this heading, "Guardian or conservator."
Nonmember of system, rights of children, **32:12C.**
Options and other rights, **32:12, 32:12B, 32:12C, 32:17.**
Payments to guardian or conservator, **32:11, 32:12, 32:100.**
Policemen or firemen, rights of children, **32:89, 32:89A, 32:89B, 32:100.**
State policeman retired for illness or injury in performance of duty, children, **32:26.**
Public charge, effect of retired employee or pensioner becoming, **32:92.**
Support payments for children, **32:92A, 235:34A.**
Survivor allowance, **32:12, 32:12B, 32:95, 32:95A, 32:100.**
Payment to surviving children of certain nonparticipating employees, **32:12C.**
Increases in pensions, etc.
Amount of allowances and pensions, increase, **32:22, 32:80, 32:90A, 32:90C, 32:96, 32:97.**
Annuities. See within this heading, "Annuities and annuity contracts."

RETIREMENT SYSTEMS AND PENSIONS —Cont'd

Increases in pensions, etc —Cont'd

Certain public employees, **32:1.**

Equalizing monthly installments, **32:13.**

Policemen and firemen, **32:80, 32:81B, 32:85E.**

Indemnification.

Boards of retirement, **32:20A, 32:20B.**

Policemen and firemen, certain hospital and medical expenses, **41:100, 41:100B.**

Independent agricultural and technical schools.

Employees, **74A:18.**

Indictments.

Effect of suspension of state employee while, **30:59.**

Municipal or county officer or employees, indictment for misconduct, **268A:25.**

Individual retirement account.

See INDIVIDUAL RETIREMENT ACCOUNT.

Industrial accidents, payments for periods interrupted, **32:14.**

Infants.

Incompetents or minors. See within this heading, "Incompetents or minors."

Inheritance tax legacy and succession taxes.

See LEGACY AND SUCCESSION TAXES.

Injunctive relief against violations of chapter, **151D:15.**

Injury in line of duty.

Accidental disability retirement. See within this heading, "Accidental disability retirement."

Insane persons.

Incompetents or minors. See within this heading, "Incompetents or minors."

Insolvency laws inapplicable to funds and allowances, **32:19, 32:41.**

Inspection.

Examination, inspection, or investigation. See within this heading, "Examination, inspection, or investigation."

Insurance.

Administrative agent for general funds, authority to act, **175:47A.**

Agents and agency employees, contributory retirement system, **175:36A.**

RETIREMENT SYSTEMS AND PENSIONS —Cont'd

Insurance —Cont'd

Annual report to show facts as to carrier or service, **151D:3.**

Commissioner of insurance.

Insurance commissioner. See within this heading, "Insurance commissioner."

Disability retirement for officers and employees, **175:36, 175:36A, 175:36B.**

Execution or attachment, benefits for officers and employees not subject, **175:36A.**

Exemptions from insurance laws and regulations, **32:39, 175:29.**

Fraternal benefit societies, employees, **176:56.**

Group insurance. See within this heading, "Group insurance."

Hospital expenses, indemnification of policemen and firemen, **41:100, 41:100B.**

Investment of retirement system funds in securities of insurance companies, **32:23, 62:8.**

Life insurance.

See LIFE INSURANCE.

Loss, insurance against, **151D:3.**

Mental illness, provisions for insurance against costs, **175:47B.**

Military service of employee counted for pension, **175:36.**

Officers and employees, benefits for, **175:36 et seq.**

Payments by carrier or service, to interested persons, forbidden, **151D:3.**

Premiums.

Insurance premiums. See within this heading, "Insurance premiums."

Private pensions associations as exempt from regulations governing, **32:39.**

Restrictions as to benefits for insurance company officers and employees, **175:35.**

Soldiers' homes, medical and hospital expenses paid, **175:22.**

Insurance commissioner, **32:21.**

Appointment of member of state retirement board, **10:18.**

Assessment of expenses, **32:21.**

RETIREMENT SYSTEMS AND PENSIONS —Cont'd

Insurance commissioner —Cont'd

Districts, duties in connection with acceptance of general act, **32:28.**

Duties of, **32:21.**

Enforcement of laws, **32:24.**

Examinations, **32:21.**

Financial reports filed, **32:23.**

Housing authorities, duties in connection with acceptance of general act, **32:28.**

Investments, valuation, **32:21.**

Involuntary retirement, appeal of decision concerning, **32:16.**

Massachusetts Bay Transportation Authority police retirement system, supervision, **32:21.**

Municipal systems, duties in connection with establishment, **32:28.**

Pension associations for private employees, supervision, **32:40.**

Powers as to pensions, **175:36, 175:36A.**

Reports by commissioner, **32:21.**

Rules and regulations, promulgation and approval, **32:21.**

State retirement board, appointment of member, **10:18.**

Supervision, **32:21, 32:40.**

Insurance premiums.

Assignment of benefits to pay, **32:19, 32:19A, 32:92, 32A:10B.**

Group annuities, payment of premiums as regular compensation, **32:1.**

Political subdivision, contributing to retired employee's share of cost, **32B:9A.**

Interest on money.

County systems, interest on money owing, **35:24.**

Custodian of system, duties, **32:23.**

Regular interest, **32:1, 32:22.**

Sales of interest in pension, annuity, or allowance, **32:92.**

Intermittent employees.

Seasonal or intermittent employees. See within this heading, "Seasonal or intermittent employees."

RETIREMENT SYSTEMS AND PENSIONS —Cont'd

Interns in municipal hospitals electing to join, **32:3.**

Interstate commissions, retention of status by state employees transferred, **32:28, 32:28I.**

Intervals of payment of allowances, **32:13.**

Intrastate service in governmental unit where no system existed, creditable service in case, **32:3, 32:4.**

Investigation.
Examination, inspection, or investigation. See within this heading, "Examination, inspection, or investigation."

Investment advisory unit, **7:50.**

Investment division, responsibilities, **10:5C.**

Investment income account, **32:22.**
Assignment of certain pension contracts to separate investment account, **175:132F.**

Deficit, how made up, **32:22.**

Transfer of balance to pension fund, **32:22.**

Investment of funds, **32:23, 151D:16.**
Advisory unit, **7:50.**

Assets and liabilities, valuation of investment, **32:22.**

Bank, advice, **32:23.**

Boards of retirement employed as advisers, **32:23.**

Combined investment funds, establishment, **32:23.**

Commissioner of insurance, valuation of investments, **32:21.**

Committee, **32:23.**

Corporate retirement board, investment adviser, **32:23.**

County systems, **32:23.**

Data system, **32:21.**

Deputy state treasurer, investments for board of retirement, **10:5C.**

Division of investment responsibility, **10:5C.**

Income account.
Investment income account. See within this heading, "Investment income account."

Insurance securities, investment of retirement system funds, **32:23, 62:8.**

RETIREMENT SYSTEMS AND PENSIONS —Cont'd

Investment of funds —Cont'd
Mortgage pass-through securities and mortgage-backed bonds, tax exemption for certain investments, **32:23, 62:8.**

Municipal systems, **32:23.**

Northern Ireland, investments by local systems, **32:23.**

Pension fund or system credited or charged, **32:21, 32:22.**

Periodic experience investigation, retirement benefits, **32:21.**

Railroad securities, investments, **32:23.**

Regular interest, **32:22.**

South Africa, investments by local systems, **32:23.**

State treasurer's duties, **32:23.**

Stock of banks, investment, **32:23.**

Teachers' retirement system, investment of funds, **10:5C, 32:23.**

Telephone company securities, investments, **32:23.**

Trust funds, **151D:3.**

Variable pension contracts assigned to separate investment accounts, provisions, **175:132F.**

Involuntary retirement, **32:16.**
Hearing and appeal with respect, **32:16.**

School janitors, **32:44.**

Teachers, **32:43.**

United States Department of State, creditable service during leave of absence for service, **32:4.**

Janitors in schools, municipal pensions, **32:44 et seq.**

Joint and last survivor allowance, option, **32:12.**

Joint employment under two or more systems, **32:3.**
Veterans, joint employment by two towns, **32:53.**

Joint private pension associations for officers and employees of related companies, **32:39.**

Joint water boards, pensions for laborers employed, **32:78, 32:78A, 32:79.**

Judges and judicial officers, **32:65A et seq.**
Amount of allowances and pensions. See within this heading, "Amount of allowances and pensions."

RETIREMENT SYSTEMS AND PENSIONS —Cont'd

Judges and judicial officers —Cont'd
Appeals court, **32:65D, 32:65F, 211A:16.**

Application for allowances, **32:65I.**

Appointed after attaining age 60, **32:65A.**

Boston courts, pensions for judges, **32:65A, 32:65B.**

Computation of time served as, inclusion of service as special justice, **32:4, 32:65A.**

Creditable service, computation, **32:4.**

District courts. See within this heading, "District courts."

Housing court, **32:65A, 32:65D.**

January 2, 1975, judges retiring on or after, **32:65D.**

Juvenile court justices, **32:65A.**

Land court. See within this heading, "Land court."

Mandatory retirement age, **32:90F; MA Const Amend Art 98.**

Multiple membership, transfer of credits, **32:65D.**

Municipal court judge, promulgation of rule for reporting of cases upon retirement, **231:108.**

Service after Jan 2, 1975, **32:3.**

Special justices, pensions, **32:65B.**

State ballot law commission, retired judge as member, **55B:1.**

Supreme judicial court. See within this heading, "Supreme judicial court."

Temporary service by retired justice as affecting pension, **32:65F, 32:65G, 211:24, 211A:16.**

Vacation allowances and sick leave credits, **32:65J.**

Wartime service as period of service in office, **32:65C.**

Widows of certain judges, benefits, **32:65C.**

Judicial review.
Appeal. See within this heading, "Appeal."

Juvenile courts.
See JUVENILE COURTS AND DELINQUENT CHILDREN.

Laborers, pensions, **32:77 et seq.**
Fire district laborers, **32:78, 32:78A, 32:79.**

RETIREMENT SYSTEMS AND PENSIONS —Cont'd

Laborers, pensions —Cont'd

Increase in noncontributory pensions, **32:77B.**

Joint water boards, **32:78, 32:78A, 32:79.**

Options on retirement, **32:77A.**

Promotion to supervisory positions, effect, **32:77C.**

Sewer district laborers, **32:78, 32:78A.**

Water district laborers, **32:78, 32:78A, 32:79.**

Widow, payments, **32:65C, 32:77A.**

Land court.

Judges, **32:65A, 32:65D.**

Recorder and deputy recorders, **185:6.**

Widows of judges, **32:65C.**

Late entry into membership, **32:3.**

Law Commission.

Retirement Law Commission. See within this heading, "Retirement Law Commission."

Leave of absence, effect, **32:3, 32:4.**

Boards of retirement, **32:3.**

Military service, insurance company employee's length of service for pension purposes as including leave, **175:36.**

Representative of employee organizations, **32:28K.**

Superannuation retirement allowance, **32:5.**

Without pay, **32:3.**

Legacy and succession taxes, exemption, **32:19.**

Employer contributions, **65:1.**

Federal system funds, **65:1.**

Legal representative of deceased member, payments, **32:11.**

Length of service.

Annuities to certain officials not entitled to pensions, etc., **32:95.**

City firemen, **32:80, 32:81A.**

City policemen, **32:83, 32:83A.**

Court officers, **32:66.**

Death or disability caused by cancer, **32:94B.**

Increases in benefits in certain cases, **32:56, 32:96, 32:97.**

Insurance company employee's length of service for pension purposes as including leave of absence for military service, **175:36.**

RETIREMENT SYSTEMS AND PENSIONS —Cont'd

Length of service —Cont'd

Judges, **32:65A et seq.**

Laborers, **32:77, 32:78.**

Municipal pensions for teachers, **32:43.**

Prison employees, **32:47.**

Probation officers, **32:75 et seq.**

School janitors, municipal pensions, **32:44.**

Scrub women in state house, **32:74.**

Spanish and World War I veterans, **32:57, 32:58.**

State police officers and inspectors, **32:28A.**

Town policemen and firemen, **32:85E.**

Liabilities.

Assets and liabilities. See within this heading, "Assets and liabilities."

Liability fund.

Pension liability fund. See within this heading, "Pension liability fund."

Library employees, **32:1.**

Annuity savings fund, duties of treasurer in connection, **32:22.**

Licensed electricians, classification, **32:3.**

Life annuity, option, **32:12.**

Life insurance.

See LIFE INSURANCE.

Light or gas plants owned by municipality.

Municipal lighting and heating plants. See within this heading, "Municipal lighting and heating plants."

Limitation of amount, **175:36.**

Limitation of retirement allowances for judges and judicial officers, **32:65H.**

List of securities held by system, duties of custodian, **32:23.**

Loaned employee injured while aiding other governmental unit.

Accidental disability allowance, **32:7.**

Massachusetts Turnpike Authority, inapplicability of provisions, **32:7.**

Local adoption of general contributory act, **32:28.**

Logan International Airport.

Cancer as cause of death or disability, **32:94B.**

RETIREMENT SYSTEMS AND PENSIONS —Cont'd

Logan International Airport —Cont'd

Classification of employees paid by United States, **32:3.**

Crash crewmen or crash boatmen, **32:94B.**

Hypertension or heart disease, benefits on death or disability, **32:94.**

Lowell Technological Institute building authority.

Retirement system, inclusion of employees, **32:2.**

State employees, personnel defined, **32:1.**

Lump sum.

Public employees, **32:13.**

Lunch programs in schools, employees, **32:1.**

Maintenance repairmen, classification, **32:3.**

Make-up payments, **32:3, 32:22.**

Management of funds, **32:23.**

Management of retirement system, **32:20.**

Mandatory retirement age.

Age for retirement. See within this heading, "Age for retirement."

Manner of payment of benefits or allowances, **32:13, 32:23.**

Manner of registration, **151D:2.**

Massachusetts Bay transportation authority.

See MASSACHUSETTS BAY TRANSPORTATION AUTHORITY.

Massachusetts Water Resources Authority, election of workers' compensation or pension **152:73.**

Maximum age.

Attainment of maximum group age, retirement, **32:3.**

Defined, **32:1.**

Employment after retirement, age seventy exceeded, **32:3, 32:91.**

For eligibility, **32:3.**

Notice, **32:20.**

Reclassification after attaining, **32:5.**

Superannuation retirements, **32:5.**

Teachers' retirement system.

Alternative superannuation retirement benefit program, **32:5.**

Mayors.

See MAYORS.

RETIREMENT SYSTEMS AND PENSIONS —Cont'd

Medical boards to determine cause of death of public employees, chairman, **32:89, 32:89A, 32:89B.**

Medical examination.

Disability retirement, **32:6.**

Effect of passing medical examination, **32:94.**

Expenses for disability examination, **32:6.**

Medical panel. See within this heading, "Medical panel."

Reexamination of retired members, **32:8.**

Refusal to permit reexamination, **32:8.**

X-rays, authority to make, **32:6.**

Mandatory retirement age, employees working beyond as required to have annual physical examination, **32:90G, 32:90G½, 32:90J.**

Policemen and firemen. See within this heading, "Policemen and firemen."

Probation officer seeking retirement, certificate from physician, **32:75.**

Refusal to submit to examination, **32:8.**

Spanish and World War I veterans subject, **32:57A.**

State inspectors, annual physical examination, **32:90I.**

Suspension or discontinuance of benefits for failure to submit, **32:8.**

Medical examiners employed by state as member of systems, **32:3.**

Medical expenses, indemnification of policemen and firemen, **41:100, 41:100B.**

Medical panel, **32:6.**

Employment of registered physicians by boards, **32:20.**

Pensioner's right to payment for service, **32:91.**

Medical technicians, **111C:15.**

Meetings.

Boards, meetings, **32:20.**

Town meetings.

See TOWN MEETINGS.

Members and membership, **32:3.**

Administrator of deceased member, payments, **32:11.**

Age limit for eligibility, **32:3.**

RETIREMENT SYSTEMS AND PENSIONS —Cont'd

Members and membership —Cont'd

Annual statement or report, **32:20, 32:22D.**

Annuity saving fund, **32:22.**

Appointive officials, previous retirement as affecting right to become member of contributory retirement system, **32:5.**

Boards of retirement.

Certificates of membership, issuance, **32:4.**

Eligibility of retired employees as members, **32:20.**

Removal or discharge of members, hearing, **32:16.**

Certificates, **32:4.**

Continued employment after age seventy, **32:91.**

Contributory systems for public employees, retirement rights of members, **32:3.**

Death and death benefits. See within this heading, "Death and death benefits."

Deductions of members. See within this heading, "Deductions of members."

Defined, **32:1.**

Dereliction of duties by members. See within this heading, "Dereliction of duty by members."

Dual membership. See within this heading, "Dual membership."

Election as to membership in plan, **32:3.**

Eligibility, **32:3.**

Employee in active service, application, **32:3.**

Female members, survivorship benefits to children, **32:12B.**

Filing of members' records, **32:18.**

Inactive members, **32:3.**

Kind of membership, **32:3.**

Late entry into, **32:3.**

Member in service, **32:3.**

Nonmembers, **32:2, 32:12C.**

Other states or federal government, **32:3.**

Payroll deductions from compensation of members. See within this heading, "Payroll deductions from compensation of members."

Reestablishment of membership, **32:3.**

RETIREMENT SYSTEMS AND PENSIONS —Cont'd

Members and membership —Cont'd

Remarriage of widow of member as affecting allowance, **32:12.**

Retired members, reexamination, **32:8.**

Special act, acceptance of general act by city or town as affecting membership in system, **32:28.**

State employees' retirement system, right to membership by district officers or employees, **32:2, 32:28.**

Teachers' retirement system, members of board, **15:16.**

Transfer of membership. See within this heading, "Transfer of membership."

Turnpike Authority, **32:3.**

Waiver of benefits by one electing not to become member, **32:3.**

Watershed guards, membership, **32:3.**

Withdrawal of member. See within this heading, "Withdrawal of member."

Mental capacity.

Physical or mental incapacity. See within this heading, "Physical or mental incapacity."

Mental health department payment for services of certain retired employees, **32:91.**

Withholding of certain employees' retirement deductions, **32:22.**

Mental retardation department, **32:91.**

Methods of financing, **32:22.**

Metropolitan district commission.

Administration of pensions for widows of fire fighters or police officers, **32:20.**

Annuities to dependents of certain employees dying in performance of duty, **32:89A, 32:100.**

Budget estimates of commission to include certain pension contributions by Commonwealth, **29:9A.**

Contributions by state, **29:9A.**

Death of certain employees dying in line of duty, annuities to dependents in case, **32:89A, 32:100.**

RETIREMENT SYSTEMS AND PENSIONS —Cont'd

Metropolitan district commission —Cont'd

Employees, inclusion, **32:1, 32:2.**

Group classification of police force members, **32:3.**

Police.

Metropolitan police. See within this heading, "Metropolitan police."

Metropolitan districts.

Acceptance of general act, **32:28.**

Annuities to dependents of employee dying in performance of duty, **32:89A, 32:100.**

Commission.

Metropolitan district commission. See within this heading, "Metropolitan district commission."

Pensions for widows of firefighters or police officers, administration, **32:71, 32:100.**

Sewer districts, pensions for laborers, **32:78, 32:78A.**

State system, contributions to districts, **29:9A.**

Metropolitan parks maintenance fund, payment of police pensions and annuities out of appropriations, **32:72.**

Metropolitan police, **32:71, 32:72.**

Administration of pensions for widows, **32:71, 32:100.**

Annuities to dependents, **32:71.**

Appropriations, **32:72.**

Classification for retirement, **32:3.**

Death, **32:71.**

Medical examination for retirement for disability, **32:85F.**

Pensions and retirement benefits, **32:72.**

Retirement allowance for disability incurred in performance of duty, **32:90A.**

Source of payment of benefits, **32:72.**

Military service.

Active duty, creditable service for members of reserve units called, **32:58A.**

Credit, **32:22.**

Divorce and alimony, marital property defined, **208:34.**

RETIREMENT SYSTEMS AND PENSIONS —Cont'd

Military service —Cont'd

Dual membership, effect on military service credit fund, **32:22.**

Income tax.

Adjusted gross income, **62:2.**

Insurance company employee, military service counted for pension, **175:36.**

Militia.

See MILITIA.

Observance of Retired Members of Armed Forces Day, **6:15CC.**

Public officers and employees.

Appropriations of funds to effectuate crediting of military service, **Spec L 35:9A.**

Creditable service, military service credited, **Spec L 35:9.**

Reinstatement, retirement without, **Spec L 35:9B.**

Separation from position as affecting membership, **Spec L 35:8.**

Teachers' retirement associations, **Spec L 35:9.**

Special fund for military service credit. See within this heading, "Special fund for military service credit."

State employees' and teachers' retirement systems, military credit, **32:22.**

Veterans. See within this heading, "Veterans."

Minimum guaranteed allowance, **32:25.**

Minimum wage law as affected by payments, **32:22, 149:26, 149:27.**

Penalty for receiving rebate, refund, etc., **149:27.**

Minors.

Incompetents or minors. See within this heading, "Incompetents or minors."

Misappropriation of funds or property, **32:15, 151D:6.**

Misconduct, effect of suspension after indictment for on retirement benefits of municipal or county officer or employee, **268A:25.**

Misrepresentation.

Fraud. See within this heading, "Fraud."

RETIREMENT SYSTEMS AND PENSIONS —Cont'd

Model water and sewer commission, transferred employee's membership in system protected, **40N:7.**

Modification or change.

Amendments. See within this heading, "Amendments, modifications, or alterations of plans."

Mortality experience, investigation, **32:21.**

Mortgage-backed securities, investments, **32:23, 62:8.**

Mortgage of allowances, annuities, or pensions, invalidity, **32:92.**

Mosquito control districts or projects, **32:1, 32:2, 32:28.**

Motor vehicles.

Group classification of registry employees, **32:3.**

Investigator of registry, **32:89.**

Lessee-contractor employees, **159B:6A.**

Multiple membership by judges, transfer of credits, **32:65D.**

Municipal court justices, promulgation of rule for reporting cases upon retirement or removal, **231:108.**

Municipal court of Boston.

Age 60, retirement benefits of justices appointed after attaining, **32:65A.**

Judge or justice deemed appointed to trial court for purpose of retirement, **32:65A, 32:65D.**

Municipal lighting and heating plants.

Cadet engineers, **164:69E.**

Group classification of certain employees, **32:3.**

Municipal systems and pensions.

Acceptance of act. See within this heading, "Acceptance of act by cities, towns, and districts."

Administration, **32:20.**

Advance payment to employees eligible for retirement, **32:99.**

Aldermen.

Selectmen or aldermen. See within this heading, "Selectmen or aldermen."

Annual reports of boards, **32:20.**

Annuities. See within this heading, "Annuities and annuity contracts."

RETIREMENT SYSTEMS AND PENSIONS —Cont'd

Municipal systems and pensions —Cont'd

Appropriations. See within this heading, "Appropriations."

Assessment of supervision expenses, **32:21.**

Auditor, compensation for service rendered in connection with contributory retirement system, **32:20.**

Beach employees of cities and towns, retention of rights, **40:12F.**

Boards of retirement. See within this heading, "Boards of retirement."

Boston. See within this heading, "Boston."

Budget provisions, **32:22.**

City council. See within this heading, "City council."

Clerks.

City and town clerks. See within this heading, "City and town clerks."

County systems, inclusion of town employees, **32:28.**

Creditable service for elected officers, **32:4.**

Credit unions, deposit of allowances, **35:19C, 41:41C.**

Credit unions, deposit of pension and retirement funds, **35:19C, 41:41C.**

Custodian of retirement system funds, compensation of city or town treasurer for services, **32:20.**

Death benefits, **32:89A.**

Defined, **32:1.**

Dental assistants and interns in municipalities, retirement, **32:3, 32:44C.**

Deposit of employees' pension and retirement allow-ances, **35:19C, 41:41C.**

Description, **32:2.**

Elected officers, **32:3, 32:4.**

Eligibility, **32:3, 32:20.**

Establishment, **32:28, 40:5D.**

Expense fund, time for payment, **32:22.**

RETIREMENT SYSTEMS AND PENSIONS —Cont'd

Municipal systems and pensions —Cont'd

Federal savings and loan associations, investment in share accounts, **32:23.**

Fiscal year, **32:22.**

Gas or electric plant owned by municipality.

Municipal lighting and heating plants. See within this heading, "Municipal lighting and heating plants."

General act, adoption of retirement system for officers and employees, **32:28.**

Group insurance for municipal employees.

See GROUP INSURANCE FOR MUNICIPAL EMPLOYEES.

Guaranty of allowances by municipality, **32:25.**

Hospital operated or owned by municipality. See within this heading, "Hospital operated or owned by municipality."

Housing authorities, acceptance of general act, **32:28.**

Increase of benefits in certain cases, **32:90A, 32:96, 32:97.**

Indictment for misconduct, effect on retirement benefits, **268A:25.**

Investment of funds, **32:23.**

Laborers. See within this heading, "Laborers, pensions."

Library employees included, **32:1.**

Light or gas plants owned by municipality, employees of.

Municipal lighting and heating plants. See within this heading, "Municipal lighting and heating plants."

Notice of vacancy in retirement boards, **32:20.**

Ordinary disability, authority to increase allowances of employees retired, **32:90D.**

Pensioners rendering services to city, compensation, **32:91.**

RETIREMENT SYSTEMS AND PENSIONS —Cont'd

Municipal systems and pensions —Cont'd

Policemen and firemen. See within this heading, "Policemen and firemen."

Powers and duties of boards, **32:20.**

Retired employees whose former classification has been abolished, benefits, **32:90E.**

Retirement Law Commission, town agencies, **10:35I.**

Revocation by municipalities of acceptance of statute. See within this heading, "Revocation by municipalities of acceptance of statute."

School janitors, **32:44 et seq.**

Selectmen or aldermen. See within this heading, "Selectmen or aldermen."

Special funds, **40:5D.**

Suspension after indictment for misconduct, effect on retirement benefits, **268A:25.**

Tax, **32:22.**

Teachers, **32:42, 32:43.**

Time for payment into funds, **32:22.**

Town accountant, compensation, **32:20.**

Town election for acceptance, **32:28.**

Town meetings.

See TOWN MEETINGS.

Treasurers.

Compensation in connection with retirement system duties, **32:20.**

Corporate nominee partnerships, establishment, **32:23.**

Custodian of retirement system's funds, treasurer, **32:23, 32:42.**

Deposit in credit unions, **41:41C.**

Deposit of funds, **41:41C.**

Unfunded pensions, pension reserve fund, **58:25.**

Vacancy in retirement boards, notice, **32:20.**

Vacation pay upon retirement of municipal employees, **41:111E.**

RETIREMENT SYSTEMS AND PENSIONS —Cont'd

Municipal systems and pensions —Cont'd

Veterans. See within this heading, "Veterans."

Nantucket, establishment of system, **32:28.**

National Guard.

See MILITIA.

Natural resources department coastal wardens, group classification, **32:3.**

Naval service.

Military service. See within this heading, "Military service."

Negligence.

Dereliction of duty by members. See within this heading, "Dereliction of duty by members."

New Bedford Institute of Technology, privileges of officers and employees, **71:16F, 74:42O.**

Nomination of beneficiaries, **32:11.**

Noncontributory pension.

Cost of living adjustments for noncontributory retirees, **32:102, 32:103.**

Eligibility of person having inchoate rights, **32:3.**

Guaranty of allowances at least equal, **32:25.**

Payment, **35:11.**

Policemen and firemen. See within this heading, "Policemen and firemen."

Nonmember of system, rights of widow and children, **32:12C.**

Nonresident trustee, service of process, **151D:3.**

"Normal retirement age" defined, **151D:1.**

"Normal retirement benefit" defined, **151D:1.**

Notices.

Accidental death, **32:9.**

Accidental injury, **32:7.**

Appropriations, **32:22.**

Benefits, **32:20.**

Benefit withholding, **32:91.**

Criminal record offender information, notice access to retirement boards, **32:91C.**

Deductions, **149:150A.**

Annuity savings fund, **32:22.**

Retirement or pension fund, **149:150A.**

Election not to become member, **32:3.**

RETIREMENT SYSTEMS AND PENSIONS —Cont'd

Notices —Cont'd

Involuntary retirement, **32:16.**

Mandatory retirement age, notice of option to continue working after reaching, **32:90G¾.**

Maximum age of member, board to give notice, **32:20.**

Old age assistance or public welfare, availability, **32:20.**

Options, notification by board, **32:12, 32:90G¾.**

Port authority employees retirement system, notice of violations of contributory retirement law, **32:24.**

Probation officers, notice of retirement, **276:103.**

Removal or discharge, notice, **32:16.**

Statements and records of members, notice of failure to file, **32:18.**

Termination of plan, notice, **151D:14.**

Vacancies on municipal retirement boards, **32:20.**

Violations of contributory retirement laws, **32:24.**

Number of memberships.

Dual membership. See within this heading, "Dual membership."

Nurses.

See NURSES AND NURSING SERVICES.

Offenses.

Criminal offenses. See within this heading, "Criminal offenses."

Old colony planning council employees, membership in state employees' retirement system, **32:1.**

Operation expenses.

Expenses of administration and operation. See within this heading, "Expenses of administration and operation."

Options.

Election or option. See within this heading, "Election or option."

Options on retirement, **32:12.**

Annuities, options with respect, **32:12.**

City fireman's pension, **32:81A, 32:81B.**

RETIREMENT SYSTEMS AND PENSIONS —Cont'd

Options on retirement —Cont'd

City police pensions, **32:83A.**

Death without naming beneficiary, effect, **32:12.**

Incompetent members, exercise on behalf, **32:12, 32:12B, 32:12C, 32:17.**

Joint and last survivor allowance, **32:12.**

Judges, benefits for widows, **32:65C.**

Laborers' pensions, **32:77A.**

Member survivor allowance, election of spouse, **32:12.**

Notification by board, **32:12.**

Policemen and firemen, **32:81A, 32:81B, 32:83A, 32:85, 32:85B, 32:85E, 32:85J.**

Spouse receiving allowance as beneficiary under option, death, **32:12.**

State police, **32:12.**

Veteran, option in favor of wife, **32:58B.**

Optometric services, provisions, **151D:4.**

Ordinary disability retirement, **32:6.**

Organization of private pension associations, **32:39.**

Orphans.

Incompetents or minors. See within this heading, "Incompetents or minors."

Other governmental unit, proration for injuries received while employed, **32:7.**

Other laws, trustees, etc., as subject, **151D:10.**

Other states or federal government.

Affidavit of membership in federal civil service retirement system, **32:3.**

Classification of military department employees whose compensation is paid, **32:3.**

Consumer Price Index, cost-of-living adjustment, **32:102, 118A:2.**

Establishment of calculation, **32:103.**

Credit for out-of-state or federally funded service, **32:3, 32:4.**

Department of State, creditable service during leave of absence for service, **32:4.**

RETIREMENT SYSTEMS AND PENSIONS —Cont'd

Other states or federal government —Cont'd

Eligibility for membership in state system of employees paid by federal funds, **32:3.**

Grants by, employee compensation derived, **29:2C, 32:3, 32:22.**

Interstate commissions, retention of status of employees transferred, **32:28, 32:28I.**

Legacy and succession tax, federal government retirement fund as exempt, **65:1.**

Pension to wives and children of pensioners residing in other jurisdictions, **32:92A.**

Social security.

See SOCIAL SECURITY.

Support payments to wife or children of pensioner residing outside United States, **32:92A.**

Teachers.

Creditable service of teacher formerly employed in state education department and paid by Federal Funds, **32:4.**

Service out of state, **32:3, 32:4.**

Trustees operating under law, **151D:8, 151D:12.**

Veterans. See within this heading, "Veterans."

Waiver as to funds administered under laws, **151D:8.**

Owner-employees' funds, exceptions, **151D:7.**

Owner-operator of leased motor vehicle equipment as employee of lessee-contractor for welfare and retirement purposes, **159B:6A.**

Parking authority employees, **32:1, 32:2.**

Park police, **32:3, 32:85B, 32:94.**

Parolees' supervision, group classification of employees charged, **32:3.**

Partial invalidity of law as to, severability of provisions in event, **151D:18.**

Partnerships.

See PARTNERSHIPS.

Part-time employees.

Creditable service, **32:4.**

Deferred compensation program established, **29:64, 29:64D.**

RETIREMENT SYSTEMS AND PENSIONS —Cont'd

Part-time employees —Cont'd

Eligibility, **32:3.**

Superannuation retirement allowance, **32:5.**

Payment of allowances and funds, **32:11, 32:13, 32:22, 32:23, 32:25.**

Advance payments. See within this heading, "Advance payments."

Beneficiaries of deceased members, **32:11.**

Child support enforcement.

Checking for arrearages before issuance of benefits, **32:11i9C.**

Special payment. See within this heading, "Special payment."

Payroll deductions from compensation of members, **32:19, 32:19A, 32:22, 32:92.**

Mandatory retirement age, deductions from salaries of employees working past, **32:90G, 32:90G½, 32:90G¾, 32:95A.**

Penal institutions.

See CORRECTIONAL INSTITUTIONS.

Penalties.

Fines and penalties. See within this heading, "Fines and penalties."

"Pension" defined, **32:1.**

Pension liability fund, **32:11, 32:22.**

Appropriations, **32:22C.**

Definitions, **32:1.**

Establishment, **29:6B.**

PRIM board, **32:1.**

"Pension plan" defined, **151D:1.**

Pension reserve fund, **29:6B, 32:1, 32:22, 40:5D.**

Pension reserves investment management (PRIM) board, **32:1, 32:22, 32:23.**

Pension reserves investment trust (PRIT) fund, **32:1, 32:22, 32:22B, 40:5D.**

Periodic experience investigation, **32:21.**

Perjury as to statements in regard, **32:18.**

Natural guardian's account of accidental death benefit, **32:9.**

Permanent disability, **32:6.**

Permanent watershed guards, membership, **32:3.**

RETIREMENT SYSTEMS AND PENSIONS —Cont'd

Perpetuities, trust plans for employee welfare and retirement funds as exempt from rule against, **203:3A.**

Pharmacies for use by retirees, **112:39A, 112:40.**

Philippine Insurrection, veterans of.

Spanish and World War I veterans. See within this heading, "Spanish and World War I veterans."

Physical education teachers included, **32:1.**

Physical examination.

Medical examination. See within this heading, "Medical examination."

Physical or mental incapacity.

Accidental death benefits, eligibility of member upon recovery from disability, **32:3.**

Annual evaluation of employees working beyond mandatory retirement age, **32:90G½.**

Auditor of state, **221:62A.**

Call firemen, **32:7.**

Cancer, death or disability in line of duty, **32:94B.**

City firemen, **32:80, 32:81A.**

City police pensions, **32:83, 32:83A.**

Court officers, pension, **32:66, 32:67.**

Disability retirement. See within this heading, "Disability retirement."

Disease contracted in line of duty, **32:94A.**

Failure to file, **151D:3.**

Incompetents or minors. See within this heading, "Incompetents or minors."

Insurance against mental illness costs, provisions, **175:47B.**

Laborers, pensions, **32:77 et seq.**

Line of duty, **32:7, 32:8.**

Medical examination, effect of passing, **32:94.**

Offices and employees of insurance companies, disability benefits, **175:36 et seq.**

Park police in cities and towns, **32:85B.**

Physicians and nurses, payment for services, **32:91.**

RETIREMENT SYSTEMS AND PENSIONS —Cont'd

Physical or mental incapacity —Cont'd

Probation officers, pensions, **32:75 et seq.**

Public employees having care custody, or control over mentally ill persons, classification for retirement purposes, **32:3.**

Return to service.

Evaluation of ability to perform, **32:26.**

School janitors, municipal pension, **32:44.**

Scrub women in state house, pensions, **32:74.**

Spanish and World War I veterans, **32:56, 32:57.**

State police officers and inspectors, **32:26.**

Teachers, municipal pensions, **32:42, 32:43.**

Town policemen and firemen, pensions, **32:85, 32:85A et seq.**

Withholding of retirement deductions from employees of department of mental health, **32:22.**

Physician.

Contributory retirement appeal board may employ, **32:16.**

Emergency employment of retired physicians by health department, **32:91.**

Interning in municipal hospitals, election to join contributory retirement system, **32:3.**

Medical examination. See within this heading, "Medical examination."

Medical panel. See within this heading, "Medical panel."

Mentally ill persons, payment for services of physicians and nurses, **32:91.**

Municipal hospitals, contributory retirement system, **32:3.**

Pensioned or retired public employee's service as, effect, **32:91.**

Visual services, reimbursement, **151D:4.**

Plan administrators.

Administrators of plan. See within this heading, "Administrators of plan."

Pledge of allowances, annuities, or pensions, **32:92.**

RETIREMENT SYSTEMS AND PENSIONS —Cont'd

Policemen and firemen, **32:80 et seq.**

Acceptance of statute as to retirement, **32:57B.**

Accidental disability retirement. See within this heading, "Accidental disability retirement."

Additional allowance depending on period of service, **32:56.**

Adjustment of pensions, **32:85E.**

Age for retirement, **32:80, 32:81A, 32:83, 32:83A.**

Aiding police officer or fireman, payments to dependents of persons dying while, **32:88.**

Ambulance attendants in fire departments, classification, **32:3.**

Amount of allowances and pensions. See within this heading, "Amount of allowances and pensions."

Annuities. See within this heading, "Annuities and annuity contracts."

Boards of retirement. See within this heading, "Boards of retirement."

Building police of public works department, **32:3.**

Cadets, retirement benefits, **147:21A.**

Call firemen. See within this heading, "Call firemen."

Capitol police, classification, **32:3.**

Cause of death to be determined by board, **32:89, 32:89A, 32:89B.**

Certain laws inapplicable to aged officers, **32:90.**

Children.

Incompetents or minors. See within this heading, "Incompetents or minors."

City fire departments, **32:80 et seq.**

City police departments, **32:83 et seq.**

Classification of signal operators, **32:3.**

Computation of full time service of reserve and permanent-intermittent, **32:4.**

Contributory retirement system, retirement age for policemen not members, **32:83A.**

RETIREMENT SYSTEMS AND PENSIONS —Cont'd

Policemen and firemen —Cont'd

Creditable service. See within this heading, "Creditable service."

Death benefits to dependents.

Death and death benefits. See within this heading, "Death and death benefits."

Dependents. See within this heading, "Dependents."

Disability retirement, **32:6, 32:81B, 32:85E.**

Districts.

Classification of fire wardens, **32:3.**

Fire district laborers, pensions, **32:78, 32:78A, 32:79.**

Veterans' retirement act, allowances of firemen retiring, **32:58C.**

Eligibility for pension, **32:85C.**

Emergency temporary service by pensioners, **32:83A, 32:85B.**

Evidence as to fireman's death or disability resulting from disease as suffered in line of duty, **32:94A.**

Fire wardens, classification, **32:3.**

Group classification, **32:3, 32:4.**

Heart disease by firemen suffered in line of duty, **32:94.**

Holiday pay as regular compensation, **32:1.**

Hypertension, death or disability, **32:94.**

Incompetents or minors. See within this heading, "Incompetents or minors."

Increase in pensions, **32:80, 32:81B, 32:85E.**

Indemnification for certain hospital and medical expenses, **41:100, 41:100B.**

Intermittent police officers, **32:85H.**

Involuntary retirement, effect on allowances, **32:16.**

Length of service. See within this heading, "Length of service."

Lung disease contracted by fireman as suffered in line of duty, **32:94A.**

Massachusetts Bay Transportation Authority police, **32:20.**

RETIREMENT SYSTEMS AND PENSIONS —Cont'd
Policemen and firemen —Cont'd
Medical examination.
For disability retirement, **32:85F.**
Passing of examination by firemen subsequent to entry into service, **32:94, 32:94A.**
Mentally ill.
Incompetents or minors. See within this heading, "Incompetents or minors."
Metropolitan police. See within this heading, "Metropolitan police."
Municipal park police, benefits for death or disability of certain, **32:94.**
Non-contributory pension.
Computation, **32:81B.**
Retired policeman, payable, **32:83A.**
Optional provisions, **32:81A, 32:81B, 32:83A, 32:85E, 32:85J.**
Ordinary disability retirement, **32:6.**
Overtime compensation, payment, **147:17E.**
Park police, **32:3, 32:85B, 32:94.**
Payment of death benefits to dependents of person aiding, **32:88.**
Physical fitness standards, **32:5.**
Presumptions.
Death or disability having occurred in line of duty, presumptions arising, **32:94, 32:94A, 32:100.**
Passing medical examination subsequent to employment, presumptions arising, **32:94.**
Public works building police. See within this heading, "Public works building police."
Relief for firemen injured or killed, pension system annuity as affecting, **48:83.**
Removal, discharge, or failure of reappointment, retirement allowances in event, **32:10.**
Reserve policemen. See within this heading, "Reserve policemen."
Retirement in absence of pension system, **32:84.**
Selectmen or aldermen. See within this heading, "Selectmen or aldermen."

RETIREMENT SYSTEMS AND PENSIONS —Cont'd
Policemen and firemen —Cont'd
Signal operators.
Compensation, **32:1.**
Group classification, **32:3.**
Special police officers.
Compensation of full-time service, **32:7.**
Temporary compensation before retirement, **32:85H.**
State police. See within this heading, "State police."
State relief as affected by pension system annuity, **48:83.**
Superannuation retirements, **32:5.**
Surviving spouses of officers killed in performance of duty, **32:100.**
Temporary compensation before retirement, **32:85H.**
Town policemen and firemen, **32:85, 32:85A, 32:85E.**
Veterans' retirement act, allowances of firemen retiring, **32:58C.**
Widows, rights, **32:20, 32:71, 32:85J, 32:89 et seq., 32:100.**
Political subdivision.
Defined, **32:1.**
Municipal systems and pensions. See within this heading, "Municipal systems and pensions."
Port authority.
See PORT AUTHORITY.
Port of Boston commission employees, classification, **32:3.**
Post-retirement employment.
Employment after retirement. See within this heading, "Employment after retirement."
Potential earnings, **32:8.**
Premiums.
Insurance premiums. See within this heading, "Insurance premiums."
Presence.
Absence. See within this heading, "Absence."
Presumptions.
Abandonment of employee benefit trust distribution, presumption, **200A:5C.**
Policemen and firemen. See within this heading, "Policemen and firemen."

RETIREMENT SYSTEMS AND PENSIONS —Cont'd
PRIM (Pension Reserves Investment Management) board, **32:1, 32:22, 32:23.**
Prior service.
Certificates, **32:4.**
Creditable service. See within this heading, "Creditable service."
Defined, **32:1.**
Prior systems.
Existing systems. See within this heading, "Existing systems, effect."
Prison employees.
See CORRECTIONAL INSTITUTIONS.
PRIT (Pension Reserves Investment Trust) fund, **32:1, 32:22, 32:22B, 40:5D.**
Private pension associations or plans, **32:39 et seq., 151D:1 et seq.**
Privation contracts, **7:54.**
Probate.
See PROBATE AND FAMILY COURT.
Probate and insolvency judges, pensions, **32:65A et seq.**
Probation officers, **32:3, 32:75 et seq.**
Boston, **32:75 et seq., 276:86.**
Juvenile courts.
See JUVENILE COURTS AND DELINQUENT CHILDREN.
Notice of retirement, **276:103.**
"Profit-sharing retirement plan" defined, **151D:1.**
Promotions.
Laborers, promotion to supervisory position as affecting, **32:77C.**
School janitor or custodian promotions as affecting retirement, **32:45B.**
Proration for injuries sustained in other governmental unit, **32:7.**
Provisional employees.
Creditable prior service, **32:4.**
Eligibility, **32:3.**
Superannuation retirement allowance, **32:5.**
Public beach district employees, retention of rights, **40:12F.**
Public charge, effect of retired employee or pensioner becoming, **32:92.**
Public employee pension deductions, **32:11, 32:22.**

RETIREMENT SYSTEMS AND PENSIONS —Cont'd

Public employee retirement administration, **7:49.**

Commissioner.

Investment, purchase, sale or reinvestment of funds, consent, **32:23.**

Mortality and morbidity, program to reduce incidence among general public, **111:206.**

Notice of violations, **32:24.**

Powers and duties, **7:50.**

Contributory retirement law, **32:1 et seq.**

Criminal record offender information, access to, **32:91C.**

Intragovernmental service fund, workers' compensation chargeback, **29:2Q.**

Wage reporting system and computer match files, **32:91B.**

Public employee retirement and disability data system, **32:21.**

Public health department.

Health department. See within this heading, "Health department."

Public safety department employees.

Annuities to dependents of, for death in performance of duty, **32:89A.**

Classification, **32:3.**

Rating board, **32:26.**

Retirement, **32:26.**

State police. See within this heading, "State police."

Public service companies, investments in securities, **32:23.**

Public utilities.

See TELECOMMUNICATIONS AND ENERGY DEPARTMENT.

Public works and department.

Minimum wages, **149:26, 149:27.**

Plans as affecting wages, **149:26, 149:27.**

Police.

Public works building police. See within this heading, "Public works building police."

Restoration of employees' rights on termination of service in unclassified positions, **16:4.**

RETIREMENT SYSTEMS AND PENSIONS —Cont'd

Public works and department —Cont'd

Transfer of officers and employees, **16:1.**

Public works building police.

Eligibility for retirement, **32:3.**

Hypertension or heart disease, death or disability, **32:94.**

Purchase of investment securities by trustees or plan administrators at fair market value as authorized investment, **151D:3.**

Qualification and disqualification.

Eligibility. See within this heading, "Eligibility."

Railroads.

Employment security.

See EMPLOYMENT SECURITY.

Tax deductions, **62:3.**

Rating board with regard to retirement of officers and inspectors in department of public safety, **32:26.**

Rebate, penalty for receipt in connection with payments to pension plan, **149:27.**

Reclassification in group after attaining maximum age, superannuation retirement as affected, **32:5.**

Recorder and deputy recorders of land court, **185:6.**

Records.

Assets and liabilities of plans, boards to keep data relating, **32:20.**

Child support enforcement reports, **32:20.**

Copies. See within this heading, "Copies."

Correction of errors, **32:20.**

Employees' records to be kept by boards, **32:20.**

Examination, inspection or investigation. See within this heading, "Examination, inspection, or investigation."

False reports or statements. See within this heading, "False reports or statements."

Filing. See within this heading, "Filing."

Private pension association, violation by custodian of books and papers, **32:40.**

Protection against fraud, **32:18, 32:91A.**

RETIREMENT SYSTEMS AND PENSIONS —Cont'd

Records —Cont'd

Statements and reports. See within this heading, "Statements and reports."

Redevelopment authorities, acceptance of act, **32:28.**

Re-employed persons, eligibility, **32:3.**

Reentry into active service.

Creditable service. See within this heading, "Creditable service."

Reestablishment of membership, **32:3.**

Reformatory institutions, **32:46 et seq.**

See CORRECTIONAL INSTITUTIONS.

Refund.

Cash refund annuity, option, **32:12.**

Disability retirement benefits in case of excess earnings, **32:91A.**

Part of payment to pension plan, refund or rebate by employee, **149:27.**

Teachers, refund of military service credit fund, **32:22.**

Regional health district offices and positions to be placed in county system, **111:27B.**

Regional school districts.

Acceptance of Veterans' Retirement Law, **32:60.**

Blue Hills regional vocational school employees, system, **32:1 et seq.**

Nonteaching employees, contributory retirement system, **71:16F.**

Retiring authority, **32:59.**

Teachers' retirement system. See within this heading, "Teachers' retirement system."

Registers of probate included in county systems, **32:2.**

Registration, **151D:2.**

Exceptions, **151D:7.**

Filing fees, **151D:5.**

Registry of motor vehicles, employees of.

Motor vehicles. See within this heading, "Motor vehicles."

"Regular compensation" defined, **32:1.**

"Regular deductions" defined, **32:1.**

Regular interest, **32:1, 32:22.**

RETIREMENT SYSTEMS AND PENSIONS —Cont'd

Rehabilitation, **32:8, 32:21.**

Rehabilitation commission of Massachusetts, rights of employees, **6:75.**

Reimbursement.

Actions. See within this heading, "Actions."

Boards of retirement. See within this heading, "Boards of retirement."

Loaned employee injured while aiding other governmental unit, **32:7.**

Teacher's pension paid to ineligible person, **32:20.**

Transfer of membership, **32:3.**

Veterans' pension based upon creditable service performed with other governmental unit, **32:59A.**

Visual services, reimbursement of optometrist or physician, **151D:4.**

Reinstatement to active service.

After discharge or removal, **32:16.**

Creditable service. See within this heading, "Creditable service."

Justices, **32:65D½.**

Public works department, **16:4.**

Removal or discharge from office or employment, **32:10.**

Deferral of receipt of allowance due on removal, etc., **32:10.**

Hearing, **32:16.**

Judicial review, **32:16.**

Termination retirement allowance. See within this heading, "Termination retirement allowance."

Veterans, **32:16.**

Repeal of laws, **32:25.**

Reports.

Statements and reports. See within this heading, "Statements and reports."

Representative of employee organizations, leaves of absence, **32:28K.**

Reserve fund.

Annuity reserve fund. See within this heading, "Annuity reserve fund."

Pension reserve fund, **29:6B, 32:1, 32:22, 40:5D.**

Pension reserves investment management board, indemnification, **32:20B.**

RETIREMENT SYSTEMS AND PENSIONS —Cont'd

Reserve fund —Cont'd

Pension reserves investment trust (PRIT) fund, **32:1, 32:22, 32:22B, 32:23, 40:5D.**

Reserve policemen.

Amount of accidental disability allowance, **32:7.**

Annuities to dependents for death in performance of duty, **32:89 et seq.**

Computation of full time service, **32:4.**

Creditable service, **32:57B, 32:85G.**

Injured police officer, retirement, **32:85H.**

Resident agent, appointment by nonresident plan administrator or trustee, **151D:3.**

Resignation from office, **32:10.**

Deferral of allowance due on resignation, etc., **32:10.**

Superannuation retirements, resignation as affecting, **32:10.**

Restoration.

Reinstatement to active service. See within this heading, "Reinstatement to active service."

"Retirement allowance" defined, **32:1.**

Retirement boards.

Boards of retirement. See within this heading, "Boards of retirement."

Retirement certificates, **32:4.**

Retirement Law Commission, **10:35I.**

Administration and finance executive office, agency within, **7:4G.**

Administrative rules, **7:50.**

Employment dislocations and assistance in reemployment of dislocated workers, **6:17.**

Establishment, **10:35I.**

Governor and council, supervision, **6:17.**

Retiring authority, defined, **32:59.**

Return of accumulated total deductions, **32:10, 32:11, 32:15.**

Additional deductions, **32:22.**

Failure to file statements, **32:18.**

Return to service.

Evaluation of ability to perform, **32:26.**

RETIREMENT SYSTEMS AND PENSIONS —Cont'd

Revenue commissioner to appoint member of unpaid contributory retirement appeal board, **32:16.**

Review of plan by certified public accountant or public accountant, **151D:3A.**

Revocation.

Suspension or discontinuance of benefits. See within this heading, "Suspension or discontinuance of benefits."

Revocation by municipalities of acceptance of statute.

Effect, **4:4A.**

Funding system, irrevocability of acceptance, **32:22D.**

Revocation of election by member to continue working beyond mandatory retirement age, **32:90G¾.**

Rules and regulations of boards, **32:20, 32:21, 32:24.**

Safety department.

Public safety departments. See within this heading, "Public safety department employees."

Salary.

Compensation. See within this heading, "Compensation."

Sales.

Interest in pension, annuity, or allowance, **32:92.**

Securities held by system, **32:23.**

Savings banks.

See SAVINGS BANKS.

Savings fund.

Annuity savings fund. See within this heading, "Annuity saving fund."

Schools and education.

Athletic instructors, retirement, **32:1.**

Board of higher education, **15A:40.**

Colleges and universities. See within this heading, "Colleges and universities."

Crossing guard as eligible for retirement benefits, **32:1.**

Employment of retired teachers, **32:91.**

Janitors, municipal pensions, **32:44 et seq.**

Lunch program employees, included, **32:1.**

Regional school districts. See within this heading, "Regional school districts."

RETIREMENT SYSTEMS AND PENSIONS —Cont'd

Schools and education —Cont'd
Social workers.
Teachers' retirement system.
See within this heading,
"Teachers' retirement
system."
Student survivor benefits, **32:7,
32:9, 32:26.**
Teachers' retirement system. See
within this heading,
"Teachers' retirement
system."
Scrubwomen in state house,
pensions, **32:74.**
Seasonal or intermittent
employees.
Call firemen. See within this
heading, "Call firemen."
Creditable prior service, **32:4.**
Eligibility, **32:3.**
Injured intermittent police
officers, retirement, **32:85H.**
Soldiers' homes, performance of
emergency services by
retired personnel, **32:91.**
Superannuation retirement
allowance, **32:5.**
Selectmen or aldermen.
Laborers, pensions, **32:77.**
Nonsalaried service as affecting
retirement, **32:4.**
Notice of retirement, **50:6A.**
Police and firemen, authority as
to pensions, **32:85, 32:85B,
32:85E.**
Optional provisions as to
pensions, **32:85E.**
Seventy, retention in service
after, **32:91.**
Vote of acceptance of retirement
act in towns having system
under special act, **32:28.**
Self-employed individuals.
Funds, exceptions, **151D:7.**
Individual retirement account.
See INDIVIDUAL
RETIREMENT
ACCOUNT.
Separate maintenance, pension not
exempt from attachment or
execution in case, **235:34A.**
"Service" defined, **32:1.**
Services by retired employee.
Employment after retirement.
See within this heading,
"Employment after
retirement."
Sewer district laborers, **32:78,
32:78A.**

RETIREMENT SYSTEMS AND PENSIONS —Cont'd

Sheriffs, duty with respect to
retirement of certain court
officers, **32:66.**
Sick leave credits for judges,
32:65J.
Signal operators.
Policemen and firemen. See
within this heading,
"Policemen and firemen."
Social security.
See SOCIAL SECURITY.
Social workers for schools.
Teachers' retirement system. See
within this heading,
"Teachers' retirement
system."
Soldiers' homes.
Employment of retired persons,
32:91.
Medical and hospital expense
payments, **175:22.**
South Africa, investment of public
pension funds, **32:23.**
Southeastern Massachusetts
Regional Planning District
employees, transfer to
successor district without loss
of rights, **40B:11.**
Spanish and World War I
veterans, **32:56 et seq.**
Acceptance of statutes, **32:60.**
Appeal to contributory
retirement appeal board,
32:57A.
Army nurses, **32:57 et seq.**
Creditable service for period of
military or naval service,
32:58A.
Guaranty of rights as
retirement, **32:25.**
Half pay, retirement from public
service, **32:56 et seq.**
Incapacitation, retirement,
32:56, 32:57.
Medical examination before or
during retirement, **32:57A.**
Option for benefit of surviving
spouse, **32:58B.**
Retiring authority, defined,
32:59.
Thirty-year service, retirement
after, **32:58.**
Where law in effect, **32:60.**
Special district court judges,
32:65B.
Special education personnel in
school department of certain
institutions, **71B:12.**
Special fund for military service
credit, **32:22.**
Appropriations, **32:22.**

RETIREMENT SYSTEMS AND PENSIONS —Cont'd

Special fund for military service
credit —Cont'd
Creditable service for period of
military or naval service,
32:4, 32:5, 32:58A.
Death of member before
retirement, **32:22.**
Defined, **32:1.**
Disposition of funds as of Jan. 1,
1946, **32:27.**
Disposition of military service
deductions of members,
32:12B, 32:22.
Dual membership in more than
one system, effect, **32:22.**
Regular interest, **32:22.**
Reinstatement after withdrawal,
32:22.
Reserve units called to active
duty, creditable service,
32:58A.
Teachers, refund of military
service credit fund, **32:22.**
Time for payments by towns and
districts, **32:22.**
Transfer of account to annuity
reserve fund on retirement,
32:22.
Withdrawal of member, effect,
32:22.
Special laws, prior systems under.
Existing systems. See within
this heading, "Existing
systems, effect."
Special master or auditor, payment
for services rendered by
pensioner acting, **32:91.**
Special payment.
Defined, **151D:1.**
Experience deficiency, special
payments in cases, **151D:13.**
"Split-funded plan" defined,
151D:1.
Spouses.
Husband and wife. See within
this heading, "Husband and
wife."
State actuary, duties, **32:21.**
State ballot law commission,
retired supreme judicial court
justice as member, **55B:1.**
State board.
Boards of retirement. See within
this heading, "Boards of
retirement."
State-Boston retirement system,
temporary teachers as
members, **32:3.**
State college building authority.
Retirement system, inclusion of
employees, **32:2.**

RETIREMENT SYSTEMS AND PENSIONS —Cont'd

State college building authority —Cont'd

State employees, personnel defined, **32:1.**

State colleges, **75:14.**

Building authority.

State college building authority, **32:1, 32:2.**

Privileges of state college personnel, **73:16.**

Reemployment as substitute teachers of retired teachers, **32:91.**

State house.

See STATE HOUSE.

Statements and reports.

Accountants, review of plan and report, **151D:3A.**

Amendments, modifications, or alterations of plans, reports, **151D:3.**

Annual statement or report. See within this heading, "Annual statement or report."

Boards, financial statements, **32:20, 32:23.**

District court justices, report of removal or retirement, **218:43, 231:108.**

Education commissioner, report concerning state teachers' retirement system, **32:20.**

False reports or statements. See within this heading, "False reports or statements."

Financial report by state treasurer, **32:23.**

Financial reports of pension associations, **32:40.**

Fraud, protection against with respect to filed statements, **32:18.**

Insurance commissioner, financial reports filed, **32:23.**

Members' statements, filing, **32:18.**

Natural guardian of minor dependent, report, **32:9.**

Perjury. See within this heading, "Perjury as to statements in regard."

Private pension associations, **32:40.**

State boards of retirement, **32:20.**

State treasurer's report as to financial condition of retirement systems, **32:23.**

RETIREMENT SYSTEMS AND PENSIONS —Cont'd

Statements and reports —Cont'd

Verification of statements of service, **32:4.**

State police, **32:26.**

Accidental disability retirement benefits, **32:26.**

Additional retirement allowance to war veterans, **32:26.**

Amount of allowances and pensions. See within this heading, "Amount of allowances and pensions."

Annuities to dependents for death in performance of duty, **32:89A.**

Attainment of retirement age, **32:26.**

Children of state policeman retired for illness or injury in performance of duty, **32:26.**

Classification of members, **32:3, 32:26.**

Disability retirement.

Reinstatement after disability retirement, **22C:24A.**

Group classification, **32:3, 32:26.**

Heart disease, death or disability, **32:94.**

Hypertension, death or disability, **32:94.**

Illness or injury incurred in performance of duty, dependents of state policeman retired, **32:26.**

Length of service of state police officers and inspectors, **32:28A.**

Options available on retirement, **32:12.**

Ordinary disability, retirement, **32:3, 32:6.**

Physical or mental incapacity, retirement, **32:26.**

Request, retirement, **32:28A.**

Widows and children, **32:12B.**

State system, **32:1 et seq.**

State treasurer.

Administrator, employment, **10:5.**

Advance payments of retirement allowance to state employees, **32:98.**

Chairman of state board of retirement, treasurer, **10:18.**

Combined investment funds for state employees' retirement system, **32:23.**

Co-operative nominee partnerships for benefit of employee systems, **32:23.**

RETIREMENT SYSTEMS AND PENSIONS —Cont'd

State treasurer —Cont'd

Direct deposit of retirement benefits, **29:31.**

Funds, custody and management, **32:23.**

Group insurance, elderly retired government employees, **32A:10B.**

Investments for state board of retirement by deputy state treasurer, **10:5C.**

Issuance of warrant to assess tax for expenses of system, **32:21.**

Report as to financial condition of retirement systems, **32:23.**

Right of prisoner to payment for service in treasury department, **32:91.**

Teachers' retirement funds, management, **32:23.**

"Statutory vested benefit" defined, **151D:1.**

Students as eligible for survivors benefits, **32:7, 32:9, 32:26.**

Substitute teachers, employment of retired teaching personnel, **32:9, 32:91.**

Succession tax.

Legacy and succession taxes. See within this heading, "Legacy and succession taxes, exemption."

Suffolk County.

Co-operative service, employees, **32:1, 32:28.**

Dual membership provisions as applicable to person employed, **32:3.**

Prison employees, pensions, **32:46.**

Probation officers, pensions, **32:75.**

Summary of fund and amendments to plan to be furnished to participants, **151D:3.**

Superannuation retirements, **32:5, 32:90G½.**

Abolition of office, **32:10.**

Absence, superannuation retirement allowance, **32:5.**

Additional amounts, **32:5, 32:90C.**

Increase for 20 years of service, **32:90C3/4.**

Alternate method of computing allowance, **32:5.**

RETIREMENT SYSTEMS AND PENSIONS —Cont'd

Superannuation retirements —Cont'd

Amount, **32:5, 32:10.**

Increase for 20 years of service, **32:90C¾.**

Appeal of involuntary retirement to contributory retirement appeals board, retirement pending, **32:16.**

Civil service employees, age discrimination, **32:90H.**

Compensation, allowance in case of unavailable rates, **32:5.**

Conditions, **32:5.**

Deferral of, right, **32:10.**

Elective officials. See within this heading, "Elective officials."

Failure of reappointment or reelection, **32:10.**

Firefighters and police officers, physical examinations, termination of employment, **31:61A.**

Hearing, **32:16.**

Husband and wife in same or different systems, **32:5.**

Inactive members, **32:3, 32:5.**

Increase for 20 years of service, **32:90C¾.**

Increase for 25 years of service, **32:90C½.**

Increase in retirement allowance of certain municipal employees, **32:90C.**

Involuntary retirement, **32:16.**

Late entry into membership, **32:3.**

Leave or period of absence, **32:5.**

Limit as to total normal yearly amount, **32:5.**

Mandatory retirement age, members continuing to work after reaching, **32:90G½, 32:90G¾.**

Maximum age, **32:5.**

Minimum benefits, **32:5.**

Part-time employees, **32:5.**

Probation officers, **32:75 et seq.**

Reclassification after attaining maximum age, **32:5.**

Reestablishment or reinstatement, effect, **32:3.**

Removal or discharge as affecting, **32:10.**

Resignation as affecting, **32:10.**

Suspended employee, retirement, **32:18.**

Teachers, **32:5.**

RETIREMENT SYSTEMS AND PENSIONS —Cont'd

Superannuation retirements —Cont'd

Teachers' retirement system. Alternative superannuation retirement benefit program, **32:5.**

Transferee of membership, eligibility, **32:3.**

Veterans, amount of allowance, **32:5.**

Superior court.

Judges of, pension, **32:65A et seq.**

Jurisdiction of enforcement, **32:24.**

Officers and employees of, pensions, **32:66, 32:67.**

Pensioners, payment for services as auditor or special master, **32:91.**

Superseded systems.

Existing systems. See within this heading, "Existing systems, effect."

Supervisor of school janitorial service, pension, **32:45B.**

Supplemental dependent allowance, **32:7.**

Support obligations.

Divorce.

See DIVORCE AND ALIMONY.

Incompetents or minors, **32:92A, 235:34A.**

Supreme judicial court.

Auditor or special master, payment for services, **32:91.**

Justices of, pension, **32:65A et seq.**

Temporary and retired justices, **211:24.**

List of retired justices, posting of names, **32:65E.**

Officers and employees, **32:66, 32:67.**

Pensioners, payment for services as auditor or special master, **32:91.**

Reinstatement in service, **32:65D½.**

State ballot law commission, retired supreme judicial court justice as member, **55B:1.**

Survivor allowance, **32:12, 32:12B, 32:12C.**

Accidental death benefits, **32:9.**

Accumulated deductions as affecting, **32:12B.**

RETIREMENT SYSTEMS AND PENSIONS —Cont'd

Survivor allowance —Cont'd

Annuities and annuity contracts. See within this heading, "Annuities and annuity contracts."

Children.

Incompetents or minors. See within this heading, "Incompetents or minors."

Death of spouse receiving allowance as beneficiary under option, **32:12.**

Disability, widows of public employees retired, **32:101.**

Firefighter's or police officer's widow, **32:85J, 32:89, 32:89A, 32:89B, 32:100.**

Group insurance coverage for surviving spouse, **32A:10, 32B:9B.**

Incompetents or minors. See within this heading, "Incompetents or minors."

Janitor's widow, **32:44B.**

Joint and last survivor allowance, option, **32:12.**

Judge's widow, **32:65C.**

Laborer's widow, **32:77A.**

Limitation on total annual allowance of survivorship benefits under contributory retirement law, **32:12B.**

Mandatory retirement age, deductions from salaries of employees working past, **32:90G.**

Maximum pension for surviving spouse of deceased public official or employee, **32:95B.**

Mentally ill.

Incompetents or minors. See within this heading, "Incompetents or minors."

Municipal employees, widows, payment of annuities, **32:89D, 32:95, 32:95A, 32:100.**

National guard technicians, group health insurance for survivors, **32A:10.**

Nonparticipating employee's surviving widow, **32:12C.**

Payment to beneficiaries pending determination of claims for accidental death benefits, **32:12A.**

Policeman's or fireman's widow, **32:85J, 32:89, 32:89A, 32:89B, 32:100.**

RETIREMENT SYSTEMS AND PENSIONS —Cont'd

Survivor allowance —Cont'd

Reimbursement of one retirement system by another, **32:3, 32:59A.**

School janitors' widows, **32:44B.**

Veteran's widow, **32:25, 32:58B.**

Suspension from employment of municipal or county officer or employee upon indictment for misconduct, effect on retirement benefits, **268A:25.**

Suspension or discontinuance of benefits.

Failing to file statements or records, **32:18.**

Refusal to submit to medical examination, **32:8.**

Taxation.

Alcoholic beverage tax, crediting of receipts, **138:21.**

Assessment for municipal system, **32:22.**

Exemption from attachment, execution, taxation. See within this heading, "Exemption from attachment, execution, or taxation."

Exemption from income tax, **32:19, 62:3, 62:5.**

Income tax.

See INCOME TAX.

Individual retirement account, Income tax, **62:2, 62:5.**

Legacy and succession taxes, exemption, **32:19, 65:1.**

Levy for pension and retirement funds, **32:22.**

Private pension associations, **32:41, 59:5.**

Railroads, deductions and exemptions allowed in determining taxable income, **62:3.**

Warrant to assess tax for expenses of system, issuance by state treasurer, **32:21.**

Teachers.

Alternative superannuation retirement benefit program, **32:104.**

Teachers' retirement system, **32:10.**

Actuary, information, **32:22.**

Administration and finance executive office, teachers' retirement board as within, **7:4G.**

Administration by board, **15:16, 32:20.**

RETIREMENT SYSTEMS AND PENSIONS —Cont'd

Teachers' retirement system —Cont'd

Alternative superannuation retirement benefit program, **32:5.**

Annual report of board, **32:20.**

Annuities purchased for employees of education department and public educational institutions, **15:18A.**

Appropriations, **32:22, 32:42, 32:43.**

Assignability of benefits, **32:19.**

Athletic programs, teachers engaged, **32:1.**

Board of retirement, **15:16 to 15:18A, 32:20, 32:43.**

Bond for secretary of board, **15:18.**

Boston.

Application to teachers in schools, **32:1.**

State-Boston system, **32:3.**

Clerical assistants to board, **15:18.**

Commissioner of education, report, **32:20.**

Committee on investments, **32:23.**

Commonwealth checks, payment, **29:32.**

Compensation of member of board, **15:17, 32:22.**

Consultants, retired teachers employed, **32:91.**

Continued service after retirement age, **32:5.**

Contributions to be paid by governmental unit, **32:22.**

Co-operative nominee partnership for Massachusetts teachers' retirement fund, establishment, **32:23.**

Creditable service, **32:3, 32:4.**

Critical shortage of teachers.

Employment of retired teachers, **32:91.**

Deductions transmitted to annuity savings fund, **32:22.**

Defined, **32:1.**

Deputy state treasurer, investments for board of retirement, **10:5C.**

Description of system, **32:2.**

Education commissioner, report concerning state teachers' retirement system, **32:20.**

RETIREMENT SYSTEMS AND PENSIONS —Cont'd

Teachers' retirement system —Cont'd

Employment after retirement, without loss of pension, **32:91.**

Equalizing monthly installments, increase, **32:13.**

Expense fund, **32:22.**

Expenses of board, **15:17.**

Federal government.

Other states or federal government. See within this heading, "Other states or federal government."

Financial reports, **32:23.**

Funds, investment of retirement funds by deputy state treasurer, **10:5C.**

Governor, board members appointed, **15:16.**

Group life and health insurance for retired teachers, procedures for termination, **32B:11E.**

Guaranty of allowances by Commonwealth, **32:25.**

Indemnification, teachers' retirement board, **32:20B.**

Ineligible person, reimbursement of teacher's pension paid, **32:20.**

Investment of funds, **10:5C, 32:23.**

Involuntary retirement, **32:43.**

Maximum age.

Alternative superannuation retirement benefit program, **32:5.**

Medical panel, selection, **32:6.**

Members of board, **15:16.**

Military service credit fund, refund, **32:22.**

Municipal pensions, **32:42, 32:43.**

Out-of-state service credit.

Other states or federal government. See within this heading, "Other states or federal government."

Part-time professional consultants, employment of retired teachers, **32:91.**

Payment of allowance, **32:13.**

Physical education teachers included, **32:1.**

Powers and duties of board, **32:20.**

RETIREMENT SYSTEMS AND PENSIONS —Cont'd

Teachers' retirement system —Cont'd

PRIT Fund, participation, **32:22.**

Reemployment of retired teachers, **32:91.**

Refund of military service credit fund, **32:22.**

Reimbursement for pension paid to one ineligible, **32:20.**

Retirement Law Commission, **10:35I.**

School social workers, **32:1.**

Social workers for schools, **32:1.**

Special education personnel, **71B:12.**

State-Boston retirement system, **32:3.**

State treasurer, **32:23.**

Substitute teachers, retired teachers, **32:9, 32:91.**

Superannuation retirements, **32:5.**

Temporary teachers as members of State-Boston retirement system, **32:3.**

Transfer of reestablishment of membership, effect, **32:3.**

Telephone companies, investment in securities, **32:23.**

Temporary employees.

Creditable prior service, **32:4.**

Deferred compensation program established, **29:64, 29:64D.**

Eligibility, **32:3.**

Emergency employment. See within this heading, "Emergency employment."

Judge or justice, temporary service after retirement as affecting pension, **32:65F, 32:65G, 211:24, 211A:16.**

Seasonal or intermittent employees. See within this heading, "Seasonal or intermittent employees."

State-Boston retirement system, temporary teachers as members, **32:3.**

Superannuation retirement allowance, **32:5.**

Ten years of creditable service, vesting of accrued benefits after, **32:10.**

Termination of plan, **151D:14.**

Termination retirement allowance.

Abolition of office, **32:10.**

Amount, **32:10.**

Collusion or conspiracy, effect, **32:10.**

RETIREMENT SYSTEMS AND PENSIONS —Cont'd

Termination retirement allowance —Cont'd

Deference of, right, **32:10.**

Eligibility, **32:3.**

Failure of reappointment or reelection, **32:10.**

Removal or discharge as affecting right to, **32:10.**

Violation of law or rules, effect of removal or discharge, **32:10.**

Term of service before person may receive retirement benefits, **32:5.**

Terms of options, **32:12.**

Third party beneficiaries, **32:14A.**

Time or date.

Allowances, intervals of payment, **32:13.**

Annual statements, date for filing, **32:20, 32:23.**

Appeals as to retirement, pensions, etc., **32:16.**

Checks for benefits, time for presentation, **32:11.**

Fiscal year changes, conforming, **32:22.**

Housing authorities, time for acceptance of Veteran's Retirement Law, **32:60.**

Involuntary retirement hearing, time for assigning hearing officers, **32:16.**

Judge or judicial officers, computation of time served, **32:65A, 32:65D.**

Length of service. See within this heading, "Length of service."

Registration, time, **151D:2.**

Termination of plan, allocation of benefits in event, **151D:14.**

Towns and districts, payments, **32:22.**

Vesting of rights in pension fund, length of service required, **151D:13.**

Waiver of vested benefits provisions requirements, limitation on length of time, **151D:9.**

Withdrawal of certain deductions, time, **32:22.**

Total deductions.

Accumulated total deductions. See within this heading, "Accumulated total deductions."

RETIREMENT SYSTEMS AND PENSIONS —Cont'd

Total disability, **32:6.**

Town clerks.

City and town clerks. See within this heading, "City and town clerks."

Town meetings.

See TOWN MEETINGS.

Towns.

Municipal systems and pensions. See within this heading, "Municipal systems and pensions."

Traffic supervisor as eligible for retirement benefits, **32:1.**

Transfer of funds, **32:22.**

Accumulated total deductions, to annuity reserve fund, on retirement, **32:22.**

Annuity reserve fund, **32:22.**

Annuity savings fund. See within this heading, "Annuity saving fund."

Deficiency appropriation for annuity reserve fund, **32:22.**

Disposition of funds as of Jan 1, 1946, **32:27.**

Investment income account, **32:22.**

Military service credit fund accounts, **32:22.**

Pension fund, **32:11, 32:22.**

Excess in annuity reserve fund transferred, **32:22.**

Restoration after retirement disability as effecting transfer to annuity savings fund, **32:22.**

Transfer of membership, **32:3, 32:22.**

Reimbursement, **32:3.**

Superannuation retirements, eligibility of transferee of membership, **32:3.**

Termination of service in one of two or more governmental units, **32:3.**

Transfer of rights or interests, invalidity, **32:92.**

Transportation areas, rights of former employees of private companies acquired, **161:147.**

Treasurers.

Municipal systems. See within this heading, "Municipal systems and pensions."

State treasurer. See within this heading, "State treasurer."

Trial or hearings.

Hearings. See within this heading, "Hearings."

RETIREMENT SYSTEMS AND PENSIONS —Cont'd

Trust companies.
See TRUST COMPANIES.
Tuberculosis hospital personnel transferred to state service, rights, **111:83.**
Turnpike Authority employees' retirement and pensions.
Acceptance of act, **32:28.**
Administration, **32:20.**
Allowance, deposit in credit union, **32:20.**
Checks for benefits, time for presentation, **32:11.**
Cost-of-living adjustments, **32:102.**
Credit union, deposit of allowance, **32:20.**
Deferred compensation programs, **81A:21.**
Definitions, **32:1.**
Dereliction of members, initiation of proceedings, **32:15.**
Description of system, **32:2.**
Election between compensation and pension, **152:73.**
Establishment of system, **32:20.**
Guaranty of allowances, **32:25.**
Individual retirement accounts, **81A:22.**
Loaned employee injured while aiding other governmental unit, inapplicability of provision, **32:7.**
Management of fund, **32:23.**
Membership, **32:3.**
Methods of financing, **32:22.**
Notice of violations, Public Employee Retirement Commissioner, **32:24.**
Reimbursement of retirement costs, **81A:24.**
Superannuation retirement, **32:5.**
Supervision, **32:21.**
Violations, **32:24.**
Workers' compensation benefits, effect, **32:14.**
Two or more systems, membership in.
Dual membership. See within this heading, "Dual membership."
Unclaimed benefits transferred to pension funds, **32:11.**
Unemployment compensation benefits as affected by, **151A:25, 151A:28.**
See EMPLOYMENT SECURITY.

RETIREMENT SYSTEMS AND PENSIONS —Cont'd

Uniform Securities Act, exemptions, **110A:402.**
United States consumer price index, cost-of-living adjustments determined on basis, **32:102, 118A:2.**
Calculation, **32:103.**
Universities.
Colleges and universities. See within this heading, "Colleges and universities."
Vacation pay.
Accumulated vacation allowances upon separation from service, payment, **29:31A.**
Judges, vacation allowances and sick leave credits for judges, **32:65J.**
Municipal employees, vacation pay upon retirement, **41:111E.**
Valuation of assets and liabilities by actuary, annual, **32:21.**
Variable pension contracts assigned to separate investment accounts, provisions, **175:132F.**
Venue of complaints for failure to pay contributions or benefits, **151D:11.**
Verification, **32:4.**
Vesting of fund participants, **32:10, 151D:13.**
Veterans.
Acceptance of pension law by municipalities, **32:54, 32:55.**
Adjustments in retirement allowances, **32:102.**
Allowance on retirement before reaching age fifty-five, **32:10.**
Previously retired veterans, **32:10.**
Allowances under act, **32:58C, 32:58D.**
Amount of permissible income for veterans retired because of disability, **32:56.**
Army nurses in public service, **32:57 et seq.**
Beneficiaries other than spouse, eligibility, **32:58B.**
Commissioner of veterans' services, **7:4M.**
Creditable service, **32:4, 32:5, 32:58A, 32:59A.**
Deductions from military service credit, disposition on death of member before retirement, **32:22.**

RETIREMENT SYSTEMS AND PENSIONS —Cont'd

Veterans —Cont'd
Defined, **32:1.**
Dependents, right under retirement system, **32:25, 32:58B.**
Disability retirement, amount of permissible income for veterans, **32:56.**
Disposition of military service credit deductions of members, **32:12B, 32:22.**
Employment service, state retirement credit for former employees of veterans' employment service, **32:4.**
Extension of time for acceptance by municipalities, **32:60.**
Former employees of United States, employment service of state retirement credit, **32:4.**
Further allowance dependent upon period of service, **32:56, 32:57.**
Guaranteed rights on retirement, **32:25.**
Half pay, retirement from public service, **32:56 et seq.**
Housing authorities, veterans employed, **32:56 et seq.**
Increase in pension allowance of veterans retiring after 30 years' service, **32:58.**
Insurance company employees, military service counted for company pension, **175:36.**
Joint employment by two towns, **32:53.**
Mandatory retirement age, continued employment after, **32:90G, 32:90G¾.**
Military service credit deductions, disposition on death of member before retirement, **32:22.**
Optional benefits of surviving spouse, **32:58B.**
Ordinary disability retirement, **32:6.**
Provisional training regiments, persons serving, **32:1.**
Reimbursement for payment of pension based upon creditable service performed in other governmental unit, **32:59A.**
Removal or discharge, **32:16.**
Rights on retirement, **32:25.**
Services districts, acceptance of act, **32:28.**

RETIREMENT SYSTEMS AND PENSIONS —Cont'd

Veterans —Cont'd

Soldiers' homes. See within this heading, "Soldiers' homes."

Spanish and World War I veterans. See within this heading, "Spanish and World War I veterans."

Special fund for military service credit. See within this heading, "Special fund for military service credit."

State police, additional retirement allowance, **32:26.**

Superannuation retirement allowances, **32:5.**

Surviving spouse, rights, **32:25, 32:58B.**

Termination date of certain laws relating, **32:4, 32:58A.**

Towns.

Extension of time for acceptance by town, **32:56.**

Veterans in service, **32:52 et seq., 32:58D.**

United States, payment over of compensation or pension, **115:5.**

Veterans Employment Service of United States Employment Service, creditable service credit for former employees, **32:4.**

Wartime service of judge as period of service in office, **32:65C.**

World War I veterans.

Spanish and World War I veterans. See within this heading, "Spanish and World War I veterans."

Veterans Employment Service of United States, **32:4.**

Victims of violent crime.

See VICTIMS OF VIOLENT CRIMES.

Violations of retirement laws, **32:24, 151D:5, 151D:10.**

Visual services, reimbursement of optometrist or physician, **151D:4.**

Vocational rehabilitation program, **32:8.**

Voluntary retirement after 10 years creditable service, vesting of accrued retirement benefits after, **32:10.**

Voting rights of retired public employees, **32:3.**

RETIREMENT SYSTEMS AND PENSIONS —Cont'd

Vouchers for payments from funds of retirement systems, **32:23.**

Wages.

Compensation. See within this heading, "Compensation."

Waiver.

Benefits waived by one electing not to become member, **32:3.**

Other states or United States, funds administered under laws, **151D:8.**

Portions of retirement allowance, waiver of rights, **32:90B.**

Requirements of vested benefits provisions of law, provision for waiver of in economic hardship cases, **151D:9.**

Retired public employee appointed to public office, waiver of rights, **32:91.**

Warrant to assess tax for expenses of system, issuance by state treasurer, **32:21.**

Water district laborers, pensions, **32:78, 32:78A, 32:79.**

Water pollution control division, employees, **21:26.**

Watershed guards, membership, **32:3.**

Welfare funds.

Board of health, welfare, and retirement trust funds, **151D:1 to 151D:18.**

Widow.

Survivor allowance. See within this heading, "Survivor allowance."

Wife.

Husband and wife. See within this heading, "Husband and wife."

Withdrawal from service, public employee pension deductions, **32:11.**

Withdrawal of deductions, time, **32:22.**

Withdrawal of member.

As affecting military service credit fund, **32:22.**

Return of accumulated total deductions. See within this heading, "Return of accumulated total deductions."

Withholding.

Allowances for payment of medical or hospital insurance premiums, **32:19A.**

RETIREMENT SYSTEMS AND PENSIONS —Cont'd

Withholding —Cont'd

Deductions from compensation of members, **32:22.**

Payroll deductions from compensation of members, **32:19, 32:19A, 32:22, 32:92.**

Mandatory retirement age, deductions from salaries of employees working past, **32:90G, 32:90G½, 32:90G¾, 32:95A.**

Pension funds, **32:22.**

Teachers' retirement system, **32:19B.**

Subject to child support liens, **32:19C.**

Witnesses.

Before contributory retirement appeal board, **32:16, 32:20.**

Before retirement boards, **32:16, 32:20.**

Fees. See within this heading, "Fees."

Health, welfare, and retirement funds, witnesses at investigation, **151D:3.**

Workers' compensation.

See WORKERS' COMPENSATION.

Worksharing, continuation of health benefits, **151A:29D.**

World War I veterans.

Spanish and World War I veterans. See within this heading, "Spanish and World War I veterans."

RETRACTION ACT.

Libel, **231:93, 260:32.**

RETRAINING PROGRAMS.

Disabled public employees returning to work, **31:39.**

RETREADED TIRE.

Defined, **90:1.**

Sale, **90:7M.**

RETROACTIVE OR PROSPECTIVE OPERATION.

Absentee trust beneficiaries, settlement of trust estates involving, **203:39.**

Building code, **143:92.**

Employment security director, rulings, **151A:70.**

Ex post facto laws, **US Const Art 1 Sec 9 cl 3 and Art 1 Sec 10 cl 1.**

Fraternal benefit societies.

Law inapplicable to existing societies, **176:51.**

RETROACTIVE OR PROSPECTIVE OPERATION —Cont'd

Group hospital service plans, **176A:10.**

Life or endowment insurance policy, **175:130.**

Recorded instruments as to land titles, statutes as to indefinite references, **184:25.**

Small loans, determination of maximum rate of charge, **140:100.**

RETROCESSION.

Jurisdiction over land formally ceded to government, **1:7A.**

Notice, **1:7A.**

Reinsurance Intermediary Act, **175:177T.**

RETURN DAY.
See RETURN OF PROCESS.

RETURN OF PROCESS.

Absentee's estate, time for return of process against, **200:3.**

Absentee trust beneficiaries, proceedings for transfer of estates, **203:29.**

Attachment of property.
See ATTACHMENT OF PROPERTY.

Citation, return, **228:5.**

Collection of local taxes, affidavit as to service in proceedings, **60:1, 60:57.**

Constable, return, **41:94, 262:9.**

Criminal proceedings, return of expense under oath, **262:47.**

Day of return.
Absentee's estate, process against, **200:3.**
Absent trust beneficiaries, proceedings for transfer of estates, **203:29.**

Deputy sheriffs.
Sheriffs and deputies. See within this heading, "Sheriffs and deputies."

District court actions, service by mail, **223:31.**

Executions.
See EXECUTIONS.

Fees.
Indorsement of fees on writ of process, **262:19.**
Magistrate, refusal of fees for negligence in certifying and returning recognizance, **262:63.**
Specification of items of fees for service of process, **262:18.**

RETURN OF PROCESS —Cont'd

Habeas corpus, **248:10.**
See HABEAS CORPUS.

Indorsement of fees on writ of process, **262:19.**

Land court, process, **185:1.**

Leaving, service by, return to state place leaving, **223:35.**

Magistrate, refusal of fees for negligence in certifying and returning recognizance, **262:63.**

Mail or express, mileage on return, **262:9.**

Place of leaving process, statement of officers in return, **223:35.**

Registration of land title, notice of petition, **185:39.**

Replevin.
See REPLEVIN.

Return day.
Day of return. See within this heading, "Day of return."

Sheriffs and deputies.
Mail or express, return, **262:9.**
Return after going out of office, **37:14.**

Specification of items of fees for service of process, **262:18.**

Taxation.
Collection of local taxes, affidavit as to service in proceedings, **60:1, 60:57.**
Foreclosure of rights of redemption under tax titles, **60:67.**

Unfair insurance practices proceedings, **176D:6.**

Vacancy in office of sheriff, effect, **37:14.**

Venire, return, **234:24.**

Voters, proceedings as to improper registration, **51:48.**

Warrants.
See WARRANTS.

RETURN OF PROPERTY.

Aircraft financial responsibility act.
See AIRCRAFT FINANCIAL RESPONSIBILITY ACT.

Banks.
See BANKS AND BANKING.

Credit slips, time limitation on use, **93:14S.**

Executor or administrator, judgment for return of property rendered against, **230:4.**

Purchase of goods with privilege, **106:2-326, 106:2-327.**

RETURN OF PROPERTY —Cont'd

Retail installment sales and services, **255D:11A, 255D:11B, 255D:14.**

Merchandise certificate or coupons, buyer's right to return for credit, **255D:11A, 255D:11B.**

RETURN OF VERDICT.
See VERDICT.

RETURNS AND RECORDS.
See RECORDS, REPORTS, AND RETURNS.

REUSE RESTRICTIONS.

Surplus state property, disposition, **7:40F, 7:40F½.**

REVENUE BILLS.

United States.
See CONSTITUTION OF THE UNITED STATES.

REVENUE CUTTER SERVICE.

Uniforms, unlawful use, **101:30, 264:10A.**

REVENUE DEPARTMENT AND COMMISSIONER, 14:1 et seq., 58:1 et seq.

Abatement of penalty attributable to erroneous advice of department employee, **62C:36B.**

Abatement of taxes, **62C:37.**
Appearance by commissioner, **58:1.**
Application.
Form of application, approval, **59:59.**
Statement of processing procedures, **14:6.**
Cigarette tax, **64C:6.**
Corporations subject to franchise tax, notice of abatement, **59:74.**
Income tax.
Additional tax as penalty for failure to file return on time, **62C:33, 62C:34.**
Appeal and review, **62C:39.**
Federal court action for abatement, statutory remedies as affecting right, **62C:41.**
Filing return prior to application for abatement, **62C:38.**
Forms, application for abatement, **62C:37.**
Refunds, **62C:36, 62C:40.**

REVENUE DEPARTMENT AND COMMISSIONER —Cont'd

Abatement of taxes —Cont'd

Real estate taxes, abatement where assessed value insufficient to pay collection charges, **59:72.**

Refunds, issuance, **14:6.**

Returns in abatement proceedings, **62C:38.**

Telephone or telegraph companies, **59:39.**

Timely rendering of decisions and issuance of refunds, **14:6.**

Uncollected taxes, **58:8.**

Abolition of county governments, **34B:1 to 34B:22.**

See ABOLITION OF COUNTY GOVERNMENTS.

Absentees' estates, settlement, **200:13.**

Abstracts, preparation, **58:10.**

Accounts, bureau and director, **14:1.**

City and town auditors, **44:40, 44:43, 44:56A.**

Counties, **35:32, 35:44, 35:45, 35:47, 35:50.**

County commissioners, **34:8, 34:10, 35:27.**

Emergency finance board, member, **10:47.**

Establishment, **14:1.**

Local assessments, **59:23.**

Public beach districts, audit of accounts, **40:12B.**

Records, destruction or sale, **44:45.**

Town accountants to use classifications and forms prescribed, **41:57.**

Administration.

See ADMINISTRATION AND FINANCE EXECUTIVE OFFICE.

Administration division, establishment, **14:1.**

Administration of estates, application, **193:3.**

Administrators.

Executors and administrators. See within this heading, "Executors and administrators."

Notice of foreign executor's sale or real property, **202:32, 203:17A.**

Party to proceedings for receipt and sale of personal property, **204:3.**

REVENUE DEPARTMENT AND COMMISSIONER —Cont'd

Agreement with taxpayer to make installment payments, **62C:37B.**

Agricultural and horticultural property.

Annual determinations of eligibility, approval by commissioner of application form, **61A:6.**

Equalization, valuation by commissioner, **61A:20.**

Excise on certain farm machinery, animals, fowl, determination by commissioner of revenue, **59:8A.**

Farmland valuation advisory commission, membership and duties, **61A:11.**

Rules and regulations, promulgation by commissioner, **61A:22.**

Aid or assistance, **58:3.**

Alcoholic beverage taxes, **63A:1, 63A:2, 138:21.**

Abatement of taxes, **138:21.**

Excise taxes, powers, **138:21.**

Public warehousemen's storage permits, **138:20A.**

Revenue commissioner defined for purposes of alcoholic beverage taxes, **63A:1.**

Alcoholic liquors.

Storage permits for warehousemen, **138:20A.**

Taxes.

Alcoholic beverage taxes. See within this heading, "Alcoholic beverage taxes."

Annual report.

Business trusts, filing and examination, **182:12-182:14, 182:12 et seq.**

Exemptions, state-owned land, **58:15.**

Governor and to general court, annual report, **35:46.**

Municipal corporations, **44:44.**

Requirement to file, **14:5, 14:6.**

Appeals.

Appellate tax board. See within this heading, "Appellate tax board."

Classifications by commissioner, appeals, **58:2.**

Registration or license, appeal from denial, **62C:67.**

Statement of procedure, **14:6.**

Appellate tax board.

Establishment, **14:1.**

Reports concerning, **58:10C.**

REVENUE DEPARTMENT AND COMMISSIONER —Cont'd

Application.

Abatement of taxes. See within this heading, "Abatement of taxes."

Appointment.

Assistant collector, **41:39C.**

Secretary of administration and finance, appointment, **14:2.**

Apportionment.

Equalized valuations for cities and towns, **44:1, 58:9-58:10C.**

Expenses of removal of causes of water pollution, **111:165.**

Use certificate, services sold at retail outside Commonwealth, **64H:6.**

Approval of appropriation for care and maintenance of forfeited property, **40:5.**

Approval of bonds.

City clerk, **41:13A.**

Public beach district treasurer's bond, **40:12E.**

Treasurer and assistants, **41:35, 41:39A.**

Approval of certificates, **158:9, 158:41.**

Approval of forms, **58:31, 62C:3.**

Application for tax abatement, **59:59.**

Forms, prescription and approval of. See within this heading, "Forms, prescription and approval."

Statements and lists, **58:5, 59:54.**

Aqueduct companies duties of commissioner, **165:12-165:14, 166:4, 166:5.**

Assessment of local taxes, powers and duties as to, **58:1, 58:1A, 58:2, 58:8B.**

Assessors.

Tax assessors. See within this heading, "Tax assessors."

Assistance of counsel, CPA, agent or actuary at in-person interviews, request by taxpayer, **62C:80.**

Assistant city or town treasurer, **41:35, 41:39A.**

Audits.

City and town accounts, **41:99H.**

Division, establishment, **14:1.**

Public beach districts, **40:12B.**

Taxpayer information regarding audit process, **62C:80.**

Bad checks, abating penalty for tendering, **60:57A.**

REVENUE DEPARTMENT AND COMMISSIONER —Cont'd

Banking, membership on incorporation board, **26:5.**

Beaches.
Annual audit, **40:12B.**
Treasurer of district, approval of bond, **40:12E.**

Bond issues.
Failure to make payments.
Abolition of county governments, **34B:1 to 34B:22.**
See ABOLITION OF COUNTY GOVERNMENTS.
Regulations as to qualified bonds, **44A:10.**

Bonds and undertakings.
Failure to make payments.
Abolition of county governments, **34B:1 to 34B:22.**
See ABOLITION OF COUNTY GOVERNMENTS.

Bonds, surety.
Approval of bonds, **40:12E, 41:13A, 41:35, 41:39A.**
Assistant city or town treasurer, bond, **41:35, 41:39A, 41:123A.**
City clerk, approval of bond, **41:13A.**
Commissioner of revenue to supply bond for faithful performance, **14:2.**
Deputy collectors, tender of faithful performance bond, **14:3.**
Enforcement of violations, **107:8.**
Fidelity or surety companies, approval of bonds, **175:105.**
State treasurer, giving of bond, **14:2.**
Town clerk, approval of bond, **41:13.**

Branches and bureaus to be established by commissioner, **14:5.**

Verification of corporate deposits with state treasurer, **10:6.**

Bucket shopping, dissolution of corporation convicted, **271:36.**

Bureau of account.
Account, bureau and director of. See within this heading, "Accounts, bureau and director."

Bureau of local assessment, establishment, **14:1.**

REVENUE DEPARTMENT AND COMMISSIONER —Cont'd

Bureau of special investigations, **14:10.**

Business trusts' annual reports, **182:12 et seq.**

Certificates and certification.
Approval of organization certificate, **158:9.**
Colleges and universities, submission of certificate of organization to of collegiate authority, **69:30.**

Charities.
See CHARITIES AND CHARITABLE CONTRIBUTIONS.

Child support enforcement, **14:1, 14:1A, 119A:1, 271:43.**

Cigarette tax.
Adhesive stamps and metering machines, authority, **64C:29, 64C:30.**
Appointment of stampers, **64C:30.**
Inspection of records, **64C:5, 64C:6, 64C:11.**
Issuance of licenses, **64C:2.**
Powers and duties, **64C:29 et seq.**
Premises, search, **64C:11.**
Refund of tax, **64C:6.**
Reports from carriers, warehousemen, or bailees may be required, **64C:6.**
Returns filed, **64C:6.**
Searches and seizures, **64C:8, 64C:11.**
Special police officers, appointment, **64C:26.**
State tax commission.
Abatement of tax, **64C:6.**
Refunds for unused cigarette tax stamps, **64C:31.**

Cities and towns.
Municipal finance. See within this heading, "Municipal finance."

City and town treasurers.
Approval of bonds, **41:35, 41:39A, 41:123A.**
Suspension or removal, **41:39B.**

City clerk, approval of bond, **41:13A, 41:123A.**

Civil service, **14:1-14:4, 14:6, 14:7, 62C:36B, 62C:80.**

Employees. See within this heading, "Employees."

Classification of real property for tax purposes.
Appeals from classification by commissioner, **58:2.**

REVENUE DEPARTMENT AND COMMISSIONER —Cont'd

Classification of real property for tax purposes —Cont'd
Recreational land.
Determination of value of land, **61B:16.**
Forms for valuation of land, **61B:3.**
Rules and regulations of commissioner, **61B:18.**
Use classification for local assessment purposes, **40:56.**

Collectors.
Tax collectors. See within this heading, "Tax collectors."

Colleges and universities.
Board of collegiate authority, submission of certificate of organization to, **69:30.**
Valuation of University of Massachusetts lands, **58:13.**

Commissioner of corporations and taxation, references as meaning commissioner of revenue, **14:1 (note).**

Compensation.
Wages, salaries, and compensation. See within this heading, "Wages, salaries, and compensation."

Complaints by taxpayers, statement of filing procedure, **14:6.**

Compromise and settlement.
Settlement for amount less than assessment, **62C:37C.**

Construction and interpretation.
Departmental regulations, **14:1.**
Interpretation and construction. See within this heading, "Interpretation and construction."
Tax laws, **14:6.**

Contributory retirement appeal board, commissioner to appoint member, **32:16.**

Controlled substances tax, **64K:1.**

Copies.
Eligible business facility, copy of certificate to be furnished, **23B:15.**
Federal withholding tax, copy of statements, **58:28B.**

Corporations.
Abatement of franchise taxes, notice, **59:74.**
Annual certificate of condition, failure to file, **158:38.**
Applications for incorporation, list of to be furnished, **155:2.**

REVENUE DEPARTMENT AND COMMISSIONER —Cont'd

Corporations —Cont'd

Aqueduct companies, duties of commissioner, **165:12 et seq., 166:4, 166:5.**

Banking, membership on incorporation board, **26:5.**

Banks.
See BANKS AND BANKING.

Changes in corporate structure or powers, list of to be furnished, **155:2.**

Classification made by tax commissioner, filing application for review by corporation objecting, **58:2.**

Corporation taxes.
See CORPORATION TAXES.

Declaration of estimated tax by corporations, **63B:3.**

Deposits with state treasurer, assessment, **58:28.**

Director for corporation division, appointment, **9:2.**

Dissolution of corporation.
Bucket shopping, dissolution of corporation convicted, **271:36.**
Duties, **156B:100, 156B:101.**
List of proposed dissolutions to be furnished, **155:2.**
Notice as to distribution of assets of dissolved corporations, **156B:103.**
Notice of dissolution to commissioner, **156B:100.**
On application, **155:50A.**

Foreign corporations. See within this heading, "Foreign corporations."

Insurance companies, **26:8D, 175:49.**

Merger of corporations, list of proposed mergers to be furnished, **155:2.**

Property and motor vehicles, assessor's report, **59:83.**

Public charitable corporations involuntarily dissolved, transmission of listing, **180:11B.**

Revival of corporations, list of to be furnished, **155:2.**

Secretary of Commonwealth to furnish certain information and documents, **155:2.**

Telegraph and telephone companies. See within this heading, "Telegraph and telephone companies."

REVENUE DEPARTMENT AND COMMISSIONER —Cont'd

Corporations —Cont'd

Urban redevelopment corporations. See within this heading, "Urban redevelopment corporations."

Verification of corporate deposits with state treasurer, **10:6.**

Corporations and taxation department, change of name to department of revenue effective Aug 1, 1978, **14:1 (note).**

Corporation taxes.
See CORPORATION TAXES.

Correcting improper methods of assessment, **58:4.**

County accounts, annual report, **35:46.**

County and county hospital appropriations, duties of director of accounts, **35:32.**

County budgets, submission of copies to accounts director, **35:28, 35:28B.**

County treasurers.
Annual report to governor and to general court, **35:46.**
Apportionment, assessment, and collection of county taxes according to equalization and apportionment reported by commissioner of revenue, **35:31.**

County tuberculosis hospital, taxation of land, **58:17A.**

Criminal investigations, interviews with taxpayers, **62C:80.**

Date.
Time or date. See within this heading, "Time or date."

Declaration of estimated income tax.
"Commissioner" as meaning, **62B:1.**
Contents of declaration, power to prescribe, **62B:13.**
Corporations.
Declaration of estimated tax by corporations. See within this heading, "Declaration of estimated tax by corporations."
Filing requirements, **62C:45A.**

Declaration of estimated tax by corporations.
Extension of time for filing, **63B:3.**
Form for declarations, prescribing, **63B:2.**

REVENUE DEPARTMENT AND COMMISSIONER —Cont'd

Deduction of estimated receipts of towns, approval, **59:23.**

Deed and document stamp tax, duties, **64D:3, 64D:4, 64D:6.**

Defective procedure, certificate, **158:36.**

Deputy collectors, appointment, **14:3.**

Description of organization, commissioner of revenue required to prepare, **14:5.**

Director of special investigations, **14:10, 14:11.**

Disability of Bureau of accounts director, appointee to act in absence, **14:1.**

Disclosure of information, **58:3, 62C:21, 271:43.**

Dissolution of corporations.
Corporations. See within this heading, "Corporations."

Divisions within, **14:1.**

Domicile for death tax purposes, settlement of disputes, **65B:1, 65B:3, 65B:4.**

Education.
Schools and education. See within this heading, "Schools and education."

Electronic transfer of funds for payments, **62C:85.**

Eligibility and qualification.
Eligible business facility. See within this heading, "Eligible business facility."
Employees. See within this heading, "Employees."

Eligible business facility.
Contents of certificate of eligibility, **23B:15.**
Definition, **23B:11.**

Emergency finance board, membership, **10:47.**

Employees.
Career advancement and promotion policy, **14:1, 14:6, 14:7.**
Civil service, **14:1 et seq.**
Erroneous advice of employee, waiver or abatement of taxpayer penalty, **62C:36B.**
Ethical conduct, investigation of employees, **62C:80.**
Performance evaluations, **14:7.**
Production goals or quotas for individual employees, **14:7.**
Professional standards and conduct, **14:1.**
Qualification, **14:6.**
Advancement and promotion, **14:6, 14:7.**

397

REVENUE DEPARTMENT AND COMMISSIONER —Cont'd

Employees —Cont'd
Tax collectors. See within this heading, "Tax collectors."
Training programs, **14:8.**
Employment.
Employees. See within this heading, "Employees."
Employment security, confidential information, **151A:46.**
Labor organizations, approval, **180:15, 180:16.**
Endorsement of statement concerning property exchange for capital stock, **158:33.**
Enforcement procedures, statement to taxpayers, **14:6.**
Equalized valuations for cities and towns.
Appeals, **58:10B.**
Failure of municipality to submit information for use in determining, **58:10.**
Final equalization and apportionment, establishment, **58:10C.**
Hearing on proposed equalized valuations, **58:10A.**
Proposed equalized valuation, duties of department, **58:9.**
Report, **44:1.**
Estate taxes.
Compliance with rules and regulations, **65C:8.**
Defined, **65C:1.**
Executor, discharge, **65C:7.**
Federal estate tax credit surcharge, **65A:1 et seq.**
Form of return to be prescribed, **65C:8.**
Issuance of documents, **65C:24.**
Lien, discharge or release, **65C:14.**
Town assessor, information furnished, **58:3.**
Estimated taxes.
Declaration of estimated income tax. See within this heading, "Declaration of estimated income tax."
Declaration of estimated tax by corporations. See within this heading, "Declaration of estimated tax by corporations."
Estimates to local assessors, **59:21.**
Examination.
Inspection or examination. See within this heading, "Inspection or examination."

REVENUE DEPARTMENT AND COMMISSIONER —Cont'd

Excess of net state tax revenues, reports to state auditor, **62F:5.**
Excise taxes.
Alcoholic liquors, **138:21.**
Effect of unconstitutionality, **63:52.**
Gasoline and motor fuel taxes, **64A:7.**
Motor vehicle registration, notice to commissioner for purpose of, collecting excise tax, **60A:2.**
Executors and administrators.
Notice of foreign executor's sale or real property, **202:32, 203:17A.**
Party to proceedings for receipt and sale of personal property, **204:3.**
Exemptions.
Annual report. See within this heading, "Annual report."
Exempt property, **58:15, 59:2A, 59:5D, 59:5F, 59:86.**
Fair cash value of publicly owned lands, determination, **58:13.**
Falsely assuming to be official of bureau of special investigations, **268:33.**
False reports to, penalty, **268:6.**
Fidelity or surety companies, approval of bonds, **175:105.**
Final equalization and apportionment on cities and towns, establishment, **58:10C.**
Fines and penalties, **280.2.**
Abatement of penalties, **62C:33.**
Certificates, failure to file, **158:42.**
Erroneous advice of department employee, waiver of penalty attributable to, **62C:36B.**
False reports, **268:6.**
Fire district, notices of establishment, **48:63.**
Foreign corporations.
Agent for service of process, **181:3, 181:4.**
Annual certificate of condition, approval of, **181:13.**
"Commissioner" as meaning, **181:1.**
Construction work in Commonwealth, report, **30:39L.**
Domestic business subject to tax, **63:32D.**
Trustee process against foreign corporation, **246:6.**

REVENUE DEPARTMENT AND COMMISSIONER —Cont'd

Foreign fiduciaries to file proof of authority, **199A:2.**
Foreign states or countries, establishment of offices of department, **14:3.**
Forests and forestry.
Application for abatement, approval of form by commissioner, **61:2.**
Certification of forest products removed, forests and parks director, **58:15.**
Forms, prescription and approval, **58:31, 62C:3.**
Application for tax abatement, **59:59.**
Statements and lists, **58:5, 59:54.**
Fraud and deceit.
Bureau of special investigations, **14:10.**
Fraudulent claims commission, **14:9.**
Investigations, **14:9 to 14:11.**
Functions transferred to Department of Revenue, **14:1 et seq.**
Gasoline.
See GASOLINE AND MOTOR FUEL TAXES.
Gasoline and motor fuels tax.
Bill to restrain collection of tax on sales exempt by federal law against, **64A:12.**
Claims for reimbursement, approval, **64A:7.**
Computation of tax, **64E:4.**
Inspection of records and statement, **64A:3.**
Licenses to distributors and unclassified importers granted, **64A:2.**
Mass transportation facilities and services, determination of amounts payable, **58:25B.**
Out-of-state purchaser of fuel or special fuel, **64F:1.**
Quarterly tax return forms, approval, **64F:6.**
Reimbursement of excise, form of affidavit prescribed by commissioner, **64A:7.**
Special fuels, **64E:1.**
Suspension of license of distributor, **64A:9.**
Tax free sales of fuels, regulation, **64A:8A.**
General court, reports filed, **14:5, 14:6, 35:46, 58:10C.**

REVENUE DEPARTMENT AND COMMISSIONER —Cont'd

Governor.
Annual reports filed, **14:5, 14:6, 35:46.**
Commissioner, appointment, **14:1.**
County accounts, report, **35:46.**
Hearing on proposed equalized valuations for cities and towns, **58:10A.**
Highway fund, duties, **58:18B, 81:31, 81:32.**
Horticultural property.
Annual determinations of eligibility, approval by commissioner of application form, **61A:6.**
Equalization, valuation by commissioner, **61A:20.**
Excise on certain farm machinery, animals, fowl, determination by commissioner of revenue, **59:8A.**
Farmland valuation advisory commission, membership and duties, **61A:11.**
Rules and regulations, promulgation by commissioner, **61A:22.**
Housing and community development department, **23B:15.**
Income tax.
See INCOME TAX.
Information, obtaining, **14:6.**
Commissioner of revenue, information to record deed to real property, **36:24B.**
Corporations, listing, **58:2.**
Erroneous advice of employee, waiver or abatement of taxpayer penalty, **62C:36B.**
Interviews with taxpayers, **62C:80.**
Real estate values, **58:6.**
Taxable estate property, furnishing town assessors with information concerning, **58:3.**
Taxpayers' rights and procedural information, distribution by department, **62C:80.**
Unpaid taxes, **58:7.**
Inspection or examination.
Audits.
City and town accounts, **41:99H.**
Division, establishment, **14:1.**
Public beach districts, **40:12B.**

REVENUE DEPARTMENT AND COMMISSIONER —Cont'd

Inspection or examination —Cont'd
Audits —Cont'd
Taxpayer information regarding audit process, **62C:80.**
Bureau of special investigations, **14:10.**
Corporation taxes.
See CORPORATION TAXES.
Criminal investigations, **62C:80.**
Director of special investigations, **14:10.**
Employees, investigation of integrity, **62C:80.**
Ethical conduct of employees, **62C:80.**
Fraudulent claims commission, **14:9.**
Municipal accounts, **44:46A.**
Procedure, **14:11.**
Sales at retail division established, **14:1.**
Tax lists, **59:32.**
Taxpayers, in-person interviews, **62C:80.**
Installment payments, written agreement with taxpayer, **62C:37B.**
Instructions to assessors, **58:1, 58:3, 58:5.**
Insurance companies.
Commissioner of insurance to act, **175:49.**
Notice and collection of assessment, **26:8D.**
Interest on overdue taxes, **62C:32, 62C:40.**
Interpretation and construction.
Departmental regulations, **14:1.**
Tax laws, **14:6.**
Interviews with taxpayers, **62C:80.**
Investigations, **14:9 to 14:11.**
Bureau of special investigations, **14:10.**
Director of special investigations, **14:10, 14:11.**
Fraudulent claims commission, **14:9.**
Inspection or examination. See within this heading, "Inspection or examination."
Procedure, **14:11.**
Labor.
Employment. See within this heading, "Employment."
Labor organizations, approval, **180:15, 180:16.**
Legacy and succession taxes.
Abatement, application, **65:27A.**

REVENUE DEPARTMENT AND COMMISSIONER —Cont'd

Legacy and succession taxes —Cont'd
Additional tax, determination, **65:27.**
Alteration of valuations of property made, **65:26.**
Amount due, certification, **65:27.**
Approval of settlement of tax on future interest by commissioner, **65:14.**
Assessment of taxes, powers and duties, **65:27, 65:29.**
Deposits in lieu of tax upon future interest, determination of amount, **65:15.**
Determination of amount of tax, **65:27, 65:29.**
Domicile of decedents, settlement of disputes, **65B:3, 65B:4.**
Fees for issuance of certain documents, **65:35A.**
Future interests, valuation, **65:14.**
Informing and instructing assessors as to assessments, **58:3.**
Inventory and appraisal of estates, filing, **65:22.**
Issuance of certain documents, **65:35A.**
Notice of proceedings before appellate tax board, **65:26.**
Payment, certificate of commissioner as to, **65:23, 65:35A.**
Recommendation of abatement of uncollectible taxes, **65:32.**
Refunds of excess, certificate, **65:27, 65A:6.**
Representative of Commonwealth in proceedings, **65:30.**
Sale of property for collection of taxes, **65:31.**
Settlement of tax upon future interest for present value impossible to compute, **65:14.**
Taxes in dispute, extension of time for assessments and collection, **65:33A.**
Taxes payable, **65:7.**
Time for instituting proceedings for collection, **65:32, 65:33A.**
Valuation of property subject to tax, **65:14, 65:25, 65:26, 65:35A.**

REVENUE DEPARTMENT AND COMMISSIONER —Cont'd

Letter rulings, **62C:3.**

Levy of taxes, commissioner to keep records of sales of real property pursuant, **62C:61.**

Limitation of time for reimbursement claims, filing with commissioner of revenue, **58:8B.**

Local services.

Appeals from local tax classification, **58:2.**

Assessment bureau as within department, **14:1.**

Long range capital facilities agencies, submission, **29:7D.**

Mass transportation facilities and services, certification of amounts payable, **58:25B.**

Medical care and assistance, lien on decedent's estate, **118E:16C.**

Medical service corporation, formation, **176B:2.**

Methods for determining value of property, **58:10.**

Minority Business Assistance, coordination of programs and services, **23A:44.**

Motor vehicles.

Abatement when valuation excessive, **60A:1, 60A:2.**

Collection of tax, **60A:2.**

Determination of value, **60A:1.**

Notice, **60A:2.**

Owner, notice, **60A:2.**

Registrar of motor vehicles, notice, **60A:2A.**

Religious corporations as exempt, **60A:1.**

Remedies, **60A:3.**

Suspension of certificate of registration for nonpayment of excise, approval of form, **60A:2A.**

Municipal finance, **58:1A.**

Amounts distributable to cities and towns, determination, **58:25A.**

Annual estimates of returns, **58:25A.**

Annual reports of affairs, **44:44.**

Appropriations, commissioner's approval of mayor's or selectman's certificate stating town's interest in real estate not reasonably protected, **40:5.**

Assessors.

Tax assessors. See within this heading, "Tax assessors."

REVENUE DEPARTMENT AND COMMISSIONER —Cont'd

Municipal finance —Cont'd

Audit of accounts, **41:99H.**

Clerk, approval of bond, **41:13A, 41:123A.**

Collectors of taxes.

Tax collectors. See within this heading, "Tax collectors."

Determination of amounts due and partial distributions, **41:99I, 58:25.**

Equalized valuations for cities and towns. See within this heading, "Equalized valuations for cities and towns."

Flood control, reimbursement for loss of taxes on property taken, **58:17B.**

Foreclosure against city, **60:77.**

Investigations by director of municipal accounts and financial transactions, commissioner to fix compensation for temporary investigators, **44:46A.**

Joint or co-operative assessment of property, regulation, **41:30B.**

Officers and employees of cities, towns and districts, audit of accounts and apportionment of costs by department, **41:99H.**

Old persons, real property owned by, reimbursements of municipalities, **59:5.**

Qualified bonds, regulations, **44A:10.**

Reimbursement of towns for loss of tax on public lands, duties with respect, **58:13 et seq., 58:25A.**

Tax rates, change, **59:23.**

Transfer of land purchased by municipality, approval, **60:52.**

Treasurer of city or town, **41:35, 41:39A, 41:39B, 41:123A.**

Names of resident wage earners reported to commissioner, **62C:8.**

Neglect of assessors, appointment of others in case, **59:27.**

Non-profit medical service plans, annual returns, **176C:15.**

Notice.

Assessors, instructions as to notices and lists, **58:5.**

Changes in law, notice to taxpayers, **62C:3.**

REVENUE DEPARTMENT AND COMMISSIONER —Cont'd

Notice —Cont'd

Dissolution of corporation, **156B:100, 156B:103.**

Fire districts, notices of establishment, **48:63.**

Foreign executor's sale of real property, notice, **202:32, 203:17A.**

Insurance companies, notice and collection of assessments, **26:8D.**

Modification or revocation of eligibility of business facility, **23B:15.**

Motor vehicle, notice of registration to revenue commissioner for excise tax collection purposes, **60A:2.**

Register of probate and insolvency to send notices and inventories, **217:16.**

Trust instruments, notice of recording, **36:31A.**

Old persons, real property owned by, reimbursement of municipalities, **59:5.**

Operations division, establishment, **14:1.**

Out-of-state employees, **14:3.**

Overdue taxes, interest, **62C:32, 62C:40.**

Owner of real estate.

Authorizing assessment of taxes, **59:11.**

Furnishing assessor information, **58:3.**

Old persons, reimbursement of municipalities, **59:5.**

Paraplegic veteran, reimbursement of municipalities for loss of taxes through abatement as authorized by commissioner, **58:8A.**

Penalties, **280.2.**

Abatement of penalties, **62C:33.**

Certificates, failure to file, **158:42.**

Electronic transfer of funds for payments, **62C:85.**

Erroneous advice of department employee, waiver of penalty attributable to, **62C:36B.**

False reports, **268:6.**

Performance evaluation, collection employees, **14:7.**

Pipelines, duties as to valuation, **59:38A.**

Policy statement, **14:1.**

Political influence and partiality prohibited, **14:1.**

REVENUE DEPARTMENT AND COMMISSIONER —Cont'd

Powers and duties, **62C:3.**

Problem resolution office established, **14:1.**

Procedure manual furnished to assessors, information relative to determination of eligibility of charitable organizations for property tax exemptions, **58:3.**

Process and service of process and papers, summons issued by department, **58:25B.**

Processing division, establishment, **14:1.**

Production goals or quotas, individual employees, **14:7.**

Professional standards and conduct of employees, **14:1.**

Promoters of shows, records and reports filed, **62C:8A, 62C:67A.**

Property values and ownership, furnishing assessors information, **58:3.**

Proposed equalized valuation for cities and towns, duties, **58:9.**

Public beach districts, commissioner to approve of bond for district treasurer, **40:12E.**

Public charitable corporations involuntarily dissolved, transmission of listing, **180:11B.**

Public lands, determination of fair cash value, **58:13.**

Public meetings and records, inapplicability of law, **30A:11A.**

Qualification.
Eligibility and qualification. See within this heading, "Eligibility and qualification."

Qualified bonds, regulations, **44A:10.**

Quotas, employee evaluation, **14:7.**

Railroad stock, filing of vote creating preferred class, **160:44.**

Ratio studies as to local assessments, **58:10.**

Reciprocal enforcement of tax liabilities between Commonwealth and other states, certificate by commissioner, **58:28C.**

Records, reports, and returns.
Abatement proceedings, returns, **62C:38.**

REVENUE DEPARTMENT AND COMMISSIONER —Cont'd

Records, reports, and returns —Cont'd
Annual report. See within this heading, "Annual report."

Appellate tax board, commissioner's reports concerning, **58:10C.**

Certificates and certification. See within this heading, "Certificates and certification."

Commissioner, reports, **14:5, 14:6, 58:9.**

Declaration of estimated income tax, filing requirements, **62C:45A.**

Enforcement procedures, statement to taxpayers, **14:6.**

Equalizing valuations for cities and towns, report, **44:1.**

Excess of net state tax revenues, reports to state auditor, **62F:5.**

Extension of time for filing declaration of estimated tax by corporation, **63B:3.**

Failure to keep proper records of local assessments, **58:4 et seq.**

False reports, **268:6.**

General Court reports, **14:5, 14:6, 35:46, 58:10, 58:10C.**

Local property assessment, expenses of keeping record, **58:4C.**

Promoters of shows, **62C:8A, 62C:67A.**

Promoters of shows, records and reports, **62C:8A, 62C:67A.**

Settlement agreements, **62C:37C.**

Town taxable property returns, **58:3.**

Recreational land.
Classification of real property for tax purposes. See within this heading, "Classification of real property for tax purposes."

Refunds, timely payment to taxpayers, **14:6.**

Regional police districts, **41:99H, 41:99I.**

Register of probate and insolvency to send notices and inventories, **217:16.**

Registers of deeds, notice to commissioner of revenue of trust deeds and declarations of trust, **36:31A.**

REVENUE DEPARTMENT AND COMMISSIONER —Cont'd

Registration or license, grounds for denial, suspension, or revocation by commissioner, **62C:67, 62C:68.**

Regulatory authority, **14:6, 62C:3, 62C:4.**

Reimbursement.
Gasoline and motor fuel excise taxes, reimbursement, **64A:7.**

Taxpayers, timely payment of reimbursements or refunds, **14:6.**

Towns for loss of tax on public lands, duties with respect to reimbursement, **58:13 et seq., 58:25A.**

Removal or suspension of treasurer of municipality, district or regional school district, **41:39B.**

Reports and returns.
Records, reports, and returns. See within this heading, "Records, reports, and returns."

Representation, taxpayer's right at in-person interviews, **62C:80.**

Retirement systems, commissioner to appoint member of contributory retirement appeal board, **32:16.**

Returns.
Records, reports, and returns. See within this heading, "Records, reports, and returns."

Revision of assessments, **59:59, 59:76.**

Safe deposit boxes, duties as to unclaimed contents, **158:17.**

Salaries and compensation.
Wages, salaries, and compensation. See within this heading, "Wages, salaries, and compensation."

Sales taxes.
See SALES TAXES.

Schools and education.
Certification to commissioner of amount of school aid payable to city and town, **70:5.**

Colleges and universities.
Board of collegiate authority, submission of certificate of organization to, **69:30.**

Valuation of University of Massachusetts lands, **58:13.**

REVENUE DEPARTMENT AND COMMISSIONER —Cont'd

Schools and education —Cont'd

Colleges and universities. See within this heading, "Colleges and universities."

Local assessors, authority to conduct and sponsor training programs, **58:1.**

Removal of treasurer or regional school district, **41:39B.**

State aid, filing statements, **70:5.**

Transportation of school pupils, certification of tax allowance payable, **71:7B.**

Secretary of commissioner of revenue, appointment, **14:2.**

Set-off debt collection, **62D:1 et seq.**

See SET-OFF DEBT COLLECTION.

Settlement for amount less than assessment, **62C:37C.**

Sexual offender registration and community notification.

Authority to examine information to confirm registration, **6:178F.**

Southeastern Regional Planning and Economic Development District Commission, audit of accounts, **40B:18.**

Special assessments.

See SPECIAL ASSESSMENTS.

Special fields tax, powers and duties, **64E:5, 64E:10.**

State auditor.

See STATE AUDITOR.

Statements.

Records, reports, and returns. See within this heading, "Records, reports, and returns."

State tax commission abolished and replaced by commissioner of revenue, **14:1 (note).**

State taxes, estimates, **59:21.**

Storage permits for warehousemen, **138:20A.**

Submission of certificate of increase of capital stock not filed in time, **158:39.**

Supervision of local taxation, **58:1 et seq.**

Suspension of treasurer of municipality, district or regional school district, **41:39B.**

Tax assessors.

Appointment, **41:27.**

REVENUE DEPARTMENT AND COMMISSIONER —Cont'd

Tax assessors —Cont'd

Assistance to local assessors, **58:3.**

Blank forms provided, **58:1.**

Books, approval of form, **59:45.**

Corporate property and motor vehicles, assessor's report, **59:83.**

Correction of improper methods, **58:4.**

Delinquent taxes, reports to commissioner, **58:7.**

Estimates to local assessors, furnishing, **59:21.**

Exempt property, assessor's returns, **59:86.**

Information, **36:24B, 58:2, 58:3.**

Instructions to assessors, **58:1, 58:3, 58:5.**

List of corporations furnished, **58:2.**

Neglect of assessors, appointment of others in case, **59:27.**

Notices and lists of assessors, instructions, **58:5.**

Powers and duties, **58:1.**

Procedural manual for assessors, commissioner to prepare, **58:3.**

Property values and ownership, furnishing information, **58:3.**

Prosecution of assessors, **58:1.**

Qualification standards, **58:1.**

Revision of assessment, time for filing for abatement of taxes, **59:59.**

State taxes, **59:20, 59:21, 59:26, 59:27.**

Supervision, **58:1.**

Taxable estate property, commissioner to furnish town assessors with information, **58:3.**

Training programs for local assessors, **58:1.**

Unknown persons, authority to assess taxes upon real property, **59:11.**

Unpaid taxes, reports, **58:7.**

Tax collection process, taxpayer information, **62C:80.**

Tax collectors.

Appointees of city or town treasurer, approval, **41:37.**

Bonds of collectors, approval, **60:13.**

Books of collectors, approval of form, **60:8.**

REVENUE DEPARTMENT AND COMMISSIONER —Cont'd

Tax collectors —Cont'd

Deputy collectors, appointment and removal, **60:92.**

Forms, approval, **59:54, 60:8, 60:105.**

Lists of collectors, approval of method of preparation, **59:54, 60:6.**

Preparation and distribution of manuals outlining procedures for use in performance of duties, **58:3.**

Prosecution of delinquent collectors, **58:8.**

Salaries of local tax collectors, **41:108B.**

Suspension and removal, **41:39B.**

Unpaid taxes, reports, **58:7.**

Tax deeds.

See TAX DEEDS AND TITLES.

Tax liens.

Business corporation, powers and duties as to tax lien in conjunction with sale or transfer, **62C:51, 62C:52.**

Notice requirement, **62C:50.**

Waiver or release of lien, **62C:50.**

Tax list committed to collector, approval of form, **59:54.**

Taxpayer rights, **62C:80.**

Tax sales.

Extension of time as to nonenforcement of covenants against municipal purchaser, **60:77.**

Records of redemption from tax sales, commissioner to keep, **62C:61.**

Transfer of land purchased by municipality, approval, **60:52.**

Tax stamps, exaction or abatement of penalty for failure to affix, **64D:6A.**

Technical information releases, **62C:3.**

Telegraph and telephone companies.

Abatement of taxes, **59:39.**

Assessors to inform commission, **59:40.**

Estimate by commission in default of return, **59:42.**

Returns by companies to be made, **59:41.**

Time or date.

Commissioner's annual report by commissioner, **14:6.**

REVENUE DEPARTMENT AND COMMISSIONER —Cont'd

Time or date —Cont'd

Declaration of estimated tax by corporations, extension of time for filing, **63B:3.**

Installment payment agreement, notice of modification or termination, **62C:37B.**

Refund or reimbursement, timely payment to taxpayer, **14:6.**

Reimbursement claims, limitation of time, **58:8B.**

Submission of certificate of increase of capital stock not filed in time, **158:39.**

Town clerk, approval of bond, **41:13.**

Towns.

Municipal finance. See within this heading, "Municipal finance."

Town treasurers.

City and town treasurers. See within this heading, "City and town treasurers."

Trade organizations, approval, **180:15, 180:16.**

Training programs for employees, **14:8.**

Training programs for local assessors, authority to conduct and sponsor, **58:1.**

Transfer of land purchased by municipality, approval, **60:52.**

Transfer of officials, agents, clerks and other employees, **14:3.**

Transportation of school pupils, certification of tax allowance payable, **71:7B.**

Treasurer.

City and town treasurer. See within this heading, "City and town treasurers."

County treasurer. See within this heading, "County treasurers."

Trustee process against foreign corporation, **246:6.**

Trusts and trustees.

Annual report, filing and examination of business trusts, **182:12, 182:13.**

Notice of recording of trust instruments, **36:31A.**

Universities.

Colleges and universities. See within this heading, "Colleges and universities."

Unknown persons, authority to assess taxes upon real property, **59:11.**

REVENUE DEPARTMENT AND COMMISSIONER —Cont'd

Unpaid contributory retirement appeal board, appointment of members, **32:16.**

Unpaid taxes, obtaining information, **58:7.**

Urban redevelopment corporations.

Approval of agreements of association, **121A:18B.**

Filing of certificate, **121A:16.**

Valuation.

Agricultural and horticultural property, basis for valuation, **61A:20.**

Certain state and county lands, **38:13 et seq.**

Equalized valuations for cities and towns. See within this heading, "Equalized valuations for cities and towns."

Local assessments, commissioner's duties, **58:1A.**

Massachusetts Water Resources Authority, valuation of land for purpose of payment to division of watershed management, **59:5G.**

Pipelines, **59:38A.**

Reconciliation of valuation of business corporation, **63:68A.**

Recreational land, **61B:3, 61B:16.**

Revisions in valuation, commissioner may recommend, **59:76.**

State and county lands, valuation by revenue department of certain, **38:13 et seq.**

Telephone and telegraph companies' machinery, poles, and wires, valuation, **59:39.**

Veterans.

Reimbursement of municipalities for loss of revenue through abatement for paraplegic veterans, **58:8A.**

Services districts, audit of accounts, **115:15.**

Wage reporting system, **62B:2, 62E:1 et seq.**

See WAGE REPORTING SYSTEM.

Wages, salaries, and compensation.

Commissioner, **7:4A, 14:2.**

Department employees, **14:3.**

Income tax.

See INCOME TAX.

REVENUE DEPARTMENT AND COMMISSIONER —Cont'd

Wages, salaries, and compensation —Cont'd

Wage reporting system.

See WAGE REPORTING SYSTEM.

Withholding exemption certificates, power to prescribe form and contents, **62B:4.**

Wage withholding exemption certificates, power to prescribe form and contents, **62B:4.**

Waiver of penalty attributable to erroneous advice of department employee, **62C:36B.**

Warehousemen, storage permits, **138:20A.**

Water pollution, apportionment of expenses of removal of causes, **111:165.**

Withholding of tax.

Amount to be withheld, determination, **62B:2.**

Assessment against employer for failure to withhold and pay over to commissioner, **62B:6.**

Commissioner as meaning, **62B:1.**

Federal withholding tax, copy of statements, **58:28B.**

Returns, approval of form, **62B:5.**

Withholding exemption and deduction certificate, power to prescribe form and contents, **62B:4.**

Witnesses, attendance, **62C:70.**

Writing.

Advice of department employee, erroneous, **62C:36B.**

Installment payment agreement with taxpayer, **62C:37B.**

REVENUE LOANS.
See LOANS.

REVENUE RETENTION ACCOUNT.
Defined, **29:1.**

REVERE.
District court, **218:1.**

Metropolitan air pollution control district, membership, **111:142B.**

Parks, provision by metropolitan commission, **92:33.**

Record of votes for register of deeds, transmission, **54:112.**

REVERE —Cont'd
Refuse disposal, **92:9A.**
Senatorial district, **57:3.**
Suffolk county extension service budget, **128:44A.**

REVERSAL.
See APPEAL AND REVIEW.

REVERSE GEAR.
Audible warning signals to be used when gasoline trucks are in reverse, **90:7.**

REVERSE MORTGAGES.
Credit unions, **171:65.**
Regulation, **167E:2, 183:67.**

REVERSIONS.
See LIFE ESTATES, REMAINDERS, AND REVERSIONS.

REVIEW.
See APPEAL AND REVIEW.

REVISED UNIFORM LIMITED PARTNERSHIP ACT, 109:1 et seq.

REVIVAL.
Action or suit, **228:1-228:14.**
See ABATEMENT, SURVIVAL, AND REVIVAL.
Corporations, **155:56, 156B:108.**
Certificate of revival, **155:56, 156B:2, 156B:108.**
Petition to general court for revival, **3:5, 3:7.**
Special commissions, revival or continuation, **4:2A.**

REVOCATION OR SUSPENSION.
Pharmacists and pharmacies.
See PHARMACISTS AND PHARMACIES.

REVOLVERS.
Firearms and weapons, **140:121 et seq.**
See FIREARMS AND WEAPONS.

REVOLVING CREDIT AGREEMENT.
Open-end credit.
See OPEN-END CREDIT.
Retail installment sales.
See RETAIL INSTALLMENT SALES AND SERVICES.

REWARDS.
Assassination of police officer, reward for information concerning, **276:10.**
Bomb threats, persons supplying information concerning, **269:14.**

REWARDS —Cont'd
Bonus, leave of absence from private employment for military training as affecting, **149:52A.**
Bounties.
See BOUNTIES.
False alarm of fire, reward for information leading to arrest and conviction of person making, **276:10.**
Felons, apprehension, **276:9, 276:10.**
Killing of dog found injuring domestic animals, **140:162.**
Motor vehicle theft, **175A:10A.**
Payment by state treasurer, **280:16.**
Prosecuting officers forbidden to receive, **12:30.**
Public safety officers or inspectors forbidden to receive, **147:3.**
State police.
See STATE POLICE.

REYES SYNDROME.
Health and sanitation, reporting of Reyes syndrome by persons examining or treating disease, **111:110B.**

RHEUMATIC FEVER.
State health department to furnish drugs for treatment of patients, **111:14A.**

RHEUMATISM.
Chronic, hospitalization of persons suffering, **111:116A.**

RHODE ISLAND.
Bays System Commission, **Spec L 137:1.**
Commonwealth may invest in obligations of counties, towns, and cities, **29:38.**
First Congress, representation in, **US Const Art 1 Sec 2 cl 3.**
Marine boundary, **1:3.**
Marine fisheries, reciprocal enforcement of laws relating, **130:15A.**
Police and fire vehicles as exempt from registration, **90:9B.**
Statewide branch banking, notice and hearing for establishment of branch offices or depots, **167C:3.**

RHODE ISLAND SOUND.
Territorial limit of Commonwealth, **1:3.**

RHODONITE.
Gem of Commonwealth, **2:15.**

RHUBARB.
Sale by bunch permissible, **94:96.**

RIBES.
Protection against white pine blister rust, **128:23.**

RICHMOND.
District court held, **218:1.**
Medical examiner district, **38:1.**
Senatorial district, **57:3.**

RIDERS.
Insurance riders.
See INSURANCE.

RIDING SCHOOLS.
Fines and penalties, **128:2B.**
Instructors, licensing, **128:2A.**
License to operate, **128:2A, 128:2B.**
Operator, defined, **128:1.**

RIFLES.
See FIREARMS AND WEAPONS.

RIGHT OF ENTRY.
See ENTRY INTO LAND AND PREMISES.

RIGHT OF WAY.
Easements.
See EASEMENTS.
Militia, drills or parades, **33:50.**
Railroads.
See RAILROADS.
Through ways.
See THROUGH WAYS AND ROUTES.
Traffic regulations and rules of the road.
See TRAFFIC REGULATIONS AND RULES OF THE ROAD.

RIGHT ON RED, 89:8.

RIGHTS OF ACCUSED, US Const 5th Amend, 6th Amend.
See CRIMINAL PROCEDURE.

RIGHTS OF VICTIMS AND WITNESSES OF CRIME, 258B:1 to 258B:13.
Assessments against persons convicted of crimes, **258B:8.**
Communication of information to victims, requirements, **258B:12.**
Convicted persons, loss of rights, **258B:13.**
Co-operation among courts, agencies, and district attorney, **258B:7.**
Definitions, **258B:1.**

**RIGHTS OF VICTIMS AND
WITNESSES OF CRIME**
—Cont'd
Employer, discharge or other
penalty imposed, **258B:3,
268:14B.**
Final disposition of charges,
enforcement of provisions
until time of, **258B:11.**
Notice requirements, **258B:3.**
Presence of victims and families at
court proceedings, **258B:3.**
Private cause of action for
enforcement of chapter
prohibited, **258B:10.**
Program.
Creation and maintenance by
district attorney, **258B:5.**
Submission of plan to victim and
witness assistance board,
258B:6.
Prompt disposition of actions,
258B:3.
Prosecutor.
Duties with regard to victims
and families of victims,
258B:3.
Family members, prosecutors
not precluded from
providing services to family
members, **258B:2.**
Family requesting assistance,
258B:12.
Reporting of crime as prerequisite
to exercise of rights, **258B:2.**
Reversal of conviction, victim
retaining rights, **258B:11.**
Security of victims and families
during court proceedings,
258B:3.
Victim and witness assistance
board, **258B:4.**
Victim and witness assistance
fund, deposit of assessments,
258B:9.
Words and phrases, **258B:1.**

RIGHT TO BARGAIN ACT.
Labor relations, **150A:3.**

RIGHT TO COUNSEL.
Attorneys at law.
See ATTORNEYS AT LAW.

**RIGHT TO KNOW, 111F:1 et
seq.**

RIGHT TO LIFE.
Pregnancy maintenance services,
establishment, **111:51B.**

**RIGHT TO ORGANIZE ACT,
150A:1 et seq.**
Labor, **150A:1 et seq.**

RIGHT TURN, 90:14.
Red light, turn, **89:8.**
Signal, **90:14B.**

RING BUOYS.
Motorboats, required equipment,
90B:5, 90B:11.

RINKS.
Skating rinks.
See SKATING RINKS.

RIOTS AND MOBS, 269:1-269:8.
Aid and assistance in suppressing,
269:1, 269:2, 269:4, 269:6.
Alcoholic liquors.
Licensee whose business is
damaged by riot, relief,
138:25.
Order not to sell, give away, or
deliver liquor, **138:68.**
Arrest, **269:2, 269:4, 269:5.**
Fingerprinting and
photographing participants,
41:98.
Bystanders.
Refusal to assist in suppression
of riots, **269:2.**
Suppression of riots with
assistance, **269:1, 269:2,
269:4, 269:6.**
Capitol police, duty, **269:1-269:6.**
Correctional institutions.
See CORRECTIONAL
INSTITUTIONS.
Curfew, imposition upon threat of
civil disorder, **40:37A.**
Destruction of property, **269:7,
269:8.**
Dispersion, duty, **269:1-269:6.**
Emergency police officers, powers
and duties, **149:176.**
Fingerprinting and photographing
of persons arrested for
offenses committed during riot
or similar disturbance, **41:98.**
Force used in suppression,
269:4-269:6.
Homicide during riots, **269:6.**
Indictment, **277:79.**
Intoxicating liquors.
Alcoholic liquors. See within this
heading, "Alcoholic liquors."
Militia.
See MILITIA.
Municipal liability for property
damage caused, **269:8.**
Neglect of officers in suppression,
269:3.
Notice to disperse, **269:1 et seq.**
Number of participants, effect,
269:1, 269:6, 269:8.

RIOTS AND MOBS —Cont'd
Police.
See POLICE.
Public officers' and employees'
duties and powers, **269:1 et
seq.**
Refusal to disperse or assist in
dispersal, **269:2.**
Sheriffs.
See SHERIFFS AND
DEPUTIES.
Suppression of, **269:1-269:6.**
Third persons.
Bystanders. See within this
heading, "Bystanders."
Unlawful assembly, **269:1, 269:2.**
Weapons, unlawful assembly of
persons armed, **269:1.**

RIPARIAN OWNERS.
**See WATERS AND
WATERWAYS.**

RISK OF LOSS.
Accident.
See ACCIDENT AND
SICKNESS INSURANCE.
Collateral security, risk of loss,
106:9-207.
Insurance.
See INSURANCE.
Leases under Commercial Code,
106:2A-219, 106:2A-220.
Sales under commercial code.
See SALES UNDER
COMMERCIAL CODE.

RITUAL.
Fraternal benefit societies, lodge
system defined, **176:2.**
Humane slaughtering of livestock,
94:139G.

RIVERS.
**See WATERS AND
WATERWAYS.**

R.N.
Nurses, use of abbreviation,
112:80.

ROADHOUSE.
Discrimination because of race,
color, in places of public
accommodation or resort,
272:92A, 272:98.

ROADS.
**See HIGHWAYS AND
STREETS.**

ROADSIDE STANDS.
Marking grade of potatoes sold,
94:117H.

ROAD TO BOSTON, THE.
Official ceremonial march of
Commonwealth, designation,
2:27.

ROBBERY, 265:17-265:21.
Armed robbery, **265:17.**
  Assault with intent to rob, **265:18, 265:18A.**
Assault with intent to rob.
  Armed, **265:17, 265:18, 265:18A.**
  Unarmed, **265:20.**
Bank robberies, **265:21.**
Dangerous weapon, robbery, **265:17.**
Dwelling house, armed assault with intent to commit felony, **265:18A.**
Firearms.
  See FIREARMS AND WEAPONS.
Grand jury investigation, immunity of witness appearing during, **233:20D.**
Indictment.
  Form, **277:79.**
  Meaning of term, **277:39.**
Insurance, kinds, **175:47, 175:93A, 175:93C.**
Larceny from the person, **266:25.**
Limitation of prosecution, **277:63.**
Mask, robbery while wearing, **265:17.**
Motor vehicle physical damage insurance policy, notice provision, **175:191A.**
Parole of persons convicted, **127:133.**
Punishment, **265:17.**
Restoration of stolen goods to owner, **266:48.**
State employees, additional insurance coverage where death occurs as result of robbery, **32A:10A.**
Stealing, putting in fear for purpose, **265:21.**
Surrender of stolen property after conviction, **266:21.**
Threats, **265:21.**
Unarmed robbery, **265:19.**

ROBERT FROST DAY.
Governor's proclamation, **6:15CCCC.**

ROBERT GODDARD DAY, 6:15AAAA.

ROCHESTER.
Congressional district, **57:1.**
District court, **218:1.**
Medical examiner district, **38:1.**
Senatorial district, **57:3.**

ROCK CLIMBING.
Experiential education program, physical education departments, **69:1A.**

ROCKETS.
Fireworks, sale or use, **148:39.**

ROCKLAND.
Congressional district, **57:1.**
District court, **218:1.**
Senatorial district, **57:3.**

ROCKPORT.
Congressional district, **57:1.**
District court held, **218:1.**
Medical examiner district, **38:1.**
Senatorial district, **57:3.**

ROCKS.
See STONE OR ROCK.

RODENTS.
Beavers, town appropriation for control, **40:5.**
Chipmunk.
  See CHIPMUNK.
Destruction or control, **128:8A, 131:43.**
Rats.
  See RATS AND MICE.
Rodenticides.
  See PESTICIDES.
Squirrels.
  See SQUIRRELS.
Youth conservation and service corps, **78A:3.**

ROGATORY LETTER.
See LETTER ROGATORY.

ROGERS FUND.
Expenditure of income by superintendent of industrial school for girls, **120:9.**

ROGUE'S GALLERY.
Photographing of prisoners, **127:23-127:30.**

ROLL-BACK TAXES.
Agricultural and horticultural property.
  Bases for assessment, collection, and payment, **61A:19.**
  Certificate of amount, application, **61A:19A.**
  Lands no longer qualified for privileged uses, **61A:13.**
  Modification or abatement, application, **61A:19.**
  Qualification of land as dependent upon actual use, **61A:16.**
Recreational lands.
  Land subject, **61B:8.**
  Liability, **61B:11, 61B:12.**
  Liens on land, **61B:6.**
  Procedures for payment, **61B:14.**

ROLL DAMS.
Boats and boating, warning signs, **253:50A.**

ROLLER SKATING.
Motor vehicles, attaching to outside of prohibited, **90:13.**
Skating rinks.
  See SKATING RINKS.

ROLLING MILL MACHINERY.
Minors under sixteen not to work on certain machines, **149:61.**

ROLLING STOCK.
See RAILROADS.

ROMAN CANDLES.
Fireworks, sale or use, **148:39.**

ROMAN CATHOLIC CHURCHES.
See CATHOLIC CHURCHES.

ROOFS AND ROOFING.
Fire prevention, **148:1.**
Inspection of buildings, **143:1.**
Public contract bids, categories of specifications, **149:44F.**
Special assessments, granting tax abatements for improvements to real estate, **59:38.**
Town bylaws requiring removal of snow, **40:21.**

ROOMINGHOUSES.
See HOTELS, MOTELS, AND ROOMINGHOUSES.

ROOM OCCUPANCY TAX, 64G:1 et seq.
Abatement of excise paid on worthless accounts, **64G:7A.**
Administrative tax provisions as applicable, **62C:2.**
Amount.
  Reimbursement of operator of establishment for amount of tax, **64G:4.**
  Rent, amount of tax collected to be stated and charged separately, **64G:5.**
Bed and breakfast establishments, **64G:1, 64G:3, 64G:3A, 64G:6.**
Certificate or registration, **64G:6.**
Collection of tax.
  Amount of tax collected to be stated and charged separately from rent, **64G:5.**
  By commissioner of corporations and taxation, **64G:4.**
  From occupant by operator, **64G:4.**
Definitions, **64G:1.**
Exemptions, **64G:2, 64G:3.**
Imposition, **64G:3.**
Lodging houses, **64G:3.**
Military exemption, **64G:12.**
Payment of tax, time, **64G:3.**

ROOM OCCUPANCY TAX
—Cont'd
Rate, **64G:3.**
Records, **64G:5.**
Reimbursement of operator of
establishment for amount,
64G:4.
Surtax, **64G:3.**
Tax collection.
Collection of tax. See within this
heading, "Collection of tax."
Worthless account, abatement of
excise paid, **64G:7A.**

ROOMS.
Board.
See BOARD AND LODGING.
Hotels.
See HOTELS, MOTELS, AND
ROOMINGHOUSES.
Occupancy tax, **64G:1 et seq.**
See ROOM OCCUPANCY TAX.
Reading rooms.
See READING ROOMS.
Registering bets, **271:10, 271:17.**
State house.
See STATE HOUSE.

ROOTS.
Digging up or carrying away as
criminal offense, **266:113.**

ROPE.
Automatic sprinklers in buildings
for manufacturing, etc.,
148:26, 148:27.
Fire alarm signal system, **166:11,
166:12.**
Longshore and waterfront
employees, **149:18D.**

ROPE INFECTION.
Bakery products, prevention, **94:5.**

**ROSE FITZGERALD
KENNEDY DAY.**
Annual observance, **6:12SS.**

ROSETTE.
Unlawful use, **266:69, 266:70.**

ROTARIES.
Motor vehicles entering,
regulating, **89:8.**

ROTH IRA'S.
Taxation.
Exemption from income tax,
62:5.

ROUTES.
Carriers.
See CARRIERS.
Electric railroads.
See ELECTRIC RAILROADS.
Street railways.
See STREET RAILWAYS.

**ROUTES OF REASONABLE
ACCESS.**
Definition, **90:1.**
Tandem units, **90:19G.**

ROWE.
Medical examiner district, **38:1.**

ROWLEY.
Congressional district, **57:1.**
District court, **218:1.**
Medical examiner district, **38:1.**
Senatorial district, **57:3.**

ROXBURY.
District court.
Assistant clerks, **218:10.**
Classification of clerk, **35:49.**
Municipal court, **218:1.**
Additional justice, **218:6.**
Assistant clerks, **218:10.**
Jurisdiction as to juvenile
offenders and offenses,
119:52, 218:1.
Justices, **218:6.**
School attendance, jurisdiction
over, **76:2.**

ROXBURY DISTRICT.
Justices of municipal court,
231:108.

ROXBURY PUDDINGSTONE.
Rock emblem of the
Commonwealth, **2:22.**

ROYALSTON.
Congressional district, **57:1.**
District court, **218:1.**
Medical examiner district, **38:1.**
Senatorial district, **57:3.**

ROYALTIES.
Machinery operated under
agreement for, place of
taxation, **59:18.**

R.S.
Use of title restricted to registered
sanitarians, **112:87OO.**

RUBBER.
Automatic sprinklers in buildings
for manufacturing, etc.,
148:26, 148:27.
Removal of waste rubber, **148:5.**

RUBBER BOOTS.
Municipalities authorized to
furnish to employees, **40:6J.**

RUBBISH.
See GARBAGE AND RUBBISH.

RUBELLA.
College students, immunization,
76:15C.

RUBELLA —Cont'd
Female seeking certificate of
intention to marry,
requirements, **207:28A.**

RUFFED GROUSE.
Damage to agricultural property,
killing, **131:37.**

**RULE AGAINST
PERPETUITIES, 184A:1 et
seq.**
**See PERPETUITIES, RULE
AGAINST.**

RULE IN SHELLEY'S CASE.
Applicability, **184:5.**

RULES COMMITTEE.
See GENERAL COURT.

RULES OF CONSTRUCTION.
**See CONSTRUCTION AND
INTERPRETATION.**

RULES OF COURT.
Appeals court.
See APPEALS COURT.
Appellate procedure rules.
See APPELLATE PROCEDURE
RULES.
Appellate tax board rules of
practice and procedure.
See APPELLATE TAX BOARD
RULES OF PRACTICE
AND PROCEDURE.
Bail and recognizance rules.
See BAIL AND
RECOGNIZANCE RULES.
Bar overseers board rules.
See BAR OVERSEERS BOARD
RULES.
Boston municipal court rules.
See BOSTON MUNICIPAL
COURT RULES.
Child support guidelines.
See CHILD SUPPORT
GUIDELINES.
Civil motor vehicle infractions,
uniform rules on.
See CIVIL MOTOR VEHICLE
INFRANCTIONS,
UNIFORM RULES ON.
Civil procedure rules.
See CIVIL PROCEDURE
RULES.
Clerks of courts.
See COMMITTEE ON
PROFESSIONAL
RESPONSIBILITY FOR
CLERKS OF COURTS
RULES.
Clients' security board.
See CLIENTS' SECURITY
BOARD RULES.

RULES OF COURT —Cont'd
Committee on professional
responsibility for clerks of
courts rules.
See COMMITTEE ON
PROFESSIONAL
RESPONSIBILITY FOR
CLERKS OF COURTS
RULES.
Criminal procedure rules.
See CRIMINAL PROCEDURE
RULES.
Depositions, taking, **233:40,
233:43, 233:57.**
Destruction of obsolete and useless
papers and records, **221:27A.**
District and municipal court
supplemental rules of civil
procedure.
See DISTRICT AND
MUNICIPAL COURT
SUPPLEMENTAL RULES
OF CIVIL PROCEDURE.
District courts, **218:19C, 218:43.**
District and municipal court
rules of civil procedure.
Appellate division appeals
rules.
See DISTRICT/MUNICIPAL
COURT RULES
APPELLATE DIVISION
APPEAL.
Special rules.
See DISTRICT COURT
SPECIAL RULES.
Supplemental rules.
See DISTRICT AND
MUNICIPAL COURT
SUPPLEMENTAL
RULES OF CIVIL
PROCEDURE.
District court special rules.
See DISTRICT COURT
SPECIAL RULES.
District court standing orders.
See DISTRICT COURT
STANDING ORDERS.
District/Municipal courts rules for
appellate division appeal.
See DISTRICT/MUNICIPAL
COURTS RULES FOR
APPELLATE DIVISION
APPEAL.
District/Municipal courts rules of
criminal procedure.
See DISTRICT/MUNICIPAL
COURTS RULES OF
CRIMINAL PROCEDURE.
Domestic relations rules of
procedure.
See DOMESTIC RELATIONS
RULES OF PROCEDURE.

RULES OF COURT —Cont'd
Executions.
See EXECUTIONS.
Extension of papers on records,
221:27.
Housing court rules.
See HOUSING COURT RULES.
Impoundment procedure, uniform
rules on.
See IMPOUNDMENT
PROCEDURE, UNIFORM
RULES ON.
Judicial conduct commission rules.
See JUDICIAL CONDUCT
COMMISSION RULES.
Judicial ethics committee rules.
See JUDICIAL ETHICS
COMMITTEE RULES.
Juvenile court rules.
See JUVENILE COURT
RULES.
Land court, **185:1.**
Rules.
See LAND COURT RULES.
Magistrates, uniform rules.
See MAGISTRATES, UNIFORM
RULES.
Motions and orders, **231:71.**
Motor vehicle infractions.
See CIVIL MOTOR VEHICLE
INFRACTIONS, UNIFORM
RULES ON.
Municipal courts rules.
See MUNICIPAL COURTS.
Pecuniary legacies, interest rate,
197:20.
Pretrial orders and sales, **231:71.**
Probate and family court rules.
See PROBATE AND FAMILY
COURT RULES.
Probation and parole, **127:133C.**
Professional conduct, rules of.
See PROFESSIONAL
CONDUCT, RULES OF.
Small claims, uniform rules.
See SMALL CLAIMS,
UNIFORM RULES.
Subpoenas to court officials,
uniform rules of.
See SUBPOENAS TO COURT
OFFICIALS, UNIFORM
RULES OF.
Substitute care review hearings,
uniform rules for.
See SUBSTITUTE CARE
REVIEW HEARINGS,
UNIFORM RULES FOR.
Summary process, uniform rules.
See SUMMARY PROCESS,
UNIFORM RULES.
Superior courts rules.
See SUPERIOR COURTS
RULES.

RULES OF COURT —Cont'd
Support guidelines.
See CHILD SUPPORT
GUIDELINES.
Supreme Judicial court, **213:3,
213:3A.**
See SUPREME JUDICIAL
COURT RULES.
Tax board.
See APPELLATE TAX BOARD
RULES OF PRACTICE
AND PROCEDURE.
Trust instrument, interest rate
upon pecuniary distributions,
197:20.
Uniform magistrate rules.
See MAGISTRATES, UNIFORM
RULES.
Uniform rules for substitute care
review hearings.
See SUBSTITUTE CARE
REVIEW HEARINGS,
UNIFORM RULES FOR.
Uniform rules of subpoenas to
court officials.
See SUBPOENAS TO COURT
OFFICIALS, UNIFORM
RULES OF.
Uniform rules on civil motor
vehicle infractions.
See CIVIL MOTOR VEHICLE
INFRACTIONS, UNIFORM
RULES ON.
Uniform rules on impoundment
procedure.
See IMPOUNDMENT
PROCEDURE, UNIFORM
RULES ON.
Uniform small claims rules.
See SMALL CLAIMS,
UNIFORM RULES.
Uniform summary process rules.
See SUMMARY PROCESS,
UNIFORM RULES.
Waiver of indictment, application,
263:4A.

**RULES OF THE ROAD,
81:1-81:10.**
**See TRAFFIC REGULATIONS
AND RULES OF THE
ROAD.**

RUNAWAY CHILD.
Probable cause for arrest,
119:39H.

RUNWAYS.
Airports.
See AIRPORTS AND LANDING
FIELDS.
Longshore and waterfront
employees, protection,
149:18A.

RURAL HIGHWAYS.
Federal aid for construction, **81:30.**

RURAL HOUSING.
Housing authority powers and duties, **121B:27.**

RUSSELL.
Congressional district, **57:1.**
District court, **218:1.**
Medical examiner district, **38:1.**
Senatorial district, **57:3.**

RUTLAND.
Congressional district, **57:1.**
District court, **218:1.**
Medical examiner district, **38:1.**
Senatorial district, **57:3.**

RUTLAND HOSPITAL.
Admission of patients, **111:69E.**

S

SABBATH, 6:12A et seq., 136:5 et seq., 149:45 et seq.

SABBATH SCHOOL.
Correctional institutions, maintenance, **127:89.**

SABOTAGE.
Contracts awarded under emergency conditions without competitive bidding, **30:39M, 149:44A.**
Insurance against, corporations, **175:47.**

SACRED MUSIC.
Religious society appropriating money, **67:17, 67:27.**

SADDLED PROMINENT BEETLES.
Suppression, **132:11 et seq.**
Transporting insect pests, **266:119.**

SADDLE PATHS.
Reserved spaces in public ways, **82:34.**

SAFE DEPOSIT BOXES AND COMPANIES.
Abandoned, lost, and unclaimed property, **158:17, 171:75.**
Business corporation provisions inapplicable to safe deposit companies, **156:2, 156B:3.**
Certain miscellaneous corporations, organization under law, **158:1.**
Commission for the Blind, requirement as to furnishing certain information, **6:131.**
County retirement systems, deposit of securities, **32:23.**

SAFE DEPOSIT BOXES AND COMPANIES —Cont'd
Credit unions, **171:75.**
Income tax, deduction of rentals by trustees, **62:10.**
Insurance on contents of box, notice to lessees, **158:17.**
Municipal retirement systems, deposit of securities, **32:23.**
Notaries public, opening of box in presence, **158:17, 171:75.**
Public welfare officials, information as to deposits to be given, **18:15, 122:22.**
Rent of boxes, proceedings when unpaid, **158:17.**
Veteran, giving information as to financial condition, **115:2.**
Wage reporting system, **62E:4, 62E:5.**

SAFE DRINKING WATER ACT.
Environmental affairs executive office, **21A:18.**

SAFE DRIVER INSURANCE PLAN, 175:113P.

SAFE ROADS ACT, 90:23 et seq., 90C:2, 218:26.

SAFES AND VAULTS.
Attempt to compel person to surrender means of opening, **165:21.**
Boxes.
See SAFE DEPOSIT BOXES AND COMPANIES.
Breaking and entering.
Intent to blow up or destroy safe or vault, **266:16.**
Making and repairing tools for, penalty, **266:49.**
Columbarium.
See COLUMBARIUM.
Confining or intimidating persons for purpose of stealing, **265:21.**
District court's storage of documents, **218:13.**
Insurance.
Banks, insurance, **175:47.**
Life insurance companies' annual statements, disbursements listed, **175:25.**
Notice as to insurance on contents of safe deposit boxes, **158:17.**
Making and repairing tools for breaking into, penalty, **266:49.**
Small loan business, access to vaults, **140:97.**

SAFETY AND SAFETY DEVICES.
Abuse protection, location of safe place, **209C:6.**
Ammonia compressors.
Penalty for nonuse of safety valves, **146:55.**
Use of safety valves, **146:42.**
Asbestos, protective equipment requirements, **149:6C.**
Bicycles.
See BICYCLES.
Boxing matches, requirement of protective gear, **147:38.**
Brake drums, safety standards to be marked, **90:7G.**
Building code of state.
See BUILDING CODE OF STATE.
Building regulations and standards board, **143:93 et seq.**
Buildings and structures, **143:1 et seq.**
Burns, reporting of treatment, **112:12A.**
Business demonstration projects to be subject to safety regulations, **71:37K.**
Cans, inflammable liquids stored, **148:23.**
Carriers.
See CARRIERS.
Charitable homes for the aged, fire and safety regulations, **111:71, 143:3Q.**
Coal mining operations, imminent danger, **21B:8 et seq.**
Compressed air tanks, **146:35.**
Compressors.
Ammonia compressors, **146:42, 146:55.**
Construction workers, safety inspections for personnel and equipment, **149:6.**
Criminal history systems board, student housing safety, **6:168C.**
Dangerous buildings.
See DANGEROUS BUILDINGS AND STRUCTURES.
Department of public safety, **22:1 et seq.**
Dogs, dangerous.
See DOGS.
Drinking water as safe, **111:17.**
Education.
Schools. See within this heading, "Schools."
Elevators.
Amendment of regulations, **143:68.**

SAFETY AND SAFETY DEVICES —Cont'd

Elevators —Cont'd
Report of tests, **143:64.**
Testing, **143:63, 143:64.**
Exclusion of persons and vehicles from state highways by public works department, **85:2E.**
Ferries, safety requirements, **88:3.**
Film, penalty for sale, lease, or false marking of combustible, **143:87.**
Firearms.
See FIREARMS AND WEAPONS.
Fire escapes.
See FIRE ESCAPES.
Fire extinguishers.
See FIRE EXTINGUISHERS.
Fire in public buildings, **143:3 et seq.**
Fire marshal's suggestions, **148:33.**
Glazing material in buildings, **143:3T.**
Hazardous location, **143:3V.**
Labeling, **143:3U.**
Governor's highway safety committee, **6A:18, 90A:1 et seq.**
Hazardous waste facilities siting.
See HAZARDOUS WASTE FACILITIES SITING.
Hazardous waste management.
See HAZARDOUS WASTE MANAGEMENT.
Hazards.
See HAZARDS AND HAZARDOUS OR TOXIC SUBSTANCES.
Highways.
See HIGHWAYS AND STREETS.
Hot water heating boilers.
See HOT WATER HEATING BOILERS.
Insurance.
See INSURANCE.
Jet skis, surf jets, or wetbikes, safety skills necessary, **90B:9A, 90B:9B.**
Labor.
Defined under labor and workforce development law, **149:1.**
Health and safety.
See LABOR AND WORKFORCE DEVELOPMENT.
Life preservers.
See LIFE PRESERVERS OR VESTS.

SAFETY AND SAFETY DEVICES —Cont'd

Linemen's working in manner other than with insulated hot line tools, penalty, **149:129C.**
Longshore.
Requirements, **149:18A.**
Mentally ill and retarded persons, transportation, **19B:17.**
Missing children, **22A:1 et seq.**
Motorboat or vessel in unsafe condition, operation, **90B:12A.**
Motorcycles, wearing of protective head gear when riding, **90:7.**
Motor vehicles.
See MOTOR VEHICLES.
Physical fitness standards, police officers and firefighters, **31:61A.**
Police stations, lockups, houses of detention, jails, houses of correction, prisons and reformatories, inspection and general sanitary condition, **40:36B, 111:20 et seq.**
Power lawnmowers, safety devices as required equipment, **147:56.**
Public safety department, **22:1 et seq.**
Railroads.
See RAILROADS.
Recreation and snow vehicles, **90B:24, 90B:26.**
Riot, peace officers' duty to approach as near as safety permits, **269:1, 269:3.**
Safe workplace, liability for injuries and damages for failure to provide, **143:51.**
Schools, **71:37H, 71:37H½.**
Buses.
See SCHOOL BUSES AND TRANSPORTATION OF PUPILS.
Criminal history systems board, student housing safety, **6:168C.**
Crossings, protection, **85:21A.**
Highway safety, promotion in public schools, **6:15P, 71:48A.**
Instruction in public school, **71:1.**
Public safety executive office, board of schoolhouse structural standards as agency within, **6A:18.**
Safety patrol and stations, **71:48A, 71:71A.**
Students' rights regarding personal dress and appearance, **71:83.**

SAFETY AND SAFETY DEVICES —Cont'd

Smoke.
See SMOKE AND HEAT DETECTORS.
Social worker and client, safety of client requiring disclosure of confidential communications, **112:135A, 112:135B.**
State building code.
See BUILDING CODE OF STATE.
State parks, recreation areas, and reservations, safety rest areas as part of planning, **132A:2D.**
Steam boilers.
See STEAM BOILERS AND ENGINES.
Street cars or railways, requirement, **161:98.**
Swimming pool equipment, **140:206.**
Throwing or dropping objects endangering public safety, **265:35.**
Traffic regulations.
See TRAFFIC REGULATIONS AND RULES OF THE ROAD.
Traffic Safety week, **6:15P.**
Trailers to be attached to towing vehicle by safety chains, **90:7.**
Transportation of mentally retarded persons, **19B:17.**
Workers' compensation insurers may prescribe rules, **152:64.**

SAFETY BELTS.
Motor vehicles.
See MOTOR VEHICLES.

SAFETY FUND.
Life insurance companies, **175:141.**

SAFETY LOCKING DEVICES.
Firearms.
Required, **140:123.**
Sale without functioning device. Liability of dealer, **140:131K.**

SAFETY REST AREAS.
Advertising, **93D:1, 93D:6.**
Federal-aid highways, acquisition and use of lands adjacent, **81:13B.**

SAILING.
See SHIPS AND OTHER WATERCRAFT.

SAILMAKER SHOPS.
Fire insurance, classification, **175:99C.**

SAILORS.
See SEAMEN.

SAINT JEAN DE BAPTISTE DAY, 6:15OO.

SALAMANDERS.
Use regulated, **148:25.**

SALARIES.
See WAGES, SALARIES, AND COMPENSATION.

SALEM.
Alcoholic beverage licenses, hearings on appeals to commission, **138:67.**
City marshal, additional day's pay for duty on holidays, **147:17F.**
Congressional district, **57:1.**
County commissioners, meeting, **34:9.**
District court, **218:1.**
Medical examiner district, **38:1.**
Metropolitan area planning district, membership, **40B:26.**
Probate court sessions for Essex county, **215:62.**
Senatorial district, **57:3.**
Superior court sittings, **212:14.**

SALEM HARBOR.
Boarding vessel without leave prohibited, **102:1.**
Penalty, **102:3.**
Limits for purpose of certain statutes, **102:4.**

SALEM STATE COLLEGE.
Management, **73:1.**
Trustees of state colleges, jurisdiction, **73:19.**

SALE OF SECURITIES ACT, 110A:1 et seq.

SALE OR TRANSFER OF PROPERTY.
Abandoned property.
See ABANDONED, LOST, AND UNCLAIMED PROPERTY.
Abandoned spouse, conveyance of property by, **209:30, 209:31, 209:36.**
Absentees, estates of.
See ABSENTEES' ESTATES.
Acceptance of offer.
Offer and acceptance. See within this heading, "Offer and acceptance."
Accountant's right to sell working papers, etc., **112:87E.**
Adjournment of sale.
See ADJOURNMENT OF SALE.
Administrative regulations of state agencies, sale of copies, **30A:6.**
Administrators.
See EXECUTORS AND ADMINISTRATORS.

SALE OR TRANSFER OF PROPERTY —Cont'd
Agents.
See SALESPERSONS.
Agreements for purchase, **184:17A.**
Agriculture, **94:117A to 94:117F, 106:2-105, 106:2-107.**
See AGRICULTURE.
Aircraft.
Fuel, **64A:8A, 64J:3, 64J:8.**
Sales taxes.
See SALES TAXES.
Suspended registration, **90:49L.**
Air rifles or BB guns, sale or furnishing to minor, **269:12A, 269:12B.**
Alcoholic beverages control commission.
See ALCOHOLIC BEVERAGES CONTROL COMMISSION.
Alcoholic liquors.
Candy containing alcohol, **270:8.**
Generally.
See ALCOHOLIC LIQUORS.
Aliens, **184:1.**
Ammunition.
See AMMUNITION.
Animals, **128:10.**
Generally.
See ANIMALS.
Horses. See within this heading, "Horses."
Annual reports, sale, **5:6, 12:11.**
Antifreeze solutions, **94:303G et seq.**
See ANTIFREEZE SOLUTIONS.
Apportionment of tax on realty divided by sale, **59:81.**
Appropriations.
House of Representatives, transfer of funds among items, **29:7M.**
Municipal departments, transfer between, **44:33B.**
Approval, sales, **106:2-326, 106:2-327.**
Aqueduct companies, notice of sale of shares for failure to pay assessment, **165:18.**
Archaeological sites, reservation from sale, **9:26A.**
Arrest on mesne process.
See ARREST ON MESNE PROCESS AND SUPPLEMENTARY PROCEEDINGS.
Arrowheads, sale to children or minors, **269:16.**
Arsenic, articles containing, **114:51, 270:10 et seq.**
Attached property, **223:87 et seq.**
See ATTACHMENT OF PROPERTY.

SALE OR TRANSFER OF PROPERTY —Cont'd
Attempts to commit crime.
Device or machine with defaced serial number, sale, **266:139A.**
Motor vehicle or trailer with defaced serial number, sale, **266:139.**
Attorney general, sale of annual report, **12:11.**
Auctions and auctioneers, **100:1 et seq., 106:2-328.**
See AUCTIONS AND AUCTIONEERS.
Automobiles.
See MOTOR VEHICLES.
Aviation.
Aircraft. See within this heading, "Aircraft."
Bail and recognizance.
Property deposited in lieu of bond, **276:80.**
Surety's sale, **276:61A.**
Bailments, **266:84 et seq.**
Delivery of goods in possession of bailee, risk of loss, **106:2-509.**
Sales tax, property purchased for rental, **64H:8.**
Stoppage of delivery in transit of goods held by bailee, **106:2-705.**
Tender of delivery of goods in possession of bailee, **106:2-503.**
Use, consumption, or storage tax on property or services purchased for rental, **64I:8.**
Bankruptcy.
See INSOLVENCY AND BANKRUPTCY.
Banks.
See BANKS AND BANKING.
Bees which are diseased, **128:33.**
Beverages, **94:10A et seq., 140:21A et seq.**
Bicycles.
See BICYCLES.
Bills of lading, **106:7, 106:101 et seq.**
See BILLS OF LADING.
Bills of sale.
See BILLS OF SALE.
Biographical sketches of members of general court, **5:18.**
Blind persons.
Discrimination in realty sales, **151B:4.**
License for sales, **6:139.**
Products and services, **6:134, 6:143, 7:22.**

SALE OR TRANSFER OF PROPERTY —Cont'd

Boats.
Motorboats. See within this heading, "Motorboats."
Ships.
See SHIPS AND OTHER WATERCRAFT.
Bombs.
Explosions and explosives. See within this heading, "Explosions and explosives."
Bona fide purchasers.
See BONA FIDE PURCHASERS.
Bond as required in action for possession after sale, **239:6.**
Bonds.
See BONDS AND DEBENTURES.
Bradford Durfee College of Technology, purchases, **74:42N.**
Bribery of agent, **271:39.**
Brokers, **112:87PP et seq.**
Bulk transfers.
See BULK TRANSFERS.
Burden of proof.
Presumptions and burden of proof. See within this heading, "Presumptions and burden of proof."
Burned and dangerous buildings, sale to cover expense of removing, **139:3A.**
Business corporations.
See CORPORATIONS.
Camp meetings, peddling, **272:39.**
Cancellation of contract.
Commercial code provisions as to.
See SALES UNDER COMMERCIAL CODE.
Retail installment sales agreements, cancellation prior to delivery of copy, **255D:14.**
Seller's place of business, cancellation of contracts not executed, **93:48.**
Candy containing alcohol, **270:8.**
Carriers.
See CARRIERS.
Case books, **5:8.**
Cash buyers, prohibition as to discrimination against, **255D:10A.**
Cattle transport, bill of sale, **129:41.**
Cemeteries.
See CEMETERIES.

SALE OR TRANSFER OF PROPERTY —Cont'd

Certificates.
Mortgage transaction, requirements as to certification of title, **93:70.**
Motorboats, evidence of payment of taxes on sales or use as prerequisite to certification, **64H:25A, 64I:26A.**
Registration. See within this heading, "Registration."
Resale certificates.
Resale. See within this heading, "Resale."
Vendors, certificate of registration, **62C:67.**
Charcoal, **94:244.**
Charities and charitable contributions.
Representations in connection with public solicitation of funds, prohibitions, **68:27.**
Transient sale from charitable purposes, city and town licensing board or officers authorized to issue special licenses, **101:12A.**
Checks, **172A:15.**
Cigarettes, prohibition as to sale or distribution of tobacco products to persons under 18, **270:6.**
Cigarette tax, **64C:1 et seq.**
City council.
See CITY COUNCIL.
Civil rights.
Real property.
See CIVIL RIGHTS AND DISCRIMINATION.
Clam and clam bait, **94:85, 94:88B, 94:92B.**
Clearance sales.
See CLEARANCE SALES.
Clinical thermometers, sale, **98:13, 98:14.**
Clinics.
Transfer of ownership.
See DISPENSARIES OR CLINICS.
Closing out sales, **93:28A et seq.**
Clothing or household goods, sale to enforce lien of person working on, **255:31D.**
C.O.D., **106:2-513, 266:38.**
See C.O.D. SALES.
Cold storage articles, **94:69.**
Collateral, premature sale, **266:85.**
Colleges.
See COLLEGES AND UNIVERSITIES.

SALE OR TRANSFER OF PROPERTY —Cont'd

Commercial Code provisions, **106:2-101 et seq.**
Commodities defined, **137:7.**
Community antenna television systems.
License, transfer of.
See COMMUNITY ANTENNA TELEVISION SYSTEMS.
Television or radio sets, licensee's duty to refrain from sale, **166A:5.**
Community colleges, **40:14.**
Complaint.
Forms. See within this heading, "Forms."
Conditional sale.
See SECURED TRANSACTIONS.
Conditions and restrictions, **184:23 et seq.**
Condominiums.
Bylaws of organization of unit owners, **183A:12.**
Sex discrimination in sale, **183A:12.**
Unit as subject to sale, **183A:3.**
Conservation restrictions, **184:31 et seq.**
Consignment, **104:1 et seq.**
Constitution of Massachusetts.
Excess taken for construction of highways and streets, **MA Const Part 1 Art 10.**
General court to regulate sale of land by Commonwealth, **MA Const Amend Art 43.**
Convalescent and nursing homes, transfer of ownership and licenses, **111:71.**
Conveyances, **183:1 et seq.**
Cooperative banks.
See COOPERATIVE BANKS.
Cordwood, **94:299.**
Corporations.
See CORPORATIONS.
Corpses.
Dead bodies. See within this heading, "Dead bodies, sale."
Cost of goods construed, **93:14E.**
Counties.
See COUNTIES.
Cranberries, **94:115 et seq.**
Credit slips, time limitation on use, **93:14S.**
Credit unions.
See CREDIT UNIONS.
Crops, **106:2-105, 106:2-107.**
See AGRICULTURE.
Cumulative tables of changes in general statutes, **5:4A.**

SALE OR TRANSFER OF PROPERTY —Cont'd

Damaged goods, **93:14G.**

Dead bodies, sale, **112:84, 272:72.**

Commercial Code, **106:2-316.**

Dealers.

See DEALERS AND DISTRIBUTORS.

Debtors.

See DEBTORS AND CREDITORS.

Decedents' estates.

Debts or claims, right of purchaser to sue in own name, **231:6.**

Executors.

See EXECUTORS AND ADMINISTRATORS.

Deceit.

See FRAUD AND DECEIT.

Deeds, **183:1 et seq.**

Delivery.

Commercial code, sales under.

See SALES UNDER COMMERCIAL CODE.

Invoices.

See INVOICES AND DELIVERY TICKETS.

Retail installment sales agreements, cancellation prior to delivery of copy, **255D:14.**

"Short sales," prima facie evidence as to intent concerning delivery, **137:6.**

Tax stamps, penalty for failure to affix to deed prior to delivery to purchaser, **64D:6A.**

Demonstration sheep farms, sale of sheep, **128:10.**

Dies, molds, or forms, **94:320.**

Dietetic ice cream, **94:65L, 94:65T.**

Disclaimer rights, bar, **191A:8.**

Discrimination.

Real property.

See CIVIL RIGHTS AND DISCRIMINATION.

Dispensaries.

Transfer of ownership.

See DISPENSARIES OR CLINICS.

Divorce action, assignment or conveyance of encumbered real estate, **208:34A.**

Dogs, **140:151A.**

Drinking water protection commission, authority to buy or sell property, **40:39J½.**

SALE OR TRANSFER OF PROPERTY —Cont'd

Economic development.

See ECONOMIC DEVELOPMENT AND INDUSTRIAL CORPORATIONS.

Eggs, grading, **94:90C et seq.**

Electric companies.

See GAS AND ELECTRIC COMPANIES.

Embalming fluid containing arsenic, **114:51.**

Eminent domain, sale of buildings not removed from property taken, **79:13.**

Employment and training division in labor and workforce department, rental-purchase agreements, **7:40G.**

Employment security.

Contributions, transfer of business as affecting, **151A:14.**

Equipment, custody of money received from sale, **151A:58.**

Obligation of seller, transfer of business, **62C:44.**

Equal rights under law, **93:102.**

Escrow agents.

Actions on entitlement escrowed funds, **184:17A.**

Estate taxes.

Estate property, probate court's approval of sale, **65C:6.**

Lien as affected, **65C:14.**

Payment of tax, sale of real property, **65C:14, 202:20.**

Prerequisites, **65C:14.**

Returns, sale of bonds on obligations given to secure taxes, **65C:10.**

Executive session of governmental body held to discuss purchase or exchange of realty, **30A:11A½, 34:9G, 39:23B.**

Explosions and explosives.

Bombs, **266:102B.**

Regulation and licensing, **148:9, 148:13, 148:16.**

Stink bombs, **269:15.**

Extension of land contract, recording, **184:17A.**

Fair trade law, **93:14E et seq.**

Falsely labeling commercial fertilizer, **128:74.**

Family or personal use, civil remedies of purchaser of real estate, **93A:9.**

Farm products, **94:117A to 94:117F, 106:2-105, 106:2-107.**

See AGRICULTURE.

SALE OR TRANSFER OF PROPERTY —Cont'd

Federal-aid highways, public works department's purchase of land or rights within or adjacent, **81:13B.**

Fertilizers, regulation, **128:64 et seq.**

Fiduciaries.

See FIDUCIARIES.

Firearms, **140:121 et seq.**

See FIREARMS AND WEAPONS.

Fireworks.

See FIREWORKS.

Fishermen.

See MARINE FISH AND FISHERIES.

Flammable children's sleepwear, sale, **111:186B.**

Forcible entry on land, **184:18.**

Foreclosure sales, **244:11 et seq.**

See MORTGAGE FORECLOSURE.

Foreign fiduciaries.

See FOREIGN FIDUCIARIES.

Foreign substance, distributing, selling or giving food containing, **270:8A.**

Forest land of state, **132:34A.**

Forfeitures, **257:7, 257:8, 257:15.**

Attached personal property, forfeiture of bond given in lieu of sale, **223:94.**

Criminal cases, forfeitures, **94C:47.**

Forged archaeological artifacts, penalties for sale, **9:27C.**

Forms.

Petition for sale of real estate, form, **202:7.**

Retail installment sales and services.

Disclosure as to extension or modification of credit, **255D:18A.**

Notice of cancellation, **255D:9.**

Title and rights, procedure for transfer, **94:320.**

Vending machines, application for license for sale of food through, **94:309.**

Fraud.

See FRAUD AND DECEIT.

Frauds, statute of.

See STATUTE OF FRAUDS.

Fraudulent conveyances.

See FRAUDULENT CONVEYANCES OR TRANSFERS.

Fruit, use of term "native" in connection with sale, **94:99B.**

SALE OR TRANSFER OF PROPERTY —Cont'd

Fuel oil, **94:303F.**

Furs, **94:277A.**

Gambling devices, sale penalized, **271:5A.**

Garageman's lien, sale of vehicle to enforce, **255:39A.**

Gas.
　See GAS AND ELECTRIC COMPANIES.

Gasoline.
　See GASOLINE AND MOTOR FUELS.

General Court manual, **5:11.**

Gift enterprises prohibited, **271:6C, 271:29, 271:30.**

Gifts to minors.
　Uniform transfers to minors act, **201A:1 to 201A:24.**
　See TRANSFERS TO MINORS.

Glue or cement, sales to minors of certain, **270:19.**

Going out of business sale, **93:28A et seq.**
　See CLOSING OUT SALES.

Grain and meal, **94:222.**

Greeting cards, retail sale on Sunday, **136:6.**

Guardians.
　See GUARDIANS, CONSERVATORS, AND COMMITTEES.

Hairdressers' and cosmetologists' sales of beauty preparations, regulation, **112:87CC.**

Hawkers and peddlers, **101:1 et seq.**
　See TRANSIENT VENDORS.

Hazards.
　See HAZARDS AND HAZARDOUS OR TOXIC SUBSTANCES.

Health and Education Facilities Authority, sale of property acquired, **15A:5E.**

Health spa contracts, buyer's right to relief, **93:86.**

Highways.
　See HIGHWAYS AND STREETS.

Hired goods.
　Bailments. See within this heading, "Bailments."

Historic interest, reservation from sale of lands containing items, **9:26A.**

Honey, **128:36B.**

SALE OR TRANSFER OF PROPERTY —Cont'd

Horse and dog racing meetings, commission to approve transfers of more than 10 percent of value or stock of facility or corporation, **128A:11C.**

Horses.
　Disabled horses, sale as criminal offense, **272:78.**
　Foals, **272:78A.**
　Horsemeat, sale regulated, **94:151A.**

Hospitals.
　Transfer of ownership.
　　See HOSPITALS AND HEALTH CARE FACILITIES.

Hospital service corporations, sales, **176A:16.**

Housing.
　See HOUSING AND URBAN RENEWAL.

Husband and wife.
　Deeds.
　　See DEEDS AND CONVEYANCES.
　Disposition of proceeds of sale, **209:16.**

Ice, sale of, **94:157 et seq.**
　See SNOW AND ICE.

Imported goods, regulation as to sale, **94:277B.**

Income taxes, certificate as to sale, **62C:59, 62C:60.**

Incompetent's land contract, specific performance, **204:1.**

Inflammables.
　License, **148:13, 148:16.**
　Regulation of sales, **148:9, 148:16, 148:39.**
　Sleepwear, **111:186B, 148:25D.**

Injunctions.
　See INJUNCTIONS.

Insolvency.
　See INSOLVENCY AND BANKRUPTCY.

Insurance.
　See INSURANCE.

Investment securities under commercial code.
　Transfer.
　　See INVESTMENT SECURITIES UNDER COMMERCIAL CODE.

Jewelers' liens, sale to enforce, **255:31C.**

Joint tenants.
　See JOINT TENANTS AND TENANTS IN COMMON.

SALE OR TRANSFER OF PROPERTY —Cont'd

Judicial sales.
　See JUDICIAL SALES.

Knives and other dangerous weapons, **269:12.**

Kosher food, **94:156.**

Labeling of copied paintings, **94:277C.**

Land contracts, **202:14, 204:1.**

Lead-based paints and glazes, sale, **111:196.**

Leased or rented personalty.
　Bailments. See within this heading, "Bailments."

Legacy and succession taxes, sale of realty to pay, **65:21, 202:20.**
　Enforcement of tax lien, **65:31.**
　Refusal or neglect to pay tax by person entitled in realty, **65:17.**

Legislative documents, **5:12, 5:13.**

Letters of credit, **106:5-101 to 106:5-117.**
　See LETTERS OF CREDIT.

Libel and slander, defense, **231:91B.**

Liens, sales to enforce, **255:26 et seq.**

Life estates.
　Sale of trust property affecting, **203:17.**

Life insurance.
　Sales of securities or property, restrictions on, **175:66, 175:121.**

Limitation of action on condition broken, **260:31A.**

Limitations and restrictions, **184:23 et seq.**

Limited access ways, sale of property acquired, **81:7E.**

Linseed oil, sale, **94:291.**

Loan transactions by retail seller of goods or services, **255D:22A.**

Lobsters, **94:77G, 94:77H, 130:47 et seq.**
　See LOBSTERS.

Logs and timber, **96:11A, 106:2-107.**

Lost property.
　See ABANDONED, LOST, AND UNCLAIMED PROPERTY.

Lottery tickets or sales.
　See LOTTERIES.

Machine guns.
　See MACHINE GUNS.

Manufactured homes and manufactured housing communities, **140:32L, 140:32M, 140:32R.**

SALE OR TRANSFER OF PROPERTY —Cont'd

Mapping commissions in cities and towns, **40:8K.**

Maps prepared by public works department, sale, **91:33.**

Marine fish.
See MARINE FISH AND FISHERIES.

Markets.
See MARKETS AND MARKETING.

Master keys for motor vehicles, sale of for illegal purpose, **266:140.**

Matches, **148:52.**

Measure.
See WEIGHTS AND MEASURES.

Meat, retail sale by weight, **94:92B.**

Mechanics' lien.
Enforcement.
See MECHANICS' LIENS.

Medical care and assistance.
Eligibility as conditioned on sale or transfer of property, **118E:13.**
Fraud and deceit in connection with sale or transfer of property, **18:5D.**
Recipients, **118E:13A.**

Medical service corporations, property sales, **176B:10.**

Mentally ill persons, **123:29, 204:1.**

Merchandising schemes of trading stamps, **271:29, 271:30.**

Methyl alcohol, **94:303A et seq., 270:4.**

Metropolitan districts.
See METROPOLITAN DISTRICTS.

Milk, **94:12 et seq.**

Misrepresentation.
See FRAUD AND DECEIT.

Mobile vending vehicles, sales, **101:22A.**

Molotov cocktails, possession, sale or use, **266:102B.**

Money advanced by seller to buyer as loan, **140:96.**

Monopolies, **93:14E et seq.**

Morris plan banks.
See MORRIS PLAN BANKS.

Mortgages.
See MORTGAGES AND DEEDS OF TRUST.

Motion pictures.
See MOTION PICTURES.

SALE OR TRANSFER OF PROPERTY —Cont'd

Motorboats, **90B:3.**
Taxes on sales or use, evidence of payment as prerequisite to certification, **64H:25A, 64I:26A.**

Motor carriers' purchase of commodities from shippers for immediate resale, **159B:6D.**

Motor vehicles.
See MOTOR VEHICLES.

Moving pictures, **143:87.**

Multi-level distribution companies, **93:69.**

Municipal finance.
See MUNICIPAL FINANCE.

Municipal lighting.
Purchase and sale.
See MUNICIPAL LIGHTING AND HEATING PLANTS.

Natural gas, purchase or sale by municipalities, **164:69A.**

New Bedford Institute of Technology, purchases, **74:42N.**

New England power pool.
By-products, sale, **164A:6.**
Foreign utility companies, powers, **164A:4.**
Power of purchase and sale, **164A:3.**

Newspapers, license not required for sale, **101:17.**

Notice.
Amendment of pleadings, purchaser of property attached as affected by absence of notice, **231:138.**
Aqueduct companies, notice of sale of shares for failure to pay assessment, **165:18.**
Clothing or household goods, sale to enforce lien of person working on, **255:31D.**
Garageman's lien, sale of vehicle to enforce, **255:39A.**
Gasoline sales, notice of failure to renew dealers' agreement, **93E:5.**
Imported footwear, tools or hardware, restrictions on sales, **94:277B.**
Jewelers' liens, notice of sale to enforce, **255:31C.**
Minors, notice prohibiting sale of cigarettes, **270:7.**
Mortgaged personal property, sale by mortgagor without notice of mortgage, **266:83.**
Personal property, sale by hirer or lessee without notice to buyer, **266:84.**

SALE OR TRANSFER OF PROPERTY —Cont'd

Notice —Cont'd
Pictures or photographs, sale to enforce lien of person working on, **255:31F.**
Posting.
See POSTING.
Promoters of shows, notice to revenue commissioner, **62C:8A, 62C:67A.**
Public building, notice of purchase or sale of land, **7:40I.**
Real property, sale or conveyance without notice of encumbrance, **266:80, 266:81.**
Retail installment sales.
See RETAIL INSTALLMENT SALES AND SERVICES.
Spinners' liens, notice of sale to enforce, **255:31B.**
Taxation. See within this heading, "Taxation."
Trust in land, rights of purchasers without notice, **203:3.**
Vending machine sales of food, notice as to violations, **94:311.**

Nuisances.
See NUISANCES.

Nursery stock, **128:19.**

Nursing.
Change of ownership.
See NURSING OR REST HOMES.

Obscene literature, sale to minors, **272:28.**

Ocean cruises, restriction on sale of passenger tickets, **94:277B.**

Offer and acceptance.
Commercial Code.
See SALES UNDER COMMERCIAL CODE.
Definition of offer to sell under Uniform Securities Act, **110A:401.**

Tax sale, offer to surrender and discharge deed in case of invalidity, **60:46.**

Official textbooks, case books, and technical reports, **5:8.**

Oleomargarine, labeling for sale, **94:49, 94:55.**

Option to purchase.
See OPTION TO PURCHASE.

Optometrists.
See OPTOMETRISTS AND OPTOMETRY.

SALE OR TRANSFER OF PROPERTY —Cont'd

Ordinary course of business.
See SALES TAXES.
Outdoor advertising adjacent to interstate and primary highway systems, application of regulations to signs advertising sale of property, **93D:2.**
Out-of-state property, regulations as to sales by real estate brokers, **112:87AAA.**
Paint, sale, **94:291 et seq.**
Lead-based paints and glazes, **111:196.**
Licenses to paint dealers for sale of alcohol, **138:76.**
Pamphlet edition of session laws, **5:4.**
Paramount title to realty, effect of irregularities in fiduciary sales claimed by claimant, **204:20.**
Parol evidence.
See PAROL EVIDENCE.
Partition.
See PARTITION.
Partnerships.
See PARTNERSHIPS.
Pawnbrokers.
See PAWNBROKERS.
Pensions.
Retirement systems and pensions. See within this heading, "Retirement systems and pensions."
Perpetuities, rule against.
See PERPETUITIES, RULE AGAINST.
Personal or family use, civil remedies of purchaser of real estate, **93A:9.**
Pesticides, **64H:6.**
Pharmacists and pharmacies.
See PHARMACISTS AND PHARMACIES.
Phonograph records.
See PHONOGRAPH RECORDS.
Photographic film, retail sale on Sunday, **136:6.**
Pledge, **106:9-102, 140:87 to 140:89.**
See SECURED TRANSACTIONS.
Poisons.
Arsenic, articles containing, **114:51, 270:10 et seq.**
Toxic vapors, use, possession, or sale of substances releasing, **270:18, 270:19.**
Police.
See POLICE.

SALE OR TRANSFER OF PROPERTY —Cont'd

Portraits of members of general court, books containing, **5:18.**
Posting.
See POSTING.
Poultry and poultry products, **94:152A et seq.**
See POULTRY AND POULTRY PRODUCTS.
Powers of sale.
See POWERS OF SALE.
Prepackaged commodities sold at retail, labeling, **94:181.**
Presumptions and burden of proof.
Burden of proving breach with respect to accepted goods, **106:2-607.**
Fiduciary's sale of realty, presumption of highest obtainable price, **202:38.**
International log rule, contracts for purchase and sale of logs presumed made on basis, **96:11A.**
Privation contracts, purchase of state services, **7:52 et seq.**
Probate.
See PROBATE AND FAMILY COURT.
Probate bonds.
See PROBATE BONDS.
Professional corporations, purchase of stock on death or disqualification of shareholder, **156A:12.**
Promoters of shows, notice to revenue commissioner, **62C:8A, 62C:67A.**
Propane gas dealers and subsequent home purchasers, binding agreements, **93:94.**
Public administrator, sale of land, **194:9.**
Public convenience certificates.
See CERTIFICATES OF PUBLIC CONVENIENCE AND NECESSITY.
Public records and documents, **5:4, 5:6, 5:8, 5:11, 30:42.**
Purchase or purchased defined, **64I:1.**
Purchaser defined, **64H:1, 64I:1.**
Quahaugs, **94:88B.**
Radio.
See RADIO AND TELEVISION.
Railroads.
See RAILROADS.
Reassessment of taxes after transfer, **59:77.**
Receivers, land contracts of.
See ABSENTEES' ESTATES.

SALE OR TRANSFER OF PROPERTY —Cont'd

Recognizance.
Bail and recognizance. See within this heading, "Bail and recognizance."
Records, **5:6, 9:19, 30:42.**
Recreational areas, sale of land or wood, **132A:3.**
Recreation and snow traveling vehicles, transfer of ownership, **90B:23.**
Recycled paper materials, **7:22.**
Refrigerators kept for sale, removal of doors, **271:46.**
Regional community colleges, city's authority to acquire land for use, **40:14.**
Regional refuse disposal districts, **40:44F, 40:44J.**
Regional transportation authority, sale of property, **161B:6.**
Registration.
Aircraft and aviation, suspended registration, **90:49L.**
Land titles.
See REGISTRATION OF LAND TITLES.
Motor vehicles.
See MOTOR VEHICLES.
Resale and exempt use certificate, **64H:8, 64I:8.**
Vendors, **62C:67, 64H:7, 64I:9.**
Religion.
See RELIGION AND RELIGIOUS SOCIETIES.
Removal sale.
See CLOSING OUT SALES.
Repurchase.
Banned hazardous substances, repurchase by manufacturer, distributor, or dealer, **94B:8.**
Credit unions, **171:67, 171:71.**
Petroleum supplier's offer to repurchase products from dealer upon termination of lease, **93E:4.**
State funds, investment in repurchase agreements, **29:38.**
Warranty provisions of used motor vehicles, repurchase price defined, **90:7N¼.**
Resale.
Alcoholic beverages, minimum consumer resale price list, **138:25C.**
Certificates, **64H:8, 64I:8.**
Sales tax exempt use certificate, effect on vendor, **64H:8.**

SALE OR TRANSFER OF PROPERTY —Cont'd

Resale —Cont'd

Certificates —Cont'd

Use, consumption, or storage tax, **64I:8.**

Form and contents, **64I:8.**

Storage or use other than as certified, **64I:8.**

Vendor's liability, release by execution, **64I:8.**

Coffin or casket used for disposition of dead human body, **112:84.**

Commercial Code.

See SALES UNDER COMMERCIAL CODE.

Energy resources, reseller defined for purposes, **25A:3.**

Insurance company's authority to resell goods to employees, **175:64.**

Motor carriers' purchase from shippers from immediate resale, **159B:6D.**

Price maintenance, **94:15 et seq.**

See UNFAIR SALES ACT.

Registration, **64H:8, 64I:8.**

Sales taxes.

See SALES TAXES.

Tickets, **140:185A et seq.**

See TICKETS.

Uniform Commercial Code, sales under, **106:2-706, 106:2-711.**

See SALES UNDER COMMERCIAL CODE.

Use, consumption.

See USE, CONSUMPTION, OR STORAGE TAX.

Residential dwellings insulated with formaldehyde foam insulation, disclosure, **255:12I.**

Restraints of trade and monopolies, **93:14E et seq.**

Restrictions, **184:23 et seq.**

Retail installment sales.

See RETAIL INSTALLMENT SALES AND SERVICES.

Retail or wholesale sale defined, **93:14E.**

Retirement systems and pensions.

Interest in pension, annuity, or allowance, **32:92.**

Securities held by system, **32:23.**

Safe deposit boxes, disposition of unclaimed contents, **158:17.**

Sale defined, **64H:1, 64I:1.**

Salespersons.

See SALESPERSONS.

Sales price defined, **64H:1, 64I:1.**

SALE OR TRANSFER OF PROPERTY —Cont'd

Sales taxes, **64H:1 et seq.**

See SALES TAXES.

Sales under commercial code.

See SALES UNDER COMMERCIAL CODE.

Secondary boycott defined, **149:20C.**

Secured transactions, **106:9-101 to 106:9-507.**

See SECURED TRANSACTIONS.

Securities.

Transfer of securities.

See SECURITIES AND SECURITIES REGULATIONS.

Securities act.

See SECURITIES ACT.

Seeds.

See SEEDS.

Self-abuse, sale of articles, **272:21.**

Self-storage facilities, enforcement of operator's lien, **105A:4.**

Session laws, **5:3, 5:4.**

Sex discrimination, **151B:4.**

Condominiums, sex discrimination in sales, **183A:12.**

Conveyance of realty, **184:23B.**

Shellfish.

See SHELLFISH.

Sheriffs.

Auctions.

See AUCTIONS AND AUCTIONEERS.

Seized property, **276:7, 276:8.**

Tax sales.

Fees, **60:89.**

Tax collector, sheriff, **60:88, 60:89.**

Ships.

See SHIPS AND OTHER WATERCRAFT.

"Short sales," prima facie evidence of intent, **137:6.**

Shotguns.

Licenses, **140:123, 140:131A.**

Serial number requirements, **269:11E.**

Unlicensed resident selling not more than four firearms within single year, sale, **140:128A.**

Sidewalk, sale of merchandise, **93:40.**

Smoke detectors, sale and installation, **148:26F.**

Snow.

See SNOW AND ICE.

SALE OR TRANSFER OF PROPERTY —Cont'd

Snow traveling and recreational vehicles, transfer of ownership, **90B:2.**

Soaked goods, **94:155.**

Social services.

Welfare and social services. See within this heading, "Welfare and social services."

Soft drinks, **94:10A et seq.**

Soil conditioners, **128:64 et seq.**

Solid waste disposal, public works department's acquisition of land and facilities, **16:19.**

Space heaters, restriction as to sale, **148:5A, 148:25A, 148:25B.**

Special assessments.

See SPECIAL ASSESSMENTS.

Specific performance of sales contract, **106:2-716.**

Spinners' liens, **255:31A, 255:31B.**

State, **81:7E.**

Administrative regulations, sale of copies, **30A:6.**

Agencies, acquiring buildings for use, **7:40F.**

Bonds.

See STATE BONDS AND OBLIGATIONS.

Colleges, **73:15, 74:42N, 75:13.**

Employees not to act in connection with sale of land, **30:44.**

Forest lands, **132:34A.**

Highways, sales without permit, **85:17A.**

Institutions of state accounts of sales of property, **30:41.**

Itemized accounts of sale of state property, **30:41.**

Privatization contracts, **7:52 et seq.**

Records of no value, **9:19.**

Recreation areas, sale of land or products, **132A:3.**

Surplus state property, **7:40F, 7:40F½.**

Textbooks, state publications, **5:8.**

Treasurer.

See STATE TREASURER.

Underwater archaeological resources, Commonwealth and private museums as having first option to purchase, **91:63.**

State treasurer.

See STATE TREASURER.

SALE OR TRANSFER OF PROPERTY —Cont'd

Statute of frauds.
See STATUTE OF FRAUDS.
Stink bombs, penalty for sale, **269:15.**
Stock.
See CORPORATIONS.
Stop sale order, adulterated commercial feed, **128:60.**
Stores.
See STORES AND MERCHANTS.
Stray beasts, **134:5.**
Street railways.
See STREET RAILWAYS.
Subdivision control law, vendor's liability for failure to comply, **41:81Y.**
Succession taxes.
Legacy and succession taxes. See within this heading, "Legacy and succession taxes, sale of realty to pay."
Summary process to recover land.
See SUMMARY PROCESS TO RECOVER LAND.
Sunday, sales, **136:5, 136:6.**
Superior court.
See SUPERIOR COURTS.
Supplementary proceedings, sale of unredeemed property at public auction, **224:17.**
Supreme judicial court.
See SUPREME JUDICIAL COURT.
Surety on bail or recognizance, real property sold, **276:61A.**
Surplus state property, **7:40F, 7:40F½.**
Taxation.
Aircraft fuel, tax free sale, **64A:8A.**
Apportioned use certificate, services sold at retail outside of Commonwealth, **64H:6.**
Disqualification system for sale of certain and town properties, **60:77B.**
Estate taxes. See within this heading, "Estate taxes."
Income tax, certificate as to sale, **62C:59, 62C:60.**
Legacy and succession taxes. See within this heading, "Legacy and succession taxes, sale of realty to pay."
Motor vehicle excise tax, **60A:1 et seq.**
See MOTOR VEHICLES.

SALE OR TRANSFER OF PROPERTY —Cont'd

Taxation —Cont'd
Notice, **60:25, 60:26.**
Sales and use taxes, **62C:67A, 64H:29, 64H:32, 64I:33.**
Tax sales.
See TAX SALES.
Sales taxes, **64H:1 et seq.**
See SALES TAXES.
Services sold at retail, tax exemptions, **64H:6, 64I:7.**
Stamps, penalty for failure to affix to deed prior to delivery to purchaser, **64D:6A.**
Tax sales generally.
See TAX SALES.
Use, consumption or storage tax, **62C:16, 64I:1 et seq.**
See USE, CONSUMPTION, OR STORAGE TAX.
Tax collectors.
Auction sale provisions inapplicable, **100:11.**
Personal property, distress and sale, **60:20-60:28.**
Taking of property, tax collection after sale or, **60:61, 60:61A.**
Tax sales, **60:37 et seq.**
See TAX SALES.
Technical reports and textbooks, **5:8.**
Telephone.
See TELEPHONE AND TELEGRAPH COMPANIES.
Television.
See RADIO AND TELEVISION.
Term papers and themes to be used by another for academic credit, **271:50.**
Textbooks, state publications, **5:8.**
Thread, **94:285 et seq.**
Tickets.
See TICKETS.
Timber, **106:2-107.**
Title.
See TITLE AND OWNERSHIP.
Tobacco.
See TOBACCO.
Toxic substances.
Poisons. See within this heading, "Poisons."
Trackless trolleys, purchase of property, **163:11.**
Trade-in.
See TRADE-IN.
Transfers to minors act, **201A:1 to 201A:24.**
See TRANSFERS TO MINORS.
Transient vendors, **101:1 et seq.**

SALE OR TRANSFER OF PROPERTY —Cont'd

Trees.
Fee simple, sale of trees from property in which seller owns less than, **184:14.**
Forest land of state, **132:34A.**
Logs.
Contract for sale.
See LOGS AND TIMBER.
Nursery stock, sale, **128:19.**
Trust companies.
Assets and property.
See TRUST COMPANIES.
Trustee process.
See TRUSTEE PROCESS.
Trusts.
See TRUSTS AND TRUSTEES.
Truth in lending, transfer of debtor's bank funds in satisfaction of debt, **140D:21, 140D:23.**
Turpentine, sale, **94:289.**
Unclaimed property.
See ABANDONED, LOST, AND UNCLAIMED PROPERTY.
Unfair sales act.
See UNFAIR SALES ACT.
Uniform Commercial Code, **106:2-101 to 106:2-725.**
See SALES UNDER COMMERCIAL CODE.
Uniform Procurement Act, **30B:1 et seq.**
Uniform Securities Act.
See SECURITIES ACT.
United States uniforms, misuse, **264:10A.**
University.
See COLLEGES AND UNIVERSITIES.
Unwed mothers, institutions for.
See UNWED MOTHERS.
Unwholesome food or beverage, **94:150, 94:150A.**
Urban redevelopment corporations, real property, **121A:11, 121A:16A.**
Urban renewal projects.
See HOUSING AND URBAN RENEWAL.
Use, consumption, or storage tax, **62C:16, 64I:1 et seq.**
Used car sales, **140:57 et seq.**
Vending machines, **94:308 et seq.**
Vessel.
See SHIPS AND OTHER WATERCRAFT.
Warehouse receipts, **106:7-101 et seq.**
See WAREHOUSE RECEIPTS.

SALE OR TRANSFER OF PROPERTY —Cont'd

Warehouses.
See WAREHOUSES.
Water impoundment sites, acquisition, **21:9A.**
Water rights, **40:38, 165:4B.**
Waterworks and water supply.
Lands not needed, sale, **40:15B.**
Stock in water companies, sale of new issue of preferred stock, **164:19, 165:2.**
Weapons, **140:121 et seq.**
See FIREARMS AND WEAPONS.
Welfare and social services.
Procuring payment by false or fraudulent means, **18:5D.**
Services rendered, provisions as to bills, **18:5C.**
Wetland protection, **131:40.**
Wharves and real estate lying in common, sale by proprietors, **179:14.**
Wife.
Husband and wife. See within this heading, "Husband and wife."
Wildflowers, **266:116A.**
Wills.
See WILLS.
Wines.
Hawkers and peddlers prohibited from selling, **101:16.**
Pharmacist selling on prescription, **138:29.**
Wholesalers importers, **138:18.**
Wood.
See WOOD.
Wood alcohol, **94:303A et seq., 270:4.**
Written statement on sale of securities or commodities, **271:38.**

SALES ACT.
Motor fuel, **94:295A et seq.**

SALES FINANCE COMPANIES.
Retail installment sales and services.
See RETAIL INSTALLMENT SALES AND SERVICES.

SALESPERSONS.
Alcoholic liquors.
Solicitation of licensees, **138:19A.**
Transportation of samples, **138:22.**

SALESPERSONS —Cont'd

Attorneys at law.
Real estate brokers and salespersons.
See ATTORNEYS AT LAW.
Bribery, **271:39.**
Commissions of sales representatives, **104:7 et seq.**
Contracts and agreements, **104:8, 104:9.**
Correctional institutions, appointment of sales agent, **127:68.**
Correspondence school salesmen, licensing, **75C:1, 75C:3, 75C:9.**
Earnings, wages, and other compensation, sales representatives commission, **104:7 et seq.**
Hawkers, **101:1 to 101:30.**
See TRANSIENT VENDORS, **101:1 et seq.**
Insurance agents or brokers, **175:162-175:177.**
See INSURANCE AGENTS AND BROKERS.
Minimum wage law, applicability, **151:2.**
Overtime pay, **151:1A.**
Peddlers, **101:1 to 101:30.**
See TRANSIENT VENDORS.
Private business schools, training in sales techniques, **75D:1.**
Professional engineers and land surveyors, exemption from law, **112:81R.**
Real estate brokers, **112:87PP to 112:87DDD.**
See REAL ESTATE BROKERS AND SALESPERSONS.
Transient vendors, **101:1 to 101:30.**
Traveling salesmen, **101:2, 101:15.**

SALES TAXES, 64H:1 et seq.
Accounting, auditing and bookkeeping services, **64H:1, 64H:6.**
Advertising.
Assumption or absorption of tax by vendor, advertisement, **64H:23.**
Direct mail promotional advertising materials, **64H:6.**
Exclusion of advertising agents from tax on persons furnishing information, **64H:1.**
Promoters of shows. See within this heading, "Promoters of shows."

SALES TAXES —Cont'd

Advertising —Cont'd
Unlawful for vendor to advertise that he will assume or absorb tax, **64H:23.**
Aged persons, exemption for meals furnished to certain organizations of, **64H:6.**
Aircraft.
Casual sales, **64H:6.**
Evidence of payment of taxes prerequisite to registration, **64H:25A.**
Fuels, exemption from sales tax, **64A:8A, 64H:6.**
Meals, exemption for meals prepared while transporting passengers for hire, **64H:6.**
Alcoholic beverage taxes.
Exemptions, **64H:6.**
Separate statement of sales tax, **64H:5.**
Amendment of classified permits, **64H:9.**
Amount of sale, determination of tax, **64H:4.**
Amusements and exhibitions.
Shows. See within this heading, "Shows."
Animals used for research, exemption from sales tax, **64H:6.**
Apportioned use certificate, services sold at retail outside of Commonwealth, **64H:6.**
Architectural services, **64H:1, 64H:6.**
Armored car services, exemptions, **64H:1.**
Art services, commercial, **64H:1.**
Assumption of tax by vendor, unlawful advertising, **64H:23.**
Auctioneer's responsibilities, **100:8.**
Auditing services, exemptions, **64H:6.**
Automobiles.
Motor vehicles. See within this heading, "Motor vehicles."
Boarding home for aged, exemption for meals prepared and served, **64H:6.**
Boats, **64H:27A, 64I:28.**
See SHIPS AND OTHER WATERCRAFT.
Bookkeeping services, exemptions, **64H:6.**
Burden of proof, gross receipts from sale of tangible personal property as sales subject to tax, **64H:8.**

SALES TAXES —Cont'd
Certificates.
  Apportioned use certificate,
    services sold at retail
    outside of Commonwealth,
    64H:6.
  Exempt use certificate, **64H:6 et
    seq.**
  Levy of taxes, **62C:59, 62C:60.**
  Motor vehicle certificate or
    registration, **64H:25.**
  Permits and registration.
    Aircraft, evidence of payment
      of taxes prerequisite to
      registration, **64H:25A.**
    Classified permits, **64H:9.**
    Direct payment permit, **64H:3.**
    Increasing fees for certificates,
      62C:67.
    Promoter's certificate,
      requirements, **62C:67A.**
    Resale and exempt use
      certificate, **64H:8.**
    Vendors, **64H:7.**
  Resale certificates, **64H:6.**
Churches, exemption for meals
  prepared and served on
  premises, **64H:6.**
Claim for reimbursement of excise
  paid by vendor on worthless
  account, **64H:33.**
Classified permits.
  Amendment upon determination
    that percentage of exempt
    sales inaccurate, **64H:9.**
  Revocation of classification upon
    determination that
    percentage of exempt sales
    inappropriate, **64H:9.**
Clothing or footwear as exempt
  from tax, **64H:6.**
Collection.
  Credit reporting and collection
    services, **64H:1.**
  Formula, **64H:4.**
  Motor vehicles, method of
    collecting tax, **64H:3.**
  Statement and charge of tax,
    64H:5.
  Unpaid tax, **64H:16.**
Commuter passenger service
  vessels, exemption from sales
  tax, **64H:6.**
Computer maintenance and repair
  services, exemptions, **64H:1.**
Concrete mixing units, exemption
  as to replacement parts,
  64H:6.
Construction contracts and works.
  Bond or deposit to secure
    payment, **64H:30A,
    64I:31A.**

SALES TAXES —Cont'd
Construction contracts and works
  —Cont'd
  Definition of contractor,
    64H:30A.
  Exemptions, **64H:6.**
Convalescent home, exemption for
  meals prepared and served,
  64H:6.
Corporations, lien for taxes upon
  sale or transfer other than in
  ordinary course of business,
  62C:51.
Costs of performance defined,
  64H:1.
Court reporting and stenographic
  services, exemption, **64H:1.**
Credit reporting and collection
  services, **64H:1.**
Dealer contract, form of clause
  relative to tax, **106:2-201.**
Definitions, **64H:1, 64H:30A.**
Designees or purchasers outside
  state, exemption, **64H:6.**
Detectives, exemptions, **64H:1.**
Direct mail promotional
  advertising materials, **64H:6.**
Direct payment permit, issuance
  and effect, **64H:3.**
Educational services, exemption
  form sales tax, **64C:6, 64H:6.**
Election or option.
  Purchaser, reporting of gross
    receipts from rented
    personalty, **64H:8.**
  Services sold at retail, **64H:2.**
Electricity, residential service
  exempt from sales tax, **64H:6.**
Energy systems exempt from tax
  on retail sales, certain, **64H:6.**
"Engaged in business of the
  Commonwealth," definition,
  64H:1.
Engineering and surveying
  services, **64H:1, 64H:6.**
Exemptions.
  Accounting services, **64H:6.**
  Advertising agents, **64H:1.**
  Aircraft fuel, **64H:6.**
  Alcoholic beverage sales tax as
    exempt from separate
    statement of taxes, **64H:5,
    64H:6.**
  Animals for research, **64H:6.**
  Architectural services, **64H:6.**
  Art and graphic design services,
    commercial, **64H:1.**
  Auditing services, **64H:6.**
  Blood, blood plasma, and human
    tissues and organs, **64H:6.**
  Bookkeeping services, **64H:6.**

SALES TAXES —Cont'd
Exemptions —Cont'd
  Certificates, exempt use
    certificate, **64H:8.**
  Classified permits, **64H:9.**
  Clothing, **64H:6.**
  Commercial fishing vessels,
    machinery, and equipment,
    64H:6.
  Commuter passenger service
    vessels, **64H:6.**
  Composed type or the like,
    64H:6.
  Computer maintenance and
    repair services, **64H:1.**
  Concrete mixing units,
    replacement parts, **64H:6.**
  Construction contracts and
    works, **64H:6.**
  Court reporting and
    stenographic services,
    64H:1.
  Credit reporting and collection
    services, **64H:1.**
  Detective, guard, armored car
    services, **64H:1.**
  Educational services, **64C:6,
    64H:6.**
  Electricity, residential service,
    64H:6.
  Energy systems exempt from tax
    on retail sales, certain,
    64H:6.
  Engineering services, **64H:6.**
  Federal exemptions, **64H:6.**
  Gasoline and motor fuel taxes,
    64A:12, 64E:12, 64F:13.
  Feed for fur-bearing animals,
    64H:6.
  Fire trucks and ambulances,
    64H:6.
  Foreign state or country,
    designees or purchasers,
    64H:6.
  Fuels, exemption of certain
    fuels, **64H:6.**
  Gas service, residential, **64G:6.**
  Gun safes, **64H:6.**
  Insulin, **64H:6.**
  Legal services, **64H:6.**
  Manufacturing equipment,
    64H:6.
  Marine fish and fisheries, **64H:6,
    64I:7.**
  Medical devices or equipment,
    64H:6.
  Motor vehicles purchased by
    certain disabled persons,
    64H:6.
  Photographic studios, **64H:1.**
  Piped-in music, **64H:1.**

SALES TAXES —Cont'd
Exemptions —Cont'd
Precious metals, **64H:6.**
Printed matter, **64H:6.**
Public utilities, **64H:6.**
Railroad fuels, **64H:6.**
Regional transportation
authorities' properties,
64H:6.
Research and development
corporations, **64H:6.**
Research animals, **64H:6.**
Retail, services sold, **64H:3,
64H:6.**
Security system services, **64H:1.**
Steam, **64H:6.**
Surveying services, **64H:1.**
Trigger locks, **64H:6.**
Typographer, compositor or color
separator, **64H:6.**
United States flags, **64H:6.**
Use tax exemptions, **64I:7.**
Utility services, residential,
64H:6.
Vessels used for scheduled
commuter passenger service,
64H:6.
Waste service firms, service
contracts, **64H:6.**
Water, residential service,
64H:6.
Exempt use certificate, **64H:6.**
Federal exemptions, **64H:6.**
Gasoline and motor fuel taxes,
64A:12, 64E:12, 64F:13.
Fines and penalties.
Assumption of tax by vendor,
unlawful advertising,
64H:23.
Evasion of tax by means of
exempt use certificate,
64H:8.
Resale certificate, wrongful
giving, **64H:8.**
Foreign state or country, services
used outside of
Commonwealth, **64H:6.**
Forms.
Dealer contract clause relative
to sales taxes, **106:202.**
Exempt use certificate, **64H:8.**
Formula for imposition and
collection, **64H:4.**
Fuel.
Exemptions, **64H:6.**
Gasoline and motor fuel taxes,
64A:1 et seq.
See GASOLINE AND MOTOR
FUEL TAXES.
Residential service exempt from
sales tax, **64G:6.**

SALES TAXES —Cont'd
Goods in transit, exemption for,
64H:6.
Graphic design services,
exemptions, **64H:1.**
Gross receipts.
Defined, **64H:1.**
Tax as measured, **64H:2.**
Guards, exemptions, **64H:1.**
Gun safes.
Exemptions, **64H:6.**
Hearing, revocation of promoter's
registration certificate,
62C:67A.
Heating fuel, residential, exempt
from sales tax, **64H:6.**
Hospitals and asylums, exemption
for meals prepared and
served, **64H:6.**
Imposition, **64H:2.**
Information, furnishing, collecting,
compiling, or analyzing subject
to tax, **64H:1.**
Insulin and insulin items,
exemption, **64H:6.**
Intoxicating liquor.
Exemptions, **64H:6.**
Separate statement of sales tax,
64H:5.
Legal services, **64H:1, 64H:6.**
Liability for failure to pay
commissioner, **64H:16.**
Licenses.
Permits and registration. See
within this heading,
"Permits and registration."
Marine fish and fisheries.
Materials, equipment, and
machinery used in
commercial fishing, sales tax
exemption, **64H:6.**
Vessels used in commercial
fishing, sales tax exemption,
64I:7.
Medical devices or equipment,
exemption, **64H:6.**
Motorboats, evidence of payment
of tax on sales or use as
prerequisite to certification,
64H:25A, 64I:26A.
Motor vehicles, **64H:3, 64H:25,
64H:26.**
Certificate of registration,
restriction on issuance,
64H:25.
Revocation, **64H:25.**
Defined, **64H:3, 64H:26, 64I:27.**
Exemption of sales to certain
disabled persons, **64H:6.**
Fire trucks, exemption, **64H:6.**

SALES TAXES —Cont'd
Motor vehicles —Cont'd
Gasoline and motor fuel taxes,
64A:1 et seq.
See GASOLINE AND MOTOR
FUEL TAXES.
Materials, equipment and
machinery used in
manufacture of vehicle as
exempt, **64H:6.**
Method of paying and collecting
tax, **64H:3.**
Paraplegic's vehicle, tax
exemption, **64H:6.**
Presumption of sale, **64H:25.**
Registrar's duties, **64H:3.**
Revocation of certificate of
registration, **64H:25.**
Vendor's statement of sale,
64H:3.
Moving pictures, exemption,
64H:6.
Newspapers, **64H:1.**
Nonresidents.
Continuance of proceedings,
64I:33.
Contractor, filing of bond or
deposit by, for payment of
tax, **64H:30A.**
Service of process, **64H:32.**
Notices.
Manner of service, **64H:29,
64H:32, 64I:33.**
Resale and exempt use
certificate, notice to produce,
64H:8.
Shows, filing of notice, **62C:67A.**
Nursing home, exemption for
meals prepared and served,
64H:6.
Option or election.
Purchaser, reporting of gross
receipts from rented
personalty, **64H:8.**
Services sold at retail, **64H:2.**
Ordinary course of business.
Corporations, lien for taxes on
sales other than in ordinary
course of business, **62C:51.**
Exemption of manufacturing
equipment and tools from
sales and use tax where
sold, **64H:6.**
Payment, **64H:3, 64H:4.**
Aircraft, evidence of payment of
taxes prerequisite to
registration, **64H:25A.**
Construction contracts and
works, bond or deposit to
secure payment of sales tax,
64H:30A, 64I:31A.

SALES TAXES —Cont'd
Payment —Cont'd
  Direct payment permit, **64H:3.**
  Nonresidents, filing of bond or
    deposit by contractor,
    64H:30A.
  Purchaser to pay, **64H:3, 64H:4.**
  Reimbursement, **64H:3, 64H:33.**
Penalties.
  Assumption of tax by vendor,
    unlawful advertising,
    64H:23.
  Evasion of tax by means of
    exempt use certificate,
    64H:8.
  Resale certificate, wrongful
    giving, **64H:8.**
Percentage of exempt sales,
  issuance of classified permit
  establishing, **64H:9.**
Permits and registration.
  Aircraft, evidence of payment of
    taxes prerequisite to
    registration, **64H:25A.**
  Classified permits, **64H:9.**
  Direct payment permit, **64H:3.**
  Increasing fees for certificates,
    62C:67.
  Promoter's certificate,
    requirements, **62C:67A.**
  Resale and exempt use
    certificate, **64H:8.**
  Vendors, **64H:7.**
Person, defined, **64H:16.**
Photography studios or services,
  exemption, **64H:1.**
Piped-in music, exemption, **64H:1.**
Precious metals, exemptions,
  64H:6.
Presumptions, gross receipts from
  sale of tangible personal
  property as sales subject to
  tax, **64H:8.**
Printed matter, exemption, **64H:6.**
Printers and printing.
  Exemption from sales taxes,
    64H:6.
  Furnishing printed information
    as subject to taxes, **64H:1.**
Promoters of shows.
  Defined, **62C:1.**
  Notice of shows, filing, **62C:67A.**
  Registration certificate,
    requirement, **62C:67A.**
  Reports and records of shows,
    62C:8A.
    Failure to report, penalty,
      62C:34.
  Revenue commissioner, filing of
    reports in records, **62C:8A,**
    62C:67A.

SALES TAXES —Cont'd
Public utilities, **64H:1, 64H:6.**
Purchaser to pay, **64H:3, 64H:4.**
Radio and television, exemptions.
  Information services used by
    broadcasters, **64H:1.**
  Transmission and broadcasting
    equipment, **64H:1, 64H:6.**
Railroads, exemption of fuel used,
  64H:6.
Rate of tax, **64H:2.**
Records, auctions and auctioneers,
  100:8.
Regional transportation
  authorities' properties,
  exemption, **64H:6.**
Registration.
  Motor vehicles. See within this
    heading, "Motor vehicles."
  Permits and registration. See
    within this heading,
    "Permits and registration."
Reimbursement.
  Tax, reimbursement by
    purchaser to vendor, **64H:3.**
  Worthless accounts,
    reimbursement of sales tax
    paid by vendor, **64H:33.**
Rental, property purchased,
  64H:8.
Reports.
  Information reports as subject to
    sales tax, **64H:1.**
  Promoters of shows, **62C:8A,**
    62C:34.
  Rental property, reporting of
    gross receipts, **64H:8.**
Resale certificates, **64H:8.**
  Exempt use certificate, effect on
    vendor, **64H:8.**
Research animals, exemption,
  64H:6.
Retail.
  Defined, **64H:1.**
  Services sold at retail,
    64H:1-64H:3, 64H:6,
    64H:23.
Returns, **62C:16.**
  Worthless accounts, recovery by
    vendor, **64H:33.**
Revenue Department and
  Commissioner.
  Information analysis, **64H:1.**
  Records in reports filed, **62C:8A,**
    62C:67A.
Revocation.
  Classified permit, **64H:9.**
  Motor vehicle certificate of
    registration, **64H:25.**
  Promoter's registration
    certificate, **62C:67A.**

SALES TAXES —Cont'd
Schools and education, **64C:6,**
  64H:6.
Security systems, exemptions,
  64H:1.
Separate charge and statement of
  tax collected, **64H:5.**
Services defined, **64H:1.**
Services sold at retail, **64H:2.**
  Apportioned use certificates,
    64H:6.
  Assumption or absorption of tax
    by vendor, advertisement,
    64H:23.
  Definitions, **64H:1.**
  Election or option, **64H:2.**
  Exceptions and exemptions,
    64H:3, 64H:6.
  Foreign state or country, tax on
    services used outside of
    Commonwealth, **64H:6.**
  Reimbursement for tax by
    purchaser to vendor, **64H:3.**
  Resale and exempt use
    certificates, **64H:8.**
  Sales at retail defined, **64H:1.**
  SIC defined, **64H:1.**
  Time of sale, **64H:2.**
Ships, **64H:6, 64H:25A, 64H:27A,**
  64I:26A.
Shows.
  Defined, **62C:1.**
  Exemptions, **64H:1.**
  Promoters.
    Notice of shows, filing,
      62C:67A.
    Registration certificate,
      requirement, **62C:67A.**
    Reports and records of shows,
      62C:8A, 62C:34.
    Revenue commissioner, filing
      of reports in records,
      62C:8A, 62C:67A.
  Tickets, tax, **64H:1.**
SIC defined, **64H:1.**
Special act of 1966, extension of
  effect, **64H:1.**
Steam, residential service exempt
  from sales tax, **64H:6.**
Surveying and engineering
  services, **64H:1, 64H:6.**
Synagogue, exemption for meals
  prepared and served on
  premises, **64H:6.**
Tangible personal property,
  defined, **64H:1.**
Telecommunications, service
  defined, **64H:1.**
Television, exemptions.
  Information services used by
    broadcasters, **64H:1.**

SALES TAXES —Cont'd

Television, exemptions —Cont'd
Transmission and broadcasting equipment, **64H:1, 64H:6.**
Time or date.
Claim for reimbursement of sales tax paid by vendor on worthless account, **64H:33.**
Resale and exempt use certificate, time limit for vendor to produce, **64H:8.**
Services sold at retail, **64H:2.**
Trade-ins, **64C:6, 64H:26, 64H:27A.**
Transfer of business as affecting sales tax liability, **62C:44.**
Transportation.
Commuter passenger service vessels, exemption, **64H:6.**
Goods in transit, exemption for, **64H:6.**
Trigger locks.
Exemptions, **64H:6.**
Typographer, compositor or color separator, exemption, **64H:6.**
United States flags, exemption of sale, **64H:6.**
Use of a service defined, **64H:1.**
Utility services, **64H:1, 64H:6.**
Vessels, **64H:27A, 64I:28.**
See SHIPS AND OTHER WATERCRAFT.
Waste service firms, service contracts, **64H:6.**
Watercraft, **64H:6, 64H:25A, 64H:27A, 64I:26A.**
Water, residential service exempt from sales tax, **64H:6.**
Wood fuel heating systems, sales of equipment, **64H:6.**

SALES UNDER COMMERCIAL CODE, 106:2-101 to 106:2-725.

Acceptance of contract.
Offer and acceptance. See within this heading, "Offer and acceptance."
Acceptance of draft, document deliverable, **106:2-514.**
Acceptance or rejection of goods, **106:2-602, 106:2-606, 106:2-607, 106:2-608.**
Additional terms in acceptance or confirmation, **106:2-207.**
Approval, acceptance under sale, **106:2-327.**
Conduct subsequent to rejection, **106:2-603, 106:2-604, 106:2-606.**
Damages.
Breach in regard to accepted goods, **106:2-714.**

SALES UNDER COMMERCIAL CODE —Cont'd

Acceptance or rejection of goods —Cont'd
Damages —Cont'd
Nonacceptance, **106:2-708, 106:2-709.**
Expenses of buyer, reimbursement, **106:2-603.**
Fraud, rejection of goods as precluding remedies, **106:2-721.**
Good faith conduct with respect to rejected goods as acceptance, **106:2-603.**
Improperly delivered goods, **106:2-601, 106:2-609.**
Instructions to buyer with respect to rejected goods, **106:2-603.**
Manner, **106:2-602.**
Merchant buyer's duty, **106:2-603.**
Nonconforming goods. See within this heading, "Nonconforming goods."
Partial acceptance or rejection, **106:2-601, 106:2-606.**
Reservation of security interest, **106:2-401.**
Revocation in part, **106:2-607, 106:2-608.**
Payment for goods accepted, **106:2-607.**
Prior to inspection as acceptance, **106:2-512.**
Remedies of seller, **106:2-703, 106:2-704.**
Reservation of rights, **106:1-207.**
Revocation, **106:2-608.**
Partial revocation of acceptance of goods, **106:2-401, 106:2-607, 106:2-608.**
Remedies of sellers, **106:2-703, 106:2-704.**
Revesting of title in seller, **106:2-401.**
Risk of loss, **106:2-510.**
Salvage of rejected goods, buyer's option, **106:2-604.**
Sample or part, **106:2-606.**
Security interest arising from rightful rejection, **106:2-711.**
Time, **106:2-602.**
Waiver of objections, **106:2-605.**
Accounts, sales of, **106:9-101 et seq.**
See SECURED TRANSACTIONS.

SALES UNDER COMMERCIAL CODE —Cont'd

Acknowledgment that goods are held for buyer as precluding stoppage of delivery, **106:2-705.**
Action or suit, **106:2-701 to 106:2-725.**
Breach of warranty, buyer's duty to advise seller of action, **106:2-607.**
Buyer's, **106:2-310, 106:2-711 to 106:2-717.**
Consumer goods and services, disclaimer or waiver by agreement of warranties or remedies by sale, **106:2-316A.**
Creditors, goods held on approval or on sale or return as subject to claims, **106:2-326.**
Creditor's remedies, **106:2-402.**
Cumulative remedies, form for clause in sales contract authorizing, **106:2-317.**
Damages. See within this heading, "Damages."
Fraudulent conveyances.
See FRAUDULENT CONVEYANCES OR TRANSFERS.
Good faith. See within this heading, "Good faith."
Infringement, duties of buyer with respect to claim, **106:2-607.**
Preserving evidence of goods in adjustment of claim, **106:2-515.**
Price, action for recovery, **106:2-709.**
Privity of contract abolished as defense in actions concerning goods sold, **106:2-318.**
Replevin, buyer's right, **106:2-716.**
Specific performance, buyer's right, **106:2-716.**
Statute of limitations, **106:2-725.**
Third parties, action for injuries to goods against, **106:2-722.**
Unconscionable contract or clause, recovery, **106:2-302.**
Waiver of claim arising from breach of contract.
Waiver and estoppel. See within this heading, "Waiver and estoppel."

SALES UNDER COMMERCIAL CODE —Cont'd

Additional terms in acceptance or confirmation, **106:2-207.**

Agent, remedies, **106:2-707.**

Agriculture.
See AGRICULTURE.

Allocation.
Production and delivery, **106:2-615, 106:2-616.**
Risk of loss, **106:2-303.**

Alteration.
Modification. See within this heading, "Modification."

Ancillary contract, remedies for breach, **106:2-701.**

Antecedent breach, cancellation or rescission of contract as affecting, **106:2-720.**

Anticipatory repudiation of contract, **106:2-610, 106:2-611.**
Proof of market price in action, **106:2-723.**

Approval, sale, **106:2-326, 106:2-327.**

Assignment of rights under contract, **106:2-210.**

Assurance of performance.
Performance. See within this heading, "Performance."

Auctions and auctioneers.
See AUCTIONS AND AUCTIONEERS.

Bailments, **266:84 et seq.**
Delivery of goods in possession of bailee, risk of loss, **106:2-509.**
Leases under UCC.
See LEASES UNDER COMMERCIAL CODE.
Stoppage of delivery in transit of goods held by bailee, **106:2-705.**
Tender of delivery of goods in possession of bailee, **106:2-503.**

Banker's credit defined, **106:2-325.**

Bankruptcy.
See INSOLVENCY AND BANKRUPTCY.

Benefits received as reducing damages, **106:2-718.**

Bill of sale, form, **106:2-201.**

Bills of lading, **106:7-101 et seq.**
See BILLS OF LADING.

Blood, blood plasma, and human tissues and organs.
Applicability of sale articles to sales from blood banks or reservoirs, **106:2-316.**

SALES UNDER COMMERCIAL CODE —Cont'd

Blood, blood plasma, and human tissues and organs —Cont'd
Not to be regarded as commodities for purposes of certain implied warranties, **106:2-316.**

Bona fide purchasers.
See BONA FIDE PURCHASERS.

Breach of contract, **106:2-601, 106:2-616.**
Acceptance of goods as affecting right to assert, **106:2-607.**
Antecedent breach, cancellation or rescission of contract as affecting, **106:2-720.**
Assignment of right to damages, **106:2-210.**
Buyer's remedies, **106:2-711 to 106:2-717.**
Cancellation of contract, breach of contract by buyer as entitling seller, **106:2-703.**
Collateral contracts, remedies for breach, **106:2-701.**
Damages. See within this heading, "Damages."
Delegation of performance as relieving liability, **106:2-210.**
Delivery, seller as entitled to withhold delivery upon breach by buyer, **106:2-703.**
Failure to specify or cooperate in performance, **106:2-311.**
Installment contracts, **106:2-612.**
Letter of credit, failure to furnish, **106:2-325.**
Limitation of actions, **106:2-725.**
Risk of loss as affected, **106:2-510.**
Seller's remedies, **106:2-702 to 106:2-710.**
Waiver and estoppel. See within this heading, "Waiver and estoppel."

Breach of warranty.
See WARRANTIES.

Bulk transfers.
See BULK TRANSFERS.

Burden of proving breach with respect to accepted goods, **106:2-607.**

Cancellation, repudiation, or rescission, **106:2-209.**
Antecedent breach, **106:2-720.**
Assurance, failure to provide, **106:2-609.**

SALES UNDER COMMERCIAL CODE —Cont'd

Cancellation, repudiation, or rescission —Cont'd
Breach of contract by buyer as entitling seller, **106:2-703.**
Buyer, cancellation, **106:2-711.**
Claims for antecedent breach as affected, **106:2-720.**
Damages recoverable by seller, **106:2-708, 106:2-713.**
Defined, **106:2-106.**
Fraud, effect on remedy, **106:2-721.**
Notice of termination of contract, **106:2-309.**
Installment contracts, **106:2-612.**
Seller's remedies, **106:2-703, 106:2-704, 106:2-708, 106:2-713.**

C & F sales.
See C & F SALES.

Carrier.
Lien of carrier, sale to enforce, **106:7-308.**
Motor carrier's purchase of commodities from shippers for immediate resale, **159B:6D.**
Shipment of goods. See within this heading, "Shipment of goods."

Cash sale.
Good faith purchase, **106:2-403.**
Insolvency of buyer as entitling seller, **106:2-702.**

Casualty to identified goods, **106:2-613.**

Change.
Modification. See within this heading, "Modification."

Check, payment, **106:2-511.**

C.I.F. sales.
See C.I.F. SALES.

Claims.
Action or suit. See within this heading, "Action or suit."

C.O.D. terms, inspection of goods prior to payment, **106:2-513.**

Collateral contracts, remedies for breach, **106:2-701.**

Commercial unit.
Acceptance of part as acceptance of whole, **106:2-606.**
Defined, **106:2-105.**

Commission on sale of rejected goods, buyer's right, **106:2-603.**

Conditions and terms.
Additional terms, **106:2-107.**

SALES UNDER COMMERCIAL CODE —Cont'd

Conditions and terms —Cont'd
Excuse for delivery or nondelivery based on failure, **106:2-615, 106:2-616.**
Installment contract, **106:2-612.**
Modification. See within this heading, "Modification."
Payment. See within this heading, "Payment."
Tender of goods upon conditions, **106:2-507.**
Conduct of parties.
Course of dealing as affecting construction of contract, **106:2-208.**
Existence of contract, conduct of parties as recognition, **106:2-204, 106:2-207.**
Good faith. See within this heading, "Good faith."
Ratification of wrongful acceptance of goods, **106:2-606.**
Confirmation of acceptance, **106:2-207.**
Confirmed credit defined, **106:2-325.**
Consequential or incidental damages.
Action for price, **106:2-709.**
Buyer's right, **106:2-715.**
Contractual limitation or exclusion, **106:2-719.**
Representative of seller, **106:2-707.**
Restrictions, **106:1-106.**
Seller's, **106:2-710.**
Consignment sales, sale or return, **106:2-326.**
Construction or interpretation of sales contracts, **106:2-302 to 106:2-328.**
Conversion.
Good faith conduct with respect to rejected goods, **106:2-603.**
Salvage of rejected goods, **106:2-604.**
Cooperation respecting performance, **106:2-311.**
Course of dealing, **106:2-208.**
"Cover," buyer's right, **106:2-711, 106:2-712.**
Creditors.
Goods held on approval or on sale or return as subject to claims, **106:2-326.**
Lien creditor, seller's right to reclaim goods as subject to rights, **106:2-702.**

SALES UNDER COMMERCIAL CODE —Cont'd

Creditors —Cont'd
Reclamation of goods on insolvency of buyer, **106:2-702.**
Seller's creditors' rights against sold goods, **106:2-402.**
Crops, **106:2-105, 106:2-107.**
Cumulative remedies, form for clause in sales contract authorizing, **106:2-317.**
Custom or usage.
Construction of sales contract, aid, **106:2-202, 106:2-208.**
Implied warranties arising, **106:2-314.**
Exclusion or modification, **106:2-316.**
Damages.
Acceptance or rejection of goods. See within this heading, "Acceptance or rejection of goods."
Assignment, **106:2-210.**
"Cancellation" or "rescission" of contract as affecting claim, **106:2-720.**
Consequential or incidental damages. See within this heading, "Consequential or incidental damages."
Contractual modification or limitation, **106:2-719.**
Deduction from price, **106:2-717.**
Expenses of seller as element, **106:2-710.**
Incidental damages.
Consequential or incidental damages. See within this heading, "Consequential or incidental damages."
Limitation on damages for breach of sales contract, **106:2-718, 106:2-719.**
Liquidation, **106:2-718.**
Market price as determining factor, **106:2-713.**
Nonacceptance of goods, damages, **106:2-708, 106:2-709.**
Nondelivery of goods, **106:2-713.**
Repudiation of contract, damages, **106:2-708, 106:2-713.**
Substitute goods, buyer's procurement, **106:2-712.**
Date.
Time. See within this heading, "Time."
Dealer contract, form containing clause relative to tax on sales, **106:2-201.**

SALES UNDER COMMERCIAL CODE —Cont'd

Debtors and creditors.
Creditors. See within this heading, "Creditors."
Defects.
Documents, payment as waiver in defects, **106:2-605.**
Financing agency's right to reimbursement, defects in relevant document as affecting, **106:2-506.**
Objections to defects in goods, waiver, **106:2-605.**
Definiteness of contract, **106:2-204.**
Definitions, **106:2-103 to 106:2-106.**
Delay.
Allowance to aggrieved party for delay occasioned by repudiation of contract, **106:2-611.**
Delivery, excuse for delay, **106:2-311, 106:2-615, 106:2-616.**
Delegation of performance, **106:2-210.**
Delivery.
Acceptance of draft, document deliverable, **106:2-514.**
Allocation of production and delivery, **106:2-615, 106:2-616.**
Assurance of performance, acceptance of improper delivery as affecting right, **106:2-609.**
Bills of lading.
See BILLS OF LADING.
Buyer's rights on improper delivery, **106:2-601.**
Conditional delivery, **106:2-507.**
Conditions, excuse for delivery or nondelivery based on failure, **106:2-615, 106:2-616.**
Cure of improper delivery, **106:2-508.**
Damages, nondelivery of goods, **106:2-713.**
Delay in delivery, excuse, **106:2-311, 106:2-615, 106:2-616.**
Documents of title. See within this heading, "Documents of title."
Ex-ship delivery, **106:2-322.**
F.A.S. sales, **106:2-319.**
Financing agency's right to stop, **106:2-506.**

SALES UNDER COMMERCIAL CODE —Cont'd

Delivery —Cont'd

F.O.B. sales.
See F.O.B. SALES.

Insolvency of buyer, refusal of delivery upon discovery, **106:2-702.**

Installment contracts, **106:2-612.**

Invoices and delivery tickets. See within this heading, "Invoices and delivery tickets."

Notice, **106:2-503.**

Obligations of parties, **106:2-301.**

Place for delivery, failure to specify, **106:2-308.**

Previous sale in enforcement of lien or on termination of storage as excusing, **106:7-403.**

Remedies of buyer for failure of seller to make, **106:2-711.**

Risk of loss. See within this heading, "Risk of loss."

Seller as entitled to withhold delivery upon breach by buyer, **106:2-703.**

Shipment by seller, **106:2-504.**

Single or several lots, **106:2-307.**

Stoppage of delivery in transit. See within this heading, "Stoppage of delivery in transit."

Substituted performance, **106:2-614.**

Tender of delivery, **106:2-503.**
Conditional delivery, **106:2-507.**
Cure of improper tender, **106:2-508.**
Effect, **106:2-507.**
Risk of loss, **106:2-509, 106:2-510.**

Tickets.
Invoices and delivery tickets. See within this heading, "Invoices and delivery tickets."

Time, **106:2-309.**

Title.
Documents of title. See within this heading, "Documents of title."
Passing of title on delivery, **106:2-401.**
Power to transfer title as affected by mode of delivery, **106:2-403.**

SALES UNDER COMMERCIAL CODE —Cont'd

Department store, form for agreement for sale of manufacturer's or distributor's products, **106:2-201.**

Deposit, breach as affecting buyer's right to return, **106:2-718.**

Description.
Express warranty created, **106:2-313.**
Goods to contract.
Identification of goods to contract. See within this heading, "Identification of goods to contract."
Sample as superseding description in considering inconsistent warranties, **106:2-317.**
Specifications as superseding description in considering inconsistent warranties, **106:2-317.**

Destruction of goods.
Loss or destruction of goods. See within this heading, "Loss or destruction of goods."

Deterioration of goods.
C.I.F. or C & F terms, imposition of risk upon seller, **106:2-321.**
"No arrival, no sale" term, liability for deterioration, **106:2-324.**
Option of buyer, **106:2-613.**
Warehouseman's right to sell goods in danger, **106:7-206.**

Dishonor.
See PRESENTMENT, DISHONOR, AND PROTEST.

Disputes, preserving evidence of goods in adjustment, **106:2-515.**

Documents of title.
Delivery of goods by way, **106:2-310, 106:2-401.**
Dishonor of as affecting tender of delivery, **106:2-503.**
Inspection of goods prior to payment against, **106:2-513.**
Manner of delivery of documents, **106:2-308.**
Payment.
Inspection of goods prior to payment against document, **106:2-513.**
Waiver of defects on face of document, payment without reservation, **106:2-605.**

SALES UNDER COMMERCIAL CODE —Cont'd

Documents of title —Cont'd
Stoppage of delivery in transit after issuance, **106:2-705.**
Tender of delivery by means, **106:2-503.**

Duration.
Time. See within this heading, "Time."

Election or option.
Options respecting performance. See within this heading, "Options respecting performance."

Encumbered property.
See LIENS AND ENCUMBRANCES.

Entrusting.
Defined, **106:2-403.**
Transfer of title by merchant in possession, **106:2-403.**

Estoppel.
Waiver and estoppel. See within this heading, "Waiver and estoppel."

Evidence.
Burden of proving breach with respect to accepted goods, **106:2-607.**
Market price, proof, **106:2-723.**
Market quotations, admissibility, **106:2-724.**
Parol evidence. See within this heading, "Parol evidence."
Preservation of evidence of goods in dispute, **106:2-515.**
Unconscionable contract or clause, proof, **106:2-302.**

Examination of goods.
Inspection of goods. See within this heading, "Inspection of goods."

Exclusive dealings, agreement, **106:2-306.**

Excuse for nonperformance, **106:2-311, 106:2-615, 106:2-616.**

Expenses.
Damages, expenses of seller as element, **106:2-710.**
Inspection of goods. See within this heading, "Inspection of goods."
Rejected goods, buyer's right to reimbursement for care and sale, **106:2-603.**

Ex-ship delivery, **106:2-322.**

Farm products.
See AGRICULTURE.

F.A.S. terms, **106:2-319.**

SALES UNDER COMMERCIAL CODE —Cont'd

Financing agency.
   Defined, **106:2-104.**
   Rights, **106:2-506.**
Firm offers, **106:2-205.**
F.O.B. sales, **106:2-319, 106:2-323.**
Formation of contract, **106:2-201, 106:2-204.**
   Offer and acceptance. See within this heading, "Offer and acceptance."
Form of contract, **106:2-201 to 106:2-210, 106:2-317.**
Fraudulent conveyances.
   See FRAUDULENT CONVEYANCES OR TRANSFERS.
Future goods, **106:2-105, 106:2-501.**
Gas and oil, severance from real property, **106:2-107.**
Good faith.
   Action or suit.
      Fraud, remedies, **106:2-721.**
      Rejected goods, good faith conduct with respect, **106:2-603.**
      Seller's creditors remedies against sold goods, **106:2-402.**
   Defined, **106:2-103.**
   Open price term in sales contract, **106:2-305.**
   Purchaser in good faith, **106:2-403.**
   Rejected goods, merchant buyer's duty, **106:2-603.**
   Solvency, buyer's misrepresentation, **106:2-702.**
   Specification of performance by party, **106:2-311.**
   Transferability of title to goods obtained by sales, **106:2-403.**
Human tissues.
   Blood, etc. See within this heading, "Blood, blood plasma, and human tissues and organs."
Identification of goods to contract.
   Action for price, **106:2-709.**
   Casualty to identified goods, **106:2-613.**
   Description. See within this heading, "Description."
   Insolvency of seller, buyer's right to goods, **106:2-502.**
   Insurable interest, ascertainment, **106:2-501.**

SALES UNDER COMMERCIAL CODE —Cont'd

Identification of goods to contract —Cont'd
   Passing of title as dependent, **106:2-401.**
   Resale of goods by seller, **106:2-706.**
   Seller's right to identify goods notwithstanding breach, **106:2-704.**
Implied warranties, **106:2-314, 106:2-315.**
   See WARRANTIES.
Incidental damages.
   Consequential or incidental damages. See within this heading, "Consequential or incidental damages."
Infringement.
   Duties of buyer with respect to claim, **106:2-607.**
   Warranty against, **106:2-312.**
Insolvency.
   See INSOLVENCY AND BANKRUPTCY.
Inspection of goods.
   Buyer's right to, **106:2-513.**
   C.I.F. or C & F terms, inspection of goods shipped, **106:2-321.**
   Documents of title, inspection of goods prior to payment against, **106:2-513.**
   Expenses of inspection, **106:2-513.**
      Security interest of buyer, **106:2-711.**
   Implied warranty as affected by opportunity of buyer to examine goods, **106:2-316.**
   Payment prior, **106:2-512.**
   Place of inspection, **106:2-513.**
   Preserving evidence of goods in dispute, **106:2-515.**
   Resale of goods by seller, necessity of providing for inspection by prospective bidders, **106:2-706.**
Installment contract, **106:2-612.**
Instructions.
   F.A.S. or F.O.B. terms, delivery instructions by buyer, **106:2-319.**
   Rejected goods, instructions from seller, **106:2-603.**
Insurance.
   See INSURANCE.
Investment securities under commercial code.
   See INVESTMENT SECURITIES UNDER COMMERCIAL CODE.

SALES UNDER COMMERCIAL CODE —Cont'd

Invoices and delivery tickets.
   C.I.F. terms, **106:2-320.**
   Consular invoice as prima facie evidence, **106:1-202.**
   Postdating as affecting credit period, **106:2-310.**
Judicial sales.
   See JUDICIAL SALES.
Knowledge.
   Notice or knowledge. See within this heading, "Notice or knowledge."
Laches.
   Delay. See within this heading, "Delay."
Lack of privity in action against manufacturer, seller, etc., **106:2-318.**
Lease of personal property.
   Bailments. See within this heading, "Bailments."
Letter of credit, provision, **106:2-325.**
Liens.
   See LIENS AND ENCUMBRANCES.
Limitation of actions, **106:2-725.**
Limitation of remedy, **106:2-718, 106:2-719.**
Limitations.
   Conditions and terms. See within this heading, "Conditions and terms."
Liquidated damages for breach, **106:2-718.**
Location.
   Place. See within this heading, "Place."
Logs and timber, contracts for sale, **96:11A, 106:2-107.**
Loss or destruction of goods.
   Delivery as excused, **106:7-403.**
   Partial loss, **106:2-613.**
   Payment under C.I.F. or C & F terms, **106:2-320.**
   Risk of loss. See within this heading, "Risk of loss."
Market quotations, admissibility, **106:2-724.**
Minerals, contract for sale, **106:2-107.**
Modification.
   Readjustment, **106:2-201 to 106:2-210.**
   Remedies, modification, **106:2-719.**
   Terms, modification, **106:2-209.**
      Course of performance as relevant to establish, **106:2-208.**

SALES UNDER COMMERCIAL CODE —Cont'd
Modification —Cont'd
Terms, modification —Cont'd
Parol evidence to vary terms of final written contract, **106:2-202.**
Warranties, security agreement as affecting modification, **106:9-206.**
Money, price payable, **106:2-304.**
Negotiable instruments.
See NEGOTIABLE INSTRUMENTS.
"No arrival, no sale" term, **106:2-324.**
Risk of loss, **106:2-613.**
Nonacceptance of goods.
Acceptance or rejection of goods. See within this heading, "Acceptance or rejection of goods."
Nonconforming goods.
Acceptance, **106:2-607.**
Revocation of acceptance, **106:2-608.**
Shipment, acceptance of sales contract, **106:2-206.**
Identification for purpose of ascertaining insurable interest, **106:2-501.**
Installment contracts, **106:2-612.**
Payment prior to inspection, **106:2-512.**
Nonconforming tender.
Risk of loss, **106:2-510.**
Substitution of conforming tender, **106:2-508.**
Notice or knowledge.
Approval sales, failure to notify seller of election to return goods as acceptance, **106:2-327.**
Breach of warranty, buyer's duty to advise seller of action, **106:2-607.**
Cancellation, repudiation, or rescission. See within this heading, "Cancellation, repudiation, or rescission."
Creditor's claims against goods held on sale or return as affected, **106:2-326.**
Delay or nondelivery, notice, **106:2-615, 106:2-616.**
Delivery, notice, **106:2-503.**
Excuse for nonperformance, notice, **106:2-616.**
Installment contracts, notice of cancellation, **106:2-612.**

SALES UNDER COMMERCIAL CODE —Cont'd
Notice or knowledge —Cont'd
Rejection of goods, notice, **106:2-602.**
Resale of goods by seller, notice, **106:2-706.**
Revocation of acceptance of goods, **106:2-608.**
Shipment of goods, notice, **106:2-504.**
Stoppage of delivery in transit, **106:2-705.**
Termination of contract, notice of.
Cancellation of contract. See within this heading, "Cancellation, repudiation, or rescission."
Title of seller, buyer's knowledge of limitations, **106:2-312.**
Obligation of parties, **106:2-301.**
Offer and acceptance, **106:2-206, 106:2-207.**
Auction sales, **106:2-328.**
Firm offers, **106:2-205.**
Recipient of goods offered for sale but not ordered, rights, **93:43.**
Open price term, **106:2-305.**
Options respecting performance, **106:2-311.**
Acceleration of payment or performance, **106:1-208.**
Deterioration of goods, option of buyer, **106:2-613.**
Lease as security, option to purchase as affecting, **106:1-201.**
Notification of seller of election to return goods as acceptance, approval sale, **106:2-327.**
Salvage. See within this heading, "Salvage."
Overseas shipment, bill of lading required, **106:2-323.**
Ownership.
Title. See within this heading, "Title."
Parol evidence.
Admissibility to vary terms of final written contract, **106:2-202.**
"Or return" term of sales contract, **106:2-326.**
Partial acceptance or rejection of goods.
Acceptance or rejection of goods. See within this heading, "Acceptance or rejection of goods."

SALES UNDER COMMERCIAL CODE —Cont'd
Partial loss of goods, **106:2-613.**
Payment.
Acceleration, **106:1-208.**
Acceptance or rejection of goods. See within this heading, "Acceptance or rejection of goods."
Action to recover, **106:2-709.**
Assurance of performance, payment as affecting right, **106:2-609.**
Buyer's right to recover, **106:2-711.**
Cash payment, insolvency of buyer as entitling seller, **106:2-702.**
Check, payment, **106:2-511.**
C.I.F. or C. & F. terms, **106:2-320, 106:2-321.**
C.O.D. terms, inspection of goods prior to payment, **106:2-513.**
Damages as deductible from price, **106:2-717.**
Delivery, buyer's duty to make payment upon tender, **106:2-507.**
Deposits, breach by buyer as affecting right to return, **106:2-718.**
Documents deliverable, **106:2-514.**
Documents of title. See within this heading, "Documents of title."
F.A.S. or F.O.B. terms, payment, **106:2-319.**
Financing agency, rights, **106:2-506.**
Goods, price payable, **106:2-304.**
Damages as reduced by payments in form of goods, **106:2-718.**
Inspection, payment prior, **106:2-512.**
Money, price payable, **106:2-304.**
Obligation of parties, **106:2-301.**
Open price term, **106:2-305.**
Place, **106:2-310.**
Realty, price payable, **106:2-304.**
Remedies of seller upon buyer's failure to make, **106:2-703, 106:2-704.**
Statute of frauds as rendered inapplicable, **106:2-201.**
Stoppage of delivery in transit for buyer's failure to make, **106:2-705.**
Substituted performance, **106:2-614.**

SALES UNDER COMMERCIAL CODE —Cont'd

Payment —Cont'd
Tender, **106:2-511.**
Time, **106:2-310.**
Waiver of defects in documents, **106:2-605.**
Performance, **106:2-501 to 106:2-515.**
Acceptance of sales contract, **106:2-206.**
Assurance.
Assignment delegating performance, as grounds for demand, **106:2-210.**
Cooperation respecting, **106:2-311.**
F.A.S. or F.O.B. terms, **106:2-319.**
Retraction of anticipatory repudiation, assurance, **106:2-611.**
Right to assurance, **106:2-609.**
Delegation, **106:2-210.**
Excuse for nonperformance, **106:2-311, 106:2-615, 106:2-616.**
Modification of terms, course of performance as relevant to establish, **106:2-208.**
Options respecting performance. See within this heading, "Options respecting performance."
Repudiation of contract.
Cancellation, repudiation, or rescission. See within this heading, "Cancellation, repudiation, or rescission."
Specific performance, buyer's right, **106:2-716.**
Substituted performance, **106:2-614.**
Time, **106:2-309.**
Personal injuries, limitation of damages, **106:2-719.**
Person in the position of a seller, remedies, **106:2-707.**
Place.
Delivery, place, **106:2-308.**
Inspection, place, **106:2-513.**
Market price, place for determining, **106:2-713, 106:2-723.**
Payment, place, **106:2-310.**
Resale of goods by seller, place, **106:2-706.**
Tender of delivery, place, **106:2-503.**
Title, place of passing, **106:2-401.**

SALES UNDER COMMERCIAL CODE —Cont'd

Plasma.
Blood, blood plasma, and human tissues and organs. See within this heading, "Blood, blood plasma, and human tissues and organs."
Presentment.
See PRESENTMENT, DISHONOR, AND PROTEST.
Price.
Payment. See within this heading, "Payment."
Privity of contract, lack of abolished as defense in actions concerning goods sold, **106:2-318.**
Profit on resale of goods by seller, accountability to buyer, **106:2-706.**
Public sale.
Auctions.
See AUCTIONS AND AUCTIONEERS.
Judicial sales.
See JUDICIAL SALES.
Resale by seller, **106:2-706.**
"Purchase" defined, **106:1-201.**
Quota, allocation, **106:2-615, 106:2-616.**
Ratification of wrongful acceptance of goods, **106:2-606.**
Readjustment of contract, **106:2-201 to 106:2-210.**
Reasonable time.
Assurance of performance, time for providing, **106:2-609.**
Rejection of goods, time, **106:2-602.**
What constitutes under Commercial Code, **106:1-204.**
Receipts.
C.I.F. sales, **106:2-320.**
Defined, **106:2-103.**
F.A.S. terms, **106:2-319.**
Invoices and delivery tickets. See within this heading, "Invoices and delivery tickets."
Recording contract for sale of goods to be severed from realty, **106:2-107.**
Rejection of goods.
Acceptance or rejection of goods. See within this heading, "Acceptance or rejection of goods."
Remedies.
Action or suit. See within this heading, "Action or suit."

SALES UNDER COMMERCIAL CODE —Cont'd

Replacement as curing improper tender or delivery, **106:2-508.**
Replevin, buyer's right, **106:2-716.**
Repudiation of contract.
Cancellation, repudiation, or rescission. See within this heading, "Cancellation, repudiation, or rescission."
Requirements of buyer, contract based, **106:2-306.**
Resale, **106:2-706, 106:2-711.**
Judgment in action for price as reduced by proceeds, **106:2-709.**
Motor carriers' purchase of commodities from shippers for immediate resale, **159B:6D.**
Person in position of seller, **106:2-707.**
Rescission of contract.
Cancellation, repudiation, or rescission. See within this heading, "Cancellation, repudiation, or rescission."
Reservation, shipment of goods, **106:2-310, 106:2-505.**
Restrictions.
Conditions and terms. See within this heading, "Conditions and terms."
Retraction of anticipatory repudiation of contract, **106:2-611.**
Return, sale or return, **106:2-326, 106:2-327.**
Revesting of title in seller, **106:2-401.**
Revocation of acceptance of goods.
Acceptance or rejection of goods. See within this heading, "Acceptance or rejection of goods."
Risk of loss, **106:2-509.**
Allocating or dividing, **106:2-303.**
Approval, sale, **106:2-327.**
Casualty to identified goods, **106:2-613.**
C. & F. terms, **106:2-320, 106:2-321.**
C.I.F. terms, **106:2-320, 106:2-321.**
Ex-ship terms, **106:2-322.**
F.A.S. terms, **106:2-319.**
F.O.B. terms, **106:2-319.**
No arrival, no sale term, **106:2-324.**
Return, sale with privilege, **106:2-327.**

SALES UNDER COMMERCIAL CODE —Cont'd

Risk of loss —Cont'd

Revocation of acceptance, **106:2-510.**

Tender of delivery, **106:2-509, 106:2-510.**

Salvage.

Rejected goods, buyer's option as to salvage, **106:2-604.**

Seller's right to salvage unfinished goods, **106:2-704.**

Scope of article, **106:2-102.**

Seal affixed to sales contract, **106:2-203.**

Secured transactions, **106:9-113 et seq.**

Generally.

See SECURED TRANSACTIONS.

Inspection of goods, security interest of buyer for expenses, **106:2-711.**

Liens.

See LIENS AND ENCUMBRANCES.

Reservation of title, **106:2-401.**

Sales article as governing, **106:9-113.**

Several lots, delivery, **106:2-307.**

Severance from real property.

Oil and gas, **106:2-107.**

Timber to be cut, **106:2-107.**

Shipment of goods, **106:2-504.**

Acceptance of sales contract, **106:2-206.**

Bills of lading, **106:7-101 to 106:7-105, 106:7-301 to 106:7-603, 108:42 et seq.**

See BILLS OF LADING.

Delivery. See within this heading, "Delivery."

Option, **106:2-311.**

Overseas shipment, bill of lading required, **106:2-323.**

Resale, carrier's purchase, **159B:6D.**

Reservation, shipment, **106:2-310, 106:2-505.**

Sale to enforce lien of carrier, **106:7-308.**

Short title, **106:2-101.**

Signature to firm offer, **106:2-205.**

Single lots, delivery, **106:2-307.**

Special property interest in goods, obtaining, **106:2-501, 106:2-502.**

Specific performance, buyer's right, **106:2-716.**

Statute of limitations, **106:2-725.**

Stoppage of delivery in transit, **106:2-705.**

Delivery as excused, **106:7-403.**

SALES UNDER COMMERCIAL CODE —Cont'd

Stoppage of delivery in transit —Cont'd

Financing agency's right, **106:2-506.**

Incidental damages resulting, **106:2-710.**

Person in position of seller, **106:2-707.**

Substitute goods, buyer's procurement, **106:2-712.**

Tax on sales, form for clause in dealer contract relative, **106:2-201.**

Tender.

Delivery. See within this heading, "Delivery."

Nonconforming tender. See within this heading, "Nonconforming tender."

Payment, tender, **106:2-511.**

Termination.

Contract.

Cancellation, repudiation, or rescission. See within this heading, "Cancellation, repudiation, or rescission."

Delivery, previous sale in enforcement of lien or on termination of storage as excusing, **106:7-403.**

Warehouses, sale of goods upon termination of storage, **106:7-206.**

Terms.

Conditions and terms. See within this heading, "Conditions and terms."

Third parties as liable for injury to goods, **106:2-722.**

Timber, contract for sale of, **96:11A, 106:2-107.**

Time.

Accrual of cause of action for breach of contract, **106:2-725.**

Contract, duration, **106:2-309.**

Credit period, commencement of running, **106:2-310.**

Delay. See within this heading, "Delay."

Firm offers, period of irrevocability, **106:2-205.**

Indeterminate time of making of contract, **106:2-204.**

Market price, establishment, **106:2-723.**

Payment, time, **106:2-310.**

Performance, time, **106:2-309.**

Reasonable time. See within this heading, "Reasonable time."

SALES UNDER COMMERCIAL CODE —Cont'd

Time —Cont'd

Rejection of goods, **106:2-602.**

Revocation of acceptance, **106:2-608.**

Stoppage of delivery in transit, time, **106:2-705.**

Tender of delivery, time, **106:2-503.**

Title, time of passing, **106:2-401.**

Title.

Acceptance of goods by acts inconsistent with seller's ownership, **106:2-606.**

Approval, passing of title on sale, **106:2-327.**

Delivery. See within this heading, "Delivery."

Documents of title. See within this heading, "Documents of title."

Good faith purchaser, transfer of title, **106:2-403.**

Passing, **106:2-401.**

Power to transfer, **106:2-403.**

Rejection of goods, buyer's exercise of ownership after, **106:2-602.**

Special property interest in goods, obtaining, **106:2-501, 106:2-502.**

Time of passing of title, **106:2-401.**

Voidable title, transfer, **106:2-403.**

Warranty, **106:2-312.**

Transferability of goods, **106:2-105.**

Unconscionable contract or clause, **106:2-302.**

Unfinished goods, seller's rights upon breach, **106:2-704.**

Unique goods, specific performance in case, **106:2-716.**

Usage.

Custom or usage. See within this heading, "Custom or usage."

Waiver and estoppel.

Breach of contract, waiver of claim or right arising, **106:1 et seq.**

Objection, waiver of breach by failure to particularize, **106:2-605.**

Consumer goods and services, disclaimer or waiver by agreement of warranties or remedies by sale, **106:2-316A.**

SALES UNDER COMMERCIAL CODE —Cont'd
Waiver and estoppel —Cont'd
Objections to goods, buyer's waive, **106:2-605.**
Provisions of contract, waiver, **106:2-208, 106:2-209.**
Warehouse receipts, **106:7-101 et seq.**
See WAREHOUSE RECEIPTS.
Warehouses.
Enforcement of warehouseman's lien by sale of goods, **106:7-210.**
Receipts.
See WAREHOUSE RECEIPTS.
Termination of storage, sale, **106:7-206.**
Warranties, **106:2-312 to 106:2-318.**
See WARRANTIES.

SALISBURY.
Congressional district, **57:1.**
District court, **218:1.**
Medical examiner district, **38:1.**
Senatorial district, **57:3.**

SALMON.
Atlantic salmon.
Connecticut River Atlantic Salmon Compact, **S133:1.**
Sale regulated, **131:22.**

SALMONELLA PULLORUM.
Testing of birds, **131:19A.**

SALOONS.
See TAVERNS.

SALT.
Commercial feed labels, **128:53.**
Drugs and narcotics, **75:36B.**
Snow removal.
Contract quantity, increase, **85:7A.**
Storage, **85:7A.**
Watershed, **92:107A.**

SALVAGE.
Bureau.
Accident and health insurance, blanket policies authorized, **175:110.**
Foreign corporations engaged in salvage business, **91:50, 91:51.**
Motor vehicles.
Junkyards and junked vehicles.
See MOTOR VEHICLES.
Railroad wreckage, **160:241A.**
Sales under Commercial Code.
Rejected goods, buyer's option as to salvage, **106:2-604.**

SALVAGE —Cont'd
Sales under Commercial Code —Cont'd
Seller's right to salvage unfinished goods, **106:2-704.**
State property, rules for disposal, **7:22.**
Underwater archaeological resources, salvage, **6:180, 91:63.**

SALVES.
Sale of, by hairdressers, etc., **112:87CC.**

SAMPLE OR MODEL.
Alcoholic liquors.
Analysis, **138:37, 138:63.**
Tampering with samples of seized liquor, **138:39.**
Transportation by salesmen, **138:22.**
Apples, power of commissioner of agriculture to take samples, **94:106.**
Ballots for election.
See ELECTIONS.
Bedding or upholstery, materials used, **94:276.**
Cosmetics.
Examination of samples, **94:189.**
Vendor to furnish for analysis, **94:304.**
Description as superseded by sample in considering inconsistent warranties, **106:2-317.**
Drugs and narcotics, **94:188, 94:189, 94:304, 94C:9, 111:12, 111:13.**
Election ballots.
See ELECTIONS.
Evidence.
Chemical analysis.
See EVIDENCE.
Hazardous substances, **94B:6.**
Fertilizer, collection of samples for analysis, **128:77.**
Food.
See FOOD.
Hazardous substances, use of samples in evidence, **94B:6.**
Hazardous waste management act, **21C:8, 21C:9.**
Hazardous waste site cleanup professionals, order requiring production or analysis of samples, **21A:19F.**
Health department's sampling and analysis of various products, **94:188, 94:189, 111:11 et seq.**
Implied warranty as affected by opportunity to inspect, **106:2-316.**

SAMPLE OR MODEL —Cont'd
Intoxicating liquors.
Alcoholic liquors. See within this heading, "Alcoholic liquors."
Lead poisoning detection, **111:195.**
Milk.
See MILK AND MILK PRODUCTS.
Motor fuel, manufacturers or distributors to submit samples, **94:295G.**
Real estate time-shares, **183B:16.**
Seeds, taking and testing, **128:95.**
Specifications as superseding sample or model in considering inconsistent warranties, **106:2-317.**
Surgical devices.
Examination of sample, **94:189.**
Vendor to furnish sample for analysis, **94:304.**
Vinegar, sampling for analysis, **94:166 et seq.**
Voting machine sample ballots, **53:33.**
Wage reporting system, sampling technique, **62E:13.**
Warranty created, **106:2-313, 106:2-316.**

SAMUEL GRAY.
Commemoration of, death, **6:12D.**

SAMUEL MAVERICK.
Commemoration of, death, **6:12D.**

SAMUEL SLATER DAY.
Annual observance, **6:15PPP.**

SANATORIA, 111:94A et seq.
See TUBERCULOSIS AND TUBERCULIN.

SANCTUARIES.
Fish.
See FISH AND GAME.
Ocean sanctuaries.
See OCEAN SANCTUARIES.
Wildlife.
Establishment, **131:7.**
Rules, **131:8.**

SAND AND GRAVEL.
Beaches or shore line, removal penalized, **91:30, 91:30A.**
Digging up and carrying away as criminal offense, **266:113.**
Eminent domain, acquisition of pits, **82:38.**
Harbors, illegal deposit, **102:17.**
Highways and streets.
Oil and sand pavement, **84:6.**
Pits, acquisition by eminent domain, **82:38.**

SAND AND GRAVEL —Cont'd

Highways and streets —Cont'd

Town ways, cost of sanding, **81:26, 84:5A.**

Ocean sanctuaries, removal, **132A:15, 132A:16.**

Oil and gravel surfacing, **84:6.**

Ordinances and bylaws prohibiting removal, **40:21.**

Public works, transportation of gravel or fill, **149:27.**

Sales and use tax, exemption of sand-handling equipment and tools, **64H:6.**

Ships.

See SHIPS AND OTHER WATERCRAFT.

Snow and ice removal, **81:26, 84:5A, 85:7A.**

Street railways, transportation, **161:50.**

Public ways, regulations concerning transportation, **85:36.**

Town ways, **81:26, 84:5A.**

Weights and measures.

Certificates in connection with sale, **94:244, 94:245.**

Vessels transporting to be weighed and marked, **102:6 et seq.**

SANDISFIELD.

District court, **218:1.**

Medical examiner district, **38:1.**

Senatorial district, **57:3.**

SANDWICH.

District court, **218:1.**

Medical examiner district, **38:1.**

SANITARIANS, 112:87LL et seq.

Application for registration, **112:87MM.**

Board of registration, **13:51 et seq.**

Engineering board of registration to recognize sanitarians, **112:81E.**

Rules and regulations, **112:88.**

Certificate of registration, **112:87MM.**

Duplicate certificate, **112:88.**

General provisions as to furnishing, **112:88.**

Temporary certificate, **112:87NN.**

Continuing education requirement for registration renewal, **112:87MM.**

Definitions, **112:87LL.**

Drinking water supply facilities board of certification, sanitary engineer as member, **13:66B.**

SANITARIANS —Cont'd

Engineering board of registration to recognize, **112:81E.**

Environmental code, duties regarding, **21A:13.**

Examination, inspection, or investigation.

Registration, examination, **112:87MM.**

Issuance of certificate without examination, **112:87NN.**

Reports of investigations or inspection for violations, **111:127B.**

Tenant's petition for enforcement in absence of inspection, **111:127C.**

Fee for registration, **112:87MM.**

General provisions, **112:88.**

Qualifications for registration, **112:87NN.**

"Registered sanitarian," use of title, **112:87OO.**

Registration, **112:87MM, 112:87NN.**

Board of registration. See within this heading, "Board of registration."

Certificate of registration. See within this heading, "Certificate of registration."

Examination, inspection, or investigation. See within this heading, "Examination, inspection, or investigation."

Fee. See within this heading, "Fee for registration."

School sanitary engineers.

Janitors and custodians.

See SCHOOLS AND EDUCATION.

Secretary of board of registration, **13:52.**

SANITARY CODES.

Barbers.

See BARBERS.

Beaches, state sanitary code, **111:127A.**

Cambridge, enforcement by housing inspection commissioner, **111:127A, 111:127B, 111:127C, 111:127E, 111:127L.**

Camps, state sanitary code, **111:127A.**

District courts.

See DISTRICT COURTS.

Environmental protection department, **111:127A.**

Health.

See HEALTH AND HEALTH DEPARTMENTS.

SANITARY CODES —Cont'd

Lead poisoning, violations of sanitary code, **111:198.**

Records and reports.

Central file for sanitary codes of cities and towns, **21A:8, 111:31.**

Investigations or inspections for violations, reports, **111:16, 111:127B.**

Swimming and swimming pools, state sanitary code, **111:127A.**

SANITARY FILL.

Common nuisances, duty of owner or agent, **139:3A.**

SAN JOSE SCALE, 128:24.

SARSAPARILLA.

Nonintoxicating beverages derived, **140:21A et seq.**

SATELLITE CLINICS.

University of Massachusetts, **75:36C.**

SATELLITE TRANSMISSIONS.

Board of higher education, Massachusetts corporation for educational telecommunication, **15A:3A.**

Retail sales tax.

Definitions, **64H:1.**

SATISFACTION.

Acknowledgment.

Injured person's acknowledgment of satisfaction as discharging civil liability of wrongdoer, **276:55, 276:56.**

Legacy, **197:25A.**

Bills of lading.

Excusing nondelivery, **106:7-403.**

Lien satisfied by person claiming goods, **106:7-403.**

Contracts.

See ACCORD AND SATISFACTION.

Criminal and civil proceedings as affected, **276:55, 276:56.**

Delivery of goods as excused, **106:7-403.**

Executions.

See EXECUTIONS.

Judgments.

See JUDGMENTS, ORDERS, AND DECREES.

Legacy, acknowledgment of satisfaction, **197:25A.**

Levy of taxes, **62C:54.**

Executors and administrators, **60:36.**

SATISFACTION —Cont'd

Mortgages.
    Discharge or release.
        See MORTGAGES AND
            DEEDS OF TRUST.
Negotiable instruments.
    Bills of lading, **106:7-403.**
Tax title account, satisfaction,
    60:62.
Warehouse receipts.
    Excusing nondelivery,
        106:7-403.
    Person claiming goods,
        satisfaction of lien,
        106:7-403.

SATURDAY NIGHT SPECIALS.

Restrictions on sales, **140:123.**

SATURDAYS.

Banks, closing, **167:21.**
Bidders on building construction
    work, times excluded in
    computing time for return of
    bid deposits of unsuccessful
    bidders, **149:44B.**
City and town employees, half
    holiday, **41:110, 149:33.**
Civil service.
    Sundays and holidays.
        See CIVIL SERVICE.
County offices may be closed,
    34:16.
Courts open for business,
    213:4.
Electricity not to be shut off,
    164:124.
Equivalent time off for public
    employees required to work,
    30:24, 147:17A.
Gas not to be shut off,
    164:124.
Half holiday, **92:65, 149:33,
    149:41.**
    Civil service.
        Sundays and holidays.
            See CIVIL SERVICE.
    Metropolitan district
        commission, employees,
        92:65.
    Municipal employees, **41:110,
        149:33.**
    State employees, **149:33,
        149:41.**
Legal holiday falling on Saturday,
    time off for state employees in
    case, **30:24A.**
Municipal offices may be closed on
    Saturday, **41:110A.**
Police officer's regular day off
    falling on Saturday holiday,
    147:17A.

SATURDAYS —Cont'd

Probate court sessions, **215:58.**
Public officers and employees.
    Half holiday, **41:110, 92:65,
        92:67, 149:33, 149:41.**
    Legal holiday falling on
        Saturday, **30:24A.**
    Office hours, **30:24.**
Registration of voters.
    Sessions for registration.
        See REGISTRATION OF
            VOTERS.
Sentence to be served on
    weekends, **279:6A.**
State officers.
    Public officers and employees.
        See within this heading,
        "Public officers and
        employees."
Sunday work by persons observing
    Sabbath on Saturday,
    136:6.

SAUGUS.

Congressional district, **57:1.**
District court, **218:1.**
Medical examiner district, **38:1.**
Metropolitan air pollution control
    district, membership,
    111:142B.
Parks, provision by metropolitan
    commission, **92:33.**
Refuse disposal, **92:9A.**
Senatorial district, **57:3.**

SAUSAGE.

Adulteration.
    Penalty for manufacture or sale
        of adulterated sausage,
        94:143.
    What constitutes, **94:142.**
Cereal content, maximum
    permissible, **94:142.**
Coloring matter, **94:142.**
Defined, **94:1.**
Fine or penalty for violations as to
    manufacture or sale, **94:142 et
    seq.**
Ingredients, **94:142.**
Offal, **94:142.**
Permissible ingredients,
    94:142.
Sale regulated, **94:143.**
Sulphur compounds, containing,
    94:153A.
Unwholesome or contaminated
    ingredients, **94:142.**
Vegetable sausage, requirements
    concerning, **94:143A.**
Water, permissible maximum,
    94:142.

SAVINGS ACT.

Statute of limitations, **260:32.**

**SAVINGS AND LOAN
    ASSOCIATIONS.**

Abandoned property.
    Federal savings and loan
        associations.
        See ABANDONED, LOST,
            AND UNCLAIMED
            PROPERTY.
Accounts.
    Agreements with cities and
        towns to collect accounts
        payable, **60:2A.**
    Consumer account disclosure,
        140E:1-140E:4.
        See TRUTH IN SAVINGS.
Authorized depository for credit
    union deductions from pay,
    federal savings and loan
    association, **149:178B.**
Burial expenses of ward, increase
    of limitation on amounts
    deposited, **201:48A.**
Commissioner of social services to
    deposit trust funds,
    18B:18.
Consumer account disclosure,
    140E:1-140E:4.
    See TRUTH IN SAVINGS.
Cooperative banks.
    See COOPERATIVE BANKS.
Corporation taxes.
    See CORPORATION TAXES.
Credit unions.
    See CREDIT UNIONS.
Direct deposit of public employees'
    wages, etc., **41:41B.**
Dissolution or liquidation,
    178A:5.
Eminent domain proceedings,
    investment of amounts
    awarded as damages, **79:7D.**
Executors and administrators,
    deposits, **205:19A, 206:25 et
    seq.**
Federal savings.
    See FEDERAL SAVINGS AND
        LOAN ASSOCIATIONS.
Foreign corporations.
    Advertising to show place of
        origin, **181:7.**
    Name, **181:7.**
Income tax, **62:2, 62C:12.**
Industrial Finance Agency bonds
    as legal public investments,
    23A:39.
Medical director, savings bank life
    insurance, **178A:8.**

SAVINGS AND LOAN ASSOCIATIONS —Cont'd

Partition proceedings, investment of unclaimed proceeds, **241:34.**

Recycling funds of cities and towns, deposit, **40:5.**

Sales finance company, association, **255D:1.**

Secured transactions article as applicable to transfer of accounts maintained, **106:9-104.**

Small business assistance division, co-operation, **23A:17.**

State.
See COOPERATIVE BANKS.

Trust companies.
See TRUST COMPANIES.

Trustee process against, bond may be required of plaintiff, **246:31.**

Uniform Securities Act, securities exempt from provisions, **110A:402.**

Veterans' deposits, furnishing information, **115:2.**

Wage reporting system, **62E:4, 62E:5.**

SAVINGS AND SAVINGS ACCOUNTS.

Consumer account disclosure, **140E:1-140E:4.**
See TRUTH IN SAVINGS.

Cooperative banks.
See COOPERATIVE BANKS.

Dormant accounts, prohibition of service charges, **200A:15C.**

Inmate savings accounts, use of interest-bearing accounts, **127:48A.**

Persons over 65 or under 18 years of age, prohibition of fees against savings accounts, **167D:2.**

Savings banks.
See SAVINGS BANKS.

Secured transactions article as applicable to transfer, **106:9-104.**

Trust companies.
See TRUST COMPANIES.

Verification, **167:20.**

Withdrawal, **167D:16.**

Workers' compensation, savings of injured employee not deductible, **152:38.**

SAVINGS BANK LIFE INSURANCE.

Accounts and records, **30A:11A.**

Annuity contracts and policies, **175:25.**

SAVINGS BANK LIFE INSURANCE —Cont'd

Appeal and review, **178A:6.**

Bylaws, **178A:9.**

Classes of stock, **178A:4.**

Compensation of directors, **178A:9.**

Consumer affairs and business regulation office, **178A:9.**

Contracts and policies, **175:25.**

Council on savings bank life insurance.
Insurance departments assumed, **178A:2.**
Termination, **178A:7, 178A:8.**

Definitions, **178A:1.**

Deputy commissioner, office abolished, **178A:8.**

Directors.
Election, **178A:3.**
Plan of assumption, **178A:4 et seq.**
Policyholders protective board, **178A:9.**

Discrimination, **178A:7.**

Dividends.
Approval by policyholders protective board, **178A:10.**
Postmortem, **178A:5.**

Division of savings bank life insurance, **30:1.**
Commissioner of savings bank life insurance, **26:1.**
Group insurance for state employees, membership of employees, **32A:2, 32A:8.**

Election of directors, **178A:3.**

Federal savings and loan associations, **175:63.**

General insurance guaranty fund.
Abolishment, **178A:8.**
Public meetings and records, inapplicability of law, **30A:11A.**

Governor, **178A:9.**

Group insurance for state employees, membership of savings bank life insurance division employees, **32A:2, 32A:8.**

Guaranty fund.
General insurance guaranty fund. See within this heading, "General insurance guaranty fund."

Hearings.
Dividends, payment, **178A:6.**
Plan of assumption, **178A:6.**

Investments, **178A:7.**
Federal savings and loan associations, **175:63.**

License, **178A:4.**

SAVINGS BANK LIFE INSURANCE —Cont'd

Limitation of actions for contract actions, **178A:11.**

Liquidation, **178A:5.**

Medical director of state, office abolished, **178A:8.**

Policies and annuity contracts, **175:25.**

Policyholders protective board.
Approval of dividend distribution, **178A:10.**
Establishment, **178A:9.**

Publication, notice of hearing, **178A:6.**

Records, reports and returns, **30A:11A.**

Reinsurance.
See REINSURANCE.

State actuary, office abolished, **178A:8.**

Stocks and bonds, ownership, **178A:4.**

Surplus.
Consultants, cost, **178A:6.**
Defined, **178A:1.**
Distribution as dividends, **178A:5.**
Issuance of stock, **178A:4.**

SAVINGS BANKS, 168:1 et seq.

Abandoned and unclaimed deposits and funds, deposit of, **171:29.**

Absentees, estates of.
See ABSENTEES' ESTATES.

Absent officers-elect, notice, **168:15.**

Accountant, selection by auditing committee, **168:25.**

Accounts, **167D:1 et seq.**
Audit of books and accounts. See within this heading, "Audit of books and accounts."
Consumer account disclosure, **140E:1-140E:4.**
See TRUTH IN SAVINGS.
Deposits and depositors. See within this heading, "Deposits and depositors."

Adjustable or flexible mortgages, **183:28A.**

Advancements.
Loans. See within this heading, "Loans."

Affirmation.
Oath or affirmation. See within this heading, "Oath or affirmation."

Agents.
Officers, agents, and employees. See within this heading, "Officers, agents, and employees."

SAVINGS BANKS —Cont'd

Age restrictions, corporators, **168:9.**

Appeal from decisions of board of bank incorporation as to bank holding companies, **167A:4.**

Application, submission to board of bank incorporation, **168:5.**

Armed services, information as to veteran's financial condition, **115:2.**

Articles, filing, **168:7.**

Assessments.
  Local or special assessments, exemption, **59:5.**

Assets.
  Bank holding company, acquisition of assets of subsidiaries, **167A:2.**
  Insurance company assets, savings deposits included, **175:11.**
  State or federally chartered banks, loan upon or purchase of assets, **168:35.**

Associations.
  Retirement association for savings bank employees. See within this heading, "Retirement association for savings bank employees."

Attachment.
  Exemption from.
    Exemption from process. See within this heading, "Exemption from process."
  Trustee process. See within this heading, "Trustee process."

Auditing committee, **168:16.**
  Dividends, report, **168:28.**
  Examination and audit of books, securities, etc., **168:25.**
  Powers and duties, **168:25, 168:26.**
  Reports, **168:25.**

Audit of books and accounts, **168:25, 168:26, 170:14.**
  Committee for.
    Auditing committee. See within this heading, "Auditing committee."

Authorized depository for credit union deductions from pay of public employees, **149:178B.**

Bank commissioner.
  Annual report, submission, **168:26.**
  Deficit, written notice, **168:27.**
  State or federally-chartered bank, notice of purchase of assets or stock, **168:35.**

SAVINGS BANKS —Cont'd

Bank holding companies.
  See BANK HOLDING COMPANIES.

Bank incorporation, board.
  Application, submission, **168:5.**
  Bank holding companies, appeal from decision of board, **167A:4.**

Bequests to counties, deposit, **34:23.**

Blind persons, requirement as to furnishing information as to certain deposits to commission, **6:131.**

Board of bank incorporation.
  Bank incorporation, board of. See within this heading, "Bank incorporation, board."

Board of investments, **168:12.**
  Corporate surety on bond, **175:105.**
  Election, **168:14.**
  Meetings, **168:8, 168:12.**

Board of trustees.
  Trustees. See within this heading, "Trustees."

Bonds and other securities.
  Investments. See within this heading, "Investments."

Bonds and undertakings.
  Corporate surety on bond, **175:105.**
  Guaranty and suretyship. See within this heading, "Guaranty and suretyship."
  Officers and employees, **168:18.**
  Trustee process bond, **246:31.**

Books and records.
  Records, reports, and returns. See within this heading, "Records, reports, and returns."

Borrowing money.
  Loans. See within this heading, "Loans."

Branch banks or offices.
  Community needs, obligation to meet, **168:34-168:34B, 168:34D, 168:35, 170:26B.**
  Divestment, **168:38.**

Brokerage for loan made by corporation, **168:23.**

Burial expenses of wards, deposits, **201:48A.**

Business corporation law as applicable to savings banks, **156:2, 156B:3.**

Bylaws.
  Adoption and amendment, **168:6, 168:16.**

SAVINGS BANKS —Cont'd

Bylaws —Cont'd
  Contents, **168:17.**

Campaign funds, investment, **55:6.**

Cemetery funds, deposits, **114:43K.**

Certificates and certification.
  Board of bank incorporation, issuance, **168:5.**
  Commissioner, annual report, **168:26.**
  Incorporation, certificate, **168:7.**

Chapter, applicability, **168:3.**

Charter.
  Federal savings bank charter, **168:36.**
  State-chartered stockholder-owned bank, change of control, **168:34C, 170:26C, 172:26A.**

Checks.
  Wage checks, cashing by savings banks, **168:56.**

Cities and towns.
  Claims trust for municipal self-insurance, **32B:3A.**
  Conservation funds, investment, **40:5.**
  Recycling funds, deposit, **40:5.**
  Stabilization fund, deposit, **40:5B.**
  Trust funds, deposit or investment, **44:54.**

Claims trust for municipal self-insurance, **32B:3A.**

Clerk, appointment at first meeting of subscribers, **168:6.**

Commissioner of banks.
  Bank commissioner. See within this heading, "Bank commissioner."

Commissions, **168:23, 186:20.**

Committees.
  Auditing committee. See within this heading, "Auditing committee."

Community needs, obligation to meet, **167:38, 168:34-168:34B, 168:34D, 168:35, 170:26A, 170:26B.**

Compensation.
  Wages, salaries, and compensation. See within this heading, "Wages, salaries, and compensation."

Competition among banking institutions, **167:38, 168:34 et seq.**

Consent to merger and consolidation, time of existence affecting, **168:35A.**

SAVINGS BANKS —Cont'd
Consolidation or merger, **168:34.**
Approval, time of existence
affecting, **168:35A.**
Bank holding companies,
167A:2.
Competition among banking
institutions, **167:38, 168:34
et seq.**
Consent, time of existence
affecting, **168:35A.**
Co-operative bank, merger or
consolidation, **168:34A,
170:26A, 170:26B.**
Depositors insurance fund,
consolidation or merger
affecting **168:34B, 168:34D.**
Net new benefits defined, **168:34
et seq.**
Residency requirements for
corporators, trustees and
directors, **168:34B, 168:34D,
172:36.**
Thrift institution, merger or
consolidation, **168:34B.**
Consumer account disclosure,
140E:1-140E:4.
See TRUTH IN SAVINGS.
Contract as to formation of
corporation, **168:4.**
Contributions.
Employees' retirement
association, contributions,
168:39.
Gifts. See within this heading,
"Gifts."
Conversion or purchase.
Assets or stock of state or
federally-chartered bank,
purchase, **168:35.**
Federal savings and loan
association, conversion
involving, **168:37, 168:38.**
Federal savings bank charter,
168:36.
State or federally-chartered
stock corporation, **168:34D.**
Stockholder-owned corporation,
168:34C, 168:34E.
Co-operative banks, consolidation
or merger with savings banks,
168:34A, 170:26A, 170:26B.
Corporation taxes.
See CORPORATION TAXES.
Corporators, **168:4.**
Annual meeting, **168:9A.**
Election and term of office,
168:9.
Meetings, **168:6, 168:8, 168:9A.**
Residency requirements on
consolidation or merger,
168:34B, 168:34D, 172:36.

SAVINGS BANKS —Cont'd
Corporators —Cont'd
Stockholders, formation of
corporations owned, **168:4,
170:2.**
County finance.
Capitol Improvement Fund,
deposit of proceeds, **35:28B.**
Gifts or bequests to counties,
deposit, **34:23.**
Credit, extension to officers, etc.,
168:19, 168:20.
Credit unions.
See CREDIT UNIONS.
Decedents' estates, deposit of
funds, **206:25 et seq.**
Deductions from wages.
Payroll and payroll deductions.
See within this heading,
"Payroll and payroll
deductions."
Deficit, written notice to
commissioner, **168:27.**
Definitions, **4:7, 168:1.**
Deposit books, putting up for bail,
276:57.
Deposits and depositors, **167D:1 et
seq.**
Bequests or gifts to counties,
deposit, **34:23.**
Books of deposit, **276:57.**
Borrowing money.
Loans. See within this
heading, "Loans."
Burial expenses for ward,
deposit, **201:48A.**
Cemetery funds, **114:43K.**
Cities and towns. See within
this heading, "Cities and
towns."
Consumer account disclosure,
140E:1-140E:4.
See TRUTH IN SAVINGS.
Corporation taxes.
See CORPORATION TAXES.
Counties, deposit of gifts or
bequests, **34:23.**
Credit unions.
See CREDIT UNIONS.
Decedents' estates, **206:25 et
seq.**
Direct deposit of public
employees' wages, etc.,
41:41B.
Dividends on.
Dividends and interest. See
within this heading,
"Dividends and interest."
Exemption from process. See
within this heading,
"Exemption from process."

SAVINGS BANKS —Cont'd
Deposits and depositors —Cont'd
Exemption from taxation. See
within this heading,
"Exemption from taxation."
Federal deposit insurance
coverage, **168:36.**
Federal savings and loan
association or federal
savings bank converting to
state-chartered savings
bank, deposits into
Depositors insurance fund,
168:38.
Fiduciaries, deposits, **201:48A,
205:19A, 206:25 et seq.**
Group insurance commission
trust fund, investments and
deposits, **32A:9A.**
Guardian, **201:48A, 205:19A,
206:25 et seq.**
Industrial development and
health care and educational
development funds, deposit
in savings banks, **40D:9.**
Insolvent bank receiving
deposits, penalty, **266:54.**
Insurance company assets,
savings deposits included,
175:11.
Interest.
Dividends and interest. See
within this heading,
"Dividends and interest."
Investments. See within this
heading, "Investments."
Motor vehicle sold for storage
charges, deposit of proceeds,
255:39A.
Municipal funds.
Cities and towns. See within
this heading, "Cities and
towns."
Mutual insurance companies,
funds, **175:80, 175:90.**
Passbooks, **276:57.**
Payroll deduction deposits,
154:8.
Pension system funds, **32:23.**
Public administrator, when not
to act with regard to
deposits, **194:5, 200:8.**
Public employees' wages, direct
deposit, **41:41B.**
Records of deposits, **276:57.**
Retirement system funds, **32:23.**
Schools and school systems,
accounts and deposits of,
71:16G½.
Stabilization funds, **40:5B.**
State moneys, deposit, **29:34A.**

SAVINGS BANKS —Cont'd
Deposits and depositors —Cont'd
Taxation. See within this
heading, "Taxation."
Trust funds. See within this
heading, "Trust funds."
Unknown legatees, deposit of
legacies, **206:26.**
Wage deductions, **154:8.**
Direct deposit of public employees'
wages, etc., **41:41B.**
Directors.
Trustees. See within this
heading, "Trustees."
Dissolution, **168:33.**
Distribution, participation, **168:36.**
Dividends and interest, **168:28.**
Federal savings banks, taxation
of interest, **62:2.**
Income tax, **62:2.**
Ordinary dividends, **168:29.**
Unauthorized dividends, **168:24.**
Duties.
Powers and duties. See within
this heading, "Powers and
duties."
Economic development and
industrial corporations, sales
of real property, **121C:9.**
Elections.
Auditing committee, **168:16.**
Board of investment, **168:14.**
Board of trustees, **168:10.**
Corporators, **168:9.**
Officers and trustees, **168:6,
168:14.**
Electronic banking, **167B:1 et seq.**
Eminent domain proceedings,
investments of amounts
awarded as damages, **79:7D.**
Employees.
Officers, agents, and employees.
See within this heading,
"Officers, agents, and
employees."
Employees retirement association.
Retirement association for
savings bank employees. See
within this heading,
"Retirement association for
savings bank employees."
Estates of decedents, deposit of
funds, **206:25 et seq.**
Examination, inspection, and
investigation.
Audit of books and accounts. See
within this heading, "Audit
of books and accounts."
Fee, **168:5.**
Exception as to fee or brokerage
for loan by corporation,
168:23.

SAVINGS BANKS —Cont'd
Exemption from process.
Deposits exempt, amount,
235:34, 246:28A.
Employees' retirement
association, **168:41.**
Exemption from taxation.
Employees benefit association,
168:42 et seq.
Employees' retirement
association, **168:41.**
Local taxes, exemption, **59:5.**
Expenses.
Fees. See within this heading,
"Fees."
Federal deposit insurance
coverage, **168:36.**
Federal savings and loan
association, conversion
involving, **168:37, 168:38.**
Federal savings bank, **62:2,
168:36.**
Fees.
Investigation fee, **168:5.**
Loan made by corporation, fee,
168:23.
Fiduciaries.
Deposits, **201:48A, 205:19A,
206:25 et seq.**
Guardians, deposits, **201:48A,
205:19A, 206:25 et seq.**
Trustees. See within this
heading, "Trustees."
Fines and penalties, **168:23A.**
Bank holding company law,
violations, **167A:6.**
Imprisonment. See within this
heading, "Imprisonment."
Insolvent bank receiving
deposits, **266:54.**
Proscribed acts, **168:22.**
Publication of notice of elected
officers and trustees, **168:15.**
Unauthorized dividends, **168:24.**
Fire insurance company's profits,
deposit, **175:80.**
Flexible or adjustable mortgages,
183:28A.
Formation, **168:4.**
Funeral expenses of ward,
guardian's deposit, **201:48A.**
Garnishment.
Trustee process. See within this
heading, "Trustee process."
Gifts.
Counties, deposit of gifts or
bequests, **34:23.**
Loan made by corporation, gifts,
168:23.
Government land bank, **Spec L
9:8E.**

SAVINGS BANKS —Cont'd
Group insurance.
Debtors, life insurance on lives,
167F:2.
Trust fund investments and
deposits, **32A:9A.**
Guaranty and suretyship.
Bond, corporate surety, **175:105.**
Fund.
See SAVINGS BANK LIFE
INSURANCE.
Guardians, deposits, **201:48A,
205:19A, 206:25 et seq.**
Holding companies, **167A:1 et seq.**
See BANK HOLDING
COMPANIES.
Housing and urban renewal.
Investments. See within this
heading, "Investments."
Local community needs,
obligation to meet, **167:38,
168:34-168:34B, 168:34D,
168:35, 170:26A, 170:26B.**
Urban redevelopment
corporations. See within this
heading, "Urban
redevelopment
corporations."
Imprisonment.
Proscribed acts, **168:22.**
Unauthorized dividends, **168:24.**
Income or earnings.
Dividends and interest. See
within this heading,
"Dividends and interest."
Income tax.
See INCOME TAX.
Wages, salaries, and
compensation. See within
this heading, "Wages,
salaries, and compensation."
Income tax.
See INCOME TAX.
Incorporation.
Bank incorporation, board of.
See within this heading,
"Bank incorporation, board."
Certificate, **168:7.**
Corporators. See within this
heading, "Corporators."
Industrial development agencies,
deposit of funds, **40D:9,
40D:13, 40D:18.**
Industrial finance agency, bonds as
legal public investments,
23A:39.
Inheritance, decedents' estates,
206:25 et seq.
Insolvent bank, penalty for
receiving deposits, **266:54.**

437

SAVINGS BANKS —Cont'd
Inspection.
Examination, inspection, and investigation. See within this heading, "Examination, inspection, and investigation."
Insurance.
Assets of insurance company, savings deposits included, **175:11.**
Federal deposit insurance coverage, **168:36.**
Life insurance. See within this heading, "Life insurance."
Mutual insurance companies, deposit of funds, **175:80, 175:90.**
Savings bank life insurance. See SAVINGS BANK LIFE INSURANCE.
Interest.
Dividends and interest. See within this heading, "Dividends and interest."
Interlocking restrictions relative to board of trustees, **168:10.**
Investigation.
Examination, inspection, and investigation. See within this heading, "Examination, inspection, and investigation."
Investments, **167E:1 et seq.**
Board of investments. See within this heading, "Board of investments."
Bonds, **167F:2.**
Campaign funds, investment, **55:6.**
Eminent domain proceedings, investment of amount awarded as damages, **79:7D.**
Group insurance commission trust fund, investments, **32A:9A.**
Housing and urban renewal.
Bonds and notes of operating agencies, investment, **121B:15.**
Investments of operating agencies, securities legal for investment by savings banks, **121B:11.**
Urban redevelopment corporations. See within this heading, "Urban redevelopment corporations."
Loans. See within this heading, "Loans."

SAVINGS BANKS —Cont'd
Investments —Cont'd
Mortgage-backed securities, investments, **32:23.**
Municipal funds or bonds, **40:5B, 44:54.**
January 1, 1955, applicability of chapter to corporations formed before and after, **168:3.**
Jurisdiction of Supreme Judicial Court to enforce bank holding company law, **167A:7.**
Legal investments, **167:15A.**
License requirements for lending, exemption, **140:114A.**
Liens and encumbrances.
Mortgages. See within this heading, "Mortgages."
Life insurance.
Debtors, group life insurance on lives, **167F:2.**
Savings bank life insurance. See SAVINGS BANK LIFE INSURANCE.
Limitations and restrictions.
Age restrictions, corporators, **168:9.**
Liquidation and dissolution, **168:33.**
Loan by corporation, brokerage fee, **168:23.**
Ordinary dividends, **168:29.**
Liquidation, **168:33.**
Loans, **167E:1 et seq.**
Assets of state or federally chartered banks, loan upon or purchase, **168:35.**
Brokerage fees for loan made by corporation, **168:23.**
Credit unions. See CREDIT UNIONS.
Dividends and interest. See within this heading, "Dividends and interest."
Legal investments, **167:15A.**
License for lending, exemption, **140:114A.**
Mortgages. See within this heading, "Mortgages."
Officers of corporation, loans, **168:19, 168:20.**
Savings. See SAVINGS AND LOAN ASSOCIATIONS.
Trustees, loans, **168:19.**
Local community needs, obligation to meet, **167:38, 168:34-168:34B, 168:34D, 168:35, 170:26A, 170:26B.**
Local or special assessments, exemption, **59:5.**

SAVINGS BANKS —Cont'd
Locations of banks, **167C:1 et seq., 168:4, 168:8.**
Meetings.
Corporators, **168:8, 168:9A.**
Investment, board, **168:8, 168:12.**
Quorum. See within this heading, "Quorum."
Subscribers, first meeting, **168:6.**
Trustees, board, **168:8, 168:11.**
Membership.
Employees' retirement association, **168:39.**
Investment, board, **168:12.**
Merger.
Consolidation or merger. See within this heading, "Consolidation or merger."
Military affairs, information as to veteran's financial condition, **115:2.**
Mortgage-backed securities, investments, **32:23.**
Mortgages, **167E:1 et seq.**
Adjustable or flexible mortgages, **183:28A.**
Flexible mortgages, **183:28A.**
Officers, mortgages granted, **168:19, 168:20.**
Trust companies. See TRUST COMPANIES.
Motor vehicle sold for storage charges, deposit of proceeds, **255:39A.**
Municipal funds.
Cities and towns. See within this heading, "Cities and towns."
Mutual insurance companies, deposit of funds, **175:80, 175:90.**
Mutual savings banks, merger or consolidation of savings banks, providing for residency requirements for corporators, trustees and directors, **168:34B.**
Name by which corporation to be known, **168:4.**
National banks.
Tax on income, **62:1.**
Trustees, restrictions upon interlocking, **40:5.**
Negotiable instruments.
Checks. See within this heading, "Checks."
Investments. See within this heading, "Investments."
Net new benefits defined, **168:34 et seq.**

SAVINGS BANKS —Cont'd
Notice.
Absent officers-elect, notice, **168:15.**
Audits, **168:25, 170:14.**
Balance sheet, posting, **168:26.**
Board of bank in corporation, submission of application, **168:5.**
Corporators, annual meeting, **168:9A.**
Elected officers, trustees, notice by publication, **168:15.**
Federal savings and loan association, conversion involving savings bank, **168:37, 168:38.**
Subscribers, first meeting, **168:6.**
Trustees, regular meetings, **168:11.**
Oath or affirmation.
Auditing committee, **168:16.**
Officers, trustees and board of investment, **168:14.**
President and trustees, **168:7.**
Officers, agents, and employees, **168:13.**
Absent officers-elect, notice, **168:15.**
Bank commissioner. See within this heading, "Bank commissioner."
Benefit association established, powers, by-laws, terms, tax exemption of property, **168:42 et seq.**
Bond requirement, **168:18.**
Clerk, appointment at first meeting of subscribers, **168:6.**
Election, **168:6, 168:14.**
Loans or mortgages, **168:19, 168:20.**
Oaths, **168:7.**
Payroll deductions as to public employees, **149:178B.**
Retirement of.
Retirement association for savings bank employees. See within this heading, "Retirement association for savings bank employees."
Terms of office. See within this heading, "Terms of office."
Treasurers, powers and duties, **168:21.**
Trustees. See within this heading, "Trustees."
Vacancies in office, trustees and board of investment, **168:14.**

SAVINGS BANKS —Cont'd
Officers, agents, and employees —Cont'd
Wages, salaries, and compensation. See within this heading, "Wages, salaries, and compensation."
Operation as redevelopment corporation, acquisition of site from housing authority, **121A:7A.**
Ordinary dividends, **168:29.**
Organization.
Incorporation. See within this heading, "Incorporation."
Other banks.
Consolidation or merger. See within this heading, "Consolidation or merger."
Partition of land, disposition of unclaimed proceeds, **241:34.**
Passbooks, **276:57.**
Payroll and payroll deductions.
Deposits, **154:8.**
Public employees, **149:178B.**
Penalties.
Fines and penalties. See within this heading, "Fines and penalties."
Pensions.
Retirement systems and pensions. See within this heading, "Retirement systems and pensions."
Poor persons, information as to deposits, **18:15, 122:22.**
Powers and duties, **168:2.**
Investment, board, **168:12.**
Property.
Employees' retirement association, **168:41.**
Investments in real estate, **167F:2.**
Mortgages. See within this heading, "Mortgages."
Proscribed acts, **168:22.**
Public administrator's activities not required when savings bank deposit is sole asset of estate, **194:5, 200:8.**
Public moneys, deposit by treasurer, **29:34A.**
Public utilities, deposit of funds, **155:3A.**
Public welfare.
Welfare and welfare department. See within this heading, "Welfare and welfare department."
Purpose, **168:4.**
Qualifications for board of trustees, **168:10.**

SAVINGS BANKS —Cont'd
Quorum.
Corporators, annual meeting, **168:9A.**
Trustees, meetings, **168:11.**
Real property.
Investments, **167F:2.**
Mortgages. See within this heading, "Mortgages."
Records, reports, and returns.
Auditing committee, reports, **168:25.**
Bank holding companies, **167A:5.**
Commissioner, annual report, **168:26.**
Deposit books, **276:57.**
Employees' retirement association, annual report, **168:40.**
Federal savings and loan association, conversion involving savings bank, **168:37, 168:38.**
Income tax returns, **62C:12.**
Loans or extension of credit to officers, etc., **168:20.**
Notice of elected officers and trustees, **168:15.**
Savings bank life insurance, **30A:11A.**
Wage reporting system, **62E:4, 62E:5.**
Recycling funds of cities and towns, deposit, **40:5.**
Reports.
Records, reports, and returns. See within this heading, "Records, reports, and returns."
Reserve balances, **168:27A.**
Residency requirements of corporators and trustees on consolidation or merger, **168:34B, 168:34D, 172:36.**
Retirement association for savings bank employees, **168:39 et seq.**
Annual report, **168:40.**
Bylaws of association, **168:40.**
Employee deduction, **168:41.**
Membership, **168:39.**
Property of association, **168:41.**
Retirement systems and pensions.
Deposit of pension or retirement system funds, **32:23.**
Employees' benefit association, **168:42 et seq.**
Investments in, **167F:2.**

SAVINGS BANKS —Cont'd
Retirement systems and pensions —Cont'd
Retirement association for savings bank employees. See within this heading, "Retirement association for savings bank employees."
Returns.
Records, reports and returns. See within this heading, "Records, reports, and returns."
Review of decisions of board of bank incorporation as to bank holding companies, **167A:4.**
Salaries.
Wages, salaries, and compensation.
Payroll and payroll deductions. See within this heading, "Payroll and payroll deductions."
Reporting system, **62E:4, 62E:5.**
Sales, **255:39A.**
Sales finance company, bank, **255D:1.**
Savings.
See SAVINGS AND LOAN ASSOCIATIONS.
Savings bank life insurance.
See SAVINGS BANK LIFE INSURANCE.
Schools and school systems, accounts and deposits, **71:16G½.**
Securities.
Investments. See within this heading, "Investments."
Stock and stockholders. See within this heading, "Stock and stockholders."
Sentence and punishment.
Imprisonment. See within this heading, "Imprisonment."
Social services.
Welfare and welfare department. See within this heading, "Welfare and welfare department."
Special assessments, exemption, **59:5.**
Special guaranty fund, formation of corporation, **168:5.**
Stabilization funds, deposit, **40:5B.**
State-chartered stockholder-owned bank, change of control, **168:34C, 170:26C, 172:26A.**
State funds, deposit of, **29:34A.**

SAVINGS BANKS —Cont'd
Statements.
Records, reports and returns. See within this heading, "Records, reports, and returns."
State or federally-chartered bank, purchase of assets or stock, **168:35.**
State or federally-chartered stock corporation, conversion of stock corporation, **168:34D.**
State treasurer, deposit of public moneys, **29:34A.**
Stock and stockholders.
Corporators. See within this heading, "Corporators."
Holding companies.
See BANK HOLDING COMPANIES.
Investments in stock, **167F:2, 167F:3.**
Savings bank, conversion to stockholder-owned corporation, **168:34C, 168:34E.**
State-chartered stockholder-owned bank, change of control, **168:34C, 170:26C, 172:26A.**
Stock corporation, conversion to state or federally-chartered stock corporation, **168:34D.**
Subscribers.
Corporators. See within this heading, "Corporators."
Supreme Judicial Court, jurisdiction to enforce bank holding company law, **167A:7.**
Sureties and suretyship.
Guaranty and suretyship. See within this heading, "Guaranty and suretyship."
Surplus, **168:27.**
Life insurance.
See SAVINGS BANK LIFE INSURANCE.
Taxation.
Corporation taxes.
See CORPORATION TAXES.
Exemption from taxation, **59:5, 168:41, 168:42-168:44.**
Federal savings banks, taxation of interest, **62:2.**
Income tax.
See INCOME TAX.
Local or special assessments, exemption, **59:5.**
Terms of office.
Board of trustees, **168:10.**
Corporators, **168:9.**

SAVINGS BANKS —Cont'd
Tewksbury Hospital, deposit of patient funds, **122:6, 122:9.**
Thrift institution, merger or consolidation, **168:34B.**
Time or date, audit, **168:25, 170:14.**
Towns.
Cities and towns. See within this heading, "Cities and towns."
Treasurer of bank, powers and duties, **168:21.**
Treasurer of state, deposit of public moneys, **29:34A.**
Trust companies.
See TRUST COMPANIES.
Trust departments, **167G:1 et seq.** See BANKS AND BANKING.
Trust deposits.
Trust funds. See within this heading, "Trust funds."
Trustee process.
Bond may be required of plaintiff, **246:31.**
Exemption from process. See within this heading, "Exemption from process."
Trustees, **168:10.**
Bank holding company law, penalties for violations, **167A:6.**
Co-operative bank director not to serve, **168:9.**
Election, **168:6, 168:14.**
Loans to trustees, **168:19.**
Meetings, **168:8, 168:11.**
Oaths, **168:7.**
Qualifications, **168:10.**
Residency requirement on consolidation or merger, **168:34B, 168:34D, 172:36.**
Vacancy in office, **168:14.**
Trust funds.
Cities and towns, deposit or investment trust funds, **44:54.**
Group insurance commission trust fund, investments and deposits, **32A:9A.**
Social services commissioner, deposit of funds held in trust in bank, **18B:18.**
Unknown legatees, deposit of legacies, **206:26.**
Urban redevelopment corporations.
Investment of deposits in projects, **121A:18A.**
Operating as redevelopment corporation, acquisition of site from housing authority, **121A:7A.**

SAVINGS BANKS —Cont'd
Urban renewal.
Housing and urban renewal. See within this heading, "Housing and urban renewal."
Utilities, deposit of funds, **155:3A.**
Vacancies in office, trustees and board of investment, **168:14.**
Veterans, information as to financial condition of, **115:2.**
Voting.
Bank holding company stock, **167A:2, 167A:3.**
Elections. See within this heading, "Elections."
Wages, salaries, and compensation.
Payroll and payroll deduction. See within this heading, "Payroll and payroll deductions."
Reporting system, **62E:4, 62E:5.**
Welfare and welfare department.
Disclosure of deposits of poor persons, **18:15, 122:22.**
Social services department, deposit of funds held in trust by commissioner in savings banks, **18B:18.**
Wills, deposit of bequests to counties, **34:23.**

SAVINGS CLAUSES.
Severability.
See SEVERABILITY OF ACT.

SAVOY.
District court, **218:1.**
Medical examiner district, **38:1.**
Senatorial district, **57:3.**

SAWDUST AND SHAVINGS.
Automatic sprinklers, **148:26.**
Coastal waters, pollution, **130:23, 130:24.**
Removal, **148:5.**
Storage or handling, **148:24.**

SAWED-OFF SHOTGUNS, 269:10.
Certificate by ballistics expert as prima facie evidence, **140:121A.**
Firearms and weapons generally.
See FIREARMS AND WEAPONS.

SAWMILLS.
Dust removal provisions for emery wheels inapplicable, **149:121.**
Stationary steam engine.
License, **140:115.**

SAY HELLO TO SOMEONE IN MASSACHUSETTS.
Official polka of Commonwealth, **2:44.**

SCAFFOLDING.
Minors under sixteen not to work, **149:61.**

SCALES.
See WEIGHTS AND MEASURES.

SCALLOPS, 130:73.
Adult scallops, defined, **130:70.**
Bag limit, **130:72.**
Brands and labels.
Labels or tags. See within this heading, "Labels or tags."
Closed seasons.
Seasons. See within this heading, "Seasons."
Commercial certificate or permit, **130:80.**
Contamination regulations, **130:74.**
Culling required, **130:70.**
Defined, **130:1.**
Director of division of marine fisheries, powers and duties, **130:70 et seq.**
Fines and penalties.
Tags or labels, violations, **130:92.**
Taking, **130:70, 130:72.**
Imported fish products, sale and advertising, **94:277B.**
Labels or tags, **130:92.**
Inapplicable provisions, **130:81, 130:82.**
Penalties, **130:92.**
Licenses and permits, **130:70, 130:73.**
Commercial permit or certificate, **130:80.**
Penalties.
Fines and penalties. See within this heading, "Fines and penalties."
Sales, **94:88B, 94:92B, 130:92.**
Seasons, **130:71, 130:73.**
Modification, **130:73.**
Seed scallops defined, **130:70.**
Shellfish, definition of, **130:1.**
Tags.
Labels or tags. See within this heading, "Labels or tags."
Violation of regulations, penalty, **130:70, 130:72.**
Weight, sale, **94:88B, 94:92B.**

SCALP HAIR PROSTHESIS.
Accident and sickness insurance.
Required coverage, **175:47T.**
Group insurance for state employees.
Required coverage, **32A:17E.**

SCALP HAIR PROSTHESIS —Cont'd
Health maintenance organizations.
Required coverage, **176G:4J.**
Medical service corporations.
Required coverage, **176A:8T.**
Group coverage, **176B:4R.**

SCALPING.
Lottery tickets, **10:29.**
Railroad tickets, **160:198B.**

SCAVENGERS.
Minors, employment, **149:69 et seq.**

SCENERY.
City and town road improvement, **40:15C.**
Control of outdoor advertising adjacent to interstate and primary highway systems, **93D:2.**
Defacing by advertisements, **266:126.**
Federal-aid highways, restoration and preservation of scenic beauty adjacent, **81:13B.**
Rivers and streams, establishment of system of scenic and recreational, **21:17B.**

SCHEDULE BONDS.
Militia officers, bonds, **33:109.**
State officers and employees arranging, **30:16.**

SCHEDULE INSURANCE.
Automobile insurance.
Blanket policies.
See AUTOMOBILE INSURANCE.

SCHEMATIC LIST.
Offices and departments of state, **30:45.**

SCHOLARSHIPS AND FELLOWSHIPS.
"Accredited educational institution" defined for survivors' benefits under contributory retirement law, **32:26.**
Agriculture department, intern scholarship program, **20:6A.**
Aliens.
Citizens and aliens. See within this heading, "Citizens and aliens."
Board of higher education, **15A:16.**
Bradford Durfee College of Technology, disposition of fines for violations of regulations, **74:42Q.**

**SCHOLARSHIPS AND
   FELLOWSHIPS** —Cont'd
Child Care Affordability
   Scholarship Assistance Fund,
   28A:5A.
Christa McAuliffe teacher
   incentive program, **15A:7.**
Christian A. Herter memorial
   scholarship program.
      See CHRISTIAN A. HERTER
         MEMORIAL
         SCHOLARSHIP
         PROGRAM.
Citizens and aliens.
   Clean waters scholarship
      program, **21:38A.**
   Food and Agriculture
      Department, requirements,
      20:6A.
Clean waters scholarship intern
   program, **21:38A.**
Consortium scholarships, **15A:7,
   15A:16.**
Contracts and agreements.
   Clean waters scholarship intern
      program, **21:38A.**
   Services under contract for
      intern program, **20:6A.**
Correctional employees killed in
   line of duty, award to children,
   15A:7.
Dentistry, **6:17, 15A:7.**
Education department.
   Higher education board.
      See EDUCATION
         DEPARTMENT.
Fines for violation of regulations,
   disposition, **73:18.**
Firefighters, award of scholarships
   to children of deceased, **15A:7.**
Food and Agriculture Department,
   intern scholarship program,
   20:6A.
General Court Fellowship
   Program, **75:33A.**
Higher education assistance
   corporation.
      See HIGHER EDUCATION
         ASSISTANCE
         CORPORATION.
Intern scholarship programs.
   Citizens and aliens. See within
      this heading, "Citizens and
      aliens."
   Clean waters scholarship intern
      program, **21:38A.**
   Contracts and agreements. See
      within this heading,
      "Contracts and agreements."
   Food and agriculture
      department, scholarship
      program, **20:6A.**

**SCHOLARSHIPS AND
   FELLOWSHIPS** —Cont'd
Matching scholarship grant
   program, **15A:7, 69:31B.**
Medical, dental and nursing
   scholarship board, **6:17.**
Medical specialties residents,
   grants and fellowships for
   hospital training, **17:6A.**
Medicine and related fields, **15A:7,
   115A:10.**
Military affairs.
   Selective Service Act, compliance
      by applicants for scholarship
      or other financial aid, **15A:7.**
   Veterans. See within this
      heading, "Veterans."
National Defense Education Act,
   Scholarships at University of
   Massachusetts, **75:33.**
National guard educational
   assistance program, **33:137.**
New Bedford Institute of
   Technology, **74:42Q.**
Nursing, **6:17, 15A:7.**
Parking fines on campus to be
   deposited in scholarship trust
   funds, **75:32A.**
Police officers and fire fighters,
   award of scholarships to
   children of deceased, **15A:7.**
Prisoners of war or servicemen
   missing in action,
   establishment of scholarships
   for children, **15A:7.**
Qualified state tuition program,
   180:17L.
Residence requirements for college
   and university scholarships,
   75:33.
Selective Service Act, compliance
   by applicants for scholarship
   or other financial aid, **15A:7.**
Soldiers.
   Veterans. See within this
      heading, "Veterans."
Surgery, training grants for
   fellows, **115A:10.**
Tax bill, donations to scholarship
   fund by taxpayers of cities and
   towns, **60:3C.**
Teachers.
   Tomorrow's teachers scholarship
      program, **15A:19D.**
University of Massachusetts,
   75:33.
   General Court Fellowship
      Program, **75:33A.**
   University scholarships, **75:33.**
Urology, training grants for
   fellows, **115A:10.**

**SCHOLARSHIPS AND
   FELLOWSHIPS** —Cont'd
Veterans.
   Prisoners of war or servicemen
      missing in action,
      establishment of
      scholarships for children,
      15A:7.
   Vietnam veterans, aid, **67:7A.**
Veterinary medicine, **15A:7.**
Vocational education programs at
   post-secondary level, **74:37C.**

**SCHOOL AGE CHILD CARE
   PROGRAM.**
Licenses, regulations, **28A:4,
   28A:9 et seq.**

SCHOOL AID.
**See SCHOOLS AND
   EDUCATION.**

**SCHOOL ATTENDANCE ACT,
   76:1 et seq.**

**SCHOOL BUSES AND
   TRANSPORTATION OF
   PUPILS, 71:7A, 90:7A et
   seq.**
Age of operator, **90:8A.**
Agricultural and technical
   institutes, **74A:11.**
   Independent agricultural and
      technical schools, **74A:11.**
Agricultural schools of counties,
   74:31A, 74:31B.
Aid.
   State aid or reimbursement. See
      within this heading, "State
      aid or reimbursement."
Air brakes, exception from
   requirement, **90:7.**
Allowances for transportation,
   payment to cities and towns,
   58:25B.
Application for license to operate
   school bus, **90:8A½.**
Appropriations by cities and
   towns, **40:5.**
   Games, transportation, **71:47.**
Athletic or extracurricular
   activities and events, **90:7D,
   159A:11A.**
Automobile insurance.
   Contract with cities or towns,
      school buses operated, **40:4.**
   Exemption from compulsory
      insurance, **90:1A.**
Bands of schools, transportation,
   71:47.
Bidders and bidding on school bus
   contracts, **71:7A.**
Blinker lights, **90:14.**

SCHOOL BUSES AND TRANSPORTATION OF PUPILS —Cont'd

Brakes, exception from requirement as to air brakes, **90:7.**

Camp buses as included in definition, **90:1.**

Certificate of insurance, **40:4.**

Charges.
Rates and charges. See within this heading, "Rates and charges."

Charter school students, **71:89.**

"Charter service" or "special service" as used in Motor Carriers of Passenger Law, transportation of children as within terms, **159A:11A.**

Chassis model year requirements, **90:1A, 90:7B.**

Cities and towns, **71:68.**
Appropriations by cities and towns. See within this heading, "Appropriations by cities and towns."
Education department may compel towns to furnish, **71:68.**
High school pupils of towns not maintaining high schools, payment of cost of transporting, **71:6.**
May contract, **40:4.**
Payment of transportation allowances to cities and towns, **58:25B.**

Civil rights.
Racial imbalance as affected by. See within this heading, "Racial imbalance as affected."

Committees, **71:7A.**
Discretion as to expending appropriations for transportation of pupils, **40:5.**
Power to contract for transportation of pupils, **40:4.**
Private way, committee not compelled to furnish transportation, **71:68.**

Community groups, vehicles used for transporting, **159A:32.**

Compulsory liability insurance, **40:4, 90:1A.**

Contracts and agreements.
Cities and towns may contract for transportation, **40:4.**

SCHOOL BUSES AND TRANSPORTATION OF PUPILS —Cont'd

Contracts and agreements —Cont'd
Motor carriers of passengers, transportation of school children as charter or special service, **159A:11A.**
Requirement as to contracts, **71:7A.**

Costs and expenses.
Appropriations by cities and towns. See within this heading, "Appropriations by cities and towns."
High school pupils of towns not maintaining high schools, payment of cost of transporting, **71:6.**
Non-white and minority pupils, transportation expenses, **15:1I.**
Private schools, **76:1.**
Racial imbalance. See within this heading, "Racial imbalance as affected."
Registration fee, **90:33.**
State aid or reimbursement. See within this heading, "State aid or reimbursement."

County agricultural schools, **74:31B, 74:31A.**

Crossing guards as exempt from civil service requirements, **31:48.**

Date.
Time or date. See within this heading, "Time or date."

Defined under motor vehicles law, **90:1.**

Designation as, to be painted on vehicle, **90:7D.**

Drivers, **90:8A.**

Education department.
See EDUCATION DEPARTMENT.

Elevated railways, tickets for pupils, **161:108.**

Emergency first aid or transportation rendered to injured students, exemption from liability, **71:55A.**

Emergency vehicles to stop, **89:7B.**

Equipment, **71:7A, 90:7 et seq.**

Examinations.
Applicant for operator's license, examination, **90:8A.**
Drivers, examination, **90:8A½.**

Expenses and expenditures.
Costs and expenses. See within this heading, "Costs and expenses."

SCHOOL BUSES AND TRANSPORTATION OF PUPILS —Cont'd

Extra-curricular school-sponsored activities, use to transport pupils, **90:7D, 159A:11A.**

Fee for registration, **90:33.**

Fines and penalties.
Overloading, **90:20.**
Permitting standees, **90:7L.**
Subsequent offenses, **71:7A, 90:14.**
Throwing or shooting missiles. See within this heading, "Throwing or shooting missiles."
Wages, operator accepting less than prescribed rates, **71:7A.**

Fire extinguisher, vehicle equipped, **90:7D.**

Flashing lights, **90:14.**

Games, transportation, **71:47.**

Grades or standards for equipment, minimum, **90:7C.**

Grants for cost of transportation to magnet school facilities, application, **71:37I.**

Guards at school crossings as exempt from civil service requirements, **31:48.**

Headlights to be illuminated while bus is in operation, **90:7B.**

High school pupils of towns not maintaining high schools, payment of cost, **71:6.**

Highway safety stations for children awaiting, **71:71A.**

Indemnity coverage for buses operated under city or town contract, **40:4.**

Independent agricultural and technical schools, **74A:11.**

Inspections.
Daily inspection by driver required, **90:7B.**

Insurance.
Automobile insurance. See within this heading, "Automobile insurance."

Interfering with driver, **159:104.**

Investigations.
Periodic inspection of buses, **90:7A.**

Islands, pupils living, **76:14.**

Lettering, **90:7D.**

License plates for vehicles used for transportation of pupils, **90:2.**

Licenses and permits.
Application for license to operate school bus, **90:8A½.**

**SCHOOL BUSES AND
  TRANSPORTATION OF
  PUPILS** —Cont'd
Licenses and permits —Cont'd
  Operators' licenses, **90:8A.**
  School service permits,
    159A:11A.
Lights, **90:7.**
  Flashing lights, **90:14.**
  Headlights to be illuminated
    while bus is in operation,
    90:7B.
Machinery and equipment, **71:7A,
  90:7 et seq.**
Magnet school facilities,
  application for grants to cover
  cost of transportation, **71:37I.**
Mentally ill and retarded persons,
  19B:17.
  Special education. See within
    this heading, "Special
    education."
Mileage rates for carriers
  furnishing special service or
  school service, **159A:11A.**
Minimum standards for
  equipment, **90:7C.**
Minors, bus driver's license not
  issued, **159A:9.**
Mirrors and other exterior devices,
  lateral projection, **90:19.**
Missiles.
  Throwing or shooting missiles.
    See within this heading,
    "Throwing or shooting
    missiles."
Motor vehicles, operation in
  vicinity of school buses, **90:14.**
Municipal finance.
  Appropriations by cities and
    towns. See within this
    heading, "Appropriations by
    cities and towns."
Municipalities.
  Cities and towns. See within
    this heading, "Cities and
    towns."
Non-white and minority pupils,
  transportation expenses,
  15:1I.
Operation of, rules governing,
  90:8A.
Operators' licenses, **90:8A.**
Overloading, penalty, **90:20.**
Painting, **90:7D.**
Passing school buses, **90:14.**
Payment of transportation
  allowances to cities and towns,
  58:25B.
Penalties.
  Fines and penalties. See within
    this heading, "Fines and
    penalties."

**SCHOOL BUSES AND
  TRANSPORTATION OF
  PUPILS** —Cont'd
Permits.
  Licenses and permits. See
    within this heading,
    "Licenses and permits."
Physically disabled pupils, state
  reimbursement to small
  towns, **71:10, 71:11.**
Private schools, **40:5.**
  Public expense, **76:1.**
  Street or elevated railways,
    special rates, **161:108.**
Private way, committee not
  compelled to furnish
  transportation, **71:68.**
Pupil, defined, **90:1.**
Qualifications for operators, **90:8A.**
Racial imbalance as affected,
  71:37D.
  Magnet school facilities,
    application for grants, cost
    of transportation, **71:37I.**
  Transportation fees of busing
    children to achieve racial
    balance, **15:1I.**
Railroad crossings, stopping,
  90:15.
Rates and charges.
  Elevated railways, tickets for
    pupils, **161:108.**
  Mileage rates for carriers
    furnishing special service or
    school service, **159A:11A.**
  Special rates by carriers, **159:18,
    161:107, 161:108.**
Red blinker lights, **90:14.**
Regional school districts, **71:16C,
  71:16D.**
Registrar of motor vehicles.
  Equipment, registrar may adopt
    special regulations, **90:7A.**
  Licensing of school bus
    operators, duties, **90:8A.**
  Periodic inspections, **90:7A.**
Registration, **90:1A, 90:2, 90:5,
  90:9.**
  Fee, **90:33.**
Reimbursement.
  State aid or reimbursement. See
    within this heading, "State
    aid or reimbursement."
Retarded persons.
  Mentally ill and retarded
    persons. See within this
    heading, "Mentally ill and
    retarded persons."
Safety equipment, **71:7A, 90:7 et
  seq.**
School service permits, **159A:11A.**

**SCHOOL BUSES AND
  TRANSPORTATION OF
  PUPILS** —Cont'd
Sealed bids, contracts to be
  awarded only, **71:7A.**
Seatbelts, **90:7D.**
Semiannual safety inspections of
  vehicles, **90:7A.**
Service vehicles, licensing and
  registration, **159A:11A.**
Sex offense conviction as affecting
  licensing of driver, **90:8A.**
Shooting missiles at.
  Throwing or shooting missiles.
    See within this heading,
    "Throwing or shooting
    missiles."
Signaling, **90:14B.**
Solicitation of funds, stopping for
  purpose, **85:17A.**
Special education, **71B:8, 71B:10.**
  Special needs, transportation of
    children, **71:11, 71B:8.**
  Display of name of owner,
    90:7CC.
Special rates for school children,
  159:18, 161:107, 161:108.
Special regulations as to
  equipment, registrar of motor
  vehicles may adopt, **90:7A.**
"Special service" or "charter
  service," transportation of
  school pupils as within terms
  under motor carrier of
  passengers law, **159A:11A.**
Speed restrictions, **90:17.**
  Passing stopped school bus,
    speed permitted, **90:14.**
Standards, failure to conform to,
  penalty, **90:7C.**
Standees, restrictions, **90:7L.**
State aid or reimbursement,
  71:7A, 71:16C, 71A:8, 71B:14.
  Magnet school facilities,
    application for grants for
    cost of transportation,
    71:37I.
  Physically disabled pupils,
    71:10.
  Private enterprises, aid for
    school buses in competition,
    71:7C.
  Public transportation used for
    transporting pupils, costs
    incurred in maintaining,
    71:7B.
  Regional school districts,
    71:16C, 71:16D.
  See REGIONAL SCHOOL
    DISTRICTS.
Stopping.
  Other vehicle stopping, **89:7B,
    90:14.**

SCHOOL BUSES AND TRANSPORTATION OF PUPILS —Cont'd

Stopping —Cont'd
Passing stopped school bus, **90:14.**
Railroad crossings, stopping, **90:15.**
Street railways, special service cars and special rates, **161:107, 161:108.**
Summer school, use of school busses to transport pupils to and, **159A:11A.**
Telecommunications and energy department, supervision of school service motor carriers, **159A:11A.**
Throwing or shooting missiles, **159:104.**
Arrest and jurisdiction, **159:93, 159:94, 159:104.**
Time or date.
Duration of contracts for service, **40:4.**
Operator's license, **90:8A.**
Periodic inspections, **90:7A.**
Towns.
Cities and towns. See within this heading, "Cities and towns."
Trespass, **266:120.**
Vocational education and schools, **74:8A, 161:108.**
Requirements as to vehicles used in transportation of vocational school students, **90:1, 90:7D½.**
Special rates on street or elevated railways, **161:108.**
Wage rates for operators as effected by Massachusetts Bay transportation authority wages, **71:7A.**
Width limitation, **90:19.**

SCHOOL DISCRIMINATION LAW, 76:5, 151C:1 et seq.

**SCHOOL DISTRICTS.
See SCHOOLS AND EDUCATION.**

SCHOOLHOUSE STRUCTURAL STANDARDS BOARD.
Public safety executive office, agencies within, **6A:18.**

**SCHOOL NURSES.
See NURSES AND NURSING SERVICES.**

SCHOOLS AND EDUCATION, 71:1 et seq.

Abortion, discrimination against medical school applicants opposing, **112:12I.**
Absence or presence, **76:1 et seq.**
Education commissioner, **15:1F.**
Emergency medical care, presence of person trained in.
Athletic activities. See within this heading, "Athletic activities."
Leaves of absence. See within this heading, "Leaves of absence."
Pupils.
Attendance. See within this heading, "Attendance."
Teachers.
See TEACHERS.
Abused and neglected children, committee's notice of reporting requirements to school personnel, **71:37L.**
Academically talented children.
Advisory commission on academically talented pupils, **15:6C.**
Special programs, **71:1.**
Academies, penalty for burning, **266:2.**
Accident.
See ACCIDENT AND SICKNESS INSURANCE.
Accountants of cities and towns, committees to prescribe forms and designations used, **41:57.**
Accounts and accounting.
Colleges.
See COLLEGES AND UNIVERSITIES.
Districts.
See REGIONAL SCHOOL DISTRICTS.
Education department.
See EDUCATION DEPARTMENT.
Savings accounts, **71:16G½.**
Accreditation of all schools of higher learning, accepted applicants for admission to be given notice, **69:31C.**
Accredited educational institution defined for purposes of survivors' benefits under contributory retirement law, **32:26.**
Acquisition of property, approval by vote at town meeting, **71:16.**

SCHOOLS AND EDUCATION —Cont'd

Actions.
Correspondence school bond, **75C:4.**
Escaping inmates of state training schools, action for damages, **120:13A.**
Exclusion of pupil, action, **76:16.**
Racial imbalance in schools, actions concerning, **71:37D.**
Regional school districts.
See REGIONAL SCHOOL DISTRICTS.
Special jurisdiction, action to compel city or town to appropriate for support of public education, **214:3.**
Adjustment counselors.
Psychology-related professions or occupations excluded from regulations, **112:125.**
Tenure for, **71:41.**
Administration.
See ADMINISTRATION AND FINANCE EXECUTIVE OFFICE.
Administrative aides and interns, **71:38, 71:38G.**
Administrative procedure.
Proceedings to revoke or suspend power to grant degrees, **69:30A.**
Teachers, dismissal, **71:42.**
Administrator.
Employment contract, **71:38.**
Reports of abused and neglected children under 16 to be made, **119:51A.**
Special education administrator appointed, **71B:3A.**
Admission to bar, educational requirements for.
See ATTORNEYS AT LAW.
Adult educational programs.
See ADULT EDUCATIONAL PROGRAMS.
Advertising.
See ADVERTISING AND ADVERTISEMENTS.
Aeronautics, **6:57, 64H:1, 64I:1.**
After school programs, licensing or approval, **28A:9 et seq.**
Age.
See AGE.
Agreements.
Contracts and agreements. See within this heading, "Contracts and agreements."

SCHOOLS AND EDUCATION
—Cont'd

Agricultural and technical institutes, independent, **74A:1 to 74A:23.**
See AGRICULTURAL AND TECHNICAL INSTITUTES.

Agriculture.
See AGRICULTURE.

Aid and assistance.
Agricultural and technical institutes.
State aid, **74A:12.**
Building assistance. See within this heading, "Building assistance."
Colleges.
See COLLEGES AND UNIVERSITIES.
Department.
See EDUCATION DEPARTMENT.
Distribution, **10:35, 58:18B et seq., 59:20.**
Federal aid or funds. See within this heading, "Federal aid or funds."
Gifts, grants, and gratuities. See within this heading, "Gifts, grants, and gratuities."
Higher education assistance corporation.
See HIGHER EDUCATION ASSISTANCE CORPORATION.
Loans to students. See within this heading, "Loans to students."
Municipal finance. See within this heading, "Municipal finance."
Racial imbalance. See within this heading, "Racial imbalance."
State aid or reimbursement. See within this heading, "State aid or reimbursement."
Teachers.
See TEACHERS.
Transportation of pupils.
See SCHOOL BUSES AND TRANSPORTATION OF PUPILS.

Alcohol education program.
See ALCOHOL EDUCATION PROGRAMS.

Alcoholic liquors.
Educational corporations and institutions.
See ALCOHOLIC LIQUORS.

SCHOOLS AND EDUCATION
—Cont'd

Aldermen and selectmen.
Approval of fees paid counsel for school committee, **71:37E, 71:37F.**
Employment of counsel for general purposes, approval of expenditures, **71:37F.**

Alteration or amendment.
Change. See within this heading, "Change."

Ambulance operators and attendants to be trained in emergency medical care, **111C:6.**

American and Canadian French cultural exchange commission, duties, **6:157.**

American citizenship, education as to.
See EDUCATION DEPARTMENT.

American history month, observance, **6:15C.**

American Medical Association, approval of schools or courses for physical therapists, **112:23C.**

American sign language recognized as independent language, **71:2B.**

Animals.
See ANIMALS.

Annual budgets, public viewing, **71:38N.**

Annual report.
Records, reports, and returns. See within this heading, "Records, reports, and returns."

Annuities.
See ANNUITIES AND ANNUITY CONTRACTS.

Appeal.
See APPEAL AND REVIEW.

Appearance and dress of students, limitation on school officials' right to regulate, **71:83.**

Apprentice training division of labor and workforce development department, **23:11E-23:11L, 74:7B.**

Appropriations.
Allocations of, prohibition against, **71:34.**
Board of higher education, **15A:15.**
Cities or towns, appropriations by.
Municipal finance. See within this heading, "Municipal finance."

SCHOOLS AND EDUCATION
—Cont'd

Appropriations —Cont'd
Colleges.
See COLLEGES AND UNIVERSITIES.
Defined for purpose of school tax provision, **59:23C.**
Eyeglasses and hearing aids, **40:5.**
Regional school districts, **71:16B.**
Expenses of planning board, **71:14.**
Illegal appropriations by, restraint, **40:53.**
Teachers and other professional employees, salaries, **71:16 (note), 71:42B.**
Reimbursement appropriation, **59:23.**
Special education, **71B:5.**
State aid or reimbursement. See within this heading, "State aid or reimbursement."

Arbitration of discharge of teachers or other employees of school district, **71:42.**

Arbor and Bird Day, observance, **6:15.**

Archeological resources under water, preservation, **91:63.**

Architects, training experience required for examination for registration, **112:60C.**

Arithmetic required to be taught, **71:1, 71:18.**

Armed forces.
Military. See within this heading, "Military affairs."

Assault and battery, **71:37G, 265:13D.**
Physical restraint.
Use on students, **71:37G.**

Assessors of taxes.
Training programs, **58:1, 58:21A.**

Assistance.
Aid and assistance. See within this heading, "Aid and assistance."

Athletic activities.
Appropriations by municipalities, **40:5, 71:47.**
Borrowing by municipality for construction of facility, **44:7.**
Boxing instruction.
See BOXING AND BOXING MATCHES.

Calisthenics, **71:3.**

SCHOOLS AND EDUCATION
—Cont'd
Athletic activities —Cont'd
Cheerleaders' uniforms,
payment, **71:47.**
Coaches, contract for
employment, **71:47A.**
Committees. See within this
heading, "Committees."
County and other agricultural
schools.
Employment of athletic
director, coaches, faculty
member and physician in
connection with program,
74:31B.
Rental of facilities for practice
sessions of teams, **74:31B.**
Supervision of athletics and
expenditures, **74:31B.**
Disposition of receipts, **71:47.**
Education in.
See PHYSICAL EDUCATION
AND FITNESS.
Emergency medical care,
presence at school football
games, **71:54A.**
Interscholastic athletics,
71:47.
Insurance plan covering.
Administration, **175:29.**
Cities and towns to make
appropriations, **40:5.**
Intercollegiate sailing programs,
exemption from lifesaving
equipment requirements for
vessels used, **90B:5A.**
Municipal appropriations, **40:5,
71:47.**
Physicians.
Employment in connection
with athletic program of
county agricultural school,
74:31B.
Football games, attendance,
71:54A.
Retirement of teachers, **32:1.**
Supervision and control of
athletic and other
organizations, **71:47.**
Attendance, **76:1 et seq.**
Abuse prevention, reporting
requirements for attendance
officer, **119:51A.**
Age for attendance,
establishment of maximum
and minimum, **76:1.**
Civil service, attendance
supervisors as subject,
31:52.
Committee.
Enforcement, **76:1.**

SCHOOLS AND EDUCATION
—Cont'd
Attendance —Cont'd
Committee —Cont'd
Plans for attendance of child
outside place of residence,
76:12, 76:12A.
Powers and duties, **71:37.**
Religious education, absence
for excused, **76:1.**
Compulsory attendance, **76:1 et
seq.**
Continuation schools or
courses, **71:22.**
Continuation schools and
courses. See within this
heading, "Continuation
schools and courses."
Deaf children, **76:2A.**
Dependent children. See within
this heading, "Dependent
children."
Diseased children, attendance,
71:55, 71:56.
Employment permit, **76:1.**
Enforcement of attendance rules
and parental duties, **76:1,
76:2.**
Establishment of minimum and
maximum ages, **76:1.**
Evening schools, attendance by
certain illiterate minors,
76:3.
Excused absences, **76:1.**
Experimental school project,
15:1G, 76:1.
Illiterate minors, attendance at
evening schools, **76:3.**
Inducing unlawful absence, **76:4.**
Jurisdiction, **76:2.**
Juvenile courts.
See JUVENILE COURTS
AND DELINQUENT
CHILDREN.
Married women, evening school
attendance by certain, **76:3.**
Maximum and minimum ages
for attendance,
establishment, **76:1.**
Mental condition of child, **76:1.**
Nautical schools, excuse from
other schools of boys
attending, **74:52.**
Nonresident pupils, **76:6, 76:12
et seq.**
Notice of absence, **76:1A, 76:18,
76:19.**
Non-custodial parents,
71:34H.
Number of absences permitted,
76:1.

SCHOOLS AND EDUCATION
—Cont'd
Attendance —Cont'd
Parents, duties, **76:2.**
Penalties, **76:2 et seq.**
Physical condition of child, **76:1.**
Place, **76:1, 76:5, 76:6.**
Private schools, **72:2, 76:1.**
Procedure for permanent
absence, **76:19.**
Racial imbalance. See within
this heading, "Racial
imbalance."
Regional school districts, duty of
temporary secretary,
71:16A.
Religious matters, **76:1,
151C:2B.**
Required, when, **76:1.**
Residence of parent or guardian,
attendance in places other
than, **76:6, 76:12 et seq.**
Special education programs,
76:1, 76:2A.
Supervisors of attendance. See
within this heading,
"Supervisors of attendance."
Training programs for tax
assessor, attendance
required, **59:21A.**
Twelve month school year plan,
pupil attendance
requirement, **76:1.**
Where child may attend, **76:1,
76:5, 76:6.**
Attorney general.
See ATTORNEY GENERAL.
Attorneys at law.
See ATTORNEYS AT LAW.
Attorneys' fees.
Collective bargaining, limit on
fee expended by regional
school district, **71:16,
71:37E.**
Committee of school, fees of
counsel, **71:37F.**
Record, fees in proceedings to
compel furnishing, **71:34B.**
Audio-visual materials.
Procurement, contracts awarded
without bids, **30B:7.**
Audio-visual media specialists,
certification, **71:38G.**
Automobiles.
Motor vehicles. See within this
heading, "Motor vehicles."
Bands, equipment and
transportation, **71:47.**
Banks and banking.
Colleges.
See COLLEGES AND
UNIVERSITIES.

SCHOOLS AND EDUCATION
—Cont'd

Banks and banking —Cont'd
  Co-operative banks, school loans
    or savings accounts, **170:13,
    170:16, 170:19.**
  Deposits and accounts,
    71:16G½.
  Municipalities, **71:71C,
    71:71E.**
  School savings deposit
    programs, **167D:10.**
  Holding companies, exemption of
    educational corporations
    from laws, **167A:1.**
  Massachusetts Higher Education
    Assistance Corporation,
    guarantees, **167D:12.**
  Students, establishment of
    banks, **167:37B.**
  Trust company officers,
    education loans extended,
    172:18.
Barbers, **112:87K, 112:87P.**
  See BARBERS.
Bilingual education, **71A:1-71A:9.**
  See BILINGUAL EDUCATION.
Bill of rights, required teaching,
  71:2.
Blind persons, **6:134, 6:143.**
  See BLIND PERSONS.
Board of education.
  See EDUCATION
    DEPARTMENT.
Board of higher education, **15A:1
  to 15A:36.**
  See BOARD OF HIGHER
    EDUCATION.
Boards of trustees of state
  institutions of higher learning,
  student members, **268A:23A.**
Bonds and debentures.
  Municipal finance. See within
    this heading, "Municipal
    finance."
Books.
  See TEXTBOOKS.
Bootblacking, regulation, **101:19.**
Boston.
  See BOSTON.
Boxing instruction.
  See BOXING AND BOXING
    MATCHES.
Breakfast program for needy
  children, **15:1G.**
Budgets.
  See BUDGETS.
Building assistance, **70B:1 to
  70B:19.**
  Advisory board.
    Composition, **70B:3.**
    Powers, **70B:3.**

SCHOOLS AND EDUCATION
—Cont'd

Building assistance —Cont'd
  Alternative projects.
    Projects neither construction
      nor renovation, **70B:14.**
  Applications for reimbursement,
    70B:4.
  Applications for school facilities
    grants, **70B:6.**
  Appropriations, annual, **70B:7.**
  Approval.
    Priorities, **70B:8.**
  Bond issues.
    Interest rate, **70B:19.**
    Refunding, **70B:13.**
    School facilities grants.
      Payments, projects financed
        with, **70B:11.**
  Certification of payments,
    70B:10.
  Cost criteria.
    Alternative projects, **70B:14.**
  Defined terms, **70B:2.**
  Effect on existing loans, **70B:18.**
  Establishment of program,
    70B:3.
  Financing.
    Study and review, **70B:7.**
  First annual estimated
    payments, **70B:7.**
  Interest rate, **70B:19.**
  Maintenance assessment
    program, **70B:16.**
  Maximum eligible cost and size
    standards for projects,
    70B:9.
  Newly admitted cities or towns,
    70B:12.
  Notice of interest rate, **70B:19.**
  Policy and review standards,
    70B:3.
  Priorities for approval, **70B:8.**
  Purpose, **70B:1, 70B:3.**
  Regional school districts.
    See REGIONAL SCHOOL
      DISTRICTS.
  Reimbursement for surveys of
    school conditions, **70B:4.**
  Reports, **70B:17.**
  Sale or lease of assisted
    structure or facility, **70B:15.**
  School facilities grants, **70B:5.**
    Applications, best interest
      determination, **70B:6.**
    Effect on existing loans,
      70B:18.
    Payments, **70B:10.**
      Bond issues, projects
        financed with, **70B:11.**
  Standards and procedures,
    70B:9.

SCHOOLS AND EDUCATION
—Cont'd

Building assistance —Cont'd
  Temporary loans.
    Bond issues, refunding,
      70B:13.
Building assistance commission,
  increase in membership and
  grants for approved school
  projects, **71:1. (note)**
Building regulations and
  standards board, continuing
  educational program, **143:99.**
Buildings, **71:68 et seq.**
  Assistance.
    Building assistance. See
      within this heading,
      "Building assistance."
  Charter schools, **71:89.**
  Citizenship classes, **69:8, 69:9.**
  Committees. See within this
    heading, "Committees."
  Construction.
    Grants, **44:19.**
    Regional school districts.
      See REGIONAL SCHOOL
        DISTRICTS.
    State aid or reimbursement.
      See within this heading,
        "State aid or
        reimbursement."
  Damaging or defacing school
    buildings.
    Penalties, **266:98.**
  Examination by school
    physician, **71:54.**
  Insurance. See within this
    heading, "Insurance."
  Maintenance assessment
    program, **70B:16.**
  Nursing or convalescent homes,
    requirements as to
    licensing, **111:71.**
  Regional school districts.
    See REGIONAL SCHOOL
      DISTRICTS.
  Renting or leasing storage space,
    71:16.
  School building assistance
    program, **70B:1 to 70B:19.**
  Schoolhouse structural
    standards board as agency
    within public safety
    executive office, **6A:18.**
  Spitting, **270:14, 270:15.**
  State aid for construction.
    State aid or reimbursement.
      See within this heading,
        "State aid or
        reimbursement."
  State building code as applicable
    to school buildings, **15:1G.**

SCHOOLS AND EDUCATION
—Cont'd

Buildings —Cont'd
Vocational education.
  See VOCATIONAL
    EDUCATION AND
    SCHOOLS.
Buses, **71:7A, 90:7A-90:7D.**
  See SCHOOL BUSES AND
    TRANSPORTATION OF
    PUPILS.
Business administrators, **71:38,
  71:41, 71:41A, 71:42, 71:42D,
  71:43 et seq.**
Business demonstration projects
  authorized, **71:37K.**
Business schools.
  See BUSINESS SCHOOLS.
Bylaws of educational corporation,
  180:7.
Cable television company's duty to
  provide cable drop, **166A:5.**
Calisthenics, **71:3.**
Camps, duties of school
  superintendent with regard to
  children's health camps,
  111:62B, 111:62C.
Canada.
  American and Canadian French
    cultural exchange
    commission, duties, **6:17,
    6:157.**
  Licensing of Canadian medical
    school graduates, **112:2.**
Cancer in women, schools
  providing programs of
  instruction for early detection
  of certain types, **71:1.**
Cardiopulmonary resuscitation to
  be taught, **71:1.**
Carnegie School Grant Program,
  15:63 et seq.
Carrying weapons, display of
  posters on laws, **269:11.**
Census, **71:2, 71:3.**
Centralized weekly payroll system
  for teachers and supervisors,
  establishment, **29:31.**
Certificates and certification.
  Administrative interns, **71:38G.**
  Annuity contracts for public
    educational institution
    employees, certification as to
    premiums payable, **15:18A.**
  Chiropractors, educational
    requirement for issuance of
    license renewal certificate,
    112:96.
  Co-operative education
    programs, certification to
    civil service director of
    students enrolled, **30:60.**

SCHOOLS AND EDUCATION
—Cont'd

Certificates and certification
  —Cont'd
  Department of education.
    See EDUCATION
      DEPARTMENT.
  Educational certificates.
    See LABOR AND
      WORKFORCE
      DEVELOPMENT.
  Educational personnel.
    See INTERSTATE
      COMPACTS AND
      AGREEMENTS.
  Evening classes and schools,
    certificate violations, **149:98.**
  Health certificate for return to
    school, **71:55.**
  High school pupil, certificate to
    attend school in another
    town, **71:6.**
  Insurance on buses, certificate,
    40:4.
  Interstate compacts.
    See INTERSTATE
      COMPACTS AND
      AGREEMENTS.
  Loan defaulters denied issuance
    or renewal of certificates,
    30A:13, 112:61.
  Principals, and supervisory
    personnel, certification,
    71:38G.
  Provisional educators, **71:38G.**
  Revenue commissioner, amount
    of aid payable to each city
    and town certified, **70:2.**
  Special education, **131:13.**
  Teachers, **71:38G.**
    See TEACHERS.
Chairmen of committees.
  Committees. See within this
    heading, "Committees."
Change.
  Charter cities, notice of changes
    in plans for construction or
    alteration of school building,
    43:34.
  Charter of educational
    institutions, approval of
    amendments, **69:30, 69:31.**
  Marital status of teacher or
    superintendent, change of,
    as cause for dismissal,
    71:42.
  Name of educational
    corporation, change, **180:11.**
  Purposes of educational
    corporation, change, **180:10,
    180:11.**

SCHOOLS AND EDUCATION
—Cont'd

Change —Cont'd
  Racial imbalance, change in
    district to eliminate,
    71:37D.
Charities.
  See CHARITIES AND
    CHARITABLE
    CONTRIBUTIONS.
Charters.
  Amendments to charters of
    educational institutions,
    approval, **69:30, 69:31.**
  City charters.
    See CITY CHARTERS.
  Forfeiture of educational
    corporation's charter for
    violations as to gaming laws
    or boxing matches, **180:27,
    180:28.**
Charter schools, schoolhouses,
  71:89.
Cheerleaders' uniforms, payment,
  71:47.
Chiropractors, requirements for
  issuance of license renewal
  certificate, **112:96.**
Christa McAuliffe teacher
  incentive program.
  See CHRISTA MCAULIFFE
    TEACHER INCENTIVE
    PROGRAM.
Christian A. Herter memorial
  scholarship program.
  See CHRISTIAN A. HERTER
    MEMORIAL
    SCHOLARSHIP
    PROGRAM.
Christmas and other festivals,
  guidelines for celebration,
  71:31A.
Cities and towns, distribution of
  school aid, **10:35, 58:18B,
  58:18F, 59:20.**
Citizens.
  See EDUCATION COUNCIL
    FOR FOREIGN MEDICAL
    GRADUATES.
Citizenship classes.
  American citizenship.
    See EDUCATION
      DEPARTMENT.
Citizenship, discrimination against
  child's attendance on basis of
  national origin, **76:5.**
City charters.
  See CITY CHARTERS.
City council.
  Collective bargaining, **71:16.**
  Eyeglasses and hearing aids for
    school children,
    appropriations, **40:5.**

SCHOOLS AND EDUCATION
—Cont'd
City department of education.
See EDUCATION
DEPARTMENT.
City finance.
Municipal finance. See within
this heading, "Municipal
finance."
Civics, required subject, **71:2.**
Civil rights, **76:5.**
Accommodation or resort,
exemption from laws as to
discrimination in places,
272:92A.
Commission against
discrimination advisory
board, membership, **6:56.**
Disciplinary programs and codes
of conduct, public schools,
71:37H.
Education department.
Racial imbalance in schools.
See EDUCATION
DEPARTMENT.
Equal education improvement
fund, **15:1I.**
Fair educational practices,
151C:1 et seq.
See FAIR EDUCATIONAL
PRACTICES.
Medical school applicants
opposing abortion,
discrimination against,
112:12I.
Notice and knowledge.
Racial imbalance. See within
this heading, "Racial
imbalance."
Private school, discrimination as
affecting availability of
public health services for
students, **71:57.**
Programs against discrimination
in employment, education,
151B:3.
Racial imbalance. See within
this heading, "Racial
imbalance."
Schoolhouse construction grants
to reduce or eliminate racial
imbalance, **15:1I.**
Sex discrimination. See within
this heading, "Sex
discrimination."
Special education, **71B:6.**
Teachers.
See TEACHERS.
Civil rights week, observance,
6:12P.
Civil service.
See CIVIL SERVICE.

SCHOOLS AND EDUCATION
—Cont'd
Clinics, excepting as to licensing,
111:52.
Closing for teachers' meetings,
71:73.
Coaches.
See ATHLETICS.
Collaborative education programs,
40:4E, 71:40.
Emergency first aid or
transportation rendered to
injured students, exemption
of employees from civil
liability, **71:55A.**
Pensions and retirement
systems, reimbursements,
32:28.
Private school tuition paid,
71:71D.
Public employer as including
educational collaborative,
258:1.
Regional school districts.
See REGIONAL SCHOOL
DISTRICTS.
School committees to prepay
tuition, **41:56, 71:71D.**
Teacher's salary and
compensation, **71:40.**
Collective bargaining, **71:16,
71:37E, 71:37F, 71:41.**
Colleges.
See COLLEGES AND
UNIVERSITIES.
Commission against discrimination
advisory board, membership,
6:56.
Commissioner of education.
See EDUCATION
DEPARTMENT.
Committees, **71:35 et seq.**
Abused and neglected children,
notice of reporting
requirements to school
personnel, **71:37L.**
Admission of students from
outside of Commonwealth,
71:6A.
Adult physical fitness programs,
use of school gymnasiums,
71:71B.
Aldermen and selectmen. See
within this heading,
"Aldermen and selectmen."
American citizenship, classes,
69:9, 69:9A, 69:10.
Annuity contracts, purchase,
71:37B, 71:43.
Athletics.
Coaches, contracts for
employment, **71:47A.**

SCHOOLS AND EDUCATION
—Cont'd
Committees —Cont'd
Athletics —Cont'd
Expending appropriations for
students injured, **40:5.**
Supervision and control of
athletic organization,
71:47.
Trainers, hiring, **112:23E.**
At-large members, incumbent
candidates, **54:41, 54:42.**
Attendance. See within this
heading, "Attendance."
Attorneys, **71:37A, 71:37E,
71:37F.**
Ballot statement of prior holding
of office, **53:34.**
Bilingual education.
See BILINGUAL
EDUCATION.
Books.
See TEXTBOOKS.
Bootblacking, regulation, **101:19.**
Building committee, school
committee representation,
71:68.
Business demonstration projects,
authorization, **71:37K.**
Cardiopulmonary resuscitation,
decision that instruction
shall not be offered, **71:1.**
Certificate to attend high school
of another town, **71:6.**
Christmas and other festivals,
establishment of guidelines
for celebration, **71:31A.**
Citizenship, classes, **69:9, 69:9A,
69:10.**
City charters, **43:31-43:36.**
See CITY CHARTERS.
Collaborative educational
programs, committees to
prepay tuition, **41:56,
71:71D.**
Commencement of term of office
of committee members in
cities, **71:35.**
Community interest, committee
to allow use of property for
purposes, **71:71.**
Community school programs,
handling of moneys
received, **71:71C, 71:71E.**
Compensation of members,
71:52.
Treasurers of regional
vocational school
committees, **71:16A.**
Compensation of superintendent
fixed, **71:59.**

SCHOOLS AND EDUCATION
—Cont'd
Committees —Cont'd
Compliance with law by, duty of education board, **15:1G.**
Conservation of soil, water and related resources committee, **21:20.**
Consolidation of functions with cities or towns, **71:37M.**
Contagious diseases, notice to committee, **111:113.**
Contracts and agreements.
Charter cities, interest in contracts by committee members, **43:27.**
Ensuing fiscal year, committee's contracts, **71:49A.**
Expenditure of federal funds, contracts with other committees as to programs involving, **40:4A.**
Counsel, **71:37A, 71:37E, 71:37F.**
Course of study in industrial or vocational schools, **74:37A.**
Degrees, authority to grant, **71:79.**
Director of occupational guidance and placement, appointment, **71:38A, 71:38D.**
District representation, **43:129 et seq.**
Duties, **71:37.**
Educational collaboratives, committees to prepay tuition, **41:56, 71:71D.**
Educational television, school committees may budget funds, **71:13F.**
Elections.
See ELECTIONS.
Emergency care at football games, payment of cost of providing, **71:54A.**
Establishment and maintenance of course on junior college level, **71:75.**
Estimates, state aid to be included, **70:10.**
Evening classes.
See EVENING CLASSES AND SCHOOLS.
Exclusion of certain children, **76:16 et seq.**
Executive officer, superintendent, **71:59.**
Exhibitions and expositions, **71:51.**

SCHOOLS AND EDUCATION
—Cont'd
Committees —Cont'd
Extended services for children of employed mothers.
Establishment, **71:26A.**
Expenditure of funds, **71:26C.**
Operation, **71:26B.**
Eye protective devices, requirement as to wearing, **71:55C.**
Federal aid or funds. See within this heading, "Federal aid or funds."
Fiscal year, contracts for services in ensuing year, **71:49A.**
Flags to be furnished, **71:69.**
Food services.
See FOOD SERVICES AND FREE LUNCH PROGRAMS.
Forms and designations prescribed to be used by town accountants, **41:57.**
Free lectures, committee may provide, **71:27.**
Funds for services for children of employed mothers, duties, **71:26B.**
Gifts.
Acceptance and disbursement of gift, **71:37A.**
Compensation to employees granted leaves of absence from grants or gifts, **71:41A.**
Patriotic plaques, acceptance, **71:69A.**
Government, classes in principles, **69:9, 69:9A, 69:10.**
Hawking and peddling by certain minors, regulated, **101:19.**
Health board to notify concerning contagious diseases, **111:113.**
High schools.
See HIGH SCHOOLS.
Highway safety stations, designation and discontinuance, **71:71A.**
Hiring of employees, **43:32, 71:38, 112:23E.**
Illegal employment of children, report, **149:92.**
Incumbent candidates, at-large members, **54:41, 54:42.**
Initiative petitions, filing of objections, **43:38.**

SCHOOLS AND EDUCATION
—Cont'd
Committees —Cont'd
Instructional aide, definition and appointment, **71:38.**
Interest in contracts, **43:27.**
Janitors or custodians, appointment and removal, **43:32.**
Joint committee for superintendence unions, **71:63.**
Junior college level courses.
See COLLEGES AND UNIVERSITIES.
Labor relations and disputes, expenditure of funds for collective bargaining legal services, **71:16, 71:37E, 71:37F.**
Leaves of absence for teachers, school nurses, etc., **71:41A.**
Lectures, may provide without charge, **71:27.**
Legal counsel, **71:37A, 71:37E, 71:37F.**
Lists of all persons 3 through 21 years of age to be transmitted by board of registrars of voters, **51:4, 51:14A.**
Lunches for pupils, duty to prepare and sell, **71:72.**
Magnet school facilities, application for grants, **71:37I.**
Management and conduct of public schools vested, **43:81.**
Meetings, **39:23A-39:23C, 43:35.**
Members.
Ineligible to hold position of teacher or superintendent, **71:52.**
Municipal offices, holding, **43:32.**
Prior holding of office, **53:34, 53:45.**
Mentally retarded children, approval of transportation to special schools, **71B:8.**
Model education programs, agreement, **40:4E.**
Nomination papers to state, **53:45.**
Nonresident pupils, plans for attendance, **76:12, 76:12A.**
Notice.
Disease or defect found in child, notice to parent or guardian, **71:56.**
Evening schools, duty to give notice, **71:20.**

SCHOOLS AND EDUCATION
—Cont'd

Committees —Cont'd

Notice —Cont'd

Meeting, **39:23A.**

Prior offices of members, **53:34, 53:45.**

School building, change in plans for construction or alteration, **43:34.**

Occupational guidance and placement director, appointment, **71:38A, 71:38D.**

Operation of services for children of employed mothers, **71:26B.**

Organizations of pupils, supervision and control, **71:47.**

Parents of children found to be suffering from disease or defect to be notified by committee, **71:56.**

Peddling by certain minors, regulated, **101:19.**

Permits to minors to peddle goods or act as bootblacks, control over, **101:19 et seq.**

Physical record of each pupil, committee to require to be kept, **71:57.**

Physician.

Appointment and assignment, **71:53.**

Employment and assignment to certain football games, **71:54A.**

Playgrounds, control over, **45:14.**

Printing of reports, **40:49.**

Priorities in hiring, **112:23E.**

Private schools, **76:1.**

Private ways, committee not compelled to furnish transportation for pupils, **71:68.**

Proposed annual budgets, public hearings, **71:38N.**

Public relations bureau, authority to establish in school department, **71:38K.**

Quorum for budget hearing, **71:38N.**

Racial imbalance. See within this heading, "Racial imbalance."

Receipts from certain programs, expenditure, **71:71E.**

Recommendations with respect to nature and extent of insurance of buildings and personal property, **40:5.**

SCHOOLS AND EDUCATION
—Cont'd

Committees —Cont'd

Records, public nature, **39:23A et seq.**

Regional school districts, **71:16A-71:16G.**

See REGIONAL SCHOOL DISTRICTS.

Regulations.

Attendance, **71:37, 76:1.**

Conduct of teachers or students, **71:37H.**

Removal, demotion, or dismissal of school personnel. See within this heading, "Removal, demotion, or dismissal of school personnel."

Residency requirements for teachers and professional employees, restrictions, **71:38.**

Safety patrols, establishment, **71:48A.**

Schoolhouses.

City charters.

See CITY CHARTERS.

Committee to have general charge, **71:68.**

Secretary, appointment and duties, **71:36.**

Selectmen.

Aldermen and selectmen. See within this heading, "Aldermen and selectmen."

Sex education committees to be appointed, **71:38O.**

Special education.

See SPECIAL EDUCATION.

Student advisory committees, **71:38M.**

Subjects for evening schools, selection, **71:18.**

Summer school. See within this heading, "Summer school."

Superintendents.

Committee members ineligible to hold position, **71:52.**

Employed by committees, **71:59.**

Suspension or discharge by committee, **71:42.**

Supplementary education centers and innovative educational programs, authority to make expenditures, **40:4A.**

Teachers.

See TEACHERS.

Term of office, **41:1, 71:35.**

SCHOOLS AND EDUCATION
—Cont'd

Committees —Cont'd

Textbooks.

See TEXTBOOKS.

Tools, implements, materials and supplies necessary, to be furnished, **71:48.**

Traffic belts for safety patrol leaders, expenditures, **71:48A.**

Transportation of pupils.

See SCHOOL BUSES AND TRANSPORTATION OF PUPILS.

Treasurer of collaborative board, appointment, **40:4E.**

Tuition.

Prepayment by committees to educational collaboratives and other institutions, **71:71D.**

Waiver, **71:6A, 76:6.**

Twelve-month school year, acceptance, **71:1.**

Uniforms, furnishing to employees, **71:48B.**

Vacancies in office, **43:36.**

Vacation schools, committee may establish, **71:28.**

Vocational education.

See VOCATIONAL EDUCATION AND SCHOOLS.

Voluntary prayer, children participating, **71:1B.**

Commonwealth scholars program, **15A:7.**

Commonwealth service corps, purpose of creation, **6:121.**

Communications commission educational, **6:17, 6:158.**

See EDUCATIONAL COMMUNICATIONS COMMISSION.

Community colleges.

See COLLEGES AND UNIVERSITIES.

Community health, instruction, **71:1.**

Community school programs, handling of moneys received, **71:71C, 71:71E.**

Compensation.

Salaries and compensation. See within this heading, "Salaries and compensation."

Complaint.

Degrees, revocation or suspension of educational institution's power to grant, **69:30A.**

SCHOOLS AND EDUCATION
—Cont'd
Complaint —Cont'd
Fair educational practices
violations, **151C:3.**
Teachers and superintendents,
disciplinary procedure
against, **71:42D.**
Comptroller of state.
See COMPTROLLER OF
STATE.
Compulsory attendance.
Attendance. See within this
heading, "Attendance."
Computers.
Software.
Procurement, contracts
awarded without bids,
30B:7.
Conservation education, duties of
supervisor, **15:4A.**
Conservation of soil, water and
related resources committee,
powers and duties, **21:20.**
Consolidation of functions of school
committees with cities or
towns, **71:37M.**
Constitution Day, observance,
6:14B, 6:15A.
Constitution of Massachusetts.
See CONSTITUTION OF
MASSACHUSETTS.
Construction of buildings.
Buildings. See within this
heading, "Buildings."
Consumer health, instruction,
71:1.
Contagious and infectious
diseases.
Disease or illness. See within
this heading, "Disease or
illness."
Continuation schools and courses,
71:21 et seq.
Attendance.
Compulsory attendance, **71:22.**
Employer's duty to discharge
child failing to attend,
149:91.
Temporarily unemployed
minors working elsewhere
than in town of residence,
attendance, **71:25.**
Tuition for attendance of pupil
in another town, **71:24.**
Authority, **71:21.**
Cities and towns.
Municipal finance. See within
this heading, "Municipal
finance."
Compulsory attendance, **71:22.**

SCHOOLS AND EDUCATION
—Cont'd
Continuation schools and courses
—Cont'd
Deposit of moneys received by
school committee, **71:71E.**
Employer's duty to discharge
child failing to attend,
149:91.
Establishment, **71:21.**
Fines and penalties of towns
failing to raise funds, **71:26.**
Hours of sessions, **71:21.**
Minors compelled to attend,
71:22.
Municipal finance. See within
this heading, "Municipal
finance."
Number of weeks to be in
session, **71:21.**
Part of public school system,
71:23.
Penalty on town for failure to
raise funds, **71:26.**
Reimbursement of towns by
Commonwealth, **71:24.**
Required in certain towns,
71:21.
Teachers, **71:38G.**
Classes for training, **74:18.**
Tuition for attendance of pupil
in another town, **71:24.**
Continuing education, **71:21 to
71:26.**
Acupuncturists, **112:154.**
Dieticians, **112:207.**
Elevator mechanics.
License renewal, **143:71C.**
Nurses.
See NURSES AND NURSING
SERVICES.
Pharmacies, **112:24A.**
Weights and measures.
Sealers, **98:35.**
Sealers, inspectors and
deputies, **98:29.**
Contracts and agreements.
Annuities.
See ANNUITIES AND
ANNUITY CONTRACTS.
Athletic coaches, contracts of
employment, **71:47A.**
Colleges.
See COLLEGES AND
UNIVERSITIES.
Committees. See within this
heading, "Committees."
Educational materials and
equipment, lease or
purchase, **40:4.**
Education department.
See EDUCATION
DEPARTMENT.

SCHOOLS AND EDUCATION
—Cont'd
Contracts and agreements
—Cont'd
Employment contracts. See
within this heading,
"Employment contracts."
Interest of school committee
members, **43:27.**
Interstate compacts and
agreements.
See INTERSTATE
COMPACTS AND
AGREEMENTS.
Labor.
Employment contracts. See
within this heading,
"Employment contracts."
Maintenance services for school
property, periods of
contracts authorized, **40:4.**
Model education programs,
agreements, **40:4E.**
Officers and employees, **71:38.**
Photography services, **30B:1.**
State colleges, agreements as to
practice schools, **73:3.**
Superior court contracts for
continuing education of
court personnel, **7:28A.**
Teachers.
See TEACHERS.
Transportation of pupils.
See SCHOOL BUSES AND
TRANSPORTATION OF
PUPILS.
Contributions.
Charities.
See CHARITIES AND
CHARITABLE
CONTRIBUTIONS.
Gifts, grants, and gratuities. See
within this heading, "Gifts,
grants, and gratuities."
Cooking.
Home economics and cooking.
See within this heading,
"Home economics and
cooking."
Co-operating employment.
See LABOR AND WORKFORCE
DEVELOPMENT.
Co-operative banks, **170:13,
170:16, 170:19.**
Co-operative plan students,
employment of.
See LABOR AND WORKFORCE
DEVELOPMENT.
Corporal punishment of pupils,
prohibition against, **71:37G.**
Corporations.
Annual return of educational
corporations, **180:26A.**

SCHOOLS AND EDUCATION
—Cont'd

Corporations —Cont'd

Bank holding companies, exemption of educational corporations from laws, **167A:1.**

Bylaws of educational corporation, **180:7.**

Change of purpose or name, **180:10, 180:11.**

Charities.

Business corporations, gifts. See CHARITIES AND CHARITABLE CONTRIBUTIONS.

Contributions of educational purposes, **155:12C.**

Higher education assistance corporation. See HIGHER EDUCATION ASSISTANCE CORPORATION.

Incorporation, **180:1 et seq.**

Management of school funds, provisions of chapter not to affect such management, **71:74.**

Promotion of education purposes, **180:2.**

Correctional institutions, programs, **127:48 et seq.**

Commissioner of corrections, duties, **124:1.**

County prisons, **41:96B, 127:48.** Work release programs, **127:86F.**

General education development tests, certain inmates may be permitted to take, **127:92A.**

Good conduct, reduction of sentence of prisoner, **127:129D.**

High school equivalency certificate, reduction of sentence, **127:129D.**

Inmates of correctional institutions, **127:48, 127:49, 127:49A.**

Labor of prisoners, instructors, **127:52.**

Mentally retarded persons, **123:2.**

Mental retardation department, officers and inmates of penal and reformatory institutions receiving educational, training and employment programs, **127:49B.**

Moral instruction, prisoners' assemblies, **127:22.**

SCHOOLS AND EDUCATION
—Cont'd

Correctional institutions, programs —Cont'd

Personnel of correctional institutions, **124:1, 125:9.**

Reading and writing.

Inmates' ability, ascertainment, **127:21.**

Instruction and facilities, **127:92, 127:93.**

Sabbath school for prisoners, **127:89.**

Special education for school aged children with special needs who are incarcerated in county houses of detention, **71B:11A.**

Vocational training, good conduct reduction of sentence, **127:129D.**

Youth services department programs, **120:2, 120:3, 120:12.**

See YOUTH SERVICES DEPARTMENT AND MASSACHUSETTS TRAINING SCHOOLS.

Correspondence schools, **75C:1-75C:11.**

See CORRESPONDENCE SCHOOLS.

Costs and expenses.

Expenses and expenditures. See within this heading, "Expenses and expenditures."

Councils, **71:59C.**

Counsel.

See ATTORNEYS AT LAW.

Counselors.

Adjustment counselors. See within this heading, "Adjustment counselors."

Guidance counselor. See GUIDANCE COUNSELORS.

County aid, acceptance, **71:37A.**

County co-operative extension service, **128:40 et seq.**

County, correspondence school operated, **75C:1.**

County prisons.

Correctional institutions. See within this heading, "Correctional institutions, programs."

Courses of study.

Curriculum and courses of study. See within this heading, "Curriculum and courses of study."

SCHOOLS AND EDUCATION
—Cont'd

Court personnel, continuing education, **7:28A.**

Credit life insurance for educational loans, **175:133.**

Credit unions.

See CREDIT UNIONS.

Crimes and offenses.

Alcoholic beverages, sale, delivery, or possession in school buildings, **272:40A.**

Assault and battery on school system, employees, **265:13D.**

Colleges.

See COLLEGES AND UNIVERSITIES.

Disturbance of school, **272:40.**

Employees of school systems, assault and battery, **265:13D.**

Endorsement by educational institution, false assertion, **266:90.**

Expulsion of students, **71:37H½.**

Fines and penalties. See within this heading, "Fines and penalties."

Property, injury, **266:98.**

Criminal justice training council, **6:116-6:119.**

See CRIMINAL JUSTICE TRAINING COUNCIL.

Criminal offender record information of applicants for positions, **71:38R.**

Crossings, protection by erection of figures or objects, **85:21A.**

Culinary arts program.

See CULINARY ARTS PROGRAM.

Curriculum accommodation plans, **71:38Q½.**

Curriculum and courses of study, **71:1 et seq.**

Citizenship and government, cities and towns to establish classes, **69:9, 69:9A, 69:10.**

Continuation schools and courses. See within this heading, "Continuation schools and courses."

Education department.

See EDUCATION DEPARTMENT.

English. See within this heading, "English."

Foreign languages. See within this heading, "Foreign languages."

Health education. See within this heading, "Health education."

SCHOOLS AND EDUCATION
—Cont'd
Curriculum and courses of study
—Cont'd
High schools.
See HIGH SCHOOLS.
History, **6:15C, 71:1, 71:2, 71:18.**
Home economics and cooking.
See within this heading, "Home economics and cooking."
Industrial schools, committee to establish courses of study, **74:37A.**
New courses, requirements, **71:13.**
Special education, **71B:9, 71B:10.**
Superintendent, recommended, **71:59.**
Swimming instruction, **40:12.**
Vocational education.
See VOCATIONAL EDUCATION AND SCHOOLS.
Custodians.
Janitors and custodians. See within this heading, "Janitors and custodians."
Damaging or defacing school buildings or property.
Penalties, **266:98.**
Day care.
Extended services for children of employed mothers. See within this heading, "Extended services for children of employed mothers."
Daylight saving time, **4:10.**
Deaf school children.
Hearing of pupils. See within this heading, "Hearing of pupils."
Death.
Scholarships for survivors of decedents, **152:31.**
Workers' compensation death benefits, extension to deceased employee's full-time student child over 18, **152:31.**
Debt, approval of acquisition of property and incurring of debt, **71:16.**
Debt limit of municipality, exceeding in anticipation of public funds, **71:26D.**
Deceit.
Fraud and deceit. See within this heading, "Fraud and deceit."

SCHOOLS AND EDUCATION
—Cont'd
Declaration of Independence, required teaching, **71:2.**
Defacing school buildings or property.
Damaging or defacing school buildings or property.
Penalties, **266:98.**
Defenses.
Assault, use of force as protection from in public school, **71:37G.**
Degrees and diplomas.
See COLLEGES AND UNIVERSITIES.
Delinquent children.
See JUVENILE COURTS AND DELINQUENT CHILDREN.
Demonstration projects operated by students, **71:37K.**
Demotion of school personnel.
Removal, demotion or dismissal. See within this heading, "Removal, demotion, or dismissal of school personnel."
Dental health, instruction, **71:1.**
Dentists.
See DENTISTS.
Department of education.
See EDUCATION DEPARTMENT.
Dependent children.
Attendance in school as condition, **118:1.**
Vocational training course, effect of applicant's attendance, **118:3.**
Deposits.
Banks and banking. See within this heading, "Banks and banking."
Development and industrial commission of city or town to aid in establishment of educational projects, **40:8A.**
Dieticians.
Continuing education, **112:207.**
Educational requirements, **112:203.**
Directors.
Elections, contracts, and promotions, **71:38.**
Leaves of absence for study or research, **71:41A.**
Loans, **170:19.**
Disabled or handicapped persons.
Blind persons.
See BLIND PERSONS.

SCHOOLS AND EDUCATION
—Cont'd
Disabled or handicapped persons
—Cont'd
Deaf school children.
Hearing of pupils. See within this heading, "Hearing of pupils."
Mentally ill.
See MENTALLY ILL AND RETARDED PERSONS.
Special education.
See SPECIAL EDUCATION.
Disadvantaged children, special programs, **71:1.**
Disciplinary programs and codes of conduct, **71:37H.**
Discontinuance of certain regional school districts, **71:42B.**
Discrimination.
Civil rights. See within this heading, "Civil rights."
Disease or illness.
Accident.
See ACCIDENT AND SICKNESS INSURANCE.
Cancer in women, schools providing programs for early detection, **71:1.**
Child showing signs of illness to be sent home, **71:55A.**
Emergency first aid or transportation, exemption from liability, **71:55A.**
Notice. See within this heading, "Notice."
Pupils exposed to or infected with dangerous disease not to attend without certificate, **71:55, 71:55A, 71:56.**
Sickle cell anemia, testing of children, **76:15A.**
Tuberculosis. See within this heading, "Tuberculosis."
Vaccination of pupils against, **76:15.**
Dismissal of school personnel.
Removal, demotion or dismissal. See within this heading, "Removal, demotion, or dismissal of school personnel."
Disqualification.
Qualification. See within this heading, "Qualification or disqualification."
Dissection of animals in, regulated, **272:80G.**
Districts.
Abused and neglected children, committee's notice of reporting requirements to school personnel, **71:37L.**

SCHOOLS AND EDUCATION
—Cont'd
Districts —Cont'd
Budgets.
See BUDGETS.
Driver education courses, contracts, **40:4.**
Fiscal year. See within this heading, "Fiscal year."
Formation of district by two or more towns, purpose, **71:38D.**
Health insurance, payment of municipal employees' surviving spouses' premiums, **32B:9D¾.**
Minimum state standards, **15:1G.**
Postural defects, testing by school districts, **71:57.**
Racial imbalance, change in district to eliminate, **71:37D.**
Regional school districts, **71:14-71:20.**
See REGIONAL SCHOOL DISTRICTS.
School committees, district representation, **43:129 et seq.**
Student government day, districts for observance, **6:12M.**
Superintendence districts and unions. See within this heading, "Superintendence districts and unions."
Traffic safety week, costs, **6:15P.**
Vocational education.
See VOCATIONAL EDUCATION AND SCHOOLS.
Disturbing or interrupting, **272:40.**
Diversity awareness education trust fund, **10:35Q.**
Diversity of learning styles.
Curriculum accommodation plans, **71:38Q½.**
Domicile.
Residence. See within this heading, "Residence."
Dormitories, listing of residents for purposes of voter registration, **51:10A.**
Double sessions, **71:1.**
Drawing required to be taught, **71:1, 71:18.**
Dress and appearance of students, **71:83, 71:85, 71:86.**
Driver education.
See DRIVER EDUCATION.
Dropouts, procedures, **76:18.**

SCHOOLS AND EDUCATION
—Cont'd
Drugs.
See DRUGS AND NARCOTICS.
Early childhood intervention services, **111G:1-111G:6.**
See EARLY CHILDHOOD INTERVENTION SERVICES.
Ecology, instruction, **71:1.**
Economic diversification program, **23F:6.**
Educational affairs executive office.
See EDUCATIONAL AFFAIRS EXECUTIVE OFFICE.
Educational certificates.
See LABOR AND WORKFORCE DEVELOPMENT.
Educational collaborative board.
Collaborative educational programs. See within this heading, "Collaborative education programs."
Educational Commissioner as member of advisory groups, **18A:9, 120:10.**
Educational communications commission.
See EDUCATIONAL COMMUNICATIONS COMMISSION.
Educational development commission.
Membership and purposes, **15:1G.**
Educational excellence and equity, **15:49A et seq.**
Educational institution, defined, **40J:12, 151C:1.**
Educational materials.
Procurement, contracts awarded without bids, **30B:7.**
Textbooks.
See TEXTBOOKS.
Educational services, children in need, **119:39E, 119:39G.**
Educational television, **71:13F et seq.**
See EDUCATIONAL TELEVISION.
Education department, **15:1 et seq.**
See EDUCATION DEPARTMENT.
Education week, observance, **6:12G.**
Elections.
See ELECTIONS.
Electrolysis, schools, **112:87LLL.**
Elementary schools, number of days in school year, **71:1.**

SCHOOLS AND EDUCATION
—Cont'd
Eligibility.
Qualification or disqualification. See within this heading, "Qualification or disqualification."
Emergencies.
First aid. See within this heading, "First aid."
High schools, emergency as affecting requirement as to minimum number of days, **71:4.**
Transportation expenses of non-white and minority pupils, emergency school aid act, **15:1I.**
Transportation rendered to injured students, exemption from liability, **71:55A.**
Emotional development, instruction, **71:1.**
Employed mothers, extended services for children, **71:26A et seq.**
Employees.
Agricultural and technical institutes, **74A:16.**
Criminal offender record information of applicants for positions, **71:38R.**
Teachers.
See TEACHERS.
Employment.
See EMPLOYMENT AND TRAINING DIVISION IN LABOR AND WORKFORCE DEPARTMENT.
Employment contracts.
Superintendents, **71:16.**
Training, **71:38.**
Employment security.
See EMPLOYMENT SECURITY.
Endorsement by, false assertion, **266:90.**
Energy Resources Executive Office, powers and duties, **25A:6.**
Enforcement of municipal duty to provide support for schools, **71:34.**
Engineers.
See ENGINEERS AND SURVEYORS.
English.
Adults, instruction, **69:9 et seq.**
Buildings to be used for classes, **69:9.**
Reimbursement of cities and towns for expense of holding classes, **69:10.**

SCHOOLS AND EDUCATION
—Cont'd
English —Cont'd
Required to be taught, **71:1,
71:18.**
Environmental management
department, educational
outreach programs, **21:20.**
Equal educational opportunity
grant, **70A:2 et seq.**
Equality in education.
Civil rights. See within this
heading, "Civil rights."
Equipment.
Machinery and equipment. See
within this heading,
"Machinery and equipment."
Estimates of state aid, **70:5, 70:10.**
Estoppel.
Waiver and estoppel. See within
this heading, "Waiver and
estoppel."
Evening classes and schools,
71:18-71:20.
See EVENING CLASSES AND
SCHOOLS.
Examination, inspection, or
investigation.
Attorneys at law, general
education examination as
requirement for admission
to bar, **221:36.**
Barbers, **13:40.**
Bilingual language program,
examination of pupils
enrolled, **71A:2.**
Buildings, examination by school
physician, **71:54.**
Buses.
See SCHOOL BUSES AND
TRANSPORTATION OF
PUPILS.
Correspondence schools,
issuance of license, **75C:2.**
Dental hygienists, examination
of certain dental students
for registration, **112:51.**
Education department.
See EDUCATION
DEPARTMENT.
Education department records
open to public inspection,
69:2.
Eyesight of pupils, testing,
71:57.
Hospital school, **58:25B.**
Incorporation, investigation
prior, **180:5, 180:6.**
Medical laboratory technologists,
schools, **112:2B.**

SCHOOLS AND EDUCATION
—Cont'd
Examination, inspection, or
investigation —Cont'd
Medical or physical examination.
See within this heading,
"Medical or physical
examination."
Nursing schools, **112:81A.**
School buses.
See SCHOOL BUSES AND
TRANSPORTATION OF
PUPILS.
School personnel.
School teacher's right to
inspect his records,
71:42C.
Tuberculosis, tests of
personnel, **71:55B.**
Special education.
Hearings and investigations.
See SPECIAL EDUCATION.
Student records. See within this
heading, "Student records."
Taking of examinations for
another, **271:50.**
University of Massachusetts,
testing fees.
See UNIVERSITY OF
MASSACHUSETTS.
Youth services department.
See YOUTH SERVICES
DEPARTMENT AND
MASSACHUSETTS
TRAINING SCHOOLS.
Exceptions, exemptions or
exclusions.
Bank holding companies,
educational corporations as
exempt from laws, **167A:1.**
Certain children, exclusion, **76:5,
76:16 et seq.**
Certification of teachers,
exemption in case of
hardship in securing
teachers, **71:38G.**
Clinics, exception as to licensing,
111:52.
Employment security laws,
students employed in
organized camps exempted,
151A:6.
Lobbying laws, exemption
regarding employees or
agents of regional school
districts, **3:50.**
Model organizations and
operations for educational
purposes exception from law
against unauthorized
banking, **167:12.**

SCHOOLS AND EDUCATION
—Cont'd
Exceptions, exemptions or
exclusions —Cont'd
Nurses as exempt from laws
governing health educators,
112:80B.
State aid or reimbursement,
70:14.
Tax exemption.
Taxes. See within this
heading, "Taxation."
Uniform Securities Act,
exemptions, **110A:402.**
Vaccination requirement,
exemption or religious
grounds, **76:15.**
Veterinary students, exemption
from licensing provisions for
clinical training, **112:56E.**
Excuse of absences, **76:1.**
Executive committee for
educational television
programs, **71:13I.**
Exemptions.
Exceptions, exemptions or
exclusions. See within this
heading, "Exceptions,
exemptions or exclusions."
Exhibitions of school work at
expositions, **71:51.**
Expenses and expenditures.
Advisory commission on
academically talented
pupils, members, **15:6C.**
Attorneys, authority of school
committee to expend funds
for employment, **71:37E.**
Colleges.
See COLLEGES AND
UNIVERSITIES.
Educational communications
commission, powers, **6:158.**
Federal aid or funds. See within
this heading, "Federal aid or
funds."
Fees. See within this heading,
"Fees."
Football games, attendance of
physicians or persons
trained in emergency
medical care, **71:54A.**
Industrial school and workshop
for the blind, lodging and
support for workmen or
pupils, **6:144.**
Intern scholarship program,
expenses to be paid from
agricultural purposes fund,
20:6A.

SCHOOLS AND EDUCATION
—Cont'd

Expenses and expenditures
—Cont'd

Labor relations and disputes, expenditure of funds for collective bargaining legal services, **71:16, 71:37E, 71:37F.**

Medical care or treatment. See within this heading, "Medical care or treatment."

Municipal finance. See within this heading, "Municipal finance."

Racial imbalance, cost of establishing magnet school facility, **71:37J.**

Receipts from certain programs, expenditure by school committee, **71:71E.**

Regional school districts, **71:64.**

Reimbursement. See within this heading, "Reimbursement."

Special awards to pupils for meritorious performance as school purpose expenditures, **71:47.**

Superintendence unions, payment of expenses of superintendent, **71:64.**

Supplementary education centers and innovative educational programs, municipal expenditures, **40:4A.**

Traffic belts for safety patrol leaders, **71:48A.**

Experimental schools, attendance of pupils, **15:1G, 76:1.**

Expulsion, **71:37H, 71:37H½.**

Marriage or parenthood as ground, **71:84.**

Notice to non-custodial parents, **71:34H.**

Procedures, **76:16.**

Extended services for children of employed mothers, **71:26A et seq.**

Eyes.

Glasses for school children, town appropriations, **40:5.**

Protective devices, requirement as to wearing, **71:55C.**

Teachers.

Blind persons.

See BLIND PERSONS.

Protective devices for eyes, requirement as to wearing, **71:55C.**

Testing of pupils' eyesight, **71:57.**

SCHOOLS AND EDUCATION
—Cont'd

Eyes —Cont'd

Testing of vision, **71:57.**

Fair educational practices, **151C:1-151C:5.**

See FAIR EDUCATIONAL PRACTICES.

False pretenses.

Fraud and deceit. See within this heading, "Fraud and deceit."

Family members of superintendent, employment of, **71:59.**

Federal aid or funds.

Acceptance and expenditure of federal funds by cities and towns, **44:53A.**

Apprentice training division of labor and workforce development department, use of federal funds, **23:11F.**

Colleges.

Veterans.

See VETERANS AND VETERANS' ORGANIZATIONS.

Contracts as to aid programs involving expenditure of federal funds, **40:4A.**

Educational communications commission, duties, **6:158.**

Education department.

See EDUCATION DEPARTMENT.

Extended services for children of employed mothers, exceeding debt limit in anticipation, **71:26D.**

Nonresident pupils, education, **76:12B.**

Racial imbalance, expenditure by school committee of federal funds to relieve, **76:12A.**

Retirement systems, creditable service of teacher formerly employed and paid by federal government, **32:4.**

School committees' expenditure of federal funds.

Contracts as to aid programs involving, **40:4A.**

Extended services for children of employed mothers, **71:26C.**

Racial imbalance, elimination, **76:12A.**

Student loans insured by federal government, banks' authority, **167E:9.**

SCHOOLS AND EDUCATION
—Cont'd

Federal aid or funds —Cont'd

Vocational education.

See VOCATIONAL EDUCATION AND SCHOOLS.

Federal Constitution, required teaching, **71:2.**

Federal government.

City participation in programs, **264:14A.**

Colleges.

See COLLEGES AND UNIVERSITIES.

Funds.

Federal aid or funds. See within this heading, "Federal aid or funds."

Lease of schools to federal government for rehabilitation of veterans, **74:41.**

Training programs of Federal Bureau of Investigation, attendance of local police, **40:5.**

Federal savings and loan associations, exception from statute against unauthorized banking for model organizations and operations for educational purposes, **167:12.**

Fees.

Aldermen and selectmen, approval of fees paid, **71:37E, 71:37F.**

Attorneys' fees. See within this heading, "Attorneys' fees."

Colleges.

See COLLEGES AND UNIVERSITIES.

Correspondence school pupil mislead by representations, recovery of fees, **75C:10.**

Driver schools, application and license fees, **90:32G.**

Evening schools, **71:20, 74:33.**

Extended services for children of employed mothers, **71:26B.**

Maritime Academy of Massachusetts.

Activity fees, **73:1B.**

Service fees, **73:1.**

Massachusetts Educational Financial Authority bonds, issuance, **15C:5A, 15C:5B, 29:49C.**

Occupational guidance and placement director, acceptance, **71:38F.**

SCHOOLS AND EDUCATION
—Cont'd
Fees —Cont'd
Pilots federal certificates, exceptions from fees for instructors, **90:49.**
Procuring positions for teachers, **71:45.**
Regional community colleges, **40:8H.**
Regional school district employees' collective bargaining agency service fees, provisions as to payment, **180:17G.**
State colleges, **73:1 et seq.**
Superintendent prohibited from receiving for obtaining teaching position, **71:67.**
Teachers.
  See TEACHERS.
Technical colleges or institutes, **74:33, 74:46A.**
Tuition. See within this heading, "Tuition."
University of Massachusetts.
  Milk tests in laboratory, **75:16A.**
  Poultry, testing, **75:21.**
Feet of pupils, examination, **71:57.**
Females.
Board of education, appointment of women, **15:1E.**
Cancer, instruction for early detection, **71:1.**
Evening schools, attendance by certain married women, **76:3.**
Husband.
  See HUSBAND AND WIFE.
Sex discrimination. See within this heading, "Sex discrimination."
Finances and funds, **70:1 et seq.**
Aid and assistance. See within this heading, "Aid and assistance."
Athletic activities, disposition of receipts, **71:47.**
Building assistance. See within this heading, "Building assistance."
Business demonstration projects, disposition of funds, **71:37K.**
Cities.
  Municipal finance. See within this heading, "Municipal finance."
Deposits of funds by municipalities in connection with certain programs, **71:71C, 71:71E.**

SCHOOLS AND EDUCATION
—Cont'd
Finances and funds —Cont'd
Diversity awareness education trust fund, **10:35Q.**
Educational television.
  Educational television program fund, **71:13H.**
  School committees may budget funds for educational television, **71:13F.**
Federal aid or funds. See within this heading, "Federal aid or funds."
Health.
  See HEALTH AND EDUCATION FACILITIES AUTHORITY.
Improvement fund, **10:35F.**
Institutional fund management, **180A:1 et seq.**
  See INSTITUTIONAL FUND MANAGEMENT.
Labor relations and disputes, expenditure of funds for collective bargaining legal services, **71:16, 71:37E, 71:37F.**
Management of school funds by corporations not affected by chapter, **71:74.**
Massachusetts Educational Financial Authority Act. See within this heading, "Massachusetts Educational Financial Authority Act."
Municipal finance. See within this heading, "Municipal finance."
Records, reports, and returns. See within this heading, "Records, reports, and returns."
Reimbursement. See within this heading, "Reimbursement."
School choice tuition trust fund, **76:12C.**
Special education.
  See SPECIAL EDUCATION.
Stabilization fund. See within this heading, "Stabilization fund."
State aid or reimbursement. See within this heading, "State aid or reimbursement."
State comptroller's duties, **7A:9, 7A:12.**
State fund, receipt and handling, **10:15, 10:16.**
State treasurer to manage trust funds of department of education, **10:16.**

SCHOOLS AND EDUCATION
—Cont'd
Finances and funds —Cont'd
Student government day, observance, **6:12M.**
Teacher, principal and superintendent quality endowment fund, **10:35S.**
Treasurer of regional school district, removal from office, **41:39B.**
Vocational education.
  See VOCATIONAL EDUCATION AND SCHOOLS.
Fines and penalties.
Academies, penalty for burning, **266:2.**
Aid deductions, **71:4A.**
Assault and battery on employees, **265:13D.**
Buses.
  See SCHOOL BUSES AND TRANSPORTATION OF PUPILS.
Colleges.
  See COLLEGES AND UNIVERSITIES.
Continuation schools and courses, towns failing to raise funds, **71:26.**
Correspondence schools, **75C:9.**
  Operation without license, **75C:1A, 75C:9.**
Deaf children, parent failing to send to school, **76:2A.**
Director of occupational guidance and placement, acceptance of commission or fee, **71:38F.**
Educational certificate to be used for evening schools, fines for violations, **149:98.**
Evening classes and schools.
  Certificate violations, **149:98.**
  Illiterate minors, failure to attend evening classes and schools, **76:3.**
False pretenses as to graduation or holding degree, **266:89.**
Flag, violations, **71:69.**
Furniture, injury, **266:98.**
High schools not kept open for required number of days during school year, **71:4A.**
Illiterate minors, failure to attend evening school, **76:3.**
Inducing unlawful absence, **76:4.**
Medical laboratory technologists' schools, violations, **112:2B.**
Parents failing to send child to school, **76:2 et seq.**

SCHOOLS AND EDUCATION
—Cont'd

Fines and penalties —Cont'd
Politics of candidates for
teaching positions, inquiries,
71:39.
Private schools.
Business or correspondence
schools, operation without
license, **75C:1A, 75D:3.**
Trade schools, violations of
regulations, **93:21B.**
Procuring teachers' positions,
violation of regulations as to
fees, **71:45.**
Religion of candidates for
teaching positions, inquiries,
71:39.
Sale of themes, term papers,
etc., **271:50.**
Schoolhouse, injury, **266:98.**
Spitting in school buildings,
270:14, 270:15.
Superintendent accepting
commission or fee for
obtaining teaching position,
71:67.
Teachers.
Assault and battery on
teachers, **265:13D.**
Fees for procuring teaching
positions, acceptance by
certain persons, **71:45,
71:67.**
Trustees of educational
institutions, authority,
15A:13.
Firearms and other weapons.
Blank cartridges, sale for
instruction to use firearms,
148:39.
Carrying on school grounds,
written authorization,
269:10.
Display of posters on laws as to
carrying, **269:11.**
Insurance for firearms
instructors, **131:14.**
Report of incident involving
student possession or use of
dangerous weapon, **71:37L.**
Fire departments.
See FIRE DEPARTMENTS.
Fire escapes for school houses in
cities, **143:32.**
Fire safety, treatment and
prevention of burns, education
relative, **71:1.**
First aid.
Athletic activities. See within
this heading, "Athletic
activities."

SCHOOLS AND EDUCATION
—Cont'd

First aid —Cont'd
Curriculum to include
instruction, **71:1.**
Football games, presence of
person trained in emergency
medical care.
Athletic activities. See within
this heading, "Athletic
activities."
Immunity of teachers, principals
and nurses from damages
arising from first aid or
transportation provided to
pupils on emergency basis,
71:55A.
First arrests and convictions of
certain misdemeanors,
inquiries as unfair practices,
151C:2.
Fiscal year.
Regional school district
committees, authority to
amend agreements to
conform to change in dates
of fiscal year, **71:16B.**
Teachers' salaries as exception,
44:56A.
Fishing licenses, free issuance to
persons classified as mentally
retarded by public school
officials, **131:11.**
Flags.
See FLAGS.
Food services.
See FOOD SERVICES AND
FREE LUNCH
PROGRAMS.
Football games.
Athletic activities. See within
this heading, "Athletic
activities."
Foreign languages.
French language programs,
6:157.
High school programs, **71:13.**
Programs for non-English
speaking students,
71A:1-71A:9.
See BILINGUAL
EDUCATION.
Spanish, **71:13.**
Foreign states.
See FOREIGN STATES OR
COUNTRIES.
Forest and wood products
education and development
center established, **132:51.**
Forfeiture of rights under annuity
contracts for public
educational institution
employees, **15:18A, 71:37B.**

SCHOOLS AND EDUCATION
—Cont'd

Formula for determining state aid,
70:3, 70:3A.
Foster care, superintendent's
annual report as to number of
school age children, **76:7.**
Fraternal benefit societies.
Exemption from school tax,
176:49.
Operation of schools, **176:14.**
Fraternities.
See SORORITIES AND
FRATERNITIES.
Fraud and deceit.
Colleges.
See FRAUD AND DECEIT.
Correspondence school student
mislead by representations,
recovery of fees, **75C:10.**
Endorsement, false assertion,
266:90.
Graduation or degrees conferred,
fraud, **266:89.**
Trade schools, treble damages,
93:21.
Freedom of speech or expression.
Student rights. See within this
heading, "Student rights."
Free or gratuitous programs or
services.
Gifts, grants, and gratuities. See
within this heading, "Gifts,
grants, and gratuities."
French language programs, duties
of American and Canadian
French cultural exchange
commission, **6:157.**
Full-time students.
Defined, **32:26.**
Survivors benefits under
contributory retirement law
for certain, **32:7, 32:9.**
Funds.
Finances and funds. See within
this heading, "Finances and
funds."
Gaming laws, forfeiture of charter
for violation, **180:27.**
General court.
See GENERAL COURT.
Geographic education awareness
week, **6:15MMM.**
Geography required to be taught,
71:1, 71:18.
Gifted and talented education,
advisory councils for, **15:1G.**
Gifts, grants, and gratuities.
Acceptance of gifts or grants
from governmental sources,
71:37A.

SCHOOLS AND EDUCATION
—Cont'd
Gifts, grants, and gratuities
—Cont'd
Agriculture department, acceptance, **128:4.**
Building assistance commission, grants for approved school projects, **71:1.**
Building assistance. See within this heading, "Building assistance."
Charitable gifts.
See CHARITIES AND CHARITABLE CONTRIBUTIONS.
Colleges.
See COLLEGES AND UNIVERSITIES.
Committees. See within this heading, "Committees."
Corporations, contributions for educational purposes, **155:12C.**
County agricultural schools, receipt and use of gifts, **74:31.**
Early childhood discretionary grant program, **15:54.**
Educational Communications Commission, **6:158.**
Education department.
See EDUCATION DEPARTMENT.
Equal educational opportunity grant, **70A:2 et seq.**
Extended services for children of employed mothers, acceptance of contributions, **71:26C.**
Federal aid or funds. See within this heading, "Federal aid or funds."
Free lunch programs.
See FOOD SERVICES AND FREE LUNCH PROGRAMS.
Grants-in-aid, effect on school aid, **70:8.**
Instructional materials grant program, **15:57.**
Lectures, school committee may provide free lectures, **71:27.**
Medicine, surgery, and urology, training grants for fellows, **115A:10.**
Municipal finance. See within this heading, "Municipal finance."
Part-time student, grant program, **15A:7, 15A:16.**

SCHOOLS AND EDUCATION
—Cont'd
Gifts, grants, and gratuities
—Cont'd
Patriotic plaque, acceptance by schools, **71:69A.**
Racial imbalance, magnet school facility, application for grants, **71:37I.**
REACH Awards for educational achievement, **15:55.**
Regional school districts.
See REGIONAL SCHOOL DISTRICTS.
Scholarships.
See SCHOLARSHIPS AND FELLOWSHIPS.
State funds and state aid, **70:8.**
Student government day, observance, **6:12M.**
Teachers' leaves of absence, source of compensation, **71:41A.**
Trustees of educational gifts, **68:13 et seq.**
Waste prevention institute, establishment of, **71:38 et seq.**
Global Education, Center for, model curriculum, **71:1.**
Good behavior required to be taught, **71:1, 71:18.**
Government, classes of instruction in principles, **69:9, 69:9A, 69:10, 71:2.**
Governor.
See GOVERNOR.
Governor's council.
See GOVERNOR'S COUNCIL.
Governor's proclamations, school library media month, **6:15AAA.**
Grants.
Gifts, grants, and gratuities. See within this heading, "Gifts, grants, and gratuities."
Group annuity contracts, investments, **71:37B.**
Group care children, reimbursement for tuition, **76:7.**
Guardians.
See GUARDIANS, CONSERVATORS, AND COMMITTEES.
Guidance counselor.
See GUIDANCE COUNSELORS.
Hairdressers.
See HAIRDRESSERS AND COSMETOLOGISTS.

SCHOOLS AND EDUCATION
—Cont'd
Handicapped persons.
Disabled or handicapped persons. See within this heading, "Disabled or handicapped persons."
Hardship in securing teachers, exemption of municipalities from certification requirement in event, **71:38G.**
Hazardous waste site cleanup professionals, rules regarding education of, **21A:19B.**
Hazing, prohibition of practice, **269:17, 269:18, 269:19.**
Health.
Accident.
See ACCIDENT AND SICKNESS INSURANCE.
Authority.
See HEALTH AND EDUCATION FACILITIES AUTHORITY.
Certificate for return to school, **71:55.**
Children's health camps, superintendents' duties, **111:62B, 111:62C.**
Disease or illness. See within this heading, "Disease or illness."
Education in matters pertaining to.
Health education. See within this heading, "Health education."
Electrolysis schools, supervision, **112:87LLL.**
Employed mothers, standards for extended services for children, **71:26B.**
Exclusion by reason of disease dangerous to public health, notification of board of health, **71:55A.**
Facilities authority.
See HEALTH AND EDUCATION FACILITIES AUTHORITY.
Hospital school, supervision, **111:62I.**
Medical or physical examination. See within this heading, "Medical or physical examination."
Personal dress and appearance of students violating health, standards, **71:83.**

SCHOOLS AND EDUCATION
—Cont'd
Health —Cont'd
Physicians and surgeons. See
within this heading,
"Physicians and surgeons."
Teacher employed by health
department, tenure, **30:9D.**
Health care finance and policy
division, training department,
151A:46.
Health education.
Authority, **Spec L 53:1 et seq.**
See HEALTH AND
EDUCATION
FACILITIES
AUTHORITY.
Campaigns for health education,
111:50.
Education department, **69:1L.**
Nurses as exempt from laws
governing health educators,
112:80B.
Private business schools,
training, **75D:1.**
Public schools, required courses,
71:1.
Hearing of pupils.
Attendance of pupils with
hearing impairments, **76:2A.**
Municipal appropriations for
hearing aids for pupils, **40:5.**
Special education.
See SPECIAL EDUCATION.
Teachers.
Eligibility for certification as
teachers of the deaf,
71:38G.
Testing of pupils' hearing,
71:57.
Testing, **71:57, 111:185A.**
Hearings.
Fair educational practices
proceedings, **151C:3.**
Misconduct, hearings to exclude
pupils, **76:17.**
Proposed annual budgets, public
hearing, **71:38N.**
Racial imbalance, public hearing
required prior to changing
school district to eliminate,
71:37D.
Rights of pupils, **71:85.**
Special education.
See SPECIAL EDUCATION.
Superintendents, discharge or
suspension, **71:42, 71:42D.**
Teachers.
Certification, **71:38G.**
Discharge or suspension,
71:42, 71:42D.

SCHOOLS AND EDUCATION
—Cont'd
Hearings —Cont'd
Teachers —Cont'd
Maximum time period of
suspension without
hearing, **71:42D.**
Veterinarian schools, revocation
or suspension of
institutional license,
112:56D.
Higher education.
See COLLEGES AND
UNIVERSITIES.
Higher education assistance
corporation.
See HIGHER EDUCATION
ASSISTANCE
CORPORATION.
High schools.
See HIGH SCHOOLS.
Highways and streets.
Erection of figures or objects by
municipalities at school
crossings, **85:21A.**
Motor vehicles. See within this
heading, "Motor vehicles."
Protection of school children,
85:21A.
Safety patrols, **71:48A.**
Safety stations, **71:71A.**
Traffic regulations and rules of
the road. See within this
heading, "Traffic regulations
and rules of the road."
Hiring practices by school
committees, **112:23E.**
Historic districts and sites,
Archivist of Commonwealth
exhibiting or using records for
educational purposes, **9:2.**
History, **6:15C, 71:1, 71:2, 71:18.**
Hoisting and hoisting machinery,
146:53.
Holidays.
Establishment of guidelines for
celebration of Christmas
and other festivals, **71:31A.**
Lincoln's birthday, observance,
6:13.
Memorial Day, observance,
71:32.
Sabbath schools maintained in
correctional institutions,
127:89.
School Principals' Recognition
Day, **6:12UU.**
Home economics and cooking.
Culinary arts program.
See CULINARY ARTS
PROGRAM.

SCHOOLS AND EDUCATION
—Cont'd
Home economics and cooking
—Cont'd
Vocational education.
See VOCATIONAL
EDUCATION AND
SCHOOLS.
Home improvement contractors,
students exempt from
registration, **142A:14.**
Horace Mann charter schools,
71:89.
Horse and dog racing meetings,
Massachusetts bred
greyhounds, **128A:9.**
Hospital, medical, and surgical
expenses.
Municipal finance. See within
this heading, "Municipal
finance."
Hospital school of Massachusetts.
See HOSPITAL SCHOOL OF
MASSACHUSETTS.
Housing and community
development department,
powers and duties, **23B:3.**
Housing and urban renewal
projects, municipal
construction of buildings in
aid, **121B:23.**
Husband.
See HUSBAND AND WIFE.
Hygiene required to be taught,
71:18.
Illiterate minors required to
attend evening school, **76:3.**
Illness.
Disease or illness. See within
this heading, "Disease or
illness."
Immunity from civil liability for
rendering emergency first aid
or transportation to a student,
71:55A.
Immunization of pupils, **41:99,
76:15, 76:15C.**
Impersonation of officer of school,
266:89.
Income taxes, deduction for
children attending education
institutions, **62:6.**
Incorporation, **180:1 et seq.**
Indemnity and indemnification of
personnel.
Actions and claims,
indemnification of school
personnel against, **258:1.**
Insurance, **40:4, 40:5.**
Regional school district
committee members,
indemnification, **71:16.**

SCHOOLS AND EDUCATION
—Cont'd

Indemnity and indemnification of personnel —Cont'd

Students.
See LETTERS OF CREDIT.

Teachers.
Liability insurance for indemnification of school personnel, **40:5.**

Town appropriations for indemnity insurance, **40:5.**

Independent agricultural and technical institutes, **74A:1 to 74A:23.**
See AGRICULTURAL AND TECHNICAL INSTITUTES.

Industrial accidents division, **23E:10.**

Industrial schools, reformatories, **120:1 et seq.**
See YOUTH SERVICES DEPARTMENT AND MASSACHUSETTS TRAINING SCHOOLS.

Infectious diseases.
Disease or illness. See within this heading, "Disease or illness."

Information.
See INFORMATION OR INFORMATION SERVICES.

Initiative petitions, filing of school committee's objections, **43:38.**

Injured students.
First aid. See within this heading, "First aid."

Inmates of certain institutions, tuition, **76:11.**

Innovative educational programs.
Experimental projects for establishment, **15:1G.**

Supplementary educational centers and innovative educational programs, agreements concerning, **40:4A.**

Inspection.
Examination, inspection, or investigation. See within this heading, "Examination, inspection, or investigation."

Institutional funds, management of, **180A:1 et seq.**
See INSTITUTIONAL FUND MANAGEMENT.

Instructional aides, hiring, **71:38.**

Instructional materials grant program, **15:57.**

SCHOOLS AND EDUCATION
—Cont'd

Instruction Materials Trust Fund, **71:20A.**

Instructors.
See TEACHERS.

Insurance.
Accident.
See ACCIDENT AND SICKNESS INSURANCE.

Athletic activities. See within this heading, "Athletic activities."

Committee recommendations with respect to nature and extent of coverage for buildings and personal property, **40:5.**

Firearms instructors, **131:14.**

Fraternal benefit societies. See within this heading, "Fraternal benefit societies."

Group insurance for state employees, **73:16, 74:42O.**

Indemnity insurance, **40:4, 40:5, 71:16.**

Laboratory or shop work, student injured, **40:5.**

Life insurance. See within this heading, "Life insurance."

New Bedford Institute of Technology, privileges of personnel, **74:42O.**

School buses.
See SCHOOL BUSES AND TRANSPORTATION OF PUPILS.

State college personnel, insurance coverage, **73:16.**

Superintendents, liability insurance, **71:16, 71:41, 71:63.**

Teachers' paychecks, transmittal of premiums deducted, **71:37B.**

Technical colleges' or institutes' buildings and contents, **74:45.**

University of Massachusetts memorial building and contents, insurance, **75:9.**

Intelligence test scores, purging students' records, **71:87.**

International education, Global Education, Center for, model curriculum, **71:1.**

Interscholastic athletics, participation, **71:47.**

Investigation.
Examination, inspection, or investigation. See within this heading, "Examination, inspection, or investigation."

SCHOOLS AND EDUCATION
—Cont'd

Investments.
Colleges.
See COLLEGES AND UNIVERSITIES.

Group annuity contracts for employees, **71:37B.**

Municipal deposits, **44:55B.**

Regional school district bonds and notes, proceeds, **44:55.**

School fund monies, **70:9.**

State bond sinking funds, student loan marketing association as permissible investment, **29:49.**

Trust funds of Education Department, **10:16.**

Italian American War Veterans of the United States, Inc Day, observance, **6:15J.**

Jails.
Correctional institutions. See within this heading, "Correctional institutions, programs."

Janitors and custodians.
Charter city, appointment and removal by school committee, **43:32.**

Physical examination by school physician, **71:54.**

Promotion as affecting pension, **32:45B.**

Regional school district to give preference to veterans in employing persons, **41:112.**

Removal by school committee of charter city, **43:32.**

Retirement and pension, **32:44 et seq.**

Town meetings, acceptance of statute providing for janitor's pension, **32:45.**

Tuberculosis examination, **71:55B.**

Uniforms, **71:48B.**

Widows of janitors and custodians, pensions, **32:44B.**

Job training.
Occupational guidance and placement. See within this heading, "Occupational guidance and placement."

Joint maintenance by cities and towns of course on junior college level, **71:77.**

Joint school union committees, organizational procedure, **71:63.**

SCHOOLS AND EDUCATION
—Cont'd
Judges.
  Training.
    See JUDGES.
Judicial review.
  See APPEAL AND REVIEW.
Junior colleges.
  See COLLEGES AND
    UNIVERSITIES.
Jurisdiction.
  Racial imbalance in schools,
    court jurisdiction, **15:1J,
    71:37D.**
  School attendance, jurisdiction,
    76:2.
Juvenile courts.
  See JUVENILE COURTS AND
    DELINQUENT CHILDREN.
Labor.
  Employees. See within this
    heading, "Employees."
Laboratory technologists, schools,
  112:2B.
Laboratory work, municipal
  appropriations for hospital or
  medical expenses of students
  injured, **40:5.**
Land court judges and personnel,
  agreements for programs of
  continuing education, **7:28A.**
Landlord and tenant.
  Lease of schools or property. See
    within this heading, "Lease
    of schools or property."
Landscape architects, **112:101.**
Languages.
  English. See within this
    heading, "English."
  Foreign language. See within
    this heading, "Foreign
    languages."
Leadership academy for training
  principals and supervisory
  personnel, **15:58.**
Lead poisoning prevention and
  control program, **111:192.**
Learning disabled students,
  admission, **15A:5, 15A:10,
  15A:19.**
Lease of schools or property.
  Cities and towns' authority to
    lease land and buildings for
    educational purposes, **40:4.**
  Education collaboratives, **40:4E.**
  Massachusetts educational
    communications
    commission, leases, **6:158.**
  Regional school districts.
    See REGIONAL SCHOOL
      DISTRICTS.

SCHOOLS AND EDUCATION
—Cont'd
Lease of schools or property
  —Cont'd
  Rehabilitation of veterans, lease
    to federal government,
    74:41.
  State colleges and universities,
    75:26-75:28.
  Surplus space or property, **40:3,
    71:16.**
  Vocational schools and
    education.
    Land for certain schools, lease,
      74:17.
    Veterans, lease of schools to
      federal government for
      rehabilitation, **74:41.**
Leaves of absence, **71:41A,
  71:41B, 73:4A, 75:14.**
  Justices, education leave,
    211B:4.
  Militia, leave of absence for
    training, **149:52A.**
  School personnel, **71:41A.**
  Superintendent of schools,
    71:16, 71:41, 71:63.
Legacy and succession taxes,
  exemption, **65:1.**
Legal counsel.
  See ATTORNEYS AT LAW.
Legislative agent or organization
  attempting to influence
  legislation, student
  government association
  excluded from definition of
  terms, **15A:18.**
Letters of credit.
  See LETTERS OF CREDIT.
Libraries and librarians, **15:1R.**
  Appeal from dismissal or
    discharge, **71:38H.**
  Governor's proclamation setting
    apart April as library media
    month, **6:15AAA.**
  Leaves of absence for study or
    research, **71:41A.**
  Tenure, **71:38H, 71:41.**
Life insurance.
  Credit life insurance on
    educational loans, **175:133.**
  Educational corporation as life
    insurance company,
    175:118.
  Loans to students as part of life
    insurance policies, **175:182.**
Lincoln's birthday, observance,
  6:13.
Liquor.
  Educational corporations and
    institutions.
    See ALCOHOLIC LIQUORS.

SCHOOLS AND EDUCATION
—Cont'd
Loans to students.
  Board of higher education,
    student loan repayment
    program attracting
    excellence to teaching
    program, **15A:19A.**
  Collection by Commonwealth,
    **62D:1, 62D:4, 62D:8,
    62D:10, 62D:13, 62D:14,
    62E:3 et seq.**
  Colleges.
    See COLLEGES AND
      UNIVERSITIES.
  Credit life insurance on
    educational loans, **175:133.**
  Garnishment of wages,
    compliance by state with,
    29:31.
  Life insurance policies, loans to
    students as part, **175:182.**
  Massachusetts Educational
    Financial Authority Act. See
    within this heading,
    "Massachusetts Educational
    Financial Authority Act."
  Revocation or suspension of
    license, default on loan,
    30A:13, 112:61.
  State bond sinking funds,
    permissible investments,
    29:49.
  Trust company officers,
    education loans extended,
    172:18.
Lobbying laws, exemptions, **3:50.**
Local history and government as
  required courses, **71:2.**
Location or place.
  Attendance, place, **76:1, 76:5,
    76:6.**
  Buildings, location, **71:70.**
  Highway safety stations for
    school children, **71:71A.**
Lodging house law inapplicable,
  140:22.
Lunches.
  See FOOD SERVICES AND
    FREE LUNCH
    PROGRAMS.
Lyman school.
  See LYMAN SCHOOL.
Machinery and equipment.
  Commissioner of education to
    collect apparatus, **69:1.**
  Community school programs,
    deposit and expenditure of
    money received by school
    committee, **71:71C.**
  Furnishing of tools, implements,
    materials, and supplies,
    71:48.

SCHOOLS AND EDUCATION
—Cont'd
Machinery and equipment
—Cont'd
Hoisting and hoisting
machinery, **146:53.**
Regional school districts.
See REGIONAL SCHOOL
DISTRICTS.
School buses, **71:7A, 90:7-90:7C.**
See SCHOOL BUSES AND
TRANSPORTATION OF
PUPILS.
Transportation of pupils, duties
of education department as
to, **71:7A, 90:7-90:7C.**
See SCHOOL BUSES AND
TRANSPORTATION OF
PUPILS.
Magazines and periodicals.
Procurement, contracts awarded
without bids, **30B:7.**
Magnet school facility.
Racial imbalance. See within
this heading, "Racial
imbalance."
Maintenance.
Repairs and maintenance. See
within this heading,
"Repairs and maintenance."
Maintenance assessment program.
Building assistance, **70B:16.**
Manpower development training.
See MANPOWER
DEVELOPMENT
TRAINING.
Maritime academy of
Massachusetts.
See MARITIME ACADEMY OF
MASSACHUSETTS.
Marriage.
Change of marital status as
ground for dismissal of
school personnel, **71:42,
71:42B.**
Disciplinary action against
student because of
marriage, **46:2, 71:84.**
School record as evidence of age
for purpose, **207:33A.**
Massachusetts college student loan
authority, establishment,
15C:1.
Massachusetts Educational
Financial Authority Act.
Bonds and notes, **15C:5A,
15C:5B.**
College opportunity fund,
creation, **15C:14B.**
College opportunity program
established, **15C:5A,
15C:5B.**

SCHOOLS AND EDUCATION
—Cont'd
Massachusetts Educational
Financial Authority Act
—Cont'd
Defaulters denied issuance or
renewal of licenses, **30A:13,
112:61.**
Definitions, **15C:3.**
Fees for issuance of bonds,
15C:5A, 15C:5B, 29:49C.
Financial agreements, **15C:5A,
15C:5B, 29:38C.**
Members of authority, **15C:4.**
Recordkeeping requirements,
15C:5A, 15C:5B.
Redemption of bonds, **15C:5A,
15C:5B.**
Savings programs, development,
15C:5.
Tuition agreements, **15C:5.**
Maximum age for attendance,
establishment, **76:1.**
Mayors.
See MAYORS.
Meals.
See FOOD SERVICES AND
FREE LUNCH
PROGRAMS.
Medical care or treatment.
Acupuncturists, **112:154.**
Examination.
Medical or physical
examination. See within
this heading, "Medical or
physical examination."
First aid. See within this
heading, "First aid."
Municipal finance. See within
this heading, "Municipal
finance."
Physicians and surgeons. See
within this heading,
"Physicians and surgeons."
Public safety department
trainees, **22:7A.**
Medical corporations, conferring of
degrees, **180:13.**
Medical laboratory technologists,
defined, **112:2B.**
Medical malpractice insurance,
remedial action requiring
additional training, **175A:5C.**
Medical or physical examination,
71:54, 71:57.
Postural defects in students,
testing by school districts,
71:57.
School bus operator's license,
applicant, **90:8A.**
Sickle cell anemia, testing of
children, **76:15A.**

SCHOOLS AND EDUCATION
—Cont'd
Medical or physical examination
—Cont'd
Test cards, state health
department to furnish,
111:185A.
Tuberculosis. See within this
heading, "Tuberculosis."
Medical schools.
See MEDICAL SCHOOLS.
Medical X-ray technicians, school
for training, **112:2C.**
Medicine, veterinary medicine,
dentistry, or nursing,
scholarships, **15A:7.**
Meditation, silent.
Prayer. See within this heading,
"Prayer."
Meetings.
State board of education, **15:1E.**
Memorial Day, observance, **71:32.**
Mentally ill.
See MENTALLY ILL AND
RETARDED PERSONS.
Meritorious performance in certain
fields, special award to pupils,
71:47.
Metropolitan district commission,
co-operative engineering
program, **28:4B, 28:4C.**
Migrant farm workers, educational
opportunities, **111:128H.**
Military affairs.
Military academy.
See MILITARY ACADEMY
OR SCHOOL.
Militia, training for. See within
this heading, "Militia,
training."
Missing in action, scholarships
for children of certain
servicemen, **15A:7.**
Recruiting on school campus,
71:88.
Scholarships.
See SCHOLARSHIPS AND
FELLOWSHIPS.
Military drill, **71:3.**
Military recruiting on campus,
71:88.
Militia, training, **33:38 et seq.**
Authority for training reserved
to states, **US Const Art 1
Sec 8 cl 15.**
Leave of absence for employees
for active duty training,
149:52A.
Summer camp, **33:60.**
Milk dealer license, **94A:4.**
Minimum age for attendance,
establishment, **76:1.**

SCHOOLS AND EDUCATION
—Cont'd

Minimum number of days required in each school year, **71:1, 71:4.**

Minimum state standards for school districts, **15:1G.**

Minimum wage law as inapplicable to persons undergoing rehabilitation or training in certain institutions, **151:2.**

Misconduct, exclusion of pupils, **76:17.**

Misrepresentation.
Fraud and deceit. See within this heading, "Fraud and deceit."

Missing children, notice to school, **22A:9.**

Model education programs, agreements, **40:4E.**

Modification.
Change. See within this heading, "Change."

Motion pictures, special license for showing, **143:85.**

Motor vehicles.
Colleges.
See COLLEGES AND UNIVERSITIES.
Driver education.
See DRIVER EDUCATION.
High schools, driving may be taught, **71:13D.**
Junior operator's license, application, **90:8.**
License plates used in the transportation of school children, **90:2.**
Nonresident students operating, **90:3.**
Safety patrols, establishment, **71:48A.**
School buses.
See SCHOOL BUSES AND TRANSPORTATION OF PUPILS.
Service vehicles, licensing and regulation, **159A:11A.**
Speed in school zones, **90:17.**
Traffic regulations and rules of the road. See within this heading, "Traffic regulations and rules of the road."

SCHOOLS AND EDUCATION
—Cont'd

Motor vehicles —Cont'd
Traffic safety week, educational programs, **6:15P.**

Municipal finance.
Adult education, continuing education, summer school, and community school programs, deposit of moneys received by school committee in connection with conduct, **71:71C, 71:71E.**
Allocations of education appropriations, prohibition against, **71:34.**
Athletic activities in schools, appropriations, **40:5, 44:7, 71:47.**
Breakfast programs, **15:1G.**
Budgets, notification of regional schools of vote concerning, **71:16B.**
Classes in citizenship, government, and English, reimbursement for expense, **69:10.**
Continuation schools and courses.
Fines and penalties of towns failing to raise funds, **71:26.**
Reimbursement of towns by Commonwealth, **71:24.**
Deaf school children, appropriations for hearing aids, **40:5.**
Deposit of moneys for certain programs, **71:71C, 71:71E.**
Enforcement of municipal obligation to provide funds to support schools, **71:34.**
Exceeding debt limit in anticipation of public funds, **71:26D.**
Eyeglasses for school children, appropriations, **40:5.**
Federal Bureau of Investigation training schools, appropriations for expense of local police officers attending, **40:5.**
Federal funds expended to aid schools, **44:53A.**

SCHOOLS AND EDUCATION
—Cont'd

Municipal finance —Cont'd
Gifts, grants, and gratuities.
Construction grants, **44:19.**
Trustees, cities and towns, **68:13, 68:14.**
In-service training for municipal officers and employees, **40:5.**
Investment of municipal deposits, **44:55B.**
Laboratory or shop, appropriation for insurance coverage for student injured, **40:5.**
Machinery or equipment, deposit and expenditure of money received, **71:71C.**
Magnet programs, reimbursement, **71:37J.**
Medical, hospital, and surgical expenses of public school students.
Appropriations for payment of reasonable, **40:5.**
Athletic contest, student injured, **40:5.**
Public transportation system used for transporting school students, reimbursement for cost incurred in maintaining, **71:7B.**
Refunding bonds, **44:21A.**
Regional school districts.
See REGIONAL SCHOOL DISTRICTS.
Reimbursement for tuition, **76:7, 76:9.**
Residence of school physician, appropriation, **40:13B.**
School buses and transportation of pupils, **40:5, 71:47.**
Shop injuries to students, appropriations for insurance against, **40:5.**
Special education reimbursements, **59:23, 71B:5.**
Stabilization fund, appropriation for approved school project, **40:5B.**
State aid or reimbursement.
See within this heading, "State aid or reimbursement."
Superintendence union employees, compensation, **71:53A.**

SCHOOLS AND EDUCATION
—Cont'd

Municipal finance —Cont'd

Supplementary education centers, authority to expend money, **40:4A.**

Support of schools, duty to furnish funds, **71:34.**

Teachers.

See TEACHERS.

Training schools for police officers, appropriations for police attending, **40:5.**

Trustees of gifts for educational purposes, municipalities, **68:13, 68:14.**

Trust property, power to hold and convey, **40:3.**

Tuition.

Certain instances, towns may be required to pay tuition, **71:6.**

Educational collaboratives and other schools, school committees to pay tuition, **71:71D.**

High school students, payment of tuition, **71:6.**

Nonresident students, **71:6A, 71:24, 76:6.**

Other town, tuition for attendance of pupil, **71:24.**

Reimbursement for tuition, **76:7, 76:9.**

Separate accounts, deposit of tuition, **71:71F.**

Waiver of tuition charges for child temporarily residing in town, **76:6.**

Municipal lighting and heating plants, training and employment of cadet engineers, **164:69B et seq.**

Music required to be taught, **71:1.**

Narcotics.

See DRUGS AND NARCOTICS.

National Defense Education Act, scholarships at University of Massachusetts, **75:33.**

National origin, discrimination against students based, **76:5.**

Nature study, state parks, recreation areas, and reservations, **132A:2D.**

Nautical schools, establishment by towns, **74:52.**

New Bedford institute of technology.

See NEW BEDFORD INSTITUTE OF TECHNOLOGY.

SCHOOLS AND EDUCATION
—Cont'd

New courses, requirements, **71:13.**

Newspapers.

Minors selling or delivering during school hours, **149:69, 149:73, 149:78, 149:83.**

Procurement, contracts awarded without bids, **30B:7.**

Nonresident students.

Aliens, tuition charges, **15A:5A.**

Attendance, **71:25, 76:6, 76:12 et seq.**

Bilingual education programs, enrollment of nonresident child, **71A:4.**

Colleges.

See COLLEGES AND UNIVERSITIES.

Deposit of tuition in separate accounts, **71:16D½, 71:71F.**

Federal funds for education, **76:12B.**

Motor vehicles nonresident students operating, **90:3.**

Racial imbalance, attendance to alleviate.

Racial imbalance. See within this heading, "Racial imbalance."

State colleges, **73:6.**

Temporarily unemployed minors working elsewhere than in town of residence, attendance at continuation schools, **71:25.**

Tuition, **15A:5A, 71:6A, 76:6.**

Continuation schools and courses, attending in another town, **71:24.**

Deposit in separate accounts, **71:16D½, 71:71F.**

Vocational education and schools, **74:7A.**

Waiver of tuition, **71:6A, 76:6.**

Vocational education and schools, **74:37C, 74:37F.**

Admission, **74:7.**

Transportation, **74:8A.**

Tuition, **74:7A.**

Norfolk county agricultural school.

See NORFOLK COUNTY AGRICULTURAL SCHOOL.

Notice.

Absence notification, **76:1A, 76:18, 76:19.**

Accreditation of all schools of higher learning, accepted applicants for admission to be given notice, **69:31C.**

SCHOOLS AND EDUCATION
—Cont'd

Notice —Cont'd

Annuity contracts for employees of public educational institutions, **71:37B.**

Bilingual program, notice to parents of child's enrollment, **71A:3.**

Budgets, hearings on proposed, **71:38N.**

Charter cities, notice as to construction work, **43:34.**

Colleges.

See COLLEGES AND UNIVERSITIES.

Committees. See within this heading, "Committees."

Correspondence schools, service of process, **75C:11.**

Degrees, notice as to revocation or suspension of institution's power to grant, **69:30A.**

Discipline of student, notice to non-custodial parent, **71:34H.**

Disease.

Exclusion of school children by reason, **71:55A.**

Notice, **71:56, 111:113.**

District's proposed annual budget, notice of public hearing, **71:38N.**

Dropouts, notice to parents, **76:18.**

Evening schools, **71:20.**

Fair educational practices proceedings, notice of hearing, **151C:3.**

Health board notified where child sent home by reason of dangerous disease, **71:55A.**

Intent to dismiss superintendent or teacher, **71:42, 71:63.**

Massachusetts training schools, notice of claims for damages by escaping inmates, **120:13A.**

Meetings of regional school district committees, **39:23B.**

Missing children, **22A:9.**

Parent or guardian.

Absences, notice, **76:18, 76:19.**

Custodial or non-custodial parent requesting information about child enrolled in school **71:34H.**

SCHOOLS AND EDUCATION
—Cont'd
Notice —Cont'd
Parent or guardian —Cont'd
Disease or defect found in
child, notice, **71:56.**
Racial imbalance, notice of
intention to transfer to
another school, **71:37D.**
Sex education, parental
notification regarding,
71:32A.
Racial imbalance. See within
this heading, "Racial
imbalance."
Reemployment of teachers or
superintendent, **71:41.**
Regional school districts.
See REGIONAL SCHOOL
DISTRICTS.
Sex education, parental
notification regarding,
71:32A.
Student rights, notice to public
school students of
regulations in defining and
clarifying, **71:85.**
Superintendents. See within this
heading, "Superintendents."
Teachers.
Certification, **71:38G.**
Intent to dismiss teacher,
71:42.
Reemployment of teachers,
71:41.
Transitional bilingual program.
Notice to parents of child's
enrollment, **71A:3.**
Union superintendents of
schools, intent to remove,
71:63.
Weapons, posting of notices
regarding, **269:11.**
Youth Services Department and
Massachusetts Training
Schools.
Claims for damage by
escaping inmates of
institutions, **120:13A.**
Furnishing information to
board, **119:69A.**
Number.
Absences, permitted, **76:1.**
Days in school year, **71:1, 71:4,
71:4A.**
Weeks in session, **71:21, 71:37.**
Nurses.
See NURSES AND NURSING
SERVICES.
Nursing or rest home.
Administrators, training,
112:110, 112:115.

SCHOOLS AND EDUCATION
—Cont'd
Nursing or rest home —Cont'd
Licensing requirements, **111:71.**
Nurses, schools for.
See NURSES AND NURSING
SERVICES.
Nutritional standards and
regulations for school food
services, establishment,
15:1G.
Occupational guidance and
placement.
Children in need of services,
119:39E, 119:39G.
Job training and retraining
centers, **15:1F.**
Supervisor, **15:6B.**
Town directors.
Appointment, **71:38A, 71:38D.**
Commission, fee,
compensation or reward,
acceptance of prohibited,
71:38F.
Duties, **71:38A.**
Formation of district for
employment, **71:38D.**
Provisions as to teachers
applicable, **71:38C.**
Vocational education.
See VOCATIONAL
EDUCATION AND
SCHOOLS.
Ocean sanctuaries, activities
permitted, **132A:16.**
Offenses.
Crimes and offenses. See within
this heading, "Crimes and
offenses."
Office of educational quality and
accountability, **15:55A.**
Oil and hazardous material
release prevention and
response act, priority disposal
site defined, **21E:2, 21E:3A.**
Older persons.
Education programs, **40:5.**
Hot lunches served to older
persons at schools, **19A:37.**
On-campus recruiting
opportunities offered to armed
services, **15A:38.**
Optometrists, annual participation
in educational programs as
condition precedent to renewal
of registration, **112:69.**
Orders for education and support
of minors under 21 years of
age, **208:28, 209:37.**
Organization of educational
corporation, **180:3.**

SCHOOLS AND EDUCATION
—Cont'd
Organizations of pupils,
supervision and control, **71:47.**
Orthography required to be
taught, **71:1, 71:18.**
Out-of-state teachers at public
academies, **32:3.**
Outside educational resources,
utilization, **69:36.**
Overburden aid, **70:5.**
Overtime pay for employee,
151:1A.
Parent and child.
Parental involvement.
Curriculum accommodation
plans, **71:38Q1/2.**
Parenthood as ground for
expulsion or disciplinary
action, **71:84.**
Parking control officers,
appointment, **147:10F.**
Partnerships, school-community
partnerships, **71:59D.**
Part-time student.
See PART-TIME STUDENT.
Patriotic plaque may be installed
on building, **71:69A.**
Payroll, establishment of
centralized weekly system for
teachers and supervisors,
29:31.
Penal institutions.
Correctional institutions. See
within this heading,
"Correctional institutions,
programs."
Penalties.
Fines and penalties. See within
this heading, "Fines and
penalties."
Pensions.
See RETIREMENT SYSTEMS
AND PENSIONS.
Permanent absence from school,
procedure, **76:19.**
Permanent employment.
See TENURE AND SENIORITY.
Personnel.
Employees. See within this
heading, "Employees."
Personnel administrator, training
programs for state employees,
7:28A.
Persons and properties, prohibition
of acts against, **265:39,
266:127A, 266:127B.**
Pesticides.
Anti-microbial pesticides.
Review for applicability,
132B:6K.

SCHOOLS AND EDUCATION
—Cont'd

Pesticides —Cont'd
Application restrictions,
132B:6C.
Compliance with application
requirements, **71:68.**
Emergency applications,
132B:6H.
Indoor use, products eligible,
132B:6F.
Integrated pest management
plans, **132B:6E.**
Notice of application, **132B:6C.**
Outdoor use, products eligible,
132B:6G.
Records of applications, **132B:6I.**
Training programs exempted,
132B:6J.
Pharmacists and pharmacies.
See PHARMACISTS AND
PHARMACIES.
Photography services, purchase of,
30B:1.
Physical education.
See PHYSICAL EDUCATION
AND FITNESS.
Physical examination.
Medical or physical examination.
See within this heading,
"Medical or physical
examination."
Physically handicapped pupils.
Disabled or handicapped
persons. See within this
heading, "Disabled or
handicapped persons."
Physical restraint.
Use on students, **71:37G.**
Physical therapy schools, **112:23C.**
Physician assistants, educational
requirements for registration,
112:9I, 112:9K.
Physicians and surgeons.
American Medical Association,
approval of schools or
courses for physical
therapists, **112:23C.**
Appointment and assignment,
71:53.
Appropriation for quarters for
school physician, **40:13B.**
Assistants, programs of training
and qualification,
certificates of registration,
112:9G.
Athletic activities. See within
this heading, "Athletic
activities."
Buildings, examination, **71:54.**
Canadian medical school
graduates, licensing, **112:2.**

SCHOOLS AND EDUCATION
—Cont'd

Physicians and surgeons —Cont'd
Cities and towns.
Certain towns, town
physician, **41:106A.**
Residence of school physician,
appropriations, **40:13B.**
Committees. See within this
heading, "Committees."
County agricultural school
athletic program,
employment of physician,
74:31B.
Dangerous disease, examination
of child infected with or
exposed, **71:55.**
Employment permits.
See LABOR AND
WORKFORCE
DEVELOPMENT.
Feet of pupils, examination,
71:57.
Fellows in medicine, surgery,
and urology, training grants,
115A:10.
Football games of public
secondary schools, physician
to be in attendance, **71:54A.**
Foreign medical graduates,
necessity of obtaining
certificate from educational
council, **112:2.**
Health inspector, appointment,
41:102A.
Industrial schools, **120:3.**
Laboratory technologists,
schools, **112:2B.**
Malpractice insurance, remedial
action requiring additional
training, **175A:5C.**
Medical corporations, conferring
of degrees, **180:13.**
Medical or physical examination.
See within this heading,
"Medical or physical
examination."
Medical schools.
See MEDICAL SCHOOLS.
Physical examination.
Medical or physical
examination. See within
this heading, "Medical or
physical examination."
Podiatry and podiatrists. See
within this heading,
"Podiatry and podiatrists."
Psychotropic drugs,
administration, **71:54B.**
Pupils showing signs of ill
health to be sent home,
71:55A.

SCHOOLS AND EDUCATION
—Cont'd

Physicians and surgeons —Cont'd
Residence quarters, **40:13B.**
Residents in medical specialties,
establishment of training
programs for, under health
department, **17:6A.**
Superintendence district or
union, employment, **71:53A,
71:53B.**
Teachers, temporary registration
of physicians holding faculty
appointment, **112:9B.**
Technologist or technician
schools, fines and penalties
for violations, **112:2B,
112:2C.**
Tuberculosis examination,
71:55B.
University of Massachusetts,
75:36C.
Physiology required to be taught,
71:18.
Place.
Location or place. See within
this heading, "Location or
place."
Pledge of allegiance to the flag,
71:69.
Plumbers and gas fitters, **142:3A.**
Inspections and inspectors,
142:11B.
Podiatry and podiatrists.
Approval of schools for
podiatrists, **112:16.**
Facilities for students, **112:16B.**
Pupils' feet, examination, **71:57.**
Police.
See POLICE.
Poliomyelitis, immunization
against, **41:99, 76:15.**
Politics of candidates for teaching
positions, inquiries forbidden,
71:39.
Postural defects in students,
testing by school districts,
71:57.
Practical arts classes.
See PRACTICAL ART
CLASSES.
Practical nurses.
See NURSES AND NURSING
SERVICES.
Prayer.
Children participating in when
voluntary, **71:1B.**
Period of silence for prayer or
meditation, **71:1A.**
Pregnancy, prohibition against
disciplinary action based
solely, **71:84.**

SCHOOLS AND EDUCATION
—Cont'd

Presence or absence.
Absence or presence. See within this heading, "Absence or presence."
Principals.
Certification, **71:38G.**
Curriculum accommodation plans, **71:38Q1/2.**
Elections, contracts, and promotions, **71:38.**
Emergency first aid or transportation provided to pupils, immunity from liability, **71:55A.**
Employment and duties, **71:59B.**
Failure to display flag or to salute or have pupils salute flag, penalty, **71:69.**
Finances and funds.
Teacher, principal and superintendent quality endowment fund, **10:35S.**
Leadership academy for training principals and supervisory personnel, **15:58.**
Leaves of absence, **71:41A.**
Morals and competency requirements, **71:4.**
Recruiting program, **15A:19E.**
Residency requirements, **71:38.**
School Principals' Recognition Day, **6:12UU.**
Tenure, **71:41.**
Tuberculosis examinations, **71:55B.**
Printing of tax bill for school tax, **60:3A.**
Priorities in hiring school committees, **112:23E.**
Prisons.
Correctional institutions. See within this heading, "Correctional institutions, programs."
Private schools.
See PRIVATE SCHOOLS.
Probate court orders for support and education of children under 21 years of age, **208:28, 209:37.**
Probation officers, **276:85, 276:99.**
Probation reports, accessibility, **276:100.**
Professional development plans, **71:38Q.**
Professional development schools grant program, **15A:20, 15A:21.**
Promotion of employee, **32:45B, 71:38.**

SCHOOLS AND EDUCATION
—Cont'd

Provisional educators, **71:38G.**
Psychotropic drugs, **71:54B.**
Public charges.
See WELFARE AND SOCIAL SERVICES.
Public health services for private school students as affected by school's discrimination, **71:57.**
Public office, leaves of absences for school personnel elected, **71:41A.**
Public officers and employees.
Employees. See within this heading, "Employees."
Public relations bureau, establishment, **71:38K.**
Public safety department trainees, medical expenses, **22:7A.**
Public safety executive office, board of schoolhouse structural standards as agency within, **6A:18.**
Public school, defined, **32:1.**
Public use of property or buildings, **71:71.**
Public welfare.
See WELFARE AND SOCIAL SERVICES.
Public works and department.
Co-operative engineering students' program, **16:4B.**
Crossings, specifications and standards for objects erected, **85:21A.**
Speed of motor vehicles in school zones, **90:17.**
Purchasing consortium.
Board of higher education and board of trustees, **15A:24A.**
Qualification or disqualification.
Board of higher education, qualifications for scholarship recipients, **15A:16.**
Civil service by commitment, disqualification, **120:21.**
Colleges.
See COLLEGES AND UNIVERSITIES.
Correspondence school license, proceedings to obtain, **75C:2.**
Education department.
See EDUCATION DEPARTMENT.
School bus operators, qualifications, **90:7B, 90:8A.**
Quorum for school budget hearing, **71:38N.**
Race.
Civil rights. See within this heading, "Civil rights."

SCHOOLS AND EDUCATION
—Cont'd

Racial imbalance, **15:1J, 71:37, 71:37D.**
Aid and assistance.
Magnet school facility, application for grants, **71:37I.**
State aid withheld from schools failing to eliminate, **15:1I.**
Attendance of nonresident children to correct, **76:12A, 76:12B.**
Busing.
See SCHOOL BUSES AND TRANSPORTATION OF PUPILS.
Board of education, authority and duties, **71:30.**
Busing to alleviate.
See SCHOOL BUSES AND TRANSPORTATION OF PUPILS.
Declaration of public policy, **71:37C.**
Definition, **71:37D.**
Education department.
See EDUCATION DEPARTMENT.
Federal funds, expenditures by school committee, **76:12A.**
Grants to magnet schools, **71:37I.**
Jurisdiction, **15:1J, 71:37D.**
Magnet school facility.
Application for grants, **71:37I.**
Establishment, **71:37I, 71:37J.**
Payment of costs, **71:37J.**
Notice.
Change in district, notice of hearing, **71:37D.**
Parents or guardian, written notice of intention to transfer to another school, **71:37D.**
School committee or regional district school committee finding that racial imbalance exists, **71:37D.**
Public hearing required prior to changing school district to eliminate, **71:37D.**
Reports on progress of plan for elimination, **71:37B.**
School buses and transportation of pupils.
See SCHOOL BUSES AND TRANSPORTATION OF PUPILS.

SCHOOLS AND EDUCATION
—Cont'd

Racial imbalance —Cont'd
School committees.
Duties, **15:1I, 15:1J, 71:37D.**
Expenditure of federal funds
to relieve, **76:12A.**
Magnet school facilities,
application for grants,
71:37I.
Non-white pupils,
determination of
percentage, **71:37D.**
Plans for elimination of racial
imbalance, **71:37D.**
Supreme judicial and superior
courts, jurisdiction, **15:1J,
71:37D.**
Transfer of pupils to alleviate,
71:37D.
Radio and television.
Board of higher education,
Massachusetts corporation
for educational
telecommunication, **15A:3A.**
Educational television, **71:13F
et seq.**
See EDUCATIONAL
TELEVISION.
Technicians registration law,
applicability, **112:87QQQ.**
Raffles and bazaars, conduct,
271:7A.
REACH Awards for educational
achievement, **15:55.**
Reading and writing.
Correctional institutions. See
within this heading,
"Correctional institutions,
programs."
Real property, **40:3, 40:14, 71:16,
128:45.**
Records, reports, and returns.
Abused and neglected children
under 16, reports to be
made by administrator,
119:51A.
Annual report.
Education department.
See EDUCATION
DEPARTMENT.
Superintendents. See within
this heading,
"Superintendents."
Trustees of trust funds, **68:13,
68:14.**
Attorneys' fees in proceedings to
compel furnishing of record,
71:34B.
Chief executive office of cities
and towns in district, copies
of reports to be filed with,
72:9.

SCHOOLS AND EDUCATION
—Cont'd

Records, reports, and returns
—Cont'd
Colleges.
See COLLEGES AND
UNIVERSITIES.
Committees. See within this
heading, "Committees."
Criminal offender record
information of applicants for
positions, **71:38R.**
Department of education.
See EDUCATION
DEPARTMENT.
Districts, end-of-year reports,
72:3, 72:6.
Educational trust funds of
towns, **68:13, 68:14.**
Fair educational practice
proceedings, reports,
151C:3.
Financial statement of school
athletic accident, health,
and benefit plan, duties of
treasurer, **175:29.**
Labor.
See LABOR AND
WORKFORCE
DEVELOPMENT.
Massachusetts Educational
Financial Authority
requirements, **15C:5A,
15C:5B.**
Missing children, **22A:9.**
Parents with or without custody
of child, requesting
information from school
71:34H.
Pesticides.
Records of applications,
132B:6I.
Private school students, transfer
of records, **71:34G.**
Probation reports, accessibility,
276:100.
Racial imbalance in schools,
reports on progress of plan
for elimination, **71:37B.**
Regional school districts.
See REGIONAL SCHOOL
DISTRICTS.
Registers and returns generally,
72:1 to 72:9.
Retention, duplication, storage,
and destruction of school
records, **71:50.**
Rules and regulations as to
recordkeeping, **71:34D.**
School building assistance,
70B:17.

SCHOOLS AND EDUCATION
—Cont'd

Records, reports, and returns
—Cont'd
State aid, **70:8.**
Reports to commissioner, **70:4.**
Student records. See within this
heading, "Student records."
Superintendents. See within this
heading, "Superintendents."
Teacher's right to inspect own
record, **71:42C.**
Trust funds, **68:13, 68:14.**
Tuberculosis examination of
employees, **71:55B.**
Weapons, report of incident
involving student possession
or use of, **71:37L.**
Youth services department.
See YOUTH SERVICES
DEPARTMENT AND
MASSACHUSETTS
TRAINING SCHOOLS.
Recruitment for armed forces on
campus, **71:88.**
Reduction.
Salaries of teachers and
superintendents, **71:43.**
State aid or reimbursement. See
within this heading, "State
aid or reimbursement."
Reformatories.
See YOUTH SERVICES
DEPARTMENT AND
MASSACHUSETTS
TRAINING SCHOOLS.
Regional community colleges.
See REGIONAL COMMUNITY
COLLEGES.
Regional school districts,
71:14-71:20.
See REGIONAL SCHOOL
DISTRICTS.
Registered nurses, employment in
schools, **71:53, 71:53A,
71:53B.**
Registers and returns, **72:1 to
72:9.**
Attendance registers, **72:8.**
Condition of schools.
School committee, annual
report, **72:4.**
Copies of reports, **72:9.**
Enrollment report, annual, **72:3.**
Extension of time to file, **72:6.**
Failure to file, **72:5.**
Penalties, **72:6, 72:7.**
Forms, furnishing, **72:1.**
Registration information
required, **72:2.**
School committee, annual report,
72:4.

SCHOOLS AND EDUCATION
—Cont'd
Registers and returns —Cont'd
School returns, annual report, **72:4.**
Registration.
Annual enrollment report, **72:3.**
Driver education.
Courses, content, **71:13D.**
Motor vehicles registrar's power as to driver schools, **90:32G.**
Education council for foreign medical graduates.
See EDUCATION COUNCIL FOR FOREIGN MEDICAL GRADUATES.
Enrollment report, annual, **72:3.**
Forms, furnishing, **72:1.**
Information required, **72:2.**
Registration of voters.
Assistant registrar of voters at high schools and vocational schools, **51:42E.**
Dormitories, listing of residents for purposes of voter registration, **51:10A.**
Employees as registered voters, **51:42E.**
School committee, board of registrars of voters to transmit lists of persons up to 21 years of age, **51:4, 51:14A.**
Sessions in schools, **51:42C et seq.**
Regulations.
Rules and regulations. See within this heading, "Rules and regulations."
Rehabilitation commission, supervisor of education, **6:79.**
Reimbursement.
Appropriation, **59:23.**
Attendance of nonresident students, **76:12A.**
Breakfast programs, **15:1G.**
Cities and towns.
Education department.
See EDUCATION DEPARTMENT.
Municipal finance. See within this heading, "Municipal finance."
State aid or reimbursement. See within this heading, "State aid or reimbursement."
Taxes. See within this heading, "Taxation."

SCHOOLS AND EDUCATION
—Cont'd
Reimbursement —Cont'd
Cities and towns —Cont'd
Working committee established to draft guidelines for reimbursement, **15:60.**
Model educational programs, services, **40:4E.**
Pensions and retirement systems, collaborative education programs, **32:28.**
Regional school districts.
See REGIONAL SCHOOL DISTRICTS.
Special education.
See SPECIAL EDUCATION.
State aid or reimbursement. See within this heading, "State aid or reimbursement."
Superintendent of schools.
District superintendent, expenses, **71:64.**
Employment contract, **71:16, 71:41, 71:63.**
Salary, reimbursement in certain small towns, **71:59A.**
Teachers.
See TEACHERS.
Transportation of students, reimbursement for expenses, **71:7A, 71:16C.**
Tuition. See within this heading, "Tuition."
Vocational education.
See VOCATIONAL EDUCATION AND SCHOOLS.
Religion.
Absences, **76:1, 151C:2B.**
Books not to favor tenets of any particular sect, **71:31.**
Candidates for teaching positions, inquiries, **71:39.**
Discrimination on account of.
Civil rights. See within this heading, "Civil rights."
Educational television, sponsorship of programs, **71:13I.**
Fair educational practices.
See FAIR EDUCATIONAL PRACTICES.
Injury to buildings used for religious instruction, **266:98.**
Minimum wage law as applicable to rehabilitation and training programs, in religious institutions, **151:2.**

SCHOOLS AND EDUCATION
—Cont'd
Religion —Cont'd
Prayer. See within this heading, "Prayer."
Sabbath schools maintained in correctional institutions, **127:89.**
Silent meditation period, **71:1A.**
Sponsorship of religion by executive committee for educational television programs as prohibited, **71:13I.**
Teachers.
See TEACHERS.
Use of school property by religious organization, **71:71.**
Vaccination of pupils, exemption on religious grounds, **76:15.**
Removal, demotion, or dismissal of school personnel, **43:32, 71:42.**
Janitors and custodians, **43:32.**
Judicial review of.
See APPEAL AND REVIEW.
Librarians, appeal from discharge, **71:38H.**
Marriage as ground, **71:42, 71:42B.**
Superintendents. See within this heading, "Superintendents."
Teachers.
See TEACHERS.
Treasurers of regional school districts, **41:39B.**
Union superintendent, removal, **71:63.**
Removal of minor from employment for failure to attend continuation school or course, **149:91.**
Repairs and maintenance.
Cities and towns to provide and maintain buildings, **71:1, 71:4, 71:68.**
Colleges.
See COLLEGES AND UNIVERSITIES.
Contracts for, periods authorized, **40:4.**
Janitors and custodians. See within this heading, "Janitors and custodians."
Regional school districts building committee, powers and duties, **71:16A.**
Traffic control devices, **85:2.**
Reports.
Records, reports, and returns. See within this heading, "Records, reports, and returns."

472

SCHOOLS AND EDUCATION
—Cont'd
Requested courses, school committee approval, **71:13.**
Residence.
Colleges.
See COLLEGES AND UNIVERSITIES.
Correspondence schools, service of process, **75C:11.**
Dormitories to list residents for purposes of voter registration, **51:10A.**
Nonresident students. See within this heading, "Nonresident students."
Physician, town appropriation for residence, **40:13B.**
Restrictions on residency requirements for principals, teachers, and professional employees, **71:38.**
Special education, residential schools, **71B:2, 71B:3, 71B:5.**
Superintendent.
Effect on ability to address local appropriating authority, **71:34.**
Teachers' aides, **71:38.**
Tuition charges for child temporarily residing in town, waiver, **76:6.**
Residents in medical specialties.
Physicians and surgeons. See within this heading, "Physicians and surgeons."
Rest home.
Nursing or rest home. See within this heading, "Nursing or rest home."
Retail sales tax, exemptions, **64C:6.**
Retarded persons.
See MENTALLY ILL AND RETARDED PERSONS.
Retirement systems.
See RETIREMENT SYSTEMS AND PENSIONS.
Revenue department.
See REVENUE DEPARTMENT AND COMMISSIONER.
Review.
See APPEAL AND REVIEW.
Revocation or suspension.
Default on education loan, revocation or suspension of license, **30A:13, 112:61.**
Institution's power to grant degrees, **69:30A.**

SCHOOLS AND EDUCATION
—Cont'd
Revocation or suspension —Cont'd
Revenue Department and Commissioner, treasurer of municipality, district, or regional school district, **41:39B.**
Teachers and superintendents, suspension, **71:42, 71:42D.**
Weapons, report of incident involving student possession or use of, **37:L.**
Riding schools.
See RIDING SCHOOLS.
Rights of students.
Student rights. See within this heading, "Student rights."
Rules and regulations.
Attendance. See within this heading, "Attendance."
Committees. See within this heading, "Committees."
Food services, establishment of nutritional standards and regulations, **15:1G.**
Publication of rules and regulations pertaining to teachers and students, **71:37.**
Racial imbalance transfers, **71:37D.**
Recordkeeping, **71:34D.**
Student rights, adoption after student hearings of rules and regulations defining and clarifying rules, **71:85.**
Supervisor of attendance, appointment, compensation, **76:19.**
Traffic regulations and rules of the road. See within this heading, "Traffic regulations and rules of the road."
Tuition, waiver, **76:6.**
Sabbath schools maintained in correctional institutions, **127:89.**
Safety.
See SAFETY AND SAFETY DEVICES.
Salaries and compensation, **15:1G, 71:40, 71:42, 71:43.**
Advisory commission on academically talented pupils, compensation for members, **15:6C.**
Centralized weekly payroll system for supervisors and teachers, establishment, **29:31.**

SCHOOLS AND EDUCATION
—Cont'd
Salaries and compensation
—Cont'd
Chancellor of Board of Regents of Higher Education, **15A:4.**
Clean water scholarship intern program, services provided, **20:6A.**
Colleges.
See COLLEGES AND UNIVERSITIES.
Committees. See within this heading, "Committees."
County agricultural school trustees, **74:27.**
Dismissed personnel, **71:42.**
Education department.
See EDUCATION DEPARTMENT.
Fees. See within this heading, "Fees."
Food and agriculture department's scholarship intern program, services provided, **21:3.**
Minimum wage law as inapplicable to persons undergoing rehabilitation or training in certain institutions, **151:2.**
Occupational guidance and placement director, **71:38F.**
Overtime pay, **151:1A.**
Reduction of teachers' and superintendents' salaries, **71:43.**
Regional school districts, **71:16, 71:42B, 71:64.**
Regional vocational school committees, compensation of treasurers, **71:16A.**
School bus contracts bidders, employees, **71:7A.**
Special education personnel in school departments of certain institutions, **71B:12.**
State employees in training schools, pay plan, **30:45.**
Superintendence districts and unions. See within this heading, "Superintendence districts and unions."
Superintendents. See within this heading, "Superintendents."
Supervisors, **29:31, 30:46.**
Supervisors of attendance, **76:19.**
Teachers, **29:31, 29:31B, 71:40, 71:42B.**
See TEACHERS.

SCHOOLS AND EDUCATION
—Cont'd
Salaries and compensation
—Cont'd
Transportation of pupils, wage rates under contracts, **71:7A.**
Union superintendent, **71:63, 71:64.**
Voluntary services at public schools during working hours without loss of salary, state employees authorized to provide, **29:31E.**
Withholding tax on wages of students employed in personal employment, **62B:1.**
Workers' compensation. See within this heading, "Workers' compensation."
Sales tax exemptions, **64C:6, 64H:6.**
Sanitarians, continuing education requirements for registration renewals, **112:87MM.**
Sanitary engineers.
Janitors and custodians. See within this heading, "Janitors and custodians."
Savings banks, accounts, and deposits, **71:16G½, 167:D:11.**
Scholarships.
See SCHOLARSHIPS AND FELLOWSHIPS.
School aid.
Aid and assistance. See within this heading, "Aid and assistance."
School buses.
See SCHOOL BUSES AND TRANSPORTATION OF PUPILS.
School Choice Tuition Trust Fund, **76:12C.**
School committees.
Committees. See within this heading, "Committees."
School districts.
Districts. See within this heading, "Districts."
Schoolhouses.
Buildings. See within this heading, "Buildings."
School improvement fund, **10:35F.**
School readiness office, **15:54.**
School social workers.
Social workers. See within this heading, "Social workers."
School teachers.
See TEACHERS.

SCHOOLS AND EDUCATION
—Cont'd
Schooner Ernestina Commission, duties, **6:182B.**
Securities Act, exemptions, **110A:402.**
Selectmen.
Aldermen and selectmen. See within this heading, "Aldermen and selectmen."
Senior citizens, **40:5.**
Sentence.
See SENTENCE AND PUNISHMENT.
Sex discrimination.
Change of marital status of superintendent as cause for dismissal, **71:42.**
Pupils, discrimination against, **76:5.**
Sexual orientation, **151B:1, 151B:4.**
Teachers.
See TEACHERS.
Unfair educational practice, sex discrimination, **151C:2.**
Vocational training schools, discrimination, **151C:2A.**
Sex education.
Committees, appointment, powers, and duties, **71:38O.**
Parental notification regarding, **71:32A.**
Sexual harassment of students, **151C:2.**
Ships.
Colleges and universities.
See SHIPS AND OTHER WATERCRAFT.
Shirley industrial school.
See SHIRLEY INDUSTRIAL SCHOOL.
Shop work, municipal appropriation for medical or hospital expenses of student injured, **40:5.**
Sickle cell anemia, testing pupils, **76:15A.**
Sickness.
Disease or illness. See within this heading, "Disease or illness."
Sight of pupils.
Eyes. See within this heading, "Eyes."
Silent meditation period, observance, **71:1A.**
Situation of schoolhouses, determination of by cities and towns, **71:70.**
Smith's agricultural school.
See SMITH'S AGRICULTURAL SCHOOL.

SCHOOLS AND EDUCATION
—Cont'd
Smoking in schools, prohibition, **71:2A.**
Social services department.
See WELFARE AND SOCIAL SERVICES.
Social workers.
Retirement systems.
See RETIREMENT SYSTEMS AND PENSIONS.
Teacher, included in definition, **32:1.**
Tenure rights, **74:22E.**
Vocational schools, **74:22E.**
Software.
Procurement, contracts awarded without bids, **30B:7.**
Solid waste management, environmental Protection Department, **16:18. (note)**
Sororities.
See SORORITIES AND FRATERNITIES.
Spanish required to be taught in certain high schools, **71:13.**
Special education.
See SPECIAL EDUCATION.
Speech, freedom of.
Student rights. See within this heading, "Student rights."
Speed in school zones, **90:17.**
Spelling required to be taught, **71:1, 71:18.**
Spitting in school building, **270:14, 270:15.**
Sports.
Athletic activities. See within this heading, "Athletic activities."
Stabilization fund.
Appropriation by municipality for approved school project, **40:5B.**
Establishment, **71:16G½.**
State aid or reimbursement, **70:1 et seq.**
Acceptance, **71:37A.**
Adjusted prior year amount, **70:12.**
Allocation of funds appropriated for state school aid, **70:13.**
Amount of aid, determination, **70:3, 70:6, 70:7, 70:11.**
Amount of state aid, determination of, **70:12.**
Application of funds, **70:8.**
Budget guidelines compiled by board of education, **15:1G.**
Building assistance. See within this heading, "Building assistance."

SCHOOLS AND EDUCATION
—Cont'd
State aid or reimbursement
—Cont'd
Classes in citizenship,
government and English,
69:10.
Construction of school buildings,
financial assistance for.
Building assistance. See
within this heading,
"Building assistance."
Continuation schools or courses,
71:24.
Deductions for schools not kept
open for required number of
days, **71:4A.**
Definitions, **70:2.**
English, reimbursement of
expenses for providing class,
69:10.
Estimates, **70:5, 70:10.**
Excess school aid carried over
from previous year,
treatment, **70:8.**
Exemption of certain districts,
70:14.
Expenditure of funds, **70:8.**
Formula for determining state
aid, **70:3, 70:3A.**
Gifts, **70:8.**
Government theory,
reimbursement of expenses
for providing classes, **69:10.**
Grants, **70:8.**
High schools, reimbursement,
71:11.
Ineligibility, **70:8.**
Legislative purpose, **70:1.**
Management of funds, **70:8.**
Physically disabled pupils,
tuition and transportation,
71:10.
Professional development plans,
71:38Q.
Public charges, payment of
tuition, **76:7, 76:10.**
Racial imbalance, withholding
state aid from schools
failing to eliminate, **15:1I.**
Reduction.
Automatic reductions of school
appropriations, **70:7.**
Overburden aid, **70:5.**
Regional school districts,
71:16B-71:16D.
See REGIONAL SCHOOL
DISTRICTS.
Reports, **70:4, 70:8.**
Revenue commissioner, amount
of aid certified, **70:2.**

SCHOOLS AND EDUCATION
—Cont'd
State aid or reimbursement
—Cont'd
School buses and transportation
of pupils, **71:7A, 71A:8,
71B:14.**
See SCHOOL BUSES AND
TRANSPORTATION OF
PUPILS.
Special education, **15:1M, 70:4,
71B:14.**
State treasurer.
See STATE TREASURER.
Student government day, state
funds not to be used, **6:12M.**
Superintendence unions, **71:64.**
Superintendents. See within this
heading, "Superintendents."
Todd fund, income, **70:10, 70:11.**
Transitional bilingual education,
reimbursement of costs of
programs, **71A:8.**
Transportation of pupils, **71:7A,
71A:8, 71B:14.**
See SCHOOL BUSES AND
TRANSPORTATION OF
PUPILS.
Tuition. See within this heading,
"Tuition."
Union superintendents of
schools, **71:64.**
Vocational education.
See VOCATIONAL
EDUCATION AND
SCHOOLS.
Voluntary services at public
schools during working
hours without loss of salary,
state employees authorized
to provide, **29:31E.**
State bond sinking funds,
investment in student loan
marketing association, **29:49.**
State building code as applicable
to school buildings, **15:1G.**
State colleges, **73:1 et seq.**
See COLLEGES AND
UNIVERSITIES.
State comptroller's duties as to
funds, **7A:9, 7A:12.**
State constitution day, observance,
6:14B.
State employees in training
schools, pay plan, **30:45.**
State finance.
State aid or reimbursement. See
within this heading, "State
aid or reimbursement."
State police.
See STATE POLICE.

SCHOOLS AND EDUCATION
—Cont'd
State schools.
Annuity contracts for employees,
notice, **15:18A.**
Colleges, **73:1 et seq.**
See COLLEGES AND
UNIVERSITIES.
Correspondence schools, schools
operated by state, **75C:1.**
Mentally ill.
See MENTALLY ILL AND
RETARDED PERSONS.
Youth services department.
See YOUTH SERVICES
DEPARTMENT AND
MASSACHUSETTS
TRAINING SCHOOLS.
State treasurer.
See STATE TREASURER.
Statutes distributed to schools,
5:3.
Stimulants, teaching effects, **71:1.**
Streets.
Highways and streets. See
within this heading,
"Highways and streets."
Structures.
Buildings. See within this
heading, "Buildings."
Student advisory committee,
election, **71:38M.**
Student conduct handbooks, **71:37.**
Annual review by committee,
71:37H.
Student defined, **90:1.**
Student government associations
excluded from definition of
legislative agent or
organization attempting to
influence legislation, **15A:18.**
Student government day,
observance, **6:12M.**
Student loans.
Loans to students. See within
this heading, "Loans to
students."
Student records, **71:34D, 71:34E.**
Intelligence test scores, purging
from student records, **71:87.**
Physical record of each child to
be kept, **71:57.**
Transcript of record, furnishing,
71:34A, 71:34B.
Waiver of school record for
employment permit, **149:88.**
Student rights, **71:82.**
Rules and regulations defining
and clarifying, **71:85.**
Sexual harassment of students,
151C:2.

SCHOOLS AND EDUCATION
—Cont'd
Student rights —Cont'd
Speech, freedom, **71:82.**
Guidelines, rules, and
regulations, **71:85.**
Municipalities accepting
provisions, **71:86.**
Subjects required to be taught.
Curriculum and courses of study.
See within this heading,
"Curriculum and courses of
study."
Suicide prevention, training of
police officers, **40:36C.**
Summer school.
Deposit of money received by
school committee, **71:71E.**
Establishment by school
committee, **71:28.**
School buses, use to transport
pupils to and, **159A:11A.**
Twelve-month school year. See
within this heading,
"Twelve-month school year."
Sundays and holidays.
Holidays. See within this
heading, "Holidays."
Superintendence districts and
unions.
Annual meeting of joint
committee for unions, **71:63.**
Clerical help, employment,
71:53A.
Education department,
formation or readjustment
of unions, **71:62.**
Employees, **71:53A, 71:53B,
71:63.**
Expenses of union
superintendent, payment,
71:64.
Joint committee for union,
71:63.
Nurses, employment, **71:53A,
71:53B.**
Organization of joint committee
for union, **71:63.**
Physicians, employment,
71:53A, 71:53B.
Reimbursement of
superintendent for expenses,
71:64.
Removal of union
superintendent, **71:63.**
Salary.
Employees of union, **71:53A.**
Union superintendent, **71:63,
71:64.**
Special teachers, employment,
71:53A.

SCHOOLS AND EDUCATION
—Cont'd
Superintendence districts and
unions —Cont'd
Supervisors, employment,
71:53A.
Tenure of union
superintendents, **71:63.**
Superintendents.
Absences, power to excuse, **76:1.**
Annual budget, public viewing,
71:38N.
Annual report.
Foster care, number of school
age children, **76:7.**
Students permanently leaving
school, annual reports to
education department,
76:18.
Appeal from dismissal.
See APPEAL AND REVIEW.
Attorneys at law.
See ATTORNEYS AT LAW.
Board of health to be notified by
superintendent of pupils
showing signs of ill health,
71:55A.
Closing schools for teachers'
meetings, **71:73.**
Commission or fee for obtaining
teaching position,
acceptance prohibited,
71:67.
Committees. See within this
heading, "Committees."
Complaint in disciplinary
procedure against, **71:42D.**
Contracts, elections, and
promotions, **71:38.**
Duties, **71:59.**
Education department.
See EDUCATION
DEPARTMENT.
Elections.
See ELECTIONS.
Employment of minors, duties
regarding.
See LABOR AND
WORKFORCE
DEVELOPMENT.
Employment of superintendent,
71:59.
Executive officer of school
committee, **71:59.**
Finances and funds.
Teacher, principal and
superintendent quality
endowment fund, **10:35S.**
Firearms, posting of notices
regarding, **269:11.**
Foster care, annual report as to
number of school age
children, **76:7.**

SCHOOLS AND EDUCATION
—Cont'd
Superintendents —Cont'd
Fringe benefits, **71:16, 71:41,
71:63.**
Health camps for children,
duties of superintendent,
111:62B, 111:62C.
Ill health of students, notice to
board of health concerning,
71:55A.
Judicial review of dismissals.
See APPEAL AND REVIEW.
Leave of absence, **71:16, 71:41,
71:41A, 71:63.**
Liability insurance, **71:16, 71:41,
71:63.**
Notice.
Board of health, notice as to
student showing signs of
ill health, **71:55A.**
Firearms, posting of notices
regarding, **269:11.**
Intent to dismiss, **71:42,
71:63.**
Reemployment, notice prior,
71:41.
Period of employment, **71:41.**
Discharge of superintendent,
71:42.
Posting of notices regarding
firearms, **269:11.**
Records, reports, and returns.
State aid, filing of data
necessary to determine
amount, **70:4.**
Recruiting program, **15A:19E.**
Reduction of salaries, **71:43.**
Reemployment for next year,
notice required, **71:41.**
Regional school districts, **71:16.**
Salary and expenses, **71:64.**
Reimbursement. See within this
heading, "Reimbursement."
Relocation expenses, **71:16,
71:41, 71:63.**
Removal, demotion, or dismissal,
71:42.
Judicial review of dismissal.
See APPEAL AND
REVIEW.
Suspension, **71:42D.**
Salaries and compensation.
Employment contract, **71:16,
71:41, 71:63.**
Fixed by committee, **71:59.**
Reduction, **71:43.**
Reimbursement. See within
this heading,
"Reimbursement."
Services after discharge,
71:42.

SCHOOLS AND EDUCATION
—Cont'd
Superintendents —Cont'd
Salaries and compensation
—Cont'd
Union and regional school
districts, **71:64.**
Severance pay, **71:16, 71:41,
71:63.**
Small towns, superintendent in
certain, **71:59A.**
State aid.
Filing of data necessary to
determine amount, **70:4.**
Small town superintendents,
71:59A.
Suspension, **71:42, 71:42D.**
Teachers.
Commission or fee for
obtaining position,
acceptance, **71:67.**
Maximum period of
suspension of teacher
without hearing, **71:42D.**
Recommendation, **71:59.**
Teacher's meetings, closing
schools, **71:73.**
Tenure and seniority, **71:41,
71:63.**
Transfer cards furnished, **76:6,
76:13.**
Tuberculosis, examinations,
71:55B.
Union of towns for employment
of.
Superintendence districts and
unions. See within this
heading,
"Superintendence districts
and unions."
Vacations, removal of
superintendents from office,
71:42.
Women superintendents, change
of marital status not cause
for dismissal, **71:42.**
Superior court.
Chief justice of superior court,
continuing education of
judges and court personnel,
agreements concerning
programs, **7:28A.**
Compelling cities and towns to
furnish funds for support of
schools, **71:34.**
Compelling issuance of
transcript of record of
student, **71:34B.**
Jurisdiction as to racial
imbalance, **15:1J.**
Trade school licenses, review of
refusal or revocation,
93:21C.

SCHOOLS AND EDUCATION
—Cont'd
Supervisors.
Attendance supervisors.
Supervisors of attendance. See
within this heading,
"Supervisors of
attendance."
Certification of supervisory
personnel, **71:38G.**
Conservation education, duties
of supervisor, **15:4A.**
Leadership academy for training
principals and supervisory
personnel, **15:58.**
Leave of absence for study or
research, **71:41A.**
Rehabilitation commission,
supervisor of education,
6:79.
Residency requirements, **71:38.**
Salaries, **29:31, 30:46.**
Superintendence union,
employment, **71:53A.**
Supervisors of attendance.
Appointment, compensation,
76:19.
Duties and authority, **76:20.**
Labor.
Minors.
See LABOR AND
WORKFORCE
DEVELOPMENT.
Lists of persons 3 to 21 years of
age, assistance in making,
51:14A.
Minimum age, **76:19.**
Petition seeking determination
that child is in need of
services, power to apply,
119:39E.
Supplementary education centers,
municipal authority to expend
money, **40:4A.**
Surgeons.
Physicians and surgeons. See
within this heading,
"Physicians and surgeons."
Surplus space or property, renting
or leasing, **40:3, 71:16.**
Survivors' benefits under
contributory retirement law,
eligibility of students, **32:26.**
Suspension.
Revocation or suspension. See
within this heading,
"Revocation or suspension."
Swimming, **40:12.**
Taxation.
Assessors' training programs,
58:1, 59:21A.

SCHOOLS AND EDUCATION
—Cont'd
Taxation —Cont'd
Buildings on land leased from
state universities, taxation,
75:28.
Employment and training
division in labor and
workforce department.
Fair information practice,
62C:21.
Federal unemployment taxes,
151A:46.
Set-off debt collection,
liabilities, **62D:13.**
Wage reporting system, **62B:2,
62E:1 et seq.**
Exemptions.
Fraternal benefit societies,
exemption from school
tax, **176:49.**
Legacy and succession taxes,
exemption, **65:1.**
Meals served to students as
exempt from taxation,
64H:6.
Sales tax exemptions, **64C:6,
64H:6.**
Income tax deduction for
children attending
educational institutions,
62:6.
Off-campus residence buildings
for officers of educational
institutions, **59:5.**
Printing of tax bill for school
tax, **60:3A.**
Regional school districts.
Exemption of bonds or notes
issued by school district,
59:5.
Reduction in local taxes,
71:16B, 71:16B½.
State aid or reimbursement,
71:14B, 71:16B-71:16D.
Revenue department.
See REVENUE
DEPARTMENT AND
COMMISSIONER.
Sales tax exemptions, **64C:6,
64H:6.**
Withholding tax on wages of
students employed in
seasonal employment,
62B:1.
Teacher mentoring.
Curriculum accommodation
plans, **71:38Q1/2.**
Teachers.
See TEACHERS.
Teachers' aides, residency
requirements, **71:38.**

SCHOOLS AND EDUCATION
—Cont'd

Technologist or technician schools, **112:2B, 112:2C.**

Television.
  Radio and television. See within this heading, "Radio and television."

Tenure.
  See TENURE AND SENIORITY.

Term of office.
  Regional district school committee members, **54:162.**
  Superintendent of schools, **71:41.**

Term papers, sale for academic credit, **271:50.**

Test cards, blanks, and the like, state health department to furnish, **111:185A.**

Tests or examinations.
  Examination, inspection, or investigation. See within this heading, "Examination, inspection, or investigation."

Textbooks.
  See TEXTBOOKS.

Tickets, issuance by carriers, **159:18, 161:107, 161:108.**

Tobacco, prohibition of use in public schools, **71:2A.**

Todd fund, income, **70:10, 70:11.**

Tools, implements, materials, and supplies to be furnished, **71:48.**

Tort liability of cities and towns for unlawful exclusion from schools, **76:16.**

Town meetings.
  Acquisition of property, approval by vote at town meeting, **71:16.**
  Janitor's municipal pension, acceptance of statute providing, **32:45.**
  Location of schoolhouse to be determined, **71:70.**

Towns and cities, distribution of school aid, **10:35, 58:18B, 58:18F, 59:20.**

Trade schools.
  See TRADE SCHOOLS.

Traffic regulations and rules of the road.
  Buses.
    See SCHOOL BUSES AND TRANSPORTATION OF PUPILS.
  Control signals to protect schoolchildren, **85:21A.**
  Maintenance and repair of traffic control devices, **85:2.**

SCHOOLS AND EDUCATION
—Cont'd

Traffic regulations and rules of the road —Cont'd
  Safety patrol leaders, traffic direction, **71:48A.**
  Speed of motor vehicles in school zones, **90:17.**

Traffic safety week, observance, **6:15P.**

Training division of labor and workforce development department for apprentices, **23:11E-23:11L, 74:7B.**

Training schools, **120:1 et seq.**
  See YOUTH SERVICES DEPARTMENT AND MASSACHUSETTS TRAINING SCHOOLS.

Transcript of record of student, furnishing, **71:34A, 71:34B.**

Transfer of pupils.
  Furnishing transfer cards, **76:6, 76:13.**
  Racial imbalance, transfer to alleviate, **71:37D.**

Transportation of pupils.
  See SCHOOL BUSES AND TRANSPORTATION OF PUPILS.

Treasurers.
  Collaborative education board, appointment of treasurer, **40:4E.**
  Regional school district treasurers, removal from office, **41:39B.**
  Regional vocational school committee treasurers, compensation, **71:16A.**
  State treasurer.
    See STATE TREASURER.

Trial or hearing.
  Hearings. See within this heading, "Hearings."

Trust company officers, education loans extended, **172:18.**

Trusts and trustees.
  Annual reports of trustees, **68:13, 68:14.**
  Board of higher education, student loan repayment program attracting excellence to teaching program, **15A:19A.**
  Colleges.
    See COLLEGES AND UNIVERSITIES.
  County agricultural school trustees, **74:27.**
  Educational television, trust fund, **71:13H.**

SCHOOLS AND EDUCATION
—Cont'd

Trusts and trustees —Cont'd
  Education department.
    See EDUCATION DEPARTMENT.
  Fines and penalties, **15A:13.**
  Records and reports of trustees of educational trust funds of towns, **68:13, 68:14.**
  Removal of trustees of educational trust funds of towns, **68:14.**
  Student trustees at institutions of higher learning, **268A:23A.**
  Towns, administration of trust funds, **68:13, 68:14.**

Tuberculosis.
  Colleges, **71:55B.**
  Examination of school personnel, **71:55B.**
  Instruction as to prevention, **71:1.**
  Prohibition against employment of tubercular persons, **71:55B.**

Tuition.
  Aliens, tuition charges for nonresident aliens, **15A:5A.**
  Clean waters scholarship intern program, **21:38A.**
  Collaborative education programs, prepayment of tuition by school committees, **41:56, 71:71D.**
  Colleges.
    See COLLEGES AND UNIVERSITIES.
  Committees. See within this heading, "Committees."
  Continuation schools or courses, pupils attending in another town, **71:24.**
  County and other agricultural schools.
    Free tuition for residents of certain counties, **74:33.**
    Income from tuition, disposition, **74:30.**
  Educational collaboratives, school committees to prepay tuition, **41:56, 71:71D.**
  Education department.
    See EDUCATION DEPARTMENT.
  Evening schools, **71:20.**
  Food and Agriculture Department, intern scholarship program, **20:6A.**
  High school pupils of towns not maintaining high schools, payment of tuition, **71:6.**

SCHOOLS AND EDUCATION
—Cont'd

Tuition —Cont'd

Inmates of certain institutions, **76:11.**

Massachusetts Educational Financial Authority, tuition agreements, **15C:5.**

Municipal finance. See within this heading, "Municipal finance."

Nonresidents. See within this heading, "Nonresident students."

Payment of, **76:9.**

Physically handicapped pupils, state reimbursement to small towns, **71:10.**

Prepayment to educational collaboratives and other institutions by school committees, **71:71D.**

Public charges, **76:7, 76:10.**

Regional school districts.
See REGIONAL SCHOOL DISTRICTS.

Reimbursements.
Inmates of certain institutions, **76:11.**
Public school students, reimbursement to certain cities and towns, **71:10, 76:7, 76:9.**
Taxation. See within this heading, "Taxation."
Towns reimbursement in certain cases, **71:68.**

Scholarships.
See SCHOLARSHIPS AND FELLOWSHIPS.

Separate accounts, nonresident and other students, **71:16D½, 71:71F.**

Settlement of accounts for tuition of public charges, **76:10.**

Special education.
See SPECIAL EDUCATION.

Technical colleges or institutes, **74:46.**

Vietnam veterans, **15A:16.**

Vocational education.
See VOCATIONAL EDUCATION AND SCHOOLS.

Waiver, **71:6A, 76:6.**

Tutoring.
Curriculum accommodation plans, **71:38Q1/2.**

Twelve-month school year plan.
Adoption by cities and towns, **71:1, 71:4.**

SCHOOLS AND EDUCATION
—Cont'd

Twelve-month school year plan —Cont'd

Pupil attendance requirements, **76:1.**

Underwater archaeological resources, preservation, **91:63.**

Unemployment compensation.
See EMPLOYMENT SECURITY.

Uniforms.
Cheerleaders' uniforms, payment, **71:47.**
Employees, furnishing of uniforms, **71:48B.**

Uniform Securities Act, exemptions, **110A:402.**

United Nations Day, observance, **6:12N.**

United States.
Federal government. See within this heading, "Federal government."

Universities.
See COLLEGES AND UNIVERSITIES.

Urban redevelopment corporations contracting with municipality to establish, **121A:14.**

Vacancies in office.
School committees, **43:36.**

Vacations.
Nonteaching positions, vacations of certain persons holding, **29:31C.**
Summer school. See within this heading, "Summer school."
Superintendents and teachers, vacation periods in computation of time for notice of dismissal, **71:42.**
Twelve-month school year plan. See within this heading, "Twelve-month school year plan."

Vacation school.
Summer school. See within this heading, "Summer school."

Vaccination of school children, **76:15, 76:15C.**

Veterans.
See VETERANS AND VETERANS' ORGANIZATIONS.

Veterinarians.
Colleges.
See VETERINARIANS.

Vietnam veterans.
See VETERANS AND VETERANS' ORGANIZATIONS.

SCHOOLS AND EDUCATION
—Cont'd

Vision.
Eyes. See within this heading, "Eyes."

Vivisection prohibited, **272:80G.**

Vocational education, **74:1 et seq.**
See VOCATIONAL EDUCATION AND SCHOOLS.

Voluntary prayer, parental permission for schoolchildren to participate, **71:1B.**

Voluntary services at public schools during working hours without loss of salary, state employees authorized to provide, **29:31E.**

Wages.
Salaries and compensation. See within this heading, "Salaries and compensation."

Waiver and estoppel.
Certification of teachers, exemption from requirements in case of hardship in securing teachers for town's schools, **71:38G.**
Chiropractors, waiver of educational requirements for license renewal certificate, **112:96.**
Employment permit, waiver of school record, **149:88.**
Tuition charges, **71:6A, 76:6.**

Waste prevention institute, **71:38 et seq.**

Water pollution control division, instruction and education of personnel, **21:27, 21:38.**

Weapons.
Firearms and other weapons. See within this heading, "Firearms and other weapons."

Welfare.
See WELFARE AND SOCIAL SERVICES.

Wife.
See HUSBAND AND WIFE.

Wines, **138:14, 138:19B.**

Withholding tax on wages, student engaged in seasonal employment, **62B:1.**

Witnesses before school boards, summoning, **233:8.**

Women.
Females. See within this heading, "Females."

SCHOOLS AND EDUCATION
 —Cont'd
Workers' compensation.
 Death benefits, extension of to
  deceased employee's
  dependent child over 18 who
  is full-time student, **152:31.**
 Dependents and employees
  defined, **152:1.**
 Injured employee, additional
  compensation for dependent
  child over 18 who is
  full-time student, **152:35A.**
 Regional school district
  employees, **152:69.**
 Vocational rehabilitation office,
  152:30G.
Writing.
 Reading and writing. See within
  this heading, "Reading and
  writing."
Year.
 Fiscal year. See within this
  heading, "Fiscal year."
 Twelve-month school year. See
  within this heading,
  "Twelve-month school year."
Youth conservation and service
 corps, **78A:1 et seq.**
 See YOUTH CONSERVATION
  AND SERVICE CORPS.
Youth honor day, observance,
 6:15G.
Youth services department and
 Massachusetts training
 schools, **18A:1 et seq., 120:1
 et seq.**
 See YOUTH SERVICES
  DEPARTMENT AND
  MASSACHUSETTS
  TRAINING SCHOOLS.
Zoning regulations, **40A:3.**

SCHOOL TEACHERS.
See TEACHERS.

SCHOONER ERNESTINA
 COMMISSION, 6:182A,
 6:182B.
Employment dislocations and
 assistance in reemployment of
 dislocated workers, **6:17.**
Governor, supervision, **6:17.**

SCIENCE AND SCIENTISTS.
Alcoholic liquors delivered to state
 departments or agencies for
 scientific purposes, **138:51.**
Anatomical science, **113:1 et seq.**
Animals for research, sales tax
 exemption, **64H:6.**
Antitrust laws, **93:2.**

SCIENCE AND SCIENTISTS
 —Cont'd
Archeologist's duty to examine
 scientific information, **9:27.**
Breathalyzer test to be
 administered to intoxicated
 persons taken into custody,
 111B:8.
Civil service appointments to
 scientific positions, **31:16.**
Congress may promote, by
 granting exclusive rights, **US
 Const Act 1 Sec 8 cl 8.**
Constitution of Massachusetts,
 encouragement of sciences,
 **MA Const Part 2 Ch 5 Sec
 2.**
Corporations.
 See SCIENTIFIC
  CORPORATIONS AND
  ORGANIZATIONS.
Dogs and cats, use in scientific
 investigation, experiment or
 instruction, **140:174D.**
Drugs.
 Research and study projects.
  See DRUGS AND
   NARCOTICS.
Economic diversification program,
 production of scientific
 instruments as defense-related
 commercial activity, **23F:1.**
Education department.
 Advance placement courses,
  board's duties as to, **69:1D.**
 Advisory councils to board,
  15:1G.
Experiment stations.
 Agricultural experiment station.
  See UNIVERSITY OF
   MASSACHUSETTS.
Fireworks, **148:39.**
Hospitals and health care
 facilities, supplying of
 information for scientific
 studies to reduce morbidity
 and mortality, **111:24A.**
Morbidity and mortality, studies
 for reduction, **111:24A.**
Motorcycle noise emissions,
 measurement, **90:7T.**
Sales tax exemption, animals for
 research, **64H:6.**
Senate committee on science and
 technology, compensation of,
 3:9.
Taxation.
 Animals for research, sales tax
  exemption, **64H:6.**
 Lists of property held for
  scientific purposes, **59:29.**

SCIENCE AND SCIENTISTS
 —Cont'd
Toxics use reduction, **21I:6.**
Underwater archaeological
 resources, preservation, **91:63.**
Zoning, **40A:9.**

SCIENCE AND TECHNOLOGY
 COMMITTEE.
General court members,
 compensation of, **3:9.**

SCIENCE AND TECHNOLOGY
 OFFICE.
Reorganization of department of
 economic development, **23A:46
 et seq.**

SCIENTIFIC CORPORATIONS
 AND ORGANIZATIONS.
Alcoholic liquors.
 See ALCOHOLIC LIQUORS.
Annual return, **180:26A.**
Antitrust laws, scientific
 information, **93:2.**
Boxing matches, forfeiture of
 charter for violations, **180:28.**
Bylaws, **180:7.**
Change of name, **180:11.**
Change of purposes, **180:10,
 180:11.**
Contributions by corporations,
 155:12C.
Directors, officers, and agents,
 180:7.
False personation of official,
 94:187D.
Forfeiture of charter, **180:27,
 180:28.**
Gaming laws, forfeiture of charter
 for violation, **180:27.**
Incorporation, **180:2.**
Intoxicating liquors.
 See ALCOHOLIC LIQUORS.
Investigation before incorporation,
 180:5, 180:6.
Massachusetts science and
 technology foundation,
 appointment of board
 members of Massachusetts
 technology development
 corporation, **40G:9.**
Massachusetts technology park
 corporation.
 See MASSACHUSETTS
  TECHNOLOGY PARK
  CORPORATION.
Organization, **180:3.**
Restraints of trade and
 monopolies, scientific
 information, **93:2.**
Sales tax exemptions on sale of
 services, **64H:6.**

SCIENTIFIC CORPORATIONS AND ORGANIZATIONS
—Cont'd
Services, sales tax exemptions, **64H:6.**
Zoning and planning, special permits for scientific research and development, **40A:9.**

SCIRE FACIAS.
Administrators.
Executors and administrators. See within this heading, "Executors and administrators."
District courts, **218:20.**
Invalid levy, scire facias, **236:51.**
Issuance of writs, **218:20.**
Executions, **235:19 et seq.**
Further breach of bond or condition after judgment, **235:11.**
Ineffectual sale, **235:20, 235:21.**
Real estate, invalid levy, **236:51, 236:52.**
Trustee process, **246:45-246:49.** See TRUSTEE PROCESS.
Executors and administrators, **218:20, 230:10.**
Administrator de bonis non, issuance of scire facias in favor of or against, **230:12.**
District court jurisdiction, **218:20.**
Fees for service, **262:8.**
Nonresidents, endorsement of writ or bill by responsible inhabitant in actions by or against, **231:42.**
Special judgments against bankrupts or insolvents, **235:24.**
Trustee process, **246:45-246:49.** See TRUSTEE PROCESS.

SCITUATE.
Congressional district, **57:1.**
District court, **218:1.**
Medical examiner district, **38:1.**
Senatorial district, **57:3.**
Superior court jurisdiction of crimes committed in parts, **212:6.**

SCOTT, GENERAL WINFIELD.
Flag standard, **8:17A.**

SCOUTING.
Corporations to promote, **180:2.**

SCOWS.
Penalty for mooring to buoys, **266:135.**

SCRAPIE.
Sheep, destruction of infected sheep, **129:13A.**

SCRAPPED VEHICLES.
See MOTOR VEHICLES.

SCREENS.
Gaming houses, taverns, etc., **271:25, 271:26.**
Motor vehicle junkyards, screening, **140B:3.**
Taverns and restaurants, **138:1.**

SCRIP.
Issuance and rights of holders, **156B:28.**

SCRUBWOMEN.
Hours of labor or services.
Regulations inapplicable, **149:30A.**
State House, **8:5.**
State house, **8:4, 8:5.**
Retirement and pensions, **32:74.**

SCUBA DIVERS.
Commonwealth tidelands, access, **91:10D.**
Flags, display, **90B:13A.**
Motorboat speed near divers' flags, **90B:13A.**
Penalty for failure to display required flag, **90B:14.**
Tanks for divers.
See AIR, COMPRESSED.

SCULPIN.
Taking for bait, **131:52.**

SEA.
See OCEAN OR SEA.

SEABEE VETERANS OF AMERICA.
Insignia, unlawful use, **266:70.**
Patriotic holiday observances, municipal appropriations, **40:5.**
Uniform, unlawful use, **264:10A.**

SEAFOOD.
See MARINE FISH AND FISHERIES.

SEALERS OF WEIGHTS AND MEASURES, 98:34-98:56.
See WEIGHTS AND MEASURES.

SEALING CONTAINERS.
Frozen desserts, **98:20, 98:21.**
See FROZEN DESSERTS.
Milk products, **98:18, 98:19, 98:51.**
See MILK AND MILK PRODUCTS.

SEALS AND SEALED INSTRUMENTS.
Actions on instruments, limitation of actions on sealed instruments, **260:1.**

SEALS AND SEALED INSTRUMENTS —Cont'd
Affixation of official seals, necessity, **4:9A.**
Amherst economic development and industrial corporation, **Spec L 23:4.**
Antidiscrimination commission, **151B:3.**
Architects.
See ARCHITECTS AND ARCHITECTURE.
Ballots, sealing of.
See ELECTIONS.
Barbers registration board, use of seal, **13:40.**
Bonds or notes.
State bonds and notes, facsimile of state seal, **29:48A.**
Water pollution abatement districts, **21:35 et seq.**
Business trusts, **182:6.**
Caucuses.
Official ballots.
See CAUCUSES.
Central Massachusetts Economic Development Authority, description of seal of, **Spec L 22:18.**
Cigarette vending machines, sealing of unlicensed machines, **64C:10.**
City and town seals, **40:47.**
Penalty for misuse, **268:35.**
Commissioners to qualify public officers, seal, **222:5.**
Community economic development assistance corporation, **40H:3, 40H:4.**
Conservation district supervisors, seal, **21:24.**
Co-operative banks employees benefit association, **170:33.**
Copies, **9:11, 46:19C.**
Corporations.
See CORPORATIONS.
Counterfeiting.
See FORGERY AND COUNTERFEITING.
Counties, **34:14.**
Facsimile seals and signatures, use on county obligations, **35:39G, 35:39H.**
Court seal, **4:9A, 4:9B.**
District court. See within this heading, "District court."
Credit unions, contents of safe deposit box, **171:75.**
Criminal records, provisions as to sealing certain, **94C:34, 94C:44.**

SEALS AND SEALED INSTRUMENTS —Cont'd

Death record or certificate, **9:11, 46:19C.**

Deeds, validation ten years after recording, **184:24.**

Deposition, sealing of, **233:34.**

District court, **218:4.**

Process to be issued under seal of court, **218:44.**

Drugs and narcotics, sealing of record as to arrest or first conviction, **94C:34, 94C:44.**

Elections.

See ELECTIONS.

Extradition, governor's warrant of arrest, **276:16.**

Facsimile seals.

See FACSIMILE SEALS AND SIGNATURES.

Forgery.

See FORGERY AND COUNTERFEITING.

Gas meters, sealing, **164:103, 164:113 et seq.**

Great seal.

See STATE SEAL.

Hairdressers' registration board, **13:43.**

Hazardous substances, access to records of movement in commerce or holding, **94B:7.**

Health and health departments, seal used to authenticate copies of birth, marriage and death records, **46:19C.**

Housing court department, **185C:6.**

Impression of seal as sufficient, **4:9B.**

Insurance companies, use of seal on agreement for consolidation, **175:19A, 175:19B.**

Interest in land, instrument purporting to affect, **183:1A.**

Labor relations commission, **23:9O.**

Labor union seals, fraudulent display or use, **266:69, 266:69A.**

Landscape architects' seal, **112:100.**

Limitation of actions on sealed instruments, **260:1.**

Metering machines in connection with sale of deed or document tax stamps, sealing, **64D:3.**

Milk.

See MILK AND MILK PRODUCTS.

SEALS AND SEALED INSTRUMENTS —Cont'd

Municipal seals.

City and town seals. See within this heading, "City and town seals."

Narcotics, sealing of record as to arrest or first conviction, **94C:34, 94C:44.**

Notes.

Bonds and notes. See within this heading, "Bonds or notes."

Person defined, **4:9A.**

Precinct seals, custody and use, **54:30.**

Public health department authentication of copies of birth, marriage and death records, **46:19C.**

Public officers, **4:9A, 4:9B.**

Public works commission, duties of secretary, **16:5.**

Railroads.

Stock certificate to bear seal, **160:38.**

Street railways. See within this heading, "Street railways."

Real estate brokers and salesmen, board of registration, **13:56.**

Reciting of sealing as equivalent to seal, **4:9A.**

Records, sealing.

Caucuses, sealing records of.

Official ballots.

See CAUCUSES.

Criminal records, **94C:34, 94C:44, 276:100A-276:100C.**

See DRUGS AND NARCOTICS.

Depositions, **233:34.**

Hazardous substances, access to records of movement in commerce or holding, **94B:7.**

Unsealed instruments, when given effect of sealed instruments, **4:9A.**

Regional planning districts, seals, **40B:4B.**

Registered professional engineers and registered professional land surveyors, **112:81M.**

Requisites for seal, **4:9B.**

Sales contract, effect of affixing of seal, **106:2-203.**

Secretary of state, authority of Commonwealth as to arms, seal and flags, **2:5.**

State bonds and notes, facsimile of state seal, **29:48A.**

State college division, common seal, **73:1D.**

SEALS AND SEALED INSTRUMENTS —Cont'd

State seal.

See STATE SEAL.

Street railways.

Commonwealth seal to be affixed to certificate of incorporation, **161:9.**

Company seal, stock certificates to bear, **161:19.**

Tax collection warrants, **60:34.**

Technology development corporation.

Power to adopt seal, **40G:3.**

Secretary as custodian of seal, **40G:2.**

Telecommunications and energy department, **25:1.**

Town seals.

City and town seals. See within this heading, "City and town seals."

Trademarks and trade names, state seal on certificate of registration, **110B:4.**

University of Massachusetts, common seal, **75:5.**

Unsealed instruments, when given effect of sealed instruments, **4:9A.**

Water pollution abatement district.

See WATER POLLUTION.

What constitutes seal, **4:9B.**

Zoning, seals of regional planning districts, **40B:4B.**

SEAMEN.

Arrest, **102:2 et seq.**

Compensation.

Wages or compensation. See within this heading, "Wages or compensation."

Employment security laws, application, **151A:6.**

Exemption.

Arrest for board or lodging after signing for voyage, exemption, **102:2.**

Trustee process, wages due seaman as exempt, **246:32.**

Holding property or luggage for board or lodging, penalty, **102:2.**

Landlord and tenant.

Lien of landlord, **102:2.**

Rights as against, **102:23.**

Maritime academy of Massachusetts.

See MARITIME ACADEMY OF MASSACHUSETTS.

Nuncupative wills, **191:6.**

Overtime pay, **151:1A.**

SEAMEN —Cont'd

Trustee process, wages due
seaman exempt, **246:32.**
Wages or compensation.
Overtime pay, **151:1A.**
Trustee process, wages due
seaman as exempt, **246:32.**
Workers' compensation, **152:1.**
Workers' compensation, **152:1.**

**SEARCH AND RESCUE
VOLUNTEERS.**
Good Samaritan law, **231:85AA.**

SEARCHES AND SEIZURES.
Adulterated commercial feed,
128:58.
Affidavits for warrants, **276:2B.**
Air pollution emergency orders,
violations, **111:2B.**
Alcoholic liquors.
See ALCOHOLIC LIQUORS.
Animals.
Animal Rescue League request,
272:88.
Cruelty to animals complaint,
search warrant for
investigation, **272:83.**
Disposition of property seized
under search warrant,
276:3.
Fighting birds and animals. See
within this heading,
"Fighting birds and
animals."
Appeal and review.
Cigarette tax, claims to seized
cigarettes, vehicles, or
containers, **64C:8.**
Forfeiture, appeal, **276:8.**
Arrest.
Possession of seized property,
arrest, **276:2.**
Regulation of searches
conducted incident, **276:1.**
Warrant outstanding, issuance
of search warrant, **276:1.**
Assault weapons, **269:10.**
Baskets containing less than
standard measure, seizure,
94:98.
Bedding and upholstered
furniture, **94:273, 94:276.**
Bottles and other containers
bearing registered devices,
search warrant, **110:25.**
Cigarette tax.
See CIGARETTE TAX.
Clinical thermometers, seizure,
98:12.
Coal, condemnation of unfit,
94:249A.
Sale of condemned coal
penalized, **94:249C.**

SEARCHES AND SEIZURES
—Cont'd

Commercial feed, **128:58, 128:60.**
Complaints to obtain warrants,
276:1.
Concealment.
Disposition of seized property,
276:3.
Warrant, **276:1.**
Confidential relationships having
custody of property, search
and seizure prohibited, **276:1.**
Constables.
See CONSTABLES.
Constitution of Massachusetts,
MA Const Part 1 Art 15.
Initiative or referendum
petition, right not subject to,
**MA Const Amend Art 48
Init Part 2 Sec 2.**
Controlled Substances Act,
administrative inspection
warrants, **94C:30.**
Controlled substances, seized
property management office
established, **94C:47.**
Counterfeiting.
Forgery and counterfeiting. See
within this heading,
"Forgery and
counterfeiting."
Cruelty to animals, entry of
premises for prevention,
272:83.
Damages for forfeiture proceedings
on seizure of property without
probable cause, **257:9.**
Dangerous weapons,
269:10-269:12B, 276:3.
Police search of person
suspected of possessing,
41:98.
Delivery of seized property to
rightful owner, **276:3, 276:7.**
Description of property or articles
sought, **276:2.**
Destruction of property seized,
94:124, 276:3, 276:7.
Diseases.
Animals, diseased, **129:27,
276:3.**
Carcasses or products, seizure
and destruction of diseased,
94:124, 94:146.
Powers of health officers
examining premises and
unwholesome conditions,
111:131.
Disposition of property seized,
**94:124, 98:54, 98:55, 130:48,
135:7, 135:8, 271:23, 276:3,
276:7.**

SEARCHES AND SEIZURES
—Cont'd

District courts.
See DISTRICT COURTS.
Drug manufacturer, probable
cause for administrative
inspection, **94C:30.**
Drunks taken into protective
custody, searches, **111B:8.**
Embezzled property, **276:1.**
Evidence.
Inadmissibility of illegally seized
property, **276:1.**
Motion to suppress illegally
seized evidence, **276:1 Form
1.**
Property seized under search
warrant, **276:3.**
Weighing and measuring
devices, seizure as evidence,
98:54, 98:55.
Exemption from seizure, antique
slot machine, **271:5A.**
Explosives, etc., **148:36, 148:50,
148:51, 266:102A.**
False pretenses, property obtained,
276:1.
Fees for making search of person
named in process, **262:20.**
Fertilizer, condemnation of
commercial, **128:78.**
Fighting birds and animals,
272:88, 272:89.
Expense of care, **272:93.**
Judgment of forfeiture, **272:91.**
Search warrants, **272:88,
272:89.**
Firearms.
Dangerous weapons. See within
this heading, "Dangerous
weapons."
Fire escapes, seizure of articles
obstructing, **143:22.**
Fish.
See FISH AND GAME.
Food, **94:88D, 94:146.**
Lobsters. See within this
heading, "Lobsters."
Meat. See within this heading,
"Meat."
Warrant, disposition of food
seized, **276:3.**
Forfeiture of property seized.
Appeal, **276:8.**
Civilly forfeited property.
See FORFEITURES.
Disposition, **94:124, 271:23,
276:3, 276:7.**
Enforcement of provisions by
superior court as to seizure
and labeling of forfeited
property, **257:1 et seq.**

SEARCHES AND SEIZURES
—Cont'd

Forfeiture of property seized
—Cont'd

Fighting birds and animals, judgment of forfeiture, **272:91.**

Infernal machine, seizure and forfeiture, **266:102A.**

Marine fish.
See MARINE FISH AND FISHERIES.

Notice. See within this heading, "Notice as to seizure of property or forfeiture of seized property."

Postponement of trial, **276:6.**

Probable cause, damages for forfeiture proceedings on seizure of property without, **257:9.**

Recognizance as prerequisite to appeal from decree of forfeiture, **276:8.**

Service of notice, **276:5.**

Forgery and counterfeiting, **267:30.**

Disposition of property after seizure, **267:3, 267:7.**

Form of search warrant, **276:2, 276:2A.**

Fuel oils, warrantless inspection or seizure of vehicles, **94:303F.**

Furniture and bedding, **94:273, 94:276.**

Gaming and games of chance, **271:23.**

Antique slot machines, exemption from seizure, **271:5A.**

Arrest without warrant for gaming, **272:2, 272:6.**

Fighting birds and animals. See within this heading, "Fighting birds and animals."

Hazardous waste management act, seizure of property with respect, **21C:14.**

Hazards and hazardous substances.
See HAZARDS AND HAZARDOUS OR TOXIC SUBSTANCES.

Health.
Diseases. See within this heading, "Diseases."

Health officers examining premises and unwholesome conditions, powers, **111:131.**

Houses of prostitution, search warrants, **272:9.**

SEARCHES AND SEIZURES
—Cont'd

Identification of property or articles sought, **276:2.**

Illegally seized property, inadmissibility as evidence, **276:1.**

Infernal machine, seizure and forfeiture, **266:102A.**

Interception of wire and oral communications, warrants authorizing, **272:99.**

Judges issuing search warrants, **138:42, 271:23, 276:1.**

Labor relations and disputes.
Commonwealth, seizure and operation of facilities by, in dispute dangerous to public health or safety, **150B:4.**

Private property, seizure or occupation of, as unfair labor practice, **150A:4A.**

Lead poisoning, search warrants for inspection of premises for detection, **111:194.**

Lobsters.
Disposal after seizure, **130:48.**

Undersized lobsters, **130:44, 130:48.**

Unmarked containers, **130:47, 130:50.**

Lotteries, disposition of seized item, **271:23.**

Marine fish.
See MARINE FISH AND FISHERIES.

Measures.
Weights and measures. See within this heading, "Weights and measures."

Meat, **94:146.**
Unwholesome meat, **276:3.**

Milk and ice cream containers, warrant in case of unlawful use, **110:25.**

Moneys seized, disposition, **276:3, 276:7.**

Motor vehicles.
See MOTOR VEHICLES.

Night-time searches, **276:2.**

Notice as to seizure of property or forfeiture of seized property, **276:4, 276:5.**

Animal carcass, notice of seizure and condemnation, **94:146.**

Bombs and explosives, notice of seizure, **148:36.**

Infernal machine, notice of seizure, **266:102A.**

Oath for issuance of search warrant, **276:1; US Const Amend 4.**

SEARCHES AND SEIZURES
—Cont'd

Papers.
Constitutional security of papers from unreasonable search, **US Const Amend 4.**

"Property" as defined in search warrant law, papers, **276:1.**

Service of process and papers. See within this heading, "Process and service of process and papers."

Personal appearance by person seeking warrant required, **276:2B.**

Pesticide control, **132B:15.**

Police, duties of, **276:2.**

Possession of property seized, arrest of persons having, **276:2.**

Probable cause for issuance of search warrant, **MA Const Part 1 Art 14; US Const Amend 4.**

Process and service of process and papers.
Fees for making search of person named in process, **262:20.**

Forfeiture of property seized, service of notice, **276:5.**

Penalty for delay in service of search warrants, **268:22.**

Return of warrant, time, **276:3A.**

Property and articles for which search warrant may issue, **276:1.**

Prostitution, houses, **272:9.**

Protective custody, search of drunks taken into, **111:8.**

Public safety department.
Disposition by commissioner of property seized under search warrant, **276:3.**

Infernal machine, notice of seizure, **266:102A.**

Receptacles holding less than standard measure, seizure, **94:98.**

Recognizance as prerequisite to appeal from decree of forfeiture of property seized, **276:8.**

Records, reports, and returns.
Papers. See within this heading, "Papers."

Search warrants. See within this heading, "Search warrants."

Registered bottles and other containers, search warrants, **110:20 et seq.**

SEARCHES AND SEIZURES
—Cont'd

Restoration of property to owner, **276:3, 276:7.**

Return of warrant, time, **276:3A.**

Review.
  Appeal and review. See within this heading, "Appeal and review."

Rifles, **276:3.**

Sale of property seized, **276:7, 276:8.**

Search warrants, **276:1-276:8; US Const Amend 4.**
  Affidavits, **276:2B.**
  Alcoholic liquors.
    See ALCOHOLIC LIQUORS.
  Animals. See within this heading, "Animals."
  Arrest warrant outstanding, issuance of search warrant for person for whom, **276:1.**
  Bottles and other containers bearing registered devices, search warrant, **110:25.**
  Complaints to obtain, **276:1.**
  Concealment, **276:1.**
  Constitutional security from unreasonable searches, **US Const Amend 4.**
  Contents, **276:2, 276:2A.**
  Controlled Substances Act, **94C:30.**
  Delay in service of warrant, penalty, **268:22.**
  Description of property and articles, **276:2.**
  Disposition of property seized, **276:3, 276:7.**
  District courts.
    See DISTRICT COURTS.
  Evidence, property seized under warrant, **276:3.**
  Explosives, etc., **148:50.**
  Fighting birds and animals, **272:88.**
    Entry without warrant, **272:89.**
  Fish and game law violations, **130:9 et seq., 131:87, 131:89.**
  Food, **276:3.**
  Form, **276:2, 276:2A.**
  Hazardous waste management act, enforcement, **21C:8.**
  Interception of wire and oral communications, warrants authorizing, **272:99.**
  Issuance, **276:1 et seq.**
  Judges issuing, **138:42, 271:23, 276:1.**

SEARCHES AND SEIZURES
—Cont'd

Search warrants —Cont'd
  Lead poisoning, search warrants for inspection of premises for detection, **111:194.**
  Marine fish and fisheries, **276:2C.**
  Milk and ice cream containers, warrant in case of unlawful use, **110:25.**
  Motor vehicles, **130:10, 276:1.**
  Oath for issuance, **US Const Amend 4.**
  Officers to whom directed, **276:2.**
  Personal appearance by person seeking warrant required, **276:2B.**
  Pesticide control, **132B:15.**
  Police, duties of, **276:2.**
  Probable cause for issuance, **MA Const Part 1 Art 14; US Const Amend 4.**
  Property and articles for which issued, **276:1.**
  Prostitution, houses, **272:9.**
  Records, reports, and returns.
    "Property" as including records, **276:1.**
    Subversive organizations, warrants for records, **276:1A.**
    Time for return of warrant, **276:3A.**
  Registered bottles and other containers, search warrants, **110:20 et seq.**
  Sheriffs and deputies.
    Duties as to search warrants, **276:2.**
    Gaming, arrest without warrant, **272:2, 272:6.**
    Sale of property, seized under search warrants, **276:7, 276:8.**
  Ships and other watercraft, warrants for search, **130:9 et seq., 138:42, 276:1.**
  Subversive organizations, warrants for records, **276:1A.**
  Time for return of warrant, **276:3A.**
  Security from, **US Const Amend 4.**
  Seeds, **128:96.**
    Definition, **128:84.**
  Service of process.
    Process and service of process and papers. See within this heading, "Process and service of process and papers."

SEARCHES AND SEIZURES
—Cont'd

Sheriffs.
  Search warrants. See within this heading, "Search warrants."
Ships and other watercraft, warrants for search, **130:9 et seq., 138:42, 276:1.**
Show cause notice as to forfeiture of seized property, **276:4, 276:5.**
Slot machines, **271:5A.**
State treasurer, moneys seized to be paid, **276:3, 276:7.**
Stolen property, **276:1, 276:3.**
Subversive organizations, search warrants for books, **276:1A.**
Superior courts.
  Alcoholic liquors, appeals on seizure, **138:55.**
  Appeal from decree of forfeiture of seized property, **276:8.**
  Search warrants returnable in district court, **276:3A.**
Suppression of evidence illegally seized, motion, **276:1 Form 1.**
Taxes, seizure of property for, **60:53-60:56.**
  See TAX LIENS.
Telecommunication services, seizure of apparatus designed to obtain services by fraud, **166:42B.**
Thermometers, seizure of clinical, **98:12.**
Time of making searches, **276:2.**
Time of return of warrant, **276:3A.**
Trial as to seized property, postponement, **276:6.**
Unwholesome meat or provisions, **276:3.**
Warrants.
  Search warrants. See within this heading, "Search warrants."
Weapons.
  Dangerous weapons. See within this heading, "Dangerous weapons."
Weights and measures.
  Baskets containing less than standard measure, seizure, **94:98.**
  Disposition of condemned weighing or measuring devices, **98:54, 98:55.**
  Penalty for use of condemned weighing or measuring devices, **98:25 et seq.**

SEARCH WARRANTS.
See SEARCHES AND SEIZURES.

SEASHORE.
See COAST OR SHORE.

SEASONAL EMPLOYMENT.
See LABOR AND WORKFORCE
DEVELOPMENT.

SEASONS FOR HUNTING,
130:1, 131:1.

SEASON TICKETS.
Railroads.
Tickets.
See RAILROADS.
State lottery.
Telephone sales, 10:24.

SEATBELTS.
Motor vehicles.
Safety belts.
See MOTOR VEHICLES.

SEA WALLS.
Connecticut River, 91:13.
License for construction, 91:14 et
seq.

SEAWEED, 130:102.

SEA WORMS.
Municipal regulations of taking,
130:52.

SECONDARY BOYCOTT.
Legality, 149:20C, 149:24.

SECOND DEGREE MURDER.
Murder.
See MURDER OR HOMICIDE.

SECONDHAND ARTICLES.
Bedding.
Sterilization.
See BEDDING AND
UPHOLSTERED
FURNITURE.
Definition of "secondhand," 94:270.
Junk collectors or dealers, 140:54,
140:54A, 140:55,
140:202-140:205.
See JUNK COLLECTORS AND
DEALERS.
Motor vehicles.
See USED CAR SALES.
Prohibition as to servicing or sale
of used brake drums, 90:7G.
Registered bottles, unlawful
dealings, 110:19, 110:20.
Space heaters, 148:25A.

SECOND OFFENSE.
Sentence.
See SENTENCE AND
PUNISHMENT.

**SECRETARY OF
AGRICULTURE.**
Water resources.
Improvement works regulated,
21:14.
Funding, 21:15.

**SECRETARY OF ECONOMIC
AFFAIRS.**
See ECONOMIC AFFAIRS
SECRETARY.

**SECRETARY OF HEALTH,
EDUCATION AND
WELFARE.**
Aged and disabled assistance.
Advances to the secretary.
Covering supplementary
payments to the
Commonwealth, 118A:5.
Transitional assistance.
Agreement with secretary to
administer payments,
118A:3.
Aid to families with dependent
children.
Institutions applying for
payment for care given.
Rules and regulations, 118:11.

**SECRETARY OF HOUSING
AND URBAN
DEVELOPMENT.**
Mortgage loans.
Classes of permissible loans,
167E:2.
National flood insurance act.
Terms and conditions, 175:102D.
Urban area insurance placement.
Assessment of insurance
companies, 175C:8.
Definitions, 175C:1.

SECRETARY OF LABOR.
Director of labor and workforce
development.
See LABOR AND WORKFORCE
DEVELOPMENT.

**SECRETARY OF STATE, 9:1 et
seq.**
Absent defendants, state secretary
to give notice of action to
certain, 64I:33, 227:5.
Absent voters.
See ELECTIONS.
Acceptance or rejection of laws by
municipalities, reports
concerning, 4:5.
Accountants, inspection of
duplicate list, 13:34.
Accounting of moneys received,
bond, 9:1.
Administrative procedure.
See ADMINISTRATIVE
PROCEDURE.
Adoption of children, furnishing
forms, 46:16.
Air pollution, filing of regulations
for prevention, 111:142A.

SECRETARY OF STATE
—Cont'd
Alcoholic liquor questions to be
placed upon ballot, 138:11.
Annual reports, 9:2B, 9:17, 30:32.
Aqueduct companies, filing
certificate of payment of
capital stock, 165:13.
Archeological, historical, and
scientific information,
secretary's duty to publish,
9:26.
Archives and archivists.
Advisory committee,
appointment of members,
9:2A.
Division chief, appointment, 9:2.
Arguments as to initiative or
referendum measures, filing,
54:54.
Arms, seal and flags of
Commonwealth, authority and
duties, 2:5, 9:11.
Articles of organization or
amendment thereto for health
related corporations, approval,
155:2B.
Asset management and
maintenance, regulations of
commissioner, 7:39B.
Associations and societies.
Co-operative corporations and
associations. See within this
heading, "Co-operative
corporations and
associations."
Fraternal benefit societies.
Filing change of location or
purpose, 176:6.
Professional corporations and
associations, 156A:7.
Records.
Authority to destroy originals
previously permanently
reproduced, 9:19.
Registration of insignia of
societies, associations, or
labor unions, 266:69.
Attachment of bulky goods, writ to
be filed with state secretary,
223:50.
Authentication of records and
documents for use as evidence,
9:11.
Ballot law commission.
State ballot law commission. See
within this heading, "State
ballot law commission."
Ballots.
See ELECTIONS.

SECRETARY OF STATE
—Cont'd
Banks and banking.
  Trust companies, submission of
    articles of organization,
    172:8.
Biennial count of voters, **53:38A.**
Biographical sketches of general
  court members, sale of books
  containing, **5:18.**
Births.
  See BIRTHS.
Boarding and lodging houses,
  record of conviction of offenses
  sent to secretary of state,
  140:32, 140:183C.
Board of commissioners on
  uniform state laws within
  department, **12:11B.**
Bonds and undertakings.
  Secretary's bond, **9:1.**
  State treasurer's bond, deposit,
    10:3.
Books and papers, **4:5, 9:2A, 9:2B,
  9:4, 9:17, 9:19, 54:54.**
  Biographical sketches and
    portraits of general court
    members, sale of books
    containing, **5:18.**
  Birth reports, **46:17.**
  Casebooks and textbooks,
    distribution, **5:8.**
  Distribution of state
    publications, **5:1.**
  Indexes and indexing. See
    within this heading,
    "Indexes and indexing."
  Law reports and books to be
    furnished to towns and
    cities, duties regarding,
    5:14, 5:15.
  State library, deposit of books
    and documents, **6:39, 30A:6.**
Boundaries.
  Changes of boundary markers,
    report, **1:5.**
  Marine boundaries, reports, **1:3.**
  Town lines, preservation of
    records concerning, **42:10.**
Bulletins.
  Pamphlets, circulars, or
    bulletins. See within this
    heading, "Pamphlets,
    circulars, or bulletins."
Business trust reports to be filed
  with secretary, **182:13.**
Casebooks, distribution, **5:8.**
Cashier, appointment, **9:2.**
Caucuses, notice of adoption or
  revocation of law as to use of
  official ballots, **53:90.**

SECRETARY OF STATE
—Cont'd
Certificates and certification.
  Aqueduct companies, filing
    certificate of payment of
    capital stock, **165:13.**
  City and town clerks, certificates
    of election, **41:19A.**
  Decision of department upon
    issue or bonds filed,
    certificate, **166:4.**
  Dental service corporations,
    certificate of incorporation,
    176E:2.
  Dissolution, certificate, **121B:4.**
  District officers, filing certificate
    of appointment or election,
    41:19A.
  Election, certification of.
    See ELECTIONS.
  Good standing certificate,
    corporations, **156B:116.**
  Housing and community
    development department,
    23B:9.
  Municipal charters adopted,
    revised or amended, filing of
    certified copy, **43B:12.**
  Municipal industrial
    development financing
    authorities, certificate of
    organization, **40D:2.**
  Municipal solid waste disposal
    facility, certificate of
    organization, **40D:21.**
  Optometric service corporations,
    certificate of incorporation,
    176F:2.
  Registered voters, certification of
    number, **51:61.**
  Representatives to general court,
    certificates of election, **3:1.**
  Vacancy in office, certificate as to
    nomination of candidate in
    case, **53:15.**
Cession of state land to United
  States, filing of plan of tract,
  1:7.
Charities.
  See CHARITIES AND
    CHARITABLE
    CONTRIBUTIONS.
Circulars.
  Pamphlets, circulars, or
    bulletins. See within this
    heading, "Pamphlets,
    circulars, or bulletins."
Cities and towns.
  Acceptance or rejection of laws
    by municipalities, reports
    concerning, **4:5.**

SECRETARY OF STATE
—Cont'd
Cities and towns —Cont'd
  Boundaries between towns,
    preservation of records
    concerning, **42:10.**
  Certificates and certification. See
    within this heading,
    "Certificates and
    certification."
  Solid waste disposal powers,
    certification by state
    secretary in connection with
    industrial development,
    40D:21.
  Welfare compensation plans,
    filing of rules and
    regulations concerning,
    30:37.
Civil service laws, department
  officers and employees as
  exempt, **9:2, 30:45.**
Clerks and clerical assistants to
  secretary, appointment, **9:2.**
Coat of arms, duties, **2:5.**
Commercial fisherman permits,
  applicant list, **130:38B.**
Commissioner of asset
  management and
  maintenance, regulations,
  7:39B.
Commissioners to qualify public
  officers, returns, **222:3.**
Commissions, fee for issuance of
  certain, **30:13.**
Communist organization,
  adjudication, **264:18.**
Compensation.
  Salaries and compensation. See
    within this heading,
    "Salaries and
    compensation."
Conservation board as within
  department, **9:29.**
Constitution of Massachusetts.
  State secretary.
    See CONSTITUTION OF
      MASSACHUSETTS.
Co-operative corporations and
  associations.
  Filing certificate of organization
    of certain co-operatives,
    157:7.
  Recovery of penalty for use of
    term co-operative, **157:8.**
Copies.
  See COPIES.
Corporations.
  See CORPORATIONS.
County Charter Procedures Act,
  34A:3.

SECRETARY OF STATE
—Cont'd
County officers.
  See COUNTY OFFICERS AND
    EMPLOYEES.
Credit unions.
  See CREDIT UNIONS.
Criminal history systems board,
  annual report, **6:168.**
Custody of documents, **66:7.**
Death of secretary of state, flag to
  be flown at half-mast, **2:6A.**
Death of treasurer of state, duties,
  10:12, 10:13.
Death records, duties as to.
  See DEATH.
Defined, **4:7.**
Dental service corporations,
  certificate of incorporation,
  176E:2.
Deputies, **9:2, 9:3, 9:10A.**
Destruction or sale of records,
  9:19.
Disposal of documents, **9:19.**
Distribution of documents, **5:7,
  5:8.**
District officers.
  Filing of certificate of
    appointment or election,
    41:19A.
  Furnishing supplies for election,
    41:118.
Division heads, appointment, **9:2.**
Dockets of lobbyists, **3:41, 3:45,
  3:47.**
Economic development
  department, filing of
  description of organization,
  23A:5.
Educational institution's power to
  grant degrees, notice as to
  revocation or suspension,
  69:30A.
Elder affairs department,
  description of organization of,
  filing, **19A:3.**
Election.
  See ELECTIONS.
Electrical wiring in buildings,
  deposit of regulations, **143:3L.**
Electricity.
  See GAS AND ELECTRIC
    COMPANIES.
Electronic voting systems, powers
  and duties with respect, **54:32,
  54:34, 54:37, 54:45.**
Elevator regulations, depositing,
  143:69.
Employees and officers of
  department as excepted from
  labor relations laws, **150E:1.**

SECRETARY OF STATE
—Cont'd
Employment security regulations,
  filing of copy, **23:9J.**
Energy resources executive office,
  filing description of
  organization, **25A:2.**
Engrossment of copies of bills and
  resolves, **3:23.**
Environmental management
  board, filing of charges and
  records of proceedings for
  removal of member, **21:2B.**
Estimates of costs of regulatory
  compliance, filing, **30A:5.**
Ethics commission.
  Major policymaking positions
    reported to commission,
    268B:3.
  Members, removal, **268B:2.**
Evidence, authentication of records
  and documents for use, **9:11.**
Examination, inspection, or
  investigation.
  Accountants, inspection of
    duplicate list, **13:34.**
  Election apparatus, **54:32.**
  Fees for examining records,
    262:37.
  Filing of regulations by inspector
    general, **12A:6.**
Exchanges and disposition of laws
  and documents to which
  members of general court are
  entitled, **5:16.**
Express companies, filing of power
  of attorney appointing general
  agent for foreign company,
  159:5, 159:7.
Extradition, filing application for
  requisition, **276:20L.**
Fees, **262:36, 262:37.**
Fire prevention regulations
  deposited, **148:10.**
Fish and game.
  Commercial fisherman permits,
    applicant list, **130:38B.**
  Fisheries and wildlife board,
    record of proceedings
    regarding, **21:7B.**
Flag.
  Death of secretary, flag to be
    flown at half-staff, **2:6A.**
  State flag, authority, **2:5.**
Foreign corporations.
  See FOREIGN
    CORPORATIONS.
Foreign insurance companies.
  Domestic companies, duties,
    175:19A.
  Foreign company, duties as to
    consolidation to form,
    175:19B.

SECRETARY OF STATE
—Cont'd
Fraternal benefit societies, filing
  change of location or purposes
  with secretary, **176:6.**
Game.
  Fish and game. See within this
    heading, "Fish and game."
Gas.
  See GAS AND ELECTRIC
    COMPANIES.
General court.
  See GENERAL COURT.
Gifts to Massachusetts Historical
  Commission, powers of
  secretary of state, **9:26.**
Great seal, duties and authority,
  2:5, 9:11.
Historical commission, duties,
  9:26, 9:27.
Hotels and lodging houses.
  Furnishing of summary of
    license laws, **140:19.**
  Record of conviction of offenses
    sent to secretary of state,
    140:32, 140:183C.
Housing and community
  development department.
  Copy of description of
    organization filed, **23B:4.**
  Filing of authority to certify
    instruments and documents,
    23B:9.
Housing and urban renewal.
  Housing authority, certificate of
    dissolution, **121B:4.**
  Redevelopment authority,
    certificate of dissolution,
    121B:4.
Human habitation standards and
  regulations, duties, **111:127A.**
Indexes and indexing.
  Massachusetts reports,
    index-digest, **5:14.**
  State departments and officials,
    indexing rules and
    regulations, **30:37.**
  State statutes, deposit of copies
    of indexes, **3:51.**
Initiative.
  See INITIATIVE AND
    REFERENDUM.
Inspection.
  Examination, inspection, or
    investigation. See within
    this heading, "Examination,
    inspection, or investigation."
Inspector general, filing of
  regulations, **12A:6.**
Insurance.
  See INSURANCE.

SECRETARY OF STATE
—Cont'd

Inventory of treasury funds upon vacancy in office of state treasurer, **10:13.**

Investigation.
Examination, inspection, or investigation. See within this heading, "Examination, inspection, or investigation."

Issuance of certain commissions, fee, **30:13.**

Journals and records of general court, duties regarding, **3:22, 5:10.**

Jurisdiction over land ceded to United States, filing of plan of tract, **1:7.**

Jury service, exemption, **234:1.**

Justices of the peace.
Annual listing of justices of the peace for town clerks and registrars, **9:16.**
Notice of expiration of commission, **9:15.**

Labor relations and disputes.
Insignia of labor unions, registration, **266:69.**
Officers and employees of department as excepted from labor relations laws, **150E:1.**

Law enforcement division, filing of rules and regulations, **21:6B.**

Law reports, index-digest, **5:14.**

Legislative agents, duties, **3:41, 3:45, 3:47.**

Legislative bills and resolves, duties, **3:23.**

Legislative committees, furnishing copies of rules and regulations, **30A:6.**

Library associations exempted from filing annual reports, **180:26A.**

Limited partnerships.
See LIMITED PARTNERSHIPS.

Lobbying, regulations and duties regarding, **3:39 et seq.**

Lodging houses.
Hotels and lodging houses. See within this heading, "Hotels and lodging houses."

Lottery commission's rules and regulations filed, **10:24.**

Maine lands, custody of records, **9:12.**

Major policymaking positions reported to State Ethics Commission, **268B:3.**

Manual of General Court, distribution, **5:11.**

SECRETARY OF STATE
—Cont'd

Marine boundaries, reports, **1:3.**

Marriage.
Fees for copies of marriage records, **262:36.**
Solemnization, authorization of nonresidents, **207:39.**
Transmission of copies of marriage records to secretary of state, **46:12, 46:17A, 46:17C, 46:17D, 46:18.**

Medical examiners, duty to supply records, **38:2.**

Medical schools, annual returns, **180:26A.**

Meetings of boards and commissions, notice to be filed with secretary, **30A:11A.**

Messengers of department, **9:2.**

Mining stock, statement to be filed before offering for sale, **93:15, 93:16.**

Municipal corporations.
Cities and towns. See within this heading, "Cities and towns."

Name change of state official, registration with state secretary, **30:7B.**

National Guard Week, duties regarding proclamation, **6:15BB.**

National presidential conventions, time for giving notice of number of delegates, **53:70B.**

Nomination papers.
See ELECTIONS.

Notaries public.
Expiration of commission, secretary's duty to notify, **9:15.**
Validation of acts of notary, **9:15A.**

Notices.
Absent defendants failing to appoint agents for service of process, notice of action, **227:5.**
Acceptance or rejection of statutes, return of notice to state secretary, **4:5.**
Attorney general notice to regarding petition for pardon, **127:153.**
Caucuses, notice of adoption or revocation of law as to use of official ballots, **53:90.**
Educational institution's power to grant degrees, notice as to revocation or suspension, **69:30A.**

SECRETARY OF STATE
—Cont'd

Notices —Cont'd
Hearings, transmission to clerks of house of representatives and senate and to counsel thereof, **30A:6.**
Justices and notaries of expiration of commission, secretary's duty to give notice, **9:15.**
Meetings, boards and commissions to file notice, **30A:11A.**
Presidential conventions, time for giving notice of number of delegates, **53:70B.**
Publication. See within this heading, "Publication."
Public hearings, transmission of notice regarding to clerks of house of representatives and senate and to counsel thereof, **30A:6.**
Retrocession, filing of notice, **1:7A.**
Suspension of state employees, filing copy of notice, **30:59.**
Vacancies in office, notices to secretary, **54:146, 221:13.**

Oath of office of public officers, **30:11, 34:15.**

Objections to nomination, **53:11, 55B:5.**

Official textbooks, distribution, **5:8.**

Optometric service corporations, certificate of incorporation, **176F:2.**

Original records permanently reproduced, authority to destroy, **9:19.**

Pamphlets, circulars, or bulletins.
Laws, publication of pamphlet edition, **5:4.**
Legislative committee hearings, sale of bulletins, **5:12.**

Pardons, duties with respect, **127:152, 127:153.**

Pensioner's right to payment for service in department, **32:91.**

Petitions for initiative or referendum to state time of filing writs, **53:22A.**

Petitions to general court, **3:1, 3:5, 3:7.**

Plan of tract of land ceded to United States, filing for jurisdiction purposes, **1:7.**

Political committees.
See POLITICAL COMMITTEES.

SECRETARY OF STATE
—Cont'd
Portraits.
Photographs of portraits and art objects in state house, availability, **9:28.**
Sale of books containing portraits and biographical sketches of members of general court, **5:18.**
Power of attorney appointing general agent for foreign express company, filing, **159:5, 159:7.**
Preservation of public records concerning town lines, **42:10.**
Presidential conventions, time for giving notice of number of delegates, **53:70B.**
Presidential electors.
Contents and filing of lists of electors, **54:78A.**
Meeting of electors, duties with respect, **54:148.**
Presidential primaries.
See PRESIDENTIAL PRIMARIES.
Primary elections.
See PRIMARY ELECTIONS.
Process.
Foreign corporations.
See FOREIGN CORPORATIONS.
Service on state secretary as agent of absent defendant, **64I:33, 227:5.**
Professional corporations and associations, organization, **156A:7.**
Publication.
Distribution of state publications, **5:1.**
Duties regarding certain petitions to the general court, **3:5.**
Laws, publication, **5:2, 5:4.**
Provision of copies of publications of state agencies to state secretary, **5:6A.**
Veteran's organizations, copies of proceedings, **5:9.**
Public buildings, advertising prior to sale or rental, **7:40H.**
Public works department, filing copy of description of organization, **16:3.**
Quarterly reports of fees received, **9:1.**
Railroads.
State secretary.
See RAILROADS.

SECRETARY OF STATE
—Cont'd
Records, reports, and returns.
Books and papers. See within this heading, "Books and papers."
Recounts of state primaries or elections, **54:135.**
Registers of probate and insolvency, duty to report vacancy in office of assistant register to secretary, **217:17.**
Registration of insignia of societies, associations or labor unions, **266:69.**
Registration of voters.
Certification of number of registered voters, **51:61.**
English and Spanish, provision of, affidavits, **51:36.**
Receipt of copies of affidavits, **51:46A.**
Report to general court, **54:133.**
Transmission to state secretary of copy of registration affidavits, **51:46A.**
Rejection of statute by city or town, return, **4:5.**
Representatives to general court, duties with respect to certificates of election, **3:1.**
Reproduction of records, **46:19A.**
Retired pensioner's right to compensation for service in department, **32:91.**
Retrocession, filing of notice, **1:7A.**
Rules and regulations, **10:24, 30A:6, 110B:9.**
Salaries and compensation, **9:1.**
Fees, **262:36, 262:37.**
Legislative and constitutional officers' compensation advisory board, duties, **6:162.**
Pensioner's right to payment for service in department of state, **32:91.**
Sale or destruction of records, **9:19.**
Sales and use tax laws, service of process in judicial proceedings against nonresidents, **64I:33.**
Schools or other educational institutions, notice as to revocation or suspension of power to grant degrees, **69:30A.**
Seal of Commonwealth, authority and duties, **2:5, 9:11.**
Securities Act.
See SECURITIES ACT.

SECRETARY OF STATE
—Cont'd
Service of process.
Process. See within this heading, "Process."
Session laws, distribution, **5:3.**
Solid waste disposal powers of municipalities, certification in connection with industrial development, **40D:21.**
Special sheriffs, record, **37:4.**
State ballot law commission.
Commission as within department of state secretary, **9:29.**
Printing of ballots, **55B:4.**
Time for objection to nomination of secretary, **55B:5.**
State departments and officials.
Annual report, **30:32.**
Filing and indexing rules and regulations, **30:37.**
State library, deposit of books and documents, **6:39, 30A:6.**
State lottery commission, filing of rules and regulations, **10:24.**
State political committees, filing list of members and officers, **52:1.**
State printing.
See STATE PRINTING.
State publications, distribution, **5:1.**
State secretary as referring to secretary of state, **4:7.**
State treasurer.
Bond, deposit, **10:3.**
Death or vacancy in office, **10:12, 10:13.**
State universities, filing of annual report with secretary, **75:15.**
Steam boilers and engines, filing regulations, **146:2.**
Stereotype and other plates owned by state, custody and disposition, **9:13.**
Street railways.
See STREET RAILWAYS.
Student government day, observance, **6:12M.**
Subversive organization, adjudication, **264:18.**
Supervisor of public records, appointment and supervision, **9:4, 9:5.**
Suspension of state employees, filing of copy of notice, **30:59.**
Take-over bids in acquisition of corporation, responsibilities, **110C:2 et seq.**

SECRETARY OF STATE
—Cont'd
Taxation.
Sales and use taxes, service of
process against
nonresidents, **64I:33.**
Suit by officer of another state
for enforcement of tax
liabilities, prerequisites,
58:28C.
Technical reports, distribution, **5:8.**
Telephone and telegraph
companies.
Certificate of decision of
department upon issue of
stock or bonds filed, **166:4.**
Statement of capital stock
subscribed and paid filed,
166:1.
Term limits, **10:1, 53:48.**
Textbooks, casebooks, and
technical reports, distribution,
5:8.
Towns.
Cities and towns. See within
this heading, "Cities and
towns."
Trademarks.
See TRADEMARKS AND
TRADE NAMES.
Treasurer of state.
State treasurer. See within this
heading, "State treasurer."
Trust company, submission of
articles of organization, **172:8.**
Unemployment compensation
regulations, filing copy, **23:9J.**
Uniform Securities Act.
See SECURITIES ACT.
Uniform state laws, board of
commissioners, **12:11B.**
United Nations day, observance,
6:12N.
Urban redevelopment corporations,
certificate of organization,
121A:6.
Urban renewal.
Housing and urban renewal. See
within this heading,
"Housing and urban
renewal."
Vacancies in office.
Assistant clerk, notice to
secretary of state of
vacancy, **221:13.**
Certificate as to nomination of
candidate to fill vacancy,
53:15.
County offices, notice concerning
vacancies in certain, **54:146.**
Deputies to act in case of
vacancy in office of
secretary, **9:3.**

SECRETARY OF STATE
—Cont'd
Vacancies in office —Cont'd
Registers of probate and
insolvency, duty to report
vacancy in office of assistant
register, **217:17.**
Treasurer of state, duties upon
vacancy in office, **10:12,
10:13.**
Validation of acts of notary, **9:15A.**
Veterans' organizations,
publication and distribution of
copies of proceedings, **5:9.**
Vital statistics, authority of
secretary as to records, **111:2.**
Voting machines and election
equipment, powers concerning,
54:28.
Wages.
Salaries and compensation. See
within this heading,
"Salaries and
compensation."
Wards and voting precincts,
notices, **54:1, 54:7A, 54:10.**
Welfare compensation plans of
municipalities, filing of rules
and regulations concerning,
30:37.

**SECRETARY OF TREASURY
OF UNITED STATES.**
Sworn certificate as evidence in
prosecution for counterfeiting,
267:15.

SECRETS AND SECRECY.
Confidential information.
See PRIVILEGED AND
CONFIDENTIAL
MATTERS.
Elections.
See ELECTIONS.
Insurance, prohibition against
secret inducements, **175:182
et seq.**
Trade secrets.
See TRADE SECRETS.

SECTIONMEN.
Fires.
See FIRES AND FIRE
PREVENTION.
Notification of discovery of fine,
railroad sectionmen to receive,
160:237.
Railroads, **160:237, 160:238.**

**SECURED TRANSACTIONS,
106:9-101 to 106:9-507.**
Accessions, priority of security
interest, **106:9-314.**

SECURED TRANSACTIONS
—Cont'd
Account debtor defined, **106:9-105.**
Accounts and accounting.
Application of article to
accounts, **106:9-102.**
Attachment of encumbered
personalty, statement of
account by secured party,
223:75.
Defined, **106:9-106.**
Exclusion of sale of accounts
from article, **106:9-104.**
Filing assignment, **106:9-302.**
Foreign state or country.
Application of article where
assignor keeps records,
106:9-103.
Perfection, **106:9-103.**
Preexisting indebtedness,
exception as to transfer of
single account in
satisfaction, **106:9-104.**
Priorities, **106:9-301.**
Resale for excess of amount over
security interest,
accountability, **106:2-706.**
Security agreement covering
revolving loans on accounts,
form, **106:9-507.**
Time of attachment of security
interest in accounts,
106:9-204.
Use or disposition of collateral
as requiring accounting,
106:9-205.
Advances.
Future advances. See within this
heading, "Future advances."
After-acquired property, security
interest, **106:9-108, 106:9-204.**
Form, **106:9-507.**
Agreements.
Contract liability. See within
this heading, "Contract
liability of secured party for
debtor's acts or omissions."
Financing agreement, definition,
23D:1.
Agriculture.
See AGRICULTURE.
Airplanes as subject, **106:9-103.**
Air rights leases over highways,
pledge, **81:7L.**
Alcoholic liquors.
Liens and encumbrances.
See ALCOHOLIC LIQUORS.
Pledges.
See ALCOHOLIC LIQUORS.
Alienability of debtor's rights,
106:9-311.

SECURED TRANSACTIONS
—Cont'd

Amendment or modification.
  Assignment, modification after notice, **106:9-318.**
  Contract, modification after notice of assignment, **106:9-318.**
  Financing statement, **106:9-402.**
    Form, **106:9-507.**
  Sales warranties, **106:9-206.**
Animals, secured transactions involving, **106:9-109, 106:9-204.**
Antecedent debt, pledge by consignee or factor, **104:5.**
Assembled goods, priorities, **106:9-315.**
Assessment of mortgaged goods for taxation, **59:19.**
Assets of insurance companies, collateral security included, **175:11.**
Assignments and transfers.
  Agreement not to assert defenses against assignee, **106:9-206.**
  Bulk transfers.
    See BULK TRANSFERS.
  Compensation of employee, exclusion of assignment of claim, **106:9-104.**
  Continuation statement to be accompanied by statement, **106:9-403.**
  Credit union accounts, transfer, **106:9-104.**
  Debtors' rights, transferability, **106:9-311.**
  Filing of assignment of security interest, **106:9-302, 106:9-405, 106:9-507.**
  Financing statement. See within this heading, "Financing statement."
  General intangibles, validity of contracts prohibiting assignment, **106:9-318.**
  Modification after notice of assignment, **106:9-318.**
  Motor vehicles.
    See MOTOR VEHICLES.
  Notice or knowledge. See within this heading, "Notice or knowledge."
  Oil, gas, or minerals, indexing of assignment of interest, **106:9-405.**
  Perfection where assignor keeps records in foreign country, **106:9-103.**

SECURED TRANSACTIONS
—Cont'd

Assignments and transfers
  —Cont'd
  Release, statement of assignment to accompany, **106:9-406.**
  Termination statement, duty on presentation, **106:9-404.**
  Timber, indexing of assignment of interests, **106:9-405.**
  Trust or estate, security interest created by assignment of interest, **106:9-302.**
  Wage assignments. See within this heading, "Wage assignments."
Attachment of property.
  See ATTACHMENT OF PROPERTY.
Attachment of security interest, **106:9-203.**
  Accounts, time of attachment of security interest, **106:9-204.**
  After-acquired property as subject, **106:9-204.**
  Index of definition, **106:9-105.**
  Time of attachment of security interest, **106:9-204.**
  Trustee process. See within this heading, "Trustee process."
Attorneys' fees.
  Payment of attorney's fees from proceeds from sale of collateral after default, **106:9-504.**
  Redemption of collateral, debtor's liability for attorney's fees, **106:9-506.**
Automotive equipment as subject, **106:9-103.**
Bailees' lien on goods sold, priority against security interest of seller or lessor, **255:35.**
Bailments.
  Leases. See within this heading, "Leases."
Bank deposits and collections.
  Depositary and collecting banks.
    Collection of items.
      Security interests of collecting banks.
      Items accompanying documents and proceeds, **106:4-210.**
  Documentary drafts.
    Dishonor.
      Privilege of presenting bank to deal with goods.
      Security interest for expenses, **106:4-504.**

SECURED TRANSACTIONS
—Cont'd

Bankruptcy, insolvency proceedings as affecting rights of secured party, **106:9-306.**
Banks.
  See BANKS AND BANKING.
Bills of lading.
  See BILLS OF LADING.
Bona fide purchasers.
  Buyer in ordinary course of business. See within this heading, "Buyer in ordinary course of business."
  Certificates of title, perfection of interest by bona fide purchasers in multi-state transactions, **106:9-103.**
  Priority, **106:9-309.**
  Sale of collateral upon default, **106:9-504.**
Bulk transfers.
  See BULK TRANSFERS.
Buyer in ordinary course of business.
  Farm products, priority as to buyer, **106:9-301.**
  Personal or family use, protection as to goods purchased, **106:9-307.**
Buyers of goods under sales article of Commercial Code.
  Sales under Commercial Code. See within this heading, "Sales under Commercial Code."
Buying or receiving personal property knowing it to be hired, leased, or collateral security, **266:86.**
Cancellation.
  Termination statements. See within this heading, "Termination statements."
Carriers.
  Shipping contracts. See within this heading, "Shipping contracts or charters."
Cash proceeds.
  Defined, **106:9-306.**
  Deposit accounts, **106:9-306.**
  Purchase money security interest, priority, **106:9-312.**
  Secured party's rights, **106:9-306.**
Cemetery lot, conveyance as security, forbidden, **114:43B.**
Certificates and certification.
  Filing officer, certification of papers, **106:9-407.**
  Multi-state transactions, perfection of security interests, **106:9-103.**

SECURED TRANSACTIONS
—Cont'd
Certificates and certification
—Cont'd
Title certificate.
Financing statements,
exception as to filing,
106:9-302.
Indication of security interest,
106:9-302.
Law governing security
interest in property
covered, **106:9-103.**
Multi-state transactions,
perfection of security
interests, **106:9-103.**
Change.
Amendment or modification. See
within this heading,
"Amendment or
modification."
Charge for additional statements
of account, **106:9-208.**
Charters.
Shipping contracts or charters.
See within this heading,
"Shipping contracts or
charters."
Chattel mortgages, **4:7, 106:9-102.**
Chattel paper.
Application of article, **106:9-102.**
Defined, **106:9-105.**
Exclusion of sale of chattel
paper from article,
106:9-104.
Filing to perfect security
interest, **106:9-304.**
Multi-state transactions,
perfection of security
interests, **106:9-103.**
Perfecting security interest,
106:9-103, 106:9-305.
Priorities, **106:9-301, 106:9-308.**
Shipping contracts or charters,
106:9-105.
Chattel trust, application of article
to generally, **106:9-102.**
Checks as included in cash
proceeds, **106:9-306.**
Chief executive office, multi-state
transactions as affected by
location, **106:9-103.**
Choice of law, **106:1-105.**
Classification of goods, **106:9-109.**
Coercion in placing of insurance,
175:193E.
Collateral.
Accounting as required upon use
or disposition, **106:9-205.**
After-acquired collateral,
106:9-204.

SECURED TRANSACTIONS
—Cont'd
Collateral —Cont'd
Attachment as affected by
debtor's rights, **106:9-203.**
Banks receiving public deposits
in excess of insurance
amount, **29:34A.**
Commingling of collateral. See
within this heading,
"Commingling of collateral."
Compulsory disposition,
106:9-505.
Consent of non-debtor owner of
collateral to pledge, form,
106:9-507.
Default. See within this heading,
"Default."
Defined, **106:9-105.**
Description of. See within this
heading, "Description of."
Discharge of obligation by
acceptance, **106:9-505.**
Disposition of collateral. See
within this heading,
"Disposition of collateral."
Duties of secured party in
possession, **106:9-207.**
Form for collateral note,
106:9-507.
Fraudulent substitution, **266:33.**
Fungible collateral,
commingling, **106:9-207.**
Garnishment of debtor's rights
in collateral, **106:9-311.**
Guarantee of payment by
non-debtor owner of
collateral, form, **106:9-507.**
Hydroelectric company, pledge of
prior bonds to secure
refunding mortgage bonds,
164:9.
Insurance. See within this
heading, "Insurance."
Judgment taken on right to
payment as subject to
Article 9, **106:9-104.**
Lapsed filing, sufficiency of
financing statement,
106:9-402.
Lists and schedules of collateral,
request for. See within this
heading, "Lists and
schedules of collateral,
request."
Loan of collateral security by
secured party, **266:85.**
Massachusetts Bay
transportation authority.
See MASSACHUSETTS BAY
TRANSPORTATION
AUTHORITY.

SECURED TRANSACTIONS
—Cont'd
Collateral —Cont'd
Multi-state transactions,
perfection, **106:9-103.**
Pawnbrokers.
See PAWNBROKERS.
Priorities of secured party filing
after collateral comes into
possession of debtor,
106:9-301.
"Proceeds" as including
insurance, **106:9-306.**
Proposal to retain collateral in
satisfaction of obligation,
forms for notice, **106:9-507.**
Receipts, **140:86.**
Redemption of collateral. See
within this heading,
"Redemption of collateral."
Release of collateral. See within
this heading, "Release of
collateral."
Renunciation by debtor of rights
in, form, **106:9-507.**
Repossession and intent to
dispose of collateral.
Notice or knowledge. See
within this heading,
"Notice or knowledge."
Rights of secured party in
possession, **106:9-207.**
Sale of collateral. See within
this heading, "Sale of
collateral."
Secured party in possession,
rights, **106:9-207.**
Substitution, **266:33.**
Taking possession of, after
default, **106:9-503, 255:13J,
255B:20B, 255D:22.**
Title to collateral, materiality,
106:9-112, 106:9-202.
Collection right of secured party
upon default, **106:9-502.**
Collections, secured transaction as
subject to laws governing,
106:9-203.
Commercial Code, **106:9-101 et
seq.**
Commingling of collateral,
106:9-205.
Fungible collateral, **106:9-207.**
Priority as to commingled
collateral, **106:9-315.**
Compensation, exclusion from
article of assignment of claim,
106:9-104.
Compulsory disposition of
collateral, **106:9-505.**
Concealment of goods, **266:82,
266:87.**
Indictment, form, **277:79.**

SECURED TRANSACTIONS
—Cont'd
Conditional sales, **106:9-102.**
Attachment of property, **223:74.**
Construction of statutes, **4:7.**
Retail installment sales.
See RETAIL INSTALLMENT SALES AND SERVICES.
Termination of personal service contracts, **255:13K.**
Consent to security interest in existing fixtures, form, **106:9-507.**
Consignment.
See CONSIGNMENT.
Construction machinery as subject, **106:9-103.**
Construction mortgage, index of definition, **106:9-105.**
Construction of statute, meaning of terms, **4:7.**
Consumer goods and consumer protection, **106:9-203.**
After-acquired property clause, attachment of security interest, **106:9-204.**
Buyer as taking free of security interest, **106:9-307.**
Criminal violations as to consumer notes, **255:12C.**
Default. See within this heading, "Default."
Defined, **106:9-109.**
Filing security interest, **106:9-302, 106:9-401.**
Installment sale contract, form, **106:9-507.**
Limitation on consumer protection actions, **260:5A.**
Repossession and disposition of consumer goods after default, **255:13I, 255B:20B, 255D:22.**
Consumer notes, violations, **255:12C.**
Redemption, **255:13J.**
Security agreement covering loans on, form, **106:9-507.**
Continuation statement, statement of assignment to accompany, **106:9-403.**
Contract liability of secured party for debtor's acts or omissions, **106:9-317.**
Application of article, **106:9-102.**
Defined, **106:9-106.**
Exclusion of sale of contract rights from article, **106:9-104.**
Filing assignment, **106:9-302.**
Filing security interest, **106:9-401.**

SECURED TRANSACTIONS
—Cont'd
Contract liability of secured party for debtor's acts or omissions —Cont'd
Priorities, **106:9-301.**
Time of attachment of security interest, **106:9-204.**
Contracts.
Agreements. See within this heading, "Agreements."
Conversion, failure to dispose of collateral upon default, **106:9-505.**
Cooperative banks.
See COOPERATIVE BANKS.
Copies.
Assignment, copy, **106:9-405.**
Duty of filing officer to certify, **106:9-407.**
Financing statements, sufficiency of copies, **106:9-402.**
Public inspection, **106:9-403.**
Sufficiency of copies of financing statement, **106:9-402.**
Corporations.
Pledge and collateral security. See CORPORATIONS.
Credit disclosure, effect of laws governing, **106:9-203.**
Creditor's claims on goods delivered for sale or return. Effect of Article 9, **106:2-326.**
Credit unions.
See CREDIT UNIONS.
Crimes and offenses.
Buying or receiving of pledged chattels, **266:86.**
Concealment of goods, **266:82, 266:87.**
Consignee or factor, pledging property, **266:88.**
Fines and penalties. See within this heading, "Fines and penalties."
Fraudulent substitution of collateral, **266:33.**
Mortgagor selling collateral without notice to or consent of secured party, **266:83.**
Selling or loaning pledged property before debt due, **266:85.**
Violations as to consumer notes, violations, **255:12C.**
Crops.
See AGRICULTURE.
Damages on improper disposition of collateral, **106:9-507.**
Debtor defined, **106:9-105.**

SECURED TRANSACTIONS
—Cont'd
Deed registers.
Registers and registries of deeds. See within this heading, "Registers and registries of deeds."
Deeds, special provisions as to fixture filings and registries, **106:9-410.**
Default, **106:9-501 to 106:9-507.**
Acceptance of collateral as discharging obligation, **106:9-505.**
Collection rights of secured party, **106:9-502.**
Consumer goods, **255B:20B, 255D:22.**
Notice or knowledge. See within this heading, "Notice or knowledge."
Disposal of collateral, **106:9-504.**
Compulsory disposition of collateral, **106:9-505.**
Foreclosure of security interest, **106:9-501.**
Lease, allocation of proceeds to expense of preparing, **106:9-504.**
Notice or knowledge. See within this heading, "Notice or knowledge."
Possession after default, secured party's right, **106:9-503.**
Repossession. See within this heading, "Repossession."
Real and personal property, security agreement covering, **106:9-501.**
Sale of collateral. See within this heading, "Sale of collateral."
Sales articles, security interest arising, **106:9-113.**
Secured party's liability for failure to comply with article, **106:9-507.**
Waiver, **106:9-501.**
Defenses.
Agreement not to assert defenses against assignee, **106:9-206.**
Assignee, defenses against, **106:9-318.**
Automobile damage claims defenses available against registered owner as available against holder of security interest, **231:85E.**
Waiver, **106:9-206.**

SECURED TRANSACTIONS
—Cont'd
Deficiency.
  Consumer goods, debtor's
    liability for deficiency after
    repossession and sale,
    255:13I.
  Debtor's liability, **106:9-502,**
    106:9-504.
  Owner of collateral other than
    debtor as liable, **106:9-112.**
  Deficiency judgments, **255:13J.**
  Definitions, **23D:1, 106:9-105,**
    106:9-115, 175:180A.
Delivery of financial asset, security
  interest arising in, **106:9-116.**
Demand.
  Secured party. See within this
    heading, "Secured party."
Deposit accounts.
  See BANKS AND BANKING.
Deposits, exclusion of transfer,
  106:9-104.
Description of assignment,
  106:9-318.
Description of collateral.
  Financing statement,
    description, **106:9-402.**
  Security agreement, description,
    106:9-203.
  Sufficiency, **106:9-110.**
Destruction of old records,
  106:9-408, 106:9-409.
Diamonds, requirements as to
  loans, **140:86.**
Discharge or release.
  Acceptance of collateral,
    106:9-505.
  Assignment, release to be
    accompanied by statement,
    106:9-406.
  Chattel mortgages.
    Payment or tender of legal
      amount, **140:91, 140:103,**
      140:107.
    Redemption, provisions
      regarding loans under
      1000 dollars inapplicable,
      140:95.
    Refusal to discharge, liability,
      140:94.
  Collateral.
    Release of collateral. See
      within this heading,
      "Release of collateral."
Disclaimer, pledge of interest on
  money as bar, **191A:8.**
Disclosure of terms, effect of laws
  governing, **106:9-203.**
Disposition of collateral.
  Default. See within this heading,
    "Default."

SECURED TRANSACTIONS
—Cont'd
Disposition of collateral —Cont'd
  Lack of accounting, **106:9-205.**
  Repossession and intent to
    dispose of collateral.
  Notice. See within this
    heading, "Notice or
    knowledge."
  Secured party's rights,
    106:9-306.
Documents.
  Application of article, **106:9-102.**
  Controlling in goods as against
    person holding security
    interest, document of title,
    106:7-502.
  Defined, **106:9-105.**
  Filing to perfect security
    interest, **106:9-304.**
  Multi-state transactions,
    perfection of security
    interests, **106:9-103.**
  Priorities, **106:9-301.**
Drug-related cases, security
  interest unaffected by
  forfeiture, **94C:47.**
Duration of filing, **106:9-403.**
Employment security benefits not
  to be pledged, **151A:36.**
Encumbrances.
  See LIENS AND
    ENCUMBRANCES.
Enforceability of security interest,
  106:9-203.
Equipment.
  Defined, **106:9-109.**
  Farm equipment.
    See AGRICULTURE.
  Forms of security agreement
    covering, **106:9-507.**
  Railroads.
    Cars and rolling stock.
      See RAILROADS.
    Liens and encumbrances.
      See RAILROADS.
  Equipment trust, **106:9-102.**
    Life insurance companies'
      investments in equipment
      trust certificates secured by
      aircraft or aircraft
      equipment, **175:63.**
    Rolling stock, exclusion from
      article of equipment trust
      covering, **106:9-104.**
Errors.
  Mistake. See within this
    heading, "Mistake or error."
Estate interest, exception as to
  assignment, **106:9-302.**
Estate tax lien as applicable to
  property transferred to
  pledgee, **65C:14.**

SECURED TRANSACTIONS
—Cont'd
Evidence.
  Assignment, proof, **106:9-318.**
  Subordinate security interest,
    evidence, **106:9-504.**
Examination or inspection.
  Goods sold under sales article of
    Commercial Code, buyer's
    security interest for
    expenses of examination or
    inspection, **106:2-711.**
  Pledge, examination or
    inspection of records
    concerning, **140:87 et seq.**
Excluded transactions, **106:9-104.**
Exemptions.
  Assignments for benefit of
    creditors, **106:9-302.**
  Certificates of title, **106:9-302.**
  Chattel mortgages, exemption
    under Uniform Securities
    Act, **110A:402.**
  Financing statement, exception
    as to filing, **106:9-302.**
  Governmental entities,
    transactions, **106:9-104.**
  Insurance proceeds, **106:9-104.**
  Preexisting indebtedness,
    transfer of single account in
    satisfaction, **106:9-104.**
  Shipping charter or contract,
    106:9-105.
  Trust or estate, assignment of
    beneficial interest,
    106:9-302.
Expenses and expenditures.
  Inspection of goods sold under
    sales article of Commercial
    Code, buyer's security
    interest for expenses,
    106:2-711.
  Preserving collateral as
    chargeable to debtor,
    106:9-207.
Expiration of security interests
  perfected in multi-state
  transactions, **106:9-103.**
Factors and commission
  merchants, **106:9-102.**
Farm equipment.
  See AGRICULTURE.
Federal statutes, exclusion of
  security interests subject,
  106:9-104.
Fees.
  Attorneys' fees. See within this
    heading, "Attorneys' fees."
  Filing. See within this heading,
    "Filing."
Filing, **106:9-401 to 106:9-408.**
  Assignment, filing statement,
    106:9-405.

SECURED TRANSACTIONS
—Cont'd
Filing —Cont'd
Contract liability. See within this heading, "Contract liability of secured party for debtor's acts or omissions."
Crop mortgages, **255:7D.**
Destruction of old records, **106:9-408.**
Duration, **106:9-403.**
Duties of filing officer, **106:9-403-106:9-406.**
Information, filing officer's duty to give. See within this heading, "Information, filing officer's duty to give."
Erroneous filing, **106:9-401.**
Fees for filing, **106:9-403, 106:9-404.**
Assignment, filing statement, **106:9-405.**
Copies of documents, fee for making, **106:9-407.**
Financing statement, filing fees, **106:9-403.**
Release of collateral, **106:9-406.**
Termination statement, filing, **106:9-404.**
Financing statement. See within this heading, "Financing statement."
Fixtures, special provisions for filing, **106:9-409.**
Information, filing officer's duty to give. See within this heading, "Information, filing officer's duty to give."
Intangibles, **106:9-401.**
Lapsed filing. See within this heading, "Lapsed filing."
Notice of security interest, filing, **106:9-309.**
Other state, filing to perfect security interest, **106:9-103.**
Perfection of security interest, **106:9-302, 106:9-304, 106:9-305.**
Foreign country, perfection of security interest where assignor keeps records, **106:9-103.**
Proceeds, security interest, **106:9-306.**
Place, **106:9-401.**
Priorities as determined by order, **106:9-301, 106:9-312.**
Sales article, security interest arising, **106:9-113, 106:9-302.**

SECURED TRANSACTIONS
—Cont'd
Filing —Cont'd
Subordination agreements as to sharecropping, **255:7D.**
Termination statement, filing, **106:9-404.**
What constitutes, **106:9-403.**
Financing agreement, definition, **23D:1.**
Financing statement.
Amendment. See within this heading, "Amendment or modification."
Assignment for benefit of creditors, exception, **106:9-302.**
Assignment of security interest in collateral, disclosure, **106:9-405.**
Certificates of titles, exception, **106:9-302.**
Commingled goods, financing statement as covering, **106:9-315.**
Consignments, requirements of statements covering, **106:9-408.**
Copies, sufficiency, **106:9-402.**
Errors, **106:9-402.**
Exceptions as to filing, **106:9-302.**
Exemption of filing officer from duty as to giving of information, **106:9-407.**
Filing of, **106:9-302, 106:9-402, 106:9-403.**
Fixture filing, sufficiency, **106:9-402.**
Formal requisites, **106:9-402.**
Forms, **106:9-402, 106:9-507.**
Indexing, **106:9-403.**
Lapsed filing, sufficiency, **106:9-402.**
Leased goods, requirements of statements covering, **106:9-408.**
Mistake, **106:9-402.**
Mortgages, **106:9-402.**
Multi-state transactions, exceptions as to filing, **106:9-302.**
Name of debtor, effect of change, **106:9-402.**
Oil, gas, and minerals, sufficiency of statement, **106:9-401.**
Registers and registries of deeds. See within this heading, "Registers and registries of deeds."

SECURED TRANSACTIONS
—Cont'd
Financing statement —Cont'd
Statement of continuation, form for partial release or assignment, **106:9-507.**
Timber to be cut, sufficiency of statement, **106:9-402.**
Fines and penalties.
Deposited property, penalty for pledging, **105:62.**
Inspection of pledge, failure to allow, **140:89.**
Insurance, coercion in placing, **175:193E.**
Leased chattels, buying and selling of, **266:84, 266:86, 266:87.**
Liquor container, illegal sale, **266:82.**
Sale of chattel mortgaged property without consent of mortgagee, **266:83.**
Fish, time of attachment of security interest, **106:9-204.**
Fixtures.
See FIXTURES.
Foreclosure sale.
Judicial sales. See within this heading, "Judicial sales."
Foreign insurance companies.
Pledge and collateral security. See FOREIGN INSURANCE COMPANIES.
Foreign state or country.
Accounts and accounting. See within this heading, "Accounts and accounting."
Financing statement relating to property brought, **106:9-402.**
Perfection in multi-state transactions. See within this heading, "Perfection in multi-state transactions."
Place of business of foreign air carrier for purpose of determining validity of security interest in airplane, **106:9-103.**
Formal requisites, **106:9-203.**
Form of financing statement, **106:9-402, 106:9-507.**
Fraudulent substitution of collateral, **266:33.**
Fraudulent transfers.
See FRAUDULENT CONVEYANCES OR TRANSFERS.
Fungible collateral, commingling, **106:9-207.**
Future advances.
Buyers interests, **106:9-307.**

SECURED TRANSACTIONS
—Cont'd
Future advances —Cont'd
Covered obligations, future advances, **106:9-204.**
Discharge of security when provision made, **140:107.**
Form, **106:9-507.**
Priority as to, **106:9-312.**
Security agreement including, **106:9-204.**
Small loan providing for, release of security, **140:107.**
Garnishment.
Trustee process. See within this heading, "Trustee process."
Gas.
See GAS AND OIL.
General intangibles.
Assignment, validity of contracts prohibiting, **106:9-318.**
Money as included in term, **106:9-106.**
Multi-state transactions, perfection of security interests, **106:9-103.**
Good faith purchasers.
Bona fide purchasers. See within this heading, "Bona fide purchasers."
Goods, **106:9-101 et seq.**
Accessions, priority of security interest, **106:9-314.**
Application of article, **106:9-102.**
Buyers of goods.
Sales under Commercial Code. See within this heading, "Sales under Commercial Code."
Concealment of goods. See within this heading, "Concealment of goods."
Consumer goods. See within this heading, "Consumer goods and consumer protection."
Defined, **106:9-105.**
Incoming goods already subject to security interest, law governing, **106:9-103.**
Perfecting security interest, **106:9-304, 106:9-305.**
Person in possession furnishing services or materials, **106:9-310.**
Priorities, **106:9-301.**
Termination statement, **106:9-404.**
Governmental entities as exempt from laws governing, **106:9-104.**
Guaranty by third person, form, **106:9-507.**

SECURED TRANSACTIONS
—Cont'd
Hazardous waste insolvency fund, power to provide pledges, **21C:18.**
Highways and streets, **29:2O, 81:7L.**
Hydroelectric company, pledge of prior bonds to secure refunding mortgage bonds, **164:9.**
Identification of assignment, **106:9-318.**
Identification of collateral.
Description of collateral. See within this heading, "Description of collateral."
Income tax as to corporation holding property as security under pledge, **62:14.**
Indexing of financing statements, **106:9-403.**
Indictment, form for concealing mortgaged personal property, **277:79.**
Information, filing officer's duty to give, **106:9-407.**
Registers of deeds and assistant recorders of land court, exemption from duty to issue certificate, **106:9-407.**
Injunctive relief, owner of collateral other than debtor as entitled, **106:9-112.**
Insolvency proceedings as affecting rights of secured party, **106:9-306.**
Inspection.
Examination or inspection. See within this heading, "Examination or inspection."
Installment sales, article as affecting regulation governing, **106:9-201, 106:9-203.**
Instruments.
Application of article, **106:9-102.**
Defined, **106:9-105.**
Filing to perfect security interest, **106:9-304.**
Multi-state transactions, perfection of security interests, **106:9-103.**
Perfecting security interest, **106:9-305.**
Priorities, **106:9-301.**
Insurance, **106:9-104, 175:63, 175:180A.**
Assets, pledge and collateral security included, **175:11.**
Banks receiving public deposits in excess of insurance amount, **29:34A.**

SECURED TRANSACTIONS
—Cont'd
Insurance —Cont'd
Coercion in placing of insurance, **175:193E.**
Debtor as liable for insurance, **106:9-207.**
Disclosure of information with respect to insurance required as collateral security to loan, prohibition against, **176D:4.**
Equipment trust certificates secured by aircraft or aircraft equipment, life insurance companies' investments, **175:63.**
Exclusion of interest or claim in insurance, **106:9-104.**
Foreign insurance companies.
Pledge and collateral security. See FOREIGN INSURANCE COMPANIES.
Investments in equipment or chattels, **175:63.**
Liquidation proceedings, secured claims, **175:180K.**
Loan or lien, unreasonable disapproval of insurance policy provided by borrower as security, **176D:4.**
Personalty, penalty for coercion in placing of insurance, **175:193E.**
Premium finance agencies.
Insurance premium finance agencies. See within this heading, "Insurance premium finance agencies."
"Proceeds" as including casualty insurance on collateral, **106:9-306.**
Schedule of loans secured, **175:25.**
Insurance premium finance agencies.
Effect of laws governing, **106:9-203.**
Perfection of insurance premium finance agreement as secured transaction, **255C:12.**
Intangibles, **106:9-102, 106:9-103, 106:9-401.**
Defined, **106:9-106.**
Filing, **106:9-401.**
General intangibles. See within this heading, "General intangibles."

SECURED TRANSACTIONS
—Cont'd
Intangibles —Cont'd
Priority, **106:9-301.**
Interest on money.
See INTEREST ON MONEY.
Inventory.
Defined, **106:9-109.**
Form for security agreement
covering loans, **106:9-507.**
Mobile goods, perfection in
multi-state transactions as
to inventory, **106:9-103.**
Priorities, **106:9-308, 106:9-312.**
Investment securities.
Chattel mortgage exemption
under Securities Act,
110A:402.
Commercial code, securities
under.
See INVESTMENT
SECURITIES UNDER
COMMERCIAL CODE.
Hydroelectric company bonds,
164:9.
Municipal industrial
development projects,
40D:9, 40D:14.
State refunding bonds, security
for issuance, **29:53A.**
Joint bank deposits.
See BANKS AND BANKING.
Judgments, exclusion from article
of rights represented,
106:9-104.
Judicial sales.
Foreclosure of security interest
by judicial sale, **106:9-311,
106:9-501.**
Foreclosure sale, priorities of
purchaser, **106:9-313,
106:9-314.**
Knowledge.
Notice or knowledge. See within
this heading, "Notice or
knowledge."
Land as security for debt, **183:18
et seq., 244:1 et seq.**
Landlord and tenant.
Leases. See within this heading,
"Leases."
Lapsed filing.
Effect, **106:9-403.**
Removal from records,
106:9-403.
Sufficiency of financing
statement, **106:9-402.**
Law governing, **106:9-103.**
Leases, **106:1-201.**
Application of article to leases,
106:9-102, 106:9-104.

SECURED TRANSACTIONS
—Cont'd
Leases —Cont'd
Bailee's lien, priority against
lessor's security interest,
255:35.
Crops, security interest in crops
given in conjunction with
lease, **106:9-204.**
Default, allocation of proceeds
pursuant, **106:9-504.**
Financing statements covering
leased goods, **106:9-408.**
Lien of landlord excluded from
article, **106:9-104.**
Penalty for buying or selling of
leased chattels, **266:84,
266:86, 266:87.**
Waiver.
Defenses by lessees, waiver,
106:9-206.
Priority, form for landlord's
waiver, **106:9-507.**
Letters of credit.
Assignment of proceeds,
106:5-114.
Perfecting security interests,
106:9-304, 106:9-305.
Transfer of interest in letter
excluded from article,
106:9-104.
Licensed lenders, effect of laws
governing, **106:9-203.**
Limitations, consumer protection
actions, **260:5A.**
Liquidation proceedings involving
insurance companies, secured
claims, **175:180K.**
Lists and schedules of collateral,
request, **106:9-208.**
Insurance, schedule of loans
secured, **175:25.**
Livestock, secured transactions
involving, **106:9-109,
106:9-204.**
Loans of collateral unauthorized,
266:85.
Logs and timber.
Timber. See within this heading,
"Timber."
Losses.
Owner of collateral other than
debtor as having right to
recover, **106:9-112.**
Secured party's liability,
106:9-207.
Machinery.
Equipment. See within this
heading, "Equipment."
Manufactured goods, priorities,
106:9-315.

SECURED TRANSACTIONS
—Cont'd
Materialman's lien, exclusion from
article, **106:9-104.**
Mechanics' liens, exclusion from
article, **106:9-104.**
Minehead, multi-state transaction
as governed by location,
106:9-103.
Mines.
See MINES AND MINERALS.
Miscellaneous corporations,
approval of stockholders
required as to chattel
mortgages, **158:10.**
Mistake or error.
Filing of security interest in
error, **106:9-401.**
Financing statement, **106:9-402.**
Mobile goods, multi-state secured
transactions, **106:9-103.**
Modification.
Amendment or modification. See
within this heading,
"Amendment or
modification."
Money.
Cash proceeds. See within this
heading, "Cash proceeds."
"General intangibles" as
including, **106:9-106.**
Morris plan banks.
See MORRIS PLAN BANKS.
Mortgages of real property, **183:18
et seq., 244:1 et seq.**
See MORTGAGES AND DEEDS
OF TRUST.
Motor vehicles.
See MOTOR VEHICLES.
Municipal industrial development
projects, pledge of rentals and
other revenues to secure
bonds, **40D:9, 40D:14.**
Negotiable instruments.
See NEGOTIABLE
INSTRUMENTS.
Noncash proceeds defined,
106:9-306.
Notice or knowledge.
Acceptance of collateral as
discharge of obligation,
notice to debtor, **106:9-505.**
Assignee's notice to account
debtor, form, **106:9-507.**
Assignment, notice, **106:9-318.**
Default, **255:13I.**
Automobile, creditor's notice
to police as to
repossession, **255B:20C.**
Filing as notice, **106:9-309.**

SECURED TRANSACTIONS
—Cont'd
Notice or knowledge —Cont'd
Intent to retain collateral, owner
of collateral other than
debtor as entitled to notice,
106:9-112.
Lien creditor of unperfected
security interests, effect of
knowledge, **106:9-301.**
Proposal to retain collateral in
satisfaction of obligation,
form for giving notice,
106:9-507.
Repossession and intent to
dispose of collateral, form
for giving notice, **106:9-507.**
Sale of collateral.
Default, notice of sale by
secured party, **106:9-504.**
Form, **106:9-507.**
Mortgagor, sale of collateral
by, without notice to
secured party, **266:83.**
Offenses.
Crimes and offenses. See within
this heading, "Crimes and
offenses."
Oil.
See GAS AND OIL.
Old records, destruction of,
106:9-409.
One thousand dollars, loans
secured by pledge for amounts
less than, **140:91.**
Ordinary goods in multi-state
transactions, perfection of
security interests, **106:9-103.**
Other state.
Foreign state or country. See
within this heading,
"Foreign state or country."
Passbooks, exclusion of transfers,
106:9-104.
Pawnbrokers, **140:70 et seq.,**
140:202-140:205.
See PAWNBROKERS.
Penalties.
Fines and penalties. See within
this heading, "Fines and
penalties."
Perfected security interest.
Accessions, **106:9-314.**
Conflict of laws, **106:9-103.**
Filing. See within this heading,
"Filing."
Highway infrastructure fund,
security for bonds issued,
29:2O.
Instruments, documents, and
goods, perfection of security
interest, **106:9-304.**

SECURED TRANSACTIONS
—Cont'd
Perfected security interest
—Cont'd
Insurance premium finance
agreement, perfection as
secured transaction,
255C:12.
Letters of credit, **106:9-304,**
106:9-305.
Motor vehicle certificates of title,
90D:21, 90D:37.
Multi-state transactions.
Perfection in multi-state
transactions. See within
this heading, "Perfection
in multi-state
transactions."
Possession by secured party,
106:9-305.
Proceeds, security interest,
106:9-306.
Temporary perfection, **106:9-304.**
Time of perfecting, **106:9-303.**
Motor vehicle, time of
perfection of security
interest, **90D:21.**
Unperfected security interest,
priority over, **106:9-301.**
Perfection in multi-state
transactions, **106:9-103.**
Accounts, interests, **106:9-103.**
Certificates of title, interests,
106:9-103.
Chattel paper, interests,
106:9-103.
Documents, interests, **106:9-103.**
Financing statement, exception
as to filing, **106:9-302.**
Foreign countries, laws
governing perfection,
106:9-103.
Instruments, interests,
106:9-103.
Intangibles, interests, **106:9-103.**
Minerals, interests, **106:9-103.**
Mobile goods, interests,
106:9-103.
Ordinary goods, interests,
106:9-103.
Title, certificates, **106:9-103.**
Personal property, default
involving security covering
real and personal property,
106:9-501.
Place of filing, **106:9-401.**
Pledges, **106:9-102, 140:87-140:89.**
Highway infrastructure fund,
funds pledged as security for
bonds or notes, **29:2O.**
Statutory definition, **4:7.**

SECURED TRANSACTIONS
—Cont'd
Policy of article, **106:9-102.**
Possession.
Default. See within this heading,
"Default."
Perfecting security interest,
106:9-305, 106:9-503.
Repossession. See within this
heading, "Repossession."
Secured party.
Default, right to possession,
106:9-503.
Demand for possession, form,
106:9-507.
Preexisting indebtedness,
exception as to single account
transferred in satisfaction,
106:9-104.
Preferences.
Priorities. See within this
heading, "Priorities."
Premature sale of pledge, **266:85.**
Premium finance agencies.
Insurance premium finance
agencies. See within this
heading, "Insurance
premium finance agencies."
Preservation of collateral security,
liability for expenses,
106:9-207.
Priorities.
Accessions, **106:9-314.**
Bailee's lien on goods, priority
against security interest or
seller or lessor, **255:35.**
Cash proceeds, priority of
purchase money security
interest, **106:9-312.**
Chattel paper, priorities of
purchaser, **106:9-308.**
Commingled goods, **106:9-315.**
Conflicting security interests,
106:9-312.
Consignment as affecting,
106:9-114, 106:9-302,
106:9-312.
Farm products, buyers in
ordinary course of business,
106:9-301.
Fixtures, priority of security
interests, **106:9-313.**
Foreclosure sale, priorities of
purchaser, **106:9-313,**
106:9-314.
Future advances, **106:9-307,**
106:9-312.
Good faith purchaser in
multi-state transaction as to
goods covered by certificates
of title, **106:9-103.**

SECURED TRANSACTIONS
—Cont'd
Priorities —Cont'd
Insurance proceeds.
Article 9 as governing priority
as to proceeds, **106:9-104.**
Intangibles, **106:9-301.**
Leasehold interest, form for
waiver of priority,
106:9-507.
Lien arising by operation of law,
106:9-310.
Multi-state transactions,
interests perfected,
106:9-103.
Non-negotiable instruments,
priority of purchaser,
106:9-308.
Personal use, buyers of goods,
106:9-307.
Processed goods, **106:9-315.**
Purchase money security
interest, **106:9-301,
106:9-312.**
Purchasers of instrument and
documents, **106:9-309.**
Sale of goods resulting in
account or chattel paper
transfer to secured party,
106:9-306.
Security without filing, conflicts
involving, **106:9-304.**
Subordination of priorities. See
within this heading,
"Subordination of priorities."
Unperfected security interest,
106:9-301.
Waiver of priority as to
leasehold interest, form,
106:9-507.
Private sale of collateral after
default, form for giving notice,
106:9-507.
Proceeds.
Attachment as affected by
secured party's rights,
106:9-203.
Cash proceeds. See within this
heading, "Cash proceeds."
Collateral, casualty insurance,
106:9-306.
Defined, **106:9-306.**
Description of collateral by term,
106:9-203.
Insurance proceeds as subject to
laws governing secured
transactions, **106:9-104.**
Money or instruments, laws
governing perfection,
106:9-304.
Perfection as limited by nature
of collateral producing,
106:9-306.

SECURED TRANSACTIONS
—Cont'd
Processed goods, priorities,
106:9-315.
Profits.
Losses. See within this heading,
"Losses."
Secured party's right to hold
profits on security,
106:9-207.
Proof of assignment, **106:9-318.**
Public sale of collateral after
default, form for giving notice,
106:9-507.
Public utilities.
Transmitting utilities. See
within this heading,
"Transmitting utilities."
"Purchase" as including taking by
pledges, **106:1-201.**
Purchase money security interest.
Cash proceeds, priority,
106:9-312.
Defined, **106:9-107.**
Multi-state transactions,
perfection, **106:9-103.**
Priority, **106:9-301, 106:9-312.**
Purchase of financial asset,
security interest arising in,
106:9-116.
Purchaser for value.
Bona fide purchasers. See within
this heading, "Bona fide
purchasers."
Railroads.
Cars and rolling stock.
See RAILROADS.
Liens and encumbrances.
See RAILROADS.
Receipts.
Pledges, receipts to borrowers,
140:86.
Trust receipts. See within this
heading, "Trust receipts."
Warehouse receipts. See within
this heading, "Warehouse
receipts."
Records and recording.
Filing. See within this heading,
"Filing."
Pledges, records concerning,
140:86 et seq.
Redemption of collateral.
Consumer goods, **255:13J.**
Debtor's right, **106:9-506.**
Mortgage foreclosure.
See MORTGAGE
FORECLOSURE.
Owner of collateral other than
debtor as entitled,
106:9-112.

SECURED TRANSACTIONS
—Cont'd
Registers and registries of deeds.
Fees, **106:9-403-106:9-406.**
Filing officer register, **106:9-403.**
Financing statement.
Exemption from duty as to
giving of information,
106:9-407.
What constitutes filing,
106:9-403.
Fixtures, special provisions for
filing, **106:9-409, 106:9-410.**
Special provisions as to filings,
106:9-410.
Regulations governing loans, effect
of Commercial Code articles,
106:9-201.
Reimbursement for removal of
accessions, **106:9-314.**
Rejected goods in contract for sale
under Commercial Code,
security interest, **106:2-711.**
Release.
Discharge or release. See within
this heading, "Discharge or
release."
Release of collateral, **106:9-406.**
Form, **106:9-507.**
Legal amount, payment or
tender, **140:91, 140:103,
140:107.**
Statements, furnishing to
secured party on filing of
termination statement,
106:9-404.
Removal of collateral from realty,
106:9-313.
Removal or concealment of
mortgaged goods, **266:82,
266:87.**
Rents, exclusion, **106:9-104.**
Renunciation of rights in collateral
by debtor, form, **106:9-507.**
Repossession.
Consumer goods and consumer
protection. See within this
heading, "Consumer goods
and consumer protection."
Motor vehicle retail installment
sales.
See MOTOR VEHICLE
RETAIL INSTALLMENT
SALES.
Notice. See within this heading,
"Notice or knowledge."
Retail installment sales and
services.
See RETAIL INSTALLMENT
SALES AND SERVICES.
Reservation of security interest,
106:7-209.

SECURED TRANSACTIONS
—Cont'd

Reservation of title as taking of
security interest, **106:1-201,
106:2-401.**

Retail installment sales and
services, **255D:1-255D:32.**
See RETAIL INSTALLMENT
SALES AND SERVICES.

Retirement allowance or pension
of public employee as subject
to chattel mortgage, **32:92.**

Risk of loss of collateral security,
106:9-207.

Road building equipment as
subject, **106:9-103.**

Rolling stock.
See RAILROADS.

Salary, assignment of.
Wage assignments. See within
this heading, "Wage
assignments."

Sale of collateral.
Consent of mortgagee of chattel
mortgaged property, sale of
property without, **266:83.**
Criminal offense, **266:83,
266:85, 266:87.**
Default, disposal of collateral,
106:9-504.
Forms for giving notice,
106:9-507.
Deficiency, owner other than
debtor as liable, **106:9-112.**
Notice or knowledge. See within
this heading, "Notice or
knowledge."
Prior to default, **266:85.**
Resale for excess of amount over
security interest,
accountability, **106:2-706.**
Trustee's sale of collateral,
246:63.

Sales under Commercial Code,
106:9-113.
Expenses of inspection, security
interest of buyer, **106:2-711.**
Option to purchase as affecting
lease as security, **106:1-201.**
Partial revocation of acceptance
of goods, reservation of
security interest as
affecting, **106:2-401.**
Protection of buyers, **106:9-307.**
Purchase money security
interest. See within this
heading, "Purchase money
security interest."
Rejected goods, security interest,
106:2-711.

SECURED TRANSACTIONS
—Cont'd

Sales under Commercial Code
—Cont'd
Sale or return.
Effect of article 9 on creditor's
claims on goods delivered,
106:2-326.
Shipment with reservation of
security interest, **106:2-505.**
Savings and loan associations,
exclusion of accounts
maintained, **106:9-104.**
Savings, exclusion of transfer,
106:9-104.
Schedules.
Lists and schedules. See within
this heading, "Lists and
schedules of collateral,
request."
Scope of article, **106:9-102.**
Search warrant, delivery of seized
property to mortgagee, **276:7.**
Secretary of state, filing of security
interests in transmitting
utility, **106:9-401.**
Secured party.
Answer to debtor's request for
information, form,
106:9-507.
Defined, **106:9-105.**
Demand, forms for making.
For possession, **106:9-507.**
Subsequent secured party's
demand to share in
proceeds of sale,
106:9-507.
Liability for failure to comply
with article, **106:9-507.**
Objection to retention of
collateral by, form,
106:9-507.
Possession. See within this
heading, "Possession."
Proposal to retain collateral in
satisfaction of obligation,
form for giving notice,
106:9-507.
Request for information by
debtor, form, **106:9-507.**
Securities.
Investment securities. See
within this heading,
"Investment securities."
Securities Act, exemption of
chattel mortgages, **110A:402.**
Security agreement.
Defined, **106:9-105.**
Description of collateral,
106:9-203.
Forms, **106:9-507.**

SECURED TRANSACTIONS
—Cont'd

Security agreement —Cont'd
Future advances. See within this
heading, "Future advances."
Validity of, **106:9-201.**
Security interest.
Defined, **4:7, 106:1-201.**
Purchase or delivery of financial
asset, security interest
arising in, **106:9-116.**
Setoff, excluding right, **106:9-104.**
Shipment of goods for sale with
reservation of security
interest, **106:2-505.**
Ship Mortgage Act, exclusion of
security interest subject,
106:9-104.
Shipping contracts or charters.
Chattel paper as excluding,
106:9-105.
"General intangibles" as
including, **106:9-106.**
Ships and other watercraft,
106:9-104, 106:9-105.
Liens.
See SHIPS AND OTHER
WATERCRAFT.
Short title, **106:9-101.**
Signing.
Financing statement, **106:9-402.**
Termination statement,
106:9-404.
Small loans.
Commercial code article as
affecting regulations
governing, **106:9-201.**
Discharge of security, **140:107.**
One thousand dollars, pledge
securing loan for amount,
140:91.
Redemption, provisions for loans
under 1000 dollars
inapplicable, **140:95.**
State auditor defined in connection
with contracts and security
agreements, **4:7.**
Statements.
Attachment of encumbered
personalty, statement of
account by secured party,
223:75.
Destruction of old records,
106:9-408.
Filing officer to furnish,
106:9-404, 106:9-407.
Financing statement. See within
this heading, "Financing
statement."
Owner other than debtor as
entitled to receive,
106:9-112.

SECURED TRANSACTIONS
—Cont'd

Statements —Cont'd

Request, **106:9-208.**

Secured party as entitled to receive, **106:9-404.**

Termination statements. See within this heading, "Termination statements."

State refunding bonds, security for issuance, **29:53A.**

State secretary defined in connection with contracts and security agreements, **4:7.**

State treasurer, **4:7, 29:2O.**

Statutory construction of terms referring to security interests, **4:7.**

Stolen property pledged, proceedings, **140:88.**

Storage charges, priority against secured party of, lien, **255:35.**

Subordination of priorities, **106:9-316.**

Agreements as to sharecropping, recording, **255:7D.**

Forms, **106:9-507.**

Subordination obligations as security interests, **106:1-209.**

Subrogation to rights of secured party, **106:9-504.**

Substitution for contract after notification of assignment, **106:9-318.**

Substitution of collateral, **266:33.**

Successor in interest, liability for failure to provide list of collateral, **106:9-208.**

Surplus.

Debtor's right, **106:9-502, 106:9-504.**

Owner of collateral as entitled, **106:9-112.**

Taxes.

Debtor as liable for payment, **106:9-207.**

Estate tax lien as applicable to property transferred to pledgee, **65C:14.**

Pledged property, tax, **59:19, 62:14.**

Tenant.

Leases. See within this heading, "Leases."

Termination statements, **106:9-404.**

Failure to provide termination statement within proper time, penalty, **106:9-404.**

Fixtures, special provisions for filing, **106:9-409.**

SECURED TRANSACTIONS
—Cont'd

Termination statements —Cont'd

Forms, **106:9-507.**

Term prohibiting assignment, effectiveness, **106:9-318.**

Tickets or receipts to depositors of pledges, **140:86.**

Timber.

Assignment, indexing, **106:9-404.**

Description of land in security agreement covering, **106:9-203.**

Filing, place, **106:9-401.**

Financing statement, sufficiency, **106:9-402.**

"Goods" as excluding, **106:9-105.**

Time of attachment of security interest, **106:9-204.**

Time.

Attachment of security interests, **106:9-203, 106:9-204.**

Goods coming into state, **106:9-103.**

Lapsed filing. See within this heading, "Lapsed filing."

Multi-state transactions, perfection, **106:9-103.**

Perfected security interest. See within this heading, "Perfected security interest."

Title.

Certificate of title.

Certificates and certification. See within this heading, "Certificates and certification."

Document of title as controlling right in goods, **106:7-502.**

Materiality of title to collateral, **106:9-202.**

Reservation of security interest, title retained, **106:1-201, 106:2-401.**

Torts.

Exclusion of tort claims, **106:9-104.**

Liability of secured party for acts or omission of debtor, **106:9-317.**

Transfers.

Assignments and transfers. See within this heading, "Assignments and transfers."

Transmitting utilities.

Defined, **106:9-105.**

Duration of filing, **106:9-403.**

Filing, place, **106:9-401.**

Trust deed, application of article, **106:9-102.**

SECURED TRANSACTIONS
—Cont'd

Trustee process.

Collateral, garnishment of debtor's rights, **106:9-311.**

Judgment and execution in case of property held as security, **246:34.**

Sale of property by trustee where held as security, **246:63.**

Trust interests, exception as to assignment, **106:9-302.**

Trust receipts.

Application of article, **106:9-102.**

Form for, trust receipt type security agreement, **106:7-104, 106:9-507.**

Truth in lending, effect of laws governing, **106:9-203.**

Unemployment compensation benefits not to be pledged, **151A:36.**

Uniform Securities Act, exemption of chattel mortgages, **110A:402.**

Unperfected security interests, priority over, **106:9-301.**

Use of collateral without accounting, **106:9-205.**

Usury, article as affecting regulations governing, **106:9-201.**

Validity of security agreement, **106:9-201.**

Value, attachment as affected by giving, **106:9-203.**

Wage assignments.

Exclusion from article, **106:9-104.**

Validity of wage assignment as security for loan, **140:108, 154:2.**

Waiver.

Default, **106:9-501.**

Defenses against assignee, **106:9-206.**

Leases. See within this heading, "Leases."

Warehouse receipts.

Document of title as controlling right in goods as against person holding security interest, **106:7-502.**

Penalty for pledging deposited property, **105:62.**

Reservation of security interest, **106:7-209.**

Warranties.

Modification of sales warranties as affected by existence of security agreement, **106:9-206.**

SECURED TRANSACTIONS
—Cont'd
Watercraft. **106:9-104, 106:9-105.**
Liens.
  See SHIPS AND OTHER
    WATERCRAFT.
Waterworks and water supply,
  drinking water protection
  commission, **40:39K.**
Wellhead, multi-state transaction
  as governed by location,
  106:9-103.
Wills, security interests as
  affecting devises of property,
  191:23.

**SECURITIES ACT, 110A:101 et
seq.**
Actions.
  Injunctions. See within this
    heading, "Injunctions."
  Limitation of actions, **110A:410.**
  Summary proceedings. See
    within this heading,
    "Summary proceedings."
  Survival of actions for civil
    liabilities, **110A:410.**
Administration of statutory
  provisions by secretary of
  state, **9:10A, 110A:406.**
Administrative files and opinions,
  110A:413.
Advertising literature, filing,
  110A:403.
Agents.
  Definition, **110A:401.**
  Registration of broker-dealers
    and agents. See within this
    heading, "Registration of
    broker-dealers and agents."
  Service of process and papers.
    See within this heading,
    "Service of process and
    papers."
Applications of broker-dealers.
  Examination of applicant for
    registration, **110A:406.**
  Registration of broker-dealer or
    agent, **110A:202.**
  Withdrawal from registration as
    broker-dealer or agent,
    110A:204.
Assistants and others, state
  secretary to employ for
  enforcement, **12:15.**
Attorneys' fees, **110A:410.**
Automatic registration as agent
  under uniform securities act,
  restrictions placed, **110A:202.**
Bankruptcy.
  Insolvency and bankruptcy. See
    within this heading,
    "Insolvency and
    bankruptcy."

SECURITIES ACT —Cont'd
Banks.
  See BANKS AND BANKING.
Broker-dealers, **110A:202,
  110A:401.**
Burden of proof.
  Civil liabilities, **110A:410.**
  Exemption or exception from
    definitions, **110A:402.**
Cease and desist orders,
  110A:407A.
Civil liabilities, **110A:410.**
Commercial code provisions for
  dealings in securities.
  See INVESTMENT
    SECURITIES UNDER
    COMMERCIAL CODE.
Commission of securities.
  See SECURITIES AND
    SECURITIES
    REGULATIONS.
Contempt in connection with
  investigations by secretary of
  state, **110A:407.**
Copies.
  Administrative files and
    opinions, **110A:413.**
  Registration statements,
    110A:302, 110A:303.
Costs of actions, **110A:407A.**
Criminal penalties, **110A:409.**
Damages, **110A:410.**
Date.
  Time or date. See within this
    heading, "Time or date."
Dealers.
  Broker-dealers, **110A:202,
    110A:401.**
Definitions, **110A:302, 110A:401.**
Disclosure of information received
  by secretary of state and
  employees, **110A:406.**
Evidence.
  Burden of proof. See within this
    heading, "Burden of proof."
  Investigations and subpoenas,
    110A:407.
  Privilege of secretary of state or
    his officers or employees,
    110A:406.
Examination, inspection, or
  investigation.
  Administrative files, inspection,
    110A:413.
  Investigations, **110A:407.**
  Registration as broker-dealer,
    examination, **110A:204,
    110A:406.**
Exceptions, exemptions, and
  exclusions, **110A:402,
    110A:405.**

SECURITIES ACT —Cont'd
False or misleading statements or
  fraud.
  Advisory activities, **110A:102.**
  Civil liabilities, **110A:410.**
  Criminal penalties, **110A:409.**
  Denial, suspension, revocation of
    registration of security,
    110A:305.
  Filings, **110A:404.**
  Registration of broker-dealers or
    agents, denial or
    cancellation, **110A:204.**
  Registration or exemption of
    securities, unlawful
    representation concerning,
    110A:405.
  Sales and purchase, **110A:101.**
Federal government.
  Exemptions, **110A:402.**
  Registration by coordination,
    110A:302.
Fees.
  Attorneys' fees, **110A:410.**
  Registration of broker-dealers
    and agents. See within this
    heading, "Registration of
    broker-dealers and agents."
  Registration of securities, filing
    fee, **110A:304.**
Filing.
  Administrative files, **110A:413.**
  Brokers and agents, registration,
    110A:202.
  Denial of registration of
    broker-dealer or agent,
    failure to pay filing fee as
    ground, **110A:204.**
  Investigations by secretary of
    state, filing of written
    statement, **110A:407.**
  Misleading filings, **110A:404.**
  Post-registration provisions
    governing broker-dealers,
    110A:203.
  Registration of securities,
    110A:304.
  Sales and advertising literature,
    110A:403.
Financial statement or condition.
  Filing by registered
    broker-dealer, **110A:203.**
  Information to be included in
    application for registration
    as broker-dealer or agent,
    110A:202.
  Insolvency and bankruptcy. See
    within this heading,
    "Insolvency and
    bankruptcy."
Fines and penalties, **110A:407A.**

SECURITIES ACT —Cont'd
Fraud.
False or misleading statements
or fraud. See within this
heading, "False or
misleading statements or
fraud."
Hearings, **110A:412.**
Injunctions, **110A:407A, 110A:408.**
Applications for registration as
broker-dealer or agent,
information, **110A:202.**
Registration of broker-dealers or
agents, denial or
cancellation, **110A:204.**
Registration of securities,
110A:305.
Insolvency and bankruptcy.
Denial or suspension of
registration of broker-dealer,
110A:204.
Exemptions, **110A:402.**
Inspection or investigation.
Examination, inspection or
investigation. See within
this heading, "Examination,
inspection, or investigation."
Judicial review of orders,
110A:411.
Jurisdiction, **110A:414.**
Licensing.
Registration of broker-dealers
and agents. See within this
heading, "Registration of
broker-dealers and agents."
Limitation of actions, **110A:410.**
Limitations and restrictions on
automatic registration as
agent under uniform securities
act, **110A:202.**
Misleading statements.
False or misleading statements
or fraud. See within this
heading, "False or
misleading statements or
fraud."
Notice.
Agent, notice of beginning or
termination of association
with broker-dealer or issuer,
110A:201.
Denial or suspension of
registration as broker,
dealer or agent, orders,
110A:204.
Exemptions, order for denial or
revocation, **110A:402.**
Initial application for
registration as broker-dealer
or agent, publication,
110A:202.

SECURITIES ACT —Cont'd
Notice —Cont'd
Summary postponement or
suspension of registration of
broker-dealer or agent
under, notice of order,
110A:204.
Oath or affirmation in connection
with investigations or
proceedings, **110A:407.**
Offer to sell defined, **110A:401.**
Omissions.
Civil liabilities, **110A:410.**
Denial or suspension of
registration as broker-dealer
based on omissions from
application, **110A:204.**
Registration statement, omission
of information, **110A:304.**
Sales and purchases, fraudulent
and other prohibited
practices, **110A:101.**
Orders by secretary of state,
110A:412.
Cease and desist orders,
110A:407A.
Enforcement of orders,
employment by secretary of
assistants, **9:10A.**
Judicial review, **110A:411.**
Policy of statute, **110A:415.**
Presumptions and burden of proof.
Burden of proof. See within this
heading, "Burden of proof."
Price amendment defined,
110A:302.
Privilege of secretary of state or
his officers or employees in
case of subpoena, **110A:406.**
Process and service of process.
Service of process and papers.
See within this heading,
"Service of process and
papers."
Prospectus.
Criminal offense, false
statements, **266:92.**
Filing of sales and advertising
literature, **110A:403.**
Qualification, registration of
securities, **110A:303.**
Registration statements,
110A:302, 110A:303.
Records, reports, and returns.
Broker-dealers, records
maintained, **110A:203.**
False or misleading statements
or fraud. See within this
heading, "False or
misleading statements or
fraud."

SECURITIES ACT —Cont'd
Records, reports, and returns
—Cont'd
Filing. See within this heading,
"Filing."
Financial statement or
condition. See within this
heading, "Financial
statement or condition."
Registration of broker-dealers and
agents, **110A:203A.**
Applications. See within this
heading, "Applications of
broker-dealers."
Denial, revocation, suspension,
cancellation, and
withdrawal of registration,
110A:204.
Examination, **110A:204,**
110A:406.
Fees.
Examination of applicant, fee,
110A:406.
Failure to pay filing fee as
ground for denial of
registration, **110A:204.**
Procedures for registration,
110A:202.
Financial statement or
condition. See within this
heading, "Financial
statement or condition."
Post-registration procedures,
110A:203.
Procedure, **110A:202.**
Registration requirement,
110A:201.
Registration of securities,
110A:301 et seq.
Commercial Code provisions,
106:8-101 et seq.
See INVESTMENT
SECURITIES UNDER
COMMERCIAL CODE.
Coordination, registration,
110A:302.
Copies of registration
statements, **110A:302,**
110A:303.
Denial, suspension, and
revocation, **110A:305.**
Exemptions, **110A:402.**
Provisions applicable to
registration, **110A:304.**
Qualification, registration,
110A:303.
Registration requirement,
110A:301.
Service of process and papers.
See within this heading,
"Service of process and
papers."

SECURITIES ACT —Cont'd
Registration of securities —Cont'd
Unlawful representations concerning registration or exemption, **110A:405.**
Reports.
Records, reports, and returns. See within this heading, "Records, reports, and returns."
Revocation or suspension.
Exemptions, order for denial or revocation, **110A:402.**
Registration of broker-dealers and agents, **110A:204.**
Registration of securities, **110A:305.**
Rules, **110A:412.**
Sales and transfers.
Definition, **110A:401.**
Filing of literature, **110A:403.**
Fraud, **110A:101.**
Unregistered securities, offense of sale, **110A:301.**
Scope of statute, **110A:414.**
Secretary of state, **110A:412.**
Administration of statutory provisions by, **9:10A, 110A:406.**
Orders by secretary of state. See within this heading, "Orders by secretary of state."
Securities.
See SECURITIES AND SECURITIES REGULATIONS.
Service of process and papers, **110A:414.**
Consent to service of process, **110A:414.**
Registration of broker-dealers or agents, consent to service of process, **110A:202.**
Registration of securities by co-ordination, consent to service of process, **110A:302.**
Registration of securities by qualification, consent to service of process, **110A:303.**
Severability of statutory provisions, **110A:417.**
Short title of statute, **110A:416.**
State, county and municipal securities, filing, **110A:402, 110A:403.**
Subpoenas, **110A:407.**
Investigations or proceedings by secretary of state, **110A:407.**

SECURITIES ACT —Cont'd
Subpoenas —Cont'd
Privilege of secretary of state or his officers or employees, **110A:406.**
Summary proceedings.
Broker-dealer, postponement or suspension of registration, **110A:204.**
Registration statement, postponement or suspension of effectiveness, **110A:305.**
Survival of actions for civil liabilities, **110A:410.**
Suspension or revocation.
Revocation or suspension. See within this heading, "Revocation or suspension."
Time or date.
Broker-dealers and agents, expiration of registration, **110A:201.**
Civil liabilities, matters involving, **110A:410.**
Denial, suspension, and revocation of registration of securities, **110A:305.**
Preservation of records by registered broker-dealer, **110A:203.**
Registration of securities, **110A:302 et seq.**
Withdrawal from registration as broker-dealer or agent, **110A:204.**
Transfer of agent, fees, **110A:202.**
Transfers of securities.
Sales and transfer. See within this heading, "Sales and transfers."
Trial or hearings, **110A:412.**
Uniform Commercial Code provisions.
See INVESTMENT SECURITIES UNDER COMMERCIAL CODE.
United States.
Federal government. See within this heading, "Federal government."
Unlawful representations concerning registration or exemption, **110A:405.**
Waiver of compliance with provisions of statute, **110A:410.**

SECURITIES AND EXCHANGE COMMISSION.
See SECURITIES AND SECURITIES REGULATIONS.

SECURITIES AND SECURITIES REGULATIONS.
Abandoned property.
Bonds and other securities. See ABANDONED, LOST, AND UNCLAIMED PROPERTY.
Actual purchases and sales, definition, **137:4.**
Annuity contracts.
Variable annuity contracts. See within this heading, "Variable annuity contracts, laws applicable."
Automobile insurance, deposit of securities in lieu of. See AUTOMOBILE INSURANCE.
Banks.
See BANKS AND BANKING.
Blue sky act, **110A:101-110A:417.**
See SECURITIES ACT.
Broker-dealers, registration with securities and exchange commission, **110A:202, 110A:401.**
See SECURITIES ACT.
Bucket shops, **137:4-137:7, 271:35-271:38.**
See BUCKET SHOPS.
Capital.
See CAPITAL AND CAPITAL STOCK.
Commercial Code, investment securities under, **106:8-101 et seq.**
See INVESTMENT SECURITIES UNDER COMMERCIAL CODE.
Commission.
Securities and exchange commission. See within this heading, "Securities and Exchange Commission."
Common trust funds, amortization of premiums paid on purchase of interest-bearing securities for investment, **203A:1.**
Consumer protection, securities and commodities transactions, **93A:1, 93A:4, 93A:9.**
Corporate stock.
See CORPORATIONS.

SECURITIES AND SECURITIES REGULATIONS —Cont'd

Corporation taxes.
See CORPORATION TAXES.
Creditors.
Debtors and creditors. See within this heading, "Debtors and creditors."
Credit unions.
See CREDIT UNIONS.
Crimes and offenses.
Embezzlement by broker, **266:56.**
Fraud and deceit. See within this heading, "Fraud and deceit."
Transactions without actual sales of securities, recovery, **137:5.**
Uniform securities act violations, injunction against, **110A:407A.**
Death.
Transfer on death security registration, **201E:101 to 201E:402.**
See TRANSFER ON DEATH SECURITY REGISTRATION.
Debtors and creditors.
Evidence of debt, securities, **137:7.**
Deceased person, transfer of securities owned, **196:9.**
Deceit.
Fraud and deceit. See within this heading, "Fraud and deceit."
Definitions, **65C:14, 137:7.**
Delivery, purchases without, **137:4.**
Dental service corporations, investments, **176E:10.**
Deposits and depositories.
Banks.
See BANKS AND BANKING.
Disclosure of information to public regarding financial institutions, accounts and services, **167D:34.**
Dividends, presumption of abandonment, **200A:5.**
Embezzlement by broker or corporation doing business of broker, **266:56.**
Enforcement of contract for sale or transfer, **259:6.**
Equity securities.
See CORPORATIONS.
Estate taxes.
See ESTATE TAXES.

SECURITIES AND SECURITIES REGULATIONS —Cont'd

Evidence of intent not to complete transactions, **137:6.**
False advertising, **266:91, 266:92.**
False and misleading statements.
Fraud and deceit. See within this heading, "Fraud and deceit."
Fiduciaries.
See FIDUCIARIES.
Financial disclosure.
False statements as to issuer's financial condition, **266:92.**
Public officers and employees, **268B:5.**
Fines and penalties.
Secured transactions.
See SECURED TRANSACTIONS.
Securities Act, **110A:407A.**
Stock, fraudulent issuance, **266:66.**
Foreign fiduciary, deliveries or payments, **199A:2.**
Forgery.
See FORGERY AND COUNTERFEITING.
Fraud and deceit.
False advertising, **266:91, 266:92.**
Financial condition of issuer, false statements, **266:92.**
Issuance or transfer of stock or securities, penalties, **266:65, 266:66.**
Securities Act as to false statements.
See SECURITIES ACT.
Gas.
Bonds and debentures.
See GAS AND ELECTRIC COMPANIES.
Stock and stockholders.
See GAS AND ELECTRIC COMPANIES.
Gift.
Minors.
Uniform transfers to minors act, **201A:1 to 201A:24.**
See TRANSFERS TO MINORS.
Guaranty.
See GUARANTY.
Guardians and conservators, **196:9, 201:38, 206:4.**
Health, welfare, and retirement trusts or funds, purchase by or investment securities at fair market price authorized, **151D:3.**

SECURITIES AND SECURITIES REGULATIONS —Cont'd

Income tax.
See INCOME TAX.
Indictments, description, **277:23.**
Industrial finance agency.
Bonds and notes.
See INDUSTRIAL FINANCE AGENCY.
Insurance against loss, **175:47.**
Investment partnership, exemption of nonresident limited partner from payment of personal income tax, **62:17.**
Investment securities under commercial code.
See INVESTMENT SECURITIES UNDER COMMERCIAL CODE.
Life insurance.
See LIFE INSURANCE.
Mining stock, sale, **93:15 et seq.**
Misrepresentation.
Fraud and deceit. See within this heading, "Fraud and deceit."
Morris plan banks.
See MORRIS PLAN BANKS.
Mortgages.
See MORTGAGES AND DEEDS OF TRUST.
Mutual funds as persons required to file annual reports concerning unclaimed or abandoned property, **200A:1, 200A:7.**
National securities exchange.
See NATIONAL SECURITIES EXCHANGE.
Necessity of sale of securities, **271:35 et seq.**
Offenses.
Crimes and offenses. See within this heading, "Crimes and offenses."
Optometric service corporations, investments, **176F:10.**
Pledge of securities.
See SECURED TRANSACTIONS.
Presumption of abandonment, **200A:5, 200A:5B.**
Probate and Family Court, **196:9, 215:41.**
Public utilities.
Bonds and debentures.
See TELECOMMUNICATIONS AND ENERGY DEPARTMENT.

SECURITIES AND SECURITIES REGULATIONS —Cont'd

Public utilities —Cont'd
Stock and stockholders.
See TELECOMMUNICATIONS AND ENERGY DEPARTMENT.
Real estate brokers' and salesmen's registration law not applicable, **112:87QQ.**
Registration, **107:4.**
Bonds.
See BONDS AND DEBENTURES.
Broker-dealers.
See SECURITIES ACT.
Commercial code provisions.
See INVESTMENT SECURITIES UNDER COMMERCIAL CODE.
Commonwealth, securities, **29:39, 29:58.**
Municipal bonds, **44:52, 44:61.**
Uniform securities act provisions.
See SECURITIES ACT.
Uniform transfer on death security registration act, **201E:101 to 201E:402.**
See TRANSFER ON DEATH SECURITY REGISTRATION.
Sale or transfer.
Transfer. See within this heading, "Transfer of securities."
Savings banks.
Investments.
See SAVINGS BANKS.
Stock and stockholders.
See SAVINGS BANKS.
Secured transactions.
Investment securities.
See SECURED TRANSACTIONS.
Securities and Exchange Commission.
Co-ordination, registration of securities under Uniform Securities Act, **110A:302.**
Copies of documents filed with, as evidence, **233:76A.**
Denial or suspension of registration of broker-dealer based on order entered, **110A:204.**
Examination of records of registered broker-dealers, co-operation, **110A:203.**

SECURITIES AND SECURITIES REGULATIONS —Cont'd

Securities and Exchange Commission —Cont'd
Insurance company's stock, sale or transfer of as affected, **175:193I.**
Real estate time shares.
Public offering, registration, **183B:40.**
Registration of broker-dealers, **110A:201 to 110A:204, 110A:401, 110A:406.**
See SECURITIES ACT.
Segregation by trust department, **167G:4.**
Small loan companies, registration, **140:96A.**
State bonds.
See STATE BONDS AND OBLIGATIONS.
State funds, investment in certain corporate securities, **29:38.**
Statements.
Broker's refusal of statement of dealings, **271:38.**
False or misleading statements. Fraud and deceit. See within this heading, "Fraud and deceit."
Stock.
See CORPORATIONS.
Stolen property in connection with pretended sales of securities, recovery, **137:5.**
Subdivision control law, requirement prior to approval of definitive plan, **41:81U.**
Takeover bids.
See CORPORATIONS.
Taxation.
See TAXATION.
Technology development corporation.
Investment fund, **40G:4.**
Power to buy, hold and sell, **40G:3.**
TOD security registration, **201E:101 to 201E:402.**
See TRANSFER ON DEATH SECURITY REGISTRATION.
Transfer of securities.
Commercial Code.
See INVESTMENT SECURITIES UNDER COMMERCIAL CODE.
Insurance companies, **175:59.**
Securities act.
See SECURITIES ACT.

SECURITIES AND SECURITIES REGULATIONS —Cont'd

Transfer of securities —Cont'd
Uniform transfer on death security registration act, **201E:101 to 201E:402.**
See TRANSFER ON DEATH SECURITY REGISTRATION.
Validity of contract, **259:6.**
Transfers to minors, **201A:1 to 201A:24.**
See TRANSFERS TO MINORS.
Trust companies.
See TRUST COMPANIES.
Trusts and trustees.
Common trust funds, amortization of premiums paid on purchase of interest-bearing investment securities, **203A:1.**
Corporation or corporate agents, liability in connection with stock transfer, **203:21.**
Distributions of securities as trust income or principal, **203:21A.**
Execution of trust involving, **203:21.**
Fiduciaries, manner in which fiduciaries may hold securities, **203:14B.**
Investment securities under commercial code.
See INVESTMENT SECURITIES UNDER COMMERCIAL CODE.
Production of securities on accounting, **206:4.**
Unclaimed securities by beneficiaries, presumption of abandonment, **200A:5.**
Unclaimed.
Bonds and other securities.
See ABANDONED, LOST, AND UNCLAIMED PROPERTY.
Uniform Acts.
Investment securities under commercial code, **106:8-101 et seq.**
See INVESTMENT SECURITIES UNDER COMMERCIAL CODE.
Securities act, **110A:101 et seq.**
See SECURITIES ACT.
Variable annuity contracts, laws applicable.
Sales, **175:3.**
Wills, regulation of securities bequeathed, **191:1A.**

SECURITY.

Carriers.

Bond or undertaking.

See CARRIERS.

Costs of action.

See COSTS OF ACTION.

Defined, **93:90.**

Eminent domain.

See EMINENT DOMAIN.

Executors.

See EXECUTORS AND
ADMINISTRATORS.

SECURITY AGREEMENT.
See SECURED
TRANSACTIONS.

SECURITY AND PRIVACY
COUNCIL.
See CRIMINAL OFFENDER
RECORD INFORMATION
SYSTEM.

SECURITY FOR
PERFORMANCE.

Bonds.

See BONDS AND
UNDERTAKINGS.

Deposits and depositories.

See DEPOSITS AND
DEPOSITORIES.

SECURITY GUARDS.
See GUARDS OR WATCHMEN.

SECURITY INTERESTS.

After-acquired property.

See AFTER-ACQUIRED
PROPERTY.

Defined, **93:90.**

Investment securities under
commercial code.

See INVESTMENT
SECURITIES UNDER
COMMERCIAL CODE.

Secured transactions.

See SECURED
TRANSACTIONS.

SECURITY OF PRISONERS.

Duties of commissioner of
correction, **124:1.**

SECURITY SYSTEMS.

Defined, **141:1.**

Electronic security devices.

See ELECTRONIC SECURITY
DEVICES.

Licenses, **147:57 et seq.**

Contractors and technicians,
141:3.

Conviction of crime, **147:59.**

Definitions, **147:57.**

Employees of licensees, **147:60.**

Fees, **147:61.**

SECURITY SYSTEMS —Cont'd

Licenses —Cont'd

Oath, certification, and proof of
qualifications, **147:58.**

Renewal or revocation, **147:59.**

Term, **147:59.**

Sales tax exemptions, **64H:1.**

Taxing of security services, **64H:1,**
64I:1.

SEDGE.

Cutting or carrying away as
criminal offense, **266:113.**

SEDIMENT CONTROL
MEASURES.

Soil Conservation Service of
United States, co-operative
agreements, **91:11.**

SEDITION ACT, 264:11.

SEDUCTION.

Drugs, seduction by use, **272:3.**

Evidence, corroboration required,
272:11.

Limitation of time for prosecution,
272:11.

Persons under eighteen, seduction,
272:4.

Public excluded from trial
involving minors, **278:16A.**

Sentence and punishment, **272:3,**
272:4.

SEED ACT, 128:84 et seq.

SEEDLINGS.

Cities and towns, furnishing,
132:35.

SEEDS, 128:84 et seq.

Administration of seed laws,
128:98.

Advertising and advertisements.

Definition, **128:84.**

False or misleading advertising,
128:90, 128:91.

Affirmance of stop-sale order by
superior court, **128:95.**

Agricultural seeds.

Defined, **128:84.**

False or misleading advertising,
128:91.

Label requirements, **128:85,**
128:93.

Penalties for improper sales,
prerequisites to imposition,
128:93, 128:100.

Seizure and condemnation,
128:96.

Stop-sale orders, **128:95.**

Testing requirements prior to
sales, **128:90.**

Agriculture, Commissioner.

Enforcement of seed laws,
128:94.

SEEDS —Cont'd

Agriculture, Commissioner
—Cont'd

Germination standards, **128:98.**

Inspection, **128:95.**

Penalty for violation of order,
128:100.

Seizure and condemnation of
seeds on complaint, **128:96.**

Stop-sale order or tag, issuance,
128:95.

Test records, **128:90.**

Agriculture Experiments Station.

Definition, **128:84.**

Germination standards, **128:98.**

Penalties for obstruction,
128:100.

Rules and regulations, **128:98.**

Sale of seeds not meeting
germination standards,
128:90.

Sample of seeds taken by
agriculture commissioner,
analysis, **128:95, 128:97,**
128:99.

Tests and analysis, **128:97,**
128:99.

Voluntary submission of seeds
for testing, **128:99.**

Alfalfa seed, label to indicate to lot
number and origin, **128:86.**

Alteration of labels as violation,
128:91.

Analysis, **128:95, 128:97.**

Animals, label requirements as to
seeds harmful, **128:85.**

Annual sort of flower seeds to be
indicated on label, **128:88.**

Appeal of stop-sale order, **128:95.**

Application to court for release of
seeds, **128:96.**

Association of official seed
analysts, pure seed and
germination as defined by
rules for testing seeds
published, **128:84.**

Bean seeds, label requirements,
128:87.

"Below standard" caption to
appear on labels, **128:87,**
128:88.

Biennial sort of flower seeds to be
indicated on label, **128:88.**

Brands and labels.

Labels. See within this heading,
"Labels."

Certified seed.

Defined, **128:84.**

Sale of seeds labeled, **128:90.**

Chemicals on seeds, label to
indicate nature, **128:85.**

SEEDS —Cont'd

Cleaning, **128:92.**

Clover seeds, label to indicate lot number and origin, **128:86.**

Condemnation and seizure of seeds, **128:96.**

Corn seeds, label requirements, **128:87.**

Date of test.
  Tests. See within this heading, "Tests."

Defacing of labels, **128:91.**

Definitions, **128:84.**

Department of agriculture, sale of seed potatoes in violation of regulations, **128:101.**

Destruction of property.
  Labels, **128:91.**
  Order for destruction, **128:96.**

Detachment of labels, **128:91.**

Division of markets, waiver of seed potato requirements by director, **128:101.**

Enforcement of seed laws, **128:94, 128:96.**

Equity practice, appeal from stop-sale orders to comply, **128:95.**

Examination.
  Inspection of seeds. See within this heading, "Inspection of seeds."
  Tests. See within this heading, "Tests."

False label, sale of seeds having, **128:90, 128:100.**

False or misleading advertising, **128:90, 128:91.**

Fees for testing of seeds by director of Massachusetts agricultural experiment station, **128:99.**

Field testing of seeds by director of Massachusetts agricultural experiment station, **128:97.**

Fines and penalties, **128:94.**
  Prerequisites to imposition, **128:93.**
  Sales in violation of law, penalties, **128:100.**
  Seed potatoes, penalties for violations, **128:101.**

Flower seeds.
  Defined, **128:84.**
  False or misleading advertising, **128:91.**
  Germination standards, **128:98.**
  Inspections by agriculture commissioner, **128:95.**
  Label requirements, **128:85, 128:88, 128:93.**

SEEDS —Cont'd

Flower seeds —Cont'd
  Mixtures of seeds, manner of sale, **128:91.**
  Penalties for improper sales, prerequisites to imposition, **128:93, 128:100.**
  Rules and regulations as to tree and shrub seeds, **128:98.**
  Seizure and condemnation, **128:96.**
  Stop-sale order, **128:95.**
  Tests, **128:88, 128:90, 128:97.**

Food and agriculture department, commissioner of.

Agriculture, Commissioner of. See within this heading, "Agriculture, Commissioner."

Foundation seed.
  Defined, **128:84.**
  Sale of seeds labeled, **128:90.**

Gardens, requirements as to labels of seeds for use, **128:88.**

Germination.
  Defined, **128:84.**
  Director of Massachusetts agricultural experiment station to set standards, **128:90.**
  Flower seeds, label to indicate percentage of germination, **128:88.**
  Label requirements, **128:86.**
  Standards, establishment, **128:98.**
  Test for germination required prior to sale, **128:90.**
  Tree and shrub seed germination to be indicated on label, **128:89.**
  Vegetable seed germination standards to appear on label, **128:87.**
  Voluntary submission of seeds for tests, **128:99.**

Grass seed, sale other than by weight, **94:237.**

Grower's declaration, imposition of penalty upon failure to obtain, **128:93.**

Hard seed, label requirements, **128:86 et seq.**

Harvest, tree and shrub seed packages to indicate year, **128:89.**

Hearing and notice as to violation of seed laws, **128:94.**

Home flower gardens, requirements as to labels of flowers sold for use, **128:88.**

SEEDS —Cont'd

Humans, label requirements as to seeds harmful, **128:85.**

Hybrid seed.
  Definition, **128:84.**
  Regulation of sale, **128:90.**

Inert matter, labels to indicate percentage, **128:86.**

Inspection of seeds.
  Agriculture commissioner, inspections, **128:95.**
  Rules and regulations, **128:98.**

Interstate commerce, rules and regulations as to seed laws to accord, **128:98.**

Invoice, imposition of penalty upon failure to obtain, **128:93.**

Judicial enforcement of seed laws, **128:96.**

Judicial review of stop-sale order or tags, **128:95.**

Jurisdiction.
  Complaint for seizure and condemnation of seeds, **128:96.**
  Stop-sale order, appeal, **128:95.**

Labels, **128:85, 128:86.**
  Agricultural seed packages, **128:85, 128:93.**
  Alteration or destruction, **128:91.**
  Cleaning, label requirements as applicable to seeds consigned, **128:92.**
  Cultivar of vegetable seeds, **128:88.**
  Definition, **128:84.**
  False labels, **128:90, 128:100.**
  Flower seed packages, **128:88.**
  Germination, percentage, **128:86 et seq.**
  Hard seed, percentage, **128:86, 128:87.**
  Harvesting, label to indicate year, **128:89.**
  Inert matter, percentage, **128:86.**
  Kind, variety, or cultivar to appear, **128:86 et seq.**
  Lawn seeding mixture, **128:86.**
  Lot number to appear, **128:86 et seq.**
  Mixtures, indication of percentages, **128:86.**
  Origin to appear, **128:86, 128:89.**
  Penalties for violations, **128:93, 128:100.**
  Relabeling pursuant to court order, **128:96.**
  Requirements, **128:85, 128:86.**
  Sale, proper label required prior, **128:90.**

SEEDS —Cont'd
Labels —Cont'd
Shrub and tree seed packages, **128:89.**
Sort of flower seed to be indicated, **128:88.**
Sowing, label requirements, **128:92.**
Stop-sale order or tags. See within this heading, "Stop-sale order or tags."
Storage, label requirements, **128:92.**
Test date, **128:86.**
"Trace," **128:90.**
Uncleaned seeds, representations, **128:92.**
Vegetable seed packages, **128:87, 128:88.**
Weed seeds, percentage, **128:86.**
Weight, percentage, **128:86, 128:89.**
Lawn seeding mixture, labeling, **128:86.**
Lots, **128:86.**
Defined, **128:84.**
Flower seed lot number to appear on label, **128:88.**
Vegetable seed lot number to appear on label, **128:87.**
Maize seeds, label requirements, **128:87.**
Manufacturer or seller, label to indicate name and address, **128:85.**
Measurement.
Weights and measures. See within this heading, "Weights and measures."
Misleading or false advertising, **128:90, 128:91.**
Mixed seeds.
Flower seeds, manner of sale, **128:91.**
Inspections by agriculture commissioner, **128:95.**
Label requirements, **128:86, 128:93.**
Penalty for illegal sale, **128:100.**
Stop-sale order, **128:95.**
Modification of stop-sale order by superior court, **128:95.**
Name and address of seller or manufacturer to appear on labels, **128:85.**
Notice and hearing as to violation of seed laws, **128:94.**
Noxious-weed seeds.
Defined, **128:84.**
Label requirements, **128:85.**
Sale of seed packages containing, **128:90.**

SEEDS —Cont'd
Obstruction of officials, **128:91, 128:100.**
Officially recognized, defined, **128:84.**
Official orders, **128:91.**
Orders.
Condemnation of seeds by court of competent jurisdiction, **128:96.**
Official orders, **128:91.**
Penalties for violations, **128:100.**
Stop-sale order. See within this heading, "Stop-sale order or tags."
Origin of seeds, imposition of penalty upon failure to obtain statement, **128:89, 128:93.**
Parties having standing to appeal stop-sale order, **128:95.**
Pea seeds, requirements of labels, **128:87.**
Penalties.
Fines and penalties. See within this heading, "Fines and penalties."
Perennial sort of flowers to be indicated on label, **128:88.**
Persons aggrieved, appeal of stop-sale order, **128:95.**
Poisonous seed, label warnings, **128:85.**
Potatoes.
Definition, **128:84.**
Sales, **128:101.**
Prohibited sales practices, **128:90, 128:91.**
Prosecution of violations by agriculture commissioner or assistant, **128:94.**
Publication of seed test results, **128:97.**
Purchaser, labeling requirements as met by removing seeds from properly-labeled container in presence, **128:93.**
Pure seed.
Defined, **128:84.**
Label for tree and shrub seeds to indicate percentage, **128:89.**
Records of germination test, **128:90.**
Registered seed.
Defined, **128:84.**
Sale of seeds labels, **128:90.**
Release of seeds, application to court, **128:96.**
Revocation of stop-sale order by superior court, **128:95.**
Rules and regulations, adoption, **128:98.**

SEEDS —Cont'd
Sales.
Agriculture commissioner's issuance of stop-sale order or tag, **128:95.**
Label requirements, necessity of compliance, **128:90.**
Name and address of seller or manufacturer to appear on label, **128:85.**
Penalties for violations, **128:93, 128:100.**
Prohibited sales practices, **128:91.**
Seed potatoes, regulation of sale, **128:101.**
Stop-sale order or tags. See within this heading, "Stop-sale order or tags."
Testing requirements, **128:90.**
Samples of seeds, **128:95.**
Searches and seizures.
Seizure. See within this heading, "Seizure."
Seed potatoes.
Potatoes. See within this heading, "Potatoes."
Seizure, **128:96.**
Definition, **128:84.**
Seller or manufacturer, label to indicate name and address, **128:85.**
Shrubs.
Trees and shrubs. See within this heading, "Trees and shrubs."
Sowing, **128:85 et seq.**
Standing to appeal stop-sale order, **128:95.**
Stop-sale order or tags, **128:91.**
Agriculture commissioner's issuance, **128:95.**
Definition, **128:84.**
Substitution of seeds prohibited, **128:91.**
Suffolk County, appeal of stop-sale order to Superior Court, **128:95.**
Superior court.
Appeal of stop-sale order, **128:95.**
Penalties for violation of orders, **128:100.**
Sweet corn, label requirements, **128:87.**
Tests.
Agricultural experiment station, tests and analyses, **128:95, 128:97.**
Agriculture commissioner's tests and inspections, **128:95.**

SEEDS —Cont'd
Tests —Cont'd
Date of test.
Flower seeds, **128:88.**
Label requirements, **128:86,**
128:87.
Tree and shrub seeds, **128:89.**
Flower seeds, **128:88.**
Label requirements, **128:86,**
128:87.
Rules and regulations, **128:98,**
128:99.
Sales, testing requirements
prior, **128:90.**
Tree and shrub seed, **128:89.**
Vegetables and vegetable
products. See within this
heading, "Vegetables and
vegetable products."
Voluntary submission of seeds,
128:99.
Time or date.
Date of test.
Tests. See within this heading,
"Tests."
Hearing on violation of seed
laws, **128:94.**
Toxic seeds, warnings, **128:85.**
"Trace" prohibited on label, **128:90.**
Treated seeds.
Definition, **128:84.**
Label information, **128:85.**
Trees and shrubs.
Definition, **128:84.**
False or misleading advertising,
128:91.
Inspections by agriculture
commissioner, **128:95.**
Label requirements, **128:85,**
128:89, 128:93.
Penalty for illegal sale, **128:93,**
128:100.
Rules and regulations, adoption,
128:98.
Sales, testing requirements
prior, **128:90.**
Seizure and condemnation,
128:96.
Stop-sale order, **128:95.**
Tests, **128:89.**
Type, defined, **128:84.**
Uncleaned seeds, label
representations, **128:92.**
United States Department of
Agriculture, agriculture
commissioner's co-operation in
seed law enforcement, **128:95.**

SEEDS —Cont'd
University of Massachusetts
agriculture experiment
station.
Agriculture experiment station.
See within this heading,
"Agriculture Experiments
Station."
Variety-cultivar.
Definition, **128:84.**
Labels requirements, **128:86 et**
seq.
Penalties for incorrect label,
128:93.
Vegetable seeds, label
requirements, **128:89.**
Vegetables and vegetable products.
Defined, **128:84.**
False or misleading advertising,
128:91.
Germination standards to be
adopted, **128:98.**
Inspections by agriculture
commissioner, **128:95.**
Label requirements, **128:85,**
128:87, 128:93.
Penalty for illegal sale, **128:93,**
128:100.
Potatoes. See within this
heading, "Potatoes."
Sales, testing requirements
prior, **128:90.**
Seizure and condemnation,
128:96.
Stop-sale order, **128:95.**
Tests, **128:87.**
Director of Massachusetts
agricultural experiment
station to conduct, **128:97.**
Sales, tests required prior,
128:90.
Venue of appeal of stop-sale order,
128:95.
Violations, agriculture
commissioner's prosecution,
128:94.
Voluntary submission of seeds for
testing by director of
Massachusetts agricultural
experiment station, **128:99.**
Waiver of seed potato
requirements by director of
division of markets, **128:101.**
Warnings, poisonous seeds, **128:85.**
Water chestnut seeds, **128:20A.**

SEEDS —Cont'd
Weeds.
Definition, **128:84.**
Label to indicate percentage,
128:86.
Noxious-weed seeds. See within
this heading, "Noxious-weed
seeds."
Sale of seed packages
containing, **128:90.**
Weights and measures.
Container, label requirements as
affected by weight, **128:87,**
128:89.
Label requirements, **128:86.**
Percentage by weight of pure
seed to be indicated on
label, **128:89.**
Weed seeds, sale of seeds having
certain percentage by
weight, **128:90.**

SEEING EYE DOGS.
Certificate by commission for blind
required for free license,
140:139.
Discrimination in housing, **151B:4.**
Privileges extended to persons
using, **272:98A.**

SEEKONK.
Congressional district, **57:1.**
District court, **218:1.**
Medical examiner district, **38:1.**
Senatorial district, **57:3.**

SEGREGATION OF FUNDS.
Commingling.
See COMMINGLING.
Money, property or securities of
trust department, **167G:4.**
Out-of-state banks, **167:42.**
Trust department as separate from
general business of bank,
167G:2.

SEINES.
See FISH AND GAME.

SEISIN.
Entry, writs of.
See ENTRY, WRITS.
Title.
Disseisin.
See TITLE AND
OWNERSHIP.

SEIZURE.
See SEARCHES AND
SEIZURES.

SEIZURE ACT.
Public utilities, **150B:1 et seq.**

SELECTMEN.
**See ALDERMEN AND
 SELECTMEN.**

SELF-ABUSE.
Sale of articles, **272:21.**

SELF-ACTING MULES.
Cotton factories.
 Traversing carriages, **149:128.**

SELF-CLOSING HATCHES.
Industrial safety, **149:129.**

**SELF-CONTAINED
 BREATHING APPARATUS.**
Firefighters, **48:51A.**

SELF-DEFENSE.
Evidence.
 Reasonableness of use of force,
  233:23F.
Resisting arrest, **268:32B.**

SELF-EMPLOYMENT.
Child support obligations.
 Orders of support, **119A:112.**
Health care finance and policy.
 Definitions, **118G:1.**
Health insurance.
 Nongroup health reinsurance.
  Definition of "eligible
   individual," **176M:1.**
Health, welfare, and retirement
 funds.
 Self-employed not subject to
  chapter, **151D:7.**
Jury duty.
 Compensation, **234A:48.**
  Extreme financial hardship,
   234A:49.
Public assistance overpayment.
 Repayment, **19:30.**
Public welfare.
 Medical assistance.
  Insurance reimbursement,
   18E-9C.
Retirement plans.
 Funds, exceptions, **151D:7.**
Worker's compensation.
 Duty to report earnings,
  152:11D.

**SELF-INCRIMINATION, 233:20;
 US Const Amend 5.**
Administration and finance
 commissioner, testimony
 before, **7:11.**
Antitrust laws, **93:8.**
Bribery of agent testimony
 concerning, **271:39.**
Constitution of Massachusetts,
 protection against
 self-incrimination, **MA Const
 Part 1 Art 12.**

SELF-INCRIMINATION
 —Cont'd
Desertion of spouse or children,
 273:7.
Discovery proceedings, answering
 interrogatories, **231:63.**
Discrimination commission,
 testimony before, **151B:3.**
Employment security proceedings,
 151A:43.
Failure of accused to testify,
 278:23.
General Court, testimony before,
 3:28.
Grand jury, witness with
 immunity called before,
 233:20E.
Immunity from suit.
 See IMMUNITY.
Inspector general, rights of
 witnesses in proceedings
 called, **12A:7.**
Insurance, hearings with respect
 to unfair practices, **176D:13.**
 Rebates of insurance premiums,
  testimony, **175:183.**
Interstate Family Support Act,
 refusal to testify, **209D:3-316.**
Labor relations commission,
 testimony before, **150A:7.**
Legislative committees, testimony
 before, **3:28.**
Milk control law hearings, **94A:18.**
Presidential electors, contest of
 election, **54:120.**
Restraints of trade and
 monopolies, **93:8.**
Will, destruction, **266:39.**

SELF-INSURANCE.
Aircraft Financial Responsibility
 Act.
 Law not applicable to self
  insurer, **90:49D.**
 Self-insurance, **90:49G.**
Automobile insurance.
 Deposit of cash or securities in
  lieu of insurance.
  See AUTOMOBILE
   INSURANCE.
Claims against Commonwealth,
 municipal self-insurance trust
 fund for payment of claims,
 32B:3A.
Medical malpractice, **175F:1 et
 seq.**
 See MALPRACTICE.
Municipal electric departments,
 164:129 et seq.
Risk retention and risk purchasing
 groups, **176L:8.**

SELF-INSURANCE —Cont'd
Workers' compensation,
 152:25A-152:25D.
 See WORKERS'
  COMPENSATION.

**SELF-SERVICE AUTO REPAIR
 CENTER.**
Sunday operation, **136:6.**

SELF-SERVICE LAUNDRIES.
Sunday operation, **136:6.**

**SELF-STORAGE FACILITIES,
 105A:1 et seq.**
Access to leased space, denial,
 105A:5.
Default, **105A:4, 105A:5.**
Definitions, **105A:1.**
Exclusive care, custody, and
 control of property, **105A:7.**
Lien on stored property, **105A:3.**
Notice, **105A:4, 105A:6.**
Residential purposes, **105A:2.**
Unfair or deceptive acts or trade
 practices, **105A:8.**

**SELF-SURRENDER OF
 PRINCIPAL.**
Bail.
 See BAIL AND
  RECOGNIZANCE.

SEMIAUTOMATIC WEAPONS.
Licenses.
 Clubs with on-site shooting
  ranges or galleries, **140:131.**
Restrictions on firing capacity,
 140:123.
Roster of large capacity weapons
 and feeding devices,
 140:131¾.
Sales, **140:131M.**
Unlawful carrying or possession,
 269:10.

SEMICONDUCTORS.
Massachusetts technology park
 corporation.
 Definitions, **40J:2.**

SEMINAL FLUID.
State police, prima facie evidence
 of sperm cells or seminal fluid,
 22C:41.

SEMINOLE WAR VETERANS.
Town appropriations for
 memorials, **40:5.**

SEMI-SOLID COMMODITIES.
Containers, **98:22 et seq.**

SEMI-TRAILERS.
**See TRAILERS AND
 SEMI-TRAILERS.**

SENATE ART COMMITTEE.
Membership and duties, **3:65.**

SENATE OF STATE, 3:9 et seq.;
MA Const Part 2 Ch 1 Sec
2.
See **GENERAL COURT.**

SENATE OF UNITED STATES.
Adjournment over three days
requiring consent of House,
US Const Art 1 Sec 5 cl 4.
Advice and consent of, when
President must have, **US**
Const Art 2 Sec 2 cl 2.
Appointment of senators
temporarily by executives of
states, **US Const Art 1 Sec 3**
cl 2; 17th Amend.
Appointments made by President,
power in respect of, **US Const**
Art 2 Sec 2 cl 2.
Arrest, privilege of senators from,
US Const Art 1 Sec 6 cl 1.
Attendance of absent members,
power to compel, **US Const**
Art 1 Sec 5 cl 1.
Breach of peace, arrest of senator
for, **US Const Art 1 Sec 6 cl**
1.
Certificates of electors of President
and Vice President to be
opened by president of, **US**
Const Amend 12.
Classification of senators, **US**
Const Art 1 Sec 3 cl 2.
Compensation of senators, **US**
Const Art 1 Sec 6 cl 1.
Composition of, **US Const Art 1**
Sec 3 cl 1; Amend 17.
Disorderly conduct, punishment of
senators for, **US Const Art 1**
Sec 5 cl 2.
Disqualifications of senators.
Qualifications and
disqualifications of senators.
See within this heading,
"Qualifications and
disqualifications of
senators."
Districts.
See **SENATORIAL DISTRICTS.**
Election of senators, **54:152.**
Judge of election of own
members, Senate as, **US**
Const Art 1 Sec 5 cl 1.
Legislature of state, prior to
constitutional amendment
for election directly by the
people, **US Const Art 1 Sec**
3 cl 1.
Nominations. See within this
heading, "Nominations."

SENATE OF UNITED STATES
—Cont'd
Election of senators —Cont'd
People, election by, **US Const**
Amend 17.
Qualifications of voters, **US**
Const 17th Amend, 24th
Amend.
Transmission of records, **54:112.**
Vacancy, election to fill, **54:139.**
Emoluments not to be enjoyed by
senators, **US Const Art 1 Sec**
6 cl 2.
Equal suffrage of states in, **US**
Const Art 5.
Expulsion of member, **US Const**
Art 1 Sec 5 cl 2.
Flag to be flown at half-mast on
death of senator, **2:6A.**
Impeachment.
Effect of judgment of, **US Const**
Art 1 Sec 3 cl 7.
Sole power to try, **US Const Art**
1 Sec 3 cl 6.
Jury service, exemption of
members and officers, **234:1.**
Legislative powers as vested in,
US Const Art 1 Sec 1.
List of votes for President and Vice
President sent to president of,
US Const Amend 12.
Manual of general court delivered
to senators, **5:11.**
Motor vehicle plate bearing
facsimile of seal, **90:2.**
Nominations.
Filing of nomination papers,
time, **53:10, 53:48.**
Objection to nomination, time
for filing, **55B:5.**
President, powers in respect of
nominations made by, **US**
Const Art 2 Sec 2 cl 2.
Objection to nomination, time for
filing, **55B:5.**
Officers of, power to choose, **US**
Const Art 1 Sec 3 cl 5.
Other office, senators not to hold,
US Const Art 1 Sec 6.
President of Senate.
Vice President of the United
States. See within this
heading, "Vice President of
the United States."
Punishment of senators for
disorderly behavior, **US Const**
Art 1 Sec 5 cl 2.
Qualifications and disqualifications
of senators.
Age, **US Const Art 1 Sec 3 cl**
3.

SENATE OF UNITED STATES
—Cont'd
Qualifications and disqualifications
of senators —Cont'd
Aid and comfort given to
enemies of United States,
US Const Amend 14 Sec
3.
Citizenship, **US Const Art 1**
Sec 3 cl 3.
Inhabitancy of state, **US Const**
Art 1 Sec 3 cl 3.
Other offices, senators not to
hold, **US Const Art 1 Sec 6**
cl 2.
Rebellion, participation in, **US**
Const Amend 14 Sec 3.
Qualifications of voters in elections
for, **US Const Amend 17,**
24th Amend.
Quorum, **US Const Art 1 Sec 5 cl**
1 and Art 12; 12th Amend.
Records, reports, and returns.
Elections, transmission of
records, **54:112.**
List of votes for President and
Vice President seat to
president of senate, **US**
Const Amend 12.
Members returns, Senate as
judge of, **US Const Art 1**
Sec 5 cl 1.
Revenue bills, powers in respect of,
US Const Art 1 Sec 7 cl 1.
Rules of procedure, power to
determine, **US Const Art 1**
Sec 5 cl 2.
Seats of senators, terms at which
vacated, **US Const Art 1 Sec**
3 cl 2.
State statutes distributed to
senators, **5:3.**
Terms of office of senators, **US**
Const Art 1 Sec 3 cl 2; 17th
Amend, 20th Amend.
Tie vote as entitling Vice President
to vote, **US Const Art 1 Sec**
3 cl 4.
Treason, arrest of senator for, **US**
Const Art 1 Sec 6 cl 1.
Treaties, powers in respect of, **US**
Const Art 2 Sec 2 cl 2.
Two senators from each state, **US**
Const Art 1 Sec 3 cl 2; 17th
Amend.
Two-thirds vote.
See **TWO-THIRDS**
ATTENDANCE OR VOTE.
Vacancies, **54:139; US Const**
Art 1 Sec 3 cl 2; 20th Amend.

SENATE OF UNITED STATES
—Cont'd

Vice President of the United States.

Choice of vice-president by Senate, **US Const 12th Amend, 20th Amend Sec 4.**

Circumstances requiring, **US Const Amend 12.**

President of Senate,

Vice-president as, **US Const Art 1 Sec 3 cl 4.**

Voting.

Each senator to have one vote, **US Const Art 1 Sec 3 cl 2; 17th Amend.**

Two-thirds attendance.

See TWO-THIRDS ATTENDANCE OR VOTE.

Vice President to vote in case of tie, **US Const Art 1 Sec 3 cl 4.**

SENATORIAL DISTRICTS.

Bristol, Norfolk and Plymouth district, designation, **57:3.**

Constitution of Massachusetts, determination of senatorial districts, **MA Const Amend Art 101.**

Determination, **57:3.**

Elections.

See ELECTIONS.

General court, **57:3; MA Const Amend Art 101.**

Instruction of senators by submission of questions of public policy to voters, **53:19 et seq.**

Instruction of senators by submission of questions of public policy to voters, **53:19 et seq.**

Plymouth included in Norfolk and Bristol district, **57:3.**

State committee members, **52:1, 53:17A.**

Worcester, Hampden and Hampshire senatorial district, designation, **57:2, 57:3.**

SENATORS.

Federal.

See SENATE OF UNITED STATES.

State.

See GENERAL COURT.

SENIOR CITIZENS.
See OLDER PERSONS.

SENIORITY.
See TENURE AND SENIORITY.

SENTENCE AND PUNISHMENT, 279:1 et seq.

Abduction, **272:1, 272:2.**

Abortion, **272:19, 272:20.**

Absence of specific statute, **279:4, 279:5.**

Accessory after the fact, **274:4, 274:5.**

Accessory before the fact, **274:2, 274:3.**

Accountant, unauthorized use of title of certified public accountant, **112:87D.**

Adulteration of food, drugs, or cosmetics, **94:190.**

Adultery, **272:14, 279:18.**

Getting woman with child, **279:5 et seq.**

Advertising offenses, **266:89 et seq.**

Aiding or abetting delinquency of child, **119:63.**

Alcoholic liquors.

See ALCOHOLIC LIQUORS.

Alteration of sentence.

Revision or revocation of sentence. See within this heading, "Revision or revocation of sentence."

Ammonia compressors, violations, **146:55.**

Anarchy, promotion, **264:11.**

Animals, cruelty, **272:77.**

Appeal.

See APPEAL AND REVIEW.

Arrest of judgment, motions, **278:34.**

Arson, **266:1 et seq.**

Assault and battery, **265:13A.**

See ASSAULT AND BATTERY.

Attached land, selling without notice, **266:81.**

Attachment of dead body, **272:70.**

Attempts.

See ATTEMPT TO COMMIT CRIME.

Attorneys at law.

See ATTORNEYS AT LAW.

Auctioneers, licensing, **100:12.**

Automobile violations.

See MOTOR VEHICLES.

Baby chickens or ducks, sale, **272:80D.**

Bail.

See BAIL AND RECOGNIZANCE.

Barbers, violations, **112:87R.**

Bastardy, **273:16.**

SENTENCE AND PUNISHMENT —Cont'd

Bedding and upholstered furniture, violations, **94:277.**

Begging by children, **272:58.**

Bicycle theft, second or subsequent offense, **266:41.**

Bigamy, **272:15.**

Birth, false notice, **272:96.**

Blasphemy, **272:36.**

Blind persons with seeing eye dogs, discrimination against, **272:98A.**

Blood donations, reduction in sentence, **127:133.**

Bookmaking, **128A:13.**

Booths, enclosed booths in restaurants, **272:25 et seq.**

Breach of peace.

See BREACH OF PEACE AND DISORDERLY CONDUCT.

Bribery.

See BRIBERY.

Bucket shops, second and subsequent offenses, **271:36, 271:37.**

Buggery, **272:34.**

Building code enforcement, conveyances to avoid, **111:127O.**

Burglary and related offenses, **266:14 et seq.**

Cafes, enclosing booths, **272:25 et seq.**

Camp meeting, peddling or gaming, **272:39.**

Capital cases.

See CAPITAL CASES.

Cattle, malicious injury, **266:112.**

Caucus of political party, illegal participation, **53:76.**

Certificate of termination, **127:130, 127:130A.**

Certified public accountant, unauthorized use of title, **112:87D.**

Change in place of imprisonment as affecting, **127:116.**

Change in sentence.

Revision or revocation of sentence. See within this heading, "Revision or revocation of sentence."

Chicks, sale, **272:80D.**

Child pornography, penalties, **272:29A, 272:29B.**

Children and minors.

Accessory after the fact, **274:4.**

Adultery, getting woman with child, **279:5 et seq.**

Aiding or abetting delinquency of child, **119:63.**

**SENTENCE AND
  PUNISHMENT** —Cont'd
Children and minors —Cont'd
  Begging by children, **272:58.**
  Child prostitution, mandatory
    sentence for offenses
    involving, **272:4A, 272:4B.**
  Contributing to delinquency,
    119:63.
  Desertion and nonsupport of
    children or spouse, **273:15A.**
  Concealing assets to avoid
    payment, **273:15B.**
  Indecent assault on child,
    265:13B.
  Juvenile courts.
    See JUVENILE COURTS
      AND DELINQUENT
      CHILDREN.
  Lascivious acts with child under
    sixteen, **272:35A.**
  Motor vehicle violations,
    119:58B.
  Pornography, **272:29A, 272:29B.**
  Pupils in schools, corporal
    punishment, **71:37G.**
  Rape of child, **265:22A, 265:23.**
  Runaways, **272:61.**
  Sporting events, conduct,
    272:36A.
  Stubborn children, **272:61.**
  Unnatural act with child,
    272:35A.
Civil rights.
  See CIVIL RIGHTS AND
    DISCRIMINATION.
Civil service law for firefighter or
  police officer, **31:62, 31:62A.**
Class of crime as determined,
  274:1.
Clerk of court to notify sheriff,
  279:34.
Coal mining, violations regarding,
  21B:15.
Cockfighting, **272:94, 272:95.**
Commercial bribery, penalties,
  271:39.
Commercial driver license.
  See UNIFORM OPERATION OF
    COMMERCIAL MOTOR
    VEHICLES.
Commission for sentencing, **211E:1
  to 211E:4.**
Commitment.
  See CORRECTIONAL
    INSTITUTIONS.
Common nightwalkers, **272:61,
  272:62.**
Common railers and brawlers,
  272:53, 272:61.
Compressed air tanks, violations,
  146:61.

**SENTENCE AND
  PUNISHMENT** —Cont'd
Concealing criminals, **274:4.**
Concealing death of illegitimate
  child, **272:22.**
Concealing felony, **268:36.**
Concurrent and consecutive
  sentences, **127:38B, 279:8,
  279:8A, 279:9.**
  Assault by prisoner on officer,
    guard, etc., **127:38B.**
Conditional sentences, **279:10.**
Confinement and holding in
  accordance with sentence or
  order of court, **125:12.**
Consecutive sentences.
  Concurrent and consecutive
    sentences. See within this
    heading, "Concurrent and
    consecutive sentences."
Conspiracy, punishment, **274:7.**
Constitution of Massachusetts.
  See CONSTITUTION OF
    MASSACHUSETTS.
Contempt.
  See CONTEMPT.
Controlled substances.
  See DRUGS AND NARCOTICS.
Co-operative banks, proscribed
  acts, **170:16.**
Correctional institutions.
  See CORRECTIONAL
    INSTITUTIONS.
Counsel.
  See ATTORNEYS AT LAW.
Counterfeiting and forgery, **267:11,
  267:19.**
County jail, sentence, **279:15.**
Credit card offenses, **266:37B,
  266:37C.**
  Identity fraud, **266:37E.**
Credit on sentence for
  imprisonment pending trial,
  127:129B, 279:33A.
Crime against nature, **272:34,
  272:35, 272:35A.**
Cruel and unusual punishment
  not to be inflicted, **US Const
  Amend 8.**
Dance marathons, **272:103.**
Death.
  Capital cases.
    See CAPITAL CASES.
  Concealing illegitimate child's
    death, **272:22.**
  Dead bodies, offenses, **112:87,
    272:70 et seq.**
  False notices of deaths, **272:96.**
  Murder or homicide.
    See MURDER OR
      HOMICIDE.

**SENTENCE AND
  PUNISHMENT** —Cont'd
Death —Cont'd
  Reckless operation of motor
    vehicles, penalties for
    causing death, **90:24G.**
Death penalty.
  See CAPITAL CASES.
Deductions.
  Reductions or deductions. See
    within this heading,
    "Reductions or deductions."
Deer Island, sentences to by
  municipal courts, **218:48.**
Deformities, exhibition, **272:33.**
Delinquency of child.
  Children and minors. See within
    this heading, "Children and
    minors."
Dentists' registration law,
  violation, **112:52.**
Desertion and nonsupport.
  See DESERTION AND
    NONSUPPORT.
Dictaphones, eavesdropping,
  272:99, 272:99A.
Direction to carry out sentence,
  279:34.
Disabled horses, offenses, **272:78.**
Disorderly conduct.
  See BREACH OF PEACE AND
    DISORDERLY CONDUCT.
District courts.
  See DISTRICT COURTS.
Divorce, sentence as ground,
  208:2.
Dogs, offenses against, **266:47,
  272:77A, 272:80A et seq.**
Drive-it-yourself automobile rental
  agency, defrauding, **90:32F.**
Drugs.
  See DRUGS AND NARCOTICS.
Drunken driving, penalty, **90:21,
  90:22, 90:24.**
Ducklings, sale, **272:80D.**
Dueling, **265:4.**
Eavesdropping, **272:99, 272:99A.**
Education.
  Schools. See within this heading,
    "Schools."
Elderly persons, mandatory
  minimum sentences for violent
  crimes committed against,
  **265:15A, 265:15B, 265:18,
  265:19, 266:25, 276A:4.**
Electricians, violations, **141:5.**
Embalming without registration,
  112:87.
Embezzlement, **266:23, 266:30,
  266:50 et seq.**
Emergency housing, food, or fuel
  regulations, violations, **23:9H.**

515

SENTENCE AND PUNISHMENT —Cont'd

Employment agency sending person to house of prostitution, **272:12.**

Employment security violations, **151A:47.**

Engineer's registration law, violations, **112:81T.**

Equal rights under law, relief for violation, **93:102.**

Escape, **268:15 et seq.**

Estate taxes.
 See ESTATE TAXES.

Excessive punishment.
 Cruel and unusual punishment, **US Const Amend 8.**

Execution of sentence, **126:10, 279:1 et seq.**

Expedition of sentence, **279:3A.**

Expiration date of previous sentence, **279:8A.**

Explosives, crimes involving, **266:102-266:102B, 269:14.**

Exposure, indecent, **272:53, 272:61.**

Extortion, **265:25.**

Failure to stop after automobile accident, **90:24.**

Fair employment practice violations, **151B:7, 151B:8.**

False arrest or imprisonment, **263:2.**
 Recovery of penalties under habeas corpus provisions as bar to false arrest action, **248:33.**

False notices of marriages, births, or deaths, **272:96.**

False or fraudulent claims affecting Commonwealth, **266:67A, 266:67B.**

False personation.
 See FALSE PERSONATION.

Federal correctional institutions, effect of transfer of state prisoner, **127:97A.**

Females.
 Women. See within this heading, "Women."

Fighting birds and animals, **272:94, 272:95.**

Fines.
 See FINES AND PENALTIES.

Firearms and weapons.
 Fines, penalties, and forfeitures.
  See FIREARMS AND WEAPONS.

First offenders.
 Remission of fine or imprisonment, **279:11.**

SENTENCE AND PUNISHMENT —Cont'd

First offenders —Cont'd
 Special sentences of imprisonment, **279:6A.**

Fish and game violations, noncriminal disposition, **21:6F.**

Flood plains, violations of law for protection, **131:40, 131:40A.**

Food, drugs, and cosmetics, misbranding or adulteration, **94:190.**

Forfeiture of office by sentence to state prison, **279:30.**

Forgery and counterfeiting, **267:11, 267:19.**

Fornication, **272:18.**
 Unnatural methods, **272:35, 272:35A.**

Framingham Correctional Institution.
 Hard labor, confinement, **279:20.**
 Term of sentence, **279:17, 279:18.**
 Women, place of imprisonment, **279:16 et seq.**

Fraud and deceit.
 False name or Social Security number to law enforcement officer, **268:34A.**
 Identity fraud, **266:37E.**

Freaks, exhibitions, **272:33.**

"From and after" sentence, when effective, **279:8A.**

Funeral directing without license, **112:87.**

Funeral, disturbance, **272:42.**

Furniture and bedding, violations, **94:277.**

Further sentences of prisoners, **279:26 et seq.**
 Service of new mittimus, **279:40.**

Gaming offenses, **271:1 et seq., 272:39.**

General provisions absent other statute, **279:4, 279:5.**

Guidelines for sentencing, **211E:3.**

Guilty plea, withdrawal prior, **278:29B.**

Habitual offenders.
 Second and subsequent offenses.
  See within this heading, "Second and subsequent offenses."

Harboring criminals, **274:4.**

Hard labor, place of confinement of women sentenced, **279:20.**

Harmful drug violations.
 See DRUGS AND NARCOTICS.

Hawking, peddling, or gaming at camp meeting, **272:39.**

SENTENCE AND PUNISHMENT —Cont'd

Hazardous waste management act, violations, **21C:10.**

Health and sanitation, offenses against, **270:1 et seq.**
 See HEALTH AND HEALTH DEPARTMENTS.

High school equivalency certificate, reduction of sentence for prisoners receiving, **127:129D.**

Hoisting machinery, unlicensed operation, **146:55.**

Holidays, special sentences to be served, **279:6A.**

Homicide.
 See MURDER OR HOMICIDE.

Horses, crimes, **272:77A et seq.**

Hospitals.
 See HOSPITALS AND HEALTH CARE FACILITIES.

Hostages, prisoners holding, **127:38A.**

House of ill fame.
 See DISORDERLY HOUSES.

Husband or father failing to obey support decree, provisions as to jail sentence, **215:34.**

Identity fraud, **266:37E.**

Immoral solicitation in cafes, etc., **272:26, 272:27.**

Imposition of regardless of appeal taken, **279:4.**

Imprisonment.
 Crime against person, record to contain reasons for not imposing imprisonment, **265:41.**
 Pending trial to be credited, **127:129B.**
 Savings banks.
  Proscribed acts, **168:22.**
  Unauthorized dividends, **168:24.**
 Trust companies.
  Proscribed acts, **172:21.**
  Sections 18 and 20, violation, **172:23.**

Incest, **272:17.**

Included offenses, sentence on conviction, **278:12.**

Increase of penalty prohibited, **279:1A.**

Indeterminate sentences, **279:24, 279:31, 279:32.**
 State farm, **279:36.**
 State prison, **279:24.**
 Women, **279:17, 279:18, 279:32, 279:33.**

Insignia, misuse, **266:69-266:70, 268:35.**

SENTENCE AND PUNISHMENT —Cont'd

Inspector general, failure to file report, **12A:13.**

Intercepting communications, **272:99, 272:99A.**

Jury or jury room, wiretapping, **272:99A.**

Juveniles.
  Children and minors. See within this heading, "Children and minors."

Keys, offenses involving, **266:49, 266:140.**

Kidnapping, **265:26.**

Labor and workforce development department, acceptance of reward by inspectors, **149:16.**

Land surveyors' registration law, violations, **112:81T.**

Larceny.
  See LARCENY AND THEFT.

Lascivious acts with child under sixteen, **272:35A.**

Lascivious behavior, **272:16.**

Leaving scene of accident, **90:24.**

Length of sentence, **279:33.**

Lesser included offenses, sentence on conviction, **278:12.**

Lewdness.
  See OBSCENITY AND LEWDNESS.

Libel of groups of certain classes, **272:98C.**

Liberty permit, effect of revocation on term of sentence, **127:149.**

Life imprisonment.
  See LIFE IMPRISONMENT.

Limitations on sentence to jail or house of correction, **279:23.**

Littering, **265:32, 265:35, 265:36.**

Live birds, use for target practice, **272:87.**

Lotteries, offenses involving, **271:10.**

Manslaughter, **265:13.**

Marathons and walkathons, **272:103.**

Marine fish and fisheries violations, **130:2.**

Marriage.
  See MARRIAGE.

Massachusetts civil rights act, enforcement of court orders, **12:11J.**

Mayhem, **265:14.**

Meetings.
  Camp meetings, peddling or gaming, **272:39.**
  Disturbance of public meetings, **272:40.**

SENTENCE AND PUNISHMENT —Cont'd

Mentally ill and retarded persons, crime against, **19:10, 19:19, 19B:10, 19B:15.**

Militia.
  See MILITIA.

Minimum period, service, **127:133.**

Minimum wage violations, **151:19.**

Minors.
  Children and minors. See within this heading, "Children and minors."

Misbranding food, drugs, cosmetics, or surgical devices, **94:190.**

Misdemeanors, **274:1, 279:5, 279:13, 279:14.**

Misprision of felony, **264:3.**

Mitigation of punishment by restitution, receiving stolen property, **266:61.**

Mittimus.
  See CORRECTIONAL INSTITUTIONS.

Modification of sentence.
  Revision or revocation of sentence. See within this heading, "Revision or revocation of sentence."

Morris plan banks.
  See MORRIS PLAN BANKS.

Motion.
  Arrest of judgment, motion, **278:34.**
  Sentence, motion, **279:3A.**

Motorcycle regulation, violation, **90:7J.**

Motor vehicles.
  See MOTOR VEHICLES.

Mules, stabling offenses, **272:86-272:86F.**

Multiple offenders.
  Second and subsequent offenses. See within this heading, "Second and subsequent offenses."

Municipal courts, sentences to Deer Island, **218:48.**

Murder.
  See MURDER OR HOMICIDE.

Names.
  False name or Social Security number to law enforcement officer, **268:34A.**

Narcotics.
  See DRUGS AND NARCOTICS.

Nonpayment of fine, sentence, **279:7, 279:9, 279:10.**

Nonsupport of spouse of children, **273:15A.**
  Concealing assets to avoid payment, **273:15B.**

SENTENCE AND PUNISHMENT —Cont'd

Notice.
  Birth, false notice, **272:96.**
  Clerk of court to notify sheriff, **279:34.**

Nursing home administrator's acting without license or making misrepresentation as to registration, **112:116.**

Obscenity.
  See OBSCENITY AND LEWDNESS.

Office of community corrections, **211F:1 to 211F:6.**

Offices forfeited by sentence to state prison, **279:30.**

Oil pollution of waters, punishment, **21:27.**

Order of serving sentences, **279:8, 279:8A, 279:9.**

Other states, habitual criminal status because of sentence, **279:25.**

Overdue taxes, imprisonment, **60:29, 60:30, 60:34.**

Overtime compensation, failure to pay, **151:1B.**

Pandering and pimping, **272:6-272:8.**

Pardons.
  See PARDONS.

Parole.
  See PROBATION AND PAROLE.

Partial suspension authorized, **279:1, 279:1A.**

Peddling near or at camp meeting, **272:39.**

Periodic service of sentence, **279:6A.**

Perjury, **268:1, 268:2, 268:3.**

Pharmacy schools and courses, violations, **112:24B.**

Pigeons, killing or frightening, **266:132, 272:87.**

Pimping, **272:6-272:8.**

Place or location for service of sentence, **279:6, 279:7.**

Pleas.
  Guilty plea, withdrawal prior, **278:29B.**
  Time to sentence after plea or verdict, **279:3A.**

Podiatrist's registration law, violation, **112:22.**

Poison, use with intent to kill or injure, **265:16, 265:28.**

Pollution of waters, **21:27, 21:42, 111:164, 111:169.**

Polygamy, **272:15.**

SENTENCE AND PUNISHMENT —Cont'd

Poor prisoner, release, **127:146.**

Poultry, sale of immature, **272:80D.**

Pounds, injury, **49:23.**

Pregnant women, adultery, getting woman with child, **279:5 to 279:7.**

Presentence investigation, inspection of record by defendant and counsel prior to sentence, prior criminal prosecutions, **276:85.**

Pretrial diversion of selected offenders.
See PRETRIAL DIVERSION OF SELECTED OFFENDERS.

Prior offenses.
Second and subsequent offenses. See within this heading, "Second and subsequent offenses."

Prize fighting, **265:9-265:12.**

Probation.
See PROBATION AND PAROLE.

Profanity, **272:36, 272:36A.**

Professional engineers' registration law, violations, **112:81T.**

Profession, practice after revocation or suspension of registration, **112:65.**

Prostitution.
See PROSTITUTION.

Public health, offenses against, **270:1 et seq.**
See HEALTH AND HEALTH DEPARTMENTS.

Public meetings, disturbance, **272:40.**

Public safety department inspectors receiving rewards, **147:3.**

Pupils in schools, corporal punishment, **71:37G.**

Racing corporations having interlocking directorate with fair, **128A:11A.**

Racing information, punishment for transmitting, **271:31A.**

Rape, **265:22 et seq.**
Child, **265:22A, 265:23.**
Parole and discharge, **127:133.**
Second and subsequent offense, **265:22, 265:23.**

Real property.
See REAL PROPERTY.

Receiving stolen property.
See RECEIVING STOLEN PROPERTY.

SENTENCE AND PUNISHMENT —Cont'd

Recidivists.
Second and subsequent offenses. See within this heading, "Second and subsequent offenses."

Reckless driving, **90:24.**

Recognizance.
Bail and recognizance.
See BAIL AND RECOGNIZANCE.

Recording devices, electronic, eavesdropping, **272:99, 272:99A.**

Reductions or deductions.
Blood, prisoners donating, **127:133.**
Commercial motor vehicle license, reduction of lifetime disqualification, **90F:9.**
Confinement awaiting trial, **127:129B.**
Credit for imprisonment awaiting trial, **127:129B, 279:33A.**
Drug offense, good conduct deductions, **94C:32H.**
Good conduct deductions, **94C:32H, 127:129C, 127:129D.**
High school equivalency certificate, prisoners receiving, **127:129D.**
Reforestation camp, **127:83B.**

Reforestation camp, **127:83A-127:83E.**
See CORRECTIONAL INSTITUTIONS.

Reformatories, suspension of commitment, **279:2.**

Refrigerator, failure to remove doors from discarded, **271:46.**

Registration of voters, interference with supervisors, **51:54.**

Religion and religious organizations.
Blasphemy, **272:36.**
Worship, disturbance, **272:38, 272:39.**

Remission.
See REMISSION.

Removal of prisoner from one penal institution to another as affecting, **127:116.**

Repeal of statute as affecting, **281:5, 281:6.**

Reproductive health facilities.
Obstruction of access, **266:120E1/2.**

Resentencing by appellate division, **278:28C.**

SENTENCE AND PUNISHMENT —Cont'd

Respite from sentence.
See STAY OR SUPERSEDEAS.

Restaurants, inclosing booths in and immoral use, **272:25-272:27.**

Restitution.
Payments to probation officer, **276:92.**
Receiving stolen property, restitution as mitigating punishment, **266:61.**

Revision or revocation of sentence.
Registration, practice of profession after revocation, **112:65.**
Suspension or stay of sentence, revocation, **279:1-279:3.**
Withdrawal of appeal, **278:25.**

Revocation of sentence.
Revision or revocation of sentence. See within this heading, "Revision or revocation of sentence."

Rifles, violation of fisheries and game director's order prohibiting possession or use, **131:4.**

Riots and unlawful assemblies, offenses, **269:2, 269:3, 269:7.**

Robbery, **265:17, 265:18, 265:19.**

Runaways, **272:61.**

Sales, unlawful, **266:80-266:87, 266:92A, 269:10A.**

Saloons, enclosing booths in or immoral use, **272:25-272:27.**

Saturdays, **279:6A.**

Savings banks, proscribed acts and unauthorized dividends, **168:22, 168:24.**

Scenic road designation by city or town, fines, **40:15C.**

School bus, subsequent offense, **71:7A, 90:14.**

Schools.
Cheating, **271:50.**
Civil service examination, offenses in connection with operation of school, **271:48.**
Disturbance, **272:40.**
High school equivalency certificate, reduction of sentence, **127:129D.**
Pharmacy schools and courses, violations, **112:24B.**
Pupils in schools, corporal punishment, **71:37G.**
School bus, **71:7A, 90:14.**
Second and subsequent offenses, **94C:34, 279:8, 279:8A, 279:9, 279:25.**
Air pollution, **111:31C.**

SENTENCE AND PUNISHMENT —Cont'd

Second and subsequent offenses —Cont'd

Alcoholic beverages, nuisances, **139:16A.**

Armed burglary, suspension of sentence or probation after second conviction, **266:14.**

Assault with intent to commit rape, penalties, **265:24.**

Atmospheric pollution, violation of regulations for control, **111:31C.**

Bicycle theft, **266:41.**

Breach of peace and disorderly conduct, **272:56, 272:61.**

Bucket shops, **271:36.**

Common and notorious thief, **266:40.**

Common nightwalkers, **272:61, 272:62.**

Common railers and brawlers, **272:61.**

Common receiver of stolen goods, **266:62.**

Common victuallers, **140:21.**

Conviction of prior offenses, separate trial of issue, **278:11A.**

Corporations issuing obligations redeemable in numerical order, **107:8.**

Dangerous weapons, carrying or possessing, **269:10.**

Distinct offense, successive violations, **4:6.**

Dog control violations, **140:173A.**

Drivers license, suspension, **90:20.**

Driving while intoxicated, **90:21, 90:22, 90:24.**

Drugs and narcotics, minimum terms for offenses with respect, **94C:32-94C:32H.**

Employment security violations, **151A:47.**

Fine or imprisonment as affected, **279:11.**

Firearms, carrying or possessing, **269:10.**

Forgery and counterfeiting, **267:11, 267:19.**

Gaming and lottery laws, second offenses against, **271:10.**

Habitual offenders, **279:25.**

Health laws, **111:87.**

Hospital, occupancy of building, **111:75.**

Ice, review of order, **94:162.**

SENTENCE AND PUNISHMENT —Cont'd

Second and subsequent offenses —Cont'd

Indecent assault and battery, penalties, **265:13B.**

Indecent exposure, **272:61.**

Innholders, **140:21.**

Inspection of record of prior criminal prosecutions by defendant and counsel prior to sentencing, **276:85.**

Lascivious acts with child, **272:35A.**

Lewd and lascivious persons, **272:61.**

Lotteries, **271:10.**

Motorcycle handlebar regulations, violations, **90:7J.**

Motor vehicle driving offenses, **90:20, 90:22-90:24.**

Motor vehicle junkyard act violations, **140B:8.**

Motor vehicle thefts and fraudulent insurance claims, penalties, **266:27A, 266:29.**

Parole or probation, **127:133B, 265:13C, 266:14, 276:87.**

Pimps or purveyors, imprisonment, **272:7.**

Pollution, **111:31C, 111:164, 111:169.**

Public contractor's violation of laws as to preferences, wages, etc., **149:27C.**

Rape, penalties, **265:22, 265:23.**

Receiving or concealing stolen automobiles, punishment, **266:28.**

Recognizance, breach, **272:56.**

Runaways, **272:61.**

School bus, **71:7A, 90:14.**

Separate trial on issue of conviction of prior offense, **278:11A.**

Stilts, violations as to use of in employment, **149:129B.**

Stubborn children, **272:61.**

Suspended sentence in felony cases, prohibition against, **279:1, 279:1A.**

Theater tickets, resale, **140:185F.**

Theft of tools from building, **266:27.**

Traffic violations, **90:20-90:24.**

Unauthorized use of motor vehicle, **90:24.**

Unnatural act with child, **272:35A.**

SENTENCE AND PUNISHMENT —Cont'd

Second and subsequent offenses —Cont'd

Vagrants and tramps, **272:56, 272:61.**

Water pollution, **111:164, 111:169.**

Water supply, **111:164, 111:169.**

Seduction, **272:3, 272:4.**

Seeing eye dogs, discrimination against persons, **272:98A.**

Sepulture, violation, **272:71.**

Several offenses, sentence, **279:8, 279:8A, 279:9.**

Sheriffs.
See SHERIFFS AND DEPUTIES.

Ships and other watercraft, offenses involving, **266:108-266:111, 266:135.**

Shoplifting, **266:30A.**

Smoking in public conveyances, **272:43A.**

Social Security numbers.
Providing false name or Social Security number to law enforcement officer **268:34A.**

Sodomy, **272:34, 272:35, 272:35A.**

Solitary confinement, **127:39-127:41.**

Sound recordings, offenses, **266:143.**

Special sentences of imprisonment, **279:6A.**

Stabling horses and mules, offenses, **272:86-272:86F.**

Stalls enclosed in restaurants, **272:25, 272:27.**

State farm, sentences, **279:36.**

State finance laws, violations, **29:66.**

Statutory provisions.
Effect of lack, **279:4, 279:5.**
Repeal of statute as affecting, **281:5, 281:6.**

Stay of execution.
See CAPITAL CASES.

Steamboat, gross negligence in management, **265:30.**

Steam boilers and engines, violations, **146:33.**

Stilts, violations involving use in employment, **149:129B.**

Stock, crimes as to issuance, **266:65, 266:66.**

Stubborn children, **272:61.**

Subsequent offenses.
Second and subsequent offenses.
See within this heading, "Second and subsequent offenses."

SENTENCE AND PUNISHMENT —Cont'd

Subversive organizations, crimes involving, **264:19, 264:21-264:23.**

Successive sentences, **279:8, 279:8A, 279:9.**

Sunday law violations, **136:5.**

Sunday service of sentence, **279:6A.**

Superior court.

Appeal to superior court not entered, district court sentence in event, **278:24.**

Appellate division, resentencing of defendants, **278:28C.**

Supervisors of registration of voters, interference, **51:54.**

Supplementary proceedings as affected by sentence for contempt, **224:18.**

Supreme judicial court, transfer of cases to and, **211:4A.**

Sureties on bail disposing of real estate, **276:61A.**

Surgical devices, misbranding, **94:190.**

Surveyors' registration law, violation, **112:81T.**

Suspension of sentence, **279:1, 279:1A, 279:2.**

Armed burglary, suspension of sentence or probation after second conviction, **266:14.**

Arrest of person on probation, **279:3.**

Certain sentences not to be suspended, **279:1, 279:1A.**

Commitment to certain institutions, **279:2.**

Dangerous weapons, suspension of sentence, **279:1, 279:1A.**

Delinquency of child, aiding or abetting, **119:63.**

Election offense, **56:58.**

Life imprisonment, sentence, **279:1, 279:1A.**

Partial suspension, **279:1, 279:1A.**

Probation, **279:1, 279:1A.**

Armed burglary, **266:14.**

Arrest of person on probation, **279:3.**

Prohibited, when, **279:1, 279:1A.**

Reformatories, commitment, **279:2.**

Revision or revocation. See within this heading, "Revision or revocation of sentence."

SENTENCE AND PUNISHMENT —Cont'd

Suspension of sentence —Cont'd

Second or subsequent felony cases, prohibition against suspended sentence, **279:1, 279:1A.**

Tattooing, **265:34.**

Taverns, inclosing booths in or immoral use, **272:25, 272:27.**

Telecommunications, publishing information as to avoidance of lawful charges for use, **266:37D.**

Term or duration of sentence, **279:33.**

Threatening to commit crime, **275:4.**

Three strikes.

Firearms, unlawful possession. Augmented sentence for prior conviction of violent crime or serious drug offense, **269:10G.**

Throwing or shooting at train, bus, etc., **159:104.**

Timber and trees, offenses involving injury, **266:113-266:115.**

Time.

Length of sentence, **279:33.**

Periodic service of sentence of imprisonment, time, **279:6A.**

Plea or verdict, sentence after, **279:3A.**

Previous sentence, expiration time, **279:8A.**

Tombs or memorials, penalties for damage or defacement, **272:73.**

Tools, theft from building, **266:27.**

Traffic regulations.

See TRAFFIC REGULATIONS AND RULES OF THE ROAD.

Transfer of prisoners between penal institutions, **127:116.**

Treason, **264:2, 264:3, 265:1.**

Trespass, criminal, **266:118, 266:120.**

Trial.

Credit for imprisonment awaiting, **127:129B, 279:33A.**

Separate trial of issue of conviction of prior offenses, **278:11A.**

Trust companies, proscribed acts, **172:21.**

Truth in sentencing, **6:168A, 6A:18¾, 279:1, 279:24.**

SENTENCE AND PUNISHMENT —Cont'd

Two or more sentences, **279:8, 279:8A, 279:9.**

Unemployment compensation violations, **151A:47.**

Uniform operation of commercial motor vehicles.

See UNIFORM OPERATION OF COMMERCIAL MOTOR VEHICLES.

Uniforms, unlawful use, **264:10A.**

Unnatural acts, **272:34, 272:35, 272:35A.**

Unusual punishment.

Cruel and unusual punishment, **US Const Amend 8.**

Upholstered furniture and bedding, offenses, **94:277.**

Usury, **271:49.**

Vacation of office, sentence as causing, **279:30.**

Vagrants and tramps, **272:56, 272:61.**

Vandalism, **266:94-266:99, 266:103-266:107, 266:114, 266:122, 266:124-266:130, 266:133, 266:137-266:139, 269:7, 272:74.**

Veterinarians' registration law, violation, **112:59.**

Victim and witness assistance, assessments, **258B:8.**

Wage violations, **151:19.**

Walkathons, **272:103.**

Water pollution, punishment, **21:27, 21:42, 111:164, 111:169.**

Weapons.

See FIREARMS AND WEAPONS.

Weekend, special sentences to be served, **279:6A.**

Wiretapping, **272:99, 272:99A.**

Withdrawals.

Appeal, revising sentence on withdrawal, **278:25.**

Guilty plea, withdrawal of, prior to sentence, **278:29B.**

Suspension, withdrawal of prohibited while appeal pending, **279:1A.**

Witnesses.

Assessments, victim and witness assistance, **258B:8.**

Capital cases.

Perjury in capital case, **268:1.**

Summons of witnesses, **277:66.**

Credibility, record of conviction as affecting, **233:21.**

Refusal to testify before General Court, **3:28A.**

SENTENCE AND PUNISHMENT —Cont'd
Women, **279:16-279:20.**
Adultery, getting woman with child, **279:5 to 279:7.**
Desertion and nonsupport of spouse, **273:15A.**
Concealing assets to avoid payment, **273:15B.**
Indeterminate sentences, **279:17, 279:18, 279:32, 279:33.**
Place of confinement, **279:16-279:20.**
See CORRECTIONAL INSTITUTIONS.
Work deductions, **127:48A, 127:129D.**
Work release prisoner, punishment for escape, **127:86F.**
Youth services department, suspension of commitment, **279:2.**

SENTENCING COMMISSION, **211E:1 to 211E:4.**

SENTENCING GUIDELINES, **211E:3.**

SEPARABILITY.
See SEVERABILITY OF ACT.

SEPARATE MAINTENANCE OR SUPPORT, 209:32.
Appeal, effect upon act appealed from in probate court, **215:24.**
Attachment of property, **209:33, 235:34A.**
Children, custody and maintenance, **209:32, 209:37.**
Contempt citation and capias, service, **215:34A.**
Deeds and conveyances, **209:30, 209:31, 209:36.**
Effect of judgment directing conveyance, of real property, **209:32D.**
Judgment, conveyance after, **209:36.**
Desertion.
See DESERTION AND NONSUPPORT.
Injunctions in proceedings, **209:32.**
Interstate Family Support Act.
See INTERSTATE FAMILY SUPPORT ACT.
Investigations and reports in proceedings, **209:32.**
Judgments.
Conveyance after judgment, **209:36.**
Effect of judgment directing conveyance, **209:32D.**

SEPARATE MAINTENANCE OR SUPPORT —Cont'd
Jurisdiction of absentee spouse, **223A:3.**
Retirement systems and pensions not exempt from attachment or execution, **235:34A.**
Set-off debt collection, priority of unpaid spousal support, **62D:13.**
Venue of proceedings, **209:34.**
Will affected by separation, **191:9, 209:36.**

SEPARATE PROPERTY.
See HUSBAND AND WIFE.

SEPARATION OF ACTIONS.
See JOINDER OF ACTIONS OR ISSUES.

SEPARATION OF SPOUSES.
See DIVORCE AND ALIMONY.

SEPARATION PAY.
See WAGES, SALARIES, AND COMPENSATION.

SEPTIC TANKS.
Definitions, **148:38B.**
Facilities for disposal of contents, **111:31D.**
Income tax credit.
Design and construction expenses, **62:6.**
Installers appointed or elected to board of health, **111:26G.**

SEPULTURE.
Penalty for violation, **272:71.**

SEQUESTRATION OF PROPERTY.
See INSOLVENCY AND BANKRUPTCY.

SERGEANT AT ARMS OF GENERAL COURT, 3:15 et seq.
See GENERAL COURT.

SERIAL NUMBERS.
Bedding and upholstered furniture, **94:271, 94:272.**
Defacement or mutilation of, **266:139.**
Firearms.
See FIREARMS AND WEAPONS.
Insurance policy, rider to show number, **175:33.**
Motorboats, **90:5, 90B:3, 90B:4B.**
See MOTORBOATS.
Motor vehicles.
See MOTOR VEHICLES.
Police identification badge to show officer's number, **41:98C.**

SERIAL NUMBERS —Cont'd
Warehouse receipts, necessity of numbering, **106:7-202.**

SERIAL PAYMENT PLAN.
County bonds, **35:37A.**
Municipal bonds, **4:8, 44:19.**
State bonds, **29:49.**

SERIAL SHARES.
Cooperative banks.
See COOPERATIVE BANKS.

SERPENTS.
Fireworks, sale or use, **148:39.**

SERVICE AT COST ACT, **161:115 et seq.**

SERVICE CHARGES.
See RATES AND CHARGES.

SERVICE CORPS COMMISSION.
Abolition and transfer of powers, **23B:1.**
Administrative procedure.
See ADMINISTRATIVE PROCEDURE.
Commonwealth Service Corps, **6:121.**
Employment dislocations and assistance in reemployment of dislocated workers, **6:17.**
Governor and council, supervision, **6:17.**

SERVICE FACILITIES.
Limited access ways.
See LIMITED ACCESS WAYS.

SERVICE FORCES.
Alcoholism treatment and rehabilitation, service forces established to perform police functions, **111B:12.**

SERVICEMEN.
Military affairs.
See MILITARY AFFAIRS.
Veterans.
See VETERANS AND VETERANS' ORGANIZATIONS.

SERVICE OF PROCESS AND PAPERS.
Process.
See PROCESS AND SERVICE OF PROCESS AND PAPERS.

SERVICE STATIONS.
See FILLING STATIONS.

SERVIENT ESTATES.
See EASEMENTS.

SESSION LAWS.
See STATUTES.

SESSIONS OF CONGRESS, US
Const Art 1 Sec 4 Cl 2;
Amend 20 Sec 2.

SESSIONS OF COURT.
Appeals court, **211A:4.**
Boston municipal court, **218:15.**
Additional sessions, **218:52.**
Change of time and place, **220:5.**
Daylight savings time as affecting,
4:10.
District courts.
See DISTRICT COURTS.
First day of sitting, **220:4.**
Juvenile sessions, **119:65.**
Sheriff or deputy, attendance,
37:16, 262:22, 262:50.
Superior courts.
See SUPERIOR COURTS.
Supreme judicial court.
See SUPREME JUDICIAL
COURT.

SET NETS.
Use in inland waters, **131:54.**

SETOFF AND
COUNTERCLAIM.
Absent defendants, proceedings
against, **227:2, 227:3.**
"Action" as including, **106:1-201.**
Administrators.
See EXECUTORS AND
ADMINISTRATORS.
Arrearages in rent as reduced or
eliminated by tenant's
counterclaim for breach of
warranty or other violation,
239:8A.
Attachment of property.
See ATTACHMENT OF
PROPERTY.
Bank deposits and collections,
167D:20.
Commercial code, setoff by
beneficiary's bank,
106:4A-502.
Child support, assistance in
collection, **62D:4, 62D:9.**
City or town money payable to tax
delinquent, withholding,
60:93.
Collection of support or
educational obligation, **62D:1**
et seq.
See SET-OFF DEBT
COLLECTION.
Commercial code, setoff by
beneficiary's bank,
106:4A-502.

SETOFF AND
COUNTERCLAIM —Cont'd
Consumer protection actions for
damages, **93A:11.**
Credit unions, **171:48.**
Dam, damages caused, **253:8.**
Death of defendant, setoff based
on dissolution of attachment,
223:119.
Dissolution of attachment by death
of defendant, setoff in action
based, **223:119.**
District courts.
See DISTRICT COURTS.
Dower.
See DOWER AND CURTESY.
Exclusion from secured
transactions article of right,
106:9-104.
Executions.
Levy on real property by setoff,
236:6-236:25.
Set-off of executions, **235:27.**
Trustee process. See within this
heading, "Trustee process."
Executors.
See EXECUTORS AND
ADMINISTRATORS.
Fair value of use and occupancy of
premises unfit for human
habitation as reduced, **239:8A.**
Frivolous claims, award of costs
and attorneys' fees, **231:6F.**
Health violations, rent arrearages
as reduced or eliminated by
tenant's counterclaim,
111:127F.
Homestead property, **188:9.**
Insurance claims, setoff of unpaid
premiums against, **175:22I.**
Jurisdictional amount of
counterclaims entitling parties
to file claim of trial in superior
court, **231:104.**
Limitation of actions, application,
260:36.
Mine entry by public officials,
mitigation of damages arising,
21B:10.
Nonresident plaintiffs as
answerable to counterclaims,
227:2.
Public bodies and officers.
Claims against, **258:4.**
Mine entry by public officials,
mitigation of damages
arising, **21B:10.**
Removal of cause of action as
affecting, **231:103.**

SETOFF AND
COUNTERCLAIM —Cont'd
Rent arrearages as eliminated or
reduced by tenant's
counterclaim for breach of
warranty or other violation of
law, **111:127F.**
Secured transactions article of
Commercial Code, exclusion of
setoff or counterclaim right,
106:9-104.
Summary process actions,
landlord's conduct as basis for
counterclaim, **239:8A.**
Superior court, jurisdictional
amount of counterclaims
permitting parties to file claim
of trial, **231:104.**
Tax delinquents, withholding
money payable by city or
town, **60:93.**
Tenant's counterclaim for breach of
warranty or other violation of
law as reducing or eliminating
rent arrearages, **111:127F,**
239:8A.
Transfer or removal of cause of
action as affecting, **231:103.**
Trustee process.
Attachment of setoff asserted in
pending action, **246:38.**
Trustee's right to assert setoff,
246:26.
Water pollution abatement
districts' bonds and notes,
payments, **21:36.**
Weekly wage payment law, defense
to complaint for violation,
149:150.
Writs of entry.
See ENTRY, WRITS.

SET-OFF DEBT COLLECTION,
62D:1 et seq.
Administrative hearing to contest
claim, **62D:6.**
Appeal, right, **62D:7.**
Assistance of transitional
assistance department by
revenue department in
collection of debts, **62D:3.**
Child support.
Assistance in collection, **62D:4,**
62D:9.
Priority of unpaid support,
62D:13.
Claimant agency, defined, **62D:1.**
Commissioner, defined, **62D:1.**
Contesting validity of claim,
62D:6.
Debt, defined, **62D:1.**
Debtor, defined, **62D:1.**

SET-OFF DEBT COLLECTION
—Cont'd

Definitions, **62D:1.**

Employment and training division in labor and workforce department, **62D:13, 151A:69B.**

Escrow account, transfer of funds, **62D:5.**

Escrow amount credited to debtor's obligation, **62D:8.**

Exclusivity of remedy, **62D:12.**

Finalization of set-off, **62D:8.**

Information.
Exchange, legality, **62D:10.**
Revenue department, furnishing to by claimant agency, **62D:4.**

Joint return, **62D:5.**

Legality of exchange of information, **62D:10.**

Minimum debt and refund, **62D:2.**

Notice.
Finalization of set-off, **62D:9.**
Revenue department, notification by claimant agency, **62D:4.**
Transfer to escrow account, **62D:5.**

Priorities.
Child support, priority of unpaid support, **62D:13.**
Unpaid taxes, priority of unpaid taxes against refund, **62D:13.**

Refund, minimum, **62D:2.**

Remedy not exclusive, **62D:12.**

Revenue department to assist transitional assistance department, **62D:3.**

Rules, regulations and forms, **62D:11.**

Separate maintenance or support, priority of unpaid spousal support, **62D:13.**

Transfer of funds to escrow account, **62D:5.**

SETTING ASIDE.

Abuse prevention, vacating order, **208:34C, 209A:1 to 209A:7.**

Administrative adjudicatory decision, court's power to set aside, **30A:14.**

Arbitration.
See ARBITRATION.

Bank commissioner's order to cease and desist unfair or deceitful consumer transaction practices, **167:2D, 167:2E.**

Confession of judgment on power of attorney, **231:13A.**

SETTING ASIDE —Cont'd

District courts.
Removal to superior court, **231:104.**
Timely request for trial, vacating judgment for failure to make, **231:59G.**

Divorce and alimony, vacating order, **208:34B, 208:34C.**

Ethics commission of state, reimbursement of employee if judgment modified, **268B:4.**

Indigency affidavit and request for waiver of costs, filing in petitions to vacate or set aside, **261:27B.**

Labor relations.
See LABOR RELATIONS AND DISPUTES.

Larceny and theft, vacating order, **276:28.**

Removal to superior court, vacating district court judgments, **231:104.**

Superior courts.
District court judgments, setting aside or vacating upon removal to superior court, **231:104.**

Motions, **213:3.**

Unfair labor practices, orders, **150A:6.**

Verdict.
See VERDICT.

SETTLEMENT.
See COMPROMISE AND SETTLEMENT.

SETTLEMENT OF TOWNS.

Appropriations for anniversaries, **40:5.**

SEVERABILITY OF ACT.

Controlled Substances Act, **94C:48.**

Economic development and industrial corporation provisions, **121C:17.**

Housing and urban renewal provisions, **121B:2.**

Housing or redevelopment projects, partial invalidity, **121A:19.**

Income tax.
Constitutionality of provisions, severability upon question, **62:54.**
Trust estates, severability of taxes, **62:16.**

Northeast Interstate Dairy Compact, **Spec L 139:22.**

Penal statutes, **4:6.**

SEVERABILITY OF ACT
—Cont'd

Provisions of act, severability, **106:1-108.**

Statutes, construction, **4:6.**

Trademarks and trade names, provisions governing, **110B:16.**

Uniform Securities Act, **110A:417.**

SEVERAL LIABILITY.
See JOINT AND SEVERAL LIABILITY.

SEVERAL TENANCY.
See JOINT TENANTS AND TENANTS IN COMMON.

SEVERANCE FROM REALTY.

Contract for sale of goods to be severed from realty, **106:2-107.**

Sales under commercial code.
Oil and gas, **106:2-107.**
Timber to be cut, **106:2-107.**

SEVERANCE OF PROCEEDINGS.
See JOINDER OF ACTIONS OR ISSUES.

SEVERANCE PAY.
See WAGES, SALARIES, AND COMPENSATION.

SEWAGE DISPOSAL, 83:5-83:7.
See SEWERS AND DRAINS.

SEWER COMMISSIONERS.

Abolition of office, **41:63.**

Construction of sewer systems, powers and duties, **83:1.**

Election and term, **41:1, 41:63.**

Powers and duties, **41:65, 83:1.**

Road commissioners acting, **41:1.**

Selectmen acting, **41:21, 41:23.**

Term of office, **41:1, 41:63.**

Town public works board as successor, **41:69D.**

SEWER DISTRICTS.

Annual financial statement of state treasurer, **10:11.**

Assessment limitations, **59:20A, 59:20B.**

Bonds and certificates of indebtedness, exemption from taxation, **59:5.**

"Districts" defined as to include, **40:1A, 41:1A, 44:1.**

Environmental protection department, disposal of privy, cesspool, and septic tank contents, **111:31D.**

Group insurance for employees, **32B:2.**

SEWER DISTRICTS —Cont'd

Planning commission's plans and recommendations as to location of sewers and drains, **40B:5.**

Privy, cesspool, and septic tank contents, provision of facilities for disposal, **111:31D.**

Work clothes for employees, **28:4A.**

SEWERS AND DRAINS, 83:1-83:29.

Abandonment or discontinuance of easement taken for highway drains, **83:4.**

Abatement of charges, **83:16E.**

Abutting owners.

More than one way, assessment of land abutting, **83:21.**

Municipal indebtedness for sewer connections, **44:7.**

Aldermen.

See ALDERMEN AND SELECTMEN.

Annual reports and recommendations.

Environmental protection department, **111:23.**

Health commissioner's annual report and recommendations as to sewers, **111:23.**

State treasurer's annual financial statement as to sewer districts, **10:11.**

Applications.

Discharge permit, **21:43-21:46A.**

Disposal system applications, uniform procedures, **111:31E.**

Assessments, **83:15.**

Betterment law, **83:28.**

Bonds or notes, use to pay assessments, **83:3.**

Connecting sewers, **83:24.**

Construction of sewers, **83:14, 83:27, 83:28.**

Cities and towns, construction, repair, and maintenance of sewers, **83:1.**

Contracts for construction of sewer systems for prevention of pollution, **40:41, 83:1.**

Costs of, assessments to pay, **83:23.**

Digging up public ways, **83:8.**

Filing fees, statement of amount due for labor in construction of sewers, **262:34.**

Financing of, laws applicable, **83:23.**

SEWERS AND DRAINS —Cont'd

Assessments —Cont'd

Construction of sewers —Cont'd

Health department, approval, **111:127N.**

Highway drains, entry upon private land for purpose of constructing, **83:4.**

Particular sewers, regulation as to construction and use, **83:10.**

Railroads, construction of sewers, **83:1.**

Construction of water pollution facilities, **83:15B.**

Contracts for construction of sewer systems for prevention of pollution, **40:41, 83:1.**

Debt service charges, **59:21C.**

Determination of method, **83:18.**

Duration of lien created under special act, **83:29.**

Extension of time of payment, **83:19.**

Fee for use by owners not liable to assessment, **83:20.**

Financing of construction through assessments, **83:23.**

Interest, **83:19.**

Land abutting on more than one way, **83:21.**

Land court, filing, **262:39.**

Landowners, sewers built, **83:22.**

Lien, **83:16A et seq., 83:27, 83:29.**

Limitations, **59:20A, 59:20B.**

Method, determination, **83:18.**

Particular sewers, **83:24.**

Permanent privilege for particular sewer, **83:24.**

Private sewers or drains, **83:22.**

Record of, keeping, **83:2.**

Redetermination of fixed rate, **83:15A.**

Repairs and maintenance, money received from assessments to be used, **83:16.**

Sewage systems, **83:15, 83:15A.**

Special assessments, provisions applicable, **83:28.**

Statement of assessments, recording, **83:27.**

Uniform method.

Assessing sewerage costs, **83:15.**

Computation of uniform unit method, **40:42K.**

Use of sewers, **83:16.**

SEWERS AND DRAINS —Cont'd

Automobiles, complaint of motorist for injuries from defective sewer cover, **Spec L 17:3 Form 1.**

Bakeries, sanitary requirements, **94:9G.**

Bonds or notes.

Cost of connections, use of assessments to pay bonds or notes issued, **83:3.**

Exemption from taxation of sewer district bonds and certificates of indebtedness, **59:5.**

Borrowing by municipality, **44:7, 44:8, 83:16.**

Bonds or notes. See within this heading, "Bonds or notes."

Collection of sewer construction costs, **83:23.**

Debt limit, borrowing beyond, **44:8.**

Environmental protection department, borrowing within debt limit for reconstruction of sewers, **44:7.**

Fee for filing statement of amount due for labor in sewer construction, **262:34.**

School districts borrowing for sewers, **71:16.**

Standpipes, indebtedness, **44:8.**

Boston.

See METROPOLITAN DISTRICTS.

Boston water.

See BOSTON WATER AND SEWER REORGANIZATION ACT.

Bylaws of cities and towns, **40:21.**

Canals, fencing, **88:12, 88:13.**

Cemetery land, ground drainage entering public water supply, **114:35.**

Charles River.

Connection, **92:76.**

Pollution and drainage into, **111:175.**

Cities.

See CITIES AND TOWNS.

Coal mines, drainage requirements, **21B:11.**

Commissioners.

See SEWER COMMISSIONERS.

Common sewers.

Misuse, **83:13.**

Municipal indebtedness for connection of dwellings or buildings, **44:7.**

SEWERS AND DRAINS —Cont'd

Common sewers —Cont'd

Notice requirements regarding use, common sewers in cities and towns, **83:10.**

Condemnation.

Eminent domain. See within this heading, "Eminent domain."

Connections, **83:1, 83:3, 83:7, 83:10, 83:11.**

Assessment of connecting sewers, **83:24.**

Charles River, **92:76.**

Municipal indebtedness for connection of dwellings or buildings with common sewer, **44:7.**

Outdoor toilets where sewer connections available, **111:126.**

Particular sewers connecting house or building, **83:3.**

Violations, **111:127.**

Construction of sewers, financial aspects of, **83:1, 83:14, 83:16, 83:23.**

Assessments. See within this heading, "Assessments."

Construction of water pollution facilities, assessments, **83:15B.**

Contracts.

Construction of sewer systems for prevention of pollution, **40:41, 83:1.**

Debts contracted for sewer purposes.

Borrowing. See within this heading, "Borrowing by municipality."

Municipality's power to enter into, **83:1.**

Other governmental units, construction contracts, **40:4.**

Public works contracts, payment of sums due contractors after completion, **30:39G.**

Pumping stations, competitive bidding on contracts, **149:44A.**

Costs.

Abatement of charges, **83:16E.**

Fees. See within this heading, "Fees."

Lien for construction costs, **83:23.**

Payment of part by city or town, **83:23.**

Covers, complaint of motorist for injuries from defective sewer cover, **Spec L 17:3 Form 1.**

SEWERS AND DRAINS —Cont'd

Cranberry land, flooding and drainage, **253:39, 253:40.**

Debt limit.

Borrowing by municipality. See within this heading, "Borrowing by municipality."

Defective sewer cover, complaint of motorist for injuries, **Spec L 17:3 Form 1.**

Descriptions, keeping, **83:2.**

Determination of method of assessment, **83:18.**

Digging up public ways, **83:8.**

Discharge.

Permits, **21:43-21:46A.**

Watercraft, adoption of regulations as to discharge, **21:27.**

Disposal systems.

Sewage disposal works. See within this heading, "Sewage disposal works."

Districts.

See SEWER DISTRICTS.

Easements, **252:15-252:23.**

Construction of sewer system, acquisition of easements, **83:1.**

Highway drains, abandonment or discontinuance of easement taken, **83:4.**

Eminent domain, **83:1.**

Damages for construction of sewer systems, recovery, **83:1.**

Drainage of highways and streets, taking, **83:4.**

Lowlands, right of way for drainage or access, **252:15-252:23.**

Sewage disposal works, **83:6.**

Encumbrances.

Liens and encumbrances. See within this heading, "Liens and encumbrances."

Enforcement of laws, **83:13.**

Entry upon private land for purpose of constructing or maintaining highway drains, **83:4.**

Environment.

Actions for purpose of protecting natural resources and, **214:7A.**

Attorney general's office, authority as to improper sewage disposal of environmental protection division, **12:11D.**

Environmental affairs executive office, duties and functions, **21A:2.**

SEWERS AND DRAINS —Cont'd

Environment —Cont'd

Health department's duties under state environmental code regarding sewage disposal systems, **21A:13.**

State environmental code, **21A:13.**

Environmental protection department.

Annual reports and recommendations, **111:23.**

Construction to be approved, **83:1.**

On-site sewage disposal system inspections, **21A:13A.**

Powers and duties, **111:17.**

Reconstruction of sewers, borrowing within debt limit, **44:7.**

Sewage disposal works. See within this heading, "Sewage disposal works."

Sewer districts, disposal of privy, cesspool, and septic tank contents, **111:31D.**

Estates, connecting, **83:3.**

Expenses.

Costs. See within this heading, "Costs."

Extension of time of payment of assessments, **83:19.**

Fees.

Base rates, **21:53A.**

Ditch, fees for application to construct drainage ditch, **252:22.**

Filing fees. See within this heading, "Filing fees."

Liens, **83:16A et seq.**

Use of sewers and drains, fees for owners not subject to assessment, **83:20.**

Wastewater treatment facilities operators, fee for certification, **21:34B.**

Fencing of canals, **88:12, 88:13.**

Filing fees.

Sewer assessment, filing in land court, **262:39.**

Statement of amount due for labor in construction of sewers, **262:34.**

Financing construction by cities and towns, laws applicable to, **44:7, 44:8, 83:1, 83:14, 83:16, 83:23.**

Fines and penalties.

Connection with sewers, violations, **111:127.**

Digging up public ways without consent, **83:8.**

SEWERS AND DRAINS —Cont'd

Fines and penalties —Cont'd

Failure of owner to comply with order, **83:10, 83:12.**

Obstruction of ditches or drains, **83:9, 83:10.**

Use of sewers, violation of regulations, **83:10.**

Fixed rate assessment, redetermination, **83:15A.**

Grade crossings, change or relocation on abolition, **159:75.**

Group insurance for employees of sewer districts, **32B:2.**

Health department.

Annual report and recommendations of commissioner as to sewers, **111:23.**

Approval by department as to location, construction, and maintenance, **111:31D, 111:127N.**

Connections.

Agreements and contracts, Water Resources Authority, **83:1.**

Orders, **83:3, 83:11.**

House drainage, health regulations, **111:127.**

Private drain, orders to owners to repair, **83:12.**

Sewage disposal works, duties under state environmental code, **21A:13.**

Hearings, notice, **83:6, 111:31.**

Highways and streets.

Abutting owners, municipal indebtedness for sewer connections, **44:7.**

Digging up, **83:8.**

Ditches along, **84:9.**

Drainage, **83:4.**

Easements, **83:4.**

Eminent domain, **83:4.**

Laying out, **83:1, 83:25.**

Private ways. See within this heading, "Private ways."

Repairs and maintenance. See within this heading, "Repairs and maintenance."

Reservation of space, **82:34.**

Road commissioners, powers, **41:1, 41:64.**

Superintendent of streets, duties, **41:68.**

Unaccepted town ways, sewers and pipes, **82:25.**

Hospital for state minor wards and Massachusetts hospital school, joint use of sewage system, **111:62R.**

SEWERS AND DRAINS —Cont'd

House drainage, health regulations, **111:127.**

Housing and community development department.

Assistance program for low-income homeowners, **23B:24B.**

Powers and duties in general, **23B:3.**

Housing and urban renewal projects, municipal construction in aid, **121B:23.**

Improvement associations, powers, **45:12.**

Indebtedness of city or town for.

Borrowing. See within this heading, "Borrowing by municipality."

Infiltration and inflow, grant program to remove from sewage systems of towns, cities, and sewage districts, **21:30A. (note)**

Injunctions.

Misuse of common sewers, injunction restraining, **83:13.**

Permit for discharge of sewage and waste, injunction against, **21:43-21:46A.**

Injuries of motorist caused by defective sewer cover, complaint, **Spec L 17:3 Form 1.**

Inspections.

On-site sewage disposal systems, **21A:13A.**

Insurance for employees of sewer districts, **32B:2.**

Interest upon assessments, **83:19.**

Laying out, **82:25, 83:1.**

Licenses and permits.

Discharge of sewage and waste, permit, **21:43-21:46A.**

Marinas, requirements to obtain license to operate, **91:59B.**

Liens and encumbrances.

Assessment for sewers and drains, **83:16A et seq., 83:27, 83:29.**

Charges, lien, **83:16A et seq.**

Construction costs, lien, **83:23.**

Fees, **83:16A et seq.**

Limitation of municipal debt.

Borrowing by municipality. See within this heading, "Borrowing by municipality."

Loans.

Borrowing by municipality. See within this heading, "Borrowing by municipality."

SEWERS AND DRAINS —Cont'd

Local officials' authority to lay out, **83:1.**

Lowlands and swamps, **252:15-252:23.**

See LOWLANDS AND SWAMPS.

Maintenance.

Repairs and maintenance. See within this heading, "Repairs and maintenance."

Map for municipal planning, effect of adoption, **41:81E.**

Marinas, requirements to obtain license to operate, **91:59B.**

Master plan of municipal planning boards as to location, **41:81D.**

Materials to be used, **83:1.**

Method of assessment for, determination, **83:18.**

Metropolitan district commission. See METROPOLITAN DISTRICT COMMISSION.

Mortgagees, notification of water or sewer service provider of change in possession, **244:15A.**

Municipal borrowing.

Borrowing by municipality. See within this heading, "Borrowing by municipality."

Natural resources and environment, actions for purpose of protecting, **214:7A.**

Notes.

Bonds or notes. See within this heading, "Bonds or notes."

Notice.

Common sewers in cities and towns, notice requirements regarding use, **83:10.**

Hearings, **83:6, 111:31.**

Mortgagees, notification of water or sewer service provider of change in possession, **244:15A.**

Permit for discharge of sewage and waste, **21:43-21:46A.**

Nuisance.

House drainage regulated, **111:127.**

Lowlands.

See LOWLANDS AND SWAMPS.

Operation of sewage disposal works, **83:6, 83:7.**

Obstruction, **83:9, 83:10.**

Oil pollution, waste oil retention facilities for prevention, **21:52A.**

Ordinances of cities and towns, **40:21.**

SEWERS AND DRAINS —Cont'd
Other governmental units,
    contracts for construction,
    40:4.
Outdoor toilets where sewer
    connections available, **111:126.**
Payments.
    Assessments, extension of time
      for payment, **83:19.**
    Costs, payment in whole or in
      part by city or town, **83:23.**
    Permanent privilege of using
      sewers, **83:17.**
    Public works contracts, payment
      of sums due contractors
      after completion, **30:39G.**
Penalties.
    Fines and penalties. See within
      this heading, "Fines and
      penalties."
Permanent privilege of using.
    Particular services, **83:24.**
    Payment, **83:17.**
Permits.
    Licenses and permits. See
      within this heading,
      "Licenses and permits."
Plans and specifications.
    Construction, plans, **83:1.**
    Keeping, **83:2.**
    Location of sewers and drains,
      planning commission's
      plans, **40B:5.**
    Sewage disposal systems, state
      environmental code
      requirements, **21A:13.**
    Study plan of municipal
      planning board, **41:81D,**
      41:81E.
    Survey board plans, necessity of
      municipal conforming,
      41:77.
Plumbers, exemption from
    drainage regulations, **111:127.**
Plumbing systems.
    Drain layers, **142:3.**
    Regulations, **142:13.**
    Separate systems for sewage
      and storm waters, **83:5.**
Pollutants, regulation of disposal
    from sewage treatment
    facilities, **92:107A.**
Prescriptive drainage rights as
    affected by provisions as to
    protection of water supply
    sources, **111:168.**
Preservation of reports, **66:8.**
Private sewers or drains.
    Assessment, **83:22.**
    Repair, **83:3A, 83:12.**
Private ways.
    Laying out, **83:1.**

SEWERS AND DRAINS —Cont'd
Private ways —Cont'd
    Plans, effect on municipal
      authority to lay sewers of
      construction not in
      accordance, **41:77.**
    Repair of sewers, **83:3A.**
Privileges.
    Permanent privilege of using.
      See within this heading,
      "Permanent privilege of
      using."
Privy.
    Environmental protection
      department, sewer districts,
      disposal of privy, cesspool,
      and septic tank contents,
      111:31D.
    Location of privy vaults,
      111:126.
Proposed subdivisions which will
    be serviced by municipal
    sewerage system, approval,
    41:81U.
Public construction contracts,
    competitive bidding, **149:44A.**
Public works board of town as
    successor to offices of sewer
    commissioners, **41:69D.**
Railroads.
    Abolition of grade crossings,
      expenses of changing or
      relocating, **159:75.**
    Construction of sewers, **83:1.**
    Entry upon land, **83:4.**
    Recording of assessments, **83:27.**
Rates and charges.
    Abatement, **83:16E.**
    Assessments, **59:21C.**
    Base rates, **21:53A.**
    Deferral of charges, **83:16G.**
    Sewer Rate Relief Fund, **29:2Z.**
    Tax title accounts, **60:62,**
      60:76B.
Reconstruction of sewers,
    municipal borrowing, **44:7.**
Records, reports, and returns.
    Annual report. See within this
      heading, "Annual reports
      and recommendations."
    Filing fees. See within this
      heading, "Filing fees."
    Health board or officer, approval
      of sewage system, **41:81U.**
    Health commissioner's annual
      report and recommendations
      as to sewers, **111:23.**
    Keeping records, **83:2.**
    Permit for discharge of sewage
      and waste, **21:43-21:46A.**
    Preparatory work to
      construction of sewer
      systems, **83:1.**

SEWERS AND DRAINS —Cont'd
Records, reports, and returns
    —Cont'd
    Preservation of reports, **66:8.**
    Statement of assessments,
      83:27.
    State treasurer, annual financial
      statement regarding sewer
      district, **10:11.**
Repairs and maintenance, **83:1.**
    Health department approval,
      111:127N.
    Highway drains, entry upon
      private land for purpose of
      maintaining, **83:4.**
    Money received from
      assessments to be used,
      83:16.
    Private drains, **83:3A, 83:12.**
    Private ways, sewers, **83:3A.**
    Way of municipalities, laying of
      sewers upon construction,
      alteration, or repair, **83:25.**
Reports.
    Records, reports, and returns.
      See within this heading,
      "Records, reports, and
      returns."
Revocation or suspension of permit
    for discharge of sewage and
    waste, **21:43-21:46A.**
Right of way.
    Easements. See within this
      heading, "Easements."
Rivers, prescriptive drainage
    rights and use, **111:168.**
Roads.
    Highways and streets. See
      within this heading,
      "Highways and streets."
School districts, borrowing, **71:16.**
Selectmen.
    See ALDERMEN AND
      SELECTMEN.
Sewage disposal works, **83:5-83:7.**
    Applications, procedure,
      111:31E.
    Attorney general's office,
      environmental protection
      division in office of,
      authority as to improper
      sewage disposal, **12:11D.**
    Borrowing by municipalities,
      44:7, 44:8.
    Eminent domain, **83:6.**
    Environmental protection
      department.
      Approval of establishment,
      83:6.
      Consultation with town
      officers, **111:17.**

SEWERS AND DRAINS —Cont'd
Sewage disposal works —Cont'd
Environmental protection
department —Cont'd
Prevention of nuisance arising
from sewage disposal
works, **83:7.**
Sewer districts, disposal of
privy, cesspool, and septic
tank contents, **111:31D.**
Establishment, **83:6.**
Facilities for disposal of privy,
cesspool, and septic tank
contents, provision of by
cities and towns, **111:31D.**
Health department duties under
state environmental code,
21A:13.
Nuisance, operation of works to
avoid, **83:6, 83:7.**
On-site sewage disposal systems.
Inspection, **21A:13A.**
Separate plumbing systems for
sewage and storm waters,
83:5.
State environmental code
provisions, **21A:13.**
Ships and other watercraft,
adoption of regulations as to
discharge, **21:27.**
Special assessments.
Assessments. See within this
heading, "Assessments."
Specifications.
Plans and specifications. See
within this heading, "Plans
and specifications."
Standpipes.
Municipal indebtedness, **44:8.**
Reservoirs, inapplicability of
statute, **253:44.**
State environmental code, **21A:13.**
Storm waters to be kept separate
from sewage, **83:5.**
Streets.
Highways and streets. See
within this heading,
"Highways and streets."
Study plan of municipal planning
board to provide, **41:81D.**
Subdivision control.
See ZONING AND PLANNING.
Superintendent of streets, duties,
41:68.
Superintendents of town sewer
departments, **41:69.**
Superior court, **81:13.**
Supreme judicial court,
enforcement of laws as to
sewers and drains, **83:13.**
Survey board plans, necessity of
conforming, **41:77.**

SEWERS AND DRAINS —Cont'd
Taxation.
Annual sewer use charge added
to tax, **59:57.**
Assessments. See within this
heading, "Assessments."
Exemptions, **59:5.**
Exemptions for local property,
59:5D, 59:5E.
Liens, **83:16A et seq.**
Tax title accounts for sewer use
rates, **60:62, 60:76B.**
Tort liability for obstruction of
ditch or drain, **83:9.**
Trial or hearing, **83:6, 111:31.**
Uniform unit method, **40:42K,
83:15.**
Urban redevelopment corporations
contracting with municipality
for construction, **121A:14.**
Waste oil retention facilities to
prevent oil pollution, **21:52A.**
Wastewater treatment facilities
operators, board of
certification, **21:34A, 21:34B,
21:34C.**
Watercraft, adoption of regulations
as to discharge, **21:27.**
Water pollution.
See WATER POLLUTION.
Water Resources Authority,
agreements and contracts for
making connections for
collection, treatment, and
disposal of sewage, **83:1.**
Waterways, fencing, **88:12, 88:13.**
Waterworks and water supply.
Cemetery land, ground drainage
entering public water
supply, **114:35.**
Construction of sewerage
systems to protect, **40:41.**
Prescriptive drainage rights as
affected by provisions as to
protection of water supply
sources, **111:168.**
Work clothes for employees of
sewer districts, **28:4A.**
Works for treatment, purification,
and disposal.
Sewage disposal works. See
within this heading,
"Sewage disposal works."
Zoning.
See ZONING AND PLANNING.

SEWER USE CHARGES.
Preliminary tax bills, **59:23D.**

SEWING MACHINE.
Execution, exemption from seizure,
235:34.

SEX CHANGE OPERATIONS.
Amendment of birth certificate
upon completion of sex
reassignment surgery, **46:13.**

SEX DISCRIMINATION.
**See CIVIL RIGHTS AND
DISCRIMINATION.**

SEX EDUCATION.
Committees on sex education,
appointment, powers, and
duties, **71:38O.**
Notice to parents or guardians as
to sex education courses,
71:32A.

SEX OF PERSON.
Civil service.
See CIVIL SERVICE.
Statutory construction of gender,
4:6.

**SEXUAL ASSAULT
COUNSELOR.**
Definition, **233:20J.**
Privileged communications,
233:20B.

SEXUAL CONDUCT.
Defined, **272:31.**

SEXUAL HARASSMENT.
Abuse of disabled persons,
discharge or discipline of
public officers or employees
for, **30:9B.**
Defined, **151A:25, 151B:1, 151C:1.**
Education and training in the
workplace, **151B:3A.**
Employer, sexual harassment,
151B:4.
Employment security benefits,
sexual harassment, **151A:25.**
Equity, freedom from sexual
harassment, **214:1C.**
Housing accommodations, **151B:4.**
Prohibition, **151A:25, 151B:1.**
Students, sexual harassment,
151C:2.

**SEXUALLY DANGEROUS
PERSONS, 123A:1 et seq.**
Agency with jurisdiction.
Defined, **123A:1.**
Juvenile offenders, duty to
identify, **123A:12.**
Examination and diagnosis.
Juvenile offenders, **123A:13.**
Juvenile offenders.
Examination and diagnosis,
123A:13.
Identification of potentially
dangerous offenders,
123A:12.

SEXUALLY DANGEROUS PERSONS —Cont'd
Juvenile offenders —Cont'd
Incompetent offenders.
Fact-finding trial, **123A:15.**
Jury trial to determine, **123A:14.**
Reports of treatment, **123A:16.**
Segregation from adults at detention facilities, **123A:6A.**
Temporary commitment pending determination, **123A:14.**
Records, reports, and returns.
Juvenile offenders.
Reports of treatment, **123A:16.**

SEXUAL OFFENSES AND OFFENDERS, 123A:1 et seq.
Abduction.
See ABDUCTION.
Abuse of children.
See ABUSED AND NEGLECTED CHILDREN.
Abusive relationships, expert testimony as to, **233:23F.**
Address confidentiality of domestic violence victims, **9A:1 to 9A:7.**
See ADDRESS CONFIDENTIALITY OF DOMESTIC VIOLENCE VICTIMS.
Adultery, **272:14.**
See ADULTERY.
Attorneys.
District and prosecuting attorneys. See within this heading, "District and prosecuting attorneys."
Autopsy required in event of death, **38:6.**
Bigamy, **272:15.**
See POLYGAMY.
Center for treatment of dangerous persons.
Treatment facilities and programs. See within this heading, "Treatment facilities and programs."
Central computerized registry of all sex offenders, **6:178D.**
Challenge of risk level determined by registry board, **6:178M.**
Chaste person under eighteen, unlawful intercourse, **272:4.**
Children.
Abused.
See ABUSED AND NEGLECTED CHILDREN.

SEXUAL OFFENSES AND OFFENDERS —Cont'd
Children —Cont'd
Assault with intent to rape, **265:24B.**
Dangerous persons, **123A:1 et seq.**
District attorney, reporting of sexual offenses against children, **119:51B.**
Expedited trial involving minor victim or witness, **278:16F.**
Pornography, **272:29A.**
See CHILD PORNOGRAPHY.
Prostitution, **272:4A, 272:4B.**
See PROSTITUTION.
Rape, **265:22A-265:24B.**
See RAPE.
Release of sex offenders and youth offenders committing crimes against children, **120:12.**
Restrictions on placement of child adjudicated for sex offense, **119:33B.**
Statute of limitations relative to rape, **277:63.**
Testimony in proceeding involving abuse, **233:20.**
Unlawful intercourse, **272:4.**
Unnatural and lascivious acts with minor, **272:35A.**
Commissioner of mental health, duties, **123A:2.**
Commitment and retention.
New commitment, application, **120:14.**
Community notification.
Registration and community notification. See within this heading, "Registration and community notification."
Community parole supervision for life, **265:45, 275:18.**
Certificate of termination of sentence, **127:133D.**
Jurisdiction of parole board, **127:133D.**
Conditional release, **123A:9.**
Continuance in trial involving minor victim or witness, **278:16F.**
Correctional institutions.
Bridgewater treatment center, **123A:1 et seq.**
Discharge of offenders.
Examination and discharge of sexually dangerous persons, **123A:9.**
Next friend, application for release of sexually dangerous person, **123A:9.**

SEXUAL OFFENSES AND OFFENDERS —Cont'd
Correctional institutions —Cont'd
Discharge of offenders —Cont'd
Notice of discharge, **123A:9.**
State police, notice of release of prisoners convicted of sexual crimes, **22C:37.**
Escape from confinement, sexually dangerous persons, **268:16.**
Expenditure of money earned by inmate, **127:48A.**
Crimes redefined in sex-neutral terms, **265:24, 265:24B, 269:14A.**
Criminal history systems board, **6:178K.**
Criminal procedure, **278:16A.**
Dangerous persons, **123A:1 et seq.**
Definitions, **6:178C, 123A:1, 265:24, 265:24B, 269:14A, 277:39, 277:79.**
Discharge of offenders from correctional institutions.
Correctional institutions. See within this heading, "Correctional institutions."
District and prosecuting attorneys.
Children, reporting sexual offenses against, **119:51B.**
Duties in prosecution of sexually dangerous persons, **123A:9.**
Notice required prior to discharge of conditionally released sexually dangerous persons, **123A:9.**
DNA database, **22E:1 to 22E:15.**
See DNA DATABASE.
Drivers' licenses, obligation of sex offenders to register with police, **6:178E.**
Drugs, **272:3.**
Enticing to unlawful intercourse, **272:4.**
Escape from confinement, prosecution of sexually dangerous persons, **268:16.**
Evidence, **272:11.**
Abusive relationships, expert testimony as to, **233:23F.**
Children, testimony in proceeding involving abuse, **233:20.**
Corroboration, **272:11.**
Rape.
See RAPE.
Examinations, **123A:9.**
Expedited trial involving minor victim or witness, **278:16F.**
FBI, transmission of registration data to, **6:178E.**

SEXUAL OFFENSES AND OFFENDERS —Cont'd

Feeble-minded person, venue, **265:24A.**

Fee, penalty for engaging in sexual conduct, **272:53, 272:53A, 272:54.**

Filing, computerized files on all sex offenders, **6:178D.**

Fornication.
　See FORNICATION.

Harassment.
　See SEXUAL HARASSMENT.

Hearings.
　See TRIAL OR HEARINGS.

Hospitals and health care facilities, reporting requirements as to sexual crime victims, **112:12A½.**

Husband and wife, application for release, **123A:9.**

Idiot, venue, **265:24A.**

Incest.
　See INCEST.

Indecent exposure.
　See INDECENT EXPOSURE.

Indictments and information.
　Cohabitation, lewd and lascivious, **277:79.**
　Form, **277:79.**
　Indecent exposure, **277:79.**
　Meaning of term, **277:39.**
　Unnatural and lascivious acts, **277:45.**

Kidnapping.
　Enhanced sentence for sexual assault of victim, **265:26.**

Knowledge, discharge or release of sexually dangerous person, **22C:37, 123A:9.**

Lascivious cohabitation, **272:16.**
　Indictment, **277:79.**

Limitation of time for prosecution in certain cases, **272:11.**

Mentally ill persons.
　Mental health commissioner or department, **123A:2, 123A:9.**
　Professionals, sexual contact with patients or clients, **12:11L.**
　Venue, **265:24A.**

Minors.
　Children. See within this heading, "Children."

Next friend, application for release of sexually dangerous person, **123A:9.**

SEXUAL OFFENSES AND OFFENDERS —Cont'd

Notice and knowledge.
　Community notification.
　　Registration and community notification. See within this heading, "Registration and community notification."

Discharge or release of sexually dangerous person, **22C:37, 123A:9.**

Obscenity and lewdness, **272:16, 272:28-272:32, 272:53, 272:61, 277:45, 277:79.**
　See OBSCENITY AND LEWDNESS.

Outpatient treatment, **123A:9.**

Owner of premises permitting use for unlawful intercourse, **272:6.**

Periodic examinations, **123A:9.**

Petitions.
　Examination and discharge, **123A:9.**

Physicians attending victims, reporting requirements, **112:12A½.**

Police.
　Notice or information, **22C:37, 123A:9.**
　Registration and community notification. See within this heading, "Registration and community notification."

Polygamy.
　See POLYGAMY.

Pornography, **272:16, 272:28 to 272:32, 272:53, 272:61, 277:45, 277:79.**
　See OBSCENITY AND LEWDNESS.

Prisoners.
　State police, notice of release of prisoners convicted of sexual crimes, **22C:37.**

Probation.
　See PROBATION AND PAROLE.

Probation and parole.
　Community parole supervision for life, **265:45, 275:18.**
　Jurisdiction of parole board, **127:133D.**

Prosecuting attorneys.
　District and prosecuting attorneys. See within this heading, "District and prosecuting attorneys."

SEXUAL OFFENSES AND OFFENDERS —Cont'd

Prostitution, **272:53, 277:79.**
　See PROSTITUTION.

Public counsel services committee.
　Sex offense registry.
　　Indigent services, provision, **211D:16.**

Public excluded from trials involving, **278:16A, 278:16C.**

Rape, **265:22 et seq.**
　See RAPE.

Recommitment of sexually dangerous inmate, **120:14.**

Registration and community notification, **6:178C et seq.**
　Agency defined, **6:178C.**
　Arrest of sex offender, **6:178P.**
　Challenge of risk level determined by registry board, **6:178M.**
　Change of address, **6:178E.**
　Commissioner of revenue.
　　Authority to examine information to confirm registration, **6:178F.**
　Crimes against offenders.
　　Illegal use of registry information, **6:178N.**
　Criminal history systems board, **6:178K.**
　Definitions, **6:178C.**
　Duration of registration, **6:178G.**
　Failure to register.
　　Authority to arrest, **6:178P.**
　　Penalties, **6:178H.**
　Fines and penalties.
　　Failure to register, **6:178H.**
　　Register of sex offenders, illegal use of information in, **6:178N.**
　Harassment of offenders.
　　Illegal use of registry information, **6:178N.**
　Homeless shelters.
　　Failure to register or verify, penalty, **6:178H.**
　　Verification of residence, **6:178F.**
　Indigent services, provision, **211D:16.**

SEXUAL OFFENSES AND OFFENDERS —Cont'd

Registration and community notification —Cont'd

Police or other public employees.
Liability for providing information, **6:178O.**
Probable cause to arrest sex offender, **6:178P.**
Transmission of registration data to, **6:178E.**
Public access to registry information, **6:178I.**
Registration and verification forms, **6:178D.**
Registration data, **6:178D.**
Verification, **6:178F.**
Report identifying offenders, **6:178I.**
Request of registry information, qualifications, **6:178J.**
Revocation of parole for failure to register, **6:178E.**
Risk of reoffense, determination, **6:178L.**
Challenge to determination, **6:178M.**
Sex offender registry, **6:178D.**
Illegal use of registry information, **6:178N.**
Public access, **6:178I.**
Requests for information, procedures, **6:178J.**
Sex offender registry board, **6:178D, 6:178J.**
Sex offense registry.
Public counsel services committee, **211D:16.**
Time or duration, **6:178E, 6:178G.**
Verification, appearance at police station, **6:178F.**
Level 2 or 3 sexual offenders, **6:178F½.**
Youthful offenders, **6:178E.**
Release of offenders.
Children, release of sex offenders and youth offenders committing crimes against, **120:12.**
Correctional institutions. See within this heading, "Correctional institutions."
Husband and wife, application for release, **123A:9.**
Next friend, application for release of sexually dangerous person, **123A:9.**
Registration and community notification. See within this heading, "Registration and community notification."

SEXUAL OFFENSES AND OFFENDERS —Cont'd

Release of offenders —Cont'd
State police, notice of release of prisoners convicted of sexual crimes, **22C:37.**
Reports and returns, **123A:9.**
Registered offenders, **6:178I.**
Retention.
Commitment and retention. See within this heading, "Commitment and retention."
Revocation of parole for failure to register, **6:178E.**
Risk of reoffense, determination, **6:178L.**
Challenge to determination, **6:178M.**
School bus drivers, disqualification, **90:8A.**
Search of registry of offenders, **6:178J.**
Seduction.
See SEDUCTION.
Sex offender registry board, **6:178D, 6:178J, 6:178K.**
Sodomy.
See SODOMY.
Spectators may be excluded from courtroom, **278:16A, 278:16C.**
Spouses, application for releases, **123A:9.**
State police, notice of release of prisoners convicted of sexual crimes, **22C:37.**
Superior court.
See SUPERIOR COURTS.
Support of prostitution, **272:7.**
Time or date, registration and community notification, **6:178E, 6:178G.**
Treatment facilities and programs, **123A:2.**
Bridgewater treatment center, **123A:1 et seq.**
Trial.
See TRIAL OR HEARINGS.
Two witness rule, **272:11.**
Verification of registration of offenders, **6:178F.**
Level 2 or 3 sexual offenders, **6:178F½.**
Victims.
Reporting requirements as to sexual crime victims, **112:12A½.**
Warning on reports of registered offenders as to use of list, **6:178I.**
Warrantless arrest for engaging in illegal sexual conduct for fee, **272:54.**

SEXUAL OFFENSES AND OFFENDERS —Cont'd

Wife and husband, application for release, **123A:9.**
Work release ineligibility, **127:49.**
Youth Services Department and Massachusetts Training Schools, recommitment of sexually dangerous persons, **120:14.**

SEXUAL ORIENTATION.

Discrimination on basis, **151B:1, 151B:3, 151B:4, 272:92A, 272:98.**
Hate crimes.
See HATE CRIMES.

SEXUAL PSYCHOPATHS ACT, **123A:1 et seq.**

SEXUAL STERILIZATION. See STERILIZATION.

SHACKLE LIFT KITS.

Altering height of motor vehicles, regulation, **90:7P.**

SHAD.

Manner of taking, limitations, **130:100C.**
Palmer River, **130:100C.**

SHADE TREE MANAGEMENT AND PEST CONTROL BUREAU.

Entry on land for certain purposes, **132:8.**
Gypsy and brown tail moths, suppression, **132:11.**
Local superintendents, **132:13.**
Nuisances, state assistance to municipalities in suppression, **132:16.**
Superintendents, **132:13.**

SHADE TREES, **87:1-87:13.**

Appropriations by towns and cities for planting, **40:5.**
Consolidated hearings as to removal, **40:15C, 87:3.**
Cutting of another's privately owned trees, penalty, **87:11.**
Cutting of public shade trees, **87:3-87:6.**
Approval of mayor or selectmen upon objection, **87:4.**
Buildings, cutting trees to expedite moving, **87:5.**
Hearing, **87:3.**
Highways and streets, trees along, **87:3-87:6, 87:8.**
Penalty for violations, **87:6.**
Definition of public shade tree, **87:1.**

SHADE TREES —Cont'd

Fines and penalties.

Cutting of public shade trees, **87:6.**

Injuries to shade trees, **87:10-87:12.**

Privately owned trees, cutting or damaging, **87:11.**

Signs and marks on shade trees, **87:9.**

Highways and streets, shade trees along.

Authorized town expenditures, **87:7.**

Boundaries, shade trees presumptively, **87:1.**

Cutting or trimming where obstructing highway, **87:5.**

Cutting or trimming, **87:3-87:6, 87:8.**

Highway fund as available for care of, on state highways, **90:34.**

Insect pests, cutting or trimming trees to suppress, **87:5.**

Obstruction of travel, cutting or trimming in case, **87:5.**

Officers charged with protection in cities, **87:13.**

Planting and location, **87:7.**

Posting signs on, cutting or marking, penalty, **87:9.**

Road commissioners, powers, **41:64.**

Small trees and brush, **87:5.**

State highways. See within this heading, "State highways."

Improvement associations, powers, **45:12.**

Municipal appropriations for planting, **40:5.**

Parks and reservations, **45:12.**

Function of tree warden concerning, **87:2.**

Penalties.

Fines and penalties. See within this heading, "Fines and penalties."

Pest Control Bureau.

See SHADE TREE MANAGEMENT AND PEST CONTROL BUREAU.

Planting.

Appropriations by cities and towns for planting, **40:5.**

Town, planting, **87:7.**

Posting notice or advertisement on, as offense, **87:9.**

Privately owned trees, cutting or damaging, **87:11.**

Public shade trees, defined, **87:1.**

SHADE TREES —Cont'd

Reservations.

Parks and reservations. See within this heading, "Parks and reservations."

Roads.

Highways and streets. See within this heading, "Highways and streets, shade trees along."

Signs and marks, **87:9.**

State highways.

Highway fund as available for care of shade trees, **90:34.**

Trees, **87:8, 87:10.**

Streets.

Highways and streets. See within this heading, "Highways and streets, shade trees along."

Tree wardens' duties, **87:2-87:5, 87:7.**

SHAFTING.

Safeguards in factories, **149:127.**

SHALE.

Coal containing, **94:248.**

SHARE ACCOUNT.

Truth-In-Savings law, definition of "account" for purposes, **140E:1.**

SHARECROPPERS.

Mortgages, **255:7D.**

SHAREHOLDERS APPRAISAL ACT, 156:46.

SHARES AND SHAREHOLDERS.

Corporations.

See CORPORATIONS.

Credit unions.

See CREDIT UNIONS.

Professional corporations.

Issuance and transfer, **156A:10.**

Liability, **156A:6.**

Proxies and vote in trusts, **156A:11.**

Redemption, **156A:12, 156A:13.**

SHARON.

Congressional district, **57:1.**

District court, **218:1.**

Medical examiner district, **38:1.**

Senatorial district, **57:3.**

SHARPS INJURY PREVENTION, 111:53D.

SHEEP.

Certificate of healthy condition, **129:20.**

Demonstration sheep farms, **128:9-128:11.**

SHEEP —Cont'd

Distraint for doing damage, **49:29.**

Driving along highways, power of town to regulate, **85:10.**

Excise tax, **59:8A.**

False pedigree, **266:93.**

Inspection, **129:19.**

Prizes and exhibits, **128:2.**

Sausage, definition, **94:1.**

Scrapie, destruction and partial reimbursement for sheep affected with or exposed, **129:13A.**

Slaughtering, humanely, **94:139C-94:139G.**

Society for Prevention of Cruelty to Animals, duties of agents, **129:9.**

Taking up and impounding, **49:24, 49:25.**

Taxation.

Excise tax, **59:8A.**

Exemption from local taxes, **59:5.**

Trespass by, penalty, **266:118.**

SHEFFIELD.

District court, **218:1.**

Medical examiner district, **38:1.**

Senatorial district, **57:3.**

SHELBURNE.

Medical examiner district, **38:1.**

SHELBURNE FALLS.

District court, **218:1.**

SHELL.

New England Neptune as shell of Commonwealth, **2:29.**

SHELLEY'S CASE.

Applicability of rule, **184:5.**

SHELLFISH, 130:37 et seq.

Adulterated or contaminated shellfish, defense against charge of selling, **94:194A.**

Alderman and selectmen.

Constable for shellfish, appointment, **130:98.**

License to propagate and take shellfish, **130:57.**

Aliens, permit, **130:55.**

Appearances before clerks of district court, **21:6F.**

Appointment, powers, and duties of deputy constables, **130:98.**

Appropriations.

Cultivation of shellfish, **130:54, 130:56.**

Expenditure of appropriated funds for increasing shellfish supply, **130:20.**

SHELLFISH —Cont'd
Appropriations —Cont'd
Local control of shellfisheries.
See within this heading,
"Local control of
shellfisheries."
Propagation, **130:20A.**
Purification plants, **130:76.**
Bacteriological counts as
determination of contaminated
areas, **130:74.**
Bag limits, **130:52.**
Family purposes, taking, **130:52.**
Scallops, **130:72.**
Seed quahaugs or clams, **130:69.**
Bait.
Claim bait, sale by barrel, **94:85.**
Crabs, taking for bait, **130:37,
130:37A.**
Permit, **130:75.**
Biologist, increase of supply of
shellfish with advice, **130:20.**
Boats or vessels, penalty for
fastening to marks or bounds,
130:66.
Bounds.
Private shellfish grants. See
within this heading,
"Private shellfish grants."
Brands and labels.
Labels or tags. See within this
heading, "Labels or tags."
Canned lobster meat or crabmeat
defined, **130:1.**
Carriers.
Importation regulations
inapplicable, **130:81.**
Labeling requirements as to
scallops inapplicable,
130:92.
Sale of shellfish, **135:5.**
Certification as to contaminated
areas, **130:74, 130:74A.**
Clams.
See CLAMS AND CLAM BAIT.
Cockles, disposal, **130:103.**
Commercial fisherman permits,
130:80-130:83.
Aliens, **130:55.**
Fees, **130:83.**
Importation of shellfish for
consumption as food,
130:81.
Revocation or suspension,
130:80.
Rules and regulations, **130:80.**
Commercial fishing, withdrawal of
areas for individual use,
130:52.
Commissioner of environmental
quality engineering.
Certification of contaminated
areas, **130:74, 130:74A.**

SHELLFISH —Cont'd
Commissioner of environmental
quality engineering —Cont'd
Conservation and management
plans, **130:17, 130:52,
130:75.**
Purification methods, **130:75.**
Common carrier.
Carriers. See within this
heading, "Carriers."
Conch contamination, tests for
determination, purification
plants, **130:74, 130:74A,
130:75-130:77, 130:80.**
Conservation and management
plans, development, **130:17,
130:52, 130:75, 130:98.**
Constables in cities and towns,
appointment and duties,
130:98.
Containers or packages, marking
of.
Labels or tags. See within this
heading, "Labels or tags."
Contaminated areas, **130:74 et
seq.**
Bait permit, **130:75.**
Determination and certification
by department of health,
130:74, 130:74A.
Digger's permit, **130:75, 130:83.**
Document as prima facie
evidence of contamination,
130:74.
Environmental protection
department, **130:74.**
Illegal taking, penalty, **130:75.**
Immediate designation as
emergency, **130:74A.**
Master digger's permit, **130:75,
130:83.**
Municipal authority, **130:52.**
Penalties, **130:75.**
Permits, **130:75.**
Possession as evidence of
violation, **130:75.**
Posting of notice, **130:74.**
Contaminated shellfish, defense
against rule, **94:194A.**
Crabs.
See CRABS.
Cultch, planting, **130:57.**
Cultivation.
Municipal appropriations,
130:54.
Damages.
Double damages. See within this
heading, "Double damages."
Treble damages, **130:27.**
Dealers.
Certificate, **130:80, 130:83.**

SHELLFISH —Cont'd
Dealers —Cont'd
Labeling requirements with
respect, **130:82.**
Sales, **130:82.**
Shipping certificate, **130:80.**
Definitions, **130:1.**
Deputy constables, appointment
and duties, **130:98.**
Diggers permit, **130:75.**
Digger's shellfish shipping
certificate, **130:80, 130:83.**
Double damages.
Pollution of shellfish areas,
130:27.
Private shellfish grants,
trespassers, **130:63.**
Dredges, use without consent of
licensee of private shellfish
grants, **130:67.**
Emergencies, immediate
designation of contaminated
areas, **130:74A.**
Environmental Protection
Department.
Commissioner of environmental
quality engineering. See
within this heading,
"Commissioner of
environmental quality
engineering."
Evidence.
Contaminated areas, document
as prima facie evidence of
contamination, **130:74.**
Control and regulation of
shellfisheries, **130:52,
130:74.**
Importation for consumption as
food, label on container,
130:81.
Examination, inspection, or
investigation.
Constable, authority, **130:98.**
Imported shellfish intended for
consumption as food,
130:81.
Private shellfish grants, **130:57.**
Exclusive license to private
shellfish grantees, **130:63.**
Extermination of enemies of
shellfish, **130:20.**
Fees.
Commercial permits and
certificates, **130:83.**
Private shellfish grants. See
within this heading,
"Private shellfish grants."
Purification plants, **130:77.**
Fines and penalties.
Boat or vessel, fastening to
marks or bounds, **130:66.**

SHELLFISH —Cont'd
Fines and penalties —Cont'd
Contaminated areas, illegal taking of shellfish, **130:75.**
Dealers receiving unlabeled shellfish, **130:82.**
Destruction of marks or bounds of licenses or grants, **130:66.**
Forfeiture. See within this heading, "Forfeiture."
Hours for taking from private grounds, **130:68.**
Importation of shellfish for consumption as food, **130:81.**
License and permit violations, **130:64.**
Pollution of water by sewage, **130:27.**
Private shellfish grants. See within this heading, "Private shellfish grants."
Scallops, **130:70, 130:72, 130:92.**
Seed clams, quahaugs, or oysters, taking, **130:69.**
Unauthorized taking from private grounds, **130:67, 130:68.**
Weight, violations as to sale by measure other than, **94:88B, 94:92B.**
Fisheries, Wildlife, and Recreational Vehicles commissioner, powers and duties as to purification plants, **130:76.**
Food, shellfish.
Determination of fitness for public consumption, **130:74.**
Importation of shellfish intended for consumption, **130:81.**
Forfeiture.
Illegally taken shellfish, **130:12.**
Private shellfish grants. See within this heading, "Private shellfish grants."
Form, permit or license, **130:12, 130:53, 130:62.**
Grants.
Private shellfish grants. See within this heading, "Private shellfish grants."
Purification plants, acquisition of land and buildings, **130:76.**
Health and health department, **130:76.**
Certification or designation of contaminated areas, **130:74, 130:74A.**
Drainage causing pollution of, shellfish areas, **130:25.**

SHELLFISH —Cont'd
Health and health department —Cont'd
Imported shellfish as food, enforcement of provisions, **130:81.**
Penalty for transportation of shellfish taken from contaminated areas, **130:75.**
Sanitary rules and regulations, **130:80.**
Impact of work on nearby land, **131:40.**
Importation for consumption as food, **130:81.**
Increasing supply, co-operation of director with coastal cities and towns, **130:20.**
Inspections.
Examination, inspection, or investigation. See within this heading, "Examination, inspection, or investigation."
Interstate commerce, **130:80, 130:81.**
Labels or tags, **94:181, 130:82.**
Contaminated shellfish, counterfeiting, altering, defacing or tampering with tags or labels, **130:81, 130:82.**
Imported shellfish, **130:81.**
Sales by dealers, **130:82.**
Scallops, **130:92.**
Licenses and permits.
Aliens taking shellfish for commercial purposes, **130:55.**
Area or territory covered.
Private shellfish grants. See within this heading, "Private shellfish grants."
Bait permit, **130:75.**
Commercial fisherman permit. See within this heading, "Commercial fisherman permits."
Contaminated areas, taking shellfish, **130:75.**
Death of licensee, continuation for benefit of family, **130:57.**
Diggers permit, **130:75.**
Family use permits, **130:52, 130:53.**
Fees for commercial permits, **130:83.**
Forfeiture for nonpayment of fees, **130:64.**
Form, **130:12, 130:53, 130:62.**
Individuals, permits, **130:52, 130:53.**

SHELLFISH —Cont'd
Licenses and permits —Cont'd
Inspection and certification by division of marine fisheries, **130:57.**
Limitations, **130:52.**
Master diggers permit, **130:75.**
Private shellfish grants. See within this heading, "Private shellfish grants."
Propagation and taking of shellfish from certain coastal waters, license, **130:57.**
Scallops, taking, **130:70, 130:73, 130:80.**
Seed clams, quahaugs or oysters, taking for planting, **130:69.**
Lobsters.
See LOBSTERS.
Local control of shellfisheries, **130:52-130:56.**
Alien, issuance of permit, **130:55.**
Appropriations.
Cultivation, propagation, and protection, **130:54.**
Joint control by two or more municipalities, **130:56.**
Purification plants, **130:76.**
Areas for family use, **130:52.**
Bag limit, **130:52.**
Close seasons, declaration, **130:54.**
Expenditure of funds for increase of shellfish, **130:20.**
Failure or neglect to take control, **130:52.**
Joint control by two or more municipalities, **130:56.**
Licensing, **130:52.**
Regulations authorized, **130:52.**
Maintenance of purification plants, **130:76.**
Marine fisheries division.
Commercial fisherman permits. See within this heading, "Commercial fisherman permits."
Expenditure of funds for increase of supply of shellfish, **130:20.**
Importation certificates, **130:81.**
Imported shellfish to be consumed as food, **130:81.**
Increasing supply of shellfish, **130:20.**
Inspection and certification, **130:57.**
Local control, **130:52.**
Programs to enhance population, **130:20.**

SHELLFISH —Cont'd
Marine fisheries division —Cont'd
Purification plants, **130:76, 130:77.**
Scallops, powers and duties with respect, **130:70-130:73.**
Temporary local control, **130:52.**
Treatment and purification of shellfish, **130:20.**
Marine worms or shellfish, permit required for taking or digging, **130:80.**
Marks.
Package marking.
Labels or tags. See within this heading, "Labels or tags."
Private shellfish grants. See within this heading, "Private shellfish grants."
Master diggers permit, **130:75.**
Matching city or town funds, **130:20A.**
Minimum size regulations, **130:60.**
Ocean sanctuaries, activities permitted, **132A:16.**
Oysters.
See OYSTERS.
Penalties.
Fines and penalties. See within this heading, "Fines and penalties."
Permits.
Licenses and permits. See within this heading, "Licenses and permits."
Pollution of waters, **130:25-130:27.**
Contaminated areas. See within this heading, "Contaminated areas."
Criminal liability, **130:27.**
Jurisdiction of proceedings, **130:26.**
Sewage, **130:25, 130:27.**
Treble damages, **130:27.**
Posting notice of contamination areas, **130:74.**
Private shellfish grants, **130:57-130:68.**
Application for license, **130:59.**
Area or territory covered by license.
Destruction of marks or bounds, penalty, **130:66.**
Marking, **130:61.**
Record, **130:62.**
Survey and plan, **130:61.**
Cities and towns, **130:54, 130:57.**
Deficiency in planting shellfish, forfeiture of license, **130:65.**
Director's authority, **130:52.**

SHELLFISH —Cont'd
Private shellfish grants —Cont'd
Double damages against trespassers, **130:63.**
Examination or inspection, **130:57.**
Exclusive rights of licensee or transferee, **130:63.**
Fastening boat to marks or bounds, penalty, **130:66.**
Fees.
Annual license fee, **130:64.**
Forfeiture of license for nonpayment, **130:64.**
Recording fees, **130:62.**
Fines and penalties.
Fastening boats to marks or bounds, **130:66.**
Hours for taking shellfish, regulations, **130:68.**
Unauthorized taking of shellfish, **130:67, 130:68.**
Unlawful use of grounds or beds, **130:67.**
Forfeiture of license.
Deficiency in planting shellfish, **130:65.**
Hours for taking, violation, **130:68.**
Nonpayment of fees, **130:64.**
Grounds or beds, unauthorized use of or injury, **130:67.**
Hearing as to issuance, transfer or renewal of license, **130:60.**
Hours for taking shellfish, **130:68.**
Inefficiency in planting shellfish, forfeiture of license, **130:65.**
Inspection and certification, **130:57.**
Licenses and permits, **130:57.**
Annual fee, **130:64.**
Application, **130:59.**
Forms, **130:62.**
Hearing, **130:60.**
Marks or bounds, **130:61.**
Fastening boat, **130:66.**
Injury or destruction, penalty, **130:66.**
Revocation of license for failure to maintain, **130:61.**
Municipal cultivation, **130:54, 130:57.**
Reports of shellfish planted, **130:65.**
Survey and plan of territory covered by license, **130:61.**
Transfer or renewal of licenses, **130:58.**
Exclusive rights of transferee, **130:63.**

SHELLFISH —Cont'd
Private shellfish grants —Cont'd
Transfer or renewal of licenses —Cont'd
Forms, **130:62.**
Hearing, **130:60.**
Records, **130:62.**
Trespass, **130:63.**
Unauthorized taking of shellfish, penalty, **130:67, 130:68.**
Use of grounds or beds without consent of licensee, **130:67.**
Propagation.
Biologist's advice and opinion, **130:20.**
Cooperation with Federal Government or private institution, **130:20.**
Expenditure of funds, **130:20.**
License, **130:57.**
Municipality, **130:54, 130:56.**
Purification plants, **130:76, 130:77.**
Acquisition, **130:76.**
Appropriations, **130:76.**
Approval, **130:76.**
Construction of new plants, **130:76.**
Cooperation with Federal Government and private institutions, **130:20.**
Environmental Protection Department, **130:76.**
Existing plants, authority to maintain, **130:76.**
Fisheries, wildlife, and recreational vehicles department's powers and duties with respect, **130:76, 130:77.**
Investigations by directors, **130:20.**
Maintenance and operation, **130:76.**
Municipal appropriations, **130:76.**
Permits for taking shellfish from contaminated areas, **130:75.**
Petition of local authorities, **130:76.**
Report of director of marine fisheries, **130:76.**
Revocation of approval, **130:76.**
Service charges, **130:77.**
Tagging of shellfish proceeding, **130:82.**
Quahaugs.
See QUAHAUGS.
Records.
Reports and returns. See within this heading, "Reports and returns."

535

SHELLFISH —Cont'd
Renewal of license.
Private shellfish grants. See within this heading, "Private shellfish grants."
Reports and returns.
Contaminated areas, **130:74A.**
Director of marine fisheries, reports, **130:76.**
Shellfish planted, **130:65.**
Sales.
Adulterated or contaminated shellfish, defense against charge of selling, **94:194A.**
Common carrier, **135:5.**
Dealers. See within this heading, "Dealers."
Weight, requirement as to sales, **94:88B, 94:92B.**
Wholesalers, exemption from certification of fishermen and lobstermen selling, **130:80.**
Sanitary conditions of processing establishments and vessels used for transportation, regulations, **94:88C.**
Scallops.
See SCALLOPS.
Seasons.
Municipal cultivation, **130:54.**
Scallops, **130:71, 130:73.**
Seed clams, quahaugs, or oysters, **130:69.**
Selectmen.
Alderman and selectmen. See within this heading, "Alderman and selectmen."
Service charges for use of shellfish purification facilities, **130:77.**
Sewage, pollution of waters, **130:25, 130:27.**
Shipping plant, dealer's certificate required, **130:80.**
Shucking plant, certificate required, **130:80.**
South Essex ocean sanctuary, activities permitted, **132A:16.**
Special statutes, **130:104.**
State program for matching city or town funds for shellfish propagation, **130:20A.**
Tagging.
Labels or tags. See within this heading, "Labels or tags."
Transfer or renewal of license.
Private shellfish grants. See within this heading, "Private shellfish grants."
Transportation.
Carriers. See within this heading, "Carriers."

SHELLFISH —Cont'd
Transportation —Cont'd
Certificate required, **130:80.**
Labels or tags required, **130:81, 130:82.**
Treble damages for pollution of waters, **130:27.**
Vessel or boat, penalty for fastening to marks or bounds, **130:66.**
Victuallers, labeling requirements, **130:82.**
Water pollution.
Pollution of waters. See within this heading, "Pollution of waters."
Weight, requirement as to sale, **94:88B, 94:92B.**
Winkles, disposition, **130:103.**
Work on nearby land, impact, **131:40.**

SHELTERED WORKSHOP PROGRAM.
Handicapped persons, employment, **6:78A.**

SHELTERS.
Animals.
See ANIMALS.
Constitution of Massachusetts, regulation of shelters in time of war or public emergency, **MA Const Amend Art 47.**
Defined, mandatory sterilization of shelter animals, **140:136A.**
Emergency temporary housing, **41:125, 44:8.**
Park shelters, **45:7.**
Welfare.
See HOUSING AND URBAN RENEWAL.

SHERBORN.
Burial place for prisoners, **125:17.**
Congressional district, **57:1.**
District court, **218:1.**
Medical examiner district, **38:1.**
Senatorial district, **57:3.**

SHERIFFS AND DEPUTIES, 37:1 et seq.
Abolition of county governments.
Rights and duties upon transfer, **34B:12.**
Employees, **34B:13, 34B:14.**
Absence or presence.
County commissioners. See within this heading, "County commissioners, attendance at meetings."
Negligence, survival of action, **228:1.**

SHERIFFS AND DEPUTIES —Cont'd
Accounting for fees and money received, **37:22, 262:8A.**
Actions by or against.
Bond of, actions, **97:8.**
Champerty prohibited, **220:8.**
Conversion of property, time to sue, **260:4.**
Local actions brought in wrong county issuance to sheriff in proper county, **235:15.**
Misconduct or negligence of deputies, time to sue, **260:3, 260:4.**
Recovery of fine, actions against sheriffs and deputies, **280:13.**
Service of writ, **37:15.**
Aid and assistance.
Power to require in criminal matters, **37:13.**
Summoning aid or assistance, penalty for refusal to aid, **268:24.**
Alcoholic liquors.
See ALCOHOLIC LIQUORS.
Animals.
Disease control, assistance of sheriff, **129:6.**
Disposal of old and infirm animals by sheriff, **133:1-133:4.**
Duty to prosecute offenses, **272:84.**
Annual reports, **127:10.**
Appeals court.
See APPEALS COURT.
Appointment.
Court officers, appointment by sheriffs, **221:70.**
Deputies, **37:3.**
Special sheriffs, **37:4.**
Armed forces' orders as to suppression of riots, **269:5.**
Arrest.
See ARREST.
Arrest on mesne process and supplementary proceedings, **224:23.**
Exemption of sheriff, **37:10.**
Fees of sheriff, **262:8.**
Assault and battery, **265:13D.**
Assistance.
Aid and assistance. See within this heading, "Aid and assistance."
Assistant chief deputy sheriffs, **221:71A.**
Attachment, sheriff as obligee on bond for release of property, **223:125.**

SHERIFFS AND DEPUTIES
—Cont'd
Attendance at meetings of county commissioners, **37:16, 262:16.**

Attendance on courts, **37:16.**

Compensation for court attendance, **221:75.**

Fees for court attendance, **262:22, 262:27.**

Attorney general relationship with sheriffs, **12:6A.**

Attorney, sheriff or deputy sheriff not to act, **221:45.**

Auctions and auctioneers.

Fees of sheriff or deputy serving as auctioneer, **262:8.**

Sheriffs as exempt from laws governing, **100:11.**

Bail.

See BAIL AND RECOGNIZANCE.

Bailments, service of notice of termination of lease of personalty, **231:85H.**

Banks, deposit of surplus cash, **35:22.**

Body executions against, forbidden, **37:10.**

Bonds and undertakings, **37:2.**

Actions, **37:8.**

Acts of deputies or jailers as covered, **37:2.**

Attachment, sheriff as obligee on bond for release of property, **223:125.**

Constable's bond, execution for costs against endorser, **41:93.**

Copies of, as evidence, **37:9.**

Death, removal or resignation of sheriff as affecting liability, **37:2.**

Fee for administration of oaths by sheriffs, deputy sheriffs, and constables, **262:8.**

Penalty for neglecting or refusing to give, **37:7.**

Premiums on bonds of deputy sheriffs in certain counties, payment, **221:77.**

Removal from office.

Breach of bond, removal from office, **37:2.**

Failure to give bond removal, **37:7.**

Special sheriffs, **37:4, 37:5.**

Who may sue, **37:8.**

Boston terminal corporation, arrest of person unlawfully riding on property, **160:220.**

Calling for assistance, **37:13.**

SHERIFFS AND DEPUTIES
—Cont'd
Capias from probate court, service by deputy sheriff, **215:34A.**

Capital cases, powers and duties with respect, **279:57 et seq.**

Certificates and certification.

Election of sheriff, issuance of certificate, **54:116.**

Party enrollment of candidate for, certificate, **53:48.**

Traveling expenses, certification as to use of conveyance, **262:19.**

Champerty prohibited, **220:8.**

Change of venue, transfer of custody of prisoner in case, **277:54.**

Chief deputy sheriffs, **221:71.**

Chief justice for administration and management, appointment of deputy sheriffs as court officers, **221:5.**

Chief justice of superior court's issuance of order to, for special sitting of criminal case jury, **212:21.**

Citations, service of copies, **37:12.**

Civil arrest, exemption, **37:10.**

Commercial driver license.

See UNIFORM OPERATION OF COMMERCIAL MOTOR VEHICLES.

Commitment, executing warrant, **279:38.**

Compensation.

Salaries and compensation. See within this heading, "Salaries and compensation."

Conditional sentence, execution of remainder, **279:10.**

Conduct of public officials.

Misconduct. See within this heading, "Misconduct."

Constables.

See CONSTABLES.

Constitution of Massachusetts.

Election of sheriff, **MA Const Amend Arts 14, 19.**

Plurality of offices regulated, **MA Const Part 2 Ch 6 Art 2; Amend Art 8.**

Conversion of property by, time to bring suit, **260:4.**

Correctional institutions.

See CORRECTIONAL INSTITUTIONS.

Counterfeit bills and coins, seizure, **267:30.**

SHERIFFS AND DEPUTIES
—Cont'd
County commissioners, attendance at meetings, **37:16.**

Sheriff's fee for attending meetings, **262:12.**

County personnel review board, sheriff as member, **35:51B.**

County prisons.

See COUNTY PRISONS.

County treasurer.

Accounting by sheriff for fees and moneys received, **37:22, 262:8A.**

Disqualified to serve as treasurer, sheriff, **35:1.**

Courts.

Attendance on courts. See within this heading, "Attendance on courts."

District courts. See within this heading, "District courts."

House of prostitution, court authorizing sheriff to enter, **272:9.**

Land court. See within this heading, "Land court."

Officers.

Appointment by sheriffs, **221:70.**

Number of deputies to serve as court officers, **221:69.**

Retirement of, sheriff's judgment, **32:66.**

Service of process and papers. See within this heading, "Service of process and papers."

Superior courts.

See SUPERIOR COURTS.

Supreme judicial court.

See SUPREME JUDICIAL COURT.

Criers, sheriffs to perform duties, **220:9.**

Criminal history systems board, membership, **6:168.**

Criminal justice committee, membership, **6:156.**

Criminal Justice Training Council, membership, **6:116.**

Cruelty to animals, duty to prosecute offenses, **272:84.**

Dead body, penalty for attachment, **272:70.**

Death.

Bonds, death of sheriff as affecting liability, **37:2.**

Capital cases, powers and duties with respect, **279:57 et seq.**

Election of sheriff, effect of death before beginning term of office, **54:145.**

SHERIFFS AND DEPUTIES
—Cont'd
Death —Cont'd
Status of jailer, superintendent or keeper of house of correction, status, **126:24.**
Warrants and processes delivered to successor, **127:7.**
Demands, service of copy, **37:12.**
Depositing surplus cash in banks, **35:22.**
Deputies, **37:3.**
Disability or disqualification.
Alcoholic beverages, furnishing prisoners, **268:29.**
County treasurer, disqualification to act, **35:1.**
Special sheriff to act, **37:4, 37:5.**
Diseased or sick persons, powers and duties, **111:96, 111:99-111:101.**
District courts.
Adjournment of court by sheriff, **218:42.**
Inquest, fees, **262:26.**
Service of writs, precepts or process, sheriff's fees, **262:8.**
Ejectment, fees for service of execution, **262:17.**
Election, **37:1, 54:159.**
Certificates and certification. See within this heading, "Certificates and certification."
Constables, report of election, **41:15.**
Death before beginning term of office, **54:145.**
Failure to elect sheriff, proceedings, **54:142.**
Nomination papers, number of signatures, **53:44.**
Party enrollment of candidate, certificate, **53:48.**
Record of votes, transmission, **54:112.**
State constitution, **MA Const Amend Arts 14, 19.**
Vacancy in office, election to fill, **54:142.**
Election examiners, member of board, **54:122.**
Election precepts, fees for service, **262:13.**
Eminent domain, execution of warrant for taking possession of property, **79:3.**
Escape.
Call for aid by sheriff, **37:13.**
Liability for fines of escaped persons, **280:12.**

SHERIFFS AND DEPUTIES
—Cont'd
Escape —Cont'd
Refusal to aid sheriff, **268:24.**
Exceptions.
Exemptions. See within this heading, "Exemptions."
Executions, **37:10, 235:23.**
Conditional sentence, execution of remainder, **279:10.**
Constable's bond, execution for costs against endorser, **41:93.**
Deputies, execution and return of process during vacancy in office of sheriff, **37:14.**
Ejectment, service of execution, **262:17.**
Eminent domain, execution of warrant for taking possession of property, **79:3.**
Fees, **262:8.**
Indemnification before leaving on personal property, right, **235:35.**
Local actions brought in wrong county, issuance to sheriff in proper county, **235:15.**
Money received on, liability for failure to turn over, **235:52.**
Sentences, execution of.
Sentence and punishment. See within this heading, "Sentence and punishment, execution."
Warrant of commitment, execution, **279:38.**
Exemptions.
Auctioneers, sheriffs as exempt from laws governing, **100:11.**
Civil arrest, exemption, **37:10.**
Jury service, exemption, **234:1.**
Uniform Securities Act, exemptions, **110A:402.**
Expenses.
Maintenance allowance, limitation, **37:17.**
Quarters and subsistence when acting as jail keeper, **37:17.**
Traveling expenses. See within this heading, "Traveling expenses."
Extra-county powers as to execution of mittimuses, **279:38.**
False claim as to identity, **268:33.**
Fees, **262:8-262:22.**
Accounting for fees, **37:22, 262:8A.**
Attachment cases, **262:8.**

SHERIFFS AND DEPUTIES
—Cont'd
Fees —Cont'd
Attendance as witness against juvenile offenders, **262:27.**
Auctioneer, fees of sheriff or deputy serving, **262:8.**
Bail, fees for taking, **262:8.**
Care and custody of property, **262:8.**
Charges for copies of process left or delivered, **262:11.**
Civil arrests, **262:8.**
Copies of writ or process, **262:11, 262:15.**
County commissioners' meetings, charges for attending, **262:12.**
Court attendance, **262:22.**
Criminal cases, **262:8, 262:21, 262:48.**
Extra compensation for meritorious service, **262:47.**
Itemization and oath to expenses, **262:47.**
Limitation where several processes served or prisoners conveyed, **262:48.**
Ejectment, fees for service of execution, **262:17.**
Election precepts, service, **262:13.**
Indorsement on writ, **262:19.**
Inquests by district courts, **262:26.**
Itemization, **262:18, 262:19.**
Judicial sales, fee for service of notice, **262:8.**
Land court.
Expenses of deputy, **185:11.**
Process, service, **262:16.**
Limitation where several process served or prisoners conveyed, **262:48.**
Militia called by sheriff, expense of service, **33:49.**
Nantucket county, **37:17.**
Oaths, fee for administration by sheriffs, deputy sheriffs, and constables, **262:8.**
Penalty for refusing or falsifying statement, **262:18, 262:19.**
Reciprocal Enforcement of Support Act, service of process, **262:8.**
Registration of land proceedings, **262:39.**
Replevin suits, **262:8.**
Salaried sheriffs, **262:50, 262:53A.**

SHERIFFS AND DEPUTIES
—Cont'd
Fees —Cont'd
Sale of property, **262:8.**
Schedule, **262:8.**
Searching for persons named in process, **262:20.**
Service of process, **262:8, 262:8A, 262:48.**
Specification of items, **262:18, 262:19.**
Subpoenas issued by general court, service, **262:8, 262:13.**
Supplementary process, **262:14.**
Traveling expenses, **37:21.**
Financing of judicial system, exemption as to sheriffs' offices, **29A:1.**
Fines and penalties.
Action for recovery of fine against sheriff, **280:13.**
Attachment of dead body, penalty, **272:70.**
Bonds, penalty for refusing or neglecting to give, **37:7.**
Fees, penalty for refusing or falsifying statement, **262:18, 262:19.**
Forfeitures. See within this heading, "Forfeitures."
Money received on execution, liability for failure to turn over, **235:52.**
Probation officer's payment, **279:1.**
Sentence and punishment. See within this heading, "Sentence and punishment, execution."
Suffering escape, liability to pay fines, **280:12.**
Summoning aid or assistance, penalty for refusal to aid, **268:24.**
Willfully delaying service of warrant, **268:22.**
Firearms, authority to carry, **147:8A.**
Forfeitures.
Failure to give bond, forfeiture, **37:7.**
Recognizances, liability for forfeited, **280:12, 280:13.**
Gaming.
Arrest without warrant, **271:2, 271:6.**
Houses, searches of gaming houses, **271:23.**
Gas and electric company employee prevented from entering premises, duty to accompany, **164:116.**

SHERIFFS AND DEPUTIES
—Cont'd
General court.
Fees, sheriffs serving subpoenas issued by court, **262:13.**
Manual of general court delivered to sheriff, **5:11.**
Hampden county, designation of chief deputy sheriff, **221:71.**
House of prostitution, court authorizing entry, **272:9.**
Humane society, complaint against persons injuring property, **266:133.**
Indemnification before levying on personal property, right, **235:35.**
Indictment for murder, service of copy on defendant, **277:65.**
Jails.
See CORRECTIONAL INSTITUTIONS.
Jury.
See JURY AND JURY TRIAL.
Land court.
Assignment of deputy to court, **185:13.**
Expenses of deputy, **185:11.**
Fees. See within this heading, "Fees."
Orders, precepts and processes issued by court, service, **185:25A, 262:16.**
Leaving copy of writ, fees, **262:11.**
Limitation of action for misconduct or negligence of deputies, **260:3, 260:4.**
Lockups accessible, **40:37.**
Maintenance allowance for, limiting, **37:17.**
Manual of General Court delivered, **5:11.**
Meetings of county commissioners.
County commissioners, attending at meetings of. See within this heading, "County commissioners, attendance at meetings."
Mesne process and supplementary proceedings.
Arrest on mesne process and supplementary proceedings. See within this heading, "Arrest on mesne process and supplementary proceedings."
Middlesex County, chief deputy sheriff, **221:71.**
Mileage allowance.
Traveling expenses. See within this heading, "Traveling expenses."

SHERIFFS AND DEPUTIES
—Cont'd
Militia called by, expense of service, **33:49.**
Misconduct.
Deputies, time to sue for misconduct or negligence, **260:3, 260:4.**
Survival of action, **228:1.**
Mittimuses, extra-county powers as to execution, **279:38.**
Money received.
Accounting, **37:22, 262:8A.**
Depositing surplus cash in banks, **35:22.**
Execution, liability for failure to turn over money received, **235:52.**
Motor vehicles.
Commercial driver license.
See UNIFORM OPERATION OF COMMERCIAL MOTOR VEHICLES.
Registration, enforcement of suspension for nonpayment of tax, **60A:2A.**
Uniform operation of commercial motor vehicles.
See UNIFORM OPERATION OF COMMERCIAL MOTOR VEHICLES.
Murder indictment, service of copy on defendant, **277:65.**
Nantucket County.
Salary and fees of sheriff, **37:17.**
Traveling expenses of sheriff, **37:21.**
Neglect of duty.
Bonds, penalty for refusing or neglecting to give, **37:7.**
Performance of duties under criminal process, neglect of or refusal, **268:20-268:25.**
Suppression of unlawful assembly, **269:3.**
Negligence.
Deputies, time to sue for negligence, **260:3, 260:4.**
Survival of action, **228:1.**
Nomination papers, number of signatures, **53:44.**
Nonsupport contempt proceedings, service of citation by deputy sheriff, **215:34A.**
Notice.
Judicial sales, fee for service of notice, **262:8.**
Laws enacted, notice of by Attorney General, **12:6A.**
Personal property, notice of termination of lease, **231:85H.**

SHERIFFS AND DEPUTIES
—Cont'd
Notice —Cont'd
Service of copies of notices, **37:12.**
Special jury for sitting for criminal business in superior court, notice, **212:21.**
Number of deputy sheriffs to serve as court officers, **221:69.**
Oaths, **37:2-37:4.**
Criminal cases, itemization and oath to expenses, **262:47.**
Official bond.
Bonds and undertakings. See within this heading, "Bonds and undertakings."
Pamphlet edition of session laws sent, **5:4.**
Penalties.
Fines and penalties. See within this heading, "Fines and penalties."
Personnel review board, sheriff as member, **35:51B.**
Political party enrollment of candidate for sheriff's office, certificate, **53:48.**
Posse.
See POSSE.
Poundage, **262:8.**
Precepts, sheriffs and deputies to serve, **37:11.**
Premiums on bonds of deputy sheriffs in certain counties, payment, **221:77.**
Presence.
Absence or presence. See within this heading, "Absence or presence."
Prisons.
See CORRECTIONAL INSTITUTIONS.
Probate court, service of copies, **215:34A.**
Probationers and parolees, deputizing probation officers of other state for supervision, **127:151H.**
Process.
Service of process and papers. See within this heading, "Service of process and papers."
Province lands, enforcement of regulations, **91:27.**
Punishment.
Sentence and punishment. See within this heading, "Sentence and punishment, execution."

SHERIFFS AND DEPUTIES
—Cont'd
Qualification.
Disability or disqualification. See within this heading, "Disability or disqualification."
Quarters and subsistence where acting as jail keeper, **37:17.**
Railroads, arrest of persons riding unlawfully, **160:220.**
Reciprocal Enforcement of Support Act, fees for service of process, **262:8.**
Recognizances, forfeited, liability, **280:12, 280:13.**
Records, reports, and returns.
Annual reports, **127:10.**
Civil process, deputies to account for fees received for service, **262:8A.**
Constables, report of election, **41:15.**
County prison inmates, report concerning, **126:12.**
Registry of deeds, sheriff's fee for depositing copies, **262:8.**
Votes for sheriff, transmission of record, **54:112.**
Refusals.
Aid, penalty for refusal or neglect, **268:24.**
Bonds, penalty for refusal or neglect to give, **37:7.**
Removal.
Bonds and undertakings. See within this heading, "Bonds and undertakings."
Failure to pay judgment, **37:10.**
Intoxicants, **127:14.**
Resignation. See within this heading, "Resignation."
Service of writs and process after, **37:14.**
Unsatisfied execution on judgment against sheriff, **37:10.**
Resignation.
Prisoner to be delivered to successor, **126:23.**
Warrants, official papers to be delivered to successor, **127:7.**
Retirement and pensions of certain court officers, duty with respect, **32:66.**
Returns of service.
After going out of office, **37:14.**
Mail or express, return, **262:9.**
Riots and mobs.
Unlawful assemblies. See within this heading, "Unlawful assemblies, suppression."

SHERIFFS AND DEPUTIES
—Cont'd
Salaries and compensation, **37:17.**
Attendance on courts. See within this heading, "Attendance on courts."
Criminal cases, extra compensation for meritorious service, **262:47.**
Deputies, **262:50, 262:53A.**
Double pay, officers not to draw, **221:81.**
Expenses. See within this heading, "Expenses."
Payment by Commonwealth, **37:21A.**
Special sheriffs, **37:5.**
Sales.
Auctions and auctioneers. See within this heading, "Auctions and auctioneers."
Seized property, **276:7, 276:8.**
Tax sales. See within this heading, "Tax sales."
Search for person, fees, **262:20.**
Search warrants.
Duties, **276:2.**
Gaming, arrest without warrant, **272:2, 272:6.**
Sale of property, seized, **276:7, 276:8.**
Sentence and punishment, execution, **279:34.**
Conditional sentences, execution of remainder, **279:10.**
Service of process and papers, **220:7.**
Accounting for fees received by deputy sheriffs, time, **37:22, 262:8A.**
Arrest on mesne process and supplementary proceedings. See within this heading, "Arrest on mesne process and supplementary proceedings."
Authority to serve papers not required to be served by an officer, **37:12.**
Bailment, service of notice of termination, **231:85H.**
Citations, service of copies, **37:12.**
Copies of process, fees, **262:11, 262:15.**
Criminal cases.
Fees. See within this heading, "Fees."
Demands not requiring service by officer, sheriff may serve, **37:12.**

SHERIFFS AND DEPUTIES
—Cont'd
Service of process and papers
—Cont'd

District courts, **262:8.**

Ejectment, fees for service of execution, **262:17.**

Indictment for murder, service of copy on defendant, **277:65.**

Indorsement on writ, fee, **262:19.**

Interest as inhabitant of political subdivision, **37:11.**

Land court, service of orders, precepts, and processes issued, **185:25A, 262:16.**

Nonsupport contempt proceedings, service of citation by deputy sheriff, **215:34A.**

Powers of sheriffs, **37:11, 37:12.**

Precepts, service, **37:11.**

Probate court, service by deputy of copies, **215:34A.**

Reciprocal Enforcement of Support Act, fee for service, **262:8.**

Removal or vacancy in office, **37:14.**

Returns of service. See within this heading, "Returns of service."

Search for person named in process, fee, **262:20.**

Subpoena, fee for serving, **262:8, 262:13.**

Supplementary process, **262:14.**

Traveling expenses, **262:8-262:21, 262:48.**

Vacancy in sheriff's office as affecting return of process, **37:14.**

Willful delay in service of warrant, **268:22.**

Writ for or against sheriffs and deputies, service, **37:15.**

Signatures, number on nomination papers, **53:44.**

Special election upon failure to elect or vacancies, **54:142.**

Special sheriffs, **37:4, 37:5.**

Appointment and qualification, **37:4.**

Duties, **37:5.**

How paid, **37:5.**

Oath, **37:4.**

Powers, **37:4.**

Vacancies in office, special sheriff to act, **37:5.**

State treasurer.

Bonds of sheriffs, furnishing copies, **37:9.**

SHERIFFS AND DEPUTIES
—Cont'd
State treasurer —Cont'd

Warrants of treasurer, sheriffs' fees of disbursing, **262:8.**

Statutes distributed, **5:3, 5:4.**

Subpoena, fee for serving, **262:8, 262:13.**

Successor in office.

Jails, delivery of prisoners, **126:23, 126:24.**

Warrants and processes delivered, **127:7.**

Suffolk county.

See SUFFOLK COUNTY.

Summoning aid or assistance, penalty for refusal to aid, **268:24.**

Superior court.

See SUPERIOR COURTS.

Supplementary proceedings.

Arrest on mesne process and supplementary proceedings. See within this heading, "Arrest on mesne process and supplementary proceedings."

Supreme judicial court.

See SUPREME JUDICIAL COURT.

Surplus funds in hands of, deposit, **35:22.**

Survival of action for misconduct or negligence, **228:1.**

Tax collectors.

See TAX COLLECTORS.

Tax sales.

Fees of sheriff, **60:89.**

Tax collector, sheriff, **60:88, 60:89.**

Term of office, **37:1, 54:159.**

Transportation of prisoners.

See CORRECTIONAL INSTITUTIONS.

Traveling expenses, **37:21.**

Certification as to use of conveyance, **262:19.**

Criminal cases, **262:21, 262:48.**

Deputy sheriff, fees for attendance of meetings of county commissioners, **262:12.**

Payment by Commonwealth, **37:21A.**

Return of process by mail or express, **262:9.**

Salaried officers, **262:50.**

Service of process, **262:8-262:21, 262:48.**

Use or hiring of conveyance, **262:19.**

SHERIFFS AND DEPUTIES
—Cont'd

Trespass, arrest, **266:120, 266:131.**

Uniform operation of commercial motor vehicles.

See UNIFORM OPERATION OF COMMERCIAL MOTOR VEHICLES.

Uniform Securities Act, exemptions, **110A:402.**

Uniforms to be worn, **221:80.**

Unlawful assemblies, suppression, **269:1-269:6.**

Armed forces' orders, **269:5.**

Neglect of duty, **269:3.**

Vacancies in office.

Deputies may execute process during, **37:14.**

How filled, **54:142.**

Special sheriff to act, **27:5.**

Venue, transfer of custody of prisoner in case of change, **277:54.**

Wages.

Salaries and compensation. See within this heading, "Salaries and compensation."

Weapons, authority to carry, **147:8A.**

Willfully delaying service of warrant, penalty, **268:22.**

SHIFTING USES.
Contingent remainders taking effect in manner, **184:3.**

SHINERS.
Enclosing waters for artificial propagation, **131:47.**

SHIPMASTERS.
Births and deaths, duty to report, **46:7, 46:8.**

Fraudulent conversion or embezzlement of property by captain of vessel, **266:32.**

Railroad drawbridge, duties in passing through, **160:122.**

Workers' compensation, **152:1.**

SHIPMENT OF GOODS.
See CARRIERS.

SHIP MORTGAGE ACT.
Exclusion from secured transactions article of security interest subject, **106:9-104.**

SHIPPING BASKETS.
Bakery products, requirements, **94:2.**

SHIPS AND OTHER WATERCRAFT.
Abandonment.

Motorboat, **90B:3.**

Unfloatable vessels, **91:49.**

SHIPS AND OTHER WATERCRAFT —Cont'd

Abatement of excise tax, **60B:2.**
　Excuse for failure to file returns for ships in interstate or foreign trade, **59:8.**
Accident reports as evidence, **90B:9.**
Accidents, **91:38 et seq.**
　See SHIPWRECKS.
Admiralty.
　See ADMIRALTY.
Affidavits.
　Attachment of ship, affidavit, **223:44.**
　False affidavit used to defraud ship's insurer, **266:111.**
Alcoholic liquors.
　See ALCOHOLIC LIQUORS.
Amount of excise tax in lieu of local tax, **60B:2.**
Anchoring vessel.
　See ANCHORING VESSEL.
Annual inspection of marks on vessels transporting stone, gravel or sand, **102:11.**
Arson, **266:2, 266:5.**
　To defraud owner or insurer, **266:108, 266:109.**
Attachment of property, **223:43, 223:44.**
　Affidavit, **223:44.**
　Lien, attachment to enforce, **255:17.**
Baggage of seaman, unlawful holding, **102:2.**
Barges.
　See BARGES.
Beacons.
　See BEACONS.
Bilge water, discharging, **91:59.**
Bills of lading, **106:7-101 to 106:7-105, 106:7-301 to 106:7-603, 108:42 et seq.**
　See BILLS OF LADING.
Births, duty of master to report, **46:7, 46:8.**
Boarding vessel without permission, **102:1, 102:1A, 102:3.**
Board of assessors, duties, **60B:4.**
Bonds and undertakings.
　Dismantling of unfloatable vessels, **91:47.**
　Pilots of vessels, **103:6.**
　　Discharge of surety, **103:15.**
　　New bond, **103:15, 103:16.**
　Vessels receiving or discharging petroleum products, **21:50B.**
Boston may incur debt to acquire boats, **44:7.**

SHIPS AND OTHER WATERCRAFT —Cont'd

Breaking and entering, **218:26, 266:16 et seq.**
Bridges, passing under or through, **85:26 et seq.**
Building as including ship as to certain crimes, **271:1A.**
Buoys.
　See BUOYS.
Burden of proof.
　Presumptions and burden of proof. See within this heading, "Presumptions and burden of proof."
Burning.
　Fires and fire prevention. See within this heading, "Fires and fire prevention."
Canals, **88:9 et seq.**
Canoes.
　See CANOES, KAYAKS, ETC.
Captains.
　See SHIPMASTERS.
Cargo.
　Bills of lading, **106:7-101 to 106:7-105, 106:7-301 to 106:7-603, 108:42 et seq.**
　　See BILLS OF LADING.
　Fraud, **88:9, 88:10, 266:110.**
　Sale of unclaimed good, **135:6.**
Charles River basin, **92:72 et seq.**
Charles River dam, **92:70, 92:71.**
Chattel paper, shipping contract or charter, **106:9-105.**
Cities and towns.
　Drawbridge regulations, **85:26.**
　Excise tax in lieu of local tax. See within this heading, "Excise tax in lieu of local tax."
　Insurance on, appropriations, **40:5.**
　Lien on vessel, filing statement for lien with city or town clerk, **255:15.**
　Lighters, regulation of marking and weighing, **102:14.**
　Municipal finance.
　　Excise tax in lieu of local tax. See within this heading, "Excise tax in lieu of local tax."
　Nautical schools, appropriations for establishment, **74:52.**
　Park district, boating, **92:41.**
　Powers of town health authorities, **111:122.**
　Weighing of vessels carrying stone, **102:10.**
Clearance of vessels from or to one state, **US Const Art 1 Sec 9 cl 6.**

SHIPS AND OTHER WATERCRAFT —Cont'd

Coal tar, defacing vessels, **266:103.**
Collector of taxes, duties, **60B:4.**
Colleges and universities.
　Intercollegiate sailing programs, exemption from requirements as to life saving devices of vessels used, **90B:5A.**
　Massachusetts Maritime Academy, duties of state college board of trustees, **73:1.**
Commercial fishing vessels.
　See MARINE FISH AND FISHERIES.
Commercial vessels, stationing to public commercial dock, **91:10C.**
Commuter passenger service vessels, sales tax exemption, **64H:6.**
Consent, boarding vessel without, **102:1, 102:1A, 102:3.**
Constitution of the United States.
　See CONSTITUTION OF THE UNITED STATES.
Construction contracts.
　See CONSTRUCTION CONTRACTS AND WORK.
Corporations.
　See CORPORATIONS.
County commissioners, powers of regulating use of drawbridges, **85:26.**
Credit unions, loans, **171:62.**
Crimes.
　Offenses and penalties. See within this heading, "Offenses and penalties."
Dealers, **90:5, 90B:3.**
Death, **32:94B, 46:7, 46:8.**
Deceit.
　Fraud and deceit. See within this heading, "Fraud and deceit."
Delivery ex-ship, seller's duty to discharge liens, **106:2-322.**
Destruction.
　Restitution, penalty for destruction of ship, **266:108.**
　Riots, destruction during, **269:7, 269:8.**
　Shipwrecks, **91:38 et seq.**
　　See SHIPWRECKS.
　To defraud owner or insurer, **266:108.**
　Unfloatable vessels, dismantling, **91:46 et seq.**
Discharges from vessels into waters, **21:27, 91:59.**

SHIPS AND OTHER WATERCRAFT —Cont'd

Dismantling of unfloatable vessels, **91:46 et seq.**

Distribution of lien sale proceeds to persons providing storage, **255:20.**

Docks and piers, **88:14 et seq.** See WHARVES, PIERS, AND DOCKS.

Drawbridges, ships passing through, **85:26 et seq.**

Dredging operations and dumping of material in tidewaters, **91:52 et seq.**

Dumping articles likely to obstruct navigation, **102:17.**

Economic diversification program, ship and boat building as defense-related commercial activity, **23F:1.**

Embezzlement by masters, **266:32.**

Employment security. See EMPLOYMENT SECURITY.

Encumbrances. Liens. See within this heading, "Liens."

Environmental affairs executive office, duties of law enforcement division, **90B:12.**

Equipment. Taxation. See within this heading, "Taxation."

Ernestina commission, **6:182A et seq.**

Evidence. Accident reports, **90B:9.** Presumptions and burden of proof. See within this heading, "Presumptions and burden of proof." Steamboats. See STEAMBOATS AND STEAMBOAT COMPANIES.

Exceptions. Exemptions and exceptions. See within this heading, "Exemptions and exceptions."

Excise tax in lieu of local tax, **60B:2.** Abatement of excise tax, **59:8, 60B:2.** Amount of tax, **60B:2.** Assessors, board of, assessment or abatement of tax, **60B:2, 60B:4.** Boat list transmitted to marine and educational vehicle director, **60B:6.**

SHIPS AND OTHER WATERCRAFT —Cont'd

Excise tax in lieu of local tax —Cont'd Cities and towns. Assessment of excise tax on vessels, **60B:2.** Payment of tax to municipal waterways improvement and maintenance fund, **60B:2.** Treasury, excise taxes paid into, **60B:2.** Vessels owned by, exemption from tax, **60B:3.** Collector of taxes, duties, **60B:4.** Commercial fishing vessels, **63:31A, 63:67.** See MARINE FISH AND FISHERIES. Exemptions. Local tax, exemption from upon payment of excise tax, **60B:2, 60B:3.** Public vessels exempt from excise tax, **60B:3.** Ferries, exemption from tax, **60B:3.** Habitually moored or docked, defined, **60B:1.** Interstate commerce, **59:8, 63:67.** Law enforcement vessels, exemption from tax, **60B:3.** Motor vehicle excise tax, administrative provisions as governing tax on vessels, **60B:5.** Oaths and affirmations, returns made, **60B:2.** Principally situated, defined, **60B:1.** Sales or transfers, abatement of tax upon sale of boat within designated time, **60B:2.** State vessels exempt from tax, **60B:3.** Tax returns, **60B:2.** Treasury of municipality, payment of excise tax into, **60B:2.** Valuation of vessels, **60B:2.** Vessel, defined, **60B:1.** Warrant for collection, issuance by board of assessors, **60B:4.**

Execution. Attachment of property. See within this heading, "Attachment of property." Exemption, **235:34.**

SHIPS AND OTHER WATERCRAFT —Cont'd

Exemptions and exceptions. Excise tax. See within this heading, "Excise tax in lieu of local tax."

Execution, exemption, **235:34.**

Intercollegiate sailing programs, exemption from lifesaving device requirements for vessels used, **90B:5A.**

Paraplegics, exception permitting carrying of firearms, **131:63.**

Sales and use taxes, exemption of fishing boats and equipment, **64H:6, 64I:7, 64M:6.**

Expectoration in or upon ship, **270:14, 270:15.**

Express business, steamboat lines engaging, **159:9.**

Ex-ship delivery, seller's duty to discharge liens, **106:2-322.**

False. Fraud and deceit. See within this heading, "Fraud and deceit."

Federal government. United States. See within this heading, "United States."

Ferries. See FERRIES.

Fines and penalties. Offenses and penalties. See within this heading, "Offenses and penalties."

Firearms, carrying loaded in boats, **131:63.**

Fires and fire prevention. Arson. See within this heading, "Arson." Boston, boats required, **44:7.** Entry for inspection or investigation, **148:1, 148:4.**

Fireworks, flares, and lanterns, **148:39, 148:44.**

Fish. See FISH AND GAME.

Fitting out with intent to destroy, **266:109.**

Foreign states and countries. Fish taken from state waters by foreign vessels, penalties, **130:99.** Nonstatutory liens on foreign vessels, **255:22.** Salvaging corporations, **91:50, 91:51.** Taxation of vessels engaged in foreign trade, **59:8, 63:67.**

SHIPS AND OTHER WATERCRAFT —Cont'd

Fraud and deceit.
Canals, false reports as to cargo on boat, **88:9, 88:10.**
Cargo on vessel, **266:110.**
Conversion of property by ship captain, **266:32.**
Fitting out vessel with intent to defraud insurer, **266:109.**
Fraud in connection with cargo, **266:108 et seq.**
Invoice of cargo of vessel to defraud insurer, **266:110.**
Owner or insurer, fraud and deceit against, **266:108 et seq.**
Pilots of vessels, false return as to fees, **103:5.**
Protest or affidavit of masters, **266:111.**

Freight.
Cargo. See within this heading, "Cargo."
Gasoline and motor fuel taxes, **64A:7, 64A:13.**

Gravel.
Marks on vessels. See within this heading, "Marks on vessels transporting stone, gravel or sand."

Great ponds, regulation of boating, **131:45.**
Grounding of unfloatable vessels, **91:49.**
Habitually moored or docked, defined, **60B:1.**

Harbor masters.
See HARBOR MASTERS.

Harbors.
See PORTS AND HARBORS.
Hazardous waste site cleanup professionals, entry for purposes of investigation, **21A:19E.**

Health.
Death, notice, **46:7, 46:8.**
Examination, **111:122.**
Food fish, **94:88C.**
"House" as including ship as to certain crimes, **271:1A.**
Houseboats, waste discharge, **21:27.**
Humane society, pilots to make complaint against persons injuring property, **266:133.**
Incineration of refuse prohibited aboard vessels in ocean sanctuaries, **132A:15.**
Inflammable fluids in motorboat tanks, **148:23.**

SHIPS AND OTHER WATERCRAFT —Cont'd

Insurance.
See MARINE INSURANCE.
Intercollegiate sailing programs, exemption from requirements as to life saving devices of vessels used, **90B:5A.**

Interference.
Obstructions. See within this heading, "Obstructions."
Interstate commerce, excise tax on vessels, **59:8, 63:67.**
Jurisdiction of telecommunications and energy department, **159:12.**

Kayaks.
See CANOES, KAYAKS, ETC.
Lakes, regulation of boating, **131:45.**

Larceny and theft.
Boats, taking, **266:63.**
Fraudulent conversion of property by captain, **266:32.**
Stealing from vessels, **266:20.**
Law enforcement vessels, exemption from excise tax, **60B:3.**

Licenses and permits.
Dismantling floating structures, **91:46, 91:46A, 91:47.**
Dredging operations and dumping of material in tidewaters, **91:52 et seq.**
Foreign salvaging or wrecking corporations, **91:50, 91:51.**
Grounding, burden of proof of permit, **91:49.**
Lumber, unloading, **102:2.**
Marina, license to operate, **91:59B.**
Pilots of vessels, fines or penalties for acting without license, **103:35.**
Terminals used for loading or discharge of petroleum products from vessels, licensing, **21:50.**

Liens.
Attachment of property to enforce lien, **255:17.**
Distribution of lien sale proceeds to person providing storage, **255:20.**
Ex-ship delivery, seller's duty to discharge liens, **106:2-322.**
Fee for recording, **262:34.**
Filing statement of demand for lien, **255:15.**
Mortgage act, **106:9-104.**
Pilotage fees for vessels, **103:17.**

SHIPS AND OTHER WATERCRAFT —Cont'd

Liens —Cont'd
Preferred status of liens on vessels 40 feet or less in length, **255:14A.**
Repairs and supplies. See within this heading, "Repairs and supplies, liens."

Lifeboats.
See LIFEBOATS.
Lifesaving devices, **90B:5, 90B:5A, 90B:11, 90B:14.**

Lists.
Registered owners of boats moored or docked in municipalities, information, **90B:11.**
Transfer of list to marine and recreational vehicle director, **60B:6.**

Livery boats.
See LIVERY BOATS.
Loans, credit unions, **171:62.**
Lobsters, marking of boats used for taking, **130:38A.**

Longshore.
See LONGSHORE AND WATERFRONT EMPLOYMENT.
Lumber, permit to unload, **102:22.**

Machinery and equipment.
Taxation. See within this heading, "Taxation."

Marinas.
See MARINAS.

Marine fish.
See MARINE FISH AND FISHERIES.

Marine insurance.
See MARINE INSURANCE.
Maritime Academy, duties of state college board of trustees, **73:1.**
Marks on vessels transporting stone, gravel or sand, **102:7.**
Annual examination, **102:11.**
Penalties, **102:13.**

Masters.
Harbor masters.
See HARBOR MASTERS.
Shipmasters.
See SHIPMASTERS.
Metropolitan park districts, boating, **92:41.**
Minor, employment as fireman or engineer, **149:62, 149:78.**

Misrepresentation.
Fraud and deceit. See within this heading, "Fraud and deceit."
Mistake or inaccuracy in lien statement as to repairs or supplies, **255:16.**

SHIPS AND OTHER WATERCRAFT —Cont'd

Mooring.
See MOORING.
Mortgage act, **106:9-104.**
Motorboats, **90B:1 et seq.**
See MOTORBOATS.
Motor vehicle excise tax administrative provisions as governing tax imposed on vessels, **60B:5.**
Municipalities.
Cities and towns. See within this heading, "Cities and towns."
Naval vessels, transfer of ships to U.S.S. Massachusetts Memorial Committee, Inc for use as memorial to veterans of armed forces, **6:124A.**
Noxious substances, damaging ship, **266:103.**
Oaths and affirmations.
Affidavits. See within this heading, "Affidavits."
Tax returns made, **60B:2.**
Obstructions.
Drawbridges, penalty for obstructing, **85:26.**
Dumping articles likely to obstruct navigation, **102:17.**
Notice to remove vessel obstructing harbor or waterway, **91:40.**
Ocean cruises.
See OCEAN CRUISES.
Ocean sanctuaries, incineration of refuse prohibited on vessels within, **132A:15.**
Offenses and penalties.
Baggage of seaman, holding, **102:2.**
Boarding or remaining on vessel without leave, **102:1, 102:1A, 102:3.**
Breaking and entering, **266:16 et seq.**
Building as including ship as to certain crimes, **271:1A.**
Coal tar, injuring vessel, **266:103.**
Conduct of persons aboard during weighing and marking, **102:10.**
Destroying to defraud owner or insurer, **266:108 et seq.**
Discharging oil or bilge water, **21:27, 91:59.**
Dumping objects tending to obstruct navigation, **102:17.**
Embezzlement by captain of vessel, **266:32.**

SHIPS AND OTHER WATERCRAFT —Cont'd

Offenses and penalties —Cont'd
Failure to obtain license to break up, **91:46A.**
Fitting out with intent to destroy, **266:109.**
Fraud and deceit. See within this heading, "Fraud and deceit."
Grounding or abandoning vessels, **91:49.**
"House" as including ship as to certain crimes, **271:1A.**
Landing places, violations as to use, **88:19.**
Master, false protest or affidavit, **266:111.**
Mooring to buoy, beacon, etc., **266:135.**
Motorboats, **90B:2, 90B:4A, 90B:4B, 90B:12, 90B:14.**
Noxious substances, injury, **266:103.**
Petroleum products, receiving or unloading without furnishing bond or a natural security, **21:50B.**
Pilots of vessels.
See PILOTS OF VESSELS.
"Place" as including ship as to certain crimes, **271:1A.**
Public policy, crimes against, **271:1A.**
Restitution, penalty for destruction of ship, **266:108.**
Riots, destruction during, **269:7, 269:8.**
Spitting on ship, **270:14, 270:15.**
Steamboats.
See STEAMBOATS AND STEAMBOAT COMPANIES.
Tar, injury to vessel, **266:103.**
Trespassing, **266:120.**
Unauthorized use of boats, **266:63.**
Unlawful entry, placing person therein in fear, **266:17, 266:18.**
Unlicensed foreign salvage or wrecking corporation, **91:50, 91:51.**
Vitriol, injuring ship, **266:103.**
Weighing and marking violations, **102:10, 102:13, 102:14.**
Oil, pollution of waters by.
See WATER POLLUTION.
Paraplegics, exception permitting carrying of firearms, **131:63.**

SHIPS AND OTHER WATERCRAFT —Cont'd

Partnership interests, taxation, **59:8, 59:18.**
Penal institutions, illicit conveyance of articles to or, **268:31.**
Penalties.
Offenses and penalties. See within this heading, "Offenses and penalties."
Permits.
Licenses and permits. See within this heading, "Licenses and permits."
Personal flotation devices acceptable on boats, **90B:1, 90B:5.**
Piers, **88:14 et seq.**
See WHARVES, PIERS, AND DOCKS.
Pilots of vessels.
See PILOTS OF VESSELS.
"Place" as including ship as to certain crimes, **271:1A.**
Police.
Excise taxes, law enforcement vessels exempt, **60B:3.**
Steamboat police, **159:92 et seq.**
See STEAMBOATS AND STEAMBOAT COMPANIES.
Pollution by.
See WATER POLLUTION.
Ports.
See PORTS AND HARBORS.
Presumptions and burden of proof.
Grounding, burden of proof of permit, **91:49.**
Motorboats, burden of proof in prosecution as to numbering, **90B:2.**
Principally situated, defined, **60B:1.**
Public policy, crimes against, **271:1A.**
Public works department, dismantling unfloatable vessels, **91:48.**
Pyrotechnic signals or fireworks, **148:39, 148:44.**
Quabbin watershed advisory committee, advice regarding boating and other recreational activities, **92:114.**
Reclamation districts may provide insurance coverage for vessels, **252:6A.**
Records.
Accident reports as public records, **90B:9.**

SHIPS AND OTHER WATERCRAFT —Cont'd

Records —Cont'd
Division of motorboat records, **90B:3.**
Remaining on vessel without leave, **102:1.**
Removal of vessel obstructing harbor or waterway, notice to require, **91:40.**
Rental of boats.
See LIVERY BOATS.
Repairs and supplies, liens, **255:14 et seq.**
Attachment of vessel, **255:17.**
Claiming lien, **255:15.**
Enforcement, **255:17.**
Filing and recording, **255:15, 255:16.**
Foreign vessels, nonstatutory liens, **255:22.**
Inaccuracies in lien statement, **255:16.**
Marshaling claims, **255:20.**
Owner paying obligations of contractor or subcontractor, **255:21.**
Sale of vessel and distribution of proceeds, **255:20.**
Subcontractor's rights, **255:14.**
Venue for enforcement, **255:17.**
Reports of accidents as public records, **90B:9.**
Restitution, penalty for destruction of ship, **266:108.**
Riots, destruction during, **269:7, 269:8.**
Roll dams, warning signs in vicinity, **253:50A.**
Rowing clubs in Charles River Basin, **92:74A.**
Rules and regulations.
Fire insurance.
See INSURANCE RATES AND RATING ORGANIZATIONS.
Houseboats, waste discharge, **21:27.**
Marine and recreational vehicles director's authority, **90B:11.**
Sailing.
Exemption from requirements as to lifesaving devices aboard vessels used in intercollegiate sailing programs, **90B:5A.**
Racing committees, liability, **231:85R.**
Tort liability, **231:85V.**
Yachting corporations.
See YACHTING CORPORATIONS.

SHIPS AND OTHER WATERCRAFT —Cont'd

Sales.
Commercial Code, seller's duty under ex-ship delivery contract to discharge liens, **106:2-322.**
Excise tax, abatement, **60B:2.**
Motorboats.
See MOTORBOATS.
Obstruction of water, sale to cover expenses of removal, **91:43.**
Secured transactions. See within this heading, "Secured transactions."
Unclaimed goods, **135:6.**
Sales tax.
Casual sales, **64H:6.**
Commuter passenger service vessels, **64H:6.**
Exemptions, **64H:6.**
Motorboats, certification upon payment of use or sales tax, **64H:25A, 64I:26A.**
Trade-in of boat, sales tax, **64H:27A.**
Salvaging business, licenses required of foreign corporations, **91:50, 91:51.**
Sand and gravel.
Marks on vessels. See within this heading, "Marks on vessels transporting stone, gravel or sand."
Sanitary requirements for vessels used for transportation of food fish, regulations, **94:88C.**
Schools.
Colleges and universities. See within this heading, "Colleges and universities."
Scows, penalty for mooring to buoys, **266:135.**
Seamen.
See SEAMEN.
Search warrants, **130:9 et seq., 138:42, 276:1.**
Secured transactions, **106:9-104, 106:9-105.**
Liens. See within this heading, "Liens."
Shipwrecks, **91:38 et seq.**
See SHIPWRECKS.
South Essex ocean sanctuary, activities prohibited, **132A:15.**
State.
See STATE AND STATE DEPARTMENTS.
Steamboats.
See STEAMBOATS AND STEAMBOAT COMPANIES.

SHIPS AND OTHER WATERCRAFT —Cont'd

Steamship authority.
See STEAMSHIP AUTHORITY.
Stone.
Weighing of vessels transporting stone or other ballast. See within this heading, "Weights and measures."
Storage of vessels, distribution of lien sale proceeds to persons providing, **255:20.**
Sunday, boating activities permitted, **136:6.**
Supplies.
Repairs and supplies. See within this heading, "Repairs and supplies, liens."
Tar, injury to vessel, **266:103.**
Taxation, **59:4, 59:8.**
Assessment as personal property, **59:18.**
Board of assessors, duties, **60B:2.**
Collector of taxes, duties, **60B:4.**
Corporation's interest in vessel, taxation, **63:67.**
Equipment.
Assessments on, **59:4, 59:18.**
Commercial fishing equipment, exemption, **59:5.**
Excise tax in lieu of local tax, **60B:2 et seq.**
Fishing, ships engaged, **59:5, 59:8, 64H:6, 64I:7.**
Foreign trade, ships engaged, **59:8, 63:67.**
Gasoline and motor fuel taxes, **64A:7, 64A:13.**
Interstate commerce, ships engaged, **59:8, 63:7.**
Partnership interest, **59:8, 59:18.**
Returns, **59:8, 62C:12.**
Sales taxes, **64H:6, 64H:25A, 64H:27A, 64I:26A.**
Telecommunications and energy department, jurisdiction, **159:12.**
Terminals used for loading or discharge of petroleum products from vessels, licensing, **21:50.**
Theft.
Larceny and theft. See within this heading, "Larceny and theft."
Towns.
Cities and towns. See within this heading, "Cities and towns."

SHIPS AND OTHER WATERCRAFT —Cont'd

Trade-in of boat, sales tax, **64H:27A.**

Trailers for boats.
See TRAILERS AND SEMI-TRAILERS.

Treasury of municipality, payment of excise tax into, **60B:2.**

Trespass.
Criminal offense, **266:120.**
Notices, removal or defacing, **266:122.**

Unauthorized use, **266:63.**

Unemployment compensation.
See EMPLOYMENT SECURITY.

Unfloatable vessels.
Dismantling, **91:47.**
Grounding and abandonment, **91:49.**

United States.
Federal service personnel defined for purposes of absentee voting, **54:103B.**
Information on request, **90B:10.**
Motorboats, **90B:1 et seq.**
See MOTORBOATS.
Transfer of vessels to U.S.S. Massachusetts Memorial Committee, **6:124A.**
Vessel having valid marine document issued, **90B:1, 90B:2.**

Universities.
Colleges and universities. See within this heading, "Colleges and universities."

Unlawful entry, placing person lawfully therein in fear, **266:17, 266:18.**

Unsafe condition, operation of motorboat or vessel, **90B:12A.**

Valuation of vessels for purposes of excise tax, **60B:2.**

Vessel defined in motorboat law, **90B:5.**

Vitriol, injuring ship, **266:103.**

Wages due seamen not subject to trustee process, **246:32.**

Warrant for collection of excise taxes, issuance by board of assessors, **60B:4.**

Warships.
State not to keep without consent of Congress, **US Const Art 1 Sec 10 cl 3.**
Transfer of naval vessels to U.S.S. Massachusetts Memorial Committee for use as memorial to veterans of armed forces, **6:124A.**

SHIPS AND OTHER WATERCRAFT —Cont'd

Water pollution.
See WATER POLLUTION.

Watershed system advisory committee, advice regarding boating and other recreational activities, **92:115.**

Weights and measures.
Canal toll collector weighing load on boat, **88:11.**
Fish landed from vessel or boat, weighing, **94:86 et seq.**
Stone or other ballast, weighing of vessels transporting, **102:6 et seq.**
Deductions from tonnage, **102:9.**
Fees, **102:11, 102:12.**
Marks. See within this heading, "Marks on vessels transporting stone, gravel or sand."
Penalties, **102:13, 102:14.**
Persons on board during weighing, **102:10.**
Town ordinances, **102:14.**
Weighers.
Appointment, **102:6.**
Duties, **102:8.**
Fees, **102:12.**

Wharves, **88:14 et seq.**
See WHARVES, PIERS, AND DOCKS.

Workers' compensation, seamen as not eligible, **152:1.**

Wrecks, **91:38 et seq.**
See SHIPWRECKS.

Yachting corporations.
See YACHTING CORPORATIONS.

SHIPWRECKS, 91:38-91:49.

Abandoned or wrecked vessels and property.
Grounding vessels, scows, or the like, abandonment within harbor limits, **91:49.**
Removal, **91:39, 91:41, 91:43.**
Taking possession, **91:38.**
Unlicensed foreign salvage or wrecking operations, **91:50, 91:51.**

Application for Federal reimbursement, **91:45.**

Charles River basin, wrecks, **92:72, 92:73.**

Foreign salvage corporations, **91:50, 91:51.**

Harbor masters, report, **102:27.**

Insurer as liable for expense of removal, **91:44.**

SHIPWRECKS —Cont'd

Notice to owner of vessel, **91:40.**

Owner's liability for expense of removal, **91:42.**

Sale of vessel to pay cost of removal, **91:43.**

SHIRE TOWNS.

Costs as affected by fixing place of trial, **261:24.**

Place of trial at, fixing, **231:82.**

Registries of deeds, **36:1.**

SHIRLEY.

Congressional district, **57:1.**

District court, **218:1.**

Medical examiner district, **38:1.**

Senatorial district, **57:3.**

Squannacook and Nissitissit Rivers Sanctuary established, **132A:17.**

SHIRLEY INDUSTRIAL SCHOOL.

Compensation for property damaged by escaping inmates, **120:13A.**

Control by youth service division, **120:2.**

SHOCHTIM.

Humane slaughter of livestock according to ritual requirements of Jewish faith, **94:139C-94:139G.**

SHOCK TREATMENT.

Intensive care unit for women, electroconvulsive treatment not to be performed, **123:23.**

Mental health department.
Rights of patients, **123:23.**

Mental retardation.
Rights of residents, **123B:9.**

SHOES AND FOOTWEAR.

Bootblacks.
See BOOTBLACKS.

Fluoroscopic shoe-fitting machines, **111:186A.**

Imported goods, restrictions as to advertising or sale, **94:277B.**

Independent industrial shoe-making school of city of Lynn, **74:23.**

Municipalities authorized to purchase, **40:6B.**

Sales tax, exemptions, **64H:6.**

SHOOTING GALLERIES AND PRESERVES, 131:31.

Ammunition, sale, **148:39.**

Assault weapons.
Licenses.
Clubs with on-site shooting ranges or galleries, **140:131.**

SHOOTING GALLERIES AND PRESERVES —Cont'd

Birds, **131:65, 272:87.**

Buildings, discharge of firearms, **269:12E.**

Commercial shooting preserves, posting of notices, **131:31.**

Crossbows, **131:64.**

Damage or injury from sportsman's weapon, **131:60, 131:61.**

Intoxicating liquor or drugs, shooting under influence, **131:62.**

Licensing, **140:56A.**

Firearms licenses.

Clubs with on-site shooting ranges or galleries, **140:131.**

Militia.

See MILITIA.

Minor, issuance of sporting license, **131:14.**

Noise pollution, liability, **214:7B.**

Nuisances, liability for noise pollution, **214:7B.**

Public shooting grounds, **131:6.**

Rifles and shotguns, carrying on public way of loaded weapon, exceptions, **269:12D.**

Sunday, shooting at artificial targets, **131:57.**

Wounded migratory game birds from powerboat, shooting, **131:65.**

SHOP BILLS.

Engraving or printing bills or advertisements to resemble bank bills, **267:29.**

SHOPLIFTING.

Elements of crime and penalties therefor, **231:94B, 266:30A.**

Parents, liability, **231:85G.**

SHOP LIGHT.

Defined, **25B:1, 25B:2.**

SHOPPING CENTERS.

Architectural barriers against handicapped persons regulated, **22:13A.**

Municipal authority for establishment of shopping centers, plazas, or malls, **40:5.**

SHOPS.

See STORES AND MERCHANTS.

SHORE.

See COAST OR SHORE.

SHORING.

Excavations, requirement, **149:129A.**

SHORT FORM OF DEED ACT, 183:8 et seq.

See DEEDS AND CONVEYANCES.

SHORT HAUL RATES.

Regulation, **159:14.**

SHOTGUNS.

Bailments.

Sales and rental. See within this heading, "Sales and rental."

BB shot, regulations prescribing type and size, **131:66.**

Carrying.

Sawed-off shotgun, **269:10.**

Shotgun containing shells, on public way, **269:12D.**

Certificate by ballistics expert as prima facie evidence, **140:121A.**

Children or aliens, penalty for furnishing, **140:130.**

Discharge within certain distance of building, **269:12E.**

Failure to surrender shotgun, **269:10.**

Identification card, penalty for failure to comply with provisions, **140:128A.**

Leases.

Sales and rentals. See within this heading, "Sales and rentals."

Licenses and permits, **140:123, 140:131A.**

Offense committed while using a firearm, **265:18B.**

Permits.

Licenses and permits, **140:123, 140:131A.**

Possession.

Carrying. See within this heading, "Carrying."

Restrictions, **140:129C.**

Sawed-off shotguns, **269:10.**

Public ways, carrying loaded shotgun, **269:12D.**

Purchasers or donees, reports involving, **140:128B.**

Recovery of stolen shotgun, notice, **140:129C.**

Rentals.

Sales and rentals. See within this heading, "Sales and rentals."

Reports and reporting.

Calendar year, **140:128A.**

Purchasers or donees, **140:128B.**

Sales and rentals.

Licenses, **140:123, 140:131A.**

Serial number requirements, **269:11E.**

SHOTGUNS —Cont'd

Sales and rentals —Cont'd

Unlicensed resident selling not more than four firearms within single year, sale, **140:128A.**

Sawed-off shotguns.

Regulation, **269:10.**

Search warrants, disposition of property seized, **276:3.**

Serial numbers, requirements in sales of shotguns, **269:10, 269:11E, 269:14.**

Surrender, **140:129D.**

Unlawful possession, penalties, **269:10.**

SHOW CAUSE.

Absentee's estates, notice of petition for receiver's appointment and disposal of property, **200:2.**

Contempt generally.

See CONTEMPT.

Contracts and agreements.

Motion as to damages upon further breach, **235:11.**

Declaratory judgments, **231A:5.**

Minimum wages.

Why name should not be published for nonobservance of wage rates, **151:11.**

Seized property, forfeiture, **276:4, 276:5.**

SHOWS, 140:181 et seq.

See AMUSEMENTS AND EXHIBITIONS.

SHREWSBURY.

Congressional district, **57:1.**

District court, **218:1.**

Medical examiner district, **38:1.**

Senatorial district, **57:3.**

SHRINE.

Grand Army of Republic, **8:16A.**

SHRINKAGE.

Imposition of risk upon seller under C.I.F. or C & F terms, **106:2-321.**

SHRUBS AND SHRUBBERY.

Appeals to commissioner of agriculture, **128:25, 128:26.**

Cutting or destroying on land of another, as criminal offense, **266:113.**

Inspections, **128:24.**

Nurseries and nursery stock, **128:17-128:21.**

See NURSERIES AND NURSERY STOCK.

SHRUBS AND SHRUBBERY
—Cont'd
Plants.
　See PLANTS AND PLANT
　　DISEASES AND PESTS.
Sale as nursery stock, **128:19.**
San Jose scale, protection against,
　128:24.
Seeds.
　See SEEDS.
Trespass to destroy or take away,
　penalty, **266:115.**

SHUCKING PLANTS.
Shellfish shucking plants, **130:80.**

SHURIKEN.
Dangerous weapons.
　Sale or manufacture, **269:12.**
　Unlawful possession, **269:10,**
　　269:12.

SHUTESBURY.
Medical examiner district, **38:1.**

SHUTOFF.
Gas and electric.
　See GAS AND ELECTRIC
　　COMPANIES.
Hot water tanks, **142:19.**
Waterworks.
　See WATERWORKS AND
　　WATER SUPPLY.

SHUTTLES.
Textile factories, **149:131, 149:132,**
　149:156.

SIBLINGS.
See BROTHERS AND SISTERS.

SIC CODE.
Toxics use reduction.
　Annual reports, **21I:10.**
　Identification code, **21I:2.**
　Use fee, **21I:19.**

SICK.
See DISEASE OR ILLNESS.

SICK BENEFITS.
Fraternal societies.
　See FRATERNAL BENEFIT
　　SOCIETIES.
Insurance.
　See ACCIDENT AND
　　SICKNESS INSURANCE.

SICK LEAVE.
Accumulation of sick leave by
　clerks of court, **218:79.**
Assistant clerks.
　Clerks and assistant clerks of
　　court. See within this
　　heading, "Clerks and
　　assistant clerks of court."

SICK LEAVE —Cont'd
Bodily injuries, rules as to public
　officers and employees, **7:28.**
Boston juvenile court temporary
　clerks, **218:9.**
Boston municipal court.
　Assistant clerk, **218:53.**
　Clerk, **218:53.**
　Justices, **218:50.**
Civil service, **31:37.**
Clerks and assistant clerks of
　court, **218:10, 218:53,**
　　218:53A.
　Accumulation of sick leave,
　　218:79.
　District court, **218:8-218:11,**
　　218:80.
　Municipal court, **218:53,**
　　218:53A.
District Court.
　Clerks, **218:8-218:11, 218:80.**
　Judges, **218:6.**
Extended illness leave bank for
　employees of executive branch,
　Spec L 23:4P.
Firemen, **41:111F.**
Grievances of state employees,
　30:53, 30:57.
Human resources division,
　regulation, **7:28.**
Indictment, effect of suspension of
　state employee while, **30:59.**
Judges and justices.
　District court, **218:6.**
　Municipal court, **218:50, 218:52.**
Municipal courts.
　Boston municipal court. See
　　within this heading, "Boston
　　municipal court."
　Clerks and assistant clerks,
　　218:53, 218:53A.
　Justice, **218:50, 218:52.**
Municipal employees, **40:21A.**
Non-permanent civil service
　appointees, continuation of
　group insurance for state
　employees during, **32A:2.**
Police, **41:111F.**
Public officers, **7:28, 40:21A.**
Public utilities.
　See TELECOMMUNICATIONS
　　AND ENERGY
　　DEPARTMENT.
Special education personnel in
　school department of certain
　institutions, **71B:12.**
State employees, **7:28.**
　Incumbents in certain
　　managerial positions,
　　eligibility, **30:46H.**
Temporary probation officers,
　276:89.

SICK LEAVE —Cont'd
Trial court of the Commonwealth,
　sick leave for justices, **211B:4.**
Tuberculosis, teachers or
　employees afflicted, **71:55B.**
Workers' compensation of public
　employees as affected, **7:28,**
　30:58, 152:69.

SICKLE CELL ANEMIA.
Testing, treatment, and care,
　76:15A, 76:15B.

SIDEWALKS.
Abutting owners.
　Removal of snow and ice,
　　85:5-85:7.
　Right to construct sidewalks,
　　85:4.
Appropriations by municipalities,
　44:7.
Architectural barriers against
　handicapped persons, **22:13A.**
Arrest for throwing filth or
　rubbish, **272:60.**
Assessments, **83:26.**
　Lien, **83:27, 83:29.**
　Provisions applicable, **83:28.**
　Recording of statements, **83:27.**
　Snow and ice removal, **85:6.**
　Tax abatements for
　　improvements to real estate,
　　59:38.
Barbed wire fences along,
　prohibited, **86:6.**
Bicycle operated, **85:11B.**
Cable television company's duty to
　repair, **166A:5.**
Complaint against town for
　negligent maintenance, **258:2**
　Form 5.
Consent required for obstructing
　or digging up, **83:25.**
Damage from defects, liability,
　81:18, 84:15, 84:21.
Digging up, consent required,
　83:25.
Disabled and handicapped
　persons, architectural barriers
　against, **22:13A.**
District for building and
　maintenance of, town may
　establish, **40:44.**
Driving upon.
　Riding or driving upon. See
　　within this heading, "Riding
　　or driving."
Establishment, **83:25.**
Fences of barbed wire along,
　prohibition against, **86:6.**
Filth or rubbish, arrest for
　throwing on sidewalks,
　272:60.

SIDEWALKS —Cont'd

Fines and penalties.
Barbed wire fences, erecting on sidewalk, **86:6.**
Filth or rubbish thrown on sidewalk, arrest, **272:60.**
Glass thrown on sidewalk, penalty, **265:32.**
Malicious destruction, **266:94.**
Riding or driving upon sidewalk, **85:4.**
Snow and ice, failure to remove, **85:5.**
Soliciting of merchandise on sidewalk, **93:40.**
Throwing glass on sidewalk, **265:32.**
Glass, penalty for throwing on sidewalks, **265:32.**
Grade, determination, **83:25.**
Handicapped persons, architectural barriers against, **22:13A.**
Highways of state.
State highways. See within this heading, "State highways, sidewalks along."
Housing and urban renewal projects.
Municipal construction in aid, **121B:23.**
Urban redevelopment corporations contracting with municipality for construction, **121A:14.**
Ice.
See SNOW AND ICE.
Indebtedness of city or town, **44:7.**
Laying out of footways, **82:33.**
Liability for damage from defects, **84:15.**
Lien of assessments, **83:27, 83:29.**
Littering, **272:60.**
Malicious destruction, **266:94.**
Materials used for construction, determination, **83:25.**
Notice to property owner of claim for damages by reason of defective condition, **84:21.**
Obstructions, consent required, **83:25.**
Owners abutting.
Abutting owners. See within this heading, "Abutting owners."
Park sidewalks in Boston, incurring indebtedness, **44:7.**
Pedestrian crosswalks, installation of slanted curbing, **83:25.**
Penalties.
Fines and penalties. See within this heading, "Fines and penalties."

SIDEWALKS —Cont'd

Planning or laying out of footways, **82:33.**
Reconstruction of existing sidewalks, **83:25.**
Recording of assessments, **83:27.**
Riding or driving, **85:4.**
Bicycles, **85:11B.**
Road commissioners, powers, **41:64.**
Snow removal.
See SNOW AND ICE.
Soliciting sale of merchandise, **93:40.**
Special assessments.
Assessments. See within this heading, "Assessments."
Spitting, **270:14, 270:15.**
State highways, sidewalks along.
Construction and maintenance, **81:20.**
Liability for injuries sustained, **81:18.**
Taxation.
Assessments. See within this heading, "Assessments."
Urban renewal projects.
Housing and urban renewal projects. See within this heading, "Housing and urban renewal projects."

SIDE YARD.

Tenant house law, **144:2, 145:2.**
Zoning requirements as to setbacks, exemptions, **40:6.**

SIDING.

Buildings, installation of siding capable of conducting electricity, **148:57.**

SIGHT.
See EYES.

SIGHT-SAVING MONTH.
Observance, **6:12W.**

SIGHT-SEEING BUSES.
Operation of, as within terms "charter service" or "special service" in Motor Carriers of Passenger Law, **159A:11A.**

SIGNALS.
See SIGNS AND SIGNALS.

SIGNATURES.
Absent voting by federal service personnel.
See ELECTIONS.
Accountants, restrictions on designation, **112:87D, 112:87D½.**
Admission of execution of document, demand, **231:69.**

SIGNATURES —Cont'd

Alcoholic liquor analysis, judicial notice of signature, **138:36.**
Answers to interrogatories, **231:62.**
Anticipation notes of state, **29:48, 29:48A.**
Application for commercial driver license application, **90F:7.**
Application for life insurance, **175:123.**
Apprentice agreement, **23:11J.**
Arbitration and award.
Collective bargaining agreements to arbitrate, signature on arbitrators' award, **150C:7.**
Commercial disputes, **251:8.**
Attested instrument, proof of signature, **233:68.**
Authentication of signature of officer attesting public records or documents, **233:76.**
Bank deposits.
See BANKS AND BANKING.
Births.
Alteration of copies of birth record, penalty, **46:30.**
Parent to sign copies of birth reports, **46:3A.**
Bonds and debentures.
Anticipation notes of state, **29:48, 29:48A.**
Central Massachusetts Economic Development Authority, **Spec L 22:10.**
Facsimile signatures on public obligations, **29:48A, 29:49A, 35:39H, 71:16.**
Water pollution abatement districts, treasurer and executive director to sign bonds, **21:35-21:37.**
Central Massachusetts Economic Development Authority, treasurer signing bonds or notes, **Spec L 22:10.**
Certificates and certification.
Commissioner to qualify public officers, certificate of signature, **222:5.**
Resale and exempt use certificates, **64H:8, 64I:8.**
State ballot law commission.
See STATE BALLOT LAW COMMISSION.
Stock certificates, **156B:27.**
Charities, signatures required on financial reports of public charities, **12:8F.**
Cities.
See CITIES AND TOWNS.

SIGNATURES —Cont'd

Clerks of court.
  See CLERKS OF COURT.
Collective bargaining agreements to arbitrate, signature of award by arbitrators, **150C:7.**
Commercial Code definitions, **106:1-201.**
Commercial driver license and application, **90F:7, 90F:8.**
Commissioner to qualify public officers, certificate of signature, **222:5.**
Complaints.
  Indictments, informations, and complaints. See within this heading, "Indictments, informations, and complaints."
Constitution of Massachusetts.
  See CONSTITUTION OF MASSACHUSETTS.
Contracts.
  Apprentice agreement, **23:11J.**
  Insurance adviser, contract, **175:177C.**
  On which required, **255D:9, 259:1.**
  Retail installment sales contract, buyer's signature, **255D:9.**
  Written renunciation or waiver of breach, **106:1-107.**
Copies.
  Birth reports, parent to sign copies, **46:3A.**
  Marriage, birth, or death records, penalty for altering, **46:30.**
Corporations.
  See CORPORATIONS.
Countersignatures.
  See COUNTERSIGNATURE.
County bonds or notes, signatures, **35:39I.**
Debentures.
  Bonds and debentures. See within this heading, "Bonds and debentures."
Deed, proof of execution, **183:35.**
Deed registers.
  Registers and registries of deeds. See within this heading, "Registers and registries of deeds."
Demand for admission of execution of document, **231:69.**
Denial of signature.
  See PLEAS AND ANSWERS.
Depositions, signature, **233:32.**
Drug analysts, judicial notice of signatures, **111:13.**

SIGNATURES —Cont'd

Elections.
  See ELECTIONS.
Employment security division, bond of persons signing checks, **23:9K.**
Engineers and surveyors.
  Disciplinary action in connection with use of signature, **112:81P.**
  Plans, specifications and reports, requirement, **112:81M.**
Estoppel.
  Waiver and estoppel. See within this heading, "Waiver and estoppel."
Evidence.
  See EVIDENCE.
Facsimile seals.
  See FACSIMILE SEALS AND SIGNATURES.
Federal service personnel, absent voting by.
  See ELECTIONS.
Food, application for license for sale through vending machines, **94:309.**
Foreign insurance companies.
  See FOREIGN INSURANCE COMPANIES.
Forgery.
  See FORGERY AND COUNTERFEITING.
Fraud and deceit, **266:31, 266:35.**
  See FRAUD AND DECEIT.
Garnishment.
  Trustee process. See within this heading, "Trustee process."
General court.
  Nomination papers for senate or house, **53:7, 53:44.**
  Senate and house clerks, facsimiles of signatures, **3:12A.**
Governor.
  Primary elections, number of signatures required for candidates, **53:44.**
  State bonds and notes, facsimile of signature, **29:48A.**
Habeas corpus.
  Return, **248:11.**
  Writ, **248:6.**
Highway defects, notice of injury, **84:19.**
Homestead, release, **188:7.**
Illegible signature on instrument presented for recording, printing or typing name, **36:18A.**

SIGNATURES —Cont'd

Indictments, informations, and complaints.
  Obtaining signature by false pretenses, **277:79.**
  Subscribing of complaint by complainant, **276:22.**
Indorsement.
  See INDORSEMENTS.
Initials.
  Accountancy, initials indicating practice, **112:87D, 112:87D½.**
  Nomination papers, **53:46.**
  Physical therapists, initials indicating practice, **112:23L.**
Initiative and referendum, **53:7, 53:22A, 56:11.**
  Collecting signatures within 150 feet from polling place, **54:65.**
  Constitution of Massachusetts. See CONSTITUTION OF MASSACHUSETTS.
  Penalty for signing illegally, **56:11.**
Insurance.
  See INSURANCE.
Interrogatories in connection with trustee process, **246:12.**
Investment securities under commercial code.
  See INVESTMENT SECURITIES UNDER COMMERCIAL CODE.
Judicial notice of signatures of chemical analysts, **111:13, 138:36.**
Jury trial waived by signing written waiver, **263:6.**
Justice of the peace or notary public to print or type name below signature, **222:8, 222:8A.**
Land court recorder, facsimile signature, **185:9.**
Letters of credit.
  Forged signature of beneficiary, **106:5-108.**
  Formal requirements, **106:5-104.**
  Successors of beneficiaries, **106:5-113.**
Life insurance application, **175:123.**
Mark, signature, **4:7.**
Medical assistance program vouchers, signature of vendor, **6:131G.**
Method of, when required by law, **4:7.**
Motor vehicles.
  See MOTOR VEHICLES.

SIGNATURES —Cont'd
Municipal finance.
  See MUNICIPAL FINANCE.
Negotiable instruments.
  See NEGOTIABLE
    INSTRUMENTS.
Nomination papers of candidate
  for election, **50:3A, 53:7,
  53:9A, 53:44, 53:46.**
Notary public to print or type
  name below signature, **222:8,
  222:8A.**
Physical therapists, initials
  indicating practice, **112:23L.**
Pleading.
  See PLEADING.
Pleas.
  See PLEAS AND ANSWERS.
Political advertisements and
  circulars, signatures or names,
  56:39-56:41.
Presidential primaries.
  See PRESIDENTIAL
    PRIMARIES.
Primary elections.
  See PRIMARY ELECTIONS.
Process.
  See PROCESS AND SERVICE
    OF PROCESS AND
    PAPERS.
Proof of signature to attested
  instrument, **233:68.**
Public authorities' reports,
  signatures required on copies
  deposited in state library,
  6:39A.
Public charities' financial reports,
  signatures required, **12:8F.**
Records, reports, and returns.
  Birth reports, parents to sign
    copies, **46:3A.**
  Copies. See within this heading,
    "Copies."
  Engineer or land surveyor,
    requirement as to signature
    on reports stamped with
    seal, **112:81M.**
  Financial reports of public
    charities, signatures
    required, **12:8F.**
  Habeas corpus, **248:11.**
  Illegible signature, printing
    name in case, **36:18A.**
  Marriage, death, or birth
    records, penalty for altering
    copies, **46:30.**
  Public records or documents,
    authentication of signature
    of officer attesting, **233:76.**
  State library, signatures
    required on copies of public
    authorities' reports
    deposited, **6:39A.**

SIGNATURES —Cont'd
Records, reports, and returns
  —Cont'd
  Tax returns, signatures
    required, **62C:15.**
Referendum petitions.
  Initiative and referendum. See
    within this heading,
    "Initiative and referendum."
Registers and registries of deeds.
  Illegible signatures on
    instruments, authority to
    print or type name, **36:18A.**
  Nomination papers, number of
    signatures, **53:44.**
Registers of probate.
  See REGISTERS OF PROBATE
    AND INSOLVENCY.
Reports.
  Records, reports, and returns.
    See within this heading,
    "Records, reports, and
    returns."
Resale and exempt use certificates,
  64H:8, 64I:8.
Retail installment sales contracts,
  buyer's signature, **255D:9.**
Sale of food through vending
  machines, application for
  license, **94:309.**
Secured transactions.
  Financing statement, **106:9-402.**
  Termination statement,
    106:9-404.
Service of process.
  See PROCESS AND SERVICE
    OF PROCESS AND
    PAPERS.
State ballot law commission.
  See STATE BALLOT LAW
    COMMISSION.
Statute of frauds, requirements,
  259:1.
Stock certificates, **156B:27.**
Surveyors.
  Engineers and surveyors. See
    within this heading,
    "Engineers and surveyors."
Tax collector, use of facsimile
  signature on warrant issued,
  60:29.
Tax returns, signatures required,
  62C:15.
Town meeting warrants, insertion
  of subjects, **39:10.**
Traffic regulations and rules of the
  road, refusal to comply with
  officer's demand for signature,
  90:25.
Trustee process.
  Answer of trustee, **246:11.**

SIGNATURES —Cont'd
Trustee process —Cont'd
  Interrogatories, requirements,
    246:12.
Trust in land, instrument creating,
  203:1.
Unauthorized signatures.
  Commercial Code, **106:1-201.**
  Forgery, **106:1-201.**
Vending machines, application for
  license for sale of food
  through, **94:309.**
Waiver and estoppel.
  Breach of contract, signing of
    written renunciation or
    waiver, **106:1-107.**
  Jury trial, signature on written
    waiver, **263:6.**
Warehouse receipt, necessity of
  signing, **106:7-202.**
Water pollution abatement district
  bonds, treasurer and executive
  director to sign, **21:35-21:37.**
Wills.
  See WILLS.
Writs, **223:20, 248:6.**
"Written signature," construction
  of phrase, **4:7.**

SIGNING BONUS PROGRAM.
Teachers, **15A:19B.**

SIGN LANGUAGE.
College credit, **15A:9A.**
Courts.
  Interpreters for the deaf,
    221:92A.
Deaf and hard of hearing
  commissioner.
  Fluent in sign language, **6:193.**
Public higher education.
  Recognized as legitimate
    language for study, **15A:9A.**
  Course credit as foreign
    language, **15A:9A.**
Public schools.
  Recognized as standard,
    independent language,
    71:2B.
  Foreign language requirement,
    71:2B.

SIGNS AND SIGNALS.
Advertising.
  See ADVERTISING AND
    ADVERTISEMENTS.
Bells.
  See BELLS.
Bicycles, required equipment,
  85:11B.
Billboards.
  See ADVERTISING AND
    ADVERTISEMENTS.

SIGNS AND SIGNALS —Cont'd

Building restrictions, limitations on proceedings, **184:23A.**

Creditor's claims against goods held on sale or return as precluded by sign evidencing consignor's interest, **106:2-326.**

Credit unions, advertisements, **171:55.**

Dump trucks, warning systems required, **90:7.**

Electric railroads, **162:16.**

Elevator license regulation as applicable to installation of signal systems, **143:71F.**

Federal signals, penalty for injuring or removing, **1:10.**

Filling stations.

Fuel price signs along highway or on premises, prohibition against, **94:295C.**

Limited access highways, signs indicating existence of station, **81:2, 85:2D.**

Fire signal system, meddling with, false alarms, etc., **268:32.**

Fireworks used, **148:39, 148:44.**

Fish nets, identification number, **130:30.**

Hand signals.

See HAND SIGNALS.

Highways.

See HIGHWAYS AND STREETS.

Hotels, motels, and roominghouses.

Limited access highways, signs indicating availability of boarding and lodging, **85:2D.**

Violations, **140:18.**

Kosher food, labeling, **94:156.**

Limited access highways, erection of signs for public convenience, **85:2D.**

Longshore and waterfront employment.

Persons authorized to give signals, **149:18D.**

Railroad cars, signals for work done near, **149:18H.**

Malicious defacing or marking, **266:94.**

Motels.

Hotels, motels, and roominghouses. See within this heading, "Hotels, motels, and roominghouses."

No smoking signs.

Tobacco. See within this heading, "Tobacco."

SIGNS AND SIGNALS —Cont'd

Outdoor advertising.

See ADVERTISING AND ADVERTISEMENTS.

Parking spaces for handicapped persons, **22:13A.**

Pedestrian walk signals prohibited, **85:2.**

Police signal system, interference, **268:32.**

Public property, defacement, **266:126.**

Railroad crossings.

See RAILROAD CROSSINGS.

Railroads.

See RAILROADS.

Reflectors.

See REFLECTORS.

Right on red, **89:8.**

Roominghouses.

Hotels, motels, and roominghouses. See within this heading, "Hotels, motels, and roominghouses."

School crossings, erection of figures or objects by municipalities, **85:21A.**

Scuba divers required to display flag as warning device to boat operators, **90B:13A.**

Services available to public, signs advertising along limited access highways, **85:2D.**

Service stations.

Filling stations. See within this heading, "Filling stations."

Ski area operator, posting required, **143:71J, 143:71N.**

Smoking in terminal or other facility of Massachusetts Bay transportation authority where signs prohibit, **272:43A.**

Street railways.

Department may require signals, **159:22.**

Injury to or tampering with signals, **159:102, 159:103.**

Tobacco.

Regulation of posting of no smoking signs, **270:21.**

Terminal or other facility of Massachusetts Bay Transportation Authority where signs prohibit smoking, **272:43A.**

Traffic regulations.

See TRAFFIC REGULATIONS AND RULES OF THE ROAD.

Trespass notices, removal or defacing, **266:122.**

SIGNS AND SIGNALS —Cont'd

Unemployment compensation.

Employer to provide signs with instructions for filing, **151A:62A.**

Waterfront employment.

Longshore and waterfront employment. See within this heading, "Longshore and waterfront employment."

Wetland protection, **131:40.**

Whistles.

See WHISTLES.

Zoning, signs as prior nonconforming uses, **40A:6.**

SILENCERS.

Fire arms, silencers, **269:10A.**

Mufflers.

See MUFFLERS.

Sale prohibited, **269:10A.**

SILENT MEDITATION PERIOD.

Schools, **71:1A.**

SILICON BREAST IMPLANTS.

Risk factor disclosure, **111:70E.**

SILVER.

Banks.

Buying and selling silver bullion, **167F:2.**

Coins.

Counterfeiting, **267:17 to 267:20.**

Creditors.

Levy of execution, **235:32.**

Creditors.

Levy of execution.

Silver coins, **235:32.**

Misrepresentation of article, **266:77.**

Record of purchase or sale, **266:142A.**

Retail sales tax.

Exemptions, **64H:6.**

Silver goods, requirements as to content, **266:77.**

SILVER-HAIRED LEGISLATURE DAYS.

Annual observance, **6:15DDD.**

SILVICULTURAL PRACTICES.

Demonstrations in forestry practices, **132:6.**

SIMPLE LABORATORY TEST.

Defined, **111D:1.**

SIMULCAST WAGERING.

Horse and dog racing, **128C:1 et seq.**

SIMULTANEOUS DEATH ACT, 190A:1-190A:8, 190A:1 et seq.

SINGERS.
See MUSIC AND MUSICAL INSTRUMENTS.

SINGLE EMPLOYING UNIT.
Employment security law, several places of business as single unit within, **151A:9.**

SINGLE FAMILY DWELLING.
Zoning.
See ZONING AND PLANNING.

SINGULAR NUMBER.
Statute, plural in, as including singular, **4:6.**

SINKING FUNDS.
Cancellation of instruments.
Coupons, cancellation upon payment, **44:48.**
Substitution of new bonds, **44:49.**
Co-operative business corporations, **157:2.**
County finance.
Exchange of bonds held by commissioner, **35:43.**
Refusal to issue nonnegotiable bonds, penalty, **44:61.**
Registration of bonds held by commissioner, **35:43, 44:52, 44:61.**
Districts.
Bonds held by sinking fund commissioners, registration, **35:43, 44:52, 44:61.**
Inspection of records and securities, **44:48.**
Economic development and industrial corporations, **121C:7.**
Highway infrastructure fund, payments on bonds or notes issued, **29:2O.**
Housing authorities, **29:49, 121B:34, 121B:59.**
Indebtedness, exclusion, **4:7.**
Inspection of records, **44:48.**
Municipal finance, **44:47-44:52.**
See MUNICIPAL FINANCE.
Refunding bonds, provisions applicable, **29:53A.**
Registration of bonds and securities held by commissioners, **35:43, 44:52, 44:61.**
Social services department, investment of funds in securities, **18B:19.**
State finance.
See STATE FINANCE.
State treasurer, **29:2O, 29:45.**

SINKING FUNDS —Cont'd
Street railway companies, **161:25.**
Trust companies, sinking fund for state bonds, **29:49.**
Trusts and trustees, applicability to deposit of refunding bonds proceeds, **29:53A.**

SIPPIO ROOMS.
Hearing required prior to issuance of license, **140:177.**
Licenses and permits.
Penalty for keeping facilities without license, **140:178.**
Public hearing required prior to issuance, **140:177.**
Peace officers permitted to enter, **140:201.**
Penalty for keeping facilities without license, **140:178.**

SIRENS.
Bicycle regulations, **85:11B.**
Motor vehicles.
Offensive or illegal operation, **90:16, 90:16., 90:20.**

SISTERS.
See BROTHERS AND SISTERS.

SISTER STATES.
See FOREIGN STATES OR COUNTRIES.

SIX O'CLOCK LAW.
Employment of children, **149:66, 149:69, 149:73, 149:78.**

SIX PERCENT ACT, 107:3.
Disclosure of information to public regarding financial institutions, accounts and services, **167D:34.**

SIX PERSON JURY.
Administrative justices.
See ADMINISTRATIVE JUSTICES.
Appeal, **278:18.**
District courts.
Appeals, criminal jurisdiction for appeal to jury of six from finding of guilty or sentence, **278:18.**
Criminal cases, **218:27A.**
Misdemeanors, trial, **218:26.**
Trial of actions, **218:19A, 218:19B.**
Essex county.
Criminal cases, **218:27A.**
District courts, **218:19B, 218:26.**
Procedure, **234:25.**
Worcester county.
See WORCESTER COUNTY.

SIZE AND SIZE RESTRICTIONS.
Accident and sickness insurance policies, size of type for printing, **175:108.**
Apples.
See APPLES.
Bass, striped, **130:100A.**
Buildings.
See BUILDINGS AND STRUCTURES.
Carriers.
See CARRIERS.
Compressed air tanks, **146:35.**
Eels, **130:100D.**
Eggs, standard sizes, **94:90B.**
Length.
See LENGTH.
Lobsters, **130:44.**
Marine fish and fisheries.
Eels, **130:100D.**
Lobsters, **130:44.**
Striped bass, **130:100A.**
Minimum size regulations.
See MINIMUM SIZE REGULATIONS.
Motor carriers.
See CARRIERS.
Railroad crossings, lettering on signboards, **160:140.**
Steam boiler, contents of certificate of inspection, **146:27.**
Striped bass, **130:100A.**
Traffic regulations and rules of the road.
See TRAFFIC REGULATIONS AND RULES OF THE ROAD.
Trailers, **90:19.**
Weights.
See WEIGHTS AND MEASURES.

SKATES.
Rinks.
See SKATING RINKS.
Roller skating.
See ROLLER SKATING.

SKATING RINKS.
Admission of young persons, **140:198.**
Appropriations by city or town, **40:5, 44:7.**
Borrowing money within debt limit by cities and towns, **44:7.**
Discrimination because of race or color, **272:92A, 272:98.**
Emergency telephone numbers, posting, **45:25.**
Licenses, **140:186, 140:187.**
Peace officers permitted to enter, **140:201.**

554

SKATING RINKS —Cont'd
Penalties, **140:200.**
Posting copy of laws, **140:199.**
Sunday sports, licensing, **136:4.**
Transfer of operating funds,
132A:10.

SKEET SHOOTING.
See SHOOTING GALLERIES
AND PRESERVES.

SKELETONS.
See HUMAN REMAINS.

SKIING.
Assumption of risk, **143:71O.**
Conduct, responsibilities, and
duties, **143:71O.**
Cross country skiing trails in state
forests, **132:38A.**
Definitions, **143:71.**
Emergency care, treatment, or
transportation by ski patrol
members, liability, **231:85I.**
Fines, penalties, and forfeitures.
Improper conduct, **143:71O.**
Leaving scene of accident
without leaving personal
identification, **143:71Q.**
Rules and regulations, violation,
143:71R.
Water skiing violations, **90B:14.**
Forfeitures.
Fines, penalties, and forfeitures.
See within this heading,
"Fines, penalties, and
forfeitures."
Identity and identification, leaving
scene of accident without
leaving, **143:71Q.**
Jet skis.
See JET SKIS.
Liability of ski area operator,
143:71O, 143:71P.
Lifts, **143:71H-143:71S.**
See RECREATIONAL
TRAMWAYS.
Negligence of ski area operator,
143:71O, 143:71P.
Notice and knowledge, ski operator
to be given notice of injury
prior to commencement of
action, **143:71P.**
Penalties.
Fines, penalties, and forfeitures.
See within this heading,
"Fines, penalties, and
forfeitures."
Signs and signboards, regulations
requiring use of signs by ski
operators, **143:71J.**
Ski area defined, **143:71I.**

SKIING —Cont'd
Ski patrols, duties and liability,
231:85I.
Slope or trail, defined, **143:71I.**
Speed, responsibilities regarding,
90B:11, 143:71, 143:71O.
Sunday sports, licensing, **136:4.**
Touring trails, construction in
state forests, **132:38A.**
Tramways, **143:71H-143:71S.**
See RECREATIONAL
TRAMWAYS.
Water skiing regulated, **90B:8,**
90B:11.
Written statements and
instruments, requirement of
written notice to ski area
operator prior to
commencement of action,
143:71P.

SKILO.
Lottery, skilo, **271:6B.**

SKIMMED MILK.
See MILK AND MILK
PRODUCTS.

SKIN CANCER.
Tanning facilities.
Warnings, **111:209.**

SKIN DIVERS.
Compensation for services
rendered, **40:5.**
Public Safety Department,
employment, **22:6.**
Scuba divers, **90B:13A, 90B:14,**
146:34.
See SCUBA DIVERS.

SKI PATROLS.
Members rendering emergency
care, treatment, or
transportation, liability,
231:85I.

SKUNKS.
Possession without permit,
authorized, **131:5.**
Removal from hole in ground,
131:76.

SKY-ROCKETS.
Sale or use of fireworks, **148:39.**

SLAMMING.
Local and long distance telephone
service providers.
Unauthorized switching, **93:109**
to 93:113.

SLANDER.
See LIBEL AND SLANDER.

SLASH.
Clearing and disposal,
48:16-48:20.

SLAUGHTERHOUSES,
94:118-94:132.
Adulteration, **94:124, 94:125,**
94:186.
Prohibited acts, **94:127.**
Animal diseases.
See ANIMAL DISEASES.
Animal food manufacturers,
registration, **94:126.**
Brands and labels.
Labels and labeling. See within
this heading, "Labels and
labeling."
Brokers.
Defined under food and drug
inspection law, **94:118.**
Registration, **94:126.**
"Capable of use as human food,"
defined under food and drug
inspection law, **94:118.**
Commissioner of public health,
authority over
slaughterhouses and meat
processing plants, **94:119,**
94:126.
Containers.
Commissioner's powers, **94:126.**
Health department's general
powers and duties, **94:125.**
Misleading practices, **94:126.**
Definitions under food and drug
inspection law and humane
slaughtering of livestock law,
94:118, 94:139C.
Dressed poultry slaughtered in
other state, **94:139B.**
Entry on premises for purposes of
inspection, **94:124.**
Equines, slaughtering, **94:126,**
94:127, 94:139C to 94:139G.
Examination.
Inspection and supervision. See
within this heading,
"Inspection and
supervision."
Exclusion from definition of
livestock under humane
slaughter of livestock law,
94:139C.
Exempt operations, **94:130.**
Failure to appear, testify, or
produce documentary
evidence, penalty, **94:128.**
False labeling, **94:126.**
False statements and reports,
penalty for making, **94:128.**
Federally inspected
establishments, inspection,
94:131.
Fees for licenses, **94:120.**

SLAUGHTERHOUSES —Cont'd

Fines and penalties, **94:128, 94:129, 94:139F, 111:154.**

Failure to appear, testify, or produce documentary evidence, penalty, **94:128.**

False labeling, **94:126.**

False statements and reports, penalty for making, **94:128.**

Forgery of official device, mark, or certificate, **94:127.**

Records, failure to furnish, **94:127.**

Forgery of official device, mark, or certificate, **94:127.**

Health and health department, **94:121-94:124, 111:151.**

Commissioner of public health, authority over slaughterhouses and meat processing plants, **94:119, 94:126.**

Containers.

Powers and duties, **94:125, 94:126.**

General authority over slaughterhouses and meat processing plants, **94:119, 94:126.**

Humane slaughtering of livestock law, administration, **94:139C.**

Labeling regulations, **94:125, 94:126.**

Powers and duties, **94:125.**

Hearings.

Licenses, hearing on suspension or revocation, **94:121.**

Highways and streets, transporting of offal over, **85:10.**

Horses, slaughtering, **94:126, 94:127, 94:139C to 94:139G.**

Humane slaughtering of livestock, **94:139C to 94:139G.**

Identification of livestock and poultry for inspection purposes, **94:125.**

Injunctions against, **111:152, 111:153.**

Inspection and supervision, **94:124 to 94:126.**

Commissioner's authority, **94:126.**

Entry on premises, **94:124.**

Federally inspected establishment, inspection, **94:131.**

Health department, authority, **94:119, 94:125, 94:126.**

Identification of livestock and poultry for inspection purposes, **94:125.**

SLAUGHTERHOUSES —Cont'd

Inspection and supervision —Cont'd

Penalties for failure to attend and testify, **94:128.**

Records of inspection, maintenance, **94:124.**

Society for prevention of cruelty to animals, investigation by agents, **129:9.**

Inspectors, defined under food and drug inspection law, **94:118.**

Kosher food, labeling, **94:156.**

Labels and labeling.

Defined under food and drug inspection law, **94:118.**

False or misleading labeling, **94:126.**

Health department's general powers and duties, **94:125, 94:126.**

Kosher food, **94:156.**

Prohibited acts, **94:127.**

Licenses and permits, **94:121-94:124, 111:154.**

Fees, **94:120.**

Issuance, **94:119.**

Necessity for and requirements, **94:120, 111:151.**

Suspension or revocation, **94:121.**

Unsanitary conditions as ground, **94:119, 94:124.**

Marking.

Labels and labeling. See within this heading, "Labels and labeling."

"Meat food product," defined under food and drug inspection law, **94:118.**

Misleading practices in connection with labeling or containers, **94:126.**

Nuisances, **111:151, 111:153, 111:154.**

Offal transported on or over public ways, regulation, **85:10.**

Operations exempt from statute, **94:130.**

Outside Commonwealth, slaughtered dressed poultry, **94:139B.**

Own use, slaughtering and preparation of livestock and poultry for own use as exempt operation, **94:130.**

Penalties.

Fines and penalties. See within this heading, "Fines and penalties."

SLAUGHTERHOUSES —Cont'd

Permits.

Licenses and permits. See within this heading, "Licenses and permits."

Poultry and poultry products.

Definitions under food and drug inspection law, **94:118.**

Exclusion from definition of livestock under humane slaughter of livestock law, **94:139C.**

Identification, marking and labeling, **94:125.**

Inspection, **94:124.**

Outside Commonwealth, slaughtered poultry, **94:139B.**

Own use, exemption of slaughter, **94:130.**

Prohibited acts with respect, **94:127.**

Records to be kept by persons engaged in slaughtering, processing, or rendering of poultry, **94:125.**

Slaughter and processing of, necessity of license, **94:120.**

Storage and handling of livestock and poultry product, regulation of conditions of and persons engaged, **94:126.**

Prohibited acts with respect to livestock, poultry, or their products, **94:127.**

Public health and health department and commissioner.

Health and health department. See within this heading, "Health and health department."

Records, reports, and returns.

Failure to furnish, **94:127.**

False statements in, penalty, **94:128.**

Health commissioner's powers to require, **94:126.**

Inspections, **94:124.**

Maintaining, **94:124.**

Persons engaged in business of slaughtering, processing, or rendering of livestock or poultry, records to be kept, **94:125.**

Registration of brokers, renderers, animal food manufacturers, etc., **94:126.**

Regulations, **94:119 et seq.**

Renderers and rendering.

Defined under food and drug inspection law, **94:118.**

SLAUGHTERHOUSES —Cont'd
Renderers and rendering —Cont'd
Provisions, **111:151-111:154.**
Records to be kept by renderers, **94:125.**
Registration, **94:126.**
Revocation of licenses.
Licenses and permits. See within this heading, "Licenses and permits."
Rules and regulations, **94:119 et seq.**
Sanitation, health department's powers and duties as to, **94:125.**
Seizure and destruction of diseased or unwholesome carcasses or products, **94:124.**
Severability provisions of act concerning, **94:132.**
"Slaughterer" defined under food and drug inspection law, **94:139C.**
Society for Prevention of Cruelty to Animals, investigation by agents, **129:9.**
Storage and handling of livestock and poultry products, regulation of conditions of and persons engaged, **94:126.**
Supervision.
Inspection and supervision. See within this heading, "Inspection and supervision."
Suspension or revocation of licenses.
Licenses and permits. See within this heading, "Licenses and permits."
Trial.
Hearings. See within this heading, "Hearings."
Unsanitary conditions as grounds for suspension revocation of license, **94:119, 94:124.**
Unwholesome carcasses or products, seizure and destruction, **94:124.**

SLAVES.
Fugitive slaves to be delivered up, **US Const Art 4 Sec 2 cl 3.**
Importation of, how long permitted, **US Const Art 1 Sec 9 cl 1.**
Loss on emancipation of, not to be paid for, **US Const Amend 14 Sec 4.**
Prohibition of slavery or involuntary servitude, **US Const Amend 13 Sec 1.**

SLAVES —Cont'd
Right to vote not abridged by previous condition of servitude, **US Const Amend 15 Sec 1.**
Three-fifths of, included in representative numbers, **US Const Art 1 Sec 2 cl 3.**

SLEDS.
Bells on horse-drawn sleds, **89:3, 89:5.**
Coasting on highways, power to regulate, **85:10.**
Motor vehicles, attaching to outside of prohibited, **90:13.**
Recreation and snow vehicles, equipment required on sleds attached, **90B:24.**

SLEEPING CARS.
Drinking water, exception from requirement, **160:174.**
Wages may be paid less frequently than weekly, **149:148.**

SLEEPING SICKNESS.
Municipal appropriations for control of encephalitis, **40:5.**

SLEEPWEAR.
Flammable children's sleepwear, manufacture, labeling, or sale, **94B:1, 111:186B, 148:25D.**

SLEIGHT OF HAND.
Obtaining property by, penalized, **266:75.**

SLICHTER ACTS, 150A:1 et seq., 150B:1 et seq.

SLIDING FEE SCHEDULES.
Early childhood intervention services, **111G:4.**
Mentally ill and retarded persons, reimbursement of transportation costs, **19B:17.**

SLINGS.
Longshoremen.
See LONGSHORE AND WATERFRONT EMPLOYMENT.

SLINGSHOT.
Carrying as criminal offense, **269:10.**
Manufacture and sale of, penalty, **269:12.**
Sports and sporting events, sale to club or association conducting, **269:12.**

SLIP AND FALL.
Claims against Commonwealth, forms of complaints and answers, **258:2 Forms 2 et seq.**

SLOPE EASEMENT.
State highway, condemnation of easement for purpose, **81:7B.**

SLOT MACHINES.
Antique slot machines as exempt from seizure, **271:5A.**
Deputy director of standards, coin operated devices to be approved, **94:283.**
Fines and penalties for violations, **94:284, 266:75A, 266:75B.**
Fraudulent operation, **266:75A, 266:75B.**
Gambling device, **271:5A.**
Seizure and forfeiture, **271:5A.**

SLOVAK INDEPENDENCE DAY.
Annual observance of Slovak Independence Day, **6:12I.**

SLOW MOVING VEHICLES.
Emblem required, **90:7.**
Right lane ascending grade, duty to keep, **89:4.**

SLUGS.
Use in slot machines, **266:75A, 266:75B.**

SLUM CLEARANCE.
See HOUSING AND URBAN RENEWAL.

SMALL BUSINESS.
Assistance division.
See ECONOMIC DEVELOPMENT DEPARTMENT.
Definition, **23A:15.**
Department of economic development, definition, **23A:15.**
Environmental management department, educational outreach programs, **21:20.**
Film and video development office, **23A:57.**
Health care finance and policy division.
See HEALTH CARE FINANCE AND POLICY DIVISION.
Health care finance and policy, insurance for small businesses, **118G:21, 118G:22.**
Insurance.
Assistance division, co-operation, **23A:17.**
Investments and other powers, **167F:2.**
Loans.
See BANKS AND BANKING.
Rules and regulations, **30A:5, 30A:6.**

SMALL BUSINESS —Cont'd
Toxics use reduction, outreach
program, 21I:7.
Words and phrases, 23A:15.

**SMALL BUSINESS
ASSISTANCE DIVISION.**
**See ECONOMIC
DEVELOPMENT
DEPARTMENT.**

**SMALL BUSINESS
INCUBATOR FACILITIES.**
Development finance agency.
See DEVELOPMENT FINANCE
AGENCY.

**SMALL BUSINESS LOAN
REVIEW BOARDS.**
Regional review boards, 167:14C.

SMALL BUSINESS LOANS.
See BANKS AND BANKING.

**SMALL BUSINESS
PURCHASING PROGRAM,
Spec L 3:1 et seq.**
Administering purchases, **Spec L
3:5.**
Agencies of state, guidelines for
purchases, **Spec L 3:3.**
Annual report to general court,
Spec L 3:8.
Awarding of purchases, **Spec L
3:4.**
Commissioner, duties, **Spec L 3:7.**
Definitions, **Spec L 3:2.**
Deposit of funds, **Spec L 3:6.**
Eligible businesses, **Spec L 3:3.**
Funds, deposit, **Spec L 3:6.**
General court, annual reports,
Spec L 3:8.
Guidelines for purchases by state
agencies, **Spec L 3:3.**
Legislative purpose, **Spec L 3:1.**
Limitation in participation, **Spec
L 3:3.**
Paying for purchases, **Spec L 3:5.**
Procedure for administering and
paying for purchases, **Spec L
3:5.**
Reports and records, annual report
to general court, **Spec L 3:8.**
Secretary, powers and duties,
Spec L 3:6.

**SMALL CLAIMS ACTIONS
AND PROCEDURE.**
Alternative procedure established
by rule for small civil cases,
218:21.
Appeal to jury of six session in
District Court department,
218:23.

**SMALL CLAIMS ACTIONS
AND PROCEDURE** —Cont'd
Boston Municipal Court.
Fees, **218:22.**
Jurisdiction, **218:21.**
Trial by jury, **218:23.**
Discretion as to costs, **218:25.**
District and municipal courts,
claims in, **218:21-218:25.**
Entry fee, **218:22.**
Fees for actions, Boston Municipal
and District Court
departments, **218:22.**
Finality of judgment, **218:23.**
Housing authorities, actions
against, **258:4.**
Housing courts, proceedings in,
185C:19.
Jurisdiction of Boston Municipal
and District Court, **218:22.**
Jury trial, waiver, **218:23.**
Procedure, **218:22, 218:23.**
Registered mail, notice, **218:22.**
Removal, **218:23.**
Res judicata or collateral estoppel,
218:23.
Superior courts, **218:23.**
Supreme Judicial Court, approval
of small claims procedural
rules, **218:21.**
Transfer to ordinary docket,
218:24.
Uniform small claims rules.
See SMALL CLAIMS,
UNIFORM RULES.
Venue, **218:21.**
Waiver.
Jury trial, **218:23.**
Venue, **218:21.**

**SMALL CLAIMS, UNIFORM
RULES.**
Amendments, **Rule 5.**
Answer to claim, **Rule 3.**
Appeals, **Rule 10.**
Applicability, **Rule 1.**
Attachments, **Rule 6.**
Counterclaim and third party
practice, **Rule 3.**
Discovery, **Rule 5.**
Enforcement of judgments, **Rule
9.**
Fees, **Rule 3.**
Filing statement of claim, **Rule 2.**
Impleader, **Rule 3.**
Interpleader, **Rule 3.**
Judgments, **Rules 7-10.**
Jury session, transmittal to,
appeals, **Rule 10.**
Jury trial, conduct of, **Rule 10.**
Mail, claim and fee may be filed
by, **Rule 2.**

**SMALL CLAIMS, UNIFORM
RULES** —Cont'd
Notice of judgment and order to
pay, **Rule 10.**
Notice to defendant, **Rule 3.**
Orders to pay, **Rule 10.**
Relief from judgment or order,
Rule 8.
Setoff and counterclaim, **Rule 3.**
Transfer, **Rule 4.**
Trials, **Rule 7.**

SMALL ESTATES.
Administration by executor,
195:16.
Compensation.
Wages, salaries, and
compensation. See within
this heading, "Wages,
salaries, or compensation."
Delivery to parent of small funds
currently held by executor or
administrator and to which
minor is entitled, **215:41A.**
Employment security benefits
owing to deceased person,
payment without
administration, **151A:68.**
Executor named in will, voluntary
administration in event,
195:16A.
Executors and administrators.
Public administrator. See within
this heading, "Public
administrator."
Funeral expenses of small estates.
Public administrator's payment,
194:17.
Voluntary or informal
administration, **195:16,
195:16A.**
Grandchildren's administration,
195:16.
Informal and voluntary
administration, **195:16,
195:16A.**
Maximum value, **195:16.**
Mental health facility inpatients
and residents, administration
of estates, **123:28, 195:16.**
Motor vehicle title transferred by
informal administration,
195:16.
Public administrator.
Claims to small estates, **194:17.**
Disposition of small estates,
194:17, 194:18.
Relatives of decedent entitled to
act as administrator, **195:16.**
State officer or employee, payment
of salaries, wages or other
money owing to deceased,
29:31D.

SMALL ESTATES —Cont'd
Voluntary administration.
  Administrators of certain small
    estates, **195:16.**
  Defined, **195:16.**
  Executor named in will,
    195:16A.
  Fees of register of probate and
    insolvency for filing
    statement of voluntary
    administration, **262:40.**
Wages, salaries, or compensation.
  Deceased employee, payment
    without administration,
    149:178A, 149:178C.
  Employment security benefits
    owing to deceased, **151A:68.**
  State officer or employee,
    payment of salaries, wages,
    or other money owing to
    deceased, **29:31D.**

SMALL GAME LICENSE.
Hunting licenses, **131:11.**

SMALL LOANS, 26:5A, 140:90,
  140:96 et seq.
Agent for service of process,
  140:104.
Assignment of wages, **140:108,**
  154:2.
Avoidability of note while lender is
  unlicensed, **140:110.**
Banks and banking.
  Bank commissioner.
    See BANK COMMISSIONER.
  Charge for interest in excess of
    maximum rate on one or
    more portions of loan,
    140:114A.
  Regulatory board. See within
    this heading, "Regulatory
    board."
Bonus, fee or charge, forbidden,
  140:100.
Change in status of licensee,
  regulations, **140:104.**
Charges.
  Fees and charges. See within
    this heading, "Fees and
    charges."
Companies for business of, **140:90.**
Costs and expenses.
  Investigations, assessment of
    licensee for cost, **140:97.**
  Recovery of illegal interest,
    140:106.
  Small loans regulatory board,
    members, **26:5A.**
Credit life, insurance provisions,
  140:114A.
Definitions, **140:96.**

SMALL LOANS —Cont'd
Destruction of old returns,
  140:113.
Discharge of small loan secured by
  pledge or mortgage, **140:91,**
  140:94.
Equipment or chattels of insurance
  companies, limitation on
  investments, **175:63.**
Evidence in prosecutions for
  violations, **140:90, 140:110.**
Examination and inspection.
  Books and papers, fee for
    inspection, **140:97.**
  Licensees, examination, **140:99.**
Excessive charges, **140:103.**
Exemptions, **140:114.**
Expenses.
  Costs and expenses. See within
    this heading, "Costs and
    expenses."
Failure to return note or discharge
  of mortgage on loan under
  $1,000, liability, **140:94.**
Farm loans, **167:14.**
Fees and charges.
  Borrower fees, **140:100.**
  Dependence upon receipt of
    commissions, fees, bonuses
    or other consideration,
    140:96.
  Inspection of books and papers,
    140:97.
  License fees, **140:102.**
  Recording fees, charging to
    borrower, **140:100.**
Fines and penalties.
  Annual return, penalty for
    failure to make, **140:98.**
  Examination by commissioner,
    refusal to appear, **140:99.**
  Regulations, violations, **140:103.**
  Trust companies and banks,
    140:114A.
  Unlicensed persons, penalties,
    140:110.
Foreclosure of small home
  mortgages.
  See MORTGAGE
    FORECLOSURE.
Form of license, **140:101.**
Fraternal benefit societies,
  exemption from regulations,
  140:114.
Future advances, discharge of
  security when provision made,
  140:107.
Group insurance premium not
  deemed charge on loan,
  175:134.
Hearings for establishment of
  maximum rate of charge,
  140:100.

SMALL LOANS —Cont'd
Illegal interest, **140:106.**
Inspections.
  Examination and inspection. See
    within this heading,
    "Examination and
    inspection."
Insurance.
  See INSURANCE.
Interest on money.
  Absence of agreement as
    affecting law, **140:111.**
  Bonus, fee or charge, forbidden,
    140:100.
  Group insurance premium not
    deemed charge on loan,
    175:134.
  Items and expenses in
    computing, **140:96.**
  One thousand dollars, rate on
    loans, **140:90.**
  Rate, **140:90, 140:96, 140:100,**
    140:108.
  Recovery of illegal interest,
    140:106.
  Verdict, interest running to
    time, **140:90.**
  Voiding loan for excess charges,
    140:103, 140:114A.
  Waiver of interest provisions as
    against public policy,
    140:90.
Investigations, assessment of
  licensee for cost, **26:3, 140:97.**
Liabilities and assets, return to
  commissioner, **140:98.**
Licenses and permits, **140:96.**
  Application, **140:104.**
  Change in name or address,
    statement, **140:104.**
  Defined, **140:100.**
  Examination of licensee, **140:99.**
  Exemption, **140:114.**
  Fees, **140:102.**
  Form, **140:101.**
  Insurance premium finance
    agency, exception from
    licensing requirement,
    255C:2.
  One thousand dollars,
    inapplicability to small loan
    licenses of provisions for
    loans, **140:95.**
  Place of business, one for each,
    140:102.
  Posting, **140:101.**
  Prerequisites, **140:104.**
  Revocation or suspension,
    140:103, 140:104.
  Term, **140:101.**
  Unlicensed persons, penalty,
    140:110.

SMALL LOANS —Cont'd
Mortgages.
 See MORTGAGES AND DEEDS
  OF TRUST.
Notice.
 Establishment of maximum
  rates of charge, **140:100.**
 Posting of licenses, **140:101.**
One thousand dollars, loans under,
 140:90-140:95.
Part payment, receipt, **140:109.**
Pawnbrokers.
 See PAWNBROKERS.
Penalties.
 Fines and penalties. See within
  this heading, "Fines and
  penalties."
Performance assessment, **167:14.**
Permits.
 Licenses and permits. See
  within this heading,
  "Licenses and permits."
Place of business for each license,
 140:102.
Pledges, discharge of loans
 secured, **140:91.**
Police enforcement of regulations,
 140:112.
Posting of licenses, **140:101.**
Prosecution for violation, evidence,
 140:110.
Public policy, waiver of interest
 provisions as against, **140:90.**
Rate of interest on loans, **140:96,**
 140:100, 140:108.
Receipt for part payment, **140:109.**
Records.
 See RECORDS, REPORTS, AND
  RETURNS.
Regulatory board, **26:5A.**
 Establishment of maximum
  rates of charge, **140:100.**
 Public meetings and records,
  inapplicability of law,
  30A:11A.
Relocation of office, investigation
 fee, **140:102.**
Reports to commissioner of banks,
 140:98.
Retail installment sales.
 See RETAIL INSTALLMENT
  SALES AND SERVICES.
Returns to commissioner.
 See BANK COMMISSIONER.
Review boards, **167:14C.**
Revocation and suspension of
 licenses, **140:103, 140:104.**
Rules and regulation.
 Regulatory board. See within
  this heading, "Regulatory
  board."

SMALL LOANS —Cont'd
Secured transactions.
 See SECURED
  TRANSACTIONS.
Seller's advance of money to buyer
 as engaging in small loan
 business, **140:96.**
Service of process, agents,
 140:104.
State police, enforcement of
 regulations, **140:112.**
Supervisor of loan agencies,
 appointment and bond, **26:4.**
Suspension of licenses, **140:103,**
 140:104.
Term and form of license, **140:101.**
Trust companies, **140:114A.**
Unlicensed persons engaging in,
 penalties, **140:110.**
Verdict, interest on loan under
 $1,000 to time, **140:90.**
Voiding of loan for violation of
 regulations, **140:103.**
Waiver of interest provisions as
 against public policy, **140:90.**

**SMALL POWER PRODUCTION
 FACILITY.**
Defined, **164:1.**

SMALLPOX.
Expenses in caring for afflicted
 persons, responsibility,
 111:116.
Hospitals for victims, **111:92.**
Investigations, **111:7.**
Isolation hospitals, **111:92.**
Nonresident persons as victims,
 111:116.
Physicians and nurses, **111:93.**
Tewksbury Hospital, admission,
 122:4.

**SMALL VALUE CASES
 TRANSFER ACT, 231:102C.**

SMELLS.
See ODORS.

SMELT, 130:34-130:36.
Angling as permissible means of
 taking, **130:35.**
Closed areas for spawning, **130:36.**
Closed seasons, **130:34.**

**SMITH'S AGRICULTURAL
 SCHOOL.**
Net maintenance sum, how
 determined, **74:1.**
Vocational school, maintenance
 and operation, **74:24.**

SMOKE.
Damage, **93:28D-93:28F.**
Detection devices.
 See SMOKE AND HEAT
  DETECTORS.

SMOKE —Cont'd
Motor vehicles, **90:16, 90:20.**
Refuse treatment and disposal
 facilities as nuisance,
 111:150A.
Tobacco products contaminated by,
 sale, **94:307.**

**SMOKE AND HEAT
 DETECTORS.**
Apartments required to have,
 148:26C.
Approved smoke detector, defined,
 148:26D.
Cities.
 See CITIES AND TOWNS.
Definitions, electrical systems,
 141:1.
Family hotels, requirements,
 148:26C.
Fines and penalties for failure to
 comply with provisions,
 148:27.
Licenses and certificates.
 Forms, **141:3.**
 Installers of wires, **141:1A.**
 Misstatements by applicant for
  systems technician's license,
  141:9.
Private dwellings, regulations,
 148:26E.
Residential buildings,
 requirements, **148:26B.**
Sales and transfers, installation of
 smoke detectors in residential
 property, **148:26F.**
Systems contractor, **13:32.**
Systems technician, **13:32.**

SMOKELESS TOBACCO.
Cigarette excise taxes, **64C:1,**
 64C:6.
Giving or selling to minor, **270:6.**

SMOKING.
Flea markets, **270:23.**
No smoking legislation, **270:21.**
 Flea markets, **270:23.**
Public conveyances, smoking
 prohibition, **272:43A.**
 Massachusetts Bay
  transportation authority,
  161A:42.
Tobacco.
 See TOBACCO.

SMUGGLING.
Correctional institutions,
 smuggling articles into or out,
 268:31.

SNARES.
Restrictions on use, **131:79.**

SNOB ZONING LAW, 40B:20 et seq.

SNOW AND ICE.
Abutting owner.
  Liability for failure to remove under municipal ordinance, **40:21.**
  Notice of injury, **84:21.**
  Removal, **85:5-85:7.**
Adjoining towns, agreements with regarding removal, **84:5A.**
Agreement between towns for removal or sanding, **84:5A.**
Animals, when illegal to drive on snow or ice, **111:174.**
Appropriations or aid by cities and towns for removal, **40:6C, 40:6D, 40:7, 44:31D, 81:26.**
Assessment for removal of snow and ice, **85:6.**
Barriers, ordinance requiring erection, **40:21.**
Borrowing outside of debt limit by cities and towns for ice skating rink, **44:7.**
Bylaws of cities or towns.
  Ordinances or bylaws, **40:21.**
Chemicals for snow removal, regulation of storage and use, **85:7A.**
Civil service status of snow removal employees of public works department, **31:48.**
Connecting ways, removal, **84:7A.**
Contracts between towns for removal, **84:5A.**
Cutting of ice, penalty for unlawful, **266:106.**
Defect in highway or street, snow and ice, **84:18, 84:19, 84:22.**
Driving animals upon, when illegal, **111:174.**
Easement for snow fence, **82:32C.**
Environmental protection department, storage of snow and ice removal chemicals, **85:7A.**
Fire hydrants, piling snow, **148:27B.**
Health department.
  Sale of ice. See within this heading, "Sale of ice."
Highway fund available to pay cost of removal, **90:34.**
Injury from snow or ice on highway or street.
  Correction of defective notices, **84:20.**
  Defect in street, snow and ice, **84:18, 84:19, 84:22.**

SNOW AND ICE —Cont'd
Injury from snow or ice on highway or street —Cont'd
  Liability of county, city or town, **84:17, 84:18.**
  Notice of injury, **84:18-84:21.**
    To county, city or town, **84:18-84:20.**
    To owner of private property, **84:21.**
  Service of notice on county, city or town, **84:19.**
Inspection by city, **40:24.**
Joint township highway removal projects, **84:5A.**
Licenses for sale of ice, **101:17.**
Limit of expenditures for removal, **81:26.**
Local authorities, duty of, **40:7, 84:7.**
Metal studded snow tires, **90:16.**
Motor vehicles interfering with removal from highways and streets, **40:2, 85:2A, 159B:6B.**
Neglect of duty by town, liability, **84:22.**
Notice of injury.
  Injury from snow or ice on highway or street. See within this heading, "Injury from snow or ice on highway or street."
Obstruction or interference by vehicles with efforts to remove from highways and streets, **40:21, 85:2A, 85:7B, 159B:6B.**
Ordinances or bylaws.
  Barriers, ordinance requiring erection, **40:21.**
  Removal of snow and ice, ordinances and bylaws, **40:21.**
Other towns, agreements with regarding removal, **84:5A.**
Personal injury.
  Injury. See within this heading, "Injury from snow or ice on highway or street."
Ponds.
  See ICE PONDS.
Presence on highway as imposing liability, **84:17.**
Price.
  Sale of ice. See within this heading, "Sale of ice."
Private ways open to public use, appropriations by cities or towns for removal, **40:6C, 40:6D.**
Public works department.
  Civil service status of snow removal employees, **31:48.**

SNOW AND ICE —Cont'd
Public works department —Cont'd
  Duty to keep state highways clear, **81:19.**
  Storage and use of snow removal chemicals, regulations, **85:7A.**
Roofs, town bylaws providing for removal of snow, **40:21.**
Sale of ice, **94:157-94:162.**
  Cutting of ice unlawfully, penalty, **266:106.**
  Health department.
    Appeal from order, **94:162.**
    Enforcement of orders, **94:161.**
    Municipal inspections, **40:24.**
    Regulation, **111:159.**
  Impure ice, **94:160.**
  Licenses for sale of ice, **101:17.**
  Price list.
    To be filed, **94:158.**
    To be posted on ice wagons, **94:159.**
  Refusal of dealer to sell on request, penalty, **94:157.**
  Requirement of license, **101:17.**
  Scales, vehicles to be provided, **94:158.**
  Sunday, sales, **136:6.**
  Supervision by health department, **111:159.**
  Weight, sale by weight only, **94:159.**
Sanding of roads, agreements between towns, **84:5A.**
Selectmen, agreement with adjoining towns for removal from highway, **84:5A.**
Sidewalks, removal, **40:21, 84:5-84:7, 85:5-85:7A.**
  Abutting owner, removal, **85:5-85:7.**
  Agreement of owner to remove snow, **85:7.**
  Assessments, **85:6.**
  Expense where owner fails to remove, **85:6, 85:7.**
  Municipality may require, **85:5.**
  Town appropriations, **40:7.**
Skating rinks.
  See SKATING RINKS.
Skiing.
  See SKIING.
Special assessment for removal of snow and ice, **85:6.**
State aid to keep highways and streets open in winter, **84:11.**
State highways, clearing, **81:19.**
Street railways.
  Removal of snow and ice, **161:85.**

SNOW AND ICE —Cont'd
Street railways —Cont'd
  Transportation of snow and ice,
    161:50.
Sunday sale of ice, **136:6.**
Tires, metal studded snow tires,
  90:16.
Tort liability for injuries from
  snow and ice.
  Injuries. See within this
    heading, "Injury from snow
    or ice on highway or street."
Towing away motor vehicles
  during removal operations,
  85:2A, 159B:6B.
Vehicles for travel on,
  90B:20-90B:35.
  See RECREATIONAL
    VEHICLES.
Vehicles interfering with removal
  from highways and streets,
  40:21, 85:2A, 159B:6B.
Weights and measures, provisions
  as to sale of ice, **94:158,
  94:159.**

SNOW LOADERS.
Exemption from motor vehicle law,
  90:1.

SNOWMOBILES, 90B:20-90B:35.
**See RECREATIONAL
  VEHICLES.**

SNOW TIRES.
Metal studded tires, **90:16.**

SNOW VEHICLES.
Defined, **90B:20.**
Motor vehicle civil infractions,
  procedure, **90C:1.**
Sales tax.
  Calculation with trade-ins,
    64H:26.
Snowmobiles, **90B:20 to 90B:35.**
Use, consumption, or storage tax.
  Calculation with trade-ins,
    64I:27.

SNUB-NOSE PISTOLS.
Restrictions on sales of firearms
  with barrels of less than three
  inches, **140:123, 140:131N.**

SNUFF.
Excise tax, smokeless tobacco,
  64C:1, 64C:6.
Minors, giving or selling, **270:6.**

SOAP.
Automatic sprinklers in buildings
  for manufacturing, etc.,
  148:26.
Prisoners in jail or house of
  correction, furnishing, **126:34.**

SOAP —Cont'd
Term "cosmetic" as not including
  for purposes of food and drug
  inspection law, **94:1.**

SOCCER.
Volunteer services, tort liability,
  231:85V.

**SOCIAL AND ECONOMIC
  OPPORTUNITY DIVISION
  AND COUNCIL, 23B:24,
  118:2.**
**See HOUSING AND
  COMMUNITY
  DEVELOPMENT
  DEPARTMENT.**

SOCIAL CORPORATIONS.
Boxing matches, illegal, charter
  void, **180:28.**
Gaming, charter void for illegal,
  180:27.
Incorporation, **180:1-180:11.**
Liquor law violations, charter void,
  180:27.
Location, change, **180:26.**
Uniform Securities Act,
  exemptions, **110A:402.**

**SOCIAL JUSTICE FOR
  IRELAND DAY.**
Observance, **6:15U.**

SOCIAL SECURITY.
Aged.
  See AGED AND DISABLED,
    ASSISTANCE.
Annual observance of Social
  Security Day, **6:12LL.**
Blind persons.
  Co-operation of public welfare,
    public health and education
    departments in
    administration of Social
    Security Act, **69 Appx:1.**
  Definition regarding eligibility
    for medical assistance,
    6:137.
  Payments by commission for the
    blind to blind persons,
    6:131-6:131J.
Bonds or notes of Commonwealth,
  inclusion of tax information
  regarding consequences to
  recipients of social security
  benefits, **29:48B, 44:22B.**
Community mental health center
  revenues, disposition, **19:24.**
Contributory retirement law, effect
  on benefits, **32:12B, 118C:10.**
Deduction of contributions, **62:3.**
  Notice to employees, **149:150A.**

SOCIAL SECURITY —Cont'd
Dependent children, aid.
  Allowance with income earned
    under exemption from Social
    Security Act, **118:3.**
  Co-operation in administration
    of Social Security Act, **69
    Appx:1.**
  Number of applicant to be listed
    in application, **118:2B.**
  Reports to Department of
    Health, Education, and
    Welfare, **118:5.**
Disability insurance benefits.
  Effect of increase in social
    security benefits, **175:110A.**
Legal assistance to mentally or
  physically disabled persons,
  Supreme Judicial Court
  power, **211:25.**
Vocational rehabilitation
  services for persons
  receiving old age and
  survivor disability insurance
  benefits, **6:78.**
Elder service corps in elder affairs
  department, **19A:13.**
Emergency assistance program,
  matching funds, **18:2.**
Employment security.
  See EMPLOYMENT
    SECURITY.
Exemptions.
  Aid to dependent children,
    allowance with income
    earned under exemption
    from Social Security Act,
    118:3.
  Medical care and assistance,
    exempt income and
    resources, **118E:10.**
  Tax exemption, exclusion of
    social security benefits in
    determining old person's
    eligibility, **59:5.**
Health care finance and policy
  division.
  See HEALTH CARE FINANCE
    AND POLICY DIVISION.
Health records requested from
  providers by persons seeking
  benefits, **111:70, 111:70E,
  112:12CC.**
Housing and urban renewal
  operating agency employees,
  benefits, **121B:12.**
Identification number, commercial
  driver license and application
  form, **90F:7, 90F:8.**
Income standards for medical
  assistance programs, **118E:1.**

SOCIAL SECURITY —Cont'd
Income tax.
  See INCOME TAX.
Intermediate care facilities for mentally retarded persons as affected, **111:71.**
Matching funds emergency assistance programs, **18:2.**
Medical care and assistance.
  Blind persons, definition regarding eligibility for medical assistance, **6:137.**
  Exempt income and resources, **118E:10.**
  Income standards for medical assistance programs, **118E:1.**
  Registration of physicians contingent on agreement relative to Social Security Act Title XVIII health insurance, **112:2.**
Mentally ill and retarded persons.
  Community mental health center revenues, disposition, **19:24.**
  Department of mental health, effect of programs, **19:24.**
  Intermediate care facilities for mentally retarded persons as affected by social security, **111:71.**
Notice of effect on retirement benefits, **32:20.**
Public employees, application, **118C:1-118C:10.**
  Administrative expenditures, **118C:6.**
  Agreement with Federal Security Administrator, **118C:3.**
  Contribution fund, **118C:5.**
  Declaration of policy, **118C:1.**
  Definitions, **118C:2.**
  Housing and urban renewal operating agencies, employees, **121B:12.**
  Joint interstate instrumentality, **118C:3.**
  Plan submitted by instrumentality, **118C:4.**
  Reports.
    By instrumentality, **118C:4.**
    By state board, **118C:8.**
  Rights of members of other contributory retirement systems not affected, **118C:10.**
  Saving clause, **118C:9.**
  State board.
    Retirement board. See within this heading, "Retirement board."

SOCIAL SECURITY —Cont'd
Public welfare.
  Welfare and social services. See within this heading, "Welfare and social services."
Rehabilitation.
  Commission, relation to federal social security programs, **6:80.**
  Determination of disability, by rehabilitation commission, **6:80.**
  Old age and survivors disability benefits, vocational rehabilitation services for persons receiving, **6:78.**
Reports.
  Public employees, application to. See within this heading, "Public employees, application."
Retirement board.
  Functions, **118C:3-118C:8.**
  Reports and recommendations, **118C:8.**
  Rules and regulations, **118C:7.**
  State agency defined, **118C:2.**
  Studies, **118C:8.**
Social services department.
  Welfare and social services. See within this heading, "Welfare and social services."
Supplemental Security Income Commission, **6A:16.**
Taxation.
  See INCOME TAX.
Tax consequences, statement to holders of public bonds or notes, **29:48B, 44:22B.**
Unemployment compensation.
  See EMPLOYMENT SECURITY.
Victims of violent crime, **258C:10.**
Vocational rehabilitation of blind, co-operation in administration of Social Security Act, **69 Appx:1.**
Vocational rehabilitation services for persons receiving old age and survivors disability insurance benefits, **6:78.**
Welfare and social services.
  Co-operation in administration of Social Security Act, **69 Appx:1.**
  Disregarding of certain social security benefits by department, **18:1.**
  Matching funds emergency assistance program, **18:2.**

SOCIAL SECURITY —Cont'd
Welfare and social services —Cont'd
  Social services required under social security, **18B:5.**

SOCIAL SERVICES AND SOCIAL SERVICES DEPARTMENT, 18:1 et seq., 18B:1 et seq.
See WELFARE AND SOCIAL SERVICES.

SOCIAL SERVICES COMMISSIONER.
See WELFARE AND SOCIAL SERVICES.

SOCIAL SERVICES PROGRAM FUND, 29:2MM.

SOCIAL SKILLS AND HABITS.
Private business schools, teaching, **75D:1.**

SOCIAL WORKERS.
Abused or neglected children under 16, social worker's reports, **119:51A.**
Abuse of patients or residents in long-term care facilities, reports and records, **111:72G.**
Advisory council, mental health and retardation, **19:16.**
Application to obtain license, **112:131.**
Assault and battery, protection of social services employees, **265:13D.**
Board of Registration.
  Registration board. See within this heading, "Registration board."
Confidential communications, **18:21, 112:135, 119:51A.**
Corrections department, qualifications for position as psychiatric social worker, **27:2A.**
Definitions, **112:130, 123:1.**
Disclosure of information, regulation, **18:21, 112:135, 119:51A.**
Educational requirements, **112:131.**
Effective date of licenses, **112:136.**
Examinations, inspections, or investigations, **13:84, 112:132, 231:85N.**
Felony conviction, **112:137.**
Foster care review directors, appointment of by commissioner of social services, **18B:6A.**

SOCIAL WORKERS —Cont'd

Gross negligence in practice,
112:137.

Hearings.

Client communications,
disclosure, **90:20A,
90:20A½.**

Disciplining licensee, **112:137.**

Hospitals.

See HOSPITALS AND HEALTH
CARE FACILITIES.

Information acquired in
professional capacity,
disclosure, **18:21, 112:135.**

Licenses, **112:131, 112:132,
112:136, 112:137.**

Registration board. See within
this heading, "Registration
board."

Mental health and retardation.

Advisory council, **19:16.**

Communications with client,
disclosure,
112:135-112:135B.

Nurses, exemption from law,
112:80B.

Privileged and confidential
matters, disclosure of
information, **18:21,
112:135-112:135B, 119:51A.**

Psychiatric social worker in
mental health department,
19:10.

Psychology-related professions or
occupations excluded from
regulations, **112:125.**

Public welfare recipients, periodic
visits, **18:22.**

Qualification of members of
registration board, **13:80.**

Reciprocity for licensing, **112:132.**

Records.

Reports. See within this
heading, "Reports."

Registration board.

Appointment of successor to
board, **13:82.**

Expenses, reimbursement,
13:83.

Hearing for removal from office,
13:82.

Investigatory powers, **13:84,
112:132, 231:85N.**

Meetings, **13:84.**

Membership qualifications,
13:80.

Officers, **13:84.**

Powers and duties, **13:84,
231:85N.**

Term of office, **13:81.**

Reinstating license, **112:137.**

SOCIAL WORKERS —Cont'd

Renewal of licenses, **112:136.**

Reports.

Abused and neglected children
under 16, reports, **119:51A.**

Abuse of patients or residents in
long-term care facilities,
reports and records,
111:72G.

Schools.

See SCHOOLS AND
EDUCATION.

Third party payments for licensed
independent clinical social
workers, **175:47B, 176A:8A,
176B:4A.**

Unlawful or unprofessional
practice, **112:133, 112:134,
112:137.**

**SOCIETY FOR PREVENTION
OF CRUELTY TO
ANIMALS, 129:5, 129:9,
277:78-277:85A.**

See ANIMALS.

**SOCIETY FOR PREVENTION
OF CRUELTY TO
CHILDREN, 18A:9, 22C:56.**

State police, appointment of
special police, **22C:56.**

SOCIETY, LOSS OF.

Children, cause of action, **231:85X.**

Wrongful death damages, **229:2.**

**SOCIETY OF FRIENDS.
See FRIENDS, SOCIETY OF.**

**SOCIETY OF THE SONS OF
THE REVOLUTION.**

Patriotic holiday observances,
municipal appropriations,
40:5.

SOCIOLOGIST.

AIDS advisory board, **111:2F.**

SODA FOUNTAINS.

Cleanliness and sanitation of
places dealing in frozen
desserts or frozen dessert mix,
94:65N.

Lunch counters.

Butter substitute served, **94:58.**

Horse meat, **94:151A.**

Soft drinks, generally.

See SOFT DRINKS.

SODIUM CHLORIDE.

Commercial feed labels, **128:53.**

Drugs and narcotics, **75:36B.**

Generally.

See DRUGS AND
NARCOTICS.

SODIUM CHLORIDE —Cont'd

Snow removal.

Contract quantity, increase,
85:7A.

Storage, **85:7A.**

Watershed, **92:107A.**

SODOMY.

Criminal offense, **272:34.**

Indictment, **277:79.**

Parole, **127:133.**

Unnatural and lascivious acts,
parole of persons convicted,
127:133.

SOFTBALL.

Sports, generally.

See ATHLETICS.

Volunteer services, tort liability,
231:85V.

SOFT DRINKS, 94:10A-94:10G.

Bottling permit.

Licenses or permits. See within
this heading, "Licenses or
permits to bottle or
manufacture."

Containers, **94:319.**

Examination or inspection of
premises and equipment,
94:10C.

Exclusion, **94:10G.**

Health department.

Public health department. See
within this heading, "Public
health department."

Ingredients used in manufacturing
or bottling, **94:10D.**

Inspection of premises and
equipment, **94:10C.**

Licenses or permits to bottle or
manufacture, **94:10A-94:10G.**

Fees, **94:10B.**

Out-of-state manufacturers to
sell within state, permit,
94:10A.

Revocation.

Grounds, **94:10C.**

Hearing upon revocation,
94:10C.

Unlicensed manufacturer, selling
or offering to sell beverages,
94:10A.

Who may grant, **94:10B.**

Offenses and penalties by
manufacturers and bottlers,
94:10F.

Public health department.

Examination of licensee's
premises and equipment,
94:10C.

Out-of-state manufacturers to
sell within state, permit,
94:10A.

SOFT DRINKS —Cont'd

Public health department —Cont'd

Permit to manufacture or bottle, **94:10A, 94:10B.**

Regulation of manufacturing and bottling, **94:10E.**

Revocation of licenses.

Licenses or permits to bottle or manufacture. See within this heading, "Licenses or permits to bottle or manufacture."

Sanitary regulations, **94:10C-94:10E.**

Selling or offering to sell beverages of unlicensed manufacturer, **94:10A.**

Sunday, sales, **136:6.**

Vending machine sales, **94:308-94:313.**

See VENDING MACHINES.

SOFTWARE.

Campaign finance reports, **55:18C.**

Cities and towns borrowing money for, **44:7.**

Computers, generally.

See DATA PROCESSING.

Firearms record keeping fund, **29:2SS.**

Massachusetts college student loan authority, **15C:15B.**

Repurchase by equipment dealers, **93G:4.**

Schools and education.

Educational technology plan, **15A:3A.**

Procurement, contracts awarded without bids, **30B:7.**

SOIL CONSERVATION, 128B:1 et seq.

Committee for conservation of soil, **21:19, 21:20.**

County acquisition of land, **34:25.**

Erosion.

See EROSION.

Harbors and waterways, public works department's authority to enter into agreement with conservation service for improvement, **91:11.**

Restrictions on real property, **184:31-184:33.**

SOIL OR DIRT.

Burning of, as criminal offense, **266:5, 266:5A.**

Conservation.

See SOIL CONSERVATION.

Digging up and carrying away without owner's consent, **266:113.**

SOIL OR DIRT —Cont'd

Environmental Protection Department, cover and disposal of soil containing lead, **21A:17.**

Harbors, depositing, **102:17.**

Municipal regulation of removal, **40:21.**

Official soil of Commonwealth, **2:33.**

Paxton soil series, designation as official soil of Commonwealth, **2:33.**

Public works construction as including soil explorations, **149:27D.**

Registration of earth-moving vehicles, **90:9.**

Street railways, conveyance, **161:50.**

Zoning and planning, granting of variance, **40A:10.**

SOLAR ENERGY.

Credit unions, solar heating system, **171:60.**

Defined, **40A:1A.**

Easements, protection of access to sunlight, **187:1A.**

Exemption of solar systems from taxation, **59:5.**

Historic districts, protection of access to sunlight, **40C:7.**

Incentives through tax benefits for use of alternative energy resources, **63:38H.**

Long-range utility forecasts, **164:69I.**

Municipal planning, protection of access to sunlight, **41:81M, 41:81Q.**

Real property provisions, protection of access to sunlight, **184:23C.**

Zoning.

Definitions, **40A:1A.**

Special permits, protection of access to sunlight, **40A:9, 40A:9B.**

Sunlight, protection of access, **40A:3.**

SOLDIERS.
See MILITARY AFFAIRS.

SOLDIERS' AND SAILORS' CIVIL RELIEF ACT.

Mobile homes of nonresident military personnel, exemption from taxation, **59:5.**

Reinstatement of residents, **S35:14.**

SOLDIERS' HOME IN HOLYOKE, 6:70, 6:71.

Attorney general defending employees of Home in actions involving alleged civil rights violations, **12:3E.**

Dead bodies, soldiers' home in Holyoke exempt from provisions, **113:1.**

Emergency services, retired personnel performing, **32:91.**

Employment dislocations and assistance in reemployment of dislocated workers, **6:17.**

Federal aid, **10:7.**

Health and human services executive office, trustees as agency within, **6A:16.**

Hospital service corporations, contract, **176:1.**

Medical director, **6:71.**

Physical therapy law inapplicable to nurses, **112:23O.**

Reimbursement of town for tax loss, **58:13.**

Removal of employees, **30:9B.**

Subscriber's contract precluding payment to soldiers' home, **175:22.**

Superintendent, **6:17, 6:71.**

Supervision, **6:17.**

Treasurer, **6:71.**

Trustees, **6:70, 6:71.**

Unclaimed funds and bank accounts of former patients, **200A:14.**

SOLDIERS' HOME IN MASSACHUSETTS, 115A:1 et seq.

Abandoned, lost, or unclaimed funds and bank accounts of patients, **115A:6, 115A:7, 200A:14.**

Attorney general defending employee of Home in action involving alleged civil rights violations, **12:3E.**

Board of trustees, **6:40, 6:41.**

Governor and council, appointment and supervision, **6:17, 6:40.**

Holyoke, soldiers' home in, **6:70, 6:71.**

Insurance coverage for buildings and contents, trustees authorized to procure, **115A:11.**

Rules and regulations, **115A:5.**

Buildings and contents of, insurance coverage, **115A:11.**

Chapels, lease of land, **115A:8.**

SOLDIERS' HOME IN MASSACHUSETTS —Cont'd

Constitution of Massachusetts, public funds may be used for maintenance and support of Soldiers' Home in Massachusetts, **MA Const Amend Art 18.**

Dead bodies, inapplicability of law as to disposition, **113:1.**

Emergency services, employment of retired persons, **32:91.**

Employment dislocations and assistance in reemployment of dislocated workers, **6:17.**

Escheat of intestate estates of patients, **190:3.**

Exclusion or discharge of certain persons, **115A:3, 115A:5.**

Federal aid, **10:7.**

Governor and council, supervision, **6:17, 6:40.**

Health and human services executive office, trustees as agency within, **6A:16.**

Health, welfare, and retirement funds not to restrict payment of medical or hospital expenses, **175:22.**

Holyoke, Soldiers' Home in.
See SOLDIERS' HOME IN HOLYOKE.

Hospital service corporations, contracts, **176A:1.**

Hours of labor and overtime pay laws inapplicable to certain officials and employees, **149:30A, 149:30B.**

Insurance.
Building and contents of Soldier's Home in Massachusetts, issuances, **115A:11.**
Medical and surgical expenses as affected by treatment, insurer's liability, **175:22.**

Intestate estates of patients, escheat, **190:3.**

Medical and surgical expenses, treatment by soldiers' homes as affecting insurer's liability, **175:22.**

Patients' rights, **111:70E.**

Persons entitled to benefits, **115A:1, 115A:3, 115A:4.**

Polish army, admission of veterans, **115A:4.**

Religious beliefs, patients' right to worship in accordance, **115A:8.**

Removal of employees, **30:9B.**

SOLDIERS' HOME IN MASSACHUSETTS —Cont'd

Residence requirements for admission, **115A:3.**

Retirement systems and pensions.
Employment of retired persons in soldiers' homes, **32:91.**
Medical and hospital expense payments to home, **175:22.**

Rules and regulations of trustees, **115A:5.**

Service, defined, **115A:2.**

State police, special police officers, **22C:62.**

Superintendent of, appointment, **6:17.**

Supervision by governor and council, **6:17, 6:40.**

Towns, reimbursement for tax loss, **58:13.**

Trespassing or refusing to leave, **266:123.**

Trustees.
Board of trustees. See within this heading, "Board of trustees."

Unclaimed funds in bank accounts of former patients, **115A:6, 115A:7, 200A:14.**

United Nations, service under flag, **6:41.**

Voting rights of veterans residing in Chelsea Soldiers' Home, **51:4.**

Women veterans, domiciliary facilities, **115A:9.**

SOLDIERS' MEMORIALS.
Trustees, **41:105.**

SOLEMNIZATION OF MARRIAGE.
See MARRIAGE.

SOLICITOR GENERAL.
Constitution.
See CONSTITUTION OF MASSACHUSETTS.

SOLICITORS AND SOLICITATION.
Alcoholic liquors.
Foreign importers and manufacturers, **138:18A.**
Salesmen as solicitors, **138:19A.**
Alcoholism Treatment and Rehabilitation Law, solicitation of funds, **111B:5.**
Attorneys at law.
See ATTORNEYS AT LAW.
Blind persons, fund raising for benefit, **6:138-6:141.**
Bonds and undertakings, **68:23, 68:24.**

SOLICITORS AND SOLICITATION —Cont'd

Campaign expenditures.
See CAMPAIGN EXPENDITURES AND CONTRIBUTIONS.

Charities.
See CHARITIES AND CHARITABLE CONTRIBUTIONS.

Chiropractors, solicitation of patronage, **112:97.**

Cities.
See CITIES AND TOWNS.

Door-to-door sales.
See TRANSIENT VENDORS.

Embalmers and funeral directors, **112:84.**

Employment agencies prohibited from soliciting for inducing employees to leave employment, **140:46K.**

Employment security claims, soliciting employment to prosecute or oppose, **151A:37.**

Fines and penalties, **265:1, 265:2.**
Charitable organizations soliciting contributions from public, offenses, **68:30.**
Jury list, penalty for soliciting placing of name, **234:38.**
Sidewalk, sale of merchandise, **93:40.**
Vehicles, soliciting purchases or contributions from occupants, **85:17A.**
Votes or distribution of campaign literature in voter registration offices, **51:52A.**

Flags, emblems, and uniforms, misuse, **264:5, 264:10A.**

Fraternal benefit societies.
See FRATERNAL BENEFIT SOCIETIES.

Governmental units pooled insurance, solicitation of membership in group, **40M:9.**

Group health insurance for older persons, solicitation of business, **175:110C.**

Hawkers and peddlers.
Transient vendors.
See TRANSIENT VENDORS.

Hospitals and health care facilities.
Charitable contributions, **68:20.**
Conditions as to public solicitation of funds, **111:25D.**

Hospital service corporations, **176A:15.**

**SOLICITORS AND
SOLICITATION** —Cont'd
Insurance.
See INSURANCE.
Labor relations.
See LABOR RELATIONS AND
DISPUTES.
Legislative agents, gifts, **268B:6.**
Lottery tickets, **271:11.**
Medical service corporations,
176B:4.
Misuse of flags, emblems,
uniforms, etc., **264:5, 264:10A.**
Nonprofit corporations.
See NONPROFIT
CORPORATIONS AND
ORGANIZATIONS.
Peddlers.
Transient vendors.
See TRANSIENT VENDORS.
Penalties.
Fines and penalties. See within
this heading, "Fines and
penalties."
Personal jurisdiction based upon
acts or conduct within
Commonwealth, **223A:3.**
Police.
See POLICE.
Prostitution.
See PROSTITUTION.
Public employees, solicitation of
gifts or outside compensation,
**268A:2, 268A:3, 268A:11,
268A:17.**
Sidewalk sale of merchandise,
93:40.
Stopping vehicle to solicit funds,
penalty, **85:17A.**
Transient vendors.
See TRANSIENT VENDORS.
Unlawful use of flags, emblems, or
uniforms, **264:5, 264:10A.**

**SOLID WASTE, 16:18 et seq.,
270:16 et seq.
See GARBAGE AND RUBBISH.**

**SOLID WASTE FACILITIES,
21H:1 - 21H:8.**
Contracts and leases,
municipalities, **44:28C.**
Disposal, authorization, **16:19.**
Hazardous waste, generally.
See HAZARDOUS WASTE
FACILITIES SITING.
Master plans, **16:21.**
Taxation, **16:24.**

**SOLITARY CONFINEMENT.
See CORRECTIONAL
INSTITUTIONS.**

**SOLVENCY.
See INSOLVENCY AND
BANKRUPTCY.**

**SOLVENCY ACCOUNT,
151A:14, 151A:14A,
151A:14C, 151A:14G,
151A:14K, 151A:14L,
151A:30, 151A:30B,
151A:69C.**

**SOMBA.
See MINORITY BUSINESS
ASSISTANCE.**

SOMERSET.
Congressional district, **57:1.**
District court, **218:1.**
Medical examiner district, **38:1.**
Senatorial district, **57:3.**

SOMERVILLE.
Congressional district, **57:1.**
District court, **218:1.**
Embalmers' and funeral directors'
registration board,
representation, **13:29.**
Medical examiner district, **38:1.**
Metropolitan air pollution control
district, **111:142B.**
Metropolitan area planning
district, membership, **40B:26.**
Parks, provision by metropolitan
commission, **92:33.**
Refuse disposal, **92:9A.**
Senatorial district, **57:3.**
Six-man jury trial of criminal
cases, right, **218:27A.**
Snow emergency parking
violations, **397:3.**

SONGS.
Children employed as singers,
149:104, 149:105.
Glee club song, **2:43.**
Music and musical instruments.
See MUSIC AND MUSICAL
INSTRUMENTS.
Ode to Massachusetts.
Official ode of the
Commonwealth, **2:47.**
Official and folk songs of the
Commonwealth, **2:19, 2:20,
2:31.**
Patriotic song of Commonwealth,
Massachusetts (Because of You
Our Land Is Free), **2:31.**
Star Spangled Banner, manner of
playing, **264:9.**

**SONS OF AMERICAN
REVOLUTION.**
Patriotic holiday observances,
municipal appropriations,
40:5.

**SONS OF UNION VETERANS
OF CIVIL WAR.**
Flag, **264:5.**
Insignia, unlawful use, **266:70.**
Patriotic holiday observances,
municipal appropriations,
40:5.
State house, room, **8:16A.**
Uniform, unlawful use, **264:10A.**

**SORORITIES AND
FRATERNITIES.**
Ceremonial bonfires authorized,
111:142H.
Employment security as to
domestic service, **151A:6.**
Fraudulent use of names of,
penalty, **266:71, 266:71A,
266:72.**
Houses as subject to laws
regulating lodging houses,
51:10A, 140:22.
Registration of voters, fraternity
houses as lodging for purpose,
51:10A.
Sundays, activities prohibited,
136:6.
Tenancies at institutions of higher
education, termination,
186:17.
Voter registration, listing of
residents for purposes,
51:10A.

SOUNDINGS.
Boston water and sewer
commission, **S17:6.**
County highways, **82:11A.**
Highways.
State highways, **81:7F.**
Turnpike authority and
metropolitan highway
system, **81A:4.**
Massachusetts Bay transportation
authority, **161A:35.**
Massachusetts parking authority,
S71:6.
Massachusetts port authority,
S73:4.
Massachusetts water resource
authority, **S67:8.**
Metropolitan sewers, water and
parks, **92:103.**
Radioactive waste management,
111H:20.
Water and sewer commission,
powers, **40N:8.**

SOUND PRESSURE LEVELS.
Motorcycle sound emission levels,
90:7S-90:7U.
See MOTORCYCLES.

SOUND PRESSURE LEVELS
—Cont'd
Mufflers.
See MUFFLERS.
Recreation and snow vehicles,
restrictions as to noise,
90B:24.

**SOUND RECORDING
EQUIPMENT.**
Electronic recording devices and
equipment.
See ELECTRONIC
RECORDING DEVICES
AND EQUIPMENT.
Phonograph records.
See PHONOGRAPH RECORDS.

SOUTH AFRICA.
Doing business, **32:23, 40D:12.**
Pension fund investments in firms
doing business in or with
South Africa, **32:23.**
Retirement funds, investments,
32:23.

SOUTHAMPTON.
Congressional district, **57:1.**
Medical examiner district, **38:1.**
Senatorial district, **57:3.**

SOUTHBOROUGH.
Congressional district, **57:1.**
District court, **218:1.**
Medical examiner district, **38:1.**
Senatorial district, **57:3.**

SOUTH BOSTON.
Concurrent jurisdiction of
municipal court over waters
and islands, **218:3.**
Justices of municipal court,
231:108.
Municipal court of, **218:1.**

SOUTHBRIDGE.
Airport, lease, **90:51F.**
Congressional district, **57:1.**
District court, **218:1.**
Senatorial district, **57:3.**

SOUTH CAROLINA.
First Congress, representation in,
US Const Art 1 Sec 2 cl 3.

**SOUTHEASTERN
MASSACHUSETTS
TECHNOLOGICAL
INSTITUTE.**
See SOUTHEASTERN
MASSACHUSETTS
UNIVERSITY.

**SOUTHEASTERN
MASSACHUSETTS
UNIVERSITY, 75B:1 et seq.**
Annuities, purchase by employees,
15:18A.

**SOUTHEASTERN
MASSACHUSETTS
UNIVERSITY** —Cont'd
Board of trustees, traffic
violations, **90C:1.**
Contracting power of board of
trustees of colleges and
universities, **15C:14A.**
Education department of state,
board of trustees, **90C:1.**
Employees.
Officers, professional staff and
employees. See within this
heading, "Officers,
professional staff and
employees."
General court.
See GENERAL COURT.
Group annuities for employees,
15:18A.
Labor and employment.
Officers, professional staff and
employees. See within this
heading, "Officers,
professional staff and
employees."
Officers, professional staff and
employees.
Board of trustees, traffic
violations, **90C:1.**
Salaries, establishment, **30:46.**
Salaries, establishment, **30:46.**
Traffic violations, **90C:1.**
Trustees, board, **90C:1.**

**SOUTHEASTERN REGIONAL
PLANNING AND
ECONOMIC
DEVELOPMENT
DISTRICT, 40B:9-40B:19.**
Action or suit, power to bring,
40B:14.
Aldermen.
Selectmen. See within this
heading, "Selectmen."
Assessment against cities and
towns of amounts necessary to
pay costs and expenses of
district, **40B:18.**
Audit of accounts of commission,
40B:18.
Cities, and towns, membership,
40B:10.
City council, termination of city's
membership in district,
40B:10.
City manager.
Appointment of commission
members to serve interim
term, **40B:11.**
Consultation with officials of
municipality to be included
or excluded from district,
40B:10.

**SOUTHEASTERN REGIONAL
PLANNING AND
ECONOMIC
DEVELOPMENT DISTRICT**
—Cont'd
City manager —Cont'd
Membership of commission,
40B:12.
Membership of executive
committee, **40B:15.**
Report as to audits of account of
commission, **40B:18.**
Commission, **40B:12.**
Appointment of committees,
40B:15.
Appointment of members to
serve interim term, **40B:11.**
Approval of contracts, **40B:17.**
Audit of accounts, **40B:18.**
Borrowing in anticipation of
revenue, restriction, **40B:12.**
Committees, appointment and
membership, **40B:15,
40B:17.**
Election of officers, **40B:11,
40B:15.**
Executive director, **40B:16.**
Bond required, **40B:15.**
Interim terms, appointments,
40:11.
Meetings, **40B:15.**
Membership, **40B:12.**
Records to be kept, **40B:15.**
Reports, **40B:14.**
Salaries or compensation of
employees or members,
40B:15, 40B:16.
Compensation.
Salaries or compensation. See
within this heading,
"Salaries or compensation."
Contracts to receive services,
facilities, assistance or money
payments, **40B:17.**
Debt in anticipation of revenue,
40B:14.
Establishment, **40B:9.**
Estimates of costs and expenses of
district for current fiscal year,
40B:18.
Exchange of information with
districts, agencies, political
subdivisions of
Commonwealth, **40B:19.**
Executive committee, **40B:15.**
Executive director.
Commission. See within this
heading, "Commission."
Expenditures or obligations.
Assessment against cities and
towns of amounts necessary
to pay costs and expenses of
district, **40B:18.**

SOUTHEASTERN REGIONAL PLANNING AND ECONOMIC DEVELOPMENT DISTRICT —Cont'd

Expenditures or obligations
—Cont'd
Conditions and limitations, **40B:17.**
Mayors.
Consultation with officials of municipalities to be included or excluded from district, **40B:10.**
Membership of commission, **40B:12.**
Membership of executive committee, **40B:15.**
Report as to audit of commission accounts, **40B:18.**
Records.
Commission to keep, **40B:15.**
Reports. See within this heading, "Reports."
Transfer of records on dissolution of Southeastern Massachusetts Regional Planning District, **40B:11.**
Regional planning district, dissolution, **40B:11.**
Reports.
Audit of accounts of commission, reports, **40B:18.**
Commission to make and publish, **40B:14.**
Transfer to successor district or dissolution of Southeastern Massachusetts Regional Planning District, **40B:11.**
Reserve funds, accumulation, **40B:18.**
Resident population of federal military installations, exclusion of in apportioning cost on per capita basis, **40B:7.**
Salaries or compensation.
Commission members, **40B:15.**
Employees of commission, **40B:16.**
Selectmen.
Appointment of commission members to serve interim term, **40B:11.**
Consultation with officials of municipality to be included or excluded from district, **40B:10.**
Executive committee, membership, **40B:15.**
Membership of executive committee, **40B:15.**

SOUTHEASTERN REGIONAL PLANNING AND ECONOMIC DEVELOPMENT DISTRICT —Cont'd

Selectmen —Cont'd
Membership on commission, **40B:12.**
Reports of audit of accounts of commission, **40B:18.**
Southeastern Massachusetts Regional Planning District, transfer of employees, records and property on dissolution, **40B:11.**
Technical advisory committees, **40B:15.**
Termination of membership in district by cities and towns, **40B:10.**
Town meeting, termination of town's membership in district, **40B:10.**
Wages.
Salaries or compensation. See within this heading, "Salaries or compensation."

SOUTHEASTERN REGIONAL TRANSIT AUTHORITY.
Authorization, **161B:2.**
Off-street parking facilities, **S21:1.**
Transit authorities, generally. See REGIONAL TRANSIT AUTHORITIES.

SOUTHERN BERKSHIRE.
Stockbridge, district court to exercise concurrent jurisdiction in town, **218:1.**

SOUTHERN MIDDLESEX DISTRICT COURT.
Additional justice, **218:6.**
Misdemeanor trials by juries of six, **218:26.**

SOUTH ESSEX OCEAN SANCTUARY.
Activities permitted, **132A:15.**
Area included, **132A:13.**
Establishment, **132A:13.**

SOUTH HADLEY.
Congressional district, **57:1.**
District court, **218:1.**
Medical examiner district, **38:1.**
Senatorial district, **57:3.**

SOUTH SHORE TRANSPORTATION DISTRICT.
Open meeting law as applicable to board of managers' meetings, **30A:11A.**

SOUTHWICK.
Congressional district, **57:1.**
District court, **218:1.**
Medical examiner district, **38:1.**
Senatorial district, **57:3.**

SOVEREIGN IMMUNITY.
Alcoholism treatment and rehabilitation law, exemption from liability for duties performed, **111B:13.**
Commonwealth, enforcement of claims against, **258:12.**
Fire department personnel, **48:49, 48:76.**
Freedom of expression of students, officials not responsible for expressions made by students, **71:82.**
Public health programs, physicians and nurses carrying out, **112:12C.**
Trespass, governmental immunity of Commonwealth or United States for certain employees committing, **1:9.**

SPACE CRAFT.
Economic diversification program, production of space vehicles as defense-related commercial activity, **23F:1.**
Issuance and classification of policies insuring, **175:80.**

SPACE HEATERS AND STOVES.
Cities and towns, purchase of energy management services, **40:4.**
Drying of material used for construction, **148:25.**
Fines, penalties, and forfeitures, **148:5A, 148:25A, 148:25B.**
Sale or installation, **148:25A.**
Use, **148:5A, 148:25B.**
Polish, manufacture, storage, and sale of explosive polish, **148:46.**
Prohibition as to use, **148:5A, 148:25B.**
Railroad cars, heating, **160:165.**
Sale, use, or installation, **148:5A, 148:25A, 148:25B.**
Unvented liquid fired space heaters, regulation of sale and use, **148:5A, 148:25A.**

SPANISH-AMERICAN WAR.
Flags, **8:17A.**
Holiday commemorating, **6:14A.**
Insignia, improper use, **266:70.**
Military and Naval Order of the Spanish-American War, **264:10A, 266:70.**

SPANISH-AMERICAN WAR
—Cont'd
Veterans generally.
See VETERANS AND
VETERANS'
ORGANIZATIONS.

SPANISH LANGUAGE.
Bilingual English-Spanish voter
registration affidavits,
provision, **51:36.**
High schools, required teaching of
Spanish, **71:13.**

SPARK ARRESTERS.
Forest fires, spark arresters on
steam appliances to prevent,
48:21, 48:22.
Locomotives, required equipment,
160:235.

SPARKLERS.
Fireworks, generally.
See FIREWORKS.
Fireworks known as, fire
prevention regulations,
148:39.

SPARRING.
**See BOXING AND BOXING
MATCHES.**

SPAS.
**See HEALTH SPA
CONTRACTS.**

SPAWNING.
**See MARINE FISH AND
FISHERIES.**

SPEAKER OF HOUSE.
Compensation, **3:9.**

SPEAKING TUBES.
Engine rooms, requirement,
149:124, 149:125.

SPECIAL ADMINISTRATORS.
**See EXECUTORS AND
ADMINISTRATORS.**

**SPECIAL AND LOCAL
LEGISLATION.**
Advertisement of special acts,
3:33.
Alcoholic liquor law exemption for
cities with liquor license board
created, **138:10.**
Avoidance of special legislation,
policy, **3:53.**
Betterments, **80:17.**
Borrowing by cities and towns,
authorization, **4:8, 44:2, 44:15.**
City charters, **4:7, 43B:19.**
Constitution of Massachusetts,
effect of home rule article on
special laws relating to cities
and towns, **MA Const Amend
Art 2 Sec 9.**

**SPECIAL AND LOCAL
LEGISLATION** —Cont'd
Counsel of senate and house,
duties, **3:53.**
Home rule procedures act, effect as
to laws subsequently enacted,
43B:19.
Indebtedness, construction of
special acts authorizing, **4:8,
44:2, 44:15, 71:16.**
Insurance.
Amendments, **175:50.**
Conflict with general laws,
175:30-175:31A.
Notice of organization under
special act, **175:44.**
Liens, **83:29.**
Marine fish and fisheries, effect of
general law, **130:104.**
Municipal indebtedness,
authorization, **4:8, 44:2, 44:15.**
Petitions and publications of
notice, filing, **3:5, 3:7.**
Policy to avoid, **30:33A.**
Railroad corporation, **160:41.**
Recommendations by state officers
or departments, **30:33A.**
Regional school districts, **71:16D.**
State aid for construction of
regional schools, **71:16D.**
Temporary debt, power to incur
in anticipation of revenue,
71:16.
Religious society, **67:28.**

**SPECIAL ASSESSMENTS, 80:1
et seq.**
Abandonment of improvement and
discontinuance of eminent
domain proceedings, **80A:11.**
Abatement of assessments, **80:5 et
seq.**
Advancement of proceedings,
80:9.
Answer to petition, **80:9.**
Appeals.
County commissioners,
appeals, **80:10.**
Superior court, appeals, **80:7.**
Costs of proceeding, **80:9.**
Death of person entitled to
petition, **80:8.**
Defenses to proceeding to be
pleaded, **80:9.**
Extension of time for filing
petition, **80:6.**
Failure to act upon petition for,
80:10A.
Heir or devisee may petition,
80:8.
Interest, **80:5, 80:9.**
Judgment, **80:9.**

SPECIAL ASSESSMENTS
—Cont'd
Abatement of assessments
—Cont'd
Notice.
Appeal from decision as to
abatement, **80:10.**
Decision of abatement, **80:5.**
Effect of failure to act, **80:10A.**
Executor or administrator
may petition, **80:8.**
Extension of time for filing,
80:6.
Filing, **80:5, 80:6.**
Petition, **80:9.**
Petition, **80:5, 80:6.**
Answer, **80:9.**
Appeals, **80:7, 80:10.**
Decedent's estate, filing, **80:8.**
Failure of board to act,
80:10A.
Procedure, **80:9.**
Procedure, **80:9.**
Reimbursement, **80:5.**
Service of process, **80:9.**
Trial, **80:9.**
Addition to annual tax, **80:13.**
Adoption of charter by city as
affecting, **43:24.**
Advancement of abatement
proceedings, **80:9.**
Agricultural and horticultural
property, **40L:7, 61A:18.**
Airport approach hazards, expense
of obviating, **90:40F.**
Alienation of title as affecting lien
of assessment, **80:12.**
Annual tax, addition of special
assessments, **80:13.**
Answer to petition.
For abatement, **80:9.**
For eminent domain, **80A:5.**
Appeals.
Abatement of assessments, **80:7,
80:10.**
Division of assessment, **80:15.**
Eminent domain proceedings,
80A:10.
Apportionment, **80:13.**
Eminent domain proceedings,
80A:14.
Lessee, proportion to be paid,
80:11.
Reapportionment of certain
assessments, **80:13.**
Area benefited, description to be
included in order, **80:2.**
Assessors, duties, **80:13.**
Audit of municipal accounts,
assessment of tax for payment
of expenses, **44:41.**

SPECIAL ASSESSMENTS
—Cont'd
Auditor appointed by court in
proceeding for abatement,
80:9.
Authorized, **80:1, 80A:1.**
Banks, exemption of savings banks
from local tax, **59:5.**
Benefit of improvement,
assessment not to exceed,
80:1.
Bond payments, **44:16, 44:19.**
Bridges, **84:14.**
Certificates.
Dismissal or discontinuance of
eminent domain
proceedings, **80A:11.**
Fee for collector's certificate to
dissolve lien, **80:12.**
Charter, effect of city's adoption,
43:24.
Collectors of taxes.
Duties of, **80:4.**
Fee for collector's certificate to
dissolve lien, **80:12.**
Commissioners, **80A:8, 80A:10,
80A:15.**
Compensation, **21D:5, 80A:15.**
Condemnation, assessment in
course of, **80A:1 et seq.**
Eminent domain.
See EMINENT DOMAIN.
Condominiums, assessments
against, **183A:14.**
Continuation of lien, **80:12.**
Contribution by lessee, **80:11.**
Correction, **80:4.**
Costs of proceedings.
Abatement proceedings, **80:9.**
Eminent domain proceedings,
80A:13.
Lessee's proportion, petition to
superior court to determine,
80:11.
County commissioners.
Appeal of refusal to abate,
80:10.
Eminent domain proceedings,
80A:8, 80A:10, 80A:15.
Damages by taking of property
included in cost for purpose of
determining, **80:1.**
Date.
Abatement petition, filing, **80:5,
80:6.**
Appeal from decision as to
abatement, **80:7.**
Assessment, time, **80:1.**
Election to surrender land
assessed, **80:3.**
Extension of time.
Filing petition for abatement,
80:6.

SPECIAL ASSESSMENTS
—Cont'd
Date —Cont'd
Extension of time —Cont'd
Payment where land not
build, **80:13A.**
Lien, duration, **80:12.**
Reassessment, **80:16.**
Decedent's estate.
Abatement, filing, **80:8.**
Payment of assessment, **80:13B.**
Default in eminent domain
proceedings, **80A:6.**
Defenses to petition for abatement,
80:9.
Deferral and recovery agreement,
80:13B.
Demand for payment, **60:17.**
Description of affected area, **80:2.**
Eminent domain proceedings,
80A:3.
Discharge of lien, **80:12.**
Discontinuance of eminent domain
proceedings, **80A:11.**
Division of assessment upon
division of property, **80:15.**
Drains, **83:14, 83:15, 83:27, 83:28.**
See SEWERS AND DRAINS.
Elections.
Eminent domain proceedings,
election, **80A:16.**
Surrender of land assessed,
election, **80:3.**
Elevators, assessment for costs of
inspection system, **143:62.**
Eminent domain and judicial
proceedings, assessments in
course, **80A:1 et seq.**
Abandonment of improvement,
80A:11.
Amendment of commissioners'
report, **80A:10.**
Answer to petition, **80A:5.**
Appeals, **80A:10.**
Apportionment of assessments,
80A:14.
Assumption of betterments as
condition of settlement of
claim for damages, **79:39.**
Authorized, **80A:1.**
Benefit, commissioners to
determine value, **80A:8.**
Certificate of discontinuance or
dismissal of proceedings,
recording, **80A:11.**
Commissioners.
Amount of benefit,
determination, **80A:8.**
Appointment, **80A:8.**
Compensation, **80A:15.**
Confirmation of
commissioners' report,
80A:10.

SPECIAL ASSESSMENTS
—Cont'd
Eminent domain and judicial
proceedings, assessments in
course —Cont'd
Commissioners —Cont'd
Powers and duties, **80A:8.**
Confirmation of commissioners'
report, **80A:10.**
Costs, awarding, **80A:13.**
Damages included in costs for
purpose of determining
special or local assessments,
80:1.
Default, **80A:6.**
Description of area in order,
80A:3.
Discontinuance of proceedings,
80A:11.
Election to assess by this
method, **80A:16.**
Estimate of assessments, **80A:3.**
Guardian ad litem, **80A:6.**
Compensation, **80A:15.**
Hearing, **80A:7.**
Intent to take, order, **80A:2,
80A:3.**
Judgment of condemnation,
80A:10, 80A:11.
Jury, redetermination, **80A:9,
80A:10.**
Law applicable to proceedings,
80A:15.
Liens, **80A:14.**
Necessary party, effect of, failure
to join, **80A:15.**
Notice.
Adoption of order, **80A:3.**
Order, **80A:4.**
Petition instituting proceedings,
80A:4.
Answer to petition, **80A:5.**
Dismissal upon failure to
enter judgment of
condemnation, **80A:10.**
Records and reports.
Amendment or confirmation of
report of commissioners,
80A:10.
Certificate of discontinuance
or dismissal of
proceedings, **80A:11.**
Judgment of condemnation,
recording, **80A:10, 80A:11.**
Order, plan, and estimate,
recording, **80A:3.**
Redetermination by jury, **80A:9,
80A:10.**
Registry of deeds.
Certificate of discontinuance
or dismissal of
proceedings, recording,
80A:11.

SPECIAL ASSESSMENTS
—Cont'd

Eminent domain and judicial proceedings, assessments in course —Cont'd

Registry of deeds —Cont'd

Judgment or interlocutory judgment of condemnation recorded, **80A:10, 80A:11.**

Regulation of procedure, **80A:15.**

Statement as to assessment, order to contain, **79:1, 80A:2.**

Estates of decedents.

Abatement, filing, **80:8.**

Payment of assessment by estate, **80:13B.**

Estimates included in order, **80:2, 80:3, 80A:3.**

Exclusiveness of provisions, **80:17.**

Executor or administrator may petition for abatement, **80:8.**

Extension of time.

Filing petition for abatement, **80:6.**

Payment where land not built upon, **80:13A.**

Fees.

Collector's certificate to dissolve lien, **80:12.**

Filing fee, **80:13B.**

Forest lands, **61:4.**

Guardian ad litem, eminent domain proceedings, **80A:6, 80A:15.**

Hazardous waste facilities siting. See HAZARDOUS WASTE FACILITIES SITING.

Hearing of case in eminent domain or special assessment by judicial proceedings, **80A:7.**

Heir or devisee may petition for abatement, **80:8.**

Highways and streets, construction, **82:12.**

Improvement districts.

Assessments by, **59:23, 59:25.**

Liens, **252:11.**

Installment payment, **80:13.**

Interest on money.

Abatement, **80:5, 80:9.**

Assessments, **80:13, 80:13B.**

Railroad aid indebtedness, **59:24.**

Suspension of improvement assessments, effect of interest, **60:3B.**

Time of payment extended, **80:13A.**

Water rate or sewer use charge added to tax, **59:57.**

SPECIAL ASSESSMENTS
—Cont'd

Interrogatories in abatement proceedings, **80:9.**

Invalid assessments, reassessment, **80:16.**

Joinder, failure to join necessary party in eminent domain proceedings, **80A:15.**

Judgments and decrees.

Abatement proceedings, **80:9.**

Eminent domain proceedings, **80A:10, 80A:11.**

Orders, **80:1-80:3, 80A:2-80A:4.**

Jury and jury trial.

Proceedings for abatement, **80:9.**

Redetermination, **80A:9, 80A:10.**

Laying out or alteration of highways and streets, **82:12.**

Leases, contribution by lessees, **80:11.**

Liability for taxes, **80:4.**

Registration of title as affecting, **185:46, 185:84.**

Licenses and permits, municipal discretion in granting or renewing, **40:57.**

Liens, **80:12.**

Duration and termination, **80:12.**

Eminent domain proceedings, **80A:14.**

Improvement districts, **252:11.**

Mortgages, **80:15, 203:23.**

Registered land, enforcement against, **185:84.**

Street sprinkling assessments, **40:18.**

Minors entitled to real estate tax exemption, suspension of improvement assessments, **60:3B.**

Mortgages.

Division of assessment, **80:15.**

Trust property mortgaged to pay assessment, **203:23.**

Necessary party, failure to join in eminent domain proceedings, **80A:15.**

Notices.

Abatement of assessments, **80:5, 80:6, 80A:8-80A:10A.**

Division of assessment, notice of intent, **80:15.**

Election to surrender land assessed, **80:3.**

Eminent domain proceedings, **80A:3, 80A:4.**

Owners, notice, **80:4.**

Order, **80:1, 80:2.**

Eminent domain proceedings, orders, **80A:2 et seq.**

SPECIAL ASSESSMENTS
—Cont'd

Order —Cont'd

Estimates included, **80:2, 80:3, 80A:3.**

Park loans, application, **45:6.**

Partition of land assessed, division of assessment, **80:15.**

Payment.

Bond payments, **44:16, 44:19.**

Decedent's estate, payment of assessment, **80:13B.**

Demand, **60:17.**

Extension of time, **80:13A.**

Installments, **80:13.**

Mortgages, **80:15, 203:23.**

Surrendered land, payment, **80:3.**

Suspension of payment, **60:3B.**

Personal liability of owner, **80:4.**

Petitions.

Abatement of assessments, **80:5-80:10A.**

Answer to petition, **80:9, 80A:5.**

Eminent domain proceedings, **80A:4, 80A:5, 80A:10.**

Lessee, petition to determine contribution, **80:11.**

Plan of area benefits to be referred to in order, **80:2.**

Preliminary tax bills, **59:23D.**

Private roads and bridges, **84:14.**

Process and service in proceedings for abatement, **80:9.**

Proration, **80:1.**

Railroad aid indebtedness, assessments to repay, **59:24.**

Reapportionment of certain betterment assessments, **80:13.**

Reassessment, **80:16, 80:17.**

Records and reports.

Abatement petition, **80:5, 80:6.**

Betterment assessments, orders, **80:2.**

Eminent domain proceedings, **80A:3, 80A:10, 80A:11.**

Filing fee, **80:13B.**

Liens, dissolution, **80:12.**

Orders, plans, and estimates, **80:2.**

Registry of deeds. See within this heading, "Registry of deeds."

Sidewalk assessments, **83:27.**

Recreational lands as subject, **61B:13.**

Redemption of land sold for nonpayment, **80:4.**

Regional transportation authorities, exemption, **161B:13.**

SPECIAL ASSESSMENTS
—Cont'd
Registration of title as affecting
  liability, **185:46, 185:84.**
Registry of deeds.
  Deferral and recovery
    agreements pertaining to
    betterment assessments,
    recording, **80:13B.**
  Dissolution of lien, filing, **80:12.**
  Drains, sewers, and sidewalks,
    recordation of assessment
    statements, **83:27.**
  Eminent domain proceedings,
    80A:10, 80A:11.
  Order, recording of estimate and
    plan, **80:2.**
Rehabilitation of owner-occupied
  residential properties, special
  assessment policy for, **59:5J.**
Reimbursement upon abatement,
  80:5.
Review.
  Abatement of assessments, **80:7,**
    80:10.
  Division of assessment, **80:15.**
  Eminent domain proceedings,
    80A:10.
Salaries and compensation, **21D:5,**
  80A:15.
Sale of land assessed.
  Division of assessment upon
    division of land, **80:15.**
  For nonpayment of assessments,
    80:4.
  Prohibition against, where
    unpaid, **80:13B.**
  Surrendered land, **80:3.**
Savings banks, exemption from
  local tax, **59:5.**
Service of process in abatement
  proceedings, **80:9.**
Sewers, **83:14, 83:15, 83:27, 83:28.**
  See SEWERS AND DRAINS.
Sidewalks, **59:38, 83:26-83:29,**
  85:6.
Sinking funds, duties, **44:16.**
Special prior laws as to,
  superseded, **80:17.**
Speedy trial of proceedings for
  abatement, **80:9.**
Sprinkling of streets, **40:17, 40:18.**
Street railways, **161:78 et seq.**
  See STREET RAILWAYS.
Suffolk County extension service
  budget, **128:44A.**
Superior court.
  Appeal from decision as to
    abatement, **80:7.**
  Petition to determine proportion
    to be paid by lessee, **80:11.**

SPECIAL ASSESSMENTS
—Cont'd
Surrender of land assessed, **80:3.**
Surviving spouse, payment,
  80:13B.
Suspension of payment, **60:3B.**
Tax collectors.
  Duties of, **80:4.**
  Fee for collector's certificate to
    dissolve lien, **80:12.**
Termination of lien, **80:12.**
Time or date.
  Abatement petition, filing, **80:5,**
    80:6.
  Appeal from decision as to
    abatement, **80:7.**
  Assessment, time, **80:1.**
  Election to surrender land
    assessed, **80:3.**
  Extension of time.
    Filing petition for abatement,
      80:6.
    Payment where land not
      build, **80:13A.**
  Lien, duration, **80:12.**
  Reassessment, **80:16.**
Trial in proceedings for abatement,
  80:9.
Trust estate may be mortgaged to
  pay, **203:23.**
Undeveloped land, extension of
  time of payment, **80:13A.**
Urban redevelopment corporations,
  121A:10.
Validity of assessments,
  proceedings testing.
  Continuation of lien, **80:12.**
  Extension of time for filing
    petition for abatement, **80:6.**
Value, **80:1, 80:3.**
View by jury in proceedings for
  abatement, **80:9.**
Warrants, **80:4.**
Waterworks and water supply,
  40:42G, 40:42H.
Widows entitled to real estate tax
  exemption, suspension of
  improvement assessments,
  60:3B.
Zoning variance or special permit,
  recording, **40A:11.**

SPECIAL CHARTER.
Corporations.
  See CORPORATIONS.
Legislature, petition for special
  charter for county, **34A:13.**

SPECIAL COUNSEL.
Supplementary proceedings,
  224:26.

SPECIAL COURTS-MARTIAL.
Military courts, **33:69, 33:72.**

SPECIAL DAMAGES.
Commercial Code, **106:1-106.**
Real estate time-shares, **183B:7.**

SPECIAL DEPOSITS.
See BANKS AND BANKING.

SPECIAL DISTRICTS.
See METROPOLITAN
  DISTRICTS.

SPECIAL DUTY.
Indemnification of regular police
  officer assigned to special
  duty, **41:100.**
Leave without loss of pay for
  police injured on special duty,
  41:111F.
Other community assignments of
  police to special duty, **41:99.**

SPECIAL EDUCATION, 15:1F,
  15:1R et seq.
Abolition of ineffective program,
  71B:2.
Absence or presence.
  Attendance. See within this
    heading, "Attendance in
    schools as affected by
    special education programs."
Academically talented children,
  special school programs, **71:1.**
Accounting for funds under joint
  agreements between school
  committees, **71B:4.**
Additional direct or indirect
  instruction consultation
  service and equipment, **71B:2.**
Adequacy of local educational
  facilities, report, **71B:10.**
Administrator of special education
  appointed, **71B:3A.**
Admission of children of preschool
  age, **71B:2.**
Advisory bodies, **15:1G.**
  Regional advisory council. See
    within this heading,
    "Regional advisory council."
  State advisory commission,
    71B:3.
  Transitional advisory committee,
    71B:12B, 71B:12C.
Agreements for provision of special
  education by institutions
  within or without
  Commonwealth, **71B:4.**
Alteration of programs, **71B:2.**
Alternative educational
  placements recommended to
  parents etc., upon rejection of
  evaluations, **71B:3.**
Annual payments by state
  treasurer to city, town, or
  school district, **71B:14.**

SPECIAL EDUCATION —Cont'd
Appropriations, children with disabilities, **71B:5.**
Approval of education department, necessity, **71B:3, 71B:4.**
    Curriculum, **71B:10.**
Assessment of child's needs.
    Evaluation and assessment of child's needs. See within this heading, "Evaluation and assessment of child's needs."
Attendance in schools as affected by special education programs, **76:1.**
    Deaf children, attendance requirement, **76:2A.**
Benefits from programs, periodic evaluation, **71B:2.**
Budget of school committees, **71B:5.**
Certification of publicly supported schools for mentally retarded, **131:13.**
Class size, standard, **71B:9.**
Committees.
    School committee. See within this heading, "School committee."
Confidentiality of evaluations and assessments, **71B:3.**
Consent.
    Approval. See within this heading, "Approval of education department, necessity."
Constitutional limitations on agreements with private schools for special education, **71B:4.**
Consultation service or equipment, additional, **71B:2.**
Continuity of services for children with special needs, **71B:12A, 71B:12B, 71B:12C.**
Contracts or agreements between school committees and private schools or institutions, **71B:4.**
Correctional institutions, special education for school aged children with disabilities who are incarcerated in county houses of detention, **71B:11A.**
Costs.
    Extraordinary and unanticipated special education costs. Zero interest loan program, **71B:5C.**
Curriculum.
    Approval of curriculum at institutions by Department of Education, **71B:10.**

SPECIAL EDUCATION —Cont'd
Curriculum —Cont'd
    Standard, **71B:9.**
Custodians of child.
    Parents, guardians or custodians of child. See within this heading, "Parents, guardians, or custodians of child."
Day school or other facility, **71B:2.**
Deaf children, **71B:2.**
Definitions, **28A:2, 71B:1.**
Directors.
    School departments for special education in certain institutions, **71B:12.**
Disabled or handicapped persons, **15:15B.**
Disadvantaged children, special school programs, **71:1.**
Discrimination as to educational opportunities, **71B:6.**
Division of special education, **15:1F, 15:1R et seq.**
Educational personnel.
    Retirement benefits, **71B:12.**
    Salaries, **71B:12.**
    School departments for special education in certain institutions, **71B:12.**
    Standards, **71B:9.**
Equal educational opportunities, proceedings on denial, **71B:6.**
Establishment of division, **15:1F.**
Evaluation and assessment of child's needs, **71B:2, 71B:3.**
    Confidential nature, **71B:3.**
    Current educational status of child, **71B:3.**
    Hearings and investigations, **71B:3.**
    Independent evaluation, child's right, **71B:3.**
    Necessity, **71B:3.**
    Parent without custody, notification of child's referral for assessment **71:34H.**
    Qualifications of persons making assessments, **71B:3.**
    Records, **71B:3.**
    Referral and placement of child with disability, moving to other school district, **71B:5.**
    Rejection of evaluations, alternative educational placements recommended to parents etc., **71B:3.**
    School committees, duties, **71B:3.**
    Specialist, assessments, **71B:3.**
    Subsequent periodic evaluation, **71B:2.**

SPECIAL EDUCATION —Cont'd
Evaluation and assessment of child's needs —Cont'd
    Tests for, regulated, **71B:7.**
    Waiver of requirements, **71B:3.**
Examination, inspection or investigation.
    Hearings and investigations. See within this heading, "Hearings and investigations."
Excused absence from regular school for special education programs, **76:1.**
Expenses and expenditures.
    Instruction and support of child in institution within or without Commonwealth, expenses, **71B:10.**
    Municipal finance. See within this heading, "Municipal finance."
    Reimbursement. See within this heading, "Reimbursement."
Extraordinary and unanticipated special education costs.
    Pooled risk program, **71B:5B.**
    Zero interest loan program, **71B:5C.**
Family guidance or counseling services, **71B:3.**
Fishing certificate, issuance of special certificates to administration of state schools for retarded, **131:13.**
Foreign states, institutions in, **71B:10, 71B:12.**
Full-time special class teaching or treatment in public school buildings, **71B:2.**
Guardians of child.
    Parents, guardians or custodians of child. See within this heading, "Parents, guardians, or custodians of child."
Guidelines and standards for providing special education programs, **71B:9.**
Handicapped or disabled children, **15:15B.**
Health department.
    Public health department. See within this heading, "Public health department."
Hearings and investigations.
    Equal educational opportunities denial, **71B:6.**
    Evaluation and assessment of child's needs. See within this heading, "Evaluation and assessment of child's needs."

SPECIAL EDUCATION —Cont'd
Hearings and investigations
—Cont'd
Programs, inspection, **71B:3.**
Home teaching or treatment,
71B:2, 71B:3.
Hospital, teaching or treatment,
71B:2.
Implementation of law requiring
programs for children in need
of special education,
preparation of plan, **71B:2.**
Independent evaluation of needs,
child's right, **71B:3.**
Injunction against denial of equal
educational opportunities,
71B:6.
Institutions for special education,
71B:4, 71B:10, 71B:12.
Investigations or inspections.
Hearings and investigations. See
within this heading,
"Hearings and
investigations."
Joint agreements of school
committees for special
education, **71B:4.**
Labor.
Educational personnel. See
within this heading,
"Educational personnel."
Labor and workforce development
department, transitional
advisory committee, **71B:12B,
71B:12C.**
Medical treatment as part, **71B:3.**
Mental health advisory council,
19:16.
Mental health department
programs.
Access, **71B:10.**
School departments for special
education, **71B:12.**
Municipal finance.
Annual payments by state
treasurer to city, town, or
school district, **71B:14.**
Appropriations, children with
disabilities, **71B:5.**
Budget of school committees for
special education, **71B:5.**
City or town treasurers,
payment of special
education funds, **71B:14.**
Reimbursement. See within this
heading, "Reimbursement."
Nonresidents, admission to
Massachusetts hospital school,
111:62J.
Notice to parents or guardian,
71B:3.

SPECIAL EDUCATION —Cont'd
Number of students in class,
standard, **71B:9.**
Occupational training programs,
71B:2.
Organizations providing social,
rehabilitative, health, or
special education services,
contracts, **29:29B.**
Out-of-state institutions, **71B:10,
71B:12.**
Parent and child.
Workshop on rights of students
and parents, **70B:19.**
Curriculum, **71B:9A.**
Parents, guardians, or custodians
of child.
Hearing on evaluation, right,
71B:3.
Liability for expense of
placement in institution
within or without
Commonwealth, **71B:10.**
Notice of referral, **71B:3.**
Support of child in institution,
71B:10.
Periodic evaluation of benefits
from programs, **71B:2.**
Placement of child with special
needs.
Referral and placement of child
with disability. See within
this heading, "Referral and
placement of child with
disability."
Pooled risk program for
extraordinary and
unanticipated special
education costs, **71B:5B.**
Preoccupational training
programs, **71B:2.**
Preschool age children, admission,
71B:2.
Presumptions.
Existence of disability as
requirement of special
education, presumption
against, **71B:3.**
Regular education, presumption
of child's assignment, **71B:3.**
Prima facie denial of equal
educational opportunities,
71B:6.
Private schools.
Agreement for provision of
special education, **71B:4.**
Referral to private schools,
71B:10, 71B:12.
Probation officer to obtain record
of child attending special
class, **119:57.**

SPECIAL EDUCATION —Cont'd
Programs, **71B:2, 71B:3.**
Psychological treatment as part,
71B:3.
Public health department.
Programs, access, **71B:10.**
School departments for special
education, **71B:12.**
Public health institutions, school
departments for special
education, **71B:12.**
Public schools, agreements for
provision of special education,
71B:4.
Public welfare programs, access,
71B:10.
Qualifications of persons making
evaluations as to children's
needs, **71B:3.**
Reassignment of children
dependent upon benefits
derived from programs, **71B:2,
71B:3.**
Records, reports, and returns.
Adequacy of local educational
facilities, report, **71B:10.**
Evaluation and assessment of
child's needs, records,
71B:3.
Probation officer to obtain record
of child attending special
class, **119:57.**
School committees, annual
reports, **71B:6.**
Referral and placement of child
with disability, **71B:3.**
Denial of equal educational
opportunities, **71B:6.**
Institutions within or without
Commonwealth, **71B:10.**
Local schools, in institutions
other than, **71B:10.**
Notice to parent or guardian,
71B:3.
Reassignment, **71B:2, 71B:3.**
Reevaluation of needs, moving to
other school district, **71B:5.**
School committees, duties,
71B:3.
Social services department,
referral, **71B:10.**
Superior court proceedings,
71B:3.
Tests for, regulated, **71B:7.**
Regional advisory council.
Adequacy of local educational
facilities, report, **71B:10.**
Inspection of special education
programs, **71B:3.**
Regular education.
Presumption of child's
assignment, **71B:3.**

SPECIAL EDUCATION —Cont'd
Reimbursement.
Medical or psychological
treatment, **71B:3.**
Municipality, reimbursement for
special education programs,
59:23.
School departments in certain
institutions, reimbursement
of Commonwealth by school
districts, **71B:12.**
Social services, **71B:3.**
Time, **71B:14.**
Transportation costs of persons
attending special education
programs, **71B:8.**
Tuition, reimbursement by
Commonwealth, **76:11.**
Reimbursement program, **71B:5A.**
Reports.
Records, reports, and returns.
See within this heading,
"Records, reports, and
returns."
Residential schools, **71B:2, 71B:3,
71B:5.**
Retirement benefits of school
department special education
personnel in certain
institutions, **71B:12.**
Rights of students and parents.
Annual workshop, **70B:19.**
Curriculum, **71B:9A.**
Salaries of school department
personnel in certain
institutions, **71B:12.**
School buses.
Transportation of pupils. See
within this heading,
"Transportation of pupils."
School committee, **71B:3.**
Agreements with public or
private schools and
institutions, **71B:4.**
Annual reports, **71B:6.**
Budget for cost of special
education, **71B:5.**
Denial of equal educational
opportunities, **71B:6.**
Evaluation and assessment of
child's needs, duties of
school committees, **71B:3.**
Tuition, prepayment by school
committees, **71:71D.**
School departments for special
education in mental health,
public health and youth
services departments, **71B:12.**
Separate instructions for adequate
care of child, **71B:3.**
Sheltered workshops program,
6:78A.

SPECIAL EDUCATION —Cont'd
Social services.
Welfare and social services
department. See within this
heading, "Welfare and social
services department."
Special classes, standards, **71B:9.**
Specialists, evaluation and
assessment of children's needs,
71B:3.
Special resource classrooms,
71B:2.
Speech handicaps, **71B:1.**
Staff.
Educational personnel. See
within this heading,
"Educational personnel."
Standards for providing special
education programs, **71B:9.**
State advisory commission, **71B:3.**
State aid or funds, receipt and
allocation, **70:4, 71B:14.**
Superior court proceedings for
placement of child with
disability, **71B:3.**
Supplementary individual or small
group instruction, **71B:2.**
Support of child in institution,
liability, **71B:10.**
Supreme Court proceedings, denial
of equal educational
opportunities, **71B:6.**
Teachers.
Educational personnel. See
within this heading,
"Educational personnel."
Tests for referral, diagnosis or
evaluation of children, **71B:7.**
Time of payments of
reimbursements, **71B:14.**
Transfer of employees of former
bureau of special education,
15:1F.
Transitional advisory committee,
71B:12B, 71B:12C.
Transportation of pupils, **71B:8,
71B:10.**
Disabled students, **71:11.**
Trial or hearings.
Hearings. See within this
heading, "Hearings and
investigations."
Tuition.
Prepayment by school
committees, **71:71D.**
Reimbursement by
Commonwealth of tuition of
inmates of institutions,
76:11.
Waiver of assessment
requirements, **71B:3.**

SPECIAL EDUCATION —Cont'd
Welfare and social services
department.
Admission of children to
programs and evaluation of
benefits, **71B:2.**
Referral by department of
children for special
education programs, **71B:10.**
School committees, evaluation
and assessment of children
for special education
programs, **71B:3.**
Workshop on rights of students
and parents, **70B:19.**
Curriculum, **71B:9A.**
Workshops, program of sheltered
workshops, **6:78A.**
Youth services institutions, school
departments for special
education, **71B:12.**
Zero interest loan program for
extraordinary and
unanticipated special
education costs, **71B:5C.**

SPECIAL ELECTIONS.
Absent voters and voting.
Absent voting, **54:103A.**
City, and town, and county
elections, **54:103A.**
Mayor or alderman, special
elections for in certain
cases, **39:6.**
Precinct voting at special
elections, **39:20.**
Rescission of statutes, **4:4B.**
State elections, **54:86.**
Ballot law commission.
State ballot law commission. See
within this heading, "State
ballot law commission."
Campaign expenditures and
contributions, **55:18.**
Caucuses relative, **53:74.**
Certificates of nominations, time
for filing, **53:10.**
City charters.
See CITY CHARTERS.
County offices, filling vacancies,
54:142-54:144.
Federal constitutional
amendments, vote, **53:18.**
Filing of certificates of nomination
and nomination papers in
state elections, **53:10.**
Local option statutes, revocation of
approval, **4:4B.**
Primaries before state elections,
time for holding, **53:28.**
Registration of voters.
Certification meeting prior to
election, **53:46.**

SPECIAL ELECTIONS —Cont'd
Representative in Congress,
 failure to elect or vacancy in
 office, **54:140.**
Rescission of statutes by cities or
 towns, **4:4B.**
State ballot law commission,
 55B:10.
 Decisions as to election, **55B:10.**
 Objections to nominations,
 registrars' determination,
 55B:7.
State elections.
 Absent voting, **54:86.**
 Filing of certificates of
 nominations and nomination
 papers, **53:10.**
 Primaries before, time for
 holding, **53:28.**
Time or date.
 Certificate of nomination, time
 for filing, **53:10.**
 City and town elections, time for
 calling, **43:39, 43:40.**
 Failure to elect or vacancy in
 office of state
 representatives, **54:141.**
 Primaries, holding before special
 election, **53:28.**
 State representative, time for
 holding special election,
 54:141.
Voters' registration.
 Registration of voters.
 Certification meeting prior to
 election, **53:46.**

SPECIAL FUELS.
Administrative tax provisions as
 applicable, **62C:2.**
Gasoline and motor fuel taxes,
 64E:1-64E:15, 64F:1-64F:15.
 See GASOLINE AND MOTOR
 FUEL TAXES.

SPECIAL FUND.
Incorporation or settlement of
 cities and towns, **44:53I.**
Military service credit, special
 fund for.
 See RETIREMENT SYSTEMS
 AND PENSIONS.
Retirement purposes,
 establishment by counties,
 32:22.
Workers' compensation.
 See WORKERS'
 COMPENSATION.

SPECIAL GRAND JURY.
Veniremen, number, **277:2A.**

**SPECIAL INVESTIGATING
 COMMISSION.**
Coal mining operations, **21B:2,
 21B:8, 21B:9.**

**SPECIAL INVESTIGATIONS
 BUREAU.**
Public safety department, special
 investigations bureau
 established, **22:15B.**
State police, **22C:67.**
Welfare.
 See WELFARE AND SOCIAL
 SERVICES.

**SPECIAL INVESTIGATIONS
 DIRECTOR.**
Social services.
 See WELFARE AND SOCIAL
 SERVICES.

SPECIAL JUDGMENTS.
Bankrupts or insolvents, special
 judgments against,
 235:23-235:26, 246:66.
Insolvency and bankruptcy.
 See INSOLVENCY AND
 BANKRUPTCY.

**SPECIAL JUSTICES OR
 JUDGES.**
Boston juvenile court.
 Certification of intent to serve
 full time, **218:58B.**
 Per diem compensation, **218:6.**
Boston municipal court, **218:52.**
 Holding of court by part-time
 special justice, **218:40.**
District courts, **218:6, 218:7.**
 See DISTRICT COURTS.
Interest in or benefit by fees or
 emoluments arising from
 matter pending in probate
 court, **217:6B.**
Municipal courts, **218:50, 218:52.**
 Basis for computation of
 pensions, **32:65B.**
 Boston municipal court. See
 within this heading, "Boston
 municipal court."
 Holding of court, **218:40.**
Pensions, **32:65B.**
Per diem compensation, Boston
 juvenile court, **218:6.**
Probate and insolvency judges,
 217:6B.
 Pensions, **32:65B.**

**SPECIALLY MANUFACTURED
 GOODS.**
Statute of frauds as applicable to
 sale, **106:2-201.**

SPECIAL MASTERS.
See AUDITORS, MASTERS,
 AND REFEREES.

SPECIAL MEETINGS.
County commissioners, **34:9,
 34:19.**
 Costs in connection with special
 meetings, **34:19.**

SPECIAL MEETINGS —Cont'd
Credit unions.
 See CREDIT UNIONS.
Districts, **40:5B, 41:119.**
Stabilization fund at special town
 or district meeting,
 appropriation, **40:5B.**
Street railways, stockholders,
 special meetings, **161:15.**
Town meetings, **39:9, 39:10.**
 See TOWN MEETINGS.

**SPECIAL NEEDS AWARENESS
 DAY, 6:15BBBB, 6:15DDDD.**

SPECIAL NOTICE ACCOUNTS.
Cooperative banks.
 See COOPERATIVE BANKS.
Credit unions, **171:34.**

**SPECIAL NUCLEAR
 MATERIAL.**
Defined, **6:85.**
Manufacture or possession, **6:92,
 6:93.**

**SPECIAL OBLIGATION
 REFUNDING BONDS,
 29:53A.**

SPECIAL OFFICERS.
Police.
 See POLICE.

SPECIAL PERMITS.
See LICENSES AND PERMITS.

SPECIAL PRIMARIES.
See PRIMARY ELECTIONS.

SPECIAL SERVICE BUSES.
Motor carriers of passengers,
 159A:11A.

SPECIAL SHERIFFS, 37:4, 37:5.
**See SHERIFFS AND
 DEPUTIES.**

SPECIAL STOCK.
See CORPORATIONS.

SPECIAL VERDICT.
Contributory negligence, special
 verdict, **231:85.**

SPECIFICATIONS.
**See PLANS AND
 SPECIFICATIONS.**

SPECIFIC PERFORMANCE.
Damages, generally.
 See DAMAGES.
Fees for entry of petition, **262:40.**
Home improvement contractors,
 142A:20.
Land contracts, **204:1.**
Legal remedy as bar, **214:1A.**
Letters of credit, **106:5-111.**

SPECIFIC PERFORMANCE
—Cont'd

Railroads, remedy to compel construction of embankments, culverts, walls, or fences, **160:92.**

Remedy in damages as precluding action, **214:1A.**

Sales contract, specific performance, **106:2-716.**

Uniform commercial code, generally.
  See COMMERCIAL CODE.

SPECTACLES.
See EYEGLASSES.

SPECTATORS.

Amusements and exhibitions.
  See AMUSEMENTS AND EXHIBITIONS.

Courtroom, exclusion in certain cases, **278:16A-278:16C.**

SPEECH, FREEDOM OF, US Const Amend 1.

Censorship, **111B:11, 123:23, 231:91A.**

Constitution of Massachusetts, **MA Const Part 1 Art 16.**

Initiative or referendum petition, right not subject to, **MA Const Amend Art 48 Init Part 2 Sec 2.**

Legislature, freedom in, **MA Const Part 1 Art 21.**

Constitution of the United States.
  See CONSTITUTION OF THE UNITED STATES.

Students' rights, **71:82.**

Guidelines, rules, and regulations, **71:85.**

Municipalities accepting provisions, **71:86.**

SPEECH HANDICAPS.

Special education.
  See SPECIAL EDUCATION.

SPEECH PATHOLOGISTS.

Abuse of patients or residents in long-term care facilities, reports, **111:72G.**

Early intervention services, dependent coverage, **175:47C, 176A:8B, 176B:4C, 176G:4.**

Group insurance for state employees for treatment by, **32A:23.**

License to engage in practice, **13:85-13:87, 112:138-112:147.**

Psychology-related professions or occupations excluded from regulations, **112:125.**

SPEED.

Jet skis, speed limits, **90B:11.**

Motorboats.
  See MOTORBOATS.

Races.
  See RACES AND RACING.

School buses and transportation of pupils.

Passing stopped school bus, speed permitted, **90:14.**

Restrictions on speed, **90:17.**

Skiers, responsibilities, **90B:11, 143:71, 143:71O.**

Surf jets, speed limits, **90B:11.**

Traffic regulations and rules of the road, **85:20-85:24, 90:17, 90:18.**

See TRAFFIC REGULATIONS AND RULES OF THE ROAD.

Water recreational vehicles, speed limits, **90B:11.**

Wet bikes, speed limits, **90B:11.**

SPEEDY TRIAL, 231:59A, 231:59C-231:59F.

Accused's right, **220:13; US Const Amend 6.**

Appeals.

Child held in confinement, **119:27, 119:68.**

Subdivision control law, zoning appeals, **41:81BB.**

Bail, speedy trial for persons in custody for want, **212:29.**

Collectors of taxes, removal, **41:39B.**

Elderly persons, acceleration of speedy trail, **231:59F.**

Election laws, actions, **231:59D.**

Employment security contributions, actions, **151A:15.**

Examination after arrest, **276:35.**

Housing authority or redevelopment authority, speedy trial requirements to determine action taken, **231:59E.**

Labor action to recover, **231:59A.**

Lobbying, violations of laws regarding, **3:49.**

Malpractice suits, **231:59C.**

"No-fault" automobile liability insurance actions, **90:34M.**

Personal labor, actions, **231:59A.**

Pretrial motions, **231:59A.**

Public utilities commission, appeals from rulings or orders, **25:5.**

Public works, actions on contractors' bonds, **149:29.**

SPEEDY TRIAL —Cont'd

Right, **220:13A; US Const Amend 6.**

Sanitary code, speedy trial for enforcement, **111:127A.**

Special assessments, proceedings for abatement, **80:9.**

State environmental code, enforcement proceedings, **21A:13.**

Superior court, speedy trial of persons held in jail in default of bail, **212:29.**

Workers' compensation cases, **152:11.**

Zoning, appeals under subdivision control law, **41:81BB.**

SPENCER.

Congressional district, **57:1.**

District court, **218:1.**

Medical examiner district, **38:1.**

Senatorial district, **57:3.**

SPENDTHRIFTS.

Burial expenses of spendthrift, increase of limitation on amounts reserved, **201:48A.**

Debauchery, addict to, as spendthrift, **4:7.**

Appointment of guardian, **201:8.**

Disclaimer, spendthrift provisions affecting, **191A:9.**

Guardians.
  See GUARDIANS, CONSERVATORS, AND COMMITTEES.

Statutory construction, **4:7.**

Trusts.
  See TRUSTS AND TRUSTEES.

SPIRITUAL HEALERS.

Nursing home administrators certified by certain religious denominations, applicability of regulations, **112:108.**

Physicians, inapplicability of laws, **112:7.**

SPITE FENCE.

Nuisance, spite fence, **49:21.**

SPLASH GUARDS.

Motor vehicle equipment, **90:7.**

SPLIT-LOAD DELIVERY.

Underground storage tank petroleum product cleanup fund, **21J:2.**

SPLIT VERDICT.

Costs as affected, **261:9.**

SPOILED BALLOTS.
See ELECTIONS.

SPONGE TAX.
Estate tax, absorption of federal credit, **65C:2A, 65C:3.**

SPORTS.
See ATHLETICS.

SPOTLIGHTS.
Motor vehicles, **90:16, 90:20.**

SPOUSE.
See HUSBAND AND WIFE.

SPRINGFIELD.
Alcoholic liquor licenses, hearings on appeals, **138:67.**
Assigned risk plan under compulsory automobile liability insurance law, establishment of office for implementation, **175:113H.**
Automobile insurance.
    Motor vehicles. See within this heading, "Motor vehicles."
Commission against discrimination, regional office, **6:56.**
Congressional district, **57:1.**
District court, **218:1.**
    Changes in territorial jurisdiction, **218:1.**
    Justice, **218:6.**
Justices.
    District court, **218:6.**
    Juvenile court.
        See SPRINGFIELD JUVENILE COURT.
Juvenile court.
    See SPRINGFIELD JUVENILE COURT.
Medical examiner district, **38:1.**
Motor carriers of property, hearings upon certificates of public convenience and necessity, **159B:3.**
Motor vehicles.
    Assigned risk plan under compulsory automobile liability insurance law, establishment of office for implementation, **175:113H.**
    Compulsory liability insurance, notice of hearings, **175:113B.**
Nurses' examinations for registration, places for holding, **112:74.**
Police training school, expenses of policemen attending, **40:5.**
Senatorial district, **57:3.**
Steam boiler rules, notice of hearing on proposed changes, **146:3.**

SPRINGFIELD —Cont'd
Superior court sittings, **212:14.**

SPRINGFIELD JUVENILE COURT.
Adjudication of child as delinquent, proceedings after, **119:58.**
Clerical assistants to clerk, **218:70.**
Clerks, **218:58, 218:79.**
    Clerical assistants to clerk of court, **218:70.**
    Temporary clerks and assistants, **218:9, 218:11.**
Disposition of case, time, **119:68.**
District court justices, assignment, **218:58.**
Governor's appointment of clerks, **218:58.**
Judges.
    Justices. See within this heading, "Justices."
Jurisdiction over offenders, **218:60.**
    Territorial jurisdiction, **218:57.**
Justices, **218:6, 218:58.**
    Pension, **32:65A.**
Pensions for justices, **32:65A.**
Powers, duties and procedures, **218:59.**
Practice of law by justices prohibited, **218:58.**
Quarters, **218:57.**
Rules, **218:60.**
School attendance, enforcement of parental duties, **76:2.**
Special provisions relative, **218:57-218:60.**
Territorial jurisdiction, **218:57.**

SPRINGFIELD OFFICE BUILDING.
Commissioner's duties regarding use of space, **7:40F.**
Superintendent of buildings, care and operation for buildings of state, **8:9.**

SPRINGING EXECUTORY INTERESTS.
Contingent remainders taking effect in manner, **184:3.**
Generally.
    See LIFE ESTATES, REMAINDERS, AND REVERSIONS.

SPRINGS.
Bottling permit for spring water, **94:10A-94:10C.**
Defilement, **111:170, 265:28.**
Poisoning, **265:28.**
Public health department, supervision, **111:159.**

SPRINGS —Cont'd
Waterworks.
    See WATERWORKS AND WATER SUPPLY.

SPRINKLER FITTER/JOURNEYMAN SPRINKLER FITTER.
Fire sprinkler system contractors and fitters, **146:81-146:85A.**

SPRINKLER SYSTEMS.
Appeals, **148:26A, 148:26B, 148:26G.**
Automatic sprinklers.
    Boarding or lodging houses, installation, **148:26H.**
    Disconnecting, obstructing, removing, or destroying, **148:27A.**
    Grievances by head of fire department, appeals to automatic sprinkler appeals board, **148:26G.**
    Installation in high rise buildings, **6:200, 6:201, 148:26A, 148:26A½.**
    Licensing of contractors, **146:85.**
    Mercantile establishment, installation in basement, **148:26.**
    Penalty for failure to install, **148:27.**
    Required in certain buildings, **148:26, 148:26H, 148:27.**
Buildings requiring, **148:26A-148:26B, 148:26I.**
Contractors and fitters, bureau established, examination and licensing, application and fee, **22:10A, 146:81-146:85A.**
Definition, **146:81.**
Fines and penalties for failure to comply with provisions, **148:27, 148:27A.**
Housing projects, requirement, **121B:28.**
Installation or servicing, **143:3Q, 148:58.**
Installation schedule, **148:26A½.**
Insurance.
    Leakage insurance. See within this heading, "Leakage insurance."
    Sprinkler risks, **175:80.**
Leakage insurance, **175:47.**
    Combination policies, **175:22A, 175:117A.**
    Mutual insurance, **175:93A-175:93C.**
Mandatory installation, requirement, **148:26G.**

SPRINKLER SYSTEMS —Cont'd

Nursing homes, installation, **143:3Q.**

Parking structures, installation of automatic sprinkler systems, **148:26G.**

State building code requirements, **148:26A, 148:26B.**

Suppressant systems in lieu of automatic sprinkler systems, **148:26I.**

SPURS.

Railroads.
See RAILROADS.

SPUTUM.

Laboratories, examining, certificate of approval, **111:184A.**

SQUANNACOOK AND NISSITISSIT RIVERS SANCTUARY, 132A:17.

SQUARE DANCING.

Dancing, generally.
See DANCING AND DANCE HALLS.

Official folk dance of the Commonwealth, **2:32.**

Sunday, permitted activities, **136:2.**

SQUIRRELS.

Flying squirrels.
Possession without permit, **131:5.**
Removal from hole in tree, **131:76.**

Possession without permit, **131:5.**

Red squirrels.
Possession without permit, **131:5.**
Removal from hole in ground, **131:76.**

STABILIZATION FUND.

Districts, appropriation at special district meeting, **40:5B.**

Municipalities, **40:5B.**

Regional school districts establishing, **71:16G½.**

Special meetings, appropriation of stabilization fund at special town or district meeting, **40:5B.**

State finance, **29:2H.**

STABLES, 272:86 et seq.
See BARNS AND STABLES.

STADIUMS AND ARENAS.

Discrimination, **272:92A, 272:98.**

Dropping or throwing objects at sports event, penalty, **265:36.**

STADIUMS AND ARENAS —Cont'd

Gymnasiums.
Adult programs, **71:71B.**
Appropriation of money, **40:5.**
Gender discrimination, **272:92A.**
Management, **40:5.**

Handicapped persons, facilities, **22:13A.**

Restaurant liquor licensee, sales at more than one location, **138:12.**

Town appropriations, **40:5.**

STAGNANT WATERS.

Lowlands, **252:1-252:24.**
See LOWLANDS AND SWAMPS.

STAIRWAYS.

Defined or construed, **144:2, 145:2.**

Housing projects, requirements, **121B:28.**

Lease provision as to liability for injuries, **186:15.**

Moving stairways, defined or construed, **143:62, 143:71E.**

Nursing homes, lighting, **111:72C.**

Public transportation facilities, offenses on premises, **161:94A, 161:95.**

Smoke detector location in private dwellings, **148:26E.**

Street railways, loitering on stairways, **161:95.**

STALKING, 265:43.

Address confidentiality of domestic violence victims, **9A:1 to 9A:7.**
See ADDRESS CONFIDENTIALITY OF DOMESTIC VIOLENCE VICTIMS.

Criminal harassment, **265:43A.**

Harassment, generally.
See HARASSMENT.

STALLIONS.
See HORSES.

STALLS.

Restaurants, curtains or screens on stalls, **272:25.**

Stables, stalls, **111:155.**

STAMPS AND STAMPING.

Certificates of stock.
See CORPORATIONS.

Cigarette tax.
See CIGARETTE TAX.

Compressed air tanks, Interstate Commerce Commission's approval stamp, **146:34.**

Corporations.
See CORPORATIONS.

STAMPS AND STAMPING —Cont'd

Deed and document stamp tax, **64D:2-64D:4, 64D:7-64D:9.**
See DEED AND DOCUMENT STAMP TAX.

Film, falsely stamping as incombustible, **143:87.**

Fish.
See FISH AND GAME.

Forgery.
See FORGERY AND COUNTERFEITING.

Gas meters, stamping, **164:103, 164:113-164:115A.**

Insurance company's name to be stamped on riders, when, **175:33.**

Junk dealers, **140:55.**

Kosher food, **94:156.**

Migratory waterfowl stamp, **131:11, 131:13.**

Minors, employment on stamping machines, **149:61.**

Postage.
See MAIL AND MAILING.

Steam boilers inspected, stamping, **146:24.**

Tax stamps.
See TAX STAMPS.

Trading stamps, **93:14L-93:14R.**
See TRADING STAMPS.

STAMP TAX ACT.

Documents, **64D:1 et seq.**

STANDARDBRED AGRICULTURAL FAIR AND BREEDING FUND COMMITTEE, 20:10-20:12.

STANDARDIZATION BOARD.

Membership and duties, **7:26.**

STANDARDS.
See GRADES AND STANDARDS.

STANDARD TIME, 4:10.

STANDING COMMITTEES.

Religious societies.
See RELIGION AND RELIGIOUS SOCIETIES.

Service of process, **223:37.**

STANDING TO SUE.
See PARTIES TO ACTIONS.

STANDPIPES.
See SEWERS AND DRAINS.

STARFISH.

Disposal regulated, **130:103.**

STARLINGS, 131:5, 131:83.

Taking or destruction of nest or eggs, **131:74.**

STAR OF DAVID.
Kosher food, labeling, **94:156.**

STAR SPANGLED BANNER.
Manner of playing, **264:9.**

STATE ACTUARY.
Retirement systems and pensions,
duties, **32:21.**
Savings bank life insurance,
178A:8.

**STATE AIRPORT
MANAGEMENT BOARD.
See AIRPORTS AND LANDING
FIELDS.**

**STATE AND STATE
DEPARTMENTS, 1:1 et seq.**
Abandoned property.
See ABANDONED, LOST, AND
UNCLAIMED PROPERTY.
Accounts.
See ACCOUNTS AND
ACCOUNTING.
Actuary.
See STATE ACTUARY.
Administration and Finance
Executive Office, **7:1 et seq.**
See ADMINISTRATION AND
FINANCE EXECUTIVE
OFFICE.
Administrative procedure,
30A:1-30A:17.
See ADMINISTRATIVE
PROCEDURE.
Admission to union, **US Const Art
4 Sec 3 cl 1.**
Advisory standardization board,
representatives of
departments as members,
7:26.
Age, discharge or refusal to
employ because, **151B:4.**
Agency relationship of state
officers and employees to
principals.
Principal and agent. See within
this heading, "Principal and
agent."
Agriculture, **20:1 et seq.**
See AGRICULTURE.
Aid.
See AID AND ASSISTANCE.
Aircraft.
See AIRCRAFT AND AVIATION.
Alliances, not to enter into, **US
Const Art 1 Sec 10 cl 1.**
Allocation of officers, **30:45, 30:46.**
Allotment of appropriations to
departments by governor,
29:9B.
Annual reports, **7A:12,
30:32-30:33A.**
Printing and distribution,
5:6-5:8.

**STATE AND STATE
DEPARTMENTS** —Cont'd
Annual reports —Cont'd
State treasurer.
See STATE TREASURER.
Appeal.
See APPEAL AND REVIEW.
Appropriations, **29:6 et seq.**
See STATE FINANCE.
Approval of governor and council
as to establishment of
divisions, **30:3.**
Archeologist of state.
See ARCHEOLOGY AND
ARCHEOLOGISTS.
Architectural barriers against
handicapped persons, state
agencies and institutions
prohibited from maintaining,
22:13A.
Archives.
See ARCHIVES AND
ARCHIVISTS.
Arms of the Commonwealth.
Coat of arms. See within this
heading, "Coat of arms."
Assessment of taxes.
See TAXATION.
Assignment of mortgages, **29:35,
29:36.**
Assignment of unplaced boards
and agencies to departments,
30:2.
Atomic energy, studies and
recommendations by
departments, **6:91.**
Attorney General, **12:1 et seq.**
See ATTORNEY GENERAL.
Attorneys' liens, discharge of
Commonwealth from liability,
221:50A.
Audit of transit authority,
reimbursement to state of
cost, **161B:12.**
Auditor, **11:1 et seq.**
See STATE AUDITOR.
Babingtonite as mineral emblem,
2:18.
Ballot boxes.
See ELECTIONS.
Ballot Law Commission, **55B:1 et
seq.**
See STATE BALLOT LAW
COMMISSION.
Banking, Department of, **26:1 et
seq.**
See BANKING AND
INSURANCE
DEPARTMENT.
Bay transportation authority.
See MASSACHUSETTS BAY
TRANSPORTATION
AUTHORITY.

**STATE AND STATE
DEPARTMENTS** —Cont'd
Beauty shops in state institutions
and agencies, licensing,
112:87AA.
Bids.
See BIDS AND BIDDING.
Bird, **2:9.**
Blind persons, aid to.
See BLIND PERSONS.
Bond.
See BONDS AND
UNDERTAKINGS.
Bonds and debentures.
Bonds held.
See STATE TREASURER.
Bonds issued.
See STATE BONDS AND
OBLIGATIONS.
Borrowing.
See STATE FINANCE.
Boundaries, **1:2-1:5.**
Flats or land adjacent to or
covered by high water, state
not affected by
determination of boundaries,
240:26.
Inspection and repair, **1:4.**
Marine boundaries of
Commonwealth, extent, **1:3.**
Monuments and markers,
change or removal, **1:5.**
Prohibition as to removal by
officers of boundaries
established by
Commonwealth and another
state, **42:5.**
Boxing.
See BOXING AND BOXING
MATCHES.
Budget, **29:6.**
See STATE FINANCE.
Building code of state.
See BUILDING CODE OF
STATE.
Buildings.
See BUILDINGS AND
STRUCTURES.
Capitol building.
See STATE HOUSE.
Cash prizes for suggestions by
employees, **7:31A.**
Centralized purchasing, **30:51,
30:52.**
Centralized weekly payroll system,
29:31.
Central personnel register, **30:38.**
Certiorari, service where
defendant is state board or
commission, **249:4A.**
Chaplains in state institutions,
advisory committee, **6:166B.**

STATE AND STATE DEPARTMENTS —Cont'd

Charitable organizations soliciting funds from public, prohibition as to representations of indorsement by state, **68:27.**

Chickadee as state bird, **2:9.**

Children, Office for, **28A:1 et seq.**
See CHILDREN AND MINORS.

Cigarettes.
See TOBACCO.

Civil service.
See CIVIL SERVICE.

Claims against state, **258:1 et seq.**
See CLAIMS AGAINST COMMONWEALTH.

Claims of state.
Attorney general's duty to collect, **12:4, 12:5.**
Not to be prejudiced by construction of constitution, **US Const Art 4 Sec 3 cl 2.**

Coal mining regulation and reclamation, **21B:1-21B:15.**
See COAL MINING REGULATION AND RECLAMATION.

Coat of arms, **2:1 et seq.**
Manufacture of state coat of arms, regulations regarding, **2:5.**
Misuse, **264:5, 264:6.**
Secretary of state, duties, **2:5.**
Use and display of, regulations regarding, **2:5.**

Cod as fish emblem of Commonwealth, **2:13.**

Collection of amounts due to, duty of attorney general, **12:4, 12:5.**

Collective purchasing in conjunction with political subdivisions, **7:22A, 7:22B.**

Colleges, **73:1 et seq.**
See COLLEGES AND UNIVERSITIES.

Commerce among states, regulation by Congress, **US Const Art 1 Sec 8 cl 3.**

Commission to office.
See COMMISSION TO OFFICE.

Community affairs, **23B:1 et seq.**
See HOUSING AND COMMUNITY DEVELOPMENT DEPARTMENT.

Compacts.
See INTERSTATE COMPACTS AND AGREEMENTS.

Competitive bidding on contracts.
See BIDS AND BIDDING.

Comptroller of state.
See COMPTROLLER OF STATE.

STATE AND STATE DEPARTMENTS —Cont'd

Concurrent jurisdiction over places ceded to or acquired by United States, **1:2, 1:7.**

Confidential employees of heads of departments, **30:7.**

Conflicting jurisdiction or powers of state departments, appeal in case, **30:5.**

Constitution Day, **6:14B.**

Constitution of Massachusetts.
See CONSTITUTION OF MASSACHUSETTS.

Construction of public works, cities' and towns' contracts with state, **40:4D.**

Construction of statutes, definition for purpose, **4:7.**

Contracts.
Comptroller of state.
See COMPTROLLER OF STATE.
Confidentiality of contracts with Commonwealth, **30:39R.**
Copies of contracts to be filed with comptroller, **7A:5.**
Foreign corporations, contract for performance of public construction work, **30:39L.**
Labor disputes involving vendors contracting with Commonwealth, peaceful settlement, **150A:1, 150A:2.**
Payment by subcontractors on contracts for construction, **30:39F.**
Regional transit authorities, Commonwealth may provide contract assistance, **161B:23.**
Surplus state property, disposition agreements, **7:40F.**
Vocational rehabilitation services, agreement affecting eligibility, **6:78.**
Watershed management division, contractual powers, **92:120.**

Conventions, attendance by state officers or employees at public expense, **6:10, 6:11.**

Conveyances.
See DEEDS AND CONVEYANCES.

Cooperative banks.
See COOPERATIVE BANKS.

Corporations.
See CORPORATIONS.

STATE AND STATE DEPARTMENTS —Cont'd

Correctional institutions, **125:1 et seq., 126:1 et seq.**
See CORRECTIONAL INSTITUTIONS.

Correspondence schools, schools operated by state, **75C:1.**

Costs of action.
See COSTS OF ACTION.

County finance.
See COUNTY FINANCE.

County to first offer property for sale or lease to Commonwealth, **34:14.**

Cranberry juice, state beverage, **2:10.**

Credit unions, shares, deposits, and investments, **171:67.**

Custody.
Bonds held by state, **29:41.**
Departmental records, **66:6.**
Great seal, **9:11.**
Records, **66:7.**

Customs duties, power to lay, **US Const Art 1 Sec 10 cl 2.**

Damages for trespass by employees, **1:9.**

Dangerous diseases, liability for care of persons suffering, **111:116.**

Daylight-saving time, **4:10.**

Day work basis of employees, **149:42.**

Death of officer or employee.
Additional insurance coverage for death from certain causes, **32A:10A.**
Continued coverage for surviving spouse and dependents after, **32A:10B, 32A:11.**
Flag to be flown at half-staff, **2:6A.**
Payment of salary, money, or other compensation owing, **29:31, 29:31A, 29:31D.**
Return of body in case of death while traveling on duty, **30:25A.**
Tenure of substitute in event of death of department heads and commissioners, **30:6.**

Decrees.
Judgments, **245:7 to 245:10.**

Deeds.
See DEEDS AND CONVEYANCES.

Deeds of trust.
See MORTGAGES AND DEEDS OF TRUST.

Defacing buildings, **266:96.**

STATE AND STATE DEPARTMENTS —Cont'd

Defects in state highways, liability for injuries, **81:18.**

Definitions, **4:7, 6:39, 6A:1, 29:1, 30:1, 90:30B, 90F:1.**

Dental insurance for employees, **32A:1, 32A:2, 32A:5, 32A:6, 32A:10, 32A:10B, 32A:11.**

Dental service corporations authorized to contract, **176E:3.**

Departments, **29:1, 30:1 et seq.**

Deregulation and Monetary Control Act, Commonwealth exempt from usury provisions, **183:63.**

Disability or absence of department head, designation of substitute head during, **30:6, 30:6A.**

Discharge of debtors of Commonwealth, **224:24-224:26.**

Discrimination, commission against.
See CIVIL RIGHTS AND DISCRIMINATION.

Dispensary, exemption from requirement of license to operate, **111:32.**

District attorney.
Representation, **12:27.**
Unlawful entry on lands of, district attorney may bring action, **245:1, 245:2.**

District courts.
See DISTRICT COURTS.

Divisions in departments, establishment, **30:3.**

Due process requirement, **US Const 14th Amend Sec 1.**

Economic development, Department of, **23A:1 et seq.**

Education department, **15:1 et seq.**
See EDUCATION DEPARTMENT.

Elder affairs, **19A:1 et seq.**
See ELDER AFFAIRS DEPARTMENT.

Elections.
See ELECTIONS.

Electric companies.
See GAS AND ELECTRIC COMPANIES.

Electricians.
See ELECTRICIANS AND ELECTRICITY.

Elevator inspectors, retirement age, **32:90F.**

STATE AND STATE DEPARTMENTS —Cont'd

Emblems of, **2:1 et seq.**

Emergency use of state-owned vehicles, **30:36.**

Eminent domain, exemptions from consent and notice provisions, **79:5C.**

Employees.
Officers and employees.
See PUBLIC OFFICERS AND EMPLOYEES.

Employment security, **151A:1-151A:74.**
See EMPLOYMENT SECURITY.

Encumbrances.
Liens and encumbrances. See within this heading, "Liens and encumbrances."

Energy facilities siting.
Council's co-operation with state agencies, **164:69Q.**
Prohibited from imposing restrictions on certificate of environmental impact and public need, **164:69K.**

Energy resources, **25A:1 et seq.**
See ENERGY RESOURCES EXECUTIVE OFFICE.

Engineer officer of state, **33:15.**

Environmental impact.
Determination and reports, **30:61, 30:62.**
Prohibition from imposing restrictions on certificate of environmental impact and public need, **164:69K.**

Environment management and affairs, **21:1 et seq., 21A:1 et seq.**
See ENVIRONMENTAL MANAGEMENT DEPARTMENT.

Equal protection requirement, **US Const 14th Amend Sec 1.**

Equipment and supplies, **7:22, 7:25A, 30:51, 30:52.**

Escheat, notice by publication, **245:4.**

Estimates.
See STATE FINANCE.

Ethics commission, **268B:2.**
See ETHICS COMMISSION OF STATE.

Executions.
See EXECUTIONS.

Executive council, **6:3 et seq.**
See GOVERNOR'S COUNCIL.

Executive offices, **6:1 et seq.**

STATE AND STATE DEPARTMENTS —Cont'd

Executive session of governmental body to hear and discuss personal matters regarding state officer or employee, **30A:11A½.**

Exemption from taxation of state property, **59:5.**

Expenses.
See STATE FINANCE.

Exports from states, not taxable, **US Const Art 1 Sec 9 cl 5.**

Ex post facto laws may not be passed by, **US Const Art 1 Sec 10 cl 1.**

Extradition.
See EXTRADITION.

Fair.
See STATE FAIR.

Fair employment practices.
See FAIR EMPLOYMENT PRACTICES.

False reports to state departments, penalty, **268:6.**

Farm.
See STATE FARM.

Federal aid.
See FEDERAL AID OR FUNDS.

Federal penitentiary, forfeiture of state office after sentence, **279:30.**

Fees.
See FEES.

Filing.
Records, reports, and returns. See within this heading, "Records, reports, and returns of departments."

Finances.
See STATE FINANCE.

Fines.
See FINES AND PENALTIES.

Fire insurance, buildings exempt from certain requirements in application, **175:98.**

Fire marshals.
See FIRE MARSHALS.

Fires.
See FIRES AND FIRE PREVENTION.

First Congress, representation in, **US Const Art 1 Sec 2 cl 3.**

Fiscal year.
See STATE FINANCE.

Fish.
See FISH AND GAME.

Flag, **2:3 et seq.**
See FLAGS.

Flats, regulations as to coastal wetlands as affecting authority of state reclamation board, **130:105.**

**STATE AND STATE
DEPARTMENTS** —Cont'd

Flood control, reimbursement of towns for loss of taxes on property taken, **58:17B.**

Flower, mayflower, **2:7.**

Food.
See FOOD AND AGRICULTURE DEPARTMENT.

Foreclosure of mortgage.
See MORTGAGE FORECLOSURE.

Foreign corporations, contract for performance of public construction work, **30:39L.**

Foreign insurance companies.
See FOREIGN INSURANCE COMPANIES.

Foreign states.
See FOREIGN STATES OR COUNTRIES.

Foresters.
See FORESTERS AND FOREST WARDENS.

Forests.
See FORESTS AND FORESTRY.

Forfeitures.
Compensation for holding office in violation of law, forfeiture, **30:22.**
Office, forfeiture, **279:30.**
Plumbers and gas fitters, **142:16.**

Forgery.
See FORGERY AND COUNTERFEITING.

Full faith and credit requirement, **US Const Art 4 Sec 1.**

Full time service required of officers and employees, **30:32.**

Funds.
See STATE FINANCE.

Gas.
See GAS AND ELECTRIC COMPANIES.

General fund.
See STATE FINANCE.

Geologists, **21A:7A.**

Gifts.
See GIFTS, GRANTS, AND GRATUITIES.

Government land bank.
See GOVERNMENT LAND BANK.

Governor, **6:1 et seq.**
See GOVERNOR.

Governor's council, **6:3 et seq.**
See GOVERNOR'S COUNCIL.

Grade crossing elimination, settlement of barred claim, **159:76.**

**STATE AND STATE
DEPARTMENTS** —Cont'd

Great seal, **2:2, 2:3.**
See STATE SEAL.

Grievance procedure of state employees as to assignment to departments, **30:53.**

Hazardous waste insolvency fund.
See HAZARDOUS WASTE INSOLVENCY FUND.

Hazardous waste management, **21C:1 et seq.**
See HAZARDOUS WASTE MANAGEMENT.

Heads of departments.
Absence or disability, designation of substitute during, **29:65, 30:6, 30:6A.**
Confidential secretary, appointment and removal, **30:7.**
Printing, binding and procuring of stationery under direction, **30:31.**

Health and health departments, **17:1 et seq.**
See HEALTH AND HEALTH DEPARTMENTS.

Health, welfare, and retirement funds law, applicability, **151D:7.**

Higher grade positions, lower grade employee assigned duties, **30:24B.**

Highways and streets, **81:1-81:32.**
See HIGHWAYS AND STREETS.

Holding office until successor appointed, **30:8.**

Horse.
See HORSE AND DOG RACING MEETINGS.

Horse emblem of Commonwealth, Morgan horse, **2:11.**

Hospital for state minor wards.
See HOSPITAL FOR STATE MINOR WARDS.

Hospitals, **111:63-111:67.**
See STATE HOSPITALS.

Hotels.
See HOTELS, MOTELS, AND ROOMINGHOUSES.

Hours of labor.
See HOURS OF LABOR OR SERVICES.

House, state house as seat of government.
See STATE HOUSE.

Housing.
See HOUSING AND URBAN RENEWAL.

**STATE AND STATE
DEPARTMENTS** —Cont'd

Housing board abolished and duties transferred to economic development department, **23A:1.**

Housing court.
See HOUSING COURT.

Hunting and fishing fines paid, **131:3.**

Illegally parked vehicles, state as exempt from provisions as to towing, **85:2C.**

Impairment of contract obligations by, prohibited, **US Const Art 1 Sec 10 cl 1.**

Indictment, suspension of officer or employee, **30:59.**

Indigency, filing affidavit of and request for state payment of court costs, **261:27B.**

Industrial schools, **18A:8, 20:2 et seq.**
See YOUTH SERVICES DEPARTMENT AND MASSACHUSETTS TRAINING SCHOOLS.

Industries, **23:1 et seq.**
See LABOR AND WORKFORCE DEVELOPMENT.

Information on officers or employees furnished to bureau of personnel and standardization, **30:38.**

Injunction.
Fees for injunctions or restraining orders, **262:4, 262:4A.**
Unlawful exercise or abuse of power by state officer or employee, injunction against, **29:63.**

Insect control, **266:119.**

Insect emblem of state, ladybug, **2:12.**

Inspection of state boundaries, **1:4.**

Inspector, **33:15.**

Insurance, **26:1 et seq.**
See BANKING AND INSURANCE DEPARTMENT.

Insurrection, not to assume debts incurred in aid of, **US Const 14th Amend Sec 4.**

Interstate compacts.
See INTERSTATE COMPACTS AND AGREEMENTS.

Interstate Family Support Act.
See INTERSTATE FAMILY SUPPORT ACT.

Invasion, powers in case of, **US Const Art 1 Sec 10 cl 3.**

STATE AND STATE DEPARTMENTS —Cont'd

Job group, classification of employees according, **30:45, 30:46.**

Judge advocate of state, **33:15.**

Judgments, **245:7-245:10.**

Judicial power over states, extent of, **US Const Art 3 Sec 2 cl 1.**

Jurisdiction, **1:2, 1:7.**
See JURISDICTION.

Juvenile behavior, state council on.
See JUVENILE BEHAVIOR, STATE COUNCIL.

Korean emergency or war.
Official Korean war veterans memorial, **2:46.**

Labor.
See LABOR AND WORKFORCE DEVELOPMENT DEPARTMENT.

Labor council.
See MASSACHUSETTS STATE LABOR COUNCIL AFL-CIO.

Laborers employed, **30:50.**

Labor relations.
See LABOR RELATIONS AND DISPUTES.

Ladybug as state insect, **2:12.**

Land bank.
See GOVERNMENT LAND BANK.

Landlord.
See LANDLORD AND TENANT.

Lands of.
See PUBLIC LANDS.

Land title registration.
Registration of land titles. See within this heading, "Registration of land titles."

Leave of absence by employees, **30:9F, 30:9G, 30:46, 32:4.**

Legal services rendered by attorney general, **12:3.**

Legal tender, powers in respect of, **US Const Art 1 Sec 10 cl 1.**

Legislature.
See GENERAL COURT.

Letterheads and stationery, **30:30, 30:30A.**

Letters of marque and reprisal, may not grant, **US Const Art 1 Sec 10 cl 1.**

Library, **6:33-6:38.**
See STATE LIBRARY.

Liens and encumbrances.
Attorney's liens, discharge of Commonwealth from liability, **221:50A.**

STATE AND STATE DEPARTMENTS —Cont'd

Liens and encumbrances —Cont'd
Hospitals, lien for medical and other services furnished, **111:70A.**

Mortgages.
See MORTGAGES AND DEEDS OF TRUST.

Lieutenant Governor.
See LIEUTENANT GOVERNOR.

Limitation of actions.
See LIMITATION OF ACTIONS.

List of classes of positions in departments, **30:45.**

Lists of officers and employees, **7:30.**

Littoral property of, duties of department of public works, **91:2, 91:11.**

Living expenses of officers and employees, **30:25.**

Local property assessments, exemption, **59:2B.**

Lottery of, **10:22 et seq.**
See LOTTERY OF STATE.

Lower grade employees assigned duties of position in higher grade, provisions concerning, **30:24B.**

Lowlands.
See LOWLANDS AND SWAMPS.

Malicious destruction of historical monument or building of, restitution, **266:95, 266:96.**

Maps.
See MAPS, PLATS, AND SURVEYS.

Marine mammal emblem, **2:16.**

Massachusetts Bay transportation authority.
See MASSACHUSETTS BAY TRANSPORTATION AUTHORITY.

Mayflower as state flower, **2:7.**

Medical service corporations, state contracts, **176B:3.**

Mentally ill.
See MENTALLY ILL AND RETARDED PERSONS.

Merit certificates for suggestions, **7:31A.**

Metropolitan District Commission, **28:1 et seq.**
See METROPOLITAN DISTRICT COMMISSION.

Militia, **33:1 et seq.**
See MILITIA.

Milk.
See MILK AND MILK PRODUCTS.

STATE AND STATE DEPARTMENTS —Cont'd

Mining regulation and reclamation, **21B:1-21B:15.**
See COAL MINING REGULATION AND RECLAMATION.

Minority business assistance office (SOMBA).
See MINORITY BUSINESS ASSISTANCE.

Morgan horse as state horse, **2:11.**

Mortgage foreclosure.
See MORTGAGE FORECLOSURE.

Mortgages.
See MORTGAGES AND DEEDS OF TRUST.

Motor carriers of property, exemption from laws, **159B:13.**

Motor vehicles.
See MOTOR VEHICLES.

Name change of state official, registration with state secretary, **30:7B.**

New departmental divisions, establishment, **30:3.**

New states.
Admission to union, **US Const Art 4 Sec 3 cl 1.**

Not to be erected within jurisdiction of another state, **US Const Art 4 Sec 3 cl 1.**

Notice.
Acquisition by purchase or rental of real property for use of state agencies, **7:40H.**

Administrative procedure.
See ADMINISTRATIVE PROCEDURE.

Colleges.
See COLLEGES AND UNIVERSITIES.

Eminent domain, exemptions from consent and notice provisions, **79:5C.**

Escheat, notice by publication, **245:4.**

Ethics commission of state.
See ETHICS COMMISSION OF STATE.

Political committees of state, notice to of recount of ballots for statewide office, **54:135.**

Public officers.
See PUBLIC OFFICERS AND EMPLOYEES.

Purchase, sale, rental, lease, transfer, or significant change in use of real property, **7:40I.**

STATE AND STATE DEPARTMENTS —Cont'd

Notice —Cont'd

Sanatorium or hospital of state, notice of admission of needy person, **111:69F, 111:69G.**

Surplus state property, hearing to consider potential reuses and reuse restrictions, **7:40F, 7:40F½.**

Suspension of officer or employee under indictment, notice, **30:59.**

Transfer of use and responsibility for maintenance of buildings within or between state agencies, **7:40F.**

Treasurer, accounting upon notice for money received by state treasurer, **10:2.**

Nuisances.

Prosecution for nuisances on state property, **12:7.**

Suppression of moths and certain other nuisances on land under control of state, **132:12A.**

Nutrition board, report, **6:182.**

Obsolete public records, disposition, **30:42.**

Ode of Commonwealth, **2:47.**

Office building bureau, **8:1.**

Office hours, **30:24.**

Officers and employees, **30:1 et seq.**

See PUBLIC OFFICERS AND EMPLOYEES.

Official Korean war veterans memorial, **2:46.**

Old provincial state house, care and maintenance, **8:20.**

Optometric service corporations authorized to contract, **176F:3.**

Ordnance officer of state, **33:15.**

Organization of departments, report, **30:4.**

Ornithologist of state, **21:7H.**

Other states.

See FOREIGN STATES OR COUNTRIES.

Parks.

See STATE RECREATION AREAS.

Part-time teaching by officers or employees, **268A:7.**

Payment.

See STATE FINANCE.

Peace statue.

Official peace statue of Commonwealth, **2:45.**

STATE AND STATE DEPARTMENTS —Cont'd

Penal institutions.

See CORRECTIONAL INSTITUTIONS.

Personnel appeals board, **30:53, 30:57.**

See PERSONNEL APPEALS BOARD.

Petition to require action to try title, rights and interest of Commonwealth not affected, **240:5.**

Physicians.

See PHYSICIANS AND SURGEONS.

Planning board, economic development department as successor, **23A:1.**

Plumbers.

See PLUMBERS AND GAS FITTERS.

Police.

See STATE POLICE.

Political committees.

See POLITICAL COMMITTEES.

Polka.

Official polka of Commonwealth, **2:44.**

Premature infants, when chargeable with care, **111:67C.**

Primary elections.

See PRIMARY ELECTIONS.

Principal and agent, **268A:4 et seq.**

Conflict with discharge of duties, state officer or employee to avoid acting as agent in case, **268A:4.**

Fines and penalties, acting as agent on sale of land to Commonwealth, **30:44.**

Labor relations.

See LABOR RELATIONS AND DISPUTES.

Lottery ticket agent, state employee not to act, **10:27.**

Purchasing agent, **7:4A, 7:22 et seq.**

See STATE PURCHASING AGENT.

Printing, **5:1-5:18, 29:28, 30:31.**

See STATE PRINTING.

Prison.

Correctional institutions.

See CORRECTIONAL INSTITUTIONS.

Sentence to.

See SENTENCE AND PUNISHMENT.

Probate.

See PROBATE AND FAMILY COURT.

STATE AND STATE DEPARTMENTS —Cont'd

Process.

See PROCESS AND SERVICE OF PROCESS AND PAPERS.

Property officer of state, **33:15.**

Prosecuting attorney.

Attorney General, **12:1 et seq.**

See ATTORNEY GENERAL.

District attorney. See within this heading, "District attorney."

Prosecution expenses, **12:7, 280:4.**

Psychologists employed by state, penal provisions as applicable, **112:123.**

Public lands.

See PUBLIC LANDS.

Public officers and employees.

Officers and employees.

See PUBLIC OFFICERS AND EMPLOYEES.

Public utilities, **25:1 et seq.**

See TELECOMMUNICATIONS AND ENERGY DEPARTMENT.

Public works and department, **16:1 et seq.**

Publishing state publications, **5:1-5:18, 29:28, 30:31.**

See STATE PRINTING.

Purchasing agent, **7:4A, 7:22 et seq.**

See STATE PURCHASING AGENT.

Qualification for state office or employment, time to establish, **30:12.**

Racing commission.

See HORSE AND DOG RACING MEETINGS.

Radio and television technicians registration law, applicability, **112:87QQQ.**

Railroad crossings.

See RAILROAD CROSSINGS.

Railroads.

See RAILROADS.

Real property.

See PUBLIC LANDS.

Reciprocal enforcement of tax liabilities between Commonwealth and other states, **58:28C.**

Reclamation board.

See LOWLANDS AND SWAMPS.

Records, reports, and returns of departments, **30A:6, 30A:6B, 30A:11A.**

Accounting statements, in records and reports, verification, **7A:10.**

STATE AND STATE DEPARTMENTS —Cont'd

Records, reports, and returns of departments —Cont'd

Annual reports. See within this heading, "Annual reports."

Avoidance of special legislation, recommendations, **30:33A.**

Budget director, estimates made, **7:8.**

Building superintendent's records, **8:17A.**

Class of legislation to accompany recommendations, **30:33.**

Comptroller to have access to books and papers, **7A:9.**

Concealment, **231:94C, 266:145.**

Custody of departmental records, **66:6.**

Disposition of obsolete public records, **30:42.**

Environmental impact reports of state departments, agencies, etc., **30:61, 30:62.**

False reports, penalty, **268:6.**

Federal grants, report of comptroller regarding, **7A:4.**

Finance. See STATE FINANCE.

Fiscal reports. See STATE FINANCE.

Housing court, recording system, **185C:18.**

New projects involving assessment of cities and towns in metropolitan districts, **30:35A.**

Nutrition board, report, **6:182.**

Obsolete public records, disposition, **30:42.**

Organization, report, **30:4.**

Property of state, public records, **30:42.**

Recommendations for legislative action, **30:33, 30:33A.**

Rules and regulations, filing, **30:7, 30:37.**

Secretary of state, filing and indexing rules and regulations of state departments and officials, **30:37.**

Special reports to state purchasing agent, **30:35.**

State motor vehicles, reports as to use, **30:36.**

Verification of accounting statements, **7A:10.**

Vocational rehabilitation, inspection by state departments of records of applicants, **6:84.**

STATE AND STATE DEPARTMENTS —Cont'd

Recovery of land held by Commonwealth pursuant to judgment, subsequent action, **245:9, 245:10.**

Recreation areas, **132A:1 et seq.** See STATE RECREATION AREAS.

Regional community colleges, city's authority to acquire and convey land to state for use, **43:30.**

Regional transit authorities. See REGIONAL TRANSIT AUTHORITIES.

Register of personnel, central, **30:38.**

Registration of land titles. See REGISTRATION OF LAND TITLES.

Rehabilitation, **6:78, 6:84.**

Removal of employees, **30:9B.**

Rents, profits and improvements, liability, **245:6, 245:11.**

Reports. Records, reports, and returns. See within this heading, "Records, reports, and returns of departments."

Representation in suits and proceedings, **12:3-12:5, 12:27.**

Representatives to general court. See GENERAL COURT.

Reservation of jurisdiction over property acquired by United States, **1:7.**

Reserved powers, **US Const 10th Amend.**

Retirement systems. See RETIREMENT SYSTEMS AND PENSIONS.

Revenue department, **14:1 et seq.** See REVENUE DEPARTMENT AND COMMISSIONER.

Review. See APPEAL AND REVIEW.

Rewards for apprehension of criminals, **276:9.**

Safety, Department of Public Safety, **22:1 et seq.** See PUBLIC SAFETY DEPARTMENT.

Sale or transfer of property. See SALE OR TRANSFER OF PROPERTY.

Sales tax, exemptions, **64H:6.**

Sanatoria, **111:63-111:67.**

Saturdays. Half-holiday, **41:110, 92:67, 149:33, 149:41.**

STATE AND STATE DEPARTMENTS —Cont'd

Saturdays —Cont'd Legal holiday falling, **30:24A.** Office hours, **30:24.**

Schedule bonds for officers and employees, **30:16.**

School buses. See SCHOOL BUSES AND TRANSPORTATION OF PUPILS.

Schools. See SCHOOLS AND EDUCATION.

Seal of state, **2:2, 2:3.** See STATE SEAL.

Secretary of state, **9:1 et seq.** See SECRETARY OF STATE.

Senate. See GENERAL COURT.

Service corps commission. See SERVICE CORPS COMMISSION.

Service of process. See PROCESS AND SERVICE OF PROCESS AND PAPERS.

Session laws, right of departments to copy, **5:3, 5:4.**

Sheep farms, compensation, **128:11.**

Ships and other watercraft, **132A:2D.** Excise tax, state vessels exempt, **60B:3.** Warships, consent of Congress required for state to keep, **US Const Art 1 Sec 10 cl 3.**

Sinking funds. See STATE FINANCE.

Social services, **18:1 et seq., 18B:1 et seq.** See WELFARE AND SOCIAL SERVICES.

Song of state, **2:19, 2:20.**

Special examination of management or finances, **7:9-7:11.**

Spouses, surviving. See SURVIVING SPOUSE.

Stabilization fund, **29:2H.**

State glee club song, **2:43.**

State house. See STATE HOUSE.

Stationery and letterheads, **30:30, 30:30A.**

Statute of limitations. See LIMITATION OF ACTIONS.

Statutes, meaning, **4:7.**

Street railways. See STREET RAILWAYS.

STATE AND STATE DEPARTMENTS —Cont'd

Student government day, observance, **6:12M.**

Students in co-operative education programs, employment, **30:60.**

Subrogation of state in action against registered titles assurance fund, **185:105.**

Substitute department head, **29:65, 30:6, 30:6A.**

Successor in office, holding office until appointment, **30:8.**

Superintendent of buildings, **8:1 et seq.**
See STATE SUPERINTENDENT OF STATE OFFICE BUILDINGS.

Supplementary payments to blind persons.
See BLIND PERSONS.

Supplies and equipment, **7:22, 7:25A, 30:51, 30:52.**

Supreme Court's original jurisdiction over suits by or against, **US Const Art 3 Sec 2 cl 3.**

Surgeons.
Physicians and surgeons.
See PHYSICIANS AND SURGEONS.
State surgeon.
See STATE SURGEON.

Surveys.
See MAPS, PLATS, AND SURVEYS.

Surviving spouse.
See SURVIVING SPOUSE.

Suspension of officer or employee under indictment, **30:59.**

Taxation.
See TAXATION.

Tax commission.
See REVENUE DEPARTMENT AND COMMISSIONER.

Teachers.
See TEACHERS.

Telephone or telegraph companies, reduced rates, **159:15.**

Temporary officers.
Classification and allocation, **30:45.**
Suspended officers or employees, powers and duties of appointees filling positions, **30:59.**

Tidelands, **91:10D, 130:105.**

Titles of nobility not to be granted by, **US Const Art 1 Sec 10 cl 1.**

STATE AND STATE DEPARTMENTS —Cont'd

Tobacco.
Below cost sales to state institutions or agencies, **64C:15.**
Sales or solicitation of sales of cigarettes to be brought into Commonwealth, **64C:10.**

Tonnage duties not to be laid by, **US Const Art 1 Sec 10 cl 3.**

Topographical survey of, improvement, **91:33.**

Topographic maps issued by department, applicability of provisions as to state printing, **5:1.**

Training schools, **18A:1 et seq.**
See YOUTH SERVICES DEPARTMENT AND MASSACHUSETTS TRAINING SCHOOLS.

Transportation charges of motor carriers of property, exception as to requirements for payment, **159B:19A.**

Treasurer, **10:1 et seq.**
See STATE TREASURER.

Trees.
Shade tree management and pest control bureau, state assistance to municipalities, **132:16.**
State tree, **2:8.**

Trespass.
See TRESPASS.

Trial of right of possession of land as against, **245:1-245:12.**

Troops not to be kept by, **US Const Art 1 Sec 10 cl 3.**

Trust companies.
See TRUST COMPANIES.

Trustees ineligible to hold other office in same institution, **30:23A.**

Trust funds.
See STATE FINANCE.

Tuberculosis.
See TUBERCULOSIS AND TUBERCULIN.

Unclaimed.
See ABANDONED, LOST, AND UNCLAIMED PROPERTY.

Underwater archaeological resources, Commonwealth as having first option to purchase, **91:63.**

Unemployment compensation, payment of Commonwealth checks, **29:32.**

Universities, **73:1 et seq.**
See COLLEGES AND UNIVERSITIES.

STATE AND STATE DEPARTMENTS —Cont'd

Unplaced boards and agencies, assignment to departments, **30:2.**

Utilities, **25:1 et seq.**
See PUBLIC UTILITIES DEPARTMENT.

Vacancies in gubernatorial appointed offices, filling, **30:10.**

Venue of actions, **223:5.**

Veterans' services commissioner as agent, **115:2.**

Veterans, waiver of fees for copy of records to assist in proving claim against government, **262:46A.**

Vocational education.
See VOCATIONAL EDUCATION AND SCHOOLS.

Wages, salaries and compensation of state officers and employees, **29:31, 30:46.**
See WAGES, SALARIES, AND COMPENSATION.

Walking Sunday, observance, **6:15NN.**

Warships, congressional consent for state to keep, **US Const Art 1 Sec 10 cl 3.**

War, state not to engage in, **US Const Art 1 Sec 10 cl 3.**

Welfare, **18:1 et seq., 18B:1 et seq.**
See WELFARE AND SOCIAL SERVICES.

White pine blister rust, compensation with respect to suppression, **128:23.**

Willful acts of children, parents' civil liability, **231:85G.**

Witnesses in criminal cases summoned upon behalf, **233:1.**

Writs of entry against, **237:2, 245:9-245:12.**
See ENTRY, WRITS.

Youth and youth services, **18A:1 et seq.**
See YOUTH SERVICES DEPARTMENT AND MASSACHUSETTS TRAINING SCHOOLS.

Zoning and planning exemptions, **40A:3.**

STATE AUDITOR, 11:1 et seq.

Administrators of field operations, appointment, **11:5.**

Adverse findings by state auditor, required response, **111:12.**

STATE AUDITOR —Cont'd
Agreements with federal government or state agencies for audit purposes, **11:13.**
Annual reports, **11:12, 62F:5.**
Appointment of employees, **11:5-11:6A.**
Appropriations, salaries of department officers and employees as subject, **11:6.**
Ballots and voting machines, order of appearance of names of candidates, **54:43A.**
Bond or undertaking.
First deputy, **11:2.**
State auditor, **11:1.**
Book stores on property of state colleges, audit, **73:10.**
Bradford Durfee College of Technology, audit of accounts, **74:42H.**
Certificate of election, **54:116.**
Change of name of divisions in office, **11:6.**
Civil service.
Employees' status, **11:6, 30:45.**
Reports of state officers, **31:69.**
Stop-payment order as to persons illegally employed, **31:73.**
Colleges.
See COLLEGES AND UNIVERSITIES.
Compensation.
Salaries and compensation. See within this heading, "Salaries and compensation."
Constitution of Massachusetts.
See CONSTITUTION OF MASSACHUSETTS.
Contract audits division, establishment, **11:6.**
Creation of department, **11:1.**
Death of, flag to be flown at half-staff, **2:6A.**
Deferred compensation plan, audit, **29:64.**
Defined, **4:7.**
Deputies, **11:2, 11:5.**
Districts and authorities created by general court, audit of accounts, **11:12.**
Divisions in office, **11:6.**
Duties, **11:12.**
Election, **54:150.**
Certificate of election, issuance, **54:116.**
Nomination papers, time for filing, **53:10, 53:48.**
Objection to nomination, time for filing, **55B:5.**

STATE AUDITOR —Cont'd
Election —Cont'd
Order of appearance of names of candidates on ballots and voting machines, **54:43A.**
Primary elections, number of signatures required for candidates, **53:44.**
Record of votes, transmission, **54:112.**
Employees.
Civil service laws, employees as exempt, **11:6, 30:45.**
Establishment of salaries, duties, and personnel regulations, **11:6.**
Labor relations laws, department officers and employees excepted, **11:6, 150E:1.**
Environmental affairs executive office, audit of funds, **21A:9.**
Ethics Commission.
Major policy-making positions reported, **268B:3.**
Personnel and other assistants made available, **268B:2.**
Federal audits division, establishment, **11:6.**
First deputy, **11:2.**
Fish and game license records, audit and inspection, **131:18.**
Flag to be flown at half-staff on death, **2:6A.**
Fraud in audit of executive office of health and human services, reference, **11:12.**
General court, salaries of officers and employees as subject to appropriation, **11:6.**
Governor, confirmation of appointment of deputy state auditors, **11:5.**
Highway fund as available for maintenance of department, **90:34.**
Horse racing authority, annual audit, **128A:26.**
Income tax division, audit of accounts, **11:12.**
Industrial development authority, audit, **40:18, 40:19.**
Inspector general.
See INSPECTOR GENERAL.
Labor and workforce development.
Civil service law exemption, **11:6, 30:45.**
Employees. See within this heading, "Employees."
Industrial development authority, audit, **40D:18, 40D:19.**

STATE AUDITOR —Cont'd
Labor and workforce development —Cont'd
Labor relations law exemption, **11:6, 150E:11.**
Salaries and regulations for employees, establishment, **11:6.**
Legislative post audit and oversight bureau, reports, **3:63.**
Local mandates division.
Establishment, **11:6.**
Municipality submitting notice, **29:27C.**
Lottery commission accounts and transactions, audit, **10:36.**
Major policy-making positions reported to State Ethics Commission, **268B:3.**
Marine fisheries division director, audit and inspection of books and records, **130:4.**
Municipal industrial development financing authorities, audits, **40D:18.**
New Bedford Institute of Technology, audit of accounts, **74:42H.**
Nomination papers, time for filing, **53:10, 53:48.**
Objection to nomination, time for filing, **55B:5.**
Official bond.
Bond or undertaking. See within this heading, "Bond or undertaking."
Organization of state auditor's office, **11:1.**
Pensioner's right to payment for service in department, **32:91.**
Primary elections, number of signatures required for candidates, **53:44.**
Private business schools, financial statements submitted to state auditor, **75D:3.**
Privation contracts, **7:54, 7:55.**
Qualified bonds, certification as to state aid withheld due, **44A:10.**
Records and reports, **11:6A, 11:12.**
Civil service reports of state officers, **31:69.**
Excess of net state tax revenues, **62F:5.**
Records conservation board, membership, **30:42.**
Removal of employees, **11:6.**
Reports.
Records and reports. See within this heading, "Records and reports."

STATE AUDITOR —Cont'd

Retention of veterans in public employment, officers and employees of department as exempt from laws regulating, **11:6.**

Revenue Department and Commissioner.

Duties of auditor, **11:12.**

Excess of net state tax revenues, reports, **62F:5.**

Inspection of books and records, **62C:20.**

Salaries and compensation, **11:1.**

Employees, **11:6.**

Legislative and constitutional officers' compensation advisory board, duties, **6:162.**

Pensioner's right to payment for services in department, **32:91.**

State agencies, reports of audits, **7:4.**

State college accounts, audit, **73:10, 75:6.**

Bradford Durfee College of Technology, **74:42H.**

Stop-payment order as to persons illegally employed, **31:73.**

Student government day, observance, **6:12M.**

Taxation.

Revenue growth limits.

Oversight, **62F:5.**

Term limits, **11:1.**

Transmission of record of votes, **54:112.**

Veterans, officers and employees of department as exempt from laws regulating retention in public service, **11:6.**

Voting machines and ballots, order of appearance of candidates' names, **54:43A.**

Wages.

Salaries. See within this heading, "Salaries and compensation."

STATE BALLOT LAW COMMISSION, 55B:1 et seq.

Access to ballots, enforcement, **55B:4.**

Address of voter as required for objections, **55B:5.**

Alias.

See ASSUMED NAME.

Appeal.

See APPEAL AND REVIEW.

STATE BALLOT LAW COMMISSION —Cont'd

Appeals court, retired justice as commission member, **55B:1.**

Assumed name.

See ASSUMED NAME.

Attorney general, time for objection to nomination, **55B:5.**

Auditor of state, time for objection to nomination, **55B:5.**

Biennial state elections, decisions, **55B:10.**

Books and papers.

Production of books and papers. See within this heading, "Production of books and papers."

Boston, exception as to objections to nominations, **55B:7.**

Candidates, qualifications, **55B:4.**

Certificate of voter registration, form, **55B:5.**

Certificates of nomination, **55B:4.**

Decisions, **55B:10.**

Certification of signatures.

Challenging, **55B:5.**

Review, **55B:6.**

Certified mail, filing of objections, **55B:5, 55B:7.**

Chairman, **55B:1.**

City charter, petition for adoption, **43:9, 43:9B.**

City office nominations, objections, **55B:7.**

City or town elections, commission having no jurisdiction over questions regarding ballots or candidates, **55B:4.**

Clerical assistance, **55B:3.**

Compensation of members, **55B:3.**

Conflicts of interests of members, **55B:2.**

Constitutional qualifications of candidates, **55B:4.**

Copies of objections, filing, **55B:5.**

County elective offices.

Time for objection to nomination, **55B:5.**

Withdrawal of nomination, **55B:4.**

Date.

Time or date. See within this heading, "Time or date."

Deceit.

Fraud and deceit. See within this heading, "Fraud and deceit."

Decisions.

Commission, **55B:10.**

Failure to render, **55B:4.**

STATE BALLOT LAW COMMISSION —Cont'd

Decisions —Cont'd

Registrars, **55B:7.**

Discovery and disclosure.

Power to require, **55B:4.**

Records of proceedings, **55B:12.**

Registrars' power to require production of books and papers, **55B:7.**

District court, retired justice as commission member, **55B:1.**

Employment dislocations and assistance in reemployment of dislocated workers, **6:17.**

Establishment, **55B:1 et seq.**

Examination or investigation, **55B:4.**

Ballot boxes, examination, **53:32.**

Records of proceedings of, examination, **55B:12.**

Executive council, time for objection to nomination, **55B:5.**

Expiration of term, **55B:1.**

Federal office, withdrawal of nomination, **55B:4.**

Fees.

Objection, filing fee, **55B:4, 55B:5.**

Witness fees, **55B:4, 55B:7.**

Forgery.

Decisions, **55B:10.**

Jurisdiction, **55B:4.**

Objections based, **55B:5.**

Forms.

Certificate of voter registration, form, **55B:5.**

Notice of objections, contents, **55B:8.**

Fraud and deceit.

Jurisdiction, **55B:4.**

Nomination, effect of fraud, **55B:11.**

Objections based, **55B:5.**

Governor.

Appointment of commission, **6:17, 55B:1.**

Time for objection to nomination, **55B:5.**

Hearings.

Initiative and referendum petitions, **43:38, 55B:9.**

Rules, promulgation, **55B:4.**

Initiative and referendum petitions.

Fraudulent signing, **55B:4.**

Hearings, **43:38, 55B:9.**

Notice of objection, **55B:8.**

Supplemental signatures, objections, **55B:5.**

STATE BALLOT LAW COMMISSION —Cont'd
Investigations.
  Examination or investigation.
    See within this heading,
    "Examination or
    investigation."
Judges and justices.
  Justice of peace, holding of
    office, **55B:2.**
  Retired justice as member of
    commission, **55B:1.**
Jurisdiction, **55B:4.**
  Review of signatures, **55B:6.**
Lieutenant governor, time for
  objection to nomination,
  55B:5.
Mail and mailing.
  Filing of objection to
    nominations, **55B:5, 55B:7.**
  Notice of objections, **55B:8.**
  Registered mail. See within this
    heading, "Registered mail,
    filing of objections."
Membership, **55B:1.**
  Compensation, **55B:3.**
  Conflicts of interest, **55B:2.**
  Terms of offices, **55B:1.**
Nominations.
  Certificates of nomination. See
    within this heading,
    "Certificates of nomination."
  Decisions, **55B:10.**
  Fictitious name or alias, **55B:11.**
  Hearings as to nomination
    papers, **55B:9.**
  Investigations, **55B:4.**
  Membership on commission,
    nomination for public office
    as affecting, **55B:2.**
  Objections, filing, **55B:5, 55B:7.**
  Withdrawal of nominations. See
    within this heading,
    "Withdrawal of
    nominations."
Notary public, holding office,
  55B:2.
Notice of objections, **55B:8.**
Oaths.
  Administration, **55B:4.**
  Registrars authorized to
    administer, **55B:7.**
Objections, **55B:5.**
  Decisions, **55B:10.**
  Filing fee, **55B:5.**
  Hearings, **55B:9.**
  Nomination papers and
    petitions, **55B:7.**
  Notice, **55B:8.**
  Procedure, **55B:7.**
  Registered mail. See within this
    heading, "Registered mail,
    filing of objections."

STATE BALLOT LAW COMMISSION —Cont'd
Objections —Cont'd
  Sufficiency, **55B:4, 55B:5.**
  Time for filing, **55B:5.**
  Voters' objections, **55B:5.**
Penalties, failure to appear and
  testify, **55B:4, 55B:7.**
Perfecting appeal, **55B:4.**
Political party membership as
  affecting membership, **55B:1,
  55B:2.**
Powers and duties, **55B:4.**
Presidential primaries, **55B:4.**
  Decisions, **55B:10.**
  Signatures for candidates,
    review, **55B:6.**
Primary elections, **55B:4.**
  Decisions, **55B:10.**
  Hearings, **55B:9.**
  Notice of objections, **55B:8.**
  Objections to nominations,
    registrars' determination,
    55B:5, 55B:7.
  Presidential primaries. See
    within this heading,
    "Presidential primaries."
Printing of ballot.
  Registrars' failure to render
    decision as affecting, **55B:7.**
  State secretary, **55B:4.**
Printing of rules for hearings,
  55B:4.
Production of books and papers.
  Power to require, **55B:4.**
  Registrars' power to compel,
    55B:7.
Public inspection of records,
  55B:12.
Public policy questions, no
  jurisdiction over, **55B:4.**
Qualification of members, **55B:1.**
Qualifications of candidates,
  55B:4.
Receiver general, time for
  objection to nomination,
  55B:5.
Records of proceedings, **55B:12.**
  Stenographic recording, **55B:3.**
  Tape recordings, **55B:3.**
Referendum.
  Initiative and referendum
    petitions. See within this
    heading, "Initiative and
    referendum petitions."
Registered mail, filing of
  objections, **55B:5, 55B:7.**
  Certified mail, filing of
    objections, **55B:5.**
  Notice of objections, **55B:8.**
Registrars of voters.
  Certificate of registration,
    issuance, **55B:5.**

STATE BALLOT LAW COMMISSION —Cont'd
Registrars of voters —Cont'd
  Signatures, request for review of
    sufficiency, **55B:6.**
  Summons by registrars, **55B:4,
    55B:7.**
  Town offices, consideration of
    objections to nominations,
    55B:7.
Representative in Congress, time
  for filing objection to
  nomination, **55B:5.**
Retired justice as member of
  commission, **55B:1.**
Rules for hearings, distribution,
  55B:4.
Rules of procedure, notice, **55B:8.**
Secretary of state.
  State secretary. See within this
    heading, "State secretary."
Senator and Congress, time for
  objection to nomination,
  55B:5.
Senator, state, time for objection to
  nomination, **55B:5.**
Severability of provisions, **55B:1.**
Signatures.
  Certification of signatures. See
    within this heading,
    "Certification of signatures."
  Decisions, **55B:10.**
  Objections, **55B:5.**
  Presidential candidates,
    signatures, **55B:6.**
  Procedure for review of, **55B:6.**
  Supplemental signatures. See
    within this heading,
    "Supplemental signatures."
Special elections, **55B:10.**
  Decisions, **55B:10.**
  Objections to nominations,
    registrars' determination,
    55B:7.
State auditor, time for objection to
  nomination, **55B:5.**
State representative, time for
  objection to nomination,
  55B:5.
State secretary.
  Commission as within
    department, **9:29.**
  Printing of ballots, **55B:4.**
  Records of commission stored,
    55B:12.
  Time for objection to
    nomination, **55B:5.**
State senator, time for objection to
  nomination, **55B:5.**
Stenographic members,
  compensation, **55B:3.**

STATE BALLOT LAW COMMISSION —Cont'd

Stenographic recording, **55B:3.**

Suffolk County, review of signatures, **55B:6.**

Summons by registrars, **55B:4, 55B:7.**

Superior Court.
Retired justice as member, **55B:1.**
Signatures, review of sufficiency, **55B:6.**

Supplemental signatures.
Hearings, **55B:9.**
Notice of objections, **55B:8.**
Objections, **55B:5.**

Supreme judicial court, retired justice as commission member, **55B:1.**

Tape recordings of proceedings, **55B:3.**

Tenure of members, **55B:1.**

Terms of office of members, **55B:1.**

Time or date.
Decisions of commission, **55B:10.**
Hearings on objections, **55B:9.**
Judicial review, time to commence, **55B:4.**
Objections, time for filing, **55B:5, 55B:7.**
Signatures, request for review, **55B:6.**

Town clerk, transmittal of objections, **55B:7.**

Town office nominations, objections, **55B:7.**

Treasurer and receiver general, time for objection to nomination, **55B:5.**

Trial.
Hearings. See within this heading, "Hearings."

Vacancies in office, **55B:1.**

Voter registration, form of certificate, **55B:5.**

Voters, objections, **55B:5.**

Withdrawal of nominations, **55B:10.**
County elective offices, **55B:4.**
Decisions, **55B:10.**
Registrars' decisions, **55B:7.**
State office, **55B:4.**

Witnesses, summons by registrars, **55B:4, 55B:7.**

STATE BONDS AND OBLIGATIONS.

Abandoned or lost property.
Lost or destroyed bonds. See within this heading, "Lost or destroyed bonds."

STATE BONDS AND OBLIGATIONS —Cont'd

Advertising for bids, **29:53.**

Agreements with brokers for placement, **29:49B.**

Amount for payment to be included in state tax, **29:50.**

Anticipation notes.
Assessments for metropolitan districts, **29:47A.**
Execution, **29:48.**
Interest, **29:47, 29:47A.**
Issuance, **29:47, 29:47A.**
Metropolitan districts, notes, **29:47A.**
Signatures, **29:48, 29:48A.**

Appropriations as unnecessary for payment of treasury notes issued for temporary loans, **29:18.**

Assessments on metropolitan districts, **29:47A, 29:51.**

Assignment, **29:35.**

Bids and bidding.
Deposits by bidders, **29:54.**
Sale of obligations, **29:53.**

Borrowing to pay legal obligations of Commonwealth, permissibility, **29:47, 44:6A.**

Budget of state.
Inclusion of amount to be paid on bonds and debentures, **29:50.**
Serial bond and sinking fund requirements, classification to show, **29:6.**

Certification of amounts to be paid on state bonds or scrip, **29:50.**

Community preservation.
Bond issues, authorized, **44B:11.**

Consolidation of bond issues, **29:49.**

Contracts for sale of bonds.
Public contracts. See within this heading, "Public contracts for sale of state bonds or notes."

Coupon bonds, exchange of registered bonds, **29:58.**

Credit enhancement, highway fund, **29:2O.**

Denominations of bonds, **29:49.**

Deposits by bidders for bonds at public sale, **29:54.**

Destroyed or lost bonds.
Lost or destroyed bonds. See within this heading, "Lost or destroyed bonds."

Duplicates for lost, mutilated, endorsed, or destroyed bonds, **29:58, 29:59.**

STATE BONDS AND OBLIGATIONS —Cont'd

Employment security funds to be invested, **151A:56.**

Endorsed bonds, substitution, **29:58.**

Exchange of registered bonds for coupon bonds, **29:58.**

Execution, **29:48, 29:48A.**

Expenses of sale, **29:55.**

Facsimiles of signature and state seal, **29:48A, 29:49A.**

Filing of state, county and municipal securities, **110A:402, 110A:403.**

Finance advisory board to submit recommendations, **6:98.**

Forgery or counterfeiting, **267:7.**
See FORGERY AND COUNTERFEITING.

General obligations, status of certain bonds, **29:60A.**

Highway infrastructure fund, **29:2O.**

Housing authority notes issued by Commonwealth, guaranty, **121B:34B.**

Income from public obligations, taxation, **62:2.**

Indemnity bond by owner of lost or destroyed state bond, **29:60.**

Infrastructure fund, **29:2O.**

Injunctions against unlawful obligations, **29:63.**

Interest on bonds or notes, **29:47, 29:47A, 29:49.**

Issuance, **29:47, 29:47A, 29:49, 29:58.**

Loans.
Anticipation notes. See within this heading, "Anticipation notes."

Lost or destroyed bonds.
Duplicates issued, **29:59, 29:60.**
Indemnity bond by owner, **29:60.**
Payment after redemption date, **29:59.**

Massachusetts College Student Loan Authority, investments, **15C:18.**

Maturities of bonds, **29:49.**

Metropolitan districts, **29:47A, 29:51.**

Minibonds, issuance and sale, **29:49A.**

Mutilated or defaced bonds, substitution, **29:58.**

Proposals for purchase of, inviting, **29:53.**

Public contracts for sale of state bonds or notes, **259:6.**
Advertising for bids, **29:53.**
Deposits by bidders, **29:54.**

STATE BONDS AND OBLIGATIONS —Cont'd
Public works department's allocation of funds to certain cities and towns, borrowing money for purpose, **44:6A.**
Railroad crossings.
See RAILROAD CROSSINGS.
Redemption.
Issuance and sale of bonds subject to call, **29:49.**
Payment of lost or destroyed bond after redemption date, **29:59.**
Refunding bonds, highway infrastructure funds, **29:2O.**
Registered bonds, issuance and exchange for coupon bonds, **29:58.**
Registration, **29:39.**
Revenue loans.
Anticipation notes. See within this heading, "Anticipation notes."
Sale of bonds.
Bids and bidding, **29:53.**
Expense of sale, payment, **29:55.**
Proposals, **29:53.**
Public contracts. See within this heading, "Public contracts for sale of state bonds or notes."
State treasurer's duties, **29:48, 29:48A, 35:38A.**
Unexpended receipts from, transfer, **29:56.**
Secured transactions, security for issuance of state refunding bonds, **29:53A.**
Serial payment plan, **29:6, 29:49, 29:50.**
Signatures, **29:48, 29:48A.**
Sinking funds.
See STATE FINANCE.
Social security benefits, statement of tax consequences to recipients, **29:48B.**
Substitution or duplication for mutilated, defaced, lost, destroyed, or endorsed bonds, **29:58, 29:59.**
Surety on bond given by owner of lost or destroyed bond, **29:60.**
Taxation.
Acceptance of notes in payment of taxes, **29:48.**
Amount included in state tax for serial payments of bonds, **29:50.**
Income from public obligations, **62:2.**

STATE BONDS AND OBLIGATIONS —Cont'd
Transfer of unexpended receipts from sale, **29:56.**
Treasurer's signature on notes and bonds issued by Commonwealth, **29:48, 29:48A.**

STATE BUDGET, 29:6.
See STATE FINANCE.

STATE COLLEGES, 73:1 et seq.
See COLLEGES AND UNIVERSITIES.

STATE CRIER AND GREETER.
Establishment of position, **6:15FFF.**

STATE FAIR.
Racing.
See HORSE AND DOG RACING MEETINGS.
Use of term forbidden, **110:4B.**

STATE FARM.
Injury to property by prisoner, **266:130.**
Minors, **119:66.**
Prisons, generally.
See PRISONS.
Sentences to, **279:36.**
Trespass upon land, **266:123.**

STATE FINANCE, 7A:7-7A:11, 29:1-29:63.
Abandoned property.
See ABANDONED, LOST, AND UNCLAIMED PROPERTY.
Accounts and accounting.
Allotment of funds by governor, subsidiary accounts as governing, **29:27.**
Audit of state accounts, **11:12.**
Fiscal year, state officers and departments to keep accounts, **30:28.**
General court.
See GENERAL COURT.
Itemized accounts of sales of property by state institutions, **30:41.**
Keeping books at state institutions, **30:29.**
Municipal tax liability, semi-annual collection on account, **59:20.**
State library accounts, approval, **6:36.**
Subsidiary accounts. See within this heading, "Subsidiary accounts."
Systems, **7A:7, 7A:8.**
Comptroller to design and install, **7A:7, 7A:8.**

STATE FINANCE —Cont'd
Administration.
See ADMINISTRATION AND FINANCE EXECUTIVE OFFICE.
Adoption affordability assistance fund, **29:2WW.**
Advancements of funds.
Defined, **30:45.**
Officers, when advancements to officers authorized, **29:23-29:25, 29:31.**
Railroads, advancements for relocation or other work, **81:7I.**
Airports and landing fields.
Construction and improvement costs, state contribution towards, **90:39F.**
Alcoholic beverage license fees and excise taxes paid into general fund, **138:21, 138:27.**
Allotment of funds by governor, **29:9B.**
Estimate of anticipated expenditures for allotment period, **29:9B.**
Exceeding of, forbidden, **29:26.**
Increase in salaries, requirements, **29:27.**
New employees, requirement as to employment, **29:27.**
Schedule of expenditures required, **29:27.**
Subsidiary accounts as governing payments out, **29:27.**
Allowances for expenses of state officers and employees, **30:25.**
Animal inspectors, compensation, **129:17.**
Annual estimates of officers and departments, **29:3-29:5.**
Annual investigation of notes and securities held by state treasurer, **29:42.**
Annual report of expenditures by state institutions and agencies, **7A:12.**
Annuity contracts for public educational institution employees, notice, **15:18A.**
Antitrust law violations, general fund, **93:14.**
Appeal, grievances of state employees as to budget, **30:49.**
Appropriations, **29:5, 29:6, 29:20, 29:26.**
Limit on interest and principal payments on general obligation of Commonwealth, **29:60B.**

STATE FINANCE —Cont'd
Approval of governor and council, expenditures not requiring, **29:21.**
Arts lottery fund, **10:35, 10:37.**
Asset management board, general fund, **7B:8.**
Attorney general, state treasurer's transmittal to attorney general of account of overdue bonds and securities, **10:9.**
Auditor, **11:1 et seq.**
   See STATE AUDITOR.
Balances from ordinary revenue, carrying over, **29:16.**
Banks.
   Deposit of state funds, **29:34, 29:34A, 29:38, 62C:45.**
   Sinking funds for state bonds, **29:49.**
   Taxes, depositary banks, **62C:45.**
   Trust companies.
      See TRUST COMPANIES.
Beano receipts, apportionment, **10:39.**
Bonds.
   Generally.
      See STATE TREASURER.
   State bonds and obligations.
      See STATE BONDS AND OBLIGATIONS.
Borrowing money, **29:47, 29:48.**
   Annual statement as to condition of state indebtedness, **29:5.**
   Appropriations, effect of indebtedness to state by person entitled, **29:17.**
   Bonds and obligations, permissibility of borrowing to pay legal obligations of Commonwealth, **29:47, 44:6A.**
   Budget provisions, **29:7A.**
   Comptroller of state, countersigning notes, **29:48.**
   In anticipation of receipts, **29:47, 29:47A.**
   Provisions as to expenditures to be defrayed, **29:7A.**
   Requests for funds by state agencies, submission, **29:2F, 29:7A.**
   Treasurer.
      See STATE TREASURER.
   Treasury notes issued for temporary loans, appropriations as unnecessary for payment, **29:18.**
Boxers' fund, payment to Commonwealth, **147:40A.**

STATE FINANCE —Cont'd
Bradford Durfee college of technology.
   See BRADFORD DURFEE COLLEGE OF TECHNOLOGY.
Brownfields redevelopment fund, **23G:29A.**
Brownfields revitalization fund, **29:2VV.**
   Established, **29:2UU.**
Budget, **29:6.**
   Administrative expenses, classification of budget to show, **29:6.**
   Allotment period, estimate of anticipated expenditures by state officers, **29:9B.**
   Amount to be paid on bonds or scrip, inclusion in budget, **29:50.**
   Annual estimates of officers and departments, **29:3.**
   Appeals of grievances of state employees, **30:49.**
   Board of education to compile guidelines, **15:1G.**
   Bonds and obligations.
      Inclusion of amount to be paid, **29:50.**
      Serial bond and sinking fund requirements, classification to show, **29:6.**
   Bradford Durfee college of technology.
      See BRADFORD DURFEE COLLEGE OF TECHNOLOGY.
   Buildings.
      Construction and improvement estimates, **29:4, 29:6.**
      Maintenance and repairs standards and guidelines, **7:43C.**
      Rental, **7:40G.**
   Capital facilities budgets, **29:7E.**
   Classification, **29:6.**
   Colleges.
      See COLLEGES AND UNIVERSITIES.
   Confidential secretary for budget director, **30:7.**
   Deafness, budget requests of office, **6:84.**
   Deficiencies in appropriations of former years, classification to show, **29:6.**
   Department financial plans, **29:5F.**

STATE FINANCE —Cont'd
Budget —Cont'd
   Director of fiscal affairs division, **29:6.**
   Employees of bureau, **7:4D.**
   Environmental management department budget, **21:3C.**
   Estimates.
      Allotment period, submission of estimate by state officers as to anticipated expenditures, **29:9B.**
      Building construction, **29:4, 29:6.**
      Departments and officers, annual estimates, **7:8, 29:3, 29:4.**
      Extraordinary expenses, estimate, **29:4.**
      Judicial system, submission by chief justice of supreme judicial court of statement as to estimates for maintenance, **211:2A.**
      Metropolitan district commission to include certain pension contributions, **29:9A.**
      Proposed legislation, secretaries of executive offices to submit cost estimates, **29:3A.**
      Requirements in preparation, **29:6.**
      Review by secretaries of executive offices prior to submission to budget director, **29:3.**
      Secretaries of executive offices, submission, **29:3.**
      State secretary, filing estimates of cost of regulatory compliance with budget, **30A:5.**
      Total available revenue for annual budget, preparation, **29:5B.**
   Extraordinary expenditures, submission of estimate, **29:4.**
   Fisheries and wildlife division budget, **21:7G.**
   Game laws, provision for enforcement, **29:6.**
   General court, submission, **29:6.**
   Governor's cabinet, submission of executive office estimates, **29:3.**
   Governor's functions and duties in connection with budget, **29:6.**

STATE FINANCE —Cont'd
Budget —Cont'd
Inland fisheries, provision for
enforcement of laws, **29:6.**
Interest on public debt,
classification, **29:6.**
Judicial system, estimates,
211:2A.
Long range capital facilities
agencies, submission, **29:7D.**
Maintenance and operation
expenses, classification of
budget to show, **29:6.**
Mental health and retardation
services budget, **19:18,
19:20.**
Mentally ill and retarded
persons, submission of
annual budget requests of
mental health department,
19:20.
Message of governor, **29:6.**
Metropolitan district commission
estimates to include certain
pension contributions,
29:9A.
New Bedford institute of
technology.
See NEW BEDFORD
INSTITUTE OF
TECHNOLOGY.
New construction and
improvements, classification
to show, **29:6.**
Notice to budget director of
decision of personnel
appeals board, **30:57.**
Nutrition board, duties, **6:182.**
Overdrafts in appropriations of
former years, classification
to show, **29:6.**
Pension contributions to
metropolitan district
commission, **29:9A.**
Powers and duties as to, **29:6.**
Preliminary studies, estimates
for building construction
accompanied, **29:9.**
Preparation of, **29:6.**
Proposed legislation, secretaries
of executive offices to submit
cost estimates, **29:3A.**
Recommendations, **29:6, 30:45.**
Reports.
Director of fiscal affairs
division, reports as to
reallocation of position of
state employees, **30:49.**
Reallocation of position of
state employees, **30:49.**
State departments and
officers, submission of
reports, **7:8.**

STATE FINANCE —Cont'd
Budget —Cont'd
Requirements in preparation,
29:6.
Schedules for appropriation with
respect to expenses, filing,
29:27.
Schools, board of education to
compile guidelines, **15:1G.**
Secretaries of executive offices,
submission of estimates to
governor's cabinet, **29:3.**
Serial bond requirements,
classification to show, **29:6.**
Single appropriation bill, **29:6.**
Sinking fund requirements,
classification to show, **29:6.**
Social services department.
See WELFARE AND SOCIAL
SERVICES.
Submission by governor, **29:6.**
Substitution of terms in
statutes, **7:1.**
Suggestion awards board,
membership of budget
director, **7:31A.**
Supplementary budget, **29:6;
MA Const Amend Art 63
Sec 3.**
Supreme judicial court,
submission by chief justice
of statement concerning
estimate for maintenance of
judicial system, **211:2A.**
Television budgets of state
agencies, **6:158.**
Transfer of funds, approval of
budget director, **29:29.**
Universities.
See COLLEGES AND
UNIVERSITIES.
Water pollution control division
director to submit estimates
to budget director, **21:48.**
Welfare and social services.
See WELFARE AND SOCIAL
SERVICES.
Buildings.
Budget. See within this heading,
"Budget."
Construction contracts and
works. See within this
heading, "Construction
contracts and works."
Capital Expenditure Reserve Fund
established, **29:2DD.**
Capital facilities planning fund,
establishment, **29:2G.**
Caseload increase mitigation fund,
29:2NN.
Catastrophic illness in children
relief fund, **29:2ZZ.**
Commission, **111K:1 to 111K:11.**

STATE FINANCE —Cont'd
Categorical Grants Fund.
See GIFTS, GRANTS, AND
GRATUITIES.
Central artery/third harbor tunnel
project, **29:2O.**
Centralized purchasing, **30:51,
30:52.**
Centralized weekly payroll system,
establishment, **29:31.**
Certification of need for
advancement of funds, **29:24.**
Chargebacks, payment system for,
29:29I.
Checks not paid within year,
replacement checks, **29:32.**
Chelsea Information Technology
Building Management Fund,
29:2AA.
Child care fund, **29:2LL.**
Child care quality fund, **29:2JJ.**
Children's and seniors' health care
assistance fund, **29:2FF.**
Cities.
See MUNICIPAL FINANCE.
Claims for payment, **7A:3 et seq.**
Authority to contract by general
court as essential to
allowance of account, **29:19.**
Firemen's relief, **48:81.**
Grade crossing elimination,
settlement of barred claim,
159:76.
Indigency, filing affidavit of and
request for state payment of
court costs, **261:27B.**
Itemization required, **29:19.**
Oath of claimant, **29:61.**
Patient in state institution,
funds, **111:65D.**
Payment, **29:18, 29:20.**
Procedure, **258:1 et seq.**
See CLAIMS AGAINST
COMMONWEALTH.
Training schools, damage by
escapees, **120:13A.**
Trespass by state employees,
1:9.
Veterans' benefits, **115:2.**
Claims of state, **12:4, 12:5.**
Collective purchasing in
conjunction with political
subdivisions, **7:22A, 7:22B.**
Combined investment funds,
establishment, **29:38A.**
Community reinvestment act,
bank rating as affecting
eligibility to receive funds,
29:34.
Compact fund.
See COMPACT FUND.

STATE FINANCE —Cont'd

Comptroller of state.
  See COMPTROLLER OF
    STATE.
Condominium units, subsidization
  of urban redevelopment
  corporation's rental units from
  profits, **121A:18D.**
Conservation of soil, water, and
  related resources, allotment of
  appropriations to committee,
  21:20.
Consolidated net surplus.
  Operating funds.
    Certification and disbursal,
    29:5C.
Construction contracts and works.
  Airports, contribution toward
    costs of construction and
    improvement, **90:39F.**
  Appropriations, **29:9.**
  Budget classification to show
    new construction and
    improvements, **29:6.**
  Contractors constructing,
    altering, repairing, or
    demolishing buildings,
    payment, **30:39K.**
  Debarment from public
    contracts, **29:29F.**
  Subcontractors, payment,
    30:39F.
Consultants, employment, **29:29A.**
Contractors constructing, altering,
  repairing, or demolishing
  public buildings, payment,
  30:39K.
Co-operative banks, deposit of
  public funds, **29:34A.**
Corporate securities, investment,
  29:38.
Correctional institutions, **34:3,**
  126:7, 127:90.
Costs of proposed legislation,
  furnishing of estimates, **29:3A.**
Court costs, payment by state for
  indigents, **261:27B.**
Crimes and offenses, **29:29F,**
  29:66.
Criminal justice committee,
  appropriations, **6:156.**
Dairy equalization fund, **29:2V.**
Data processing equipment, lease
  or purchase, **29:27B.**
Debarment from public contracts,
  29:29F.
Deferred compensation programs,
  conforming change in law as
  to payment of salaries to
  permit, **29:31.**
Definitions, **29:1.**

STATE FINANCE —Cont'd

Departments, defined, **29:1.**
Depositing of public funds, **29:34,**
  29:34A, 29:38, 151:1B,
  151:20.
Direct debt limit for
  Commonwealth established,
  29:60A.
Direct deposit of wages and
  salaries, **29:31.**
Director of budget, **29:6.**
Disposition of funds.
  Central artery/third harbor
    tunnel project, **29:2O.**
  Checks not paid, **29:32.**
  Regional transit authorities,
    29:2O.
  State revenues, **29:2.**
  Unappropriated income of state
    funds, disposition, **29:44.**
  Unclaimed wages or salaries due
    from Commonwealth,
    29:32A.
Drinking water revolving fund,
  29:2QQ.
Dutch elm disease, municipal
  suppression, **132:14.**
  See CAMPAIGN
    EXPENDITURES AND
    CONTRIBUTIONS.
Electricians' fees and fines paid to
  Commonwealth, **141:10.**
Employment security
  administration, expenditures,
  appropriations, **151A:58.**
Energy facilities siting, general
  fund, **164:69H.**
Environmental Affairs Executive
  Office, **21A:18.**
Environmental fund, state
  recreation areas, **132A:3.**
Environmental permitting.
  See ENVIRONMENTAL
    PERMITTING AND
    COMPLIANCE
    ASSURANCE FUND.
Equipment, materials, and
  supplies, purchase of, **7:22.**
Escheated estate funds payable
  into general fund, **18B:19,**
  29:46B.
Estimates.
  Annual estimates of officers and
    departments, **29:3-29:5.**
  Budget. See within this heading,
    "Budget."
  Construction and repair,
    payment of estimates in
    absence of appropriation,
    29:9.
  Costs of proposed legislation,
    furnishing estimates, **29:3A.**

STATE FINANCE —Cont'd

Exceptions, exemptions, and
  exclusions, state reduction
  fund, **29:2I.**
Exhibits, fees for use of state
  house for, **10:35P.**
Explosives, appropriations for
  enforcement of laws, **148:11.**
Facilities and services, benefited
  private persons to pay cost,
  7:3B.
False claims prosecution fund,
  29:2YY.
Federal aid.
  See FEDERAL AID OR FUNDS.
Federal facilities reserve fund,
  29:2HH.
Federal savings and loan
  associations, investment of
  public funds in shares,
  29:34A.
Fines and penalties, **29:66.**
  Electricians, fines levied, **141:10.**
  Hunting and fishing fines, **131:3.**
  Improper deposit of state funds,
    29:34.
  Plumbing and gas fitting
    regulations, forfeitures for
    violations, **142:16.**
Firearms records keeping fund,
  29:2SS.
Firemen's relief, appropriation,
  48:81.
Fiscal year, **4:7.**
  Appropriations to be made for,
    29:12.
  Books and accounts of state
    officers kept on basis, **30:28.**
  Defined, **4:7.**
  Labor relations commission
    report, **23:9O.**
Fish.
  See FISH AND GAME.
Food and agriculture department,
  128:4.
Forests, expenditure of funds
  appropriated for state forests,
  132:32.
Free employment offices,
  appropriations, **149:166.**
Fringe benefit costs, **29:5D.**
Game laws, expense of
  enforcement, **29:6.**
General court.
  Submission of operating budget,
    capital facilities budget, and
    long range development
    plan, **29:7H.**
  Ways and means committees.
    Department financial plans,
    29:5F.

STATE FINANCE —Cont'd
General court —Cont'd
Ways and means committees
—Cont'd
Subsidiary salary account,
29:29.
General federal grants fund,
establishment, **29:2C.**
General fund.
Abandoned property.
See ABANDONED, LOST,
AND UNCLAIMED
PROPERTY.
Alcoholic beverage license fees
and excise taxes paid into,
138:21, 138:27.
Antitrust laws, **93:14.**
Asset management board, **7B:8.**
Beano receipts, apportionment,
10:39.
Cigarette tax law, **64C:6.**
Cities and towns, distributions
from general fund, **58:25,**
58:25A.
Community mental health
center revenues, disposition,
19:24.
Dividends or refunds received by
state employees group
insurance commission to be
paid into, **32A:9.**
Employers' permits, deposit of
fees for issuance, **149:147.**
Employment security
administration
expenditures, **151A:58.**
Energy facilities siting, **164:69H.**
Environmental Affairs Executive
Office, **21A:18.**
Escheated funds and unclaimed
dividends payable into,
18B:19, 29:46B.
Established, **64A:1, 64A:4,**
64C:6, 64C:28, 64E:1,
64E:4, 64F:6.
Game laws, expense of
enforcement, **29:6.**
Housing and community
development department,
reimbursement of
advancements from to be
credited to general fund,
23B:10A.
Inland fisheries law, expense of
enforcement, **29:6.**
Insurance commissioner, annual
assessments, **26:8F, 26:8I.**
Mentally ill and retarded
persons, monies remaining
in trust funds, **19:16,**
19:19B:13.

STATE FINANCE —Cont'd
General fund —Cont'd
Military and naval service fund,
transfer of balances, **18B:19.**
Municipalities, distributions
from general fund, **58:25,**
58:25A.
Payments into, **29:2.**
Prison industries, revenues,
127:71.
Receipts from licenses and
permits for structures in
waterways and for
displacement of tidewater to
go into, **91:24.**
Recipient of profits of state
lottery, **10:35, 10:36.**
Revenues to go into, **29:2.**
Second Century Fund
established, **29:2EE.**
Special funds transferable,
18B:19.
State aid for public libraries,
78:19A.
Unclaimed funds.
See ABANDONED, LOST,
AND UNCLAIMED
PROPERTY.
Unpaid check fund, transfer,
29:32.
General salary schedule, **30:46.**
Governor.
Administration and finance
executive office, request for
special examination of state
management of finances,
7:9.
Allotment of funds by governor.
See within this heading,
"Allotment of funds by
governor."
Budget information, **29:3, 29:6.**
Office expenses, when approval
of governor and council not
required, **29:21.**
Salary, appropriations
unnecessary for payment,
29:18.
Grants.
See GIFTS, GRANTS, AND
GRATUITIES.
Guaranty of housing authority
notes issued by
Commonwealth, **121B:34B.**
Health care security trust, **29D:1**
to 29D:5.
Hearings regarding debarment of
contractor from receipt of
public contracts, **29:29F.**
Highway fund.
See HIGHWAYS AND
STREETS.

STATE FINANCE —Cont'd
Housing and urban renewal
projects, grants, **121B:34,**
121B:35, 121B:37, 121B:56.
Human service programs, timely
payments, **29:23A.**
Hunting.
See FISH AND GAME.
Improper deposit of state funds,
penalty, **29:34.**
Income from funds, disposition of
unappropriated income, **29:44.**
Indebtedness.
Borrowing money. See within
this heading, "Borrowing
money."
Inflammable fluids and
compounds, appropriations for
enforcement of laws, **148:11.**
Infrastructure fund, **29:2O.**
Injunctions and restraining orders.
Fees for injunctions or
restraining orders, **262:4,**
262:4A.
Unlawful expenditures or
obligations, injunctions
against, **29:63.**
Inland fisheries.
See FISH AND GAME.
Innholder's sale of guest's
abandoned property, payment
of proceeds over to state,
140:15.
Insufficient revenue, reporting,
29:9C-29:9E.
Insurance.
Annual assessments, insurance
commissioner, **26:8F, 26:8I.**
Life insurance companies paying
over unclaimed funds to
state treasurer to be
credited to state finance,
175:149D.
Special authorization required
for insurance of property,
29:30.
Insurance commissioner, annual
assessments, **26:8F, 26:8I.**
Interchange of fund, permanent
position salary fund as
exempt, **29:29.**
Interchange of subsidiary salary
account as requiring prior
approval of ways and means
committees, **29:29.**
Interest.
Bonds issued by state, **29:49.**
Classification of budget to show
interest on public debt, etc.,
29:6.
Deposits of public funds,
payment to Commonwealth,
29:34.

STATE FINANCE —Cont'd
Interest —Cont'd
Sinking funds, appropriation unnecessary for payment of interest on bonds, **29:18.**
Intragovernmental service fund.
See INTRAGOVERNMENTAL SERVICE FUND.
Investment of state funds.
See STATE TREASURER.
Itemized bills, **29:19.**
Judicial system, financing, **29A:3, 211:2A.**
Labor and workforce development commissioner, deposit in general fund in connection with minimum fair wage claims, **151:1B, 151:20.**
Landing fields.
Airports and landing fields. See within this heading, "Airports and landing fields."
Late charges on overdue payments to Commonwealth, **29:29H.**
Later appropriation as superseding prior one, **29:15.**
Leo J. Martin recreation fund, **29:2II.**
Liability management and reduction fund.
Establishment, **29:2TT.**
Libraries.
Accounts, approval, **6:36.**
State aid for public libraries, **78:19A, 78:19B, 78:19C.**
Life insurance companies paying over unclaimed funds to state treasurer to be credited, **175:149D.**
Limitations and restrictions.
Deposit of state funds, amount, **29:34, 29:34A.**
Direct debt limit for Commonwealth, **29:60A.**
Interest and principal payments on general obligations, **29:60B.**
Unpaid checks, limitation of time, **29:32, 29:32A.**
Living expenses of state officers and employees, **30:25.**
Loans.
Borrowing money. See within this heading, "Borrowing money."
Local aid.
See COMPACT FUND.
Local Aid Fund established, **29:2C½.**
Local consumer inspection fund, **29:2OO.**

STATE FINANCE —Cont'd
Long range capital facilities agencies budget, submission of, **29:7D.**
Long range capital facility development plans, capital budget requests, **29:2F.**
Lottery of state.
See LOTTERY OF STATE.
Marine fisheries division, funding, **21:5, 130:17.**
Marine resources, obligation imposed by acceptance of trust funds for purpose of protection, **130:17.**
Massachusetts Educational Financial Authority Act.
See SCHOOLS AND EDUCATION.
Materials, supplies, and equipment, purchase of, **7:22, 7:25A, 30:51, 30:52.**
Maximization fund, **29:2R.**
Mentally ill.
See MENTALLY ILL AND RETARDED PERSONS.
Metropolitan area planning council fund, establishment, **40B:29.**
Metropolitan districts, **10:11, 29:9A.**
Metropolitan parks.
Expense fund, **92:48.**
Trust fund, **92:34.**
Minibonds, limitation on principal amount sold by state treasurer in any one fiscal year, **29:49A.**
Minimum fair wage claims, deposit in general fund by commissioner of labor and workforce development, **151:1B, 151:20.**
Morris Plan Banks, deposit of funds, **29:34.**
Moth and insect suppression, **132:14, 132:16.**
Motor vehicle fees, how used and disposed, **90:34.**
Motor vehicles owned by state, expenditure of funds for repair, **30:36A.**
Municipalities, state aid to.
See MUNICIPAL FINANCE.
Municipal tax liability, semi-annual collection on account, **59:20.**
New Bedford institute of technology.
See NEW BEDFORD INSTITUTE OF TECHNOLOGY.
New employees of department, **29:27.**

STATE FINANCE —Cont'd
Oath of claimant against state funds, **29:61.**
Office expenses, when approval of governor and council not required, **29:21.**
Operation and maintenance of state departments, offices.
Appropriations for, **29:12, 29:14.**
Budget estimates, **29:3.**
Unexpended appropriations for, disposition, **29:13.**
Parks.
Metropolitan parks. See within this heading, "Metropolitan parks."
State treasurer's annual financial statement as to park districts, **10:11.**
Participation units in combined investment funds, sale, **29:38A.**
Payment system for chargebacks, **29:29I.**
Payroll.
See PAYROLL AND PAYROLL DEDUCTIONS.
Penalties.
Fines and penalties. See within this heading, "Fines and penalties."
Permanent Assistance to Cities.
See COMPACT FUND.
Permanent position salary fund as exempt from interchange of funds, **29:29.**
Plumbing and gas fitting regulations, forfeitures by cities or towns for violations, **142:16.**
Ponkapoag recreational fund, **29:2U.**
Prison industries funds, appropriations unnecessary for payments out, **29:18.**
Private collection agencies used by state, **29:29D.**
Private persons as obligated to pay for public services or facilities, **7:3B.**
Private persons, authority to retain services of, **29:29G.**
Proposed legislation, secretaries of executive offices to submit cost estimates, **29:3A.**
Prosecution expenses, payment, **280:4.**
Public hearings by ways and means committee on appropriations, **3:38B.**

STATE FINANCE —Cont'd

Public utilities.

Appropriations for telecommunications and energy department, **25:9, 25:19.**

General fund. See within this heading, "General fund."

Publishing state publications, payment, **29:28.**

Purchasing agent, **7:4A, 7:22 et seq.**

See STATE PURCHASING AGENT.

Quarantine of animals, payment of expense, **129:29.**

Railroads, advancements for relocation or other work, **81:7I.**

Recess, expenses of committee acting during, **3:32.**

Records.

Reports. See within this heading, "Reports."

Recreation areas, **132A:3, 132A:10.**

Regional school districts.

See REGIONAL SCHOOL DISTRICTS.

Regional transit authorities, disposition of funds, **29:2O, 29:3B.**

Registration of bonds and securities held by Commonwealth, **29:39.**

Rehabilitation commission's expenditure of state funds, **6:74.**

Replacement checks for checks not paid within year, **29:32.**

Reports.

Adequacy of charges for services and facilities, report by administration secretary, **7:3B.**

Appropriations for preceding and current fiscal years, reports, **29:3.**

Budget director, reports, **7:8.**

Budget. See within this heading, "Budget."

Comptroller's report as to use made of appropriations, **29:9F.**

Federal grants, reports, **29:3.**

Insufficient revenue, reports, **29:9C-29:9E.**

Restraining orders.

Injunctions and restraining orders. See within this heading, "Injunctions and restraining orders."

STATE FINANCE —Cont'd

Retarded persons.

See MENTALLY ILL AND RETARDED PERSONS.

Retirement systems.

See RETIREMENT SYSTEMS AND PENSIONS.

Review or appeal, state employee budget grievances, **30:49.**

Safe drinking water act fund established, **29:2P½.**

Salaries.

Appropriation not required for payment of governor and justices of the supreme judicial court, **29:18.**

Increases, regulation of appropriations, **29:27.**

Payment of, **29:31.**

Unclaimed wages or salaries due from Commonwealth, disposition, **29:32A.**

Sale.

See SALE OR TRANSFER OF PROPERTY.

Savings banks.

See SAVINGS BANKS.

Schedule of expenditures required for allotment of funds by governor, **29:27.**

Schools.

See SCHOOLS AND EDUCATION.

Second Century Fund established, **29:2EE.**

Secretary of administration to report as to adequacy of charges for services and facilities, **7:3B.**

Secured transactions, security for issuance of state refunding bonds, **29:53A.**

Semi-annual collection on account of municipal tax liability, **59:20.**

Sewer districts, state treasurer's annual financial statement, **10:11.**

Sewer Rate Relief Fund, **29:2Z.**

Sinking funds, **29:49-29:51.**

Application of accumulations, **29:45.**

Appropriation necessary for payment of principal or interest of bonds, **29:18.**

Budget provisions, **29:6.**

Classification for budget to show sinking fund requirements, **29:6.**

Exceeding requirements, **29:45.**

Highway infrastructure fund, payments on bonds or notes issued, **29:2O.**

STATE FINANCE —Cont'd

Sinking funds —Cont'd

Investments of, restrictions on maturity, **29:45.**

Purchase of securities, **29:45.**

Surplus added to other funds, **29:45.**

Social services program fund, **29:2MM.**

Special appropriations, period for which available, **29:14.**

Special commission, investigation, **29:38.**

Special education.

See SPECIAL EDUCATION.

Stabilization fund, **29:2H.**

State house special event fund established, **10:35P.**

Statement of expenditures for which funds advanced, making and filing, **29:25.**

Subsidiary accounts.

Expenditures not to exceed funds, **29:29.**

Expenses set up in, appropriations to be expended in accordance, **29:27.**

Transfer of funds, **29:29.**

Successive appropriations, **29:15.**

Supplies and equipment, purchase of, **7:22.**

Supreme judicial court, **29:18, 211:2A.**

Surplus funds.

Certification and disposition of consolidated net surplus in operating funds, **29:5C.**

Suspension of contractor from receipt of public contracts, **29:29F.**

Taxation.

See TAXATION.

Tobacco settlement fund, **29:2XX.**

Tourism and industrial promotion fund, matching funds for shellfish propagation, **130:20A.**

Training schools, claims for damage done by escapees, **120:13A.**

Transfer of funds.

Appropriations for House of Representatives, transfer of funds among items, **29:7M.**

Between officers and departments, **29:29, 29:29A.**

Bonds.

See STATE TREASURER.

Speaker of house of representatives, **29:7N, 29:7O.**

STATE FINANCE —Cont'd

Transitional aid to needy families fund, **29:2KK.**

Treasurer.

See STATE TREASURER.

Treasury notes.

See STATE BONDS AND OBLIGATIONS.

Trespass by state employees, claims, **1:9.**

Trust companies.

See TRUST COMPANIES.

Trust funds.

Appropriation as unnecessary for payment of principal or income, **29:18.**

Compact fund.

See COMPACT FUND.

Food and agriculture department, **128:4.**

General fund, unclaimed dividends trust funds payable into, **18B:19, 29:46B.**

Highway fund, trust agreement as security for bonds issued through highway infrastructure fund, **29:20.**

Marine resources, obligation imposed by acceptance of trust funds for purpose of protection, **130:17.**

Metropolitan parks, **92:34.**

State treasurer.

See STATE TREASURER.

Youth services department and Massachusetts training schools, **10:15, 120:1.**

Unadjusted account of persons entitled to appropriation, **29:17.**

Unappropriated income of state funds, disposition, **29:44.**

Unclaimed funds.

See ABANDONED, LOST, AND UNCLAIMED PROPERTY.

Unemployment compensation, appropriations, **151A:58.**

Unexpended appropriations, **29:13, 29:14.**

Unexpended funds from sale of bonds, disposition, **29:56.**

Unpaid checks, disposal, etc., **29:32.**

Urban redevelopment corporations, subsidization of rental units from condominium unit profits, **121A:18D.**

Veterans' benefits.

See VETERANS AND VETERANS' ORGANIZATIONS.

STATE FINANCE —Cont'd

Violation of state finance laws, penalty, **29:66.**

Vocational rehabilitation of handicapped persons, expenditures of state funds, **6:74.**

Vocational schools.

See VOCATIONAL EDUCATION AND SCHOOLS.

Vouchers required to obtain funds, **29:20.**

Wages.

Salaries. See within this heading, "Salaries."

Warrants for payments, **7A:3, 10:10, 10:11, 29:18.**

Water districts, state treasurer's annual financial statement, **10:11.**

Water pollution abatement and drinking water projects administration fund.

Transfer of funds to, **29:2W.**

Waterways, receipts from licenses for structures, **91:24.**

Ways and means committees.

General court. See within this heading, "General court."

Welfare department, funding, **18B:7.**

White Pine blister rust, compensation with respect to suppression, **128:23.**

Wildlife sanctuaries, **131:7.**

Withdrawal of appropriations limited to expense incurred, **29:22.**

Workforce training fund, **29:2RR.**

Works of improvement, appropriations, **21:15.**

STATE GAMBLING ADVISORY COMMISSION, 12B:1, 12B:2.

STATE GUARD.
See MILITIA.

STATE HOSPITALS, 111:63-111:67.

Admission, **111:63A, 123:10.**

Billing of Medicare, **111:63B.**

Boards of trustees, meetings, **19:14.**

Bond for performance of treasurers and assistant treasurers, **19:14.**

Books and records, maintenance, **30:29.**

Children.

See CHILDREN AND MINORS.

STATE HOSPITALS —Cont'd

Claims against funds of patient, **111:65D.**

Commitment or admission of patients, designation of institutions, **123:10.**

Correctional institutions, expense of removing prisoners to state hospitals, **127:123.**

Danvers state hospital, **19:7.**

Danvers state hospital reuse fund.

State finance.

Establishment, **29:2UU.**

Deposit of patients' funds, **111:65C, 111:65D, 122:6.**

Employees.

Officers and employees. See within this heading, "Officers and employees."

Expense of removing prisoners, **127:123.**

Foxborough state hospital, **19:7.**

Gardner state hospital.

See GARDNER STATE HOSPITAL.

Gifts and trust funds, **111:67.**

Grafton state hospital.

See GRAFTON STATE HOSPITAL.

Hospital service corporations, contracts, **176A:1.**

Hypertension or heart disease, benefits for state officers and employees in case, **32:94.**

Lakeville hospital.

See LAKEVILLE HOSPITAL.

Lien for medical and other services furnished, **111:70A.**

Lottery ticket sales to mental patients, **10:27.**

Medfield.

See MEDFIELD.

Medicare, billing, **111:63B.**

Mentally ill.

See MENTALLY ILL AND RETARDED PERSONS.

Minors.

See CHILDREN AND MINORS.

Nursing service in, exempt from law as to nurses, **112:80B.**

Officers and employees.

Hypertension or heart disease, benefits in case, **32:94.**

Indemnification for damage to clothing, etc., **30:9C.**

Nurses, exemptions, **112:80B.**

Statutes distributed to superintendents, **5:3.**

Superintendents. See within this heading, "Superintendents."

STATE HOSPITALS —Cont'd

Patients' funds or property.

Deposit, **111:65C, 111:65D, 122:6.**

Unclaimed funds or property of patients, **111:65D, 122:7-122:9.**

Products of, sales, use, and disposal, **6:134, 7:22, 7:25, 7:25A.**

Public officers and employees.

Officers and employees. See within this heading, "Officers and employees."

Records, maintenance, **30:29.**

Reimbursement of employees for damage to clothing, etc., **30:9C.**

Room occupancy tax, exemption of accommodations at state institutions, **64G:2.**

Rutland hospital.

See RUTLAND HOSPITAL.

Statutes distributed to superintendents, **5:3.**

Superintendents, **19:14.**

Advisory committee on chaplains in state institutions, **6:166B.**

Health commissioner's authority to appoint, **17:6.**

Removal, **19:14.**

Statutes distributed, **5:3.**

Tewksbury hospital.

See TEWKSBURY HOSPITAL.

Trustees' consultation, **19:14.**

Taunton state hospital.

See TAUNTON STATE HOSPITAL.

Tax exemption, **59:5, 64G:2.**

Tewksbury hospital.

See TEWKSBURY HOSPITAL.

Treasurers, books and accounts, **30:29.**

Trespass upon lands, **266:123.**

Trusts and trustees.

Medfield State Hospital trustees, **19:8A, 19:10, 19:14.**

Other office in same institution, trustees ineligible to hold, **30:23A.**

Superintendent to appear and answer trustees' questions as to hospital operations, **19:14.**

Trust funds, **111:67.**

Tuberculosis treatment centers, establishment, **111:94D.**

Unclaimed funds or property of patients, **111:65D, 122:7-122:9.**

STATE HOSPITALS —Cont'd

Veterans, leases to United States for rehabilitation, **74:41.**

Vocational rehabilitation research and demonstration projects, **19:14-19:15.**

Westborough state hospital, **19:8A, 19:14.**

Western Massachusetts hospital.

See WESTERN MASSACHUSETTS HOSPITAL.

Youth service division, **120:10.**

STATE HOUSE.

Accidental death benefits for scrubwomen and cleaners, **32:74.**

Adams papers, **8:17B.**

Administration commissioner.

Approval of assignment of rooms, **8:10.**

Fire protection regulations, **143:2B.**

Physician, appointment and duties, **7:6B.**

Afro-American veterans, assignment of quarters, **8:17.**

Art.

Commission on art to have custody of historical relics and works of art in state house, **6:20.**

Photographs of portraits and art objects in state house, **9:28.**

Assignment of rooms and quarters, **8:10, 8:17.**

Criminal justice training council, **6:119.**

Special commissions, **4:2A.**

Building regulations inapplicable, **143:2A.**

Capitol police.

See POLICE.

Care and maintenance, **8:6, 8:7, 8:9, 8:20.**

Casualty damage, repairs in case, **8:7.**

Civil War nurses' hall memorial, designation, **8:16A.**

Commissioner's duties regarding use of space, **7:40F.**

Council on juvenile behavior, offices, **6:160.**

Criminal justice training council, **6:119.**

Death benefits for scrubwomen and cleaners, **32:74.**

Disasters.

Fires or other disasters. See within this heading, "Fires or other disasters."

STATE HOUSE —Cont'd

Doric Hall, exhibition of writings of John Adams, **8:17B.**

Egress from, regulations, **143:2B.**

Employees, **8:4, 8:5.**

Fees.

Photographic prints of portraits and art objects, **9:28.**

Use of state house, **10:35P.**

Fires or other disasters.

Plans for evacuation in case, **143:2C.**

Regulations as to fires, **143:2B.**

Repairs to state house, **8:7.**

Fixtures, maintenance and repair, **8:9.**

Flags, custody, care and display, **8:17A.**

Foot passengers, passageway, **8:9.**

Furniture, maintenance and repair, **8:9.**

General court.

See GENERAL COURT.

Governors, portraits, **8:19, 8:19A.**

Grand Army of the Republic.

Memorial and shrine, **8:16A.**

Rooms, **8:10.**

Grounds to remain open, **8:16.**

Guided tours, duties of secretary of state, **9:2.**

Handicapped persons, accessibility, **8:9.**

Historic districts and sites.

Bostonian Society, maintenance and preservation by, **8:20.**

Custody and care of historical relics and works of art, **6:20.**

Exhibition of writings of John Adams, **8:17B.**

Portraits and art objects in, storage of photographs, **9:28.**

Improvements, **8:6, 8:7, 8:9.**

Janitors and other employees, **8:4, 8:5.**

John Adams, display of writings, **8:17B.**

Legislative and constitutional officers' compensation advisory board, offices, **6:162.**

Legislative post audit and oversight bureau, quarters, **3:64.**

Legislative research bureau, quarters, **3:60.**

Library, **6:38.**

Meetings, **8:16A, 8:19A, 8:21, 10:35P.**

Memorials.

Civil war nurses' hall memorial, **8:16A.**

STATE HOUSE —Cont'd
Memorials —Cont'd
Former governors, memorials,
8:19A.
Grand Army of the Republic,
8:16A.
Permanent memorials, **8:21.**
Military museum, **8:14.**
Nutrition board, offices, **6:181.**
Obscene literature control
commission, quarters, **6:101.**
Old provincial state house, care
and maintenance, **8:20.**
Passageway for foot passengers,
8:9.
Permanent memorials in,
establishment, **8:21.**
Photographs and portraits.
Art objects and portraits,
photographs, **9:28.**
Former governors, portraits,
8:19, 8:19A.
Physician, **7:6B.**
Portraits.
Photographs and portraits. See
within this heading,
"Photographs and portraits."
Preservation and restoration, **3:65.**
Professional licensure division,
offices, **13:9.**
Provincial state house, care and
maintenance, **8:20.**
Railroads forbidden from land
around, **8:16.**
Receptions, fees for use of state
house for, **10:35P.**
Records of veterans' organizations,
8:18.
Repairs and improvements, **8:6,
8:7, 8:9.**
Bidding process, **149:44E½.**
Restoration, **3:65.**
Bidding process, **149:44E½.**
Retirement.
Retirement law commission,
10:35I.
Scrubwomen, retirement and
pension benefits, **32:74.**
Rooms.
Assignment of. See within this
heading, "Assignment of
rooms and quarters."
Grand Army of the Republic,
memorial and shrine, **8:16A.**
Scrubwomen and cleaners, **8:4,
8:5.**
Retirement and pensions, **32:74.**
Secretary of state, duties as to
guided tours, **9:2.**
Special commissions, offices, **4:2A.**
Special event fund established,
10:35P.

STATE HOUSE —Cont'd
Superintendent.
See STATE
SUPERINTENDENT OF
STATE OFFICE
BUILDINGS.
Surrounding land to remain open,
8:16.
United Nations Day, observance,
6:12N.
Veterans displaying memorabilia,
8:18A.
Veterans' organizations, facilities,
8:16, 8:16A, 8:17, 8:18.
Vietnam veterans, assignment of
quarters for use, **8:17.**
Window cleaners, state safety code
applicable, **143:2A.**
Women's contribution to
government, artworks as
memorial to, **8:18B.**
Writings of John Adams to be
displayed, **8:17B.**

**STATE INDUSTRIAL
SCHOOLS, 18A:8, 120:2 et
seq.
See YOUTH SERVICES
DEPARTMENT AND
MASSACHUSETTS
TRAINING SCHOOLS.**

**STATE LABOR RELATIONS
ACT, 150A:1 et seq.**

STATE LIBRARY, 6:33-6:38.
Annual report.
Cities and towns, **40:49, 40:50.**
County commissioners, **35:27.**
Trustees, **6:37.**
Approval of accounts, **6:36.**
Bequests, **6:37A.**
City and town records and reports,
copies sent, **40:50.**
Coordinator of flexible hours,
report, **7:6F.**
Copies of all published rules and
regulations filing, **30A:6.**
County commissioners' annual
report, copy, **35:27.**
Depository library for
Massachusetts state
publications.
Definitions, **6:39.**
Designation, **6:39A.**
State agencies, furnishing copies
of publications, **6:39B.**
Deposits of records, **6:39.**
Distribution of laws, **5:3.**
Expenditures authorized, **6:36.**
Funds, receipt and handling by
state treasurer, **10:16.**

STATE LIBRARY —Cont'd
General court.
See GENERAL COURT.
Gifts, **6:37A.**
Governor's council.
Librarian, appointment, **6:35.**
Trustees, supervision and
appointment, **6:17, 6:33.**
Hours for keeping open, **6:38.**
Librarian, **6:35.**
Massachusetts register to be
distributed, **30A:6.**
Records conservation board,
membership, **30:42.**
Location, **6:38.**
Massachusetts register, copy to
state librarian, **30A:6.**
Public authorities' reports, deposit,
6:39A.
Railroads, deposit of plans upon
petition for special charter,
160:9.
State books and documents,
repository, **6:39.**
State departmental rules and
regulations, filing, **30:37.**
Town reports, copies, **40:50.**
Trustees, **6:33-6:37A, 10:16.**
Annual report, **6:37.**
Approval of accounts, **6:36.**
Duties, **6:34.**
Employment dislocations and
assistance in reemployment
of dislocated workers, **6:17.**
Supervision of governor and
council, **6:17, 6:33.**
Trust funds, **6:37A.**

**STATE LOTTERY, 10:22 et seq.
See LOTTERY OF STATE.**

**STATE OFFICE OF MINORITY
AND WOMEN BUSINESS
ASSISTANCE.**
Reorganization of department of
economic development,
23A:40-23A:44.

STATE-OWNED VEHICLES.
Energy resources executive office,
fuel efficiency for new vehicles,
25A:11B.

**STATE PARKS, 132A:1 et seq.
See STATE RECREATION
AREAS.**

STATE POLICE.
Abandoned, lost or unclaimed
property.
Auction of unclaimed property,
22C:45-22C:47.
Motor vehicles, disposition of
abandoned, **90:22C.**

STATE POLICE —Cont'd

Abandoned, lost or unclaimed
    property —Cont'd
    Responsibility, **22C:45.**
    Time for keeping unclaimed
        property, **22C:45, 22C:46,
        22C:48.**
Abuse, arrest forms providing
    space to indicate offenses
    involving, **22C:49.**
Accidental disability retirement.
    Reinstatement after disability
        retirement, **22C:24A.**
Affirmative action office within
    department, **22C:23.**
Age requirements, **22C:10.**
Agreements for services, **22C:29 et
    seq.**
Air pollution emergency orders,
    enforcement, **111:2B.**
Amendment of departmental
    orders of department, **22C:43.**
Animals, special police for
    prevention of cruelty, **22C:57.**
Annuities to dependents following
    death, **32:89A.**
Appeal.
    See APPEAL AND REVIEW.
Appeal of findings of misconduct
    trial, **22C:12.**
Appearances before clerks of
    district court, **21:6F.**
Appointments, **41:87A.**
    Children, appointment of special
        police to Society for the
        Prevention of Cruelty to
        Children, **22C:56.**
    Colonel of state police, **22C:3.**
    Felony convictions affecting
        appointments, **22C:14.**
    Governor, appointment of
        personnel, **22C:3.**
    List of eligible officers,
        appointments, **22C:11.**
    Misdemeanor convictions
        affecting appointment,
        22C:14.
    Officers of department of state
        police, **22C:10 et seq.**
    Public inspection of records,
        22C:52.
    Sanatoriums, employees
        appointed as special police
        officers, **22C:65.**
    Special officers, **10:5, 22C:4,
        22C:7, 22C:50 et seq.**
    State treasurer, appointment,
        10:5.
    University of Massachusetts,
        guards appointed by
        trustees, **22C:50.**

STATE POLICE —Cont'd

Appointments —Cont'd
    Veterans and veterans'
        organizations, **10:5.**
Appropriations, **22C:17, 40:5.**
Arrests, **22C:12.**
    Forms, space to indicate offenses
        involving abuse, **22C:49.**
    Special police officers, arrest
        powers, **22C:56 et seq.**
Assignment of officers, **22:3.**
Auction of unclaimed property,
    22C:45-22C:47.
Badges, **147:2.**
Bargaining unit in labor relations,
    150E:3.
Boxing teams, **147:39.**
Captains, eligibility for promotion,
    22C:26.
Career incentive pay program,
    41:108L.
Cigarette excise tax provisions,
    enforcement, **64C:8, 64C:10.**
Civil defense agency employees as
    special police officers, **22C:64.**
Civil rights and discrimination,
    state police reporting incidents
    of hate crimes,
    22C:32-22C:35.
Civil service.
    See CIVIL SERVICE.
Collective bargaining unit for
    uniformed branch, eligibility
    for membership, **150E:3.**
Colonel of state police, **6:18B,
    6:116, 6:156, 22C:1 et seq.**
    Appointments, **22C:3.**
    Estimates forwarded by colonel,
        22C:17.
Commercial vehicle violations,
    investigation or examination,
    159B:14A.
Commissioned officers.
    Defined, **22C:1.**
    Vacancies among commissioned
        officers, filling, **22C:27.**
Commissioner of public safety.
    Assignment of officers, **22:3.**
    Duties, **147:1.**
    Housing units, purchase of land
        for state police, **147:2.**
    Massachusetts criminal justice
        training council,
        commissioner as member,
        6:116.
    Requirements and qualifications
        for officers and inspectors,
        establishment, **22:6.**
    Temporary appointment to state
        police of public safety
        department officers and
        inspectors, **147:2.**

STATE POLICE —Cont'd

Compacts.
    See INTERSTATE COMPACTS
        AND AGREEMENTS.
Compensation.
    Salaries and compensation. See
        within this heading,
        "Salaries and
        compensation."
Competitive examination for
    enlistees, **22C:10.**
Confiscation of property by police,
    responsibility, **22C:45-22C:48.**
Contributory retirement law.
    See RETIREMENT SYSTEMS
        AND PENSIONS.
Costs and expenses.
    Expenses and expenditures. See
        within this heading,
        "Expenses and
        expenditures."
Criminal identification bureau,
    22C:36.
    Information requested from,
        22C:36A.
Criminal information section.
    Corrective change in law,
        271:47.
    Duties and functions, **22C:38.**
    Narcotics unit, **22C:40.**
Department of state police
    established, **22C:1-22C:69.**
Detectives, private detective
    regulations inapplicable,
    147:23.
Detention, private detective
    regulations as inapplicable,
    147:23.
Disability retirement.
    Reinstatement after disability
        retirement, **22C:24A.**
Divorce cases, investigation,
    208:16.
DNA database for sexual
    offenders, **22E:1 to 22E:15.**
    See DNA DATABASE.
Drugs and narcotics.
    Criminal information section,
        narcotics unit, **22C:40.**
    Prima facie evidence, chemists'
        analysis, **22C:39.**
    Training programs, **12:11C.**
Education.
    Schools and education. See
        within this heading,
        "Training programs."
Eligibility, **22:6, 22C:10.**
Eligibility for promotion, **22C:26.**
Emergencies.
    Air pollution orders,
        enforcement, **111:2B.**

603

STATE POLICE —Cont'd
Emergencies —Cont'd
Working hours, **22C:18.**
Employment and training division
in labor and workforce
department, special police
officers, **22C:66.**
Evaluation reports of performance
of personnel, **22C:22.**
Evidence.
Chemists' certified reports as
prima facie evidence,
22C:39, 22C:41.
Drug analysis, **22C:39.**
Motor vehicle ownership,
22C:42.
Sperm cells or seminal fluid,
22C:41.
Traveling expenses for
appearing as witness,
262:53B.
Examination, inspection, or
investigation.
Appointments, public inspection
of records, **22C:52.**
Commercial vehicle violations,
159B:14A.
Competitive examination for
enlistees, **22C:10.**
Investigation and intelligence
division, **22C:4, 22C:6.**
Paint inspectors, **94:293.**
Pawnbroker's books, **140:81.**
Promotional examinations,
notice and knowledge,
22C:25.
Public safety commissioner,
establishment of
requirements and
qualifications for inspectors,
22:6.
Special investigations bureau,
22C:67.
Expenses and expenditures.
Estimates forwarded by colonel,
22C:17.
Highway fund available, **90:34.**
Massachusetts Turnpike
Authority, expenses of police
service, **22C:29.**
Medical and surgical expenses
paid out of travel or other
expenses, **22C:16.**
Port authority, service, **22C:30.**
Travel expenses. See within this
heading, "Travel expenses."
Water resources authority,
services, **22C:31.**
Federal reservations.
Housing units, purchase, **147:2.**
Powers, **147:2.**

STATE POLICE —Cont'd
Fees.
Mileage fees, **262:53B.**
Payment to salaried officers,
262:50.
Witness fees and travel
expenses, officer's
certification, **262:53B.**
Felony convictions affecting
appointments, **22C:14.**
Field services division, **22C:4,
22C:5.**
Findings of misconduct trial,
22C:12.
Fines and penalties.
Gifts or gratuities accepted by
officers, **22C:14.**
Refusal to perform duties,
22C:54.
Uniform worn by nonmembers of
department, **22C:19.**
Firearms, authority to carry,
22C:19, 147:2.
Fish.
See FISH AND GAME.
Fraudulent claims commission,
22C:68.
Garbage and rubbish, enforcement
of provisions against unlawful
disposal, **270:16, 270:16A.**
Gifts or gratuities accepted by
officers, **22C:14.**
Governor.
Appointment of personnel,
22C:3.
Command over police, **147:2.**
Special state police officers,
appointment, **127:127.**
Transmittal of hate crime data,
22C:34.
Guardian ad litem, state police to
give assistance, **215:56A,
215:56B.**
Hate crime, **22C:32-22C:35.**
Defined, **22C:32.**
Governor, transmittal of hate
crime data, **22C:34.**
Reports, collection and analysis,
22C:33-22C:35.
Hazardous waste, seizure and
forfeiture of property, **21C:14.**
Hearings.
Trial or hearing. See within this
heading, "Trial or hearing."
Highways.
See HIGHWAYS AND
STREETS.
Hospitals, special police officers,
22C:63.
Hours of labor and overtime pay.
Laws regulating as inapplicable
to state police, **149:30A,
149:30B, 149:36.**

STATE POLICE —Cont'd
Hours of labor and overtime pay
—Cont'd
Special rules for overtime
compensation, **149:30C.**
Housing units for, purchase of
land, **147:2.**
Indemnification, **258:9A.**
Industrial disputes.
Labor relations and disputes,
bargaining unit for
uniformed branch, **150E:3.**
Inspection.
Examination, inspection, or
investigation. See within
this heading, "Examination,
inspection, or investigation."
Interstate compacts.
See INTERSTATE COMPACTS
AND AGREEMENTS.
Investigation.
Examination, inspection, or
investigation. See within
this heading, "Examination,
inspection, or investigation."
Jurisdiction over highways of
state, **81:19.**
Justice of the peace swearing in
special officers, **22C:53.**
Juvenile courts, witness fees,
262:53B.
Labor relations and disputes,
bargaining unit for uniformed
branch, **150E:3.**
Licenses provided to special
officers, **22C:53, 22C:59,
22C:60 et seq.**
Lieutenants, eligibility for
promotion, **22C:26.**
List of eligible officers,
appointments, **22C:11.**
Lockups accessible, **40:37.**
Lost property.
Abandoned, lost or unclaimed
property. See within this
heading, "Abandoned, lost or
unclaimed property."
Lottery commission, special police
officers, **22C:67.**
Massachusetts police memorial
day, annual observance,
6:15JJJ.
Medical and surgical expenses
paid out of travel or other
expenses, **22C:16.**
Mental health department
requesting special officers,
22C:59.
Mentally ill.
See MENTALLY ILL AND
RETARDED PERSONS.

STATE POLICE —Cont'd

Mileage and witness fees,
262:53B.

Misconduct, charges, **22C:12.**

Misdemeanor convictions affecting
appointment, **22C:14.**

Misdemeanors committed in
presence, **22C:12.**

Motorboat laws, enforcement,
90B:12.

Motor vehicles.
Abandoned motor vehicles,
disposition, **90:22C.**
Commercial vehicle violations,
investigation or
examination, **159B:14A.**
Evidence of ownership, **22C:42.**
Financing law, enforcement,
255B:6.
Junkyard act, enforcement,
140B:8.
Loss prevention central
organization, reports filed,
175:1130.
Rewards, auto theft strike force,
175A:10A.
Snow traveling and recreational
vehicles, enforcement of law
and regulations, **90:32.**

Municipal or local police, training
at state police schools, **40:5.**

Narcotics.
Drugs and narcotics. See within
this heading, "Drugs and
narcotics."

Noncommissioned officers, **22C:26.**
Defined, **22C:1.**
Eligibility for promotion,
22C:26.

Notary public swearing in special
officers, **22C:53.**

Notice and knowledge.
Promotional examinations,
22C:25.
Schemes and rackets, advising
local police departments,
22C:38.
Sexual crimes, release of
prisoners convicted, **22C:37.**
Special police officers, notice of
discontinuance of service,
22C:53 et seq.

Oath of office, **22C:15.**
Special officers, **22C:53.**

Orders of department,
amendment, suspension or
revocation, **22C:43.**

Overtime.
Hours of labor and overtime pay.
See within this heading,
"Hours of labor and
overtime pay."

STATE POLICE —Cont'd

Paint inspectors, **94:293.**

Parole permits, notification of
effective date and conditions,
127:131A.

Parol of prisoners convicted of
sexual crimes, **22C:37.**

Pawnbrokers.
Entry on premises by state
police, **140:73, 140:74.**
Inspection of books by state
police, **140:81.**

Pensions, **32:26.**
See RETIREMENT SYSTEMS
AND PENSIONS.

Petitions.
Misconduct trial, petition for
review of findings, **22C:12.**
Railroad commission petitioning
for special police, **22C:51,
22C:52.**

Port authority.
Service, **22C:30.**
Special police officers, **22C:58.**

Powers and duties, **22C:3, 147:2.**

Prima facie evidence, **22C:39,
22C:41, 22C:42.**

Private detective regulations
inapplicable, **147:23.**

Proceeds of auction sales and
unclaimed money paid to
Commonwealth, **22C:47.**

Promotions, **22C:26.**
Notice and knowledge,
promotional examinations,
22C:25.
Period of service for certain
appointments, **22C:28.**
Ranking members for promotion
purposes, **22C:26.**

Province land regulations,
enforcement, **91:27.**

Public safety commissioner and
department.
Commissioner of public safety.
See within this heading,
"Commissioner of public
safety."

Purchase of land for housing units,
147:2.

Qualifications, **22:6, 22C:10.**

Railroad commission petitioning
for special police, **22C:51,
22C:52.**

Ranking members for promotion
purposes, **22C:26.**

Records and reports.
Affirmative action efforts,
22C:23.
Appointments, public inspection
of records, **22C:52.**

STATE POLICE —Cont'd

Records and reports —Cont'd
Blind persons, aid to,
information to state police,
66:17A.
Chemists' certified reports as
prima facie evidence,
22C:39, 22C:41.
Criminal identification bureau,
information from, **22C:36A.**
Evaluation reports of
performance of personnel,
22C:22.
Hate crime, collection and
analysis of reports,
22C:33-22C:35.
Identification of criminals,
transmittal of information
regarding, **22C:36.**
Injuries or burns caused by
weapons, **112:12T.**
Retention requirements, **22C:44.**
Wage reporting system,
information from, **62E:8.**

Reenlistment of officers, **22C:10.**

Reinstatement after disability
retirement, **22C:24A.**

Reinstatement of terminated
employees, **22C:24.**

Reports.
Records and reports. See within
this heading, "Records and
reports."

Reservations.
Federal reservations. See within
this heading, "Federal
reservations."

Retail installment sales and
services law, enforcement,
255D:6.

Retention of records and reports,
22C:44.

Retirement systems and pensions,
32:26.
See RETIREMENT SYSTEMS
AND PENSIONS.

Rewards.
Auto theft strike force,
175A:10A.
Penalty for receiving, **147:3.**

Riots, suppression, **147:2.**

Rules and regulations, **22C:10,
22C:19, 22C:69.**

Salaries and compensation,
22C:28A.
Additional work, **22C:18.**
Career incentive pay program,
41:108L.
Fees. See within this heading,
"Fees."
Hospital and medical expenses
for injury or death in line of
duty, **22C:16.**

STATE POLICE —Cont'd
Salaries and compensation
—Cont'd
Hours of labor and overtime pay.
See within this heading,
"Hours of labor and
overtime pay."
Retirement systems and
pensions, **32:26.**
See RETIREMENT SYSTEMS
AND PENSIONS.
Special police officers, **22C:56 et
seq.**
Witness in criminal case,
compensatory time off for
attendance in court,
262:53C.
Sanatoriums, employees appointed
as special police officers,
22C:65.
Schools and education.
Training programs. See within
this heading, "Training
programs."
University of Massachusetts,
guards appointed by
trustees, **22C:50.**
Separate maintenance
proceedings, investigations,
209:32.
Sexual crimes, notice of release of
prisoners convicted, **22C:37.**
Small loan business, enforcement
of regulations, **140:112.**
Smoking regulations, **22C:10.**
Snow traveling and recreation
vehicles, enforcement of law
and regulations, **90B:32.**
Society for the Prevention of
Cruelty to Children,
appointment of special police,
22C:56.
Soldiers' Homes, special police
officers, **22C:62.**
Special investigations bureau,
22C:67.
Special officers.
Animals, special police for
prevention of cruelty,
22C:57.
Appointments, **10:5, 22C:4,
22C:7, 22C:50 et seq.**
Children, appointment of special
police to Society for the
Prevention of Cruelty to
Children, **22C:56.**
Civil defense agency employees
as special police officers,
22C:64.
Colonel of state police,
appointment, **22C:4, 22C:7,
22C:50 et seq.**

STATE POLICE —Cont'd
Special officers —Cont'd
Education and training
programs, special police
officers, **22C:63, 22C:66.**
Hospitals, special police officers,
22C:63.
Justice of the peace swearing in
special officers, **22C:53.**
Licenses provided to special
officers, **22C:53, 22C:59,
22C:60 et seq.**
Lottery commission, special
police officers, **22C:67.**
Massachusetts Turnpike
Authority, **22C:61.**
Mental health department
requesting special officers,
22C:59.
Notary public swearing in
special officers, **22C:53.**
Notice of discontinuance of
service, **22C:53 et seq.**
Port authority, **22C:58.**
Salaries and compensation,
22C:56 et seq.
Sanatoriums, appointment of
employees, **22C:65.**
Soldiers' Homes, special police
officers, **22C:62.**
State treasurer, appointment,
10:5.
Sperm cells or seminal fluid, prima
facie evidence, **22C:41.**
Staff officers defined, **22C:1.**
Steamboat police, **22C:51, 22C:52.**
Stolen property, responsibility,
22C:45.
Street railways, enforcement of
regulations as to heating of
cars, **161:100.**
Suicide prevention training for
police officers, **40:36C.**
Support services division, **22C:4,
22C:8.**
Survivors' allowances.
See RETIREMENT SYSTEMS
AND PENSIONS.
Suspension or revocation of
departmental orders of
department, **22C:43.**
Technical services bureau, **22C:8.**
Termination of employment,
22C:24.
Time or date.
Promotions, period of service for
certain appointments,
22C:28.
Retention of records, **22C:44.**
Unclaimed property, time for
keeping, **22C:45, 22C:46,
22C:48.**

STATE POLICE —Cont'd
Training programs.
Assignment of officers, **22C:50,
22C:63.**
Drugs and narcotics, **12:11C.**
Local police, **22C:20, 40:5.**
Narcotics and harmful drug
laws, **12:11C.**
New enlistees, **22C:20.**
Special police officers, **22C:63,
22C:66.**
Suicide prevention training for
police officers, **40:36C.**
Transmittal of hate crime data to
state officials, **22C:34.**
Travel expenses.
Medical and surgical expenses
paid out of travel or other
expenses, **22C:16.**
Witness, traveling expenses for
appearing, **262:53B.**
Trial or hearing.
Appeal of findings of misconduct
trial, **22C:12.**
Misconduct trial, findings,
22C:12.
Turpentine manufacture and sale,
enforcement of regulations,
94:290.
Unclaimed property.
Abandoned, lost or unclaimed
property. See within this
heading, "Abandoned, lost or
unclaimed property."
Uniformed branch, eligibility for
membership in collective
bargaining unit, **150E:3.**
Uniforms, rules and regulations
regarding, **22C:19.**
University of Massachusetts,
guards appointed by trustees,
22C:50.
Unlawful assemblies, suppression,
269:1.
Vacancies among commissioned
officers, filling, **22C:27.**
Veterans and veterans'
organizations.
Appointment of officer, **10:5.**
Veteran defined, **22C:1.**
Wages.
Salaries and compensation. See
within this heading,
"Salaries and
compensation."
Water resources authority,
services, **22C:31.**
Weapons, authority to carry,
22C:19, 147:2.

STATE POLICE —Cont'd

Weights and measures,
appointment of state police as
weighers and measurers,
41:87A.

Turnpike authority, **81A:19.**

Witnesses.
Compensatory time off for
attendance in court as
witness in criminal cases,
262:53C.

Fees, **262:53B.**

Traveling expenses for
appearing as witness,
262:53B.

Work hours.
Hours of labor and overtime pay.
See within this heading,
"Hours of labor and
overtime pay."

**STATE PRINTING, 5:1-5:18,
29:28, 30:31.**

Administrative regulations,
publication of, **30A:6.**

Annual reports of state officers,
departments, and
commissions, **5:6-5:8.**

Archeological, historical, and
scientific information, state
secretary's duty to publish,
9:26.

Ballots, **55B:4.**

Bidding and letting of contracts,
5:1.

Bills for, checking and auditing,
7:15.

Bonds of contractors, **5:1.**

Bulletins of legislative committee
hearings, **5:12.**

Contracts and agreements.
Bidding and letting, **5:1.**
Bills, **7:15.**

Crimes and offenses, **5:1.**

Department heads, responsibilities
as to printing, binding, and
procurement of stationery,
30:31.

Depository library for
Massachusetts state
publications.
See STATE LIBRARY.

Employment.
Labor and employment. See
within this heading, "Labor
and employment."

Engrossment of bills and resolves
of general court, **3:23.**

General Court.
Engrossment of bills and
resolves, **3:23.**

STATE PRINTING —Cont'd

General Court —Cont'd
Fiscal note for proposed
legislation, **3:38A.**
Journals, **5:10.**
Lists of committees and
members, printing and
distribution, **5:10.**
Manual, **5:11.**
Portraits of members, printing
and distribution of books
containing, **5:18.**
Stationery, **3:36.**

General statutes, cumulative table
of changes, **5:4A.**

Hours of labor laws, applicability,
149:36.

Labor and employment.
Department of labor and
workforce development to
enforce laws, **5:1.**
Hours of labor laws,
applicability to state
printing, **149:36.**
Prevailing wage rates, **5:1.**

Libraries.
See LIBRARIES AND
LIBRARIANS.

Lists of general court members
and committees, **5:10.**

Manual of general court, **5:11.**

Maps, state printing, **5:11.**

Payment for publishing state
publications, **29:28.**

Portraits of general court
members, printing and
distribution of books
containing, **5:18.**

Prevailing rate of wages, **5:1.**

Purchasing agent.
See STATE PURCHASING
AGENT.

Records and reports.
Annual reports of state officers
and commissions, **5:6.**
Distribution and printing,
5:1-5:18.
Persons doing state printing,
records required, **5:1.**
Submission of reports and
documents to state
purchasing agent prior to
printing, **7:29.**

Reformatory to be supplied with
paper, **7:27.**

Regulations of administrative
agencies, publication of,
30A:6.

Reports.
Records and reports. See within
this heading, "Records and
reports."

STATE PRINTING —Cont'd

Secretary of state.
Ballots, printing, **55B:4.**
Copies of state agencies'
publications, provision to
state secretary, **5:6A.**
Cumulative tables of changes in
general statutes,
responsibilities for printing,
5:4A.
Duties, **5:1.**

Stationery.
General court, **3:36.**
State officers and departments,
30:31.

Stereotype plates, custody, **9:13.**

Submission of reports and
documents to state purchasing
agent prior to printing, **7:29.**

Supervision, **5:1, 30:31.**

Topographic maps, state printing,
5:11.

Wages, prevailing rate, **5:1.**

**STATE PURCHASING AGENT,
7:4A, 7:22 et seq.**

Administration and finance
executive office, **7:4A, 7:4D.**

Administration commissioner,
powers, **7:4.**

Advising with state institutions
making products, **7:25.**

Advisory standardization board,
7:26.

Annual reports of state officers
and commissions, printing,
5:6.

Appeals.
Action of purchasing agent,
appeals, **5:8, 7:25A, 7:29.**
Reports.
Certification of reports of
purchasing agent,
decisions regarding, **7:29.**
Special reports of officers or
departments, decision,
30:35.
State agencies, appeals of
decisions to commissioner of
administration and finance,
7:25A.

Appointment and term, **7:4A.**

Approval of purchase by state
departments and officers,
7:25A, 30:52.

Bidders on contracts for supplies
and equipment, classified list
of prospective bidders, **7:22.**

Blind-produced articles and
services, provisions as to
purchase and use, **6:134.**

Bond of state purchaser, **7:4A.**

STATE PURCHASING AGENT
—Cont'd
Bradford Durfee College of
Technology, purchases,
74:42N.
Centralized state purchasing
agency for materials and
supplies, **30:51, 30:52.**
Classified list of prospective
bidders on contracts for
supplies and equipment, **7:22.**
Collective purchases by political
subdivisions, authority, **7:22A,
7:22B.**
Compensation, **7:4A.**
Confidential secretary, **30:7.**
Contractors with state as bound by
rules and regulations, **7:23A.**
Correctional institutions.
Contracts on account of state
purchasing agent, **125:20.**
Prison-made articles, purchase,
127:57, 127:60, 127:127.
Purchase of tools and materials,
127:66, 127:66A.
Documents of state agencies,
printing and publishing of.
Printing and publication. See
within this heading,
"Printing and publication."
Employees for division,
appointment, **7:4D.**
Equipment, purchase of, **7:22.**
Governor and council to approve
contracts, **7:22.**
Letterheads, determination of
uniform style of headings,
30:30A.
List of supplies and materials to
be purchased or contracted,
7:22.
Minority Business Assistance,
coordination of programs and
services, **23A:44.**
Motor vehicles of state, regulations
as to marking, **30:36.**
New Bedford Institute of
Technology, purchases,
74:42N.
Official letterheads, determination
of uniform style of headings,
30:30A.
Official textbooks, casebooks, and
technical reports,
determination as to status of
publications, **5:8.**
Preferences in purchases, **7:22,
7:23A.**
Printing and publication.
Annual reports of state officers
and commissions, printing,
5:6.

STATE PURCHASING AGENT
—Cont'd
Printing and publication —Cont'd
Appeal from purchasing agent's
decision as to publication of
state documents, **7:29.**
Bills for, checking and
allowance, **7:15.**
Submission of state agencies'
reports to purchasing agent
prior to publication, **7:29.**
Supervision of state printing,
5:1.
Technical reports, determination
as to status of publications,
5:8.
Prison-made goods, **127:57,
127:60, 127:127.**
Publication.
Printing and publication. See
within this heading,
"Printing and publication."
Public records, **7:22.**
Quantities of purchases by state
agencies, approval, **7:25A,
30:52.**
Records, reports, and returns.
Appeals. See within this
heading, "Appeals."
List of state purchases to be
kept by state purchasing
agent, **7:22.**
Printing and publication. See
within this heading,
"Printing and publication."
Public records of purchasing
agent, **7:22.**
Special reports to purchasing
agent, **30:35.**
Reformatory of state, paper
supplied, **7:27.**
Reports.
Records, reports, and returns.
See within this heading,
"Records, reports, and
returns."
Review.
Appeals. See within this
heading, "Appeals."
Rules and regulations.
Binding other offices or
departments, **7:22.**
Contractors with state as bound,
7:23A.
State motor vehicles, marking,
30:36.
Special reports of officers and
departments, powers, **30:35.**
State colleges, purchases, **73:15.**
State institutions, advice on
making products suitable for
needs of state departments,
7:25.

STATE PURCHASING AGENT
—Cont'd
State treasurer, delivery of bond,
7:4A.
State universities, purchases,
75:13.
Stationery, letterhead,
determination of uniform
official style, **30:30A.**
Supplies, purchasing of, **7:22.**
Tools and materials for
correctional institutions,
127:66, 127:66A.
Transfer of supplies or equipment
between institutions or offices,
7:25A.
Unemployment, preference to
industries in towns having,
7:22.
Wearing apparel and clothing,
provisions and limitations as
to purchase, **7:22.**

**STATE RACING COMMISSION.
See RACING COMMISSION.**

**STATE RECLAMATION AND
MOSQUITO CONTROL
BOARD, 252:2.**

**STATE RECREATION AREAS,
132A:1 et seq.**
Acquisition of land for state parks,
132A:2A, 132A:3, 132A:3A.
Activities to be developed,
132A:2D.
Agricultural land preservation,
132A:11A.
Annual report of commissioner,
132A:9.
Appalachian Trail, protection,
132A:12.
Bequests for recreational and
conservation purposes,
acceptance, **132A:1.**
Boxing matches organized by
recreation departments,
147:39A, 147:50A.
Capital outlay program, **132A:3.**
Charges for use of facilities,
132A:2D.
Cities and towns.
Contributions for state trails or
paths, **132:39.**
Joint ownership of land with
Commonwealth, **132A:11A.**
Commercial activity within state
forest recreational areas,
132A:2B.
Concessions, **132A:7.**
Conservation commissioner, duties
and powers as to trials,
132:38.

STATE RECREATION AREAS
—Cont'd
Conservation program for cities and towns, establishment, **132A:11.**
County commissioners' approval of assumption of care by commissioner, **132A:2.**
County superintendent, discharge, **35:51.**
Department of environmental management.
Environmental Management Department. See within this heading, "Environmental Management Department."
Director, advisory capacity, **132A:8.**
Division of parks and recreation, duties transferred to division of forests and parks, **21:4.**
Electricity, construction of facilities for transmission, **132A:3.**
Eminent domain, acquisition of land, **132A:2A, 132A:3, 132A:3A.**
Enclosure of trails, **132:38.**
Environmental fund, payment of proceeds from sale of products, **132A:3.**
Environmental Management Department, **132A:2-132A:2D.**
Acceptance of gifts and bequests for purposes of recreation conservation, **132A:1.**
Acquisition of land, **132A:3.**
Advice and assistance of certain departments, **132A:2C.**
Annual report, **132A:9.**
Expenditure for care and maintenance of parks, **132A:2.**
Fish and game regulations, **132A:7.**
Preservation of state forest recreational areas in natural state, **132A:2B.**
Report, **132A:9.**
Rules and regulations, **132A:7.**
Sale of land or other wood in state areas, **132A:3.**
State parks program, **132A:2A.**
State recreation areas fund, **132A:10.**
Fees for use of facilities, **132A:2D.**
Fishing and hunting areas, **132A:2D.**
Forest supervisors to exercise powers and duties of constables and police officers, **132A:7.**

STATE RECREATION AREAS
—Cont'd
Funds, **132A:10.**
Gifts, **132:2, 132A:1.**
Governor.
Approval of exercise of power of eminent domain for state parks, reservations, and recreation areas, **132A:3A.**
Approval of regulations, **132A:7.**
Hiking, construction of trails, **132:38A.**
Horseback riding, construction of trails, **132:38A.**
Hunting and fishing areas, **132A:2D.**
Injury or damage on trails, liability, **132:38.**
Laborers of department of natural resources to exercise powers and duties of constables and police officers, **132A:7.**
Metropolitan parks district, **92:33-92:59.**
See METROPOLITAN DISTRICTS.
Money received from sale of wood or land, payment to environmental fund, **132A:3.**
Municipal corporations.
Cities and towns. See within this heading, "Cities and towns."
Natural state, policy that sites by preserved, **132A:2B.**
Ocean sanctuary, establishment, **132A:13.**
Other state departments, cooperation, **132A:2C.**
Parking of vehicles, **132A:2D, 132A:7.**
Parks, **132A:2A-132A:2D, 132A:3, 132A:3A.**
Penalty for violation of rules and regulations, **132A:7.**
Pipelines, granting rights of way through state parks or reservations, **30:44B.**
Planning, **132A:2D.**
Posting rules and regulations, **132A:7.**
Recreation facilities, admission of certain disabled veterans and handicapped persons without charge, **132A:2D.**
Refreshments, authority for selling, **132A:7.**
Report of commissioner, **132A:9.**
Rest camps and shelters, **132:38.**
Revocation of permit to enclose trails, **132:38.**

STATE RECREATION AREAS
—Cont'd
Sales, **132A:3.**
Snowmobiling, construction of trails, **132:38A.**
South Essex ocean sanctuary established, **132A:13.**
Squannacook and Nissitissit rivers sanctuary, **132A:17.**
State treasurer, gifts received to be paid, **132A:1.**
Superintendents to exercise powers and duties of constable and police officer, **132A:7.**
Tax exemption, **59:5.**
Timber in conservation and recreational areas, sale, **132A:3.**
Towns.
Cities and towns. See within this heading, "Cities and towns."
Trails or paths, **132:38-132:39.**
Wood in state conservation areas, sale, **132A:3.**

STATE SEAL, 2:2, 2:3.
Advertising or commercial purposes, use for, penalized, **264:5, 264:6.**
Custody, **9:11.**
Extradition, governor's warrant of arrest, **276:16.**
Facsimile of seal on state bonds and notes, **29:48A.**
Incorporation certificates to be attested, **156:12, 158:9, 160:24, 161:9.**
Lottery tickets to be imprinted, **10:24.**
Manufacture of state seal, regulations regarding, **2:5.**
Misuse, **264:5, 264:6.**
Public health commissioner, use of seal, **9:11.**
Secretary of state, duties, **2:5, 9:11.**
State bonds and notes, facsimile, **29:48A.**
Trademarks and trade names, state seal on certificate of registration, **110B:4.**
Use and display of state seal, regulations regarding, **2:5.**

STATE SUPERINTENDENT OF STATE OFFICE BUILDINGS, 8:1 et seq.
Adams papers and writings, exhibition, **8:17B.**
Annual report to include account of flags, **8:17A.**

STATE SUPERINTENDENT OF STATE OFFICE BUILDINGS —Cont'd

Appointment of employees, **8:4.**

Assignment of rooms in state house, **8:10.**

Bureau of state buildings, head, **8:1.**

Capitol police.
See POLICE.

Change of title, **8:1 et seq.**

Charles F. Hurley building, care and operation, **8:9.**

Commissioner of asset management and maintenance, approval of appointments and room assignments, **8:4, 8:16A.**

Confidential secretary, **30:7.**

Creation of office, **8:1.**

Direction of repairs and improvements, **8:6.**

Electricians, **8:4.**

Elevator operators, **8:4.**

Employees and assistants, **8:4, 8:5.**

Engineers, **8:4.**

Erich Lindemann building, care and operation, **8:9.**

Evacuation of state house in case of fire, **143:2C.**

Fees.
Non-governmental individuals or entities, fees or service charges for, **8:9A.**

Firemen, **8:4.**

Flags, **6:15BBB, 8:17A.**

General court chambers and lobbies, care and operation, **8:9.**

Improvements of state house, **8:6.**

Janitors, **8:4.**

John Adams, exhibition of writings, **8:17B.**

John W. McCormack state office building, care and operation, **8:9.**

Leverett Saltonstall state office building, care and operation, **8:9.**

Mechanics, **8:4.**

Military museum, duties regarding, **8:14.**

Offices outside state house, care and responsibility, **8:9.**

Oilers, **8:4.**

Old provincial state house, funds for maintenance of, **8:20.**

100 Nashua Street, care and operation of building, **8:9.**

Parking areas, care and operation, **8:9.**

STATE SUPERINTENDENT OF STATE OFFICE BUILDINGS —Cont'd

Pittsfield office building, **8:9.**

Powers and duties, **8:6, 8:10.**

POW/MIA flag, **6:15BBB.**

Records and reports, flags, **8:17A.**

Regulations transmitted, **143:2B.**

Repairs to state house, **8:6, 8:7, 8:9.**

Reports and records, flags, **8:17A.**

Room assignments, approval, **8:10.**

Scrubwomen and cleaners, **8:4, 8:5.**

Soldiers' home in Holyoke, appointment and duties of superintendent, **6:71.**

Springfield office building, care and operation, **8:9.**

Veterans' organizations, approval of facilities in state house, **8:16A.**

STATE SURGEON, 33:15.

Board to consider claims for injuries during military service, member, **33:90.**

Retirement system rating board, member, **32:26.**

State house physician, appointment, **7:6B.**

STATE TAX COMMISSION. See REVENUE DEPARTMENT AND COMMISSIONER.

STATE TREASURER, 10:1 et seq.

Abandoned property.
See ABANDONED, LOST, AND UNCLAIMED PROPERTY.

Absence of, person to act, **10:5.**

Absentees, treasurer as party to proceedings for settlement of estates, **200:1.**

Accounts and accounting, **10:2.**

Attorney general, account of overdue bonds and money transmitted, **10:9.**

Audits and auditing. See within this heading, "Audits and auditing."

Comptroller, accounting of state funds, **7A:5.**

Governor may issue warrant to treasurer for accounts and demands against Commonwealth, **7A:3.**

Registers of probate and insolvency, accounting, **217:20.**

Unadjusted account, payment withheld from person having, **29:17.**

STATE TREASURER —Cont'd

Actions against treasurer for compensation from assurance fund, **185:102, 185:103.**

Administration and finance executive office.
Annual report of commission on administration and finance as to receipts and expenditures by state treasurer, **7A:12.**

Deposit of funds of office, **7:4F.**

Advances from treasury, **29:23-29:25, 29:31.**

Certification of immediate need, **29:24.**

Commission for the Blind, working capital advancements, **6:132.**

Detailed statement to comptroller, **29:25.**

Massachusetts Maritime Academy, **73:1.**

Retirement allowance to state employees, **32:98.**

Salary payments, **29:31.**

State supplementary payments, advances to United States Health, Education, and Welfare Department, **6:131D.**

Advisory council on investments.
Investment advisory council. See within this heading, "Investment advisory council."

AIDS Fund, **10:35R.**

Alcoholic liquors.
See ALCOHOLIC LIQUORS.

Alcoholism Treatment and Rehabilitation Law, disposition of funds received, **111B:5.**

Algae, weeds and other aquatic nuisances, expenditure of municipal appropriations for control, **40:5.**

Amount of deposits in any particular institution, **29:34, 29:34A.**

Annual investigation of notes and securities, **29:42.**

Annual report, **10:5A, 10:10, 10:11.**

Receipts and expenditures, annual report of commission on administration and finances, **7A:12.**

Anthracite coal mining reclamation fund, duties regarding, **21B:5.**

STATE TREASURER —Cont'd
Anticipation of receipts, borrowing money, **21:1, 29:47, 29:47A.**
Antitrust laws, **93:14.**
Assessments.
Bond issues, assessments on metropolitan districts, **29:51.**
Garbage and rubbish, assessment of costs against municipalities, **16:24.**
Asset Management Board, **7B:8.**
Assignments.
Mortgage held by state, **29:35, 29:36.**
State bonds or securities, authority, **29:35.**
Assistants.
Employees and assistants. See within this heading, "Employees and assistants."
Assurance fund for registered lands, **185:100-185:106.**
Attorney general.
Action to enforce treasurer's bond, **10:3.**
Transmission of account of overdue money and bonds, **10:9.**
Audits and auditing.
Deferred compensation plan, audit, **29:64.**
General Court, auditing of expenses of committees, **3:37.**
Municipal accounts, duties in connection with expenses of audit, **44:41.**
Regional refuse disposal district committee accounts, duties in connection with cost of audit, **40:44, 40:44I.**
Automobile clubs, filing of bond as evidence of financial responsibility, **174B:6.**
Automobile insurance.
See AUTOMOBILE INSURANCE.
Ballots, order of candidates' names, **54:43A.**
Bankruptcy.
Insolvency. See within this heading, "Insolvency."
Banks.
See BANKS AND BANKING.
Blasting bonds, operations in more than one city or town, **148:20A.**
Blind persons, working capital advancements to commission, **6:132.**

STATE TREASURER —Cont'd
Board of Registration in Medicine Trust Fund established, **10:35M.**
Bonds and securities held by state.
Account of overdue bonds and money transmitted to attorney general, **10:9.**
Annual examination, **29:42.**
Assignment, **29:35.**
Certain corporate securities, investment, **29:38.**
Collection of notes or securities, **29:42.**
Corporate securities, investment, **29:38.**
Custody, **29:41.**
Inventory of when vacancy occurs in treasurer's office, **10:13.**
Motor vehicle insurance, deposit of securities in lieu, **90:34D.**
Political subdivisions, bonds, **29:38.**
Refunding bonds, issuance and sale, **29:53A.**
Registration, **29:39.**
Sale, **29:42.**
Sinking fund, purchase of securities, **29:45.**
Transfer of funds. See within this heading, "Transfer of funds."
Bonds and securities issued by state, **29:47, 29:47A, 29:49, 29:50.**
Infrastructure fund, bond issues, **29:20.**
Bonds and undertakings.
Automobile clubs, filing of bond as evidence of financial responsibility, **174B:6.**
Blasters' bonds, operation in more than one city or town, **148:20A.**
Fireworks bonds, duties with respect, **148:41, 148:42.**
Infrastructure fund, security for bond issues, **29:20.**
Motor carriers of property, deposits of bonds, **159A:6.**
Official bond. See within this heading, "Official bond."
Registers of probate and insolvency, bond to be filed, **217:12.**
Sheriff's bonds, furnishing copies, **37:9.**
Trackless trolleys, bond for damage, **163:12.**
Boxing and boxing matches.
Distribution of money received from matches, **147:47.**

STATE TREASURER —Cont'd
Boxing and boxing matches —Cont'd
Member of boxers' fund board, **6:99.**
Payment of tax on gross receipts of matches, **147:40.**
Bradford Durfee College of Technology expenditures, **74:42J.**
Campaign expenditures and contributions.
Expenditures by wire transfer or other electronic means, **55:19.**
Penalty for failure to file report to be paid, **55:19.**
Capital facilities projects, expenditure of funds, **35:11.**
Cemetery funds of cities and towns, care and management, **114:20, 114:21, 114:25.**
Central artery and statewide road and bridge infrastructure fund, **10:63.**
Centralized weekly payroll system, approval of rules and regulations, **29:31.**
Certificates and certification.
Advances from state treasury, **29:24.**
Amount required to pay state bonds or scrip, certification, **29:50.**
Corporations and organizations, certification of deposits, **10:6.**
Election, issuance of certificate, **54:116.**
Forgery of notes, certificates, or bills of credit issued by treasurer, **267:7.**
Payments from treasury, certification by comptroller, **29:18.**
Per diem allowances for members of general court, **3:9B.**
Regional transit authorities, certification of payments to meet expenses, **161B:11.**
Unclaimed funds of social services department, certification of information for release, **18B:19.**
Checks.
Commonwealth checks, payment, **29:32.**
Drafts or checks drawn by any state officer or agency, funding, **29:23.**

STATE TREASURER —Cont'd
Checks —Cont'd
Unpaid state treasurer's checks, procedure, **29:32, 29:32A.**
Children.
Child support trust fund, treasurer to serve as treasurer, **119A:10, 119A:11.**
Desertion of spouse or children, use of fines resulting, **273:3.**
Report by state treasurer as to amount expenditures for children in need of services, **119:39J.**
Child support trust fund, treasurer to serve as treasurer, **119A:10, 119A:11.**
Chiropractors, disposition of fees received by Board of Registration, **13:66.**
Cigarette stamps, refunds for unused, **64C:31.**
Civil service.
Exclusion of employees, **31:48.**
Payment of employees, **31:71.**
Stop-payment order as to persons illegally employed, **31:73.**
Collection of assessments on metropolitan districts for bond issues, **29:51.**
Colleges and universities.
State colleges. See within this heading, "State colleges."
Combined investment funds, establishment, **29:38A.**
Commission for the Blind, working capital advancements, **6:132.**
Committee of national association of insurance commissioners on valuation of securities, duties as to funds for use, **175:14A.**
Communist organization, escheat of funds or property, **264:18.**
Community development finance corporation, treasurer authorized to purchase stock, **40F:4, 40F:4A.**
Community Reinvestment Act, bank rating as affecting eligibility to receive funds under the Act, **29:34.**
Compact fund.
See COMPACT FUND.
Compensation.
Wages, salaries, and compensation. See within this heading, "Wages, salaries, and compensation."
Comptroller, **7A:1, 7A:5.**
Accounting of state funds, **7A:5.**

STATE TREASURER —Cont'd
Comptroller —Cont'd
Advances from treasury, detailed statement to comptroller, **29:25.**
Payments from treasury, certification, **29:18.**
Conservation districts, sums of money remaining from dissolved, **21:21.**
Conservation funds, receipt and handling, **10:16.**
Constitution of Massachusetts.
See CONSTITUTION OF MASSACHUSETTS.
Conveyances.
Deeds and conveyances. See within this heading, "Deeds and conveyances."
Co-operative banks, deposit by state treasurer of cash deposited in lieu of automobile liability insurance or bonds, **90:34D.**
Corporations, **29:40.**
Banks.
See BANKS AND BANKING.
Certification of deposit, **10:6.**
Correctional institutions, disposition of unclaimed money or property of former prisoners, **127:96A, 127:96B.**
Costs and expenses.
Campaign expenditures and contributions. See within this heading, "Campaign expenditures and contributions."
Costs of action.
See COSTS OF ACTION.
Regional transit authorities. See within this heading, "Regional transit authorities."
Costs of action.
See COSTS OF ACTION.
Counties, duties as to emergency loans, **35:36A.**
Coupon bonds, exchange of registered bonds, **29:58.**
Credit enhancement, highway fund, **29:2O.**
Credit unions.
Payroll deductions, **149:178B.**
State treasurer forwarding pension or retirement funds, **171:45.**
Criminal history systems board, duties regarding funds, **6:168.**
Criminal justice committee, duty as to funds, **6:156.**

STATE TREASURER —Cont'd
Death.
Flag of Commonwealth to be flown at half-mast when state treasurer dies, **2:6A.**
Procedure in event, **10:12, 10:13.**
Deeds and conveyances.
Custody of deeds and conveyances, **29:41.**
Foreclosed real estate, sale and conveyance, **29:37.**
Defaced state bonds, substitutions, **29:58.**
Deferred compensation program for state employees.
Committee established in office of state treasurer, **29:38B.**
Funds, investment by state treasurer, **29:38, 29:64.**
Deposits and depositories.
Administration and finance executive office, deposit of funds, **7:4F.**
Amount of deposits in any particular institution, **29:34, 29:34A.**
Assessment of local taxes, deposits with state treasurer.
See TAXATION.
Automobile liability insurance, deposits of cash in lieu, **90:34D.**
Cash or securities deposited with state treasurer in lieu of motor vehicle insurance, **90:34D.**
Cooperative banks, deposit by state treasurer of cash deposited in lieu of automobile liability insurance or bonds **90:34D.**
Corporation taxes, deposits, **58:5, 58:28.**
Direct deposit of employees' wages, etc., **29:31.**
Executive offices, deposits of gifts and grants received by secretaries, **6A:6.**
Fraternal benefit societies, deposits of foreign or alien societies with treasurer, **175:185, 176:32.**
Insurance.
See INSURANCE.
Legacy and succession taxes, deposits in lieu of tax on future estates, **65:15.**
Lowlands and swamps, deposit of estimated expense for financing of improvements, **252:10.**

STATE TREASURER —Cont'd

Deposits and depositories —Cont'd

Motor carriers of property, deposit of bonds, **159A:6.**

Public funds, depositories, **29:34, 29:34A.**

Reciprocal insurance exchanges. See RECIPROCAL INSURANCE EXCHANGES.

Savings banks, deposit of public moneys by state treasurer, **29:3A.**

Workers' compensation. See WORKERS' COMPENSATION.

Deputy sheriffs.

Sheriffs and deputies. See within this heading, "Sheriffs and deputies."

Desertion of spouse or children, use of fines resulting, **273:3.**

Development department.

Economic development department. See within this heading, "Economic development department."

Development finance corporation, purchase of shares, **40F:5.**

Direct deposit of employees' wages, etc., **29:31.**

Disabled and handicapped persons, federal aid funds for rehabilitation, **6:82.**

Discharge of mortgage, assignment in lieu, **29:36.**

District courts.

Advancement of funds, **218:49.**

Books and supplies, payment, **218:39.**

Payments and accounting to be made to state treasurer, **218:47.**

Dividends or refunds received by state employees' group insurance commission, duties, **32A:9.**

Division of Insurance Trust Fund established, **10:35L.**

Dredged material, recovery of cost of supervision of transportation and dumping in tide water, **91:54.**

Duplicate receipts by successor, **10:13, 10:14.**

Economic development department.

Bond of commissioner furnished, **23A:1.**

Custody of gifts and grants, **23A:8.**

STATE TREASURER —Cont'd

Education.

Schools and education. See within this heading, "Schools and education."

Educational television programs, reimbursement of cities and towns sharing cost, **71:13F.**

Education department.

Fire training bureau, gifts, **15:1F.**

Trust funds from department, **10:16.**

Election campaign expenditures and contributions.

Campaign expenditures and contributions. See within this heading, "Campaign expenditures and contributions."

Election of state treasurer, **54:150.**

Certificate of election, issuance, **54:116.**

Order of appearance of names of candidates on ballots and voting machines, **54:43A.**

Primary elections, number of signatures required for candidates, **53:44.**

Record of votes, transmission, **54:112.**

Embezzlement or fraud by employee, **266:50.**

Emergency appropriations, approval board with regard to indebtedness of city or town, **44:8.**

Emergency finance board, membership, **10:47.**

Emergency loans by counties, duties, **35:36A.**

Employees and assistants, **10:5.**

Civil service. See within this heading, "Civil service."

Contributions by employees to Massachusetts independent health agencies, payroll deduction and transmittal, **180:17F.**

Defined in labor relations laws, department officers and employees as excepted, **150E:1.**

Embezzlement or fraud, **266:50.**

Exempt from civil service office and position classification and pay plan, **30:45.**

Group life insurance of state employees, duties, **175:138A.**

Retirement systems. See RETIREMENT SYSTEMS AND PENSIONS.

STATE TREASURER —Cont'd

Employees and assistants —Cont'd

Wages, salaries, and compensation. See within this heading, "Wages, salaries, and compensation."

Employment security, state treasurer as treasurer of unemployment compensation fund, **151A:50.** See EMPLOYMENT SECURITY.

Endorsed bonds, substitution, **29:58.**

Environmental funds, duties regarding, **10:16, 21A:10.**

Escheated estates.

Communist organization, escheat of funds or property, **264:18.**

General fund, escheated estates fund balances payable, **18B:19.**

Reports, **200A:11.**

Ethics commission, major policymaking positions reported, **268B:3.**

Examination.

Investigation. See within this heading, "Investigation."

Exception of department officers and employees from definition of employee for purposes of labor relations laws, **150E:1.**

Exchange of registered bonds for coupon bonds, **29:58.**

Executive offices, deposits of gifts and grants received by secretaries, **6A:6.**

Executors. See EXECUTORS AND ADMINISTRATORS.

Expenses.

Costs and expenses. See within this heading, "Costs and expenses."

Federal aid funds.

Forest fund, **10:8A.**

Medical assistance program, custodian of funds allocated to Commonwealth, **118E:3.**

Outdoor recreation facilities, authority to borrow money in anticipation of receipt of federal funds, **21:1.**

Rehabilitation of handicapped persons, **6:82.**

Soldiers' home, funds, **10:7.**

State highways, funds, **10:8.**

Vocational education, custody of funds, **74:20.**

STATE TREASURER —Cont'd

Federal savings and loan
  association, investment of
  public moneys in shares,
  29:34A.
Fees.
  Chiropractors, **13:66.**
  General court, witness fees,
    3:38.
  Nursing home administrators,
    board of registration, **13:75.**
  Sheriff's fee for disbursing
    treasurer's warrant, **262:8.**
  State officers, fees paid over to
    treasurer, **30:27.**
  Telecommunications and energy
    department, bond of
    employee receiving filing
    fees, **25:10B.**
Finance advisory board, **6:97.**
Fines, forfeitures, and penalties.
  Campaign expenditure reports,
    failure, **55:19.**
  Deficient commercial fertilizer,
    128:71.
  Desertion of spouse or children,
    273:3.
  Embezzlement by employee of
    department, **266:50.**
  Higher education, parking
    violation fines, **15A:13.**
  Highway fund, **280:2.**
  Payable to treasurer, **280:2.**
Firearms surrendered to public
  safety commissioner,
  disposition of proceeds of sale,
  140:129D.
Firemen's relief commissioners,
  member, **10:21.**
Fire training bureau in education
  department, authority as to
  gifts and grants, **15:1F.**
Fireworks bonds, duties with
  respect, **148:41, 148:42.**
First deputy to act for, when, **10:4,
  10:5.**
Flag to be flown at half-mast on
  death, **2:6A.**
Foreclosed real estate, sale and
  conveyance, **29:37.**
Foreign insurance companies.
  See FOREIGN INSURANCE
    COMPANIES.
Forests and forestry.
  Payment of money received by
    sale of forest or forest
    products, **132:34A.**
  Receipt of federal aid for forest
    fire prevention, **10:8A.**
  State forester's acceptance of
    federal aid from state
    treasurer, **132:6.**

STATE TREASURER —Cont'd

Forests and forestry —Cont'd
  Transfer of gifts or bequests,
    132:2.
Forfeitures. See within this
  heading, "Fines, forfeitures,
  and penalties."
Forgery of notes, certificates, or
  bills of credit issued, **267:7.**
Fraternal benefit societies,
  deposits of foreign or alien
  societies, **175:185, 176:32.**
Fraud or embezzlement by
  employee, **266:50.**
Garbage and rubbish.
  Assessment of costs against
    municipalities, **16:24.**
  Audit of accounts of regional
    refuse disposal district
    committee, duties in
    connection with costs, **40:44,
    40:44I.**
General Court.
  Account of moneys rendering
    upon notice, **10:2.**
  Auditing of expenses of
    committees, **3:37.**
  Certification of per diem
    allowances to member, **3:9B.**
  Fees for witnesses before, **3:38.**
  Payment of compensation to
    members, **3:9.**
  Report, **10:10.**
Governor.
  See GOVERNOR.
Grounds for removal from office,
  10:4.
Handicapped persons, custodian of
  federal funds for
  rehabilitation, **6:82.**
Head Injury Treatment Services
  Trust Fund, **10:59.**
Health and welfare commission,
  funds, **6:125.**
High-accident locations,
  reimbursement of cities and
  towns for installation of traffic
  control devices, **90:33B.**
Highway fund, distribution to
  cities and towns, **58:18B.**
Highways.
  See HIGHWAYS AND
    STREETS.
Historical commission,
  administration of funds, **9:26.**
Horse and dog racing license fees,
  refunds, **128A:4.**
Hospitals of state, unclaimed
  property of patients, **111:65D.**
Income tax refunds, **62C:36,
  62C:40.**

STATE TREASURER —Cont'd

Indigent persons, record of
  payments of court costs,
  261:27G.
Industrial homework permit fees
  paid, **149:147.**
Infrastructure fund, **29:2O.**
Innholder's sale of guests'
  abandoned property, payment
  over of proceeds, **140:16.**
Insolvency.
  Registers of probate and
    insolvency. See within this
    heading, "Registers of
    probate and insolvency."
  Removal, **10:4.**
Insurance.
  See INSURANCE.
Interest on money.
  Anticipated revenue, borrowing
    against, **29:47, 29:47A.**
  Cash or securities deposited
    with state treasurer in lieu
    of motor vehicle insurance,
    90:34D.
  Head Injury Treatment Services
    Trust Fund, **10:59.**
Inventory of funds and securities
  when vacancy in office occurs,
  10:13.
Investigation.
  Annual investigation of notes
    and securities held by
    treasurer, **29:42.**
  Municipal affairs, collection and
    payment of expenses for
    investigation, **44:46A.**
Investment advisory council.
  Combined investment funds,
    advice as to establishment,
    29:38A.
  Reports furnished, **10:5B.**
Investment of funds, **6:98,
  10:15-10:17A, 29:38.**
  Advisory council on.
    Investment advisory council.
      See within this heading,
      "Investment advisory
      council."
  Annual examination of
    securities, **29:42.**
  Appropriation unnecessary,
    29:18.
  Bonds and securities held by
    state. See within this
    heading, "Bonds and
    securities held by state."
  Combined investment funds,
    establishment, **29:38A.**
  Committee for state employees'
    group insurance dividend or
    refunds, **32A:9A.**

STATE TREASURER —Cont'd

Investment of funds —Cont'd

Custody of securities held by Commonwealth, **29:41.**

Deferred compensation plan funds, investment, **29:38.**

Federal savings and loan association shares, investment, **29:34A.**

Gifts, acceptance and investment, **10:17A.**

Group insurance commission trust funds, **32A:9A.**

Head Injury Treatment Services Trust Fund, **10:59.**

Highway infrastructure fund, **29:20.**

Infrastructure fund, **29:20.**

Investment division's establishing, **10:5C.**

Marine fisheries division trust funds, **10:16.**

Recommendations of state advisory board, **6:98.**

Registration of bonds held by state, **29:39.**

Retirement system funds, **10:5C, 32:23.**

Sale of securities, **29:42.**

Sinking funds, **29:45.**

State funds, **29:38.**

Transfer of funds. See within this heading, "Transfer of funds."

Job descriptions, state treasurer to file annual report on salaries and, **10:5A.**

Judgment for costs against Commonwealth, payment, **261:16.**

Landscape architects' registration board, limitation upon salary and expenses of members, officers, and employees, **13:69.**

Legacy and succession taxes.

Deposits in lieu of tax on future estates, **65:15.**

Payment of refunds, **65:27.**

Libraries.

Custodian of library funds, **78:19.**

Payment to cities and towns for free public libraries, **78:19A.**

Trust funds, **6:37A, 10:16.**

License plates, portion of revenues to go to Massachusetts United States Olympic Fund, **10:35O.**

Life insurance.

Group insurance of state employees, duties, **175:138A.**

STATE TREASURER —Cont'd

Life insurance —Cont'd

Unclaimed funds, duties, **175:149C, 175:149D.**

Line of credit, agreements with commercial banks or trust companies to provide, **29:49B.**

Local property assessment, expenses of keeping records, **58:4C.**

Long range capital facilities agency plans, submission, **29:7D.**

Lost property, **200A:1-200A:15.**

See ABANDONED, LOST, AND UNCLAIMED PROPERTY.

Lottery of state.

Director of lottery, appointment, **10:26.**

Holders of winning tickets in excess of $600, reports, **10:28B.**

Lottery commission, chairman, **10:23.**

Quarterly credit of balance to Compact Fund, **10:35.**

Lowlands and swamps.

Approval and payment of expenses, **252:14.**

Financing of improvements, deposit of estimated expense with treasurer, **252:10.**

Major policy making positions reported to State Ethics Commission, **268B:3.**

Management of funds under control of state agencies, **29:23, 32:23.**

Marine fisheries division trust funds, receipt and investment, **10:16, 130:17.**

Maritime Academy, advances, **73:1.**

Martin Luther King commission fund established, **10:35N.**

Massachusetts Bay transportation authority state and local contribution fund, **10:35T.**

Massachusetts United States Olympic Fund, **10:35O.**

Mass transportation facilities and services, certification of amounts payable, **58:25B.**

Medical assistance program, custodian of federal funds allocated to Commonwealth, **118E:3.**

Mental illness or retardation.

Duties as to trust funds to insane or incompetent persons, **10:17.**

Removal from office for mental illness, **10:4.**

STATE TREASURER —Cont'd

Metropolitan air pollution control district expenditures, reimbursement of Commonwealth, **111:142B.**

Metropolitan area planning council fund, duties, **40B:29.**

Metropolitan districts.

See METROPOLITAN DISTRICTS.

Military funds, receipts and handling, **10:17A.**

Minors.

Children. See within this heading, "Children."

Mortgages held by Commonwealth.

Assignment, **29:35, 29:36.**

Powers and duties in respect, **244:37-244:40.**

Sale and conveyance of foreclosed real estate, **29:37.**

Motor carriers of passengers, deposit of bonds, **159A:6.**

Motorcycle safety fund established, **10:35G.**

Multi-jurisdictional lottery games, **10:24A.**

Municipal finance.

Algae, weeds and other aquatic nuisances, expenditure of appropriations for control, **40:5.**

Cemetery funds of cities and towns, care and management, **114:20, 114:21, 114:25.**

Construction of structures for protection of private property, municipal appropriations, **91:29A.**

Distribution of state funds to cities and towns, **58:18B.**

Educational television programs, reimbursement of cities and towns, **71:13F.**

Emergency appropriations, approval board with regard to indebtedness of city or town, **44:8.**

Free public libraries, payment to cities and towns, **78:19A.**

High-accident locations, reimbursement of cities and towns for installation of traffic control devices, **90:33B.**

Highway fund, distribution to cities and towns, **58:18B.**

Metropolitan air pollution control district expenditures, reimbursement of Commonwealth, **111:142B.**

STATE TREASURER —Cont'd
Municipal finance —Cont'd
Special commission investigating state and municipal finance, membership, **29:38.**
Transportation of pupils, reimbursement of cities and towns, **71:7A.**
Mutilated or defaced state bonds, substitutions, **29:58.**
Natural Heritage and Endangered Species Fund, **10:35D.**
New Bedford Institute of Technology, expenditures, **74:42J.**
Nomination, filing deadlines, **53:10, 53:48, 55B:5.**
Nongame wildlife fund, **10:35D.**
Notes and bonds issued by Commonwealth, **29:2O, 29:47, 29:47A, 29:49, 29:58.**
Nuisances in bodies of water, expenditure of municipal appropriations for control, **40:5.**
Nursing home administrators board of registration, disposition of fees received, **13:75.**
Objection to nomination, time for filing, **55B:5.**
Official bond, **10:2.**
Actions, **10:3.**
Conditions, **10:2.**
Employees, **10:5.**
Employment security, liability in respect, **151A:59.**
First deputy, **10:4.**
Public works commissioner to give bond to treasurer, **16:1.**
Purchasing agent required to give bond to treasurer, **7:4A.**
Recipient of bond, state treasurer, **9:1.**
Revenue commissioner, performance on bond, **14:2.**
Supervisor of loan agencies, bond, **26:4.**
Surety companies, power to require official bonds be secured, **30:18.**
Telecommunications and energy department, bond of employee receiving filing fees, **25:10B.**
Order of appearance of names of candidates on ballots and voting machines, **54:43A.**
Outdoor recreation facilities, authority to borrow money in anticipation of receipt of federal funds, **21:1.**

STATE TREASURER —Cont'd
Outlawing of unpaid checks, **29:32, 29:32A.**
Participation units in combined investment funds, sale, **29:38A.**
Past due bonds or securities, annual report to attorney general, **10:9.**
Patients' funds, disposition of unclaimed, **122:7-122:9.**
Payments from treasury, **29:17-29:20A, 29:23-29:25, 29:31, 29:32.**
Penalties.
Fines, forfeitures, and penalties. See within this heading, "Fines, forfeitures, and penalties."
Pensions.
See RETIREMENT SYSTEMS AND PENSIONS.
Per diem allowances of members of general court, certification, **3:9B.**
Police.
Authority of treasurer as to regional police districts, **41:99H.**
Special state police officer, appointment, **10:5.**
Poor persons, record of payment of court costs, **261:27G.**
Primary election.
Number of signatures required for candidates, **53:44.**
Probate registers.
Registers of probate and insolvency. See within this heading, "Registers of probate and insolvency."
Public administrators.
See EXECUTORS AND ADMINISTRATORS.
Public employee organizations, deduction of dues from employee payrolls, **180:17A.**
Public works commissioner to give bond, **16:1.**
Purchasing agent for state, bond, **7:4A.**
Ratepayer parity trust fund, **10:62.**
Real property.
Deeds and conveyances. See within this heading, "Deeds and conveyances."
Foreclosed real estate, sale and conveyances, **29:37.**
Metropolitan district commission, duties and powers with respect to sale of property, **92:85.**

STATE TREASURER —Cont'd
Real property —Cont'd
Mortgages held by Commonwealth. See within this heading, "Mortgages held by Commonwealth."
State property, enforcement of sale, **81:7E.**
Receiver, duty as to unclaimed funds in hands of, **175:178.**
Reclamation districts for improvement of swamps and lowlands.
Lowlands and swamps. See within this heading, "Lowlands and swamps."
Records.
Reports. See within this heading, "Reports."
Recreational areas of state, gifts received to be paid to state treasurer, **132A:1.**
Refunding bonds, issuance and sale, **29:2O, 29:53A, 29:60A.**
Refund of tax, payment, **62C:39, 62C:40, 64C:31, 65:27.**
Regional police districts, authority, **41:99H.**
Regional refuse disposal district committee accounts, duties in connection with costs of audit, **40:44I.**
Regional transit authorities.
Borrowing by state treasurer to make payments, **161B:10.**
Certification of payments to meet current expenses, **161B:11.**
Net cost of service, ratification to and actions by state treasurer, **161B:10.**
Register of state bonds, **29:58.**
Registers of probate and insolvency.
Accounting, **217:20.**
Bond to be filed, **217:12.**
Forfeiture for failure to keep records, **217:11.**
Payment of salaries and traveling expenses by state, **217:35A, 217:42.**
Rehabilitation of handicapped persons, federal aid funds, **6:82.**
Reimbursement.
Indigent persons, reimbursement of counties for court costs and fees paid, **261:27G.**
Municipal finance. See within this heading, "Municipal finance."

STATE TREASURER —Cont'd

Removal from office, **10:4.**

Replacement checks for checks not paid within year, **29:32, 29:32A.**

Reports.

Annual report. See within this heading, "Annual report."

Assurance fund, **185:100.**

Children in need of services, report by state treasurer as to amount of expenditures, **119:39J.**

Escheat of property, **200A:11.**

Investment advisory council, reports furnished, **10:5B.**

Lottery winners, reports of winning tickets in excess of $600, **10:28B.**

Metropolitan districts, financial condition, **10:11.**

Refunding bonds, sale, **29:53A.**

Retirement systems, financial condition, **32:23.**

Salaries, job classification of state employees, etc., **10:5A.**

State universities, report of expenditures, **75:8, 75B:6.**

Warrants for payment, report of unpaid, **10:11.**

Restraints of trade and monopolies, **93:14.**

Retardation.

Mental illness and retardation. See within this heading, "Mental illness or retardation."

Retirement law commission, **10:35H.**

Retirement systems.

See RETIREMENT SYSTEMS AND PENSIONS.

Revenue commissioner, bond tendered by, performance, **14:2.**

Rubbish.

Garbage and rubbish. See within this heading, "Garbage and rubbish."

Salaries.

Wages, salaries, and compensation. See within this heading, "Wages, salaries, and compensation."

Sales.

Forest or forest products, payment of money received by sale, **132:34A.**

Investment of securities, sale of securities, **29:42.**

Metropolitan district commission, sale of property, **92:85.**

STATE TREASURER —Cont'd

Sales —Cont'd

Real property. See within this heading, "Real property."

Refunding bonds, **29:53A.**

State bonds or notes, advertising for bids, **29:53.**

Transfer of funds, unexpended receipts from sales of bonds, **29:56.**

Savings banks, deposit of public moneys by state treasurer, **29:3A.**

Schools and education.

Additional assistance for local services, **29:71.**

Department of.

Education department. See within this heading, "Education department."

State colleges. See within this heading, "State colleges."

Sealing up records or funds on death or vacancy in office, **10:12.**

Search warrant, disposition of moneys seized, **276:3, 276:7.**

Secretary of state.

Bond, deposit, **10:3.**

Death or vacancy in office, **10:12, 10:13.**

Secured transactions, **4:7, 29:2O.**

Securities.

Bonds and securities. See within this heading, "Bonds and securities held by state."

Sheriffs and deputies.

Bonds of sheriffs, furnishing copies, **37:9.**

Warrants of treasurer, sheriffs' fees for disbursing, **262:8.**

Signature on bonds and notes issued by Commonwealth, **29:48, 29:48A.**

Sinking fund, **29:2O, 29:45.**

Skin divers, compensation, **22:6.**

Social services department, duties as to unclaimed funds, **18B:19.**

Soldiers' homes, receipt of federal funds, **10:7.**

Solid waste disposal.

Garbage and rubbish. See within this heading, "Garbage and rubbish."

Special commission investigating state and municipal finance, membership, **29:38.**

Special cost assessment fund, duties with respect, **280:6A.**

Special state police officer, appointment, **10:5.**

STATE TREASURER —Cont'd

State board of retirement.

See RETIREMENT SYSTEMS AND PENSIONS.

State bonds.

See STATE BONDS AND OBLIGATIONS.

State colleges.

Distribution of appropriations, **73:12.**

Expenditures, **74:42J, 75:8.**

Student activity fee funds as violating constitutional provision requiring payment of money into treasury, **73:1B.**

State forests, receipt of proceeds of sale, **132:34A.**

State recreational areas, gifts received to be paid to state treasurer, **132A:1.**

Stop-payment order as to persons illegally employed in civil service, **31:73.**

Student activity fee funds as violating constitutional provision requiring payment of money into treasury, **73:1B.**

Student government day, observance, **6:12M.**

Subversive organization, escheat of funds or property, **264:18.**

Succession taxes.

Legacy and succession taxes. See within this heading, "Legacy and succession taxes."

Successors in office, receipting for property, **10:13, 10:14.**

Supervisor of loan agencies, bond, **26:4.**

Surety companies, power to require official bonds to be secured, **30:18.**

Surplus funds, disposition, **29:44.**

Surrender to, **200A:8A.**

Swamps.

Lowlands and swamps. See within this heading, "Lowlands and swamps."

Taxation.

See TAXATION.

Teachers' retirement system, management of funds, **32:23.**

Telecommunications and energy department, bond of employee receiving filing fees, **25:10B.**

Tewksbury Hospital, disposition of unclaimed funds or property of inmates, **122:7-122:9.**

Tourism fund, **10:35J.**

Trackless trolleys, bond for damage, **163:12.**

STATE TREASURER —Cont'd

Trading stamp companies, duties, **93:14P, 93:14Q.**

Traffic Control devices at high-accident locations, reimbursement of cities and towns, **90:33B.**

Training school trust funds, receipt and handling, **10:15.**

Transfer of funds.

Beano, quarterly credit of moneys from licensed games to Compact Fund, **10:39.**

Between funds, transfer of securities, **29:46.**

Compact fund.

See COMPACT FUND.

Forests and forestry, transfer of gifts or bequests to state treasurer, **132:2.**

Lottery of state, transfer of revenues to Compact Fund, **10:35.**

Special to general, **18B:19.**

Unexpended receipts from sales of bonds, **29:56.**

Transportation of pupils, reimbursement of cities and towns, **71:7A.**

Trust companies.

See TRUST COMPANIES.

Trust funds.

Appropriation unnecessary for payment of principal or income, **29:18.**

Child support trust fund, treasurer to serve as treasurer, **119A:10, 119A:11.**

Deposit with state treasurer, **29:40.**

Group insurance commission trust funds, deposit or investment, **32A:9A.**

Head Injury Treatment Services Trust Fund, **10:59.**

Insane or incompetent persons, duties as to trust funds, **10:17.**

Schools' trust funds, receipt and handling, **10:15, 10:16.**

State library trust fund, **6:37A, 10:16.**

Unclaimed dividends of trust fund balances, disposition, **29:46.**

Unappropriated income of funds, disposition, **111:65D.**

Unclaimed property, **200A:1-200A:15.**

See ABANDONED, LOST, AND UNCLAIMED PROPERTY.

STATE TREASURER —Cont'd

Unemployment compensation fund, treasurer of.

See EMPLOYMENT SECURITY.

Unpaid checks, procedure, **29:32, 29:32A.**

Unpaid wages or salaries due from Commonwealth, procedure, **29:32A.**

Unpaid warrants, annual statement, **10:10.**

Urban renewal projects, borrowing, **121B:26A.**

Vacancy in office.

Inventory of funds and securities, **10:13.**

Sealing up funds and records, **10:12.**

Successor, receipting for property, **10:13.**

Vocational education, custody of federal funds, **74:20.**

Wages, salaries, and compensation, **10:1.**

Advances from treasury, **29:31.**

Annual report on salaries and job descriptions, **10:5A.**

Deferred compensation program for state employees. See within this heading, "Deferred compensation program for state employees."

Direct deposit, **29:31.**

General court, payment of compensation to members, **3:9.**

Job descriptions, state treasurer to file annual report on salaries, **10:5A.**

Landscape architects' registration board, limitation upon salary and expenses of members, officers and employees, **13:69.**

Legislative and constitutional officers' compensation advisory board, duties, **6:162.**

Registers of probate and insolvency, payment of salaries and traveling expenses, **217:35A, 217:42.**

Reports, salaries, job classification of state employees, etc., **10:5A.**

Retirement systems.

See RETIREMENT SYSTEMS AND PENSIONS.

STATE TREASURER —Cont'd

Wages, salaries, and compensation —Cont'd

Skin divers, **22:6.**

Unpaid wages or salaries due from Commonwealth, procedure, **29:32A.**

Weekly wage payment, treasurer exempting self or other public officer from requirements, **149:148.**

Warrants for payments, **7A:3, 10:10, 10:11, 29:18.**

Warrants for search, disposition of moneys seized, **276:3, 276:7.**

Warrants to assess tax for expenses of retirement system, issuance, **32:21.**

Waterfowl stamp fees, disposition, **131:11.**

Weeds and other aquatic nuisances, expenditure of municipal appropriations for control, **40:5.**

Weekly wage payments, treasurer exempting self or other public officer from requirements, **149:148.**

Wildlife fund, nongame, **10:35D.**

Wildlife sanctuaries, receipt of trust funds, **131:90.**

Witness fees, **3:38, 280:10.**

Workers' compensation.

See WORKERS' COMPENSATION.

STATE WALKING SUNDAY.

Observance, **6:15NN.**

STATEWIDE EMERGENCY TELECOMMUNICATIONS BOARD ACT, 6A:18B et seq.

STATIONARY ENGINEERS.

Mentally ill and retarded persons, exemption from civil service law and rules, **19:20, 19B:16.**

STATIONERY.

District attorney, stationery, **12:24.**

Executive council, **6:7.**

Flag, exception to law as to misuse, **264:6.**

Foreign corporations conducting certain businesses, **181:7.**

General Court, stationery, **3:36.**

Insurance.

Annual statements of life insurance company, disbursements listed, **175:25.**

Holding self out as insurance advisor, agent, broker, etc., **175:175, 175:177A.**

STATIONERY —Cont'd
Paper, generally.
　See PAPER AND PAPER
　　PRODUCTS.
State printing.
　General court, **3:36.**
　State officers and departments,
　　30:31.
State purchasing agent,
　letterhead, determination of
　uniform official style, **30:30A.**
Uniform style of letterheads on
　official stationery,
　determination, **30:30A.**

STATIONS AND DEPOTS.
Filling stations, **94:295B et seq.**
　See FILLING STATIONS.
Fire departments.
　Cable television in stations,
　　166A:5.
　Care of stations, **48:52.**
Highway safety stations for
　schoolchildren, **71:71A.**
Littering, **161:94A.**
Loitering, **161:95.**
Milk.
　See MILK AND MILK
　　PRODUCTS.
Parking.
　See PARKING AND PARKING
　　STATIONS.
Police.
　See POLICE.
Public transportation facilities,
　offenses on premises, **161:94A,
　161:95.**
Railroads, **160:128-160:131A.**
　See RAILROADS.
Spitting, **270:14, 270:15.**
Statewide branch banking, notice
　and hearing for establishment
　of branch offices or depots,
　167C:3.
Street railways.
　See STREET RAILWAYS.
Television stations.
　See COMMUNITY ANTENNA
　　TELEVISION SYSTEMS.
Terminals.
　See TERMINALS.

STATISTICS.
Credit Union Employees
　Retirement Association, Labor
　Statistics Bureau, **171:82.**
Credit unions, subscription for
　statistical services, **171:75.**
Criminal justice committee, duties,
　6:156.
Division of research and statistics
　in education department, **69:4.**

STATISTICS —Cont'd
Divorce statistics, **208:46.**
Employment security statistics,
　151A:44, 151A:46.
Health.
　See HEALTH AND HEALTH
　　DEPARTMENTS.
Industrial accident and accident
　reviewing board records,
　23E:6.
Insurance rates.
　See INSURANCE RATES AND
　　RATING ORGANIZATIONS.
Labor.
　See LABOR AND WORKFORCE
　　DEVELOPMENT.
Legislative research bureau,
　statistical research, **3:58, 3:59.**
Marine fish and fisheries, **130:21.**
Motor vehicle insurance rating
　bureau, employment, **26:8E.**
Publication, defined for purposes of
　depository library for
　Massachusetts state
　publications, **6:39.**
Public records, statistics, **4:7.**
Racial imbalance, school
　committees to submit
　statistics to commissioner,
　71:37D.
Rehabilitation commission may
　compile, if identity not
　disclosed, **6:84.**
Retirement and disability data
　system, **32:21.**
Street railways, tables of annual
　returns, **161:139.**
Telecommunications and energy
　department, appointment of
　statisticians, **25:7.**
Workers' compensation statistics,
　152:19.

**STATUE OF LIBERTY
　AWARENESS DAY.**
Holiday establishment, **6:12HH.**

STATUES.
Generally.
　See MONUMENTS.

**STATUTE OF DESCENT AND
　DISTRIBUTION, 190:1 et
　seq.**

**STATUTE OF FRAUDS, 259:1 et
　seq.**
Admissions by parties.
　Statute rendered inapplicable,
　　106:2-201.
Agreements not to be performed
　within year, **259:1.**
Attachment of property, statute of
　frauds as defense in action for
　dissolution of fraudulent
　attachment, **223:110.**

STATUTE OF FRAUDS —Cont'd
Bankruptcy, new promise after
　discharge, **259:3.**
Bidders on public contract, consent
　for imparting information,
　29:8B.
Brokers or finders or negotiation of
　loan or purchase, sale, or
　exchange of business,
　agreement to pay
　compensation for services,
　259:7.
Character of another,
　representations, **259:4.**
Commercial Code, general
　application, **106:1-206.**
Consent orders as to parties to
　action or proceeding, **231:72.**
Consideration need not be stated
　in writing, **259:2.**
Contracts required to be in
　writing, **259:1.**
Conveyance of land, requirement
　for writing, **183:3, 259:1.**
Corporate stock, contracts for sale
　or transfer, **259:6.**
Credit.
　Another's credit,
　　representations, **259:4.**
　Misrepresentation of ability to
　　pay or to obtain credit,
　　requirement of writing for
　　offense, **266:35.**
Debt or default of another,
　promises to answer, **259:1.**
Definitions, statutory construction
　of "written" and "in writing,"
　4:7.
Devise or bequest, promise, **259:5,
　259:5A.**
Dissolution of fraudulent
　attachment, statute of frauds
　as defense in action, **223:110.**
Executor or administrator
　assuming personal liability,
　259:1.
Federal obligations, contracts for
　sale or transfer, **259:6.**
Guaranty.
　As within requirements of
　　statute of frauds, **259:1.**
Insolvent debtor, new promise,
　259:3.
Insurance adviser's contract to be
　in writing, **175:177C.**
Interest at more than 6 percent,
　writing required for recovery,
　107:3.
Investment securities under
　commercial code, applicability,
　106:8-113.

STATUTE OF FRAUDS —Cont'd

Land contracts, **183:3, 259:1.**

Leases under Commercial Code, **106:2A-201.**

Limitations, new promise or acknowledgment tolling, **260:13.**

Marriage, agreements in consideration, **259:1.**

Memoranda, **259:1.**

Sale memorandum as satisfying, **106:2-201.**

Misrepresentation of ability to pay or to obtain credit, requirement of writing, **266:35.**

Municipal contracts, when required to be in writing, **43:29.**

Municipal obligations, contracts for sale or transfer, **259:6.**

New promise to pay, **259:3, 260:13.**

One year, contracts not to be performed within, **259:1.**

Parties to action or proceeding.

Admissions by parties. See within this heading, "Admissions by parties."

Consent orders, **231:72.**

Payment, statute of frauds rendered inapplicable, **106:2-201.**

Pleading, **106:2-201.**

Real estate, sale or conveyance of interest in, **183:3, 259:1.**

Revolving credit agreement required to be in writing, **255D:27.**

Sales contracts, application, **106:2-201, 259:1.**

Corporate stock, **259:6.**

Modification of contract, **106:2-209.**

"Or return" term of contract, **106:2-326.**

Retail installment sales extension agreement, necessity for writing, **255D:16.**

Signature, requirement, **259:1.**

State bonds or obligations, contracts for sale or transfer, **259:6.**

Stipulations, when writing required, **231:72.**

Stock, contracts for sale or transfer, **259:6.**

Trusts in land, necessity of writing, **203:1.**

Wills, agreement, **259:5, 259:5A.**

STATUTE OF FRAUDS —Cont'd

Year, agreements not to be performed within, **259:1.**

STATUTE OF LIMITATIONS, 260:1 et seq.

Abandoned, lost and unclaimed property, statute of limitations as affecting duty to report, **200A:7.**

Abatement.

Citation, limitation of time for taking, **228:5.**

Insurance cases, **175:99, 175:187A.**

Nonjoinder of party against whom action is barred, **260:17.**

Original action, time for new suit after abatement, **260:32.**

Tolling of limitation period by abatement of action, **175:187A.**

Absence from state.

Fiduciary sale of real estate, action or entry for recovery after, **204:22.**

Limitation of action based on right of entry for condition broken or possibility of reverter as affected, **260:31A.**

Nonresident defendants, **260:9.**

Trust beneficiaries, actions against trustees, **203:32, 203:35.**

Accident.

See ACCIDENT AND SICKNESS INSURANCE.

Accountants, actions against accounts, **260:4.**

Account current, action, **260:6.**

Acknowledgment of debt as affecting, **260:13.**

Joint obligor acknowledging, **260:15, 260:16.**

Mortgage debt, **260:33-260:35.**

Adoption of statute, **281:9.**

Advance payment, notice of statute of limitations to person receiving, **231:140B.**

Adverse possession, limitation on actions and possession, **260:21 et seq.**

Affidavit that mortgage is not satisfied as tolling statute, **260:33-260:35.**

Airport approach regulation, time for filing petition for damages occasioned, **90:40G.**

STATUTE OF LIMITATIONS —Cont'd

Anti-discrimination laws, limitation of civil actions, **151B:9.**

Antitrust laws, **93:13.**

Aqueduct companies, actions after dissolution, **165:21.**

Arbitration.

See ARBITRATION.

Architectural barriers board, actions, **22:13A.**

Arrest.

See ARREST.

Arrest of judgment, new action after, **260:32.**

Art, action for preservation, **260:2C.**

Asbestos removal, **260:2D.**

Assault and battery, **260:4.**

Assignees in insolvency, actions by and against, **260:4.**

Assurance fund, actions for compensation, **185:108.**

Attachment of property.

See ATTACHMENT OF PROPERTY.

Attorneys' fees paid by mortgagor or mortgagee, limitation of consumer protection actions involving, **260:5A.**

Automobile insurance.

Insurer's liability, limitation of action to reach, **260:4.**

Personal injury claims, **90:34M.**

Automobiles.

See MOTOR VEHICLES.

Back wages, actions based on new judicial interpretation of law, **260:4A.**

Banks.

See BANKS AND BANKING.

Billing practices, limitation of consumer protection actions involving, **260:5A.**

Bond, time for action.

Fireworks display, actions on bond, **148:41, 148:43.**

Guardian or conservator, time to sue, **205:35.**

Probate bonds, **260:11.**

Replevin bond, **247:18.**

Trustee process, dissolution, **246:67.**

Building restrictions, proceedings, **184:23A.**

Business schools, limitation of consumer protection actions involving, **260:5A.**

Certified public accountants, actions against accounts, **260:4.**

STATUTE OF LIMITATIONS
—Cont'd

Certiorari, time to apply, **249:4.**

Children.
See CHILDREN AND MINORS.

Citation requiring executor or administrator to appear in action, time limitation for taking, **228:5.**

Cities or towns, **60:80C, 260:2D, 260:4.**

Civil rights.
Discrimination. See within this heading, "Discrimination."

Civil service, **31:41, 31:42.**

Claims against Commonwealth.
See CLAIMS AGAINST COMMONWEALTH.

Claims against estates, **193:15, 197:9.**

Collection agencies, limitation of consumer protection actions to recover penalties, **260:5A.**

Commercial paper. **See within this heading, "Negotiable instruments."**

Commonwealth, **260:1, 260:3A, 260:4, 260:18.**
Absence from state. See within this heading, "Absence from state."
Buildings and property, **260:31A.**
Claims for unpaid wages and salaries, **29:32A.**
Condition broken or possibility of reverter, action based, **260:31A.**
Enforcement of unpaid checks, **29:32.**
Motor vehicles, tort actions arising out of operation, **260:4.**
Real property actions, **260:31.**

Concealment of facts, **260:4B, 260:12.**

Conditional sales, limitation of consumer protection actions involving, **260:5A.**

Conservation district supervisors, claims against, **21:21.**

Construction contracts and work, actions on contractor's bond, **30:39A, 149:29.**

Construction of limitation periods, **281:9.**

Consumer protection.
See CONSUMERS AND CONSUMER PROTECTION.

Contagious diseases, municipalities' recovery of expense, **111:116.**

STATUTE OF LIMITATIONS
—Cont'd

Contract actions, **260:1 et seq.**

Contracts.
Currency, introduction of Euro, **260:19A.**
Contribution among joint tortfeasors, enforcement of right, **231B:3.**

Conversion actions against sheriffs and the like, **260:4.**

Corporations.
Action to recover penalty, **277:64.**
Directors, officers, and agents, **156B:13, 156B:65, 164:6, 180:3.**
Take-over bids, **110C:9.**

Correctional institutions.
Prisoners. See within this heading, "Prisoners."

Correspondence schools, limitation of consumer protection actions involving, **260:5A.**

Counterclaims, limitation, **260:36.**

Counties.
Asbestos removal, **260:2D.**
Personal injuries or death, action, **260:4.**
Right of entry for condition broken or possibility of reverter, action based, **260:31A.**

Covenants or restrictions on land, enforcement, **184:23A, 184:27, 184:28.**

Credit transactions.
See CONSUMERS AND CONSUMER PROTECTION.

Criminal actions, **277:63.**

Criminal procedure.
See CRIMINAL PROCEDURE.

Damages.
See DAMAGES.

Dams or reservoirs, action for damages caused, **253:4.**

Daylight savings time, **4:10.**

Death.
Abatement on, new suit after, **260:32.**
Extension of time in case, **260:10.**
Fraudulent conveyance by decedent, **202:2.**
Wrongful death.
See WRONGFUL DEATH.

Debt.
Acknowledgment of debt. See within this heading, "Acknowledgment of debt as affecting."

STATUTE OF LIMITATIONS
—Cont'd

Debt —Cont'd
Limitation of consumer protection actions involving unreasonable collection, **260:5A.**
Nonprofit land conservation corporations, recovery of interest in loans, **260:21.**

Deed registers.
Registers and registries of deeds. See within this heading, "Registers and registries of deeds."

Deeds.
See DEEDS AND CONVEYANCES.

Deficiency on mortgage foreclosure, time to sue, **244:17A.**

Dentists, action against, **260:4.**

Disability, **260:7, 260:8, 260:31A-260:35.**
Discrimination against disabled or handicapped persons, **260:5B.**
Mortgage foreclosure as affected, **260:33.**

Discovery of cause of action, **260:12.**

Discrimination, **260:5B.**
Damages and injunctive relief on account, **151B:9.**
Fair employment practices, **149:105A, 260:5B.**
Sex, wage disparities based, **149:105A.**

Dismissal for failure to join parties defendant as affected, **260:17.**

Divorce and alimony, **208:4, 208:5, 208:6B.**

Dower, claiming, **189:16.**

Eminent domain action for damages, **79:19.**

Employment.
See LABOR AND WORKFORCE DEVELOPMENT.

Employment security.
Complaint as to violation, **151A:47.**
Refund of overpayment of contributions, action, **151A:18.**

Endorsements of payment, **260:14.**

Enemy aliens, **260:8.**

Entry, writs of.
Writ of entry. See within this heading, "Writ of entry."

Environmental impact reports, actions, **30:62H.**

STATUTE OF LIMITATIONS
—Cont'd

Estates tail, **260:29, 260:30.**
Estate tax liability, **62C:15, 62C:21, 62C:65.**
Excessive fees, actions to recover.
  Attorneys' fees, consumer protection actions involving, **260:5A.**
Execution.
  Fraudulent conveyance, **236:47.**
  Redemption suits, **236:39.**
  Trustee process. See within this heading, "Trustee process."
Executors.
  See EXECUTORS AND ADMINISTRATORS.
Extension of time, **260:7-260:10.**
Extradition, **276:20C, 276:20E.**
Fair educational practice proceedings, **151C:3.**
False claims against Commonwealth, **12:5K.**
False imprisonment, **260:4.**
Fees.
  Excessive fees. See within this heading, "Excessive fees, actions to recover."
Fee simple, long term lease treated, **184:19.**
Fiduciary.
  Executors.
    See EXECUTORS AND ADMINISTRATORS.
  Sale of land, limitation of action or entry for recovery after, **204:22.**
Fine or penalty, action to recover, **260:5, 260:5A.**
Fire insurance, **175:99.**
Fires, negligence in cases, **266:8.**
Fireworks manufacturers and exhibitors, action on bonds, **148:41, 148:43.**
Fish and game violations, **131:91.**
Foreclosure of mortgage.
  See MORTGAGE FORECLOSURE.
Foreign statutes as barring actions, **260:9.**
Forfeitures, actions to recover, **260:5.**
Fraudulent concealment of cause of action, **260:4B, 260:12.**
Fraudulent conveyances by deceased persons, **202:2.**
Garnishment.
  Trustee process. See within this heading, "Trustee process."
Gasoline dealer's action against supplier, limitation on bringing, **93E:8.**

STATUTE OF LIMITATIONS
—Cont'd

Hazardous waste insolvency fund, notice of civil action against licensee, **21C:19.**
Highways.
  See HIGHWAYS AND STREETS.
Hit and run accident cases, **260:4B.**
Home inspectors.
  Time for filing, **112:225.**
Hospitals and health care facilities, **260:4.**
  Lien, **111:70C.**
  Service corporations, actions against, **176A:8.**
Housing authorities, small claims against, **258:4.**
Identity of person liable for motor vehicle accident, concealment of as tolling limitations, **260:4B.**
Implied contracts, actions, **260:2.**
Improvements, action for damages arising out of, **260:28.**
Incest, **277:63.**
Income tax.
  See INCOME TAX.
Injunction as tolling, **175:187A.**
Insolvency matters, **260:4.**
Installment sales of motor vehicles, limitation of consumer protection actions involving, **260:5A.**
Insurance.
  See INSURANCE.
Insurance premium finance agencies.
  Consumer protection actions, **260:5A.**
  Recovery of finance charges, **255C:9.**
Insurance rates.
  See INSURANCE RATES AND RATING ORGANIZATIONS.
Insurance, reorganization of mutual companies.
  Actions commenced after filing of reorganization plan, **175:19L.**
  Actions on orders or transactions regarding conversion, **175:19L.**
Interest on money, **260:14, 260:21.**
Interruption of limitations.
  Tolling. See within this heading, "Tolling of limitations."
Joinder of parties defendant, limitation of actions as affecting dismissal for failure, **260:17.**

STATUTE OF LIMITATIONS
—Cont'd

Joint obligors.
  Acknowledgment by, **260:15, 260:16.**
  Action barred as to some, overruling of plea of nonjoinder, **260:17.**
  Payment on account by, **260:15, 260:16.**
Judgments.
  See JUDGMENTS, ORDERS, AND DECREES.
Labor.
  See LABOR AND WORKFORCE DEVELOPMENT.
Land court, compensation from consumer fund, **185:108.**
Land court department, appeals, **40A:17.**
Landlords, limitation of consumer protection actions involving, **260:5A.**
Legacy and succession tax lien, termination, **65:9.**
Letters of credit, **106:5-115.**
Libel actions, **260:4.**
Life insurance.
  See LIFE INSURANCE.
Loans.
  Debts. See within this heading, "Debt."
Local property taxes, actions for refunds or recoveries, **60:98.**
Long term lease treated as fee simple, reversion based, **184:19.**
Malpractice actions, **260:4.**
  Medical malpractice actions. See within this heading, "Medical malpractice actions."
Marine fisheries, actions and prosecutions under laws, **130:14.**
Marriage, **207:28, 207:57.**
Massachusetts College Student Loan Authority, civil actions against, **15C:22A.**
Mechanics' liens.
  See MECHANICS' LIENS.
Medical malpractice actions, **260:4.**
  Minors, claims, **231:60D.**
Mentally ill persons, actions, **260:7, 260:31A-260:35.**
Minimum fair wage law violations, **151:20A.**
Minors.
  See CHILDREN AND MINORS.
Morris plan banks, **172A:7A, 172A:8A.**

STATUTE OF LIMITATIONS
—Cont'd

Mortgage foreclosure.
See MORTGAGE
FORECLOSURE.
Mortgages.
See MORTGAGES AND DEEDS
OF TRUST.
Motions before trial, **277:47A.**
Motor vehicles.
See MOTOR VEHICLES.
Multi-level distribution companies,
limitation of consumer
protection actions involving,
260:5A.
Municipalities, actions against,
260:4.
Mutual current accounts, **260:6.**
Negotiable instruments, **106:3-118,
260:1, 260:13 to 260:17.**
Enforcement of unpaid checks,
actions by or against
Commonwealth, **29:32.**
Negotiable instruments. See
within this heading,
"Negotiable instruments."
New action, time, **260:32.**
New promise as affecting, **260:13,
260:15, 260:16.**
Nonprofit hospital service
corporation contract provision
as to time for bringing action,
176A:8.
Nonprofit land conservation
corporations, recovery of
interest in loans, **260:21.**
Nonresidents, actions against,
260:5B, 260:8, 260:9, 260:33.
Notes, actions, **260:1,
260:13-260:17.**
Notice.
Advance payment received by
plaintiff or claimant, statute
of limitations, **231:140B.**
Hazardous waste insolvency
fund, **21C:19.**
Novation as affecting, **260:13,
260:15, 260:16.**
Oil and hazardous material
release prevention and
response act, civil actions
under, **21E:11A.**
Optometrist, action against, **260:4.**
Overassessment or overpayment of
taxes, time to apply for
abatement, **62C:37.**
Parties defendant, limitation of
action as affecting dismissal
for failure to join, **260:17.**
Part payment, **260:14-260:16,
260:33-260:35.**

STATUTE OF LIMITATIONS
—Cont'd

Penalties, actions to recover,
260:5, 260:5A.
Personal injury actions,
260:2A-260:4, 260:4B.
Physicians and surgeons, actions
against.
Medical malpractice. See within
this heading, "Medical
malpractice actions."
Plaintiff or claimant receiving
advance payments, notice of
statute of limitations,
231:140B.
Pleading, **Civ Sec 8.**
Abatement, pleas, **260:17.**
Advance payment to tort
claimant, **231:140B.**
Nonjoinder, **260:17.**
Possibility of reverter, action
based, **260:31A.**
Pretermitted child's share, claim,
191:20.
Prisoners.
Actions by prisoners, **260:7.**
Escaping inmates of
Massachusetts training
schools, claims for damage,
120:13A.
Support, actions to recover,
260:1.
Probate, **197:9.**
Probate bond, **260:11.**
Promissory notes, actions, **260:1,
260:13-260:17.**
Public accountants, actions against
accounts, **260:4.**
Public officers.
See CLAIMS AGAINST
COMMONWEALTH.
Public works.
Action against city or town,
149:28.
Contractor's bond, action,
30:39A, 149:29.
Deficiency or neglect in design,
planning, construction, or
general administration of
improvement to real
property of public agency,
action for damages arising
out, **260:2B.**
Quieting title, **184:24.**
Railroads.
See RAILROADS.
Rape of child, **277:63.**
Real estate time-shares,
warranties, **183B:48.**
Real property actions, **260:21 et
seq.**

STATUTE OF LIMITATIONS
—Cont'd

Recognizance for debt, issue of
original execution, **256:8.**
Recording as affecting.
Condition broken, action based
on right of entry, **260:31A.**
Mortgage foreclosure,
260:33-260:35.
Possibility of reverter, action
based, **260:31A.**
Registers and registries of deeds.
See within this heading,
"Registers and registries of
deeds."
Redemption suits.
Execution, property taken or
sold, **236:39.**
Mortgage foreclosure.
See MORTGAGE
FORECLOSURE.
Registers and registries of deeds.
Defects, actions based on, as
limited to ten years after
recording, **184:24.**
Right of entry for condition
broken or possibility of
reverter as affected by
recording of claim, **260:31A.**
Religion and religious societies,
discrimination, **260:5B.**
Remainders and reversions, action
based on possibility of
reverter, **260:31A.**
Rents and profits, recovery on writ
of entry, **237:15.**
Repeal of statutes as affecting,
281:9.
Replevin, **247:18, 260:2A.**
Residential repair or remodeling
contracts, exculpatory
provisions, **143:90.**
Restraints of trade and
monopolies, **93:13.**
Retail installment sales and
service, limitation of consumer
protection actions involving,
260:5A.
Reversal, new action after, **260:32.**
Reverter, applicability to
Commonwealth of limitation
of actions based on possibility,
260:31A.
Scire facias proceedings against
person adjudged in trustee
process proceeding to be
trustee, **246:49.**
Sealed contracts, actions, **260:1.**
Service of process, new action
because of defects, **260:32.**
Sidewalk defects, actions
involving, **84:18.**

623

STATUTE OF LIMITATIONS
—Cont'd
Skiing injury, **143:71N, 143:71P.**
Slander actions, **260:4.**
Small loan businesses, limitation of consumer protection actions involving, **260:5A.**
Special limitations as controlling, **260:19.**
State.
Commonwealth. See within this heading, "Commonwealth."
Street railways.
Highway defect actions, **161:89.**
Labor and materials, actions, **159:100.**
Recovery of penalty for allowing sales by children upon cars, **161:97.**
Subdivision control law, **41:81Y.**
See ZONING AND PLANNING.
Summary process, **184:18.**
Possession of land, **239:8.**
Sundays, prosecution for penalties, **136:9.**
Suspension of limitations.
Tolling. See within this heading, "Tolling of limitations."
Take-over bids in acquisition of corporations, actions involving, **110C:9.**
Taxation.
Estate taxes, limitation period for collection, **62C:65.**
Income taxes, limitation on additional assessment, **62C:30.**
Legacy and succession tax lien, termination, **65:9.**
Local property taxes, actions for refunds or recoveries, **60:98.**
Motor vehicle excise tax, time to apply for abatement, **60A:2.**
Overassessment or overpayment of taxes, time to apply for abatement, **62C:37.**
Redemption from tax sale, **60:65, 60:69.**
Tax sales, **60:65, 60:69, 202:20.**
Telegraph company, negligence, **166:19.**
Tidelands, **260:31.**
Toilet facilities in industrial establishment, apportionment of expense of changing, **149:134.**
Tolling of limitations, **260:7-260:10, 260:28-260:35.**
Abatement of action, tolling of limitation period, **175:187A.**
Concealment, **260:4B, 260:12.**

STATUTE OF LIMITATIONS
—Cont'd
Tolling of limitations —Cont'd
Disabilities as affecting, **260:7, 260:8, 260:31A-260:35.**
Injunction, **175:187A.**
Tort actions, **260:2A-260:4, 260:4B.**
Towns or cities, actions against, **260:4.**
Trade schools, limitation of consumer protection actions involving, **260:5A.**
Training schools, claims for damage by escaping inmates, **120:13A.**
Trustee process.
Bonds to dissolve attachment, **246:67.**
Scire facias proceedings against person adjudged in trustee process proceedings to be trustee, **246:49.**
Trustees.
Actions against, **203:32, 203:35, 246:49, 260:11.**
Process.
Trustee process. See within this heading, "Trustee process."
Truth in lending, consumer protection actions involving credit disclosure, **260:5A.**
Unclaimed property, statute of limitations as affecting duty to report, **200A:7.**
Unemployment compensation.
Employment security. See within this heading, "Employment security."
Unfair trade practices, limitation of consumer protection actions involving, **260:5A.**
Uniform Securities Act, actions for civil liabilities, **110A:410.**
Wagers on horse or dog races, recovery of winning, **128A:5A.**
Wages, salaries.
See WAGES, SALARIES, AND COMPENSATION.
Wetlands laws, limitation of action against subsequent owner for preexisting violations, **131:40.**
Witnesses, action for penalty for false certification of fees and expenses, **262:62.**
Workers' compensation.
See WORKERS' COMPENSATION.
Writ of entry, **260:21 et seq.**
Action by remainderman or reversioner, **237:41.**

STATUTE OF LIMITATIONS
—Cont'd
Wrongful death, **260:10.**
See WRONGFUL DEATH.
Zoning.
See ZONING AND PLANNING.
STATUTE OF USES.
Language necessary to conveyance or devise, **183:14.**
STATUTES, 4:1 et seq.
Abatement.
See ABATEMENT, SURVIVAL, AND REVIVAL.
Acceptance, **4:4 et seq.**
Cities.
See CITIES AND TOWNS.
Civil service.
See CIVIL SERVICE.
Elections.
See ELECTIONS.
Form of question as to acceptance by cities and towns, **54:58A.**
Initiative and referendum. See within this heading, "Initiative and referendum."
Rescission of acceptance, **4:4B.**
Acknowledgments, **4:6.**
Construction, rules, **4:6.**
Federal government.
See FEDERAL GOVERNMENT AND STATUTES.
Amendments.
Corrections or amendments. See within this heading, "Corrections or amendments."
Bills.
See LEGISLATIVE BILLS AND RESOLVES.
Bylaws.
See ORDINANCES AND BYLAWS.
Carriers, special compilation by utilities commission of statutes, **25:8.**
Citation of general laws, **281:1.**
Cities.
Generally.
See CITIES AND TOWNS.
City and town clerks.
Finance.
Municipal finance. See within this heading, "Municipal finance."
Generally.
See CITY AND TOWN CLERKS.
Civil service.
See CIVIL SERVICE.

STATUTES —Cont'd
Constitution of Massachusetts.
    See CONSTITUTION OF
        MASSACHUSETTS.
Construction, **4:6-4:8.**
    See CONSTRUCTION OF
        STATUTES.
Continuous consolidation,
    3:51-3:55A.
Copies.
    Libraries, defacing copies of
        statutes, **266:99.**
    Original engrossed acts and
        resolutions, authorization
        where original illegible,
        3:23.
    Session laws, **5:3.**
Corporations, **155:1, 156:6, 175:30.**
Corrections or amendments,
    3:51-3:53, 3:55A.
    Drafting of amendments, **3:52.**
    Duties of counsel of senate and
        house, **3:53.**
    Duties of recodification counsel,
        3:55A.
    Pension and retirement system
        provisions, no loss of rights
        on amendment, **32:25.**
    Workers' compensation, **152:2A.**
Declaratory judgments.
    Construction of statute, **231A:2.**
    Purpose of statute authorizing,
        231A:9.
Deeds.
    See MORTGAGES AND DEEDS
        OF TRUST.
Definition of certain words when
    used, **4:6, 4:7.**
Distribution, **5:2-5:4.**
District court, distribution, **5:3.**
Districts, acceptance, **4:4.**
Documents of title article as
    subject, **106:7-103.**
Effect, **281:1-281:10.**
Effective date, **4:1, 281:1.**
    Rescission, **4:4B.**
    Sanitary code, **111:127A.**
    Uniform Commercial Code.
        See Appendix following Article
            9, Chapter 106.
Elections.
    See ELECTIONS.
Enacting clause, initiated
    measures, **4:3.**
Engrossment of bills and
    resolutions, **3:23.**
Former acts.
    Commercial code, **106:1-103.**
    Constitution of Massachusetts,
        continuation of former laws,
        **MA Const Part 2 Ch 6 Art
        6.**

STATUTES —Cont'd
Former acts —Cont'd
    General laws as continuation,
        281:2.
    Repeal. See within this heading,
        "Repeal."
General court, **3:1 et seq.**
General laws, **281:1 et seq.**
Housing and community
    development department,
    formulation of model housing
    and zoning codes, **23B:3.**
Incorporation of new laws in
    General laws, **3:51.**
Index, **3:51.**
Initiative and referendum.
    Acceptance by municipal
        corporation of statutes
        subject to petition, **4:1.**
    Revocation of acceptance, **4:4B.**
Insurance.
    See INSURANCE.
Judicial notice of laws of United
    States or other states, **233:70.**
Justices of the peace.
    Construction of statutes as to
        acknowledgment, rules, **4:6.**
    Distribution of statutes, **5:3.**
Keeping to date, **3:51.**
Legislative bills.
    See LEGISLATIVE BILLS AND
        RESOLVES.
Libraries and librarians.
    Defacing copies of statutes,
        266:99.
    Distribution to libraries, **5:3.**
    Public documents deposited in
        state library, **5:7.**
Liens.
    Mortgages.
        See MORTGAGES AND
            DEEDS OF TRUST.
    Tax liens. See within this
        heading, "Tax liens."
Marginal references as referring to
    general acts, **4:11.**
Marriage settlement or contract
    not invalidated by statute,
    209:13.
Mistake or error, correction of.
    Corrections or amendments. See
        within this heading,
        "Corrections or
        amendments."
Mittimus, when statement as to
    law on which conviction
    founded to accompany, **279:35.**
Morris plan banks, laws applicable
    or not applicable, **172A:3,
    172A:14.**
Mortgage foreclosure.
    See MORTGAGE
        FORECLOSURE.

STATUTES —Cont'd
Mortgages.
    See MORTGAGES AND DEEDS
        OF TRUST.
Municipal finance.
    Appropriations, **40:5.**
    Distribution of statutes, **5:3.**
    Indebtedness, authorization, **4:8,
        44:2, 44:15.**
Notice.
    Acceptance or rejection of
        optional statute by
        municipal corporation, **4:5.**
    Judicial notice of laws of United
        States or other states,
        233:70.
    Publication. See within this
        heading, "Publication."
Number of copies for distribution,
    5:3.
Officers and salaries not affected
    by repeals, **281:7, 281:8.**
Official act, definition, **268A:1.**
Ordinances.
    See ORDINANCES AND
        BYLAWS.
Original engrossed bills and
    resolutions, **3:23.**
Pamphlet edition of laws, **5:4.**
Pending criminal actions not
    affected, **281:6.**
Permit for discharge of sewage and
    waste, **21:43-21:46A.**
Prior statute.
    Former acts. See within this
        heading, "Former acts."
Probate court proceedings, law
    governing, **281:4.**
Proof, **233:75.**
Proposed statutes, submission to
    voters.
    See ELECTIONS.
Publication, **5:2.**
    City or town, no newspaper, **4:6.**
Recodification, **3:53, 3:55A.**
Reconsideration of legislation.
    See RECONSIDERATION OF
        LEGISLATION.
Referendum on.
    Initiative and referendum. See
        within this heading,
        "Initiative and referendum."
Repeal, **281:2-281:6.**
    Abatement.
        See ABATEMENT,
            SURVIVAL, AND
            REVIVAL.
    Acts done not affected, **281:4.**
    Commercial code.
        See COMMERCIAL CODE.
    Counsel for senate and house,
        duties, **3:53.**

STATUTES —Cont'd
Repeal —Cont'd
Criminal actions not affected, **281:6.**
Forfeitures not affected, **4:6, 281:5.**
Former acts not revived, **4:6, 281:3.**
Liabilities not affected, **281:4.**
Limitation of actions as affected, **281:9.**
Offenses previously committed as affected, **4:6.**
Penalties previously incurred as affected, **4:6, 281:5.**
Pension and retirement system provisions, no loss of rights, **32:25.**
Prior provisions not reviewed, **4:6, 281:3.**
Rights accrued or established not affected, **281:4.**
Salaries to continue after, **281:8.**
Sentence and punishment, repeal of statute as affecting, **281:5, 281:6.**
Tenure of office preserved despite, **281:7.**
Rescission by cities and towns of statutes previously accepted, **4:4B.**
Resolves.
See LEGISLATIVE BILLS AND RESOLVES.
Restrictions on rescission by cities or towns, **4:4B.**
Retrospective statutes, settlement of trust estates involving, **203:39.**
Revision of.
Corrections or amendments. See within this heading, "Corrections or amendments."
Revocation of acceptance of certain statutes, **4:4A, 4:4B.**
Sale, **5:3.**
Secretary of state, return to by cities and towns regarding acceptance of statutes, **4:5.**
Sentence and punishment.
Lack of statute, **279:4, 279:5.**
Repeal of statute as affecting, **281:5, 281:6.**
Session laws.
Copies, who is entitled, **5:3.**
Distribution, **5:3.**
Pamphlet editions, **5:4.**
Sale of copies, **5:3, 5:4.**
Severability, **4:6.**
Special.
See SPECIAL AND LOCAL LEGISLATION.

STATUTES —Cont'd
Special commissions to investigate and study, powers and duties, **4:2A.**
Special election for rescission of acceptance, **4:4B.**
State library, public documents deposited, **5:7.**
Statement as to law on which conviction founded to accompany mittimus, when, **279:35.**
Tables showing changes in general laws, printing and distribution, **5:2, 5:4A.**
Tax liens.
Collector's enforcement, ordinance directing, **60:87.**
Preventing enforcement, **60:37, 60:37A.**
Temporary acts not affected, **281:10.**
Time or date.
Effective date. See within this heading, "Effective date."
References to time, **4:10.**
Towns.
Generally.
See CITIES AND TOWNS.
Municipal finance. See within this heading, "Municipal finance."
Uniform acts.
See UNIFORM ACTS OR LAWS.
Waiver of statutory provisions regarding insurance, **175:22B.**

STATUTORY RAPE, 265:22A, 265:23.
Rape generally.
See RAPE.

STAY OR SUPERSEDEAS.
Agriculture commissioner, appeals, **128:25, 128:26.**
Alcoholic liquors.
See ALCOHOLIC LIQUORS.
Antitrust laws, **93:12.**
Arbitration, **251:2.**
Labor dispute.
See LABOR RELATIONS AND DISPUTES.
Automobiles.
Motor vehicles. See within this heading, "Motor vehicles."
Banks and banking, order to cease and desist unfair or deceitful consumer transaction practices, **167:2E.**
Building Code Appeals Board, appeal, **143:100.**
Capital cases.
See CAPITAL CASES.

STAY OR SUPERSEDEAS —Cont'd
Cases reported for determination by full court, **231:111 et seq.**
Child support hearing officers, orders or judgments, **221B:9.**
Clerk of trial court, stay of execution pending receipt of appellate transcript, **235:16.**
Costs of action.
Denial of relief from costs, stay pending appeal, **261:27D.**
Former action, stay for nonpayment of costs, **261:10.**
Criminal procedure, appeal as stay of proceedings, **279:4.**
Death sentence, stay, **279:4.**
Denial of relief from court costs, stays pending appeal, **261:27D.**
Divorce case, appeal as operating to stay running of nisi period, **215:24.**
Driver's license, effect of appeal or new trial motion on revocation, **266:28.**
Execution, **231:115.**
Capital cases.
See CAPITAL CASES.
Confessed judgment, stay of execution, **231:13A.**
Notice of appeal as affecting stay, **231:115.**
Transcript of appeal, stay of execution pending receipt by trial court clerk, **235:16.**
Transferability of causes, **211:4A.**
Fees and costs, appeal of award, **231:6G.**
Foreign states, stay of proceedings pending appeal in connection with money judgments, **235:23A.**
Former action, stay for nonpayment of costs, **261:10.**
Injunctions, **231:116, 249:9.**
Insolvent insurers, stay of proceedings against, **175D:15.**
Insurance, stay of proceedings, **175D:15, 176D:8.**
Labor relations.
See LABOR RELATIONS AND DISPUTES.
Money judgments of foreign states, stay of proceedings pending appeal, **235:23A.**
Motor vehicles.
Decisions of registrar, **90:28.**
Revocation of operator's license, effect of appeal or motion for new trial, **266:28.**

STAY OR SUPERSEDEAS
—Cont'd
Nonpayment of costs in former action, stay, **261:10.**
Other forum, stay on ground that action should be heard, **223A:5.**
Planning.
Zoning and planning. See within this heading, "Zoning and planning."
Pretrial diversion of selected offenders.
See PRETRIAL DIVERSION OF SELECTED OFFENDERS.
Private nuisances, abatement, **243:2.**
Public or subsidized housing, criminal activity by nonresidents, stay of action by landlord, **121B:32F.**
Railroad crossings, stay on appeal of certain proceedings, **160:111.**
Real estate brokers' or salesmen's license, stay of revocation or suspension pending appeal, **112:87BBB.**
Receivers and receiverships, **231:116.**
Registrar of motor vehicles, appeal from decisions, **90:28.**
Restraints of trade and monopolies, **93:12.**
Revocation of driver's license, effect of appeal or new trial motion, **266:28.**
Subdivision plans, effect of appeal from disapproval, **40:6.**
Subversive organization, adjudication, **264:18.**
Summary process to recover land.
See SUMMARY PROCESS TO RECOVER LAND.
Superior court, appeals, **231:97.**
Supreme judicial court.
Sentence, stay, **279:4.**
Transferability of causes, **211:4A.**
Telecommunications and energy department, effect of appeal, **25:5.**
Unfair insurance practices proceedings, pending appeal, **176D:8.**
Urban redevelopment corporations, appeals from project disapprovals, **121A:6C.**
Zoning and planning.
Disapproval of subdivision plan as affecting exemption of land from zoning law, **40:6.**

STAY OR SUPERSEDEAS
—Cont'd
Zoning and planning —Cont'd
Termination of rights pending appeal of plans, stay, **40A:6.**

STEALING.
Burglary.
See BURGLARY.
Larceny or theft.
See LARCENY AND THEFT.
Receiving stolen property.
See RECEIVING STOLEN PROPERTY.
Robbery.
See ROBBERY.

STEAM AND HOT WATER COMPANIES.
Boilers.
See STEAM BOILERS AND ENGINES.
Capital, amount, **158:3.**
Formation, **158:3.**
Highways, streets, and lanes, digging up and laying pipes, **40:43, 158:12-158:14.**
Municipal lighting.
See MUNICIPAL LIGHTING AND HEATING PLANTS.
Number of incorporators required, **158:3.**
Sales of steam exempt from tax, **64H:6.**
Sunday manufacture and distribution of steam, **136:6.**

STEAM BATHS, 140:51-140:53.

STEAMBOATS AND STEAMBOAT COMPANIES.
Alcoholic liquors, search warrant, **138:42.**
Arrests by police, **159:9, 159:93, 159:94.**
Attachment of steamboats, **223:43.**
Authority.
See STEAMSHIP AUTHORITY.
Badges of steamboat police, **159:92.**
Bonds, guaranty by railroad corporations, **160:66.**
Bylaws of relief corporations, **159:87.**
Civil rights and racial discrimination, **272:92A, 272:98.**
Disorderly or annoying conduct in steamboat, **272:43, 272:43A.**
District court's jurisdiction of persons arrested by police, **159:94.**

STEAMBOATS AND STEAMBOAT COMPANIES
—Cont'd
Employees.
Fines and penalties, employees' relief corporation's failure to allow examination of books, **159:87.**
Influencing employment or discharge, **271:40, 271:41.**
Overtime pay, **151:1A.**
Relief corporations, employees may form, **159:86.**
Evidence.
Police officers. See within this heading, "Police officers."
Examination of books of employees' relief corporation, refusal to allow, **159:87.**
Expectoration in steamboats, **270:14, 270:15.**
Express business, engaging, **159:9.**
Fare, arrest for failure to pay, **159:93, 159:94.**
Fee for license, **140:192.**
Filing and recording.
Records. See within this heading, "Records, reports, and returns."
Fines and penalties.
Employees' relief corporation's failure to allow examination of books, **159:87.**
Negligence in operation, **265:30.**
Removal from employment, improperly influencing, **271:40, 271:41.**
Unlicensed operation, **140:193.**
Foreign countries, purchase or lease of corporations to operate, **160:250.**
Gambling on steamboats, **271:2.**
Labor and employment.
Employees. See within this heading, "Employees."
Licenses, **140:191, 140:192.**
Misconduct of police, tort liability, **159:95.**
Negligent operation of steamboats, **265:30.**
Penalties.
Fines and penalties. See within this heading, "Fines and penalties."
Police officers, **159:92-159:95.**
Arrests, **159:93, 159:94.**
Badges, **159:92.**
Compensation, **159:95.**
Duties, **159:94.**
Evidence.
Badge as evidence of being on duty, **159:92.**

STEAMBOATS AND STEAMBOAT COMPANIES —Cont'd

Police officers —Cont'd
  Jurisdiction of persons arrested, **159:94.**
  Petition of water carriers of passengers, officers appointed, **22:9M.**
  Powers, **159:93.**
  State police as steamboat police, **22C:51, 22C:52.**
  Telecommunications and energy department. See within this heading, "Telecommunications and energy department."
  Tort liability for misconduct, **159:95.**
Posting of license, **140:192.**
Racial discrimination, **272:92A, 272:98.**
Railroads.
  Guaranty of bonds, **160:66.**
  Operation, **160:70A.**
  Purchase or lease of corporations to operate in foreign countries, **160:250.**
  Through routes, **159:21.**
Records, reports, and returns.
  Police officers. See within this heading, "Police officers."
  Relief corporation, **159:87.**
Relief corporations, **159:86-159:88.**
  Bylaws, **159:87.**
  Employees may form, **159:86.**
  Fine for failure to allow examination of books, **159:87.**
  Purposes, **159:86.**
  Reports and returns, **159:87.**
  Telecommunications and energy department, powers, **159:87.**
Removal from employment, improperly influencing, **271:40, 271:41.**
Search warrant for alcoholic liquor, **138:42.**
Smoking on steamboats, **272:43A.**
Spitting, **270:14, 270:15.**
State police as steamboat police, **22C:51, 22C:52.**
Telecommunications and energy department.
  Relief corporations, powers and duties, **159:87.**
Through routes with railroads, **159:21.**
Tort liability for misconduct of police, **159:95.**
Warrant, arrests by steamboat police without warrant, **159:93, 159:94.**

STEAMBOATS AND STEAMBOAT COMPANIES —Cont'd

Wharves, piers, and docks, steamboat police, **159:93.**
Wild birds, penalty for use in taking, **131:65.**

STEAM BOILERS AND ENGINES, 140:115 et seq., 146:1 et seq.

Abatement as nuisance, **140:119.**
Administration, commissioner.
  Appeal from denial of inspector's certificate, determination of fee, **146:63.**
  Boiler inspectors' certificates, determination of fee, **146:62.**
  Inspectors' certificates, determination of fee for replacement, **146:59.**
  License application fee, determination, **146:60.**
Agricultural and horticultural purposes.
  Exemption from annual inspection, **146:7.**
  Licensing exception as to use, **146:46, 146:51.**
Aldermen and selectmen.
  Abatement of steam engines as common nuisance, **140:119.**
  Alteration and regulation of steam engines, **140:116.**
  Licensing powers, **140:115.**
Alterations to conform to law, **140:116.**
American Society of Mechanical Engineers Code, determination of minimum safety valve relieving capacity, **146:48.**
Ammonia compressors, **146:42-146:45.**
  See AMMONIA COMPRESSORS.
Apartment houses, licensing exception, **146:46, 146:51.**
Appeal and review.
  Certificate of competency, **146:63.**
  Engineer's or fireman's license, **146:66.**
  Refusal or revocation of license or certificate, appeal of orders, **140:117.**
Appliances.
  Safety appliances and devices. See within this heading, "Safety appliances and devices."

STEAM BOILERS AND ENGINES —Cont'd

Appropriations for investigations and apparatus, **146:69.**
Attendance of boiler, definitions, **146:46.**
Attorney general to assist board in framing rules, **146:2.**
Board of boiler rules of public safety department, **22:10, 146:2-146:4.**
  Ammonia compressors.
    See AMMONIA COMPRESSORS.
  Appointment of persons, **22:10.**
  Changes in rules.
    Hearings, **146:3.**
    Time of taking effect, **146:4.**
  Classification of state offices and positions, **30:50.**
  Compensation of members, **22:10.**
  Compressed air tanks, rules, **146:35.**
  Duties, **146:2-146:4.**
  Enforcement, **146:5.**
  Inspectors and chiefs of inspectors as members, **22:10.**
  Insurance on boiler not conforming, **146:26.**
  Refrigeration and air conditioning systems, adoption of rules and regulations, **146:45A.**
Board of examiners, **146:61.**
Boiler, defined, **146:1.**
Boiler rules, board of.
  Board of boiler rules. See within this heading, "Board of boiler rules of public safety department."
Buildings, erection near, **140:118.**
Cancellations.
  Insurance and insurance companies. See within this heading, "Insurance and insurance companies."
Certificates and certification, **146:62, 146:79.**
  Appeal from revocation or refusal, **146:63.**
  Applicant may have person present, **146:58.**
  Boiler inspector for insurance company must hold, **146:14, 146:15.**
  Contents, **146:27.**
  Examination of applicants, **146:56, 146:61.**

STEAM BOILERS AND ENGINES —Cont'd

Certificates and certification —Cont'd

Expiration or cancellation of insurance, operation prohibited until certificate issued, **146:30, 146:33.**

Fee, **146:60.**

Form prescribed by board, **146:2.**

Insurance of boiler upon which certificate not previously issued, **146:26.**

Issuance or withholding, **146:23, 146:71, 146:76.**

Insurance company, **146:16, 146:25.**

Lost or destroyed certificate, **146:59.**

Noncertificated insurance inspector, issuance, **146:76.**

Operation without, **146:8, 146:23-146:27, 146:30, 146:33.**

Penalties, **146:16, 146:33.**

Placing, **146:8, 146:27, 146:33.**

Revocation or suspension, **146:59.**

Chief of inspectors as member of board of boiler rules, **22:10.**

Cities and towns, purchase of energy management services, **40:4.**

Civil service exemptions, mental health department stationary engineers and firemen, **19:30.**

Cleaning while engine running, **149:127.**

Condition of boiler, daily record, **146:51, 146:55.**

Construction.

Buildings, erection near, **140:118.**

Changes ordered by local authorities, **140:116.**

Illegal erection or use of boilers as nuisance, **140:119.**

Rules prescribed by board, **146:2.**

Types not covered by rules, **146:4.**

Daily record of condition and repairs to boiler, **146:51, 146:55.**

Defacing inspection number or tag, **146:24, 146:33.**

Defects in boiler, notice, **146:29, 146:33.**

Definitions, **146:1.**

STEAM BOILERS AND ENGINES —Cont'd

Devices.

Safety appliances and devices. See within this heading, "Safety appliances and devices."

Division of inspection, enforcement of rules, **146:5.**

Dwellings and dwelling houses.

Exemption from annual inspection, **146:7.**

Licensing exception, **146:46, 146:51.**

Engineers and operators.

Licenses and permits. See within this heading, "Licenses and permits."

Entry into land and premises for inspection, **146:5, 146:32, 146:33.**

Erection.

Construction. See within this heading, "Construction."

Evidence of operation by unlicensed person, **146:47.**

Examinations.

Fees. See within this heading, "Fees."

Inspections and inspectors. See within this heading, "Inspections and inspectors."

Licenses and permits. See within this heading, "Licenses and permits."

Tests and testing. See within this heading, "Tests and testing."

Federal government.

United States. See within this heading, "United States."

Fees.

Appeal from refusal to grant certificate of competency, **146:63.**

Certificate of competency, examination, **146:60.**

Compressed air tanks, advance payment of fees for inspection, **146:40.**

Engineer's or fireman's license, examination, **146:57.**

Inspection fees, **146:22, 146:40, 146:71.**

New certificate of competency, **146:59.**

Reexamination, **146:62.**

Renewal license of engineers and firemen, **146:67.**

Fines, penalties, and forfeitures.

Engineer's and fireman's licenses, violations, **146:55.**

STEAM BOILERS AND ENGINES —Cont'd

Fines, penalties, and forfeitures —Cont'd

Rules and regulations of board, violation, **146:33.**

Fire engines exempt from annual inspections, **146:7.**

Fire insurance policies, inclusion of boiler liability coverage, **175:102A.**

Firemen.

Licenses and permits. See within this heading, "Licenses and permits."

Forest fires, spark arresters required to prevent, **48:21, 48:22.**

Forfeitures.

Fines, penalties, and forfeitures. See within this heading, "Fines, penalties, and forfeitures."

Form of certificate of inspection prescribed by board, **146:2.**

Hearings on changes in rules, **146:3.**

Horsepower.

Determination, **146:48.**

Exemption from annual inspection, basis, **146:7.**

Licensing exceptions as basis, **146:46, 146:51.**

Horticultural uses.

Agricultural and horticultural purposes. See within this heading, "Agricultural and horticultural purposes."

Hot water heating boilers, **146:70-146:80.**

See HOT WATER HEATING BOILERS.

Hydrostatic pressure test, **146:31.**

Inflammable fluids in tanks, **148:23.**

Injunction against use pending appeal, **140:117.**

Inspections and inspectors, **146:5 et seq.**

American Society of Mechanical Engineers, boilers and pressure vessel code, **146:70.**

Annual inspection, **146:6, 146:7.**

Appropriations for apparatus, **146:69.**

Board of boiler rules, authority, **22:10, 146:70-146:79.**

Defective or dangerous boilers, operation, **146:78.**

Definitions, **146:1.**

Designs not covered by rules, approval, **146:70.**

STEAM BOILERS AND ENGINES —Cont'd

Inspections and inspectors —Cont'd

Division inspection and inspectors, **146:13, 146:17.**

Duties of inspectors, **146:11.**

Emergency, exemption from inspection requirements during, **146:7.**

Enforcement of rules, **146:5.**

Entry of premises, **146:5.**

Excessive pressures, operation, **146:71.**

Exemptions from annual inspection, **146:7.**

Extension of time, **146:6.**

Fees for inspection, **146:22, 146:40, 146:71.**

Fines and penalties, **146:33, 146:80.**

First inspections, **146:70.**

Hindering inspectors, **146:32, 146:33.**

Hydrostatic pressure test, **146:31, 146:72.**

Identification number, **146:71.**

Insurance companies.

Certificate of inspection issued, **146:16, 146:25.**

First inspection, **146:26.**

Inspections, **146:13.**

Inspector for, certificate of competency, **146:14-146:16, 146:33, 146:73, 146:75.**

Reinsurance of boilers and pressure vessels upon inspection, **146:14.**

Reports of inspections, **146:18, 146:33.**

Notice to prepare for inspection, **146:78.**

Numbering of inspected boilers, **146:24.**

Operation without inspection, **146:8, 146:23-146:27, 146:30, 146:71.**

Other states, inspections, **146:13.**

Persons authorized to inspect, **146:13, 146:14, 146:73.**

Pipes subject to inspection, **146:70.**

Preparation of boiler, **146:21.**

Qualifications of inspectors, **146:13, 146:14, 146:73.**

Reexamination of inspectors, **146:62.**

Rules prescribed by board, **146:2.**

STEAM BOILERS AND ENGINES —Cont'd

Inspections and inspectors —Cont'd

Safety appliances and devices. See within this heading, "Safety appliances and devices."

Stamping of inspected boilers, **146:24.**

Tagging of inspected boilers, **146:24.**

Installation, rules prescribed by board, **146:2.**

Insurance and insurance companies.

Cancellations.

Boiler not to be operated, **146:30, 146:33.**

Report by company, **146:19, 146:33.**

Expiration of, boiler not to be operated, **146:30, 146:33.**

Fire insurance policies, inclusion of boiler liability coverage, **175:102A.**

Inspections and inspectors. See within this heading, "Inspections and inspectors."

Issuance of policies by mutual companies, **175:92.**

License may be revoked for issuing improper certificate of inspection, **146:16.**

Limit of single risk, **175:21.**

Nonconforming boilers barred, **146:26.**

Notice of expiration or cancellation, **146:78.**

Powers of mutual companies, **175:55.**

Purposes or kinds of insurance, **175:47, 175:92.**

Rates, **175A:1 seq.**

See INSURANCE RATES AND RATING ORGANIZATIONS.

Refusal of, report by company, **146:19, 146:33.**

Reinsurance as prerequisite, **175:92.**

Reports and returns.

Cancellation or refusal of insurance, **146:19, 146:33.**

Inspections, **146:10, 146:18, 146:33, 146:73, 146:75.**

Representative of company employing applicant for certificate of competency to accompany applicant upon examination, **146:58.**

STEAM BOILERS AND ENGINES —Cont'd

Insurance and insurance companies —Cont'd

Term of policy, **175:117.**

Investigations.

Inspections and inspectors. See within this heading, "Inspections and inspectors."

Knowledge.

Notice and knowledge. See within this heading, "Notice and knowledge."

Licenses and permits, **140:115-140:119.**

Classification of licenses, **146:49.**

Continuing education, **146:49.**

Engineers and firemen, **146:46 et seq.**

Appeal from suspension, revocation, or failure to grant license, **146:66.**

Applications, **146:57, 146:64.**

Chemical engineers, **146:50.**

Classification of licenses, **146:49.**

Electrical engineers, **146:50.**

Examinations, **146:50, 146:50A, 146:56, 146:58, 146:64.**

Expiration of license, **146:67.**

Fee, **146:57.**

Lost or destroyed license, **146:59.**

Nuclear steam power plant operators and engineers, **146:50A.**

Posting of license, **146:51, 146:55.**

Qualifications, **146:49, 146:50.**

Renewal license, fee, **146:67.**

Revocation or suspension of license, **146:59, 146:66.**

Special licenses, **146:49, 146:64.**

Examinations.

Applicants, **146:64.**

Engineers and firemen, **146:50, 146:50A, 146:56, 146:58, 146:64.**

Nuclear steam power plant operators and engineers, **146:50A.**

Technicians, **146:67A.**

Inspectors, **146:60.**

Insurance company license, certificate of inspection issued, **146:16, 146:25.**

Number of steam plants authorized to operate, **146:49.**

**STEAM BOILERS AND
ENGINES** —Cont'd
Licenses and permits —Cont'd
Qualifications for license,
146:50.
Unlicensed person, operation,
146:46, 146:47, 146:55.
Manufacturer of type not covered
by rules, **146:4.**
Manufacturing establishments,
146:46, 149:124, 149:125.
Mental health department
stationary engineers and
firemen, civil service
exemptions, **19:30.**
Mentally ill and retarded persons,
steam firemen exempt from
civil service law and rules,
19:20, 19B:16.
Minors, employment, **149:61,
149:78.**
Motor vehicles.
Exemption from annual
inspections, **146:7.**
Licensing exception, **146:46.**
Notice and knowledge.
Change to conform to law,
notice, **140:116.**
Defects in boilers, **146:29,
146:33.**
Insurance on boiler not
previously inspected,
146:26.
Nuclear power plants.
See ATOMIC ENERGY.
Nuisances, **140:116.**
Abatement, **140:119.**
Appeal from order adjudging
engine, **140:117.**
Illegal erection or use, **140:119.**
Injunction, **140:117.**
Numbering inspected boilers,
146:24.
Operation.
Expiration or cancellation of
insurance, **146:30, 146:33.**
Inspector of division may forbid,
146:21, 146:33.
Licenses and permits. See
within this heading,
"Licenses and permits."
Prohibited without inspection
and certificate of inspection,
**146:8, 146:23-146:27,
146:30, 146:33.**
Safe pressure, **146:9, 146:33.**
Operators.
Licenses and permits. See
within this heading,
"Licenses and permits."

**STEAM BOILERS AND
ENGINES** —Cont'd
Penalties.
Fines, penalties, and forfeitures.
See within this heading,
"Fines, penalties, and
forfeitures."
Permits.
Licenses and permits. See
within this heading,
"Licenses and permits."
Petitions for changes in rules,
146:3.
Pressure.
Certificate of inspection to state
maximum, **146:23, 146:25.**
Hydrostatic test, **146:31.**
Inspector, duties, **146:11.**
Operation under excessive
pressure, **146:9, 146:33.**
Rules for ascertaining safe
working pressure prescribed
by board, **146:2.**
Pressure vessels, **146:1 et seq.**
Prima facie evidence of operation
by unlicensed person, **146:47.**
Public buildings, prohibition
against erection near, **140:118.**
Public safety department.
Board of boiler rules. See within
this heading, "Board of
boiler rules of public safety
department."
Member of steam plants which
engineers or firemen may
supervise, **146:49.**
Official of, inspection, **146:6.**
Rules transmitted to
commissioner of public
safety, **146:2.**
Technicians, examination for
certification, **146:67A.**
Qualifications.
Engineers and firemen, **146:49,
146:50.**
Inspectors, **146:13, 146:14.**
Records and reports.
Daily record of condition and
repairs, **146:51, 146:55.**
Inspectors of division, **146:17.**
Insurance and insurance
companies. See within this
heading, "Insurance and
insurance companies."
Uninsured boiler, report, **146:10.**
Removal.
Inspection number or tag,
146:24, 146:33.
Safety appliances, **146:12,
146:33.**
Repairs, daily record, **146:51,
146:55.**

**STEAM BOILERS AND
ENGINES** —Cont'd
Reports.
Records and reports. See within
this heading, "Records and
reports."
Review.
Appeal and review. See within
this heading, "Appeal and
review."
Rules board.
Board of boiler rules. See within
this heading, "Board of
boiler rules of public safety
department."
Safety appliances and devices.
Heating, boilers, **146:20, 146:33.**
Inspection, **146:11.**
Minimum relieving capacity,
determination, **146:48.**
Operation without, **146:9.**
Overloading, **146:12, 146:33.**
Relief valve, loading, **146:74.**
Requirements, **146:71.**
Rules regulating construction
and size of, formulated by
board, **146:2.**
Tampering with or removing,
146:12, 146:33, 146:74.
Valves, inspection, **146:11.**
Selectmen.
Aldermen and selectmen. See
within this heading,
"Aldermen and selectmen."
Stamping inspected boilers,
146:24.
State secretary, rules filed, **146:2.**
Students, operation of boilers,
146:50.
Superior court, appeals, **140:117.**
Supervise, regulating number of
steam plants that engineers
and firemen may, **146:49.**
Tagging inspected boilers, **146:24.**
Tampering with safety appliances,
146:12, 146:33.
Tests and testing.
Hydrostatic pressure, **146:31.**
Inspections and inspectors. See
within this heading,
"Inspections and inspectors."
Licenses and permits. See
within this heading,
"Licenses and permits."
Qualities of materials prescribed
by board, **146:2.**
Uninsured boilers, report, **146:10,
146:33.**
United States.
Exemption from annual
inspection, **146:7.**

STEAM BOILERS AND ENGINES —Cont'd

United States —Cont'd

Licensing exception, **146:46, 146:51.**

Unlawful use as common nuisance, **140:119.**

Unlicensed persons, operation, **146:46, 146:47, 146:55.**

Withholding of certificates.

Certificates and certification. See within this heading, "Certificates and certification."

Work done on boilers, daily record, **146:51, 146:55.**

STEAM PIPES.

Highways and streets, permit to lay, **40:43.**

STEAM ROAD ROLLERS.

Spark arresters required on, when, **48:21, 48:22.**

STEAM SAWMILLS.

Spark arresters required on, when, **48:21, 48:22.**

STEAMSHIP AUTHORITY, Spec L 77:1-Spec L 77:20.

Abolition of New Bedford, Woods Hole, Martha's Vineyard and Nantucket Steamship Authority, **Spec L 77:16.**

Action to enforce bondholders' rights, **Spec L 77:12.**

Advisory board for finance, **Spec L 77:14.**

Assets of New Bedford, Woods Hole, Martha's Vineyard and Nantucket Steamship Authority, transfer, **Spec L 77:16.**

Bidding on contracts, **Spec L 77:15.**

Board of advisors for finance, **Spec L 77:14.**

Bonds and notes.

Investment, eligibility, **Spec L 77:11.**

Steamship bonds, **Spec L 77:5.**

Certification of amount as reimbursement, **58:25B.**

Changes in schedule, notice, **Spec L 77:15A.**

Commonwealth.

Contracts for reimbursement, **Spec L 77:9A.**

Credit not pledged, **Spec L 77:2.**

Conflicts of interest, penalty, **Spec L 77:15.**

Constitutional construction, **Spec L 77:18.**

STEAMSHIP AUTHORITY —Cont'd

Construction of Act, **Spec L 77:17, 77:18.**

Contracts.

Bidding procedure, **Spec L 77:15.**

Conflicts of interest, **Spec L 77:15.**

Reimbursement, contracts with Commonwealth for reimbursement, **Spec L 77:9A.**

Date, effective date of law, **Spec L 77:20.**

Effective date, **Spec L 77:20.**

Eligibility for investment, bonds, **Spec L 77:11.**

Equity action to enforce bondholders' rights, **Spec L 77:12.**

Exemption from taxation, **Spec L 77:6.**

Finance advisory board, **Spec L 77:14.**

Governing law, Act, **Spec L 77:19.**

Grant of powers, **Spec L 77:4.**

Hearings on each island, **Spec L 77:15B.**

Inconsistent laws inapplicable, **Spec L 77:19.**

Indemnification, **Spec L 77:15.**

Interpretation of Act, **Spec L 77:17, 77:18.**

Investment, bonds eligible, **Spec L 77:11.**

Labor and labor relations, strike interrupting service, **Spec L 77:15.**

Liberal construction of Act, **Spec L 77:17.**

Mandamus to enforce bondholders' rights, **Spec L 77:12.**

New Bedford, Woods Hole, Martha's Vineyard and Nantucket Steamship Authority, abolition and transfer of assets, **Spec L 77:16.**

Notice of schedule changes, **Spec L 77:15A.**

Pledge of credit by Commonwealth, **Spec L 77:2.**

Powers, **Spec L 77:4.**

Publication of announcement for bids on contracts, **Spec L 77:15.**

Reimbursement.

Certification of amount as reimbursement for mass transportation facilities and services, **58:25B.**

STEAMSHIP AUTHORITY —Cont'd

Reimbursement —Cont'd

Contracts with Commonwealth, **Spec L 77:9A.**

Remedies, **Spec L 77:12.**

Reports, **Spec L 77:13.**

Revenues, **Spec L 77:9.**

Schedule changes, notice, **Spec L 77:15A.**

Steamship bonds, **Spec L 77:5.**

Strikes, interruption of service, **Spec L 77:15.**

Suit to enforce bondholders' rights, **Spec L 77:12.**

Taxation, exemption, **Spec L 77:6.**

Transfer of assets of New Bedford, Woods Hole, Martha's Vineyard and Nantucket Steamship Authority, **Spec L 77:16.**

Trusts.

Agreement, **Spec L 77:8.**

Funds, **Spec L 77:10.**

Woods Hole Steamship Authority.

Certification of amount as reimbursement for mass transportation facilities and services, **58:25B.**

STEAM SHOVELS.

Spark arresters required on, when, **48:21, 48:22.**

STEAM TRACTORS.

Spark arresters required on, when, **48:21, 48:22.**

STEEL FOUNDRIES.

Buildings used for industrial purposes, **149:1.**

Toilet facilities, **149:137.**

STEEL PLATES.

State secretary's custody of plates owned by Commonwealth, **9:13.**

STEELYARDS.

Use, permissibility, **98:8.**

STENOGRAPHERS.

Banks, record of investigative hearing of consumer transactions, **167:2C.**

Court stenographers, **221:82-221:91C.**

See COURT STENOGRAPHERS.

District attorneys, employment of persons for clerical or stenographic work, **12:19, 12:22.**

Farmer-winery license, hearing, **138:19B.**

STENOGRAPHERS —Cont'd

General court, reports of hearings,
3:29.

Governor, **6:6, 6:6A.**

Grand jury, **221:86.**

Defendant's own stenographer,
presence at proceedings,
221:91B.

Hearing on certification of
teachers, **71:38G.**

Medical depositions, stenographic
service expense, **233:24A.**

State ballot law commission
proceedings, **55B:3.**

Transcripts.
See COURT
STENOGRAPHERS.

Wages, salaries, and compensation.
Court stenographers.
See COURT
STENOGRAPHERS.

Governor, stenographers, **6:6,
6:6A.**

State ballot commission
members, **55B:3.**

STEPCHILDREN.
See CHILDREN AND MINORS.

**STEPHEN L. FRENCH
FORESTRY CAMP.**

Institutional service bureau of
youth service department to
operate, **18A:8.**

STEP-IN-RANGE.

County employees, salary range,
35:51A.

State positions, salary range,
30:45, 30:46.

STEREOTYPE PLATES.

Custody of Commonwealth plates,
9:13.

STERILIZATION.

Bedding and upholstered
furniture, **94:273.**
See BEDDING AND
UPHOLSTERED
FURNITURE.

Consent.
Minor as authorized to consent,
112:12F.

Physician to obtain written
consent, **112:12W.**

Hospitals and health care
facilities.
Furniture, sterilization before
reuse, **94:273.**

Refusal of private hospital to
admit patient for
sterilization, **272:21B.**

STERILIZATION —Cont'd

Minor as authorized to consent,
112:12F.

Physicians and surgeons.
Refusal to perform on moral or
religious grounds, **112:12I.**

Written consent necessary before
performing, **112:12W.**

Privately controlled hospital or
health care facility, effect of
refusal to admit patient for
purpose, **272:21B.**

Shelter animals, mandatory
sterilization, **140:136A,
140:139A.**

STERLING.

Congressional district, **57:1.**

District court, **218:1.**

Medical examiner district, **38:1.**

Senatorial district, **57:3.**

STEVEDORES.
**See LONGSHORE AND
WATERFRONT
EMPLOYMENT.**

STEWARDS.

Civil service appointments, **31:49.**

Horse and dog racing meetings,
128A:7, 271:39.

STICKLEBACKS.

Taking for bait, **131:52.**

STILETTO.

Carrying as criminal offense,
269:10.

STILLBORN CHILDREN.
See FETAL DEATH.

STILTS.

Prohibition as to use in
construction work, **149:129B.**

STIMULANTS.
See DRUGS AND NARCOTICS.

STIPENDS.
**See WAGES, SALARIES, AND
COMPENSATION.**

STIPULATIONS.

Administrative procedure, **30A:10.**

Amendments, **231:72.**

Antitrust laws, **93:8.**

Appellate division.
Inferences from cases stated by
agreement of parties,
appellate division's power to
draw, **231:110.**

Reporting of cases to appellate
division on agreement of
parties, **231:111, 231:112.**

Civil actions, agreements between
parties in, **231:82.**

STIPULATIONS —Cont'd

Deeds from Commonwealth,
enforcement of stipulations,
91:37.

Discrimination based on color,
prohibition against
stipulations, **175:122.**

Dismissal of action, **232A:2.**

Eminent domain proceedings,
apportionment of taxes,
79:35A.

Entry of orders pursuant, **231:72.**

Fire insurance policy, standard
form, **175:99.**

Insurance.
Fire policy, standard form,
175:99.

Void provisions of policy, **175:22.**

Registration of land titles,
stipulations on withdrawal of
petition, **185:44.**

Reporting of cases to appellate
division on agreement of
parties, **231:111, 231:112.**

Restraints of trade and
monopolies, **93:8.**

Tender, stipulation of dismissal
upon acceptance, **232A:2.**

Trial, stipulations as to site of
trial, **231:82.**

Void provisions of insurance policy,
175:22.

Writing, when required, **231:72.**

STOCK BONUS PLAN.

Adjusted gross income as affected
by employer contributions to
stock bonus plan, **62:2.**

Deductible item from gross
income, **62:2.**

Exemptions from income tax, **62:5.**

Income tax, **62:2, 62:5.**

STOCKBRIDGE.

District court, **218:1.**

Medical examiner district, **38:1.**

Senatorial district, **57:3.**

STOCK COMPANIES.

Insurance, mutual companies.
Reorganization into stock
insurer, owned by holding
company, **175:19F to
175:19W.**
See INSURANCE.

Joint stock companies.
See JOINT STOCK
COMPANIES.

Life insurance, conversion to stock
companies, **175:19E.**

STOCK EXCHANGES.
**See SECURITIES AND
SECURITIES
REGULATIONS.**

STOCKHOLDER WAGE LIABILITY ACT, 156:35.

STOCK HOLDING COMPANY.
Mutual holding companies, conversion to stock holding company, **167H:9.**

STOCK IN TRADE.
Exemption from attachment or execution, **235:34.**

STOCK NURSERY.
See NURSERIES AND NURSERY STOCK.

STOCK OFFERINGS.
Insurance, reorganization of mutual companies.
Options and grants, **175:19P.**

STOCKYARDS.
Defined, **94:139C.**
Slaughterhouses.
See SLAUGHTERHOUSES.

STOLEN PROPERTY.
Burglary.
See BURGLARY.
Firearms surrender program.
Weapons recovered through firearms surrender program, **140:131O.**
Larceny or theft.
See LARCENY AND THEFT.
Negotiable instruments, **106:3-309, 106:3-312.**
Receiving stolen property.
See RECEIVING STOLEN PROPERTY.
Robbery.
See ROBBERY.

STOMATITIS.
Eradication, **129:14A.**

STONEHAM.
Congressional district, **57:1.**
District court, **218:1.**
Medical examiner district, **38:1.**
Metropolitan air pollution control district, membership, **111:142B.**
Parks, metropolitan district, **92:33.**
Senatorial district, **57:3.**

STONE, LUCY.
Lucy Stone day, **6:15DDDD.**

STONE OR ROCK.
Advertisements illegally placed on rocks, penalty, **266:126.**
Coal containing unreasonable amount of rocks, **94:248.**
Commonwealth, rocks and stones, **2:22-2:25.**
Crimes involving, **266:113.**

STONE OR ROCK —Cont'd
Diamonds.
See JEWELRY.
Digging up or carrying away as criminal offense, **266:113.**
Erosion by sea, penalty for removal of natural barriers furnishing protection against, **91:30A.**
Gravestones.
See CEMETERIES.
Harbors, illegal deposit, **102:17.**
Motor vehicle used in unlawful digging up or carrying away of stone, report to registrar of motor vehicles, **90:24A.**
Precious stones.
See JEWELRY.
Quarries.
See QUARRIES.
Rock emblems of the Commonwealth, **3:22-3:24.**
Sand.
See SAND AND GRAVEL.
Street railways, transportation, **161:50.**
Tide waters, removal from shores or beaches of, regulated, **91:30.**
Vessels transporting stone, **102:6-102:14.**
Walls of stone, criminal offense of pulling down, **266:105.**
Waste by joint tenant or tenant in common, triple damages, **242:4, 242:5.**
Waters and watercourses, penalty for removal, **91:30, 91:30A.**
Weights and measures.
Diamonds and precious stones, standards of weight, **99:1.**
Vessels transporting stone.
See SHIPS AND OTHER WATERCRAFT.

STONE, WALTER D.
Memorial zoo, **92B:1 et seq.**

STOP AND FRISK ACT, 41:98.

STOP LIGHTS.
Equipment on vehicles, **90:7, 90:7A.**
Traffic regulations and rules of the road.
See TRAFFIC REGULATIONS AND RULES OF THE ROAD.

STOP PAYMENT ORDER.
See BANKS AND BANKING.

STOP SALE ORDER.
Commercial feed, **128:60.**

STOP SALE ORDER —Cont'd
Seeds.
See SEEDS.
Warehouse receipts, **106:7-504.**
Excusing nondelivery, **106:7-403.**
Negotiation of document of title, effect on rights acquired, **106:7-502.**

STOP SIGNS.
See TRAFFIC REGULATIONS AND RULES OF THE ROAD.

STOP WORK ORDER.
Workers' compensation, **152:25C.**

STORAGE.
Alcoholic liquors.
See ALCOHOLIC LIQUORS.
Apples.
"Controlled" or "modified" atmosphere, storage, **94:109.**
Labeling and marking requirements not applicable to apples in storage, **94:102.**
Bakeries, storage of products and ingredients, **94:3.**
Buildings.
See BUILDINGS AND STRUCTURES.
Bulk storage facilities.
See BULK STORAGE FACILITIES.
Cold storage, **94:66-94:73A.**
See COLD STORAGE.
Credit union records, **171:28.**
Definition, **64I:1.**
Election records, sealing and storage, **54:105.**
Environmental protection department, storage of snow and ice removal chemicals, **85:7A.**
Explosions.
See EXPLOSIONS AND EXPLOSIVES.
Fires.
See FIRES AND FIRE PREVENTION.
Fireworks.
See FIREWORKS.
Garages.
See GARAGES.
Gas and electric companies.
Regulation by department, storage, **164:105A.**
Reservoir companies, stocks and bonds, **164:9.**
Gas and oil, **21J:8, 94:295F, 164:105A.**

STORAGE —Cont'd
Gasoline.
  See GASOLINE AND MOTOR
    FUELS.
Hazardous waste management act,
  regulation, **21C:2, 21C:6.**
Infected articles and goods, taking
  property for storage, **111:100.**
Inflammables.
  See INFLAMMABLES.
Labeling goods and materials in
  storage, **94:102, 94:295F.**
Lease of municipal airport land
  areas for purpose, **90:51F.**
Liens.
  See LIENS AND
    ENCUMBRANCES.
Lockers, **94:66A, 149:139.**
Massachusetts Petroleum Council,
  underground storage tank
  petroleum product cleanup
  fund administrative review
  board, **21J:8.**
Metropolitan district police,
  storage of vehicles removed
  from scene of accident,
  255:39A.
Motor vehicles.
  Fuels.
    See GASOLINE AND MOTOR
      FUELS.
  Garages.
    See GARAGES.
  Illegally parked motor vehicles,
    charges for storage, **40:22D.**
  Metropolitan district police,
    storage of vehicles removed
    from scene of accident,
    255:39A.
  Parking.
    See PARKING AND
      PARKING STATIONS.
  Placed for storage and not
    claimed, sale, **255:39A.**
  Private ways, limitation of
    liability in removing
    vehicles, **266:120D.**
  Unauthorized use of motor
    vehicle, elements of civil
    damages, **90:24F.**
  Use, consumption or storage tax,
    64I:4, 64I:26, 64I:27.
Nursing home residents, secure
  storage space, **111:72V.**
Papers and records, procedure for
  storage, **221:27A.**
Railroad's storage of baggage from
  Friday to Monday, **160:195.**
Records, reports, and returns.
  Storage of records, **221:27A.**

STORAGE —Cont'd
Records, reports, and returns
    —Cont'd
  Underground storage tank
    petroleum product cleanup
    fund.
    See UNDERGROUND
      STORAGE TANK
      PETROLEUM PRODUCT
      CLEANUP FUND.
  Underground tanks.
    See UNDERGROUND
      TANKS.
Sales tax, exemption of goods in
  storage, **64H:6.**
Self-storage facilities, **105A:1 et
  seq.**
  See SELF-STORAGE
    FACILITIES.
Snow and ice removal chemicals
  and abrasives, storage, **85:7A.**
Solid waste disposal, **16:18.**
State supplies and equipment,
  rules for storage, **7:22.**
Tanks.
  See TANKS.
Taxation, **64I:1 et seq.**
  Consumption, or storage tax.
    See USE, CONSUMPTION,
      OR STORAGE TAX.
  Sales tax exemption of stored
    goods, **64H:6.**
Unauthorized use of motor vehicle,
  elements of civil damages,
  90:24F.
Underground storage tank
  petroleum product cleanup
  fund.
  See UNDERGROUND
    STORAGE TANK
    PETROLEUM PRODUCT
    CLEANUP FUND.
Underground tanks.
  See UNDERGROUND TANKS.
Use, consumption or storage tax,
  64I:1 et seq.
  See USE, CONSUMPTION, OR
    STORAGE TAX.
Warehouse receipts.
  See WAREHOUSE RECEIPTS.
Warehouses, **105:1 et seq.**
  See WAREHOUSES.

STORES AND MERCHANTS.
Airport land of municipalities,
  lease for purposes of shops,
  90:51F.
Alcoholic liquors.
  See ALCOHOLIC LIQUORS.
Architectural barriers against
  handicapped persons
  regulated, **22:13A.**

STORES AND MERCHANTS
    —Cont'd
Army business, **110:4B.**
Arson, **266:2.**
Barbers.
  See BARBERS.
Benzol, marking containers,
  149:142A-149:142G.
Blind persons' vending stands in
  public buildings, **6:133.**
Carbon tetrachloride, marking
  containers,
  149:142A-149:142G.
Childbirth, employment of women
  shortly before or after,
  149:180.
Children.
  Minors. See within this heading,
    "Minors."
Cigarette sales to minors, **270:6,
  270:7.**
Cigarette tax.
  See CIGARETTE TAX.
City, establishment of shopping
  centers, **40:5.**
Civil rights.
  See CIVIL RIGHTS AND
    DISCRIMINATION.
Commercial Code provisions as to
  sales by, **106:2-101 et seq.**
  See SALES UNDER
    COMMERCIAL CODE.
Consumers.
  See CONSUMERS AND
    CONSUMER
    PROTECTION.
Credit.
  Denial to person over age 62,
    151B:4.
  Larceny, obtaining credit by
    fraud, **266:33.**
  Retail installment sales.
    See RETAIL INSTALLMENT
      SALES AND SERVICES.
  Time limitation on use of credit
    slips, **93:14S.**
Day of rest for employees,
  149:48-149:52.
Denial of credit to person over age
  62, **151B:4.**
Employees.
  Benzol, marking containers,
    149:142A-149:142G.
  Carbon tetrachloride, marking
    containers,
    149:142A-149:142G.
  Day of rest, **149:48-149:52.**
  Defined under labor law, **149:1.**
  Hours of labor.
    See HOURS OF LABOR OR
      SERVICES.

STORES AND MERCHANTS
—Cont'd

Employees —Cont'd

Meal hours for women and children, **149:100.**

Minors, employment.

Hours of labor or services, **149:56, 149:57, 149:66, 149:67, 149:78.**

Under sixteen, **149:60, 149:69, 149:78, 149:86.**

Under twenty-one must have educational certificate, **149:95.**

Seats for employees, **149:103.**

Sunday operation, **149:48-149:52.**

Women.

Childbirth, employment shortly before or after, prohibited, **149:180.**

Hours of labor or services, **149:56, 149:57, 149:66, 149:67, 149:78.**

Females.

Employees. See within this heading, "Employees."

Flour.

See FLOUR.

Fraud and deceit.

Credit. See within this heading, "Credit."

False advertisements, **266:91.**

Nature of certain articles sold, penalty for misrepresentation, **266:77 et seq.**

Gift enterprises, **271:29, 271:30.**

Going out of business sales, regulation, **93:28A.**

Grocery stores.

See GROCERY STORES AND GROCERIES.

Hairdressers.

See HAIRDRESSERS AND COSMETOLOGISTS.

Holidays.

Sundays and holidays. See within this heading, "Sundays and holidays."

Hours of labor.

See HOURS OF LABOR OR SERVICES.

Housing for elderly and handicapped persons of low income, provisions for convenience stores, **121B:39.**

Installment sales.

See RETAIL INSTALLMENT SALES AND SERVICES.

Labor.

Employees. See within this heading, "Employees."

STORES AND MERCHANTS
—Cont'd

Labor law, mercantile establishments defined for purposes, **149:1.**

Larceny, obtaining credit by fraud, **266:33.**

Law merchant.

See LAW MERCHANT.

Lease of municipal airport land areas for purpose of shops, **90:51F.**

Licenses, **62C:67.**

Lottery in, penalty, **271:8.**

Malls.

Shopping centers. See within this heading, "Shopping centers, plazas, and malls."

Marine fish.

See MARINE FISH AND FISHERIES.

Meat.

See MEAT.

Merchant, defined, **167B:1.**

Minors.

Cigarettes, sale to minors, **270:6, 270:7.**

Employees. See within this heading, "Employees."

Misrepresentations.

Fraud and deceit. See within this heading, "Fraud and deceit."

Municipal authority for establishment of shopping malls, **40:5.**

Navy business, **110:4B.**

Pharmacists and pharmacies.

See PHARMACISTS AND PHARMACIES.

Plazas.

Shopping centers, plazas, and malls. See within this heading, "Shopping centers, plazas, and malls."

Private detective regulations inapplicable to mercantile agencies, **147:23.**

Registration of vendors, **64H:7.**

Retail installment sales.

See RETAIL INSTALLMENT SALES AND SERVICES.

Salespersons.

See SALESPERSONS.

Search warrant for alcoholic liquor, **138:42.**

Shoplifters, **231:94B, 266:30A.**

Shopping centers, plazas, and malls.

Architectural barriers against handicapped persons regulated, **22:13A.**

STORES AND MERCHANTS
—Cont'd

Shopping centers, plazas, and malls —Cont'd

Municipal authority for establishment, **40:5.**

Sidewalk solicitation, **93:40.**

Smoking in public places, regulation, **270:21.**

Sundays and holidays, **136:5-136:7.**

Opening at any time on summer holidays and Sundays, **136:16.**

Sale of foodstuffs, **136:5, 136:6.**

Thanksgiving and Christmas holiday seasons, stores to open on Sundays during, **136:6.**

Taxation.

Cigarette tax.

See CIGARETTE TAX.

Returns, **62C:16.**

Throwing noxious or filthy substance into stores, **266:103.**

Vagabonds in stores or shops, **272:68.**

Women.

Employees. See within this heading, "Employees."

STORMS.

Damage prevention, effect of work on nearby land, **131:40.**

Floods.

See FLOODS AND FLOOD CONTROL.

Hail insurance, **175:93A-175:93C.**

Inspector for storm damage as exempt from detective licensing requirement, **147:23.**

Insurance against.

See WEATHER INSURANCE.

Marine fish and fisheries.

Fishing gear swept ashore by storms, **130:31, 130:32.**

Taking up lobster or crab traps endangered by storm, **130:39.**

Motor carriers, storms as affecting hours of duty of drivers, **159B:18.**

Municipalities authorized to furnish stormy weather work clothes to employees, **40:6J.**

Repair of shore damage caused, **91:31.**

Traps for lobsters and crabs endangered by storm, taking up, **130:39.**

STOUGHTON.

Congressional district, **57:1.**

District court, **218:1.**

STOUGHTON —Cont'd
Medical examiner district, **38:1.**
Senatorial district, **57:3.**

STOVES.
Defective stoves, regulations, **48:53.**
Kitchen facilities in lodging houses, **140:22A.**
Space heaters.
See SPACE HEATERS AND STOVES.

STOW.
Congressional district, **57:1.**
District court, **218:1.**
Medical examiner district, **38:1.**
Senatorial district, **57:3.**

STRANGLING.
See CRIMES AND OFFENSES.

STRAWBERRIES.
Containers and measurements in sale, **94:98, 94:99.**

STRAY BEASTS, 134:2 et seq.
See ANIMALS.

STREAMS.
See WATERS AND WATERWAYS.

STREET COMMISSIONERS.
See HIGHWAYS AND STREETS.

STREET LIGHTS.
See HIGHWAYS AND STREETS.

STREET LISTS.
Voters.
See REGISTRATION OF VOTERS.

STREET MUSICIANS.
Town regulation, **85:10.**

STREET RAILWAYS, 161:1 et seq.
Abolition of grade crossings, **161:129, 161:130.**
Actions in connection with, how taken, **161:13.**
Agreement for, joining, **159:80.**
Apportionment of cost of changes, **159:70.**
Approval of plans by aldermen or selectmen, **161:129.**
Bonds issued, **159:73, 161:25.**
Change of location, **159:70, 159:74.**
Company considered as railroad corporation, **161:60.**
Costs as part of value of property, **159:73.**

STREET RAILWAYS —Cont'd
Abolition of grade crossings —Cont'd
Instruments in connection with, how executed, **161:13.**
Issue of stock or bonds, **159:73, 161:25.**
Public works department.
Determination of changes in location and grade, **159:70.**
Order for removal or relocation of tracks, **159:74.**
Stock or bonds, issuance, **159:73, 161:25.**
Tracks, removal or relocation, **159:74.**
Abstracts of returns of companies to be prepared by department, **161:139.**
Acceptance.
See ACCEPTANCE.
Accidents.
Death. See within this heading, "Death."
Telecommunications and energy department. See within this heading, "Telecommunications and energy department."
Trackless trolley companies, actions on bonds to enforce judgments in accident cases, **163:12.**
Accommodations for passengers.
Additional accommodations may be required by department, **161:105.**
Reasonable accommodations required, **161:104.**
Accounts, **159:31, 159:33.**
Actions.
Alteration of location upon state highway, recovery of expense, **161:82.**
Assessments upon capital stock, collection, **161:22.**
Attachment of cars and equipment, **223:43.**
Change of name of company not to defeat, **161:134.**
Compelling company to resume use of tracks, **161:86.**
Directors, actions to be taken, **161:13.**
How taken by street railway, **161:13.**
Labor and materials, actions, **159:96-159:100.**
Construction contractor not to have, **159:97.**

STREET RAILWAYS —Cont'd
Actions —Cont'd
Labor and materials, actions —Cont'd
Contract with person other than railway company, **159:96.**
Limitation of actions, **159:100.**
Notice of intention to claim right of action for materials, **159:98.**
Statement of amount due for labor, filing, **159:99.**
Limitation of actions. See within this heading, "Limitation of actions."
Penalty for allowing sales by children upon cars, recovery, **161:97.**
Purchaser upon sale by receivers, actions against, **161:135.**
Removal of railway upon revocation of location, recovery of expenses, **161:77.**
Removal of tracks, recovery of expense, **161:86.**
Trackless trolley companies, actions on bonds to enforce judgments in accident cases, **163:12.**
Advertising, exemption from requirements as to outdoor signs, **93:32.**
Advice of department as affecting duties and liabilities, **159:38.**
Affidavits, notice of first meeting, **161:10.**
Affirmation.
Oath. See within this heading, "Oath."
Agents.
Officers and agents. See within this heading, "Officers and agents."
Agreement of association.
Certificate of compliance annexed, **161:9.**
Contents, **161:4.**
Corporate name.
Name. See within this heading, "Name."
Directors. See within this heading, "Directors."
Filing and recording, **161:9, 161:136.**
Increase of capital stock beyond limit fixed, **161:25, 161:26.**

STREET RAILWAYS —Cont'd
Agreement of association —Cont'd
Inspection, examination, or investigation. See within this heading, "Inspection, examination, or investigation."
Intent. See within this heading, "Intent to be stated in agreement of association."
Length. See within this heading, "Length to be stated in agreement of association."
Name of cities, counties, and towns to be stated, **161:4.**
Presentation to department, **161:8.**
Publication, **161:6.**
Records, **161:9, 161:136.**
Sale by receivers, new company, **161:136.**
Statements.
Stock and stockholders. See within this heading, "Stock and stockholders."
Termini. See within this heading, "Termini to be stated in agreement of association."
Stock and stockholders. See within this heading, "Stock and stockholders."
Subscription, **161:4.**
Telecommunications and energy department, **161:8.**
Termini. See within this heading, "Termini to be stated in agreement of association."
Agreements.
Contracts and agreements. See within this heading, "Contracts and agreements."
Alcoholic liquors not to be sold at resorts operated, **161:42.**
Aldermen or selectmen.
Adjudication that certain private land is required, application, **161:58.**
Alteration.
Crossing between public ways and railways, application for alteration, **159:59.**
Public way to construct crossings, authorization, **161:131.**
Carriage of newspapers, baggage, express, and freight, regulation, **161:53.**
Cars, regulations as to number and routes, **161:84.**

STREET RAILWAYS —Cont'd
Aldermen or selectmen —Cont'd
Changes in rates, notice, **161:112.**
Complaints by selectmen, **159:24.**
Contracts and leases to carry out formation of transportation area, **161:145.**
Electricity, consent to use of public ways for, transmission, **161:45.**
Grade crossing elimination, approval of plans, **161:129.**
Maintenance and repair of bridges, application to compel, **159:84.**
Notice.
Approach of cars prescribed, **161:93.**
Rate changes, **161:112.**
Through routes, notice of establishment, **159:21.**
Permits for opening public ways and bridges issued, **161:89.**
Petition to compel resumption of use of tracks, **161:86.**
Private land, approval to purchase or lease, **161:55.**
Rate changes, notice to selectmen, **161:112.**
Regulation, **161:7, 161:53, 161:84.**
Revocation, **161:77.**
Speed regulations, **161:84.**
Temporary discontinuance of use of tracks may be ordered, **161:87.**
Temporary location, granting in case of repairs or alterations to bridges, **161:73.**
Through routes, establishment, **159:21.**
Tracks.
Regulation of use, **161:84.**
Removal by company upon order of aldermen or selectmen after voluntary discontinuance of use, **161:86.**
Transportation of materials in connection with streets, consent, **161:50.**
Trustees of transportation area chosen, **161:146.**
Alteration.
Change or alteration. See within this heading, "Change or alteration."

STREET RAILWAYS —Cont'd
Amusements and exhibitions.
Increase in capital stock or issuing bonds to acquire land for pleasure resorts, **161:25.**
Power to own and operate pleasure resorts, **161:42.**
Annual meeting of stockholders, **161:14, 161:15.**
Annual returns.
Reports and returns. See within this heading, "Reports and returns."
Appeals as to carrying of freight, express, newspapers, or baggage, **161:53.**
Apportionment of expenses.
Crossings, expenses.
Abolition of grade crossings, **159:70.**
Alteration, **159:59.**
Widening, altering, or changing grade of public ways, **161:78-161:80.**
Appropriations by cities and towns in aid, **40:5, 161:161.**
Arrests.
Loitering or trespassing, **161:94A, 161:95.**
Stolen or counterfeited employee transportation pass, **161:113A.**
Without warrant, **159:93, 159:94, 159:104, 161:113A.**
Arson, burning car, **266:2.**
Assaulting or interfering with employees of.
Employees. See within this heading, "Employees."
Assessments.
Betterment assessments. See within this heading, "Betterment assessments."
On capital stock, **161:21, 161:22.**
Sale by receiver, liability of purchaser for assessments, **161:135.**
Assumption of risk by passengers riding on platform, **161:106.**
Attachment of cars and equipment, **223:43.**
Auction sale of stock.
Assessment, sale for failure to pay, **161:21, 161:22.**
Notice of auction sale of new shares, **159:50-159:52.**
Baggage, railway may become carrier, **161:53.**
Bailment.
Leases. See within this heading, "Leases."

638

STREET RAILWAYS —Cont'd

Barns.

Car barns. See within this heading, "Car barns."

Betterment assessments, **161:78-161:80.**

Alteration or change in grade of public way, **161:79.**

Bonds of street railways, taxation, **59:4.**

Increase of capital stock or issue of bonds for paying, **161:25.**

Widening public way, expense, **161:78.**

Blind person accompanied by seeing eye dog, carriage, **272:98A.**

Bond or undertaking of treasurer.

Of railway company, **161:12, 161:13.**

Of transportation area, **161:148.**

Bonds, notes, etc., **161:19-161:35.**

Certain purposes, issue, **161:25, 161:26.**

Computing amount of capital stock as basis for issue, **159:53.**

Consolidated company, issue, **161:64.**

Directors of service at cost company appointed by governor not to be holders, **161:124.**

Enforcement of laws and regulations as to issuance, **161:30.**

Examination of books and financial condition upon request of bondholders, **159:35.**

Foreign corporation controlling domestic company, issuance, **181:10.**

Grade crossing elimination, issuance to pay costs, **159:73, 161:25.**

Limits upon issuance, **161:29.**

Minimum price may be prescribed by department, **161:25.**

Other corporations, holding bonds, **161:41.**

Pleasure resorts, increase in issuing bonds to acquire land, **161:25.**

Proceeds, application, **161:28.**

Purchasing company upon sale, issue, **161:64.**

Refunding bonds, **161:25.**

Reserve fund of service at cost company, issue to provide, **161:117.**

STREET RAILWAYS —Cont'd

Bonds, notes, etc. —Cont'd

Stockholders must authorize issuance, **161:29.**

Taxation, **59:4.**

Transportation area, issuance, **161:152.**

Violations as to issuance, **161:31.**

Books and papers.

Records and recording. See within this heading, "Records and recording."

Borrowing.

Indebtedness. See within this heading, "Indebtedness."

Boston.

Auction sales of new shares, **159:51.**

Elevated railway company, law inapplicable, **161:159.**

Pleasure resorts not to be operated by street railways, **161:42.**

Publication of result of examination of books and financial condition, **159:35.**

Boulevards, **92:43-92:47.**

Brakemen.

Assaulting or interfering, **159:104.**

Hours of labor, **161:103.**

Brakes on cars, **161:98.**

Branch crossings, stopping, **161:92.**

Bridges, **159:83-159:85.**

Construction of railway outside, **161:54-161:61.**

County commissioners, application to department to compel maintenance and repair, **159:84.**

Defects in, liability, **161:89, 161:90.**

Examination, **159:83.**

Guards or railings, **161:91.**

Maintenance and repair, **159:84, 159:85, 161:89.**

Obstruction, **161:96.**

Plans for construction of bridges to be submitted to department, **159:83.**

Power to transmit electricity in, over, or under bridge, **161:45.**

Railings, **161:91.**

Right to open for repairs to railway, **161:89.**

Temporary location in event of repairs or alterations, **161:73.**

STREET RAILWAYS —Cont'd

Burning car as arson, **266:2.**

Business corporations, **156:2, 156B:3, 161:2 et seq.**

Business trusts.

Control by telecommunications and energy department, **182:7-182:10.**

Rates and charges, business trust owning or controlling street railways, **182:11.**

Bylaws.

Annual meeting governed, **161:14.**

Appointments.

Directors of service at cost company appointed by governor, provision, **161:124.**

Officers, **161:13.**

Bond of treasurer prescribed, **161:13.**

First meeting, adoption, **161:11.**

Notice of meetings provided, **161:14.**

Officers and agents may be authorized, **161:12.**

Quorum provided, **161:14.**

Signing of stock certificates, **161:19.**

Vacancies in office, filling, **161:13.**

Capital stock.

Stock and stockholders. See within this heading, "Stock and stockholders."

Car barns.

Increase in capital stock or issue of bonds to acquire, **161:25.**

Use of private land to reach, **161:54.**

Cars and equipment.

Additions to rolling stock, recommendations of department, **159:23.**

Attachment, **223:43.**

Barns.

Car barns. See within this heading, "Car barns."

Brakes, **161:98.**

Coal, transportation, **161:51.**

Conveyance of own supplies, **161:51.**

Delaying passage, **161:94.**

Detaining cars of another company, **161:96.**

Emergency tools, **161:99.**

Fenders on cars, **161:98.**

Heating, **161:100.**

Increase of capital stock or issue of bonds to acquire rolling stock, **161:25.**

STREET RAILWAYS —Cont'd
Cars and equipment —Cont'd
Interchange, **161:47.**
   Materials in connection with
     streets and highways,
     transportation, **161:50.**
Notice.
   Approach, notice, **161:93.**
   Change in running, **161:111.**
Railroad crossings, stopping,
   161:92.
Regulations as to number and
   routes, **161:84.**
Riding on rear or side of cars,
   85:17B.
Safety devices, **161:98.**
Sales by minors on cars, **161:97.**
Special service cars, **161:107.**
Stopping cars. See within this
   heading, "Stopping cars."
Street sprinkling cars, **161:49.**
Tampering, **159:103.**
Telecommunications and energy
   department. See within this
   heading,
   "Telecommunications and
   energy department."
Through routes, operation,
   159:21.
Transportation areas, purchase
   of additional equipment,
   161:153.
Warning of approach, **161:93.**
Wheel guards on cars, **161:98.**
Certificates and certification.
Agreement of association,
   compliance certificate to be
   annexed, **161:9.**
Capital stock.
   Stock and stockholders. See
     within this heading,
     "Stock and stockholders."
Change of name, **161:133.**
Clerk. See within this heading,
   "Clerk."
Compliance with laws prior to
   opening, certification by
   department, **161:83.**
Decision of department upon
   issue of stock, bonds, notes,
   etc., **161:28.**
Directors. See within this
   heading, "Directors."
Incorporation.
   Forms. See within this
     heading, "Forms."
   Issuance, **161:9, 161:137.**
   Location void if certificate not
     issued, **161:7.**

STREET RAILWAYS —Cont'd
Certificates and certification
   —Cont'd
   Inspection, examination, or
     investigation. See within
     this heading, "Inspection,
     examination, or
     investigation."
   Location, **161:7, 161:73.**
   Oath of trustees of
     transportation area,
     161:146.
   Preferred stock, **161:34.**
   Presentation to department,
     161:8.
   President. See within this
     heading, "President."
   Public convenience and
     necessity.
     Extensions into other cities
       and towns, **161:39.**
     Mass transportation facilities
       and services,
       determination of amount
       payable, **58:25B.**
     Private land, taking, **161:58.**
   Reduction of capital stock,
     161:27.
   Secretary of state. See within
     this heading, "Secretary of
     state."
   Stock certificates.
     Stock and stockholders. See
       within this heading,
       "Stock and stockholders."
   Temporary location, **161:73.**
   Transfer, lease, purchase, or sale
     of franchise and property,
     certificate of approval,
     159:54.
   Treasurer. See within this
     heading, "Treasurer."
Chairman of transportation area,
   election, **161:148.**
Change or alteration.
   Grade crossings, **159:70, 159:74.**
     Abolition of grade crossings.
       See within this heading,
       "Abolition of grade
       crossings."
     Public ways, alteration of
       crossings, **159:59, 159:80.**
     Temporary tracks as part of
       cost, **161:76.**
   Highways and streets. See
     within this heading,
     "Highways and streets."
   Location. See within this
     heading, "Location."
   Name. See within this heading,
     "Name."

STREET RAILWAYS —Cont'd
Change or alteration —Cont'd
   Notice. See within this heading,
     "Notice."
   Public works department. See
     within this heading, "Public
     works department."
   Rates and charges. See within
     this heading, "Rates and
     charges."
   Rules and regulations, petition
     for change or alteration,
     159A:12.
   Service, change, **161:111.**
   Stock and stockholders. See
     within this heading, "Stock
     and stockholders."
   Telecommunications and energy
     department. See within this
     heading,
     "Telecommunications and
     energy department."
Charges.
   Rates and charges. See within
     this heading, "Rates and
     charges."
Charter, **3:5.**
   Increase of stock or issue of
     bonds beyond limits, **161:25,
     161:26.**
   Sale of railway where
     authorized, **161:62.**
Chief accounting officer, annual
   returns sworn, **161:138.**
Children or minors.
   Sales upon cars, **161:97.**
   School children, special rates,
     161:107, 161:108.
Cities and towns.
   Abatement of taxes upon
     property owned or leased by
     transportation area,
     161:158.
   Agreement for transportation
     area, **161:144, 161:145.**
   Aldermen or selectmen. See
     within this heading,
     "Aldermen or selectmen."
   Appropriations in aid of
     railways, **40:5, 161:161.**
   Auction sales of new shares of
     capital stock, towns in
     which held prescribed by
     department, **159:51.**
   Authority to establish
     transportation area,
     161:143.
   Borrowing.
     Debt limit, borrowing beyond
       for street railways, **44:8.**
     Transportation area,
       borrowing, **161:152.**

STREET RAILWAYS —Cont'd
Cities and towns —Cont'd
Boston. See within this heading, "Boston."
Clerks.
City or town clerks, filing with. See within this heading, "City and town clerks, filing."
Connecting location between, **161:40.**
Contracts for transportation of materials used in connection with streets, **161:50.**
Contributions. See within this heading, "Contributions."
Exclusion from transportation area, **161:154.**
Extensions into other cities and towns, **161:39.**
Increase of capital stock or issue of bonds for furnishing electricity to towns, **161:25.**
Mayor. See within this heading, "Mayor."
Municipal lighting plants, sale of electricity, **164:52-164:54.**
Names of cities and towns in which located to be stated in agreement of association, **161:4.**
New company upon sale by receivers, **161:136.**
Obligation of service at cost company to sell, **161:123.**
Preliminary agreement for transportation area, **161:144, 161:145.**
Rate changes, notice, **161:112.**
Recovery over against company for defects in ways and bridges, **161:90.**
Through routes, notice to aldermen or selectmen of hearing upon establishment where lines connect, **159:21.**
City and town clerks, filing.
Certificate for temporary location, **161:73.**
Metropolitan district committee's order locating street railway lines in park areas to be recorded, **92:46.**
Notice of claim for materials, **159:98.**
Petition for termination of lease by transportation area, **161:155.**
Statement of amount due for labor, **159:99.**
Civil rights, discrimination because of race or color, **272:92A, 272:98.**

STREET RAILWAYS —Cont'd
Clerk.
Affidavit of service of notice of first meeting, **161:10.**
Agreement of association and certificate presented to department, **161:8.**
Certificates.
Amount of capital stock fixed and paid in, signed and sworn to, certificate stating, **161:24.**
Capital stock fully subscribed and fifty percent paid, certificate that, **161:23.**
Publication of agreement of association, certificate, **161:6.**
City and town clerks. See within this heading, "City and town clerks, filing."
Court clerk, shares of dissenting stockholder deposited, **161:63.**
Directors to appoint prior to organization, **161:5, 161:13.**
Duties, **161:13.**
Election, **161:13.**
Notice of meetings, **161:14, 161:15.**
Oath, **161:13.**
Required, **161:12.**
Telecommunications and energy department. See within this heading, "Telecommunications and energy department."
Coal, transportation, **161:51.**
Collection of assessments on capital stock, **161:22.**
Commissioners.
Revenue commissioner, filing copy of vote creating and order approving preferred stock, **161:34.**
Review of orders as to service at cost companies, **161:128.**
Valuation of dissenting stock, **161:63.**
Committees, director appointed by governor in company rendering service at cost to be member, **161:124.**
Commonwealth.
Division into street railway districts, **161:125.**
Obligation of service at cost company to sell, **161:123.**
Operation of railways by transportation area outside, **161:154.**

STREET RAILWAYS —Cont'd
Commonwealth —Cont'd
Recovery over against company for defects in ways and bridges, **161:90.**
Secretary of state. See within this heading, "Secretary of state."
Compelling company to resume use of tracks, **161:86.**
Compensation.
Overtime pay for employees, **151:1A.**
Police, **159:95.**
Transportation area trustees, **161:146.**
Complaints.
Employees, **159:30.**
Establishment of through routes, complaints, **159:21.**
Forfeiture, recovery by complainant, **161:97.**
Indictment of director for unlawful issuance of stock or script, **161:37.**
Initiation of administrative or judicial proceedings.
Indictment of director for unlawful issuance of stock or scrip, **161:37.**
Petition. See within this heading, "Petition."
Mayor, selectmen, or voters, **159:24.**
Petition. See within this heading, "Petition."
Police officers, complaint against person arrested, **159:94.**
Complying with lawful requirements, increase of capital stock or issue of bonds, **161:25.**
Compressed air tanks used on cars, exception, **146:34.**
Condemnation.
Eminent domain. See within this heading, "Eminent domain, taking land."
Conduct of public officials and employees, **159:95, 161:89.**
Conductors.
Enclosure of platforms for protection, **161:101, 161:102.**
Hours of labor, **161:103.**
Connecting companies.
Consolidation, **161:63.**
Contracts between, **161:66.**
Foreign company, purchase by domestic company, **161:69.**
Joint use of tracks, **161:46.**

STREET RAILWAYS —Cont'd
Connecting companies —Cont'd
Lease, **161:66.**
Sale, **161:63.**
Connecting locations, **161:40.**
Connecting tracks to railroad
tracks, **161:48.**
Consolidation or merger,
161:63-161:65.
Association or trust owning
entire capital stock,
161:69A.
Bonds, issue, **161:64.**
Connecting companies, **161:63.**
Department's approval, **159:54,
161:63, 161:69A.**
Directors' approval, **161:63.**
Dissenting stockholders, **161:63.**
Duties of consolidated
companies, **161:65.**
Exchange of securities, **161:64.**
Express or freight business,
passage of right to engage,
161:65.
Filing, **161:69A.**
Increase of capital stock, **161:64.**
Legal incapacity of dissenting
stockholder, time to file
dissent extended, **161:63.**
Powers of consolidated
companies, **161:65.**
Purchase of dissenting stock,
161:63.
Telecommunications and energy
department, approval of
consolidation, **161:63,
161:69A.**
Valuation of dissenting stock,
161:63.
Construction work.
Bridges. See within this
heading, "Bridges."
Completed within 18 months,
161:38.
Contractor not to have action for
labor and materials, **159:97.**
Electricity, construction of
facilities across lands of
street railways, **164:73.**
Highways and streets. See
within this heading,
"Highways and streets."
Natural gas pipelines,
construction, **164:75C.**
Not to be commenced until
capital stock fully
subscribed and fifty per cent
paid, **161:23.**
Private land, **161:54-161:61.**
Contracts and agreements.
Abolition of grade crossings,
joining in agreement,
159:80.

STREET RAILWAYS —Cont'd
Contracts and agreements
—Cont'd
Action in contract to recover
expense of alteration of
location upon state highway,
161:82.
Annual return to set forth
copies, **159:33, 161:138.**
Association.
Agreement of association. See
within this heading,
"Agreement of
association."
Connecting companies, contracts
between, **161:66.**
Contributions toward cost of
service, agreements,
161:161.
Directors. See within this
heading, "Directors."
Express company, contracts to be
set forth in return, **159:33.**
Labor and materials furnished
under contract, action,
159:96 et seq.
Leases. See within this heading,
"Leases."
Materials used in connection
with streets and highways,
transportation, **161:50.**
Municipal lighting plants, sale of
electricity, **164:52.**
Operation, restrictions on
contract, **161:62.**
Reimburse municipalities for
financial deficits, **161:152A.**
Sale. See within this heading,
"Sale."
Street sprinklers, **161:49.**
Telecommunications and energy
department. See within this
heading,
"Telecommunications and
energy department."
Transportation areas, formation,
161:144, 161:145.
Transportation of one company
to be performed by another,
161:66.
Department's consent, **159:54,
161:66.**
Directors' approval, **161:66.**
Powers and duties of
contracting company,
161:67.
Stockholders' approval,
161:66.
Contributions.
Cost of service, **161:152,
161:161.**

STREET RAILWAYS —Cont'd
Contributions —Cont'd
Debt limit basis for contribution
toward cost of service,
161:152.
Transportation area, **161:150,
161:151.**
Corporations, **156:2, 156B:3, 161:2
et seq.**
Cost, service at.
Rates and charges. See within
this heading, "Rates and
charges."
Counterfeiting, use of stolen or
counterfeited employee
transportation pass, **161:113A.**
Counties in which located to be
stated in agreement of
association, **161:4.**
County commissioners, application
to department to compel
maintenance and repair of
bridges, **159:84.**
County medical examiner, notice of
accident resulting in loss of
life, **159:28.**
Courts.
Name to appear in agreement of
association of new company,
court ordering sale by
receivers, **161:135, 161:136.**
Superior court. See within this
heading, "Superior court."
Supreme judicial court. See
within this heading,
"Supreme judicial court."
Cream, transportation, **161:114.**
Crossings.
Apportionment of expenses. See
within this heading,
"Apportionment of
expenses."
Duty to stop cars, **161:92.**
Grade crossings. See within this
heading, "Grade crossings."
Overhead crossings and
underpasses, **161:130,
161:131.**
Regulated by public utilities
department, **159:57, 159:58.**
Damages.
Passenger riding upon platform,
recovery, **161:106.**
Trackless trolley companies to
give security for damages,
163:12.
Transportation area leases to
provide, **161:157.**
Date.
Time. See within this heading,
"Time."

STREET RAILWAYS —Cont'd

Day's work of employees.
Hours of labor. See within this heading, "Hours of labor of employees."
Death.
Investigation of accident, **159:29.**
Notice of accident, **38:8, 159:28.**
Wrongful death, liability, **229:2.**
Debts or indebtedness.
Indebtedness. See within this heading, "Indebtedness."
Defects.
Bridges, liability for defects, **161:89, 161:90.**
Complaints by employees, **159:30.**
Deficiency in price of capital stock, liability of subscriber, **161:29.**
Definitions, **161:1.**
Department of public utilities.
Telecommunications and energy department. See within this heading, "Telecommunications and energy department."
Depreciation, allowances for, included in cost of service, **161:116.**
Directors.
Actions to be taken, **161:13.**
Agreement of association, **161:4.**
Department, agreement of association and certificate presented, **161:8.**
New company upon sale by receivers, **161:136.**
Annual returns, **161:138.**
Assessments on stock, **161:21, 161:22.**
Auction sale of new shares upon increase of capital stock, **159:51.**
Certificates signed and sworn.
Capital stock fully subscribed and fifty per cent paid, **161:23.**
Stating amount of capital stock fixed and paid, **161:24.**
Vote upon change of name, **161:133.**
Clerk, appointment and election, **161:5, 161:13.**
Collection of assessments upon capital stock, **161:22.**
Connecting location, acceptance, **161:40.**
Consolidation, approval, **161:63.**
Contracts or agreements.
Transportation upon railway by another, approval required, **161:66.**

STREET RAILWAYS —Cont'd

Directors —Cont'd
Corporation may associate itself with relief corporations upon vote, **159:88.**
Election, **161:11, 161:13.**
Examination of books and financial condition upon request, **159:35.**
Filing of agreement of association and certificates, **161:9.**
Free tickets or passes, **161:107.**
Governor, appointment of directors of service at cost company, **161:124.**
Indictment for unlawful issue of stock or scrip, **161:37.**
Instruments to be signed, **161:13.**
Issue of stock or bonds unlawfully, **161:31.**
Lease of railway, approval, **161:66.**
Liability for debts and contracts of corporation, **161:27, 161:37.**
Maintenance and repair of bridges, application to compel, **159:84.**
Meetings, **161:18.**
Service at cost company, **161:124.**
Minimum number required, **161:11, 161:12.**
Notice.
First meeting of incorporators to be signed by directors, **161:10.**
Increase in capital stock, notice to stockholders, **159:50.**
Meeting, **161:18.**
Officers and agents, appointment, **161:5, 161:13.**
President elected by and, **161:13.**
Publication of agreement of association, **161:6.**
Sale of railway, approval, **161:63.**
Snow removal regulations, petition for amendment, **161:85.**
Stock and stockholders. See within this heading, "Stock and stockholders."
Temporary location, petition for and acceptance, **161:73.**
Treasurer, appointment and election, **161:5, 161:13.**

STREET RAILWAYS —Cont'd

Directors —Cont'd
Vacancies in offices, filling, **161:5, 161:13.**
Waiver of notice of meetings, **161:18.**
Dirt, transportation, **161:50.**
Discharge of employees, influencing, **271:40, 271:41.**
Discontinuance.
Line, notice to be given, **161:111.**
Public ways in which tracks located, **161:88.**
Use of tracks, **161:86, 161:87.**
Discrimination because of race or color, **272:92A, 272:98.**
Disorderly conduct in streetcar, **272:43.**
Dispatchers, hours of labor, **161:103.**
District court, jurisdiction of persons arrested by railway police, **159:94.**
Districts, division of Commonwealth into, **161:125.**
Dividends.
Preferred stock dividends included in cost of service, **161:116.**
Proceeds of sale, use for dividends, **161:68.**
Stock and scrip dividends, **161:36, 161:37.**
Dog, carriage of blind person accompanied by seeing eye dog, **272:98A.**
Drawbridges, guards or railings, **161:91.**
Duplicates, issuance of stock or obligation by street railways, duplicate of decision, **161:28.**
Duties, effect of request or advice of public utilities department, **159:38.**
Eighteen months, commencement of operation within, **161:38.**
Ejection of passenger for failure to pay fare, **159:101.**
Election.
Directors, **161:11, 161:13.**
Officers, **161:13, 161:147, 161:148.**
Stock, voting rights, **161:16, 161:17, 161:35, 161:69A.**
Transportation areas. See within this heading, "Transportation areas."
Electricians' laws inapplicable, **141:7.**

STREET RAILWAYS —Cont'd

Electricity and gas.

Construction of pipes, wires, etc., across lands of street railways, **164:72, 164:73, 164:75.**

Foreign companies furnishing to company rendering service at cost, filing of schedule of rates, **161:125.**

Increase of capital stock or issue of bonds for purpose of furnishing to town, **161:25.**

Poles or towers on land of street railway, **164:73.**

Power to manufacture and transmit, **161:45.**

Rights of way or easements in location of street railway, taking by eminent domain, **164:72.**

Sale to town operating municipal lighting plant, **164:52-164:54.**

Use as motive power, **161:43.**

Electric railroads, street railway law as applicable, **162:15.**

Emergency tools on cars, **161:99.**

Eminent domain, taking land, **161:58-161:61.**

Telecommunications and energy department. See within this heading, "Telecommunications and energy department."

Employees.

Assaulting or interfering, **159:104.**

Arrest, **159:93, 159:94, 159:104.**

Compensation. See within this heading, "Compensation."

Complaint of defects, **159:30.**

Conductors. See within this heading, "Conductors."

Enclosure of platforms for protection, **161:101, 161:102.**

Gatemen. See within this heading, "Gateman."

Hiring or discharge of employees, influencing, **271:40, 271:41.**

Hours of labor. See within this heading, "Hours of labor of employees."

Motorman. See within this heading, "Motorman."

Officers and agents. See within this heading, "Officers and agents."

STREET RAILWAYS —Cont'd

Employees —Cont'd

Relief corporations formed by employees.

Relief corporations. See within this heading, "Relief corporations."

Statement of amount due for labor, filing with city and town clerks, **159:99.**

Transportation pass of employee, use of stolen or counterfeited, **161:113A.**

Enclosure of platforms, **161:101, 161:102.**

Enforcement of laws and orders, **161:142.**

Engineer to examine bridges, **159:83.**

Equipment.

Cars and equipment. See within this heading, "Cars and equipment."

Evasion of payment of fare, **159:101.**

Arrest, **159:93, 159:94.**

Evidence.

Certificate of incorporation, or copy, conclusive evidence of existence, **161:9.**

Clerk's certificate of publication of agreement of association as conclusive evidence, **161:6.**

Compliance with orders, submission of evidence, **159:16.**

Inquest, liability for expense of evidence taken, **38:11.**

Police officers. See within this heading, "Police officers."

Witness to accident causing death, **159:29.**

Examination.

Inspection, examination, or investigation. See within this heading, "Inspection, examination, or investigation."

Executive committee, director appointed by governor to be member of, in company rendering service at cost, **161:124.**

Exhibitions.

Amusements and exhibitions. See within this heading, "Amusements and exhibitions."

Expenses.

Rates and charges. See within this heading, "Rates and charges."

STREET RAILWAYS —Cont'd

Explosives or explosions, requirement as to marking of torpedoes used by street railways, **159:102.**

Express.

Annual return of express company, **159:33.**

Consolidated companies, **161:65.**

Contract or lease not to convey right to carry, **161:67.**

Railway may carry, **161:53.**

Extension.

Defined, **161:1.**

Increase in capital stock or issuing bonds, **161:25.**

Location, **161:70.**

Other cities and towns, extension into, **161:39.**

Telecommunications and energy department. See within this heading, "Telecommunications and energy department."

Time for construction and operation, **161:38.**

Transportation areas, **161:153.**

Fares.

Rates and charges. See within this heading, "Rates and charges."

Fees.

Certificate of incorporation, **161:9.**

Debt due for labor, fee for filing statement of amount, **262:34.**

Directors of service at cost company, **161:124.**

Merger with certain associations or trusts, filings, **161:69A.**

Notice of claim for materials, filing, **159:98.**

Recording metropolitan district commission's grant of location, **262:34.**

Statement of amount due for labor, filing, **159:99.**

Fenders on cars, **161:98.**

Filing and recording.

Records and recording. See within this heading, "Records and recording."

Finance committee, director of service at cost company appointed by governor to be member, **161:124.**

Financial condition.

Contracts to reimburse municipalities for financial deficits, **161:152A.**

STREET RAILWAYS —Cont'd

Financial condition —Cont'd

Examination of, upon request of director, stockholder, or bondholder, **159:35.**

Reduction of capital stock after consideration of financial condition, **161:27.**

Fines and penalties.

Accidents, failure to give notice, **159:28.**

Accounts, failure to keep in method prescribed by department, **159:31.**

Additional accommodations for passengers required by department, failure to provide, **161:105.**

Annual return, failure to make or amend, **161:138.**

Assaulting or interfering with employees, **159:104.**

Blind person accompanied by seeing eye dog, refusal to carry, **272:98A.**

Books, refusal to submit to examination of department, **159:31.**

Cars, tampering, **159:103.**

Delaying passage of cars, **161:94.**

Detaining cars of another company, **161:96.**

Discrimination because of race or color, **272:92A, 272:98.**

Disorderly conduct in streetcar, **272:43.**

Emergency tools, violations, **161:99.**

Enclosure of platforms, violations, **161:102.**

Expectoration in cars, **270:14, 270:15.**

Express companies, failure to make or amend return, **159:33.**

Fire apparatus, failure to stop, **89:6A.**

Forfeiture. See within this heading, "Forfeiture."

Fraudulent evasion of payment of fare, **159:101.**

Free tickets or passes, violations, **161:107.**

Gambling on streetcar, **271:2.**

Garbage, filth, or rubbish, throwing on platforms, **161:94A.**

Guards or railings upon bridges and draws, failure to provide, **161:91.**

STREET RAILWAYS —Cont'd

Fines and penalties —Cont'd

Heating of cars, violations, **161:100.**

Hindering passage of vehicles, **161:96.**

Hours of labor, violations, **161:103.**

Influencing appointment or discharge of employees, **271:40, 271:41.**

Issue of stock or bonds, violations, **161:31.**

Lessee FAILING TO MAKE ANNUAL RETURN TO OWNER, **161:140.**

Loitering in or about stations, **161:95.**

Missiles, throwing or shooting at car or train, **159:93, 159:94, 159:104.**

Negligent operation of streetcar, penalty, **265:30.**

Number and routes of cars, violations, **161:84.**

Obstructing tracks or public ways, **161:94, 161:96.**

Railroad crossings, failure to stop, **161:92.**

Reasonable accommodations, failure to provide, **161:104.**

Riding on rear or side of cars, **85:17B.**

Sales by children upon cars, **161:97.**

School tickets, violations, **161:108.**

Shooting at car or train, **159:104.**

Signals, injury, **159:102.**

Smoking in streetcar, **272:43A.**

Special rates, violations, **161:107.**

Speed regulations, violations, **161:84.**

Spitting in cars, **270:14, 270:15.**

Stock or scrip dividends, liability of directors, **161:37.**

Stolen or counterfeit employee passes, **161:113A.**

Tampering with signals, tracks, or equipment, **159:103.**

Throwing filth or rubbish on platforms, **161:94A.**

Throwing missiles at car or train, **159:93, 159:94, 159:104.**

Torpedoes, failure to mark, **159:102.**

Tracks, violations, **161:84, 161:94, 161:103.**

STREET RAILWAYS —Cont'd

Fines and penalties —Cont'd

Transfer tickets, violations, **161:113.**

Fire apparatus, stopping, **89:6A.**

Firemen, free tickets or passes, **161:107.**

First meeting of incorporators, **161:10, 161:11.**

Foreign companies.

Bonds, notes, etc., issued, **181:10.**

Purchase of, by domestic company, **161:69.**

Schedule of rates of company furnishing electricity to service at cost company, **161:125.**

Forfeiture.

Complainant, recovery, **161:97.**

Failure to pay assessment, forfeiture of stock, **161:22.**

Formation of company, **161:3.**

Forms.

Account books prescribed by department, **159:31.**

Express company, **159:33.**

Annual return, form prescribed by department, **161:138.**

Certificate of incorporation, **161:9.**

New company upon sale by receivers, **161:137.**

Preferred stock, certificate, **161:34.**

Question in election upon formation of transportation area, **161:145.**

Franchise, approval by department of lease, purchase, or sale, **159:54.**

Fraud.

Evasion of payment of fare. See within this heading, "Evasion of payment of fare."

Stolen or counterfeited employee transportation pass, **161:113A.**

Free checks and transfers, withdrawal, **161:110.**

Free tickets, **161:107.**

Freight, railway may become carrier, **161:53, 161:65.**

Freight yards, use of private lands to reach, **161:54.**

Funded debt, increase of capital stock or issue of bonds for refunding, **161:25.**

Gambling on streetcar, **271:2.**

STREET RAILWAYS —Cont'd

Garbage and rubbish, throwing on platforms of public transportation facility, **161:94A.**

Gas.
Electricity and gas. See within this heading, "Electricity and gas."

Gateman.
Hours of labor, **161:103.**

Gauge, **161:4.**

General court.
Contract for operation or lease, consent, **161:62.**
Notice of hearing upon petition for location to members, **161:7.**
Petition for legislation, **3:5.**
Private land, authorization of use, **161:54.**
Sale of railway where authorized by special act, **161:62.**
Taking securities of other corporations, approval, **161:41.**

GI bill of rights, special rates for veterans attending school, **161:107.**

Governor, appointment of directors of service at cost company, **161:124.**

Grade crossings.
Abolition of grade crossings. See within this heading, "Abolition of grade crossings."
Change or alteration. See within this heading, "Change or alteration."
Laws as to local jurisdiction inapplicable, **82:20.**

Grade of public way, expense of change, **161:79.**

Grades of fare.
Rates and charges. See within this heading, "Rates and charges."

Gravel.
Sand and gravel. See within this heading, "Sand and gravel."

Guards, hours of labor, **161:103.**

Guards or railings upon bridges and draws, **161:91.**

Headlights, **161:98.**

Hearings.
Additional accommodations for passengers, **161:105.**
Alteration of location, **161:71.**
Appeals as to carrying of freight, express, newspapers, and baggage, **161:53.**

STREET RAILWAYS —Cont'd

Hearings —Cont'd
Change of name, **161:132.**
Connecting location, application, **161:40.**
Contract for all transportation upon road of one company by another, **159:54.**
Extension of location, **161:70.**
Extension of time for construction and operation, **161:38.**
Extensions into other cities and towns, **161:39.**
Interchange in traffic and cars, **161:47.**
Issue of stock, bonds, notes, etc., **161:28.**
Location, petition, **161:7.**
Maintenance and repair of bridges, **159:84.**
Notice. See within this heading, "Notice."
Preliminary agreement for transportation area, **161:145.**
Private land, purchase or lease, **161:55.**
Reduction of capital stock, **161:27.**
Revocation of location, **161:77.**
Schedules of fares and transfer privileges of service at cost company, **161:120.**
Snow removal regulations, amendment, **161:85.**
Taking land by eminent domain for grade crossing elimination, **161:129.**
Through routes, establishment, **159:21.**
Transfer, lease, purchase, or sale of franchise and property, **159:54.**

Heating of cars, **161:100.**

Height of crossings above railroad tracks, **161:130.**

Highways and streets.
Alteration.
Aldermen or selectmen. See within this heading, "Aldermen or selectmen."
Apportionment of expense, **161:79.**
Crossing with public ways, alteration, **159:59, 159:80.**
Increase of capital stock or issue of bonds to pay, **161:25.**
Railroad crossings, alteration for constructing, **161:131.**

STREET RAILWAYS —Cont'd

Highways and streets —Cont'd
Alteration —Cont'd
Ways in which tracks located, **161:88.**
Boulevards, **92:43-92:47.**
Change in grade, apportionment of expense, **161:79.**
Construction outside, **161:54-161:61.**
For railroad crossings, **161:130.**
Discontinuance of ways in which tracks located, **161:88.**
Grade crossings. See within this heading, "Grade crossings."
Liability for injuries by defects, **161:89, 161:90.**
Obstruction, **161:96.**
Pedestrian injured, rights as traveler on highway, **82:34.**
Repairs, **159:84, 159:85, 161:89.**
Reservation of space in public ways for street railways, **82:34.**
Right to transmit electricity in, over, or, **161:45.**
Sand and gravel, regulations concerning transportation on public ways, **85:36.**
Sprinkling cars, **161:49.**
State highways. See within this heading, "State highways."
Superintendent of streets. See within this heading, "Superintendent of streets."
Surface of, duty of company to repair, **161:89.**
Sweepings, transportation, **161:50.**
Taking up public way in which tracks located, **161:88.**
Widening for railway, expense, **161:78.**

Hiring employees, influencing, **271:40, 271:41.**

Holding stock.
Stock and stockholders. See within this heading, "Stock and stockholders."

Hours of labor of employees, **161:103.**
Overtime pay, **151:1A.**

Ice.
Snow and ice. See within this heading, "Snow and ice."

Improvement fund of service at cost company, **161:122.**

Improvements.
Betterment assessments. See within this heading, "Betterment assessments."

STREET RAILWAYS —Cont'd
Incorporation.
Certificates and certification. See within this heading, "Certificates and certification."
Increase of capital stock.
Stock and stockholders. See within this heading, "Stock and stockholders."
Indebtedness.
Capital stock, collection of assessment, **161:22.**
Cities and towns. See within this heading, "Cities and towns."
Increase of capital stock or issue of bonds for paying, **161:25.**
Interest on, included in cost of service, **161:116.**
Police, complaint against person arrested, **159:94.**
Reimbursement of debt service, **161B:7.**
Indictment of director for unlawful issuance of stock or scrip, **161:37.**
Informers, recovery of forfeiture for allowing children to sell articles on cars, **161:97.**
Injunction to restrain violations, **161:142.**
Inquest, liability for expense of evidence taken, **38:11.**
Inspection, examination, or investigation.
Accidents, investigation, **159:29.**
Agreement of association and certificates to be open, **161:9.**
New company upon sale by receivers, **161:137.**
Books and papers, examination.
On request of director, stockholder, or bondholder, **159:35.**
Refusal to submit to examination of department, fines and penalties, **159:31.**
Relief corporations, books and papers, **159:87.**
Bridges, examination, **159:83.**
Complaint by mayor, selectmen, or voters, examination into condition and operation, **159:24.**
Financial condition, examination on request of director, stockholder, or bondholder, **159:35.**

STREET RAILWAYS —Cont'd
Inspection, examination, or investigation —Cont'd
Opening of books for public use, examination by department prior, **161:83.**
Service at cost companies, investigation, **161:125.**
Tracks, roadbeds, and tunnels, examination, **159:83.**
Instruments, execution, **161:13.**
Intent to be stated in agreement of association, **161:4.**
New company upon sale by receivers, **161:136.**
Interchange of traffic and cars, **161:47.**
Interest as included in cost of service, **161:116, 161:118.**
Interfering with employees.
Employees. See within this heading, "Employees."
Intersecting companies.
Connecting companies. See within this heading, "Connecting companies."
Intoxicating liquors not to be sold at resorts operated, **161:42.**
Investigation.
Inspection, examination, or investigation. See within this heading, "Inspection, examination, or investigation."
Investments.
Increase of capital stock or issue of bonds for making permanent investments, **161:25.**
Rates and charges. See within this heading, "Rates and charges."
Joint and several liability, directors, **161:24, 161:27.**
Joint fares and rates, **159:21, 161:47.**
Joint use of tracks, **161:46.**
Jurisdiction.
District court, jurisdiction of persons arrested by railway police, **159:94.**
Local jurisdiction laws inapplicable to grade crossings, **82:20.**
Public utilities department, **159:12.**
Jury trial as to value of dissenting stock, **161:63.**
Labor and employment.
Employees. See within this heading, "Employees."

STREET RAILWAYS —Cont'd
Labor and materials.
Actions for.
Actions. See within this heading, "Actions."
Cars and equipment. See within this heading, "Cars and equipment."
Fee for filing statement of amount debt due for labor, **262:34.**
Transportation of materials used in connection with streets, **161:50.**
Landlord and tenant.
Leases. See within this heading, "Leases."
Law of the road, **89:6.**
Laws applicable to, **161:2.**
Leases, **161:66.**
Annual return to set forth copies, **161:138.**
Cars and equipment, certificate of approval for lease, etc., **159:54.**
Connecting companies, lease, **161:66.**
Cost of service, rentals included, **161:116.**
Department's consent, **159:54, 161:66.**
Directors' approval, **161:66.**
Duties of leasing company, **161:67.**
General court, consent, **161:62.**
Lessee to make return to owner, **161:140.**
Owning company of leased railway responsible for annual return, **161:138.**
Powers of leasing company, **161:67.**
Private land, lease, **161:55.**
Restrictions, **161:62.**
Stockholders' approval, **161:66.**
Transportation areas. See within this heading, "Transportation areas."
Legal incapacity of dissenting stockholder, time to file dissent extended, **161:63.**
Length to be stated in agreement of association, **161:4.**
New company upon sale by receivers, **161:136.**
Letter carriers, free tickets or passes, **161:107.**
Liability.
Directors, **161:24, 161:27, 161:37.**
Request or advice of department, effect on liability, **159:38.**

STREET RAILWAYS —Cont'd
Licenses and permits.
  Authority for carrying of freight,
    baggage, express, and
    newspapers, **161:53.**
  Opening public ways and
    bridges, **161:89.**
  Trackless trolley permit, **163:2,
    163:6, 163:8.**
Liens for labor and materials,
  159:98-159:100.
Lifting jack, cars to be provided,
  161:99.
Lights, headlights on cars, **161:98.**
Limitation of actions.
  Highway defect actions, **161:89.**
  Labor and materials, actions,
    159:100.
  Recovery of penalty for allowing
    sales by children upon cars,
    161:97.
Limitation or restriction.
  Assessment, limitation, **161:78,
    161:79.**
  Bonds and notes issuance, limit,
    161:29.
  Contracts for operation,
    restrictions, **161:62.**
  Debt limit, city or town
    borrowing outside in
    connection with street
    railways, **44:8.**
  Domestic corporations,
    limitation on holding of
    capital stock by street
    railways, **156B:15.**
  Stock and stockholders. See
    within this heading, "Stock
    and stockholders."
Lines or routes.
  Route or line. See within this
    heading, "Route or line."
Liquor sales at resorts operated,
  161:42.
Lists and schedules.
  Service-at-cost company,
    schedules of grades of fare
    and transfer privileges,
    161:120.
  Stockholders, list, **159:31.**
Litter, throwing or placing on
  public transportation facility
  premises, **161:94A.**
Loans, increase of capital stock
  and issuance of bonds to pay
  loan, **161:25.**
Local jurisdiction laws as
  inapplicable to grade
  crossings, **82:20.**
Location, **161:7, 161:72-161:76.**
  Actions as to, manner of taking,
    161:13.

STREET RAILWAYS —Cont'd
Location —Cont'd
  Alteration, **161:71.**
    Abolition of grade crossings,
      change, **159:70, 159:74.**
    Order of public works
      department, **161:82.**
  Amendment, **161:7.**
  Certification by department,
    161:7, 161:73.
  Connecting locations between
    cities and towns, **161:40.**
  Defined, **161:1.**
  Eminent domain, location on
    private land, **161:58-161:61.**
  Extension, **161:70.**
  Fee for recording grant of
    location to street railway,
    262:34.
  Instruments in connection with,
    execution, **161:13.**
  Metropolitan park areas, street
    railways running through,
    92:43, 92:46, 92:47.
  Obtaining, **161:7.**
  Private land, location,
    161:54-161:61.
  Public utilities department,
    certificate of location, **161:7.**
  Removal of tracks upon
    revocation, **161:77.**
  Revocation, **161:77.**
  State highways, **161:81, 161:82.**
  Switch connections, granting,
    159:21.
  Taking up public ways in which
    tracks located, **161:88.**
  Temporary location,
    161:72-161:76.
    Acceptance, **161:73.**
    Application to department,
      161:74.
    Authority to grant, **161:72.**
    Bridge repairs or alterations,
      161:73.
    Certification, **161:73.**
    Cost as part of expense of
      grade crossing alteration,
      161:76.
    Department may grant,
      161:74.
    Private land, **161:72.**
    Termination, **161:72, 161:75.**
  Time within which certain
    proceedings must be
    completed, **161:7.**
  Void locations, **161:7.**
  Widening public way, **161:78.**
Loitering or trespassing on
  premises, **161:94A, 161:95.**
Losses included in cost of service,
  161:116.

STREET RAILWAYS —Cont'd
Machinery and equipment.
  Labor and materials. See within
    this heading, "Labor and
    materials."
Mail and mail carriers.
  Free tickets or passes, **161:107.**
  Transportation of mail, **161:52.**
Maintenance.
  Repairs. See within this
    heading, "Repairs."
Massachusetts Bay transportation
  authority, **161A:1 to 161A:47.**
  See MASSACHUSETTS BAY
    TRANSPORTATION
    AUTHORITY.
Massachusetts business trusts.
  Business trusts. See within this
    heading, "Business trusts."
Materials.
  Labor and materials. See within
    this heading, "Labor and
    materials."
Mayor.
  Changes in rates, notice,
    161:112.
  Complaint, **159:24.**
  Contracts and leases to carry
    out formation of
    transportation area,
    161:145.
  Petition to compel resumption of
    use of tracks, **161:86.**
  Trustees of transportation area
    to be chosen, **161:146.**
  Veto power not affected, **161:1.**
Mechanics' liens, **159:100.**
Medical examiner, notice of fatal
  accident, **159:28.**
Meetings, **161:14-161:18.**
  Annual meeting, **161:14, 161:15.**
  Directors. See within this
    heading, "Directors."
  First meeting, **161:10, 161:11.**
  Merger with certain associations
    or trusts, approval, **161:69A.**
  Stockholders, **161:14, 161:15.**
  Trustees of transportation area,
    161:148.
Mentally ill persons, stockholder
  dissenting from sale or
  consolidation of street
  railways, **161:63.**
Merger.
  Consolidation or merger. See
    within this heading,
    "Consolidation or merger."
Metropolitan districts.
  Grant of location by
    metropolitan district
    commission, fee for
    recording, **262:34.**

STREET RAILWAYS —Cont'd
Metropolitan districts —Cont'd
Park areas of, running through,
92:43, 92:46, 92:47.
Powers of metropolitan district
commission as to location,
92:43-92:47.
Milk, transportation, **161:114.**
Minors.
Children or minors. See within
this heading, "Children or
minors."
Misconduct.
Liability of street railways for
misconduct of agents or
servants while repairing
ways and bridges, **161:89.**
Police officers, liability for
misconduct, **159:95.**
Missiles, throwing or shooting at
train, bus, etc., **159:93,
159:94, 159:104.**
Mortgages, sale by receivers as
affecting, **161:135.**
Motive power, **161:43.**
Increase in capital stock or issue
of bonds for changing,
161:25.
Motorman.
Assault, **159:93, 159:94,
159:104.**
Duty to stop cars at railroad
crossings, **161:92.**
Enclosure of platforms for
protection, **161:101,
161:102.**
Hours of labor, **161:103.**
Motor vehicles.
Passing streetcars, **90:14.**
Power to own and operate,
161:44.
Municipalities.
Cities and towns. See within
this heading, "Cities and
towns."
Municipal lighting plants, sale of
electricity, **164:52-164:54.**
Name.
Change, **161:132-161:134.**
Action not defeated, **161:134.**
Authorized, **161:132.**
Certificate of change, **161:133.**
Rights and duties of company
under new name, **161:134.**
Corporate name to be stated in
agreement of association,
161:4.
New company upon sale by
receiver, **161:135,
161:136.**
Transportation areas, **161:143.**

STREET RAILWAYS —Cont'd
Natural gas pipelines,
construction, **164:75C.**
Negligent operation of streetcar,
penalty, **265:30.**
Newspapers.
Railway may become carrier,
161:53.
Sales by minors upon cars,
161:97.
Notes.
Bonds, notes, etc. See within
this heading, "Bonds, notes,
etc."
Notice.
Accidents, **38:8, 159:28.**
Additional accommodations for
passengers, hearing,
161:105.
Aldermen or selectmen. See
within this heading,
"Aldermen or selectmen."
Appeal as to carrying of freight,
newspapers, baggage, or
express, **161:53.**
Approach of cars, **161:93.**
Assessments on capital stock,
161:21.
Auction sale of stock. See within
this heading, "Auction sale
of stock."
Authority to purchase or lease
private land, hearing on
petition, **161:55.**
Cars and equipment. See within
this heading, "Cars and
equipment."
Change or alteration.
Location, **161:71.**
Name, change, **161:132,
161:133.**
Rates, change, **161:112.**
Service, change, **161:111.**
Snow removal regulations,
amendment, **161:85.**
Stock, increase in capital
stock, **159:50.**
Connecting location, hearing,
161:40.
Construction and operation,
application for extension of
time, **161:38.**
Contract that all transportation
upon road of one company
be performed by another,
159:54.
County medical examiner, notice
of fatal accident, **159:28.**
Directors. See within this
heading, "Directors."
Examination by department
upon complaint of mayor,
selectmen, or voters, **159:24.**

STREET RAILWAYS —Cont'd
Notice —Cont'd
Extension into other cities and
towns, hearing, **161:39.**
Extension of location, **161:70.**
First meeting of incorporators,
161:10.
Increase in capital stock, **159:50.**
Intention to claim right of action
for materials, **159:98.**
Interchange of traffic and cars,
hearing on regulation,
161:47.
Location, hearing on petition,
161:7.
Maintenance and repair of
bridges, application, **159:84.**
Materials, notice of claim,
159:98.
Mayors, notice of rate changes,
161:112.
Meetings, notice, **161:10, 161:14,
161:15, 161:18.**
Merger with certain associations
or trusts, meeting, **161:69A.**
Preliminary agreement for
transportation area,
hearing, **161:145.**
Private land, hearing on
application for authority to
take by eminent domain,
161:58.
Proceeding to compel company
to resume use of tracks,
161:86.
Publication. See within this
heading, "Publication."
Renewal of lease by
transportation area,
161:155.
Revocation of location, **161:77.**
Schedules of grades and fares of
company rendering service
at cost, hearing, **161:120.**
Snow removal regulations,
amendment, **161:85.**
Stock and stockholders. See
within this heading, "Stock
and stockholders."
Taking land outside public ways
for grade crossing
elimination, **161:129.**
Telecommunications and energy
department. See within this
heading,
"Telecommunications and
energy department."
Through routes, establishment,
159:21.
Transfer, lease, purchase, or sale
of franchise and property,
159:54.

STREET RAILWAYS —Cont'd
Notice —Cont'd
Waiver of notice. See within this heading, "Waiver of notice."
Number of persons required to form company, **161:3.**
Oath.
Clerk, **161:13.**
Return of express company, **159:33.**
Statement of amount due for labor, **159:99.**
Trustees of transportation area, **161:146.**
Obligations, effect of request or advice of department, **159:38.**
Obsolescence, allowance for, included in cost of service, **161:116.**
Obstruction.
Public ways, **161:96.**
Tracks, **161:94.**
Officers and agents.
Appointment, **161:5, 161:13.**
Bylaws may authorize, **161:12.**
Chief accounting officer, annual returns sworn, **161:138.**
Election of officers, **161:13.**
Free tickets or passes for executive officers, **161:107.**
Issue of stocks or bonds unlawfully, **161:31.**
Misconduct, **161:89.**
Police officers. See within this heading, "Police officers."
President. See within this heading, "President."
Provided, **161:12.**
Secretary of transportation area, **161:148.**
Stock certificates signed, **161:19.**
Term of office, **161:13.**
Transportation area, election, **161:147, 161:148.**
Vacancies, filling, **161:5, 161:13, 161:15.**
Opening for public use, **161:83.**
Operation, **161:83-161:103.**
Orders of court for sale by receiver, **161:135.**
Ordinances, power to adopt, **85:10.**
Outdoor advertising signs, exemption from requirements, **93:32.**
Overtime pay for employees, **151:1A.**
Papers.
Records and recording. See within this heading, "Records and recording."

STREET RAILWAYS —Cont'd
Par value.
Stock and stockholders. See within this heading, "Stock and stockholders."
Passes or tickets.
Tickets or passes. See within this heading, "Tickets or passes."
Passing of streetcars by other vehicles, **90:14.**
Pedestrian injured by, rights as traveler on highway, **82:34.**
Penalties.
Fines and penalties. See within this heading, "Fines and penalties."
Permits.
Licenses and permits. See within this heading, "Licenses and permits."
Personal property.
Increase of capital stock or issue of bonds for acquiring, **161:25.**
Lease, purchase, or sale, departmental approval, **159:54.**
Power to hold, **161:41.**
Petition.
Adjudication by aldermen or selectmen that private land must be taken, **161:58.**
Alteration of location, **161:71.**
Authority to become carrier of freight, express, newspapers, or baggage, **161:53.**
Compelling resumption of use of tracks, **161:86.**
Enforcement of laws and orders, **161:142.**
Extension of location, **161:70.**
General Court, petition for legislation, **3:5.**
Interchange of traffic and cars, **161:47.**
Location, **161:7.**
Private land, purchase or lease, **161:25, 161:55.**
Reduction of capital stock, **161:27.**
Reversal or modification of orders as to service at cost companies, **161:128.**
Revocation or alteration of rules and regulations, petition, **159A:12.**
Snow removal regulations, amendment, **161:85.**
Temporary location, **161:72-161:74.**

STREET RAILWAYS —Cont'd
Petition —Cont'd
Termination of lease by transportation area, **161:155.**
Through routes, establishment, **159:21.**
Valuation of dissenting stock, **161:63.**
Plans.
Abolition of grade crossings, approval of plans by aldermen or selectmen, **161:129.**
Application for authority to purchase or lease land, plan, **161:55.**
Bridges, construction plans to be submitted to department, **159:83.**
Platform.
Station or platform. See within this heading, "Station or platform."
Pleasure resorts.
Amusements and exhibitions. See within this heading, "Amusements and exhibitions."
Police officers, **159:92-159:95.**
Appointment, **22:9M.**
Arrests, **159:93, 159:94, 159:95, 159:104, 161:113A.**
Badges, **159:92.**
Compensation, **159:95.**
Complaint against person arrested, **159:94.**
District court, jurisdiction of persons arrested, **159:94.**
Duties, **159:94.**
Evidence.
Badge, wearing as evidence that officer lawfully upon duty, **159:92.**
Filing and recording.
Records and recording. See within this heading, "Records and recording."
Free tickets or passes, **161:107.**
Misconduct, liability, **159:95.**
Powers, **159:93.**
Records and recording. See within this heading, "Records and recording."
Posting notice of change of service, **161:111.**
Postmen, free tickets or passes, **161:107.**
Power houses, increase in capital stock or issuing bonds to acquire, **161:25.**

STREET RAILWAYS —Cont'd
Powers of street railway
    corporation, **161:38-161:53,
    161:65.**
Preferred stock, **161:32-161:35.**
    Certificate, **161:34.**
    Common stock offered first to
      holders, **161:35.**
    Dividends, **161:116.**
    Exchange of common stock,
      161:33.
    Increase, **161:32.**
    Issue, **161:32.**
      Limitations, **161:35.**
      To provide reserve fund of
        service at cost company,
        161:117.
    Offered first to common
      stockholders, **161:35.**
    Voting powers, **161:35.**
President.
    Actions to be taken, **161:13.**
    Certificates.
      Amount of capital stock fixed
        and paid in, signed and
        sworn, **161:24.**
      Capital stock fully subscribed
        and fifty per cent paid,
        signed and sworn, **161:23.**
      Vote on change of name signed
        and sworn, **161:133.**
    Copy of snow removal
      regulations sent, **161:85.**
    Election, **161:13.**
    Instruments required to be
      signed by, compliance with
      requirements, **161:13.**
    Meetings called, **161:14.**
    Petition for amendment to snow
      removal regulations, **161:85.**
    Required, **161:12.**
    Stock certificates signed, **161:19.**
    Temporary location, petition,
      161:73.
Price.
    Fares.
      Rates and charges. See within
        this heading, "Rates and
        charges."
    New shares of capital stock
      established by stockholders.
      Auction sale of stock. See
        within this heading,
        "Auction sale of stock."
    Transportation area, price to be
      paid for property, **161:145.**
Private property.
    Approval by department of lease
      or purchase, **159:54.**
    Baggage, railway may become
      carrier, **161:53.**

STREET RAILWAYS —Cont'd
Private property —Cont'd
    Electricity may be transmitted
      over, **161:45.**
    Law applicable to railways
      using, **161:57.**
    Purchase or lease for location,
      161:55.
    Regulation of use, **161:56.**
    Stopping cars at private railroad
      crossings, **161:92.**
    Switch connections with private
      sidetracks, establishment,
      159:21.
    Temporary location, **161:72.**
    Use, **161:54-161:61.**
Proxy, voting, **161:17.**
Publication.
    Agreement of association, **161:6.**
    Auction sale of new shares upon
      increase in capital stock,
      notice, **159:51.**
    Hearing upon petition for
      location, notice, **161:7.**
    Result of examination of books
      and financial condition,
      159:35.
    Valuation of property upon
      formation of transportation
      area, **161:145.**
Public convenience and necessity.
    Certificates and certification. See
      within this heading,
      "Certificates and
      certification."
Public officers.
    Officers and agents. See within
      this heading, "Officers and
      agents."
Public officials, free tickets or
    passes, **161:107.**
Public ways.
    Highways and streets. See
      within this heading,
      "Highways and streets."
Public works department.
    Abolition of grade crossings. See
      within this heading,
      "Abolition of grade
      crossings."
    Alteration.
      Crossings with state
        highways, **159:59.**
      Highways for railroad
        crossings, **161:131.**
      Location upon state highways,
        161:82.
    Contracts for transportation of
      materials used in connection
      with highways, **161:50.**
    Location and grade upon state
      highways, designation,
      161:81.

STREET RAILWAYS —Cont'd
Public works department —Cont'd
    Snow removal regulations,
      161:85.
    Supervision on state highways,
      161:82.
Purchase.
    Sale. See within this heading,
      "Sale."
Quorum.
    Stockholders, **161:14.**
    Trustees of transportation area,
      161:148.
Racial discrimination, **272:92A,
    272:98.**
Railings on bridges and draws,
    161:91.
Railroad crossings.
    Crossings. See within this
      heading, "Crossings."
Rate of speed, regulation, **161:84.**
Rates and charges.
    Arrest for failure to pay fare,
      159:93, 159:94.
    Business trust owning or
      controlling street railway,
      182:11.
    Changes in rates.
      Department,
        recommendations, **159:23.**
      Laws as to railroad fares,
        applicability, **161:109.**
      Notice, **161:112.**
    Children, special rates, **161:107,
      161:108.**
    Directors, free tickets or passes,
      161:107.
    Division of rates on through
      routes, **159:21.**
    Ejection of passenger for failure
      to pay fare, **159:101.**
    Establishment of fares by
      companies, **161:104.**
    Evasion of payment of fare. See
      within this heading,
      "Evasion of payment of
      fare."
    Firemen, free passes or tickets,
      161:107.
    Fraudulent evasion of payment
      of fare.
      Evasion of payment of fare.
        See within this heading,
        "Evasion of payment of
        fare."
    Free checks and transfers,
      withdrawal, **161:110.**
    Free tickets, **161:107.**
    GI bill of rights, special rates for
      veterans attending school,
      161:107.

STREET RAILWAYS —Cont'd

Rates and charges —Cont'd

Investigations as to service at cost companies, **161:125.**

Joint fares and rates, **159:21, 161:47.**

Letter carriers, free tickets or passes, **161:107.**

Mayor to be notified of changes, **161:112.**

Notice of changes, **161:112.**

Passes, **161:107.**

Policemen, free tickets or passes, **161:107.**

Public officials, free tickets or passes, **161:107.**

Railroad fares, laws as to regulation of, applicability, **161:109.**

Reduced rates, **161:107, 161:108.**

School children, tickets, **161:107, 161:108.**

Selectmen to be given notice of changes, **161:112.**

Service at cost, **161:115-161:128.**

Acceptance of law, **161:126.**

Authorized, **161:115.**

Capital investment, **161:116, 161:126.**

Definitions, **161:116.**

Foreign company furnishing electricity, schedule of rates, **161:125.**

Governor to appoint directors of company, **161:124.**

Grades of fare.

Changes, **161:121.**

Schedules, **161:120.**

Improvement fund, **161:122.**

Investigation by department, **161:125.**

Items included in cost of service, **161:116, 161:118.**

Obligation to sell to state or municipality, **161:123.**

Operational expenses included in cost of service, **161:116.**

Reports by companies, **161:125.**

Reserve fund.

Establishment, **161:117.**

Report of condition, **161:125.**

Required, **161:117.**

Use, **161:117, 161:119.**

Reversal or modification of orders of department, **161:128.**

Schedules and tariffs.

Foreign company furnishing electricity, **161:125.**

STREET RAILWAYS —Cont'd

Rates and charges —Cont'd

Service at cost —Cont'd

Schedules and tariffs —Cont'd

Grades of fare and transfer privileges, **161:20.**

Stock investment, **161:116, 161:126.**

Interest included in cost of service, **161:116.**

Supervision of companies by department, **161:125.**

Transfer privileges, schedules, **161:120.**

Unfunded debt.

Interest on, included in cost of service, **161:118.**

Status determined by department, **161:118.**

Useless property, disposition, **161:127.**

Special rates, **161:107, 161:108.**

Transfers.

Schedules of transfer privileges, **161:120.**

Violation of conditions, **161:113.**

Withdrawal of free transfers, **161:110.**

Transportation areas, **161:156.**

Unfunded debt.

Service at cost. See within this heading, "Service at cost."

Veterans, reduced rate service, **161:107.**

Working people, special rates, **161:107.**

Zone fares, **161:156.**

Real property.

Increase of capital stock or issue of bonds for acquiring, **161:25.**

Power to hold, **161:41.**

Private property. See within this heading, "Private property."

Sale of property owned for resort purposes, **161:42.**

Telecommunications and energy department. See within this heading, "Telecommunications and energy department."

Receivers, sale, **161:135-161:137.**

Actions against purchasers, **161:135.**

Agreement of association of new company, **161:136.**

Authorized, **161:135.**

Effect, **161:135.**

Mortgage not affected, **161:135.**

New company, **161:136.**

STREET RAILWAYS —Cont'd

Receivers, sale —Cont'd

Organization of new company by purchaser, **161:136, 161:137.**

Taxes and assessments, liability of purchaser, **161:135.**

Recommendations of department for changes in operation, **159:23.**

Records and recording.

Actions for labor and materials, notice and statement, **159:98, 159:99.**

Affidavit of service of notice of first meeting of incorporators, **161:10.**

Agreement of association, **161:9.**

New company upon sale by receivers, **161:136.**

Alteration of location, acceptance, **161:71.**

Change of name, copy of authorization and certificate of vote, **161:133.**

City and town clerks, filing with. See within this heading, "City and town clerks, filing."

Connecting location, acceptance, **161:40.**

Department and commissions to keep records of proceedings, **161:141.**

Dissent of stockholder from sale or consolidation, **161:63.**

Election to accept laws as to service at cost, **161:126.**

Examination of, on request of director, stockholder, or bondholder.

Inspection, examination, or investigation. See within this heading, "Inspection, examination, or investigation."

Extension into other cities and towns, certificate, **161:39.**

Extension of location, acceptance, **161:70.**

Fees. See within this heading, "Fees."

Forms. See within this heading, "Forms."

Issue of bonds, stock, and notes, certificate of decision, **161:28.**

Location, acceptance, **161:7.**

Merger with certain associations or trusts, **161:69A.**

Oath of trustee of transportation area, certificate, **161:146.**

STREET RAILWAYS —Cont'd
Records and recording —Cont'd
Par value, application for approval of change, **161:4, 161:20A.**
Preferred stock, copy of vote creating and order approving, **161:34.**
Private land, petition and plan for purchase or lease, **161:55.**
Reduction of capital stock, certificate, **161:27.**
Reports and returns. See within this heading, "Reports and returns."
Schedule of rates of foreign company furnishing electricity to service at cost company, **161:125.**
Snow removal regulations, findings of department, **161:85.**
Temporary location, acceptance, **161:73.**
Termination of lease by transportation area, petition, **161:155.**
Through routes, petition for location necessary, **159:21.**
Transfer, lease, purchase, or sale of franchise and property, certificate of approval, **159:54.**
Valuation of dissenting stock, petition, **161:63.**
Reduction.
Stock and stockholders. See within this heading, "Stock and stockholders."
Refunding bonds, purposes for increasing capital stock or issuance of bonds by street railways, **161:25.**
Reimbursement.
Contracts to reimburse municipalities for financial deficits, **161:152A.**
Debt service, reimbursement, **161B:7.**
Relief corporations, **159:86-159:88.**
Bylaws, approval by department, **159:87.**
Examination of books and papers by department, **159:87.**
Financial transactions, statement to department, **159:87.**
Funds not liable for liability of railroad corporation or members, **159:88.**

STREET RAILWAYS —Cont'd
Relief corporations —Cont'd
Membership, statement to department, **159:87.**
Purposes for which formed, **159:86.**
Railway corporation may associate with employees in forming, **159:88.**
Representation of railway corporation, **159:88.**
Returns, **159:87.**
Removal from employment, improperly influencing, **271:40, 271:41.**
Removal upon revocation of location, **159:74, 161:77, 161:86.**
Rentals.
Leases. See within this heading, "Leases."
Repairs.
Public ways and bridges, **159:84, 159:85, 161:89.**
Recommendations by department, **159:23.**
Right to open ways or bridges, **161:89.**
Telecommunications and energy department. See within this heading, "Telecommunications and energy department."
Repair shops, use of private land to reach, **161:54.**
Replacement of surface materials on ways and bridges, **161:89.**
Reports and returns.
Abstracts of returns of companies to be prepared by department, **161:139.**
Annual returns.
Contracts and agreements, annual return to set forth copies, **159:33, 161:138.**
Lessee to make to owner, **161:140.**
Public utilities department, annual returns by companies, **161:138, 161:139.**
Trustees of transportation area, **161:148.**
Bridges, examination, **159:83.**
Commissioner's report of value of dissenting stock, **161:63.**
Companies rendering service at cost, **161:125.**
Express companies, **159:33.**
Financial report of treasurer of transportation area, **161:148.**

STREET RAILWAYS —Cont'd
Reports and returns —Cont'd
Investigation of accidents, **159:29.**
Relief corporations, **159:87.**
Trustees of transportation area, annual report, **161:148.**
Requests of department, effect on duties and liabilities of railway, **159:38.**
Reservation of space in public ways, **82:34.**
Reserve fund of service at cost company.
Rates and charges. See within this heading, "Rates and charges."
Resorts.
Amusements and exhibitions. See within this heading, "Amusements and exhibitions."
Restrictions.
Limitation or restriction. See within this heading, "Limitation or restriction."
Returns.
Reports and returns. See within this heading, "Reports and returns."
Revenue commissioner, filing of copy of vote creating order approving preferred stock, **161:34.**
Revocation.
Location, revocation, **161:77.**
Petition for revocation or alteration of rules and regulations, **159A:12.**
Riding on rear or side of car, **85:17B.**
Roadbeds, examination, **159:83.**
Rolling stock.
Cars and equipment. See within this heading, "Cars and equipment."
Route or line.
Notice of discontinuance, **161:111.**
Regulation, **161:84.**
Safety devices on cars, **161:98.**
Salaries.
Compensation. See within this heading, "Compensation."
Sale.
Additional equipment, sale to transportation area, **161:153.**
Assessments, sale of stock for failure to pay, **161:21, 161:22.**

STREET RAILWAYS —Cont'd

Sale —Cont'd

Auction sale of stock. See within this heading, "Auction sale of stock."

Certificate of approval, **159:54.**

Electricity sold to municipal lighting plants, **164:52-164:54.**

Liquor sales at resorts operated by street railways, **161:42.**

Minors, sales on cars, **161:97.**

Private land, sale to street railway, **161:55.**

Railway.

Sale of railway. See within this heading, "Sale of railway."

Receivers, sale by. See within this heading, "Receivers, sale."

Trackless trolleys, purchase of property, **163:11.**

Sale of railway.

Bonds, issue by purchasing company, **161:64.**

Capital stock, increase by purchasing company, **161:64.**

Charter, sale of railway where authorized, **161:62.**

Department's approval, **159:54, 161:63.**

Directors' approval, **161:63.**

Dissenting stockholders, **161:63.**

Dividends, use of proceeds, **161:68.**

Duties of purchasing companies, **161:65.**

Express business, passage of right to engage, **161:65.**

Foreign corporation, sale to domestic companies, **161:69.**

Legal incapacity of dissenting stockholder, time to file dissent extended, **161:63.**

Powers of purchasing company, **161:65.**

Purchase of dissenting stock, **161:63.**

Restrictions, **161:62.**

Securities, exchange, **161:64.**

Stockholders' approval, **161:63.**

Transportation area, preliminary agreement, **161:144, 161:145.**

Valuation of dissenting stock, **161:63.**

Sand and gravel.

Public ways, regulations concerning transportation, **85:36.**

STREET RAILWAYS —Cont'd

Sand and gravel —Cont'd

Transportation, **161:50.**

Schedules and lists.

Lists and schedules. See within this heading, "Lists and schedules."

Schedules and tariffs.

Rates and charges. See within this heading, "Rates and charges."

School children, special rate, **161:107, 161:108.**

Seal.

Commonwealth seal to be affixed to certificate of incorporation, **161:9.**

Company seal, stock certificates to bear, **161:19.**

Secretary of state.

Agreement of association and certificates, filing, **161:9.**

Amount of capital stock fixed and paid in, filing certificate, **161:24.**

Certificates.

Capital stock fully subscribed and fifty percent paid, filing of certificate that, **161:23.**

Incorporation, issuance of certificate, **161:9, 161:137.**

Change in name, granting certificate, **161:133.**

Copy of authorization and certificate of vote upon change of name, filing, **161:133.**

Extension into other cities and towns, filing certificate, **161:39.**

Issue of stock, bonds, and notes, filing certificate, **161:28.**

Merger with certain associations or trusts, filing documents pertaining, **161:69A.**

New company upon sale by receivers, **161:136.**

Reduction of capital stock, filing certificate, **161:27.**

Transfer, lease, purchase, or sale of franchise and property, filing certificate of approval, **159:54.**

Secretary of transportation area, election, **161:148.**

Seeing eye dog, carriage of blind person accompanied, **272:98A.**

Selectmen.

Aldermen or selectmen. See within this heading, "Aldermen or selectmen."

STREET RAILWAYS —Cont'd

Service at cost.

Rates and charges. See within this heading, "Rates and charges."

Service of notice of first meeting of incorporators, **161:10.**

Shooting at train.

Throwing or shooting at train, bus, etc. See within this heading, "Throwing or shooting at train, bus, etc."

Sidetracks and switch connections, **161:54.**

Private sidetracks, establishment of switch connections, **159:21.**

Signals.

Department may require, **159:22.**

Injury to or tampering, **159:102, 159:103.**

Sinking fund, **161:25.**

Smoking in streetcar, **272:43A.**

Snow and ice.

Removal, **161:85.**

Transportation, **161:50.**

Special assessments.

Betterment assessments. See within this heading, "Betterment assessments."

Specially chartered companies, laws applicable, **161:2.**

Special meetings of stockholders, **161:15.**

Special rates in certain instances, **161:107, 161:108.**

Special service cars, **161:107.**

Speed regulations, **161:84.**

Spitting in cars, **270:14, 270:15.**

Sprinkling cars, **161:49.**

Spurs.

Sidetracks and switch connections. See within this heading, "Sidetracks and switch connections."

Stairways, loitering, **161:95.**

State.

Commonwealth. See within this heading, "Commonwealth."

State highways.

Actions in connection with rights in, how taken, **161:13.**

Alteration of crossings, **159:59.**

Instruments in connection with rights in, how executed, **161:13.**

Location, **161:81, 161:82.**

State police, enforcement of regulations as to heating of cars, **161:100.**

STREET RAILWAYS —Cont'd
State secretary.
Secretary of state. See within this heading, "Secretary of state."
Station or platform.
Enclosure of platform during certain months, **161:101, 161:102.**
Loitering in or about station, **161:95.**
Passengers riding upon platform, not to be required to assume risk, **161:106.**
Protection at platforms, **161:98.**
Recommendations of department for additions or changes to stations, **159:23.**
Use of private land for station, **161:54.**
Statistics, table of annual returns of street railways, **161:139.**
Stock and stockholders, **161:19-161:35.**
Abolition of grade crossings, issuance of stock, **159:73, 161:25.**
Acceptance of preliminary agreement for transportation area, **161:145.**
Agreement of association. Subscription, **161:4.**
Annual meeting of stockholders, **161:14, 161:15.**
Application by stockholders for special meeting, **161:15.**
Assessments, **161:21, 161:22.**
Auction sale of stock. See within this heading, "Auction sale of stock."
Bonds, computing amount of capital stock as basis for issuance, **159:53.**
Cash premiums added to par value in computing amount as basis for issue of bonds, **159:53.**
Certificates of stock, **161:19, 161:24.**
Par value to be paid in cash before issue, **161:20.**
Preferred stock, **161:34.**
Reduction, certificates, **161:27.**
Void if issued as dividend, **161:37.**
Certificate that stock fully subscribed and fifty per cent paid, **161:23.**
Change or alteration.
Name changes, vote required, **161:132.**

STREET RAILWAYS —Cont'd
Stock and stockholders —Cont'd
Collection of assessments, **161:22.**
Computing amount as basis for bond issue, **159:53.**
Consolidation or merger. See within this heading, "Consolidation or merger."
Contract for transportation upon one railway by another, approval required, **161:66.**
Deemed to assent to sale or consolidation, **161:63.**
Directors.
Assessments on stock, **161:21, 161:22.**
Auction sale of new shares upon increase, **159:51.**
Certificates as to stock subscriptions, **161:23, 161:24.**
Elected by stockholders, **161:13.**
Indictment for unlawful issue of stock or scrip, **161:37.**
Liability for corporate debts and contracts on reduction of capital stock, **161:27.**
Liability for stock dividend, **161:37.**
Required to be stockholders, **161:13.**
Service at cost company directors appointed by governor not to be stockholders, **161:124.**
Unlawful issuance of stock, **161:31.**
Before capital stock paid, **161:24.**
Dissenting stockholder upon sale or consolidation, **161:63.**
Dividends. See within this heading, "Dividends."
Domestic corporations, limitation on holding of capital stock, **156B:5.**
Duplicates, issuance of stock by street railways, duplicate of decision, **161:28.**
Enforcement of laws and regulations as to issue, **161:30.**
Examination of books and financial condition upon request of stockholders, **159:35.**
Failure to pay assessments, forfeiture or sale of stock, **161:21, 161:22.**

STREET RAILWAYS —Cont'd
Stock and stockholders —Cont'd
Forfeiture of shares for failure to pay assessments, **161:22.**
Grade crossing elimination, issuance of stock to pay costs, **159:73.**
Increase.
Amount determined by department based upon price fixed by stockholders, **159:52.**
Betterment assessments, increase of stock to pay, **161:25.**
Consolidated company, **161:64.**
Disposition of new shares, **159:50, 159:51.**
Notice to shareholders, **159:50.**
Pleasure resort, increase in capital stock to acquire land, **161:25.**
Preferred stock, **161:32.**
Purchasing company upon sale, **161:64.**
Purposes, **161:25, 161:26.**
Rolling stock or equipment increase in capital stock to acquire, **161:25.**
Indictment of director for unlawful issue of stock or scrip, **161:37.**
Issue of bonds and notes, authorized by stockholders, **161:29.**
Issue of stock, **161:28, 161:30, 161:31.**
Lease of railway, stockholders' approval, **161:66.**
Limitations upon issue or holding, **156B:15, 161:29.**
Preferred stock, **161:35.**
List of stockholders, department to have access, **159:31.**
Merger.
Consolidation or merger. See within this heading, "Consolidation or merger."
Minimum amount, **161:4.**
Notice of sale or issuance.
Assessments, sale for failure to pay, **161:21.**
Auction sale of new shares, **159:50-159:52.**
Notice of stockholders meetings, **161:14, 161:15.**
Other corporations.
Holding stock, **156:5, 161:41.**
Par value, **161:4.**
Certificates not to be issued until paid in cash, **161:20.**

STREET RAILWAYS —Cont'd
Stock and stockholders —Cont'd
Par value —Cont'd
Changes of, regulated, **161:4, 161:20A.**
Must be fifty per cent paid in cash prior to construction, **161:23.**
Payment of fifty percent required prior to construction, **161:23.**
Pleasure resorts, increase in capital stock to acquire land, **161:25.**
Preferred stock. See within this heading, "Preferred stock."
Price.
Auction sale of stock. See within this heading, "Auction sale of stock."
Proceeds, application, **161:28.**
Proxy, voting, **161:17.**
Public utilities department.
Approval of stock issue, **159:73, 161:25, 161:28, 161:30, 161:31.**
Auction sales of new stock, **159:51.**
Clerk of department, dissenting stockholder to file, **161:63.**
Increase of capital stock, **161:25.**
List of stockholders, access, **159:31.**
Par value stock, establishment and change, **161:4, 161:20A.**
Preferred stock, approval of restrictions and preferences, **161:32, 161:35.**
Price fixed by stockholders, determination of stock amount upon basis, **159:52.**
Reduction of capital stock, **161:27.**
Service-at-cost company's stock investment determined, **161:116, 161:126.**
Purchasing company upon sale, increase, **161:64.**
Quorum of stockholders, **161:14.**
Rates and charges. See within this heading, "Rates and charges."
Reduction, **161:27.**
Liability of directors, **161:27.**
Proceeds of sale not to be used for dividends unless stock reduced, **161:68.**

STREET RAILWAYS —Cont'd
Stock and stockholders —Cont'd
Reserve fund of service at cost company, issue to provide, **161:117.**
Sale of railway, stockholders' approval required, **161:63.**
Service-at-cost company's stock investment determined by department, **161:116, 161:126.**
Special meetings of stockholders, **161:15.**
Statements as to, in agreement of association, **161:4.**
New company upon sale by receivers, **161:136.**
Subscriptions, **159:50-159:52.**
Capital stock subscriptions in full required prior to construction, **161:23.**
Failure to pay assessment, **161:21, 161:22.**
Liability of subscriber prior to incorporation, **161:4.**
Preferred stock, **161:35.**
Rights, **159:50-159:52.**
Trackless trolley companies, **161:35, 163:8.**
Supreme judicial or superior court, enforcement of laws as to issue of stock, **161:30.**
Termination of lease by transportation area, consent, **161:155.**
Transfers.
Property or money transferred to stockholders upon reduction, **161:27.**
Shares transferred upon failure of subscriber to pay assessments, **161:21, 161:22.**
Unanimous vote for merger with certain associations or trusts, requirement, **161:69A.**
Violations as to issuance of stock, **161:31.**
Voting rights, **161:16, 161:17, 161:35, 161:69A.**
Waiver of notice of meetings, **161:14.**
Stolen passes, use of stolen or counterfeited employee transportation pass, **161:113A.**
Stones, transportation, **161:50.**
Stopping cars.
Fire apparatus, stopping on approach, **89:6A.**
Railroad crossings, stopping, **161:92.**

STREET RAILWAYS —Cont'd
Streets.
Highways and streets. See within this heading, "Highways and streets."
Subscriptions.
Stock and stockholders. See within this heading, "Stock and stockholders."
Superintendent of streets.
Permits for opening public ways and bridges issued, **161:89.**
Regulations as to snow removal, **161:85.**
Superior court.
Bridges, enforcement of maintenance and repair, **159:85.**
Enforcement of laws, rules, regulations, and orders, **161:142.**
Issue of stock and bonds, enforcement of laws, **161:30.**
Review of rulings of any department or commission, **161:142.**
Supervision of service at cost companies, **161:125.**
Supplies.
Cars and equipment. See within this heading, "Cars and equipment."
Labor and materials. See within this heading, "Labor and materials."
Supreme judicial court.
Compelling company to resume use of tracks, **161:86.**
Enforcement of laws, rules, regulations, and order, **161:142.**
Issue of stock and bonds, enforcement of laws, **161:30.**
Reversal or modification of orders as to service at cost company, **161:128.**
Review of rulings of any department or commission, **161:142.**
Valuation of dissenting stock, **161:63.**
Surface of public ways, duty to repair or replace, **161:89.**
Suspension.
Revocation. See within this heading, "Revocation."
Switch connections and sidetracks.
Sidetracks and switch connections. See within this heading, "Sidetracks and switch connections."

STREET RAILWAYS —Cont'd

Tables of annual returns of companies to be prepared by department, **161:139.**

Taking securities of other corporations, **161:41.**

Taking up public ways in which tracks located, **161:88.**

Tampering with cars, **159:103.**

Tariffs.

  Rates and charges. See within this heading, "Rates and charges."

Taxation.

  Assessments. See within this heading, "Assessments."

  Assessors to include deficit from transportation area in tax levy for following year, **161:151.**

  Bonds and notes, taxation, **59:4.**

  Contributions to cost of service by city or town may be raised, **161:161.**

  Cost of service, taxes included, **161:116.**

  Liability of purchaser upon sale by receiver for taxes, **161:135.**

  Property leased by transportation area, **161:158.**

Telecommunications and energy department.

  Abstracts of returns of companies to be prepared, **161:139.**

  Accidents.

    Investigation, **159:29.**

    Notice, **38:8, 159:28.**

  Additional accommodations for passengers may be required, **161:105.**

  Additions to rolling stock, recommendations of department, **159:23.**

  Advice of, effect upon duties and liabilities of railway, **159:38.**

  Agreements.

    Approval of contract that one company will perform transportation for another, **159:54, 161:66.**

    Association and certificates presented to, agreement, **161:8.**

    Establishment of transportation area to be approved by, agreement, **161:66, 161:143.**

  Annual returns by companies, **161:39, 161:138.**

STREET RAILWAYS —Cont'd

Telecommunications and energy department —Cont'd

  Appeals as to carrying of freight, baggage, express, and newspapers, **161:53.**

  Approach of cars, approval of regulation as to notice, **161:93.**

  Basis for contribution to transportation area by cities and towns, establishment, **161:150, 161:151.**

  Boston, publication of result of examination of books and financial condition, **159:35.**

  Bridges, powers, **159:83-159:85.**

  Business trusts, supervision, **182:7-182:10.**

  Bylaws of relief corporations approved, **159:87.**

  Capital investment of companies rendering service at cost determined, **161:116, 161:126.**

  Cars.

    Additions to rolling stock, recommendations of department, **159:23.**

    Heating, **161:100.**

    Regulations as to number and routes, **161:47, 161:84.**

  Certificates and certification. See within this heading, "Certificates and certification."

  Changes or alterations.

    Grades of fare company rendering service at cost, **161:121.**

    Location, alteration, **161:71.**

    Name, authorization of change, **161:132.**

    Operations, recommendations by department for changes, **159:23.**

  Clerk.

    Certificate of compliance to be annexed to agreement of association, **161:9.**

    Stockholder's dissent to sale or consolidation, filing, **161:63.**

  Commissioner forbidden to have interest in street railways, **25:3.**

  Connecting location between cities and towns, granting, **161:40.**

  Consolidation, approval, **159:54, 161:63, 161:69A.**

STREET RAILWAYS —Cont'd

Telecommunications and energy department —Cont'd

  Contributions by cities and towns to cost of service, determination of questions, **161:161.**

  County commissioners, application to department to compel maintenance and repair of bridges, **159:84.**

  Crossings between street railways and railroads regulated, **159:57, 159:58.**

  Damages, questions under leases to transportation area to be submitted to department, **161:157.**

  Defects, complaints by employees to department, **159:30.**

  Designation of newspaper for publication of agreement of association, **161:6.**

  Determination of price or rental to be paid by transportation area, **161:145.**

  Disposing of useless property of service at cost company, **161:127.**

  Division of Commonwealth into street railway districts, **161:125.**

  Domestic trust company may be designated as trustee of sinking fund, **161:25.**

  Emergency tools, approval, **161:99.**

  Eminent domain, taking land.

    Application for certificate of public necessity and convenience, **161:58.**

    Electricity, rights of way or easements in location of street railway, **164:72.**

    Of other railway company or railroad for grade crossing elimination, approval, **161:129.**

    Transportation area, taking street railway, **161:149.**

  Enclosure of platforms, manner prescribed by department, **161:101, 161:102.**

  Evidence of compliance with orders of department, **159:16.**

  Exclusion of city or town from transportation area, **161:154.**

  Extension.

    Into other cities and towns, **161:39.**

STREET RAILWAYS —Cont'd
Telecommunications and energy
department —Cont'd
Extension —Cont'd
Lines or purchase of
additional equipment by
transportation area,
consent, **161:153.**
Location, **161:70.**
Time for construction and
operation, **161:38.**
Fares and fare zones for
transportation areas,
approval, **161:156.**
Free checks or transfers,
approval of withdrawal,
161:110.
Grade crossing abolition,
approval of stock or bond
issue, **159:73.**
Heating of cars, regulation,
161:100.
Improvement fund of company
rendering service at cost,
161:122.
Increase of capital stock, **161:25.**
Inspector to investigate
accidents, **159:29.**
Interchange of traffic and cars,
regulation, **161:47.**
Issue of capital stock, bonds, and
notes, **161:25, 161:28,
161:30, 161:31, 161:152.**
Joint use of tracks, regulation,
161:46.
Jurisdiction, **159:12.**
Lease of railways, consent,
161:66.
List of stockholders, access,
159:31.
Location, certification, **161:7.**
Manner of constructing crossings
prescribed, **161:130.**
Mergers, approval, **161:63,
161:69A.**
Milk and cream, regulation of
transportation, **161:114.**
Minimum price of bonds may be
prescribed, **161:25.**
Motive power, approval, **161:43.**
Motor vehicles, approval of use,
161:44.
Notice.
Accidents, notice, **38:8, 159:28.**
Operation of railways,
recommendations for
changes, **159:23.**
Orders, submission of evidence
of compliance, **159:16.**
Par value stock, establishment
and change, **161:4, 161:20A.**

STREET RAILWAYS —Cont'd
Telecommunications and energy
department —Cont'd
Permission to operate railways
by transportation area
outside of Commonwealth,
161:154.
Plans for new bridges submitted,
159:83.
Platforms, protection, **161:98.**
Pleasure resorts and parks,
approval of owning and
operating, **161:42.**
Preferred stock, approval of
restrictions and preferences,
161:32, 161:35.
Preliminary agreement for
transportation area,
approval, **161:144, 161:145.**
Private sidetracks,
establishment of switch
connections, **159:21.**
Railroad crossings, modification
or suspension of
requirements for stopping
cars, **161:92.**
Railroad tracks, use of,
regulated, **161:48.**
Real property.
Approval of department for
lease, purchase, or sale,
159:54.
Private land, authority to
purchase or lease, and
regulation of use, **161:55,
161:56.**
Recommendations by
department for changes in
operation, **159:23.**
Reduction of capital stock,
authorization, **161:27.**
Repairs, powers, **159:23.**
Bridge repairs, **159:84.**
Request of, effect upon duties
and liabilities of railways,
159:38.
Reversal or modification of
orders as to service at cost
companies, **161:128.**
Revocation of location, approval,
161:77.
Rolling stock, recommendations
for addition, **159:23.**
Safety devices on cars, **161:98.**
Sale of property owned for resort
purposes, approval, **161:42.**
Schedules of grades of fare and
transfer privileges of service
at cost company, approval,
161:120.
School tickets, regulation,
161:108.

STREET RAILWAYS —Cont'd
Telecommunications and energy
department —Cont'd
Signals may be required, **159:22.**
Sinking fund, establishment
may be ordered, **161:25.**
Snow removal regulations,
amendment, **161:85.**
Speed regulations, **161:84.**
Statement of relief corporations,
159:87.
Stations, recommendations for
additions to or changes,
159:23.
Stock and stockholders. See
within this heading, "Stock
and stockholders."
Street sprinkling cars, approval
of use, **161:49.**
Supervision of service at cost
companies, **161:125.**
Switch connections, granting of
location, **159:21.**
Tables of returns of companies
to be prepared, **161:139.**
Temporary location, application
for and approval, **161:72,
161:74.**
Through routes, establishment,
159:21.
Towns for holding auction sales
of new shares of capital
stock prescribed, **159:51.**
Track regulations, **161:84.**
Transfer, lease, purchase or sale
of franchise and property,
certificate of approval,
159:54.
Trustee of sinking fund
designated, **161:25.**
Unfunded debt of service at cost
company, status determined
by department, **161:118.**
Valuation of property on
establishment of
transportation area,
161:145.
Temporary discontinuance of use
of tracks, **161:87.**
Temporary location.
Location. See within this
heading, "Location."
Termination of leases.
Transportation areas. See within
this heading,
"Transportation areas."
Termini to be stated in agreement
of association, **161:4.**
New company upon sale by
receivers, **161:136.**
Through routes, establishment,
159:21.

STREET RAILWAYS —Cont'd

Throwing or shooting at train, bus, etc., **159:104.**

Arrest and jurisdiction, **159:93, 159:94, 159:104.**

Tickets or passes.
Free tickets, **161:107.**
School pupils, **161:108.**
Stolen or counterfeited employee transportation pass, **161:113A.**

Time.
Acceptance of connecting location, **161:40.**
Completion of construction and commencement of operation, **161:38.**
Limitation of actions. See within this heading, "Limitation of actions."
Receivers, date of order and sale to appear on agreement of association of new company upon sale, **161:136.**
Temporary location, time within which certain proceedings must be completed, **161:7.**

Tools, cars to be provided with emergency tools, **161:99.**

Torpedoes, marking, **159:102.**

Towns.
Cities and towns. See within this heading, "Cities and towns."

Trackless trolleys, **163:1-163:12.** See TRACKLESS TROLLEYS.

Tracks.
Aldermen or selectmen. See within this heading, "Aldermen or selectmen."
Compelling resumption of use, **161:86.**
Discontinuance of use, **161:86, 161:87.**
Examination, **159:83.**
Fines and penalties, **161:84, 161:94, 161:103.**
Joint use, **161:46.**
Location. See within this heading, "Location."
Obstruction, **161:94.**
Recovery of expense of removing, **161:86.**
Regulations as to use, **161:84.**
Removal, **159:74, 161:77, 161:86.**
Resumption of use, **161:86.**
Snow removal, **161:85.**
Temporary tracks, **161:76.**
Use of railroad tracks, **161:48.**

Traffic regulations and rules of the road, **161:47, 161:84.**

STREET RAILWAYS —Cont'd

Transfers.
Certificate of approval, **159:54.**
Franchise and property, approval of transfers, **159:54.**
Rates and charges. See within this heading, "Rates and charges."
Sale. See within this heading, "Sale."
Stock and stockholders. See within this heading, "Stock and stockholders."

Transportation areas, **161:143-161:161.**
Advertisement of valuation of property, **161:145.**
Application of law to areas previously established, **161:160.**
Assessors to include deficit in tax levy for following year, **161:151.**
Basis for computing contribution by cities and towns, **161:150, 161:151.**
Borrowing by cities and towns, **161:152.**
Boston elevated railway company, law inapplicable, **161:159.**
Chairman, election, **161:148.**
Contribution by cities and towns, **161:150, 161:151.**
Distinctive name, area to have, **161:143.**
Election.
Officers, **161:147, 161:148.**
Preliminary agreement, **161:145.**
Question of taking street railway for area, **161:149.**
Termination of lease by area, **161:155.**
Establishment, **161:143.**
Exclusion of city or town, **161:154.**
Extension of lines, **161:153.**
Fares and fare zones, **161:156.**
Finances, **161:151.**
Leases.
Damages, **161:157.**
Formation of areas, **161:145.**
Preliminary agreement for lease of properties, **161:144.**
Renewal, **161:155.**
Rentals, **161:145, 161:155.**
Taxation of property leased by transportation area, **161:158.**

STREET RAILWAYS —Cont'd

Transportation areas —Cont'd
Leases —Cont'd
Term, **161:155.**
Termination, **161:155.**
Return of property, **161:157.**
Notes, issuance, **161:152.**
Officers, election and appointment, **161:147, 161:148.**
Operation of railways outside of Commonwealth, **161:154.**
Preliminary agreement, **161:144, 161:145.**
Price to be paid by area, determination, **161:145.**
Property operated by trustees, **161:147.**
Purchase of additional equipment, **161:153.**
Rentals, **161:145, 161:155.**
Secretary, election, **161:148.**
Taking of street railway by eminent domain, **161:149.**
Taxation, **161:151, 161:158.**
Treasurer, **161:148.**
Trustees.
Annual report, **161:148.**
Appointment, **161:146.**
Compensation, **161:146.**
Fares and fare zones, fixing, **161:156.**
Issuance of notes, **161:152.**
Maintenance of property, **161:157.**
Meetings, **161:148.**
Oath, **161:146.**
Officers elected, **161:147, 161:148.**
Powers, **161:147.**
Quorum, **161:148.**
Removal, **161:146.**
Request that street railway be taken, **161:149.**
Term of office, **161:146.**
Vacancies, filling, **161:146.**
Valuation of property, **161:145.**
Vice-chairman, election, **161:148.**

Treasurer.
Agreement of association and certificates presented to department, **161:8.**
Annual return sworn, **161:138.**
Assessments on capital stock paid, **161:21.**
Bond or undertaking of treasurer. See within this heading, "Bond or undertaking of treasurer."
Certificates.
Amount of capital stock fixed and paid in, signed and sworn, **161:24.**

STREET RAILWAYS —Cont'd
Treasurer —Cont'd
Certificates —Cont'd
Capital stock fully subscribed
and fifty per cent paid,
signed and sworn, **161:23.**
Vote on change of name signed
and sworn, **161:133.**
Directors to appoint prior to
organization, **161:5.**
Election, **161:13.**
Issue of stock or bonds
unlawfully, **161:31.**
Notice of assessments on stock,
161:21.
Required, **161:12.**
Sale of capital stock for failure
to pay assessments, **161:21,
161:22.**
Stock certificates signed, **161:19.**
Transportation area, treasurer
of, election, **161:148.**
Trespass on facilities, **161:94A,
161:95.**
Trial.
Hearing. See within this
heading, "Hearings."
Jury trial as to value of
dissenting stock, **161:63.**
Trusts and trustees.
Business trusts owning or
operating street railways,
control by public utilities
department, **182:7-182:11.**
Consolidation or merger with
association or trust owning
entire capital stock,
161:69A.
Sinking fund, trustee, **161:25.**
Transportation areas. See within
this heading,
"Transportation areas."
Tunnels, examination, **159:83.**
Unanimous approval by
stockholders of merger with
certain associations or trusts,
161:69A.
Undertakings.
Bond or undertaking of
treasurer. See within this
heading, "Bond or
undertaking of treasurer."
Unfunded debt of service at cost
company, **161:118.**
Valuation.
Dissenting stock, **161:63.**
Par value of capital stock.
Stock and stockholders. See
within this heading,
"Stock and stockholders."
Transportation area, property,
161:145.

STREET RAILWAYS —Cont'd
Veterans attending school under
GI Bill of Rights, special rates,
161:107.
Veto power of mayor not affected
by provisions, **161:1.**
Vice-chairman of transportation
area, election, **161:148.**
Voluntary discontinuance of use of
tracks, **161:86.**
Voters, complaints, **159:24.**
Voting rights of stock, **161:16,
161:17, 161:35, 161:69A.**
Wages.
Compensation. See within this
heading, "Compensation."
Waiver of notice.
Directors' meetings, **161:18.**
First meeting of incorporators,
161:10.
Stockholders' meetings, **161:14.**
Warning of approach of cars,
161:93.
Warrantless arrests, **159:93,
159:94, 159:104, 161:113A.**
Wheel guards on cars, **161:98.**
Widening of public way for
location, **161:78.**
Witnesses to accident causing
death, inspector may summon
to inquest, **159:29.**
Working capital, increase of stock
or issue of bonds to provide,
161:26.
Working people, special rates,
161:107.
Wrongful death, liability, **229:2.**
Zone fares for transportation
areas, **161:156.**

STREETS.
**See HIGHWAYS AND
STREETS.**

STRICT LIABILITY.
Blasting, **148:20C.**
Hazardous waste insolvency fund,
**21C:15, 21C:19, 21E:2,
21E:16-21E:18.**
Lead poisoning, letter of
compliance, **111:197.**
Operator of low-level waste
facility, **111H:9.**
Torts, generally.
See TORTS.

STRIKES.
**See LABOR RELATIONS AND
DISPUTES.**

STRIPED BASS.
Manner of taking, **130:100B.**
Size limit, **130:100A.**

STRIP-MINING.
Youth conservation and service
corps, **78A:3.**

STROKE.
Program to reduce incidents,
111:206.

STROPHANTHIN.
Misbranding of drugs, what
constitutes, **94:187.**

STRUCTURAL ENGINEERS.
Board of registration of
professional engineers to
recognize, **112:81E.**
Engineers generally,
112:81D-112:81T.
See ENGINEERS AND
SURVEYORS.

**STRUCTURED SETTLEMENT
CONTRACTS.**
Transfer of payment rights,
231C:1 to 231C:5.

STRUCTURES.
**See BUILDINGS AND
STRUCTURES.**

STRYCHNINE.
Misbranding of drugs, what
constitutes, **94:187.**

STUDDED SNOW TIRES.
Regulation of use, **90:16.**

**STUDENT LOAN AUTHORITY
ACT, 15C:1 et seq.**

**STUDENT LOAN MARKETING
ASSOCIATION.**
Massachusetts College Student
Loan Authority, investments,
15C:18.

STUDENT LOANS.
Income tax.
Interest payments.
Deductions from taxable
income, **62:3.**

STUDENTS.
**See SCHOOLS AND
EDUCATION.**

STUMPAGE FEES.
Municipal corporations, watershed
land in another municipality,
59:5D, 59:5F.

STUMPAGE VALUE.
Taxation of forest products based,
61:2.

STURBRIDGE.
Congressional district, **57:1.**
District court, **218:1.**
Medical examiner district, **38:1.**

STURBRIDGE —Cont'd
Senatorial district, **57:3.**

SUBADJACENT SUPPORT.
Coal mining operations,
regulation, **21B:11.**

SUB-BIDS.
See BIDS AND BIDDING.

SUBCHAPTER S EARNINGS,
62:2.

SUBCONTRACTORS.
Construction.
See CONSTRUCTION
CONTRACTS AND WORK.
Medical assistance division,
118E:51.
Words and phrases, **142A:1.**

SUBDIVISION CONTROL,
41:81K to 41:81GG.
See ZONING AND PLANNING.

SUBMACHINE GUNS.
Hunting with prohibited, **131:64.**

SUBMERGED LANDS.
Public lands, **91:2, 91:11-91:18.**

SUBORDINATION OF LIEN.
See LIENS AND
ENCUMBRANCES.

SUBORNATION OF PERJURY,
268:2, 268:3.
See PERJURY.

SUBPOENA DUCES TECUM.
See PRODUCTION OF BOOKS
AND PAPERS.

SUBPOENAS, 277:68.
Administration and finance
executive office.
Commissioner, powers, **7:4E.**
Personnel administrator, powers,
7:4I.
Administrative procedure, **30A:12.**
Appellate tax board, **58A:11.**
Arbitration and award.
Disputes as to domicile of
decedent, **65B:4.**
Use in arbitration proceedings,
251:7.
Authorities empowered to issue,
277:68.
Banks and banking, investigative
hearing on consumer
transactions, **167:2C.**
Building regulations and
standards board, powers and
duties, **143:94.**
Child support hearing officer,
power to issue subpoena,
221B:6.

SUBPOENAS —Cont'd
Civil rights and discrimination.
Commission against
discrimination, powers,
151B:3.
Fair educational practices
proceedings, **151C:3.**
Civil service commission, powers,
7:4I, 31:72.
Clerks of court, fees, **262:4.**
Commercial motor vehicle division,
powers, **25:12G.**
Community antenna television
systems, division, subpoenas,
166A:17.
Constitutional right of accused to
compulsory process, **US Const**
Amend 6.
Consumer transaction practices,
investigative hearing, **167:2C.**
Costs.
Fees and costs. See within this
heading, "Fees and costs."
Court officials, uniform rules of
subpoenas.
See SUBPOENAS TO COURT
OFFICIALS, UNIFORM
RULES OF.
Courts-martial, issuance, **33:77.**
Criminal cases, **277:68.**
Depositions, **233:47.**
Discrimination.
Civil rights and discrimination.
See within this heading,
"Civil rights and
discrimination."
Duces tecum subpoena.
See PRODUCTION OF BOOKS
AND PAPERS.
Employee subpoenaed to testify at
criminal proceeding, discharge
or penalty by employer,
258B:3, 268:14B.
Employment agencies, powers of
labor and workforce
development commissioner in
connection with hearings
involving, **140:46Q.**
Employment security.
See EMPLOYMENT
SECURITY.
Engineers and land surveyors,
proceedings before board,
112:81P.
Fair educational practices
proceedings, **151C:3.**
Fees and costs, **262:53.**
Clerk of court, **262:4.**
Indigents, subpoena as extra
court cost, **261:27A.**
Inquest, fees and expenses for
service of process relative,
262:26.

SUBPOENAS —Cont'd
Fees and costs —Cont'd
Justice of the peace, **262:1.**
Service of subpoenas issued by
general court, **262:13.**
Sheriffs' fees for serving
subpoenas, **262:8, 262:13.**
Finance executive office.
Administration and finance
executive office. See within
this heading,
"Administration and finance
executive office."
Foreign insurance companies.
See FOREIGN INSURANCE
COMPANIES.
Foreign state, compelling
production of evidence for use,
223A:11.
General court, **3:28, 3:28A.**
Fees, sheriffs serving subpoenas
issued by general court,
262:13.
Post audit and oversight
committee, authority, **3:63.**
Hearing officers division, powers,
7:4H, 221B:6.
Hospital records, **111:70.**
Indigents, subpoena as extra court
cost, **261:27A.**
Inquest, fees and expenses for
service of process relative,
262:26.
Insurance.
See INSURANCE.
Judicial conduct commission,
power to issue subpoenas,
211C:2, 211C:5.
Justices of the peace, fees, **262:1.**
Labor relations and disputes.
Member of commission of labor
relations may issue
subpoenas, **150A:7.**
Refusal to obey subpoenas,
150A:7.
Liens on buildings and land, filing
of copy of subpoena, **254:12,**
254:13.
Livestock disease control,
authority of director to issue,
129:10.
Lottery commission, subpoena
power, **10:24.**
Medical peer review committee,
records and reports not
subject to subpoena or
discovery, **111:204.**
Mental health department, powers
of trustees of public
institutions under control,
19:14.

SUBPOENAS —Cont'd
Militia.
  Board of injury, **33:90.**
  Courts-martial, issuance, **33:77.**
Milk and milk products.
  Enforcement of subpoena,
    94A:18.
  Northeast Interstate Dairy
    Compact, **Spec L 139:16.**
  Service of subpoena, **94A:19.**
Motor vehicle loss prevention
  central organization, reports
  filed, **175:113O.**
Northeast Interstate Dairy
  Compact, **Spec L 139:16.**
Personnel administrator, powers,
  7:4I.
Physicians, complaints against,
  112:5.
Police officers, service, **262:53.**
Poor persons, subpoenas as extra
  court costs, **261:27A.**
Production of books.
  See PRODUCTION OF BOOKS
    AND PAPERS.
Public accountants not subject to
  subpoena, **112:87E½.**
Public utilities commission,
  witnesses before, **25:5A.**
Radiation protection advisory
  council, authority as to
  issuance, **111:4F.**
Retirement boards, witnesses
  before, **32:16, 32:20.**
Rules.
  See SUBPOENAS TO COURT
    OFFICIALS, UNIFORM
    RULES OF.
Securities Act.
  Uniform Securities Act. See
    within this heading,
    "Uniform Securities Act."
Service, **94A:19.**
Sheriff's fee for serving, **262:8,
  262:13.**
Social services, procedure for
  appeal of departmental
  decisions, **18:16.**
State agency's authority to
  prescribe form, **30A:12.**
Taxation.
  Appellate tax board, **58A:11.**
Trusts with absentee beneficiaries,
  service on trustee, **203:28.**
Unemployment compensation.
  See EMPLOYMENT
    SECURITY.
Uniform rules of subpoenas to
  court officials.
  See SUBPOENAS TO COURT
    OFFICIALS, UNIFORM
    RULES OF.

SUBPOENAS —Cont'd
Uniform Securities Act, **110A:407.**
  Investigations or proceedings by
    secretary of state, **110A:407.**
  Privilege of secretary of state or
    his officers or employees,
    110A:406.
Welfare and social services,
  procedure for appeal of
  departmental decisions, **18:16.**

**SUBPOENAS TO COURT
OFFICIALS, UNIFORM
RULES OF.**
Approval of court for service of
  subpoenas, **Rule 1.**
Court order approving subpoena to
  be served with subpoena,
  Rule 1.
Denial of request for documents,
  Rule 2.
Justice, subpoena to, **Rule 1.**
Magistrate, subpoena to, **Rule 1.**
Payment of fee for attested copy of
  court records, **Rule 2.**
Personal identifier of each record
  requested from Commissioner
  of Probate's office, **Rule 3.**
Probation Commissioner, duces
  tecum subpoena for records
  from office of, **Rule 3.**
Sealed or impounded records,
  duces tecum subpoena
  requesting, **Rule 2.**

SUBROGATION.
Automobile insurance.
  See AUTOMOBILE
    INSURANCE.
Contribution among joint
  tortfeasors law as affecting,
  231B:1.
Hazardous waste insolvency fund,
  rights, **21C:19, 21C:20,
  21C:26.**
Home improvement contractors,
  subrogation of rights to fund
  administrator, **142A:8.**
Letters of credit, **106:5-117.**
Massachusetts life and health
  insurance guaranty
  association law, **175:147.**
Medical care.
  See MEDICAL CARE AND
    ASSISTANCE.
Motor vehicle insurance.
  See AUTOMOBILE
    INSURANCE.
Personal injury protection benefit
  payments, insurers'
  subrogation rights, **90:34M.**
Property protection insurance
  coverage, subrogation rights of
  insurers, **90:34O.**

SUBROGATION —Cont'd
Real estate time-shares, insurance,
  183B:26.
Social services department's
  subrogation to rights of
  welfare recipient, **18:5G,
  18:21, 119A:3.**
Title registration assurance fund,
  Commonwealth's right to
  subrogation to plaintiff's
  rights, **185:105.**
Victims of violent crimes,
  subrogation of state to cause
  of action accruing, **258C:11.**
Welfare department subrogated to
  rights of welfare recipient,
  **18:5G, 18:21, 118E:22,
  118E:23, 119A:3.**
Workers' compensation cases,
  152:15, 152:18.

**SUBSCRIBING WITNESSES.
See ATTESTATION AND
  ATTESTING WITNESSES.**

SUBSEQUENT INJURIES.
Workers' compensation, payment
  of compensation for
  subsequent injuries, **152:35B,
  152:37.**

**SUBSEQUENT OFFENSES.
See CONVICTION OF CRIME.**

SUBSEQUENT PURCHASERS.
Bona fide purchasers.
  See BONA FIDE
    PURCHASERS.
Holder in due course.
  See HOLDER IN DUE
    COURSE.
Propane gas dealers and
  homeowners, binding
  agreements, **93:94.**

SUBSIDIARIES.
Corporations.
  See CORPORATIONS.

**SUBSIDIES.
See AID AND ASSISTANCE.**

**SUBSTANDARD DWELLINGS.
See HOUSING AND URBAN
  RENEWAL.**

**SUBSTANTIAL EVIDENCE
  RULES.
See EVIDENCE.**

**SUBSTANTIAL
  PERFORMANCE.**
Contracts, generally.
  See CONTRACTS AND
    AGREEMENTS.
Real estate time-shares, **183B:8.**

SUBSTANTIAL PERFORMANCE —Cont'd

Sales, generally.
See SALES UNDER COMMERCIAL CODE.
Uniform commercial code, generally.
See COMMERCIAL CODE.

SUBSTITUTE CARE REVIEW HEARINGS, UNIFORM RULES FOR.

Appeals, **Rule 9.**
Applicability, **Rule 1.**
Counsel, **Rule 5.**
Definitions, **Rule 2.**
Hearing, **Rule 7.**
Notice of hearing, **Rule 4.**
Orders, **Rule 8.**
Pre-hearing conference, **Rule 6.**
Purpose, **Rule 3.**
Submission of plan, **Rule 4.**

SUBSTITUTED SERVICE ACT.

Foreign corporations, 181:4, 15.

SUBSTITUTES AND SUBSTITUTION.

Attorney General, appointment of substitute, 12:26.
Bill of lading, issuance of substitute, 106:7-305.
Butter, 94:49-94:63.
See BUTTER.
Buyer's procurement of substitute goods, 106:2-712.
Drugs and narcotics, 112:12B, 112:12D.
Endorser of writ or bill of nonresident, substitution, 231:48.
Executors.
See EXECUTORS AND ADMINISTRATORS.
Facsimile seals.
See FACSIMILE SEALS AND SIGNATURES.
Food.
See FOOD.
Indigency, filing affidavit of and request for substitution of court fees and costs, 261:27B.
Insurance.
New policy substituted for one on property securing loan, 175:193E.
Policy of one insurer substituted for that of another, prohibition against separate charge, 176D:4.
Leases under Commercial Code, 106:2A-404.

SUBSTITUTES AND SUBSTITUTION —Cont'd

Parties.
See SUBSTITUTION OF PARTIES.
Process, substituted service of, 181:4.
See PROCESS AND SERVICE OF PROCESS AND PAPERS.
Registration of land titles.
Parties, substitution, 185:32, 185:44.
Seeds, 128:91.
Superior courts.
Attorney general, appointment of substitute, 12:26.
Executor or administrator, substitution of to be in accordance with rules of civil procedure, 228:4A.
Supreme judicial court.
Attorney general, appointment of substitute, 12:26.
Executor or administrator to be substituted in accordance with rules of civil procedure, 228:4A.

SUBSTITUTION OF PARTIES.

Abatement.
See ABATEMENT, SURVIVAL, AND REVIVAL.
Corporations.
Consolidation of business corporations, 156:46C, 156B:80.
Liability of officer or stockholder, substitution of executor or administrator as defendant in action to enforce, 156:39, 158:51.
Proxies.
See PROXIES.
Registration of land title, substitution of parties in proceedings, 185:32, 185:44.

SUBVERSIVE ACTIVITIES CONTROL ACT, 264:16 et seq.

SUBVERSIVE ORGANIZATIONS.

Actions against and adjudications, 264:18.
Auditorium, building, etc., 264:22.
Becoming or remaining member, 264:19.
Books.
Records. See within this heading, "Records, reports, and returns."

SUBVERSIVE ORGANIZATIONS —Cont'd

Communist Party, 50:1, 264:16A.
Contributions, 264:23.
Definition, 264:16.
Destruction or concealment of books, records, and funds, 264:21.
Election ballot, convicted person's name not to be placed, 264:20.
Fines and penalties.
Activities in connection with subversive organizations, 264:16 et seq.
Contributions, 264:23.
Destruction or concealment of property, 264:21.
Membership, 264:19.
Use of auditorium, 264:22.
Injunctions against, 264:18.
Membership lists, 264:21, 276:1A.
Offenses and penalties.
Fines and penalties. See within this heading, "Fines and penalties."
Pictures or photographs.
Search warrant for pictures and other papers used, 276:1A.
Use by subversive organizations, 264:11.
Political designation, subversive organization's name not to be used, 53:8.
Political party, subversive organization, 50:1.
Public office or employment, ineligibility to hold, 264:20.
Records, reports, and returns.
Destruction or concealment of books, 264:21.
Search warrants, 276:1A.
Search warrants for books or pictures, 276:1A.
Unlawful, 264:17.

SUBWAYS.

Massachusetts Bay transportation authority, 161A:1 to 161A:47.
See MASSACHUSETTS BAY TRANSPORTATION AUTHORITY.

SUCCESSION.
See DESCENT AND DISTRIBUTION.

SUCCESSION TAX ACT, 65:2 et seq.

SUCCESSORS-IN-INTEREST.

Marketing agreement for sale of gasoline, designation of successor-in-interest, 93E:5A.

SUCTION MACHINES.
Sales tax exemptions, **64H:6.**

SUDBURY.
Congressional district, **57:1.**
District court, **218:1.**
Medical examiner district, **38:1.**
Senatorial district, **57:3.**

SUDBURY RESERVOIR.
"Watershed system," definition for purposes of provision creating watershed management division, **92:104.**

SUDDEN INFANT DEATH.
Autopsies, **38:3.**

SUFFERANCE.
Estates.
See ESTATES BY SUFFERANCE.

SUFFOLK COUNTY.
Additional judges for probate and insolvency, **217:2.**
Administrative assistant, **221:76.**
Alcoholic liquors.
Holidays and Sundays, **138:33.**
Hours for sale, **138:12.**
Animals.
Compensation for destruction of diseased animals, action, **129:31.**
Dogs. See within this heading, "Dogs."
Appeals.
Appeals court. See within this heading, "Appeals court."
Indigents, appeals in Suffolk county from denial of relief from court costs, **261:27D.**
Motor vehicle financing, appeals from refusal of revocation of license, **255B:5, 255B:8.**
Stop order sale concerning seeds, appeal to superior court, **128:95.**
Suffolk county district courts to Boston juvenile court, appeals, **119:27, 119:56.**
Superior court. See within this heading, "Superior court."
Appeals court.
Assistant chief deputy sheriff, **221:71A.**
Automobile insurance, Supreme Judicial Court review of plan for apportionment of rejected risks, **175:113H.**
Chief deputy sheriff, **221:71.**
Clerk of supreme judicial court for Suffolk county as clerk, **211A:6.**

SUFFOLK COUNTY —Cont'd
Appeals court —Cont'd
Court officers.
Appointment, **221:69.**
Compensation, **221:73.**
Foreign insurance company license, review of suspension or revocation of in Supreme Judicial Court, **175:5.**
Messenger, **221:76.**
Sheriff to appoint court officers, **221:69.**
Appointments.
Court officers appointed by sheriff, **221:69, 221:70.**
Official stenographer for probate court in Suffolk county, **215:18.**
Assessors, register of deeds to furnish certain information, **36:24B.**
Assistants.
Administrative assistant, **221:76.**
Chief deputy sheriff, **221:71A.**
Chief probation officer, **276:83.**
Clerks of courts, **221:4-221:6, 221:15, 221:94.**
Medical examiner, salary, **38:5.**
Messenger, **221:76A.**
Register of deeds, **36:5, 36:33.**
Associate medical examiners, **38:1.**
Powers and duties, **38:2.**
Attorneys at law.
District.
See DISTRICT AND PROSECUTING ATTORNEYS.
Practice of law by district attorney, **12:15.**
Records to be kept by clerk of supreme judicial court for Suffolk County, **221:42.**
Auditor, **35:42.**
Automobile insurance.
Supreme judicial court. See within this heading, "Supreme judicial court."
Bail, **276:60, 276:62.**
Convicted prisoners, **276:60.**
Notice to district attorney, **276:60, 276:62.**
Boston.
See BOSTON.
Bunker Hill day and Evacuation day as legal holidays, **4:7, 6:12K, 136:12, 136:13.**
Chief administrative justice of trial court, offices provided at expense of Commonwealth, **211B:9.**

SUFFOLK COUNTY —Cont'd
Chief deputy sheriff, **221:71, 221:71A.**
Claims.
Approval by auditor of claims against county, **35:42.**
Indemnity procedure and claims as to public bodies and officers, jurisdiction and venue, **258:3.**
Clerks of court, **221:3.**
Accounting for fees, **221:32.**
Appeals court, **211A:6.**
Assistant clerks, **221:4-221:6.**
Clerical assistance, **221:102.**
Compensation, **221:94.**
Duties, **221:15, 221:16.**
Election, **54:155.**
Estimate of departmental maintenance and revenues, **211B:13.**
Filling vacancies in office, **54:142, 54:143.**
Probate and insolvency, clerk, **217:28.**
Records kept, **221:42.**
Removal of assistant clerks, **221:5.**
Standing of attorneys, records to be kept, **221:42.**
Superior court clerk. See within this heading, "Superior court clerk."
Supreme judicial court. See within this heading, "Supreme judicial court."
Temporary clerks, **221:8.**
Collective bargaining agreements to arbitrate, venue of actions, **150C:15.**
Commissioners.
Apportionment commissioner, certificate of party enrollment of candidate, **53:48.**
Food and agriculture, jurisdiction of appeals regarding decisions of commissioner, **20:19.**
Hospital service corporation's proposed contracts or rates of payment, appeal from commissioner's decision disapproving, **176A:5.**
Indexes to records of instruments, powers and duties, **36:28. (note)**
Nomination papers, commissioners to apportion county, **53:44.**
Officials serving, **34:4.**

SUFFOLK COUNTY —Cont'd
Commissioners —Cont'd
Probation commissioners, accommodations, **276:98.**
Compensation.
Wages, salaries, and compensation. See within this heading, "Wages, salaries, and compensation."
Cooperative services.
Budget, **128:44, 128:44A.**
Employees, **32:1, 32:28.**
Establishment of board of trustees, **128:40.**
Group insurance for employees, **32A:2, 32A:8, 128:44A.**
Coroners.
Medical examiners. See within this heading, "Medical examiners."
Corporations.
Enforcement of penalties against, **156:52, 156B:113, 158:42.**
Foreign insurance companies. See within this heading, "Foreign insurance companies."
Hospital service corporation's proposed contracts or rates of payment, appeal from commissioner's decision disapproving, **176A:5.**
Superior court clerk, fidelity insurance and corporate suretyship lists of sureties to be furnished, **175:105.**
Councilor district, **57:2.**
Courthouse.
Executive secretary to supreme judicial court to be provided with quarters, **211:3A.**
Repairs and renovations, **149:44E1/2.**
Court officers, **217:30.**
Administrative assistant, duties and salaries, **221:76.**
Appeals court. See within this heading, "Appeals court."
Appointment, **221:69, 221:70.**
Assistant chief deputy sheriffs, **221:71A.**
Assistant messenger of superior court, **221:76A.**
Chief deputy sheriff, **221:71.**
Clerks of court. See within this heading, "Clerks of court."
Interchange or transfer of officers between courts, **221:72.**
Judges and justices. See within this heading, "Judges and justices."

SUFFOLK COUNTY —Cont'd
Court officers —Cont'd
Messengers, duties and salaries, **221:76.**
Premiums on bonds, payment by county, **221:77.**
Salaries, **35:49, 221:73.**
Service of venires and processes of supreme judicial court, bond of officer designated, **221:78.**
Sheriff to appoint court officers for appeals court, **221:69.**
Summoning of witnesses by officers, **221:79.**
Court stenographer.
Appointment of official stenographer for probate court, **215:28.**
Exclusion from salary classification, **35:49.**
Criminal law administration and defense of civil actions, district, **12:13.**
Custody of records, **212:26.**
Damages caused by dogs, county's payment, **140:171.**
Dancing on Sundays in premises authorized to sell alcoholic liquors, **138:33.**
Deeds excise fund, **64D:12.**
Dental service corporations, review of decisions, **176E:12.**
Deputy assistant registers for probate and insolvency, **217:28.**
Deputy sheriffs, **221:71, 221:71A.**
Discrimination, venue for injunction, **151B:5.**
Diseased animals, action for compensation for destruction, **129:31.**
District.
See DISTRICT AND PROSECUTING ATTORNEYS.
District courts.
See DISTRICT COURTS.
Dogs.
Damages paid by county, **140:171.**
Disposition of proceeds from dog fund, **140:170, 140:172.**
Licenses or tags, disposal of dogs without, **140:151A, 140:153.**
Elections.
Nomination papers. See within this heading, "Nomination papers."
Embalmers' and funeral directors' registration board, representation, **13:29.**

SUFFOLK COUNTY —Cont'd
Evacuation day, March seventeenth, as legal holiday, **4:7, 6:12K, 136:12, 136:13.**
Fees.
Clerks of court, accounting for fees, **221:32.**
Medical examiners, accounting for fees and expenses, **38:19.**
Officers arresting persons for unlawfully riding trains, exception as to payment, **160:221.**
Fidelity insurance companies, list to clerk of superior court clerk, **175:105.**
Fines and penalties.
Accounting for and handling, **280:2, 280:8-280:11, 280:15.**
Corporations, enforcement of penalties against, **156:52, 156B:113, 158:42.**
Food and agriculture commissioner decisions, appeals, **20:19.**
Foreign insurance companies.
Review of suspension or revocation of license to be in Supreme Judicial Court, **175:5.**
Suit as to deposits in Supreme Judicial Court, **175:185.**
General court, representatives, **57:4.**
Grand jurors, **277:2, 277:2A.**
Group insurance for county cooperative extension service employees, **128:44A.**
Health care claims, filing of criminal proceedings for falsifying, **175H:4.**
Historic courthouse.
Repairs and renovations, **149:44E1/2.**
Holidays.
Sundays and holidays. See within this heading, "Sundays and holidays."
Hospital service corporation, appeal from commissioner's decision disapproving proposed contracts or rates of payment, **176:5.**
Hours for sale of alcoholic liquors, **138:12.**
Houses of correction and penal institutions.
Clothing, bedding, and fuel, **126:33.**
Commissioner to appoint superintendent of, **126:16.**
Indexes to records of instruments.
Commissioners, powers and duties, **36:28.**

SUFFOLK COUNTY —Cont'd
Indexes to records of instruments
—Cont'd
Form, **36:25.**
Indigents, appeals in Suffolk
county from denial of relief
from court costs, **261:27D.**
Insurance.
See INSURANCE.
Judges and justices.
District courts, **231:108.**
Probate and insolvency judges in
county, additional, **217:2.**
June seventeenth, Bunker Hill
day, and March seventeenth,
Evacuation day, as county
holidays, **4:7, 6:12K, 136:12,
136:13.**
Jury service.
Additional assistant to officer in
charge of jurors' assembly
rooms, **221:73.**
Grand jurors, **277:2, 277:2A.**
Limitation on period, **234:3.**
Supreme judicial court, jury
sittings at Boston, **211:17.**
Juvenile court jurisdiction, **218:57
et seq.**
Juveniles, appeals relative, **119:27,
119:56.**
Land court department of the trial
court, offices, **185:1.**
Legal holidays, **4:7, 6:12K, 136:12,
136:13.**
Liquor.
Alcoholic liquors. See within this
heading, "Alcoholic liquors."
March seventeenth, June
seventeenth, legal holidays in
Suffolk County, **4:7, 6:12K,
136:12, 136:13.**
Masters in chancery, **221:53.**
Medical examiners, **38:1.**
Accounting for fees and
expenses, **38:19.**
Associate medical examiners.
See within this heading,
"Associate medical
examiners."
Salary, quarters and equipment,
38:5.
Messengers, **221:76.**
Assistant messengers, **221:76A.**
Motor vehicle financing, appeals
from refusal or revocation of
license, **255B:5, 255B:8.**
Nomination papers.
Commissioners to apportion
county, number of
signatures, **53:44.**
Review of signatures, **55B:6.**

SUFFOLK COUNTY —Cont'd
Optometric service corporations,
review of decisions, **176F:12.**
Penalties.
Fines and penalties. See within
this heading, "Fines and
penalties."
Personnel board, sheriff excluded
from authority, **35:49.**
Podiatry registration board,
appeals, **112:16.**
Poor persons, appeals in Suffolk
county from denial of relief
from court costs, **261:27D.**
Probate.
See PROBATE AND FAMILY
COURT.
Probation commissioner,
accommodations, **276:98.**
Probation officers, **276:83.**
Prosecutors.
See DISTRICT AND
PROSECUTING
ATTORNEYS.
Real estate brokers' and
salesmen's board of
registration, appeals,
112:87BBB.
Records and recording.
Clerk of court to keep records,
221:42.
Indexes to records of
instruments. See within this
heading, "Indexes to records
of instruments."
Registers.
See REGISTERS AND
REGISTRIES OF DEEDS.
Registers of probate.
See REGISTERS OF PROBATE
AND INSOLVENCY.
Representative districts,
apportionment, **57:4.**
Representatives in general court,
57:4.
Retirement systems.
See RETIREMENT SYSTEMS
AND PENSIONS.
Review.
Appeals. See within this
heading, "Appeals."
Salaries.
Wages, salaries, and
compensation. See within
this heading, "Wages,
salaries, and compensation."
Sheriff.
Appeals court, sheriff to appoint
court officers, **221:69.**
Chief deputy and assistant chief
deputy sheriffs, **221:71,
221:71A.**

SUFFOLK COUNTY —Cont'd
Sheriff —Cont'd
Court officers for supreme
judicial court and appeals
court appointed, **221:69.**
Personnel board, exclusion from
authority, **35:49.**
Powers and duties with respect
to work release programs,
127:86G.
Salary, **37:17.**
Simulcast wagering of horse and
dog racing meetings, **128C:2.**
Special district attorney in Suffolk
and northern districts, salary,
12:20A.
Stenographer of court.
Court stenographer. See within
this heading, "Court
stenographer."
Stray or unlicensed dogs,
140:151A, 140:153.
Summoning of witnesses by
officers, **221:79.**
Sundays and holidays.
March seventeenth, Evacuation
day, and June seventeenth,
Bunker Hill day, as Suffolk
County holidays, **4:7, 6:12K,
136:12, 136:13.**
Sale of alcoholic liquors, **138:33.**
Superior court.
Accounts of clerk, examination,
35:45.
Additional court officers, **221:70.**
Architects' registration law,
enforcement, **112:60N.**
Assistant chief deputy sheriffs,
221:71A.
Assistant messenger, **221:76A.**
Chief deputy sheriff, **221:71.**
Clerk of court.
Superior court clerk. See
within this heading,
"Superior court clerk."
Commissioner of food and
agriculture decisions,
jurisdiction of appeals,
20:19.
Criminal business, clerk to be
clerk of appellate division of
superior court, **278:28A.**
Dental service corporations,
review of decisions,
176E:12.
Medical assistance division,
filing of actions, **118E:45.**
Messenger, **221:76.**
Optometric service corporations,
review of decisions,
176F:12.

SUFFOLK COUNTY —Cont'd
Superior court —Cont'd
Podiatry board of registration,
appeals, **112:16.**
Real estate brokers' and
salesmen's board of
registration, appeals,
112:87BBB.
Removal of register of deeds,
36:9.
Salaries of clerks and assistant
clerks, **221:94.**
Seeds, appeal of stop order sale
concerning, **128:95.**
Sittings, **212:14.**
Telephone company's service
observing, enforcement of
public utility department's
authority, **166:44.**
Unfair trade practices,
jurisdiction and authority as
to civil proceedings against,
93A:4.
Veterinary schools, review of
refusal to approve, **112:55.**
Voucher for expenses, **35:12.**
Superior court clerk, **221:3,
221:16, 221:94, 221:102.**
Accounts of clerk, examination
by superior court, **35:45.**
Assistant clerks, **221:5, 221:94.**
Clerical assistance, **221:102.**
Criminal business, superior
court clerk for criminal
business to be clerk of
appellate division of
superior court, **278:28A.**
Election, **54:155.**
Fidelity insurance and corporate
suretyship, list of sureties to
be furnished to clerk,
175:105.
Filling vacancy in office, **54:142.**
First assistant clerk, salary,
221:94.
Office, **212:19.**
Removal, **211:4.**
Salaries of clerks and assistant
clerks, **221:94.**
Supreme judicial court.
Accident and sickness insurance,
review as to form of policy,
175:108.
Administrative assistant,
221:76.
Assistant clerks, **221:5, 221:15,
221:94.**
Attorney records to be kept by
clerk, **221:42.**
Automobile insurance.
Jurisdiction as to premium
rates, **175:113B.**

SUFFOLK COUNTY —Cont'd
Supreme judicial court —Cont'd
Automobile insurance —Cont'd
Review of plan for
apportionment of rejected
risks, **175:113H.**
Business trust, action against,
for failure to file annual
report brought, **182:14.**
Clerical assistance for clerk,
221:102.
Clerk, **221:3, 221:15, 221:42,
221:94, 221:102.**
Appeals court, clerk of
supreme judicial court for
Suffolk county as clerk,
211A:6.
Assistant clerks, salaries,
221:94.
Attorney records to be kept,
221:42.
Compensation, **211:22.**
Election, **54:155.**
Filling vacancy in office,
54:142.
Superior court clerk for
Suffolk county, removal,
211:4.
Contested elections of
presidential electors, **54:119,
54:120.**
Executive secretary to supreme
judicial court to be provided
with quarters in courthouse,
211:3A.
Fidelity insurance and corporate
suretyship, list of sureties to
be furnished to clerk,
175:105.
Foreign insurance companies.
See within this heading,
"Foreign insurance
companies."
Fraternal benefit societies,
jurisdiction of actions as to
deposits of foreign societies,
175:185.
Group health insurance for older
persons, review of actions,
175:110C.
Hospital service corporation's
proposed contracts or rates
of payment, appeal from
commissioner's decision
disapproving, **176A:5.**
Insurance.
See INSURANCE.
Jury sittings at Boston, **211:17.**
Public utilities commission,
jurisdiction of appeals, **25:5.**
Removal from office of superior
court clerk for Suffolk
county, **211:4.**

SUFFOLK COUNTY —Cont'd
Supreme judicial court —Cont'd
Salaries of officers, clerks and
assistant clerks, **221:73,
221:94.**
Service of venires and processes,
officer designated, **221:78.**
Sheriff to appoint court officers,
221:69.
Voucher for expenses of sitting,
35:12.
Withdrawal of approval of
insurance policy forms,
review, **175:193H.**
Telephone company's service
observing activity, enforcement
in Suffolk county superior
court of public utility
department's authority,
166:44.
Temporary clerks of courts, **221:8.**
Transfer of cases from county,
223:10.
Treasurer, **35:1, 280:7.**
Filling vacancy in office, **54:143.**
General provisions inapplicable,
35:18.
Unfair trade practices, Suffolk
county superior court's
jurisdiction and authority as
to civil proceedings against,
93A:4.
Vacancies in certain offices, how
filled, **54:142, 54:143.**
Venue.
Appeals from final decisions of
agencies in adjudicatory
proceedings, **30A:14.**
Boston, transitory actions by
and against, **223:9, 223:10.**
Claims and indemnity procedure
as to public bodies and
officers, jurisdiction and
venue, **258:3.**
Collective bargaining
agreements to arbitrate,
venue of actions, **150C:15.**
Commonwealth, actions, **223:5.**
Discrimination, venue for
injunction, **151B:5.**
Transfer from Suffolk County,
223:10.
Veterinary schools, review of
refusal to approve, **112:55.**
Wages, salaries, and compensation.
Administrative court assistant,
221:76.
Assistant registers of deeds,
36:33.
Clerks of court, **221:94.**
Court officers, **35:49, 221:73.**

SUFFOLK COUNTY —Cont'd

Wages, salaries, and compensation —Cont'd

Court stenographers, exclusion from salary classification, **35:49.**

Medical examiners and assistants, **38:5.**

Messengers in courts, **221:76.**

Probation officer, **276:83.**

Retirement systems.

See RETIREMENT SYSTEMS AND PENSIONS.

Sheriff, **37:17.**

Special district attorney, **12:20A.**

Witnesses, summoning by officers, **221:79.**

Workers' compensation.

See WORKERS' COMPENSATION.

Work release programs in house of correction and county jail, establishment, **127:86G.**

SUFFRAGE.
See ELECTIONS.

SUGAR OF LEAD.

Adulteration of beverages, **270:1.**

SUGGESTION AWARDS.

Municipal employees, awards, **40:5.**

State employees, awards, **7:31A.**

SUICIDE.

Death, generally.

See DEATH.

Health care proxies, **201D:12.**

Lockup facilities, care and protection of detainees, **40:36A-40:36C.**

Medical examiner, reporting death to, **38:3.**

Real estate transactions.

Disclosures.

Psychologically impacted property.

Not deemed material fact required to be disclosed, **93:114.**

Restraint of mentally ill patient, **123:21.**

Workers' compensation.

Dependents' right to recover as affected by suicide, **152:26A.**

Insanity, suicide while in condition, **152:26A.**

Presumption as to suicide, **152:7A.**

SULFONDIETHYLMETHANE.

Controlled dangerous substances, **94C:31.**

SULFONETHYLMETHANE.

Controlled dangerous substances, **94C:31.**

SULFONMETHANE.

Controlled dangerous substances, **94C:31.**

SULPHONMETHANE.

Misbranding of drugs, what constitutes, **94:187.**

SULPHUR.

Gas, amount permitted, **164:109.**

Meat or meat product, use of sulphur compound, **94:153A.**

SUMMARY COURTS-MARTIAL.

Militia, courts, **33:69, 33:73.**

SUMMARY JUDGMENT OR PROCEEDING.

Alcohol, action for negligence in distribution, sale, or serving to minors or intoxicated persons, **231:60J.**

Arbitration and award.

Existence of agreement to arbitrate, summary determination, **251:2.**

Labor dispute, **150C:2.**

Attorney's lien for fees, summary determination of claims, **221:50B.**

Distribution of decedent's estate, enforcement of probate decree, **197:24.**

Land recovery.

See SUMMARY PROCESS TO RECOVER LAND.

Uniform Securities Act.

Broker-dealer, postponement or suspension of registration, **110A:204.**

Registration statement, postponement or suspension of effectiveness, **110A:305.**

SUMMARY PROCESS TO RECOVER LAND, 239:1-239:13.

Adverse possession for three years or more, bar to remedy, **239:8.**

Appeals, **239:5.**

Bond on appeal. See within this heading, "Bond on appeal."

Superior court. See within this heading, "Superior court."

Arrearages in rent as reduced or eliminated by tenant's counterclaim for breach of warranty or other violation of law, **239:8A.**

SUMMARY PROCESS TO RECOVER LAND —Cont'd

Attorneys' fees in summary process proceedings, recovery, **186:20.**

At will tenant, action limited, **186:13.**

Availability of remedy.

Defendant and predecessors in possession three years or more, bar to remedy, **239:8.**

Forcible entry, or detainer of land, availability of remedy in case, **239:1.**

Bond on appeal, **239:5.**

Actions, **239:5, 239:6.**

Amount where possession after mortgage foreclosure involved, **239:6.**

Condition of bond where possession after tax foreclosure sought, **239:6A.**

Costs, **239:5-239:6A.**

Necessity, **231:98.**

Boston housing court, determination of form of writ, **239:2.**

Child of deceased tenant, application for stay of proceedings, **239:9.**

Claims of tenant against landlord, **239:8A.**

Complaint, form, **239:2.**

Constable may serve process, **41:92.**

Costs, **239:13.**

Appeal bond, **239:5-239:6A.**

Defendant's right, **239:3.**

Plaintiff's right, **239:3.**

Poor person. See within this heading, "Poor persons."

Storage of property removed under summary process, **239:4.**

Counterclaims, breach of warranty or other violation, arrearages in rent as reduced or eliminated by counterclaim, **239:8A.**

Death of tenant, application for stay of proceedings by surviving spouse, parent or child, **239:9.**

Defense.

Dwellings unfit for human habitation, **239:8A.**

Reprisal against tenant for certain activities, **239:2A.**

Deposits to cover back rent and obtain stay, **239:8A, 239:11.**

Description of property in writ, **239:2.**

SUMMARY PROCESS TO RECOVER LAND —Cont'd

Determination of lease action against lessee retaining possession after, **239:1.**

District court.
  Appeal, **239:5.**
  Jurisdiction, **218:19, 239:2.**
  Time for entry of judgments, **235:3.**
  Venue, **239:2.**

Dwelling houses.
  See DWELLING HOUSES.

Elderly tenants, extension of time, **239:9.**

Eviction, **239:1 et seq.**

Execution.
  Judgment for possession, execution, **239:3.**
  Period of limitation, **235:23.**
  Residential purposes, land or tenements used, **235:23, 239:1A, 239:3, 239:10.**
  Stay of proceedings. See within this heading, "Stay of proceedings."

Fair value of use and occupancy of premises unfit for human habitation, determination, **239:8A.**

Farm laborer, application for stay of proceedings, **239:9.**

Forcible entry on or detainer of land, availability of remedy in case, **239:1.**

Foreclosures.
  Mortgage foreclosure. See within this heading, "Mortgage foreclosures."
  Tax title foreclosure. See within this heading, "Tax title foreclosure."

Forms, **239:2.**
  Uniform summary process rules. See within this heading, "Uniform summary process rules."

Goods of tenant, removal and storage, **239:4.**

Handicapped tenants, extension of time, **239:9.**

Hearing on application for stay of proceedings, **239:10.**

Hold-over tenant, method of evicting, **239:1.**

Housing court.
  Bond or security in appeals as to summary process, **239:5.**
  Boston, court, **239:2.**
  Commencement and administration of action, **185C:19.**

SUMMARY PROCESS TO RECOVER LAND —Cont'd

Housing court —Cont'd
  Uniform summary process rules. See within this heading, "Uniform summary process rules."

Housing Court of Boston, form of writ, determination, **239:2.**

Indigency.
  Poor persons. See within this heading, "Poor persons."

Instances in which available, **239:1.**

Judgment.
  Effect, **239:7.**
  Execution. See within this heading, "Execution."
  For defendant, when authorized, **239:3.**
  For possession, **239:3.**
  Stay of proceedings. See within this heading, "Stay of proceedings."
  Time for entry in district courts, **235:3.**
  Uniform summary process rules. See within this heading, "Uniform summary process rules."

Jurisdiction of courts, **239:2.**

Landlord and tenant, **239:1 et seq.**

Lead poisoning, **239:8A.**

Lien for storage charges on removed personal property, **239:4.**

Limitation of action, **184:18, 239:8.**

Mobile homes and mobile home parks, withholding of rent because of unfitness of premises for human habitation, **239:8A.**

Mortgage foreclosures.
  Bond on appeal, amount where possession after mortgage foreclosure involved, **239:6.**
  Method of obtaining possession after, **239:1.**

Notice.
  Action to recover possession by lessor of land or tenements used for residential purposes, **239:1A.**
  Uniform summary process rules. See within this heading, "Uniform summary process rules."
  Withholding of rent by tenant for unfitness of premises for human habitation, **239:8A.**

SUMMARY PROCESS TO RECOVER LAND —Cont'd

Nuisance, avoidance of lease on grounds, **139:19.**

Officer's nonliability for removing personal property of third person, **239:4.**

Organizing or joining of tenant's union, reprisal against tenant, **239:2A.**

Parent of deceased tenant, application for stay of proceedings, **239:9.**

Persons entitled, **239:1.**

Poor persons.
  Affidavit of indigency and request for waiver of court costs, filing, **261:27B.**
  Payment of rent by after waiver of appeal bond, **239:5.**
  Premises unfit for human habitation, payment to court clerk of fair value of use and occupancy by tenant claiming defense, **239:8A.**

Purchase or sale.
  Action for possession of land after, **239:6.**
  Enforcement of lien by sale of property removed, **239:4.**
  Failure of purchaser to take title, **239:1.**
  Person acquiring title to land, **239:1.**
  Public auction, sale of unredeemed property, **239:4.**

Questions adjudicated, **239:7.**

Quiet possession for three years, **239:8.**

Registration of title to land, obtaining possession of property after, **239:1.**

Removal of personal property from premises, **239:4.**

Rent.
  Allegation in writ, **239:2.**
  Appeal bond conditioned to pay, **239:5-239:6A.**
  Judgment and execution, **239:3.**
  Stay of proceedings, deposit as condition, **239:11.**
  Subsequent action, **239:7.**
  Tender of rent, **186:11.**
  Withholding of rents where premises unfit for human habitation, **239:8A.**

Reporting violations of law, reprisal against tenant, **239:2A.**

Reprisal against tenant for certain activities as defense, **239:2A.**

**SUMMARY PROCESS TO
RECOVER LAND** —Cont'd
Residential purposes, recovery of
possession by lessor of land or
tenements used, **239:1A.**
Retaliatory eviction as defense,
239:2A.
Sales.
Purchase or sale. See within this
heading, "Purchase or sale."
Service of process, **41:92.**
Stay of proceedings, **111:127F.**
Child, parent, or surviving
spouse, of deceased tenant,
application, **239:9.**
Circumstances under which
obtainable, **239:9, 239:10.**
Costs, **239:13.**
Deposit required, **239:11.**
Duration, **239:9.**
Farm laborer, application, **239:9.**
Hearing on application, **239:10.**
Power to grant, **239:9.**
Waiver as void, **239:12.**
Storage of property of evicted
tenant, **239:4.**
Summons, **239:2.**
Superior court.
Appeals, **239:5.**
Bond or security in appeal,
239:5.
Jurisdiction and venue, **239:2.**
Time for appeals, **231:97.**
Surviving spouse of deceased
tenant, application for stay of
proceedings, **239:9.**
Tax title foreclosure.
Condition of bond in action for
possession after, **239:6A.**
Fees of land court, **262:39.**
Obtaining possession after,
239:1.
Tender of rent, **186:11.**
Third person, removal and storage
of property, **239:4.**
Time.
Adverse possession for three
years or more, bar to
remedy, **239:8.**
Appeal to superior court, time,
231:97.
Elderly and handicapped
tenants, extension of time,
239:9.
Entry of judgments in district
courts, time, **235:3.**
Residential purposes, time of
action for recovery of
possession by lessor of land
or tenements used, **239:1A.**
Stay of proceedings, duration,
239:9.

**SUMMARY PROCESS TO
RECOVER LAND** —Cont'd
Time —Cont'd
Uniform summary process rules.
See within this heading,
"Uniform summary process
rules."
Trespass action not barred, **239:7.**
Uniform summary process rules.
See SUMMARY PROCESS,
UNIFORM RULES.
Use and occupancy in summary
process actions, recovering an
amount, **239:2.**
Venue, **239:2.**
Violations of landlord as defense,
239:8A.
Waiver.
Bond or security on appeal,
239:5.
Validity of lease provision
waiving right to obtain stay
of proceedings, **239:12.**
Withholding of rents where
premises unfit for human
habitation, **239:8A.**
Writ or process, **239:2.**

**SUMMARY PROCESS,
UNIFORM RULES.**
Admission requests, **Rule 7.**
Answer, **Form 2, Rule 3.**
Appeals, **Rule 12.**
Default, **Rule 10.**
Default judgments, **Rule 10.**
Delay, **Rule 7.**
Demand for jury, **Rule 4.**
Discovery, **Rule 7.**
Dismissal, **Rule 10.**
Documents, requests for
production of, **Rule 7.**
Entry of action, **Rule 2.**
Equitable relief, **Rule 9.**
Execution, **Rule 13.**
Filing, **Rule 2.**
Form of summons and complaint,
Rule 2.
Forms.
Answer, **Form 2.**
Summons and complaint, **Form
1.**
Housing court, **Rule 4.**
Interrogatories, **Rule 7.**
Judgment.
Default, **Rule 10.**
Entry of, **Rules 10, 11.**
Relief from, **Rule 11.**
Jury, **Rules 4, 8.**
Motions, **Rule 6.**
Notice, **Rules 2, 10.**
Postponement of trial date, **Rule
7.**

**SUMMARY PROCESS,
UNIFORM RULES** —Cont'd
Pretrial motions, **Rule 6.**
Production of documents, **Rule 7.**
Relief from judgment, **Rule 11.**
Removal of default or dismissal,
Rule 10.
Scheduling of trial date, **Rule 2.**
Service of motion papers, **Rule 6.**
Service of process, **Rule 2.**
Time, **Rule 2.**
Trial, date of, **Rule 2.**
Transfer of action, **Rule 4.**

SUMMER CAMPS.
Children's health camps.
See CHILDREN'S HEALTH
CAMPS.
Militia.
See MILITIA.
Tax exemptions, **64G:2, 64H:6.**

**SUMMER SCHOOL
PROGRAMS.
See SCHOOLS AND
EDUCATION.**

SUMMONS.
Agent for service of process,
leaving summons, **223:31.**
Alcoholics and drunkards, arrest
upon failure to appear in court
when summoned, **123:35.**
Arrest.
Failure to obey summons as
contempt, **276:26.**
Recognizance may be required,
276:27.
Service of summons, **276:25.**
Attachment of property, **223:79.**
Attorney general, **233:1, 277:68.**
Tax enforcement procedures,
powers, **62C:70.**
Banks and banking, investigative
hearing of consumer
transaction practices, **167:2C.**
Clerks of court.
Fees, **262:2, 262:4.**
Witnesses, summonses, **233:1.**
Complaint, indictment issuance,
276:24.
Consumer transaction practices,
investigative hearing, **167:2C.**
Contempt for failure to obey in
criminal case, **276:26.**
Criminal procedure, **262:1, 276:22,
276:25.**
Deed, proceedings for proof of
execution of unacknowledged
deed, **183:36.**
Dental service corporations' agents
or employees, **176E:9.**
Discovery, compelling, **12A:9.**

SUMMONS —Cont'd

District and prosecuting attorneys.
  Subpoena power, **277:68.**
  Witnesses, summoning upon request of prosecutor in criminal case, **233:1.**
District courts, fees of clerks, **262:2.**
Divorce.
  See DIVORCE AND ALIMONY.
Election results, summons, **54:116.**
Ethics commission, investigations, **268B:4.**
Execution of unacknowledged deed, proceedings for proof, **183:36.**
Expenses of summons witnesses, **221:79.**
Fees.
  Attendance upon certain courts, **262:22.**
  Clerks of courts, **262:2, 262:4.**
  Criminal proceeding, service, **262:8, 262:21, 262:48.**
  District court clerks, fees, **262:2.**
  Issuance of summons, **262:1-262:4.**
  Justices of the peace, fees for summons, **262:1.**
  Special justices, fees, **262:3.**
  Supplementary proceedings, service, **262:14.**
Fictitious name, commencement of action by summons and complaint using, **223:19.**
Fires, witnesses on investigation, **148:3.**
Grand jury, **277:1-277:2G.**
  See GRAND JURY.
Indictments, informations, and complaints, issuance on complaint, **276:24.**
Inspector general.
  Discovery, summons to compel, **12A:9.**
  Witnesses, compelling attendance, **12A:7.**
Insurance commissioner's powers as to witnesses, books, and papers, **175:4, 175:8A.**
Issuance, **262:1-262:4.**
Jury and jury trial, **234:24-234:24B.**
  See JURY AND JURY TRIAL.
Justices of the peace.
  See JUSTICES OF THE PEACE.
Juvenile courts.
  See JUVENILE COURTS AND DELINQUENT CHILDREN.

SUMMONS —Cont'd

Labor and workforce development department, physician's reports of occupational diseases to, not subject to summons, **149:11.**
Leaving with one of suitable age and discretion, service, **223:31, 223:35, 276:25.**
Mail, service, **276:25.**
Minimum wage orders, for employer to show cause against publication of name for nonobservance, **151:11.**
Motor vehicle violations, **90:24, 90:27.**
Optometric service corporations' officers and employees, **176F:9.**
Overdue taxes, imprisonment, **60:29.**
Pedestrians violating rules, **90:18A.**
Presidential electors, improper certification of applicant to vote, **51:48, 51:49.**
Probate.
  See PROBATE AND FAMILY COURT.
Process.
  See PROCESS AND SERVICE OF PROCESS AND PAPERS.
Prosecuting attorneys.
  District and prosecuting attorneys. See within this heading, "District and prosecuting attorneys."
Registration of voters, proceedings as to legality, **51:48.**
Residence, summons served on witness, **233:2.**
Revenue department authorized to issue, **58:25B.**
Service of summons.
  See PROCESS AND SERVICE OF PROCESS AND PAPERS.
Special justices, fees, **262:3.**
State ballot law commission, registrars, **55B:4, 55B:7.**
Summary proceedings for possession of land, **239:2.**
Supplementary proceedings, summons to appear at examination, **224:14.**
Supreme judicial court's issuance, **211:3.**
Tax enforcement procedures, powers of attorney general, **62C:70.**

SUMMONS —Cont'd

Tender of payment before or contemporaneous with commencement of action, **233:1.**
Trustee process, **246:1.**
  See TRUSTEE PROCESS.
Unacknowledged deed, proceedings for proof of execution, **183:36.**
Weekly wage payment law, summons for violation, **149:149.**
Witnesses.
  See WITNESSES.

SUNDAYS AND HOLIDAYS,
6:12A et seq., 136:1 et seq.,
149:45 et seq.

Accessories for motor vehicles, sale, **136:6.**
Acetylene, manufacture and distribution, **136:6.**
Actions, Sunday law as defense, **136:11.**
Activities permitted, **136:6.**
Acts to be performed on, time for performance, **4:9, 30:24, 34:16, 36:11, 41:110A.**
Admission fees to public entertainments, **136:4.**
Aggravation of certain offenses by commission on Sunday, **266:113.**
Agricultural fairs, transportation of livestock, commodities, and equipment, **136:6.**
Aircraft, piloting, **136:6.**
Albert Schweitzer's Reverence for Life Day, **6:12T.**
Alcoholic liquors.
  See ALCOHOLIC LIQUORS.
Aldermen and selectmen.
  Half holidays to employees, **41:110.**
  Licensing of activities, **136:7, 136:14.**
Amusements, exhibitions, shows, and resorts.
  Activities permitted, **136:14.**
  Dancing and dance halls. See within this heading, "Dancing and dance halls."
  Gaming on Sunday, **271:2, 271:6.**
  General prohibition, **136:2.**
  Licensing, **136:4.**
  Public entertainments, **136:2, 136:3.**
  Revocation of licenses, **136:4.**
  Sports and games. See within this heading, "Sports and games."

SUNDAYS AND HOLIDAYS
—Cont'd
Amusements, exhibitions, shows, and resorts —Cont'd
Transportation of livestock, commodities, amusement devices, and equipment for fairs, etc., **136:6.**
Animals.
Dog racing, **128A:2, 128A:3, 128A:5, 136:2, 136:3, 136:4.**
Horses. See within this heading, "Horses."
Poultry, **136:6.**
Sales and care, **136:6, 149:50.**
Work or activities permitted, **136:6.**
Arrest.
See ARREST.
Athletics.
Sports and games. See within this heading, "Sports and games."
Aunt's and Uncle's Day, **6:12T.**
Automobiles.
See MOTOR VEHICLES.
Bail on Sunday, admission, **276:64.**
Bakery products, sale, **136:6.**
Banks.
See BANKS AND BANKING.
Bathhouses, public, **136:6.**
Beano, conduct of game on Sunday, **10:38.**
Bidders on public building construction work, substitution of bond in lieu of bid deposits, **149:44B.**
Boarding and lodging houses, **136:6.**
Boats, operation, **136:6.**
Bootblack, carrying on business at public airport, **136:6.**
Bowling, **136:4.**
Boxing matches prohibited, **147:32.**
Bunker Hill day.
See BUNKER HILL DAY.
Business, trade, labor or work, **136:5-136:7.**
Butter, making, **136:6.**
Candle safety day, **6:12XX.**
Carbon dioxide, manufacture and distribution, **136:6.**
Caribbean week, annual observance, **6:15QQQ.**
Carriers.
Activities permitted, **136:6, 136:14.**
Transportation of petroleum products, **136:1.**
Car washing business, exceptions, **136:6.**

SUNDAYS AND HOLIDAYS
—Cont'd
Charity, **136:4, 136:5.**
Cheese, making, **136:6.**
Chickens, sale, **136:6.**
Christmas.
See CHRISTMAS.
Citation of law, **136:1.**
Cities and towns.
Municipalities. See within this heading, "Municipalities."
City council.
Enjoining violations of law relating to Sunday, **136:10.**
Licensing of sports, games and amusements, **136:4.**
Permits for work to be done on Sunday, **136:7, 136:7A.**
Civic organizations, **136:6.**
Civil process, service, **136:8.**
Civil service.
See CIVIL SERVICE.
Clara Barton week, **6:15YYY.**
Clerical and office personnel, permit for performance of work on legal holiday, **136:15.**
Closing of public offices, **136:12.**
Coin-operated car washing business, operation, **136:6.**
Collections at sports or games, **136:4.**
Commemorative exercises, parades for purpose of holding, **136:6.**
Commerce or trade on, **136:5-136:7.**
Commercial shooting preserves, **131:31, 131:57.**
Commissioner of public safety, approval of licenses, **136:4.**
Common day of rest, **136:1.**
Common victuallers, **136:6.**
Compensation.
See WAGES, SALARIES, AND COMPENSATION.
Compensatory rest days for employees working on Sunday or holiday, **30:24A, 149:51, 149:52.**
Confectionery, **136:6.**
Constitution day.
See CONSTITUTION DAY.
Contracts.
Preparation, **136:6.**
To be performed, **4:9.**
Correctional institutions.
Discharge of prisoner whose term ends on holiday, **127:150.**
School for inmates on Sabbath, **127:89.**

SUNDAYS AND HOLIDAYS
—Cont'd
Correctional institutions —Cont'd
State employees, exception from rule of time off when holiday falls on Saturday, **30:24A.**
Courts open for business, **185:1, 213:4, 215:58, 215:60, 220:6.**
Credit unions.
See CREDIT UNIONS.
Cultivation of land, **136:6.**
Damage and loss, licensing work or labor for prevention, **136:7.**
Dancing and dance halls, **136:2-136:4.**
Dancing permitted, **138:33.**
Deborah Samson, official heroine of the Commonwealth, **6:12GG.**
Defined, **136:1.**
Delivery of laundry and diapers, **136:14.**
Destroyer Escort Day, annual observance, **6:12TT.**
Discharge of prisoner where term ends, **127:150.**
District Courts, closing, **220:6.**
Dog racing, **128A:2, 128A:3, 128A:5, 136:2, 136:3, 136:4.**
Drugs, sale, **136:6.**
Elections falling, **50:4.**
Electricity.
Gas and electric companies. See within this heading, "Gas and electric companies."
Employment security benefits as affected, **151A:23.**
Enjoining violations, **136:10.**
Entering orchard with intent to destroy or injure products, **266:117.**
Entertainment on, **136:14.**
Evacuation Day, **4:7, 6:12K, 136:12, 136:13.**
Excepted from ten days allowed President to return bill, **US Const Art 1 Sec 7 cl 2.**
Exceptions or exemptions, **136:6.**
Exercise Tiger Day, **6:12OO.**
Exhibitions.
Amusements, exhibitions, shows, and resorts. See within this heading, "Amusements, exhibitions, shows, and resorts."
Farm-wineries, sales, **138:33.**
Fees, licenses for entertainments, **136:4.**
Fines and penalties.
Entertainments and amusements, **136:2.**

SUNDAYS AND HOLIDAYS
—Cont'd
Fines and penalties —Cont'd
Labor or work performed, **136:5, 149:180A.**
Limitation of actions, **136:9.**
Proprietors and managers of games and sports, punishment, **136:3.**
Public entertainments, maintaining, **136:3.**
Shops open on Sunday, **136:5.**
Warehouse or workhouse, keeping open on Sunday, **136:5.**
Firearms.
Carrying, **131:57.**
Hunting, **136:4.**
Fire departments.
See FIRE DEPARTMENTS.
Fish and game.
See FISH AND GAME.
Flowers, sale, **136:6.**
Folk or square dancing, **136:2.**
Foodstuffs, **136:5, 136:6.**
Mercantile establishments defined for purposes of labor law, **149:1.**
Former Prisoner of War Recognition Day, annual observance established, **6:12PP.**
Form of indictment or complaint charging violation of Sunday law, **277:79.**
Fraternal organizations, parades, **136:6.**
Fruit, sale, **136:6.**
Fuel, sale, **136:6.**
Funeral processions on public ways, **85:14A.**
Gaming and games of chance, **271:2, 271:6.**
Garden week, annual observance of, **6:12WW.**
Gas and electric companies.
Laws as to Sunday or day of rest as affecting gas and electric companies, **136:6.**
Manufacture and distribution, **149:49.**
Shutting off of electricity on Sunday, prohibited, **164:124.**
Gas and oil.
Sales, **136:6.**
Transportation, **136:1.**
Gasoline and motor fuels, sale, **136:6.**
Geographic Education Awareness Week established, **6:15MMM.**
Golf, **136:4.**

SUNDAYS AND HOLIDAYS
—Cont'd
Grandparents' Day, observance, **6:12EE, 6:12T.**
Greek Independence Day, **6:15RR.**
Greeting cards, sale on Sunday, **136:6.**
Gubernatorial proclamations, **6:12A et seq.**
Half holidays.
Public officers and employees, **41:110, 92:65, 149:33, 149:41.**
Saturdays.
See SATURDAYS.
Head injury awareness month, **6:15VVV.**
Home Composting Recognition Week, **6:15UUU.**
Homeless Unity Day established, **6:12QQ.**
Home video rental business, **136:6.**
Horses, **136:6.**
Racing meetings, **128A:2, 128A:3, 128A:5, 136:2, 136:3, 136:4.**
Hospitals, laundry service, **136:14.**
Hotels and innkeepers, **136:6.**
Hours of labor or service, **149:47-149:52, 160:184.**
Hunting on Sundays.
See FISH AND GAME.
Hydrogen, manufacture and distribution, **136:6.**
Ice, sale, **136:6.**
Independence day.
See INDEPENDENCE DAY.
Indictment for violation of law, **277:79.**
Injunctive relief against violations, **136:10.**
Irish-American heritage month, **6:15FFFF.**
Irish moss, transportation or processing on Sunday, **136:6.**
Italian-American heritage month, **6:15EEEE.**
Joshua James Day, **6:15XX.**
Korean War Veterans Day, **6:12MM.**
Kosher meat, sale, **136:6.**
Kosher wine sold on Sundays, **136:6, 138:33.**
Labor and workforce development, **149:47-149:52.**
Labor day.
See LABOR DAY.
Labor week, **6:12KK.**
Land court as open on Sunday, **185:1.**
Laundry.
Processing and delivery, **136:14.**
Self-service, **136:6.**

SUNDAYS AND HOLIDAYS
—Cont'd
Law Enforcement Memorial Month, May designated as, **6:15TTT.**
Lead poisoning prevention week, **6:15XXX.**
Legal holidays, **4:7, 136:12-136:15.**
Leif Erickson day, **6:15YY.**
Libraries, work permitted, **136:6.**
Licenses and permits, **136:7, 136:7A, 136:13, 136:14, 136:15.**
Alcoholic beverage licensee as exempt from requirement as to radio and television license, **136:4.**
Alderman and selectmen, **136:4, 136:7, 136:14.**
Automobile and motorcycle racing, **136:4.**
Boston police commissioner, licensing of work, **136:7.**
City council's licensing activities, **136:4, 136:7, 136:7A, 136:14.**
Clerical and office personnel, work, **136:15.**
Effective time, **136:4.**
Legal holiday, work, **136:15.**
Mayors, licensing of sports, games, and amusements, **136:4, 136:14.**
Motor transportation of merchandise, **136:14.**
Police officers, licensing certain work, **136:7.**
Public entertainments, **136:4.**
Regulations and restrictions, **136:4.**
Revocation, **136:4.**
Sports and games, license, **136:4, 136:14.**
Work or labor, **136:5, 136:7.**
Lime, calcimining, **136:6.**
Limitations for commencement of prosecutions for violations, **136:9.**
Liquor.
See ALCOHOLIC LIQUORS.
Literacy Awareness Month, **6:15NNN.**
Lithuanian Independence Day, **6:12GG.**
Lottery of state, Sunday sales, **10:24, 136:6.**
Loyalty Day, municipal appropriations for celebration, **40:5.**
Lucy Stone day, **6:15DDDD.**
Maintaining certain public exhibitions prohibited, **136:3.**

SUNDAYS AND HOLIDAYS
—Cont'd

Makeup hours of labor, requiring illegal number in connection with holidays, **149:46, 149:180.**

Managers, punishment with respect, **136:3.**

Manufacturing, mechanical, and mercantile establishments, or workshop, **149:45, 149:48-149:52.**

Martin Luther King day, **4:7, 136:13.**

Massachusetts Hospice Week, **6:15SS.**

Mayors.
  Enjoining violations of laws as to Sunday, **136:10.**
  Licensing of sports, games and amusements, **136:4, 136:14.**

Medicines, sale, **136:6.**

Memorial day.
  See MEMORIAL DAY.

Memorials, parades for purposes of dedicating, **136:6.**

Merchants.
  Stores and merchants. See within this heading, "Stores and merchants."

Military defense, licensing of certain work on Sunday, **136:7.**

Milk and milk products.
  Control act, exclusion in computing period of notice, **94A:17.**
  Manufacture or distribution of milk on Sundays, **149:49.**
  Sale, **136:6.**

Mondays, designation of certain as legal holidays, **4:7.**

Motion pictures.
  See MOTION PICTURES.

Motor vehicles.
  See MOTOR VEHICLES.

Municipalities.
  Appropriations for celebration of holidays, **40:5, 40:9.**
  Motor transportation of merchandise, **136:6, 136:14.**
  Public officers and employees. See within this heading, "Public officers and employees."
  Sports and games, permits, **136:4.**
  Town meetings, **39:9.**
  Work which may be performed on legal holidays, permits, **136:7A, 136:15.**

SUNDAYS AND HOLIDAYS
—Cont'd

Native American Day, establishment of, **6:12VV.**

News dealers, sales, **136:6.**

Newspapers.
  Service of process, **136:8.**
  Work permitted, **136:6.**

New year's day.
  See NEW YEAR'S DAY.

Nitrogen, manufacture and distribution, **136:6.**

Nonintoxicating beverages, regulations, **140:21C.**

Notice.
  Intention to marry, notice not receivable, **207:23.**
  Meetings of public bodies, notice as affected by Sunday or holiday, **30A:11A.**
  Motor transportation of merchandise on Sundays or holiday, notice of permit, **136:14.**
  Revocation of license, **136:4.**
  Service of process, **136:8.**

Nursing and rest homes, laundry, **136:14.**

Oil.
  Gas and oil. See within this heading, "Gas and oil."

Oxygen, manufacture and distribution, **136:6.**

Parades with music, **136:6.**

Parliamentary Law Month, **6:15QQ.**

Patriots' day.
  See PATRIOTS' DAY.

Penalties.
  Fines and penalties. See within this heading, "Fines and penalties."

Performance of acts on next succeeding business day, **4:9, 30:24, 34:16, 36:11, 41:110A.**

Perishable food, sale, **136:6.**

Permits.
  Licenses and permits. See within this heading, "Licenses and permits."

Petroleum products, transportation, **136:1. (note)**

Photographic film sale and processing, **136:6.**

Photographs, taking, **136:6.**

Physicians' offices, laundry service, **136:14.**

Plants, sale, **136:6.**

Pleasure boats, letting, **136:6.**

Police.
  See POLICE.

SUNDAYS AND HOLIDAYS
—Cont'd

Polish-American heritage month, **6:15WWW.**

Portuguese-American month, **6:15GGGG.**

Poultry, sale, **136:6.**

Practical nursing education week, annual observance, **6:15UU.**

Prescriptions of physicians, **136:6.**

Presidents Day, proclamation of annual observance, **6:15VV.**

Prisoners.
  Correctional institutions. See within this heading, "Correctional institutions."

Private employment, requirement of day of rest in each seven for employees, **149:47-149:52.**

Probate and Family Court.
  Sessions of court, **215:58, 215:60.**
  Summons, legal holiday as affecting, **215:60.**

Proprietors and managers of public entertainment, punishment with respect, **136:3.**

Prosecutions for penalties, **136:9.**

Public entertainments, **136:4.**

Public exhibitions, **136:3.**

Public inconvenience, permitting work or labor for prevention, **136:7.**

Public officers and employees.
  Aldermen and selectmen. See within this heading, "Aldermen and selectmen."
  Appreciation Day, **6:15TT.**
  City council. See within this heading, "City council."
  Compensation of employee required to work, **30:24A, 32:1.**
  Equivalent time off for employees required to work on Saturday, **30:24.**
  Fire departments.
    See FIRE DEPARTMENTS.
  Half holiday, **41:110, 92:65, 149:33, 149:41.**
  Legal holiday falling on Saturday, **30:24A.**
  Mayors. See within this heading, "Mayors."
  Memorial day.
    See MEMORIAL DAY.
  Regulation of leaves for municipal employees, **40:21.**
  Veterans' day.
    See VETERANS' DAY.

Public offices to be closed, **136:12.**

SUNDAYS AND HOLIDAYS
—Cont'd

Racing, licensing, **136:4.**

Radio and television, **136:4, 136:6.**

Registration of voters where last
day falls, **51:31.**

Religion and religious societies.
Kosher food, Sunday sale, **136:6.**
Labor restrictions, exemption for
Sabbatarians, **136:6.**
Parades, **136:6.**

Rental of certain vehicles, **136:6.**

Repairs on disabled motor
vehicles, **136:6.**

Requiring labor on, **149:45.**

Resorts.
Amusements, exhibitions, shows,
and resorts. See within this
heading, "Amusements,
exhibitions, shows, and
resorts."

Retail merchants to open on,
136:16.

Robert Goddard Day, **6:15AAAA.**

Sales.
Stores and merchants. See
within this heading, "Stores
and merchants."

Saturdays.
See SATURDAYS.

Schedule of employees working on
Sunday and compensatory day
of rest for each to be posted by
employer, **149:51, 149:52.**

School Principals' Recognition Day,
6:12UU.

Schools.
See SCHOOLS AND
EDUCATION.

Selectmen.
Alderman and selectmen. See
within this heading,
"Aldermen and selectmen."

Self-service auto repair center,
136:6.

Self-service laundry, **136:6.**

Sentence to be served on
weekends, **279:6A.**

Service of process, **136:8, 209A:7.**

Shooting on commercial shooting
preserves, **131:57.**

Shows.
Amusements, exhibitions, shows,
and resorts. See within this
heading, "Amusements,
exhibitions, shows, and
resorts."

Slovak Independence Day, annual
observance, **6:12II.**

Social Security day, **6:12LL.**

Soft drinks, sale, **136:6.**

SUNDAYS AND HOLIDAYS
—Cont'd

Sparring matches prohibited,
147:32.

Special needs awareness day,
6:15BBBB, 6:15DDDD.

Special sentences of imprisonment,
279:6A.

Sports and games, **136:2-136:4,
136:14.**
Activities permitted, **136:6.**
Admission fees, charging, **136:4.**
Bowling, **136:4.**
Contest involving time trial
driving of automobiles,
136:4.
Gambling.
See GAMING AND GAMES
OF CHANCE.
Golf, **136:4.**
License, **136:4.**
Proprietors or managers of,
punishment, **136:3.**
Tennis, **136:4.**

Sports equipment, rental, **136:6.**

State departments closed, **30:24.**

State library, hours, **6:38.**

State lottery sales, **136:6.**

State walking Sunday, observance,
6:15NN.

Statue of Liberty Awareness Day,
6:12HH.

Steam, manufacture and
distribution, **136:6.**

Stores and merchants,
136:5-136:7.
Sale of foodstuffs, **136:5, 136:6.**

Suffering, work or labor for
prevention, **136:7.**

Suffolk county.
March seventeenth, Evacuation
day, and June seventeenth,
Bunker Hill day, as Suffolk
County holidays, **4:7, 6:12K,
6:12, 136:12, 136:13.**
Sale of alcoholic liquors, **138:33.**

Superior courts.
Transaction of court business on
Sunday, when permitted,
213:4.

Violations of Sunday laws,
enjoining, **136:10.**

Tax returns and reports,
preparation, **136:6.**

Thanksgiving.
See THANKSGIVING.

Tobacco, sale, **136:6.**

Torts suffered on, defenses, **136:11.**

Tourists, licensing of sales, **136:14.**

Towing of disabled motor vehicles,
136:6.

SUNDAYS AND HOLIDAYS
—Cont'd

Towns.
Municipalities. See within this
heading, "Municipalities."

Transporting goods or
merchandise.
Carriers. See within this
heading, "Carriers."

Trespass.
Arrest for trespass, **266:120,
266:131.**
Penalty for trespass on land of
another, **266:113.**
Warrant, arrest and detention of
trespasser without, **266:131.**

Trial preparation by lawyers,
136:6.

Unemployment security benefits,
151A:23.

USO Appreciation Day,
proclamation, **6:12RR.**

Vegetables, sale, **136:6.**

Veterans and veterans'
organizations.
Armistice Day, **6:15R.**
Hospital day, **6:12T.**
Memorial day.
See MEMORIAL DAY.
Parades and other permitted
activities, **136:6.**
Patriotic holiday for world war
veterans, **40:5.**
Pearl Harbor Day, **6:12DD.**
Veterans day.
See VETERANS' DAY.
Vietnam veterans, **6:15MM.**

Visiting nurse association week,
6:12JJ.

Wages.
See WAGES, SALARIES, AND
COMPENSATION.

Warehouses, prohibition against
keeping open, **136:5.**

Washington's birthday.
See WASHINGTON'S
BIRTHDAY.

Water supply, **136:6.**

Weapons.
Firearms. See within this
heading, "Firearms."

Workers' Memorial Day
established, **6:15KKK.**

Workhouse, prohibition against
keeping open, **136:5.**

Works of art, exhibitions, **136:6.**

Youth in government day,
6:15WW.

SUNDAY SCHOOL.
Correctional institutions,
maintenance, **127:89.**

SUNDERLAND.
Medical examiner district, **38:1.**

SUNFISH.
Sale, regulated, **131:22.**
Stocking of private waters for
fishing by members of youth
organizations, **131:4.**

SUNGLASSES.
Distribution and sale,
requirements, **270:1A.**
Impact tests, **270:1A.**

SUNSHINE LAW.
See MEETINGS.

SUNSTROKE.
Workers' compensation payment
for injury caused, **152:26.**

**SUPERANNUATION
RETIREMENTS, 32:5.
See RETIREMENT SYSTEMS
AND PENSIONS.**

SUPERFUND, 21E:1 et seq.

**SUPERINTENDENCY
DISTRICTS AND UNIONS.
See SCHOOLS AND
EDUCATION.**

SUPERINTENDENTS.
Building superintendent, 8:1 et
seq.
See STATE
SUPERINTENDENT OF
STATE OFFICE
BUILDINGS.
Correctional institutions.
See CORRECTIONAL
INSTITUTIONS.
County industrial farms.
Appointment or removal, **126:36.**
Discharge from employment,
35:51.
Powers and duties, **126:37.**
County prisons.
See COUNTY PRISONS.
Education department.
Annual reports, **72:2A, 72:3,
76:7.**
Students leaving schools,
reports, **76:18.**
Teachers. See within this
heading, "Teachers."
Union of towns for employment
of superintendent, **71:62.**
Employer's liability for death or
injury to employees.
Negligence of superintendent,
injury, **153:1.**
Notice to superintendent as
affecting, **153:2.**

SUPERINTENDENTS —Cont'd
Free employment offices,
superintendent, **149:161.**
Highways.
See HIGHWAYS AND
STREETS.
Hospitals.
See STATE HOSPITALS.
Industrial farms.
County industrial farms. See
within this heading,
"County industrial farms."
Mentally ill.
See MENTALLY ILL AND
RETARDED PERSONS.
Plants.
See PLANTS AND PLANT
DISEASES AND PESTS.
Public employment offices, district
superintendents, **23:9M.**
Regional school districts, **71:16,
71:64.**
Schools.
See SCHOOLS AND
EDUCATION.
Shade tree management and pest
control bureau, **132:13.**
Soldier's home in Holyoke,
management, **6:17.**
State hospitals.
See STATE HOSPITALS.
State schools, grounds for removal,
19:14.
Street railways, **161:85, 161:89.**
Streets, superintendent of.
See HIGHWAYS AND
STREETS.
Teachers.
Commission or fee for obtaining
position, acceptance, **71:67.**
Maximum period of suspension
of teacher without hearing,
71:42D.
Recommendation by
superintendent, **71:59.**
Vacation, effect of discharge,
71:42.
Tewksbury hospital.
See TEWKSBURY HOSPITAL.
Town superintendent of public
works, **41:69E.**
Tuberculosis.
See TUBERCULOSIS AND
TUBERCULIN.
Vacancy and position of
superintendent of state school,
mental retardation
department, **19B:8.**
Youth services department.
See YOUTH SERVICES
DEPARTMENT AND
MASSACHUSETTS
TRAINING SCHOOLS.

**SUPERIOR COURTS,
212:1-212:30.**
Abandoned, lost, and unclaimed
property.
Appeals by claimants, **200A:10.**
Order of payment when
claimant resides in certain
foreign countries, **200A:10.**
Surrender orders, **200A:12.**
Abatement, survival.
See ABATEMENT, SURVIVAL,
AND REVIVAL.
Abortions, order authorizing or
enjoining, **112:12S, 112:12U.**
Absence or presence.
Attendance. See within this
heading, "Attendance."
Absent defendants, notice, **227:7.**
Absentee voting matters, **54:103.**
Abuses and imperfections in
practice, remedying, **213:3.**
Accident, late entry of appeal on
ground, **212:13.**
Accounts and accounting.
Allowance, **213:8.**
Special jurisdiction in actions
which cannot be settled in
district court, **214:3.**
Suffolk County, examination of
accounts of clerk, **35:45.**
Adjournments.
Absence of justice, adjournment,
213:11, 213:12.
Another shire town,
adjournment, **213:10.**
Notice, **213:11.**
Sittings of court, **212:14, 213:6.**
Adjudicatory proceedings, appeals
from final decisions of
agencies, **30A:14.**
Administrative justices.
See ADMINISTRATIVE
JUSTICES.
Administrative procedure.
See ADMINISTRATIVE
PROCEDURE.
Advertising and advertisements.
False advertising, injunction
against, **266:91B.**
Outdoor advertising adjacent to
certain highways,
jurisdiction to restrain,
93D:5.
Signs, jurisdiction to enjoin,
93:31, 93D:5.
Advisory committee on personnel
standards, administrative
justice as member, **211B:8.**
Affidavits, indigency actions,
261:27B.
Affirmation of judgment of District
Court upon nonentry of
appeal, **212:12.**

SUPERIOR COURTS —Cont'd

Agreements.
See CONTRACTS AND
AGREEMENTS.
Aircraft.
See AIRCRAFT AND AVIATION.
Air pollution control regulations,
enforcement, **111:2B, 111:31C,
111:142A, 111:142B,
111:142E.**
Airports.
See AIRPORTS AND LANDING
FIELDS.
Alcoholic liquors.
Appeals to courts upon seizure,
138:55.
Farmer-winery license, appeal of
denial, **138:19B.**
Jurisdiction in equity to enforce
surrender of license, **138:23.**
Alcoholism facilities, jurisdiction to
enforce regulations regarding,
111B:6, 111B:6A.
Alteration.
Amendments. See within this
heading, "Amendments."
Always open for business, **213:4.**
Amendments.
Judgment, amendment by
appellate division, **278:28C.**
Prescribing terms for allowance,
213:3.
Amount of claims, counterclaims,
and cross-claims permitting
parties in district court action
to file claim of trial in superior
court, **231:104.**
Animal diseases.
Bovine tuberculosis, action for
destruction of animal
affected, **129:33.**
Compensation for condemned
animals, proceedings,
129:31, 129:33.
Equitable jurisdiction to enforce
statutory provisions, **129:37.**
Answers and pleas, eminent
domain, **79:22.**
Antitrust laws.
See RESTRAINTS OF TRADE
AND MONOPOLIES.
Appeal from judgment or order in
superior court, **231:113,
231:118.**
See APPEAL AND REVIEW.
Appeals court.
See APPEALS COURT.
Appeals to superior court, **278:18
et seq.**
Abandoned, lost, and unclaimed
property, **200A:10.**

SUPERIOR COURTS —Cont'd

Appeals to superior court —Cont'd
Adjudicatory proceedings,
appeals from final decisions
of agencies in, **30A:14.**
Alcoholic liquors. See within this
heading, "Alcoholic liquors."
Appellate division. See within
this heading, "Appellate
division."
Automobile insurance,
cancellation or refusal,
175:113D.
Buildings and structures,
electrical wiring and
appliances, **143:3P.**
Commitment or bail pending
appeal, **278:18.**
Criminal cases, **278:18 et seq.**
Criminal offender record
information system, **6:176.**
District courts.
See DISTRICT COURTS.
Fees, appellant's liability,
278:18.
Historic districts and sites,
40C:12.
Housing and urban renewal,
landowners affected,
121B:47.
Jailer's fees where appeal
withdrawn, **278:26.**
Jurisdiction, **212:5.**
Crimes tried before district
court, **212:6.**
Late entry of appeal, **212:13.**
Milk Control Commission
proceedings, review, **94A:8,
94A:21.**
Municipal lighting and heating
plants board or commission
member, appeals from
removal, **164:56E.**
Nonentry of appeal from district
court judgment, affirmation
on appeal, **212:12.**
Notification of right to appeal,
278:18.
Sales finance companies, appeals
as to licensing, **255D:5,
255D:8.**
Searches and seizures. See
within this heading,
"Searches and seizures."
Seeds, appeal of stop-sale order,
128:95.
Sentence where appeal not
entered, **278:24.**
Small claims actions, **218:23.**
Special assessments, appeal
from decision as to
abatement, **80:7.**

SUPERIOR COURTS —Cont'd

Appeals to superior court —Cont'd
State ballot law commission,
review of sufficiency of
signatures, **55B:6.**
Statement of fees, **278:22.**
Stay or supersedeas, **231:97.**
Traffic offender, appeal from
designation as habitual,
90:22F.
Transmission of papers, **278:20.**
Withdrawal of appeal, **278:25.**
Witnesses, binding over, **278:19.**
Appearances, arrested person,
certificate of expenses, **276:44.**
Appellate division.
Amendment of judgment,
278:28C.
Clerk and assistant clerk,
278:28A.
Hearing outside county, clerk's
duty, **278:28D.**
Correctional institution, sitting,
278:28A.
Criminal cases,
278:28A-278:28D.
Dismissal of appeal, **278:28C.**
Disqualification of certain
justices, **278:28A.**
Duty of clerk on hearing outside
county, **278:28D.**
Hearing and determination,
278:28B, 278:28D.
Jurisdiction, **278:28A.**
Procedure for appeal, **278:28B.**
Resentencing defendant,
278:28C.
Rules.
Criminal cases, procedure and
forms, **Rule 64.**
District/Municipal Courts
Rules for Appellate
Division Appeal.
See DISTRICT/MUNICIPAL
COURTS RULES FOR
APPELLATE DIVISION
APPEAL.
Salaries and traveling expenses
of clerks, **278:28D.**
Application of term "superior
court, **212:1.**
Appointees of justices,
arrangement of names on
primary ballots, **53:34.**
Apprenticeship agreements,
appeals, **23:11K.**
Arbitration proceedings,
applications to consolidate or
sever, **251:2A.**
Architects' registration law,
enforcement, **112:60N.**

SUPERIOR COURTS —Cont'd

Arraignment of prisoner, **212:7.**

Arrest.

Appearance of arrested person, certificate of expenses, **276:44.**

Justice's power, **276:21.**

Assembling of grand jury, **212:23.**

Assessors, compensation paid for by state, **221:55.**

Assignment of cases.

Chief justice, assignments to be made, **212:2.**

Special master's duties, **212:19A.**

Assistants.

Appellate division. See within this heading, "Appellate division."

Clerical assistants, appointment, **221:89.**

Clerks of court, assistant clerks, **221:4, 221:5, 221:6K-221:6M, 221:12, 278:28A.**

Register of deeds, approval of appointment of assistant, **36:4.**

Supervisor of probation, designation of assistant, **276:83.**

Assurance fund, actions for compensation, **185:101.**

Attachments.

Appeal from decision of superior court, attachment taken for security to stand, **212:8.**

Judgments.

Attachment after, **223:86A.**

Dissolution of attachment, **223:115.**

Late entry of appeal, attachments given in original action not to be revived by allowance, **212:13.**

Special jurisdiction in actions to reach and apply debts subject, **214:3.**

Trustee process.

See TRUSTEE PROCESS.

Attendance.

Jurors summoned for attendance upon superior court, central pools, **212:20A.**

Justices, attendance, **213:9, 213:11, 213:12.**

Notice, absent defendants, **227:7.**

Revenue department, justices compelling attendance of witnesses and production of papers before, **58:25B.**

SUPERIOR COURTS —Cont'd

Attendance —Cont'd

Witnesses, enforcement of attendance, **58:25B, 233:10.**

Attorney general.

Appointment of substitute, **12:26.**

Gift or conveyance to county, city or town, special jurisdiction in Attorney General's action to enforce, **214:3.**

Transmission of indictment, **212:7.**

Attorneys at law.

Admission to bar, filing of petition for examination, **221:37.**

District attorney. See within this heading, "District attorney."

Fees in action to enforce purposes of gift or conveyance to city or town, **214:3.**

Jurisdiction to restrain violations regarding practice of law, **221:46B.**

Lien of attorney for fees and expenses, enforcement, **221:50.**

Notice of trials in civil causes to be given, **213:3.**

Practice of law, jurisdiction to restrain certain violations regarding, **221:46B.**

Removal of attorney, **221:40.**

Auditors, masters, and referees.

Boston, submission of expenses voucher to city auditor, **35:12.**

Compensation, **221:55.**

Special master. See within this heading, "Special master."

Automobile insurance.

Appeal on cancellation or refusal of insurance, **175:113D.**

Special jurisdiction, **214:3.**

Automobiles.

Motor vehicles. See within this heading, "Motor vehicles."

Bail and recognizance.

Appealed criminal cases, **278:18.**

Binding over, certificate of fees and expenses forwarded to superior court, **276:44.**

Chief justice's monthly statement, **276:61.**

Defendant released on own recognizance without surety, review of refusal to order, **276:58.**

District court bail, application to superior court bail, **276:58.**

SUPERIOR COURTS —Cont'd

Bail and recognizance —Cont'd

Justice's powers, **276:57.**

Professional bail bondsman, **276:61B.**

Return day for appeals involving recognizance in criminal cases, **212:22.**

Speedy trial of persons held in jail in default, **212:29.**

Bakery, appeal from administrative order, **94:9L, 94:9M.**

Ballot law commission.

State ballot law commission. See within this heading, "State ballot law commission."

Ballots, arrangement of names of justice-appointed incumbents on primary ballots, **53:34.**

Barbers' board of registration, appeals, **112:87N.**

Bonds and undertakings.

Assistant clerks of court, bonds, **221:12.**

Contractor's bond on public works, **149:29.**

County officers and employees, approval, **35:43A.**

Creditor's action against partnership property, effect of bond given by partner, **214:3.**

Criminal cases, return day for appeals involving bonds, **212:22.**

Late entry of appeal, security given in original action not to be revived or continued by allowance, **212:13.**

Petroleum products, enforcement of bond furnished by vessel receiving or discharging, **21:50B.**

Replevin writ returnable to superior court, bond if, **247:8.**

Security bond given in superior court action to stand on appeal, **212:8.**

Sheriff, certification of failure to give bond, **37:7.**

Small claims proceedings, defendant to furnish bond, **218:23.**

Summary process, appeals, **239:5.**

Boston.

Expenses, submission of voucher to city auditor, **35:12.**

Sittings at Boston, **212:14.**

SUPERIOR COURTS —Cont'd

Boundaries, jurisdiction and venue over matters arising within marine boundaries of Commonwealth, **1:3.**

Boxing matches, injunction against, **147:45.**

Bridges, enforcement of provisions as to repair and maintenance, **159:85.**

Bristol county, assistant clerk to perform duties of clerk for criminal proceedings, **221:6M.**

Buildings.
See BUILDINGS AND STRUCTURES.

Business trusts, jurisdiction to enjoin use of misleading name, **182:2A.**

Cage for defendants prohibited, **34:3.**

Calendars and dockets, **278:1.**
Publication, **213:3.**

Cambridge.
Jurisdiction of crimes committed in Cambridge, **212:6.**
Sittings at Cambridge, **212:14.**

Capital cases, transmission of indictment, **212:7.**

Carriers.
Bridges, enforcement of provisions as to repair and maintenance, **159:85.**
Discrimination, enforcement of law against, **159:1.**
Jurisdiction to restrain violations, **159A:15, 159B:21.**

Central pools of jurors summoned for attendance upon the superior court, **212:20A.**

Certiorari to correct errors, **249:4.**

Charities and charitable organizations.
Appeal from refusal of articles of organization, **180:6.**
Fraudulent use of name of, jurisdiction to enjoin, **266:71A.**
Jurisdiction as to, **180:11.**
Public charities' duty to file copies of instruments, **12:8E.**

Public ways, jurisdiction to enforce provisions as to collection of funds, **68:16.**

Checks for damage awards, issuance, **79:7D, 79:7E.**

Chief justice, **212:1 et seq.**
Assembling of grand jury upon written order to sheriff, **212:23.**

SUPERIOR COURTS —Cont'd

Chief justice —Cont'd
Assignments to be made, **212:2.**
Bail, monthly statement, **276:61.**
Continuing education of judges and court personnel, agreements concerning programs, **7:28A.**
Designation of clerk's offices, **212:19.**
Establishment of office, **212:1.**
Naturalization sittings, establishment, **212:14A.**
Order to sheriff for special jury for sitting of criminal business, **212:21.**
Panel of three associate justices to act upon labor dispute case, chief justice designation, **212:30.**
Sales of copies of rules, duties, **213:3A.**
Sittings, establishing, **212:14A.**
Transmission of indictment, **212:7.**
Vacancy in office, **213:1.**

Chief justice for administration and management, **212:1 et seq.**

Children or minors.
Child pornography, injunctions against, **272:30D.**
Desertion of children, **273:2.**
Juvenile courts.
See JUVENILE COURTS AND DELINQUENT CHILDREN.
Probation, **276:87.**

Church records, jurisdiction to compel delivery to city or town clerk, **66:16.**

Cigarette tax, appeal in proceedings upon seizure of cigarettes, vehicles, or containers, **64C:8.**

Cities and towns.
Boston. See within this heading, "Boston."
Charter, questions as to adoption of plan F, **43:9B.**
Clerk of, jurisdiction to compel delivery of church records, **66:16.**
Clerks of court, fees, **262:4A.**
Enforcement of municipal finance provisions, **44:59.**
Home rule procedures act, jurisdiction of superior court, **43B:14.**

SUPERIOR COURTS —Cont'd

Cities and towns —Cont'd
Lighting plants.
Municipal lighting and heating plants. See within this heading, "Municipal lighting and heating plants."
Ordinances or bylaws, jurisdiction to enforce, **40:21.**
Restraint of illegal appropriations, **40:53.**
Special jurisdiction in action to enforce gift or conveyance, **214:3.**
Treasurer, petition for removal, **41:39B.**
Wards, authority as to division into, **54:1.**

Civil rights.
See CIVIL RIGHTS AND DISCRIMINATION.

Civil service.
Enforcing submission of list of employees, **31:67.**
Mandamus, employee's right, **31:73.**

Claim of trial, **231:104.**

Claims against Commonwealth.
Enforcement of claims against Commonwealth, **258:12.**
Judge to approve award, compromise or settlement, **258:7.**
Jurisdiction, **212:3, 258:3.**

Clerk of court, **212:19.**
Appellate division. See within this heading, "Appellate division."
Assistant clerks, **221:4, 221:5, 221:6K-221:6M, 221:12, 221:94, 278:28A.**
Certification of copies of records by clerks, **212:26.**
Classification of clerk by county personnel board, **35:49.**
County treasurer, clerk's certificate of fine imposed, **280:7.**
Criminal justice training council, membership, **6:116.**
Criminal proceedings, assistant clerk of courts for certain counties to perform duties of clerk, **221:6L, 221:6M.**
Damage award checks, issuance, **79:7D, 79:7E.**
Election of clerks and term of office, **221:3.**
Entry of judgment, **213:3.**

SUPERIOR COURTS —Cont'd
Clerk of court —Cont'd
Equity clerks, **221:6A, 221:6B, 221:6K, 221:61.**
Fees, **262:4A.**
Indictment, transmission, **212:7.**
Issuance of process, **213:2.**
Land court, transmission of papers in transferred case, **212:26A.**
Removal of clerk of superior court for Suffolk county, **211:4.**
Reports of criminal proceedings, **124:8, 265:13B, 265:13H, 265:22 et seq.**
Salaries of clerk and assistant clerks, **221:94.**
Sales of copies of rules, duties, **213:3A.**
Statutes distributed, **5:3.**
Suffolk County, **221:3, 221:16, 221:94, 221:102.**
See SUFFOLK COUNTY.
Temporary clerk, appointment, **221:8.**
Transfer or removal of cases from probate court to superior court, **215:6.**
Clerks and clerical work.
Appointment and compensation of clerical assistants, **221:89.**
Clerk of court. See within this heading, "Clerk of court."
Clinical laboratories, jurisdiction of complaints, **111D:12.**
Closing out sales, restraining violations with respect, **93:28E.**
Club's unlawful use of dwelling, proceedings to restrain, **40:21.**
Coastal wetlands regulations, exclusive jurisdiction of court concerning, **130:105.**
Co-executors and co-administrators, special jurisdiction in actions between, **214:3.**
Collective bargaining agreements to arbitrate.
See LABOR RELATIONS AND DISPUTES.
Commissioners, compensation paid for by state, **221:55.**
Compensation.
Wages, salaries, and compensation. See within this heading, "Wages, salaries, and compensation."

SUPERIOR COURTS —Cont'd
Compulsory counterclaims permitting defendant in District Court action to file claim of trial, **231:104.**
Concurrent jurisdiction.
See CONCURRENT JURISDICTION.
Condemned animals.
Animal diseases. See within this heading, "Animal diseases."
Condominiums.
Enforcement of liens, **254:5.**
Improvements or restoration, proceedings by unit owner disagreeing, **183A:17, 183A:18.**
Conflict between rules of superior court and supreme judicial court, prohibition against, **213:3.**
Congestion, use of district court justices to relieve, **212:14A.**
Consolidation or severance of proceedings.
Arbitration proceedings, **251:2A.**
Cases transferred to district court, consolidation with actions pending there, **223:2A, 231RF:102C.**
Costs in cases tried together, **261:8.**
Consumers' civil remedies against unfair trade practices, **93A:9, 93A:11.**
Continuance of cases.
Adjournment. See within this heading, "Adjournments."
Special master's duties, **212:19A.**
Contracts.
See CONTRACTS AND AGREEMENTS.
Contribution by or between devisees, legatees, or heirs, special jurisdiction in actions, **214:3.**
Conveyance.
Deed or conveyance. See within this heading, "Deed or conveyance."
Convicted persons restrained from holding of public office, **264:20.**
"Co-operative," jurisdiction as to use of word by corporations, **157:8.**
Corporations.
See CORPORATIONS.
Correctional institutions.
See CORRECTIONAL INSTITUTIONS.

SUPERIOR COURTS —Cont'd
Costs of actions.
Cases tried together, **261:8.**
Diminishing, **213:3.**
Fees. See within this heading, "Fees."
Gift or conveyance to governmental unit, costs in action to enforce, **214:3.**
Indigency. See within this heading, "Indigency."
Items allowable, **261:23.**
Replevin, **261:4.**
Where recovery is under 100 dollars, **261:4.**
Counsel.
Attorneys at law. See within this heading, "Attorneys at law."
Counterclaims and cross-claims, **231:104.**
Counties.
Correctional facility, order for closing, **127:1B.**
Essex county. See within this heading, "Essex county."
Law libraries for counties, bylaws subject to approval of court, **78:2.**
Middlesex county. See within this heading, "Middlesex county."
Norfolk county. See within this heading, "Norfolk county."
Officer or employee.
Bonds and undertakings, approval, **35:43A.**
Indictment for misconduct in office, notice to clerk, **268A:25.**
Plymouth county. See within this heading, "Plymouth county."
Special jurisdiction of action to enforce gift or conveyance, **214:3.**
Suffolk county.
See SUFFOLK COUNTY.
Transaction of business in any county, **213:5.**
Treasurer.
County treasurers. See within this heading, "County treasurers."
County commissioners, fee for filing of petition, **262:4A.**
County treasurers.
Clerk's certificate of fines imposed, **280:7.**
Justice of court disqualified to act, **35:1.**
Vouchers for expenses, **35:12.**

SUPERIOR COURTS —Cont'd

Court officers and employees.

Appointment, **213:13.**

Clerk of court. See within this heading, "Clerk of court."

Continuing education of judges and court personnel, agreements concerning programs, **7:28A.**

Counties. See within this heading, "Counties."

Discharge from employment.

Removal from office or employment. See within this heading, "Removal from office or employment."

Justices. See within this heading, "Justices."

Misconduct in office, notice to clerk of indictment, **268A:25.**

Norfolk county, additional court officers, **221:70.**

Number, **221:69.**

Pensions, **32:66, 32:67.**

Temporary employees. See within this heading, "Temporary employees."

Term of office, **221:72.**

Cranberry land, review of apportionment of expense of flooding, **253:40.**

Creditors' actions, special jurisdiction, **214:3.**

Credit unions, unauthorized operation, **171:7.**

Criminal cases.

Appeals. See within this heading, "Appeals to superior court."

Appellate division, **278:28A-278:28D.**

Bail and recognizance. See within this heading, "Bail and recognizance."

Bristol county, assistant clerk to perform duties of clerk for criminal proceedings, **221:6M.**

District court justices to sit in certain cases, **212:6.**

Failure of accused to testify, comments, **278:23.**

Fees for assisting in investigations, **262:29.**

Jailers' return of list of prisoners to court, **126:7.**

Jurisdiction, **212:6.**

Police officers in attendance, **262:53A, 262:53C.**

SUPERIOR COURTS —Cont'd

Criminal cases —Cont'd

Probation and parole. See within this heading, "Probation and parole."

Reports by clerks, **124:8.**

Return day in criminal cases, **212:22.**

Rules governing.

See CRIMINAL PROCEDURE.

Separation of civil and criminal business, **212:20.**

Special sittings for criminal business, **212:21.**

Speedy trial of persons held in jail in default of bail, **212:29.**

Trial list, **278:1.**

Criminal justice training council, superior court clerk as member, **6:116.**

Criminal offender record information system.

Actions for damages or injunctions, **6:177.**

Appeals, **6:176.**

Criminal usury, voiding of transactions involving, **271:49.**

Cross actions or actions arising out of same accident, event or transaction pending in both superior and district courts, transfer to superior court, **223:2B.**

Custody of records, **212:26.**

Dams and reservoirs.

Action for damages caused, **253:4.**

Jurisdiction of safety enforcement proceedings, **253:50.**

Death sentence, transmission of indictment, **212:7.**

Deceit.

Fraud and deceit. See within this heading, "Fraud and deceit."

Declarations of intention in naturalization proceedings, fixing of time, **220:18.**

Declaratory judgments, **213:3, 231A:1, 231A:2.**

Decrees.

Judgments and decrees. See within this heading, "Judgments and decrees."

Deed or conveyance.

Action to enforce purposes of conveyance, **214:3.**

Assistant register of deeds, **36:4.**

SUPERIOR COURTS —Cont'd

Deed or conveyance —Cont'd

Decree in equity operating, **183:43.**

Fraudulent conveyances, **214:3.**

Defective service, further service after, **223:84.**

Defined, statutory construction purposes, **4:7.**

Delay, prevention, **213:3.**

Dental examiners, enforcement proceedings, **112:43.**

Dental service corporations, review of decisions involving, **176E:12.**

Depositions, **233:24.**

Deputy probation officers, appointment and duties, **276:89A.**

Desertion of wife and children, prosecution, **273:2.**

Devisees, special jurisdiction in actions for contribution by or between, **214:3.**

Discretion of court, fixing requirements, **213:3.**

Disqualification.

Appellate division criminal proceedings, certain justices, **278:28A.**

County treasurer, justice of court disqualified to act, **35:1.**

Dissolution.

Injunction issued by Supreme Judicial Court, prohibition against, dissolution, **214:15.**

Judgment, dissolution of attachment, **223:115.**

District attorney.

Appointment of substitute district attorney, **12:26.**

Expenses, approval, **12:24.**

Precedence of certain prosecutions, motion of district attorney, **212:24.**

Speedy trial of persons held in jail in default of bail, district attorney's consent, **212:29.**

Suits returnable at election, **212:22.**

District courts.

See DISTRICT COURTS.

Divorce.

See DIVORCE AND ALIMONY.

Dockets.

Calendars and dockets. See within this heading, "Calendars and dockets."

SUPERIOR COURTS —Cont'd

Drains.

Sewers and drains. See within this heading, "Sewers and drains, enforcement of provisions."

Drinking water supply facilities.

Waterworks and water supply. See within this heading, "Waterworks and water supply."

Drugs and narcotics.

Administrative inspection warrants, **94C:30.**

Injunctions, **94C:28.**

Dumping ground, enforcement of provisions as to assignment of places, **111:150A.**

Duration of sittings, **213:6.**

Dwelling houses.

See DWELLING HOUSES.

Elections.

Absent voting matters, **54:103.**

Clerks of court, **221:3.**

Incumbent candidates previously appointed by justices, arrangement on primary ballot of names, **53:34.**

Offenses, jurisdiction, **56:59.**

Precincts for voting, authority of court as to revision, **54:9A.**

Electricity.

See GAS AND ELECTRIC COMPANIES.

Electrologists' registration board, appeals, **112:87JJJ, 112:87LLL.**

Electronic recording devices, authorizing use of, to obtain evidence of crime, **272:99.**

Emergency medical care, enforcement of provisions regarding, **111C:11.**

Eminent domain.

See EMINENT DOMAIN.

Employment security laws, enforcement, **151A:72.**

Encumbrances.

Liens and encumbrances. See within this heading, "Liens and encumbrances."

Engineers and surveyors.

Certificate of, appeal from refusal or revocation, **112:81P, 112:81S.**

Professional engineers and land surveyors, enforcement of orders of board, **112:81E, 112:81P.**

Entry of judgment, **213:3, 213:5, 235:4.**

SUPERIOR COURTS —Cont'd

Entry on state land, jurisdiction to prosecute unlawful entry, **245:1.**

Environment and natural resources.

Enforcement of environmental code, **21A:13.**

Protection of, actions, **214:7A.**

Scenic and recreational rivers and streams jurisdiction, over actions affecting, **21:17B.**

Equal rights under law, civil action for violation of rights, **93:102.**

Equity.

See EQUITY.

Essex county.

Equity clerk, **221:6B.**

Jurisdiction and venue over matters arising within marine boundaries, **1:3.**

Sittings of court, **212:14.**

Ethics commission investigations, compelling attendance of witnesses, **268B:4.**

Evidentiary value in superior court of small claims finding for plaintiff in district court, **218:23.**

Excavations, jurisdiction to enforce town bylaws for safeguarding, **40:21.**

Exclusive original jurisdiction, **212:3.**

Injunctive relief, **215:6.**

Labor dispute cases, **214:1.**

Probate and Family Court, **215:3, 215:4.**

Executions.

Redemption, action, **236:39-236:41.**

Scire facias on invalid levy, **236:51.**

Time of issuance of execution, **235:16.**

Trustee process.

See TRUSTEE PROCESS.

Expenses and expenditures.

Appearance of arrested person, certificate of expenses, **276:44.**

Attorneys at law, lien for expenses, **221:50.**

Binding over, certificate of fees and expenses, **276:44.**

Costs of actions. See within this heading, "Costs of actions."

Cranberry land, review of apportionment of expense of flooding, **253:40.**

SUPERIOR COURTS —Cont'd

Expenses and expenditures —Cont'd

District attorney, approval of expenses, **12:24.**

Fees. See within this heading, "Fees."

Injunctions to restrain unlawful public expenditures or obligations, **29:63.**

Liens for.

Liens and encumbrances. See within this heading, "Liens and encumbrances."

Vouchers, **35:12.**

Witnesses, travel expenses, **262:29, 262:53A.**

Explosions and explosives.

Blasting, jurisdiction to enforce laws and regulations, **148:21.**

Power to restrain use of building in violation of regulations, **148:17.**

Extension of concurrent jurisdiction of superior court, **213:1A.**

Extension of sitting, **212:25.**

Extra compensation for meritorious service, approval, **262:47.**

Fair employment practice commission, review of orders, **151B:6.**

False advertising, injunction against, **266:91B.**

Fees.

Appellant's liability for fees, **278:18.**

Assisting in investigations of criminal cases, **262:29.**

Attorneys at law, **214:3, 221:50.**

Binding over, certificate of fees and expenses, **276:44.**

County commissioners, fee for filing of petition, **262:4A.**

Entry fee, increase, **231:104.**

Filing action, **262:4A.**

Injunctions, **262:4A.**

Jailer's fees where appeal withdrawn, **278:26.**

Sheriffs for service of writs, precepts or process, **262:8.**

Statement, **278:22.**

Witness fees, **262:53, 262:53B.**

Fictitious name, writ designating defendant, **223:19.**

Fidelity insurance companies, list to clerk in Suffolk county, **175:105.**

SUPERIOR COURTS —Cont'd
Filing.
Records and recording. See within this heading, "Records and recording."
Fire districts, excluding persons or estate, **48:79.**
Firefighters, appeal from denial of indemnification, **41:100.**
Fire insurance, review of form of appraisal or adjustment contract, **175:172.**
Fires.
See FIRES AND FIRE PREVENTION.
First assistant chief probation officer established, **276:83.**
First justice of court, **212:14A.**
Fish and game.
Fisheries and game, hearing on waste regulations by director, **131:41.**
Flood plains, jurisdiction over violation of law for protection, **131:40.**
Inland wetlands, enforcement of orders affecting, **131:40A.**
Marine fish and fisheries. See within this heading, "Marine fish and fisheries."
Flowing lands, jurisdiction involving complaints, **212:3.**
Food and agriculture, appeals from decisions of commissioner, **20:19.**
Foreclosure of mortgage actions, exclusive original jurisdiction, **212:3.**
Foreign insurance companies, enforcement of laws, **175:193A.**
Forfeited property, enforcement of provisions as to seizure and libeling, **257:1-257:15.**
Form and substance, distinguishing between, **213:3.**
Framing issues for jury in equity case, **214:13.**
Fraternal benefit societies, jurisdiction, **176:53.**
Fraud and deceit.
Discouraging, **213:3.**
Injunctions against false advertising, **266:91B.**
Special jurisdiction in actions involving fraudulent conveyances, **214:3.**
Furnaces for iron or glass, injunction restraining use, **140:117.**

SUPERIOR COURTS —Cont'd
Garbage and rubbish, enforcement of provisions as to assignment of places for dumping, **111:150A.**
Garnishment.
See TRUSTEE PROCESS.
Gas and oil.
Gas.
See GAS AND ELECTRIC COMPANIES.
Ships receiving or discharging petroleum products, enforcement of bond furnished, **21:50B.**
Gasoline and motor fuels.
Motor fuel sales act. See within this heading, "Motor fuel sales act."
Taxes on gasoline and motor fuels, jurisdiction to restrain collection, **64A:12, 64E:12, 64F:13.**
General fields, jurisdiction, **179:36-179:40.**
Gift to governmental unit, special jurisdiction in action to enforce purpose, **214:3.**
Grade crossings, abolition, **159:79.**
Grand jury.
Assembling of grand jury, **212:23.**
Granting additional time for completion of grand jury investigations, **277:1A.**
Gravel, jurisdiction to enforce municipal ordinances or bylaws as to removal, **40:21.**
Habitual traffic offender status, appeal from designation, **90:22F.**
Hampden county, **212:14.**
Hazardous waste facility sites, decisions, **111:150B.**
Hazardous waste management act, jurisdiction over violations, **21C:10, 21C:14.**
Health care facilities, jurisdiction to enforce health department's procedures for determination of need, **111:25G.**
Health maintenance organizations.
Fines and penalties assessed, **111:25G.**
Mandamus action, **111:25C.**
Health regulations, enforcement, **111:5, 111:187.**
Hearings.
Appellate division, **278:28B, 278:28D.**
Fisheries and game, hearing on waste regulations by director, **131:41.**

SUPERIOR COURTS —Cont'd
Hearings —Cont'd
Hearing officers division, powers of court regarding proceedings, **7:4H.**
Industrial homework, witnesses upon hearings and investigations, **149:147F.**
Heating plants.
Municipal lighting and heating plants. See within this heading, "Municipal lighting and heating plants."
Heirs, special jurisdiction in action for contributions by or between, **214:3.**
Highways and streets.
Enforcement of highway regulations, **85:2.**
Outdoor advertising, **93D:5.**
Traffic regulations and rules of the road. See within this heading, "Traffic regulations and rules of the road."
Unauthorized moving of buildings along highways, jurisdiction to enforce law, **85:18.**
Historic districts and sites.
Appeals from determination by historic district commission, **40C:12.**
Jurisdiction, **9:27, 9:27C, 40C:13.**
Holidays.
Sundays and holidays. See within this heading, "Sundays and holidays."
Home rule procedures act, jurisdiction, **43B:14.**
Horse or dog racing meeting employees, request for appointment or discharge, **271:40.**
Hospitals.
Enjoining unlawful occupancy of building as hospital, **111:75.**
Incorporation of hospitals, appeal, **155:2B.**
Hours for transacting business, **213:4.**
Housing and urban renewal, **121A:6, 121A:6C, 121B:47.**
Housing court.
See HOUSING COURT.
Hunting.
Fish and game. See within this heading, "Fish and game."
Ice, appeals from proceedings as to sale of impure ice, **94:162.**

SUPERIOR COURTS —Cont'd

Immunity of witnesses.

Defendant not to be convicted solely on testimony of witness granted immunity, **233:20I.**

Inactive religious societies, special jurisdiction of suits to determine disposition of property, **214:3.**

Income tax return, jurisdiction of mandamus proceedings to compel filing, **62C:9.**

Incorporation of hospitals, appeal, **155:2B.**

Incumbents appointed by justices of, order of placing names on primary ballots, **53:34.**

Indemnification of policemen or firemen, denial of appeal, **41:100.**

Indictment.

County officers or employees, indictment for misconduct in office, **268A:25.**

Transmission, **212:7.**

Waiver, **263:4A.**

Indigency.

Appeals from denial of relief from court costs by indigents in matters arising in superior court, **261:27D.**

Filing affidavit of indigency and request for waiver of cost of action arising in superior court, **261:27B.**

Industrial homework, witnesses upon hearings and investigations, **149:147F.**

Injury to employee, order for examination of premises, **153:9.**

Inquest, filing of report, **38:12.**

Insolvent estates of deceased, appeals as to claims against, **198:11-198:17.**

Inspector general.

Discovery, orders, **12A:9.**

Witnesses, compelling testimony, **12A:7. (note)**

Insurance.

See INSURANCE.

Interest on money.

Home mortgages, actions under laws as to interest, **140:90D.**

Jurisdiction to declare small loan void for excessive interest, **140:114A.**

Interlocutory appeal, criminal cases, **278:28E.**

Interlocutory orders, relief, **231:118.**

SUPERIOR COURTS —Cont'd

Interpreters, appointment, **221:92.**

Intoxicating liquor.

Alcoholic liquors. See within this heading, "Alcoholic liquors."

Issuance of process in any county, **213:2.**

Issues of fact.

Questions of law or fact. See within this heading, "Questions of law or fact."

Joinder of actions.

Consolidation or severance of proceedings. See within this heading, "Consolidation or severance of proceedings."

Joint heirs, equitable suit to recover debt, **197:31.**

Joint owners of personal property, special jurisdiction in actions between, **214:3.**

Joint trustees, special jurisdiction in actions between, **214:3.**

Judges.

Justices. See within this heading, "Justices."

Judgments and decrees.

Amendment of judgment, **278:28C.**

Attachments. See within this heading, "Attachments."

Declaratory judgments, **213:3, 231A:1.**

Dissolution of attachment by judgment, **223:115.**

Entry of judgment, **213:3, 213:5, 235:4.**

Land court, default decree, **185:16.**

Nonentry of appeal, affirmation of judgment of District Court, **212:12.**

Orders. See within this heading, "Orders."

Realty, decree in equity operating as release, **183:43.**

Setting aside of judgments or verdicts. See within this heading, "Setting aside of judgments or verdicts."

Supreme judicial court decrees to be recorded, **212:9.**

Vacating district court judgments upon removal, **231:104.**

Judicial council, composition, **221:34A.**

Jurisdiction, **212:3-212:6.**

Jury and jury trial.

Attorney, notice of trials of civil causes to be given, **213:3.**

SUPERIOR COURTS —Cont'd

Jury and jury trial —Cont'd

Central pools of jurors, **212:20A.**

Extension of sitting, **212:25.**

Grand jury. See within this heading, "Grand jury."

Interchangeable use in civil or criminal cases, **212:20.**

Land court, jury trial in superior court, **185:15, 185:16.**

List of cases for trial, **278:1.**

Protracted cases, jurors empanelled, **234:26B.**

Questions of law or fact. See within this heading, "Questions of law or fact."

Right to and waiver of jury trial, **263:6.**

Small claims, **218:23.**

Special jury for sitting of criminal business, **212:21.**

Justices.

Adjournment in absence of justice, **213:11, 213:12.**

Administrative justices.

See ADMINISTRATIVE JUSTICES.

Appellate division, disqualification of certain justices, **278:28A.**

Appointed after attaining age 60, retirement benefits, **32:65A.**

Appointees of, arrangement of names on primary ballots, **53:34.**

Arrests, power, **276:21.**

Attendance, **213:9, 213:11, 213:12.**

Bail, powers, **276:57.**

Belated decisions, **220:14A.**

Chief justice. See within this heading, "Chief justice."

Claims against Commonwealth, judge to approve award, compromise or settlement, **258:7.**

Compelling attendance of witnesses and production of papers before state tax commission, **58:25B.**

Congestion, use of district court justices to relieve, **212:14A.**

Continuous sitting in Boston for purpose of determining equitable relief, **214:14.**

County treasurer, justice of court disqualified to act, **35:1.**

Designation of officers to attend central pool of jurors, **212:20A.**

SUPERIOR COURTS —Cont'd

Justices —Cont'd

District court justices sitting in certain cases, **212:14A.**

Labor dispute cases, panel of three associate justices to act, **212:30.**

Number, **211B:2, 212:1.**

Pensions, **32:65A-32:67.**

Presiding justices serving at pleasure of administrative justice, **212:14A.**

Retirement, **32:65A.**

Revenue commissioner, compelling attendance of witnesses and production of papers before, **58:25B.**

Salaries, **211B:4.**

State ballot law commission, retired justice as member, **55B:1.**

Supervision of sales of copies of rules, **213:3A.**

Juvenile courts.

See JUVENILE COURTS AND DELINQUENT CHILDREN.

Labor and workforce development, **149:9.**

Apprenticeship agreements, **23:11K.**

Enforcement of orders of department, **149:9.**

Temporary employees. See within this heading, "Temporary employees."

Labor relations.

See LABOR RELATIONS AND DISPUTES.

Labor relations commission.

See LABOR RELATIONS COMMISSION.

Land court.

Appeals from Superior Court, **185:15.**

Cases transferred between land court and Superior Court.

Report, reservation, or transfer of cases. See within this heading, "Report, reservation, or transfer of cases or questions to or from."

Certification of determination of issues, **185:17.**

Concurrent jurisdiction, **185:1.**

Default decree, jury trial in appeal, **185:16.**

Jurisdiction of, as affecting jurisdiction of superior court, **212:3.**

Jury trial in Superior Court, **185:15, 185:16.**

SUPERIOR COURTS —Cont'd

Land court —Cont'd

Report, reservation, or transfer of cases or questions. See within this heading, "Report, reservation, or transfer of cases or questions to or from."

Landlord.

See LANDLORD AND TENANT.

Late entry of appeal, **212:13.**

Lead poisoning prevention provisions, jurisdiction to enforce, **111:198.**

Legatees, special jurisdiction in actions for contribution by or between, **214:3.**

Liability insurance, appeal as to cancellation or refusal of automobile insurance, **175:113D.**

Liens and encumbrances.

Attorney's lien for expenses and fees, **221:50.**

Mechanics' liens, enforcement, **254:5.**

Mortgages. See within this heading, "Mortgages."

Veteran's real property, enforcement of liens, **115:5A.**

Wharves, piers, and docks, enforcement of Commonwealth's lien for cost of removal when unsafe, **91:49B.**

Lighting plants.

Municipal lighting and heating plants. See within this heading, "Municipal lighting and heating plants."

Lists.

Cases for trial.

Calendars and dockets. See within this heading, "Calendars and dockets."

Civil service, enforcing submission of list of employees, **31:67.**

Publication of trial lists, **213:3.**

Surety companies, list to be furnished to clerk in Suffolk County, **175:105.**

Lobbying laws, jurisdiction over violations, **3:49.**

Lost and unclaimed property.

Abandoned, lost, and unclaimed property. See within this heading, "Abandoned, lost, and unclaimed property."

Low and moderate income housing, review of decision on application to build, **40B:22.**

SUPERIOR COURTS —Cont'd

Lowlands and swamps.

Coastal wetlands regulations, exclusive jurisdiction of court concerning, **130:105.**

Reclamation board's determinations, revision, **252:7.**

Malpractice.

Medical malpractice claims. See within this heading, "Medical malpractice claims."

Mandamus.

Appeals court's review of mandamus proceedings in superior court, **211A:10.**

Civil service employee's right, **31:73.**

Health maintenance organizations, mandamus actions, **111:25C.**

Income tax return, jurisdiction of mandamus proceeding to compel filing, **62C:9.**

Petition for action in nature, **249:5.**

Manner of holding court, **212:2.**

Marine boundaries, jurisdiction and venue over matters arising within, **1:3.**

Marine fish and fisheries.

Coastal wetlands regulations, exclusive jurisdiction of court concerning, **130:105.**

Fishways, jurisdiction, **130:19.**

Marriage, cancellation of unauthorized notice of intention, **207:26.**

Massachusetts water management act, enforcement of provisions, **21G:14.**

Masters.

Auditors, masters, and referees. See within this heading, "Auditors, masters, and referees."

Mechanics' liens, enforcement, **254:5.**

Medical care and treatment.

Emergency medical care, enforcement of provisions regarding, **111C:11.**

Facilities for health care, jurisdiction to enforce health department's procedures for determining need, **111:25G.**

Hospitals. See within this heading, "Hospitals."

SUPERIOR COURTS —Cont'd

Medical care and treatment —Cont'd

Malpractice.

Medical malpractice claims. See within this heading, "Medical malpractice claims."

Medical malpractice claims.

Justice of superior court as member of tribunal for hearing, **231:60B.**

Medical service corporations, disputes involving, **176B:12, 176C:12.**

Meetings of governmental bodies, enforcement of laws governing meetings, **30A:11A½, 34:9G, 39:23B, 39:23C, 66:17C.**

Mentally ill and retarded persons.

Appeal from order of commitment, **123:9.**

Jurisdiction of superior court over licensed facilities, **19:19, 19B:15.**

Superintendents or directors, removal, **19:14.**

Meritorious service, approval of extra compensation, **262:47.**

Metropolitan districts.

Air pollution control district rules and regulations, jurisdiction to restrain violations, **111:142B.**

Middlesex county.

Chief deputy sheriff, **221:71.**

Equity clerk, **221:6A.**

Sittings, **212:14.**

Migrant farm laborers, jurisdiction to protect visitation rights, **111:128H.**

Milk and milk products.

Enforcement of attendance of witnesses in proceedings under Milk Control Act, **94A:18.**

Review of Milk Control Commission proceedings, **94A:8, 94A:21.**

Minimum wages, appeals from decisions of commissioner of labor and workforce development, **151:14.**

Minors.

Children or minors. See within this heading, "Children or minors."

Mistake, late entry of appeal on ground, **212:13.**

Mixed actions, exclusive original jurisdiction, **212:3.**

SUPERIOR COURTS —Cont'd

Monday as return day in criminal cases, **212:22.**

Mortgages.

Action for redemption, mortgages held by state, **244:40.**

Foreclosure actions, jurisdiction, **140:90D, 212:3, 244:40.**

Interest on home mortgages, actions under laws, **140:90D.**

Motions.

Interlocutory appeal, criminal cases, **278:28E.**

Setting aside of verdicts, recording and notifying adverse parties of motions, **213:3.**

Motor carrier.

Carriers. See within this heading, "Carriers."

Motor fuel sales act.

Injunctions enjoining violations of law, **94:295L, 94:295T.**

Jurisdiction, **94:295L, 94:295P.**

Motor vehicles.

Carriers. See within this heading, "Carriers."

Fuel for.

Gasoline and motor fuels. See within this heading, "Gasoline and motor fuels."

Habitual traffic offender, appeal from designation, **90:22F.**

Insurance.

Automobile insurance. See within this heading, "Automobile insurance."

Junkyard, abatement as nuisance, **140B:7.**

Loss prevention central organization, access to records, **175:113O.**

Registrar of motor vehicles, enforcement of orders, **90:28.**

Traffic regulations and rules of the road. See within this heading, "Traffic regulations and rules of the road."

Municipality.

Cities and towns. See within this heading, "Cities and towns."

Municipal lighting and heating plants.

Appeals from removal of municipal light board or commission member, **164:56E.**

SUPERIOR COURTS —Cont'd

Municipal lighting and heating plants —Cont'd

Enforcement of laws and orders of department, **164:79.**

Mutual fire insurance company books and records, authority to permit inspection by interested persons, **175:78.**

Names.

Benevolent or charitable organization, jurisdiction to enjoin fraudulent use of name, **266:71A.**

Business trusts, jurisdiction to enjoin use of misleading name, **182:2A.**

Narcotics.

Drugs and narcotics. See within this heading, "Drugs and narcotics."

Naturalization.

Chief justice to establish sittings, **212:14A.**

Fixing time and place for clerk's reception of declarations, **220:18.**

Jurisdiction over, **220:15.**

Superior court sittings, **212:14, 212:14A.**

Natural resources.

Environment and natural resources. See within this heading, "Environment and natural resources."

Negligence, discouraging, **213:3.**

Noisome or offensive trade, prevention of exercise, **111:144, 111:153.**

Non-alcoholic beverages, enjoining sales, **140:21C.**

Nonentry of appeal from District Court judgment, affirmation on appeal, **212:12.**

Norfolk county.

Court officers, **221:70.**

Sittings, **212:14.**

Notice.

Adjournment, **213:11.**

Appeal, notification of right, **278:18.**

Attorneys, notice of trials in civil causes to be given, **213:3.**

Evidence intended to be offered by adverse party, giving notice, **213:3.**

Setting aside of verdict, notice to adverse parties of motion, **213:3.**

Nuisances.

See NUISANCES.

SUPERIOR COURTS —Cont'd

Number of justices and court officers, **211B:2, 212:1, 221:69.**

Numerical order, proceedings, against corporation issuing obligations redeemable, **107:8.**

Obscene matter, jurisdiction, **272:28C-272:31.**

Offensive trade, power to restrain use of building, **111:153.**

Officers and employees of court.

  Court officers and employees. See within this heading, "Court officers and employees."

Official bonds.

  Bonds and undertakings. See within this heading, "Bonds and undertakings."

Oil.

  Gas and oil. See within this heading, "Gas and oil."

Optometric service corporations, review of decisions involving, **176F:12.**

Orders.

  Abandoned, lost, and unclaimed property, **200A:10, 200A:12.**

  Chief justice, assembling of grand jury upon written order to sheriff, **212:23.**

  County correction facility, order for closing, **127:1B.**

  Entry in any county, **213:5.**

  Establishing or changing time of sittings, entry of orders, **212:14A.**

  Fish and game, enforcement of orders affecting inland wetlands, **131:40A.**

  Inspector general, orders as to discovery, **12A:9.**

  Labor and workforce development department, enforcement of orders, **149:9.**

  Municipal lighting and heating plants department, enforcement of laws and orders, **164:79.**

  Prisoner's record disclosed under court order, **127:29.**

  Seeds. See within this heading, "Seeds."

  Sheriff, orders, **212:12, 212:21, 212:23.**

  State regulatory agencies, actions to enforce of orders, **214:3.**

  Supreme judicial court's orders to be recorded, **212:9.**

SUPERIOR COURTS —Cont'd

Orders —Cont'd

  Water supply treatment facilities, enforcement of order requiring installation and operation, **111:5G.**

Outdoor advertising adjacent to certain highways, jurisdiction to restrain, **93D:5.**

Panel of three associate justices of superior court to act upon labor dispute cases, **212:30.**

Parole.

  Probation and parole. See within this heading, "Probation and parole."

Partnership, property as reachable in creditor's action, **109:45, 214:3.**

Pensions.

  Retirement systems and pensions. See within this heading, "Retirement systems and pensions."

Persons held for trial, removal between jails and correctional institutions, **276:52A.**

Pesticides violations, **132B:14.**

Petitions.

  See COMPLAINT.

Physician's refusal to submit to examination upon order of board of registration, **112:5H.**

Planning boards.

  See ZONING AND PLANNING.

Pleas and answers, eminent domain, **79:22.**

Plymouth county.

  Clerk for equity proceedings, **221:61.**

  Institution of proceedings as to civil and criminal matters within marine boundaries of Commonwealth, **1:3.**

Sittings, **212:14.**

Podiatry schools, review of refusal to approve, **112:16.**

Police officers.

  Attendance in criminal cases, **262:53A, 262:53C.**

  Indemnification of, appeal from, denial, **41:100.**

  State police officers, witness fees and travel allowance, **262:53B.**

Poor persons.

  Indigency. See within this heading, "Indigency."

Postponement of cases, special master's duties in connection, **212:19A.**

Adjournments. See within this heading, "Adjournments."

SUPERIOR COURTS —Cont'd

Practice of law.

  Attorneys at law. See within this heading, "Attorneys at law."

Precedence of certain prosecutions, **212:24.**

Preliminary injunction, appeal from granting or denial, **231:118.**

Presiding justices serving at pleasure of administrative justice, **212:14A.**

Primary ballots, arrangement of candidates' names, **53:34.**

Printing.

  Copies of rules, **213:3A.**

  Trial lists, **213:3.**

Prisoners.

  Cages in courtrooms abolished, **34:3.**

  Correctional institutions. See CORRECTIONAL INSTITUTIONS.

Privacy actions, jurisdiction, **214:1B.**

Private trade school, appeal from refusal of license, **93:21C.**

Privilege.

  Immunity. See within this heading, "Immunity of witnesses."

Probate and Family Court, removal of causes, **215:6.**

Probate bonds, actions, **205:30.**

Probation and parole.

  Assistant supervisor of probation, **276:80.**

  Guilty verdict, probation prior or subsequent, **276:87.**

Officers.

  See PROBATION OFFICERS.

Process.

  See PROCESS AND SERVICE OF PROCESS AND PAPERS.

Professional bail bondsman, registration, **276:61B.**

Protracted cases, jurors empanelled, **234:26B.**

Provisions common to supreme judicial court and superior courts, **213:1-213:13.**

Psychologists, enforcement of orders pertaining, **112:128.**

Publication of trial lists, **213:3.**

Public buildings, enforcement of regulations to facilitate physically handicapped persons' use, **22:13A.**

Public meetings and records of boards and commissions, compelling compliance with law, **39:23C.**

SUPERIOR COURTS —Cont'd

Public records.

Boards and commissions, compelling compliance with law as to public meetings and records of boards, **39:23C.**

Compelling delivery to public officer, **66:13.**

Enforcement of provisions forbidding certain appliances to be used in making, **66:4.**

Inspection, compliance orders, **66:10.**

Jurisdiction to enforce standards established for materials used in recording, **66:4.**

Public utilities.

Recovery of forfeiture for use of name indicating that person is public service corporation, **155:5.**

Request for appointment or discharge of employees, **271:40.**

Qualification.

Disqualification. See within this heading, "Disqualification."

Questions of law or fact.

Distinct presentation of questions to be tried by jury, **213:3.**

Equity suit, trial of fact issues, **214:11.**

Report, reservation, or transfer of cases or questions. See within this heading, "Report, reservation, or transfer of cases or questions to or from."

Quieting title.

Damages in proceedings to free property form restrictions, assessment, **240:17.**

Equity suit, **240:6-240:10C.**

Restrictions running with land, jurisdiction of action to enforce, **240:10A.**

Quo warranto, action in nature, **249:6, 249:9.**

Racial imbalance in schools, jurisdiction, **15:1J.**

Railroads.

See RAILROADS.

Rape and related offenses, clerk's reports, **265:13B, 265:13H, 265:22 et seq.**

Real actions, exclusive original jurisdiction, **212:3.**

SUPERIOR COURTS —Cont'd

Real estate.

Brokers' and salesmen's of real estate, board of registration, appeals, **112:87BBB.**

Decree in equity operating as release of realty, **183:43.**

Quieting title. See within this heading, "Quieting title."

Redemption, actions, **236:39-236:41.**

Replevin. See within this heading, "Replevin."

Restrictions running with land, jurisdiction of action to enforce, **240:10A.**

Seized property, appeal from decree of forfeiture, **276:8.**

Unlawful entry on state land, jurisdiction, **245:1.**

Veterans, enforcement of liens or real estate, **115:5A.**

Reclamation boards' determination, revision, **252:7.**

Recognizance.

Bail and recognizance. See within this heading, "Bail and recognizance."

Records and recording.

Attorneys at law, filing of petition for examination for admission to bar, **221:37.**

Certification of copies of records by clerk of court, **212:26.**

Church records, jurisdiction to compel delivery to city or town clerk, **66:16.**

Criminal offender record information system. See within this heading, "Criminal offender record information system."

Custody of records, **212:26.**

Decrees of supreme judicial court to be recorded, **212:9.**

Electronic recording devices, authorizing use, **272:99.**

Motions to set aside verdicts and notifying adverse parties thereof, **213:3.**

Motor vehicle loss prevention central organization, access to records, **175:113O.**

Mutual fire insurance company books and records, authority of court to permit inspection by interested persons, **175:78.**

SUPERIOR COURTS —Cont'd

Records and recording —Cont'd

Order establishing or changing time or place of sittings to be entered into record, **212:14A.**

Prisoner's records disclosed on order of court, **127:29.**

Public records. See within this heading, "Public records."

Recreational tramway board, appeals from orders, **143:71M.**

Redelivery of goods or chattels taken or detained from owner, special jurisdiction in action to compel, **214:3.**

Redemption.

Mortgages held by state, action, **244:40.**

Numerical order, corporation issuing obligations redeemable in, proceedings, **107:8.**

Real estate, actions, **236:39-236:41.**

Referees.

Auditors, masters, and referees. See within this heading, "Auditors, masters, and referees."

Refuse disposal incinerators, enforcement of provisions as to assignment of places, **111:150A.**

Registrar of motor vehicles, enforcement of orders, **90:28.**

Reimbursement of municipality by state, action, **29:27C.**

Release of defendant on own recognizance without surety, review of refusal to order, **276:58.**

Religious societies, special jurisdiction to determine disposition of property of inactive societies, **214:3.**

Removal from office or employment.

Attorneys at law, removal by superior court, **221:40.**

Employees or officers of court, **35:51.**

Horse and dog racing meeting employees, request for discharge, **271:40.**

Justice, substitution of justices in event of removal, **212:148.**

Special master, **212:19A.**

SUPERIOR COURTS —Cont'd

Removal from office or
employment —Cont'd

Suffolk County superior court
clerk, **211:4.**

Tax collectors, **41:39B.**

Removal of actions.

Report, reservation, or transfer
of cases or questions to. See
within this heading,
"Report, reservation, or
transfer of cases or
questions to or from."

Removal of persons held for trial
between jails and correctional
institutions, **276:52A.**

Replevin.

Bond where replevin writ
returnable, **247:8.**

Costs of action, **261:4.**

Special jurisdiction, **214:3.**

Report, reservation, or transfer of
cases or questions to or from,
213:1B, 231:102C, 231:104.

Boston municipal court or
district courts, transfers,
231:102C, 231:104.

Compulsory counterclaim,
removal to superior courts
as of right by defendant
asserting, **231:103.**

Cross actions or actions arising
out of same accident, event
or transaction pending in
both superior and district
courts, **223:2B.**

District Courts, transfers,
231:102C.

Full court, **231:111 et seq.**

Land court, **185:15, 212:26A.**

Jury trial, Superior Court
from Land Court, **185:15.**

Probate court, transfer or
removal of cases to superior
court, **215:6.**

Small claims proceeding,
removal to superior court,
218:23.

Unfit dwellings, removal to
superior court of action
involving order disposing of
rents, **111:127G.**

Vacating District Court
judgment upon removal to
superior court, **231:104.**

Worcester central district court,
removal of causes, **218:19A.**

Resentencing of defendant by
appellate division, **278:28C.**

SUPERIOR COURTS —Cont'd

Reservation of questions of law.

Report, reservation, or transfer
of cases or questions to. See
within this heading,
"Report, reservation, or
transfer of cases or
questions to or from."

Reservoirs.

Dams and reservoirs. See within
this heading, "Dams and
reservoirs."

Restraints of trade.

See RESTRAINTS OF TRADE
AND MONOPOLIES.

Restrictions running with land,
240:10A, 240:17.

Retail installment sales and
services.

Avoidance of installment sales
agreements, **255D:29.**

Licensing of sales finance
companies, appeals, **255D:5,
255D:8.**

Retarded persons.

Mentally ill and retarded
persons. See within this
heading, "Mentally ill and
retarded persons."

Retired justices, temporary
service, **32:65F, 32:91.**

Retirement systems and pensions.

Judges, pension, **32:65A-32:67.**

Jurisdiction of enforcement,
32:24.

Officers and employees of court,
pensions, **32:66, 32:67.**

Pensioners, payment for services
as auditor or special master,
32:91.

Retrial in, of cases appealed from
district court, **231:97.**

Return day in criminal cases,
212:22.

Revenue commissioner, compelling
attendance of witnesses and
production of papers before,
58:25B.

Review.

Appeal. See within this heading,
"Appeals to superior court."

Revival of actions.

See ABATEMENT, SURVIVAL,
AND REVIVAL.

Right of privacy actions,
jurisdiction, **214:1B.**

Rules, **213:3, 213:3A.**

See SUPERIOR COURTS
RULES.

SUPERIOR COURTS —Cont'd

Salaries.

Wages, salaries, and
compensation. See within
this heading, "Wages,
salaries, and compensation."

Sales.

Copies of revisions of rules to
public, **213:3A.**

Going out of business sale,
restraining violations,
93:28E.

Retail installment sales and
services. See within this
heading, "Retail installment
sales and services."

Unfair Sales Act violations,
93:14H.

Sanitary code, speedy trial for
enforcement, **111:127A.**

Saturday, when business may be
transacted, **213:4.**

Scenic and recreational rivers and
streams, jurisdiction with
reference to actions affecting,
21:17B.

Schools.

See SCHOOLS AND
EDUCATION.

Scituate, jurisdiction of crimes
committed, **212:6.**

Seal of court, **213:13.**

Searches and seizures.

Alcoholic liquors, appeals to
courts upon seizure, **138:55.**

Forfeiture of seized property,
appeal from decree, **276:8.**

Warrants returnable in district
court, **276:3A.**

Seashore, proceedings for wrongful
removal of natural barriers,
91:30A.

Securing parties from being
misled, rule making for
purposes, **213:3.**

Security.

Bonds and undertakings. See
within this heading, "Bonds
and undertakings."

Seeds.

Appeal of stop-sale order,
128:95.

Penalties for violation of court
orders, **128:100.**

Sentence.

See SENTENCE AND
PUNISHMENT.

Separation of civil and criminal
business, **212:20.**

Services, allowance of accounts,
213:8.

SUPERIOR COURTS —Cont'd
Sessions.
Sittings of court. See within this
heading, "Sittings of court."
Setting aside of judgments or
verdicts.
District court judgments, setting
aside or vacating upon
removal to superior court,
231:104.
Motions, **213:3.**
Severance of proceedings.
Consolidation or severance of
proceedings. See within this
heading, "Consolidation or
severance of proceedings."
Sewers and drains, enforcement of
provisions, **83:13.**
Sexually dangerous persons.
Applications for parole, **123A:9.**
Authority as to conditional
release, **123A:9.**
Conditional release, **123A:9.**
Level of risk of reoffense,
challenge to determination
of, **6:178M.**
Sheriff.
Adjournment by in absence of
justice, **213:11.**
Assembling of grand jury upon
written order, **212:23.**
Certification of failure to give
bond, **37:7.**
Duty to attend sessions, **37:16.**
Fees for service of writs,
precepts, or process, **262:8.**
Justice's order requiring sheriff
to adjourn court, **213:12.**
Middlesex county, chief deputy
sheriff, **221:71.**
Reporting as to prisoners in
houses of correction, **126:12.**
Special sittings for criminal
business, written order to
sheriff, **212:21.**
Suffolk county superior court,
designation of two assistant
chief deputy sheriffs,
221:71A.
Ship receiving or discharging
petroleum products,
enforcement of bond, **21:50B.**
Shire town, adjournment, **213:10.**
Simplifying and shortening
pleadings and procedure,
promulgating rules for
purpose, **213:3.**
Simultaneous sessions, **213:7.**
Sittings of court, **212:14.**
Adjournments, **212:14, 213:6.**
Calendars and dockets. See
within this heading,
"Calendars and dockets."

SUPERIOR COURTS —Cont'd
Sittings of court —Cont'd
Changing time, **212:14A.**
Chief justice to establish,
212:14A.
Correctional institution,
appellate division sitting,
278:28A.
Duration, **213:6.**
Extension, **212:25.**
Sheriff, duty to attend, **37:16.**
Simultaneous, **213:7.**
Special sittings. See within this
heading, "Special sittings."
Slaughterhouses and meat
processing plants, restraint
and prevention of violation of
operations concerning, **94:129.**
Small claims proceedings, **218:23.**
Small home mortgages, actions
under laws as to interest,
140:90D.
Soil, loam, sand, or gravel,
jurisdiction to enforce
ordinances or bylaws as to
removal, **40:21.**
Special assessments.
Appeal from decision as to
abatement, **80:7.**
Petition to determine proportion
to be paid by lessee, **80:11.**
Special master, **212:19A.**
Compensation, **32:91, 212:19A,
221:55.**
Special sittings.
Chief justice to establish,
212:14A.
Criminal business, **212:21.**
Speedy trial, securing, **212:29,
213:3.**
Squannacook and Nissitissit
Rivers Sanctuary, **132A:17.**
Stables, restraining erection or
use, **111:158.**
Standing orders.
See SUPERIOR COURTS
RULES.
State ballot law commission.
Retired justice as member,
55B:1.
Signatures, review of sufficiency,
55B:6.
State police officers, witness fees
and travel allowance,
262:53B.
Statutes distributed to clerks, **5:3.**
Steam engines, appeal from
orders, **140:117.**
Stenographers and temporary
stenographers, **221:82, 221:83,
221:91.**

SUPERIOR COURTS —Cont'd
Street railways.
See STREET RAILWAYS.
Streets.
Highways and streets. See
within this heading,
"Highways and streets."
Striking unnecessary counts in
statements, prescribing terms,
213:3.
Substitutions.
Attorney general, appointment
of substitute, **12:26.**
Executor or administrator,
substitution of to be in
accordance with rules of
civil procedure, **228:4A.**
Subversive organizations, actions
against, **264:18.**
Suffolk county.
See SUFFOLK COUNTY.
Summary process to recover land.
See SUMMARY PROCESS TO
RECOVER LAND.
Sundays and holidays.
Transaction of court business on
Sunday, when permitted,
213:4.
Violations of Sunday laws,
enjoining, **136:10.**
Supplementary proceedings
involving charge of fraud,
224:19.
Supreme judicial court.
See SUPREME JUDICIAL
COURT.
Surety companies, list to be
furnished to clerk in Suffolk
county, **175:105.**
Surprise, prevention, **213:3.**
Surveyors.
Engineers and surveyors. See
within this heading,
"Engineers and surveyors."
Survival of actions.
See ABATEMENT, SURVIVAL,
AND REVIVAL.
Swamps.
Lowlands and swamps. See
within this heading,
"Lowlands and swamps."
Taxation.
See TAXATION.
Telephone and telegraph
companies.
Discrimination, enforcement of
laws against, **166:15.**
Issue of stock or bonds,
enforcement of laws, **166:5.**
Subscriber's remedies against
interception or monitoring,
166:44.

SUPERIOR COURTS —Cont'd

Temporary employees.
Clerk of court, appointment of temporary, **221:8.**
Probation officers, **276:89.**
Tender of payment accepted in action commenced, **232A:2.**
Term.
Sittings of court. See within this heading, "Sittings of court."
Theaters, enjoining unlicensed use, **140:181.**
Time.
Adjournments. See within this heading, "Adjournments."
Appeal, late entry, **212:13.**
Execution, time of issuance, **235:16.**
Grand jury investigations, granting additional time for completion, **277:1A.**
Holding court, time and place, **212:2.**
Holiday, when court business may be transacted, **213:4.**
Records order establishing or changing time or place of sittings to be entered into, **212:14A.**
Simultaneous sessions, **213:7.**
Sittings of court, duration, **213:6.**
Towns.
Cities and towns. See within this heading, "Cities and towns."
Toxics use reduction act.
See TOXICS USE REDUCTION ACT.
Trade name, enjoining use, **155:9.**
Trade school license, review of refusal or revocation, **93:21C.**
Trade secrets, enjoining misappropriation, **93:42A.**
Trading stamp companies, jurisdiction over, **93:14R.**
Traffic regulations and rules of the road.
Enforcement, **85:2.**
Habitual traffic offender, appeal of designation, **90:22F.**
Trailer coach parks, jurisdiction, **255:26.**
Transaction of business in any county, **213:5.**
Transfer of actions.
Report, reservation, or transfer of cases or questions to or from. See within this heading, "Report, reservation, or transfer of cases or questions to or from."

SUPERIOR COURTS —Cont'd

Transmission.
Appeal and review, transmission of papers, **278:20.**
Indictments, **212:7.**
Transportation.
Charges, enforcement of claim, **149:29.**
Expenses.
Travel expenses. See within this heading, "Travel expenses."
Travel expenses.
Clerks of appellate division, **278:28D.**
Witnesses, **262:29, 262:53A.**
Treason, disclosure to superior court, **264:3.**
Treasurer of city or town, petition for removal, **41:39B.**
Treasurers.
County treasurers. See within this heading, "County treasurers."
Trial, **213:3.**
Hearing. See within this heading, "Hearings."
Jury and jury trial. See within this heading, "Jury and jury trial."
Trial lists, **213:3, 278:1.**
Trial court of Commonwealth, departments, **211B:1.**
Trustee process.
See TRUSTEE PROCESS.
Trusts.
See TRUSTS AND TRUSTEES.
Unclaimed property.
Abandoned, lost, and unclaimed property. See within this heading, "Abandoned, lost, and unclaimed property."
Undertakings.
Bonds and undertakings. See within this heading, "Bonds and undertakings."
Unemployment compensation laws, enforcement, **151A:72.**
Unfair competition against consumers, **93A:11.**
Unfair labor practice proceedings, review, **150A:6, 150A:6B.**
Unfair Sales Act violations, **93:14H.**
Unfair trade practices against consumers, **93A:4, 93A:6, 93A:7, 93A:9.**
Unfit dwellings, removal to superior court of action involving order disposing of rents, **111:127G.**

SUPERIOR COURTS —Cont'd

Unlawful entry on state land, jurisdiction, **245:1.**
Urban area insurance placement facility's denial of insurance coverage requested, review, **175C:7.**
Urban renewal.
Housing and urban renewal, **121A:6, 121A:6C, 121B:47.**
Utilities.
Public utilities. See within this heading, "Public utilities."
Vacancy in office, **213:1.**
Vacating judgments.
Setting aside of judgments or verdicts. See within this heading, "Setting aside of judgments or verdicts."
Venire facias writs, issuance, **212:20A.**
Venue.
See VENUE.
Verdicts.
Filing and hearing of motions to set aside, **213:3.**
Guilty verdicts, placing person on probation either prior or subsequent, **276:87.**
Prescribing forms, **213:3.**
Setting aside judgments or verdicts. See within this heading, "Setting aside of judgments or verdicts."
Veterans.
Enforcement of decisions of veterans' services commissioner, **115:2A.**
Lien on real estate of recipient of benefits, enforcement, **115:5A.**
Veterinarians, appeals concerning, **112:55, 112:56D.**
Votes and voting.
Elections. See within this heading, "Elections."
Wages, salaries, and compensation, **221:93 to 221:102.**
Appellate division clerks, **278:28D.**
Assistant clerks, **221:94.**
Clerical assistants in superior court, **221:89.**
Clerk of court, **221:94.**
Commissioners, assessors, referees, masters, and auditors, award of compensation, **221:55.**
Condemned animals, proceedings for compensation, **129:31, 129:33.**

SUPERIOR COURTS —Cont'd
Wages, salaries, and compensation —Cont'd
Justices, **211B:4.**
Meritorious service, approval of extra compensation, **262:47.**
Minimum wages, **151:14.**
Officers designated to attend central pool of jurors, compensation, **212:20A.**
Special master, compensation, **32:91, 212:19A, 221:55.**
Suffolk county, clerks and assistant clerks of superior courts, **221:94.**
Travel expenses. See within this heading, "Travel expenses."
Waiver.
Indictment, **263:4A.**
Jury trial, **263:6.**
Warrants.
Drugs and narcotics, administrative inspection warrants, **94C:30.**
Search warrants returnable in district court, **276:3A.**
Waters.
See WATERS AND WATERWAYS.
Waterworks and water supply.
Installation and operation of water supply treatment facilities, enforcement of order requiring, **111:5G.**
Jurisdiction to enforce employment of certified operator, drinking water supply facility, **112:87DDDD.**
Massachusetts water management act, enforcement of provisions, **21G:14.**
Wharves, piers and docks, enforcement of Commonwealth's lien for cost of removal when unsafe, **91:49B.**
Wiretapping, authorization to obtain evidence of crime, **272:99.**
Witnesses.
Binding over, **278:25.**
Criminal cases, comments on accused's failure to testify, **278:23.**
Depositions, **233:24.**
Enforcement of attendance, **94A:18, 233:10.**
Ethics commission investigations, compelling attendance of witnesses, **268B:4.**

SUPERIOR COURTS —Cont'd
Witnesses —Cont'd
Fees of certain officers, **262:53, 262:53B.**
Immunity of witnesses. See within this heading, "Immunity of witnesses."
Industrial homework investigations, **149:147F.**
Inspector general, compelling testimony of witnesses, **12A:7. (note)**
State tax commission, justices compelling attendance of witnesses and production of papers before, **58:25B.**
Travel expenses, **262:29, 262:53A.**
Worcester central district court, removal of causes, **218:19A.**
Workers' compensation.
See WORKERS' COMPENSATION.
Writs and process, issuance of, **223:20.**
See PROCESS AND SERVICE OF PROCESS AND PAPERS.
Written instruments, procedure to secure binding interpretation, **213:3.**
Zoning.
See ZONING AND PLANNING.

SUPERIOR COURTS RULES.
Affidavit, verification by, **Rule 15.**
Annulment of marriage, **Rule 76.**
Appeal.
Claim of appeal, criminal cases, **Rule 65.**
Motor vehicle liability policy appeals, **Rule 74.**
Appearances, **Rules 2, 3, 32, 48, 62.**
Appellate Division.
Criminal cases, procedure and forms, **Rule 64.**
District/municipal courts rules for appellate division appeal.
See DISTRICT/MUNICIPAL COURTS RULES FOR APPELLATE DIVISION APPEAL.
Application of verdicts to counts, **Rule 25.**
Arbitration, **Rule 52.**
Arguments, **Rules 7, 68.**
Attorneys.
Arguments, **Rules 7, 68.**
Assignment in criminal cases, **Rule 53.**

SUPERIOR COURTS RULES —Cont'd
Attorneys —Cont'd
Bail or surety, **Rule 11.**
Engagements, **Rule 34.**
Witnesses, **Rule 12.**
Bail.
Attorney as, **Rule 11.**
Authorized persons to take bail, rules governing.
See BAIL AND RECOGNIZANCE RULES.
Professional bondsmen, rules governing.
See BAIL AND RECOGNIZANCE RULES.
Certificates of readiness, **Rule 35.**
Civil actions, special provisions for, **Rules 18-48.**
Claim of appeal, **Rule 65.**
Clerk's office hours, **Rule 2.**
Commissions, criminal cases, **Rule 71.**
Compensation, receivers, deposits for expenses and compensation, **Rule 51.**
Costs, **Rule 18.**
New trial motion, hearing, **Rule 26.**
Postponements, **Rule 21.**
Taxation, **Rule 46.**
County, hearing of cases from another county, **Rules 43-45.**
Cover sheet, **Rule 29, Standing Order 1-83.**
Criminal cases, special provisions for, **Rules 53-72.**
Cross-motions, **Rule 9A.**
Damages, statement of, **Rule 29.**
Default, failure to appear, **Rule 48.**
Delinquent children cases, experts, **Rule 55.**
Depositions, criminal cases, **Rules 71, 72.**
Discovery.
Deposition, **Rules 71, 72.**
Interrogatories, **Rule 30.**
Motions, **Rule 30A.**
Settlement of disputes, **Rule 9C.**
Dismissal of old cases, **Rule 31.**
Divorce cases, **Rules 76, 77.**
Election petitions, **Rule 75.**
Engagements of counsel, **Rule 34.**
Entry of action, **Rule 19.**
Exhibits, **Rules 14, 50.**
Expenses, receivers, deposits for expenses and compensation, **Rule 51.**

SUPERIOR COURTS RULES
—Cont'd

Experts, **Rules 54, 55.**
Extra charges by officers, **Rule 10.**
Filing papers upon judgment,
    Rule 47.
Forms.
  Appeal, notice to Justice of filing
    notice of, **Standing Order
    1-80.**
  Certificate of readiness, **Rule
    35.**
  Damages, statement of, to
    prevent transfer to District
    or Municipal court, **Rule 29.**
  Master, order of reference to,
    Rule 49.
  Pre-trial order, **Standing
    Order 1-88.**
  Special assignment of justices to
    civil actions, **Standing
    Order 9-80.**
  Surcharge matters.
    Complaint seeking review of
      order or finding of Board
      of Appeal on Motor
      Vehicle Liability Policies
      and Bonds, **Standing
      Order 6-80.**
  Waiver of indictment, **Rule 59.**
Grand jury proceedings, court
    reporter in, **Rule 63.**
Hampden, hearing cases from
    Berkshire, Franklin, and
    Hampshire, **Rule 45.**
Hearings.
  Interlocutory, **Rule 23.**
  Lists, **Rule 33.**
  New trial motion, **Rule 26.**
  Other county, **Rules 43-45.**
Hospital records, **Rule 13.**
Housing Court.
  See HOUSING COURT RULES.
Indictment, waiver, **Rule 59.**
Injunction, **Rule 20.**
Instructions, requests for, criminal
    cases, **Rule 70.**
Interlocutory matters, **Rules 9,
    9A, 23.**
Interrogatories, **Rule 30.**
Judgments and decrees.
  Default for failure to appear,
    Rule 48.
  Filing of papers upon judgment,
    Rule 47.
Jury and jurors, **Rule 5.**
  Notes by, **Rule 8A.**
  Peremptory challenges, **Rule 6.**
  Trial lists, **Rules 35, 36.**
Lists, trial and hearing, **Rules 33,
    35, 36, 77.**

SUPERIOR COURTS RULES
—Cont'd

Masters, **Rules 49, 50.**
Money paid into court, **Rule 22.**
Motions, **Rules 9, 9A.**
  Discovery orders, **Rule 30A.**
  Interlocutory matters, **Rules 9,
    9A.**
  New trial, **Rule 26.**
  Reconsideration, **Rule 9D.**
  Return of property and
    suppression of evidence,
    Rule 61.
  Waiver of motions to dismiss
    and for judgment, **Rule 28.**
Motor vehicle liability policy
    appeals, **Rule 74.**
Naturalization, **Rule 73.**
New trial, motion for, **Rule 26.**
Not guilty plea, **Rule 60.**
Objections, **Rules 8, 52.**
Old cases, **Rule 31.**
Opening statements, **Rule 7.**
Payment orders, **Rule 58.**
Peremptory challenges, **Rule 6.**
Postponements, **Rules 4, 21.**
Preferences on trial lists, **Rule 36.**
Pre-trial, **Rule 27.**
Probation.
  Condition of, **Rule 56.**
  Term of, **Rule 57.**
Protection writs, **Rule 16.**
Quieting title.
  Damages in proceedings to free
    property form restrictions,
    assessment, **240:17.**
Receivers, deposits for expenses
    and compensation, **Rule 51.**
Reconsideration.
  Motion, **Rule 9D.**
Recording proceedings, **Rule 17,
    Standing Order 2-87.**
Restraining orders, **Rule 20.**
Rulings, requests for, criminal
    cases, **Rule 70.**
Special provisions for civil actions,
    Rules 18-48.
Standing orders.
  Abortion authorization petitions,
    Standing Order 5-81.
  Appeal, notices of, **Standing
    Order 1-80.**
  Cover sheets, civil action,
    Standing Order 1-83.
  Criminal case management,
    Standing Order 2-86.
  Dismissal of pending criminal
    cases, **Standing Order
    4-81.**
  Electronic recordation of
    proceedings, **Standing
    Order 2-87.**

SUPERIOR COURTS RULES
—Cont'd

Standing orders —Cont'd
  Forms. See within this heading,
    "Forms."
  Malpractice action against
    health care provider,
    Standing Order 1-82.
  Middlesex County, motion
    procedure in room list
    session, Courtroom 6B,
    Standing Order 3-84.
  Notices of appeal, **Standing
    Order 1-80.**
  Pending criminal cases subject
    to dismissal pursuant to
    Crim Proc Rule 36,
    Standing Order 4-81.
  Periodic review, call, and
    processing of certain civil
    actions with jury claims,
    Standing Order 2-81.
  Periodic review, call, and
    processing of certain
    non-jury civil actions,
    Standing Order 1-81.
  Revocation of Standing Orders
    2-78 and 3-78, **Standing
    Order 2-84.**
  Special assignment of justices to
    civil actions, requests for,
    Standing Order 9-80.
  Surcharge matters, complaints
    for judicial review of,
    Standing Order 6-80.
  Time standards, **Standing
    Order 1-88.**
  Transfer procedures, **Standing
    Order 1-86.**
  Trial session hours, **Standing
    Order 5-80.**
Suffolk.
  Divorce cases, **Rule 77.**
  Other county, cases from, **Rule
    44.**
Suppression of evidence, motion,
    Rule 61.
Surety, attorney as, **Rule 11.**
Trial lists, **Rules 33, 35, 36, 77.**
Verdicts, civil actions, **Rules 24,
    25.**
Verification by affidavit, **Rule 15.**
Waiver.
  Indictment, **Rule 59.**
  Motions to dismiss or for
    judgment, **Rule 28.**
  Withdrawal of appearance, **Rule
    62.**
Witnesses.
  Attorneys, **Rule 12.**
  Criminal cases, **Rule 69.**

SUPERIOR COURTS RULES
—Cont'd
Witnesses —Cont'd
Depositions, **Rules 71, 72.**
Experts, **Rules 54, 55.**
Interrogatories, **Rule 30.**
Writ of protection, **Rule 16.**

SUPERMARKETS.
Smoking in public places, regulation, **270:21.**

SUPERNATURAL PHENOMENON.
Real estate transactions.
Disclosures.
Not deemed material fact required to be disclosed, **93:114.**

SUPERSEDEAS.
See STAY OR SUPERSEDEAS.

SUPPLEMENTAL SECURITY INCOME.
Commission.
See SUPPLEMENTARY SECURITY INCOME COMMISSION.
Disability benefits project for legal assistance to mentally or physically disabled persons, Supreme Judicial Court power, **211:25.**

SUPPLEMENTARY AFFIDAVITS.
Indigents, filing additional requests for waiver of court costs, **261:27B.**

SUPPLEMENTARY ASSISTANCE.
Aged.
See AGED AND DISABLED, ASSISTANCE.
Credit Union Employees Retirement Association, **171:82.**

SUPPLEMENTARY EDUCATION CENTERS.
Establishment through agreements for expenditure of public funds, **40:4A.**

SUPPLEMENTARY PROCEEDINGS, 223:84-223:86A, 224:14-224:30.
See ARREST ON MESNE PROCESS AND SUPPLEMENTARY PROCEEDINGS.

SUPPLEMENTARY REGISTRATION TO VOTE.
See REGISTRATION OF VOTERS.

SUPPLEMENTARY SECURITY INCOME COMMISSION.
Health and human services executive office, agencies within, **6A:16.**

SUPPLIES AND MATERIALS.
Construction contracts.
See CONSTRUCTION CONTRACTS AND WORK.
Contracts and agreements.
Cities, towns, and districts, **40:4.**
Construction contracts.
See CONSTRUCTION CONTRACTS AND WORK.
State institutions and offices, **7:22.**
Correctional institutions.
See CORRECTIONAL INSTITUTIONS.
County prisons.
See COUNTY PRISONS.
County public institutions, recording bills for supplies, **127:9.**
Electricity.
See GAS AND ELECTRIC COMPANIES.
Financing of judicial system, supplies as property of Commonwealth for purpose, **29A:2.**
Fire insurance coverage with respect to commercial property, **175:54F.**
Gas.
See GAS AND ELECTRIC COMPANIES.
Gasoline.
See GASOLINE AND MOTOR FUELS.
Highways.
See HIGHWAYS AND STREETS.
Licenses for supplies, **62C:67.**
Life insurance companies' annual statements, **175:25.**
Massachusetts Maritime Academy, duties of state college board of trustees, **73:1.**
Material supplier defined for purposes of system of public construction, **7:40C.**
Mechanics' liens.
See MECHANICS' LIENS.
Militia, **33:98-33:116.**
See MILITIA.
Municipal finance.
See MUNICIPAL FINANCE.
Political subdivisions, collective purchasing, **7:22A, 7:22B.**

SUPPLIES AND MATERIALS
—Cont'd
Public contractors, rules, **7:23A.**
Public utilities department, expenses, **25:8.**
Railroads.
See RAILROADS.
Regional health district, state reimbursement to exclude supplies, **111:27C.**
Ships.
Marks on vessels transporting stone, gravel or sand.
See SHIPS AND OTHER WATERCRAFT.
Siding or walling capable of conducting electricity, installation, **148:57.**
State departments or commissions, **7:22, 30:51, 30:52.**
State purchasing agent.
See STATE PURCHASING AGENT.
State sanitoria, inventory of supplies, **111:63.**
Street railways.
See STREET RAILWAYS.
Transfer between institutions or offices, **7:25A.**

SUPPORT AND MAINTENANCE.
Absentee's spouse and minor children, allowance, **200:10.**
Abuse prevention.
Court orders for support, **209A:3.**
Notice to abused person of rights to support, **209A:6.**
Accident and sickness insurance, **208:28, 209:32, 209:32F, 209C:9, 273:18A.**
Acknowledgments, action may be commenced by spouse or child entitled to support, **209:32F.**
Attachment of property, **32:19, 32:41, 151A:36, 152:47, 175:135, 201:40, 209:33, 246:28.**
Bail and recognizance.
Desertion proceedings, **273:6.**
Paternity suit, **273:18.**
Boston municipal court, support when married persons living apart, jurisdiction to enter judgment against spouse chargeable with support, **209:32F.**
Charter commission, municipal obligation to support financially, **43B:8.**

SUPPORT AND
   MAINTENANCE —Cont'd
Child support, **208:28, 208:28A.**
   Access to information, **46:3C,**
      62C:21, 119A:14, 271:43.
      Paternity acknowledgments,
         46:3D.
      Request of IV-D agencies,
         46:3D.
   Accident and sickness insurance.
      Commencement of support
         action where married
         persons are living apart,
         209:32F.
      Notice from IV-D agency,
         119A:12.
      Support order, **208:28, 209:32,**
         209C:9, 273:18A.
      Withholding of past due
         support from benefit
         payment, **175:24D.**
   Acknowledgments, action may
      be commenced by child
      entitled to support, **209:32F.**
   Actions, persons who may
      commence, **119:28.**
   Administration and finance
      executive office, **119A:1.**
   Adult children enrolled in
      educational programs,
      208:28, 209:37.
   Advertisements, **119A:2.**
   Affidavits, **119A:8.**
      Other jurisdiction, affidavits
         required for filing of
         support order, **119A:8.**
      Paternity, affidavit alleging
         intercourse between
         mother and putative
         father, **209C:17.**
   Agreements between parents,
      modification affecting
      support obligations, **119A:1,**
      119A:13.
   Appeal and review, **119A:16,**
      221B:8, 221B:10.
   Assignment of estate in divorce
      proceedings, future needs of
      children considered, **208:34.**
   Assignment of support rights,
      child receiving foster care
      maintenance payments,
      119:23.
   Assignments of wages. See
      within this subheading,
      "Income withholdings."
   Attorney representing IV-D
      agency, **119A:3.**
   Birth certificates.
      Access to records, **111:24B.**
   Blood test, paternity, **209C:17.**

SUPPORT AND
   MAINTENANCE —Cont'd
Child support —Cont'd
   Bonds and undertakings,
      119A:12, 208:36, 221B:7.
   Boston Municipal Court, **209C:3,**
      215:4, 218:19.
      Concurrent jurisdiction,
         209:32F.
      Transfer of case to probate
         and family court, **209C:3.**
   Capias, **119A:6, 215:34A,**
      221B:6.
   Certified copies required for
      filing of support order of
      another jurisdiction, child
      support enforcement
      assistance by agency,
      119A:8.
   Chief administrative justice,
      221B:3.
   Civil liability for conveyance to
      avoid, **231:85Z.**
   Claimant agency, defined, **62D:1.**
   Collection procedures, **119A:6.**
      Collection of support
         obligations via tax system,
         62D:3, 119A:6.
   Commencement of action,
      119A:3.
   Commission of Child Support
      Enforcement, establishment,
      119A:1.
   Committees on child support,
      221B:2, 221B:3.
   Complaint, **209:32F, 209C:5.**
   Concealing assets to avoid
      payment, **273:15B.**
      Civil liability for conveyance
         to avoid, **231:85Z.**
   Consumer Credit Protection Act,
      93:52A, 119A:12.
   Contempt, **119A:3, 119A:6,**
      119A:12, 215:34, 221B:7.
   Continuing coverage for child,
      119A:12.
   Court rules.
      See CHILD SUPPORT
         GUIDELINES.
   Criminal liability, **273:1.**
      Concealing assets to avoid
         payment, **273:15B.**
      Sentencing, **273:15A.**
   Criminal offender record
      information system.
      Access for purposes of child
         support enforcement,
         6:172D.
   Custody of children, intervention
      as of right in action for
      support, **209:32F.**

SUPPORT AND
   MAINTENANCE —Cont'd
Child support —Cont'd
   Debt, defined, **62D:1.**
   Default, **221B:7.**
   Definitions, **119A:1A.**
   Dependent children, aid to.
      See DEPENDENT
         CHILDREN, AID TO.
   Desertion.
      See DESERTION AND
         NONSUPPORT.
   Deviation from guidelines,
      208:28.
   Disabled or handicapped
      persons, **117A:7, 273:23.**
   Dismissal on intermarriage of
      parents, **273:17.**
   Dispute resolution, **119A:17.**
   District court.
      Concurrent jurisdiction,
         209:32F.
      Transfer of case to probate
         and family court, **209C:3.**
   District courts, **119A:8, 209C:3.**
   Division of Support
      Enforcement, establishment,
      14:1.
   Divorce and alimony, **119A:3.**
   Documents required for filing of
      support order of another
      jurisdiction, **119A:8.**
   Drivers' licenses.
      Suspension or revocation for
         child support arrearages,
         90:22.
   Employment and training
      division in labor and
      workforce department,
      support obligation, **151A:46.**
   Employment security.
      See EMPLOYMENT
         SECURITY.
   Enforcement, **14:1, 14:1A,**
      62C:21, 62D:11, 62E:1,
      62E:3, 62E:4, 62E:6,
      62E:7A; 62E:11, 62E:12,
      93:51, 93:52A, 119A:1 to
      119A:17.
      Access to criminal offender
         record information
         system, **6:172D.**
      Wage reporting system, **62E:1**
         to 62E:14.
         See WAGE REPORTING
            SYSTEM.
   Expediting hearing of cases,
      procedures, **221B:4.**
   Family Support Act.
      See INTERSTATE FAMILY
         SUPPORT ACT.

**SUPPORT AND
  MAINTENANCE** —Cont'd
Child support —Cont'd
  Federal tax refund intercept
    program, **119A:6.**
  Fees and penalties, **119A:2.**
  Felony, failure to support, **273:1.**
  Foreign jurisdiction, support
    order issued by court or
    agency, **119A:8.**
  Foster care for children.
    See FOSTER CARE FOR
      CHILDREN.
  Group health insurance, child
    born out of wedlock not
    covered by private plan,
    209C:9.
  Guardian, commencement of
    action, **209:32F.**
  Guidelines.
    Generally.
      See CHILD SUPPORT
        GUIDELINES.
    Rebuttable presumption for
      use, **208:28, 209:32F,
      209:37.**
    See CHILD SUPPORT
      GUIDELINES.
  Hearing officers,
    221B:1-221B:10.
  Heirs or next of kin,
    commencement of action for
    child support, **209:32F.**
  Illegitimate children.
    See ILLEGITIMATE
      CHILDREN.
  Income withholdings.
    Arrears, assignment of portion
      of earnings, **209:32E.**
    Judgment or order for income
      assignment, **119A:12.**
    License reinstatement upon
      compliance with support
      payments, **119A:16.**
    Notification, **119A:6, 119A:7,
      119A:12.**
  Information or information
    services, assistance in
    collecting support, **62D:10A.**
  Insurance.
    Accident and sickness
      insurance. See within this
      subheading, "Accident and
      sickness insurance."
  Interest, **119A:6.**
  Interstate Family Support Act.
    See INTERSTATE FAMILY
      SUPPORT ACT.
  Issue of void marriage, **207:18.**
  IV-D agencies.
    Confidentiality of records,
      119A:5A.

**SUPPORT AND
  MAINTENANCE** —Cont'd
Child support —Cont'd
  IV-D agencies —Cont'd
    Enforcement duties, **119A:2.**
    Modification of judgment,
      order or decree.
      Periodic review of IV-D
        cases, **119A:3B.**
    Petition to disclose
      confidential information,
      119A:5B.
    Records and reports, **119A:4.**
    State disbursement unit,
      119A:5.
  Judgments, orders or decrees,
    119A:12.
    Administrative review,
      119A:6.
    Assignment, **119A:12.**
    Certified copies required for
      filing of support order of
      another jurisdiction,
      119A:8.
    Contempt proceedings,
      119A:12, 215:34.
    Enforcement procedure,
      62C:21, 119A:6, 208:36A.
    Entry notwithstanding
      default, **209:32F.**
    Expiration of order or
      judgment 6 months after
      judgment of dismissal or
      final order of commitment,
      119:28.
    Foreign jurisdiction, **119A:8.**
    Hearing officers,
      221B:7-221B:10.
    Modification, **119A:3,
      119A:3B, 119A:7,
      119A:13, 208:28, 209:32F,
      209:37, 209C:20.**
    Presentment of order of child
      support hearing officer to
      justice of division for
      approval, **221B:7A.**
    Recognizance, release from
      custody on probation,
      276:66.
    Retroactive modification,
      support payments, effect
      as judgment, **119A:13,
      215:34B.**
    Security for payment, **208:36.**
  Jurisdiction.
    Affidavits required for filing of
      support order, **119A:8.**
    Certified copies required for
      filing of support order of
      another jurisdiction,
      119A:8.

**SUPPORT AND
  MAINTENANCE** —Cont'd
Child support —Cont'd
  Jurisdiction —Cont'd
    Departure from
      Commonwealth, **223A:3.**
    Evidence, **119A:15.**
    Filing support order of
      another jurisdiction,
      119A:8.
    Long-arm, enforcement,
      208:36A.
    Modification, increase,
      decrease, or revocation of
      judgment, **209:32F.**
  Juvenile courts.
    See JUVENILE COURTS
      AND DELINQUENT
      CHILDREN.
  Levy and seizure, **119A:6.**
  License revocation, **119A:16.**
  Liens and encumbrances,
    **119A:6, 119A:12, 185:78,
    209C:19.**
  Locating persons legally
    responsible for support,
    119A:14.
  Married persons living apart,
    courts which may enter
    judgment, **209:32F.**
  Medical expenses,
    reimbursement for, **209C:9.**
  Modification of agreements
    between parents affecting
    support obligations, **119A:1,
    119A:13.**
  Notice.
    Annual review, hearing officer
      performance, **221B:2.**
    Assignments of wages, **119A:6,
      119A:7, 119A:12.**
    Delinquent determination,
      119A:6.
    Lien, notice, **119A:6.**
    Satisfaction of enforced
      judgment, **119A:5.**
    Suspended income assignment
      system, notice describing,
      119A:12.
  Obligors.
    Disclosure of information to
      IV-D agency, **62C:21.**
    Lists, **62E:4.**
    Services to be provided by
      agency, **119A:1.**
  Paternity.
    Acknowledgments.
      Access to information for
        child support purposes,
        46:3D.
    Genetic marker test to
      establish, **119A:3A.**

**SUPPORT AND
MAINTENANCE** —Cont'd
Child support —Cont'd
Penalties and fees, **119A:2.**
Personal data.
Confidentiality and disclosure,
119A:5A.
Petition to disclose
confidential information,
119A:5B.
Poor persons, parents of poor
persons as responsible for
support, **117A:7.**
Privileged and confidential
matters, **62D:10, 119A:12.**
Probate.
See PROBATE AND FAMILY
COURT.
Probate courts, **208:36A,
209C:3, 218:19, 221B:3.**
Probation and parole, **62D:3,
276:66, 276:85A.**
Payment of child support as
condition, **127:130.**
Process and service of process
and papers, **209:32F.**
Reports by agency, **119A:4.**
Retirement plans and pensions.
Authority to attach, **119A:6A.**
Not exempt from attachment
or execution, **235:34A.**
Revenue department and
commissioner, child support
enforcement, **14:1, 14:1A,
119A:1.**
Review of obligation.
Periodic review of IV-D cases,
119A:3B.
Setoff debt collection, **62D:13,
271:43.**
See SET-OFF DEBT
COLLECTION.
State case registry, **119A:4.**
State disbursement unit,
119A:5.
State treasurer, **119A:10,
119A:11.**
Stay or supersedeas, hearing
officers' orders or judgments,
221B:9.
Subpoenas, **119A:15, 221B:6.**
Suspension of assignment,
119A:12.
Temporary orders providing for
support, entry pending
action, **119:28.**
Threatening of officers, **119A:2A.**
Trustee process, **119A:12,
221B:7.**
Trust fund, **119A:9-119A:11.**
Unknown whereabouts of
support obligee, IV-D
payments, **119A:5.**

**SUPPORT AND
MAINTENANCE** —Cont'd
Child support —Cont'd
Venue, married persons living
apart, **209:32F.**
Wage reporting system, **62E:3,
271:43.**
Welfare and social services,
119:23, 209:32F, 209C:5.
Workers' compensation awards.
Liens against certain
compensation awards or
settlements, **152:46A.**
Complaint, support action,
209:32F.
Contempt of court for failure to
comply with order, **215:34.**
Correctional institutions.
See CORRECTIONAL
INSTITUTIONS.
County prisons.
See COUNTY PRISONS.
Credit Union Employees
Retirement Association,
171:84.
Custody of children, intervention
as of right in action for
support, **209:32F.**
Default, entry of order or
judgment notwithstanding,
209:32F.
Desertion.
See DESERTION AND
NONSUPPORT.
District courts, support
proceedings when married
persons living apart, judgment
against spouse chargeable
with support, **209:32F.**
Eighteen and twenty-one years of
age, requirements as to
maintenance orders for
persons between, **208:28,
209:37.**
Employment security dependency
allowances, **151A:29.**
Family or household member's
duty of support, **119:39,
209:30 et seq., 273:1 et seq.**
See DESERTION AND
NONSUPPORT.
Family Support Act.
See INTERSTATE FAMILY
SUPPORT ACT.
Guardians.
See GUARDIANS,
CONSERVATORS, AND
COMMITTEES.
Guidelines.
See CHILD SUPPORT
GUIDELINES.

**SUPPORT AND
MAINTENANCE** —Cont'd
Hearings.
See TRIAL OR HEARINGS.
Hospital school, payment for
support, **111:62M.**
Husband and wife, **209:32.**
Illegitimate children.
See ILLEGITIMATE
CHILDREN.
Interstate Family Support Act.
See INTERSTATE FAMILY
SUPPORT ACT.
Intervention by spouse, parent, or
custodian as of right, **209:32F.**
Juvenile courts and delinquent
children, **119:28.**
See JUVENILE COURTS AND
DELINQUENT CHILDREN.
Kindred, duty of, **119:39, 209:30 et
seq.**
Lemuel Shattuck hospital,
111:69H, 111:69I.
Long-arm jurisdiction to enforce
support orders, **208:36A.**
Mentally ill persons.
Husband and wife, support of
insane spouse, **201:25,
201:43, 209:32.**
Inmates, action for support,
260:1.
Necessaries, wife's liability, **209:1,
209:7.**
Nonsupport.
See DESERTION AND
NONSUPPORT.
Orders for support.
See JUDGMENTS, ORDERS,
AND DECREES.
Parents.
Child support. See within this
heading, "Child support."
Support of parents by children,
201:43A, 273:20-273:22.
Pondville hospital, **111:69H,
111:69I.**
Poor persons.
See POOR PERSONS.
Probate.
See PROBATE AND FAMILY
COURT.
Probation.
See PROBATION AND
PAROLE.
Probation officers.
See PROBATION OFFICERS.
Prostitute, deriving support from
earnings, **272:7.**
Recognizance.
Bail and recognizance. See
within this heading, "Bail
and recognizance."

SUPPORT AND MAINTENANCE —Cont'd

Retirement systems.
See RETIREMENT SYSTEMS AND PENSIONS.
Separate maintenance, **209:32.**
See SEPARATE MAINTENANCE OR SUPPORT.
Set-off debt collection, **62D:1 et seq.**
See SET-OFF DEBT COLLECTION.
Spouses, **209:32.**
Taxation, **119A:6.**
Set-off debt collection, **62D:1 et seq.**
See SET-OFF DEBT COLLECTION.
Temporary orders, **209:32F.**
Termination of public assistance due to collection of monthly support in excess of benefits, notification by department, **18:21.**
Tewksbury hospital.
Kindred's liability for support of inmates, **122:14, 122:16.**
Unclaimed funds or property used for support of inmates, **122:7-122:9.**
Trial.
See TRIAL OR HEARINGS.
Trustee process, **119A:12, 208:13, 209C:19, 221B:7.**
Uniform Interstate Family Support Act.
See INTERSTATE FAMILY SUPPORT ACT.
Welfare.
See WELFARE AND SOCIAL SERVICES.
Westfield sanatorium, **111:69H, 111:69I.**

SUPPORT SERVICES DIVISION.

State police, **22C:4, 22C:8.**

SUPREME COURT OF UNITED STATES.

Appellate jurisdiction.
Congress, power to regulate, **US Const Art 3 Sec 2 cl 2.**
Fact and law, jurisdiction as to, **US Const Art 3 Sec 2 cl 2.**
Chief justice to preside on trial of President for impeachment, **US Const Art 1 Sec 3 cl 6.**
Judges.
Compensation of, **US Const Art 3 Sec 1.**

SUPREME COURT OF UNITED STATES —Cont'd

Judges —Cont'd
Nomination and appointment, **US Const Art 2 Sec 2 cl 2.**
Term of office, **US Const Art 3 Sec 1.**
Judicial power as vested in, **US Const Art 3 Sec 1.**
Jurisdiction, **US Const Art 3 Sec 2 cl 2.**
Original jurisdiction, **US Const Art 3 Sec 2 cl 2.**
States, suits by or against as within original jurisdiction, **US Const Art 3 Sec 2 cl 2.**

SUPREME JUDICIAL COURT, **211:1-211:23.**

Abatement of nuisances, **139:16.**
Abatement, survival and revival.
Decedent's death, relief where plaintiff not apprised, **228:5B.**
Relief where plaintiff fails to take out citation, **228:5A.**
Substitution of executor or administrator to be in accordance with rules of civil procedure, **228:4A.**
Absence.
See ABSENCE OR PRESENCE.
Absentee voting matters, jurisdiction, **54:103.**
Abuses and imperfections in practice, remedying, **213:3.**
Accounts and accounting.
Allowance, **213:8.**
Audit, **211:21.**
Auditor's compensation paid by state, **221:61.**
Clerk's accounts examined by director of accounts, **35:45.**
Special jurisdiction in actions upon accounts which cannot be settled in district court, **214:3.**
Adjournment of sittings, **213:6.**
Absence of justice, **213:11, 213:12.**
Another shire town, adjournment, **213:10.**
Fall River, adjournment, **211:18.**
Notice, **213:11.**
Administration of inferior courts, superintendence, **211:3.**
Administrative assistant to justices, **211:3A.**
Administrative justice.
Chief administrative justice. See within this heading, "Chief administrative justice."

SUPREME JUDICIAL COURT —Cont'd

Administrative justice —Cont'd
Equity jurisdiction to enforce provisions of sanitary code, approval of rules and forms, **218:19C.**
Administrative officer of appeals court to transmit records, **211A:8.**
Administrative procedure law, cases, **30A:15, 30A:16.**
Administrator of courts for the trial court, approval of appointment, **211B:12.**
Adoption proceedings, appeals, **210:11.**
Advertising, jurisdiction to restrain outdoor advertising adjacent to certain highways, **93D:5.**
Advisory committee, establishment, **211C:11.**
Aggrieved person's appeal to, **215:9.**
Air pollution or contamination, enforcement of laws, **111:142A.**
Allowance of accounts, **213:8.**
Always open for business, **213:4.**
Appeals, **231:114, 278:28.**
Appeals court.
See APPEALS COURT.
Appellate division, appeal, **231:109.**
Appellate tax board.
See TAXATION.
Appointments.
Administrator of courts for the trial court, approval of appointment, **211B:12.**
Attorney General, appointment of substitutes, **12:26.**
Bar examiners, appointment, **221:35.**
Clerks of court, appointment, **221:1, 221:4.**
Commission on judicial conduct, members, **211C:1.**
Court officers, **213:13.**
Employees, **211:3B.**
Incumbents appointed by justices, elections, **53:34.**
Suffolk County, administrative assistants, **221:76.**
Apportionment of representatives, proceedings, **56:59.**
Arbitration of controversies by fiduciaries, authority, **204:14.**
Arrest warrants issued by justice, **276:21.**

SUPREME JUDICIAL COURT
—Cont'd

Assessors, compensation paid for
by state, **221:55.**

Assistant clerk of court, **221:1,
221:4, 221:5, 221:94.**

Associate justices.
Justices. See within this
heading, "Justices."

Attachment of property.
See ATTACHMENT OF
PROPERTY.

Attorney General.
Appointment of substitute,
12:26.
Gift or conveyance to county, city
or town, special jurisdiction
in Attorney General's action
to enforce, **214:3.**
Interlocutory appeals by state,
278:28E.

Attorneys, answering
questionnaires for evaluation
of judicial performance,
211:26A.

Attorneys at law.
Admission to bar, filing of
petition for examination,
221:37.
Bar examiners, appointment,
221:35.
Clients' Security Board and
Fund.
See CLIENTS' SECURITY
BOARD RULES.
District and prosecuting
attorneys. See within this
heading, "District and
prosecuting attorneys."
Executive secretary. See within
this heading, "Executive
secretary."
Fees in action to enforce purpose
of gift or conveyance to city
or town, **214:3.**
Jurisdiction to restrain
violations regarding practice
of law, **221:46B.**
Practice of law.
By justices or personnel,
211:3B, 211:22.
Jurisdiction to restrain certain
violations regarding,
221:46B.
Removal of attorney, **221:40.**
Suffolk County, records to be
kept by clerk of court,
221:42.

Audit of accounts, **211:21.**

Auditors, compensation paid for by
state, **221:61.**

SUPREME JUDICIAL COURT
—Cont'd

Automobile insurance.
See AUTOMOBILE
INSURANCE.

Automobiles.
Motor vehicles. See within this
heading, "Motor vehicles."

Bail and recognizance.
Justice's power to admit, **276:57.**
Release on own recognizance
without surety, appeal from
refusal to order, **276:58.**
Transfer of causes to and from
supreme judicial courts,
211:4A.

Bankruptcy.
See INSOLVENCY AND
BANKRUPTCY.

Banks.
See BANKS AND BANKING.

Bar examiners, appointment,
221:35.

Barred claims against estates of
decedents, relief against,
197:10.

Bond given by partner in creditor's
action against partnership
property, **214:3.**

Boston.
Bills and vouchers for expenses
of sittings, **35:12.**
Hearings in, of questions arising
in other counties, **211:16.**
Justices, continuous sittings in
Boston for purposes of
determining equitable relief,
214:14.
Sittings at, **211:17.**

Briefs for Commonwealth in
criminal appeals, expenses,
280:5.

Bristol, Dukes County, Nantucket,
or Bristol cases to be tried,
211:19.

Budget director, submission of
statement showing estimates
for maintenance of judicial
system, **211:2A.**

Buildings and structures.
Regulations, enforcement,
143:59.
Restraining illegal erection, use,
or alteration, **143:12,
143:57, 143:60.**

Business trusts.
See BUSINESS TRUSTS.

Calendars and dockets, **262:4.**

Capital cases.
See CAPITAL CASES.

Carriers.
See CARRIERS.

SUPREME JUDICIAL COURT
—Cont'd

Cemetery property held in trust,
sale or transfer, **204:12.**

Certiorari to correct errors, **249:4.**

Chain transactions, injunction
against, **271:6A.**

Charges, sale of lands subject,
185:52.

Charities and charitable
organizations.
Clerk of court, duties as to lists
of charitable corporations,
180:11B.
Dissolution of charitable
corporation, **180:11A,
180:11B.**
Jurisdiction as to charitable
corporation, **180:11,
180:11A, 180:11B.**
Purpose, enforcing laws as to
collections on public ways,
68:16.

Chief administrative justice.
Delivery of report and
recommendations, **211B:9.**
Revision of uniform schedule of
fees, **262:4B.**

Chief justice, **211:1.**
Benefits, **32:65A, 32:65C.**
Compensation, **211:22.**
Designation of member to
criminal justice committee,
6:156.
Determination of necessity for
holding court on Saturdays,
213:4.
Financing of judicial system,
recommendation that
building be acquired by
Commonwealth, **29A:5.**
Registers of probate and
insolvency, reports to be
filed with chief judge and
executive secretary, **217:8.**
Sales of copies of rules, duties,
213:3A.
Vacancy in office, **213:1.**

Child support hearing officers,
rules promulgated, **221B:5.**

Cities and towns.
Law reports, delivery of copies,
5:14, 5:15.
Municipal finance laws,
enforcement of, **44:59.**
Municipal lighting and heating
plants. See within this
heading, "Municipal lighting
and heating plants."
Reports and decisions, towns to
be supplied with sets, **5:14,
5:15.**

SUPREME JUDICIAL COURT
—Cont'd
Cities and towns —Cont'd
Restraint of illegal
appropriations, **40:53.**
Special jurisdiction in action to
enforce gift or conveyance,
214:3.
Civil rights.
See CIVIL RIGHTS AND
DISCRIMINATION.
Civil service.
See CIVIL SERVICE.
Claim of appeal from appellate
division of District Court,
increase in time for filing,
231:109.
Classification of clerk by county
personnel board, **35:49.**
Clerical assistance, **211:23, 221:23,
221:93.**
Clerks of court, **221:1, 221:2.**
Accounts of, examination by
director of accounts, **35:45.**
Appointment, **221:1.**
Assistant clerk, **221:1, 221:4,
221:5, 221:94.**
Charitable corporations, duties
as to lists, **180:11B.**
Clerical assistance, employment,
221:93.
Code of professional
responsibility, **Rule 3:12.**
County personnel board,
classification, **35:49.**
Dissolved charitable
corporations, duties as to
lists, **180:11B.**
District court clerk, removal,
211:4.
Election of clerks and term of
office, **221:3.**
Entry of judgment, **213:3.**
Fees, **262:4, 262:4B.**
Issuance of process, **213:2.**
Records, reports, and returns,
221:2, 262:4, 262:4B.
Removal from office of clerks
and assistant clerks, **211:4,
221:1.**
Rules.
See COMMITTEE ON
PROFESSIONAL
RESPONSIBILITY FOR
CLERKS OF COURTS
RULES.
Salaries of clerk and assistant
clerk, **221:2, 221:93, 221:94.**
Sales of copies of rules, duties,
213:3A.
Statutes distributed, **5:3.**

SUPREME JUDICIAL COURT
—Cont'd
Clerks of court —Cont'd
Suffolk county.
See SUFFOLK COUNTY.
Summoning jury to try issues in
equity case, **214:12.**
Temporary clerks, appointment,
221:8.
Clients' Security Board and Fund
rules.
See CLIENTS' SECURITY
BOARD RULES.
Clinical laboratories, jurisdiction
of complaints, **111D:12.**
Co-executors and
co-administrators, special
jurisdiction in actions
between, **214:3.**
Collection of funds on public ways
for charitable purposes,
jurisdiction to enforce
provisions, **68:16.**
Combustibles, restraining
violations, **148:17.**
Commissioners, compensation paid
for by state, **221:55.**
Commission on Judicial Conduct.
See JUDICIAL CONDUCT
COMMISSION.
Common carriers.
See CARRIERS.
Compensation.
Wages, salaries and
compensation. See within
this heading, "Wages,
salaries, and compensation."
Compromises and settlements,
proceedings involving.
Fiduciaries, controversies,
204:14.
Wills, **204:15-204:18.**
Concurrent jurisdiction, **119:39I,
151A:42, 211A:10, 213:1A,
218:19A, 218:19B, 231:109.**
Conduct of officers.
See JUDICIAL CONDUCT
COMMISSION.
Confidential matters.
Rules. See within this heading,
"Rules."
Conflict between rules of superior
court and supreme judicial
court, prohibition against,
213:3.
Constitutional questions, direct
appeals, **211A:10.**
Constitution of Massachusetts.
See CONSTITUTION OF
MASSACHUSETTS.
Contents of rescripts, **211:9.**

SUPREME JUDICIAL COURT
—Cont'd
Continuance or adjournment.
Adjournment. See within this
heading, "Adjournment of
sittings."
Continuing education of judges
and court personnel,
agreements concerning
programs, **7:28A.**
Contribution by or between
devisees, legatees, or heirs,
special jurisdiction in actions,
214:3.
Conveyances.
Action to enforce purposes,
214:3.
Charges, land subject, **183:52.**
Fraudulent conveyances, special
jurisdiction in actions
involving, **214:3.**
Judgment or decree operating as
deed, conveyance, or release,
183:43.
Timber, conveyance during life
estate, **184:14.**
Co-operative banks, bank holding
company law, jurisdiction to
enforce, **167A:7.**
"Co-operative," enforcing laws as
to use of word, **157:8.**
Copies of court documents,
262:4B.
Corporations.
See CORPORATIONS.
Costs.
Action to enforce gift or
conveyance to governmental
unit, **214:3.**
Appeal to, costs, **262:4.**
Diminishing, **213:3.**
Fees. See within this heading,
"Fees."
Frivolous appeal, **211:10.**
Indigency, court costs, **261:27B.**
Items allowable, **261:23.**
Probate court, costs on appeal,
215:45.
Counties.
Commissioners.
County commissioners. See
within this heading,
"County commissioners."
Personnel board, classification of
clerks, **35:49.**
Questions arising in other
counties, hearings in
Boston, **211:16.**
Representative districts. See
within this heading,
"Representative districts."

SUPREME JUDICIAL COURT
—Cont'd

Counties —Cont'd

Special jurisdiction of action to enforce gifts or conveyances, **214:3.**

Transaction of business in any county, **213:5.**

Treasurer.
See COUNTY TREASURERS.

County commissioners.
Enforcing performance of duties by commissioners, **35:35.**

Removal of commissioners, **211:4.**

Court officers and employees.
Appointment, **211:3B, 213:13.**

Attorneys at law. See within this heading, "Attorneys at law."

Benefits, **32:66, 32:67.**

Clerks of court. See within this heading, "Clerks of court."

Compensation of.
Wages, salaries, and compensation. See within this heading, "Wages, salaries, and compensation."

Continuing education, **7:28A.**

Justices. See within this heading, "Justices."

Number, **221:69.**

Stenographers. See within this heading, "Stenographers."

Temporary employees. See within this heading, "Temporary employees."

Term of office, **221:72.**

Credit insurance combination policies, review of insurance commissioner's disapproval, **175:117B.**

Creditors' actions, special jurisdiction, **214:3.**

Credit unions.
See CREDIT UNIONS.

Criminal proceedings.
Appeals, **278:28.**

Capital cases.
See CAPITAL CASES.

Criminal justice committee, member designation, **6:156.**

Eavesdropping, authority, **272:99.**

Exceptions, entry, **211:15.**

Habeas corpus. See within this heading, "Habeas corpus."

Usury, voiding of transactions, **271:49.**

Dams and reservoirs, safety enforcement proceedings, **253:50.**

SUPREME JUDICIAL COURT
—Cont'd

Deceit, discouraging, **213:3.**

Decision.
Judgments, orders, and decrees. See within this heading, "Judgments, orders, and decrees."

Declaratory judgments.
Jurisdiction, **231A:1.**

Procedure to be made effective by court, **213:3.**

Deeds.
Conveyances. See within this heading, "Conveyances."

Delay.
Decedents' estates, powers as to delayed claims against, **197:10.**

Prevention, **213:3.**

Dental service corporations, enforcement of law, **176E:16.**

Dentist's registration, appeal from revocation, **112:64.**

Destruction of papers or records, supervision, **221:27A.**

Determination of locations for sittings of appeals court, **211A:4.**

Devisees, special jurisdiction in actions for contribution by or between, **214:3.**

Direct appeals, **211A:10.**

Directions.
Full court's duty to make, **211:8.**

Issuance, **211:3.**

Direct review, **211A:12.**

Disability benefits project for legal assistance to mentally or physically disabled persons, power, **211:25.**

Discharge.
Removal. See within this heading, "Removal from office or employment."

Disciplinary procedures for justices failing to achieve evaluation standards, **211:26B.**

Disclosure of treason to supreme judicial court, **264:3.**

Discretion of court, fixing requirements, **213:3.**

Discrimination.
See CIVIL RIGHTS AND DISCRIMINATION.

Dismissal of appeals from appellate tax board, nontransferability, **211:4A.**

Dispute resolution, uniform rules, **Rule 1:18.**

Dissolution of injunction issued by superior court, prohibition against, **214:15.**

SUPREME JUDICIAL COURT
—Cont'd

District and prosecuting attorneys.
Appointment of substitute, **12:26.**

Interlocutory appeals by state to supreme judicial court, **278:28E.**

Removal, **211:4.**

District court.
Accounts, special jurisdiction in actions upon accounts which cannot be settled in district court, **214:3.**

Appellate jurisdiction over, **278:28.**

Clerk, removal, **211:4.**

Equity jurisdiction to enforce provisions of Sanitary Code, approval of rules and forms, **218:19C.**

Small claims procedure rules of administrative justices to be approved by supreme judicial court, **218:21.**

Time for appeal, **231:109.**

Dockets and docketing, fee for entry of case, **262:4.**

Double costs allowed for frivolous appeal, **211:10.**

Drains, **83:13.**
See SEWERS AND DRAINS.

Druggist, appeal from revocation of license, **112:64.**

Dukes County cases to be tried in Bristol, **211:19.**

Duration of sittings, **213:6.**

Eavesdropping to obtain evidence of crime, authorization, **166:44, 272:99.**

Elections.
Absent voting disputes, **54:103.**

Clerks of court, **221:3.**

Contest of election of presidential electors, **54:119, 54:120.**

Incumbents appointed by justices, order of placing names on primary ballots, **53:34.**

Offenses, **56:59.**

Electricity.
See GAS AND ELECTRIC COMPANIES.

Emergency medical care, enforcement of provisions regarding, **111C:11.**

Employees.
Court officers and employees. See within this heading, "Court officers and employees."

SUPREME JUDICIAL COURT
—Cont'd
Employment security.
  Appellate procedure, **151A:42.**
  Enforcement of employment
    security laws, **151A:72.**
Entry of case on docket, fee, **262:4.**
Entry of exceptions, **211:15.**
Entry of judgment, **213:3, 213:5,**
  235:4.
Equity, **231:125A.**
  See EQUITY.
Evaluation of judicial performance,
  211:26 et seq.
Exceptions.
  Entry, **211:15.**
  Full court to hear questions of
    law arising, **211:5.**
Executions.
  See EXECUTIONS.
Executive secretary, **211:3A.**
  Membership in Massachusetts
    bar as prerequisite, **211:3A.**
  Number of employees, **211:3B.**
  Practice of law prohibited,
    211:3B.
  Quarters to be provided, **211:3A.**
  Reports of registers of probate,
    217:8.
  Salary, **211:3A.**
Executors.
  See EXECUTORS AND
    ADMINISTRATORS.
Expenses and expenditures.
  Bills or vouchers for expenses of
    court, **35:12.**
  Briefs for Commonwealth in
    criminal appeals, **280:5.**
  Clerical assistance, expenses,
    211:23.
  Costs. See within this heading,
    "Costs."
  Examination of expenses
    incident to court, **211:21.**
  Fees. See within this heading,
    "Fees."
  Injunction to restrain unlawful
    expenditures, **29:63.**
  Statement, **211:2A.**
Explosives and inflammables,
  injunction against violation of
  regulation, **148:17.**
Extension of concurrent
  jurisdiction of superior court,
  213:1A.
Facilities, provision, **7:41C.**
Fact questions.
  Questions of law and fact. See
    within this heading,
    "Questions of law and fact."
Fall River, sittings, **211:18.**

SUPREME JUDICIAL COURT
—Cont'd
Fees.
  Appeal of award, **231:6G.**
  Attorneys at law, fees in action
    to enforce purpose of gift or
    conveyance to city or town,
    214:3.
  Chief administrative justice,
    revision of uniform schedule
    of fees, **262:4B.**
  Clerks of court, **262:4, 262:4B.**
  Filing action in Supreme
    Judicial Court, **262:4.**
  Habeas corpus, uniform schedule
    of court fees, **262:4B.**
  Schedule of court fees, **262:4B.**
  Sheriffs' fees for service of writs,
    precepts or process, **262:8.**
  Witness fees, **262:29.**
Fictitious name, writ designating
  defendant, **223:19.**
Fiduciaries.
  Appeals involving validity of
    acts, **215:9A.**
  Executors.
    See EXECUTORS AND
      ADMINISTRATORS.
Filing.
  Records, reports, and returns.
    See within this heading,
    "Records, reports, and
    returns."
Financing of judicial system,
  29A:1.
Fire insurance.
  Mutual companies, jurisdiction,
    175:78, 175:84.
  Review of form of combination
    policies, **175:102A,**
    175:102C.
Fire prevention, restraining
  violations of regulations,
  148:17.
First assistant clerk, appointment,
  221:4.
Fish and fisheries.
  Marine fish and fisheries. See
    within this heading,
    "Marine fish and fisheries."
Foreign corporations.
  See FOREIGN
    CORPORATIONS.
Foreign insurance companies.
  Deposits, jurisdiction, **175:185.**
  Insurance rates and rating
    organizations, jurisdiction,
    175:18.
  License, review of suspension or
    revocation, **175:5.**
Foreign legal consultants.
  Licensing, **Rule 3:05.**

SUPREME JUDICIAL COURT
—Cont'd
Form and substance,
  distinguishing between, **213:3.**
Framing issues of fact in equity
  case, **214:11.**
Fraudulent conveyances, special
  jurisdiction in actions
  involving, **214:3.**
Frivolous appeal, **211:10.**
Full court.
  Contested elections of
    presidential electors, **54:119,**
    54:120.
  Directions, full court's duty,
    211:8.
  Questions of law to be heard,
    211:5, 231:111 et seq.
  Transfer of cases, **211:14.**
Further appellate review, **211A:11.**
Further report of facts in equity
  and probate appeals to
  Supreme Judicial Court,
  231:125A.
Garnishment.
  See TRUSTEE PROCESS.
Gas.
  See GAS AND ELECTRIC
    COMPANIES.
Gasoline and motor fuel taxes,
  restraining collection, **64A:12,**
  64E:12, 64F:13.
Gift, special jurisdiction in action
  to enforce purpose, **214:3.**
Governmental units, special
  jurisdiction to enforce gifts or
  conveyances, **214:3.**
Habeas corpus.
  Powers of supreme judicial
    court, **248:25.**
  Return of writ, **248:4.**
  Uniform schedule of court fees,
    262:4B.
Health care facilities, jurisdiction
  to enforce procedures of health
  department's determination of
  need for expansion of certain,
  111:25G.
Hearings.
  Boston, hearings in, of questions
    arising in other counties,
    211:16.
  Certain criminal cases, **211:15.**
  Child support hearing officers,
    rules promulgated, **221B:5.**
  Immunity of witnesses,
    application and hearing for
    order granting, **233:20E.**
  Industrial homework, hearings
    and investigation, **149:147F.**
  Motions for setting aside
    verdicts, filing and hearing,
    213:3.

SUPREME JUDICIAL COURT
—Cont'd
Heating plants of municipality.
Municipal lighting and heating
plants. See within this
heading, "Municipal lighting
and heating plants."
Heirs, special jurisdiction in action
for contributions by or
between, **214:3.**
Holiday, when court business may
be transacted, **213:4.**
Horse or dog racing meeting
employees, interfering with
employment or discharge,
271:40.
Hospital service corporations.
See HOSPITAL SERVICE
CORPORATIONS.
Immunity of witnesses.
Grant of immunity by court,
233:20C.
Order granting immunity,
application and hearing,
233:20E.
Inactive religious societies, special
jurisdiction of suits to
determine disposition of
property, **214:3.**
Income tax returns, mandamus to
compel filing, **62C:9.**
Incumbents appointed to office by,
arrangement of names on
primary ballots, **53:34.**
Indigency, form of affidavit of
indigency and request for
waiver of court costs, **261:27B.**
Industrial homework, hearings
and investigation, **149:147F.**
Inferior courts, superintendence,
211:3, 211A:5.
Inflammables and explosives,
injunction against violations,
148:17.
Injunctions.
Appeal to supreme judicial court
from granting or denial,
231:118.
Chain transactions, injunction
against, **271:6A.**
Explosives and inflammables,
injunctions against violation
of regulations, **148:17.**
Optometric service corporations,
enjoining transaction of
business, **176F:13.**
Outdoor advertising adjacent to
certain highways,
jurisdiction to restrain,
93D:5.
Practice of law, jurisdiction to
restrain certain violations
regarding, **221:46B.**

SUPREME JUDICIAL COURT
—Cont'd
Injunctions —Cont'd
Superior court, prohibition
against dissolution of
injunction issued, **214:15.**
Trade names, injunction against
improper use, **155:9.**
Trade secrets, enjoining
misappropriation, **93:42A.**
Transfer of causes from other
courts, **211:4A.**
Unlawful public expenditures or
obligations, **29:63.**
Insurance.
See INSURANCE.
Intercepting communications.
Authorization of, to obtain
evidence of crime, **272:99.**
Subscriber's remedies against
interception or monitoring,
166:44.
Interest on money.
Criminal usury, voiding
transactions involving,
271:49.
Pecuniary legacies, fixing,
197:20.
Small loans, voiding for
excessive interest,
140:114A.
Interlocutory appeals from
superior court in criminal
cases, **278:28E.**
Issuance of process, **213:2, 223:20.**
Joint owners of personal property,
special jurisdiction in actions
between, **214:3.**
Joint trustees, special jurisdiction
in actions between, **214:3.**
Judges.
Justices. See within this
heading, "Justices."
Judgments, orders, and decrees,
211:8.
Any county, entry of orders,
213:5.
Charges, sale of land subject,
183:52.
Declaratory judgments. See
within this heading,
"Declaratory judgments."
Deed, conveyance, or release,
decree operating, **183:43.**
Direct review by court, justice's
order, **211A:10.**
Entry, **213:3, 213:5, 235:4.**
Full court's duty to make orders,
211:8.
Labor relations commission,
review of judgment
enforcing order, **150A:6,
150A:6B.**

SUPREME JUDICIAL COURT
—Cont'd
Judgments, orders, and decrees
—Cont'd
Municipal lighting and heating
plants department,
enforcement of laws and
orders, **164:69, 164:79.**
Publication.
See REPORTER OF
DECISIONS.
Quieting title, appeal from
decree registering land free
from restriction, **240:18.**
Relief from judgment,
nontransferability of
motions, **211:4A.**
Rescript after decision. See
within this heading,
"Rescript after decision."
Sheriff, justice's order requiring
sheriff to adjourn court,
213:12.
Single justice, appeal from
judgment, **231:114.**
Superior courts, supreme
judicial court decrees to be
recorded, **212:9.**
Judicial conduct.
Code of judicial conduct, **Rule
3:09.**
Judicial conduct commission.
See JUDICIAL CONDUCT
COMMISSION.
Judicial conduct commission rules.
See JUDICIAL CONDUCT
COMMISSION RULES.
Judicial conferences, **211:3B.**
Judicial council, composition,
221:34A.
Judicial institute.
Superintendence, **211B:17.**
Judicial performance, evaluation
of, **211:26 et seq.**
Jury and jury trial.
Clerk of court summoning jury
to try issues in equity case,
214:12.
Power of justices at jury sittings,
211:20.
Questions of law and fact. See
within this heading,
"Questions of law and fact."
Sittings of jury, **211:7.**
Justices.
Adjournment in absence of
justice, **213:11, 213:12.**
Administrative assistant to
justices, **211:3A.**
Administrative justice. See
within this heading,
"Administrative justice."

SUPREME JUDICIAL COURT
—Cont'd
Justices —Cont'd
Appointed after attaining age
60, retirement benefits,
32:65A.
Associate justices, **211:1.**
Attendance, **213:9, 213:11,
213:12.**
Bail, powers, **276:57.**
Benefits, **32:65A, 32:65C.**
Certification of need for
additional facilities for
probate court, **215:54.**
Chief administrative justice. See
within this heading, "Chief
administrative justice."
Chief justice. See within this
heading, "Chief justice."
Clerical assistance, **211:23,
221:23, 221:93.**
Conduct of.
See JUDICIAL CONDUCT
COMMISSION.
Continuing education, **7:28A.**
Continuous sitting in Boston for
purpose of determining
equitable relief, **214:14.**
Direct review by supreme
judicial court, justice's
issuance of order, **211A:10.**
Discharge, **271:40.**
Elections, arrangement on ballot
of names of incumbents
appointed by justices, **53:34.**
Evaluation of judicial
performance, **211:26 et seq.**
Executive secretary. See within
this heading, "Executive
secretary."
Horse or dog racing meeting
employees, interfering in
employment or discharge,
271:40.
Incumbents appointed to office
by, arrangement of names
on primary ballots, **53:34.**
Jury sittings, power of justices,
211:20.
Leaves of absence, **211:28.**
Number, **211:1.**
Power at jury and law sittings,
211:20.
Practice of law forbidden,
211:3B, 211:22.
Probate courts. See within this
heading, "Probate courts."
Retired justice as member of
state ballot law commission,
55B:1.

SUPREME JUDICIAL COURT
—Cont'd
Justices —Cont'd
Revenue commissioner,
compelling attendance of
witnesses and production of
papers before, **58:25B.**
Salaries, **211:22, 211A:2.**
Single justice. See within this
heading, "Single justice,
appeal from judgment of."
Summoning jury to try issues in
equity case, **214:12.**
Supervision of sales of copies of
rules, **213:3A.**
Wages, salaries, and
compensation, **211:22,
211A:2.**
Warrants of arrest, power to
issue, **276:21.**
Widows of justices, benefits,
32:65C.
Juvenile courts, concurrent
equitable jurisdiction, **218:59.**
Labor relations and disputes.
Report on questions of law,
214:6.
Review of judgment enforcing
order of labor relations
commission, **150A:6,
150A:6B.**
Laches or delay.
Delay. See within this heading,
"Delay."
Land court.
See LAND COURT.
Law clerks, **211:23.**
Law questions.
Questions of law and fact. See
within this heading,
"Questions of law and fact."
Law reports, **221:63-221:68.**
Cities and towns, delivery of
copies, **5:14, 5:15.**
Law sittings, **211:12.**
Power of justices, **211:20.**
Leaves of absence for justices,
211:28.
Legal consultants, foreign.
Licensing, **Rule 3:05.**
Legatees, special jurisdiction in
actions for contribution by or
between, **214:3.**
Lighting plants of municipality.
Municipal lighting and heating
plants. See within this
heading, "Municipal lighting
and heating plants."
Limitations as to claims against
decedents' estates, relief
against, **197:10.**

SUPREME JUDICIAL COURT
—Cont'd
Lobbying laws, jurisdiction over
violations, **3:48.**
Local property assessment, failure
to keep proper records, **58:4A.**
Mandamus.
Election offenses, enforcement of
law, **56:59.**
Income tax returns, mandamus
to compel filing, **62C:9.**
Jurisdiction of supreme judicial
and superior courts, **56:59.**
Petition for action in nature,
249:5.
Representative districts, division
of county into, **56:59.**
Senatorial districts,
establishment, **57:3.**
Marine fish and fisheries.
Fishways, jurisdiction, **130:19.**
Pollution of waters, jurisdiction,
130:26.
Marine insurance, review of form
of policies, **175:117A.**
Massachusetts Reports,
221:63-221:68.
Masters in chancery, compensation
paid for by state, **221:55.**
Medical care.
Emergency, enforcement of
provisions regarding medical
care, **111C:11.**
Health department's
determination of need for
expansion of certain health
care facilities, jurisdiction to
enforce procedures, **111:25G.**
Medical service corporations,
discrimination against persons
seeking to become
participating physicians,
176B:13.
Medicine, appeal from revocation
of registration to practice,
112:64.
Meetings.
Governmental bodies,
enforcement of laws
governing meetings,
**30A:11A½, 34:9G, 39:23B,
66:17C.**
Public meetings, enforcing law,
39:23C.
Mental health legal advisors
committee, appointment,
221:34E.
Mortgages held by state, action for
redemption, **244:40.**
Motions.
Appeal from motion to suppress
evidence in criminal case,
278:28E.

SUPREME JUDICIAL COURT
—Cont'd

Motions —Cont'd

Relief from judgment, nontransferability of motions, **211:4A.**

Setting aside of verdicts, filing and hearing of motions, **213:3.**

Motor carriers.
See CARRIERS.

Motor vehicles.
Automobile insurance.
See AUTOMOBILE INSURANCE.

Carriers.
See CARRIERS.

Enforcement of orders of registrar, **90:28.**

Municipal lighting and heating plants.

Enforcement of laws and orders of department, **164:69, 164:79.**

Recovery of forfeiture for failure to make or amend annual returns, **164:63.**

Recovery of penalty for supplying gas below standard, **164:110.**

Names.

Fictitious name, writ designating defendant, **223:19.**

Injunction against improper use of trade names, **155:9.**

Public service corporation, recovery of forfeiture for use of name, **155:5.**

Nantucket cases to be tried in Bristol, **211:19.**

Naturalization, jurisdiction over, **220:15.**

Negligence, discouraging, **213:3.**

New trial, ordering, **211:8, 278:33E.**

Nontransferable causes, **211:4A.**

Notice.

Adjournment, **213:11.**

Adverse parties to be notified of filing and hearing of motions to set aside verdicts, **213:3.**

Evidence intended to be offered by adverse party, giving notice, **213:3.**

Nuisance, abatement, **139:16.**

Numbers.

Court officers, number, **221:69.**

Justices, number, **211:1.**

Objections.

Exceptions. See within this heading, "Exceptions."

SUPREME JUDICIAL COURT
—Cont'd

Officers of court.

Court officers and employees. See within this heading, "Court officers and employees."

Optometric service corporations, enjoining transaction of business, **176F:13.**

Orders.

Judgments, orders, and decrees. See within this heading, "Judgments, orders, and decrees."

Other counties, hearings in Boston of questions arising, **211:16.**

Other courts.

Transfer of cases. See within this heading, "Transfer of cases."

Outdoor advertising adjacent to certain highways, jurisdiction to restrain, **93D:5.**

Partnership property as reachable in creditor's action, **214:3.**

Pecuniary distributions under trust instruments, fixing of interest, **197:20.**

Pensions.

See RETIREMENT SYSTEMS AND PENSIONS.

Pharmacist's registration, appeal from revocation, **112:64.**

Physician's registration, appeal from revocation, **112:64.**

Pleadings and procedure, rule making for purposes of simplifying and shortening, **213:3.**

Pollution of waters, jurisdiction, **130:26.**

Postponement.

Adjournment. See within this heading, "Adjournment of sittings."

Powers of, **231:124.**

Practice of law.

Attorneys at law. See within this heading, "Attorneys at law."

Presidential electors, contest of election, **54:119, 54:120.**

Primary ballots, arrangement of candidates' names, **53:34.**

Printing and disposition of copies of rules, **213:3A.**

Privilege.

Immunity of witness. See within this heading, "Immunity of witnesses."

Privileged or confidential matters.
Rules. See within this heading, "Rules."

SUPREME JUDICIAL COURT
—Cont'd

Probate courts.

Appeal, **215:9, 215:45.**

Certification by justice of Supreme Judicial Court of additional facilities for probate court, **215:54.**

Charges, sale of lands subject, **183:52.**

Concurrent equity jurisdiction with probate court, **215:6.**

Costs on appeal from probate court, **215:45.**

Further report of facts in probate appeals to Supreme Judicial Court, **231:125A.**

Justices of Supreme Judicial Court, certification of need for additional facilities for probate court, **215:54.**

Registers of probate and insolvency. See within this heading, "Registers of probate and insolvency."

Removal of register of probate, **211:4.**

Probation board to comply with requests of secretary for information, etc., **211:30.**

Procedure to secure binding interpretation of written instruments, **213:3.**

Process, issuance of, **211:3, 213:2, 223:20.**

Profession, review as to certificate of registration, **112:64.**

Prosecuting attorneys.

District and prosecuting attorneys. See within this heading, "District and prosecuting attorneys."

Provisions common to supreme judicial court and superior courts, **213:1-213:13.**

Publication of decisions.

See REPORTER OF DECISIONS.

Public expenditures or obligations, injunctions against, **29:63.**

Public meetings, enforcing law, **39:23C.**

Public records.

Enforcement of provisions forbidding certain appliances to be used in making, **66:4.**

Inspection, compliance orders, **66:10.**

Jurisdiction to enforce standards established for materials used in recording, **66:4.**

SUPREME JUDICIAL COURT
—Cont'd

Public utilities.

Commission, appeals and enforcement of orders, **25:5.**

Name indicating that person is public service corporation, forfeiture for using, **155:5.**

Rates, transferability of causes, **211:4A.**

Request for appointment of discharge of certain employees, **271:40.**

Questionnaires for evaluation of judicial performance, **211:26A.**

Questions of law and fact.

Constitutional questions, direct appeals, **211A:1D.**

Distinct presentation of questions to be tried by jury, **213:3.**

Framing fact issues in equity case, **214:11.**

Full court, **231:111 et seq.**

Law questions to be heard, **211:5.**

Labor dispute cases, report of questions of law, **214:6.**

Reservation of questions of law. See within this heading, "Reservation of questions of law."

Summoning jury to try fact issues in equity case, **214:12.**

Tax foreclosure proceedings, review of questions of law, **60:72.**

Time for arguing law questions, **211:7.**

Quieting title.

Appeal from decree registering land free from restriction, **240:18.**

Equity suit to quiet title, **240:6-240:10C.**

Quorum, **211:2.**

Quo warranto, action in nature, **249:6, 249:9.**

Racial imbalance in schools, jurisdiction, **15:1J, 71:37D.**

Railroad crossings.

See RAILROAD CROSSINGS.

Railroads.

See RAILROADS.

Recognizance.

Bail and recognizance. See within this heading, "Bail and recognizance."

Recorder of land court, removal, **211:4.**

SUPREME JUDICIAL COURT
—Cont'd

Records, reports, and returns, **5:14, 5:15.**

Administrative officer of appeals court to transmit records to supreme judicial court, **211A:8.**

Chief administrative justice, delivery of report and recommendations, **211B:9.**

Clerks of court, **221:2, 262:4, 262:4B.**

Commission on judicial conduct, report, **211C:4.**

Destruction of papers on records, supervision, **221:27A.**

Equity and probate appeals, reports, **231:125A.**

Executive secretary. See within this heading, "Executive secretary."

Filing fees, **262:4.**

Foreign corporation, jurisdiction to proceed in equity against when certificates and reports are not filed, **181:9.**

Full court to hear questions of law arising upon reports, **211:5, 214:6.**

Income tax returns, mandamus to compel filing, **62C:9.**

Law reports. See within this heading, "Law reports."

Massachusetts reports, **221:63-221:68.**

Motions to set aside verdicts and notifying adverse parties thereof, **213:3.**

Municipal lighting and heating plants, recovery of forfeiture for failure to make or amend annual returns, **164:63.**

Public records. See within this heading, "Public records."

Suffolk County, records to be kept by clerk of court, **221:42.**

Superior courts, supreme judicial court decrees to be recorded, **212:9.**

Towns to be supplied with acts of reports and decisions, **5:14, 5:15.**

Transmission of papers on criminal appeal, **278:33E.**

Redelivery of goods or chattels taken or detained from owner, special jurisdiction in action to compel, **214:3.**

SUPREME JUDICIAL COURT
—Cont'd

Redemption of real estate, actions, **236:39-236:41.**

Mortgages held by state, action for redemption, **244:40.**

Referees, compensation paid for by state, **221:55.**

Registers of probate and insolvency.

Chief judge and executive secretary, reports to be filed, **217:8.**

Removal of registers, **211:4.**

Release of defendant on own recognizance without surety, appeal from refusal to order, **276:58.**

Religious societies, sales or transfers of property involving, **204:12, 214:3.**

Remanding case to trial court, **211:8.**

Removal from office or employment.

Attorneys at law, removal, **221:40.**

Certain officers, **211:4, 221:1.**

Reporter of decisions, **221:63 et seq.**

Representative districts.

Jurisdiction of proceedings as to division of counties into, **57:4. (note)**

Mandamus for division of county into, **56:59.**

Rescript after decision, **211:8.**

Contents, **211:9.**

Reservation of questions of law, **211:6.**

Full court, reservation or report of rulings, **211:5, 231:111 et seq.**

Retail installment sales agreements, avoidance, **255D:29.**

Retirement systems.

See RETIREMENT SYSTEMS AND PENSIONS.

Revival of actions.

Abatement, survival and revival. See within this heading, "Abatement, survival and revival."

Rules, **213:3, 213:3A.**

Appellate review, **211A:13.**

Child support hearing officers, **221B:5.**

Generally.

See SUPREME JUDICIAL COURT RULES.

SUPREME JUDICIAL COURT
—Cont'd
Rules —Cont'd
Small claims procedure, district court approval of rules, **218:21.**
Salaries.
Wages, salaries, and compensation. See within this heading, "Wages, salaries, and compensation."
Sales.
Conveyances. See within this heading, "Conveyances."
Copies of revisions of rules to public, **213:3A.**
Decisions of court, **221:64A.**
Land subject to charges, proceedings for sale, **183:52.**
Retail installment sales agreements, avoidance, **255D:29.**
Saturday, when business may be transacted, **213:4.**
Savings banks.
See SAVINGS BANKS.
Schedule of court fees, **262:4B.**
Seal of court, **213:13.**
Securing parties from being misled, rule making for purposes, **213:3.**
Senatorial districts, mandamus to establish, **57:3. (note)**
Sentence, stay, **279:4.**
Services, allowance of accounts, **213:8.**
Sessions.
Sittings. See within this heading, "Sittings."
Settlements.
Compromises and settlements. See within this heading, "Compromises and settlements, proceedings involving."
Sewers and drains, enforcing laws as to, **83:13.**
See SEWERS AND DRAINS.
Sheriff.
Adjournment in absence of justice, **213:11.**
Attendance at sessions of court, **37:16.**
Fees for service of writs, precepts, or process, **262:8.**
Justice's order requiring sheriff to adjourn court, **213:12.**
Removal, **211:4.**
Shire town, adjournment, **213:10.**
Simplifying and shortening pleadings and procedure, promulgating rules for purpose, **213:3.**

SUPREME JUDICIAL COURT
—Cont'd
Simultaneous sessions, **213:7.**
Single justice, appeal from judgment of, **231:114.**
Rules.
See SUPREME JUDICIAL COURT RULES.
Sittings.
Adjournment of sittings. See within this heading, "Adjournment of sittings."
Appeals court, location for sittings, **211A:4.**
Boston. See within this heading, "Boston."
Duration, **213:6.**
Fall River, sittings, **211:18.**
Jury sittings.
Jury and jury trial. See within this heading, "Jury and jury trial."
Law sittings. See within this heading, "Law sittings."
Simultaneous sessions, **213:7.**
Small claims procedure, district court approval of rules, **218:21.**
Small loan voided for excessive interest, **140:114A.**
Special masters, compensation paid for by state, **221:55.**
Speedy trial, securing, **213:3.**
Sprinkler leakage insurance, review of form of policies, **175:117A.**
Standards for justices, establishment of, **211:26B.**
State ballot law commission, retired justice as member, **55B:1.**
Statement of expenses, costs, and salaries, **211:2A.**
Statutes distributed to clerk, **5:3.**
Stay or supersedeas.
Sentence, stay, **279:4.**
Transferability of causes, **211:4A.**
Stenographers, **211:23.**
Temporary stenographer, **221:83.**
Street railways.
See STREET RAILWAYS.
Striking unnecessary counts in statements, prescribing terms, **213:3.**
Substance and form, distinguishing between, **213:3.**
Substitutes and substitution.
Attorney General, appointment of substitute, **12:26.**

SUPREME JUDICIAL COURT
—Cont'd
Substitutes and substitution
—Cont'd
Executor or administrator to be substituted in accordance with rules of civil procedure, **228:4A.**
Suffolk county.
See SUFFOLK COUNTY.
Summons, issuance of, **211:3.**
Sunday, when court business may be transacted, **213:4.**
Superior court.
Appellate division, appeal, **231:109.**
Concurrent jurisdiction of, extension, **213:1A.**
Conflict between rules of superior court and supreme judicial court, prohibition against, **213:3.**
Decrees and orders of supreme judicial court, recording in superior courts, **212:9.**
Dissolution of injunction issued by superior court, prohibition against, **214:15.**
Interlocutory appeals from in criminal cases, **278:28E.**
Mandamus, **56:59.**
Provisions common to supreme judicial courts in superior courts, **213:1-213:13.**
Records and recording, supreme judicial court decrees to be recorded by superior courts, **212:9.**
Removal of clerk of, superior court in Suffolk county, **211:4.**
Supersedeas.
Stay or supersedeas. See within this heading, "Stay or supersedeas."
Supervision and superintendence.
Destruction of papers and records, **221:27A.**
Inferior courts, **211:3, 211A:5.**
Sale of copies of rules, **213:3A.**
Surety companies, list to be furnished to clerk for Suffolk county, **175:105.**
Surprise, prevention, **213:3.**
Survival of actions.
Abatement, survival and revival. See within this heading, "Abatement, survival and revival."
Taxation.
Generally.
See TAXATION.

SUPREME JUDICIAL COURT
—Cont'd
Telephone and telegraph
companies.
Discrimination, enforcement of
laws against, **166:15.**
Stock or bonds, enforcement of
laws as to issue, **166:5.**
Subscriber's remedies against
interception or monitoring,
166:44.
Temporary employees.
Clerks of court, appointment,
221:8.
Stenographers, **221:83.**
Term of office.
Clerk, **221:3.**
Employees, **221:72.**
Timber, conveyance during life
estate, **184:14.**
Time.
Adjournment. See within this
heading, "Adjournment of
sittings."
Adoption of rules as to time for
review, **211A:13.**
Arguing law questions, time,
211:7.
Delay. See within this heading,
"Delay."
District courts, time for appeals,
231:109.
Sittings, duration, **213:6.**
Time or date.
Evaluation of performance of
justices, **211:26A.**
Title quieting.
Quieting title. See within this
heading, "Quieting title."
Towns.
Cities and towns. See within
this heading, "Cities and
towns."
Trade name, enjoining use, **155:9.**
Trade secrets, enjoining
misappropriation, **93:42A.**
Training programs for justices,
establishment, **211:27.**
Transaction of business in any
county, **213:5.**
Transfer of cases, **211:4A,
211A:12.**
Bail and recognizance, **211:4A.**
Between supreme judicial court
and other courts, **211:4A,
211A:12.**
By full court, **211:14.**
District court, jurisdiction,
218:19, 218:26, 218:60.
Injunction proceedings, **211:4A.**
Land Court, jurisdiction, **185:1.**

SUPREME JUDICIAL COURT
—Cont'd
Transfer of cases —Cont'd
Nontransferable causes, **211:4A.**
Probate court, jurisdiction,
215:3.
Public utility rates, **211:4A.**
Transfer of justices and personnel
between departments,
appealing order of chief
administrative justice, **211B:9.**
Treason, disclosure to supreme
judicial court, **264:3.**
Trials.
Conducting, **213:3.**
Hearings. See within this
heading, "Hearings."
New trial, ordering, **211:8,
278:33E.**
Trust companies.
See TRUST COMPANIES.
Trustee process.
See TRUSTEE PROCESS.
Trusts.
See TRUSTS AND TRUSTEES.
Unemployment compensation.
See EMPLOYMENT
SECURITY.
Uniform rules on dispute
resolution, **Rule 1:18.**
Uniform schedule of court fees,
262:4B.
Urban renewal projects, appeal of
landowners affected, **121B:47.**
Utilities.
Public utilities. See within this
heading, "Public utilities."
Vacancy in office, **213:1.**
Validity of acts of certain
fiduciaries pending appeal
from decree of appointment,
215:9A.
Verdicts, **213:3.**
Veterinarian's license, appeal from
revocation, **112:64.**
Voting.
Elections. See within this
heading, "Elections."
Wages, salaries, and compensation,
211:22.
Chief justice and associate
justices, **211:22.**
Clerks and assistant clerks of
court, **221:2, 221:92-221:94.**
Commissioners, assessors,
referees, masters, and
arbitrators, award of
compensation, **221:55.**
Employees, **211:3B.**
Executive secretary,
compensation, **211:3A.**

SUPREME JUDICIAL COURT
—Cont'd
Wages, salaries, and compensation
—Cont'd
Justices, **211:22, 211A:2.**
Limitation on duties of
comptroller regarding, **7A:3.**
Waiver or court costs, affidavit of
indigency and request,
261:27B.
Warrants to arrest issued by
justice, **276:21.**
Waters.
See WATERS AND
WATERWAYS.
Watershed system, enforcement of
provisions, rules, and
regulations, or orders, **92:112.**
Waterworks.
See WATERWORKS AND
WATER SUPPLY.
Widows of justices, benefits,
32:65C.
Wills.
See WILLS.
Wiretapping, authorization to
obtain evidence of crime,
166:44, 272:99.
Witnesses.
Enforcement of attendance,
233:10.
Fees, **262:29.**
Immunity of witnesses. See
within this heading,
"Immunity of witnesses."
Worcester central district court,
review of trial of civil actions
by jury of six, **218:19A.**
Workers' compensation.
See WORKERS'
COMPENSATION.
Writs and process, issuance of,
213:2, 223:20.
Written instruments, procedure to
secure binding interpretation,
213:3.

**SUPREME JUDICIAL COURT
RULES.**
Advisory committee, ethical
opinions for clerks of court,
Rule 3:14.
Alcoholism and chemical
dependency, programs for
lawyers suffering from, **Rule
4:07.**
Alias executions, forms for all
courts, **Rule 1:10.**
Amendment, modification, repeal
of Rules, **Rule 4:08.**
Appointment docket, maintenance,
Rule 1:07.

SUPREME JUDICIAL COURT RULES —Cont'd

Assessment, periodic, of attorneys, **Rule 4:03.**

Assignment of counsel, **Rule 3:10.**

Attachment, **Rule 1:04A.**

Attorneys.

Administration of justice, **Rule 3:02.**

Admission, applications for, **Rule 3:01.**

Alcoholism and chemical dependency, programs for lawyers suffering from, **Rule 4:07.**

Amendment, modification, repeal of rules, **Rule 4:09.**

Another jurisdiction, discipline, **Rule 4:01.**

Applications for admission, **Rule 3:01.**

Appointments to Board of Bar Overseers, **Rule 4:01.**

Assessment, periodic, **Rule 4:03.**

Assignment of counsel, **Rule 3:10.**

Association not to be represented by disbarred attorney, **Rule 3:02.**

Bar discipline, **Rules 4:01-4:03.**

Bar examination, qualifications for taking, **Rule 3:01.**

Bar examiners' rules, **Rule 3:01.**

Bar Overseers Board, appointments to, **Rule 4:01.**

Clerks of court.

Definitions, **Rule 4:02.**

Fee for periodic registration, inapplicable, **Rule 4:03.**

Periodic registration, clerk status, **Rule 4:02.**

Practice of law forbidden, **Rule 3:02.**

Clients' Security Board.

See CLIENTS' SECURITY BOARD RULES.

Code of judicial conduct, **Rule 3:09.**

Confidentiality, allegations of misconduct, **Rule 4:01.**

Conviction of serious crimes, **Rule 4:01.**

Corporation not to be represented by disbarred attorney, **Rule 3:02.**

Disciplinary rules, **Rule 3:08, 4:01.**

Discipline in another jurisdiction, **Rule 4:01.**

Disposition of petitions for admission, **Rule 3:01.**

SUPREME JUDICIAL COURT RULES —Cont'd

Attorneys —Cont'd

Fees to be paid upon periodic registration, **Rule 4:03.**

Inactive attorneys, periodic registration fees inapplicable, **Rule 4:03.**

Incorporation, **Rule 3:06.**

Indigent and indigent but able to contribute, counsel for parties, **Rule 3:10.**

Interpretation of rules, **Rule 4:08.**

Investigative function of prosecutor, **Rule 3:08.**

IOLTA accounts, **Rule 3:07.**

Law students, legal assistance, **Rules 3:03, 3:04.**

Lawyers concerned for lawyers fund and oversight committee, **Rule 4:07.**

Legal assistance programs, **Rules 3:03, 3:04.**

Limited liability entities, **Rule 3:06.**

Limited practice, attorneys from other jurisdictions engaged in certain graduate law studies or legal assistance programs, **Rule 3:04.**

Motion, admissions on, **Rule 3:01.**

Periodic assessment of, **Rule 4:03.**

Periodic registration of, **Rules 4:02, 4:03.**

Professional conduct rules, **Rule 3:07.**

Prosecutor or defense lawyer, disciplinary rules applicable to practice, **Rule 3:08.**

Public notice of bar examination results, **Rule 3:01.**

Public service.

Voluntary pro bono publico service, **Rule 3:07.**

Qualification for taking bar exam, **Rule 3:01.**

Reciprocal discipline of suspended or disbarred attorneys, **Rule 4:01.**

Registration, periodic, **Rule 4:02.**

Reimbursement of losses, claims by clients, **Rule 4:05.**

Retired attorneys, periodic registration fees inapplicable, **Rule 4:03.**

Students, appearance of, **Rule 3:03.**

SUPREME JUDICIAL COURT RULES —Cont'd

Attorneys —Cont'd

Subpoena to members of Board of Bar Examiners, **Rule 3:01.**

Bar discipline, **Rules 4:01 et seq.**

Clerks of court.

Advisory opinion requests, **Rule 3:14.**

Code of professional responsibility, **Rule 3:12.**

Practice of law forbidden, **Rule 3:02.**

Proceedings of committee, **Rules 5 to 8.**

Professional responsibility.

Committee on professional responsibility. See within this heading, "Committee on professional responsibility for clerks of court."

Clients' Security Board rules.

See CLIENTS' SECURITY BOARD RULES.

Code of Judicial Conduct, **Rule 3:09.**

Code of professional responsibility for clerks of courts, **Rule 3:13.**

Generally.

See COMMITTEE ON PROFESSIONAL RESPONSIBILITY FOR CLERKS OF COURTS RULES.

Committee on Judicial Ethics, **Rule 3:11.**

Committee on professional responsibility for clerks of court, **Rule 3:13.**

Generally.

See COMMITTEE ON PROFESSIONAL RESPONSIBILITY FOR CLERKS OF COURTS RULES.

Confidentiality of materials.

Bar discipline, **Rule 4:01.**

Impounded materials, **Rule 1:15.**

Judicial performance enhancement programs, **Rule 1:16.**

Definitions, **Rule 1:01.**

Indigency, **Rule 3:10.**

Depositions and discovery, **Rule 1:02A.**

Disciplinary rules, **Rules 3:08, 4:01.**

Disposal of records and papers, **Rules 1:11, 1:12.**

SUPREME JUDICIAL COURT RULES —Cont'd

Disposition of petitions for admission of attorneys, **Rule 3:01.**

Emergency opinions, advisory committee on ethical opinions for clerks of court, **Rule 3:14.**

Ethical opinions, requests for advisory opinions, **Rule 3:14.**

Exclusive arrangement for news media coverage of proceedings, judicial conduct, **Rule 3:09.**

Executions, forms for all courts, **Rules 1:09, 1:10.**

Experts.
  Appointment docket, **Rule 1:07.**

Fiduciary activities, code of professional responsibility for clerks of courts, **Rule 3:12.**

Form, style and size, papers filed in all courts, **Rules 1:06, 1:08.**

Housing court, definition, **Rule 1:01.**

Impoundment requests, **Rule 1:15.**

Incorporation of attorneys, **Rule 3:06.**

Indigent persons, **Rules 3:03, 3:10.**

IOLTA accounts.
  Funds, maintenance of, **Rule 3:07.**

Judicial conduct.
  Discriminatory organizations, membership of justice in, **Rule 3:09.**
  Exclusive arrangement for news media coverage of proceedings, **Rule 3:09.**
  Impartial and diligent performance of duties, **Rule 3:09.**
  Membership of justice in discriminatory organizations, **Rule 3:09.**

Judicial conference, **Rule 1:04.**

Judicial officers, certain contracts, **Rule 1:05.**

Judicial performance enhancement programs, **Rule 1:16.**

Land Court Department, retention of case papers and records, **Rule 1:11.**

Law students, legal assistance to indigents, **Rule 3:03.**

Massachusetts Legal Assistance Corporation receiving IOLTA funds, **Rule 3:07.**

Material facts, Probate and Family Court, time for report, **Rule 1:13.**

SUPREME JUDICIAL COURT RULES —Cont'd

Motor vehicle equity, establishing indigency, **Rule 3:10.**

Multistate Professional Responsibility Examination, **Rule 3:01.**

Original executions, form for all courts, **Rule 1:09.**

Pecuniary legacies and trust distributions, interest, **Rule 1:14.**

Professional conduct.
  Rules of professional conduct, **Rule 3:07.**

Questions of law, uniform certification, **Rule 1:03.**

Real estate equity, establishing indigency, **Rule 3:10.**

Records, official form and style, **Rules 1:06, 1:08.**

Registration, periodic, of attorneys, **Rule 4:02.**

Reimbursement of losses, claims by attorney's clients, **Rule 4:05.**

Reports, determination of indigency report, **Rule 3:10.**

Requests for impoundment in appellate courts, **Rule 1:15.**

Retired judges, representation, **Rule 3:09.**

Sentence served in jail or correctional institution, establishing indigency, **Rule 3:10.**

Single justice, practice before.
  Adverse parties, copies, **Rule 2:09.**
  Appearances, **Rule 2:03.**
  Appellate Tax Board, appeals from decisions, **Rule 2:20.**
  Arguments, time, **Rule 2:17.**
  Commissioners, **Rule 2:13.**
  Fixing time for pleadings and proceedings, **Rules 2:01, 2:05.**
  Hearings.
    Motions grounded on facts, **Rule 2:11.**
    Notice, **Rule 2:07.**
  Interlocutory ruling, appear from single justice denial of relief on, **Rule 2:21.**
  Jury issues, **Rule 2:08.**
  Masters and commissioners, special, **Rule 2:13.**
  Money paid into court, **Rule 2:10.**
  Motions grounded on facts, hearings, **Rule 2:11.**

SUPREME JUDICIAL COURT RULES —Cont'd

Single justice, practice before —Cont'd
  Notice.
    Giving of, criminal cases, **Rule 2:04.**
    Hearing before single justice, **Rule 2:07.**
  Objections, **Rule 2:15.**
  Order of business, **Rule 2:18.**
  Papers, form and indorsement, **Rule 2:02.**
  Petitions, **Rule 2:22.**
  Pleadings and proceedings, time, **Rules 2:01, 2:05.**
  Postponement for want of evidence, **Rule 2:12.**
  Public Utilities, Department of, reviews of orders, **Rule 2:19.**
  Rulings, requests, **Rule 2:16.**
  Special masters, **Rule 2:13.**
  Time for pleadings and proceedings, fixing, **Rules 2:01, 2:05.**
  Verification by oath or affirmation, elimination of requirement, **Rule 2:06.**
  Weekends and holidays, time for pleadings and proceedings when last day of performance falls, **Rule 2:05.**
  Writ of protection, **Rule 2:14.**

Stenographic notes of testimony, disposal, **Rule 1:12.**

Trustee process, **Rule 1:03A.**

Waiver form as to counsel, **Rule 3:10.**

Worcester County Division, Housing Court, **Rule 1:01.**

SURCHARGES.

Acute hospitals, **118G:18A.**
  Definitions, **118G:1.**

Ambulatory surgical centers, **118G:18A.**
  Definitions, **118G:1.**

Automobile insurance.
  See AUTOMOBILE INSURANCE.

DUI fines, **90:24.**

Elevated structures, public easement, **162:17.**

Executors and administrators, liability for contracts and torts, **195:17.**

Pollution liability reinsurance corporation, **175G:5.**

SURETIES AND SURETY COMPANIES, 175:105-175:107.

Agents.
  Employment agencies. See within this heading, "Employment agencies."
  Laws as to insurance agents applicable to surety company agents, 175:107.
  Principal as member of issuing company, 175:90B.
  Resident agent of foreign company, applicability of requirement, 175:157.
Arrest in civil action, surrender of principal, 224:7.
Assets of surety companies as limiting amount of single risk, 175:105.
Attachment of property.
  Bond to dissolve attachment, sureties, 223:120, 223:124.
  Probate bond, surety's attachment of principal's property, 205:28.
  Trustee process, 246:1.
Auctioneer licenses, applications, 100:3.
Authorized insurance business, 175:47, 175:105.
Bail.
  See BAIL AND RECOGNIZANCE.
Bank commissioner, powers, 175:105.
Bid bond on public or private contracts, applicability of requirement as to resident agent for foreign surety company, 175:157.
Blasting.
  See BLASTING.
Brokers of fidelity insurance, laws as to insurance brokers applicable, 175:107.
Business corporation law inapplicable to surety companies, 156:2, 156B:3.
Children.
  See CHILDREN AND MINORS.
Clerks of court.
  Bonds of clerks, surety, 221:12.
  Insurance, list of corporate sureties to be furnished each clerk of court, 175:105.
  Release of defendant on own recognizance without surety, procedure, 276:58.
Collection agencies, bonds, 93:26.
Combination with other classes of insurance, 175:48, 175:48A, 175:51, 175:54.

SURETIES AND SURETY COMPANIES —Cont'd

Co-operative banks, 170:15, 175:105.
Corporations and taxation commissioner, powers, 175:105.
County officers and employees to furnish surety company bonds, 35:43A.
Court clerks.
  Clerks of court. See within this heading, "Clerks of court."
Defined for purposes of general statutory construction, 4:7.
Deposits.
  Federal savings and loan associations, deposits by fiduciaries by agreement with their sureties, 205:19A.
  Foreign company, 175:106.
  Uniform Commercial Code, 106:1-201.
Discharge.
  See DISCHARGE OR RELEASE.
Discrimination by surety companies, 151B:4.
Employment agencies.
  Bonds for license, 140:46F, 140:46H.
  Securing performance of certain statutory duties, 140:46J.
  Service of process in actions against, 140:46G.
Employment security.
  See EMPLOYMENT SECURITY.
Federal savings and loan associations, deposits by fiduciaries by agreement with their sureties, 205:19A.
Fireworks.
  See FIREWORKS.
Foreign companies.
  Authority to do business, 175:106.
  Bid bonds issued on public or private contracts, applicability of requirement as to resident agent, 175:157.
  Conditions to admission, 175:151.
  Deposit required, 175:106.
  Probate bond, acceptability as surety, 175:105.
Health spa contracts, 93:79, 93:88.
Incorporation, 175:47-175:49.
Insurance commissioner.
  See INSURANCE COMMISSIONER.

SURETIES AND SURETY COMPANIES —Cont'd

Insurance contracts, bonds as, 175:107.
Issuing company, principal as member, 175:90B.
Joint surety companies.
  Acceptability in lieu of two or more sureties, 175:105.
  Power to act, 175:105.
Limitation of amount of single risk, surety companies, 175:105.
Model water and sewer commission, notes of, 40N:10.
Municipal officers and employees to furnish surety company bonds, 35:43A, 41:109A.
Mutual surety, liability, and casualty companies, 175:90B, 175:93B-175:93D.
Officers and employees.
  Employment agencies. See within this heading, "Employment agencies."
  Insurance companies, qualification of sureties on bonds, 175:60.
  Mutual insurance company officers, 175:94.
Oral recognizance, fidelity bond or insurance in lieu, 175:105.
Pawnbroker's bonds, 140:77.
Powers of fidelity and corporate surety companies, 175:105.
Private business schools, liability of sureties on bonds to be posted, 75D:14.
Probate bonds.
  See PROBATE BONDS.
Professional bondsmen, registration, 276:61B.
Qualified bonds, state as surety, 44A:12.
Rates, 175A:1 et seq.
  See INSURANCE RATES AND RATING ORGANIZATIONS.
Registers of probate and insolvency, list of corporate sureties to be furnished, 175:105.
Reinsuring risks, 175:54B.
Replevin, 247:14, 247:15.
  Fees, 247:16, 262:8.
  Notice and hearing, 247:15.
Revenue commissioner to approve form of surety companies, 175:105.
Savings banks.
  See SAVINGS BANKS.
Sole surety, power of surety company to act, 175:105.

SURETIES AND SURETY COMPANIES —Cont'd

Southeastern Regional Planning and Economic Development District, bond of treasurer, **40B:15.**

State treasurer's power to require bonds secured by surety companies, **30:18.**

Status of surety bonds, surety companies, **175:107.**

Statute of frauds, written promise required, **259:1.**

Stock certificate of business corporation, bond on replacement when lost or destroyed, **156:34, 156B:29.**

Stock or mutual plan, **175:48, 175:48A.**

Suffolk county, supreme judicial court and superior court, list of corporate sureties to be furnished, **175:105.**

Transportation charges on public works projects, bond, **30:39A.**

Trust companies.
See TRUST COMPANIES.

Trustee process, qualification of sureties in action commenced, **246:1.**

Use of word "surety" as requiring surety company bond for certain offices, **4:7.**

SURFBOARDING.

Use regulated, **90B:8, 90B:11, 90B:14.**

SURF JETS.

Regulation, **90B:1, 90B:11.**

SURGEONS.

See PHYSICIANS AND SURGEONS.

SURGICAL DEVICES, 94:1, 94:189-94:194.

Adulteration, **94:186.**

Complaints and proceedings, **94:189, 94:189A.**

Manufacturers of adulterated devices, **94:190.**

Brands.
Misbranding. See within this heading, "Misbranding."

Complaints as to adulterated or misbranded device, **94:189, 94:189A.**

Dealer, prosecution, **94:193, 94:194.**

Definition of term "device, **94:1.**

Examination of samples, **94:189.**

Fines or penalties.
Failure to furnish sample for analysis, **94:304.**

SURGICAL DEVICES —Cont'd

Fines or penalties —Cont'd
Manufacturers of adulterated or misbranded devices, **94:190.**

Manufacturers of adulterated or misbranded devices, **94:190.**

Misbranding, **94:187.**

Complaints and proceedings, **94:189, 94:189A.**

Manufacturers of misbranded devices, **94:190.**

Penalties.
Fines or penalties. See within this heading, "Fines or penalties."

Proceedings when devices suspected of being adulterated or misbranded, **94:189A.**

Rules and regulations, **94:192, 94:193.**

Sample.
Examination, **94:189.**

Vendor to furnish sample for analysis, **94:304.**

SURPLUS.

Banks.
See BANKS AND BANKING.

Co-operative banks, **170:21.**

Credit unions.
See CREDIT UNIONS.

Fraternal benefit societies, **176:12.**

Distribution of surplus, **176:25.**

False statements, **176:47.**

Waiver of mortuary contributions as affected by surplus, **176:25.**

Government land bank.
See GOVERNMENT LAND BANK.

Insurance.
See INSURANCE.

Life insurance.
See LIFE INSURANCE.

Morris plan banks.
See MORRIS PLAN BANKS.

Mortgage foreclosure sale, disposition of surplus proceeds, **183:27.**

Real estate time-shares, **183B:27.**

Reciprocal insurance exchanges.
See RECIPROCAL INSURANCE EXCHANGES.

Savings bank life insurance.
See SAVINGS BANK LIFE INSURANCE.

Savings banks.
See SAVINGS BANKS.

Schools, renting or leasing of surplus space or property, **40:3, 71:16.**

SURPLUS —Cont'd

Secured transactions.
Debtor's right to surplus, **106:9-502, 106:9-504.**

Owner of collateral as entitled to surplus, **106:9-112.**

State property, disposition, **7:40F, 7:40F½.**

Taxation.
Accounting for surplus after distress and sale of personal estate, **60:28.**

Low value lands held by city or town under tax title, surplus from sale, **60:79.**

Town water works, disposition of surplus revenues, **41:69B.**

Trust companies.
See TRUST COMPANIES.

SURRENDER.

Bail.
See BAIL AND RECOGNIZANCE.

Extradition, **276:11 et seq.; US Const Art 4 Sec 2 cl 2.**
See EXTRADITION.

Property, surrender of.
See SURRENDER OF PROPERTY.

SURRENDER OF PROPERTY.

Abandoned property.
See ABANDONED, LOST, AND UNCLAIMED PROPERTY.

Accident and sickness insurance policy, surrender, **175:108.**

Alcoholic liquors license, equitable enforcement of surrender, **138:23.**

Arrest on mesne process and supplementary proceedings, surrender of principal, **224:7.**

Bail.
See BAIL AND RECOGNIZANCE.

Certificate of incorporation, surrender, **155:54.**

Corporations.
Certification of incorporation, **155:54.**

Stock certificate upon sale for unpaid installments, **156:20.**

Expectant estates not defeated by surrender of precedent estate, **184:10, 184:11.**

Firearms, **140:129D.**

Possession by person with intent to surrender, **140:129C.**

Forfeitures.
See FORFEITURES.

Insolvent estate of decedent, surrender of voidable preferences, **198:7A.**

SURRENDER OF PROPERTY
—Cont'd
Insurance agent's, adjuster's, or
broker's license, **175:174B.**
Motor vehicle license.
See MOTOR VEHICLES.
Public administrator, surrender of
letters and property on
appointment of successor,
194:12.
Rent as affected by surrender of
lease or premises, **186:8.**
State treasurer.
See STATE TREASURER.
Stolen property, refusal to
surrender as criminal offense,
266:21.
Telephone party line, refusal to
surrender use of, for
emergency call, offense and
penalty, **166:15C.**
Voluntary administrator, surrender
of policy or passbook, **195:16.**
Weapons.
Firearms. See within this
heading, "Firearms."

SURTAX.
Corporation taxes.
See CORPORATION TAXES.

SURVEYORS, 112:81D-112:81T.
See ENGINEERS AND
SURVEYORS.

SURVEYS AND SURVEY
BOARDS, 97:1 et seq.
See MAPS, PLATS, AND
SURVEYS.

SURVIVAL OF ACTIONS,
228:1-228:14.
See ABATEMENT, SURVIVAL,
AND REVIVAL.

SURVIVING CHILDREN.
See ORPHANS.

SURVIVING SPOUSE.
Absentees, estates.
Allowance, **200:10.**
Petition for appointment of
receiver, **200:1.**
Accident and sickness insurance.
Common disaster, presumption
as to survivorship in deaths
caused, **190A:4, 190A:5.**
Continuation by widow of
fireman killed in
performance of duty,
32B:9C, 32B:9D.
Facility of payment of small
amounts, **175:187E.**
Firefighter's health insurance,
continuation, **32B:9C,**
32B:9D, 32B:11D.

SURVIVING SPOUSE —Cont'd
Accident and sickness insurance
—Cont'd
Retired employee's widow,
political subdivision's
contribution toward health
insurance premiums,
32B:9D.
State employee's premiums paid
for surviving spouse,
32A:11.
Administration of estate, payment
of decedent's earnings due to
surviving spouse without,
29:31D, 149:178A, 149:178C.
Alcoholic liquors, widow's
continuation of pharmacy
business involving dealings,
138:30B, 138:30C.
Allowance, **200:10.**
Amount of allowances to widows of
deceased public employees,
32:12B.
Annuity to surviving spouse of
county, city, or town officers or
employees, **32:95A.**
Apparel of surviving spouse, **196:1.**
Blind insurance broker's widow as
exempt from license fees,
175:167A.
Burial and funeral expenses,
guardian or conservator power
to pay, **201:38A.**
Burial plots, rights, powers, and
duties, **114:29.**
Cities and towns.
Municipal officer or employee.
See within this heading,
"Municipal officer or
employee."
Civil rights.
See CIVIL RIGHTS AND
DISCRIMINATION.
Civil service preference for widows
or widowed mothers of
veterans, **31:26, 31:28.**
Common disaster, presumption of
survivorship in deaths caused,
190A:1 et seq.
Consequential damages aspect of
personal injury action,
survival, **228:1.**
Credit unions.
See CREDIT UNIONS.
Dead bodies.
See DEAD BODIES.
Dentists, continuing practice,
112:53.
Depositor, payment to surviving
spouse, **167D:33.**
Descent and distribution.
Share of spouse, **190:1.**

SURVIVING SPOUSE —Cont'd
Descent and distribution —Cont'd
Waiver of will provisions,
191:15.
Disposition of property of spouses
of certain deceased persons,
196:1, 196:2, 200:1, 200:10.
Dower.
See DOWER AND CURTESY.
Earnings, payment to surviving
spouse without
administration, **29:31D,**
149:178A, 149:178C.
Executors.
See EXECUTORS AND
ADMINISTRATORS.
Fire departments.
Group health insurance,
contributions for widow's
continuation of after
firefighter's death, **32B:9C,**
32B:9D, 32B:11D.
Pensions of widows of
firefighters, **32:100.**
Tax exemption for widows of
firefighters, **59:5.**
Gifts of human bodies, organs and
tissue, **113:8.**
Group insurance, **175:134.**
Accident and health coverage
extended to surviving
spouses, **175:110G,**
176A:8D, 176B:6A.
Contents of group life policies,
175:134.
Continuing coverage, **32A:10B,**
32A:10C.
County officers and employees,
health insurance for
surviving spouse, **32B:9C,**
32B:9D.
Elderly retired governmental
employees, continuance of
coverage, **32A:10B.**
Firemen killed in line of duty,
conversion privilege,
32B:9C, 32B:9D.
Governmental employees,
continuation, **32A:10B,**
32A:10C, 32A:11, 32B:9B,
32B:11C.
Municipal employee, **32B:9B.**
State employee, **32A:11,**
32B:1.
Health insurance premiums of
surviving spouse, **32B:9C,**
32B:9D, 32B:9D½,
32B:9D¾, 32B:11D.
Police officer, conversion
privilege as to insurance,
32B:9E.

SURVIVING SPOUSE —Cont'd
Health insurance.
Accident and sickness insurance.
See within this heading,
"Accident and sickness
insurance."
Homesteads.
See HOMESTEADS.
Improvement assessments,
suspension as to widows
entitled to exemption, **60:3B.**
Insurance agent or broker,
continuance of business by
surviving spouse, **175:174D.**
License fees, exemption of
certain widows, **175:167A.**
Judges, benefits for widows of
certain, **32:65C.**
Legacy and succession tax
exemption of real estate to
surviving spouse in joint
tenancy or tenancy by
entirety, **65:1.**
Life insurance, facility of payment
of small amounts, **175:187E.**
Group life insurance, **175:134.**
Limitation of time as to claim for
interest in realty, **189:16.**
Mandatory retirement age,
deductions from salaries of
employees working past,
32:90G.
Motor vehicle distinctive
registration plates, deceased
prisoner of war, **60A:1, 90:2.**
Municipal officer or employee.
Contribution, health insurance
premiums, **32B:9D.**
Payment of health insurance
premiums, **32B:9D¾.**
Payment of salary, **41:111I.**
Necessaries, allowance, **196:2.**
Optometry, continuing practice,
112:73.
Pensions.
See RETIREMENT SYSTEMS
AND PENSIONS.
Personal injury action, survival of
action for consequential
damages, **228:1.**
Pharmacist, widow's continuation
of business, **112:36, 138:30B,
138:30C.**
Police.
See POLICE.
Public administrators.
See EXECUTORS AND
ADMINISTRATORS.
Qualified terminable interest
property, **65C:3A.**
Real estate tax exemption of
certain widows after change of
domicile, **59:5.**

SURVIVING SPOUSE —Cont'd
Remarriage.
See REMARRIAGE.
Retirement systems.
See RETIREMENT SYSTEMS
AND PENSIONS.
Salary.
Wages. See within this heading,
"Wages due deceased
employee, payment to
surviving spouse."
Securities owned by a deceased
person, transfer, **196:9.**
State officer or employee.
Accident and sickness insurance,
state employee's premiums
paid for surviving spouse,
32A:11, 32B:1.
Payment of earnings without
administration, **29:31D.**
Summary process for possession of
land, stay upon application of
tenant's surviving spouse,
239:9.
Taxation.
See TAXATION.
Trusts.
See TRUSTS AND TRUSTEES.
Uniform Statutory Will Act,
191B:5-191B:7, 191B:13.
Veterans.
See VETERANS AND
VETERANS'
ORGANIZATIONS.
Wages due deceased employee,
payment to surviving spouse.
County officer or employee,
35:19B.
Municipal officer or employee,
41:111I.
Without administration, **29:31D,
149:178A, 149:178C.**
Wearing apparel of surviving
spouse, **196:1.**
Wills.
See WILLS.
Workers' compensation.
See WORKERS'
COMPENSATION.

**SURVIVORS AND
SURVIVORSHIP.**
Civil service preference to
veterans' surviving spouse or
parent, **31:26, 31:28.**
Group life insurance policy
provisions as to payment,
175:134.
Joint owners, legacy and
succession taxes of survivor,
65:1, 65:6.
See LEGACY AND
SUCCESSION TAXES.

**SURVIVORS AND
SURVIVORSHIP** —Cont'd
Legacy.
See LEGACY AND
SUCCESSION TAXES.
Partnerships.
See PARTNERSHIPS.
Real estate tax exemptions for
widows and certain children of
firefighters, **59:5. (note)**
Retirement systems and pensions,
32:1, 32:12B, 32:12C.
See RETIREMENT SYSTEMS
AND PENSIONS.
Simultaneous death law,
presumption, **190A:1 et seq.**
Spouse.
See SURVIVING SPOUSE.

**SUSAN B. ANTHONY
AMENDMENT.**
Women's suffrage, **US Const
Amend 19.**

SUSAN B. ANTHONY DAY.
Observance, **6:15E.**

SUTTON.
Congressional district, **57:1.**
District court, **218:1.**
Medical examiner district, **38:1.**
Senatorial district, **57:3.**

SWAMPS, 252:1-252:24.
**See LOWLANDS AND
SWAMPS.**

SWAMPSCOTT.
Buoying of lobster or crab pots in
water, **130:37.**
Congressional district, **57:1.**
District court, **218:1.**
Maintenance of reservations and
boulevards, assessments,
92:55.
Medical examiner district, **38:1.**
Metropolitan area planning
district, membership, **40B:26.**
Parks, provision by metropolitan
commission, **92:33.**
Refuse disposal, **92:9A.**
Senatorial district, **57:3.**
South Essex ocean sanctuary
established, **132A:13.**

SWANSEA.
Congressional district, **57:1.**
District court, **218:1.**
Medical examiner district, **38:1.**
Senatorial district, **57:3.**

SWEARING.
Oath.
See OATH OR AFFIRMATION.
Profanity.
See ABUSIVE OR OFFENSIVE
LANGUAGE.

SWIMMING AND SWIMMING POOLS, 140:206.
Beaches.
  See BEACHES.
Charles River basin, swimming pools along, **92:74A.**
Cities.
  See CITIES AND TOWNS.
Discrimination because of race, color, etc., **272:92A, 272:98.**
Home improvement contractors constructing, **142A:14.**
Instructions in, towns may provide, **40:12.**
Rental of bathing suits, licenses, **140:194-140:196.**
State environmental code to prescribe standards for pools, **21A:13.**
State parks, recreation areas, and reservations, part of planning, **132A:2D.**
State sanitary code, **111:127A.**
Town appropriations for swimming pools, **40:5, 44:7.**
Transfer of operating funds, **132A:10.**
Water supply, penalty for swimming, **111:171.**

SWINE.
Animal diseases.
  See ANIMAL DISEASES.
Dairying and animal husbandry division to report unsanitary condition of barn, stable, etc., **128:13.**
Dealers.
  License, **129:39.**
  License plates for vehicles used, **129:40.**
Diseases.
  See ANIMAL DISEASES.
Distraint for doing damage, **49:29.**
Driving or herding along highways, power of town to regulate, **85:10.**
Excise tax, **59:8A.**
False pedigree, **266:93.**
"Farmer" defined for purpose of registration of farm motor vehicles, **90:1.**
Fees.
  License for porcine animals, **129:39.**
  Permit for feeding garbage to swine, **129:14B.**
Garbage, feeding, **129:14B.**
Humane slaughtering, **94:139C-94:139G.**
Imported swine, serum neutralization test for pseudorabies, **129:14E.**

SWINE —Cont'd
Inspection, **129:19.**
Licenses and permits.
  Dealers, **129:39.**
  Fees. See within this heading, "Fees."
  Garbage, feeding, **129:14B.**
Massachusetts Society for Prevention of Cruelty to Animals, duties of agents, **129:9.**
Prizes and exhibits, **128:2.**
Sales tax, exemptions, **64H:6.**
Sausage.
  See SAUSAGE.
Taking up and impounding, **49:24, 49:25.**
Taxation.
  Excise tax on swine, **59:8A.**
  Exemption of local taxes, **59:5.**
  Sales tax exemption, **64H:6.**
Terms "agriculture" and "farming" as including raising, **128:1A.**
Trespass by, penalty, **266:118.**
Unsanitary conditions, division of dairying and animal husbandry to report, **128:13.**

SWITCHES.
Railroads.
  See RAILROADS.

SWITCH KNIFE, 269:10, 269:12.
See KNIVES AND DAGGERS.

SWIVEL GUN.
Use in taking of birds forbidden, **131:68.**

SWORD CANE.
Manufacture and sale of, penalty, **269:12.**

SWORN STATEMENT.
See OATH OR AFFIRMATION.

SYNAGOGUES.
See RELIGION AND RELIGIOUS SOCIETIES.

SYNDICATES.
Gambling syndicate, penalty for organization, **271:16A.**
Insurance policies underwritten, **175:99.**

SYNTHETIC FIBERS.
Lien on account of labor and materials furnished in processing, **255:31A, 255:31B.**

SYNTHETIC NATURAL GAS.
Definition, **164:69G.**

SYPHILIS.
See VENEREAL DISEASES.

SYRINGE.
See DRUGS AND NARCOTICS.

SYRUP.
Candy containing alcoholic syrup, sale, **270:8.**

T

TABBY CAT.
Official cat of Commonwealth, **2:30.**

TADEUSZ KOSCIUSZKO DAY.
Holiday, **6:12BB.**

TAG ACT, 90:20C.

TAG DAYS.
Charities and veteran organizations, special permit for sale of flags, medals, buttons, etc., **101:33.**

TAGGING LAW.
Graffiti, **266:126A, 266:126B.**

TAGLIABUE OPEN CUP TESTER.
Hazardous substances, testing, **94B:1.**

TAGS.
Brands.
  See BRANDS AND LABELS.
Dogs.
  See DOGS.
Shellfish.
  See SHELLFISH.

TAIL, ESTATES.
See ESTATES TAIL.

TAIL LIGHTS.
Motorboats, **90B:5.**
Motor vehicles and trailers, **90:7.**
Track motor cars, **160:176A.**

TAIL OF HORSE.
Docking tail of horse, **272:79A, 272:79B.**

TAKE-OVER BIDS.
See CORPORATIONS.

TAKING OF PROPERTY.
Eminent domain.
  See EMINENT DOMAIN.
Nonpayment of taxes, taking of land for, **60:53-60:56.**
  See TAX LIENS.
Searches.
  See SEARCHES AND SEIZURES.

TAKING OR DIVERTING WATER.
Watershed system, **92:109, 92:111.**

TALESMEN, 234:27.

TALKING BOOKS.
Libraries and librarians, **78:19.**

TALLY OF ELECTION.
See ELECTIONS.

TAMPERING.
Alcoholic liquors.
  Content or composition of
    alcoholic liquors, **138:16.**
  Samples of seized liquor, **138:39.**
Automobile rental agencies,
  tampering with mileage
  registration device, **90:32C.**
Ballot boxes, apparatus, and
  supplies, penalty for
  tampering, **54:27.**
Commercial driver license,
  tampering, **90F:8.**
Contaminated shellfish, tags or
  labels, **130:81, 130:82.**
Fire laws, penalty for tampering
  with or destruction of notice of
  violation, **148:30A.**
Motor vehicles.
  See MOTOR VEHICLES.
Railroads.
  See RAILROADS.
Steam boilers and engines, safety
  appliances, **146:12, 146:33.**
Telephone or telegraph facilities or
  equipment, penalty for
  tampering, **166:42A.**

TANDEM UNIT.
Definition, **90:1.**
Routes of reasonable access,
  90:19G.

TANKS.
Air, compressed, **146:34-146:41.**
  See AIR, COMPRESSED.
Bulk storage facilities.
  See BULK STORAGE
    FACILITIES.
Burning, **266:2, 266:5A.**
Fees of sealers, **98:56.**
Gasoline tanks, removal, **148:38A.**
Hot water tanks.
  See HOT WATER TANKS.
Inflammable fluids stored, **148:37,
  148:38.**
Massachusetts Petroleum Council,
  underground storage tank
  petroleum product cleanup
  fund administrative review
  board, **21J:8.**
Milk and milk products.
  Calibrating, sealing, and
    checking of bulk milk tanks,
    98:46A.
  Licensing and regulation of
    receiver of raw milk from
    producer for inclusion in
    loan of bulk tank truck,
    94:27A, 94:28A, 94:30.

TANKS —Cont'd
Pressure tanks.
  See PRESSURE TANKS.
Septic tanks.
  See SEPTIC TANKS.
Testing by sealer, frequency, **98:42.**
Underground tanks.
  See UNDERGROUND TANKS.

**TANNING FACILITIES, 111:207
  et seq.**
Children and minors, **111:211.**
Definitions, **111:207.**
Fines and penalties, **111:214.**
Licenses and permits, **111:208.**
Reports, **111:212.**
Warnings, **111:209, 111:211,
  111:212.**

TAPE.
Standards and testing of
  surveyor's tape, **97:3.**

TAPE RECORDINGS.
**See ELECTRONIC
  RECORDING DEVICES
  AND EQUIPMENT.**

TAR.
Buildings, criminal offense for
  throwing into, **266:103.**
Ways spread with, regulations,
  84:6.

TARDINESS.
Deductions from wages, **149:152.**

TARGET PRACTICE.
**See SHOOTING GALLERIES
  AND PRESERVES.**

TARIFFS.
See RATES AND CHARGES.

TATTOOING.
Penalty, **265:34.**

TAUNTON.
Congressional district, **57:1.**
District court, **218:1.**
Medical examiner district, **38:1.**
Probate court sessions for Bristol
  county, **215:62.**
Senatorial district, **57:3.**
State hospital.
  See TAUNTON STATE
    HOSPITAL.
Superior court sittings, **212:14.**

TAUNTON RIVER.
Pilotage district four, **103:1.**

TAUNTON STATE HOSPITAL.
Board of trustees, **19:8A.**
Control, **19:14.**
Trustees to serve in mental health
  department, **19:14.**

TAVERNS.
Alcoholic beverage control
  generally, **138:1 to 138:78.**
  See ALCOHOLIC LIQUORS.
Barred or barricaded entrances or
  exits, **272:25, 272:27.**
Children.
  Minors. See within this heading,
    "Minors."
Convictions of certain offenses to
  be reported to licensing
  authority, **272:27.**
Cover charge for persons under 13
  years of age, prohibition,
  140:183D.
Defined, **138:1.**
Discrimination, **272:92A, 272:98.**
Dram shop act, **138:69.**
Driving while intoxicated.
  Dram shop act, **138:69.**
  Killer Bar Law, **90:24J.**
Enclosed booths or stalls, **272:25,
  272:27.**
Immoral solicitation, **272:26,
  272:27.**
Killer Bar Law, **90:24J.**
Labor and employment.
  Minors. See within this heading,
    "Minors."
Licenses, **140:2 et seq.**
  See COMMON VICTUALLERS.
Minors, employment, **149:64.**
  Cover charge for persons under
    13 years of age, prohibition,
    140:183D.
  Penalty, **149:78.**
Tax information as to residence,
  penalty against keepers for
  violations as to giving, **59:92.**
Tips or gratuities, misleading
  patrons as to beneficiaries,
  149:159A.

**TAX ADMINISTRATION, 62C:1
  et seq.**
See TAXATION.

**TAX AND BUDGET LIMITS
  FOR LOCAL
  GOVERNMENT, 59:21C.**
Appropriations, limitations on
  departmental appropriations,
  44:30, 44:31A.
Assessment rates, limitations on,
  59:21C.
Debt limit, **41:30, 44:10.**
Elections, increases in real
  property tax rate, **59:21C.**
Equalized valuation as
  determining debt limit, **44:10.**
Local mandates division, **11:6,
  29:27C.**

TAX AND BUDGET LIMITS FOR LOCAL GOVERNMENT —Cont'd

Local option statutes.

Laws and regulations involving cost obligations for municipalities, acceptance, **29:27C.**

Revocation of acceptance, **4:4B.**

Notice to local mandates division, **29:27C.**

Other governmental entities, assessment of costs on municipalities, **59:20A.**

Proposition 2½, **59:21C.**

Public schools, support, **71:34.**

Regional veterans' districts included, **59:20B.**

Rent, tax deduction, **62:3.**

Rules and regulations imposing additional costs on municipalities, **29:27C.**

TAX ASSESSORS, 41:24-41:30A, 59:20 et seq.

Abatement of taxes, **59:38G.**

Certificate of abatement, issuance, **59:70.**

Complaints, **59:64.**

Lands acquired by town by purchase or gift, abatement of taxes, **59:72A.**

Notice.

Applicant, notice of decision, **59:63.**

Application for abatement, notice, **61B:14.**

Collector, notice, **59:70A.**

Corporations, **59:74.**

Municipal financial officers, notice, **59:23A, 59:23B, 59:70A.**

Telephone or telegraph companies, applications for abatement, **59:39.**

Penalty for false valuation by assessor, **41:30.**

Prepaying of costs in proceedings, **59:62.**

Real estate taxes where assessed value insufficient to pay collection charges, **59:72.**

Records, **59:60.**

Recreational land, **61B:5, 61B:14.**

Revision of assessment, time for filing for abatement of taxes, **59:59.**

Town auditors, notice, **59:23B, 59:70A.**

Uncollectible taxes, **58:8, 59:71.**

TAX ASSESSORS —Cont'd

Abstract cards furnished by registers of deeds, **36:24B, 262:38.**

Additional assessments, powers, **59:25.**

Additional duties, **59:83, 59:86.**

Address.

Failure to furnish assessor with name and address of grantee of real estate, **184:8A.**

Records or property owners' names and addresses, assessors to maintain, **184:8A.**

Agricultural and horticultural uses.

Appeal of determinations to appellate tax board, **61A:19.**

Certificate of taxes due or paid, issuance, **61A:19A.**

Conclusive proof of land use, **61A:14.**

Notice to assessor of land claimed, **61A:6.**

Powers and duties with respect to liens, **61A:9.**

Amount of annual assessment, **59:23.**

Annual instruction and information by tax commissioner, **58:3.**

Annual notice to assessors of total city and town receipts, **41:54A.**

Appeals, valuation of property.

Appellate tax board, appeals, **59:38.**

Public lands, **58:14.**

Appellate tax board.

Agricultural and horticultural uses, appeal of determination, **61A:19.**

Legal counsel for tax assessors before appellate tax board, **41:26A.**

Valuation of property, appeals to appellate tax board, **59:38.**

Appointment or election of assessors.

Assistant assessors, **41:1, 41:25A.**

Commissioner of revenue, appointment, **41:27.**

Failure to choose assessors, penalty, **41:4.**

Number of assessors, **41:24.**

Oath of office, **41:29.**

Selectmen acting as assessors, **41:20, 41:21.**

Elections with respect, **41:20, 41:23.**

TAX ASSESSORS —Cont'd

Appointment or election of assessors —Cont'd

Selectmen acting as assessors —Cont'd

Rescission of selectmen's authority, **41:23.**

Salary, **41:22.**

Term of office, **41:22.**

Selectmen, appointment, **41:25, 41:26.**

Election authorizing, **41:26.**

Term of office, **41:1, 41:22, 41:24, 41:25.**

Town officers, assistant assessors, **41:1.**

Appraisal of taxable property, **58:1A, 59:38-59:42.**

Appropriations.

Compensation and expenses of assessor, **41:108B.**

Fire districts, appropriation for compensation and expenses, **41:108B.**

Orders certified, **41:15A.**

Assessment districts in cities, may establish, **59:38.**

Assessment of taxes, **59:20-59:28.**

Assignment of tax title held by city or town, notice, **60:76C.**

Assistant assessors.

Appointment, **41:25A.**

Election, **41:1.**

Oath of office, **41:29.**

Powers and duties, **41:28.**

Removal, **41:25A.**

Salary, **41:25A.**

Term of office, **41:1, 41:25A.**

Attorneys, employment, **41:26A.**

Auditors and auditing.

Abatement of taxes, notice to town auditor, **59:23B, 59:70A.**

Municipal accounts, assessment of tax for expense of audit, **44:41.**

Blank lists, furnishing, **59:30.**

Boardinghouse keepers to give information, **59:92.**

Board of tax appeals.

Appellate tax board. See within this heading, "Appellate tax board."

Boards of assessors of cities and towns, organization of, **41:24.**

Bond issues of municipalities, notice, **44:16.**

Books and lists, **59:29-59:37, 59:43-59:48, 59:50-59:52, 59:52B, 60:12.**

Abatements, records, **59:60.**

Appeal and review, **59:52B.**

TAX ASSESSORS —Cont'd
Books and lists —Cont'd
Assistance of assessors in making lists of persons from 3 to 21 years of age, **51:14A.**
Blank lists, furnishing, **59:30.**
Buildings, statements, **59:46.**
City or town to furnish, **59:45.**
Classification of estates and total valuation of each classification of property, **59:44, 59:46.**
Commissioner and department of revenue, approval of form of books, **59:45.**
Contents, **59:43, 59:44.**
Copies of law, books to contain, **59:50.**
Corporations, revenue department to furnish list, **58:2.**
Deposit for public inspection, **59:43.**
Diminished valuation, statement of cause of, penalty for neglect by assessor, **59:94.**
Directions to assessors in making lists, **59:46.**
District taxes, separate list and warrant, **59:53.**
Error in name, **60:21.**
Estimate of value in default of list, **59:36, 59:37.**
Exempt property, entry of, **59:51, 59:86.**
Form, **59:45.**
Furnishing of books, **59:45.**
Inspection.
Abatement record, **59:60.**
Deposit for public inspection, **59:43.**
Lists for taxation, **59:32.**
Real estate owners, public inspection of records of names and addresses, **184:8A.**
Warehouse records, **59:33.**
Instructions by commissioner, **58:5.**
Motorboats, snow vehicles, and recreation vehicles, registration lists to be furnished to assessors, **90B:11.**
Name in assessor's books, effect of error, **60:21.**
Nonresident property owners, **59:44.**
Notice of requirement of tax lists, **59:29.**
Payment of taxes prior to receipt of tax lists and warrants from assessors, **60:19.**

TAX ASSESSORS —Cont'd
Books and lists —Cont'd
Penalty for neglect of duty by assessor, **59:94.**
Persons subject to tax, lists, **59:29.**
Posting notices, **59:29, 60:88.**
Recreational lands, **61B:17.**
Registration lists of motorboats, snow vehicles and recreation vehicles, to be furnished, **90B:11.**
Rights to books and records, **59:60, 60:12.**
Table of aggregates, penalty for neglect of duty by assessor, **59:94.**
Valuation books and lists.
Diminished valuation, penalty for neglect as to statement of cause, **59:94.**
Estimate of value in default of list, **59:36, 59:37.**
Exempt property, entry of, **59:51, 59:86.**
Parcels of real estate, notice to give collector information as to valuation list, **60:22A.**
Statement of assessors, **59:52.**
Verification of tax lists, **59:31.**
Water wheels, description, **59:46.**
Borrowing within debt limit for appraisal of taxable property, **44:7.**
Boundary locations, delivery to land court department, **59:52A.**
Buildings.
Permits to erect, notice to assessors of issuance, **143:61.**
Statements, **59:46.**
Burned or dangerous buildings or other structures, enforcement of lien for expense for removal, **139:3A.**
Children and minors.
Lists of persons between 3 and 21 years of age, **51:14A.**
Cities and towns, **41:24 et seq., 59:20 et seq.**
City charters.
Administration of oath to assessors, **43:17.**
Removal of assessors by mayor, exemption, **43:54.**
Classification.
Books and lists of classification of estates and total valuation, **59:44, 59:46, 61B:17.**

TAX ASSESSORS —Cont'd
Classification —Cont'd
Corporations, time for filing objections to classification, **58:2.**
Forest lands, classification for taxation, **61:1.**
Recreational land, **61B:2-61B:8, 61B:14, 61B:17.**
Clerical or data processing error, time for taxation of property omitted through, **59:75, 59:76.**
Collector of taxes, **60:1 et seq., 62C:46 et seq.**
Abatement of taxes, notice to collector, **59:70A.**
Assessor not to hold office, **41:24.**
Invalid tax sale, collector to give notice, **60:46.**
Issuance of warrants for, **59:53-59:56.**
Records, **59:43, 59:60.**
Reports and returns, **60:2.**
Tax collectors.
See TAX COLLECTORS.
Warrants, **59:53-59:56.**
Commissioner and department of revenue.
Appointment, **41:27.**
Assistance to local assessors, **58:3.**
Blank forms provided, **58:1.**
Books, approval of form, **59:45.**
Corporate property and motor vehicles, assessor's report, **59:83.**
Correction of improper methods, **58:4.**
Delinquent taxes, reports to commissioner, **58:7.**
Estimates to local assessors, furnishing, **59:21.**
Exempt property, assessor's returns, **59:86.**
Information, **36:24B, 58:2, 58:3.**
Instructions to assessors, **58:1, 58:3, 58:5.**
List of corporations furnished, **58:2.**
Neglect of assessors, appointment of others in case, **59:27.**
Notices and lists of assessors, instructions, **58:5.**
Powers and duties, **58:1.**
Procedural manual for assessors, commissioner to prepare, **58:3.**
Property values and ownership, furnishing information, **58:3.**

TAX ASSESSORS —Cont'd
Commissioner and department of revenue —Cont'd
Prosecution of assessors, **58:1.**
Qualification standards, **58:1.**
Revision of assessment, time for filing for abatement of taxes, **59:59.**
State taxes, **59:20, 59:21, 59:26, 59:27.**
Supervision, **58:1.**
Taxable estate property, commissioner to furnish town assessors with information, **58:3.**
Training programs for local assessors, **58:1.**
Unknown persons, authority to assess taxes upon real property, **59:11.**
Unpaid taxes, reports, **58:7.**
Commitment of tax lists for collection, **59:53, 59:54.**
See TAX COLLECTORS.
Compensation, **41:22, 221:55.**
Complaints as to abatement, **59:64.**
Compromise of assessments to keep residence, proposals, **59:89.**
Construction of statutory references, **4:7.**
Contracts for preparation of assessment maps, **44:4.**
Corporations.
Abatement of taxes, notice, **59:74.**
Annual report as to property and motor vehicles, **59:83.**
Duties in assessment of, **58:2, 59:83.**
Fixed property and vehicles, statements to commissioner of assessed value, **59:83.**
Time for filing objections to classification, **58:2.**
Correction of improper methods by commissioner, **58:4.**
Costs and expenses.
dings, prepayment, **59:62.**
Appropriations for expenses of tax assessors, **41:108B.**
Group insurance for municipal employees, certification of costs to board of assessors, **32B:3.**
County taxes, duties with respect, **35:31.**
Debt limit of city or town, equalized valuation as determining, **44:10.**

TAX ASSESSORS —Cont'd
Deductions in determining amount of annual assessments, **59:23.**
Deferral and recovery agreements with respect to taxes of certain persons 65 years of age or over, **59:5.**
Defined for statutory construction purposes, **4:7.**
Delinquent taxes, reports to commissioner, **58:7, 59:20.**
Deposit of books and lists for public inspection, **59:43.**
Deputy assessors, automatic promotion, **30:46.**
Deputy tax collector, assessor prohibited from holding office, **41:24.**
Determination of tax rate, **59:21.**
Diminished valuation, penalty for neglect as to statement of cause, **59:94.**
Distress or imprisonment without demand, special warrant, **60:19.**
Distribution of taxes to cities and towns, duties, **58:25A.**
District tax matters, **59:21.**
Dwelling house masters to give information, **59:92.**
Education, training programs, **58:1.**
Elections.
Assessment pursuant to vote, responsibility, **59:87.**
Maps or descriptions of new voting precincts, aldermen to furnish copies to assessors, **54:5.**
Of assessors, **41:1, 41:20, 41:23.**
Eminent domain proceedings, valuation by assessor as evidence, **79:35.**
Enforcement of municipal finance provisions, **44:59.**
Equalized valuations for cities and town, notice, **58:10A.**
Estate taxes.
Bank deposit to defeat assessment, **65C:28.**
Classification of estates, **59:44, 59:46.**
Commission to furnish town assessors information, **58:3.**
Duplicate copy of notice, **65C:24.**
Information as to taxable estate property, assessors of taxes to be furnished, **58:3.**
Penalties for failure to comply with assessment provisions, **62C:26.**

TAX ASSESSORS —Cont'd
Estate taxes —Cont'd
Transferee's liability, **65C:14, 65C:15.**
Valuation, **59:44, 59:64, 65C:4, 65C:5.**
Examination, inspection, and investigation.
Books and lists, **59:32, 59:33, 59:43, 59:60, 184:8A.**
Municipal affairs, assessment of tax to pay expenses of investigating, **44:46A.**
Excise tax on ships and vessels, **59:8.**
Exempt property.
Entry on valuation list, **59:51.**
Returns, **59:86.**
Veterans' exemptions, **59:5.**
Expenses.
Abatement proceedings, prepayment, **59:62.**
Appropriations for expenses of tax assessors, **41:108B.**
Group insurance for municipal employees, certification of costs to board of assessors, **32B:3.**
Failure to choose, penalty, **41:4.**
False valuation by, penalty, **41:30.**
Fees for copies of abatement records, **59:60.**
Financial officers in cities and towns, notices, **59:23A, 59:23B, 59:70A.**
Fines and penalties.
Compromise of assessments to keep residence, making or assenting to proposal, **59:89.**
Corporate property and motor vehicles, assessor's failure to report, **59:83.**
Delinquent state taxes, assessment with respect, **59:20.**
Failure to choose assessors, **41:4.**
False valuation, **41:30.**
Forfeiture for failure to take oath, **41:29.**
Grantee of real estate, failure to furnish owner's name and address to assessor, **184:8A.**
Keepers of taverns, boardinghouses or dwelling houses failing to give information, **59:92.**
Neglect of duty, **59:93, 59:94.**
Storage warehouses failing to give information, **59:33.**
Fire districts.
Additional assessments, **59:25.**

TAX ASSESSORS —Cont'd
Fire districts —Cont'd
Amount of annual assessment, **59:23.**
Appropriation for compensation and expenses, **41:108B.**
Assessment of taxes, **59:21.**
Clerks, certification to assessors, **48:73.**
Overlay assessments, **59:25.**
Powers and duties with respect to, **48:73.**
Separate list and warrant for district taxes, **59:53.**
Fishing vessels, excise tax, **59:8.**
Foreclosure of tax title held by city or town.
Assessment for cost, **60:50B.**
Notice, **60:76C.**
Forest lands and products tax, duties, **61:1-61:6.**
Forms.
Books, **59:45.**
Commissioner of revenue, blank forms provided, **58:1.**
Valuation lists, assessors' statement, **59:52.**
Warrants for collection, **59:55.**
Gas and electric bills collected, **164:58D, 164:58E.**
Group insurance for municipal employees, cost certified to assessors, **32B:3.**
Health districts, assessment of taxes, **59:21.**
Horticultural uses, **61A:6, 61A:9, 61A:14, 61A:19, 61A:19A.**
Imprisonment or distress without demand, special warrant, **60:19.**
Improvement districts, **59:21, 59:25.**
Separate list and warrant for district taxes, **59:53.**
Improvement of lowlands and swamps, duties, **252:11.**
Inclusion of state, county, and town taxes in one assessment, **59:26.**
Incompatible offices, assessors and collectors, **41:24.**
Inspection and investigation.
Books and lists, **59:32, 59:33, 59:43, 59:60, 184:8A.**
Municipal affairs, assessment of tax to pay expenses of investigating, **44:46A.**
Insurance, certification to assessors of cost of group insurance for municipal employees, **32B:3.**

TAX ASSESSORS —Cont'd
Interest on deferred taxes, **59:5, 83:16G.**
Invalid tax sale, collector to give notice, **60:46.**
Land court department, delivery of real property boundary locations, **59:52A.**
Lands acquired by town by purchase or gift, abatement of taxes, **59:72A.**
Legal counsel, employment, **41:26A.**
Legal opinions on local property assessment, **58:1A.**
Liens on agricultural and horticultural land, powers and duties with respect, **61A:9.**
Light districts, assessment of taxes, **59:21.**
Separate list and warrant for district taxes, **59:53.**
Limits on local government taxes, increases in real property tax rate, **59:21C.**
Lists, **59:29-59:37, 59:43-59:48, 59:50-59:52, 59:52B, 60:12.**
Local aid fund, notice of amounts due to cities and towns, **58:25A.**
Loss or destruction of warrant for collection, issuance of new warrant, **59:56.**
Lowlands and swamps, duties in connection with improvement, **252:11.**
Mandamus to enforce municipal finance provisions, **44:59.**
Maps for assessment purposes, **40:4.**
Borrowing within debt limit, **44:7.**
Contracts for preparation, **44:4.**
Mortgagors or mortgagees to make statements, **59:34.**
Municipal corporations in general, **41:24 et seq., 59:20 et seq.**
Names.
Books and lists, error in name, **60:21.**
Failure to furnish assessor with name and address of grantee of real estate, **184:8A.**
Records or property owners' names and addresses, assessors to maintain, **184:8A.**
Neglect of duties, **59:93, 59:94.**
Appointment of others in case, **59:27.**

TAX ASSESSORS —Cont'd
Neglect of duties —Cont'd
Corporate property and motor vehicles, failure to report, **59:83.**
News and reference bulletins, **58:3.**
Nonresident owners, listing valuation and assessment of property, **59:44.**
Notice.
Abatement of taxes, **59:63.**
Agricultural and horticultural uses, notice to assessor of land claimed, **61A:6.**
Annual instructions of commissioner as to notices and lists, **58:5.**
Assessment of taxes, **59:23A, 59:29.**
Bond issues of municipalities, **44:16.**
Books and lists, **59:29, 60:88.**
Building permits issued, notice to assessors, **143:61.**
Equalized valuations for cities and towns, **58:10A.**
Financial officers in cities and town, notices, **59:23A, 59:23B, 59:70A.**
Foreclosure or assignment of tax title held by city or town, notice, **60:76C.**
Invalid tax sale, collector to give notice, **60:46.**
Lists of persons subject to tax, **59:29.**
Local aid fund, notice of amounts due cities and towns, **58:25A.**
Persons appearing upon assessor's recent valuation list when alcoholic liquor license application for transfer is sought, notice, **138:15A.**
Proposed equalized valuations for cities and towns, **58:10A.**
Public lands, valuation, **58:14.**
Receipts of cities and towns, **41:54A.**
Sewer charges, deferral notice, **83:16G.**
Tax lists, notice of requirement, **59:29.**
Tax rate, notice to local officers, **59:23A.**
Total local receipts, annual notice to assessors, **41:54A.**
Treasurers of cities and towns.
Abatements, **59:23A, 59:23B, 59:70A.**

TAX ASSESSORS —Cont'd
Notice —Cont'd
Treasurers of cities and towns
—Cont'd
Amount and rate of taxes,
59:23A, 59:23B.
Annual receipts, **41:54A.**
Tax titles, **60:76C.**
Valuation list of parcels of real
estate, notice to give
collector information,
60:22A.
Water charges, deferral notice,
40:42J.
Number in each city or town,
41:24.
Oaths and affirmation, **41:29,
43:17.**
Older person, deferral and
recovery provisions with
respect to taxes, **59:5.**
Omitted or unassessed property.
Liability of town for, **59:28.**
Warrant for assessment on,
59:75.
Organization of boards, **41:24.**
Overlay account, additional
assessments, **59:25.**
Owner of real estate.
Commissioner furnishing
information as to property
values and ownership, **58:3.**
Information, owner or lessee's
failure to submit, **59:38D.**
Lessee or owner of real property
failing to submit
information, **59:38D.**
Procurement of name and
address, **184:8A.**
Parcels of real estate, notice to
give collector information as to
valuation list, **60:22A.**
Pipelines.
Assessed to owner, **59:3C, 59:83.**
Corporations, assessment of
taxes, **59:83.**
Valuation, **59:38A.**
Preliminary taxes, **59:57C.**
Probate courts, local property
assessment, **59:12B.**
Procedural manual for, revenue
commissioner to prepare, **58:3.**
Process, **223:37.**
Professional association, additional
compensation for tax assessor
certificated, **59:21A.**
Promotion of deputy assessors,
30:46.
Public lands.
Appeal from valuation, **58:14.**
Assessment, **58:17A.**

TAX ASSESSORS —Cont'd
Public lands —Cont'd
Notice as to valuation, **58:14.**
Qualification standards of revenue
commissioner, **58:1.**
Railroad aid, assessment, **59:24.**
Rate of tax.
Change, **59:23.**
Determination, **59:21, 59:23.**
Distribution of estimate of
among towns, **58:25A.**
Factors to be considered in
setting, **59:23.**
Notice to financial officers of
municipalities, **59:23A,
59:23B.**
Receipts of cities and towns.
Annual notice, **41:54A.**
Setting annual tax rate, receipts
used by assessors, **59:23.**
Records, **59:43-59:48, 59:50-59:52.**
Abatement of taxes, records,
59:60.
Books and lists, **59:29-59:37,
59:43-59:48, 59:50-59:52,
59:52B, 60:12.**
Commissioner of revenue to
record deed to real property,
information determined,
36:24B.
Owners of real estate, tax
assessors to maintain
records of names and
addresses, **184:8A.**
Registers of deeds to furnish
abstract cards or copies of
records to tax assessors,
36:24B.
Warehouse records, right to
inspect, **59:33.**
Recreational land, classification for
tax purposes.
Abatement of tax, notice of
application, **61B:14.**
Change in use of land, **61B:4.**
Purchaser of land, affidavits,
61B:7.
Registry of deeds, change of
record of ownership of land,
61B:6.
Revaluation of property,
abatement of tax, **61B:5.**
Roll-back of taxes,
determination, **61B:8.**
Tax list, **61B:17.**
Valuation of land, **61B:2, 61B:3.**
Redemption of tax title held by
city or town, notice, **60:76C.**
Registration of land titles.
Abstract cards or copies of
records furnished, **36:24B,
61B:6.**

TAX ASSESSORS —Cont'd
Registration of land titles —Cont'd
Assessed valuation as
controlling for purposes of
assurance fund, **185:109.**
Betterments as affected, **185:46.**
Removal.
Appointees of selectmen, **41:25.**
Assistant assessors, **41:25A.**
City charters, exemption from
removal of assessor by
mayor, **43:54.**
Reports.
Boardinghouse keepers, **59:92.**
Corporate property and motor
vehicles, **59:83.**
Delinquent taxes, reports, **58:7.**
Dwelling house masters and
mistresses, **59:92.**
Inspection by officials of
Commonwealth, **59:52B.**
Tavern keepers, **59:92.**
Reserve fund for balance of overlay
account, **59:25.**
Responsibility, **59:87.**
Retirement systems of
municipalities, assessment of
tax for supervision expenses,
32:21.
Returns.
Collectors, **60:2.**
Exempt property, **59:86.**
Fair cash value of property,
return containing
information, **59:38F,
59:38G.**
Inspection by officials of
Commonwealth, **59:52B.**
Pipeline owners, **59:38A.**
Sworn, written returns,
submission to assessors,
59:38D, 59:38E.
Telephone and telegraph lines
and equipment, informing
commission concerning,
59:41.
Revenue department, **58:1.**
Revision of assessment, time for
filing for abatement of taxes,
59:59.
Ripeness.
Finality of judgment where
board of assessors takes no
action, **58A:6.**
Roll-back of taxes on recreational
property, determinations,
61B:8.
Salary or compensation, **41:22,
221:55.**
Appropriations, **41:108B.**
Assistant assessors, **41:25A.**

TAX ASSESSORS —Cont'd
Salary or compensation —Cont'd
City and town assessors,
59:21A½.
Commissioner of revenue,
appointees, **41:27.**
District taxes, assessors,
41:108B.
Professional association,
additional compensation for
tax assessor certificated,
59:21A.
Selectmen, appointment or election
of assessors, **41:20-41:27.**
Service of process, **223:37.**
Sewer charges, notice of deferral,
83:16G.
Sheriff, posting of warrants, **60:88.**
Ships and vessels, excise tax, **59:8,
60B:2, 60B:4.**
Single assessment, inclusion of
state, county, and town taxes,
59:26.
Special assessments, duties
regarding, **80:13.**
Sprinkling of streets, assessments,
40:17, 40:18.
State taxes.
Duties with respect, **59:20,
59:21.**
Excessive assessment, **59:21.**
Inclusion of state, county, and
town taxes in one
assessment, **59:26.**
Neglect of assessors,
appointment of others in
case, **59:27.**
Underestimate of assessments,
59:21.
State treasurer, warrants, **59:20.**
Storage warehouses to give
information, **59:33.**
Suffolk County assessors, register
of deeds required to furnish
certain information, **36:24B.**
Supervision of tax commissioner
over, **58:1.**
Tavern keepers to give
information, **59:92.**
Tax collectors.
Collector of taxes. See within
this heading, "Collector of
taxes."
Tax title held by city or town.
Assignment, **60:76C.**
Foreclosure, **60:50B, 60:76C.**
Redemption, **60:76C.**
Telephone and telegraph
companies, duties as to
valuation of machinery, poles,
wires, etc., **59:39, 59:40.**

TAX ASSESSORS —Cont'd
Term of office, **41:1, 41:22, 41:24,
41:25.**
Assistant assessors, **41:25A.**
Title to property.
Owner of real estate. See within
this heading, "Owner of real
estate."
Registration of land titles. See
within this heading,
"Registration of land titles."
Tax title. See within this
heading, "Tax title held by
city or town."
Training programs.
Attendance at required, **59:21A.**
Authority of revenue
commissioner, **58:1.**
Treasurers of cities and towns,
44:16.
Abatements, notice, **59:23A,
59:23B, 59:70A.**
Amount and rate of taxes,
notice, **59:23A, 59:23B.**
Annual receipts, notice, **41:54A.**
Tax titles, notice pertaining,
60:76C.
Warrant of town treasurer,
60:90.
Unassessed property.
Liability of town, **59:28.**
Warrant for assessment, **59:75.**
Uncollectible taxes, abatement,
58:8, 59:71.
Unpaid taxes, reports, **58:7.**
Vacancy not to affect powers of
remaining assessors, **41:30A.**
Valuation of property, **58:1A,
59:38-59:42.**
Appeals, **58:14, 59:38.**
Board of assessors, **59:38F,
59:38G.**
Books and lists.
Diminished valuation, penalty
for neglect as to statement
of cause, **59:94.**
Estimate of value in default of
list, **59:36, 59:37.**
Exempt property, entry of,
59:51, 59:86.
Parcels of real estate, notice to
give collector information
as to valuation list,
60:22A.
Statement of assessors, **59:52.**
Borrowing within debt limit for
appraisal of taxable
property, **44:7.**
Contracting for appraisal, **40:4.**
Duty of assessors, **59:38.**
Eminent domain proceedings,
assessor's valuation as
evidence, **79:35.**

TAX ASSESSORS —Cont'd
Valuation of property —Cont'd
Equalized valuations for cities
and towns, notice, **58:10A.**
False valuation, **41:30.**
Pipelines, **59:38A.**
Public lands, **58:14.**
Recreational land, **61B:2, 61B:3,
61B:5.**
Returns, **59:38F, 59:38G,
59:52B.**
Revaluation of recreational
lands, abatement of tax,
61B:5.
Statement of assessors on
valuation list, **59:52.**
Telephone and telegraph
companies, property, **59:39,
59:40.**
Verification of tax lists, **59:31.**
Veterans' tax exemptions, duties,
59:5.
Visitation, **58:3.**
Warehouses to give information,
59:33.
Warrants.
Assessment of state taxes, **59:20.**
Collection warrants, issuance,
59:53-59:56.
Form and contents, **59:55.**
New warrant upon loss or
destruction of original,
59:56.
District taxes, separate list and
warrant, **59:53.**
Omitted property, assessments,
59:75.
Payments of taxes prior to
receipt of warrants from
assessors, acceptance, **60:19.**
Posting by sheriff, **60:88.**
Special warrant for distress or
imprisonment without
demand, **60:19.**
State treasurer, warrants, **59:20.**
Town treasurer's warrant, **60:90.**
Water charges, notice of deferral,
40:42J.
Water districts, assessment of
taxes, **59:21, 59:25.**
Separate list and warrant for
district taxes, **59:53.**
Water wheels, descriptions, **59:46.**
Zoning and planning.
Certification of parties in
interest, **40A:11.**
Plans of assessors as basis for
district maps, **40A:4.**

TAXATION, 58:1 et seq.
Abandoned property.
Abatement of taxes, **58:8.**

TAXATION —Cont'd

Abandoned property —Cont'd

Determination of claims against surrendered property, **200A:10.**

Abatement of penalty attributable to written advice of revenue department employee, **62C:36B.**

Abatement of taxes, **59:59-59:74, 62C:37-62C:43.**

Abandoned real property, **58:8.**

Absence of taxpayer, **59:71.**

Addition of subsequent taxes as affecting, **59:65A.**

Amount of annual assessment as affected, **59:23.**

Amount of tax as affecting abatement of local assessments, **59:64.**

Amounts under one dollar, refunds, **59:58A.**

Animals on farm, excise tax, **59:8A.**

Appeals, **62C:39.**

Appellate tax board, appeals to, **58:13, 59:64, 59:65, 62C:39.**

Assessed valuation of property, **58A:12D.**

Commission's refusal to abate tax, **62C:39.**

Costs, **59:64.**

County commissioners appeals, **59:64.**

Damages for improper assessment, **58A:14.**

Insufficient payment on account of taxes as affecting, **59:65D.**

Jurisdiction, **62C:39.**

Late entry, **59:65C.**

Public transportation corporations, abatement of local taxes assessed against, **59:64 (note), 59:65.**

Real estate tax, **59:65B.**

Telephone or telegraph companies, appeals, **59:39.**

Time to appeal, **59:64, 59:65C.**

Transfer from county commissioners to appellate tax board, **59:64.**

Appellate tax board.

Applications, **59:59, 62C:37.**

Date of delivery, **59:59.**

Notice of application to board of assessors, **61B:14.**

Open to inspection of assessors, etc., **59:60.**

TAXATION —Cont'd

Abatement of taxes —Cont'd

Applications —Cont'd

Revenue department and commissioner.

Form of application, approval, **59:59.**

Statement of processing procedures, **14:6.**

Assessment.

Appeals of assessed valuation, **58A:12D, 58A:14.**

Effect of abatement on annual assessment amount, **59:23, 59:64, 59:65B.**

Special assessments, **80:5-80:10A.**

See SPECIAL ASSESSMENTS.

Value of land insufficient to pay collection charges, **59:72.**

Assessors, **59:38G.**

See TAX ASSESSORS.

Bad checks, penalty for tendering, **60:57A.**

Blind person's realty, abatement of tax, **59:5.**

Certificate of abatement, **59:70, 60:20.**

Charitable corporations and trusts, abatement of taxes, **59:5.**

Cigarette tax, **64C:6.**

Cities and towns, **59:64, 59:72A.**

Abatement of unpaid taxes on lands acquired by purchase or gift, **59:72A.**

Election by town as to hearing by appellate tax board on abatement, **59:64.**

Lands acquired by town other than eminent domain, **59:72A.**

Light board, petitions for abatement filed, **164:58F.**

Notice, **59:23B, 59:70A.**

Treasurers.

Notice, **59:23B, 59:70A.**

Collection fees as affected, **60:20.**

Collectors.

Assessors, records furnished, **59:60.**

Books and records, **60:7.**

Certificates of abatement, exhibition to collector, **60:20.**

Clerical error, **58:8.**

Credit for sums abated, **60:95.**

Fees for collection as affected, **60:20.**

TAXATION —Cont'd

Abatement of taxes —Cont'd

Collectors —Cont'd

Mistake, **58:8.**

Notice, **59:70A.**

Uncollectible taxes, **59:71.**

Complaint upon refusal, **59:64.**

Conditions, **59:61.**

Corporation taxes.

Manufacturing corporations, provisions applicable to, **63:38C, 63:42B.**

Costs in proceedings, **59:62, 59:64.**

Appellate proceedings, **59:64.**

Prepayment required, **59:62.**

County commissioners.

Appeals, **59:64.**

Certificate, **59:70.**

Death of taxpayer as cause, **59:71.**

Deed and document stamp tax, abatement for erroneous payment of tax, **64D:4.**

Delinquent taxes, abatement, **58:8.**

Discovery in proceedings, **59:60, 59:61A.**

Display of abatement certificate, **60:20.**

Distribution of taxes as affected, **58:25.**

Election of town as to hearing by appellate tax board on abatement proceedings, **59:64.**

Entry on tax title account, **59:70A.**

Excuse for delay, **59:61, 59:64.**

Executors or administrators, application, **59:59.**

Exhibition or viewing of property, **59:61A.**

Extension of time, **59:5 (note), 80:6.**

Failure of assessors to act, **59:64.**

Failure to list personal estate, **59:5.**

Farm animals, excise tax, **59:8A.**

Federal court, existence of statutory remedies as affecting right of action, **62C:41.**

Fees for collection as affected, **60:20.**

Filing, **59:59.**

Special assessments, extension of time for filing petition for abatement, **80:6.**

Veterans and dependents, **59:5.**

TAXATION —Cont'd
Abatement of taxes —Cont'd
Forbidden or limited in certain cases, **62C:38.**
Forest lands and products, abatement of taxes, **61:2.**
Form for application, **59:59, 62C:37.**
Houses of worship, eligibility for property tax exemption and application for abatement, **59:5.**
Inability to pay as condition to appeal from denial, **59:65B.**
Income tax.
Additional tax as penalty for failure to file return on time, **62C:33, 62C:34.**
Appeal and review, **62C:39.**
Federal court action for abatement, statutory remedies as affecting right, **62C:41.**
Filing return prior to application for abatement, **62C:38.**
Forms, application for abatement, **62C:37.**
Refunds, **62C:36, 62C:40.**
Insolvency as cause, **59:71.**
Inspection and discovery, **59:60, 59:61A.**
Interest allowed, **59:64, 59:65B, 59:69, 61:2, 62C:36, 62C:40, 62C:69.**
Motor vehicle excise tax, **60A:2.**
On unpaid taxes, **58:8.**
Lands acquired by town other than by eminent domain, **59:72A.**
Late entry of appeals in certain cases, **59:65C.**
Legacy and succession taxes, **65:27, 65:27A.**
See LEGACY AND SUCCESSION TAXES.
Lists of property, requirements with respect, **59:61, 59:64.**
Mistake.
Insufficient payments due to mistake, **59:65D.**
Late appeal, **59:65C.**
Tax collectors, **58:8.**
More than one thousand dollars on real estate, appeal from refusal to abate tax, **59:65B.**
Mortgaged realty, application with respect, **59:59.**
Motor vehicle excise tax, abatement, **60A:1, 60A:2.**

TAXATION —Cont'd
Abatement of taxes —Cont'd
Municipal corporations.
Cities and towns. See within this heading, "City and town auditors."
Notice, **59:70A, 59:74.**
Assessors.
Applicant, notice of decision, **59:63.**
Application for abatement, notice, **61B:14.**
Collector, notice, **59:70A.**
Corporations, **59:74.**
Municipal financial officers, notice, **59:23A, 59:23B, 59:70A.**
Telephone or telegraph companies, applications for abatement, **59:39.**
Collectors and other officers, notice, **59:70A.**
Corporations liable to franchise tax, notice, **59:74.**
Decision in abatement proceedings, **59:63, 62C:37.**
Municipal financial officers, notice, **59:23B, 59:70A.**
Telephone or telegraph companies, application for abatement, **59:39, 59:74.**
Old persons, application, **59:5.**
Omitted assessments, application with respect, **59:59.**
Overlay of tax.
Abatement chargeable against, **59:70A.**
Assessment, **59:25.**
Reserve funds for balance of overlay account, **59:25.**
Overpayments, exceptions, **62C:40.**
Payment of taxes.
Assessed value insufficient to pay collection charges, **59:72.**
Exceptions as to overpayments, **62C:40.**
Inability to pay as condition to appeal from denial of abatement, **59:65B.**
Insufficient payment because of mistake, **59:65D.**
Necessity of, to obtain review of decision, **59:64.**
Poverty as basis for abatement, **59:71.**
Penalty for false valuation by assessor, **41:30.**

TAXATION —Cont'd
Abatement of taxes —Cont'd
Personal property.
Failure to file list, **59:5, 59:61.**
Inability to pay tax, **59:71.**
Record, **59:60.**
Restrictions, **59:61.**
Poverty as cause, **59:71.**
Private auditors, abatement proceedings open, **59:60.**
Probate courts, **62C:39.**
Procedure after abatement, **59:70A.**
Proceedings for, **62C:37.**
Property tax exemption eligibility and application for abatement of taxes, **59:5.**
Public transportation corporations, appeal for abatement of local taxes assessed against, **59:64 (note), 59:65 (note).**
Reassessment of taxes, abatement, **59:59.**
Records, **59:60.**
Collectors, furnished, **59:60.**
Entries upon abatement by reviewing board, **59:70A.**
Filing, **59:5, 59:59, 80:6.**
Land valuation insufficient to pay collection charges, authorization of abatement in case, **59:72.**
Right to inspect, **59:60.**
Recreational lands.
Notice of application, **61B:14.**
Revaluation of land, **61B:5.**
Refund of abated taxes, **59:58A, 59:69, 62C:36, 62C:40.**
Reimbursement, **59:69.**
Release of oil or hazardous materials, **59:59A.**
Reserve funds for balance of overlay account, **59:25.**
Residential land, change in use, **61B:5.**
Restrictions as to personal property tax, **59:61.**
Return as prerequisite, **62C:38.**
Revenue department and commissioner, **62C:37.**
See REVENUE DEPARTMENT AND COMMISSIONER.
Room occupancy excise paid on worthless accounts, **64G:7A.**
Rounding off to whole numbers, **62C:4.**
Sale for taxes as affecting, **59:65A.**
Senior citizens, **59:5.**

TAXATION —Cont'd

Abatement of taxes —Cont'd

Sewer charges, **83:16E.**

Ships in interstate or foreign trade, **59:8, 60B:2.**

Small amounts due, **62C:43.**

Special assessments, **80:5-10A.** See SPECIAL ASSESSMENTS.

Stamps, penalty for failure to affix, **64D:6A.**

State treasurer, refund, **62C:40.**

Street sprinkling assessments, **40:18.**

Supreme judicial court, order on appeal, **58A:13.**

Taking of land for nonpayment of taxes, **59:65A.**

Telegraph and telephone companies, appeal, **59:39.**

Tenant's application, **59:59.**

Time limitation.

Appeal, **59:59, 59:64, 59:65C, 62C:39.**

Application for abatement, **59:59, 62C:37.**

Excuse for delay, **59:61, 59:64.**

Extension, **59:5. (note)**

Treasurers of cities and towns. Notice, **59:23B, 59:70A.**

Trustees, application, **59:59.**

Uncollected or uncollectible taxes, abatement, **58:8, 59:71, 62:42, 62C:42.**

Unpaid property tax bills, **60:2.**

Use of residential land, change, **61B:5.**

Valuation of property, **59:38F, 59:38G.**

Veterans and dependents, filing for abatement, **59:5.**

Water rate added to tax bill, **40:42E.**

Withholding tax on wages, effect of abatement, **62C:37.**

Absence of taxpayer.

Abatement of taxes uncollectible on account, **59:71.**

Estate, **200:13.**

Inheritance taxes paid out of absentee's estate, **200:13.**

Abstract cards and records furnished to assessors, **36:24B.**

Accountants.

Service defined for tax purposes, **6HA:1, 64I:1.**

Accounts and accounting.

Cigarette tax, examination of retailers by commissioner, **64C:11.**

TAXATION —Cont'd

Accounts and accounting —Cont'd

Director of accounts, duties as to local assessments, **59:23.**

Exemption of personal property used in accounting function, **59:5.**

Income tax.

Income tax division, audit of accounts, **11:12.**

Individual retirement account, **62:2, 62:5.**

Method required, **62:62.**

Refunds credited directly to bank accounts, **62C:36.**

Overlay tax account, **59:25.**

Tax collectors, **60:2, 60:8, 60:15, 60:94, 60:97-60:102.**

Tax title account, **60:50.** See TAX DEEDS AND TITLES.

Treasurer of city accounting for tax redemption money, **60:63.**

Withholding tax on wages, use of accounting machines to calculate, **62B:2.**

Additional property, levy against, **62C:53.**

Additional tax.

Abatement, addition of subsequent taxes as affecting, **59:65A.**

Declarations of corporate estimated income tax, **62B:14.**

Assessment and collection, **63B:10.**

Fractional divisions, addition to tax to avoid, **59:25.**

Income taxes.

Assessment, **62C:26.**

Campaign financing, voluntary additional tax, **62:6C.**

Decedents' estates, **62C:30.**

Declarations of estimated income tax, **62B:14, 63B:10.**

Penalty for failure to file tax on time, **62C:33, 62C:34.**

Legacy and succession taxes, **65:27.**

Federal estate tax laws, additional tax upon change in laws, **65A:6.**

State activities, additional taxes for support, **65:1.**

Local taxes, assessment, **59:25.**

Adjournment of sale of personal property, notice, **60:26.**

TAXATION —Cont'd

Administration and finance executive office.

Appellate tax board, **7:4G.**

Revenue department, **7:4A, 14:2.**

Special examination of state finance for appropriations to be met by assessment of taxes, **7:9-7:11.**

Administration of taxes, **62C:1 et seq.**

Administrative function, exemption of personal property used, **59:5.**

Administrative policy statement, **14:1.**

Administrative procedure law, applicability, **30A:1.**

Adoption of charter by city as affecting existing taxes, **43:24.**

Adoption of children.

Exemption for children of deceased police officers or firefighters, **59:5.**

Income tax deduction for fees of agency, **62:3.**

Legacy and succession taxes of adopted persons their heirs and beneficiaries, **65:1.**

Advertising.

Bonds and notes of Commonwealth, information regarding tax consequences to social security recipients, **29:48B, 44:22B.**

Collection notices, **60:1.**

Sale of low value land held by municipality under tax title, **60:79.**

Sales taxes.

Assumption or absorption of tax by vendor, advertising of, **64H:23.**

Exclusion of advertising agents from tax on persons furnishing information, **64H:1.**

Promoters of show, **62C:1, 62C:8A, 62C:34, 62C:67A.**

Service defined for tax purposes, **64H:1, 64I:1.**

Tax sales, **60:40.**

Demand for payment as affecting time for, **60:39.**

Low value land held by municipality, **60:79.**

Use, consumption, or storage tax, unlawful advertising, **64I:24.**

TAXATION —Cont'd
Affidavits.
Agricultural and horticultural property.
Agricultural or horticultural use affidavit to be filed upon conveyance of land, **61A:12.**
Municipality's notice of intent to exercise purchase option, **61A:14.**
Assessment of preliminary taxes, affidavit of name and address of owner of property to be included with notice, **59:57D.**
Collector of taxes, affidavit of, **60:1, 60:57.**
Notice to holder of invalid tax title, recording of affidavit, **60:83.**
Religious societies and parishes, posting notice of sale of pews for nonpayment of taxes, **67:32.**
Sale for taxes, effect as prima facie evidence of affidavit, **60:57.**
Tax collectors.
Evidence of demand, affidavit as notice and service, **60:1, 60:57.**
Sale, effect of affidavit, **60:57.**
Tax deeds and titles.
Invalid tax title, affidavit of notice to holder, **60:83.**
Low value of land held by city or town under tax title, affidavit of value, **60:79.**
Aged persons.
Older persons. See within this heading, "Older persons."
Agreements.
Appraisal, **40:4, 44:7, 58:1A.**
Installment payments, written agreement with taxpayer, **62C:37B.**
Agricultural and horticultural property, **61A:1-61A:24.**
Affidavit.
Agricultural or horticultural use affidavit to be filed upon conveyance of land, **61A:12.**
Municipality's notice of intent to exercise purchase option, **61A:14.**
Agricultural societies, loss of real property exemption, **59:5.**
Agricultural use defined, **61A:1.**

TAXATION —Cont'd
Agricultural and horticultural property —Cont'd
Aid to agriculture, levy, **128:44.**
Animals, excise tax, **59:8A.**
Appellate tax board, appeal of board of assessors' determinations, **61A:19.**
Assessors, **61A:6, 61A:9, 61A:14, 61A:19, 61A:19A.**
Associations and societies, property, **59:5, 63:31A.**
Betterment assessments, basis for application, **61A:18.**
Buildings, basis for taxation, **61A:15.**
Certificate of roll-back or conveyance taxes due or paid, **61A:19A.**
Change in use of land, effect on assessment of land, **61A:6, 61A:7.**
Cities and towns, first option on land to be sold and converted, **61A:14.**
Classification, **61A:4.**
Collection of taxes, **61A:12, 61A:19.**
Contiguous land, what constitutes, **61A:4, 61A:5.**
Continuation of tax benefits based exclusively on use rather than ownership, **61A:16.**
Conveyance taxes.
Appeal, payment as prerequisite, **61A:19.**
Certificate of amount, application, **61A:19A.**
Death, tax applicable, **61A:9.**
Exemption, **61A:12.**
Liens, **61A:9.**
Unpaid taxes, collection, **61A:12.**
Co-operative corporations and associations, **157:7.**
Credit, carrying over portion of excise tax credit, **63:31A.**
Demand for payment prior to distress of stock or produce on land, **60:27.**
Details shown by tax lists for agricultural and horticultural lands, **61A:21.**
Disallowance of application for assessment of property for agricultural or horticultural uses, **61A:9.**
Eligibility of land, determination, **61A:6.**

TAXATION —Cont'd
Agricultural and horticultural property —Cont'd
Equipment and machinery, **59:5, 59:8A.**
Exemption, **59:5, 59:8A, 60:24.**
Sales tax, **64H:6, 64H:26, 64I:27.**
Estate taxes, **65C:5, 65C:14.**
Evasion of payment, penalty, **61A:23.**
Excise tax.
Animals owned by minors, taxation, **59:8A.**
Carrying over portion of excise tax credit, **63:31A.**
Machinery and equipment, **59:5, 59:8A.**
Exemptions, **59:5, 59:8A, 60:24.**
Chapter 59 provisions, effect of exemption, **61A:20.**
Conveyance tax, **61A:12.**
Equipment and machinery, **59:5, 59:8A, 60:24, 64H:6, 64I:27.**
Sales tax, **64H:6.**
Farm land valuation advisory commission, **61A:11.**
Fee for certificate of taxes due or paid, **61A:19A.**
Forest products, raising as horticultural use, **61A:2.**
Form of notice of municipality's intent to exercise purchase option, **61A:14.**
Horticultural use defined for taxation purposes, **61A:2.**
Incentive areas, assessments, **40L:5, 40L:7.**
Income tax, declaration of estimated tax, **62B:14.**
Indicia for use in valuing land, **61A:10.**
Interest on reimbursement of overpaid taxes, **61A:19.**
Leased land, **61A:6.**
Liens, **61A:9.**
Certificate of taxes paid or due as terminating lien, **61A:19A.**
Warrant for levy on stock or produce, **60:27.**
Limitation on allowance or disallowance of application for valuation, assessment, and taxation, **61A:9.**
Machinery, **59:5, 59:8A.**
Exemption, **59:5, 59:8A, 60:24.**
Sales tax, **64H:6, 64H:26, 64I:27.**
Modification of roll-back taxes, application, **61A:19.**

TAXATION —Cont'd
Agricultural and horticultural
property —Cont'd
Mortgage foreclosure sales.
Exemption from conveyance
tax, **61A:12.**
Subject to municipality's
option to purchase,
61A:14.
Notary public's affidavit of
municipality's notice of
intent to exercise purchase
option, **61A:14.**
Organizations dealing with
agriculture and horticulture,
59:5, 63:31A.
Overpayment, reimbursement on
account, **61A:19.**
Partial payment, authorized
amount, **61A:19.**
Payment of tax as prerequisite
to appeal, **61A:19.**
Perfection of lien, **61A:9.**
Preservation restrictions,
132A:11D.
Presumptions.
Allowance of application for
valuation, assessment,
and taxation, **61A:9.**
Date of acquisition of property
for purpose of conveyance
tax, **61A:12.**
Notice of intent to exercise
purchase option, **61A:14.**
Use, board of assessor's
certificate, **61A:14.**
Qualification.
Actual use as determinative,
61A:16.
Certificate of taxes due or paid
as affected by
termination, **61A:19A.**
Real property, **61A:1-61A:24.**
Recording.
Certificate of roll-back taxes or
conveyance taxes due,
61A:19A.
Notice of municipality's intent
to exercise purchase
option, **61A:14.**
Redemption from sale for
nonpayment of conveyance
taxes, **61A:12.**
Reimbursement on account of
overpaid taxes, **61A:19.**
Release of lien, **61A:9.**
Residential use of agricultural or
horticultural land as
constituting conversion of
use, **61A:14.**

TAXATION —Cont'd
Agricultural and horticultural
property —Cont'd
Revaluation by city or town of
all property prior to final
date for filing application for
reassessment, **61A:8.**
Revenue department and
commissioner.
Annual determinations of
eligibility, approval by
commissioner of
application form, **61A:6.**
Equalization, valuation by
commissioner, **61A:20.**
Excise on certain farm
machinery, animals, fowl,
determination by
commissioner of revenue,
59:8A.
Farmland valuation advisory
commission, membership
and duties, **61A:11.**
Rules and regulations,
promulgation by
commissioner, **61A:22.**
Roll-back taxes.
Bases for assessment,
collection, and payment,
61A:19.
Certificate of amount,
application, **61A:19A.**
Lands no longer qualified for
privileged uses, **61A:13.**
Modification or abatement,
application, **61A:19.**
Qualification of land as
dependent upon actual
use, **61A:16.**
Sale of equipment, machinery,
and materials, exemption
from tax, **64H:6.**
Sale of land.
Agricultural or horticultural
uses, effect on tax rate of
sale for other than,
61A:12.
Notification of city of sale or
conversion to
nonagricultural use,
61A:14.
Tax sales, **61A:12.**
Animals, distress and sale,
60:24, 60:27.
City or town, option to
purchase on notification
of sale or conversion to
nonagricultural use,
61A:14.
Produce, **60:27.**
Stay pending appeal,
61A:19.

TAXATION —Cont'd
Agricultural and horticultural
property —Cont'd
Separation from agricultural
use, **61A:17.**
Societies, tax exemption of
property of agricultural
societies, **59:5.**
Special or betterment
assessments, **40L:7, 61A:9,
61A:18.**
Standing to apply for
modification or abatement of
roll-back taxes, **61A:19.**
Stay of collection pending
appeal, **61A:19.**
Tax collectors.
Stay of collection pending
appeal, **61A:19.**
Unpaid conveyance taxes,
61A:12.
Tax liens, **61A:9.**
Certificate of taxes paid or due
as terminating lien,
61A:19A.
Warrant for levy on stock or
produce, **60:27.**
Termination of valuation as
agricultural or horticultural
land, filing of statement,
61A:9.
Test for determining whether
land devoted to agricultural
use, **61A:3, 61A:4.**
Town treasury to receive fee for
certificate of taxes due or
paid, **61A:19A.**
Unpaid conveyance taxes,
collection, **61A:12.**
Valuation, **61A:4, 61A:9.**
Estate taxes, dates, **65C:5.**
Farm land valuation advisory
commission, **61A:11.**
General property tax
purposes, criteria for
determination of value of
land, **61A:4.**
Indicia for use in valuing land,
61A:10.
Limitation on allowance or
disallowance of
application for valuation,
taxation, and assessment,
61A:9.
Revaluation by city or town,
61A:8.
Air conditioning of premises,
exemption, **59:5.**
Aircraft and aviation.
Airports.
Development project funding,
gasoline and motor fuel
taxes, **64A:13.**

TAXATION —Cont'd
Aircraft and aviation —Cont'd
Airports —Cont'd
    Exemptions, **59:5,
        59:5D-59:5F.**
    Private airports, **59:5.**
  Certificate fees in lieu of
    taxation, **90:49.**
  Distributor, **64A:8A.**
  Excise tax, **64J:4, 64J:5, 64J:12.**
  Flight instruction, service
    defined for tax purposes,
    64H:1, 64I:1.
  Gasoline tax, **64J:1 et seq.**
    See AIRCRAFT AND
       AVIATION.
  Meals, exemption from taxation,
    64H:6.
  Sales tax, **64A:8A, 64H:6,
    64H:25A.**
  Use, consumption, and storage
    tax, **64I:7, 64I:26A.**
Air pollution.
  Deduction of expenditures for
    construction of air pollution
    control facilities, **63:38D.**
  Exemption from taxation of
    pollution control devices,
    59:5.
  Reimbursement of
    Commonwealth for
    metropolitan air pollution
    control expenditures, tax,
    111:142B.
Airports.
  Development project funding,
    gasoline and motor fuel
    taxes, **64A:13.**
  Exemptions, **59:5, 59:5D-59:5F.**
  Private airports, **59:5.**
Air raid shelters, exemption, **59:5.**
Air rights over highways, taxation
  of leasehold improvements,
  81:7L.
Air space leases, **40:22E.**
Alcoholic beverage taxes, **63A:1,
  63A:2, 138:21.**
  See ALCOHOLIC BEVERAGE
    TAXES.
Amherst economic development
  and industrial corporation, tax
  exempt status, **Spec L 23:9.**
Amount of tax.
  Abatement of local assessments
    as affected, **59:64.**
  Rate establishing amount of tax,
    factors considered when
    setting, **59:23.**
  Room occupancy tax, **64G:4,
    64G:5.**

TAXATION —Cont'd
Amount of tax —Cont'd
  State bonds and obligations,
    amount included in state
    tax for serial payments of
    bonds, **29:50.**
  Valuation of property to
    determine, **4:7, 58:1,
    59:38-59:42.**
Animals.
  Distress and sale for taxes,
    60:24, 60:27.
  Excise tax on farm animals,
    59:8A.
  Exemption, **59:5.**
    In other states, **59:5.**
    Neat cattle, exemption,
      59:5.
    Research animals, sales tax
      exemption, **64H:6.**
    Sales tax exemption, **64H:6.**
  Feed for fur-bearing animals as
    exempt from sales tax,
    64H:6.
  Minors, taxation of farm animals
    owned, **59:8A.**
  Research animals, sales tax
    exemption, **64H:6.**
Annual assessments, amount,
  59:23.
Annuities.
  Estate tax valuation dates,
    65C:5.
  Exemption of annuity
    associations, **59:5.**
  Public employee retirement, tax
    sheltered annuity program,
    29:64D.
Appeal and review.
  Abatement, **62C:39.**
  Administrative procedure act,
    applicability, **30A:1,
    58:13.**
  Agricultural and horticultural
    land, taxes on, appellate
    procedure, **61A:19.**
  Appearance by commissioner,
    58:1.
  Appellate Tax Board, **14:1.**
  Apportionment of taxes upon
    division of property after
    assessment, appeal, **59:81.**
  Assessors.
    Appellate tax board, **41:26A,
      59:38, 61A:19.**
    Valuation of property, **58:14,
      59:38.**
  Books, lists, tables and returns
    of assessors, **59:52B.**

TAXATION —Cont'd
Appeal and review —Cont'd
  Cigarette tax.
    Claims to seized cigarettes,
      vehicles, or containers,
      64C:8.
    Forfeiture proceedings,
      64C:8.
  Classification.
    Commissioner, appeals from
      classification, **58:2.**
    Recreational land, appeal of
      assessment of tax to
      appellate tax board,
      61B:14.
  Collection of taxes as affected,
    61A:19.
  Commissioner of revenue,
    reports, **58:10C.**
  Consolidation of appeals,
    59:39.
  Corporation taxes, appeal to
    appellate tax board.
    Classification of corporation,
      appeal, **58:2.**
    Urban redevelopment
      corporations, appeal from
      valuation, **121A:10.**
  County commissioners, **59:5,
    59:64.**
  Dismissal of appeal from board,
    211:4A.
  Division of property after
    assessment, appeal from
    apportionment of taxes,
    59:81.
  Duties of appellate tax board
    with respect to valuation of
    public lands, **58:14.**
  Eligibility or noneligibility of
    property tax exemption for
    charitable organizations,
    appeal from determination,
    59:5B.
  Employees and assistants of
    appellate tax board, **58A:5.**
  Equalized valuations for cities
    and towns, appeals, **58:10B.**
  Establishment of final
    equalization and
    apportionment on cities and
    towns, **58:10C.**
  Excuse for failure to timely file,
    59:64, 59:65B, 59:65C.
  Fees on appeal to appellate tax
    board, **59:64.**
  Foreclosure proceedings, appeal
    of questions of law or fact,
    60:72.
  Forest lands and products,
    refusal to abate taxes,
    61:2.

TAXATION —Cont'd
Appeal and review —Cont'd
  Generally, **58A:1 to 58A:14.** See
    within this heading,
    "Appellate tax board."
  Rules.
    See APPELLATE TAX
      BOARD RULES OF
      PRACTICE AND
      PROCEDURE.
  Hearings, **59:65.**
  Income tax.
    Abatement proceedings,
      62C:39.
    Payment as prerequisite to
      appeal, **61A:19.**
  Jurisdiction of appellate tax
    board, **62C:39.**
  Legacy and succession taxes,
    appeal to appellate tax
    board.
    Commissioner, appeal from
      valuation of property,
      65:26.
  Legal counsel for tax assessors
    in proceedings before
    appellate tax board, **41:26A.**
  License or registration, appeal
    from commissioner's refusal
    to grant, **62C:67.**
  Local property assessment,
    review, **58:1A, 58:14 (note),
    59:5D, 59:5E.**
  Minor's exemption, denial, **59:5.**
  Mortgagee's application for
    abatement, **59:59.**
  Motor vehicle excise tax, interest
    on abatement, **60A:2.**
  Municipalities, **58:1A, 58:14
    (note), 59:5D, 59:5E.**
    Excuse for untimely filing of
      appeal of local
      assessment, **59:65C.**
    Extension of time to appeal,
      51:14.
    Failure to submit sworn
      statements concerning
      local assessment, **59:38D.**
    Notice of proposed
      equalization values,
      58:10A.
    Proposed equalization
      valuations, appeals,
      58:10B.
    Right of appeal to as affected
      by failure to furnish
      information, **58:10.**
  Nontransferability of dismissal
    of appeals from board,
    211:4A.

TAXATION —Cont'd
Appeal and review —Cont'd
  Oaths.
    Local property assessment,
      failure to submit sworn
      statements concerning,
      59:38D.
  Petition, **59:65.**
  Phone companies, **59:39.**
  Pipeline valuation by tax
    commission, **59:38A.**
  Proceedings on appeal to
    appellate tax board, **59:65.**
  Public lands, determination of
    value, **58:14.**
  Records and recording.
    Excuse for failure to timely
      file appeal, **59:64, 59:65B,
      59:65C.**
  Recreational land, appeal of
    assessment, **61B:14.**
  Registration or license, appeal
    from refusal of
    commissioner to grant,
    62C:67.
  Reports and opinions.
    Ratio of assessment to value
      of property, report to
      appellate tax board,
      58:10C.
    Revenue commissioner's
      reports, **58:10C.**
  Residential property tax
    exemption, appeal from
    denial, **59:5C.**
  Return statement falsely made,
    59:38F.
  Revenue Department and
    Commissioner.
    Appellate tax board.
      Establishment, **14:1.**
      Reports concerning, **58:10C.**
    Classifications by
      commissioner, appeals,
      58:2.
    Registration or license, appeal
      from denial, **62C:67.**
  Rules of practice and procedure
    of Appellate Tax Board.
    See APPELLATE TAX BOARD
      RULES OF PRACTICE
      AND PROCEDURE.
  Special assessments.
    Abatement of assessments,
      80:7, 80:10.
    Division of assessment, **80:15.**
    Eminent domain proceedings,
      80A:10.
  State administrative procedure
    act, applicability, **30A:1,
    58:13.**

TAXATION —Cont'd
Appeal and review —Cont'd
  Supreme judicial court, appeals.
    Foreclosure proceedings,
      review of questions of law,
      60:72.
    Nontransferability of dismissal
      of appeal, **211:4A.**
  Surviving spouse's exemption,
    denial, **59:5.**
  Telephone or telegraph
    companies, appeals, **59:39.**
  Time for appeal to appellate tax
    board, **59:65C.**
    Extension of time to appeal,
      51:14.
    Failure to timely file appeals,
      59:64, 59:65B, 59:65C.
  Transferability of dismissal of
    appeals from board, **211:4A.**
  Transfer of abatement appeals
    from county commissioners,
    59:64.
  Valuation of property.
    Valuation of property. See
      within this heading,
      "Valuation of property."
  Veterans' tax exemption, appeals
    with respect, **59:5.**
  Water rates, **40:42E.**
Appellate tax board, **58A:1 to
  58A:14.**
  Alternative dispute resolution.
    Authority to employ, **58A:8A.**
  Alternative procedures.
    Informal procedure, **58A:7A.**
    Small claims procedure,
      58A:7A.
  Appeal and review. See within
    this heading, "Appeal and
    review."
  Appeals of board decisions,
    58A:13.
  Arrest and imprisonment.
    Special warrant for distress or
      imprisonment without
      demand for payments,
      60:19.
    Warrant for imprisonment for
      nonpayment of taxes,
      60:29, 60:30, 60:34.
  Assessed value of real property.
    Abatement of local taxes,
      58A:12D.
    Comprehensive assessment
      ratio, **58A:12C.**
    Costs of action, **58A:12A.**
    Damages of improper
      assessment, **58A:14.**
    Evidence of fair valuation,
      58A:12B.

TAXATION —Cont'd
Appellate tax board —Cont'd
Assessors, **223:37.**
Attorneys, **58A:5A.**
Cigarette tax, service of process
  in forfeiture proceedings,
  64C:8.
Clerks.
  Appointment, **58A:5A.**
Costs of action.
  Assessed value of real
    property, **58A:12A.**
  Taxed against unsuccessful
    party, **58A:12.**
Damages for improper
  assessment, **58A:14.**
Decisions by single member of
  board, **58A:1A.**
Demand for payment, **60:16,
  60:39.**
Denial.
  Deemed denied for failure to
    take action, **58A:6.**
Employees, **58A:5A.**
Established, **58A:1.**
Expenditures of board, **58A:5A.**
  Travelling expenses for
    members, **58A:5.**
Expense statement.
  Filed with petition, when
    required, **58A:7.**
Fees.
  Entry fee, **58A:7.**
    Informal procedure, **58A:7A.**
    Small claims procedure,
      58A:7B.
  Witness fees, **58A:11, 58A:12.**
Foreclosure proceedings, **60:66.**
Forms.
  Informal procedure, **58A:7A.**
Hearings, **58A:8.**
Imprisonment for overdue taxes,
  60:29.
Income tax return, writ of
  mandamus to compel filing,
  62C:9.
Informal procedure, **58A:7A.**
Inspection of personal property.
  Prior to hearing, **58A:8A.**
Interest on awards or payments,
  58A:13.
Jurisdiction, **58A:6.**
Low value tax land, proceedings
  to establish title, **60:80B.**
Mediation.
  Authority to employ, **58A:8A.**
Meetings, **58A:2.**
Members, **58A:1.**
  Travelling expenses, **58A:5.**
Nonresident tax title owners,
  agents, **60:47.**

TAXATION —Cont'd
Appellate tax board —Cont'd
Oaths, **58A:11.**
Office, **58A:2.**
Opinions.
  Publication, sale and
    distribution, **58A:3.**
  Time for delivery, **58A:13.**
Papers and documents,
  production, **58A:11.**
Performance evaluations, **58A:1.**
Petitions, **58A:7.**
Quorum, **58A:1A.**
Real property.
  Assessed valuation, **58A:12A
    to 58A:12D.**
Recordation of proceedings,
  58A:10.
Records.
  Open to public, **58A:13.**
Reports.
  Annual report of
    recommendations and
    matters handled, **58A:4.**
  Publication, sale and
    distribution, **58A:3.**
  Time for delivery, **58A:13.**
Return of process.
  Collection of local taxes,
    affidavit as to service in
    proceedings, **60:1, 60:57.**
  Foreclosure of rights of
    redemption under tax
    titles, **60:67.**
Revenue departments, service of
  summons issued, **58:25B.**
Ripeness.
  Finality of judgment where
    board of assessors takes
    no action, **58A:6.**
Rules of practice and procedure
  of Appellate Tax Board.
  See APPELLATE TAX BOARD
    RULES OF PRACTICE
    AND PROCEDURE.
Sales and use tax laws, service
  of nonresidents in judicial
  proceedings, **64H:29,
  64H:32, 64I:33.**
Service of process and papers,
  58A:9.
  Petitions, **58A:7.**
Single member of board.
  Decisions authorized, **58A:1A.**
Small claims procedure, **58A:7B.**
Subpoenas, **58A:11.**
Temporary members, **58A:1.**
Transcripts, **58A:10.**
Travelling expenses for
  members, **58A:5.**
Warrants for arrest of
  delinquent taxpayers, **60:34.**

TAXATION —Cont'd
Appellate tax board —Cont'd
Withholding tax on wages,
  employer failing to withhold,
  62B:7.
Witnesses, **58A:11.**
  Fees, **58A:11, 58A:12.**
Applications for abatement, **59:59,
  59:60, 61B:14, 62C:37.**
Apportioned use certificate,
  services sold at retail outside
  of Commonwealth, **64H:6.**
Apportionment or equalization of
  taxes, **58:9, 58:10; US Const
  Art 1 Sec 2 cl 3.**
  Abstracts and information
    furnished to general court,
    58:9, 58:10.
  Returns or statements as to
    taxable property,
    commissioner may
    require, **58:3.**
Collector, payments, **60:95.**
Commissioner's duties, **58:3,
  58:9, 58:10.**
Counties, **35:31.**
Division of realty after
  assessment, **59:78A, 59:81.**
Eminent domain proceedings,
  79:7D.
Exemptions, apportionment of
  certain, **59:5.**
Forest lands and products tax,
  61:4.
Mortgagor and mortgagee,
  apportionment as between,
  59:12.
Motor vehicles, excise tax upon
  late registration, **60A:1.**
Regional refuse disposal
  districts, agreement with as
  to apportionment or
  equalization of taxes,
  40:44H.
Report to general court, **58:9,
  58:10.**
Special assessments, **80:13.**
  Eminent domain proceedings,
    80A:14.
  Lessee, proportion to be paid,
    80:11.
  Reapportionment of certain
    assessments, **80:13.**
Surviving spouse and minor
  heirs of decedent,
  apportionment of tax
  exemption among, **59:5.**
Valuations for cities and towns.
  Appeals, **58:10B.**
  Appeals to appellate tax
    board, **58A:12C.**

TAXATION —Cont'd
Apportionment or equalization of
taxes —Cont'd
Valuations for cities and towns
—Cont'd
As basis for municipal debt
limit computation, **44:10.**
Damages for improper
assessment, **58A:14.**
Data to be utilized in
determining, **58:10.**
Definition under law
governing municipal
finance, **44:1.**
Failure of municipality to
submit information for
use in determining, **58:10.**
Final equalization and
apportionment,
establishment, **58:10C.**
Hearing on proposed equalized
valuations, **58:10A.**
Notice, **58:10A.**
Proposed equalized valuation,
duties of department,
58:9.
Regional school districts,
equalized valuation for
purposes of computing
regional valuation
percentage for state aid,
71:16D.
Report, **44:1.**
State Administrative
Procedure Law,
proceedings to determine,
as adjudicatory
proceedings within
meaning, **30A:1.**
Veterans' benefits and services,
115:11.
Appraisal, **4:7, 58:1, 58:10,
59:38-59:42.**
Approval by voters to assess taxes,
59:21C, 62C:27.
Aqueduct companies, utility
company franchise tax,
63:52A.
Armed forces, **62C:81.**
Militia, **58:13-58:17A, 59:5,
60:24.**
Arrest and imprisonment.
Cigarette tax, **64C:8.**
Collectors, **60:29-60:34A.**
See TAX COLLECTORS.
Credit for taxes assessed upon
person jailed for
nonpayment, **60:95.**
Discharge of persons committed
to jail for nonpayment,
60:31, 224:28.

TAXATION —Cont'd
Arrest and imprisonment —Cont'd
Special warrant for distress or
imprisonment without
demand for payments,
60:19.
Town treasurer's powers, **41:37.**
Warrant for imprisonment for
nonpayment of taxes, **60:29,
60:30, 60:34.**
Artwork and artists.
Exemption for works of art,
59:5.
Service defined for tax purposes,
64H:1, 64I:1.
Assessments, **41:24-41:30A, 59:1
et seq.**
Affidavit of name and address of
owner of property to be
included with notice of
preliminary tax, **59:57D.**
Agricultural and horticultural
property, **61A:1.**
See SPECIAL
ASSESSMENTS.
Consent or approval, **59:21C,
62C:27.**
Corporation taxes, **63:38C,
63:38N, 63:52, 63:52A.**
See CORPORATION TAXES.
County tax assessments, use of
federal funds to reduce,
35:30.
Eminent domain proceedings,
apportionment of tax in,
79:35A.
Inspection of information,
59:52C.
Legacy and succession taxes,
65:27-65:29, 65:33A.
See LEGACY AND
SUCCESSION TAXES.
Notice.
Assessors.
See TAX ASSESSORS.
Division of assessment, notice
of intent, **80:15.**
Preliminary tax for real estate
and personal property,
affidavit of address to be
included, **59:57D.**
Preliminary tax for real estate
and personal property,
affidavit of address to be
included, **59:57D.**
Rates, limitations on, **59:21C.**
Reassessment, **59:57, 59:59,
59:76-59:78, 60:46, 60:84,
60:84A.**

TAXATION —Cont'd
Assessments —Cont'd
Special assessments for
betterments, **80:1 et seq.,
80A:1 et seq.**
See SPECIAL
ASSESSMENTS.
Valuation of land, determining,
**59:5D, 59:5F, 59:5G,
121B:16.**
Vessels, assessment of excise,
60B:2.
Watershed management
districts.
Treasurer to pay municipality
difference in assessment,
59:5H.
Assessors, **41:24-41:30A, 59:20 et
seq.**
See TAX ASSESSORS.
Assignee of insolvent debtor,
demand against for payment
of delinquent taxes, **60:36.**
Assistance to aged and disabled.
Demand for payment of
assessment, **60:16.**
Exemption of hot lunch program
from taxation, **64H:6.**
Associations and societies.
Agricultural, dairy, or mercantile
associations, **157:7.**
Dividends issued, declaration of
estimated tax, **62:1.**
Exemption, **59:5, 176:49.**
Income tax, **59:5, 62C:8, 62C:77.**
Assurance fund, assessed value as
evidence in action for
compensation, **185:109.**
Athletic organizations, charitable
organizations exempt from
property tax, **59:5.**
Attendance of witnesses, **62C:70.**
Attorney general.
Agent for service of process on
business corporations
merging with foreign
corporations, **156B:79.**
Charitable and benevolent
purposes, omission to file
report with division of
public charities as affecting
tax exemption of property,
59:5.
Delinquent tax collectors,
proceedings against, **58:8.**
Enforcement powers, **62C:70.**
Suits in other states to collect
taxes, **58:28C.**
Attorneys at law.
Assessors, **41:26A.**
Request by taxpayer for
representation, **62C:80.**

TAXATION —Cont'd
Attorneys at law —Cont'd
Service defined for tax purposes, **64H:1.**
Auction, **60:43.**
Tax sales generally, **59:2B, 59:12E, 60:37 to 60:60.**
Audits and auditors.
Abandoned real property, abatement of taxes, **58:8.**
Abatement proceedings open to private auditors, **59:60.**
Assessors.
Abatement of taxes, notice to town auditor, **59:23B, 59:70A.**
Municipal accounts, assessment of tax for expense of audit, **44:41.**
Collectors, audit of accounts of tax collectors on cessation of office, **60:97.**
Cooperation among governments as to audit of taxes, **62C:23.**
Explanation of audit process, **62C:80.**
Income tax.
Cooperation of government with audit, **62C:23.**
Division, accounts, **11:12.**
State auditor, inspection of records of commissioner of revenue, **62C:20.**
Municipal accounts, tax to defray expense of audit, **44:41.**
Refund of overpayment determined after taxpayer audits, authorization, **62C:27.**
Revenue department and commissioner.
Audit division, establishment, **14:1.**
City and town accounts, audit, **41:99H.**
Public beach districts, **40:12B.**
Sales tax on audit services, **64H:1, 64H:6.**
Service defined for tax purposes, **64H:1, 64I:1.**
Statistical sample methods allowed for audit of taxpayer's books, **62C:24.**
Veterans' services department, **115:15.**
Back taxes recovery.
Action, **60:98, 62C:36 et seq.**
Repayment of tax paid by one other than fee owner, **60:60.**
Bad checks, penalty for tendering, **60:57A, 62C:35.**

TAXATION —Cont'd
Bail bond, taxpayer's release, **60:34A.**
Bailments.
Charitable organizations, exemption from excise tax of vehicles leased to, **60A:1.**
Cigarette tax records and reports, **64C:6.**
Report of leased personalty for tax administration purposes, **62C:13.**
Sales tax, property purchased for rental, **64H:8.**
Use, consumption, or storage tax on property purchased for rental, **64I:8.**
Bankruptcy trustees, **62:13, 62C:6.**
Banks and trust companies.
Agreement by cities with banks for collection of local taxes, **60:2A.**
Allocation and investment of mortgagors' periodic tax payments, **183:23.**
Cooperative banks.
Corporation taxes, **59:5, 63:2, 63:22B, 63:22C.**
Exemptions, **59:5, 170:35.**
Income tax, **62:2, 62C:12.**
Lien of tenant in common or joint tenant paying taxes, **60:85, 60:86.**
Nonpayment of taxes, taking over for, **60:56, 60:76A.**
Personal property of banks, **59:18.**
Corporation taxes, **63:1 et seq.**
Annual tax, **63:2, 63:7.**
Definitions, **63:1.**
Exemption of certain trust companies from excise, **63:2.**
Foreign banks, net income, **63:1.**
Net income, **63:1, 63:2, 63:7.**
Percentage of net income for taxation, **63:2.**
Rate of taxation, **63:2.**
Savings, co-operative banks, and associations.
Exemptions, **59:5, 63:2.**
Securities, taxation of bank holding companies dealing exclusively in, **63:38B.**
Taxable year defined, **63:1.**
Credit unions.
Credit Union Employees Retirement Association, **171:84.**
Deposit of tax receipts, **59:5, 62:2.**

TAXATION —Cont'd
Banks and trust companies —Cont'd
Credit unions —Cont'd
Exemption from tax, **59:5.**
Mobile homes, **171:61.**
Real estate loans, **171:65, 171:66.**
Retirement accounts, **171:34, 171:84.**
Definition, "Bank", **63:1.**
Deposit of taxes, **62C:45.**
Estate tax, depositing of taxable assets with intent to evade or defeat assessment or collection, **65C:28.**
Exemption from local taxes, **59:5.**
Federal savings banks, taxation of interest, **62:2.**
Income tax, interest from deposits, **62:2.**
Morris Plan banks, **60:68, 60:76A, 62:2, 172A:13.**
Mortgage loan clauses as to payment of taxes, **183:23.**
Net income determined from business carried on within the Commonwealth, **63:2A.**
Refund may be credited to taxpayer's bank account, **62C:40.**
Savings banks.
Corporation taxes, **59:5, 63:2, 63:22B, 63:22C.**
Exemption from taxation, **59:5, 168:41, 168:42-168:44.**
Federal savings banks, taxation of interest, **62:2.**
Income taxes, **62:1, 62:2, 62C:12.**
Stock exempt from local taxation, **59:5.**
Withholding tax on wages, requiring employer to deposit taxes in bank, **62B:7.**
Bazaars.
Rate of taxation on gross proceeds realized, **271:7A.**
Returns, **62C:18.**
Tax administration provisions applicable, **62C:2.**
Beano games, taxation of gross receipts, **10:39.**
Bed and breakfast establishments, taxation on meals served, **64H:6.**
Betterment assessments, **80:1 et seq., 80A:1 et seq.**
See SPECIAL ASSESSMENTS.

TAXATION —Cont'd
Biennial report of apportionment of state taxes, **58:9.**
Bill for taxes, **60:3-60:3B, 60:22A.**
See TAX COLLECTORS.
Blind persons, exemption or abatement, **59:5, 59:59, 60A:1, 62:3.**
Boardinghouse keepers to give information as to residents, **59:92.**
Board of assessors, **41:24.**
See TAX ASSESSORS.
Boats, **59:4, 59:8, 60B:1-60B:4, 64H:6.**
Assessment of tax, **90B:11.**
Fishing.
Excise tax, **59:8, 60B:3.**
Exemption from tax, **59:5, 60B:3, 64H:6, 64I:7.**
Gasoline tax, **64A:7, 64A:13.**
Payment as prerequisite to issuance of certificate of number, **64H:25A.**
Ships and other watercraft.
See SHIPS AND OTHER WATERCRAFT.
Bomb shelters, exemption, **59:5.**
Bond issues, **59:4, 59:5.**
County anticipation notes for temporary loans, **35:37.**
Districts.
Exemption, **59:5.**
Tax levy, **44:16, 44:19.**
Water pollution abatement districts, **21:36.**
Estate taxes.
Deposit of government bonds to secure payment, **65C:10.**
Exempt for lien, **65C:14.**
Exemptions from taxation, **59:5.**
Exemptions, highway infrastructure bonds, **29:2O.**
Highway infrastructure bonds, exemptions, **29:2O.**
Industrial development project bonds, **40D:20.**
Municipal corporations.
Anticipation of revenue, limitation of notes issued, **44:4.**
Exemption from tax, **59:5.**
Payment of, tax levy, **44:16, 44:19.**
Property taxes, use of notes for payment, **60:2, 183:62.**
Provision for payment, **44:16, 44:19.**
Taxation of, **62:2.**
State bonds and obligations.
Acceptance of notes in payment of taxes, **29:48.**

TAXATION —Cont'd
Bond issues —Cont'd
State bonds and obligations —Cont'd
Amount included in state tax for serial payments of bonds, **29:50.**
Income from public obligations, **29:2O, 62:2.**
Infrastructure bonds, **29:2O.**
Social security recipients, information as to tax consequences, **29:48B, 44:22B.**
Water pollution abatement districts, **21:36.**
Bonds, surety.
Bail bond for release of taxpayer, **60:34A.**
Cigarette tax.
Appeal bonds, forfeiture proceedings, **64C:8.**
Payment of tax, bond, **64C:30.**
Collection.
Mayor, fixing amount of bonds, **60:13.**
Collectors, **60:13.**
Action against delinquent collectors, **58:8.**
Amount of bond, fixing by selectmen, **60:96.**
Commitment of tax lists, required prior, **59:53.**
Deputy collectors, **14:3, 41:37, 60:92.**
Liability on for neglect of duty, **58:8.**
Reassessed taxes, applicability, **59:78.**
Special collector, **60:14.**
Temporary collector, **41:40, 41:61A.**
Town may pay expense, **40:5.**
Uncollectible taxes, **60:95.**
Commitment of tax list, prerequisite, **59:53.**
Contractor filing bond or deposit for payment of sales tax, **64H:30A.**
Deed and document stamp tax, bond of register of deeds to assure account for monies received, **64D:3.**
Reimbursement of county for premiums on bond, **64D:3B.**
Legacy and succession taxes.
Future interests, bond for payment of taxes, **65:15.**
Legacies required to be paid within one year, bond to indemnify executor or administrator, **197:21.**

TAXATION —Cont'd
Bonds, surety —Cont'd
Payment of tax, bonds to secure, **62C:66.**
Books of assessors, **59:29-59:37, 59:43-59:48, 59:50-59:52, 59:52B, 60:12.**
See TAX ASSESSORS.
Borrowing money, **59:4.**
Income tax consequences of business loans, **62:2.**
Municipal corporations. See within this heading, "Municipal corporations."
Boxing, **147:40, 147:40A, 147:47.**
Bridges.
Sales tax exemptions, **64H:6.**
Stock as personal property, **59:4.**
Buildings.
Agricultural buildings, **61A:15.**
Assessors.
Permits to erect buildings, notice to assessors of issuance, **143:61.**
Statements as to buildings, **59:46.**
Cemetery administration buildings, tax exemption, **59:5.**
Colleges and universities, taxation of buildings on land leased from state universities, **75:28.**
Commonwealth, assessment of buildings erected on land leased, **59:11.**
Exemptions.
Cemetery administration buildings, **59:5.**
Sales tax, exemptions, **64H:6.**
Recreational uses, taxation, **61B:10.**
Statements in tax assessor's books, **59:46.**
Burial rights, exemption, **59:5.**
Bus companies, franchise tax, **63:52A.**
Business carried on within the Commonwealth, determination of net income, **63:2A.**
Business leases of state property as subject, **59:5.**
Capital resource company, **Spec L 11:1 et seq.**
See CAPITAL RESOURCE COMPANY.
Capital stock, **59:4, 59:5.**
See CORPORATION TAXES.
Capitation tax, **US Const Art 1 Sec 9 cl 1, 4; 24th Amend.**

TAXATION —Cont'd
Carriers.
  Appeal for abatement of local
    taxes as assessed against,
    59:64 (note), 59:65.
  Utility company franchise tax,
    63:52A.
Cash receipts and disbursement
  method of accounting, income
  tax determined, **62:62.**
Cattle.
  Animals. See within this
    heading, "Animals."
Cemeteries.
  Exemption of property, **59:5.**
  Town raising money for care and
    maintenance, **114:16.**
Central Massachusetts Economic
  Development Authority,
  taxation of lands,
  rights-of-way, easements, etc.,
  Spec L 22:15.
Certificates and certification,
  60:23, 60:23A.
  Abatement of taxes, **59:70,
    60:20.**
  Agricultural land, taxes due or
    paid, **61A:19A.**
  Apportioned use certificate,
    services sold at retail
    outside of Commonwealth,
    64H:6.
  Appropriations, orders certified
    to tax assessors, **41:15A.**
  Collectors, **40:42C, 41:43A,
    60:23, 60:36, 60:60, 60:63,
    80:12.**
    See TAX COLLECTORS.
  Estate taxes on nonresident's
    estate, forms, **65C:21.**
  Federal tax laws, certificate of
    similarity, **62C:23.**
  Housing for elderly, exemptions,
    59:5.
  Income tax.
    Sale for taxes, **62C:59,
      62C:60.**
    Similarity to federal tax laws,
      certificates, **62C:23.**
    Withholding of tax, **62B:4.**
  Levy of taxes, certificate of sale
    for property levied, **62C:59,
      62C:60.**
  Liens, **60:23, 60:23A, 60:86.**
    Agricultural lands, certificate
      of taxes paid or due as
      terminating lien,
      61A:19A.
    Amount of taxes due,
      certification as necessary
      to taking for nonpayment,
      60:37B.

TAXATION —Cont'd
Certificates and certification
  —Cont'd
  Liens —Cont'd
    Federal tax liens, **36:24.**
    Fees, **60:23B.**
    Municipal lien certificates
      furnished by tax
      collectors, **60:23.**
    Proceeding on certificate of
      title and registration
      subject to lien, **185:46.**
  Registration certificate for
    taxpayer, **62C:67.**
  Resale or exempt use certificate,
    notice to produce, **64I:8.**
  Room occupancy tax, certificate
    of registration required,
    64G:6.
  Sales taxes.
    Apportioned use certificate,
      services sold at retail
      outside of Commonwealth,
      64H:6.
    Exempt use certificate,
      64H:6-64H:8.
    Levy of taxes, **62C:59, 62C:60.**
    Motor vehicle certificate or
      registration, **64H:25.**
    Permits and registration.
      Aircraft, evidence of
        payment of taxes
        prerequisite to
        registration, **64H:25A.**
      Classified permits, **64H:9.**
      Direct payment permit,
        64H:3.
      Increasing fees for
        certificates, **62C:67.**
      Promoter's certificate,
        requirements, **62C:67A.**
      Resale and exempt use
        certificate, **64H:8.**
      Vendors, **64H:7.**
    Resale certificates, **64H:6.**
  Special assessments, **80:12,
    80A:11.**
  Title, certificates of, noted
    encumbrances, **185:46.**
  Trailers, suspension of
    registration certificate for
    nonpayment of tax, **60A:2A.**
  Use, consumption, or storage
    tax.
    Exempt use certificates, **64I:8.**
    Motor vehicles or trailers,
      revocation of certificate of
      registration, **64I:26.**
    Resale certificates, **64I:8.**
  Withholding exemption and
    deduction, **62B:4.**

TAXATION —Cont'd
Charitable trusts, tax exemptions,
  59:5, 62:3.
Charity, **68:1 et seq., 180:1 et
  seq.**
  See CHARITIES AND
    CHARITABLE
    CONTRIBUTIONS.
Charter cities.
  Assessors, **43:17, 43:54.**
  Existing taxes as affected by
    city's adoption of charter,
    43:24.
  Support of charter commission,
    43B:8.
Chattel mortgages, tax on property
  subject, **59:19.**
Chicken.
  Excise tax on domestic fowl,
    59:8A.
  Exemption, **59:5, 64H:6.**
  Sales tax, exemptions, **64H:6.**
Children and minors.
  Adoption, **59:5, 62:3, 65:1.**
  Exemptions, **59:5, 60:3B, 64G:2.**
  Farm animals owned by minors,
    59:8A.
  Income tax, **62:2, 62:3, 62D:1,
    62D:3, 62E:1.**
  Local assessments for child care
    facilities, **59:3F.**
  Support collection.
    Procedures by IV-D agency for
      accrued arrearages,
      119A:6.
    Set-off debt collection,
      transitional assistance
      department to assist
      public welfare department
      in collecting support
      obligations, **62D:3.**
Churches and religious
  organizations.
  Affidavit as to posting notice of
    sale of pews for nonpayment
    of taxes, **67:32.**
  Eligibility for property tax
    exemption and application
    for abatement, **59:5.**
  Land assessed where and to
    whom, **59:11.**
  Legacy and succession taxes,
    exemption, **65:1.**
  Meals, tax exemption, **64H:6.**
  Ministerial fund, real estate,
    59:11.
  Property as exempt from local
    taxes, **59:5.**
  Room occupancy tax, exemption,
    64G:2.
  Sales tax, exemption, **64H:6.**

TAXATION —Cont'd
Churches and religious
  organizations —Cont'd
  Services sold at retail, sales tax
    exemptions, **64H:6.**
Cigarette taxes, **64C:1-39.**
  See CIGARETTE TAX.
Cities, **44:1 et seq., 59:1 et seq.**
City and town auditors.
  Expenses for audits of accounts,
    tax for, **44:41.**
  Notice of abatement of tax,
    59:23B.
  Rate, notice of tax rate, **59:23A.**
City council.
  Exemption of local property from
    taxation, **59:5C.**
  Usage classification of real
    property for taxation
    purposes, **40:56.**
Civic center financing surcharges,
  62C:86.
Claims against public bodies and
  officers as to collection of tax,
  application of provisions
  concerning, **258:10.**
Classification.
  Agricultural and horticultural
    property, **61A:4.**
  Assessors.
    Books and lists of
      classification of estates
      and total valuation, **59:44,**
      59:46, 61B:17.
    Corporations, time for filing
      objections to classification,
      58:2.
    Forest lands, classification for
      taxation, **61:1.**
    Recreational land,
      61B:2-61B:8, 61B:14,
      61B:17.
  Forest lands and products, **59:5,**
    61:1 to 61.8.
  Withdrawal from
    classification, **61:7.**
  Local property assessments,
    59:2A.
  Municipal corporations, **40:56.**
    Criminal jurisdiction,
      218:26A.
  Usage classification, **59:2A.**
  Recreational lands,
    61B:1-61B:18.
  Revenue commissioner,
    classification, **58:2.**
  Use, consumption, or storage
    tax, classified permit
    establishing percentage of
    exempt sales, **64I:11.**
  Valuation of property,
    classification, **59:38, 61B:2,**
    61B:3.

TAXATION —Cont'd
Clerk of city or town, **60:12,**
  60:77B.
Clothing.
  Distress and sale, exemption,
    60:24.
  Exemption, **59:5.**
Cluster housing development,
  assessment of taxes on
  common lands within, **59:11.**
Collateral security, debtor as liable
  for payment of taxes,
  106:9-207.
Collection agencies and agents,
  60:2B, 64H:1, 64I:1.
Collection of support.
  Set-off debt collection, revenue
    department to assist
    transitional assistance
    department in collecting
    support obligations, **62D:3.**
Collection of taxes, **60:1-60:105,**
  62C:46 et seq.
  See TAX COLLECTORS.
Combat zones, soldiers serving,
  62C:81.
Comity, reciprocal enforcement of
  tax liabilities between
  Commonwealth and other
  states, **58:28C.**
Commercial fishing gear and
  equipment, exemption, **59:5.**
Commissioner, **14:1 et seq., 58:1**
  et seq.
  See REVENUE DEPARTMENT
    AND COMMISSIONER.
Commitment of tax list, **59:53,**
  59:54.
  See TAX COLLECTORS.
Common lands within a cluster
  development, assessment of
  taxes, **59:11.**
Comprehensive assessment ratios.
  Valuation of real property,
    58:10.
    Appeals to appellate tax
      board, **58A:12C.**
    Damages for improper
      assessment, **58A:14.**
Computation of tax.
  Business carried on within the
    Commonwealth,
    determination of net income
    from, **63:2A.**
  Prohibition of rounding off
    figures used, **62C:4.**
Condominiums, **183A:14.**
Congress, power of, **US Const Art**
  18 cl 1.
Consent to tax assessment,
  59:21C, 62C:27.

TAXATION —Cont'd
Conservation.
  Alternative energy resources,
    tax incentive for use,
    63:38H.
  Conservation lands,
    reimbursement for tax loss,
    58:13-58:17A.
Consolidation or merger.
  Appeals, consolidation.
    Pipeline valuations, appeals
      involving, **59:38A.**
    Telephone and telegraph
      company property,
      valuation, **59:39.**
  Corporations, effect of merger,
    156:46A, 156:46C, 156:46D.
Constables acting as tax collectors,
  41:39, 59:53.
Constitution of Massachusetts.
  See CONSTITUTION OF
    MASSACHUSETTS.
Constitution of the United States.
  See CONSTITUTION OF THE
    UNITED STATES.
Construction contracts and work,
  bond or deposit to secure
  payment, **64H:6, 64H:30A,**
  64I:31A.
Consumption tax, **62C:16, 64I:1 et**
  seq.
  See USE, CONSUMPTION, OR
    STORAGE TAX.
Containers or packages.
  Cigarette tax.
    Marking, **64C:5.**
    Possession of unmarked
      container, penalty,
      64C:10.
    Seizure and forfeiture for
      illegal transportation or
      possession, **64C:8.**
  Imported goods in original
    package, tax information,
    59:33.
  Sales tax, exemption of
    containers, **64H:6.**
Contested tax.
  Bar on collection while tax being
    contested, **62C:32.**
Contracts and agreements for
  appraisal of taxable real
  estate, **40:4, 44:7, 58:1A.**
  Banks, cities' contracts for
    collection of local taxes,
    60:2A.
  Dealer contract clause relative
    to sales taxes, **106:2-201.**
  Dividends, taxation upon failure
    to file agreement with
    revenue commissioner, **62:1.**

TAXATION —Cont'd
Conversion of agricultural land to
other use, first option on sale,
61A:14.
Conversion of funds, penalties,
62C:73.
Conveyance taxes.
Agricultural and horticultural
property.
Appeal, payment as
prerequisite, **61A:19.**
Certificate of amount,
application, **61A:19A.**
Death, tax applicable, **61A:9.**
Exemption, **61A:12.**
Liens, **61A:9.**
Unpaid taxes, collection,
61A:12.
Deed and document stamp tax,
64D:1 et seq.
See DEED AND DOCUMENT
STAMP TAX.
Effect of deed in tax sale,
62C:59, 62C:60.
Income from property in estate
under terms of deed set
aside for charity, **62:3.**
Recreational lands.
Land subject, **61B:7, 61B:12.**
Liens, **61B:6.**
Redemption of real estate levied
on, delivery of deed of
release upon, **236:33.**
Cooperation of governments as to
assessments and audits,
62C:23.
Cooperative banks.
Corporation taxes, **59:5, 63:2,
63:22B, 63:22C.**
Exemptions, **59:5, 170:35.**
Income tax, **62:2, 62C:12.**
Lien of tenant in common or
joint tenant paying taxes,
60:85, 60:86.
Nonpayment of taxes, taking
over for, **60:56, 60:76A.**
Personal property of banks,
59:18.
Co-operative corporations, **157:18.**
Agricultural, dairy, or mercantile
associations, submission of
certificate of organization
for approval of commissioner
of corporations and taxation,
157:7.
Corporate trusts, **62:8.**
Corporation taxes, **63:1 et seq.**
See CORPORATION TAXES.
Corrections department,
reimbursement of towns for
loss of taxes on land used,
58:13.

TAXATION —Cont'd
Costs of action.
Abatement of taxes, **59:62,
59:64.**
Appellate proceedings, **59:64.**
Prepayment required, **59:62.**
Assessors.
Abatement proceedings,
prepayment, **59:62.**
Appropriations for expenses of
tax assessors, **41:108B.**
Group insurance for municipal
employees, certification of
costs to board of
assessors, **32B:3.**
Foreclosure proceedings, deposit
in court, **60:73.**
Taxation of costs, **261:19,
261:20.**
Appeal from taxation by clerk
of court, **261:20-261:22.**
Double or treble costs, **261:11.**
Fee for taxing not required,
202:4.
Notice of application, **261:19.**
Counties and county taxes, **35:31.**
Action against town for
nonassessment or
nonpayment, **59:28.**
Agricultural schools, amount to
be taxed, **74:29.**
Amount regulated, **35:30.**
Anticipation notes for temporary
loans, **35:37.**
Apportionment and equalization
among towns, **35:31, 58:9,
58:10.**
Deduction of previous year's
unappropriated balance
prior, **35:30.**
Assessment, **35:31, 59:21.**
Collection, **35:31.**
Commissioners.
County commissioners. See
within this heading,
"County commissioners."
Debt and interest payments,
levy, **35:30.**
Deduction of prior fiscal year's
unappropriated balance
prior to apportionment or
assessment, **35:30.**
Failure to certify, **59:21.**
Federal funds used to reduce
assessments, **35:30.**
Formerly owned property,
taxation, **59:2C.**
Gasoline sales tax receipts,
construction and
improvement of county
roads, **64A:13.**

TAXATION —Cont'd
Counties and county taxes
—Cont'd
Hospital land, reimbursement of
towns for loss of taxes,
58:13-58:17A.
Inclusion in assessment of other
taxes, **59:26.**
Indexes of records of
instruments, estimate of
expense, **36:30.**
Industrial farms, levy, **126:39.**
Interest on county obligations,
35:30, 62:2.
Liability of city or town for,
35:31, 59:28.
Neglect of assessors,
appointment of others in
case, **59:27.**
Revenue department's biennial
report of apportionment
among towns, **58:9, 58:10.**
Time for payment by towns,
35:31.
Tuberculosis hospitals, taxation
of land, **58:13-58:17A.**
Warrant for collection, **35:31.**
County commissioners.
Abatement of taxes.
Appeals, **59:64.**
Certificate, **59:70.**
Aged persons, appeal from
denial of tax exemption,
59:5.
Appeal.
Abatement of taxes, **59:64.**
Aged persons, denial of
exemption, **59:5.**
Apportionment and assessment
of county taxes among
towns, **35:31.**
Fraternal benefit societies as
exempt, **176:49.**
Minor's exemption, denial, **59:5.**
Reimbursement of cities or
towns for loss of tax on
lands held by commissioners
for hospital purposes,
58:13-58:17A.
Surviving spouse's exemption,
denial, **59:5.**
Veteran's tax exemption, **59:5.**
Credit bureaus, **64H:1, 64I:1,
93:52.**
Credits against tax.
Corporation taxes.
Job incentive credit, **63:30,
63:38F.**
Declaration of estimated income
tax.
Estimated tax payments,
62B:13-62B:15.

TAXATION —Cont'd
Credits against tax —Cont'd
Declaration of estimated income tax —Cont'd
Overpayment, **62C:79.**
Statement of estimated credits in declaration, **62B:13.**
Energy conservation for residential property, credit, **62:6.**
Estate taxes.
Federal estate tax credit surcharge, **65A:1-65A:6.**
See ESTATE TAXES.
State death tax, credit as affecting tax rate, **65C:2.**
Federal estate tax, **65A:3.**
Gasoline and motor fuel taxes.
Highway Fund, credit of part of tax, **64A:13.**
Other state, application for credits for taxes paid, **64F:4.**
Receipts, crediting, **64A:13.**
Income tax, **62:6.**
See INCOME TAX.
Lead paint law, credit for expense of complying, **62:6.**
Prisoners, credits, **62:6.**
Revenue growth limit.
Amounts in excess of growth limit, **62F:6.**
Rounding off to whole numbers, **62C:4.**
Withholding of tax.
Amount withheld as credit on income tax of employee, **62B:9, 62B:12.**
Estimated income tax, **62B:13.**
Credit unions.
Credit Union Employees Retirement Association, exemptions, **171:84.**
Deposit of tax receipts, **59:5, 62:2.**
Exemption from tax, **59:5.**
Mobile homes, **171:61.**
Real estate loans, **171:65, 171:66.**
Retirement accounts, **171:34, 171:84.**
Custodian of tax-foreclosed property, appointment, **60:77B.**
Customs duties.
Congress' power to lay and collect, **US Const Art 1 Sec 8 cl 1.**
Exportations from any state, duties not to be laid on, **US Const Art 1 Sec 9 cl 5.**

TAXATION —Cont'd
Customs duties —Cont'd
Importation of persons, **US Const Art 1 Sec 9 cl 1.**
State may not impose without consent of Congress, **US Const Art 1 Sec 10 cl 2.**
Customs office.
Concurrent jurisdiction in land acquired, **1:7.**
Federal jurisdiction over lands ceded, **1:7.**
Motorboats, numbering, **90B:2.**
Damages.
Disproportionate assessment, **58A:14.**
Death.
Collector of taxes, effect of death, **60:97.**
Special assessments, death of person entitled to petition for abatement, **80:8.**
Taxpayer's death, abatement of uncollectible poll and personal property taxes, **59:71.**
Debts, **59:4.**
Borrowing money, **59:4.**
Income tax consequences of business loans, **62:2.**
Collateral security in commercial code secured transaction, debtor as liable for payment of taxes, **106:9-207.**
Insolvent debtor, collection from, **60:19, 60:36.**
Municipal corporations. See within this heading, "Municipal corporations."
Set-off debt collection, revenue department to assist transitional assistance department in collecting support obligations, **62D:3.**
Decedents' estates.
Actions against estates, **60:36.**
Estate taxes, **62C:1 et seq., 65A:1 et seq., 65B:1 et seq., 65C:1 et seq.**
See ESTATE TAXES.
Executors and administrators, **59:18, 59:75, 62C:17, 202:20.**
See EXECUTORS AND ADMINISTRATORS.
Heir's liability for local taxes, **59:12D.**
Heirs, service of demand for local taxes, **60:16.**
Income tax, **62:9, 62C:8, 62C:26.**
See INCOME TAX.

TAXATION —Cont'd
Decedents' estates —Cont'd
Insolvent estates, priority in payment in taxes due from, **198:1.**
Insolvent estates, priority in payment of taxes due, **198:1.**
Legacy and succession taxes, **65:2 et seq.**
See LEGACY AND SUCCESSION TAXES.
Removal of property to evade taxes, **193:3.**
Repayment of exempted taxes of widows, poor persons, etc., **59:5.**
Sale of real property for payment, **202:20.**
Special assessments, **80:8, 80:13B.**
Declaration of estimated income tax, **61B:1, 62B:13-62B:21, 63B:1 et seq.**
See DECLARATION OF ESTIMATED INCOME TAX.
Declaration of estimated tax by corporations, **63B:1 et seq.**
See DECLARATION OF ESTIMATED TAX BY CORPORATIONS.
Deductions.
Capital gains, amendments to, **62:2.**
Energy conservation patent, **62:6.**
Estate taxes, **65C:3, 65C:3A.**
Income tax, **62:3.**
See INCOME TAX.
Insurance company taxation, **63:24.**
Legacy and succession taxes, **65:17, 65:18, 65:27.**
Local assessments, **59:23.**
Municipalities.
Local assessment, deduction of appropriations in determining, **59:23.**
Sums due Commonwealth, deduction of, **58:20A.**
Social security, **62:3, 149:150A.**
Withholding of tax, **62B:2, 62B:4, 62B:9, 62B:12.**
Deeds and conveyances.
Agricultural land conveyance taxes, **61A:9, 61A:12, 61A:19, 61A:19A.**
Effect of deed in tax sale, **62C:59, 62C:60.**
Income from property in estate under terms of deed set aside for charity, taxation of, **62:3.**

TAXATION —Cont'd
Deeds and conveyances —Cont'd
Recreational land, tax on
conveyance of, **61B:6,
61B:12.**
Registers and registry of deeds,
60:23, 60:62, 60:63.
See REGISTERS AND
REGISTRIES OF DEEDS.
Special assessments, registry of
deeds, **80:2, 80:12, 80:13B,
83:27.**
Eminent domain proceedings,
80A:1 et seq.
See SPECIAL
ASSESSMENTS.
Stamp tax, **64D:1 et seq.**
See DEED AND DOCUMENT
STAMP TAX.
Default of city or town as to state
taxes, enforcement in case,
59:20.
Deferral of taxes, **40:42J, 59:5,
83:16G.**
Deficiency assessment, interest,
62B:14, 62C:26.
Deficiency notice, **59:12F.**
Definitions, **61B:1, 62C:1, 64H:1,
64I:1.**
Delinquent taxes.
Abatement, **58:8.**
City or town delinquent in
paying state tax, penalty,
59:20.
Collection of information by
commissioner, **58:7.**
Demand for payment,
60:16-60:22A.
Disclosure of list of delinquent
taxpayers, **62C:21.**
Employment security, **62C:21.**
Foreclosure, **60:64 et seq.**
Notice to delinquent taxpayers,
62C:21.
Property taxes, interest
penalties on overdue, **59:57.**
Registration of title to land as
affecting, **185:46.**
Sale for taxes, **59:2B, 59:12E,
60:37-60:60.**
See TAX SALES.
Uncollectible taxes, **59:71.**
Water rates, **40:42C.**
Demand for payment,
60:16-60:22A.
Abatement claimants to exhibit
certificate, **60:20.**
Betterments, **60:17.**
Collectors, **60:1, 60:57.**
Decedents' estates, **60:36.**
Error in name on tax list not to
prevent collection of tax,
60:21.

TAXATION —Cont'd
Demand for payment —Cont'd
Executors and administrators,
demands against, **60:36.**
Fees to be paid by delinquent
taxpayer, **60:15.**
Insolvent debtors, demand
against assignee, **60:36.**
Mortgagees, demand, **60:38.**
Motor vehicle excise tax, **60:16.**
Notice of place for service, **60:39.**
Old age assistance tax, **60:16.**
Part payment, **60:22, 60:22A.**
Prior to sale or distraint, **60:16.**
Service, **60:16, 60:39.**
Special assessments, **60:17.**
Special warrant for distress or
imprisonment without,
60:19.
Stock or produce on land,
demand prior to distress,
60:27.
Tax collectors, demand for
payment.
Evidence, **60:1, 60:57.**
Mailing, **60:16.**
Special warrant for arrest,
60:19.
Time for advertisement of tax
sale, demand for payment as
affecting, **60:39.**
Dental service corporation, tax
exemption, **176E:14.**
Department of revenue, **14:1 et
seq., 58:1 et seq.**
See REVENUE DEPARTMENT
AND COMMISSIONER.
Deposit of taxes.
Banks and trust companies,
62C:45.
Government bonds, deposit to
secure payment of estate
taxes, **65C:10.**
Interest on by mortgagees,
183:61.
Descent of property.
Estate tax, **62C:1 et seq., 65A:1
et seq., 65B:1 et seq.,
65C:1 et seq.**
See ESTATE TAXES.
Legacy and succession tax, **65:2
et seq.**
See LEGACY AND
SUCCESSION TAXES.
Destruction of returns and
documents, **62C:69.**
Diminished valuation, **59:94.**
Director of accounts, powers and
duties as to local tax
assessments, **59:23.**

TAXATION —Cont'd
Disabilities.
Assistance to aged and disabled.
Demand for payment of
assessment, **60:16.**
Elderly and disabled tax fund.
Voluntary check off, **60:3D.**
Exemption of hot lunch
program from taxation,
64H:6.
Veterans, **58:8A, 59:5.**
Disabled veterans.
Exemption of property, **59:5.**
Paraplegic veterans or their
surviving spouses,
reimbursement of
municipalities for abatement
of taxes, **58:8A.**
Disclosure of tax information,
62C:21.
Discount on taxes, **59:58.**
Disqualification system for sale of
certain and town properties,
60:77B.
Dissolution, **41:43A, 156B:101.**
Distress and sale of personal
estate, **59:20, 60:24-60:28.**
See TAX SALES.
Distribution of taxes, **29:18,
58:18B et seq.**
Amount of, determination,
58:25, 58:25A.
Annual estimates, **58:25A.**
Cities and towns, distributions,
58:18B, 58:25.
Deductions of sums due to
Commonwealth, **58:20A.**
Highway fund, distributions to
cities and towns, **58:18B.**
Notice to town treasurers of
amount available, **58:25.**
Partial distributions, **58:25.**
Revenue department to
determine amounts, **58:25.**
Districts, **59:21, 62:1.**
Amount of annual assessment
with respect, **59:23, 59:25.**
Assessment districts,
establishment, **59:38.**
Bonds and notes.
Exemption, **59:5.**
Tax levy, **44:16, 44:19.**
Water pollution abatement
districts, **21:36.**
Commitment of separate lists
and warrants, **59:53.**
Debt limit as determined by
assessed valuation, **44:10.**
Fire districts, **48:61, 59:5.**
Light districts, **59:5, 59:21,
59:53.**

TAXATION —Cont'd
Districts —Cont'd
Lists of property, **59:53.**
Overlay assessments, **59:25.**
Regional school districts.
Exemption of bonds or notes
issued by school districts,
59:5.
Reduction in local taxes,
71:16B, 71:16B½.
State aid or reimbursement,
71:14B, 71:16B-71:16D.
See REGIONAL SCHOOL
DISTRICTS.
Reserve funds, establishment,
40:5C.
Salary and expenses of assessors
and collectors, **41:108B.**
Subject to law with respect to
assessment and collection of
town taxes, **59:21.**
Tax collectors.
Fire district taxes, **48:73.**
Salary and expenses of
collectors of district taxes,
41:108B.
Separate list and warrant for
district taxes, **59:53.**
Water and sewer districts,
exemption from taxation of
bonds, **59:5.**
Division of realty after
assessment.
Apportionment, **59:78A, 59:81.**
Appeal, **59:81.**
Foreclosure, partition as
affecting redemption, **60:68.**
Partial redemption from tax
sale, **60:76A.**
Dog racing, **61B:1, 128A:5,
128A:5B, 128A:23.**
Domestic animals and fowl, **59:5,
59:8A.**
Dwelling houses.
Residence generally. See within
this heading, "Residence."
Easements.
Central Massachusetts Economic
Development Authority,
Spec L 22:15.
Effect of tax deeds, **60:45.**
Taking of land for nonpayment
of taxes as subject to
easements, **60:54.**
Economic development and
industrial corporation,
property, **59:5, 121C:9.**
Education.
Schools and education. See
within this heading,
"Schools and education."

TAXATION —Cont'd
Elderly and disabled tax fund.
Voluntary check off on municipal
tax form, **60:3D.**
Elderly persons. See within this
heading, "Older persons."
Election or option.
Abatement proceedings, town
electing to have hearing by
appellate tax board, **59:64.**
Agricultural use, option of
municipality on land to be
sold or converted, **61A:14.**
Income tax.
Installments, **62:63.**
Taxable year, choice, **62:62.**
Installment transactions,
election for tax purposes,
62:63.
Local option statutes, **4:4B,
29:27C.**
Sales taxes.
Purchaser, reporting of gross
receipts from rented
personalty, **64H:8.**
Services sold at retail, **64H:2.**
Use, consumption, or storage
tax, reporting by purchaser
of gross receipts from rented
personalty, **64I:8.**
Electric and gas companies.
Condensed return to state,
164:84A.
Overdue bills collected as tax,
164:58E.
Residential service exempt from
sales tax, **64H:6.**
Returns, **62C:12.**
Sales tax exemptions, **64H:6.**
Transmission lines, **59:5, 59:18.**
Underground facilities, **59:5,
59:83.**
Eminent domain.
Apportionment, **79:7D, 79:35A.**
Collector of taxes, copy of notice
or petition to be furnished
to, **79:7F.**
Corporate realty, **59:3B.**
Damages or compensation.
Exemptions, effect of, **79:12.**
Liens for taxes, payment from
damages, **79:44A.**
Proration of taxes, **79:12.**
Settlement, assumption of
betterment assessment as
condition of, **79:39.**
Time for filing petition for,
79:16.
Evidence of assessed value,
79:35.

TAXATION —Cont'd
Eminent domain —Cont'd
Flood control reservoirs,
reimbursement of towns for
loss of taxes by taking of,
58:17B.
Lien for taxes, notice, **79:44A.**
Proration of taxes, **79:12.**
Recreational land, effect of tax
on, **61B:7.**
Special assessments, registry of
deeds, **80A:1 et seq.**
See SPECIAL
ASSESSMENTS.
Employers' report of income paid,
penalty for late filing, **62C:34.**
Employment and training
department.
Fair information practices,
62C:21.
Federal unemployment taxes,
151:46.
Set-off debt collection, liabilities,
62D:13.
Wage reporting, **62E:1 et seq.**
See WAGE REPORTING
SYSTEM.
Employment security.
Delinquent taxes, **62C:21.**
Excise tax, compromise,
151A:20.
Income tax.
Contributions, deductibility
from income, **151A:21.**
Exemptions.
Benefits, **151A:22.**
Federal exemptions, **151A:6.**
Federal internal revenue code.
Compromise of unpaid
unemployment excise
tax due, **151A:20.**
Exemptions under, **151A:6.**
Endowment associations,
exemption of property, **59:5.**
Energy systems.
Alternative energy resources,
tax incentive for use,
63:38H.
Exemptions.
Corporate taxes, tax
incentives for conservation
of energy resources,
63:38H.
Sales tax, **64H:6.**
Patents for, tax deductions, **62:2,
63:30.**
Solar energy, **59:5, 63:38H.**
Tax credit for energy
conservation expenditures,
62:6.
Wind powered facilities, **59:5,
62:6, 63:38H.**

TAXATION —Cont'd
Enterprise funds, tax levy for
fiscal year, **40:39K.**
Environmental fund of
environmental affairs
executive office, public funds,
21A:10.
Environmental management
department.
Annual certification as to forest
products removed to be
made by director of forests
and parks, **58:15.**
Forester's regulations as to
taxation of forest lands,
approval, **61:1.**
Lands as exempt, **59:5.**
Reimbursement of towns for loss
of revenue on lands
controlled, **58:13-58:17A.**
Valuation by revenue
commissioner of lands,
58:13.
Environmental pollution.
Pollution. See within this
heading, "Pollution."
Environmental protection
department, **58:13, 59:5.**
Equalization of taxes, **5:10, 58:3,
58:9.**
Equipment, **59:18.**
Errors or irregularities.
Abatement of taxes.
Insufficient payments due to
mistake, **59:65D.**
Late appeal, **59:65C.**
Tax collectors, **58:8.**
Clerical or data processing error,
time for taxation of property
omitted through, **59:75,
59:76.**
Names of taxpayers, **60:21.**
Reassessment in case, **59:77.**
Redemption amount as affected,
60:62.
Tax sales.
Effect of errors, **60:37.**
Reimbursement of purchaser
at invalid sale, **60:46.**
Water rates and charges,
redemption as affected by
errors, **60:76B.**
Waiver, penalty attributable to
erroneous advice of revenue
department employee,
62C:36B.
Escrow accounts for taxes on
mortgaged property, payment
of interest, **183:61.**
Estate planning by guardians and
conservators to minimize
taxes, **201:38.**

TAXATION —Cont'd
Estate taxes, **62C:1 et seq., 65C:1
et seq.**
Generally.
See ESTATE TAXES.
Legacy taxes, **65:2 et seq.**
See LEGACY AND
SUCCESSION TAXES.
Estimated tax.
Declaration of estimated income
tax, **61B:1, 62B:13-62B:21,
63B:1 et seq.**
See DECLARATION OF
ESTIMATED INCOME
TAX.
Estimate of value of property in
default of list, **59:36, 59:37.**
Evasion of tax, **59:89-59:92.**
Agricultural land, **61A:23.**
Assessment in event, **62C:26.**
Change of residence for purpose,
59:90.
Compromising assessment to
keep residence, penalized,
59:89.
Concealment of residence, **59:90.**
Deposit of assets with intent to
evade or defeat assessment
or collection of estate tax,
65C:28.
Estate tax, **65C:13, 65C:26,
65C:28.**
Exemption, inapplicability in
cases of evasion, **59:5.**
False lists for purpose of,
penalty, **59:91.**
False reports to commissioner,
268:6.
False valuation by assessors,
penalty, **41:30.**
Income tax, fraudulent returns,
62C:28.
See INCOME TAX.
Motor vehicle fuel tax, **64E:11,
64F:12.**
Penalties for, **41:30, 59:89-59:92,
62C:73, 64H:8.**
Return statement falsely made,
59:38F.
Venue for prosecution, **59:90.**
Veterans' exemption inapplicable
in case, **59:5.**
Evidence.
Appeal and review.
Assessed value, **79:35, 185:109.**
Attorney general's powers
relating to tax enforcement
procedures, **62C:70. (note)**
Bills, prima facie evidence as to
sending, **60:3.**

TAXATION —Cont'd
Evidence —Cont'd
Cigarette tax.
Advertisement offering to sell
or sale at less than cost as
evidence of intent to
injure competitors or
destroy or lessen
competition, evidence,
64C:14.
Cost, evidence, **64C:13,
64C:18, 64C:20.**
Counterfeit impression,
manufacture or possession
as evidence of
counterfeiting stamps,
64C:37.
Intent to destroy or lessen
competition, sales at less
than cost as evidence,
64C:14.
Manufacture or possession of
cigarette excise stamp or
dye or device not
authorized by
commissioner, evidence of
counterfeiting stamps,
64C:37.
Purchase at fictitious price,
evidence as to, discounts,
64C:18.
Searches and seizures, **64C:8,
64C:10, 64C:11, 64C:35,
64C:37.**
Unstamped cigarettes, **64C:34,
64C:36.**
Collector's affidavit as evidence
of demand, notice, and
service, **60:1, 60:57.**
Disability of veteran, evidence
for tax exemptions, **59:5.**
Instrument of assignment of tax
title, as prima facie
evidence, **60:52.**
Legacy or succession taxes,
discharge of lien, **65:9.**
Mass transportation facilities
payments, powers of state
tax commission in
determination, **58:25B.**
Presumptions and burden of
proof.
Agricultural and horticultural
property, **61A:9, 61A:12,
61A:14.**
Assessment of taxes, **62C:26.**
Horticultural property, **61A:9,
61A:12, 61A:14.**
Sales for taxes, circumstances
where municipality
deemed to be purchaser,
60:49.

TAXATION —Cont'd

Evidence —Cont'd

Presumptions and burden of
proof —Cont'd

Sales taxes, **64H:8, 64H:25.**

Use, consumption, or storage
tax, **64I:8, 64I:26.**

Registered lands, assurance
fund for, assessed value as
evidence in actions for
compensation, **185:109.**

Taking of land for nonpayment
of taxes, instrument prima
facie evidence of validity,
60:54.

Tax deeds and titles.

Assignment of title,
instrument of as prima
facie evidence, **60:52.**

Deed, tax deed as prima facie
evidence of tax title,
60:45.

Redemption, tax title account
as prima facie evidence of
amount necessary, **60:50.**

Tax sales.

City or town deemed
purchaser, **60:49.**

Collector's affidavit as
evidence of notice, **60:57.**

Redemption, tax title account
as evidence of amount
necessary, **60:50.**

Town treasurer's statement in
connection with low value
lands, **60:79.**

Veteran's disability, evidence for
tax exemption, **59:5.**

Waiver or release of tax lien,
62C:50, 62C:51.

Witnesses.

Attendance of witnesses in tax
proceedings, **62C:70.**

Revenue department's
authority to require
attendance and testimony,
58:25B.

Examination, inspection, or
investigation.

Abatement of taxes, **59:60,
59:61A.**

Administration and finance
executive office, special
examination of need for
appropriations to be met by
assessment of taxes,
7:9-7:11.

Assessments, **44:46A, 59:52B.**

Assessors.

Books and lists, **59:32, 59:33,
59:43, 59:60, 184:8A.**

TAXATION —Cont'd

Examination, inspection, or
investigation —Cont'd

Assessors —Cont'd

Municipal affairs, assessment
of tax to pay expenses of
investigating, **44:46A.**

Cigarette tax.

Books, papers and records,
64C:5, 64C:6, 64C:11.

Carriers, bailees, or
warehousemen, records,
64C:6.

Premises where cigarettes
possessed, stored, or sold,
64C:8, 64C:11.

Stampers, examination of
stocks, **62C:24.**

Tax stamps and metering
machines, **64C:33.**

Collector's books, **60:8.**

Co-operation as to examination
of records and returns,
62C:23.

Corporation taxes.

Books and papers, **63:26,
63:69, 63:79.**

Deed and document stamp tax,
64D:6.

Gasoline and motor fuel tax
licensees, inspection of
records, **64E:3.**

Income tax.

Returns, **62C:20 et seq.**

Revenue department and
commissioner, **62C:20,
62C:24.**

United States Secretary of the
Treasury, **62C:22, 62C:23.**

Verification of return, books
and papers examined,
62C:24.

In-person interviews with
taxpayers, **62C:80.**

Insurance companies,
examination of books, **63:26.**

Lists, **59:32.**

Mass transportation service
payments, powers of state
tax commission in
determination, **58:25B.**

Pipeline owners' returns to tax
commission, **59:38A.**

Records, **59:43, 62C:20,
62C:23-62C:25, 62C:70.**

Regulation of disclosure, **62C:21.**

Title, examination under
foreclosure or redemption
rights, **60:66.**

Valuation of property, inspection
of tax information, **59:52C.**

TAXATION —Cont'd

Excise taxes.

See EXCISE TAXES.

Excuses for failure to timely file
appeal, **59:64, 59:65B, 59:65C.**

Executions.

Cigarette tax proceeding,
execution for costs of, **64C:8.**

Collector of taxes, judgment
against, **41:43A.**

Legacy and succession taxes,
execution for collection of,
65:30.

Reimbursement of execution
creditor, **236:33.**

Executors and administrators,
59:18, 59:75, 62C:17, 202:20.

See EXECUTORS AND
ADMINISTRATORS.

Exemptions, **32:19, 59:2, 59:5 to
59:5K, 59:59, 60:3A.**

Additional exemptions, exempt
property not to receive, **59:5.**

Aged persons, **59:5.**

Additional exemptions, **62:3.**

Hot lunch program, **64H:6.**

Volunteers providing
municipal services, **59:5K.**

Agricultural property, **59:5,
59:8A, 60:24.**

Air conditioning of premises,
59:5.

Air Force Cross, holder, **59:5.**

Air pollution control devices,
59:5.

Airports, **59:5, 59:5D-59:5F.**

Air raid shelters, **59:5.**

Alterations or improvements for
elderly nonowners, **59:5.**

Amherst economic development
and industrial corporation,
Spec L 23:9.

Animals, **59:5, 64H:6.**

Annual report of commission,
58:15.

Annuity associations, **59:5.**

Appeal from denial of residential
property tax exemption,
59:5C.

Application, **59:5. (note)**

Apportionment of certain, **59:5.**

Assessors.

Entry on valuation list of
exempt property, **59:51,
59:86.**

Veterans' property exemptions,
59:5.

Athletics, charitable corporation
as exempt from property
tax, **59:5.**

Banks and trust companies,
59:5.

TAXATION —Cont'd
Exemptions —Cont'd
Blind persons, **59:5, 59:59, 60A:1, 62:3.**
Bomb shelters, **59:5.**
Bonds and certificates of indebtedness of certain governmental entities, **59:5.**
Boston public health commission, **Spec L 70:9.**
Bridges, exemption from sales tax, **64H:6.**
Buildings and structures.
Cemetery administration buildings, **59:5.**
Sales tax, exemptions, **64H:6.**
Burial rights, **59:5.**
Cemetery property, **59:5.**
Certificates and certification, housing for elderly, **59:5.**
Charitable trusts.
Effect of failure to file annual report with division of public charities, **59:5.**
Income tax exemption, **62:3.**
Charities and charitable contributions, **66:1, 66:18.**
See CHARITIES AND CHARITABLE CONTRIBUTIONS.
Children of deceased policemen or fire fighters, property, **59:5.**
Churches and religious organizations.
Legacy and succession taxes, **65:1.**
Meals, **64H:6.**
Property exempt from local taxes, **59:5.**
Room occupancy tax, exemption, **64G:2.**
Sales tax, **64H:6.**
Clothing, **59:5.**
Distress and sale, exemption, **60:24.**
Commercial fishing gear and equipment, **59:5.**
Containers or packages, sales tax exemptions, **64H:6.**
Contracts for extension of tax exemption, **121A:6A.**
Co-operative banks, **59:5, 170:35.**
Corporation taxes.
Machinery and equipment, **59:5, 63:30.**
Savings, co-operative banks, and associations. See within this heading, "Savings bank."

TAXATION —Cont'd
Exemptions —Cont'd
Credit Union Employees Retirement Association, **171:84.**
Credit unions, **59:5.**
Deed and document stamp tax exemptions, **64D:1.**
Deeds and documents, excise tax, **64D:1.**
Dental service corporations, **176E:14.**
Deposit insurance fund, **168 Appx (1934):8.**
Depositors insurance fund, **168 Appx (1932):9.**
Savings bank investment fund, **168 Appx (1945):11.**
Disabled veterans and their spouses and parents, **59:5.**
Distress and sale, property exempt, **60:24.**
Dividends from federal S corporation trusts, **62:8.**
Economic development corporations, **59:5, 121C:9.**
Elderly persons, **59:5.**
Employees benefit association established, **168:42-168:44.**
Employment security benefits, **151A:22.**
Energy systems.
Corporate taxes, tax incentives for conservation of energy resources, **63:38H.**
Sales tax, **64H:6.**
Entry on valuation list, **59:51.**
Equipment.
Corporation taxes, **59:5, 63:30.**
Machinery situated in other state, **59:5.**
Sales tax exemption for manufacturing equipment, **64H:6.**
Estate taxes, **65C:2, 65C:3.**
Exceptions, **59:5.**
Express exemption, necessity, **59:2.**
Extension of time within which certain persons may apply, **59:5.**
Fallout shelters, **59:5.**
Farm tractors, sales tax exemption, **64H:23, 64I:27.**
Fathers and mothers of soldiers and sailors, **59:5.**
Federal government, **59:5.**
Fiduciaries, exemption of intangible property, **59:5.**

TAXATION —Cont'd
Exemptions —Cont'd
Fire departments.
Fire trucks sold to certain organizations as exempt from sales tax, **64H:6.**
Surviving spouses and minor children of deceased fire fighters, **59:5.**
Fire district bonds and certificates, **59:5.**
Fishing gear and equipment, commercial, **59:5.**
Foreign states or countries, property, **59:5.**
Forest lands, **59:5.**
Fraternal benefit societies, **59:5, 176:49.**
Fuel used by railroads, sales tax exemption, **64H:6.**
Gasoline and motor fuel taxes.
Excise tax on fuel bought out of state, exceptions from as affected by fuel tank capacity, **64F:3.**
Licensing requirement, noncommercial vehicles exempted, **64E:2.**
Restraining collection of gasoline tax on exempt federal sales, **64A:12, 64E:12, 64F:13.**
Gun safes, **64H:6.**
Hawkers, peddlers, and transient vendors, exemption from statutory requirements, **101:2.**
Hazardous waste insolvency fund, **21C:28.**
Highway infrastructure bonds, **29:2O.**
Homesteads of old persons, **59:5, 188:1A.**
Horticultural property, **59:5, 59:8A, 60:24.**
Horticultural societies, **59:5.**
Hospitals and health care.
Local taxes, **59:5.**
Room occupancy tax, **64G:2.**
Sales tax on meals, **64H:6.**
Hospital service corporations' real estate investments, **176A:16, 176A:19.**
Household furniture and effects, exemption from personal property tax, **59:5.**
Housing and urban renewal, **121A:6A, 121A:10, 121A:15, 121A:18A, 121A:18C, 121B:15, 121B:16.**
Hydroelectric plants, **59:5.**

TAXATION —Cont'd
Exemptions —Cont'd
Income producing property, **59:5.**
Income tax, **62:1 et seq.**
See INCOME TAX.
Increase in real property tax exemptions, acceptance of laws effecting, **29:27C.**
Industrial waste, **59:5, 63:38D.**
Infrastructure bonds, **29:2O.**
Insurers insolvency fund, exemptions, **175D:11.**
Intangible property held by fiduciaries, **59:5.**
Laundry equipment, **59:5.**
Legacy and succession taxes, **65:1.**
Charitable purposes, **62:3, 65:1.**
Lien, exemptions, **65:9.**
Retirement systems and pensions, **32:19, 65:1.**
Library associations relieved from requirement as to filing annual reports with Secretary of State, **180:26A.**
Lists required, **59:29, 59:51.**
Local property assessment, **59:2B, 59:5, 59:59, 60:3A.**
Machinery and equipment.
Corporation taxes, **59:5, 63:30.**
Machinery situated in other state, **59:5.**
Sales tax exemption for manufacturing equipment, **64H:6.**
Manufacturing equipment, sales tax exemption, **64H:6.**
Massachusetts Bay transportation authority, **161A:24.**
Mayors, **59:5C, 59:5E.**
Meals at churches, **64H:6.**
Medical care and assistance, exempt income and resources of applicant, **118E:10.**
Militia, **59:5, 60:24.**
Minor children of policemen or fire fighters, exemptions, **59:5.**
Mobile homes of nonresident military personnel, **59:5.**
Model water and sewer commission, **40N:19.**
Motor vehicles, **59:5, 60A:1, 64H:6.**
Music and musical instruments, **59:5, 64H:1.**
Neat cattle, **59:5.**
Nets, **59:5.**
Issuance of notices requiring lists, **59:29.**

TAXATION —Cont'd
Exemptions —Cont'd
New England power pool, **164A:8, 164A:20.**
Old persons, **59:5.**
Additional exemptions, **62:3.**
Hot lunch program, **64H:6.**
Optometric service corporations, **176F:14.**
Parsonages and residences of officials of religious faiths, **59:5.**
Partnership shares, **59:5.**
Policeman killed in line of duty, real property of surviving spouse or minor children, **59:5.**
Poll tax bills to contain notice of persons entitled, **59:5.**
Poultry and poultry products, **59:5, 64H:6.**
Precious metals, sales tax exemption for certain metals, **64H:6.**
Property taxes, **59:2A, 59:5, 59:5C to 59:5K, 164A:8.**
Public lands, **59:5.**
Radio and television, **59:5, 64H:1, 64H:6.**
Railroads.
Fuel used by railroads, sales tax exemption, **64H:6.**
Real property, limited exemption, **160:87.**
Record of abatement for purpose, **59:60.**
Recreational land, **59:5, 61B:7.**
Regional incinerator district bonds and notes, **59:5.**
Regional transportation authorities, **161B:13.**
Religious organizations.
Legacy and succession taxes, **65:1.**
Meals, **64H:6.**
Property exempt from local taxes, **59:5.**
Room occupancy tax, exemption, **64G:2.**
Sales tax, **64H:6.**
Resale or exempt use certificate, notice to produce, **64I:8.**
Research and development corporations, exemption from sales tax for certain sales, **64H:6.**
Residence.
District executive of southern New England District of Assemblies of God, residence, **59:5.**

TAXATION —Cont'd
Exemptions —Cont'd
Residence —Cont'd
Educational institutions, removal of exemption from officers' residences which are not on campuses of such institutions, **59:5.**
Methodist Church, residence occupied by district superintendent, **59:5.**
Old persons, residential property, **59:5.**
Widows' and minors' exemption as affected by change, **59:5.**
Retail sales tax exemptions, **64H:6, 64I:7.**
Retirement systems and pensions, **32:19, 32:23, 32:41, 59:5, 62:8, 171:84.**
Revaluation of real estate, relief, **59:5.**
Room occupancy tax, **64G:2, 64G:3.**
Military personnel, **64G:12.**
Sale and distress, property exempt, **60:24.**
Savings banks, **59:5, 168:41, 168:42-168:44.**
Services sold at retail, tax exemptions, **64H:6, 64I:7.**
Sewers.
Local property, **59:5D, 59:5E.**
Model sewer and water commission, **40N:19.**
Ships and vessels, excise tax, **60B:2, 60B:3.**
Short taxable year, **62:3.**
Small businesses.
Exemption for certain property, **59:5I.**
Social security payments, excluded in determining old persons' eligibility, **59:5.**
Solar energy systems, **59:5.**
Soldiers and sailors and their spouses, **59:5.**
"Specially adapted housing" occupied by disabled veteran, **59:5.**
Specific exemption as affecting state tax return, **62C:17.**
State-owned land or property, **58:15A, 59:5, 64G:2, 64H:6.**
Stock of certain corporations, **59:5.**
Storage warehouses, **59:5.**
Nonresident's personalty stored in original packages, **59:2.**

TAXATION —Cont'd
Exemptions —Cont'd
Surviving spouses, **59:5, 60:3B, 65:1.**
Swine exempt from sales tax, **64H:6.**
Television and radio, **59:5, 64H:1, 64H:6.**
Time.
Application, extension of time, **59:5, 59:59.**
Short taxable year, **62:3.**
Tools, **59:5.**
Distress and sale, exemption, **60:24.**
Sales and use tax, **64H:6.**
Trailer coaches in certain parks, **59:5.**
Trigger locks, **64H:6.**
Turnpike authority, **59:2B, 81A:8.**
Underground wires and conduits, **59:5.**
United States. See within this heading, "United States."
Urban redevelopment corporations, **59:5, 121A:6A, 121A:6C, 121A:10, 121A:18A, 121B:15, 121B:16.**
Application of gross receipts to reduce exemption, **121A:15.**
Charitable corporations undertaking urban renewal projects, **121A:15.**
Use, consumption or storage tax, **64I:7.**
See USE, CONSUMPTION, OR STORAGE TAX.
Veterans, **59:5, 60A:1, 62:1.**
Water companies, **59:5.**
Water pollution, property used for abatement or prevention, **59:5.**
Wearing apparel, **59:5.**
Distress and sale, exemption, **60:24.**
Widows and widowers, **59:5, 60:3B, 65:1.**
Wind powered energy systems, **59:5.**
Withholding of tax.
Dependency deductions or exemptions, **62B:2, 62B:9, 62B:12.**
Students in seasonal or temporary employment, **62B:1.**
Exorbitant charge for redemption from tax title, penalty, **60:104.**

TAXATION —Cont'd
Expenses incurred in conjunction.
Levy and sale, expenses, **60:25, 62C:62.**
Liens for property tax deficiency, **59:12F.**
Mortgagee in possession, taxes and other expenditures, **244:20.**
Partition property, apportion of tax, **59:78A.**
State treasurer, expenses of keeping records of local property assessment, **58:4C.**
Tax assessors, appropriations for compensation and expenses, **41:108B.**
Exports from any state not to be taxed, **US Const Art 1 9 cl 5.**
Extension of time.
Abatements or exemptions, extension of time within which certain persons may apply, **59:5. (note)**
City or town, increase in time for appeal, **51:14.**
Combat zones, soldiers serving, **62C:81.**
Corporation taxes.
Assessment of taxes in case of revival of certain sections, extension of time, **63:52.**
Declaration of estimated tax by corporations.
Filing of declarations, **63B:3.**
Payment of tax, **63B:4.**
Estate taxes.
Filing of return, **64C:8.**
Interest for extending time for payment, **65A:2.**
Payment, **65A:2, 65C:10, 65C:13.**
Federal estate tax laws, **65A:2.**
Foreclosure of tax title, **60:62.**
Income tax.
Assessment of tax, **62C:27.**
Declaration of estimated tax, **62B:13.**
Filing of returns and payment of tax, **62C:19.**
Legacy and succession taxes, **65:32.**
Sale for taxes, **60:37A, 60:77.**
Special assessments.
Filing petition for abatement, **80:6.**
Payment where land not built, **80:13A.**
Tax title foreclosure, **60:62.**
Extent of levy, **62C:53.**
Fair cash value in assessing local taxes, **58:9, 59:2A, 59:21C, 59:38, 59:38F, 59:38G.**

TAXATION —Cont'd
Fair information practices, **62C:21, 62C:22, 62C:74.**
Fallout shelters, **59:5.**
False tax lists, penalty, **59:91.**
Farm property, **61A:1-61A:24.**
Federal government.
United States. See within this heading, "United States."
Federal savings banks, taxation of interest, **62:2.**
Fees.
Abatement records, fees for copies, **59:60.**
Adoption of children, income tax deduction for fees of agency, **62:3.**
Agricultural or horticultural land, fee for issuance of certificate of taxes due or paid, **61A:19A.**
Appellate tax board.
Witness fees, **58A:11, 58A:12.**
Cigarette tax, refund or reimbursement of license fees, **64C:5.**
Collection of taxes, **60:15, 60:95.**
See TAX COLLECTORS.
Deeds and titles, **60:15, 60:73, 262:39.**
Estate taxes.
Issuance of documents by commissioner, **65C:24.**
Returns, fees for filing, **62C:17, 65C:8.**
Federal tax lien, fee for filing notice or certificate of discharge, **36:24.**
Foreclosure of tax title, land court's fees, **262:39.**
Gasoline and motor fuel tax law, fees for licenses, **64A:2.**
Income tax.
Adopted children, exemption of fees paid to adoption agency, **62:3.**
Warrant for collection, fees to officer executing, **62C:46.**
Licenses, **62C:67, 62C:68.**
Liens.
Business corporation sale or transfer, fee for waiver of tax lien, **62C:52.**
Certificates, **60:23A, 60:23B.**
Collector's fees in connection with taking for nonpayment, **60:55.**
Federal tax liens, filing notice of certificate of discharge, **36:24.**
Preservation statements, recording fees, **60:37A.**

TAXATION —Cont'd
Fees —Cont'd
Liens —Cont'd
Register of deeds entering
instrument of taking of
land for nonpayment,
262:38.
Taking of land for
nonpayment, fees, **60:55,
262:38, 262:39.**
Waivers by commissioners,
fees, **62C:52.**
Municipal corporations, **59:5D,
59:5F, 262:4.**
Register of deeds furnishing
abstract cards or copies of
recorded instruments,
262:38.
Revenue department, fees for
licenses charged, **62C:67.**
Sales.
Legal fees, **60:79.**
Sheriff, **60:89.**
Tax collector, **60:15.**
State employees, compensation
for filing state tax returns,
268A:4.
Taking of land for nonpayment
of taxes, entering
instrument, **262:38, 262:39.**
Warrant for taxes, fee for
issuance, **262:4.**
Filing.
Records and recording. See
within this heading,
"Records and recording."
Financial officers of municipalities,
notice to, **59:23A, 59:23B,
59:70A.**
Fines and penalties.
Abatement of penalty
attributable to written
advice of revenue
department employee,
62C:36B.
Arrest and imprisonment,
60:29-60:31.
Assessors.
Compromise of assessments to
keep residence, making or
assenting to proposal,
59:89.
Corporate property and motor
vehicles, assessor's failure
to report, **59:83.**
Delinquent state taxes,
assessment with respect,
59:20.
Failure to choose assessors,
41:4.
False valuation, **41:30.**

TAXATION —Cont'd
Fines and penalties —Cont'd
Assessors —Cont'd
Forfeiture for failure to take
oath, **41:29.**
Grantee of real estate, failure
to furnish owner's name
and address to assessor,
184:8A.
Keepers of taverns,
boardinghouses or
dwelling houses failing to
give information, **59:92.**
Neglect of duty, **59:93, 59:94.**
Storage warehouses failing to
give information, **59:33.**
Bad checks, **60:57A, 62C:35.**
Boardinghouse keepers,
information to be given,
59:92.
Cigarette tax, **64C:5.**
See CIGARETTE TAX.
Collectors, **60:99-60:104, 62C:33.**
See TAX COLLECTORS.
Conducting business without
license or registration,
62C:76.
Conversion of funds, **62C:73.**
Disclosure of tax information by
public employees, **62C:21.**
Dwelling house masters and
mistresses, information to
be given, **59:92.**
Estate taxes, **62C:21, 62C:26 to
62C:28, 65C:13.**
Estimated income taxes,
62C:45A.
Evasion of tax, **41:30,
59:89-59:92, 62C:73, 64H:8.**
False list of property, **59:91.**
Forest products tax, failure to
make return, **61:5.**
Fraud, evasion of tax, **41:30,
59:89-59:92, 62C:73, 64H:8.**
Gasoline and motor fuel taxes.
False return or statement,
64A:11, 64E:11, 64F:12.
Forfeiture, **64E:10-64E:14.**
Income paid, late reporting,
62C:34.
Income tax, **62C:21, 62C:28,
62C:33, 62C:34, 62C:73.**
See INCOME TAX.
Juror as taxpayer in action for
recovery of forfeiture,
234:30.
Late filing, **62C:33, 62C:34.**
Legacy and succession taxes.
Apportionment, **65A:5.**
Domicile of decedent, penalties
and interest as affected by
determination, **65B:5.**

TAXATION —Cont'd
Fines and penalties —Cont'd
Legacy and succession taxes
—Cont'd
Inventory and appraisal of
estates, failure to file,
65:22.
Neglect or refusal to furnish
information to
commissioner, **65:29.**
Other state, penalty as part of
tax imposed, **58:28C.**
Partnership returns, late filing,
62C:34.
Property taxes, interest
penalties on overdue, **59:57.**
Sales tax.
Assumption of tax by vendor,
unlawful advertising,
64H:23.
Evasion of tax by means of
exempt use certificate,
64H:8.
Resale certificate, wrongful
giving, **64H:8.**
Special warrant for distress or
imprisonment without
demand for payment, **60:19.**
Stamps, failure to affix, **64D:6A.**
Storage warehouses, failure to
give information, **59:33.**
Tavern keepers, information to
be given, **59:92.**
Telephone and telegraph
companies failing to provide
required information, **59:42.**
Underpayment based on fraud,
65C:13.
Use, consumption and storage
tax.
Evasion of tax by means of
exempt use certificate,
64I:8.
Resale certificate, wrongful
giving, **64I:8.**
Unlawful advertising, **64I:24.**
Waiver, penalty attributable to
erroneous advice of revenue
department employee,
62C:36B.
Fire departments, exemptions.
Fire trucks sold to certain
organizations as exempt
from sales tax, **64H:6.**
Surviving spouses and minor
children of deceased fire
fighters, **59:5.**
Fire districts.
Assessments and collections,
48:73.
Assessors, **41:108B, 48:73,
59:21, 59:23, 59:25, 59:53.**

TAXATION —Cont'd
Fire districts —Cont'd
Bonds and notes of, exemption, **59:5.**
Establishment and maintenance of, taxes, **48:61.**
Excluded persons or estates, exemption, **48:79.**
Purchase of engines and equipment, **48:69.**
Purpose of raising money by taxes, **48:61, 48:69.**
Firefighters killed in line of duty, tax exemptions for surviving spouses and minor children, **59:5.**
Fire prevention orders as to additions or changes limited by assessed valuation, **148:29.**
Fiscal year.
Conforming changes in law in recognition of adoption, **59:21, 59:23, 59:23A, 59:25, 59:27.**
Municipalities.
Assessment of taxes, **59:21, 59:23, 59:23A, 59:25, 59:27.**
Collection of taxes, **60:3, 60:17.**
Payments in lieu of taxes, **44:64.**
Fish and game.
Boats.
Excise tax, **59:8, 60B:3.**
Exemption from tax, **59:5, 60B:3, 64H:6, 64I:7.**
Conservation, reimbursement for loss of tax on land used for, **58:13-58:17A.**
Land of fisheries and wildlife division exempt, **58:15A.**
Marine fish and fisheries.
Excise tax on interests in fishing vessels, **63:31A, 63:67.**
Gasoline tax receipts, crediting, **64A:13.**
Sales tax exemption, **64H:6, 64I:7.**
Nongame wildlife program, contribution from tax liability, **62:6E.**
Flood control reservoirs, towns reimbursed for loss of taxes by taking, **58:17B.**
Foreclosure.
Assessors, foreclosure of tax title held by city or town.
Assessment for cost, **60:50B.**
Notice, **60:76C.**

TAXATION —Cont'd
Foreclosure —Cont'd
Legal fees, payment to city or town, **60:65.**
Liens.
Agricultural and horticultural property.
Exemption from conveyance tax, **61A:12.**
Subject to municipality's option to purchase, **61A:14.**
Deed as subject to taxes, mortgaged lands, **244:14.**
Mortgagee in possession, taxes and other expenditures, **244:20.**
Personal property, distress and sale of for payment of taxes, **60:24-60:28.**
See TAX SALES.
Real property, **60:53-60:56.**
Tax liens generally.
See TAX LIENS.
Real property sale, foreclosure by, **60:37-60:60.**
See TAX SALES.
Redemption, foreclosure of right of, **60:64-60:75.**
See TAX DEEDS AND TITLES.
Supreme judicial court, review of questions of law in tax foreclosure proceedings, **60:72.**
Tax sales.
Lien for taxes, foreclosure by sale, **60:37-60:60.**
Redemption of tax title created by sale, foreclosure of right to, **60:64-60:75.**
See TAX DEEDS AND TITLES.
Titles, foreclosure of redemption right on, **60:64-60:75.**
See TAX DEEDS AND TITLES.
Unoccupied or abandoned building, petition to vacate decree of foreclosure, **60:69A.**
Foreign corporations, **63:39-63:42B.**
See CORPORATION TAXES.
Foreign states or countries.
Apportioned use certificate, services sold at retail outside of Commonwealth, **64H:6.**
Deduction for capital stock taxes by foreign state or country as disallowed, **63:1.**

TAXATION —Cont'd
Foreign states or countries —Cont'd
Enforcement of tax liability, bringing suit in foreign state, **58:28C.**
Exemption of property, **59:5.**
Income tax.
Credit or deduction for taxes due or paid to other state or country, **62:6.**
Exemptions.
Beneficiaries, income received, **62:3.**
Pensions received from other state, **62:3.**
Gross income, inclusion of income from foreign sources, **62:2.**
Reciprocity, **62:3, 62C:22, 62C:23.**
Residents of, taxation of income, **62:5A.**
Interstate co-operation commission, function, **9:23.**
Reciprocity, **58:28C.**
Services sold at retail outside of Commonwealth, sales tax exemption, **64H:6.**
Ships engaged in foreign trade, excise tax, **59:8, 63:67.**
Special warrant for taxpayer about to enter, **60:19.**
Use, consumption, or storage tax.
Bond or deposit, filing by nonresident contractor to secure payment of tax, **64I:31A.**
Exemptions, **64I:7.**
Presumption as to property brought into Commonwealth from another state, **64I:8.**
Proceedings against nonresident defendants, **64I:33.**
Forest lands and products, **61:1-61:8.**
Abatement of taxes, application, **61:3.**
Appeal from refusal to abate taxes, **61:3.**
Application for classification, **61:2.**
Apportionment of tax, **61:5.**
Assignment to nonprofit agency, **61:8.**
Classification for taxation, **59:5, 61:2.**
Withdrawal from classification, **61:7.**

TAXATION —Cont'd
Forest lands and products
—Cont'd
Collection of taxes, **61:3.**
Definitions, **61:1.**
Determination of tax upon
owner's failure to file
return, **61:4.**
Environmental management
department, **58:13-58:17A,
59:5.**
Failure to file return, **61:4, 61:6.**
Fires, assessment for state
expenditures with respect,
48:24.
Imposition of tax, **61:3.**
Interest upon abatement, **61:3.**
Notice of classification, **61:2.**
Notice of tax, **61:3.**
Option to purchase classified
land.
City or town, **61:8.**
Penalty for failure to make
return, **61:6.**
Refund of taxes upon abatement,
61:3.
Returns required of taxpayer,
61:3.
Sale of classified land,
restrictions, **61:8.**
Special and betterment
assessments, **61:5.**
State forest land.
Evaluation, **58:15.**
Reimbursement of towns for
loss of tax, **58:13-58:17A.**
Structures erected by
licensees, **59:5.**
Withdrawal of land from
classification, **61:7.**
Forms.
Abatement application, **59:59,
61:2, 62C:37.**
Agricultural land, municipality's
intent to exercise purchase
option, **61A:14.**
Appellate tax board.
Informal procedure, **58A:7A.**
Approval by commissioner and
department of revenue,
58:31.
Assessment, **60:105.**
Assessors.
Books, **59:45.**
Commissioner of revenue,
blank forms provided,
58:1.
Valuation lists, assessors'
statement, **59:52.**
Warrants for collection, **59:55.**
Bills, **60:3A.**

TAXATION —Cont'd
Forms —Cont'd
Collectors, **60:105.**
Approval by commissioner,
59:54, 60:8, 60:105.
Warrant issued to collector,
form and contents, **59:55.**
Estate taxes.
Certificate for proving
payment of taxes on
nonresident's estate,
65C:21.
Return, **65C:8.**
Income tax.
Abatement, application,
62C:37.
Commissioner to promulgate,
62C:3.
Furnishing and distribution,
62C:5.
Returns, **62C:5.**
Withholding of tax, **62B:4,
62B:5.**
List committed to collector,
59:54.
Return, form, **62C:5.**
Revenue department and
commissioner, prescription
and approval of forms,
58:31, 62C:3.
Statements and lists, **58:5,
59:54.**
Sales taxes.
Dealer contract clause relative
to sales taxes, **106:201.**
Exempt use certificate, **64H:8.**
Warrants for collection, **59:55.**
Withholding of tax.
Returns, approval of form,
62B:5.
Withholding exemption and
deduction certificate,
prescribing form, **62B:4.**
Fowl.
Excise tax on domestic fowl,
59:8A.
Exemption, **59:5, 64H:6.**
Sales tax, exemptions, **64H:6.**
Fractional divisions, addition to
tax to avoid, **59:25.**
Fraternal societies, exemptions,
59:5, 176:49.
Fraud, **59:89-59:92.**
Free public libraries, use of tax
revenues, **78:19A.**
Fuel distributors, **64A:1 et seq.**
See GASOLINE AND MOTOR
FUEL TAXES.
Furniture, exemption, **59:5.**
Future interests, settlement and
payment of certain taxes,
65:15A.

TAXATION —Cont'd
Game.
Fish and game. See within this
heading, "Fish and game."
Garage accessories, exemption,
59:5.
Garbage and rubbish.
Assessments, **16:22.**
Appropriations in districts to
meet, **16:24.**
Environmental Protection
Department, solid waste
disposal facilities owned,
58:13.
Cities and towns,
reimbursement for loss of
tax on land used for disposal
facilities, **58:13.**
Corporation taxes, exemptions,
63:38D.
Operator of privately owned
facility, **16:24A.**
Privately owned or operated
resource recovery facilities,
taxation, **16:24, 16:24A.**
Reimbursement for tax loss on
lands used, **21H:3, 58:13.**
Resource recovery facilities.
Owner taxed by town or city
in which facility located,
16:24A.
Residue as solid waste for
purpose of landfill fee,
111:150A.
Solid waste disposal.
As manufacturing activity,
58:2.
Operator of privately owned
facility, **16:24A.**
Gas and electric companies.
Condensed return to state,
164:84A.
Overdue bills collected as tax,
164:58E.
Residential service exempt from
sales tax, **64H:6.**
Returns, **62C:12.**
Sales tax exemptions, **64H:6.**
Transmission lines, **59:5, 59:18.**
Underground facilities, **59:5,
59:83.**
Gasoline, **64A:1-64A:13.**
See GASOLINE AND MOTOR
FUEL TAXES.
General court, **MA Const Part 2
Ch 1 Sec 1 Art 4.**
Gifts, grants, and gratuities.
Charitable contributions,
68:1-68:16, 180:1 et seq.
See CHARITIES AND
CHARITABLE
CONTRIBUTIONS.

TAXATION —Cont'd
Gifts, grants, and gratuities
—Cont'd
Death taxes.
Estate taxes, **62C:1 et seq.,
65A:1 et seq., 65B:1 et
seq., 65C:1 et seq.**
See ESTATE TAXES.
Legacy taxes, **65:2 et seq.**
See LEGACY AND
SUCCESSION TAXES.
Income tax, training grants for
residents in psychiatry as
subject, **19:10.**
Lands acquired by
municipalities through gift,
abatement of unpaid tax,
59:72A.
Nongame wildlife fund,
contributions, **62:6D.**
Organ transplant fund,
contributions, **62:6E.**
Goods, chattels, etc., **59:4.**
Government entity or
instrumentality thereof,
taxation of real property
formerly owned, **59:2C.**
Grand army associations,
exemption, **59:5.**
Gross receipts tax for games at
elderly housing projects,
10:38.
Group insurance for municipal
employees, cost included tax
rate, **32B:3.**
Growth.
State tax revenues, limitation on
growth, **62F:1 to 62F:8.**
Guardians, conservators, and
committees.
Exemption of intangible
property held by guardian,
59:5.
Income tax, **62:13, 62C:62.**
Gun safes.
Exemptions, **64H:6.**
Hawkers, peddlers, and transient
vendors, stock in trade.
Exemption from statutory
requirements, creation,
101:2.
Payment before obtaining local
license, **101:5.**
Hazardous waste insolvency fund,
exemptions, **21C:28.**
Head tax, **US Const Art 1 9 cl 1,
4; 24th Amend.**
Health.
Exempt income and resources of
applicant for assistance,
118E:10.

TAXATION —Cont'd
Health —Cont'd
Exemption as to infirm persons,
59:5.
Medical malpractice
self-insurance trust funds,
exemption from taxation,
175F:16.
Reimbursement of towns for loss
of taxes on land used by
health department, **58:13.**
Research animals, sales tax
exemption, **64H:6.**
Service plans and corporations,
**176B:10, 176B:14, 176C:14,
176C:15.**
Hearings.
Appeal and review, **59:65.**
Heavy vehicle use tax, proof of
payment accompanying
registration application,
90:1A.
Highway fund, **90:34.**
See HIGHWAYS AND
STREETS.
Highways and streets.
Abatement of street sprinkling
assessment, **40:18.**
Additional expenditures covered,
81:25.
Easement for landscaping along
state highways, **81:13A.**
Gasoline and motor fuel taxes.
Administrative expenses as
payable from fund, **90:34.**
Constitution of Massachusetts,
expenditure of motor
vehicle and fuel revenue
on highways, **MA Const
Amend Art 78.**
Disposition, **64A:13, 64E:13,
64F:14.**
Infrastructure bonds, **29:2O.**
Out-of-state purchase of fuel or
special fuels, disposition of
tax receipts, **64F:14.**
Poles and wires in public ways,
how and where assessed,
59:18.
Repairs of private ways or
bridges, financing, **84:14.**
Special motor fuels tax,
distribution, **64E:13.**
Hogs.
Excise tax, **59:8A.**
Exemption of local taxes, **59:5.**
Sales tax exemption, **64H:6.**
Horse racing, **61B:1, 128A:5,
128A:5B, 128A:23.**
Horses.
Excise tax, **59:8A.**
Exemption, **59:5.**

TAXATION —Cont'd
Horticultural property,
61A:1-61A:24.
Hospitals and health care
facilities, exemptions, **59:5,
64G:2, 64H:6.**
Hospital service corporations,
taxation of real estate owned,
176A:16.
Hotels, motels, and
roominghouses.
Information as to residents of
boarding houses, refusal to
give or falsity in giving,
59:92.
Returns of innkeepers, **62C:16.**
Room occupancy tax, **64G:1 et
seq.**
See ROOM OCCUPANCY
TAX.
Household furniture, exemption,
59:5.
Housekeeping utensils exempt
from distress and sale, **60:24.**
Housing and redevelopment
authorities, payments in lieu
of taxes where revaluation
occurs, **121B:16.**
Housing and urban renewal.
Exemptions, **121A:6A, 121A:10,
121A:15, 121A:18A,
121A:18C, 121B:15,
121B:16.**
Generally.
See URBAN
REDEVELOPMENT
CORPORATIONS.
Husband and wife.
Support obligations, collection
via taxation system, **62D:3,
119A:6.**
Use of names of both spouses,
14:6.
Hydroelectric plants, property tax
exemptions, **59:5.**
Identification of property on tax
bills, **60:3A.**
Illegal taxes, partial validity of
assessment, **59:82.**
Imports.
Federal taxation, **US Const Art
1 Sec 8 cl 1.**
State may not tax without
consent of Congress, **US
Const Art 1 Sec 10 cl 2.**
Imprisonment, **60:29, 60:30, 60:34.**
Improvements.
Assessments, **80:1 et seq.,
80A:1 et seq.**
See SPECIAL
ASSESSMENTS.

TAXATION —Cont'd
Improvements —Cont'd
Assessors.
  Improvement districts, **59:21, 59:25.**
    Separate list and warrant for district taxes, **59:53.**
  Lowlands and swamps, duties in connection with improvement, **252:11.**
  Housing for elderly, **59:5.**
  Limited tax abatements for improvements to real estate, **59:38.**
  Lowlands and swamps, taxation for improvement, **252:11.**
  Special assessments, **80:1 et seq., 80A:1 et seq.**
    See SPECIAL ASSESSMENTS.
Improvements raising assessment by over 50 percent.
  Pro rata tax, **59:2D.**
Inability to pay tax.
  Abatement of certain taxes, **59:65B, 59:71.**
  Imprisonment for nonpayment, grounds for release, **60:31.**
Inclusion of state taxes in assessment of other taxes, **59:26.**
Income producing property, exemption, **59:5.**
Income tax, **62:1 et seq., 62B:1 et seq.**
  See INCOME TAX.
Increase in real property tax exemptions, acceptance of statutes effecting, **29:27C.**
Indians not taxed excluded from representative numbers, **US Const Art 1 Sec 2 cl 3; 14th Amend 2.**
Indigent persons.
  Poor persons. See within this heading, "Poor persons."
Individual retirement accounts, income tax, **62:2, 62:5.**
  Turnpike authority employees, **81A:22.**
Industrial development of cities and towns.
  Authority, property, **40E:18.**
  Lessee or occupant of development project, **40D:20.**
Industrial or commercial use, conversion of recreational land, **61B:9.**
Industrial waste, tax exemption or deduction for facilities dealing, **59:5, 63:38D.**

TAXATION —Cont'd
Infirm persons, exemption, **59:5.**
Inheritance tax, **65:27-65:29, 65:33A.**
  See LEGACY AND SUCCESSION TAXES.
Injunctions.
  Collectors, dissolution of injunction against, **41:43A, 60:91.**
  Corporation taxes, **60:91, 63:80.**
  Gasoline tax on exempt federal sales, restraining collection of, **64A:12, 64E:12, 64F:13.**
  License or registration, enjoining conduct of business without, **62C:76.**
Inland wetlands protection, assessed owner of lands deemed "owner" for purpose, **131:40A.**
In lieu payments and taxes.
  Housing and redevelopment authorities, payments in lieu of taxes where revaluation occurs, **121B:16.**
  Motor vehicle excise tax, **60A:1-60A:6.**
    See MOTOR VEHICLES.
  Municipal borrowing in anticipation, **44:4.**
  Parking meter receipts, **40:22B.**
  Sale of real estate by municipality, **44:63A.**
  Ships and other watercraft, **60B:2-60B:4, 60B:6.**
Innkeepers.
  Information as to residents of boarding houses, refusal to give or falsity in giving, **59:92.**
  Returns of innkeepers, **62C:16.**
  Room occupancy tax, **64G:1 et seq.**
    See ROOM OCCUPANCY TAX.
Insolvency.
  Abatement of uncollectible taxes, **59:71, 90:49R.**
  Bankruptcy trustees, **62:13, 62C:6.**
  Collection from insolvent debtor, **60:19, 60:36.**
  Hazardous waste insolvency fund, exemptions, **21C:28.**
  Notice of commissioner from register of probate and insolvency, **217:16.**
Inspection.
  Examination, inspection or investigation. See within this heading, "Examination, inspection, or investigation."

TAXATION —Cont'd
Installment payments, written agreement with taxpayer, **62C:37B.**
Insurance.
  Declaration of estimated tax by corporations, additional tax, **63B:10.**
  Housing projects, **121A:18.**
  Income tax, **62C:12.**
    Exemption of interest from business loans, **62:2.**
  Mortgaged lands, allocation of investment of mortgagor's periodic payments for taxes and insurance premiums, **167:58, 183:23.**
  Municipal corporations.
    Group insurance for municipal employees, cost included in determination of tax rate, **32B:3.**
    Stock of insurance companies, exemption from local taxes, **59:5.**
  Returns by insurance companies, **62C:12.**
  Revenue department and commissioner.
    Commissioner of insurance to act as to companies, **175:49.**
  Notice and collection of assessment from companies, **26:8D.**
Intangible property held by fiduciaries, exemption, **59:5.**
Interest on money.
  Abatement of taxes, **59:64, 59:65B, 59:69, 61:2, 62C:36, 62C:40, 62C:69.**
  Motor vehicle excise tax, **60A:2.**
  On unpaid taxes, **58:8.**
  Agricultural or horticultural lands, interest on reimbursement of taxes, **61A:19.**
  Books showing interest, tax collector to keep, **60:7.**
  Business loans, income tax consequences, **62:2.**
  Cigarette tax law, crediting of funds received, **62C:28.**
  Collectors.
    Books showing interest, tax collector to keep, **60:7.**
    Unpaid taxes, **62C:26, 62C:32.**
    Waiver, **59:57.**
  Deferred taxes, **59:5, 83:16G.**
  Deficiency assessment, **62C:26.**

TAXATION —Cont'd
Interest on money —Cont'd
Estate taxes.
Coupons as exempt from lien, **65C:14.**
Delayed payment of taxes due on reversionary or remainder interest, **65C:10.**
Extending time for payment, **65A:2.**
Federal estate tax credit surcharge, **65A:2, 65A:5.**
Nonresident's estate, proof of taxes, penalty, or interest paid or secured, **65C:21.**
Reversions and remainder interest, **65C:10.**
Extension of time for payment of estate taxes, **65A:2.**
Federal savings banks, taxation of interest, **62:2.**
Forest lands and products, refunds of taxes, **61:2.**
Income tax.
Bank deposits, **62:1, 62:2.**
Commonwealth obligations, taxation of interest, **62:2.**
Debts, deduction of interest, **62:2, 62:3.**
Deficiency, **62B:14, 62C:26.**
Estimated income tax, **62B:14.**
Exemption of interest from business loans, **62:2.**
Governmental obligations, deduction of interest, **62:2.**
Massachusetts gross income, inclusion, **62:2.**
Overpayment of taxes, **62C:36, 62C:40.**
Refunds to taxpayer, **62C:36, 62C:40.**
Savings, deduction of interest, **62:3.**
Unpaid taxes, **62C:26, 62C:32.**
Abatement by commissioner after granting additional time for payment, **62C:33.**
Judgment in case of insufficient part payment, **60:22.**
Landlord and tenant.
Failure to pay rent on residential lease, **186:15B.**
Overages in taxes charged by lessor under escalation clauses, **186:15C.**
Security deposit on residential property, **186:15B.**

TAXATION —Cont'd
Interest on money —Cont'd
Legacy and succession taxes, **65:6.**
Deposits in lieu of tax upon future interests, **65:15.**
Domicile of decedent, penalties and interest as affected by determination, **65B:5.**
Federal estate tax laws, **65A:1-65A:6, 191B:13, 200:13.**
Lien, **65:9.**
Refunds of abatements, **65:27.**
Local tax collectors, **60:2.**
Mortgagees, payment of interest of tax deposits, **183:61.**
Motor vehicle excise tax, **60A:2.**
Omitted assessments, **59:57.**
Overdue taxes, **59:57, 59:57A, 62C:32, 62C:40.**
Overpaid taxes.
Agricultural land, **61A:19.**
Refund of taxes, **59:64, 62C:40.**
Tenant, overages in taxes paid under tax escalation clause, **186:15C.**
Property taxes, late payment, **59:57, 59:57B.**
Railroad aid, local tax levied to pay interest on indebtedness, **44:57, 59:24.**
Rate payable after due date, **59:57.**
Real estate tax deposits with mortgagees, payment of interest, **183:61.**
Reassessed taxes, **59:57, 59:78.**
Recreational lands, **61B:8.**
Redemption of tax sales, rate of interest, **51:52, 60:62, 60:63, 60:68.**
Refund of taxes, **59:64, 62C:40.**
Revised assessments, **59:57, 59:78.**
Savings and loan associations, income tax on interest, **62:2.**
Special assessments.
Abatement, **80:5, 80:9.**
Assessments, **80:13, 80:13B.**
Railroad aid indebtedness, **59:24.**
Suspension of improvement assessments, effect of interest, **60:3B.**
Time of payment extended, **80:13A.**
Water rate or sewer use charge added to tax, **59:57.**

TAXATION —Cont'd
Interest on money —Cont'd
Suspension of improvement assessments, effect of interest, **60:3B.**
Unpaid taxes, **62C:26, 62C:32.**
Waiver, **59:57, 59:69.**
Water rates, **40:42D, 59:57.**
Internal Revenue Service.
Copy of statements of federal withholding tax given to, **58:28B.**
Inspection of returns, **62C:23.**
Prima facie evidence, certificate of similarity to federal tax laws as, **62C:23.**
State income tax information disclosed to, **62C:22.**
State tax administration, cooperation with, **62C:23.**
Interstate co-operation commission, function, **9:23.**
Interstate ships and vessels subject to excise tax, **59:8, 63:67.**
Investigation.
Examination, inspection or investigation. See within this heading, "Examination, inspection, or investigation."
Jewelry, tax exemption of personal effects, **59:5.**
Joint airport projects, **90:51N.**
Joint committee on taxation in general court, compensation of chairman, **3:9.**
Joint tenants and tenants in common.
Estate taxes, surviving tenant as liable for, **65C:14.**
Exemption for certain realty of blind persons, **59:5.**
Legacy and succession taxes, **65:1, 65:6, 65:7, 65A:2.**
Lien for taxes paid by one of joint tenant, **60:85, 60:86.**
Local property assessments, liability for, **59:12B.**
Old persons, exemption for realty owned by, **59:5.**
Personal property taxes, assessment and liability, **59:18.**
Redemption of property from tax sale, **60:76A.**
Judgments, orders, and decrees.
Gasoline and motor fuel taxes.
Collection of taxes on sales exempt by federal law, jurisdiction of supreme judicial or superior court to restrain, **64E:12, 64F:13.**

TAXATION —Cont'd
Judgments, orders, and decrees
—Cont'd
Income tax.
Superior court, jurisdiction in
mandamus to compel
filing of return, **62C:9.**
Legacy and succession taxes.
Probate court, **65:30.**
Municipal corporations.
Amount of tax assessed,
judgment against town
affecting, **59:23.**
Treasurer or tax collector, tax
for payment of judgment
against, **41:43A.**
Special assessments.
Abatement proceedings, **80:9.**
Eminent domain proceedings,
80A:10, 80A:11.
Tax collectors.
Against collectors, **41:43A.**
Part payment, judgment for
amount due after, **60:22.**
Juror as taxpayer in action for
recovery of forfeiture, **234:30.**
Lambs.
Excise tax, **59:8A.**
Exemption from local taxes,
59:5.
Landlord and tenant.
Abatement of taxes, tenant's
right to apply, **59:59.**
Commonwealth land and
buildings, assessment of
leases of lands of
Commonwealth, **59:11.**
Contributions by lessees, **80:11.**
Deduction of rent from taxable
income, **62:3.**
Escalation clause, **186:15B,
186:15C.**
Interest on money.
Failure to pay rent on
residential lease, **186:15B.**
Overages in taxes charged by
lessor under escalation
clauses, **186:15C.**
Security deposit on residential
property, **186:15B.**
Liability of lessee, **62C:48.**
Local tax assessment of
leasehold interest, **40:22E,
59:3E, 59:11.**
Local taxes.
Authority of municipalities to
reach rent of land taken
for delinquent, **60:53.**
Liability, **59:12C.**
Rights of tenants, **59:59.**
Special assessments,
contribution by lessees,
80:11.

TAXATION —Cont'd
Landlord and tenant —Cont'd
State colleges, **75:28.**
United States, lease for or by,
59:3E, 59:11.
Late penalties, **62C:33, 62C:34.**
Late reporting of income paid,
penalty, **62C:34.**
Laundry equipment, exemption,
59:5.
Lead paint law, income tax credit
for expense of complying, **62:6.**
Leasehold interests.
Personal property leases.
Bailments. See within this
heading, "Bailments."
Real property.
Landlord and tenant. See
within this heading,
"Landlord and tenant."
Legacy and succession taxes, **65:2
et seq.**
Estate taxes, **62C:1 et seq.,
65A:1 et seq., 65B:1 et
seq., 65C:1 et seq.**
See ESTATE TAXES.
Generally.
See LEGACY AND
SUCCESSION TAXES.
Levy of taxes, **62C:53-62C:64.**
Licenses and permits, taxation of,
62C:67, 62C:68.
See LICENSES AND PERMITS.
Liens, **59:2B, 59:12E, 59:12F,
60:37, 60:50-60:56,
62C:50-62C:52.**
See TAX LIENS.
Lieu payments.
In lieu payments and taxes. See
within this heading, "In lieu
payments and taxes."
Life insurance.
Investment privilege, **63:22B,
63:22C.**
Legacy and succession taxes on
proceeds, **65:1, 65:7.**
Merger assets, adjustment of
basis as to, **63:22D.**
Qualifying cosmetic life
company, **63:22D.**
Light districts, **59:5, 59:21, 59:53.**
Limitation of actions.
Abatement of unpaid and
uncollectible taxes, **62C:42.**
Estate taxes, limitation period
for collection, **62C:65.**
Income taxes, limitation on
additional assessment,
62C:30.
Legacy and succession tax lien,
termination, **65:9.**

TAXATION —Cont'd
Limitation of actions —Cont'd
Local property taxes, actions for
refunds or recoveries, **60:98.**
Motor vehicle excise tax, time to
apply for abatement, **60A:2.**
Overassessment or overpayment
of taxes, time to apply for
abatement, **62C:37.**
Redemption from tax sale,
60:65, 60:69.
Refund applications, **62C:36.**
Limitations and restrictions.
Agricultural preservation
restrictions, **132A:11D.**
Land subject to permanent
restriction, assessment,
59:11.
Municipal debt limits.
Assessed valuation as
determining, **44:10.**
Avoidance through assessor's
valuation of property,
41:30.
Municipal tax rate limit,
59:21C.
See TAX AND BUDGET
LIMITS FOR LOCAL
GOVERNMENT.
Nonpayment of taxes, taking of
land for nonpayment as
subject to restrictions,
60:54.
State tax revenues, limitation on
growth, **62F:1 to 62F:8.**
Limited investment partnership,
exemption of nonresident
limited partner from payment
of personal income tax, **62:17.**
Lists.
Abatement of taxes, **59:61,
59:64.**
Agricultural or horticultural
land, details shown by tax
lists, **61A:21.**
Appeal in abatement cases,
failure to list as affecting
rights, **59:64.**
Assessors, **59:29-59:37,
59:43-59:48, 59:50-59:52,
59:52B, 60:12.**
See TAX ASSESSORS.
Bonds required prior to
commitment, **59:53.**
Classified forest land, **61:1.**
Collectors.
Bonds required prior to
commitment, **59:53.**
Collectors to keep book
containing tax list, **60:6.**
Commitment of tax lists, **58:5,
59:29, 59:43, 59:53, 59:54,
59:78.**

TAXATION —Cont'd
Lists —Cont'd
Collectors —Cont'd
Payment of taxes prior to receipt of tax list, acceptance, **60:19.**
Posting, **60:88.**
Successor collector, turning over lists, **60:97.**
Commitment of tax lists for collection, **59:53, 59:54.**
See TAX COLLECTORS.
Delinquent taxpayers, disclosure, **62C:21.**
Estimate of value of property in default of list, **59:36, 59:37.**
Exemptions, lists required, **59:29, 59:51.**
Failure to list, **59:5, 59:36, 59:37, 59:61, 59:64.**
False or fraudulent lists, penalized, **59:91.**
Form and contents of tax list, **59:54.**
Inspection, **59:32.**
Mortgagors or mortgagees, statements, **59:34.**
Notice.
Assessors to furnish, **58:5, 59:30.**
Posting notices, **59:29, 60:88.**
Oath required, **59:31.**
Personal property, **59:5, 59:29.**
Posting of tax lists, **59:29, 60:88.**
Preservation, **59:32.**
Property, **59:29-59:37.**
Lists of property. See within this heading, "Lists."
Real estate, **59:29.**
Recreational lands, **61B:17.**
Storage warehouses, property stored, **59:33.**
Treasurers of cities and towns, bonds required prior to commitment of lists, **59:53.**
Verification, **59:31.**
Warehouses, **59:33.**
Loans, **59:4.**
Income tax consequences of business loans, **62:2.**
Municipal corporations. See within this heading, "Municipal corporations."
Local assessments, **80:1 et seq., 80A:1 et seq.**
See SPECIAL ASSESSMENTS.
Local option statutes.
Increase of real property tax exemptions, acceptance of laws effecting, **29:27C.**

TAXATION —Cont'd
Local option statutes —Cont'd
Tax and budget limits for local government.
Laws and regulations involving cost obligations for municipalities, acceptance, **29:27C.**
Revocation of acceptance, **4:4B.**
Local taxes.
Counties and county taxes. See within this heading, "Counties and county taxes."
Municipal corporations. See within this heading, "Municipal corporations."
Location, **59:11 et seq.**
Lodges and societies, exemptions, **59:5, 176:49.**
Lottery prizes, assignment of funds of winning ticket for payment of estate and inheritance taxes, **10:28.**
Lowlands and swamps.
Improvement of lowlands and swamps, taxation, **252:11.**
Protection of inland wetlands, person to whom tax assessed deemed "owner" for purposes, **131:40A.**
Low value lands acquired without foreclosure by municipalities, sale, **60:79.**
Machinery and equipment, **59:18.**
Abatement of taxes, notice, **59:74.**
Agricultural and horticultural property, **59:5, 59:8A, 60:24, 64H:6, 64H:26, 64I:27.**
Corporation taxes.
Exemptions.
Manufacturing corporations, **59:5.**
Exemptions.
Corporation taxes, **63:30, 63:38C, 63:42B.**
Machinery situated in other state, **59:5.**
Sales tax exemption for manufacturing equipment, **64H:6.**
Fire districts, purchase of engines and equipment, **48:69.**
Other state, tax exemption of machinery situated, **59:5.**
Transmission lines and equipment, **59:18, 59:83.**
Abatement of taxes, notice, **59:74.**

TAXATION —Cont'd
Machinery and equipment —Cont'd
Transmission lines and equipment —Cont'd
Corporations, assessment of taxes, **59:83.**
Public ways, how and where assessed, **59:18.**
Underground utilities, **59:5.**
Transportation and carriage of goods, assessment of machinery employed, **59:18.**
Water pollution, tax exemption for machinery used for abatement or prevention, **59:5.**
Mail and mailing.
Notices, **60:3.**
Postmark date as payment date, **62C:33A.**
Mandamus to compel filing of income tax return, **62C:9.**
Manual outlining procedures tax collectors should use in performance of duties, **58:3.**
Manufacturing corporations, **59:5, 63:38C, 63:42B.**
See CORPORATION TAXES.
Maps for assessment purposes, **40:4, 44:7.**
Marine fish and fisheries.
Excise tax on interests in fishing vessels, **63:31A, 63:67.**
Gasoline tax receipts, crediting, **64A:13.**
Sales tax exemption, **64H:6, 64I:7.**
Massachusetts Bay Transportation Authority.
Abatement appeals of public transportation corporations, **59:64, 59:65.**
Cigarette tax, **58:25B.**
Mass transportation facilities and services.
Cigarette tax, **58:25B, 64C:1, 64C:6, 64C:28.**
Gasoline and motor fuel tax increases, **64A:1, 64A:4, 64E:1, 64E:4, 64F.**
Mayors.
Assessments, failure to keep proper records, **58:4A.**
Classification for tax purposes, **40:56.**
Custodian of tax-foreclosed property, appointment, **60:77B.**
Exemption from taxation, **59:5C, 59:5E.**

TAXATION —Cont'd
Mayors —Cont'd
Tax collectors.
Accounting to mayor, **60:94.**
Bonds, fixing amount, **60:13.**
Temporary tax collector,
appointment, **41:61A.**
Meals, excise tax on meals served
to public, **62C:16, 64H:6.**
Medical care.
Exempt income and resources of
applicant for assistance,
118E:10.
Hospitals and health care
facilities, exemptions, **59:5,
64G:2, 64H:6.**
Service plans and corporations,
**176B:10, 176B:14, 176C:14,
176C:15.**
Medical malpractice self-insurance
trust funds, exemption from
taxation, **175F:16.**
Mentally ill and retarded persons.
Collectors, removal for insanity,
60:96.
Exemption of institution from,
59:5.
Meals, exemption from taxation,
64H:6.
Reimbursement of towns for loss
of taxes on lands used by
department, **58:13.**
Merchandise in other state,
exemption, **59:5.**
Merger.
Consolidation of appeals,
59:38A, 59:39.
Corporations, effect of merger,
156:46A, 156:46C, 156:46D.
Metropolitan districts.
Air pollution control, **111:142B.**
Assessments, **40B:29.**
Sewer district taxation.
Bonds of sewer district,
exemption from taxation,
59:5.
Property held for sewage
disposal purposes,
56:6-56:7A.
Water districts, **59:5D et seq.**
Military and militia, **62C:81.**
Camp grounds of militia,
reimbursement for loss of
tax, **58:13-58:17A.**
Exemption of militia property,
equipment, and supplies,
59:5, 60:24.
Room occupancy excise tax,
64G:12.
Minimum residential factors,
calculation, **58:1A.**

TAXATION —Cont'd
Minks, tax, **59:8A, 128:8B.**
Minors.
Adoption, **59:5, 62:3, 65:1.**
Exemptions, **59:5, 60:3B, 64G:2.**
Farm animals owned by minors,
59:8A.
Income tax, **62:2, 62:3, 62D:1,
62D:3, 62E:1.**
Local assessments for child care
facilities, **59:3F.**
Support collection.
Federal tax refund intercept
program, **119A:6.**
Procedures by IV-D agency for
accrued arrearages,
119A:6.
Set-off debt collection, revenue
department to assist
transitional assistance
department in collecting
support obligations,
62D:3.
Mistake.
Errors or irregularities. See
within this heading, "Errors
or irregularities."
Mobile homes and mobile home
parks.
Assessment of trailers owned by
corporations, **59:83.**
Exemption from local property
taxes, **59:5.**
Lien of operator, **255:26-255:31.**
Money taxable as personalty, **59:4.**
Monthly returns from persons
required to file, **62C:16.**
Morris Plan banks, **172A:13.**
Income tax on deposits, **62:2.**
Tax sale redemption, **60:68,
60:76A.**
Mortgaged lands, **59:12-59:14.**
Abatement of taxes, mortgagee's
application, **59:59.**
Addition to debt, tax payment by
mortgagee, **60:58.**
Advancement by mortgagee,
183:28A.
Allocation of investment of
mortgagor's periodic
payments for taxes and
insurance premiums,
183:23.
Allowance to mortgagee for
taxes, **244:20.**
Apportionment of tax between
mortgagor and mortgagee,
59:12.
Bank mortgage loan clause as to
payment of taxes, **183:23.**
Betterment assessments,
mortgage of trust estate to
pay, **203:23.**

TAXATION —Cont'd
Mortgaged lands —Cont'd
Chattel mortgages, tax on
property subject, **59:19.**
Cities and towns.
Situs of property in two or
more towns, **59:12.**
Tax payments by mortgagees,
183:62.
Co-tenant's lien for taxes as
subject to mortgage, **60:86.**
Deduction from debt, tax
payment, **60:59.**
Demand for payment of
mortgagor, when, **60:38.**
Estate tax lien, **65C:14.**
Excess above assessed value
taxable as personalty, **59:4.**
Foreclosure.
Agricultural and horticultural
property.
Exemption from conveyance
tax, **61A:12.**
Subject to municipality's
option to purchase,
61A:14.
Deed as subject to taxes,
244:14.
Mortgagee in possession, taxes
and other expenditures,
244:20.
Sales.
Lien for taxes, foreclosure
by sale, **60:37-60:60.**
Redemption of tax title
created by sale,
foreclosure of right to.
Interest on tax deposits with
mortgagees, payment,
183:61.
Municipalities.
Situs of property in two or
more towns, **59:12.**
Tax payments by mortgagees,
183:62.
Payment by mortgagor or
mortgagee, **60:58, 60:59.**
Payments for taxes as secured,
183:28A.
Redemption, **60:54, 60:62, 60:63,
62C:57, 62C:58.**
See TAX SALES.
Situs of property situated in two
or more towns, **59:12.**
State as mortgagee in
possession, **59:5.**
Statements to assessors, **59:34.**
Motels.
Information as to residents of
boarding houses, refusal to
give or falsity in giving,
59:92.

TAXATION —Cont'd
Motels —Cont'd
Returns of innkeepers, **62C:16.**
Room occupancy tax, **64G:1 et seq.**
See ROOM OCCUPANCY TAX.
Motorboats.
Assessment of tax, **90B:11.**
Gasoline tax, **64A:7, 64A:13.**
Payment as prerequisite to issuance of certificate of number, **64H:25A.**
Motor fuel taxes, **64A:1-64A:13.**
See GASOLINE AND MOTOR FUEL TAXES.
Motor vehicles.
Cigarette tax.
Place of business, vehicle, **64C:1.**
Seizure and forfeiture of vehicle for illegal transportation or possession of cigarettes, **64C:8.**
Constitution of Massachusetts, expenditure of revenue from fees and taxes relating to motor vehicles, **MA Const Amend Art 78.**
Corporation taxes.
Excise tax in lieu of local tax, **60A:1-60A:6.**
See MOTOR VEHICLES.
Local taxation, **59:83.**
Display of proof of payment, **64H:25, 64H:26.**
Excise tax in lieu of local tax, **60A:1-60A:6.**
See MOTOR VEHICLES.
Exemptions, **59:5, 60A:1, 64H:6.**
Franchise tax on foreign bus company, **63:52A.**
Fuel taxes, **64A:1-64A:13.**
See GASOLINE AND MOTOR FUEL TAXES.
Garages, **59:5, 60A:1.**
Gasoline taxes, **64A:1-64A:13.**
See GASOLINE AND MOTOR FUEL TAXES.
Manufacturers, distributors, and dealers.
Excise tax, **60A:1.**
Foreign corporation, franchise tax, **63:52A.**
Free association with other franchisees, rights, **93B:10.**
Notice of cancellation or termination of dealer's franchise, **93B:4.**

TAXATION —Cont'd
Motor vehicles —Cont'd
Manufacturers, distributors, and dealers —Cont'd
Foreign corporation, franchise tax —Cont'd
Right to damages of franchisees, **93B:12.**
Unfair competition or deceptive practices, **93B:4.**
Sales tax exemption of materials, equipment, and machinery used in manufacture of tangible personal property, **64H:6.**
Tax exemptions.
Excise tax, **60A:1.**
Sales tax, **64H:6.**
Mobile homes, **59:5.**
Motor fuel taxes, **64A:1-64A:13.**
See GASOLINE AND MOTOR FUEL TAXES.
Repairs and maintenance.
Exemption of vehicles under control of repairmen, **60A:1.**
Garages, **59:5, 60A:1.**
Service defined for tax purposes, **64H:1, 64I:1.**
Sales taxes, **64H:3, 64H:25, 64H:26.**
See SALES TAXES.
Suspension or revocation of registration for failure to pay, **60A:2A.**
Trailers, **60A:1, 60A:2A.**
Military personnel, **59:5.**
Use, consumption, or storage tax, **64I:4, 64I:7, 64I:26, 64I:27.**
See USE, CONSUMPTION, OR STORAGE TAX.
Veterans, **60A:1.**
Weight permit sticker, fee for issuance, **90:33.**
Mules, exemption, **59:5.**
Municipal corporations, **44:1 et seq., 59:1 et seq.**
Abatement of taxes, **59:64, 59:72A.**
Absence of appropriations, amount of tax to be assessed in event, **59:23.**
Additional local taxes, assessment, **59:25.**
Adoption of charter as affecting existing taxes, **43:24.**
Agricultural and horticultural property, first option on property proposed to be sold or converted, **61A:14.**

TAXATION —Cont'd
Municipal corporations —Cont'd
Airports owned by, taxation in connection with joint projects, **90:51N.**
Amount of assessment, determination, **59:23.**
Appeal and review, **58:1A, 58:14 (note), 59:5D, 59:5E.**
Excuse for untimely filing of appeal of local assessment, **59:65C.**
Extension of time to appeal, **51:14.**
Failure to submit sworn statements concerning local assessment, **59:38D.**
Notice of proposed equalization values, **58:10A.**
Proposed equalization valuations, appeals, **58:10B.**
Right of appeal to as affected by failure to furnish information, **58:10.**
Appropriate financial official, **60:2C.**
Appropriations.
Departmental appropriations, limitations on, **44:30, 44:31A.**
For care and maintenance of tax forfeited real estate, **40:5.**
Assessment rates, limitations on, **59:21C.**
Assessor of taxes, **41:24 et seq., 59:20 et seq.**
See TAX ASSESSORS.
Auditors of city and town.
Expenses for audits of accounts, tax for, **44:41.**
Notice of abatement of tax, **59:23B.**
Rate, notice of tax rate, **59:23A.**
Available funds deficit, **60:2C.**
Banks, cities' agreements with for collection of local taxes, **60:2A.**
Bond or undertaking required prior to commitment of tax lists, **59:53.**
Bonds and notes.
Anticipation of revenue, limitation of notes issued, **44:4.**
Exemption from tax, **59:5.**
Payment of, tax levy, **44:16, 44:19.**

TAXATION —Cont'd
Municipal corporations —Cont'd
Bonds and notes —Cont'd
Property taxes, use of notes
for payment, **60:2, 183:62.**
Provision for payment, **44:16,
44:19.**
Taxation of, **62:2.**
Budget limitations set by limits
to taxing authority, **44:10,
59:21C.**
See TAX AND BUDGET
LIMITS FOR LOCAL
GOVERNMENT.
Care and maintenance of real
property forfeited for taxes,
40:5.
Cemeteries, raising money,
114:16.
Certificates of lien, **60:23,
60:23A.**
Charter cities.
Assessors, **43:17, 43:54.**
Existing taxes as affected by
city's adoption of charter,
43:24.
Support of charter
commission, **43B:8.**
Claims or accounts against,
60:93, 258:10.
Classification of property, **40:56.**
Criminal jurisdiction,
218:26A.
Usage classification, **59:2A.**
Clerk of city or town.
Records of tax collector, **60:12.**
Collectors, **60:1-60:105.**
See TAX COLLECTORS.
Commissioner defined, **60:2C.**
Conservation lands,
reimbursement of
municipalities for tax loss,
58:13-58:17A.
Corporation taxes, distribution.
Amount for distribution,
determination, **58:25,
58:25A.**
Annual estimates of returns to
cities and towns, **58:25A.**
Business corporation tax,
58:25, 58:25A.
Deduction of sums due
Commonwealth from
business corporation
taxes, **58:20A.**
Partial distributions, **58:25.**
Council, city.
Exemption of local property
from taxation, **59:5C.**
Usage classification of real
property for taxation
purposes, **40:56.**

TAXATION —Cont'd
Municipal corporations —Cont'd
Counties and county taxes. See
within this heading,
"Counties and county taxes."
Current tax receivables, **60:2C.**
Debt limit.
Assessed valuation as
determining, **44:10.**
Avoidance through assessor's
valuation of property,
41:30.
Maps and appraisals,
borrowing beyond debt
limit, **44:7.**
Deductions.
Local annual tax assessment,
deduction of
appropriations in
determining, **59:23.**
Sums due Commonwealth,
deduction, **58:20A.**
Deeds, tax titles acquired by
municipalities, **60:50, 60:79.**
See TAX DEEDS AND
TITLES.
Delinquent state taxes,
collection, **59:20.**
Director of accounts, powers and
duties as to local tax
assessments, **59:23.**
Disclosure of tax information,
62C:21.
Discount on taxes, towns
forbidden to allow, **59:58.**
Disqualification system for sale
of properties, **60:77B.**
Distress proceedings against,
59:20.
Distribution of taxes among,
29:18, 58:18B, 58:25A.
Division of cities into
assessment districts, **59:38.**
Donations to scholarship fund,
tax bill, **58:9, 59:25, 60:3C.**
Entity defined, **60:2C.**
Equalized valuations for cities
and towns.
Appeal, **58:10B.**
As basis for municipal debt
limit computation, **44:10.**
Data to be utilized in
determining, **58:10.**
Debt limit as determined by,
44:10.
Definition of, under law
governing municipal
finance, **44:1.**
Failure to submit information
for use in determining,
58:10.

TAXATION —Cont'd
Municipal corporations —Cont'd
Equalized valuations for cities
and towns —Cont'd
Notice, **58:10A.**
Regional school districts,
equalized valuation for
purposes of computing
regional valuation
percentage for state aid,
71:16D.
Revenue Department and
Commissioner, **44:1,
58:9-58:10C.**
State Administrative
Procedure Law,
proceedings to determine,
as adjudicatory
proceedings within
meaning, **30A:1.**
Estimated tax, authorization for
notice and payment, **59:2A.
(note)**
Exemptions from local taxation,
59:2B, 59:5, 59:5C-59:5F.
Facsimile signatures on
warrants issued by tax
collectors, **60:29.**
Failure of towns to pay certain
state and county taxes,
action based, **59:28.**
Failure to keep proper records,
58:4-58:4B.
Fees, **59:5D, 59:5F, 262:4.**
Financial officers, notices.
Abatement of taxes, **59:23B,
59:70A.**
Tax rate, **59:23A.**
First option on land to be sold
and converted, **61A:14.**
Fiscal year.
Assessment of taxes, **59:21,
59:23, 59:23A, 59:25,
59:27.**
Collection of taxes, **60:3,
60:17.**
Payments in lieu of taxes,
44:64.
Foreclosure, tax on, property
acquired, **60:77.**
Forfeited property, care and
maintenance, **40:5.**
Fraternal benefit societies
exempt from taxation, **59:5,
176:49.**
Gift of land to municipality,
abatement of unpaid tax,
59:72A.
Group insurance for municipal
employees, cost included in
tax rate, **32B:3.**

TAXATION —Cont'd
Municipal corporations —Cont'd
Health department,
reimbursement of towns for
loss of taxes on land used,
58:13.
Inclusion in assessment of other
taxes, **59:26.**
Income tax.
Lands taken for delinquent
taxes, authority of
municipality to reach
income, **60:53.**
Proportionate share of income
tax revenues as factor in
determination of
appropriations, **44:30.**
Individual taxpayer receivable
defined, **60:2C.**
Industrial development of cities
and towns.
Authority, property, **40E:18.**
Lessee or occupant of
development project,
40D:20.
In lieu payments and taxes.
Motor vehicle excise tax,
60A:1-60A:6.
See MOTOR VEHICLES.
Municipal borrowing in
anticipation, **44:4.**
Parking meter receipts,
40:22B.
Sale of real estate by
municipality, **44:63A.**
Ships and other watercraft,
60B:2-60B:4, 60B:6.
Insurance.
Group insurance for municipal
employees, cost included
in determination of tax
rate, **32B:3.**
Stock of insurance companies,
exemption from local
taxes, **59:5.**
Interest on late payment,
property taxes, **59:57B.**
Investigation of municipal
affairs, tax for expense,
44:46A.
Joint or co-operative assessment,
41:30B.
Judgment.
Amount of tax assessed,
judgment against town
affecting, **59:23.**
Treasurer or tax collector, tax
for payment of judgment
against, **41:43A.**
Legacy and succession taxes,
exemption of property, **65:1.**

TAXATION —Cont'd
Municipal corporations —Cont'd
Licenses and permits, municipal
discretion in granting or
renewing, **40:57.**
Lighting plants.
Levy to include estimated cost,
164:57.
Liens as included in tax,
164:58D, 164:58E.
New England Power Pool,
164A:8, 164A:20.
Tax title accounts for
municipal light rates,
60:62, 60:76B.
Limitation of actions for
recovery of local property
taxes, **60:98.**
Limitation on amount
appropriated or assessed,
44:10, 59:21C.
See TAX AND BUDGET
LIMITS FOR LOCAL
GOVERNMENT.
Limitation on indebtedness,
41:30, 44:10.
Loans.
Anticipation of taxes,
borrowing, **44:4.**
Determination of amount of
assessment, **59:23.**
Limit of indebtedness.
Assessed valuation as
determining, **44:10.**
Avoidance through
assessor's valuation of
property, **41:30.**
Maps and appraisals,
borrowing beyond debt
limit, **44:7.**
Railroad aid, local tax levied
to pay interest, **44:57,
59:24.**
Setoff of taxes and charges
against municipal
indebtedness, **60:93.**
Local option statutes.
Laws and regulations
involving cost obligations
for municipalities,
acceptance, **29:27C.**
Revocation of acceptance,
4:4B.
Low value lands, sale of without
foreclosure, **60:79.**
Maps and appraisals of taxable
property, municipal debt
limitations as affecting
contracts, **44:7.**
Mayors.
Assessments, failure to keep
proper records, **58:4A.**

TAXATION —Cont'd
Municipal corporations —Cont'd
Mayors —Cont'd
Classification for tax purposes,
40:56.
Custodian of tax-foreclosed
property, appointment,
60:77B.
Exemption from taxation,
59:5C, 59:5E.
Tax collectors.
Accounting to mayor, **60:94.**
Bonds, fixing amount, **60:13.**
Temporary tax collector,
appointment, **41:61A.**
Mortgaged lands.
Situs of property in two or
more towns, **59:12.**
Tax payments by mortgagees,
183:62.
Municipality defined, **60:2C.**
Notice.
Equalized valuations, notice,
58:10A.
Estimated tax, **59:2A. (note)**
Financial officers, **59:23A,
59:23B, 59:70A.**
Proposed equalization values,
58:10A.
Redemption of tax title held
by city or town, notice,
60:76C.
Obligations of.
Bonds and notes. See within
this heading, "Bond
issues."
Officers and employees,
collection of federal
withholding tax, **58:28A,
58:28B.**
Offsetting unpaid taxes against
amounts due, **60:93.**
Ordinance or bylaw directing
collector to sell or take
property for nonpayment of
taxes, **60:87.**
Parcel defined, **60:2C.**
Payment of taxes with municipal
notes, **60:2.**
Pipelines, taxation, **40:43,
59:3C.**
Preliminary tax payments,
authorization, **59:23D.**
Proposition 2½, **59:21C.**
Public lands, reimbursement of
towns for loss of tax,
58:13-58:17B.
Purchaser as tax sale,
60:48-60:52.
See TAX SALES.
Purchaser defined, **60:2C.**

TAXATION —Cont'd
Municipal corporations —Cont'd
Railroad aid, tax levied to pay
interest on indebtedness,
44:57, 59:24.
Rate of tax, **59:23, 59:23A.**
Ratio studies, **58:10.**
Real estate.
Elderly and disabled tax fund.
Voluntary check off, **60:3D.**
Real property formerly owned by
city or town, taxation,
59:2C.
Records, failure to keep proper,
58:4-58:4B.
Referendum, appropriations
from tax levy, **59:21C.**
Refund or reimbursement.
Conservation lands,
reimbursement of
municipalities for tax loss,
58:13-58:17A.
Public lands, reimbursement
for loss of tax on,
58:13-58:17B.
Time limit for filing claims,
58:8B.
Veterans, taxes lost, **58:8A,
59:5.**
Regional police district operating
costs, local assessment,
41:99H.
Rehabilitation of owner-occupied
residential properties,
special assessment policy
for, **59:5J.**
Related tax, **60:2C.**
Rents and other income of lands
taken for delinquent taxes,
authority to reach, **60:53.**
Reserve fund, limit, **40:5A, 40:6.**
Revenue department and
commissioner, **58:1A.**
See REVENUE
DEPARTMENT AND
COMMISSIONER.
Sale for taxes, purchaser at,
60:48-60:52.
See TAX SALES.
Scholarship fund, donations,
58:9, 59:25, 60:3C.
Semi-annual payment of
liability, **59:20.**
Service agent, **60:2C.**
Setoff of taxes and charges
against municipal
indebtedness, **60:93.**
Sinking funds, addition of
unexpended tax moneys,
44:11.
Situs of property in two or more
towns, **59:12.**

TAXATION —Cont'd
Municipal corporations —Cont'd
Special assessments, **80:1-80:17.**
See SPECIAL
ASSESSMENTS.
Stabilization fund, limitation,
40:5B.
State taxes, assessment and
collection, **59:20, 59:21,
59:28.**
Statutory notice third party,
60:2C.
Stumpage fee, watershed land in
another municipality,
59:5D, 59:5F.
Subsequent individual taxpayer
receivable, **60:2C.**
Subsequent taxes after sale or
taking for nonpayment,
treasurer's duties with
respect, **60:61, 60:61A.**
Supervision of local taxation,
58:1-58:8.
Taking of land for nonpayment
of taxes, **60:53-60:56.**
See TAX LIENS.
Tax and budget limits, **44:10,
59:21C.**
See TAX AND BUDGET
LIMITS FOR LOCAL
GOVERNMENT.
Tax assessors, **41:24 et seq.,
59:20 et seq.**
See TAX ASSESSORS.
Taxes defined, **60:2C.**
Taxpayer receivable defined,
60:2C.
Tax receivable defined, **60:2C.**
Tax titles acquired by
municipalities, **60:50, 60:79.**
See TAX DEEDS AND
TITLES.
Time for city or town to appeal
assessments, **51:14.**
Transportation and carriage of
goods, assessment of
machinery employed, **59:18.**
Treasurers of cities and towns.
Abatement of taxes, **59:23B,
59:70A.**
Accounting for tax redemption
money, **60:63.**
Affidavit of notice to holder of
invalid tax title, notice to
treasurer of recording,
60:83.
Agricultural or horticultural
land, certificate of taxes
due or paid, **61A:19A.**
Assessors of taxes, **44:16.**
See TAX ASSESSORS.

TAXATION —Cont'd
Municipal corporations —Cont'd
Treasurers of cities and towns
—Cont'd
Collectors of taxes, **41:1,
41:37, 41:39B, 60:2,
60:90.**
See TAX COLLECTORS.
County taxes, payment, **35:31.**
Deeds, **60:50, 60:50B, 60:52,
60:61-60:63.**
Deputy collectors of taxes,
appointment, **41:37.**
Distress and sale for taxes,
powers of town treasurers,
41:37.
Judgment against, tax for
payment, **41:43A.**
Lists, bonds required prior to
commitment, **59:53.**
Rate of taxes, notice, **59:23A.**
Redemption from tax, duties,
60:62, 60:63.
Revenue Department and
Commissioner, **41:35,
41:39A, 41:39B, 41:123A.**
Subsequent taxes after sale of
taking for nonpayment,
duties, **60:61, 60:61A.**
Urban redevelopment
corporations, local taxation,
121A:10.
Usage classification, **59:2A.**
Veterans' services, local
departments of, **115:15.**
Waiver of charges by local tax
collectors, **60:15.**
Warrants, **59:20, 60:29.**
Waterways improvement and
maintenance fund, receipt of
revenues for improvements
of harbor and shipping
facilities, **40:5.**
Withholding money payable to
persons owing taxes, etc.,
60:93.
Municipal heating and lighting
plants.
Levy to include estimate cost,
164:57.
Liens as included in tax,
164:58D, 164:58E.
New England power pool,
164A:7, 164A:8, 164A:20.
Tax title accounts for municipal
light rates, **60:62, 60:76B.**
Musical instruments, exemption,
59:5, 64H:1.
Name.
Enforcement of tax liability,
bringing of suit in another
state, **58:28C.**

TAXATION —Cont'd
Name —Cont'd
Error on tax list, collection of taxes as affected, **60:21.**
Husband and wife, use of names of both, **14:6.**
Owners of real property, tax assessors' duties as to maintenance of record of names and addresses, **184:8A.**
Resident wage earners, names to be reported to commissioner, **62C:8.**
Tax assessors.
Books and lists, error in name, **60:21.**
Failure to furnish assessor with name and address of grantee of real estate, **184:8A.**
Records or property owners' names and addresses, assessors to maintain, **184:8A.**
Whole estate taken in name of one or more of several owners for nonpayment, **60:56.**
National bank, income tax on savings, **62:2.**
Neat cattle, exemption, **59:5.**
Neglect by assessors, appointment of others in case, **59:27.**
Nets, tax exemption, **59:5.**
Issuance of notices requiring lists, **59:29.**
New England Power Pool.
Bonds and notes, **164A:20.**
Exemptions from taxation, **164A:8, 164A:20.**
Foreign companies, **164A:7.**
Municipal electric departments, **164A:8, 164A:20.**
Newly acquired public lands, valuation, **58:15.**
Nongame wildlife fund, contribution of all or part of tax return, **62:6D.**
Nonresidents.
Assessors' lists to show valuation and assessment of property, **59:44.**
Estate taxes.
Computation of tax, **65C:2.**
Federal estate taxes, **65A:1.**
Liability, **65C:2.**
Proof of taxes paid or secured by nonresident's estate, **65C:21.**
Foreign corporations, **63:39-63:42B.**
See CORPORATION TAXES.

TAXATION —Cont'd
Nonresidents —Cont'd
Foreign states or countries. See within this heading, "Foreign states or countries."
Form for proving payment of estate taxes, **65C:21.**
Gasoline and motor fuel taxes, exemption, **64F:3.**
Income tax, **62:1, 62:4-62:6.**
See INCOME TAX.
Injunction against doing business by, upon failure to pay tax, **60:91.**
Legacy and succession taxes, **65:1.**
See LEGACY AND SUCCESSION TAXES.
Limited investment partnership, exemption of nonresident partner, **62:17.**
Lists, **59:29, 59:44.**
Mobile homes of nonresident military personnel, exemption, **59:5.**
Public storage warehouse, exemption of personalty stored in original packages, **59:2.**
Sales taxes.
Continuance of proceedings, **64I:33.**
Contractor, filing of bond or deposit by, for payment of tax, **64H:30A.**
Service of process on nonresidents, **64H:32, 64I:33.**
Statements and appointment of agent by tax title owners, **60:47.**
Notaries public.
Professional service, taxing of, **64H:1, 64I:1.**
Verification of tax lists, **59:31.**
Notes.
Bonds and securities. See within this heading, "Bond issues."
Notice.
Abatement of taxes, **59:70A, 59:74.**
Assessors.
Applicant, notice of decision, **59:63.**
Application for abatement, notice, **61B:14.**
Collector, notice, **59:70A.**
Corporations, **59:74.**
Municipal financial officers, notice, **59:23A, 59:23B, 59:70A.**

TAXATION —Cont'd
Notice —Cont'd
Abatement of taxes —Cont'd
Assessors —Cont'd
Telephone or telegraph companies, applications for abatement, **59:39.**
Adjournment of sale of personal property, **60:26.**
Administration provisions, notice authorized, **62C:71.**
Amount of tax, notice, **62C:26.**
Assessments.
Division of assessment, notice of intent, **80:15.**
Assessors.
See TAX ASSESSORS.
Bill, notice, **60:3.**
Blank lists, assessors to furnish, **59:30.**
Cigarette tax.
Forfeiture proceedings upon seizure of cigarettes, vehicles and containers for illegal transportation or possession, **64C:8.**
Minors, notice prohibiting sales, **64C:10.**
Classification by commissioner, **58:2.**
Collectors, bill or notice, **60:3-60:3B, 60:22A.**
See TAX COLLECTORS.
Contents, **60:3A.**
Corporations and taxation commissioner, notice, **60A:2.**
Corporation taxes.
Abatement of taxes, **59:74.**
Utility company franchise tax, **63:52A.**
Deeds and titles.
Affidavit of notice to holder of invalid tax title, recording, **60:83.**
Assignment or transfer by municipality, **60:52.**
Foreclosure, **60:66.**
Instruments affecting tax deed, notation on record, **36:22.**
Invalid title, **60:82.**
Low value lands, sale by municipality, **60:80A.**
Petition for foreclosure, recording notice of filing and disposition, **60:75.**
Protection of municipal tax title, **60:50A.**
Deficiency notice, **59:12F.**
Delinquent taxpayers, notice, **60A:2A, 62C:21.**

TAXATION —Cont'd
Notice —Cont'd
Demands for payment, **60:16,
60:39.**
Designation of place of service,
60:39.
Distress and sale, **60:25, 60:26.**
Distribution of taxes, notice to
assessors with respect,
58:25A.
Equalization and apportionment
of state and county taxes,
58:10.
Estimated real property tax,
authorization for notice and
payment, **59:2A. (note)**
Exemptions, poll tax bills to
contain notice, **59:5.**
Fees charged by tax collectors,
60:15.
Financial officers of municipal
corporations, **59:23A,
59:23B, 59:70A.**
Forest lands and products, **61:1,
61:2.**
Gasoline and motor fuel taxes,
notice of discontinuance,
sale, or transfer of business
of licensee, **64E:14, 64F:15.**
Income tax.
Assessment of additional tax
upon verification of
return, **62C:26.**
Decision upon application for
abatement, **62C:37.**
Withholding of tax, **62B:7,
62C:10.**
Installment payments, notice of
modification or termination
of written agreement with
taxpayer, **62C:37B.**
Insurance companies, notice and
collection of assessment,
26:8D.
Invalid tax sales, collector to
give notice, **60:46.**
Legacy and succession taxes.
Abatement, notice to applicant
of commission's decision,
65:27A.
Alterations of valuations made
by commissioner, **65:26.**
Appellate tax board, notice of
proceedings before, **65:26.**
Conveyance of real estate of
nonresident decedent,
65:9.
Death, presumption of notice,
65:33A.
Domicile of decedent,
settlement of disputes as
to, **65B:2, 65B:4.**

TAXATION —Cont'd
Notice —Cont'd
Legacy and succession taxes
—Cont'd
Official of state of domicile of
nonresident by register of
probate, notice, **65:24C.**
Receiving additional property
after tax determined,
65:27.
Register of probate to give
notice to official of state of
domicile of nonresident
decedent, **65:24C.**
Valuation and appraisal of
property, **65:25, 65:26.**
Liens.
Business corporations, notice
to commissioner of sale or
transfer, **62C:51.**
Collector, notice by town
officers or boards, **60:23.**
Federal tax lien, recording
notice, **36:24.**
Fixtures, **62C:50.**
Personal property, **62C:50.**
Real property, **62C:50.**
Taking, notice, **60:53, 62C:56.**
Lists.
Assessors to furnish, **58:5,
59:30.**
Posting notices, **59:29, 60:88.**
Mailing, **60:3, 60:15.**
Motor vehicles, notice to owners,
60A:2.
Municipal corporations.
Equalized valuations, notice,
58:10A.
Estimated tax, **59:2A. (note)**
Proposed equalization values,
58:10A.
Redemption of tax title held
by city or town, notice,
60:76C.
Partitioned property, notice of
apportionment of tax,
59:78A.
Preliminary tax, notices, **59:57C.**
Probate and insolvency register,
notices to commissioner,
217:16.
Public lands, notice to assessors
of valuation, **58:14.**
Rate of taxation, notice, **59:23A.**
Resale or exempt use certificate,
notice to produce, **64I:8.**
Sale or transfer of property,
60:25, 60:26.
Sales and use taxes, **62C:67A,
64H:29, 64H:32, 64I:33.**
Tax sales.
See TAX SALES.
Seizure, notice, **62C:56.**

TAXATION —Cont'd
Notice —Cont'd
Service, **60:1.**
Special assessments.
Abatement of assessments,
80:5, 80:6, 80:8-80:10A.
Election to surrender land
assessed, **80:3.**
Eminent domain proceedings,
80A:3, 80A:4.
Taking of land for nonpayment
of taxes, **60:53.**
Tax assessors.
See TAX ASSESSORS.
Tax collectors, fees charged,
60:15.
Use, consumption, or storage
tax.
License to sell, notice of
revocation, **140:50.**
Resale or exempt use
certificate, notice to
produce, **64I:8.**
Verification of lists, **59:31.**
Withholding of tax, filing
returns, or paying taxes,
employer failure, **62B:7.**
Cancellation of notice, **62B:7.**
Returns required, **62C:10.**
Oath or affirmation.
Appeal and review.
Local property assessment,
failure to submit sworn
statements concerning,
59:38D.
Appellate tax board, **58A:11.**
Assessors, oath, **41:29, 43:17.**
Corporation taxes.
Estimated tax, **63B:2.**
Examination of treasurer and
directors under oath by
commissioner of
corporations and taxation,
63:69.
Foreign corporations,
alternative method of
determining net income
from business in state,
filing statement under
oath with commissioner,
63:42.
Income tax returns, **62C:5.**
Lists, oath required, **51:31,
51:35.**
Mortgage holder's oath, **59:12A.**
Revenue department's authority
to take testimony and proofs
under oath, **58:25B.**
Valuation of real estate.
Sworn written returns
concerning local
assessments, **59:38D,
59:38E.**

TAXATION —Cont'd

Occupancy tax, **64G:1 et seq.**
See ROOM OCCUPANCY TAX.

Oil and hazardous material release prevention and response act.

Tax credits.

Emergency response actions, **63:38Q.**

Environmental response actions, remediation efforts, **62:6.**

Older persons.

Abatement of taxes, **59:5.**

Assistance to aged and disabled.

Demand for payment of assessment, **60:16.**

Elderly and disabled tax fund.

Voluntary check off, **60:3D.**

Exemption of hot lunch program from taxation, **64H:6.**

Deferral and recovery agreements allowing postponement of real estate tax payment, **59:5.**

Exemption, **59:5.**

Additional exemptions, **62:3.**

Hot lunch program, **64H:6.**

Volunteers providing municipal services, **59:5K.**

Gross receipts tax for games at elderly housing projects, **10:38.**

Housing for elderly, alterations or improvements, **59:5.**

Real estate tax assistance.

Elderly and disabled tax fund.

Voluntary check off, **60:3D.**

Retirement. See within this heading, "Retirement."

Room occupancy tax, exemption of certain institutions, **64G:2.**

Sales tax, exemption for meals prepared and served in boarding home for aged, **64H:6.**

Suspension of assessments, **60:3B.**

Omitted property, **59:75.**

Abatement of assessments, application, **59:59.**

Charitable institutions, omission as affecting exemption, **59:5.**

Interest, **59:57.**

Time for assessment, **59:75.**

Option.

Election or option. See within this heading, "Election or option."

TAXATION —Cont'd

Optometric service corporations, tax exemption, **176F:14.**

Organ transplant fund, voluntary contributions, **62:6E.**

Orphans, tax exemption, **59:5.**

Other corporations, exemption of capital stock, **59:5.**

Overlay of tax, **59:25, 59:70A.**

Packages or containers.

Cigarette tax.

Marking, **64C:5.**

Possession of unmarked container, penalty, **64C:10.**

Seizure and forfeiture for illegal transportation or possession, **64C:8.**

Imported goods in original package, tax information, **59:33.**

Sales tax, exemption of containers, **64H:6.**

Paraplegic veterans or their surviving spouses, reimbursement of municipalities for abatement of taxes, **58:8A.**

Parcel, defined, **59:5C.**

Parents of veterans, exemption of property, **59:5.**

Parking meter receipts, use for payment in lieu of taxes, **40:22B.**

Parsonages, exemption, **59:5.**

Partially invalid assessments, **59:82.**

Partial payment, **60:22, 60:22A.**

Abatement, insufficient payment as affecting, **59:65D.**

Agricultural land, **61A:19.**

Penalty for underpayment of estate tax based on fraud, **65C:13.**

Partition.

Division of realty after assessment. See within this heading, "Division of realty after assessment."

Partnerships.

Cigarette tax violations, liability of partner aiding in, **64C:21.**

Income tax, **62:17.**

See INCOME TAX.

Individuals liable, **62C:31A.**

Personal property tax, **59:18.**

Shares subject to income tax, exemption of, **59:5.**

Ships or vessels, assessment of, **59:8, 59:18.**

Payment of taxes.

Demand for payment, **60:16-60:22A.**

TAXATION —Cont'd

Payment of taxes —Cont'd

Hazardous waste insolvency fund, **21C:28.**

Income tax.

Amount required with return, **62C:32.**

Appeal, payment as prerequisite, **61A:19.**

Deferred payment plan income, **62:2.**

Estimated taxes, **62C:79.**

See DECLARATION OF ESTIMATED INCOME TAX.

Installment payments, written agreement with taxpayer, **62C:37B.**

Time due, **62C:29, 62C:32-62C:33A, 62C:79.**

Withholding taxes, **62B:5, 62B:7, 62B:10, 62C:10.**

Installment payments, written agreement with taxpayer, **62C:37B.**

Interest on late property tax payment, **59:57B.**

Notice of modification or termination of written agreement with taxpayer, **62C:37B.**

Partial payment, **60:22, 60:22A.**

Abatement, insufficient payment as affecting, **59:65D.**

Agricultural land, **61A:19.**

Penalty for underpayment of estate tax based on fraud, **65C:13.**

Preliminary tax payments, authorization, **59:23D.**

Redevelopment and housing authorities, tax status of real estate owned, **121B:16.**

Refund or reimbursement, timely payment to taxpayers, **14:6.**

Settlement for amount less than assessment, **62C:37C.**

Unpaid taxes.

Abatement of taxes, unpaid property tax bills, **60:2.**

Private entities providing services for collection, **14:3A.**

Payments for certain lands, determination, **59:5D, 59:5F, 59:5G, 121B:16.**

Payments in lieu of taxes.

In lieu payments and taxes. See within this heading, "In lieu payments and taxes."

TAXATION —Cont'd
Peddlers' stock in trade.
Exemption from statutory
requirements, creation,
101:2.
Payment before obtaining local
license, **101:5.**
Penalties.
Fines and penalties. See within
this heading, "Fines and
penalties."
Pensions.
Retirement. See within this
heading, "Retirement."
Perishable or hard-to-store goods,
sale for taxes, **62C:57.**
Permanent restriction, assessment
of lands, **59:11.**
Personal property, **59:2, 59:4.**
Abatement of taxes.
Failure to file list, **59:5, 59:61.**
Inability to pay tax, **59:71.**
Record, **59:60.**
Restrictions, **59:61.**
Adjournment of sale of, notice,
60:26.
Assessment, **59:18.**
Assessors' books to show, **59:43.**
Corporation taxes, foreign
corporation storing tangible
personal property, **63:39.**
Debts, **59:4.**
Distress and sale, **59:20,
60:24-60:28.**
See TAX SALES.
Exemptions, **59:5.**
Failure to list, abatement as
affected, **59:5, 59:61.**
Foreign state, exemption of
property located, **59:5.**
Household furniture and effects,
exemption from personal
property tax, **59:5.**
Lien for taxes against, **62C:50.**
Distress and sale of personalty
for taxes, **60:24-60:28.**
See TAX SALES.
Listing by taxpayer, **59:5,
59:29-59:37, 59:61.**
Literary, benevolent, charitable,
and scientific institutions,
exemptions, **59:5.**
Mortgaged property, who
deemed owner, **59:19.**
Municipal notes, payment, **60:2,
183:62.**
Payment of tax, **59:57.**
Persons subject to taxation,
59:18, 59:19.
Place for assessment, **59:18.**
Pledged property, who deemed
owner, **59:19.**

TAXATION —Cont'd
Personal property —Cont'd
Sales tax, **64H:1 et seq.**
See SALES TAXES.
Ships and vessels taxable, **59:4,
59:18.**
Tax bills, time for sending,
59:57.
Temperance societies,
exemptions, **59:5.**
Time for assessment, **59:18.**
Transient vendor's goods or
stock, **101:5.**
Uncollectible taxes on,
abatement, **59:71.**
Use, consumption, and storage
tax, **62C:16, 64I:1 et seq.**
See USE, CONSUMPTION,
OR STORAGE TAX.
When property taxable, **59:4.**
Persons subject to taxation.
Mortgagors and mortgagees of
real estate, **59:12-59:14.**
Names, effect of errors, **60:21.**
Ownership of land, time for
determination, **59:11.**
Personal property, **59:18.**
Pledged or mortgaged
personalty, **59:19.**
Record owner of real estate,
59:11.
Petition for appeal, **59:65.**
Pigs.
Excise tax, **59:8A.**
Exemption of local taxes, **59:5.**
Sales tax exemption, **64H:6.**
Pipes and pipelines, **40:43, 59:3C,
59:18.**
Assessors.
Assessed to owner of pipelines,
59:3C, 59:83.
Corporations, assessment of
taxes, **59:83.**
Valuation, **59:38A.**
Franchise tax for pipeline
companies, **63:52A.**
Valuation, **59:38A.**
Place, **59:11-59:19.**
Plateware, exemption, **59:5.**
Pledged property, who deemed
owner, **59:19.**
Poles and wires.
Transmission lines and
equipment. See within this
heading, "Transmission lines
and equipment."
Police.
Cigarette tax, **64C:8, 64C:10,
64C:26.**
Exemption for surviving spouse
or children, **59:5.**

TAXATION —Cont'd
Pollution.
Air pollution.
Deduction of expenditures for
construction of air
pollution control facilities,
63:38D.
Exemption from taxation of
pollution control devices,
59:5.
Reimbursement of
Commonwealth for
metropolitan air pollution
control expenditures, tax,
111:142B.
Water pollution.
Bonds and notes issued by
water pollution abatement
districts, **21:36.**
Corporations, tax benefits for
pollution abatement or
control measures, **59:5,
63:38D.**
Poor persons.
Abatement of tax, **59:71.**
Bankruptcy trustees, **62:13,
62C:6.**
Collection from insolvent debtor,
60:19, 60:36.
Exemption, **59:5.**
Hazardous waste insolvency
fund, exemptions, **21C:28.**
Imprisonment for nonpayment of
taxes, poverty as grounds
for release, **60:31.**
Inability to pay tax.
Abatement of certain taxes,
59:65B, 59:71.
Imprisonment for
nonpayment, grounds for
release, **60:31.**
Notice of commissioner from
register of probate and
insolvency, **217:16.**
Port facilities, tax exemption, **59:5.**
Posting.
Lists, tax lists, **59:29, 60:88.**
Sales, tax sales, **60:42.**
Titles, sale of land held under
tax titles, **60:79.**
Postmark date as payment date,
62C:33A.
Poultry and poultry products.
Excise tax on domestic fowl,
59:8A.
Exemption, **59:5, 64H:6.**
Sales tax, exemptions, **64H:6.**
Practice and procedure, rules of
Appellate Tax Board.
See APPELLATE TAX BOARD
RULES OF PRACTICE
AND PROCEDURE.

TAXATION —Cont'd

Preferences and priorities, insolvent estates of deceased persons, tax claims against, **198:1, 206:31.**

Preparers of returns.
Confidentiality of personal data, **62C:74.**
Crimes and penalties, **62C:73, 268A:4.**
State employee not to receive outside compensation, **268A:4.**

Presumptions and burden of proof.
Agricultural and horticultural property.
Allowance of application for valuation, assessment, and taxation, **61A:9.**
Date of acquisition of property for purpose of conveyance tax, **61A:12.**
Notice of intent to exercise purchase option, **61A:14.**
Use, board of assessor's certificate, **61A:14.**
Assessment of taxes, **62C:26.**
Sales for taxes, circumstances where municipality deemed to be purchaser, **60:49.**
Sales taxes, **64H:8, 64H:25.**
Use, consumption, or storage tax, **64I:8, 64I:26.**

Private airports, exemption of certain, **59:5.**

Private auditors, abatement proceedings open, **59:60.**

Private pension associations, **32:41, 59:5.**

Private way or bridge, financing repairs, **84:14.**

Privileged and confidential matters, **62C:21, 62C:77.**

Probate and Family Court.
Abatement proceedings, jurisdiction of appeals, **62C:39.**

Local property assessment, persons liable for tax, **59:12B.**

Process.
Service of process and papers. See within this heading, "Service of process and papers."

Procurement.
Contractors providing goods, services or real estate space. Certification of tax compliance, **62C:49A.**

Production of papers and documents.
Appellate tax board, **58A:11.**

TAXATION —Cont'd

Promoters of shows, **62C:1, 62C:8A, 62C:67A, 62C:76.**

Property.
Community preservation. Surcharge, **44B:4.**
Personal property. See within this heading, "Personal property."
Real estate, **59:2 et seq., 60:1 et seq.**

Proposition 2½, **59:21C.**
See TAX AND BUDGET LIMITS FOR LOCAL GOVERNMENT.

Protesting payment of tax, **60:98.**

Provincetown harbor, persons occupying state land, **59:5.**

Public lands.
Assessors.
Appeal from valuation, **58:14.**
Assessment, **58:17A.**
Notice as to valuation of public lands, **58:14.**
Boston, Commonwealth flats, **59:5.**
Exemption from taxation, **59:5.**
Reimbursement of towns for loss of tax, **58:13-58:17B.**
Amount, determination, **58:25A.**
Annual statement to state treasurer, **58:16.**
Appeal from valuation by assessors, **58:14.**
County tuberculosis hospitals, **58:17A.**
Exempt state land, inclusion in valuation of property, **58:15A.**
Flood control, property taken, **58:17B.**
Newly acquired lands, valuation, **58:15.**
Notice to assessors, **58:14.**
Rate of reimbursement, **58:17.**
Solid waste disposal facilities of public works department, **58:13.**

Public officers and employees.
Federal withholding tax on wages and salaries of, collection, **58:28A, 58:28B.**
Penalties for disclosure of tax information, **62C:21.**
Tax deferred investments, state and county employees, **15:18A.**

Public works department, real estate, **59:5.**

Purchasers' returns, **62C:16.**

TAXATION —Cont'd

Quarterly installment of estimated corporate taxes, **63B:4.**

Rabbis' residences, exemption, **59:5.**

Radio and television, **59:5, 64H:1, 64H:6.**

Raffles and bazaars.
Rate of taxation on gross proceeds realized, **271:7A.**
Returns, **62C:18.**
Tax administration provisions applicable, **62C:2.**

Railroads.
Bonds, **59:4.**
Exemptions.
Fuel used by railroads, sales tax exemption, **64H:6.**
Real property, limited exemption, **160:87.**
Fuel used, sales tax exemption, **64H:6.**
Levy by city or town to pay interest on debts incurred in aid, **44:57, 59:24.**
Subscription indebtedness, assessment for interest, **59:24.**
Utility company franchise tax, **63:52A.**

Rate of taxation.
Assessors.
Change, **59:23.**
Determination, **59:21, 59:23.**
Distribution of estimate of among towns, **58:25A.**
Factors to be considered in setting, **59:23.**
Notice to financial officers of municipalities, **59:23A, 59:23B.**
Factors to be considered when setting, **32B:3, 59:23.**
Gasoline and motor fuel taxes, **64A:4, 64E:4, 64F:3.**
Out-of-state purchase of fuel or special fuel, **64F:1, 64F:3, 64F:6.**
Prior to effective date, **64A:1, 64F:1.**
Special fuels, **64E:4, 64F:1, 64F:3, 64F:6.**
Insurance included in determining, cost, **32B:3.**
Limits on local government, **59:21C.**
See TAX AND BUDGET LIMITS FOR LOCAL GOVERNMENT.
Municipal lighting charges, overdue, **164:58D, 164:58E.**

TAXATION —Cont'd

Rate of taxation —Cont'd

Notice to municipal financial officers, **59:23A.**

Printing on tax bill, **60:3A.**

Trailers, maximum rate of excise tax, **60A:1.**

Use, consumption, or storage tax, **64I:2.**

Formula for collection, **64I:5.**

Ratio studies for local property assessment, **58:10.**

Real estate, **59:2 et seq., 60:1 et seq.**

Elderly and disabled tax fund. Voluntary check off, **60:3D.**

Real estate time-shares, **183B:3, 183B:29.**

Real property.

Appellate tax board.

Assessed valuation, **58A:12A to 58A:12D.**

Damages for improper assessment, **58A:14.**

Reassessment or revision of tax assessment, **59:76-59:78.**

Abatement as to, application, **59:59.**

Alienation of land as affecting, **59:77.**

Collection, **59:78.**

Interest on revision of assessment, **59:57, 59:78.**

Invalid sale or tax titles, **60:46, 60:84, 60:84A.**

Lien, reassessed tax, **59:77.**

List of property, **59:78.**

Reciprocity, **58:28C.**

Disclosure of tax information, reciprocity, **62C:22.**

Exemption of certain corporate property under reciprocity provisions, **59:5.**

Foreign insurance companies, reciprocity provisions, **175:159.**

Gasoline and motor fuel taxes, **64F:4, 64F:5.**

Income tax, **62:3, 62C:22, 62C:23.**

Recognizance, taxpayer's release on bail bond, **60:34A.**

Records and recording, **59:43-59:48, 59:50-59:52, 62C:25.**

Abatement of taxes, **59:5, 59:59, 59:60, 59:70A, 59:72, 80:6.**

Abstract cards of records to be furnished to assessors, **36:24B.**

Administration, **62C:1-62C:77.**

TAXATION —Cont'd

Records and recording —Cont'd

Agricultural and horticultural property.

Certificate of roll-back taxes or conveyance taxes due, **61A:19A.**

Notice of municipality's intent to exercise purchase option, **61A:14.**

Appeal and review, **59:64, 59:65B, 59:65C.**

Appellate tax board.

Open to public, **58A:13.**

Recordation of proceedings, **58A:10.**

Assessors, books and lists of, **59:43-59:48, 59:50-59:52.**

See TAX ASSESSORS.

Certificate of payment by one other than owner of fee, **60:60.**

Cigarette tax, **65C:1, 65C:5, 65C:6, 65C:8.**

Collectors, **60:6 et seq.**

See TAX COLLECTORS.

Combat zones, soldiers serving, **62C:81.**

Contracts for extension of tax exemption, **121A:6A.**

Cooperation with federal government and other states, **62C:23.**

Deeds, **60:45, 60:54.**

See TAX DEEDS AND TITLES.

Destruction, **62C:69.**

Disclosure, **62C:70.**

Examination, inspection, or investigation. See within this heading, "Examination, inspection, or investigation."

Extensions of time, filing, **62C:19, 63B:3, 65C:8, 80:6.**

Fair information practices, **62C:21.**

Gasoline and motor fuel taxes, **64A:3, 64E:3.**

Inventory of fuels on hand, filing, **64A:1.**

Receipts and invoices, **64A:7, 64A:13, 64E:5, 64E:13, 64F:14.**

Returns by distributors, **64A:11, 64E:4, 64E:11, 64F:6, 64F:12.**

Sales and collections, report, **64A:4, 64E:4, 64F:6.**

Income tax, **62C:4-20.**

See INCOME TAX.

Legacy and succession taxes.

Inventory and appraisal of estates, **65:22.**

TAXATION —Cont'd

Records and recording —Cont'd

Legacy and succession taxes —Cont'd

Payment of federal tax, record, **36:16.**

Petition for accounting in estate of nonresident by official of state of domicile, **65:24C.**

Proof of payment of taxes and state of domicile of nonresident decedent, **65:24B.**

Liens, **40:42A, 40:42B.**

See TAX LIENS.

Municipal property assessment, failure to keep proper records, **58:4-58:4B.**

Redemption certificates, **60:63.**

Registers of deeds, records furnished, **36:24B.**

Sales for taxes.

Collector's deeds, **60:45.**

Conveyances, effect of recording, **60:37.**

Redemption certificates, **60:63.**

Sale and redemption, commissioner to keep records, **62C:61.**

Surrender and discharge of invalid tax title, **60:46.**

Sales taxes, filing of notice of shows, **62C:67A.**

Special assessments.

Abatement petition, **80:5, 80:6.**

Betterment assessments, orders, **80:2.**

Eminent domain proceedings, **80A:3, 80A:10, 80A:11.**

Filing fee, **80:13B.**

Liens, dissolution, **80:12.**

Orders, plans, and estimates, **80:2.**

Registry of deeds, **80:2, 80:12, 80:13B, 80A:3, 80A:10, 80A:11, 83:27.**

Sidewalk assessments, **83:27.**

Stamps, penalty for failure to affix prior to leaving instrument for recording, **64D:6A.**

State treasurer, expenses of keeping records of local property assessments, **58:4C.**

Taking of land for nonpayment of taxes, instrument, **60:54.**

Titles, **60:45, 60:54.**

See TAX DEEDS AND TITLES.

TAXATION —Cont'd

Records and recording —Cont'd
Verification of returns by
examination of books,
62C:24.
Recovery back of taxes.
Action, **60:98, 62C:36 et seq.**
Repayment of tax paid by one
other than fee owner, **60:60.**
Recreational lands, **61B:1-61B:18,
64H:1, 64I:1.**
Abatement of tax.
Notice of application, **61B:14.**
Revaluation of land, **61B:5.**
Appellate tax board, appeal of
assessment of tax, **61B:14.**
Board of assessors, **61B:2-61B:8,
61B:14, 61B:17.**
Buildings, valuation, **61B:10.**
Change in use of land, **61B:4.**
Classification, **61B:1-61B:18.**
Commissioner of revenue,
classification, **61B:3,
61B:16, 61B:18.**
Conveyance tax.
Land subject, **61B:7.**
Liens, **61B:6.**
Definitions, **61B:1.**
Eminent domain, effect on tax,
61B:7.
Exemption from certain taxes,
59:5, 61B:7.
Interest on taxes, **61B:8.**
List, **61B:17.**
Registry of deeds, change in
ownership of land, **61B:6.**
Residential, industrial, or
commercial use, conversion
of land, **61B:9.**
Roll-back tax.
Land subject, **61B:8.**
Liability, **61B:11, 61B:12.**
Liens on land, **61B:6.**
Procedures for payment,
61B:14.
Sale or conveyance of land,
liability for tax, **61B:12.**
Special or betterment
assessments, land subject,
61B:13.
Valuation of land, **61B:2, 61B:3.**
Recreational services, **64H:1,
64I:1.**
Redevelopment and housing
authorities, tax status of real
estate owned, **121B:16.**
Reduction of tax.
Corporation taxes, reduction of
taxes on account of excess
as affected by minimum tax
rate, **63:31B.**

TAXATION —Cont'd

Reduction of tax —Cont'd
Income tax dependency
deductions, **62B:4.**
State finance, reduction fund,
29:2I.
Refrigeration, exemption of
personal property used, **59:5.**
Refund or reimbursement, **62C:40.**
Abated taxes, **59:58A, 59:69,
62C:36, 62C:40.**
Actions to recover, **60:98,
62C:36 et seq.**
Agricultural land, overpaid
taxes, **61A:19.**
Air pollution control
expenditures,
reimbursement of
Commonwealth, **111:142B.**
Applications for refunds, **62C:36.**
Appropriation unnecessary for
payment, **29:18.**
Audit, authorization of refund
determined after, **62C:27.**
Bank account of taxpayer, direct
credit of refund, **62C:40.**
Child support collection.
Procedures by IV-D agency for
accrued arrearages,
119A:6.
Set-off debt collection, revenue
department to assist
transitional assistance
department in collecting
support obligations,
62D:3.
Cigarette tax.
License fees, **64C:5.**
Tax, **64C:6.**
Unused stamps and meter
settings, **64C:31.**
Cities and towns.
Conservation lands,
reimbursement of
municipalities for tax loss,
58:13 et seq.
Public lands, reimbursement
of towns for loss of tax,
58:13 et seq.
Time limit for filing claims,
58:8B.
Veterans, taxes lost, **58:8A,
59:5.**
Corrections department,
reimbursement of towns for
loss of taxes on land used,
58:13.
Counties containing state-owned
land, exception as to
reimbursement, **58:15A.**
Deed and document stamp tax,
64D:4.

TAXATION —Cont'd

Refund or reimbursement —Cont'd
Distribution, withholding, **58:25.**
Education reimbursement
appropriation, **59:23.**
Excise tax on motor vehicles,
60A:2.
Execution creditor paying taxes,
right to reimbursement,
236:33.
Expenses of tax collector, **60:15.**
Federal estate tax, **65A:2,
65A:4.**
See ESTATE TAXES.
Forest lands and products,
abatement of taxes, **61:2.**
Gasoline and motor fuel taxes.
Farming, fuel used by persons
engaged, **64A:7A.**
Form of affidavit prescribed by
revenue commissioner,
64A:7.
Other than farming or
highway operation, fuels
used, **64A:7.**
Out-of-state purchase of fuel
or special fuels, **64F:4.**
Receipts and invoices to
accompany
reimbursement claims,
64A:7, 64E:5, 64E:13.
Special fuels, **64E:5, 64F:4.**
Time for filing, **64A:7.**
Health department,
reimbursement of towns for
loss of taxes on land used,
58:13.
Income tax, **62C:36.**
See INCOME TAX.
Interest on money, **59:64,
61A:19, 62C:40, 186:15C.**
Invalid tax sale, reimbursement
of purchaser, **60:46.**
Legacy and succession taxes,
65:20.
See LEGACY AND
SUCCESSION TAXES.
Mass transportation facilities
and services, certification of
amounts as reimbursement,
58:25B.
Metropolitan air pollution
control district expenditures,
tax to reimburse
Commonwealth, **111:142B.**
Municipalities, **58:8A, 58:8B,
58:13 et seq., 59:5.**
One dollar, amounts under,
property tax refunds,
59:58A.
Owner repaying tax paid by
another, right of recovery,
60:60.

TAXATION —Cont'd
Refund or reimbursement —Cont'd
Part payment in excess of tax, **60:22.**
Public lands, reimbursement of towns for loss of tax, **58:13-58:17B.**
Purchaser at invalid tax sale, **60:46.**
Reassessment as affected, **59:77.**
Room occupancy tax, reimbursement of operator of establishment, **64G:4.**
Rounding off to whole numbers, **62C:4.**
Sales taxes.
Tax, reimbursement by purchaser to vendor, **64H:3.**
Worthless accounts, reimbursement of sales tax paid by vendor, **64H:33.**
Set-off debt collection, revenue department to assist transitional assistance department in collecting support obligations, **62D:3.**
Ships and vessels, filing of claim for reimbursement of gasoline tax, **64A:7.**
Solid waste disposal facilities, reimbursement of municipalities for tax loss on lands used, **58:13.**
Special education reimbursement appropriation as part of estimated receipts, **59:23.**
Specially adapted housing for disabled veteran, reimbursement of cities and towns for taxes lost, **59:5.**
State treasurer, payment of refund, **62C:39, 62C:40.**
Support obligation collection.
Procedures by IV-D agency for accrued arrearages, **119A:6.**
Set-off debt collection, revenue department to assist transitional assistance department in collecting support obligations, **62D:3.**
Time limit on refund applications, **62C:36.**

TAXATION —Cont'd
Refund or reimbursement —Cont'd
Timely payment to taxpayers, **14:6.**
Turnpike authority, reimbursement for tax paid on fuel used for other than highway operation, **64A:7, 64E:5.**
University of Massachusetts, reimbursement of loss of taxes on land used, **58:13-58:17A.**
Regional incinerator districts, bonds and notes as exempt from taxation, **59:5.**
Regional police district operating costs, assessment of local taxes to pay, **41:99H.**
Regional refuse disposal districts, assessments to pay apportionments pursuant to agreement, **40:44H.**
Regional school districts.
Exemption of bonds or notes issued by school districts, **59:5.**
Reduction in local taxes, **71:16B, 71:16B½.**
State aid or reimbursement, **71:14B, 71:16B-71:16D.**
See REGIONAL SCHOOL DISTRICTS.
Regional transportation authorities, exemption, **161B:13.**
Registered land.
Assessors.
Abstract cards or copies of records furnished, **36:24B, 61B:6.**
Assessed valuation as controlling for purposes of assurance fund, **185:109.**
Betterments as affected, **185:46.**
Assurance fund, assessed value as evidence in action for compensation, **185:109.**
Effect of taxes, **185:46.**
Enforcement of tax liens, **185:84.**
Register of probate and insolvency to send notices and copies to revenue commissioner, **217:16.**
Registers.
See REGISTERS AND REGISTRIES OF DEEDS.

TAXATION —Cont'd
Registration lists of motorboats, snow vehicles and recreation vehicles, transmittal to local assessors, **90B:11.**
Rehabilitation of owner-occupied residential properties, special assessment policy for, **59:5J.**
Reimbursement of towns for loss of tax on public lands, **58:13 et seq.**
Release of levy, **62C:64.**
Release of person imprisoned for nonpayment of taxes, **60:31, 224:28.**
Repairs and maintenance.
Motor vehicles, **59:5, 60A:1, 64H:1, 64I:1.**
Private ways or bridges, financing of repairs, **84:14.**
Services, taxing of, **64H:1, 64H:6, 64I:1.**
Reports.
Appellate tax board.
Annual report of recommendations and matters handled, **58A:4.**
Publication, sale and distribution, **58A:3.**
Time for delivery, **58A:13.**
Apportionment of state and county taxes, **58:9, 58:10.**
Commissioner of revenue, false reports, **268:6.**
Equalized valuations for cities and towns, furnishing of information for determining, **58:10.**
Income tax.
Inspection of reports, **64C:20.**
Leased personalty, **64C:13.**
Payment of income, **64C:8.**
Promoters of shows, **62C:8A.**
Revenue department.
See REVENUE DEPARTMENT AND COMMISSIONER.
Sales tax, information reports as subject, **64H:1.**
Use, consumption, or storage tax, rental property receipts, **64I:8.**
Research science, **59:29, 64H:6.**
Reserve funds for balance of overlay account, **59:25.**
Residence.
Abatement of tax based on change in use of residential land, **61B:5.**
Address of owner, assessor's duties, **184:8A.**

TAXATION —Cont'd
Residence —Cont'd
Agricultural land, residential use as constituting conversion, **61A:14.**
Air raid or fallout shelters, exemption for, **59:5.**
Cluster housing, common land, **59:11.**
Compromising assessment to keep residence, penalty, **59:89.**
Determination of residential factor, **58:1A.**
District executive of southern New England District of Assemblies of God, residence, **59:5.**
Educational institutions, off-campus residence for officers, **59:5.**
Evasion of taxation by concealment or change of, penalty, **59:90.**
Lease of residence, provisions as to tax escalation clauses, **186:15C.**
Methodist Church, residence occupied by district superintendent, **59:5.**
Mobile homes and mobile home parks, **59:5, 59:83, 255:26-255:31.**
Names of resident wage earners reported to revenue commissioner, **62C:8.**
Older persons, residential property, **59:5.**
Penalty in refusal to give or falsity in giving tax information, **59:92.**
Recreational land, conversion to residential use, **61B:9.**
Specially adapted housing of disabled veterans, tax exemption of, **59:5.**
Statements required of owners of tax titles, **60:47.**
Valuation for abatement of tax upon change in use, **61B:5.**
Widows' and minors' exemption as affected by change, **59:5.**
Resource recovery facilities.
Owner taxed by town or city in which facility located, **16:24A.**
Residue as solid waste for purpose of landfill fee, **111:150A.**
Restaurateurs, returns, **62C:16.**

TAXATION —Cont'd
Retail merchants.
Stores and merchants. See within this heading, "Stores and merchants."
Retirement.
Alcoholic beverage tax, crediting of receipts, **138:21.**
Assessment for municipal system, **32:22.**
Exemption from taxation, **32:19, 32:41, 59:5, 62:3.**
Legacy and succession taxes, **32:19, 65:1.**
Income tax.
Individual retirement account, **62:2, 62:5.**
Internal Revenue Code, receipt of unemployment compensation, **151A:29.**
Pension plan income.
Deductible from gross income, **62:2, 62:3.**
Exemption from tax, **32:19, 62:3, 62:5.**
Federal government pensions, **62:3.**
Massachusetts gross income, **62:2.**
Other states, taxation of retirement pensions, **62:3.**
Part B adjusted gross income as affected by employer contributions, **62:2.**
Withholding by retiree or annuitant of sums assigned for payment of income taxes, **32:19, 32:19A.**
Legacy and succession taxes, exemption, **32:19, 65:1.**
Levy for pension and retirement funds, **32:22.**
Private pension associations, **32:41, 59:5.**
Railroads, deductions and exemptions allowed in determining taxable income, **62:3.**
Warrant to assess tax for expenses of system, issuance by state treasurer, **32:21.**
Return of process, **50:1, 60:57, 60:67.**
Return of property following release of levy of taxes, **62C:64.**
Returns.
Abatement, **62C:38.**

TAXATION —Cont'd
Returns —Cont'd
Alcoholic beverage taxes, **62C:14, 62C:16.**
Appeal and review, return statement falsely made, **59:38F.**
Assessors, **60:2.**
Banks, **62C:12.**
Beano, raffle, or bazaar, **62C:18.**
Cigarette tax, **64C:6.**
False returns, penalties, **64C:10.**
Retailers and stampers, **62C:16.**
Collectors, **60:2.**
Compensation of state employees for filing state tax returns, **268A:4.**
Corporation taxes, **62C:11, 62C:12.**
Destruction, **62C:69.**
Estate taxes, **62C:17, 65C:8.**
See ESTATE TAXES.
Executors, administrators, and other fiduciaries, returns, **62C:6, 62C:8, 62C:17.**
Failure to make or file.
Forest products, returns, **61:4.**
Telephone and telegraph companies, **59:42.**
Foreign corporations, **62C:11.**
Forest products tax, **61:3, 61:4.**
Forms, **62C:5.**
Fuel distributors, **62C:16.**
Gas and electric companies, condensed return to state amount accrued for taxes, **164:84A.**
Gasoline and motor fuel taxes, **64A:4.**
See GASOLINE AND MOTOR FUEL TAXES.
General court members, compensation for filing tax returns, **268A:4.**
Income tax, **62C:4 et seq.**
See INCOME TAX.
Innkeepers, **62C:16.**
Insurance companies, **62C:12.**
Notice, returns required, **62C:10.**
Partnership returns, penalty for late filing, **62C:34.**
Penalty for fraudulent, **62C:28.**
Pipeline owners' return to state tax commission, **59:38A.**
Preparers.
Confidentiality of personal data, **62C:74.**
Crimes and penalties, **62C:73, 268A:4.**

TAXATION —Cont'd
Returns —Cont'd
Preparers —Cont'd
State employee not to receive
outside compensation,
268A:4.
Purchasers, **62C:16.**
Restaurateurs, **62C:16.**
Retail merchants, **62C:16.**
Revenue department.
See REVENUE
DEPARTMENT AND
COMMISSIONER.
Sales taxes, **62C:16.**
Shipping companies, **62C:12.**
Ships, **59:8, 62C:12.**
Telephone and telegraph
companies, **59:41, 59:42.**
Urban redevelopment
companies, **62C:12.**
Utility companies, **62C:12.**
Verification.
Cooperation of governments,
62C:23.
Corporation taxes.
Insurance companies, **63:26.**
Income tax returns, **62C:24,
62C:26.**
Withholding tax, **62B:5, 62C:10.**
Failure to file, **62B:7.**
Revenue Department and
Commissioner, **14:1 et seq.,
58:1 et seq.**
See REVENUE DEPARTMENT
AND COMMISSIONER.
Revenue growth limit, **62F:1 to
62F:8.**
Adjustments, **62F:4.**
Budget restrictions, **62F:3.**
Credit for amounts in excess of
growth limit, **62F:6.**
Defined terms, **62F:2.**
Imposition, **62F:3.**
Oversight, **62F:5.**
Preamble, **62F:1.**
Purpose, **62F:1.**
Severability of provisions, **62F:8.**
Taxpayer suits, **62F:7.**
Roll-back taxes.
Agricultural and horticultural
property.
Bases for assessment,
collection, and payment,
61A:19.
Certificate of amount,
application, **61A:19A.**
Lands no longer qualified for
privileged uses, **61A:13.**
Modification or abatement,
application, **61A:19.**
Qualification of land as
dependent upon actual
use, **61A:16.**

TAXATION —Cont'd
Roll-back taxes —Cont'd
Recreational lands.
Land subject, **61B:8.**
Liability, **61B:11, 61B:12.**
Liens on land, **61B:6.**
Procedures for payment,
61B:14.
Room occupancy tax, **64G:1 et
seq.**
See ROOM OCCUPANCY TAX.
Rounding off to whole numbers,
62C:4.
Rules and regulations, **62C:3.**
Sale for taxes, **59:2B, 59:12E,
60:37-60:60.**
See TAX SALES.
Sales tax, **64H:1 et seq.**
See SALES TAXES.
Satisfaction of levy, **62C:54.**
Executors and administrators,
60:36.
Savings and loan associations,
income tax on interest, **62:2.**
Savings banks.
Corporation taxes, **59:5, 63:2,
63:22B, 63:22C.**
Exemption from taxation, **59:5,
168:41, 168:42-168:44.**
Federal savings banks, taxation
of interest, **62:2.**
Income taxes, **62:1, 62:2,
62C:12.**
Schools and education.
Assessors' training programs,
58:1, 59:21A.
Buildings on land leased from
state universities, taxation
of, **75:28.**
Employment and training
department.
Fair information practices,
62C:21.
Federal unemployment taxes,
151A:46.
Set-off debt collection,
liabilities, **62D:13.**
Wage reporting system, **62B:2,
62E:1 et seq.**
Exemptions.
Fraternal benefit societies,
exemption from school
tax, **176:49.**
Legacy and succession taxes,
65:1.
Meals served to students,
64H:6.
Sales tax, **64C:6, 64H:6.**
Income tax deduction for
children attending
educational institutions,
62:6.

TAXATION —Cont'd
Schools and education —Cont'd
Off-campus residence buildings
for officers of educational
institutions, **59:5.**
Printing of tax bill for school
tax, **60:3A.**
Regional school districts.
Exemption of bonds or notes
issued by school districts,
59:5.
Reduction in local taxes,
71:16B, 71:16B½.
State aid or reimbursement,
71:14B, 71:16B-71:16D.
See REGIONAL SCHOOL
DISTRICTS.
Revenue department and
commissioner.
Certification to commissioner
of amount of school aid
payable to city and town,
70:5.
Local assessors, authority to
conduct and sponsor
training programs, **58:1.**
Removal of treasurer of
regional school district,
41:39B.
State aid, filing statements,
70:5.
Sales tax exemptions, **64C:6,
64H:6.**
Tax assessors training programs,
58:1, 59:21A.
Withholding tax on wages of
students in seasonal
employment, **62B:1.**
Science, **59:29, 64H:6.**
Secretary of state.
Sales and use taxes, service of
process against
nonresidents, **64I:33.**
Suit of officer of another state
for enforcement of tax
liabilities, prerequisites,
58:28C.
Securities.
Bonds and securities. See within
this heading, "Bond issues."
Seizure of property for taxes,
60:53-60:56.
See TAX LIENS.
Semi-annual installments on
account of municipal liability,
59:20.
Senior citizens, **60:3D.**
Separate bill or notice for each
parcel of real estate, **60:3,
60:22A.**

TAXATION —Cont'd
Service of process and papers.
  Appellate tax board.
    Affidavit as notice and service,
      60:57.
    Appeals to, **58A:7, 58A:9,**
      58A:13.
    Cigarette tax forfeiture
      proceedings, **64C:8.**
    Fees, **64C:23.**
    Return of process, **60:1, 60:57,**
      60:67.
    Revenue department.
      Service of summons,
        58:25B.
    Sales and use taxes,
      nonresidents, **64H:29,**
      64H:32, 64I:33.
  Arrest and imprisonment.
    Collection by imprisonment,
      service of warrant, **60:29,**
      60:34.
  Assessors, **223:37.**
  Attorney general.
    Agent for service of process for
      foreign corporations,
      156B:79.
  Cigarette tax forfeiture
    proceedings, **64C:8.**
    Fees, **64C:23.**
  Collector's affidavit as evidence
    of service, **60:1, 60:57.**
  Decedents' estates.
    Heirs, demand for local taxes,
      60:16.
  Demand for payment.
    Decedents' estates, local taxes,
      60:16.
    Notice of place for service,
      60:39.
  Foreclosure proceedings, **60:66.**
  Income tax return.
    Writ of mandamus to compel
      filing, **62C:9.**
  Low value lands, proceedings to
    establish title, **60:80B.**
  Municipal corporations.
    Service agent, **60:2C.**
  Nonresidents.
    Sales and use taxes, **64H:29,**
      64H:32, 64I:33.
    Tax title owners or agents,
      60:47.
  Notice, **60:1.**
  Place of service, designation,
    60:39.
  Return of process.
    Appellate tax board, **60:1,**
      60:57, 60:67.
  Revenue department.
    Service of summons, **58:25B.**

TAXATION —Cont'd
Service of process and papers
  —Cont'd
  Sales and use taxes.
    Nonresidents, **64H:29,**
      64H:32, 64I:33.
  Tax collectors.
    Affidavit as notice and service,
      60:1, 60:57.
  Withholding tax on wages,
    employer's failure to
    withhold, **62B:7.**
Services sold at retail.
  Apportioned use certificate,
    services sold at retail
    outside of Commonwealth,
    64H:6.
  Exemptions, **64H:6, 64I:7.**
  Sales taxes, **64H:1-64H:3,**
    64H:6, 64H:8, 64H:23.
  Use, consumption, or storage
    tax, **64I:1-64I:8, 64I:24.**
Set-off debt collection, revenue
  department to assist
  transitional assistance
  department in collecting
  support obligations, **62D:3.**
Setoff of taxes and charges against
  municipal indebtedness, **60:93.**
Sewers.
  Annual use charge added to tax,
    59:57.
  Assessments, **83:15.**
    See SEWERS AND DRAINS.
  Exemptions.
    Local property, **59:5D, 59:5E.**
    Model sewer and water
      commission, **40N:19.**
  Liens, **83:16A et seq.**
  Tax title accounts for sewer use
    rates, **60:62, 60:76B.**
Sheep.
  Excise tax, **59:8A.**
  Exemption from local taxes,
    59:5.
Sheriffs.
  See TAX COLLECTORS.
Ships and vessels, **59:4, 59:8,**
  60B:1-60B:4, 64H:6.
  See SHIPS AND OTHER
    WATERCRAFT.
Short taxable year, effect on
  income tax exemptions, **62:3.**
Sidewalk assessments, **59:38,**
  83:26-83:29, 85:6.
Sinking funds, addition of
  unexpended tax moneys,
  44:11.
Situs for taxation, **59:11-59:19.**
  Mortgaged land, **59:12.**
  Motor vehicles excise tax, **60A:6.**

TAXATION —Cont'd
Situs for taxation —Cont'd
  Personal property, **59:18.**
  Resource recovery facilities,
    16:24A.
Small amounts of tax, abatement,
  62C:43.
Small businesses.
  Exemption for certain property,
    59:5I.
Snow traveling and recreation
  vehicles, **90B:31.**
Solar energy.
  Exemption of solar or
    wind-powered systems from
    taxation, **59:5.**
  Incentives through tax benefits
    for use of alternative energy
    resources, **63:38H.**
Solid waste disposal.
  As manufacturing activity, **58:2.**
  Operator of privately owned
    facility, **16:24A.**
Southeastern Regional Planning
  and Economic Development
  District, annual tax levy for
  expenses, **40B:18.**
Special assessments, **80:1 et seq.,**
  80A:1 et seq.
  See SPECIAL ASSESSMENTS.
Special collection warrant as to
  taxpayer insolvent or about to
  leave state, **60:19.**
Special education reimbursement
  appropriation as part of
  estimated receipts for purpose,
  59:23.
Specific exemption as affecting
  state tax return, **62C:17.**
Split-interest trusts, **68:1 et seq.**
Sponge tax on estates, absorption
  of federal credit, **65C:2A,**
  65C:3.
Spouses.
  Support obligations, collection
    via taxation system, **62D:3,**
    119A:6.
  Use of names of both, **14:6.**
Stable accessories, exemption,
  59:5.
Stamps.
  Cigarette tax, **64C:1, 64C:29 et**
    seq.
  Deeds and documents,
    64D:2-64D:4, 64D:7-64D:9.
    See DEED AND DOCUMENT
      STAMP TAX.
  Federal tax stamp, notation,
    36:15.
State Administrative Procedure
  Law, applicability, **30A:1,**
  58:13.

TAXATION —Cont'd
State bonds and obligations.
  Acceptance of notes in payment
    of taxes, **29:48.**
  Amount included in state tax for
    serial payments of bonds,
    29:50.
  Income from public obligations,
    29:2O, 62:2.
  Infrastructure bonds, **29:2O.**
  Social security recipients,
    information as to tax
    consequences, **29:48B,
    44:22B.**
State forest land.
  Evaluation, **58:15.**
  Reimbursement of towns for loss
    of tax, **58:13-58:17A.**
  Structures erected by licensees,
    59:5.
State hospitals, exemption, **59:5,
  64G:2.**
Statements.
  Administrative policy statement,
    14:1.
  Agricultural property, affidavits,
    61A:12, 61A:14.
  Appeal and review, return
    statement falsely made,
    59:38F.
  Destruction of documents,
    62C:69.
  Failure to make or file lists of
    property, **59:36, 59:37.**
  Forest products tax, **61:2.**
  Listing of property, **59:29-59:37.**
  Mass transportation facilities
    and services, submission of
    statements for
    determination, **58:25B.**
  Mortgagor's or mortgagee's
    statements concerning
    assessment, **59:34.**
  Raffles and bazaars, statements
    concerning, **62C:18, 271:7A.**
  Taking of land for nonpayment,
    statement that taking
    cannot be legally made,
    60:37A.
  Tax deeds and titles.
    Release of town from liability
      on warranties in deed,
      recording statement
      giving, **60:82.**
    Residence and place of
      business of owner, filing
      and recording statement,
      60:47.
State military camp ground,
  reimbursement of towns for
  loss of tax on land used,
  58:13-58:17A.

TAXATION —Cont'd
State property.
  Deductions from distributions to
    towns, **58:20A.**
  Exemption from local taxes,
    59:5.
  Interest upon obligations,
    taxation, **62:2.**
  Offset of obligations owing to
    delinquent municipalities,
    59:20.
State tax commission.
  Abolition and replacement by
    commissioner of revenue,
    14:1. (note)
State tax revenues, limitation on
  growth, **62F:1 to 62F:8.**
State treasurer.
  Action against town for
    nonassessment or
    nonpayment of state tax,
    59:28.
  Deductions of sums due
    Commonwealth from
    distributions, **58:20A.**
  Deposits by corporations, **58:5,
    58:28.**
  Distribution of state funds,
    58:18B.
  Federal withholding tax,
    collection, **58:28A, 58:28B.**
  Flood control, reimbursement of
    towns for loss of tax on
    property taken, **58:17B.**
  Highway fund, distribution,
    58:18B.
  Income tax refunds, **62C:36,
    62C:40.**
  Legacy and succession taxes.
    Deposits in lieu of tax on
      future estates, **65:15.**
    Payment of refunds, **65:27.**
  Local collections, payment to
    state treasurer, **59:20.**
  Local property assessment,
    expenses of keeping records,
    58:4C.
  Loss of tax on public lands,
    reimbursement of towns,
    58:16, 58:17, 58:17B.
  Mass transportation,
    certification of amounts
    payable, **58:25B.**
  Paraplegic veterans or their
    surviving spouses,
    reimbursement of
    municipalities for
    abatements of taxes, **58:8A.**
  Payment for distribution of
    taxes, **58:25.**

TAXATION —Cont'd
State treasurer —Cont'd
  Pension and retirement systems,
    issuance of warrant to
    assess tax for expenses,
    32:21.
  Public lands, reimbursement of
    towns for loss of tax, **58:13,
    58:16, 58:17, 58:17B.**
  Refund, payment, **62C:39,
    62C:40.**
  Town's liability, **59:28.**
  Warrants for state taxes sent to
    assessors, **59:20.**
Statistical sample methods
  allowed for audit of taxpayer's
  books, **62C:24.**
Statute of limitations.
  Abatement of unpaid and
    uncollectible taxes, **62C:42.**
  Estate taxes, limitation period
    for collection, **62C:65.**
  Income taxes, limitation on
    additional assessment,
    62C:30.
  Legacy and succession tax lien,
    termination, **65:9.**
  Local property taxes, actions for
    refunds or recoveries, **60:98.**
  Motor vehicle excise tax, time to
    apply for abatement, **60A:2.**
  Overassessment or overpayment
    of taxes, time to apply for
    abatement, **62C:37.**
  Redemption from tax sale,
    60:65, 60:69.
  Refund applications, **62C:36.**
Stocks of corporations, **59:4.**
  See CORPORATION TAXES.
Storage tax, **62C:16, 64I:1 et seq.**
  See USE, CONSUMPTION, OR
    STORAGE TAX.
Storage warehouses.
  Assessors, giving information,
    59:33.
  Cigarette tax, examination of
    warehouse's records and
    reports, **64C:6.**
  Corporation taxes, foreign
    corporation storing tangible
    personal property, **63:39.**
  Exemption of property, **59:5.**
    Nonresident's personalty
      stored in original
      packages, **59:2.**
  Listing property for taxation,
    59:33.
  Sales tax exemption of stored
    goods, **64H:6.**

TAXATION —Cont'd
Stores and merchants.
Apportioned use certificate, services sold at retail outside of Commonwealth, **64H:6.**
Cigarette tax, **62C:10-62C:21.** See CIGARETTE TAX.
Exemptions, **64H:6, 64I:7.**
Returns, **62C:16.**
Sales taxes, **64H:1 et seq.** See SALES TAXES.
Street railways.
Assessments, **161:21, 161:22, 161:135.**
Betterment assessments, **59:4, 161:78-161:80.**
Bonds and notes, taxation of, **59:4.**
Cost of service, **161:116, 161:161.**
Liability of purchaser upon sale by receiver for taxes, **161:135.**
Property leased by transportation area, **161:158.**
Stumpage fees, municipal corporations, watershed land in another municipality, **59:5D, 59:5F.**
Subpoenas.
Appellate tax board, **58A:11.**
Subsequent taxes.
Abatement as affected, **59:65A.**
Liens, taking of land or property for nonpayment of taxes, **60:61, 60:61A.**
Succession taxes, **65:2 et seq.**
Estate taxes, **62C:1 et seq.** See ESTATE TAXES.
Legacy and succession taxes. See LEGACY AND SUCCESSION TAXES.
Sunday, execution of returns or reports, **136:6.**
Superior courts.
Compelling attendance of witnesses and production of papers in proceedings before revenue commissioner, **58:25B.**
Jurisdiction, **62C:9, 64E:12, 64F:13.**
Removal of tax collectors, **41:39B.**
Supervision of local taxation, **58:1-58:8.**
Support and maintenance.
Procedures by IV-D agency for accrued arrearages, **119A:6.**

TAXATION —Cont'd
Support and maintenance —Cont'd
Set-off debt collection, revenue department to assist transitional assistance department in collecting support obligations, **62D:3.**
Supreme judicial court.
Compelling attendance of witnesses and production of papers before commission, **58:25.**
Delinquent municipalities, proceedings against, **59:20.**
Failure to keep proper records of local property assessment, **58:4A.**
Foreclosure proceedings, review of questions of law, **60:72.**
Gasoline and motor fuel taxes, restraining collection, **64A:12, 64E:12, 64F:13.**
Income tax returns, mandamus to compel filing, **62C:9.**
Jurisdiction, **64E:12, 64F:13.**
Nontransferability of dismissal of appeal, **211:4A.**
Pipelines, valuation, **59:38A.**
Surplus.
Accounting for surplus after distress and sale of personal estate, **60:28.**
Low value lands held by city or town under tax title, surplus from sale, **60:79.**
Surviving spouses.
Appeal from denial of exemption, **59:5.**
Apportionment of exemption of surviving spouse and minor heirs, **59:5.**
Exemption from certain assessments, **59:5, 60:3B, 65:1.**
Legacy and succession tax exemption of real estate to surviving spouse in joint tenancy or tenancy by entirety, **65:1.**
Police or firefighters killed in line of duty, exemption for spouses, **59:5.**
Qualified terminal interest property, **65C:3A.**
Veterans, **58:8A, 59:5.**
Swamps.
Improvement of lowlands and swamps, taxation, **252:11.**
Protection of inland wetlands, person to whom tax assessed deemed "owner" for purposes, **131:40A.**

TAXATION —Cont'd
Swine.
Excise tax, **59:8A.**
Exemption of local taxes, **59:5.**
Sales tax exemption, **64H:6.**
Tables.
Income tax liability determined, **62:64.**
Withholding tax on wages, **62B:2.**
Taking of land for nonpayment of taxes, **60:53-60:56.** See TAX LIENS.
Tavern keepers, penalty for refusal or falsity in giving tax information, **59:92.**
Tax collectors, **60:1 et seq., 62C:46 et seq.** See TAX COLLECTORS.
Taxpayer defined, **64H:1, 64I:1.**
Taxpayer information, **14:6, 62C:80.**
Taxpayer suits.
Revenue growth limit, **62F:7.**
Telecommunications and energy department.
Assessment, **25:18, 164:61.** See TELECOMMUNICATIONS AND ENERGY DEPARTMENT.
Corporations owning and operating railroad terminal facilities, **63:52A.**
Exemptions, **59:2B.**
Franchise tax, **63:52A.**
Returns, **62C:12.**
Sales tax exemption for production facilities, **64H:6.**
Telegraph and telephone companies.
Abatement appeals, **59:39.**
Assessors to give information to commissioner, **59:40.**
Double valuation of property on failure to provide required tax information, **59:42.**
Estimate of property value by department in default of returns, **59:42.**
Failure to provide required information, double valuation of property, **59:42.**
Franchise tax, **63:52A.**
Poles, wires, and conduits, **59:18, 59:39-59:42.**
Returns, **59:41, 59:42.**
Valuation of machinery, poles, wires, etc., **59:18, 59:39-59:42.**
Television and radio, **59:5, 64H:1, 64H:6.**

TAXATION —Cont'd

Temperance societies.

Lists of property, **59:29.**

Tax exemptions, **59:5.**

Third persons, payment of real property tax, **60:60.**

Thrift institutions, **63:1, 63B:1.**

Time.

Abatement of taxes.

Appeal, **59:59, 59:64, 59:65C, 62C:39.**

Application for abatement, **59:59, 62C:37.**

Excuse for delay, **59:61, 59:64.**

Extension, **59:5. (note)**

Appellate tax board, time for appeal to, **59:65C.**

Extension of time to appeal, **51:14.**

Failure to timely file appeals, **59:64, 59:65B, 59:65C.**

Bills for taxes, **59:57, 60:3.**

Corporation taxes.

Extension of time, **62C:19, 63:52, 63B:3, 63B:4.**

Taxable year, **63:1, 63:30, 63:32, 63:39.**

Declaration of estimated income tax.

Corporations, **63B:3, 63B:4.**

Extension of time for filing, **62B:13, 63B:3, 63B:4.**

Filing of declaration, time, **62B:13.**

Farming, declaration of estimated income, **62B:14.**

Payment of estimated tax, time, **62C:79.**

Farming, estimated income, **62B:14.**

Declaration of estimated tax by corporations, **62B:13, 63B:3, 63B:4.**

Deeds, foreclosure of right of redemption, **60:65, 60:69A.**

Delinquent taxes. See within this heading, "Delinquent taxes."

Due date, **62C:32.**

Exemption.

Application, extension of time, **59:5, 59:59.**

Short taxable year, **62:3.**

Extension of time. See within this heading, "Extension of time."

Fiscal year. See within this heading, "Fiscal year."

Gasoline and motor fuel taxes, **64A:4, 64A:7, 64A:7A, 64F:6.**

TAXATION —Cont'd

Time —Cont'd

Income tax due date, **62C:32, 62C:79.**

See INCOME TAX.

Installment payments, notice of modification or termination of written agreement with taxpayer, **62C:37B.**

Late filing, penalty, **62C:33, 62C:34.**

Legacy or succession tax due date, **65:7.**

See LEGACY AND SUCCESSION TAXES.

Levy of taxes, time requirements, **62C:53.**

Limitation of actions. See within this heading, "Limitation of actions."

Local assessments due to Commonwealth, **59:20.**

Motor vehicle excise tax in lieu of local tax, due date, **60A:2.**

Municipalities, time for appeal as to assessments, **51:14.**

Omitted property, date for assessment, **59:75, 59:76.**

Ownership of realty, determination, **59:11.**

Postmark date as payment date, **62C:33A.**

Refund or reimbursement, timely payment to taxpayers, **14:6.**

Revenue department.

See REVENUE DEPARTMENT AND COMMISSIONER.

Sale for taxes.

Bid, time to pay, **60:49.**

Extension by commissioner of time as to nonenforcement of covenants against municipal purchaser, **60:77.**

Notice of time and place of sale, **60:40.**

Redemption, **60:65, 60:69.**

Time in which real estate liable, **202:20.**

Sales taxes.

Claim for reimbursement of sales tax paid by vendor on worthless account, **64H:33.**

Resale and exempt use certificate, time limit for vendor to produce, **64H:8.**

Services sold at retail, **64H:2.**

Special assessments.

Abatement petition, filing, **80:5, 80:6.**

TAXATION —Cont'd

Time —Cont'd

Special assessments —Cont'd

Appeal from decision as to abatement, **80:7.**

Assessment, time, **80:1.**

Election to surrender land assessed, **80:3.**

Extension of time, **80:6, 80:13A.**

Lien, duration, **80:12.**

Reassessment, **80:16.**

Withholding of tax.

Effective dates of withholding exemption and deduction certificates, **62B:4.**

Payment of tax, time, **62B:5, 62B:7.**

Payroll periods, use in computing amount to be withheld, **62B:2.**

"Status determination date" defined under withholding tax law, **62B:4.**

Withholding tax statement to employee, time for furnishing, **62B:5.**

Titles, **60:45, 60:54, 60:64-60:83.**

See TAX DEEDS AND TITLES.

Tobacco, **64C:1-39.**

See CIGARETTE TAX.

Tools, exemption, **59:5.**

Distress and sale, exemption, **60:24.**

Sales and use tax, **64H:6.**

Towns.

Municipal corporations. See within this heading, "Municipal corporations."

Trailer coach park operators, lien, **255:25A.**

Trailers and semi-trailers.

Maximum rate of excise tax on registered motor vehicles and trailers, **60A:1.**

Military personnel, exemption from taxation of nonresident, **59:5.**

Suspension of registration certificate for nonpayment of tax, **60A:2A.**

Transfer of case from district court, **231:104.**

Transient vendors, stock in trade, **101:2, 101:5.**

Transmission lines and equipment, **59:18, 59:83.**

Abatement of taxes, notice, **59:74.**

Corporations, assessment of taxes, **59:83.**

TAXATION —Cont'd
Transmission lines and equipment —Cont'd
Public ways, how and where assessed, **59:18.**
Underground utilities, **59:5.**
Transportation facilities, abatement appeals of public transportation corporations, **59:64, 59:65.**
Treasurers of cities and towns.
Abatement of taxes.
Notice, **59:23B, 59:70A.**
Accounting for tax redemption money, **60:63.**
Affidavit of notice to holder of invalid tax title, notice to treasurer of recording, **60:83.**
Agricultural or horticultural land, certificate of taxes due or paid, **61A:19A.**
Assessors of taxes, **44:16.**
See TAX ASSESSORS.
Collectors of taxes.
See TAX COLLECTORS.
County taxes, payment, **35:31.**
Deeds.
See TAX DEEDS AND TITLES.
Deputy collectors of taxes, appointment, **41:37.**
Distress and sale for taxes, powers of town treasurers, **41:37.**
Judgment against, tax for payment, **41:43A.**
Lists, bonds required prior to commitment, **59:53.**
Rate of taxes, notice, **59:23A.**
Redemption from tax, duties, **60:62, 60:63.**
Revenue department and commissioner.
Approval of bonds, **41:35, 41:39A, 41:123A.**
Suspension or removal, **41:39B.**
Subsequent taxes after sale of taking for nonpayment, duties, **60:61, 60:61A.**
Trigger locks.
Exemptions, **64H:6.**
Trusts and trustees.
Abatement, application, **59:59.**
Charitable trusts.
Tax exemption, **59:5, 62:3.**
Corporate trusts, **62:8.**
Estate taxes, trustees as liable for payment, **65C:14.**
Future interests, authority of fiduciaries to pay taxes, **65:15A.**

TAXATION —Cont'd
Trusts and trustees —Cont'd
Income tax.
See INCOME TAX.
Legacy and succession taxes.
Trustees, **65:6, 65:17, 65:21, 65:30, 202:20.**
See LEGACY AND SUCCESSION TAXES.
Trust property subject to, **65:a.**
Parsonages held in irrevocable trust for religious corporations, local assessment, **59:5.**
Split-interest trusts, **68:1 et seq.**
Turnpike authority.
Exemption from taxation, **59:2B, 81A:8.**
Mass transportation facilities and services, determination by revenue department of amounts payable, **58:25B.**
Real property tax on leased, etc., land, **81A:14.**
Reimbursement for tax paid on fuel used for other than highway operation, **64A:7, 64E:5.**
Turnpikes, stocks, **59:4.**
Unassessed real estate, **59:28, 59:75.**
Uncollectible taxes.
Abatement, **58:8, 59:71, 62C:42.**
Bond required with respect, **60:95.**
Personal property taxes, **59:71.**
Statement of impossibility, **60:37A.**
Underground wires, conduits, and equipment, **59:5.**
Underpayment, **60:22, 60:22A.**
Abatement, insufficient payment as affecting, **59:65D.**
Agricultural land, **61A:19.**
Penalty for underpayment of estate tax based on fraud, **65C:13.**
Undertakings.
Bonds and undertakings. See within this heading, "Bond issues."
Unemployment compensation.
Delinquent taxes, **62C:21.**
Excise tax, compromise, **151A:20.**
Income tax.
Contributions, deductibility from income, **151A:21.**
Exemptions.
Benefits, **151A:22.**
Federal exemptions, **151A:6.**

TAXATION —Cont'd
Unemployment compensation —Cont'd
Income tax —Cont'd
Federal internal revenue code.
Compromise of unpaid unemployment excise tax due, **151A:20.**
Exemptions under, **151A:6.**
Uniformity, requirement of, **US Const Art 1 Sec 8 cl 1.**
United States.
Bonds and obligations of, exemption, **59:5.**
Certificate of similarity to federal tax laws, **62C:23.**
Child support collection, **119A:6.**
Congress, taxation power, **US Const Art 1 Sec 8 cl 1.**
Constitution of the United States.
See CONSTITUTION OF THE UNITED STATES.
Cooperation with federal government as to taxes, **62C:23.**
Corporation taxes, filing federal return, **63:30, 63:32B, 63:39.**
County taxes, federal funds used to reduce assessments, **35:30.**
Estate tax, federal, **65A:1-65A:6.**
See ESTATE TAXES.
Exemption of federal property, **59:5.**
Gasoline and motor fuel taxes, **64A:12, 64E:12, 64F:13.**
Heavy vehicle use tax, proof of payment accompanying registration application, **90:1A.**
Interest from savings and loan associations, income tax, **62:2.**
Lease, taxes on land leased from or, **59:3E, 59:11.**
Lien of federal government for taxes, **36:24, 185:46, 185:78, 185:80.**
Room occupancy tax, exemption, **64G:2.**
Sales tax, exemptions, **64H:6.**
Support collection, **119A:6.**
Withholding tax, collection, **58:28A, 58:28B.**
University of Massachusetts.
Leased land, **59:11, 75:28.**
Loss of taxes on lands used by University, reimbursement of, **58:13-58:17A.**

TAXATION —Cont'd
Unknown persons, assessment of
    taxes on property, **59:11.**
Unpaid taxes.
    Abatement of taxes, unpaid
        property tax bills, **60:2.**
    Private entities providing
        services for collection,
        14:3A.
Urban renewal and housing.
    Exemptions, **121A:6A, 121A:10,
        121A:15, 121A:18A,
        121A:18C, 121B:15,
        121B:16.**
    Redevelopment corporation,
        121A:10, 121A:15, 121B:16.
    Redevelopment corporations.
        See URBAN
            REDEVELOPMENT
            CORPORATIONS.
Usage classification of real
    property, **59:2A, 59:38.**
Use, consumption, and storage,
    62C:16, 64I:1 et seq.
    See USE, CONSUMPTION, OR
        STORAGE TAX.
Utilities.
    Telecommunications and energy
        department. See within this
        heading,
        "Telecommunications and
        energy department."
Valuation of property, **4:7, 58:1,
    58:10, 59:38-59:42.**
    Abatements, **59:38F, 59:38G.**
    Affidavit of value of land held by
        city or town under tax title,
        60:79.
    Agricultural and horticultural
        property, **61A:4, 61A:5,
        61A:9-61A:11.**
    Appeals, **59:38, 59:39.**
        Equalization of valuations for
            cities and towns, **58:10B.**
        Pipeline, valuation of, appeal
            from commissioner's
            determination, telephone
            and telegraph companies,
            59:38A, 59:41, 59:42.
        Public lands, appeal from
            valuation, **58:14.**
        Urban redevelopment
            corporation, **121A:10.**
    Appraisal reports, **58A:8A.**
    Assessor's duties, **58:1A,
        59:38-58:42.**
        See TAX ASSESSORS.
    Classification of property for
        purposes of valuation, **59:38,
        61B:2, 61B:3.**
    Collection charges, abatement
        where value of realty
        insufficient to pay, **59:72.**

TAXATION —Cont'd
Valuation of property —Cont'd
    Collection of information by
        commissioner as to real
        estate values, **58:6.**
    Contracts for appraisal of
        taxable real estate, **40:4,
        44:7.**
    Corporation taxes.
        See CORPORATION TAXES.
    County tuberculosis hospitals,
        land, **58:17A.**
    Debt limit of municipality as
        determined, **44:10.**
    Entries on record, **59:43.**
    Equalized validation for cities
        and towns.
        Appeal, **58:10B.**
        Appeals to appellate tax
            board, **58A:12C.**
        As basis for municipal debt
            limit computation, **44:10.**
        Damages for improper
            assessment, **58A:14.**
        Data to be utilized in
            determining, **58:10.**
        Debt limit as determined by,
            44:10.
        Definition of, under law
            governing municipal
            finance, **44:1.**
        Failure to submit information
            for use in determining,
            58:10.
        Notice, **58:10A.**
        Regional school districts,
            equalized valuation for
            purposes of computing
            regional valuation
            percentage for state aid,
            71:16D.
        Revenue Department and
            Commissioner, **44:1,
            58:9-58:10C.**
        State Administrative
            Procedure Law,
            proceedings to determine,
            as adjudicatory
            proceedings within
            meaning, **30A:1.**
    Estate taxes.
        Alternate valuation of federal
            estate tax as affecting,
            65C:5.
        Classification of estates, **59:44,
            59:64.**
        Date of valuation, **65C:5.**
        Estimate of value of property in
            default of list, **59:36, 59:37.**
        Evidence of assessed value,
            79:35, 185:109.

TAXATION —Cont'd
Valuation of property —Cont'd
    Exempt property, **59:5, 59:51.**
    Fair cash value, **59:38, 59:38F,
        59:38G.**
    Fire prevention orders as to
        additions or changes
        limited, **148:29.**
    Flood control, property taken,
        58:17B.
    Forest lands and products tax,
        61:1-61:3.
    Inspection of tax information,
        59:52C.
    Legacy and succession taxes,
        65:13, 65:25, 65:26.
        Alteration of valuations,
            65:26.
        Future interests, **65:14.**
        Revenue department and
            commissioner, **65:14,
            65:25, 65:26, 65:35A.**
    Meaning of term "valuation"
        with regard to town
        property, **4:7.**
    Motor vehicles for purpose of
        excise tax, **60A:1.**
    Newly acquired public lands,
        58:15.
    Oath or affirmation, **59:38D,
        59:38E.**
    Pipelines, **59:38A.**
    Public land, with respect to
        reimbursement of towns,
        58:13-58:17B.
    Ratio valuations for local
        property assessments,
        58:10.
    Records concerning, **58:4A,
        59:43-59:48, 59:50-59:52.**
    Recreational land, **61B:2, 61B:3.**
    Residential land, abatement of
        tax upon change in use,
        61B:5.
    Return containing information
        determining actual fair cash
        value of property, **59:38F,
        59:38G.**
    Revaluation of real estate,
        exemption, **59:5.**
    Revenue department and
        commissioner.
        Agricultural and horticultural
            property, basis for
            valuation, **61A:20.**
        Certain state and county
            lands, **38:13 et seq.**
        Equalized valuations for cities
            and towns, **44:1,
            58:9-58:10C.**
        Local assessments,
            commissioner's duties,
            58:1A.

TAXATION —Cont'd
Valuation of property —Cont'd
Revenue department and
commissioner —Cont'd
Massachusetts Water
Resources Authority,
valuation of land for
purpose of payment to
division of watershed
management, **59:5G.**
Pipelines, **59:38A.**
Reconciliation of valuation of
business corporation,
63:68A.
Recreational land, **61B:3,
61B:16.**
Revisions in valuation,
commissioner may
recommend, **59:76.**
State and county lands,
valuation by revenue
department of certain,
38:13 et seq.
Telephone and telegraph
companies' machinery,
poles, and wires,
valuation, **59:39.**
Revision of taxes, **59:76.**
Ships and vessels, excise tax,
60B:2.
Special assessments, **80:1, 80:3.**
State forests, **58:15.**
Sworn written returns
concerning local
assessments, **59:38D,
59:38E.**
Telephone and telegraph
companies, double valuation
on failure to provide
required tax information,
59:42.
Test of value, **59:38.**
Urban redevelopment
corporation, appeal from
valuation, **121A:10.**
Usage classification, **59:2A,
59:38.**
Venue.
Assessors violating laws,
prosecutions, **58:1.**
Delinquent tax collectors,
actions against, **58:8.**
Evasion of taxes, venue of
criminal prosecution, **59:90.**
Income tax return, mandamus to
compel filing, **62C:9.**
Verification.
Cooperation of governments as
to, **62C:23.**
Corporation taxes, **63:26,
63:38B, 63:38C.**

TAXATION —Cont'd
Verification —Cont'd
Income tax returns, **62C:24,
62C:26.**
Lists, **59:31.**
Vessels, **59:4, 59:8, 60B:1-60B:4,
64H:6.**
See SHIPS AND OTHER
WATERCRAFT.
Veterans.
Abatement of taxes, **58:8A, 59:5.**
Alcoholic beverages tax,
veterans' organizations,
63A:1.
Apportionment of cost of district
departments of veterans'
services, **115:11.**
Associations and organizations
of veterans, **59:5, 63A:1.**
Benefits and services.
Apportionment of cost of
district apartments of
veterans' services, **115:11.**
Assessments, **115:11.**
Expense of audit of accounts
of districts for veterans'
services, **115:15.**
Blind or with impaired vision,
exemption from taxation,
59:5.
Disabled veterans, **58:8A, 59:5.**
Evidence of disability, proof for
tax exemptions, **59:5.**
Exemptions, **59:5, 60A:1, 62:1.**
Local departments of veterans'
services.
Apportionment of tax
assessments, **115:15.**
Expense of audit of district
accounts, **115:15.**
Missing in action or taken
prisoner during Vietnam
war, exemptions, **62:1.**
Motor vehicle excise taxes,
60A:1.
Municipalities, local
departments of veterans'
services, **115:15.**
One hundred percent disabled
veterans, **59:5.**
Organizations, exemption, **59:5.**
Parents of soldiers dying in
service, exemption, **59:5.**
Real property tax exemptions,
59:5.
Surviving spouses of soldiers
dying in service.
Exemption, **59:5.**
Paraplegic veterans, widows
of, reimbursement of
municipalities for loss of
taxes, **58:8A.**

TAXATION —Cont'd
Veterans —Cont'd
Time to apply for tax exemption,
59:5.
Vietnam veterans, exemptions,
59:5, 60A:1, 62:1.
Wachusett Mountain State
Reservation, reimbursement of
town for loss of tax, **58:13.**
Waiver.
Cities and towns, waiver of
charges by local tax
collectors, **60:15.**
Foreclosure proceedings, jury
trial, **60:71.**
Gasoline and motor fuel taxes,
reciprocal agreements with
other states waiving
requirement, **64F:5.**
Interest on unpaid taxes, **59:57,
59:69.**
Legacy and succession taxes.
Issuance of waiver, **65:35A.**
Penalty for late filing of taxes,
65:22.
Lien, waiver, **60:50, 62C:52.**
Penalty attributable to
erroneous advice of revenue
department employee,
62C:36B.
Tax collectors, **59:57, 60:15.**
Warehouses.
Storage warehouses. See within
this heading, "Storage
warehouses."
Warrants, **62C:46.**
See TAX COLLECTORS.
Water pollution.
Bonds and notes issued by water
pollution abatement
districts, **21:36.**
Corporations, tax benefits for
pollution abatement or
control measures, **59:5,
63:38D.**
Watershed management districts.
Assessments.
Treasurer to pay municipality
difference in assessment,
59:5H.
Watershed management division,
59:5D, 59:5F, 59:5G.
Waterworks and water supply.
Assessments.
Districts and tax assessors,
59:21, 59:25, 59:53.
Special assessments to meet
cost of laying pipes,
40:42G et seq.
Collection, **40:42A et seq.,
60:23.**

TAXATION —Cont'd
Waterworks and water supply
—Cont'd
Corporation taxes.
Franchise taxes, **63:52A.**
Local taxes on water
companies, **59:5.**
Deferral of charges for water
supplied to tax exempt
property, **40:42J.**
Exemption from taxation, **59:5.**
Impoundment sites acquired by
water resources commission,
21:9A.
Lien, termination for inaction as
to tax, **40:42B.**
Rates and charges.
Collection, **40:42A et seq.,
60:23.**
Tax bill, addition of unpaid
accounts, **40:42C et seq.**
Tax sales for nonpayment of
water rates, **40:42D,
60:76B.**
Tax title as affected by errors
or irregularities, **60:76B.**
Sales tax exemption, **64H:6.**
Special assessments to meet cost
of laying pipes, **40:42G,
40:42H.**
Commissioners, duty, **40:42I.**
Fixed uniform rate, **40:42H.**
Liens, assessments, **40:42I.**
Procedure, **40:42G.**
Recording of determination,
40:42I.
Wearing apparel, exemption, **59:5.**
Distress and sale, exemption,
60:24.
Whole estate taken in name of one
or more of several owners for
nonpayment of taxes, **60:56.**
Whole numbers, rounding off,
62C:4.
Widow or widower.
Appeal from denial of
exemption, **59:5.**
Apportionment of exemption of
surviving spouse and minor
heirs, **59:5.**
Exemption from certain
assessments, **59:5, 60:3B,
65:1.**
Legacy and succession tax
exemption of real estate to
surviving spouse in joint
tenancy or tenancy by
entirety, **65:1.**
Police or firefighters killed in
line of duty, exemption for
spouses, **59:5.**

TAXATION —Cont'd
Widow or widower —Cont'd
Qualified terminal interest
property, **65C:3A.**
Veterans, **58:8A, 59:5.**
Wife.
Support obligations, collection
via taxation system, **62D:3,
119A:6.**
Surviving spouses.
Widow or widower. See within
this heading, "Widow or
widower."
Use of names of both spouses,
14:6.
Wildlife sanctuary, reimbursement
of towns for loss of tax on land
used, **58:13-58:17A.**
Wind powered facilities.
Alternative energy resources,
tax incentive for use,
63:38H.
Exemption of solar or
wind-powered systems, **59:5.**
Residential property tax credit,
62:6.
Withholding by city or town of
money payable to person
owing assessments, **60:93.**
Withholding tax on wages,
62B:1-12.
See WITHHOLDING OF TAX.
Witnesses.
Appellate tax board, **58A:11.**
Fees, **58A:11, 58A:12.**
Attendance of witnesses in tax
proceedings, **62C:70.**
Revenue department's authority
to require attendance and
testimony, **58:25B.**
Works of art, tax exemption, **59:5.**
Wounded veterans, exemption of
real estate, **59:5.**
Writing.
Advice of revenue department
employee found to be
erroneous, **62C:36B.**
Installment payment agreement
with taxpayer, **62C:37B.**
Zoning, notice provisions as to
adoption or change of
ordinance or bylaw to be
contained in tax bills, **40A:5.**

**TAXATION OF COSTS, 261:1 et
seq.**
See COSTS OF ACTION.

**TAX COLLECTORS, 60:1-60:105,
62C:46 et seq.**
Abandoned property, definition,
60:1.

TAX COLLECTORS —Cont'd
Abatement of taxes.
Assessors, records furnished,
59:60.
Books and records, **60:7.**
Certificates of abatement,
exhibition to collector,
60:20.
Clerical error, **58:8.**
Credit for sums abated, **60:95.**
Fees for collection as affected,
60:20.
Mistake, **58:8.**
Notice, **59:70A.**
Uncollectible taxes, **59:71.**
Absence of, appointment of
temporary collector in case,
41:40, 41:61A.
Accounts and accounting.
Aldermen, accounting, **60:94.**
Cessation of office, **60:97.**
Cities, collection of accounts due,
41:38A.
Distress and sale of personal
estate, accounting of surplus
to owner, **60:28.**
Examination, **60:8.**
Executor or administrator,
accounting, **60:97-60:100.**
Fees and charges, **60:2, 60:15.**
Fine or penalty for neglect of
duty, **60:96, 60:99-60:102.**
Mayor, accounting, **60:94.**
Municipal treasurer, accounting,
60:2.
Open to inspection, **60:8.**
Removal for failure or refusal,
60:96.
Selectmen, accounting, **60:94.**
Taxes received, **60:2, 60:94.**
Turning over of accounts to
successor, **60:97.**
Actions by and against, **41:43A,
58:8, 60:35, 60:36.**
Additional tax assessed, collection,
62C:26.
Affidavits.
Evidence of demand, affidavit as
notice and service, **60:1,
60:57.**
Sale, effect of affidavit, **60:57.**
After sale or taking of property,
60:61, 60:61A.
Agricultural or horticultural
property.
Farm equipment or utensils,
59:8A.
Stay of collection pending
appeal, **61A:19.**
Unpaid conveyance taxes,
61A:12.

TAX COLLECTORS —Cont'd
Aid in arresting delinquent
taxpayers, **60:33, 60:103.**
Aldermen.
Selectmen. See within this
heading, "Selectmen."
Appeal, stay of collection pending,
61A:19.
Arrest and imprisonment,
collection of taxes,
60:29-60:34A.
Assistance, collector may
require, **60:33.**
Penalty for failure to assist,
60:103.
Bond for release from custody,
60:34A.
Certificate of tax collector to be
given to jail keeper, **60:30.**
Demand for payment prior,
60:16.
Discharge or release, **60:34,
224:28.**
Bond, **60:34A.**
Liability of collector after,
60:32.
Notice, **60:31.**
Rearrest after discharge,
60:34.
Supplementary proceedings,
discharge after
examination of debtor,
60:31.
Fees of collectors, **60:15, 60:95.**
Forms, **60:105.**
Jail keeper, delivery of
certificate, **60:30.**
Liability of collector for tax,
60:32.
Limit of detention, **60:29.**
Proceedings prior, **60:16-60:22A.**
Sheriff's fees, **60:89.**
Special warrant for, without
demand, **60:19.**
Supplementary proceedings for
release, **60:31.**
Warrant, **60:29, 60:34.**
Assessment list.
Lists. See within this heading,
"Lists."
Assessors.
Abatement of taxes, notice to
collector, **59:70A.**
Invalid tax sale, collector to give
notice, **60:46.**
Office, assessor not to hold,
41:24.
Records, **59:43, 59:60.**
Reports and returns, **60:2.**
Warrants, **59:53-59:56.**
Assignment of tax title held by city
or town, notice, **60:76C.**

TAX COLLECTORS —Cont'd
Assistance in arresting delinquent
taxpayers, **60:33, 60:103.**
Assistant collector, appointment,
41:39C.
Attachment in damage actions
against, dissolution, **41:43A.**
Auction sale provisions as
inapplicable to sales, **100:11.**
Banks, cities' agreements with for
collection of taxes, **60:2A.**
Bidding in property at tax sale,
when authorized, **60:48.**
Bill or notice, **60:3-60:3B, 60:22A.**
Abatement of taxes, notice to
collector, **59:70A.**
Changes in assessed valuation,
inclusion of information
about, **60:3A.**
Contents, **60:3, 60:3A.**
Delinquent taxpayers, notice of
warrant, **60A:2A.**
Failure to send or receive, **60:3.**
Fees charged, **60:15.**
Form, **60:3A.**
General tax rate, printing,
60:3A.
Liability for payment of bill,
59:12B.
Mailing, **60:3.**
Parcels of real estate, tax bills
with respect, **60:3, 60:22A.**
Payments with insufficient funds
checks, notice by tax
collector regarding, **60:57A.**
Poll tax bills to contain notice of
persons entitled to
exemptions, **59:5.**
Printing, **60:3A.**
Private entities hired to collect
unpaid taxes, **14:3A.**
Proof of mailing, **60:3.**
School tax rate, printing, **60:3A.**
Sending out by collector, **60:3.**
Separate tax bill for parcels of
land separately assessed or
listed, **60:3, 60:22A.**
Time for sending, **59:57, 60:3.**
Total tax rate of town, printing,
60:3A.
Bond of arrested taxpayer for
release from custody, **60:34A.**
Bond or note of municipality,
payment of tax, **60:2.**
Bonds of collectors, **60:13.**
Action against delinquent
collectors, **58:8.**
Amount of bond, fixing by
selectmen, **60:96.**
Commitment of tax lists,
required prior, **59:53.**

TAX COLLECTORS —Cont'd
Bonds of collectors —Cont'd
Deputy collectors, **14:3, 41:37,
60:92.**
Liability on for neglect of duty,
58:8.
Reassessed taxes, applicability,
59:78.
Special collector, **60:14.**
Temporary collector, **41:40,
41:61A.**
Town may pay expense, **40:5.**
Uncollectible taxes, **60:95.**
Books and papers, **60:6-60:12.**
Abatement of taxes, **59:60,
59:70A, 60:7.**
Affidavits, **60:1, 60:57.**
Assessors, **59:60, 60:12.**
Cash books, **60:7.**
Certificates. See within this
heading, "Certificates."
Deposit with assessor upon
cessation of office, **60:97.**
Impossibility of taking for sale
for taxes, statement,
60:37A.
Monthly report of uncollected
funds, **60:92.**
Open for inspection, **60:8.**
Payment, books showing, **60:7.**
Penalty for failure or refusal to
exhibit books, **60:102.**
Property of towns, **60:8.**
Tax book, collector to keep, **60:6.**
Town auditor may examine,
60:8.
Town clerk may demand
custody, **60:12.**
Unpaid taxes reported to
commissioner, **58:7.**
Burned and dangerous buildings
or other structures,
enforcement of lien for
expense of removal, **139:3A.**
Cash books, **60:7.**
Certificates.
Attachment or injunction suit
against collector, **41:43A.**
Keeper of jail, delivery of
certificate, **60:30.**
Liens, certificate, **60:23.**
Municipal lien certificates, tax
collectors furnishing, **60:23.**
Payment of taxes by person
other than owner, **60:60.**
Real estate taxes and
assessments, **60:63.**
Registers and registries of deeds,
recording of certificate of
taxes and assessments,
60:23.

TAX COLLECTORS —Cont'd
Certificates —Cont'd
  Special assessments, fee for
    collector's certificate to
    dissolve lien, **80:12.**
  Water charges owing to
    municipalities, **40:42C.**
Charges.
  Fees and charges. See within
    this heading, "Fees and
    charges."
Child support obligations,
    collection via taxation system,
    62D:3, 119A:6.
Cities and towns, collection of
    taxes for, **60:1-60:105.**
Collection agencies, tax collectors
    entering into agreements,
    60:2B.
Commissioner of revenue.
  Appointees of city or town
    treasurer, approval, **41:37.**
  Bonds of collectors, approval,
    60:13.
  Books of collectors, approval of
    form, **60:8.**
  Deputy collectors, appointment
    and removal, **60:92.**
  Forms, approval, **59:54, 60:8,
    60:105.**
  Lists of collectors, approval of
    method of preparation,
    59:54, 60:6.
  Preparation and distribution of
    manuals outlining
    procedures for use in
    performance of duties, **58:3.**
  Prosecution of delinquent
    collectors, **58:8.**
  Salaries of local tax collectors,
    41:108B.
  Suspension and removal,
    41:39B.
  Unpaid taxes, reports, **58:7.**
Commitment of tax lists, **59:53,
    59:54.**
  Bonds required, **59:53.**
  Contents of lists, **59:29.**
  Deposit of assessor's books prior,
    59:43.
  Furnishing, **58:5.**
  Reassessed taxes, **59:78.**
  Separate lists and warrant for
    district taxes, **59:53.**
Conforming changes in laws due to
    adoption of fiscal year, **60:3,
    60:17.**
Constables, **41:39, 59:53.**
Contracts or agreements.
  Banks, contracts of cities, **60:2A.**
  Collection agencies, contracts of
    tax collectors, **60:2B.**

TAX COLLECTORS —Cont'd
Conveyance taxes, collection of
    unpaid, **61A:12.**
County taxes, collection, **35:31.**
Credits, sums credited to collector,
    60:95.
Custodian for tax foreclosed
    property, appointment by
    selectmen, **60:77B.**
Damage actions against, defense,
    41:43A.
Death, **60:97.**
Deeds, **60:45, 60:54, 60:64-60:83.**
  See TAX DEEDS AND TITLES.
Defenses to actions against,
    41:43A.
Defined for purposes of law
    governing collection of local
    taxes, **60:1.**
Delinquent collectors, proceedings
    against, **58:8.**
Demands for payment.
  Evidence, **60:1, 60:57.**
  Mailing out, **60:16.**
  Special warrant for arrest
    without, **60:19.**
Deposit of collected funds in town
    treasury, **60:92.**
Deputy collectors.
  Appointment and bond, **14:3,
    41:37, 60:92.**
  Assessors prohibited from
    holding office, **41:24.**
  Income taxes, **62C:46.**
Direction from municipality as to
    taking sale, **60:87.**
Disability, appointment of
    temporary collector in case,
    41:40, 41:61A.
Discharge or release.
  Arrest and imprisonment. See
    within this heading, "Arrest
    and imprisonment,
    collection of taxes."
Disposition of funds collected,
    60:2.
  Sale proceeds, **62C:63.**
Dissolution.
  Attachment or injunction
    against tax collector,
    dissolution, **41:43A.**
  Special assessments, fee for
    collector's certificate to
    dissolve lien, **80:12.**
Distress and sale of personal
    estate, **60:20-60:28.**
  Fees of collectors, **60:15.**
District taxes.
  Fire districts, **48:73.**
  Salary and expenses of
    collectors, **41:108B.**

TAX COLLECTORS —Cont'd
District taxes —Cont'd
  Separate list and warrant,
    59:53.
Duties, **60:2, 60:50A, 80:4.**
Election of town collectors, **41:1.**
Eminent domain proceedings,
    furnishing of copies of
    petitions or notice to tax
    collector, **79:7F.**
Enforcement of municipal finance
    provisions, **44:59.**
Error.
  Abatement of taxes, **58:8.**
  Name on tax list, effect of error,
    60:21.
Estate tax collection, **62C:36.**
  See ESTATE TAXES.
Examination or inspection,
    collector's books open, **60:8.**
Execution on judgments against,
    41:43A.
Executor or administrator of,
    accounting, **60:97-60:100.**
Exhibition of books and accounts,
    penalty for failure or neglect,
    60:99-60:102.
Facsimile signatures, use on
    warrants issued in cities and
    towns, **60:29.**
Fees and charges, **60:15, 60:95.**
  Abatement of taxes as affecting,
    60:20.
  Accounting, **60:2, 60:15.**
  Agricultural and horticultural
    lands, evasion of full and
    proper taxes, **61A:23.**
  Certificate of lien, city tax
    collector's fee for as
    compensation, **60:23.**
  Delinquent taxpayers, fees to be
    paid, **60:15.**
  Distress and sale, **60:15, 60:89.**
  Estate tax assessments,
    violations, **62C:26.**
  Excessive fees, redemption of tax
    title, **60:104.**
  Forest lands and products,
    penalty for failure to make
    tax return, **61:5.**
  Notice of issuance of warrant to
    collect, **60:15.**
  Officer executing warrant for
    collection, fees, **62C:46.**
  One other than owner of fee
    paying tax, certificate,
    60:60.
  Real estate taxes and other
    assessments, certificate,
    60:23.
  Redemption certificate, fee,
    60:93.

TAX COLLECTORS —Cont'd
Fees and charges —Cont'd
Registered mailing of written
demands or collection notice,
60:15.
Sheriff's fees for collecting,
60:89.
Special assessment, certificate
for dissolution, **80:12.**
Statement that sale cannot be
legally made, fees for
recording, **60:37A.**
Taking of land for nonpayment
of taxes, **60:55.**
Tax liens, certificates, **60:23.**
Waiver of charges by local tax
collectors, **60:15.**
Warrant for collection of taxes,
60:15, 62C:46.
Fiduciaries.
Accounting by executors and
administrators,
60:97-60:100.
Personal liability, **62:13, 62:42.**
Fines and penalties, **60:99-60:104,
62C:33.**
Books, failure or refusal to
exhibit, **60:96, 60:99-60:102.**
Demand, failure to give up
accounts, **60:101.**
Excessive fees and charges of
collector, redemption of tax
title, **60:104.**
Exhibition of accounts or
receipts, failure or refusal,
60:99.
Payment over of money, failure,
60:102.
Redemption from tax title,
exorbitant charge, **60:104.**
Turning over accounts to
successor, failure or refusal,
60:100.
Fire districts, powers and duties
with respect, **48:73.**
Fiscal year, conforming changes in
laws in recognition of
adoption, **60:3, 60:17.**
Foreclosure of tax title, notice,
60:76C.
Foreign corporations failing to pay
tax, injunction against doing
business, **60:91.**
Forest lands and products tax,
61:2, 61:5.
Forms, **60:105.**
Approval by commissioner,
59:54, 60:8, 60:105.
Warrant issued to collector, form
and contents, **59:55.**
Gas and electric bills, collection,
164:58E.

TAX COLLECTORS —Cont'd
Gasoline and motor fuel taxes.
Disposition of receipts, **64A:13.**
Distributors and unclassified
importers, payments, **64A:4.**
Jurisdiction of supreme judicial,
or superior court to restrain
collection on sales exempt
by federal law, **64F:13.**
Reports, **64A:4, 64E:4, 64F:6.**
Restraining collection of taxes
on sales exempt by federal
law, **64A:12, 64A:13.**
Horticultural property.
Farm equipment or utensils,
59:8A.
Stay of collection pending
appeal, **61A:19.**
Unpaid conveyance taxes,
61A:12.
Impossibility of taking or sale for
taxes, statement, **60:37A.**
Imprisonment, collection of taxes
by.
Arrest and imprisonment. See
within this heading, "Arrest
and imprisonment,
collection of taxes."
Income taxes.
Deputy collectors, **62C:46.**
Remedies for collection of taxes,
62C:47 et seq.
Warrant for collection, **62C:46.**
Incompatible offices, assessor and
collector, **41:24.**
Indemnification by municipalities,
40:5, 41:43A.
Information, collection, **62C:49.**
Injunctions.
Corporation taxes, **60:91, 63:80.**
Dissolution of, **41:43A, 60:91.**
Gasoline tax on exempt federal
sales, **64A:12, 64E:12,
64F:13.**
Insanity, removal, **60:96.**
Insolvent debtors, collection, **60:36.**
Inspection, books and records
available, **60:8.**
Interest.
Books showing interest, tax
collector to keep, **60:7.**
Late property tax payment, tax
bills, **59:57B.**
Unpaid taxes, interest, **62C:26,
62C:32.**
Waiver, **59:57.**
Invalid sale, **60:46.**
Invalid tax titles, duties with
respect, **60:82-60:84A.**
Jail keeper, delivery of certificate,
60:30.

TAX COLLECTORS —Cont'd
Jeopardy collection, **60:19.**
Judgments.
Against collectors, **41:43A.**
Part payment, judgment for
amount due after, **60:22.**
Land court, certificate for
dissolution of attachment or
injunction against collector to
be filed, **41:43A.**
Legacy and succession taxes.
Enforcement of lien, **65:31.**
Execution, **65:30.**
Executors and administrators to
collect tax from person
entitled to property, **65:17.**
Federal estate tax laws, tax
upon estates subject, **65A:4.**
Removal of assets from
Commonwealth to thwart
collection, **193:3.**
Sale of real property, **65:31.**
Time for instituting proceedings,
65:32, 65:33A.
Trustees to collect from persons
entitled to property, **65:17.**
Levy, collection, **62C:53.**
Liens for taxes, **59:2B, 59:12E,
59:12F, 60:37, 60:53-60:56,
62C:50-62C:52.**
Limitation period, **62C:65.**
Lists.
Bonds required prior to
commitment, **59:53.**
Collectors to keep book
containing tax list, **60:6.**
Commitment of tax lists, **59:53,
59:54.**
Bonds required, **59:53.**
Contents of lists, **59:29.**
Deposit of assessor's books
prior, **59:43.**
Furnishing, **58:5.**
Reassessed taxes, **59:78.**
Separate lists and warrant for
district taxes, **59:53.**
Payment of taxes prior to receipt
of tax list, acceptance,
60:19.
Posting, **60:88.**
Successor collector, turning over
lists, **60:97.**
Local tax collection, **60:1-60:105.**
Loss or destruction of warrant
issued to, new warrant, **59:56.**
Mandamus to enforce municipal
finance provisions, **44:59.**
Manual outlining procedures for
use of tax collectors in
performance of duties,
preparation and distribution
by commissioner of revenue,
58:3.

TAX COLLECTORS —Cont'd

Mayor.

Accounting, **60:94.**

Bonds, fixing amount, **60:13.**

Temporary tax collector, appointment, **41:61A.**

Mental illness, removal, **60:96.**

Mistake or error.

Abatement of taxes, **58:8.**

Name on tax list, effect of error, **60:21.**

Motor vehicle excise tax, **60A:2-60A:3.**

Municipal or local taxes, collection of, **60:1-60:105.**

Name errors, **60:21.**

Neglect of duty, liability, **58:8, 60:96, 60:99-60:102.**

Nonresident failing to pay tax, injunction against doing business, **60:91.**

Notes of governmental bodies to be accepted in payment, **60:2.**

Notice, **60:3-60:3B, 60:22A.**

Oath of temporary collectors, **41:40, 41:61A.**

Omitted property, assessments, **59:75.**

Ordinance or bylaw directing sale or taking of property for nonpayment of taxes, **60:87.**

Overdue gas and electric bills collected as tax, **164:58E.**

Overdue taxes, arrest and imprisonment for.

Arrest and imprisonment. See within this heading, "Arrest and imprisonment, collection of taxes."

Partial payment, effect of acceptance, **60:22.**

Payment, **60:95.**

Demands for payment.

Evidence, **60:1, 60:57.**

Mailing out, **60:16.**

Special warrant for arrest without, **60:19.**

Insufficient funds check, notice as to payment, **60:57A.**

Partial payment, **60:22.**

Penalties.

Fines and penalties. See within this heading, "Fines and penalties."

Performance evaluation, **14:7.**

Powers, **60:29.**

Private collectors, **14:3A, 60:2A, 60:2B.**

Publication of notices, **60:1.**

Purchase for city or town at tax sale, **60:48, 60:50A.**

TAX COLLECTORS —Cont'd

Quotas, employee evaluations by commissioner, **14:7.**

Reassessed taxes, collection, **59:78.**

Records.

Books and papers. See within this heading, "Books and papers."

Redemption of tax title held by city or town, notice, **60:76C.**

Registers and registries of deeds.

Affidavit of tax collector filed in registry as evidence, **60:57.**

Certificate of taxes and assessments on real estate, recording, **60:23.**

Statement by tax collector as to impossibility of sale for liens, **60:37A.**

Reimbursement for expenses, **60:15.**

Release from custody.

Arrest and imprisonment. See within this heading, "Arrest and imprisonment, collection of taxes."

Remedies of commissioner, **62C:47 et seq.**

Removal from office, **41:39B, 60:96.**

Deputies, **60:92.**

Renunciation of rights under statement of impossibility of sale, **60:37A.**

Return of collection to assessors, **60:2.**

Revenue department.

Commissioner of revenue. See within this heading, "Commissioner of revenue."

Room occupancy tax, **64G:4, 64G:5.**

Sales.

Auction sale provisions inapplicable, **100:11.**

Land, **59:2B, 59:12E, 60:37-60:60.**

See TAX SALES.

Personal property, distress and sale, **60:20-60:28.**

Taking of property, tax collection after sale or, **60:61, 60:61A.**

Selectmen.

Accounting, **60:94.**

Appointment of temporary tax collectors, **41:40.**

Bonds, fixing amount, **60:96.**

Custodian for tax foreclosed property, appointment, **60:77B.**

Removal of tax collectors, **60:96.**

TAX COLLECTORS —Cont'd

Selectmen —Cont'd

Special collectors, appointment, **60:14.**

Sending of bills by collector, **60:3.**

Service of demands, notices and process, **60:1, 60:15, 60:16.**

Set-off debt collection, revenue department to assist transitional assistance department in collecting support obligations, **62D:3.**

Setoff of monies due from municipalities to tax delinquents, **60:93.**

Sheriff or deputy.

Appointment, **60:92.**

Bond, **60:92.**

Collection and payment over of taxes, **60:2, 62C:46.**

Commitment of tax lists, **59:53.**

Fees for collecting, **60:89.**

Income tax, warrant for collection, **62C:46.**

Motor vehicle registration, enforcement of suspension for nonpayment of tax, **60A:2A.**

Posting of warrant, **60:88.**

Tax sales.

Fees of sheriff, **60:89.**

Sheriff as tax collector, **60:88, 60:89.**

Warrant issued to, **60:34, 60:90, 62C:46.**

Signatures, use of facsimile signature on warrant issued by tax collector, **60:29.**

Special assessments.

Duties of tax collectors, **80:4.**

Fee for collector's certificate to dissolve lien, **80:12.**

Special collectors, **60:14.**

Special warrant, **60:19.**

Statement of impossibility, **60:37A.**

Stay of collection pending appeal, **61A:19.**

Street sprinkling assessments, **40:18.**

Subsequent taxes after sale or taking for nonpayment, collection, **60:61, 60:61A.**

Successors, turning over records and papers, **60:97.**

Superior courts, removal of tax collectors, **41:39B.**

Support obligations, collection via taxation system, **62D:3, 119A:6.**

Suspension or removal from office, **41:39B, 60:96.**

Deputies, **60:92.**

TAX COLLECTORS —Cont'd
Temporary collectors.
  City collector, appointment,
    bond, oath, **41:61A.**
  Term of office for city appointee
    limited, **41:61A.**
  Town collectors, appointment,
    bond, oath, **41:40.**
Term of office of town collectors,
  41:1.
Titles, **60:45, 60:54, 60:64-60:83.**
  See TAX DEEDS AND TITLES.
Towns, collection of taxes for,
  60:1-60:105.
Treasurer of city or town.
  Accounting by collector for fees,
    60:15.
  As collector of taxes, **41:1, 41:37.**
    Suspension or removal,
      41:39B.
  Deputy collectors, appointment,
    41:37.
  Exercise of powers of, by
    collector, **41:38.**
  Issuance of warrants, **41:37,**
    60:90.
  Judgment against collector,
    payment, **41:43A.**
  Payment of taxes, **60:2.**
    Penalty for failure, **60:102.**
Uncollectible taxes.
  Abatement, **58:8, 59:71, 62C:42.**
  Bond required with respect,
    60:95.
  Personal property taxes, **59:71.**
  Statement of impossibility,
    60:37A.
Use, consumption, or storage tax.
  Formula, **64I:5.**
  Records, amount of tax collected
    by vendor to be shown
    separately from sales price,
    64I:6.
  Vendor' collection, **64I:4.**
Vacancy in office.
  Constable may act, **41:39.**
  Failure to give bond as grounds,
    60:13.
  Temporary collector,
    appointment, **41:40, 41:61A.**
Wages, salaries, and compensation,
  14:3, 41:39B, 41:108B, 60:15,
  60:23.
  Income taxes. See within this
    heading, "Income taxes."
Waivers, **59:57, 60:15.**
Warrants for collection, **62C:46.**
  Assessors, issuance of collection
    warrants, **59:53-59:56.**
  Cities and towns, **59:20, 60:29.**
  City treasurer, issuance, **41:37,**
    60:90.

TAX COLLECTORS —Cont'd
Warrants for collection —Cont'd
  Contents and form, **59:55.**
  County taxes, **35:31.**
  Distress and sale, **59:20, 60:34.**
  Facsimile signatures on
    warrants issued by tax
    collectors in cities and
    towns, **60:29.**
  Fees, **60:15, 62C:46, 262:4.**
  Imprisonment of tax debtor,
    60:29, 60:30, 60:34.
  Levy on stock or produce, **60:27.**
  Loss or destruction, **59:56,**
    183:62.
  Notice to delinquent taxpayer,
    60A:2A.
  Personal property, sale, **59:20,**
    60:34.
  Posting by sheriff, **60:88.**
  Retirement system expenses,
    32:21.
  Sale for taxes.
    Distress and sale, **59:20,**
      60:34.
    Payment without demand,
      special warrant to compel,
      60:19.
  Ships and vessels, taxes, **60B:4.**
  Special assessments, **80:4.**
  Special warrants, **60:19.**
  State taxes, **59:20, 59:21.**
  Town treasurer, issuance, **41:37,**
    60:90.
Water rates, collection,
  40:42A-40:42I.
  Certificate, **60:23.**
Withholding money payable by city
  or town to person owing taxes,
  60:93.
Withholding of tax.
  Bank, requiring employer to
    make deposit, **62B:7.**
  Federal withholding tax, **58:28A,**
    58:28B.
  Remedies, **62B:6.**

TAX DEEDS AND TITLES,
  60:45, 60:54, 60:64-60:83.
Abandoned property,
  determination that property
  acquired under tax sales was
  abandoned, **60:81A.**
Abatement of taxes, entry on tax
  title account, **59:70A.**
Absolute after sale or foreclosure,
  right of redemption made,
  60:62, 60:64.
Accounts.
  Abatement of items, **59:70A.**
  Addition of subsequent taxes to,
    as affecting abatement
    proceedings, **59:65A.**

TAX DEEDS AND TITLES
  —Cont'd
Accounts —Cont'd
  Collector's certificate as
    affecting, **60:23.**
  Errors or irregularities, **60:37.**
  Other tax titles in municipality,
    60:61A.
  Prima facie evidence of amount
    necessary for redemption,
    60:50.
  Protection of municipality's
    interest, inclusion of
    expense incurred, **60:50A.**
  Redemption, amount required,
    60:62.
  Required to be kept, **60:50.**
  Subsequent taxes after sale or
    taking for nonpayment,
    addition, **60:61, 60:61A.**
  Water rates and charges, effect
    of errors, **60:76B.**
Advertising sales of low value
  lands held by municipality,
  60:79.
Affidavits.
  Invalid tax title, affidavit of
    notice to holder, **60:83.**
  Low value of land held by city or
    town under tax title,
    affidavit of value, **60:79.**
Appropriation of sums necessary
  for foreclosure by city or
  town, **60:50B.**
Assessors, tax title held by city or
  town, **60:50B, 60:76C.**
Assignment or transfer by
  municipality.
  Approval by commissioner,
    60:52.
  Notice to collectors and
    assessors, **60:76C.**
  Recording assignment, **36:22.**
  Redemption from assignee,
    60:62.
  Subsequent taxes and
    assessments, **60:61.**
Auction sale of lands acquired by
  cities and towns through
  foreclosure, **60:52, 60:77B.**
Cancellation by recording
  redemption certificates, **60:63.**
Cities.
  Municipalities. See within this
    heading, "Municipalities,
    titles acquired by."
City treasurer.
  Treasurer of city or town. See
    within this heading,
    "Treasurer of city or town."
Commissioner of revenue.
  Foreclosure proceedings,
    institution, **60:50.**

TAX DEEDS AND TITLES
—Cont'd
Commissioner of revenue —Cont'd
Sale of lands of low value held
by city or town under tax
titles, **60:79.**
Conditions and restrictions, tax
titles subject, **60:45.**
Contents and effect of tax deeds,
60:45, 60:54.
Municipality as purchaser, deed,
60:50.
Costs, **60:73.**
Covenants running with land as
enforceable against town
acquiring property, **60:77.**
Default decree for foreclosure,
60:67, 60:69.
Discharge of tax deed.
Irregularities, **60:46.**
Marginal notation of discharge
of tax deed, **36:22.**
Recording redemption certificate,
60:63.
Easements and restrictions, deed
subject, **60:45.**
Effect of tax deed, **62C:59, 62C:60.**
Errors or irregularities, **60:37,
60:76B.**
Evidence.
Assignment of title, instrument
of as prima facie evidence,
60:52.
Deed, tax deed as prima facie
evidence of tax title, **60:45.**
Redemption, tax title account as
prima facie evidence of
amount necessary, **60:50.**
Execution by collectors, **60:45,
60:54.**
Exorbitant charge for redemption
from, penalty, **60:104.**
Fees, **60:15, 60:73, 60:79, 262:39.**
Foreclosure of right of redemption,
60:64-60:75.
Absolute title after, **60:64.**
Answer, **60:68.**
Appropriation of sums necessary
for foreclosure by cities and
towns, **60:50B.**
Assessors of taxes, notice,
60:76C.
Collectors, notice, **60:76C.**
Costs and fees, **60:73.**
Default judgment, **60:67, 60:79.**
Discretion as to vacation of tax
foreclosure decree barring
redemption, **60:69.**
Division by sale, mortgage or
upon petition for partition,
60:68.

TAX DEEDS AND TITLES
—Cont'd
Foreclosure of right of redemption
—Cont'd
Examination of title, **60:66.**
Extension of time by installment
payments, **60:62.**
Finding of court for redemption,
60:68.
Hearing of court, **60:68.**
Holder of tax deed, foreclosure,
60:65.
Installment redemption
payments as grounds for
extension, **60:62.**
Judgments and decrees.
Barring redemption, **60:69.**
Default decree, **60:67, 60:69.**
Vacation of decree barring
redemption, **60:69,
60:69A.**
Validity of title, **60:70.**
Jurisdiction of land court, **60:64.**
Jury trial of issues, **60:71.**
Land court, proceedings in,
60:64-60:75.
Low value lands, **60:80A.**
Municipalities, foreclosure.
Appropriation of sums
necessary, **60:50B.**
Care and disposal of land
acquired by cities and
towns, **60:52, 60:77B.**
Conveyances after, recording,
60:77A.
Sale after, **60:52, 60:77B.**
Title after, **60:77.**
Treasurer of town to institute
proceedings on behalf of
town, **60:50.**
Notice to interested party, **60:66.**
Offer to redeem, **60:68.**
Part owner or person interested
in part of property,
redemption, **60:76A.**
Petition, **60:65.**
Practice and procedure, **60:75.**
Prerequisite to possession of
property, **60:45.**
Questions of law, report, **60:72.**
Recording of notice of filing and
disposition of petition,
60:75.
Redemption prior to, right,
60:62.
Sale without foreclosure of lands
held by city or town under
tax title, **60:79.**
Summary process to recover
land, **239:1, 239:6A, 262:39.**
Supreme judicial court, report of
questions of law, **60:72.**

TAX DEEDS AND TITLES
—Cont'd
Foreclosure of right of redemption
—Cont'd
Time.
Petition for foreclosure, **60:65.**
Vacation of decree of
foreclosure, **60:69A.**
Title after, **60:77.**
Town treasurer to institute
proceedings on behalf of
town, **60:50.**
Two or more parcels included in
petition by two, **60:65.**
Vacation of decree barring
redemption, **60:69, 60:69A.**
Validity of title, how raised,
60:70.
Water rates and charges, effect
of errors or irregularities,
60:76B.
Housing and community
development department,
foreclosure of rights of
redemption in abandoned
property, **60:81A.**
Immaterial irregularities in sale
proceedings, **60:37.**
Inclusion of several parcels in
same deed, when permissible,
60:51.
Insurance on property acquired by
city or town, requirement,
60:50A.
Invalid titles, proceedings in case,
60:82-60:84A.
Collection of taxes, **60:84.**
Disclaimer of title held by city or
town, **60:84.**
Judicial proceedings, refunds to
holders of titles held invalid,
60:84A.
Liability of town, **60:82.**
Notice to holder by tax collector,
60:82.
Reassessment of taxes, **60:84.**
Refunds to holders, **60:46, 60:82,
60:83.**
Judicial proceedings, where
title held invalid, **60:84A.**
Refusal to release interest by
holder, **60:82.**
Reimbursement of purchaser,
60:46.
Judgments.
Foreclosure. See within this
heading, "Foreclosure of
right of redemption."
Jurisdiction of land court, **60:64,
185:1.**
Jury trial of issues in foreclosure
proceedings, **60:71.**

TAX DEEDS AND TITLES
—Cont'd

Land Court, **60:50B, 60:64, 185:1.**

Legal fees, **60:79.**

Limitation of action to vacate decree of foreclosure, **60:69A.**

Low value lands, acquisition by municipalities, **60:1, 60:79-60:80B.**

Mistakes, errors, and irregularities, **60:37, 60:76B.**

Municipalities, titles acquired by, **60:50, 60:79.**

Auction sale, **60:52, 60:77B.**

Care and disposal of land acquired by foreclosure, **40:5, 60:52, 60:77B.**

Conveyances of, recording deeds, **60:77A.**

Covenants running with land, enforcement, **60:77.**

Custodian, appointment, **60:77B.**

Deduction of proceeds of sale in determining amount of annual local tax assessment, **59:23.**

Extension of enforcement of covenants running with land, **60:77.**

Foreclosure of right of redemption, **60:64-60:75.**

Insurance of interest, **60:50A.**

Invalid title, disclaimer, **60:84.**

Low value lands, sale, **60:79-60:80B.**

Deeds for, execution and recording, **60:79, 60:80.**

Interested persons served with notice barred from questioning title conveyed by recorded deed, **60:80A.**

Lack of bids, proceedings, **60:80.**

Petition to establish title after, **60:80B.**

Several parcels of low value may be conveyed in one deed, **60:51.**

Management and transfer, **40:5, 60:52.**

Notice to collectors and assessors of assignments, redemptions and foreclosures, **60:76C.**

Proceeds of redemption or sale, disposition, **60:43.**

Statement releasing town from liability on warranties in deed, recording, **60:82.**

Subsequent taxes, collection, **60:61, 60:61A.**

TAX DEEDS AND TITLES
—Cont'd

Municipalities, titles acquired by —Cont'd

Taking of land for nonpayment of taxes, **60:54.**

Tax sales generally.
See TAX SALES.

Treasurer. See within this heading, "Treasurer of city or town."

Validity, inquiry into, **60:79.**

Nature of title acquired, **60:45.**

Nonresident owner to appoint agent, **60:47.**

Notice.

Affidavit of notice to holder of invalid tax title, recording, **60:83.**

Assignment or transfer by municipality, **60:52.**

Foreclosure, **60:66.**

Instruments affecting tax deed, notation on record, **36:22.**

Invalid title, **60:82.**

Low value lands, sale by municipality, **60:80A.**

Petition for foreclosure, recording notice of filing and disposition, **60:75.**

Protection of municipal tax title, **60:50A.**

Offer to surrender deed, where sale invalid, **60:46.**

Petitions.

Foreclosure of rights of redemption, petition, **60:65, 60:75.**

Low value lands sold by municipality, petition to establish title, **60:80B.**

Protection of municipal interest, **60:50A.**

Records and recording, **60:45, 60:54.**

Affidavit of notice to holder of invalid title, recording, **60:83.**

Assignment of tax titles, notation, **36:22.**

Deed, notation on record of instruments affecting, **36:22.**

Disclaimers, **36:22.**

Foreclosure petition, notice of filing and disposition, **60:75.**

Instrument of taking of land for nonpayment of taxes, **60:54.**

Invalid title, affidavit of notice to holder, **60:83.**

Low value lands held by city or town, deeds with respect to sale, **60:79, 60:80.**

TAX DEEDS AND TITLES
—Cont'd

Records and recording —Cont'd

Notice. See within this heading, "Notice."

Redemption certificates, **60:63.**

Registers and registries of deeds. See within this heading, "Registers and registries of deeds."

Release or discharge affecting tax titles, **36:22.**

Surrender and discharge of invalid tax deed, **60:46.**

Tax title owners to file statement of residence and place of business, **60:47.**

Redemption, **60:54, 60:62, 60:63, 62C:57, 62C:58.**

Foreclosure, **60:64-60:75.**

Tax sales.
See TAX SALES.

Refunds to holders of invalid titles, **60:46, 60:82, 60:83, 60:84A.**

Registers and registries of deeds.

Affidavits, **60:57, 60:83.**

Certificate of redemption from, recording, **60:62, 60:63.**

Conveyances of tax titles held by city, record, **60:77A.**

Foreclosure of right of redemption from, recording notice of filing and disposition of petition, **60:75.**

Invalid deed or title, **60:46, 60:83.**

Low value lands held by city or town under, recording in connection with sale, **60:79.**

Marginal notation, instruments affecting tax deeds, **36:22.**

Notice to holder of invalid tax title, recording affidavit, **60:83.**

Record of tax deed from city, **60:79.**

Statement of residence to be filed by owner, **60:47.**

Surrender and discharge of invalid tax deed, **60:46.**

Warranties in deeds, recording of statement releasing town from liability, **60:82.**

Release.

Discharge of tax deed, **36:22, 60:46, 60:63.**

Liability on warranties in deed, release of town, **60:82.**

Redemption, release, **60:63.**

Revenue commissioner.

Foreclosure proceedings, institution, **60:50.**

TAX DEEDS AND TITLES
—Cont'd
Revenue commissioner —Cont'd
Sale of lands of low value held
by city or town under tax
titles, **60:79.**
Sale of tax title property,
60:37-60:60.
See TAX SALES.
Sale without foreclosure of lands
held under tax title by city or
town, **60:79.**
Several parcels of small value may
be conveyed in one deed,
60:51.
Sewer use or municipal light rates,
tax title accounts, **60:62,**
60:76B.
Statements.
Release of town from liability on
warranties in deed,
recording statement giving,
60:82.
Residence and place of business
of owner, filing and
recording statement, **60:47.**
Summary process to recover land.
Condition of bond in action for
possession after tax title
foreclosure, **239:6A.**
Fees of land court on tax title
foreclosure, **262:39.**
Obtaining possession after tax
title foreclosure, **239:1.**
Surplus from sale of low value
lands held by city or town,
60:79.
Surrender and discharge of invalid
tax deed and title, **60:46.**
Time, foreclosure of right of
redemption, **60:65, 60:69A.**
Towns.
Municipalities. See within this
heading, "Municipalities,
titles acquired by."
Transfer or assignment by
municipality.
Approval by commissioner,
60:52.
Notice to collectors and
assessors, **60:76C.**
Recording assignment, **36:22.**
Redemption from assignee,
60:62.
Subsequent taxes and
assessments, **60:61.**
Treasurer of city or town.
Appropriations in connection
with tax title foreclosure,
60:50B.
Custody of tax deeds, **60:50.**

TAX DEEDS AND TITLES
—Cont'd
Treasurer of city or town —Cont'd
Error or irregularity in tax title
account, duties with respect,
60:62.
Institution of foreclosure
proceeding on behalf of
town, **60:50.**
Redemption duties, **60:62, 60:63.**
Subsequent taxes, duties with
respect, **60:61, 60:61A.**
Tax title account, to keep, **60:50.**
Transfer of tax titles, **60:52.**
Vacation of decree barring
redemption, **60:69, 60:69A.**
Validity.
Errors or irregularities as
affecting, **60:37.**
Foreclosure proceedings, raising,
60:70.
Inquiry into validity of tax titles
on land acquired by
municipality, **60:79.**
Invalid titles, **60:46,**
60:82-60:84A.
Water rates and charges, effect
of errors or irregularities,
60:76B.
Warranty in collector's deeds,
60:45.
Statement releasing town from
warranties, recording, **60:82.**
Water rates and charges, effect of
errors or irregularities,
60:76B.

TAX EXEMPTIONS, 32:19, 59:2,
59:5, 59:5C-59:5F, 59:59,
60:3A.
See TAXATION.

TAXICABS.
Liability insurance, complaints as
to cancellation for nonpayment
of premium, **175:113D.**
Markings required, **40:22.**
Meters.
Deputy director of standards,
accuracy of meters, **98:45.**
Fee for sealing, **98:56.**
Testing and penalty for use of
untested meters, **98:45.**
Municipal regulation of, **40:22.**
Name of owner and name of city
or town, display, **40:22.**
Parking violations by cab drivers,
owner's avoidance of liability,
90:20E.
Registration fees, **90:33.**
Sale of vehicles used, **266:92A.**
Town council, regulation, **40:22.**

TAXIDERMIST.
Deer heads and hides, buying and
selling, **131:22.**
Defined, **131:1.**
Regulation of business, **131:27.**
TAX LIENS, 59:2B, 59:12E,
59:12F, 60:37, 60:53-60:56,
62C:50-62C:52.
Abatement of taxes, effect on
taking for nonpayment,
59:65A.
Actions for enforcement, **62C:50.**
Administrative action preventing
sale, **60:37, 60:37A.**
Agricultural or horticultural lands,
61A:9.
Certificate of taxes paid or due
as terminating lien,
61A:19A.
Warrant for levy on stock or
produce, **60:27.**
Alienation, termination, **60:37.**
Assignment of tax by municipality
as affecting taking for
subsequent taxes, **60:61.**
Bulk sales, lien for taxes upon,
62C:51.
Burned or dangerous buildings or
other structures, enforcement
of lien for expense of removal,
139:3A.
Business corporation, lien upon
sale or transfer of, **62C:51,**
62C:52.
Care and maintenance of
tax-forfeited property,
appropriation, **40:5.**
Certificates, **60:23, 60:23A, 60:86.**
Agricultural lands, certificate of
taxes paid or due as
terminating lien, **61A:19A.**
Amount of taxes due,
certification as necessary to
taking for nonpayment,
60:37B.
Federal tax liens, **36:24.**
Fees, **60:23B.**
Municipal lien certificates
furnished by tax collectors,
60:23.
Proceeding on certificate of title
and registration subject to
lien, **185:46.**
Civil actions to enforce liens,
62C:50.
Collectors of taxes, **59:12E,**
59:12F, 60:37, 60:53-60:56,
62C:50-62C:52.
Commissioner.
Business corporation, powers
and duties as to tax lien in
conjunction with sale or
transfer, **62C:51, 62C:52.**

TAX LIENS —Cont'd
Commissioner —Cont'd
Notice requirement, **62C:50.**
Waiver or release of lien,
62C:50.
Consumer reports containing
information, **93:52.**
Continuance in case of invalid
taking or sale of property,
60:37.
Conveyance of recreational land,
lien for tax, **61B:6.**
Co-owner paying taxes, **60:85,**
60:86.
Corporations, **62C:51, 62C:52.**
Cotenant's payment of tax, **60:85,**
60:86.
Custodian of tax-foreclosed
property, appointment,
60:77B.
Deferral and recovery agreements,
statement of action
constituting lien, **59:5.**
Discharge or release, **60:22A.**
Agricultural or horticultural
property, **61A:9.**
Commissioner, issuance of
waiver or release, **62C:50.**
Eminent domain, payment from
discharges for property
taken, **79:44A.**
Federal tax lien, record of
discharge, **36:24.**
Notice, **36:24.**
Disclosure of information
concerning liens, **62C:50.**
Eminent domain, payment of liens
from discharges for property
taken, **79:44A.**
Enforcement.
Actions for, **62C:50.**
Foreclosure. See within this
heading, "Foreclosure."
Ordinance directing, **60:87.**
Registered land, **185:84.**
Establishment, **60:37.**
Estate taxes, **65C:14.**
See ESTATE TAXES.
Expenses in connection with lien
for property tax deficiency,
59:12F.
Expiration, **60:37.**
Farm lands, **61A:9.**
Certificate of taxes paid or due
as terminating lien,
61A:19A.
Warrant for levy on stock or
produce, **60:27.**
Federal tax liens.
Certificates and certification,
real property or fixtures,
36:24.

TAX LIENS —Cont'd
Federal tax liens —Cont'd
Discharge or release, **36:24.**
Fees for filing, notice of
certificate of discharge,
36:24.
Filing notice of lien or of
discharge of lien, **36:24.**
Real property or fixtures, lien,
36:24.
Registration of land titles.
Effect, **185:46.**
Filing of instruments intended
to affect registered land,
185:78, 185:80.
Release or discharge as to real
property or fixtures, **36:24.**
Uniform recording procedure,
36:24, 185:46, 185:78,
185:80.
Fees.
Business corporation sale or
transfer, fee for waiver of
tax lien, **62C:52.**
Certificates, **60:23A, 60:23B.**
Collector's fees in connection
with taking for nonpayment,
60:55.
Federal tax liens, filing notice of
certificate of discharge,
36:24.
Preservation statements,
recording fees, **60:37A.**
Register of deeds entering
instrument of taking of land
for nonpayment, **262:38.**
Taking of land for nonpayment,
fees, **60:55, 262:38, 262:39.**
Waivers by commissioners, fees,
62C:52.
Foreclosure.
Personal property, distress and
sale of for payment of taxes,
60:24-60:28.
See TAX SALES.
Real property, foreclosure of tax
lien.
Sale, foreclosure by,
60:37-60:60.
See TAX SALES.
Taking of land for nonpayment
of taxes. See within this
heading, "Taking of land
or property for
nonpayment of taxes."
Redemption, foreclosure of right
of, **60:64-60:75.**
See TAX DEEDS AND
TITLES.
Supreme judicial court, review of
questions of law in tax
foreclosure proceedings,
60:72.

TAX LIENS —Cont'd
Gas and electric bills overdue,
164:58C.
Impossibility of legal sale as
affecting, **60:37, 60:37A.**
Injunction against sale, **60:37,**
60:37A.
Invalid sale or taking, **60:37.**
Irregularity in sale as affecting,
60:37.
Joint tenant's payment of tax,
60:85, 60:86.
Judgment creditor, validity
against, **62C:50.**
Jurisdiction of enforcement
actions, **62C:50.**
Land Court, recording tax lien
certificates, **60:23.**
Legacy and succession taxes, **65:9.**
Certificate of commissioner,
65:35A.
Discharge, **65:9.**
Enforcement, **65:31.**
Estates subject to federal estate
tax laws, no lien to attach
on account of tax, **65A:4.**
Exempt property, **65:9.**
Legacy payable out of real
estate, tax, **65:18.**
Lighting plant liens included in
local tax, **164:58D, 164:58E.**
Mortgagee, validity against,
62C:50.
Notices.
Business corporations, notice to
commissioner of sale or
transfer, **62C:51.**
Collector, notice by town officers
or boards, **60:23.**
Federal tax lien, recording
notice, **36:24.**
Fixtures, **62C:50.**
Personal property, **62C:50.**
Real property, **62C:50.**
Taking, notice, **60:53, 62C:56.**
Option of municipality whether to
take or sell property for taxes,
60:87.
Ordinance or bylaw of
municipality directing
collector to sell or take
property to enforce, **60:87.**
Parcels of real estate, effect of
payment or part payment of
tax, **60:22A.**
Partition of land.
Apportionment of taxes on real
estate subsequently divided,
59:78A.
Municipal tax title on part of
land, **60:61A.**

TAX LIENS —Cont'd
Part payment of tax, **60:22A.**
Perfection of lien on agricultural
  or horticultural property,
  61A:9.
Period of lien, **60:37.**
Personal property, lien, **62C:50.**
  Distress and sale of personalty
    for taxes, **60:24-60:28.**
  See TAX SALES.
Pledgee, validity against, **62C:50.**
Preservation of lien where sale
  prevented, **60:37A.**
Priority, **62C:50.**
Purchaser, validity against,
  62C:50.
Race, color, or national origin,
  federal requirement for
  recordkeeping regarding
  federal tax lien notices, **36:24.**
Reassessed tax on land, **59:77.**
Records and recording, **40:42A,**
  40:42B.
  Certificate of collector as to liens
    and charges, **60:23.**
  Conveyances, effect of recording,
    60:37.
  Federal tax liens. See within
    this heading, "Federal tax
    liens."
  Impossibility of sale, collector's
    statement, **60:37A.**
  Instrument of taking for
    nonpayment, **60:54.**
  Notice or discharge of federal
    lien, recording, **36:24.**
Recreational land, lien for tax on
  conveyance, **61B:6.**
Redemption from foreclosure of tax
  lien, **60:54, 60:62, 60:63,**
  60:68, 60:76, 60:76A, 62C:57,
  62C:58.
  See TAX SALES.
Registered land.
  Enforcement against, **185:84.**
  Federal tax liens, **185:46,**
    185:78, 185:80.
Registers and registries of deeds.
  Certificates of liens on real
    estate, recording or
    registering, **60:23.**
  Deficiency, liens, **59:12F.**
  Federal tax liens and discharges
    thereof, filing, **36:24.**
  Tax collector's statement as to
    impossibility of sale for
    liens, **60:37A.**
Release.
  Discharge or release. See within
    this heading, "Discharge or
    release."

TAX LIENS —Cont'd
Revenue commissioner.
  Business corporation, powers
    and duties as to tax lien in
    conjunction with sale or
    transfer, **62C:51, 62C:52.**
  Notice requirement, **62C:50.**
  Waiver or release of lien,
    62C:50.
Sale of property for nonpayment of
  taxes, **60:24-60:28,**
  60:37-60:60.
  See TAX SALES.
Security defined, **62C:50.**
Seizure of property for taxes.
  Taking of land or property for
    nonpayment of taxes. See
    within this heading, "Taking
    of land or property for
    nonpayment of taxes."
Several owners, taking in name of
  one, **60:56.**
Sewer charges, tax lines imposed
  for unpaid annual, **83:16A et**
  seq.
Special assessments, **80:12.**
  Duration and termination,
    80:12.
  Eminent domain proceedings,
    80A:14.
  Improvement districts, **252:11.**
  Mortgages, **80:15, 203:23.**
  Registered land, enforcement
    against, **185:84.**
  Street sprinkling assessments,
    40:18.
Statutes.
  Collector's enforcement,
    ordinance directing, **60:87.**
  Preventing enforcement, **60:37,**
    60:37A.
Street sprinkling assessments,
  40:18.
Supreme judicial court, review of
  questions of law in tax
  foreclosure proceedings, **60:72.**
Suspension of improvement
  assessments, continuance of
  lien in case, **60:3B.**
Taking of land or property for
  nonpayment of taxes,
  60:53-60:56.
  Abatement, **59:65A.**
  Assignment of tax by
    municipality as affecting
    taking for subsequent taxes,
    60:61.
  Authorized, **60:53.**
  Care and maintenance of
    tax-forfeited property,
    appropriations, **40:5.**

TAX LIENS —Cont'd
Taking of land or property for
  nonpayment of taxes —Cont'd
  Certification of amount
    necessary, **60:37B.**
  Collector's fees, **60:55.**
  Custodian of foreclosed property,
    appointment, **60:77B.**
  Deed and title to land sold after
    taking for nonpayment,
    60:45, 60:54, 60:64-60:83.
    See TAX DEEDS AND
      TITLES.
  Distress and sale of personalty,
    60:24-60:28.
    See TAX SALES.
  Execution of instrument, **60:54.**
  Fees, **60:55, 262:38, 262:39.**
  Instrument, **60:54.**
  Invalid taking, **60:37.**
  Low value lands, sale,
    60:79-60:80B.
  Municipality may direct whether
    to take or sell property,
    60:87.
  Notice, **60:53.**
  Ordinance or bylaw directing
    collector with respect, **60:87.**
  Procedure, **60:53-60:54.**
  Recording instrument of taking,
    60:54.
  Redemption from taking, **60:54,**
    60:62, 60:63, 60:68, 60:76,
    60:76A, 62C:57, 62C:58.
    See TAX SALES.
  Rents and income of land taken
    for taxes, authority to reach,
    60:53.
  Rights acquired, **60:54.**
  Sale of land taken, **60:24-60:28,**
    60:37-60:60.
    See TAX SALES.
  Several owners, taking in name
    of one, **60:56.**
  Statement that taking cannot be
    legally made, filing and
    recording, **60:37A.**
  Subsequent taxes, **60:61,**
    60:61A.
  Sale unnecessary, **60:61.**
  Tax title of municipality on
    part of land as affecting,
    60:61A.
Tenant in common, payment of
  tax, **60:85, 60:86.**
Termination, **60:37, 61A:19A,**
  62C:50, 62C:51.
Time, **62C:50, 62C:51.**
United States.
  Federal tax liens. See within
    this heading, "Federal tax
    liens."

TAX LIENS —Cont'd
Validity, **62C:50.**
Waiver by commissioner of lien on
sale or transfer of business
corporation, **62C:51, 62C:52.**
Warrant for levy on stock or
produce, **60:27.**

TAXPAYERS' ACTIONS.
County commissioner's
performance of duties, **35:35,
35:36.**
Emergency medical care,
enforcement of provisions
regarding, **111C:11.**
Gas and electric plant, **164:69.**
Illegal appropriations, restraint,
40:53.
Municipal finance, compliance
with laws, **44:59.**
Taxpayer's rights, **62C:80.**

**TAX SALES, 59:2B, 59:12E,
60:37-60:60.**
Abatement proceedings as affected,
59:65A.
Absolute title after sale without
foreclosure, **60:62.**
Accounting for surplus after sale of
personalty, **60:28.**
Adjournment of sales, **60:26,
60:44.**
Administrative action preventing
sale, **60:37, 60:37A.**
Advertisement, **60:40.**
Demand for payment as
affecting time, **60:39.**
Low value land held by
municipality, **60:79.**
Affidavit of collector, **60:57.**
Agricultural or horticultural
property, **61A:12.**
Animals, distress and sale,
60:24, 60:27.
City or town, option to purchase
on notification of sale or
conversion to
nonagricultural use, **61A:14.**
Produce, **60:27.**
Stay pending appeal, **61A:19.**
Animals, distress and sale, **60:24,
60:27.**
Auction, **60:43.**
Exemption of sales by tax
collectors, **100:11.**
Foreclosure of taxes, auction
sale of land acquired by
cities and towns through,
60:52, 60:77B.
Notice required, **60:52.**
Bidding.
Collector, bidding in of property,
60:48.

TAX SALES —Cont'd
Bidding —Cont'd
Time for payment, **60:49.**
Change of name of town, notice in
case, **60:41.**
Church pews, sale of for
nonpayment of taxes, **67:32.**
Cities and towns.
Municipality as purchaser. See
within this heading,
"Municipality as purchaser."
Collectors of taxes.
Auction sale provisions
inapplicable, **100:11.**
Land, **59:2B, 59:12E,
60:37-60:60.**
Personal property, distress and
sale, **60:20-60:28.**
Taking of property, tax collection
after sale or, **60:61, 60:61A.**
Commissioner.
Extension of time as to
nonenforcement of
covenants against municipal
purchaser, **60:77.**
Records of redemption from tax
sales, commissioner to keep,
62C:61.
Transfer of land purchased by
municipality, approval,
60:52.
Conduct of sale in general, **60:43,
62C:56, 62C:57.**
Conveyance tax, exemption for
foreclosure sales on
agricultural or horticultural
property, **61A:12.**
Cost of sale of several parcels of
small value, apportionment,
60:51.
Covenants running with land.
Collector's deed as affecting,
60:45.
Municipality as purchaser,
enforceability against,
60:77.
Cumbersome property, sale and
redemption, **62C:57.**
Deeds and titles given upon sale,
60:45, 60:54, 60:64-60:83.
See TAX DEEDS AND TITLES.
Definitions, **60:43.**
Demand for payment prior to sale,
60:16-60:22A.
See TAXATION.
Deposit by purchaser required,
60:43.
Detention of personalty at expense
of owner, **60:25.**
Devisees, notice, **60:40.**
Disposition of sale proceeds,
62C:63.

TAX SALES —Cont'd
Distress and sale of personal
estate, **59:20, 60:24-60:28.**
Division of land, effect on
redemption, **60:68, 60:76A.**
Easements, effect of collector's
deed, **60:45.**
Errors and irregularities.
Effect, **60:37.**
Reimbursement of purchaser at
invalid sale, **60:46.**
Water rates and charges,
redemption as affected by
errors, **60:76B.**
Evidence.
City or town deemed purchaser,
60:49.
Collector's affidavit as evidence
of notice, **60:57.**
Redemption, tax title account as
evidence of amount
necessary, **60:50.**
Exemptions.
Conveyance tax of foreclosure
sales on agricultural or
horticultural property,
61A:12.
Distress and sale, **60:24.**
Exorbitant charge for redemption,
penalty, **60:104.**
Extension of time, **60:37A, 60:77.**
Fees.
Legal fees, **60:79.**
Sheriff, **60:89.**
Tax collector, **60:15.**
Foreclosure.
Lien for taxes, foreclosure by
sale, **60:37-60:60.**
Redemption of tax title created
by sale, foreclosure of right
to, **60:64-60:75.**
See TAX DEEDS AND
TITLES.
Hard to store property, sale and
redemption, **62C:57.**
Heirs of decedents, notice, **60:40.**
Homesteads, exemption, **188:1.**
Horticultural property, **61A:12.**
Animals, distress and sale,
60:24, 60:27.
City or town, option to purchase
on notification of sale or
conversion to
nonagricultural use, **61A:14.**
Produce, **60:27.**
Stay pending appeal, **61A:19.**
Immaterial irregularities, **60:37.**
Impossibility of legal sale as
affecting lien for taxes, **60:37.**
Collector's statement as to,
recording, **60:37A.**

TAX SALES —Cont'd

Income tax, certificate as to sale, **62C:59, 62C:60.**

Interest on tax owed, rate for redemption, **60:62, 60:63, 60:68.**

Invalidity of title of land sold for nonpayment of assessments, proceedings in event of, **60:82 et seq.**

See TAX DEEDS AND TITLES.

Invalid sale.

   Continuance of lien, **60:37.**

   Deposit, purchaser's failure to make, **60:43.**

   Nonpayment by purchaser, **60:49.**

   Reimbursement of purchaser, **60:46.**

   Town, effect of assignment or transfer of invalid tax deed, **60:46.**

Land Court, **60:76, 185:1.**

Legacy and succession taxes.

   Personal property, sale to pay taxes, **202:20.**

   Real estate, sale for payment of taxes, **65:21, 202:20.**

   Enforcement of lien of tax, **65:31.**

   Refusal or neglect to pay tax by person entitled to realty, **65:17.**

Levy of taxes, sale pursuant, **60:27, 62C:53, 62C:56, 62C:57.**

Limitation of time.

   Redemption, **60:65, 60:69.**

   Sale for taxes, time in which real estate liable, **202:20.**

Lots, sale, **60:43.**

   Small value parcels to be sold together, **60:51.**

Low value lands, **60:51, 60:79-60:80B.**

Mistake.

   Effect, **60:37.**

   Reimbursement of purchaser at invalid sale, **60:46.**

   Water rates and charges, redemption as affected by errors, **60:76B.**

Mortgage, redemption, **60:62, 60:68.**

Municipality as purchaser, **60:48 et seq.**

   Agricultural land, **61A:14.**

   Covenants running with land, enforceability, **60:77.**

   Demand upon owner of record to protect interest of municipality as purchaser, **60:50A.**

TAX SALES —Cont'd

Municipality as purchaser —Cont'd

   Duties of building inspector with respect, **60:81A.**

   Inquiry as to value of property and validity of tax titles held thereon, **60:79.**

   Management and sale of lands after purchase, **60:52.**

   Nonpayment by purchaser, municipality deemed purchaser in case, **60:49.**

   Protection of interest of municipality, **60:50A.**

   Redemption, **60:62, 60:63.**

   Subsequent taxes, collection, **60:61.**

   Tax on property acquired by municipality by foreclosure, **60:77.**

Notice, **60:40.**

   Adjournment of sale, **60:26, 60:44.**

   Change of name of town, **60:41.**

   Collector's affidavit as evidence, **60:57.**

   Distress and sale of personalty, **60:25, 60:26.**

   Heirs and devisees, **60:40.**

   Parcels of small value sold together, **60:51.**

   Personal property, sale, **60:25.**

   Posting, **60:42.**

   Protection of municipality's interest, demand upon owner of record, **60:50A.**

   Publication, **60:1, 60:40.**

   Public auction, **60:52.**

   Purchase at tax sale, collector's notice, **60:48.**

   Redemption, notice to collectors, **60:76C.**

   Service.

      Affidavit of collector as evidence, **60:57.**

      Designation of place, **60:39.**

   Time and place of sale, **60:40.**

Option of municipality to purchase agricultural or horticultural property, **61A:14.**

Ordinance or bylaw directing collector to sell property for taxes, **60:87.**

Parcels, sale, **60:43.**

   Small value parcels to be sold together, **60:51.**

Partial redemption from tax sale after division of real estate, **60:76A.**

Partition of land, effect on redemption, **60:68, 60:76A.**

TAX SALES —Cont'd

Payment of bid, time, **60:49.**

Payment or part payment of tax upon real estate parcels prior, **60:22, 60:22A.**

Perishable property, sale and redemption, **62C:57.**

Personal property, distress and sale of, **60:24-60:28.**

Preservation of lien where sale prevented, **60:37A.**

Proceeds of sale, disposition, **62C:63.**

Produce, distress and sale, **60:27.**

Public auction, **60:43.**

   Exemption of sales by tax collectors, **100:11.**

   Foreclosure of taxes, auction sale of land acquired by cities and towns through, **60:52, 60:77B.**

   Low value lands held by city or town under tax title, **60:79.**

   Notice required, **60:52.**

Rate of interest to redeem, **51:52, 60:62, 60:63, 60:68.**

Records and recording.

   Collector's deeds, **60:45.**

   Conveyances, effect of recording, **60:37.**

   Redemption certificates, **60:63.**

   Sale and redemption, commissioner to keep records, **62C:61.**

   Surrender and discharge of invalid tax title, **60:46.**

Redemption, **60:54, 60:62, 60:63, 60:68, 60:76, 60:76A, 62C:57, 62C:58.**

   Abatement of taxes as affecting, **59:65A.**

   Adjustment of errors and amounts, **60:62.**

   After foreclosure proceedings instituted, **60:68.**

   Agricultural or horticultural property, **61A:12.**

   Amount required, **60:50, 60:62.**

   Answer in foreclosure under tax title, **60:68.**

   Assessors of taxes, notice to, when, **60:76C.**

   Assignees of purchaser, redemption, **60:62.**

   Barring, time limit, **60:69.**

   Certificates of redemption, **60:62, 60:63.**

   City or town, redemption, **60:62, 60:63.**

   Commissioner to keep records, **62C:61.**

TAX SALES —Cont'd
Redemption —Cont'd
Deed of collector subject to right, **60:45.**
Discharge of tax title, redemption, **60:63.**
Division of land by sale, mortgage, or upon petition for partition, **60:68.**
Partial redemption after division, **60:76A.**
Duration of right, **60:65.**
Enforcement of redemption, suit, **60:65-60:76.**
Errors or irregularities as affecting amount, **60:62.**
Evidence of amount necessary, **60:50.**
Excess amount, forbidden, **60:62.**
Execution, right of redemption of land sold, **236:36.**
Exorbitant charge for, penalty, **60:104.**
Finding of court for redemption in foreclosure under tax title, **60:68.**
Foreclosure of right of redemption from tax sale, **60:64-60:75.**
See TAX DEEDS AND TITLES.
Installment payment, **60:62.**
Insufficient amount paid, action to recover balance, **60:63.**
Interest charged, **60:62, 60:63, 60:68.**
Jurisdiction of land court of proceedings, **60:76, 185:1.**
Limitation of time, **60:65, 60:69.**
Mortgage as affecting, **60:68.**
Mortgagee, effect of redemption, **60:62.**
Municipality as purchaser, application of proceeds received in case, **60:43.**
Notice to collectors and assessors, **60:76C.**
Offer to redeem in foreclosure under tax title, **60:68.**
Partial redemption after division of real estate by sale, mortgage, or upon petition for partition, **60:76A.**
Partition proceedings as affecting, **60:68.**
Part owner or person interested in part of property, redemption, **60:76A.**
Payments required, **60:62.**
Person other than owner redeeming, **60:62.**

TAX SALES —Cont'd
Redemption —Cont'd
Portion of recorded plat or subdivision, **60:76A.**
Purchasers other than municipality, redemption, **60:62.**
Rate of interest to redeem, **60:62, 60:63, 60:68.**
Records of, commissioner to keep, **62C:61.**
Registers and registries of deeds, certificate of redemption, **60:62, 60:63.**
Release, **60:63.**
Sale as affecting, **60:68.**
Subsequent taxes and assessments as charge with respect, **60:61.**
Taking of land for taxes by municipality as subject, **60:54.**
Tax collectors, notice, when, **60:76C.**
Tax deed, redemption as discharge, **60:63.**
Tax title account as prima facie evidence of amount necessary, **60:50.**
Tender of payment, where and to whom made, **60:47.**
Time limitation, **60:65, 60:69.**
Treasurer of city or town, duties as to redemption, **60:62, 60:63.**
Vacation of decree barring, **60:69, 60:69A.**
Water rates, sale for nonpayment, **40:42D, 60:76B.**
Who may redeem, **60:62.**
Registered land, **185:84.**
Reimbursement in case of invalid sale, **60:46.**
Revenue commissioner.
Extension of time as to nonenforcement of covenants against municipal purchaser, **60:77.**
Records of redemption from tax sales, commissioner to keep, **62C:61.**
Transfer of land purchased by municipality, approval, **60:52.**
Service of notice.
Affidavit of collector as evidence, **60:57.**
Designation of place, **60:39.**
Several parcels of small value, inclusion in same sale, **60:51.**

TAX SALES —Cont'd
Sheriff.
As tax collector, **60:88, 60:89.**
Fees, **60:89.**
Small value parcels, sale, **60:51, 60:79-60:80B.**
Special warrant to compel payment without demand, **60:19.**
Subsequent taxes, lien for to continue after tax sale, **60:61.**
Surplus after sale of personalty, accounting, **60:28.**
Tax title, **60:45, 60:54, 60:64-60:83.**
See TAX DEEDS AND TITLES.
Time.
Bid, time to pay, **60:49.**
Extension by commissioner of time as to nonenforcement of covenants against municipal purchaser, **60:77.**
Notice of time and place of sale, **60:40.**
Redemption, **60:65, 60:69.**
Sale for taxes, time in which real estate liable, **202:20.**
Title given upon sale, **60:45, 60:54, 60:64-60:83.**
See TAX DEEDS AND TITLES.
Treasurer of city or town, powers, **41:37.**
Undivided realty of decedents assessed to heirs or devisees, notice with respect, **60:40.**
Void sale.
Invalid sale. See within this heading, "Invalid sale."
Warrants.
Distress and sale, **59:20, 60:34.**
Payment without demand, special warrant to compel, **60:19.**
Warranty in deed of collectors, **60:45.**
Water rates, sale for nonpayment, **40:42D, 60:76B.**
Zoning and planning, partial redemption from tax sale under subdivision control law, **60:76A.**

TAX STAMPS.
Cigarette tax, **64C:29-64C:31.**
See CIGARETTE TAX.
Deeds and documents, **64D:2-4, 64D:7-9.**
See DEED AND DOCUMENT STAMP TAX.
Federal tax stamp, notation, **36:15.**

TAX TITLES, 60:45, 60:54, 60:64-60:83.
See TAX DEEDS AND TITLES.

TAY-SACHS DISEASE.
Testing, treatment, and care of persons susceptible, **76:15B.**

TDD/TTY.
Defined, **166:15E.**

TEACHERS.
Absences.
　Authority to excuse, **76:1.**
　Leaves of absence for teachers, **71:41A.**
Abused and neglected children, reports, **71:37L, 119:51A.**
Academies.
　Duties of instructors, **71:30.**
　Jury service, exemption, **234:1.**
Advisory commission on academically talented pupils, members, **15:6C.**
Affirmation.
　Oath or affirmation. See within this heading, "Oath or affirmation."
Agricultural and technical institutes.
　Conduct of public officials and employees, **74A:20.**
　Equal pay for women teachers at Essex Agricultural and Technical Institute, **71:40.**
　Group insurance, **74A:17.**
　Retirement, **74A:18.**
　Rights, **74A:16.**
　Special duties of teachers, **74:37.**
　Tort liability, status, **74A:19.**
Aid or assistance.
　Counsel, assistance of.
　　Attorneys. See within this heading, "Attorneys at law."
　Education department.
　　See EDUCATION DEPARTMENT.
Air rifles or BB guns, sale or furnishing to minor, **269:12A.**
Aliens, certification as teachers, **71:38G.**
Anarchy, effect of conviction, **264:11.**
Appeal.
　See APPEAL AND REVIEW.
Application for certificate prior to effective date of rules and regulations promulgated, **71:38G.**
Apprenticeships.
　Master teacher corps program, **15A:19C.**

TEACHERS —Cont'd
Appropriations.
　Pensions, appropriations by cities and towns, **32:42, 32:43.**
　Private schools, appropriations for support of teachers, **67:17, 67:27.**
　Regional school district teachers' salaries, **71:16, 71:42B.**
Assault and battery, **71:37G, 265:13D.**
Assistance.
　Aid or assistance. See within this heading, "Aid or assistance."
Assistants in medicine as permitted to practice under supervision of instructors, **112:9A.**
Associations of teachers.
　Professional educational organizations. See within this heading, "Professional educational organizations."
Athletic instructors, retirement, **32:1.**
Attorneys at law.
　Certification proceedings, representation of applicant counsel, **71:38G.**
　Disciplinary proceedings, representation by counsel, **71:42D.**
Barbers.
　Defined, **112:87F.**
　Examination and registration, **112:87P.**
Bilingual education teachers, qualification and certification, **71A:6.**
Blind persons.
　Commission for the blind, teachers, **6:130.**
　Eligibility for teaching positions, **71:38, 71:38G.**
Board of higher education, student loan repayment program attracting excellence to teaching program, **15A:19A.**
Bradford Durfee College of Technology, **74:42C, 74:42O.**
　See BRADFORD DURFEE COLLEGE OF TECHNOLOGY.
Centralized weekly payroll system for, establishment, **29:31.**
Certification, **71:38G.**
　Bilingual education teachers, **71A:6.**
　Hardship in securing teachers, exemption from certification requirement, **71:38G.**

TEACHERS —Cont'd
Certification —Cont'd
　Interstate compacts.
　　See INTERSTATE COMPACTS AND AGREEMENTS.
　Issued prior to effective date of rules for provisional certification, **71:38G.**
Charter schools, **71:89.**
Checks, retirement board, **29:32.**
Christa McAuliffe teacher incentive program.
　See CHRISTA MCAULIFFE TEACHER INCENTIVE PROGRAM.
Civil rights and discrimination.
　Religion or political involvement of teachers, inquiry into, **71:39.**
　Women teachers. See within this heading, "Women teachers."
Classes for training teachers in continuation or vocational schools, **74:18.**
Closing schools for meetings, **71:73.**
Collaborative educational programs, **40:4E, 71:40.**
Colleges.
　See COLLEGES AND UNIVERSITIES.
Commission for the blind, employment, **6:130.**
Committees.
　Blind person who is candidate for teaching position, contracting, **71:38.**
　Duties of, **32:43.**
　Election of teachers, **71:38.**
　Hiring of teachers by, **71:38.**
　Ineligibility of members to hold teaching position, **71:52.**
　Leaves of absence for teachers, **71:41A.**
　Lunches for teachers.
　　Acceptance of provision, **71:80.**
　　Duty to prepare and sell, **71:72.**
　Politics of candidates for teachers, inquiry as to forbidden, **71:39.**
　Publication of policies of conduct, **71:37.**
　Religion of candidates for teachers, inquiry as to forbidden, **71:39.**
　Rights of teachers not to be restricted, **71:44.**
　Suspension of teachers, **71:42, 71:42D.**

TEACHERS —Cont'd
Committees —Cont'd
Tenure to be given to certain teachers, **71:41.**
Compact on certification.
See INTERSTATE COMPACTS AND AGREEMENTS.
Compensation.
Salaries and compensation. See within this heading, "Salaries and compensation."
Competency requirements, **71:1.**
Complaint in disciplinary proceedings against teacher, **71:42D.**
Conduct of teachers.
Publication of rules or regulations pertaining to conduct, **71:37H.**
Suspension for unbecoming conduct, **71:42D.**
Conservation education supervisor to encourage training, **15:4A.**
Continuation schools and courses, **71:38G.**
Classes for teacher training, **74:18.**
Contract.
Election or promotion of teachers, **71:38.**
Leaves of absence, teachers obtaining, **71:41A.**
Conviction of crime, eligibility for employment after, **264:11, 264:20.**
Co-operative corporations, appropriations for teaching co-operation, **157:6.**
Corps, establishment and purposes of teachers, **71:1.**
Correspondence schools, proceedings to obtain license, **75C:2.**
Critical shortage.
Employment of retired teachers, **32:91.**
Deaf persons.
Eligibility for certification as teachers, **71:38G.**
Testing of pupils' hearing, **71:57.**
Deferral of payment, **44:56, 44:56A, 71:40.**
Director of occupational guidance and placement, provisions as to teachers applicable, **71:38C.**
Discharge, dismissal, and suspension, **71:42, 71:42D.**
Massachusetts Maritime Academy, **73:4B.**
Services rendered after, **71:42.**

TEACHERS —Cont'd
Discharge, dismissal, and suspension —Cont'd
Vacation for school teachers and superintendents, effect of discharge, **71:42.**
Discrimination.
Civil rights and discrimination. See within this heading, "Civil rights and discrimination."
Driver education.
See DRIVER EDUCATION.
Dues of professional associations, **180:17C.**
Duties, **71:32.**
Education department.
See EDUCATION DEPARTMENT.
Elections.
See ELECTIONS.
Electrolysis, instructors, **112:87LLL.**
Eligibility.
Qualification or eligibility. See within this heading, "Qualification or eligibility."
Emergency first aid or transportation to student, immunity from civil liability, **71:55A.**
Employment security law, election by nonprofit institutions as to providing coverage, **151A:6.**
Endorsement by, false assertion, **266:90.**
Engineers, teaching experience considered for purposes of registration, **112:81J.**
Equal educational opportunity funds, **15:49A-15:49E.**
Equal pay, **71:40.**
Exchange teachers from abroad, **264:14A.**
Expanded responsibilities, **15:1G.**
Eyesight.
Blind persons. See within this heading, "Blind persons."
Protective devices for eyes, requirement as to wearing, **71:55C.**
Testing of pupils' eyesight, **71:57.**
False pretenses as to status, **266:89.**
Fees.
Applications for teachers positions, **69:6.**
Certification of teachers, **71:38G.**
Procuring positions for teachers, regulation of fees, **71:45, 71:67.**

TEACHERS —Cont'd
Fees —Cont'd
Registration of federal certificates of pilots, exceptions in law, **90:49.**
Females.
Women teachers. See within this heading, "Women teachers."
Finances and funds.
Teacher, principal and superintendent quality endowment fund, **10:35S.**
Fines and penalties.
Assault and battery on teachers, **265:13D.**
Fees for procuring teaching positions, acceptance by certain persons, **71:45, 71:67.**
First aid or transportation of students on emergency basis, immunity from damages, **71:55A.**
Flag, duties, **71:69.**
Food.
Membership on nutrition board, **6:181.**
Hairdressers.
See HAIRDRESSERS AND COSMETOLOGISTS.
Hardship in securing teachers, exemption from certification requirement, **71:38G.**
Hearing and deafness.
Deaf persons. See within this heading, "Deaf persons."
Hearings.
Certification of teachers, **71:38G.**
Discharge or suspension, **71:42, 71:42D.**
Hiring.
Incoming teacher signing bonus program, **15A:19B.**
Master teacher corps program, **15A:19C.**
Tomorrow's teachers scholarship program, **15A:19D.**
Horace Mann teachers, **71:38.**
Immunity from damages for rendering emergency first aid or transportation of students, **71:55A.**
Incoming teacher signing bonus program, **15A:19B.**
Indemnity and indemnification.
Liability insurance for indemnification of school personnel, **40:5.**
Town appropriations for indemnity insurance, **40:5.**
Inspection of records, teacher's right, **71:42C.**

TEACHERS —Cont'd
Instructional aides, hiring, **71:38.**
Insurance.
  Income protection insurance
    premiums, deduction from
    salaries, **180:17D.**
  Indemnity and indemnification.
    See within this heading,
    "Indemnity and
    indemnification."
  Premiums deducted form pay,
    transmittal, **71:37B.**
Interns, necessity for certification
  by board of education, **71:38G.**
Interstate compacts.
  See INTERSTATE COMPACTS
  AND AGREEMENTS.
Jury duty, exemption, **234:1.**
Leaves of absence for, **71:41A,**
  71:41B.
Literacy services and adult basic
  education.
  Certification of teacher, **69:1H.**
Lunch for teachers.
  Committees. See within this
    heading, "Committees."
  Manner of voting for election,
    71:38.
Maritime Academy, selection and
  dismissal of teachers, **73:4B.**
Massachusetts board of education,
  education professionals
  authorized to serve, **15:1E.**
Master teacher corps program,
  15A:19C.
Maximum period of suspension
  without hearing, **71:42D.**
Meetings, closing of school, **71:73.**
Mental health.
  See MENTALLY ILL AND
  RETARDED PERSONS.
Mentors.
  Master teacher corps program,
    15A:19C.
Minimum salaries, **71:40.**
Moral requirements, **71:1.**
Most at risk schools, equal
  educational opportunity funds,
  15:49A-15:49E.
Motor vehicles.
  See MOTOR VEHICLES.
Municipal finance.
  Pensions, appropriations, **32:42,**
    32:43.
  Treasurers of cities and towns.
    See within this heading,
    "Treasurers of cities and
    towns."
New Bedford Institute of
  Technology.
  Salaries for personnel, **74:42O.**
  Tenure, **74:42C.**

TEACHERS —Cont'd
Nominating papers, right to sign
  not to be restricted, **71:44.**
Notice.
  Certification, **71:38G.**
  Intent to dismiss teacher, **71:42.**
  Reemployment of teachers,
    71:41.
Nurses in schools, payroll
  deductions for dues to
  teachers' associations,
  180:17E.
Nutrition board, membership,
  6:181.
Oath or affirmation, **71:30.**
  Exemption of exchange teachers,
    264:14A.
Observance of Teachers' Day,
  6:12X.
Occupational guidance and
  placement director, provisions
  as to teachers applicable,
  71:38C.
Out-of-state service as creditable
  for retirement purposes, **32:3.**
Out-of-state teachers at public
  academies, **32:3.**
Part-time teachers, state
  employees, **268A:7.**
Payroll deductions, **180:17I.**
  Association dues, **180:17C.**
  Bargaining association charges,
    180:17G.
  Income protection insurance
    premiums, **180:17D.**
  Nurses, dues, **180:17E.**
  Professional association dues,
    180:17C, 180:17E.
  Time for transmittal of funds
    withheld, **71:37B, 149:178B.**
  Treasurers of cities and towns.
    See within this heading,
    "Treasurers of cities and
    towns."
Penalties.
  Fines and penalties. See within
    this heading, "Fines and
    penalties."
Pensions.
  See RETIREMENT SYSTEMS
  AND PENSIONS.
Performance evaluation, **71:38.**
Permanent employment.
  See TENURE AND SENIORITY.
Physical examination by school
  physician, **71:54, 71:55B.**
Physicians holding faculty
  appointment, temporary
  registration, **112:9B.**
Playgrounds, appointment, **45:14.**
Politics of candidates, inquiries as
  to, forbidden, **71:39.**

TEACHERS —Cont'd
Prayer or meditation, announcing
  period of silence, **71:1A.**
Private schools.
  Academies. See within this
    heading, "Academies."
  Appropriations for support,
    67:17, 67:27.
  Conviction of crime, ineligibility
    for employment, **264:20.**
Professional educational
  organizations.
  Bargaining association charges,
    payroll deductions, **180:17G.**
  Dues, payroll deductions,
    180:17C, 180:17E.
  Leave of absence for service,
    71:41A.
Psychology-related professions or
  occupations excluded from
  regulations, **112:125.**
Publication of rules and
  regulations, **71:37.**
Qualification or eligibility.
  Certification. See within this
    heading, "Certification."
  Retirement board, eligibility of
    retired employees as
    members, **15:16.**
  School committee members
    ineligible to be teachers,
    71:52.
Records concerning teachers or
  their work, school officials to
  permit teachers to inspect,
  71:42C.
Recruiting.
  Incoming teacher signing bonus
    program, **15A:19B.**
  Master teacher corps program,
    15A:19C.
  Tomorrow's teachers scholarship
    program, **15A:19D.**
Reduction of salaries, **71:43.**
Reemployment for next year,
  notice required, **71:41.**
Refund or reimbursement.
  Failing to return after
    termination of leave of
    absence, teacher to make
    refund, **71:41A.**
  Fees and tuition expended in
    upgrading skills,
    reimbursement, **71:38I.**
  Indemnity. See within this
    heading, "Indemnity and
    indemnification."
  Leave of absence,
    reimbursement of salary
    during, **71:41A.**
  Military service credit fund,
    32:22.

TEACHERS —Cont'd
Refund or reimbursement —Cont'd
Retirement board, expenses,
15:17.
Regionally licensed teachers,
employment, **71:38G.**
Regional school districts.
See REGIONAL SCHOOL
DISTRICTS.
Reimbursement.
Refund or reimbursement. See
within this heading,
"Refund or reimbursement."
Religion.
Candidates for teaching
positions, inquiries as to
religion forbidden, **71:39.**
Prayer or meditation,
announcing period of
silence, **71:1A.**
Support of teachers, religious
societies and parishes may
appropriate money, **67:17,
67:27.**
Removal.
Discharge. See within this
heading, "Discharge,
dismissal, and suspension."
Residency requirements,
restrictions, **71:38.**
Retirement systems.
See RETIREMENT SYSTEMS
AND PENSIONS.
Salaries and compensation, **29:31,
29:31B, 71:40, 71:42B.**
Centralized weekly payroll
system for teachers,
establishment, **29:31.**
Deductions.
Payroll deductions. See within
this heading, "Payroll
deductions."
Deferral in payment, **44:56,
44:56A, 71:40.**
Discharge of teachers, services
rendered after dismissal,
71:42.
Educational collaborative, **71:40.**
Equal pay, **32:91, 71:40.**
Essex Agricultural and Technical
Institute, equal pay for
women teachers, **71:40.**
Exchange teachers, **264:14A.**
Expanded responsibilities,
financial incentives, **15:1G,
71:40.**
Fully earned, **71:40.**
Institutions of higher education,
salary, **30:46.**
Leaves of absence, source of
compensation, **71:41A.**

TEACHERS —Cont'd
Salaries and compensation
—Cont'd
Method of payment, **29:31.**
Minimum, **71:40.**
New Bedford Institute of
Technology, compensation of
personnel, **74:42O.**
Payroll deductions. See within
this heading, "Payroll
deductions."
Reduction, **71:43.**
Refund or reimbursement. See
within this heading,
"Refund or reimbursement."
Regional school district teachers,
compensation, **71:16,
71:42B.**
Retired teachers, effect of
compensation as substitute
on pension, **32:9.**
Schedule, **30:46.**
State positions, **30:46.**
Method of payment, **29:31,
29:31B.**
Weekly payment in state
institutions, **29:31B.**
Supervising teachers of practice
schools, payment in
connection with state
teachers colleges, **73:3.**
Teachers' retirement board,
members, **15:17.**
Vocational education board's
powers in disposal of federal
funds, **74:22.**
Scholarships and fellowships.
Tomorrow's teachers scholarship
program, **15A:19D.**
School bus driver training,
instructors, **90:8A.**
School committees.
Committees. See within this
heading, "Committees."
School improvement fund,
improvement of school
buildings, **10:35F.**
Sex discrimination.
Women teachers. See within this
heading, "Women teachers."
Signing bonus program, **15A:19B.**
Special education.
See SPECIAL EDUCATION.
State colleges.
See COLLEGES AND
UNIVERSITIES.
State positions.
Colleges.
See COLLEGES AND
UNIVERSITIES.
Part-time teachers, state
employees, **268A:7.**

TEACHERS —Cont'd
State positions —Cont'd
Recruitment, **30:46.**
Salaries and compensation. See
within this heading,
"Salaries and
compensation."
Tenure, **30:9D, 74:42C.**
Student advisory committee,
meetings, **71:38M.**
Student rights, adoption after
student hearings of rules and
regulations defining and
clarifying, **71:85.**
Substitute teachers.
Reemployment of retired
personnel, **32:91.**
Temporary substitute defined,
71:38G.
Superintendence unions,
employment of special
teachers, **71:53A.**
Superintendent.
Commission or fee for obtaining
position, acceptance, **71:67.**
Maximum period of suspension
of teacher without hearing,
71:42D.
Recommendation, **71:59.**
Vacation, effect of discharge,
71:42.
Suspension.
Discharge. See within this
heading, "Discharge,
dismissal, and suspension."
Teachers corps, establishment,
purposes, etc., **71:1.**
Teaching learning corps, **15A:7A.**
Teaching or administrative intern
defined, **71:38G.**
Temporary certificates, **71:38G.**
Temporary substitute defined,
71:38G.
Tenure.
See TENURE AND SENIORITY.
Time or date.
Effective date of provisional
certification rules,
applications for certification
made prior, **71:38G.**
Paychecks, time for transmittal
of funds withheld, **71:37B,
149:178B.**
Suspension for unbecoming
conduct, period, **71:42D.**
Tomorrow's teachers scholarship
program, **15A:19D.**
Training courses, continuation or
vocational schools, **74:18.**
Transportation of students in
emergency, immunity from
damages, **71:55A.**

TEACHERS —Cont'd

Treasurers of cities and towns.
  Payroll deductions.
    Insurance premiums,
      deduction and
      transmittal, **180:17D.**
    Teachers' associations,
      transmission of payroll
      deductions, **180:17C.**
  Pension fund for teachers,
    custodian, **32:42.**
Trials.
  Hearings. See within this
    heading, "Hearings."
Tuberculosis in school personnel,
  examination, **71:55B.**
Unbecoming conduct, period of
  suspension, **71:42D.**
Unemployment compensation,
  151A:6.
University of Massachusetts.
  See UNIVERSITY OF
    MASSACHUSETTS.
Vacations, effect of discharge of
  teacher or superintendent,
  71:42.
Vocational education.
  See VOCATIONAL
    EDUCATION AND
    SCHOOLS.
Voting.
  See ELECTIONS.
Wages.
  Salaries and compensation. See
    within this heading,
    "Salaries and
    compensation."
Weapons and firearms, instructor
  furnishing to pupils under
  eighteen, **140:130.**
Women teachers.
  Change of marital status not
    cause for dismissal, **71:42.**
  Payment at same rate as men,
    71:40.

TEACHERS' EQUAL PAY ACT,
  71:40.

TEA HOUSES.

Licensing, **140:47.**

TEAMSTERS.

Public works, employment, **149:26,**
  149:27, 149:27B.

TEAR GAS.

Unlawful use, **269:10C.**

TECHNICAL CODE COUNCIL,
  143:94.

TECHNICAL COLLEGES OR
  INSTITUTES,
  74:42A-74:46B.

Agricultural and technical
  institutes, **74A:1 to 74A:23.**
  See AGRICULTURAL AND
    TECHNICAL INSTITUTES.

TECHNICAL COLLEGES OR
  INSTITUTES —Cont'd

Annual reports, **74:44.**
Bradford Durfee College of
  Technology, **74:42A et seq.**
  See BRADFORD DURFEE
    COLLEGE OF
    TECHNOLOGY.
Contracts with, notice to
  beneficiary of right of
  termination, **255:13K.**
Cost of tests performed by college
  or institute, payment, **74:46A.**
Degrees, granting, **74:42A,**
  74:42B.
Fees, **74:46A.**
Honorary doctorates, granting,
  74:42B.
Insurance on buildings and
  contents, **74:45.**
Master of science, authority to
  grant honorary degree,
  74:42A.
Nonresidents, tuition, **74:46.**
Reports, annual, **74:44.**
Research foundation, **74:46B.**
Tenure of teachers or professors,
  74:42C.
Tests authorized, **74:46A.**
Trusts and trustees.
  Corporation for purpose of
    taking and holding property,
    74:43.
  Granting of honorary degrees,
    74:42A, 74:42B.
  Property, power to take and
    hold, **74:43.**
Tuition for nonresident pupils,
  74:46.
Vocational education.
  See VOCATIONAL
    EDUCATION AND
    SCHOOLS.

TECHNICAL REFERENCE
  CENTERS.

Hazardous waste disposal
  recycling practices, reference
  centers, **21C:4.**

TECHNOLOGY
  DEVELOPMENT
  CORPORATION, 40G:1 et
  seq.

Accounting records, treasurer to be
  in charge, **40G:2.**
Administration secretary as
  member of board of directors,
  40G:2.
Annual report, **40G:6.**
Appointment of officers and
  employees, **40G:3.**

TECHNOLOGY
  DEVELOPMENT
  CORPORATION —Cont'd

Audit, **40G:7.**
Banks, deposit of moneys, **40G:4.**
Bequests, power to accept, **40G:3.**
Board.
  Composition, **40G:2.**
  Defined, **40G:1.**
Bond, officers and employees to
  give, **40G:2.**
Books of account, treasurer to be
  in charge, **40G:2.**
Borrowing of money, power, **40G:3.**
Bylaws, power to make, amend
  and repeal, **40G:3.**
Chairman of board of directors,
  designation, **40G:2.**
Co-investment funds, **40G:4B.**
Commonwealth Fund,
  establishment of, **40G:4B.**
Compensation, **40G:2.**
Contracts, power to make, **40G:3.**
Corporation, defined, **40G:1.**
Co-venture, defined, **40G:1.**
Definitions, **40G:1.**
Devises, power to accept, **40G:3.**
Direct investment, defined, **40G:1.**
Disclosure of interest or
  involvement of director,
  40G:2.
Documents, secretary as custodian,
  40G:2.
Donations, power to accept, **40G:3.**
Economic development
  department, secretary to serve
  as director, **40G:2.**
Economic diversification program,
  23F:4.
Employment opportunities,
  co-investment funds, **40G:4B.**
Enterprise, defined, **40G:1.**
Federal aid, receipt, **40G:5A.**
Film and video development office
  membership, **23A:56.**
Governor's appointments to board
  of directors, **40G:2, 40G:7.**
Grants, power to accept, **40G:3.**
House of representatives, annual
  report to clerk, **40G:6.**
Indemnification of officers and
  employees, **40G:2.**
Insurance, power to procure,
  40G:3.
Interest or involvement of director,
  disclosure, **40G:2.**
Investment fund, establishment,
  40G:4.
Investment powers, **40G:3.**
Liability insurance, board to
  purchase, **40G:2.**

**TECHNOLOGY
DEVELOPMENT
CORPORATION** —Cont'd

Manpower affairs, corporation as
included in executive office,
40G:2.

Members of board of directors,
40G:2.

Minutes of board, recording
interest or involvement of
director, **40G:2.**

Paid-in capital, defined, **40G:1.**

Papers, secretary as custodian,
40G:2.

Personal property, power to
acquire, own, hold and
dispose, **40G:3.**

Powers, **40G:3.**

President, duties and salary,
40G:2.

Primary employment, defined,
40G:1.

Professional investor, defined,
40G:1.

Public records, information
received by board, **40G:10.**

Qualified security, defined, **40G:1.**

Quorum of board of directors,
40G:2.

Real property, power to acquire,
40G:3.

Records and reports.
  Annual report, **40G:6.**
  Donation or grant, details in
    annual report, **40G:3.**
  Secretary to keep records of
    board, **40G:2.**

Reimbursement of directors'
expenses, **40G:2.**

Rules and regulations, power to
make, amend and repeal,
40G:3.

Salary of president, **40G:2.**

Seal.
  Power to adopt, **40G:3.**
  Secretary as custodian, **40G:2.**

Secretary, election, **40G:2.**

Securities.
  Investment fund, **40G:4.**
  Power to buy, hold and sell,
    40G:3, 40G:4B.

Seed capital, defined, **40G:1.**

Senate, annual report to clerk,
40G:6.

Small business investment
corporation, license to operate,
40G:5.

Substandard areas, use of funds,
40G:4.

Treasurer.
  Election, **40G:2.**
  Moneys payable, **40G:4.**

**TECHNOLOGY
DEVELOPMENT
CORPORATION** —Cont'd

Trust companies, deposit of
moneys, **40G:4.**

Vacancies on board of directors,
40G:2.

Vice-chairman, election, **40G:2.**

Wages, **40G:2.**

Willful dishonesty, liability of
board members and officers,
40G:2.

**TECHNOLOGY PARK
CORPORATION.
See MASSACHUSETTS
TECHNOLOGY PARK
CORPORATION.**

**TECHNOLOGY 2000
PARTNERSHIP, 23F:1 et
seq.**

Bay State Skills Corporation,
23F:1 et seq.

Contracts and agreements, **23F:5.**

Defense Conversion, Reinvestment
and Transition Act of 1993,
23F:9.

Economic affairs secretary, **23F:2.**

TELECOMMUNICATIONS.

Board of higher education,
Massachusetts corporation for
educational
telecommunication, **15A:3A.**

Deaf persons, availability of
telecommunication devices,
6:197.

Educational Telecommunications,
Corporation For.
  See EDUCATIONAL
    TELEVISION.

Education and vocational
rehabilitation office,
maintenance of toll-free
number, **23E:10.**

Fire warning and security
systems, applicability of
provisions, **141:7.**

Interception of.
  See EAVESDROPPING AND
    WIRETAPPING.

Larceny and theft,
telecommunications service
and equipment, **166:42A,
166:42B, 175A:10A.**

Mental health patients, rights,
123:23.

Municipal lighting and heating
plants.
  Authority to establish, **164:47E.**

Radio.
  See RADIO AND TELEVISION.

TELECOMMUNICATIONS
  —Cont'd

Service defined for tax purposes,
64H:1, 64I:1.

Taxing of telecommunications
services, **64H:1, 64I:1.**

Telephone.
  See TELEPHONE AND
    TELEGRAPH COMPANIES.

Theft, telecommunications service
and equipment, **166:42A,
166:42B, 175A:10A.**

Watershed management division,
licenses or permits for
installation and operation of
telecommunications
transmission facilities, **92:107.**

**TELECOMMUNICATIONS AND
ENERGY DEPARTMENT,
25:1 et seq.**

Abandoned or unclaimed property,
public utility companies as
persons required to file annual
reports, **200A:1, 200A:7.**

Abstracts of returns of companies
under jurisdiction of
telecommunications and
energy department, report
containing, **161:139, 164:77,
165:7.**

Accountants, **25:7.**

Advertising, recovery from
ratepayer of direct or indirect
expenditure, **164:33A.**

Air carriers, rates or tariffs,
159:14A.

Aldermen and selectmen.
  Appointment or discharge of
    employees of utilities,
    271:40.
  Municipal lighting.
    See MUNICIPAL LIGHTING
      AND HEATING PLANTS.
  Rate change or reduction in
    service, **25:4A.**

Alteration, amendment, or change.
  Rates and charges. See within
    this heading, "Rates and
    charges."

Annual reports.
  Records, reports, and returns.
    See within this heading,
    "Records, reports, and
    returns."

Appeal.
  See APPEAL AND REVIEW.

Applications, fees for filing,
25:10B.

Appropriations, **25:9, 40:5.**

Aqueducts.
  See AQUEDUCTS AND
    AQUEDUCT COMPANIES.

TELECOMMUNICATIONS AND ENERGY DEPARTMENT
—Cont'd

Assessments, **25:18 et seq., 164:61.**

Assistants.
Employees and officers. See within this heading, "Employees and officers."

Atomic energy, studies and recommendations, **6:91.**

Attachments, power to regulate, **166:25A.**

Attorney general.
Gas.
See GAS AND ELECTRIC COMPANIES.
Municipal lighting.
See MUNICIPAL LIGHTING AND HEATING PLANTS.
Rates or tariffs.
Notice of rate schedule changes, **159:1.20.**
Proceedings, **12:11E.**
Supervision of litigation relative to common carriers, **25:7.**
Water companies, recovery of penalty for failure to file copies of contracts with affiliated companies, **165:4A.**

Attorneys and counsel, **25:7, 159:40.**

Bond issues, **25:3, 25:5, 25:7, 25:10B.**
Depreciation fund, **155:5A.**
Investments. See within this heading, "Investments."
Mortgage to secure bonds of gas companies, **164:9, 164:13.**
Stock and stockholders. See within this heading, "Stock and stockholders."
Validity of securities issued pending appeal of decisions, **25:5.**

Bonds, surety.
Employees receiving filing fees, bond, **25:10B.**
Zoning and planning, bond given to secure installation of utilities, **41:81U.**

Boston terminal corporation.
See BOSTON TERMINAL CORPORATION.

Boston water.
See BOSTON WATER AND SEWER REORGANIZATION ACT.

Burden of proof on appeal, **25:5.**

Business corporation, control, **182:8.**

TELECOMMUNICATIONS AND ENERGY DEPARTMENT
—Cont'd

Business trusts.
See BUSINESS TRUSTS.

Carriers, **25:7, 25:8.**
See CARRIERS.

Certificates and certification.
Appeals, **25:5.**
Hazardous waste, transportation, **21C:7.**
Public convenience and necessity, filing fees for certificate, **25:10B.**

Chairmen, duties and functions, **25:4.**

Changes.
Rates and charges. See within this heading, "Rates and charges."

Charitable purposes approved by department, free or reduced rate service by carriers, **159:15.**

Charter, amendment or extension, **3:5.**

Children under twelve months of age, shutoffs to residences housing, **164:124H.**

Cities and towns.
Aldermen and selectmen. See within this heading, "Aldermen and selectmen."
Appropriations by towns in connection with proceedings before department, **40:5.**
Municipal lighting and heating plants, **164:34-164:69F.**
See MUNICIPAL LIGHTING AND HEATING PLANTS.
Planning, **41:81D, 41:81E.**
Rate changes, selectmen to be notified as time and place of hearing, **25:4A.**

Civil penalties in relation to theft of electricity or gas, **164:127A.**

Civil service status of employees, **31:48.**

Coal mining licenses, contents of application, **21B:5.**

Cogeneration, small power production facilities and industrial energy conservation, financing incentives, **40D:1, 40D:7, 40D:23.**

Coin machines, obtaining utility services by fraudulent operation, **266:75A.**

Commercial motor vehicle division, **25:12F, 25:12G.**
See CARRIERS.

TELECOMMUNICATIONS AND ENERGY DEPARTMENT
—Cont'd

Commission, **25:2-25:5A.**
Conflicts of interest.
Employment by regulated industry, **268A:8B.**
Employment by regulated industry, **268A:8B.**
Metropolitan district commission. See within this heading, "Metropolitan district commission."
Reorganization, **25:2, 25:4.**

Commonwealth Service Corps, **6:121.**

Community antenna television system.
Attachments to utility facilities, regulation, **166:25A.**
Underground plant damage prevention system, participation, **164:76D.**

"Company," defined, **25:3.**

Compensation.
Salary. See within this heading, "Salary."

Condominiums, gas and electricity furnished, **164:94H.**

Conflicts of interest of commissioners forbidden, **25:3.**

Consent and notice provisions for eminent domain proceedings, exemptions, **79:5C.**

Consumer affairs.
See CONSUMER AFFAIRS AND BUSINESS REGULATION EXECUTIVE OFFICE.

Consumer protests, rates, **12:11E.**

Contracts of department, **25:3, 25:10B.**
Gas.
See GAS AND ELECTRIC COMPANIES.

Procurement contracts, **30B:7.**

Control by business corporation, **182:8.**

Conversion of oil to coal by electric generating facilities, **164:94G ½.**

Co-operative banks, deposit of funds of public service corporations, **155:3A.**

Corporation, as owning utility, **182:8.**
Stock and stockholders. See within this heading, "Stock and stockholders."

Costs, **25:5, 25:8, 25:9.**

Coupon notes, department may order depreciation fund, **155:5A.**

TELECOMMUNICATIONS AND ENERGY DEPARTMENT
—Cont'd

Credit unions.
  See CREDIT UNIONS.
Death.
  Inquests into deaths. See within this heading, "Inquests into deaths."
Deceit.
  See FRAUD AND DECEIT.
Decisions.
  Rulings and orders. See within this heading, "Rulings and orders."
Deeds of trust.
  Mortgages and deeds of trust. See within this heading, "Mortgages and deeds of trust."
Definitions, **25:3, 166:25A.**
Deposits.
  See DEPOSITS AND DEPOSITORIES.
Depreciation funds, provision, **155:5A.**
Directory assistance, charge, **159:19, 159:19A.**
Discontinuance of services, **25:4A, 164:124A, 164:124F, 164:124H, 164:124I.**
Discriminatory rate, complaint, **159:14, 159:14A.**
Easements.
  See EASEMENTS.
Electric companies.
  See GAS AND ELECTRIC COMPANIES.
Electricians law inapplicable, **141:7.**
Electric railroads.
  See ELECTRIC RAILROADS.
Elevated railways.
  See ELEVATED RAILWAYS.
Emergency mutual aid among foreign and domestic utilities, **164:133.**
Eminent domain, exemptions from consent and notice provisions, **79:5C.**
Employees and officers, **25:7, 25:9, 25:12F.**
  Additional assessments to pay for benefits, **25:18 et seq.**
  Bonds of employees receiving filing fees, **25:10B.**
  Civil service status of employees, **31:48.**
  Common carriers, appointment in connection, **25:7.**
  Control over, **25:10.**

TELECOMMUNICATIONS AND ENERGY DEPARTMENT
—Cont'd

Employees and officers —Cont'd
  Duties, **25:4.**
  Electric companies, appointment for duties in connection, **25:9.**
  False claims as to identity, **268:33.**
  Free railroad transportation, **159:15.**
  Gas companies, appointment for duties in connection, **25:9.**
  Hanging outside of or on rear of vehicle by employee permitted, **90:13.**
  Influencing appointment and discharge, **271:40, 271:41.**
  Motor carriers, appointment for duties relating, **25:12F.**
  Sick leave. See within this heading, "Sick leave."
  Water companies, appointment for duties relative, **25:9.**
Energy advisory board, **25:2A.**
  Membership, **25A:10.**
Engineers and land surveyors.
  Land surveys. See within this heading, "Land surveys."
Entry into land, **21C:8.**
Environmental impact reports, exceptions, **30:62A.**
Evidence.
  Appeals from public utilities commission, **25:5.**
  Burden of proof on appeal, **25:5.**
  Carriers' submission of evidence of compliance with departmental orders, **159:16.**
  Interstate commerce commission, department may present evidence, **159:41.**
  Witnesses. See within this heading, "Witnesses."
Examination, inspections, and investigations, **25:4.**
Expenses, **25:8.**
Inquests into deaths. See within this heading, "Inquests into deaths."
Inspectors, **25:7.**
Reports of examiners, **25:4.**
Underground plant damage prevention systems for public utilities, investigations into, **164:76D.**

TELECOMMUNICATIONS AND ENERGY DEPARTMENT
—Cont'd

Examination, inspections, and investigations —Cont'd
  Use of name indicating that person is a public service corporation, investigation, **155:5.**
Execution, money to pay for utilities as exempt, **235:34.**
Expenses, **25:5, 25:8, 25:9.**
  Fees. See within this heading, "Fees."
  Municipal light commissions, increase in purchase costs without bids, **164:56D.**
  Underground plant damage prevention system, maintenance, **164:76D.**
Experts, **25:7, 25:9.**
Express companies.
  See EXPRESS COMPANIES.
Failure to restore full service, fine, **164:124G.**
False.
  See FRAUD AND DECEIT.
Fees.
  Copies of documents and orders, **262:44.**
  Filing applications or documents, **25:10B.**
  Witnesses, **25:5A.**
Financial hardship, discontinuance of utility service because, **164:124A, 164:124F.**
Fire warning and security systems, applicability of provisions, **141:7.**
Foreign commerce.
  Interstate and foreign commerce. See within this heading, "Interstate and foreign commerce."
Foreign states.
  Emergency mutual aid, **164:133.**
  Interstate and foreign commerce. See within this heading, "Interstate and foreign commerce."
Representation of department at hearings, **159:41.**
Forest cutting regulations, clearing on rights of way as exempt, **132:34A, 132:44.**
Franchise tax, **63:52A.**
Fraud.
  See FRAUD AND DECEIT.
Free railroad transportation, **159:15.**
Gas.
  See GAS AND ELECTRIC COMPANIES.

TELECOMMUNICATIONS AND ENERGY DEPARTMENT
—Cont'd

General court.
Appointment or discharge of employees, request, **271:40.**
Appropriations, **25:9.**
Committee hearings, **159:41.**
Petitions for legislation, **3:5.**
Rate changes, request for hearings, **25:4A.**
Hazardous materials, safety standards for rail transport, **25:5C.**
Hazardous waste management act, duties regarding, **21C:5, 21C:7, 21C:8.**
Hearings, **25:4, 25:4A, 40:5, 159:20, 159:41.**
Heat.
See GAS AND ELECTRIC COMPANIES.
Herbicides, regulation of application, **132B:6B.**
Highway drains, approval to enter for construction, **83:4.**
Hospitals and nursing homes, notice required before shutting off utilities services, **164:124C.**
Incorporation, **158:1.**
Injunctions.
Gas.
See GAS AND ELECTRIC COMPANIES.
Landlord's failure to supply utility services, injunctive relief against, **186:14.**
Telephone.
See TELEPHONE AND TELEGRAPH COMPANIES.
Inquests into deaths.
Magistrate's report to department, **38:11.**
Notice to department as to deaths on carriers, **38:8, 159:28.**
Inspections.
Examination, inspections, and investigations. See within this heading, "Examination, inspections, and investigations."
Installation of services prior to approval of plan by planning boards, requirement, **41:81U.**
Insurance.
See INSURANCE.
Interest on money.
See INTEREST ON MONEY.

TELECOMMUNICATIONS AND ENERGY DEPARTMENT
—Cont'd

Interstate and foreign commerce.
Forms prescribed by department to conform to forms prescribed by commission, **159:31.**
Petition for relief from violations of interstate commerce law, **159:41.**
Investigations.
Examination, inspections, and investigations. See within this heading, "Examination, inspections, and investigations."
Investments.
Retirement system funds, **32:23.**
State funds invested in notes of certain utility companies, **29:38.**
Judgments, decrees, and orders.
Rulings and orders. See within this heading, "Rulings and orders."
Jurisdiction.
Abstracts of returns of companies under jurisdiction, report containing, **161:139, 164:77, 165:7.**
Carriers subject to jurisdiction, **159:12.**
Provisions of chapter, jurisdiction not limited, **159:105.**
Street railways, **159:12.**
Labor.
See LABOR AND WORKFORCE DEVELOPMENT.
Landlord and tenant, injunction against failure to supply utility services, **186:14.**
Land surveys.
Entry onto adjoining land by surveyor, **266:120C.**
Exemption from law as to engineers and land surveyors, **112:81R.**
Legislation concerning.
General court. See within this heading, "General court."
Legislative committees, representation of department at hearings before, **159:41.**
License required for, pipelines, conduits and cables under tidewater, **91:14.**
Lien on real property, municipal light charges, **60:23, 164:58B.**

TELECOMMUNICATIONS AND ENERGY DEPARTMENT
—Cont'd

Life and health insurance.
Additional assessments, **25:18 et seq.**
Lighting.
Gas.
See GAS AND ELECTRIC COMPANIES.
Metropolitan district commission, payment for lighting, boulevards and reservations on expiration of agreement thereto, **92:67.**
Municipal lighting.
See MUNICIPAL LIGHTING AND HEATING PLANTS.
Lists and schedules.
Rates and charges. See within this heading, "Rates and charges."
Tables. See within this heading, "Tables."
Magistrates report to department upon inquest into death, **38:11.**
Mapping commissions in cities and towns, location of lines, **40:8K.**
Maps, plats, and surveys.
Land surveys. See within this heading, "Land surveys."
Massachusetts Bay transportation authority.
Classification as domestic electric utility, **161A:41.**
Conflict of regulations, **161A:39.**
Procurement of electric utility services, **161A:40.**
Public utilities relocation, construction projects, **161A:5.**
Massachusetts water management act, water rates as considering fee schedules, **21G:19.**
Master plan of planning boards, **41:81D.**
Metropolitan district commission.
Payment for lighting boulevards and reservations on expiration of agreement thereto, **92:67.**
Questions as to quality and price of gas and electricity sold, **92:68.**
Metropolitan districts.
Park districts. See within this heading, "Park districts."
Metropolitan park areas.
Park districts. See within this heading, "Park districts."

TELECOMMUNICATIONS AND ENERGY DEPARTMENT
—Cont'd

Milk, department to fix tariff, **160:213.**

Minimum rate for carriers may be prescribed by department, **159:20.**

Mobile radio telephone utility companies.

See MOBILE RADIO TELEPHONE UTILITY COMPANIES.

Mortgages and deeds of trust.

Bonds of gas companies, mortgages to secure, **164:9, 164:13.**

Estates less than fee simple, registration and cancellation of mortgages including, **185:59.**

New England power pool, powers of foreign utility companies, **164A:4.**

Motor carriers.

See CARRIERS.

Motor vehicles.

Hanging outside of or on rear of vehicle by employee permitted, **90:13.**

Registration, **90:1A.**

Storage and towing, amounts authorized, **159B:6B, 266:120D.**

Municipalities.

Cities and towns. See within this heading, "Cities and towns."

Name, **155:4, 155:5.**

Notice.

Deaths on carriers, notice to department, **38:8, 159:28.**

Eminent domain, exemptions from consent and notice provision, **79:5C.**

Hospitals, notice required before shutting off service, **164:124C.**

Rate changes or service reductions, **25:4A, 159:20.**

Service of process and papers. See within this heading, "Service of process and papers."

Ocean sanctuaries, activities, **132A:15, 132A:16.**

Officers.

Employees and officers. See within this heading, "Employees and officers."

TELECOMMUNICATIONS AND ENERGY DEPARTMENT
—Cont'd

Orders.

Rulings and orders. See within this heading, "Rulings and orders."

Organization of companies, **158:1.**

Overhead wires and poles, department's authority as to removal and replacement with underground facilities, **166:22H.**

Park districts.

Location of public utilities in park area, **92:43-92:47, 262:34.**

Payment for lighting after expiration of agreement, **92:67.**

Right to cross and manner of crossing railroad, **92:51.**

Petitions.

Appeals petitions to be filed with secretary of commission, **25:5.**

Corporate matters, petitions to general court, **3:5.**

Interstate commerce law, petition for relief from violations, **159:41.**

Pipes.

See PIPES AND PIPELINES.

Plant damage prevention systems, **82:40, 164:76D.**

Police services from Public Safety Department, **22:9M.**

Prices.

Rates and charges. See within this heading, "Rates and charges."

Process.

Service of process and papers. See within this heading, "Service of process and papers."

Procurement contracts, **30B:7.**

Production of books and papers, power, **159:34, 159B:16A.**

Protective orders, **25:5D.**

Public hearings, representation, **159:41.**

Public officers and employees.

Employees and officers. See within this heading, "Employees and officers."

Radio and television technicians registration law, applicability, **112:87QQQ.**

Radio telephone.

See MOBILE RADIO TELEPHONE UTILITY COMPANIES.

TELECOMMUNICATIONS AND ENERGY DEPARTMENT
—Cont'd

Railroads.

See RAILROADS.

Rates and charges.

Affiliated companies of carriers, department to keep informed, **159:34A.**

Air carriers, rates or tariffs, **159:14A.**

Aldermen and selectmen, rate change or reduction in service, **Spec L 35:4A.**

Applications, fees for filing, **25:10B.**

Attorney general. See within this heading, "Attorney general."

Business customers, assistance service, **159:19A.**

Business trust, ownership or control, **182:11.**

Changes in rates of carrier, **159:19, 159:20.**

Recommendations by department, **159:23.**

Selectmen to be notified as to time and place of hearing, **25:4A.**

Charitable purposes approved by, free or reduced rate service by carriers, **159:15.**

Consumer protests, **12:11E.**

Deposits of utility customers, rate of interest, **158:16, 164:58A.**

Depreciation fund, ordering establishment of, upon approving rates, **155:5A.**

Determination of just and reasonable rates, **159:14.**

Directory assistance, **159:19, 159:19A.**

Discriminatory rate, complaint, **159:14, 159:14A.**

Division of rates between railroads upon through routes, **159:21.**

Fees for filing applications with department, **25:10B.**

Financial hardship, discontinuance of utility service due, **164:124A, 164:124F.**

Fixing rates, **159:14, 159:18.**

Free transportation of department officials and personnel, **159:15.**

Gas.

See GAS AND ELECTRIC COMPANIES.

**TELECOMMUNICATIONS AND
ENERGY DEPARTMENT**
—Cont'd

Rates and charges —Cont'd
Hearings, **25:4A, 159:20.**
Interest rates on deposits of
customers of franchised
corporations, **158:16.**
Joint rates of railroads,
establishment, **159:21.**
Lien on real property, municipal
lighting charges, **60:23,
164:58B.**
Massachusetts water
management act, **21G:19.**
Milk, department to fix tariff,
160:213.
Minimum rate for carriers may
be prescribed, **159:20.**
Orders.
Changes in schedule rates of
carriers, **159:20.**
Depreciation fund, ordering
establishment of, upon
approving rates, **155:5A.**
Fixing rates of carriers,
159:14.
Joint rates of railroads,
159:21.
Minimum rate for carriers,
159:20.
Reparation to person paying
discriminatory rate,
159:14.
Suspension of taking effect of
changes in schedule rates
of carriers, **159:20.**
Reduction in price or
improvement in quality of
service enforced, **164:93.**
Regulation, **159:14.**
Rejection of tariffs of air
carriers, **159:14A.**
Reparation to persons paying
discriminatory rates,
159:14.
Sales tax exemption, residential
service, **64H:6.**
Schedules of rates of carriers to
be filed, **159:19.**
Changes in rates, **159:19,
159:20.**
Season tickets of carriers subject
to approval, **159:18.**
Shares and interest in
controlling organizations not
to be considered in fixing
rates, **182:11.**
Supreme judicial court,
transferability of causes,
211:4A.

**TELECOMMUNICATIONS AND
ENERGY DEPARTMENT**
—Cont'd

Rates and charges —Cont'd
Town appropriation in
connection with proceedings
before department, **40:5.**
Real property assessments,
exemption, **59:2B.**
Records, reports, and returns.
Abstracts of returns of
companies under
jurisdiction of department,
reports containing, **161:139,
164:77, 165:7.**
Annual reports.
Aqueducts and aqueduct
companies, **165:7.**
Department, **159:43.**
Express companies, **159:33.**
Appeals, **25:5.**
Commercial motor vehicle
division, **25:12F.**
Death, magistrate's report to
department regarding,
38:11.
Examiners, reports, **25:4.**
False reports, **268:6.**
Fees for filing documents,
25:10B.
Inquests into deaths. See within
this heading, "Inquests into
deaths."
Name indicating that person is a
public service corporation,
use of report containing,
155:5.
Production of books and papers,
powers, **159:34.**
Public records, **25:12F.**
Railroad company stocks and
bonds, reports by public
utilities commission, **25:7.**
Telecommunications division,
25:12E½.
Recreational tramways,
jurisdiction over, **143:71S.**
Reduction in price or improvement
in quality of services enforced,
164:93.
Reduction of service, venue of
hearing, **25:4A.**
Regional transportation
authorities, resolution of
conflicts, **161B:16.**
Registered land, certificates of title
as to easements, **185:59.**
Reorganization of public utilities
commission, **25:2.**
Reparation to person paying
discriminatory rate, **159:14.**

**TELECOMMUNICATIONS AND
ENERGY DEPARTMENT**
—Cont'd

Reports.
Records, reports, and returns.
See within this heading,
"Records, reports, and
returns."
Restoration of services, fine for
failure to complete, **164:124G.**
Rules and regulations.
Authority to establish, **164:76C.**
Discontinuance of utility service,
164:124A, 164:124F.
Rulings and orders, **25:5, 25:12F.**
Appeal. See within this heading,
"Appeal."
Compliance, **159:16.**
Depreciation fund, **155:5A.**
Enforcement, **159:40.**
Fees for copies, **262:44.**
Rates and charges. See within
this heading, "Rates and
charges."
Securities issued pending
appeals of decisions,
validity, **25:5.**
Service, **159:37.**
Salary.
Commissioners, **25:2, 25:3.**
Frequency of payment, **149:148.**
Sales tax, exemption of production
facilities, **64H:6.**
Savings banks, deposit of funds,
155:3A.
Schedules.
Rates and charges. See within
this heading, "Rates and
charges."
School service motor carriers,
supervision, **159A:11A.**
Seal, **25:1.**
Season tickets of carriers subject
to approval of department,
159:18.
Secretary of commission, petition
for appeals to be filed, **25:5.**
Secretary of energy resources,
power and authority for
commercial and apartments
conservation service programs,
25A:11a.
Secured transactions.
See SECURED
TRANSACTIONS.
Securities.
Bonds and debentures. See
within this heading, "Bond
issues."
Stock and stockholders. See
within this heading, "Stock
and stockholders."

TELECOMMUNICATIONS AND ENERGY DEPARTMENT
—Cont'd

Seizure, **150B:4.**

Selectmen.

Aldermen and selectmen. See within this heading, "Aldermen and selectmen."

Service of process and papers.

Appeals from decision of department, **25:5.**

Carriers, service of orders of telecommunications and energy department, **159:37.**

Commission, service by employees, **159B:14.**

Rulings and orders, service on parties in interest, **25:5, 159:37.**

Subpoenas, **25:5A.**

Sick leave.

Additional assessments, **25:18 et seq.**

Special service or school service, regulation of carriers furnishing, **159A:11A.**

State finance.

See STATE FINANCE.

Statutes relating to carriers, compilation and annotation, **25:8.**

Steamboats.

See STEAMBOATS AND STEAMBOAT COMPANIES.

Stock and stockholders.

Amount which may be held by business corporations, **156:5.**

Auction sales of new shares of capital stock, **159:51.**

Determination by department as to amount of stock, **159:52.**

Exemption from securities act, **110A:402.**

Foreign corporations' securities based on holdings of local utilities, **181:10.**

Increase or reduction of, certificate, **158:39, 158:40.**

Ordering depreciation fund upon approval, **155:5A.**

Takeover bids, **110C:8, 110C:12.**

Validity of securities issued pending appeal of decisions, **25:5.**

Street railways, **161:1 et seq.**

See STREET RAILWAYS.

Subdivision control law, requirement prior to approval of plan, **41:81U.**

TELECOMMUNICATIONS AND ENERGY DEPARTMENT
—Cont'd

Subpoena, issuance, **25:5A.**

Superior courts.

Recovery of forfeiture for use of name indicating that person is public service corporation, **155:5.**

Request for appointment or discharge of employees, **271:40.**

Surveys.

Land surveys. See within this heading, "Land surveys."

Tables.

Expenditures, **25:8.**

Rate schedules, **159:19, 159:20.**

Street railway companies, tables and abstracts of returns, **161:139.**

Take-over bids as to banks, **110C:8, 110C:12.**

Tariffs.

Rates and charges. See within this heading, "Rates and charges."

Taxation.

Assessments. See within this heading, "Assessments."

Corporations owning and operating railway terminal facilities, **63:52A.**

Exemptions, **59:2B.**

Franchise tax, **63:52A.**

Returns, **62C:12.**

Sales tax, exemption of production facilities, **64H:6.**

Telecommunications and energy department, **25:1 et seq.**

Telecommunications division, **25:12E½.**

Telephone and telegraph companies, **166:1-166:43.**

See TELEPHONE AND TELEGRAPH COMPANIES.

Towing fees and rates, amounts authorized, **159B:6B, 266:120D.**

Towns.

Cities and towns. See within this heading, "Cities and towns."

Trackless trolleys, **163:1 et seq.**

See TRACKLESS TROLLEYS.

Transportation area board of trustees, powers, **161:147.**

Transport of hazardous waste, certification of licenses, **21C:7.**

Traveling expenses, **25:8.**

TELECOMMUNICATIONS AND ENERGY DEPARTMENT
—Cont'd

Trusts owning.

See BUSINESS TRUSTS.

Unclaimed or abandoned property, utility companies as persons required to file annual reports, **200A:1, 200A:7.**

Underground plant damage prevention system, investigations into, **164:76D.**

Uniform Securities Act, securities exempt from provisions, **110A:402.**

Venue of hearing for increase in rates or reduction of service, **25:4A.**

Wages.

Salary. See within this heading, "Salary."

Waterworks, **40:38-40:42, 165:1-165:11C.**

See WATERWORKS AND WATER SUPPLY.

Welfare and social services, financial services for utilities, **18:2.**

Wetlands, maintaining, repairing or replacing public utility lines through, **131:40.**

Wholesale electric company.

See WHOLESALE ELECTRIC COMPANY.

Witnesses, **25:5A, 25:12G.**

Commercial motor vehicle division, **25:12G.**

Oaths, **25:3, 25:5A.**

Wrongful use of name indicating public service, **155:4, 155:5.**

Zoning regulations.

Bond given to secure installation, **41:81U.**

Exemption, **25:10B, 40A:3.**

Filing fees for exemptions, **25:10B.**

Master plan, **41:81D.**

Municipal planning map, **41:81D, 41:81E.**

Subdivision control law, requirement prior to approval of plan, **41:81U.**

TELEPHONE AND TELEGRAPH COMPANIES, **166:1-166:43.**

Abuse prevention, emergency orders, **209A:5.**

Accounts and services, disclosure of information to public regarding, **167D:34.**

**TELEPHONE AND
TELEGRAPH COMPANIES**
—Cont'd

Aid, priority of emergency calls
for.
Party lines. See within this
heading, "Party lines,
priority of emergency calls
for aid."
Alcoholism treatment and
rehabilitation facilities, right
of patient to use telephone,
111B:11.
Aldermen and selectmen,
complaints, **159:24.**
Ambulance attendants, liability of
physicians and nurses for
emergency medical advice
communicated, **111C:13.**
Annoying calls, criminal offense,
269:14A.
Annual returns, **166:11-166:12A.**
Apparatus adapted to obtain
telecommunication services
fraudulently, manufacture,
166:42B.
Appropriations by municipal
corporations for telegraph
lines, **40:5.**
Arrested person, right to use
telephone, **276:33A.**
Assessments.
Special assessments.
See SPECIAL
ASSESSMENTS.
Telecommunications and energy
department. See within this
heading,
"Telecommunications and
energy department."
Attorney General.
Duties as to issuance of stock or
bonds, **166:5.**
Emergency services, proceedings
to require, **6A:18E.**
Rates and charges, **12:11E.**
Service records, right to demand
certain, **271:17B.**
Attorneys.
Attorney General. See within
this heading, "Attorney
General."
District and prosecuting
attorneys. See within this
heading, "District and
prosecuting attorneys."
Auction sale of new shares of
stock, **166:8.**
Automatic telephone dialing
system, common carriers,
159:19B to 159:19E.

**TELEPHONE AND
TELEGRAPH COMPANIES**
—Cont'd

Berkshire Mountains, protection of
watershed resources and
natural scenic qualities,
131:39A.
Bonds, notes, etc.
Attorney General's duties as to
issuance, **166:5.**
Disposition of proceeds,
166:4-166:6.
Enforcement of laws as to issue,
166:5.
Issue, **166:4-166:6.**
Penalty for violations as to
issue, **166:6.**
Pension and retirement system
funds, investment, **32:23.**
Stock and stockholders. See
within this heading, "Stock
and stockholders."
Borrowing money.
Debts. See within this heading,
"Debts."
Boston, sale of new shares of
stock, **166:7, 166:8.**
Business corporation law,
applicability, **156:2, 156B:3.**
Business statement as to in
returns, **166:11, 166:12A.**
Carriers, **159:19B-159:19E,
159B:2.**
Carrying charges for capital,
statement in condensed
return, **166:12A.**
Cellular telephones, radio utility
rates, **159:12C.**
Certain miscellaneous
corporations, organization
under chapter, **158:1.**
Charges.
Rates and charges. See within
this heading, "Rates and
charges."
Charitable organizations soliciting
contributions from public,
restrictions as to use of paid
telephone operators, **68:28.**
Chief accounting officer, returns
sworn, **166:11, 166:12A.**
Children and minors.
Employees and officers. See
within this heading,
"Employees and officers."
Cities.
Municipal corporations. See
within this heading,
"Municipal corporations."
Civil rights and discrimination.
Discrimination. See within this
heading, "Discrimination."

**TELEPHONE AND
TELEGRAPH COMPANIES**
—Cont'd

Clerks of cities and towns.
Certificate of sale or transfer of
locations filed, **166:15B.**
Copy of condensed return filed,
166:12A.
Coin-operated phones.
Pay phones. See within this
heading, "Pay phones."
Complaints by mayor, selectmen,
or customers, **159:24.**
Condensed returns, **166:12,
166:12A.**
"Conspicuous" nature of term or
clause in telegram, **106:1-201.**
Contract limiting liability for
negligence in transmitting,
receiving, or delivering
telegrams, **166:19.**
Convalescent or nursing homes to
install telephone, **111:72D.**
Credit unions.
See CREDIT UNIONS.
Crimes.
Offenses and penalties. See
within this heading,
"Offenses and penalties."
Damages for negligence in
transmitting, receiving, or
delivering telegrams, **166:19.**
Deaf persons, **166:15E.**
Debts.
Liability of president and
treasurer, **166:3.**
Limit, **166:2.**
Penalty upon director or officer
incurring illegally, **166:6.**
Statement of in annual return,
166:11.
Deceit.
Fraud and deceit. See within
this heading, "Fraud and
deceit."
Definitions, **6A:18A, 106:1-201,
149:1, 166:15E.**
Deposits and depositories, **158:16.**
Depreciation, statement in
condensed return, **166:12A.**
Directories.
Charge for directory assistance,
159:19, 159:19A.
Dental advertising, **112:52C.**
Priority of emergency calls on
party lines, directory to
contain copy of law,
166:15C.
Directors.
Debt, penalty for incurring
illegally, **166:6.**

TELEPHONE AND TELEGRAPH COMPANIES
—Cont'd

Directors —Cont'd
Dividends, penalty for issuance, **166:10.**
Issue of stock and bonds, penalty for violations, **166:6.**
Meeting of business corporation directors, authority to hold by telephone, **156B:59.**
Proceeds from issue of stock or bonds, violations as to disposition, **166:6.**
Disabled persons, **166:15E.**
Discrimination.
Telegraph company, **166:16-166:18.**
Telephone company, **166:13-166:15.**
District and prosecuting attorneys.
Interception of telephone communications to obtain evidence of crime, **272:99.**
Telephone company service records, right to demand, **271:17B.**
Dividends, **166:9, 166:10.**
Statement in returns, **166:11, 166:12A.**
Duty to receive and transmit telegrams, **166:16-166:18.**
Dwellings, posting notice of telephone number of owner or agent, **143:3S.**
Easements, **166:37.**
Private ways, easements for construction of electricity and telephone lines, **187:5.**
State forests, granting right of way through, **132:34A.**
Eavesdropping and wiretapping, **166:44, 272:99-272:101.**
Educational telecommunications.
See EDUCATIONAL COMMUNICATIONS COMMISSION.
Elections, telephone authorization to issue certificate to voter in polling place, **54:100.**
Electricians' law, applicability, **141:7.**
Elevators, installation, **143:71F.**
Emergencies.
Abuse prevention, emergency orders, **209A:5.**
Ambulance attendants, liability for medical advice communicated, **111C:13.**
Attorney General, proceedings to require emergency services, **6A:18E.**

TELEPHONE AND TELEGRAPH COMPANIES
—Cont'd

Emergencies —Cont'd
Definitions, **6A:18A.**
Enhanced 911 service, **6A:18A et seq.**
Party lines, **166:15C.**
Posting of emergency numbers at ice skating facilities, **45:25.**
Rates, fares, tolls, and charges, **159:19A.**
Schedule of services, **6A:18D, 166:14A.**
Statewide emergency telecommunications board, **6A:18B.**
Transmissions for requests for services, **6A:18C.**
Uniform number for emergency service, **166:14A.**
Employees and officers.
Directors. See within this heading, "Directors."
Influencing appointment or discharge, **271:40, 271:41.**
Joint trenches, work, **166:15D.**
President's liability for debts, **166:3.**
Railroad telegraphers, days of rest, **160:184.**
Telegraph offices, employment of children under sixteen, **149:60, 149:68, 149:78, 149:86.**
Telephone exchanges.
Girls under twenty-one, night employment, **149:66, 149:78.**
Hours of labor of women and children, **149:56, 149:57.**
Children under eighteen, **149:66, 149:67, 149:68, 149:78.**
Overtime pay, **151:1A.**
Treasurers. See within this heading, "Treasurer."
Enhanced 911 service, **6A:18A et seq.**
Examination or inspection.
Condensed return open to inspection, **166:12A.**
Utility department's inspection of, telephone company's service observing, **166:44.**
False.
Fraud and deceit. See within this heading, "Fraud and deceit."

TELEPHONE AND TELEGRAPH COMPANIES
—Cont'd

Females.
Employees and officers. See within this heading, "Employees and officers."
Filing and recording.
Annual returns, **166:11.**
Attorney general or district attorney, demand, **271:17B.**
Capital stock subscribed and paid, statement, **166:1.**
Certificate of sale or transfer of locations, **166:15B.**
Condensed return, **166:12A.**
Decision and certificate of department authorizing issue of stock or bonds, **166:4.**
Finances and financial matters, **166:1-166:10.**
Statement in returns of financial condition, **166:11, 166:12A.**
Fines.
Offenses and penalties. See within this heading, "Offenses and penalties."
Forests and forestry.
Clearance and disposal of slash, **48:18-48:20.**
Right of way through state forests, grant, **132:34A.**
Fraud and deceit.
Evasion of payment of telecommunication services, **266:37D, 266:75A, 266:75B.**
Explosives, use of telephone for false alarm, **269:14.**
Obtaining telecommunication services, **166:42A, 166:42B.**
Party line, false claim of emergency to secure use, **166:15C.**
Gaming purposes, **271:17, 271:17A, 271:47.**
Attorney General demanding telephone records, **271:17B.**
Occupant permitting use of telephone for, punishment, **271:17A.**
Racing information, **271:31A.**
Reinstallation after, **271:47.**
Second conviction, **271:10.**
General court, petition, **3:5.**
Hand telephone sets, charges for use, **166:15A.**
Hearings upon complaint by mayor, selectmen, or customers, **159:24.**
Herbicides, regulation of application, **132B:6B.**

**TELEPHONE AND
TELEGRAPH COMPANIES**
—Cont'd

Highways and streets.
Public ways. See within this
heading, "Public ways."
Ice-skating rinks, posting of
emergency numbers, **45:25.**
Incorporation and organization
under law as to certain
miscellaneous corporations,
158:1.
Indictments, informations, and
complaints.
Accused's right to use of
telephone, **276:33A.**
Stock or scrip, indictment of
telephone and telegraph
company directors for
unlawful issuance, **166:10.**
Injunctions.
Lines unlawfully erected,
166:26, 166:33.
Remedies against service
observing interception or
monitoring, **166:44.**
Injury caused by poles, liability,
166:42.
Inspection.
Examination or inspection. See
within this heading,
"Examination or inspection."
Instruments adapted to obtain
fraudulent telecommunication
service, **166:42B.**
Insurance company investments,
175:63.
Interest in company, public
utilities commissioners
forbidden to have, **25:3.**
Interest on money.
Capital, condensed return to
show amount accrued for
interest, **166:12A.**
Deposits of customers, interest,
158:16.
Intoxication, right to phone call of
person detained, **111B:8.**
Joint trench, employees engaged to
perform work, **166:15D.**
Jurisdiction of telecommunications
and energy department,
159:12.
Jury commissioner for
Commonwealth.
See JURY COMMISSIONER
FOR COMMONWEALTH.
Landlord's failure to furnish
telephone service, penalty,
186:14.

**TELEPHONE AND
TELEGRAPH COMPANIES**
—Cont'd

Licenses and permits.
Metropolitan District
Commission, maintenance of
transmission lines, **92:43.**
Public ways, telephones and
booths, **85:8.**
Limitation of liability for
negligence in transmitting,
receiving, or delivering
telegrams, **166:19.**
Limited-access ways, pay phones,
85:2D.
Limit of debt, **166:2.**
Local service providers.
Unauthorized switching, **93:109
to 93:113.**
Locations, sale or transfer,
166:15B.
Long distance service providers.
Unauthorized switching, **93:109
to 93:113.**
Lottery ticket sales by telephone,
10:24.
Mayor, complaint, **159:24.**
Metropolitan districts, licensing
maintenance of transmission
lines, **92:43.**
Mobile radio telephone utility
companies, **159:12A to
159:12E.**
See MOBILE RADIO
TELEPHONE UTILITY
COMPANIES.
Motor carriers of property,
exception from laws, **159B:2.**
Motor vehicles.
See MOTOR VEHICLES.
Municipal corporations.
Appropriations for telegraph
lines, **40:5.**
Clerks of cities and towns. See
within this heading, "Clerks
of cities and towns."
Emergency telephone service,
contracts, **166:14A.**
Hearings on complaints, **159:24.**
Reduced rates, **159:15.**
Negligence in transmitting,
receiving or delivering
telegrams, liability, **166:19.**
Newspapers, publication of notice
of sale of new stock, **166:8.**
Notes.
Bonds, notes, etc. See within
this heading, "Bonds, notes,
etc."
Notice.
Cellular telephones, notice in
fluctuation in radio utility
rates, **159:12C.**

**TELEPHONE AND
TELEGRAPH COMPANIES**
—Cont'd

Notice —Cont'd
Cutting wires, notice before,
166:39-166:41.
Hearing upon complaint by
mayor, selectmen, or
customers, **159:24.**
Increase of capital stock, **166:7.**
Notice of switch in local or long
distance exchange carriers,
93:111.
Sale of new shares of stock,
166:8.
Nursing home residents, access to
telephones, **111:72D.**
Offenses and penalties.
Annoying phone calls, **269:14A.**
Arrested person's right to use
telephone, **276:33A.**
Avoiding payment for
telecommunication services,
266:37D.
Cutting wires without notice,
166:40, 166:41.
Debt, director or officer
incurring illegally, **166:6.**
Disclosure or publication of
information as to fraudulent
evasion of payment for
telecommunication systems,
266:37D.
Discrimination by telegraph
company, **166:18.**
District and prosecuting
attorneys, interception of
telephone communications
to obtain evidence of crime,
272:99.
Eavesdropping, **166:44,
272:99-272:101.**
False claim of emergency to
secure use of party line,
166:15C.
Fraud and deceit. See within
this heading, "Fraud and
deceit."
Gaming purposes. See within
this heading, "Gaming
purposes."
High voltage lines, prohibited
acts close, **166:21B.**
Indictments, informations and
complaints. See within this
heading, "Indictments,
informations, and
complaints."
Issue of stock, bonds, or scrip
dividends, **166:6, 166:10.**
Negligence in delivering,
receiving, or transmitting
messages, damages, **166:19.**

**TELEPHONE AND
TELEGRAPH COMPANIES**
—Cont'd

Offenses and penalties —Cont'd
Proceeds from issue of stock and
bonds, violations as to
disposition, **166:6.**
Refusal to yield use of party line
for emergency call, **166:15C.**
Returns, failure to make,
166:12.
Time of filing and receipt of
messages, failure of
telegraph company to place
upon copies, **166:20.**
Use to make annoying calls,
269:14A.
Wiretapping, **166:44,
272:99-272:101.**
Officers.
Employees and officers. See
within this heading,
"Employees and officers."
Operating expenses, statement in
condensed return, **166:12A.**
Other telegraph companies not to
be discriminated against,
166:16-166:18.
Party lines, priority of emergency
calls for aid.
False claim of emergency,
offense and penalty,
166:15C.
Refusal to yield use of line,
offense and penalty,
166:15C.
Par value of stock must be paid in
cash prior to issue, **166:9,
166:10.**
Pay phones.
Convalescent or nursing homes,
111:72D.
Definition, public coin and
coinless telephone service,
166:15E.
Fraud, **266:75, 266:75B.**
Limited-access ways, **85:2D.**
Penalties.
Offenses and penalties. See
within this heading,
"Offenses and penalties."
Permits.
Licenses and permits. See
within this heading,
"Licenses and permits."
Petition to general court as to
corporate matters, **3:5.**
Pipelines, appeal from
commissioner's determination
as to valuation, **59:38A, 59:41,
59:42.**

**TELEPHONE AND
TELEGRAPH COMPANIES**
—Cont'd

Poles.
Installation of new poles,
164:34B.
Police.
Gambling, approval of
reinstallation of telephones
used, **271:47.**
Persons held by police, telephone
calls, **276:33A.**
Utility poles, removal of
communication equipment,
166:22J.
Preferences and priorities.
Party lines, priority of
emergency calls on. See
within this heading, "Party
lines, priority of emergency
calls for aid."
President's liability for debts,
166:3.
Private ways, construction of
electricity and telephone
service lines, **187:5.**
Property, telegraphic messages,
159B:2.
Prosecuting attorneys.
District and prosecuting
attorneys. See within this
heading, "District and
prosecuting attorneys."
Publication of notice of sale of new
stock upon increase, **166:8.**
Public coin and coinless telephone
service, defined, **166:15E.**
Public telephones.
Pay phones. See within this
heading, "Pay phones."
Public ways.
Permit for maintaining public
telephones and booths, **85:8.**
Signs on limited access
highways indicating
availability of telephones,
85:2D.
Wires under streets, regulations,
166:30, 166:32.
Racing information, prohibition as
to transmission, **271:31A.**
Railroads.
See RAILROADS.
Rates and charges.
Another telegraph company,
charges for messages
received, **166:17, 166:18.**
Attorney general, **12:11E.**
Cellular telephones, radio utility
rates, **159:12C.**
Changes in schedule rates,
159:20.

**TELEPHONE AND
TELEGRAPH COMPANIES**
—Cont'd

Rates and charges —Cont'd
Cities, reduced rates, **159:15.**
Commonwealth, reduced rates,
159:15.
Complaint by mayor, selectmen,
or customers, public
hearing, **159:24.**
Directory assistance, **159:19,
159:19A.**
Discrimination prohibited,
166:16-166:18.
Emergencies, **159:19A.**
Free or reduced rate service,
159:15.
Hand telephone sets, charges,
166:15A.
Hearing on complaint, notice,
159:24.
Mail, charges for dispatches
received, **166:17, 166:18.**
Reduced direct dialed directory
assistance call allowance,
159:19A.
Schedules of rates, **159:19,
159:20.**
Towns, reduced rates, **159:15.**
Receipts and expenditures,
statement in returns, **166:11,
166:12A.**
Records, reports, and returns.
Annual returns, **166:11-166:12A.**
Attorney general or district
attorneys may demand
certain, **271:17B.**
Condensed returns, **166:12,
166:12A.**
Filing and recording. See within
this heading, "Filing and
recording."
Service observing activity,
annual reports, **166:44.**
Retail installment sales by catalog,
255D:9.
Retirement systems and pensions,
investment of funds, **32:23.**
Revenue department.
See REVENUE DEPARTMENT
AND COMMISSIONER.
Sale.
Exemptions from sales tax,
64H:6.
Lottery tickets sold by phone,
10:24.
New shares of stock, **166:7,
166:8.**
Property to another company,
sale, **166:15B.**
Retail installment sales by
catalog, **255D:9.**

TELEPHONE AND TELEGRAPH COMPANIES
—Cont'd

Sales tax, exemptions, **64H:6.**

Scrip dividends, **166:9, 166:10.**

Secretary of state.

State secretary. See within this heading, "State secretary."

Security deposits.

Deposits, **158:16.**

Selectmen and aldermen, complaints, **159:24.**

Sentence and punishment.

Offenses and penalties. See within this heading, "Offenses and penalties."

Signs on limited access highways indicating availability of telephone, **85:2D.**

Slash, clearance and disposal, **48:18-48:20.**

State forests, granting right of way through, **132:34A.**

State secretary.

Certificate of decision of department upon issue of stock or bonds filed, **166:4.**

Statement of capital stock subscribed and paid filed, **166:1.**

Statewide emergency telecommunications board, **6A:18B.**

Stock and stockholders.

Amount authorized to be stated in annual return, **166:11.**

Attorney general's enforcement of laws as to issuance, **166:5, 166:6.**

Boston, sale of new shares of stock, **166:7, 166:8.**

Carrying charges, statement in condensed return of amounts accrued, **166:12A.**

Consent to sale or transfer of property, **166:15B.**

Debt limited to one half amount paid, **166:2.**

Dividends. See within this heading, "Dividends."

Enforcement of laws as to issue of stock or bonds, **166:5.**

Increase of, disposition of new shares, **166:7, 166:8.**

Indictment of telephone and telegraph company directors for unlawful issuance of stock or scrip, **166:10.**

Issue, **166:4-166:6.**

New shares of capital stock to be offered to stockholders, **166:7, 166:8.**

TELEPHONE AND TELEGRAPH COMPANIES
—Cont'd

Stock and stockholders —Cont'd

Par value must be paid in cash prior to issue, **166:9, 166:10.**

Penalty for violations as to issue, **166:6.**

Proceeds from issue, disposition, **166:4-166:6.**

Not to be divided among stockholders, **166:9, 166:10.**

Proportion which must be subscribed and paid prior to construction, **166:1.**

Railroad corporations, holding stock of telegraph companies, **160:65.**

Statement of capital stock subscribed and paid to be filed with secretary of state, **166:1.**

Subscription rights to new shares, **166:7.**

Subscriber's remedies against service observing, interception, or monitoring, **166:44.**

Sunday, work permitted, **136:6.**

Superior and supreme judicial courts.

Discrimination, enforcement of laws against, **166:15.**

Issue of stock or bonds, enforcement of laws, **166:5.**

Subscriber's remedies against interception or monitoring, **166:44.**

Surrender of use of party line for emergency call, refusal of, offense and penalty, **166:15C.**

Taxation.

See TAXATION.

TDD/TTY device for deaf persons, **166:15E.**

Telecommunications and energy department.

Attachments to facilities of utilities, regulation, **166:25A.**

Consent to issue of stock, bonds, etc., **166:4.**

Hearings upon complaint by mayor, selectmen, or customers, **159:24.**

Interest in company, commissioner for bidder to have, **25:3.**

Jurisdiction, **159:12.**

Returns, filing, **166:11, 166:12A.**

TELEPHONE AND TELEGRAPH COMPANIES
—Cont'd

Telecommunications and energy department —Cont'd

Service observing, interception, on monitoring of conversations, rights and remedies, **166:44.**

Universal emergency telephone service, filing of rates, rules and regulations, **166:14A.**

Theft of telecommunications service and equipment, **166:42A, 166:42B.**

Time of filing and receipt of telegram to appear on copies, **166:20.**

Towns.

Municipal corporations. See within this heading, "Municipal corporations."

Transfer.

Sale. See within this heading, "Sale."

Treasurer.

Issue of stock or bonds, violations, **166:6.**

Liability for indebtedness of company, **166:3.**

Penalty for incurring debt illegally, **166:6.**

Proceeds from issue of stock or bonds, violations as to disposition, **166:6.**

Returns sworn, **166:11, 166:12A.**

Underground location used jointly with electric company, performance of work by employees, **166:15D.**

Uniform emergency service number, assignment, **166:14A.**

Unincorporated owners, application of chapter, **166:43.**

Universal emergency telephone service, contracts, **166:14A.**

Wetlands, maintenance, repair, or replacement of telephone or telegraph lines, **131:40.**

Wiretapping, **166:44, 272:99-272:101.**

Yielding use of party line for emergency call, refusal of, offense and penalty, **166:15C.**

TELEPHONE OPERATORS.

District attorney, appointment, **12:19.**

TELEVISION.

See RADIO AND TELEVISION.

TELLERS CHECKS.

Defined, **106:3-104.**

TELLERS CHECKS —Cont'd
Effect on obligation for which taken, **106:3-310.**
Lost, destroyed or stolen, **106:3-309, 106:3-312.**
Negotiable instruments.
　Generally, **106:3-101 to 106:3-605.**
　　See NEGOTIABLE INSTRUMENTS.
Refusal to pay, **106:3-411.**

TELLERS OF ELECTIONS.
Appointment to court ballots, **54:12.**
Primaries, **53:29.**
Salaries and compensation, **53:29.**

TEMPERANCE SOCIETIES, 180:1-180:11.
Incorporation, **180:1 et seq.**
Taxation.
　Lists of property, **59:29.**
　Tax exemptions, **59:5.**

TEMPERATURE.
Tanning facilities, **111:210.**

TEMPLETON.
Congressional district, **57:1.**
District court, **218:1.**
Medical examiner district, **38:1.**
Senatorial district, **57:3.**

TEMPORARY INJUNCTIONS. See INJUNCTIONS.

TENANTS.
Estates.
　Joint tenants.
　　See JOINT TENANTS AND TENANTS IN COMMON.
Landlord and tenant.
　See LANDLORD AND TENANT.

TENDER OFFER.
Corporations.
　See CORPORATIONS.

TENDER OF PAYMENT.
Acceptance, **232A:2.**
Breach of condition of mortgage, tender after, **244:19.**
Cosmetics, tender as affecting duty of vendor to furnish sample, **94:304.**
Costs of actions.
　See COSTS OF ACTION.
Dismissal of action by stipulation upon acceptance, **232A:2.**
Effect, **232A:1.**
Execution, tender on redemption from levy, **236:33, 236:34, 236:40.**
Legal tender, states' power to define, restricted to gold and silver coin, **US Const Art 1 Sec 10 cl 1.**

TENDER OF PAYMENT —Cont'd
Lien cases, tender, **232A:3.**
Loans of less than one thousand dollars, discharge, **140:91.**
Mortgage foreclosure.
　See MORTGAGE FORECLOSURE.
Motor vehicle sales contracts, tender required for redemption after repossession, **255B:20B.**
Nonresident tax title owners, effect of tender of payment to agent, **60:47.**
Rent after notice to quit, effect of tender, **186:11, 186:12.**
Sales under commercial code.
　See SALES UNDER COMMERCIAL CODE.
Stipulation of dismissal upon acceptance, **232A:2.**
Tax redemption, tender, **60:47, 60:62.**
Towns, tender as to claims against, **41:51.**
Trespass, involuntary, effect of tender, **242:8.**
Trustee process proceeding, tender, **246:29.**
Weekly wage payment provisions, defense to complaint for violation, **149:150.**

TENDER RAILROAD.
Drawbridges.
　See DRAWBRIDGES.
Unlawful riding, **160:220.**

TENEMENT HOUSES, 144:2 et seq., 145:2 et seq.
Acceptance of chapter, defined, **144:2, 145:2.**
Alcoves, defined, **144:2.**
Arson, **266:1.**
　Attempts, **266:5A.**
Attic defined, **144:2.**
Basements and cellars, defined, **144:2, 145:2.**
Boarding house, defined, **145:2.**
Board of health, defined, **144:2, 145:2.**
Building department, defined, **144:2, 145:2.**
Building inspector, defined, **144:2, 145:2.**
Bylaws, defined, **145:2.**
Cellar, defined, **144:2, 145:2.**
Charter, defined, **144:2.**
Cities, tenement houses in, **144:2 et seq.**
City and town clerks.
　Agent for service of process, **145:60B.**

TENEMENT HOUSES —Cont'd
City and town clerks —Cont'd
　Filing and indexing of owner and lessee names, **145:59.**
　Registration of name of owner of tenement posted for violations, **145:60A.**
City solicitor, defined, **144:2.**
Corner lots, defined, **144:2, 145:2.**
Courts, defined, **144:2, 145:2.**
Definitions, **144:2, 145:2.**
Discrimination in leasing on account of age, sex, or ancestry, **151B:4.**
Existing, defined, **144:2, 145:2ql.**
Expectoration, **270:14, 270:15.**
Fee for registration of owners or lessee's name, **145:59, 262:34.**
Fire.
　Arson. See within this heading, "Arson."
Fireproofing, defined, **145:2.**
Fireproof tenement house, defined, **145:2.**
First class construction, defined, **144:2.**
First story, defined, **144:2.**
Front, defined, **144:2, 145:2.**
Front yard, defined, **144:2, 145:2.**
Half story, defined, **144:2, 145:2.**
Health department, defined, **144:2.**
Height, defined, **144:2.**
Height regulations, defined, **144:2, 145:2.**
Industrial establishments, tenement house workrooms, **149:1.**
Interior lot, defined, **144:2, 145:2.**
Is occupied, defined, **144:2, 145:2.**
Knowledge.
　Notice and knowledge. See within this heading, "Notice and knowledge."
Life insurance companies, housing projects, **175:66A.**
Lodging house, defined, **145:2.**
Lots, defined, **144:2.**
Notice and knowledge.
　Fee for filing notice by owners or lessee of tenement house, **262:34.**
　Name, address, and telephone number of owner or agent, posting, **143:3S.**
　Posting of notice of name, address, and telephone number of owner or agent, **143:3S.**
Service of process and papers.
　See within this heading, "Service of process and papers."

TENEMENT HOUSES —Cont'd

Nuisances.

Definitions, **144:2, 145:2.**

Prostitution, **139:4.**

Occupied spaces, defined, **144:2, 145:2.**

Ordinances, defined, **144:2.**

Owner's name to be registered, **145:59.**

Papers.

Service of process and papers. See within this heading, "Service of process and papers."

Prostitution, tenement houses used, **139:4.**

Public halls, defined, **144:2, 145:2.**

Rear of lot defined, **145:2.**

Rear tenements, defined, **144:2.**

Registered mail, service of process and notices, **145:60.**

Registration of name of owner or lessee, **145:59, 262:34.**

Regulations, defined, **144:2, 145:2.**

Second class construction, defined, **144:2.**

Service of process and papers.

Agents, service, **145:60.**

Notices, **145:60.**

Owner, **145:60, 145:60A-145:60C.**

Shall, defined, **145:2.**

Share, defined, **144:2.**

Side yard, defined, **144:2, 145:2.**

Stair halls, defined, **144:2, 145:2.**

Street defined, **145:2.**

Temporary playgrounds in neighborhood, **45:17.**

Thereafter, defined, **144:2, 145:2.**

Third class construction, defined, **144:2.**

Town clerks.

City and town clerks. See within this heading, "City and town clerks."

Towns, tenement houses in, **145:2 et seq.**

Utility service, procedure for discontinuation, **164:124D.**

Wooden buildings defined, **145:2.**

Yards, defined, **144:2, 145:2.**

TENNESSEE VALLEY AUTHORITY.

Sinking funds for state bonds, permissible investments, **29:49.**

TENNIS.

Bribery, **271:39A.**

Municipal indebtedness, tennis court construction, **44:7.**

TENNIS —Cont'd

Sunday sports, licensing, **136:4.**

TENT CATERPILLARS.

Suppression, **132:11-132:27.**

Transportation, **266:119.**

TENTS.

Peddling or gaming near camp meeting, **272:39.**

TENURE AND SENIORITY.

Appeals court clerks, **211A:6.**

Applications for tenure by local officeholders, **41:127-41:131.**

Appointive officers of cities, towns, and districts, **41:126-41:132.**

Cities and towns, appointive officers, **41:126-41:132.**

City and town clerks, **41:19B-41:19E.**

See CITY AND TOWN CLERKS.

Civil service.

See CIVIL SERVICE.

Corporate officers, determination of tenure, **155:7, 156:13.**

Death of department head or commissioner, tenure of substitute in event, **30:6.**

Department heads in cities and towns, applications for tenure for persons serving, **41:131.**

Discrimination, observance of terms of bona fide seniority system, **151B:4.**

District offices, applications for tenure by persons holding, **41:130.**

Education.

Schools and education. See within this heading, "Schools and education."

Eligibility for tenure, **41:127.**

Fire departments.

See FIRE DEPARTMENTS.

House of representatives in general court, presiding officer pending election of speaker to be senior member, **3:3.**

Librarians, **71:38H.**

Limitations on tenure for local appointive officers, **41:132.**

Military affairs.

See MILITARY AFFAIRS.

Militia officers, **33:27.**

Office, tenure of.

See TERM OF OFFICE.

Public officers and employees, exemption of certain managerial positions, **30:46F.**

Regional school districts, **71:42B.**

Revocation of acceptance of statute by city or town as affecting tenure of teachers, **4:4A.**

TENURE AND SENIORITY —Cont'd

Schools and education.

Librarians, **71:38H.**

Regional school districts, **71:42B.**

Revocation of acceptance of statute as affecting tenure for tenures, **4:4A.**

State college presidents, rights acquired, **73:16.**

State-operated schools, tenure of faculty, **74:42C, 75:4, 75:14, 75B:10.**

Superintendents of schools, **71:41, 71:63.**

Teachers. See within this heading, "Teachers."

Vocational schools, **74:22E.**

State college presidents, rights acquired, **73:16.**

State-operated schools, tenure for faculty, **74:42C, 75:4, 75:14.**

Superintendents of schools, **71:41, 71:63.**

Teachers.

School committee granting tenure to certain teachers, **71:41.**

State-operated schools, **74:42C, 75:4, 75:14.**

Towns, effect of revocation of acceptance of statute, **4:4A.**

Trustees of higher education, award of tenure, **15A:10, 75:4, 75:14.**

University of Massachusetts. See within this heading, "University of Massachusetts."

Vocational school teachers and employees, **74:22E.**

Towns, effect of revocation of acceptance of statute, **4:4A.**

Trustees of higher educational institutions, award of tenure, **15A:10, 75:4, 75:14.**

Union superintendents of schools, **71:63.**

University of Massachusetts.

Executive sessions of trustees may consider faculty tenure, **75:4.**

Trustees to establish policy on faculty tenure, **75:14.**

TERM DEPOSITS.

See CERTIFICATES OF DEPOSIT.

TERM FEE.

See COSTS OF ACTION.

TERMINAL ILLNESS.

Registered nurses, pronouncement of death of terminally ill patients, **46:9.**

Viatical settlements, **175:212 to 175:223.**

See VIATICAL SETTLEMENTS.

TERMINALS.

Architectural barriers against handicapped persons, prohibition, **22:13A.**

Aviation terminals, **90:35 et seq.**

See AIRPORTS AND LANDING FIELDS.

Definition, **90:1.**

Discrimination, **272:92A, 272:98.**

Express company terminals, lighting, ventilation, and cleanliness, **149:113.**

Offenses on premises, **161:94A, 161:95.**

Railroads.

Boston terminal corporation.

See BOSTON TERMINAL CORPORATION.

Taking stock and securities, **160:70.**

Street railways, termini to be stated in agreement of association, **161:4.**

See STREET RAILWAYS.

Taxation of corporations owning and operating railway terminals, **63:52A.**

Trackless trolleys, termini to be stated in agreement of association, **163:4.**

TERMINATION OF PARENTAL RIGHTS.

Abused and neglected children, **119:26.**

Adoption of children, **210:3.**

TERMINATION STATEMENTS FOR SECURED TRANSACTIONS, 106:9-404.

Failure to provide termination statement within proper time, penalty, **106:9-404.**

Fixtures, special provisions for filing, **106:9-409.**

Forms, **106:9-507.**

TERM INSURANCE.
See LIFE INSURANCE.

TERM OF COURT.
See SESSIONS OF COURT.

TERM OF OFFICE.

Accident and sickness insurance company, directors' term of office as affected by conversion to mutual company, **175:19D.**

TERM OF OFFICE —Cont'd

Alcoholic liquors, terms of members of local licensing boards regulating, **138:5.**

Aldermen.

See ALDERMEN AND SELECTMEN.

Appeals Court clerk, **211A:6.**

Attorney general, **12:1.**

Auditors, masters, and referees, **221:53.**

Completion of business upon expiration of commission, **221:54.**

Bar examiners, **221:35.**

Building regulations and standards, state board, **143:93.**

Capital planning commission, **41:106B.**

City and town auditors, **41:1, 41:48.**

City and town clerks, **41:1, 41:12.**

Beginning of term, **41:107.**

Permanent tenure, **41:19B-41:19E.**

Clerks of court, **221:3.**

Assistant clerks, **221:4.**

Conservation of soil, water and related resources, commission, **21:19.**

Constitution of Massachusetts.

See CONSTITUTION OF MASSACHUSETTS.

Constitution of the United States.

See CONSTITUTION OF THE UNITED STATES.

Co-operative bank board of directors, **170:9.**

Corporations.

Clerk or secretary, **156:22, 158:18-158:20.**

Determination of tenure, **155:7, 156:13.**

Officers and directors, **156:22, 156B:50, 158:19.**

County commissioners, **34:4, 54:158.**

Court officers, **221:72.**

Credit unions, term of office of directors, **171:9.**

Death of elected officer prior to beginning of term, **54:145.**

Disability commissions, cities and towns, **40:8J.**

District attorney, **12:12.**

Elections, **53:48.**

Emergency medical care advisory board members, **111C:7.**

Fire service commission members, **6:165B.**

TERM OF OFFICE —Cont'd

Gambling advisory commission members, **12B:2.**

General Court.

Clerks, **3:12, 3:13.**

Members, **3:9.**

Governor, **53:48.**

See GOVERNOR.

Grand jury.

See GRAND JURY.

Hazardous waste advisory committee, members, **21C:3.**

Hazardous waste site cleanup professionals, board members, **21A:19A.**

Highways.

See HIGHWAYS AND STREETS.

Lieutenant governor, **6:2 et seq., 53:48.**

Low-level radioactive waste management board, **111H:3.**

Massachusetts Centers of Excellence Corporation, Board of Directors, **40J:12.**

Masters.

Auditors, masters, and referees. See within this heading, "Auditors, masters, and referees."

Medical examiners, **38:1, 38:2.**

Mentally ill.

See MENTALLY ILL AND RETARDED PERSONS.

Model water and sewer commission board members, **40N:4.**

Mortgage review board members, **167:14A.**

Municipal officers, charter provisions, **43B:20.**

Municipal planning board member, vacancy in unexpired term, **41:81A.**

Pesticide control.

Board of pesticide control, **132B:3.**

Programs director, pesticide, **132B:4.**

Physician assistant programs, term of members of board of approval and certification, **112:9F.**

President of United States, **US Const Art 2 Sec 2 cl 1.**

Beginning and ending, **US Const Art 2 Sec 2 cl 1; Amend 20 Sec 1.**

Compensation not to be altered, **US Const Art 2 Sec 1 cl 7.**

More than two terms, forbidden, **US Const Amend 22.**

TERM OF OFFICE —Cont'd
Public administrators.
   See EXECUTORS AND
      ADMINISTRATORS.
Public health council members,
   17:3.
Racing commission of state, **6:48.**
Referees.
   Auditors, masters, and referees.
      See within this heading,
      "Auditors, masters, and
      referees."
Registers and registries of deeds,
   36:2, 54:157.
Registrar of voters, **51:15, 51:17,
   51:21.**
   Assistant registrars, **51:22.**
Repeal as affecting, **281:7.**
Representative in Congress, **US
   Const Art 1 Sec 2 cl 1; 20th
   Amend.**
Savings banks, **168:9, 168:10.**
Schools and education.
   Regional district school
      committee members, **54:162.**
   Superintendent of schools,
      71:41.
Secretary of state, **10:1, 53:48.**
Senator, **US Const Art 1 Sec 3 cl
   1; 17th Amend, 20th Amend.**
Sheriffs, **37:1, 54:159.**
Small business loan review boards,
   167:14C.
State auditor, **11:1.**
State Ethics Commission, **268B:2.**
Supreme court justice, **US Const
   Art 3 Sec 1.**
Supreme judicial court.
   Clerk, **221:3.**
   Employees, **221:72.**
Tax assessors, **41:1, 41:22, 41:24,
   41:25.**
   Assistant assessors, **41:1,
   41:25A.**
Trust company directors, **172:13.**
United States President.
   President of United States. See
      within this heading,
      "President of United States."
Vice-President, **US Const Art 2
   Sec 1 cl 1; 20th Amend.**
Women veterans advisory
   committee, members, **115:2.**
Zoning and planning or survey
   board members, **41:73,
   41:81A.**

TERM PAPERS.
Sale or preparation of term paper
   to be used by another, **271:50.**

TERMS FOR YEARS.
Estates for years.
   See ESTATES FOR YEARS.

TERMS FOR YEARS —Cont'd
Life estates.
   See LIFE ESTATES,
      REMAINDERS, AND
      REVERSIONS.

TERM SHARES OR DEPOSITS.
Credit unions, **171:32.**

TERNS.
Defiling water supply, prevention,
   111:174A.

**TERRITORIES AND
   DEPENDENCIES OF
   UNITED STATES.**
Branch offices of banks, **167C:7.**
Congress to have exclusive
   jurisdiction over territories,
   US Const Art 4 Sec 3 cl 2.
Employment security dependency
   allowances for children,
   151A:29.
Income tax credit or deduction for
   taxes due, **62:6.**
Judicial notice of law, **233:70.**
Life insurance companies,
   investments, **175:66B.**
State as including, **4:7.**
United States as including, **4:7.**
Use tax exemptions, **64I:7.**

**TESTAMENTARY ADDITIONS
   TO TRUSTS ACT, 203:3B.**

TESTATOR.
See WILLS.

TEST BORINGS.
Construction of public works as
   including, **149:27D.**

TESTE.
Land court processes, teste, **185:4.**
Writs, issuance, **223:20.**

TESTIMONIAL DINNERS.
Public officers and employees,
   268:9A.

TESTIMONY, 233:1 et seq.
See WITNESSES.

TESTS.
See EXAMINATION,
   INSPECTION, OR
   INVESTIGATION.

TETANUS.
College students, immunization,
   76:15C.
School children, immunization,
   76:15.

TETRAHYDROCANNABINOLS.
Controlled dangerous substance,
   94C:1, 94C:31.

TEWKSBURY.
Birth and death records, transfer
   to town clerk, **46:20.**
Congressional district, **57:1.**
District court, **218:1.**
Hospital.
   See TEWKSBURY HOSPITAL.
Medical examiner district, **38:1.**
Senatorial district, **57:3.**

**TEWKSBURY HOSPITAL, 122:1
   et seq.**
Abandoned, lost, and unclaimed
   property.
   Funds of patients, disposition,
      122:6-122:9.
   Moneys represented by
      bankbooks, **122:9.**
   Valuables of patients, **122:8.**
Admission to, **122:11, 122:14.**
Agents and agency.
   Delegation of power, **122:1.**
   Investment of funds, **122:5.**
Banks and banking.
   Cooperative banks, deposit of
      patient funds, **122:6.**
   Duty to give information as to
      inmate funds, **122:22.**
   Inmate funds, deposit and
      disposition, **122:6-122:9.**
   Trust companies. See within this
      heading, "Trust companies."
Bequests, **122:5.**
Board of trustees.
   See TRUSTS AND TRUSTEES.
Certificates from appropriate
   department as to admission,
   122:11.
Children and minors.
   Correctional institutions. See
      within this heading,
      "Correctional institutions."
Contagious diseases.
   Diseased persons. See within
      this heading, "Diseased
      persons."
Contracts and agreements, **40:4,
   122:15.**
Correctional institutions.
   Care of prisoner disabled at time
      of discharge, **127:151.**
   Pregnant female prisoners not to
      be removed to hospital,
      127:118.
Dead bodies of inmates, disposition
   of, for anatomical purposes,
   113:1-113:5.
Deaths, record and returns, **46:20.**
Department of public health,
   regulation by, **122:1.**
Devises, **122:5.**

TEWKSBURY HOSPITAL
—Cont'd

Discharge and release, **122:10-122:15.**
Contract for employment, **122:15.**
Diseased persons.
Admission and removal, **122:13, 122:14.**
Dangerous diseases, **122:13.**
Employees.
Officers and employees. See within this heading, "Officers and employees."
Enforcement of rules, **122:4.**
Executor or administrator, payment of expenses, **122:14.**
Friends, removal for support, **122:12.**
Funds and property of inmates.
Banks and banking. See within this heading, "Banks and banking."
Control and investment, **122:5.**
Trust companies. See within this heading, "Trust companies."
Unclaimed funds and property, **122:7, 122:8.**
Gifts, **122:5.**
Governor and council, appointment of trustees, **122:2.**
Health boards, departments, and officers.
Certificate of health board or officer for admission, **122:11.**
Number and terms of board of trustees, **122:2.**
Superintendent of hospital, **122:3.**
Inpatient and outpatient services authorized, **122:1.**
Intoxicating liquors or articles, penalty for possession, **122:23.**
Investments, **122:5, 122:6.**
Legacies, **122:5.**
Legal settlement, removal to place, **122:12.**
Local health board, admission of person on certificate, **122:11.**
Lost property.
Abandoned, lost, and unclaimed property. See within this heading, "Abandoned, lost, and unclaimed property."
Medical director, superintendent may be, **122:3.**
Minors.
Correctional institutions. See within this heading, "Correctional institutions."
Officers and employees, **122:3.**
Agents. See within this heading, "Agents and agency."

TEWKSBURY HOSPITAL
—Cont'd

Officers and employees —Cont'd
Inmates as employees, **122:15.**
Transfer, **18:4.**
Payment of expenses for maintenance, **122:14, 122:16.**
Penal institutions.
Correctional institutions. See within this heading, "Correctional institutions."
Property.
Funds and property of inmates. See within this heading, "Funds and property of inmates."
Public officers and employees.
Officers and employees. See within this heading, "Officers and employees."
Records of disposition of patients' unclaimed valuables, **122:8.**
Release.
Discharge and release. See within this heading, "Discharge and release."
Removal and transfer of patients.
Dangerous disease, patients infected, **122:13.**
Legal settlement, patient removal to place, **122:12.**
Rules and regulations, **122:4.**
Sale of unclaimed property of patient, **122:8.**
Settlement, removal to place of legal settlement, **122:12.**
Smallpox, admission of victims, **122:4.**
Statutes distributed to superintendent, **5:3.**
Superintendent, **122:3.**
Records and returns, **46:20.**
Statutes distributed, **5:3.**
Vital statistic blank forms to be furnished, **46:16.**
Support of inmates.
Kindred's liability, **122:14, 122:16.**
Unclaimed funds or property used, **122:7-122:9.**
Town's power to contract for treatment of patient, **40:4.**
Transfer.
Officers or employees, **18:4.**
Patients.
Removal and transfer of patients. See within this heading, "Removal and transfer of patients."
Transitional assistance department.
Admission on certificate, **122:11.**

TEWKSBURY HOSPITAL
—Cont'd

Transitional assistance department —Cont'd
Payment from appropriations for diseased persons, **122:13.**
Removal of patient to place of legal settlement, **122:12.**
Trespassing upon lands, **266:123.**
Trust companies.
Deposit of funds of patients, **122:6-122:9.**
Handling funds and investments, **122:5.**
Trusts.
See TRUSTS AND TRUSTEES.
Unclaimed property.
Abandoned, lost, and unclaimed property. See within this heading, "Abandoned, lost, and unclaimed property."
Welfare.
Transitional assistance department. See within this heading, "Transitional assistance department."

TEXAS CATTLE.

Driving on highway or street, forbidden, **129:35.**

TEXTBOOKS.

Audit of account of person doing business as book store on property of state college, **73:10.**
Bradford Durfee College of Technology, purchases, **74:42N.**
Change of books used, **71:50.**
Colleges and universities.
State colleges. See within this heading, "State colleges."
Commissioner of education to collect school books in his office, **69:1.**
Correspondence or trade schools, fraudulent sale, **93:21.**
Execution, exemption of school books, **235:34.**
Fraudulent sale, **93:21.**
Maritime Academy, duties of state college board of trustees, **73:1.**
New Bedford Institute of Technology, purchases, **74:42N.**
Official text and case books, sale and distribution, **5:8.**
Private school pupils, availability of public school textbooks, **71:48.**
Procurement of textbooks, contracts awarded without bids, **30B:7.**

TEXTBOOKS —Cont'd
Purchase by pupils, **71:49.**
Religious sect, not to further
  tenets of particular sect,
  71:31.
Replacement of books and certain
  materials, use of money
  recovered from pupils, **44:53.**
Sales tax, exemptions, **64H:6.**
State colleges.
  Audit of account of person doing
    business as book store on
    property of state college,
    73:10.
  Purchases, **73:15, 74:42N, 75:13.**
State library, expenditures, **6:36.**
Superintendent to recommend,
  71:59.
Supply, **71:48.**
Trustees of state colleges and
  universities, authority to
  purchase books, **75:13.**

TEXTILES.
See FABRICS.

THAMES RIVER COMPACT.
See INTERSTATE COMPACTS
  AND AGREEMENTS.

THANKSGIVING.
Alcoholic liquor sales, **138:33.**
Firemen working on, additional
  pay or time off, **48:57A,**
  48:57D, 48:57E.
Police, day off or extra pay,
  147:17A.
State employees, additional day off
  or extra pay, **30:24A.**
Stores permitted to open on
  Sundays during Thanksgiving
  and Christmas season, **136:6.**

THEATERS.
Actors.
  See ACTORS.
Agents and managers, **140:180A**
  et seq.
  Application for license,
    140:180C.
  Bond, **140:180E, 140:180F.**
  Contracts for engagements,
    140:180D.
  Definitions, **140:180A.**
  Fees for licenses, **140:180C.**
  Fines and penalties, **140:180B.**
  Licenses and permits, **140:46B,**
    140:180B.
    Application, **140:180C.**
    Bond, **140:180E, 140:180F.**
    Fees, **140:180C.**
    Renewal, **140:180C.**
    Revocation of license,
      140:180C, 140:181.

THEATERS —Cont'd
Agents and managers —Cont'd
  Licenses and permits —Cont'd
    Term, **140:180C.**
  Applications for agent's license,
    140:180C.
Arrest for expectorating, **270:14,**
  270:15.
Blank cartridges for use in, sale,
  148:39.
Bond of agent or manager,
  140:180E, 140:180F.
Booking agents.
  Agents and managers. See
    within this heading, "Agents
    and managers."
Children, employment of.
  Hours of labor of women and
    children. See within this
    heading, "Hours of labor of
    women and children."
Contracts for engagements,
  140:180D.
Counterfeiting of tickets and
  passes, **267:2, 267:4-267:6.**
Defined, **143:1, 149:1.**
Definition in labor and workforce
  development law, theater as
  within, **149:1.**
Discrimination because of race,
  color, etc., **272:92A, 272:98.**
Distribution practices for motion
  pictures, **93F:1-93F:4.**
Electricians, **141:8.**
Examination, inspection, or
  investigation, **143:35.**
Fees for licenses, **140:180C,**
  140:185B.
Fines, penalties, and forfeitures.
  Agents and managers,
    140:180B.
  Building laws, violations,
    143:35.
  Show bills, damage, **266:125.**
  Thirty-five millimeter film,
    storage or exhibition,
    143:89.
Firearms.
  Blank cartridges, sale, **148:39.**
  Possession and handling,
    140:129C, 269:10.
Fireworks.
  Blank cartridges for theatrical
    uses, **148:39.**
  Manufacturers located within
    specified distance of, bonds
    required, **148:40.**
  Storage, **148:40, 148:41.**
Forfeitures.
  Fines, penalties, and forfeitures.
    See within this heading,
    "Fines, penalties, and
    forfeitures."

THEATERS —Cont'd
Forgery of tickets and passes,
  267:2, 267:4-267:6.
Hours of labor of women and
  children, **149:56, 149:57,**
  149:78, 151:1A.
  Children under eighteen, **149:66,**
    149:67, 149:78.
  Children under fifteen, **149:104,**
    149:105.
Injuring of showbills, **266:125.**
Inspections and inspectors, **143:35.**
Labor and employment.
  Actors.
    See ACTORS.
  Agents and managers. See
    within this heading, "Agents
    and managers."
  Definitions, **149:1.**
  Electricians, employment, **141:8.**
  Hours of labor of women and
    children. See within this
    heading, "Hours of labor of
    women and children."
Licenses and permits, **140:181.**
  Agents and managers. See
    within this heading, "Agents
    and managers."
  Civil liability of license for
    noncompliance with building
    laws, **143:35.**
  Criminal liability of licensee for
    noncompliance with
    buildings laws, **143:35.**
  Fees, **140:180, 140:185B.**
  Malicious injury to notice of
    licensed theater or
    exhibition, **266:125.**
  Municipal discretion granting or
    renewing permit, **40:57.**
  Resale of theater tickets,
    140:185A.
Managers.
  Agents and managers. See
    within this heading, "Agents
    and managers."
Marquees.
  See MARQUEES.
Motion pictures.
  See MOTION PICTURES.
National Anthem, manner of
  performing, **264:9.**
Penalties.
  Fines, penalties, and forfeitures.
    See within this heading,
    "Fines, penalties, and
    forfeitures."
Permits.
  Licenses and permits. See
    within this heading,
    "Licenses and permits."

THEATERS —Cont'd

Plays.

See PLAYS.

Posted advertisements, malicious injury, **266:125.**

Spitting, **270:14, 270:15.**

Thirty-five millimeter film, storage or exhibition, **143:89.**

Tickets or passes counterfeited, **267:2, 267:4-267:6.**

Unlicensed use, penalty, **140:182.**

Violation of building laws, **143:51.**

Women.

Hours of labor of women and children. See within this heading, "Hours of labor of women and children."

THEBACON.

Controlled dangerous substance, **94C:31.**

THEFT.

Insurance.

See THEFT INSURANCE.

Larceny and theft.

See LARCENY AND THEFT.

THEFT INSURANCE.

Authorized, **175:47.**

Automobile insurance.

See AUTOMOBILE INSURANCE.

Combination with other classes, **175:48, 175:48A, 175:51, 175:54.**

Controlled dangerous substances, possession and distribution without registration, **94C:7.**

Defrauding insurer by removing or concealing vehicle, **266:27A et seq.**

Municipal building insurance fund, use to replace stolen property, **40:13.**

Personal property in motor vehicle, theft of vehicle as prima facie evidence of forcible entry in action to recover, **233:79I.**

Physical damage insurance policy, notice provision, **175:191A.**

Police form required in insurance theft claims, **175:113O.**

Rates and rating organizations applied to theft insurance, **175A:4.**

Reinsuring risks, **175:54B.**

Standard form of fire policy, exception from requirements, **175:99.**

Stock or mutual plan, **175:48, 175:48A.**

THEFT INSURANCE —Cont'd

Warehousing of family, personal, or household goods, notice to depositor as to insurance, **105:4.**

THERAPEUTICS.

Drugs.

See DRUGS AND NARCOTICS.

Family therapists.

See FAMILY THERAPISTS AND THERAPY.

Fluoroscopic shoe fitting machines, therapeutic use, **111:186A.**

Health department's powers as to sale and distribution of therapeutic substances, **111:5.**

Occupational therapists.

Abuse of patients or residents in long-term care facilities, reports, **111:72G.**

Allied health professions.

See ALLIED HEALTH PROFESSIONS.

Physical therapists.

See PHYSICAL THERAPISTS.

Veterinarians' examination, subject, **112:56.**

THERMOMETERS.

Clinical thermometers, **98:9-98:14.**

See CLINICAL THERMOMETERS.

Humidity control in textile factories, **149:108-149:110, 149:112.**

THESPIANS.

See ACTORS.

THIEF.

See LARCENY AND THEFT.

THINNING OF TREES.

Demonstration in forestry practices, **132:6.**

THIRD-PARTY BENEFICIARIES.

Retirement benefits, **32:14A.**

Warranties, third-party beneficiaries, **106:2-318.**

THIRD PARTY PRACTICE.

Impleader.

See IMPLEADER.

Interpleader.

See INTERPLEADER.

THIRD PARTY RECOVERY.

Transitional assistance department, **18:5H.**

Underground tanks.

See UNDERGROUND TANKS.

THIRD PERSONS.

Alimony.

Divorce and alimony. See within this heading, "Divorce and alimony."

Arrest under extradition warrant, bystanders to assist if required, **276:18.**

Assisting police officer, **263:3, 268:24, 276:18, 276:23.**

Communication of fact of debt to person other than one liable as unfair collection procedure, **93:49.**

Dismissal.

See DISMISSAL AND NONSUIT.

Divorce and alimony.

Awarding custody of children, **208:28.**

Naming in connection with derogatory allegations, **208:11.**

Documents as prima facie evidence, **106:1-202.**

Earnings of wife from services for third persons, **209:4.**

Employee's right of action against for injuries, **152:15.**

Entry, writs.

Notice of registered land to bind third parties, **185:86.**

Rights of action for damages against third parties, **237:43.**

Gifts to minors, liability, **201A:16, 201A:17.**

Indictment, misnomer in as variance, **277:35.**

Injury to goods, action against third person, **106:2-722.**

Inspection of goods, **106:2-515.**

Jury, impaneling from bystanders, **234:27.**

Medical service corporation, charges and fees for services, **176B:7.**

Negotiable instruments.

Notice of right to defend action, **106:3-119.**

Police officers, rendering assistance, **263:3, 268:24, 276:18, 276:23.**

Riots and mobs.

Refusal to assist in suppression of riots, **269:2.**

Suppression of riots with assistance of bystanders, **269:1, 269:2, 269:4, 269:6.**

Service of warrants, assistance of officer, **276:23.**

THIRD PERSONS —Cont'd

Summary process to recover land, removal and storage of personal property of third person, **239:4.**

Tuberculosis patients, collection of charges from third party liable for cost of treatment, **111:80.**

Uniform Custodial Trust Act, **203B:11, 203B:12.**

Variance, misnomer in indictment, **277:35.**

Welfare and social services, **18:5G, 18:5H, 18:21.**

Workers' compensation.
See WORKERS' COMPENSATION.

Writs of entry.
Entry, writs of. See within this heading, "Entry, writs."

THIRTY-FIVE MILLIMETER NITRATE FILM.

Storage, public exhibition, etc., **143:89.**

THREAD, 94:285-94:288.

Automatic sprinklers in buildings for manufacturing, etc., **148:26.**

Deputy director of standards, filing of trademarks of brands of thread, **94:286.**

Sale, regulated, **94:285-94:288.**

Spinner's lien, **255:31A, 255:31B.**

THREATS.

Appeal and review.
Failure to prosecute appeal, bond to remain in force, **275:11.**
Order requiring bond to keep peace, **275:8, 275:13.**
Proceedings on appeal, **275:10.**

Arrest for threat to commit crime, **275:3.**

Bail and recognizance.
Bond to keep peace. See within this heading, "Bond to keep peace."

Bomb threats, **126:27, 269:14.**

Bond to keep peace, **275:4.**
Action upon breach of condition, **275:13.**
Appeal of order requiring, **275:8, 275:13.**
Breach of condition, **275:13.**
Commitment on failure to give, **275:5.**
Discharge upon giving, **275:12.**
Failure to prosecute appeal, bond to remain in force, **275:11.**

THREATS —Cont'd

Bond to keep peace —Cont'd
Family trouble cases, additional terms of recognizances and conditions of probation, **276:42A.**
Forfeiture in certain cases, **279:14.**
Husband assaulting wife, bond, **279:12.**
Justices authorized to keep the peace, **275:1.**
Misdemeanor, bond in addition to other punishment, **279:13, 279:14.**
Order of court, **275:4.**
Remission of penalty, **275:16.**
Surrender of principal by surety, **275:17.**
Transmission to jury session, **275:13.**

Breach of peace.
Bond to keep peace. See within this heading, "Bond to keep peace."

Child support, threatening of officers, **119A:2A.**

Civil service, penalty for coercing person to refuse appointment or promotion, **268:8B.**

Collection procedures, **93:49.**

Complaint of threat to commit crime, examination to be conducted, **275:2.**

Court or justice.
Justice or court. See within this heading, "Justice or court."

Employment, interference with.
Labor and workforce development. See within this heading, "Labor and employment, interfering."

Employment security rights, obtaining waiver by threats, **151A:47.**

Evidence.
Witnesses. See within this heading, "Witnesses."

Expenses of prosecution, liability, **275:6, 275:7.**

Explosives, threats to detonate, **126:27, 269:14.**

Extortion, **265:25.**
See EXTORTION.

Family trouble cases, additional terms of recognizance and conditions of probation, **276:42A.**

Fines and penalties, **275:4.**

Gasoline supplier preventing dealers from joining trade association by threats, **93E:6.**

THREATS —Cont'd

Hate crimes.
See HATE CRIMES.

Injunctions in labor disputes, **214:6.**

Insurance on property, intimidation, **175:193E.**

Judge.
Justice. See within this heading, "Justice or court."

Jurors in trials or other criminal proceedings, threats, **233:20D.**

Justice or court.
Bond to keep peace, justices may require, **275:1.**
Threats in presence, **275:14.**

Kidnapping, consent obtained by threats as defense to charge, **265:27.**

Labor and employment, interfering, **149:19.**
Civil service, coercing person to refuse appointment or promotion, **268:8B.**
Gasoline supplier preventing dealer from joining trade association, **93E:6.**
Injunctions in labor disputes, **214:6.**
Penalty for prevention of employment, **149:180.**

Mental patient, threats of violence, **112:129A, 123:36B.**

Peace bond.
Bond to keep peace. See within this heading, "Bond to keep peace."

Prohibition in family trouble cases, additional terms of recognizance and conditions, **276:42A.**

Rape by means, **265:22, 265:22A.**

Religious property, threats to damage, **266:127A.**

Review.
Appeal and review. See within this heading, "Appeal and review."

Security.
Bond. See within this heading, "Bond to keep peace."

Sentence and punishment, **275:4.**

Social worker, threats by client requiring disclosure of confidential communications, **112:135A, 112:135B.**

Stealing by means, **265:21.**

Trials or other criminal proceedings, threatening jurors or witnesses, **233:20D, 268:13B.**

THREATS —Cont'd
Unfair, deceptive or unreasonable collection procedures, **93:49.**
Voters, influencing, **56:33-56:36.**
Witnesses.
Grand jury investigation of intimidation of juror or witness, grant of immunity to witness appearing before, **233:20D.**
Recognizance required of witness to offense of threat to commit crime, **275:9.**
Trials or other criminal proceedings, threats, **268:13B.**

THREE DAY MARRIAGE ACT, **207:19 et seq.**

THREE DAY PLAYER.
Defined, **231:85P½.**

THREE JUDGE ACT.
Labor disputes, **212:30.**

3,4-METHYLENEDIOXY METHAMPHETAMINE, **94C:31.**

THREE STRIKES.
Firearms, unlawful possession.
Augmented sentence for prior conviction of violent crime or serious drug offense, **269:10G.**

THRIFT FUND FOR ECONOMIC DEVELOPMENT.
Film and video development office membership, **23A:56.**

THRIFT INSTITUTIONS.
See BANKS AND BANKING.

THRIFT INSTITUTIONS FUND FOR ECONOMIC DEVELOPMENT, 63:1. (note)

THROUGH BILLS OF LADING, **106:7-302.**

THROUGH WAYS AND ROUTES.
Railroads, through routes, **159:21.**
Street railways, **159:21.**
Traffic regulations.
See TRAFFIC REGULATIONS AND RULES OF THE ROAD.

THROWING OR DROPPING OBJECTS.
Beaches and ways, **265:32.**

THROWING OR DROPPING OBJECTS —Cont'd
Buses, **159:104.**
School buses, **159:93, 159:94, 159:104.**
Arrest and jurisdiction, **159:93, 159:94, 159:104.**
Explosives, penalty for throwing at person or onto property, **266:102.**
Highways.
See HIGHWAYS AND STREETS.
Littering, **270:16, 270:16A.**
See GARBAGE AND RUBBISH.
Public ways, **265:35.**
School buses.
Buses. See within this heading, "Buses."
Sports events, **265:36.**
Street railways, **159:104.**
Arrest and jurisdiction, **159:93, 159:94, 159:104.**
Trains, **159:104.**
See RAILROADS.

THROWING THREAD.
Spinner's lien, **255:31A, 255:31B.**

THYROID.
Misbranding of drugs, **94:187.**

TICKETS.
Boxing and boxing matches.
Number to be limited to capacity of hall, **147:41.**
Taxes, **147:40.**
Brokers, resale prices charged, **140:185D.**
Citations for traffic violations.
See TRAFFIC REGULATIONS AND RULES OF THE ROAD.
Delivery tickets.
See INVOICES AND DELIVERY TICKETS.
Exceptions under resale provisions, **140:185G.**
Excursion tickets, carriers may issue, **159:18.**
Fines and penalties.
Forgery or counterfeiting, **267:2, 267:4-267:6.**
See FORGERY AND COUNTERFEITING.
Price not printed on face of ticket, **140:182A.**
Resale, **140:185F.**
Firewood or bark, tickets showing quantity in load, **94:302.**
Forgery.
See FORGERY AND COUNTERFEITING.

TICKETS —Cont'd
Invoices.
See INVOICES AND DELIVERY TICKETS.
Lift tickets, **143:71N, 143:71O.**
Loans on personal property, requirements, **140:86.**
Lotteries.
See LOTTERIES.
Lottery of state.
See LOTTERY OF STATE.
Mileage tickets.
See MILEAGE TICKETS.
Ocean cruises, advertising or sale of tickets, **94:277B.**
Passes.
See PASSES.
Pawn tickets, **140:86.**
Penalties.
Fines and penalties. See within this heading, "Fines and penalties."
Prices.
Penalty for failure to have price printed on face of ticket, **140:182A.**
Resale price of tickets regulated, **140:185D.**
Street railways, free tickets, **161:107.**
Raffles and bazaars, liability of persons producing tickets, **271:7A.**
Railroads.
See RAILROADS.
Rates.
See RATES AND CHARGES.
Resale, **140:185A.**
Exceptions, **140:185G.**
Penalty, **140:185F.**
Scalping, regulation, **140:185D.**
Scalping, regulation, **140:185D.**
Small loan company borrowers, requirements as to tickets, **140:86.**
Street railways.
Free tickets, **161:107.**
School pupils, **161:108.**
Stolen or counterfeited employee transportation pass, **161:113A.**
Testimonial dinners for public officers and employees, prohibitions, **268:9A.**
Traffic tickets.
See TRAFFIC REGULATIONS AND RULES OF THE ROAD.

TICKS.
Transportation, **266:119.**

TIDAL FLATS.
See TIDE LANDS AND
WATERS.

TIDE GATES.
Drainage improvement, penalty for
obstructing gate, **252:14C.**

TIDE LANDS AND WATERS.
Access to Commonwealth
tidelands, **91:10D.**
Acquisition and maintenance of
tidal marshes and estuaries by
cities and towns, **40:5, 40:8C.**
Appeal procedures as to coastal
wetlands, actions of
commissioner, **130:105.**
Boston Harbor improvement,
91:2-91:9.
Boundaries of flats or tidewaters,
185:1, 240:19-240:26.
Adjacent coastal municipalities,
boundaries, **42:1.**
Commissioners, **240:20-240:22.**
Commonwealth, rights, **240:26.**
Concurrent determination of
boundaries and registration,
240:25.
Costs, **240:22.**
County boundaries, **34:1.**
Court, determination of
boundaries, **240:23.**
Determination of, **131:4, 185:1,**
240:19-240:26.
Jurisdiction of land court, **185:1.**
Notice, **240:20.**
Parties, **240:24.**
Petition to land court, **240:19.**
Proceedings, **240:20.**
Public lands, **91:25-91:27.**
Public works department,
establishment, **131:4.**
Report and plan, **240:21.**
Subsequent purchasers or
persons acquiring interest in
flats as parties, **240:24.**
Bridges.
Drawbridges, repair, **84:2.**
License for construction,
91:12-91:14, 91:18.
Restrictions on construction,
91:14.
Buildings and structures in or
over.
Bridges. See within this
heading, "Bridges."
Displacing of tidewater, **91:21,**
91:22.
Licenses, **91:14.**
Petition to General Court
regarding, **3:5.**
Piles below high water mark,
91:12-91:14, 91:19.

TIDE LANDS AND WATERS
—Cont'd
Burning of refuse within marine
boundaries or near shoreline,
prohibition, **270:20.**
Cities, appropriations, **40:5, 91:29.**
Coastal wetlands defined, **130:105,**
131:40.
Compensation for tidewater
displaced by filling, **91:21,**
91:22.
Disposition, **91:6, 91:24.**
County boundaries in tidewater,
34:1.
Displacement of tidewater.
Compensation. See within this
heading, "Compensation for
tidewater displaced by
filling."
Drawbridges, repair by several
towns, **84:2.**
Dredging and dumping of dredged
materials, **91:52-91:56.**
Liens on flats reclaimed by
dredging, **254:27-254:30.**
Driveways, limitations upon
construction on coastal
wetlands, **130:105.**
Encroachments upon, licenses,
91:14.
Environmental fund to receive
moneys pertaining to tide
lands, **91:24.**
Environmental management
commissioner, protection of
coastal wetlands, **130:105.**
Environmental Protection
Department, responsibilities
for coastal wetlands, **131:40.**
Fines and penalties.
Dumping, **91:55.**
Pollution of coastal waters,
130:23.
Protection of flood plains and
seacoasts, penalties for
violation of laws, **131:40.**
Regulations concerning coastal
wetlands, penalties for
violation, **40:8C, 130:105.**
Improvements.
Borrowing by cities and towns,
44:7.
Boston Harbor improvement,
91:2-91:9.
Legislative grants, filling flats
pursuant, **91:20.**
Licenses.
Bridges, construction,
91:12-91:14, 91:18.
Dredging operations and
dumping of material in
tidewater, **91:52-91:56.**

TIDE LANDS AND WATERS
—Cont'd
Licenses —Cont'd
Flats, licenses for filing,
91:12-91:18.
Structures in tide lands,
licensing and control by
public works department,
91:14.
Liens on flats reclaimed by
dredging, **254:27-254:30.**
Limitation of actions by
Commonwealth for recovery of
tide lands, **260:31.**
Limitations and restrictions.
Restrictions. See within this
heading, "Restrictions."
Mailing notices of coastal wetlands
regulations to affected
property owners, **130:105.**
Maps, plats, and surveys, public
works department's powers
and duties, **91:10.**
Municipal appropriations for tidal
estuaries, shores, etc., **40:5,**
91:29.
Notice.
Boundaries of flats,
determination, **240:20.**
Mailing notices of coastal
wetlands regulations to
affected property owners,
130:105.
Proposed bridge, dam, etc.,
91:18.
Occupation of tide waters or work
done therein, **130:16.**
Penalties.
Fines and penalties. See within
this heading, "Fines and
penalties."
Permits.
Licenses. See within this
heading, "Licenses."
Piles, driving of below high water
mark, **91:12-91:14, 91:19.**
Pollution by oil, etc., **91:59,**
91:59A, 130:23.
Public works department.
Duties, **91:2-91:6, 91:11,**
91:25-91:27, 130:28,
130:105.
Establishment of tidal bounds,
131:4.
Licensing and control of
structures, **91:14.**
Maps, plats, and surveys, **91:10.**
Tide flats, care and supervision,
91:10.
Quieting title to flats, land court's
jurisdiction, **185:1.**

TIDE LANDS AND WATERS
—Cont'd
Railroad crossings, **160:96.**
Reclamation projects for coastal wetlands, **130:105.**
Restrictions.
  Bridges, restrictions on construction over, **91:14.**
  Construction of driveways on coastal wetlands, **130:105.**
State reclamation board, regulations as to coastal wetlands as affecting authority, **130:105.**
Structures.
  Buildings and structures. See within this heading, "Buildings and structures in or over."
Superior court, exclusive jurisdiction of matters concerning coastal wetlands regulations, **130:105.**
Supervision, etc., **91:10.**
Wages or compensation.
  Compensation. See within this heading, "Compensation for tidewater displaced by filling."
Whales or other mammals, removal, **91:49A.**

TIE-IN AGREEMENTS OR SALES.
See RESTRAINTS OF TRADE AND MONOPOLIES.

TIE VOTE.
Caucuses.
  See CAUCUSES.
Elections.
  See ELECTIONS.
Political committees.
  See POLITICAL COMMITTEES.
Political parties.
  See POLITICAL PARTIES.
Primary elections.
  See PRIMARY ELECTIONS.
Senate, Vice-President as entitled to vote in case of tie vote in, **US Const Art 1 Sec 3 cl 4.**

TIMBER.
See LOGS AND TIMBER.

TIME DEPOSITS.
See CERTIFICATES OF DEPOSIT.

TIMEKEEPER.
Boxing matches, licensing timekeeper, **147:35.**

TIME OR DATE.
Abandoned property, time for liquidation by treasurer, **200A:9.**

TIME OR DATE —Cont'd
Abandonment period automatically renewable, commencement, **200A:3A.**
Abortions, informed consent of pregnant women prior, **112:12S.**
Accident.
  See ACCIDENT AND SICKNESS INSURANCE.
Accountant's permit, duration, **112:87B½.**
Administrative procedure, filing of standard rules, **30A:9.**
Admission of fact or of execution of paper, time requirements, **231:69.**
Adoption inquiry, notice of motion to extend time for conducting, **210:5A.**
Alcoholic liquors.
  See ALCOHOLIC LIQUORS.
American Education Week, dates for observance, **6:12G.**
Anatomical gift, determination of time of death for purposes, **113:13.**
Answer.
  See PLEAS AND ANSWERS.
Antedating, **175:130.**
Antitrust laws, **93:8.**
Appeal, time for, **41:81BB.**
  See APPEAL AND REVIEW.
Arbitration.
  See ARBITRATION.
Architectural Barriers Board, time limits on actions, **22:13A.**
Armistice Day, date for observance, **6:15R.**
Arrest.
  See ARREST.
Arrest on mesne process.
  See ARREST ON MESNE PROCESS AND SUPPLEMENTARY PROCEEDINGS.
Assignment for benefit of creditors, furnishing statement of assets of trust as part, **203:41.**
Assignment of wages, period of validity, **154:2.**
Attachment of property.
  See ATTACHMENT OF PROPERTY.
Audits, **11:12.**
Automobile clubs, date for filing statements of financial condition, **174B:7.**
Automobile insurance.
  See AUTOMOBILE INSURANCE.

TIME OR DATE —Cont'd
Banks.
  See BANKS AND BANKING.
Beano, hours regulated, **10:38.**
Bill of lading, misdating, **106:7-301.**
Borrowing by cities and towns in anticipation of grants or reimbursements from Commonwealth, **44:6A.**
Budgets in cities, time for submission, **44:32.**
Building permit issuance, notice to tax assessors, **143:61.**
Burglary.
  See BURGLARY.
Buses.
  School buses and transportation of pupils. See within this heading, "School buses and transportation of pupils."
Business development corporations.
  See BUSINESS DEVELOPMENT CORPORATIONS.
Capital punishment, various time limits applicable, **279:57 et seq.**
Caucuses, time for holding, **50:4, 53:72A, 53:91.**
  Duration of caucus, **53:84.**
Cell checks, frequency, **40:36B.**
Central Massachusetts economic development.
  See CENTRAL MASSACHUSETTS ECONOMIC DEVELOPMENT AUTHORITY.
Certification, date of, defined, **151A:71A.**
Certiorari, time to apply, **249:4.**
Charities.
  See CHARITIES AND CHARITABLE CONTRIBUTIONS.
Charter commission meeting to be called by city or town clerk within 10 days after election, **43B:7.**
Child abuse and neglect, investigations and reports, **119:51B.**
Cigarettes, excise tax requirements, **62C:67.**
Cities.
  See CITIES AND TOWNS.
City and town clerks.
  See CITY AND TOWN CLERKS.
City charters.
  See CITY CHARTERS.

TIME OR DATE —Cont'd

City council district representation, dates of election, **43:133.**

Civil service.
See CIVIL SERVICE.

Coal mining regulation.
See COAL MINING REGULATION AND RECLAMATION.

Cold storage.
Limit of time food may be kept in cold storage, **94:70.**
Marking date of receipt of food in cold storage, **94:71.**

Collection agency, time for accounting, **93:28.**

Collection procedures conducted at unreasonable hour as unfair, deceptive or unreasonable collection procedure, **93:49.**

Collective bargaining agreements to arbitrate.
See LABOR RELATIONS AND DISPUTES.

Commercial code.
See COMMERCIAL CODE.

Commercial driver license.
See UNIFORM OPERATION OF COMMERCIAL MOTOR VEHICLES.

Common-law right of employee, notice of retention, **152:24.**

Common victuallers to keep business open, **140:9A.**

Compensation.
See WAGES, SALARIES, AND COMPENSATION.

Computer hardware and software, payment by cities and towns, **44:7.**

Conservation restrictions, duration, **184:26, 184:33.**

Conservators.
Guardians, conservators, and committees. See within this heading, "Guardians, conservators, and committees."

Consumer transactions.
See BANKS AND BANKING.

Contracts.
See CONTRACTS AND AGREEMENTS.

Contributory retirement systems of public employees, extending time to withdraw certain funds, **32:22.**

Co-operative banks, time of audit, **168:25, 170:14.**

Corporations.
See CORPORATIONS.

TIME OR DATE —Cont'd

Corporation taxes.
See CORPORATION TAXES.

County accounts of receipts and expenditures, time for delivery, **35:36.**

County debtor, time required for treasurer to give notice, **35:24.**

County tuberculosis hospitals, time of apportionment of maintenance costs, **111:85.**

Crabs or lobster, hours for catching or taking, etc., **130:39.**

Credit slips, time limitation for redemption, **93:14S.**

Credit unions.
See CREDIT UNIONS.

Crime victims' compensation.
See VICTIMS OF VIOLENT CRIMES.

Criminal procedure.
See CRIMINAL PROCEDURE.

Dam, determination by jury as to times of opening, **253:9.**

Daylight saving, **4:10.**

Death.
See DEATH.

Declaration of estimated income tax.
See DECLARATION OF ESTIMATED INCOME TAX.

Decrees.
See JUDGMENTS, ORDERS, AND DECREES.

Deeds.
See DEEDS AND CONVEYANCES.

Demurrer, time limitation as to amendment of pleadings after, **231:52.**

Depositions, time of taking, notice, **233:61.**

District and prosecuting attorneys, duties as to administration after time limit, executors and administrators, **193:5.**

District courts.
See DISTRICT COURTS.

District meetings, time for holding, **41:119.**

Divorce.
See DIVORCE AND ALIMONY.

Dog and horse racing meetings, holding, **128A:2, 128A:3, 128A:5.**

Dogs.
See DOGS.

TIME OR DATE —Cont'd

Drivers and drivers' licenses.
Commercial vehicles.
See UNIFORM OPERATION OF COMMERCIAL MOTOR VEHICLES.
Operators' licenses generally.
See MOTOR VEHICLES.
Suspension or revocation.
See MOTOR VEHICLES.

Eastern standard time, **4:10.**

Eavesdropping to obtain evidence of crime, **272:99.**

Effective date.
Automobile insurance.
See AUTOMOBILE INSURANCE.
Gas and electric companies, effective date of articles of consolidation or merger, **164:102A.**
Insurance.
See INSURANCE.
Labor and workforce development department, rules and regulations, **149:8.**
State officers and employees, salary increases, **30:46.**
Statutes.
See STATUTES.
Teachers, effective date of provisional certification rules, **71:38G. (note)**

Elections.
See ELECTIONS.

Electric companies.
Gas and electric companies. See within this heading, "Gas and electric companies."

Electric railroads.
See ELECTRIC RAILROADS.

Electrologists' examinations, time for holding, **112:87GGG.**

Elevator appeals board, meetings, **22:11A.**

Elevators.
Appeal of elevator regulations, time, **143:70.**
Inspection for safety, **143:64.**
Meetings of elevator appeals board, **22:11A.**

Eminent domain.
See EMINENT DOMAIN.

Employer closing facility, report, **151A:71B.**

Employ Handicapped Persons Week, **6:15F.**

Employment security.
See EMPLOYMENT SECURITY.

Endorsement on marine fishing licenses, **130:4.**

TIME OR DATE —Cont'd

Energy conservation debts of city or town, payment, **44:7.**

Energy Resources Executive Office, regulations, **25A:12.**

Entry, writs of.
See ENTRY, WRITS.

Environmental impact reports.
See ENVIRONMENTAL IMPACT REPORTS.

Estate taxes.
See ESTATE TAXES.

Excise tax on motor vehicles, abatement, **60A:2.**

Executions.
See EXECUTIONS.

Executors.
See EXECUTORS AND ADMINISTRATORS.

Extension of time.
See EXTENSION OF TIME.

Extradition.
See EXTRADITION.

Family Support Act.
See INTERSTATE FAMILY SUPPORT ACT.

Farm equipment or vehicles, operation on highways, **90:7.**

Fee simple determinable or fee simple subject to right of entry for condition broken, when to become fee simple absolute, **184A:3.**

Financial disclosure by public officers and employees, **268B:5.**

Fines.
See FINES AND PENALTIES.

Firearms.
See FIREARMS AND WEAPONS.

Fire insurance.
Certification changes, time, **175:95.**
Limitation of time, fire insurance policy provisions, **175:99.**
Rates.
See INSURANCE RATES AND RATING ORGANIZATIONS.

Fire prevention regulations, hearings upon petition for changes, **148:10.**

First aid training of emergency personnel, extending date, **111:201.**

Food and agriculture commissioner, appeals, **128:25, 128:26.**

Foreclosure.
See MORTGAGE FORECLOSURE.

TIME OR DATE —Cont'd

Foreign fiduciaries.
Payment or delivery to fiduciary, **199A:3.**
Service of process, response, **199A:11.**

Foreign insurance companies.
Certification of certain changes to commissioner, time, **175:23A.**
Revocation or suspension of license, effective date, **175:5.**

Foster care review directors, appointment of by commissioner of social services, **18B:6A.**

Fraternal benefit societies.
Organization, time limit to complete, **176:4.**

Fraudulent claims board, proceedings, **26:8B.**

Fraudulent Transfer Act, **109A:1 et seq.**

Fuel oils, time and date noted on delivery ticket, **94:303F.**

Gas and electric companies.
Articles of consolidation or merger, effective date, **164:102A.**
Filing applications for consolidation or purchase on sale of property, **164:101.**

Gasoline.
See GASOLINE AND MOTOR FUEL TAXES.

Grace period.
See GRACE PERIOD.

Guardians, conservators, and committees.
Accounting, time, **206:1.**
License to sell property, duration, **204:8.**
Minor, duration of guardianship, **201:4.**

Hazardous waste management act, license proceedings, **21C:7, 21C:11.**

Health care finance.
See HEALTH CARE FINANCE AND POLICY.

Health Facilities Appeals Board, effect of failure to issue decision, **111:25E.**

Hearings.
Bank consumer transaction practices, **167:2C.**
Mentally ill and retarded persons, **123:6, 123:7, 123:8B.**
Motor vehicles, infraction hearings on assessments, **90C:3.**

TIME OR DATE —Cont'd

Hearings —Cont'd
Time limit for assigning hearing officers to involuntary retirement, **32:16.**

Highways.
See HIGHWAYS AND STREETS.

Historic districts.
See HISTORIC DISTRICTS AND SITES.

Holidays, **4:7.**

Home improvement contractors, time for filing claims, **142A:7.**

Home mortgages showing due date of payments, **140:90B.**

Horse or dog racing meetings, holding, **128A:2, 128A:3, 128A:5.**

Hours of labor.
See HOURS OF LABOR OR SERVICES.

Housing and community development department, certification of eligible business facilities, **23B:15.**

Human services programs, timely payments, **29:23A.**

Income tax.
See INCOME TAX.

Indictments.
See INDICTMENTS, INFORMATIONS, AND COMPLAINTS.

Industrial activity board, reports, **6:190.**

Initial conversion, date of, defined, **164:94G½.**

Insurance.
See INSURANCE.

Insurance rates.
See INSURANCE RATES AND RATING ORGANIZATIONS.

Interrogatories.
See INTERROGATORIES.

Interstate Family Support Act.
See INTERSTATE FAMILY SUPPORT ACT.

Investment securities under commercial code.
See INVESTMENT SECURITIES UNDER COMMERCIAL CODE.

Involuntary retirement hearing, time limit for assigning hearing officers, **32:16.**

Judgments.
See JUDGMENTS, ORDERS, AND DECREES.

Judicial conduct commission, hearing without undue delay, **211C:7.**

TIME OR DATE —Cont'd
Jury.
See JURY AND JURY TRIAL.
Jury commissioner for
Commonwealth, **234A:17,
234A:72.**
Justices of the peace, expiration of
commissions.
Acknowledgment, date of
expiration to be affixed,
222:8.
Notice of expiration, **9:15.**
Penalty for acting as justice of
peace after expiration of
commission, **222:9.**
Juvenile courts.
See JUVENILE COURTS AND
DELINQUENT CHILDREN.
Labor.
See LABOR AND WORKFORCE
DEVELOPMENT.
Labor relations.
See LABOR RELATIONS AND
DISPUTES.
Leased personal property,
presumption of conversion for
failure as to return, **231:85H.**
Lease relating to notice to quit,
time limitations for payment
of rent concerning written,
186:12.
Leases under UCC.
See LEASES UNDER
COMMERCIAL CODE.
Legacies and trust distributions,
accrual date of interest,
197:20.
Legacy.
See LEGACY AND
SUCCESSION TAXES.
Legal holidays, dates for
observance of certain, **4:7.**
Length of service.
See RETIREMENT SYSTEMS
AND PENSIONS.
Licenses.
See LICENSES AND PERMITS.
Lien on pictures or photographs,
time for payment before
notice, **255:31F.**
Life insurance.
See LIFE INSURANCE.
Limitation of actions.
See LIMITATION OF ACTIONS.
Limited liability companies.
See LIMITED LIABILITY
COMPANIES.
Lobster or crabs, hours for
catching or taking, etc.,
130:39.
Magazines and periodicals
purchased by towns for
designated time periods, **40:4.**

TIME OR DATE —Cont'd
Marriage.
See MARRIAGE.
Maturity.
See MATURITY.
Mechanics' liens.
See MECHANICS' LIENS.
Medical care.
See MEDICAL CARE AND
ASSISTANCE.
Medical examiners.
See MEDICAL EXAMINERS
AND INQUESTS.
Membership camping contract or
agreement, time for
cancellation, **93:48A.**
Mentally ill.
See MENTALLY ILL AND
RETARDED PERSONS.
Mesne process.
See ARREST ON MESNE
PROCESS AND
SUPPLEMENTARY
PROCEEDINGS.
Metropolitan district, time for
cities and towns to pay
assessments, **92:59A.**
Military affairs.
See MILITARY AFFAIRS.
Milk plant, time to apply for
license, **94:42A.**
Month, defined, **4:7.**
Morris plan banks.
See MORRIS PLAN BANKS.
Mortgages.
See MORTGAGES AND DEEDS
OF TRUST.
Motor vehicles.
See MOTOR VEHICLES.
Municipal finance.
See MUNICIPAL FINANCE.
Nighttime.
See NIGHTTIME.
"No-fault" automobile liability
insurance, time for
commencement of medical
payments by insurer, **90:34M.**
Nonprofit hospital service
corporation subscriber
qualifications, enrollment
period, **176A:1A.**
North shore ocean sanctuary,
application for permit to
discharge waste water,
132A:16.
Notaries public.
See NOTARIES PUBLIC.
Notification.
Date of notification defined,
151A:71A.
Tax installment payment
agreement, modification or
termination, **62C:37B.**

TIME OR DATE —Cont'd
Nursing home administrators,
change in renewal date of
certification, **112:111.**
Obsolete papers and records, time
requirements regarding
destruction, **221:27A.**
Old age assistance, residency
requirements, **118A:1.**
Open end credit accounts, billing
periods, **140:114B.**
Parking violations, time for owner
to forward required
information to clerk of court,
90:20E.
Partnerships, expiration of term.
Continuation of business after,
108A:23.
Dissolution, **108A:31, 108A:32.**
Pawnbroker's retention of articles,
140:71.
Pensions.
See RETIREMENT SYSTEMS
AND PENSIONS.
Peremptory challenges of jurors,
time for making, **234:29.**
Perpetuation of testimony.
See DEPOSITIONS.
Petition to general court, **3:5.**
Physician assistants, time for
registration with board,
112:9I.
Physicians and surgeons, bill
submitted to transitional
assistance department within
90 days after service rendered,
118E:20.
Pleas.
Dilatory pleas.
Appeals.
See APPEAL AND
REVIEW.
Plea in abatement.
See ABATEMENT,
SURVIVAL, AND
REVIVAL.
Interrogatories, answers to.
See INTERROGATORIES.
Political committees of
municipalities, time for giving
notice as to number of
members, **52:9.**
Political conventions.
Nomination of candidates for
presidential conventions,
time for holding, **53:4.**
Number of delegates to national
presidential conventions,
time for giving notice,
53:70B.
Postdating, **106:2-310.**

TIME OR DATE —Cont'd

Predating.

Life or endowment insurance policy, §175:130.

Presidential electors.

See PRESIDENTIAL ELECTORS.

Presidential primaries.

Candidates, time for submission of lists, 53:70E.

Nomination papers, 53:7, 53:46, 53:48.

Place of holding, 53:28, 53:70C.

Town elections, authorization to change date, 53:28.

Pretrial discovery.

See DISCOVERY AND DISCLOSURE.

Primary elections, 53:28.

See PRIMARY ELECTIONS.

Prior convictions of witness, use of in trial, 233:21.

Private ways and parking areas, unlimited duration of special regulations governing, 90:18.

Procurement contracts, 30B:5, 30B:6, 30B:12.

Public assistance.

Welfare and social services, date of application for medical assistance 118E:30.

Public charities.

See CHARITIES AND CHARITABLE CONTRIBUTIONS.

Public contract actions, filing requirements, 30:39Q.

Public employees.

Civil service.

See CIVIL SERVICE.

Resignation from position prior to separation from payroll, 30:46.

Public utilities.

Utilities. See within this heading, "Utilities."

Public welfare.

Welfare and social services, date of application for medical assistance 118E:30.

Punishments.

See SENTENCE AND PUNISHMENT.

Qualified bonds.

See MUNICIPAL FINANCE.

Quarantine of diseased or infected animals, 129:21, 129:30.

Railroads.

See RAILROADS.

Rape, preservation of evidence, 41:97B.

TIME OR DATE —Cont'd

Real estate broker or salesman, licensing, 112:87SS.

Real property.

See REAL PROPERTY.

Reasonable time.

See REASONABLE TIME.

Records.

See RECORDS, REPORTS, AND RETURNS.

Recount in primaries, filing petitions, 54:135.

Recreational land, filing deadlines for classification, 61B:3.

Refunding bonds, term, 29:53A.

Refuse vehicles, hours of operation, 111:31A.

Regional refuse disposal districts.

Disapproving incurring of indebtedness by district, time, 40:44F.

Terms of payment for sale or lease of property, 40:44J.

Regional transit authority, time when deemed established, 161B:14.

Registration of land titles.

See REGISTRATION OF LAND TITLES.

Registration of voters.

See REGISTRATION OF VOTERS.

Removal or repair of unsafe structure, 143:7.

Restraint of mentally ill patient, 123:21.

Restraints of trade and monopolies, 93:8.

Retarded persons.

Mentally ill and retarded persons.

See MENTALLY ILL AND RETARDED PERSONS.

Retirement systems.

See RETIREMENT SYSTEMS AND PENSIONS.

Return of process.

Absentee's estate, time for return of process against, 200:3.

Revenue department.

See REVENUE DEPARTMENT AND COMMISSIONER.

Review, time for, 41:81BB.

See APPEAL AND REVIEW.

Salaries.

See WAGES, SALARIES, AND COMPENSATION.

Sales for taxes.

See TAX SALES.

Sales taxes.

See SALES TAXES.

TIME OR DATE —Cont'd

Sales under commercial code.

See SALES UNDER COMMERCIAL CODE.

Sanitary code, effective date, 111:127A.

Saturdays.

See SATURDAYS.

Savings banks.

See SAVINGS BANKS.

School buses and transportation of pupils.

Duration of contracts for service, 40:4.

Operator's license, 90:8A.

Periodic inspections, 90:7A.

Searches.

See SEARCHES AND SEIZURES.

Secured transactions.

See SECURED TRANSACTIONS.

Securities act.

See SECURITIES ACT.

Seeds.

See SEEDS.

Sentence.

See SENTENCE AND PUNISHMENT.

Sexual offenses.

See SEXUAL OFFENSES AND OFFENDERS.

Shellfish, hours for taking from private grounds, 130:68.

Six O'Clock Law, 149:66, 149:69, 149:73, 149:78.

Slovak Independence Day, annual observance, 6:12II.

Social services.

Welfare and social services, date of application for medical assistance 118E:30.

Solid waste management, contracts may be for such periods as agreed upon by the parties, 40D:21.

Special assessments.

See SPECIAL ASSESSMENTS.

Special commissions to investigate and study, filing of report, 4:2A.

Special education, time of payments of reimbursements, 71:14.

Special elections.

See SPECIAL ELECTIONS.

Special zoning permits, approval, 40A:9.

Speedy trial.

See SPEEDY TRIAL.

Standard time, 4:10.

TIME OR DATE —Cont'd

State ballot law commission.
   See STATE BALLOT LAW
      COMMISSION.
State police.
   See STATE POLICE.
Statutes.
   See STATUTES.
Steam boilers, extension of time
   for inspection, **146:6.**
Street railways.
   See STREET RAILWAYS.
Subdivision control law, time for
   approval or disapproval of
   preliminary plans, **41:81S.**
Suit, time for.
   See LIMITATION OF ACTIONS.
Summary process to recover land.
   See SUMMARY PROCESS TO
      RECOVER LAND.
Sunset, arrest after, **224:6, 224:18.**
Superior court.
   See SUPERIOR COURTS.
Supplemental Medicare health
   plans, common enrollment
   dates, **176A:1A, 176A:10,
   176B:4, 176G:17A.**
Supplementary proceedings.
   See ARREST ON MESNE
      PROCESS AND
      SUPPLEMENTARY
      PROCEEDINGS.
Supreme judicial court.
   See SUPREME JUDICIAL
      COURT.
Supreme judicial court justices,
   time for evaluation of
   performance, **211:26A.**
Taxation.
   See TAXATION.
Tax deeds.
   See TAX DEEDS AND TITLES.
Tax sales.
   See TAX SALES.
Teachers.
   Effective date of provisional
      certification rules,
      applications for certification
      made prior, **71:38G. (note)**
   Paychecks, time for transmittal
      of funds withheld, **71:37B,
      149:178B.**
   Suspension for unbecoming
      conduct, period, **71:42D.**
Temporary loans made by
   municipalities in anticipation
   of money to be derived from
   sale of bonds and notes, time
   for payment of, **44:17.**
Tenancy at will, time limitations
   for payment of rent, **186:12.**

TIME OR DATE —Cont'd

Total and permanent incapacity,
   review date, **152:34B.**
Town meetings, **39:9.**
   Annual meeting, **39:9, 39:20.**
   Establishment of town meeting
      day, **6:15PP.**
Trademarks.
   See TRADEMARKS AND
      TRADE NAMES.
Traffic regulations.
   See TRAFFIC REGULATIONS
      AND RULES OF THE
      ROAD.
Transportation charges for
   materials, petition to enforce
   claim, **149:29.**
Trial.
   Hearings. See within this
      heading, "Hearings."
Trust companies.
   See TRUST COMPANIES.
Trust deeds.
   Mortgages and deeds of trust.
      See within this heading,
      "Mortgages."
Trustee process.
   See TRUSTEE PROCESS.
Tuberculosis hospitals for counties,
   time of apportionment of
   maintenance costs, **111:85.**
Unemployment compensation.
   See EMPLOYMENT
      SECURITY.
Unfair labor practices, hearing by
   labor relations commission
   member, time for filing appeal
   to full commission, **150A:6.**
Unfair trade practices, notice of
   intended action to restrain,
   93A:4.
Uniform operation of commercial
   motor vehicles.
   See UNIFORM OPERATION OF
      COMMERCIAL MOTOR
      VEHICLES.
Uniform rules of adjudicatory
   procedure, time of taking
   effect, **30A:10.**
Unpaid checks of state treasurer,
   payment, **29:32, 29:32A.**
Use classification of property for
   tax purposes, **40:56.**
Used car sales.
   See USED CAR SALES.
Utilities.
   Gas and electric companies. See
      within this heading, "Gas
      and electric companies."
   Telecommunications and energy
      department, time for taking
      appeal from rulings and
      orders, **25:5.**

TIME OR DATE —Cont'd

Variable annuity contract forms,
   approval or disapproval,
   175:134B.
Veterans benefits, appeal process
   on claims, **115:2.**
Victims of violent crimes.
   See VICTIMS OF VIOLENT
      CRIMES.
Wages, salaries.
   See WAGES, SALARIES, AND
      COMPENSATION.
Waiting period.
   See WAITING PERIOD.
Warehouse receipts.
   Claims, time of presenting,
      106:7-204.
   Date of issuance, requirement of
      showing, **106:7-202.**
   Limitation period, **106:7-204.**
   Form for pleading, **106:7-204.**
Weekends.
   See WEEKENDS.
Welfare and social services, date of
   application for medical
   assistance, **118E:30.**
Well diggers' or drillers' reports,
   21:16.
Wetlands, time for approval of
   projects, **131:40.**
Withholding of tax.
   See WITHHOLDING OF TAX.
Witnesses.
   See WITNESSES.
Women, infants, and children
   program, time for public
   hearing to review plan, **111I:3.**
Workers' compensation.
   See WORKERS'
      COMPENSATION.
Writs of entry.
   See ENTRY, WRITS.
Year.
   See YEAR.
Zoning.
   See ZONING AND PLANNING.

TIMEPIECES.

Clocks.
   See CLOCKS.

TIME-SHARES.

Real estate time-shares,
   183B:1-183B:55.

TIMOTHY SEED.

Sale to be by weight, **94:237.**

TIPPING FEE.
See GARBAGE AND RUBBISH.

TIRES.

Commercial vehicle tire rims,
   servicing, **90:9C.**

TIRES —Cont'd

Grades and standards for motor vehicle tires, **90:7K.**

Heavy vehicles, **85:30-85:32.**

Inspection, **90:7A.**

Lateral projection, **90:19.**

Registrar of motor vehicles, establishment of safety standards, **90:7K.**

Retreaded, recapped, or other than first quality tires.

Defined, **90:1.**

Sale, **90:7M.**

Safety standards, **90:7K.**

Sizes, power of municipality to regulate width, **40:21.**

Snow tires with metal studs, **90:16.**

Sunday sales, **136:6.**

Tread depth regulations, noncompliance, **90:7Q.**

Weight per inch of tire or supporting surface, **85:30.**

Width.

Regulation of tire width, **40:21.**

Truck and trailer widths as affected by tires, **90:19.**

Written instrument on sale of recapped, retreaded, or substandard tires, **90:7M.**

TISBURY.

District court, **218:1.**

Medical examiner district, **38:1.**

TITLE AND OWNERSHIP.

Abandoned property.

See ABANDONED, LOST, AND UNCLAIMED PROPERTY.

Abstracts of title.

See ABSTRACTS OF TITLE.

Abuse prevention, orders of court affecting title to real property, **209A:3.**

Accountants, working papers as property, **112:87E.**

Action to establish title, **223:127.**

Affidavits, **183:5A, 183:5B.**

Registration of land titles.

See REGISTRATION OF LAND TITLES.

Tax deeds.

See TAX DEEDS AND TITLES.

Aircraft financial responsibility act.

See AIRCRAFT FINANCIAL RESPONSIBILITY ACT.

Appraisers and appraisals, **112:174, 112:187.**

Attorneys at law.

Certification of relevancy of affidavits concerning, **183:5B.**

TITLE AND OWNERSHIP —Cont'd

Attorneys at law —Cont'd

Land court title examiners, **185:12.**

Automobile insurance.

See AUTOMOBILE INSURANCE.

Automobiles.

See MOTOR VEHICLES.

Banks and banking.

Documents of title, delivery in connection with sales through banking channels, **106:2-308.**

Federal savings and loan association or federal savings bank converting to state-chartered savings bank, property, **168:38.**

Bills of lading.

See BILLS OF LADING.

Buildings.

See BUILDINGS AND STRUCTURES.

Certificates of title.

See CERTIFICATES OF TITLE.

Certified copies.

Affidavits relating to land titles, **183:5A.**

Registration of land titles.

See REGISTRATION OF LAND TITLES.

Civil service.

See CIVIL SERVICE.

Commissioner of revenue.

Revenue department and commissioner. See within this heading, "Revenue department and commissioner."

Common property, fees for receiving records of proprietors, **262:34.**

Commonwealth, issuance of certificate of title to real property title to which is registered in name of state agency, **7:40E.**

Condominiums.

See CONDOMINIUMS.

Confirmation, **239:1.**

Registration of land titles.

See REGISTRATION OF LAND TITLES.

Consignment, reservation of title, **106:1-201.**

Control share acquisitions, **110D:1-110D:8, 110E:1-110E:7.**

Counterfeiting or forgery of muniments of title, **267:1, 267:3, 267:5.**

TITLE AND OWNERSHIP —Cont'd

Court for settlement of real property title issues, **60:64-60:75, 185:1 et seq.**

See LAND COURT.

Deeds.

See DEEDS AND CONVEYANCES.

Defects in title, **184:24.**

Definitions, **142A:1, 148:38B.**

Dies, molds or forms, procedure for transfer of title, **94:320.**

Discovery and disclosure, **231:63.**

Dishonor.

Presentment, dishonor, and protest. See within this heading, "Presentment, dishonor, and protest."

Disseisin.

Conveyance of land, effect of disseisin, **183:7.**

Entry, writs, **237:3, 237:6, 237:7.**

Expectant estates, disseisin of precedent estate as barring, **184:10, 184:11.**

Testator, effect of disseisin, **191:24.**

Documents of title.

See DOCUMENTS OF TITLE.

Dog racing meetings.

Horse and dog racing meetings. See within this heading, "Horse and dog racing meetings."

Dogs.

See DOGS.

Elevators, duty of owners as to inspection, **143:64.**

Eminent domain, vesting of title to property or interest taken, **79:3, 81:7H.**

Endangered species, alteration of significant habitat, **131A:4.**

Entirety, protection from defective discharges of mortgages, **183:54A.**

Entry, writs of.

See ENTRY, WRITS.

Environmental Protection Department, **130:105, 183A:2.**

Evidence.

Burial grounds, title, **272:74.**

Criminal prosecution, **278:9.**

Delivery of instrument affecting land title, record as conclusive evidence, **183:5.**

Environmental Protection Department licensee, presumptions and burden of proof, **183A:2.**

TITLE AND OWNERSHIP
—Cont'd

Evidence —Cont'd

Record of affidavits relating to property title, **183:5A.**

Tax deeds and titles, prima facie evidence, **60:45, 60:50, 60:52.**

Examination of title.

See TITLE EXAMINATION.

Expectant estates, disseisin of precedent estate as barring, **184:10, 184:11.**

Federal savings and loan association or federal savings bank converting to state-chartered savings bank, property, **168:38.**

Firearms, transfer of title by owner of surrendered firearms, **140:129D.**

Fire insurance, information as to actual ownership of property in fire insurance application, **175:98.**

Fires and fire prevention.

Orders affecting owner of premises, **148:5, 148:29.**

Report of investigations to owner of premises, **148:8.**

Fish.

See FISH AND GAME.

Forgery or counterfeiting of muniments of title, **267:1, 267:3, 267:5.**

Gaming house owners.

See GAMING AND GAMES OF CHANCE.

Gifts to minors, indefeasibility of minors' title, **201A:11.**

Guardians.

See GUARDIANS, CONSERVATORS, AND COMMITTEES.

Historic landmarks, consent of persons claiming ownership, **9:27.**

Horse and dog racing meetings.

Barring or suspending owners for misconduct, **128A:13.**

Influencing persons connected with race to affect result, owner penalized, **128A:13C.**

Licensing or registering, **128A:9A.**

Hospitals.

See HOSPITALS AND HEALTH CARE FACILITIES.

Improvements, allowance to defendant for as affected by possession under supposedly good title, **237:17.**

TITLE AND OWNERSHIP
—Cont'd

Indictment, description, **277:25.**

Industrial development financing authority, title to property upon dissolution, **40D:2.**

Insurance, **175:114-175:116A.**

See TITLE INSURANCE.

Interest on small home mortgages, exclusion of cost of title examination in computing, **140:90A.**

Interrogatories disclosing, **231:63.**

Joinder of parties.

Petition to require action to try title, **240:1.**

Quieting title, **240:1.**

See QUIETING TITLE.

Registration of land titles, joinder in proceedings, **185:32.**

Land court, **60:64-60:75, 185:1 et seq.**

See LAND COURT.

Land title registration, **185:26 et seq.**

See REGISTRATION OF LAND TITLES.

Lead-based substances at dangerous levels, duties of owner of residential premises in which detected, **111:197.**

Lead poisoning, **111:197D.**

Liens of spinner, definition of term owner, **255:31A.**

Limitation of action to foreclose ancient mortgage, **260:33-260:35.**

Marriage.

See MARRIAGE.

Massachusetts Centers of Excellence Corporation, powers, **40J:12.**

Mobile homes, exemption from title requirement, **90D:2.**

Mortgages and deeds of trust, **93:70.**

Motor vehicles.

See MOTOR VEHICLES.

Nursing.

See NURSING OR REST HOMES.

Partnership property, title acquired by conveyance, **108A:10.**

Personal jurisdiction over person having interest in real property in Commonwealth, **223A:3.**

TITLE AND OWNERSHIP
—Cont'd

Presentment, dishonor, and protest.

Document of title, dishonor as affecting tender of delivery, **106:2-503.**

Transferability of title obtained in exchange for check later dishonored, **106:2-403.**

Probate and Family Court.

Registration of land titles as affecting sales or mortgages by fiduciaries, **185:98.**

Title acquired from sale affected by adjudication of owners, **204:21.**

Professional corporations, ownership of property, **156A:4.**

Proof.

Evidence. See within this heading, "Evidence."

Protection of coastal and inland wetlands, **131:40A.**

Protection of land titles from uncertain and obsolete restrictions, **184:26-184:30.**

Protest.

Presentment, dishonor, and protest. See within this heading, "Presentment, dishonor, and protest."

Public domain, **45:19.**

Quieting title, **240:1-240:29.**

See QUIETING TITLE.

Real estate brokers' and salesmen's registration law not applicable to transaction in connection with own property, **112:87QQ.**

Registers or assistant registers of deeds, no compensation for title work, **36:37.**

Registration of land titles, **185:26 et seq.**

See REGISTRATION OF LAND TITLES.

Reservation of title.

Sales contract, reservation for security, **106:2-401.**

Security interest, reservation of title, **106:1-201.**

Rest homes.

See NURSING OR REST HOMES.

Revenue department and commissioner.

Authorizing assessment of taxes upon owner of real estate, **59:11.**

Furnishing assessor information as to owner of real estate, **58:3.**

TITLE AND OWNERSHIP
—Cont'd
Revenue department and
commissioner —Cont'd
Old persons owning real estate,
reimbursement of
municipalities, **59:5.**
Riparian owners.
See WATERS AND
WATERWAYS.
Sales under commercial code.
See SALES UNDER
COMMERCIAL CODE.
Secured transactions.
See SECURED
TRANSACTIONS.
Seisin.
Disseisin. See within this
heading, "Disseisin."
Sound and sound recordings,
defined, **266:143.**
Standard of care owed by owners
to children, **231:85Q.**
State agency or board of state
agency, real property held in
name of, as property of
Commonwealth, **7:40E.**
Stray beasts.
See ANIMALS.
Supposedly good title, allowance to
defendant for improvements
as affected by possession,
237:17.
Tax assessors.
See TAX ASSESSORS.
Tax deeds and titles, **60:45 et seq.**
See TAX DEEDS AND TITLES.
Testators.
See WILLS.
Third persons as bound by
proceedings affecting title to
real property, **184:15.**
Trademark, registration or
renewal as constructive notice
of claim of ownership, **110B:4.**
Unclaimed.
See ABANDONED, LOST, AND
UNCLAIMED PROPERTY.
Uniform Gifts to Minors Act,
indefeasibility of minor's title,
201A:11.
Warehouse receipts.
See WAREHOUSE RECEIPTS.
Warranty of title, **106:2-312.**
Deeds.
See DEEDS AND
CONVEYANCES.
Water management act, planning
and regulation for future
water needs, **21G:3.**
Waters.
See WATERS AND
WATERWAYS.

TITLE AND OWNERSHIP
—Cont'd
Wills.
Approval of title to devised land,
132:2.
Disseisin of testator, **191:24.**
Registration, **185:97, 185:98.**
See REGISTRATION OF
LAND TITLES.
Worthier title to property doctrine,
abolition, **184:33A, 184:33B.**
Writ of entry.
See ENTRY, WRITS.

TITLE DEFECTS ACT, 184:24.

TITLE EXAMINATION.
Abstracts of title.
See ABSTRACTS OF TITLE.
Defects in title, **184:24.**
Fees.
Maximum mortgage interest
rate, fees allowable in
addition, **140:90A.**
Mortgagor paying attorney's fees
for mortgagee, liability of
examining attorney, **93:70.**
Petition to register land by land
court, examining title,
262:39.
Land court proceedings, title
examiners in, **185:12.**
See LAND COURT.
Mortgage transactions, certificates
of title, **93:70.**
Partition proceedings, **241:17.**
Costs, **241:22.**
Relocation assistance payments of
title examination fee, **79A:7.**
Tax title, examination on
foreclosure of redemption
rights, **60:66.**

TITLE INSURANCE,
175:114-175:116A.
Certificate for resumption of
business, **175:116.**
Domestic companies not subject to
certain provisions, **175:114.**
Foreign companies not subject to
certain provisions, **175:116A.**
Guaranty fund, **175:116.**
Insurance laws, applicability,
175:29.
Tax title acquired by city or town,
insurance, **60:50A.**
Title guaranty fund, investments,
175:116.

TITLES OF NOBILITY.
Not to be conferred by United
States or accepted without
consent, **US Const Art 1 Sec
9 cl 8.**

TITLES OF NOBILITY —Cont'd
State may not grant, **US Const
Art 1 Sec 10 cl 1.**

TOBACCO.
Advisory committee on health care
and tobacco control, **29D:5.**
Annual report by manufacturers of
tobacco products, **94:305B,
94:307A.**
Below cost sale, **64C:15, 64C:17.**
Board of higher education, **15A:27.**
Cessation of smoking, programs,
111:206.
Children.
Minors. See within this heading,
"Minors."
Cigarette tax, **64C:1-64C:39.**
See CIGARETTE TAX.
Cigarette wholesaler's mark-up,
64C:13.
Cities.
See CITIES AND TOWNS.
Contamination by fire or water,
sale after, **94:307.**
Controlled Substances Act,
exclusions, **94C:2.**
Education department, tobacco
education programs, **69:1I.**
Exploding cigars or cigarettes, sale
or storage, **148:52A.**
Fire or water, sale after
contamination, **94:307.**
Fire prevention.
No smoking signs. See within
this heading, "No smoking
signs."
Forest lands, smoking, **148:54.**
Health care security trust, **29D:1
to 29D:5.**
Industrial homework, **149:144,
149:147G.**
Instruction on effects of tobacco on
human system, **71:1.**
Jury deliberations or meetings,
smoking, **234:34C.**
Manufacturers.
Master settlement agreement,
participation, **94E:1, 94E:2.**
Master settlement agreement.
Participation by manufacturers,
94E:1, 94E:2.
Minors.
Employment in manufacturing,
packing, etc., **149:61.**
Rolling papers, sale of, **270:6A.**
Selling or giving, **64C:10, 270:6,
270:6A, 270:7.**
Mortality and morbidity, program
to reduce incidence among
general public, **111:206.**

TOBACCO —Cont'd
Motor vehicles.
  Size of trailer transporting,
    90:19.
Nicotine yield ratings, **94:305B,
  94:307A.**
No smoking signs.
  Regulation of posting, **270:21.**
  Terminal or other facility of
    Massachusetts Bay
    Transportation Authority
    where signs prohibit
    smoking, **272:43A.**
Notice prohibiting cigarette sales
  to minors, **64C:10, 270:7.**
Open fields, smoking, **148:54.**
Participating manufacturers.
  Master settlement agreement,
    94E:2.
Police.
  Capitol Police Force, **31:64.**
  Cities, towns, and districts,
    41:101A.
  Investigator or examiner,
    smoker as ineligible to
    serve, **90:29.**
  Massachusetts Bay
    Transportation Authority
    Police Force, **31:64.**
  Metropolitan district police,
    31:64.
  Public Works Building Police,
    31:64.
  State police, smoking
    regulations, **22C:10.**
Polling places, prohibition against
  smoking, **54:73, 54:75.**
Prison employees, **27:2.**
Public places, regulation of
  smoking, **15A:16A, 111:72X,
  270:21, 270:22, 272:43A.**
  Flea markets, **270:23.**
Railroads.
  See RAILROADS.
Reports by manufacturers of
  tobacco products, **94:305B,
  94:307A.**
Rolling papers.
  Sales to minors, **270:6A.**
  Warning against use with
    controlled substances,
    94C:32I.
Sale.
  After contamination by fire or
    water, **94:307.**
  Below cost, **64C:15, 64C:17.**
  Cigarette tax, **64C:1-64C:39.**
    See CIGARETTE TAX.
  Exploding cigars or cigarettes,
    148:52A.
  Minors, sales, **64C:10, 270:6,
    270:6A, 270:7.**

TOBACCO —Cont'd
Sale —Cont'd
  Rolling papers, **270:6A.**
  Sales tax, exemptions, **64H:6.**
  Single unpackaged cigarettes,
    94:307A.
  Solicitation of sales of cigarettes
    to be brought into state,
    64C:10.
  Sunday sales, **136:6.**
School buses, smoking, **90:7B.**
Schools and education, **15A:27,
  71:2A.**
Settlement agreement.
  Participation by manufacturers,
    94E:1, 94E:2.
Signs.
  No smoking signs. See within
    this heading, "No smoking
    signs."
Single unpackaged cigarettes, sale
  of, **94:307A.**
Smokeless tobacco, cigarette excise
  taxes, **64C:1, 64C:6.**
Stables, smoking, **272:86C.**
State.
  Below cost sales to state
    institutions or agencies,
    64C:15.
  Sales or solicitation of sales of
    cigarettes to be brought into
    Commonwealth, **64C:10.**
  State police, smoking
    regulations, **22C:10.**
Sunday sales, **136:6.**
Tax, **64C:1-64C:39.**
Tobacco settlement fund, **29:2XX.**
  Health care security trust,
    29D:1 to 29D:5.
Town meetings, smoking, **54:73.**
University of Massachusetts,
  experimental work in planting
  and growing, **75:23.**

**TOBACCO SETTLEMENT
  FUND.**
Established, **29:2XX.**
Health care security trust, **29D:1
  to 29D:5.**

TODD FUND.
Income, **70:10, 70:11.**

**TOD SECURITY
  REGISTRATION, 201E:101
  to 201E:402.**
**See TRANSFER ON DEATH
  SECURITY
  REGISTRATION.**

TOE.
Podiatrists not to amputate,
  112:13.

TOE —Cont'd
Workers' compensation, **152:36.**

TOGGLE FISHING, 131:53.

TOILETRIES.
Hairdressers' registration board,
  rules or regulations as to sale,
  112:87CC.

TOILETS.
Appropriations for comfort stations
  by cities and towns, **40:5.**
Architectural barriers against
  handicapped persons, **22:13A.**
Bakeries, **94:9G.**
Construction and maintenance by
  municipalities for use by
  public, **111:33.**
Discrimination, **272:92A, 272:98.**
Disposal of contents, facilities,
  111:31D.
Factories, toilets, **149:133.**
Jails and houses of correction,
  facilities, **126:25.**
Labor.
  See LABOR AND WORKFORCE
    DEVELOPMENT.
Limited access ways, location of
  comfort facilities, **81:7C,
  85:2D.**
Location of privy vaults, **111:126.**
Marina, requirements to obtain
  license to operate toilet
  facilities, **91:59B.**
Nursing or convalescent homes,
  lighting, **111:72C.**
Outdoor toilets, restrictions,
  111:126.
Public lodging houses, **140:36.**
Railroad cabooses and locomotives,
  160:172A.
State parks, reservations, and
  recreation areas, part of
  planning, **132A:2D.**

TOKENS.
Coin machines, false tokens,
  266:75A, 266:75B.

TOLLAND.
Congressional district, **57:1.**
District court, **218:1.**
Medical examiner district, **38:1.**
Senatorial district, **57:3.**

TOLL BRIDGES.
Report of accidents, **90:29.**

**TOLL FREE INFORMATION
  NUMBER.**
Workers' compensation, **23E:3.**

**TOLLING OF STATUTE OF
  LIMITATIONS, 260:7 et
  seq., 260:28 et seq.**
See LIMITATION OF ACTIONS.

TOLL ROADS.
See TURNPIKES AND TOLL ROADS.

TOLLS.
Bridges.
  Report of accidents, **90:29.**
Canals, tolls, **88:9, 88:11.**
Ferries, fares or tolls, **88:2.**
Turnpikes.
  See TURNPIKES AND TOLL ROADS.

TOLUENE.
Driving under influence, **90:21.**

TOMATOES.
Massachusetts lug, **94:99A.**

TOMBS.
See CEMETERIES.

TON.
Coal, standard, **94:240.**
Defined, commercial fertilizers, **128:64.**
Refrigeration, ton of, definition, fire sprinkler system contractors and fitters, **146:81.**
Unit of measure, **98:2.**

TONGUE.
Maiming or assault with intent to maim, **265:14, 265:15.**

TONIC, 94:10A-94:10G.
See SOFT DRINKS.

TONNAGE DUTIES.
States not to lay without consent of Congress, **US Const Art 1 Sec 10 cl 3.**

TOOLS.
Burglary.
  Indictment for possession of burglary tools, form, **277:79.**
  Making or repairing burglarious instrument, **266:49.**
Construction contracts and work.
  Pawnbrokers' loans on tools, **140:83, 140:84.**
  Theft of tools, **266:27.**
Correctional institutions.
  See CORRECTIONAL INSTITUTIONS.
Counterfeiting.
  Forgery or counterfeiting. See within this heading, "Forgery or counterfeiting."
County prisons.
  Payment of bills for tools and materials, **127:72.**
  Purchase of tools and materials, **127:66A.**
Discharged prisoners, furnishing, **127:161, 127:165.**

TOOLS —Cont'd
Escaping prisoners, furnishing, **268:15.**
Execution, exemption, **235:34.**
Forgery or counterfeiting, **267:13, 267:20.**
  Seizure of tools, **267:30.**
Insurance, **175:47.**
Larceny.
  Theft. See within this heading, "Theft."
Mechanics.
  Loans on tools of, penalty for violations, **140:83, 140:84.**
  Theft of mechanics' tools, penalty, **266:27.**
Pawnbroker's loans, **140:83, 140:84.**
Public works, security for rental of tools, **149:29.**
Railroads.
  See RAILROADS.
Sales and use tax, exemption, **64H:6.**
Storage on abutting land entered for maintenance of building, **266:120B.**
Surgical devices.
  See SURGICAL DEVICES.
Tax exemption, **59:5.**
  Distress and sale, exemption, **60:24.**
  Sales and use tax, exemption of tools, **64H:6.**
Theft.
  Burglary. See within this heading, "Burglary."
  Contractors and builders, theft of tools, **266:27.**

TOPOGRAPHICAL SURVEYS AND MAPS.
Improvement of survey of Commonwealth, **91:33.**
Printing provisions, applicability to topographic maps issued by state departments, **5:1.**

TOPSFIELD.
Congressional district, **57:1.**
District court, **218:1.**
Medical examiner district, **38:1.**
Senatorial district, **57:3.**

TORNADO.
Contracts awarded under emergency conditions, bidding requirements, **30:39M, 149:44A.**
Weather insurance, **175:47.**

TORPEDOES.
Fireworks, **148:39.**

TORPEDOES —Cont'd
Possession with intent to injure persons or property, **266:102.**

TORRENS ACT, 185:26 et seq.
Land title registration, **185:1 et seq.**

TORT CLAIMS ACT, 258:2.
Massachusetts Tort Claims Act, **258:2.**

TORTS.
Abatement, survival and revival, **228:1, 228:2.**
Absent defendants, tort actions against, **227:13.**
Admissibility in evidence of advance payments to claimant or plaintiff in tort on issue of liability or to mitigate damages, **231:140B.**
Amherst economic development and industrial corporation, **Spec L 23:8.**
Boston terminal police, misconduct, **159:95.**
Certified mail, **233:79G.**
Charitable corporations, institutions, or organizations, tort liability, **231:85K.**
Children.
  See CHILDREN AND MINORS.
Cities.
  See CITIES AND TOWNS.
Conservator's or guardian's personal liability, **201:37.**
Contribution among joint tortfeasors.
  See CONTRIBUTION AMONG JOINT TORTFEASORS.
Contributory fault.
  Bank deposits and collections.
    Unauthorized signature or alteration, customer's duty to report, **106:4-406.**
  Negotiable instruments.
    Forged signature or alteration of instrument, **106:3-406.**
Recovery of damages, **231:85.**
Credit reporting agencies and report users, consumer actions against, **93:57, 93:64.**
Criminal proceedings as bar to action, **277:78.**
Damages.
  See DAMAGES.
Disclaimer of liability as parking facility owner's or operator's defense, **231:85.**
Dog-bite actions, burden of proof, **140:155.**

TORTS —Cont'd

Economic development and industrial corporation, liability, **121C:8.**

Evidence of advance payments to party claiming or suing for damages, **231:140B.**

Executors and administrators, actions by or against, **230:2.**

Express company police, misconduct, **159:95.**

Federal property, injuring or removing, **1:10.**

Fines and penalties, tort actions involving, **280:1.**

Fraud.
  Tort liability for sale of personal property, **231:85J.**

Gas.
  See GAS AND ELECTRIC COMPANIES.

Guardian's or conservator's personal liability, **201:37.**

Guest passenger's grounds for recovery against operator of motor vehicle, **231:85L.**

Housing and urban renewal operating agencies, liability, **121B:13.**

Indemnification of public employees, **258:9A.**

Innholder's liability, negligence as defense, **140:17.**

Interest on verdict or findings, **231:6B.**

Jurisdiction of person based on acts or conduct within Commonwealth, **223A:3.**

Juvenile delinquent, restitution, **119:62.**

Landowners, standard of care owed to children, **231:85Q.**

Limitation of actions, **260:2A-260:4, 260:4B, 260:10.**

Loan, failure to discharge security on payment, **140:107.**

"Long-arm" jurisdiction, **223A:3.**

Mail and mailing, tort in contract actions, use of certified mail only, **233:79G.**

Massachusetts College Student Loan Authority, liability, **15C:22A.**

Medical records in tort actions for personal injuries, **233:79G, 233:79H.**

Motor vehicle guest passenger's grounds for recovery against operator, **231:85L.**

Non-domiciliaries, personal jurisdiction based on tortuous injury within or without Commonwealth, **223A:3.**

TORTS —Cont'd

Parents' liability for willful acts of children, **231:85G.**

Parking facility, disclaimer of liability as defense in action against owner or operator, **231:85.**

Partnership liability, **108A:13.**

Penalties and fines, tort actions involving, **280:1.**

Personal jurisdiction based upon acts or conduct within Commonwealth, **223A:3.**

Pesticides for insect control, exception from tort liability for discharge of petroleum products, **91:59A.**

Physician rendering emergency treatment, liability, **112:12B.**

Police, misconduct of certain, **159:95.**

Protection of property, liability of persons requesting and rendering assistance, **149:177.**

Railroads and other carriers, misconduct of police, **159:95.**

Release or statement obtained from person confined in hospital, validity, **271:44.**

Representation of public employee by public attorney, **258:2.**

Riots, liability for property destroyed, **269:8.**

Sailing programs, **231:85V.**

Secured transactions.
  Exclusion of tort claims, **106:9-104.**
  Liability of secured party for acts or omission of debtor, **106:9-317.**

Snow.
  See SNOW AND ICE.

Sovereign immunity.
  See SOVEREIGN IMMUNITY.

Sports program volunteers, **231:85V.**

Trademark infringement, **110:4.**

Trade secrets, liability for theft, **93:42.**

Transfer of cases from superior court, **231:102C.**

Trustees as personally liable, **203:14A.**

Turnpike authority.
  Liability for bodily injury or property damage, **81A:20.**

Unsafe condition of rented or leased premises, landlord's liability in damages after notice, **186:19.**

TORTS —Cont'd

Waters and waterways, liability for property damage resulting from discharge of petroleum products or bilge water, **91:59A.**

Watershed system, wanton or malicious destruction or injury to property, **92:111.**

Witness failing to obey summons, liability in tort, **233:4.**

TOTAL DISABILITY.

Life insurance.
  See LIFE INSURANCE.

Retirement, **32:6.**

Workers' compensation, **152:34, 152:34A.**
  See WORKERS' COMPENSATION.

TOTALIZATOR MACHINES.

Horse or dog racing meetings, **128A:5.**

TOURISTS AND TOURISM.

Central Massachusetts Tourist Council, Inc.
  Financial assistance and promotion services from economic development department, **23A:14.**

Economic development department, tourism division, **23A:3.**
  Bureau of vacation travel, **23A:1.**
  Promotion fund, **23A:14.**
  Transfer of personnel to vacation travel bureau, **23A:1.**

Executive director of tourism, appointment, powers and duties, **23A:13A-23A:13E, 23A:14.**

Financial assistance to regional and local tourist promotion agencies and communities, establishment of program, **23A:14.**

Massachusetts Tourism Fund, **10:35J.**

Middlesex County, tourist and development council.
  Financial assistance and promotion services from economic development department, **23A:14.**

Regional tourism facilities fund, **23G:42.**
  Board, **23G:43.**

Shellfish propagation, matching funds from tourism and industrial production fund with local expenditures, **130:20A.**

TOURISTS AND TOURISM
—Cont'd
Turnpike authority.
  Local tourism grant programs,
    81A:18.

TOWELS.
Health regulations, **111:8.**
Registration and rental,
  110:25A-110:25C, 110:29.
Tanning facilities, **111:210.**

TOWERS.
Electricity, construction of facilities
  for transmission, **132A:3.**
Forest fires.
  See FOREST FIRES.
Railroad employees, days of rest,
  160:184.
Skiers' duty to avoid, **143:71O.**

TOWING, 40:22D.
Abandoned motor vehicles.
  Disposition, **40:5, 90:22C,**
    121B:32A.
  Unregistered or abandoned
    vehicle, towing, **90:24H,**
    121B:32A.
Anchorage of vessels in tow,
  102:21.
Bicycles, towing, **85:11B.**
Bids and bidding by contractors,
  40:22, 85:2C, 92:35A.
Chains, standard set by registrar
  of motor vehicles for safety
  towing chains on trailers,
  90:7.
Charge or fee for towing or storing
  motor vehicle, **40:22D,**
  159B:6B, 266:120D.
Cities and towns, **40:22D.**
Consent to towing abandoned
  vehicle, **90:24H.**
Diplomatic or consular officers
  excepted from provisions as to
  towing of illegally parked
  vehicles, **40:22D, 85:2C.**
Exceptions, exemptions, or
  exclusions.
  Diplomatic or consular officers
    excepted from towing
    regulations, **40:22D, 85:2C.**
  Private carrier, exception from
    definition, **159B:2.**
Excise tax on tow trucks, **60A:1.**
Exemptions.
  Exceptions, exemptions, or
    exclusions. See within this
    heading, "Exceptions,
    exemptions, or exclusions."
Fee for towing or storing motor
  vehicle, **40:22D, 159B:6B,**
  266:120D.

TOWING —Cont'd
Illegally parked or standing
  vehicles, **40:22D, 85:2C,**
  159B:6B.
Length limitations for motor
  vehicles inapplicable to
  disabled vehicles, **90:19.**
License requirement for tow
  trucks, **90:24H.**
Metropolitan parks district
  parkways, vehicles illegally
  parked, **92:35A.**
Municipal appropriations, **40:5.**
Occupancy of towed vehicle while
  in motion, **90:13.**
Parked or standing vehicles,
  40:22D, 85:2C.
Persons engaged in towing
  vehicles, financial statements
  required, **159B:6.**
Police, **40:22D, 92:35A, 159B:6B.**
Private motor carrier, person
  towing vehicles of another,
  159B:2.
Private property, town
  appropriations for towing of
  abandoned vehicles, **40:5.**
Private ways, limitation of liability
  in removing vehicles,
  266:120D.
Public works department, towing
  of illegally parked or standing
  vehicles, **85:2C.**
Refuse collection, removal of
  vehicles on municipal ways for
  interfering, **40:21.**
Registered owner, liability for
  towing and storage, **266:120D.**
Registrar of motor vehicles,
  standard for safety chains for
  trailers, **90:7.**
Rental agreements, collision
  damage waiver, **90:32E½.**
Safety chains, required use, **90:7.**
Snow removal operation, towing or
  removal of vehicle during,
  40:21, 85:2A, 159B:6B.
State highways, bidding on
  contracts for towing of
  illegally parked or standing
  vehicles, **85:2C.**
Sunday, towing boat or vehicle,
  136:6.
Trailers, **90:1, 90:7, 90:13, 90:19.**
Unauthorized use of motor vehicle,
  elements of civil damages,
  90:24F.
Unregistered vehicles, **121B:32A.**
Waterways, burning and towing of
  rubbish, **91:52.**
Wrecker plates for tow truck
  operators, **90:2.**

TOWN AND COUNTRY
  PLANNING ACT, 41:81D.

TOWN CLERKS.
See CITY AND TOWN CLERKS.

TOWN COUNSEL.
Appearances before town agencies,
  restrictions, **268A:18.**
Assessors of taxes, representation,
  41:26A.
Ballots, statement of prior holding
  of offices, **53:34.**
Conflict of interest law, opinions,
  268A:22.
Employment of, **40:5.**
General Court, representation
  before, **3:50, 40:5.**
Indemnification of municipal
  officers and employees for
  damages and expenses,
  41:100.
Municipal employee's right to
  opinion as to duties, **268A:22.**
Nomination papers, statement of
  public offices candidate, **53:45.**
Prior offices, statements, **53:34,**
  53:45.
Retirement board, legal adviser,
  32:20.
Tax collector, defense of action
  against, **41:43A.**
Treasurer, defense of actions
  against, **41:43A.**

TOWN HOUSE.
Burning as arson, **266:2, 266:5A.**
Spitting, **270:14, 270:15.**

TOWN MEETINGS, 39:9 et seq.
Absent voting law, adoption or
  revocation, **54:103A.**
Adjournments, **39:9, 39:10.**
Advisory boards or committees.
  Committees. See within this
    heading, "Committees."
Airports, joint enterprises, **90:51N.**
Alcoholic liquors, possession at
  town meetings prohibited,
  54:73-54:75.
Aldermen and selectmen.
  Selectmen. See within this
    heading, "Selectmen."
Annual meeting, **4:7, 39:9.**
  Election subsequent to, as part
    of such meeting, **39:20.**
  Matters other than election of
    town officers, **39:20.**
Annuity to surviving spouse, of
  officials or employees,
  acceptance of statute, **32:89C,**
  32:95A.
Appointment of certain officers by
  selectmen, election, **41:21.**

TOWN MEETINGS —Cont'd

Appropriation committees, provision for appointment or election, **39:16.**

Armories used, **33:122.**

Art commission, acceptance of statute, **41:82.**

Assistant moderators in case of meeting in separate places, **39:14.**

Board members, approval of appointment to another town office, **41:4A.**

Board of election commissioners, adoption of statute providing, **51:16A.**

Boundaries of voting precincts, **43A:3.**

Breach of peace.
  Disorderly conduct. See within this heading, "Disorderly conduct."

Budget, submission, **39:16.**

Bylaws.
  Proceedings at town meetings, bylaws to regulate, **39:15.**
  Referendum, bylaws subject, **43A:10.**
  Representatives at large, bylaw provisions with respect, **43A:4, 43A:5.**
  Time for submission to Attorney General for approval, **40:32.**

Canvass of returns from precincts, **39:21.**

Caucus, voting for holding, **53:121.**

Challenging registrations of voters, **51:48, 51:49.**

Challenging result of vote, **39:15.**

Changes in voting precincts, **54:7.**

Charter amendments.
  Home rule for cities and towns. See within this heading, "Home rule for cities and towns."

Clerks of towns.
  Acceptance of permanent tenure act, **41:19C.**
  Compensation for additional services, **41:19I.**
  Duties of town clerk under representative system, **43A:2-43A:9.**
  Moderator.
    Acting as moderator, **39:14.**
    Administering oath of office to clerk, **41:107.**
  Proprietors of private ways and bridges, calling meetings, **84:12.**
  Reelection of town meeting member, notice, **53:10.**

TOWN MEETINGS —Cont'd

Clerks of towns —Cont'd
  Submission of bylaws to attorney general for approval, **40:32.**
  Temporary clerk, election, **41:14.**
  Vacancy in office of selectman, calling meeting to fill, **39:11.**
  Vote at town meetings, recording, **39:15.**

Coastal wetlands, approval of acquisition, **40:8C.**

Committees, **39:16.**
  Meetings of committees to be public, **39:23A.**
  Regional refuse disposal district, creation of planning committee, **40:44A.**
  Reports and recommendations, **39:16.**

Compensation.
  Wages, salaries, and compensation. See within this heading, "Wages, salaries, and compensation."

Conservation or preservation restrictions, approval, **184:32.**

Constables, service of notice, **41:94.**

Constitution of Massachusetts. See CONSTITUTION OF MASSACHUSETTS.

Contents of notice or warrant, **39:10.**

Curfew, revocation or modification, **40:37A.**

Disability commissions, **40:8J.**

Discharge and removal.
  Removal. See within this heading, "Removal."

Discontinuance of voting precincts, **54:9.**

Disorderly conduct, **54:73-54:75.**
  Disobeying moderator, **39:17.**
  Smoking or having liquor, **54:73.**

Districts.
  Applicability of town meeting procedures, **39:24.**
  Regional refuse disposal districts. See within this heading, "Regional refuse disposal districts."

Eight-hour day for certain employees, election, **149:30.**

Ejecting disorderly persons, **39:17.**

Elderly retirees, acceptance of group insurance, **32B:10, 32B:11A, 32B:11B.**

Election commissioners, adoption of statute providing for board, **51:16A.**

TOWN MEETINGS —Cont'd

Elections.
  Procedures for voting and elections at town meetings. Voting. See within this heading, "Voting."
  Town officers, election of. See ELECTIONS.

Eligibility of voters, **39:10, 39:18.**

Eminent domain taking of land subject to vote of town, **40:14.**

Employees.
  Officers and employees of town. See within this heading, "Officers and employees of town."

Finance committee, provision for appointment or election, **39:16.**

Fire department, hours of duty of members, **48:58A, 48:58D.**

Forty-eight hour week for certain public employees, election, **149:30.**

Group insurance for employees, acceptance of provisions, **32B:10, 32B:11A, 32B:11B.**

Highways and streets of town, acceptance of laying out, relocation, or alteration, **82:23.**

Holding of primaries, submission of question, **53:56.**

Holidays, meetings falling, **39:9.**

Home rule for cities and towns.
  Proposal or consideration of charter amendments, **43B:9.**
  Special meetings as to charter amendments, **43B:10.**

Horse and dog racing meetings, approval, **128A:13A.**

Hours of public employment, election, **48:58A, 48:58D, 149:30.**

Increase in membership of boards, **41:2.**

Industrial development financing authorities, determination of necessity, **40D:2.**

Intoxicating liquors in, prohibition against, **54:73-54:75.**

Joint enterprises, airports, **90:51N.**

Judicial enforcement proceedings, **66:17C.**

Jurors drawn, **234:22, 234:23.**

Justices of the peace.
  Power to call meeting, **39:11, 39:12.**
  Presiding officer in absence of moderator, **39:14.**

Leases. See LANDLORD AND TENANT.

TOWN MEETINGS —Cont'd

Lighting plants, acquisition, **164:36, 164:42, 164:43.**

Limited application of chapter on municipal government, **39:24.**

Malicious injury to warrant for, penalty, **266:124.**

Map of voting precincts for representative form, posting, **43A:3.**

Medicare extension program for employees, acceptance, **32B:11C.**

Moderator.

Acting moderator, **39:14.**

Administering oath of office to town clerk, **41:107.**

Clerks of towns. See within this heading, "Clerks of towns."

Control over meeting, **39:17.**

Disorderly conduct, powers, **39:17.**

Duties of, **39:15.**

Election, **39:14, 39:20, 43A:7, 43A:8.**

Election officer, ineligibility to act, **54:15.**

Preservation of order, **39:17.**

Presiding officer, **39:15.**

Public declaration of votes, moderator to make, **39:15.**

Receipt of votes, **39:18, 41:8.**

Regional refuse disposal planning committee, appointment of members, **40:44A.**

Sealing of ballots, **41:9.**

Separate locations, assistant moderators for meetings, **39:14.**

Temporary moderator, **39:14.**

Term of office, **39:14.**

Vacancies in office, **39:14.**

Municipal industrial development financing authorities, determination of necessity, **40D:2.**

New board or officers, termination of existing officers by election, **41:2.**

Notices.

Constables, service of notice, **41:94.**

Contents of notice, **39:10.**

Reelection of town meeting member, **53:10.**

Representative government, standard form of. See within this heading, "Representative government, standard form."

TOWN MEETINGS —Cont'd

Notices —Cont'd

Special meetings, notice, **39:12.**

Warrant for. See within this heading, "Warrant."

Oath of office of town officers, **41:107.**

Officers and employees of town.

Annuity to surviving spouses of certain officials or employees, acceptance of statute, **32:89C, 32:95A.**

Appointment by selectmen, election, **41:21.**

Group insurance for employees, acceptance of provisions, **32B:10, 32B:11A, 32B:11B.**

Hours of employment, elections as to provisions, **48:58A, 48:58D, 149:30.**

Payroll deductions for contributions to community chest, acceptance of statute, **180:17B. (note)**

Retirement systems and pensions. See within this heading, "Retirement systems and pensions."

Salary plans for employees, **41:108A.**

Official ballots, provision for use, **41:6.**

Official maps.

See ZONING AND PLANNING.

Ordinances.

Bylaws. See within this heading, "Bylaws."

Park commissioners, removal, **45:2.**

Payroll deductions for municipal employees' contributions to community chest, acceptance of statute, **180:17B.**

Pensions.

Retirement systems and pensions. See within this heading, "Retirement systems and pensions."

Place, **33:122, 39:10, 39:14.**

Planning boards.

See ZONING AND PLANNING.

Platoon system in fire departments, adoption, **48:59.**

Playgrounds or recreation centers, **45:14, 45:16.**

Police.

See POLICE.

Precincts.

Representative government, standard form of. See within this heading, "Representative government, standard form."

TOWN MEETINGS —Cont'd

Preliminary meeting to elect moderator, when, **39:14.**

Preservation or conservation restrictions, approval, **184:32.**

Presidential electors, restoration to register of voters, **51:49.**

Presidential primary, rescheduling annual meeting, **39:9A, 39:10.**

Primary elections, submission of question of holding, **53:56.**

Procedure for meetings of governmental bodies, **39:23A, 39:23B, 39:23C.**

Judicial enforcement, **66:17C.**

Public baths or washhouses, authorizing appropriations, **40:12.**

Public declaration of votes, moderator to make, **39:15.**

Public nature of meetings, **39:23A, 43A:5.**

Public ways, acceptance of laying out, relocation or alteration, **82:23.**

Public works board, **16:5.**

Acceptance of statutes, **41:69C.**

Revocation of acceptance, **41:69F.**

Purchase of land subject to vote of town, **40:14.**

Purpose of meeting, notice to state, **39:10.**

Qualified bonds, regulations restricting future issues, **44A:3.**

Quorum, **39:13, 43A:5.**

Recording of votes.

Voting. See within this heading, "Voting."

Recreation commission elected at, exercise of powers, **45:14.**

Reelection of members, **53:10.**

Referendum on vote providing for abolition of board or office under standard form of representative government, **43A:10.**

Refusal by selectmen to call, procedure in case, **39:12.**

Regional planning districts, vote to establish, **40B:3.**

Regional refuse disposal districts.

Determination of question of establishment of district, **40:44E.**

Planning committee, creation, **40:44A.**

Regional school districts.

See REGIONAL SCHOOL DISTRICTS.

TOWN MEETINGS —Cont'd

Registration of voters.

Candidates for town meetings, registrars, **51:25.**

Challenging registrations of voters, **51:48, 51:49.**

Representative government, standard form of. See within this heading, "Representative government, standard form."

Warrants, duties, **39:10.**

Removal.

Disorderly persons, removal and confinement, **39:17.**

Park commissioners, **45:2.**

Representative to town meeting from town or precinct, effect of removal, **43A:5.**

Representative government, standard form, **43A:1 et seq.**

Abolition of board or office, referendum on vote providing, **43A:10.**

Acceptance of law, **43A:11.**

Action on articles in warrant, **43A:7.**

Adoption, **43A:1, 43A:2.**

Applicable laws, **43A:3.**

Boards or offices, referendum on votes with respect, **43A:10.**

Boundaries of voting precinct, **43A:3.**

Bylaws. See within this heading, "Bylaws."

Elections.

Adoption of representative town meeting government, **43A:2.**

Moderator, election, **43A:7, 43A:8.**

Nomination of candidates for town meeting members, **43A:6.**

Referendum to voters, **43A:10.**

Representative, election, **43A:4.**

Time and place of holding, **43A:3.**

Expenditure of money, referendum on measure authorizing, **43A:10.**

Force and effect of action at representative town meeting, **43A:11.**

General meetings, right to hold, **43A:12.**

Map of precincts, posting, **43A:3.**

Meetings of representatives, **43A:5.**

Limitation of powers, **43A:12.**

TOWN MEETINGS —Cont'd

Representative government, standard form —Cont'd

Meetings of representatives —Cont'd

Limited to elected members and members at large, **43A:5.**

Notice, **43A:5.**

Open to public, **43A:5.**

Quorum, **43A:5.**

Registered voters, participation, **43A:5.**

Meetings of voters, regulated, **43A:3.**

Merger of boards or offices, referendum on vote authorizing, **43A:10.**

Moderator, election and term, **43A:7, 43A:8.**

Municipal existence, matters affecting, **43A:12.**

New boards or offices, referendum on vote establishing, **43A:10.**

Nomination of candidates for town meeting members, **43A:6.**

Notices.

Election of representatives, **43A:4.**

Meeting, **43A:5.**

Reelection, town meeting member seeking, **53:10.**

Number of representatives, **43A:4.**

Primaries, time and place of holding, **43A:3.**

Procedure for adoption, **43A:2.**

Pro tempore moderator, election, **43A:8.**

Quorum, **43A:5.**

Referendum to voters, **43A:10.**

Registered voters.

Articles in warrant determined exclusively, **43A:7.**

Officers elected, **43A:7.**

Referendum of certain votes, **43A:10.**

Right to hold general meetings, **43A:12.**

Town meetings, participation, **43A:5.**

Removal of representative from town or precinct, **43A:5.**

Representatives.

Articles in warrant, action, **43A:7.**

At large, bylaw provisions with respect, **43A:4, 43A:5.**

TOWN MEETINGS —Cont'd

Representative government, standard form —Cont'd

Representatives —Cont'd

Compensation, **43A:5.**

Election, **43A:4.**

Judges of election, **43A:5.**

Limitation of powers, **43A:12.**

Moderator pro tempore, election, **43A:8.**

Nominations, **43A:6.**

Notice of election, **43A:4.**

Number, **43A:4.**

Powers, **43A:7, 43A:11.**

Removal from precinct or town, **43A:5.**

Resignation, **43A:5.**

Term of office, **43A:4.**

Vacancies, how filled, **43A:9.**

Resignation of representatives, **43A:5.**

Revision of precincts, **43A:3, 54:7.**

Special appropriations, referendum, **43A:10.**

Special statute establishing representative form, revocation, **39:20, 43A:2.**

Town clerk's duties, **43A:2-43A:9.**

Town officers, election by registered voters, **43A:7.**

Voting precincts, **39:20, 39:21, 43A:3.**

Boundaries, **43A:3.**

Canvas of returns, **39:21.**

Discontinuance, **54:9.**

Establishment, **43A:3.**

Representatives from, election, **43A:4.**

Revision or change, **43A:3, 54:7.**

Selectmen's powers and duties, **43A:3, 54:6-54:8.**

Vacancies as to representatives from, meeting to fill, **43A:9.**

Warrant, action on articles, **43A:7.**

Requests for special meetings, **39:10.**

Reserve funds, appropriation, **40:6.**

Residence, effect of precinct representative's change, **43A:5.**

Resignation of representatives, **43A:5.**

Retirement systems and pensions.

Elderly retirees, acceptance of group insurance, **32B:11B.**

Policemen and firemen, acceptance of provision as to retirement, **32:57B.**

TOWN MEETINGS —Cont'd

Retirement systems and pensions —Cont'd

School janitor's municipal pension, acceptance of statute providing, **32:45.**

Superannuated employees, provision for approval of additional retirement benefits, **32:90C.**

Revocation of precinct voting, **39:20, 43A:2.**

Right to address meeting, leave from moderator required, **39:17.**

Right to vote, **39:18, 51:1.**

Salaries.

Wages, salaries, and compensation. See within this heading, "Wages, salaries, and compensation."

Schools.

See SCHOOLS AND EDUCATION.

Sealing of ballots, **41:9.**

Secret ballot, **39:15.**

Selectmen.

Chairman as presiding officer of meeting, **39:14.**

Powers, **39:9.**

Refusal to call town meeting, procedure in case, **39:12.**

Rescission of vote authorizing selectmen to appoint or act as other officers, **41:23.**

Special meetings, calling, **39:10.**

Vacancy in office of selectman, meeting with respect, **39:11.**

Vote authorizing appointment of or personal performance of duties of other officers, **41:21.**

Voting precincts, powers and duties, **43A:3, 54:6-54:8.**

Separate places, holding, **39:10, 39:14.**

Sewer systems, payment of costs of construction, **83:23.**

Shore reservations, authorizing petition for establishment, **45:23A.**

Smoking at meeting as disorderly conduct, **54:73.**

Southeastern Regional Planning and Economic Development district, termination of towns' membership, **40B:10.**

Special meetings, **39:9, 39:10.**

Calling, **39:10.**

Conduct of, notice, **39:12.**

Duty to call upon request, **39:10.**

TOWN MEETINGS —Cont'd

Special meetings —Cont'd

Home rule for cities and towns, special meetings as to charter amendments, **43B:10.**

Selectmen, meeting called, **39:10.**

Stabilization fund at special town or district meeting, appropriation, **40:5B.**

Stabilization fund, appropriations, **40:5B.**

Subject matter to be stated in warrant, **39:10.**

Submission of budget, **39:16.**

Superannuated employees, provision for approval of additional retirement benefits, **32:90C.**

Surviving spouses' annuities, acceptance of statute, **32:89C, 32:95A.**

Taking of land subject to vote of town, **40:14.**

Temporary moderator, **39:14.**

Temporary town clerk, election, **41:14.**

Time for holding, **39:9.**

Annual meeting, **39:20.**

Establishment of town meeting day, **6:15PP.**

Tobacco smoking prohibited, **54:73.**

Towing of illegally parked or standing vehicles, authority, **40:22D.**

Transfer of appropriations, **44:33B.**

Two or more meetings called by same warrant, **39:10.**

Two-thirds vote, defined, **44:1.**

Unanimous votes, **39:15.**

Unpaid bills of previous years, vote to appropriate money to pay, **44:64.**

Vacancies in office.

Moderator, vacancy in office, **39:14.**

Representative, vacancy in office, **43A:9.**

Selectman, calling meeting to fill vacancy in office, **39:11.**

Town clerk, **41:14.**

Voting, **39:15.**

Absent voting law, adoption or revocation, **54:103A.**

Canvass of returns from precincts, **39:21.**

Counting and recording of votes, **39:15.**

Eligible voters, **39:10, 39:18.**

TOWN MEETINGS —Cont'd

Voting —Cont'd

Precincts.

Representative voting government. See within this heading, "Representative government, standard form."

Receipt of votes by moderator, **39:18, 41:8.**

Records, reports, and returns, **39:15, 41:15.**

Registration of voters. See within this heading, "Registration of voters."

Representative government, standard form of. See within this heading, "Representative government, standard form."

Right to vote, **39:18, 51:1.**

Sealing of ballots, **41:9.**

Secret ballot, **39:15.**

Two-thirds vote defined, **44:1.**

Unanimous votes, **39:15.**

Voting machines, purchase or lease, **54:34.**

Voting precincts.

Representative government, standard form of. See within this heading, "Representative government, standard form."

Wages, salaries, and compensation.

Representatives, **43A:5.**

Town employees, salary plans, **41:108A.**

Warrant, **39:10.**

Action on articles in warrant under representative form, **43A:7.**

Malicious injury to warrant, penalty, **266:124.**

Matters other than election of town officers, meeting, **39:20.**

Subject matter inserted, **39:10.**

Water and waterways, expenditure of appropriations for control of algae, weeds and aquatic nuisances, **40:5.**

Water pollution abatement district, approval or disapproval of establishment, **21:28.**

Water supply, acquisition, **40:38, 40:39A.**

Wetlands along coast, approval of acquisition, **40:8C.**

Widows of deceased officers or employees, acceptance of provision as to granting annuities, **32:89C, 32:95A.**

TOWN MEETINGS —Cont'd
Zoning.
See ZONING AND PLANNING.

TOWNSEND.
Congressional district, **57:1.**
District court, **218:1.**
Medical examiner district, **38:1.**
Senatorial district, **57:3.**
Squannacook and Nissitissit
Rivers Sanctuary established,
132A:17.

TOXIC SPILLS.
Hazardous materials mitigation,
21K:1 to 21K:9.
See MITIGATION OF
HAZARDOUS MATERIALS.

**TOXIC SUBSTANCES, 94B:1 et
seq., 111F:1 et seq.**
**See HAZARDS AND
HAZARDOUS OR TOXIC
SUBSTANCES.**

**TOXICS USE REDUCTION
ACT, 21I:1 et seq.**
Action and proceedings.
Fees, collection, **21I:19.**
Injunctive relief, **21I:18, 21I:20,
21I:22.**
Penalties, collection, **21I:21.**
Residents, actions, **21I:18.**
Superior Court. See within this
heading, "Superior Court."
Administrative council on toxics
use reduction, **21I:4, 21I:5,
21I:9, 21I:13-21I:15, 21I:19,
29:2K.**
Advisory board on toxics use
reduction, **21I:5.**
Appeal and review.
Performance standards, **21I:15.**
Trade secret protection, **21I:20.**
Assistance and Technology Office.
Office of Toxics Use Reduction
Assistance and Technology.
See within this heading,
"Office of Toxics Use
Reduction Assistance and
Technology."
Attorney general.
Advisory board, membership,
21I:5.
Injunctive relief, action, **21I:22.**
Attorneys' fees.
Employees' right, **21I:23.**
Residents, actions, **21I:18.**
Byproduct reduction index, **21I:10,
21I:11.**
Certified reduction planner, **21I:6,
21I:12.**
Citizen involvement, **21I:18.**

TOXICS USE REDUCTION ACT
—Cont'd
Comprehensive Environmental
Response, Compensation and
Liability Act, **21I:2-21I:4,
21I:9, 21I:19.**
Criteria.
Assistance for users, criteria for
prioritizing, **21I:7.**
Reduction plans, **21I:11.**
Emergency Planning and
Community Right to Know
Act, **21I:2, 21I:9, 21I:10,
21I:19.**
Employee rights, protection,
21I:23.
Enforcement, **21I:3, 21I:16,
21I:18, 21I:22.**
Environmental Protection
Department.
Administrative council,
commissioner as member,
21I:4.
Criteria for toxics use reduction
plans, establishment,
21I:11.
Enforcement, **21I:3, 21I:16.**
Fees, **21I:19.**
Fund, division among agencies,
29:2K.
Goals of reduction plans, annual
compilation, **21I:13.**
Information from Office of Toxics
Use Reduction Assistance
and Technology, **21I:7.**
Injunction, request to attorney
general, **21I:22.**
List of toxic or hazardous
substances,
recommendations, **21I:9.**
Performance standards,
regulations, **21I:15.**
Planners, examinations and
regulations, **21I:12.**
Priorities, recommendations,
21I:14.
Reports comparing large
quantity user goals to
statewide goal, **21I:13.**
Reports for facilities in certain
SIC codes, **21I:10, 21I:18.**
Reports from users to EPA, filing
of copies, **21I:19.**
Reports to residents within ten
miles and users, **21I:18.**
Responsibilities, **21I:3, 21I:8.**
Trade secrets, protection, **21I:20,
21I:21.**
Waiver, **21I:15, 21I:17.**
Fees.
Attorneys' fees. See within this
heading, "Attorneys' fees."

TOXICS USE REDUCTION ACT
—Cont'd
Fees —Cont'd
Establishment of toxics use fee,
21I:19.
State tax revenues, **29:2K.
(note)**
Toxics Use Reduction Institute,
fees for programs, **21I:6.**
Fines and penalties, **21I:16,
21I:18, 21I:19, 21I:21.**
Goals of state, **21I:13.**
Hearing.
Performance standards,
adjudicatory hearing,
21I:15.
Study, council to hold public
hearing, **21I:6.**
Trade secret protection, **21I:20.**
Injunctive relief, **21I:18, 21I:20,
21I:22.**
Inspections and inspectors, **21I:8.**
Laboratories, activities, **21I:10.**
List of toxic or hazardous
substances, **21I:9.**
Notice as prerequisite to action by
residents, **21I:18.**
Office of Toxics Use Reduction
Assistance and Technology.
Establishment, **21I:2, 21I:7.**
Fund, division among agencies,
29:2K.
Performance standards, **21I:15.**
Planners for reduction, **21I:6,
21I:12.**
Plans for reduction, **21I:11.**
Prioritization of user segments,
21I:14.
Reports.
Council, annual policy
recommendations, **21I:4.**
Environmental Protection
Department. See within this
heading, "Environmental
Protection Department."
Fund, expenditures, **29:2K.**
Users of large quantity toxics,
21I:10.
Residents.
Actions commenced, **21I:18.**
Within ten miles, involvement,
21I:18.
Responsibilities of department,
21I:3.
Science advisory board, **21I:6.**
Small businesses, outreach
program, **21I:7.**
State agencies, responsibilities,
21I:8.
Superior Court.
Employee rights proceedings,
21I:23.

TOXICS USE REDUCTION ACT
—Cont'd
Superior Court —Cont'd
Jurisdiction to enforce, **21I:18, 21I:22.**
Toxics Use Reduction Institute, **21I:2, 21I:6, 21I:14, 29:2K.**
Trade secret protection, **21I:2, 21I:20, 21I:21.**
Waiver of toxics use reduction, **21I:16, 21I:17, 21I:19.**

TOXICS USE REDUCTION FUND, 29:2K.

TOYS.
Arsenic, selling toys containing, **270:10, 270:11.**
Blank cartridges for toy pistols, **148:39.**
Lead-based substances, regulation, **111:196.**
Materials used in filling stuffed toys, **94:270.**
Wholesalers of stuffed toys, licensing, **94:271.**

TRACER AMMUNITION.
Hunting with prohibited, **131:64.**

TRACKLESS TROLLEYS,
163:1-163:12.
Action on security for damage caused, **163:12.**
Agreement of association.
Contents, **163:4.**
Number of associates, **163:3.**
Subscription by associates, **163:4.**
Applicability of street railway laws, **163:2, 163:5, 163:8.**
Articles of organization, **164:6.**
Bond for damage caused, **163:12.**
Bonds or stock, issue, **163:8.**
Business corporations law inapplicable, **156:2, 156B:3.**
Capital stock.
Stock and stockholders. See within this heading, "Stock and stockholders."
Certain miscellaneous corporations, exception from law, **158:1.**
Cities in which situated to be named in agreement of association, **163:4.**
Common carriers, subject to duties and liabilities, **163:7.**
Compressed air tanks, **146:34.**
Consolidation, **163:8.**
Contracts or agreements.
Agreement of association. See within this heading, "Agreement of association."

TRACKLESS TROLLEYS
—Cont'd
Contracts or agreements —Cont'd
Poles and other structures, contracts for use, **163:10.**
Counties in which situated to be named in agreement of association, **163:4.**
Curtailment of service, **163:7.**
Damage caused by, security, **163:12.**
Definitions, **163:1.**
Directors, agreement of association to designate, **163:4.**
Ejection for nonpayment of fare, **159:101.**
Electricity.
Companies may maintain structures for transmission, **163:2.**
Power to purchase, **163:10.**
Evasion of payment of fare, **159:101.**
Exception from law as to certain miscellaneous corporations, **158:1.**
Extension of service, **163:7.**
Exterior of cars, riding, **85:17B.**
Filing reports and information, **163:8.**
Fines and penalties.
Nonpayment of fare, **159:101.**
Obstruction of passage, **161:94.**
Riding on side or rear of trolley, **85:17B.**
Tampering with trolleys, **159:103.**
Throwing or shooting missiles at vehicles, **159:93, 159:94, 159:104.**
Hearing upon petition to compel giving of security, **163:12.**
Holding stock in, by corporations, **156:5.**
Incorporation, **163:3.**
Intent to be stated in agreement of association, **163:4.**
Jurisdiction of telecommunications and energy department, **159:12, 163:7.**
Leases, **163:8.**
Length of route to be stated in agreement of association, **163:4.**
Licenses or permits.
Permits. See within this heading, "Permits."
Missiles, throwing or shooting at vehicles, **159:93, 159:94, 159:104.**
Motor carriers of passengers, inapplicability of laws, **159A:14.**

TRACKLESS TROLLEYS
—Cont'd
Name to be stated in agreement of association, **163:4.**
Nonpayment of fare, ejection, **159:101.**
Notice of hearing upon petition to compel giving of security, **163:12.**
Obstruction of passage of, penalty, **161:94.**
Operation, **89:9.**
Par value of shares, **163:4.**
Penalties.
Fines and penalties. See within this heading, "Fines and penalties."
Permits, **163:2, 163:6.**
Revocation, **163:8.**
Personal property, power to hold, **163:11.**
Petition to compel giving of security for damage caused, **163:12.**
Preferred stock, subscription rights, **161:35.**
Private lands, **163:2.**
Property, power to hold, **163:11.**
Public ways, **163:2.**
Real estate, power to hold, **163:11.**
Reports, **163:8.**
Revocation of permits and locations, **163:8.**
Riding on side or rear of, penalty, **85:17B.**
Sale or transfer of property, **163:11.**
Security for damage caused, **163:12.**
Shooting, **159:93, 159:94, 159:104.**
State treasurer, bond as security for damage to run, **163:12.**
Stock and stockholders.
Agreement of association, statement as to capital stock, **163:4.**
Corporations, holding of stock, **156:5.**
Issue of stock, **163:8.**
Preferred stock, subscription rights, **161:35.**
Subscription rights, **159:50, 161:35, 163:8.**
Street railways.
Applicability of street railway laws, **163:2, 163:5, 163:8.**
Operation, **163:2.**
Suspension of service, **163:7.**
Tampering, **159:103.**

TRACKLESS TROLLEYS
—Cont'd
Telecommunications and energy
department.
Approval.
  Contracts for use of poles and
    other structures, **163:10.**
  Granting of permit, **163:6.**
  Purchase of electricity, **163:10.**
Articles of organization, **164:6.**
Filing reports and information,
  163:8.
Jurisdiction, **159:12, 163:7.**
Security, power to require,
  163:12.
Suspension or curtailment of
  service, **163:7.**
Termini to be stated in agreement
  of association, **163:4.**
Throwing missiles, **159:93, 159:94,
  159:104.**
Time within which poles and other
  appliances must be erected,
  163:9.
Towns in which situated to be
  named in agreement of
  association, **163:4.**

TRACKS.
Electric railroad, penalty for
  walking on tracks, **162:18.**
Horse.
  See HORSE AND DOG RACING
    MEETINGS.
Railroads.
  See RAILROADS.
Street railways.
  See STREET RAILWAYS.

TRACT INDEXES, 184:33.

TRACTION.
Chiropractors, **112:89.**

TRACTION ENGINES.
Use on highways, **85:30-85:32.**

TRACTORS.
See MOTOR VEHICLES.

TRADE.
See COMMERCE OR TRADE.

TRADE ASSOCIATIONS.
Commission against discrimination
  advisory board, membership,
  6:56.
Dairies, conversion of milk
  containers, **266:144.**
Gasoline dealers' right to join,
  93E:6.
Private detective or investigator,
  exception to licensing
  requirement, **147:23.**

TRADE BOARDS.
See BOARDS OF TRADE.

TRADE-IN.
Motor vehicle sales contract,
  description, **255B:9.**
Sales taxes, **64C:6, 64H:26,
  64H:27A.**

TRADE JOURNALS.
Dental advertising, **112:52C.**

TRADEMARK DILUTION
ACTION, **110:1 et seq.**

TRADEMARKS AND TRADE
NAMES, **110:1-110:29, 110B:1
et seq.**
Accountants, use of term "certified
  public accountant," **112:87D,
  112:87D½.**
Aiding or abetting violations of
  statutes, **110:27.**
Alcoholic liquors.
  Draught malt beverages, name
    to appear on tap, **138:12.**
  Schedule of beverages sold to
    wholesalers or retailers,
    138:25B, 138:25C.
Apothecaries' measures,
  trademark, **98:47.**
Army, use of word restricted,
  110:4B.
Assignment of mark and
  registration, **110B:6.**
Assumed name, doing business,
  110:5, 110:6.
Business corporations,
  prohibition as to assumption
  of name, **156B:11.**
Fee for filing statement, **262:34.**
Bottles and containers,
  110:17-110:25.
Business certificate, evidence of
  identity of person filing, **110:5.**
Business corporations.
  Corporations. See within this
    heading, "Corporations."
Business trusts, exemption from
  requirement of certificate
  stating real name of person
  transacting business, **110:6.**
Cancellation of registration,
  110B:8.
Can, defined, **110:1.**
Certificates.
  Business certificate, evidence of
    identity of person filing,
    110:5.
  Registration. See within this
    heading, "Registration."
Certified public accountant, use of
  term, **112:87D, 112:87D½.**
Clinical thermometers, **98:13.**
Coast guard, use of term
  restricted, **110:4B.**

TRADEMARKS AND TRADE
NAMES —Cont'd
Common law, validity and
  protection of marks acquired,
  110B:14.
Containers and bottles,
  110:17-110:25.
Copying or counterfeiting,
  110B:10-110B:13.
Corporations, **155:9.**
  Assumption of name by business
    corporations, prohibition,
    156B:11.
  Exempt from requirement of
    certificate stating real name
    of person transacting
    business, **110:6.**
  Misuse of term, **110:4A.**
Counterfeit marks, **266:147.**
Damages.
  Imitation or counterfeiting,
    110B:13.
  Name of person, improper use,
    110:4.
Definitions of statutory terms in
  trademark law, **110:1.**
Dentistry, practice, **112:44, 112:49.**
Druggists and pharmacists.
  Apothecaries' measures,
    trademarks, **98:47.**
  Drugstore, use of terms, **112:38.**
  "Wholesale druggists" use of
    term, **112:36C, 112:36D.**
Evidence.
  Business certificate, evidence of
    identity of person filing,
    110:5.
  Certificate of registration,
    110B:4.
Fabric clothing and equipment,
  violation of provisions as to
  trademark registration of
  rented, **110:29.**
Federal government or agency, use
  of term creating impression
  place of business is owned,
  operated, or managed, by,
  prohibited, **110:4B.**
Fees.
  Application fee, **110B:2.**
  Assignment of registration
    certificate, **110B:6.**
  Assumed name, fee for filing
    statement in connection
    with doing business, **262:34.**
  Filing beverage manufacturer's
    or seller's description of
    name, **262:34.**
  Renewal of registration, **110B:5.**

TRADEMARKS AND TRADE NAMES —Cont'd

Fictitious name.

Assumed name, doing business in. See within this heading, "Assumed name, doing business."

Filling station and motor fuel dispensing equipment to show trademark, **94:295F.**

Fines and penalties.

Aiding or abetting violation of statutory provisions, **110:27.**

Assumed or fictitious name, failure to file certificate of one doing business, **110:5.**

Bottles and containers, unlawful use, **110:18.**

Certificate of one doing business under assumed or fictitious name, failure to file, **110:5.**

Fences or structures, placing or fixing, **266:126.**

Milk cans, defacing of trademark, **266:128.**

Registered mark or name, unlawful use of, **110:4, 110:26-110:28.**

Registration of rented towels, garments, aprons, and linens, violation of provisions, **110:29.**

Unauthorized use of certain names or performances of musical compositions, **110:4A, 110:4B, 110:27.**

United States, creating improper impression of federal ownership, management, or operation, **110:4B.**

Unlawful use of trademark or name, **110:4, 110:26-110:28.**

Food.

Frozen dessert or ice cream containers, trademark, **98:20.**

Health department, publication of trademark with certificate of examination for food analyzed, **111:25.**

Milk and milk products. See within this heading, "Milk and milk products."

Forgery or counterfeiting, **110B:10-110B:13.**

Furs, **94:277A.**

Gasoline and motor fuels, trademarks to be shown on filling stations and dispensing equipment, **94:295F.**

G.I., use of term, **110:4B.**

TRADEMARKS AND TRADE NAMES —Cont'd

Government, use of term restricted, **110:4B.**

Health department, publication of trademark with certificate of examination for food analyzed, **111:25.**

Hot water tanks, manufacturer's trademark, **142:17, 142:19.**

Ice cream containers, trademark, **98:20.**

Imitation or counterfeiting prohibited, **110B:10-110B:13.**

"Incorporated," misuse of term, **110:4A.**

Infringement, imitation, or counterfeiting prohibited, **110B:10-110B:13.**

Injunction against unlawful use, **110B:12.**

Insurance policies issued by insurance company groups, heading, **175:18.**

Intoxicating liquors.

Alcoholic liquors. See within this heading, "Alcoholic liquors."

Labor unions' trademarks, fraudulent display or use, **266:69A.**

Linen supply business, **110:25A-110:25C, 110:29.**

Marine Corps, use of term restricted, **110:4B.**

Marks not registerable, **110B:3.**

Massachusetts State Fair, use of term prohibited, **110:4B.**

Milk and milk products.

Containers for milk, cream, and ice cream, registration of trademarks, **98:15, 110:21-110:25, 110:28.**

Defacing of trademark on milk cans, **266:128.**

Motor oil, sale required to be under trade name, **94:295G.**

Musical compositions, unauthorized of certain names or performances, **110:4A, 110:4B, 110:27.**

Navy, use of word restricted, **110:4B.**

Notice.

Registration or renewal as constructive notice of claim of ownership, **110B:4.**

Renewal, notice from secretary of state concerning, **110B:5.**

Optometry, practice, **112:72.**

Penalties.

Fines and penalties. See within this heading, "Fines and penalties."

TRADEMARKS AND TRADE NAMES —Cont'd

Pharmacists.

Druggists and pharmacists. See within this heading, "Druggists and pharmacists."

Physical therapist, words indicating practice, **112:23L.**

Placing or fixing illegally, penalty, **266:126.**

Post exchange or P X., **110:4B.**

Recording.

Registration. See within this heading, "Registration."

"Registered sanitarian," use of title, **112:87OO.**

Registration, **110:1 et seq., 110B:1 et seq.**

Application for registration, **110B:2.**

Assignment of mark and registration, **110B:6.**

Bottles and containers, marks and devices, **110:17-110:25, 110:28.**

Cancellation, **110B:8.**

Certificate, **110B:4.**

Exemptions from requirement of certificate showing real name of person transacting business, **110:6.**

Definitions under trademark law, **110B:1.**

Effective term, **110B:5.**

Fraudulent procurement, **110B:10.**

Linen and towel supply business, **110:25A-110:25C, 110:29.**

Milk, cream, and ice cream containers, **98:15, 110:21-110:25, 110:28.**

Penalty provisions, **110:26-110:29.**

Public record, **110B:5, 110B:7.**

Renewal of registration, **110B:5.**

Constructive notice of claim of ownership, renewal, **110B:4.**

Rules and regulations, promulgation, **110B:9.**

Towels, garments, aprons, and linens, **110:25A-110:25C, 110:29.**

Unregisterable marks, **110B:3.**

Rules and regulations.

Proceedings, rules for conduct, **110B:15.**

Secretary of state to promulgate, **110B:9.**

TRADEMARKS AND TRADE NAMES —Cont'd

Sanitarians, use of title "registered sanitarian" controlled, **112:87OO.**

Search warrants for registered bottles and other containers, **110:20-110:25.**

Secretary of state.

Application for registration, filing, **110B:2.**

Assignment of registration certificate, filing, **110B:6.**

Cancellation of registration, **110B:8.**

Record of registered marks, **110B:7.**

Registration certificate, issuance, **110B:4.**

Renewal, **110B:5.**

Rules and regulations, promulgation, **110B:9.**

Severability of statutory provisions, **110B:16.**

Silver content of articles sold, trademark indicating, **266:77.**

Similar marks or names, use of by others, **110:4.**

Taxicabs to display trade name of owner, **40:22.**

Thermometers, clinical, **98:13.**

Thread, sale regulated, **94:286, 94:288.**

Time or date.

Application for registration, information concerning use of mark, **110B:2.**

Assignment of mark or registration, recording, **110B:6.**

Renewal, notice of necessity, **110B:5.**

Term of registration, **110B:5.**

Towel supply business, **110:25A-110:25C, 110:29.**

United States, use of terms indicating ownership, operation, or management, **110:4B.**

Use without consent of registrant, **110B:11.**

Vessel, scope of term, **110:1.**

"Wholesale druggists," use of term, **112:36C, 112:36D.**

TRADE SCHOOLS, 93:21-93:21C.

Advertising.

Filing in office of commissioner of education, **93:21B.**

Fraudulent advertising, **93:21.**

TRADE SCHOOLS —Cont'd

Appeal of refusal of license to private trade school, **93:21C.**

Approval of courses and facilities, requirement to obtain license, **93:21B.**

Bond or surety, **93:21F.**

Business schools, provision relating to private trade schools inapplicable, **93:21A.**

Conditions to obtaining license, **93:21B.**

Contracts with, notice to beneficiary of right of termination, **255:13K.**

Education department.

Licensing, **93:21B.**

Fraud and deceit, treble damages, **93:21.**

Licensing, **93:21B.**

Bond or indemnification for students, **93:21F.**

Refusal to grant, or revocation of license, right of review, **93:21C.**

Limitation of consumer protection actions involving, **260:5A.**

Nonprofit endowed school as not within statutory definition, **93:21A.**

Power to regulate, **93:21B.**

Private trade schools defined under trade regulation law, **93:21A.**

Recovery of damages for fraud or misrepresentation, **93:21.**

Refusal to grant or revocation of license, right of review, **93:21C.**

Regulations concerning, **93:21 et seq.**

Reports required, **93:21B.**

Superior court review of refusal or revocation of license, **93:21C.**

Suspension or revocation of license, **93:21B, 93:21C.**

Textbooks, seller's liability for misrepresentation to pupil regarding school, **93:21.**

Training schools as not within definition, **93:21A.**

Treble damages, **93:21.**

Vocational education.

See VOCATIONAL EDUCATION AND SCHOOLS.

Witnesses, power of board of education to summon, **93:21B.**

TRADE SECRETS.

Air pollution inspections, secret processes discovered during, **111:2B, 111:142B.**

TRADE SECRETS —Cont'd

Antitrust laws, **93:2, 93:8.**

Attorney General, disclosure of information, **93A:6.**

Buying or receiving stolen secrets, **266:60A.**

Commercial and financial information corporation, confidentiality of trade secrets, **40J:12.**

Controlled dangerous substances, **94C:25, 94C:38.**

Conversion of funds or property, **93:42, 93:42A.**

Criminal penalties for theft, **266:30.**

Defined, **148:38B, 266:30, 266:60A.**

Environmental Protection Department, protection of records, **21C:12.**

Fires.

See FIRES AND FIRE PREVENTION.

Hazardous and toxic substances, **94B:3.**

Hazardous Waste Management Act, protection of information, **21C:4, 21C:12.**

Labels, omissions, **111F:7.**

MSDS, withheld information, **111F:5, 111F:12, 111F:20.**

Revelation of trade secret, **94B:3.**

Toxics Use Reduction Act, trade secret protection, **21I:2, 21I:20, 21I:21.**

Injunctive relief against misappropriation of trade secrets, **93:42A.**

Larceny, **266:30.**

Buying or receiving stolen trade secrets, **266:60A.**

Tort liability, **93:42.**

Podiatrist's betrayal of professional secret as unprofessional conduct, **112:19.**

Preliminary injunctive relief for misappropriation, **93:42A.**

Public records, exceptions as to disclosures, **4:7.**

Restraints of trade, **93:2.**

Technology Development Corporation, materials made or received, **40G:10.**

Theft of.

Larceny of. See within this heading, "Larceny."

Tort liability for theft, **93:42.**

Underground storage tanks.

See FIRES AND FIRE PREVENTION.

TRADE SECRETS —Cont'd
Water pollution control division
director as having access,
21:40.

**TRADES, OCCUPATIONS, AND
PROFESSIONS, 112:1 et
seq.**
Accident and sickness insurance.
Change of occupation, **175:108.**
Illegal occupation, **175:108.**
Associations.
Professional corporations.
See PROFESSIONAL
CORPORATIONS AND
ASSOCIATIONS.
Trade associations.
See TRADE ASSOCIATIONS.
Unions.
See LABOR RELATIONS
AND DISPUTES.
Automobile insurance, prohibitions
as to issuance or renewal,
175:22E.
Definition or construction of
"occupation," minimum wage
law, **151:2.**
Fees.
See FEES.
Group liability insurance coverage,
175:111E.
Hours of labor rules inapplicable
to certain, **149:56.**
Injunctions against operating
unlicensed or unregistered
business, **62C:76.**
Insurance for accident and
sickness.
Accident and sickness insurance.
See within this heading,
"Accident and sickness
insurance."
Jurors, business or occupation of
juror's spouse to be listed,
234:4, 234A:70.
Labor relations.
See LABOR RELATIONS AND
DISPUTES.
Licenses and registration
certificates, **62C:67.**
List of residents to contain
occupation, **51:4.**
Motion picture distribution
business practices, **93F:1,
93F:2.**
Occupational education division,
13:32.
Offensive trades.
See NUISANCES.
Professional corporations.
See PROFESSIONAL
CORPORATIONS AND
ASSOCIATIONS.

**TRADES, OCCUPATIONS, AND
PROFESSIONS** —Cont'd
Public official or employee,
engaging in professional
activity requiring disclosure of
confidential information,
268A:23.
Registration of professions and
occupations, **112:1 et seq.**
See REGISTRATION OF
PROFESSIONS AND
OCCUPATIONS.
Schools.
Trade schools.
See TRADE SCHOOLS.
Vocational education.
See VOCATIONAL
EDUCATION AND
SCHOOLS.
Secrets of trade.
See TRADE SECRETS.
Societies of certain professions or
occupations, **176:51, 231:85N.**
Unions.
See LABOR RELATIONS AND
DISPUTES.
Vocational education.
See VOCATIONAL
EDUCATION AND
SCHOOLS.
Wastewater treatment facilities
operators, board of
certification, **21:34A, 21:34B,
21:34C.**

TRADE UNIONS.
**See LABOR RELATIONS AND
DISPUTES.**

TRADE ZONES.
Foreign trade zones,
establishment, **23A:28A.**

**TRADING STAMPS,
93:14L-93:14R.**
Bond of trading stamp company,
93:14N, 93:14O.
Cash value, **93:14M.**
Crimes and offenses, **93:14R,
271:29, 271:30.**
Definitions, **93:14L.**
Enforcement of law, **93:14R.**
Fines and penalties for violations,
93:14R, 271:29, 271:30.
Merchandising schemes by,
prohibited, **271:29, 271:30.**
Milk dealers, use of trading
stamps, **94A:14.**
Notice.
Cessation of business, **93:14P.**
Default in redemption, **93:14Q.**
Penalties or fines for violations,
93:14R, 271:29, 271:30.

TRADING STAMPS —Cont'd
Redemption.
Cash, redemption, **93:14M.**
Default, **93:14Q.**
Notice of cessation of business,
93:14P.
Registration, **93:14N.**

TRAFFIC CONGESTION.
Alleviation, excise credit, shuttle
vans, **63:31D-63:31F.**
Growth and development policy
committees, cities and towns,
40:4I.

**TRAFFIC REGULATIONS AND
RULES OF THE ROAD,
89:1 et seq.**
Abandoned vehicles, authority of
police, **90:22C.**
Accidents.
Prevention of accidents, **89:1 et
seq.**
Address, driver at night to give,
85:16, 85:17.
Administrative justices,
appearance ticket for parking
violations, **90:20A, 90:20C.**
Agreements for control, failure to
comply, **81:26.**
Agricultural vehicles.
Use of flashing red light, **90:7.**
Weight limit of farm and
agricultural trailers, **90:19.**
Alcohol, driving under influence of.
See DRIVING WHILE UNDER
INFLUENCE OF
ALCOHOL OR DRUGS.
Aldermen and selectmen, **40:22.**
Ambulances, right to proceed
through intersections
regardless of traffic signals,
89:7B.
Animals.
See ANIMALS.
Appeals.
Clerk-magistrates' decision
appealed to justice, **90C:3.**
Habitual offender status,
90:22F.
Appearances.
See APPEARANCES.
Appropriations by cities and towns
to prevent automobile
accidents, **40:7A.**
Arrest for violations, **90:20C,
90:21, 90:27, 90:29.**
Fast or dangerous driving,
85:11.
Hit-and-run accidents, **90:21.**
License, display to conceal
identity, **90:23.**

TRAFFIC REGULATIONS AND RULES OF THE ROAD
—Cont'd

Arrest for violations —Cont'd

Operation of vehicle while under influence of drugs or intoxicants, **90:21.**

Pedestrians violating rules as to use of ways, **90:18A.**

Summons in lieu, **90:24.**

Without warrant, **85:11, 90:18A, 90:21, 90:27.**

Audit of records of traffic violations, **90:27.**

Automobile insurance.

Classification of risks based on accident involvement, **175:113B.**

Comprehensive insurance as affected by traffic violations, **175:113O.**

Contents, **90C:2.**

Copies, **90C:2.**

Definitions, **90C:1.**

Falsification, **90C:10.**

Fine as conviction, payment, **90C:4.**

Invalidity of part of chapter, **90C:11.**

Issuance, **90C:2.**

Noncriminal trial, contesting violation, **90C:3.**

Parking violations, **90:20A, 90:20C.**

Penalty for falsification, **90C:10.**

Person other than police officer, criminal complaint, **90C:4.**

Processing, **90C:2.**

Registrar of motor vehicles, citation books to be printed, **90:7, 90:7A, 90:8, 90:C6.**

Unlawful disposition, **90:19A.**

Axles, weight, **90:19A.**

Bell, use, **90:7, 90:16.**

Betting, driving on public way, **90:24.**

Bicycles.

See BICYCLES.

Blind persons crossing way, **90:14A.**

Boston traffic and parking commission, **90:18 et seq.**

See BOSTON.

Brakes, **90:7, 90:7A, 90:13.**

Bridges, **85:20 et seq.**

See BRIDGES.

Bulk food trucks, permit, **90:19A.**

Business district.

Defined, **90:1.**

Speed, **90:17.**

TRAFFIC REGULATIONS AND RULES OF THE ROAD
—Cont'd

Camp buses stopped on highway to pick up or discharge passengers, prohibition as to passing, **90:14.**

Certificate of registration, exhibition at scene of accident, **90:11.**

Citations, **90C:1 et seq.**

Application for complaint, indication by police officer on citation, **90C:3.**

Audit sheets, **90C:6.**

Citation books, **90C:6.**

Confess or contest violation, failure, **90C:3.**

Constitution, citation not deemed to be writ, **90C:5.**

Contents, **90C:2.**

Copies, **90C:2.**

Definitions, **90C:1.**

Falsification, **90C:10.**

Fine as conviction, payment, **90C:4.**

Invalidity of part of chapter, **90C:11.**

Issuance, **90C:2.**

Noncriminal trial, contesting violation, **90C:3.**

Parking violations, **90:20A, 90:20C.**

Penalty for falsification, **90C:10.**

Person other than police officer, criminal complaint, **90C:4.**

Processing, **90C:2.**

Registrar of motor vehicles, citation books to be printed, **90:7, 90:7A, 90:8, 90:C6.**

Unlawful disposition, **90C:9.**

Waiver of trial, **90C:3.**

Warrantless arrest not prohibited, **90C:4.**

Writ under constitution, citation not deemed, **90C:5.**

Cities and towns.

Appropriations for prevention of accidents, **40:7A.**

Control signals.

Signs and signals. See within this heading, "Signs and signals."

Failure to comply with standards as to control of traffic, **90:34.**

High-accident locations, reimbursement of cities and towns for cost of installing traffic control devices, **90:33B.**

TRAFFIC REGULATIONS AND RULES OF THE ROAD
—Cont'd

Cities and towns —Cont'd

Local speed regulations, **85:10, 90:18, 90:20.**

Ordinances and regulations require approval of department of public works, **85:2.**

Powers of regulation, **40:22-40:22C, 85:10, 85:10A.**

Receipts from municipal parking lots, **40:22C.**

Right turn on red, regulation, **89:8.**

Safety campaigns, municipal appropriations, **40:7A.**

Selectmen, **40:22.**

Signs and signals. See within this heading, "Signs and signals."

Snow and ice removal, town regulations, **40:21.**

Special constables of towns and certain cities, **90:29.**

Standards as to traffic control, withholding of funds on failure to comply, **81:26, 90:34.**

Stop and yield signs, regulating operation of vehicles, **89:9.**

Through streets, right to establish and designate, **89:9.**

Clear view.

View of driver. See within this heading, "View of driver."

Clerk-magistrate, duties as to hearings, **90C:3.**

Colleges.

See COLLEGES AND UNIVERSITIES.

Commercial driver license.

See UNIFORM OPERATION OF COMMERCIAL MOTOR VEHICLES.

Comprehensive automobile insurance as affected by violations, **175:113O.**

Confession, pedestrians violating rules as to use of ways, **90:18A.**

Constables appointed in connection with motor vehicle offenses and investigations, **90:29.**

Contracts and agreements for control of traffic, failure to comply, **81:26.**

**TRAFFIC REGULATIONS AND
RULES OF THE ROAD**
—Cont'd
Control signals.
  Signs and signals. See within
    this heading, "Signs and
    signals."
Conviction of crime.
  See CONVICTION OF CRIME.
Corners.
  Intersections. See within this
    heading, "Intersections."
Court records of offenses and
  offenders, **90:27.**
Cranes mounted on trucks,
  restrictions as to operation,
  90:19.
Criminal offenses and procedure,
  89:5, 90:20, 90:27, 90C:3.
Crosswalks.
  Pedestrian walk signals
    prohibited, **85:2.**
  Slanted curbing installed, **83:25.**
  Violation of regulations
    concerning vehicles
    approaching, **89:11.**
Curves, care and speed, **90:14,
  90:17.**
Dangerous driving.
  Reckless driving. See within this
    heading, "Reckless driving."
Death resulting from accident,
  suspension or revocation of
  driver's right to operate,
  90:24G, 90:29.
Definitions, **90:22.**
Directional signals, **90:7A, 90:14B.**
Disabled vehicles, flares, **85:14B.**
Disabled veteran, parking, **40:22,
  40:22A.**
Disobeying officer, **90:25.**
Districts.
  Business district. See within
    this heading, "Business
    district."
Drag racing.
  Racing upon public ways. See
    within this heading, "Racing
    upon public ways."
Driving records.
  Records and reports. See within
    this heading, "Records and
    reports."
Drunken.
  See DRIVING WHILE UNDER
    INFLUENCE OF
    ALCOHOL OR DRUGS.
Education.
  Schools and education. See
    within this heading,
    "Schools and education."

**TRAFFIC REGULATIONS AND
RULES OF THE ROAD**
—Cont'd
Emergency vehicles.
  See EMERGENCY VEHICLES.
Endangering public safety, fine
  and or imprisonment, **90:24.**
Environmental management
  department roads, right to
  regulate use of vehicles, **90:18.**
Equipment, driving improperly
  equipped vehicles, **90:9.**
Examination or inspection.
  Motor vehicles, **90:7A.**
  Police inspectors or
    investigators, **90:29.**
  Registry examiners or
    investigators, **90:27.**
Failure to stop after accident.
  See HIT AND RUN
    ACCIDENTS.
Farm and agricultural vehicles.
  Agricultural vehicles. See within
    this heading, "Agricultural
    vehicles."
Fast driving.
  Speed. See within this heading,
    "Speed."
Filing.
  Records and reports. See within
    this heading, "Records and
    reports."
Fines and penalties, **89:4B, 89:5,
  89:11, 90:20, 90:27.**
Fire apparatus.
  Keeping to right on approach of
    fire apparatus, **89:7A.**
  Right of way for fire vehicles,
    89:7-89:7B.
  Signals, fire vehicles may move
    contrary, **89:7B.**
Flares, **85:14B.**
Forest warden's vehicle, red lights
  on front, **90:7E.**
Forfeitures, fines, and penalties,
  89:5, 89:11, 90:20, 90:27.
Frightened animals, passing,
  90:14.
Funeral processions, **85:14A.**
Gaming, prohibition against
  driving on public way on bet,
  90:24.
Garbage and refuse, improper
  disposal, **270:16, 270:16A.**
Governor and council, powers,
  85:23.
Guards to reduce spray or splash
  caused by rear wheels,
  requirement, **90:7.**
Guilty plea.
  Habitual traffic offenders,
    hearings, **90:22F.**

**TRAFFIC REGULATIONS AND
RULES OF THE ROAD**
—Cont'd
Guilty plea —Cont'd
  License, **90:24.**
Habitual traffic offenders, **90:22F,
  90:23, 90:24.**
Hand signals, **85:11B, 90:14B.**
Headphones, wearing of while
  operating vehicle, **90:13.**
Hearing.
  Notice by clerk-magistrate to
    officer and violator of date,
    90C:3.
  Parking violation challenged by
    mail, right to hearing,
    90:20A, 90:20A½.
Heavy commercial trucks,
  restriction to use of right-hand
  lane on multi-lane highways,
  89:4C, 89:5.
Height of vehicles, printed
  designation required, **90:19.**
High-accident locations,
  reimbursement of cities and
  towns for cost of installing
  traffic control devices, **90:33B.**
Highway safety committee.
  Governor's highway safety
    committee or bureau, **6A:18,
    90A:1-90A:4.**
Hit.
  See HIT AND RUN
    ACCIDENTS.
Horns, **90:7, 90:16, 149:18G.**
Horses, frightening, **90:14.**
Housing and community
  development department,
  powers and duties, **23B:3.**
Illegally parked motor vehicles.
  See PARKING AND PARKING
    STATIONS.
Indication of course to be traveled
  by vehicles turning at certain
  intersections, **90:14.**
Inflammable fluids, vehicles
  carrying to stop at railroad
  crossings, **90:15.**
Inspections.
  Examination or inspection. See
    within this heading,
    "Examination or inspection."
Insurance.
  Automobile insurance. See
    within this heading,
    "Automobile insurance."
Intersections.
  Ambulances may proceed
    through contrary to traffic
    signals, **89:7B.**
  Crosswalks. See within this
    heading, "Crosswalks."

TRAFFIC REGULATIONS AND RULES OF THE ROAD
—Cont'd

Intersections —Cont'd
Defined, **89:8, 89:9, 90:1.**
Entering, **89:8.**
Making left turn into, **90:14.**
Operation, **90:14.**
Right of way, **89:7B, 89:8.**
Right on red, **89:8.**
Signs and signals. See within this heading, "Signs and signals."
Speed, **90:17.**
Through ways, intersections, **89:9.**
Turning within, **89:8.**
Intoxicating liquor, driving under influence of.
See DRIVING WHILE UNDER INFLUENCE OF ALCOHOL OR DRUGS.
Investigation of accidents, **90:26.**
Judgment by agreement in motor vehicle accident case as bar to action by defendant, **231:140A.**
Jurisdiction, accident reports where police have concurrent jurisdiction, **90:29.**
Justices of the peace, summonses for violations, **90:27.**
Lanes, regulation of driving on ways divided into, **89:4A, 89:4B, 89:4C, 89:5.**
Leaving scene of accident.
See HIT AND RUN ACCIDENTS.
Left, passing, **89:2, 89:5.**
Left turn, **90:14.**
Crossing center line during left turn into or from private way, **89:1.**
One-way street, left turn on red, **89:8.**
Signal, **90:14B.**
Licenses.
See MOTOR VEHICLES.
Lights, **85:15, 90:7.**
Control signals.
Signs and signals. See within this heading, "Signs and signals."
Fines and penalties for violations as to lights on vehicles, **85:15, 85:17, 90:7, 90:20.**
Flares, when required, **85:14B.**
Malicious destruction of lights on highway, **266:94.**
Number plate illumination, **90:6, 90:7.**

TRAFFIC REGULATIONS AND RULES OF THE ROAD
—Cont'd

Lights —Cont'd
Parking on way, **90:7.**
Red lights on front of vehicles, **90:7, 90:7E.**
Signs and signals. See within this heading, "Signs and signals."
Spot lights, **89:8, 90:16, 90:20.**
Tail lights, **90:7.**
Time for display of lights, **90:7.**
Locking parked vehicles, **90:13.**
Longshore and waterfront employees, horn on truck or tractor used, **149:18G.**
Magistrate, time for offender to be brought before, **90:21.**
Mail and mailing.
Notice, **90:20A, 90:20C.**
Pedestrians violating rules, notice, **90:18A.**
Malicious destruction of lights, signs, and signals on highway, **266:94.**
Mechanical or electrical signals for stopping or turning, **90:14B.**
Meeting other vehicle, keeping to right, **89:1, 89:5.**
Minors under age 17 violating motor vehicle laws, proceedings against, **119:74.**
Motorcycle handlebar regulations, violations, **90:7J.**
Motor to be stopped on parked vehicle, **90:13.**
Motor vehicle and fuel revenue, expenditure for enforcement of traffic laws, **90:34; MA Const Amend Art 78.**
Muffler.
See MOTOR VEHICLES.
Municipalities and municipal finance.
Cities and towns. See within this heading, "Cities and towns."
Name, driver at night to give, **85:16, 85:17.**
Negligence of operator.
Fine and/or imprisonment, **90:24.**
Owner's liability, **231:85F.**
Night, giving of name and address by person driving during, **85:16, 85:17.**
Noise, unnecessary noise prohibited, **90:16.**
Noncriminal disposition of violations, **90:20A, 90C:3.**

TRAFFIC REGULATIONS AND RULES OF THE ROAD
—Cont'd

Obstructed view.
Keeping to right in case, **89:4, 89:5.**
Precautions to be taken, **90:14.**
Speed limit, **90:17.**
Obstruction of police vehicles, **89:7A.**
Offenses and penalties, **89:5, 89:11, 90:20, 90:27.**
Off-street parking areas, installation of meters in leased, **40:22C.**
One-way streets.
Driving the wrong way, **89:10.**
Left turns, **89:8, 90:14.**
Operators' licenses.
See MOTOR VEHICLES.
Overtaking.
Passing. See within this heading, "Passing."
Owner's liability for motor vehicle operator's negligence, **231:85F.**
Parking violations.
See PARKING AND PARKING STATIONS.
Passing, **89:1, 89:2.**
Animals, **90:14.**
Bicycle passing motor vehicle, **85:11B.**
Heavy commercial vehicles, **89:4C.**
Left, passing, **89:2, 89:5.**
Pedestrian crosswalk, passing of vehicles stopped, **89:11.**
Penalties for violations, **89:2, 89:5, 90:14, 90:20.**
School buses, **90:14.**
Streetcars, **90:14.**
Pedestrians, **90:14.**
Bicycle operator to yield right of way, **85:11B.**
Blind persons, **90:14A.**
Construction of public ways, access to pedestrians during, **90E:2A.**
Crosswalks. See within this heading, "Crosswalks."
Defined under motor vehicle law, **90:34A.**
Limited access and express state highways, **85:2B.**
Speed limit as affected, **90:17.**
Traffic safety week, educational programs, **6:15P.**
Use of ways by, **90:18A.**
Walk signals prohibited, **85:2.**
Penalties and fines, **89:5, 89:11, 90:20, 90:27.**

TRAFFIC REGULATIONS AND RULES OF THE ROAD
—Cont'd

Personal property, regulations as to transporting, **90:31A.**

Police officers and vehicles.

Abandoned vehicles, authority, **90:22C.**

Application for complaint, indication by police officer on citation, **90C:3.**

Arrest of person believed to be drunk driver, officer's liability, **90:24.**

Blood or breath test to determine intoxication of driver, **90:24.**

Disobeying or refusing information, **90:25.**

Duties of, **90:27.**

Inspectors and investigators, powers and statutes, **90:29.**

Obeying signals, **89:8.**

Obstruction of police vehicles, **89:7A.**

Operation of police vehicles, **89:7-89:7B.**

Parking violations, handling, **90:20A.**

Patrol wagons, right of way, **89:7.**

Pedestrians violating rules, duties, **90:18A.**

Registration certificate, refusal to display at officer's request, **90:21.**

Right of way, **89:7, 89:7A.**

Show traveling and recreation vehicles, police enforcement of laws and regulations, **90B:32.**

Special constables to enforce motor vehicle law, appointment, **90:29.**

Speed restrictions, right of police to violate, **89:7B.**

State highways, jurisdiction of police over, **81:19.**

Towing away illegally parked or standing vehicles, **85:2C.**

Violation of rules of the road on direction of police officer, **89:5.**

Violators, procedure against, **90:21, 90:27.**

Presumption of unreasonable or improper speed, **90:17.**

Prevention of accidents by traffic regulation and rules of the road, **89:1 et seq.**

Private ways.

Abandonment of motor vehicle, penalty, **90:22B.**

TRAFFIC REGULATIONS AND RULES OF THE ROAD
—Cont'd

Private ways —Cont'd

Leaving vehicles in private ways, town bylaws, **40:21.**

Narcotics, driving on way while under influence, **90:24.**

Removal of motor vehicles from private ways or improved or enclosed property, **266:120D.**

Speed, regulation, **85:22, 90:18.**

Property damage accidents, reporting, **90:26.**

Public grounds, driving, **45:13.**

Public works department, powers, **85:2, 89:1, 89:4, 89:9, 90:18, 90:18A, 90:31A.**

Racing upon public ways, **90:24.**

Speed. See within this heading, "Speed."

Railroad crossings, precautions, **90:15.**

Rear vision mirrors, **90:7.**

Reckless driving, **90:24.**

Arrest, **85:11.**

Guilty plea, **90:24.**

Motorboats, **90B:8.**

Subsequent offenses, **90:24.**

Records and reports.

Accident reports, **90:26, 90:29, 272:80G.**

Convictions of traffic violations to be reported to registrar, **90:24, 90:24A.**

Insurance, fixing and establishing classification of risks, **175:113B.**

Medical examiner's report of death to registrar, **38:7.**

Pedestrian violations, **90:18A.**

Probation officers, access to driving records, **90C:4.**

Traffic citations, **90:27.**

Recreation vehicles, pushing across highway, **90B:25.**

Red lights on vehicles, **90:7, 90:7E.**

Red, right turn, **89:8.**

Reflectors on rear of vehicles, **90:7.**

Registrar of motor vehicles.

Driving without registration, penalty, **90:23.**

Powers, **90:31, 90C:8.**

Reports to.

Records and reports. See within this heading, "Records and reports."

Supervisors, investigators or examiners, duties, **90:27.**

TRAFFIC REGULATIONS AND RULES OF THE ROAD
—Cont'd

Reimbursement of cities and towns for cost of installing traffic control devices at high accident locations, **90:33B.**

Reports.

Records and reports. See within this heading, "Records and reports."

Revocation.

See MOTOR VEHICLES.

Right, keeping, **89:1, 89:4B, 89:5.**

Commercial vehicles on multi-lane highways, **89:4C.**

Fire apparatus, on approach, **89:7A.**

Slow moving vehicles, **89:4.**

When view obstructed, **89:4, 89:5.**

Right of way, **89:8.**

Ambulances, **89:7.**

Bicycle operator to yield to pedestrians, **85:11B.**

Fire and police vehicles, **89:7-89:7B.**

Intersections, **89:7B, 89:8.**

Pedestrians, **89:11.**

Red, right, **89:8.**

Snow traveling and recreation vehicles crossing public ways to yield to vehicles thereon, **90B:25.**

Through ways, **89:9.**

Yielding when making left turn at intersection, alley, or driveway, **90:14.**

Right turn, **90:14.**

Red light, turn, **89:8.**

Signal, **90:14B.**

Rotaries, regulating vehicles entering, **89:8.**

Route restrictions, fine or penalty for motor vehicles violating, **90:31A.**

Safety.

Safe driving regulations, **90:13-90:15.**

Safety campaigns, municipal appropriations, **40:7A.**

Safety week, **6:15P.**

Unsafe vehicles. See within this heading, "Unsafe vehicles, operation."

School buses.

See SCHOOL BUSES AND TRANSPORTATION OF PUPILS.

TRAFFIC REGULATIONS AND RULES OF THE ROAD
—Cont'd

Schools and education.
Buses.
See SCHOOL BUSES AND TRANSPORTATION OF PUPILS.
Colleges.
See COLLEGES AND UNIVERSITIES.
Control signals to protect schoolchildren, **85:2, 85:21A.**
Safety patrol leaders, traffic direction, **71:48A.**
Speed in school zones, **90:17.**
Second offense.
See CONVICTION OF CRIME.
Selectmen and aldermen, **40:22.**
Sentence and punishment, **89:5, 89:11, 90:20, 90:27.**
Signals.
Signs and signals. See within this heading, "Signs and signals."
Signature, refusal to comply with officer's demand, **90:25.**
Signs and signals.
Authority of cities and towns to contract or incur debt, **40:4, 44:6, 44:6A, 44:7, 85:2, 85:21A, 89:9.**
Bicycle operator, turn signal, **85:11B.**
Cities and towns, erection and maintenance, **40:4, 44:6, 44:6A, 44:7, 85:2, 85:21A, 89:9.**
Fire or police vehicles or ambulances may move contrary to, when, **89:7B.**
Flashing device for directional signals for emergency use as required equipment on motor vehicles, **90:7.**
Gasoline delivery trucks, use of audible warning signals when in reverse gear, **90:7.**
Handicapped persons, signs indicating parking spaces, **22:13A.**
Hand signals, giving, **85:11B, 90:14B.**
High accident locations, installation of traffic control devices, **90:33B.**
Highway fund, disposition of fees, **90:34.**
Indebtedness of cities and towns for acquisition, erection, or maintenance, **44:6A, 44:7.**

TRAFFIC REGULATIONS AND RULES OF THE ROAD
—Cont'd

Signs and signals —Cont'd
Malicious destruction, **266:94.**
Mechanical or electrical signals for stopping or turning, **90:14B.**
Parking in front of dwelling house, signs, **40:32.**
Police signals, obedience, **89:8.**
Public works department's powers, **85:2.**
Red light, illegal right, **89:8.**
Reimbursement of cities and towns for cost of installation at high-accident locations, **90:33B.**
Right of way as controlled, **89:8, 89:9.**
Right on red light, **89:8.**
School children, control signals to protect, **85:2, 85:21A.**
Stop signs and yield signs, regulating operation of motor vehicles, **89:9.**
Termini and angles of ways, erection of monuments and markers, **86:1.**
Through ways, stop signs, **89:9.**
Use of way where prohibited by warning signs, **90:16.**
Single lane, vehicle entirely within, **89:4A.**
Sirens on motor vehicles, **90:16, 90:20.**
Size, restrictions, **90:19.**
Lights on large vehicles, **90:7.**
Penalties, **90:20.**
Special permits for unusual vehicles, **90:19.**
Sleigh bells, **89:3, 89:5.**
Slow moving vehicles.
Duty to keep right while ascending grade, **89:4.**
Emblem required, **90:7.**
Smoke, permitting escape of excessive smoke, **90:16.**
Snow and ice removal, town regulations, **40:21.**
Snow tires with metal studs, use in certain months prohibited, **90:16.**
Snow traveling and recreational vehicles, **90B:25, 90B:32.**
Solicitation of funds, stopping vehicles, **85:17A.**
Special constables of towns and small cities, **90:29.**
Speed, **85:20-85:24, 90:17, 90:18.**
Arrest for speeding, **85:11.**

TRAFFIC REGULATIONS AND RULES OF THE ROAD
—Cont'd

Speed —Cont'd
Bicycle, speed to be reduced by motorist approaching person, **90:14.**
Bridges, **85:20-85:25.**
See BRIDGES.
Business district, speed, **90:17.**
Construction vehicles, **90:19A.**
Curves, **90:14, 90:17.**
Divided highway, speed limit for certain vehicles, **90:17.**
Fire and police vehicles, **89:7B.**
Governor and council, powers, **85:23.**
Hawking or peddling merchandise, speed near vehicle used, **90:17.**
Heavy vehicles, **85:31, 85:32, 90:17.**
Intersections, speed, **90:17.**
Issuance of local regulations, **90:18.**
Local regulations, **85:10, 90:18, 90:20.**
Metallic tires, heavy vehicles, **85:31, 85:32.**
Obstructed view, **90:17.**
Pedestrians, effect of presence, **90:17.**
Police may violate certain restrictions, **89:7B.**
Presumption of unreasonable or improper speed, **90:17.**
Private ways, regulation of speed, **85:22, 90:18.**
Railroad crossings, speed, **90:15.**
Record, using public way to make, **90:24.**
Safe speed in certain cases, **90:14.**
School buses.
See SCHOOL BUSES AND TRANSPORTATION OF PUPILS.
Slow moving vehicles. See within this heading, "Slow moving vehicles."
State ways, **85:23, 90:17A.**
Thickly settled or business district, speed, **90:17.**
Town regulations, **85:10.**
Trucks, powers of department of public works, **90:31A.**
Violations, **90:17, 90:18, 90:20.**
Warrant, arrest without warrant for speeding, **85:11.**
Weight, speed restrictions for vehicles carrying excessive, **90:17.**

TRAFFIC REGULATIONS AND RULES OF THE ROAD
—Cont'd

Spot lights, **90:16, 90:20.**
State highways.
  Grade crossing, clear view in each direction on state highway on which abolished, **159:72.**
  Jurisdiction of police over, **81:19.**
  Speed, **85:23.**
State treasurer, reimbursement of cities and towns for installation of traffic control devices at high-accident locations, **90:33B.**
State universities.
  See COLLEGES AND UNIVERSITIES.
Stopping.
  After accident, **90:24.**
  Bicycle, stop signal, **85:11B.**
  Disobeying police officer's signal to stop, **90:25.**
  Fires, stopping vehicle for fire apparatus and stopping near, **89:6A, 89:7A.**
  Hand signal, **90:14B.**
  Railroad crossings, **90:15.**
  Right on red, **89:8.**
  School buses.
    See SCHOOL BUSES AND TRANSPORTATION OF PUPILS.
  Street railways, **89:6A, 161:92.**
  Through ways, **89:9.**
Stop signs, regulating operation of motor vehicles at, **89:9.**
Storage of vehicles removed by metropolitan district police from scene of accident, **255:39A.**
Street railways.
  See STREET RAILWAYS.
Subdivision control law, general purposes, **41:81M.**
Subsequent offenses.
  See CONVICTION OF CRIME.
Summons for violations, **90:24, 90:27.**
Superior courts.
  Enforcement of traffic regulations, **85:2.**
  Habitual traffic offender, appeal of designation, **90:22F.**
Supervisor.
  See TRAFFIC SUPERVISOR.
Suspension of license.
  See MOTOR VEHICLES.
Tail lights, **90:7.**
Taxicabs, markings required, **40:22.**

TRAFFIC REGULATIONS AND RULES OF THE ROAD
—Cont'd

Television sets in vehicles, **90:13.**
Thickly settled districts.
  Defined under motor vehicle law, **90:1.**
  Speed, **90:17.**
Through ways, **89:9.**
  Designation, **85:2, 89:9.**
  Dimensions of motor trucks and trailers, **90:19.**
  State highways, designation, **89:9.**
  Weight of loads, regulated, **85:30, 85:32.**
Tickets and citations for traffic violations.
  Citations. See within this heading, "Citations."
Time.
  Accidents, time for reporting to registrar of motor vehicles, **90:29.**
  Appearances on summons for violations, **90:27.**
  Hearing date, notice by clerk-magistrate to officer and violator, **90C:3.**
  Lights, time for display or use, **90:7.**
  Offender to be brought before magistrate, **90:21.**
  Violations within same 12-month period, **90:20.**
Toll roads or bridges, police reports of accidents, **90:29.**
Towing.
  See TOWING.
Towns.
  Cities and towns. See within this heading, "Cities and towns."
Traffic signs.
  Signs and signals. See within this heading, "Signs and signals."
Trailers.
  See TRAILERS AND SEMI-TRAILERS.
Transportation of goods, violations of regulations, **90:31A.**
Trucks.
  Department of public works, powers as to speed of trucks, **90:31A.**
  Following truck cranes with projecting booms by another vehicle, requirement, **90:19.**
  Lights, **90:7.**
  Longshore and waterfront employees, horn on trucks used, **149:18G.**

TRAFFIC REGULATIONS AND RULES OF THE ROAD
—Cont'd

Trucks —Cont'd
  Right-hand lane on multi-lane highways, restriction, **89:4C, 89:5.**
  Trailers.
    See TRAILERS AND SEMI-TRAILERS.
Tunnels, traffic, **85:2B.**
Turning, **90:14, 90:14B.**
  Bicycle operator, signal, **85:11B.**
  Left turn. See within this heading, "Left turn."
  Right turn. See within this heading, "Right turn."
TV sets in vehicles, **90:13.**
Unattended vehicles, locking and removal of keys, **90:13.**
Unauthorized driving, plea of guilty to offense, **90:24.**
Uniform operation of commercial motor vehicles.
  See UNIFORM OPERATION OF COMMERCIAL MOTOR VEHICLES.
Uniform traffic tickets and citations, **90:27.**
Unintentional offenses, disposition of proceedings, **90:20.**
United States secretary of commerce, failure to comply with traffic control agreement, **81:26, 90:34.**
Universities.
  See COLLEGES AND UNIVERSITIES.
Unsafe vehicles, operation, **90:9.**
  Procedure on discovery of unsafe vehicle, **90:27.**
Veterans, parking for disabled, **40:22, 40:22A.**
View of driver.
  Obstructed view. See within this heading, "Obstructed view."
  State highways on which grade crossings abolished, clear view in each direction, **159:72.**
Violation defined, **90:22.**
Wager, driving on public way on bet prohibited, **90:24.**
Waiver of trial, **90C:3.**
Warrant, arrest without, **85:11, 90:18A, 90:21, 90:27, 90C:4.**
Weights and measures, **90:19, 90:19A.**
  Certain heavy vehicles, **85:30-85:32.**
  Size restrictions. See within this heading, "Size, restrictions."

TRAFFIC REGULATIONS AND RULES OF THE ROAD —Cont'd

Weights and measures —Cont'd
Speed restrictions on vehicles carrying heavy weight, **90:17.**
Turnpike authority, **81A:19.**
Witnesses, credibility of as affected by record of conviction of certain traffic violations, **233:21.**
Wrecks.
Accidents. See within this heading, "Accidents."
Yield signs, regulating operation of motor vehicles, **89:9.**
Zoning and planning, special permit as predicated upon traffic improvements, **40A:9.**

TRAFFIC SAFETY WEEK, **6:15P.**

TRAFFIC SIGNS AND SIGNALS.
See TRAFFIC REGULATIONS AND RULES OF THE ROAD.

TRAFFIC SUPERVISOR.
Group or blanket insurance coverage, **32B:2A.**
Retirement benefits, eligibility, **32:1.**

TRAILER COACH PARKS.
See MANUFACTURED HOMES AND MANUFACTURED HOUSING COMMUNITIES.

TRAILERS AND SEMI-TRAILERS.
Agricultural vehicles.
Farm or agricultural trailers. See within this heading, "Farm or agricultural trailers."
Air brakes, **90:7.**
Altering trailer registration certificate, **90:24B.**
Bailment.
Rental trailers. See within this heading, "Rental trailers."
Boat trailers.
Boat list, information as to registry of trailered boat, **90B:11.**
Definition of boat transporters, **90:1.**
Exemption from permit, **90:19.**
Number plates, dealers in boats and boat trailers, **90:5.**
Permit to operate, when required, **90:19.**

TRAILERS AND SEMI-TRAILERS —Cont'd

Boat trailers —Cont'd
Registration certificate dealers not required to carry, **90:11.**
Regulations applicable to dealers, **90B:3.**
Size requirements, **90:19.**
Truck-trailer boat transporter, **90:1.**
Brakes, **90:7.**
Air brakes, **90:7.**
Drums, prohibition against installation of certain brake drums, **90:7G.**
Burglary.
Theft. See within this heading, "Theft."
Certificates and certification.
Exemption of certain trailers from motor vehicle certificate of title law, **90D:2.**
Registration of trailers. See within this heading, "Registration of trailers."
Chains for safety in towing, **90:7.**
Children.
Minors. See within this heading, "Minors."
Compulsory liability insurance, continuation to cover newly acquired vehicles, **175:113A.**
Concealment, **266:27A, 266:28, 266:29, 277:58A.**
Construction materials, trailers hauling, **90:19A.**
Crane or boom, restrictions on operation of vehicle carrying, **90:19.**
Credit unions, loans, **171:62.**
Dealers.
Manufacturers, distributors and dealers. See within this heading, "Manufacturers, distributors, and dealers."
Defacing or mutilating identifying numbers on trailers, **90:32A, 266:139.**
Definitions under motor vehicle law, **90:1.**
Domicile.
Residence. See within this heading, "Residence."
Driver's license.
Licenses and permits. See within this heading, "Licenses and permits."
Emergency disaster service vehicles, registration, **90:7I.**
Equipment, **90:7.**
Improperly equipped trailers, operation, **90:9.**

TRAILERS AND SEMI-TRAILERS —Cont'd

Equipment —Cont'd
Lateral projection of mirrors and other exterior devices, **90:19.**
Recreational vehicle trailers, required equipment, **90B:24.**
Excise tax in lieu of local tax, imposition and abatement under staggered registrations, **60A:1.**
Exemptions.
Military personnel, exemption from taxation, **59:5.**
Milk and milk products, transporting bulk milk exempt from certain weight limitations, **90:19.**
Motor vehicle certificate of title law, certain trailers exempt, **90D:2.**
Special permit requirements, exemption, **90:19A.**
Farm or agricultural trailers.
Farmers, trailers owned or controlled, **90:5.**
Minors, operation, **149:62.**
Weight limit, **90:19.**
Filing.
Records and reports. See within this heading, "Records and reports."
Fines and penalties for violations, **90:20.**
Firefighters may occupy trailers in motion, **90:13.**
Forged or altered registration, possession, **90:24B.**
Fraud in leasing of trailers, **90:32F.**
Heavy duty platform trailer, defined under motor vehicle law, **90:1.**
Height of vehicles to be printed thereon, **90:19.**
Horses, trailers used for transportation, **90:19.**
House trailers.
See MANUFACTURED HOMES AND MANUFACTURED HOUSING COMMUNITIES.
Identifying numbers.
Defacement or mutilation, **90:32A, 266:139.**
Plates, **90:5, 90:6, 90:7R.**
Restoration or substitution, **90:32A.**
Inspection, **90:7A.**

TRAILERS AND
SEMI-TRAILERS —Cont'd

Insurance, continuation of compulsory liability insurance to cover newly acquired vehicles, **175:113A.**

Joint owners, issuance of certified copy of registration certificate or license, **90:30.**

Labor.
Manufacturers. See within this heading, "Manufacturers, distributors, and dealers."

Larceny.
Theft. See within this heading, "Theft."

Leased trailers.
Rental trailers. See within this heading, "Rental trailers."

Length of trailers, **90:19, 90:19F.**

Liability insurance as covering newly acquired trailers, **175:113A.**

Licenses and permits.
As to registration of trailers.
Registration. See within this heading, "Registration of trailers."
Boat trailers, **90:19.**
Classifications, **90:8.**
Joint owners, issuance of certified copy of license, **90:30.**
Public works department. See within this heading, "Public works department."
Revocation of operator's license for theft of trailer, **266:28.**

Lights on trailers, **90:7.**

Liquid petroleum products, vehicle or semi-trailer unit carrying, **90:19A.**

Machinery and equipment.
Equipment. See within this heading, "Equipment."

Manufacturers, distributors, and dealers.
Boat trailers. See within this heading, "Boat trailers."
Delivery of new vehicles without registration, **90:9.**
Not required to carry registration certificate on person, **90:11.**
Regulations applicable, **90B:3.**
Vehicles owned or controlled, **90:5.**

Maximum over-all length, **90:19.**

Milk and milk products, transporting bulk milk exempt from certain weight limitations, **90:19.**

TRAILERS AND
SEMI-TRAILERS —Cont'd

Minors.
Farm vehicles, operation, **149:62.**
Registration of trailers owned, **90:2A.**

Mirrors and other exterior devices, lateral projection, **90:19.**

Misstatements in applications, **90:9.**

Motor vehicle.
Certificate of title law, certain trailers as exempt, **90D:2.**
Registrar of motor vehicles. See within this heading, "Registrar of motor vehicles."
Trailer as motor vehicle, **90:20C.**
"Trailer" dollies used for towing registered motor vehicles, **90:1.**

Municipal debt limits, value of trailers as basis for computation, **44:10.**

Mutilation or defacing of identifying numbers, **90:32A, 266:139.**

Name and address of registered owner, report of change, **90:26A.**

National network, **90:19F.**

Newly acquired trailers, transfer of registration, **90:2.**

Nonresidents.
Agent for service of process, **90:3A-90:3D.**
Military personnel, exemption from taxation, **59:5.**

Number identification.
Identifying numbers. See within this heading, "Identifying numbers."

Occupancy while trailer in motion, **90:13.**

Oil and gas, vehicle or semi-trailer unit carrying liquid petroleum products, **90:19A.**

Owner-repairman, definition of under motor vehicle law, **90:1.**

Parking spaces and garages, reports required, **90:32.**

Permits.
Licenses and permits. See within this heading, "Licenses and permits."

Posting.
Mobile homes and mobile home parks, **140:32D.**

Private business schools, training in operating skills, **75D:1.**

TRAILERS AND
SEMI-TRAILERS —Cont'd

Process, registrar as nonresident's agent for service, **90:3A-90:3D.**

Publicly owned vehicles, registration without fee, **90:33.**

Public works department.
Exemption from special permit requirements, **90:19A.**
Permits, **90:8, 90:19, 90:19A, 90:30.**

Records and reports.
Garages and open air parking spaces, records required, **90:32.**
Registered owner, report of change in name or address, **90:26A.**
Rental records, **90:32C, 90:32D.**

Recreational vehicle trailers.
Boat trailers. See within this heading, "Boat trailers."
Registration of dealers, **90:5.**
Required equipment, **90B:24.**

Red flag, display, **90:7.**

Registrar of motor vehicles.
As attorney for service of process, **90:3A-90:3D.**
Regulatory authority, **90:31.**
Safety towing chains, establishment of standards, **90:7.**

Registration of dealers in recreational vehicle trailers, **90:5.**

Registration of trailers, **90:1A, 90:2.**
Application, information required, **90:2.**
Boat trailers. See within this heading, "Boat trailers."
Change in name or address of registered owner, report, **90:26A.**
Fees, **90:33.**
Forging registration certificate, **90:24B.**
General distinguishing number or mark, revocation of registration certificate improperly issued, **90:5.**
Joint owners, issuance of certified copy of registration certificate or license, **90:30.**
Minors, trailers owned, **90:2A.**
Misstatements in application, **90:9.**
Penalty for possession of forged certificate, **90:24B.**

TRAILERS AND SEMI-TRAILERS —Cont'd

Registration of trailers —Cont'd

Publicly-owned vehicles, registration without fee, **90:33.**

Semi-trailers, **90:33.**

Suspension of certificate for nonpayment of tax, **60A:2A.**

Temporary use on public ways following expiration, **90:6.**

Transfer of registration to newly acquired trailer, **90:2.**

Unregistered trailers, operation, **90:9.**

Rental trailers.

Personal operation by lessee, **90:32E.**

Records, **90:32C, 90:32D.**

Reports.

Records and reports. See within this heading, "Records and reports."

Residence.

Nonresidents. See within this heading, "Nonresidents."

Report of change in residence of registered owner, **90:26A.**

Restoration or substitution of identifying numbers, **90:32A.**

Revocation of operator's license for theft, **266:28.**

Safety towing chains, **90:7.**

Schools, training in operating skills by private business schools, **75D:1.**

Security interests in multi-state transactions, perfection, **106:9-103.**

Semi-trailers defined under motor vehicle law, **90:1.**

Service of process on nonresident, appointment of registrar as agent or attorney, **90:3A-90:3D.**

Ships and other watercraft.

Boat trailers. See within this heading, "Boat trailers."

Size and weight restrictions, **90:19, 90:19A.**

Snow traveling and recreation vehicles.

Recreational vehicle trailers. See within this heading, "Recreational vehicle trailers."

Stealing.

Theft. See within this heading, "Theft."

Sunday, activities permitted, **136:6.**

TRAILERS AND SEMI-TRAILERS —Cont'd

Taxation.

Maximum rate of excise tax on registered motor vehicles and trailers, **60A:1.**

Military personnel, exemption from taxation of nonresident, **59:5.**

Suspension of registration certificate for nonpayment of tax, **60A:2A.**

Theft.

Burglary from trailer, **266:20A, 266:20B.**

Revocation of operator's license for theft of trailer, **266:28.**

Vehicle, theft, **266:27A-266:29.**

Venue of criminal proceeding for buying, receiving or concealing stolen trailer, **277:58A.**

Through ways, dimensions of trailers, **90:19.**

Tires, provisions as to safety standards, **90:7K.**

Tobacco, size of trailer hauling, **90:19.**

Towing, **90:1, 90:7, 90:13, 90:19.**

Tow truck dolly, definition under motor vehicle law, **90:1.**

Training by private business schools in operation, **75D:1.**

United States Department of Transportation, conformity to equipment regulations, **90:7.**

Unregistered or improperly equipped trailers, operation, **90:9.**

Weight and size restrictions, **90:19, 90:19A.**

Wheel safety chock block, parking on hill or grade, **90:13.**

Width, **90:19, 90:19F.**

TRAINERS FOR HORSE OR DOG RACES.

Barring or suspending for misconduct, **128A:13.**

Influencing persons connected with race to affect result, penalized, **128A:13C.**

Licensing or registering, **128A:9A.**

TRAINING PROGRAMS OR SCHOOLS.

Judicial institute established for training of judicial and non-judicial personnel, **211B:16.**

Schools.

See SCHOOLS AND EDUCATION.

TRAINS.

See RAILROADS.

TRAMPS, 272:63-272:69.

See VAGRANTS AND TRAMPS.

TRAMWAYS.

See RECREATIONAL TRAMWAYS.

TRANSCRIPTS.

Administrative proceedings, standard rules, **30A:9.**

Antitrust laws, changes by witnesses and transcript of investigation by Attorney General, **93:8.**

Appeal and review.

See APPEAL AND REVIEW.

Appellate tax board, **58A:10.**

Auditor or master, admissibility of transcripts in civil proceeding before, **221:91C.**

Certified copies, **167:2E, 233:20G.**

Court stenographers.

See COURT STENOGRAPHERS.

Criminal proceedings, transcripts, **221:88, 221:91B.**

District court.

Electronic recording of proceedings, **218:27A.**

Trial by jury of six of certain criminal cases, **218:27A.**

Evidence, transcript as, **233:80.**

Executions.

Appellate transcript, stay of execution pending trial court clerk's receipt, **235:16.**

Filing as prerequisite to execution on judgment rendered by court outside of Commonwealth, **235:14.**

Fees, **221:83.**

Foreign guardian, transcript from record of appointing court, **201:30.**

Grand jury testimony, **221:86.**

Immunity for witness, transcript of proceedings at hearing, **233:20E.**

Inquest proceedings, **38:9, 38:10.**

Insurance competitive practices violations, **176D:7-176D:9.**

Interception of wire or oral communications, transcript of proceedings for issuance of warrant authorizing, **272:99.**

Nursing home administrators, transcripts of records of registration board as evidence, **112:114.**

TRANSCRIPTS —Cont'd

Physician, complaint against, recording of testimony, **112:5.**

Restraint of trade, changes by witnesses and transcript of investigation by Attorney General, **93:8.**

Stenographers.
See COURT STENOGRAPHERS.

Taxation.
Appellate tax board, **58A:10.**

Temporary court stenographers appointed, **221:83.**

Uniform rules of adjudicatory procedure, **30A:10.**

Workers' compensation.
Board proceedings, **152:11B.**
Evidence at hearings, transcript, **152:8.**
Recorded statement, transcript to be furnished to claimant, **152:7B.**

TRANSFER ACT.

Small value cases, **231:102C.**

TRANSFER AGENT.

Cooperative banks.
See COOPERATIVE BANKS.

Defined, Uniform Gifts to Minors Act, **201A:1.**

Stock certificates, signing, **156:33.**

TRANSFER BOOKS.

Corporations, **155:22, 156B:32.**

TRANSFER OF CASES.

Appeals court, transfer of causes to or from, by supreme judicial court, **211:4A, 211A:12.**

Attorney general.
See ATTORNEY GENERAL.

Bonds and undertakings.
District court, bond on removal of actions from, **231:104-231:107.**
Superior court to Boston municipal court or other district court, required for transfer of cases, **231:102C, 231:104.**

Clerks of court, **231:102C.**

District courts, **231:104.**
See DISTRICT COURTS.

Equity cases in probate and family court department, **215:6.**

Fees not required for removal of action defended by Attorney General, **262:2.**

Housing court, removal of actions to or, **185C:20.**

Judgment, effect of removal or transfer, **215:6, 231:102C, 231:104.**

TRANSFER OF CASES —Cont'd

Jurisdictional amount increased in certain courts, **231:104.**

Jury and jury trial.
Right to jury trial, removal of action from district to superior court as affecting, **231:103.**
Waiver of jury trial on transferred case, **231:102C.**

Land court, removal to superior court of actions not within exclusive jurisdiction, **185:15.**

Notice as to removal or transfer of case, **231:102C.**
District court, notice of removal, **231:107.**

Order disposing of rents from unfit dwellings, removal of action to superior court, **111:127G.**

Partial removal of case as affecting jurisdiction, **231:104A.**

Probate and Family Court, **211:4A.**
Equity proceedings, **215:6.**
Superior court, procedure as to transfers, **215:6.**

Small claims, **218:21, 218:23, 231:102C.**

Superior courts, **213:1B, 231:104.**
See SUPERIOR COURTS.

Supreme judicial court, **211:4A, 211A:12.**
See SUPREME JUDICIAL COURT.

Venue, **223:13.**
See VENUE.

Worcester Central District Court, removal of trial of civil actions, **218:19A.**

TRANSFER OF PROPERTY OR TITLE.

See SALE OR TRANSFER OF PROPERTY.

TRANSFER OF VENUE ACT, 223:15.

TRANSFER ON DEATH SECURITY REGISTRATION.

Beneficiary form.
Cancellation or change of registration in, **201E:107.**
Defined, **201E:102.**
Designation of beneficiary.
Effect, **201E:105, 201E:107.**
Examples of registrations in, **201E:401.**
How registration in beneficiary form showed, **201E:106.**
Multiple owners of security registered in, **201E:103.**

TRANSFER ON DEATH SECURITY REGISTRATION —Cont'd

Beneficiary form —Cont'd
Requirements for registration of security in, **201E:104.**
Terms and conditions for registration in.
Registering entity may establish, **201E:401.**
When security deemed registered in, **201E:105.**
Who may obtain registration in, **201E:103.**

Citation of act, **201E:101.**

Construction of provisions, **201E:101.**

Creditors of security owners.
Rights, **201E:402.**
Rights not limited by provisions, **201E:302.**

Death of all owners.
Effect, **201E:201.**

Definitions, **201E:102.**

Discharge of registering entity from claims to security, **201E:301.**

Request for registration in beneficiary form.
Acceptance by registering entity, **201E:301.**

Supplemental principles of law and equity, **201E:101.**

Survivor rights, **201E:201.**

Terms and conditions.
Registering entity may establish, **201E:401.**

Testamentary transfers.
Transfer under provisions not testamentary, **201E:302.**

Title act, **201E:101.**

TRANSFER STATION.

Hazardous waste management, **21C:2.**

TRANSFERS TO MINORS, 201A:1 to 201A:24.

Accounts and accounting.
Legal representatives and custodians, **201A:19.**
Petition, **201A:19.**
Probate court, powers, **201A:19.**

Annuities.
Life or endowment insurance policies and annuity contracts. See within

Applicability, **201A:21.**

Bank deposits and collections, **201A:1, 201A:9.**

Brokers, defined, **201A:1.**

Care and control of custodial property, **201A:9, 201A:12.**

TRANSFERS TO MINORS
—Cont'd
Citation of law, **201A:24.**
Conservators.
Guardians and conservators. See within this heading, "Guardians and
Construction of law, **201A:23.**
Corporations.
Securities. See within this heading, "Securities."
Creating custodial property and effecting transfer, **201A:9.**
Credit union as bank within meaning of act, **201A:1.**
Custodial property, **201A:8, 201A:9.**
Accounting by custodians, **201A:19.**
Care and control of custodial property, **201A:9, 201A:12.**
Defined, **201A:1.**
Use, **201A:14.**
Custody and custodian.
Accounts and accounting. See within this heading, "Accounts and
Bond, **201A:15, 201A:18.**
Defined, **201A:1.**
Existing custodianship, **201A:22.**
Expenses and compensation, **201A:15.**
Initial custodian, designation, **201A:9.**
Investment of ward's property, **201A:9.**
Nomination of custodian, **201A:3.**
Powers of custodian, **201A:13.**
Property.
Custodial property. See within this heading, "Custodial
Renunciation, removal, or resignation, **201A:18.**
Rights, powers, and duties, **201A:11.**
Securities in registered form given to minors, **201A:9.**
Single custodianship, **201A:9, 201A:10.**
Successor custodian, **201A:18.**
Termination of custodianship, **201A:20.**
Definitions, **201A:1.**
Endowment insurance policies.
Life or endowment insurance policies and annuity contracts. See within
Existing custodianships, **201A:22.**
Forms, **201A:9.**
Guardians and conservators.
Limitation of powers, **201A:11.**
Successor custodian, **201A:18.**

TRANSFERS TO MINORS
—Cont'd
Initial custodian, designation, **201A:9.**
Irrevocability of gift, **201A:11.**
Jurisdiction, **201A:2.**
Life or endowment insurance policies and annuity contracts, **201A:9.**
Custodial property, **201A:1.**
Defined, **201A:1.**
Delivery to custodian, **201A:9.**
Gifts of, **201A:9.**
Irrevocability of gift, **201A:11.**
Money, gift of, **201A:9.**
Nomination of custodian, **201A:3.**
Obligor, transfer, **201A:7.**
Personal liability of uncompensated custodian for losses, **201A:15.**
Power of appointment, transfer by exercise, **201A:4.**
Probate and family court.
Accounting, powers, **201A:19.**
Bond of custodian, powers, **201A:18.**
Successor custodian, appointment, **201A:18.**
Receipt for custodial property, **201A:8.**
Registration.
Gift of registered or unregistered security or money, method of **201A:9.**
Registered form, "What is security, **201A:1.**
Successor custodian, registration in name, **201A:18.**
Renunciation, resignation, death, or removal of custodian, **201A:18.**
Responsibility of person dealing with purported donor or custodian, **201A:6.**
Securities.
Defined, **201A:1.**
Form of gift, **201A:2.**
Gift of, **201A:9.**
Method of making gift, **201A:2.**
Registration. See within this heading, "Registration."
Short title, **201A:24.**
Single custodianship, **201A:10.**
Successor custodian, **201A:18.**
Termination of custodianship, **201A:20.**
Third persons, liability, **201A:16, 201A:17.**
Title of minors indefeasible, **201A:11.**
Trust, transfer authorized, **201A:5.**

TRANSFERS TO MINORS
—Cont'd
Uniformity of application and construction, **201A:23.**
Use of custodial property, **201A:14.**
Validity and effect of transfer, **201A:11.**
Will, transfer authorized, **201A:5.**

TRANSIENTS.
"Chronically nonresident person," defined under public health law, **111:116.**
Vagrants, **272:63-272:69.**
See VAGRANTS AND TRAMPS.
Vendors, **101:1-101:30.**
See TRANSIENT VENDORS.

TRANSIENT VENDORS, 101:1-101:30.
Advertising by, restrictions, **101:7, 101:8.**
Alcoholic liquors, **101:16, 138:32.**
Aliens and persons who have not declared intention to become citizens, **101:22.**
Arrest and prosecution of violators, **101:32.**
Artificial flowers, sale, **101:16, 101:33.**
Assignees' sales, restrictions, **101:7.**
Assistants, permissibility of employment, **101:3.**
Badges.
Charities or veterans' organizations, temporary license to sell badges, **101:33.**
Marks and badges required, **101:27.**
Bankrupt sales, restrictions, **101:7.**
Berries, wild, license to sell not required, **101:17.**
Blind persons, licensing, **101:24.**
Bond or undertaking, **101:3.**
Cancellation and refunds, **101:11.**
Payment of claims against, **101:12.**
Recourse against, **101:3.**
When subject to attachment, **101:12.**
Butter.
Licensing, **101:15, 101:17, 101:22.**
Statute as inapplicable to persons licensed to sell butter, **101:15.**
Camp meetings, peddling, **272:39.**
Certificates of registration, **101:34.**

TRANSIENT VENDORS
—Cont'd

Charities and charitable purposes.
  Inapplicability of statutes to person selling for charitable purposes, **101:15.**
  Temporary licensing of charities selling flags, badges, etc., **101:33.**
Cheese, sale, **101:17, 101:18, 101:22.**
Children and minors, **101:19-101:21, 101:31, 101:32, 101:34.**
Closing out sale, restrictions, **101:7.**
Commercial travelers, inapplicability of statute, **101:2, 101:15.**
Counterfeiting of licenses, **101:31.**
Definitions, **101:1, 101:13.**
Deposit.
  Bond or undertaking. See within this heading, "Bond or undertaking."
Deputy director of standards.
  Agent for service of process, **101:6A.**
  Arrest, power to make, **101:32.**
  Definition, **101:1.**
  Licensing, **101:3, 101:22.**
Doing business in name of another, **101:2.**
Domestic corporations, statutory provisions as inapplicable, **101:2.**
Emblems.
  Badges. See within this heading, "Badges."
Enforcement of provisions, **101:32.**
Executor's or administrator's sales, restrictions, **101:7.**
Exemptions.
  Application of statute, **101:15, 101:17, 101:18.**
  Bond or deposit of transient vendor, **101:12.**
  Local regulation, license as not conferring exemption, **101:22.**
Fees.
  Licenses. See within this heading, "Licenses."
Fines and penalties, **101:9.**
  Counterfeiting of licenses, **101:31.**
  Deposit as subject to payment, **101:12.**
  Minors, encouraging violation of permit requirements, **101:20, 101:21.**

TRANSIENT VENDORS
—Cont'd

Fines and penalties —Cont'd
  Sales organizations, **101:34.**
  Unauthorized selling, **101:14.**
Fire sale, restrictions, **101:7.**
Fish and game, **101:17, 101:22.**
  Statute inapplicable to peddling of fish obtained by own efforts, **101:15.**
Flags.
  Sale of miniature flags, **101:16, 101:33.**
  Temporary licenses, **101:33.**
Flea markets.
  See FLEA MARKETS.
Flowers.
  Artificial, sale of restricted, **101:16, 101:33.**
  Wild, license not required for sale, **101:17.**
Fruits, wild, license not required for sale, **101:17.**
Fuel oil, inapplicability of statute to suppliers, **101:15.**
Furs not to be sold, **101:16.**
Game.
  Fish and game. See within this heading, "Fish and game."
Grades and standards.
  Deputy director of standards. See within this heading, "Deputy director of standards."
Ice, license to sell not required, **101:17.**
Insolvent sales, restrictions, **101:7.**
Insurance sales, restrictions, **101:7.**
Jewelry not to be sold, **101:16.**
Jobbers, inapplicability of statute, **101:15.**
Licenses, **101:3-101:6A, 101:17, 101:22-101:30.**
  Applications for, to appoint agent for service of process, **101:6A.**
  Auctioneer's license, **101:29.**
  Begging not covered, **101:30.**
  Blind persons, **101:24.**
  Butter, **101:15, 101:17, 101:22.**
  Certificate of loss, filing, **101:11.**
  Counterfeiting of, penalized, **101:31.**
  Fees, **101:22.**
    Special licenses to certain veterans or blind persons without fee, **101:24.**
  Local licenses, **101:5, 101:6.**
    Actions to recover fee, **101:10.**
    Authority conferred, **101:22.**

TRANSIENT VENDORS
—Cont'd

Licenses —Cont'd
  Minors, permits, **101:19-101:21.**
  Misuse, **101:31.**
  Necessity of obtaining, **101:16-101:18.**
  No defense against certain violations, **101:28.**
  Not required, when, **101:17, 101:18.**
  Period for which effective, **101:26.**
  Poultry dealers, **94:152A, 94:152D.**
  Records concerning, **101:26.**
  Revocation, **101:30.**
  Selling or advertising goods without license, **101:8.**
  Signing and production on demand, **101:27.**
  State license, **101:22.**
    Application for license, filing, **101:4.**
    Records concerning, **101:3, 101:4.**
  Surrender and cancellation of licenses, **101:11.**
  Temporary licenses to sell artificial flowers and miniature flags, **101:16, 101:33.**
  Territory covered, **101:22.**
  War veterans, **101:24.**
Limited application of statute, **101:2, 101:15, 101:17, 101:18.**
Liquors, sale, **101:16.**
Local dealers, temporary association with, as not relieving from statutory requirements, **101:2.**
Local regulations, **101:19.**
  Licenses. See within this heading, "Licenses."
Magazines, sale by minors, **101:19.**
Manufacturer's sales, restriction, **101:7.**
Meats, license to sell, when required, **101:17.**
Military.
  Revocation of license for unlawful use of uniform, **101:30.**
Veterans. See within this heading, "Veterans."
Milk and milk products, inapplicability of statute, **101:15.**
Miniature flags, sale, **101:16, 101:33.**
Minors, **101:19-101:21, 101:31, 101:32, 101:34.**

TRANSIENT VENDORS
—Cont'd

Mobile vending vehicles, **101:22A.**
Display of plate or tag, **101:27.**
Municipal regulation, powers,
101:17.
Newsboys.
See NEWSBOYS.
Nuts, wild, license for sale not
required, **101:17.**
Penalties.
Fines and penalties. See within
this heading, "Fines and
penalties."
Permits.
Licenses. See within this
heading, "Licenses."
Poultry and poultry products.
Crimes and offenses, **94:152C.**
Licenses and bond, **94:152A,
94:152D.**
Produce, own, persons peddling,
101:15.
Prohibited sales, **101:16.**
Receivers' sales, restrictions,
101:7.
Records and accounts of sales
organizations, **101:34.**
Religious publications, license to
sell not required, **101:17.**
Reputation of applicant for license,
certification, **101:22.**
Samples, sales by, inapplicability
of statute, **101:2, 101:15.**
Service of process, **101:6A.**
Solicitors and solicitation.
See SOLICITORS AND
SOLICITATION.
Song sheets, sale by minors,
101:19.
Speed when driving near, vehicle
used in hawking or peddling
merchandise, **90:17.**
Spirituous liquors, sale, **101:16.**
Standards, director of.
Deputy director of standards.
See within this heading,
"Deputy director of
standards."
State license.
Licenses. See within this
heading, "Licenses."
Statement required.
Advertising or holding bankrupt
or other special sale, **101:7.**
Doing business in town, **101:5.**
Neglect to file or fraud, **101:6.**
Taxation of stock in trade.
Exemption from statutory
requirements, creation,
101:2.

TRANSIENT VENDORS
—Cont'd

Taxation of stock in trade —Cont'd
Payment before obtaining local
license, **101:5.**
Temporary license to sell artificial
flowers and miniature flags,
101:16, 101:33.
Temporary or transient business,
what constitutes, **101:1.**
Territory covered by license,
101:22.
Traveling salesmen, inapplicability
of statute, **101:2, 101:15.**
Trustee's sales, restrictions, **101:7.**
Vegetables and vegetable products,
license to sell, **101:15, 101:17,
101:22.**
Vehicle used to sell frozen deserts,
flashing lights to be installed,
101:16A.
Veterans.
Special licenses, **101:24.**
Temporary licensing of veterans'
organizations selling flags,
badges, etc., **101:33.**
Who are, **101:13-101:15.**
Wholesalers, inapplicability of
statute, **101:15.**
Wholesale sale, restrictions, **101:7.**
Wines not to be sold, **101:16.**
Without license, sales regulated,
101:17, 101:18.

TRANSIT AUTHORITIES.

Advancement by public works
department for work on
property, **81:7I.**
Massachusetts Bay transportation
authority, **161A:1 to 161A:47.**
See MASSACHUSETTS BAY
TRANSPORTATION
AUTHORITY.
Mass transportation facilities and
services.
See MASS TRANSPORTATION
FACILITIES AND
SERVICES.
Regional transit authorities,
161B:1 et seq.
See REGIONAL TRANSIT
AUTHORITIES.

TRANSITIONAL AID TO
NEEDY FAMILIES FUND,
29:2KK.

TRANSITIONAL ASSISTANCE
DEPARTMENT.

Change of name of transitional
assistance department, **18:1.**
Welfare and social services.
See WELFARE AND SOCIAL
SERVICES.

TRANSITIONAL EDUCATION.

Bilingual education.
See BILINGUAL EDUCATION.

TRANSITORY ACTIONS.

Venue, **223:1-223:3.**
See VENUE.

TRANSMISSION LINES AND
EQUIPMENT.

Abatement of taxes, notice, **59:74.**
Aqueduct companies,
165:12-165:28.
See AQUEDUCTS AND
AQUEDUCT COMPANIES.
Buildings.
See BUILDINGS AND
STRUCTURES.
Cables.
Gas.
See GAS AND ELECTRIC
COMPANIES.
Ocean sanctuaries, **132A:16.**
Civil service appointment, wire
inspector, **31:57.**
Corporations, assessment of taxes,
59:83.
Defacing, **266:126.**
Elevator license regulations as
applicable to installation,
143:71F.
Environmental impact reports,
exceptions, **30:62A.**
Gas and electric companies,
166:21-166:43.
See GAS AND ELECTRIC
COMPANIES.
Grade crossings, removal or
relocation, **159:74, 160:104A.**
Motor vehicles transporting poles,
dimensions, **90:19.**
Municipal light commission,
purchase of transmission
equipment without bids,
164:56D.
Ocean sanctuaries, activities
permitted, **132A:16.**
Pipes.
See PIPES AND PIPELINES.
Taxes and taxation, **59:18, 59:83.**
Abatement of taxes, notice,
59:74.
Corporations, assessment of
taxes, **59:83.**
Public ways, where and how
assessed, **59:18.**
Underground facilities, **59:5.**
Telephone.
See TELEPHONE AND
TELEGRAPH COMPANIES.
Underground facilities, assessment
and taxation, **59:5.**

851

TRANSMISSION LINES AND EQUIPMENT —Cont'd

Waterways, poles and wires included in term "structure" for purpose of statutes, **91:7.**

Waterworks.
See WATERWORKS AND WATER SUPPLY.

Zoning and planning, overhead wires and poles, prohibition of new construction or progressive removal, **166:22B.**

TRANSPLANTATION.

Anatomical contracts.
See ANATOMICAL CONTRACTS AND GIFTS.

TRANSPORTATION.

Additional services, transportation areas authorized to provide, **161:143.**

Administration.
See ADMINISTRATION AND FINANCE EXECUTIVE OFFICE.

Aging persons, transporting patients to or from clinics, **111:57C.**

Aircraft.
See AIRCRAFT AND AVIATION.

Airports.
See AIRPORTS AND LANDING FIELDS.

Alcoholic liquors.
See ALCOHOLIC LIQUORS.

Animal diseases.
See ANIMAL DISEASES.

Animals.
See ANIMALS.

Architectural barriers against handicapped persons, prohibition, **22:13A.**

Arrest.
See ARREST.

Assault and battery upon public transportation employees, **265:13D.**

Assessments.
Machinery used in transportation and carriage of goods, **59:18.**
Projects, assessments, **80:4, 80:13, 80:13B.**

Audits.
See AUDITS AND AUDITORS.

Bakery products, transportation, **94:3, 136:6.**

Bees, transportation, **128:35.**

Bills of lading, **106:7-101 to 106:7-105, 106:7-301 to 106:7-603, 108:42 et seq.**
See BILLS OF LADING.

TRANSPORTATION —Cont'd

Bonds and debentures, bonds of agencies concerned with transportation, **10:9A.**

Borrowing money.
Loans. See within this heading, "Loans."

Budgets.
See BUDGETS.

Bureau of transportation planning and development, **16:3A.**

Cancer clinics, transporting patients to or, **111:57A.**

Carriers, **159:1 et seq., 159A:1 et seq., 159B:1 et seq.**
See CARRIERS.

Cattle.
See ANIMALS.

Central Massachusetts tourist council, Inc.
Financial assistance and promotion services from economic development department, **23A:14.**

Cigarette tax.
See CIGARETTE TAX.

Cities.
See CITIES AND TOWNS.

Commercial driver license.
See UNIFORM OPERATION OF COMMERCIAL MOTOR VEHICLES.

Commissioner of transportation promulgating writing request for playground purposes, **45:17A.**

Commuter passenger service vessels, sales tax exemption, **64H:6.**

Consignment, **131:26, 131:28.**

Contagious and infectious diseases.
Infected dead bodies, **111:107.**
Sufferer transported to another town, permit, **111:96A.**
Tubercular persons. See within this heading, "Tubercular persons."

Contracts.
See CONTRACTS AND AGREEMENTS.

Correctional institutions.
See CORRECTIONAL INSTITUTIONS.

Credit unions, transportation expenses for mobile homes, **171:61.**

Dead bodies.
See DEAD BODIES.

Debentures.
Bonds and debentures, bonds of agencies concerned with transportation, **10:9A.**

TRANSPORTATION —Cont'd

Debts.
Loans. See within this heading, "Loans."

Disabled.
See DISABLED OR HANDICAPPED PERSONS.

Discharged prisoners, furnishing, **127:165.**

Dispensaries.
See DISPENSARIES OR CLINICS.

Dump trucks.
See DUMP TRUCKS.

Early childhood intervention services, **111G:6.**

Educational certificates required for employment of minors under eighteen, **149:95.**

Education department.
See EDUCATION DEPARTMENT.

Elderly persons.
Older persons. See within this heading, "Older persons."

Electric railroads, **162:1-162:18.**
See ELECTRIC RAILROADS.

Elevated railways, **59:50 et seq.**
See ELEVATED RAILWAYS.

Emergency transportation.
Schoolchildren, immunity of teachers, principals, or nurses from liability for providing, **71:55A.**
Ski patrol members, liability, **231:85-I.**

Employment agency, duties as to transportation of applicants for employment, **140:46J.**

Executive office of transportation.
See TRANSPORTATION AND CONSTRUCTION EXECUTIVE OFFICE.

Expenses and expenditures, **261:9, 261:23, 261:26.**

Credit unions, transportation expenses for mobile homes, **171:61.**

Federal aid or funds. See within this heading, "Federal aid or funds."

Rates.
See RATES AND CHARGES.

Students, transportation of, reimbursement for expenses, **71:7A, 71:16C.**

Transporting mentally ill and retarded persons, **19:28, 19B:17.**

Traveling expenses.
See TRAVELING EXPENSES.

TRANSPORTATION —Cont'd

Explosives.

Fireworks. See within this heading, "Fireworks."

Injury by explosives illegally transported, **148:22.**

Regulation of transportation, **148:9, 148:15.**

Federal aid or funds.

Executive office of transportation and construction, acceptance and use, **6A:19A.**

Profit or loss of transportation areas, computation, **161:151.**

Regional transportation authorities, federal aid, **161B:22.**

Firearms.

See FIREARMS AND WEAPONS.

Fires and fire prevention, **148:15, 148:56.**

Fireworks.

Agencies, exception as to use, **148:39.**

Regulation of transportation, **148:9, 148:15.**

Fish.

See FISH AND GAME.

Forgery of transportation passes.

See FORGERY AND COUNTERFEITING.

Frozen food, **94:73A, 94:77G, 111:57C.**

Gaming, parcels used, **271:22.**

Garbage.

See GARBAGE AND RUBBISH.

Gasoline sales tax, receipts credited toward matching fund, **64A:13.**

Habeas corpus.

See HABEAS CORPUS.

Hazardous waste.

Illegal transportation, forfeitures, **21C:14.**

Licenses for transportation, **21C:7.**

Uniform operation of commercial motor vehicles.

See UNIFORM OPERATION OF COMMERCIAL MOTOR VEHICLES.

High schools.

See HIGH SCHOOLS.

Highways and streets, **82:1 et seq.**

See HIGHWAYS AND STREETS.

Holidays, transportation of merchandise, **136:14.**

TRANSPORTATION —Cont'd

Hospitals and health care facilities.

Indigent patients, transfer, **111:70E.**

Ski patrol members providing emergency care, treatment, or transportation, liability to hospital for expenses, **231:85I.**

Tubercular persons, **111:94A, 111:94B.**

Hours of labor.

Carriers.

See CARRIERS.

Children under eighteen, **149:66-149:68, 149:78.**

Women and children employed in transportation, **149:56, 149:57.**

Infectious diseases.

Contagious and infectious diseases. See within this heading, "Contagious and infectious diseases."

Insect pests, violations, **266:119.**

Insurance companies' investment, **175:63.**

Intensive care unit for mentally ill women, transportation of persons to and, **123:21.**

Interagency agreements, mental retardation department, **19B:18.**

Intermodal transportation terminals, authority to construct, **121B:46.**

Length and width provisions, Federal Surface Transportation Assistance Act of 1982, **85:2B.**

Loans.

Bonds and debentures, bonds of agencies concerned with transportation, **10:9A.**

Debt statement by transportation agencies, **10:9A.**

Executive office of transportation and construction, acceptance and use of federal loans, **6A:19A.**

Regional transit authority, borrowing by state treasurer to make payments, **161B:10.**

Lobsters.

See LOBSTERS.

Lotteries, letters or parcels used, **271:22.**

Mass transportation facilities.

See MASS TRANSPORTATION FACILITIES AND SERVICES.

TRANSPORTATION —Cont'd

Medical care and assistance program, services for which financial assistance provided, **118E:6, 118E:7.**

Mentally ill.

See MENTALLY ILL AND RETARDED PERSONS.

Metropolitan transit authority.

See METROPOLITAN TRANSIT AUTHORITY.

Milk.

See MILK AND MILK PRODUCTS.

Minority pupils, expense for transportation, **15:1I.**

Motor vehicles, **90:1 et seq.**

See MOTOR VEHICLES.

Municipal finance.

See MUNICIPAL FINANCE.

Muscular dystrophy clinics, transporting patients to or, **111:57B.**

Non-white pupils, expense for transportation, **15:1I.**

Nursery stock, **128:20.**

Older persons.

Allowances to old age assistance recipients, **118A:1.**

Clinics for aging persons, transporting patients to or, **111:57C.**

Police.

See POLICE.

Poultry.

See POULTRY AND POULTRY PRODUCTS.

Prisoners, transportation of.

See CORRECTIONAL INSTITUTIONS.

Private schools.

See PRIVATE SCHOOLS.

Public officers and employees, assault and battery, **265:13D.**

Pupils, **71:7A, 90:7A-90:7D.**

See SCHOOL BUSES AND TRANSPORTATION OF PUPILS.

Railroads, **160:1-160:252.**

See RAILROADS.

Rates.

See RATES AND CHARGES.

Recreational tramways.

See RECREATIONAL TRAMWAYS.

Regional transit authorities, **161B:1-161B:25.**

See REGIONAL TRANSIT AUTHORITIES.

Removal from office.

See REMOVAL FROM OFFICE OR EMPLOYMENT.

TRANSPORTATION —Cont'd
Reptiles, transporting into or out of state, **131:85.**
Restraint of person during transportation, **123:21.**
Retarded persons.
  See MENTALLY ILL AND RETARDED PERSONS.
Sales tax.
  Commuter passenger service vessels, sales tax exemption, **64H:6.**
  Goods in transit, exemption, **64H:6.**
Sand.
  See SAND AND GRAVEL.
School buses and transportation of pupils, **71:7A, 90:7A-90:7D.**
  See SCHOOL BUSES AND TRANSPORTATION OF PUPILS.
Shellfish.
  See SHELLFISH.
Sheriffs, transportation of prisoners, **37:21, 37:24, 37:25.**
Ski patrol members providing emergency transportation, liability, **231:85-I.**
Smoking prohibition, **272:43A.**
Social services department, reciprocal agreements with other states as to transportation of welfare recipients, **18:14.**
Special education.
  See SPECIAL EDUCATION.
Street railways, **161:1-161:161.**
  See STREET RAILWAYS.
Students.
  See SCHOOL BUSES AND TRANSPORTATION OF PUPILS.
Summer school, use of school buses to transport pupils to and, **159A:11A.**
Sunday transportation of certain articles, **136:6.**
Superior courts.
  See SUPERIOR COURTS.
Towns.
  See CITIES AND TOWNS.
Trackless trolleys, **163:1-163:12.**
  See TRACKLESS TROLLEYS.
Tubercular persons.
  Hospitalization of persons with active tuberculosis, **111:94A.**

TRANSPORTATION —Cont'd
Tubercular persons —Cont'd
  State sanatorium treatment center, transportation, **111:94B.**
Uniform operation of commercial motor vehicles.
  See UNIFORM OPERATION OF COMMERCIAL MOTOR VEHICLES.
United States.
  Federal aid or funds. See within this heading, "Federal aid or funds."

TRANSPORTATION AND CONSTRUCTION EXECUTIVE OFFICE, 6A:19 et seq.
Aeronautics commission as agency within, **6A:19.**
  See AIRCRAFT AND AVIATION.
Agencies within, **6A:19.**
Building construction, **7:38A½.**
Designer, notification of appointment by commissioner of administration, **7:38A½.**
Establishment, **6A:2.**
Federal aid, acceptance, **6A:19A.**
Gifts, acceptance and use of funds, **6A:19A.**
Governor.
  Appointment of secretary, **6A:3.**
  Massachusetts Bay Transportation Authority as agency within, **6A:19.**
Grants-in-aid, acceptance and use, **6A:19A.**
Improved transportation management, federal aid, **6A:19A.**
Loans, acceptance and use of federal, **6A:19A.**
Railroads.
  See RAILROADS.
Regional transit authorities.
  As agency within, **6A:19.**
  Bond issues to be approved by secretary, **161B:17.**
  Reports to be submitted to secretary, **161B:8.**
Secretary.
  Appointment by governor, **6A:3.**
  Regional transit authorities. See within this heading, "Regional transit authorities."
Undersecretary, appointment, **6A:3.**

TRANSPORTATION AND CONSTRUCTION EXECUTIVE OFFICE —Cont'd
United States, use and acceptance of funds, **6A:19A.**
TRANSPORTATION BOND AUTHORIZATION ACT, Spec L 79:1-Spec L 79:30.
Aeronautics commission's expenditures for airport systems planning and reimbursements to municipalities, **Spec L 79:27.**
Airport Outlay Loan Act, issuance and sale of bonds, **Spec L 79:28.**
Airport systems planning and reimbursements to cities and towns, **Spec L 79:27.**
Amendment of certain laws, **Spec L 79:1-79:15, 79:17, 79:25.**
Apportionment of sums, **Spec L 79:20-Spec L 79:22.**
Appropriation from Highway Fund Debt Service, **Spec L 79:24.**
Assistance by Commonwealth to aid MBTA to pay portion of net cost of service, **Spec L 79:16.**
Bonds and notes.
  Airport Outlay Loan Act, **Spec L 79:28.**
  Highway Improvement Loan Act of 1973, **Spec L 79:23.**
Commonwealth to enter into contracts of assistance with MBTA to pay portion of net cost of service, **Spec L 79:16.**
Contracts entered into by Commonwealth to assist with MBTA to pay portion of net cost of service, **Spec L 79:16.**
Cost of service, contracts between Commonwealth and MBTA to pay portion, **Spec L 79:16.**
Date, effective date of law, **Spec L 79:30.**
Employees of MBTA, transfer, **Spec L 79:19.**
Expenditures.
  Based on federal support, **Spec L 79:29.**
  For airport systems planning and reimbursements, **Spec L 79:27.**
Federal support, expenditures based, **Spec L 79:29.**
Generators, altering or changing power source, **Spec L 79:26.**

TRANSPORTATION BOND AUTHORIZATION ACT
—Cont'd

Highway Fund Debt Service, appropriations, **Spec L 79:24.**

Highway Improvement Loan Act, issuance and sale of bonds, **Spec L 79:23.**

Issuance of bonds, **Spec L 79:23, 79:28.**

List of municipalities aided, **Spec L 79:20, 79:21.**

MBTA.

  Contracts with Commonwealth to pay portion of net cost of service, **Spec L 79:16.**

  Generators, altering or changing power sources, **Spec L 79:26.**

  Program for transportation, **Spec L 79:18.**

  Transfer of officers and employees, **Spec L 79:19.**

Names of municipalities aided, **Spec L 79:20, 79:21.**

Officers of MBTA, transfer, **Spec L 79:19.**

Power source for generators, alteration or changing, **Spec L 79:26.**

Reimbursements for airport systems planning, **Spec L 79:27.**

Sale of bonds, **Spec L 79:23, 79:28.**

Service, contracts between Commonwealth and MBTA to pay portion of net cost of service, **Spec L 79:16.**

Sums.

  Apportionment, **Spec L 79:20 et seq.**

  Use, **Spec L 79:20 et seq.**

Terms of office, termination, **Spec L 79:30.**

Towns, aeronautics commission's expenditures for airport systems planning and reimbursements, **Spec L 79:27.**

Transfer of officers and employees of MBTA, **Spec L 79:19.**

TRANSPORTATION COMPANY.

Carriers, **159:1 et seq., 159A:1 et seq., 159B:1 et seq.**

See CARRIERS.

TRANSPORTATION DEPARTMENT OF UNITED STATES.

Motor vehicles or trailers complying with equipment regulations, **90:7.**

TRANSPORTATION DIVISION.
See CARRIERS.

TRANSSEXUALS.

Amendment of birth certificate upon completion of sex reassignment surgery, **46:13.**

TRAPA NATANS, 128:20A.

TRAP DOORS.

Openings of hoistways, **149:129.**

TRAPPER TRAINING COURSE.

Effective use of box, cage and conibear type traps, **131:11.**

TRAPS AND TRAPPING.

Crabs.

  See CRABS.

Hunting, **131:11, 131:14, 131:38, 131:79, 131:80, 131:80A.**

  See FISH AND GAME.

Lobsters.

  See LOBSTERS.

Marine fish and fisheries, **130:29-130:32, 130:38, 130:38A.**

  See MARINE FISH AND FISHERIES.

Snares, **131:79.**

TRAP SHOOTING.
See SHOOTING GALLERIES AND PRESERVES.

TRAVEL AND TRAVELERS.

Advisory commission on travel and tourism, **23A:13C.**

Amusements and exhibitions.

  Notification as to location and dates in Commonwealth, **140:205A.**

  Workers' compensation and liability insurance as prerequisite to licensing traveling amusements **140:181.**

Arrest bond certificates guaranteed by certain travel clubs, **276:61B.**

Bodies of deceased travelers not to be used for anatomical purposes, **113:2.**

Checks.

  See TRAVELERS' CHECKS.

Commerce.

  See ECONOMIC DEVELOPMENT DEPARTMENT.

Common victuallers, **140:5.**

Employment agency duties with respect to applicants, **140:46J.**

Expenses, **261:9, 261:23, 261:26.**

  See TRAVELING EXPENSES.

TRAVEL AND TRAVELERS
—Cont'd

Hotels, motels.

  See HOTELS, MOTELS, AND ROOMINGHOUSES.

Infected places, licensing of travelers, **111:106.**

Passport, **149:87, 207:33A.**

Personnel and standardization director to make rules as to travel by state officers and employees, **7:28.**

Public ways to be kept safe, **84:1.**

Salesmen, **101:2, 101:15.**

Tourists.

  See TOURISTS AND TOURISM.

TRAVELERS' CHECKS.

Abandoned, lost, and unclaimed property.

  Escheat to other states, **200A:8B.**

  Issuers of travelers checks as persons required to file annual report, **200A:1, 200A:7.**

  Notice by holder of property, **200A:8.**

  Presumption of abandonment, **200A:6B.**

  Sellers of checks, reports, **200A:6C.**

  Surrender to state treasurer, **200A:8A.**

Credit unions, selling, issuing or registering, **171:75.**

Defined, **106:3-104.**

Morris plan banks, sale, **172A:15.**

Negotiable instruments generally, **106:3-101 to 106:3-605.**

  See NEGOTIABLE INSTRUMENTS.

Presumption of abandonment, **200A:6B.**

Records of seller to be maintained for 5 years, **200A:6C.**

TRAVELING EXPENSES, 261:9, 261:23, 261:26.

Administration and Finance Executive Office personnel, **7:4D.**

Aeronautics commission members and employees, expenses, **6:59.**

Anti-discrimination laws, advisory agencies and conciliation councils, **151B:3.**

Antitrust laws, **93:8.**

Architects' registration board, **13:44D.**

Archives advisory committee members, **9:2A.**

855

TRAVELING EXPENSES
—Cont'd

Attorneys at law.
  See ATTORNEYS AT LAW.
Auditors, **221:55, 221:61.**
Bedding and upholstered furniture
  advisory board, expenses of
  members, **94:274.**
Boxing commission members,
  22:12.
Bradford Durfee College of
  Technology travel policy,
  74:42P.
Building regulations and
  standards, state board,
  143:93.
Certificates and certification.
  False travel certificates by
    witnesses, forfeiture paid to
    Commonwealth, **262:62.**
  Law enforcement officers,
    expenses, **262:19, 262:53A,
    262:53B.**
  State police officers' certification
    of witness fees and travel
    allowance, **262:53B.**
Civil rights and discrimination,
  travel expenses of advisory
  agencies and conciliation
  councils under
  antidiscrimination laws, **6:56,
  151B:3.**
Clerks of courts, **218:81, 221:99,
  278:28D.**
Colleges and universities of state,
  travel policy for personnel,
  **73:17, 74:42P, 75:32,
  75B:12A-75B:16.**
Commission against discrimination
  advisory board, **6:56.**
Conservation.
  Committee for conservation of
    soil, water, and related
    resources, members, **21:19.**
  Supervisors of conservation
    districts, **21:22.**
Constables, **262:8-262:21, 262:48.**
Conventions.
  Delegates appointed by
    governor, **6:10, 6:11.**
  Forest wardens attending, **132:3.**
Costs in court actions, travel
  expenses as, **261:23, 261:26.**
Counties.
  Commissioners, **34:7, 34:8.**
  Habeas corpus, county to pay
    expense of bringing prisoner
    up, **248:40.**
  Nantucket County. See within
    this heading, "Nantucket
    County."

TRAVELING EXPENSES
—Cont'd

Counties —Cont'd
  Officers and employees, **35:32.**
  Treasurers, **35:8.**
Criminal cases, allowance, **127:30,
  262:14, 262:19, 262:21,
  262:29, 262:48, 262:50,
  262:53A, 262:53B.**
Dentistry, members of board of
  registration, **13:21.**
Dispensing opticians, board of
  registration, **13:50.**
District and prosecuting attorneys,
  12:23, 12:24.
District courts, **218:81, 262:53B.**
  Appellate division, acting
    justices, **231:108.**
Economic development
  department, limitations on
  expenditures, **23A:14.**
Election examiners, county board,
  54:122.
Electricians' examining board,
  13:32.
Electrologists, board of
  registration, **13:60.**
Embalming and funeral directing,
  board of registration, **13:31.**
Employment agency, payment,
  140:46J.
Employment security advisory
  council, **23:9N.**
Executive council, **6:4.**
False travel certificates of
  witnesses, forfeiture paid to
  Commonwealth, **262:62.**
Food and agriculture department,
  members and employees, **20:1.**
Forests and forestry.
  State forestry committee on
    cutting practices, **132:41.**
  Wardens attending conventions,
    132:3.
Furniture, expenses of members of
  advisory board on bedding and
  upholstered furniture, **94:274.**
General court.
  See GENERAL COURT.
Governor.
  Convention delegates appointed
    by governor, **6:10, 6:11.**
  Highway safety committee
    members, **90A:3.**
  Judges of probate and
    insolvency, **217:8.**
Habeas corpus, expense for
  bringing up prisoner.
  Advancement required, **248:9.**
  County to pay, when, **248:40.**
Highway safety committee
  members, **90A:3.**

TRAVELING EXPENSES
—Cont'd

Hospital licensing, surveys and
  construction planning advisory
  council, members, **111:55.**
Insurance premium finance
  companies, payment of
  mileage to witnesses attending
  hearings, **255C:8.**
Judges.
  See JUDGES.
Judicial council, **221:34C.**
Jury members, municipal
  employees, **234:1B.**
Justices.
  See JUDGES.
Land court orders, fees for service,
  262:16.
Landscape architects, travel
  expenses of members of board
  of registration, **13:69.**
Legislative research council, **3:56.**
Lieutenant governor, **6:4.**
Lowlands and swamps.
  Reclamation district
    commissioners, **252:5,
    252:5A.**
  State reclamation board
    members, **252:2.**
Manufactured home commission,
  6:108.
Medical examiners and associates,
  38:5.
Medical registration board, **13:10.**
Medicolegal investigations
  committee, members, **6:184.**
Mental health legal advisors
  committee, reimbursement of
  members, **221:34E.**
Militia.
  Allowance, **33:84.**
  Meetings, mileage, **33:62.**
Mobile homes commission
  members, **6:108.**
Nantucket County.
  Probate judge, **217:42.**
  Sheriff, **37:21.**
New Bedford Institute of
  Technology, travel policy,
  74:42P.
Nursing registration board, **13:15,
  13:15D.**
Obscene literature control
  commission, **6:101.**
Official representatives of state
  otherwise unpaid, **6:11.**
Optometry registration board,
  13:18.
Outside Commonwealth, state
  officers and employees
  traveling, **6:10, 12:24, 30:25B.**

TRAVELING EXPENSES
—Cont'd

Overtime payment to state employees on full travel status, **149:30B.**

Pharmacy registration board and its agents, **13:24, 13:25.**

Police.

Attendance as witness, **262:19, 262:53A, 262:53B.**

Service in other places on requisition, **41:99.**

Sheriffs and deputies, **37:21.** See SHERIFFS AND DEPUTIES.

State police. See STATE POLICE.

Presidential electors, **54:149.**

Prisoners.

Allowances for transportation, **262:21, 262:48.**

Correctional facility officers, expenses in performance of duty, **127:30.**

Habeas corpus. See within this heading, "Habeas corpus, expense for bringing up prisoner."

Probate and insolvency judges, **217:8, 217:42.**

Probation commissioner, **276:98.**

Probation officers, **276:94, 276:99.**

Process and service of process and papers, **262:8, 262:10, 262:16, 262:48.**

Criminal cases, **262:14, 262:19, 262:21.**

Habeas corpus. See within this heading, "Habeas corpus, expense for bringing up prisoner."

Return by mail or express, **262:9.**

Public health council members, **17:3.**

Public officers and employees, **6:10, 30:25.**

Public Safety Department, officers and inspectors, **22:7.**

Radio and television technicians registration board, **13:63.**

Reclamation districts.

Lowlands and swamps. See within this heading, "Lowlands and swamps."

Resigned member of general court as entitled, **3:10.**

Restraints of trade and monopolies, **93:8.**

Return of process by mail or express, **262:9.**

TRAVELING EXPENSES
—Cont'd

Salaried officers serving in criminal cases, **262:50.**

Sanitarians, board of registration, **13:53.**

Service of process.

Process and service of process and papers. See within this heading, "Process and service of process and papers."

Sheriffs and deputies, **37:21.** See SHERIFFS AND DEPUTIES.

Small business assistance division, experts and consultants, **23A:20.**

Special commissions of general court, **3:32A.**

State colleges and universities, personnel, **73:17, 74:42P, 75:32, 75B:16.**

State officers and employees, **6:10, 30:25.**

State police. See STATE POLICE.

Stenographers, **221:90A, 221:91.**

Superior courts.

Clerks of appellate division, **278:28D.**

Witnesses, **262:29, 262:53A.**

Supreme judicial and superior court actions, allowance, **261:23.**

Swamps.

Lowlands and swamps. See within this heading, "Lowlands and swamps."

Telecommunications and energy department, **25:8.**

Trial court of the Commonwealth, expenses of justices, **211B:4.**

Uniform state laws, commissioners, **6:28.**

Universities and colleges of state, travel policy for personnel, **73:17, 74:42P, 75:32, 75B:12A-75B:16.**

Vacancy in general court, member chosen to fill, **3:10.**

Veterans' services, commissioner, **6:23, 7:4N.**

Witnesses, **233:3, 233:13-233:13B.** See WITNESSES.

Workers' compensation.

Medical examination, reimbursement for travel, **152:45.**

Witnesses, **152:5.**

TRAVELING EXPENSES
—Cont'd

World War II, Korean Emergency, and Vietnam Conflict Memorial Commission, expenses of members, **6:124A.**

TRAVELING SALESMEN.

Hawkers, peddlers, and transient vendors statutes as inapplicable, **101:2, 101:15.**

TRAVERSING CARRIAGES.

Cotton factories, operation, **149:128.**

TRAWLS.
See FISH AND GAME.

TREASON, 264:1-264:4.

Adhering to enemies of United States, **US Const Art 3 Sec 3 cl 1.**

Aid and comfort to enemies of United States, giving of, **US Const Art 3 Sec 3 cl 1.**

Attainder of, not to work corruption of blood, **US Const Art 3 Sec 3 cl 2.**

Bail not obtainable, **264:1.**

Civil officers to be removed on conviction of, **US Const Art 2 Sec 4.**

Concealment of treason, **264:3.**

Confession in open court as basis for conviction, **US Const Art 3 Sec 3 cl 1.**

Congress.

Power of Congress to punish, **US Const Art 3 Sec 3 cl 2.**

Senator or Representative may be arrested for, **US Const Art 1 Sec 6 cl 1.**

Constitution of Massachusetts, legislature may not convict of treason, **MA Const Part 1 Art 25.**

Extradition, **276:12.**

Fines and penalties, **264:1-264:3.**

Habeas corpus, **248:1.**

Misprision of treason, **264:3.**

Overt act, necessity of proof of, **US Const Art 3 Sec 3 cl 1.**

Petit treason, **265:1.**

Proof, **264:4; US Const Art 3 Sec 3 cl 1.**

Representative in Congress may be arrested for, **US Const Art 1 Sec 6 cl 1.**

Senator may be arrested for, **US Const Art 1 Sec 6 cl 1.**

Sentence or punishment, **264:2, 264:3; US Const Art 3 Sec 3 cl 2.**

TREASON —Cont'd

Two witnesses, necessity of testimony of, **US Const Art 3 Sec 3 cl 1.**

War, levying against United States, **US Const Art 3 Sec 3 cl 1.**

What constitutes, **US Const Art 3 Sec 3 cl 1.**

TREASURER OR TREASURY.

Abandoned property, reports required, **200A:7.**

Annual reports.
See ANNUAL REPORTS OR STATEMENTS.

Attachment of property.
See ATTACHMENT OF PROPERTY.

Attorney general.
See ATTORNEY GENERAL.

Bail.
See BAIL AND RECOGNIZANCE.

Banks.
See BANKS AND BANKING.

Beach districts, **40:12E.**

Campaign expenditures.
See CAMPAIGN EXPENDITURES AND CONTRIBUTIONS.

Charitable corporations, **180:7.**

Checks by treasurers of public bodies, facsimile signatures, **107:45A.**

City treasurers.
See MUNICIPAL FINANCE.

Civil service.
See CIVIL SERVICE.

Collaborative educational board, appointment of treasurer, **40:4E.**

Colleges.
See COLLEGES AND UNIVERSITIES.

Commonwealth, **10:1 et seq.**
See STATE TREASURER.

Conflicts of interest prohibited, **44:55.**

Cooperative banks.
See COOPERATIVE BANKS.

Corporations.
See CORPORATIONS.

Correctional institutions, **125:6.**

County treasurers.
See COUNTY TREASURERS.

Credit unions.
See CREDIT UNIONS.

Discharge.
Removal from office or employment. See within this heading, "Removal from office or employment."

TREASURER OR TREASURY —Cont'd

Districts.
See DISTRICTS.

Economic development and industrial corporations, **121C:3.**

Electric companies.
See GAS AND ELECTRIC COMPANIES.

Eminent domain, treasurer of body politic or corporate on behalf of which taking is made.
Issuance of new check, **79:7E.**
Payment for damages, **79:7D.**

Engraving advertisement to resemble treasury bill of credit, penalty, **267:29.**

Executors.
See EXECUTORS AND ADMINISTRATORS.

Fire districts, temporary treasurer, **48:72.**

Fire insurance.
See FIRE INSURANCE.

Foreign insurance companies.
See FOREIGN INSURANCE COMPANIES.

Fund-raisers, exception as to regulation, **68:33.**

Gas.
See GAS AND ELECTRIC COMPANIES.

Governor.
See GOVERNOR.

Hospital School of Massachusetts, treasurer.
Inspection of accounts by trustees, **111:62O.**
Reports, **111:62N.**

Hospital service corporations, **176A:11.**

Insurance.
See INSURANCE.

Lowlands.
See LOWLANDS AND SWAMPS.

Mentally ill.
See MENTALLY ILL AND RETARDED PERSONS.

Morris plan banks.
See MORRIS PLAN BANKS.

Municipal finance.
See MUNICIPAL FINANCE.

Proprietors of wharves and real estate lying in common, **179:3, 179:5.**

Railroads.
See RAILROADS.

Reclamation district, treasurer, **252:6.**

TREASURER OR TREASURY —Cont'd

Regional health districts, **111:27B.**

Regional planning districts.
Bond of treasurer or assistant treasurer, **40B:4.**
Payments to treasurer, **40B:7.**
Southeastern Regional Planning and Economic Development District, treasurer, **40B:15.**

Regional police districts.
See REGIONAL POLICE DISTRICTS.

Regional refuse disposal districts.
Appointment, duties and compensation of treasurer, **40:44G.**
General law provisions applicable to treasurer, **40:44G.**

Regional school districts.
See REGIONAL SCHOOL DISTRICTS.

Religious societies, treasurers, **67:7, 67:8.**

Removal from office or employment.
Districts and regional school districts treasurers, removal, **41:39B.**
State treasurer, **10:4.**
Town treasurer as collector, **41:39B.**

Retirement systems.
See RETIREMENT SYSTEMS AND PENSIONS.

Revenue department.
See REVENUE DEPARTMENT AND COMMISSIONER.

Savings banks.
See SAVINGS BANKS.

Schools.
See SCHOOLS AND EDUCATION.

Secretary of treasury of United States.
Income tax.
See INCOME TAX.

Sworn certificate as evidence in prosecution for counterfeiting, **267:15.**

Service of process on treasurer of political subdivision, **223:37.**

Sinking fund commissioners.
See MUNICIPAL FINANCE.

Southeastern Regional Planning and Economic Development District, treasurer, **40B:15.**

State hospital treasurer, books and accounts, **30:29.**

State treasurer, **10:1 et seq.**
See STATE TREASURER.

TREASURER OR TREASURY
—Cont'd

Street railways.
　See STREET RAILWAYS.
Swamps.
　See LOWLANDS AND
　　SWAMPS.
Tax assessors.
　See TAX ASSESSORS.
Taxation.
　See TAXATION.
Tax collectors.
　See TAX COLLECTORS.
Tax deeds.
　See TAX DEEDS AND TITLES.
Technology development
　corporation.
　Election of treasurer, **40G:2.**
　Moneys payable to treasurer,
　　40G:4.
Telephone.
　See TELEPHONE AND
　　TELEGRAPH COMPANIES.
Town treasurers.
　See MUNICIPAL FINANCE.
Trust companies.
　See TRUST COMPANIES.
Underground storage tank
　petroleum product cleanup
　fund, **21J:2.**
United States Treasurer.
　Income tax.
　　See INCOME TAX.
　Sworn certificate as evidence in
　　prosecution for
　　counterfeiting, **267:15.**
United States treasury bills and
　obligations, **44:55, 267:29.**
Veterans' services districts, **115:10.**

TREASURERS CHECKS.
Presentment for encashment,
　service charges for failure,
　200A:15C.
Presumption of abandonment,
　200A:6B.

TREASURE TROVE.
Underwater archeological
　resources, **6:180.**

TREATIES.
Documents of title article of
　Commercial Code as subject,
　106:7-103.
Judicial power to extend to cases
　under, **US Const Art 3 Sec 2
　cl 1.**
Marine boundaries, United States
　as a party to treaties as
　affecting, **1:3.**
President to make with advice and
　consent of Senate, **US Const
　Art 2 Sec 2 cl 2.**

TREATIES —Cont'd
State may not make, **US Const
　Art 1 Sec 10 cl 1.**
Supreme law of the land, **US
　Const Art 6 cl 2.**

TREATMENT PROGRAM
UNIT, 111B:6B.
Defined, **111B:3.**

TREBLE DAMAGES.
Animals.
　Dogs. See within this heading,
　　"Dogs."
　Wrongfully killing or enticing
　　away, **272:85A.**
Antitrust laws.
　See RESTRAINTS OF TRADE
　　AND MONOPOLIES.
Aqueduct company, injuring
　aqueduct, **165:24.**
Coastal waters, pollution, **130:24.**
Consumer protection, civil
　remedies, **93A:9, 93A:11.**
Dogs.
　Notice, dog causing injury after,
　　140:159.
　Wrongfully killing or enticing
　　away dog, **272:85A.**
Employer discriminating against
　person providing child abuse
　information, **119:51B.**
False claims against
　Commonwealth, **12:5B.**
Fraternal benefit insurance, false
　statements, **176:47.**
Fraud.
　Fraternal benefit societies, false
　　statements, **176:47.**
　Mileage changes on motor
　　vehicle odometers, persons
　　defrauded, **266:141.**
　Personal property, damages for
　　fraudulent sales, **231:85J.**
　Private business schools,
　　misrepresentations to
　　students, **75D:14.**
　Textbooks, fraudulent sale,
　　93:21.
Hazardous materials mitigation,
　costs, **21K:5.**
Items excluded in computing,
　261:11.
Lead poisoning prevention
　violations, civil liability,
　111:199.
Long term care ombudsman,
　retaliation for complaining or
　giving information, **19A:33A.**
Motor vehicle odometers, damages
　to persons defrauded from
　changing mileage, **266:141.**

TREBLE DAMAGES —Cont'd
Name, portrait, or picture of
　person, treble damages for
　unauthorized use, **214:3A.**
Optional motor vehicle insurance,
　treble damages for persons
　injured by monopolistic
　practices as to rates, **175E:6.**
Private business schools, liability
　for treble damages for
　misrepresentations to
　students, **75D:14.**
Railroads.
　Endangering safety of persons
　　upon trains, **160:226.**
　Malicious injury, **160:225.**
　Obstructing engine or car,
　　160:226.
Restraints of trade.
　See RESTRAINTS OF TRADE
　　AND MONOPOLIES.
Small claims procedure, award,
　218:21.
Tenant's right of recovery against
　landlord for unlawful removal
　or exclusion from residential
　premises, **186:15F.**
Textbooks, fraudulent sale, **93:21.**
Unfair trade practices or methods
　of competition, damages in
　actions, **93A:9, 93A:11.**
Waste of property.
　Cutting or damaging timber on
　　land of another, **242:7,
　　242:8.**
　Distribution of damages among
　　cotenants, **242:5.**
　When recoverable, **242:4-242:7.**
Water supply of town, pollution or
　diversion, **40:39G.**

TREES.
Airports, height of trees near,
　90:40D, 90:40F.
American elm, state tree, **2:8.**
Cities and towns, furnishing of
　seedlings, **132:35.**
Civil service exemption of tree
　climbers, **31:48.**
Consolidated hearings as to
　removal, **40:15C, 87:3.**
Corporations for planting and
　cultivating, **180:4.**
Cutting or damaging.
　Highways.
　　See HIGHWAYS AND
　　　STREETS.
　Shade trees.
　　See SHADE TREES.
Waste, liability, **242:4, 242:7,
　242:8.**

TREES —Cont'd

Department of agriculture, annual leaflet, **128:2.**

Diseases.

See PLANTS AND PLANT DISEASES AND PESTS.

Elm as state tree, **2:8.**

Eminent domain.

See EMINENT DOMAIN.

Fee simple, sale where trees on land held by person owning less than, **184:14.**

Fines and penalties, **87:6, 87:9-87:12.**

Injuring or destroying trees, **266:113-266:115, 266:117.**

Shade trees.

See SHADE TREES.

Fires, burning tree prunings, diseased plant materials, and brush from land clearing operations, **111:142L.**

Forests.

See FORESTS AND FORESTRY.

Fruits.

See FRUITS AND FRUIT TREES.

Highways.

See HIGHWAYS AND STREETS.

Inspections, **128:24.**

Logs.

See LOGS AND TIMBER.

Malicious mischief or injury, **87:9-87:12, 266:13 et seq.**

Moths.

See MOTHS.

Nursery stock, **128:17-128:21.**

See NURSERIES AND NURSERY STOCK.

Paper.

See PAPER AND PAPER PRODUCTS.

Parks.

See PARKS AND RESERVATIONS.

Penalties.

Fines and penalties. See within this heading, "Fines and penalties."

Pest control bureau.

See SHADE TREE MANAGEMENT AND PEST CONTROL BUREAU.

Pine loopers.

See PINE LOOPERS.

Public works and departments.

Regulation of planting or removing trees upon state highways, **81:13, 81:13A, 81:21.**

TREES —Cont'd

Public works and departments —Cont'd

Removal of trees obstructing view upon state highway, **81:14.**

Railroads.

See RAILROADS.

Sale or transfer of property.

Fee simple, seller owning less than, **184:14.**

Forest land of state, **132:34A.**

Logs.

See LOGS AND TIMBER.

Nursery stock, sale, **128:19.**

Tax exemption, **64H:6.**

Sales tax exemption for fruit trees, **64H:6.**

Seeds.

See SEEDS.

Shade trees, **87:1-87:13.**

See SHADE TREES.

State highways.

See HIGHWAYS AND STREETS.

State tree, **2:8.**

Sunday, sales, **136:6.**

Timber.

See LOGS AND TIMBER.

University of Massachusetts experiments, **75:17.**

Wardens.

See TREE WARDENS.

White pine blister rust.

See WHITE PINE BLISTER RUST.

TREE WARDENS.

Abolishment of office of, in event office of land and natural resources office established, **41:69G.**

Absence, temporary appointment in case, **41:40.**

Appointment by selectmen, **41:1, 41:106.**

Election authorizing, **41:21.**

Rescission of selectmen's power of appointment, **41:23.**

Temporary wardens, **41:40.**

Compensation, **87:2.**

Cutting or trimming of shade trees, **87:3-87:5.**

Disability, temporary appointment in case, **41:40.**

Diseases and pests.

Assisting in suppression of moths and insect pests, **132:13.**

Foliage-destroying pests, duties, **132:25.**

Duties, **87:2, 87:13.**

TREE WARDENS —Cont'd

Election and term, **41:1.**

Forest warden, tree warden may hold office, **48:8.**

Lands and natural resources office, tree wardens office abolished upon establishment, **41:69G.**

Oath of office, **41:107.**

Pests.

Diseases and pests. See within this heading, "Diseases and pests."

Planting of shade trees, **87:7.**

Powers, **87:2.**

Public shade trees, cutting or trimming, **87:3, 87:4.**

Selectmen.

Appointment. See within this heading, "Appointment by selectmen."

Temporary warden, appointment, **41:40.**

Term of office, **41:1.**

Town public works board as successor, **41:69D.**

Towns may appoint, **41:1, 41:21, 41:106.**

TRESPASS.

Abuse prevention, violation of court order, **266:120.**

Abutting owners.

Adjoining or adjacent property. See within this heading, "Adjoining or adjacent property."

Adjoining or adjacent property.

County jail, house of correction, or courthouse, land appurtenant, **266:123.**

Exceptions as to certain entries upon land of another, **266:120B, 266:120C.**

Railroad clearing land adjoining tracks as trespass, **160:236.**

Agriculture Commissioner, posters as to farm and forest lands, **128:7.**

Aircraft flying over property, **90:46.**

Alcoholic liquor licensees' premises, entry into, **138:63.**

Animals, trespass, **266:118.**

Arrest.

See ARREST.

Attaching officer as trespasser, **223:117.**

Attorney General.

Action to recover state land, **245:1, 245:2.**

Prosecution of trespassers on state property, **12:7.**

TRESPASS —Cont'd

Automobiles.
  Motor vehicles. See within this heading, "Motor vehicles."
Boats.
  Ships and other watercraft. See within this heading, "Ships and other watercraft."
Buildings, violations as to, **266:114, 266:120, 266:122.**
Carrying goods from wharf or landing place, **266:113.**
Cattle, trespass, **266:118.**
Cemetery, trespass, **114:42.**
Cities or towns, buildings, **41:36.**
Closing of private lands to prevent fire hazards, **48:28C.**
Colleges and universities, trespass on land or premises, **266:123.**
Common nuisances, duty of owner or agent, **139:3A.**
Correctional institutions.
  Confinement of trespassers, **266:120, 266:131.**
  Land of institution, trespass, **266:123, 266:132.**
Costs, casual trespass cases, tender of damages as avoiding costs, **242:8.**
County property.
  Buildings, trespass, **41:36.**
  Land appurtenant to jail, house of correction or courthouse, **266:123.**
Court order, trespass as result of violation, **266:120.**
Cranberry meadow, entering, **266:115.**
Criminal offenses and procedure, **266:113 et seq.**
Crops, taking, **266:113.**
Cutting or damaging timber, liability, **242:7, 242:8, 266:113, 266:115.**
Death of trespassers on railroad property, liability, **229:2.**
Docks.
  Wharves and piers. See within this heading, "Wharves and piers."
Dog-bite actions, burden of proof, **140:155.**
Dwelling houses, notice to trespasser, **266:122.**
Exceptions to certain entries upon land, **266:120B, 266:120C.**
Family trouble cases, additional terms of recognizance and conditions of probation, **276:42A.**
Federal employees, trespass, **1:9.**
  Trespassing on private land, **266:121A.**

TRESPASS —Cont'd

Firearms, trespass while bearing, **266:121.**
Fires and fire prevention.
  Closing private land for prevention of fire hazard, **48:28C.**
  Entry of premises for inspection or investigation as trespass, **148:4.**
  Liability of fire wardens, **48:27.**
Fish and game licenses as affecting laws, **131:13.**
Fish experiments or propagation, entry on property maintained, **130:18.**
Fishing gear swept ashore by natural causes, owner's right to recover, **130:32.**
Flowers, cutting or carrying away, **266:113, 266:115, 266:116A.**
Flying over property, **90:46.**
Forest wardens, liability, **48:27.**
Fowl.
  Poultry. See within this heading, "Poultry."
Fruit, cutting or carrying away, **266:113, 266:115.**
Gambling by trespassers on private place, **271:2.**
Gardens, entering, **266:115, 266:117, 266:118.**
Gates, opening or breaking down, **266:114.**
General fields, proprietor as trespasser, **179:24.**
Glass in building, breaking, **266:114.**
Goats, trespass, **266:118.**
Grain or grass, entering another's land to destroy or carry away, **266:117.**
Gravel, carrying away, **266:113.**
Hay, entering another's land to cut or carry away, **266:117.**
Higher education institutions, trespass on land or premises, **266:123.**
Highways and streets.
  Intersections, exceptions as to trespass on private property, **266:121A.**
  Parking of motor vehicle as trespass, **266:120A.**
Hog, trespass, **266:118.**
Holidays.
  Sundays and holidays. See within this heading, "Sundays and holidays."
Horse or dog racing meeting premises, entry, **128A:10A.**

TRESPASS —Cont'd

Horses, trespass, **266:118.**
Humane society, property, **266:133.**
Improved or enclosed lands, notice to trespasser, **266:122.**
Indictments.
  See INDICTMENTS, INFORMATIONS, AND COMPLAINTS.
Injuring trespasser, **278:8A.**
Institution of higher education, land or premises, **266:123.**
Jail.
  Correctional institutions. See within this heading, "Correctional institutions."
Land court's jurisdiction of trespass actions involving title to real estate, **185:1.**
Logs and timber, cutting, **242:7, 242:8, 266:113, 266:115.**
Militia.
  Liability of, for entering upon private lands, **33:51, 33:52.**
  Parades and encampments, intruding, **33:65, 33:66.**
Motor vehicles.
  Parking, **266:120A.**
  Penalty for unauthorized use on private land, **266:121A.**
  Sales contract authorizing trespass, forbidden, **255B:20.**
  Unregistered or improperly equipped vehicle, effect of operation, **90:9.**
  Use in commission of trespass, **90:24A.**
  Violator of one-way street regulations as trespasser, **89:10.**
Municipal buildings, **41:36.**
Notice to trespassers, **266:118, 266:120, 266:122.**
Nuisances, duty of owner or agent, **139:3A.**
Nurseries, entering, **266:115.**
Orchards, entering, **266:115, 266:117, 266:118.**
Ore, carrying away, **266:113.**
Penal and reformatory institutions.
  Correctional institutions. See within this heading, "Correctional institutions."
Piers.
  Wharves and piers. See within this heading, "Wharves and piers."
Pigs, trespass, **266:118.**

TRESPASS —Cont'd

Police.

Arrest, **266:120, 266:131.**

Public transportation facility premises, power of arrest for loitering or trespassing, **161:94A, 161:95.**

Towns, prosecutions of trespasses against, **41:36.**

Posted notice, **128:7, 266:118, 266:120, 266:122.**

Poultry, **266:118.**

Where poultry kept, **266:22.**

Powered devices, trespass on private land, **266:121A.**

Presumptions and burden of proof, dog-bite actions, **140:155.**

Public lands, **12:7, 41:36, 45:13, 91:2, 245:1, 245:2, 245:9, 266:123.**

Attorney General. See within this heading, "Attorney General."

Indictments.

See INDICTMENTS, INFORMATIONS, AND COMPLAINTS.

Shore and tidal lands belonging to state, duty of public works department in connection with trespasses, **91:2.**

State buildings, **266:123.**

Public transportation facility, trespass on premises, **161:94A, 161:95.**

Railroads.

Clearing land adjoining tracks as trespass, **160:236.**

Death of trespassers on railroad property, liability, **229:2.**

Penalty, **90:15, 159:93, 160:218, 160:220.**

Removing or defacing posted notice, **266:122.**

Sheep, trespass, **266:118.**

Ships and other watercraft.

Criminal offense, **266:120.**

Notices, removal or defacing, **266:122.**

Snow traveling and recreational vehicles, **90B:33, 266:121A.**

Soldiers' Home in Massachusetts, trespassing on land, **266:123.**

State buildings and property.

Public lands. See within this heading, "Public lands."

State employees, damages for trespass, **1:9.**

Stone, carrying away, **266:113.**

TRESPASS —Cont'd

Streets.

Highways and streets. See within this heading, "Highways and streets."

Summary process to recover land, trespass action as barred by judgment, **239:7.**

Sundays and holidays.

Arrest for trespass, **266:120, 266:131.**

Penalty for trespass on land of another, **266:113.**

Warrant, arrest and detention of trespasser without, **266:131.**

Surveyor's entry upon land of another for purpose of making survey, **266:120C.**

Swine, trespass, **266:118.**

Tender of damages in action for casual trespass, **242:8.**

Timber, cutting or destroying, **266:113, 266:115.**

Title to real estate, land court's jurisdiction of trespass actions involving, **185:1.**

United States, trespass by employees, **1:9.**

Universities and colleges, trespass on land or premises, **266:123.**

Vegetables, entering another's land to destroy or carry away, **266:117.**

Vessels.

Ships and other watercraft. See within this heading, "Ships and other watercraft."

Water resources authority, **Spec L 67:1, 67:2, 67:4-67:6, 67:8-67:10, 67:12, 67:18, 67:23, 67:26, 83:11.**

Water sources, aiding or abetting trespasses, **111:170.**

Wharves and piers.

Notice to trespasser, **266:122.**

Violations, **266:113, 266:120.**

Wild flowers, digging up plant of, **266:116A.**

Writ of entry, right of plaintiff against trespassers as affected by statutory provisions, **237:43.**

TRIAL COURT OF COMMONWEALTH.

Administrative justices, **211B:1-211B:14.**

See ADMINISTRATIVE JUSTICES.

Alternative dispute resolution programs for civil actions, **211B:19.**

TRIAL COURT OF COMMONWEALTH —Cont'd

Associate justices, salary, **211B:4.**

Boston municipal court department, **4:7.**

Case management system, **211B:9.**

Chief Administrative Justice, salary, **211B:4.**

Child Support Guidelines.

See CHILD SUPPORT GUIDELINES.

Civil Motor Vehicle Infractions, Uniform Rules On.

See CIVIL MOTOR VEHICLE INFRACTIONS, UNIFORM RULES ON.

Criminal Justice Training Council, membership of administrator of trial court, **6:116.**

Departments of, **211B:1.**

District court department, divisions, **4:7.**

Electronic access and retrieval of information, fee-based system and schedule of fees, **29A:3A.**

Estimate of budgetary requirements for ordinary maintenance of court, **211B:9.**

Housing court as division, **4:7.**

Impoundment Procedure, Uniform Rules On.

See IMPOUNDMENT PROCEDURE, UNIFORM RULES ON.

Interpreters, **221C:1 et seq.**

Administration and coordination, **221C:7.**

Assistant interpreter, **221C:2.**

Definitions, **221C:1.**

Impartial interpretations, **221C:4.**

Reimbursement of expenses, **221C:6.**

Removal, **221C:5.**

Waiver of interpreter, **221C:3.**

Juvenile court as department, **4:7.**

Land court as department, **4:7.**

Leave of absence, justices, **211B:19.**

Magistrates, Uniform Rules.

See MAGISTRATES, UNIFORM RULES.

Personnel standards, advisory committee on, **211B:8.**

Probate and insolvency court as department, **4:7.**

Reserve fund for secretarial and administrative support staff and services, **211B:9.**

Rules.

Consolidation of cases, **Part XII.**

TRIAL COURT OF COMMONWEALTH —Cont'd

Rules —Cont'd

Interdepartmental judicial assignments, **Part XII.**

Probable cause determinations for person arrested without warrant, **Rule XI.**

Uniform schedule of fees, **262:4B.**

Salary schedule for justices, **211B:4.**

Small Claims, Uniform Rules. See SMALL CLAIMS, UNIFORM RULES.

Standards for personnel, advisory committee on, **211B:8.**

Subpoenas To Court Officials, Uniform Rules Of. See SUBPOENAS TO COURT OFFICIALS, UNIFORM RULES OF.

Substitute Care Review Hearings, Uniform Rules For. See SUBSTITUTE CARE REVIEW HEARINGS, UNIFORM RULES FOR.

Summary Process, Uniform Rules. See SUMMARY PROCESS, UNIFORM RULES.

Superior court as department, **4:7.**

Training program for judicial and nonjudicial personnel, **211B:16.**

TRIAL LISTS.
See CALENDARS AND DOCKETS.

TRIAL OR HEARINGS.

Abandoned motor vehicles, hearings to stay imposition of fines and costs, **90:22B.**

Accessory before the fact, **274:2.**

Adjournment. See CONTINUANCE OR ADJOURNMENT.

Administration. See ADMINISTRATION AND FINANCE EXECUTIVE OFFICE.

Administrative hearings, **30A:2, 30A:3, 30A:9, 30A:10, 30A:11, 30A:13.** See ADMINISTRATIVE PROCEDURE.

Admissions in advance of trial, demands, **231:69.**

Adoption of children.

Hearing in chambers, **210:6.**

Removal of child from proposed adoption home, hearing, **210:5A.**

TRIAL OR HEARINGS —Cont'd

Aged and disabled, hearings in connection with assistance, **118A:3.**

Aircraft. See AIRCRAFT AND AVIATION.

Air pollution orders, hearing, **111:142B, 111:142E.**

Alcoholic liquors. See ALCOHOLIC LIQUORS.

Ambulances.

Deficiencies in ambulance service, hearing, **111C:9.**

Suspension, revocation, or refusal to renew license or certificate, hearing, **111C:10.**

Amherst economic development and industrial corporation, hearing procedures relating to undertaking projects, **Spec L 23:6.**

Amusement devises, public hearing prior to issuance of license, **140:177.**

Antipsychotic medication hearings, **123:9.**

Appeal from decision at. See APPEAL AND REVIEW.

Appellate tax board, **58A:8, 59:65.**

Apples.

Grades, hearings as to establishment or modification, **94:101.**

Prosecution for violations, hearings before, **94:107.**

Appointed officials, rights, **4:7.**

Appraisers and appraisals, **112:190.**

Arbitration hearings, **251:5.**

Arbitrators' conduct of, as ground for vacating award, **251:12.**

Collective bargaining agreements to arbitrate. See LABOR RELATIONS AND DISPUTES.

Rehearings, **251:12.**

Arrest on mesne process. See ARREST ON MESNE PROCESS AND SUPPLEMENTARY PROCEEDINGS.

Assistance to the aged and disabled, hearings, **118A:3.**

Attachment of property. See ATTACHMENT OF PROPERTY.

Attorney General's report of cases litigated, **12:11.**

Attorneys at law. See ATTORNEYS AT LAW.

TRIAL OR HEARINGS —Cont'd

Authority, hearing authority defined, **121A:6C, 131:39A.**

Automobile insurance. See AUTOMOBILE INSURANCE.

Bail, hearings.

Amount of bail, **276:58.**

Necessity for sureties, **276:47.**

Ballot law commission.

State ballot law commission. See within this heading, "State ballot law commission hearings."

Banks. See BANKS AND BANKING.

Berkshire Mountains, protection of watershed resources and natural scenic qualities, **131:39A.**

Blood tests, power of hearing officer in child support case to order, **221B:6.**

Boiler rules board, hearings, **146:3.**

Bonds and undertakings, order by hearing officer in child support case to post bond and security, **221B:7.**

Breath test, hearing on suspension or revocation of license for refusal to submit, **90:24.**

Bridgewater State Hospital, hearing for commitment waived, **123:5, 123:6, 123:8.**

Building Code Appeals Board, appeal, **143:100.**

Building regulations and standards board, powers and duties, **143:94, 143:98.**

Campaign expenditures and contributions.

Corrupt practices, hearing on charges, **55:33.**

Director of campaign and political finance, investigations and hearings, **55:3.**

Carriers, **159B:2.** See CARRIERS.

Chief administrative justice, hearing officers in child support cases, **221B:3.**

Chief administrative justice, hearings for dispute settlement, **211B:9.**

Children. See CHILDREN AND MINORS.

Chiropractors, hearing on revocation of certificate, **112:93.**

TRIAL OR HEARINGS —Cont'd
Civil rights.
See CIVIL RIGHTS AND
DISCRIMINATION.
Civil service.
See CIVIL SERVICE.
Coal mining regulation.
See COAL MINING
REGULATION AND
RECLAMATION.
Collective bargaining agreements
to arbitrate.
See LABOR RELATIONS AND
DISPUTES.
Collectors of taxes, removal,
41:39B.
Commercial driver license, hearing
on disqualification, **90F:11.**
Common carriers, hearings on
discontinuance of service,
25:4A.
Commonwealth, purchase, sale,
rental, lease, transfer, or
significant change in use of
real property on behalf of
state agencies, **7:40I.**
Community antenna television
systems.
See COMMUNITY ANTENNA
TELEVISION SYSTEMS.
Competency of person to stand
trial, mental health, **123:15.**
Confinement of persons awaiting
trial, **276:42.**
Conservation districts.
Bylaws, adoption, **21:24.**
Establishment, change of
boundaries, or dissolution,
21:21.
Consolidation of cases, **223:2A.**
Constitution of Massachusetts.
See CONSTITUTION OF
MASSACHUSETTS.
Constitution of the United States.
See CONSTITUTION OF THE
UNITED STATES.
Consumers' council, hearings,
6:115A.
Consumer transaction practices.
See BANKS AND BANKING.
Contempt, **224:18.**
Continuance.
See CONTINUANCE OR
ADJOURNMENT.
Corporations.
Dissolution petition, hearing,
155:50, 156:50, 158:38.
Removal of director or officer,
hearing, **156B:51.**
Take-over bids, proceedings
concerning, **110C:2, 110C:6.**

TRIAL OR HEARINGS —Cont'd
Costs of actions.
See COSTS OF ACTION.
County charter study commission,
public hearings and forms,
34A:11.
County-owned real estate, sale or
lease, **34:14.**
Court rules for conducting, **213:3.**
Credit unions.
See CREDIT UNIONS.
Crime victims' compensation
proceedings.
Rehearing in appellate division
of district court, **231:108.**
Criminal cases.
See CRIMINAL PROCEDURE.
Criminal history systems board,
promulgation of rules and
regulations, **6:168.**
Criminal offender record
information system, hearings.
De novo hearing on appeal,
6:176.
Record of individual alleged to
be inaccurate or incomplete,
6:175.
Cultural Council of Massachusetts,
10:54.
Dams and reservoirs.
Alteration, repairs or change of
grade of public way, hearing,
253:35.
Notice of hearing upon petition
when public way is to be
overflowed, **253:34.**
Delay of trial.
Failure to answer demand for
admission of fact or of
execution of paper, **231:69.**
Speedy trial.
See SPEEDY TRIAL.
De novo hearing, motor vehicle
infractions, **90C:3.**
Dependent children, aid to,
institution's right to hearing,
118:11.
Discrimination.
See CIVIL RIGHTS AND
DISCRIMINATION.
Dissolution of attachment.
See ATTACHMENT OF
PROPERTY.
Drugs.
See DRUGS AND NARCOTICS.
Dwellings unfit for human
habitation, hearing, **111:127B.**
Economic development projects,
proposals, **121C:6.**
Elections, objections to nomination
papers and the like, **55B:8,
55B:9.**

TRIAL OR HEARINGS —Cont'd
Electric Companies.
See GAS AND ELECTRIC
COMPANIES.
Electric railroads.
See ELECTRIC RAILROADS.
Elevators.
Amendment of regulations,
hearing, **143:69.**
Variance, request, **143:70.**
Employer closing facility, report,
151A:71B.
Employment agencies and
bureaus.
Complaint against licensee,
140:46Q.
Issuance of license, **140:46D.**
Notice of hearings, **140:46D,
140:46Q.**
Employment and training
department, reconsideration of
determination, **151A:71.**
Employment security.
See EMPLOYMENT
SECURITY.
Energy facilities siting.
See ENERGY FACILITIES
SITING.
Energy resources executive office.
Appointment of members of
energy resources
commission, **40:8I.**
Regulations of office, procedures,
25A:12.
Entry, writs of.
See ENTRY, WRITS.
Environmental management
board, hearings as to removal
of members, **21:2B.**
Environmental protection
department, **21A:16, 21C:4.**
Equity.
One justice, hearing, **214:8.**
Pending cases in another
country, **214:10.**
Evidence.
See EVIDENCE.
Executions.
See EXECUTIONS.
Fair educational practices.
See FAIR EDUCATIONAL
PRACTICES.
Feed and feeding of animals,
hearings.
License, refusal, **128:52.**
Violations, **128:57.**
Fire insurance.
See FIRE INSURANCE.
Fires.
See FIRES AND FIRE
PREVENTION.

TRIAL OR HEARINGS —Cont'd

Fisheries and wildlife board, hearing on removal of members, **21:7B.**

Food.
Food and agriculture department.
See FOOD AND AGRICULTURE DEPARTMENT.
Generally.
See FOOD.

Foreign insurance companies.
See FOREIGN INSURANCE COMPANIES.

Forfeiture of property in criminal cases, hearing to determine, **94C:47.**

Foster care placement of children, **119:24.**

Gas.
See GAS AND ELECTRIC COMPANIES.

General court.
See GENERAL COURT.

Government land bank.
See GOVERNMENT LAND BANK.

Grievances of state employees, hearings on.
See LABOR RELATIONS AND DISPUTES.

Guardian appointed for mentally ill person, **201:6.**

Habeas corpus.
See HABEAS CORPUS.

Hazardous waste facilities siting.
Environmental management department, exercise of eminent domain authority, **21D:7.**

Hazardous waste management hearings, **21C:4, 21C:11.**
License requirements, **21C:4.**
Transportation vehicles, **21C:5.**
Vehicle identification devices, **21C:7.**

Hazardous waste site cleanup professionals, appeal of board determinations, **21A:19H.**

Health.
See HEALTH AND HEALTH DEPARTMENTS.

Highways.
See HIGHWAYS AND STREETS.

Historic districts, application for certificate of appropriateness, **40C:10, 40C:11.**

Horse and dog racing meetings, right of person refused admission to appeal and hearing, **128A:10A.**

TRIAL OR HEARINGS —Cont'd

Housing appeals committee, duties of as to hearings, **23B:5A.**

Housing authority.
Charges against member, **121B:6.**
Eviction, waiver of hearing, **121B:32.**

Illegitimate children.
See ILLEGITIMATE CHILDREN.

Immunity for witness in hearing.
See WITNESSES.

Impartial trial, change of venue to secure, **223:13.**

Impeachment of officer.
See IMPEACHMENT OF OFFICER.

Imprisonment pending, to be credited on sentence, **127:129B, 279:33A.**

Indigency, judicial determination, **261:27B.**

Industries.
See LABOR AND WORKFORCE DEVELOPMENT.

Initiative and referendum petitions, hearings, **43:38.**

Injunctions, **214:6.**

Inland wetlands protection, **131:40, 131:40A.**

Insurance.
See INSURANCE.

Insurance agents.
See INSURANCE AGENTS AND BROKERS.

Insurance rates.
See INSURANCE RATES AND RATING ORGANIZATIONS.

Joinder of parties, consolidation of cases in trial court, **223:2A.**

Judges.
See JUDGES.

Judicial conduct commission, power to conduct hearings, **211C:2.**

Jury.
See JURY AND JURY TRIAL.

Jury commissioner for Commonwealth.
See JURY COMMISSIONER FOR COMMONWEALTH.

Juvenile courts.
See JUVENILE COURTS AND DELINQUENT CHILDREN.

Labor.
See LABOR AND WORKFORCE DEVELOPMENT.

Labor relations.
See LABOR RELATIONS AND DISPUTES.

TRIAL OR HEARINGS —Cont'd

Labor relations commission.
See LABOR RELATIONS COMMISSION.

Laches.
Delay of trial. See within this heading, "Delay of trial."

Landscape architects, hearing as to revocation or suspension of registration, **112:106.**

Levy on execution, hearing as to partial invalidity, **236:52.**

Lowlands and swamps.
Improvements, **252:3, 252:5.**
Order affecting inland wetlands, notice of public hearing, **131:40, 131:40A.**
Organization of reclamation districts, **252:5.**

Marine fisheries.
Advisory commission, hearings, **21:5A.**
Management proposals, **130:17A.**
Shellfish licenses, **130:57, 130:60.**
Spawning fish, passageways open, **130:19.**

Massachusetts water management act, adjudicatory hearings, **21G:12.**

Masters appointed by probate and family court department, conduct of hearings, **221:58.**

Medex, prior public hearing and approval of rates charged directly to subscribers by contract known, **176A:10.**

Medical care and assistance, **118E:22, 123:9.**

Medical depositions, **233:24A.**

Medical malpractice insurance, **175A:5C.**

Mentally ill and retarded persons, advisory council hearings, **19:11.**

Metropolitan districts.
See METROPOLITAN DISTRICTS.

Milk.
Investigation and hearings.
See MILK AND MILK PRODUCTS.

Mineral resources division to conduct hearings regarding exploration and extraction of mineral resources, **21:54.**

Minimum wages.
Determination of whether contract or agreement deprives employee of status as such, hearing, **151:19.**

TRIAL OR HEARINGS —Cont'd
Minimum wages —Cont'd
Discrimination against
employees participating in
board hearing, **151:19.**
Nonobservance of wage rates
and regulations, hearing,
151:11.
Minors.
See CHILDREN AND MINORS.
Motions.
See MOTIONS.
Motor carriers.
See CARRIERS.
Motor vehicle retail installment
sales.
See MOTOR VEHICLE RETAIL
INSTALLMENT SALES.
Motor vehicles.
See MOTOR VEHICLES.
Municipal courts.
See MUNICIPAL COURTS.
Municipal lighting.
Notice and hearings.
See MUNICIPAL LIGHTING
AND HEATING PLANTS.
New trial.
See NEW TRIAL.
Nomination papers and the like,
objections, **55B:8, 55B:9.**
Nonintoxicating beverage licenses,
revocation or suspension,
140:21B.
Nonresident defendants, notice,
227:5A.
Normal fees and costs, necessity of
hearing in case, **261:27C.**
Notice of public hearings, **30A:2,**
30A:3, 30A:6, 30A:10, 30A:11.
Nuisances.
See NUISANCES.
Nursing or rest homes.
Health department, duties of
hearing officers, **111:3.**
License, hearings on revocation
or refusal to renew, **111:71.**
Obscenity, proceedings to
determine, **272:28D, 272:28F.**
Ocean sanctuaries, hearing on
application for variance to
permit waste disposal,
132A:16E.
Office of child care services,
hearings, **28A:7, 28A:13.**
Official stenographer taking
testimony as precluding other
persons from interrupting
examination to take notes,
231:83.
Overdue taxes, imprisonment,
60:29.

TRIAL OR HEARINGS —Cont'd
Parking violations, challenge by
mail, right to hearing, **90:20A,**
90:20A½.
Parole hearings.
See PROBATION AND
PAROLE.
Payments to claimant or plaintiff
in tort in advance of trial,
231:140B.
Periodic review of person found
incompetent to stand trial,
mental health, **123:17.**
Pesticide control, **132B:13.**
Pet shop licenses, suspension,
140:138A.
Physician assistants, hearings
relating to complaints,
112:9H.
Pictures or photographs.
Admission in evidence of
photographic copies,
151A:44, 233:79, 233:79A,
233:79D, 233:79E.
Expense of photographs used,
261:25A.
Place of trial or hearings,
30A:11C, 231:82; US Const
Art 3 Sec 2 cl 3.
Planning.
See ZONING AND PLANNING.
Plans, drawings, photographs and
copies used at trial, expense,
261:25A.
Pollutants in or near watersheds,
informational hearings
regarding regulation of,
92:107A.
Postponement or delay.
Delay. See within this heading,
"Delay of trial."
Pretrial proceedings.
See PRETRIAL
PROCEEDINGS.
Probate.
See PROBATE AND FAMILY
COURT.
Probation.
See PROBATION AND
PAROLE.
Promoters of shows, revocation of
registration certificate,
62C:67A.
Public buildings construction and
repair, notice of claim for
adjudicatory hearing, **30:39Q.**
Public health department,
appointment and
qualifications of hearing
officers, **17:6B.**
Public officers, grievances of.
See LABOR RELATIONS AND
DISPUTES.

TRIAL OR HEARINGS —Cont'd
Public records, hearings as part of
judicial enforcement of
procedures, **66:17C.**
Public trial.
Paternity proceedings, exclusion
of public, **209C:12.**
Right to, **220:13A; US Const**
6th Amend.
Punishment.
Sentence and punishment. See
within this heading,
"Sentence and punishment."
Questions of law.
See QUESTIONS OF LAW AND
FACT.
Railroad crossings.
Notice and hearing.
See RAILROAD CROSSINGS.
Railroads.
See RAILROADS.
Rates.
See RATES AND CHARGES.
Refuse treatment and disposal
facilities, hearing on
assignment of places,
111:150A.
Registration of professions and
occupations, **112:62.**
Hearings on complaints and
charges.
See REGISTRATION OF
PROFESSIONS AND
OCCUPATIONS.
Removal of municipal chief of
police, hearing prior, **41:21A.**
Reservoirs.
Dams and reservoirs. See within
this heading, "Dams and
reservoirs."
Rest homes.
Nursing or rest homes. See
within this heading,
"Nursing or rest homes."
Retirement systems.
See RETIREMENT SYSTEMS
AND PENSIONS.
Sale of real estate by executor or
administrator, notice of
hearing on petition, **202:10.**
Sanitary code, enforcement,
111:127A, 111:127B.
Savings bank life insurance.
See SAVINGS BANK LIFE
INSURANCE.
Savings or co-operative bank
merging with credit union,
168:34F, 170:26F.
Schools.
See SCHOOLS AND
EDUCATION.

TRIAL OR HEARINGS —Cont'd

Secretary of state, transmission of notices of public hearings to clerks of house of representatives and senate, **30A:6.**

Securities Act, **110A:412.**

Seed laws, violation, **128:94.**

Sentence and punishment.

Credit for imprisonment awaiting trial, **127:129B, 279:33A.**

Separate trial of issue of conviction of prior offenses, **278:11A.**

Set-off debt collection procedure, administrative hearings, **62D:6.**

Sewage and fluid waste, hearings for permit for discharge, **21:43-21:46A.**

Sewers and drains, **83:6, 111:31.**

Sexual offenses and offenders.

Application for parole, hearing, **123A:9.**

Exclusion of public, **278:16A, 278:16C.**

Expedited trial involving minor victim or witness, **278:16F.**

Hearing to challenge of risk level determined by registry board, **6:178M.**

Ships or vessels, restitution for destruction, **266:108.**

Small loans, hearings as to rates of charges, **140:100.**

Social workers.

Client communications, instructions regarding refusal to disclose, **112:135B.**

Discipline of licensee, **112:137.**

Soldiers' Home in Holyoke, removal of superintendent, **6:71.**

Solid waste disposal, hearings, **16:21, 16:24.**

Special commissions of general court, **4:2A.**

Special education.

See SPECIAL EDUCATION.

Spectators, exclusion, **278:16A-278:16C.**

Speedy trial, **231:59A et seq.**

See SPEEDY TRIAL.

State ballot law commission hearings.

Initiative and referendum petitions, **43:38, 55B:9.**

Rules, promulgation, **55B:4.**

State building code.

See BUILDING CODE OF STATE.

TRIAL OR HEARINGS —Cont'd

State finance, **29:29F.**

State police.

See STATE POLICE.

Statewide branch banking, notice and hearing for establishment of branch offices or depots, **167C:3.**

Stipulations as to site of trial, **231:81.**

Street railways.

See STREET RAILWAYS.

Streets.

See HIGHWAYS AND STREETS.

Subversive organizations, adjudication, **264:18.**

Summary process to recover land, hearing on application for stay of proceedings, **239:10.**

Superior courts.

See SUPERIOR COURTS.

Supplementary proceedings, trial of charge of fraud, **224:19.**

Supreme judicial court.

See SUPREME JUDICIAL COURT.

Surplus state property, disposition, **7:40F, 7:40F½.**

Swamps.

Lowlands and swamps. See within this heading, "Lowlands and swamps."

Taxation.

Appellate tax board, **58A:8.**

Teachers.

Certification of teachers, hearing, **71:38G.**

Discharge or suspension hearing, **71:42, 71:42D.**

Telecommunications and energy department, **25:4, 25:4A, 40:5, 159:20, 159:41.**

Theaters, application for license, **140:181.**

Time.

See TIME OR DATE.

Toxics use reduction act.

See TOXICS USE REDUCTION ACT.

Traffic regulations and rules of the road, notice by clerk-magistrate to officer and violator of hearing date, **90C:3.**

Tramway regulations, **143:71J.**

Transcripts.

See TRANSCRIPTS.

Trees, consolidated hearings as to removal, **40:15C, 87:3.**

Trustee process.

See TRUSTEE PROCESS.

TRIAL OR HEARINGS —Cont'd

Underwater archeological resources board, hearings, **6:180.**

Unemployment compensation.

See EMPLOYMENT SECURITY.

Uniform operation of commercial motor vehicles, hearing on driver disqualification, **90F:11.**

Uniform rules of adjudicatory procedure, **30A:10.**

Uniform Securities Act, **110A:412.**

See SECURITIES ACT.

Urban redevelopment projects, preference of actions for judicial review of disapproval, **121A:6C.**

Venue.

See VENUE.

Verdict.

See VERDICT.

Veterinarian schools, revocation or suspension of institutional license, **112:56D.**

Victims of violent crimes, compensation of.

Crime victims' compensation proceedings. See within this heading, "Crime victims' compensation proceedings."

Wage reporting system, **62E:5.**

Waiver.

See WAIVER AND ESTOPPEL.

Water pollution.

See WATER POLLUTION.

Water resources commission, public hearings, **21:9.**

Watershed management plans, adoption, **92:116.**

Waterworks.

See WATERWORKS AND WATER SUPPLY.

Welfare.

See WELFARE AND SOCIAL SERVICES.

Wetland protection, **131:40, 131:40A.**

Witnesses.

See WITNESSES.

Workers' compensation.

See WORKERS' COMPENSATION.

Writ of entry.

See ENTRY, WRITS.

Zoning.

See ZONING AND PLANNING.

TRICKERY.

See FRAUD AND DECEIT.

TRIGGER LOCKS.

Sales tax exemptions, **64H:6.**

TRIMEPERIDINE.
Controlled dangerous substance, **94C:31.**

TRIPLE DAMAGES.
See TREBLE DAMAGES.

TRIPOD QUAD CANES.
Sales tax exemptions, **64H:6.**

TROLLEYS.
Street railways.
　See STREET RAILWAYS.
Trackless trolleys, **163:1-163:12.**
　See TRACKLESS TROLLEYS.

TROTTING COURSES.
Betting on races not authorized by statute, **271:31.**
Harness horse racing, **271:31, 271:33, 271:34.**
Land used for, regulation of location, **271:33.**
Nuisance, unlawful courses, **271:34.**

TROUGHS.
Town appropriation for drinking troughs in public places, **40:5.**

TROUT.
Buying and selling regulations, **131:22.**
Coastal waters, taking, **131:51.**

TROUT UNLIMITED.
Quabbin watershed advisory committee, members, **92:114.**

TROVER.
See CONVERSION OF FUNDS OR PROPERTY.

TROY POUND.
Relationship to avoirdupois pound, **98:2.**

TRUCKS.
See MOTOR VEHICLES.

TRUE NAME ACT, 140:27 et seq.
Lodging-entry in register, **140:27 et seq.**

TRUMPETS.
Municipal regulation of use on highways and streets, **85:10.**

TRURO.
District court, **218:1.**
Medical examiner district, **38:1.**

TRUST COMPANIES, 172:1 et seq.
Abandoned or unclaimed funds, deposits with trust companies, **206:25, 206:27, 206:27A, 241:34.**
　Annual reports by trust companies, **200A:1, 200A:7.**

TRUST COMPANIES —Cont'd
Absentees, estates of.
　See ABSENTEES' ESTATES.
Accounts, **167D:1 et seq.**
　Deposits. See within this heading, "Deposits."
　Savings deposits. See within this heading, "Savings deposits."
　Surplus account. See within this heading, "Surplus account."
Adjustable or flexible mortgages, **183:28A.**
Agents.
　Officers, agents, and employees. See within this heading, "Officers, agents, and employees."
Annual meeting or report, **172:22.**
Appeals from decisions of board of bank incorporation as to bank holding companies, **167A:4.**
Applicability of chapter, **172:2.**
Appointments.
　See APPOINTMENTS.
Articles of organization, **172:8.**
Assets and property.
　Bank holding company, acquisition, **167A:2.**
　Loan upon or purchase of assets or stock of state or federally chartered bank, **172:38.**
　Purchase, sale, or exchange, **172:36, 172:38.**
Authorized depository for credit union deductions from pay of public employees, **149:178B.**
Bad debts, **172:24.**
Balance sheet, posting, **172:22.**
Bank commissioner.
　Annual report, **172:22.**
　Articles of organization, submission, **172:8.**
　Conflicts of interest prohibited, **26:2.**
　Officers, report as to loans or extension of credit, **172:18.**
　Reserve balances, report, **172:31.**
　Returns in form of trial balances, **172:22A.**
　Shares, assignment and transfer, **172:11, 172:26.**
Bank holding companies.
　See BANK HOLDING COMPANIES.
Bank incorporation, board.
　Bank holding companies, appeals from decision of board, **167A:4.**
　Out-of-state associations and corporations, **167:38.**
　Powers as to formation of trust company, **172:6.**

TRUST COMPANIES —Cont'd
Bank incorporation, board
　—Cont'd
　Stockholder list, filing, **172:9.**
Banks as trust companies, **255D:1.**
Board of bank incorporation.
　Bank incorporation, board of.
　　See within this heading, "Bank incorporation, board."
Board of directors.
　Directors. See within this heading, "Directors."
Bond issues.
　Economic development and industrial corporations, revenue or revenue refunding bonds, **121C:14.**
　Investments, **167F:2.**
　　County bonds, **35:37A.**
　　Housing and urban renewal operating agencies, bonds and notes, **121B:15.**
　　Industrial Finance Agency bonds, **23A:39.**
　　Municipal bonds, **44:55.**
　Issuance and sale, **172:30.**
　Municipal industrial development authorities, trust agreements securing bonds, **40D:9.**
　Sinking fund for state bonds, **29:49.**
Bonds for officers, **172:15.**
Books and records.
　Records and reports. See within this heading, "Records and reports."
Branch banks or offices, **172:36, 172:38.**
Brokerage for or in connection with business of trust company, acceptance, **172:20.**
Burial expenses of ward, increase of limitation on amounts deposited, **201:48A.**
Business corporation law, applicability to trust companies, **156:2, 156B:3.**
Bylaws.
　Adoption, **172:7.**
　Shares, control of assignment and transfer, **172:11.**
Capital notes, issuance and sale, **172:30.**
Capital stock, **172:9, 172:24, 172:25.**
Capital structure required for incorporation, **172:4.**
Certificates and certification.
　Deposit certificates.
　　Term deposits. See within this heading, "Term deposits."

TRUST COMPANIES —Cont'd
Certificates and certification
—Cont'd
Formation, **172:6.**
Incorporation, certificate, **172:8.**
Investment in municipal bonds
and notes, **44:55.**
Transaction of business, **172:9.**
Children, gifts to minors, **201A:1,
201A:9.**
Cities and towns.
Bonds or notes, authentication,
registration, transfer,
exchange, record and paying
agent functions, **44:16.**
Certificates of deposit,
investment of municipal and
district funds, **44:55.**
Claims trust for municipal
self-insurance, **32B:3A.**
Deposits, city and town trust
fund, **44:54, 44:55.**
Industrial development
authorities.
Bonds, trust agreements
securing, **40D:9.**
Deposit of monies, **40D:18.**
Investment of funds.
Bonds and notes, proceeds,
44:55.
Conservation funds, **40:5.**
Loans to, limit, **75C:1.**
Registered bonds, signature,
44:16A.
Treasurers of cities and towns,
prohibition against having
interest in trust companies,
44:55.
Trust funds of, deposit, **44:54.**
Claims trust for municipal
self-insurance, **32B:3A.**
Classes of stock, **172:24.**
Clerk or secretary, selection.
Incorporators, election, **172:7.**
Stockholders, election, **172:14.**
Commissioner of banking.
Bank commissioner. See within
this heading, "Bank
commissioner."
Commissions for or in connection
with business of trust
company, acceptance, **172:20.**
Compensation.
Wages, salaries, and
compensation. See within
this heading, "Wages,
salaries, and compensation."
Competition among banking
institutions, **172:36, 172:38.**
Conflict of interests, commissioner
of banks, **26:2.**

TRUST COMPANIES —Cont'd
Conservation funds of towns,
investment, **40:5.**
Conservators.
Inadequate reserve balances,
172:33.
Consolidation or merger, **172:36,
172:38.**
Approval, time of existence
affecting, **172:38A.**
Bank holding companies,
167A:2.
Contracts, formation of trust
company, **172:5.**
Conversion involving trust
company, **172:36, 172:37.**
Co-operative banks, **167A:2.**
Corporation taxes, **63:1-63:19.**
See CORPORATION TAXES.
Corrective changes in related laws,
40D:9, 40E:10, 183:28A.
Costs and expenses.
Fees and expenses. See within
this heading, "Fees and
expenses."
County finance.
See COUNTY FINANCE.
Courts.
Liquidation. See within this
heading, "Liquidation."
Probate courts, savings deposits
in name of probate judge,
241:34.
Supreme judicial court. See
within this heading,
"Supreme judicial court."
Unclaimed funds, deposits by
court of.
Abandoned or unclaimed
funds. See within this
heading, "Abandoned or
unclaimed funds, deposits
with trust companies."
Credit.
Loans. See within this heading,
"Loans."
Credit unions.
See CREDIT UNIONS.
Custodian.
Securities in registered form
given to minors, **201A:9.**
Successor custodian,
appointment as, **201A:18.**
Date.
Time or date. See within this
heading, "Time or date."
Decedents' estates, deposit by
fiduciaries of unclaimed funds,
206:25-206:27A.
Definitions, **172:1, 172:36, 172:38,
201A:1, 203:4A.**

TRUST COMPANIES —Cont'd
Deposits, **167D:1 et seq.**
Abandoned or unclaimed funds.
See within this heading,
"Abandoned or unclaimed
funds, deposits with trust
companies."
Certificate of deposits.
Term deposits. See within this
heading, "Term deposits."
City or town trust fund, **44:54,
44:55.**
Corporation taxes.
See CORPORATION TAXES.
Counties, gifts, **34:23.**
County officers, surplus funds,
35:22.
Credit union deductions from
pay of public employees,
trust company as authorized
depository, **149:178B.**
Direct deposit of public
employees' wages, **41:41B.**
Group insurance commission
funds, **32A:9A.**
Insolvent bank, acceptance of
deposits, **266:54.**
Insurance. See within this
heading, "Insurance."
Interest.
Dividends or interest. See
within this heading,
"Dividends or interest."
Municipal industrial
development authorities,
40D:18.
Mutual insurance company
funds, **175:80, 175:90.**
Poor persons on relief, disclosure
of information as to
deposits, **18:15.**
Public service corporations,
deposit of funds, **155:3A.**
Savings deposits. See within this
heading, "Savings deposits."
Technology development
corporation moneys, **40G:4.**
Term deposits. See within this
heading, "Term deposits."
Trust funds of cities and towns,
44:54.
Unclaimed funds.
Abandoned of unclaimed
funds. See within this
heading, "Abandoned or
unclaimed funds, deposits
with trust companies."
Veterans' deposits, disclosure,
115:2.
Direct deposit of public employees'
wages, etc., **41:41B.**

TRUST COMPANIES —Cont'd
Directors, **172:13.**
  Acceptance of fee or commission, **172:20.**
  Bank holding company law, penalties for violations, **167A:6.**
  Loans, **172:18.**
  Meetings, **172:16.**
  Multiple positions, holding, **172:19.**
  Officers, election, **172:14.**
  Qualifications, **172:13.**
  Selection, **172:7.**
  Stock or bond collateral, involvement in making loans secured, **172:19.**
Disclosure.
  Poor persons on relief, deposits, **18:15.**
  Veterans, information as to financial condition, **115:2.**
Dissolution.
  Liquidation. See within this heading, "Liquidation."
District funds, deposit, **44:55.**
District notes, delivery, **44:24.**
Dividends or interest, **172:28.**
  Income tax on interest, **62:2.**
  Savings deposits, **172:35.**
Earnings.
  Income or earnings. See within this heading, "Income or earnings."
Economic development and industrial corporations, revenue or revenue refunding bonds, **121C:14.**
Education loans to officers, **172:18.**
Elections, **172:7, 172:13, 172:14.**
Electronic banking, **167B:1 et seq.**
Eminent domain proceedings, investment of amounts awarded as damages, **79:7D.**
Employees.
  Officers, agents, and employees. See within this heading, "Officers, agents, and employees."
Evidence, records, books, and accounts as, **233:77, 233:79A.**
Exceptions.
  Net profits to surplus account, transfers, **172:34.**
  Officers, loans or extension of credit, **172:18.**
Executive committee of board of directors, **172:13.**
Expenses.
  Fees and expenses. See within this heading, "Fees and expenses."

TRUST COMPANIES —Cont'd
Federal reserve system, reserve balances for members, **172:32.**
Fees and expenses.
  Business of trust company, acceptance of fee for or, **172:20.**
  Formation, **172:6.**
Fiduciaries.
  Deposits of unclaimed funds, **206:25, 206:27, 206:27A.**
  Guardians. See within this heading, "Guardians."
  Public administrator, when not to act as to savings deposits, **200:8.**
Fines and penalties.
  Bank holding company law, violations, **167A:6.**
  Imprisonment. See within this heading, "Imprisonment."
  Insolvent bank, acceptance of deposits, **266:54.**
  Proscribed acts, **172:21.**
  Sections 18 and 20, violation, **172:23.**
  "Trust company," restriction on use, **172:3.**
Fire insurance, deposit of fire insurance companies' profits, **175:80.**
Foreign state or country.
  Bank incorporation board, out-of-state associations and corporations, **167:38.**
  Corporation engaging in trust business, **181:7.**
  Out-of-state banks. See BANKS AND BANKING.
Formation, **172:5.**
Fraternal benefit societies. See FRATERNAL BENEFIT SOCIETIES.
Funeral expenses of ward, guardian's deposits, **201:48A.**
Gifts.
  Acceptance in connection with business of trust company, **172:20.**
  Counties, deposit of gifts, **34:23.**
  Minors, **201A:9.**
Government land bank, **Spec L 9:8E.**
Group insurance.
  Commission funds, deposits, **32A:9A.**
  Purchase on lives of debtors, **167F:2.**
Guardians.
  Burial expenses of ward, increase of limitation on amounts deposited, **201:48A.**

TRUST COMPANIES —Cont'd
Guardians —Cont'd
  Conservators. See within this heading, "Conservators."
Holding companies.
  See BANK HOLDING COMPANIES.
Housing and urban renewal.
  Operating authorities' bonds and debentures, **121B:15.**
  Urban redevelopment corporations' securities, **121A:7.**
Imprisonment.
  Proscribed acts, **172:21.**
  Sections 18 and 20, violation, **172:23.**
Income or earnings.
  Dividends or interest. See within this heading, "Dividends or interest."
  Salaries, deductions for deposit, **149:178B, 154:8.**
Income tax, interest from deposits, **62:2.**
Incorporation and organization.
  Articles of organization, submission to secretary of state, **172:8.**
  Bank incorporation, board of. See within this heading, "Bank incorporation, board."
  Incorporators, **172:7.**
Incorporators, **172:7.**
Industrial development authorities.
  Cities and towns. See within this heading, "Cities and towns."
Industrial Finance Agency bonds as legal public investments, **23A:39.**
Insolvent bank, acceptance of deposits by, **266:54.**
Insurance.
  Deposits of profits of insurance companies.
    Fire companies, **175:80.**
    Liability companies, **175:111B.**
    Other companies, **175:90.**
  Fraternal benefit societies, trust company deposits, **176:40.**
  Life insurance. See within this heading, "Life insurance."
  Mutual insurance companies, deposit of funds, **175:80, 175:90.**
Interest.
  Dividends or interest. See within this heading, "Dividends or interest."

TRUST COMPANIES —Cont'd
Investigation fee for formation of trust company, **172:6.**
Investments, **167F:1 et seq.**
Bond issues, **167F:2.**
County bonds, **35:37A.**
Housing and urban renewal operating agency bonds, **121B:15.**
Industrial finance agency bonds, **23A:39.**
Municipal bonds, **44:55.**
Cities and towns. See within this heading, "Cities and towns."
Eminent domain proceedings, amount awarded as damages, **79:7D.**
Housing and urban renewal operating agencies, investment in bonds and notes, **121B:15.**
Industrial finance agency bonds as legal public investments, **23A:39.**
Loans. See within this heading, "Loans."
Mortgage-backed securities, investment, **32:23.**
Mortgage loans. See within this heading, "Mortgage loans."
Municipal corporations.
Cities and towns. See within this heading, "Cities and towns."
Retirement and pension systems, **32:23.**
Stock, **167F:3.**
Urban redevelopment corporations' securities, investment of trust funds, **121A:7.**
Issue of stock, **172:24.**
Judges of probate, savings deposits in name, **241:34.**
Jurisdiction.
Supreme judicial court. See within this heading, "Supreme judicial court."
Licenses, **140:114A.**
Life insurance.
Investments in stock of trust companies, **175:66.**
Schedule of bank balances, filing, **175:25.**
Limitations and restrictions.
Acceptance of fee or commission, **172:20.**
District funds, limitation on deposits, **44:55.**
Municipal corporations, limitations on loans, **75C:1.**

TRUST COMPANIES —Cont'd
Limitations and restrictions —Cont'd
Officers, loans or extension of credit, **172:18.**
"Trust company," restriction on use, **172:3.**
Liquidation, **172:39.**
Conservators. See within this heading, "Conservators."
Inadequate reserve balances, **172:33.**
Stockholders' liability, **167:24, 167:25.**
Loans, **167E:1 et seq.**
Mortgage loans. See within this heading, "Mortgage loans."
Municipal corporations, limitations on loans, **75C:1.**
Officers, loans, **172:18.**
State- or federally-chartered bank, loan on assets acquired, **172:38.**
Local community needs, **172:36, 172:38.**
Location, **167C:1 et seq.**
Meetings.
Directors, **172:16.**
Incorporators, first meeting, **172:7.**
Merger.
Consolidation or merger. See within this heading, "Consolidation or merger."
Minors, gifts, **201A:1, 201A:9.**
Morris plan banks.
See MORRIS PLAN BANKS.
Mortgage-backed securities, investments, **32:23.**
Mortgage loans, **167E:1 et seq.**
Adjustable or flexible mortgages, **183:28A.**
Officers, loans, **172:18.**
Municipal corporations.
Cities and towns. See within this heading, "Cities and towns."
Mutual insurance companies, deposit of funds, **175:80, 175:90.**
Name.
Judges of probate, savings deposits in name, **241:34.**
Restriction on use of "trust company," **172:3.**
Net new benefits defined, **172:36, 172:38.**
Net profits, transfers from to surplus account, **172:34.**
Notice.
Balance sheet, posting, **172:22.**

TRUST COMPANIES —Cont'd
Notice —Cont'd
Capital notes and debentures, issuance and sale, **172:30.**
Form trust company, intent, **172:6.**
Incorporators, first meeting, **172:7.**
Returns, publication in newspaper in form of trial balances, **172:22A.**
Oaths of officers, **172:15.**
Officers, agents, and employees, **172:15.**
Acceptance of fee or commission, **172:20.**
Bank holding company law, penalties for violations, **167A:6.**
Clerk or secretary. See within this heading, "Clerk or secretary, selection."
Conservators. See within this heading, "Conservators."
Directors. See within this heading, "Directors."
Loans or extension of credit, **172:18.**
Multiple positions, holding, **172:19.**
Oaths, **172:15.**
President, election by board of directors, **172:14.**
Public officers and employees. See within this heading, "Public officers and employees."
Secretary.
Clerk or secretary. See within this heading, "Clerk or secretary, selection."
Selection, **172:7, 172:13, 172:14.**
Stock options, **172:25.**
Stock or bond collateral, involvement in making loans secured, **172:19.**
Surety bonds, **172:15.**
Treasurer. See within this heading, "Treasurer of bank."
Options to purchase, issue and sell capital stock, **172:25, 172:25A.**
Organization.
Incorporation and organization. See within this heading, "Incorporation and organization."
Other state or country.
Foreign state or country. See within this heading, "Foreign state or country."

TRUST COMPANIES —Cont'd
Papers and documents.
  Records and reports. See within
    this heading, "Records and
    reports."
Partition of land, disposition of
  unclaimed proceeds, **241:34.**
Par value of stock, **172:24.**
Payrolls, deductions for deposit,
  149:178B, 154:8.
Penalties.
  Fines and penalties. See within
    this heading, "Fines and
    penalties."
Pensions.
  Retirement and pension
    systems. See within this
    heading, "Retirement and
    pensions systems."
Place, **167C:1 et seq.**
Poor persons on relief, information
  as to deposits, **18:15, 122:22.**
Powers, **172:1A.**
Preferred stock, **172:24.**
President, election by board of
  directors, **172:14.**
Probate judge, savings deposits in
  name of, **241:34.**
Proof, records, books, and accounts
  as evidence, **233:77, 233:79A.**
Proscribed acts, **172:21.**
Public administrator, when not to
  act as to savings deposits,
  194:5, 200:8.
Public assistance, information as
  to deposits of persons
  receiving, **18:15, 122:22.**
Publication of returns in form of
  trial balances, **172:22A.**
Public officers and employees.
  Depository for credit union
    deductions from pay,
    149:178B.
  Direct deposit of wages and
    salaries, **41:41B.**
Public securities.
  Bonds and debentures. See
    within this heading, "Bond
    issues."
Public service corporations, deposit
  of funds, **155:3A.**
Purchase of assets.
  Assets and property. See within
    this heading, "Assets and
    property."
Qualifications for directors,
  172:13.
Quorum as to assignment and
  transfer of shares, **172:11.**
Records and reports.
  Annual report, **172:22.**

TRUST COMPANIES —Cont'd
Records and reports —Cont'd
  Bank commissioner. See within
    this heading, "Bank
    commissioner."
  Bank holding companies,
    167A:5.
  Certificates and certification. See
    within this heading,
    "Certificates and
    certification."
  Directors, submission of reports,
    172:16.
  Evidence, records, books, and
    accounts, **233:77, 233:79A.**
  Life insurance companies, filing
    schedule of bank balances,
    175:25.
  Trial balances, returns in form,
    172:22A.
  Unclaimed or abandoned
    property deposited in trust
    company accounts, reports,
    200A:1, 200A:7.
  Wage reporting system, **62E:5.**
Recycling funds of cities and
  towns, deposit, **40:5.**
Redevelopment.
  Housing and urban renewal. See
    within this heading,
    "Housing and urban
    renewal."
Reports.
  Records and reports. See within
    this heading, "Records and
    reports."
Reserve balances, **172:31-172:33.**
  Commissioner, reports, **172:31.**
  Composition of reserve, **172:31.**
  Conservator, appointment,
    172:33.
  Federal reserve system, reserve
    balances for members,
    172:31.
  Inadequate reserve balances,
    172:33.
  Minimum reserve balances,
    172:31.
Residency requirement for
  directors, **172:13.**
Restrictions.
  Limitations and restrictions. See
    within this heading,
    "Limitations and
    restrictions."
Retirement and pensions systems.
  Advice as to investment of
    funds, **32:23.**
  Custody of securities, **32:23.**
  Honoring and cashing checks of
    pensioners and retirees,
    167:46.

TRUST COMPANIES —Cont'd
Retirement and pensions systems
  —Cont'd
  Investment of funds, **32:23.**
  Returns to be in form of trial
    balances, **172:22A.**
Revenue department.
  See REVENUE DEPARTMENT
    AND COMMISSIONER.
Salaries.
  Wages, salaries, and
    compensation. See within
    this heading, "Wages,
    salaries, and compensation."
Sales and purchases.
  Assets and property. See within
    this heading, "Assets and
    property."
Sales finance company, banks,
  255D:1.
Savings banks.
  Mortgage loans on real estate.
    See within this heading,
    "Mortgage loans."
Savings deposits, **172:35.**
  Group insurance commission
    funds, **32A:9A.**
  Interest, **172:35.**
  Probate judge, savings deposits
    in name, **241:34.**
Secretary of company.
  Clerk or secretary. See within
    this heading, "Clerk or
    secretary, selection."
Secretary of state, submission of
  articles of organization, **172:8.**
Securities.
  Bond issues. See within this
    heading, "Bond issues."
  Investments in, **167F:2.**
  Mortgage-backed securities,
    investments, **32:23.**
  Public securities.
    Bonds and debentures. See
      within this heading,
      "Bond issues."
  Retirement and pension
    systems, custody of
    securities, **32:23.**
  Stock and stockholders. See
    within this heading, "Stock
    and stockholders."
  Urban redevelopment
    corporations' securities,
    investment, **121A:7.**
Sentence and punishment.
  Fines and penalties. See within
    this heading, "Fines and
    penalties."
Sinking fund for state bonds,
  29:49.

TRUST COMPANIES —Cont'd
Small loans, **140:114A.**
Social services department requesting financial information, **18:15.**
State-chartered stockholder-owned bank, change of control, **168:34C, 170:26C, 172:26A.**
State finance.
  Funds, deposit, **29:34.**
  Sinking fund for state bonds, **29:49.**
State or federally-chartered bank, purchase of assets or stock, **172:38.**
State secretary, submission of articles of organization, **172:8.**
State treasurer, entering into agreement with trust company to provide line of credit, **29:49B.**
Stock and stockholders.
  Annual report and books, examination, **172:22.**
  Assignment and transfer of stock, control, **172:11.**
  Board of bank incorporation, filing of list, **172:9.**
  Capital notes or debentures, vote, **172:30.**
  Capital stock, **172:9, 172:24, 172:25.**
  Dividends, **172:28.**
  Investments in stocks, **167F:3.**
  Life insurance company investing in stock, **175:66.**
  Liquidation, liability, **167:24, 167:25.**
  Loan upon or purchase of assets or stock of state or federally chartered bank, **172:38.**
  Options to purchase, issue and sell capital stock, **172:25, 172:25A.**
  Preferred stock, **172:24.**
  Record date, **172:27.**
  Secretary, election, **172:14.**
  State-chartered stockholder-owned bank, change of control, **168:34C, 170:26C, 172:26A.**
  Voting, **172:12.**
Subscribers, minimum number, **172:5.**
Subsidiaries, acquisition of assets by bank holding company, **167A:2.**
Supreme judicial court.
  Bank holding company law, jurisdiction to enforce, **167A:7.**

TRUST COMPANIES —Cont'd
Surety bonds for officers, **172:15.**
Surplus account.
  County officers, deposit of surplus funds, **35:22.**
  Transfers from net profits, **172:34.**
Taxation.
  See TAXATION.
Technology development corporation, deposit of moneys, **40G:4.**
Temporary clerk, selection for first meeting of incorporators, **172:7.**
Term deposits.
  Income tax on interest, **62:2.**
  Municipal and district funds, investment in certificates of deposit, **44:55.**
Terms of office of directors, **172:13.**
Tewksbury hospital.
  See TEWKSBURY HOSPITAL.
Time deposits.
  Term deposits. See within this heading, "Term deposits."
Time or date.
  Consolidation or merger approval, time of existence affecting, **172:38A.**
  Directors' terms of office, **172:13.**
  Stockholders of record, record date, **172:27.**
  Term deposits. See within this heading, "Term deposits."
Towns.
  Cities and towns. See within this heading, "Cities and towns."
Treasurer of bank.
  Duties, **172:17.**
  Election by board of directors, **172:14.**
Treasurer of state, agreement with trust company to provide line of credit, **29:49B.**
Treasurers, municipal, prohibition from having interest in trust company, **44:55.**
Trial balances, returns to be in form, **172:22A.**
Trust departments, **167G:1 et seq.**
  See BANKS AND BANKING.
Trust funds.
  Cities and towns, deposit of trust funds, **44:54, 172:51.**
  Municipal industrial development authority bonds, trust agreement securing, **40D:9.**

TRUST COMPANIES —Cont'd
Unclaimed funds.
  Abandoned or unclaimed funds. See within this heading, "Abandoned or unclaimed funds, deposits with trust companies."
Uniform Custodial Trust Act, **203B:1, 203B:5.**
Uniform Gifts to Minors Act, **201A:1, 201A:9.**
Urban renewal.
  Housing and urban renewal. See within this heading, "Housing and urban renewal."
Vacancies, directors, **172:13.**
Veteran, giving information as to financial condition, **115:2.**
Violations.
  Fines and penalties. See within this heading, "Fines and penalties."
Wages, salaries, and compensation.
  Payroll deductions for deposit, **149:178B, 154:8.**
  Records and reports, wage reporting system, **62E:5.**
Welfare, information as to deposits of poor persons on relief, **18:15, 122:22.**

TRUST DEEDS.
See MORTGAGES AND DEEDS OF TRUST.

TRUST DEPARTMENTS, 167G:1 et seq.
See BANKS AND BANKING.

TRUSTEE PROCESS, 246:1-246:83.
Absent defendants.
  See ABSENT DEFENDANTS.
Additional trustees, bringing, **246:8.**
Administrators.
  Executors and administrators. See within this heading, "Executors and administrators, trustee process against."
Admission by trustee's answer to interrogatories, **246:14.**
Adverse claims to property, **246:33, 246:34.**
  Costs, **246:76, 246:82.**
  Right to assert, **246:33.**
  Trial and determination of rights, **246:33.**
Alteration or change, venue, **246:3, 246:4A.**

TRUSTEE PROCESS —Cont'd

Amount sought as affecting bond requirement, **246:1.**

Answer of trustee.

Absent trustee, costs where trustee appears and answers after return, **246:71.**

Admission of funds, **246:14.**

Corporation summoned as trustee, **246:15, 246:19.**

Disclosure to be made, **246:10.**

Failure to answer.

Default judgment, **246:18.**

Liability for costs, **246:73.**

Scire facias, **246:46-246:48.**

False answer, penalty, **246:19.**

Interrogatories, making and filing answers, **246:12, 246:18.**

Scire facias, **246:46-246:48.**

Signature and verification, **246:11.**

Stating facts to court, **246:14.**

Time to file, **246:10.**

Truth of, presumption, **246:16.**

Appearance by trustee, **246:10-246:19.**

Answer of trustee. See within this heading, "Answer of trustee."

Scire facias, **246:46-246:48.**

Time to file, **246:10.**

Assault and battery action may not be commenced, **246:1.**

Assigned claims held as security, **246:34.**

Assignee in insolvency, against, **246:22.**

Assignment of wages as valid against trustee process, **154:6, 154:8.**

Assumption of liability by trustee to third person before knowledge of service, **246:27.**

Attachment by trustee process, **223:67, 246:5, 246:20.**

Attorneys' fees, allowance to trustee, **246:68.**

Automobile liability insurance, exemption of deposit in lieu, **90:34D.**

Automobile registered in foreign state, action to recover damages on account, **246:1.**

Availability of remedy, **246:1.**

Bond.

Dissolution, **246:66, 246:67.**

Required of plaintiff, **246:1, 246:31.**

Transient vendor's bond or deposit as exempt from process, **101:12.**

TRUSTEE PROCESS —Cont'd

Bond —Cont'd

Workers' compensation self-insurers, bonds deposited by as exempt from process **152:25A.**

Boston municipal court, time for trustee to file answer, **246:10.**

Bringing in parties.

Additional trustees, **246:8.**

Adverse claimants, **246:33.**

Carrier served with, nonliability for delay in shipment or delivery, **246:65.**

Change of venue, **246:3, 246:4A.**

Children, **119A:12, 209C:19, 221B:7, 246:32.**

Cities.

See CITIES AND TOWNS.

Claims of third persons.

Adverse claims. See within this heading, "Adverse claims to property."

Collector of taxes, dissolution of attachment against, **41:43A.**

Commencement of actions by, **246:1.**

Compensation, **246:28-246:30, 246:32.**

Complaint.

Declaration in lieu of oath and trustee's answer, **246:11.**

Filing of bond to be indorsed, **246:1.**

Conditions under which property held, performance of by creditor, **246:61.**

Contingent obligations, **246:32.**

Continuance of action, defendant's action pending against trustee, **246:35.**

Contract obligations, **246:1, 246:24.**

Delivery under contract, trustee process as affecting, **246:59.**

Co-operative banks, wage deductions for deposits, **154:8.**

Corporation.

Answer, **246:15, 246:19.**

Banks.

See BANKS AND BANKING.

False answer by person appearing for corporation, **246:19.**

Foreign corporations. See within this heading, "Foreign corporations."

Money in bank account as exempt, **246:28A.**

Officers as liable for placing funds in payroll account to avoid attachment, **246:20.**

TRUSTEE PROCESS —Cont'd

Costs.

Absent trustee appearing and answering on return, **246:71.**

Adverse claimant admitted as party, **246:76, 246:82.**

Attorneys' fees, allowance to trustee, **246:68.**

Bond, expense, **246:1.**

Charging against property or effects, **246:69.**

Claim of trustee or third person, costs in action, **246:76.**

Damages less than ten dollars, **246:83.**

Default of trustee, **246:73.**

Discharged trustee, **246:70.**

District court proceedings, **261:26.**

Execution against trustee, **246:80.**

When issuable, **246:74.**

Failure of trustee to answer, liability for costs, **246:73.**

Fees. See within this heading, "Fees."

Offer of judgment, **246:29.**

Persons summoned outside of county, **246:72.**

Property or assets insufficient to pay, liability of plaintiff to trustee, **246:69.**

Scire facias proceedings against trustee, **246:77-246:81.**

Several trustees summoned, liability for costs, **246:75.**

Summons. See within this heading, "Summons."

Tender of amount due after wages trusted, **246:29.**

Trial of fact issue, **246:68.**

Trustee, allowable, **246:68.**

Counterclaim or setoff.

Setoff and counterclaim. See within this heading, "Setoff and counterclaim."

Credit for trustee's payments under trustee process during pendency of action, **246:37.**

Credit unions.

Account as exempt, **246:28A.**

Wage deductions for deposits, purchase of shares, or repayment of loans, public employees, **149:178B.**

Death of trustee.

After judgment, **246:53, 246:54.**

Before judgment, **246:50.**

Further proceedings, **246:51, 246:52.**

TRUSTEE PROCESS —Cont'd
Death of trustee —Cont'd
Effect and procedure,
246:50-246:54.
Debtors and creditors.
Indebtedness. See within this
heading, "Indebtedness of
defendant to trustee."
Debts of defendant owed to
trustee.
Indebtedness. See within this
heading, "Indebtedness of
defendant to trustee."
Decedent's estates.
Executors and administrators.
See within this heading,
"Executors and
administrators, trustee
process against."
Legacies as subject to trustee
process, **246:21.**
Deceit.
Fraud and deceit. See within
this heading, "Fraud and
deceit."
Decree.
Judgment. See within this
heading, "Judgment."
Defamation, trustee process not
available in action, **246:1.**
Default of trustee.
Costs, **246:73.**
Judgment, **246:18, 246:34.**
Scire facias, rendering and
amount of judgment, **246:46,
246:47.**
Defendant.
Pendency of action of defendant
against trustee. See within
this heading, "Pendency of
action of defendant against
trustee."
Delivery.
Carrier not liable for failure in
delivery attributable to
trustee process, **246:65.**
Dissolution, delivery over of
property or money by
trustee, **246:67.**
Failure of trustee to deliver
specific property, liability,
246:64.
Nondelivery after judgment,
remedy, **246:45-246:49.**
Officer, delivery, **246:57.**
Sale. See within this heading,
"Sale."
Scire facias for neglect to deliver
property for which he is
charged, **246:64.**
Deposits.
Amount in banking institutions
as exempt, **246:28A.**

TRUSTEE PROCESS —Cont'd
Deposits —Cont'd
Credit unions, wage deductions
for deposits, **149:178B.**
Fines and penalties, deposit in
payroll account to avoid
attachment, **246:20.**
Workers' compensation
self-insurers, bonds
deposited, **152:25A.**
Discharge of trustee, **246:13.**
Costs against plaintiff, **246:70.**
Defendant not barred from suing
for same demand, **246:44.**
Right to proceed against
defendant notwithstanding,
246:9.
Dissolution, **246:66, 246:67.**
Bond, **246:66, 246:67.**
City or town treasurer, trustee
process against, **41:43A.**
Collector of taxes, trustee
process against, **41:43A.**
Delivery over of property or
money by trustee, **246:67.**
Who may seek, **246:66.**
District court.
Absent trustee summoned,
246:4.
Commencement of action, **246:1.**
Costs allowable for trustees,
261:26.
Service of district court writs,
time, **246:7.**
Time.
Filing of trustee's answer,
246:10.
Service of district court writs,
246:7.
Venue, **223:2, 246:4, 246:4A.**
Divorce suits, use to obtain
support money, **208:13.**
Employee of foreign corporation,
action against, **246:6.**
Employment security benefits
exempt, **151A:36.**
Evidence.
Admissibility against trustee,
246:16.
Matters not stated or denied by
trustee, **246:16.**
Negotiable instruments,
obligations evidenced,
246:32.
Scire facias, **246:48.**
Unauthorized exemption,
246:28A.
Examination of trustee, **246:12,
246:14.**
Corporate trustee, **246:15.**
Scire facias proceedings, **246:48.**

TRUSTEE PROCESS —Cont'd
Execution against trustee.
Costs. See within this heading,
"Costs."
Failure to take out within thirty
days, **246:40, 246:41.**
Letting in other attachments by
delay in issuing, **246:40.**
Procuring issuance by scire
facias proceedings, **246:45.**
Service of, or making demand,
246:40, 246:42.
Executors and administrators,
trustee process against,
246:21.
Enforcement of liability, **246:56.**
Extent of liability, **246:55.**
False answer by executor or
administrator of trustee,
246:19.
Taking over or continuance of
proceedings against
decedent, **246:50-246:54.**
Exemption from.
See EXEMPTION FROM
CLAIMS OF CREDITORS.
Failure of trustee to answer.
Answer of trustee. See within
this heading, "Answer of
trustee."
Fees.
Attorney's fees of trustee,
246:68.
Service of trustee process, **262:8.**
Fines and penalties.
Deposit in payroll account to
avoid attachment by trustee
process, **246:20.**
Exempt wages, penalty for
attaching, **246:30.**
False answer by trustee, **246:19.**
Fisherman's wages or pay as
attachable by trustee process,
246:32.
Foreign corporations.
See FOREIGN
CORPORATIONS.
Fraternal benefits exempt, **176:22.**
Fraud and deceit.
Answer by trustee, penalty for
false, **246:19.**
Fraudulently conveyed property
or credits. See within this
heading, "Fraudulently
conveyed property or
credits."
Fraudulently conveyed property or
credits.
Deposit in payroll account to
avoid attachment, **246:20.**
Reaching, **109A:8, 246:25.**

TRUSTEE PROCESS —Cont'd

Goods sold and delivered, action, **246:1.**

Hearing.
  Trial or hearing. See within this heading, "Trial or hearings."

Illegitimate children, enforcement of judgment of support, **209C:19.**

Immature obligations, **246:24.**

Indebtedness of defendant to trustee, **246:26.**
  Not presently payable, **246:24.**
  Payroll accounts as exempt from attachment, **246:20.**

Indemnification of attaching creditor for redemption, **246:62.**

Insolvency funds, when subject, **246:22.**

Inspection of trustee.
  Examination of trustee. See within this heading, "Examination of trustee."

Insurance.
  Automobile, liability insurance, exemption of deposit in lieu, **90:34D.**
  Foreign insurance company as trustee, **246:6.**
  Workers' compensation self-insurer, bonds deposited, **152:25A.**

Interrogatories, answers, **246:12, 246:14.**

Intervention by adverse claimants, **246:33.**

Issues as against trustee, **246:16, 246:17.**

Joinder of parties.
  Additional trustees, **246:8.**
  Adverse claimants, **246:33.**

Judgment, **246:39-246:44.**
  Action on judgment, **246:1.**
  Against trustee.
    Amount for which chargeable need not be specified, **246:39.**
    Death of trustee. See within this heading, "Death of trustee."
    Defaulting trustee, **246:18, 246:34.**
    Delay in enforcing, **246:40, 246:41.**
    Demand for payment, **246:40-246:42.**
    Effect, **246:43.**
    Failure to appear and answer in scire facias, **246:46, 246:47.**

TRUSTEE PROCESS —Cont'd

Judgment —Cont'd
  Against trustee —Cont'd
    Payment as releasing liability to defendant, **246:43.**
    Scire facias to enforce, **246:45-246:49.**
  Death of trustee. See within this heading, "Death of trustee."
  Defendant's action against trustee, effect of judgment against defendant, **246:36.**
  Illegitimate children, enforcement of judgment of support, **209C:19.**
  Offer of judgment as affecting costs, **246:29.**

Judgment debts, reaching, **246:32.**

Jury trial of fact questions, **246:17.**

Legacies as subject, **246:21.**

Liability of trustee.
  After thirty days after judgment, **246:40, 246:41.**
  Assumption of liability by trustee to third person before knowledge of service, **246:27.**
  Delivery of property, **246:64.**
  Failure to answer, liability for costs, **246:73.**
  Making false disclosure, **246:19.**
  Several trustees summoned, liability for costs, **246:75.**

Libel or slander action may not be commenced, **246:1.**

Limitation of actions.
  Bonds to dissolve attachment, **246:67.**
  Scire facias proceedings against person adjudged in trustee process proceedings to be trustee, **246:49.**

Liquidation.
  Dissolution. See within this heading, "Dissolution."

Malicious prosecution action may not be commenced, **246:1.**

Maturity of trusted obligations, **246:24.**

Medical malpractice self-insurance trust funds not liable, **175F:15.**

Minor child or wife of defendant, wages due for labor, **246:32.**

Modification or change, venue, **246:3, 246:4A.**

Money collected on execution or process, to reach, **246:32.**

Mortgaged or pledged property.
  Indemnification of attaching creditor for redemption, **246:62.**

TRUSTEE PROCESS —Cont'd

Mortgaged or pledged property —Cont'd
  Payment of debt to obtain property, **246:60.**
  Sale of property by trustee to satisfy claim, **246:63.**

Municipal corporations.
  See CITIES AND TOWNS.

Municipal court.
  Venue, **223:2.**
  When to file trustee process, **246:10.**

Mutual demands between defendant and trustee, setting off, **246:26.**

Negotiable instruments, obligations evidenced, **246:32.**

New trustees, bringing, **246:8.**

Nonpayment or nondelivery by trustee after judgment, remedy, **246:45-246:49.**

Nonresidents, against, **246:1.**

Notice and knowledge.
  Attachment of wages for personal services, notice, **246:32.**
  Payment by trustee to defendant or third person before knowledge of service of writ, **246:27.**

Oath.
  Admission of funds by trustees, **246:14.**
  Answer and examination of corporate trustee, **246:15.**

Offer of judgment, costs as affected, **246:29.**

Officer.
  Delivery of specific property, **246:57, 246:58.**
  Sale. See within this heading, "Sale."

Partnerships, service, **246:7.**

Paymaster of foreign corporation as officer for service, **246:6.**

Payment by creditor of obligation for which specific property, **246:60.**

Payments by trustee.
  Nonpayment by trustee after judgment, remedy, **246:45-246:49.**
  To defendant or third person before knowledge of service of writ, **246:27.**
  To plaintiff.
    As discharging obligation to defendant, after judgment, **246:43.**
    Credit for, in action pending against trustee, **246:37.**

TRUSTEE PROCESS —Cont'd
Payroll and payroll deductions.
  Deposit, effect of wage
    deductions, **149:178B,
    154:8.**
  Exemption of payroll accounts
    from attachment, **246:20.**
  Valid assignment, payroll
    deductions and
    contributions, **154:8.**
Penalties.
  Fines and penalties. See within
    this heading, "Fines and
    penalties."
Pendency of action of defendant
  against trustee.
  Adjudication of trusteeship,
    246:36, 246:37.
  Continuance or proceeding with
    action, **246:35.**
  Effect, **246:35-246:38.**
  Judgment against defendant,
    246:36.
  Payments by trustee under
    trustee process, credit,
    246:37.
Pensions.
  See RETIREMENT SYSTEMS
    AND PENSIONS.
Personal services, restriction as to
  money or credit due, **246:32.**
Plea and answer.
  Answer of trustee. See within
    this heading, "Answer of
    trustee."
Pledged property.
  Mortgaged or pledged property.
    See within this heading,
    "Mortgaged or pledged
    property."
Presumption of truth of trustee's
  answer, **246:16.**
Property subject to, **246:20-246:32.**
Public officers, **246:32.**
Questions of law or fact, **246:17,
  246:68.**
Receivers, funds in hands of as
  subject to process, **246:23.**
Redemption, indemnifying
  attaching creditor, **246:62.**
Relocation assistance payments,
  exemption, **79:6A, 79A:7.**
Removal.
  Discharge. See within this
    heading, "Discharge of
    trustee."
Replevin action may not be
  commenced, **246:1.**
Residence of trustees as
  determinative of venue in
  District and Municipal Courts,
  223:2.

TRUSTEE PROCESS —Cont'd
Retirement systems.
  See RETIREMENT SYSTEMS
    AND PENSIONS.
Revenue commissioner as agent
  for service on foreign
  corporation, **246:6.**
Sale.
  Delivery, trustee process against
    seller as affecting, **246:59.**
  Goods sold and delivered,
    commencement of action,
    246:1.
  Officer, sale of specific property,
    246:57.
  Disposition of proceeds in
    certain cases, **246:62.**
  Trustee, sale of property held as
    security, **246:63.**
Savings banks.
  See SAVINGS BANKS.
Scire facias, **246:45-246:49.**
  Appearance and answer,
    246:46-246:48.
  Availability of remedy, **246:45.**
  Costs, **246:77-246:81.**
  Default by trustee, rendering
    and amount of judgment,
    246:46, 246:47.
  Defenses and evidence, **246:48.**
  Examination of trustee, **246:48.**
  Executor or administrator of
    person summoned as
    trustee, scire facias against,
    246:52.
  For neglect to deliver property
    with which he is charged,
    246:64.
  Judgment against trustee to
    state amount, **246:48.**
  Jurisdiction to issue, **246:45.**
  Separate writs against different
    trustees, effect on costs,
    246:81.
  Time to apply, **246:45, 246:49.**
Seamen, wages due, **246:32.**
Secured transactions.
  Collateral, garnishment of
    debtor's rights, **106:9-311.**
  Judgment and execution in case
    of property held as security,
    246:34.
  Sale of property by trustee
    where held as security,
    246:63.
Service, **246:5-246:8.**
  Absent defendants.
    See ABSENT DEFENDANTS.
  Assumption of liability by
    trustee to third person
    before knowledge of service,
    246:27.

TRUSTEE PROCESS —Cont'd
Service —Cont'd
  Business trusts, **182:6.**
  Carrier, nonliability for delay in
    shipment or delivery,
    246:65.
  Defendant to be served again if
    new trustee served, **246:8.**
  Effect, **246:20.**
  Execution against trustee,
    246:40, 246:42.
  Foreign corporation, **246:6.**
  New or additional trustees,
    246:8.
  Notice of attachment of wages
    for personal services,
    246:32.
  Partnerships, **246:7.**
  Payment or assumption of
    liability to third party before
    service, **246:27.**
  Summons. See within this
    heading, "Summons."
  Time for service of district court
    writs, **246:7.**
Setoff and counterclaim.
  Attachment of setoff asserted in
    pending action, **246:38.**
  Trustee's right to assert, **246:26.**
Signature and verification.
  Answer of trustee, **246:11.**
  Interrogatories, requirements,
    246:12.
Slander, trustee process not
  available to commence action,
  246:1.
Specific property, **246:57-246:65.**
Spouse of defendant, wages due,
  246:32.
Successive attachments, delay in
  enforcing judgment against
  trustee as letting, **246:40.**
Summons, **246:1.**
  Absent trustee summoned in
    district court, **246:4.**
  Corporation, appearance and
    answer, **246:15.**
  Costs.
    Persons summoned outside of
      county, **246:72.**
    Several trustees summoned,
      liability for costs, **246:75.**
  Failure of trustee to appear,
    246:18.
Superior court, commencement of
  personal action in, **246:1.**
Support and maintenance,
  **119A:12, 208:13, 209C:19,
  221B:7.**
Supreme Judicial Court,
  commencement of personal
  action in, **246:1.**

877

TRUSTEE PROCESS —Cont'd
Sureties, **246:1.**
Tax collector, dissolution of trustee process against, **41:43A.**
Tax delinquents, effect on withholding of moneys due from municipality, **60:93.**
Tender, effect on costs, **246:29.**
Third person claiming property or assets.
  Adverse claims. See within this heading, "Adverse claims to property."
Time.
  Answer of trustee, **246:10.**
  Appearance of trustee, **246:10.**
  Bond of plaintiff, **246:1.**
  District court. See within this heading, "District court."
  Filing of written interrogatories, **246:12.**
  Limitation of actions. See within this heading, "Limitation of actions."
  Pendency of action of defendant against trustee. See within this heading, "Pendency of action of defendant against trustee."
  Scire facias, application, **246:45, 246:49.**
  Service of district court writs, **246:7.**
Towns.
  See CITIES AND TOWNS.
Transient vendor's bond or deposit as not subject, **101:12.**
Transitory actions, venue, **223:2.**
Trial or hearings.
  Adverse claims determined, **246:33.**
  Questions of fact, **246:17, 246:68.**
Unemployment compensation benefits exempt, **151A:36.**
Valuation by court of specific property held by trustee, **246:58.**
Venue, **223:2, 246:2, 246:3.**
  Change, **246:3, 246:4A.**
  District court actions, **246:4, 246:4A.**
  Supreme judicial or superior court, **246:2.**
Verification.
  Signature and verification. See within this heading, "Signature and verification."
Veterans' benefits, **115:5.**

TRUSTEE PROCESS —Cont'd
Wages, **246:28-246:30, 246:32.**
  Payroll and payroll deductions. See within this heading, "Payroll and payroll deductions."
Waiver of bond requirement in action commenced, **246:1.**
Workers' compensation.
  See WORKERS' COMPENSATION.
Writ.
  Bond, filing of, to be endorsed, **246:1.**
  Exemptions, statement required, **246:28, 246:28A.**
  Information required to appear, **246:16A.**
  Permission of court to attach wages to be endorsed, **246:32.**
  Return day on district court writs, **246:7.**
  Scire facias, separate writs against different trustees, effect on costs, **246:81.**
  Service of. See within this heading, "Service."
  Wage and pension exemptions to be stated, **246:28.**
Written contract, action for money due, **246:1.**

TRUST RECEIPTS.
See SECURED TRANSACTIONS.

TRUSTS AND TRUSTEES, 203:1 et seq.
Abandoned, lost, and unclaimed property.
  Balances of trust funds, disposition of unclaimed dividends, **18B:19.**
  Presumption of abandonment of securities unclaimed by beneficiary, **200A:5, 200A:5B.**
  Unclaimed funds in hands of trustee, **206:25-206:28.**
Abatement of taxes, application, **59:59.**
Abatement, survival, and revival of actions, effect of removal of public officer or trustee under statute, **228:14.**
Absentee beneficiaries, settlement of estates, **203:26-203:39.**
  Appointment of new trustees, **203:32.**
  Bond of trustee, **203:33.**
  Death, **203:32, 203:34.**

TRUSTS AND TRUSTEES
—Cont'd
Absentee beneficiaries, settlement of estates —Cont'd
  Decree of court, contents and effect, **203:30, 203:32.**
  Definition of absentee, **203:26.**
  Distribution of trust estate, **203:32, 203:36-203:38.**
  Fees, **262:40.**
  Filing of petition for transfer of trust estate, **203:27.**
  Findings of court, **203:32.**
  Guardian ad litem, appointment, **203:31.**
  Income, decree for payment, **203:38.**
  Liability of trustee, **203:34.**
  Limitation of actions against new trustees, **203:32, 203:35.**
  New trustees.
    Action on bond, **203:33.**
    Appointment by court, **203:32.**
    Bond, **203:33.**
    Death of, **203:34.**
    Liability and powers, **203:34.**
    Limitation of actions against, **203:32, 203:35.**
    Powers, **203:34.**
    Transfer of estate, **203:32.**
  Notice of proceedings for transfer of trust estate, **203:28-203:30.**
  Order of transfer of trust estate, **203:32.**
  Parties to proceedings for transfer of trust, **203:30, 203:31.**
  Petition for sale or transfer of trust estate, **203:27.**
    Appearance and answer, **203:30, 203:31.**
    Decree of court, contents and effect, **203:30, 203:32.**
    Filing, **203:27.**
    Findings of court, **203:32.**
    Form and contents, **203:27.**
    Guardian ad litem, appointment, **203:31.**
    Notice, **203:28, 203:29.**
    Parties to proceedings, **203:30, 203:31.**
    Presumption of death, finding, **203:32.**
    Return day of notice, **203:29.**
    Service of notice, **203:29.**
  Presumption of death, **203:32.**
  Retroactive application of law, **203:39.**
  Return day of notice, **203:29.**

TRUSTS AND TRUSTEES
—Cont'd

Absentee beneficiaries, settlement of estates —Cont'd

Service of notice of petition for transfer of trust estate, **203:29.**

Subpoena to trustee, when, **203:28.**

Trust companies, **200:8.**

Venue of proceedings, **203:29, 203:37.**

Accounts and accounting, **206:1 et seq.**

Absentee beneficiaries, settlement of estates of. See within this hearing, "Absentee beneficiaries, settlement of estates."

Agriculture, accounts of trustees for county aid, **128:40.**

Annual accounts, **206:1.**

Appraised value used to appraise personal property, **206:5.**

Arbitration of controversies, **204:14.**

Auditing of public trusts, **41:53.**

Bond of trustee, conditions, **205:1.**

Citation on application of interested person, **206:23A.**

Common trust funds, **203A:3.**

Compromise of controversies as to, **204:13-204:18.**

Conclusiveness of decrees as to trustees' accounts and settlements, **192:3, 206:24.**

Contents and form, **206:2.**

Costs, allowance, **206:16.**

Counsel fees, allowance, **206:16.**

County aid to agriculture, accounts of trustees, **128:40.**

Decrees as to, conclusiveness, **192:3, 206:24.**

Examination under oath, **206:3.**

Expenses, allowance, **206:16.**

Final account and discharge of trustees, **206:22.**

Form and contents, **206:2.**

Irregularity in appointment as affecting, **204:25.**

Joint trustees, allowance on oath of one, **206:20.**

Mental health department, trustees of public institutions under control, **19:14.**

Mental health facilities.
See MENTALLY ILL AND RETARDED PERSONS.

TRUSTS AND TRUSTEES
—Cont'd

Accounts and accounting —Cont'd

Mental retardation department, **206:7, 206:24.**

Mortgage proceeds, **206:6.**

Noninventory personal property, liability, **206:6.**

Notice of application for allowance, **206:24.**

Personal liability, proceedings to determine, **203:14A.**

Personal property.
Appraised value, **206:5.**
Income, **206:6.**
Noninventory property, liability, **206:6.**
Profit or loss on sale, **206:5.**

Proceeds of sale or mortgage of real estate, **206:6.**

Production of securities and moneys, **206:4.**

Profit or loss on sale of personal property, **206:5.**

Representation of unborn, unascertained, or incompetent persons in proceedings for allowance of accounts, **206:24.**

Sales of real property, examination, **204:11.**

Schedules, **206:2.**

Securities, production, **206:4.**

Social services commissioner to deposit trust funds, **18B:18.**

Trust companies.
See TRUST COMPANIES.

Uncollected debts, **206:5.**

Uniform Custodial Trust Act, **203B:15, 203B:16.**

Action on trustee's bond.
Bond of trustee. See within this heading, "Bond of trustee."

Administration and finance commissioner's report as to trust funds of Commonwealth, **7A:12.**

Administrators.
See EXECUTORS AND ADMINISTRATORS.

Adopted child, rights under trust settlement, **210:8.**

African Methodist Episcopal Church societies' trust property, annual allowable income, **67:41.**

Agents and agency.
Nonresident trustees, **203:15.**
Prudent investor act.
Delegation of investment and management function, **203C:10.**

TRUSTS AND TRUSTEES
—Cont'd

Agricultural schools of counties, compensation of trustees, **74:27.**

Agriculture.
See AGRICULTURE.

Alcohol.
Continuation of liquor business, **138:2, 138:23.**
Sale, storage, or transportation of alcoholic beverages, **138:2.**

Aldermen and selectmen.
Duties as to public trusts, **41:45A.**
Fraud, reporting, **41:53.**

Amortization of premiums.
Bond premiums, **62:10, 203:21B.**
Interest-bearing securities, purchase, **203A:1.**

Annual reports of certain trustees etc., **68:13, 68:14.**

Annuities.
See ANNUITIES AND ANNUITY CONTRACTS.

Answer in proceedings for transfer of estates of absentee beneficiaries, **203:30.**

Appeal from appointment of certain fiduciaries, validity of acts pending appeal, **215:9A.**

Appearance in proceeding to transfer estates of absentee beneficiaries, **203:30, 203:31.**

Appointment of trustee, **203:5.**
Bond required where court makes appointment, **203:7.**
Expenses chargeable to principal, **203:22.**
Foreign fiduciaries, **199A:2, 199A:5, 199A:8.**
Irregularity in appointment as affecting duty to account, **204:25.**
Jurisdiction of courts, **203:5, 203:12.**
New trustees, appointment by court, **203:32.**
Notice, remedy in case of failure to proof, **204:26.**
Surviving spouse's share upon waiver of will, appointment of trustee to hold, **191:16.**
Testamentary trustee, **203:4.**
Vacancy, appointment to fill, **203:5, 203:12.**
Vesting of estate in successor trustee, **203:6.**

TRUSTS AND TRUSTEES
—Cont'd
Apportionment as between
principal and income.
Principal and income. See within
this heading, "Principal and
income, apportionment
between."
Appraisal of trust estate.
Inventory and appraisal. See
within this heading,
"Inventory and appraisal."
Arbitration of claims for or against
estate, **204:13-204:18.**
Arrest on mesne process.
See ARREST ON MESNE
PROCESS AND
SUPPLEMENTARY
PROCEEDINGS.
Asset management board, **7B:7,
7B:8.**
Assignment for benefit of creditors.
See ASSIGNMENT FOR
BENEFIT OF CREDITORS.
Assignment of funds from lottery
tickets, **10:28.**
Associations.
See ASSOCIATIONS AND
SOCIETIES.
Attachment of property.
See ATTACHMENT OF
PROPERTY.
Attorney general.
See ATTORNEY GENERAL.
Attorneys at law.
Higher educational institutions,
provision for indemnification
of trustees, **15A:14.**
Land, attorney's signature
required on trust
instruments, **203:1.**
Attorneys' fees.
Allowance, **206:16.**
Apportionment between
principal and income,
206:16.
Trustees process, fees of trustee,
246:68.
Auditing of public trusts in favor
of towns, **41:53.**
Bankruptcy.
See INSOLVENCY AND
BANKRUPTCY.
Banks.
See BANKS AND BANKING.
Betterment assessments, mortgage
of trust estate to pay, **203:23.**
Board of higher education, **15A:11.**
Bona fide purchasers of land
subject to trust, rights, **203:3.**
Bond of trustee.
Absentee beneficiaries, trustee,
203:33.

TRUSTS AND TRUSTEES
—Cont'd
Bond of trustee —Cont'd
Actions on bonds, **203:7.**
Probate bonds.
See PROBATE BONDS.
Successor trustee's bond,
203:7.
Amortization of premiums,
62:10, 203:21B.
Charges for payment of money,
trustee appointed for sale of
land subject, **183:52.**
Conditions of distribution, **205:1.**
Conveyance of estate subject to
remainders, **183:51.**
Court appointee, **203:6, 203:7.**
Deduction of premiums in
determining tax on income
for trust estates, **62:10.**
Enforcement, **203:7.**
Health, welfare, and retirement
funds, **151D:2.**
Highway infrastructure fund,
trust agreement as security
for bonds issued through,
29:2O.
Partition proceedings, **241:35.**
Probate bonds.
See PROBATE BONDS.
Sale of standing timber during
life estate, bond in
proceedings, **184:14.**
Successor trustee, **203:6, 203:7.**
Uniform Statutory Will Act,
191B:14.
Bradford Durfee College of
Technology, **74:42B.**
See BRADFORD DURFEE
COLLEGE OF
TECHNOLOGY.
Brokers.
Real estate brokers. See within
this heading, "Real estate
brokers."
Business corporations.
See CORPORATIONS.
Business trusts, **181:1-181:14.**
See BUSINESS TRUSTS.
Cancellation or rescission.
Termination of trust. See within
this heading, "Termination
of trust."
Carrier's certificate, transfer.
Passenger, motor carrier,
159A:7.
Property, motor carrier,
159B:11.
Cemeteries.
See CEMETERIES.
Charges for payment of money,
appointment of trustee for sale
of land subject, **183:52.**

TRUSTS AND TRUSTEES
—Cont'd
Charitable trusts, **12:8 et seq.**
See CHARITABLE TRUSTS.
Chattel trust, **106:9-102.**
See SECURED
TRANSACTIONS.
Child Abuse Prevention Fund and
board established, **6:202,
6:203, 10:50.**
Children and minors, **18B:18,
119A:9-119A:11, 191B:8,
191B:9, 201A:5, 203:18,
209C:19.**
Cities.
See CITIES AND TOWNS.
Collective investment of small
trust funds.
Common trust funds. See within
this heading, "Common
trust funds."
Colleges.
See COLLEGES AND
UNIVERSITIES.
Combined investment fund,
participation by cities and
towns, **44:54.**
Commercial paper.
See NEGOTIABLE
INSTRUMENTS.
Commissions.
Wages, salaries, and
compensation. See within
this heading, "Wages,
salaries, and compensation."
Common trust funds, **203A:1 et
seq.**
Accounting, **203A:3.**
Amortization of premiums paid
on purchase of
interest-bearing securities,
203A:1.
Annual account, **203A:3.**
Authority to establish and invest
therein, **203A:1.**
Bank's use, **167G:3.**
Consent to participate in or
withdraw from fund,
203A:2.
Conservators may establish and
invest, **203A:1.**
Co-operative banks, investment,
205:19A, 206:25, 206:27.
Corporations.
See CORPORATIONS.
Declaration of trusts, **203A:1.**
Equal proportion of interest,
participations, **203A:1.**
Establishment, **203A:1.**
Federal savings and loan
associations, investment,
205:19A, 206:25, 206:27.

TRUSTS AND TRUSTEES
—Cont'd

Common trust funds —Cont'd

Fiduciaries, participation in funds, **203A:1, 203A:1A, 203A:2.**

Filing of accounts and reports, **203A:3.**

Guardians may establish and invest, **203A:1.**

Investment of collective trust funds by fiduciary, **167G:3.**

Participation, **203A:1, 203A:1A, 203A:2.**

Probate and insolvency registers.

Annual account, filing, **203A:3.**

Declaration of trust, filing, **203A:1.**

Filing and allowance of account, **203A:3.**

Savings and loan associations, investment, **205:19A, 206:25, 206:27.**

Short title of act concerning, **203A:5.**

Taxation, **62:17.**

Uniformity of construction of act, **203A:5.**

Community mental health center revenues, disposition, **19:24.**

Compact fund.

See COMPACT FUND.

Compensation.

Wages, salaries, and compensation. See within this heading, "Wages, salaries, and compensation."

Compromise and settlement.

Accounts and accounting. See within this heading, "Accounts and accounting."

Conclusiveness of decrees as to trustee's accounts and settlements, **192:3, 206:24.**

Condominium unit as subject of trust, **183A:3.**

Confirmation or ratification of trustee's acts.

Doubtful acts, **204:24.**

Irregularity in appointment, **204:25.**

Void acts, **204:23.**

Consent to participate in common trust funds, given by fiduciaries, **203A:2.**

Conservators.

Guardians and conservators. See within this heading, "Guardians and conservators."

TRUSTS AND TRUSTEES
—Cont'd

Consignment.

See CONSIGNMENT.

Construction of trust instruments.

Arbitration or compromise of controversies, **204:14.**

"Child" as including adopted child, **210:8.**

Constructive trusts.

See CONSTRUCTIVE TRUSTS.

Consumptives, public health department as successor to trustees of hospitals, **111:67.**

Contingent interests, release, **204:4.**

Contracts.

See CONTRACTS AND AGREEMENTS.

Contracts, trustee personally liable, **203:14A.**

Conversion, venue of prosecution, **277:58B.**

Conveyances.

Deeds and conveyances. See within this heading, "Deeds and conveyances."

Cooperative banks.

See COOPERATIVE BANKS.

Corporations.

See CORPORATIONS.

Corpus.

Principal and income. See within this heading, "Principal and income, apportionment between."

Costs and expenses.

Absentee beneficiaries, action on bond of trustee, **203:33.**

Allowance, **206:16, 261:26.**

Appointment expenses chargeable to principal, **203:22.**

Apportionment between principal and income.

Principal and income. See within this heading, "Principal and income, apportionment between."

District court costs, amounts allowed, **261:26.**

Fees. See within this heading, "Fees."

Prudent investor act.

Limitations on costs, **203C:8.**

Sale of real estate, costs in case of unreasonable petition or objection thereto, **204:10.**

Surety, expense of procuring as chargeable against estate, **206:17.**

TRUSTS AND TRUSTEES
—Cont'd

Creation of trust, **203:1-203:3A.**

Declination of trust. See within this heading, "Declination of trust."

Creditors.

Notice of trust in land, rights of creditors without, **203:3.**

Trusts for creditors.

See ASSIGNMENT FOR BENEFIT OF CREDITORS.

Credit unions.

See CREDIT UNIONS.

Customers, information of trust business required to be furnished, **203:4B.**

Dalkon Shield Claimants Trust, limitation of actions for claims, **260:2E.**

Death of absentee beneficiary, presumption, **203:32.**

Death of trustee.

Abatement, survival, and revival of actions, effect of death of trustee under statute, **228:14.**

Absentee beneficiary, trustee of estate, **203:34.**

Executor or administrator not required to accept trust, **203:14.**

Uniform Statutory Will Act, **191B:12.**

Vacancy, filling, **203:5.**

Debtors.

Creditors. See within this heading, "Creditors."

Declination of trust.

Bond, failure to give, **205:8.**

Vacancy, filling, **203:5.**

Decrees.

Absentee beneficiaries, trust estates, **203:30, 203:32, 203:38.**

Conclusiveness of decrees regarding accounts, **206:24.**

Third persons, decrees with respect to payment to trustee, **192:3.**

Deduction of trustees' compensation, **62:10.**

Deeds and conveyances, **203:16.**

Conclusiveness upon represented persons, **203:17.**

Guardian of incompetent holding property in trust, **203:18.**

Insane trustee, conveyances on behalf, **203:18.**

Minor trustee, conveyances on behalf, **203:18.**

TRUSTS AND TRUSTEES
—Cont'd
Deeds and conveyances —Cont'd
Nonresident trustee,
    conveyances on behalf,
    203:18.
Ratification, **204:24.**
Registers and registries of deeds.
    See within this heading,
    "Registers and registries of
    deeds."
Sale, conveyance after, **203:16.**
Deeds of trust.
    Mortgages. See within this
    heading, "Mortgages."
Definition.
    Trustee, **23D:1, 191B:1.**
    Trust fund, **29:1.**
Deposits.
    Children, social services
    commissioner to deposit
    trust funds, **18B:18.**
    Combined investment funds,
    liquidation of depository as
    affecting, **44:55A.**
    Fraternal benefit societies,
    deposits of foreign or alien
    society as trust funds,
    175:85, 176:32.
    Sinking funds established with
    trustees, applicability to
    deposit of refunding bonds
    proceeds, **29:53A.**
    Unclaimed funds, deposit and
    disposition, **206:25-206:28.**
Descent and distribution.
    Distribution. See within this
    heading, "Distribution of
    trust estates."
Discharge.
    Release and discharge. See
    within this heading,
    "Release and discharge."
Disclaimer.
    Equitable interest as interest in
    property for purposes,
    191A:1.
    Nontestamentary trusts,
    interest, **191A:2.**
    Testamentary trusts, interest,
    191A:2.
Discretionary powers, **184B:3.**
Disposition of assets by trustees,
    conclusiveness of decrees with
    respect, **192:3.**
Distribution of trust estates,
    203:25.
    Absentee beneficiaries, estates
    involving, **203:32,**
    203:36-203:38.
    Arbitration or compromise of
    controversies, **204:14.**

TRUSTS AND TRUSTEES
—Cont'd
Distribution of trust estates
    —Cont'd
Assignments for benefit of
    creditors created by persons
    since deceased, **203:42.**
Bond conditions as to
    distribution, **205:1.**
Conversion of property into cash,
    203:25.
Employee benefit trust
    distributions, presumption
    of abandonment, **200A:5C.**
Enforcement of decree, **197:24.**
Foreign guardian, distribution,
    201:31.
Foreign trustee, distribution,
    206:29-206:32.
Interest on pecuniary
    distributions under trust
    instruments, fixing of by
    supreme judicial court,
    197:20.
Summary enforcement of
    decrees, **197:24.**
Surviving spouse's share upon
    waiver of will, **191:18.**
Unclaimed funds or dividends,
    18B:19, 206:28.
District courts, costs, **261:26.**
Dividends.
    Claims trust for municipal
    self-insurance, **32B:3A.**
    Group insurance for state
    employees, dividends
    received by commission paid
    into trust fund, **32A:9,**
    32A:10B, 32A:10C.
    Principal or income of trust,
    dividends, **203:21A.**
    Unclaimed dividends of balances
    of trust funds, disposition,
    18B:19.
Doubtful acts of trustees,
    ratification, **204:24.**
Dower, sale of decedent's realty
    free, **202:3.**
Economic development and
    industrial corporations, trust
    agreements.
    Debentures of corporations,
    121C:10.
    Resolution authorizing revenue
    books, **121C:13.**
Economic diversification program,
    23F:7.
Education.
    See SCHOOLS AND
    EDUCATION.
Education Department, **10:16.**

TRUSTS AND TRUSTEES
—Cont'd
Embezzlement by trustee, **266:57.**
    Venue for prosecution, **277:58B.**
Eminent domain.
    See EMINENT DOMAIN.
Employee retirement.
    See RETIREMENT SYSTEMS
    AND PENSIONS.
Employment within public higher
    education system, **15A:9.**
Enforcement by beneficiary where
    fiduciary unable to act, **230:5.**
Entailed equitable estate, barring,
    183:47, 183:48.
Estate tax, **65A:2, 65C:3A,**
    65C:14.
Execution of trust, **203:20, 203:21.**
Executions against trust interests,
    203:2, 203:3, 236:1.
    Return of execution against
    trustee, **235:23.**
Executors.
    See EXECUTORS AND
    ADMINISTRATORS.
Expenses.
    Costs and expenses. See within
    this heading, "Costs and
    expenses."
Federal aid or funds.
    General federal grants fund,
    29:2C.
    Unemployment trust fund of
    federal government, fund
    upon discontinuance,
    151A:56, 151A:57.
Federal savings.
    See FEDERAL SAVINGS AND
    LOAN ASSOCIATIONS.
Fees.
    Attorneys' fees. See within this
    heading, "Attorneys' fees."
    Business trusts, fee for filing
    declaration of trust or
    amendments, **262:34.**
    Registers, fees for entry of
    petition for appointment of
    administrator, conservator,
    trustee or receiver of
    absentee's estate, **262:40.**
Female trustee, effect of marriage,
    205:19, 209:5.
Filing.
    Records and recording. See
    within this heading,
    "Records and recording."
Findings of court with regard to
    absentee beneficiaries, **203:32.**
Fine art, consignment of.
    See CONSIGNMENT.

TRUSTS AND TRUSTEES
—Cont'd
Foreclosure of mortgage by
trustee.
Apportionment of proceeds as
between principal and
income, **203:24A, 203:24B.**
Instruction of court as to
application of proceeds,
203:24B.
Power of sale in mortgages by
fiduciaries, **204:6.**
Foreign corporations, **181:7.**
Common trust funds, investment
by foreign corporations
qualified as fiduciaries,
203A:1A.
Deposits of foreign fraternal
benefit societies as trust
funds, **175:185, 176:32.**
Insurance.
See FOREIGN INSURANCE
COMPANIES.
Foreign insurance companies.
See FOREIGN INSURANCE
COMPANIES.
Foreign trustees, **203:10, 203:11.**
Agent for service of process,
203:15.
Appointment, **199A:2, 199A:5,
199A:8.**
Distribution of property to, when
authorized, **206:29, 206:30.**
Letters required, **203:10.**
New trustee for, appointment,
203:10.
Notice to take out letters,
203:11.
Personal property, license to
receive and dispose, **204:3.**
Proceeds of sale of nonresident
ward's realty, transfer,
202:27.
Resignation of, by guardian or
conservator of trustee,
204:37.
Revenue commissioner as party
to proceedings to receive
and dispose of personal
property, **204:3.**
Sales.
Benefiting foreign trustee,
203:18.
Notice of sale by foreign
testamentary trustee,
203:17A.
Personal property, **204:3.**
Venue of petitions for sales of
real property by foreign
trustees, **204:7.**
Service of process, **203:15.**

TRUSTS AND TRUSTEES
—Cont'd
Foreign trustees —Cont'd
Transfer of personal property
involving, **201:31, 204:3A,
204:18.**
Venue of petitions for sales,
204:7.
Forests.
See FORESTS AND
FORESTRY.
Forfeited property in criminal
cases, trust fund for proceeds
from disposition, **94C:47.**
Forms, **183:14.**
Fraternal benefit societies.
Foreign society deposits as trust
funds, **175:185, 176:32.**
Investments in business trusts,
176:40.
Frauds, statute of, trust
instruments as within, **203:1.**
Fraudulent conversion, venue of
prosecution, **277:58B.**
Future interests, authority of
fiduciaries to pay taxes,
65:15A.
General federal grants fund,
29:2C.
Good faith purchasers of land
subject to trust, rights, **203:3.**
Governmental units pooled
insurance, board of trustees,
40M:7.
Government land bank, **Spec L
9:8E.**
Grafton State Hospital, **19:14.**
Group creditor accident and health
insurance, persons eligible,
175:110.
Group insurance for state
employees.
Creation of trust fund, **32A:9.**
Dividends or refunds received by
commission paid into trust
fund, **32A:9, 32A:10B,
32A:10C.**
Investment of trust fund,
32A:9A.
Guardian ad litem.
Foreign trustees, payment,
206:30.
Proceedings for sale of trust
estate, **203:16, 203:17.**
Settlement of trust estate where
absentee beneficiaries exist,
203:31.
Guardians and conservators.
Ad litem.
Guardian ad litem. See within
this heading, "Guardian
ad litem."

TRUSTS AND TRUSTEES
—Cont'd
Guardians and conservators
—Cont'd
Common trust funds,
establishment, **203A:1.**
Incapacity of trustee, conveyance
by guardian in case, **203:18.**
Minority of trustee, conveyance
by guardian in case, **203:18.**
Power to create trusts in
management of estate of
ward, **201:38.**
Resignation performed, **204:37.**
Uniform Custodial Trust Act,
203B:1.
Health and Education Facilities
Authority establishing trust
funds for income received from
projects, **15A:5C.**
Health care finance and policy
division.
See HEALTH CARE FINANCE
AND POLICY DIVISION.
Highway Fund, trust agreement as
security for bonds issued
through highway
infrastructure fund, **29:2O.**
Hospitals.
Massachusetts Hospital School,
111:3A.
See HOSPITAL SCHOOL OF
MASSACHUSETTS.
Membership of health facilities
appeals board regarding,
6:166.
State hospitals.
See STATE HOSPITALS.
Tewksbury Hospital. See within
this heading, "Tewksbury
Hospital."
Hospital service corporation
trustees, compensation,
176A:26.
Husband and wife.
Surviving spouse. See within
this heading, "Surviving
spouse."
Illegitimate children, **18B:18,
209C:19.**
Improvements, mortgage to pay
assessments, **203:23.**
Incapacity of trustee, conveyances
by guardian in case, **203:1A.**
Income.
Absentee beneficiaries,
distribution of income of
estate, **203:38.**
Accounting as to receipt, **206:2.**
Apportionment, **197:27.**
Dividends, **203:21A.**

TRUSTS AND TRUSTEES
  —Cont'd
Income —Cont'd
  Payable from death of testator,
    197:26.
  Principal and income. See within
    this heading, "Principal and
    income, apportionment
    between."
  Rents and profits. See within
    this heading, "Rents and
    profits."
  Tax on.
    See INCOME TAX.
  United Methodist Church,
    allowable annual trust
    income, **67:41.**
Income tax.
  See INCOME TAX.
Industrial development of cities.
  See INDUSTRIAL
    DEVELOPMENT OF
    CITIES AND TOWNS.
Infrastructure fund, trust
    agreement to secure bonds
    issued, **29:2O.**
Insane trustee.
  See MENTALLY ILL AND
    RETARDED PERSONS.
Insolvency.
  See INSOLVENCY AND
    BANKRUPTCY.
Insolvency registers, common trust
    funds, **203A:1, 203A:3.**
Inspection of buildings, **143:35.**
Instruction of court as to
    application of proceeds of
    mortgage foreclosure sale,
    203:24B.
Insurance.
  See INSURANCE.
Intent of settlor as affecting
    applicability of simultaneous
    death act, **190A:5.**
Interest and interest rates.
  Apportionment, **197:27.**
  Fixing, **197:20.**
  Payable from death of testator,
    197:26.
  Penalty for trustee's false
    answer on trustee process,
    interest, **246:19.**
Interest in or benefit by fees or
    emoluments arising from
    matter pending in probate
    court, **217:6B.**
Interpretation.
  Construction of trust
    instruments. See within this
    heading, "Construction of
    trust instruments."

TRUSTS AND TRUSTEES
  —Cont'd
Inventory and appraisal, **203:9.**
  Bond of trustee, conditions,
    205:1.
  Information as to real property,
    recording, **217:15B.**
  Necessity, **203:8.**
  Personal property accounting,
    206:5.
  Probate and insolvency courts,
    217:16.
Investments.
  Absentee beneficiaries, estates,
    203:34.
  Annuity contracts, **203:25A.**
  Cemetery property, proceeds of
    sale, **204:12.**
  Change of investment, power,
    203:19.
  Church property, proceeds of
    sale, **204:12.**
  Commercial code provisions as
    to investment securities.
    See INVESTMENT
      SECURITIES UNDER
      COMMERCIAL CODE.
  Common trust funds. See within
    this heading, "Common
    trust funds."
  Co-operative banks, investment,
    205:19A, 206:25-
    206:27.
  Federal savings and loans
    associations, investment,
    205:19A, 206:25-
    206:27.
  Fraternal benefit societies,
    business trust investments,
    176:40.
  Group insurance for state
    employees, investment of
    trust fund, **32A:9A.**
  Life insurance policies, **203:25A.**
  Mortgages, investments,
    203:24A, 203:24B.
  Proceeds of sales of trust
    property, **203:16, 203:17A,**
    204:12.
  Prudent investor act, **203C:1 to**
    203C:11. See within this
    heading, "Prudent
    investor act."
  Savings and loans associations,
    investment, **205:19A,**
    206:25-206:27.
  Successor trustees, powers,
    203:34.
  Unclaimed funds after probate
    decree, **206:26.**

TRUSTS AND TRUSTEES
  —Cont'd
Investment securities under
    commercial code.
  Authenticating trustee.
    See INVESTMENT
      SECURITIES UNDER
      COMMERCIAL CODE.
  Irregularities to sales of real
    estate, **204:19-204:26.**
Joint control of surety and
    trustee, agreements,
    205:19A.
Joint trustees.
  Account of joint trustees allowed
    upon oath of one trustee,
    206:20.
  Bond, **205:11.**
  Jurisdiction of suits between,
    185:1, 214:3.
Judgments.
  Decrees. See within this
    heading, "Decrees."
Judicial ratification of acts of
    trustees, **204:23, 204:24.**
Jurisdiction for appointment of
    trustee, **203:5, 203:12.**
Land and land titles.
  Accounting for proceeds of sale
    or mortgage, **206:4.**
  Brokers.
    Real estate brokers. See
      within this heading, "Real
      estate brokers."
  Business trusts for investment
    in and management of
    realty, **182:1-182:14.**
    See BUSINESS TRUSTS.
  Condominium unit as subject of
    trust, **183A:3.**
  Creation of trusts, **203:1.**
  Creditors without notice of trust,
    rights, **203:3.**
  Deeds and conveyances. See
    within this heading, "Deeds
    and conveyances."
  Entailed equitable estate,
    barring, **183:47, 183:48.**
  Expenses of leases chargeable to
    principal, **203:22.**
  Guaranty fund as trust for
    protection of title
    policyholders, **175:116.**
  Improvement assessments,
    mortgage of trust property
    to pay, **203:23.**
  Leases. See within this heading,
    "Leases of trust property."

TRUSTS AND TRUSTEES
—Cont'd
Land and land titles —Cont'd
Legacy and succession taxes,
  sale of trust property to pay,
  202:20.
Mortgages. See within this
  heading, "Mortgages."
Purchasers without notice of
  trust, rights, **203:3.**
Recording as notice of trust,
  203:2.
Registers and registries of deeds.
  See within this heading,
  "Registers and registries of
  deeds."
Registration of land titles,
  185:72-185:76.
  See REGISTRATION OF
    LAND TITLES.
Sales and transfers. See within
  this heading, "Sales and
  transfers."
Leases of trust property.
  Expenses chargeable to
    principal, **203:22.**
  Rents and profits. See within
    this heading, "Rents and
    profits."
Legacy.
  Executors, administrators, and
    trustees.
    See LEGACY AND
      SUCCESSION TAXES.
Libraries, **78:10-78:12.**
  See LIBRARIES AND
    LIBRARIANS.
License to sell property.
  Sales and transfers. See within
    this heading, "Sales and
    transfers."
Lien for labor performed, inclusion
  of certain fringe benefits,
  **254:1, 254:4, 254:13, 254:27,
  254:28.**
Life insurance.
  Investment by trustee in life
    insurance, **203:25A.**
  Trustee for benefit of creditors
    may not change beneficiary,
    175:125.
Limitation of actions, **203:32,
  203:35, 246:49, 260:2E,
  260:11.**
Liquor.
  Alcohol. See within this heading,
    "Alcohol."
Loan by bank to insolvent trust,
  penalty, **266:53A.**
Local assessments, mortgage of
  trust property to pay, **203:23.**

TRUSTS AND TRUSTEES
—Cont'd
Logs and timber, trust as to
  proceeds from sale of standing
  timber, **184:14.**
Long-term care trust fund.
  See LONG-TERM CARE TRUST
    FUND.
Lost property.
  Abandoned, lost, and unclaimed
    property. See within this
    heading, "Abandoned, lost,
    and unclaimed property."
Lottery tickets, assignment of
  funds, **10:28.**
Lowell University.
  See UNIVERSITY OF LOWELL.
Low-level radioactive waste, trust
  funds, **10:35I.**
Marine fisheries division, trust
  fund, **10:16.**
Maritime Academy of
  Massachusetts.
  Board of trustees, powers and
    duties, **73:1.**
  Jurisdiction of trustee of state
    colleges, institutions, **73:19.**
Married woman's capacity to act
  as trustee, **205:19, 209:5.**
Massachusetts Industrial Service
  Program, **23D:9-23D:15.**
Mayors.
  See MAYORS.
Medfield State Hospital, **19:10,
  19:14.**
  Board of trustees, **19:8A.**
Mentally ill.
  See MENTALLY ILL AND
    RETARDED PERSONS.
Methodist Episcopal churches,
  trustees, **67:41, 67:42.**
MetroZoos Zoological Trust,
  92:34A.
Minor trustee, sale or transfer on
  behalf, **203:18.**
Missing persons.
  Absentee beneficiaries. See
    within this heading,
    "Absentee beneficiaries,
    settlement of estates."
Money, conversion of estate into,
  203:25.
Mortgage foreclosure.
  Foreclosure. See within this
    heading, "Foreclosure of
    mortgage by trustee."
Mortgages, **203:23, 203:24.**
  Accounting for proceeds, **206:6.**
  Additional bond required, when,
    205:13.
  Bond of trustee.
    See PROBATE BONDS.
  Decree, **203:24.**

TRUSTS AND TRUSTEES
—Cont'd
Mortgages —Cont'd
  Extension or renewal, **203:23.**
  Finality of adjudications as to
    debts, **204:21.**
  Foreclosure by trustee.
    Foreclosure. See within this
      heading, "Foreclosure of
      mortgage by trustee."
  Form, **204:6.**
  Investment of funds in
    mortgages, **203:24A,
    203:24B.**
  Notice of hearing, **203:23.**
  Payment of, mortgage of trust
    estate, **203:23.**
  Petition for, form, **203:24.**
  Power of sale, **204:6.**
  Probate bonds.
    See PROBATE BONDS.
  Purchasers under trustees'
    deeds, rights, **184:34.**
  Repairs as purpose, **203:23.**
Motor carriers.
  Carriers. See within this
    heading, "Carrier's
    certificate, transfer."
Motor vehicle dealer, exclusions
  from definitions in motor
  vehicle business practices law,
  93B:1.
Motor vehicles.
  Dealer, exclusion of motor
    vehicle dealer from
    definitions in motor vehicle
    business practices law,
    93B:1.
  Local regulation of private ways
    and parking areas, **90:18.**
  Process in commencing action to
    recover damages on account
    of foreign automobile, **246:1.**
  Southeastern Massachusetts
    University board of trustees,
    traffic violations, **90C:1.**
Municipal finance.
  See MUNICIPAL FINANCE.
Municipalities.
  See CITIES AND TOWNS.
National banks.
  See NATIONAL BANKS.
New Bedford institute of
  technology.
  See NEW BEDFORD
    INSTITUTE OF
    TECHNOLOGY.
New England power pool, trust
  agreement, **164A:13.**

TRUSTS AND TRUSTEES
—Cont'd

New trustees.
  Absentee beneficiaries. See within this heading, "Absentee beneficiaries, settlement of estates."
  Successor trustee. See within this heading, "Successor trustees."
Nonresidents.
  Beneficiaries, distribution to foreign trustee, **206:29, 206:30.**
  Corporations.
    Foreign corporations. See within this heading, "Foreign corporations."
  Trustees.
    Foreign trustees. See within this heading, "Foreign trustees."
Notice.
  Appointment of successor upon removal of trustee, **203:12.**
  Common trust fund, notice of intention to invest, **203A:2.**
  Creditors without notice, rights, **203:3.**
  Foreign trustee's taking out of letters, notice, **203:11.**
  Purchasers without notice of trust in land, rights, **203:3.**
  Recording of trust instruments, **36:31A, 203:2.**
  Registers and registries of deeds. See within this heading, "Registers and registries of deeds."
  Removal of trustee, **203:12.**
  Sales and transfers. See within this heading, "Sales and transfers."
  Uniform Custodial Trust Act, notice of declination to service as trustee, **203B:13.**
Objections to investments in common trust funds, **203A:2.**
Order for transfer of trust estate of absentee beneficiaries, **203:32.**
Parks and reservations, city or town may take and hold trust for purpose of parks and reservations, **45:3.**
Parsonages held in irrevocable trust for religious corporations, local assessment, **59:5.**
Participations in mortgages, **203:24B.**

TRUSTS AND TRUSTEES
—Cont'd

Parties to proceeding to transfer estate of absentee beneficiaries, **203:30, 203:31.**
Partition.
  Bond of trustee, **241:35.**
  Share held by trustee, **241:30.**
  Successive interests, trustees, **241:35.**
Partnerships.
  See PARTNERSHIPS.
Payment.
  Decrees with respect to payment to trustee by third persons, **192:3.**
  Distribution of trust estates. See within this heading, "Distribution of trust estates."
  Finality of adjudication as to payment of debts, **204:21.**
  Trustee, enforcement of decree for payment, **197:24.**
Pecuniary distributions under trust instrument, rate and accrual date of interest, **197:20.**
Pensions.
  See RETIREMENT SYSTEMS AND PENSIONS.
Perjury in report or answer by trustee, **182:12.**
Permanent Assistance to Cities. See COMPACT FUND.
Perpetuities, applicability to equitable interests of rule against, **184A:4, 203:3A.**
Personal property.
  Accounts and accounting. See within this heading, "Accounts and accounting."
  Sales and transfers. See within this heading, "Sales and transfers."
Petition for transfer of trust estate.
  Absentee beneficiaries. See within this heading, "Absentee beneficiaries, settlement of estates."
Pour-over trust provisions, **203:3B.**
Powers of appointment, fulfillment of intent of creator, **191:1B.**
Premiums.
  Amortization of premiums. See within this heading, "Amortization of premiums."
Presumptions.
  Abandonment of securities unclaimed by beneficiary, **200A:5, 200A:5B, 200A:5C.**

TRUSTS AND TRUSTEES
—Cont'd

Presumptions —Cont'd
  Death of absentee beneficiary, **203:32.**
Principal and income, apportionment between.
  Appointment of trustee, expenses, **203:22.**
  Broker's commissions, **203:22.**
  Cash proceeds of sale of mortgaged real estate, **203:24A, 203:24B.**
  Costs.
    Of litigation, **206:16.**
  Default and foreclosure of mortgage, income received, **203:24A, 203:24B.**
  Dividends, **203:21A.**
  Expenses, **203:22.**
    Litigation, costs, **206:16.**
    Trustee's expenses, **206:16.**
  Foreclosure sale, cash proceeds, **203:24A, 203:24B.**
  Leases, expenses in negotiating, **203:22.**
  Procuring surety, expense, **206:17.**
  Removal of trustees, expenses, **203:22.**
  Sale, exchange or purchase of property, expenses, **203:22.**
  Securities and obligations, distribution, **203:21A.**
  Testamentary trusts, **203:21A.**
Private foundations, **68A:3.**
  See PRIVATE FOUNDATIONS.
Probate and Family Court, **203:1 et seq.**
  See PROBATE AND FAMILY COURT.
Probate and insolvency registers.
  Common trust funds. See within this heading, "Common trust funds."
Restrictions on appointment as trustee under will, **217:7.**
Probate bonds.
  See PROBATE BONDS.
Process and service of process on trustees, **223:40.**
  See PROCESS AND SERVICE OF PROCESS AND PAPERS.
Process in nature of garnishment to place holder of property in position of trustee, **246:1-246:83.**
  See TRUSTEE PROCESS.
Profits.
  Accounting for profit or loss on sale of personal property, **206:5.**

TRUSTS AND TRUSTEES
—Cont'd

Profits —Cont'd

Rents and profits. See within
this heading, "Rents and
profits."

Property.

Personal property. See within
this heading, "Personal
property."

Real property.

Land and land titles. See
within this heading,
"Land and land titles."

Prudent investor act, **203C:1 to
203C:11.**

Agents.

Delegation of investment and
management functions,
203C:10.

Beneficiaries' interest to guide
strategy, **203C:6.**

Conflicting interests among
beneficiaries, **203C:7.**

Citation of chapter, **203C:1.**

Compliance.

Determination, **203C:9.**

Compliance required, **203C:2.**

Context of portfolio considered,
203C:3.

Costs, limitations, **203C:8.**

Delegation of investment and
management functions,
203C:10.

Diversification required, **203C:4.**

Factors to be considered by
trustee, **203C:3.**

Impartiality.

Conflicting interests among
beneficiaries, **203C:7.**

Invocation of rule.

Language of trust, **203C:11.**

Language of trust which invoke
rule, **203C:11.**

Reasonable care required,
203C:3.

Review of assets.

Acceptance of trusteeship,
203C:5.

Trust provisions may defined or
alter, **203C:2.**

Public employee as trustee, **268A:4
et seq.**

Deferred compensation,
investment, **29:64, 35:57,
44:67.**

Public health department or
hospitals, trust funds, **111:67.**

Public improvement assessments,
mortgage of trust estate to
pay, **203:23.**

TRUSTS AND TRUSTEES
—Cont'd

Purchasers.

Notice of trust in land, rights of
purchasers without, **203:3.**

Rights under deed executed by
trustee, **184:34.**

Trustee as purchaser at own
sale, **203:16.**

Racing commission, **128A:3,
128A:5 notes.**

Railroads, **160:51-160:54.**

See RAILROADS.

Ratification of trustee's acts.

Confirmation or ratification. See
within this heading,
"Confirmation or ratification
of trustee's acts."

Real estate.

Land and land titles. See within
this heading, "Land and
land titles."

Real estate brokers.

Commissions, apportionment,
203:22.

Registration law not applicable
to sales by trustee,
112:87QQ.

Real estate time-shares.

See REAL ESTATE
TIME-SHARES.

Receipt of trustee, **203:20.**

Reciprocal insurance exchanges,
trustees for assets, **175:94H.**

Records and recording.

Commissioner of corporations
and taxation, notice,
36:31A.

Common trust funds, **203A:1.**

Economic development and
industrial corporation, trust
agreements, **121C:13.**

Final account and discharge of
trustee, **206:22.**

Inventory information as to real
property, **217:15B.**

Notice of trust in land provided
by recording, **203:2.**

Registers and registries of deeds.
See within this heading,
"Registers and registries of
deeds."

Reports. See within this
heading, "Reports and
returns."

Transfer of trust estate, filing
petition, **203:27.**

Transitional assistance
department, notice, **36:32.**

Uniform Custodial Trust Act,
203B:7.

TRUSTS AND TRUSTEES
—Cont'd

Regents of higher education, board
of.

Summer and evening sessions.
Conduct, **15A:16.**

Tuition waiver program,
15A:7C.

Registers and registries of deeds.

Charitable trusts, notice to
transitional assistance
department as to recording,
36:32.

Effect of recording trust
concerning land, **203:2.**

Revenue department, notice as
to recording of trust
instruments, **36:31A.**

Registers of probate, **203A:1,
203A:3.**

Registration of land titles,
185:72-185:76.

See REGISTRATION OF LAND
TITLES.

Regulation of trust business,
203:4A, 203:4B.

Release and discharge.

Cemetery lots, **204:5, 204:12.**

Final accounting, discharge of
trustee, **206:22.**

Receipt as discharge of trustee's
obligations, **203:20.**

Removal of trustees. See within
this heading, "Removal of
trustee."

Vested or contingent interests,
204:4.

Religion.

See RELIGION AND
RELIGIOUS SOCIETIES.

Remainders, conveyance of estate
subject to, **183:49-183:51.**

Removal of trustee, **203:12.**

Apportionment, as between
principal and income, of
expenses, **203:22.**

Notice, **203:12.**

Uniform Custodial Trust Act,
203B:15.

Rents and profits.

Apportionment, **197:27.**

Payable from death of testator,
197:26.

Repairs, mortgage of trust estate,
203:23.

Reports and returns.

Absentee beneficiaries, return of
notice of proceedings to
transfer estate, **203:29.**

Administration and finance
commissioner's report as to
trust funds of
Commonwealth, **7A:12.**

TRUSTS AND TRUSTEES
—Cont'd

Reports and returns —Cont'd
Aldermen and selectmen, report of fraud, **41:53.**
Business trusts, annual report, **182:4, 182:12-182:14.**
Charitable, religious, or educational purposes, annual reports of trustees, **68:13, 68:14.**
Common trust funds, accounts and reports of, filing, **203A:3.**
Perjury in trustee's report or answer, **182:12.**
Reservations.
Parks and reservations, city or town may take and hold trust for purpose of parks and reservations **45:3.**
Resignation of trustee, **203:13.**
Bond, failure to give, **205:8.**
Guardian or conservator of trustee, resignation, **204:37.**
Uniform Custodial Trust Act, **203B:13.**
Vacancy, filling, **203:5.**
Res judicata, decrees as to trustees' accounts and settlements, **192:3, 206:24.**
Retirement systems.
See RETIREMENT SYSTEMS AND PENSIONS.
Retroactive application of law as to absentee beneficiaries, **203:39.**
Returns.
Reports and returns. See within this heading, "Reports and returns."
Revenue department and commissioner.
Annual report, filing and examination of business trusts, **182:12, 182:13.**
Notice of recording of trust instruments, **36:31A.**
Salaries.
Wages, salaries, and compensation. See within this heading, "Wages, salaries, and compensation."
Sales and transfers, **183:14, 203:16.**
Absentee beneficiaries. See within this heading, "Absentee beneficiaries, settlement of estates."
Accounting for proceeds of sale, **206:16.**
Additional bond required, **205:13.**

TRUSTS AND TRUSTEES
—Cont'd

Sales and transfers —Cont'd
Adverse claimant, contest, **204:20.**
Application for license to sell real property, **203:16.**
Appointment for sale of land subject to charge, **183:52.**
Bond of trustee.
See PROBATE BONDS.
Brokers' and salesmen's registration law not applicable to sales by trustees, **112:87QQ.**
Carrier's certificate. See within this heading, "Carrier's certificate, transfer."
Cemetery lots and property, **204:5, 204:12.**
Church property, **204:12.**
Conclusiveness of sale, **192:3, 203:17.**
Confirmation or setting aside of void or voidable sales, **204:23.**
Consent of deceased persons, proceedings where sale of real estate dependent, **204:2.**
Contingent interests, **203:17.**
Deed executed by trustee, right of purchaser, **184:34.**
Disposition of proceeds of sale of real property, **203:16, 204:12.**
Dower or curtesy, transfer free, **202:3.**
Duration of license to sell real property, **204:8.**
Estate subject to remainders, appointment of trustee for conveyance, **183:49-183:51.**
Examination of fiduciary as to sale of real estate, **204:11.**
Expenses chargeable to principal, **203:22.**
Finality of adjudication as to debts, **204:21.**
Foreign trustees. See within this heading, "Foreign trustees."
Future interests, **203:17.**
Grounds authorizing sale of real property, **203:16.**
Guardian ad litem, proceedings for sale of trust estate, **203:16, 203:17.**
Insane trustee, sale on behalf, **203:18.**
Investment of proceeds, **203:16, 203:17A, 204:12.**

TRUSTS AND TRUSTEES
—Cont'd

Sales and transfers —Cont'd
Irregular and invalid sales, **204:19-204:26.**
Language as to uses, **183:14.**
License to sell.
Application, **203:16.**
Costs in case of unreasonable petition or objections thereto, **204:10.**
Duration, **204:8.**
Examination as to exercise, **204:11.**
Minor trustee, sale on behalf, **203:18.**
Mortgages. See within this heading, "Mortgages."
Neglect or misconduct in sale, action on bond, **204:11.**
Next friend, appointment where sale of personalty contemplated, **203:17.**
Notice of proceedings, **203:16, 203:17, 203:17A, 203:28-203:30.**
Failure of proof of, remedy in case, **204:26.**
Foreign testamentary trustees, sales, **203:17A.**
Personal property, **203:16, 203:17.**
Rights of purchaser without notice of trust in land, **203:3.**
Order for sale, **203:16.**
Own sale, trustee as purchaser, **203:16.**
Paramount title, irregularity in sale not available to contestant, **204:20.**
Personal property, **203:16, 203:19.**
Petitioner as purchaser, **203:16.**
Power of sale in trust instrument, **203:16.**
Proceeds of sale.
Accounting, **203:16.**
Disposition, **203:16, 204:12.**
Foreign testamentary trustees, sales, **203:17A.**
Mortgaged realty, application of cash proceeds of sale, **203:24A, 203:24B.**
Purchasers. See within this heading, "Purchasers."
Real estate, **203:16.**
Registers.
See REGISTERS AND REGISTRIES OF DEEDS.
Remainders, sale and conveyance of property subject, **183:49-183:51.**

TRUSTS AND TRUSTEES
—Cont'd
Sales and transfers —Cont'd
Rights under deed executed by
trustee, **184:34.**
Setting aside void or voidable
sales, **204:23.**
Transient vendors,
inapplicability to trustees of
restrictions on sales, **101:7.**
Unborn or unascertained
persons, representation,
203:17.
Venue of petitions for sales of
real property, **204:7.**
Void or voidable sales,
confirmation or setting
aside, **204:23.**
Salesman charges with respect to
sale of real property
chargeable to trust corpus,
203:22.
Salvage operation of trustees
holding mortgage, **203:24A,
203:24B.**
Savings and loan associations,
investment, **44:54, 205:19A,
206:25-206:27A.**
Savings banks.
See SAVINGS BANKS.
Schedules for accounting, **206:2.**
Schools.
See SCHOOLS AND
EDUCATION.
Seals and sealed instruments,
4:9A.
Securities.
Commercial code provisions.
See INVESTMENT
SECURITIES UNDER
COMMERCIAL CODE.
Common trust funds,
amortization of premiums
paid on purchase of
interest-bearing investment
securities, **203A:1.**
Corporation or corporate agents,
liability in connection with
stock transfer, **203:21.**
Distributions as trust income or
principal, **203:21A.**
Execution of trust involving,
203:21.
Highway infrastructure fund,
trust agreement as security
for bonds issued through,
29:2O.
Manner in which fiduciaries may
hold securities, **203:14B.**
Production on accounting, **206:4.**
Unclaimed by beneficiaries,
presumption of
abandonment, **200A:5.**

TRUSTS AND TRUSTEES
—Cont'd
Security interest in beneficial
interest, exception as to
perfecting, **106:9-302.**
Selectmen.
Aldermen and selectmen. See
within this heading,
"Aldermen and selectmen."
Service of process and papers,
223:40.
See PROCESS AND SERVICE
OF PROCESS AND
PAPERS.
Setting aside void or voidable acts
of trustees, **204:23.**
Settlement of trust estate.
Accounts and accounting. See
within this heading,
"Accounts and accounting."
Short form terms for trusts,
184B:1 to 184B:4.
Applicability, **184B:1.**
Statutory disability
discretionary powers,
184B:3.
Statutory optional fiduciary
powers, **184B:2.**
Statutory principal discretionary
powers, **184B:4.**
Signing of instrument creating
trust, necessity, **203:1.**
Simulcast wagering on horse and
dog racing, daily payments
into trust fund, **128C:4 et
seq.**
Simultaneous death act as
affecting disposition of
property, **190A:2, 190A:5.**
Sinking funds established with
trustees, applicability to
deposit of refunding bonds
proceeds, **29:53A.**
Small trust funds, collective
investment of.
Common trust funds. See within
this heading, "Common
trust funds."
Societies.
Associations and societies.
See ASSOCIATIONS AND
SOCIETIES.
Soldiers' Home in Holyoke, board,
6:70.
Soldiers' home in Massachusetts.
See SOLDIERS' HOME IN
MASSACHUSETTS.
Soldiers' memorials in towns,
trustees, **41:105.**
Southeastern Massachusetts
University board of trustees,
traffic violations, **90C:1.**

TRUSTS AND TRUSTEES
—Cont'd
Special assessments, trust estate
may be mortgaged to pay,
203:23.
State colleges.
See COLLEGES AND
UNIVERSITIES.
State finance.
See STATE FINANCE.
State hospitals.
See STATE HOSPITALS.
State library.
See STATE LIBRARY.
State treasurer.
See STATE TREASURER.
Statute of frauds, trust
instruments as within, **203:1.**
Statutory custodianship trusts,
201C:1 to 201C:3.
Street railways.
See STREET RAILWAYS.
Subpoena served on trustee of
trust with absentee
beneficiaries, **203:28.**
Successor trustees.
Appointment, **203:5, 203:10,
203:12.**
Bond, **203:6, 203:7.**
Delivery of property, **203:6.**
Executor or administrator of
former trustee, **203:14.**
Foreign trustee's failure to take
out letters, appointment,
203:10.
Inventory dispensed, **203:8.**
Investments, powers, **203:34.**
Jurisdiction to appoint, **203:5,
203:12.**
Powers and duties, **203:6.**
Transfer of assets, **203:6.**
Vesting of estate, **203:6.**
Superior courts.
Appointment of trustee, **203:5.**
Business trusts, jurisdiction to
enjoin use of misleading
name, **182:2A.**
Joint trustees, special
jurisdiction in actions
between, **214:3.**
Removal of trustee, **203:12.**
Vacancies, filling, **203:5, 203:12.**
Supreme judicial court.
Appointment of trustee, **203:5.**
Cemetery property held in trust,
sale or transfer, **204:12.**
Compromise of controversies by
fiduciaries, **204:14.**
Interest on pecuniary
distributions under trust
instruments, fixing, **197:20.**

TRUSTS AND TRUSTEES
—Cont'd
Supreme judicial court —Cont'd
Joint trustees, special
jurisdiction in actions
between, **214:3.**
Religious or cemetery purposes,
sale or transfer of property
held in trust, **204:12.**
Removal of trustee, **203:12.**
Vacancy, filling, **203:5, 203:12.**
Validity of acts of certain
fiduciaries pending appeal
from decree of appointment,
215:9A.
Void or voidable acts of trustees,
confirming or setting aside,
204:23.
Surety, expense of procuring,
206:17.
Survival of action against trustee
appointed under statute
following removal, resignation
or death, **228:14.**
Surviving spouse.
Uniform Custodial Trust Act,
203B:6.
Uniform Statutory Will Act. See
within this heading,
"Uniform Statutory Will
Act."
Waiver of will, appointment of
trustees to hold share,
191:16.
Taxation.
See TAXATION.
Technical colleges or institutes.
Corporation for purpose of
taking and holding property,
74:43.
Granting of honorary degrees,
74:42A, 74:42B.
Property, power to take and
hold, **74:43.**
Television, educational television
program fund, **71:13H.**
Termination of trust.
Uniform Custodial Trust Act,
203B:17.
Termination of trust created by
assignment for benefit of
creditors by person deceased,
203:42.
Testamentary trusts.
Wills. See within this heading,
"Wills."
Tewksbury Hospital, **122:2-122:4.**
Beneficiary, **122:5.**
Corporation for certain purposes,
122:5.
Finality of decisions, **122:5.**

TRUSTS AND TRUSTEES
—Cont'd
Tewksbury Hospital —Cont'd
Liability, **122:5.**
Meetings, **122:3.**
Powers and duties, **122:5,
122:10.**
Rules, **122:4.**
Visitation by trustee, **122:3.**
Timber, standing, trust as to
proceeds of sale of during life
estate, **184:14.**
Title guaranty fund as trust for
protection of title
policyholders, **175:116.**
Towns.
See CITIES AND TOWNS.
Training schools, trust funds,
10:15.
Transfer of property.
Sales and transfers. See within
this heading, "Sales and
transfers."
Transient vendors, inapplicability
of restrictions on sales, **101:7.**
Trust companies.
See TRUST COMPANIES.
Trustee process, **246:1-246:83.**
See TRUSTEE PROCESS.
Tuberculosis hospitals, trustees,
111:87.
Turnpike authority.
Money received deemed trust
funds, **81A:11.**
Notes or bonds secured by trust
agreement, **81A:6.**
Unborn, unascertained, or
incompetent persons,
representation in proceedings
for allowance of accounts,
206:24.
Unclaimed funds.
Abandoned, lost, and unclaimed
property. See within this
heading, "Abandoned, lost,
and unclaimed property."
Uncollected debts, accountability
of trustee, **206:5.**
Uniform Common Trust Fund Act.
Common trust funds. See within
this heading, "Common
trust funds."
Uniform Custodial Trust Act,
203B:1 et seq.
See UNIFORM CUSTODIAL
TRUST ACT.
Uniform Gifts to Minors Act,
201A:5.
Uniform Statutory Will Act.
Bond or surety of trustee,
191B:14.

TRUSTS AND TRUSTEES
—Cont'd
Uniform Statutory Will Act
—Cont'd
Child, underage, **191B:8,
191B:9.**
Death or unwillingness of
trustee to serve, **191B:12.**
Definition of trustee, **191B:1.**
Incompetent person, **191B:9.**
Powers and duties of trustee,
191B:13.
Surviving spouse.
Defined, **191B:1.**
Share of, **191B:6.**
Successor trustee,
appointment, **191B:12.**
United Methodist Church.
Allowable annual trust income,
67:41.
First meeting of trustees, **67:42.**
Powers of trustees, **67:41.**
United States.
Federal. See within this
heading, "Federal aid or
funds."
Universities.
See COLLEGES AND
UNIVERSITIES.
University of Massachusetts.
See UNIVERSITY OF
MASSACHUSETTS.
Urban redevelopment projects,
authority as to undertaking
and acquisition, **121A:18C.**
Vacancies, **203:5, 203:10, 203:12.**
Cities and towns, trust fund
commissioners, **41:45.**
Declination of trustee, vacancy,
203:5.
Foreign trustee failing to obtain
letters, vacancy, **203:10.**
Successor trustees. See within
this heading, "Successor
trustees."
Valuation of property.
Inventory and appraisal. See
within this heading,
"Inventory and appraisal."
Venue.
Absentee beneficiaries, transfer
of estates, **203:29, 203:37.**
Foreign trustees, petitions for
sales, **204:7.**
Prosecution for embezzlement or
fraudulent conversion,
277:58B.
Vested interests, release, **204:4.**
Veterans' Administration to
represent certain persons in
allowance of probate accounts,
206:24.

TRUSTS AND TRUSTEES
—Cont'd
Vocational education and schools, **74:3-74:6.**
  See VOCATIONAL
    EDUCATION AND
    SCHOOLS.
Void or voidable acts of trustees, confirmation or setting aside, **204:23, 204:24.**
Wages, salaries, and compensation.
  Allowance of compensation, **206:16.**
  Apportionment as between principal and income, **206:16.**
  Deduction by trustees of employees' compensation, **62:10.**
  Trustee process, **246:1 et seq.**
    See TRUSTEE PROCESS.
  Workers' compensation.
    See WORKERS'
      COMPENSATION.
Walter E. Fernald State School.
  Membership and term of office of board of trustees, **19:15.**
  Mental health department, trustees to serve, **19:14.**
Water pollution abatement trust.
  See WATER POLLUTION
    ABATEMENT TRUST.
Wife, appointment of trustee to hold surviving spouse's share upon waiver of will, **191:16.**
Wills, **183:14.**
  Annuities payable from death of testator, trustee's duties, **197:26.**
  Appointment of trustees, **203:4.**
  Embezzlement by trustee, **266:57.**
  Foreign testamentary trustee, sale of real estate, **203:17A.**
  Income, determination, **203:21A.**
  Probate and insolvency judges, restrictions on appointment as trustee under will, **217:7.**
  Sale powers, **203:16.**
  Surviving spouse. See within this heading, "Surviving spouse."
  Termination or consolidation of certain trusts under wills, **203:25.**
  Uniform Statutory Will Act. See within this heading, "Uniform Statutory Will Act."
  Validity of testamentary additions to existing inter vivos trusts, **203:3B.**

TRUSTS AND TRUSTEES
—Cont'd
Workers' compensation.
  See WORKERS'
    COMPENSATION.
Writing as necessary to create trust in land, **203:1.**
Youth service division as corporation, **120:1.**

TRUTH.
False reports.
  See FRAUD AND DECEIT.
False swearing.
  See PERJURY.
Libel and slander, truth as justification or defense, **231:91, 231:92.**
  Criminal cases, **278:8.**
  Suspicion of truth, **231:94.**
Lie detector tests as condition of employment, prohibited, **149:19B.**
Loans.
  See TRUTH IN LENDING.

TRUTH IN LENDING, 140:114B, 140D:1-140D:34.
Adjustment in accounts for inaccurate disclosure, **140D:6.**
Advertising and advertisements, **140D:14-140D:16.**
  Mortgage loan application disclosures as advertisements, **184:17B.**
Agricultural products and purposes, **140D:1, 140D:2.**
Annual percentage rate.
  Finance charges. See within this heading, "Finance charges."
Applicability of Act, **140D:2.**
Assignees, actions by or against, **140D:33.**
Bank funds of debtor, transfer to satisfy debt, **140D:21, 140D:23.**
Cancellation.
  Rescission. See within this heading, "Rescission."
Cash payment discount, **140D:1, 140D:28A.**
Certified mail, disclosure, **93:57.**
Credit cards, **140D:1, 140D:21, 140D:25-140D:28B.**
Credit extension.
  Extension of credit. See within this heading, "Extension of credit."
Default, notice of transfer of bank funds pursuant, **140D:23.**
Definitions, **140D:1.**
Discounts for payment by cash or check, **140D:1, 140D:28A.**

TRUTH IN LENDING —Cont'd
Employees, businesses providing credit cards, **140D:28.**
Excess payment of installment sales, **255D:27.**
Extended rescission rights for consumer credit transactions, **140D:35.**
Extension of credit.
  Disclosures, **255D:27.**
  Form as to retail installment sales and services credit extensions, **255D:18A.**
  Installment sales, **255D:27.**
Federal Credit Billing Act, rules consistent, **140D:29.**
Finance charges, **140D:1 et seq.**
  Advertisement, **140D:14-140D:16.**
  Annual percentage rate, **140D:5.**
  Credit cards, **140D:1, 140D:21, 140D:25-140D:28B.**
  Inaccurate disclosures, **140D:6, 140D:9.**
  Items included, **140D:4.**
  Model disclosure forms, **140D:18.**
  Open end credit, **140D:10, 140D:11, 140D:19, 140D:20, 140D:22-140D:24, 255D:27.**
  Representative annual rate in certain metropolitan areas, **140D:13.**
  Response of creditor to inquiries, **140D:17.**
Fines and penalties.
  Penalties. See within this heading, "Penalties."
Forms for disclosure, **140D:18.**
Franchised or licensed sellers as related to creditor, **255D:27.**
Guarantor's liability, **140D:24.**
Identification of items in statement, **255D:27.**
Inspection of creditors' records to determine compliance, **140D:30.**
Installment sales, **255D:27.**
Insurance premium financing agreement subject, **255C:23.**
Interest.
  Credit balance, interest to customer, **140D:22.**
  Finance charges. See within this heading, "Finance charges."
Knowledge.
  Notice and knowledge. See within this heading, "Notice and knowledge."
Limitation of actions, consumer protection actions involving credit disclosure, **260:5A.**

TRUTH IN LENDING —Cont'd

Mail, disclosure by certified mail, **93:57.**

Manner of disclosure, **140D:8.**

Media, liability arising out of advertisement, **140D:16.**

Model forms for disclosure, **140D:18.**

Mortgages, **140D:1, 140D:2, 140D:10.**

Advertisements, mortgage loan application disclosures, **184:17B.**

Motor vehicle retail installment sales subject to truth in lending, **255B:25.**

Multiple creditors or obligors, disclosure requirements involving, **140D:7.**

Newspapers, liability arising out of advertisement, **140D:16.**

Notice and knowledge.

Certified mail, disclosure, **93:57.**

Default on loan, transfer of funds pursuant, **140D:23.**

Rights of obligor, written notice of, **140D:35.**

Open end credit accounts, **140D:1, 140D:10, 140D:11, 140D:19-140D:24.**

Finance charges, computation, **255D:27.**

Optometrist's advertisements containing inaccurate statements about credit, **112:73A.**

Penalties, **140D:31.**

Unauthorized use of credit cards, **140D:27.**

Primary obligor, disclosure, **140D:7.**

Radio and television, liability arising out of advertisement, **140D:16.**

Refunds.

Credit balance, refund, **140D:22.**

Installment sales overpayment, **255D:27.**

Rescission.

Extended rescission rights for consumer credit transactions, **140D:35.**

Obligor's right of, **140D:10.**

Retail installment sales agreements, **255D:9.**

Rules and regulations, **140D:3, 140D:29.**

Secured transactions, effect of laws governing, **106:9-203.**

Securities and exchange transactions, **140D:2.**

TRUTH IN LENDING —Cont'd

Subsequent events affecting accuracy of disclosure, **140D:9.**

Television and radio, liability arising out of advertisement, **140D:16.**

Transfer of debtor's bank funds to satisfy debt, **140D:21, 140D:23.**

Unauthorized use of credit cards, liability, **140D:1, 140D:26-140D:28.**

Violations of Act as also violation of chapter business practices for consumer's protection, **140D:34.**

TRUTH-IN-NEGOTIATION CERTIFICATES.

Designer selection board, issuance of certificates, **7:38H.**

TRUTH IN SAVINGS, 140E:1 et seq.

Definitions, **140E:1.**

Disclosure of information by financial institution to consumer, **140E:2.**

Short title, **140E:4.**

Violation of provisions, **140E:3.**

TRUTH IN SENTENCING, 6:168A, 6A:18¾, 279:1, 279:24.

TRYING TITLE.
See QUIETING TITLE.

TUBERCULOSIS AND TUBERCULIN.

Accounts of county hospitals, examination, **35:45.**

Active cases, care and treatment, **111:94A-111:94H.**

Admissions to hospitals, etc.

Chronic disease patients, **111:78A, 111:82, 111:88.**

Compulsory hospitalization, **111:94A-111:94H.**

Control, **111:79.**

Homes for the aged, **111:82, 111:88.**

Lakeville sanatorium, **111:65A.**

State treatment center, **111:94A-111:94C.**

Animal diseases.
See ANIMAL DISEASES.

Appeal and review.

"Chronically non-resident," refusal to classify, **111:80.**

Teachers, appeal as to communicability of tuberculosis, **71:55B.**

TUBERCULOSIS AND TUBERCULIN —Cont'd

Assessments for establishment of county hospitals, payment of costs by cities and towns failing to pay, **111:83B.**

Borrowing for hospitals, **44:8, 111:83B, 111:85A.**

Certification for hospitalization, **111:94A.**

Charges for care and treatment.

Fixing, **111:78, 111:78A, 111:79, 111:82, 111:88, 111:91C.**

Isolation hospitals, **111:116.**

Payment, **111:78, 111:79, 111:80, 111:94E, 111:121.**

Chest diseases other than tuberculosis, treatment, **111:91C.**

Chronically nonresident patients, **111:80.**

Chronic disease hospitals.

Charges for patients, **111:82.**

Conversion to chronic disease hospitals.

County hospitals, **111:82.**

Municipal hospitals, **111:88.**

Tuberculosis hospitals, treatment of chronic disease patients, **111:78A.**

Cities and towns.

Assessments for establishment of county tuberculosis hospitals, **111:83B.**

Borrowing outside debt limit for hospitals, **44:8.**

Charges for hospital care, payment, **111:80, 111:121.**

Contracts for hospitalization, **111:79, 111:91.**

County hospitals. See within this heading, "County hospitals."

Dispensaries, operation, **111:57.**

Health boards and officers. See within this heading, "Health boards and officers."

Municipal hospitals. See within this heading, "Municipal hospitals."

Civil service status of personnel of tuberculosis hospital, **111:83.**

College and university employees, test for persons employed in colleges, **71:55B.**

Commonwealth.

State. See within this heading, "State."

Compulsory treatment or hospitalization, **111:94A-111:94H.**

TUBERCULOSIS AND TUBERCULIN —Cont'd

Contracts for care and treatment, **111:77, 111:78, 111:79, 111:82, 111:91.**

Correctional institutions.
See CORRECTIONAL INSTITUTIONS.

Costs.
Expenses and expenditures. See within this heading, "Expenses and expenditures."

County hospitals, **111:82.**
Accounts, examination, **35:45.**
Acquisition of land, **111:86.**
Aging persons, conversion to homes, **111:82.**
Apportionment of cost of maintenance, **111:85.**
Borrowing money for, by counties, **111:83B, 111:85A.**
Charges, determination, **111:78, 111:78A, 111:79, 111:80, 111:82, 111:88.**
Chronic diseases, treatment, **111:78A, 111:82.**
Cities and towns.
Inclusion in county hospital districts, **111:91.**
Payments to county hospitals, **111:80, 111:83B, 111:85, 111:91.**
Reimbursement for tax loss on lands of county hospitals, **58:13-58:17A.**
Contracts for care and treatment, **111:78, 111:79, 111:82, 111:91.**
Conveyance to Commonwealth, **111:83.**
County commissioners, powers and duties, **111:85, 111:87.**
Discharge from employment of superintendent and assistant superintendent, **35:51.**
Discontinuance and liquidation, **111:82.**
Examination, inspection, and investigation. See within this heading, "Examination, inspection, and investigation."
Expenses and expenditures.
Apportionment of maintenance costs, **111:85.**
Assessments for establishment of, payment of costs by cities or towns failing to pay, **111:83B.**

TUBERCULOSIS AND TUBERCULIN —Cont'd

County hospitals —Cont'd
Expenses and expenditures —Cont'd
Determination of charges, **111:78.**
Maintenance and repairs, expenditure of cash balances, **111:85A.**
Inclusion of cities and towns in hospital districts, **111:91.**
Officers and employees.
Appointment, **111:87.**
Civil service status, **111:83.**
Indemnity insurance, **111:83A.**
Transfer to public health department, **111:83.**
Operation and maintenance of, **111:82.**
Physicians, appointment, **111:87.**
Receipts, disposition, **111:85A.**
Reimbursement of cities and towns for tax loss on lands of county hospitals, **58:13-58:17A.**
Superintendents.
Appointment, **111:87.**
Discharge from employment of superintendent and assistant superintendent, **35:51.**
Treasurer of county.
Agreement of tax assessed, **58:17A.**
Hospital receipts paid, **111:85A.**
Trustees of, county commissioners, **111:87.**
Workers' compensation.
See WORKERS' COMPENSATION.
Declassification of active cases, **111:94F.**
Deed or conveyance of hospital property to Commonwealth, **111:83.**
Detention of patient in hospital, **111:94B.**
Diagnostic facilities, **111:81.**
Discharge of patients, **111:79, 111:94F, 111:94G.**
Dispensaries, **111:57.**
District courts.
Commitments to state treatment center, **111:94A-111:94C.**
Discharges from state treatment center, **111:94G.**
Domicile and residence.
Residents. See within this heading, "Residents."

TUBERCULOSIS AND TUBERCULIN —Cont'd

Employees.
County hospitals. See within this heading, "County hospitals."
Sanatoria employees, appointment, **17:6.**
Examination, inspection, and investigation.
Accounts of county sanatoria, examination, **35:45.**
Intradermal tuberculin tests to show freedom from tuberculosis, **111:81A.**
Licensing of county tuberculosis hospitals for treatment of chronic diseases, **111:78A.**
School personnel, testing, **71:55B.**
Veterinarian's fraud as to tuberculin test results, **112:59.**
Expenses and expenditures.
Charges for care and treatment. See within this heading, "Charges for care and treatment."
County hospitals. See within this heading, "County hospitals."
Extra-pulmonary tuberculosis treated at Lakeville Hospital, **111:65A.**
Financially responsible patients, **111:80.**
Fire prevention, inspection of premises for purpose, **148:4.**
Fraud by veterinarian as to tuberculin test results, **112:59.**
Hairdressers to be free, **112:87CC.**
Health boards and officers.
Compulsory hospitalization, certification, **111:94A, 111:94H.**
Dispensaries, regulation, **111:57.**
Health department to work, **111:81.**
Isolation hospitals, control, **111:92-111:94.**
Health department of state, **17:6, 111:77 et seq.**
Homes for aged persons.
Nursing or rest homes. See within this heading, "Nursing or rest homes."
Hospitals and health care facilities, **111:94A et seq.**
Indemnity insurance for officers and employees of county hospitals, **111:83A.**

TUBERCULOSIS AND TUBERCULIN —Cont'd

Indigents.
Poor persons. See within this heading, "Poor persons."
Information as to, gathering and dissemination, **111:63, 111:81.**
Inspection.
Examination, inspection, and investigation. See within this heading, "Examination, inspection, and investigation."
Instruction as to prevention, **71:1.**
Intradermal tuberculin tests to show freedom from tuberculosis, **111:81A.**
Isolation hospitals, **111:65A.**
Charges for treatment, **111:116.**
Local health boards, control and regulation, **111:92-111:94.**
Warrant against city or town failing to pay assessment for tuberculosis hospitals, **111:83B.**
Lakeville hospital, treatment of extra-pulmonary tuberculosis, **111:65A.**
Licenses for hospitals and health care facilities.
Conversion to chronic disease hospitals or homes for the aged, **111:82.**
Division for other chest diseases, **111:91C.**
Hearings on revocation or refusal to renew, **111:71.**
Temporary, provisional, or probationary licenses, **111:71.**
Treatment of chronic diseases, licensing of county tuberculosis hospitals, **111:78A.**
Manicurists to be free, **112:87CC.**
Medical care and assistance, furnishing, **118E:6.**
Municipal dispensaries, **111:57.**
Municipal hospitals.
Chronic disease hospitals, conversion, **111:82, 111:88.**
Civil service status of personnel, **111:83.**
Conveyance to Commonwealth, **111:83.**
Exemption from inclusion in hospital district of cities and towns maintaining, **111:91.**
Homes for aged, conversion, **111:88.**
Other chest diseases, treatment, **111:91C.**

TUBERCULOSIS AND TUBERCULIN —Cont'd

Municipal hospitals —Cont'd
Transfer of officers and employees to public health department, **111:83.**
Municipalities.
Cities and towns. See within this heading, "Cities and towns."
Nonresidents, chronically nonresident patients, **111:80.**
Notice.
Of discontinuance of use of county hospital, **111:78.**
Of proceedings for commitment to state treatment center, **111:94C.**
To city or town to pay assessment of county hospital, **111:83B.**
Nursing or rest homes.
Hospitals converted into, **111:82, 111:88.**
Patients, liability for cost of care, **111:80.**
Officers and employees.
County hospitals. See within this heading, "County hospitals."
Old persons, homes for.
Nursing or rest homes. See within this heading, "Nursing or rest homes."
Out-patient facilities, **111:63, 111:81, 111:82.**
Physicians.
Appointment, **17:6, 111:87.**
Indemnity insurance, **111:83A.**
Poor persons.
Legal settlement, **111:94E, 111:121.**
Payment for care and treatment, **111:78-111:80, 111:94E.**
Public institutions, treatment of persons, **111:121.**
Prisoners, isolation and treatment, **111:121.**
Public health council.
Appeal as to chronically nonresident classification, appointment of board, **111:80.**
Compulsory treatment or hospitalization, powers, **111:94H.**
Public health department, **111:77 et seq.**
Rates and charges.
Charges for care and treatment. See within this heading, "Charges for care and treatment."

TUBERCULOSIS AND TUBERCULIN —Cont'd

Real estate for hospitals.
Acquisition, **111:86.**
Conveyance to Commonwealth, **111:83.**
Reimbursement of cities and towns for tax loss, **58:13-58:17A.**
Records of sanatoria, destruction, **111:70.**
Regulations.
Rules and regulations. See within this heading, "Rules and regulations."
Reimbursement of cities and towns for tax loss on lands of county hospitals, **58:13-58:17A.**
Release of patients, **111:79, 111:94F, 111:94G.**
Removal or discharge from employment of county hospital superintendents and assistant superintendents, **35:51.**
Residents.
Definition under public health law, **111:80.**
Hospital care and treatment, **111:77.**
Rest homes.
Nursing or rest homes. See within this heading, "Nursing or rest homes."
Review.
Appeal and review. See within this heading, "Appeal and review."
Rules and regulations.
Admissions to hospitals, **111:78A, 111:79, 111:82, 111:88.**
Care and treatment in hospitals, **111:78.**
Chronic disease hospitals, **111:78A, 111:82, 111:88.**
Compulsory treatment or hospitalization, **111:94H.**
Discharge from hospitals, **111:79.**
Homes for the aged, **111:82, 111:88.**
Other chest diseases, treatment, **111:91C.**
Transfers of persons in hospitals, **111:79.**
Trustees or county commissioners, powers, **111:82, 111:87.**
Sanatoria, **111:94A et seq.**
Schools and education, **71:55B.**
See SCHOOLS AND EDUCATION.

**TUBERCULOSIS AND
TUBERCULIN** —Cont'd
State.
Admission to state treatment
center, **111:94A-111:94C.**
Conveyance of county and
municipal hospitals, **111:83.**
Discharge or release of patient
from state treatment center,
111:94G.
Financial responsibility for care
and treatment at state
treatment center, **111:94E.**
Superintendent.
County hospitals. See within
this heading, "County
hospitals."
Tax loss of cities and towns on
lands of county tuberculosis
hospitals, reimbursement,
58:13-58:17A.
Testing for.
Examination. See within this
heading, "Examination,
inspection, and
investigation."
Third party liable for cost of
treatment, collection, **111:80.**
Towns.
Cities and towns. See within
this heading, "Cities and
towns."
Transfers of patients in hospitals,
111:79, 111:94F.
Transportation of tubercular
persons.
Hospitalization of persons with
active tuberculosis, **111:94A.**
State sanatorium treatment
center, transportation,
111:94B.
Treasurer of county.
County hospitals. See within
this heading, "County
hospitals."
Treatment center for,
111:94A-111:94G.
Trustees of hospitals for
consumptives, public health
department as successor,
111:67.
Universities.
Colleges and university
employees, test for persons
employed in colleges,
71:55B.
Veterinarians, fraud as to
tuberculin test reports, **112:59.**
Workers' compensation.
See WORKERS'
COMPENSATION.

TUBEROUS SCLEROSIS.
Testing newborn children,
111:110A.

TUESDAY.
City elections, **50:3.**

TUGBOATS.
Anchorage of vessels in tow,
102:21.

TUITION.
**See SCHOOLS AND
EDUCATION.**

TUNNELS.
Boston excepted from restriction
as to debts, **44:2.**
Central artery/third harbor tunnel
project, **29:2O.**
Coal mining operations.
Maps of tunnels, **21B:8.**
Rules and regulations as to
tunnels, **21B:11.**
Dropping or throwing objects,
penalty, **265:35.**
Lowlands and swamps,
252:15-252:23.
See LOWLANDS AND
SWAMPS.
Maps of coal mines' tunnels,
21B:8.
Municipal planning, **41:81D.**
Railroad tunnels, examination,
159:83.
Regional planning, **40B:5.**
Traffic regulations, **85:2B.**

TURBINES.
Economic diversification program,
production of turbines as
defense-related commercial
activity, **23F:1.**

TURKEYS.
Domestic turkeys.
See POULTRY AND POULTRY
PRODUCTS.
Wild turkeys, **131:75.**
Licenses to hunt, **131:11.**

TURNAROUNDS.
Dead-end ways, **41:81Q.**

TURNERS FALLS.
District court, **218:1.**

TURNING OF VEHICLE.
Traffic regulations.
See TRAFFIC REGULATIONS
AND RULES OF THE
ROAD.

TURNIPS.
Sale by bunch, **94:96.**

**TURNPIKE ADVISORY
BOARD, 81A:29, 81A:30.**

**TURNPIKE AUTHORITY, 81A:1
to 81A:31.**
Abandoned property on turnpike,
81A:20.
Accidents on turnpike, report,
90:29.
Air rights leases, **81A:15.**
Review of contracts, agreements,
etc., **81A:27, 81A:29.**
Audits, **81A:20.**
Bonds and notes, **81A:5 to 81A:7.**
Legal investment, **81A:9.**
Power to issue, **81A:4.**
Buildings and structures defined
as public buildings, **22:13A.**
Carriers, licensing of certain,
159A:1.
Chairman as member of
metropolitan area planning
council, **40B:24.**
Construction of chapter, **81A:31.**
Contracts, agreements, etc.
Duration, **81A:25.**
Metropolitan highway system
advisory board review,
81A:27.
Turnpike advisory board review,
81A:29.
Corporate existence.
Termination by law, **81A:23.**
Creation, **81A:1.**
Deferred compensation for
employees, **29:64, 29:64A,
35:57, 35:57A, 44:67, 44:67A,
81A:21.**
Definitions, **81A:3, 81A:5.**
Deposit of funds, **81A:11.**
Drivers' licenses.
Failure to appear or pay,
penalty, **90:20G.**
Dropping or throwing objects on
public way, penalty, **265:35.**
Eminent domain, **81A:13.**
Employee organization, leave of
absence for full-time
representative, **32:28K.**
Employees.
Authority to employ, **81A:4.**
Deferred compensation program,
**29:64, 29:64A, 35:57,
35:57A, 44:67, 44:67A,
81A:21.**
Individual retirement accounts
(IRA), **81A:22.**
Failure to appear or pay, **90:20G.**
Hitchhiking on turnpike, **81A:20.**
Individual retirement accounts,
81A:22.
Labor relations, leave of absence
for full-time representative of
employee organization,
32:28K.

TURNPIKE AUTHORITY

—Cont'd

Leased property, **81A:16.**

Air rights, **81A:15.**

Taxation of property, **81A:14.**

Liability for bodily injury or property damage, **81A:20.**

Licensing of certain motor carriers, **159A:1.**

Local inspection, bridges belonging to excluded, **143:3 et seq.**

Mass transportation facilities and services, determination by revenue department of amounts payable, **58:25B.**

Members, **81A:2.**

Metropolitan area planning council, chairman as member, **40B:24.**

Metropolitan highway system advisory board, **81A:27, 81A:28.**

Notes and bonds, **81A:5 to 81A:7.**

Legal investment, **81A:9.**

Power to issue, **81A:4.**

Out-of-state purchase of fuel or special fuels for use on highways of Commonwealth, **64F:3.**

Penalties, **81A:4.**

Disposition of fines paid to authority, **280:2.**

Failure to appear or pay, **90:20G.**

Plumbers and gas fitters, **142:21.**

Powers generally, **81A:4.**

Privation contracts, definition, **7:53.**

Public buildings, structures defined, **22:13A.**

Reimbursement for tax paid on fuel used for other than highway operation, **64A:7, 64E:5.**

Reimbursement of retirement costs, **81A:24.**

Reports, **81A:17, 81A:20, 90:29.**

Retirement costs reimbursement, **81A:24.**

Special police, **22C:61.**

State police, **22C:29.**

Special police officers, **22C:61.**

Taxation.

Exemption, **59:2B, 81A:8.**

Mass transportation facilities and services, determination by revenue department of amounts payable, **58:25B.**

Real property tax on leased, etc., land, **81A:14.**

TURNPIKE AUTHORITY

—Cont'd

Taxation —Cont'd

Reimbursement for tax paid on fuel used for other than highway operation, **64A:7, 64E:5.**

Throwing or dropping objects on public way, penalty, **265:35.**

Tolls, **81A:4, 81A:10.**

Failure to pay, **81A:20.**

No tolls after transfer to highway department, **81A:26.**

Tourism grant programs for localities, **81A:18.**

Transfer of facilities from highway department, **81A:12.**

Transfer of turnpike to highway department, **81A:25.**

Transportation and construction executive office, agencies within, **6A:19.**

Turnpike advisory board, **81A:29, 81A:30.**

Unclaimed property left on turnpike, **81A:20.**

Violations.

Failure to appear or pay, **90:20G.**

Wages, salaries, and compensation, deferred compensation, **29:64, 29:64A, 35:57, 35:57A, 44:67, 44:67A, 81A:21, 161:19H, 161:19I.**

Weight of vehicles, **81A:19.**

TURNPIKES AND TOLL ROADS.

Evading toll, **81A:20.**

Massachusetts Turnpike Authority, **81A:1 to 81A:31.**

See TURNPIKE AUTHORITY.

Police to make reports as to accidents, **90:29.**

Power to charge and collect tolls on turnpike, **81A:4, 81A:10.**

Speed limit, increase of, **90:17A.**

Streetcars, emergency tools, **161:99.**

Taxation of stock as personal property, **59:4.**

Transfer of turnpike to highway department.

Operation of highway without tolls, **81A:26.**

Weight of vehicles, **81A:19.**

TURNSTILES.

Fraudulent operation, **266:75A, 266:75B.**

TURPENTINE.

Adulteration, **94:289.**

TURPENTINE —Cont'd

Fines and penalties, **94:289, 94:294.**

Inspection, **94:293, 94:294.**

Manufacture and sale of, **94:289.**

Possession as prima facie evidence of violations, **94:292.**

TWELVE MONTH SCHOOL YEAR PLAN.

Adoption by cities and towns, **71:1, 71:4.**

Pupil attendance requirements, **76:1.**

TWINE.

Automatic sprinklers in buildings for manufacturing, etc., **148:26.**

TWISTERS.

Police officers equipment, **147:2, 147:8A.**

TWO PLATOON SYSTEM.

Fire departments, adoption, **48:59.**

TWO-THIRDS ATTENDANCE OR VOTE.

Borrowings by districts, **44:8, 44:9.**

Cities.

See CITIES AND TOWNS.

City council, **44:1, 44:33B.**

Constitutional amendment, proposal by Congress, **US Const Art 5.**

Disability to hold office, removal of, **US Const Amend 14 Sec 3.**

Eminent domain, **40:14.**

Expulsion of member of Congress, **US Const Art 1 Sec 5 cl 2.**

Fraternal benefit societies.

Consolidation or merger, **176:7.**

Conversion to mutual life company, **176:8.**

Impeachment, conviction on, **US Const Art 1 Sec 3 cl 6.**

Mayor's veto, overriding, **39:4.**

Municipal finance.

See MUNICIPAL FINANCE.

Park commissioner, removal, **45:2.**

President elected by House of Representatives, **US Const Amend 12.**

Town meetings, **39:15.**

Transfer of appropriations, **44:33B.**

Treaties, ratification by Senate, **US Const Art 2 Sec 2 cl 2.**

Veto by President, passing bill over, **US Const Art 1 Sec 7 cl 2.**

TWO-THIRDS ATTENDANCE OR VOTE —Cont'd
Vice-President elected by Senate, **US Const Amend 12.**

TWO-WAY MIRRORS.
Clothing store dressing rooms, **93:89.**

TWO-WITNESS RULE.
See **WITNESSES.**

TYING-IN AGREEMENTS.
See **RESTRAINTS OF TRADE AND MONOPOLIES.**

TYNGSBOROUGH.
Congressional district, **57:1.**
District court, **218:1.**
Medical examiner district, **38:1.**
Senatorial district, **57:3.**

U

ULCERATIVE COLITIS.
Health insurance coverage, **32A:17A, 175:47I, 176A:8L, 176B:4K, 176B:4L, 176G:4D.**

ULMUS AMERICANA.
State tree, **2:8.**

ULTRASONIC NEBULIZERS.
Sales tax exemptions, **64H:6.**

ULTRAVIOLET RADIATION.
Tanning facilities.
See **TANNING FACILITIES.**

ULTRA VIRES ACTS.
Insurance companies.
Merger of insurance company with foreign corporation, **175:193.**
Proceedings against insurance companies, **175:6.**

UMPIRES.
Bribery, **268:13, 268:14.**

UNAUTHORIZED INSURERS PROCESS ACT, 175B:1 et seq.

UNBORN CHILDREN.
See **CHILDREN AND MINORS.**

UNCLAIMED OR ABANDONED PROPERTY, 134:1, 135:1 et seq., 200A:1 et seq.
See **ABANDONED, LOST, AND UNCLAIMED PROPERTY.**

UNCLES AND AUNTS.
Adoption of aunt or uncle, **210:1.**
Annual recognition day, **6:12T.**
Federal service personnel absent voting law, definitions, **54:103B.**

UNCLES AND AUNTS —Cont'd
Funeral of, prisoner's permission to attend, **127:90A.**
Marriages between, **207:2.**
Small estates, decedent's relatives authorized to administer, **195:16.**

UNCOLLECTIBLE TAXES.
See **TAX COLLECTORS.**

UNCONSCIONABLE CONTRACT OR CLAUSE.
Commercial Code sales, **106:2-302.**
Real estate time-shares, **183B:5.**

UNDECLARED WARS.
Action or suit on behalf of Commonwealth inhabitants compelled to serve, **Spec L 33:2.**
Attorney general to bring action on behalf of Commonwealth Inhabitants, **Spec L 33:2.**
Class action, **Spec L 33:2.**
Federal court jurisdiction, **Spec L 33:2.**
Foreign countries protection against service, **Spec L 33:2.**
Service in military forces by Commonwealth inhabitants in event, **Spec L 33:1.**
War powers clause, **Spec L 33:2.**

UNDERGROUND CONDUITS.
Gas and electric companies, **166:22A.**
See **GAS AND ELECTRIC COMPANIES.**
Tunnels.
See **TUNNELS.**

UNDERGROUND STORAGE TANK PETROLEUM PRODUCT CLEANUP FUND.
Administration and finance secretary.
Majority vote of board authorizing payments, **21J:6.**
Negligence, **21J:10.**
Appeal and review.
Certiorari, **21J:11.**
Review board, **21J:8.**
Waiver of appeal, **21J:9.**
Certiorari, **21J:11.**
Deductible, **21J:5.**
Definitions, **21J:1.**
Delay of reimbursement, **21J:3.**
Eligibility for reimbursement, **21J:9.**
Environmental protection department.
Funds, **21J:4.**

UNDERGROUND STORAGE TANK PETROLEUM PRODUCT CLEANUP FUND —Cont'd
Environmental protection department —Cont'd
Review board, membership, **21J:8.**
Fees, **21J:2.**
Fines and penalties, **21J:13.**
Gifts, grants, and gratuities, **21J:4, 29:2S.**
Interest on money, **21J:4.**
Invoices.
Copies open for public inspection, **21J:7.**
Exchange statement not considered invoice, **21J:1.**
Massachusetts Petroleum Council, underground storage tank petroleum product cleanup fund administrative review board, **21J:8.**
Purpose of fund, **21J:4.**
Reports.
Monthly report submitted by Public Safety Department, **21J:2.**
Penalty for late filing, **21J:12.**
Review board, **21J:8.**
Removal or replacement of fuel storage tanks, **148:37A.**
Testing, **21J:4, 148:37A.**
Third party recovery, **21J:3, 21J:4, 21J:9.**
Waiver.
Appeal, **21J:9.**
Penalties, **21J:12.**

UNDERGROUND TANKS.
Agriculture.
See **AGRICULTURE.**
Cleanup.
See **UNDERGROUND STORAGE TANK PETROLEUM PRODUCT CLEANUP FUND.**
Discharge.
Release. See within this heading, "Release."
Examination.
Inspection. See within this heading, "Inspection."
Fines and penalties.
Fires and fire prevention, **148:38H.**
Underground storage tank petroleum product cleanup fund.
See **UNDERGROUND STORAGE TANK PETROLEUM PRODUCT CLEANUP FUND.**

UNDERGROUND TANKS
—Cont'd
Fire marshals.
See FIRE MARSHALS.
Fires.
See FIRES AND FIRE
PREVENTION.
Gifts, grants, and gratuities.
Fires and fire prevention,
148:38D.
Underground storage tank
petroleum product cleanup
fund, **21J:4, 29:2S.**
Inspection.
Fires and fire prevention,
148:38F.
Testing. See within this heading,
"Testing."
Underground storage tank
petroleum product cleanup
fund, public inspection of
invoices, **21J:7.**
Massachusetts Petroleum Council,
underground storage tank
petroleum product cleanup
fund administrative review
board, **21J:8.**
Permit, **148:37.**
Property damage.
Fires and fire prevention,
148:38E.
Underground storage tank
petroleum product cleanup
fund.
See UNDERGROUND
STORAGE TANK
PETROLEUM PRODUCT
CLEANUP FUND.
Release.
Defined, **148:38B.**
Underground storage tank
petroleum product cleanup
fund.
See UNDERGROUND
STORAGE TANK
PETROLEUM PRODUCT
CLEANUP FUND.
Removal.
See FIRES AND FIRE
PREVENTION.
Reports.
Fires and fire prevention,
reporting releases from
tanks, **148:38E.**
Underground storage tank
petroleum product cleanup
fund.
See UNDERGROUND
STORAGE TANK
PETROLEUM PRODUCT
CLEANUP FUND.

UNDERGROUND TANKS
—Cont'd
Testing.
Fires and fire prevention,
148:38E.
Underground storage tank
petroleum product cleanup
fund, **21J:4, 148:37A.**
Third party recovery.
Fires and fire prevention,
148:38E.
Underground storage tank
petroleum product cleanup
fund, **21J:3, 21J:4, 21J:9.**
Underground storage tank
petroleum product cleanup
fund.
See UNDERGROUND
STORAGE TANK
PETROLEUM PRODUCT
CLEANUP FUND.

UNDER PROTEST.
Reservation of rights under
Commercial Code by use of
term, **106:1-207.**

UNDERTAKERS.
**See EMBALMERS AND
FUNERAL DIRECTORS.**

UNDERTAKINGS.
**See BONDS AND
UNDERTAKINGS.**

UNDERVALUATION.
Tax assessors, penalty for
undervaluation, **41:30.**

**UNDERWATER
ARCHAEOLOGICAL
RESOURCES BOARD,
6:179, 6:180.**
Metropolitan district commission,
cooperation in salvage of
resources, **92:72.**
Preservation of resources, **91:63.**

UNDERWEIGHT CHILDREN.
Town appropriations for care, **40:5.**

UNDERWRITERS.
See INSURANCE.

**UNDILUTED LIQUEFIED
PETROLEUM GAS
INSTALLER.**
Fees, licensing and examination,
142:1, 142:5.

UNDIVIDED EARNINGS.
Credit unions.
See CREDIT UNIONS.

UNDUE HARDSHIP.
Defined under fair labor practices
law, **151B:4.**

UNDUE INFLUENCE.
See COERCION AND DURESS.

UNEARNED PREMIUMS.
See INSURANCE.

UNEMPLOYMENT.
Compensation for unemployed
persons, **151A:48-151A:57.**
See EMPLOYMENT
SECURITY.
Economic assistance coordinating
council, **23A:3A, 23A:3D.**
Preference by state purchasing
agent to localities having,
7:22.
Town appropriations for
unemployment projects, **40:5.**

**UNEMPLOYMENT
COMPENSATION ACT,
151A:1 et seq.**

**UNFAIR COMPETITION, 93:14
et seq.**
**See UNFAIR OR DECEPTIVE
TRADE PRACTICES.**

**UNFAIR EDUCATIONAL
PRACTICES, 151C:1-151C:5.**
**See FAIR EDUCATIONAL
PRACTICES.**

**UNFAIR EMPLOYMENT
PRACTICES,
149:24A-149:24J, 149:43,
149:105A-149:105D,
151B:1-151B:10.**
**See FAIR EMPLOYMENT
PRACTICES.**

**UNFAIR INSURANCE
PRACTICES,
176D:1-176D:14.**
See INSURANCE.

**UNFAIR LABOR PRACTICES,
150A:4, 150A:4A, 150A:4B.**
**See LABOR RELATIONS AND
DISPUTES.**

**UNFAIR OR DECEPTIVE
TRADE PRACTICES, 93:14
et seq.**
Antitrust laws.
See RESTRAINTS OF TRADE
AND MONOPOLIES.
Assurance of discontinuance,
acceptance in lieu of judicial
proceedings, **93A:5.**
Attorney General's duties as to
unfair competition, **12:10,
93A:2, 93A:4.**
Bank consumer transactions,
167:2A-167:2G.
Bids.
See BIDS AND BIDDING.

UNFAIR OR DECEPTIVE TRADE PRACTICES
—Cont'd

Burden of proof, transactions and actions occurring primarily within Commonwealth, **93A:11.**

Collection agencies, violation of certain provisions regarding, **93:28, 93:49.**

Competition, **93:14 et seq.**

Consumers and consumer protection, **93A:2, 93A:4-93A:6, 93A:11.**
See CONSUMERS AND CONSUMER PROTECTION.

Credit bureaus.
Failure to disclose data to subject of credit report, **93:49A.**
Judgments or decrees in consumer actions involving to be sent to attorney general, **93A:10.**
Noncompliance with regulatory act, **93:68.**

Damages, **93A:9, 93A:11.**

Declaration of unlawfulness, **93A:2.**

Dentists, deceptive advertising, **112:52A.**

Employment practices.
See FAIR EMPLOYMENT PRACTICES.

Eyeglasses, sale, **112:73A.**

Firearms and weapons.
Sale without functioning safety lock, **140:131K.**

Gasoline dealers' agreements, regulation, **93E:5, 93E:5A.**

Health spa contracts, **93:84.**

Hearing aids, deceptive practices in sale, **93:75.**

Injunctions.
See INJUNCTIONS.

Insurance, **176D:1-176D:14.**
See INSURANCE.

Manufactured homes and manufactured housing communities, **140:32L, 140:32M.**

Milk, prohibited practices in sale and distribution, **94A:14.**

Motion picture distributions, **93F:1-93F:4.**
See MOTION PICTURE DISTRIBUTION BUSINESS PRACTICES.

UNFAIR OR DECEPTIVE TRADE PRACTICES
—Cont'd

Motor vehicle manufacturers, distributors, and dealers, business practices between, **93B:3, 93B:4.**
See MOTOR VEHICLES.

Notice of proceedings to restrain, **93A:4.**

Ophthalmic goods, regulation of advertisement, **112:73A.**

Personal service contracts, failure to give notice to beneficiary of right of termination as unfair and deceptive practice, **255:13K.**

Price cutting to meet competition, Unfair Sales Act as applicable, **93:14G.**

Proceedings to restrain, notice of, **93A:4.**

Public works, bidding on contracts for, **149:44A-149:44J.**
See BIDS AND BIDDING.

Real estate time-shares, **183B:49.**

Restraints of trade.
See RESTRAINTS OF TRADE AND MONOPOLIES.

Sales, unfair practices in, **93:14E-93:14K.**
See UNFAIR SALES ACT.

Self-storage facilities, violation of provisions regarding, **105A:8.**

Trademark or tradename infringement, **110B:10-110B:13.**

Truck dealers as exempt from regulation, **93B:4.**

Viatical settlements, **175:222.**

UNFAIR SALES ACT, 93:14E-93:14K, 93:14E et seq.

Alcoholic liquor license, violation as ground for suspension, **138:23A.**

Cartage as part of cost, **93:14E.**

Charitable purposes, inapplicability to sales, **93:14G.**

Citation, form, **93:14K.**

Clearance sales, inapplicability, **93:14G.**

Combinations of two or more items, **93:14E.**

Competition, price cutting to meet, **93:14G.**

Conflict with other acts, **93:14I.**

Cost to retailer or wholesaler defined, **93:14E.**

UNFAIR SALES ACT —Cont'd

Court, inapplicability to sales by order, **93:14G.**

Damaged merchandise, inapplicability of sale, **93:14G.**

Definitions, **93:14E.**

Discontinued line, **93:14G.**

Enforcement of provisions, **93:14H.**

Evidence of unlawful intent, advertisement, offer to sell, or sale, **93:14F.**

Excepted sales, **93:14G.**

Fines and penalties for violation, **93:14F.**

Freight charges as part of cost, **93:14E.**

Gasoline.
See GASOLINE AND MOTOR FUELS.

Governmental agency or subdivision, inapplicability to sales, **93:14G.**

Imperfect merchandise, inapplicability of sale, **93:14G.**

Injunction to enforce, **93:14H.**

Isolated transactions, **93:14G.**

Judicial sales, act inapplicable, **93:14G.**

Liquidation sales, inapplicability, **93:14G.**

Marked down merchandise, applicability, **93:14G.**

Mark-up, permissible maximum, **93:14E.**

Motor fuel retail sales, **94:295P-94:295W.**

Motor vehicles, **94:295P et seq.**

Order of court, act as inapplicable to sales, **93:14G.**

Partial invalidity, severability clause, **93:14J.**

Perishable merchandise, sale, **93:14G.**

Relief agencies, inapplicability to sales, **93:14G.**

Replacement cost, basis for computing, **93:14E.**

Retailer defined, **93:14E.**

Retail sale defined, **93:14E.**

Sales at wholesale defined, **93:14E.**

Title retaining sale, **93:14E.**

Wholesaler defined, **93:14E.**

UNFAIR SALES ACT FOR THE RETAIL SALE OF MOTOR FUELS, 94:295P et seq.

UNFINISHED GOODS.
Seller's rights upon breach of sales contracts, **106:2-704.**

UNIDENTIFIED OR UNCLAIMED BODIES.
Medical examiners.
See MEDICAL EXAMINERS AND INQUESTS.

UNIFIED MEDIA SPECIALISTS.
Certificates, granting or denial, 71:38G.

UNIFORM ACKNOWLEDGMENT ACT, 183:30, 183:31, 183:33, 183:41, 183:42.

UNIFORM ACTS OR LAWS.
Acknowledgment act, 183:30-183:33, 183:41, 183:42.
Adjudicatory procedure rules, 30A:10.
Aircraft financial responsibility act.
See AIRCRAFT FINANCIAL RESPONSIBILITY ACT.
Arbitration act, 251:1 et seq.
See ARBITRATION.
Arrests on fresh pursuit, 276:10A-276:10D.
Attorney General.
Commissioner of uniform sate laws as within department, 12:11B.
Criminal proceedings instituted under Uniform Securities Act, 110A:409.
Bank deposits and collections, 106:4-101 to 106:4-504.
See BANKS AND BANKING.
Bills of lading, 106:7-101 to 106:7-105, 106:7-301 to 106:7-603, 108:42 et seq.
See BILLS OF LADING.
Board of commissioners, 6:26-6:28, 12:11B.
Children or minors.
Transfers to minors, 201A:1 to 201A:24.
See TRANSFERS TO MINORS.
Civil motor vehicle infractions rules.
See CIVIL MOTOR VEHICLE INFRACTIONS, UNIFORM RULES ON.
Commercial code.
Bank deposits and collections, 106:4-101 to 106:4-504.
See BANKS AND BANKING.
Generally, 106:1 et seq.
See COMMERCIAL CODE.
Negotiable instruments, 106:3-101 to 106:3-605.
See NEGOTIABLE INSTRUMENTS.

UNIFORM ACTS OR LAWS
—Cont'd
Commissioners on uniform state laws, 6:26 et seq., 12:11B.
Employment dislocations and assistance in reemployment of dislocated workers, 6:17.
Common trust funds act, 203A:1 et seq.
See TRUSTS AND TRUSTEES.
Contribution among tortfeasors act, 231B:1 et seq.
See CONTRIBUTIONS.
Criminal extradition act, 276:11 et seq.
Criminal interstate rendition act, 276:11 et seq.
Criminal witnesses from other states, 233:13A-233:13D.
Custodial trust act, 203B:1 to 203B:18.
See UNIFORM CUSTODIAL TRUST ACT.
Declaratory judgments act, 231A:1 et seq.
See DECLARATORY JUDGMENTS.
Desertion and nonsupport act, 273:1 et seq.
Durable power of attorney act, 201B:1-7.
Extradition.
See EXTRADITION.
Foreign executed wills act, 191:5.
Foreign money judgments recognition act, 235:23A.
Fraudulent conveyances, 109A:1 et seq.
See FRAUDULENT CONVEYANCES OR TRANSFERS.
Gifts to minors.
Uniform transfers to minors act, 201A:1 to 201A:24.
See TRANSFERS TO MINORS.
Impoundment procedure rules.
See IMPOUNDMENT PROCEDURE, UNIFORM RULES ON.
Insurance.
See INSURANCE.
Insurers liquidation act, 175:180A et seq.
Interstate and international procedure act, 223A:1-223A:11.
Interstate cooperation commission, commissioners as members, 9:21.
Interstate family support, 209D:1 to 209D:101.

UNIFORM ACTS OR LAWS
—Cont'd
Limited partnerships.
See LIMITED PARTNERSHIPS.
Magistrate rules.
See MAGISTRATES, UNIFORM RULES.
Management of institutional funds act, 180A:1 et seq.
See INSTITUTIONAL FUND MANAGEMENT.
Marriage evasion act, 207:10-207:13, 207:50.
See MARRIAGE.
Motor vehicle certificate of title and antitheft act, 90D:1 et seq.
Negotiable instruments, 106:3-101 to 106:3-605.
See NEGOTIABLE INSTRUMENTS.
Operation of commercial motor vehicles.
See UNIFORM OPERATION OF COMMERCIAL MOTOR VEHICLES.
Partnership act, 108A:1 et seq.
See PARTNERSHIPS.
Photographic copies of business and public records as evidence act, 233:79E.
Procurement.
See UNIFORM PROCUREMENT ACT.
Reciprocal enforcement of support act.
See RECIPROCAL ENFORCEMENT OF SUPPORT ACT.
Securities Act, 110A:101-110A:417.
See SECURITIES ACT.
Simultaneous death act, 190A:1 et seq.
Small claims rules.
See SMALL CLAIMS, UNIFORM RULES.
Statutory Wills Act, 191B:1 to 191B:15.
See WILLS.
Subpoenas to court officials rules.
See SUBPOENAS TO COURT OFFICIALS, UNIFORM RULES OF.
Substitute care review hearings rules.
See SUBSTITUTE CARE REVIEW HEARINGS, UNIFORM RULES FOR.

UNIFORM ACTS OR LAWS
—Cont'd

Transfer on death security registration, **201E:101 to 201E:402.**

  See TRANSFER ON DEATH SECURITY REGISTRATION.

Transfers to minors, **201A:1 et seq.**

  See TRANSFERS TO MINORS, **201A:1 to 201A:24.**

Warehouse receipts act, **106:7-101 to 106:7-603.**

  See WAREHOUSE RECEIPTS.

Wills.

  See WILLS.

Witnesses in criminal proceedings, securing attendance from other states, **233:13A-233:13D.**

UNIFORM ACT TO SECURE THE ATTENDANCE OF WITNESSES FROM WITHOUT A STATE IN CRIMINAL PROCEEDINGS, 233:13A et seq.

UNIFORM CUSTODIAL TRUST ACT, 203B:1 et seq.

Acceptance and receipt by custodial trustee, **203B:4.**

Accounts and accounting, **203B:15, 203B:16.**

Contracts, **203B:12.**

Creation, **203B:2.**

Definitions, **203B:1.**

Description of trust property, **203B:15.**

Designation of beneficiaries, **203B:3.**

Forms, **203B:4, 203B:18.**

Guardian, defined, **203B:1.**

Incapacity of beneficiary, **203B:9, 203B:10.**

Multiple beneficiaries, **203B:6.**

Notice of declination to serve as trustee, **203B:13.**

Recordation, **203B:7.**

Reimbursement, **203B:14.**

Removal of trustee, **203B:15.**

Resignation of trustee, **203B:13.**

Rights and powers, **203B:8.**

Surviving spouse, **203B:6.**

Termination of trust, **203B:17.**

Third persons, **203B:11, 203B:12.**

Trust companies, **203B:1, 203B:5.**

UNIFORMED AND OVERSEAS CITIZENS ABSENTEE VOTING ACT, 54:95.

UNIFORM OPERATION OF COMMERCIAL MOTOR VEHICLES.

Address.

  Name or address. See within this heading, "Name or address."

Alcohol concentration defined, **90F:1.**

Alcoholic liquors.

  Definitions, **90F:1.**

  Driving while under influence of alcohol or drugs. See within this heading, "Driving while under influence of alcohol or drugs."

Application, commercial driver license, **90F:3, 90F:7, 90F:8.**

Blood, breath, or urine tests.

  Alcohol concentration defined, **90F:1.**

  Assumed consent, **90F:11.**

  Definitions, **90F:1.**

  Fines and penalties, **90F:10.**

  Percentage of alcohol in system, **90F:9-90F:11.**

  Refusal to take test, **90F:10, 90F:11.**

  Report by law enforcement officer of results or refusals, **90F:11.**

Certificates and certification.

  Application for commercial driver license, **90F:3, 90F:7.**

  Previous employment, certification of information, **90F:3.**

Change of name or address, **90F:7.**

Class "C" driver license, **90F:6.**

Classification of licenses, **90F:8.**

Commerce defined, **90F:1.**

Commercial driver license application, **90F:3, 90F:7.**

Commercial driver license system (CDLIS) defined, **90F:1.**

Commercial motor vehicle defined, **90F:1.**

Concentration of alcohol or drugs in system.

  Blood, breath or urine tests. See within this heading, "Blood, breath, or urine tests."

Consent.

  Driving record, consent by commercial driver license applicant to release information, **90F:7.**

  Drug and alcohol testing, assumed consent, **90F:11.**

Controlled substances.

  Alcoholic liquors. See within this heading, "Alcoholic liquors."

UNIFORM OPERATION OF COMMERCIAL MOTOR VEHICLES —Cont'd

Controlled substances —Cont'd

  Defined, **90F:1.**

Conviction of crime.

  Definitions, **90F:1.**

  Fines and penalties. See within this heading, "Fines and penalties."

  Foreign jurisdiction, notification, **90F:3, 90F:4, 90F:8, 90F:9, 90F:12.**

  Notification, **90F:3, 90F:4, 90F:8, 90F:9, 90F:12.**

  Traffic violations.

    Fines and penalties. See within this heading, "Fines and penalties."

    Nonresident licenseholder, notification of licensing authority, **90F:12.**

    Notification of employer and licensing authority, **90F:3, 90F:12.**

    Serious traffic violation defined, **90F:1.**

Crimes and offenses.

  Conviction of crime. See within this heading, "Conviction of crime."

  Felony. See within this heading, "Felony."

  Fines and penalties. See within this heading, "Fines and penalties."

  Second or subsequent offenses. See within this heading, "Second or subsequent offenses."

Definitions, **90F:1.**

Description or identification of licensee, **90F:7, 90F:8.**

Disqualification of driver, **90F:10, 90F:11.**

  Defined, **90F:1.**

  Hearing on driver disqualification, **90F:11.**

  License or learner's permit, issuance during disqualification, **90F:6.**

  Lifetime disqualification, **90F:9, 90F:11.**

  Notification to employer and registrar of motor vehicles, **90F:3, 90F:4.**

  Operation in violation, **90F:5, 90F:9.**

  Out-of-service order. See within this heading, "Out-of-service order."

UNIFORM OPERATION OF COMMERCIAL MOTOR VEHICLES —Cont'd

Disqualification of driver —Cont'd
  Penalty for violations, **90F:5, 90F:9.**
Domicile and residence.
  Address change, commercial vehicle license, **90F:7.**
  Foreign jurisdiction. See within this heading, "Foreign jurisdiction."
  Nonresidents. See within this heading, "Nonresidents."
  Residency requirement, commercial driver license, **90F:6.**
Drivers' license, **90F:1-90F:16.**
Driving record of licensee or applicant, **90F:7-90F:9, 90F:13.**
Driving while under influence of alcohol or drugs, **90F:9-90F:11, 159B:14.**
  Assumed consent, drug and alcohol testing, **90F:11.**
  Blood, breath, or urine tests. See within this heading, "Blood, breath, or urine tests."
  Disqualification of driver. See within this heading, "Disqualification of driver."
  Fines and penalties, **90F:9, 90F:10.**
  Hazardous materials, transporting, **90F:11.**
  Penalties, **90F:9, 90F:10.**
  Suspension from driving commercial vehicle, **90F:11.**
Electronic records and transmissions, **90F:8.**
Employer and employee.
  Conviction of crime, notification of employer and licensing authority, **90F:3, 90F:12.**
  Defined, **90F:1.**
  Disqualification of driver, notification to employer and registrar of motor vehicles, **90F:3, 90F:4.**
  Driving records, release of information to employer, **90F:13.**
  Notification, required, to employer, **90F:3, 90F:4.**
  Previous employment, verification, **90F:3.**
  Traffic violation convictions, notification of employer, **90F:3.**
Endorsements.
  Hazardous materials endorsement, **90F:8.**

UNIFORM OPERATION OF COMMERCIAL MOTOR VEHICLES —Cont'd

Endorsements —Cont'd
  Listing on license, **90F:8.**
  Testing and examination, **90F:6.**
Enforcement, **90F:14, 90F:15.**
Examinations.
  Tests and examinations. See within this heading, "Tests and examinations."
Expiration of commercial driver license, **90F:8.**
Fee for driving record information, **90F:13.**
Felony.
  Commercial motor vehicle, use in commission of felony, **90F:9.**
  Defined, **90F:1.**
Fines and penalties, **90F:9.**
  Blood, breath, or urine test, refusal, **90F:10.**
  Disqualification of driver. See within this heading, "Disqualification of driver."
  Driving while under influence of alcohol or drugs, **90F:9, 90F:10.**
  Hazardous materials, **90F:9.**
  Out-of-service order. See within this heading, "Out-of-service order."
  Revocation or suspension. See within this heading, "Revocation or suspension."
  Second or subsequent offenses, **90F:9.**
Foreign jurisdiction.
  Conviction of nonresident licenseholder, notification of licensing authority, **90F:8, 90F:9, 90F:12.**
  Defined, **90F:1.**
  Driving records, release of information, **90F:13.**
  Licensing authority, notification of conviction or license revocation or suspension, **90F:3, 90F:4, 90F:8, 90F:9, 90F:12.**
  Multiple licenses, **90F:2, 90F:4, 90F:6.**
  Notification of convictions or license revocation or suspension, **90F:3, 90F:4, 90F:8, 90F:9, 90F:12.**
  Reinstatement of license, **90F:8.**
  Resident operating under license issued, **90F:7.**
  Suspension or revocation of nonresident license, **90F:6, 90F:8, 90F:9, 90F:12.**

UNIFORM OPERATION OF COMMERCIAL MOTOR VEHICLES —Cont'd

Gross vehicle weight rating (GVWR) defined, **90F:1.**
Hazardous materials.
  Defined, **90F:1.**
  Endorsement, commercial driver license, **90F:8.**
  Out-of-service order, **90F:1, 90F:9.**
  Penalty for violations, **90F:9.**
  Tests and examinations, **90F:8, 90F:11.**
  Transporting, driver's refusal to submit to alcohol or drug testing, **90F:11.**
Hearing on driver disqualification, **90F:11.**
Identity or description of licensee, **90F:7, 90F:8.**
Information.
  Records and reports. See within this heading, "Records and reports."
Insurers, access to driving record information, **90F:13.**
Jurisdiction.
  Foreign jurisdiction. See within this heading, "Foreign jurisdiction."
Knowledge and skill of licensee or applicant, **90F:6, 90F:8.**
Learner's permit, **90F:6.**
  Application, **90F:7.**
  Defined, **90F:1.**
  Disqualification of driver, issuance of learner's permit during, **90F:6.**
  Exception to operator's license requirement, **90F:5.**
  Persons holding valid Class "D" driver's license, **90F:6.**
Leaving scene of accident, **90F:9.**
Licenses and permits, **90F:1-90F:16.**
  Address change, commercial vehicle license, **90F:7.**
  Authority.
    Licensing authority. See within this heading, "Licensing authority."
  Class "C" driver license, **90F:6.**
  Classification of licenses, **90F:8.**
  Consent by commercial driver license applicant to release information, **90F:7.**
  Conviction of crime, notification of licensing authority, **90F:12.**
  Definitions, **90F:1.**

UNIFORM OPERATION OF COMMERCIAL MOTOR VEHICLES —Cont'd

Licenses and permits —Cont'd
Disqualification, issuance of license during, **90F:6.**
Expiration of commercial driver license, **90F:8.**
Foreign jurisdiction. See within this heading, "Foreign jurisdiction."
Hazardous materials, transportation, **90F:8.**
Identity or description of licensee, **90F:7, 90F:8.**
Learner's permit. See within this heading, "Learner's permit."
Multiple licenses, **90F:2, 90F:4, 90F:6.**
Name and address of previous employers required on commercial driver license application, **90F:3.**
Out-of-state licenses.
Nonresidents. See within this heading, "Nonresidents."
Record of licensee or applicant, **90F:7-90F:9, 90F:13.**
Renewal of commercial driver license, **90F:8.**
Residency requirement, commercial driver license, **90F:6.**
Restrictions to license, **90F:8.**
Revocation or suspension. See within this heading, "Revocation or suspension."
Suspension.
Revocation or suspension. See within this heading, "Revocation or suspension."
Licensing authority.
Foreign jurisdiction. See within this heading, "Foreign jurisdiction."
Registrar of motor vehicles. See within this heading, "Registrar of motor vehicles."
Lifetime disqualification, **90F:9, 90F:11.**
Motor vehicle defined, **90F:1.**
Multiple licenses, **90F:2, 90F:4, 90F:6.**
Name or address.
Application, commercial driver license, **90F:3, 90F:8.**
Change in name or address, **90F:7.**

UNIFORM OPERATION OF COMMERCIAL MOTOR VEHICLES —Cont'd

Name or address —Cont'd
Previous employers, **90F:3.**
National driver register, **90F:8.**
Nonresident CDL defined, **90F:1.**
Nonresidents.
Conviction of nonresident licenseholder, notification of licensing authority, **90F:12.**
Definitions, **90F:1.**
Foreign jurisdiction. See within this heading, "Foreign jurisdiction."
Multiple licenses, **90F:2, 90F:4, 90F:6.**
Residency requirement for commercial driver license, **90F:6.**
Suspension or revocation of nonresident driver license, **90F:6, 90F:8, 90F:9, 90F:12.**
Notice and notification.
Conviction, notification, **90F:3, 90F:4, 90F:8, 90F:9, 90F:12.**
Electronic records and transmissions, **90F:8.**
Employer, notification of conviction or license suspension or revocation, **90F:3, 90F:4.**
Foreign jurisdiction, **90F:3, 90F:4, 90F:8, 90F:9, 90F:12.**
Information system, commercial driver license, **90F:8.**
Registrar of motor vehicles, notification, **90F:3, 90F:4, 90F:12.**
Revocation or suspension, **90F:3, 90F:4, 90F:8, 90F:9, 90F:12.**
Oath or affirmation, sworn report of law enforcement officer results of blood, breath or urine test, **90F:11.**
Operate defined, **90F:1.**
Operator defined, **90F:1.**
Orders.
Out-of-service order. See within this heading, "Out-of-service order."
Out-of-service order, **90F:1, 90F:9, 90F:10.**
Defined, **90F:1.**
Operation in violation, **90F:5.**
Out-of-state licenses.
Nonresidents. See within this heading, "Nonresidents."

UNIFORM OPERATION OF COMMERCIAL MOTOR VEHICLES —Cont'd

Penalties.
Fines and penalties. See within this heading, "Fines and penalties."
Permits.
Licenses and permits. See within this heading, "Licenses and permits."
Photograph of licensee or applicant, **90F:7, 90F:8.**
Police.
Blood, breath, or urine tests. See within this heading, "Blood, breath, or urine tests."
Previous employment, verification, **90F:3.**
Qualification.
Disqualification of driver. See within this heading, "Disqualification of driver."
Recidivists.
Second or subsequent offenses. See within this heading, "Second or subsequent offenses."
Records and reports.
Alcohol and drug testing, report by law enforcement officers of results or refusals, **90F:11.**
Applicant or licensee, driving record, **90F:7-90F:9, 90F:13.**
Consent by commercial driver license applicant to release driving record information, **90F:7.**
Electronic records and transmissions, **90F:8.**
Employer, release of driving record information, **90F:13.**
Fee for driving record information, **90F:13.**
Foreign jurisdiction, release of driving record information, **90F:13.**
Information system, commercial driver licenses, **90F:8.**
Insurers, access to driving record information, **90F:13.**
Oath or affirmation, sworn report of law enforcement officer results of blood, breath or urine test, **90F:11.**
Previous employment, certification of information, **90F:3.**
Suspension or revocation of nonresident operator, **90F:9.**

UNIFORM OPERATION OF COMMERCIAL MOTOR VEHICLES —Cont'd

Reduction of lifetime disqualification, **90F:9.**

Refusal to take blood, breath, or urine test, **90F:10, 90F:11.**

Registrar of motor vehicles, **90F:14, 90F:15.**

Defined, **90F:1.**

Notification, **90F:3, 90F:4, 90F:12.**

Registration, name and address of previous employers required on commercial driver license application, **90F:3.**

Registry of motor vehicles, electronic record as official record, **90F:8.**

Reinstatement of commercial driver license, **90F:8.**

Release of information, **90F:7, 90F:13.**

Renewal of commercial driver license, **90F:8.**

Reports.

Records and reports. See within this heading, "Records and reports."

Residence.

Domicile and residence. See within this heading, "Domicile and residence."

Restrictions to license, **90F:8.**

Revocation or suspension.

Foreign jurisdiction, **90F:6, 90F:8, 90F:9, 90F:12.**

Issuance of driver license or learner's permit while license revoked or suspended, **90F:6.**

Nonresident license, **90F:6, 90F:8, 90F:9, 90F:12.**

Notification, **90F:3, 90F:4, 90F:8, 90F:9, 90F:12.**

Operation in violation, **90F:5.**

Rules and regulations, **90F:14.**

Second or subsequent offenses.

Drug or alcohol concentration, refusal to submit to testing, **90F:11.**

Penalties, **90F:9.**

Sentence and punishment.

Fines and penalties. See within this heading, "Fines and penalties."

Serious traffic violation defined, **90F:1.**

Sheriffs and deputies.

Blood, breath or urine tests. See within this heading, "Blood, breath, or urine tests."

UNIFORM OPERATION OF COMMERCIAL MOTOR VEHICLES —Cont'd

State defined, **90F:1.**

Suspension.

Revocation or suspension. See within this heading, "Revocation or suspension."

Tests and examinations.

Blood, breath, or urine tests. See within this heading, "Blood, breath, or urine tests."

Endorsements, **90F:6.**

Hazardous materials, **90F:8, 90F:11.**

Knowledge and skill of licensee or applicant, **90F:6, 90F:8.**

Time or date.

Disqualification period, **90F:9.**

Expiration of commercial driver license, **90F:8.**

Learner's permit, validity period, **90F:6.**

Nonresident licenseholder, notification of conviction or license suspension or revocation, **90F:9, 90F:12.**

Notification of commercial driver license information system of issuance of commercial driver license, **90F:8.**

Out-of-state license, resident operating, **90F:7.**

Revocation or suspension of driver license, notification of employer or licensing authority, **90F:3, 90F:9.**

Traffic violations.

Conviction of crime. See within this heading, "Conviction of crime."

Types of vehicles to be operated, **90F:8.**

Urine test.

Blood, breath, or urine tests. See within this heading, "Blood, breath, or urine tests."

Verification of previous employment, **90F:3.**

Waiver of licensing regulations, **90F:5, 90F:6.**

UNIFORM PROCUREMENT ACT, 30B:1 et seq.

Advertising requirements, **30B:16.**

Amendment or modification of contracts for recycling services, **30B:13A.**

Awarding of contracts, **30B:5, 30B:6.**

Bids for contracts, **30B:5, 30B:6.**

UNIFORM PROCUREMENT ACT —Cont'd

Cancellation of invitation for bids, **30B:9.**

Certification of bids, **30B:10.**

Definitions, **30B:2, 30B:18.**

Delegation of duties by procurement officers, **30B:19.**

Disadvantaged vendors, **30B:18.**

Disposal of supplies or property, **30B:15, 30B:16.**

Division of procurements, **30B:11.**

Emergency procurements, **30B:8.**

Fines and penalties for violations in award of contracts, **30B:17.**

Gas and electric service, **30B:7.**

Increase in quantity of supplies or services, **30B:13.**

Inspection of records by public, **30B:3.**

Library books, contract awarded without bids, **30B:7.**

Notice of invitation for bids, **30B:5, 30B:6.**

Price quotations, necessity, **30B:4.**

Private persons, authority to enter into agreements for services of, **29:29G, 30B:1, 30B:6, 30B:13A.**

Real property, disposal, **30B:16.**

Recordkeeping requirements, **30B:3.**

Recycling, composting, or disposal of solid waste, private persons retained for, **30B:1, 30B:6.**

Sale of excess supplies, **30B:15.**

School textbooks, contract awarded without bids, **30B:7.**

Sewer service, **30B:7.**

Sheltered market programs, **30B:18.**

Telephone service, **30B:7.**

Time or date.

Bids, **30B:5, 30B:6.**

Term of contracts, **30B:12.**

Violations in award of contracts, **30B:17.**

Water services, **30B:7.**

UNIFORMS.

Cheerleaders' uniforms, **71:47.**

City.

Municipal finance. See within this heading, "Municipal finance."

Correctional institution officers and employees, **125:8, 126:9A.**

County penal institutions, officers and employees, **126:9A.**

Court officers, **217:30, 221:80.**

Deputy sheriffs attending certain courts, uniforms paid for by Commonwealth, **221:80.**

UNIFORMS —Cont'd
Education.
Schools and education. See
within this heading,
"Schools and education."
Execution, exemption, **235:34.**
Financing of judicial system,
uniforms as property of
Commonwealth for purpose,
29A:2.
Fire and police departments,
appropriations, **40:6B.**
General Court, uniforms of
sergeant-at-arms and
employees, **3:20A.**
Housing court department, officers,
185C:15.
Metropolitan district commission,
work clothes for certain
employees, **28:4A.**
Militia.
See MILITIA.
Municipal finance.
Cheerleaders, appropriations,
71:47.
Police and fire department,
appropriations, **40:6B.**
Public health nurses, purchase,
40:6K.
Plymouth County probate court
officer, **217:30.**
Police.
See POLICE.
Public health nurses, **40:6K.**
Railroads, caps for employees,
160:177.
Reimbursement of employee for
damage to uniform by patient
in institution, **30:9C.**
Schools and education.
Cheerleaders' uniforms,
payment, **71:47.**
Employees, furnishing of
uniforms, **71:48B.**
Town.
Municipal finance. See
within this heading,
"Municipal finance."
State police, **22C:19.**
Unlawful use, **264:10A.**

UNIFORM STATE LAWS
COMMISSIONER.
See UNIFORM ACTS OR LAWS.

UNINSURED MOTOR
VEHICLES.
See AUTOMOBILE
INSURANCE.

UNION CHILDREN'S HEALTH
CAMPS.
Establishment, **111:62F, 111:62G.**

UNION LABEL.
Wearing apparel and clothing
purchased by state, union
label as evidence of wage and
hour standards, **7:22.**

UNIONS.
Credit unions.
See CREDIT UNIONS.
Labor relations.
See LABOR RELATIONS AND
DISPUTES.
Tenants' union, **186:18, 239:2A.**

UNION VETERAN LEGION.
Insignia, unlawful use, **266:70.**
Uniform, unlawful use, **264:10A.**

UNIQUE GOODS.
Specific performance of contract
for sale, **106:2-716.**

UNITARIAN-UNIVERSALIST
CHURCHES.
Marriages, solemnization, **207:38,**
207:40.
Tax exemption for official
residences of district
executives, **59:5.**

UNITED METHODIST
CHURCH, 59:5, 67:40-67:43,
207:38.
Allowable annual income of trust
property, **67:41.**
Charge conference.
See CHARGE CONFERENCE.
Conveyance of church land
regulated, **68:6.**
Deacons, wardens, or similar
officers.
Bodies corporate, officers of
churches made, **68:1.**
Conveyance of church land
regulated, **68:6.**
Election of officers, **67:42.**
Exemption from taxation of
residence occupied by district
superintendent, **59:5.**
Filing record of organization,
67:43.
Limitation upon income from
property, **67:41.**
Marriage solemnization by
minister, **207:38.**
Name of Methodist Church and
Methodist Episcopal Church
changed, **59:5, 67:40, 68:1,**
68:6.
Officers of churches made bodies
corporate, **68:1.**
Organization, **67:40.**
Trusts and trustees.
Allowable annual trust income,
67:41.

UNITED METHODIST
CHURCH —Cont'd
Trusts and trustees —Cont'd
First meeting, **67:42.**
Powers, **67:41.**
Wardens.
Deacons, wardens, or similar
officers. See within this
heading, "Deacons, wardens,
or similar officers."

UNITED NATIONS.
Annual observance of United
Nations' Day, **6:12N, 40:5.**
Veterans and veterans'
organizations.
Admission to soldiers' home for
service with United Nations
forces, **6:41.**
Flag of United Nations, serving,
115:5.

UNITED SPANISH WAR
VETERANS.
Flag, permissible inscriptions,
264:5.
Headquarters for camp of, power
of city or town to provide,
40:9.
Insignia, unlawful use, **266:70.**
Patriotic holiday observances,
municipal appropriations,
40:5.
Public charities division,
exemption from requirement
of filing copy of charter, **12:8E.**
Uniform, unlawful use, **264:10A.**

UNITED STATES.
See FEDERAL GOVERNMENT
AND STATUTES.

UNITY WAR VETERANS
ASSOCIATIONS.
Provision of headquarters, **40:9.**

UNIVERSAL EMERGENCY
TELEPHONE SERVICE.
Cities and towns, contracts,
166:14A.

UNIVERSITY OF LOWELL.
Annuity contracts for employees,
15:18A.
Building authority.
Inclusion of building authority
employees in retirement
system, **32:2.**
State employees for retirement
or pension purposes,
personnel defined, **32:1.**
Chelsea center for materials reuse,
75:41.
Contracting power of board of
trustees of colleges and
universities, **15C:14A.**

UNIVERSITY OF LOWELL
—Cont'd
Employees.
  Labor and employment. See
    within this heading, "Labor
    and employment."
Free tuition for certain senior
  citizens etc., **70:30R.**
Labor and employment.
  Annuity contracts, **15:18A.**
  Building authority. See within
    this heading, "Building
    authority."
Management, **73:1.**
Officers and employees.
  Labor and employment. See
    within this heading, "Labor
    and employment."
Practice schools in connection with
  state college, agreements,
  73:3.
Retirement systems and pensions.
  Building authority. See within
    this heading, "Building
    authority."
State colleges, agreements as to
  practice schools, **73:3.**
Toxics Use Reduction Institute,
  21I:2, 21I:6, 21I:14, 29:2K.

**UNIVERSITY OF
  MASSACHUSETTS,
  75:1-75:37.**
Accounts, **75:6, 75:10.**
  Expenditures, **75:8.**
Administration by trustees, **75:9.**
Admissions, **75:2.**
Adoption.
  Center for adoption research and
    policy, **75:15A.**
Adulteration of food, investigations
  and experiments, **75:17.**
Agricultural experiment station,
  75:16-75:23.
  Adulteration of food,
    investigations and
    experiments, **75:17.**
  Bulletins of results of
    experiments and
    investigations, **75:19.**
  Commercial fertilizer, collection
    of samples for analysis,
    128:77.
  Cranberry growing, **75:23.**
  Director.
    Appointment, **75:18.**
    Milk and cream testing
      machines, powers and
      duties, **94:25-94:31.**
    Transfer of certain authority
      to commissioner of
      agriculture, **94:1.**

**UNIVERSITY OF
  MASSACHUSETTS** —Cont'd
Agricultural experiment station
  —Cont'd
  Farms and branch stations,
    75:22, 75:23.
  Fertilizers, investigations and
    experiments, **75:17, 128:77.**
  Forage, investigations and
    experiments, **75:17.**
  Insects, investigations and
    experiments, **75:17.**
  Labor of students, **75:22.**
  Market gardening, **75:23.**
  Mastitis, control and
    elimination, **75:16A.**
  Milk testing, **75:16A,
    94:25-94:31.**
  Officers, appointment, **75:18.**
  Poultry investigations and
    experiments, **75:17.**
  Seeds.
    See SEEDS.
  Tobacco growing, **75:23.**
  Trees and plants, investigations
    and experiments, **75:17.**
Agricultural lands preservation
  committee, **132A:11B.**
Agriculture college dean as
  member of committee for
  conservation of soil, water and
  related resources, **21:19.**
Agriculture to be taught, **75:2,
  75:16-75:23.**
Ambulatory care centers, satellite
  clinics, **75:36C.**
Amherst, sale or lease of land in
  town, **75:25, 75:26.**
Analysis of drugs, poisons,
  medicines, and chemicals,
  75:36B, 111:13.
Animal diseases.
  Experiments and investigations,
    75:17.
  Laboratory dealing with diseases
    of domestic animals, **75:16A.**
Annual reports, **75:15, 75:36D.**
Annuities for employees, **15:18A.**
Appliances for agricultural
  experiment station, provision,
  75:18.
Appropriations, **75:8.**
Associations and societies, sale or
  lease of land, **75:25-75:27.**
Audit of accounts, **75:6.**
Authority, delegation, **75:3A.**
Automobiles, control of movement
  and parking, **75:32A.**
Bank branches on grounds, **75:2A.**
Biologic laboratories established,
  75:43.

**UNIVERSITY OF
  MASSACHUSETTS** —Cont'd
Board of trustees.
  Trusts and trustees. See within
    this heading, "Trusts and
    trustees."
Boston, establishment of facilities
  in vicinity, **75:2.**
Branches, **75:2.**
Budget.
  Preparation and submission,
    75:7.
  Reports, **75:14.**
  Separate budget for medical
    school, **75:36.**
Bulletins containing results of
  experiments and
  investigations by experiment
  station, **75:19.**
Bureau of wildlife research and
  management, cooperation,
  21:7H.
Campus council appointed by
  board of trustees, **75:14B.**
Center for adoption research and
  policy, **75:15A.**
Chelsea center for materials reuse,
  75:41.
Childhood vaccines, biologic labs
  established for research,
  development and production
  of, **75:43.**
Civil service status of officers and
  employees, **75:14, 75:24.**
Commercial fertilizer, collection of
  samples for analysis, **128:77.**
Compensation.
  Salaries and wages. See within
    this heading, "Salaries and
    wages."
Comptroller.
  Accounting system for
    university, **75:10.**
  Expenditure of appropriations,
    75:8.
  Personnel report, **75:14.**
Conservation of soil, water, and
  related resources, agriculture
  college dean as member of
  committee, **21:19.**
Consultants and lecturers,
  employment, **75:14.**
Contracting power of board of
  trustees of colleges and
  universities, **15C:14A.**
Contracts, **75:11.**
Copies of personnel reports, **75:14.**
Cranberries, experimental work in
  planting and growing, **75:23.**
Curriculum, **75:2.**

UNIVERSITY OF MASSACHUSETTS —Cont'd

David I. Walsh-Leverett Saltonstall visiting lectureship program, establishment, **75:32B.**

Dead bodies, cremation and disposal of medical school cadavers, **75:36A.**

Deans of schools.
  Agriculture college dean as member of committee for conservation of soil, water and related resources, **21:19.**
  Medical school. See within this heading, "Medical school."

Degrees and diplomas, **75:2, 75:4, 75:12.**

Delegation of authority, **75:3A.**

Diagnostic laboratory dealing with diseases of domestic animals, **75:16A.**

Director of agriculture experiment station.
  Agricultural experiment station. See within this heading, "Agricultural experiment station."

Domestic animals, diseases of.
  Animal diseases. See within this heading, "Animal diseases."

Drugs, poison, medicines and chemicals, analysis, **75:36B, 111:13.**

Educational communications commission, trustees as members, **6:158.**

Education department, university as part, **75:1.**

Election of officers by trustees, **75:14.**

Employees.
  Labor and employment. See within this heading, "Labor and employment."

Endowed chairs established, trust fund, University of Massachusetts, **75:14. (note)**

Environmental business center, **75:39.**

Environmental management department, cooperation, **21:1.**

Environmental technology testing facility, **75:39.**

Environment and ecology.
  Chelsea center for materials reuse, **75:41.**
  Environmental business center, **75:39.**
  Environmental technology testing facility, **75:39.**

UNIVERSITY OF MASSACHUSETTS —Cont'd

Environment and ecology —Cont'd
  Funding for entities, **75:42.**
  Marine technology, environmental and engineering programs at U Mass Dartmouth, **75:40.**
  National environmental technology institute (NETI), **75:38.**

Examination, inspection, or investigation.
  Agricultural experiment station. See within this heading, "Agricultural experiment station."

Audit of accounts, **75:6.**

Medicolegal investigations committee, membership, **6:184.**

Exclusive jurisdiction as agricultural school, **75:2.**

Expenditures, **75:6, 75:8.**

Experiment stations.
  Agricultural experiment station. See within this heading, "Agricultural experiment station."

Extension board of public overseers, **75:14D.**

Faculty tenure.
  Executive sessions of trustees may consider, **75:4.**
  Trustees to establish policy, **75:14.**

Fee for testing.
  Milk in laboratory, **75:16A.**
  Poultry, **75:21.**

Fellowships and scholarships, **75:33.**
  See SCHOLARSHIPS AND FELLOWSHIPS.

Fertilizers, investigations and experiments, **75:17, 128:77.**

Fines and penalties for violating regulations, **75:3, 75:32A.**

Fires, leaves of absence to fight, **75:14.**

Fitness centers, **75:36C.**

Food adulteration, investigations and experiments, **75:17.**

Forage, investigations and experiments, **75:17.**

Forester of state.
  State forester. See within this heading, "State forester."

Forestry.
  Cutting practices, performance of duties, **132:45.**
  Instruction, **75:29, 75:30, 132:1, 132:45.**

UNIVERSITY OF MASSACHUSETTS —Cont'd

Forestry —Cont'd
  State forester. See within this heading, "State forester."
  Trees, investigations, experiments, and tests as to diseases, **75:17, 132:26A.**

Fraternities, sale or lease of land, **75:25-75:27.**

General court.
  See GENERAL COURT.

Gifts, grants or devises, **75:11.**

Gifts or bequests to Research Foundation, **75:14C.**

Governor's council.
  See GOVERNOR'S COUNCIL.

Group annuities for employees, **15:18A.**

Hadley, sale or lease of land, **75:25, 75:26.**

Health care facilities, **75:36C.**

Home health care programs, **75:36C.**

Honorary degrees, executive sessions of trustees to consider, **75:4.**

Injuries sustained in fighting fires as sustained in course of employment, **75:14.**

Insects destructive to vegetation, experiments and investigations as to history and habits, **75:17.**

Inspection.
  Examination, inspection, or investigation. See within this heading, "Examination, inspection, or investigation."

Instruction, regulation, **75:11.**

Instructors.
  Professors and instructors. See within this heading, "Professors and instructors."

Insurance, **75:9.**

Investment of funds, **75:11.**

Labor and employment.
  Annuities, **15:18A.**
  Civil service, employees exempt, **75:24.**
  Classification of employees, **75:14.**
  Faculty tenure. See within this heading, "Faculty tenure."
  Lease or sale of land to employees, **75:26, 75:27.**
  Taxation, **75:28.**
  Lecturers. See within this heading, "Lecturers, employment."
  Officers. See within this heading, "Officers."

UNIVERSITY OF MASSACHUSETTS —Cont'd

Labor and employment —Cont'd

President. See within this heading, "President."

Professors and instructors. See within this heading, "Professors and instructors."

Salaries and wages. See within this heading, "Salaries and wages."

Students employed on experimental farm, **75:22.**

Land.

Real property. See within this heading, "Real property."

Lease of land.

Acquisition of real property, **75:36C.**

Commonwealth land, sale or lease, **75:25-75:27.**

Labor and employment. See within this heading, "Labor and employment."

Taxation, **59:11, 75:28.**

Lecturers, employment, **75:14.**

David I. Walsh-Leverett Saltonstall visiting lectureship program, **75:32B.**

Legal services, student-supported, trust funds, **75:11.**

Long-term care facilities, **75:36C.**

Loss of taxes on land used for, reimbursement, **58:13-58:17A.**

Management of property, **75:11, 75:12.**

Marine technology, environmental and engineering programs at U Mass Dartmouth, **75:40.**

Market gardening, experiment station for practical demonstration, **75:23.**

Mastitis, laboratory to be used for purpose of controlling and eliminating, **75:16A.**

Medical school.

Acquisition of facilities, practices, clinics, and programs, **75:36C.**

Analysis of narcotic drugs, poison, drugs, medicines, or chemicals at University of Massachusetts Medical School, costs, **75:36B.**

Board of trustees, authority of, **75:35, 75:36C.**

Cremation and disposal of dissected bodies, **75:36A.**

Dean, **75:35.**

Medicolegal investigations committee, dean as member, **6:184.**

UNIVERSITY OF MASSACHUSETTS —Cont'd

Medical school —Cont'd

Group practice plan, establishment, **75:34.**

Maintenance and operation, **75:34.**

Mental retardation in children, program to combat, **111:4E.**

Separate budget and forecasts required, **75:36.**

Trustees, board, **75:35.**

Medicolegal investigations committee, membership, **6:184.**

Meetings of trustees, **75:3, 75:4.**

Mental health care programs or facilities, **75:36C.**

Mental retardation in children, program to combat, **111:4E.**

Milk testing, **75:16A, 94:25-94:31.**

Motor vehicles, control of movement and parking, **75:32A.**

Mount Toby state demonstration forest, maintenance and use, **75:29, 75:30.**

National environmental technology institute (NETI), **75:38.**

National Pollution Control Technology Research and Development Institute, **75:132.**

Nature and scope of experimental work with agricultural experiment stations, **75:17.**

Notes, investment of funds, **75:11.**

Notice.

Board of trustees meetings, **75:4.**

Personnel action taken, notice, **75:14.**

Publication. See within this heading, "Publication."

Objects and purpose of University, **75:2.**

Officers.

Agriculture experiment station, appointment, **75:18.**

Election by trustees, **75:14.**

Professional staff and employees, **75:14.**

Trusts and trustees. See within this heading, "Trusts and trustees."

Outpatient diagnostic or treatment centers, **75:36C.**

Payback learning contracts, time for community service payback, **75:36D.**

Physicians practices, **75:36C.**

Plants, experiments and investigations as to the diseases, **75:17.**

UNIVERSITY OF MASSACHUSETTS —Cont'd

Police, **22C:50.**

Poultry, investigation and experiments, **75:17.**

Fee, **75:21.**

President.

Delegation of authority, **75:3A.**

Election, salary, duties and tenure of office, **75:14.**

Personnel, duties, **75:14.**

Professors and instructors.

Duties of, **71:30.**

Faculty tenure. See within this heading, "Faculty tenure."

Lease or sale of land, **75:26, 75:27.**

Lecturers. See within this heading, "Lecturers, employment."

Trustees to elect and define duties and tenure of office, **75:14.**

Property, management of, **75:11, 75:12.**

Publication.

Annual reports, **75:15.**

Rules and regulations, **75:3.**

Public overseers board, **75:14D.**

Purchases, **75:13.**

Purpose of institution, **75:2.**

Quorum of trustees, number constituting, **75:4.**

Real property.

Acquisition of, **75:36C.**

Board of trustees, administration of devises, **75:11.**

Lease of land. See within this heading, "Lease of land."

Taxation. See within this heading, "Taxation."

Vehicles on property of University, **75:32A.**

Receipts.

Accounting of receipts and expenditures, **75:6.**

Student activities, **75:11.**

Records and reports.

Annual reports, **75:15, 75:36D.**

Comptroller, personnel report, **75:14.**

Financial reports, **75:10.**

Rules and regulations, filing, **74:3.**

Rehabilitation facilities, **75:36C.**

Research.

Agricultural experiment station. See within this heading, "Agricultural experiment station."

UNIVERSITY OF MASSACHUSETTS —Cont'd

Research —Cont'd

Center for, **75:2.**

Institutes and foundations, operation, **75:11.**

Research Foundation established, **75:14C.**

Rules and regulations, **75:3, 75:14A.**

Salaries and wages.

Medical school dean and officers, **75:35.**

President, **75:14.**

Professional staff, **75:14.**

Satellite clinics, **75:36C.**

Scholarships and fellowships, **75:33.**

See SCHOLARSHIPS AND FELLOWSHIPS.

Seal, **75:5.**

Societies or associations, sale or lease of land, **75:25-75:27.**

Special trust, management and investment, **75:11.**

State colleges, co-operation, **73:1.**

State forester, **132:45.**

Instructions to students, **132:1.**

State institution, continuance, **75:1.**

State police, **22C:50.**

Status of employees, **75:24.**

Taxation.

Leased land, **59:11, 75:28.**

Loss of taxes on land used for University, reimbursement, **58:13-58:17A.**

Television center, establishment and maintenance, **75:37.**

Tenure.

Faculty tenure. See within this heading, "Faculty tenure."

Tobacco, experimental work in planting and growing, **75:23.**

Travel policy, **75:32.**

Trees.

Forestry. See within this heading, "Forestry."

Trusts and trustees.

Administration by trustees, **75:9, 75:12.**

Agriculture experiment station to be maintained, **75:16, 75:16A.**

Alumni representation, board of trustees, **15A:9.**

Annual report, **75:15.**

Audit of accounts upon direction, **75:6.**

Authority, delegation, **75:3A.**

UNIVERSITY OF MASSACHUSETTS —Cont'd

Trusts and trustees —Cont'd

Bulletins containing results of experiments and investigations by experiment station, **75:19.**

Campus council appointed by board of trustees, **75:14B.**

Degrees, power to grant, **75:4, 75:12.**

Delegation of authority, **75:3A.**

Director of experiment station, appointment, **75:18.**

Educational communications commission, membership, **6:158.**

Endowed chairs established, **75:14. (note)**

Establishment of board of trustees, **6:18B, 75:1A.**

Experimental farm and branch stations, maintenance, **75:22, 75:23.**

Experiments and investigations, trustees to cause to be made, **75:17.**

Health care facilities, **75:36C.**

Honorary degrees, executive sessions of trustees to consider, **75:4.**

Instruction, determination and regulation, **75:11.**

Insurance upon buildings and contents, power to obtain, **75:9.**

Laboratory dealing with diseases of domestic animals, establishment, **75:16A.**

Lease of land, **75:26, 75:27.**

Legal services, student-supported, trust funds, **75:11.**

Management and investment of property, **75:11, 75:12.**

Massachusetts educational communications commission, membership, **6:158.**

Medical school, board of trustees, authority, **75:35.**

Meetings, **75:3, 75:4.**

Mount Toby state demonstration forest, maintenance and use, **75:29, 75:30.**

Officers.

Appointment and tenure, **75:14, 75:18.**

Duties and tenure of office, trustees to elect and define, **75:14.**

UNIVERSITY OF MASSACHUSETTS —Cont'd

Trusts and trustees —Cont'd

Open meeting law applicable, **75:3, 75:4.**

Quorum, **75:4.**

Rules and by-laws, power to make, **75:3.**

Sale of land, **75:25, 75:27.**

Seal may be altered, **75:5.**

Special trust, management and investment, **75:11.**

Student-supported activities, trust funds, **75:11.**

Vaccines, biologic labs established for research, development and production of, **75:43.**

Valuation of lands owned, **58:13.**

Veterinarians, determination of qualifications of applicants for registration, **112:55.**

Wages.

Salaries and wages. See within this heading, "Salaries and wages."

Waste prevention institute, establishment of, **71:38 et seq.**

Worchester campus.

Appointment of corporation trustees, **75:44.**

UNKNOWN PERSONS.

Absentees, estates of.

See ABSENTEES' ESTATES.

Fiduciary's account, representation in proceedings for allowance, **206:24.**

Indictments.

See INDICTMENTS, INFORMATIONS, AND COMPLAINTS.

Partner, liability after partnership dissolution of unknown partner, **108A:35.**

Real property of, assessment of taxes, **59:11.**

Writ, proceedings for issuance where defendant's name unknown, **223:19.**

UNLAWFUL ASSEMBLIES.
See RIOTS AND MOBS.

UNLIMITED TIME ACT.

Real property, **184:23.**

UNNATURAL AND LASCIVIOUS ACTS, 272:35, 272:35A, 277:45.
See OBSCENITY AND LEWDNESS.

UNORGANIZED MILITIA, 33:3.
See MILITIA.

UNSOLICITED MERCHANDISE.
Recipient, rights and obligations, **93:43.**

UNWED MOTHERS, 119:23A, 119:23B.
Audit of records, **111:54.**
Certificate of inspection, approval or disapproval, **111:51.**
Definition under public health law, **111:52.**
Licensing, **111:51, 111:52.**
Penalties for violations, **111:56.**
Records.
   Audit, **111:54.**
   Maintenance on transfer of ownership of institution, **111:70.**
   Requirement as to keeping, **111:53.**
Rules and regulations for conduct, **111:53.**
Sale or transfer of ownership of institutions.
   Licensing by new owner, **111:51.**
   Maintenance of records, **111:70.**
Transfer of patients on revocation of license, **111:51.**
Transitional assistance department, services to unwed mothers, **18:2.**

UNWHOLESOME FOOD, 94:186, 94:305A.
See FOOD.

UPHOLSTERED FURNITURE, 94:270-94:277.
See BEDDING AND UPHOLSTERED FURNITURE.

UPTON.
Congressional district, **57:1.**
District court, **218:1.**
Medical examiner district, **38:1.**
Senatorial district, **57:3.**

URBAN AREA INSURANCE PLACEMENT FACILITY, 175C:1-175C:7.
Administrative and judicial review of refusal of insurance coverage requested, **175C:7.**
Agents' commissions, establishment, **175C:3.**
Basic property insurance.
   Inspection of property of applicant for basic property insurance. See within this heading, "Inspection of property of applicant for basic property insurance."

URBAN AREA INSURANCE PLACEMENT FACILITY —Cont'd
Definitions, **175C:1.**
Inspection of property of applicant for basic property insurance.
   Liability, **175C:6.**
   Refusal of request for by agent or broker, **175C:3.**
Insurability of property, liability for statements, reports, or communications concerning, **175C:6.**
Insurance commissioner.
   Agents' commissions, establishment, **175C:3.**
   Approval, supervision and regulation of facility, **175C:5.**
   Assessment of insurance companies, **175C:8.**
   Denial of insurance coverage, review, **175C:7.**
   Joint underwriting and reinsurance association, approval, supervision, and regulation, **175C:4, 175C:5.**
Joint underwriting and reinsurance association.
   Directors, **175C:4.**
   Reports and communications, **175C:6.**
   Supervision and regulation, **175C:5.**
Liability of directors or officers, **175C:6A.**
Reports.
   Insurability of property, liability for statements in reports concerning, **175C:6.**
Solicitation of business through facility, **175C:3.**
Supervision and regulation, **175C:4, 175C:5.**

URBAN DEVELOPMENT.
See URBAN RENEWAL.

URBAN JOB INCENTIVE BUREAU, 23B:11-23B:15.
Housing and community development department.
   See HOUSING AND COMMUNITY DEVELOPMENT DEPARTMENT.

URBAN JOB INCENTIVE PROGRAM, 23B:11-23B:15.
Appeal and review, **23B:15.**
Bureau, **23B:11.**
Certificate of eligibility, **23B:13-23B:15, 63:38F.**

URBAN JOB INCENTIVE PROGRAM —Cont'd
Credit.
   Corporation taxes.
     See CORPORATION TAXES.
Definitions, **23B:11.**
Eligible business facility.
   Application for certification, **23B:14.**
   Certification, **23B:13-23B:15.**
   Contents of certificate, **23B:15.**
   Deductions in determining net income, **63:38F.**
   Definition, **23B:11.**
   Eminent domain, **23B:13.**
   Requirements to become, **23B:13.**
   Revocation, suspension or modification of **23B:15.**
   Suspension or revocation of certificate of **23B:15.**
Establishment, **23B:12.**
Functions and duties, **23B:12.**
Job incentive credit.
   Corporation taxes.
     See CORPORATION TAXES.
Manpower employment assistance and training program, **23B:12.**
Reports and recommendations, **23B:12.**

URBAN MASS TRANSPORTATION ACT OF 1964.
Regional transit authority, assistance to private carriers, **161B:8.**

URBAN PLANNING.
See ZONING AND PLANNING.

URBAN REDEVELOPMENT CORPORATIONS, 121A:1 et seq.
Acquisition of existing development, formation of corporation, **121A:18B.**
Acquisition of land, **121A:11.**
   Contracts with municipalities, **121A:14.**
   Eminent domain. See within this heading, "Eminent domain."
   From housing authority, **121A:7A.**
   Lease, gift or purchase, **121A:11.**
Alderman and selectmen, **121A:6, 121A:13.**
Appeal and review.
   Disapproval of project, appeal, **121A:6, 121A:6C.**
   Valuation for tax purposes, appeal, **121A:10.**

URBAN REDEVELOPMENT CORPORATIONS —Cont'd

Applications.
  Approval of projects, **121A:5, 121A:6, 121A:13.**
  Extension of tax exemption, **121A:10.**
Approvals.
  Housing and community development department. See within this heading, "Housing and community development department."
Bank commissioner's powers as to successor in interest, **121A:16A.**
Banks.
  See BANKS AND BANKING.
Bonds and debentures.
  Domestic insurance companies, **175:65.**
  Legal investments, **121A:7.**
  Life insurance companies, **175:66 et seq.**
  Limitation of dividends, **121A:9.**
  Power to issue, **121A:12.**
Borrowing money, **121A:12.**
  Limitation, **121A:7.**
Boston, formation of corporation, **121A:3.**
Business corporations, assumption of rights, privileges and duties, **121A:16.**
Change in type and character of buildings, application, **121A:13.**
Charitable corporations.
  Authority to participate as developers under urban renewal law, **121A:3, 121A:5, 121A:9.**
  Redevelopment, authority to undertake, **121A:18C.**
Commonwealth's liability for debts, **121A:15.**
Complaint for judicial review of disapproval of projects, requirements, **121A:6C.**
Condemnation.
  Eminent domain. See within this heading, "Eminent domain."
Conditional certificates, **121A:6.**
Condominiums, **121A:18D, 183A:2.**
Constitutionality, **121A:19.**
Contracts.
  Municipalities for construction of public improvements, contracts, **121A:14.**
  Tax exemption extension, housing board's filing, **121A:6.**

URBAN REDEVELOPMENT CORPORATIONS —Cont'd

Contracts —Cont'd
  Wholly or partially developed project, taking over, **121A:18B.**
Co-operative banks.
  Limitation of investments, **121A:18A.**
  Undertaking of projects, **121A:18A.**
Co-operative corporation operation, **121A:3.**
Debentures.
  Bonds and debentures. See within this heading, "Bonds and debentures."
Deeds of trust.
  See MORTGAGES AND DEEDS OF TRUST.
Definitions, **121A:1.**
Disapproval of projects, appeals, **121A:6, 121A:6C.**
Dividends.
  Condominium developments, **121A:18D.**
  Limitation, **121A:9.**
Economic development and industrial corporation, transfers of real property, **121C:9.**
Eminent domain.
  Filing of relocation plan, **121A:5, 121A:6.**
  Powers, **121A:2, 121A:11, 121A:14.**
Equalized valuation of property, **58:10C.**
Exemptions, tax, **59:5, 121A:6A, 121A:6C, 121A:10, 121A:18A, 121B:15, 121B:16.**
  Application of gross receipts to reduce exemption, **121A:15.**
  Charitable corporations undertaking urban renewal projects, **121A:15.**
Federal aid.
  As affecting tax exempt status, **121A:10.**
  Lump sum payments by cities and towns of funds received under federal housing and community development act, **41:56.**
  Power to receive, **121A:12.**
Gross receipts in excess of expenditures, application, **121A:15.**
Hearing authority, defined, **121A:6C.**
Hearings on projects, notice, **121A:6B.**

URBAN REDEVELOPMENT CORPORATIONS —Cont'd

Housing and community development department.
  Approval.
    Agreement of association to take over authorized urban renewal projects, **121A:18B.**
    Financing, **121A:7.**
    Projects, **121A:5, 121A:6, 121A:13.**
  Change of type and character of buildings, approval, **121A:13.**
  Contracts for extension of tax exemption, filing, **121A:6A.**
  Defined or construed, **121A:1.**
  Economic development department, substituted, **121A:18C.**
  Financing of urban renewal, approval, **121A:7.**
  Housing board, substituted, **121A:1.**
  Individual authorized to undertake housing and urban renewal projects, **121A:18C.**
  Insurance company activities defined for purposes, **121A:18.**
  Partnerships authorized to undertake projects, **121A:18C.**
  Projects.
    Approval of projects, **121A:5, 121A:6, 121A:13.**
    Authorization of undertaking, **121A:18 et seq.**
    Condominiums, **121A:18D.**
    Standards, **121A:4.**
  Proration of low income housing, **121A:18D.**
  Rules and regulations, **121A:4.**
  Standards for urban renewal projects, **121A:4.**
  Successor in interest to corporation, powers, **121A:16A, 121A:18B.**
  Tax exemption, extension, **121A:6A.**
Injunction against violations of law, **121A:8.**
Inspection of buildings and construction, **121A:8.**
Instrumentalities of Commonwealth, **121A:3.**
Insurance.
  See INSURANCE.
Investments.
  See INVESTMENTS.
Joint enterprises, **121A:18C.**

URBAN REDEVELOPMENT CORPORATIONS —Cont'd

Labor requirements under municipal contracts, **121A:14.**
Land.
　Acquisition of land. See within this heading, "Acquisition of land."
Legislative declaration of necessity, **121A:2.**
Limitations.
　Borrowing, **121A:7.**
　Dividends, **121A:9.**
　Number of projects for each corporation, **121A:3.**
Loans.
　Borrowing money. See within this heading, "Borrowing money."
Master plan, necessity for urban redevelopment, **121A:2.**
Maximum fair cash value for taxation purposes, determination, **121A:10.**
Mayors.
　Approval of projects, **121A:6.**
　Change of type and character of buildings, approval, **121A:13.**
Mixed use properties, loans for rehabilitation, **121B:59.**
Mortgages.
　See MORTGAGES AND DEEDS OF TRUST.
Nature of project, **121A:3.**
Notes.
　Bonds and debentures. See within this heading, "Bonds and debentures."
Operation and maintenance charges, **121A:15.**
Organization, **121A:3.**
　New corporation taking over existing project, **121A:18B.**
Partial invalidity of law, **121A:19.**
Partnerships as undertaking projects, **121A:18C.**
Planning boards, approval of projects, **121A:6, 121A:6B.**
Projects.
　Application for approval, **121A:5, 121A:6, 121A:13.**
　Change of type and character of buildings, application, **121A:13.**
　Cooperative banks authorized to invest deposits, **121A:18A.**
　Defined, **121A:1.**
　Disapproval of projects, appeals, **121A:6, 121A:6C.**
　Hearings on, publication of notice, **121A:6B.**

URBAN REDEVELOPMENT CORPORATIONS —Cont'd

Projects —Cont'd
　Housing and community development department. See within this heading, "Housing and community development department."
　Insurance companies authorized to undertake, **121A:18.**
　Limitation to one, **121A:3.**
　Nature, **121A:3.**
　Partially or wholly completed, new corporation undertaking, **121A:18B.**
　Partnerships undertaking, **121A:18C.**
　Savings banks authorized to invest deposits, **121A:18A.**
　Standards for plans, **121A:4, 121B:48.**
　Transfer from housing authorities, **121B:51.**
Publication of notice of hearing on projects, **121A:6B.**
Public improvements, contracts with municipalities for construction, **121A:14.**
Rate for such year defined for purposes of taxation, **121A:10.**
Redevelopment authority, acquisition of site, **121A:7A.**
Reserves, **121A:15.**
Restrictions.
　Limitations. See within this heading, "Limitations."
Revenue department and commissioner.
　Approval of agreements of association, **121A:18B.**
　Filing of certificate, **121A:16.**
Review.
　Appeal and review. See within this heading, "Appeal and review."
Rules and regulations, **121A:4.**
Sales of real property, **121A:11, 121A:16A.**
Savings banks.
　See SAVINGS BANKS.
Schedule of amenities required for tax exempt status, **121A:10.**
Securities as legal investments, **121A:7.**
Selectmen and aldermen, **121A:6, 121A:13.**
Severability of provisions, **121A:19.**
Site acquisitions, **121A:7A.**
Special or local assessments, **121A:10.**

URBAN REDEVELOPMENT CORPORATIONS —Cont'd

Standards for project plans, **121A:4.**
State aid to projects as affecting tax exempt status, **121A:10.**
State housing board or housing and community development department.
　Housing and community development department. See within this heading, "Housing and community development department."
Successors in interest, **121A:16A, 121A:18B.**
Taxation.
　Administrative tax provisions applicable, **62C:2.**
　Appeal from valuation, **121A:10.**
　Charitable corporations undertaking urban redevelopment projects, effect upon exemptions, **121A:18C.**
　Determining maximum fair cash value of urban redevelopment corporations for tax purposes, **121A:10.**
　Equalized value, **58:10C.**
　Exemptions. See within this heading, "Exemptions, tax."
　Gross receipts in excess of expenditures, application by urban redevelopment corporation, **121A:15.**
　Insurance companies undertaking housing projects, **121A:18.**
　Maximum fair cash value of urban redevelopment corporation, determination, **121A:10.**
　Payments by operating agencies in lieu of taxes, **121B:16.**
　Rate for such year defined for urban redevelopment corporation tax purposes, **121A:10.**
　Returns, **62C:12.**
　Revenue department and commissioner.
　　Approval of agreements of association, **121A:18B.**
　　Filing of certificate, **121A:16.**
　Valuation of, appeal, **121A:10.**
Violations of law by, proceedings in case, **121A:8.**
War veterans employed by, retirement rights, **32:56-32:58A, 32:59, 32:60.**

URBAN REDEVELOPMENT CORPORATIONS —Cont'd

Workers' compensation benefits, effect of payment, **32:28.**

URBAN RENEWAL, 121B:1 to 121B:59.

Commercial area revitalization plans, **40D:12.**

Housing.

   See HOUSING AND URBAN RENEWAL.

Housing programs, **121B:25 to 121B:33.**

   Elderly and handicapped, **121B:38 to 121B:40.**

   Veterans and relocation housing, **121B:34 to 121B:37.**

Municipal powers and liabilities, **121B:17 to 121B:24.**

Operating agencies, **121B:3 to 121B:7.**

   Powers and liabilities, **121B:8 to 121B:16.**

Planning.

   See ZONING AND PLANNING.

Programs, **121B:45 to 121B:52.**

Redevelopment corporations, **121A:1-121A:19.**

   See URBAN REDEVELOPMENT CORPORATIONS.

Rental assistance program, **121B:42 to 121B:44A.**

State aid, **121B:53 to 121B:57A.**

State guarantee of bonds and notes, **121B:41, 121B:41A.**

UREA FORMALDEHYDE FOAM INSULATION.
See INSULATION.

URINALYSIS.

Animals participating in contests, urine test to determine presence of drugs, **128:2C.**

Bacteriological laboratory, **111:184A.**

Driving while under influence of alcohol or drugs.

   Blood, breath or urine tests.

     See DRIVING WHILE UNDER INFLUENCE OF ALCOHOL OR DRUGS.

Uniform operation of commercial motor vehicles.

   See UNIFORM OPERATION OF COMMERCIAL MOTOR VEHICLES.

USE, CONSUMPTION, OR STORAGE TAX, 62C:16, 64I:1 et seq.

Administrative tax provisions as applicable, **62C:2.**

USE, CONSUMPTION, OR STORAGE TAX —Cont'd

Advertisement of assumption or absorption of tax by vendor prohibited, **64I:24.**

Aircraft.

   Evidence of payment of tax as prerequisite to registration, **64I:26A.**

   Tax exemption, **64I:7.**

Amendment, classified permit establishing percentage of exempt sales, **64I:11.**

Auctioneer's responsibilities, **100:8.**

Bond or deposit, filing by nonresident contractor to secure payment of tax, **64I:31A.**

Business defined, **64I:1.**

Certificates.

   Exempt use certificates, **64I:8.**

   Motor vehicles or trailers, revocation of certificate of registration, **64I:26.**

   Resale certificates, **64I:8.**

Claim for reimbursement of tax paid by vendor on worthless account, **64I:34.**

Classified permit establishing percentage of exempt sales, **64I:11.**

Collection of tax.

   By vendor, **64I:4.**

   Formula, **64I:5.**

   Records, amount of tax collected by vendor to be shown separately from sales price, **64I:6.**

Commissioner defined, **64I:1.**

Continuance of proceedings against nonresident defendants, **64I:33.**

Contractor, defined, **64I:31A.**

Costs of performance defined, **64I:1.**

Date.

   Claim for reimbursement of excise paid by vendor on worthless account, **64I:34.**

   Resale and exempt use certificate, time limit for vendor to produce, **64I:8.**

Definitions, **64H:1, 64I:1, 64I:17, 64I:27.**

Election or option, reporting by purchaser of gross receipts from rented personalty, **64I:8.**

Engaged in business defined, **64I:1.**

Exemptions, **64I:7.**

   Certificates, **64I:8.**

USE, CONSUMPTION, OR STORAGE TAX —Cont'd

Exemptions —Cont'd

   Classified permit establishing vendor's percentage of exempt sales, **64I:11.**

   Sales upon which taxes have been collected under sales tax law, **64I:7.**

   Sales upon which tax was paid to another state, **64I:7.**

   Services, **64I:7.**

   Trade-in transactions, computation of tax on transactions, **64I:27.**

Farm tractors, imposition of tax on trade-in transactions, **64I:27.**

Fines or penalties.

   Evasion of tax by means of exempt use certificate, **64I:8.**

   Resale certificate, wrongful giving, **64I:8.**

   Unlawful advertising, **64I:24.**

Foreign states or countries.

   Bond or deposit, filing by nonresident contractor to secure payment of tax, **64I:31A.**

   Exemptions, **64I:7.**

   Presumption as to property brought into Commonwealth from another state, **64I:8.**

   Proceedings against nonresident defendants, **64I:33.**

Formula for collection of tax, **64I:5.**

Good faith, vendor's taking of resale and exempt use certificate, **64I:8.**

Gross receipts.

   Defined, **64I:1.**

   Election or option, reporting by purchaser of gross receipts from rented personalty, **64I:8.**

Imposition, **64I:2.**

Liability for tax, **64I:3.**

Licenses and permits.

   Classified permit establishing percentage of exempt sales, **64I:11.**

   Notice of revocation of license to sell, **140:50.**

Local tax bill to show estimated amount to be received by town from proceeds, **60:3A.**

Motorboats, evidence of payment of tax on sales or use as prerequisite to certification, **64H:25A, 64I:26A.**

USE, CONSUMPTION, OR STORAGE TAX —Cont'd

Motor vehicles or trailers.
  Definition, **64I:27.**
  Imposition of tax on trade-in transactions, **64I:27.**
  Liability for tax, **64I:4, 64I:7.**
  Payment of tax, **64I:4.**
  Presumption that transfers of registration are for storage, use, or other consumption in Commonwealth, **64I:26.**
  Registrar, duties, **64I:4.**
  Revocation of certificate of registration, **64I:26.**
  Services, tax liability, **64I:4.**
  Tractors, imposition of use tax on trade-in transactions, **64I:27.**
  Transfer of registration, **64I:26.**
Nonresidents, **64I:31A, 64I:33.**
Notice.
  License to sell, notice of revocation, **140:50.**
  Resale or exempt use certificate, notice to produce, **64I:8.**
Option or election, reporting by purchaser of gross receipts from rented personalty, **64I:8.**
Penalties.
  Evasion of tax by means of exempt use certificate, **64I:8.**
  Resale certificate, wrongful giving, **64I:8.**
  Unlawful advertising, **64I:24.**
Permits, classified permit establishing percentage of exempt sales, **64I:11.**
Personal liability of person failing to pay tax, **64I:17.**
Person defined, **64H:1, 64I:1.**
Presumptions.
  Motor vehicles or trailers, presumption that transfers of registration are for storage, use, or other consumption in Commonwealth, **64I:26.**
  Tax liability, presumptions, **64I:8.**
Price.
  Amount of tax collected by vendor to be shown apart, **64I:6.**
  Sales price defined, **64I:1.**
Printers, **64H:1, 64H:6.**
Process and service of process against nonresident defendants, **64I:33.**
Purchase or purchased defined, **64I:1.**

USE, CONSUMPTION, OR STORAGE TAX —Cont'd

Purchaser defined, **64I:1.**
Rate of tax, **64I:2.**
  Formula for collection, **64I:5.**
Receipts.
  Election or option, reporting by purchaser of gross receipts from rented personalty, **64I:8.**
  Extinguishment of user's liability for use tax, **64I:3.**
Records, amount of tax collected by vendor to be shown separately from sales price, **64I:6.**
Registrar of motor vehicles, duties, **64I:4.**
Registration.
  Resale and exempt use certificate, **64I:8.**
  Vendor registration, **64I:9.**
Reimbursement of tax paid by vendor on worthless account, **64I:34.**
Rental, property purchased, **64I:8.**
Reporting of gross receipts of rental property, **64I:8.**
Resale certificates, **64I:8.**
Retailer defined, **64I:1.**
Retail establishment defined, **64I:1.**
Retail sale defined, **64H:1, 64I:1.**
Returns, **62C:16.**
  Monthly returns of vendors, **64I:11.**
Reversions.
  Contractor's bond or deposit to secure payment of tax, increase, **64I:31A.**
  Rate of tax, increase, **64I:2, 64I:5.**
Revocation, classified permit establishing percentage of exempt sales, **64I:11.**
Sale at retail defined, **64I:1.**
Sale defined, **64I:1.**
Sales price.
  Amount of tax collected by vendor to be shown apart, **64I:6.**
  Defined, **64I:1.**
Sales tax law, exemption for sales upon which taxes have been collected, **64I:7.**
Selling defined, **64I:1.**
Services, sales at retail, **64I:2.**
  Assumption or absorption of tax by vendor, advertisement, **64I:24.**
  Definitions, **64I:1.**

USE, CONSUMPTION, OR STORAGE TAX —Cont'd

Services, sales at retail —Cont'd
  Exemptions, **64I:7, 64I:8, 64I:27.**
  Exempt use certificates, **64I:8.**
  Foreign sales, tax was paid to another state, **64I:7.**
  Liability for tax, **64I:3.**
  Motor vehicles or trailers, tax liability, **64I:4.**
  Presumptions of tax liability, **64I:8.**
  Records, amount of tax collected by vendor to be shown separately from sales price, **64I:6.**
  Resale certificates, **64I:8.**
Special act of 1966, effect and extension, **64H:1.**
Store or storage defined, **64I:1.**
Tangible personal property.
  Defined, **64I:1.**
  Liability of person as to storing, using, or consuming tangible personal property purchased from vendor, **64I:3.**
Tax defined, **64I:1.**
Taxpayer defined, **64I:1.**
Tax returns, **62C:16.**
Time and date.
  Claim for reimbursement of excise paid by vendor on worthless account, **64I:34.**
  Resale and exempt use certificate, time limit for vendor to produce, **64I:8.**
Tractors, imposition of tax on trade-in transactions, **64I:27.**
Trade-in transactions, imposition of tax, **64I:27.**
Unlawful advertising, **64I:24.**
Use defined, **64I:1.**
Vendor.
  Advertisement of assumption or absorption of tax by vendor prohibited, **64I:24.**
  Defined, **64I:1.**
  Good faith, vendor's taking of resale and exempt use certificate, **64I:8.**
  Liability, **64I:4, 64I:8.**
  Registration, **64I:9.**
  Sales price, amount of tax collected by vendor to be shown apart, **64I:6.**
  Worthless account, claim for reimbursement of tax paid by vendor, **64I:34.**

USED ARTICLES.
  See SECONDHAND ARTICLES.

USED CAR SALES, 140:57 et seq.

Appeals from licensing board, **140:59.**

Attorney general or designee authorized to enter into licensed premises, **140:66.**

Auction sales, license, **140:57.**

Certificates of title, **90D:34-90D:36.**

Date.
　Time and date. See within this heading, "Time and date."

Disposition or sale of vehicles with altered identifying numbers, **266:139.**

Entry onto land or premises where secondhand motor vehicles sold, **140:66, 140:67.**

Exceptions, exemptions, and exclusions.
　License requirements, **140:57.**

Fees of licenses, **140:59.**

Fines and penalties.
　Breach of regulations, **140:69.**
　Obstructing inspections, **140:67.**
　Operating without license, **140:68.**

Fraudulent representation of used car as new, **93B:4.**

Identifying numbers, description of vehicle in records to contain, **140:62.**

Inspection, **90:7A.**
　Certain sales voidable where vehicle fails to pass inspection test, **90:7N.**
　Obstructing inspections, fines and penalties, **140:67.**
　Premises, **140:66, 140:67.**

Junk dealers of used cars, **140:58.**

Leasing and renting businesses, licensing, **140:57.**

Liability insurance, continuation in force after transfer of vehicle, **175:113A.**

Licenses and permits, **140:57, 140:59, 140:67A.**
　Appeals from order of licensing board, **140:59.**
　Authority to grant, **140:59.**
　Classes, **140:58.**
　Fees, **140:59.**
　Necessity, **140:57.**
　Operating without license, **140:68.**
　Revocation and suspension, **140:59, 140:67A, 140:68.**
　Term, **140:59.**

Manufacturers engaged, **140:57, 140:58.**

Representation of used vehicle as new, **93B:4.**

USED CAR SALES —Cont'd

Notice of revocation of license to sell, **140:59.**

Numbers.
　Identifying numbers, **140:62.**
　Plates.
　　Registration and number plates. See within this heading, "Registration and number plates."

Obstructing inspections, fines and penalties, **140:67.**

Operation without license, penalty, **140:68.**

Penalties.
　Fines and penalties. See within this heading, "Fines and penalties."

Permits.
　Licenses and permits. See within this heading, "Licenses and permits."

Police.
　See POLICE.

Records, reports, and returns.
　Record books, **140:62.**
　Reports by licensees, **140:57.**

Registrar of motor vehicles.
　Inspection of premises, **140:66.**
　Notice of revocation of license given, **140:59.**
　Record book, approval, **140:62.**
　Reports by licensees, **140:57.**
　Rules and regulations, **140:60.**

Registration and number plates.
　Dealer plates, **90:5.**
　Removal of before junking vehicle, **140:67A.**
　Revocation or suspension of certificate of registration, **140:69.**
　Transferred vehicles, time for registration, **90:2.**

Rental vehicle, information on bill of sale, **266:92A.**

Repair facilities, license dependent on access, **140:58.**

Reports.
　Records, reports, and returns. See within this heading, "Records, reports, and returns."

Revocation and suspension.
　Certificate of registration, **140:69.**
　Licenses, **140:59, 140:67A, 140:68.**

Selectmen, inspections, **140:66, 140:67.**

Serial numbers in records, **140:62.**

USED CAR SALES —Cont'd

Suspension of licenses.
　Revocation and suspension. See within this heading, "Revocation and suspension."

Taxicabs, police cars, or rental cars, violation of law as to sale of cars used, **266:92A.**

Term of licenses, **140:59.**

Time and date.
　Term of licenses, **140:59.**
　Warranty provisions of used motor vehicles, **90:7N¼.**

Transfer of ownership, minimum age, **90:2.**

Unfair trade practice, representation and sale of used motor vehicle as new as constituting, **93B:4.**

Voidability of sale of motor vehicle failing inspection test as affected by cost of repair, **90:7N.**

Warranty provisions, **90:7N¼.**

Water, sale of vehicle previously submerged, **266:92A.**

USO APPRECIATION DAY.

Annual observance, **6:12RR.**

U.S.S. MASSACHUSETTS MEMORIAL COMMITTEE, INC., 6:124A.

USURY.

Criminal usury, offense, **271:49.**

Maximum allowable interest rates. See INTEREST ON MONEY.

UTERINE CANCER.

Schools providing programs of instruction for early detection, **71:1.**

UTILITIES.

See TELECOMMUNICATIONS AND ENERGY DEPARTMENT.

UTTERING.

Forgery.
　See FORGERY AND COUNTERFEITING.

UXBRIDGE.

Congressional district, **57:1.**

District court, **218:1.**

Medical examiner district, **38:1.**

Senatorial district, **57:3.**

V

VACATING JUDGMENT OR ORDER.

See SETTING ASIDE.

VACATION OF COURT.
See COURTS.

VACATIONS.
School.
  See SCHOOLS AND
    EDUCATION.
Work.
  See LABOR AND WORKFORCE
    DEVELOPMENT.

VACCINATION, 76:15,
    111:181-111:183.
Animal diseases.
  See ANIMAL DISEASES.
Children.
  See CHILDREN AND MINORS.
Children's and senior's health care
  assistance fund.
    Immunization program, **111:24I.**
College students, immunization,
  76:15C.
Dogs.
  See DOGS.
Education department,
  immunization against
  Hepatitis B, **69:1C.**
Exemption.
  How obtained, **111:183.**
  Religious beliefs, exemption of
    school children based, **76:15.**
Free services, **111:5A, 111:181.**
Hepatitis B immunization required
  by education department,
  69:1C.
Hog cholera, **129:40A.**
Persons in factories and
  institutions, **111:182.**
Physicians and nurses as immune
  from civil liability in carrying
  out public health programs,
  112:12C.
Power to require, **111:181.**
Production and distribution of
  vaccine, **111:5, 111:5A.**
Public institution's vaccination of
  inmates, **111:182.**
Rabies, vaccine or inoculation
  against, **140:145A, 140:145B.**
Veterinarians.
  See VETERINARIANS.

VACUUM BRAKES.
Locomotives, **160:169.**

VAGRANTS AND TRAMPS,
    272:63-272:69, 277:79.
Arrest, **272:54, 272:59,**
    272:65-272:67, 272:69.
Begging.
  See BEGGING.
Breach of peace, **272:38 et seq.**
Burglars, **272:68.**

VAGRANTS AND TRAMPS
  —Cont'd
Discharge on recognizance, **272:57.**
Disorderly conduct, **272:38 et seq.**
Dwelling place of another, persons
  acting suspiciously around,
  272:68.
Indictment, forms for vagabonds
  and vagrants, **277:79.**
Lack of visible means of support,
  272:63, 272:66.
Pickpockets, **272:68.**
Punishment, **272:64, 272:66,**
  272:68.
Second conviction, **272:61.**
Suspicious loafers, **272:68.**
Thieves, **272:68.**
Tramps, **272:63-272:65.**
Vagabonds, **272:68, 272:69,**
  277:79.

VALVES.
Safety valves.
  See SAFETY AND SAFETY
    DEVICES.

VANDALISM, 131:61, 266:11,
    266:12, 266:13, 266:94 et seq.
See MALICIOUS MISCHIEF
    OR INJURY.

VANPOOL.
Definition, **63:31D.**

VARIABLE ANNUITY
    INSURANCE.
Authorized, **175:3, 175:47.**
Basis on which contract may be
  written, **175:132G.**
Benefits under, **175:132B,**
  175:132G.
Business that may be transacted
  by variable annuity insurance
  company, **175:51.**
Capital and reserve, investment,
  175:63.
Capital stock, **175:48.**
Contracts other than annuities.
  Conforming changes in law,
    175:3, 175:94, 175:132,
    175:132B, 175:132F,
    175:132G, 175:140, 175:142,
    175:144.
  Defined, **175:1.**
Definition of insurance company,
  175:1.
Forms, approval or disapproval,
  175:132G, 175:134B.
Group contracts, nature and basis
  of benefits to be paid,
  175:132B, 175:134B.
Individual contracts.
  Insurance commissioner,
    approval, **175:132H.**

VARIABLE ANNUITY
    INSURANCE —Cont'd
Individual contracts —Cont'd
  Statement of nature and basis of
    rights of annuitant,
    175:144.
Insurance commissioner.
  Group contracts, approval of
    nature and basis of benefits
    to be paid, **175:132B.**
  Individual contracts, approval,
    175:132H.
  Powers and duties, **175:132G.**
Investments.
  See INVESTMENTS.
Life insurance, **175:47, 175:48,**
  175:49, 175:63.
Name of company, "Variable
  annuity" to be included,
  175:49.
Pension contracts assigned to
  separate investment accounts,
  approval and regulation of
  companies issuing, **175:132F.**
Purpose of incorporation, **175:47.**
Restriction as to making, **175:3.**
Securities and securities
  regulations.
  Sales, **175:3.**
Standards for contracts,
  establishment, **175:134B.**
Stock.
  Capital stock, **175:48.**
  Investments.
    See INVESTMENTS.
Time or date, approval or
  disapproval of forms,
  175:134B.
Voting rights of holders, **175:94.**
Writing of variable annuity
  contracts, **175:48, 175:51.**

VARIANCE.
Airport approach regulations,
  permits for variances, **90:40D.**
Commercial Code provisions,
  agreement varying effect,
  106:1-102.
Indictment, variance from, **277:35.**
  See INDICTMENTS,
    INFORMATIONS, AND
    COMPLAINTS.
Zoning.
  See ZONING AND PLANNING.

VARNISH.
Automatic sprinklers in buildings
  for manufacturing, etc.,
  148:26.

VAULTS.
See SAFES AND VAULTS.

VEAL.
Calves, minimum age, **94:146,**
94:151.
Packing plants, violations,
94:121-94:124.
Sale of "neat veal," **94:151.**

VEGETABLES AND
VEGETABLE PRODUCTS.
Advertising, "Native," use of word,
94:99B, 94:107.
Brands and labels.
Frozen blanched potatoes,
94:117H.
"Native" in connection with sale
or packaging, **94:99B.**
Weight or count, containers to
show, **94:96.**
Burning or destroying, offense,
266:5.
Certificate of registration,
exemption from requirement,
94:305C.
Entering garden or other land
with intent to cut or carry
away, penalty, **266:117.**
Health boards, powers and duties,
94:146, 94:149, 94:152.
Inspection where offered or
exposed for sale, **94:146,**
94:149.
Labels.
Brands and labels. See within
this heading, "Brands and
labels."
Milk cans, penalty for placing
vegetable matter, **94:48.**
Motor vehicle used in stealing of,
report, **90:24A.**
"Native," use of word in
advertising, **94:99B, 94:107.**
Prizes for and exhibits, **128:2.**
Sausages composed, **94:143A.**
Seeds.
See SEEDS.
Sunday sale, **136:6.**
Unclaimed property, disposition,
135:5.
Unwholesome vegetables, penalty
for sale, **94:150.**
Weights and measures,
94:96-94:99B.
See WEIGHTS AND
MEASURES.

VEHICLES.
Bicycles.
See BICYCLES.
Generally.
See MOTOR VEHICLES.
Horse-drawn vehicles.
See HORSE-DRAWN
VEHICLES.

VEHICLES —Cont'd
Unauthorized use of vehicle other
than motor vehicle, penalty,
266:63.
Vending vehicles.
See MOBILE VENDING
VEHICLES.

VENDING MACHINES.
Accident insurance issued through,
facsimile signature, **175:157.**
Approval of deputy director of
standards required for
coin-operated devices, **94:283.**
Beverages sold through,
94:308-94:313.
Cigarette tax.
See CIGARETTE TAX.
Commissaries located outside of
Commonwealth, **94:312.**
Definitions under food and drug
inspection law, **94:308.**
Fees, **94:309.**
Fines and penalties, **266:75A,**
266:75B.
Food, sale, **94:284, 94:305A,**
94:313.
Food sold through, **94:308-94:313.**
Forms, application for license for
sale of food through vending
machines, **94:309.**
Fraudulent operation, **266:75A,**
266:75B.
Inspection, **94:310, 94:311.**
Insurance issued through,
facsimile signature, **175:157.**
License for operation, **62C:67,**
94:309.
Reinstatement, **94:311.**
Suspension or revocation,
94:311.
List of locations and commissaries,
94:310.
Non-alcoholic beverages, retail
sales, **140:21A.**
Notice as to violations, **94:311.**
Sale of food and beverages
through, **94:308-94:313.**
Sales tax, exemptions, **64H:6.**
Slugs or false tokens, use in
operation, **266:75A, 266:75B.**
Soft drinks sold through,
94:308-94:313.

VENDOR AND PURCHASER.
See SALE OR TRANSFER OF
PROPERTY.

VENEREAL DISEASES,
111:117-111:121A.
Assault and battery, physical
examination not constituting,
111:117.

VENEREAL DISEASES —Cont'd
Births.
See BIRTHS.
Clinics, establishment, **111:117.**
Correctional institutions,
examination, isolation, and
treatment of prisoners,
111:121, 127:16-127:18.
Examination.
Assault and battery, physical
examination not
constituting, **111:117.**
Correctional institutions,
examination of prisoners,
111:121, 127:16-127:18.
Marriage license applicants,
207:28A.
Pregnant women, **111:121A.**
Wassermann test. See within
this heading, "Wassermann
test."
Fiancee of infected person,
physician's disclosure, **112:12.**
Hairdressers, requirement of
physician's certificate,
112:87CC.
Health department's power to
define, **111:6.**
Hospitals not to discriminate
against treatment, **111:118.**
Libel or slander, disclosure by
physician, **112:12.**
Manicurist, requirement of
physician's certificate,
112:87CC.
Marriage license, examination of
applicants, **207:28A.**
Newborn children, duties as to.
See BIRTHS.
Parent or guardian of minor
infected with, physician's
disclosure, **112:12.**
Physicians, **112:12.**
Pregnant women, testing,
111:121A.
Public health department,
communicable and venereal
diseases division created, **17:4.**
Records and reports as to,
inspection, **111:119.**
Tests.
Examination. See within this
heading, "Examination."
Treatment at public expense,
111:117.
Veterans' benefits not payable
where paraplegia caused,
115:6B.
Wassermann test, **111:121A.**
Marriage license applicants,
207:28A.

VENIRE, 234:10-234:16.
Grand jury.
See GRAND JURY.
Jury and jury trial.
See JURY AND JURY TRIAL.

VENIRE FACIAS WRITS,
212:20A, 234:10, 234:32.
Worcester county, empanelling of
grand jury, 277:2E.

VENTILATION.
Cattle barns, examination, 129:23.
Coal mining operations, 21B:7,
21B:8.
Labor.
See LABOR AND WORKFORCE
DEVELOPMENT.
Nursing or convalescent homes,
111:72C, 111:73.
Police stations, lockups, penal and
reformatory institutions,
111:21.
Professional engineers, exemption
from laws, 112:81R.
Public contract bids, categories of
specification, 149:44F.
Space heaters, requirement for
vents, 148:25A.

VENUE, 223:1-223:15.
Abandoned spouse's petition for
leave to receive or convey
property, 209:30, 209:31.
Absentee trust beneficiaries,
proceedings for transfer of
estates, 203:29, 203:37.
Abuse prevention, venue of actions
concerning, 209A:2, 277:62A.
Administrators.
See EXECUTORS AND
ADMINISTRATORS.
Adoption proceedings, 210:1.
Alcohol, action for negligence in
distribution, sale, or serving to
minors or intoxicated persons,
231:60J.
Alteration or change.
Transfer. See within this
heading, "Transfer of
action."
Animals, action for damages for
destruction of diseased
animals, 129:31.
Antitrust laws.
See RESTRAINTS OF TRADE
AND MONOPOLIES.
Appeal.
See APPEAL AND REVIEW.
Arbitration.
See ARBITRATION.
Arrest on mesne process and
supplementary proceedings,
224:6.

VENUE —Cont'd
Automobile liability insurance,
appeals from refusal or
cancellation, 175:113D.
Bonds, actions, 205:30.
Boston.
Defect in way, action, 223:7.
Municipal court.
Boston Municipal Court. See
within this heading,
"Boston Municipal Court."
Transfer from Suffolk County of
actions by or against,
223:10.
Transitory actions by and
against, 223:9, 223:10.
Municipal court, 223:2.
Boston Municipal Court.
Health, welfare, and retirement
funds, complaints for failure
to pay contribution or
benefits, 151D:11.
Transitory actions, 223:2.
Breach of covenant, transitory
nature of action, 223:3.
Capital cases, 277:53, 277:54,
277:60-277:62.
Death outside state by injury in
state, 277:62.
Death within state by injury
elsewhere, 277:61.
Injury in one county and death
in another, 277:60.
Carriers.
Motor carriers of property,
proceedings against,
159B:21.
Rate increases or reduction of
service, hearings, 25:4A.
Certified copy of order directing
change of venue, 223:13.
Change of venue.
Transfer of action. See within
this heading, "Transfer of
action."
Child support proceedings,
married persons living apart,
209:32F.
City or town clerk, judicial review
of removal or suspension,
41:19D.
Civil rights and discrimination.
Commission against
discrimination, hearings,
6:56.
Injunction against
discriminatory practices,
151B:5.
Claims and indemnity procedure
as to public bodies and
officers, 258:3.

VENUE —Cont'd
Clerk of court, duties in connection
with change of venue, 223:13.
Commission against
discrimination, hearings, 6:56.
Commonwealth, actions, 223:5.
Conservators.
Guardians, conservators, and
committees. See within this
heading, "Guardians,
conservators, and
committees."
Consolidation of cross actions or
actions arising out of same
accident, event, or transaction.
District courts, 223:2A-223:2C.
Procedure after transfer of
action, 223:2C.
Transfer to superior court where
actions pending in both
superior and district courts,
223:2B.
Consumers and consumer
protection actions, 93A:4,
93A:11, 223:1.
Corporations.
See CORPORATIONS.
Costs, double costs on dismissal of
action pursuant to objection to
venue, 223:1.
Counties.
See COUNTIES.
Credit card fraud, transitory
action, 223:1.
Criminal offender record
information system, appeal of
decisions of board or counsel,
6:176.
Criminal procedure.
See CRIMINAL PROCEDURE.
Cross actions, consolidation of.
Consolidation. See within this
heading, "Consolidation of
cross actions or actions
arising out of same accident,
event, or transaction."
Dams, action for damages caused,
253:4.
Desertion and nonsupport.
Civil proceedings to compel
support, 209:34.
Criminal proceedings, 273:2.
Destitute parents, action against
child, 273:21.
Discrimination.
Civil rights and discrimination.
See within this heading,
"Civil rights and
discrimination."

VENUE —Cont'd

District court.

Consolidation of cross actions between same parties or actions arising out of same accident, event or transaction, **223:2A-223:2C.**

Health, welfare, and retirement funds, venue for complaints for failure to pay contributions to or benefits, **151D:11.**

Transitory actions, **218:54, 223:2.**

Divorce suits, **208:6.**

Domicile or residence affecting venue of transitory actions, **223:2.**

Embezzlement, **277:58.**

Fiduciaries, **277:58B.**

Receiving embezzled property, **277:58A.**

Equity, **214:5.**

Erroneous venue, **223:15.**

Double costs on dismissal, **223:1.**

Essex County.

Superior court, **1:3.**

Transitory actions by and against city of Boston, **223:9.**

Executions.

Local action improper, directing writ to sheriff of proper county, **235:15.**

Redemption suits, **235:39.**

Trustee process, **223:2, 246:2, 246:3.**

See TRUSTEE PROCESS.

Executors.

See EXECUTORS AND ADMINISTRATORS.

False weights and measures, complaint, **94:180.**

Farmer-winery licenses, appeal of denial, **138:19B.**

Food and agriculture department, appeals from decisions of commissioner, **20:19.**

Forfeitures.

Recovery of forfeiture, **223:14.**

Seizure and libeling of forfeited property, **257:2, 257:3.**

Garnishment, **223:2, 223:3.**

See TRUSTEE PROCESS.

Guardians, conservators, and committees.

License to sell real estate, **202:6.**

Petitions for sales by foreign guardians or conservators, **204:7.**

VENUE —Cont'd

Health, welfare, and retirement funds, venue of complaints for failure to pay contributions or benefits, **151D:11.**

Highways and streets, action for defect, **223:7.**

Homestead, release of rights of insane spouse, **209:24.**

Husband.

See HUSBAND AND WIFE.

Illegitimate children, complaints to establish paternity, support, custody or visitation and acknowledgments of parentage, **209C:4.**

Income tax return, mandamus to compel filing, **62C:9.**

Insurance, actions by or against subscribers to inter-insurance or reciprocal insurance exchange, **223:8A.**

Kidnapping case, **265:27.**

Land in different counties, actions relative, **223:12.**

Landlords, small claims actions against, **218:21.**

Larceny, **277:58, 277:58A.**

Letters of credit.

Choice of law and forum, **106:5-116.**

Marine boundaries of Commonwealth, institution of proceedings as to civil or criminal matters within, **1:3.**

Mechanics' liens, enforcement, **254:5.**

Mentally incompetent spouse, release of dower, curtesy or homestead rights, **209:24.**

Mill dam, action for damages caused, **253:4.**

Mineral resources regulations, prosecutions for violations, **21:56.**

Minors.

See CHILDREN AND MINORS.

Mistake.

Erroneous venue. See within this heading, "Erroneous venue."

Mortgage, suit to redeem, **244:26.**

Motor carriers of property, proceedings against, **159B:21.**

Municipal courts, **223:2.**

Murder in duel outside Commonwealth, **265:4.**

Negligence, actions, **223:7.**

Negotiable instruments, action by assignee, **223:1.**

Nonresidents, actions against, **223:1, 223:2.**

VENUE —Cont'd

Nonsupport cases.

Desertion and nonsupport. See within this heading, "Desertion and nonsupport."

Objection to venue, double costs allowed on dismissal pursuant, **223:1.**

Partition proceedings, **241:2.**

Personal injuries, actions, **223:7.**

Place of commission of crime as place of trial, **US Const Art 3 Sec 2 cl 3.**

Probate.

See PROBATE AND FAMILY COURT.

Quo warranto, action in nature, **249:6.**

Rape, **265:24A.**

Reciprocal insurance exchange, actions by or against subscribers, **223:8A.**

Redemption suits, **235:39, 244:26.**

Release of dower, curtesy, or homestead rights of insane spouse, **209:24.**

Removal of action.

Transfer of action. See within this heading, "Transfer of action."

Rent, transitory nature of action, **223:3.**

Replevin actions, **223:4.**

Reservoirs, action for damages caused, **253:4.**

Restraints of trade.

See RESTRAINTS OF TRADE AND MONOPOLIES.

Review.

See APPEAL AND REVIEW.

Sales by fiduciaries, **202:6, 204:7.**

Same accident, event or transactions.

Consolidation of cross actions. See within this heading, "Consolidation of cross actions or actions arising out of same accident, event, or transactions."

Seeds, appeal of stop sale order, **128:95.**

Separate maintenance proceedings, **209:34.**

Sexual offenses with feebleminded persons, **265:24A.**

Ships or vessels, enforcement of liens, **255:17.**

Small claims action and procedure, **218:21.**

State, claims against, **258:3.**

Suffolk county.

See SUFFOLK COUNTY.

VENUE —Cont'd

Summary process for possession of land, **239:2.**

Support of persons.

Desertion and nonsupport. See within this heading, "Desertion and nonsupport."

Taxation.

See TAXATION.

Towns, actions against, **223:7.**

Transfer of action, **223:13.**

Boston, transfer from Suffolk County of actions by or against city, **223:10.**

Collective bargaining agreements, actions, **150C:15.**

Consolidation of cross actions. See within this heading, "Consolidation of cross actions or actions arising out of same accident, event, or transaction."

Dissolution of fraudulent attachment, transfer of action in which attachment was made as affecting action, **223:112.**

Erroneous venue, **223:15.**

Probate court jurisdiction, **215:8A.**

Superior and district courts, transfer of actions pending in both, **223:2B.**

Transitory actions, **223:1-223:3.**

Boston. See within this heading, "Boston."

Corporations, actions by and against, **223:8.**

District courts, transitory action, **218:54, 223:2.**

Subscribers to reciprocal or inter-insurance exchange, actions by or against, **223:8A.**

Trustee process, **223:2, 246:2, 246:3.**

See TRUSTEE PROCESS.

Trusts and trustees.

Absentee beneficiaries, transfer of estates, **203:29, 203:37.**

Foreign trustees, petitions for sales, **204:7.**

Prosecution for embezzlement or fraudulent conversion, **277:58B.**

Use and occupation, transitory nature of action, **223:3.**

Vessels, enforcement of liens, **255:17.**

Way, action for defect, **223:7.**

VENUE —Cont'd

Wife.

See HUSBAND AND WIFE.

Workers' compensation, venue of prosecution for failure to provide, **152:25C.**

VERACRUZ EXPEDITION.

Hospital benefits of veteran serving, **115A:2.**

VERDICT.

Alternate jurors participating in, **234:26B.**

Contributory negligence, special verdict in actions involving, **231:85.**

Damages, **231:6B, 231:60G.**

Death sentence in murder case, jury recommendation, **265:2.**

Directed verdict, criminal case, motion for, renewal after verdict, **278:11.**

Disagreement of jury, sending back to reconsider case, **234:34.**

District courts.

See DISTRICT COURTS.

Five sixths of jurors, verdict, **234:34A.**

Frivolous actions, award of costs and attorneys' fees, **231:6F.**

Gifts or gratuities to jurors as affecting, **234:33.**

Impaneling new jury prior to rendering of verdict, **234:25.**

Interest, **235:8.**

Tort cases, inclusion, **231:6B.**

Malpractice, verdict as to damages in medical malpractice action, **231:60G.**

Partial acquittals and convictions, **278:12.**

Power of court on return of guilty verdict, **278:11.**

Setting aside.

Bribery of jurors, setting aside verdict, **234:33.**

Gratuities to jury, setting aside, **234:33.**

Irregularities in connection with drawing, summoning, etc., of jurors, setting aside verdict, **234:32.**

Superior courts, **213:3, 231:104.**

Six person jury, verdicts, **234:26B.**

Sixteen-member jury, **234:26B.**

Small home mortgages, actions under laws as to interest, **140:90D.**

Special verdict or questions, special verdict in contributory negligence case, **231:85.**

VERDICT —Cont'd

Split verdict, costs as affected, **261:9.**

Superior courts.

See SUPERIOR COURTS.

VERMONT.

Appalachian trial, protection, **132A:12.**

Electric company may acquire stock or obligations of corporation owning storage reservoir, **164:9.**

Police and fire vehicles as exempt from registration, **90:9B.**

State funds may be invested in obligations, **29:38.**

Statewide branch banking, notice and hearing for establishment of branch offices or depots, **167C:3.**

Witnesses, summoning to testify in criminal cases, **233:12.**

VESICULAR STOMATITIS, 129:14A.

VESICULAR XANTHEMIA, 129:14A.

VESSELS.

See SHIPS AND OTHER WATERCRAFT.

VESTED RIGHTS.

Conveyance of land subject, **183:49-183:52.**

Disclaimed interest, vesting, **191A:7.**

Fiduciaries, release, **204:4.**

Fraternal benefit insurance, interest, **176:21.**

Guardian or conservator may obtain release, **201:44.**

Register's fees for entry of petition for sale of estate subject to vested remainder, **262:40.**

VESTRY.

See RELIGION AND RELIGIOUS SOCIETIES.

VETERAN FIREMEN'S ASSOCIATIONS.

Expenditure of certain municipal funds, **40:5.**

VETERAN FIREMEN'S MUSTER DAY.

Annual observance, **6:12L.**

VETERANS AND VETERANS' ORGANIZATIONS, 115:1-115:15.

Accounts and accounting.

Fiduciary's account. See within this heading, "Fiduciary's account."

**VETERANS AND VETERANS'
ORGANIZATIONS** —Cont'd

"Active service in the Armed
Forces" defined, **4:7.**

Administration, powers and duties
of commissioner, **115:2.**

Adoption of children.
Fee for copy of record waived,
262:46A.
Newspaper advertisements by
veterans' service
department, **210:11A.**

Advertisements.
Adoption of children, newspaper
advertisements by veterans'
service department,
210:11A.
Civil service courses for disabled
veterans, **271:48.**

Advisory boards to commissioner
of veterans' services, **115:12.**

Afro-American veterans,
assignment of quarters in
State House, **8:17.**

Agents of veterans.
Appeal by, to governor and
council, **115:2, 115:2A.**
Appointment, **115:3.**
As burial agents, **115:7.**
Certification for reimbursement,
115:6.
Commissioner of veterans'
services, **115:2.**
Defined, **115:1.**
Municipalities, agents in, **115:1,
115:3 et seq.**
Notice of application for benefits,
115:5.
Powers and duties, **115:3.**
Subordination of veterans'
agents liens, **115:5A.**

Air force members, attendance at
funerals, **41:112A.**

Alcoholic liquor license, **138:12.**

Aldermen and selectmen.
Agents, appointment, **115:3.**
Graves officer, appointment,
115:9.

American Gold Star Mothers, Inc.
See AMERICAN GOLD STAR
MOTHERS, INC.

American legion.
See AMERICAN LEGION.

American officers of the great war.
See AMERICAN OFFICERS OF
THE GREAT WAR.

American Portuguese war veterans
association.
See AMERICAN PORTUGUESE
WAR VETERANS
ASSOCIATION.

**VETERANS AND VETERANS'
ORGANIZATIONS** —Cont'd

American veterans' committee.
See AMERICAN VETERANS'
COMMITTEE, INC.

Amount of benefits, **115:5.**
Determination, **115:6.**

Amputees, annuities, **115:6B.**

AMVETS.
See AMERICAN VETERANS
OF WORLD WAR II,
KOREA, AND VIETNAM,
AMVETS.

Anemia, annuity to veterans
paralyzed, **115:6A-115:6C.**

Appeal.
See APPEAL AND REVIEW.

Application for benefits,
115:3-115:5.

Armistice Day, observance, **6:15R.**

Armories, use of quarters and
facilities, **33:122.**

Army.
See ARMY AND NAVY UNION
OF THE UNITED STATES
OF AMERICA.

Assignment of benefits, prohibition
against, **115:5.**

Attorneys at law.
Commissioner of veteran's
services as attorney for
other state agencies, **115:2.**
World War II veterans,
educational requirements
for admission to bar,
221:36A.

Audit of veterans' services
districts, **115:15.**

Auditor of state, laws regulating
retention of veterans in public
service as applicable to officers
and employees, **11:6.**

Back benefits, **115:5.**

Banks and banking.
Co-operative banks, deposits and
loans, duty to furnish
information to veterans'
commissioner **115:2.**
Deposits, investigation, **115:2.**
Savings and loan associations to
furnish information to
commissioner, **115:2.**
Savings banks.
See SAVINGS BANKS.

Beano, game, **10:38.**

Benefits and services,
115:1-115:15.

Blank cartridges for use of
veterans' organizations, sale,
148:39.

Blindness or impaired vision,
benefits, **115:6A-115:6C.**

**VETERANS AND VETERANS'
ORGANIZATIONS** —Cont'd

Bonus for Vietnam veterans.
Vietnam veterans, bonus for. See
within this heading,
"Vietnam veterans, bonus."

Borrowing money.
Loans. See within this heading,
"Loans."

Burials, **114:45-114:47,
115:7-115:9.**
Affidavit prerequisite to permit,
114:46A.
Anatomical purposes, veteran's
body not to be delivered,
113:2.
Body brought into state, **114:46.**
Burial agents, **115:7.**
Citizenship requirements for
burial benefits, **115:7.**
Commissioner's duties, **115:8.**
Flags to be placed on veterans'
graves, **115:9, 272:75.**
Grave marker or metal plaque,
offense of defacing or
mutilating, **272:73.**
Graves, care, **40:5, 115:9.**
Graves officer, appointment and
duties, **115:9.**
Marking of veteran's graves,
115:9.
Municipal appropriations for
care of graves, **40:5, 115:9.**
Municipal officers and
employees, attendance at
funerals or memorial
services, **41:111C.**
Payment of expenses, **115:8.**
Permit required, **114:45-114:47.**
Record of burial in another
town, **46:12.**
Vietnam veterans, municipal
appropriations for
gravestones, **40:5.**

Celebrations for, town
appropriations, **40:5.**

Cemeteries.
Burials. See within this heading,
"Burials."

Ceremonial bonfires authorized,
111:142H.

Certificates and certification.
Death certificate, **46:10.**
Reimbursement, agents'
certification, **115:6.**

Change of name, no fee for copies
or records, **262:46A.**

Chelsea soldiers' home, repeal of
obsolete provision as to voting
rights of veterans, **51:4.**

Children.
Dependents. See within this
heading, "Dependents."

VETERANS AND VETERANS' ORGANIZATIONS —Cont'd

Cities and towns.
Municipalities. See within this heading, "Municipalities."
Citizenship as prerequisite to burial benefits, **115:7.**
Civil rights and discrimination, **151B:3-151B:5.**
Civil service.
See CIVIL SERVICE.
Civil war veterans.
Flag, **264:5.**
Town's power to make appropriations for memorials, **40:5.**
Union veteran legion.
See UNION VETERAN LEGION.
Claims for benefits, **115:2, 115:2A.**
Clerks of cities and towns.
Municipal officers and employees. See within this heading, "Municipal officers and employees."
Colleges and universities.
Vietnam veterans. See within this heading, "Vietnam veterans."
Commissioner of veterans' services, **7:4G, 7:4M et seq.**
Advisory boards, **115:12.**
Appeal from decision, **115:2, 115:2A.**
Burial benefits, duties, **115:8.**
Claims for benefits, duties, **115:2, 115:2A.**
Compelling payment of benefits, powers, **115:2.**
Co-operation with federal government, **115:2.**
Defined, **115:1.**
Employment. See within this heading, "Employment."
Enforcement of decisions, **115:2A.**
Governor.
Supervision by governor, **6:17.**
Governor's council, appointment and supervision of commission, **6:17, 115:2, 115:2A.**
Health and human services executive office, agencies within, **6A:16.**
Orders for payment of benefits, **115:5.**
Powers and duties, **115:2.**
Records not public, **66:18.**
Removal from office, **7:4O.**
Salary, **7:4M.**

VETERANS AND VETERANS' ORGANIZATIONS —Cont'd

Commissioner of veterans' services —Cont'd
Savings and loan associations to furnish information, **115:2.**
Superior court, enforcement of decision, **115:2A.**
Supervision of local departments, **115:14.**
Traveling expenses, **7:4N.**
World War II, Korean Emergency, and Vietnam Conflict Memorial Commission, member, **6:124A.**
Commission on the employment of people with disabilities, **6:105.**
Community war memorials, **40:5, 448.**
Compelling city or town to pay benefits, commissioner's powers with respect, **115:2.**
Comptroller's duties as to veterans' benefits.
Paraplegic veterans, **115:6C.**
Transmission of certificates of benefits, **115:6.**
Conscientious objectors, **115:7.**
Consent to receipt of benefits, **115:5.**
Conservators.
Guardians and conservators. See within this heading, "Guardians and conservators."
Constitution of Massachusetts, veterans not disqualified to vote by reason of receiving public aid or nonpayment of poll tax, **MA Const Amend Art 28.**
Conventions of veterans' organizations, delegates may attend without loss of pay or vacation, **41:111J.**
Co-operative banks, deposits and loans, duty to furnish information to veterans' commissioner, **115:2.**
Corrections department.
See CORRECTIONS DEPARTMENT.
Credit unions.
See CREDIT UNIONS.
Dead bodies.
Burials. See within this heading, "Burials."
Not to be delivered for anatomical purposes, **113:2.**
Soldiers' home in Holyoke exempt from provisions, **113:1.**

VETERANS AND VETERANS' ORGANIZATIONS —Cont'd

Death certificate, **46:10.**
Deceit.
Fraud and deceit, benefit payments, **62C:21.**
Decoration of graves, **115:9.**
Defacing or mutilating grave marker or memorial plaque, **272:73.**
Definitions, **4:7, 32:1, 115:1, 115:6A, 121B:1.**
Department of veterans' services.
Commissioner of veterans' services. See within this heading, "Commissioner of veterans' services."
Dependents.
Adoption of children. See within this heading, "Adoption of children."
Aid in case of dependent children, **118:10.**
Civil service to mothers and widows, preference, **31:26, 31:28.**
Compensation as to military personnel injured in line of duty, **33:88.**
Copies of certain records to be furnished free to spouse of veteran, **262:46A.**
Defined, **115:1.**
Health insurance premiums, contribution toward, **32B:9D.**
Minors, **201:2.**
Payments, **115:5.**
Real estate, discharge of lien on certain, **115:5A.**
Retirement system, rights, **32:25, 32:58B.**
Services by municipal service departments, **115:10.**
Tax exemption for disabled veterans and spouses, **59:5.**
Widower included within meaning, **115:1.**
Disability of commissioner of veterans' services, **7:4O.**
Disabled veterans.
Anemia, veterans paralyzed, **115:6A-115:6C.**
Annuities to veterans suffering loss of both legs, payment, **115:6B.**
Blindness or impaired vision, **115A:6A-115A:6C.**
Civil service.
See CIVIL SERVICE.
Commission on employment of people with disabilities, **6:105.**

**VETERANS AND VETERANS'
ORGANIZATIONS** —Cont'd
Disabled veterans —Cont'd
Hospital Day, observance, **6:12T.**
Insignia, unlawful use, **266:70.**
Lease of state property to
federal government for
rehabilitation, **74:41.**
Memorial Day observance by,
town appropriations, **40:5.**
Mentally ill. See within this
heading, "Mentally ill and
retarded persons."
Metropolitan park district's
boating and bathing
facilities, admission, **92:41.**
Motor vehicles.
See MOTOR VEHICLES.
Paraplegic veterans. See within
this heading, "Paraplegic
veterans."
Parking, special provisions,
40:22, 40:22A.
Publication and distribution of
copies of proceedings, **5:9.**
Public charities division,
exception from requirement
of filing copy of charter,
12:8E.
Quarters for, cities and towns
may appropriate money to
provide, **40:9.**
Real estate broker's license,
exemption from fees,
112:87ZZ.
Records, **8:18.**
Recreation areas outside
metropolitan parks district,
admission without charge,
132A:2D.
Rehabilitation. See within this
heading, "Rehabilitation."
Retirement benefits, permanent
disability, **32:6.**
State house, quarters, **8:17.**
Tax exemption, evidence, **59:5.**
Uniform, unlawful use, **264:10A.**
University extension and
correspondence courses,
enrollment, **6:7, 6:7A.**
Vocational schools and
education. See within this
heading, "Vocational schools
and education."
Discharge of lien on property of
dependents, **115:5A.**
Discharge papers.
Photostatic copies, **115:3A.**
Recording for municipal benefit,
115:3.

**VETERANS AND VETERANS'
ORGANIZATIONS** —Cont'd
Disclosure of information
concerning abuses in relation
to veterans' benefits payments,
62C:21.
Discrimination and civil rights,
151B:3-151B:5.
Disease, annuity to veteran
paralyzed, **115:6A-115:6C.**
Disqualification for benefits, **115:5.**
Districts.
Services districts. See within
this heading, "Services
districts."
Domicile.
Residence of veterans. See
within this heading,
"Residence of veterans."
Drills and parades by veterans'
organizations, **33:129.**
Education.
Schools and education. See
within this heading,
"Schools and education."
Elections.
Constitution of Massachusetts,
veterans not disqualified to
vote by reason of receiving
public aid or nonpayment of
poll tax, **MA Const Amend
Art 28.**
Nomination papers, contents,
53:45.
Quarters for veterans'
organizations, authority to
appropriate money to
provide, **40:9.**
Soldiers' home, voting rights of
veterans residing, **51:4.**
Use of word "veteran" by
candidate, **56:43A.**
City and town primaries,
53:34.
Presidential primaries,
53:70D.
State primaries, **53:45.**
Electricians' examination,
preference, **141:2A.**
Embezzlement of funds, **266:59.**
Emergency grant of benefits,
115:5.
Employment.
Auditor of state, employees,
11:6.
Civil service.
See CIVIL SERVICE.
Commissioner of veterans'
services.
Employment security
information as available,
151A:46.

**VETERANS AND VETERANS'
ORGANIZATIONS** —Cont'd
Employment —Cont'd
Commission on employment of
people with disabilities,
6:105.
Confidential records, **151A:46.**
Fair employment practices
regarding, **151B:4.**
Former employees of United
States employment service,
employment service of state
retirement credit, **32:4.**
Holidays, **30:9H, 40:21C½,
149:44, 149:52A½.**
Information as to veterans,
employer's duty to give,
115:2.
Insurance.
See INSURANCE.
Municipal officers and
employees. See within this
heading, "Municipal officers
and employees."
Preference rights. See within
this heading, "Preference
rights in employment."
Promotional list, special, public
officers and employees in
military service, **Spec L
35:3F, Spec L 35:4A.**
Public works, preference for
employment, **149:26,
149:27C.**
Removal. See within this
heading, "Removal from
office or employment."
Retirement systems.
See RETIREMENT SYSTEMS
AND PENSIONS.
Services districts. See within
this heading, "Services
districts."
Tenure, **30:9A.**
Wages and salaries. See within
this heading, "Wages and
salaries."
Encumbrances.
Liens. See within this heading,
"Liens."
Escheat to Commonwealth of
veteran's property, **8:18,
190:3.**
Evidence.
Disability of veteran, evidence
for tax exemption, **59:5.**
Discharge, certified copy of
record, **115:3.**
Paraplegic veterans, proof of
service and disability,
115:6C.

**VETERANS AND VETERANS'
ORGANIZATIONS** —Cont'd
Evidence —Cont'd
Soldiers' homes, burden of proof
of right to benefits, **115A:3.**
Tax exemptions, evidence of
disability, **59:5.**
Examination, inspection, or
investigation.
Claims for benefits,
investigation, **115:2, 115:3.**
Financial condition,
investigation into, **115:2.**
Plumbers and gas fitters, credit
on examination, **142:4.**
Radio and television technician,
additional credit granted to
veteran on examination,
112:87SSS.
Records of veterans
organizations, **8:18.**
Facilities.
Quarters and facilities. See
within this heading,
"Quarters and facilities."
Fair employment practices,
151B:4.
False.
Fraud and deceit, benefits
payments, **62C:21.**
Federal aid or funds.
Homes for veterans, **10:7.**
Orders to pay judgments as
applicable to benefits,
224:16.
Pension or compensation from
federal government,
payment over, **115:5.**
Soldiers' homes, aid, **10:7.**
Federal government.
Aid or support from.
Federal aid or funds. See
within this heading,
"Federal aid or funds."
Retirement benefits, veterans
employment service, **32:4.**
United States Veterans
Administration. See within
this heading, "United States
Veterans Administration."
Fees.
Copies of records and
documents, no fee, **262:46A.**
Insurance broker's license fee,
exemption, **175:167A.**
Real estate broker's license fee,
exemption from payment,
112:87ZZ.
Females.
Admission to soldiers' home,
115A:9.

**VETERANS AND VETERANS'
ORGANIZATIONS** —Cont'd
Females —Cont'd
Preference in civil service to
mother and widows, **31:26,
31:28.**
Women veterans advisory
committee, members, **115:2.**
Fences around graves, **115:9.**
Fiduciary's account.
Allowance of or application for
allowance of accounts,
206:24.
Notice of account or discharge,
206:7.
Representing certain persons in
allowance, **206:24.**
Sureties on bonds, **205:9.**
Financial condition of,
investigation into, **115:2.**
Fire departments.
Appropriations in honor of
deceased firemen paid to
veteran firemen's
associations, **40:5.**
Memorial Day holiday for
veterans, **149:44.**
Retirement allowances of
firemen retiring under
veterans' retirement act,
32:58C.
Flags.
See FLAGS.
Franco-American war veterans.
See FRANCO-AMERICAN WAR
VETERANS.
Fraud and deceit, benefits
payments, **62C:21.**
Funeral expenses.
Burials. See within this heading,
"Burials."
Game of Beano, organizations may
conduct, **10:38.**
Garnishment, benefits exempt,
115:5.
Gas fitters.
Plumbers and gas fitters. See
within this heading,
"Plumbers and gas fitters."
General court, manual delivered to
veterans' organizations, **5:11.**
G.I. loans, insurance companies,
175:65.
Governor.
Appeal on issue of veterans'
benefits, **115:2, 115:2A.**
Commissioner of veterans'
services. See within this
heading, "Commissioner of
veterans' services."

**VETERANS AND VETERANS'
ORGANIZATIONS** —Cont'd
Governor —Cont'd
Council.
Governor's council. See within
this heading, "Governor's
council."
Governor's council.
Commissioner of veterans'
services, appointment and
supervision of commissioner,
6:17, 115:2, 115:2A.
State property leased to federal
government for
rehabilitation of veterans,
74:41.
Graves.
Burials. See within this heading,
"Burials."
Group insurance for employees of
veterans' organizations, **32B:2,
32B:10.**
Guardians and conservators.
Appointment, **201:17.**
United States Veterans'
Administration. See within
this heading, "United States
Veterans Administration."
Handicapped.
Disabled veterans. See within
this heading, "Disabled
veterans."
Hawkers, peddlers, and transient
vendors.
Special licenses for veterans,
101:24.
Temporary licensing of veterans'
organizations selling flags,
badges, etc., **101:33.**
Holidays.
See SUNDAYS AND
HOLIDAYS.
Homes for veterans, **121B:32,
121B:34-121B:37, 121B:39.**
Burden of proof of right to
benefits, **115A:3.**
Discrimination in sale or
leasing, **151B:4, 151B:5.**
Female veterans, admission to
soldiers' home, **115A:9.**
Hospitals and hospital care,
115A:1-115A:7.
Nonprofit corporations for
veterans' homes. See within
this heading, "Nonprofit
corporations for veterans'
homes."
Soldiers' Home in Holyoke, **6:70,
6:71.**
See SOLDIERS' HOME IN
HOLYOKE.

VETERANS AND VETERANS' ORGANIZATIONS —Cont'd

Homes for veterans —Cont'd
Soldiers' Home in
Massachusetts,
115A:1-115A:11.
See SOLDIERS' HOME IN
MASSACHUSETTS.
United Nations, admission to
soldiers' home for service
with forces, **6:41.**
Voting rights of veterans
residing in soldiers' home,
51:4.
Women veterans, admission to
soldiers home, **115A:9.**
Honor rolls for, town
appropriation, **40:5.**
Hospital day, observance, **6:12T.**
Hospitals and hospital care.
Benefits not forfeited because of
hospital treatment, **115:5.**
Commissioner to provide
hospital care, **115:2.**
Lease at state hospitals to
United States for
rehabilitation of veterans,
74:41.
Lien for medical and other
services, **111:70A.**
Local departments to enlist
hospital support, **115:13.**
Mentally ill and retarded
persons. See within this
heading, "Mentally ill and
retarded persons."
Soldiers' homes, **115A:1-115A:7.**
Special hunting, trapping, and
fishing license for
hospitalized veterans,
131:13.
Housing.
Homes for veterans. See within
this heading, "Homes for
veterans."
Retirement provisions as to
housing authority
employees, **32:56-32:60.**
Husband and wife.
Dependents. See within this
heading, "Dependents."
Insignia of disabled veterans,
unlawful use, **266:70.**
Institution, definition of term,
115:1.
Insurance.
See INSURANCE.
Investigation.
Examination, inspection, or
investigation. See within
this heading, "Examination,
inspection, or investigation."

VETERANS AND VETERANS' ORGANIZATIONS —Cont'd

Involuntary separation from
employment at redevelopment
agency, **121B:52.**
Italian American War Veterans of
the United States, Inc., Day,
observance, **6:15J.**
Janitors and custodians, regional
school district to give
preference to veterans for
positions, **41:112.**
Jewish war veterans.
See JEWISH WAR VETERANS.
Judgment, veterans' benefits as
subject to order to pay,
224:16.
Korean emergency.
See KOREAN EMERGENCY
OR WAR.
Labor.
Employment. See within this
heading, "Employment."
Landlord and tenant.
Discrimination against veterans
in leasing of residential
property, **151B:4, 151B:5.**
Low rent housing projects,
tenant selection, **121B:32.**
Mental health facilities leased to
federal government, **74:41.**
Municipalities may lease
quarters for veterans'
organizations, **40:9.**
State property leased to federal
government for
rehabilitation of veterans,
74:41.
Legal settlement.
See POOR PERSONS.
Legion of National Guard Veterans
of Massachusetts, Inc., **8:17.**
Licenses or permits.
Burial, license or permit
required, **114:45-114:47.**
Hawkers, peddlers, and
transient vendors. See
within this heading,
"Hawkers, peddlers, and
transient vendors."
Liens.
Hospitals, lien for medical and
other services, **111:70A.**
Mortgages, **183:63.**
Property or funds of recipient of
benefits, liens, **115:5,
115:5A.**
Subordination of veterans'
agents' liens, **115:5A.**
Loans.
Co-operative banks, information
to insurance commissioner,
115:2.

VETERANS AND VETERANS' ORGANIZATIONS —Cont'd

Loans —Cont'd
G.I. loans, insurance companies,
175:65.
Mortgages, charging fees and
points, **183:63.**
Municipal borrowing, authority,
44:8, 44:10.
Local departments of veterans'
services, **115:10-115:15.**
Advisory board, **115:12.**
Apportionment of tax
assessments, **115:11.**
Assistance from other
departments, **115:13.**
Audit of accounts of districts,
115:15.
Co-operation with federal
agencies, **115:13.**
Creation, **115:10.**
Dependents, services, **115:10.**
Directors of veterans' services,
115:10.
Districts.
Services districts. See within
this heading, "Services
districts."
Enlisting support of hospitals,
115:13.
Located separate from other
agencies, **115:14.**
Payment of costs and expenses
by district boards, **115:11.**
Powers of district boards,
115:11.
Service departments, **115:10.**
Statutory rights of veterans,
printed copies, **115:13.**
Supervision by commissioner of
veterans' services, **115:14.**
Taxation.
See TAXATION.
Lottery tickets, sale, **10:27.**
Low rent housing projects, tenant
selection, **121B:32.**
Malaria, annuity to veterans
paralyzed, **115:6A-115:6C.**
Manual of General Court delivered
to veterans' organizations,
5:11.
Massachusetts veterans,
alphabetical roster, **33:15.**
Massachusetts Vietnam-era
veterans association, lease of
property, **40:9.**
Mayors.
See MAYORS.
Medicaid, veterans' benefits as
exempt income in determining
eligibility, **118E:10.**

**VETERANS AND VETERANS'
ORGANIZATIONS** —Cont'd
Memorial day.
See MEMORIAL DAY.
Memorials.
Change in designation of,
procedure, **44:8.**
Commissioner of veterans'
services as member of World
War II, Korean Emergency,
and Vietnam Conflict
Memorial Commission,
6:124A.
Community war memorials,
40:5, 44:8.
Defacing or mutilating memorial
plaque, offense, **272:73.**
Municipal appropriations and
indebtedness, **40:3, 40:5,
44:8.**
Municipal employees' attendance
at memorial services,
41:111C.
Naval vessels, transfer of ships
to U.S.S. Massachusetts
Memorial Committee, Inc.,
for use as memorial to
veterans of armed forces,
6:124A.
Official Korean war veterans
memorial, **2:46.**
Power of municipal corporations
to establish, **40:3.**
Town or city appropriations,
40:3, 40:5, 44:8.
Trustees, **41:105.**
World War II veterans, **6:17,
6:124A.**
Mentally ill and retarded persons.
Admission to Veterans'
Administration facility,
123:10, 123:28, 123:34.
Appointment of guardian for,
United States veterans'
administration as interested
party, **201:7.**
Commitment and transfer of
veteran to facility of
Veterans' Administration,
123:34.
Lease of mental health facilities
to federal government,
74:41.
Officers and employees of
department of mental
health, exempt employees,
30:9H.
Probate accounts, representation
of veterans in allowance,
206:24.

**VETERANS AND VETERANS'
ORGANIZATIONS** —Cont'd
Mentally ill and retarded persons
—Cont'd
Release or withdrawal of
voluntary admittees to
Veterans' Administration
facilities, **123:11.**
Voluntary admission, **123:10.**
Metropolitan park district's
boating and bathing facilities,
admission of disabled
veterans, **92:41.**
Mexican border service.
See MEXICAN BORDER
SERVICE.
Military order of foreign wars of
the United States.
See MILITARY ORDER OF
FOREIGN WARS OF THE
UNITED STATES.
Military order of the loyal legion of
the United States.
See MILITARY ORDER OF THE
LOYAL LEGION OF THE
UNITED STATES.
Military service, public officers and
employees in, special
promotional list, **Spec L
35:3F, Spec L 35:4A.**
Minors.
Dependents. See within this
heading, "Dependents."
Minutemen, Massachusetts
Council, **40:5.**
Mortgages, charging fees and
points, **183:63.**
Mothers.
American Gold Star Mothers,
Inc.
See AMERICAN GOLD STAR
MOTHERS, INC.
Payment of benefits, **115:5.**
Preference in civil service to
mothers and widows, **31:26,
31:28.**
Motor vehicles.
See MOTOR VEHICLES.
Municipalities.
Aldermen and selectmen. See
within this heading,
"Aldermen and selectmen."
Appeal process, adequacy of
benefits, **115:2.**
Audit of veterans' services
districts, **115:15.**
Borrowing for veterans' benefits,
44:10.
Burial in another town, record,
46:12.
Celebrations, appropriations,
40:5.

**VETERANS AND VETERANS'
ORGANIZATIONS** —Cont'd
Municipalities —Cont'd
Clerks of.
Municipal officers and
employees. See within this
heading, "Municipal
officers and employees."
Commissioner of veterans'
services, supervision of local
departments, **115:14.**
Compelling city or town to pay
benefits, commissioner's
powers with respect, **115:2.**
Dependents, services by
municipal service
departments, **115:10.**
Discharge papers, recording for
municipal benefit, **115:3.**
Graves, care, **40:5, 115:9.**
Local departments of veterans'
services. See within this
heading, "Local departments
of veterans' services."
Marking of graves in
mausoleums, **115:9.**
Memorials. See within this
heading, "Memorials."
Officers and employees.
Municipal officers and
employees. See within this
heading, "Municipal
officers and employees."
Organizations, providing
quarters, **40:9.**
Parking for disabled veterans,
40:22A.
Polish Legion of American
Veterans, appropriation for
observances of certain
patriotic holidays, **40:5.**
Primary elections, use of work
"veteran" by candidate,
53:34.
Reimbursement, **58:8A, 115:2,
115:5, 115:6, 115:8.**
Relief or aid of veterans, **40:5.**
Yankee Division Veterans
Association, quarters, **40:9.**
Municipal officers and employees.
Agents of veterans. See within
this heading, "Agents of
veterans."
Aldermen and selectmen. See
within this heading,
"Aldermen and selectmen."
Change in designation of
memorials, **44:8.**
Civil service preference rights to
veterans in public
employment, **41:112.**

**VETERANS AND VETERANS'
ORGANIZATIONS** —Cont'd
Municipal officers and employees
—Cont'd
Clerk of city or town.
Benefits for veterans, duties,
115:3.
Memorials for veterans, notice
of change in designation,
44:8.
Conventions, attendance,
41:111J.
Election to municipal office,
candidate's use of word
"veteran," **53:34.**
Employment of veterans, **41:112.**
Funerals or memorial services,
attendance, **41:111C.**
Graves officer, appointment and
duties, **115:9.**
Mayors.
See MAYORS.
Retirement systems.
See RETIREMENT SYSTEMS
AND PENSIONS.
Separation from service of
veterans holding
unclassified offices or
positions, **41:112A.**
Name.
Change of name, free furnishing
of records, **262:46A.**
Persons receiving relief, names
not to be disclosed, **40:51.**
National commander of veterans'
organizations, creditable
service, public retirement
system, **32:4.**
Navy club of the United States.
See NAVY CLUB OF THE
UNITED STATES.
Nonprofit corporations for
veterans' homes, **Spec L 37:1
et seq.**
Annual reports, **Spec L 37:7.**
Approval by state board of
housing, **Spec L 37:6.**
Assets.
Division, **Spec L 37:1.**
Remaining, **Spec L 37:9.**
Capital stock, prohibition
against, **Spec L 37:1.**
Conveyance of land by
municipality to corporation,
Spec L 37:2.
Cooperation with federal
government, **Spec L 37:8.**
Costs, estimation, **Spec L 37:6.**
Creation of veterans' housing
corporations, **Spec L 37:1.**
Dwelling units.
Rental, **Spec L 37:4.**
Sale, **Spec L 37:4.**

**VETERANS AND VETERANS'
ORGANIZATIONS** —Cont'd
Nonprofit corporations for
veterans' homes —Cont'd
Dwelling units —Cont'd
State housing board, approval,
Spec L 37:1.
Earnings, division, **Spec L 37:1.**
Estimation.
Of costs, **Spec L 37:6.**
Of expenses and revenue,
Spec L 37:6.
Expenditures, records, **Spec L
37:7.**
Expenses, estimation, **Spec L
37:6.**
Extension of public ways,
sewers, and other municipal
services, **Spec L 37:2.**
Federal government.
Cooperation, **Spec L 37:8.**
Grants, **Spec L 37:8.**
Loans, **Spec L 37:8.**
Financing, proposed method of,
Spec L 37:6.
Grants from federal government,
Spec L 37:8.
Highways, extension, **Spec L
37:2.**
Indebtedness.
Corporation, **Spec L 37:3.**
Payment, **Spec L 37:9.**
Stock, prohibition, **Spec L
37:1.**
Jurisdiction of superior court,
Spec L 37:7.
Land, reconveyance to city or
town, **Spec L 37:9.**
Layout, **Spec L 37:6.**
Loans from federal government,
Spec L 37:8.
Municipalities.
Conveyance of land to
corporation, **Spec L 37:2.**
Reconveyance of land, **Spec L
37:9.**
Nonprofit corporations to
provide, **Spec L 37:1 et
seq.**
Plans, **Spec L 37:6.**
Property, division, **Spec L 37:1.**
Receipts, records, **Spec L 37:7.**
Reconveyance of land to city or
town, **Spec L 37:9.**
Records and reports.
Annual report, **Spec L 37:7.**
Receipts and expenditures,
Spec L 37:7.
Remaining assets, **Spec L 37:9.**
Rental or dwelling units, **Spec L
37:4.**

**VETERANS AND VETERANS'
ORGANIZATIONS** —Cont'd
Nonprofit corporations for
veterans' homes —Cont'd
Revenue, estimation, **Spec L
37:6.**
Roads, extension, **Spec L 37:2.**
Sale or exchange of dwelling
units, **Spec L 37:4.**
Separate projects, **Spec L 37:1.**
Sewers, extension, **Spec L 37:2.**
State board of housing,
approval, **Spec L 37:6.**
Stock, prohibition against, **Spec
L 37:1.**
Streets, extension, **Spec L 37:2.**
Superior court jurisdiction, **Spec
L 37:7.**
Taxation, **Spec L 37:5.**
Towns.
Municipalities. See within this
heading, "Municipalities."
Notice.
Application for benefits, notice,
115:5.
Benefits, notice of wage
reporting system sent to
recipients, **115:1.**
Cities and towns, notice to pay
veterans' benefits, **115:2.**
Memorials, change in
designation, **44:8.**
Removal or discharge of veteran,
notice, **32:16.**
Nurses, retirement from public
service, **32:57-32:60.**
On-farm agricultural schools,
establishment, **74:54.**
Out-of-state commitment order,
123:34.
Outpatient treatment at soldiers'
homes, **115A:1-115A:7.**
Panamanian intervention force
veteran defined, **4:7.**
Paraplegic veterans,
115:6A-115:6C.
Real estate broker's license,
exemption from fees,
112:87ZZ.
Reimbursement of cities and
towns for loss of tax revenue
through abatement, **58:8A.**
Parking penalty, exemption, **40:21,
40:22, 40:22A, 40:22B,
40:22D.**
Patriotic holiday observances by
veterans of world wars,
municipal appropriation, **40:5.**
Payment of benefits, **115:5.**
Pearl Harbor Day, observance,
6:12DD.

VETERANS AND VETERANS' ORGANIZATIONS —Cont'd

Peddlers.
Hawkers, peddlers, and transient vendors. See within this heading, "Hawkers, peddlers, and transient vendors."
Pensions.
See RETIREMENT SYSTEMS AND PENSIONS.
Permits.
Licenses or permits. See within this heading, "Licenses or permits."
Persian Gulf veteran defined, **4:7.**
Pharmacists, right to registration, **112:24.**
Photostatic copies of discharge papers, **115:3A.**
Plumbers and gas fitters.
Credit on examination, **142:4.**
Preferences, **142:4.**
Time of service counted as experience for purposes of appointment of inspector, **142:11.**
Poisoning, annuity to veteran paralyzed, **115:6A-115:6C.**
Police.
Memorial Day as holiday for veterans, **149:44.**
State police.
See STATE POLICE.
Veterans' Retirement Act, allowances, **32:58C.**
Polish-American veterans.
See POLISH-AMERICAN VETERANS.
Poor persons.
See POOR PERSONS.
Preference rights in employment.
Cities and towns, **41:112.**
Civil service, **31:26, 31:28, 41:112.**
Mothers and widows of veterans, **31:26, 31:28.**
Plumbers and gas fitters, **142:4.**
Public works, **149:26, 149:27C.**
Regional school districts, **41:112.**
Presidential primaries.
See PRESIDENTIAL PRIMARIES.
Printers and printing.
Copies of printed matter showing veterans' rights, **115:13.**
Proceedings of veterans' organization, **5:9.**
Prisoners of war, distinctive license plates, **60A:1, 90:2, 90:33.**

VETERANS AND VETERANS' ORGANIZATIONS —Cont'd

Proceedings of organizations, preservation, printing, and distribution of copies, **5:9.**
Proposition 2½, regional veterans' districts included, **59:20B.**
Public charities division, exception from requirement of filing copy of charter, **12:8E, 12:8F.**
Public employees.
Employment. See within this heading, "Employment."
Public works, preferences in employment, **149:26, 149:27C.**
Publishing of copies of proceedings of organizations, **5:9.**
Quarters and facilities.
Appropriations by cities and town to provide, **40:9.**
Armories, use of quarters and facilities, **33:122.**
State house, **8:16A, 8:17, 8:18.**
Radio and television technician examination, extra credits for veteran, **112:87SSS.**
Raffles and bazaars, conduct, **271:7A.**
Real estate broker or salesman's license, exemption from fee, **112:87ZZ.**
Real property.
Discrimination in sale, leasing, etc., against veterans, **151B:4, 151B:5.**
Homes for veterans. See within this heading, "Homes for veterans."
Landlord and tenant. See within this heading, "Landlord and tenant."
Mortgages. See within this heading, "Mortgages."
Parents receiving veterans' benefits, lien on real estate, **115:5A.**
Tax exemptions, **59:5.**
Records and reports, **5:9, 8:18.**
Burial in another town, **46:12.**
Commissioner of veterans' services, records not public, **66:18.**
Disabled American Veterans of the World War, printing and distribution of proceedings, **5:9.**
Discharge papers, **115:3.**
Employment, confidential records, **151A:46.**
Escheat to Commonwealth of veterans' property, **8:18.**

VETERANS AND VETERANS' ORGANIZATIONS —Cont'd

Records and reports —Cont'd
Lien on real estate of recipient of veterans' benefits, **115:5A.**
Roster of Massachusetts veterans, **33:15.**
Spouse of veteran, copies of certain records to be furnished free, **262:46A.**
Veterans' organizations and services, **8:18.**
Wage reporting system.
Wages and salaries. See within this heading, "Wages and salaries."
Waiver of fees for copies of records to assist in proving claim against government, **262:46A.**
Recreation areas outside metropolitan park district, admission of certain disabled veterans without charge, **132A:2D.**
Regents of higher education, board of.
See REGENTS OF HIGHER EDUCATION, BOARD.
Regional school districts.
Preference in labor service of schools, **41:112.**
Retirement law for veterans, acceptance, **32:60.**
Registration, registers, and registrars.
Lease of rehabilitation facilities, **74:41.**
Roster of veterans, **33:15.**
Rehabilitation, **74:22D.**
Co-operation of state board for vocational education with veterans' administration, **74:22D.**
Institutional on-farm agricultural schools, **74:54.**
Lease of state property to federal government, **74:41.**
Reimbursement.
Burial expenses, **115:8.**
Cities and towns, reimbursement, **58:8A, 115:2, 115:5, 115:6.**
Removal from office or employment, **30:9A, 30:41.**
Commissioner of veterans' services, **7:4O.**
Superintendent of soldiers' home in Holyoke, **6:71.**
Unclassified offices or positions, veterans holding, **30:9A.**

VETERANS AND VETERANS' ORGANIZATIONS —Cont'd
Reports.
Records and reports. See within this heading, "Records and reports."
Representation of persons in allowance of probate accounts, **206:24.**
Residence of veterans.
Benefits furnished to veterans, **115:2, 115:5, 115:6, 115:8.**
Decision in controversies between towns, **115:2.**
Definitions, **115:1.**
Homes for veterans. See within this heading, "Homes for veterans."
Requirements for benefits, **115:5.**
Tuition benefits, Vietnam veterans, **15A:16.**
Retarded persons.
Mentally ill and retarded persons. See within this heading, "Mentally ill and retarded persons."
Retirement systems.
See RETIREMENT SYSTEMS AND PENSIONS.
Revenue department and commissioner.
Reimbursement of municipalities for loss of tax revenue through abatement for paraplegic veterans, **58:8A.**
Services districts, audit of accounts, **115:15.**
Review.
See APPEAL AND REVIEW.
Rosters of veterans, provision, **33:15.**
Salaries.
Wages and salaries. See within this heading, "Wages and salaries."
Savings and loan associations to furnish information to commissioner of veterans' services, **115:2.**
Savings banks.
See SAVINGS BANKS.
Scholarships.
See SCHOLARSHIPS AND FELLOWSHIPS.
Schools and education.
Admission to bar of veterans of World War II, educational requirements, **221:36A.**
Colleges and universities.
Vietnam veterans. See within this heading, "Vietnam veterans."

VETERANS AND VETERANS' ORGANIZATIONS —Cont'd
Schools and education —Cont'd
Department of education.
See EDUCATION DEPARTMENT.
Disabled veterans, advertisements of civil service courses, **271:48.**
Education department, establishment of institutional on-farm agricultural schools for veterans, **74:54.**
Gifts of patriotic plaques, **71:69A.**
Italian American War Veterans of the United States, Inc., Day, observance, **6:15J.**
Lease of schools to federal government for rehabilitation purposes, **74:41.**
On-farm agricultural schools, establishment, **74:54.**
Preference in employing custodians or janitors, **41:112.**
Regional school districts. See within this heading, "Regional school districts."
Scholarships.
See SCHOLARSHIPS AND FELLOWSHIPS.
Street railways, special rates for attending school, **161:107.**
Vietnam veterans. See within this heading, "Vietnam veterans."
Vocational schools and education. See within this heading, "Vocational schools and education."
Seabee veterans of America.
See SEABEE VETERANS OF AMERICA.
Selectmen.
Aldermen and selectmen. See within this heading, "Aldermen and selectmen."
Service-connected disability, certification of veteran's loss of both legs, **115:6B.**
Services districts.
Advisory boards, **115:12.**
Audit, **115:15.**
Boards, **115:11.**
Formation, **115:10.**
Group insurance for employees, **32B:2, 32B:7A, 32B:9D¾, 32B:9E, 32B:10.**

VETERANS AND VETERANS' ORGANIZATIONS —Cont'd
Services districts —Cont'd
Payment of costs and expenses by boards, **115:11.**
Surviving spouse of insured employee, contribution toward health insurance premiums, **32B:9D, 32B:9D½.**
Treasurer, **115:10.**
Withdrawal, **115:10.**
Services for, **115:1-115:15.**
Social services.
Welfare and social services. See within this heading, "Welfare and social services."
Soldiers' homes.
Homes for veterans. See within this heading, "Homes for veterans."
Southwest Asia war veterans, official state monument for, **2:37.**
Spanish American war.
See MILITARY AND NAVAL ORDER OF THE SPANISH AMERICAN WAR.
Special state police officer, appointment, **10:5.**
Spouse.
Dependents. See within this heading, "Dependents."
State auditor's officers and employees as subject to laws regulating retention in public service, **11:6.**
State comptroller.
Comptroller. See within this heading, "Comptroller's duties as to veterans' benefits."
State departments, commissioner as agent, **115:2.**
State house facilities, **8:16A, 8:17, 8:18.**
State lottery tickets, sales, **10:27.**
State police.
See STATE POLICE.
Status, town appropriation, **40:5.**
Street railways, special rates for veterans attending school, **161:107.**
Sundays.
See SUNDAYS AND HOLIDAYS.
Superior courts.
Enforcement of decisions of veterans' services commissioner, **115:2A.**

VETERANS AND VETERANS'
ORGANIZATIONS —Cont'd
Superior courts —Cont'd
Lien on real estate of recipient
of benefits, enforcement,
115:5A.
Surety on bonds relating to
probate accounts, **205:9.**
Surviving spouse.
Dependents. See within this
heading, "Dependents."
Taxation.
See TAXATION.
Teachers, retirement, **32:10.**
Tenant.
Landlord and tenant. See within
this heading, "Landlord and
tenant."
Tenure in state employment,
30:9A.
Towns.
Municipalities. See within this
heading, "Municipalities."
Transient vendors.
Hawkers, peddlers, and
transient vendors. See
within this heading,
"Hawkers, peddlers, and
transient vendors."
Traveling expenses of
commissioner of veterans'
services, **7:4N.**
Trustee process, exemption, **115:5.**
Tumors, annuity to veterans
paralyzed, **115:6A-115:6C.**
Uniforms and insignia, unlawful
use, **264:10A, 266:69, 266:70.**
United American Veterans, **40:5.**
Leasing of building space by
cities and towns, **40:9.**
United Nations.
Admission to soldiers' home for
service with forces, **6:41.**
Serving under flag, **115:5.**
United Spanish war veterans.
See UNITED SPANISH WAR
VETERANS.
United States Veterans
Administration.
Guardians and conservators.
Mentally ill or retarded
persons, administration as
interested party in cases
concerning, **201:7.**
Minors, administration as
interested party in cases
concerning, **201:2.**
Sureties in cases concerning
administration, **205:9.**
Hospitals and hospital care. See
within this heading,
"Hospitals and hospital
care."

VETERANS AND VETERANS'
ORGANIZATIONS —Cont'd
United States Veterans
Administration —Cont'd
Liens for medical and other
services furnished in
hospitals, **111:70A.**
State board for vocational
education to co-operate,
74:22D.
United States Veterans
Employment Service,
retirement benefits, **32:4.**
Unity War Veterans Association,
headquarters, **40:9.**
Universities and colleges.
Vietnam veterans. See within
this heading, "Vietnam
veterans."
Vacation, delegates may attend
conventions of veterans'
organizations without loss,
41:111J.
Victims of violent crime,
compensation for, **258C:10.**
Vietnam veterans.
Assignment of quarters in state
house, **8:17.**
Bonus.
Vietnam veterans, bonus for.
See within this heading,
"Vietnam veterans,
bonus."
Civil service examination for
Vietnam veterans.
See CIVIL SERVICE.
Colleges and universities.
Exemption from tuition,
15A:16.
Summer and evening sessions,
15A:16.
Combat veterans combined
armed forces quarters,
cities' and towns'
appropriations to provide,
40:9.
Commissioner of veterans'
services as member of World
War II, Korean Emergency,
and Vietnam Conflict
Memorial Commission,
6:124A.
Death certificate, matters to be
stated, **46:10.**
Definition, **4:7.**
Gravestones, municipal
appropriations, **40:5.**
Hawkers and peddlers,
licensing, **101:24.**
Holiday, **6:15MM.**
Income tax exemption, **62:1.**

VETERANS AND VETERANS'
ORGANIZATIONS —Cont'd
Vietnam veterans —Cont'd
Memorial, official, **2:34.**
Motor vehicle excise taxes,
exemption, **60A:1.**
Municipal appropriations for
gravestones, **40:5.**
Public charities division,
exemption from filing copy
of charter, **12:8E.**
Tax exemption, **59:5, 60A:1,**
62:1.
Tuition-free attendance at
certain educational
institutions, **15A:16.**
Women veterans advisory
committee, members, **115:2.**
Vietnam veterans, bonus, **Spec L**
39:1 et seq.
Active service in Armed Forces.
Defined, **Spec L 39:1.**
Persons deceased while, **Spec**
L 39:4.
Adjutant general to certify
information, **Spec L 39:7.**
Amount of bonus, **Spec L 39:1.**
Appeal to board from state
treasurer, **Spec L 39:10.**
Application, **Spec L 39:6.**
State treasurer to act, **Spec L**
39:9.
Armed Forces, defined, **Spec L**
39:2.
Benefits.
Application, **Spec L 39:6,**
39:9.
Eligibility, **Spec L 39:1, 39:3,**
39:5.
Mental incompetents entitled,
Spec L 39:5.
Bonds and notes, issuance, **Spec**
L 39:11, 39:12.
Certification of information by
adjutant general, **Spec L**
39:7.
Death while in active military
service, **Spec L 39:4.**
Eligibility, **Spec L 39:1, 39:3,**
39:5.
False statements, **Spec L 39:8.**
Fines, **Spec L 39:8.**
Heirs-at-law, eligibility for
benefits, **Spec L 39:3.**
Incompetents entitled to
benefits, **Spec L 39:5.**
Insane persons entitled to
benefits, **Spec L 39:5.**
Interest bearing notes, issuance,
Spec L 39:11.
Mental incompetents entitled to
benefits, **Spec L 39:5.**

VETERANS AND VETERANS' ORGANIZATIONS —Cont'd

Vietnam veterans, bonus —Cont'd
Penalties, **Spec L 39:8.**
Perjury, **Spec L 39:8.**
Treasurer of state.
Appeal to board from decision, **Spec L 39:10.**
Application processing, **Spec L 39:9.**
Vocational schools and education.
Co-operation of state board for vocational education with veterans' administration, **74:22D.**
Institutional on-farm agricultural schools for veterans, **74:54.**
Lease of schools to federal government for rehabilitation of veterans, **74:41.**
Rehabilitation of disabled veterans, **74:22D.**
Wages and salaries.
Commissioner of veterans services, compensation of, **7:4M.**
Conventions, attendance without loss of pay, **41:111J.**
Employer's duty to give information, **115:2.**
Reporting system, **62E:3.**
Lists of recipients, veterans' services department to provide, **62E:4.**
Notice sent to recipients, **115:1.**
Reporting of benefits, **115:1, 151:1, 151A:1.**
Soldiers' home in Holyoke, board of trustees, **6:70.**
Soldiers' home in Massachusetts, board of trustees, **6:40.**
Vietnam veterans, bonus for. See within this heading, "Vietnam veterans, bonus."
Workers' compensation.
See WORKERS' COMPENSATION.
World War II, Korean Emergency, and Vietnam Conflict Memorial Commission members, **6:124A.**
Waiver of fees for copies of records to assist in proving claim against government, **262:46A.**
Wartime service, defined, **4:7.**

VETERANS AND VETERANS' ORGANIZATIONS —Cont'd

Welfare and social services.
Abuses in relation to veterans' benefits payments, disclosure of information, **62C:21.**
Constitution of Massachusetts, veterans not disqualified to vote by reason of receiving public aid or nonpayment of poll tax, **MA Const Amend Art 28.**
Order to pay judgments, exemption, **224:16.**
Widows.
Dependents. See within this heading, "Dependents."
Women.
Females. See within this heading, "Females."
Women veterans advisory committee, **115:2.**
Workers' compensation.
See WORKERS' COMPENSATION.
World War I Hospital Day, observance, **6:12T.**
World War II Memorial Commission, **6:17, 6:124A.**
World War II veterans.
Death certificate, **46:10.**
Defined, **4:7.**
Educational requirements for admission to bar, **221:36A.**
Memorial commission, **6:17, 6:124A.**
Patriotic holidays, municipal applications, **40:5.**
World War I veterans.
Death certificate, **46:10.**
Defined, **4:7.**
Flags, **264:5.**
Insignia, unlawful use, **266:70.**
Orange peace statue.
Official peace statue of Commonwealth, **2:45.**
Public charities division, exemption from requirement of filing copy of charter, **12:8E.**
Uniform, unlawful use, **264:10A.**
Yankee division veterans association.
See YANKEE DIVISION VETERANS ASSOCIATION.

VETERANS' DAY, 4:7, 6:12A, 136:13.
Firemen, **30:9H, 48:57A, 48:57D, 48:57E.**

VETERANS' DAY —Cont'd
Police, day off or extra pay, **147:17A.**
State employees, day off or extra pay, **30:24A.**
Town appropriations for observance, **40:5.**
Veterans granted time off to observe, **30:9H, 40:21C½, 149:52A½.**
Vietnam Veterans' day, **6:15MM.**

VETERANS HOUSING ACT, 121B:34 et seq.

VETERANS' PREFERENCE ACT, 31:3.

VETERANS' RETIREMENT ACT, 32:56 et seq.

VETERANS SERVICES COMMISSION.
Employment dislocations and assistance in reemployment of dislocated workers, **6:17.**

VETERANS' TENURE ACT, 30:9A, 31:21 et seq.

VETERINARIANS, 112:54-112:60.
Advertising, revocation of certificate for misrepresentation, **112:59.**
Aliens, registration, **112:55.**
Animal health division.
Inspectors as practicing veterinary medicine, **112:58.**
Schools, approval, **112:55.**
Annual report of registration board, **112:57.**
Appeal and review.
Refusal or revocation of license of veterinarian, **112:55, 112:64.**
School for veterinarians, institutional licenses, **112:56D.**
Review of disapproval, **112:55.**
Applicants for examination or re-examination, **112:55.**
Biology, education or research.
College education, **112:55.**
Fraud in biological research, revocation of license, **112:59.**
Board of registration, **13:26 et seq., 112:54-112:60.**
Bovine animals, tagging, **129:42.**
Brucellosis testing and vaccination, **112:58, 129:36B, 129:36D, 129:36F.**
Bylaws and rules of registration board, **112:54, 112:61.**

VETERINARIANS —Cont'd

Cancellation of registration, **112:55.**

Cats.
  Fees for emergency treatment of dogs and cats, **140:151B.**
  Health certificates for cats, **140:138A.**

Certificate of registration.
  Duplicate certificate, **112:88.**
  General provisions as to furnishing, **112:88.**
  Issuance, **112:55.**
  Renewal, **112:55.**
  Revocation or suspension. See within this heading, "Revocation or suspension of certificate or license."

Certificates, rabies.
  Tag and certificate issued after rabies vaccination of dogs and cats, **140:145B.**

Charges and complaints against.
  Hearing, **112:61, 112:62.**
  Investigation, **112:57.**
  Notice of hearing, **112:62.**
  Pendency of criminal action, **112:63.**
  Rules and regulations, **112:61.**
  Witnesses on hearing, **112:62.**

Chief veterinary officer of animal health division, **112:55.**

Clinical training for veterinary students, exemption from licensing provisions, **112:56E.**

Colleges.
  Approval, **112:55.**
  Clinical training for veterinary students, **112:56E.**
  Institutional licenses, **112:56D.**
  Registration of graduates of unapproved veterinary schools, **112:55, 112:55A, 112:56A, 112:59.**
  Scholarship program, **15A:7.**

Complaint.
  Charges and complaints. See within this heading, "Charges and complaints against."

Conviction of crime, revocation of certificate, **112:55, 112:59.**

Cruelty to animals.
  Grounds for revocation of certificate, **112:59.**
  Reporting.
    Civil liability, **112:58B.**

Deceit.
  Fraud and deceit. See within this heading, "Fraud and deceit."

VETERINARIANS —Cont'd

Definitions, **112:54A.**

Dogs and cats, rabies vaccination required, **140:145B.**

Drugs, druggists, and pharmacists.
  Addiction as ground for revocation of registration, **112:55, 112:59.**
  Authorized possession, dispensation, etc., **94C:9.**
  Evading or violating regulations, **94:187D.**
  Examined in subject of pharmacology, veterinarians, **112:56.**
  Practitioner defined, **94C:1.**
  Prescriptions. See within this heading, "Prescriptions."
  Reduction of oral prescription to writing, **94C:20.**
  Registration, **94C:7.**
  Required information on label, **94C:21, 94C:39.**
  Revocation of license, **112:55, 112:59.**
  Veterinarian registration law as inapplicable, **112:60.**

Emergency care or treatment of domestic animal, **112:58A, 140:151B.**

Emergency registration law inapplicable, **112:60.**

Employment of unregistered persons, penalty, **112:59.**

Examination.
  Registration. See within this heading, "Registration."

Farmers, registration law inapplicable, **112:60.**

Fees.
  Annual license fee, amount, **112:55.**
  Emergency care or treatment of dogs and cats, **140:151B.**
  Examination fee, amount, **112:55.**
  Other states, fee for licensing of veterinarians, **112:56C.**
  Registration, **112:55, 112:88.**
  Schools, fees for institutional licenses, **112:56D.**

Food and agriculture department.
  Animal health inspectors as practicing veterinary medicine, **112:58.**
  Schools of veterinary medicine, approval, **112:55.**

Foreign states and countries.
  Examination of out-of-state license applicant, **112:56C.**
  Issuance of license to veterinarians licensed in other states, **112:56A.**

VETERINARIANS —Cont'd

Foreign states and countries —Cont'd
  Practice by nonresident veterinarian, **112:60.**
  Reciprocity of licensing provisions, **112:56C.**
  Schools chartered by, registration of aliens and persons receiving degrees, **112:55.**

Fraud and deceit.
  Drugs, **94:187D.**
  Revocation of certificate or license, **112:59, 112:61.**

Gross misconduct, revocation or suspension of certificate, **112:61.**

Hearing on charges or complaints, **112:61, 112:62.**

Horse and dog racing meetings.
  Employment, **6:48, 128A:8.**
  Licensing and registration of veterinarians, **128A:9A.**
  State racing commission, veterinarian as employee, **6:48.**

Hospitals.
  Prescription blanks of hospitals or clinics, **112:56B.**
  Revocation of license for unlawful practices, **112:59.**

Humane disposition of greyhounds, **128C:7.**

Imported cattle, blood test for brucellosis, **129:36D, 129:36F.**

Incorporated veterinarian hospital employing unregistered persons, **112:59.**

Insanity, revocation or suspension of certificate, **112:61.**

Insurance companies may furnish veterinary service, **175:47.**

Investigation of complaint by registration board, **112:57.**

Judicial review, refusal or revocation of license, **112:55, 112:64.**

License.
  Registration. See within this heading, "Registration."

Limited application of registration law, **112:60.**

Malpractice, revocation or suspension of license, **112:61.**

Meetings of registration board, **13:27.**

Militia, eligibility of veterinary officer, **33:21.**

VETERINARIANS —Cont'd

Narcotics.

Drugs, druggists, and pharmacists. See within this heading, "Drugs, druggists, and pharmacists."

Nonresidents.

Foreign states and countries. See within this heading, "Foreign states and countries."

Notice to city and town clerks of vaccinations of dogs against rabies, **140:145B.**

Organization of registration board, **13:27.**

Other states.

Foreign states and countries. See within this heading, "Foreign states and countries."

Pharmacology.

Drugs, druggists, and pharmacists. See within this heading, "Drugs, druggists, and pharmacists."

"Practice of veterinary medicine" defined, **112:58.**

Prescriptions.

Blanks of hospitals or clinics, **112:56B.**

Writing, reduction of oral prescription, **94C:20.**

Professional services within professional corporations law, **156A:2.**

Public or lay member of registration board, provision, **13:26.**

Qualifications of registration board members, **13:26.**

Quorum of registration board, **112:54.**

Races.

Horse and dog racing meetings. See within this heading, "Horse and dog racing meetings."

Reciprocity with other states as to licensing, **112:56C.**

Records, reports, and returns.

Board of registration of veterinary medicine, annual report, **112:57.**

Institutional licenses for veterinarian schools, **112:56D.**

Register of veterinarians, **112:57.**

Registration, **112:54-112:60.**

Appeal and review. See within this heading, "Appeal and review."

VETERINARIANS —Cont'd

Registration —Cont'd

Approval of colleges and universities, **112:55.**

Approving authority, defined, **112:54A.**

Board of registration, **13:26 et seq., 112:54-112:60.**

Cancellation, **112:55.**

Certificate of registration. See within this heading, "Certificate of registration."

Drugs, **94C:7.**

Examination, **112:55.**

Fees, **112:55.**

Out-of-state license applicant, **112:56C.**

Subjects, **112:56.**

Exemption from licensing provisions for clinical training of students, **112:56E.**

Fees, **112:55, 112:88.**

Graduates of non-approved veterinary schools, **112:55, 112:55A, 112:56A, 112:59.**

Grounds for refusal, revocation, or suspension, **112:55, 112:59.**

Horse and dog racing meetings, **128A:9A.**

Mandatory sterilization of shelter animals by licensed veterinarian, **140:139A.**

Other states, veterinarians, **112:56C.**

Qualifications, **112:55.**

Quorum of board of registration in veterinary medicine for revocation, **112:54.**

Reciprocity with other states, **112:56C.**

Re-examination, **112:55.**

Register of veterinarians, **112:57.**

Renewal, **112:55.**

Revocation or suspension. See within this heading, "Revocation or suspension of certificate or license."

Temporary permit, **112:56A.**

Reports.

Records, reports, and returns. See within this heading, "Records, reports, and returns."

Review.

Appeal and review. See within this heading, "Appeal and review."

VETERINARIANS —Cont'd

Revocation or suspension of certificate or license, **112:61.**

Addiction to vice or narcotics, **112:55, 112:59.**

Charges and complaints. See within this heading, "Charges and complaints against."

Conviction of crime, **112:55, 112:59.**

Fee, default in payment, **112:55.**

Penalty for practicing after, **112:65.**

Powers of board, **112:61.**

Reissuance of certificate after, **112:55.**

Revision or reversal by supreme judicial court, **112:64.**

Violation of law, revocation, **112:59.**

Rules and regulations, **112:54, 112:61, 112:88.**

Salaries and expenses of registration board members, **13:28.**

Sanitation of office and equipment, penalty for failure to maintain, **112:59.**

Scholarship program, **15A:7.**

Schools for.

Colleges. See within this heading, "Colleges."

Secretary to registration board, **13:27, 13:28.**

State racing commission, employee, **6:48.**

Sterilization of shelter animals by licensed veterinarian, **140:139A.**

Superior courts, appeals, **112:55, 112:56D.**

Suspension.

Revocation or suspension. See within this heading, "Revocation or suspension of certificate or license."

Tagging of bovine animals, **129:42.**

Temporary permits, **112:56A.**

Tuberculin test, **129:33.**

Unlawful practices, penalties, **112:59.**

Unregistered person, penalty for practice, **112:59.**

Vaccinations.

Brucellosis, **129:36B, 129:36D, 129:36F.**

Rabies, notice to city and town clerks, **140:145B.**

Witnesses in hearings before registration board, **112:62.**

VETO.
Adjournment, question of, excepted from veto power, **US Const Art 1 Sec 7 cl 3.**
Bills passed by Congress, **US Const Art 1 Sec 7 cl 2.**
Constitution of Massachusetts.
See CONSTITUTION OF MASSACHUSETTS.
Constitution of the United States.
See CONSTITUTION OF THE UNITED STATES.
Mayors, **39:4.**
Plan A charter cities, **43:55.**
Plan B charter cities, **43:63.**
Veterans, veto of acceptance of law as to pensions, **32:55.**
Passing bills over, **US Const Art 1 Sec 7 cl 2, 3.**
Pocket veto, **US Const Art 1 Sec 7 cl 2.**
Two-thirds vote required to pass bill over, **US Const Art 1 Sec 7 cl 2, 3.**

VIATICAL SETTLEMENTS, 175:212 to 175:223.
Annual statements, **175:217.**
Approval by commissioner, **175:216.**
Authority of commissioner, **175:221.**
Complaint procedures, **175:223.**
Definitions, **175:213.**
Disclosure, **175:219.**
Examination of business affairs of licensee, **175:218.**
Licensing of loan providers and agents, **175:214.**
Required information, **175:220.**
Short title, **175:212.**
Unfair trade practice, **175:222.**
Violations, **175:215.**

VIBRATING STEELYARDS.
Use regulated, **98:8.**

VICE-PRESIDENT OF UNITED STATES.
Absence, Senate to choose president pro tempore in case of, **US Const Art 1 Sec 3 cl 5.**
Constitution of the United States.
See CONSTITUTION OF THE UNITED STATES.
Disability of Vice-President, person to act in case of, **US Const Art 2 Sec 1 cl 6; Amend 25.**
Election.
Electoral college.
See ELECTORAL COLLEGE.

VICE-PRESIDENT OF UNITED STATES —Cont'd
Election —Cont'd
List of votes for Vice-President sent to president of Senate, **US Const Amend 12.**
Senate, election by, **US Const Amend 12; Amend 20 Sec 4.**
Electoral votes, functions in counting of, **US Const Amend 12.**
Insurance.
See INSURANCE.
President of Senate, Vice-President as, **US Const Art 1 Sec 3 cl 4.**
President of United States.
Succession to Presidency, **US Const Art 2 Sec 1 cl 6; 20th Amend, 25th Amend.**
Vice-President to act as, circumstances requiring, **US Const Art 2 Sec 1 cl 6; 20th Amend, 25th Amend Sec 3.**
Qualifications.
Age, **US Const Amend 12.**
Alien not eligible, **US Const Amend 12.**
Residence, **US Const Amend 12.**
Senate of United States.
Choice of vice-president by, **US Const 12th Amend, 20th Amend Sec 4.**
President of Senate, Vice-president as, **US Const Art 1 Sec 3 cl 4.**
Succession to Presidency, **US Const Art 2 Sec 1 cl 6; 20th Amend, 25th Amend.**
Term of office, **US Const Art 2 Sec 1 cl 1; Amend 20 Sec 1.**
Tie vote, power to resolve, **US Const Art 1 Sec 3 cl 4.**
Vacancy in office, **US Const Amend 20 Sec 3, 4, Amend 25 Sec 2.**
Vice-President-elect, succession to office of President, **US Const Amend 20 Sec 3.**

VICTIM AND WITNESS ASSISTANCE FUND, 258B:9.

VICTIMS OF VIOLENT CRIMES, 258B:2 et seq., 258C:1 et seq.
Ambulance services, **258C:3.**
Appeal of award or denial of compensation, **258C:9.**

VICTIMS OF VIOLENT CRIMES —Cont'd
Appellate division of district court, rehearing on compensation matters, **231:108.**
Burial expenses, **258C:3.**
Change of address, notice of, **258C:6.**
Children and minors, **258C:3.**
Dependent children, aid to, **258C:10.**
Claims for compensation, **258C:1 et seq.**
Compensation, **258C:1 et seq.**
Definitions, **127:1, 233:20J, 258C:1.**
Dental services, **258C:3.**
Dependent children, aid to, **258C:10.**
District courts.
See DISTRICT COURTS.
Division of victim compensation and assistance, **12:11K, 258C:4.**
Employer, discharge or other penalty imposed, **258B:3, 268:14B.**
Family and relatives, **258C:1.**
Fraudulent applications, penalties for, **258C:12.**
Good faith in attempt to provide or obtain assistance, **258C:13.**
Hearing on claim for compensation.
Rehearing in appellate division of district court, **231:108.**
Hospitals and health care facilities, **112:12A½.**
Insurance, **258C:10.**
Limitation of actions.
Claims, filing of, **258C:5.**
Maximum award of compensation, **258C:3.**
Medicaid, **258C:3, 258C:10.**
Medical care and services, compensation for, **258C:1, 258C:3, 258C:10.**
Murder or homicide.
Survivors of homicide victims awareness month, **6:15HHHH.**
Notice and knowledge.
Amount of compensation, **258C:7.**
Change of address, **258C:6.**
Reconsideration of award or denial of compensation, **258C:8.**
Sexually dangerous persons, discharge, **123A:9.**
Out-of-pocket loss, **258C:1, 258C:3, 258C:10.**

VICTIMS OF VIOLENT CRIMES —Cont'd

Parole hearings, appearances at or recommendations, **127:1, 127:133A.**

    Family members of deceased victims, **127:133C.**

Physicians and surgeons, reports concerning victims, **112:12A½.**

Rape.

    See RAPE.

Reconsideration of award or denial of compensation, **258C:8.**

Rehearing in appellate division of district court on matters affecting compensation, **231:108.**

Report.

    Promptness of crime report, **258B:2, 258C:2.**

Restitution, **258C:10.**

Retirement systems and pensions, **258C:10.**

    Attachment or execution in order to make restitution, not exempt from, **235:34A.**

Rights, **258B:2 et seq.**

    See RIGHTS OF VICTIMS AND WITNESSES OF CRIME.

Sexual offenses.

    See SEXUAL OFFENSES AND OFFENDERS.

Social security benefits, **258C:10.**

Statute of limitations.

    Limitation of actions, **258C:5.**

Subrogation of state to compensation claim of victim, **258C:11.**

Survivors of homicide victims awareness month, **6:15HHHH.**

Time or date.

    Limitation of actions, **258C:5.**

    Report of crime, promptness, **258B:2.**

Trial or hearings.

    Hearing on claim for compensation, **231:108.**

Unemployment compensation, **258C:10.**

Veteran's benefits, **258C:10.**

Worker's compensation, **258C:10.**

VICTUALLERS.

See COMMON VICTUALLERS.

VIDEOTAPING.

Child witness, testimony of, **278:16D.**

Consent of mentally ill and retarded persons, **19B:15.**

VIETNAM VETERANS.

See VETERANS AND VETERANS' ORGANIZATIONS.

VIEW.

Eminent domain cases, jury view, **79:22.**

Highways.

    See HIGHWAYS AND STREETS.

Jury view, **234:35.**

    Eminent domain cases, **79:22.**

    Overflow cases caused by dams or reservoirs, **253:7.**

Lowlands, proceedings by commissioners to obtain view, **252:13.**

Medical examiners, **38:6.**

    See AUTOPSY.

VILLAGES.

Towns may establish village for improvements, **40:44.**

VINEGAR, 94:163-94:171.

Acetic acid content, minimum, **94:163.**

Adulteration, **94:163, 94:171.**

Brands and labels, requirements, **94:165, 94:168, 94:171.**

Coloring matter prohibited, **94:163.**

Containers, violation of requirements, **94:165.**

Defined under food and drug inspection law, **94:163.**

Enforcement of provisions, **94:169.**

Examination, methods, **94:164.**

Fines and penalties, **94:163-94:171.**

Harmful ingredients, **94:170.**

Imitation or counterfeit inspection seal, or tampering with official samples, **94:168.**

Impure and unwholesome, **94:170, 94:171.**

Inspector's seal, manufacturer's use or possession, **94:165, 94:168.**

Marks and labels on containers, **94:165, 94:168, 94:171.**

Mislabeling or misbranding, **94:171.**

Sale of adulterated, **94:171.**

Sampling for analysis, **94:166-94:168.**

Standards and ingredients, **94:163.**

VINES.

Destruction or mutilation of, as criminal offense, **266:115.**

VIOLATION OF PAROLE.

See PROBATION AND PAROLE.

VIOLENCE PREVENTION ADVISORY COUNCIL, 15:1G.

Model curriculum on violence prevention.

    Recommendation to board of education, **71:1.**

VIRGINIA.

First Congress, representation in, **US Const Art 1 Sec 2 cl 3.**

VIRUSES.

Health department's power as to preparation and distribution, **111:5A.**

VISCOUS COMMODITIES.

Cartons for the sale, **98:22-98:24.**

VISION.

See EYES.

VISITATION.

Alcoholism treatment and rehabilitation facilities, regulation of visiting hours for patients, **111B:11.**

Annual observance, visiting nurse association week, **6:12JJ.**

Cemeteries, hours for visitation, **114:42A.**

Children.

    See CHILDREN AND MINORS.

Correctional institutions.

    See CORRECTIONAL INSTITUTIONS.

Guardians, conservators, and committees, **119:35, 209C:5.**

Hospital facilities division personnel, visitation, **111:53.**

Illegitimate children, visitation rights, **209C:1, 209C:3-209C:5, 209C:15, 209C:20.**

Lists of persons from 3 through 21 years of age, visiting buildings or residences in order to make, **51:4, 51:14A.**

Mental retardation, visitation privileges, **123B:9.**

Migrant farm workers, rights, **111:128H.**

Siblings in foster care, **119:23, 119:26.**

Sundays and holidays, visiting nurse association week, **6:12JJ.**

Tax assessors, **58:3.**

Welfare and social services, **119:35, 209C:5.**

VISITING NURSE ASSOCIATION.

Death of terminally ill patient, pronouncement by nurses, **46:9.**

VISITING PHYSICIANS.
Good Samaritan law, temporary
    licensees entitled to
    protection, **112:12B, 112:12C.**
Temporary registration, **112:9B.**

VISUAL TAG ACT, 90:20C.
Vehicles, **90:20C.**

VITAL STATISTICS.
Births, establishment of registry of
    vital statistics and records,
    17:4.
Copies.
    See COPIES.
Death.
    See DEATH.
Evidence, copies authenticated by
    seal, **46:19C.**
Examination of records in custody
    of public health commissioner,
    46:2A.
Fees pertaining to copies of
    records, **262:34, 262:44A.**
    Birth records, **46:13, 46:26.**
    See BIRTHS.
Fines and penalties.
    Payment and disposition in vital
        statistics cases, **46:25.**
    Registrar of vital statistics,
        neglect of duty, **46:27.**
Forms for information of birth to
    be provided by public health
    commissioner, **46:16, 111:24B.**
Health.
    See HEALTH AND HEALTH
        DEPARTMENTS.
Marriage.
    See MARRIAGE.
Neglect of duty by registrar, **46:27.**
Registry of vital records and
    statistics, establishment, **17:4.**
Secretary of state, authority as to
    vital statistics records, **111:2.**
Tables, **111:2.**

VITAMINS.
Milk, addition to.
    See MILK AND MILK
        PRODUCTS.
Misbranding of food, what
    constitutes, **94:187.**

VITRIOL.
Adulteration of beverages, **270:1.**
Criminal offense of injuring
    buildings or vessels with oil,
    266:103.

VIVISECTION.
Schools, prohibition against
    vivisection, **272:80G.**

**VOCATIONAL EDUCATION
    AND SCHOOLS, 74:1 et seq.**
Absent voter laws as applicable to
    vocational school district
    elections, **54:103A.**
Administration of district
    vocational schools under
    direction of board of education,
    74:5.
Admission.
    Discrimination, **151C:2A.**
    Other city or town, students
        residing, **74:37C, 74:D.**
Advertisement of purpose of
    certain schools, **74:16.**
Advisory committees, **15:1G, 74:6.**
Agricultural and technical
    institutes.
    Applicability, **74A:14.**
    Generally, **74A:1 to 74A:23.**
        See AGRICULTURAL AND
            TECHNICAL
            INSTITUTES.
    Independent agricultural and
        technical schools.
        Applicability of vocational
            education provisions,
            74A:14.
Agriculture.
    Cities, establishment of schools
        to teach horticulture and
        animal husbandry, **74:15,
        74:17.**
    University of Massachusetts,
        teaching, **75:2.**
Aid.
    Funds. See within this heading,
        "Funds."
Aid to dependent children
    applicant in attendance at
    vocational training course,
    118:3.
Allied health occupations schools.
    Advisory committees, **74:6.**
    Boards of regional school district
        trustees, **74:5A.**
    Commissioner, powers, **74:2.**
    Day classes, **74:13.**
    Defined, **74:1.**
    Establishment.
        Districts, **74:4.**
        Towns, **74:3.**
    Evening classes, **74:13.**
    Federal funds, state treasurer to
        be custodian, **74:20.**
    Non-resident pupils, admission,
        74:7.
    Part time classes, **74:13.**
    State treasurer to be custodian
        of federal funds, **74:20.**
    Work projects, employment of
        students on city or town,
        74:2A.

**VOCATIONAL EDUCATION
    AND SCHOOLS** —Cont'd
Animal husbandry, cities may
    establish and maintain schools
    for instruction, **74:15, 74:17.**
Annual reports, culinary arts
    program, report of
    superintendent of school
    district, **74:14B.**
Annuity contracts for employees,
    purchase, **15:18A, 71:37B.**
Applications for instruction to be
    requested before
    establishment of certain
    schools, **74:16.**
Apprentices and apprenticeships.
    Labor and workforce
        development department,
        division of apprentice
        training, **23:11F, 23:11H.**
    Provisions as to apprenticeship
        program, **74:7B.**
Approval by commissioner of
    nondegree granting vocational
    education programs, **74:37B.**
Assistant registrar of voters at
    vocational schools, **51:42E.**
Blue Hills regional vocational
    school, retirement systems for
    employees, **32:1 et seq.**
Board of education.
    Procurement of vocational
        education, **15:1G.**
    State board for vocational
        education. See within this
        heading, "State board for
        vocational education."
Board of higher education, **15A:2.**
Board of trustees.
    Trustees. See within this
        heading, "Trustees."
Bond issue election, absent voter
    laws as applicable, **54:103A.**
Bonds or undertakings of licenses,
    requirements, **93:21F.**
Bradford Durfee College of
    Technology, **74:42A et seq.**
    See BRADFORD DURFEE
        COLLEGE OF
        TECHNOLOGY.
Buildings.
    School buildings. See within this
        heading, "School buildings."
Bureau of vocational education,
    coordination of manpower
    employment assistance and
    training program, **23B:12.**
Bureau or section of department of
    education, **15:1F.**
Buses.
    School buses. See within this
        heading, "School buses and
        transportation of pupils."

VOCATIONAL EDUCATION AND SCHOOLS —Cont'd

Cities and towns.
  Allied health occupational schools, establishment, **74:3.**
  Classes for training teachers, power to establish, **74:18.**
  Collaborative programs, participation, **74:5B.**
  Employment of vocational education students, **74:2, 74:2A.**
  Establishment and maintenance of schools, **74:3, 74:15, 74:17.**
  Lynn, shoemaking school in city, **74:23.**
  Nautical schools, towns may establish, **74:52.**
  Practical art classes, towns may establish and maintain, **74:14.**
  Reimbursement by state. See within this heading, "Reimbursement by state."
  Students, employment, **74:2A.**
  Wards of cities, payment of tuition, **74:7A.**
Civil rights and discrimination.
  Unfair educational practices. See within this heading, "Unfair educational practices."
Classes, **74:13.**
  Districts, power to establish classes for training teacher, **74:18.**
  Evening classes. See within this heading, "Evening classes."
  Part-time classes. See within this heading, "Part-time classes."
Collaborative programs, participation by cities and towns, **74:5B.**
Commissioner of education.
  See EDUCATION DEPARTMENT.
Commission for occupational education, establishment, membership, functions, **15:1F, 74:2.**
Committees.
  School committees. See within this heading, "School committee."
Consumer protection actions involving trade schools, limitation, **260:5A.**
Continuation schools or courses of instruction, **71:21.**
Contracts and agreements, **152:30E, 152:30H, 255:13K.**

VOCATIONAL EDUCATION AND SCHOOLS —Cont'd

Cooking, **74:14B.**
Co-operative courses defined for purpose of labor law, **149:1.**
Coordination of programs, **23B:12, 74:24B.**
Costs and expenses, vocational rehabilitation services, **152:30H.**
Courses of study.
  Continuation schools or courses of instruction, **71:21.**
  Co-operative courses defined for purposes of labor law, **149:1.**
  Secondary school level, establishment of courses of study beyond, **74:37A.**
Culinary arts program, special fund, **74:14B.**
Day classes, **74:13.**
Definitions under vocational schools law, **74:1.**
Discrimination.
  Unfair educational practices. See within this heading, "Unfair educational practices."
Districts.
  Absent voter laws as applicable to vocational school district elections, **54:103A.**
  Allied health occupations schools, establishment, **74:4.**
  Classes for training teachers, power to establish, **74:18.**
  Establishment of schools, **74:4.**
  Organization, administration and support of schools, **74:5.**
Division of occupational education, **15:1F.**
Educational institution, vocational school as, **151C:1.**
Education and vocational rehabilitation office, vocational rehabilitation procedures, **152:30G.**
Education department.
  See EDUCATION DEPARTMENT.
Elections.
  Vocational school districts, absent voter laws as applicable to elections, **54:103A.**
  Voter registration sessions in vocational schools, **51:42C, 51:42E.**
Eminent domain, **74:17, 79:5.**
Employees.
  Labor and employment. See within this heading, "Labor and employment."

VOCATIONAL EDUCATION AND SCHOOLS —Cont'd

Employment security benefits to students, **151A:24, 151A:30.**
Evening classes, **74:13.**
  Defined under vocational schools law, **74:1.**
  Practical art courses, establishment and maintenance, **74:14.**
Eye protective devices, requirement as to wearing, **71:55C.**
Fair educational practices.
  Unfair educational practices. See within this heading, "Unfair educational practices."
Federal funds.
  Apprentice training division of labor and workforce development department, use of federal funds, **23:11F.**
  Board of education, authority as to federal funds, **74:20.**
  Expenditure, **74:20, 74:22.**
  Powers of state board for vocational education as to expenditure, **74:21, 74:22.**
  State treasurer to be custodian, **74:20.**
  Use for practical art classes, **74:14A.**
Finances.
  Funds. See within this heading, "Funds."
Floriculture, cities may establish and maintain schools for instruction, **74:15, 74:17.**
Fruit growing, cities may establish and maintain schools for instruction, **74:15, 74:17.**
Funds.
  Federal funds. See within this heading, "Federal funds."
  Receipt and disposition of funds, **15:1G.**
  State aid.
    Reimbursement by state. See within this heading, "Reimbursement by state."
Gardening, cities may establish and maintain schools for instruction, **74:15, 74:17.**
Health occupations.
  Allied health occupations schools. See within this heading, "Allied health occupations schools."
Home economics schools.
  Advisory committees, **74:6.**
  Boards of regional school district trustees, **74:5A.**

VOCATIONAL EDUCATION AND SCHOOLS —Cont'd

Home economics schools —Cont'd
Commissioner, powers, **74:2.**
Day classes, **74:13.**
Defined, **74:1.**
Establishment.
Districts, **74:4.**
Towns, **74:3.**
Evening classes, **74:13.**
Federal funds, state treasurer to be custodian, **74:20.**
Non-resident pupils, admission, **74:7.**
Part time classes, **74:13.**
State treasurer to be custodian of federal funds, **74:20.**
Work projects, employment of students on city or town, **74:2A.**
Household arts.
County agricultural schools, instruction, **74:35.**
Definitions under vocational schools law, **74:1.**
Regional school district, maintenance, **74:5A.**
Housing, construction by students, **74:2B.**
Housing of pupils, erection of buildings, **74:17.**
Independent allied health occupations school.
Allied health occupations schools. See within this heading, "Allied health occupations schools."
Independent distributive occupations maintained by regional school district, **74:5A.**
Independent vocational home economics schools.
Home economics schools. See within this heading, "Home economics schools."
Independent vocational-technical schools, **74:3-74:6.**
Industrial accidents division, **23E:10.**
Industrial arts and schools maintained by regional school districts, **74:5A.**
Industrial or vocational training to realize employment, benefits, **151A:30.**
Institutional on-farm agricultural schools for veterans, **74:54.**
Labor and employment.
Annuity contracts for employees of vocational schools, purchase, **15:18A, 71:37B.**

VOCATIONAL EDUCATION AND SCHOOLS —Cont'd

Labor and employment —Cont'd
Cities and towns, employment of students, **74:2, 74:2A.**
Employment security benefits to students, **151A:24, 151A:30.**
Teachers. See within this heading, "Teachers."
Training for, **74:1 et seq.**
Landlord and tenant, **74:17, 74:41.**
Leasing.
Land for vocational schools, **74:17.**
Veterans, lease of schools to federal government for rehabilitation, **74:41.**
Licenses.
See LICENSES AND PERMITS.
Limitation of consumer protection actions involving trade schools, **260:5A.**
Lobsters, period during which student-licensees may take, **130:38.**
Lynn, independent industrial shoemaking school in city, **74:23.**
Manpower employment assistance and training program, coordination by vocational education bureau, **23B:12.**
Mentally retarded children, training programs, **71:45.**
Municipalities.
Cities and towns. See within this heading, "Cities and towns."
Nautical schools, establishment by towns, **74:52.**
Night classes.
Evening classes. See within this heading, "Evening classes."
Nondegree granting vocational education programs at post-secondary level, approval by commissioner, **74:37B.**
Nonresident pupils.
Admission, **74:7.**
Transportation, **74:8A.**
Tuition, **74:7A, 74:7C.**
Nurses.
See NURSES AND NURSING SERVICES.
On-farm agricultural schools for veterans, **74:54.**
Part-time classes, **74:13.**
Defined under vocational schools law, **74:1.**
Placement services, discrimination, **151C:2A.**

VOCATIONAL EDUCATION AND SCHOOLS —Cont'd

Plumbing, training program, **142:3A.**
Poultry raising, cities may establish and maintain schools for instruction, **74:15, 74:17.**
Powers and duties of commissioner of education, **74:2.**
Practical art classes.
See PRACTICAL ART CLASSES.
Practical nurse training schools.
See NURSES AND NURSING SERVICES.
Prisoners completing program, reduction of sentence, **127:129D.**
Radio and television technicians registration law, applicability, **112:87QQQ.**
Records and reports, **152:30F.**
Annual reports, **74:14B.**
Culinary arts program, **74:14B.**
Eligibility of persons, **6:79.**
Regional school districts.
See REGIONAL SCHOOL DISTRICTS.
Registration of voters, sessions in vocational schools, **51:42C, 51:42E.**
Rehabilitation.
Retirement benefits, **32:8, 32:21.**
Veterans Administration, cooperation, **74:22D.**
Rehabilitation commission of Massachusetts.
See REHABILITATION COMMISSION OF MASSACHUSETTS.
Reimbursement by state.
Certification, **70:4.**
Transportation of pupils, **74:8A.**
Reports.
Records and reports. See within this heading, "Records and reports."
Representatives.
Licensing, **93:21G.**
Regulations, **93:21E.**
Resident of city or town not offering approved vocational education programs at post-secondary level, admission to program in other city, town, or regional district, **74:37C.**
Res judicata, finality of determination as to vocational rehabilitation services, **152:30H.**

**VOCATIONAL EDUCATION
AND SCHOOLS** —Cont'd

Rules and regulations to promote
employment of students,
74:2A.

Sales tax exemptions, **64H:6.**

School buildings.
Leasing. See within this
heading, "Leasing."
Power to build schools for
vocational purposes, **74:17.**

School buses and transportation of
pupils, **74:8A, 161:108.**
Requirements as to vehicles
used in transportation of
vocational school students,
90:1, 90:7D½.
Special rates on street or
elevated railways, **161:108.**

School committee.
Courses of study in vocational
schools, **74:37A.**
Duties of, **71:37, 71:37A.**
Establishment of schools
through, **74:3.**

School teachers.
Teachers. See within this
heading, "Teachers."
Secondary school level,
establishment of courses of
study beyond, **74:37A.**

Shoemaking school in city of Lynn,
74:23.

Smith Agricultural School as
approved vocational-technical
school, **74:24.**

Social services department.
Nonresident pupils, admission to
vocational training school,
74:7.
Transportation of pupils
attending outside schools,
reimbursement for expenses,
74:8A.
Tuition of state and city wards,
payment, **74:7A.**

Social workers, tenure rights,
74:22E.

State aid.
Reimbursement. See within this
heading, "Reimbursement
by state."

State board for vocational
education.
Co-operation with veterans'
administration, **74:22D.**
Defined under vocational schools
law, **74:1.**
District vocational schools, duty
as to organization,
administration, and support,
74:5.

**VOCATIONAL EDUCATION
AND SCHOOLS** —Cont'd

State board for vocational
education —Cont'd
Federal funds, powers to use,
74:21, 74:22.
Institutional on-farm
agricultural schools for
veterans, **74:54.**

State board of education, purposes
and duties, **15:1G.**

State treasurer to be custodian of
federal funds, **74:20.**

Steam boilers and engines,
qualification of certain
students to operate, **146:50.**

Street railways, special rates for
school pupils, **161:108.**

Supervision of schools by
commissioner of education,
74:2.

Supervisor of guidance and
placement, **15:6B.**

Teachers.
Establishment of training
classes, **74:18.**
Federal funds, powers of state
board for vocational
education in disposal, **74:22.**
Rights and benefits, **74:22E.**
Salaries, **71:40.**
Tenure, **74:22E.**
Training standards, **74:18.**

Technology scholar advisory
council, **74:2. (note)**

Telecommunications, maintenance
of toll-free number to
education and vocational
rehabilitation office, **23E:10.**

Tenure and seniority, vocational
school teachers and
employees, **74:22E.**

Towns.
Cities and towns. See within
this heading, "Cities and
towns."

Training schools of Massachusetts.
See YOUTH SERVICES
DEPARTMENTS AND
MASSACHUSETTS
TRAINING SCHOOLS.

Transportation of pupils.
School buses and transportation
of pupils. See within this
heading, "School buses and
transportation of pupils."

Trustees, **74:3-74:6.**
Advisory committees,
appointment, **74:6.**
Annuity contracts for employees,
purchase by trustees,
71:37B.

**VOCATIONAL EDUCATION
AND SCHOOLS** —Cont'd

Trustees —Cont'd
Continuation schools or courses
of instruction, **71:21.**
Establishment of schools
through, **74:3, 74:4.**
Independent industrial
shoemaking school of city of
Lynn, **74:23.**
Plans for organization,
administration and support
of district schools, **74:5.**
Regional school district trustees,
boards, **74:5A.**

Tuition of pupils, **74:7A, 74:37B,
74:37C, 74:37F.**
City wards, payment of tuition,
74:7A.
Nonresident pupils, **74:7C.**

Regional school districts.
See REGIONAL SCHOOL
DISTRICTS.

Technical colleges or institutes,
74:46.

Unemployment compensation
benefits to students, **151A:24,
151A:30.**

Unfair educational practices,
151C:2A.
Admission, discrimination
because of race, religion,
creed, color, age, sex or
national origin as unfair
practice, **151C:2A.**
Benefits, discrimination because
of race, religion, creed, color,
age, sex or national origin
as unfair practice, **151C:2A.**
Definitions, **151C:1.**
Inquiry concerning race,
religion, creed, color, age,
sex or national origin of
applicant as unfair practice,
151C:2A.
Religious educational
institution, exception,
151C:2A.
Participation in proceedings
under anti-discrimination
laws, penalizing student
because of as unfair
practice, **151C:2A.**
Placement services,
discrimination because of
race, religion, creed, color,
age, sex or national origin
as unfair practice, **151C:2A.**
Proceedings in case of alleged
unfair practices, **151C:3.**
Trade schools, **151C:1.**

939

VOCATIONAL EDUCATION AND SCHOOLS —Cont'd

Veterans and veterans' organizations.

Co-operation of state board for vocational education with veterans' administration, **74:22D.**

Institutional on-farm agricultural schools for veterans, **74:54.**

Lease of schools to federal government for rehabilitation of veterans, **74:41.**

Vocational-technical learning and teaching institute, **74:2. (note)**

Voters and voter registration.

Elections. See within this heading, "Elections."

Welfare.

Social services department. See within this heading, "Social services department."

Workers' compensation, vocational rehabilitation, **152:30E-152:30I.**

Youth services department.

See YOUTH SERVICES DEPARTMENT AND MASSACHUSETTS TRAINING SCHOOLS.

VOCATIONAL REHABILITATION. See REHABILITATION.

VOID OR VOIDABLE.

Credit unions.

See CREDIT UNIONS.

Health spa contracts, **93:85.**

Landlord and tenant.

Children, lease provisions, **186:16.**

Indemnification of lesser against his own negligence or fault, **186:15.**

Marriage.

See MARRIAGE.

Sales, transfer of voidable title, **106:2-403.**

Student loans, minors' obligations, **167E:10.**

VOIR DIRE. See JURY AND JURY TRIAL.

VOLCANIC INSURANCE.

Incorporation of companies, **175:47.**

VOLUNTARY ADMINISTRATION.

Small estates.

See SMALL ESTATES.

VOLUNTEERISM ADVISORY COUNCIL, 6:213.

VOLUNTEERISM OFFICE, 6:209 to 6:213.

Advisory council of volunteerism, **6:213.**

Contracting powers, **6:210.**

Duties generally, **6:211.**

Establishment, **6:209.**

Grants and gifts, **6:210.**

Information made available to director, **6:212.**

Organization, **6:209.**

Powers generally, **6:211.**

VOLUNTEERS.

Age of children performing, **149:60.**

Associations of.

See ASSOCIATIONS AND SOCIETIES.

Children performing volunteer services, regulation of age, **149:60.**

Civil defense volunteers.

Indemnification, **40:5.**

Snow vehicles, permits to operate during emergency, **90B:25.**

Commonwealth Service Corps, volunteers and workers, **6:121.**

Corps of elder volunteers in elder affairs department, **19A:4.**

County co-operative extension services, payment of volunteers expenses, **128:42.**

Employment experience, volunteer work as qualifying, **149:52B.**

Firemen.

See FIRE DEPARTMENTS.

Mental health legal advisors committee, **221:34E.**

Militia, enlisted personnel of.

See MILITIA.

Office of volunteerism, **6:209 to 6:213.**

Physicians and nurses as exempt from civil liability for emergency care or treatment, **112:12B.**

Sports program volunteers, tort liability, **231:85V.**

State officers authorized to provide voluntary services at public schools during working hours without loss of salary, **29:31E.**

Veterinarians rendering emergency care to domestic animals, exemption from civil liability, **112:58A.**

VOTERS' REGISTRATION ACT, 51:1 et seq. See REGISTRATION OF VOTERS.

VOTES AND VOTING, 51:1 et seq.

Banks.

See BANKS AND BANKING.

Cities and towns, voting by board to determine method of securing bonds and notes issued by, **44:22C.**

City.

Elections.

See CITY AND TOWN CLERKS.

Clerks.

See CITY AND TOWN CLERKS.

Condominiums.

See CONDOMINIUMS.

Constitution of Massachusetts.

See CONSTITUTION OF MASSACHUSETTS.

Constitution of the United States.

See CONSTITUTION OF THE UNITED STATES.

Cooperative banks.

See COOPERATIVE BANKS.

Cooperative corporations.

See COOPERATIVE CORPORATIONS AND ASSOCIATIONS.

Corporations.

See CORPORATIONS.

Credit unions.

See CREDIT UNIONS.

Elections.

See ELECTIONS.

Fire districts.

See FIRE DISTRICTS.

Foreign states.

See FOREIGN STATES OR COUNTRIES.

Fraternal benefit societies.

See FRATERNAL BENEFIT SOCIETIES.

Gas.

See GAS AND ELECTRIC COMPANIES.

Horse.

See HORSE AND DOG RACING MEETINGS.

Hospitals.

Elections.

See HOSPITALS AND HEALTH CARE FACILITIES.

House of representatives of United States.

See HOUSE OF REPRESENTATIVES OF UNITED STATES.

VOTES AND VOTING —Cont'd

Industrial accidents division, advisory council on workers' compensation, **23E:15.**

Insurance.
See INSURANCE.

Joint labor-management committee, **150E:9. (note)**

Loans for voting equipment replacement, **9:30, 29:2PP.**

Mentally ill.
See MENTALLY ILL AND RETARDED PERSONS.

Morris plan banks.
See MORRIS PLAN BANKS.

Multiple dwellings.
See MULTIPLE DWELLINGS.

Municipal clerks.
See CITY AND TOWN CLERKS.

Municipal finance.
See MUNICIPAL FINANCE.

Northeast Interstate Dairy Compact, **Spec L 139:5.**

Optional forms of municipal administration, submission to voters, conflicting provisions adopted, **43C:6-43C:8.**

Plurality vote.
See PLURALITY VOTE.

Proxies.
See PROXIES.

Railroads.
See RAILROADS.

Real estate time-shares, **183B:11, 183B:13, 183B:32-183B:35.**

Reclamation districts, voting at meetings, **252:6.**

Registration of voters.
See REGISTRATION OF VOTERS.

Retarded persons.
See MENTALLY ILL AND RETARDED PERSONS.

Retirement systems and pensions, voting rights of retired public employees, **32:3.**

Roll call vote, where required of membership of state boards and commissions, **30A:11A.**

Savings banks.
See SAVINGS BANKS.

Secret ballots at meetings of governmental bodies, **30A:11A½, 34:9G, 39:23B.**

Senate of United States.
See SENATE OF UNITED STATES.

Street railways, voting rights of stock, **161:16, 161:17.**

Tie vote.
See TIE VOTE.

VOTES AND VOTING —Cont'd

Town clerks.
See CITY AND TOWN CLERKS.

Town meetings.
See TOWN MEETINGS.

Two-thirds attendance.
See TWO-THIRDS ATTENDANCE OR VOTE.

Workers' compensation advisory council, meetings, **23E:15.**

Yeas.
See YEAS AND NAYS.

Zoning.
See ZONING AND PLANNING.

VOTING EQUIPMENT LOAN PROGRAM, 9:30, 29:2PP.

VOTING TIME ACT, 149:178.
Employees, **149:178.**

VOTING TRUST.
Business trusts distinguished, **182:1.**
Professional corporations, **156A:11.**

VOUCHERS.
Appellate tax board, vouchers required for expenditures, **58A:5.**

Comptroller of state, **7A:5.**
Condition to payments from appropriations, **29:20.**
Interstate cooperation commission, certification of bills and vouchers, **9:21.**

County finance.
Examination of accounts of county officers, **35:44.**
Payrolls of counties, certification, **35:19.**
Treasurers.
See COUNTY TREASURERS.

County treasurers.
See COUNTY TREASURERS.

Credit unions.
See CREDIT UNIONS.

Fraternal benefit societies, vouchers for disbursements, **176:13.**

Hospital service corporations may be required to keep, **176A:6.**

Insect pest control local superintendents, vouchers showing expenditures, **132:15.**

Insurance companies, vouchers for disbursements, **175:37.**

Interstate cooperation commission, **9:21.**

Marriage solemnization fees, vouchers, **207:44.**

Medical service corporations may be required to keep, **176B:9.**

VOUCHERS —Cont'd

Medical service plans may be required to keep, **176C:10.**

Militia officers making payments in cash to obtain, **33:86.**

Payments from appropriations, filing of vouchers required, **29:20.**

Prisons expenditures, vouchers, **126:32.**

Probation officers, vouchers for expenses, **276:94, 276:95.**

Public Safety Department, vouchers for compensation of skin divers employed, **22:6.**

Retirement systems, payments from funds, **32:23.**

Sale or destruction of state vouchers, **30:42.**

State comptroller.
Comptroller of state. See within this heading, "Comptroller of state."

Superior court, vouchers for expenses, **35:12.**

Supreme Judicial Court, vouchers for expenses, **35:12.**

Transitional assistance department's disbursements for public assistance, vouchers substantiating, **18:17.**

Wagner-Peyser Act, co-operation of state bureau of public employment offices with United States Employment Service, **23:9L.**

VULTURE.
Hunting or possession, **131:75A.**

W

WAAC.
Statutory construction, **4:7.**

WACHUSETT MOUNTAIN STATE RESERVATION.
Loss of tax on, reimbursement of town, **58:13.**

WACHUSETT RESERVOIR.
"Watershed system," definition for purposes of provision creating watershed management division, **92:104.**

WACHUSETT WATERSHED.
"Watershed system," definition for purposes of provision creating watershed management division, **92:104.**

WADING.
State parks, recreation areas, and reservations, part of planning, **132A:2D.**

WAGE REPORTING SYSTEM,
  62B:2, 62E:1 et seq.
Administration and finance
  executive office, fraudulent
  claim commission, **62E:5,**
  62E:6.
Advisory committee on wage
  reporting system, **62E:10.**
Benefit associations, **62E:4, 62E:5.**
Certified mail, treasurer notified of
  reporting requirements,
  62E:9.
Child support enforcement, **62E:3,**
  271:43.
Commercial banks, **62E:4, 62E:5.**
Comparison of lists to identify
  individuals receiving wages,
  62E:5.
Cooperative banks, **62E:4, 62E:5.**
Credit unions, **62E:4, 62E:5.**
Definitions, **62E:1.**
Design, development,
  implementation and operation
  of system, **62E:3.**
Disclosure of information,
  restriction, **62E:8.**
Employers to submit information
  to revenue commissioner,
  62E:2.
Employment security division to
  provide lists of claimants,
  62E:4.
Error, action to correct erroneous
  payments, **62E:6.**
Failure of employer to submit
  required information, **62E:9.**
Fines and penalties.
  Reporting requirements, **62E:9.**
  Unauthorized release of
    information, **62E:8.**
Fraud and deceit, **62E:3-62E:6B,**
  62E:8.
Hearings, **62E:5.**
Housing authorities, **62E:3, 62E:5.**
Identification of persons receiving
  both wages and benefits,
  62E:5.
Insurance companies, **62E:4,**
  62E:5.
Lists of persons receiving benefits
  furnished to commissioner,
  62E:4.
Massachusetts Higher Education
  Assistance Corporation, **62E:3.**
National banking associations,
  62E:5.
Notice.
  Hearing to contest adverse
    action in case of fraud,
    62E:5.
  Other state agencies notified in
    cases of fraud, **62E:6B.**

WAGE REPORTING SYSTEM
  —Cont'd
Notice —Cont'd
  Reporting requirements, **62E:9.**
  Sampling technique, notification
    provided to ways and means
    committees, **62E:13.**
Penalties.
  Fines and penalties. See within
    this heading, "Fines and
    penalties."
Production of books and
  documents, special
  investigations bureau,
  62E:6A.
Purpose of wage reporting system,
  62E:3.
Recoupment, **62E:6.**
Remote terminal units, **62E:7.**
Reporting system, defined, **62E:1.**
Safe deposit companies, **62E:4,**
  62E:5.
Savings and loan associations,
  62E:4, 62E:5.
Savings banks, **62E:4, 62E:5.**
Special investigations bureau,
  62E:6-62E:6B.
Treasurer of bank, **62E:4, 62E:9.**
Verification of information, **62E:6.**
Veterans' services department,
  62E:3, 62E:4.
Welfare.
  Salaries and compensation.
    See WELFARE AND SOCIAL
    SERVICES.

WAGERING.
See GAMING AND GAMES OF
  CHANCE.

WAGES, SALARIES, AND
  COMPENSATION, 29:31,
  30:45 et seq., 41:108,
  41:108A, 151:1 et seq.
Abandoned property, wage payers
  as persons required to file
  annual reports, **200A:1,**
  200A:7.
Absentee's estate, compensation of
  receiver, **200:12.**
Absent voter registration officers,
  51:23.
Abuse, compensation.
  Court orders, **209A:3.**
  Notice to abused person of
    rights, **209A:6.**
Academically talented pupils,
  members of advisory
  commission, **15:6C.**
Accountant of city or town.
  Municipal officers and
    employees. See within this
    heading, "Municipal officers
    and employees."

WAGES, SALARIES, AND
  COMPENSATION —Cont'd
Accounts and accounting.
  Accountancy board members,
    13:35.
  Delivery to employer of account
    of wage assignment, **154:4.**
  Withholding tax on wages, use of
    accounting machines to
    calculate, **62B:2.**
Accused persons confined awaiting
  trial, compensation upon
  acquittal, **277:73.**
Acupuncture committee, **112:150.**
Administration and finance
  executive office.
  Salaries.
    See ADMINISTRATION AND
      FINANCE EXECUTIVE
      OFFICE.
Administrative assistant in Suffolk
  County, **221:76.**
Administrative committee,
  members, **13:35.**
Administrative secretary of
  governor, **6:6A.**
Administrators.
  See EXECUTORS AND
    ADMINISTRATORS.
Advancements against salary,
  29:31, 44:64-44:66.
Advertising, members of outdoor
  advertising board, **16:14.**
Aeronautics commission, **6:57,**
  6:58.
Age discrimination, **151B:4.**
Agricultural schools, trustees of
  county schools, **74:27.**
Agriculture.
  Wages.
    See AGRICULTURE.
Aircraft.
  See AIRCRAFT AND AVIATION.
Alcoholic beverages control
  commission, **6:43.**
Alcoholic liquor licensing boards,
  138:7, 138:8.
Aldermen.
  See ALDERMEN AND
    SELECTMEN.
American and Canadian French
  cultural exchange commission
  members, **6:157.**
Animal diseases.
  See ANIMAL DISEASES.
Animal inspectors, **129:17.**
Annuities.
  See ANNUITIES AND
    ANNUITY CONTRACTS.
Anti-discrimination laws, advisory
  agencies and conciliation
  councils, **151B:3.**

WAGES, SALARIES, AND COMPENSATION —Cont'd

Appeals court.
See APPEALS COURT.
Appointed officials, right to compensation during removal or termination from office, **4:7.**
Apprentices.
See APPRENTICES.
Appropriations.
Increase in salary of state officers or employees, when effective, **30:46.**
Municipal officers and employees. See within this heading, "Municipal officers and employees."
Regional school districts, **71:16, 71:42B.**
Arbitration.
See ARBITRATION.
Architects.
See ARCHITECTS AND ARCHITECTURE.
Architectural Barriers Board, members, **22:13A.**
Archives advisory committee members, salary, **9:2A.**
Armed forces.
Military affairs.
See MILITARY AFFAIRS.
Militia.
See MILITIA.
Armory commission, members, **6:18.**
Art commission, members, **6:19.**
Assessors, **41:22, 221:55.**
See TAX ASSESSORS.
Assignment of wages, **154:1-154:8.**
Acceptance by employer, **154:2, 154:3.**
Account to be delivered to employer, **154:4.**
Attorney, execution, **154:3.**
Balance due to be stated in account, **154:4.**
Change of assignment, motions, **208:36, 209:32E.**
Charge, payments on, to be stated in account, **154:4.**
Children.
See CHILDREN AND MINORS.
Copy to be delivered to assignor and to employer, **154:4.**
Date of execution to be stated, **154:3.**
Defense to complaint for violation of weekly wage payment laws, assignment, **149:150.**

WAGES, SALARIES, AND COMPENSATION —Cont'd

Assignment of wages —Cont'd
Defined under wage assignment law, **154:1.**
Effect, **154:7.**
Employer.
Acceptance, **154:2, 154:3.**
Account to be delivered, **154:4.**
Copy to be delivered, **154:4.**
Exclusion from secured transactions article of assignments of claims for salary, **106:9-104.**
Exemption.
From assignment, **154:2, 154:3.**
From trustee process, **154:6, 154:8.**
Fees for filing and recording, **154:2, 262:34.**
Filing and recording, **154:2.**
Fee, **154:2, 262:34.**
Form, standard, **154:5.**
Hearing on arrears as prerequisite, **208:36, 209:32E.**
Interest.
Payment to be stated, **154:4.**
Rate to be stated, **154:3.**
Loans subject to laws, **154:2.**
Money or value of goods furnished to be stated, **154:3.**
Motions for change, **208:36, 209:32E.**
Notice to employer, **208:36, 209:32E.**
Payments to be stated in account, **154:4.**
Portion of earnings, assignment when support payments in arrears, **209:32E.**
Principal payments to be stated in account, **154:4.**
Prohibited provisions in retail installment sales agreement, **255D:10.**
Rate of interest to be stated, **154:3.**
Secured transactions. See within this heading, "Secured transactions."
Standard form, **154:5.**
Support payments, assignment, **209:32E.**
Time, **154:2, 154:3, 154:8.**
Trustee process, validity against, **154:6, 154:8.**
Validity.
Against trustee process, **154:6, 154:8.**

WAGES, SALARIES, AND COMPENSATION —Cont'd

Assignment of wages —Cont'd
Validity —Cont'd
Loans, security, **140:108, 154:2.**
Requisites for, **154:2-4.**
Weekly wage payment laws, defense to complaint for violation, **149:150.**
Wife's consent, **154:2, 154:3.**
Assistant adjutants general, **33:15.**
Assistant clerks of senate and house, **3:13.**
Assistant district attorneys, **12:16 et seq.**
Assistant harbor masters, **102:19.**
Assistant registers of probate, **217:35B.**
Associated Firefighters of Massachusetts conventions, attendance of delegates at, without loss of pay, **48:57B.**
Associate medical examiner, **38:2.**
Attachment, **246:28-246:30.**
See TRUSTEE PROCESS.
Attorney general, **12:1.**
Assistants, **12:2.**
Attorneys at law.
See ATTORNEYS AT LAW.
Auditors, masters, and referees, **221:55, 221:61.**
See AUDITORS, MASTERS, AND REFEREES.
Audits and auditors.
See AUDITS AND AUDITORS.
Automobile insurance.
Classification of persons entitled to wages or salary under wage continuation plan, abolition, **175:113B.**
Service charges for securing automobile insurance, **175:113I.**
Wage continuation programs, reimbursement of, by insurers after accident, **90:34A.**
Average weekly wage.
Employment security law, defined or construed in context, **151A:1.**
Workers' compensation.
Agreement for compensation, questioning wages, **152:6.**
Defined, **152:1.**
Determination, **152:1.**
Back wages, actions based on new judicial interpretation, time to sue, **260:4A.**
Banks.
See BANKS AND BANKING.
Bar examiners, **221:36.**

WAGES, SALARIES, AND COMPENSATION —Cont'd

Bedding and upholstered furniture, members of advisory board as to regulation, **94:274.**

Biweekly payment, **149:148.**

Blind persons.

Commission for the blind, **6:129, 6:130.**

Employees of schools and workshops for the blind, **6:143.**

Fund raising, **6:140.**

Workers' compensation, **152:36.**

Board of registration of psychologists, **13:79.**

Boiler Rules Board, members, **22:10.**

Bonus.

See BONUS.

Boston juvenile court.

Clerks of court and assistants, **218:79.**

Special justice, per diem compensation, **218:6.**

Boston municipal court, **218:52.**

See BOSTON MUNICIPAL COURT.

Boston public health commission, compensation of executive director of Board, **Spec L 70:4.**

Boston terminal company police, **159:95.**

Boxer's fund board, **6:99.**

Boxing commission members, **22:12.**

Bradford Durfee College of Technology personnel, compensation, **74:420.**

Building regulations and standards, state board, **143:93.**

Bus operators, **71:7A.**

Bylaws of municipality.

Ordinances and bylaws. See within this heading, "Ordinances and bylaws."

Campaign and political finance, director, **55:3.**

Capital cases, compensation for assistance of counsel, **276:37A, 277:55, 277:56.**

Capitol police.

See POLICE.

Career incentive pay program for police officers, **41:108L.**

Centralized weekly payroll system for state employees, establishment, **29:31.**

WAGES, SALARIES, AND COMPENSATION —Cont'd

Central services division head, **7:4A.**

Challenger of voters, **54:85A.**

Chaplains of senate and house, **3:14.**

Charitable contributions, **68:21, 149:148, 150E:12, 154:8, 180:17B.**

Charter cities.

See CITY CHARTERS.

Checks.

See CHECKS.

Chief engineers of fire departments, annual rate of compensation of certain, **48:57G.**

Chief justice of district court, **218:6.**

Chief medical examiner, **38:2.**

Children.

See CHILDREN AND MINORS.

Chiropractors, compensation of members of board of registration, **13:66.**

Cigarette tax stampers, compensation, **64C:30.**

Citizen advisory boards in elder affairs department, members, **19A:5.**

City and town clerks.

See CITY AND TOWN CLERKS.

City council.

See CITY COUNCIL.

City employees.

Municipal officers and employees. See within this heading, "Municipal officers and employees."

Civil rights.

See CIVIL RIGHTS AND DISCRIMINATION.

Civil service.

See CIVIL SERVICE.

Cleaners employed by state, **8:5.**

Clean water scholarship intern program, services provided, **21:38A.**

Clerical assistants in superior court, **221:89.**

Clerks of cities.

See CITY AND TOWN CLERKS.

Clerks of court, **218:10, 218:79, 218:80, 221:93, 221:94, 221:100.**

See CLERKS OF COURT.

Clerks of senate and house of representatives, **3:12, 3:13.**

Collective bargaining, **149:181, 150A:5, 150C:1, 150E:2.**

WAGES, SALARIES, AND COMPENSATION —Cont'd

Colleges.

See COLLEGES AND UNIVERSITIES.

Commerce.

See ECONOMIC DEVELOPMENT DEPARTMENT.

Commonwealth service corps personnel, **6:121.**

Community Chest, payroll deductions for contributions of state, county, or town employees, **180:17B.**

Comptroller of state, **7:4A.**

See COMPTROLLER OF STATE.

Conduct of public officials and employees, **268A:1.**

Conflict of interest as affecting state or county employees' receipt, **268A:4, 268A:11.**

Congress, members of, **US Const Art 1 Sec 6 cl 1.**

Conservation district, **21:19, 21:22.**

Conservation of soil, water and related resources, commission, **21:19.**

Constables.

See CONSTABLES.

Constitution of Massachusetts.

See CONSTITUTION OF MASSACHUSETTS.

Constitution of the United States.

See CONSTITUTION OF THE UNITED STATES.

Construction contracts and work, **149:26, 149:27, 149:29.**

See CONSTRUCTION CONTRACTS AND WORK.

Consultants employed by Commonwealth, **29:29A.**

Consumer affairs and business regulation office, director, **24A:1.**

Contagious diseases.

See CONTAGIOUS AND INFECTIOUS DISEASES.

Cooperative banks.

Payroll and payroll deductions. See COOPERATIVE BANKS.

Co-operative corporations and associations.

Dividends on employees' wages, **157:6.**

Weekly wage payment requirement inapplicable to employee-stockholders, **149:148.**

Corporations.

See CORPORATIONS.

WAGES, SALARIES, AND COMPENSATION —Cont'd

Correctional institutions.
See CORRECTIONAL INSTITUTIONS.
Corrections department.
Commissioner and deputies, **27:1, 27:2.**
Cost of living adjustments, **30:46, 35:51B.**
Cotton factories, specifications as to rate of compensation to be furnished employees, **149:155, 149:157.**
County agricultural schools, trustees, **74:27.**
County charter study commission, **34A:7.**
County commissioners.
See COUNTY COMMISSIONERS.
County finance.
See COUNTY FINANCE.
County officers and employees, **35:19, 35:49-35:56.**
See COUNTY OFFICERS AND EMPLOYEES.
County treasurers, **35:4.**
See COUNTY TREASURERS.
Court officers.
See COURT OFFICERS.
Court stenographers.
See COURT STENOGRAPHERS.
Credit services organizations, **93:68A-93:68C.**
Credit unions.
See CREDIT UNIONS.
Crime victims, compensation of.
See VICTIMS OF VIOLENT CRIMES.
Criminal defendant confined while awaiting trial, compensation upon acquittal of charges, **277:73.**
Criminal history systems board, members, **6:168.**
Criminal justice committee, **6:156, 6:156A, 6:156B.**
Criminal justice training council members, **6:117.**
Criminal offender record information system employees, **6:168.**
Criminal procedure.
See CRIMINAL PROCEDURE.
Custodians.
Retirement system funds, **32:20.**
Uniform gifts to minors act, custodian, **201A:15.**
Daily rates of pay of state employees, computation, **30:46.**

WAGES, SALARIES, AND COMPENSATION —Cont'd

Date.
Time or date. See within this heading, "Time or date."
Deceased employees.
Administration, payment of deceased employee's wages without, **29:31D, 149:178A, 149:178C.**
County officers or employees, payment of unpaid salary or wages, **35:19B.**
Heirs or next of kin. See within this heading, "Heirs or next of kin."
Immediate payment on death, **29:31.**
Municipal officers or employees. See within this heading, "Municipal officers and employees."
State officer or employee, payment of salaries or wages owing, **29:31, 29:31A, 29:31D, 149:178A, 149:178C.**
Deductions.
See PAYROLL AND PAYROLL DEDUCTIONS.
Deferred compensation programs.
See DEFERRED COMPENSATION PROGRAMS.
Definition.
Child support, **62E:1.**
Severance pay, **151A:71A.**
Demonstration sheep farms, compensation from Commonwealth, **128:11.**
Demotion of state employee as affecting salary, **30:46.**
Dental service corporations.
See DENTAL SERVICE CORPORATIONS.
Dentists.
See DENTISTS.
Deputy collector, revenue department, **14:3.**
Deputy correction commissioners, salaries, **27:2.**
Designer selection board, members, **7:38A½.**
Direct deposit in accounts with financial institutions, **29:31, 35:19, 41:41B.**
Disabled.
See DISABLED OR HANDICAPPED PERSONS.

WAGES, SALARIES, AND COMPENSATION —Cont'd

Discharge of employee.
Appointed officials, right to compensation during removal or termination from office, **4:7.**
Day of discharge, discharged employee to be paid, **149:148.**
Severance pay. See within this heading, "Severance pay."
Teachers and superintendents, services rendered after dismissed, **71:42.**
Discrimination.
See CIVIL RIGHTS AND DISCRIMINATION.
Dispensing opticians, board of registration, **13:50.**
Disputes as to.
See LABOR RELATIONS AND DISPUTES.
District and prosecuting attorneys, **12:15, 12:16, 12:20A, 280:16.**
See DISTRICT AND PROSECUTING ATTORNEYS.
District courts, **218:74, 218:75B, 218:78-218:84.**
See DISTRICT COURTS.
Divorce.
Costs and fees.
See DIVORCE AND ALIMONY.
Dog officers, allowance for care of dogs, **140:151A.**
Dog racing, police officers assigned, **128A:8.**
Domestic insurance companies, board of directors approval, **175:35.**
Dual employment with Commonwealth and county, prohibition against, **30:46.**
Dukes county.
See DUKES COUNTY.
Eastern Hampden district court, salary of clerk, **218:79.**
Economic development and industrial corporation, members, **121C:3.**
Economic diversification program, **23F:6.**
Editor of general court bulletins of committee hearings, **5:12.**
Education.
See SCHOOLS AND EDUCATION.
Educational measurement audit council, **15:55A.**

WAGES, SALARIES, AND COMPENSATION —Cont'd

Education department.
See EDUCATION DEPARTMENT.

Effective date of salary increases of state employees, **30:46.**

Elder service corpsmen, stipends and allowances, **19A:13.**

Election officers.
See ELECTIONS.

Electricians, state examiners, **13:32.**

Electrologists' registration board members, **13:60.**

Elevators.
See ELEVATORS.

Embalmers' and funeral directors' registration board members, **13:31.**

Emergency finance board, **10:47, 40:5B.**

Emergency medical technician incapacitated during performance of duty, leave without loss of pay, **41:111M.**

Eminent domain.
Damages and compensation.
See EMINENT DOMAIN.

Employment agencies.
See EMPLOYMENT AGENCIES AND BUREAUS.

Employment and training division.
See EMPLOYMENT AND TRAINING DIVISION IN LABOR AND WORKFORCE DEPARTMENT.

Employment security, **151A:1-151A:74.**
See EMPLOYMENT SECURITY.

Energy Advisory Board, members, **25A:10.**

Energy Resources Executive Office, **25A:1, 25A:5.**

Engineers.
See ENGINEERS AND SURVEYORS.

Environmental affairs executive office, **21A:5, 21A:7, 21A:9, 21A:10.**
See ENVIRONMENTAL AFFAIRS EXECUTIVE OFFICE.

Environmental management department, **21:6E.**
See ENVIRONMENTAL MANAGEMENT DEPARTMENT.

Environmental Protection Department, commissioner, **21A:7.**

WAGES, SALARIES, AND COMPENSATION —Cont'd

Essex Agricultural and Technical Institute, equal pay for women teachers, **71:40.**

Essex county.
See ESSEX COUNTY.

Ethics commission of state.
Annual report, employees' salaries included, **268B:2.**
Outside employment, regulation, **268A:4, 268A:5, 268A:11, 268A:12.**

Examination, inspection, and investigation.
Citizen's reports and recommendations as to wages, **151:7.**
Domestic service in home of employer, exceptions from inspection requirement, **149:105C, 151:3.**
Fair employment practices.
Wages, discrimination based on sex.
See FAIR EMPLOYMENT PRACTICES.
Inspector general. See within this heading, "Inspector general."
Labor and workforce development department, investigations, **149:105C, 151:3.**
Minimum wages, **151:3, 151:15, 151:17.**

Executions.
See EXECUTIONS.

Executive council, **6:3, 7A:3, 29:18.**

Executive director of Boston public health commission, **Spec L 70:4.**

Executive secretary of governor, **6:6.**

Executive secretary to justices of Supreme Judicial Court, **211:3A.**

Executive stenographer of governor, **6:6A.**

Executors.
See EXECUTORS AND ADMINISTRATORS.

Exemptions.
Assignment of wages. See within this heading, "Assignment of wages."
Claims of creditors, exemption from, **235:34, 246:28-246:30.**
See EXEMPTION FROM CLAIMS OF CREDITORS.

WAGES, SALARIES, AND COMPENSATION —Cont'd

Exemptions —Cont'd
Weekly wage payments, contract may not exempt, **149:148.**

Express company police, **159:95.**

Fair employment practices.
Wages, discrimination based on sex.
See FAIR EMPLOYMENT PRACTICES.

Fair wage records, place of keeping, **151:15.**

Family.
Heirs or next of kin. See within this heading, "Heirs or next of kin."

Federal grants, prohibition against supplementing salary or compensation of state officers or employees, **29:2C.**

Federal income tax, withholding, **58:28A, 58:28B.**

Fees.
See FEES.

Females, wage discrimination against.
Wages, discrimination based on sex.
See FAIR EMPLOYMENT PRACTICES.

Finance advisory board, **6:97.**

Financial disclosure by public officers and employees.
Compensation defined, **268B:1.**
Disclosure statement as prerequisite, **268B:5.**
Ethics commission members, **268B:2.**

Fines and penalties.
Attachment of exempt wages, **246:30.**
Attorney in action for recovery, **280:3.**
Construction contracts.
See CONSTRUCTION CONTRACTS AND WORK.
Cotton factories, failure to furnish specifications as to rate of wages, **149:157.**
Deductions.
See PAYROLL AND PAYROLL DEDUCTIONS.
Failure to pay wages as required, **149:148.**
Minimum wages.
See MINIMUM WAGES.
Probationary period for women or children, failure to pay compensation, **149:158A.**

WAGES, SALARIES, AND COMPENSATION —Cont'd

Fines and penalties —Cont'd

Retaliation by employer against employee seeking rights under wage and hour law, **149:148A.**

Return of wages resulting in net below minimum, penalties for duress resulting, **151:19.**

Specifications as to work and rate of wages, failure to post, **149:156, 149:157.**

Weavers' fines, regulated, **149:153, 149:154.**

Weekly payment, failure to make, **149:148.**

Withholding of tax.
See WITHHOLDING OF TAX.

Fire departments.
See FIRE DEPARTMENTS.

Fire insurance.
See FIRE INSURANCE.

Firemen.
See FIRE DEPARTMENTS.

Fire services department, executive officer, **22D:3.**

Fires, forest.
Forest fires. See within this heading, "Forest fires."

Fire training council, members, **6:164.**

Fiscal affairs division head, **7:4A.**

Fisheries and wildlife board, members, **21:7D.**

Fisheries, wildlife and recreational vehicles department, **21A:7, 21A:8.**

Flats, **91:21, 91:22.**
See TIDE LANDS AND WATERS.

Food and agriculture department, **20:2, 21A:7.**
Assistant commissioner, **20:5.**
Directors of divisions, **20:6.**
Student interns, compensation, **20:6A.**

Foreign countries, public officers and employees not to accept emoluments from without consent of Congress, **US Const Art 1 Sec 9 cl 8.**

Foreign insurance companies, salaries of officers and employees included in annual statement, **175:25.**

Forest fires.
Fighting, compensation, **48:12.**
Observation, compensation, **149:30A, 149:30B.**

Forest wardens, **48:12.**

WAGES, SALARIES, AND COMPENSATION —Cont'd

Forfeiture for holding office in violation of law or collecting more than one salary, **30:22.**

Forms.
Withholding tax on wages.
See FORMS.

Full time service, salaried employees required to give, **30:23.**

Gambling advisory commission, compensation of members, **12B:2.**

Gambling syndicates, organization or management, **271:16A.**

Garnishment, **246:28-246:30.**
See TRUSTEE PROCESS.

Gas.
See GAS AND ELECTRIC COMPANIES.

General court, **3:9.**
See GENERAL COURT.

General schedule of state employees' salaries, **30:46.**

Governor, **6:1.**
See GOVERNOR.

Governor's council members, **6:3, 7A:3, 29:18.**

Governor's highway safety committee, compensation of members, **90A:1, 90A:3.**

Group insurance for municipal employees, salary withholding, **32B:4, 32B:7, 175:138A.**

Group insurance for state employees.
Additional coverage, salary or wages as affecting, **32A:10A.**
Investment committee, **32A:9A.**
Withholdings, **32A:8, 32A:10A-32A:10C, 175:138A.**

Guardian ad litem.
See GUARDIAN AD LITEM.

Guardians.
See GUARDIANS, CONSERVATORS, AND COMMITTEES.

Hairdressers' registration board, **13:44.**

Hampshire County.
Clerks of court, **221:94.**
District court justices, **218:78.**
Registers of probate and insolvency, **217:35A.**

Handicapped persons.
See DISABLED OR HANDICAPPED PERSONS.

Harbor masters, **102:19.**

WAGES, SALARIES, AND COMPENSATION —Cont'd

Hazardous waste facilities sites, compensation for arbitrator of negotiation impasses, **21D:15.**

Health.
See HEALTH AND HEALTH DEPARTMENTS.

Health and human services executive office, senior staff, **6A:16.**

Health and welfare commission, compensation of members, **6:125.**

Health facilities appeals board, members, **6:166.**

Heirs or next of kin.
Deceased county officer or employee, payment to next of kin, **35:19B.**
Payment of salary of deceased municipal officer or employee, **41:111I.**
Political subdivision employee, payment of compensation to next of kin, **149:178C.**
Surviving spouse.
Wages due deceased employee, payment to surviving spouse.
See SURVIVING SPOUSE.
Tidewater displaced, heirs of person responsible to make compensation, **91:21.**

Highways.
Damages or compensation.
See HIGHWAYS AND STREETS.

Historical commission members, **9:26.**

Holidays, **136:13.**
Metropolitan district employees, half holidays, **92:65.**
Police officers and firefighters, holiday pay as regular compensation, **32:1.**
Schedule of compensatory rest days for employees working on Sunday, posting by employer, **149:51, 149:52.**
State employees, compensation or additional time off for holiday work, **30:24A.**
Vacation or holiday pay due employee under oral or written agreement as wages, **149:148.**

Horse and dog racing meetings, police officers assigned, **128A:8.**

Hospitals.
See HOSPITALS AND HEALTH CARE FACILITIES.

WAGES, SALARIES, AND COMPENSATION —Cont'd

Hospital service corporations.
See HOSPITAL SERVICE CORPORATIONS.

Hours of labor.
See HOURS OF LABOR OR SERVICES.

House of representatives.
See GENERAL COURT.

Housing appeals committee, members, **23B:5A.**

Housing authorities, elected municipal officials employed, **39:6A, 268A:20.**

Husband.
See HUSBAND AND WIFE.

Immediate payment on death, retirement, etc., **29:31.**

Increases, **30:46.**
Cost-of-living adjustments for public officers and employees, provision, **30:46, 35:51B.**
County officers and employees, **35:34, 35:53, 35:54.**
Municipal officers and employees. See within this heading, "Municipal officers and employees."
State officers and employees, etc., **29:31.**
Appropriation and allotment for, necessity, **29:27.**
Effective date of increases, **30:46.**
Length of service, **30:46.**

Independent insurance agents, premium commissions, **175:162D, 175:162E.**

Indictment, effect of suspension of state officer or employee while, **30:59.**

Industrial accident department, compensation of various board members, **23E:4, 23E:5, 23E:7.**

Industrial safety division may inspect records pertaining, **149:17.**

Initiative and referendum.
Mayors and city councilors, ordinance making pro-visions as to salaries, **39:6A.**
Police, distribution of literature for referendum pertaining to compensation, **54:65.**

WAGES, SALARIES, AND COMPENSATION —Cont'd

Inspections, chief, **22:4A.**

Inspections or investigations.
Examination, inspection, and investigation. See within this heading, "Examination, inspection, and investigation."

Inspector general.
Members of inspector general council, **12A:3.**
Salary of inspector general, **12A:5.**

Insurance.
See INSURANCE.

Insurance agents.
See INSURANCE AGENTS AND BROKERS.

Interest.
Assignment of wages. See within this heading, "Assignment of wages."
Group insurance for state employees paid directly into interest bearing accounts, salary withholdings, **32A:8.**

Intern scholarship program.
See SCHOOLS AND EDUCATION.

Interpreters, **221:92, 221:92A, 262:32.**

Interstate co-operation commission, **9:21.**

Interstate reporting of drivers' license convictions, additional compensation of compact administrator, **90:30B.**

Investigations.
Examination, inspection, and investigation. See within this heading, "Examination, inspection, and investigation."

Investigations committee, members, **6:184.**

Investment advisory council, members, **10:5B.**

Investment committee for state group insurance commission trust fund, **32A:9A.**

Judges.
See JUDGES.

Judicial council, compensation of members and secretary, **221:34C.**

Juror pools in Middlesex County, salaries of officers in charge, **212:20A.**

WAGES, SALARIES, AND COMPENSATION —Cont'd

Jurors, payment of compensation by employer, **234A:48 et seq.**

Jury commissioner for Commonwealth.
See JURY COMMISSIONER FOR COMMONWEALTH.

Justices of Commonwealth, **211:22, 211A:2, 211B:4.**

Juvenile behavior, executive secretary of council, **6:159.**

Labor and workforce development department.
Complaint by department for violation of weekly payment provisions, **149:150.**

Fair employment practices.
See FAIR EMPLOYMENT PRACTICES.

Investigations, **149:105C, 151:3.**

Members of department, **23:2, 23:9N, 23:9P.**

Minimum wages.
See MINIMUM WAGES.

School bus operators, determination of wages, **71:7A.**

Labor relations.
See LABOR RELATIONS AND DISPUTES.

Labor relations commission.
See LABOR RELATIONS COMMISSION.

Land court.
See LAND COURT.

Landing places, custodian, **88:14.**

Landscape architects, compensation of members, officers, and employees of board of registration, **13:69.**

Leave of absence for state officers and employees, credit for salary increments during, **30:46.**

Legislative agents, **3:42, 3:47.**
See LOBBYING.

Legislative and constitutional officers' compensation advisory board, members and duties, **6:162.**

Legislative document room, employees, **3:18A.**

Legislative post audit and oversight bureau, **3:9, 3:64.**

Legislative research bureau, director and employees, **3:58.**

WAGES, SALARIES, AND COMPENSATION —Cont'd

Legislative research council, **3:56.**

Length of service increases for state employees, **30:46.**

Librarian, state, **6:35.**

Library staff member granted leave of absence, **78:32.**

Lieutenant governor, **6:2.**

Legislative and constitutional officers' compensation advisory board, duties, **6:162.**

Traveling expenses, **6:4.**

Life insurance.
Officers, agents, and employees.
See LIFE INSURANCE.

Limitation of actions to recover wages.
Discrimination based on sex, **149:105A.**

Minimum fair wage violations, **151:20A.**

New judicial interpretation of law, limitation of actions based, **260:4A.**

State, wages due, **29:32A.**

Lists.
Schedules. See within this heading, "Schedules of salaries or wages."

Loan agencies, supervisor, **26:4.**

Loan collateral or security, validity of wage assignment, **140:108, 154:2.**

Lobbying, **3:42, 3:47.**

General court member accepting compensation for promotion or opposition to measures, **56:37.**

Lottery of state.
Commission members, **10:23.**
Director, **10:26.**
Tickets, payroll deductions prohibited for purchase, **10:27.**

Low.
See LOW OR MODERATE INCOME.

Lowland and swamp improvement district commissioners, **252:5, 252:6.**

Management salary schedule of Commonwealth, **30:46C.**

Mandatory retirement age, deductions from salaries of employees working past, **32:90G.**

Marine fish.
See MARINE FISH AND FISHERIES.

WAGES, SALARIES, AND COMPENSATION —Cont'd

Married women, right to earnings, **209:4.**

Massachusetts Centers of Excellence Corporation, Board of Directors, **40J:12.**

Massachusetts office on disability, director's salary, **6:185.**

Masters in chancery.
See AUDITORS, MASTERS, AND REFEREES.

Mayors, **39:6A, 43:17A, 43:17B.**

Measuring devices used in determining, testing, **98:46.**

Meat and meat products, state contracts for, as limited to places paying prevailing wage rate, **7:22.**

Medical examiners.
See MEDICAL EXAMINERS AND INQUESTS.

Medical malpractice, instructions to jury as to lost wages, **231:60J.**

Medical milk commission, **180:22.**

Medical registration board, **13:10.**

Medical service corporations.
See MEDICAL SERVICE CORPORATIONS.

Mentally ill.
See MENTALLY ILL AND RETARDED PERSONS.

Meritorious service, extra compensation, **262:47.**

Messengers in Suffolk County, **221:76.**

Metropolitan districts.
Commission.
See METROPOLITAN DISTRICT COMMISSION.
Half holidays and days off with pay, **92:65.**
Temporary laborers, wage scale, **92:64.**

Metropolitan police.
Commission.
See METROPOLITAN POLICE.

Middlesex county.
See MIDDLESEX COUNTY.

Military affairs.
See MILITARY AFFAIRS.

Militia, **33:83-33:87.**
See MILITIA.

Minimum wages, **151:1 et seq.**
See MINIMUM WAGES.

Mobile homes commission members, **6:108.**

Monthly payment, **29:31, 149:148.**

WAGES, SALARIES, AND COMPENSATION —Cont'd

More than one salary from state, prohibition against receiving, **30:21, 30:22.**

Mortgage review board members, **167:14A.**

Motor vehicles.
See MOTOR VEHICLES.

Multiple elective offices, towns, **268A:20.**

Municipal officers and employees, **41:108, 41:108A.**
Accountant of city or town.
Annual estimate to accountant, **41:59.**
Assistant accountant, salary, **41:49A.**
Retirement system, compensation for administration, **32:20.**
Adoption of charter as affecting, **43:5.**
Advances, **44:64-44:66.**
Aldermen.
See ALDERMEN AND SELECTMEN.
Annual budget, **44:32, 44:33A.**
Annual estimate to accountant, **41:59.**
Appropriations for payment of compensation, **40:5.**
Specific salaries of employees or boards, appropriations, **44:33.**
Supplemental appropriation for increase in salaries, **44:33A.**
Assistant treasurer, **41:39A.**
Auditors of cities and towns.
Assistant auditor, salary, **41:49A.**
Retirement system, compensation for administration, **32:20.**
Authority to make retroactive salary increases for certain, **41:108, 41:108A.**
Charter cities.
See CITY CHARTERS.
City and town clerks.
See CITY AND TOWN CLERKS.
City council, **39:6A, 43:17A, 43:17B.**
See CITY COUNCIL.
City manager, **43:17A, 43:103.**
Civil service.
See CIVIL SERVICE.
Classification of employees for purpose, **41:108A.**

WAGES, SALARIES, AND COMPENSATION —Cont'd

Municipal officers and employees —Cont'd

Clerks of cities.
See CITY AND TOWN CLERKS.

Deceased officer or employee.
Payment of salary to surviving spouse or next of kin, **41:111I.**

Vacation pay, death as affecting, **41:111E.**

Direct deposit, **41:41B.**

Discrimination based on sex, **41:108J.**

Emergency finance board with regard to municipal stabilization funds, **40:5B.**

Equality of compensation between sexes, **41:108G, 41:108J.**

Fair employment practices act, applicability, **151B:1.**

Group insurance, salary withholding, **32B:4, 32B:7, 175:138A.**

Hospital technicians temporarily reemployed without make-up payments, **32:3.**

Increases in salaries, **44:33A.**
Authority of municipal officers to pay increases upon removal of federal restrictions, **44:33A. (note)**

Retroactive, **41:108, 41:108A.**

Industrial development financing authorities, compensation of directors, **40D:6.**

Jurors, compensation for serving, **234:1B.**

Mayor, **39:6A, 43:17A, 43:17B.**

Militia service, no loss of pay while, **33:59.**

Multiple elective offices, **268A:20.**

Municipal lighting.
See MUNICIPAL LIGHTING AND HEATING PLANTS.

Oath to payrolls, persons designated to make, **41:41.**

Off-duty work, **44:53C.**

Ordinances and bylaws. See within this heading, "Ordinances and bylaws."

Overtime pay, **149:33A-149:33C.**

Payroll.
See PAYROLL AND PAYROLL DEDUCTIONS.

WAGES, SALARIES, AND COMPENSATION —Cont'd

Municipal officers and employees —Cont'd

Personnel advisory board, members, **7:4K.**

Plan for compensation to include minimum and maximum salary by class and grade, **41:108A.**

Purchasing agents, **41:103.**

Receipt of equal pay for equal work irrespective of sex, **41:108J, 41:108K.**

Request for appropriations, **44:31A.**

Retroactive salary or wage increases, **41:108, 41:108A, 44:68.**

Sex discrimination in wages prohibited, **41:108J.**

Sinking fund commission's secretary and treasurer, compensation, **44:48.**

Skin divers, compensation for services rendered, **40:5.**

Specific salaries of board employees, appropriations, **44:33.**

Superintendent of public works, **41:69E.**

Supplemental appropriation for salary increases, **44:33A.**

Suspension, compensation during, **268A:25.**

Town council member as employed by same municipality, **39:6A, 43:17A, 268A:20.**

Town meetings. See within this heading, "Town meetings."

Treasurers of cities and towns.
Assistant treasurer, **41:39A.**
Certification as Massachusetts municipal or district treasurer.
Additional compensation, **41:108P.**
Custodian of retirement system funds, salaries or compensation for services, **32:20.**
Deceased officer or employee, payment of salary to designated beneficiary, **41:111I.**
Deferred compensation programs, provisions as to contracts with employees for establishment, **44:67.**
Payment of, regulated, **41:52.**

WAGES, SALARIES, AND COMPENSATION —Cont'd

Municipal officers and employees —Cont'd

Treasurers of cities and towns —Cont'd
Payroll.
See PAYROLL AND PAYROLL DEDUCTIONS.
Union conventions, attendance, **40:21C.**
Vacation pay, **41:110, 41:111, 41:111A, 41:111D, 41:111E, 41:111G, 41:111G½, 41:111K, 41:111L, 44:65, 48:57D, 48:57E.**
Weekly payment of wages, **149:148.**

Nantucket county.
See NANTUCKET COUNTY.

National banks.
See NATIONAL BANKS.

New Bedford Institute of Technology.
Positions in public institutions of higher education, **30:46.**
Professional staff, **74:42O.**

Next friend, compensation, **201:35, 240:9.**

Next of kin.
Heirs or next of kin. See within this heading, "Heirs or next of kin."

Notice and knowledge.
Assignment of wages, notice to employer, **208:36, 209:32E.**
Deductions, **149:150A.**
Posting. See within this heading, "Posting."
Workers' compensation.
See WORKERS' COMPENSATION.

Nursing home administrators board of registration, **13:75.**

Nursing registration board, **13:14, 13:15, 13:15D.**

Nutrition board, members and employees, **6:181.**

Obscene literature control commission, **6:101.**

Office of child care services, director, **28A:3.**

Opticians, board of registration, **13:50.**

Optometric service corporation, officers or employees, **176F:11.**

Optometry registration board, **13:18.**

Ordinances and bylaws.
Increases in salaries, enactment of ordinances, **44:33A.**

WAGES, SALARIES, AND COMPENSATION —Cont'd

Ordinances and bylaws —Cont'd

Mayor and city councilors, ordinances making provisions for salaries, **39:6A, 43:17A, 43:17B.**

Outdoor advertising board members, **16:14.**

Overtime pay.

See HOURS OF LABOR OR SERVICES.

Parole.

Probation and parole. See within this heading, "Probation and parole."

Partnerships.

Workers' compensation.

See PARTNERSHIPS.

Part-time state employees, salary schedule, **30:46.**

Payroll.

See PAYROLL AND PAYROLL DEDUCTIONS.

Pay slip requirements, **149:148, 149:150A.**

Penalties.

Fines and penalties. See within this heading, "Fines and penalties."

Pensions.

See RETIREMENT SYSTEMS AND PENSIONS.

Personnel board, county, **35:48.**

Pesticide control board, **132B:3.**

Pharmacy registration board, **13:24.**

Physicians.

See PHYSICIANS AND SURGEONS.

Piece work, ticket showing amount of remuneration, **149:157A.**

Pipefitters' and refrigeration technicians' bureau members, **22:10A.**

Plan for Commonwealth, **30:46.**

Plumbers and gas fitters, state board of examiners, **13:38.**

Plymouth county.

See PLYMOUTH COUNTY.

Police.

See POLICE.

Posting.

Minimum wages, **151:10, 151:16.**

Schedule of wages during life of contract, **149:27.**

Postponement of pay increases of state employees, **30:46.**

President, compensation not to be altered during term of office, **US Const Art 2 Sec 1 cl 7.**

WAGES, SALARIES, AND COMPENSATION —Cont'd

Presidential electors, **54:149.**

Printing contractors for state, wage and hour laws regarding, **5:1.**

Priority of wage claims in settlement of estates held by receivers, **206:31.**

Private secretary of governor, **6:5.**

Prize fighting for reward, **265:12.**

Probate.

Probate and family court.

See PROBATE AND FAMILY COURT.

Probate and insolvency judges.

See PROBATE AND INSOLVENCY JUDGES.

Probation and parole.

Commissioner and deputy commissioners of probation, **276:98.**

Parole board members, **27:4.**

Temporary appointments to parole board, **27:7.**

Probation officers, **276:83, 276:83A.**

See PROBATION OFFICERS.

Probationary period of employment without compensation for woman or child, prohibited, **149:158A.**

Probation officers, **276:83, 276:83A.**

See PROBATION OFFICERS.

Professional employees of state, **30:46.**

Professional engineers and land surveyors, members of board of registration, **13:47.**

Professional solicitors, compensation, **68:21.**

Proposed laws and constitutional amendments, public officers or employees not to promote for compensation, **56:37.**

Prosecuting attorneys, **12:15, 12:16, 12:20A, 280:16.**

See DISTRICT AND PROSECUTING ATTORNEYS.

Public administrators.

See EXECUTORS AND ADMINISTRATORS.

Public buildings, prescribed rates of wages for cleaning and maintenance, **149:27H.**

Public health department.

See HEALTH AND HEALTH DEPARTMENTS.

Public officers and employees, **29:31, 30:45 et seq., 35:49, 35:51B, 41:108, 41:108A.**

WAGES, SALARIES, AND COMPENSATION —Cont'd

Purchasing agent.

Municipal, **41:103.**

Overtime pay for purchasing agent, **151:1A.**

State, **7:4A.**

Quarantined wage earner, compensation for loss of time, **111:95.**

Questioning of employees must be permitted, **151:17.**

Domestic service in employer's home, exception, **151:16.**

Quiet title action, compensation of guardian ad litem or next friend, **240:9.**

Racing commission, **6:48.**

Radiation.

Low-level radioactive waste facility installation, **111H:34.**

Protection advisory council, compensation of members, **111:4F.**

Radio and television.

Technicians' registration board, **13:62, 13:63.**

Railroads.

See RAILROADS.

Range of salary.

Defined or construed, **30:45, 35:51A.**

Minimum wages, **151:1 et seq.**

See MINIMUM WAGES.

Schedules of salaries or wages.

See within this heading, "Schedules of salaries or wages."

State classified service, change in job group of certain positions, **30:45.**

Step-in-range, **30:45, 30:46, 35:51A.**

Real estate brokers.

See REAL ESTATE BROKERS AND SALESPERSONS.

Receivers, priority of wage claims in settlement of estates, **206:31.**

Reclamation board members, **252:2.**

Records, reports, and returns.

Annual report by state treasurer as to salaries and job descriptions of state officers and employees, **10:5A.**

Assignment of wages. See within this heading, "Assignment of wages."

Criminal offender record information system employees, **6:168.**

WAGES, SALARIES, AND COMPENSATION —Cont'd

Records, reports, and returns —Cont'd

Employers to keep, **151:15.**

Ethics commission of state, annual report, **268B:2.**

Industrial safety division may inspect, **149:17.**

Interstate reporting of drivers' license convictions, compact administrator, **90:30B.**

Machine readable form of reports by employers with twenty-five hundred employees or more, **62E:2.**

Minimum wages.
See MINIMUM WAGES.

Place of keeping pay records under fair wage law, **151:15.**

Public works, wages paid, **149:27B.**

State officers and employees, publication of records of salaries, **7:30.**

Wage reporting system.
See WAGE REPORTING SYSTEM.

Workers' compensation.
See WORKERS' COMPENSATION.

Recreational tramway board, compensation of members, **143:71H.**

Reemployment assistance programs defined, **151A:71A.**

Referees.
See AUDITORS, MASTERS, AND REFEREES.

Referendum.
Initiative and referendum. See within this heading, "Initiative and referendum."

Refrigeration technicians' and pipe fitters' bureau members, **22:10A.**

Regional health district officers and employees, **111:27B.**

Regional school districts.
See REGIONAL SCHOOL DISTRICTS.

Regional transit authorities.
Administrator, **161B:4.**
Employees, **161B:6.**

Regional vocational school committees, compensation of treasurers and assistant treasurers, **71:16A.**

Registers of deeds, **36:33, 217:35A, 217:35B.**
See REGISTERS AND REGISTRIES OF DEEDS.

WAGES, SALARIES, AND COMPENSATION —Cont'd

Registers of probate.
See REGISTERS OF PROBATE AND INSOLVENCY.

Registrar of motor vehicles, **16:5, 16:9.**

Registration of voters, **51:23.**
City or town clerk serving on board of registrars, additional compensation, **41:19G, 41:19H.**

Rehabilitation commission, members, **6:75, 6:76.**

Reinstatement to office or employment.
State officer or employee, **30:46.**

Removal of employee.
Discharge of employee. See within this heading, "Discharge of employee."

Repeal by general law as affecting, **281:8.**

Reporter of decisions, **221:68.**

Reports.
Records, reports, and returns. See within this heading, "Records, reports, and returns."

Reserve police officers, rate of pay, **149:34B.**

Retail installment sales agreement, prohibition against wage assignment provision, **255D:10.**

Retaliation by employer against employee seeking rights under wage and hour law, prohibition, **149:148A.**

Retirement systems.
See RETIREMENT SYSTEMS AND PENSIONS.

Retroactive salary or wage increases, **41:108, 41:108A.**

Return of wages or compensation resulting in employee retaining less than minimum, duress resulting, **151:19.**

Revenue department.
See REVENUE DEPARTMENT AND COMMISSIONER.

Sales representatives, commission, **104:7.**

Sanitarians' board of registration, **13:53.**

Savings bank life insurance, directors, **178A:9.**

Savings banks.
See SAVINGS BANKS.

Schedules of salaries or wages.
Contract, posting schedule of wages during life, **149:27.**

WAGES, SALARIES, AND COMPENSATION —Cont'd

Schedules of salaries or wages —Cont'd

County offices and positions, **35:51B.**

Definition of salary schedules, **35:51B. (note)**

Posting. See within this heading, "Posting."

Rest days, **149:51, 149:52.**

School bus contracts, employees of bidders, **71:7A.**

State officers and employees, **30:46, 30:46C.**

Schools.
See SCHOOLS AND EDUCATION.

Schooner Ernestina Commission, members, **6:182A.**

Scrubwomen and cleaners employed by state, **8:5.**

Seamen.
Overtime pay, **151:1A.**
Trustee process, wages due seaman as exempt, **246:32.**
Workers' compensation, **152:1.**

Secretary of state, **9:1.**
See SECRETARY OF STATE.

Secured transactions.
Exclusion of wage assignments, **106:9-104.**
Validity of wage assignment as security for loan, **140:108, 154:2.**

Selectmen.
See ALDERMEN AND SELECTMEN.

Semi-monthly payment, **149:148.**

Senate committee on ways and means, compensation of vice chairman, **3:9.**

Separation pay.
Severance pay. See within this heading, "Severance pay."

Service charges to be paid to employees, **149:152A.**

Severance pay, **149:184.**
Collective bargaining agreement, penalty for violation of employee benefit provisions, **149:181.**
Defined, **151A:71A.**
Employment security benefits as affected by public employee's separation pay, **151A:28.**

School superintendent, **71:16, 71:41, 71:63.**

Sex discrimination.
Wages, discrimination based on sex.
See FAIR EMPLOYMENT PRACTICES.

WAGES, SALARIES, AND COMPENSATION —Cont'd

Sheltered workshop program, handicapped persons employed, **6:78A.**

Sheriffs and deputies, **37:17.**
See SHERIFFS AND DEPUTIES.

Shift differentials for county employees, establishment of rules and regulations governing, **35:51.**

Skin divers, compensation for services, **40:5.**

Small estates.
Deceased employee, payment without administration, **149:178A, 149:178C.**
Employment security benefits owing to deceased, **151A:68.**
State officer or employee, payment of salaries, wages, or other money owing to deceased, **29:31D.**

Small loan business regulatory board, **26:5A.**

Social services department.
See WELFARE AND SOCIAL SERVICES.

Soldiers' Home in Holyoke, board of trustees, **6:70.**

Soldiers' Home in Massachusetts, trustees, **6:40.**

Southeastern regional planning and economic development district.
Commission members, **40B:15.**
Employees of commission, **40B:16.**

Special assessments, **21D:5, 80A:15.**

Special district attorney in Suffolk and northern districts, **12:20A.**

Special education personnel in school departments of certain institutions, **71B:12.**

Special justices in district courts, per diem compensation, **218:6.**

Special masters, **221:55.**

Special state or county employees, regulation by ethics commission of outside employment, **268A:4, 268A:11.**

Specifications to be furnished employees, **149:155-149:157.**

Sports program volunteers, tort liability, **231:85V.**

Spouse.
See HUSBAND AND WIFE.

Standardbred agricultural fair and breeding fund committee, members, **20:10.**

WAGES, SALARIES, AND COMPENSATION —Cont'd

State auditor, **11:1.**
Employees, **11:6.**
Legislative and constitutional officers' compensation advisory board, duties, **6:162.**
Pensioner's right to payment for services in department, **32:91.**

State ballot law commission members, **55B:3.**

State boxing commission members, **22:12.**

State comptroller.
See COMPTROLLER OF STATE.

State ethics commission.
Ethics commission. See within this heading, "Ethics commission of state."

State finance.
See STATE FINANCE.

State lottery.
Lottery of state. See within this heading, "Lottery of state."

State office buildings physician, **7:6E.**

State officers and employees, **29:31, 30:46.**

State police.
See STATE POLICE.

State printing contractors, wage and hour laws regarding, **5:1.**

State purchasing agent, **7:4A.**

State reclamation board members, **252:2.**

State tax returns, compensation of state employees for filing, **268A:4.**

State treasurer.
See STATE TREASURER.

Statute of frauds, brokers, finders, or negotiation of loan or purchase, sale, or exchange of business, **259:7.**

Statute of limitations.
Limitation of actions. See within this heading, "Limitation of actions to recover wages."

Statutory positions, monthly payment of salaries of state officials, **29:31.**

Statutory provision as referring to annual salary, **4:7.**

Steamboat police, **159:95.**

Stenographers.
Court stenographers.
See COURT STENOGRAPHERS.

WAGES, SALARIES, AND COMPENSATION —Cont'd

Stenographers —Cont'd
Governor, stenographers, **6:6, 6:6A.**
State ballot commission members, **55B:3.**

Step-in-range, **30:45, 30:46, 35:51A.**

Street railways.
Overtime pay for employees, **151:1A.**
Police, **159:95.**
Transportation area trustees, **161:146.**

Streets.
Damages or compensation.
See HIGHWAYS AND STREETS.

Suffolk county.
See SUFFOLK COUNTY.

Summons for violation of weekly payment requirements, **149:149.**

Sundays.
Holidays. See within this heading, "Holidays."

Superintendent of schools.
See SCHOOLS AND EDUCATION.

Superintendent of streets.
Damages or compensation.
See HIGHWAYS AND STREETS.

Superior courts.
See SUPERIOR COURTS.

Supervisors of elections, **54:23.**

Supervisors of state employees, method of paying, **29:31.**

Supplementary security income commission.
Health and human services executive office, agencies within, **6A:16.**

Support payments.
Assignment of wages, **209:32E.**
Information sharing, child support collection enforcement, **14:1, 14:1A, 62C:21, 62D:11, 62E:1, 62E:3, 62E:4, 62E:6, 62E:7A, 62E:11, 62E:12, 93:51, 93:52A, 119A:1, 119A:2, 119A:6, 119A:10, 119A:12.**

Supreme judicial court.
See SUPREME JUDICIAL COURT.

Surveyors.
See ENGINEERS AND SURVEYORS.

WAGES, SALARIES, AND COMPENSATION —Cont'd

Surviving spouse, payment of deceased's wages.

County officer or employee, **35:19B.**

Municipal officer or employee, **41:111I.**

Without administration, **29:31D, 149:178A, 149:178C.**

Suspension of state officer or employee while under indictment, **30:59.**

Tax assessors, **41:22, 221:55.**

See TAX ASSESSORS.

Tax collectors, **14:3, 60:2B, 60:15, 60:23.**

Tax withholding.

See WITHHOLDING OF TAX.

Teachers, **29:31, 29:31B, 71:40, 71:42B.**

See TEACHERS.

Technology development corporation, members of board, **40G:2.**

Telecommunications and energy department.

Commissioners, **25:2, 25:3.**

Frequency of payment, **149:148.**

Television.

Radio and television. See within this heading, "Radio and television."

Tellers at primaries, **53:29.**

Tewksbury Hospital, employment of patients, **122:15.**

Textiles, **149:155-149:157.**

Thrift Institutions Fund for Economic Development, Board of Directors, **63:1. (note)**

Tide waters displaced by filling, compensation, **91:21, 91:22.**

Disposition of moneys, **91:6, 91:24.**

Time or date.

Assigned wages, time, **154:2, 154:3, 154:8.**

Back wages, actions based on new judicial interpretation, time to sue, **260:4A.**

Discharged employee, time for payment, **149:148.**

Limitation of actions. See within this heading, "Limitation of actions to recover wages."

Public officers and employees, final day for filing proposed ordinance as to salaried, **39:6A.**

Quarantined wage earner, compensation for loss of time, **111:95.**

WAGES, SALARIES, AND COMPENSATION —Cont'd

Time or date —Cont'd

State officers and employees, **29:31, 30:46.**

Weekly compensation, defined, **149:184.**

Weekly wage payment laws, complaint for violation, **149:150.**

Withholding of tax.

See WITHHOLDING OF TAX.

Workers' compensation.

See WORKERS' COMPENSATION.

Year of service, defined, **149:184.**

Tips.

See GIFTS, GRANTS, AND GRATUITIES.

Town meetings.

Representatives, **43A:5.**

Salary plans for town employees, **41:108A.**

Town officers and employees.

Municipal officers and employees. See within this heading, "Municipal officers and employees."

Training, pay plan for state employees, **30:45.**

Transitional department.

See WELFARE AND SOCIAL SERVICES.

Transportation areas, compensation of employees, **161:147.**

Traveling expenses.

See TRAVELING EXPENSES.

Treasurer of state.

See STATE TREASURER.

Treasurers of cities and towns.

Municipal officers and employees. See within this heading, "Municipal officers and employees."

Treasurers of counties.

See COUNTY TREASURERS.

Trust companies.

See TRUST COMPANIES.

Trustee process, **246:28-246:30.**

See TRUSTEE PROCESS.

Trusts.

See TRUSTS AND TRUSTEES.

Turnpike authority.

Deferred compensation program, **81A:21.**

Individual retirement accounts, **81A:22.**

Turnpike authority, deferred compensation, **29:64, 29:64A, 35:57, 35:57A, 44:67, 44:67A, 81A:21, 161:19H, 161:19I.**

WAGES, SALARIES, AND COMPENSATION —Cont'd

Turnpike authority individual retirement accounts, **81A:22.**

Turnpike authority members, **81A:2.**

Unclaimed or unpaid wages and salaries due from Commonwealth, **29:31, 29:31A, 29:31D, 29:32A.**

Underwater archeological resources board, members, **6:179.**

Unemployment compensation, **151A:1-151A:74.**

See EMPLOYMENT SECURITY.

Union conventions, municipal employees attending, **40:21C.**

Union dues, deduction of.

See LABOR RELATIONS AND DISPUTES.

United Fund, payroll deductions for contributions of state, county, or town employees, **180:17B.**

University of Massachusetts.

See UNIVERSITY OF MASSACHUSETTS.

Unpaid or unclaimed wages and salaries due from Commonwealth, **29:31, 29:31A, 29:31D, 29:32A.**

Urban area insurance placement facility, compensation of agents or brokers procuring coverage through, **175C:3.**

Vacation pay.

Accumulated vacation allowances upon death or separation from service, **29:31A, 41:111E.**

Contract, vacation pay due employee under oral or written contract as wages, **149:148.**

County employees, **35:19A.**

Deductions from payroll, **149:150A.**

Firefighters, **41:111A et seq.**

See FIRE DEPARTMENTS.

Municipal officers and employees, **41:110-41:111L, 44:65.**

Police, **41:111A et seq.**

See POLICE.

Public utilities.

See

TELECOMMUNICATIONS AND ENERGY DEPARTMENT.

WAGES, SALARIES, AND COMPENSATION —Cont'd

Vacation pay —Cont'd
  Retirement systems.
    See RETIREMENT SYSTEMS
      AND PENSIONS.
Veterans.
  See VETERANS AND
    VETERANS'
    ORGANIZATIONS.
Veterinarians' registration board,
  13:28.
Volunteer firemen, insurance
  compensation for injuries,
  32:85H.
Warrant for violation of weekly
  payment provisions, **149:149.**
Water pollution.
  Abatement district employees
    and commission, **21:29.**
  Limitations on outside income of
    director of water pollution
    control division, **21:26.**
Waterworks.
  See WATERWORKS AND
    WATER SUPPLY.
Wearing apparel and clothing
  purchased by state, wage rates
  required to be paid by
  manufacturers, **7:22.**
Weavers' fines, regulated, **149:153,**
  149:154.
Weekly payment, **29:31,**
  149:148-149:150.
  Average weekly wage. See
    within this heading,
    "Average weekly wage."
  Centralized weekly payroll
    system for state employees,
    establishment, **29:31.**
  Defenses to charge of violation of
    requirement, **149:150.**
  Defined, **149:184.**
  Discharge or termination,
    payment upon, **149:148.**
  Employment security benefit,
    151A:1.
Workers' compensation.
  See WORKERS'
    COMPENSATION.
Welfare.
  See WELFARE AND SOCIAL
    SERVICES.
White pine blister rust,
  compensation to owner with
  respect to suppression, **128:23.**
Withholding from wages, **62B:1 et**
  seq.
  Child support, **119A:7.**
  Withholding of tax.
    See WITHHOLDING OF TAX.

WAGES, SALARIES, AND COMPENSATION —Cont'd

Withholding of tax.
  See WITHHOLDING OF TAX.
Witnesses.
  See WITNESSES.
Women, infants, and children
  program, compensation of
  advisory board members
  prohibited, **111I:4.**
Worcester County.
  Clerks of courts, **221:94.**
  District court judges, **218:78.**
Workers' compensation,
  152:1-152:75A.
  See WORKERS'
    COMPENSATION.
Workforce development system,
  wage reporting data used for,
  62E:12.
World War II, Korean Emergency,
  and Vietnam Conflict
  Memorial Commission,
  members, **6:124A.**
Year of service defined for
  purposes of increments to
  state employees, **30:46.**
Youth services advisory committee,
  compensation of members,
  18A:9.

WAGNER-PEYSER ACT.
Money received, **151A:58.**
Segregating money from Act to
  special employment service
  accounts, **151A:61.**

WAGONS.
Municipal regulation, **40:22.**
Station wagons.
  See MOTOR VEHICLES.

WAIT AND SEE ACT, 184A:1 et
  seq.
Perpetuities, **184A:1 et seq.**

WAITING PERIOD.
Accident and sickness insurance,
  176J:5.
Defined, **176J:1.**
Divorce, commencement of period,
  208:1B.
Employment security.
  See EMPLOYMENT
    SECURITY.
Motor vehicle sales, waiting
  periods for group accident and
  health insurance issued,
  255B:10.
Workers' compensation, **152:29.**

WAITING ROOMS.
Stations.
  See STATIONS AND DEPOTS.

WAIVER AND ESTOPPEL.
Accident and sickness insurance.
  Investigation of claim, waiver of
    rights of insurer, **175:108.**
  Policy provisions, waiver,
    175:108.
Adoption of children, waiver of
  residency requirement,
  210:5A.
Aid to dependent children as
  affected by right to veterans'
  benefit, **118:9.**
Aircraft financial responsibility
  act, **90:49D.**
Alimony.
  Divorce and alimony. See within
    this heading, "Divorce and
    alimony."
Animal diseases, waiver of
  compliance with regulations
  concerning brucellosis,
  129:36H.
Antitrust laws, **93:11.**
Appeal.
  See APPEAL AND REVIEW.
Appraisal as waiver of insurer's
  rights, **175:191A.**
Arbitration.
  See ARBITRATION.
Arraignment, indictment, waiver,
  263:4A.
Art, preservation, **231:85S.**
Asbestos, waiver of damages
  caused by exposure, **149:6G.**
Ash, public health department's
  requirements as to use and
  storage, **111:150A.**
Attorneys fees.
  See ATTORNEYS' FEES.
Automobile insurance.
  See AUTOMOBILE
    INSURANCE.
Automobiles.
  Motor vehicles. See within this
    heading, "Motor vehicles."
Bank commissioner.
  See BANK COMMISSIONER.
Banks.
  See BANKS AND BANKING.
Board of higher education, **15A:19.**
Bonds.
  See BONDS AND
    UNDERTAKINGS.
Breach of contract under
  Commercial Code.
  See SALES UNDER
    COMMERCIAL CODE.
Capital cases.
  Indictment, waiver of right to be
    proceeded against, **263:4A.**
  Jury trial, **263:6.**

WAIVER AND ESTOPPEL
—Cont'd

Carnegie school grant program, **15:63.**

Certificates and certification.
Chiropractors, waiver of educational requirements for license renewal certificate, **112:96.**
Dentists certified, **112:48.**
Teachers, exemption from requirements in case of hardship in securing teachers for schools of town, **71:38G.**

Children.
See CHILDREN AND MINORS.

Chiropractors, waiver of educational requirements for license renewal certificate, **112:96.**

Collective bargaining, arbitration award, timeliness, **150C:7.**

Commercial Code, applicability of estoppel law generally, **106:1-103, 106:1-107.**

Commercial driver license.
See UNIFORM OPERATION OF COMMERCIAL MOTOR VEHICLES.

Commitment or retention hearings, **123:6, 123:8.**

Competitive bidding, notice requirement, **149:44J.**

Condemnation.
Eminent domain. See within this heading, "Eminent domain."

Consumer rights, waiver, **93:101.**

Controlled dangerous substances, waiver of records and reports, **94C:8.**

Corporations.
See CORPORATIONS.

Credit unions.
See CREDIT UNIONS.

Criminal procedure.
See CRIMINAL PROCEDURE.

Curtesy.
Dower and curtesy, **189:1, 189:9.**

Deaf persons.
Arrest for alleged violation of criminal law, **221:92A.**
Interpreters, waiver of appointment, **221:92A.**

Decrees.
Judgments and decrees. See within this heading, "Judgments and decrees."

Defenses, **175:101E, 277:47A.**

Definitions, **15A:29.**

WAIVER AND ESTOPPEL
—Cont'd

Dentists certified by National Board of Dental Examiners, waiver of examination, **112:48.**

Deposition, waiver as to notice of taking, **233:29.**

Disability, waiver of life insurance premiums as total and permanent disability benefit, **175:24.**

Disclaimer.
See DISCLAIMER.

District courts.
See DISTRICT COURTS.

Divorce and alimony.
Cooling off period, waiver, **208:6B.**
Costs, affidavit of indigency and request for waiver, **261:27B.**

Dower and curtesy, **189:1, 189:9.**

Dwellings unfit for human habitation, tenant's waiver of statutory benefits provided, **111:127K.**

Education.
See SCHOOLS AND EDUCATION.

Electric companies' property held as tenants in common, waiver of rights to partition, **164:99A.**

Eminent domain.
Acceptance of payment as waiver of claim to larger sum, **79:7G.**
Payment of judgment or award after waiver of right of appeal, **79:36A.**

Employment permit, school record, **149:88.**

Employment security.
See EMPLOYMENT SECURITY.

Environmental protection department, waiver of hearing, **21A:16.**

Equipment dealers, waiver of compliance with provisions, **93G:10.**

Eviction hearing by housing authority, **121B:32.**

Executors and administrators, consent in writing to appointment, **192:2.**

Extradition.
Nonwaiver by Commonwealth, **276:20P.**
Warrant of arrest, **276:20J.**

Federal aid or funds.
Relocation assistance, waiver of statutory provisions barring federal reimbursement, **79A:12.**

WAIVER AND ESTOPPEL
—Cont'd

Federal aid or funds —Cont'd
Utilization of federal grants by state organizations and institutions, waiver of provisions, **29:2C.**

Fines.
See FINES AND PENALTIES.

Firefighters and police officers waiving workers' compensation provisions, leave **41:111F.**

Fire insurance.
Landlord, disclosure, **186:21.**
Name of insurer, waiver of disclosure requirement, **186:21.**
Policy provisions, clause as to waiver, **175:99.**
Reference proceedings as waiver of legal defenses, **175:101E.**

Foreign insurance companies.
Insurance rates and rating organizations, waiver of hearing on application for deviation, **175A:9.**
Provisions of chapter prohibited unless authorized thereby, **175:22B.**

Fraternal benefit societies.
Mortuary contributions, waiver, **176:25.**
Provisions of constitution and bylaws, waiver, **176:27.**
Statute making statements of members representations and not warranties, waiver, **176:23.**

Gasoline and motor fuel taxes, reciprocal agreements with other states waiving requirement, **64F:5.**

Guardian's waiver on behalf of ward, **201:45.**

Hazardous waste management act, waiver of provisions, **21C:4.**

Health maintenance organization bond requirement, waiver, **176G:15.**

Hearings.
Blood or breath test, **90B:8.**
Bridgewater State Hospital, **123:6, 123:8.**
Commitment of person waived, mental health, **123:6, 123:8.**
Environmental protection department, waiver of hearing, **21A:16.**

Higher education, waiver allocation formulas for developmentally disabled persons, **15A:19.**

WAIVER AND ESTOPPEL
—Cont'd

Highway, estoppel as to location of by making repairs, **84:25.**

Housing court department, waiver of fees, **185C:19.**

Housing, pet ownership by elderly persons in public housing, **23B:3.**

Indictment, waiver, **263:4A, 276:38.**

Indigents.
  Appeal bond, payment of rent after waiver, **239:5.**
  Filing affidavit of indigency and request for waiver of court costs, **261:27B.**
  Limits of indigency for waiver of costs of actions, **261:27C.**

Insurance.
  See INSURANCE.

Insurance agents.
  See INSURANCE AGENTS AND BROKERS.

Interest on money.
  Overdue taxes, prohibition of waiver, **59:69.**
  Small home mortgages, waiver of benefit of laws as to, void as contrary to public policy, **140:90D.**

Interpreters, **221:92A, 221C:3.**

Interstate reciprocal agreements waiving gasoline and motor fuel tax, **64F:5.**

Judgments and decrees.
  Amount of recovery, waiver of costs as affected, **261:27E.**
  Vacation of judgment, filing affidavit of indigency and request for waiver of costs in petitions to vacate, **261:27B.**

Jury.
  See JURY AND JURY TRIAL.

Labor and workforce development, **149:19B, 149:29B, 149:88.**

Labor relations.
  Conciliation and arbitration.
    See LABOR RELATIONS AND DISPUTES.

Landlord.
  See LANDLORD AND TENANT.

Leases under UCC.
  See LEASES UNDER COMMERCIAL CODE.

Legacy and succession taxes.
  Issuance of waiver, **65:35A.**
  Penalty for late filing of taxes, waiver, **65:22.**

Levy, waiver, **236:50.**

WAIVER AND ESTOPPEL
—Cont'd

Lie detector tests, use by employers, **149:19B.**

Liens, waiver, **254:32.**

Life insurance premiums, waiver of, as total and permanent disability benefit, **175:24.**

Loans, regulations, **140:90.**

Lobbying, waiver of reporting penalties by secretary of state, **3:47.**

Local tax collectors, waiver of charges, **60:15.**

Marriage.
  Notice of intention to marry.
    See MARRIAGE.

Medical clearance as prerequisite to hearing aid purchase, **93:73, 93:74.**

Membership camping contract or agreement, **93:48A.**

Mental health, waiver of hearing for commitment to facility, **123:6, 123:8.**

Minors.
  See CHILDREN AND MINORS.

Morris plan banks, waiver of notice of withdrawals, **172A:6.**

Mortgage foreclosure, waiver of statutory provisions as to deficiency, **244:17C.**

Motor vehicles.
  Automobile insurance.
    See AUTOMOBILE INSURANCE.
  Commercial driver license.
    See UNIFORM OPERATION OF COMMERCIAL MOTOR VEHICLES.
  Financing law, waiver or provisions, **255B:20, 255B:23.**

Liability insurer's estoppel to deny liability, **90:34B.**

Movies, effect of waiver of trade screening, **93F:2.**

New England power pool, waiver of right to partition, **164A:5.**

Objections in criminal cases, **277:47A.**

Partition of property, waiver of right.
  Electric companies' property held as tenants in common, **164:99A.**
  New England power pool, **164A:5.**

Partnerships.
  Applicability of law of estoppel and waiver, **108A:4.**

WAIVER AND ESTOPPEL
—Cont'd

Partnerships —Cont'd
  Partnership, estoppel to deny, **108A:16.**

Payment bond, agreement between owner and contractor to waive as constituting false and deceptive act, **149:29B.**

Pensions.
  See RETIREMENT SYSTEMS AND PENSIONS.

Physicians, removal of registration waivers for certain, **112:9.**

Planning.
  Zoning and planning. See within this heading, "Zoning and planning."

Pleading.
  Indictment, application for waiver, **263:4A.**
  Indigency, filing affidavit of and request for waiver of court costs, **261:27B.**

Police officers or firefighters waiving workers' compensation provisions, leave for certain **41:111F.**

Poor persons.
  Indigents. See within this heading, "Indigents."

Premium finance agreements, provisions prohibited, **255C:16.**

Probate.
  See PROBATE AND FAMILY COURT.

Probate bonds, **205:4, 205:5.**

Probation fee, waiver, **276:87A.**

Process and service of process and papers.
  Contract action, waiver, **231:13A.**
  Indictment, service of complaint upon waiver, **263:4A.**
  Written instrument, waiver, **231:13A.**

Psychotherapists, disclosure of patient information, **233:20B.**

Public charities, waiver of notice regarding disposition of property, **180:8A.**

Public counsel services committee, waiver of fee, **211D:2A.**

Qualified bonds, information certified with respect, **44A:9.**

Railroads.
  See RAILROADS.

Rates and charges.
  Insurance rating organizations, waiver of hearing on application for deviation, **174A:9, 175A:9.**

WAIVER AND ESTOPPEL
—Cont'd
Real estate time-shares.
See REAL ESTATE
TIME-SHARES.
Relocation assistance, waiver of
statutory provisions barring
federal reimbursement,
79A:12.
Restraints of trade, **93:11.**
Retail installment sales and
services.
Buyer's waiver of protection
afforded by law, **255D:24.**
Installment sales agreements,
255D:10, 255D:24.
Retirement systems.
See RETIREMENT SYSTEMS
AND PENSIONS.
Sales under commercial code.
See SALES UNDER
COMMERCIAL CODE.
Schools.
See SCHOOLS AND
EDUCATION.
Secured transactions.
See SECURED
TRANSACTIONS.
Securities Act, civil liabilities,
110A:410.
Service of process and papers.
Process and service of process
and papers. See within this
heading, "Process and
service of process and
papers."
Sickness insurance.
Accident and sickness insurance.
See within this heading,
"Accident and sickness
insurance."
Signatures.
Breach of contract, signing of
written renunciation or
waiver, **106:1-107.**
Jury trial, signature on written
waiver, **263:6.**
Small claims actions and
procedure.
Jury trial, waiver, **218:23.**
Venue, waiver, **218:21.**
Social worker, disclosure of
information, **112:135,
112:135B.**
State purchase of supplies and
equipment, provision for
waiver of rules with regard,
7:22.
Street railways, waiver of notice.
Directors' meetings, **161:18.**
First meeting of incorporators,
161:10.

WAIVER AND ESTOPPEL
—Cont'd
Street railways, waiver of notice
—Cont'd
Stockholders' meetings, **161:14.**
Subdivision control law, waiver of
strict compliance with rules,
41:81R.
Succession taxes.
Legacy and succession taxes. See
within this heading, "Legacy
and succession taxes."
Summary process to recover land.
Bond or security on appeal,
waiver, **239:5.**
Validity of lease provision
waiving right to obtain stay
of proceedings, **239:12.**
Superior courts.
Indictment in, waiver, **263:4A.**
Jury trial, waiver, **263:6.**
Taxation.
See TAXATION.
Tax collectors, **59:57, 60:15.**
Teacher certification requirement,
waiver in case of hardship in
securing teachers, **71:38G.**
Tenant.
See LANDLORD AND TENANT.
Toxics Use Reduction Act, waivers,
21I:16, 21I:17, 21I:19.
Tuition, waiver, **71:6A, 76:6.**
Underground storage tank
petroleum product cleanup
fund.
See UNDERGROUND
STORAGE TANK
PETROLEUM PRODUCT
CLEANUP FUND.
Unemployment compensation.
See EMPLOYMENT
SECURITY.
Uniform operation of commercial
motor vehicles.
See UNIFORM OPERATION OF
COMMERCIAL MOTOR
VEHICLES.
Uniform Securities Act, civil
liabilities, **110A:410.**
Veterans' benefits, aid to
dependent children as affected
by right, **118:9.**
Victims and witness assistance
programs, waiver of
assessment due to financial
hardship, **258B:8.**
Warehouse receipts, negotiation as
working estoppel, **106:7-502.**
Water, validity of waiver of notice
of discontinuance of service,
165:11E.

WAIVER AND ESTOPPEL
—Cont'd
Way, location of, estoppel by
making repairs, **84:25.**
Wills, waiver of provisions.
Guardian's waiver, **201:45.**
Surviving spouses, waiver,
191:15.
Workers' compensation.
See WORKERS'
COMPENSATION.
Zoning and planning.
Exemption provisions, **40A:6.**
Notice of public hearing, **40A:11.**
Subdivision control law, waiver
of strict compliance, **41:81R.**

WAKEFIELD.
Congressional district, **57:1.**
District court, **218:1.**
Medical examiner district, **38:1.**
Metropolitan air pollution control
district, membership,
111:142B.
Parks, provisions by metropolitan
commission, **92:33.**
Senatorial district, **57:3.**

WALES.
Congressional district, **57:1.**
District court, **218:1.**
Medical examiner district, **38:1.**
Senatorial district, **57:3.**

WALKATHONS.
Operating or participating,
272:103.

WALKS.
See SIDEWALKS.

WALL-EYED PIKE.
Prohibition against sale, **131:22.**

WALLS.
Bakery rooms, construction, **94:9A.**
Criminal offense of destruction or
removal of stone walls,
266:105.
Deeds and conveyances, property
abutting, **183:58.**
Electricity, installation of walling
or siding capable of
conducting, **148:57.**
Highways.
Guardrails and barriers.
See HIGHWAYS AND
STREETS.
Land of another, removal of
mammal, **131:76.**
Municipal indebtedness for
construction of walls to protect
highways or property, **44:7.**
Public buildings, injury to walls,
266:96, 266:97.

WALLS —Cont'd

Railroads.

County commissioners may order construction, **160:91, 160:92.**

Double damages for failure to construct, **160:91, 160:92.**

Real estate abutting a wall, construction of instrument conveying, **183:58.**

Sea walls, **91:13-91:18.**

Show bills and placards on, malicious injury, **266:125.**

WALPOLE.

Congressional district, **57:1.**

District court, **218:1.**

Medical examiner district, **38:1.**

Prison.

See WALPOLE CORRECTIONAL INSTITUTION.

Senatorial district, **57:3.**

WALPOLE CORRECTIONAL INSTITUTION, 125:1-125.21.

Civil service status of employees, **31:48.**

Communication with prisoners contrary to regulations, penalty, **268:21.**

Death penalty, dissection of body after, **113:6.**

Fees and expenses in serving state prison warrant, **262:48.**

Officers and employees leaving prisoner at large, penalty, **268:21.**

Public officials violating conflict of interest law, punishment, **268A:2.**

State prison designated, **125:1.**

Statutes distributed to warden, **5:3.**

Transfers from or, **127:97.**

Trespassing upon land of, penalty, **266:123.**

Visitors, penalty for allowing unlawful visitation, **268:21.**

WALTER D. STONE MEMORIAL ZOO, 92B:1 et seq.

WALTHAM.

Congressional district, **57:1.**

District court, **218:1.**

Medical examiner district, **38:1.**

Metropolitan air pollution control district, membership, **111:142B.**

Parks, provisions by metropolitan commission, **92:33.**

WALTHAM —Cont'd

Senatorial district, **57:3.**

WANTON CONDUCT.

See RECKLESS CONDUCT.

WAR.

Aliens.

Admission to bar, alien claiming exemption during wartime as eligible, **221:38A.**

Time for enemy alien to commence action, **260:8.**

Banks and banking.

Collections, war causing delay, **106:4-108.**

Foreign branches.

Limitations on repayment of deposits seized or lost during war or strife, **167D:36.**

Citizens.

Aliens. See within this heading, "Aliens."

Civil service, wartime service, definition, **31:1.**

Civil war.

See CIVIL WAR.

Congress to declare, **US Const Art 1 Sec 8 cl 11.**

Constitution of Massachusetts.

Commonwealth may borrow money to assist United States in case of war, **MA Const Amend Art 62 Sec 2.**

Food, shelter, and necessaries of life, regulation in time of war, **MA Const Amend Art 47.**

Constitution of the United States.

See CONSTITUTION OF THE UNITED STATES.

Death certificate to contain statement of war service, **46:10.**

Foreign insurance policies, **175:158.**

Grand jury presentment or indictment as dispensable in certain cases in time of, **US Const 5th Amend.**

Inspectors of plumbing and gas fitting, war services experience qualification, **142:11.**

Insurance.

Foreign insurance policies, **175:158.**

Life insurance. See within this heading, "Life insurance."

War, invasion, or insurrection insurance.

See WAR, INVASION, OR INSURRECTION INSURANCE.

WAR —Cont'd

Invasion.

See WAR, INVASION, OR INSURRECTION INSURANCE.

Life insurance.

Extra premium, policy statements, **175:118.**

Foreign companies, effect on policies, **175:158.**

Mexican war, **8:17A, 40:5.**

Military and naval orders, **264:10A, 266:70.**

Missing in action, conservator appointed for estate of missing person, **201:16A.**

Necessities in time of war, **40:19, 40:20; MA Const Amend Art 47.**

Parading or drilling with firearms in time, **33:130.**

Prisoners of war, **60A:1, 90:2, 90:33, 201:16A.**

Public health department's duties in event, **111:5A.**

Quartering of soldiers in houses in time of, **US Const 3rd Amend.**

Ships.

State not to keep warships without consent of Congress, **US Const Art 1 Sec 10 cl 3.**

Transfer of naval vessels to U.S.S. Massachusetts Memorial Committee for use as memorial to veterans of armed forces, **6:124A.**

State may not make, without consent of Congress, **US Const Art 1 Sec 10 cl 3.**

Time for enemy alien to commence action, **260:8.**

Treason, levying war against United States as, **US Const Art 3 Sec 3 cl 1.**

Undeclared wars.

See UNDECLARED WARS.

U.S.S. Massachusetts Honor Roll for citizens who died in Persian Gulf War, **6:124A.**

Vessels.

Ships. See within this heading, "Ships."

Veterans.

See VETERANS AND VETERANS' ORGANIZATIONS.

War of 1812.

See WAR OF 1812.

World war I.

See WORLD WAR I.

WAR —Cont'd
World war II.
  See WORLD WAR II.

WARD COMMITTEES.
See POLITICAL
    COMMITTEES.

WARDENS.
Arrest and seizure without
  warrant, **48:15.**
Churches.
  See RELIGION AND
    RELIGIOUS SOCIETIES.
Extradition, application by warden
  for requisition, **276:20L.**
Fish.
  See FISH AND GAME.
Foresters.
  See FORESTERS AND FOREST
    WARDENS.
Forest fires.
  Fish and game wardens, duties,
    48:15.
  Foresters and forest wardens.
    See FORESTERS AND
      FOREST WARDENS.
Law enforcement division,
  wardens to exercise authority
  of police officers, **21:6B.**
Religion.
  See RELIGION AND
    RELIGIOUS SOCIETIES.
Tree wardens.
  See TREE WARDENS.

WARE.
Congressional district, **57:1.**
District court, **218:1.**
Medical examiner district, **38:1.**
Senatorial district, **57:3.**

WAREHAM.
Congressional district, **57:1.**
District court, **218:1.**
Medical examiner district, **38:1.**
Schooner Ernestina commission,
  resident as member, **6:182A.**
Senatorial district, **57:3.**

WAREHOUSE RECEIPTS,
  105:55-105:64, 106:7-101 to
  106:7-210, 106:7-401 to
  106:7-603.
Acknowledgment by depositor of
  warehouse receipt, form,
  106:7-202.
Actions, provisions as to
  institution, **106:7-204.**
Advances by warehouseman,
  statement, **106:7-202.**
Agency, negotiation of document as
  passing rights accruing under
  law, **106:7-502.**

WAREHOUSE RECEIPTS
  —Cont'd
Agricultural commodities, issuance
  of receipt for goods stored
  under bond, **106:7-201.**
Alcohol, issuance of receipt for
  distilled spirits, **106:7-201.**
Alteration, **106:7-208.**
Attachment of property.
  See ATTACHMENT OF
    PROPERTY.
Bailee defined, **106:7-102.**
Blanks, unauthorized filling,
  106:7-208.
Bona fide purchaser, **106:7-501.**
  Attachment of goods as
    affecting, **106:7-602.**
  Sale to enforce warehouseman's
    lien, rights of good faith
    purchaser, **106:7-210.**
  Unauthorized filling of blank as
    affecting rights, **106:7-208.**
Bond, issuance of receipt for goods
  stored, **106:7-201.**
Cancellation of receipt upon
  delivery of goods, **106:7-403.**
Change of shipping instructions,
  consignee's rights as affected,
  106:7-504.
Claims.
  Conflicting claims, **106:7-603.**
  Provisions as to presentment,
    106:7-204.
Collecting bank, warranties,
  106:7-508.
Commercial contract, compliance,
  106:7-509.
Conflicting claims, **106:7-603.**
Consignee defined, **106:7-102.**
Consignor defined, **106:7-102.**
Construction against negative
  implication, **106:7-105.**
Conversion.
  Delivery to person claiming
    under missing document,
    106:7-601.
  Negotiation of document
    obtained by conversion,
    106:7-502.
  Warehouseman's liability,
    106:7-210.
  Limitation, **106:7-204.**
Copies, **106:7-402.**
  Crime in failing to mark,
    105:57.
Counterfeiting, **105:63.**
Criminal offenses and penalties,
  105:55-105:64.
Damages.
  Contractual limitation of
    liability, **106:7-204.**

WAREHOUSE RECEIPTS
  —Cont'd
Damages —Cont'd
  Excuse for delay in delivery,
    106:7-403.
  Nonreceipt or misdescription of
    goods, **106:7-203.**
  Overissue, liability, **106:7-402.**
  Warehouseman's liability for
    failure to comply with
    requirements of sale in
    enforcing lien, **106:7-210.**
Date.
  Time or date. See within this
    heading, "Time or date."
Deceit.
  Fraud and deceit. See within
    this heading, "Fraud and
    deceit."
Definitions, **106:1-201, 106:7-102.**
Delay in delivery, liability of
  bailee, **106:7-403.**
Delivery of goods.
  Attachment, delivery after,
    105:64.
  Cancellation of receipt,
    106:7-403.
  Change of shipping instructions
    as affecting rights of
    consignee, **106:7-504.**
  Conflicting claims, **106:7-603.**
  Conversion as resulting from
    delivery to person claiming
    under missing document,
    106:7-601.
  Delay, liability of bailee,
    106:7-403.
  Excuse of nondelivery,
    106:7-403.
  Form for warehouse delivery
    order, **106:7-403.**
  Good faith delivery pursuant to
    warehouse receipt,
    106:7-404.
  Indorsement, delivery without,
    106:7-506.
  Loss of lien by delivery or
    refusal to deliver, **106:7-209.**
  Negotiation of warehouse
    receipt, **106:7-501.**
  Nonreceipt, issuer's liability,
    106:7-203.
  Obligation of warehouseman,
    106:7-403.
  Obtaining receipt, criminal
    offense in delivering
    without, **105:59.**
  Partial delivery, cancellation or
    notation upon document,
    106:7-403.
  Statement on warehouse receipt
    as to consignee, **106:7-202.**

WAREHOUSE RECEIPTS
—Cont'd
Delivery of goods —Cont'd
Stoppage of delivery. See within
this heading, "Stoppage of
delivery."
Surrender of receipt, criminal
offense in making delivery
without, **105:59.**
Title based on unaccepted
delivery order as subject to
right of holder of negotiated
warehouse receipt,
106:7-503.
Delivery order defined, **106:7-102.**
Description of goods.
Liability for misdescription,
106:7-203.
Misdescription of property in
warehouse receipt, **105:55,
105:56, 106:7-203.**
Receipt, description of goods,
106:7-202.
Sale to enforce warehouseman's
lien, description of goods in
notice, **106:7-210.**
Destroyed documents.
Lost or destroyed documents.
See within this heading,
"Lost or destroyed
document."
Deterioration, warehouseman's
right to sell goods in danger,
106:7-206.
Disposing of receipt after
attachment, etc., **105:64.**
Distilled spirits, issuance of
receipt, **106:7-201.**
Document defined, **106:1-201,
106:7-102.**
Document of title as including,
106:1-201.
Duplicates.
Copies. See within this heading,
"Copies."
Duress, negotiation of document
obtained, **106:7-502.**
Duty of care imposed on
warehousemen, **106:7-204.**
Endorsement.
Indorsement. See within this
heading, "Indorsement."
Enforcement of lien, **106:7-210.**
Essential terms, **106:7-202.**
Estoppel, negotiation as working,
106:7-502.
Excuse of nondelivery, **106:7-403.**
False statement, issuing receipt
containing, **105:56.**
Forgery or counterfeiting, penalty,
105:63.

WAREHOUSE RECEIPTS
—Cont'd
Forms, **106:7-202.**
Delivery order, **106:7-403.**
Liability of warehouseman,
106:7-204.
Negotiation or transfer,
106:7-501.
Sale, enforcement of lien,
106:7-210.
Fraud and deceit.
Criminal offense in issuing or
passing fraudulent receipts,
105:55, 105:60, 105:61.
False statement, issuing receipt
containing, **105:56.**
Negotiation of document
obtained, **105:60, 105:61,
106:7-502.**
Sale of property with
outstanding warehouse
receipt, **105:62.**
Fungible goods.
Commingling, **106:7-207.**
Title under warehouse receipt,
defeat, **106:7-205.**
Good faith.
Bona fide purchaser. See within
this heading, "Bona fide
purchaser."
Delivery of goods, **106:7-404.**
Goods defined, **106:7-102.**
Government bond, receipt issued
for goods stored, **106:7-201.**
Handling charges, statement,
106:7-202.
Identity.
Description of goods. See within
this heading, "Description of
goods."
Indemnification of bailee upon
stoppage of delivery by seller,
106:7-504.
Indorsement.
Delivery without indorsement,
106:7-506.
Liability of indorser for default
by bailee or previous
indorsers, **106:7-505.**
Negotiation by indorsement,
106:7-501.
Right to compel indorsement,
106:7-506.
Injunction against negotiation or
transfer, **106:7-602.**
Insurance.
Charges, warehouseman's lien,
106:7-209.
Loss of receipt, insurance
companies organized to
insure against, **175:47.**

WAREHOUSE RECEIPTS
—Cont'd
Interpleader in case of conflicting
claims, **106:7-603.**
Irregularities in issue, **106:7-401.**
Issuer defined, **106:7-102.**
Labor charges, warehouseman's
lien, **106:7-209.**
Levy on goods, negotiation of
receipt after, **105:64.**
Liability of warehouseman,
**105:55, 105:56, 106:7-203,
106:7-204.**
License for issuance of receipt for
distilled spirits or agricultural
commodities, **106:7-201.**
Lien of warehouseman.
See WAREHOUSES.
Limitation period for bringing
action, **106:7-204.**
Form for pleading, **106:7-204.**
Location of warehouse, statement,
106:7-202.
Loss or destruction of goods as
excusing nondelivery,
106:7-403.
Lost or destroyed document,
106:7-601.
Insurance companies organized
to insure against loss of
receipt, **175:47.**
Negotiation, **106:7-502.**
Misdescription of property,
liability, **105:55, 105:56,
106:7-203.**
Misrepresentation.
Fraud and deceit. See within
this heading, "Fraud and
deceit."
Missing document.
Lost or destroyed document. See
within this heading, "Lost or
destroyed document."
Mistake, negotiation of document
obtained, **106:7-502.**
Mortgages.
Mortgaging goods where receipt
outstanding, **105:62.**
Negotiation of receipt for
mortgaged goods, **105:60.**
Negative implication, construction
against, **106:7-105.**
Negotiable warehouse receipts,
106:7-104.
Negotiation or transfer, **106:7-501
to 106:7-509.**
Agency, negotiation of document
as passing rights accruing
under law, **106:7-502.**
Form, **106:7-501.**
Fraudulent negotiation or
transfer, **105:60, 105:61,
106:7-502.**

WAREHOUSE RECEIPTS
—Cont'd

Negotiation or transfer —Cont'd
Injunction against, **106:7-602.**
Levy on goods, negotiation of receipt after, **105:64.**
Lien, negotiation of warehouse receipt for goods covered, **105:60.**
Non-negotiable warehouse receipts. See within this heading, "Non-negotiable warehouse receipts."
Rights acquired, **106:7-502.**
Rights acquired in absence, **106:7-504.**
Title to goods.
Negotiation as passing, **106:7-502.**
Unaccepted delivery order, title to goods based on as subject to holder of negotiated warehouse receipt, **106:7-503.**
Warranties, **106:7-507.**
Nondelivery.
Delivery. See within this heading, "Delivery of goods."
Non-negotiable warehouse receipts, **106:7-104.**
Forms, **106:7-202.**
Indorsement, **106:7-501.**
Notice.
Naming of person to be notified of arrival of goods as notice to purchaser of bill, **106:7-501.**
Purchaser for value without notice of attachment, **106:7-602.**
Sale in enforcement of warehouseman's lien, notice, **106:7-210.**
Termination of storage, **106:7-206.**
Warehouseman's lien, manner of giving notice, **106:7-210.**
Numbering receipts, requirement, **106:7-202.**
Optional terms, **106:7-202.**
Option of warehouseman, termination of storage, **106:7-206.**
Overissue, **106:7-402.**
Receipts for fungible goods, **106:7-207.**
Ownership.
Title. See within this heading, "Title."
Own goods of warehouseman, issuance without statement, **105:58.**

WAREHOUSE RECEIPTS
—Cont'd

Partial delivery, cancellation or notation of document, **106:7-403.**
Payment for storage notwithstanding loss, form, **106:7-204.**
Penalties, **105:55-105:64.**
Pledging of property deposited, penalty, **105:62.**
Purchaser for value.
Bona fide purchaser. See within this heading, "Bona fide purchaser."
Reconsignment as excusing nondelivery, **106:7-403.**
Release as excuse for nondelivery, **106:7-403.**
Sale.
Deterioration, warehouseman's right to sell goods in danger, **106:7-206.**
Enforcement of lien, **106:7-210.**
Outstanding warehouse receipt, fraudulent sale of property, **105:62.**
Receipt, sale of.
Negotiation or transfer. See within this heading, "Negotiation or transfer."
Termination of storage, sale of goods, **106:7-206.**
Satisfaction.
Excusing nondelivery, **106:7-403.**
Person claiming goods, satisfaction of lien, **106:7-403.**
Security interest.
Document of title as controlling right in goods as against person holding, **106:7-502.**
Penalty for pledging deposited property, **105:62.**
Reservation, **106:7-209.**
Separation of goods, **106:7-207.**
Short title, **106:7-101.**
Signature of warehouseman, necessity, **106:7-202.**
Statutes, relation of article to other, **106:7-103.**
Stoppage of delivery, **106:7-504.**
As excusing nondelivery, **106:7-403.**
Rights acquired by negotiation of document of title as affected, **106:7-502.**
Storage charges.
Carrier's lien, **106:7-307.**
Lien of warehouseman.
See WAREHOUSES.
Statement, **106:7-202.**

WAREHOUSE RECEIPTS
—Cont'd

Surrender of receipt, criminal offense in making delivery without, **105:59.**
Termination of storage at warehouseman's option, **106:7-206.**
Theft, negotiation of document obtained, **106:7-502.**
Time or date.
Claims, time of presenting, **106:7-204.**
Date of issuance, requirement of showing, **106:7-202.**
Limitation period. See within this heading, "Limitation period for bringing action."
Title.
Bailee's ownership of goods, **106:7-401.**
Defeat, **106:7-205.**
Document of title as including warehouse receipt, **106:1-201.**
Negotiation or transfer. See within this heading, "Negotiation or transfer."
Statement, **106:7-202.**
Stoppage of delivery, rights acquired by negotiation of document of title as affected, **106:7-502.**
Transfer.
Negotiation or transfer. See within this heading, "Negotiation or transfer."
Transportation charges, warehouseman's lien for. See WAREHOUSES.
Treaty, relation of article, **106:7-103.**
Violation of law by issuer, **106:7-401.**
Waiver or estoppel, negotiation as working, **106:7-502.**
Warehouseman defined, **106:7-102.**
Warranties.
Collecting bank, warranties, **106:7-508.**
Negotiation or transfer, warranties, **106:7-507.**
Who may issue, **106:7-201.**

WAREHOUSES, 105:1 et seq.
Actions.
Bond of warehouseman, action, **105:3.**
Receipt, provisions in warehouse receipt concerning actions, **106:7-204.**

WAREHOUSES —Cont'd

Advances made, statement of lien, **106:7-202.**

Alcoholic liquors, storage permit, **138:20A.**

Arson, **266:2.**

Attachment of property.

Penalty for disposal after attachment, **105:64.**

Possession of warehousemen, property, **223:73.**

Receipts, goods covered, **106:7-602.**

Delivery after attachment, **105:64.**

Bond of warehouseman, **105:1.**

Actions, **105:3.**

Discharge of surety, **105:2A.**

New bond, **105:2A.**

Penalty for failure to give, **105:2.**

Publication of license, amount of bond, etc., **105:1, 105:6.**

Termination of surety's liability, **105:2A.**

Books and records.

Examination in connection with cigarette tax, **64C:6.**

Required, **105:5.**

Building on premises of another, contracts for storage, **105:2C.**

Cancellation and rescission.

Option to terminate storage, **106:7-206.**

Receipt, cancellation upon delivery of goods, **106:7-403.**

Charitable corporations, donations, **255:31D.**

Cigarette tax.

Examination of warehousemen's records, **64C:6.**

Reports required of warehousemen, **64C:6.**

Clothing, lien for storage, **255:31D.**

Cold storage warehouses, licenses, **94:66.**

Conditional vendor, bailee's rights against, **255:35-255:39.**

Co-operative corporations, calculating dividends, **157:6.**

Corporation taxes, foreign corporation storing tangible personal property in warehouse, **63:39.**

Costs in action on bond, **105:3.**

Definitions, **105:1, 106:7-102.**

Discharge of surety on warehouseman's bond, **105:2A.**

Disposal of property after attachment, penalty, **105:64.**

Dissolution of warehouseman's lien, **255:32, 255:33.**

WAREHOUSES —Cont'd

Enforcement of warehousemen's lien, **106:7-210.**

Exemptions from license requirements, **105:2C.**

Fee for license, **105:1.**

Cold storage warehouse, **94:66.**

Fertilizers, storage, **128:66.**

Fines and penalties.

Attached property, penalty for disposal after attachment, **105:64.**

Bond, failure to file, **105:2.**

License, failure to procure, **105:2.**

Receipts, **105:55-105:64.**

Gifts or donations to charitable corporations, **255:31D.**

Household goods, lien for storage, **255:31D.**

Injunctions.

Negotiation or transfer of warehouse receipt, **106:7-602.**

Operation where no bond or license, **105:2.**

Insurance.

Duty to insure goods, **105:4.**

Receipts.

Charges, warehouseman's lien, **106:7-209.**

Loss of receipt, insurance companies organized to insure against, **175:47.**

Leases.

Public works department, lease of warehouses, **91:6.**

Summary proceedings, lien for charges for storing property of tenant evicted, **239:4.**

Liability on bond, **105:3.**

Licenses and permits, **105:1.**

Advance publication of notice of application, **105:1.**

Alcoholic beverages, storage permit, **138:20A.**

Bond, failure to provide as ground for revoking, **105:2A.**

Building on another's premises, not required as to storage, **105:2C.**

Cold storage warehouses, **94:66.**

Duties on revocation of license, **105:2B.**

Exemptions from license requirements, **105:2C.**

Failure to procure license, penalty, **105:2.**

Fee for license. See within this heading, "Fee for license."

Lien as continuing after revocation of license, **105:2B.**

WAREHOUSES —Cont'd

Licenses and permits —Cont'd

Notice.

Application, **105:1.**

Issuance and discontinuance, **105:6.**

Penalty for doing business without license, **105:2.**

Public safety department, licensing, **105:1, 105:2A, 105:6.**

Revocation of, continuation of lien notwithstanding, **105:2B.**

Warehouse receipt issued for goods requiring license for issuance, **106:7-201.**

Lien of warehousemen, **106:7-209.**

Advances made, statement, **106:7-202.**

Clothing, storage, **255:31D.**

Conditional vendor, bailee's rights against, **255:35-255:39.**

Continuing after revocation of license, **105:2B.**

Delivery or refusal to deliver, loss of lien, **106:7-209.**

Dissolution, **255:32, 255:33.**

Enforcement, **106:7-210.**

Household goods, storage, **255:31D.**

Insurance, warehouseman's lien for charges, **106:7-209.**

Manner of giving notice, **106:7-210.**

Negotiation of warehouse receipt for goods covered by lien, **105:60.**

Priority of lien over conditional vendor, **255:35.**

Property worth more than twenty dollars, required contract provisions, **255:36.**

Sale, enforcement of lien, **106:7-210.**

Delivery as excused by sale, **106:7-403.**

Forms, **106:7-210.**

Satisfaction by person claiming goods, **106:7-403.**

Summary proceedings, lien for charges for storing property of tenant evicted, **239:4.**

Termination or storage, sale of goods, **106:7-206.**

Listing property for taxation, **59:33.**

Motor vehicle removed from private property, storage fees, **266:120D.**

WAREHOUSES —Cont'd
Notice.
   Insurance on family, personal, or household goods, **105:4.**
   Licenses and permits. See within this heading, "Licenses and permits."
   Lien of warehouseman, manner of giving notice, **106:7-210.**
   Receipts.
      See WAREHOUSE RECEIPTS.
Penalties.
   Fines and penalties. See within this heading, "Fines and penalties."
Permits.
   Licenses and permits. See within this heading, "Licenses and permits."
Personal, family, or household goods, notice to depositors as to insurance, **105:4.**
Pesticides, **132B:6, 132B:11.**
Port of Boston commission.
   See PORT OF BOSTON COMMISSION.
Priority of lien over conditional vendor, **255:35.**
Public safety department, licensing, **105:1, 105:2A, 105:6.**
"Public warehouseman" defined, **105:1.**
Public works department.
   Leasing of warehouses, **91:6.**
   Plans for utilization of acquired property, etc., **91:9.**
   Port of Boston harbor, powers, **91:3.**
   Taking and holding real estate and building thereon, powers, **91:5.**
Railroads.
   Holding stock in warehouse companies, **160:65B.**
   Licensed as public warehouseman need not receive property, **105:1.**
Receipts, **106:7-101 to 106:7-210, 106:7-401 to 106:7-603.**
   See WAREHOUSE RECEIPTS.
Receipts for insurance.
   Insurance. See within this heading, "Insurance."
Records.
   Books and records. See within this heading, "Books and records."

WAREHOUSES —Cont'd
Rescission.
   Cancellation and rescission. See within this heading, "Cancellation and rescission."
Sale of goods.
   Enforcement of warehouseman's lien, **106:7-210.**
   Receipts.
      See WAREHOUSE RECEIPTS.
   Upon termination of storage, **106:7-206.**
Satisfaction of warehouseman's lien by person claiming goods, **106:7-403.**
Self-storage facilities, **105A:1 et seq.**
   See SELF-STORAGE FACILITIES.
Statement as to lien for advances made, **106:7-202.**
Storage fees for removal of motor vehicle from private property, **266:120D.**
Sunday opening, **136:5.**
Taxation.
   See TAXATION.
Tenant evicted in summary proceedings, lien for charges for storing property of tenant evicted, **239:4.**
Transportation charges, lien for.
   Lien of warehouseman. See within this heading, "Lien of warehousemen."
Twenty dollars, required contract provisions for lien on property worth more than, **255:36.**
Warehouseman defined, **105:1.**
Wines, storage by innholders, **138:20.**

WARE RIVER WATERSHED.
Advisory committee established, **92:114A.**
Quabbin watershed advisory committee, purpose, **92:114.**
"Watershed system," definition for purposes of provision creating watershed management division, **92:104.**

WAR, INVASION, OR INSURRECTION INSURANCE.
Authorized, **175:47.**
C.I.F. sales, **106:2-320.**
Combination with other classes, **175:48, 175:48A, 175:51, 175:54.**

WAR, INVASION, OR INSURRECTION INSURANCE —Cont'd
Fire companies may transact, **175:51, 175:54.**
Special brokers, **175:168.**
Stock or mutual plan, **175:48, 175:48A.**

WARNINGS.
Breast implantation, **111:70E.**
Drugs.
   Impure drugs, Boston health department's warnings, **94:194.**
   Instruction as to use, containers to bear, **94:187.**
   Paraphernalia, warning against use of tobacco rolling papers in conjunction with possession of controlled substance, **94C:32I.**
Foresters.
   Notices.
      See FORESTERS AND FOREST WARDENS.
Forest fires.
   See FOREST FIRES.
Gasoline delivery trucks, use of audible warning signals when in reverse gear, **90:7.**
Hazardous substance label, **94B:1.**
Highways.
   Signs and signals.
      See HIGHWAYS AND STREETS.
Ordinance or by-law, violation of, **140:173A.**
Seed package labels, **128:85.**
Signs.
   See SIGNS AND SIGNALS.
Tanning facilities, **111:209, 111:211, 111:212.**
Voting list, warning that failure to respond to mailing may result in removal, **51:4.**

WAR OF 1812.
Holiday, anniversary of Battle of New Orleans, **6:12F.**
Society of the War of 1812, appropriation for patriotic holiday observances, **40:5.**
Town appropriation for headstones or monuments to deceased veterans, **40:5.**

WARP.
Channel or dock, prohibition against passing warp across, **102:18.**

WARRANTIES, 106:2-312 to 106:2-318.
Affirmation, express warranties created, **106:2-313.**

WARRANTIES —Cont'd

Alteration, etc.
Exclusions. See within this heading, "Exclusion, disclaimer, or modification of warranties."
Automobiles.
Motor vehicles. See within this heading, "Motor vehicles."
Bank deposits.
Deposits and collections.
See BANKS AND BANKING.
Bills of lading.
Collecting bank, warranties, **106:7-508.**
Negotiation or transfer of document of title, **106:7-507.**
Blood and blood plasma, **106:2-316.**
Breach of warranty.
Damages, **106:2-714, 106:2-715.**
Death resulting, **229:2.**
Duties of buyer where seller is answerable over, **106:2-607.**
Firearms and weapons.
Sale without functioning safety lock, **140:131K.**
Limitation of remedies, **106:2-316, 106:2-318, 106:2-725.**
Notice of action, **106:2-607.**
Privity of contract abolished as defense to action for breach of warranty of goods sold, **106:2-318.**
Statute of limitations, **106:2-318, 106:2-725.**
Summary process action, tenant's claim for breach of warranty, **239:8A.**
Third party beneficiaries as entitled to assert, **106:2-318.**
C.I.F. or C & F terms, warranty of condition on arrival, **106:2-321.**
Commercial Code, **106:2-312 to 106:2-318.**
Negotiable instruments.
Presentment warranties, **106:3-417.**
Transfer warranties, **106:3-416.**
Conflict of warranties, **106:2-317.**
Construction or interpretation as to warranties under Commercial Code, **106:2-316, 106:2-317.**
Consumer goods, exception to seller's right to exclude or modify warranty, **106:2-316A.**
Course of dealing as creating implied warranty, **106:2-314.**

WARRANTIES —Cont'd

Covenant warranties, defined, **183:10, 183:16.**
Creation of express warranties, **106:2-313.**
Credit, letters of.
Letters of credit, **106:5-110.**
Cumulation of warranties, **106:2-317.**
Damages for breach of warranty, **106:2-714, 106:2-715.**
Death resulting from breach of warranty, **229:2.**
Deeds.
See DEEDS AND CONVEYANCES.
Description.
Express warranties created, **106:2-313.**
Sample as superseding description in considering inconsistent warranties, **106:2-317.**
Specifications as superseding description in considering inconsistent warranties, **106:2-317.**
Disclaimer of warranty.
Exclusion, disclaimer, or modification. See within this heading, "Exclusion, disclaimer, or modification of warranties."
Document of title, warranties, **106:7-507, 106:7-508.**
Equipment dealers, **93G:8.**
Examination or inspection.
Implied warranties as affected by opportunity given to buyer, **106:2-316.**
Motor vehicle inspection, effect of failure, **90:7N.**
Exclusion, disclaimer, or modification of warranties, **106:2-316.**
Consumer goods, exception as to exclusion or modification of warranties in sales, **106:2-316A.**
Forms for exclusion, disclaimer, or modification of warranty, **106:2-316.**
Implied warranties, **106:2-316.**
Limitation on exclusions, **106:2-316A.**
Security agreement as affecting modification of warranty, **106:9-206.**
Express warranties, **106:2-313.**
Fire insurance.
Application for insurance as warranty, **175:98.**

WARRANTIES —Cont'd

Fire insurance —Cont'd
Defenses, warranty reference proceedings, **175:101E.**
Fitness for particular use, implied warranty, **106:2-314, 106:2-315.**
Food.
Implied warranty of fitness, **106:2-314.**
Pure Food and Drug Act, guarantee, **94:193, 94:194.**
Formal words in creating, necessity, **106:2-313.**
Fraternal benefit societies, statements of members as warranties or representations, **176:23.**
Goods sold, **106:2-312 to 106:2-318.**
Home warranty contracts.
See INSURANCE.
Human tissue and organs, **106:2-316.**
Identity.
Description. See within this heading, "Description."
Implied warranties, **106:2-314, 106:2-315.**
Certain medical items, exclusion of from definition of commodities subject to sale or barter, for purposes of implied warranties of merchantability and fitness, **106:2-316.**
Conflict with express warranties, **106:2-317.**
Course of dealing as creating, **106:2-314.**
Exclusion or modification, **106:2-316.**
Express warranties as superseding, **106:2-317.**
Fitness for particular use, **106:2-314, 106:2-315.**
Merchantability, warranty, **106:2-314.**
Opportunity to inspect as affecting, **106:2-316.**
Usage of trade as creating, **106:2-314.**
Infringement, warranty against, **106:2-312.**
Inspection.
Examination or inspection. See within this heading, "Examination or inspection."
Insurance. **175:186.**
See INSURANCE.
Investment securities under commercial code, **106:8-109.**

WARRANTIES —Cont'd
Lack of privity in action against seller or lessor of goods for breach of warranty, **106:2-318.**
Landlord and tenant, claim of tenant for breach of warranty in summary process action, **239:8A.**
Leases under UCC.
See LEASES UNDER COMMERCIAL CODE.
Letters of credit, **106:5-110.**
Liens, warranties of absence, **106:2-312.**
Limitation of actions on warranties of goods sold, **106:2-316, 106:2-318, 106:2-725.**
Limitation of warranty, form, **106:2-316.**
Limitation on exclusion or modification of, **106:2-316A.**
Manner of creating express warranties, **106:2-313.**
Medical items, **106:2-316.**
Merchantability, implied warranty, **106:2-314.**
Modification of warranties.
Exclusion, disclaimer, or modification. See within this heading, "Exclusion, disclaimer, or modification of warranties."
Motor vehicles.
Agreement for warranty, obligations as to fulfillment, **93B:6.**
Inspections, effect of failure, **90:7N.**
Replacement of, or refund of moneys paid, **90:7N½.**
Used motor vehicles, **90:7N¼.**
Negotiable instruments.
Presentment warranties, **106:3-417.**
Transfer warranties, **106:3-416.**
Opinion of seller as creating express warranties, **106:2-313.**
Ownership.
Title and ownership. See within this heading, "Title and ownership."
Plans and specifications.
Compliance with specifications, seller's warranty as affected by compliance, **106:2-312.**
Sample or description as superseded by specifications in considering inconsistent warranties, **106:2-317.**
Presentment.
Negotiable instruments.
Warranties, **106:3-407.**

WARRANTIES —Cont'd
Privity of contract abolished as defense in action for breach of warranty against seller, lessor, etc., of goods, **106:2-318.**
Promise, express warranty created, **106:2-313.**
Real estate time-shares, **183B:22, 183B:45-183B:48.**
Replacement of defective parts, form for limitation of warranty, **106:2-316.**
Retail installment sales agreements, official fees, **255D:1, 255D:11.**
Sales under Commercial Code, **106:2-312 to 106:2-318.**
Sample or model, warranty created, **106:2-313, 106:2-316.**
Secured transactions.
Modification of sales warranties as affected by existence of security agreement, **106:9-206.**
Specifications.
Plans and specifications. See within this heading, "Plans and specifications."
Summary process to recover land, tenant's claim for breach of warranty, **239:8A.**
Tax deeds, warranty, **60:45.**
Statement releasing town from warranties, recording, **60:82.**
Third-party beneficiaries, **106:2-318.**
Title and ownership, **106:2-312.**
Deeds.
See DEEDS AND CONVEYANCES.
Usage of trade as creating implied warranties, **106:2-314.**
Value of goods, affirmation, **106:2-313.**
Warehouse receipts.
Collecting bank, warranties, **106:7-508.**
Negotiation or transfer, warranties, **106:7-507.**
Warranty deeds.
See DEEDS AND CONVEYANCES.

WARRANTS.
Access.
Investigations of abuse of disabled person, **19C:7.**
Accounts and demands against Commonwealth, issuance with respect, **7A:3.**
Air pollution, warrant for inspection of premises in connection with enforcement of regulations, **111:142B.**

WARRANTS —Cont'd
Alcoholic liquors.
See ALCOHOLIC LIQUORS.
Animals.
Searches.
See SEARCHES AND SEIZURES.
Arrest warrants, **90:21, 276:23.**
See ARREST.
Automobiles.
Motor vehicles. See within this heading, "Motor vehicles."
Capital punishment, warrant of conviction, **276:20B, 279:57, 279:58, 279:67.**
Children and minors.
Juvenile courts and delinquent children. See within this heading, "Juvenile courts and delinquent children."
Collection of taxes.
See TAX COLLECTORS.
Constables.
See CONSTABLES.
Constitution of Massachusetts, warrants must be supported by oath and contain designation of persons or objects of search, arrest, or seizure, **MA Const Part 1 Art 14.**
Contagious.
See CONTAGIOUS AND INFECTIOUS DISEASES.
Copy of warrant, penalty for refusal by officer, **248:26.**
Corporations.
See CORPORATIONS.
Correctional institutions.
See CORRECTIONAL INSTITUTIONS.
County taxes, warrants for collection, **35:31.**
Delay of service of, penalty, **268:22.**
Delinquent children.
Juvenile courts and delinquent children. See within this heading, "Juvenile courts and delinquent children."
Distress warrant to compel payment of penalty by corporations, **279:42.**
District courts, **218:32-218:35.**
See DISTRICT COURTS.
Districts.
Meeting, warrant, **41:119.**
Taxes, separate list and warrant for district taxes, **59:53.**
Dog officers, form of warrant, **140:153.**

WARRANTS —Cont'd

Dower and curtesy, probate court's revocation of warrant or commission for assignment, **215:35.**

Drugs.
See DRUGS AND NARCOTICS.

Elections, notices, **54:64.**

Examination, inspection, or investigation.

Diesels carrying fuel oil, examination or inspection without warrant, **94:303F.**

Drugs and narcotics, administrative inspection warrants, **94C:30.**

Insolvency and bankruptcy, registration of notice of issuance of warrant, **262:39.**

Execution of warrant.

Service or execution. See within this heading, "Service or execution."

Extradition.
See EXTRADITION.

Facsimile signatures used on warrants issued by tax collectors in cities and towns, **60:29.**

Fees.

Attendance upon certain courts, **262:22.**

Clerks of district courts, fees for order of precept, **262:2.**

Damages by impounded animals, warrant to determine, **262:34.**

District court, special justice, **262:3.**

Improvident issuance of warrant, no fee allowed, **262:49.**

Local taxes, fees for issuing warrant for collection, **262:4.**

Records, **127:7.**

Sheriffs, **262:8.**

Filing, **127:7.**

Fines and penalties.

Delay of service of warrants, **268:22.**

Distress warrant to compel payment of penalty by corporations, **279:42.**

Officer refusing copy of warrant, **248:26.**

Town meeting, removing or defacing of warrant, **266:124.**

Fireworks, arrest without warrant of persons unlawfully possessing or selling, **148:39.**

WARRANTS —Cont'd

Forest fires.
See FOREST FIRES.

Gaming and games of chance.

Arrest, **271:2, 271:6, 271:10, 271:10A.**

Search warrants, **271:23.**

Gas and electric company, warrant directing sheriff or constable to accompany officer or employee prevented from entering premises, **164:116.**

Governor.
See GOVERNOR.

Hazardous waste management act, enforcement, **21C:8.**

Hazardous waste site cleanup professionals, warrants authorizing entry for purposes of investigation, **21A:19E.**

Housing court department, court officers, service of warrants, **185C:15.**

Impounded beasts, damages, **49:36, 262:34.**

Insolvency.
See INSOLVENCY AND BANKRUPTCY.

Inspection.

Examination, inspection, or investigation. See within this heading, "Examination, inspection, or investigation."

Interception of wire or oral communications, warrants authorizing, **272:99.**

Investigation.

Examination, inspection, or investigation. See within this heading, "Examination, inspection, or investigation."

Judges issuance of search warrant, **138:42, 271:23, 276:1.**

Justices of the peace.
See JUSTICES OF THE PEACE.

Juvenile courts and delinquent children, **119:54.**

Commitment, warrant, **119:84.**

Management system, **18:2.**

Motor vehicles.

Fuel oils, examination and inspection without warrant of vehicles carrying, **94:303F.**

Parking violations, **90:20C.**

Search warrants, **130:10, 276:1.**

Municipal finance.

Expenditures, approval of warrants for during vacancy in office of selectman, **41:56.**

WARRANTS —Cont'd

Municipal finance —Cont'd

Taxes, issuance by city or town treasurer of warrant for collection, **60:90.**

Nuisances, **111:131, 243:1-243:3.**

Arrest of persons found in places of prostitution, **139:13.**

Pardons, **127:152.**

Execution and return of warrant of pardon, **127:157.**

Revocation of pardon, execution of warrant, **127:152.**

Parking violations, **90:20C.**

Parole.

Probation and parole. See within this heading, "Probation and parole."

Partition, **241:12, 241:13, 241:35.**

Pedestrians violating rules as to use of ways, **90:18A.**

Penalties.

Fines and penalties. See within this heading, "Fines and penalties."

Pesticide control, warrants, **132B:15.**

Police.

Infected articles of goods, executing warrant for removal, **111:101.**

Search warrants, duties as to.
See SEARCHES AND SEIZURES.

Special state police officer for service of warrants, **127:127.**

Precepts.
See PRECEPTS.

Private nuisances, **243:1-243:3.**

Probate.
See PROBATE AND FAMILY COURT.

Probation and parole.

Retaking of parolee under interstate compact, **127:151J.**

Temporary custody of parolee arrested on parole officer's warrant, length, **127:149A.**

Prostitution, warrantless arrest of person for engaging in illegal sexual conduct for fee, **272:54.**

Religious societies and corporations, warrants for meetings, **67:14, 67:22, 67:23.**

Safekeeping of writ, **127:7.**

Searches and seizures, **276:1-276:8.**

See SEARCHES AND SEIZURES.

WARRANTS —Cont'd
Service or execution.
Delay, penalty, **268:22.**
Fees of sheriffs for service of
process, **262:8.**
Interception of communications,
272:99.
Pardon, warrant, **127:152,
127:157.**
Searches.
See SEARCHES AND
SEIZURES.
Shellfish constable, **130:98.**
Special state police officer for
service of warrants, **127:127.**
State treasurer.
See STATE TREASURER.
Superior courts.
District court, search warrant
returnable, **276:3A.**
Drugs and narcotics,
administrative inspection
warrants, **94C:30.**
Supplementary proceedings,
warrants to secure attendance
of parties, **224:18.**
Tax assessors.
See TAX ASSESSORS.
Taxation.
See TAX COLLECTORS.
Tax sales.
See TAX SALES.
Town meetings, **39:10.**
See TOWN MEETINGS.
Towns delinquent in paying for
bridge repairs, warrants
against, **84:4.**
Toxics use reduction, **21I:3.**
Treasurer of state.
See STATE TREASURER.
Tuberculosis hospitals, warrants
for assessments, **111:83B,
111:85.**
Warrant management system,
18:2.
Witnesses.
See WITNESSES.

WARRANTY COVENANTS.
Defined under statute governing
alienation of land, **183:10,
183:16.**

WARRANTY DEEDS.
**See DEEDS AND
CONVEYANCES.**

**WAR RECORDS
COMMISSIONER.**
Adjutant general to serve under
governor, **6:16.**

WARREN.
Congressional district, **57:1.**
District court, **218:1.**

WARREN —Cont'd
Medical examiner district, **38:1.**
Senatorial district, **57:3.**

WAR RISK INSURANCE.
**See WAR, INVASION, OR
INSURRECTION
INSURANCE.**

**WAR VETERANS CIVIC
ASSOCIATION.**
Lease of property for use as post
headquarters, **40:9.**

WARWICK.
District court, **218:1.**
Medical examiner district, **38:1.**

WASH HOUSES.
Town appropriation, **40:12.**

WASHING FACILITIES.
Labor.
Health and safety conditions.
See LABOR AND
WORKFORCE
DEVELOPMENT.

WASHING MACHINERY.
Minors under sixteen not to work,
149:61.

WASHINGTON.
District court, **218:1.**
Medical examiner district, **38:1.**
Senatorial district, **57:3.**

WASHINGTON, D.C.
See DISTRICT OF COLUMBIA.

WASHINGTON'S BIRTHDAY.
Firemen working on, additional
pay or time off, **48:57A,
48:57D, 48:57E.**
Legal holiday, **4:7.**
Observance, **6:12T.**
Police, day off or extra pay,
147:17A.
Sunday laws as applicable, **136:13.**

WASSERMAN TEST, 111:121A.
Marriage certificate, test as
prerequisite to issuance,
207:28A.

**WASTE DISPOSAL, 16:18 et
seq.**
Air pollution.
See AIR POLLUTION.
Appropriations for establishment
of waste prevention institute,
71:42.
Biology, penalties for disposal of
biological waste material,
111:127A.
Boston water.
See BOSTON WATER AND
SEWER
REORGANIZATION ACT.

WASTE DISPOSAL —Cont'd
Cesspools, facilities for disposal of
contents, **111:31D.**
Chelsea center for material reuse,
71:41.
Coal mining licenses, contents of
application, **21B:5.**
Contagious and infectious
diseases, penalties for disposal
of infectious waste material,
111:127A.
Fire hazards, removal, **148:5.**
Garbage and rubbish, **16:18 et
seq.**
See GARBAGE AND RUBBISH.
Hazardous waste insolvency fund.
See HAZARDOUS WASTE
INSOLVENCY FUND.
Hazardous Waste Management
Act, **21C:1-21C:12.**
See HAZARDOUS WASTE
MANAGEMENT.
Housing and community
development department,
powers and duties, **23B:3.**
Industrial development of cities.
See INDUSTRIAL
DEVELOPMENT OF
CITIES AND TOWNS.
Insurance.
Pollution liability reinsurance
corporation, waste facility,
175G:1-175G:7.
Logs.
See LOGS AND TIMBER.
Low-level radioactive waste.
See LOW-LEVEL
RADIOACTIVE WASTE.
Marine technology, environmental,
and engineering grants, **71:40.**
Medical waste, penalties for
improper disposal, **111:127A.**
Ocean sanctuaries, **132A:15,
132A:16-132A:16F.**
Pollution.
Air pollution.
See AIR POLLUTION.
Water pollution.
See WATER POLLUTION.
Recycling fund, appropriations,
40:8H.
Sewers and drains, **83:1-83:29.**
See SEWERS AND DRAINS.
Solid waste disposal, **16:18 et seq.**
See GARBAGE AND RUBBISH.
Testing facilities for Waste
Prevention Institute, **71:39.**
Transportation charges of motor
carriers of property, exemption
of waste materials from
requirement as to payment,
159B:19A.

WASTE DISPOSAL —Cont'd

Waste prevention institute, establishment of, **71:38 et seq.**

Appropriations, **71:42.**

Chelsea center for material reuse, **71:41.**

Marine technology, environmental, and engineering grants, **71:40.**

Testing facilities, **71:39.**

Water pollution.
See WATER POLLUTION.

Weighting bale with foreign substance or waste as offense, **94:305.**

WASTELANDS.

Lowlands.
See LOWLANDS AND SWAMPS.

Prison labor, **127:83, 127:84.**

WASTE OF PROPERTY, 242:1-242:9.

Abutting land, entry on to prevent waste, **266:120B.**

Actions for, **242:1 et seq.**

Ancestor, action during lifetime, **242:1.**

Attachment of property, enjoining waste during pendency of action, **242:9.**

Bond to obtain restraining order, **242:9.**

Co-operative bank mortgage statutory condition, **183:23.**

Costs, casual trespass cases, tender of damages as avoiding costs, **242:8.**

Criminal offenses, **266:113 et seq.**

Damages, **237:12.**

Tender of damages as avoiding costs in casual trespass case, **242:8.**

Treble damages. See within this heading, "Treble damages."

Writ of entry proceedings, **237:12, 242:6.**

Dower, waste committed by tenant, **242:1.**

Entry, writs of.
See ENTRY, WRITS.

Executor or administrator, liability for waste, **230:10, 242:3.**

Farm property, treble damages assessed for damage to, **242:7A.**

Form of action, **242:5.**

Improvement by joint tenant or tenant in common without notice of intention, **242:4.**

WASTE OF PROPERTY —Cont'd

Injunction against, during pendency of action, **242:9.**

Jailers, masters, or keepers of jails, removal for wasteful use of supplies, **127:13.**

Judgment in writ against registered land, registration, **185:90.**

Jury trial in action, **242:1.**

Mortgages.

Foreclosure, enjoining waste during pendency of action, **242:9.**

Statutory condition, **183:20, 183:23.**

Notice of intention to commit, **242:4.**

Ore, removal, **242:4.**

Parties to action, **242:1, 242:2, 242:5.**

Partition of land, waste during petition, **242:4.**

Pendency of action, waste during, **242:6.**

Partition, waste during petition, **242:4.**

Stay of waste, **242:9.**

Persons entitled to maintain action, **242:1, 242:2.**

Prevention of, entry on abutting land, **266:120B.**

Recovery of land, liability of person in possession pending, **242:6.**

Registered land, registration of judgment in writ against, **185:90.**

Restraining during pendency of action, **242:9.**

Stone, removal, **242:4.**

Tender of damages as avoiding costs in casual trespass case, **242:8.**

Timber, cutting or destroying, **242:4, 242:7, 242:8.**

Tort action in nature of waste, **242:2, 242:3.**

Treble damages.

Cutting or damaging timber on land of another, **242:7, 242:8.**

Distribution of damages among co-tenants, **242:5.**

Farm property, **242:7A.**

When recoverable, **242:4-242:7.**

Trespass for cutting of timber, **242:7, 242:8.**

Urban redevelopment corporation, waste in buildings constructed, **121A:8.**

WASTE OF PROPERTY —Cont'd

Writ of entry.
See ENTRY, WRITS.

WASTE OIL.

Fires and fire prevention, waste oil as regulated substance, **148:38B.**

Retention facilities, **21:52A.**

Underground storage tank petroleum product cleanup fund, exemption, **21J:2.**

WASTE TREATMENT.
See WASTE DISPOSAL.

WASTEWATER MANAGEMENT.

Board of certification of operators of wastewater treatment facilities, **21:34A to 21:34C.**

Environmental management department to implement protection programs, **21:38.**

Water pollution generally.
See WATER POLLUTION.

WATCHES.
See CLOCKS.

WATCHMEN.
See GUARDS OR WATCHMEN.

WATER CHESTNUTS, 128:20A.

WATER COMPANIES, 40:38-40:42, 165:1-165:11C.
See WATERWORKS AND WATER SUPPLY.

WATERCOURSES.
See WATERS AND WATERWAYS.

WATERCRAFT.
See SHIPS AND OTHER WATERCRAFT.

WATER DISTRICTS AND COMMISSIONERS.
See WATERWORKS AND WATER SUPPLY.

WATERFOWL.
See FISH AND GAME.

WATERFRONT EMPLOYMENT, 149:18A et seq.
See LONGSHORE AND WATERFRONT EMPLOYMENT.

WATER LIEN ACT, 40:42A to 40:42F.
See WATERWORKS AND WATER SUPPLY.

WATER MANAGEMENT ACT,
21G:1 et seq.
Adjudicatory hearings, **21G:12.**
Appeal procedures, **21G:12.**
Attorney general, enforcement of
provisions, **21G:14.**
Costs of action, **21G:14.**
Criminal and civil penalties,
21G:14.
Definitions, **21G:2.**
Easement restrictions, **21G:8.**
Emergencies, **21G:15-21G:17.**
Eminent domain, water
emergencies, **21G:16.**
Environmental Protection
Department, powers and
duties, **21G:2 et seq.**
Fees, **21G:18, 21G:19.**
Fines and penalties, **21G:14.**
Future water needs, planning and
regulation, **21G:3.**
Injunctions and restraining orders,
21G:14.
Inspections, **21G:13.**
Issuance or denial of permits,
21G:11.
Licenses and permits,
**21G:7-21G:11, 21G:18,
21G:19.**
Notice, permit application
procedures, **21G:9.**
Orders of department enforcing
provisions, **21G:14.**
Permits and permit applications,
**21G:7-21G:11, 21G:18,
21G:19.**
Powers of department in water
emergencies, **21G:17.**
Privileged and confidential
information, **21G:13.**
Procedures for processing permit
applications, **21G:9.**
Rates and charges, **21G:19.**
Recommendations and statements
as to permit applications,
21G:10.
Records, confidentiality, **21G:13.**
Registration of persons taking
excess of threshold volume,
21G:5, 21G:6, 21G:17-21G:19.
Renewals registration, **21G:5.**
Schedule of permit expiration
dates, **21G:11.**
Short title, **21G:1.**
Superior court, **21G:14.**
Telecommunications and energy
department, fee schedules,
21G:19.
Water resources authority, **21G:14,
21G:16.**
Water resources commission,
duties, **21G:2, 21G:3, 21G:16.**

WATER MANAGEMENT ACT
—Cont'd
Withdrawal of volume thresholds,
21G:4, 21G:5.

**WATER POLLUTION, 21:26 et
seq.**
Abatement, **21:26 et seq.; Spec L
15:1 et seq.**
Bonds and notes of pollution
abatement districts, **Spec L
15:2.**
Financial assistance for
abatement, **Spec L 15:1 et
seq.**
Grants for costs, **21:33E.**
Industrial wastes, financial
assistance for abatement,
Spec L 15:1 et seq.
Loans to construct treatment
facilities, **Spec L 15:1.**
Revolving loan program.
See WATER POLLUTION
ABATEMENT TRUST.
Rules and regulations, **Spec L
15:3.**
Trust.
See WATER POLLUTION
ABATEMENT TRUST.
Waste water treatment facilities,
loans to construct, **Spec L
15:1.**
Abatement districts, **21:28-21:30A.**
Abatement facilities, district
commission to maintain and
operate, **21:30.**
Annual apportionment of
amounts required, **21:36.**
Anticipation spending for water
treatment plants, **44:6A.**
Approval of water pollution
abatement plan, requisites,
21:32, 21:33.
Cities and towns. See within
this heading, "Cities and
towns."
City council, establishment of
districts, **21:28.**
Contractual powers of district
commission, **21:30.**
Definition, **44:1.**
District commission, **21:29.**
"District" defined under law as
to cities, towns, and districts
to include, **40:1A, 41:1A.**
Executive director, **21:29.**
Exemption from taxation of
bonds and certificate of
indebtedness, **59:5.**
Expenses of district, failure of
city or town to contribute,
21:36.

WATER POLLUTION —Cont'd
Abatement districts —Cont'd
Financial assistance in defraying
costs of projects, **21:33.**
Hearings, **21:28.**
Loans, powers of districts,
21:35-21:37.
Mandatory creation, **21:28.**
Oil pollution of waters, water
pollution control division to
represent Commonwealth
with respect, **21:51.**
Plans and specifications. See
within this heading, "Plans
and specifications."
Real property, abatement district
commissions' powers, **21:29.**
Reimbursement.
By federal government to
municipalities and
districts which have
constructed water
pollution projects, **21:37.**
To Commonwealth for
financial assistance
granted, **21:33.**
Reports. See within this
heading, "Reports."
Resources commission,
approvals, **21:28.**
Salaries and compensation of
employees and commission,
21:29.
Seals.
Adoption by district
commission, **21:30.**
Bonds and notes of district to
bear, **21:35-21:37.**
Selectmen, powers and duties,
21:28, 21:29.
Supervision of operation and
maintenance of facilities,
21:34.
Treasurer, **21:29.**
United States.
Financial assistance,
21:30-21:33A.
Reimbursement for
construction of water
pollution abatement
project, deductions, **21:37.**
Reservoirs, agreements as to
federal grants, **21:39.**
Abatement projects administration
fund, **29:2W.**
Accelerated water pollution control
program, provision, **21:26.**
Acids.
Coal mines, water quality as
affected, **21B:11.**
Coastal waters, pollution,
130:23, 130:24.

WATER POLLUTION —Cont'd
Acids —Cont'd
Inland waters, pollution, **131:42.**
Actions and proceedings.
Cities and towns, action against
for pollution or diversion,
40:39G.
Coastal waters, action for
pollution, **130:24, 130:27.**
Continuation of action
commenced by health
department, **21:26.**
Hazardous Waste Management
Act, enforcement, **21C:9.**
Injunctions, attorney general to
bring action, **21:44.**
Municipal water supply, action
for pollution or diversion,
40:39G.
Natural resources and
environment, actions for
purpose of protecting,
214:7A.
Oil pollution of waters, action
against persons causing,
21:27.
Water pollution abatement
district commission, powers,
21:30.
Advisory functions of state health
department, **111:17.**
Aldermen and selectmen, powers
and duties as to abatement
districts, **21:28, 21:29.**
Algae, weeds, and aquatic
nuisances, control, **111:5F.**
Appeal and review.
Health department rulings,
111:163.
Nuisances, appeal from denial of
license for control, **111:5E.**
Water pollution control director,
judicial review of
determinations, **21:46,
21:46A.**
Applications for discharge permits,
21:43-21:46A.
Aquatic nuisances, license to apply
chemicals to waters for
control, **111:5E.**
Arrest, **91:58.**
Oils or crude petroleum,
discharging, **91:59.**
Water supply, **111:171,
111:173A.**
Attorney general.
See ATTORNEY GENERAL.
Berkshire Mountains, protection of
watershed resources and
natural scenic qualities,
131:39A.

WATER POLLUTION —Cont'd
Board of certification of
wastewater treatment
facilities operators, **21:34A,
21:34B, 21:34C.**
Bond issues.
Pollution abatement districts.
Cities and towns. See within
this heading, "Cities and
towns."
Exemption from taxation,
21:36, 59:5.
Financing control facilities,
21:33C, 40D:22.
Issuance, **21:29, 21:35-21:37.**
Reservoirs, proceeds of bonds
for construction, **21:39.**
Water pollution abatement trust,
29C:9.
Bonds, surety.
Vessel receiving or discharging
petroleum products, **21:50B.**
Boundaries for generation, storage,
disposal or discharge of
pollutants, **92:107A.**
Certificates and certification.
Abatement districts,
apportionment of amounts
due on bonds and notes,
21:36.
Treatment facilities operators.
Waste water treatment
facilities. See within this
heading, "Waste water
treatment facilities."
Cesspools, facilities for disposal of
contents, **111:31D.**
Charles river, **92:76, 111:175.**
Metropolitan parks districts,
92:39.
Chemicals.
See CHEMICALS AND
CHEMISTRY.
Cities and towns, **21:27, 21:29,
21:32.**
Abatement districts.
City council, establishment of
districts, **21:28.**
Issuance of bonds or notes by
as affecting computation
of indebtedness, **21:35.**
Payment on bonds, **21:36.**
Selectmen, powers and duties,
21:28, 21:29.
Action for pollution or diversion,
40:39G.
Application of payments made
by Commonwealth for useful
public works project,
44:53B.

WATER POLLUTION —Cont'd
Cities and towns —Cont'd
Apportionment among cities and
towns of costs of district
plans for pollution control,
21:32.
Borrowing money for pollution
control purposes in
anticipation of state
reimbursement, **44:6A.**
Engineering reports and plans.
District plans for control of
pollution, apportionment
of costs, **21:32.**
Preparation by director of
division, **21:33B.**
Failure of municipality to
contribute toward cost of
abatement district, **21:36.**
Grants, **21:33A, 21H:3.**
Imposition of user charges,
21:36.
Industrial development of cities.
See INDUSTRIAL
DEVELOPMENT OF
CITIES AND TOWNS.
Issuance of bonds or notes by
district as affecting
computation of
indebtedness, **21:35.**
Order directing construction of
necessary facilities for which
construction grants are
authorized, **21:33D.**
Penalty for pollution, **40:39G.**
Permit for discharge of sewage
and waste, **21:43-21:46A.**
Rates and charges for users,
21:36.
Reimbursement for construction
of water pollution control
project, **21:37, 44:6A.**
Selectmen or aldermen, duties
as to pollution of water
supply, **111:162, 111:163,
111:169.**
Use without specific
appropriation of sums
allotted by state for
pollution control, **44:53.**
Waste water treatment facilities,
21:27, 21:29, 21:32.
City council, establishment of
districts, **21:28.**
Civil service law.
Control division employees,
21:26.
Exemption for clean waters
scholarship interns, **21:38A.**

WATER POLLUTION —Cont'd
Clean Waters Act.
Division of water pollution control. See within this heading, "Division of water pollution control."
Coal mining regulation.
See COAL MINING REGULATION AND RECLAMATION.
Coastal waters, discharge of refuse or pollutants, **91:59, 130:23, 130:24, 130:27, 270:16, 270:16A.**
Collection systems, grants to public entities for construction, **21:30A.**
Commissioner of Public Health, approval of adoption of standards of water quality, **21:27.**
Commissioner of water pollution control.
Division of water pollution control. See within this heading, "Division of water pollution control."
Compensation.
Salaries and compensation. See within this heading, "Salaries and compensation of employees."
Complaints to health department, **111:162.**
Continuation of action or suit commenced by health department, **21:26.**
Contracts.
Abatement district commission, powers, **21:30.**
Construction of sewer systems for prevention of pollution, contracts, **40:41.**
Pollution control division, **21:33C, 21:38, 21:51.**
Water resources commission.
Reservoirs, construction, **21:39.**
Soil conservation contracts, **21:13.**
Control by health department, **111:5.**
Control compact.
See INTERSTATE COMPACTS AND AGREEMENTS.
Control districts.
Abatement districts. See within this heading, "Abatement districts."

WATER POLLUTION —Cont'd
Control facilities.
Waste water treatment facilities. See within this heading, "Waste water treatment facilities."
Corporations.
See CORPORATIONS.
Corporation taxes, exemption for construction or improvement of waste treatment facilities, **63:38D.**
County finance, **21:37, 21H:3.**
Crimes and offenses.
Fines and penalties. See within this heading, "Fines and penalties."
Damages.
Clean water act violations, **131:42.**
Inland fisheries polluted, **131:42.**
Obviating causes, **111:162.**
Oil pollution of waters. See within this heading, "Oil pollution of waters."
Dams and reservoirs, **21:13, 21:39.**
Decrees.
Judgments, decrees, and orders. See within this heading, "Judgments, decrees, and orders."
Definitions, **21:26A, 21E:2.**
Disposal facilities for pollutants.
Waste water treatment facilities. See within this heading, "Waste water treatment facilities."
Districts.
Abatement districts. See within this heading, "Abatement districts."
Division of water pollution control, **21:26-21:53.**
Abatement of water pollution.
Duties and responsibilities, **21:27.**
Enforcement of laws, **21:26.** (note)
Grants, **21:31.**
Allocation of cost for preparation of preliminary or final reports and plans by director, **21:33B.**
Allocation to municipality of pollution control funds, **44:6A.**
Appropriations for expenditures, **21:26.**
Assistant director, appointment and qualifications, **21:26.**
Bond of ships and vessels handling petroleum products, **21:50B.**

WATER POLLUTION —Cont'd
Division of water pollution control —Cont'd
Civil service status of employees, **21:26.**
Clean Waters Act, **21:26-21:53.**
Clean waters scholarship intern program, **21:38A.**
Commissioner defined, **21:26A.**
Commissioner of environmental protection department, **21:26, 21:26A.**
Compliance with conditions of supplemental grants for water pollution abatement plans, **21:33.**
Contracts, **21:33C, 21:38, 21:51.**
Control districts, **21:28.**
Corporate tax deduction and exemption, **63:38D.**
Corrective changes in law, **21:26.**
Counsel, appointment and qualifications, **21:26.**
Damages for violation of clean waters act, **131:42.**
Definitions under law governing divisions of environmental management department, **21:26A.**
Director.
Annual report, **21:48.**
Appointment and qualifications, **21:26.**
Contracts for research and demonstrations, **21:38.**
Discharges of pollutants without permit or in violation of permit, director's authority, **21:44.**
Engineering reports and plans, preparation, **21:33B.**
Entry on property to investigate conditions relating to water pollution, **21:40.**
Examination of books and records, **21:40.**
Notice as to spillage, seepage or discharge of oil into waters, **21:27.**
Permit for outlet for discharge of sewage or waste, issuance, **21:43.**
District commissions, powers and duties, **21:30.**
District plans for control, apportionment of costs among cities and towns, **21:32.**

WATER POLLUTION —Cont'd
Division of water pollution control
—Cont'd
Duties and responsibilities of,
21:27.
Employees.
Civil service status, **21:26.**
Public health department
employees, transfer to
water pollution control
division, **21:26.**
Qualification, training and
education, **21:26, 21:27.**
Entry on property to investigate
conditions relating to
pollution, **21:40.**
Environmental quality
engineering commissioner,
appointment of director of
division, **21:26.**
Establishment of in
environmental Protection
Department, **21:26.**
Failure of municipality to
contribute toward cost of
district, **21:36.**
Federal Water Pollution Control
Act, applicability, **21:27.**
Graduate study program,
21:38A.
Grants for construction of
collection systems, **21:30A.**
Hydropower generation,
development, **164:69H½.**
Industrial development of cities
and towns, **40D:22.**
Injunctive relief against
violators, **21:46, 21:46A.**
Inland fisheries, protection,
131:41.
Interns, **21:38A.**
Licenses and permits for
treatment works, **21:34.**
Membership, **21:29.**
New England Interstate Water
Pollution Control
Commission, contracts,
21:38.
Oil pollution, **21:27, 21:50-21:52.**
Order directing municipalities to
construct necessary facilities
for which construction
grants are authorized,
21:33D.
Permit for discharge of
pollutants, proceedings in
connection with grant or
refusal, **21:43.**
Plan for control, apportionment
of costs among cities and
towns as prerequisite for
approval, **21:32.**

WATER POLLUTION —Cont'd
Division of water pollution control
—Cont'd
Pollution control facilities in
certain towns, financing,
21:33A.
Preliminary engineering report
of final engineering plant,
submission and approval,
21:33B, 21:33C.
Qualification of employees,
21:26.
Regulations regarding treatment
works, **21:34.**
Representation of
Commonwealth in relations
with other governmental
units, **21:51.**
Research and demonstration
projects and facilities, **21:38.**
Reservoirs, proceeds of bonds for
construction, **21:39.**
River basin water quality
management or waste
treatment management
plans, contracts, **21:38.**
Rules and regulations, powers,
21:27.
Supplemental grants to public
entities for planning,
designing and building
projects, **21:33, 21:33A.**
Suspension of revocation of
permit, notice and hearing
prior, **21:45.**
Training and education of
personnel, **21:27, 21:38.**
Treatment works.
Waste water treatment
facilities. See within this
heading, "Waste water
treatment facilities."
Water pollution abatement trust.
See WATER POLLUTION
ABATEMENT TRUST.
Withdrawal of approval of
project, **21:33.**
Drains.
Sewers and drains. See within
this heading, "Sewers and
drains."
Dredged materials, dumping,
21A:14, 91:52-91:56.
Cost of supervision, **91:52-91:54.**
Disposal and transportation of
dredged materials, permits,
21A:14.
Federal government, regulations
inapplicable, **91:56.**
Fines and penalties, **91:55.**
Disposal permit violations,
21A:14.

WATER POLLUTION —Cont'd
Dredged materials, dumping
—Cont'd
Licenses and permits, **21A:14,
91:53.**
Notice before commencing,
91:54.
United States, regulations
inapplicable, **91:56.**
Drinking water and ice supply
sources, **21:H3, 111:5G,
111:17, 111:160, 111:167.**
Drinking water revolving fund,
29:2QQ.
Administration, **29C:18.**
Economic development and
industrial corporations.
See ECONOMIC
DEVELOPMENT AND
INDUSTRIAL
CORPORATIONS.
Effluent limitations regarding
discharge permits,
21:43-21:46A.
Eminent domain.
See EMINENT DOMAIN.
Employment.
Labor and employment. See
within this heading, "Labor
and employment."
Enforcement of laws and
regulations concerning, **21:46,
21:46A, 111:2C.**
Engineers.
See ENGINEERS AND
SURVEYORS.
Entry into land.
See ENTRY INTO LAND AND
PREMISES.
Environmental affairs executive
office, duties and functions of,
21A:2.
Environmental impact reports,
30:62A et seq.
See ENVIRONMENTAL
IMPACT REPORTS.
Environmental Protection
Department, **21:26 et seq.**
Approval of abatement facilities,
40D:22.
Board of certification for
wastewater treatment
operators, **21:34A.**
Charles River, **111:175.**
Defilement of domestic water
supply, **111:174A.**
Division of water pollution
control. See within this
heading, "Division of water
pollution control."
Examination, inspection, or
investigation, **111:160.**
Conditions, **21:27, 21:40.**

WATER POLLUTION —Cont'd
Examination, inspection, or
    investigation —Cont'd
  Entry for purpose of
    investigation and correction
    of pollution, **21:40.**
  Expense of investigation of
    possible pollution, how
    borne, **111:165.**
  Grand jury investigation of
    environmental control law
    violations, immunity for
    witness, **233:20D.**
  Metropolitan district
    commission, investigation,
    21:40, 92:110.
  Oil pollution of waters,
    inspection to curb, **21:40,
    21:50.**
  Powers of health officers,
    111:165.
  Research and demonstration
    projects, contracts, **21:38.**
  Source, testing for toxic
    substances, **21G:3. (note)**
  Treatment facilities' records,
    21:40.
Exemptions from permit
    requirements, **21:43-21:46A.**
Expenses and expenditures.
  Abatement plans, cost, **21:32.**
  Abatement trust, **29C:4-29C:6.**
  Action by attorney general for
    recovery of costs, **21:27.**
  Appropriations for expenditures
    by water pollution control
    division, **21:26.**
  Control facilities, reimbursement
    for cost of chemicals, **21:37.**
  Engineering reports and plans,
    21:33B.
  Failure of city or town to
    contribute to abatement
    district costs, **21:36.**
  Federal aid in defraying, **21:30,
    21:31, 21:33A.**
  Financial assistance to public
    entities for collection
    system, costs as factor in
    determining, **21:30A.**
  Investigation of possible
    pollution, **111:165.**
Federal government and statutes,
    21:32, 21:38, 21:51.
  Abatement districts. See within
    this heading, "Abatement
    districts."
  Aid, **21:30-21:33A.**
  Dredging regulations
    inapplicable, **91:56.**
Fees, **21:43-21:46A, 29C:12.**

WATER POLLUTION —Cont'd
Filter beds, **83:7, 111:167, 111:168.**
Fines and penalties, **21:42, 91:59.**
  Aquatic nuisances, unlicensed
    persons applying chemicals
    to waters for control,
    111:5E.
  Bilge water, discharge, **91:59,
    91:59A.**
  Charles River, pollution,
    111:175.
  Cities and towns, pollution,
    40:39G.
  Defilement of water supply,
    111:170, 111:171.
  Dredged materials, dumping of.
    See within this heading,
    "Dredged materials,
    dumping."
  Fish, causing injury or
    destruction to by pollution
    of waters, **130:23-130:27,
    131:42.**
    See MARINE FISH AND
        FISHERIES.
  Health department order,
    violation, **111:162.**
  Oil pollution, **21:27, 21:50A,
    91:59, 91:59A.**
  Records required under water
    pollution laws, offenses,
    21:42.
  Rules and regulations, **21:27.**
  Spring, poisoning, **265:28.**
Fish, liability for destruction by
    introduction of deleterious
    materials into waters, **131:42.**
Forms for discharge permits,
    21:43-21:46A.
Foul or decaying matter, dumping
    or depositing, **111:171.**
Funds.
  Drinking water revolving fund,
    29:2QQ.
    Administration, **29C:18.**
  Water pollution abatement and
    drinking water projects
    administration fund, **29:2W.**
Garbage and refuse, **91:52, 91:59.**
  Coastal waters, discharge of
    refuse, **270:16, 270:16A.**
  Hazardous waste. See within
    this heading, "Hazardous
    waste."
  Industrial waste. See within this
    heading, "Industrial
    wastes."
  Waste water treatment facilities.
    See within this heading,
    "Waste water treatment
    facilities."

WATER POLLUTION —Cont'd
Garbage and refuse —Cont'd
  Watercraft, regulations to
    control discharge of garbage,
    21:27.
Gas and oil.
  Oil pollution. See within this
    heading, "Oil pollution of
    waters."
General court, **21:28.**
Gifts, grants, and gratuities,
    21:27A et seq., 29C:1-29C:17.
  Abatement projects, **21H:3.**
  Clean waters scholarship intern
    program, **21:38A.**
  Collection systems, construction,
    21:30A.
  Control of pollution,
    21:30-21:33A, 21:33B.
  Federal Water Pollution Control
    Act, supplemental grants to
    public entities, **21:33.**
  Order directing municipalities to
    construct necessary facilities
    for which construction
    grants are authorized,
    21:33D.
  Reservoirs, agreements as to
    federal grants, **21:39.**
Grand jury investigating violations
    of environmental control laws,
    granting of immunity to
    witness appearing before,
    233:20D.
Grants.
  Gifts, grants, and gratuities. See
    within this heading, "Gifts,
    grants, and gratuities."
Gulls, defilement, **111:174A.**
Harbors and waterways, **91:59.**
Hazardous waste, **21:27.**
  Industrial wastes. See within
    this heading, "Industrial
    wastes."
  Management act, **21C:1-21C:12.**
    See HAZARDOUS WASTE
        MANAGEMENT.
  Research as to control of
    discharge, **21:38.**
  Underground waters. See within
    this heading, "Underground
    waters."
  Waste water treatment facilities.
    See within this heading,
    "Waste water treatment
    facilities."
Health department, **111:5,
    111:159-111:175.**
  Employees transferred to water
    pollution control division,
    21:26.

WATER POLLUTION —Cont'd

Hearings.

Abatement districts, matter concerning, **21:28.**

Health department hearings, **111:162.**

Rules and regulations, hearings, **21:27.**

Wrongful discharge of waste, **21:44, 21:45.**

Ice ponds or streams, **111:167.**

Industrial development of cities.

See INDUSTRIAL DEVELOPMENT OF CITIES AND TOWNS.

Industrial wastes, **130:23, 130:24, 131:41.**

Ocean sanctuaries, **132A:15.**

Tax exemption or deduction for pollution abatement measures, **59:5, 63:38D.**

Injunctions, **21:46, 21:46A, 111:169.**

Attorney general to bring action, **21:44.**

Enforcing health department regulations and orders, **111:164.**

Hazardous waste management act, enforcement, **21C:9, 21C:10.**

Outlet for discharge of sewage or waste, making without required permit, **21:43.**

Inland fishing waters, **131:41, 131:42.**

Inspection.

Examination, inspection, or investigation. See within this heading, "Examination, inspection, or investigation."

Interns, clean waters scholarship intern, **21:38A.**

Interstate compacts and agreements, **21:38, 21:41.**

Judgments, decrees, and orders.

Construction of necessary facilities for which construction grants are authorized, **21:33D.**

Discharge of waste, issuance of order to discontinue, **21:44, 21:45.**

Injunctions. See within this heading, "Injunctions."

Penalty for violation of health department order, **111:162.**

Judicial enforcement of orders and regulations, **111:164.**

Judicial review.

Appeal and review. See within this heading, "Appeal and review."

WATER POLLUTION —Cont'd

Jurisdiction.

Coastal waters, **130:26.**

Orders for control of pollution, enforcement, **21:46, 21:46A, 111:164, 111:169.**

Labor and employment.

Division of water pollution control. See within this heading, "Division of water pollution control."

Salaries and compensation of employees. See within this heading, "Salaries and compensation of employees."

Lakes, **91:59 et seq.**

Equipment exempt from taxation, **59:5.**

Lead poisoning, regulations, **111:160.**

Licenses and permits.

Aquatic nuisances, unlicensed persons applying chemicals to water for control, **111:5E.**

Camps, revocation or suspension of license for water pollution, **140:32B.**

Chemicals, licenses for application, **111:5E.**

Division of water pollution control, duties of, **21:27, 21:43.**

Dredging materials, dumping, **21A:14, 91:53.**

Hazardous waste management act, **21C:7.**

Marinas, requirements to obtain license to operate, **91:59B.**

Nuisances, appeal from denial of license for control, **111:5E.**

Oil pollution of waters, revocation of terminal operator's license for violations, **21:50A.**

Oil terminals, **21:50.**

Waste water treatment facilities. See within this heading, "Waste water treatment facilities."

Loans.

Abatement districts, powers, **21:35-21:37.**

Cities and towns. See within this heading, "Cities and towns."

Economic development and industrial corporation, power to borrow money to abate water pollution, **121C:5.**

Revolving loan program.

See WATER POLLUTION ABATEMENT TRUST.

WATER POLLUTION —Cont'd

Local aid fund, reimbursement for water pollution for water pollution abatement projects, **21:37.**

Mandatory construction of pollution control facilities by public entities, **21:33D.**

Marinas, requirements to obtain license to operate, **91:59B.**

Marine fish and fisheries, **130:23-130:27, 131:42.**

See MARINE FISH AND FISHERIES.

Metropolitan district commission.

Boundaries for generation, storage, disposal or discharge of pollutants, **92:107A.**

Engineering reports and plans, **21:33B.**

Entry on property to investigate conditions relating to water pollution, **21:40.**

Pollutants in or near watersheds, regulation of, **92:107A.**

Reimbursement for construction of water pollution project, **21:37.**

Watersheds, regulation of pollutants near, **92:107A.**

Mining.

See COAL MINING REGULATION AND RECLAMATION.

Motorboats.

See MOTORBOATS.

Motor vehicles, **21:27.**

Municipalities.

Cities and towns. See within this heading, "Cities and towns."

Natural resources, action to protect.

Actions and proceedings. See within this heading, "Actions and proceedings."

Negligent causing of oil spill, **21:50A.**

New England interstate water pollution control commission.

Recommendations of water resources commission, **21:41.**

Research and demonstration project contracts, **21:38.**

Notice.

Attorney general, notice of pollution of water supply, **111:159.**

WATER POLLUTION —Cont'd
Notice —Cont'd
Discharge of pollutants, notice and hearings regarding, **21:43-21:46A.**
Dredging, notice before commencing, **91:54.**
Final decision of division director, notice, **21:46A.**
Oil, notice as to seepage, spillage or discharge, **21:27, 21:44.**
Ocean sanctuaries, waste disposal, **132A:16-132A:16F.**
Offenses.
Fines and penalties. See within this heading, "Fines and penalties."
Offensive matter, discharging or dumping in water supply sources, **111:167.**
Oil and Hazardous Material Release Prevention and Response Act, **21E:1 et seq.** See OIL AND HAZARDOUS MATERIAL RELEASE PREVENTION AND RESPONSE ACT.
Oil Pollution Act, defined, **21E:2.**
Oil pollution of waters, **21:27, 91:59, 91:59A, 130:23, 130:24.**
Bond required to be furnished by vessels receiving or discharging petroleum products, **21:50B.**
Booms to encircle ships discharging oil cargo at terminals, requirement, **21:50A.**
Contracts for protective and clean-up services, **21:51.**
Damages.
Person assisting in removing oil, liability, **21:27.**
Property damage resulting from discharge of petroleum products or bilge water, tort liability, **91:59A.**
Division of water pollution control, **21:27, 21:50-21:52.**
Entry on vessel or premises, **21:40, 21E:8.**
Examination, inspection, or investigation, **21:40, 21:50.**
Liabilities of persons responsible, **21:27, 21E:13.**
License of terminal operator, revocation for violations, **21:50A.**
Negligent causing, **21:50A.**
Notice as to spillage, seepage or discharge into waters, **21:27, 21:44, 21E:7.**

WATER POLLUTION —Cont'd
Oil pollution of waters —Cont'd
Oil and Hazardous Material Release Prevention and Response Act, **21E:1 et seq.** See OIL AND HAZARDOUS MATERIAL RELEASE PREVENTION AND RESPONSE ACT.
Powers and duties of division of water pollution control to curb, **21:27, 21:50-21:52.**
Reimbursement of person removing oil from waters of Commonwealth, **21:27.**
Rules and regulations, **21:50.**
Terminals use for loading or discharging of petroleum products from vessels, licensing, **21:50.**
Waste oil retention facilities, **21:52A.**
Orders.
Judgments, decrees, and orders. See within this heading, "Judgments, decrees, and orders."
Penalties.
Fines and penalties. See within this heading, "Fines and penalties."
Permits.
Licenses and permits. See within this heading, "Licenses and permits."
Plans and specifications.
Abatement facilities, submission of plans for approval, **21:27.**
Abatement plans, **21:31, 21:32.**
Cities and towns. See within this heading, "Cities and towns."
Contracts with water pollution control division, **21:38.**
Control facilities, contracts for reports and plans, **21:33C.**
Grants, **21:31, 21:33.**
Ports and harbors, **91:59.**
Prescriptive drainage rights and use of certain rivers, **111:168.**
Prosecution or suit, immunity of witness appearing before grand jury in investigation of environmental law violations, **233:20D.**
Public entities required to construct pollution control facilities, **21:33D.**
Public officers and employees.
Division of water pollution control. See within this heading, "Division of water pollution control."

WATER POLLUTION —Cont'd
Qualification, pollution control division employees, **21:26.**
Quality standards for water, enforcement by environmental Protection Department, **111:160B.**
Radioactive substances, **21:27.**
Recommendations.
Public health commissioner, recommendations for prevention of water pollution, **111:23.**
Water resources commission, duty to make recommendations, **21:41.**
Records and data.
Director of division, examination, **21:40.**
Reports. See within this heading, "Reports."
Required, **21:27, 21:42.**
Water pollution abatement trust, **29C:17.**
Refuse.
Garbage and refuse. See within this heading, "Garbage and refuse."
Regulations.
Rules and regulations. See within this heading, "Rules and regulations."
Reimbursement for water pollution projects, **21:27, 21:31, 21:33, 21:37, 44:6A.**
Renewal of discharge permits, **21:43-21:46A.**
Reports, **21:33B, 21:33C.**
Compliance with conditions of grants, reports, **21:33.**
Control facilities, contracts for reports and plans, **21:33C.**
Director of pollution control division, annual report, **21:48.**
Engineering plans, reports, **21:32, 21:33B, 21:33C.**
Joint action with other states on abatement districts, **21:28.**
Submission for approval of reports as to abatement facilities, **21:27.**
Research and demonstration projects, contracts with federal government and New England interstate water pollution control commission, **21:38.**
Residual waste treatment.
Waste water treatment facilities. See within this heading, "Waste water treatment facilities."

WATER POLLUTION —Cont'd

Resource commission.
Water resources commission. See within this heading, "Water resources commission."
Review.
Appeal and review. See within this heading, "Appeal and review."
Revolving loan program, **29C:1-29C:17.**
River basin quality management plans, contracts, **21:38.**
Rules and regulations, **21:27, 21:50.**
Lead poisoning, **111:160.**
Salaries and compensation of employees.
Abatement district employees and commission, **21:29.**
Limitations on outside income of director of water pollution control division, **21:26.**
Scholarship intern program under clean waters act, **21:38A.**
Seals.
Abatement districts. See within this heading, "Abatement districts."
Sewers and drains.
Assessments for construction of water pollution facilities, **83:15B.**
Duties of water pollution control division, **21:27.**
Shellfish.
See SHELLFISH.
Ships and other watercraft.
Bilge water, discharging, **91:59.**
Liability for, **21:27.**
Oil pollution of waters. See within this heading, "Oil pollution of waters."
Snow and ice removal chemicals, storage to prevent contamination of water supply, **85:7A.**
Specifications.
Plans and specifications. See within this heading, "Plans and specifications."
Springs, **111:170, 265:28.**
Squannacook and Nissitissit Rivers Sanctuary, **132A:17.**
Superior court, jurisdiction, **21:46, 21:46A, 111:164, 111:169.**
Supply sources, discharging or dumping offensive matter in, **111:167.**
Suspension or revocation of discharge permits, **21:43-21:46A.**

WATER POLLUTION —Cont'd

Taxation.
Bonds and notes issued by water pollution abatement districts, **21:36.**
Corporations, tax benefits for pollution abatement or control measures, **59:5, 63:38D.**
Terns, defilement, **111:174.**
Towns.
Cities and towns. See within this heading, "Cities and towns."
Training programs, **21:37, 21:38.**
Treasurer of abatement district, **21:29.**
Treatment works.
Waste water treatment facilities. See within this heading, "Waste water treatment facilities."
Trial or hearing.
Hearing. See within this heading, "Hearing."
Underground waters.
Coal mining regulation.
See COAL MINING REGULATION AND RECLAMATION.
Hazardous Waste Management Act.
Definition of "underground drinking water source" for purposes of Act, **21C:2.**
License requirements, **21C:7.**
Removal of causes of pollution, **111:162.**
United States.
Federal government and statutes. See within this heading, "Federal government and statutes."
Wages.
Salaries and compensation. See within this heading, "Salaries and compensation of employees."
Waste water treatment facilities.
Anticipatory spending by districts, **44:6A.**
Approval of by environmental Protection Department, **40:39C.**
Board of certification of waste water treatment facilities operators, **21:34A, 21:34B, 21:34C.**
Cities and towns. See within this heading, "Cities and towns."

WATER POLLUTION —Cont'd

Waste water treatment facilities —Cont'd
Corporation taxes, exemption for construction or improvement of waste treatment facilities, **59:5, 63:38D.**
Discharge permits, **21:43-21:46A.**
Division of water pollution control, duties of, **21:27.**
Inspection of records, **21:40.**
Licensing and operation of, **21:34, 21:43-21:46A.**
Ocean sanctuaries, treatment plants, **132A:16.**
Plans and specifications, **21:27, 21:33C.**
Regulations regarding, **21:34.**
Rules and regulations concerning, **21:34.**
Tax exemption or deduction for industrial waste treatment facilities, **59:5, 63:38D.**
Training of operators, **21:38.**
Watercraft.
Ships and other watercraft. See within this heading, "Ships and other watercraft."
Water management act.
See WATER MANAGEMENT ACT.
Water resources commission.
Approvals as to abatement districts, **21:28.**
Contracts. See within this heading, "Contracts."
Enforcement of Clean Waters Act, **21:53.**
Interstate compacts, recommendations, **21:41.**
Off-site reservoirs, construction, **21:39.**
Recommendations to governor and interstate water pollution control commission, duty to make, **21:41.**
Reservoirs, construction and acquisition of land, **21:39.**
Watershed management division as public entity, **92:118.**
Watershed system, **92:109, 92:111.**
Wetlands, protection, **131:40A.**
Witnesses in grand jury investigations of environmental law violations, immunity, **233:20D.**
Youth conservation and service corps, **78A:3.**

WATER POLLUTION ABATEMENT AND DRINKING WATER PROJECTS ADMINISTRATION ACT, 29:2W.

WATER POLLUTION ABATEMENT PROJECTS ADMINISTRATION FUND ACT, 21:27A, 29:2W.

WATER POLLUTION ABATEMENT REVOLVING FUND, 29:2L.

WATER POLLUTION ABATEMENT TRUST, 21C:1 et seq., 29C:1 et seq.
Annual report, 29C:17.
Board, 29C:3.
Bonds, issuance, 29C:9.
Cooperation with Environmental Protection Department, 21:27A.
Default by local government unit, 29C:11.
Definitions, 29C:1.
Deposits, 29C:8.
Disbursement of monies and revenues, 29C:4-29C:6.
Drinking water revolving fund, 29C:18.
Fees, collection and enforcement by local government, 29C:12.
Interest rates, 29C:13.
Investment securities, 29C:9.
Lines of credit, 29C:9.
Loans, 21:27A, 29C:6A.
Meetings, 29C:2.
Membership, 29C:2.
Powers and duties, 29C:3.
    Drinking water revolving fund, 29C:18.
Records, 29C:17.
Refunding bonds, 29C:9.
Security for bonds, 29C:9, 29C:15.
Segregation of Title VI funds, 29C:4.
Sources of monies to be disbursed, 29C:4.
Subsidy to local governments units for payment of debt service costs on loans, 29C:6A.
Temporary bonds and notes, 29C:9.
Termination of trust, 29C:16.
Title VI of Clean Water Act, 29C:7.
Transfer of funds to, 21:27A, 29:2W.

WATER RESOURCES AUTHORITY, Spec L 67:1 et seq.
Accounts of Authority, **Spec L** 67:22.

WATER RESOURCES AUTHORITY —Cont'd
Acquisition of property, **Spec L** 67:9.
Action or suit.
    Attorney general, appearance, **Spec L** 67:24.
    Consent decree, power of Authority to enter into, **Spec L** 67:27.
    Jurisdiction of courts, **Spec L** 67:24.
Advisory board to Authority, **Spec L** 67:23.
Affirmative action program for employees, **Spec L** 67:7.
Agencies, powers and duties, **Spec L** 67:26.
Appropriations, **Spec L** 67:5.
Assessment of damages, protection of coastal and inland wetlands, 130:105.
Assessment of local taxes, 59:5D.
    Exemption of land acquired for public purpose, 59:5F.
Assessments, establishment and adjustment of charges which may be denominated, **Spec L** 67:10.
Assumption of debt of Commonwealth, **Spec L** 67:11.
Attorney General, appearance in lawsuits involving pollution, **Spec L** 67:24.
Audit, internal unit, **Spec L** 67:7.
Bonds.
    Consent of governing body, necessity, **Spec L** 67:15.
    Definition, **Spec L** 67:2.
    Issuance, **Spec L** 67:12.
    Pledge of Commonwealth, bonds of Authority, **Spec L** 67:16.
    Refunding bonds, **Spec L** 67:12, 67:13, 67:16.
    Securities, bonds, **Spec L** 67:14, 67:17.
    Trust fund, revenues, **Spec L** 67:18.
Budget of Authority, **Spec L** 67:8.
Charges for services, **Spec L** 67:10.
Cities.
    Municipalities. See within this heading, "Municipalities."
Coastal and inland wetlands protection, 130:105, 131:40A.
Commonwealth, bonds issuance as predicated on consent, **Spec L** 67:15.
Compensation for water diverted from watershed system, **Spec L** 67:26.

WATER RESOURCES AUTHORITY —Cont'd
Consent decree, power of Authority to enter into, **Spec L** 67:27.
Construction of Act, **Spec L** 67:25, 67:29.
Costs, definition, **Spec L** 67:2.
Costs of reports, **Spec L** 67:22.
Current expenses, defined, **Spec L** 67:2.
Debt of Authority, **Spec L** 67:5.
Debt of Commonwealth, assumption, **Spec L** 67:11.
Deferred compensation plans for employees and officers, **Spec L** 67:7.
Definitions, **Spec L** 67:2.
Disposal services, exclusivity, **Spec L** 67:20.
Diversion of water from watershed system, compensation, **Spec L** 67:26.
Division, defined, **Spec L** 67:2.
Employer, definition, 150E:1.
Entry on property to investigate water pollution, 21:40, **Spec L** 67:1 et seq.
Environmental Affairs Office, Authority as within, **Spec L** 67:3.
Environmental protection department, **Spec L** 67:8.
Environmental remedies, reimbursing communities involved, **Spec L** 67:8.
Equal opportunity employment, **Spec L** 67:7.
Established, **Spec L** 67:1.
Estimated bills, **Spec L** 67:9A.
Exclusive service areas, **Spec L** 67:20.
Executive director, appointment, **Spec L** 67:5, 67:7.
Exemption from taxation, **Spec L** 67:19.
Expenses of Authority, **Spec L** 67:3.
Fees for services, **Spec L** 67:10.
Financing of Authority, **Spec L** 67:5.
    Bonds. See within this heading, "Bonds."
Fiscal year charges, 92:113.
Governing law, **Spec L** 67:28.
Group insurance for employees, **Spec L** 67:7.
Indemnification of officers and employees, **Spec L** 67:7.
Individual retirement accounts for officers and employees, **Spec L** 67:7.

WATER RESOURCES AUTHORITY —Cont'd

Inland wetlands protection, notice of public hearing, **131:40A.**

Insurance, group, for employees, **Spec L 67:7.**

Interests in realty, acquisition, **Spec L 67:9.**

Internal audit special unit, **Spec L 67:7.**

Investment securities, bonds of Authority, **Spec L 67:14, 67:17.**

Jurisdiction of enforcement actions, **Spec L 67:24.**

Labor representation of officers and employees, **Spec L 67:7.**

Lawsuits.

Action or suit. See within this heading, "Action or suit."

Local tax assessment.

Assessment of local taxes. See within this heading, "Assessment of local taxes."

Massachusetts Water Management Act, **21G:14, 21G:16.**

MDC sewer system, defined, **Spec L 67:2.**

Members of Authority, **Spec L 67:3, 67:8.**

Metropolitan District Commission, definition, **Spec L 67:2.**

Municipalities.

Consent to bond issuance, necessity, **Spec L 67:15.**

Definitions, **Spec L 67:2.**

Estimated bills, **Spec L 67:9A.**

Pledge of credit, bond issuance, **Spec L 67:16.**

Powers and duties of, **Spec L 67:26.**

Oath of office of Authority members, **Spec L 67:3.**

Payments to division of watershed management, **59:5G.**

Pledge of Commonwealth's credit prohibited, **Spec L 67:16.**

Political subdivisions.

Municipalities. See within this heading, "Municipalities."

Pollution, Attorney General's appearance in lawsuits regarding, **Spec L 67:24.**

Powers and duties of appointees, **Spec L 67:7.**

Powers and duties of Authority, **Spec L 67:6.**

Preliminary engineering reports, failure to comply with order to submit, **21:33B.**

WATER RESOURCES AUTHORITY —Cont'd

Property management and disposal, **Spec L 67:9.**

Property, transfer to Authority, **Spec L 67:4.**

Quorum for meetings, **Spec L 67:3.**

Rates for services, **21:53A, Spec L 67:10, Spec L 67:10A.**

Records, transfer to Authority, **Spec L 67:4.**

Refunding bonds, **Spec L 67:12, 67:13, 67:16.**

Regional planning, **40B:24.**

Reimbursing communities involved in remedying total coliform level violations, **Spec L 67:8.**

Removal of members of Authority, **Spec L 67:3.**

Reports, **Spec L 67:22.**

Retirement system for Authority, **Spec L 67:7.**

Revenues from bonds as trust funds, **Spec L 67:18.**

Rules and regulations, **Spec L 67:5.**

Secretary, appointment, **Spec L 67:7.**

Securities, bonds of Authority, **Spec L 67:14, 67:17.**

Service areas for divisions, designation, **Spec L 67:8.**

Severability of provisions of Act, **Spec L 67:29.**

Sewage, agreements and contracts for making connection for collection, treatment, and disposal, **83:1.**

Sewer system, **Spec L 67:4.**

Defined, **Spec L 67:2.**

Estimated bills, **Spec L 67:9A.**

Exclusive services, **Spec L 67:20.**

Operation, **Spec L 67:7.**

Rates for services, **21:53A, Spec L 10A.**

Service area division designation, **Spec L 67:8.**

Special assessments, **Spec L 67:10.**

Special audit unit, internal, **Spec L 67:7.**

Staff of Authority, appointment, **Spec L 67:5.**

State police, **22C:31.**

Suit.

Action or suit. See within this heading, "Action or suit."

WATER RESOURCES AUTHORITY —Cont'd

Superior Court jurisdiction of enforcement actions, **Spec L 67:24.**

Supreme Judicial Court, jurisdiction of enforcement actions, **Spec L 67:24.**

Tax assessments, **Spec L 67:10.**

Tax exemption of Authority, **Spec L 67:19.**

Termination of Authority, **Spec L 67:21.**

Term of office of Authority members, **Spec L 67:3.**

Total coliform levels, reimbursing communities involved in remedying, **Spec L 67:8.**

Towns.

Municipalities. See within this heading, "Municipalities."

Toxics use reduction, advisory board, **21I:5.**

Transfer of property to Authority, **Spec L 67:4.**

Treasurer of Authority, appointment, **Spec L 67:7.**

Treatment of sewage, exclusivity of services, **Spec L 67:20.**

Trespass, entry upon lands, notice, **Spec L 67:1 et seq.**

Trust funds, revenues from bonds, **Spec L 67:18.**

Use of water by city, town, or political subdivision in contravention of Massachusetts Water Resources Authority Act or purchase of water from municipalities, **40:38.**

Valuation of land, **59:5E.**

Vice-chairman of Authority, **Spec L 67:3.**

Watershed management division, supply of pure water to Massachusetts Water Resources Authority, **92:105.**

Watershed system, compensation for water diverted, **Spec L 67:26.**

Watershed system, defined, **Spec L 67:2.**

Waterworks systems, **Spec L 67:4.**

Estimated bills, **Spec L 67:9A.**

Exclusive services, **Spec L 67:20.**

Operation, **Spec L 67:8.**

Rates for services, **Spec L 10A.**

Service areas division designation, **Spec L 67:8.**

WATER RESOURCES AUTHORITY —Cont'd

Witnesses and evidence, **233:8.**
Workers' compensation or pension, election, **152:73.**

WATER RESOURCES DIVISION AND COMMISSION, 21:1, 21:8 et seq., 21A:8A et seq.

Acquisition of land for water resources development, **21:9A, 44:8.**
Advice to environmental quality engineering commissioner, **21:26.**
Agents for contracts, designation, **21:14.**
Annual report, **21:11.**
Applications for federal aid, approval, **21:12, 21:13.**
Appropriations from general court for improvements, requests, **21:15.**
Aquatic nuisances, establishment of priorities for work of controlling, **111:5F.**
Associations and societies.
　Local organization. See within this heading, "Local organizations."
Budget estimates, **21:11.**
Clean Waters Act, enforcement, **21:53.**
Commissioner of environmental quality engineering as member and chairman of water resources commission, **21:8, 21:9.**
Contracts, **21:9, 21:14.**
　Soil conservation, agreements regarding, **21:13.**
Co-operation with state committee for conservation of soil, water, and related resources, **21:20.**
Costs, **21:14, 21:15, 44:8.**
Creation, **21A:8A.**
Dams and reservoirs, powers, **21:13, 21:39.**
Definition of "works of improvement" in context of water resources division, **21:9.**
Director.
　Appointment, **21A:8E.**
　Designation of person to act in disability or absence, **21:26.**
Division of waterways as contracting agent, **21:14.**
Drinking water supply facilities board of certification, chairman as member, **13:66B.**

WATER RESOURCES DIVISION AND COMMISSION —Cont'd

Easements or rights of way, acquisition, **21:13.**
Eminent domain, exercise, **21:9A.**
Employees, **21:11.**
Entry into land and premises by employees, **21:9, 21:9A.**
Environmental management department, **21:1 et seq.**
Environmental Protection Department, division and commission as within, **21:8.**
Establishment of water resources commission, **21:1.**
Federal, state or local funds, **21:12, 21:13, 21:15.**
Fees for registration of well drillers, **21:16.**
General court, requests for appropriations, **21:15.**
Governor.
　Appointments to commission, **21:8.**
　Impoundment sites, approval of acquisition, **21:9A.**
　Recommendations, **21:41.**
Ground water, representation of ground water industry on commission, **21:8.**
Hazardous waste management act, license requirements of, **21C:7.**
Hearings, **21:9.**
Impoundment sites, acquisition, **21:9A.**
Improvements, **21:9, 21:13-21:15.**
Local organizations.
　Defined, **21:9.**
　Responsibilities, **21:13, 21:14.**
Maintenance and operation of works of improvement, **21:14.**
Massachusetts water management act, duties, **21G:2, 21G:3, 21G:16.**
Massachusetts water supply policy statement, update, **21A:8C.**
Meetings of commission, **21A:8F.**
Members and duties, **21:8.**
Metropolitan district commission as contracting agent, **21:14.**
Pollution of waters.
　See WATER POLLUTION.
Public funds, acceptance and disbursement, **21:9.**
Registration of persons engaged in business of digging or drilling wells, **21:16.**
Reports.
　Annual report, **21:11.**

WATER RESOURCES DIVISION AND COMMISSION —Cont'd

Reports —Cont'd
　Digging or drilling of wells, **21:16.**
Responsibilities and duties, **21A:8B.**
Rules and regulations, **21:11.**
　Promulgation, **21A:8D.**
Sharing cost of improvements, **21:14, 21:15.**
Soil conversation, agreements regarding, **21:13.**
State committee for conservation of soil, water, and related resources, co-operation, **21:20.**
Surveys and other geologic investigation, **21:9A.**
Suspension or revocation of certificate of well drillers, **21:16.**
Technical and clerical staff, **21A:8E.**
Underground waters.
　Ground water, representation of ground water industry on commission, **21:8.**
Underwater archaeological resources board, membership and duties, **6:179.**
United States Secretary of Agriculture, agreements, **21:14.**
Violations regarding registration of persons digging or drilling wells, **21:16.**
Water rights, acquisition, **21:13.**
Watershed Protection and Flood Prevention Act, duties of commission, **21:9, 21:12, 21:13.**
Wells, registration of persons in business of digging or drilling, **21:16.**
Works of improvement, **21:9, 21:13-21:15.**

WATERS AND WATERWAYS, 91:1-91:59.

Access.
　Effect of state licenses, **91:17.**
　Great ponds, **91:18A.**
Acquisition of sites by United States for navigation aids, **1:6.**
Acquisition of watershed, approval by environmental Protection Department, **40:41.**
Agriculture, damage to machinery used in transmission of water, **266:138A.**

WATERS AND WATERWAYS
—Cont'd
Aircraft.
Aeronautics commission.
See AIRCRAFT AND
AVIATION.
Algae.
See ALGAE.
Animal disease control, **129:23,
129:34.**
Animals.
See ANIMALS.
Annual report of public works
commission, **16:5.**
Appropriations.
Municipal finance.
See MUNICIPAL FINANCE.
Aquatic nuisances.
See NUISANCES.
Arrest.
See ARREST.
Barns in which cattle kept,
examination, **129:23.**
Beaches.
See BEACHES.
Berkshire county, protection of
watershed resources and
natural scenery, **131:39A.**
Boats.
See SHIPS AND OTHER
WATERCRAFT.
Borrowing money.
Improvement of waters and
waterways, municipal
borrowing, **44:7.**
Pollution.
See WATER POLLUTION.
Boston courts, jurisdiction, **218:2,
218:3.**
Boundaries.
County boundaries, **34:1.**
Geological.
See GEOLOGICAL AND
COAST SURVEYS.
Municipalities, **42:1, 42:8.**
Province lands, bounds and
regulations, **91:25-91:27.**
State marine boundaries, **1:3.**
Tide lands.
See TIDE LANDS AND
WATERS.
Wharves.
See WHARVES, PIERS, AND
DOCKS.
Bridges.
See BRIDGES.
Buildings in or over.
Structures in or along. See
within this heading,
"Structures in or along."
Buoys placed by United States in
navigable waters, offenses
involving, **266:135.**

WATERS AND WATERWAYS
—Cont'd
Burials in vicinity of, regulated,
114:35.
Cables or conduits, **91:14.**
Canals, **88:9-88:13.**
See CANALS.
Ceded or acquired lands,
concurrent state and federal
jurisdiction, **1:7.**
Channels.
Encroachment Act, **91:12A.**
Ocean sanctuaries, channel
protection projects as
permissible activities,
132A:16.
Passing line across, prohibited,
102:18.
Charles river.
See CHARLES RIVER.
Cities.
Municipalities. See within this
heading, "Municipalities."
Coal mining regulation.
See COAL MINING
REGULATION AND
RECLAMATION.
Coast.
See COAST OR SHORE.
Commission and division of water
resources, **21:1, 21:8 et seq.**
See WATER RESOURCES
DIVISION AND
COMMISSION.
Committee for conservation of soil,
water and related resources,
powers and duties, **21:20.**
Concurrent jurisdiction of state
and United States in ceded or
acquired lands, **1:7.**
Connecticut river.
See CONNECTICUT RIVER.
Conservation.
Committee for conservation of
soil, water, and related
resources, powers and
duties, **21:20.**
District supervisors in
conservation districts,
powers and duties, **21:23.**
Municipalities. See within this
heading, "Municipalities."
Pollution.
See WATER POLLUTION.
Resources division and
commission, **21:1,
21:8-21:16.**
See WATER RESOURCES
DIVISION AND
COMMISSION.
Squannacook and Nissitissit
rivers sanctuary, **132A:17.**

WATERS AND WATERWAYS
—Cont'd
Constitution of Massachusetts,
environmental protection, **MA
Const Amend Art 49.**
Construction contracts.
See CONSTRUCTION
CONTRACTS AND WORK.
Contracts.
See CONTRACTS AND
AGREEMENTS.
Conveyances.
See DEEDS AND
CONVEYANCES.
Counties, appropriation for
waterway improvements,
91:29.
Criminal offenses and penalties.
Aquatic nuisances, unlicensed
person applying chemicals
to waters for control,
111:5E.
Buoys, etc., placed by United
States in navigable waters,
offenses concerning,
266:135.
Dumping materials, **91:55,
102:17.**
Gravel, removing, **91:30, 91:30A.**
Injuring canals or
embankments, **266:107.**
Jurisdiction, **91:57.**
Lowering waters of great pond,
91:19A.
Millpond, drawing water,
266:138.
Motor vehicle which has been
submerged in water, sale of,
266:92A.
Poisoning, **265:28.**
Pollution.
See WATER POLLUTION.
Raising water to injure mill,
266:137.
Refusal to supply water, **270:13.**
Scenic and recreational river or
stream, penalties for
violating order establishing,
21:17B.
Surfboarding and water skiing,
offenses, **90B:14.**
Watershed system, taking or
diverting water or
corrupting or defiling water
supply, **92:111.**
Waterworks.
See WATERWORKS AND
WATER SUPPLY.
Wells, injury, **266:98.**
Damages from taking or
improvements, town may
assume liability, **91:29.**

WATERS AND WATERWAYS
—Cont'd

Dams.
See DAMS AND RESERVOIRS.
Deeds.
See DEEDS AND
CONVEYANCES.
Definitions, **21:26A, 91:1.**
Department of public works.
Public works department. See
within this heading, "Public
works department."
District courts.
Concurrent jurisdiction of
Boston municipal courts,
218:2.
Criminal jurisdiction of certain
courts in Boston, **218:3.**
Districts.
See WATERWORKS AND
WATER SUPPLY.
Diversion of water.
See DIVERSION OF WATER.
Division and commission of water
resources, **21:1, 21:8 et seq.**
See WATER RESOURCES
DIVISION AND
COMMISSION.
Division of water pollution control.
See WATER POLLUTION.
Division of waterways.
Civil service status of director,
21A:7A.
Contracting agent for works of
improvement, **21:14.**
Deputy chief engineer as
member of public access
board of department of
fisheries, wildlife, and
recreational vehicles,
21:17A.
Director, appointment, **21A:7A.**
Environmental Protection
Department, functions and
duties, **21A:8.**
Floats and rafts, authority as to
temporary mooring, **91:10A.**
Public works department,
division as arm of, **16:2.**
Docks, **88:14-88:19.**
See WHARVES, PIERS, AND
DOCKS.
Draining of ponds and other
waters, regulation, **91:19A,
131:48.**
Dredging.
See DREDGING.
Eminent domain.
See EMINENT DOMAIN.
Encroachments, **91:12-91:23,
92:74, 92:74A.**

WATERS AND WATERWAYS
—Cont'd

Entry on land.
Coast surveys, entry for making,
1:8, 1:9.
County commissioners and their
agents, **82:11A.**
Motorboat law enforcement
officers, **90B:13.**
Pollution of water.
See ENTRY INTO LAND AND
PREMISES.
Public works department agents
and employees for purpose
of making surveys or
soundings, **81:7F.**
Water resource commission
employees, **21:9.**
Watershed management
division, entry upon or over
waters, **92:106.**
Environmental affairs executive
office.
See ENVIRONMENTAL
AFFAIRS EXECUTIVE
OFFICE.
Environmental management
department.
See ENVIRONMENTAL
MANAGEMENT
DEPARTMENT.
Environmental Protection
Department, **91:1 et seq.**
See ENVIRONMENTAL
PROTECTION
DEPARTMENT.
Equipment.
Machinery and equipment. See
within this heading,
"Machinery and equipment."
Estuaries.
See TIDE LANDS AND
WATERS.
Federal aid or funds.
Harbors, applications for aid,
91:36.
Pollution control, **21:30-21:33A.**
Underwater archeological
resources board, funding,
6:180.
Federal government and statutes.
Aid.
Federal aid or funds. See
within this heading,
"Federal aid or funds."
Buoys, etc., placed by United
States in navigable waters,
offenses concerning,
266:135.
Ceded or acquired lands,
concurrent state and federal
jurisdiction, **1:7.**

WATERS AND WATERWAYS
—Cont'd

Federal government and statutes
—Cont'd
Conservation, relationships with
federal government of
committee for conservation
of soil, water, and related
resources, **21:19, 21:20.**
Dredging regulations
inapplicable to federal
government, **91:56.**
Flood control reservoirs, towns
reimbursed for loss of taxes
by taking, **58:17B.**
Navigation. See within this
heading, "Navigation."
Pollution control.
See WATER POLLUTION.
Surveys, governor and council to
represent Commonwealth,
6:9.
Territorial waters, **1:3.**
Fences.
Local authorities' powers, **88:12,
88:13.**
Partition fences, **49:9.**
Repair and rebuilding of, duty,
49:17.
Fines and penalties.
Criminal offenses and penalties.
See within this heading,
"Criminal offenses and
penalties."
Fish.
See FISH AND GAME.
Flats.
See TIDE LANDS AND
WATERS.
Floods.
See FLOODS AND FLOOD
CONTROL.
Foreign corporation engaged in
construction or repair of,
attorney for service of process,
181:3.
Foreshores.
See COAST OR SHORE.
Forests.
Cutting practices,
Commonwealth policy,
132:40.
Reforestation, **132:6.**
State forester to protect by
replanting, **132:33.**
State forests, management of,
132:31.
Form of state licenses for
structures, **91:18.**
Garbage and refuse, **91:52, 91:59.**
See WATER POLLUTION.

WATERS AND WATERWAYS
—Cont'd

General court.
See GENERAL COURT.

Geological.
See GEOLOGICAL AND COAST SURVEYS.

Geoscience data of the Commonwealth, duties of public works department, **81:1.**

Gifts, grants, and gratuities.
Impoundment sites, acquisition by water resources commission, **21:9A.**
Pollution.
See WATER POLLUTION.
Reservoirs, grants to water resources commission for construction, **21:39.**
Underwater archaeological resources board, funding, **6:180.**

Governor.
See GOVERNOR.

Governor's council.
See GOVERNOR'S COUNCIL.

Grade crossings, relocation on change or abolition, **159:75.**

Gravel, penalty for removal, **91:30, 91:30A.**

Great ponds.
See LAKES.

Ground water.
See WATERWORKS AND WATER SUPPLY.

Harbors.
See PORTS AND HARBORS.

Hazardous waste management.
See HAZARDOUS WASTE MANAGEMENT.

Health.
See HEALTH AND HEALTH DEPARTMENTS.

Highways.
Licensing construction or extension of road, **91:12 et seq.**
Piers, taking, holding, and utilization of property, **91:5, 91:9.**

Housing and community development department.
Assistance program for low-income homeowners, **23B:24B.**
Powers and duties in general, **23B:3.**

Ice ponds.
See ICE PONDS.

Impact of work on nearby land, **131:40.**

WATERS AND WATERWAYS
—Cont'd

Impoundment sites, acquisition by water resources commission, **21:9A.**

Improvements.
Division of waterways, contracting agent for works of improvement, **21:14.**
Municipal finance.
See MUNICIPAL FINANCE.
Prescriptive right not to result from improvement of lowlands and swamps, **252:14B.**
Public works department's powers, **91:11.**
Tide lands and waters.
Borrowing by cities and towns, **44:7.**
Boston Harbor improvement, **91:2-91:9.**
Water resources commission, **21:9, 21:14, 21:15.**
See WATER RESOURCES DIVISION AND COMMISSION.

Injunctions.
Massachusetts Water Management Act, enforcement of provisions, **21G:14.**
Pollution of waters.
See WATER POLLUTION.
Scenic and recreational rivers and streams, proceedings to restrain taking of real property for establishment, **21:17B.**
Unauthorized structures in waterways, **91:23.**

Inland waters, **111:159.**

Interbasin transfers of surface or groundwaters, **21:8B, 21:8C, 21:8D.**

Interstate compacts.
See INTERSTATE COMPACTS AND AGREEMENTS.

Jurisdiction.
Boston courts, **218:2, 218:3.**
Ceded or acquired lands, concurrent state and federal jurisdiction, **1:7.**
Counties, waters between, **34:1.**
District courts. See within this heading, "District courts."
Over violations, **91:57.**
Pollution.
Coastal waters, **130:26.**
Orders for control of pollution, enforcement, **21:46, 21:46A, 111:164, 111:169.**

WATERS AND WATERWAYS
—Cont'd

Jurisdiction —Cont'd
Superior courts. See within this heading, "Superior court."
Supreme judicial court. See within this heading, "Supreme judicial court."

Lakes.
See LAKES.

Landing places, **88:14 et seq.**
See WHARVES, PIERS, AND DOCKS.

Licenses and permits.
Access to waters, effect of state licenses, **91:17.**
Aquatic nuisances, license to apply chemicals to waters for control, **111:5E.**
Charles River basin.
Encroachments, **92:74.**
Recreational facilities, **92:74A.**
Water, taking, **92:76A-92:76E.**
Discharge of pollutants into waters and facilities for treating effluents, **21:34, 21:43-21:46A.**
See WATER POLLUTION.
Dredging operations and dumping of material in tidewater, **91:52-91:56.**
Highways, license for construction or extension, **91:12 et seq.**
Lumber, permit required for unloading, **102:22.**
Massachusetts Water Management Act, **21G:7-21G:11, 21G:18, 21G:19.**
Structures in.
Licenses for structures. See within this heading, "Licenses for structures in and encroachments."
Tide lands and waters.
Dredging operations and dumping of material in tidewater, **91:52-91:56.**
Flats, licenses for filing, **91:12-91:18.**
Structures in tide lands, licensing and control by public works department, **91:14.**
Licenses for structures in and encroachments, **91:12-91:18.**
Certain rivers, **91:12, 91:12A.**
Charles River Basin, **92:74.**
Control of things done under license, **91:17.**

WATERS AND WATERWAYS
—Cont'd
Licenses for structures in and
encroachments —Cont'd
Form of license, **91:18.**
Great ponds.
Below high water mark, **91:13.**
Construction with reference to
rights of others, **91:17.**
Revocable and to expire in five
years except as acted,
91:15.
Harbors and waterways,
revocability of licenses,
91:15.
Notice to local authorities,
91:18.
Period of license, **91:15.**
Pipelines, cables, or conduits,
91:14.
Receipts, disposition, **91:24.**
Shore and tidewater lands,
91:14.
Unlicensed structures as
nuisances, **91:12, 91:12A.**
Wharves, piers and structures in
waterways, **91:12-91:15.**
See WHARVES, PIERS, AND
DOCKS.
Littoral or riparian owners.
Coast.
See COAST OR SHORE.
Conveyance of real property
abutting on watercourse,
construction of instrument
effecting, **183:58.**
Marine fish.
See MARINE FISH AND
FISHERIES.
Natural barriers on seashore,
proceedings for wrongful
removal, **91:30A.**
Partition of rights of ways of
riparian owners, **241:36.**
Pesticides, exception from tort
liability for discharge of
petroleum products, **91:59A.**
Ponds and navigable streams,
regulation of enclosure,
131:47.
Railroad crossings cutting off
access to sea, **160:96.**
Tort liability for property
damage resulting from
discharge of petroleum
products or bilge water,
91:59A.
Loans.
Borrowing money. See within
this heading, "Borrowing
money."

WATERS AND WATERWAYS
—Cont'd
Lowering waters of great pond,
91:19A.
Lowlands.
See LOWLANDS AND
SWAMPS.
Lumber, permit required for
unloading, **102:22.**
Machinery and equipment.
Pollution abatement or
prevention machinery, tax
exemption, **59:5.**
Transmission machinery,
damage, **266:138A.**
Maintenance fund established,
91:10A½.
Maps, plats, and surveys, **91:10,
91:11, 91:31-91:34.**
Aquatic nuisances in certain
waters, survey prior to
proposed work to control,
111:5F.
Connecticut river, official survey
and plotting of portion,
91:32.
Public works department, **91:10,
91:33.**
Entry on land by department
employees for purpose of
making survey on
soundings, **81:7F.**
Improving topographical
survey of Commonwealth,
91:33.
Sale of maps, **91:33.**
Showing navigable waters in
map, plan, or certificate,
160:18.
Electric company, **164:72.**
Electric railroad, **162:7.**
Natural gas pipeline, **164:75C.**
Town survey of land for purpose
of water supply or water
distributing system, **40:39D.**
Marinas.
License to operate, **91:59B.**
Waste oil retention facilities,
21:52A.
Marine boundaries of
Commonwealth, **1:3.**
Marine fish and fisheries, **130:1 et
seq.**
See MARINE FISH AND
FISHERIES.
Marine resources, control of flow of
water for purpose of protecting
and improving, **130:17.**
Maritime Academy to be
maintained as institution for
study of navigation, **73:1.**

WATERS AND WATERWAYS
—Cont'd
Master plan of municipal planning
boards, **41:81D.**
Merrimack river.
See MERRIMACK RIVER.
Metropolitan district commission,
joining with city, town, or
county in laying out,
improvement, relocation,
widening, repairing,
maintaining, or caring for
public way, bridge, or stream,
92:88.
Metropolitan districts' powers,
92:69.
Metropolitan park districts, **92:33,
92:37-92:39.**
Mills, raising water to injure mill,
266:137.
Mineral resources, exploration for
and extraction of from coastal
waters for public purposes,
21:54.
Mineral waters.
Beverages derived from,
regulations, **110:1,
140:21A-140:21D.**
Bottling permit, **94:10A-94:10G.**
Mooring.
See MOORING.
Mosquito control and other
projects affecting scenic and
recreational rivers and
streams, **21:17B.**
Motorboats.
Discharge and disposal.
See MOTORBOATS.
Motor vehicle which has been
submerged in water, sale,
266:92A.
Municipalities.
Authorized to participate in
development of waters and
watercourses, **40:5, 44:8.**
Borrowing for improvement of
waters, **44:7.**
Boundaries, **42:1, 42:8.**
Coast.
See COAST OR SHORE.
Conservation, **21:20.**
Acquisition of water rights by
city and town
conservation commissions,
40:8C.
Council.
See CITY COUNCIL.
Dams.
See DAMS AND
RESERVOIRS.
Fences. See within this heading,
"Fences."

WATERS AND WATERWAYS
—Cont'd
Municipalities —Cont'd
Finance.
See MUNICIPAL FINANCE.
Harbor and shipping
improvements,
establishment of waterways
improvement and
maintenance fund to receive
revenues, **40:5.**
Landing places, powers with
respect, **88:14-88:19.**
Master plans of planning boards,
41:81D.
Shore reservations,
45:23A-45:23C.
Supply of water.
See WATERWORKS AND
WATER SUPPLY.
Tide lands.
See TIDE LANDS AND
WATERS.
Natural barriers, removal, **91:30,
91:30A.**
Navigation.
Acquisition of sites for
navigational aids by federal
government, **1:6.**
Beacons.
See BEACONS.
Buoys placed by United States
in navigable waters,
offenses involving, **266:135.**
Maritime Academy to be
maintained as institution
for study of navigation, **73:1.**
Obstructions to navigation. See
within this heading,
"Obstructions to navigation."
Showing navigable waters in
maps, plan, or certificate.
Maps, plats, and surveys. See
within this heading,
"Maps, plats, and
surveys."
Notice.
Buildings and structures in or
over navigable waters,
notice, **3:5.**
Dredging operations in
tidewater, **91:54.**
Massachusetts Water
Management Act, permit
application procedures,
21G:9.
Pollution.
See WATER POLLUTION.
Scenic and recreational river or
stream, notice required to
abutting owners prior to
establishment, **21:17B.**

WATERS AND WATERWAYS
—Cont'd
Notice —Cont'd
State licenses for structures,
notice to local authorities,
91:18.
Vessel obstructing harbor or
waterway, notice to remove,
91:40.
Nuisances.
See NUISANCES.
Obstructions to navigation.
Dumping materials likely to
cause, **102:17.**
In certain rivers, **91:10, 91:12.**
Nuisances, **91:12, 91:12A.**
Organization of reclamation
district for removal, **252:1.**
Ports and harbors, obstruction,
102:17, 102:18.
Notice to remove, **91:40.**
Reimbursement of
Commonwealth for cost of
removal, **91:45.**
Removal of, **252:1.**
Shipwrecks.
See SHIPWRECKS.
Structures in or along. See
within this heading,
"Structures in or along."
Telecommunications and energy
department's powers, **91:10.**
Unsafe wharves, piers and
docks, removal, **91:49B.**
Ocean.
See OCEAN OR SEA.
Offenses.
Criminal offenses and penalties.
See within this heading,
"Criminal offenses and
penalties."
Oil pollution.
See WATER POLLUTION.
Overflowing of lands, **253:42,
253:43.**
Partition fences, **49:9.**
Partition of water rights, **241:36,
241:37.**
Penalties.
Criminal offenses and penalties.
See within this heading,
"Criminal offenses and
penalties."
Permits.
Licenses. See within this
heading, "Licenses and
permits."
Petition to general court, **3:5.**
Petroleum pipelines under, state
grant of right of way, **30:44B.**
Piers, **88:14-88:19.**
See WHARVES, PIERS, AND
DOCKS.

WATERS AND WATERWAYS
—Cont'd
Piles, driving of below high water
mark, **91:12-91:14, 91:19.**
Pipelines, **91:14.**
Natural gas pipeline, showing
navigable waters in map,
plan, or certificate, **164:75C.**
Petroleum pipelines, state grant
of right of way, **30:44B.**
Waterworks.
See WATERWORKS AND
WATER SUPPLY.
Poisoning as criminal offense,
265:28.
Pollution of waters.
See WATER POLLUTION.
Ponds.
See PONDS.
Ports.
See PORTS AND HARBORS.
Prescriptive right not to result
from improvement of lowlands
and swamps, **252:14B.**
Private property along shores,
structures for protection,
91:29A.
Projects for water resources,
approval by environmental
Protection Department, **44:8.**
Public beaches.
See BEACHES.
Public landing places, **88:14 et
seq.**
See WHARVES, PIERS, AND
DOCKS.
Public lands, **91:25-91:27.**
Public works department.
Annual report of public works
commission, **16:5.**
Division of waterways. See
within this heading,
"Division of waterways."
Drawbridges, regulation of
passage of vessels through,
85:26.
Dredged material,
transportation and dumping
in tidewaters, **91:52-91:56.**
Entry on land for purpose of
making surveys or
soundings, **81:7F.**
Foreshores, control, **91:2, 91:11.**
Functions and powers,
91:10-91:12.
Geoscience data of the
Commonwealth, duties,
81:1.
Improving topographical survey
of Commonwealth, **91:33.**
Jurisdiction, **91:2.**

WATERS AND WATERWAYS
—Cont'd
Public works department —Cont'd
Lakes.
See LAKES.
Maps, plats, and surveys. See
within this heading, "Maps,
plats, and surveys."
Merrimack River, control over,
91:1.
Mineral resources, exploration
for and extraction of from
coastal waters for public
purposes, **21:54.**
Mosquito control and other
projects affecting scenic and
recreational rivers and
streams, **21:17B.**
Plans for structures, approval,
91:20.
Reports as to marine
boundaries, **1:3.**
Sale of maps, **91:33.**
Structures at public expense,
control over, **91:12A.**
Surveys.
Maps, plats, and surveys. See
within this heading,
"Maps, plats, and
surveys."
Railroads.
See RAILROADS.
Reclamation districts for removal
of obstructions to navigation,
organization, **252:1.**
Reforestation of lands, **132:6.**
Refusal to supply water as
criminal offense, **270:13.**
Refuse, **91:52, 91:59.**
See WATER POLLUTION.
Regional district planning
commission's plans and
recommendations, **40B:5.**
Registers.
See REGISTERS AND
REGISTRIES OF DEEDS.
Relocation on change or abolition
of grade crossings, **159:75.**
Reservoirs.
See DAMS AND RESERVOIRS.
Resources division, **21:1, 21:8 et
seq.**
See WATER RESOURCES
DIVISION AND
COMMISSION.
Riparian owners.
Littoral or riparian owners. See
within this heading,
"Littoral or riparian
owners."
Rivers, **91:1 et seq.**

WATERS AND WATERWAYS
—Cont'd
Rowing clubs in Charles River
basin, **92:74A.**
Sanctuaries, **132A:13-132A:16.**
Sand, removing from shores or
harbors, **91:30.**
Sanitation.
See HEALTH AND HEALTH
DEPARTMENTS.
Scenic and recreational rivers and
streams, establishment of
system, **21:17B.**
Schooner Ernestina Commission,
powers and duties, **6:182B.**
Ships.
See SHIPS AND OTHER
WATERCRAFT.
Shipwrecks.
See SHIPWRECKS.
Shore.
See COAST OR SHORE.
Skiing, **90B:8, 90B:11, 90B:14,
131:45.**
Speed limits, water recreational
vehicles, **90B:11.**
Squannacook and Nissitissit rivers
sanctuary, **132A:17.**
State forests.
Forests. See within this heading,
"Forests."
State health department, powers
and duties, **111:5, 111:17.**
State licenses.
Licenses. See within this
heading, "Licenses and
permits."
State public works department.
Public works department. See
within this heading, "Public
works department."
Steamboat police, powers, **159:93.**
Steamship authority.
See STEAMSHIP AUTHORITY.
Stones and gravel, penalty for
removal, **91:30, 91:30A.**
Storm damage to coast line of
river banks, repair, **91:31.**
Streams, **91:1 et seq.**
Streets.
Highways. See within this
heading, "Highways."
Structures in or along,
91:12-91:15.
Abatement of unauthorized
structures, **91:23.**
Boston harbor, structures,
91:1-91:9A.
Charles River basin,
92:72-92:74.
Connecticut river.
See CONNECTICUT RIVER.

WATERS AND WATERWAYS
—Cont'd
Structures in or along —Cont'd
Control of structures erected at
public expense, **91:12A.**
Displacing of tidewater, **91:21,
91:22.**
Existing structures not
legalized, **91:28.**
Great ponds, **91:19.**
Injunctions against
unauthorized structures,
91:23.
Landing places, structures at,
88:14.
See WHARVES, PIERS, AND
DOCKS.
Licenses for structures in and
encroachments. See within
this heading, "Licenses for
structures in and
encroachments."
Nuisance, unauthorized
structures, **91:23.**
Petition to general court
regarding, **3:5.**
Plans for, approval, **91:20.**
Private property, structures for
protection, **91:29A.**
Removal where contrary to
restrictions in deed, **91:37.**
Shore and tidewater lands,
91:14.
Unauthorized structures, **91:12,
91:12A, 91:23.**
Wharves, piers, and docks, **88:14
et seq.**
See WHARVES, PIERS, AND
DOCKS.
Subdivision control law, general
purposes, **41:81M.**
Sunday, activities permitted,
136:6.
Superior court.
Natural barriers on seashore,
proceedings for wrongful
removal, **91:30A.**
Pollution of waters, jurisdiction,
**21:46, 21:46A, 111:164,
111:169.**
Scenic and recreational rivers
and streams, jurisdiction of
actions affecting, **21:17B.**
Wharves, piers, and docks,
jurisdiction to enforce
Commonwealth's lien for
cost of removal of unsafe,
91:49B.
Supreme judicial court, **91:57.**
Entry on adjoining land for
making, **266:120C.**

WATERS AND WATERWAYS
—Cont'd
Supreme judicial court —Cont'd
Pollution, **130:26.**
United States government
survey, governor and council
to represent
Commonwealth, **6:9.**
Surveys.
Maps, plats, and surveys. See
within this heading, "Maps,
plats, and surveys."
Telecommunications and energy
department's powers as to
obstructions to navigation,
91:10.
Temporary mooring of floats or
rafts, **91:10A.**
Tide lands.
See TIDE LANDS AND
WATERS.
Timber carried away by floods,
claim of owner, **135:12.**
Title and ownership.
Littoral or riparian owners. See
within this heading,
"Littoral or riparian
owners."
Tobacco products contaminated by
water, sale, **94:307.**
Towns.
Municipalities. See within this
heading, "Municipalities."
Treatment plants.
See WATER POLLUTION.
Trees or vegetation along, penalty
for destroying, **91:30.**
Underground water.
See WATERWORKS AND
WATER SUPPLY.
Underwater Archaeological
Resources Board, **6:179, 6:180.**
See UNDERWATER
ARCHAEOLOGICAL
RESOURCES BOARD.
United States.
Federal government and
statutes. See within this
heading, "Federal
government and statutes."
Unlawful cutting of ice, **266:105.**
Waste water treatment facilities.
See WATER POLLUTION.
Water management act.
See WATER MANAGEMENT
ACT.
Watershed management division.
See METROPOLITAN
DISTRICT COMMISSION.
Wells.
See WELLS.

WATERS AND WATERWAYS
—Cont'd
Westfield River, structures in or
along, **91:12.**
Wharves, piers, and docks,
88:14-88:19.
See WHARVES, PIERS, AND
DOCKS.
Zoning and planning, purposes of
subdivision control law,
41:81M.

**WATERSHED LANDS
PRESERVATION
COMMITTEE.**
Environmental Protection
Department, commissioner as
member, **28:8.**

**WATERSHED MANAGEMENT
DIVISION.**
**See METROPOLITAN
DISTRICT COMMISSION.**

**WATERSHED MANAGEMENT
PLANS.**
Adoption, **92:116.**

**WATERSHED PROTECTION
AND FLOOD
PREVENTION ACT, 21:12,
21:13.**
Acquisition of watershed area,
approval by environmental
Protection Department, **40:41.**
Authority to enter premises within
watershed area, **111:173B.**
Restrictions, **184:32, 184:33.**
Water Resources commission,
duties, **21:9, 21:12, 21:13.**

WATERSHED SYSTEM.
Defined, for purposes of provisions
establishing watershed
management division, **92:104.**

**WATERSHED SYSTEM
ADVISORY COMMITTEE.**
Creation, purpose, and meetings,
92:115.
Periodic watershed management
plans, participation of
committee, **92:116.**

WATER SKIING.
Dangerous operation of vessel,
90B:8.
Jet skis, surf jets, or wetbikes, age
requirements for operators,
90B:9A, 90B:9B.
Nighttime use prohibited, **90B:8.**
Regulation, **90B:8, 90B:11,
90B:14, 131:45.**

WATER SUPPLY.
**See WATERWORKS AND
WATER SUPPLY.**

WATERTOWN.
Congressional district, **57:1.**
District court, **218:1.**
Medical examiner district, **38:1.**
Metropolitan air pollution control
district, membership,
111:142B.
Parks, provision by metropolitan
commission, **92:33.**
Refuse disposal, **92:9A.**
Senatorial district, **57:3.**
Superior court jurisdiction of
crimes committed, **212:6.**

WATER WHEELS.
Tax assessors' books, listing, **59:46.**

**WATERWORKS AND WATER
SUPPLY, 40:38 et seq., 165:1
et seq.**
Abandoned, lost, and unclaimed
property.
Well, appropriation for covering
abandoned wells, **40:21.**
Acquisition by water companies of
waters, water rights, flowage
rights, etc., **165:4B.**
Affiliated companies.
Contracts with, copies to be
filed, **165:4A.**
Defined, **165:4A.**
Agriculture, damage to machinery
used in transmission of water,
266:138A.
Aiding of one municipality by
another, **40:39H.**
Aldermen.
Selectmen or aldermen. See
within this heading,
"Selectmen or aldermen."
Animals.
See ANIMALS.
Annual returns of water
companies, **164:83, 164:84,
165:2.**
Appeals.
Decision of aldermen or
selectmen as to opening of
streets, appeal, **165:9.**
Massachusetts Water
Management Act
procedures, **21G:12.**
Rates and charges, **40:42E.**
Applicability of other chapters to
water companies, **165:2.**
Aqueduct companies, **165:12 et
seq.**
See AQUEDUCTS AND
AQUEDUCT COMPANIES.
Assessment limitations of regional
water districts, **59:20A,
59:20B.**

WATERWORKS AND WATER SUPPLY —Cont'd

Assessment of taxes.
Districts and tax assessors, **59:21, 59:25.**
Separate list and warrant for district taxes, **59:53.**
Service charges, **59:21C.**
Special assessments to meet cost of laying pipes, **40:42G, 40:42H.**
Commissioners, duty, **40:42I.**
Fixed uniform rate, **40:42H.**
Liens, assessments, **40:42I.**
Procedure, **40:42G.**
Recording of determination, **40:42I.**
Attorney general, recovery of penalty for failure to file copies of contracts with affiliated companies, **165:4A.**
Badges for employees of water companies, **165:11D.**
Board of certification of drinking water supply facility operators, appointment of members, **13:66B.**
Board of water commissioners.
Account of receipts and expenditures, **41:69B.**
Application of law as to powers and duties, **41:69B.**
Authority and duties, **41:69B.**
Control of systems, **40:39E.**
Establishment, **41:69A.**
Protection of water supply, control over lands acquired, **40:41.**
Report, **41:69B.**
Rescission of vote authorizing selectmen to act, **41:23.**
Selectmen, **40:39A, 41:21, 41:23, 41:69A.**
Special assessments to meet cost of laying pipes, duties, **40:42I.**
Superintendent, appointment, **41:69.**
Term of office, **41:69A.**
Town public works board as successor, **41:69D.**
Bonds and obligations.
Drinking water protection commission, **40:39K.**
Metropolitan districts.
See METROPOLITAN DISTRICTS.
Payment of interest, principal, and damages from income, **40:41, 41:69B.**
Provision for payment, **44:19.**

WATERWORKS AND WATER SUPPLY —Cont'd

Bonds and obligations —Cont'd
Water companies' bonds and obligations.
Insurance company investments in securities of water companies, **175:63.**
Issuance of, **164:13, 164:14, 164:17, 165:2.**
Mortgages to secure bond issues, **164:13, 165:2.**
Books and records.
Records, reports, and returns.
See within this heading, "Records, reports, and returns."
Borrowing money.
Aqueducts and mains, municipal borrowing outside debt limit for construction, **44:8.**
Cities and towns, borrowing for water supply, **44:8.**
Water companies, loans, **164:17A, 165:2.**
Boston.
See METROPOLITAN DISTRICTS.
Boston water.
See BOSTON WATER AND SEWER REORGANIZATION ACT.
Bottled water testing, certification of laboratory, **94:10D½.**
Bottling works, permits required, **94:10A et seq.**
Building permits, availability of water as affecting issuance, **40:54.**
Buildings and equipment, power to acquire, erect, and maintain, **40:39C.**
Business corporation law as inapplicable to water companies, **156:2, 156B:3.**
Business trusts owning or operating water companies, **182:7 et seq.**
Capital stock.
Stock. See within this heading, "Stock."
Certificates and certification.
Bottled water, certification of laboratory testing, **94:10D½.**
Environmental Protection Department membership on drinking water supply facilities board of certification, **13:66B.**

WATERWORKS AND WATER SUPPLY —Cont'd

Certificates and certification —Cont'd
Meters, certification of result of testing, **165:10.**
Operators of supply facilities, certification of. See within this heading, "Operators of supply facilities, certification."
Tax collector's certificate as to collection of water rates, **60:23.**
Well diggers or drillers, **21:16.**
Chapter as to certain miscellaneous corporations, water companies organized, **158:1.**
Charges or rates.
Rates and charges. See within this heading, "Rates and charges."
Charles River basin, taking water, **92:76A.**
Chemicals.
See CHEMICALS AND CHEMISTRY.
Cities and towns, **40:39A et seq.**
Aiding of one municipality by another, **40:39H.**
Appropriations, **40:5.**
Approval, **40:39B.**
Authority to participate in development of water resources, **40:5, 40:54, 44:8.**
Board of water commissioners.
See within this heading, "Board of water commissioners."
Bond payments, **44:19.**
Borrowing money. See within this heading, "Borrowing money."
Bylaws regulating pipes, **40:21.**
Certificated operator required for drinking water supply facility, **112:87DDDD.**
Charles River basin, borrowing to establish water supply, **92:76E.**
Chemicals in water supply, notice, **111:26F.**
Claims in connection with waterworks, **40:39F.**
Conservation, **21:20, 40:8C, 40:39J.**
Damages for injuries, **40:39F.**
Dams and reservoirs, **40:21, 40:39C, 58:17B.**
See DAMS AND RESERVOIRS.

WATERWORKS AND WATER SUPPLY —Cont'd

Cities and towns —Cont'd

Development of water supply by, **40:5, 40:38, 40:54, 44:8.**

Disposition of unneeded lands located in another city or town, **40:15B.**

Diversion of waters, penalty, **40:39G.**

Drinking troughs, wells, and fountains in public places, appropriations, **40:5.**

Drinking water protection district and commission, **40:39K.**

Elections. See within this heading, "Elections."

Emergencies, environmental Protection Department approval of water shut off, **40:41A.**

Eminent domain, exercise of power, **40:39B, 165:5.**

Entry upon lands to make surveys, **40:39D.**

Environmental Protection Department.

Acquisition of watersheds, departmental approval, **40:41.**

Disposition of unneeded lands located in another city or town, departmental approval, **40:15B.**

Emergencies, shutting off of water, departmental approval, **40:41A.**

Projects, department to approve, **44:8.**

Sources to be approved by department, **40:38, 40:39B.**

Treatment plants, departmental approval, **40:39C.**

Favorability studies as to water, appropriations for payment of town's share of cost, **40:5.**

Fee for filing statement of amount of debt due for labor performed in construction of waterworks, **262:34.**

Filter beds, borrowing beyond debt limit for construction or repair, **44:8.**

Growth and development policy committees, **40:4I.**

High volume users of water, **165:2B.**

Income of town water works, disposition, **41:69B.**

WATERWORKS AND WATER SUPPLY —Cont'd

Cities and towns —Cont'd

Indebtedness, **44:8.**

Laying of water pipes upon laying out, relocation, or alteration of town ways, **82:25.**

Limit on real estate holdings, authority to exceed, **165:28.**

Mains and aqueducts, borrowing outside debt limit for purpose of reconstructing, laying, and relaying, **44:8.**

Master plan of planning board in respect to location of pipes, **41:81D.**

Meters, borrowing for purchases, **44:8.**

Ordinances, **40:21.**

Other cities and towns. See within this heading, "Other cities or towns."

Penalty for injury to water meters, **165:11.**

Pipes, construction and maintenance, **40:39C.**

Planning map, effect of adoption, **41:81E.**

Pollution, penalty, **40:39G.**

Pricing system, water conservation, **40:39J.**

Protection of water supply, sue of bond proceeds to pay damages arising, **40:41.**

Pumping stations, municipal indebtedness, **44:8.**

Purchase of rights, **40:38.**

Rates and charges. See within this heading, "Rates and charges."

Reservoirs, construction, maintenance, and use of, **40:21, 40:39C, 58:17B.**

See DAMS AND RESERVOIRS.

Sources and lands, **40:39B.**

Streets and highways, consent to opening, **165:8, 165:9.**

Surveys.

Entry upon lands to make, **40:39D.**

Necessity of conforming to survey board plans, **41:77.**

Taking, **40:39B, 165:5.**

Treatment facilities.

Anticipation spending, **44:6A.**

Authority of public health department to require installation and operation, **111:5G.**

WATERWORKS AND WATER SUPPLY —Cont'd

Cities and towns —Cont'd

Treatment facilities —Cont'd

Borrowing, **44:8.**

Environmental Protection Department, approval, **40:39C.**

Reimbursement of construction costs to cities and towns, **21:30A.**

Cleaning products containing phosphorus, regulation of, **111:5R.**

Coal mining regulation.

See COAL MINING REGULATION AND RECLAMATION.

Commissioners.

Board of water commissioners. See within this heading, "Board of water commissioners."

Companies, **165:1 et seq.**

"Company" defined under water company law, **165:1.**

Compensation, **40:39H.**

Drinking water protection commission, **40:39K.**

Other supply systems, aid, **40:39H.**

Condemnation.

Eminent domain. See within this heading, "Eminent domain."

Conduits.

Pipes and conduits. See within this heading, "Pipes and conduits."

Consolidation or merger of water companies, **164:96, 164:98, 164:99, 164:101, 165:2.**

Construction contracts.

See CONSTRUCTION CONTRACTS AND WORK.

Contracts.

Affiliated companies, filing copies of water companies' contracts, **165:4A.**

Environmental Protection Department as contract agent for construction of public access to water, **21:17A.**

Other cities or towns, contracts to supply, **40:38.**

Control over property used, **40:39E.**

"Corporation" defined under water company law, **165:1.**

Corporation taxes.

Franchise taxes, **63:52A.**

989

WATERWORKS AND WATER SUPPLY —Cont'd

Corporation taxes —Cont'd

Local taxes on water companies, **59:5.**

Crimes and offenses.

Fines and penalties. See within this heading, "Fines and penalties."

Cross connections, **111:160A.**

Damages.

Aiding other supply systems, damages, **40:39H.**

Bond issues, payment of damages from income, **40:41, 41:69B.**

Coastal and inland wetlands, assessment of damages, **130:105, 131:40A.**

Injuries in acquiring and constructing system, **40:39F.**

Laying pipes in another town, **40:39.**

Protection of water supply, damages, **40:41.**

Damage to sources or equipment, **40:39F, 111:170, 111:171.**

Dams and reservoirs, **253:1 et seq.**

See DAMS AND RESERVOIRS.

Debt.

Indebtedness. See within this heading, "Indebtedness."

Definitions, **165:1.**

Departmental equipment, municipal indebtedness, **44:8.**

Depreciation fund, water company rates as affected, **155:5A.**

Descending unit rate basis, **40:39J½, 40:39L.**

Development by city or town, **40:5, 40:38, 40:54, 44:8.**

Discharging or dumping offensive matter in water supply sources, **111:167.**

Disconnecting or destroying water mains, **148:27A.**

Discontinuance or shutting off service, **40:42B.**

Cities and towns, environmental Protection Department to approve shutting off water in emergencies, **40:41A.**

Health and sanitation, discontinuance of use of unsafe or inadequate water supply, **111:122A.**

Hot water tanks, shutoff device, **142:19.**

Mains, shutting off, disconnecting, obstructing, removing or destroying, **148:27A.**

WATERWORKS AND WATER SUPPLY —Cont'd

Discontinuance or shutting off service —Cont'd

Nonpayment of charges, **165:11A.**

Occupants' rights to pay arrears, **165:11E.**

Prior notice required, **165:11E.**

Prior owner, effect of nonpayment of charges, **165:11C.**

Serious illness, **165:11B.**

Dissolution of liens for unpaid bills, **40:42B.**

Distribution systems, adequacy of, **165:1A.**

Districts.

Aid, **40:39H.**

Annual financial statement of state treasurer, **10:11.**

Badges for employees, **165:11D.**

Borrowing money in anticipation of revenue, **44:4.**

Commissioners of water, authority and duties as to water department and system, **41:69B.**

Definition of water district, **4:7, 44:1.**

Disposition of unneeded lands located in another city or town, **40:15B.**

"Districts" defined to include water districts, **4:7, 40:1A, 41:1A.**

Gifts of funds, acceptance and expenditure, **44:53A.**

Indemnification of policemen or firemen, **41:100, 41:111F.**

Insurance companies investing in obligations, **175:63.**

Liens on land or buildings, **254:6.**

Meters.

Borrowing for purchase and installation, **44:9.**

Testing, **40:39I.**

Metropolitan districts, **92:33 et seq.**

See METROPOLITAN DISTRICTS.

Police employed by, jurisdiction, **111:173A.**

Protection of water supply, **40:39K, 40:41.**

Reclamation districts, development, **252:14B.**

Schedule of rates, filing, **165:2A.**

Statutory construction, **4:7.**

WATERWORKS AND WATER SUPPLY —Cont'd

Districts —Cont'd

Studies as to water feasibility, district planning commission may enter into agreements, **40B:5A.**

Tax assessors, **59:21, 59:25.**

Separate list and warrant for district taxes, **59:53.**

Treatment facilities, authority of public health department to require installation and operation, **111:5G.**

Diversion of water, **40:39G.**

Aqueduct company's liability, **165:27.**

Town water supply, penalty, **40:39G.**

Dividends of water companies, prohibition of stock or scrip dividends, **164:11, 164:12, 165:2.**

Drinking troughs in public places, town appropriation, **40:5.**

Drinking water protection fund, **40:39J½, 40:39K.**

Easements.

Acquisition for protection of water supply, **40:41, 165:4B.**

Grant of easements in certain lands not needed for public water supply, **40:15B.**

Elections.

Acquisition of water supply, **40:38, 40:39A.**

Emergency.

Certification of operators of drinking water supply facilities, **112:87CCCC.**

Cities and towns, approval of shutting off water, **40:41A.**

Draining of certain ponds and reservoirs, **131:48.**

Environmental Protection Department, **21:8C.**

Fire districts, emergency water supply, **40:41A, 90:10.**

Massachusetts Water Management Act, **21G:15 et seq.**

Public water supply, **40:38.**

Restraint of use of water during, **40:41A.**

Shutting off water, **40:41A.**

Eminent domain, **165:4B.**

Acquisition of sources and lands by cities and towns, **40:39B, 165:5.**

Damages, recovery, **40:39F.**

Environmental protection department, **40:41, 165:4B.**

WATERWORKS AND WATER SUPPLY —Cont'd

Eminent domain —Cont'd

Purity of supply, acquisition of lands and sources for protection, **40:41.**

Employees.

See LABOR AND WORKFORCE DEVELOPMENT.

Enforcement of supply of water, **164:92, 165:2.**

Entry into land and premises.

Customer, entry on premises, **165:11D.**

Impoundment sites, surveys and investigations, **21:9A.**

Officers and officials in charge of water supply, entry on property, **111:173B.**

Surveys, entry on lands to make, **21:9A, 40:39D.**

Environmental Protection Department.

Acquisition of watersheds, approval, **40:41.**

Assistance to telecommunications and energy department, **165:6.**

Board of certification for operators of drinking water supply facilities, **13:66B.**

Bottled water, certification of laboratory testing, **94:10D½.**

Certification board for drinking water facilities, membership, **13:66B.**

Charles river, department to receive notice of taking of water, **92:76A.**

Cities and towns. See within this heading, "Cities and towns."

Conservation of groundwater aquifers, recharge areas, surface water resources and watersheds, **111:160.**

Contract agent for construction of public access to water, department, **21:17A.**

Cross connections between public water supplies and other supplies, regulation, **111:160A.**

Distribution system, approval, **165:1A.**

Drinking water protection commission, **40:39K.**

Emergency.

Cities and towns. See within this heading, "Cities and towns."

WATERWORKS AND WATER SUPPLY —Cont'd

Environmental Protection Department —Cont'd

Emergency. See within this heading, "Emergency."

Eminent domain, **40:41, 165:4B.**

Enforcement of regulations as to purity of supply, **111:160B.**

Engineering services furnished, **165:6.**

Examination of water supply, **111:160.**

Pollution.

See WATER POLLUTION.

Powers and duties not affected by chapter, **165:3.**

Powers and duties not impaired, **165:3.**

Projects for water supply, approval, **40:39C, 44:8.**

Quality standards for water, enforcement, **111:160B.**

Safe drinking water, powers to regulate, **111:5G, 111:17, 111:160.**

Sale by cities or towns of lands no longer required for water supply, approval, **40:15B.**

Shedding of water supply in emergency, approval, **40:41A.**

Sources of water, approval, **40:38, 40:39B.**

Taking water rights by eminent domain, **165:4B.**

Treatment plant, approval, **40:39.**

Watersheds, approval of acquisition, **40:41.**

Established systems, town not to compete, **40:39A.**

Examination, inspection, or investigation, **111:160.**

Bottled water, testing of water, **94:10A, 94:10D½, 94:10E, 94:10E½, 94:10F.**

Certification board examinations, **13:66B.**

Environmental protection department, examination of water supply, **111:160.**

Home water treatment devices, **111:160C et seq.**

Laboratory tests, provision, **94:10D½, 111:184A.**

Meters, inspection and testing, **40:39I, 165:10.**

Fees, **165:10.**

Operators of drinking water supply facilities, examinations qualifying, **112:87CCC.**

WATERWORKS AND WATER SUPPLY —Cont'd

Examination, inspection, or investigation —Cont'd

Plastic pipe connections, inspection, **165:1C.**

Reforestation, inspection of water supply lands, **132:6.**

Toxic substances, testing, **21G:3. (note)**

Excavations, **82:40 to 82:40E.**

See EXCAVATIONS.

Exemption of water companies from taxation, **59:5.**

Extraordinary maintenance or repairs, authorization by water commissioners, **41:69B.**

Favorability or feasibility studies.

Studies. See within this heading, "Studies as to water favorability or feasibility."

Federal Safe Drinking Act Assessment, **21A:18A.**

Fees.

Constructing waterworks, fee for filing statement of amount due for labor performed, **262:34.**

Drinking water protection commission, **40:39K.**

Environmental affairs executive office, federal safe drinking water assessment act, **21A:18A.**

Massachusetts Water Management Act, registration and permit application fees, **21G:18, 21G:19.**

Operators of supply facilities, certification, **112:87CCCC.**

Rates and charges. See within this heading, "Rates and charges."

Testing meters, **165:10.**

Filing.

Records, reports, and returns. See within this heading, "Records, reports, and returns."

Filter beds, incurring indebtedness for construction, **44:8.**

Finances and funds.

Depreciation fund, rates as affected, **155:5A.**

Districts, acceptance and expenditure of gifts of funds, **44:53A.**

Drinking water protection fund, **40:39J½, 40:39K.**

WATERWORKS AND WATER SUPPLY —Cont'd

Fines and penalties.
Cross connection to supply, wrongful maintenance, **111:160A.**
Dams.
See DAMS AND RESERVOIRS.
Defilement of water supply, **111:170, 111:171.**
Diversion of town water supply, **40:39G.**
Employees, failure to provide drinking water, **149:106.**
Environmental protection department, examination of water supply, **111:160.**
Failure to file copy of contracts with affiliated companies, **165:4A.**
Grounding requirements, violation, **165:1C.**
Hydrants, blocking access, **90:20A½, 184:27B.**
Ice ponds and streams, **111:167, 111:170 et seq.**
Mains, shutting off, disconnection, obstruction, removal, or destruction, **148:27A.**
Massachusetts Water Management Act, enforcement of provisions, **21G:14.**
Meters.
Injury to meters, **165:11.**
Interference with meters, **165:11.**
Millponds, drawing water, **266:138.**
Notice of discontinuance of water, **111:122A, 165:11E.**
Plastic pipe connections, **165:1C.**
Poisoning of spring, **265:28.**
Pollution.
See WATER POLLUTION.
Refusal to supply water as criminal offense, **270:13.**
Shutting off service in cases of serious illness, **165:11B.**
Swimming in water supply, **111:171.**
Unauthorized use of water, **165:11.**
Uncertified operator, operation of drinking water supply facilities, **112:8DDDD.**
Fire districts.
See FIRE DISTRICTS.
Fire hydrants.
Hydrants. See within this heading, "Hydrants."

WATERWORKS AND WATER SUPPLY —Cont'd

Fish.
See FISH AND GAME.
Flowage rights, acquisition, **165:4B.**
Foreign.
Other. See within this heading, "Other cities or towns."
Forests and forestry.
Inspection of water supply lands for reforestation, **132:6.**
Protection of water supply, replanting of woodland for purposes, **132:33.**
Forms.
Records, reports, and returns. See within this heading, "Records, reports, and returns."
Franchise, transfer, **164:21, 165:2.**
Game.
See FISH AND GAME.
General court, amendment or revival to petition for incorporation, **3:5.**
Governor, appointment of members of board of certification of operators of drinking water supply facilities, **13:66B.**
Grounding requirements, **165:1C.**
Ground water.
Underground waters. See within this heading, "Underground waters."
Gulls, prevention of defilement, **111:174A.**
Health.
See HEALTH AND HEALTH DEPARTMENTS.
Hearings.
Appeal from decision of aldermen or selectmen as to opening of streets, **165:9.**
Eminent domain, public convenience and necessity as to exercise, **165:4B.**
Notice. See within this heading, "Notice."
Rate hearings, **164:93, 164:94, 165:2.**
Upon opening of streets and highways, **165:8, 165:9.**
Highways and streets.
Aldermen, consent to opening streets and highways, **165:8, 165:9.**
Authorization for laying of pipes, **40:42.**
Construction of systems under or near, **40:39C.**

WATERWORKS AND WATER SUPPLY —Cont'd

Highways and streets —Cont'd
Digging up and laying water pipes, **40:42, 40:43, 82:25, 165:8, 165:9.**
Sprinkling of streets, **40:16 et seq.**
Home water treatment devices, **111:160C et seq.**
Hospital for state minor wards and Massachusetts hospital, joint use, **111:62R.**
Hot water heating boilers, **146:70 et seq.**
See HOT WATER HEATING BOILERS.
Hot water tanks.
See HOT WATER TANKS.
Household cleaning products containing phosphorus, regulation of, **111:5R.**
Housing and urban renewal projects, municipal construction in aid, **121B:23.**
Hydrants.
Aqueduct corporations, selectmen may take water for protection against fire, **165:26.**
Board of water commissioners may establish, **41:69B.**
Inflammable fluid as antifreeze, **148:23A.**
Parking regulations, **40:21, 90:20A½.**
Ski areas, warning requirement, **143:71N.**
Snow, prohibition as to piling on fire hydrants, **148:27A.**
Standardization, **48:87.**
Tampering with fire hydrants, **148:27A.**
Illness, discontinuance of service in cases of, prohibited, **165:11B.**
Impaired capital of water companies to be made good, **164:16, 164:17, 165:2.**
Impoundment sites.
See DAMS AND RESERVOIRS.
Improvement in quality of water, **164:93, 165:2.**
Indebtedness.
Borrowing money. See within this heading, "Borrowing money."
Debts created for supplying water as included, **4:7.**
Fee for filing statement of amount of debt due for labor, **262:34.**

WATERWORKS AND WATER SUPPLY —Cont'd

Indemnification of policemen or firemen by water districts, **41:100, 41:111F.**

Injunction against use of water supply during emergency, **40:41A.**

Injury to town water system, penalty, **40:39G.**

Inspection.
Examination, inspection or investigation. See within this heading, "Examination, inspection, or investigation."

Insurance.
Investments by insurance companies in securities of water companies, **175:63.**
Rates and rating organizations applied, **175A:4.**

Interest on money.
Bond issues, payment of interest from income, **40:41, 41:69B.**
Deposits of customers, **158:16, 164:128.**
Unpaid water bills, **40:42D.**

Interstate compacts.
See INTERSTATE COMPACTS AND AGREEMENTS.

Investigation.
Examination, inspection, or investigation. See within this heading, "Examination, inspection, or investigation."

Investments, **164:17A, 165:2.**
Bonds and obligations. See within this heading, "Bonds and obligations."

Labor.
See LABOR AND WORKFORCE DEVELOPMENT.

Laboratory tests, **94:10D½, 111:184A.**

Landlord.
See LANDLORD AND TENANT.

Laws applicable to water companies, **165:2.**

Leases.
See LANDLORD AND TENANT.

Lending of money.
Borrowing money. See within this heading, "Borrowing money."

Licenses for cross connections between companies, **111:160A.**

Liens.
Districts, liens on land or buildings, **254:6.**
Mortgage to secure bond issue, **164:13, 165:2.**

WATERWORKS AND WATER SUPPLY —Cont'd

Liens —Cont'd
Nonpayment of charges, **40:42A, 40:42B.**
Dissolution, **40:42B.**
Duration, **40:42B.**
Effective date, **40:42B.**
Recording, **40:42A, 40:42B.**
Termination for inaction as to tax, **40:42B.**

Special assessments for cost of laying pipes, **40:42I.**

Limit on real estate holdings, authority for water company to exceed, **165:28.**

Loans.
Borrowing money. See within this heading, "Borrowing money."

Lodging houses, hot and cold running water to be provided, **140:22A.**

Mains.
Pipes and conduits. See within this heading, "Pipes and conduits."

Manufacturing establishments, **92:76B, 92:76C.**

Maps.
Surveys. See within this heading, "Surveys."

Massachusetts Water Management Act.
See WATER MANAGEMENT ACT.

Meters.
Charles River basin, water taken, **92:76A.**
Cities and towns borrowing for purchases, **44:8.**
Districts. See within this heading, "Districts."
Entry on premises to repair, test, etc., **165:11D.**
Fines and penalties. See within this heading, "Fines and penalties."
Injury, **165:11.**
Interference with, penalty, **165:11.**
Refund where meter inaccurate, **165:10.**
Telecommunications and energy department, testing, **165:10.**
Testing of meters.
Examination, inspection, or investigation. See within this heading, "Examination, inspection, or investigation."

WATERWORKS AND WATER SUPPLY —Cont'd

Metropolitan district commission.
See METROPOLITAN DISTRICT COMMISSION.

Mineral waters.
See MINERAL WATERS.

Mortgagees, notification of water or sewer service provider of change in possession, **244:15A.**

Mortgages to secure bond issues, **164:13, 165:2.**

Motels, mobile home parks, and camps, **140:32B.**

Municipalities and municipal finances.
Cities and towns. See within this heading, "Cities and towns."

New construction from surplus revenues, **41:69B.**

New shares, disposition, **164:18, 164:19, 165:2.**

Nonpayment of charges.
Discontinuance or shutting off service. See within this heading, "Discontinuance or shutting off service."
Liens. See within this heading, "Liens."

Notice.
Chemicals in water supply, **111:26F.**
Contractors to give notice of excavations to water companies, **82:40.**
Discontinuance of water in residential building, **165:11E.**
Hearing.
Appeal from decision of aldermen or selectmen as to opening of streets and highways, **165:8, 165:9.**
Public convenience and necessity, eminent domain, **165:4B.**
Penalty for disobeying notice to discontinue use of unsafe water, **111:122A.**
Plastic pipe connections, notice of installation, **165:1C.**

Obstructing or destroying water mains, **148:27A.**

Offensive matter, pollution of water supply by.
See WATER POLLUTION.

Office where works located, **164:80, 165:2.**

Operators of supply facilities, certification.
Application for certification, form, content, **112:87CCCC.**

WATERWORKS AND WATER SUPPLY —Cont'd

Operators of supply facilities, certification —Cont'd
Board of certification, **13:66B.**
Certificate, issuance of original and renewals, **112:87CCCC.**
Fees, **112:87CCCC.**
Operation of facilities by uncertified person, **112:87DDDD.**
Penalties, **112:87DDDD.**
Qualifications and examination, **112:87CCCC.**
Temporary emergency certification, **112:87CCCC.**
Other cities or towns.
Contracts to supply, **40:38.**
Damages for laying of pipe through, **40:39.**
Disposition of unneeded land, **40:15B.**
Other water supply systems, aid, **40:39H.**
Payment.
Nonpayment. See within this heading, "Nonpayment of charges."
Penalties.
Fines and penalties. See within this heading, "Fines and penalties."
Pensions for retiring laborers of joint water boards, **32:78, 32:78A, 32:79.**
Phosphorus, household cleaning products containing phosphorus, regulation of, **111:5R.**
Photograph on badges of employees of water companies, districts, etc., **165:11D.**
Pipes and conduits.
Aqueduct companies, **165:12 et seq.**
See AQUEDUCTS AND AQUEDUCT COMPANIES.
Authority for laying, **40:42.**
Borrowing by municipalities for construction, laying, or relaying, **44:8.**
Bylaws regulating, **40:21.**
Damage, **148:27A, 266:138A.**
Disconnecting or destroying water mains, **148:27A.**
Extension of mains, indebtedness, **44:8.**
Fixed uniform rates for laying water pipes, **40:42H.**
Highways and streets, laying of water pipes, **40:42, 40:43, 82:25, 165:8, 165:9.**

WATERWORKS AND WATER SUPPLY —Cont'd

Pipes and conduits —Cont'd
Indebtedness of city or town, **44:8.**
Laid through another town, damages, **40:39.**
Master plan of municipal planning boards with respect to locations, **41:81D.**
Obstructing or destroying water mains, **148:27A.**
Plastic pipe connections, inspection, **165:1C.**
Regulation of payment of sums due contractors after completion of certain public works, **30:39G.**
Special assessments to meet cost of laying pipes. See within this heading, "Special assessments to meet cost of laying pipes."
Tidewater license to lay pipelines, **91:14.**
Town system, **40:39C.**
Waterways, pipes and conduits, **91:14.**
Plastic pipe connections, grounding of electrical systems upon installation, **165:1C.**
Plumbers.
See PLUMBERS AND GAS FITTERS.
Police.
Arrest of person found in act of corrupting or bathing in water supply, **111:171.**
Indemnification by water districts, **41:100, 41:111F.**
Territorial jurisdiction of police employed by water boards or districts, **111:173A.**
Pollution.
See WATER POLLUTION.
Power of town to establish water supply, **40:39A.**
Preferred stock, sale of new issue, **164:19, 165:2.**
Price of water.
Rates and charges. See within this heading, "Rates and charges."
Projects for water resources, approval by environmental Protection Department, **40:39C, 44:8.**
Protection of.
Purity of supply. See within this heading, "Purity of supply, protection."

WATERWORKS AND WATER SUPPLY —Cont'd

Public acquisition of water company.
See METROPOLITAN DISTRICTS.
Public domain, **45:19 et seq.**
Public health department.
See HEALTH AND HEALTH DEPARTMENTS.
Pumping stations, municipal indebtedness, **44:8.**
Purchase of rights, **40:38, 165:4B.**
Purity of supply, protection, **40:41.**
Adoption of regulations by health department, **111:160.**
Advice of health department as to protection, **111:17.**
Pollution.
See WATER POLLUTION.
Replanting of woodland for protection of water supply, **132:33.**
Qualification of drinking water supply facilities operators, **112:87CCCC.**
Railroad locomotives, pure refrigerated drinking water, **160:172A.**
Rates and charges.
Abatement, **40:42E.**
Acceptance of law by municipalities, **40:42A.**
Appeals, **40:42E.**
Assessments, **59:21C.**
Base rates, **165:2B.**
Board of tax appeals, appeals, **40:42E.**
Board of water commissioners, powers and duties, **41:69B.**
Change, **164:93, 164:94, 165:2.**
Collection of, **40:42A et seq., 60:23.**
Depreciation fund, rates as affected, **155:5A.**
Descending unit rate basis, **40:39J½, 40:39L.**
Disconnection of fittings where charges not paid, **165:11A.**
Drinking water, **40:39J½, 40:39K.**
Filing of schedules, **164:94, 165:2, 165:2A.**
Hearings, **164:93, 164:94, 165:2.**
Interest on unpaid account, **40:42D.**
Liens. See within this heading, "Liens."
Metropolitan districts.
See METROPOLITAN DISTRICTS.

WATERWORKS AND WATER SUPPLY —Cont'd
Rates and charges —Cont'd
Nonpayment of charge.
Discontinuance or shutting off service. See within this heading, "Discontinuance or shutting off service."
Liens. See within this heading, "Liens."
Owner's recovery from tenants, 40:42F.
Pipes, fixed uniform rates for laying, 40:42H.
Preliminary tax bills, 59:23D.
Pricing system, water conservation, 40:39J.
Recovery from tenant by owners paying, 40:42F.
Reduction, 165:2.
Refusal of water supply, 270:13.
Schedule, 164:94, 165:2, 165:2A.
Surplus revenues applied in reduction, 41:69B.
Tax bill, addition of unpaid accounts, 40:42C et seq.
Tax collectors, collection, 40:42A et seq.
Certificate, 60:23.
Tax sales for nonpayment of water rates, 40:42D, 60:76B.
Tax title as affected by errors or irregularities, 60:76B.
Reclamation districts, development by water districts, 252:14B.
Records, reports, and returns.
Access by department, 164:80, 165:2.
Affiliated companies, copies of contracts, 165:4A.
Annual report of department, 165:7.
Annual returns of companies, 164:83, 164:84, 165:2.
Board of water commissioners, 41:69B.
Determination to lay water pipes, 40:42I.
Drinking water protection commission, 40:39K.
Drinking water supply facilities certification board to keep records, 13:66B.
Fee for filing statement of amount of debt due for labor performed in constructing waterworks, 262:34.
Forms.
Books and accounts of water companies, 164:81, 165:2.

WATERWORKS AND WATER SUPPLY —Cont'd
Records, reports, and returns —Cont'd
Forms —Cont'd
Station records, 164:82, 165:2.
Lien for unpaid water bills, 40:42A, 40:42B.
Meters, reports of test results, 40:39I.
Result of test of meters, 165:10.
Schedule of rates, filing, 164:94, 165:2, 165:2A.
State treasurer's annual financial statement as to districts, 10:11.
Water rate law, certificate of acceptance, 40:42A.
Recovery from tenants by owners paying charges, 40:42F.
Reforestation.
Forests and forestry. See within this heading, "Forests and forestry."
Refund where meter inaccurate, 165:10.
Refusal to supply water, penalty, 270:13.
Regional waterworks non-profit association, 21A:18.
Reports.
Records, reports, and returns. See within this heading, "Records, reports, and returns."
Reservoirs, 253:1 et seq.
See DAMS AND RESERVOIRS.
Review.
Appeals. See within this heading, "Appeals."
Rights of way.
Easements. See within this heading, "Easements."
Rules and regulations, establishment of, 165:1B.
Safety of drinking water.
Household cleaning products containing phosphorus, regulation of, 111:5R.
Safety of drinking water, regulation by environmental Protection Department, 111:5G, 111:17, 111:160.
Salaries.
Compensation. See within this heading, "Compensation."
Sales.
Lands not needed, 40:15B.
Stock in water companies, sale of new issue of preferred stock, 164:19, 165:2.

WATERWORKS AND WATER SUPPLY —Cont'd
Sales tax, exemptions, 64H:6.
Schedule of rates, 164:94, 165:2, 165:2A.
Scrip dividends of water companies, 164:11, 164:12, 165:2.
Security deposits of customers, payment of interest, 164:128.
Security interests, drinking water protection commission, 40:39K.
Selectmen or aldermen.
Commissioners, selectmen, 40:39A, 41:21, 41:23, 41:69A.
Consent to opening of streets and highways, 165:8, 165:9.
Control of system, 40:39E.
Drinking water, failure to provide, 149:106.
Hydrants, selectmen may take water for protection against fire, 165:26.
Impoundment sites, approval, 21:9A.
Laying of pipes under public ways, authorization, 40:42, 40:43.
Municipal water and light commissioners, acting, 41:21, 41:23.
Pollution of water supply, duties, 111:162, 111:163, 111:169.
Streets and highways, consent to opening, 165:8, 165:9.
Superintendent of local board, acting, 41:69.
Water department supervisor, appointment, 41:69.
Sewers.
See SEWERS AND DRAINS.
Shutting off service.
Discontinuance or shutting off service. See within this heading, "Discontinuance or shutting off service."
Snow removal chemicals, regulations as to storage and use to prevent contamination, 85:7A.
Special assessments to meet cost of laying pipes, 40:42G, 40:42H.
Commissioners, duty, 40:42I.
Fixed uniform rate, 40:42H.
Liens, assessments, 40:42I.
Procedure, 40:42G.
Recording of determination, 40:42I.

WATERWORKS AND WATER SUPPLY —Cont'd

Springs.
Defilement, **111:170, 265:28.**
Permit for bottling spring water, **94:10A et seq.**
Poisoning, **265:28.**
Public Health Department Supervision, **111:159.**
Sprinkler leakage insurance.
See SPRINKLER SYSTEMS.
Stables to be equipped with pails of water, etc., **272:86D, 272:86F.**
Stand pipes, municipal indebtedness, **44:8.**
State treasurer's annual financial statement as to water districts, **10:11.**
Station records, **164:82, 165:2.**
Stock.
Dividends, stock or scrip, **164:11, 164:12, 165:2.**
Increase or reduction of capital stock, **164:10, 164:99, 165:2.**
Issues, **165:2.**
New shares, disposition, **164:18, 164:19, 165:2.**
Preferred stock, sale of new issue, **164:19, 165:2.**
Subscription rights, **165:2.**
Streets.
Highways and streets. See within this heading, "Highways and streets."
Studies as to water favorability or feasibility.
Cities and towns, appropriations for studies, **40:5.**
Contracts and agreements, **21:9, 40B:5A.**
District planning commissions may enter into agreements, **40B:5A.**
Fire and water districts, appropriations for studies, **41:124.**
Superintendent of water department, appointment, **41:69.**
Superior courts.
Drinking water supply facility, jurisdiction to enforce employment of certified operator, **112:87DDDD.**
Installation and operation of water supply treatment facilities, enforcement of order requiring, **111:5G.**
Supervision of water companies by telecommunications and energy department, **165:4.**

WATERWORKS AND WATER SUPPLY —Cont'd

Supreme Judicial Court.
Contracts with affiliated companies, recovery of penalty for failure to file copies, **165:4A.**
Metropolitan water districts, enforcing law, **165:4A.**
Surplus revenues, disposition, **41:69B.**
Surveys.
Cities and towns. See within this heading, "Cities and towns."
Entry into land and premises, **21:9A, 40:39D.**
Swimming in water supply, penalty, **111:171.**
Taking of property.
Eminent domain. See within this heading, "Eminent domain."
Taxation.
Assessments.
Districts and tax assessors, **59:21, 59:25, 59:53.**
Special assessments to meet cost of laying pipes, **40:42G et seq.**
Collection, **40:42A et seq., 60:23.**
Corporation taxes.
Franchise taxes, **63:52A.**
Local taxes on water companies, **59:5.**
Deferral of charges for water supplied to tax exempt property, **40:42J.**
Exemption from taxation, **59:5.**
Exemptions, **59:5.**
Impoundment sites acquired by water resources commission, **21:9A.**
Lien, termination for inaction as to tax, **40:42B.**
Rates and charges.
Collection, **40:42A et seq., 60:23.**
Tax bill, addition of unpaid accounts, **40:42C et seq.**
Tax sales for nonpayment of water rates, **40:42D, 60:76B.**
Tax title as affected by errors or irregularities, **60:76B.**
Sales tax exemption, **64H:6.**
Special assessments to meet cost of laying pipes, **40:42G, 40:42H.**
Commissioners, duty, **40:42I.**
Fixed uniform rate, **40:42H.**

WATERWORKS AND WATER SUPPLY —Cont'd

Taxation —Cont'd
Special assessments to meet cost of laying pipes —Cont'd
Liens, assessments, **40:42I.**
Procedure, **40:42G.**
Recording of determination, **40:42I.**
Taxes.
Utility company franchise tax, **63:52A.**
Telecommunications and energy department.
Access to water company records, **164:80, 165:2.**
Annual report, **165:7.**
Appeals by water companies from decision of aldermen or selectmen as to opening of streets and highways, **165:9.**
Application by water company for authority to hold real estate in excess of limits, **165:28.**
Business trusts, supervision, **182:7 et seq.**
Commissioners forbidden to have interest in water companies, **25:3.**
Copies of contracts with affiliated water companies, filing, **165:4A.**
Eminent domain, functions as to water companies' exercise, **165:4B.**
Employees and assistants, **25:9.**
Enforcement of orders, **164:79, 165:2.**
Environmental Protection Department's assistance to telecommunications and energy department, **165:6.**
Establishment of rules and regulations, **165:1B.**
Expenses, **25:9.**
Meters, testing, **165:10.**
Public health department to render assistance, **165:6.**
Rates, supervision, **164:93, 164:94, 165:2.**
Supervision of water companies by, **165:4.**
To act as commissioners in taking by city or town, **165:5.**
Tenant.
See LANDLORD AND TENANT.
Termination of lien for water rates, **40:42B.**
Terns, prevention of defilement, **111:174A.**

WATERWORKS AND WATER SUPPLY —Cont'd

Testing.
Examination, inspection, or investigation. See within this heading, "Examination, inspection, or investigation."
Tidewater, license to lay pipelines, **91:14.**
Towers, municipal indebtedness, **44:8.**
Towns.
Cities and towns. See within this heading, "Cities and towns."
Transfer of franchise, **164:21, 165:2.**
Transmission facilities.
Pipes and conduits. See within this heading, "Pipes and conduits."
Transportation of animals, watering during, **272:81.**
Treatment devices for home water, **111:160C et seq.**
Treatment facilities.
Cities and towns. See within this heading, "Cities and towns."
Supply treatment facilities, authority of public health department to require installation and operation, **111:5G.**
Waste water treatment facilities. See WATER POLLUTION.
Trial or hearing.
Hearings. See within this heading, "Hearings."
Troughs, municipal appropriations, **40:5.**
Unauthorized use of water, **165:11.**
Unclaimed property.
Abandoned, lost, and unclaimed property. See within this heading, "Abandoned, lost, and unclaimed property."
Underground waters.
Coal mines to insure against polluting, **21B:5.**
Definitions, **21C:2.**
Growth and development policy committees, cities and towns, **40:4I.**
Pollution of.
See WATER POLLUTION.
Supervision by public health department, **111:159.**
Water resources division.
See WATER RESOURCES DIVISION AND COMMISSION.

WATERWORKS AND WATER SUPPLY —Cont'd

Underground waters —Cont'd
Wells.
See WELLS.
Uniform municipal accounting system, **40:39J.**
Urban redevelopment corporations may contract with municipality to establish, **121A:14.**
Use of lands not needed, **40:15B.**
Use of resources by city or town, **40:38.**
Violations of law by water companies, **164:78, 165:2.**
Wages.
Compensation. See within this heading, "Compensation."
Water management act.
See WATER MANAGEMENT ACT.
Watershed protection.
See WATERSHED PROTECTION AND FLOOD PREVENTION ACT.
Water treatment.
See WATER POLLUTION.
Water works association, membership on drinking water supply facilities board of certification, **13:66B.**
Wells.
See WELLS.
Zoning and planning, cemeteries at water supply, **114:35.**

WAY BILLS.
Bills of lading.
See BILLS OF LADING.
Motor carriers of property, submission for examination, **159B:14-159B:14B.**

WAYLAND.
Congressional district, **57:1.**
District court, **218:1.**
Medical examiner district, **38:1.**
Senatorial district, **57:3.**

WAY OF NECESSITY.
Registered land, not implied against, **185:53.**

WAYS AND MEANS COMMITTEE.
See STATE FINANCE.

WAYWARD CHILDREN, 119:1 et seq., 120:1 et seq., 218:57 et seq.
See JUVENILE COURTS AND DELINQUENT CHILDREN.

WEAPONS, 140:121 et seq.
See FIREARMS AND WEAPONS.

WEARING APPAREL.
Arsenic, penalty for sale of articles containing, **270:12.**
Caps.
Hats. See within this heading, "Hats."
Charitable corporation, donation, **255:31D.**
Children's sleepwear.
Flammable apparel. See within this heading, "Flammable apparel."
Correctional institutions.
See CORRECTIONAL INSTITUTIONS.
Distress and sale, exemption, **60:24.**
Dressing rooms in clothing stores, two-way mirror or electronic video camera, **93:89.**
Encumbrances.
Liens. See within this heading, "Liens."
Execution, exemption, **235:34.**
Fines and penalties, two-way mirror or electronic video camera in clothing store, **93:89.**
Flammable apparel.
Children's sleepwear.
Labeling requirements, **94B:1.**
Manufacture or sale, **111:186B, 148:25D.**
Eyewear, distribution and sale, **270:1A.**
Public instruction relative to flammable qualities of certain fabrics, **71:1.**
Hats.
Helmets.
See HELMETS OR HARD HATS.
Railroad employees, uniform hats, **160:177.**
United States military forces, restriction as to wearing hats, **264:10A.**
Hazardous substances.
Flammable apparel. See within this heading, "Flammable apparel."
Headgear.
Hats. See within this heading, "Hats."
Helmets.
See HELMETS OR HARD HATS.

WEARING APPAREL —Cont'd
Hotels, motels, and
roominghouses.
Loss, liability, **140:10, 140:11.**
Sale of unclaimed apparel,
140:14-140:16.
Hunter's clothing to include
certain colors, **131:71.**
Imported goods, sale and
advertising, **94:277B.**
Industrial homework, prohibition,
149:144.
Infected articles, seizure and
removal, **111:99-111:102.**
Inflammables.
Flammable apparel. See within
this heading, "Flammable
apparel."
Liens.
Seamen's apparel exempt, **102:2.**
Work and storage, **255:31A,
255:31B, 255:31D.**
Metropolitan district commission,
work clothes for certain
employees, **28:4A.**
Militia.
See MILITIA.
Motels.
Hotels, motels, and
roominghouses. See within
this heading, "Hotels,
motels, and roominghouses."
Motorcycles, wearing of protective
head gear when riding, **90:7.**
Municipal finance.
See MUNICIPAL FINANCE.
Nursing or rest homes,
responsibility for loss of or
damage to patient's clothing,
111:72.
Pawnbrokers.
See PAWNBROKERS.
Police.
See POLICE.
Public assistance recipients,
retention of income, **118E:10
(note), 177:8 (note).**
Registration and use,
110:25A-110:25C, 110:29.
Reimbursement of employee for
damages to, by patient in
state institution, **30:9C.**
Roominghouses.
Hotels, motels, and
roominghouses. See within
this heading, "Hotels,
motels, and roominghouses."
Sales tax, exemptions, **64H:6.**
Schools, wearing apparel of
students, **71:83, 71:85, 71:86.**
Seamen's apparel exempt from
lien, **102:2.**

WEARING APPAREL —Cont'd
Shoes.
See SHOES AND FOOTWEAR.
State purchases of, requirements,
7:22.
Students, **71:83, 71:85, 71:86.**
Surviving spouse and minor
children, rights, **196:1.**
Taxation exemption, **59:5.**
See TAXATION.
Trademark registration of rented
towels, aprons, garments, and
linens, violation of provisions,
110:29.
Two-way mirror, clothing store
dressing room, **93:89.**
Uniforms.
See UNIFORMS.
Video camera, clothing store
dressing room, **93:89.**

WEASELS.
Possession without permit,
authorized, **131:5.**
Removal from hole in ground,
131:76.

WEATHER.
Floods.
See FLOODS AND FLOOD
CONTROL.
Fuel assistance programs, notice
to recipients of weatherization
assistance programs of
existence, **23B:24A.**
Insurance.
See WEATHER INSURANCE.
Public works contractors, weather
protection required for
employees during certain
months, **149:44G.**
Railroad track motor cars,
protection of occupants,
160:163A.
Storms.
See STORMS.

**WEATHER AMENDMENT
BOARD.**
Employment dislocations and
assistance in reemployment of
dislocated workers, **6:17.**
Supervision by governor and
council, **6:17.**

WEATHER INSURANCE.
Authorized, **175:47.**
Capital of stock companies,
175:48, 175:51.
Combination with other classes,
**175:48, 175:48A, 175:51,
175:54.**
Fire insurance clause in policy as
to lightning, **175:99,
175:102A.**

WEATHER INSURANCE
—Cont'd
Floods.
Dividends on insurance, **175:80.**
National Flood Insurance Act,
175:102D.
Foreign insurance companies,
175:151, 175:152.
Formation of corporations, **175:49.**
Guaranty capital of mutual
companies, **175:90A, 175:93D.**
Hail insurance.
See HAIL INSURANCE.
Lightning clause.
In combination policy, **175:102A.**
In standard fire policy, **175:99.**
National Flood Insurance Act,
issuance of "association"
policies by companies
participating in programs,
175:102D.
Number of risks in mutual
companies, **175:90A, 175:93D.**
Rates and rating organizations
applied, **174A:4, 175A:4.**
Reinsuring risks, **175:54B.**
Stock or mutual plan, **175:48,
175:48A.**

WEAVERS.
Fines, regulated, **149:153,
149:154.**
Specifications as to work to be
done and rate of wages to be
furnished, **149:155-149:157.**

WEBSTER.
Congressional district, **57:1.**
District court, **218:1.**
Medical examiner district, **38:1.**
Senatorial district, **57:3.**

WEBWORMS.
Suppression, **132:11.**

WEEDS.
Algae.
See ALGAE.
Appropriations by town for
suppression, **40:5.**
Aquatic nuisances, control, **40:5,
111:5E, 111:5F.**
Forestry practices, demonstrations
of weeding, **132:6.**
Orchards, inspection for and
control of weeds within,
128:24.
Pest control definitions, **132B:3.**
Seeds.
See SEEDS.
Veterans' graves, care, **115:9.**

WEEKENDS.
Saturday.
See SATURDAYS.

WEEKENDS —Cont'd
Special sentences to served,
279:6A.
Sundays.
See SUNDAYS AND
HOLIDAYS.

**WEEKLY PAYMENT OF
WAGES, 29:31,
149:148-149:150.**
See WAGES, SALARIES, AND
COMPENSATION.

WEIGHT REDUCING SALON.
Employment of women and
minors, **149:56, 149:66.**
Health spas, weight loss and
controlled services, **93:79.**
Hours of labor, **149:56, 149:57,
149:67, 149:68, 149:78.**

**WEIGHTS AND MEASURES,
94:176-94:180, 98:1 et seq.,
99:1 et seq.**
Agricultural products.
Farm products, **94:117A to
94:117F.**
Aircraft certificates, weight as
factor in determining fees for
registration, **90:49.**
Aldermen.
See ALDERMEN AND
SELECTMEN.
Annual testing of devices, **94:41,
94:42, 98:33, 98:33A.**
Anthracite coal, standard sizes,
94:239A.
Antifreeze solutions, statement of
weight or measure on
containers, **94:303I.**
Appeal from civil citation, **98:29A.**
Appeal from order of deputy
director of standards, **98:29.**
Appointment of weighers and
surveyors of goods and
commodities, **41:85, 41:87A,
94:219.**
Arrest of hawker, peddler, or
transient vendor, power of
sealer, **101:32.**
Automatic weighing and
measuring machines, devices
for testing accuracy, **98:46.**
Avoirdupois, what constitutes,
98:2.
Axles.
See MOTOR VEHICLES.
Bark, **94:296-94:303.**
Fees, **94:300.**
Barrel, what constitutes, **94:172.**
Baskets.
Fuel, records concerning baskets
used in soil, **94:246.**

WEIGHTS AND MEASURES
—Cont'd
Baskets —Cont'd
Less than standard measure,
seizure of baskets
containing, **94:98.**
Bass, **130:100A.**
Beef cattle, weighing, **94:140,
94:141.**
Berries.
Containers, **94:98.**
Cranberry containers,
94:115-94:117.
Strike or level measure required
with respect, **94:99.**
Bicycle weight counted as part of
baggage of railroad passenger,
160:196.
Board measure presumed rule for
evidentiary purposes, **96:11A.**
Bond of fish weigher, **41:88, 41:89.**
Boxing gloves, required weight,
147:38.
Box measurements for farm
product sold at wholesale,
94:99A.
Bread.
Bakery product regulations,
power to adopt, **94:9.**
Loaves, weight, **94:7-94:9.**
Bridges.
See BRIDGES.
Bulk milk trailers as exempt from
certain weight limitations,
90:19.
Bushel measure for coke, charcoal
and kindling wood, **94:242.**
Canal toll collector weighing load
on boat, **88:11.**
Capacity, metric measurement,
99:2.
Cargoes of certain vessels,
determining weight,
102:6-102:14.
Carriers.
See CARRIERS.
Cental, **94:174, 94:222.**
Certificates and certification.
Aircraft certificates, weight as
factor in determining fees
for registration, **90:49.**
Approval, certificate, **98:53.**
Fuel, weight certificate required
in sale, **94:244.**
Hundredweight, certificate of
weigher where grain or feed
is sold, **94:222.**
Inspections, **94:244.**
Oil delivery certificates or
memoranda, examination or
inspection, **94:303F.**

WEIGHTS AND MEASURES
—Cont'd
Certificates and certification
—Cont'd
Prima facie evidence, weighers
and measurers certificate,
106:1-202.
Sand and gravel, certificates in
connection with sale,
94:244, 94:245.
Charcoal and coke, **94:244-94:246,
94:248, 94:249.**
Bushel measure, **94:242.**
Citations.
Civil citations for violations,
98:29A.
Cities and towns.
Aldermen.
See ALDERMEN AND
SELECTMEN.
Annual testing of devices used
in certain towns, **98:33A.**
Fuel, weighing of loads or
containers, **94:245.**
Lighters, regulation of marking
and weighing, **102:14.**
Logs.
See LOGS AND TIMBER.
Standards, **98:5, 98:6, 98:32.**
Weighers and measurers,
41:85-41:90.
Civil service status of inspectors
and deputies, **31:48, 31:52.**
Clams and clam bait.
Bait, **94:85.**
Quahaugs, sale by weight,
94:88B.
Soft shell claims exemption from
requirement of sale by
weight, **94:92B.**
Clinical thermometers, **98:9-98:14.**
See CLINICAL
THERMOMETERS.
Coal.
See COAL.
Coke.
Charcoal and coke. See within
this heading, "Charcoal and
coke."
Commercial fertilizer, short
weight, **128:72.**
Complaint.
Complainants.
Informers. See within this
heading, "Informers."
Inspection and testing upon
complaint, **98:52.**
Violation of law, **98:32.**
Condemned weighing or
measuring devices.
Disposition, **98:54, 98:55.**

WEIGHTS AND MEASURES
—Cont'd
Condemned weighing or
measuring devices —Cont'd
Penalty for use, **98:25-98:27,
98:55.**
Congress may prescribe standards
of, **US Const Art 1 Sec 8 cl
5.**
Consumer affairs and business
regulation office, division and
deputy director of standards
in.
Deputy director of standards.
See within this heading,
"Deputy director of
standards."
Containers.
Antifreeze solutions, statement
of weight or measure on
containers, **94:303I.**
Barrel, what constitutes, **94:172.**
Baskets. See within this
heading, "Baskets."
Berries. See within this heading,
"Berries."
False substances in, to increase
weight or measure, **94:305.**
Fruit, nut, and vegetable
containers. See within this
heading, "Fruit, nut, and
vegetable containers,
standards."
Fuels, power of certain officers
to require weighing of
containers, **94:245.**
Grain and meal, **94:96, 94:174A.**
Hogshead, what constitutes,
94:172.
Lubricating oil, **98:14A.**
Milk and milk products, **98:15,
98:51.**
Nails, **94:278, 94:279.**
Net contents to appear on
container, **94:181-94:184.**
Prepackaged commodities. See
within this heading,
"Prepackaged commodities."
Standard box and half box for
sale of farm produce at
wholesale, **94:99A.**
Testing by sealers, **98:23.**
Unauthorized marking, **98:24.**
Viscous or semisolid
commodities, cartons used
for sale, **98:22-98:24.**
Conviction of crime.
See CONVICTION OF CRIME.
Cordwood measurers,
94:296-94:298.

WEIGHTS AND MEASURES
—Cont'd
Counterfeiting.
Forgery and counterfeiting. See
within this heading,
"Forgery and
counterfeiting."
Cranberry containers,
94:115-94:117.
Cubic foot as unit of measure for
gas sold by meter, **164:111,
164:115.**
Customers, weighing of articles
sold to be in view, **98:56A.**
Dairy products.
Milk and milk products. See
within this heading, "Milk
and milk products."
Definitions, **94:176, 98:1.**
Deputies and inspectors, civil
service status, **31:48, 31:52.**
Deputy director of standards,
98:29 et seq.
Appeal from rule or order, **98:29.**
Bulk milk tanks, calibration and
inspection, **98:46A.**
Certification, **98:29.**
Custody of standard weighing
and measuring devices,
98:3.
Defined, **94:295A, 98:1.**
Discretion as to testing various
kinds of measuring devices,
98:46.
Enforcement of law by, **94:248,
94:249F.**
Fines and penalties,
establishment by director,
98:29.
Glass easures used by
apothecaries, specifications,
98:47.
Investigators, examiners, and
other employees having
police powers, may upon
request of registrar of motor
vehicles, be appointed
weighers and measurers,
41:87A.
Laboratory testing of weights
and measures, director may
establish fee schedule,
98:46.
Leather.
See LEATHER.
Meters for measuring heating
oil, regulations for heating
and testing, **98:28A.**
Metric weights and measures,
duties, **99:3, 99:4.**
Milk and milk products, **98:15,
98:46A.**

WEIGHTS AND MEASURES
—Cont'd
Deputy director of standards
—Cont'd
Municipal weighers, measurers
and surveyors, form and
inspection of records, **41:86.**
Powers and duties, **98:29-98:33.**
Taxi meters, accuracy, **98:45.**
Textile looms, pick clocks, **98:41.**
Weighers and surveyors of goods
and commodities,
inspections of records,
41:86.
Diamonds and precious stones,
standards of weight, **99:1.**
District sealers, **98:36.**
Druggists.
Pharmacists and druggists. See
within this heading,
"Pharmacists and
druggists."
Duplicate set of weights and
balances to be provided, **98:38,
98:40.**
Edgings, sale, **94:247.**
Egg grades, **94:90B.**
Electric companies.
See GAS AND ELECTRIC
COMPANIES.
Enforcement of provisions relating
to, **98:29.**
Comprehensive enforcement
programs.
Annual reports by
municipalities on, **98:37.**
Comprehensive weights and
measures enforcement
systems, **98:35.**
Inadequate weights and
measures enforcement
systems, **98:36A.**
Engineers and surveyors.
Surveyors. See within this
heading, "Surveyors."
Entry on premises, when
authorized, **98:52.**
Evidence.
Board measure, presumed rule,
96:11A.
False or condemned device,
possession, **98:26, 98:55.**
Illegal devices, possession,
98:55.
Metric equivalents,
determination, **99:2.**
Seizure of illegal devices, **98:54,
98:55.**
Weighers and measurers,
certificate as prima facie
evidence, **106:1-202.**

WEIGHTS AND MEASURES
—Cont'd
Examination.
  Inspection and testing. See
    within this heading,
    "Inspection and testing."
False weights and measures.
  Fines and penalties. See within
    this heading, "Fines and
    penalties."
  Jurisdiction over prosecution,
    94:180.
Farm products, **94:117A-94:117F.**
Fees.
  Aircraft certificates, weight as
    factor in determining fees
    for registration, **90:49.**
  Bark, **94:300.**
  Bulk milk tank, recalibration
    fee, **98:46A.**
  Fish, fees for weighing, **94:88.**
  Inspection and testing of
    weighing and measuring
    devices, **98:56.**
  Laboratory testing of weights
    and measures, director may
    establish fee schedule,
    98:46.
  Sealers. See within this heading,
    "Sealers."
  Taxi meter, sealing, **98:56.**
  Vehicle tanks, sealing, **98:56.**
  Weighers, **94:221.**
  Wood and bark, measurers,
    94:300.
Female employees, eligibility to
  appointment as coal weighers,
  94:238.
Fertilizer, short weight, **128:72.**
Fines and penalties, **98:1-98:57.**
  Apothecaries' weights or
    measures, use of untested,
    98:48.
  Civil citations for violations,
    98:29A.
  Condemned weighing or
    measuring devices,
    98:25-98:27, 98:55.
  Deputy director of standards,
    establishment, **98:29.**
  False weight or measure,
    94:176, 94:177, 94:305.
  Devices, **98:25-98:27, 98:55.**
  Fuel, dealer possessing
    fraudulent measuring
    devices for sale, **94:249.**
  Grain and meal, **94:224.**
  Metric system, **99:5.**
  Minimum penalties, **94:177.**
  Municipal weighers and
    measurers of goods and
    commodities,
    misrepresentation, **41:86.**

WEIGHTS AND MEASURES
—Cont'd
Fines and penalties —Cont'd
  False weight or measure
    —Cont'd
    Sales, **94:177, 98:25 et seq.**
  Fish landed from vessel, **94:86.**
  Foreign substances in containers
    to increase weight, **94:305.**
  Fuels, penalty for short weight
    or measure, **94:243, 94:248,
    94:249.**
  Grain and meal. See within this
    heading, "Grain and meal."
  Grass seed, sale other than by
    weight, **94:237.**
  Hindering municipal weighers of
    fish, **41:90A.**
  Ice cream containers, violation of
    provisions, **98:24.**
  Incorrect or inaccurate devices,
    98:25-98:28, 98:48.
  Interference with inspector,
    94:249B.
  Leather not officially measured,
    sale, **95:4.**
  Metric weights and measures,
    illegal use, **99:5.**
  Misrepresentation.
    Price of commodity or service
      sold by weights or
      measure,
      misrepresentation, **94:177.**
  Motor vehicles.
    See MOTOR VEHICLES.
  Neglect of duty.
    Sealer, **98:7, 98:32.**
    Weigher, **94:178.**
  Obstruction of or interference
    with inspector, **94:249B.**
  Paper cartons, violation of
    provisions, **98:24.**
  Placing scale or weighing device
    so weight indicator may not
    be read and weighing
    operations be observed by
    purchaser, **98:56A.**
  Possession of illegal weighing
    and measuring devices,
    98:26, 98:55.
  Public weigher, refusal or
    neglect to act, **94:178.**
  Quahogs in the shell, sale
    otherwise than by weight,
    94:88B.
  Refusal to permit testing of
    weighing or measuring
    device, **98:52.**
  Removal of marking of incorrect
    or unsealed device, **98:25.**
  Removal of notice of
    nonconformity to standards,
    98:53.

WEIGHTS AND MEASURES
—Cont'd
Fines and penalties —Cont'd
  Sales, violations, **94:174A,
    94:222.**
  Sealer.
    Failure to comply with
      direction, **98:42.**
    Hindering or obstruction,
      98:34, 98:42.
    Impersonation, **98:31.**
    Neglect, penalty, **98:7, 98:32.**
    Seal, violations concerning,
      98:31.
  Shellfish, violations as to sales
    by weight, **94:88B, 94:92B.**
  Short weight, giving of, **94:177.**
  Statutory requirements,
    violation, **98:31, 98:32.**
  Taxi meters, failure to comply
    with rules and regulations
    to insure accuracy, **98:45.**
  Thread, illegal sale, **94:288.**
  Unauthorized marking of
    containers, **98:24.**
  Unsealed devices, **98:24-98:28,
    98:48.**
  Untested or inaccurate devices,
    98:24-98:28.
  Violating oath of office by
    weigher or surveyor, **41:90.**
  Weighers, violations by, **94:224.**
Firewood.
  See FIREWOOD.
Fish.
  Clams and clam bait. See within
    this heading, "Clams and
    clam bait."
  Landed from vessel or boat,
    weighing of fish,
    94:86-94:88.
  Marine fish.
    See MARINE FISH AND
      FISHERIES.
  Quintal of fish, what constitutes,
    94:84.
  Sale by weight, **94:77F, 94:92B.**
  Weighers.
    Fish, weighers of. See within
      this heading, "Fish,
      weighers."
Fish, weighers, **41:88.**
  Bonds, **41:88, 41:89.**
  Deputy, **41:89.**
  Hindering, etc., **41:90A.**
Flour.
  See FLOUR.
Food, **94:176-94:180.**
Foreign substances placed in
  containers to increase weight,
  94:305.

WEIGHTS AND MEASURES
—Cont'd

Forgery and counterfeiting.
  Leather measurer's marks, **95:5.**
  Seal of sealer, **98:31.**
Fraud and deceit.
  False weights and measures. See
    within this heading, "False
    weights and measures."
  Fines and penalties. See within
    this heading, "Fines and
    penalties."
  Forgery and counterfeiting. See
    within this heading,
    "Forgery and
    counterfeiting."
  Price of commodities or services
    sold by weight or measure,
    misrepresentation, **94:177.**
Fruit, nut, and vegetable
  containers, standards,
  94:96-94:99B.
  Berries. See within this heading,
    "Berries."
  Dealer possessing fraudulent
    measuring devices for sale,
    94:249.
  Inspection, **94:245, 94:249A.**
  Paper bags used in sale, **94:243.**
  Records concerning baskets used
    in sale, **94:246.**
  Short measure in sale, **94:243,**
    94:248.
  Weight certificate, requirement
    in connection with sale,
    94:244.
Fuel.
  Bushel measurement, **94:242.**
  Charcoal and coke. See within
    this heading, "Charcoal and
    coke."
  Coal.
    See COAL.
  Cubic foot as measure unit for
    gas sold by meter, **164:111,**
    164:115.
  Dealer possessing fraudulent
    measuring devices for sale,
    94:249.
  Firewood.
    See FIREWOOD.
  Inspection, **94:245, 94:249A,**
    94:303F.
  Meters.
    See METERS AND
      METERING.
  Oil delivery certificates or
    memoranda, examination or
    inspection, **94:303F.**
  Paper bags used in sale, **94:243.**
  Records concerning baskets used
    in sale, **94:246.**

WEIGHTS AND MEASURES
—Cont'd

Fuel —Cont'd
  Sealers, enforcement of
    provisions as to sale, **94:248,**
    94:249A.
  Short measure in sale, **94:243,**
    94:248, 94:249.
  Tickets showing quantity in load
    hauled from wharf or
    landing place, **94:302.**
  Weight certificate, requirement
    in connection with sale,
    94:244.
Gems, standards of weight, **99:1.**
Goods and commodities, weighers
  and surveyors of, **41:85-41:90.**
Grades and standards, **98:2-98:11.**
Grain and meal, **94:219-94:224.**
  Aldermen and selectmen.
    Appointment of grain
      weighers, **94:219.**
    Fixing fees of grain weighers,
      94:221.
  False or inaccurate weighing
    devices, **94:224.**
  Retail sale to be by weight or in
    standard container, **94:96.**
  Short weight, **94:222.**
  Standard weights of containers,
    94:174A.
  Testing of grain or measuring
    device, refusal to permit,
    98:52.
  Weighers, **94:219, 94:221,**
    94:224.
Gravel.
  Sand and gravel. See within this
    heading, "Sand and gravel."
Guarantee by supplier as
  exonerating dealer, **94:184.**
Hawkers, peddlers, and transient
  vendors, power of sealer to
  arrest for violations, **101:32.**
Hay, **94:236.**
  Scales, testing, **98:49.**
Heating oil, sealing and testing of
  meters for measuring, **98:28A.**
Herdsgrass seed, sale, **94:237.**
Highways and streets, weight of
  vehicles, **85:3-85:32, 90:19A.**
  Turnpike authority, **81A:19.**
Hogshead, what constitutes,
  94:172.
Hundredweight, **94:174.**
  Certificate of weigher where
    grain or feed is sold, **94:222.**
  What constitutes, **98:2.**
Ice cream containers, **98:20, 98:21,**
  98:24.
Imitation of seal used by sealer or
  deputy, possession, **98:31.**

WEIGHTS AND MEASURES
—Cont'd

Impersonation of sealer, **98:31.**
Incorrect measuring devices,
  penalty, **98:25-98:28, 98:48.**
Informers.
  Notice forbidding use of
    weighing device, reward to
    complainant as to removal,
    98:53.
  Unsealed weighing devices,
    complainant may recover
    forfeiture for use, **98:27.**
Inspection and testing.
  Annual testing of devices, **98:33,**
    98:33A, 98:41, 98:42.
  Apothecaries' weights and
    measures, **98:32, 98:47,**
    98:48.
  Automated electronic retail
    check out systems, **98:56D.**
  Berry containers, **94:98.**
  Charcoal scales, **94:244, 94:245.**
  Clinical thermometers,
    98:12-98:14.
  Coal scales, **94:244, 94:245.**
  Coke scales, **94:244, 94:245.**
  Complaint, **98:52.**
  Containers, **98:23.**
  Devices used in standardizing
    production, determining
    wages, etc., **98:46.**
  Fees, **98:56.**
  Fuel, **94:245, 94:249A, 94:303F.**
  Glass milk or cream bottles,
    98:51.
  Hay scales, **98:49.**
  Ice cream cans, molds, and
    containers, **98:21.**
  Impersonating sealer or
    counterfeiting seal, **98:31.**
  Inspectors.
    Weighers and measurers. See
      within this heading,
      "Weighers and
      measurers."
  Interference with inspectors,
    penalties, **94:249B.**
  Leather measuring devices,
    98:44.
  Local standards and testing
    devices, **98:32.**
  Lubricating oil, glass jars and
    bottles used for sale,
    98:14A.
  Manufacturer may request,
    98:29.
  Marks and certificates, **98:53.**
  Meters for measuring heating
    oil, **98:28A.**
  Metric system devices, **99:4.**

WEIGHTS AND MEASURES
—Cont'd
Inspection and testing —Cont'd
Milk and milk products, **98:51.**
Motor vehicle registrar's request, inspectors, examiners, and other employees having police powers may be appointed weighers and measurers, **41:87A.**
Municipal weighers, inspection of records, **41:86.**
Obstruction or interference. See within this heading, "Obstruction or interference."
Official seals, **98:31.**
Pharmacists' and druggists' weights and measures, **98:32, 98:47, 98:48.**
Price registering devices, **98:43.**
Records of weighers and surveyors of goods and commodities, **41:86.**
Refusal to permit testing of weighing or measuring device, **98:52.**
Request, **98:50.**
Road materials, checking of weights, **94:245.**
Sealers. See within this heading, "Sealers."
State institutions, devices used, **98:33.**
Steelyards, annual inspection, **98:8.**
Taximeters, **98:45.**
Towns, devices used in certain, **98:33A.**
Untested or inaccurate devices, **98:24-98:28.**
Interference.
Obstruction or interference. See within this heading, "Obstruction or interference."
Jurisdiction over prosecutions for false weights and measures, **94:180.**
Labor and workforce development department.
Deputy director of standards. See within this heading, "Deputy director of standards."
Leather, **94:5.**
Generally.
See LEATHER.
Length, metric measurement, **99:2.**
Lighters, weighing, **102:6-102:14.**

WEIGHTS AND MEASURES
—Cont'd
Lime casks, **94:265.**
Liquefied petroleum gas meters, sealing and testing, **98:28A.**
Liquid measures, fees for sealing, **98:56.**
Loaves of bread, weight, **94:7-94:9.**
Lobsters, short, **130:44, 130:48.**
Location of weighing devices, **98:56A.**
Logs and timber, **94:296-94:303, 96:7 et seq.**
See LOGS AND TIMBER.
Lubricating oil, containers for sale, **98:14A.**
Marine fish.
See MARINE FISH AND FISHERIES.
Meal.
Grain and meal. See within this heading, "Grain and meal."
Measurers.
Weighers and measurers. See within this heading, "Weighers and measurers."
Meat.
Beef cattle offered for sale, **94:140, 94:141.**
Prepackaged meat, **98:56B.**
Retail sale by weight, **94:92B.**
Meters.
See METERS AND METERING.
Metric system, **99:1-99:5.**
See METRIC SYSTEM.
Milk and milk products, **98:15 et seq.**
Bulk milk trailers as exempt from certain weight limitations, **90:19.**
Deputy director of standards, calibration and inspection of bulk milk tanks, **98:46A.**
Inspection and testing of bottles, **98:51.**
Misbranding of food, **94:187.**
Misrepresentations.
Fraud and deceit. See within this heading, "Fraud and deceit."
Motor carriers.
See CARRIERS.
Motor vehicles, **41:87A, 85:19 et seq., 85:30 et seq.**
See MOTOR VEHICLES.
Municipalities.
Cities and towns. See within this heading, "Cities and towns."
Nails.
Marking weight of containers, **94:279.**

WEIGHTS AND MEASURES
—Cont'd
Nails —Cont'd
Maximum weight of containers, **94:278.**
National bureau of standards.
Metric equivalents for weights and measures, determination, **99:2.**
Surveyor, testing tape, **97:3.**
Neglect of duty.
Fines and penalties. See within this heading, "Fines and penalties."
Net contents to appear on food packages, **94:181-94:184.**
Nonconformity to statutory provisions as affecting right to recover for goods sold, **98:28.**
Notice forbidding use of device, **98:53.**
Nuts.
Fruit, nut, and vegetable containers. See within this heading, "Fruit, nut, and vegetable containers, standards."
Oath of weighers and surveyors of goods and commodities, **41:85.**
Violation, **41:90.**
Obstruction or interference.
Inspector of division of standards, **94:249B.**
Municipal fish weighers, hindering, **41:90A.**
Sealer or deputy, obstructing in performance of duty, **98:34, 98:42.**
Office clinical thermometer, **98:10.**
Packages.
Containers. See within this heading, "Containers."
Paper or fiber cartons, standards where used for sale of viscous or semi-solid commodities, **98:22-98:24.**
Particular commodities, certain laws inapplicable to weighers, **41:87.**
Penalties.
Fines and penalties. See within this heading, "Fines and penalties."
Pharmacists and druggists.
Duplicate sets of weights, etc., to be provided upon request, **98:38.**
Glass measures, **98:47.**
Standard for apothecary's weight, **98:3.**
Testing of weights and measures, **98:32, 98:47, 98:48.**

WEIGHTS AND MEASURES
—Cont'd
Pharmacists and druggists
—Cont'd
Untested weight or measure,
98:48.
Ponds, measuring, **131:46.**
Possession of illegal weighing and
measuring devices, **98:26,**
98:55.
Poultry.
See POULTRY AND POULTRY
PRODUCTS.
Pound, relationship between
avoirdupois and troy pound,
98:2.
Prepackaged commodities.
Labeling to show weight, **94:181.**
Meat, poultry or fish, **98:56B.**
Price of commodities sold by
weight or measure, penalty for
misrepresentations, **94:177.**
Price-registering devices,
inspection and testing, **98:43.**
Public institutions, weighing and
measuring devices used,
98:33.
Public weighers.
Weighers and measurers. See
within this heading,
"Weighers and measurers."
Quahaugs, sale by weight only,
94:88B.
Qualifications of weighers and
surveyors of goods and
commodities, **41:85.**
Quintal of fish, what constitutes,
94:84.
Records and reports.
Bulk milk tanks, calibrating,
sealing and checking,
98:46A.
Commodities, records of
weighers, measurers and
surveyors, **41:86.**
Consumer affairs, office of.
Annual report of director,
98:57.
Findings of annual tests of
devices used in state
institutions, etc., **98:33.**
Fish landed from vessel, record
of weight, **94:87.**
Fuel, baskets used in sale,
94:246.
Municipalities.
Annual report on weights and
measures program, **98:37.**
Road material, weighing or
measuring, **94:246.**
Sealers, annual report, **98:34.**

WEIGHTS AND MEASURES
—Cont'd
Removal from employment of
weighers, measurers, and
surveyors of goods and
commodities, **41:85.**
Reports.
Records and reports. See within
this heading, "Records and
reports."
Retail sale of meat by weight,
94:92B.
Reweighing, **94:245.**
Safekeeping of municipal
standards, **98:6.**
Sales by weight or measure,
94:176-94:180.
Salt water fish weighers.
Fish, weighers of. See within
this heading, "Fish,
weighers."
Sand and gravel.
Certificates in connection with
sale, **94:244, 94:245.**
Vessels transporting to be
weighed and marked,
102:6-102:14.
Saw logs, rule for determining
number of board feet, **96:11A.**
Scallops sold by weight, **94:88B.**
Sealers, **98:34-98:56.**
Appointment, **98:34-98:36.**
Failure to appoint as
inadequate enforcement
system, **98:36A.**
Arrest of hawker, peddler or
transient vendor, power to
make, **101:32.**
Certification, **98:29, 98:35,**
98:36.
Coal, inspection and
condemnation, **94:249F.**
Custody and accountability for
standards and seal received,
98:31, 98:39.
Deputies, **98:35.**
Devices for weighing and
measuring, testing,
98:12-98:28.
District sealers, **98:36.**
Duplicate sets of measures,
98:38, 98:40.
Duty as to safekeeping on
municipal standards, **98:6.**
Expenses, allowance, **98:34,**
98:35.
Fees, **98:56.**
Accountability, **98:34-98:36.**
Fines and penalties. See within
this heading, "Fines and
penalties."

WEIGHTS AND MEASURES
—Cont'd
Sealers —Cont'd
Fuel, enforcement of provisions
as to sale, **94:248, 94:249A.**
Impersonation, **98:31.**
Inspection and testing.
Annual testing of devices,
98:41, 98:42.
Coal, **94:249F.**
Devices for weighing and
measuring, **98:12-98:28.**
Municipal standards, **98:32.**
Metric weights and measures,
99:3, 99:4.
Municipal, appointment and
deputies, **98:34, 98:35.**
Neglect, **98:7, 98:32.**
Penalties.
Fines and penalties. See
within this heading,
"Fines and penalties."
Repairs and adjustments,
compensation, **98:56.**
Report, annual, **98:34.**
Salary, how determined, **98:34,**
98:35.
Selectmen may appoint, when,
98:35.
Small towns, **98:35.**
Stencil, use for sealer's
inspection mark, **98:53.**
Testing by sealers, **98:23.**
Searches and seizures.
Baskets containing less than
standard measure, seizure,
94:98.
Evidence, seizure of weighing
and measuring devices,
98:54, 98:55.
Penalty for use of condemned
weighing or measuring
devices, **98:25-98:27, 98:55.**
Second and subsequent offenses of
misrepresenting price of
commodity or service sold by
weight or measure, **94:177.**
Seeds.
See SEEDS.
Seizure.
Searches and seizures. See
within this heading,
"Searches and seizures."
Selectmen.
See ALDERMEN AND
SELECTMEN.
Semisolid commodities, sale,
98:22-98:24.
Sewing thread, **94:285, 94:287,**
94:288.
Ships.
See SHIPS AND OTHER
WATERCRAFT.

WEIGHTS AND MEASURES
—Cont'd

Short lobsters, **130:44, 130:48.**

Shucked scallops and quahaugs, sale by weight only, **94:88B.**

Special deputies to check receipt or disbursement of supplies in state institutions or departments, **98:33.**

Standards, **98:2-98:11.**

State police, appointment of state police as weighers and measurers, **41:87A.**

Turnpike authority, **81A:19.**

State standards, **98:3, 98:4.**

Steelyards, annual inspection, **98:8.**

Stencil, certain devices to be marked, **98:53.**

Stone.

Diamonds and precious stones, standards of weight, **99:1.**

Vessels or lighters transporting, **102:6-102:14.**

Strike or level measure required with respect to berries, **94:99.**

Surface, metric measurement, **99:2.**

Surveyors.

Goods and commodities, weighers and surveyors of, **41:85-41:90.**

Measuring devices other than standardized measuring tapes, **97:3.**

Tapes, annual comparison, **97:3.**

Table of equivalents between metric system and other weights and measures, **99:2.**

Taxicabs.

See TAXICABS.

Term of office for weighers, measurers, and surveyors of goods and commodities, **41:85.**

Testing.

Inspection and testing. See within this heading, "Inspection and testing."

Textile factory employees lifting objects over certain weight, **149:141A.**

Thread for sewing, etc., **94:285, 94:287, 94:288.**

Timber, **94:296-94:303, 96:7 et seq.**

See LOGS AND TIMBER.

Timothy seed, sale, **94:237.**

Tolerances and exemptions with respect to marked net contents of food packages, **94:182.**

Tomatoes sold at wholesale or retail, Massachusetts lug, **94:99A.**

WEIGHTS AND MEASURES
—Cont'd

Ton.

See TON.

Towns.

Cities and towns. See within this heading, "Cities and towns."

Traffic regulations.

See TRAFFIC REGULATIONS AND RULES OF THE ROAD.

Trailers and semi-trailers, **90:19, 90:19A.**

Troy pound, relationship to avoirdupois pound, **98:2.**

Trucks and trailers, dimensions and weights, **90:19, 90:19A.**

Unsealed weighing devices, complainant may recover forfeiture for use, **98:27.**

Value of goods sold by unsealed devices, **98:28.**

Vegetables.

Fruit, nut, and vegetable containers. See within this heading, "Fruit, nut, and vegetable containers, standards."

Venue of prosecution for false weight or measure, **94:180.**

Vessels.

See SHIPS AND OTHER WATERCRAFT.

Vibrating steelyards, annual inspection, **98:8.**

View of customer, weighing of articles sold to be done, **98:56A.**

Viscous commodities, sale, **98:22-98:24.**

Weighers and measurers.

Aldermen.

See ALDERMEN AND SELECTMEN.

Appointment, duties and penalties, **41:87A, 94:178.**

Beef cattle, **94:140, 94:141.**

Bond of fish weighers and deputy weighers, **41:88, 41:89.**

Certificate as prima facie evidence, **106:1-202.**

Certification of inspectors, sealers and deputies, **98:29.**

Coal, weighers, **94:238.**

Fees, **94:221.**

Goods and commodities, weighers and surveyors of, **41:85-41:90.**

Grain, weighers, **94:219-94:221, 94:224.**

WEIGHTS AND MEASURES
—Cont'd

Weighers and measurers —Cont'd

Gravel, vessel or lighters transporting, **102:6-102:14.**

Hay weighers, **94:236.**

Leather.

See LEATHER.

Lumber, **96:7-96:11A.**

Motor vehicles.

See MOTOR VEHICLES.

Neglect of duty, **94:178.**

Records, **41:86.**

Sealers. See within this heading, "Sealers."

Vessel weighers.

See SHIPS AND OTHER WATERCRAFT.

Wood and bark, **94:296-94:303.**

"Weighing or measuring device" defined, **98:1.**

Width.

See WIDTH.

Women employees, eligibility to appointment as coal weighers, **94:238.**

Wood, **94:296-94:303, 96:7-96:11A.**

Firewood.

See FIREWOOD.

Logs.

See LOGS AND TIMBER.

WEIRS.
See MARINE FISH AND FISHERIES.

WELDING.

Eye protective devices to be worn while attending classes in public schools, **71:55C.**

Motor vehicles, reassembling vehicle from other vehicles, **90D:20F.**

WELFARE AND SOCIAL SERVICES, 18:1 et seq., 18B:1 et seq.

Abandoned children, increase in age limitation as to reports and care concerning, **119:23.**

Abandoned property law, exceptions, **200A:14.**

Ability to pay, consideration, **18B:4.**

Abused.

See ABUSED AND NEGLECTED CHILDREN.

Accounts and accounting.

Separate accounts of department, **18B:7.**

Trust funds of department, commissioner to deposit, **18B:18.**

WELFARE AND SOCIAL SERVICES —Cont'd

Acknowledgment of illegitimate children, motion for approval, **209C:11.**

Administration and finance executive office, advertisements prior to rental of public building, **7:40H.**

Administration of programs, **18B:2.**

Administrators and executors, **195:16.**

Adoption of children.
See ADOPTION OF CHILDREN.

Advancement of funds, **18:17, 18B:20.**

Advisory boards, **18:7, 111:4.**
Commissioners, **18:3, 18B:6, 18B:6A.**
Community service boards, appointment, membership, and duties, **18:7.**
Medical assistance division, **118E:6.**
Social services department, **18B:16.**

Affordable housing trust fund, **121D:1 to 121D:5.**

Age.
See AGE.

Aged.
See AGED AND DISABLED, ASSISTANCE.

Agencies, authority of area boards to receive funds, **18B:15.**

Aliens, receipt of benefits, **6A:16C.**
Medicaid, **118E:16D.**

Allocation of social services, priorities, **18B:4.**

Annual budgets and plans, preparation and submission to commissioner by area social services directors, **18B:12.**

Annual report to general court by commissioner, **18B:7.**

Appeals.
Applicants for or recipients of public aid, **18:16.**
Medical assistance division, **118E:25, 118E:38, 118E:47, 118E:48.**
Placement of children, orders, **119:29B.**

Appropriations.
Advancements, **18B:20.**
Limitation, **18B:7.**
Services subject, **18B:4.**
Tewksburg hospital, payment from appropriation for diseased persons, **122:13.**

WELFARE AND SOCIAL SERVICES —Cont'd

Approval of services by medical assistance division, **118E:19.**

Area boards.
Budgets, **18B:12, 18B:15.**
Contracts and agreements, **18B:15.**
Directors.
Area directors. See within this heading, "Area directors."
Duties and powers, **18B:15.**
Establishment, **18:7.**
Meetings of area board, selection of officers, **18B:15.**
Members, appointment, **18B:13, 18B:14.**
Salaries and compensation of members, **18B:13.**
Selection committees, recommendations for appointment of members to board, **18B:14.**
Statewide advisory council, membership, **18B:16.**
Terms of office and filling of vacancies, **18B:13.**

Area directors.
Appointment, qualifications, and duties, **18B:12.**
Assistant area directors, **18B:15.**
Recruitment and selection, **18B:15.**

Artificial ponds of coastal waters, plans by public welfare boards and officers, **130:28.**

Assault and battery, protection of employees in performance of their duties, **265:13D.**

Assessments.
Annual assessment by commissioner of social services as to needs, **18B:7.**
Prematurely born infants, liability and assessments for care, **111:67C.**

Assignment of support rights on behalf of child receiving foster care maintenance payments, **119:23.**

Assignments.
Certain funds by persons receiving relief or support, assignment, **118:11.**
Medical assistance division, **118E:28.**
Repayment of overpayment of financial assistance, **18:30.**
Wage assignment for support, persons entitled to receive, **208:36, 209:32E.**

WELFARE AND SOCIAL SERVICES —Cont'd

Assistant area social services director, recruitment and selection, **18B:15.**

Assistant commissioners, **18:4, 18B:9.**

Attorney general.
See ATTORNEY GENERAL.

Attorneys at law.
Appointment of attorney by commissioner, **18B:10.**
Medical assistance division, **118E:4.**
Programs for legal services, administration by department, **18B:2.**

Auditing bureau.
Special investigations bureau. See within this heading, "Special investigations bureau."

Banks.
See BANKS AND BANKING.

Birth control, comprehensive family planning program, **111:24E.**

Births.
See BIRTHS.

Blind persons.
See BLIND PERSONS.

Borrowing money for, authority of cities and towns, **44:10.**

Boston juvenile court's administrative assistant to coordinate activities, **218:58A.**

Breakfast programs for needy school children.
See FOOD SERVICES AND FREE LUNCH PROGRAMS.

Bribery, medical assistance division, **118E:41.**

Budget, **18:1, 18:2, 18B:7.**
Area boards, **18B:12, 18B:15.**
Departmental budget estimates, **18B:7.**
Standard budget of assistance, formulation, **18:2.**

Burial expenses, payment of, **118:2, 119:23.**
See POOR PERSONS.

Case work, administration of programs, **18B:2, 18B:7.**

Cemetery plots, **118E:25.**

Centers of social services, location, **18B:17.**

Certification.
Advancements of appropriations, **18B:20.**
Release of unclaimed funds, **18B:19.**

WELFARE AND SOCIAL SERVICES —Cont'd

Certification —Cont'd
  Tewksbury hospital, admission on certificate, **122:11.**
Charges.
  Fees and charges. See within this heading, "Fees and charges."
Charities and charitable contributions.
  Contracts with department, **6:126.**
  Health, welfare and retirement funds law, applicability, **151D:7.**
  Information as to public assistance may be disclosed to Catholic charity, **66:17A.**
  License to sell articles for charitable purposes, power to issue, **101:33.**
  Notice to social services department as to charitable trusts, **36:32, 217:19.**
Children.
  See CHILDREN AND MINORS.
Cities.
  See CITIES AND TOWNS.
Citizens or aliens, receipt of benefits, **6A:16C.**
Medicaid, **118E:16D.**
Civil rights.
  Discrimination. See within this heading, "Discrimination."
Civil service.
  City welfare employees' compensation plan, rules concerning, **30:37.**
  Commissioner, deputy and assistants, applicability of civil service law, **18:8.**
  Compensation plan for welfare employees, filing of rules and regulations concerning, **30:37.**
  Employees as included under civil service laws, **31:48.**
  Exemption of regional directors, **31:48.**
  Reallocation of positions, **30:46.**
  Retirement deductions of employees not subject, **32:22.**
Collection of overpayments of financial assistance, **18:30.**
Collection of program and fiscal data annually, **18B:7.**
Commissioners, **18:3, 18B:6, 18B:6A.**
Community or private agencies, authority of area boards to receive funds, **18B:15.**

WELFARE AND SOCIAL SERVICES —Cont'd

Community service area, **18:5, 18:7.**
  Administration, **18:5.**
  Boards.
    Area boards. See within this heading, "Area boards."
  Centers, change of name to areas, **18:5.**
  Directors.
    Area directors. See within this heading, "Area directors."
Compensation.
  Salaries and compensation. See within this heading, "Salaries and compensation."
Complaint to establish paternity, support, visitation, or custody, illegitimate children, **209C:5.**
Comprehensive family planning program, **111:24E.**
Comprehensive welfare program, **18:2, 18:18B:3.**
Comptroller of state.
  See COMPTROLLER OF STATE.
Confidential matters, medical assistance division, **118E:49.**
Consumers, membership on social services area board, **18B:13.**
Contracts and agreements.
  Area boards, contracts, **18B:15.**
  Assumption or reimbursement of municipal contracts, **18:1.**
  Federal Health, Education and Welfare Secretary, commissioner's agreements with concerning assistance to aged and disabled, **118A:3.**
  Medical assistance division, **118E:7, 118E:10, 118E:50.**
  Overpayments, repayment of, **18:30.**
Convicts.
  See CORRECTIONAL INSTITUTIONS.
Co-operation with other departments, **18B:3.**
Co-operative banks, requests for financial information, **18:15.**
Corporations may make contributions to relief committee or agency approved by commissioner, **155:12A.**
Correctional institutions.
  See CORRECTIONAL INSTITUTIONS.
Counseling, administration of programs, **18B:2.**

WELFARE AND SOCIAL SERVICES —Cont'd

Creation, **18:1, 18:18B:1.**
Crimes and offenses.
  Applicants for public assistance, offenses as to information regarding, **40:51, 271:43.**
  Assault and battery, protection of employees in performance of their duties, **265:13D.**
  Blind persons, false representation relating to financial assistance, **6:131F.**
  Fines and penalties. See within this heading, "Fines and penalties."
  Fraud and deceit. See within this heading, "Fraud and deceit."
  Information as to application for public assistance, offenses, **40:51, 271:43.**
  Leaving family to qualify them for public assistance, **18:5F.**
  Perjury. See within this heading, "Perjury."
Damages, medical assistance division, **118E:44.**
Date of application for medical assistance, **118E:30.**
Day care facilities, administration of programs, **18B:2.**
Dead bodies, disposition, **38:15, 113:1-113:5.**
Death certificates, provisions as to when bodies delivered to department for burial, **38:15.**
Definitions, **18:29, 62E:1, 118E:8.**
Delegation by commissioner of responsibilities as appointing authority, **18:9.**
Department of social services, **18B:1 et seq.**
Department of transitional assistance.
  Transitional assistance department. See within this heading, "Transitional assistance department."
Dependent children, aid to, **118:1-118:11.**
  See DEPENDENT CHILDREN, AID TO.
Deposits.
  Banks.
    See BANKS AND BANKING.
  Health and welfare commission, deposit of federal funds received, **6:125.**
  Savings banks. See within this heading, "Savings banks."

WELFARE AND SOCIAL
  SERVICES —Cont'd
Deposits —Cont'd
  Social services commissioner to
    deposit trust funds for
    children, **18B:18.**
Deputy commissioner,
  appointment, qualifications,
  salary, **18:4, 18B:8.**
Description of departmental
  organization, preparation and
  maintenance, **18:5.**
Disabled persons, assistance to.
  See AGED AND DISABLED,
    ASSISTANCE.
Disclosing information as to
  recipients of relief, **18:15,
  18:18A, 40:51, 62C:21,
  271:43.**
Discrimination.
  Minority business assistance,
    23A:39-23A:44.
    See MINORITY BUSINESS
      ASSISTANCE.
  Race, color or religion,
    discrimination in granting
    relief on account, **272:98B.**
  Sexual equality relating to
    receipt of certain public
    assistance benefits, **118:3,
    118E:10.**
Disposal of obsolete departmental
  records, **66:17A.**
District employees.
  Group insurance, **32B:7A,
    32B:9E, 32B:10.**
  Workers' compensation, **152:74.**
Division of Medical Assistance.
  See MEDICAL ASSISTANCE
    DIVISION.
Divisions, bureaus, establishment,
  18:5, 18:16.
Drugs and narcotics, **17:13,
  111E:13A, 118E:17, 118E:25.**
Early childhood intervention
  services, social services
  department as member,
  111G:3.
Education.
  Schools and education. See
    within this heading,
    "Schools and education."
Eligibility.
  Qualification. See within this
    heading, "Qualification."
Emergency assistance to needy
  families with children, **18:2.**
Emergency food, fuel, and housing
  regulations or assistance,
  23:9H, 118:2. (note)
Employees of department.
  Appointment and removal, **18:9.**

WELFARE AND SOCIAL
  SERVICES —Cont'd
Employees of department —Cont'd
  Auditing bureau. See within this
    heading, "Auditing bureau."
  Civil service. See within this
    heading, "Civil service."
  District employees. See within
    this heading, "District
    employees."
  Exception in law, **271:41.**
  Group insurance, **32B:7A,
    32B:9E, 32B:10.**
  Protection against arbitrary
    removal, **30:9B.**
  Reallocation of positions, **30:46.**
  Removal from office. See within
    this heading, "Removal from
    office."
  Retirement systems, employee
    contributions required,
    32:22.
  Salaries and compensation. See
    within this heading,
    "Salaries and
    compensation."
  State employee providing
    services or materials to
    recipient of public
    assistance, promulgation of
    schedule of charges, **268A:7.**
  Teacher's tenure, **30:9D.**
  Tenure, seniority, and retirement
    rights, **30:9A, 30:9D.**
  Training.
    Schools and education. See
      within this heading,
      "Schools and education."
  Withholding of retirement
    deductions of certain
    employees, **32:22.**
Employment.
  Labor and employment. See
    within this heading, "Labor
    and employment."
Energy crisis, emergency grants to
  assist, **18:2.**
Equality between sexes relating to
  receipt of certain public
  assistance benefits, **118:3,
  118E:10.**
Evidence.
  See EVIDENCE.
Examination, inspection, or
  investigation.
  Health, welfare, and retirement
    funds, **151D:3.**
  Labor controversies,
    investigation upon request
    by governor, **150:3.**
  Missing parents, investigation
    by department concerning,
    118:3.

WELFARE AND SOCIAL
  SERVICES —Cont'd
Examination, inspection, or
  investigation —Cont'd
  Records, **66:17A.**
Excess payments, reimbursement,
  18:18.
Execution, public assistance
  payments as exempt, **235:34.**
Executors.
  See EXECUTORS AND
    ADMINISTRATORS.
False representations.
  Fraud and deceit. See within
    this heading, "Fraud and
    deceit."
Family Support Act.
  See INTERSTATE FAMILY
    SUPPORT ACT.
Federal aid.
  Acceptance of funds, **18:2.**
  Benefits as subject to orders to
    pay judgment, **224:16.**
  Commissioner of social services
    to apply for and receive,
    18B:7.
  Conformity of employment
    policies with federal
    requirements, **18:9.**
  Health and welfare commission,
    deposit of funds received,
    6:125.
  Medical assistance division,
    118E:11.
  Social services department,
    acceptance and use, **18B:7.**
Federal savings and loan
  associations, deposit by
  commissioner of funds held in
  trust, **18B:18.**
Fees and charges.
  Ability of recipient of services to
    pay, **18B:4.**
  General court, determination,
    18B:5.
  Medical assistance division,
    118E:7.
  Medical assistance division,
    liens and encumbrances,
    118E:34.
  State employee providing
    services or materials to
    recipient of public
    assistance, formulation of
    schedule of charges, **268A:7.**
Financial or business professions,
  membership on area boards,
  18B:13.
Fines and penalties.
  Banks' failure to give
    information as to deposits of
    welfare recipients, **18:15,
    122:22.**

WELFARE AND SOCIAL SERVICES —Cont'd

Fines and penalties —Cont'd

Disclosure of information, hearing to contest sanctions, **18:18A.**

False representations.

Fraud and deceit. See within this heading, "Fraud and deceit."

Financial institutions' failure to furnish information as to deposits of applicants for or recipients of public aid, **18:15, 122:22.**

Medical assistance division, **118E:37, 118E:40 et seq.**

Names of persons on welfare, disclosure or publishing, **40:51.**

Fire departments.

See FIRE DEPARTMENTS.

Food services.

See FOOD SERVICES AND FREE LUNCH PROGRAMS.

Forwarding of recipients checks, **18:27A.**

Foster care.

Appointment of foster care review directors by commissioner of social services, **18B:6A.**

Provision, **18B:2, 119:23.**

Fraud and deceit.

Aid to dependent children, fraud in obtaining, **118:10.**

Assistance programs, **18:5B.**

Blind persons, false representation relating to financial assistance, **6:131F.**

Disclosure of information by bureau of special investigation, **18:11.**

Financial institutions furnishing false information, **18:15.**

Improper payments to applicant for public assistance, **271:43.**

Lien created by repayment of fraudulently received benefits, **18:29.**

Medical assistance division, **118E:36, 118E:39, 118E:40.**

Vendors procuring payment by means of fraud, **18:5D.**

Veterans' benefit payments, disclosure of fraud or abuse in relation, **62C:21.**

Fuel assistance program for certain low income households, emergency, **118:2.**

WELFARE AND SOCIAL SERVICES —Cont'd

Funding of social services department, **18B:7.**

Furniture purchased by transitional assistance department, **18:17-18:19.**

General Court.

Commissioner, reports, **18:10, 18B:7.**

Duties, **18B:5, 18B:7.**

Gifts, grants, or gratuities.

Charities and charitable contributions. See within this heading, "Charities and charitable contributions."

Federal aid. See within this heading, "Federal aid."

Medical assistance division, **118E:7, 118E:27, 118E:43.**

Private grants, bequests, or contributions, commissioner authorized to apply for and accept, **18B:7.**

Governor.

See GOVERNOR.

Group activities, administration of programs, **18B:2.**

Guardians.

See GUARDIANS, CONSERVATORS, AND COMMITTEES.

Handicapped assistance to.

See AGED AND DISABLED, ASSISTANCE.

Health and human services executive office, agencies within, **6A:16.**

Health and welfare commission, social services commissioner as member, **6:125.**

Health care finance and policy division.

See HEALTH CARE FINANCE AND POLICY DIVISION.

Hearings.

Applicant's right, **18:16.**

Children in need of services, notice of hearing, **119:39E.**

Collection of overpayments of financial assistance, **18:30.**

Disclosure of information, hearing to contest sanctions, **18:18A.**

Division of hearings, establishment, **18:16.**

Medical assistance division, **118E:47, 118E:48.**

Referee to conduct, **18:16.**

Termination or reduction of assistance, **18:16.**

WELFARE AND SOCIAL SERVICES —Cont'd

Heating assistance, **18:2.**

High school, recipients with youngest child, **118:3.**

Home for welfare recipient, purchase, **18:20.**

Homemaker services.

Board of accreditation, **18:28.**

Social services department, administration of programs, **18B:2.**

Hospitals.

See HOSPITALS AND HEALTH CARE FACILITIES.

Hours of labor and overtime pay laws inapplicable in field, **149:30A, 149:30B.**

Housing.

See HOUSING AND URBAN RENEWAL.

Identification of medical assistance recipients, **26:8H, 118E:26.**

Illegitimate children, **18B:18, 209C:5, 209C:11.**

Infirmaries, **47:2, 47:8.**

Informal education, administration of programs, **18B:2.**

Information or information services, **18:21, 18B:2, 112:135.**

Inspection.

Examination, inspection, or investigation. See within this heading, "Examination, inspection, or investigation."

Insurance.

Disclosure of information as to insurance, **18:15.**

Group insurance for welfare district employees, **32B:7A, 32B:9D¾, 32B:9E, 32B:10.**

Information as to deposits of poor persons, **18:15, 122:22.**

Levy on life insurance for repayment of fraudulently received benefits, **18:29.**

Medical assistance division, **118E:18.**

Insurance reimbursement program, **118E:9C.**

Rates and rating organizations, purpose, **174A:2, 175A:2.**

Interest income paid to public assistance recipients, disclosure, **62C:21.**

Investigation.

Examination, inspection, or investigation. See within this heading, "Examination, inspection, or investigation."

WELFARE AND SOCIAL SERVICES —Cont'd

Judgments.
Collection of overpayments of financial assistance, **18:30.**
Public welfare benefits as subject to orders to pay, **224:16.**
Juvenile Court, **119:21 et seq.**
See JUVENILE COURTS AND DELINQUENT CHILDREN.
Labor and employment.
Controversies affecting public welfare, investigation upon request by governor, **150:3.**
Department of social services, employees of.
Employees of department. See within this heading, "Employees of department."
Employment.
See EMPLOYMENT AND TRAINING DIVISION IN LABOR AND WORKFORCE DEPARTMENT.
Employment of people with disabilities commission, **6:105.**
Information on employment security available to commissioner of social services, **151A:46.**
Multiple employer welfare arrangement, life and health insurance guaranty association law, **175:147.**
Public works, welfare plans as affecting wages, **149:26, 149:27.**
Larceny, medical assistance division, **118E:36.**
Leaving persons in Commonwealth for purpose of qualifying them for public assistance as criminal offense, **18:5F.**
Legal services, administration of programs, **18B:2.**
Licenses.
Charitable purposes, power to issue licenses to sell articles, **101:33.**
Hospital licensing surveys and construction planning, membership on advisory council, **111:55.**
Social workers.
See SOCIAL WORKERS.
Liens and encumbrances.
Medical assistance division, **118E:34.**

WELFARE AND SOCIAL SERVICES —Cont'd

Liens and encumbrances —Cont'd
Repayment of fraudulently received benefits, **18:29.**
Workers' compensation payments, liens to extent of welfare benefits paid to employees **152:46A.**
Lists of selection committee filed with social services commissioner, **18B:14.**
Long-term care trust fund.
See LONG-TERM CARE TRUST FUND.
Loss of taxes on land used by, reimbursement of cities and towns, **58:13.**
Management information system, commissioner to develop and implement, **18B:7.**
Medicaid.
See MEDICAL CARE AND ASSISTANCE.
Medical assistance division.
See MEDICAL ASSISTANCE DIVISION.
Medical service corporation, consent to formation, **176C:3.**
Meetings of area board, selection of officers, **18B:15.**
Mentally ill and retarded persons, **18B:13.**
Minors.
See CHILDREN AND MINORS.
Missing children, report to central register for missing children, **22A:7.**
Missing parents, investigation into, **118:3.**
Monitoring and evaluation system, development and implementation by commissioner, **18B:7.**
Municipalities.
See CITIES AND TOWNS.
Names of recipients of public assistance, disclosure, **18:11, 40:51, 66:17A, 271:43.**
Neglected children.
See ABUSED AND NEGLECTED CHILDREN.
Notice.
Charitable trusts, notice of recording, **36:32, 217:19.**
Children in need of services, notice of hearing, **119:39E.**
Collection of overpayments of financial assistance, **18:30.**
Medical assistance division, **118E:25, 118E:29, 118E:32, 118E:47.**

WELFARE AND SOCIAL SERVICES —Cont'd

Notice —Cont'd
Placement of children committed to training schools, **120:12.**
Register of deeds to notify of recording of certain instruments, **36:32.**
Register of probate and insolvency to send notice of charitable trust to department, **217:19.**
Repayment of fraudulently received benefits, **18:29.**
State hospital or sanatorium, notice to board of admission, **111:69F.**
Nursing.
See NURSING OR REST HOMES.
Nutrition board, member, **6:181.**
Offices, location and number, **18:5.**
Older persons.
See AGED AND DISABLED, ASSISTANCE.
Organizations providing social, rehabilitative, health, or special education services, contracts, **29:29B.**
Orientation of area-based staff, **18B:7.**
Outreach arrangements, establishment, **18:5.**
Outstanding default warrants, prohibition of payments to persons with, **18:2.**
Overpayments, collection of, **18:30.**
Over-the-counter drugs, **118E:25.**
Parent.
See CHILDREN AND MINORS.
Paternity affirmation as evidence, **273:15.**
Penalties.
Fines and penalties. See within this heading, "Fines and penalties."
Perjury.
Absent father, **118:3.**
Attorney general, investigation, **12:8H.**
Dependent children, application for aid to be signed under penalty of perjury, **118:2B, 118:3.**
Medical assistance vouchers, **6:131G, 118E:20.**
Vendor's vouchers to be signed under penalty, **18:5C.**
Physicians and surgeons, bill submitted within 90 days after service rendered, **118E:20.**

WELFARE AND SOCIAL SERVICES —Cont'd

Placement of certain publicly supported poor persons, **120:12.**

Planned parenthood programs, administration, **18B:2.**

Poor persons, assistance to and support of, **18:1 et seq., 18B:1 et seq.**

Pregnant women, medical assistance for, **118E:10.**

Priorities for allocation of services, **18B:4.**

Private grants, bequests, gifts or contributions, commissioner authorized to apply for and accept, **18B:7.**

Private social service providers, membership on area boards, **18B:13.**

Privileged and confidential matters, medical assistance division, **118E:49.**

Privileged communications between worker and client, **112:135A, 112:135B.**

Probate and Family Court.
Custody of child on order of probate court, **119:23.**
Subrogation rights, proceedings to enforce, **18:21.**
Visitation of child by parent, guardian, or next of kin, power to compel department to permit, **119:35.**

Probate of wills, medical assistance division, **118E:32.**

Protection of children, **18B:2, 119:51D.**

Public assistance division, prescribing forms of infirmary records of admission, **47:8.**

Qualification.
Commissioner, **18:3.**
Deputy commissioners, **18:4, 18B:8.**
Directors, **18:1.**
Medical assistance division. See within this heading, "Medical assistance division."

Rebates, medical assistance division, **118E:41.**
Secondary discounts by manufacturers or suppliers of durable medical equipment, **118E:41A.**

Recipients, financial assets or income of, **18B:4.**

Reciprocal agreements with other states, **18:14.**

WELFARE AND SOCIAL SERVICES —Cont'd

Recommendations.
Health and welfare commission for coordination of services, **6:126.**
Social services, recommendations for improving quality, **18B:3.**

Records, **18B:7, 18B:20, 66:17A.**
Charitable trusts, notice of recording, **36:32.**
Federal government, examination, **18B:5.**
Financial records of public assistance applicants or recipients, department's request, **18:5.**
Public assistance division, prescribing forms of infirmary records of admission, **47:8.**
Register of deeds to notify of recording of certain instruments, **36:32.**
Reports. See within this heading, "Reports."
Social services department, **18B:20.**
Wage reporting system, public records, **66:17A.**

Referral services, administration of programs, **18B:2.**

Regional offices.
Commissioner, establishment, **18B:11.**
Medical assistance division, **118E:5.**
Supervisory functions, **18:5.**

Regions, division of Commonwealth, **18B:3.**

Register of deeds to notify of recording of certain instruments, **36:32.**

Register of probate and insolvency to send notice of charitable trust, **217:19.**

Registration.
See SOCIAL WORKERS.

Rehabilitation commission of Massachusetts, **6:74-6:84.**
Advisory council, member, **6:76.**
Co-operation, **6:81.**

Reimbursement.
Disabled or handicapped persons, assignment of reimbursement, **118:11.**
Excess payments, reimbursement of department, **18:18, 18:30.**
Fraudulently received benefits, repayment of, **18:29.**

WELFARE AND SOCIAL SERVICES —Cont'd

Reimbursement —Cont'd
Loss of taxes on land used by department, reimbursement of cities and towns, **58:13.**
Medical assistance division, **118E:35.**
Medical care and assistance, **118E:16.**

Relatives, contributions for medical services by, **118E:31.**

Release of lien by bureau of special investigations, **18:29.**

Removal from office.
Deputy commissioner of social services, **18B:8.**
Protection against arbitrary removal, **30:9B.**
Superintendents of department institutions, **18:9.**

Removal of patient to place of legal settlement, **122:12.**

Rent.
Administration and finance executive office, advertisements prior to rental of public building, **7:40H.**
Direct payment, **18:26, 18:27.**

Renting and leasing space for social services centers, **18B:17.**

Reports, **118:5, 118:10.**
Commissioner, reports, **18:10, 18B:7.**
Comptroller, reports, **18:17.**
Salaries and compensation. See within this heading, "Salaries and compensation."
Social services department, **18B:7, 18B:20.**
Social workers.
See SOCIAL WORKERS.
Wage reporting system.
Salaries and compensation. See within this heading, "Salaries and compensation."

Residential care for children with special needs or aging persons, **18B:2.**

Rest home.
See NURSING OR REST HOMES.

Retired public employee becoming public charge, **32:92.**

Retirement systems, employee contributions required, **32:22.**

Return of unjustified payments, **18:5E.**

WELFARE AND SOCIAL SERVICES —Cont'd

Rules and regulations, promulgation of, **18:10, 18B:3, 18B:4, 18B:7, 30:37, 118A:8.**
Salaries and compensation.
Area boards, **18B:13.**
Area directors, **18B:2.**
Assignment of wages for support, persons entitled to receive, **208:36, 209:32E.**
Civil service, compensation plan for welfare employees, **30:37.**
Commissioner of social services, **18:3, 18B:6.**
Deputy and assistant commissioners, salaries, **18:4, 18:18B:8.**
Hours of labor and overtime laws inapplicable, **149:30A, 149:30B.**
Legal counsel, **18B:10.**
Public works, welfare plans as affecting wages, **149:26, 149:27.**
Reporting system.
Crime as relating to use of information, **271:43.**
Eligibility of participants, **62E:3.**
Fraud, **62E:5.**
Furnishing information to bureau of special investigations, **62E:5.**
List of recipients, provision of by department, **62E:4.**
Public records, **66:17A.**
Sale.
See SALE OR TRANSFER OF PROPERTY.
Savings banks.
Disclosure of information as to deposits of poor persons, **18:15, 122:22.**
Social services department, deposit of funds held in trust by commissioner in savings banks, **18B:18.**
Schools and education.
Area-based staff of department, training, **18B:7.**
Assistant commissioners, educational requirements, **18B:9.**
Deputy or assistant commissioner, education, **18B:8, 18B:9.**
Informal education, administration of programs, **18B:2.**

WELFARE AND SOCIAL SERVICES —Cont'd

Schools and education —Cont'd
Placement of children committed to training schools, notice, **120:12.**
Placing of certain children in schools by department, **119:32.**
Social services centers located in schools, **18B:7.**
Special education. See within this heading, "Special education."
Teacher employer by department, tenure, **30:9D.**
Tuition, payment, **76:7, 76:10.**
Vocational education.
See VOCATIONAL EDUCATION AND SCHOOLS.
Securities, authority of state treasurer to invest or reinvest proceeds, **18B:19.**
Seizure of property for repayment of fraudulently received benefits, **18:29.**
Selection committees for area boards, appointment by commissioner, **18B:14.**
Self-employed persons repaying overpayments of financial assistance, **19:30.**
Service of process and papers, **18:16.**
Service planning of department, commissioner to co-ordinate, **18B:7.**
Services to be provided by, **18:2, 18B:2.**
Set-off debt collection, **62D:1 et seq.**
See SET-OFF DEBT COLLECTION.
Sexual equality relating to receipt of certain public assistance benefits, **118:3, 118E:10.**
Shelters.
See HOUSING AND URBAN RENEWAL.
Shutoff or resumption of utility services, financial services, **18:2.**
Sinking funds, investment of funds in securities, legality, **18B:19.**
Social security.
Disregarding of certain benefits by department, **18:1.**
Matching funds emergency assistance program, **18:2.**
Social services required, **18B:5.**

WELFARE AND SOCIAL SERVICES —Cont'd

Social services department, **18B:1 et seq.**
Early childhood intervention services, **111G:3.**
Social workers.
See SOCIAL WORKERS.
Special education.
Admission of children to programs and evaluation of benefits, **71B:2.**
Referral by department of children for special education programs, **71B:10.**
School committees, evaluation and assessment of children for special education programs, **71B:3.**
Special investigations bureau.
Child support, **62E:1.**
Defined, **62E:1.**
Falsely assuming to be official, **268:33.**
Fraudulently received benefits, repayment of, **18:29.**
Information, furnishing to bureau, **62E:5.**
Wage reporting system, **62E:6 to 62E:6B.**
Specialized foster family care, administration of programs, **18B:2.**
Standard budget of assistance, formulation, **18:2.**
State comptroller.
See COMPTROLLER OF STATE.
State employee providing services or materials to recipient of public assistance, promulgation of schedule of charges, **268A:7.**
State hospital or sanatorium, admission to, notice to board, **111:69F.**
State treasurer, receipt and distribution of unclaimed money held by department, **18B:19.**
Statewide advisory council, advice to commissioner of social services concerning delivery of social services, **18B:16.**
Studies of social and economic problems, **18B:3.**
Subcontractors, **118E:51.**
Subpoenas, **18:16.**
Subrogation, **18:5G, 18:21, 118E:22, 118E:23, 119A:3.**
Supervision of employees by area social services directors, **18B:12.**

WELFARE AND SOCIAL SERVICES —Cont'd

Surrender of levied property for repayment of fraudulently received benefits, **18:29.**

Suspension of commitment to social services department, **279:2.**

Teacher employed by department, tenure, **30:9D.**

Terms of office and filling of vacancies in area social services board, **18:3, 18B:13.**

Tewksbury hospital.
Admission on certificate of welfare department, **122:11.**
Payment from appropriations for diseased persons, **122:13.**
Removal of patient to place of legal settlement, **122:12.**

Third parties.
Recovery, **18:5H.**
Subrogation of department to recipients' claims against, **18:5G, 18:21.**

Towns.
See CITIES AND TOWNS.

Training of area-based staff, **18B:7.**

Transfer of social service functions and property of transitional assistance department to social services department, **18B:1.**

Transitional assistance department, **18:1 et seq.**
Change of name to department of transitional assistance, **18:1.**
Early childhood intervention service member, **111G:3.**
Employment security, confidentiality of records, **151A:46.**
Hearings, Division, **18:16.**
Medical care.
See MEDICAL CARE AND ASSISTANCE.
Public welfare department changed to, **18:1 et seq.**
Transfer of social service functions to department of social services, **18B:1.**
Warrant management system, **18:2.**

Transportation of children to court or institution, provision of suitable vehicle, **119:34.**

Trial.
Hearings. See within this heading, "Hearings."

WELFARE AND SOCIAL SERVICES —Cont'd

Trust companies, requesting information, **18:15.**

Unidentified or unclaimed bodies released by medical examiner to department, **38:13.**

Unlicensed funds held by department, **18B:19.**

Vacancy in office of medical assistance commissioner, **118E:3.**

Veterans.
See VETERANS AND VETERANS' ORGANIZATIONS.

Visitation, **119:35, 209C:5.**

Vocational education.
See VOCATIONAL EDUCATION AND SCHOOLS.

Wage reporting system.
Salaries and compensation. See within this heading, "Salaries and compensation."

Wages.
Salaries and compensation. See within this heading, "Salaries and compensation."

Warrant management system, names of persons with outstanding default warrants reported to, **18:2.**

Wedlock, services to mothers bearing children out, **18B:2, 119:23B.**

Welfare department.
Transitional assistance department. See within this heading, "Transitional assistance department."

Workers' compensation.
Assignment of benefit payments in reimbursement, **118:11.**
Liens on workers' compensation payments, **152:46A.**

Youth services coordinating committee, membership of commissioner, **120:10.**

WELFARE FUNDS DISCLOSURE ACT, 151D:1 et seq.

WELLESLEY.
Congressional district, **57:1.**
District court, **218:1.**
Medical examiner district, **38:1.**
Parks, provision by metropolitan commission, **92:33.**

WELLESLEY —Cont'd
Senatorial district, **57:3.**

WELLFLEET.
District court, **218:1.**
Medical examiner district, **38:1.**

WELLHEAD.
Security interest in multi-state transaction as governed by law of locality, **106:9-103.**

WELLNESS PROGRAMS.
Accident and sickness insurance, **176J:3.**
Firefighters and police officers, **31:61A, 32:5A.**
Mortality and morbidity, program to reduce incidence among general public, **111:206.**
Physical fitness standards for police officers and firefighters, **32:5A.**
Retirement and disability data system, **32:21.**

WELLS.
Appropriation by town for wells in public places, **40:5.**
Banking institutions in which devises and bequests to counties may be deposited, **34:23.**
Building permits, availability of water supply from wells as affecting issuance, **40:54.**
Certification of diggers or drillers, **21:16.**
Church wells, injuries, **266:98.**
Coal mining operations, regulation, **21B:11.**
Covering, **40:21.**
Crimes and offenses.
Drillers' registration, violations, **21:16.**
Poisoning, **265:28.**
School or church well, injury, **266:98.**
Diggers or drillers, regulation, **21:16.**
Indebtedness by municipality, **44:8.**
Openings to be guarded in factory or mercantile building, **149:129, 149:180.**
Poisoning as criminal offense, **265:28.**
Schoolhouse wells, injuries, **266:98.**
Water resources commission, registration of diggers or drillers, **21:16.**

WENDELL.
District court, **218:1.**
Medical examiner district, **38:1.**

WENHAM.
Congressional district, **57:1.**
District court, **218:1.**
Medical examiner district, **38:1.**
Senatorial district, **57:3.**

WESTBOROUGH.
Congressional district, **57:1.**
Medical examiner district, **38:1.**
Senatorial district, **57:3.**

WESTBOROUGH STATE HOSPITAL, 19:8A, 19:14.

WEST BOYLSTON.
Congressional district, **57:1.**
District court, **218:1.**
Medical examiner district, **38:1.**
Senatorial district, **57:3.**

WEST BRIDGEWATER.
Congressional district, **57:1.**
District court, **218:1.**
Medical examiner district, **38:1.**
Senatorial district, **57:3.**

WEST BROOKFIELD.
Congressional district, **57:1.**
District court, **218:1.**
Medical examiner district, **38:1.**
Senatorial district, **57:3.**

WESTERN APPELLATE DIVISION DISTRICT.
District courts within, **231:108.**

WESTERN MASSACHUSETTS HOSPITAL, 111:63, 111:64, 111:69E-111:69I.
Admissions, **111:69E.**
Cancer patients, **111:65C.**
Notice of admission of needy person, **111:69F, 111:69G.**
Charges for support, **111:69H, 111:69I.**
Eligibility for admission as needy person, determination, **111:69G.**
Evidence in proceedings to collect charges, **111:69I.**
Institution's name changed, **111:63.**

WESTERN WORCESTER DISTRICT COURT.
Rental of facility, **7:40G (note), 29A:4 (note).**

WESTFIELD.
Clinical services bureau of youth service department to operate detention center, **18A:5.**
Congressional district, **57:1.**
District court, **218:1.**
Medical examiner district, **38:1.**
Sanatorium.
  See WESTERN MASSACHUSETTS HOSPITAL.

WESTFIELD —Cont'd
Senatorial district, **57:3.**
Trustees of state colleges, institutions under jurisdiction, **73:19.**

WESTFIELD RIVER.
Public works department, control over, **91:12.**

WESTFORD.
Congressional district, **57:1.**
District court, **218:1.**
Medical examiner district, **38:1.**
Senatorial district, **57:3.**

WESTHAMPTON.
Congressional district, **57:1.**
Medical examiner district, **38:1.**
Senatorial district, **57:3.**

WEST INDIES.
Fire or marine insurance company agents' balances representing business written in, deduction from assets, **175:25.**

WESTMINSTER.
Congressional district, **57:1.**
District court, **218:1.**
Medical examiner district, **38:1.**
Senatorial district, **57:3.**

WEST NEWBURY.
Congressional district, **57:1.**
District court, **218:1.**
Medical examiner district, **38:1.**
Senatorial district, **57:3.**

WESTON.
Congressional district, **57:1.**
District court, **218:1.**
Medical examiner district, **38:1.**
Parks, provision by metropolitan commission, **92:33.**
Senatorial district, **57:3.**

WESTON RESERVOIR.
"Watershed system," definition for purposes of provision creating watershed management division, **92:104.**

WESTPORT.
Congressional district, **57:1.**
District court, **218:1.**
Marine boundary of Commonwealth in area, **1:3.**
Medical examiner district, **38:1.**
Senatorial district, **57:3.**

WEST ROXBURY.
Assistant clerk for municipal court, **218:10.**
Clerk of municipal court, classification, **35:49.**

WEST ROXBURY —Cont'd
Justices of District Courts within, **231:108.**
Municipal court of, **218:1, 218:10.**

WEST SPRINGFIELD.
Congressional district, **57:1.**
Medical examiner district, **38:1.**
Senatorial district, **57:3.**
State agricultural and industrial building, **128:2.**

WEST STOCKBRIDGE.
District court, **218:1.**
Medical examiner district, **38:1.**
Senatorial district, **57:3.**

WEST TISBURY.
Medical examiner district, **38:1.**

WESTWOOD.
Congressional district, **57:1.**
District court, **218:1.**
Medical examiner district, **38:1.**
Parks, provision by metropolitan commission, **92:33.**
Senatorial district, **57:3.**

WETBIKES.
Regulation, **90B:1, 90B:11.**

WETLANDS.
See LOWLANDS AND SWAMPS.

WETLANDS PROTECTION ACT, 131:40, 131:40A.

WEYMOUTH.
Congressional district, **57:1.**
District court, **218:1.**
Medical examiner district, **38:1.**
Metropolitan air pollution control district, membership, **111:142B.**
Parks, provision by metropolitan commission, **92:33.**
Senatorial district, **57:3.**

WHALE AWARENESS DAY.
Governor, proclamation, **6:15ZZ, 6:16AAA.**

WHARVES, PIERS, AND DOCKS, 88:14-88:19.
Acquisition of property, **91:5.**
Alterations, **88:14.**
Appeals to county commissioners, **88:15, 88:17, 88:18.**
Booms and other equipment required to prevent oil pollution, **21:50A.**
Boundaries.
  Ascertainment, **88:16.**
  Fence taken as, when, **86:2.**
Buildings and structures, **88:14.**

WHARVES, PIERS, AND DOCKS —Cont'd

Burying of refuse within marine boundaries or near shoreline, prohibition against, **270:20.**

Carrying away goods of another, **266:113.**

Charges for use, **91:2A, 91:6, 91:7.**

Cockbilling and bracing yards, power of harbor master to require, **102:23.**

Commercial vessel, stationing to public commercial dock, **91:10C.**

Common landing places, **88:14-88:19.**

Condemnation of property for.
Eminent domain. See within this heading, "Eminent domain."

Congress' exclusive power over dockyards, **US Const Art 1 Sec 8 cl 17.**

Construction of, licenses, **91:12-91:15.**

Control over, **88:14, 88:19.**

County commissioners, appeals, **88:15, 88:17, 88:18.**

Criminal trespass.
Trespass. See within this heading, "Trespass."

Custodian, **88:14.**

Damages to private property, **88:14.**

Discontinuance, **88:17, 88:18.**

Eminent domain, **91:5.**
Highways, taking, holding, and utilization of property in connection with piers, **91:5, 91:9.**
Public landing places, **88:14.**

Extension beyond established harbor line, **91:34.**

Fence as boundary when true boundaries unknown, **86:2.**

Harbormaster, powers, **102:23-102:25.**

Harbors and inland waters maintenance fund, credit of costs of state for removal of wharves, piers, and docks, **91:49B.**

Highways, taking, holding, and utilization of property in connection with piers, **91:5, 91:9.**

Landing places, **88:14-88:19.**

Laying out, **88:14, 88:15.**

Licenses.
Construction, licenses, **91:12-91:15.**

WHARVES, PIERS, AND DOCKS —Cont'd

Licenses —Cont'd
Marinas, **91:59B.**
Oil terminals, **21:50.**

Marinas.
License to operate, **91:59B.**
Waste oil retention facilities, **21:52A.**

Mineral resources division, duties, **21:54.**

Mooring.
See MOORING.

Municipal borrowing for improvements, **44:7.**

Notice.
Proprietors of wharves and real estate lying in common.
Agenda to be set forth in notice of meeting, **179:9.**
First meeting, **179:2.**
Trespasser, notice, **266:122.**

Oil pollution of waters, **21:50A.**

Oil terminals, licensing and inspection, **21:50.**

Piles, **91:14 et seq.**
See PILES.

Plan and description, filing and recording, **88:14.**

Port of Boston commission.
See PORT OF BOSTON COMMISSION.

Proprietors of wharves and real estate lying in common, **179:1-179:17.**
See PROPRIETORS OF WHARVES AND REAL ESTATE LYING IN COMMON.

Public landing places, **88:14-88:19.**

Railroads.
See RAILROADS.

Recognizance for costs on appeal to county commissioners, **88:18.**

Regulation of use of, **88:19.**

Removal of vessel from berth, harbor master's power, **102:24, 102:25.**

Removal when unsafe, **91:49B.**

Steamboat police, **159:93.**

Structures upon, building and leasing, **88:14.**

Taking property for.
Eminent domain. See within this heading, "Eminent domain."

Tidewater, compensation to Commonwealth for displacing, **91:21, 91:22.**

Trespass.
Notice to trespasser, **266:122.**
Violations, **266:113, 266:120.**

WHARVES, PIERS, AND DOCKS —Cont'd

Unsafe premises, notice to owners to remove, **91:49B.**

Warps or lines obstructing vessels, **102:18.**

Water pollution by oil or petroleum products, **21:50A.**

WHATELY.

Medical examiner district, **38:1.**

WHEELCHAIRS.

Collateral costs, **93:107.**

Consumer protection, **93:107.**

Customized wheelchairs, sale and warranty of, **93:107.**

Definitions, **93:107.**

Early termination of lease of customized wheelchairs, **93:107.**

Leasing of customized wheelchairs, **93:107.**

Motor vehicle certificate of title law, self-propelled wheelchair as exempt, **90D:2.**

Reasonable attempt to repair customized wheelchairs, **93:107.**

Sales tax, exemptions, **64H:6.**

WHEEL GUARDS.

Street cars, **161:98.**

WHEELS.

Fireworks known as, sale or use, **148:39.**

Tires.
See TIRES.

WHIPPING.

Schools, prohibition against corporal punishment, **71:37G.**

WHIST.

Exemption from gaming laws, **271:22A.**

WHISTLEBLOWERS.

Protection, **149:185.**
Abuse or neglect of patients in long-term care facilities.
Retaliation against persons reporting, **111:72G.**
False claims against Commonwealth, **12:5J.**
Health care workers, **149:187.**
Wage and hour law, **149:148A.**

WHISTLES.

Bicycles, whistles, **85:11B.**

Electric railroads, **162:16.**

Employers, **149:175.**

Motorboats, required equipment, **90B:5.**

WHISTLES —Cont'd
Railroads.
Crossings, sounding, **160:138, 160:139.**
Electric railroads, **162:16.**

WHITE CANE SAFETY DAY.
Observance, **6:15V.**

WHITE LIGHTS.
Motorboats, display, **90B:5.**

WHITE PERCH.
Regulations, **131:22.**

WHITE PINE BLISTER RUST.
Arbitration and award, **128:23.**
Elimination, **128:23, 128:25, 128:29, 128:30.**

WHITMAN.
Congressional district, **57:1.**
District court, **218:1.**
Medical examiner district, **38:1.**
Senatorial district, **57:3.**

WHOLESALE ELECTRIC COMPANY, Spec L 13:1 et seq.
Acquisition of property by eminent domain, **Spec L 13:7.**
Act as supplemental to other laws, **Spec L 13:22.**
Actions upon bonds, **Spec L 13:14.**
Application for issuance of bonds, **Spec L 13:17.**
Bids, purchasing fuel and other supplies without, **Spec L 13:19.**
Board of directors, **Spec L 13:4.**
Bonds and notes.
Applications for issuance, **Spec L 13:17.**
Consent necessary to issue, **Spec L 13:18.**
Decisions on application for issuance of bonds, **Spec L 13:17.**
Investments, bonds as proper and legal investment, **Spec L 13:15.**
Investment securities under Uniform Commercial Code, bonds, **Spec L 13:16.**
Issuance of, **Spec L 13:9.**
Obligation of state, cities, or towns, **Spec L 13:12.**
Refunding bonds, issuance, **Spec L 13:11.**
Suits, **Spec L 13:14.**
Trust agreement securing bonds, **Spec L 13:10.**
Uniform Commercial Code, bonds as investment securities, **Spec L 13:16.**

WHOLESALE ELECTRIC COMPANY —Cont'd
Charges.
Fees and charges. See within this heading, "Fees and charges."
Cities.
Municipalities. See within this heading, "Municipalities."
Commonwealth, bonds not obligation, **Spec L 13:12.**
Condemnation, acquisition of property, **Spec L 13:7.**
Consent necessary to issue bonds, **Spec L 13:18.**
Construction and interpretation, **Spec L 13:23.**
Contracts to sell or purchase electrical output, **Spec L 13:6.**
Controlling nature of Act, **Spec L 13:22.**
Definitions, **Spec L 13:1.**
Directors, **Spec L 13:4.**
Dissolution, vesting of title to funds and properties, **Spec L 13:21.**
Electric services.
Contracts to sell or purchase electric output, **Spec L 13:6.**
Fees and charges. See within this heading, "Fees and charges."
Eminent domain, acquisition of property, **Spec L 13:7.**
Expenses of members, **Spec L 13:3.**
Fees and charges, **Spec L 13:6.**
Electric services, **Spec L 13:10.**
Fuel or supplies, purchase without bidding, **Spec L 13:19.**
Funds.
Trust, **Spec L 13:13.**
Trust funds, **Spec L 13:13.**
Vesting of title upon termination or dissolution, **Spec L 13:21.**
Interpretation, **Spec L 13:23.**
Investments, bonds, **Spec L 13:15.**
Investment securities under Uniform Commercial Code, bonds, **Spec L 13:16.**
Laws applicable to corporation, **Spec L 13:19.**
Liberal construction to be given Act, **Spec L 13:23.**
Massachusetts Wholesale Electric Company Trust, termination, **Spec L 13:25.**
Members and membership.
Expenses, **Spec L 13:3.**
Powers, **Spec L 13:3.**

WHOLESALE ELECTRIC COMPANY —Cont'd
Members and membership —Cont'd
Representatives of members, **Spec L 13:3.**
Voting, **Spec L 13:3.**
Municipalities.
Bonds not obligations, **Spec L 13:12.**
Special obligation, **Spec L 13:6.**
Notes.
Bonds and notes. See within this heading, "Bonds and notes."
Officers, **Spec L 13:4.**
Powers of corporation, **Spec L 13:5.**
Property.
Acquisition by eminent domain, **Spec L 13:7.**
Vesting of title upon termination or dissolution, **Spec L 13:21.**
Public nature of corporation, **Spec L 13:2.**
Public official as director or officer of corporation, **Spec L 13:4.**
Rates, **Spec L 13:6, 13:10.**
Refunding bonds, issuance, **Spec L 13:11.**
Reports and records, annual report, **Spec L 13:20.**
Representatives of members, **Spec L 13:3.**
Rights and powers of corporation, **Spec L 13:5.**
Sales or exchanges of electrical output, contracts, **Spec L 13:6.**
Severability, **Spec L 13:24.**
State, bonds not obligation, **Spec L 13:12.**
Suits upon bonds, **Spec L 13:14.**
Supplemental nature of Act, **Spec L 13:22.**
Taxation, **Spec L 13:9.**
Termination.
Massachusetts Wholesale Electric Company Trust, **Spec L 13:25.**
Vesting of title to funds and properties, **Spec L 13:21.**
Title to funds and properties, vesting upon termination and dissolution, **Spec L 13:21.**
Towns, special obligation, **Spec L 13:6.**
Trusts and trust funds, **Spec L 13:13.**
Agreement securing bonds, **Spec L 13:10.**

WHOLESALE ELECTRIC COMPANY —Cont'd

Trusts and trust funds —Cont'd
Termination of Massachusetts Wholesale Electric Company Trust, **Spec L 13:25.**
Vesting of title to funds and properties upon termination or dissolution, **Spec L 13:21.**
Voting by members, **Spec L 13:3.**
Wholesale Electric Company Trust, termination, **Spec L 13:25.**

WHOLESALERS.

Alcoholic liquors.
  See ALCOHOLIC LIQUORS.
Bedding, upholstery jobber as exempt from license law, **94:270.**
Cigarette tax.
  See CIGARETTE TAX.
Energy Resources Department, **25A:3, 25A:7.**
Hawkers and peddlers statute as inapplicable, **101:15.**
Housing and community development department, eligible business facilities under programs, **23B:13.**
Licenses for, **62C:67.**
Marine fish.
  See MARINE FISH AND FISHERIES.
Milk jobbers, registration, **94:16F.**
Petroleum products, records and reports of Energy Resources Department regarding, **25A:7.**
Pharmacists and pharmacies, **112:36A-112:36D.**
  See PHARMACISTS AND PHARMACIES.
Shellfish, contaminated, increase in penalties for selling, **130:75.**
Stuffed toys, licenses required, **94:271.**
Transient vendors, restrictions on sales, **101:7.**

WIC PROGRAM ACT, 111I:1 et seq.

WIDOW OR WIDOWER.
See SURVIVING SPOUSE.

WIDTH.

Buses, limitation of width, **90:19.**
Federal Surface Transportation Assistance Act of 1982, motor vehicle requirements, **85:2B.**
Tires, **40:21, 90:19.**
Trailers and semi-trailers, **90:19, 90:19F.**

WIDTH —Cont'd

Zoning requirements as to, exemptions, **40:6.**

WIFE.
See HUSBAND AND WIFE.

WIGS.

Accident and sickness insurance.
  Required coverage, **175:47T.**
Group insurance for state employees.
  Required coverage, **32A:17E.**
Health maintenance organizations.
  Required coverage, **176G:4J.**
Medical service corporations.
  Required coverage, **176A:8T.**
  Group coverage, **176B:4R.**

WILBRAHAM.

Congressional district, **57:1.**
District court, **218:1.**
Medical examiner district, **38:1.**
Senatorial district, **57:3.**

WILD AZALEAS.

Digging up plant as criminal offense, **266:116A.**

WILD BERRIES.

License to peddle not required, **101:17.**

WILD CATS, 131:5, 131:76.

WILD FLOWERS.

License to peddle not required, **101:17.**
Protection, **266:116A.**

WILDLIFE.
See FISH AND GAME.

WILD TURKEY.

Designation as game bird of the Commonwealth, **2:36.**

WILLIAMSBURG.

Congressional district, **57:1.**
Medical examiner district, **38:1.**
Senatorial district, **57:3.**

WILLIAMSTOWN.

District court, **218:1.**
Medical examiner district, **38:1.**
Salaries of district court justices, **218:78.**
Senatorial district, **57:3.**

WILLS, 191:1 et seq.

Abandoned property.
  See ABANDONED, LOST, AND UNCLAIMED PROPERTY.
Abatement, survival.
  See ABATEMENT, SURVIVAL, AND REVIVAL.
Accountant, transfer of working papers, **112:87E.**

WILLS —Cont'd

Actions to recover legacies, **197:19.**
Administrator with will annexed, appointment, **193:9.**
Adoption of children.
  Inclusion of adopted persons in statute against lapsed legacies, **191:22.**
  Rights of adopted children, **210:7-210:9.**
  Taxation of property passing to adopted persons, their heirs, and beneficiaries, **65:1.**
Advancements.
  See ADVANCEMENTS.
Affidavits.
  Probate and Family Court. See within this heading, "Probate and Family Court."
After acquired real estate, passing, **191:19.**
Age of person who may make, **191:1.**
Agreements.
  Contracts and agreements. See within this heading, "Contracts and agreements."
Agriculture department, authority tc accept bequests, **128:4.**
Alienability of estates subject to contingent remainders, executory devises, or other estates in expectancy, **184:2.**
Amortization of bond premiums, **203:21B.**
Anatomical contracts and gifts, **113:7-113:13.**
  Delivery, deposit, and production of will, **113:11.**
  Form and execution, **113:10.**
Annuities and annuity contracts.
  Apportionment, **197:27.**
  Payable from death of testator, **197:26.**
  Trustee's duties as to annuities payable from death of testator, **197:26.**
Annulment of marriage as revoking, **191:9.**
Antilapse statute, **191:22.**
Appeals from allowance or disallowance of claims in insolvent estates, **198:14.**
Appointment and disposal.
  Powers of appointment and disposal. See within this heading, "Powers of appointment and disposal."
Appointment of guardian in proceedings for arbitration or compromise of wills, **204:16, 204:18.**

WILLS —Cont'd
Arbitration of controversies
    involving, **204:14-204:18.**
Attestation.
  Subscribing witnesses. See
    within this heading,
    "Subscribing witnesses."
Attorney general as party to
    probate proceedings, **192:1A.**
Attorneys' fees in connection with
    will construction case,
    215:39B.
Blind, gifts by will to commission,
    6:148.
Bond.
  See EXECUTORS AND
    ADMINISTRATORS.
Bonds and securities.
  Amortization of bond premiums,
    203:21B.
  Regulation of bequest, **191:1A.**
  Uniform Statutory Will Act,
    powers and duties of
    personal representative or
    trustee, **191B:13.**
Bradford Durfee College of
    Technology, devises.
  Management, **74:42L.**
  Research foundation's powers,
    74:46B.
Burning, revocation, **191:8.**
Business corporations.
  Corporations. See within this
    heading, "Corporations."
Cancellation, revocation, **191:8.**
Capacity.
  Mentally ill.
    See MENTALLY ILL AND
      RETARDED PERSONS.
  Testator's capacity, **123B:10,
    191:1.**
  Witnesses' capacity, **191:2,
    191:3.**
Cemeteries.
  See CEMETERIES.
Change in condition or
    circumstances as revocation,
    191:8.
Charges, proceedings for sale of
    lands subject, **183:52.**
Charities and charitable
    contributions.
  Charitable corporations'
    authority to accept bequests,
    180:6, 180:9.
  Compromise of will contest as to
    charitable bequests, **204:16,
    204:17.**
  Income from charitable devise or
    bequest, taxation, **62:3.**

WILLS —Cont'd
Children and minors.
  Adoption of children. See within
    this heading, "Adoption of
    children."
  Distribution of property, **201A:5.**
  Guardians and conservators. See
    within this heading,
    "Guardians and
    conservators."
  Posthumous children, rights and
    liabilities, **191:20, 191:25,
    191:28, 191:29.**
  Pretermitted children. See
    within this heading,
    "Pretermitted children."
  Uniform Statutory Will Act,
    distribution to minor child,
    191B:9.
Cities and towns.
  Acceptance of lands for
    forestation purposes, **132:35.**
  Conservation commissions
    authorized to acquire
    interest in land, **40:8C.**
  Historical commissions, powers,
    40:8D.
  Jurisdiction of land court to
    enforce purposes of bequest,
    185:1.
  Mapping commissions in cities
    and towns, **40:8K.**
  Park purposes, acceptance of
    devise or bequest, **45:3.**
  Shore reservations in towns,
    acceptance of devise,
    45:23C.
  Veterans memorial hospitals,
    acceptance of devise or
    bequest, **40:3.**
Claims under trustee process,
    246:21.
Class gifts.
  Death of legatee before testator
    as affecting, **191:22.**
  Determination of class, **184:6A.**
  Distribution, **197:23.**
  "Heirs" or "next of kin,"
    ascertainment of class in
    limitation of property to
    class described, **184:6A.**
Codicils.
  Definition including, **4:7.**
  Fraudulent destruction or
    concealment, **266:39.**
  Guardian as custodian, **201:38.**
  Larceny, **266:39.**
Common disaster, presumptions in
    use, **190A:1 et seq.**
Communist country, payment of
    legacy of resident, **206:27B.**

WILLS —Cont'd
Competency.
  See MENTALLY ILL AND
    RETARDED PERSONS.
Compromise of controversies as to
    wills, **192:3, 204:14-204:18.**
Concealment of wills.
  Codicil to will, **266:39.**
  Penalty, **191:13, 191:14, 266:39.**
  Proceedings in case, **191:14.**
Conclusiveness of decrees as
    against devisees and legatees,
    192:3.
Concurrent jurisdiction of probate
    courts with supreme judicial
    and superior courts, **215:6.**
Conditional fee, when to become
    fee simple absolute, **184A:3.**
Conditional limitations, sale and
    conveyance of property
    subject, **183:49-183:51.**
Condominium unit as subject to
    devise, **183A:3.**
Conservation commissions and
    commissioners, acceptance of
    bequests, **40:8C, 132:2.**
Conservators.
  Guardians and conservators. See
    within this heading,
    "Guardians and
    conservators."
Construction and interpretation,
    191:1A.
  Arbitration or compromise of
    controversies, **204:14.**
  "Child" as including adopted
    child, **210:8.**
  Compromises and settlements,
    204:14-204:18.
  Counsel fees, **215:39B.**
  Declaratory judgment for
    construction of will, **231A:2.**
  Devisee or legatee dying before
    testator, **191:22.**
  "Die without issue" under real
    property law, **184:6.**
Contempt for failure to present
    will for probate, **191:13,
    191:14.**
Contesting probate.
  Arbitration, compromise, or
    settlement, **204:14-204:18.**
  Election to take under or against
    will, extension of time,
    191:15.
Contingent interests.
  Executory devises. See within
    this heading, "Executory
    devises."
  Perpetuities, rule against.
    See PERPETUITIES, RULE
      AGAINST.

WILLS —Cont'd
Contingent interests —Cont'd
Protection, **204:16, 204:17.**
Contracts and agreements.
Anatomical contracts and gifts.
See within this heading,
"Anatomical contracts and
gifts."
Annuities and annuity contracts.
See within this heading,
"Annuities and annuity
contracts."
Bequest, necessity of writing,
259:5, 259:5A.
Contribution, **191:25-191:30.**
Dower, contribution for loss
occasioned by allowance,
191:30.
Exemption provided by wills,
191:27, 191:30.
Insolvency of devisee OR
LEGATEE, **191:29.**
Omitted children, right and
liability, **191:25, 191:28,
191:29.**
Payment of debts, **197:34.**
Decedent's debts, recovery
upon liability, **197:30.**
Property is taken, **191:26,
191:27 29.**
Personal representative liable in
case of death of devisee or
legatee, **191:29.**
Posthumous children, right and
liability, **191:25, 191:28,
191:29.**
Special appropriation of estate
made by testator, **191:27.**
Conveyance of realty.
Sale and conveyance of realty.
See within this heading,
"Sale and conveyance of
realty."
Corporations.
Not to practice law by drawing
wills, **221:46.**
Recipient of gift under will,
business corporation,
156B:9.
Corrections department,
acceptance of legacies and
devises, **124:10.**
Costs of action.
Concealed wills, proceedings
with respect, **191:14.**
Fees. See within this heading,
"Fees."
Counties, devises or bequests,
34:23.
Crimes.
Offenses and penalties. See
within this heading,
"Offenses and penalties."

WILLS —Cont'd
Criminal history systems board,
bequests, **6:168.**
Criminal justice committee,
bequests of funds, **6:156.**
Curtesy.
Dower. See within this heading,
"Dower."
Custodian's production in court,
191:10-191:14.
Death of devisee or legatee.
Issue to take in case of death
before testator, **191:22.**
Liability for decedent's debts,
197:30.
Debts.
Contribution. See within this
heading, "Contribution."
Liability of devisees and
legatees. See within this
heading, "Liability of
devisees and legatees."
Marshaling assets, **202:9.**
Undevised real estate to be first
sold, **202:4.**
Declaratory judgment for
construction, **231A:2.**
Deeds.
Sale and conveyance. See within
this heading, "Sale and
conveyance of realty."
Defined or construed for general
statutory purposes, **4:7.**
Deposits.
Anatomical contracts and gifts,
113:11.
Custody and delivery, **191:11,
191:12.**
Opened at first probate court
after notice of death, **191:12.**
Probate court, deposit of will,
191:10-191:14.
Unknown legatees, deposit of
legacies, **206:26.**
Unpaid legacies deposited in
co-operative banks,
206:25-206:27A.
Descent.
See DESCENT AND
DISTRIBUTION.
Destruction.
As revocation, **191:8.**
Criminal offense, **266:39.**
Determinable fee, when to become
fee simple absolute, **184A:3.**
"Die without issue," effect of
words, **184:6.**
Disability or incapacity.
Capacity. See within this
heading, "Capacity."

WILLS —Cont'd
Disabled persons.
Handicapped persons. See
within this heading,
"Handicapped persons."
Disclaimer of property received,
191A:2, 191A:10.
Discovery proceedings to obtain
production, **191:14.**
Disposal powers.
Powers of appointment and
disposal. See within this
heading, "Powers of
appointment and disposal."
Disseisin of testator as affecting
devise, **191:24.**
Distribution of unclaimed funds.
Residuary legatees. See within
this heading, "Residuary
legatees."
Divorce, automatic revocation,
191:9.
Domicile of testator, law of, as
governing sufficiency of
execution, **191:5.**
Dower.
Appointment of trustee to hold
share of surviving spouse,
191:16.
Assignment of dower or other
undivided interests, **189:10.**
Contribution for loss due to
allowance, **191:30.**
Election to take against will,
191:15.
Guardian ad litem for
incompetent spouse in
probate of will, **192:1B.**
Rights of surviving spouse,
191:15-191:17.
Waiver of testamentary
provisions, **191:15.**
Will provisions, dower or curtesy
in addition, **191:17.**
Drug rehabilitation division,
acceptance of legacies or
devises, **124:10.**
Effective, when, **191:7.**
Election to take under or against,
191:15.
Eligibility.
Qualification or eligibility. See
within this heading,
"Qualification or eligibility."
Embezzlement by trustee under
trust created by will, **266:57.**
Eminent domain, taking of
property subject to executory
devise, **79:24-79:26.**
Energy resources executive office,
acceptance of bequests, **25A:6.**

WILLS —Cont'd

Enforcement of claim by legatee where executor or administrator refuses or is unable to do so, **230:5.**

Entirety, devise to husband and wife as creating tenancy, **184:7.**

Environmental affairs executive office, acceptance of bequests, **21A:2.**

Estate taxes.
See ESTATE TAXES.

Evidence.
Destruction or concealment of will, **266:39.**
Joint grantees, presumption from conveyance or devise, **184:7.**
Presumption. See within this heading, "Presumption."
Proof of wills, **192:2.**
Public administrators powers to cease on proof, **194:7.**
Subscribing witnesses. See within this heading, "Subscribing witnesses."

Execution of will, **191:1 et seq.**
Anatomical contracts and gifts, **113:10.**
Compliance with statutes, necessity, **191:7.**
Law at time of execution, compliance, **191:4.**
Outside of Commonwealth.
Governing law, **191:5.**
Probate and administration, **192:9-192:11.**
Probate as conclusive as to execution, **191:7.**
Uniform Statutory Will Act, **191B:2.**

Execution sale, redemption, **236:54.**

Executors.
See EXECUTORS AND ADMINISTRATORS.

Executory devises.
Alienability of land subject, **184:2.**
Contingent remainder taking effect in manner, **184:3.**
Conveyances subject, **183:49-183:51.**
Eminent domain, taking of property subject to executory devise, **79:24-79:26.**
Mortgage of property subject, **183:49-183:51.**
Precedent estate, effect of alienation or destruction, **184:10.**

WILLS —Cont'd

Exemptions from giving sureties on bonds, **205:5.**

Failure of issue in lifetime, "Die without issue" as meaning, **184:6.**

Fees.
Attorneys' fees in will construction case, **215:39B.**
Probate, **191:10, 262:40.**

Fee simple.
Long-term estate to be construed, **186:1.**
Presumption of devise, **191:18.**
When determinable fee to become fee simple absolute, **184A:3.**

Fines and penalties.
Offenses and penalties. See within this heading, "Offenses and penalties."

Firearms, permissible transfer to legatees on death of owner, **140:129C.**

Fixtures, effect of will provisions as to removal by life tenant, **184:12.**

Foreign wills.
Execution of will. See within this heading, "Execution of will."
Probate of courts.
Probate and Family Court. See within this heading, "Probate and Family Court."

Forgery, **267:1, 267:5.**

Fraudulent destruction or concealment, **191:13, 191:14, 266:39.**

Future contingent interests.
Contingent interests. See within this heading, "Contingent interests."

Gifts to minors, transfer authorized by will, **201A:5.**

Governor, approval of acceptance of funds given or bequeathed to Commonwealth, **10:17B.**

Guardian ad litem, appointment for incompetent surviving spouse, **192:1B.**

Guardians and conservators.
Appointment in proceedings for arbitration or compromise, **204:16, 204:18.**
Custody of will or codicil, **201:38.**
Election or waiver of rights on behalf of ward, **201:45.**
Exemption from giving sureties on bond, **205:5.**

WILLS —Cont'd

Guardians and conservators —Cont'd
Minor children, **192:1B.**
Nomination by will, **201:3.**
Waiver of rights under wills, **201:45.**

Handicapped persons.
Gifts to commission on employment, **6:107.**
Rehabilitation commission to administer gifts made, **6:83.**

Historical commission's power to accept bequests, **9:27A, 40:8D.**

Homestead as subject to devise and payment of legacies, **188:1, 188:4.**

Hospital school and hospital for state minor wards, acceptance of devises or bequests, **111:62K.**

Housing and urban renewal agencies, acceptance of bequests, **121B:11.**

Human bodies, organs, and tissue.
Anatomical contracts and gifts. See within this heading, "Anatomical contracts and gifts."

Husband and wife.
Annulment, effect on will, **191:9.**
Attesting witness, bequest to spouse, **191:2.**
Devise to spouses as tenancy in common, joint tenancy, or tenancy by entirety, **184:7.**
Dower. See within this heading, "Dower."
Election to take against will, **191:16.**
Marriage as revoking prior will, **191:9.**
Separation, **191:9.**
Simultaneous death, **190A:1 et seq.**
Uniform Statutory Will Act, share of surviving spouse, **191B:5-191B:7, 191B:13.**
Waiver of will provisions, **191:15.**

Implied revocation, **191:8.**

Incapacity.
Capacity. See within this heading, "Capacity."

Income.
Apportionment, **197:27.**
Bequests set aside for charitable purposes, taxation of income, **62:3.**
Legacy or succession tax as chargeable against capital or income, **65:12.**

WILLS —Cont'd
Incompetency.
　See MENTALLY ILL AND
　　RETARDED PERSONS.
Incorporation by reference,
　Uniform Statutory Will Act,
　191B:3.
Indefinite failure of issue, "Die
　without issue" not to be
　construed, **184:6.**
Ineffective wills, **191:7.**
Infants.
　Children and minors. See within
　　this heading, "Children and
　　minors."
Insolvency of legatee or devisee, as
　affecting liability for
　contribution, **191:29.**
Insurance company conversion to
　mutual company, acquisition
　by bequest of own capital
　stock, **175:19D.**
Intention of testator.
　After-acquired real estate,
　　passing, **191:19.**
　Devise of fee as affected, **191:18.**
　Dower in addition to will
　　provisions, **191:17.**
　Revocation as requiring, **191:8.**
　Simultaneous Death Act,
　　190A:5.
Interest and interest rates.
　Apportionment, **197:27.**
　Legacies, rate of interest,
　　197:20.
　Payable from death of testator,
　　197:26.
Interpretation.
　Construction and interpretation.
　　See within this heading,
　　"Construction and
　　interpretation."
Inter vivos gifts in satisfaction of
　legacy.
　See ADVANCEMENTS.
Intestacy.
　See DESCENT AND
　　DISTRIBUTION.
Intestate succession absent valid
　will.
　See DESCENT AND
　　DISTRIBUTION.
"In trust," effect of words, **183:14.**
Issue, adopted children, **191:22.**
Judges of probate and insolvency,
　restrictions on appointment as
　trustee under will, **217:7.**
Land court, jurisdiction to enforce
　purpose of bequest to city or
　town, **185:1.**
Lapse on death of devisee or
　legatee before testator, statute
　against, **191:22.**

WILLS —Cont'd
Larceny and destruction of wills,
　266:39.
Law at time of execution, effect of
　wills made in conformity,
　191:4.
Legacy.
　See LEGACY AND
　　SUCCESSION TAXES.
Letters testamentary.
　See EXECUTORS AND
　　ADMINISTRATORS.
Liability of devisees and legatees.
　Contribution. See within this
　　heading, "Contribution."
　Creditors who may enforce,
　　197:29.
　Death, estate liable, **197:30.**
　Debts of decedent,
　　197:28-197:34.
　　Amount recoverable,
　　　197:29-197:34.
　　Contribution. See within this
　　　heading, "Contribution."
　　Enforcement, **197:29.**
　　Equity suit, when, **197:31,**
　　　197:32.
　　Insolvency, **197:33, 197:34.**
　　Limitation of actions, **197:29.**
　　Marshaling assets, **202:9.**
　　Reversal of probate decree as
　　　affecting, **192:3.**
　　Undevised real estate to be
　　　first sold, **202:4.**
　Decrees affecting, **192:3.**
　Purchasers from devisees or
　　legatees, conclusiveness of
　　decrees in favor, **192:3.**
　Repayment upon reversal of
　　decree, **192:3.**
Life estates, remainders, and
　reversions.
　Alienability of estates subject to
　　contingent remainders,
　　executory devises, or other
　　estates in expectancy, **184:2.**
　Contingent interests. See within
　　this heading, "Contingent
　　interests."
　Devise of life estate with
　　remainder to heirs, **184:5.**
　Executory devises. See within
　　this heading, "Executory
　　devises."
　Limitation of taking effect of
　　contingent remainders,
　　184:3.
　Removal of fixtures by life
　　tenant, effect of will
　　provision, **184:12.**
　Sale and conveyance,
　　183:49-183:51.

WILLS —Cont'd
Life estates, remainders, and
　reversions —Cont'd
　Time for conditional fee or fee
　　subject to reversionary
　　interest to become absolute,
　　184A:3.
Life insurance, company
　converting into mutual
　company, acquisition by
　bequest of own capital stock,
　175:19D.
Limitation of actions, devises and
　legacies, actions to recover,
　197:19.
Limitation of property to class
　described as "heirs" or "next of
　kin," determination of class,
　184:6A.
"Living wills."
　Health care proxies.
　See HEALTH CARE
　　PROXIES.
　Uniform Durable Power of
　　Attorney Act,
　　201B:1-201B:7.
Lost wills.
　See ABANDONED, LOST, AND
　　UNCLAIMED PROPERTY.
Manufactured homes and
　manufactured housing
　communities, **140:32R.**
Marriage or annulment of
　marriage as revoking, **191:9.**
Married women.
　Husband and wife. See within
　　this heading, "Husband and
　　wife."
Marshaling assets to pay debts,
　202:9.
Massachusetts Centers of
　Excellence Corporation,
　powers, **40J:12.**
Mentally ill.
　See MENTALLY ILL AND
　　RETARDED PERSONS.
Minors.
　Children and minors. See within
　　this heading, "Children and
　　minors."
Mortgages of real property.
　Devise of mortgaged property,
　　191:23.
　Executory devise, mortgage of
　　property subject,
　　183:49-183:51.
　Payment of legacies, mortgage,
　　202:28.
Municipalities.
　Cities and towns. See within
　　this heading, "Cities and
　　towns."

WILLS —Cont'd

Mutilation as criminal offense, **266:39.**

Natural resources commissioner, acceptance of bequests, **132A:1.**

New Bedford Institute of Technology, management of devises, **74:42L.**

Nonresident decedent, disposition of property, **199:1.**

Notice.

Allowance of will, **192:12.**

Probate and Family Court. See within this heading, "Probate and Family Court."

Questions under wills, **214:7.**

Tax sale of undivided realty, notice, **60:40.**

Nuncupative wills, **191:6.**

Obliteration, revocation, **191:8.**

Offenses and penalties.

Concealment of will, **191:13, 191:14, 266:39.**

Destruction of will, **266:39.**

Failure to present will for probate, **191:13, 191:14.**

Forgery of will, **267:1, 267:5.**

Omitted children, rights of.

Pretermitted children. See within this heading, "Pretermitted children."

Oral will, **191:6.**

Park purposes, city or town may accept devises and bequests, **45:3.**

Parties to actions.

Arbitration of controversies, actions concerning, **204:15.**

Attorney general as party to certain probate proceedings, **192:1A.**

Creditors of decedent, actions, **197:32.**

Payment of debts.

Debts. See within this heading, "Debts."

Payment of legacies.

Action, **197:19.**

Homestead as subject, **188:1, 188:4.**

Indemnification of executor or administrator, when, **197:21.**

Mortgage of real estate, **202:28.**

Repayment of legacies on reversal of decree, **192:3.**

Sale of real property, **202:1 et seq.**

Pecuniary legacies, rate and accrual date of interest, **197:20.**

WILLS —Cont'd

Penalties.

Offenses and penalties. See within this heading, "Offenses and penalties."

Perpetuities, rule against, **184A:1-184A:6.**

See PERPETUITIES, RULE AGAINST.

Petitions.

Probate and Family Court. See within this heading, "Probate and Family Court."

Pleading.

Probate and Family Court. See within this heading, "Probate and Family Court."

Possessor to present for probate, **191:13.**

Posthumous children, rights and liabilities, **191:20, 191:25, 191:28, 191:29.**

Power of sale of real estate given trustees, **203:16.**

Powers of appointment and disposal.

Exercise of powers, **191:1A, 191:9.**

General bequest exercising power, **191:1A.**

Marriage of testator, will not revoked, **191:9.**

Premiums, amortization of bond, **203:21B.**

Presumption.

Abandoned bequest, arising, **200A:2.**

Common disaster, survivorship, **190A:1 et seq.**

Pretermitted children.

Appointment of guardian ad litem in probate proceedings, **192:1C.**

Contribution, rights and liabilities, **191:25, 191:28, 191:29.**

Right to share in estate, **191:20.**

Probate and Family Court, **192:1 et seq., 215:1 et seq.**

Affidavits.

Accompanying petition for probate, **192:1.**

Subscribing witness affidavit as evidence, **192:2.**

Attorney general as party, **192:1A.**

Conclusiveness of decrees, **191:7, 192:3.**

Concurrent jurisdiction with supreme judicial and superior courts, **215:6.**

WILLS —Cont'd

Probate and Family Court —Cont'd

Consent, probate, **192:2.**

Construction cases, counsel fees, **215:39B.**

Contesting probate. See within this heading, "Contesting probate."

Deposit of will with probate court, **191:10-191:14.**

Executory devises, sale subject, **183:49-183:51.**

Fee for probate, **191:10, 262:40.**

Foreign wills, **192:9-192:11.**

Execution, **192:9-192:11.**

Foreign fiduciaries as affected by admission of will to probate in foreign jurisdiction, **199A:2.**

Notice and hearing, **192:9, 192:10.**

Guardian ad litem for incompetent surviving spouse, **192:1B.**

Judges, restrictions on appointment as trustee under will, **217:7.**

Jurisdiction, **215:3, 215:6.**

Medical assistance division, **118E:32.**

Necessity, **191:7.**

Notice.

Persons interested in foreign will, **192:9.**

To attorney general, **192:1A.**

To devisees and legatees, **192:12.**

Parties to actions. See within this heading, "Parties to actions."

Penalty for failure to present will for probate, **191:13, 191:14.**

Petition.

Affidavit to accompany, **192:1.**

Attorney general to be made party to, when, **192:1A.**

Verification, **192:1.**

Production for probate, duty, **191:12-191:14.**

Proof of will, **192:2.**

Registers of probate and insolvency. See within this heading, "Registers of probate and insolvency."

Restrictions on land contained in will, recording, **184:16, 184:19, 184:29.**

Revocation of letters of administration, **193:6.**

WILLS —Cont'd
Probate and Family Court
—Cont'd
Taking wills from registry,
215:52.
Testimony required, **192:2.**
Verification of petition for
probate, **192:1.**
Probate and insolvency registers.
Registers of probate and
insolvency. See within this
heading, "Registers of
probate and insolvency."
Production for probate,
191:12-191:14.
Proof of will.
Evidence. See within this
heading, "Evidence."
Qualification or eligibility.
Maker of will, **191:1.**
Uniform Statutory Will Act,
191B:2.
Witnesses, **191:2, 191:3.**
Redemption from mortgage, right
to make, **244:33.**
Registers of probate and
insolvency.
Affidavit of subscribing witness
taken before will proved,
192:2.
Copies of wills, **217:15C.**
Furnishing to revenue
department, **217:17.**
Deposit of wills, **191:10-191:12.**
Original will may be taken from
register, **215:2.**
Registration of land titles, **185:97,
185:98.**
See REGISTRATION OF LAND
TITLES.
Rehabilitation commission, gifts,
6:83.
Remainders.
Life estates, remainders, and
reversions. See within this
heading, "Life estates,
remainders, and reversions."
Residuary legatees.
Bond of legatee as executor,
205:3.
Cemetery lot of family not
affected by residuary clause,
114:31.
Distribution of unclaimed funds,
206:28.
Failure of residuary gift,
proportionate distribution,
191:1A.
Res judicata as against devisees
and legatees, **192:3.**
Restriction running with land
contained in will, recordation,
184:16, 184:19, 184:29.

WILLS —Cont'd
Retarded persons.
See MENTALLY ILL AND
RETARDED PERSONS.
Reversions.
Life estates, remainders, and
reversions. See within this
heading, "Life estates,
remainders, and reversions."
Revival of action.
See ABATEMENT, SURVIVAL,
AND REVIVAL.
Revocation, **191:8, 191:9.**
Agreement, **259:5A.**
Right of entry, devise of land to
which testator has only,
191:24.
Rule against perpetuities.
See PERPETUITIES, RULE
AGAINST.
Rules of construction.
Construction and interpretation.
See within this heading,
"Construction and
interpretation."
Sale and conveyance of realty.
Charges, proceedings for sale of
lands subject, **183:52.**
Conclusiveness of decrees as
affecting, **192:3.**
Debts of decedent, sale to pay,
202:4.
Estate at will, **183:3.**
Execution sale, redemption,
236:54.
Executory devises, sale subject,
183:49-183:51.
Legacies, sale to pay, **202:1 et
seq.**
Life estates, remainders, and
reversions, **183:49-183:51.**
Tax sale of undivided realty,
notice, **60:40.**
Undevised real property sold
first to pay debts, **202:4.**
Savings banks.
See SAVINGS BANKS.
Security interest on devised or
bequeathed property as
affecting passing, **191:23.**
Self-proving affidavit, effect and
form, **192:2.**
Separation of spouses as affecting,
191:9.
Setoff of debts due from
beneficiaries, **197:25.**
Settlements involving wills, **192:3,
204:14-204:18.**
Shore reservations in towns,
acceptance of devise, **45:23C.**
Short form terms for wills, **184B:1
to 184B:4.**
Applicability, **184B:1.**

WILLS —Cont'd
Short form terms for wills
—Cont'd
Statutory disability
discretionary powers,
184B:3.
Statutory optional fiduciary
powers, **184B:2.**
Statutory principal discretionary
powers, **184B:4.**
Signature, **191:1.**
Revocation by signed writing,
191:8.
Witnesses.
Subscribing witnesses. See
within this heading,
"Subscribing witnesses."
Simultaneous death act as
affecting disposition of
property under will, **190A:1 et
seq.**
Small estates, procedure where
executor named in will,
195:16A.
Social services department,
acceptance and use of
bequests, **18B:7.**
Special jurisdiction of supreme
judicial and superior courts in
actions for contributions by or
between devisees, **214:3.**
Spouses.
Husband and wife. See within
this heading, "Husband and
wife."
State agencies, acquiring buildings
for use, **7:40F.**
State colleges, management of
grants or devises, **73:14,
75:11.**
State library, bequests, **6:37A.**
Statute of frauds for contract or
agreement as to bequests,
259:5, 259:5A.
Subscribing witnesses, **191:1.**
Affidavit in support of will,
192:2.
Competency, **191:2, 191:3.**
Devises or bequests, **191:2.**
Number required, **191:1.**
Spouse of, devise or bequest,
191:2.
Subsequent incompetency,
191:3.
Testimony required for probate,
192:2.
Subsequent will as revoking prior
one, **191:8.**
Sunday, activities permitted,
136:6.
Superior court, concurrent
jurisdiction with probate
court, **215:6.**

WILLS —Cont'd
Supreme judicial court.
Compromise of wills,
    204:14-204:18.
Concurrent jurisdiction with
    probate court, **215:6.**
Exemption from giving sureties
    on bond, when, **205:5.**
Fixing of interest rate on
    pecuniary legacies, **197:20.**
Survival of action.
    See ABATEMENT, SURVIVAL,
      AND REVIVAL.
Surviving spouse.
    Husband and wife. See within
      this heading, "Husband and
      wife."
Survivorship in common disaster,
    presumption, **190A:1 et seq.**
Taxation.
    Estate taxes.
      See ESTATE TAXES.
    Legacy.
      See LEGACY AND
        SUCCESSION TAXES.
Tax sale of undivided realty,
    notice, **60:40.**
Tearing, revocation, **191:8.**
Technology development
    corporation, acceptance of
    bequests, **40G:3.**
Temporary administrators or
    administrators with will
    annexed, request, **193:7A.**
Tenancy by entirety may be
    created by devises, **184:7.**
Tewksbury Hospital,
    administration of property
    received by bequest, **122:5.**
Time as of which effective, **191:7.**
Time limitations on conditions or
    restrictions attached to devise,
    184:23.
Title to devised land.
    Approval, **132:2.**
    Disseisin of testator, **191:24.**
    Registration, **185:97, 185:98.**
    See REGISTRATION OF
      LAND TITLES.
Towns.
    Cities and towns. See within
      this heading, "Cities and
      towns."
Trusts.
    See TRUSTS AND TRUSTEES.
Two or more persons, effect of
    devise, **184:7.**
Unclaimed property, will as
    affecting presumption as to
    abandonment, **200A:2.**
Uniform Statutory Will Act,
    191B:1 et seq.
    Conflicts, **191B:3.**

WILLS —Cont'd
Uniform Statutory Will Act
  —Cont'd
Construction and application,
    191B:15.
Eligibility to make statutory
    will, **191B:2.**
Execution, **191B:2.**
Executors.
    See EXECUTORS AND
      ADMINISTRATORS.
Mentally disabled person,
    distribution, **191B:9.**
Minor child, distribution,
    191B:9.
Passing of statutory will estate,
    191B:4.
Personal representative.
    Defined, **191B:1.**
    Executors.
      See EXECUTORS AND
        ADMINISTRATORS.
    Trusts.
      See TRUSTS AND
        TRUSTEES.
Surviving spouse, share,
    191B:5-191B:7, 191B:13.
Trusts.
    See TRUSTS AND
      TRUSTEES.
Unknown legatees, deposit of
    legacies, **206:26.**
Uses and trusts, **183:14.**
Veterans' memorials, cities and
    towns may accept bequests or
    devises, **40:3.**
Waiver of provisions.
    Guardian's waiver, **201:45.**
    Surviving spouses, waiver,
      191:15.
Who may make, **191:1.**
Wildlife sanctuaries, acceptance of
    bequests, **131:7.**
Witnesses.
    Subscribing witnesses. See
      within this heading,
      "Subscribing witnesses."
Worthier title to property doctrine,
    abolition, **184:33A, 184:33B.**
Writing.
    Agreement as to bequests, **259:5,**
      259:5A.
    Instrument, **191:1.**
    Revocation, **191:8.**
    Signature. See within this
      heading, "Signature."
Years, estate for long term, **186:1.**
Youth service division, taking of
    bequests or devises, **120:1.**

WILMINGTON.
Congressional district, **57:1.**
District court, **218:1.**

WILMINGTON —Cont'd
Medical examiner district, **38:1.**
Senatorial district, **57:3.**

WINCHENDON.
Congressional district, **57:1.**
District court, **218:1, 218:79.**
Medical examiner district, **38:1.**
Salaries of district court justices,
    218:78.
Senatorial district, **57:3.**

WINCHESTER.
Congressional district, **57:1.**
District court, **218:1.**
Medical examiner district, **38:1.**
Metropolitan air pollution control
    district, membership,
    111:142B.
Parks, provision by metropolitan
    commission, **92:33.**
Senatorial district, **57:3.**

WINDING UP.
Limited liability companies,
    156C:45.

WIND INSURANCE.
See WEATHER INSURANCE.

WINDOWS.
Advertising matter on windows of
    building, **138:1.**
Easement of light and air not
    acquired, **187:1.**
Gaming houses, obstructions,
    271:25.
Motor vehicles.
    See MOTOR VEHICLES.
Public contract bids, categories of
    specifications, **149:44F.**
Railroad passenger cars,
    installation of safety windows,
    160:163.
State House, state safety code
    applicable to window cleaners,
    143:2A.
Taverns and restaurants, **138:1.**
Windshields.
    See WINDSHIELDS.

WIND POWER.
Credit unions, real estate loans,
    171:60.
Public works and contracts, solar
    energy estimates required,
    149:44M.
Taxation.
    Alternative energy resources,
      tax incentive for use,
      63:38H.
    Exemption of solar or
      wind-powered systems, **59:5.**
    Residential property tax credit,
      62:6.

WINDSHIELDS.
Motor vehicles.
  See MOTOR VEHICLES.
Track motor cars, **160:163A.**

WINDSOR.
District court, **218:1.**
Medical examiner district, **38:1.**
Senatorial district, **57:3.**

WINES.
Auctioning wine, temporary liquor
  licenses for, **138:15D,**
  138:15E.
Charitable organizations,
  auctioning of wine, **138:15D.**
Covering of wines on Sunday,
  138:23.
Defined, **138:1.**
Education corporations and
  institutions.
  Farmer-winery license as
    affected by proximity of
    schools, **138:19B.**
  Special license for dispensing,
    138:14.
Excise tax, **138:21.**
Farmer-wineries, **138:1, 138:19B.**
  See FARMER-WINERIES.
Hawkers and peddlers forbidden to
  sell, **101:16.**
Innholders, storage of wines in
  warehouses, **138:20.**
Kosher food, **94:156.**
  Sundays, kosher wine sold on
    Sundays, **136:6, 138:33.**
Licenses and permits.
  Auctions, temporary liquor
    licenses for wine auctions,
    138:15D, 138:15E.
  Restaurants, wine tastings,
    138:12, 138:15.
Manufacturers' sale, **138:19.**
Number of licenses for sale,
  138:17.
Pharmacist on prescription, sale,
  138:29.
Reduction in proof of certain wines
  for tax purposes, **138:21.**
Restaurants, wine tastings,
  138:12, 138:15.
Sales and transfers.
  Auction sales, temporary liquor
    licenses for, **138:15D,**
    138:15E.
  Hawkers and peddlers
    prohibited, **101:16.**
  Kosher wine sold on Sundays,
    136:6, 138:33.
  Pharmacist selling on
    prescription, **138:29.**
  Wholesalers importers, **138:18.**

WINES —Cont'd
Schools.
  Education corporations and
    institutions. See within this
    heading, "Education
    corporations and
    institutions."
Sunday, wines and malt liquors
  not required to be covered,
  138:23.
Wholesalers and importers, sale,
  138:18.
Zoning restrictions, exemption of
  viticulture, **40A:3.**

WINFIELD SCOTT.
Flag standard of General Scott,
  8:17A.

WINKLES.
Disposal, **130:103.**

WINTHROP.
Congressional district, **57:1.**
Metropolitan air pollution control
  district, membership,
  111:142B.
Parks, provision by metropolitan
  commission, **92:33.**
Refuse disposal, **92:9A.**
Register of deeds, transmission of
  record of votes, **54:112.**
Senatorial district, **57:3.**
Suffolk County extension service
  budget, **128:44A.**

WIRES.
See TRANSMISSION LINES
AND EQUIPMENT.

WIRETAPPING, 272:99.
See EAVESDROPPING AND
WIRETAPPING.

WITHHOLDING OF TAX, 62B:1
et seq.
Abatement of tax, **62C:37.**
Accelerated collection of withheld
  taxes, **62B:5.**
Accounting machines to calculate
  amount to be withheld, **62B:2.**
Additional tax, estimate, **62B:2.**
Additional withholdings,
  agreement between employer
  and employee, **62B:2.**
Amounts to be deducted and
  withheld, **62B:2, 62B:9,**
  62B:12.
Assessment against employer
  failing to withhold or pay tax,
  62B:6.
Bank, requiring employer to
  deposit taxes, **62B:7.**
Cancellation of notice to employer
  failing to withhold taxes, file
  returns, or pay taxes, **62B:7.**

WITHHOLDING OF TAX
—Cont'd
Certificates as to withholding
  exemption and deduction,
  62B:4.
Changes in dependency
  deductions, new withholding
  exemption and deduction
  certificate, **62B:4.**
Circumstances beyond control of
  employer as excusing failure
  to deposit taxes in bank,
  62B:7.
Collection.
  Bank, requiring employer to
    make deposit, **62B:7.**
  Federal withholding tax, **58:28A,**
    58:28B.
  Remedies, **62B:6.**
Commissioner.
  Revenue department and
    commissioner. See within
    this heading, "Revenue
    department and
    commissioner."
Contract between employer and
  employee for additional
  withholdings, **62B:2.**
Correction of withholding
  exemption and deduction
  certificate upon change in
  number of dependency
  deductions, **62B:4.**
Credits.
  Amount withheld as credit on
    income tax of employee,
    62B:9, 62B:12.
  Estimated income tax.
    Declaration of, statement of
      estimated credits for
      withholding taxes,
      62B:13.
Date.
  Effective dates of withholding
    exemption and deduction
    certificates, **62B:4.**
  Payment of tax, time, **62B:5,**
    62B:7.
  Payroll periods, use in
    computing amount to be
    withheld, **62B:2.**
  "Status determination date"
    defined under withholding
    tax law, **62B:4.**
  Withholding tax statement to
    employee, time for
    furnishing, **62B:5.**
Deductions or exemptions for
  dependents, **62B:2, 62B:4,**
  62B:9, 62B:12.
Deemed date of payment as to
  withheld taxes, **62C:79.**

WITHHOLDING OF TAX
　—Cont'd
Definitions under tax law, **62B:1, 62E:1.**
Delivery of notice in hand to require employer to deposit taxes in bank, **62B:7.**
Dependency deductions or exemptions.
　Defined, **62B:4.**
　Rate of taxation, **62B:2, 62B:9, 62B:12.**
　Withholding exemption and deduction certificates, **62B:4.**
Duration of effectiveness of withholding exemption and deduction certificates, **62B:4.**
Employee defined, **62B:1.**
Employer.
　Additional withholdings, agreement between employer and employee, **62B:2.**
　Assessment against, for failure to withhold and pay over to commissioner, **62B:6.**
　Bank, requiring employer to deposit taxes, **62B:7.**
　Defined under withholding tax law, **62B:1, 62B:5.**
　Liability for payment of tax, **62B:5, 62B:10, 62C:10.**
　Notice to employer, **62B:7, 62C:10.**
　Report as wages paid, penalty for late filing, **62C:34.**
　Statement of wages, failing, **62B:5.**
　Wage reporting system, **62B:2, 62E:1 et seq.**
　　See WAGE REPORTING SYSTEM.
Estimates.
　Credits for estimated tax, **62B:13.**
　Dependency deductions, estimate of future, **62B:4.**
　Quarterly earnings, **62B:2.**
Exemptions.
　Dependency deductions or exemptions, **62B:2, 62B:4, 62B:9, 62B:12.**
　Students in seasonal or temporary employment, **62B:1.**
　Withholding exemption and deduction certificates, **62B:4.**
Extension of time for filing returns, **62B:5.**

WITHHOLDING OF TAX
　—Cont'd
Federal Internal Revenue Code, **62B:1, 62B:5.**
Federal withholding tax.
　Collection of withholding tax by state officers, **58:28A, 58:28B.**
　Employer liability, withholding tax laws as affecting, **62C:10.**
　Federal commissioner of internal revenue to be given copy of statements, **58:28B.**
　Public officers and employees, withholding with respect to salaries, **58:28A, 58:28B.**
Filing of statements by employer, **62B:5.**
Fines and penalties.
　Bank, employer failing to deposit taxes, **62B:7.**
　Failure to withhold, **149:148B.**
　Report of wages paid, penalty for late filing, **62C:34.**
　Wage reporting system, **62E:8, 62E:9.**
Forms.
　Returns, approval of form, **62B:5.**
　Withholding exemption and deduction certificate, prescribing form, **62B:4.**
Increase in number of dependency deductions, new withholding exemption and deduction certificate, **62B:4.**
Internal Revenue Code of United States.
　Application of definitions, **62B:1.**
　Conformity of state law to federal law, **62B:1.**
　Federal withholding tax, **58:28A, 58:28B, 62C:10.**
　Payment of withholding tax, **62B:5.**
Lack of funds as excuse for failure to deposit taxes in bank, **62B:7.**
Miscellaneous payroll periods, as basis of computing amount to be withheld, **62B:2.**
Monthly returns and payments, **62B:5.**
Municipal officers and employees, collection of federal withholding tax, **58:28A, 58:28B.**
National bank, requiring employer to deposit taxes, **62B:7.**
Nearest dollar, rounding off computation, **62B:2.**

WITHHOLDING OF TAX
　—Cont'd
Notice to employer, **62B:7.**
　Cancellation of notice, **62B:7.**
　Returns required, **62C:10.**
Other than wages, remuneration paid, **62B:3.**
Payment of tax.
　Employer's liability, **62B:5, 62B:10, 62C:10.**
　Time, **62B:5, 62B:7.**
Payroll periods, use in computing amount to be withheld, **62B:2.**
Personal liability of employer, **62B:5, 62B:10.**
Public employees' federal withholdings, **58:28A, 58:28B.**
Quarterly earnings, calculating amount to be withheld on estimate, **62B:2.**
Reasonable doubt as to requirement of withholding of tax, as excusing failure to deposit taxes in bank, **62B:7.**
Reduction in number of dependency deductions, new withholding exemption and deduction certificate, **62B:4.**
Remuneration other than wages, **62B:3.**
Reports of wages, **62B:2, 62E:1 et seq.**
　See WAGE REPORTING SYSTEM.
Returns, **62B:5, 62C:10.**
　Failure to file, **62B:7.**
Revenue department and commissioner.
　Amount to be withheld, determination, **62B:2.**
　Assessment against employer for failure to withhold and pay over to commissioner, **62B:6.**
　Commissioner as meaning, **62B:1.**
　Federal withholding tax, copy of statements, **58:28B.**
　Returns, approval of form, **62B:5.**
　Withholding exemption and deduction certificate, power to prescribe form and contents, **62B:4.**
Rounding off amount to nearest dollar, **62B:2.**
Seasonal employment, students in, excluded, **62B:1.**
Service of notice to employer failing to withhold taxes, file returns, or pay taxes, **62B:7.**

WITHHOLDING OF TAX
—Cont'd
Special bank deposit of taxes in trust for Commonwealth, **62B:7.**
Statement of wages to employee, **62B:5.**
"Status determination date" defined under withholding tax law, **62B:4.**
Students in seasonal or temporary employment, excluded, **62B:1.**
Surtaxes and additional taxes, inclusion, **62B:2.**
Tables for computing amount to be withheld, **62B:2.**
Tax administration provisions as applicable, **62C:2.**
Temporary employment, students in, excluded, **62B:1.**
Time.
Effective dates of withholding exemption and deduction certificates, **62B:4.**
Payment of tax, time, **62B:5, 62B:7.**
Payroll periods, use in computing amount to be withheld, **62B:2.**
"Status determination date" defined under withholding tax law, **62B:4.**
Withholding tax statement to employee, time for furnishing, **62B:5.**
Trust, amounts withheld as held in trust for Commonwealth, **62B:5, 62B:7.**
Trust company, requiring employer to deposit taxes, **62B:7.**
Underpayment defined under withholding tax law, **62B:14.**
United States.
Federal withholding tax, **58:28A, 58:28B, 62C:10.**
Internal Revenue Code, **62B:1, 62B:5.**
Wage reporting system., **62B:2, 62E:1 et seq.**
See WAGE REPORTING SYSTEM.
Wages defined under withholding tax law, **62B:1.**

WITHHOLDING RENTS.
Unfitness of residential property, **239:8A.**

WITHHOLDINGS FROM WAGES.
Payroll.
See PAYROLL AND PAYROLL DEDUCTIONS.

WITHHOLDINGS FROM WAGES —Cont'd
Withholding of tax.
See WITHHOLDING OF TAX.

WITHOUT PREJUDICE.
Reservation of rights under Commercial Code by use of term, **106:1-207.**

WITNESSES, 233:1 et seq.
Abused children, out of court statements by victims, sexual contact, **233:81-233:83.**
Accessory after the fact, limitation of cross-examination, **274:4.**
Accidents causing death, investigation, **159:29.**
Accused.
Failure to testify, **278:23.**
Fees. See within this heading, "Fees."
Immunity, defendant not to be convicted solely on testimony or evidence of witness granted, **233:20I.**
Psychiatric examination, admissibility of statements of accused while undergoing, **233:23B.**
Right to be faced by witnesses, **263:5; MA Const Part 1 Art 12; US Const Amend 6.**
Right to testify voluntarily, **233:20.**
Self-incrimination.
See SELF-INCRIMINATION.
Addresses of, discovery proceedings to obtain, **231:63.**
Adjoining states.
Other states. See within this heading, "Other states, attendance of witnesses in or from."
Adjournment or continuance, fees of certain officers, **262:53.**
Administration and finance commission hearings, **7:11.**
Administrative proceedings, **30A:9-30A:12, 233:8-233:11.**
Adverse party, cross-examination, **233:22.**
Aeronautics commission, attendance before, **90:42.**
Affirmation.
Oath or affirmation. See within this heading, "Oath or affirmation."
Alcoholic liquors.
Complainants of illegal dealing as witnesses, **138:44.**

WITNESSES —Cont'd
Alcoholic liquors —Cont'd
Grand jury investigation of violations, grant of immunity, **233:20D.**
Places illegally keeping or selling liquor, persons found, **139:13, 139:16A.**
Ancient criminal offenses, showing, **233:21.**
Antitrust laws.
See RESTRAINTS OF TRADE AND MONOPOLIES.
Appeal.
See APPEAL AND REVIEW.
Appellate tax board, **58A:11.**
Witness fees, **58A:11, 58A:12.**
Arbitration.
See ARBITRATION.
Architects' registration board, summons, **13:44C.**
Arrest.
Constitution of Massachusetts, power of governor, house of representatives or senate to punish assault upon or arrest of witness, **MA Const Part 2 Ch 1 Sec 2 Arts 10, 11.**
Generally.
See ARREST.
Material witness, commitment of.
Commitment. See within this heading, "Commitment."
Assault and battery.
Binding over after inquest, **38:13.**
Constitution of Massachusetts, power of governor, house of representatives or senate to punish assault upon or arrest of witness, **MA Const Part 2 Ch 1 Sec 2 Arts 10, 11.**
Grand jury, immunity of witnesses before, **233:20D.**
Assistant of bank commissioner sent in lieu of commissioner, **233:3A.**
Atheism as affecting credibility, **233:19.**
Attendance, **233:1 et seq.**
Attestation.
See ATTESTATION AND ATTESTING WITNESSES.
Attorney general.
See ATTORNEY GENERAL.
Attorneys at law.
Inspector general, compelling testimony by witness, **12A:7.**

WITNESSES —Cont'd
Attorneys at law —Cont'd
Right to counsel on issues of
materiality of testimony and
of recognizance with or
without surety, **276:47.**
Audit of municipal accounts,
powers of director to accounts
with respect to, **44:45.**
Auditors.
See AUDITORS, MASTERS,
AND REFEREES.
Automobiles.
Motor vehicles. See within this
heading, "Motor vehicles."
Autopsies by medical examiners,
attendance, **38:6.**
Award.
See ARBITRATION.
Bail and recognizance, **38:13,
276:45-276:51, 277:70.**
See BAIL AND
RECOGNIZANCE.
Banks.
See BANKS AND BANKING.
Barbers' board of registration,
powers, **112:87M.**
Binding over.
See BAIL AND
RECOGNIZANCE.
Boards, commissions, and
commissioners, administrative
proceedings before,
30A:9-30A:12, 233:8-233:11.
Boxing commission, summoning
before, **147:44.**
Bribery.
Grand jury, witness appearing
before, **233:20D.**
Immunity, **234:33, 268:13,
268:13B, 268:14.**
Participant not excused from
testifying in prosecution for
bribery of agent or servant,
271:39.
Building regulations and
standards board, powers and
duties, **143:94.**
Campaign expenditures.
See CAMPAIGN
EXPENDITURES AND
CONTRIBUTIONS.
Capital cases.
See MURDER OR HOMICIDE.
Carriers.
See CARRIERS.
Certificates and certification.
False certification liability,
262:62.
Fees. See within this heading,
"Fees."

WITNESSES —Cont'd
Certificates and certification
—Cont'd
Land surveyors or professional
engineers, proceedings to
revoke certificate, **112:81P.**
State police officer's certification
of witness fees and travel
expenses, **262:53B.**
Teachers' certification, hearing,
71:38G.
Character, credibility as affected,
233:21A, 233:23.
Charities and charitable
organizations, **12:8H, 12:8I,
68:30.**
Children.
See CHILDREN AND MINORS.
City clerk, proceedings for review
of removal or suspension,
41:19D.
City council, witnesses before,
233:8.
Civil service investigations.
Oaths, **31:72.**
Perjury.
See PERJURY.
Summoning for investigations,
7:4I, 31:72.
Clerks of court.
Fees. See within this heading,
"Fees."
Collective bargaining agreements
to arbitrate, cross-examination
of witness at hearings,
150C:5.
Commercial motor vehicle division,
25:12G.
Commitment.
Bail.
See BAIL AND
RECOGNIZANCE.
Discharge in misdemeanor case
where injured party is
satisfied, **276:55, 276:56.**
Discharge on recognizance,
276:49, 276:51.
Fees, **262:30.**
Handcuffing witness to prisoner,
penalty, **276:54.**
Impossibility of procuring
sureties, **277:70.**
Presumption of perjury, **268:4.**
Treatment of witnesses during
confinement, **276:52.**
Communications lawfully
intercepted, testimony, **272:99.**
Compelling attendance and
testimony, **233:11.**
Accused's right of compulsory
process to obtain attendance
of witness, **US Const
Amend 6.**

WITNESSES —Cont'd
Compelling attendance and
testimony —Cont'd
Boards and commissions,
testimony before, **233:6,
233:8-233:11.**
Deponents, **233:38.**
Employment security, **151A:43.**
Executive council and
committee, **233:7.**
Penalty for failure to appear at
criminal proceeding in
adjoining state, **233:13,
233:13A.**
Reciprocity with other states,
233:13A-233:13D.
Subpoenas, **277:68.**
See SUBPOENAS.
Summoning. See within this
heading, "Summoning."
Town officers, commissions, and
so forth, witnesses before,
233:9.
Warrant. See within this
heading, "Warrant."
Workers' compensation, **152:5.**
Compensation.
Fees. See within this heading,
"Fees."
Traveling expenses. See within
this heading, "Traveling
expenses."
Competency, **233:20.**
Comptroller of state.
Fees. See within this heading,
"Fees."
Compulsory attendance.
Compelling attendance and
testimony. See within this
heading, "Compelling
attendance and testimony."
Conciliation and arbitration board,
proceedings before, **150:8,
262:29.**
Confrontation by, accused's right,
**263:5; MA Const Part 1 Art
12; US Const Amend 6.**
Constitution of Massachusetts.
Assault upon or arrest of
witness, power of governor,
house of representatives or
senate to punish, **MA Const
Part 2 Ch 1 Sec 2 Arts 10,
11.**
Right of accused to confront, **MA
Const Part 1 Art 12.**
Self-incrimination, **MA Const
Part 1 Art 12.**
Constitution of the United States.
See CONSTITUTION OF THE
UNITED STATES.

WITNESSES —Cont'd
Contempt, **233:5, 233:6.**
  See CONTEMPT.
Contest of elections of presidential
  electors, witnesses testifying,
  54:120.
Continuance or adjournment, fees
  of certain officers, **262:53.**
Conviction of crime as affecting
  credibility, showing of record,
  233:21.
Coroner's inquest, certain officers
  not to receive witness fees for
  appearance, **262:50.**
Corrections, duty of commissioner,
  276:52.
Corroboration.
  Sexual offenses, **233:82, 272:11.**
  Treason, proof, **264:4; US Const
    Art 3 Sec 3 cl 1.**
Costs.
  Expenses and costs. See within
    this heading, "Expenses and
    costs."
Counterfeiting, testimony, **267:14.**
County commissioners.
  Fees for appearing before,
    262:29.
  Nonattendance of witnesses,
    233:5.
Courts-martial.
  See MILITIA.
Credibility.
  Impeachment. See within this
    heading, "Impeachment."
Criminal offender record
  information system, **6:175,
    6:178A.**
Cross-examination.
  Accessory after fact, limitation
    on cross-examination, **274:4.**
  Adverse party called as witness,
    233:22.
  Collective bargaining
    agreements to arbitrate,
    cross examination of
    witnesses at hearings,
    150C:5.
  Criminal cases, **276:38.**
  Employment security, **151A:41.**
  Impeachment. See within this
    heading, "Impeachment."
  Officer or agent of corporate
    party, **233:22.**
  Opportunity for, as essential to
    admissibility of deposition
    or affidavit, **233:44.**
  Rape victim, confidential
    communications, **233:20J.**
  Registration of voters, illegal or
    incorrect proceedings, **51:49.**

WITNESSES —Cont'd
Damages, liability for, from failure
  to obey summons, **233:4.**
Deaf witnesses, appointment of
  interpreters, **221:92A.**
Death sentence.
  Capital cases. See within this
    heading, "Capital cases."
Definitions, **233:23E.**
Delinquent children, **119:54,
    119:58.**
  See JUVENILE COURTS AND
    DELINQUENT CHILDREN.
Depositions, **233:24-233:63.**
  See DEPOSITIONS.
Desertion and nonsupport
  proceedings, **273:7.**
Detectives, witness fees, **262:53B.**
Disability or incapacity to act,
  233:20.
Disbelief in God as affecting
  credibility, **233:19.**
Discovery.
  See DISCOVERY AND
    DISCLOSURE.
Discrimination, witnesses before
  commission against, **151B:3.**
District.
  See DISTRICT AND
    PROSECUTING
    ATTORNEYS.
District courts.
  See DISTRICT COURTS.
Domicile and residence.
  Other states, attendance of
    witnesses in or from. See
    within this heading, "Other
    states, attendance of
    witnesses in or from."
  Picketing of building or
    residence occupied by
    witness, **268:13A.**
  Police witnesses attending court
    outside domiciliary area,
    fees and expenses, **262:53A,
    262:53B.**
  Service of summons on witness,
    233:2.
Druggists and pharmacists.
  Hearings on complaints before
    board of registration,
    112:27, 112:62.
  Revocation or suspension of
    registration or permit,
    proceedings, **112:40,
    112:42A.**
Election offenses.
  See ELECTION OFFENSES.
Elections.
  See ELECTIONS.

WITNESSES —Cont'd
Employment agencies, powers of
  labor and workforce
  development commissioner as
  to hearings involving,
  140:46D, 140:46Q.
Employment security.
  Compelling attendance of
    witnesses, **151A:43.**
  Cross-examination, **151A:41.**
  Fees, **151A:43.**
Ethics commission, investigations,
  268B:4.
Examination.
  Criminal cases, **276:38.**
  Cross-examination. See within
    this heading,
    "Cross-examination."
  Fraternal benefit societies,
    witnesses on examination by
    insurance commissioner,
    176:44.
  Habeas corpus, **248:38, 248:39.**
  Health maintenance
    organizations, summons of
    witnesses in examination of
    affairs, **176G:10.**
  Interruption for purpose of
    taking notes forbidden
    where official stenographer
    is functioning, **231:83.**
  Presidential electors, **51:33,
    51:49.**
  Psychiatric examination of
    defendant, admissibility of
    statements of defendant
    made while undergoing,
    233:23B.
  Public works department,
    powers of hearing examiner,
    16:5.
  Testimony reduced to writing,
    276:40.
Excuse for failure to attend,
  failure to pay or tender fees
  and mileage, **233:3.**
Executive council and committees,
  compelling attendance and
  testimony before, **233:7.**
Exemption from arrest and
  process, witnesses in criminal
  proceedings required to attend
  in or brought in from other
  states, **233:13C.**
Expenses and costs.
  Campaign expenditures.
    See CAMPAIGN
      EXPENDITURES AND
      CONTRIBUTIONS.
  False certification, liability,
    262:62.

WITNESSES —Cont'd
Expenses and costs —Cont'd
Fees. See within this heading,
"Fees."
Habeas corpus proceedings,
Commonwealth to pay
expense of procuring
witnesses, **248:40.**
Indigents. See within this
heading, "Indigents."
Police officers off duty, as
witnesses in criminal cases,
262:53A.
Public employees called as
witnesses, **268A:2, 268A:3.**
Railroad police, **262:55.**
Reduction of costs in cases tried
together, **261:8.**
Summons, payment of expenses,
221:79.
Traveling expenses. See within
this heading, "Traveling
expenses."
Expert.
See EXPERT AND OPINION
EVIDENCE.
Extradition, **233:13A-233:13D.**
Fair education practices
proceedings, **151C:3.**
Fair employment practices.
See FAIR EMPLOYMENT
PRACTICES.
False travel certificates of
witnesses, forfeiture, **262:62.**
Fees, **3:38, 90:28, 90B:11.**
Accused, payment of witness
fees, **262:53.**
Legal conviction, **263:9.**
Apportioned in two or more
criminal cases pending,
262:59.
Arbitration and award, **251:7,
262:29.**
Attendance of witness excused
by failure to pay or tender,
233:3.
Attorney general's
investigations, fees of
witnesses, **262:2.**
Auditors, masters, and referees,
fees of witnesses in cases
before, **262:29.**
Autopsies, **38:6.**
Certification, **262:29, 262:53B,
262:62.**
Foreign insurance companies,
filing of certificate as to
fees, **175:8A.**
Clerks of court.
Reduction or apportionment of
fees, **262:59.**

WITNESSES —Cont'd
Fees —Cont'd
Clerks of court —Cont'd
Report of improperly charged
fees and expenses to
district attorney, **262:58.**
Commercial motor vehicle
division, **25:12G.**
Commitment of witness as
affecting, **262:30.**
Comptroller of state.
Foreign insurance companies,
filing of certificate as to
witness fees, **175:8A.**
Public utilities commission,
appearance before, **25:5A.**
Conciliation and arbitration
board, proceedings before,
262:29.
Coroner's inquest, certain
witnesses not to receive fees
for appearing, **262:50.**
Costs, reduction of in cases tried
together, **261:8.**
Criminal cases, **262:29, 262:30,
262:32, 262:33.**
Apportionment, same witness
attending for two or more
cases, **262:59.**
Commission of crime, witness
inducing, **262:60.**
Investigations, fees of persons
assisting, **262:29.**
Off duty, **262:53-262:53C.**
Officers not to purchase or
discount orders for
payment, **262:61.**
Outside state, witness coming,
262:32.
Police officers,
262:50-262:53C.
Salaried officers,
262:50-262:58.
State treasurer, fees to be
paid, **280:10.**
Delinquent and neglected
children, proceedings,
262:27, 262:33, 262:53.
Detectives, **262:53B.**
Double or treble costs, items
excluded in computing,
261:11.
Employees of carriers testifying
at inquest, **38:11.**
Employment security
proceedings, **151A:43.**
Ethics commission
investigations, **268B:4.**
Executive counsel, witnesses
before, **233:7.**
False, liability, **262:62.**

WITNESSES —Cont'd
Fees —Cont'd
Foreign insurance company,
175:8A.
General court, witnesses before,
262:29.
Indigents, witnesses' fees as
extra court cost, **261:27A.**
Inquests, **38:5, 38:11, 262:50.**
Insurance commissioner, witness
fees, **175:8A.**
Jail, witnesses confined, **262:30.**
Juvenile court proceedings,
262:27, 262:33, 262:53.
Labor relations or disputes,
proceedings, **150:8, 150A:7,
262:29.**
Land court proceedings, **262:29.**
Local and municipal boards and
commissions, witnesses
before, **233:8.**
Medical examiners, **38:5.**
Militia courts-martial, witnesses
appearing before, **33:82.**
Motor vehicle liability policies
and bonds, witnesses before
board of appeal, **26:8A.**
Neglect and delinquent cases,
fees, **262:27, 262:33, 262:53.**
Other state, witness summoned
to attend in or,
233:13-233:13B, 262:32.
Payment by state treasurer,
3:38, 280:10.
Penalty for improper charge,
262:58.
Police officers, **262:50-262:53C,
262:55, 262:56.**
Probate court, proceedings,
262:29.
Public officers and employees,
262:50-262:58.
Public utilities commission,
appearing before, **25:5A.**
Railroad police, **262:55.**
Refusal where witness induced
commission of crime,
262:60.
Registrars, persons appearing
before, **55B:7.**
Restraints of trade and
monopolies, **93:8.**
Retirement boards, appearance
before, **32:16, 32:20.**
Salaried officer attending trial
as witness in behalf of
Commonwealth, **262:57.**
State administrative
proceedings, **30A:12.**
State police officers, **262:53B,
262:53C.**

WITNESSES —Cont'd
Fees —Cont'd
Summoning witnesses, **233:3, 262:8.**
State ballot law commission, **55B:4.**
Tender as condition of requiring attendance, **233:3.**
Toxics use reduction action, **21I:18.**
Workers' compensation, **152:5, 152:11B, 262:29.**
Financial disclosure by public officers.
See FINANCIAL DISCLOSURE BY PUBLIC OFFICERS AND EMPLOYEES.
Fines and penalties.
Capital cases, **277:66.**
Credibility, showing of right of conviction of crime as affecting, **233:21.**
Failure of witness to attend, **233:5.**
Immunity, after grant, **233:20H.**
Out of state prosecution, **233:13-233:13B.**
False certification of fees, **262:62.**
General court, witness to appeal and testify before, **3:28, 3:28A.**
Handcuffing witness to prisoners, **276:54.**
Local and municipal boards and commissions, failure of witnesses to appear before, **233:8.**
Obstruction or interference with witnesses in criminal cases, **268:13B.**
Perjury.
See PERJURY.
Public officer's improper charge for fees and expenses as witness, **262:58.**
Refusal to testify before general court, **3:28A.**
State ballot law commission, witnesses before, **55B:4.**
Summoning witnesses, **233:4, 233:5, 276:22, 276:30.**
Transporting witnesses in same vehicle with prisoner, **276:54.**
Treason, requirement of two witnesses, **264:4.**
Fires, investigation, **148:3, 148:32.**
Foreign insurance companies.
See FOREIGN INSURANCE COMPANIES.

WITNESSES —Cont'd
Foreign states.
Other states, attendance of witnesses in or from. See within this heading, "Other states, attendance of witnesses in or from."
Fraternal benefit societies, witnesses on examination by insurance commissioner, **176:44.**
General court.
See GENERAL COURT.
Gifts.
Human bodies, organs, and tissues, execution of instruments making gifts, **113:10.**
Prohibition as to acceptance or solicitation, **268A:2, 268A:3.**
Grand jury.
Immunity of witnesses, grant, **233:20C et seq.**
Habeas corpus.
Examination of witnesses, **248:38, 248:39.**
Expense of procuring witnesses, Commonwealth to pay, **248:40.**
Permissible use of writ to bring in witnesses, **248:25.**
Hairdressers' board of registration, powers, **112:87EE.**
Handcuffing witness to prisoner, penalty, **276:54.**
Health care proxies, **201D:2.**
Health maintenance organizations, summons of witnesses in examination of affairs, **176G:10.**
Health, welfare, and retirement funds, witnesses at investigation, **151D:3.**
Hearing officers division, powers, **7:4H.**
Homicide.
See MURDER OR HOMICIDE.
Hospital service corporations, witnesses in proceedings involving, **176A:7.**
Human bodies, organs, and tissue, execution of instruments making gifts, **113:10.**
Husband or wife as witness against opposite spouse, **233:20.**
Illegitimate children, **209C:16.**
Immunities.
See IMMUNITY.
Impeachment.
Conviction of crime as affecting credibility, **233:21.**

WITNESSES —Cont'd
Impeachment —Cont'd
Disbelief in God as receivable to affect credibility, **233:19.**
Inconsistent statements out of court, impeachment by showing, **233:23.**
Own witness, **233:23.**
Reputation, **233:21A, 233:23.**
Traffic violation convictions, credibility as affected by certain, **233:21.**
Inconsistency of testimony with statements out of court, party producing witness may show, **233:23.**
Indigents.
Fees as extra court cost, **261:27A.**
Travel expenses for witnesses paid by Commonwealth for indigent defendant, **262:29.**
Industrial accidents board, depositions of medical witnesses, **152:5.**
Industrial homework, investigations, **149:147F.**
Inquests.
See INQUESTS.
Inspector general.
Request of testimony, **12A:9.**
Summons, compelling testimony, **12A:7.**
Insurance.
See INSURANCE.
Interference with or obstruction of witnesses at trial or other criminal proceeding, **268:13B.**
Interpreters, **221:92A.**
Interrogatories.
See INTERROGATORIES.
Intimidation.
Threats. See within this heading, "Threats."
Intoxicating liquor.
Alcoholic liquor. See within this heading, "Alcoholic liquors."
Jail.
Commitment. See within this heading, "Commitment."
Judge's reduction or apportionment of witness fees, **262:59.**
Judicial conduct commission, power to subpoena witnesses, **211C:2.**
Jury session, recognizance before, **275:9.**
Justices of the peace, summons, **233:1.**
Contempt powers of justice for nonattendance of witness, **233:5.**

WITNESSES —Cont'd

Justices of the peace, summons —Cont'd

Criminal cases in other states, **233:12.**

Warrant to compel attendance, **233:6.**

Juvenile courts and delinquent children, **119:54, 119:58.**

See JUVENILE COURTS AND DELINQUENT CHILDREN.

Labor and workforce development, removal or penalty of employee for attendance as witness, **258B:3, 268:14B.**

Labor relations.

See LABOR RELATIONS AND DISPUTES.

Land court, proceedings, **262:29.**

Land surveyors, proceedings to revoke certificate, **112:81P.**

Licensing authorities and boards, summoning and administration of oath to witnesses before, **233:8.**

Livestock disease control director, proceedings before, **129:10.**

Local and municipal boards and commissions, witnesses before, **233:8-233:11.**

Marine fish industries, witnesses with respect to compiling information, **130:21.**

Masters.

See AUDITORS, MASTERS, AND REFEREES.

Materiality of testimony, hearing, **276:47.**

Material witnesses.

Commitment. See within this heading, "Commitment."

Medical care and assistance, attendance at hearings on appeal by person aggrieved by decision, **118E:22.**

Medical examiners.

Autopsies, attendance, **38:6.**

Fees for services, **38:5.**

Medical malpractice claims, expert and opinion evidence, **231:60E.**

Medical peer review committee, testifying before, **111:204.**

Mental condition of witnesses, **123:19.**

Mentally retarded witness, **233:23E.**

Metropolitan district commission.

Police, witness fees, **262:56.**

Summoning and administration of oath, **233:8.**

WITNESSES —Cont'd

Mileage allowance.

Traveling expenses. See within this heading, "Traveling expenses."

Militia.

See MILITIA.

Milk control law hearings, **94A:18.**

Minors.

See CHILDREN AND MINORS.

Motorboat accident inquiries, **90B:11.**

Motor carriers.

See CARRIERS.

Motor vehicles.

Commercial motor vehicle division, powers of director, **25:12G.**

Financing, witnesses in investigation, **255B:4, 255B:6.**

Fraudulent insurance claims, proceedings, **278:6A.**

Liability policies and bonds, powers of board of appeal, **26:8A.**

Public works department, **90:28.**

Registrar.

Employees as witnesses, fees, **262:53, 262:53A.**

Power to summon, **90:28.**

Theft prosecutions, **278:6A.**

Transporting witnesses in vehicles carrying prisoners, **276:54.**

Municipal boards and commissions, witnesses before, **30A:9-30A:12, 233:8-233:11.**

Municipal courts, payment of witness fees, **280:10.**

Murder.

See MURDER OR HOMICIDE.

Names and addresses of, discovery proceedings to obtain, **231:63.**

Nonresidents.

Other states. See within this heading, "Other states, attendance of witnesses in or from."

Notice.

Compelling attendance, **12A:7.**

Employer notified of subpoena to testify, **258B:3, 268:14B.**

Nuisances.

Alcoholic beverages, persons found in places illegally keeping or selling, **139:13, 139:16A.**

Prostitution, persons found in places, **139:13.**

WITNESSES —Cont'd

Oath or affirmation, **233:14 et seq.**

Accounts, examination on oath before court upon matters relevant, **206:3.**

Arbitrators, referees, and the like may administer, **233:14.**

Boards and commissions, summoning and administration of oaths, to witnesses before, **233:8-233:11.**

Circumstances when affirmation authorized, **233:17, 233:18.**

Civil service, **31:72.**

Commission on judicial conduct, power to administer oaths and affirmations to witnesses, **211C:2.**

Depositions, **233:30.**

Employment agency license hearing, powers of labor and workforce development commissioner, **140:46E.**

Ethics commission investigations, swearing of witnesses, **268B:4.**

Fires, witnesses in investigation, **148:3.**

General court, refusal of appearance or testimony before general court, **3:28A.**

Industrial homework, witnesses upon investigations, **149:147F.**

Livestock disease control, examinations under oath, **129:10.**

Manner of administering oath, **233:15, 233:16.**

Non-Christians, **233:19.**

Public employees, **268A:4, 268A:11, 268A:17.**

Public works department hearing examiner authorized to take testimony under oath, **16:5.**

Revenue commissioner authorized to take testimony and proofs under oath, **58:25B.**

State tax commission authorized to take testimony and proofs under oath, **58:25B.**

Telecommunications and energy department, **25:3, 25:5A.**

Variances from usual form, **233:16, 233:17.**

Obstruction or interference with witnesses at trials or other criminal proceedings, **268:13B.**

WITNESSES —Cont'd

Opinion evidence.
　See EXPERT AND OPINION
　　EVIDENCE.
Optometrists' board of registration,
　powers, **112:71.**
Other states, attendance of
　witnesses in or from,
　233:12-233:13D, 233:45.
　Depositions.
　　See DEPOSITIONS.
　Exemption from arrest or service
　　of process, **233:13C.**
　Fees for witnesses from without
　　Commonwealth,
　　233:13-233:13B, 262:32.
Own witnesses, impeachment,
　233:23.
Pardons, proceedings before
　advisory board, **127:154.**
Parking violations, adjudication by
　mail, **90:20A, 90:20A½.**
Parole board, summons of
　witnesses, **233:8.**
Parties.
　Accused. See within this
　　heading, "Accused."
　Competency, **233:20.**
　Cross-examination of adverse
　　party called as witness,
　　233:22.
　Inconsistency of testimony with
　　statements out of court,
　　party producing witness
　　may show, **233:23.**
　Indigents. See within this
　　heading, "Indigents."
Penalties.
　Fines and penalties. See within
　　this heading, "Fines and
　　penalties."
Pensions.
　See RETIREMENT SYSTEMS
　　AND PENSIONS.
Perjury, **26:1-26:6.**
　See PERJURY.
Perpetuation of testimony.
　See DEPOSITIONS.
Personal injuries, written
　statements of persons
　sustaining, **233:23A, 271:44.**
Pharmacists.
　Druggists and pharmacists. See
　　within this heading,
　　"Druggists and
　　pharmacists."
Picketing of building or residence
　occupied, **268:13A.**
Police commissioners, witnesses
　before, **233:8.**

WITNESSES —Cont'd

Police officers.
　Compensatory time off for
　　attendance in criminal
　　cases, **262:53C.**
　Fees and expenses,
　　**262:50-262:53C, 262:55,
　　262:56.**
　Railroad police, fees and
　　expenses, **262:55.**
　State police. See within this
　　heading, "State police."
Poor persons.
　Indigents. See within this
　　heading, "Indigents."
Pornography, testimony of child
　pornography prosecution,
　272:29A.
Presidential electors.
　Contest of election of
　　presidential electors, **54:120.**
　Examination of applicants and
　　witnesses, **51:33, 51:49.**
Prior convictions, extension of time
　limits as to use of in criminal
　trial, **233:21.**
Privileged.
　See PRIVILEGED AND
　　CONFIDENTIAL
　　MATTERS.
Privileges.
　See IMMUNITY.
Probate.
　See PROBATE AND FAMILY
　　COURT.
Process.
　Summoning. See within this
　　heading, "Summoning."
Production of books and papers,
　grant of immunity to witness,
　233:20C et seq.
Professional engineers,
　proceedings to revoke
　certificate, **112:81P.**
Professions and occupations,
　powers of boards of
　registration of, **112:62.**
Prosecuting attorneys.
　See DISTRICT AND
　　PROSECUTING
　　ATTORNEYS.
Prostitution, persons found in
　places, **139:13.**
Psychiatry and psychiatrists.
　Admissibility of defendant's
　　statements made while
　　undergoing psychiatric
　　examination, **233:23B.**
　Communication of
　　psychotherapist with
　　patient, privilege, **233:20B.**

WITNESSES —Cont'd

Public accountants, testimony by,
　112:87E½.
Public charities division, testimony
　before, **12:8H, 12:8I.**
Public employees as witnesses.
　Civil service investigations. See
　　within this heading, "Civil
　　service investigations."
　Fees. See within this heading,
　　"Fees."
　Financial disclosure by public
　　officers.
　　See FINANCIAL
　　　DISCLOSURE BY
　　　PUBLIC OFFICERS AND
　　　EMPLOYEES.
　Penalty for perjury, **268A:4,
　　268A:11, 268A:17.**
Public safety department.
　Inspector general, compelling
　　testimony, **12A:7.**
　Summoning and administration
　　of oath, **233:8.**
Public welfare hearings, **18:16.**
Public works and departments.
　Powers of hearing examiner,
　　16:5.
　Summoning of witnesses on
　　appeal from decision of
　　registrar of motor vehicles
　　as to public works
　　department, **90:28.**
Racing commission, witnesses
　before, **233:8.**
Railroads.
　Accident causing death,
　　inspector may summon to
　　inquest, **159:29.**
　Fees for police attending as
　　witnesses, **262:55.**
　Reciprocity provisions between
　　states with respect to
　　witnesses in criminal cases
　　and investigations,
　　233:13A-233:13D.
Recognizance by, **38:13,
　276:45-276:51, 277:70.**
　See BAIL AND
　　RECOGNIZANCE.
Recount of votes, summoning in
　case, **54:135.**
Referees.
　See AUDITORS, MASTERS,
　　AND REFEREES.
Reform school inmates as
　witnesses in criminal cases,
　278:16.
Registrar of motor vehicles,
　proceedings on appeal, **90:28.**
Registration of voters, illegal or
　incorrect proceedings, **51:49.**

WITNESSES —Cont'd
Removal or penalty by employer
for being witness, **258B:3,
268:14B.**
Reputation, credibility as affected,
233:21A, 233:23.
Residence.
Domicile and residence. See
within this heading,
"Domicile and residence."
Restraints of trade.
See RESTRAINTS OF TRADE
AND MONOPOLIES.
Retirement systems.
See RETIREMENT SYSTEMS
AND PENSIONS.
Revenue department's authority to
attendance and testimony,
58:25B.
Review.
See APPEAL AND REVIEW.
Rights, **258B:2 et seq.**
See RIGHTS OF VICTIMS AND
WITNESSES OF CRIME.
Satisfaction of injured party in
misdemeanor case, discharge
of witnesses, **276:55, 276:56.**
School boards, witnesses before,
233:8.
Self-incrimination.
See SELF-INCRIMINATION.
Sentence.
See SENTENCE AND
PUNISHMENT.
Service.
Summoning. See within this
heading, "Summoning."
Social worker and client
communications, preventing
witness from disclosure,
112:135B.
Spouse as witness against opposite
spouse, **233:20.**
State administrative proceedings,
30A:11, 30A:12.
State ballot law commission,
appearance of witnesses before
registrars, **55B:4, 55B:7.**
State police.
Compensatory time off for
attendance in court as
witness in criminal cases,
262:53C.
Fees, **262:53B.**
State racing commission,
witnesses before, **233:8.**
State treasurer, witness fees, **3:38,
280:10.**
Statute of frauds, effect of
admissions of party,
106:2-201.

WITNESSES —Cont'd
Subdivision control appeals
boards, powers of chairman,
41:81AA.
Subpoenas.
See SUBPOENAS.
Subscribing witnesses.
See ATTESTATION AND
ATTESTING WITNESSES.
Suffolk county, summoning of
witnesses by officers, **221:79.**
Summoning.
Architects' registration board,
summons, **13:44C.**
Attorney general, summoning of
witness on request, **233:1.**
Boards and commissions,
summoning and
administration of oaths to
witnesses before,
233:8-233:11.
Capital cases, **277:66.**
Civil service, **7:4I, 31:72.**
Clerks of court, summons for
witnesses, **233:1.**
Criminal cases, **233:1, 233:2.**
Depositions, summoning and
compelling witness for
deposition to perpetuate
testimony, **233:38, 233:39,
233:45, 233:47.**
Expenses, payment, **221:79.**
Fees. See within this heading,
"Fees."
Foreign state or country.
Other states, attendance of
witnesses in or from. See
within this heading,
"Other states, attendance
of witnesses in or from."
Form of summons, **233:1.**
Habeas corpus proceedings,
248:40.
Health maintenance
organizations, summons of
witnesses in examination of
affairs, **176G:10.**
Immunity of witnesses, proof of
service on application,
233:20E.
Inspector general, **12A:7.**
Justices of the peace. See within
this heading, "Justices of
the peace, summons."
Other states, witnesses, **233:12,
233:13B, 233:13C, 233:45.**
Parole board, summons, **233:8.**
Payment or tender of fees in
connection with.
Fees. See within this heading,
"Fees."

WITNESSES —Cont'd
Summoning —Cont'd
Penalties, **233:4, 233:5, 276:22,
276:30.**
Public works department,
summoning of witnesses,
16:5, 90:28.
Railroads, inspector may
summon to inquest, **159:29.**
Recount of votes, summoning in
case, **54:135.**
Residence, service of summons,
233:2.
Service, **223:2.**
Immunity of witnesses, proof
of service on application,
233:20E.
Other states, attendance of
witnesses in or, **233:13C.**
Place, **223:2.**
Subpoenas.
See SUBPOENAS.
Suffolk and Worcester Counties,
summoning of witnesses by
officers, **221:79.**
Who may issue summons, **233:1.**
Superior court.
See SUPERIOR COURTS.
Supreme judicial court.
See SUPREME JUDICIAL
COURT.
Sureties for witnesses, **38:13,
276:45-276:51, 277:70.**
See BAIL AND
RECOGNIZANCE.
Taxation.
Appellate tax board, **58A:11.**
Witness fees, **58A:11, 58A:12.**
Attendance of witnesses in tax
proceedings, **62C:70.**
Revenue department's authority
to require attendance and
testimony, **58:25B.**
Teachers, certification hearing,
71:38G.
Telecommunications and energy
department, **25:5A, 25:12G.**
Commercial motor vehicle
division, **25:12G.**
Oaths, **25:3, 25:5A.**
Teste.
See TESTE.
Threats.
Grand jury investigation of
intimidation of juror or
witness, grant of immunity
to witness appearing before,
233:20D.
Recognizance required of
witness to offense of threat
to commit crime, **275:9.**

WITNESSES —Cont'd
Threats —Cont'd
Trials or other criminal
proceedings, threats,
268:13B.
Time or date.
Conviction of crime, time
limitation as to use of
evidence, **233:21.**
Town clerk, proceedings to review
removal or suspension,
41:19D.
Traffic violations on which only a
fine was imposed, effect upon
credibility of witness, **233:21.**
Transcripts.
See TRANSCRIPTS.
Transporting witness in same
vehicle with prisoner, **276:54.**
Traveling expenses, **233:3,**
233:13-233:13B, 262:29.
Criminal cases, witnesses,
262:29.
False travel certificates, **262:62.**
Identification of criminals,
127:30.
Insurance, **175:8A, 255C:8.**
Officer serving writ, **262:8.**
Police officers, **262:53A.**
Probate court witnesses, **262:29.**
Public officers, **262:57.**
Railroad police, **262:55.**
State police officers, **262:53B.**
Workers' compensation, **152:5.**
Treason, two witnesses necessary
for conviction, **264:4; US**
Const Art 3 Sec 3 cl 1.
Trials or other criminal
proceedings, obstruction or
interference with witnesses,
268:13B.
Trust department officers, **167G:7.**
Two-witness rule.
Corroboration. See within this
heading, "Corroboration."
Unemployment compensation.
Employment security. See within
this heading, "Employment
security."
Uniform law to secure attendance
in criminal proceedings of
witnesses from outside a state,
233:13A-233:13D.
Uniform rules of adjudicatory
procedure, **30A:10.**
Utilities.
Telecommunications and energy
department. See within this
heading,
"Telecommunications and
energy department."

WITNESSES —Cont'd
Victim and witness assistance
board, **258B:4.**
Victim and witness assistance
fund, deposit of assessments,
258B:9.
Videotaping.
Consent of mentally ill and
retarded persons, **19B:15.**
Testimony of child witness,
278:16D.
Wages and compensation.
Compensation. See within this
heading, "Compensation."
Waiver of court costs for indigents,
261:27A.
Warrant.
Arrest warrant, summoning
witnesses, **276:22, 276:30.**
Boards and commissions,
warrant to compel
attendance before, **233:6.**
Contempt, warrant, **233:6.**
To compel attendance, **233:6,**
233:9.
Water Resources Authority, **233:8.**
Wife as witness against husband,
233:20.
Worcester county, summoning of
witnesses by officers, **221:79.**
Workers' compensation.
Compelling attendance, **152:5.**
Fees for attending, **152:5,**
152:11B, 262:29.
Travel pay, **152:5.**
Writ and process.
Summoning. See within this
heading, "Summoning."
Zoning, powers of chairman of
subdivision control appeals
board, **41:81AA.**

WOBURN.
Congressional district, **57:1.**
District court, **218:1.**
Medical examiner district, **38:1.**
Metropolitan air pollution control
district, **111:142B.**
Senatorial district, **57:3.**

WOLVES.
Hybrids, possession of, **131:77A,**
131:90.

WOMEN.
Females.
See FEMALES.

WOMEN, COMMISSION ON
THE STATUS OF, 3:66.

WOMEN-OWNED
BUSINESSES.
Public construction, **7:40C, 7:40N.**

WOMEN-OWNED BUSINESSES
—Cont'd
State office of minority business
assistance (SOMBA), **7:40N.**

WOMEN'S, INFANTS AND
CHILDREN PROGRAM,
111I:1 et seq.
Advisory board, **111I:4.**
Appropriation of funds, **111I:7.**
Availability of funds, **111I:6.**
Compensation of advisory board
members prohibited, **111I:4.**
Delivery of food to participants,
111I:5.
Director, **111I:3.**
Federal WIC program,
administration consistent
with, **111I:1 et seq.**
Financial eligibility of
participants, **111I:5.**
Funds, supplementation of federal
funds, **111I:2.**
Members of advisory board, **111I:4.**
Monthly food packages supplied to
participants, **111I:5.**
Notice of public hearing to review
plan, **111I:3.**
Public hearing to review plan,
111I:3.
Purpose, **111I:1.**
Reimbursement of expenses of
advisory board members,
111I:4.
Supplemental food and nutrition
education, **111I:1 et seq.**
Time and place for public hearing
to review plan, **111I:3.**

WOMEN'S RELIEF CORPS.
Insignia, unlawful use, **266:70.**
Uniform, unlawful use, **264:10A.**

WOOD.
Burning of, criminal offense,
266:5, 266:5A.
Carpenter shops.
See CARPENTER SHOPS.
Firewood, **94:242, 94:243, 94:296**
et seq.
See FIREWOOD.
Forests and forestry, **132:1 et seq.**
See FORESTS AND
FORESTRY.
Lien on account of labor and
materials furnished in
processing, **255:31A, 255:31B.**
Logs.
See LOGS AND TIMBER.
Pollution of coastal waters by
wood shavings, **130:23-130:27.**
Sale.
Firewood, **94:242, 94:243,**
94:296 et seq.
See FIREWOOD.

WOOD —Cont'd
Sale —Cont'd
Logs and timber, **106:2-107.**
See LOGS AND TIMBER.
State forest, sale of wood,
132:34A.
Tax exemption of sales of wood
heating systems equipment,
64H:6.
State forest, sale of wood,
132:34A.
Tax exemption of sales of wood
heating systems equipment,
64H:6.
Weights and measures,
94:296-94:303, 97:7-97:11A.
Firewood.
See FIREWOOD.
Logs.
See LOGS AND TIMBER.
Woodworking establishments.
See WOODWORKING
ESTABLISHMENTS.

WOOD ALCOHOL.
See ALCOHOL.

WOODCHUCK.
Control and destruction, **128:8A.**
Poison, **131:43.**
Possession without permit, **131:5.**
Removal from hole in ground,
131:76.

WOODCUTS.
State secretary's custody of
woodcuts owned by
Commonwealth, **9:13.**

WOODLANDS, 132:1 et seq.
See FORESTS AND
FORESTRY.

WOOD SHAPERS OR
JOINTERS.
Minors, operation, **149:6.**

WOODS HOLE STEAMSHIP
AUTHORITY.
See STEAMSHIP AUTHORITY.

WOOD TICKS.
Poison for suppression, **131:43.**
Suppression, **131:43, 132:11.**
Transportation, **266:119.**

WOODWORKING
ESTABLISHMENTS.
Automatic sprinklers, **148:26.**
Carpenter shops.
See CARPENTER SHOPS.
Dust removal provisions for emery
wheels inapplicable, **149:121.**
Minors under sixteen not to work
on certain machines, **149:61.**

WOOL.
Spinning, lien, **255:31A, 255:31B.**
Weighting bale with foreign
substance as offense, **94:305.**

WOOL PICKING MACHINES.
Minors, operation, **149:61.**

WORCESTER.
Additional assistant register of
deeds, **36:6.**
Alcoholic liquor licenses, hearings
on appeals, **138:67.**
Chief clerk of registry district,
36:7.
Congressional district, **57:1.**
Councilor district, **57:2.**
County.
See WORCESTER COUNTY.
Discrimination commission, office
in Worcester, **6:56, 151B:3.**
Housing commissioner, duties,
111:127A, 111:127B,
111:127C, 111:127E,
111:127L.
Juvenile court.
See WORCESTER JUVENILE
COURT.
Medical examiner district, **38:1.**
Motor carriers of property,
hearings upon certificates of
public convenience and
necessity, **159B:3.**
Motor vehicle liability insurance,
notice of hearings, **175:113B.**
Nurses' examinations for
registration, places for
holding, **112:74.**
Plan E charter government
provisions repealed, **43:93.**
Police training schools, expenses of
policemen attending, **40:5.**
Regional transit authority, **161B:2.**
Senatorial district, **57:3.**
Southwest Asia war veterans,
official state monument for,
2:37.
State college.
See WORCESTER STATE
COLLEGE.
Steam boiler rules, notice of
hearing on proposed changes,
146:3.

WORCESTER COUNTY.
Abolition of county governments,
34B:1 to 34B:22.
See ABOLITION OF COUNTY
GOVERNMENTS.
Administration of criminal law
and defense of civil actions,
district, **12:13.**

WORCESTER COUNTY
—Cont'd
Bellingham, jurisdiction of
Worcester County Housing
Court, **185C:1.**
Bond of court officer, premium to
be paid by county, **221:77.**
Bonds and undertakings, failure to
pay.
Abolition of county governments,
34B:1 to 34B:22.
See ABOLITION OF COUNTY
GOVERNMENTS.
Central District Court,
Massachusetts Rules of
Appellate Procedure as
applicable, **218:19A.**
Clerks of courts.
Assistant clerks, **221:4, 221:5,**
221:6E, 221:6F.
Criminal proceedings, assistant
clerk, **221:6F.**
Equity proceedings, assistant
clerk, **221:6E, 221:6F.**
Grand jury, empanelling,
277:2E.
Salary, **218:79, 221:94.**
Compensation.
Salaries. See within this
heading, "Salaries."
Court officers, **217:30.**
Appointment, **221:70.**
Chief court officers, **221:71.**
Clerks of courts. See within this
heading, "Clerks of courts."
Judges and justices. See within
this heading, "Judges and
justices."
Masters in chancery, **221:53.**
Premiums on bonds of court
officers to be paid by county,
221:77.
Summoning of witnesses,
221:79.
District courts, **218:1.**
Athol as included, **12:13.**
Bellingham, jurisdiction over,
218:1.
Clerks of courts. See within this
heading, "Clerks of courts."
Juries.
Six person jury. See within
this heading, "Six person
jury."
Justices, **218:6, 231:108.**
Number of justices, **218:6.**
Salaries of justices, **218:78.**
Second district court of Southern
Worcester, place for holding
sessions, **218:1.**
Six person jury. See within this
heading, "Six person jury."

WORCESTER COUNTY
—Cont'd
Eastern Worcester, provision for appointment of assistant clerk for First District Court, **218:10.**
Economic development authority.
See CENTRAL MASSACHUSETTS ECONOMIC DEVELOPMENT AUTHORITY.
Embalmers' and funeral directors' registration board, representation, **13:29.**
General court, representatives, **57:4.**
Grand jurors, **277:2E.**
Group insurance coverage for employees, **32A:2, 32A:8, 32B:1 et seq.**
Housing court division, **185C:1 et seq.**
Judges and justices.
District courts. See within this heading, "District courts."
Juvenile court, **218:57-218:60.**
Pension, **32:65A.**
Jury and jury trial.
Six person jury. See within this heading, "Six person jury."
Juvenile court.
See WORCESTER JUVENILE COURT.
Masters in chancery, **221:53.**
Medical examiner district, **38:1.**
Meeting of county commissioners, **34:9.**
Misdemeanor, jury trial, **218:26.**
Probate court.
Additional judges or officers, **217:30.**
Registers of probate.
See REGISTERS OF PROBATE AND INSOLVENCY.
Sessions for Worcester County, **215:62.**
Recording of instruments, registry districts, **36:1.**
Registers of probate.
See REGISTERS OF PROBATE AND INSOLVENCY.
Representatives in general court, **57:4.**
Salaries.
Clerks of courts, **221:94.**
District court judges, **218:78.**
Six person jury.
Civil actions, **218:19A.**
In central District Court, **218:19A.**

WORCESTER COUNTY
—Cont'd
Six person jury —Cont'd
Misdemeanor trials, **218:26.**
Trial of criminal cases, right, **218:27A.**
Summoning of witnesses by officers, **221:79.**
Superior court sittings, **212:14.**
Surveys in co-ordinate system, **97:8.**
Wages.
Salaries. See within this heading, "Salaries."
Witnesses, summoning by court officers, **221:79.**

WORCESTER COUNTY LEAGUE OF SPORTSMEN.
Quabbin watershed advisory committee, members, **92:114.**

WORCESTER JUVENILE COURT.
Adjudication of child as delinquent, proceedings after, **119:58.**
Assignment of justice of district court to sit, **218:58.**
Clerical assistants to clerk, **218:70.**
Clerks, **218:57-218:60, 218:79.**
Temporary clerks and assistants, **218:9, 218:11.**
Court officers.
Clerks. See within this heading, "Clerks of court."
Disposition of case, time, **119:68.**
Governor's appointment of clerks, **218:58.**
Jurisdiction over offenders, **218:57, 218:60.**
Justices, **218:57-218:60.**
Pension, **32:65A.**
Powers, duties and procedures, **218:59.**
Practice of law by justices prohibited, **218:58.**
Retirement system and pension for justices, **32:65A.**
Rules, **218:60.**
School attendance, enforcement of parental duties, **76:2.**
Special provisions relative, **218:57-218:60.**
Territorial jurisdiction, **218:57.**

WORCESTER STATE COLLEGE.
Management, **73:1.**
Trustees of state colleges, institutions under jurisdiction, **73:19.**

WORCESTER STATE HOSPITAL, 19:8A, 19:14.

WORDS AND PHRASES.
Abandoned property, **60:1, 200A:1.**
Abandoned workings, **21B:2.**
Abatement, **111:189A.**
Abatement facilities, **21:26A.**
Abortion, **112:12K.**
Above foundation reimbursement amount, **76:12B.**
Absentee, **203:26.**
Absent parent, child support, **62E:1.**
Absorbed through skin, **94B:1.**
Abuse, **19C:1, 209A:1, 233:20K.**
Abuse or neglect of patients in long-term care facilities, **111:72F.**
Address confidentiality of domestic violence victims, **9A:1.**
Child custody, **208:31A.**
Husband and wife, **209:38.**
Illegitimate children, **209C:10.**
Abusive parent.
Abuse prevention, **209A:3.**
Abutting community, **21D:1.**
Accelerated benefits.
Viatical settlements, **175:213.**
Acceptance, **106:4A-209.**
Negotiable instruments, **106:3-409.**
Acceptance, written, **50:1.**
Acceptor.
Negotiable instruments, **106:3-103.**
Accessible, **22:13A, 151B:1.**
Accessions, **106:2A-310(1), 106:9-314.**
Accessory after the fact, **274:4.**
Accessory before the fact, **274:2, 274:3.**
Accident, **233:23D.**
Accidental discharge.
Sales of firearms, **140:123.**
Accident and sickness insurance, **175:108.**
Accident, boating, **90B:1.**
Account, **106:9-106, 140E:1, 167D:34, 167D:35, 171:53, 175:117C.**
Bank deposits and collections, **106:4-104.**
Accountants, **112:87A.**
Accountant's report, **30:39R.**
Account debtor, **106:9-105.**
Accredited educational institution, **32:7, 32:9, 32:26.**
Accredited state, **175:174G.**
Accrued portion of normal retirement benefit, **151D:1.**

WORDS AND PHRASES
—Cont'd

Accumulated additional
deductions, **32:1.**
Accumulated regular deductions,
32:1.
Accumulated total deductions,
32:1.
Acquire.
  Community preservation, **44B:2.**
Acquisition, **79A:1.**
Acquisition, capital facilities or
  projects, **7:39A.**
Acquisition costs, **121B:1.**
Act, **21A:18, 21A:18A.**
Acting within the scope of his
  office or employment, **258:1.**
Action, Commercial Code,
  106:1-201.
Active ingredient, **132B:2.**
Active service, **32A:8, 32B:9I.**
Active service in the Armed
  Forces, **4:7.**
Activity and use limitation.
  Oil and hazardous material
    release prevention and
    response, **21E:2.**
Act of God.
  Hazardous materials mitigation,
    21K:1.
Actor's manager, **140:180A.**
Act to communicate directly with a
  covered executive official to
  influence a decision concerning
  policy or procurement defined,
  3:39.
Actual costs, **118G:1.**
Actual loss, **142A:1.**
Actual purchase of securities,
  137:4.
Actuarial equivalent, **32:1.**
Actuarial opinion, **176J:1, 176K:9.**
Actuary, **32:1, 175:177G,
  175:177N.**
Acupuncture, **112:148.**
Acute care hospitals, **111:25B.**
Acute hospital, **118G:1.**
Acute psychiatric service, **111:25B.**
Adaptable, **22:13A.**
Addition, **7:39A, 78:19G-78:19K.**
Additional deductions, **32:1.**
Address.
  Address confidentiality of
    domestic violence victims,
    9A:1.
Adjudicatory proceedings, **30A:1.**
Adjustable mortgages, **183:28A.**
Adjusted average market premium
  price, **176J:1.**
Adjusted composite rate, **176M:1.**
Adjusted for inflation.
  Tobacco master settlement
    agreement, **94E:1.**

WORDS AND PHRASES
—Cont'd

Adjusted gross income, **62:1, 62:2.**
Adjusted premiums, **175:144.**
Adjusted property valuation, **70:2.**
Adjuster, insurance, **175:162.**
Administer, **94C:1.**
Administering agency, **7:39A.**
Administration, **171:1.**
Administrative inspection
  warrants, **94C:30.**
Administrator, **125:1.**
Administrator, voluntary, **195:16.**
Admitted assets, **175:63A.**
Adopted child as included in term
  child, **210:8.**
Adoption date.
  Insurance, reorganization of
    mutual insurers, **175:19G.**
Adult, **4:7, 203B:1.**
Adulterated or adulteration,
  94:65O, 94:186, 132B:2.
Adultery, **277:39.**
Adult paraphernalia store,
  40A:9A.
Adult scallop, **130:70.**
Adult video store, **40A:9A.**
Advance, **63:30.**
Advance notification, **151A:71A.**
Adverse claim, **106:8-102.**
Adverse underwriting decision,
  175I:2.
Advertise, **112:163.**
Advertisement, **128:84, 140D:1,
  171:55.**
Advertising, **164:33A.**
Adviser, insurance, **175:177A.**
Advisor.
  Letters of credit, **106:5-102.**
Advisory board.
  Hazardous materials mitigation,
    21K:1.
  Horse racing, **128:17.**
Advisory committee, **21A:18,
  21A:18A, 92:104, 111:189A,
  111G:1.**
Advisory committee on hazardous
  waste, **21C:2.**
Advisory council, **132B:2.**
Advisory organization, insurance
  rates, **174A:12, 175A:12.**
AED.
  Good Samaritan provisions,
    112:12V½.
AED agency.
  Good Samaritan provisions,
    112:12V½.
AED medical director.
  Good Samaritan provisions,
    112:12V½.
AED provider.
  Good Samaritan provisions,
    112:12V½.

WORDS AND PHRASES
—Cont'd

Aeronautics, **90:35.**
Aeronautics instructor, **90:35.**
Aesthetician, **112:87T.**
Affected community, low-level
  radioactive waste, **111H:1.**
Affiliate, **23A:3A, 94A:1, 109A:2,
  110F:3, 175:206, 175I:2.**
Affiliate of an offeror, **110C:1.**
Affiliates.
  Tobacco master settlement
    agreement, **94E:1.**
Affirmation, use of word in
  indictment, **277:36.**
Affirmative choice.
  Gas and electric companies,
    164:1F.
Affray, **277:39.**
Afternoon.
  Bank deposits and collections,
    106:4-104.
After school program, **28A:9-12.**
Age, fair employment practices,
  151B:1.
Agency, **3:63, 6:39, 7:53, 7B:1,
  21I:2, 23A:57, 30A:1.**
  Business development office,
    23A:60.
  Sex offender registration and
    community notification,
    6:178C.
Agency with jurisdiction.
  Sexually dangerous persons act,
    123A:1.
Agent, **94C:1, 110A:401, 129:1.**
Agent, legislative, **3:39.**
Age of majority, **4:7.**
Aggravated rape, **277:39.**
Aggregate amount of medium
  grade and lower grade
  obligations, **175:63A.**
Aggregator, **164:1.**
Aggrieved parties, **106:1-201.**
Agreement, **106:1-201.**
Agreement for electronic
  presentment.
  Bank deposits and collections,
    106:4-110.
Agreement funding, **175:132F.**
Agricultural carrier by motor
  vehicle, **159B:2.**
Agricultural commodity, **132B:2.**
Agricultural education, **74:1.**
Agricultural incentive areas,
  40L:1.
Agricultural lime, **128:64.**
Agricultural preservation
  restrictions, **184:31.**
Agricultural school, independent,
  74:1.

WORDS AND PHRASES
—Cont'd

Agricultural seeds, **128:84.**
Agriculture, **128:1A.**
Aiding.
  Bear hunting, **131:21A.**
Aid or assist the dentist, **112:43A.**
AIDS, **111:2D.**
AIDS advisory board, **111:2D.**
AIDS education, **111:2D.**
AIDS Fund, **111:2D.**
AIDS research, **111:2D.**
AIDS treatment defined, **111:2D.**
Aid to families with dependent
  children, **118:1.**
Airbill, **106:1-201.**
Aircraft and aviation, **64J:1,
  90:35, 90:49B.**
Airman, **90:35.**
Air navigation facility, **90:35.**
Airport, **90:35.**
Airport hazard, **90:35.**
Air school, **90:35.**
Air space, navigable, **90:35.**
Alcohol, **90F:1, 138:1.**
Alcohol concentration, **90F:1.**
Alcoholic beverages, **138:1.**
Alcoholics, **111B:3, 123:35.**
Alcoholism, **111B:3.**
Alcove, **144:2.**
Aldermen and mayor, **4:7, 50:1.**
Alien insurer, **175:161A.**
Allied health occupations, **74:1.**
Allied mental health and human
  services professional, **112:163.**
All my rights under the contract,
  106:2-210.
Allocable shares.
  Tobacco master settlement
    agreement, **94 E:1.**
Allowable contribution.
  Clean elections law, **55A:1.**
Allowance, **149:44G.**
Alter, **131A:1.**
Alteration, **22:13A, 143:1.**
  Capital facilities projects, **7:39A.**
  Negotiable instruments,
    106:3-407.
Altered, **40C:5.**
Alternate energy producer, **164:1.**
Alternative energy development,
  25A:3.
Alternative energy property,
  25A:3.
Alternatives to construction.
  School building assistance,
    70B:2.
Ambulance, **90:1.**
  Emergency medical services
    system, **111C:1.**
Ambulance service.
  Emergency medical services
    system, **111C:1.**

WORDS AND PHRASES
—Cont'd

Ambulatory surgery, **111:25B.**
Ambulatory surgical center.
  Health care finance and policy,
    118G:1.
Ambulatory surgical center
  services.
  Health care finance and policy,
    118G:1.
American aircraft, **151A:1.**
American board of cardiovascular
  perfusion, **112:211.**
American cheese, **94:61A.**
American employer, **151A:4A.**
American vessel, employment
  security law, **151A:1.**
Ammunition.
  Gun control, **140:121.**
Amount, **268B:1.**
Amount financed, **255B:1, 255D:1.**
Amount invested in condominium,
  121A:18D.
Amount of underpayment, **62B:14.**
Analyst, insurance, **175:177A.**
Ancillary services, **164:1.**
Ancillary state, **175:180A.**
And up, **112:73A.**
Angling, **130:1, 131:1.**
Animal, **131A:1, 132B:2.**
Annual election, **4:7.**
Annual finance charge formula,
  255D:1.
Annual income.
  Community preservation, **44B:2.**
Annually, **94:270.**
Annual meeting, **156B:50A.**
Annual percentage rate, **255B:1,
  255C:1, 255D:1.**
Annual town meeting, **4:7.**
Annuity, **32:1.**
Annuity contract, group,
  175:132A.
Annuity contracts, **201A:1.**
Annuity issuer.
  Structured settlement contracts,
    231C:1.
Annuity reserve, **32:1.**
Annuity reserve fund, **32:1.**
Annuity savings fund, **32:1.**
Anomalous indorsement.
  Negotiable instruments,
    106:3-205.
Antifreeze, **94:303G.**
Anti-microbial pesticide.
  Pesticides, **132B:2.**
Antique motor car, **90:1.**
Appellate division, **90C:1.**
Appliance, **94:314.**
Applicable federal rate.
  Structured settlement contracts,
    231C:1.

WORDS AND PHRASES
—Cont'd

Applicable law.
  Structured settlement contracts,
    231C:1.
Applicant.
  Letters of credit, **106:5-102.**
  Tourism facilities fund, **23G:42.**
Application assistant.
  Address confidentiality of
    domestic violence victims,
    9A:1.
Application, motor vehicle
  provisions, **90:1.**
Application statement, **41:126.**
Appointing authority, **4:7, 31:1.**
Appointing officer, **31:1.**
Appointive office, **41:126.**
Appointment, **31:1.**
Appraisal, **112:173.**
Appraisal assignment, **112:173.**
Appraisal Foundation, **112:173.**
Appraisal report, **112:173.**
Apprentice, **23:11H, 142:1, 146:81.**
  Hearing instrument specialists,
    112:196.
Appropriate corrective actions.
  Banks, compliance review,
    167:49.
Appropriate person, **106:8-107.**
Appropriate public authority with
  respect to group insurance for
  municipal employees, **32B:2.**
Appropriate regional
  comprehensive health
  planning agency, **111:25B.**
Appropriate supervision, **112:43A.**
Appropriation, **29:1.**
Approved continuing education,
  112:163.
Approved program, **112:9C.**
Approved public library project,
  78:19G-78:19K.
Approved school project.
  School building assistance,
    70B:2.
Approved smoke detector,
  148:26D.
Approved training or assistance
  program, **23B:11.**
Approved veterinary school,
  112:54A.
Approved worksharing program,
  151A:29D.
Approving authority, **112:54A.**
Aquifer, **92:104.**
Arbors, **20:13.**
Architects, **112:60A.**
Architectural designers, **112:60K.**
Architecture, practice, **112:60A.**

WORDS AND PHRASES
—Cont'd

Area constituting the authority.
Massachusetts Bay
transportation authority,
161A:1.
Area labor-management
committee, **23D:1.**
Area or areas to be served,
166A:1.
Armed forces, **4:7.**
Armed-site, **21D:1.**
Art dealer, **104A:1.**
Article, **266:143.**
Article of food, **94:1.**
Articles of organization, **156B:2,
164:1.**
Insurance, reorganization of
mutual insurers, **175:19G.**
Articulated bus, **90:1.**
Artificial flowers, **101:16.**
Artist, **104A:1, 231:85S.**
Art, practical art class, **74:1.**
Art, work, **6:20.**
As is, **106:2-316.**
Assault weapon, **269:10.**
Gun control, **140:121.**
Assembly, place, **143:1.**
Assessment, **21A:18, 276A:1.**
Assessor, meaning of statutory
references, **4:7.**
Asset, **7B:1, 109A:2.**
Asset management board, **7B:1.**
Asset management project, **7B:1.**
Assignee.
Structured settlement contracts,
231C:1.
Assignment, **4:7.**
Assignment of wages, **154:1.**
Assigns, **183:13, 183:28.**
Assistance, **164:133.**
Assistance with activities of daily
living, **19D:1.**
Assistance with or supervision of
instrumental activities of daily
living, **19D:1.**
Assistant clerk, **218:1.**
Assisted facility.
School building assistance,
70B:2.
Assisted living residences
residence, **19D:1.**
Assistive listening device and
system.
Hearing instrument specialists,
112:196.
Associate, **110D:1, 110E:1, 110F:3.**
Associated physician, **176C:1.**
Associate home inspectors.
Home inspectors, **112:221.**
Associate of an offeror, **110C:1.**

WORDS AND PHRASES
—Cont'd

Association group policy, **176J:1.**
Association member, **175:193R.**
Assumed in-school special
enrollment, **70:2.**
Assumed tuitioned-out special
education enrollment, **70:2.**
Athletic trainer, **112:23A.**
Atomic energy, **6:85.**
Attachment, **166:25A.**
Attempt to commit crime, **274:6.**
Attending physician, **201D:1.**
Attic, **144:2.**
Attorney, **176H:1.**
Attorney general, **93:2.**
Attorney in fact, reciprocal
insurance exchange
provisions, **175:94A.**
At will, **106:1-208.**
Auction, **100:1.**
Auctioneer, **100:1.**
Auction sale, **100:1.**
Audiologists, **93:71.**
Hearing instrument specialists,
112:196.
Audiology, **112:138.**
Audit, **3:63, 30:39R.**
Audit sheet, **90C:1.**
Authority.
Development finance agency,
23G:1.
Authority loans, **15C:3.**
Authorized account, **106:4A-105.**
Authorized driver, **90:32E½.**
Authorized insurer, **176L:1.**
Authorized person, **166:21F.**
Authorized service area, **159:12A.**
Auto home, **90:1.**
Automatic amusement device,
140:177A.
Automatic checkout system,
6:184B.
Automatic defrost, **25B:1.**
Automobile club, **174B:2.**
Automobile graveyard, **140B:1.**
Automobile law violation, **90C:1.**
Automobile transporter, **90:1.**
Automotive lubricating oils,
94:295A.
Available phosphoric acid, **128:64.**
Average annual net earnings,
79A:7.
Average current operating
expenditure per pupil in
regular day program, **70:2.**
Average direct service expenditure
per pupil in regular day
program, **70:2.**
Average group diameter test
result.
Sales of firearms, **140:123.**

WORDS AND PHRASES
—Cont'd

Average number of life years,
175:117C.
Average weekly wage, employment
security law, **151A:1, 152:1.**
A-weighted sound level, **90:7S.**
Bacteriological laboratory,
111:184A.
Bad debt, **118G:1.**
Bailee, **106:7-102.**
Bakery, **94:1.**
Balanced budget.
State finance, **29:1.**
Ballast, **25B:2.**
Ballot label, **50:1.**
Ballot, official, **50:1.**
Ballot question committee, **55:1.**
Bank, **63:1, 106:1-201,
106:4A-105, 178A:1, 201A:1.**
Commercial code, **106:1-201,
106:4-105.**
Banker, **106:1-201.**
Banker's credit, **106:2-325.**
Bank holding companies, **167A:1,
167A:2.**
Banking, **172A:3.**
Banking company, **172A:3.**
Banking day.
Commercial code, **106:4-104.**
Banking institution, **167D:34,
167D:35.**
Bank or storage facility, **113:7.**
Bankruptcy, **156C:2.**
Bankrupt, within uniform
partnership act, **108A:2.**
Banned hazardous substance,
94B:1.
Barbers and apprentice barbers,
112:87F.
Barrel, constituting measure of
quantity of clam bait, **94:85.**
Barrel length.
Gun control, **140:121.**
Base aid, **70:2.**
Base elevation, protection of
Berkshire Mountains
watershed regions, **131:39A.**
Basement, **144:2, 145:2.**
Base period, **111:70, 151A:1.**
Base period payroll level, **63:38.**
Base period property level, **63:38.**
Base revenue amount.
Massachusetts Bay
transportation authority
state and local contribution
fund, **10:35T.**
Base year foundation budget, **70:2.**
Basic property insurance, **175C:1.**
Bathing water.
Minimum sanitation standards
for bathing waters, **111:5S.**

WORDS AND PHRASES
—Cont'd

Bazaars, **271:7A.**

Bearer, **106:1-201.**

Bearer form, **106:8-102.**

Beauty shop, **112:87T.**

Bed and breakfast establishment, **64G:1.**

Bed and breakfast home, **64G:1.**

Bedding, **94:270.**

Beneficial insects, **132B:2.**

Beneficiaries, **32:1, 106:4A-103, 151D:1, 191A:1, 203B:1.**

Letters of credit, **106:5-102.**

Beneficiary form.

Transfer on death security registration, **201E:102.**

Beneficiary's bank, **106:4A-103.**

Benefit contract.

Fraternal benefit societies, **176:1.**

Benefit level, **176J:1.**

Benefit member.

Fraternal benefit societies, **176:1.**

Benefits, employment security, **151A:1.**

Benefit year, employment security, **151A:1.**

Benevolent gestures, **233:23D.**

Between merchants, **106:2-104.**

Beverages, **110:1, 138:1.**

Bicycle, **90E:1.**

Bicycle parking facility, **90E:1.**

BID, **30B:2, 40O:1, 93F:1.**

BID member, **40O:1.**

Bike lane, **90E:1.**

Bike path, **90E:1.**

Bike route, **90E:1.**

Bikeway, **90E:1.**

Bilingual enrollment, **70:2.**

Billing address, **63:1.**

Bill of lading, **106:1-201.**

Bird of prey, **131:75A.**

Birds, **131:1.**

Blanket accident or sickness insurance policy, **175:110.**

Blighted open area, **121A:1, 121B:1.**

Blind bidding, **93F:1.**

Block group, **57:1.**

Blocks, **57:1.**

Board, contributory retirement systems, **32:1.**

Board, criminal history systems, **22A:1.**

Boarding house, **145:2.**

Board, listing board, **50:1.**

Board of aldermen, **4:7, 50:1.**

Board of health, **111:1, 111:207, 144:2, 145:2.**

WORDS AND PHRASES
—Cont'd

Board of health and hospitals, **Spec L 70:2.**

Board of selectmen, **4:7.**

Board or officer in charge of the sewer department, **83:16A.**

Boat, **90B:1.**

Boating accident, **90B:1.**

Boat transporter, **90:1.**

Bodily injury, **265:13J.**

Child custody, **208:31A.**

Husband and wife, **209:38.**

Bogs, **131:40.**

Boiler, **146:1.**

Bond act, **29C:1.**

Bond fund, **29:1.**

Bond, motor vehicle liability bond, **90:34A.**

Bond resolution, **15C:3.**

Bond revenues, **29:1.**

Bonds, **15C:1, 29C:1, 92:104.**

Development finance agency, **23G:1.**

Book and equipment allotment, **70:2.**

Booking agent, **140:180A.**

Books, **4:7.**

Books and records, milk control law, **94A:1.**

Bordering vegetated wetland, **92:104.**

Borrower, **15C:3, 23A:57, 140:90A.**

Business development office, **23A:60.**

Boston City Hospital, **Spec L 70:2.**

Boston extension.

Turnpike authority, **81A:3.**

Boston harbor, **91:1.**

Boston Specialty and Rehabilitation Hospital, **Spec L 70:2.**

Bottler, **94:321.**

Boycott, secondary, **149:20C.**

Branch, **106:1-201.**

Brand, **128:64.**

Brand name, **128:51.**

Bread, **94:1.**

Breaks, horse and dog racing meetings provisions, **128A:5.**

Bridges, words deemed to include references, **4:7.**

Broker, **94:118, 106:8-102, 111H:1, 175:174G, 201A:1.**

Broker's license, motor carriers of property, **159B:2.**

Brokers of real estate, **112:87PP.**

Bucketing, **271:35.**

Bucketshop, **271:35.**

Budgetary funds, **29:1.**

Budget director, **29:1.**

WORDS AND PHRASES
—Cont'd

Budgeted revenues and other financial resources pertaining to the budgeted funds.

State finance, **29:1.**

Builder's risk policies, **175:98.**

Building authority, **7:39A, 25A:11C.**

Building inspector, **144:2, 145:2.**

Building projects, **7:39A.**

Development finance agency, **23G:35.**

Buildings, **6:20, 143:1, 148:6, 148:7, 183A:1, 271:1A.**

Buildings used for industrial purposes, **149:1.**

Bulk facility, **21J:1.**

Bulk fertilizer, **128:64.**

Bulk, supplying electricity, **164:1.**

Burden of establishing, **106:1-201.**

Bureau, **3:63, 79A:1, 146:81.**

Bureau of special investigations, **62E:1.**

Business, **23A:3A, 23A:57, 23D:1, 64H:1, 64I:1, 79A:1, 151E:1, 233:78, 268B:1.**

Business development office, **23A:60.**

Business combination transaction, **110F:3, 149:20E.**

Business day.

Child support enforcement, **62E:1, 119A:1A.**

Privation contracts, **7:53.**

Business district, motor vehicle regulation act, **90:1.**

Business improvement district board of directors, **40O:1.**

Business incubator, **23A:3A.**

Business trusts, **182:1.**

Business with which he is associated, **268B:1.**

Bus or motorbus, **90:1.**

Bus, school, **90:1.**

Butter, **94:1.**

Buyer, **106:2-103.**

Buyer in ordinary course of business, **106:1-201, 106:2A-103.**

Buying, **106:1-201.**

Bylaws, **4:7, 110D:1, 110E:1, 145:2.**

Byproduct, **21I:2.**

Byproduct material, **6:85, 111:5M.**

Cadet engineers, **164:69B.**

Callahan tunnel.

Turnpike authority, **81A:3.**

Campaign team.

Clean election slaw, **55A:11**

Cancellation, **106:2-106, 106:2-720, 106:2A-103.**

WORDS AND PHRASES
—Cont'd
C. & F., **106:2-320.**
Candidate, **55:1.**
Candidate for public office, **268B:1.**
Candidate's committee, **55:1.**
Candidate site community,
low-level radioactive waste,
111H:1.
Candidate site, low-level
radioactive waste, **111H:1.**
Can, label and trademarks law,
110:1.
Canned lobster meat or crabmeat,
130:1.
Capable of use as human food,
94:118.
Capacity to make health care
decisions, **201D:1.**
Capital asset, **62:1.**
Capital construction project.
School building assistance,
70B:2.
Capital facility, **7:39A.**
Capital facility projects, **7:39A.**
Capital gain, **62:1.**
Capital gain income, **62:1.**
Capital investment program.
Massachusetts Bay
transportation authority,
161A:1.
Capital loss, **62:1.**
Capital participation instruments,
40F:1.
Capital participation investments,
40F:1.
Cardholder, **266:37A.**
Caretaker, **19C:1.**
Carriers, **159:34A, 159A:2,
159A:11A, 159B:2, 176G:1,
176J:1, 176K:9, 176M:1.**
Accident and sickness insurance,
replacement coverage for
insolvent HMO's, **175:110.**
Health maintenance
organizations, insolvency,
176G:23.
Hospital service corporations,
replacement coverage for
insolvent HMO'S, **176A:33.**
Medical service corporations,
replacement coverage for
insolvent HMO'S, **176B:21.**
Case, **175:117C.**
Case characteristics, **176J:1.**
Case mix, **118G:1.**
Casher of checks, **169A:1.**
Cashier's check.
Negotiable instruments,
106:3-104.
Cash price, **255B:1, 255D:1.**

WORDS AND PHRASES
—Cont'd
Cash proceeds, **106:9-306.**
Casualty and surety rate
regulatory law,
175A:1-175A:20.
Catastrophic condition.
Viatical settlements, **175:213.**
Catastrophic illness.
Catastrophic illness in children
relief fund commission,
111K:1 to 111K:11.
CATV operator, **166A:1.**
Caucus, **50:1.**
Cause, **156B:50A.**
Causes burns, **94B:1.**
Caution, **94B:1.**
CDC, **40H:2.**
CEDAC, **40H:2.**
Ceding entity, **175G:1.**
Cellar, **144:2, 145:2.**
Center, **40J:12.**
Center of Excellence, **40J:12.**
Central, **94:174.**
Central artery.
Turnpike authority, **81A:3.**
Central artery north area.
Turnpike authority, **81A:3.**
Central Credit Union Fund, Inc.,
171:1.
Central register, **22A:1.**
Central routing unit, **167B:1.**
CERCLA, **21I:2.**
Certificate, **62B:4, 121A:6, 142:1,
159:12A, 164:69G, 178A:1.**
Fraternal benefit societies,
176:1.
Certificated security, **106:8-102.**
Certificate of deposit.
Negotiable instruments,
106:3-104.
Certificate of inspection, **90:1.**
Certificate of limited partnership,
109:1.
Certificate of number, **90B:1.**
Certificate of organization, **156C:2.**
Certificate of rejection, **90:1.**
Certificate of waiver, **90:1.**
Certificate, withholding exemption
and deduction certificate,
62B:4.
Certification.
Forest lands and products tax,
61:1.
Certified, **128:84.**
Certified applicator, **132B:2.**
Certified appraisal or certified
appraisal report, **112:173.**
Certified by a planning board,
41:81L.
Certified candidate.
Clean elections law, **55A:1.**

WORDS AND PHRASES
—Cont'd
Certified check.
Negotiable instruments,
106:3-409.
Certified fund, **175F:1.**
Certified inspector, **90:1.**
Certified interpreter, **221C:1.**
Certified project, **23A:3A.**
Certified public accountant, **13:33.**
Chain pharmacist, **13:22.**
Chain transactions, **271:6A.**
Change order, **7:42E.**
Charge, **118G:1.**
Charitable home for the aged,
111:71.
Charitable organization, **59:5,
60A:1.**
Charitable solicitation, **68:18.**
Charter.
Insurance, reorganization of
mutual insurers, **175:19G.**
Charter, city, **4:7, 43:1, 144:2.**
Charter schools, **71:89.**
Charter service, **159A:11A.**
Charter, special charter as
included, **4:7.**
Chattel mortgage, **4:7.**
Chattel paper, **106:9-105.**
Cheat, **266:76.**
Check, **55:9, 93:104.**
Negotiable instruments,
106:3-104, 106:3-312.
Cheddar cheese, **94:61A.**
Cheese, **94:1, 94:61A.**
Chief administrative officer, **4:7.**
Chief executive officer, **4:7, 21D:1.**
Chief justice.
Community corrections, **211F:1.**
Chief procurement officer, **30B:2.**
Child, **118G:1, 209D:1-101,
265:13J.**
Catastrophic illness in children
relief fund commission,
111K:1 to 111K:11.
Child fatality review teams,
38:2A.
Child born out of wedlock, **209C:1.**
Child in need of services, **119:21.**
Child passenger restraint, **90:1.**
Children and minors, **4:7, 28A:2,
28A:9, 32:12B, 40D:1,
54:103B, 62D:1, 119:1, 119:52,
152:28, 171:1, 184:6, 272:31.**
Children of limited
English-speaking ability,
71A:1.
Children of working parents,
15:54.
Child support order, **209D:1-101.**
Chiropractic, **112:89.**

WORDS AND PHRASES
—Cont'd
Chiropractic service, **176B:1.**
Chiropractor, **112:89.**
Chronically nonresident person,
  111:80, 111:116.
Church, **138:16C.**
C.I.F., **106:2-320.**
Cigarettes, **64C:1.**
  Tobacco master settlement
    agreement, **94E:1.**
Circulation of library materials
  within regional systems,
  78:19F.
Citation book, **90C:1.**
Citizens advisory committee,
  low-level radioactive waste,
  111H:1.
Citizenship, **1:1.**
City, **43:128, Spec L 70:2.**
City clerk, **50:1.**
City council, **4:7.**
City election, **50:1.**
City officers, meaning of statutory
  references to, where city has
  no such officers, **4:7.**
City solicitor, **4:7, 144:2.**
Civil aircraft, **90:35.**
Civil motor vehicle infraction,
  90C:1.
Civil service, **31:1.**
Claim, **109A:2, 200A:1, 258C:1.**
  False claims against
    Commonwealth, **12:5A.**
Claimant, **18:5G, 90:49B, 118E:22,
  142A:1, 258C:1.**
  Negotiable instruments,
    106:3-312.
Claimant agency, **62D:1.**
Clam, **130:1.**
Class, **30:45, 31:1, 35:51A.**
Class allocation, **30:45, 35:51A.**
Classification, **30:45, 35:51A.**
Class I milk, **Spec L 139:2.**
Class of appliances, **94:314.**
Class of business, **175:117C,
  176J:1.**
Class reallocation, **30:45, 35:51A.**
Clean election funds.
  Clean elections law, **55A:1.**
Clean Water Act, **29C:1.**
Clearance project, **121B:1.**
Clearing corporation, **106:8-102.**
Clearing house.
  Bank deposits and collections,
    106:4-104.
Clerk, **218:1, 261:27A.**
  Vital statistics, **46:1E.**
Clerk, city, **50:1.**
Clerk of court, **218:1.**
Client company, **152:14A.**

WORDS AND PHRASES
—Cont'd
Clients, **112:135.**
  Home inspectors, **112:221.**
Clinic, **155:2B.**
Clinical laboratory, **111E:1.**
Clinical social work, independent
  practice, **112:130.**
Closed plan, **176M:1.**
Closed season, **130:1, 131:1.**
Close proximity to overhead high
  voltage lines, **166:21A.**
Closure, low-level radioactive
  waste, **111H:1.**
Closure plan, low-level radioactive
  waste, **111H:1.**
Closure, solid waste facilities,
  21H:2.
Club, **138:1.**
Club agent, **174B:2.**
Cluster development, **40A:9.**
Coal, **164:94G½.**
Coastal facilities improvement,
  21F:2, 21F:3.
Coastal water, **130:1, 131:1.**
Coastal wetlands, **130:105, 131:40.**
Code, **62:1, 62C:1, 65C:1.**
  Child support enforcement,
    62E:1.
Coded, **6:184B.**
CODIS DNA database, **22E:1.**
Cogeneration facility, **164:1.**
Collateral, **106:9-105.**
Collateral costs, **93:107.**
Collect, for purposes of hazardous
  waste management act, **21C:2.**
Collecting bank.
  Commercial code, **106:4-105.**
Collection system, **21:26A.**
Collector, **60:1.**
College, **266:89.**
  Reputable dental college, **112:46.**
Collision damage waiver,
  90:32E½.
Colonel, **22C:1.**
  DNA database, **22E:1.**
Colostrum, **94:12.**
Combination of persons, **55:7.**
Combined DNA index system.
  DNA database, **22E:1.**
Combustible, **94B:1.**
Commemoration day, **4:7.**
Commerce, **90F:1, 93:2, 93A:1.**
Commercial applicator, **132B:2.**
Commercial center revitalization
  district, **23B:11.**
Commercial computer service,
  266:33A.
Commercial domicile, **63:1.**
Commercial driver license system
  (CDLIS) defined, **90F:1.**

WORDS AND PHRASES
—Cont'd
Commercial establishment,
  111:5R.
Commercial facilities.
  Tourism facilities fund, **23G:42.**
Commercial feed, **128:51.**
Commercial fertilizer, **128:64.**
Commercial motor vehicle, **90F:1,
  159B:2.**
Commercial space, **151B:1.**
Commercial unit, **106:2-105,
  106:2A-103.**
Commission, **Spec L 70:2.**
Commissioned officer, **22C:1.**
Commissioner, agriculture, **128:1.**
Commissioner, Environmental
  Affairs Executive Office,
  21A:18.
Commissioner, health care finance
  and policy division, **118G:1.**
Commissioner of health and
  hospitals, **Spec L 70:2.**
Commission marketing order,
  Spec L 139:2.
Committed, **125:1.**
Committed offender, **125:1.**
Commodities, **137:7, 271:35.**
Commodity account, **106:9-115.**
Commodity contract, **106:9-115.**
Commodity customer, **106:9-115.**
Commodity intermediary,
  106:9-115.
Common carrier, **159:19B, 159B:2,
  166:15E.**
Common hallway, **148:26D.**
Common meaning as guide, **4:6.**
Common paymaster, **175:133.**
Common receiver of stolen goods,
  266:60.
Common thief, **266:40.**
Common utterer of counterfeit
  money, **267:11, 267:19.**
Commonwealth bonds, **15C:3.**
Commonwealth contractor.
  Municipal finance.
    Federal aid for medically
      necessary expenses, **44:72.**
Commonwealth funding schedule,
  32:1.
Commonwealth, public officials,
  66:17A.
Commonwealth service corps,
  23B:10.
Commonwealth's pension liability,
  32:1.
Commonwealth's pension liability
  fund, **32:1.**
Communication common carrier,
  272:99.
Communications, **112:135,
  233:20B.**

WORDS AND PHRASES
—Cont'd
Communities and development secretary, **23B:10.**
Community access board, **123A:1.**
Community Access Program, **123A:1.**
Community action agency, **23B:24.**
Community antenna television system, **166A:1.**
Community college, **15A:5B, 15A:10.**
Community college affiliate, **15A:5B, 15A:10.**
Community compensation, low-level radioactive waste, **111H:1.**
Community corrections plan, **211F:1.**
Community corrections program, **211F:1.**
Community development block grant, **23B:29.**
Community development corporation, **40F:1.**
Oil and hazardous material release prevention and response, **21E:2.**
Community health centers, **118G:1.**
Community housing.
Community preservation, **44B:2.**
Community preservation, **44B:2.**
Community preservation committee, **44B:2.**
Community preservation fund, **44B:2.**
Community programs bureau, **23B:10.**
Community rating, **176K:9.**
Community renewal program, **121B:1.**
Community supervisory committee, low-level radioactive waste, **111H:1.**
Commuting student, **63:31D.**
Compact, **Spec L 139:2.**
Compact over-order price, **Spec L 139:2.**
Company, **26:8C, 157:3, 157:3B, 168:20, 176G:1, 178A:1.**
Excavations, **82:40.**
Company, banking, **172A:3.**
Company shuttle van, **63:31D.**
Comparable low bid or offer, **7:1, 7:22G.**
Comparable replacement dwelling, **79A:1.**
Compensable week, **151A:1.**
Compensation, **21D:1, 63:1, 268A:1.**

WORDS AND PHRASES
—Cont'd
Compensation, regular, **32:1.**
Competent interpreter services.
Interpreters for acute care psychiatric facilities, **123:23A.**
Interpreters for emergency and acute care medical services, **111:25J.**
Competitive bidding, **268A:1.**
Competitive examination, **31:1.**
Completed operations liability, **176L:1.**
Compliance period.
Low-income housing tax credit, **62:6I.**
Low-income housing tax credit, corporations, **63:31H.**
Compliance review document.
Banks, compliance review, **167:49.**
Compliance review supervisor.
Banks, compliance review, **167:49.**
Comprehensive cancer center, **118G:1.**
Comprehensive Environmental Response Compensation and Liability Act, **148:38B.**
Comprehensive operating contract, low-level radioactive waste, **111H:1.**
Computation date, **151A:14.**
Computing scale, **98:56B.**
Conditional certificate, **121A:6.**
Conditional sale, **4:7.**
Condition in mortgage, statutory, **183:20, 183:23.**
Condition of substantial release migration.
Oil and hazardous material release prevention and response, **21E:2.**
Condominium buildings, **183A:1.**
Confidential communication, **233:20J.**
Confidentiality, **110F:3.**
Confidential research information.
Genetic testing, **111:70G.**
Confirmed credit, **106:2-325.**
Confirmer.
Letters of credit, **106:5-102.**
Conforming goods, **106:2A-103.**
Conforming to contract, **106:2-106.**
Consent, **175J:1.**
Conservation restriction, **184:31.**
Conservator, **203B:1.**
Consideration.
Negotiable instruments, **106:3-303.**

WORDS AND PHRASES
—Cont'd
Consignee, **106:7-102.**
Consignment, **104A:1.**
Consignor, **106:7-102.**
Consolidated net surplus in the operating funds, **29:1.**
Conspicuous, **106:1-201.**
Constitutional officers, **32:1.**
Construct, **121A:1.**
Constructed, **40:5.**
Constructing, **81:32.**
Construction, **12A:1, 22:13A, 121A:1, 144:2, 164:69G.**
Capital facilities project, **7:39A.**
Development finance agency, **23G:1.**
Public library, **78:19G-78:19K.**
Tourism facilities fund, **23G:42.**
Construction manager, **7:38A½.**
School building assistance, **70B:2.**
Construction mortgage, **106:2A-309(1)(d).**
Construction services bureau, **23B:10.**
Consumer, **93:50, 93:107, 93A:1, 94A:1, 140E:1.**
Consumer goods, **106:9-109, 255:12C.**
Consumer lease, **93:90.**
Consumer note, **255:12C.**
Consumer report, **93:50, 175I:2.**
Consumer reporting agency, **93:50, 175I:2.**
Contagious and infectious diseases, **111:1, 111:6, 111:116, 129:1.**
Container, **94:118.**
Containment, **111:189A.**
Solid waste facilities, **21H:2.**
Contents, condition and quality unknown, **106:7-203.**
Contents or condition of contents of packages unknown, **106:7-301.**
Contested meeting, **149:184.**
Contested meeting date, **149:184.**
Contiguous land.
Forest lands and products tax, **61:1.**
Contiguously located housing, **151B:1.**
Contingent liability account, low-level radioactive waste, **111H:1.**
Continued services, **7:38A½.**
Continuing care facility, **40D:1.**
Continuity of services to developmentally disabled persons, **71B:12A, 71B:12B, 71B:12C.**

WORDS AND PHRASES
—Cont'd

Continuous attendance.
Steamboilers, **146:46.**
Continuous examination, **31:1.**
Contract, **30:39R, 30B:2,
106:1-201, 106:2-101,
106:2-210, 142A:1, 176B:4,
271:35.**
Development finance agency,
23G:1.
Contract carrier by motor vehicle,
159B:2.
Contract feeder, **128:51.**
Contract for sale, **106:2-106.**
Contract modification, **7:42E.**
Contract of insurance, **175:2.**
Contractor, **12A:1, 29:29F,
29:142A:1, 30B:2, 64H:30A,
64I:31A.**
Child support enforcement,
62E:1.
Contractor, capital facilities
projects, **30:39R.**
Contract right, **106:9-106.**
Contract termination fee, **164:1.**
Contractual producers, **94:152F.**
Contribution, **55:1, 156C:2.**
Clean elections law, **55A:1.**
Employment security provisions,
151A:1.
Contributory group hospital,
surgical, or medical insurance
plan, **175:110G.**
Contributory group non-profit
hospital service contract,
176A:8D.
Contributory group non-profit
medical service plan,
176A:8D.
Control, **106:8-106, 106:9-115.**
Control and supervision, **7:39A.**
Controlled atmosphere, **94:109.**
Controlled insurer, **175:174G.**
Controlled substances, **64K:1,
90F:1, 94C:1.**
Controlling broker, **175:174G.**
Controlling business, **23A:3A.**
Controlling person, **175:177N.**
Control of company, **168:20.**
Control or controlled, **175:174G.**
Control or controlling, **175:177N.**
Control transferee, **149:183,
149:184.**
Control transferor, **149:184.**
Convalescent or nursing home,
111:71.
Convention, **50:1.**
Conversion, **7:39A.**
Conversion nongroup health plan,
176M:1.

WORDS AND PHRASES
—Cont'd

Converted holding company.
Insurance, reorganization of
mutual insurers, **175:19G.**
Conveyances, **108A:2, 183:9.**
Conviction, **90:30B, 90F:1.**
Gun control, **140:121.**
Co-operative, **157:3, 157:8.**
Co-operative association, **94:42A,
94A:1.**
Co-operative banks, **170:1, 170
Appx:2, 170 Appx:3.**
Cooperative housing corporations,
157B:4.
Copy, as meaning certified copy,
94:1.
Corner lot, **144:2, 145:2.**
Corporate and institutional
trading partners.
Eavesdropping, wire tapping
and interception of
communications, **272:99.**
Corporate clinic, **155:2B.**
Corporate credit union, **171:1.**
Corporate trust, **62:1.**
Corps, **78A:1.**
Correctional facility, **125:1.**
Correctional institution, **125:1.**
Correct price, **6:184B.**
Corrosive, **94B:1.**
Corrupt offering or acceptance of
gift, **268A:2.**
Corrupt practices, **55:32.**
Cosmetic, **94:1.**
Cosmetologist, **112:87F, 112:87T.**
Cost items, **150E:1.**
Cost of conversion, **164:94G½.**
Cost of goods, **93:14E.**
Cost-of-living adjustment.
Income tax credits.
Older persons, credit for real
estate or rent payments,
62:6.
Cost of the project, **40F:1, 121C:1.**
Development finance agency,
23G:1.
Costs, **29C:1, 40N:3, 94A:1.**
Development finance agency,
23G:1.
Turnpike authority, **81A:5.**
Costs of a project, **40F:1.**
Costs of issuance.
Turnpike authority, **81A:5.**
Costs of performance, **64H:1,
64I:1.**
Costs of the project.
Tourism facilities fund, **23G:42.**
Cost to the retailer, **64C:13,
93:14E.**
Cost to the wholesaler, **64C:13,
93:14E.**

WORDS AND PHRASES
—Cont'd

Coterminous, **4:7.**
Council, **21D:1, 21I:2, 25A:2,
121A:6, 164:69G.**
Tourism facilities fund, **23G:42.**
Counsel, **19C:1.**
Counseling, **112:130.**
Counselor, insurance, **175:177A.**
Counterfeit substance, **94C:1.**
County agency, **268A:1.**
County correctional facility, **125:1.**
County employee, **35:51A, 268A:1.**
County or state fair, **128A:1.**
Coupon, **255D:1.**
Course of dealing, **106:1-205.**
Court, **119:52, 201A:1, 203B:1,
209A:1, 217:1, 218:1, 221C:1,
224:1.**
Rights of victims and witnesses
of crime, **258B:1.**
Tenement house law provisions,
144:2, 145:2.
Court of insolvency, **4:7, 217:1.**
Co-venture, **40G:1.**
Cover, **106:2-711, 106:2-712.**
Covered claim, **175D:1.**
Covered dependent, **176B:1,
176H:1.**
Covered executive official, **3:39.**
Covered legal services, **176H:1.**
Covered partial closing, **151A:71A.**
CP.
Community preservation, **44B:2.**
CPI.
Income tax credits.
Older persons, credit for real
estate or rent payments,
62:6.
Crabmeat, canned, **130:1.**
Cream, **94:12.**
Cream cheese, **94:1.**
Credibility factor, **175:117C.**
Credibility table, **175:117C.**
Credit, **266:37.**
Creditable prior service, **32:1.**
Creditable service, **32:1.**
Credit card, **63:1, 93:104, 266:37A.**
Credit card issuer's
reimbursement fee, **63:1.**
Credit eligible territory, **175C:1.**
Creditor, **106:1-201, 109A:2.**
Credit share.
Retaliatory tax credit for
property and casualty
companies, **63:29E.**
Credit union, **171:1, 171:82.**
Crime.
Rights of victims and witnesses
of crime, **258B:1.**
Crime reporting unit, **22C:32.**

WORDS AND PHRASES
—Cont'd

Criminal, **90C:1.**
Criminal investigator, **268:13B.**
Criminal justice agencies, **6:167,**
66A:1.
Criminal offender record
information, **6:167.**
Critical economic area, **40E:2.**
Crops, **106:9-109.**
Cultural organization.
Tourism facilities fund, **23G:42.**
Current expenses, **40N:3.**
Development finance agency,
23G:1.
Custodial trust property, **203B:1.**
Custodian, **201A:1.**
Marriage records, **46:1E.**
Custodian property, **201A:1.**
Custody, **119:21.**
Customer, **94:320, 106:4A-105.**
Bank deposits and collections,
106:4-104.
Customer-formula feed, **128:51.**
Customized wheelchair dealer,
93:107.
Customized wheelchair lessor,
93:107.
Cut.
Forest lands and products tax,
61:1.
Cutting plan.
Forest lands and products tax,
61:1.
Dairy farm, **94:16.**
Dam, **253:44.**
Damage to the environment,
12:11D, 214:7A.
Danger, **94B:1.**
Dangerous buildings, **143:6.**
Dark days, **128C:1.**
Dark season, **128C:1.**
Data processing center, **167B:1.**
Date of certification, **151A:71A.**
Date of conversion, **178A:1.**
Date of initial conversion,
164:94G½.
Date of loss, **18:5G, 118E:22.**
Date of notification, **151A:71A.**
Date of qualification, **43:40.**
Date prescribed for payment or
delivery, abandoned property,
200A:1.
Date the system becomes
operative, **32:1.**
Day, **104:7.**
Day care center.
Pesticides, **132B:2.**
Day player, **231:85P½.**
Deaf person, **166:15E.**
Dealer, **64K:1, 90:1, 90:5, 90B:36,**
90D:1, 130:1, 131:1.

WORDS AND PHRASES
—Cont'd

Death, fetal, **46:24.**
Death tax, **65:24A, 65B:1, 65C:21.**
Debarment, **29:29F.**
Debt, **109A:2.**
Spousal and child support
obligations, **62D:1.**
Debtor, **62D:1, 106:9-105, 109A:2,**
224:1.
Debt service, **44A:1.**
Decadent areas, **121B:1.**
Decedent, **113:7.**
Decibel, **90:7S.**
Declarant, **183A:1.**
Declaration of estimated income
tax, definitions, **62B:1,**
62B:13.
Declaration of intent.
Clean elections law, **55A:1.**
Declaration of loss.
Negotiable instruments,
106:3-312.
Declination of insurance coverage,
175I:2.
Dedicated revenue source.
Massachusetts Bay
transportation authority,
161A:1.
Dedicated sales tax revenue
amount.
Massachusetts Bay
transportation authority
state and local contribution
fund, **10:35T.**
Deductions, **32:1.**
Deeds and conveyances, **183:9,**
183:13.
Default, **105A:1.**
Business development office,
23A:60.
Default insurance, **15C:3.**
Default reserve fund, **15C:3.**
Default service, **164:1.**
Defendant, **106:1-201, 224:1.**
Defense corporation, **63:38.**
Defense-dependent firm, **23F:1.**
Defense-dependent industry,
23F:1.
Defense-related commercial
activities, **23F:1.**
Deferred payment price, **255D:1.**
Defined geographic area, **93F:1.**
Defoliant, **132B:2.**
Delegated procedures, **112:43A.**
Deliberation, **30A:11A, 34:9F,**
39:23A.
Delinquency proceeding, **175:180A.**
Delinquent child, **119:52.**
Deliver, **94C:1.**
Delivered weights, **106:2-321.**

WORDS AND PHRASES
—Cont'd

Delivery, **106:1-201, 106:8-301.**
Delivery order, **106:7-102.**
Delivery period, under milk control
act, **94A:13.**
Demolition burning, **48:13.**
Demonstrator, **112:87T.**
Hairdresser provisions, **112:87T.**
Dental assistant, **112:43A.**
Dental hygienist, **112:43A.**
Dentist, **233:79G.**
Dentistry, practicing, **112:50.**
Department, **21A:18, 21A:18A,**
21J:1, 22A:1, 22C:1, 70:2,
71B:1, 94D:1, 111:189A,
111G:1, 123:1, 123B:1,
148:38B, 149:184, 258C:1.
Departmental list, **30:45.**
Departmental promotional
examination, **31:1.**
Department, Environmental
Affairs Executive Office,
21A:18.
Departments of state, **30:1.**
Dependency deduction, **62B:4.**
Dependent children, **118:1,**
175:108.
Dependent funds, **123:1, 123B:1.**
Dependent or dependents, **7:53,**
32A:2, 32B:2, 115:1, 118G:1,
152:1, 176B:1, 258C:1.
Structured settlement contracts,
231C:1.
Deposit account, **106:9-105,**
140E:1.
Depositary bank, **106:4-105.**
Deposits, **167D:1, 171:48.**
Depressant or stimulant
substance, **94C:1.**
Depressed area, **7:22.**
Deputy assistant clerk, **218:1.**
Deputy commissioner, capital
facilities projects, **7:38A½,**
149:44A.
Description of excavation location.
Excavations, **82:40.**
Deserter, **33:56.**
Desiccant, **132B:2.**
Designated private auditor, **59:60.**
Designed for use.
Drug paraphernalia, **94C:1.**
Designer, **7:38A½, 30B:2.**
Designers, architectural, **112:60K.**
Design services, **7:38A½.**
Detailed site characterization,
low-level radioactive waste,
111H:1.
Detective, private, **147:22.**
Developer, Massachusetts
Hazardous Waste Facility
Siting Act, **21D:1.**

WORDS AND PHRASES
—Cont'd

Development contract, low-level radioactive waste, **111H:1.**

Development cost, **121B:1.**

Development Finance Insurance Fund.

Development finance agency, **23G:1.**

Development, low-level radioactive waste, **111H:1.**

Device, **94:1, 132B:2.**

Device, adulteration, **94:186.**

Devisee.

Transfer on death security registration, **201E:102.**

Dickey, pole dickey, **90:1.**

Die without heirs of the body, **184:6.**

Die without issue, **184:6.**

Direct appropriation, **29:1.**

Direct debt limit, **29:1.**

Direct investment, **40G:1.**

Directly or indirectly, **175:63A.**

Direct plurality vote, **50:1.**

Direct public use, for purposes of determining whether property is surplus, **7:40F.**

Direct supervision, **112:43A.**

Hearing instrument specialists, **112:198.**

Disability.

Special education, **71B:1.**

Disabled person, **3A, 6:77, 6:172C, 19C:1, 166:15E, 221.**

Disadvantaged vendor, **30B:18.**

DISC, **63:30.**

Discharge, **31:1, 183:54.**

Discontinuance.

Accident and sickness insurance, replacement coverage for insolvent HMO's, **175:110.**

Health maintenance organizations, insolvency, **176G:23.**

Hospital service corporations, replacement coverage for insolvent HMO's, **176A:33.**

Medical service corporations, replacement coverage for insolvent HMO's, **176B:21.**

Discounted present value.

Structured settlement contracts, **231C:1.**

Discount/finance charge.

Structured settlement contracts, **231C:1.**

Discover, **106:1-201.**

Disease, contagious, **129:1.**

Disease dangerous to the public health, **111:1.**

WORDS AND PHRASES
—Cont'd

Dishonor.

Letters of credit, **106:5-102.**

Dispensaries or clinics, **111:51, 155:2B.**

Dispense, **94C:1.**

Dispensing facility, **21J:1.**

Dispensing hearing instruments.

Hearing instrument specialists, **112:196.**

Dispensing optician, **112:73C.**

Displaced homemaker, **23D:26.**

Displaced person, **79A:1.**

Display, **6:184B.**

Disposal, hazardous waste management, **21C:2, 21D:1.**

Disposal, low-level radioactive waste, **111H:1.**

Disposition.

Rights of victims and witnesses of crime, **258B:1.**

Disproportionate share hospital, **118G:1.**

Disqualification, **90F:1.**

Disseminate, **272:31.**

Dissolution of partnership, **108A:29.**

Distress factor, **23A:3A.**

Distributable aid, **44A:1.**

Distribute, **94C:1.**

Distributed generation, **164:1.**

Distribution, **164:1.**

Distribution agreement, **7:22G.**

Distribution company, **164:1.**

Distribution facility, **164:1.**

Distribution service, **164:1.**

Distributive occupations, **74:1.**

Distributor, **93B:1, 93F:1, 128:64.**

Distributor branch, **93B:1.**

Distributor or wholesaler of motor vehicles, **93B:1, 93B:15.**

Distributor representative, **93B:1.**

District, **4:7, 32:1, 32B:2, 40:1A, 41:1A, 41:126, 44:4, 70:2, 90:1.**

District commission, **21:26A.**

District court, **4:7, 90C:1, 123:1, 231:59G.**

Dividend, **61:1, 62:1.**

Division, capital facilities projects, **7:38A½.**

Division, health care finance and policy, **118G:1.**

DNA analysis, **22E:1.**

DNA database, **22E:1.**

DNA record, **22E:1.**

DNA sample, **22E:1.**

Doctoral degree in psychology, **112:118.**

Document, **106:9-105, 106:9-109.**

Letters of credit, **106:5-102.**

WORDS AND PHRASES
—Cont'd

Documentary draft.

Bank deposits and collections, **106:4-104.**

Documentary material, **93A:1.**

Document of title, **106:1-201, 106:7-102.**

Dog fund, **140:136A.**

Dog officer, **140:136A.**

Doing business, **63:32, 63:39, 63:52A.**

Doing business with Burma (Myanmar), **7:22G.**

DOL, **111F:1.**

Dolly, pole, **90:1.**

Domestic animals, disease control provisions, **129:1.**

Domestication, **175:161A.**

Domestic business corporations, **63:30.**

Domestic electric utility, **164A:1.**

Domestic insurer, **175:161A.**

Domestic limited liability company, **156C:2.**

Domestic property and casualty insurer.

Retaliatory tax credit for property and casualty companies, **63:29E.**

Domestic utility, **164:133.**

Domestic violence victims' counselor, **233:20K.**

Domestic violence victims' program, **233:20K.**

Domicile, **176L:1.**

Domiciliary foreign guardian or conservator, **199A:1.**

Domiciliary foreign personal representative, **199A:1.**

Domiciliary state, **175:180A.**

Donor, **113:7.**

Draft.

Bank deposits and collections, **106:4-104.**

Drainage, **41:81L, 111:17.**

Drawee.

Bank deposits and collections, **106:4-104.**

Negotiable instruments, **106:3-103.**

Drawer.

Negotiable instruments, **106:3-103.**

DRG, **118G:1.**

Drift, **21B:2.**

Drinking water project.

Water pollution abatement trust, **29C:1.**

Drinking water supply, solid waste facilities, **21H:2.**

WORDS AND PHRASES
—Cont'd
Driver license, **90F:1.**
Drug, **94:1, 94C:1, 112:38, 128:51.**
Drug business, **112:37.**
Drug paraphernalia, **94C:1.**
Dual party TDD/TTY telephone
message relay service,
166:15E.
Dual purpose vehicle, **111C:1.**
Due diligence, **106:1-201.**
Dukes county, statutory references,
4:7.
Duly negotiated, **106:7-501.**
Dumbwaiters as within term
elevators, **143:71E.**
Duplicate of a computer data file
or program file, **233:79K.**
Duty of support, **209D:1-101.**
Dwelling, **79A:1.**
Dwelling house, **266:1.**
Dwelling, multiple, **151B:1.**
Dynamometer.
Motor vehicle emissions,
111:142M.
EACC, **23A:3A.**
Each delivery is a separate
contract, **106:2-612.**
Early childhood intervention
services, **111G:1.**
Early intervention services,
111G:1.
Early termination cost, **93:107.**
Early termination savings, **93:107.**
Earned premiums, **175:1.**
Earned premiums at rates in use,
175:117C.
Earned premiums at the nominal
rates, **175:117C.**
Economically distressed area.
Brownfields redevelopment fund,
23G:29A.
Oil and hazardous material
release prevention and
response, **21E:2.**
Economic assistance coordinating
council, **23A:3A.**
Economic development and
industrial corporation.
Oil and hazardous material
release prevention and
response, **21E:2.**
Economic development area,
121C:1.
Economic development incentive
program, **23A:3A.**
Economic development plan,
121C:1.
Economic development project,
63:1 (note), 121C:1.
Development finance agency,
23G:1.

WORDS AND PHRASES
—Cont'd
Economic hardship, **151D:1.**
Economic opportunity area,
23A:3A.
Economic target area, **23A:3A.**
EDIP, **23A:3A.**
Educational institution, **40J:12,
62:6, 151C:1.**
Educational practices, unfair
practices, **151C:1, 151C:2.**
Education loan, **15C:3.**
Education loan series portfolio,
15C:3.
Effective date.
Insurance, reorganization of
mutual insurers, **175:19G.**
Effluent limitation, **21:26A.**
Eggs, **94:90B.**
Elderly governmental retirees,
32A:2, 32B:11B.
Elderly housing, **19D:1.**
Elderly person, **6:172C.**
Elderly persons of low income,
20:13, 121B:1.
Elderly relative.
Family and medical leave,
149:52D.
Elected at large, **43:1.**
Election, **55:1.**
Election, annual, **4:7.**
Election cycle.
Clean elections law, **55A:1.**
Election officer, **50:1.**
Election year.
Clean elections law, **55A:1.**
Elector, **40O:1.**
Electric company, **164:1, 164:69G.**
Electrician, **141:1.**
Electricity, supplying electricity in
bulk, **164:1.**
Electric power facilities, **164:8,
164A:1, Spec L 13:1.**
Electric service, **164:1.**
Electric utility, **164A:1.**
Electrolysis, **112:87EEE.**
Electronic fund transfer, **167B:1.**
Electronic network.
Motor vehicle emissions,
111:142M.
Elementary enrollment, **70:2.**
Elevator, **143:62, 143:71E.**
Eligibility period, **151A:71A.**
Eligibility statement.
Low-income housing tax credit,
62:6I.
Low-income housing tax credit,
corporations, **63:31H.**
Eligible, **25A:11C, 149:44A.**
Eligible applicant.
School building assistance,
70B:2.

WORDS AND PHRASES
—Cont'd
Eligible borrower.
Water pollution abatement trust,
29C:1.
Eligible business facility, **23B:11.**
Eligible dependent, **176J:1.**
Eligible employee, **176J:1.**
Medical assistance division,
118E:9C.
Eligible employer.
Medical assistance division,
118E:9C.
Eligible list, **31:1.**
Eligible organization, **40H:2.**
Eligible person, **7:38J, 118G:1,
176K:9.**
Elder affairs department,
prescription drug insurance,
19A:39.
Oil and hazardous material
release prevention and
response, **21E:2.**
Pharmacy assistance pilot
program, **118E:16B.**
Eligible project.
Tourism facilities fund, **23G:42.**
Eligible section of substantial
poverty, **23B:11.**
Eligible self-employed husband
and wife.
Medical assistance division,
118E:9C.
Eligible self-employed single
individual.
Medical assistance division,
118E:9C.
Eligible small business or group,
176J:1.
Eligible tenant.
Oil and hazardous material
release prevention and
response, **21E:2.**
Embalmer and apprentice
embalmer, **112:82.**
Embalming, **112:82.**
Emergency, **30A:11A, 34:9F,
39:23A.**
Emergency medical services
system, **111C:1.**
Excavations, **82:40.**
Emergency appointment, civil
service provisions, **31:1.**
Emergency, city, town or district
boards, notice of meetings,
39:23A.
Emergency in city or town for
purpose of borrowing or
expending funds, **44:8, 44:31.**
Emergency medical services,
111C:1.

WORDS AND PHRASES
—Cont'd
Emergency medical technician.
Emergency medical services
system, **111C:1.**
Emergency meetings of county
boards and commissions,
34:9F.
Emergency mitigation response.
Hazardous materials mitigation,
21K:1.
Emergency mutual aid, **164:133.**
Emergency projects, wetlands
protection, **131:40.**
Emergency response.
Emergency medical services
system, **111C:1.**
Emergency services, **176J:1.**
Emigrant agent, **140:46A.**
Emission, **21I:2.**
Emissions analyzer.
Motor vehicles, **111:142M.**
Emissions inspection.
Motor vehicles, **111:142M.**
Emissions inspection and
maintenance program.
Motor vehicles, **111:142M.**
Emissions inspection certificate.
Motor vehicles, **111:142M.**
Emissions inspection facility.
Motor vehicles, **111:142M.**
Emissions inspector.
Motor vehicles, **111:142M.**
Emissions repair technician.
Motor vehicles, **111:142M.**
Emissions waiver certificate.
Motor vehicles, **111:142M.**
Emotional disturbance.
Special education, **71B:1.**
Emotional impairment.
Special education, **71B:1.**
Employee, **23D:1, 32:1, 35:51A,**
62B:1, 62E:1, 63:1, 118G:1,
142A:1, 149:183, 149:184,
149:185, 151A:71A, 151B:1,
152:1.
Child support enforcement,
119A:1A.
Massachusetts Bay
transportation authority,
161A:33, 161A:34.
Negotiable instruments,
106:3-405.
Turnpike authority, **81A:21,**
81A:22.
Employee benefit plan, **151D:1.**
Employee cooperative corporations,
157A:2.
Employee, higher education
faculty, **149:52C.**
Employee involvement, **23D:1.**

WORDS AND PHRASES
—Cont'd
Employee leasing company,
152:14A.
Employee organization, **23D:1,**
150E:1.
Employee or labor organization,
151D:1.
Employee-owned business, **23D:1.**
Employee ownership, **23D:1.**
Employee-ownership project,
23D:1.
Employee stock ownership plan,
23D:1.
Employer, **23D:1, 62B:1, 62B:5,**
62E:1, 90F:1, 118G:1, 150E:1,
151A:71A, 151B:1, 152:1.
Child support enforcement,
119A:1A.
Employer sponsored ride sharing
incentive program, **63:31D.**
Employing unit, **151A:1.**
Employment, **118C:2, 125:1, 149:1,**
149:20E, 151A:1.
Employment agency, **140:46A,**
151B:1.
Employment agreement, **30B:2.**
Employment permit, **76:1.**
Employment related expenses,
62:3.
Employment security benefits,
151A:1.
Employment security benefit year,
151A:1.
EMS.
Emergency medical services
system, **111C:1.**
EMS first responder.
Emergency medical services
system, **111C:1.**
EMS first response.
Emergency medical services
system, **111C:1.**
EMS first response service.
Emergency medical services
system, **111C:1.**
EMS first response vehicle.
Emergency medical services
system, **111C:1.**
EMS personnel.
Emergency medical services
system, **111C:1.**
EMS plan.
Emergency medical services
system, **111C:1.**
EMS provider.
Emergency medical services
system, **111C:1.**
EMS system.
Emergency medical services
system, **111C:1.**

WORDS AND PHRASES
—Cont'd
EMS vehicle.
Emergency medical services
system, **111C:1.**
EMT.
Emergency medical services
system, **111C:1.**
Encumbrance, **106:2A-309.**
End-aisle display, **6:184B.**
Endangered species, **131A:1.**
Endless chain transactions,
gambling provisions, **271:6A.**
Endorsed by a planning board,
41:81L.
Endowment fund, **180A:1.**
Endowment insurance policies,
201A:1.
End suppliers, **21A:18, 21A:18A.**
End-user, **25A:3.**
Energy audit, **25A:3.**
Energy audit, capital facilities
project, **7:39A.**
Energy conservation, **25A:3.**
Energy conservation measures,
25A:3.
Energy conservation projects,
7:39A, 25A:3.
Energy conservation systems,
Spec L 13:1.
Energy efficiency, **164:1.**
Energy efficient construction
rating.
School building assistance,
70B:2.
Energy management services,
25A:3.
Energy resources secretary, **25A:3.**
Engaged in business in the
Commonwealth, **63:1, 64H:1.**
Engaged in the operation of
aircraft, **90:35.**
Engage in an equine activity,
128:2D.
Engineering, practice, **112:81D.**
Enlisted person, **33:1.**
Enriched bread or flour, **94:1.**
Enrollee, **118G:1.**
Elder affairs department,
prescription drug insurance,
19A:39.
Enrollment categories, **70:2.**
Enterprise, **40G:1.**
Entitlement holder, **106:8-102.**
Entrusting, **106:2-403.**
Entry level, civil service, **31:1.**
Environment, **132B:2.**
Environmental Affairs Executive
Office, **21A:18.**
Environmental cleanup action.
Brownfields redevelopment fund,
23G:29A.

WORDS AND PHRASES
—Cont'd

Environmental contamination.
Business development office,
23A:60.
Environmental monitoring
program, low-level radioactive
waste, 111H:1.
Environmental response action.
Business development office,
23A:60.
Environmental site assessment.
Brownfields redevelopment fund,
23G:29A.
EPCRA, 21I:2.
Equalized property valuation,
70:2.
Equalized tax rate differential,
63:38E.
Equalized valuation, 44:1.
Equalized valuation per mile,
81:31, 81:32.
Equalized valuation per person in
a city or town, 70:2.
Equalized valuation per person in
the Commonwealth, 70:2.
Equine, 128:2D.
Equine activity, 128:2D.
Equine activity sponsor, 128:2D.
Equine professional, 128:2D.
Equipment, 23D:1, 59:8A,
106:9-109, 161B:1.
Massachusetts Bay
transportation authority,
161A:1.
Equity, 268B:1.
Equity aid, 70:2.
Equity gap, 70:2.
Equity rights.
Insurance, reorganization of
mutual insurers, 175:19G.
Equity security, 110C:1.
Equivalent, actuarial, 32:1.
Equivalent uniform amount, life
insurance provisions, 175:144.
Erect, 121A:1.
Escalators, 143:62, 143:71E.
Essential, 7:1, 7:22G.
Essential goods or services,
150B:2.
Established place of business,
90:1.
Establish, establishing,
establishment, joint municipal
airports provisions, 90:51N.
Estates, life estate, 184A:1.
Estate tax, 65C:1.
Evaluative information, 6:167.
Evaporative emissions test.
Motor vehicles, 111:142M.
Evening class, 74:1.

WORDS AND PHRASES
—Cont'd

Evidence, 119:21.
Evidence of coverage, 176G:1.
Examination of documentary
material, 93A:1.
Examiners, 142:1.
Excavation, 82:40.
Excavator, 82:40.
Exceeded its powers, 175J:1.
Excess debt service amount, 70:2.
Excess fuel, 111:142F.
Exclusive, income taxes provisions,
62C:41.
Exclusive run, 93F:1.
Executed, 106:4A-301.
Executive agent, 3:39, 55:1.
Executive authority, interstate
rendition, 276:11.
Executive director, 23D:1.
Executive head, 90:30B.
Executive office, 30A:6D.
Executive office promotional
examination, 31:1.
Executive officer of a public
employer, 258:1.
Executive officer (out-of-state bank
or bank holding company),
167:38, 167A:4.
Executive session, 30A:11A, 34:9F,
39:23A.
Executor, 65C:6.
Executor in his own wrong,
195:14-195:16.
Executor or administrator, 197:1.
Exempt school, 71:37D.
Exhibitor, 93F:1.
Exigent circumstances,
eavesdropping, wire tapping,
etc., 272:99.
Existing, 144:2, 145:2.
Existing customer, 175:113S.
Expanded program allotment,
70:2.
Expansion, public libraries,
78:19G-78:19K.
Expenditure, 55:1.
Clean elections law, 55A:1.
Expenditure minimum with
respect to expenditures for a
change in service or increase
in staff, 111:25B.
Expenditure minimum with
respect to substantial capital
expenditures, 111:25B.
Expense fund, retirement systems
and pensions, 32:1.
Expenses.
Clean election slaw, 55A:11.
Experience, 175:117C.
Experience deficiency, 151D:1.

WORDS AND PHRASES
—Cont'd

Experience period, 175:117C.
Experience rate, 151A:14.
Experimental treatment, 111:2D.
Expired credit card, 266:37A.
Exploration, 21B:2.
Express service.
Massachusetts Bay
transportation authority,
161A:1.
Ex-ship, 106:2-322.
Extended services, 7:38A½.
Extended sheltered employment,
rehabilitation commission
sheltered workshop program,
6:78A.
Extension, public libraries,
78:19G-78:19K.
Extenuating circumstances,
140:46N.
Exterior architectural feature,
40C:5.
Extracorporeal circulation.
Perfusionists, 112:211.
Extra fees and costs, 261:27A.
Extraordinary maintenance
allotment, 70:2.
Extra player, 231:85P½.
Extremely flammable, 94B:1.
Facilities, 23A:3A, 201D:1.
Abuse or neglect of patients in
long-term care facilities,
111:72F.
Development finance agency,
23G:1.
Turnpike authority, 81A:12.
Factory branch, 93B:1.
Factory representative, 93B:1.
Fair lending laws.
Banks, compliance review,
167:49.
Fair, state or county fair, 128A:1.
Fair wage, 151:2.
Falcon, 131:1.
Falconry, 131:1.
False, 175H:1.
False and deceptive act in
commerce, agreement to waive
payment bond, 149:29B.
False claims action.
False claims against
Commonwealth, 12:5A.
False claims law.
False claims against
Commonwealth, 12:5A.
Falsely embosses a credit card,
266:37A.
Falsely makes, credit card
offenses, 266:37A.
False pretenses, 277:39.

WORDS AND PHRASES
—Cont'd

Families of low income, **20:13,
121B:1.**

Families with dependent children,
118:1.

Family, **188:1, 233:23D, 258C:1.**
Catastrophic illness in children
relief fund commission,
111K:1 to 111K:11.

Family foster care, **28A:9, 76:7.**

Family member, **50:1.**
Employment security,
unemployment health
insurance contribution,
151A:14G.
Rights of victims and witnesses
of crime, **258B:1.**

Family or household member,
209A:1.

Fare revenue.
Massachusetts Bay
transportation authority,
161A:1.

Farm, **20:13.**

Farmer, **90:1, 128:1A.**

Farmer-brewery, **138:1.**

Farmer-winery, **138:1.**

Farming, **128:1A.**
Motor vehicle provisions, **90:1.**

Farm operation, **79A:1.**

Farm products, **106:9-109.**

F.A.S., **106:2-319.**

Fatality.
Child fatality review teams,
38:2A.

Father and mother, **59:5.**

Fault, **106:1-201, 106:2A-103.**

Feasibility grant.
Tourism facilities fund, **23G:42.**

Federal act, **50:1.**
Family and medical leave,
149:52D.

Federal agency, **40:4I.**
Development finance agency,
23G:1.
Tourism facilities fund, **23G:42.**

Federal Appraisal Subcommittee,
112:173.

Federal Consumer Credit
Protection Act, **140:C:1.**

Federal credit union, **171:1.**

Federal government, **4:7, 94C:1,
121B:1, 121B:34.**

Federal grant, **29:1.**

Federal gross estate, **65C:1.**

Federal gross income, **62:1.**

Federal legislation, **121B:34.**

Federal low-income housing tax
credit.
Low-income housing tax credit,
62:6I.

WORDS AND PHRASES
—Cont'd

Federal low-income housing tax
credit —Cont'd
Low-income housing tax credit,
corporations, **63:31H.**

Federally registered pesticide,
132B:2.

Federally related mortgage loan,
183:54.

Federal security administrator,
118C:2.

Federal service personnel,
54:103B.

Fees and costs, **40O:1, 140:46A,
261:27A.**

Felony, **90F:1, 274:1.**

Felony murder, **265:1.**

Fences, **49:2.**

FERC, **164:1.**

Fertilizer material, **128:64.**

Fetal death, **46:24, 111:202.**

Fiduciary, **21E:2, 123:1, 123B:1,
203:4A.**
Hazardous materials mitigation,
21K:1.
Negotiable instruments,
106:3-307.

Field investigation, **9:26B.**

Field of dietetics and nutrition,
112:201.

FIFRA, **132B:2.**

Fifty-one cities and towns.
Massachusetts Bay
transportation authority,
161A:1.

File, **93:50.**

Filling material, **94:270.**

Final determination of
delinquency.
Child support enforcement,
119A:16.

Final remedial response plan,
21A:19.

Finance charge, **255B:1, 255D:1.**

Finance committee, **7:1.**

Finance company, sales, **255B:1.**

Finance lease, **106:2A-103.**

Financial asset, **106:8-102.**

Financial assistance, **23F:1.**
Water pollution abatement trust,
29C:1.

Financial assistance bureau,
23B:10.

Financial exploitation, **19A:14.**

Financial impairment, **176J:1.**

Financial index, **15C:3.**

Financial institution, **23A:57, 63:1.**
Business development office,
23A:60.
Eavesdropping, wire tapping
and interception of
communications, **272:99.**

WORDS AND PHRASES
—Cont'd

Financial institution —Cont'd
Truth-In-Savings law, **140E:1.**

Financial law, **276:92A.**

Financial requirements, **118G:1.**

Financing agency, **106:2-104.**

Financing agreement, **23D:1.**

Financing document.
Development finance agency,
23G:1.

Financing entity.
Viatical settlements, **175:213.**

Financing statement, **106:9-402.**

Financing transaction.
Viatical settlements, **175:213.**

Fine art, **104A:1, 231:85S.**

Firearms, **269:10.**
Gun control, **140:121.**

Fire district, **48:90.**

Firefighter, **4:7, 32:94A.**

Fire insurance, Massachusetts
standard fire policy, **175:99.**

Fire loss adjuster, **175:162.**

Fireman, **4:7.**

Fire, marine, and inland marine
rate regulatory law,
174A:1-174A:19.

Fireproof tenement house, **145:2.**

Fire protection sprinkler system,
146:81.

Fire protection sprinkler system
contractor, **146:81.**

Fire sale, **93:28F.**

Firewood, **94:298.**

Fireworks, **148:39, 148:44.**

Firm offer of credit, **93:50.**

First class construction, **144:2.**

First mortgage lender, **184:17D.**

First story, **144:2.**

Fiscal year, **4:7, 118G:1, 161B:1.**

Fiscal year of Commonwealth, **4:7.**

Fish, **130:1, 131:1.**

Fish car, **130:1.**

Fisheries, marine, **130:1, 131:1.**

Fishing vessel, **175:94A.**

Fixed charges, **175:63.**

Fixture filing, **106:2A-309.**

Fixtures, **106:2A-309.**

Flammable, **94B:1.**

Flare, **85:14B.**

Fleet inspection station, **90:1.**

Flexible mortgages, **183:28A.**

Float, **131:53.**

Floater, personal property floater,
175:54D.

Flood plain, **92:104.**

Flower seeds, **128:84.**

Fluid milk, **94A:1.**

Fluorescent lamp ballast, **25B:2.**

F.O.B., **106:2-319.**

WORDS AND PHRASES
—Cont'd

Following, 4:7.

Food, 6:184B, 94:1, 94:305A, 94:305B.

Food department, 6:184B.

Food store, 6:184B.

Foreign corporations, 63:30, 181:1.

Foreign country, 175:180A.

Foreign credit unions, 171:1.

Foreign deposits, 167:38, 167A:2.

Foreign electric utility, 164A:1.

Foreign government or person, 151E:1.

Foreign guardian or conservator, 199A:1.

Foreign insurance companies, 175:1.

Foreign judgment, 235:23A.

Foreign jurisdiction, 90F:1.

Foreign limited liability company, 156C:2.

Foreign personal representative, 199A:1.

Foreign property and casualty insurer.
 Retaliatory tax credit for property and casualty companies, 63:29E.

Foreign state, 235:23A.

Foreign utility, 164:133.

Forester, 4:7.

Forest land, 61:1.
 Forest lands and products tax, 61:1.

Forest management plan.
 Forest lands and products tax, 61:1.

Forest or woods road, 48:16.

Forest products, 61:1, 61:2.
 Forest lands and products tax, 61:1.

Forestry, 132:47.

Forgery, 277:39.

Former patient, 12:11L.

Fornication, 277:39.

Foundation, 15A:37, 128:84.

Foundation aid, 70:2.

Foundation assistants, 70:2.

Foundation athletic expenses, 70:2.

Foundation budget, 70:2.

Foundation central office professional staff, 70:2.

Foundation custodial staff, 70:2.

Foundation enrollment, 70:2.

Foundation extracurricular activity expense, 70:2.

Foundation health care staff, 70:2.

Foundation miscellaneous expenses, 70:2.

WORDS AND PHRASES
—Cont'd

Foundation non-salary expenses, 70:2.

Foundation payroll, 70:2.

Foundation special education tuition, 70:2.

Foundation support staff, 70:2.

Foundation teaching staff, 70:2.

Foundation utility and ordinary maintenance expenses, 70:2.

Foundation vocational staff, 70:2.

IV-D agency, 62E:1.
 Retirement systems and pensions, 32:1.

IV-D services.
 Child support enforcement, 119A:1A.

Fourteen cities and towns.
 Massachusetts Bay transportation authority, 161A:1.

Fowls, 140:136A.

Franchise, 7:22G, 93B:1.

Franchisee, 93B:1.

Franchisor, 93B:1.

Fraternal benefit society, 26:8C, 176:1.

Fraud, 93B:1.

Fraudulent indorsement.
 Negotiable instruments, 106:3-405.

Fraudulent practices, motor vehicle driver schools provisions, 90:32G.

Free appropriate education.
 Special education, 71B:1.

Free care, 118G:1.

Freezer, 25B:2.

Fresh water wetlands, 131:40.

Fringe benefits, worksharing program, 151A:29D.

From and after sentence, 279:8A.

Front, 144:2, 145:2.

Front yard, 144:2, 145:2.

Frozen dessert mix, 94:65G, 94:65O.

Frozen desserts, 94:65G, 94:65O.

Frozen food, 94:73A.

Fuel, 64A:1, 64F:1.

Fuel cost savings, 164:94G½.

Fuel storage tank, 148:37A.

Full age, 4:7.

Fullmount, 90:1.

Full schedule of live racing performances, 128C:1.

Full-time employee, 63:31C.

Full-time equivalent pupil, 70:2.

Full-time faculty member, 112:43A.

Full-time student, 32:26.

WORDS AND PHRASES
—Cont'd

Fund, 21:J1, 29:1, 29C:1, 123:1, 123B:1, 142A:1.

Affordable housing trust fund, 121D:1.

Business development office, 23A:60.

Catastrophic illness in children relief fund commission, 111K:1 to 111K:11.

Tourism facilities fund, 23G:42.

Fund administrator, 142A:1.

Funding, 151D:1.

Funding agreement, life insurance provisions, 175:132F.

Funding system, retirement systems, 32:1.

Funds transfer, 106:4A-104.

Funds transfer business day, 106:4A-105.

Funds transfer system, 106:4A-105.

Funds transfer system rule, 106:4A-501.

Funeral directing, 112:82.

Funeral director, 112:82.

Fungi, 132B:2.

Fungible, 106:1-201.

Fur buyer, 131:1.

Future goods, 106:2-105.

FWPCA, Federal Water Pollution Control Act, 21:26A.

F40T12 lamp, 25B:2.

F96T12 lamp, 25B:2.

Gain, capital, 62:1.

Gainful employment, 125:1.

Game, 131:1.

Gaming, illegal, 4:7.

Garage, under motor vehicle regulation act, 90:1.

Garbage, 129:14B.

Garden, 20:13.

Garnetted clippings, 94:270.

Gas, 164:69G.

Gas company, 142:3B, 164:1, 164:69G.

Gas fitting, 142:1.

Gas fitting corporation, 142:3B.

Gasoline driven, 90:33.

Gender, disregard in construing statutes, 4:6.

General assets, 175:180A.

General counsel, 19C:1.

General court, employees, 32:1.

General election campaign period.
 Clean elections law, 55A:1.

General health supplies, care or rehabilitative services and accommodations, 118G:1.

General intangibles, 106:9-106.

WORDS AND PHRASES
—Cont'd

General revenues, **29C:1.**

General salary schedule, **75:14.**

General supervision, **112:43A.**

Generating facility, **164:69G.**

Generation, **164:1.**

Generation company, **164:1.**

Generation facility, **164:1.**

Generation service, **164:1.**

Generator, hazardous waste management, **21C:2, 21D:1.**

Genetic information.

  Accident and sickness insurance, **175:108H.**

  Disability insurance, **175:108I.**

  Fair employment practices, **151B:1.**

  Genetic testing, **111:70G.**

  Health maintenance organizations, **176G:24.**

  Hospital service corporations, **176A:3B.**

  Life insurance, **175:120E.**

  Medical service corporations, **176B:5B.**

  Preferred provider arrangements, **176I:4A.**

Genetic test, **111:70G.**

  Accident and sickness insurance, **175:108H.**

  Disability insurance, **175:108I.**

  Fair employment practices, **151B:1.**

  Health maintenance organizations, **176G:24.**

  Hospital service corporations, **176A:3B.**

  Life insurance, **175:120E.**

  Medical service corporations, **176B:5B.**

  Preferred provider arrangements, **176I:4A.**

Genuine, **106:1-201.**

Germination, **128:84.**

Gift, **268B:1.**

Gift certificate, **255D:1.**

Gift instrument, **180A:1.**

Gifts to minors, **201A:1.**

Gives notice, **106:1-201.**

Glass, safety, **90:9A.**

Goat's milk, **180:20.**

Good faith, **106:1-201, 106:2-103, 106:4A-105, 106:8-102, 200A:15D.**

  Letters of credit, **106:5-102.**

  Negotiable instruments, **106:3-103.**

Good moral character, **112:60A.**

Goods, **106:2-105, 106:2A-103, 106:7-102, 106:9-105, 255D:1.**

WORDS AND PHRASES
—Cont'd

Governing board, **180A:1.**

Governing body.

  Development finance agency, **23G:1.**

Governmental body, **25A:11C, 30A:11A, 30B:2, 34:9F, 39:23A, 268B:1.**

Governmental unit, **32:1, 118G:1.**

Governmental units pooled insurance, **40M:2.**

Government of Burma (Myanmar), **7:22G.**

Grade or grades, **31:1, 94:117G, 128:84.**

Granada rescue mission veteran, **4:7.**

Grant, **183:12.**

  Tourism facilities fund, **23G:42.**

Grant agreement, **30B:2.**

Grantee, **4:7.**

Grant-in-aid, **23D:1.**

Grantor, **4:7.**

Great pond, **91:35, 131:1.**

Green pelt, **131:1.**

Grievance, **40:21B.**

Grocery items, **6:184B.**

Gross error, **6:184B.**

Gross fraud, **266:76.**

Gross income, **61:2, 63:1, 63:30, 79A:1, 121A:10.**

Gross inpatient service revenue, **118G:1.**

Gross negligence, **231:85S.**

Gross overburden amounts, **70:2.**

Gross patient service revenue, **118G:1.**

Gross receipts, **63A:1.**

Gross rents, **63:1.**

Gross standard of effort, **70:2.**

Gross vehicle weight, **90:1, 90:7.**

Gross vehicle weight rating (GVWR), **90F:1.**

Gross vehicle weight rigging, **90:1.**

Ground water, **92:104.**

Group annuity contract, **175:132A.**

Group average premium rates, **176J:1.**

Group base premium rates, **176J:1.**

Group health maintenance contract, **176G:1.**

Group hospital service plan, **176A:10.**

Group insurance for municipal employees, **32B:2.**

Group insurance for state employees, **32A:2.**

Group insurance policy, **151A:71A.**

Group life insurance, **175:133.**

WORDS AND PHRASES
—Cont'd

Group marketing, **175:193R.**

Group marketing plan, **175:193R.**

Group medical service agreement, **176B:4.**

Guarantee, **106:2-313.**

Guaranteed analysis, **128:64.**

Guaranteed arrest bond certificate, **276:61B.**

Guaranteed issue managed care plan, **176M:1.**

Guaranteed issue medical plan, **176M:1.**

Guaranteed renewable, **176K:9.**

Guarantor, **148:38B.**

Guard, **147:22.**

Guard dog business, **129:1.**

Guardian, **201A:1, 203B:1.**

Guest occupant of motor vehicle, **90:34A.**

Guest track, **128C:1.**

Gunsmith.

  Gun control, **140:121.**

Gypsum or land plaster, **128:64.**

Habitual criminals, **279:25.**

Habitual traffic offenders, **90:22F.**

Hairdressers, **112:87T.**

Hairdressing, **112:87T.**

Hair dye, **94:186.**

Half and half, **94:1.**

Half-life, low-level radioactive waste, **111H:1.**

Half story, **144:2, 145:2.**

Halfway house for alcoholics, **111B:3.**

Hall, public, **144:2, 145:2.**

Handicap, **151B:1.**

Handicapped person, **6:77, 22:13A, 151B:1.**

Handicapped persons of low income, **121B:1.**

Harass.

  Identity fraud, **266:37E.**

Harbor plan, **21F:2.**

Hard of hearing person, **166:15E.**

Harmful to minors, **272:31.**

Hate crime data, **22C:32.**

Hate crimes, **22C:32.**

Have no issue, **184:6.**

Hawker, **101:13.**

Hazard, airport, **90:35.**

Hazardous financial condition, **176L:1.**

Hazardous locations, **143:3T.**

Hazardous material or waste, **21A:19, 92:104.**

Hazardous materials, **21:26A, 90F:1.**

  Hazardous materials mitigation, **21K:1.**

WORDS AND PHRASES
—Cont'd

Hazardous materials mitigation emergency response plan, **21K:1.**

Hazardous waste, **21C:2, 21D:1.**

Hazardous waste advisory committee, **21C:2.**

Hazardous waste insolvency fund, **21C:15.**

Hazardous waste licensee, **21C:2.**

Hazardous waste management, **21C:2.**

Hazardous waste management, Massachusetts Hazardous Waste Facility Siting Act, **21D:1.**

Hazardous waste site cleanup professional, **21A:19.**

Hazing, **269:17-269:19.**

Head of fire department, **148:1, 148:38B.**

Head of his department, **32:1.**

Head of household.

Income tax credits.

Older persons, credit for real estate or rent payments, **62:6.**

Headway speed, **90B:9A, 90B:9B.**

Health benefit plan, **176J:1.**

Health care agent, **201D:1.**

Health care benefit, **175H:1.**

Health care corporation, **175H:1.**

Health care facilities, **111:25B, 111:52, 111:70, 111:206, 113:7, 151A:40, 233:79G.**

Health care insurer, **175H:1.**

Health care organization, **32A:2, 32B:2.**

Health care provider, **111:1, 112:12CC, 175:193U, 175F:1, Spec L 69:1.**

Health maintenance organizations, liability of members of insolvent organization, **176G:22.**

Health care proxy, **201D:1.**

Health care resource, **111:25A.**

Health care services, **118G:1.**

Health department, **144:2.**

Health insurance benefits fund, **151A:71A.**

Health insurance company, **118G:1.**

Health insurance plan, **118G:1.**

Health maintenance contract, **176G:1.**

Health maintenance organization, **111:25B, 118G:1, 176G:1.**

Health officer, **112:87WWW.**

Health services, **12:11L, 112:118, 176G:1.**

WORDS AND PHRASES
—Cont'd

Health service training program, **112:118.**

Health spa contracts, **93:78.**

Health, welfare, and retirement funds, **149:181, 151D:1.**

Hearing aid, **93:71.**

Hearing instrument specialists, **112:196.**

Hearing authority, **121A:6C, 131:39A.**

Hearing instrument specialist, **112:196.**

Hearing screening test.

Newborn infants, **111:67F.**

Hearing test evaluation, **93:71.**

Heated milk, **94:1.**

Heater, space, **148:25B.**

Heavy commercial vehicles, **89:4C.**

Heavy duty platform trailer, under motor vehicle regulation act, **90:1.**

HEFA, **15A:5B, 15A:10.**

Height, under tenement house law, **144:2, 145:2.**

Heirs, **183:13, 184:6A.**

Transfer on death security registration, **201E:102.**

Heirs of the body, die without, **184:6.**

Hemophilia, **111:6A.**

High-accident locations, **90:33B.**

Highly protected risk, **175:98.**

Highly toxic, **94B:1.**

High school, **71:11.**

High school enrollment, **70:2.**

High voltage, **166:21F.**

Highway, **48:16.**

Highway, state, **81:13.**

Historic dollar value, **180A:1.**

Historic site, **81:7M.**

Historic structures and landscapes.

Community preservation, **44B:2.**

HIV, **111:2D.**

HIV/AIDS, **175:47O.**

Holder, **106:1-201.**

Holder in due course.

Negotiable instruments, **106:3-302.**

Holding company, bank, **167A:1.**

Holiday, legal, **4:7, 136:12.**

Home care services, **175:110.**

Home health agency.

Abuse or neglect of patients in long-term care facilities, **111:72F.**

Home health aide.

Abuse or neglect of patients in long-term care facilities, **111:72F.**

WORDS AND PHRASES
—Cont'd

Home inspection.

Home inspectors, **112:221.**

Home inspectors, **112:221.**

Homemaker.

Abuse or neglect of patients in long-term care facilities, **111:72F.**

Homemaker services, **18:28.**

Home state, **90:30B, 209D:1-101.**

Home warranty company, **175:149F.**

Home warranty contracts, **175:149F.**

Home water treatment device, **111:160C.**

Honor, **106:1-201.**

Letters of credit, **106:5-102.**

Hook, **131:1.**

Horizontal market power, **164:1.**

Horned pout, **131:1.**

Horsepower, **90B:1.**

Hospice, **111:57D.**

Hospice program.

Abuse or neglect of patients in long-term care facilities, **111:72F.**

Hospital.

Emergency medical services system, **111C:1.**

Hospital agreement, **118G:1.**

Hospital district, **32:1.**

Hospital medical officer.

Vital statistics, **46:1E.**

Hospitals and health care facilities, **111:25B, 111:52, 111:70, 111:206, 113:7, 118G:1, 151A:40, 233:79G.**

Hospital service corporation, **118G:1.**

Hospital service plan, group, **176A:10.**

Host community, **21D:1.**

Host track, **128C:1.**

Hotel, **64G:1, 138:1.**

Innkeepers' rights, **140:12A.**

House, **271:1A.**

Household arts education, **74:1.**

Household cleaning product, **111:5R.**

Household hazardous waste collection, **21E:2.**

House trailer, **90:1.**

Housing accommodation, **151B:1.**

Housing and community development department, general or special laws with respect, **23B:10.**

Housing board, **121A:18.**

Housing court, **4:7.**

WORDS AND PHRASES
—Cont'd

Housing development, **151B:1.**
Housing for the handicapped bureau, **23B:10.**
Humane method of slaughter, **94:139C.**
Hundred-weight, **98:2.**
Hybrid, **128:84.**
Hydro power generating facility, **164:69H½.**
I.C.U., intensive care unit for mentally ill women, **123:1.**
Identifying number or numbers, **90B:1, 90D:1, 266:139, 269:11A.**
Illegal gaming, **4:7.**
Illegitimate, **46:24.**
Illegitimate children, **209C:1.**
Imitation firearm.
    Gun control, **140:121.**
Imitation frozen dessert, **94:65G.**
Immediate container, **94B:1.**
Immediate family, **128A:11A, 128A:11B, 268A:1, 268B:1.**
Immediate precursor, **94C:1.**
Immediate treatment, **94C:9.**
Imminent hazard, **21A:19, 132B:2.**
Imminent threat.
    Hazardous materials mitigation, **21K:1.**
Implement of husbandry, **90D:1.**
Improvement, **40D:1.**
    Development finance agency, **23G:1.**
Improvement plan, **40O:1.**
In books, **4:7.**
Incapacitated, **111B:3, 203B:1.**
Incident commander.
    Hazardous materials mitigation, **21K:1.**
Incident report, **22C:32.**
Income, **209D:1-101, 268B:1.**
    Catastrophic illness in children relief fund commission, **111K:1 to 111K:11.**
    Child support enforcement, **119A:1A.**
Income and gains from investment of unrestricted funds, **118G:12.**
Income-withholding order, **209D:1-101.**
Incompetent person, **90:1.**
Incomplete credit card, **266:37A.**
Incomplete instrument.
    Negotiable instruments, **106:3-115.**
Incorporation by reference, **183:8.**
Increase in number of permanent full-time employees of the controlling business employed by and at the project, **23A:3A.**

WORDS AND PHRASES
—Cont'd

Increase in the number of full-time employees employed by the corporation, **63:31C.**
Increment, **30:45, 35:51A.**
Incremental cost items, **150E:1.**
Incurred claim count, **175:117C.**
Incurred claims, **175:117C.**
Indebtedness, net indebtedness, **4:7, 29:38.**
Independent agricultural school, **74:1.**
Independent allied health occupations schools, **74:1.**
Independent certified public accountant, **30:39R.**
Independent distributive occupations school, **74:1.**
Independent expenditure, **55:18A.**
Independent funds, **123:1, 123B:1.**
Independent household arts school, **74:1.**
Independent industrial school, **74:1.**
Independent living rehabilitation services, **6:77.**
Independent pharmacist, **13:22.**
Independent professional advice.
    Structured settlement contracts, **231C:1.**
Independent vocational home economic schools, **74:1.**
Indicia of ownership primarily to protect a security interest, **21E:2.**
    Hazardous materials mitigation, **21K:1.**
Indigent, **211D:2, 261:27A.**
In-district programs.
    Special education reimbursement program, **71B:5A.**
Individual, **175I:2.**
Individual policyholder, **178A:1.**
Indorsement, **106:8-102.**
    Negotiable instruments, **106:3-204.**
Indorser.
    Negotiable instruments, **106:3-204.**
Industrial advisory board, **151A:71A.**
Industrial development agency, **40E:2.**
Industrial development facilities, **40D:1.**
    Development finance agency, **23G:1.**
Industrial development fund, **40E:2.**

WORDS AND PHRASES
—Cont'd

Industrial development project, **40E:2.**
Industrial disease, **149:1.**
Industrial education, **74:1.**
Industrial enterprise, **40E:21.**
    Development finance agency, **23G:1.**
Industrial establishments, **149:1, 149:106, 149:133.**
Industrial life insurance policy, **175:1.**
Industrial occupant, **40D:1.**
Inert ingredient, **132B:2.**
Infernal machine, **266:102A.**
Infertility, **175:47H, 176A:8K, 176B:4J, 176G:4.**
Inflation index.
    Massachusetts Bay transportation authority state and local contribution fund, **10:35T.**
Information center, **93D:1.**
Informed written consent.
    Genetic testing, **111:70G.**
Infrastructure.
    Tourism facilities fund, **23G:42.**
Inhabitant, **4:7, 62:1; MA Const Part 2 Ch 1 Sec 2 Art 2.**
Inherent risks of equine activities, **128:2D.**
Initially eligible for coverage, **176K:9.**
Initiating state, **209D:1-101.**
Initiating tribunal, **209D:1-101.**
Initiation of negotiations, **79A:1.**
Initiative and referendum, **MA Const Amend Art 48 Part 1 Def.**
In-kind contribution.
    Clean elections law, **55A:1.**
Inland waters, **111:1, 131:1.**
Inland wetlands, **131:40A.**
Inmate, **125:1, Spec L 138:1.**
    Court costs of indigent persons, **261:27A.**
Inner court, **144:2, 145:2.**
Innovative community use.
    School building assistance, **70B:2.**
Innovative service, **111:25B.**
Inpatient services, **111:25B.**
Insane person, **4:7.**
Insect, **132B:2.**
Insider, **109A:2.**
Insolvency, **109A:3.**
Insolvency proceedings, **106:1-201.**
Insolvent, **106:1-201.**
Insolvent insurer, **175D:1.**
Inspection certificate.
    Motor vehicles, **111:142M.**
Inspection station, **90:1.**

WORDS AND PHRASES
—Cont'd

Inspector, **128:1, 129:1, 148:1.**

Installment buyer and seller, **255D:1.**

Installment contract, **106:2-612.**

Installment lease contract, **106:2A-103.**

Installment transaction, **62:63.**

Institution.

Development finance agency, **23G:1.**

Insurance, reorganization of mutual insurers, **175:19G.**

Institutional control account, low-level radioactive waste, **111H:1.**

Institutional control, low-level radioactive waste, **111H:1.**

Institutional fund, **180A:1.**

Institutional source, **175I:2.**

Institution for higher education, **15C:3, Spec L 53:3.**

Institution, higher education foundations, **15A:37.**

Instruction, **106:8-102.**

Instructional costs.

Special education reimbursement program, **71B:5A.**

Instructional or administrative aid, **71:38.**

Instructor, **112:87T.**

Instructor, aeronautics instructor, **90:35.**

Instructor in barber school, **112:87F.**

Instructor of hairdressers, **112:87T.**

Instrument, **106:9-105.**

Negotiable instruments, **106:3-104.**

Insurance, **175F:1, 176L:1.**

Insurance adjuster, **175:162.**

Insurance adviser, **175:177A.**

Insurance agent, **175:162, 176D:1, 176D:2, 255C:1.**

Insurance analyst, **175:177A.**

Insurance broker, **175:162, 176D:1, 176D:2, 255C:1.**

Insurance certificate, **176H:1.**

Insurance company, **175E:1.**

Insurance company group, **174A:5, 175A:5.**

Insurance contracts, **175:2, 178A:1.**

Insurance counselor, **175:177A.**

Insurance department, **26:8C, 178A:1.**

Insurance exchange, reciprocal, **175:94A.**

WORDS AND PHRASES
—Cont'd

Insurance holding company systems, **175:173L, 175:206.**

Insurance institution, **175I:2.**

Genetic testing, **111:70G.**

Insurance representative, **175I:2.**

Insurance specialist, **175:177A.**

Insurance-support organization, **175I:2.**

Insurance transaction, **175I:2.**

Insured, **152:1, 176H:1, 176K:9.**

Viatical settlements, **175:213.**

Insured legal services plan, **176H:1.**

Insured person, **152:1.**

Insurer, **152:1, 175:174G, 175:177G, 175:177N, 175:180A, 175:206, 175J:1, 176H:1.**

Intangible assets, **63:30.**

Integrated pest management. Pesticides, **132B:2.**

Intelligence information, **6:167.**

Intensive Care Unit for Mentally Ill Women, **123:1.**

Interbasin transfer, **21:8B.**

Intercepting device, **272:99.**

Interception, eavesdropping, wire tapping, **272:99.**

Interchangeable drug product, **112:12D.**

Interest, **62:1, 171:1.**

Interested party.

Structured settlement contracts, **231C:1.**

Interested person, **65B:1.**

Interested stockholder, **110F:3.**

Interest in property, **191A:1.**

Interest, regular interest, **32:1, 32:22.**

Interim remedial response, **21A:19.**

Interior lot, **144:2, 145:2.**

Intermediary, **176J:1.**

Intermediary bank, **106:4A-104.**

Commercial code, **106:4-105.**

Intermediate care facilities for mentally retarded persons, **111:71.**

Intermediate product, **211:2.**

Intermediate sanctions program.

Community corrections, **211F:1.**

Intermediate stock holding company.

Insurance, reorganization of mutual insurers, **175:19G.**

Intermittent appointment, **31:1.**

Intermodal transportation facilities, **121B:46.**

Internal Revenue Code, **62B:1, 62E:1.**

WORDS AND PHRASES
—Cont'd

International organization, **151E:1.**

Interpreter, **221C:1.**

Intersecting way, **89:8, 90:1.**

Interstate license or registration, **159B:2.**

Interstate system or systems, **6:167, 93D:1, 140B:1.**

Inter-track simulcasting, **128C:1.**

Intramural group dental practice, **112:43A.**

In trust, **183:14.**

Inventory, **106:9-109.**

Investigational allowance, **128:64.**

Investigative consumer report, **93:50, 175I:2.**

Investigator or examiner of the registry of motor vehicles, **32:89.**

Investigator, private, **147:22.**

Investment adviser, **110A:401.**

Investment adviser representative, **110A:401.**

Investment company security, **106:8-103.**

Investment property, **106:9-115.**

Investments by banks, **167F:1.**

Investment, stock, **161:116.**

Invitation for bids, **30B:2.**

Invitation to bid, **93F:1.**

In writing, **4:7, 106:1-201.**

Iron works, **149:1.**

Irregular route common carrier, **159B:2.**

Irritant, **94B:1.**

Is occupied, **144:2, 145:2.**

Isomer, **94C:1.**

Issue, **4:7, 176K:9, 191B:1.**

Negotiable instruments, **106:3-105.**

Issuer, **106:7-102, 106:8-201, 110A:401, 201A:1, 266:37A.**

Letters of credit, **106:5-102.**

Negotiable instruments, **106:3-105.**

Issuing authority, **166A:1.**

Issuing public corporation, **110D:1, 110E:1.**

Issuing state, **209D:1-101.**

Issuing tribunal, **209D:1-101.**

Item, **6:184B, 167D:34.**

Bank deposits and collections, **106:4-104.**

Job group, **30:45, 35:51A.**

Joint bond, **75D:14.**

Journeyman electrician, **141:1.**

Journeyman gas fitter, **142:1.**

Journeyman pipefitter, **146:81.**

Journeyman plumber, **142:1.**

WORDS AND PHRASES
—Cont'd

Journeyman refrigeration technician, fire sprinkler system contractors and fitters, **146:81.**

Judge, **185C:1, 217:1, 221C:1.**

Judgment, under aircraft financial responsibility act, **90:49B.**

Junior high/middle school enrollment, **70:2.**

Junk, **140B:1.**

Junk collector, **140:56.**

Junkyard, **140B:1.**

Jurisdictional disputes, **214:6A.**

Justice, **218:1.**

Juvenile court, **4:7.**

Keeper, **140:136A, 271:35.**

Keep out of the reach of children, **94B:1.**

Kennel, **140:136A.**

Keno growth revenue, **10:27A.**

Kind, **128:84.**

Kindergarten enrollment, **70:2.**

Kindling wood, **94:298.**

Knowing, **272:31.**
  False claims against Commonwealth, **12:5A.**

Knowingly.
  False claims against Commonwealth, **12:5A.**

Knowledge, **106:1-201.**

Knowledge of fact, within partnership act, **108A:3.**

Knows, **106:1-201.**

Korean emergency, **4:7.**

Korean veteran, **4:7.**

Label or labeling, **94:1, 94:118, 94:186, 94:187, 94:321, 94B:1, 128:64, 128:84, 132B:2.**

Labor disputes, **149:20C, 150A:2, 150B:2.**

Laborers, **30:50, 32:77.**

Labor organization, **150A:2, 151B:1.**
  Child support enforcement, **62E:1.**

Labor relations representative, **30B:2.**

Labor service, **31:1.**

Lamps, **25B:2.**

Land assembly and redevelopment, **121A:1.**

Land court, **4:7.**

Landfill, **21H:2.**

Land in agricultural use, **131A:1.**

Land in aquacultural use, **131A:1.**

Landing area, restricted, **90:35.**

Landlord, **121B:32B-121B:32F.**

Land or lands, **4:7, 132B:2.**

Landscape architect, **112:98.**

WORDS AND PHRASES
—Cont'd

Landscape architecture, **112:98.**

Land surveying, **112:81D.**

Land surveyor, **112:81D.**

Larceny, **277:39.**

Large capacity ammunition belt, **269:10.**

Large capacity feeding device.
  Gun control, **140:121.**

Large capacity magazine, **269:10.**

Large capacity weapon.
  Gun control, **140:121.**

Large quantity toxic user, **21I:2.**

Lascivious intent, **272:31.**

Last known address, **105A:1.**

Late-deafened deaf, **6:191.**

Late enrollee, **176J:1, 176K:9.**

Law, **209D:1-101.**

Law enforcement authority, **22A:1.**

Law enforcement officer, **6:116A, 90B:20.**

Lawful labor dispute, **149:20C.**

Law officer, **209A:1.**

Laws.
  Fraternal benefit societies, **176:1.**

Learn, **106:1-201.**

Learners permit to operate commercial motor vehicle, **90F:1.**

Lease agreement, **106:2A-103.**

Lease contract, **106:2A-103.**

Leasehold, **106:2A-103.**

Leasehold condominium, **183A:1.**

Lease, notice, **183:4.**

Lease space, **105A:1.**

Lease, UCC, **106:2A-103.**

Least restrictive environment, **71B:1.**

Lebanese peacekeeping force veteran, **4:7.**

Legal and sufficient fences, **49:2.**

Legal closing of the mine, **21B:2.**

Legal holiday, **4:7, 136:12.**

Legal representative, **201A:1, 203B:1.**

Legislation, **3:39.**

Legislative agent, **3:39, 55:1, 268B:1.**

Legislative body, **4:7, 150E:1.**
  Community preservation, **44B:2.**

Lender, **140:90A.**

Lending institution.
  Development finance agency, **23G:1.**

Length, **90B:1.**

Length of barrel.
  Gun control, **140:121.**

Lessee, **93:90, 106:2A-103, 171:75.**

Lessee in ordinary course of business, **106:2A-103.**

WORDS AND PHRASES
—Cont'd

Lessor, **93:90, 106:2A-103.**

Lessor's residual interest, **106:2A-103.**

Letter of authorization.
  Gas and electric companies, **164:1F.**

Letter of credit, **106:2-325, 106:5-102.**

Levy, **62C:53.**

Liability, **176L:1.**

Liability bond, motor vehicle, **90:34A.**

Liability insurance, motor vehicle liability policy, **90:34A.**

Librarian, **78:24.**

Library materials and property, **266:99.**

Library media center, **78:19E.**

Library premises, **266:99.**

License, **7:22G, 9:26B, 30A:13.**
  Child support enforcement, **119A:16.**

License agreement, **93F:1.**

Licensed applicator, **132B:2.**

Licensed certified social worker, **112:130.**

Licensed dietitian/nutritionist, **112:201.**

Licensed independent clinical social worker, **112:130.**

Licensed insurer, **26:8C.**

Licensed marriage and family therapist, **112:163.**

Licensed mental health counselor, **112:163.**

Licensed mental health professional, **123:1.**
  Accident and sickness insurance, **175:47B.**
  Group insurance for state employees, **32A:22.**
  Health maintenance organizations, **176G:4M.**
  Hospital service corporations, **176A:8A.**
  Medical service corporations, **176B:4A.**

Licensed perfusionists, **112:211.**

Licensed pesticide dealer, **132B:2.**

Licensed private drivers school, **90:1.**

Licensed public storage warehouse, **59:2.**

Licensed rehabilitation counselor, **112:163.**

Licensed social worker, **112:130.**

Licensee, **140:100, 147:22, 166:25A, 169A:1.**
  Community antenna television systems, **166A:1.**

WORDS AND PHRASES
—Cont'd
License fee, **166A:1.**
License period, **140:136A.**
License renewal certificate, **112:89.**
Licensing authority, **90:30B,**
138:1, 140:1.
Child support enforcement,
119A:16.
Gun control, **140:121.**
Licentiate, **13:9B.**
Lien, **4:7, 106:2A-103, 109A:2.**
Lien creditor, **106:9-301.**
Lienors, **111:127I.**
Lifeboats, **90B:1.**
Life-cycle cost estimates, **149:44M.**
Life insurance company, **175:118.**
Life or endowment insurance
policies, **201A:1.**
Likelihood of serious harm, **123:1.**
Like offense, **90:1.**
Like violation, **90:1.**
Limited access ways, **81:7C.**
Limited common areas and
facilities, **183A:1.**
Limited covenants, **183:17.**
Limited liability company, **156C:2.**
Limited liability company interest,
156C:2.
Limited partnerships, **109:1.**
Limited society.
Fraternal benefit societies,
176:1.
Limited undiluted liquefied
petroleum gas installer, **142:1.**
Line-item, **29:1.**
Line losses, **164:94G.**
Liquefied natural gas, **164:69G.**
Liqueur or cordial, **138:1.**
Liquid waste disposal facilities,
40D:1.
Listed action, **93:95.**
Listing board, **50:1.**
Listing service, **93:95.**
Livery boat, **90B:1.**
Livestock, **94:139C, 140:136A.**
Livestock product, **94:118.**
Loaded shotgun or rifle, **131:1,**
269:12D.
Loan, **23A:57, 29C:1, 63:1,**
140:90A, 167E:1.
Brownfields redevelopment fund,
23G:29A.
Business development office,
23A:60.
Development finance agency,
23G:1.
Tourism facilities fund, **23G:42.**
Loan agreement, **29C:1.**
Loan funding deposit, **15C:3.**
Loan secured by real property,
63:1.

WORDS AND PHRASES
—Cont'd
Loansharks, assault and battery
for purpose of collecting loans,
265:13C.
Lobster, **130:1.**
Local administration, **199A:1.**
Local aid distributions, **29C:1.**
Local appointing authority, **40N:3.**
Local contribution, **70:2.**
Local government, **164:69G.**
Local government obligations,
29C:1.
Local government unit, **29C:1.**
Local guardian or conservator,
199A:1.
Local jurisdiction.
Emergency medical services
system, **111C:1.**
Local licensing authority, **148:1.**
Local municipal governing body,
40O:1.
Local organization, **21:9.**
Local originating depository
institution, **167D:35, 171:53.**
Local personal representative,
199A:1.
Local service.
Massachusetts Bay
transportation authority,
161A:1.
Local support percentage, **70:2.**
Local system revenues, **29C:1.**
Local team.
Child fatality review teams,
38:2A.
Locations for banks, **167C:1.**
Locker, **94:66A.**
Lodge system, **176:2.**
Lodging house, **64G:1, 140:22,**
145:2.
Long-range forecast, **164:69G.**
Long-term care facility, **111:72W.**
Long term care services, **93:76.**
Loss, **148:42.**
Loss, capital, **62:1.**
Loss ratio, **175:117C.**
Lot, **41:81L, 106:2-105,**
106:2A-103, 128:84.
Low-boy boat transporter, **90:1.**
Lower grade obligations, **175:63A.**
Lowest responsible and eligible
bidder, **30:39M, 81:8A.**
Low-income enrollment, **70:2.**
Low income housing.
Community preservation, **44B:2.**
Low-income project.
Low-income housing tax credit,
62:6I.
Low-income housing tax credit,
corporations, **63:31H.**

WORDS AND PHRASES
—Cont'd
Low-level radioactive waste,
111H:1.
Low-level radioactive waste trust
fund, **111H:1.**
Low or moderate income housing,
40B:20.
Low or moderate income senior
housing.
Community preservation, **44B:2.**
Low rent housing project, **121B:1,**
121B:34.
Luminaire, **25B:2.**
Lunatic, **4:7.**
Machine gun.
Gun control, **140:121.**
Machinery, **90B:1.**
Made public, **30A:11A, 34:9F,**
39:23A.
Magistrate, **90C:1.**
Magnet educational program,
71:37J.
Magnet school facility, **71:37I.**
Mail, registered, **4:7, 41:81L.**
Mail service program.
Elder affairs department,
prescription drug insurance,
19A:39.
Maintain and operate, maintaining
and operating, maintenance
and operation, **90:51N.**
Maintaining, **81:32.**
Maintaining a household, **62:3.**
Maintenance, **7:39A.**
Community preservation, **44B:2.**
Net maintenance sum, **74:1.**
Maintenance drug.
Elder affairs department,
prescription drug insurance,
19A:39.
Maintenance rating.
School building assistance,
70B:2.
Majority, **50:1.**
Majority-owned subsidiary, **7:22G.**
Majority vote, **30B:2, 44:1.**
Major life activities, **151B:1.**
Major movable equipment,
111:25B.
Major policymaking position,
268B:1.
Major reconstruction project.
School building assistance,
70B:2.
Maker.
Negotiable instruments,
106:3-103.
Malfunction.
Sales of firearms, **140:123.**
Malt beverages, **138:1.**

WORDS AND PHRASES
—Cont'd
Mammals, **131:1.**
Managed health care plan, **118G:1.**
Management, **30:39R.**
Management entity, **40O:1.**
Management of hazardous waste, **21C:2.**
Management plan.
Forest lands and products tax, **61:1.**
Manager, **19D:1, 156C:1, 183A:1.**
Managing general agent, **175:177G.**
Mandated benefit, **176J:1.**
Mandated reporter, **19C:1.**
Manicuring, **112:87T.**
Manicuring shop, **112:87T.**
Manicurists, **112:87T.**
Manifest, hazardous waste management, **21C:2.**
Manufacture, **21I:2, 93:107, 94C:1.**
Manufactured home, **140:32Q.**
Manufacturer, motor vehicle regulation act, **90:1.**
Manufacturer of motor vehicles, **93B:1.**
Manufacturer under upholstered furniture and bedding law, **94:270.**
Manufacture, year, **60A:1.**
Manufacturing corporation, **63:38.**
Manufacturing establishments, **149:1.**
Manufacturing network, **23D:30.**
Maps, plats, and surveys, **97:12, 97:13.**
Marijuana, **64K:1, 94C:1, 94D:1.**
Marine fisheries, **130:1, 131:1.**
Mark, **110B:1.**
Marketing, **93:76.**
Marketing agreement, **93E:1.**
Market, milk control act provisions, **94A:1.**
Marshal, **148:1, 148:38B.**
Hazardous materials mitigation, **21K:1.**
Marshes, **131:40.**
Massachusetts adjusted gross estate, **65C:1.**
Massachusetts Bay transportation authority state and local assistance fund, **161A:1.**
Massachusetts Child Custody Jurisdiction Act, **209B:1.**
Massachusetts clean elections. Clean elections law, **55A:1.**
Massachusetts clean elections fund. Clean elections law, **55A:1.**
Massachusetts commission for deaf and hard of hearing, **6:191.**

WORDS AND PHRASES
—Cont'd
Massachusetts co-ordinate system, **97:12, 97:13.**
Massachusetts credit union share insurance corporation, **171:1.**
Massachusetts export finance fund.
Development finance agency, **23G:1.**
Massachusetts gross income, **62:2.**
Massachusetts medical malpractice reinsurance plan, **Spec L 69:1.**
Massachusetts net estate, **65C:1.**
Massachusetts Oil and Hazardous Material Release Prevention and Response Act, **21E:2.**
Massachusetts standard fire policy, **175:99.**
Massachusetts taxable estate, **65C:1.**
Massachusetts Technology Park Corporation, **40J:2.**
Massachusetts water management act, **21G:2.**
Mass marketed life or health insurance, **175:190A.**
Mass merchandising, **175:193R.**
Mass merchandising plan, **175:193R.**
Mass transportation facilities, **161B:1.**
Massachusetts Bay transportation authority, **161A:1.**
Master electrician, **141:1.**
Master gas fitter, **142:1.**
Master pipefitter, **146:81.**
Master plan, capital facilities project, **7:39A.**
Master plan, public library, **78:19G-78:19K.**
Master plumber, **142:1.**
Master refrigeration technician, fire sprinkler system contractors and fitters, **146:81.**
Master settlement agreement.
Tobacco master settlement agreement, **94E:1.**
Material supplier, **7:40C.**
Matter, **21:27, 272:31.**
Maximize.
Massachusetts Bay transportation authority, **161A:1.**
Maximum age, **32:1.**
Mayor, **4:7, 121A:1.**
Mayor and aldermen, **4:7.**
MCEC Board, **40J:12.**
Meal, **64H:6.**

WORDS AND PHRASES
—Cont'd
Measure or part thereof protested against, **43:42.**
Measuring device, **98:1.**
Meat, canned lobster meat or crabmeat, **130:1.**
Meat food products, **94:118.**
Mechanical barrier, **166:21F.**
Mechanical hazard, **94B:1.**
Mechanics, **30:50.**
Median income.
Low-income housing tax credit, **62:6I.**
Low-income housing tax credit, corporations, **63:31H.**
Media organization, **55:8A.**
Medicaid program, **118G:1.**
Medical assistance, **118E:8.**
Medical assistance for the aged, **118A:3.**
Medical assistance program, **118G:1.**
Medical care, **258C:1.**
Medical care and assistance, **111:57A-111:57C, 118E:2, 118E:16, 118E:16C.**
Medical-care institution, **175I:2.**
Medical clearance, **93:71.**
Medical control.
Emergency medical services system, **111C:1.**
Medical direction.
Emergency medical services system, **111C:1.**
Medical facility, **266:120E.**
Medical information, **93:50.**
Medical laboratory technologists, schools for training, **112:2B.**
Medical literature, **175:47K, 175:47O.**
Medically necessary services, **118G:1.**
Medical malpractice insurance, **Spec L 69:1.**
Medical malpractice insurer, **175:193U, Spec L 69:1.**
Medical malpractice reinsurance plan, **175:193U.**
Medical organization, **176C:1.**
Medical professional, **175I:2.**
Medical-record information, **175I:2.**
Medical service, **176B:1.**
Medical service agreement, **176B:4.**
Medical service corporation, **26:8C, 118G:1, 176B:1, 176C:1.**
Medical service plan, **176B:1, 176C:1.**
Medical X-ray technicians, school for training, **112:2C.**

WORDS AND PHRASES
—Cont'd

Medicare, **176K:9.**
Medicare program, **118G:1.**
Medicare select insurance, **176K:9.**
Medicare supplement insurance, **176K:9.**
Meeting, **30A:11A, 34:9F, 39:23A.**
 Racing, **128A:1.**
Member municipality, **40:4I.**
Member of minor's family, **201A:1.**
Member of the beneficiary's family, **203B:1.**
Member of the New England Power Pool, **164A:1.**
Members, **78A:1.**
 Insurance, reorganization of mutual insurers, **175:19G.**
 Legal services plan, **176H:1.**
Membership camping contract or agreement, **93:48A.**
Membership certificate, legal services plan, **176H:1.**
Membership interests.
 Insurance, reorganization of mutual insurers, **175:19G.**
Membership legal services plan, **176H:1.**
Membership service, **32:1.**
Mental abnormality.
 Sex offender registration and community notification, **6:178C.**
 Sexually dangerous persons act, **123A:1.**
Mental health services, **12:11L.**
Mentally retarded person, **123:1, 123B:1, 201:1.**
Mental retardation, **233:23E.**
Mercantile establishments, **149:1.**
Merchandise certificate, **255D:1.**
Merchant, **106:2-104, 167B:1.**
Merchant discount, **63:1.**
Merchant lessee, **106:2A-103.**
Merger assets, **63:22D.**
Merit principles, civil service, **31:1.**
Metropolitan highway system, **81A:3.**
Metropolitan highway system revenues, **81A:3.**
MEWA, **176J:1.**
Midnight deadline.
 Bank deposits and collections, **106:4-104.**
Military custodian, **33:1.**
Military forces of the Commonwealth, **33:1.**
Militia officer, **33:1.**
Militia unit, **33:1.**
Milk, **94:12, Spec L 139:2.**
Milk dealers, **94A:1.**

WORDS AND PHRASES
—Cont'd

Milk fluid, **94:1.**
Milk ice, **94:65G.**
Milk plant or manufactory, **94:1.**
Milk producer, **94:42A.**
Mined area or affected land, **21B:2.**
Mine inspector, **21B:2.**
Mineral feed, **128:51.**
Mineral resources, **21:54.**
Minimum capital, **175:48.**
Minimum required local contribution, **70:2.**
Minimum surplus, **175:48.**
Mining, **21B:2.**
Minor informalities, **25A:11C, 30B:2.**
Minority, **7:40N.**
Minority business, **7:40N.**
Minority business, capital facilities projects, **7:40C.**
Minority Business Enterprise, **23A:40.**
Minority, capital facilities projects, **7:40C.**
Minors, **4:7, 28A:2, 28A:9, 32:12B, 40D:1, 54:103B, 62D:1, 119:1, 119:52, 152:28, 171:1, 184:6, 272:31.**
Minor's family, member, **201A:1.**
Misappropriation of patient or resident property.
 Abuse or neglect of patients in long-term care facilities, **111:72F.**
Misbranded, **94:187, 132B:2.**
Misbranded hazardous substances, **94B:3.**
Misdemeanor, **274:1.**
Missing child or children, **22A:1.**
Mistreatment.
 Abuse or neglect of patients in long-term care facilities, **111:72F.**
Mitigation, **164:1.**
Mixed fertilizer, **128:64.**
Mixture, **21I:2.**
Mobile construction crane, **90:1.**
Mobile radio utility system, **159:12A.**
Mobile unit, **169A:1.**
Model rocket engine, **148:9A.**
Moderate income housing.
 Community preservation, **44B:2.**
Modified atmosphere, **94:109.**
Modular building, **149:44A.**
Molder, **94:320.**
Molotov cocktail, **266:102B.**
Monetary contribution.
 Clean elections law, **55A:1.**
Money, **106:1-201.**

WORDS AND PHRASES
—Cont'd

Money market mutual fund.
 Child support enforcement, **119A:6.**
Month, **4:7.**
Morris plan banks, **172A:1.**
Mortgage, **106:9-105.**
Mortgage borrower, **184:17D.**
Mortgage broker, **142A:1, 255E:1.**
Mortgage, chattel, **4:7.**
Mortgage covenants, **183:19.**
Mortgage deed, **183:18, 183:19.**
Mortgagees, **111:127I.**
Mortgage lender, **142A:1, 255E:1.**
Mortgage loan, **142A:1, 255E:1.**
Mortgage or mortgage holder, **183:54.**
Mortgages and deeds of trust, **106:9-105, 167E:1, 255E:1.**
Mortgage servicer, **183:54.**
Mortgages lender, **32:23.**
Motel, **64G:1, 140:32A.**
Motorboat, **90B:1.**
Motor carrier, **64F:1, 159A:2, 159B:2.**
Motorcycle, **90:1, 90:7S.**
Motor fuel, **94:295A.**
Motor vehicle, common carrier, **159B:2.**
Motor vehicle dealer, **93B:1.**
Motor vehicle liability bond, **90:34A.**
Motor vehicle liability policy, **90:34A.**
Motor vehicle repair, **100A:1.**
Motor vehicle repair shop, **100A:1.**
Motor vehicle retail installment sales, **255B:1.**
Motor vehicles, **64H:1, 64H:26, 64I:1, 90:1, 90:7N¼, 90:20A, 90:22, 90F:1, 93B:1, 255B:1.**
Motor vehicles per road mile, **81:31, 81:32.**
Motor vehicle violation, **90:22.**
Mountain regions, protection of Berkshire Mountains watershed regions, **131:39A.**
Moving stairways, **143:62, 143:71E.**
Multi-dwelling unit, **51:10A.**
Multi-level distribution company, **93:69.**
Multi-media, **21I:2.**
Multiple account case, **175:117C.**
Multiple dwelling, **22:13A, 151B:1.**
Multiple employer welfare arrangement, **176J:1.**
Multiple-use alternative fuel, **164:1.**
Municipal Administration Act, Optional Forms, **43C:2.**

WORDS AND PHRASES
—Cont'd

Municipal agency, **268A:1.**
Municipal application, **23A:3A.**
Municipal court, **4:7.**
Municipal election, regular, **43:1.**
Municipal electric department, **164A:1.**
Municipal employee, **268A:1.**
Municipality, **23A:3A, 121C:1.**
  Development finance agency, **23G:1.**
Municipal light board, **164:1, 164A:1.**
Municipal party, **50:1.**
Municipal purpose, **40:14.**
Municipal revenue growth factor, **70:2.**
Municipal service, **41:81L.**
Murder, **265:1, 277:39.**
Mutual company.
  Insurance, reorganization of mutual insurers, **175:19G.**
Mutual holding company.
  Insurance, reorganization of mutual insurers, **175:19G.**
Mutual insurer.
  Insurance, reorganization of mutual insurers, **175:19G.**
National credit union administration, **171:1.**
National pollutant discharge elimination system permit, **164:69G.**
Natural gas, **164:69G.**
Natural resource officer, fish and game division, **131:1.**
Natural resources, **21:1.**
Nature preserve, **131:1.**
Navigable air space, **90:35.**
Neglect.
  Abuse or neglect of patients in long-term care facilities, **111:72F.**
Negotiable instrument, **106:3-104.**
Negotiating, **259:7.**
Negotiation.
  Negotiable instruments, **106:3-201.**
Neighboring community, low-level radioactive waste, **111H:1.**
Nematode, **132B:2.**
Net assets, **175:1.**
Net capital gain, **62:1.**
Net cost of service, **161B:1.**
Net direct premiums, **Spec L 69:1.**
Net direct written premiums, **175D:1.**
Net earnings, **175:63.**
Net estate, **65A:5.**
Net expenditure, **62:6.**

WORDS AND PHRASES
—Cont'd

Net income, **63:1.**
Net indebtedness, **4:7.**
Net investment income, **63:22B.**
Net landed weights, **106:2-321.**
Net maintenance sum, **74:1.**
Net new benefits, **167:38, 167A:4, 167C:3, 168:34, 168:34A, 168:34B, 168:34D, 168:34F, 168:35, 170:24-170:26B, 170:26D, 170:26F, 172:36, 172:38.**
Net operating investment per passenger-mile ratio.
  Massachusetts Bay transportation authority, **161A:1.**
Net quantity, **94:181.**
Net saving, **161B:1.**
Net school spending, **70:2.**
Net value of policy, **175:1.**
Network.
  Motor vehicle emissions, **111:142M.**
New, **90B:36.**
  Under upholstered furniture and bedding law, **94:270.**
New appliance, **25B:2.**
Newborn infants.
  Hearing screening, **111:67F.**
New building, **149:44M.**
New charges, **111:70.**
New England power pool, **164A:1.**
New England Power Pool agreement, **164A:1.**
New motor vehicle, **93B:1.**
New technology, **111:25B.**
Next of kin, **118E:16, 184:6A.**
Nighttime, **278:10.**
No arrival, no sale, **106:2-324.**
Nominal rates, **175:117C.**
Nominated person.
  Letters of credit, **106:5-102.**
Non-acute hospital, **118G:1.**
Noncash proceeds, **106:9-306.**
Noncommissioned officer, **22C:1.**
Non-competitive examination, **31:1.**
Nonconformity, **93:107.**
Noncontinuous attendance.
  Steamboilers, **146:46.**
Non-election year, **55:19.**
Non-English speaker, **221C:1.**
  Interpreters for acute care psychiatric facilities, **123:23A.**
  Interpreters for emergency and acute care medical services, **111:25J.**
Non-gasoline driven, **90:33.**

WORDS AND PHRASES
—Cont'd

Nongroup medical service agreement, **176B:4.**
Non-isolated intermediate, **21I:2.**
Non-participating candidate.
  Clean elections law, **55A:1.**
Nonpartisan, **15A:29.**
Nonprofessional staff, **75:14.**
Non-profit hospital service corporation, **26:8C.**
Nonprofit medical service plan, **176B:1.**
Nonprovider, **17:3.**
Non-renewable energy supply and resource development, **25A:3.**
Nonresident CDL, **90F:1.**
Nonresident decedent, **199A:1.**
Nonresident protected person, **199A:1.**
Nonstate fundraising.
  School building assistance, **70B:2.**
Nontransportation revenues.
  Massachusetts Bay transportation authority, **161A:1.**
Normal cost, retirement systems, **32:1.**
Normal fees and costs, **261:27A.**
Normal maintenance or improvement, **131A:1.**
Normal retirement age, **151D:1.**
Normal retirement benefit, **151D:1.**
No significant risk, **21E:3A.**
Note, **140:90A.**
  Negotiable instruments, **106:3-104.**
Note holder, **183:54.**
Notes or bonds.
  Turnpike authority, **81A:3.**
Notice, **90:49B, 106:1-201, 266:120E.**
Notice of claim, **175:110.**
Notice of facts, within partnership act, **108A:3.**
Notice of intention, **164:69G.**
Notice of lease, **183:4.**
Notifies, **106:1-201.**
Notorious thief, **266:40.**
Not used for purposes incompatible with forest production.
  Forest lands and products tax, **61:1.**
Noxious-weed seeds, **128:84.**
Nuclear reactor, **111:1.**
Nudity, **272:31.**
Nuisance, **144:2, 145:2.**
Number, certificate, **90B:1.**

WORDS AND PHRASES
—Cont'd
Number plate, motor vehicle
  regulation act provisions, **90:1.**
Nurse, **94C:1.**
Nursery stock, **128:1.**
Nurses' aide, **111:72W.**
  Abuse or neglect of patients in
  long-term care facilities,
  111:72F.
Nursing, **112:80B.**
Nursing home, **111:71, 112:108.**
Nursing home administrator,
  112:108.
Nursing pool, **111:72Y.**
Nutritionists, **112:201.**
Oath, **4:7.**
Obligated bank.
  Negotiable instruments,
  106:3-312, 106:3-411.
Obligated expenditure.
  Clean elections law, **55A:1.**
Obligee, **209D:1-101.**
  Child support enforcement,
  119A:1A.
Obligor, **209D:1-101.**
  Child support enforcement,
  62E:1, 119A:1A.
OBRA 90, **176K:9.**
Obscene, **272:31.**
Occupancy, **64G:1.**
Occupancy, is occupied, **144:2,
  145:2.**
Occupant, **64G:1, 105A:1.**
Occupational disease, **149:1.**
Occupational therapy, **112:23A.**
Occupations under minimum wage
  law, **151:2.**
Occupied spaces, **144:2, 145:2.**
Odometer, **266:141.**
Offender, **258C:1.**
Offender, committed, **125:1.**
Offeree, **110C:1.**
Offeror, **110C:1.**
Offer to sell, **110A:401.**
Officer, **32:26.**
Official act, **268A:1.**
Official ballot, **50:1.**
Official compendium of drugs,
  94:186.
Official designee, **276A:1.**
Official fees, **255B:1, 255D:1.**
Official health certificate,
  140:138A.
Officially recognized, **128:84.**
Official responsibility, **268A:1.**
Official sample, **128:51, 128:64.**
Official service, **31:1.**
Official, state, **32:1.**
Official student referendum,
  15A:29.

WORDS AND PHRASES
—Cont'd
Off-label, **175:47O.**
Off-label use, **175:47K.**
Offshore oil facility, **21E:2.**
Oil, **21:27, 21A:19.**
  Hazardous materials mitigation,
  21K:1.
Oil company, gasoline or fuel
  taxes, **64A:1, 64E:1.**
Oil conservation adjustment,
  164:94G½.
Oil facility, **21E:2.**
Oil facility or company, **164:69G.**
Oil Pollution Act, **21E:2.**
Oily, **94:270.**
Oleomargarine, **94:1.**
On-camera narrator or
  spokesperson, **231:85P½.**
On consignment, **106:2-326.**
One-man units, **150A:2.**
On foot patrol, **41:98B.**
On memorandum, **106:2-326.**
On-road test.
  Motor vehicle emissions,
  111:142M.
Onshore oil facility, **21E:2.**
Open area, blighted, **121A:1.**
Open season, **130:1, 131:1.**
Open space.
  Community preservation, **44B:2.**
Operate, **90F:1.**
Operating agreement, **156C:2.**
Operating expense.
  Massachusetts Bay
  transportation authority,
  161A:1.
Operator, **21J:1, 64G:1, 64G:7B,
  90F:1, 105A:1, 112:87T,
  143:71I, 148:38B.**
  Hazardous materials mitigation,
  21K:1.
Opiate, **94C:1.**
Opium poppy, **94C:1.**
Oppressive and unreasonable
  wage, **151:1, 151:2.**
Optician, dispensing, **112:73C.**
Optional fee, **15A:29.**
Optional Medicare extension,
  32A:2, 32B:2.
Optometry, practice, **112:66.**
Oral communication, **272:99.**
Oral prescription, **94:187, 94C:1.**
Order.
  Negotiable instruments,
  106:3-103.
Ordinance, **4:7, 43:1, 144:2.**
Ordinary care.
  Negotiable instruments,
  106:3-103.
Organization, **106:1-201, 167B:1,
  255:12F.**

WORDS AND PHRASES
—Cont'd
Organization member, **171:1.**
Original painting, **94:277C.**
Original source.
  False claims against
  Commonwealth, **12:5A.**
Original standard container,
  94:96.
Originator, **106:4A-104.**
Originator's bank, **106:4A-104.**
Or return, **106:2-326.**
Other covered housing
  accommodations, **151B:1.**
Other forms of financial
  assistance.
  Water pollution abatement trust,
  29C:1.
Other served communities.
  Massachusetts Bay
  transportation authority,
  161A:1.
Other than first quality, **90:1.**
Otolaryngologist, **93:71.**
Outdoor advertising, **93D:1.**
Outer court, **144:2, 145:2.**
Out-of-district programs.
  Special education
  reimbursement program,
  71B:5A.
Out-of-pocket loss, **258C:1.**
Out of service order, **90F:1.**
Outpatient services, **111:25B.**
Out turn, **106:2-321.**
Overburden aid, **70:2.**
Overburden (mining), **21B:2.**
Overissue, **106:8-210.**
Overseas, **106:2-323.**
Oversight, **7:39A.**
Owner, **21J:1, 90:1, 90B:1, 90D:1,
  110F:3, 111:189A, 142A:1,
  148:38B, 266:143.**
  Forest lands and products tax,
  61:1.
  Hazardous materials mitigation,
  21K:1.
Owner-contractor, **90:1.**
Owner of motor vehicle, **90:22B.
  (note)**
Owner-repairman, **90:1.**
Owner's material, **94:270.**
PAC, **29:1.**
Package, **94:118.**
Packer, **94:139C.**
Paid in capital, **40F:1, 40G:1.**
Paint, **94:1.**
Panamanian intervention force
  veteran, **4:7.**
Parcel, **59:5C.**
  Forest lands and products tax,
  61:1.

WORDS AND PHRASES
—Cont'd
Pardons, **127:152.**
Parent, **15C:3, 118:1, 119:21.**
Parent corporation, **175:207.**
Park, **45:1.**
Parole board, **127:1.**
Part, **113:7.**
Partial closing, **151A:71A.**
Partially regulated plant, **Spec L 139:2.**
Partial unemployment, **151A:1.**
Participant, **128:2D, 175F:1.**
Clean elections law, **55A:1.**
Participant or participating town, **Spec L 22:11.**
Participate, **268A:1.**
Participating attorneys, **176H:1.**
Participating chiropractor, **176B:1.**
Participating financial institution, **23A:57.**
Business development office, **23A:60.**
Participating health care provider, **175F:1.**
Participating institution for higher education, **15C:3.**
Participating physician, **176B:1.**
Participating provider.
Health maintenance organizations, hold harmless provisions, **176G:21.**
Participating state, **Spec L 139:2.**
Participation, **63:1.**
Participation rate, **176J:1.**
Participation requirement, **176J:1.**
Particular matter, **268A:1.**
Parties in interest, **40A:11.**
Partnership, **108A:6.**
Partnership property, **108A:8.**
Part time class, **74:1.**
Part-time student, **15A:7B.**
Part-time veterans' agent, **115:1.**
Party, **30A:1, 106:1-201, 224:1, 231:6E.**
Negotiable instruments, **106:3-103.**
Passenger miles.
Massachusetts Bay transportation authority, **161A:1.**
Passengers, **90:49B.**
Pasteurized milk, **94:1.**
Paternal responsibility claim, **210:4A.**
Patient, **12:11L, 118G:1, 123:1, 233:20B.**
Patient care assessment coordinator, **111:205.**
Patrol agency, **147:22.**
Payee.
Structured settlement contracts, **231C:1.**

WORDS AND PHRASES
—Cont'd
Payment, amount of underpayment, **62B:14.**
Payment by beneficiary's bank to beneficiary, **106:4A-405.**
Payment by originator to beneficiary, **106:4A-406.**
Payment by sender to receiving bank, **106:4A-403.**
Payment date, **106:4A-401.**
Payment or delivery, date prescribed, **200A:1.**
Payment order, **106:4A-103.**
Payments in lieu of contributions, **151A:1.**
Payments subject to surcharge.
Health care finance and policy, **118G:1.**
Payoff statement, **183:54.**
Payor bank, **106:4-105.**
Payor of income.
Child support enforcement, **62E:1.**
Pay period, **94:42A.**
Payroll, **151A:1.**
Payroll level, **63:38.**
Peddler, **101:13.**
Pedestrians, **90:18A, 90:34A.**
Pelt, green, **131:1.**
Penal institution, **125:1.**
Pension contracts, **175:132F.**
Pension fund, **32:1, 149:181.**
Pension or retirement plan.
Child support enforcement, **119A:1A.**
Pension plan, **151D:1.**
Percent or percentage, **128:51, 128:64.**
Performance, **272:31.**
Performance auditing, **3:63.**
Performance, child pornography, **272:29A.**
Perfusion, **112:211.**
Perfusion protocols, **112:211.**
Periodic attendance.
Steamboilers, **146:46.**
Period of underpayment, **62B:14.**
Permanent employment, **140:46N.**
Permanent full time employee, **23A:3A.**
Permanent member of a fire department, **4:7.**
Permanent solution, **21A:19, 21E:3A.**
Permit, **21A:18.**
Permit application, **21A:18.**
Permit for employment, **76:1.**
Permit granting authority, **40A:1A.**
Permit proceeding or determination, **21:43.**

WORDS AND PHRASES
—Cont'd
Permitting and licensing agencies, **164:69H½.**
Persian Gulf veteran defined, **4:7.**
Person, **4:7, 7:1, 7:22G, 21A:18, 23D:1, 25A:11C, 29:29F, 63:1, 64H:1, 64I:1, 93:2, 94:277C, 100A:1, 109A:2, 111:5R, 118E:8, 131A:1, 142A:1, 148:38B, 156C:2, 156C:63, 175:206, 175H:1, 175I:2, 183:54, 203B:1.**
Development finance agency, **23G:1.**
Emergency medical services system, **111C:1.**
False claims against Commonwealth, **12:5A.**
Genetic testing, **111:70G.**
Hazardous materials mitigation, **21K:1.**
Insurance, reorganization of mutual insurers, **175:19G.**
Massachusetts Hazardous Waste Facility Siting Act, **21D:1.**
Transfer on death security registration, **201E:102.**
Viatical settlements, **175:213.**
Personal agent, **140:180A.**
Personal data.
Child support enforcement information, **119A:5A.**
Personal flotation device, **90B:1.**
Personal identifying information.
Identity fraud, **266:37E.**
Personal information, **175I:2.**
Personal injury, **152:1.**
Personal injury protection, **90:34A.**
Personality disorder.
Sexually dangerous persons act, **123A:1.**
Personal property, **79A:1, 105A:1.**
Personal representative, **191B:1, 199A:1, 203B:1.**
Transfer on death security registration, **201E:102.**
Personal risk liability, **176L:1.**
Personal services, **19D:1.**
Person entitled to enforce.
Negotiable instruments, **106:3-301.**
Person entitled under the document, **106:7-403.**
Person having care and custody, **265:13J.**
Person in the position of a seller, **106:2-707.**
Personnel record, **149:52C.**
Person participating or interested in labor dispute, **149:20C.**

WORDS AND PHRASES
—Cont'd

Person related, **255:12F.**

Person who has been selected, **268A:1.**

Person who resides in a city or town, **70:2.**

Pest, **132B:2.**

Pesticide, **132B:2.**

Pet food, **128:51.**

Petit treason, **265:1.**

Petroleum products, **21J:1, 25A:3.**

Pet shop, **129:1.**

Pharmacist, **94:187, 94C:1.**

Pharmacy, **94C:1.**

Pharmacy benefit manager.
  Elder affairs department, prescription drug insurance, **19A:39.**

Phosphoric acid, **128:64.**

Phosphorus, **111:5R.**

Phototherapy device, **111:207.**

Physically handicapped person, **22:13A.**

Physical therapist, **112:23A.**

Physical therapy, **112:23A.**

Physician, **93:71, 94D:1, 112:23A, 113:7, 123:1, 233:79G, 233:79H.**
  Vital statistics, **46:1E.**

Physician assistant, **112:9C.**

Physician assistant trainee, **112:9C.**

Pillow, **94:270.**

Pipefitting, **146:81.**

Place, **4:7, 271:1A.**

Placement employee, **140:46A.**

Placement of a restoration, **112:43A.**

Place of business, under cigarette excise tax law, **64C:1.**

Place of employment, **149:1.**

Place of public accommodation, **272:92A.**

Place of residence of the person injured, **84:18.**

Plainly and conspicuously, **94:117G.**

Plaintiff personal injury listing, **93:95.**

Plan A, **43:1.**

Plan administrator, **151D:1.**

Plan B, **43:1.**

Plan C, **43:1.**

Plan D, **43:1.**

Plan E, **43:1.**

Plan F, **43:1.**

Plan, medical service plan, **176B:1, 176C:1.**

Planned unit development, **40A:9.**

Planning assistance bureau, **23B:10.**

WORDS AND PHRASES
—Cont'd

Planning, capital facilities project, **7:39A.**

Planning, public library, **78:19G-78:19K.**

Plan of conversion.
  Insurance, reorganization of mutual insurers, **175:19G.**

Plan of insurance, **175:117C.**

Plan of operation or feasibility study, **176L:1.**

Plan of reorganization.
  Insurance, reorganization of mutual insurers, **175:19G.**

Plan of service, **276A:1.**

Plan, preliminary plan, **41:81L.**

Plant, **131A:1.**

Plant closing, **151A:71A.**

Plant regulator, **132B:2.**

Plastic, **94:321.**

Plastic bottle, **94:321.**

Platform trailer, heavy duty, **90:1.**

Pledge, **4:7.**

Plumber, journeyman, **142:1.**

Plumber, master, **142:1.**

Plumbing, **142:1.**

Plural and singular words, construction in statutes, **4:6.**

Podiatry, **112:13.**

Point-of-sale terminal, **167B:1.**

Pole dickey, **90:1.**

Pole dolly, **90:1.**

Poles and overhead wires and associated overhead structures, **166:22A.**

Police officer, motor vehicle regulation act provisions, **90:1.**

Police station, **147:21.**

Policing, **81:32.**

Policy.
  Insurance, reorganization of mutual insurers, **175:19G.**

Policyholder, **175I:2.**
  Insurance, reorganization of mutual insurers, **175:19G.**

Policyholders' adviser, **175:177A.**

Policyholders' counselor, **175:177A.**

Policy of accident and sickness insurance, **175:108.**

Policy of industrial life insurance, **175:1.**

Political action committee, **55:1.**

Political advertising, **164:33A.**

Political committee, **50:1, 55:1.**
  Clean elections law, **55A:1.**

Political contribution, **268B:1.**

Political designation, **50:1.**

Political party, **50:1.**

Political party committee, **55:1.**

Political subdivision.
  False claims against Commonwealth, **12:5A.**

WORDS AND PHRASES
—Cont'd

Political subdivision —Cont'd
  Retirement systems and pension provisions, **32:1.**

Pollutant, **21:26A, 92:104.**

Pollution control facilities, **40D:1, 121C:1.**
  Development finance agency, **23G:1.**

Pollution liability insurance policies acceptable for reinsurance, **175G:1.**

Pool.
  Health care finance and policy, **118G:1.**

Pooled account case, **175:117C.**

Pool plant, **Spec L 139:2.**

Poor persons, law governing definition of court costs, **261:27A.**

Poppy straw, **94C:1.**

Population, **4:7.**

Pose.
  Identity fraud, **266:37E.**

Position, **30:45, 35:51A.**

Position allocation, **30:45, 35:51A.**

Position classification plan, **30:45, 35:51A.**

Position reallocation, **30:45, 35:51A.**

Post-closure observation and maintenance, low-level radioactive waste, **111H:1.**

Potash, **128:64.**

POTW, **21I:2.**

Poultry, **94:118.**

Poultry producer, **94:152A.**

Poultry product, **94:118.**

Poultry sold or used for food, **94:152A.**

Poverty rate, **23A:3A.**

Power of appointment, **204:27.**

Power of sale in mortgage, statutory, **183:21, 183:24.**

Practical art class, **74:1.**

Practical nursing, **112:80B.**

Practical plumber, **142:1.**

Practice of forestry, **132:47.**

Practice of marriage and family therapy, **112:163.**

Practice of mental health counseling, **112:163.**

Practice of rehabilitation counseling, **112:163.**

Practices, fraudulent, **90:32G.**

Practitioner, **94C:1, 111:52, 112:12D.**

Preauthorized electronic fund transfers, **167B:1.**

Preceding, **4:7.**

WORDS AND PHRASES
—Cont'd

Predatory.
Sex offender registration and community notification, **6:178C.**
Preexisting conditions provision, **176J:1.**
Preferences, insolvent estates, **198:10A.**
Preferred claim, **175:180A.**
Pregnancy, **112:12K.**
Preliminary characterization, low-level radioactive waste, **111H:1.**
Preliminary local contribution, **70:2.**
Preliminary plan, **41:81L.**
Premises, **111:189A.**
Premium finance agency, **255C:1.**
Premium finance agreement, **255C:1.**
Premiums, **63:20.**
Fraternal benefit societies, **176:1.**
Prepared, **94:118.**
Preschool enrollment, **70:2.**
Prescreening, **93:50.**
Prescribed form, **32:1.**
Prescription drug, **94C:1.**
Presentation.
Letters of credit, **106:5-102.**
Presenter.
Letters of credit, **106:5-102.**
Presenting bank.
Bank deposits and collections, **106:4-105.**
Presentment.
Negotiable instruments, **106:3-501.**
Present sale, **106:2-106.**
Present value, **106:2A-103.**
Preservation.
Community preservation, **44B:2.**
Preservation restriction, **184:31.**
Presiding officer, **50:1.**
Pressure component, **90:7.**
Pressure vessels, **146:1.**
Presumed, **106:1-201.**
Presumption, **106:1-201.**
Pretenses, false, **277:39.**
Pretext interview, **175I:2.**
Previously registered vehicle, **90D:34.**
Price amendment, **110A:302.**
Primarily intended for use.
Drug paraphernalia, **94C:1.**
Primary, **50:1.**
Primary ambulance response.
Emergency medical services system, **111C:1.**

WORDS AND PHRASES
—Cont'd

Primary ambulance service.
Emergency medical services system, **111C:1.**
Primary business, **169A:1.**
Primary election campaign period.
Clean elections law, **55A:1.**
Primary employment, **40E:2, 40F:1, 40G:1, 40H:2.**
Development finance agency, **23G:1.**
Primary energy source, **164:1.**
Primary system, highways, **140B:1.**
Primary systems, **93D:1.**
Principal, **104:7, 201D:1.**
Principal base of operations, **63:1.**
Principal, law as to architects, **112:60A.**
Principal shareholder, **168:20.**
Print works, **149:1.**
Prior appropriations continued, **29:1.**
Priority list or system, **21:26A.**
Priority project.
Brownfields redevelopment fund, **23G:29A.**
Prior written consent.
Genetic testing, **111:70G.**
Prison, **125:1.**
Prisoner, **125:1.**
Private applicator, **132B:2.**
Private business school, **75D:1.**
Private carrier, **159B:2.**
Private detective, **147:22.**
Private detective business, **147:22.**
Private investigator, **147:22.**
Private passenger automobile, **90:32E½.**
Private sector charges, **118G:1.**
Private trade school, **93:21A.**
Privation contract, **7:53.**
Privileged information, **175I:2.**
Probate and insolvency court, **4:7.**
Probate court, **4:7, 123:1.**
Probation officer, **119:52, 276:83.**
Proceedings, adjudicatory, **30A:1.**
Proceeds, **106:9-203, 106:9-306.**
Proceeds of a letter of credit, **106:5-114.**
Process, **21I:2.**
Processed, **94:118.**
Procurement, **12A:1, 30B:2, 149:44A.**
Procurement officer, **30B:2.**
Produce, **132B:2.**
Producer, **175:177G, 175:177N.**
Producers, **94A:1, 132B:2.**
Product, **21I:2.**
Production, **94C:1.**

WORDS AND PHRASES
—Cont'd

Production facility, **6:85.**
Production unit, **21I:2.**
Product liability, **176L:1.**
Product name, **128:51.**
Professional bondsmen, **276:61B.**
Professional boxer, **147:35.**
Professional corporation, **156A:2.**
Professional data processing positions, **30:45.**
Professional development allotment, **70:2.**
Professional employee, **150E:1.**
Professional engineer, **112:81D.**
Professional investor, **40G:1.**
Professional land surveyor, **112:81D.**
Professional librarian, **78:24.**
Professional nursing, **112:80B.**
Professional service, **156A:2.**
Professional staff, **75:14.**
Profits, **121A:18D.**
Profit-sharing retirement plan, **151D:1.**
Program, **23A:57, 23B:29, 23D:1, 276A:1.**
Business development office, **23A:60.**
Capital facilities project, **7:39A.**
Elder affairs department, prescription drug insurance, **19A:39.**
Program for mass transportation.
Massachusetts Bay transportation authority, **161A:1.**
Program in transitional bilingual education, **71A:1.**
Programmer, **7:38A½.**
Program participant.
Address confidentiality of domestic violence victims, **9A:1.**
Prohibited noxious-weed seeds, **128:84.**
Development finance agency, **23G:1.**
Project.
Development finance agency, **23G:1.**
Project development services, **23B:10.**
Project EOA, **23A:3A.**
Project ETA, **23A:3A.**
Project manager.
School building assistance, **70B:2.**
Project proposal, **23A:3A.**
Project proposal date, **23A:3A.**

WORDS AND PHRASES
—Cont'd

Projects, **9:26B, 15A:5B, 15A:10, 23A:3A, 40F:1, 121A:1, 121B:34.**

Development finance agency, **23G:1.**

Project site.

Brownfields redevelopment fund, **23G:29A.**

Promise.

Negotiable instruments, **106:3-103.**

Promoter, **62C:1, 175:48.**

Promotion, **31:1.**

Promotional advertising, **164:33A.**

Promotional examination, competitive, **31:1.**

Proof gallon, **138:21.**

Propagator, **131:1.**

Propane air, **164:69G.**

Property, **40O:1, 109A:2, 276:1.**

Transfer on death security registration, **201E:102.**

Property and casualty insurer.

Retaliatory tax credit for property and casualty companies, **63:29E.**

Property level, **63:38.**

Property management services bureau, **23B:10.**

Property owner, **40O:1.**

Property protection insurance, **90:34O.**

Proportional representation, **43:1.**

Proposal, **30B:2.**

Proprietary environmental technology systems, **149:44A.**

Prosecutor.

Rights of victims and witnesses of crime, **258B:1.**

Prosthesis.

Accident and sickness insurance, **175:47T.**

Group insurance for state employees, **32A:17E.**

Health maintenance organizations, **176G:4J.**

Medical service corporations, **176A:8T.**

Medical service corporations, group coverage, **176B:4R.**

Protected person, **199A:1.**

Protected purchaser, **106:8-303.**

Protect health and environment, **132B:2.**

Prototype plan, **176J:1.**

Prototypical school plans.

School building assistance, **70B:2.**

Prove, **106:4A-105.**

Negotiable instruments, **106:3-103.**

WORDS AND PHRASES
—Cont'd

Provider, **118E:2, 118E:8.**

Provider of health care, **231:60B.**

Provider of travel services, **93:48B.**

Providing treatment, **111:57A, 111:57B.**

Provisional appointment, **31:1.**

Provisional educator, **71:38G.**

Provisional educator certificate, **71:38G.**

Provisional educator certificate with advanced standing, **71:38G.**

Provisional educator with advanced standing, **71:38G.**

Provisional employee, **31:1.**

Provisional licensed perfusionists, **112:211.**

Psychiatric nurse, **123:1.**

Psychiatrist, **123:1.**

Psychologists, **112:118, 123:1.**

Psychology, practice, **112:118.**

Psychotherapist, **233:20B.**

Psychotherapy of a nonmedical nature, **112:130.**

Pub brewer, **138:1.**

Pub brewery, **138:1.**

Public, **118E:2.**

Public access defibrillation program.

Good Samaritan provisions, **112:12V½.**

Public agency, **7:38A½, 7:39A, 25A:11C, 29:29F, 78:19G-78:19K, 79A:1, 149:44A.**

Public aircraft, **90:35.**

Publication, **6:39, 60:1.**

Public attorney, **258:1.**

Public auction, **100:1.**

Public authority, appropriate authority, **32:89, 32:89A, 32:89B.**

Public bathing beach.

Minimum sanitation standards for bathing waters, **111:5S.**

Public body, **149:185.**

Development finance agency, **23G:1.**

Tourism facilities fund, **23G:42.**

Public building, **22:13A, 143:1.**

Public charities division, **12:8A.**

Public charity director, **12:8A.**

Public coin and coinless telephone service, **166:15E.**

Public contract, **29:29F.**

Public employee, **150E:1, 258:1, 268B:1.**

Public entity, **21:26A.**

Public funds, **12A:1.**

WORDS AND PHRASES
—Cont'd

Public hall, **144:2, 145:2.**

Public housing development, **121B:32B-121B:32F.**

Public library, **78:19G-78:19K.**

Public library facility, **78:19G-78:19K.**

Public lodging house, **140:33.**

Publicly aided patient, **118G:1.**

Publicly assisted housing accommodations, **151B:1.**

Public medical institution, **118E:8.**

Public office, **268B:1.**

Public official, **268B:1.**

Public officials of the Commonwealth, **66:17A.**

Public payer-dependent non-acute hospital, **118G:1.**

Public record, **4:7, 66:3.**

Public school, **32:1.**

Public storage warehouse, licensed, **59:2.**

Public utility company, **25:3.**

Hazardous materials mitigation, **21K:1.**

Public vessel, **21E:2.**

Public view, **231:85S.**

Public warehouse, **105:1.**

Public warehouseman, **105:1.**

Publishing, **266:37D.**

Punishment as is provided by law, **119:52.**

Pupil, **70:2.**

Purchase, **106:1-201, 106:2A-103.**

Gun control, **140:121.**

Purchase description, **30B:2.**

Purchase money lease, **106:2A-309.**

Purchase money security interest, **106:9-107.**

Purchase of securities, **137:4, 137:7.**

Purchase or purchased, **64I:1.**

Purchaser, **64H:1, 64I:1, 106:1-201.**

Gun control, **140:121.**

Health care finance and policy, **118G:1.**

Purchasing group, **176L:1.**

Pure seed, **128:84.**

Purge, **6:167.**

Pursuant to commitment, **106:9-105.**

Quabbin watershed advisory committee, **92:104.**

Quahaug, **130:1.**

Qualified actuary, **175:9B.**

Qualified assignment agreement.

Structured settlement contracts, **231C:1.**

WORDS AND PHRASES
—Cont'd
Qualified Bond Act, **44A:1.**
Qualified bonds, **44A:1.**
Qualified candidate, **55:8A.**
Qualified dependent, **62:6.**
Qualified diagnostician.
    Juvenile courts and delinquent
      children, **119:33B.**
Qualified education loan, **15A:19A.**
Qualified escrow fund.
    Tobacco master settlement
      agreement, **94E:1.**
Qualified examiner, **123A:1.**
Qualified hospitalization, **62C:81.**
Qualified interpreter, **221C:1.**
Qualified investment.
    Tourism facilities fund, **23G:42.**
Qualified Massachusetts project.
    Low-income housing tax credit,
      62:6I.
    Low-income housing tax credit,
      corporations, **63:31H.**
Qualified medical insurance.
    Medical assistance division,
      118E:9C.
Qualified physician, **123:1.**
Qualified psychiatric nurse mental
    health clinical specialist,
    123:1.
Qualified psychologist, **123:1.**
Qualified security, **40G:1.**
Qualified taxpayer, **62:6.**
Qualified United States financial
    institution, **175:177N.**
Qualifying.
    Clean elections law, **55A:1.**
Qualifying contribution.
    Clean elections law, **55A:1.**
Qualifying domestic life insurance
    company, **63:22D.**
Qualifying examination, **31:1.**
Qualifying health plan, **176J:1.**
Qualifying individual, **62:3.**
Qualifying period.
    Clean elections law, **55A:1.**
Quarterly wage, **151A:1.**
Quitclaim covenant, **183:17.**
Quorum, **30A:11A, 34:9F, 39:23A,**
    71:38N.
Racetrack, **128:17, 128A:1.**
Racial imbalance, **71:37D.**
Racial isolation, **71:37D.**
Racing card, **128C:1.**
Racing meeting, horse racing,
    128:17.
Racing meeting licensee, **128C:1.**
Racing performance, **128C:1.**
Racing season, **128C:1.**
Radioactive substance, **94B:1.**
Radio and television master
    technical license, **112:87PPP.**

WORDS AND PHRASES
—Cont'd
Radio and television technical
    license, **112:87PPP.**
Radio and television technician,
    112:87PPP.
Radio or television receiver,
    112:87PPP.
Radiopharmaceutical drugs, **94C:1.**
Radio utility, **159:12A.**
Raffles, **271:7A.**
Rail rights-of-way, **161C:2.**
Railroad.
    Massachusetts Bay
      transportation authority.
      Commuter rail service,
        161A:43.
Railroad establishment, **149:133.**
Railroads, **160:1, 161:2.**
    Massachusetts Bay
      transportation authority.
      Commuter rail service,
        161A:43.
Railroad train, **153:1.**
Railway, Boynton bicycle railway,
    162:2.
Rape, **277:39.**
    Address confidentiality of
      domestic violence victims,
      9A:1.
Rape crisis center, **233:20J.**
Raptors, **131:1.**
Rate basis type, **176J:1.**
Rate for such year, **121A:10.**
Rating board, **32:26.**
Rating period, **176J:1.**
RCRA, **21C:2, 148:38B.**
Ready-to-eat food, **94:1.**
Real estate, **4:7, 112:87PP,**
    112:173.
Real estate appraisal trainee,
    112:173.
Real estate brokers, **112:87PP.**
Real estate project, **23A:3A.**
Real estate salesmen, **112:87PP.**
Real estate tax payment.
    Income tax credits.
      Older persons, credit for real
        estate or rent payments,
        62:6.
Real property, **7:39A, 108A:2,**
    112:173.
    Community preservation, **44B:2.**
Real property interest.
    Community preservation, **44B:2.**
Real property owned, **63:1.**
Rear, **144:2, 145:2.**
Reasonable accommodation,
    151B:4.
Reasonable attempt to repair,
    93:107.

WORDS AND PHRASES
—Cont'd
Reasonable evidence of a risk of
    harm.
    Child support enforcement data,
      119A:5A.
Reasonable insurable value,
    175C:1.
Reasonable precautions, **112:135,**
    123:1.
Receipt of goods, **106:2-103.**
Receipts, **21A:18A.**
Receipts, gross receipts, **63A:1.**
Receiver, **175:1, 175:180A.**
Receiver of stolen goods, common
    receiver, **266:60.**
Receives notice, **106:1-201.**
Receiving bank, **106:4A-103.**
Receiving, credit card offenses,
    266:37A.
Receiving district, **76:12B.**
Receiving state, **Spec L 138:1.**
Recipient, **18:5G.**
Reciprocal insurance exchange,
    175:94A.
Reciprocal state, **175:180A.**
Reciprocity of certified educators,
    71:38G.
Reclamation, **21B:2.**
Recognized association of
    physicians, **176C:1.**
Recognized educational institution,
    112:118, 112:130, 112:163.
Reconstruction, **22:13A.**
Record.
    Letters of credit, **106:5-102.**
Recordation or recorded, **183:54.**
Recorded, **4:7, 30:39R, 41:81L.**
Recorded device, **266:143.**
Records, **112:12CC.**
Records, public record, **4:7.**
Record title, **93:70.**
Recreational tramways, **143:71I.**
Recreational use.
    Community preservation, **44B:2.**
Recreation vehicle, **90B:20.**
Recruiting domestic employment
    agency, **140:46A.**
Redevelopment agency.
    Oil and hazardous material
      release prevention and
      response, **21E:2.**
Redevelopment and land assembly,
    121A:1.
Redevelopment authority, **121B:1.**
    Oil and hazardous material
      release prevention and
      response, **21E:2.**
Reemployment assistance benefits,
    151A:71A.
Reemployment assistance fund,
    151A:71A.

WORDS AND PHRASES
—Cont'd

Reemployment assistance program, **151A:71A.**

Referee station, **90:1.**

Referendum, **43:42; MA Const Amend Art 48 Part 1 Def.**

Refrigeration, **146:81.**

Refrigeration apprentice, fire sprinkler system contractors and fitters, **146:81.**

Refrigeration contractor, **146:81.**

Refrigeration technician, **146:81.**

Refrigeration trainee, **146:81.**

Refrigerator, **25B:2.**

Refrigerator-freezer, **25B:2.**

Refuse, **111:150A.**

Refuse disposal facility, **40:44B.**

Region, **Spec L 139:2.**

 Emergency medical services system, **111C:1.**

 Forest lands and products tax, **61:1.**

Regional EMS council.

 Emergency medical services system, **111C:1.**

Regional local governmental unit, **29C:1.**

Regionally licensed or certified educator, **71:38G.**

Regionally licensed or certified teacher, **71:38G.**

Regional position, **78:19C.**

Regional public libraries, **6:39.**

Regional school district.

 School building assistance, **70B:2.**

Regional schools.

 School building assistance, **70B:2.**

Regional tourism facility.

 Tourism facilities fund, **23G:42.**

Register, **209D:1-101.**

 Hearing instrument specialists, **112:196.**

 Transfer on death security registration, **201E:102.**

Registered, **128:84, 142:1.**

Registered chiropractor, **176B:1.**

Registered corporation, **149:184, 156B:50A.**

Registered dietitian, **112:201.**

Registered form, **106:8-102.**

Registered mail, **4:7, 41:81L.**

Registered motor vehicle repair shop, **100A:1.**

Registered physical therapist, **112:23A.**

Registered physician, **31:1, 176B:1.**

Registered sanitarian, **112:87OO.**

WORDS AND PHRASES
—Cont'd

Registered under the laws of the state, **130:1.**

Registering entity.

 Transfer on death security registration, **201E:102.**

Registering tribunal, **209D:1-101.**

Register number, **90:1.**

Register of deeds, **41:81L.**

Register of probate, **217:1.**

Registrant, **94C:1, 132B:2, 142A:1.**

Registrar, **50:1, 90B:1.**

 Motor vehicle emissions, **111:142M.**

Registrar of motor vehicles, **90F:1.**

Registrars of voters, **50:1.**

Registration, **90:49B, 94C:1.**

Registration agency, **50:1.**

Registration number, **94C:1.**

Registry, **217:1.**

 Motor vehicle emissions, **111:142M.**

 Vital statistics, **46:1.**

Registry of deeds, **60:1.**

Registry of motor vehicles, investigator or examiner, **32:89.**

Regular compensation, **32:1.**

Regular day program, **70:2.**

Regular deductions, **32:1.**

Regular education, **71B:1.**

Regular interest, **32:1, 32:22.**

Regular municipal election, **43:1.**

Regular place of business, **63:1.**

Regular routes, **159B:2.**

Regular work week, **32A:2.**

Regulated activities, protection of Berkshire Mountains watershed regions, **131:39A.**

Regulated area, **Spec L 139:2.**

Regulated substance, **148:38B.**

Regulating board, **156A:2.**

Regulations, **144:2, 145:2.**

Regulatory agreement.

 Low-income housing tax credit, **62:6I.**

 Low-income housing tax credit, corporations, **63:31H.**

Rehabilitation, **78:19G-78:19K.**

Rehabilitation commission, definition of terms in connection with powers and duties, **6:77.**

Rehabilitation facility, **6:77.**

Rehabilitation services, vocational, **6:77.**

Reimbursement, **21J:1.**

Reinstatement, **31:1.**

Reinsurance intermediary, **175:177N.**

WORDS AND PHRASES
—Cont'd

Reinsurance intermediary broker, **175:177N.**

Reinsurance intermediary manager, **175:177N.**

Reinsure, **175G:1.**

Reinsurer, **175:177N.**

Related facilities or equipment, **161C:2.**

Related person, **138:25D.**

Related stock insurance company, **175:66C.**

Relative, **109A:2, 118E:31.**

Relator.

 False claims against Commonwealth, **12:5A.**

Release, **21J:1, 148:38B, 204:31.**

 Hazardous materials mitigation, **21K:1.**

Released claims.

 Tobacco master settlement agreement, **94E:1.**

Releasing parties.

 Tobacco master settlement agreement, **94E:1.**

Religious accommodation.

 Abuse or neglect of patients in long-term care facilities, **111:72F.**

Relocation agency and payments, **79A:1, 121B:1.**

Relocation bureau, **23B:10.**

Relocation payments, **121B:1.**

Relocation project, **121B:1.**

Remade, **94:270.**

Remaker, **94:270.**

Remedy, **106:1-201(34).**

Remedy operation status.

 Oil and hazardous material release prevention and response, **21E:2.**

Remitter.

 Negotiable instruments, **106:3-103.**

Remodeling, **22:13A.**

Remuneration, **151A:1.**

Renderer, **94:118.**

Renewable energy, **164:1.**

Renewable energy source property, **62:6.**

Renovated, **94:270.**

Renovation, **7:39A, 78:19G-78:19K.**

Renovator, **94:270.**

Rent, **64G:1, 171:75.**

Rental agreement, **90:32E½, 105A:1.**

Rental company, **90:32E½.**

Rental housing project, **23B:25.**

WORDS AND PHRASES
—Cont'd

Rent constituting real estate tax
  payment.
  Income tax credits.
    Older persons, credit for real
      estate or rent payments,
      62:6.
Rent control, **40P:3.**
Reorganized insurer.
  Insurance, reorganization of
    mutual insurers, **175:19G.**
Reorganizing insurer.
  Insurance, reorganization of
    mutual insurers, **175:19G.**
Repair, **7:39A, 143:1.**
Repairer, **94:270.**
Repairman, **140:58.**
Repairman, defined under motor
  vehicle regulation act, **90:1.**
Replacement.
  Accident and sickness insurance,
    replacement coverage for
    insolvent HMO's, **175:110.**
  Health maintenance
    organizations, insolvency,
    176G:23.
  Hospital service corporations,
    replacement coverage for
    insolvent HMO's, **176A:33.**
  Medical service corporations,
    replacement coverage for
    insolvent HMO's, **176B:21.**
Replacement reserve fund, **183A:1.**
Reportable condition, **19C:1.**
Reporting person, **268B:1.**
Reporting system.
  Child support enforcement,
    62E:1.
Repossessor, **90:1, 140:58.**
Representation, proportional, **43:1.**
Representative, **106:1-201.**
Representative form of
  government for fraternal
  benefit society, **176:3.**
Represented person.
  Negotiable instruments,
    106:3-307.
Represented price, **6:184B.**
Reputable dental college, **112:46.**
Request for proposals, **30B:2.**
Rescission, **106:2-720.**
Research institution, **40J:12,
  140:136A.**
Reseller, petroleum products,
  25A:3.
Reserve, annuity, **32:1.**
Reserve percentage, **151A:14.**
Reserve valuation method,
  commissioner's, **175:9.**
Reside, **115:1, 118E:2, 118E:8.**

WORDS AND PHRASES
—Cont'd

Residence, **46:1.**
  Income tax credits.
    Older persons, credit for real
      estate or rent payments,
      62:6.
Residence dealer, **94:270.**
Residence of the person injured,
  place, **84:18.**
Resident, **19D:1, 23B:11, 62:1,
  65C:1, 118G:1.**
  Abuse or neglect of patients in
    long-term care facilities,
    111:72F.
  Catastrophic illness in children
    relief fund commission,
    111K:1 to 111K:11.
Resident creditor, **199A:1.**
Residential buildings.
  Home inspectors, **112:221.**
Residential contracting, **142A:1.**
Residential property, **183:67,
  255E:1.**
Resident or inhabitant, **62:1.**
Residual value, **164:1.**
Residual waste, **16:18.**
Resignation, **31:1.**
Resource recovery facility, **16:18.**
Respiratory care, **112:23R.**
Respiratory therapist, **112:23R.**
Responding state, **209D:1-101.**
Responding to an emergency,
  defined, **149:177B.**
Responding tribunal, **209D:1-101.**
Response action, **21A:19.**
Response action contract,
  hazardous waste, **21E:2.**
Response action contractor,
  hazardous waste, **21E:2.**
Responsibility.
  Negotiable instruments,
    106:3-405.
Responsible, **25A:11C, 149:44A.**
Responsible administrative
  authority.
    Structured settlement contracts,
      231C:1.
Responsible bidder or offeror,
  30B:2.
Responsible buyer, **40E:2.**
Responsible tenant, **40E:2.**
Responsive bidder or offeror,
  30B:2.
Responsive offeror, **25A:11C.**
Restaurant, **64H:6, 138:1.**
Rest home, **111:71.**
Restitution.
  Rights of victims and witnesses
    of crime, **258B:1.**
Restraint, **123:1, 123B:1.**

WORDS AND PHRASES
—Cont'd

Restricted landing area, **90:35.**
Restricted noxious-weed seeds,
  128:84.
Retail assess, **164:1.**
Retail buyer or buyer, **255B:1.**
Retail customer, **164:1, 164:94G.**
Retail dealer, marine fish and
  fisheries, **130:1.**
Retail drug business, **94C:1.**
Retailer, **64C:1, 64H:1, 64I:1,
  93:14E, 94:270.**
Retail establishment, **64H:1, 64I:1.**
Retail installment contract,
  255B:1.
Retail installment sale agreement,
  255B:1, 255D:1.
Retail motor fuel dealers, **94:295A.**
Retail sales, **64C:13, 64H:1, 64I:1,
  93:14E, 140:21A.**
Retail trade reporting agencies,
  93:49A.
Retained revenue, **29:1.**
Retaliatory action, **149:185.**
Retaliatory taxes.
  Retaliatory tax credit for
    property and casualty
    companies, **63:29E.**
Retirement allowance, **32:1,
  32:91A.**
Retirement association, **171:1.**
Retirement benefit, **151A:29.**
Retirement system funding
  schedule, **32:1.**
Retiring authority, **32:59.**
Retread or recapped, **90:1.**
Reupholsterer, **94:270.**
Revenue bonds, **15C:3.**
Revenue center, **118G:1.**
Revenue retention account, **29:1.**
Revenues, **29C:1, 40N:3, 44:1,
  92:104.**
  Development finance agency,
    23G:1.
Reverse mortgage loans, **167E:2.**
Review commission.
  Elder affairs department,
    prescription drug insurance,
    19A:39.
Reviewer, **112:87A.**
Reviewing board, **152:1.**
Revoked credit card, **266:37A.**
Revolving account, **29:1.**
Revolving credit agreement,
  255D:1.
Rewritten or refinanced mortgage
  loan, **183:63A.**
Rider.
  Massachusetts Bay
    transportation authority,
    161A:1.

WORDS AND PHRASES
—Cont'd

Ride sharing, **63:31D.**

Riding school operator, **128:1.**

Rifle, **269:10.**
Gun control, **140:121.**

Rifle or shotgun, loaded, **131:1.**

Right of representation, taking, **190:8.**

Rights, **106:1-201.**

Right to operate, **90:1.**

Rigid plastic container, **94:321.**

Riot, **269:1.**

Risk retention group, **176L:1.**

Ritual slaughter, **94:139G.**

Robbery, **277:39.**

Rolls, **94:1.**

Roof, **143:1, 148:1.**

Rooming house, **111:199B.**

Roster, **31:1.**

Routes of reasonable access, **90:1.**

R S., **112:87OO.**

Rules.
Fraternal benefit societies, **176F:1.**

Run, **93F:1.**

Saddlemount combination, **90:1.**

Safe deposit box, **171:75.**

Safe Drinking Water Act.
Water pollution abatement trust, **29C:1.**

Safety glass, **90:9A.**

Safety glazing material, **143:3T.**

Safety rest area, **93D:1.**

Safety zone.
Excavations, **82:40.**

Said to contain, **106:7-203, 106:7-301.**

Salary, **4:7.**

Salary classification of county officers and employees, **35:49.**

Salary grade, **35:51B.**

Salary range, **30:45, 35:51A.**

Salary schedule, **35:51B.**

Sale, **64C:1, 64E:1, 64H:1, 64I:1, 93B:1, 94:315, 110A:401.**
Commercial code, **106:2-106.**
Gun control, **140:121.**
Hearing instrument specialists, **112:196.**

Sale at retail, **64H:1, 64I:1.**

Sale by weight, **94:176.**

Sale on approval, **106:2-326.**

Sale or return, **106:2-326.**

Sales agent, **101:34.**

Sales finance company, **255B:1, 255D:1.**

Salesmen, real estate, **112:87PP.**

Salesperson, **142A:1.**

Sales price, **64H:1, 64I:1.**

Sales representative, **104:7.**

WORDS AND PHRASES
—Cont'd

Same class, **128C:1.**

Sanitarian, **112:87LL, 112:87OO.**

Sanitary condition, **160:172A.**

Sausage and sausage meat, **94:1.**

Savings and insurance bank, **178A:1.**

Savings bank, **4:7, 168:1, 187A:1.**

Savings bank life insurance, **178A:1.**

Savings fund, annuity, **32:1.**

Savings insurance bank, **26:8C.**

Savings program, **15C:3.**

Sawed-off shotgun, **269:10.**
Gun control, **140:121.**

Scallop, **130:1, 130:70.**

Scalp hair prosthesis.
Accident and sickness insurance, **175:47T.**
Group insurance for state employees, **32A:17E.**
Health maintenance organizations, **176G:4J.**
Medical service corporations, **176A:8T.**
Medical service corporations, group coverage, **176B:4R.**

Scenic and recreational rivers and streams, **21:17B.**

Schedule, **94C:1.**

Schematic list, **30:45.**

School, **112:87T.**
Family and medical leave, **149:52D.**

School administration.
Pesticides, **132B:2.**

School age child, **71B:1.**

School age child care program, **28A:9.**
Pesticides, **132B:2.**

School age child requiring special education, **71B:1.**

School age child with a disability.
Special education, **71B:1.**

School aid percentage, **70:2.**

School bus, **90:1.**

School district, **70:2.**

School official, **71:82.**

Schools.
Pesticides, **132B:2.**

School service motor carriers, **159A:11A.**

SCPE, **166:15E.**

Sea scallop, **130:1.**

Seasonably, **106:1-204.**

Seasonal determination, **151A:1.**

Seasonal employee, **151A:1.**

Seasonal employer, **151A:1.**

Seasonal employment, **151A:1.**

Seat, registration fee for bus, **90:33.**

WORDS AND PHRASES
—Cont'd

Secondary boycott, **149:20C.**

Second class construction, **144:2.**

Secondhand, **94:270.**

Secured claim, **175:180A.**

Secured lender.
Hazardous materials mitigation, **21K:1.**

Secured party, **106:9-105.**

Secured transactions, **106:9-105, 106:9-106, 175:108A.**

Securities, **137:4, 137:7, 271:35.**

Securities account, **106:8-501.**

Securities intermediary, **106:8-102.**

Securitization, **164:1.**

Security, **18:29, 93:90, 106:8-102, 110A:401, 201A:1.**

Security account.
Transfer on death security registration, **201E:102.**

Security agreement, **106:9-105.**

Security box, **140:10.**

Security certificate, **106:8-102.**

Security entitlement, **106:8-102.**

Securityholder, **175:206.**

Security interest, **93:90, 106:1-201, 255D:1.**

Security procedure, **106:4A-201.**

Seed capital, **40G:1.**

Seed clam, **130:1.**

Seed potatoes, **128:84.**

Seed quahaug, **130:1.**

Seizure, **128:84.**

Selectmen, **121A:6.**

Self-administered medication management, **19D:1.**

Self-employed, **118G:1.**

Self-insurance health plan, **118G:1.**

Self-service storage facility, **105A:1.**

Self testing.
Banks, compliance review, **167:49.**

Sell, **93:71, 94:270, 110A:401.**
Gun control, **140:121.**
Hearing instrument specialists, **112:196.**

Sell at retail, cigarette excise tax, **64C:13.**

Sell at wholesale, cigarette excise tax, **64C:13.**

Seller, **106:2-103.**

Selling, **64H:1, 64I:1.**

Selling price, gasoline or fuel taxes, **64A:1, 64E:1.**

Semi-automatic, **269:10.**
Gun control, **140:121.**

Semi-public bathing beach.
Minimum sanitation standards for bathing waters, **111:5S.**

WORDS AND PHRASES
—Cont'd

Semi-public outdoor inground swimming pool, **140:206.**

Semi-trailer, defined for purposes of motor vehicle regulation act, **90:1.**

Send, **106:1-201.**

Sender, **106:4A-103.**

Sending district, **76:12B.**

Sending state, **Spec L 138:1.**

Sentencing court.
Sex offender registration and community notification, **6:178C.**

Separate account agreement.
Life insurance, **175:180A.**

Separate sleeping area, **148:26D.**

Separation pay, **151A:71A.**

Serial number, **266:139, 269:11A.**

Serious assaultive behavior, **123:8.**

Serious bodily injury.
Child custody, **208:31A.**
Husband and wife, **209:38.**
Kidnapping, **265:26.**
Neglected or abused children, **119:26.**

Serious drug offense.
Firearms possession violations, **269:10G.**

Serious incident of abuse.
Child custody, **208:31A.**
Husband and wife, **209:38.**

Serious traffic violation, **90F:1.**

Seropositive, **111:2D.**

Service area, **159:12A.**

Service charges, **140:185D.**

Service mark, **110B:1.**

Service quality standards.
Massachusetts Bay transportation authority, **161A:1.**

Services, **12A:1, 30B:2, 32:1, 60:1, 64H:1, 64I:1, 159B:2, 255D:1.**
Charter service, **159A:11A.**
Emergency medical services system, **111C:1.**
Medical service, **176B:1.**
Municipal, **41:81L.**

Services and treatment, **111:57C.**

Service territory, **164:1.**

Service zone.
Emergency medical services system, **111C:1.**

Service zone provider.
Emergency medical services system, **111C:1.**

Servicing, **183:54.**

Set-off debt collection procedure, **62D:1.**

Settle.
Bank deposits and collections, **106:4-104.**

WORDS AND PHRASES
—Cont'd

Settled claim.
Structured settlement contracts, **231C:1.**

Severe economic dislocation, **23D:1.**

Sewage, **111:17.**

Sewer works system, **40N:3.**

Sex offender.
Sex offender registration and community notification, **6:178C.**

Sex offender registry.
Sex offender registration and community notification, **6:178C.**

Sex offense.
Sex offender registration and community notification, **6:178C.**

Sex offense involving a child.
Sex offender registration and community notification, **6:178C.**

Sexual assault.
Address confidentiality of domestic violence victims, **9A:1.**
Kidnapping, **265:26.**

Sexual assault counselor, **233:20J.**

Sexual conduct, **272:31.**

Sexual contact, **12:11L.**

Sexual excitement, **272:31.**

Sexual harassment, **151A:25, 151B:1, 151C:1.**

Sexually dangerous person, **123A:1.**

Sexually violent offense.
Sex offender registration and community notification, **6:178C.**

Sexually violent predator.
Sex offender registration and community notification, **6:178C.**

Sexual offense, **123A:1.**

Sexual orientation, **151B:3.**

Shade trees, public, **87:1.**

Shall as mandatory word, **144:2, 145:2.**

Shallow land burial, **111H:1.**

Share account, **171:1.**

Shared legal custody, **208:31.**

Shared physical custody, **208:31.**

Shares, **171:1, 171:48.**

Shellfish, **130:1.**

Shelter, **140:136A.**

Sheltered market program, **30B:18.**

Shipper's weight, load and count, **106:7-301.**

WORDS AND PHRASES
—Cont'd

Shipping container, **94:118.**

Ship's lifeboats, **90B:1.**

Shooting gallery, **140:56A.**

Shop, **112:87T.**

Shop light, **25B:1, 25B:2.**

Shoreline, **1:3.**

Short lobster, **130:1.**

Short term measure, **21A:19.**

Shotgun, **269:10.**
Gun control, **140:121.**

Shotgun or rifle, loaded, **131:1.**

Show, **62C:1.**

SIC, **64H:1.**

SIC code, **21I:2.**

Side yard, **144:2, 145:2.**

Signed, **106:1-201.**

Significant habitat, **131A:1.**

Significant portion of his income, **164:69G.**

Silencers, **269:10A.**

Simulcast, **128C:1.**

Simulcast wager, **128C:1.**

Single account case, **175:117C.**

Singular and plural words, construction in statutes, **4:6.**

Site, **9:26B.**
Brownfields redevelopment fund, **23G:29A.**
Business development office, **23A:60.**
Hazardous materials mitigation, **21K:1.**

Site community, low-level radioactive waste, **111H:1.**

Ski area, **143:71I.**

Ski area operator, **143:71I.**

Skier, **143:71I.**

Skilled nursing care, **19D:1.**

Skilo, **271:6B.**

Skimobile, **143:71I.**

Ski slope or trail, **143:71I.**

Slash, **48:16.**

Slaughter, **94:139C.**

Slot machines, **271:5A.**

Sludge, **16:18.**

Small artificial flowers, **101:16.**

Small business, **23A:15, 23A:57, 40F:1, 118G:1.**

Small business investment corporation, **40F:1.**

Small power production facility, **164:1.**

Small quantity toxics user, **21I:2.**

Snowmobiles, trespass, **266:121A.**

Snow vehicle, **90B:20.**

Social Security Act, **118C:2.**

Social worker, **112:130, 123:1.**

Social work, practice, **112:130.**

Society, **157:3, 157:3B.**

WORDS AND PHRASES
—Cont'd
Soil conditioner, **128:64.**
Solar access, zoning, **40A:1A.**
Solar energy, **40A:1A.**
Solar energy system, zoning, **40A:1A.**
Sole community provider, **118G:1.**
Sole legal custody, **208:31.**
Sole physical custody, **208:31.**
Solicitor, city, **4:7.**
Solid waste, **16:18, 21H:2, 266:146.**
Solid waste disposal facilities, **16:18.**
  Development finance agency, **23G:1.**
Solvency account, **151A:14.**
SOMBA, State Office of Minority Business Assistance, **23A:40.**
SOMWBA, executive office of economic affairs, **23A:40.**
Sound level, **90:7S.**
Source material, low-level radioactive waste, **111:5M.**
Source minimization, low-level radioactive waste, **111H:1.**
Space heater, **148:25B.**
Spaces, occupied, **144:2, 145:2.**
Spanish War veteran, **4:7.**
Special charter as included in term charter, **4:7.**
Special county employee, **268A:1.**
Special deposit claim, **175:180A.**
Special education, **28A:2, 71B:1.**
Special fuels, **64E:1, 64F:1.**
Special fund for military service credit, **32:1.**
Special investigating commission (mines), **21B:2.**
Specialist, insurance, **175:177A.**
Specialized code, **143:1.**
Specialized services, **112:173.**
Special justice, **218:1.**
Specially qualified voter, **50:1.**
Special mobile equipment, **90:1, 90D:1.**
Special municipal employee, **268A:1.**
Special nuclear material, **6:85.**
Special nuclear material, low-level radioactive waste, **111:5M.**
Special payment, **151D:1.**
Special permit granting authority, **40A:1A.**
Special population.
  Emergency medical services system, **111C:1.**
Special service, **159A:11A.**
Special state employee, **268A:1.**
Special-support order, **209D:1-101.**

WORDS AND PHRASES
—Cont'd
Specialty fertilizer, **128:64.**
Specialty hospital, **118G:1.**
Species, **131A:1.**
Species of special concern, **131A:1.**
Specifications, **30:45, 35:51A.**
Specific learning impairment.
  Special education, **71B:1.**
Specific license, low-level radioactive waste, **111:5M.**
Specimens, **9:26B.**
Speech-language pathology, **112:138.**
Spendthrift, **4:7, 201:8.**
Split-funded plan, **151D:1.**
Sponsor, **19D:1, 78A:1, 176H:1.**
  Development finance agency, **23G:1.**
Sprinkler fitter/journeyman sprinkler fitter, **146:81.**
Staff officer, **22C:1.**
Stair hall, **144:2, 145:2.**
Stairways, moving stairways as within term elevators, **143:62, 143:71E.**
Stalking.
  Address confidentiality of domestic violence victims, **9A:1.**
Stamper, **64C:1.**
Stamp, trading, **93:14L.**
Standard color-coded markings.
  Excavations, **82:40.**
Standard educator, **71:38G.**
Standard educator certificate, **71:38G.**
Standard fire policy, Massachusetts, **175:99.**
Standard government services, **40O1.**
Standard of care.
  Oil and hazardous material release prevention and response, **21E:2.**
Standard of effort, **70:2.**
Standard of effort gap, **70:2.**
Standard reference compendia, **175:47K, 175:47O.**
Standard rules, **30A:9, 30A:10.**
Standard written notification.
  Pesticides, **132B:2.**
State agency, doing business with Burma (Myanmar), **7:22G.**
State auditor, **4:7.**
State authority, doing business with Burma (Myanmar), **7:22G.**
State building code, **143:1.**
State-certified general real estate appraiser, **112:173.**

WORDS AND PHRASES
—Cont'd
State-certified residential real estate appraiser, **112:173.**
State correctional facility, **125:1.**
State dairy regulation, **Spec L 139:2.**
Stated deductible amount, **175:111G.**
State election, **50:1.**
State employee, **268A:1.**
State fire warden, **4:7.**
State forester, **4:7.**
State housing board, **23B:10.**
State institution, health care finance and policy, **118G:1.**
State office.
  Clean elections law, **55A:1.**
State officer, **50:1.**
State official, **32:1.**
State or county fair, **128A:1.**
State overburden obligation, **70:2.**
State plumbing code, **25B:2.**
State police surgeon.
  Retirement systems and pensions, **32:1.**
State prison, **125:1.**
State registrar.
  Vital statistics, **46:1E.**
State revenue, **29:1.**
State school aid, **70:2.**
State school choice limit, **76:12B.**
State secretary, **4:7, 156:1.**
State tax revenues.
  State finance, **29:1.**
State team.
  Child fatality review teams, **38:2A.**
State to DNA database, **22E:1.**
State treasurer, **4:7.**
Statewide office.
  Clean election slaw, **55A:1.**
Status determination date, **62B:4.**
Statutes, construction, **4:6.**
Statutory condition in mortgage, **183:20, 183:23.**
Statutory definitions, **4:7.**
Statutory power of sale in mortgage, **183:21, 183:24.**
Statutory vested benefit, **151D:1.**
Statutory will estate, **191B:1.**
Stealing, **277:39.**
Step-in-range, **30:45, 35:51A.**
Sterilizer, **94:270.**
Stink bombs, **269:15.**
Stock investment, **161:116.**
Stock purchase rights.
  Insurance, reorganization of mutual insurers, **175:19G.**
Stockyard, **94:139C.**
Stolen goods, common receiver, **266:60.**

WORDS AND PHRASES
—Cont'd

Stop and frisk, **41:98.**

Stop sale, **128:84.**

Storage, **16:18, 21C:2, 21D:1, 64I:1.**

Storage warehouse, licensed public warehouse, **59:2.**

Store, **94A:1.**

Store or storage, **64I:1.**

Street, **144:2, 145:2.**

Street railway, **161:1.**

Streets and roads in such city or town, **81:31, 81:32.**

Strike, **150E:1.**

Stringer-steered boat transporter, **90:1.**

Strong sensitizer, **94B:1.**

Structure, **40C:5, 143:1, 148:1.**

Structured settlement, **231C:1.**

Structured settlement agreement, **231C:1.**

Structured settlement obligor, **231C:1.**

Structured settlement payment rights, **231C:1.**

Structure or structures in waterways, **91:1.**

Student, **90:1, 112:87T.**

Student organization, **15A:29.**

Study, **7:39A, 78:19G-78:19K.**

Stumpage value, **61:1, 61:2.**
  Forest lands and products tax, **61:1.**

Stunt day player, **231:85P½.**

Subclass of appliances, **94:314.**

Subcontractor, **142A:1.**

Subdivision, **41:81L.**

Subdivision control, **41:81L.**

Sublease, **106:2A-103.**

Subprofessional librarian, **78:24.**

Subscriber, **93:95, 176B:1.**

Subscribing member, **176C:1.**

Subsidiary, **94A:1, 175:206.**

Subsidiary corporation, **175:207.**

Subsidized housing development, **121B:32B-121B:32F.**

Substandard area, **121A:1, 121B:1.**

Substantial bodily injury, **265:13J.**

Substantial capital expenditure, **111:25B.**

Substantial change in services, **111:25B.**

Substantial completion, **30:39G.**

Substantial evidence, **30A:1.**

Substantial interest, **128A:11B, 175:64.**

Subversive organization, **264:16.**

Successor employer, **149:179C.**

Successor-in-interest, **93E:5A.**

WORDS AND PHRASES
—Cont'd

Successor of a beneficiary.
  Letters of credit, **106:5-102.**

Sufficient and legal fences, **49:2.**

Suitable employment, **151A:25.**

Sumner tunnel.
  Turnpike authority, **81A:3.**

Sum of weighted full-time equivalent pupil, **70:2.**

Superintendent, **123:1, 123B:1, 125:1.**

Superior court, **4:7.**

Superior site, low-level radioactive waste, **111H:1.**

Supervised health service experience, **112:118.**

Supervision of activities of daily living, **19D:1.**

Supervision of instrumental activities of daily living, **19D:1.**

Supervisor, **149:185.**

Supplemental service, **40O:1.**

Supplier, **64E:1, 106:2A-103, 164:1.**

Suppliers of water, **21A:18.**

Supplies, **12A:1, 30B:2.**

Supply contract, **106:2A-103.**

Supply dealer, **94:270.**

Supplying electricity in bulk, **164:1.**

Support enforcement agency, **209D:1-101.**

Supporting documents, **90D:1.**

Support order, **209D:1-101.**
  Child support enforcement, **119A:1A.**

Surcharge payor.
  Health care finance and policy, **118G:1.**

Surety, **4:7, 106:1-201.**

Surety rate regulatory law, **175A:1-175A:20.**

Surface water, **92:104.**

Surgeon, **113:7.**

Surplus, **175:48, 178A:1.**

Surrender, extradition provisions, **276:11.**

Surviving spouse, **191B:1.**

Suspends payments.
  Bank deposits and collections, **106:4-104.**

Suspension, **29:29F.**

Swamps, **131:40.**

Swear, **4:7.**

Syndication, **63:1.**

Synthetic natural gas, **164:69G.**

System, **32:1.**
  Excavations, **82:40.**

WORDS AND PHRASES
—Cont'd

System revenues.
  Massachusetts Bay transportation authority, **161A:1.**

Take, **131A:1.**

Takeout, **128C:1.**

Take-over bid, **110C:1.**

Tampering.
  Motor vehicle emissions, **111:142M.**

Tandem unit, **90:1.**

Tangible personal property, **64H:1, 64I:1.**

Tanning device, **111:207.**

Tanning facility, **111:207.**

Target area, **40F:1, 40H:2.**

Target company, **110C:1.**

Tavern, **138:1.**

Taxable, **63:1.**

Taxable year, **62:1, 63:1, 63:30, 63:52A.**

Taxation, **60:43, 61B:1, 62:2, 62B:1, 62B:13, 62C:1, 64H:1, 64I:1, 121A:10.**

Tax expenditures, **29:1.**

Taxidermist, **131:1.**

Taxpayer, **63:1, 64H:1, 64I:1.**
  Low-income housing tax credit, **62:6I.**
  Low-income housing tax credit, corporations, **63:31H.**

Taxpayer's total income.
  Income tax credits.
    Older persons, credit for real estate or rent payments, **62:6.**

TDD/TTY, **166:15E.**

Teacher, **32:1.**

Teacher of transitional bilingual education, **71A:1.**

Teaching or administrative intern, **71:38G.**

Team leader.
  Hazardous materials mitigation, **21K:1.**

Technical assistance, **23D:1, 23F:1, 40H:2.**

Technical terms, how construed, **4:6.**

Ted Williams tunnel.
  Turnpike authority, **81A:3.**

Telecommunications services, **64H:1, 64I:1.**

Telegram, **106:1-201.**

Telephone and telegraph companies, **6A:18A, 106:1-201, 149:1, 166:15E.**

Temporary assistant clerk, **218:1.**

Temporary certificate.
  Teacher certification, **71:38G.**

Temporary clerk, **218:1.**

WORDS AND PHRASES
—Cont'd

Temporary closure, low-level radioactive waste, **111H:1.**
Temporary employment, **140:46N.**
Temporary measure, **21A:19.**
Temporary or transient business, **101:1.**
Temporary substitute, **71:38G.**
Tenant household, **121B:32B-121B:32F.**
Tenement house, **144:2, 145:2.**
Tenure, **41:126.**
Term, **106:1-201.**
Term deposit account, for purposes of Truth-In-Savings law, **140E:1.**
Term endowment, **118G:12.**
Terminal, **90:1.**
Terminated, **106:9-404.**
Termination, **104:7, 106:2-106, 106:2A-103, 151A:71A.**
Termination of employment, **149:183, 149:184.**
Termination of insurance coverage or termination of an insurance policy, **175I:2.**
Terms of the structured settlement.
  Structured settlement contracts, **231C:1.**
Territorial waters, **130:1.**
Territory, **175C:1.**
Testamentary estate, **191B:1.**
Tetrahydrocannabinol, **94C:1.**
Theatre, **93F:1, 143:1.**
Theatrical engagement, **140:180A.**
Thereafter, **144:2, 145:2.**
Thermal hazard, **94B:1.**
Thickly settled or business district, **90:1.**
Thief, **266:40.**
Third class construction, **144:2.**
Third party, **18:5G, 106:1-201, 118E:22.**
Third party payer, **118G:1.**
Third-party vanpool, **63:31D.**
Third party verification.
  Gas and electric companies, **164:1F.**
Threatened species, **131A:1.**
Threat of release, **21A:19.**
  Hazardous materials mitigation, **21K:1.**
Three day player, **231:85P½.**
Threshold amounts, **21I:2.**
Time balance, **255D:1.**
Tipping fee, solid waste facilities, **21H:2.**
Tips, **151A:1.**
Title, **30:45.**

WORDS AND PHRASES
—Cont'd

Titled motorboat, **90B:36.**
Title XI, **112:173.**
Title XIX, **118E:2, 118E:8, 118G:1.**
Title XXI.
  Social security, **118E:8.**
Tobacco action.
  Health care security trust, **29D:1.**
Tobacco product manufacturers.
  Tobacco master settlement agreement, **94E:1.**
Tobin memorial bridge.
  Turnpike authority, **81A:3.**
To fish, **130:1, 131:1.**
To hunt, **131:1.**
Ton, **98:2, 128:64.**
Ton of refrigeration, fire sprinkler system contractors and fitters, **146:81.**
Total deductions, **32:1.**
Total expenditures for all pupils enrolled in regular day programs, **70:2.**
Total facilities grant.
  School building assistance, **70B:2.**
Total foundation staff, **70:2.**
Total income, **62:5.**
Total loss salvage motor vehicle, **90D:1.**
Total patient care charges, **111:70.**
Total patient care costs, **111:70.**
Total receipts, **62:17A, 63:32D.**
Total unemployment, **151A:1.**
Town, **4:7, 44:1, 45:1, 90:34.**
Town clerk.
  Vital statistics, **46:1E.**
Town meeting, annual, **4:7.**
Town officer, **50:1.**
Tow truck dolly, **90:1.**
Tow truck-operator, **90:1.**
Toxic, **21I:2, 94B:1.**
Toxic or hazardous substance, **21I:2, 111F:1.**
Toxics user, **21I:2.**
Toxics use reduction, **21I:2.**
Trace quantity, **111:5R.**
Tract, **57:1.**
Tractor, **90:1.**
Trade, **23D:30, 93A:1.**
Trademark, **110B:1.**
Tradename, **110B:1.**
Trade or business, **62:1.**
Trade school, private, **93:21A.**
Trade screening, **93F:1.**
Trade secret, **21I:2, 93:42, 148:38B, 266:30, 266:60A.**
  Hazardous materials mitigation, **21K:1.**

WORDS AND PHRASES
—Cont'd

Trading stamp, **93:14L.**
Trading stamp company, **93:14L.**
Traffic violation citation, **90C:1.**
Trailer, **90:1.**
Tramps, **272:63.**
Transfer, **109A:2.**
  Structured settlement contracts, **231C:1.**
Transfer agent, **201A:1.**
Transfer agreement.
  Structured settlement contracts, **231C:1.**
Transferee, **65C:15.**
  Structured settlement contracts, **231C:1.**
Transfer of control, **149:183, 149:184.**
Transferor, **203B:1.**
Transfer station, hazardous waste management, **21C:2.**
Transient business, **101:1.**
Transient vendor, **101:1.**
Transition charge, **164:1.**
Transition cost, **164:1.**
Transmission, **164:1, 166:22A.**
Transmission company, **164:1.**
Transmission facility, **164:1.**
Transmission service, **164:1.**
Transmitting utility, **106:9-105.**
Transportation, **159B:2.**
Transportation charges, **30:39B.**
Transportation company, **64C:1.**
Transportation property, **63:1.**
Transporter, **90:1.**
Transport, hazardous waste management, **21C:2.**
Trap, **131:1.**
Travel agent, **93:48B.**
Traveler's check.
  Negotiable instruments, **106:3-104.**
Treason, **264:1.**
Treasurer, **200A:1.**
Treated, **128:84.**
Treatment, **16:18, 21D:1, 111:57A-111:57C.**
Treatment program unit, **111B:3.**
Treatment works, **21:26A.**
Tree and shrub seeds, **128:84.**
Trees, public shade trees, **87:1.**
Trend, **176J:1.**
Tribunal, **209D:1-101.**
Tributary, **92:104.**
Truckman, **130:1.**
Trucks, **255B:1.**
Truck-trailer boat transporter, **90:1.**
Trust, **23D:1, 29C:1, 151D:1, 156:46A.**

WORDS AND PHRASES
—Cont'd

Trust agreement, **29C:1.**
Development finance agency, **23G:1.**
Trust business, **203:4A.**
Trust companies, **172:1, 172:36, 172:38, 201A:1, 203:4A, 203B:1.**
Trust departments, **167G:1.**
Trustee, **23D:1, 151D:1, 191B:1.**
Trustees of health and hospitals, **Spec L 70:2.**
Trust fund, **29:1.**
Trusts and uses, **183:14.**
Tuition agreement, **15C:3.**
Turnpike, **81A:3.**
Turnpike corridor, **81A:3.**
Turnpike revenues, **81A:3.**
Two leading political parties, **50:1.**
Two-thirds vote, **44:1.**
Type, **128:84.**
Ultimate user, **94C:1.**
Unanticipated environmental costs.
Business development office, **23A:60.**
Unauthorized, **106:1-201.**
Unauthorized electronic fund transfer, **167B:1.**
Unauthorized insurer, **175I:2.**
Unauthorized Insurers' Process Act, **175B:6.**
Unauthorized signature.
Negotiable instruments, **106:1-201.**
Unborn child, **112:12K.**
Unbundled rates, **164:1.**
Uncertificated security, **106:8-102.**
Unclaimed funds, **175:149A.**
Unclassified acquirer, **64C:1.**
Unclassified exporter, **64A:1.**
Unclassified importer, **64A:1.**
Underground drinking water source, **21C:2.**
Underground storage tank, **21J:1, 148:38B.**
Underpayment, **65C:13.**
Underpayment, amount, **62B:14.**
Under protest, **106:1-207.**
Under the direct supervision of certified applicator, **132B:2.**
Underwater archeological resources, **6:180.**
Underway, **90B:1.**
Underwrite, **175:177G.**
Underwriting groups or pools, **174A:5.**
Undiluted liquefied petroleum gas installer, **142:1.**
Undue hardship, **151B:4.**

WORDS AND PHRASES
—Cont'd

Unearned premiums, **175:1.**
Uneconomic, **40B:20.**
Unemployed, **151A:1.**
Unemployment, **151A:1.**
Unemployment benefits, worksharing program, **151A:29D.**
Unemployment health insurance contribution wage base.
Employment security, **151A:14G.**
Unemployment insurance taxable wage base, **151A:14.**
Unexpended clean primary election funds.
Clean elections law, **55A:1.**
Unfair educational practices, **151C:1, 151C:2.**
Uniform amount, equivalent, **175:144.**
Uniformed member, **22C:1.**
Uninsured motor vehicle, **175:113L.**
Uninsured patient, **118G:1.**
Union, **157:3, 157:3B.**
Unit, **6:184B, 19D:1.**
United States, **4:7.**
United States branch, **175:161A.**
Unit, governmental unit, **32:1.**
Units sold.
Tobacco master settlement agreement, **94E:1.**
University, **266:89.**
Unlawful assembly, **269:1.**
Unlawful gaming, **4:7.**
Unlawful labor dispute, **149:20C.**
Unlawful practice, **151B:1.**
Unlawful secondary boycott, **149:20C.**
Unless otherwise agreed, **106:1-102, 106:2-303.**
Unlicensed health professional, **12:11L.**
Unlicensed mental health professional, **12:11L.**
Unobligated balance, **21J:1.**
Unprofessional conduct, **112:19.**
Unprotected exposure capable of transmitting an infectious disease dangerous to public health, **111:111C.**
Unreasonable adverse effects on environment, **132B:2.**
Unreasonable and oppressive wage, **151:1, 151:2.**
Unregistered motor vehicle repair shop, **100A:1.**
Unrestricted gifts, **118G:12.**
Unrestricted income from endowment funds, **118G:12.**

WORDS AND PHRASES
—Cont'd

Unstable drug, **94:187.**
Upholstered furniture, **94:270.**
Upholstery jobber, **94:270.**
Urban area, **93D:1, 175C:1.**
Urban renewal plan, **121B:1.**
Urban revitalization and development project, **121B:1.**
Usable space, **166:25A.**
Usage of trade, **106:1-205.**
Use, consumption, or storage tax, **64H:1, 64I:1, 64I:17, 64I:27.**
Used, **94:270.**
Used material, **94:270.**
Use of a service, **64H:1.**
User of special fuels, **64E:1.**
Users, **93:50, 21A:18, 21A:18A.**
Development finance agency, **23G:1.**
User segment, **21I:2.**
User-seller, **64E:1.**
Uses, **64E:1, 64I:1.**
Conveyancing, **183:14.**
Using agency, **7:39A.**
Utility, **166:22A, 166:25A.**
Utility corporation, **63:52A.**
Utility systems projects, **7:39A.**
Utilization facility, **6:85.**
Utterer of counterfeit money, **267:11, 267:19.**
Vacant public land, **20:13.**
Vagabonds, **272:68.**
Vagrants, **272:66.**
Valid lien, **109A:2.**
Valuation, **4:7, 4:132A:6.**
Valuation percentage, **70:2.**
Value, **106:1-201.**
Vanpool, **63:31D.**
Vapor, harmful, **94B:1.**
Variable annuity contract, **175:1.**
Variety (cultivar), **128:84.**
Variety unknown, **94:102.**
Vegetable seeds, **128:84.**
Vehicle identification number.
Motor vehicle emissions, **111:142M.**
Vending machine, **94:308.**
Vending machine operator, **64C:1.**
Vendor, **64H:1, 64I:1.**
Vertical market power, **164:1.**
Vessel, **21A:19.**
Hazardous materials mitigation, **21K:1.**
Vessel, label and trademarks law, **110:1.**
Veteran, **4:7, 22C:1, 32:1.**
Annuities to certain paraplegic veterans, **115:6A.**
Veterans' agent, **115:1.**
Veterinarian, **112:54A.**

WORDS AND PHRASES
—Cont'd

Veterinary medicine, practice, **112:54A, 112:58.**

Viatical loan borrower.
Viatical settlements, **175:213.**

Viatical loan broker.
Viatical settlements, **175:213.**

Viatical loan contract.
Viatical settlements, **175:213.**

Viatical loan provider.
Viatical settlements, **175:213.**

Viatical loan representative.
Viatical settlements, **175:213.**

Viatical settlement broker.
Viatical settlements, **175:213.**

Viatical settlement contract.
Viatical settlements, **175:213.**

Viatical settlement provider.
Viatical settlements, **175:213.**

Viatical settlement representative.
Viatical settlements, **175:213.**

Viaticated policy.
Viatical settlements, **175:213.**

Viator.
Viatical settlements, **175:213.**

Victim, **6:116A, 127:1, 233:20J, 258C:1.**
Identity fraud, **266:37E.**
Rights of victims and witnesses of crime, **258B:1.**

Victim-witness advocate.
Rights of victims and witnesses of crime, **258B:1.**

Vietnam veteran, **4:7.**

VIN.
Motor vehicle emissions, **111:142M.**

Vinegar, **94:163.**

Violator, **90C:1.**

Violent crime.
Firearms possession violations, **269:10G.**
Gun control, **140:121.**

Visible, **90B:5.**

Visual material, **272:31.**

Vocational education, **74:1.**

Vocational enrollment, **70:2.**

Vocational home economics, **74:1.**

Vocational rehabilitation services, **6:77.**

Vocational-technical education, **74:1.**

Vocational training institutions, **151C:1.**

Volume minimization, low-level radioactive waste, **111H:1.**

Vote, majority, **44:1.**

Voting power, **23D:1.**

Voting security, **175:206.**

Voting stock, **110F:3.**
Insurance, reorganization of mutual insurers, **175:19G.**

WORDS AND PHRASES
—Cont'd

Voting tabulation districts or VTD, **57:1.**

VTD, **57:1.**

Vulnerable populations, **Spec L 70:2.**

WAAC defined, **4:7.**

Wage adjustment factor, **70:2.**

Wages, **62B:1, 62E:1, 118C:2, 151:2, 151A:1, 151A:6, 151A:14.**
Employment security, unemployment health insurance contribution, **151A:14G.**

Waiting period, **176J:1.**

Waivable fee, **15A:29.**

War, **41:105.**

Warden, fish and game division, **131:1.**

Warehouseman, **105:1, 106:7-102.**

Warehouse receipt, **106:1-201.**

Ware River watershed advisory committee, **92:104.**

Warning, **94B:1.**

Warning sign, **166:21F.**

Warrant, **106:2-313.**

Warranty covenants, **183:10, 183:16.**

Warranty provisions of used motor vehicles, **90:7N¼.**

Wartime service, **4:7, 31:1.**

Waste disposal facilities, **40D:1.**

Waste, hazardous waste management, **21C:2.**

Waste management area, low-level radioactive waste, **111H:1.**

Waste site cleanup activity opinion, **21A:19.**

Watch, guard or patrol agency, **147:22.**

Water companies, **165:1.**

Water district, **4:7.**

Water heater, **25B:2.**

Water pollution abatement project, **29C:1.**

Waters, **21:26A, 130:1, 131:1.**

Watersheds, **92:104.**

Watershed system, **92:104.**

Waters of the Commonwealth, **21:26A, 90B:1.**

Water works system, **40N:3.**

Way or ways, **89:8, 90:1.**

Weapon.
Gun control, **140:121.**

Weeds, **132B:2.**

Weed seeds, **128:84.**

Week, **151A:1.**

Weekly compensation, **149:183, 149:184.**

WORDS AND PHRASES
—Cont'd

Weekly wage, **151A:1, 152:1.**

Weighing device, **98:1.**

Weighted full-time equivalent pupil, **70:2.**

Weight, sale, **94:176.**

Wet meadows, **131:40.**

When he deems himself insecure, **106:1-208.**

White bread, **94:1.**

Whoever, **4:7.**

Wholesale dealer, **130:1.**

Wholesale generation company, **164:1.**

Wholesaler, **25A:3, 64C:1, 64C:13, 93:14E, 93B:1.**

Wholesale, sales, **64C:13, 93:14E.**

Wholly-owned DISC, **63:30.**

Wildlife, **132B:2.**
Research and management bureau, **21:7H.**

Will, **4:7.**

Winegrower, **138:1.**

Wines, **138:1.**

Wire communications, **272:99.**

With all faults, **106:2-316.**

Withdrawal, **21A:18, 21A:18A.**

Withholding exemption and deduction certificate, **62B:4.**

Withholding tax on wages, **62B:1.**

Without prejudice, **106:1-207.**

Witness.
Rights of victims and witnesses of crime, **258B:1.**

Witnesses with mental retardation, **233:23E.**

Women-owned business, **7:40C, 7:40N.**

Wooden building, **145:2.**

Woodlands, fish and game division, **131:1.**

Workers' compensation, **152:1, 152:14A.**

Workers' compensation, self-insurance, **152:25E.**

Workmen, **30:50.**

Work of art, **6:20.**

Worksharing benefits, **151A:29D.**

Worksharing employer, **151A:29D.**

Workshop, **6:77, 149:1.**

Works, iron, **149:1.**

Works of improvement, **21:9.**

Work week, regular, **32A:2.**

World War I veteran, **4:7.**

World War II veteran, **4:7.**

Writing, **4:7, 106:1-201, 111:70F.**

Written, **4:7, 106:1-201.**

Written acceptance, **50:1.**

Written prescription, **94:187, 94C:1.**

WORDS AND PHRASES
—Cont'd
Written report.
Abuse or neglect of patients in long-term care facilities, **111:72G.**
X and Y co-ordinates, **97:10.**
Yard, **144:2, 145:2.**
Year, **4:7.**
Year of manufacture, **60A:1.**
Year of service, **30:46, 149:183, 149:184.**
Youthful offender, **119:52.**
Zero power costs, **164:94G.**
Zoning, **40A:1A.**
Zoning administrator, **40A:1A.**
Zoning ordinance or bylaw, **121A:1.**

WORK AND LABOR, 149:1 et seq.
See LABOR AND WORKFORCE DEVELOPMENT.

WORK CLOTHES.
See WEARING APPAREL.

WORKERS' COMPENSATION, 152:1-152:75A.
Acceptance of payment by employees, releasing employer from liability, **152:23.**
Accident and sickness insurance.
Applicability of laws as to accident and sickness insurance, **175:108.**
Effect on accident and sickness insurance, **175:108.**
Lien of insurer against lump sum settlement or award where policy contains exclusion, **152:46A.**
Actions.
Public employees, recovery of compensation paid, **152:73.**
Retirement board, action on behalf of beneficiary, **152:73.**
Third person causing injury, action against.
Third person. See within this heading, "Third person."
Additional payments.
Increased compensation, **152:35B.**
Administrative judge or justice, **152:5, 152:9A, 152:11 et seq.**
Administrators.
Executors and administrators. See within this heading, "Executors and administrators."
Admissibility of evidence.
Evidence. See within this heading, "Evidence."

WORKERS' COMPENSATION
—Cont'd
Agents.
Commission fees to agents or brokers, **152:53A.**
Enforcement of workers' compensation payment provisions, designation, powers and duties of agents **152:75.**
Insurance agents or brokers designated by employers assigned to insurer, rights, **152:65O.**
Age of young employee as affecting, **152:51.**
Agreements.
Contracts and agreements. See within this heading, "Contracts and agreements."
Agricultural laborers, **152:1.**
Aircraft financial responsibility act, **90:49E.**
Amendments of law, substantive and procedural, **152:2A.**
Amusements, licensing prerequisites, **140:181.**
Ankle, severance of foot above, **152:36.**
Annual reports and statements, litigation expenses incurred by workers' compensation insurers **175:25A.**
Appeal and review.
Board of review.
Reviewing boards. See within this heading, "Reviewing boards."
Boston municipal court, **152:11.**
Certification of question of law, **152:11.**
Commissioner of insurance. See within this heading, "Commissioner of insurance."
Costs of action. See within this heading, "Costs of action."
Decisions of board or division not suspended, **152:17.**
Deposit with state treasurer, review of orders, **152:60A.**
Dispute procedures, **152:11B et seq.**
Enforcement of orders pending appeal, **152:12.**
Expenses. See within this heading, "Expenses."
Findings on questions of fact as conclusive, **152:11.**
Hearings on appeal, **152:11.**
Industrial accidents reviewing board, **152:11, 152:11C.**

WORKERS' COMPENSATION
—Cont'd
Appeal and review —Cont'd
Insurance.
Commissioner.
Commissioner of insurance. See within this heading, "Commissioner of insurance."
Payment by insurer of expenses, **152:10.**
Interest on amount in question in appeal cases, **152:50.**
Municipal court of Boston, **152:11.**
Powers of superior court and municipal court of Boston, **152:11.**
Premiums for rejected risk policy, appeal on grounds of unreasonableness, **152:65K.**
Printing expenses, **152:11, 152:11A, 152:65.**
Rating organizations. See within this heading, "Rating organizations."
Rejected risk policy, **152:65A.**
Cancellation, **152:65B.**
Orders or rulings, **152:65M.**
Premiums, appeal on grounds of unreasonableness, **152:65K.**
Retirement board, appeals, **152:73.**
Reversal on appeal, **152:17.**
Reviewing boards. See within this heading, "Reviewing boards."
Safety rules and regulations of insured parties aggrieved, **152:64.**
Self-insurer's appeal from decision revoking license, **152:25A.**
Superior court, **152:11.**
Supreme judicial court, **152:60A.**
Suspension or modification of decrees or orders during pendency, **152:17.**
Transcript of evidence, **152:8.**
Transfer of cases to and from supreme judicial court, **211:4A.**
Applications, self-insurance group, **152:25G.**
Apportionment.
Death benefits, **152:31.**
For injury in concurrent service of two or more employers, **152:26B.**
Appropriations, cities and towns, **40:5, 40:13A.**

WORKERS' COMPENSATION
—Cont'd

Arbitration of disputes, **152:10B.**

Armed forces.

Military service. See within this heading, "Military service."

Arm, payment for loss, **152:36.**

Arrest warrant or default outstanding.

Suspension of benefits, **152:7.**

Artificial eyes or limbs, furnishing, **152:30.**

Assessments, **26:8E, 152:65.**

Assigned risk pool, **152:65A et seq.**

Amendments, **152:65C.**

Appeal to commissioner, **152:65A.**

Losses incurred, **152:65G, 152:65H.**

Reinsurance pool established, **152:65C.**

Rejected risks, assigning and pooling of. See within this heading, "Rejected risks, assigning and pooling."

Assignment.

Bonds deposited with state treasurer, prohibited, **152:25A.**

Payments of compensation, **152:47.**

Public assistance to poor persons, assignment of benefit payments in reimbursement, **118:11.**

Association as employer, **152:1.**

Assumption of risk as defense, **152:66, 152:67.**

Athletes, professional, **152:1.**

Atomic energy, studies and recommendations of industrial accidents division, **6:91.**

Attachment, exemption from.

Exemption from attachment, execution, etc. See within this heading, "Exemption from attachment, execution, etc."

Attorney General.

Claims for deposit or reimbursement, payment of expense of prosecution or defense, **152:65.**

Defending claims against workers' compensation fund, **152:37.**

Division and board of industrial accidents. See within this heading, "Division and board of industrial accidents."

WORKERS' COMPENSATION
—Cont'd

Attorney General —Cont'd

Representation of industrial accident board, **152:11.**

Attorneys.

Attorney General. See within this heading, "Attorney General."

Dispute resolution division, representation before, **152:7C.**

Fees.

Counsel fees. See within this heading, "Counsel fees."

Insurance commissioner appointed as attorney, **152:25G.**

Attorneys' fees.

Counsel fees. See within this heading, "Counsel fees."

Authorized insurance carriers and premium regulation, **152:53A.**

Automobiles.

Motor vehicles. See within this heading, "Motor vehicles."

Average weekly wages.

Agreement for compensation, questioning wages, **152:6.**

Defined, **152:1.**

Determination, **152:1.**

Bankruptcy and insolvency, **152:25K, 152:25R, 152:52B, 175:46A.**

Bidding on contract, cost advantages achieved by avoiding payment of compensation premiums, **152:25C.**

Bodily disfigurement, compensation, **152:36.**

Bonds.

Deposited by self-insurer, **152:25A.**

Foreign insurance company's bond, **152:61.**

Self insurance group, **152:25G.**

Books and records.

Records and recording. See within this heading, "Records and recording."

Boston municipal court, appeals to.

Appeal and review. See within this heading, "Appeal and review."

Briefs, costs, **152:11-152:11C, 152:65.**

Bringing employees within coverage of law, **152:25B.**

Brokers.

Agents. See within this heading, "Agents."

WORKERS' COMPENSATION
—Cont'd

Brothers, payment of balance of compensation, **152:36A.**

Bulk sum.

Payment of compensation. See within this heading, "Payment of compensation."

Burden of proof.

Presumptions and burden of proof. See within this heading, "Presumptions and burden of proof."

Business trust as employer, **152:1.**

Cadet engineers as municipal employees for purpose, **164:69E.**

Cancellation.

Contracts and agreements. See within this heading, "Contracts and agreements."

Mid-term notice of cancellation of policy, **152:55A.**

Payments, termination or modification, **152:8.**

Rejected risk policy, **152:65B.**

Self-insurance groups, **152:25H, 152:25K, 152:25U.**

Termination of disability. See within this heading, "Termination of disability."

Cause of injury.

Presumptions, **152:7A.**

Statement in claim, **152:49.**

Cease and desist orders, self-insurance groups, **152:25T.**

Certificates and certification.

Insurer's qualification, certificate, **152:60C.**

Question of law, effect of certification, **152:11.**

Self-insurance, certificate of approval, **152:25E-152:25H, 152:25K, 152:25U.**

Charges compensable under workers' compensation, establishment, **152:13.**

Charitable institutions, **152:1.**

Children.

Minors. See within this heading, "Minors."

Chiropractors, services rendered, **112:97.**

City or town.

Charges for insurance funds, payment, **40:13A.**

Employees.

Public employees. See within this heading, "Public employees."

WORKERS' COMPENSATION
—Cont'd
City or town —Cont'd
  Motor vehicle, wrongful death
    action arising out of
    municipality's operation,
    260:4.
  Reserve funds, **40:13C.**
  Treasurer, payment of
    compensation, **114:19,**
    152:70.
Civil rights and discrimination.
  Discrimination. See within this
    heading, "Discrimination."
Claims for compensation.
  Contents, **152:49.**
  Insolvent domestic insurance
    companies, preference or
    compensation claims
    against, **175:46A.**
  Limitation of time. See within
    this heading, "Limitation of
    time."
  Notice. See within this heading,
    "Notice."
  Place of injury to be stated,
    152:49.
  Priority, **152:52B, 175:46A.**
  Release of employer from
    liability by filing, **152:23.**
  Reserves for claims,
    computation, **175:12,**
    175:12A.
  Signing, **152:49.**
  Value of outstanding claims,
    computation, **152:58.**
Claims of creditors, exemption
  from.
  Exemption from attachment,
    execution, etc. See within
    this heading, "Exemption
    from attachment, execution,
    etc."
Co-employee's activities, injuries,
    152:26, 152:26B, 152:27,
    152:66, 152:67.
Collective bargaining agreements
  establishing workers'
  compensation procedures
  152:10C.
Combination policies of several
  insurers, **152:56.**
Commerce.
  Foreign commerce. See within
    this heading, "Foreign
    commerce."
Commissioner of insurance.
  Appeals, **152:65A.**
  From opinion of commissioner
    on insurance policy,
    152:55.

WORKERS' COMPENSATION
—Cont'd
Commissioner of insurance
—Cont'd
  Appeals —Cont'd
    From orders and decisions of
      commissioner, **152:52F.**
    From rating organizations'
      actions, **152:52D.**
    From unreasonable premiums
      of rejected risk policy,
      152:65K.
  Assigned risk pool. See within
    this heading, "Assigned risk
    pool."
  Attorney, insurance
    commissioner appointed,
    152:25G.
  Deposits with state treasurer.
    See within this heading,
    "Deposits with state
    treasurer."
  Foreign insurance company's
    bond, approval, **152:61.**
  Policy, approval, **152:55.**
  Rating organizations.
    Appeal to commissioner from
      actions, **152:52D.**
    Assigned risk pool, **152:65A,**
      152:65C.
    Examination, **152:52C.**
    Review of co-operative
      activities of rating
      organizations and
      insurers, **152:52C.**
    Rules and regulations,
      152:52C.
    Reinsurance pool's rules and
      regulations, approval,
      152:65H.
  Self-insurance, **152:25G,**
    152:25I.
  Service of process, **152:25G.**
  Value of outstanding claims,
    computation, **152:58.**
Common law.
  Defenses abolished, **152:66,**
    152:67.
  Liability of employer, insuring
    against, **152:54A.**
  Notice of retention by employee,
    152:24.
  Release by compensation claim,
    152:23.
  Waiver.
    By employee, **152:24.**
    By public employee, **152:72.**
Commonwealth employees.
  Public employees. See within
    this heading, "Public
    employees."

WORKERS' COMPENSATION
—Cont'd
Commonwealth Service Corps,
  eligibility of personnel, **6:121.**
Compensable fees under workers'
  compensation, establishment,
  152:13.
Complaints against employers
  failing to provide, **152:25C.**
Compulsory compensation,
  152:25A-152:25D.
Conferences, **152:10A, 152:10B.**
Consequential damages, right of
  action, **152:66.**
Conservator.
  Guardian. See within this
    heading, "Guardian."
Construction work.
  Contractors. See within this
    heading, "Contractors."
Contagious disease as personal
  injury, **152:1.**
Contractors.
  Independent contractors,
    liability of. See within this
    heading, "Independent
    contractors, liability."
  Reserve or special police
    employed, **152:1.**
  Subcontractor. See within this
    heading, "Subcontractor."
Contracts and agreements, **152:19,**
  152:25A et seq.
  Cancellation, notice required,
    149:34A, 152:22, 152:65B.
  Affidavit, prima facie evidence
    of sending notice,
    149:34A.
  Collective bargaining
    agreements establishing
    workers' compensation
    procedures **152:10C.**
  Compensation, insurer's
    agreements, **152:6, 152:7.**
  Division and board of industrial
    accidents, filing of
    compensation contracts,
    152:6.
  Evidence of notice of
    cancellation of insurance,
    affidavit, **149:34A.**
  General and special employers,
    effect of agreement between
    as to liability for
    compensation of employees,
    152:18.
  Insurer's agreement as excusing
    failure to make claim,
    152:49.
  Insuring employer but not
    insuring payment of
    compensation, void,
    152:54A.

WORKERS' COMPENSATION
—Cont'd
Contracts and agreements
—Cont'd
Settlement of actions against
third party by agreement,
152:15.
Vocational rehabilitation
services, **152:30E, 152:30H.**
Waiving right to compensation,
prohibition against, **152:46.**
Contributory negligence as
defense, **152:66, 152:67.**
Controversy or dispute, **152:10A et
seq.**
Attorney representation at
workers' compensation
proceedings, **152:7C,
152:10A et seq.**
Dispute resolution division. See
within this heading,
"Dispute resolution
division."
Senior judge responsible for
operation, **23E:3, 23E:6.**
Co-operation among rating
organizations or insurers
authorized, **152:52C.**
Copies.
Appeal, clerk of court to forward
copy of judgment to
industrial accidents division,
152:11.
Medical report, copy furnished
to claimant, **152:20A.**
Written transcript of statement,
copy furnished to claimant,
152:7B.
Corporations.
Applicability of law, **152:1.**
Liability of corporate officers for
failure to provide
compensations, **152:25C.**
Correctional institutions,
application, **152:74.**
Costs of action.
Annual reports of expenses
incurred by insurers,
175:25A.
Appeals, **152:11-152:11B,
152:12A, 152:65.**
Counsel fees. See within this
heading, "Counsel fees."
Discontinuance of compensation,
insurer's proceedings,
152:12A, 152:34A.
Fraud claims, **152:53A.**
Frivolous proceedings, **152:14.**
Hearings, payment of cost by
insurer, **152:10.**
Insurer's liability,
152:10-152:14.

WORKERS' COMPENSATION
—Cont'd
Costs of action —Cont'd
Offer to pay compensation,
152:10.
Counsel fees.
Appeal, expenses, **152:12A.**
Apportionment in ratio of
amounts received in action
against third party, **152:15.**
Approval, **152:13.**
Assessment, **152:10.**
Costs on appeal, **152:12A.**
Decedent's estate, services,
152:39.
Deduction, **152:2A.**
Discontinuing compensation,
allowance to claimant in
proceedings, **152:12A.**
Frivolous proceedings, **152:14.**
Guardianship matters, services,
152:39.
Insurer's contest of claim,
152:13A.
Record of, by department,
152:7F.
Total and permanent incapacity,
hearing to discontinue
compensation, **152:34A.**
County employees.
Public employees. See within
this heading, "Public
employees."
County tuberculosis hospital
district employees.
Public employees. See within
this heading, "Public
employees."
Covering employees not covered by
law, **152:25B.**
Co-workers' activities, injury,
**152:26, 152:26B, 152:27,
152:66, 152:67.**
Creditors' claims, exemption from.
Exemption from attachment,
execution, etc. See within
this heading, "Exemption
from attachment, execution,
etc."
Date.
Time. See within this heading,
"Time."
Deafness, compensation, **152:36.**
Death, **152:31.**
Balance due after death of
injured employee, payment,
152:36A.
Employer's negligence causing,
law applicable, **152:68.**
Executors and administrators.
See within this heading,
"Executors and
administrators."

WORKERS' COMPENSATION
—Cont'd
Death —Cont'd
Funeral expenses, payment,
152:33.
Legal expenses, payment,
152:39.
Limitation of time for claiming,
152:41.
Filing petition for rehearings
as to cause of death,
152:12.
Medical examiners, duties in
case of death, **38:6, 38:7.**
Motor vehicle, wrongful death
action arising out of
municipality's operation,
260:4.
Presumptions, **152:7A, 152:32.**
Prima facie evidence of
compensability of claim,
employee's death at place of
employment, **152:7A.**
Special fund, **152:65.**
Willful misconduct,
compensation for death,
152:27.
Suicide. See within this heading,
"Suicide."
Widows and children of
employees, benefits payable,
152:31.
Full-time students over 18,
extension of benefits,
152:31.
Posthumous children as
dependents, **152:32,
152:35A.**
Presumptions, **152:32,
152:35A.**
Separated wife as dependent,
152:32.
Suicide, effect on dependents'
right to recover, **152:26A.**
Time of death, determination
of dependency as to time,
152:31, 152:32.
Willful misconduct resulting in
death, compensation,
152:27.
Debts, exemption from liability for.
Exemption from attachment,
execution, etc. See within
this heading, "Exemption
from attachment, execution,
etc."
Decisions of industrial accidents
division or board.
Division and board of industrial
accidents. See within this
heading, "Division and
board of industrial
accidents."

WORKERS' COMPENSATION
—Cont'd

Decrees.
  Judgments, decrees, and orders.
    See within this heading,
    "Judgments, decrees, and
    orders."
Deductions.
  From award where two or more
    insurers liable, **152:15A.**
  Optional endorsements by
    insurer, **152:25A.**
  Savings or insurance of injured
    employee, **152:38.**
Defenses to actions for injuries of
  employees, **152:66, 152:67.**
Definitions, **152:1, 152:14A,
  152:25E.**
Dental service corporation,
  liability, **176E:14.**
Department of industrial
  accidents.
  Division and board of industrial
    accidents. See within this
    heading, "Division and
    board of industrial
    accidents."
Dependents.
  Additional compensation,
    152:35A.
  Apportionment of award
    between, **152:31.**
  Attachment of property to
    satisfy support obligations,
    152:47.
  Balance of lump sum
    compensation payable,
    152:36A.
  Children.
    Minors. See within this
      heading, "Minors."
  Death payments, **152:31.**
  Defined under workers'
    compensation law, **152:1.**
  Full-time students over 18,
    extension of dependents'
    benefits, **152:35A.**
  Incompetent minor children,
    152:31.
  Increasing benefits payable,
    152:31, 152:35A.
  Minors. See within this heading,
    "Minors."
  Partially dependent survivors,
    benefit payments, **152:31.**
  Posthumous children, **152:32,
    152:35A.**
  Presumption as to who are,
    152:32, 152:35A.
  Special fund in absence,
    152:36A.

WORKERS' COMPENSATION
—Cont'd

Dependents —Cont'd
  Suicide of employee,
    compensation, **152:26A.**
  Surviving spouse.
    Death. See within this
      heading, "Death."
  Time of death, determination,
    152:31, 152:32.
  Willful misconduct resulting in
    death, compensation,
    152:27.
Depositions.
  Fees, **152:5, 152:9A.**
  Physicians. See within this
    heading, "Physicians."
  Promulgation of rules, **152:11B.**
  Taking of, **152:5.**
  Trust fund, payment of costs,
    152:65.
Deposits with state treasurer.
  Computation of value of claims,
    152:58.
  Duties of state treasurer,
    152:59.
  Expenses of custody, **152:60B.**
  Foreign insurance company
    ceasing to do business,
    152:62.
  Insurance commissioner's order
    requiring, **152:57.**
    Failure to comply, **152:60C,
      152:60D.**
    Filing copy, **152:57.**
    Review, **152:60A.**
  Insurance companies' deposits in
    respect to outstanding
    claims, **152:57-152:60D.**
  License revocation for failure to
    comply with orders,
    152:60C.
  Penalty for failure to comply
    with orders, **152:60C,
    152:60D.**
  Receiver, effect of appointment,
    152:60.
  Reduction of amount by court
    order, **152:60A.**
  Revocation of license for failure
    to comply with orders,
    152:60C.
  Self-insurance, securities,
    152:25A.
    Return of to self-insurer,
      152:25A.
  Special fund, **152:65.**
  Trustee, transfer of deposits,
    152:59.
  Value, deposit, **152:57.**

WORKERS' COMPENSATION
—Cont'd

Disability.
  Incapacity or disability as to
    payment of compensation,
    152:29.
Discharge or release from liability.
  Release. See within this
    heading, "Release."
Discontinuance of action.
  Dismissal and nonsuit. See
    within this heading,
    "Dismissal and nonsuit."
Discontinuance of payments,
  152:29, 152:34A.
  Costs in proceedings, **152:12A,
    152:34A.**
  Documents to be furnished to
    employee before, **152:29.**
  Examinations. See within this
    heading, "Examinations,
    inspections, and
    investigations."
  Hearings in circumstances of
    permanent, total incapacity,
    152:34A.
Discrimination.
  Rating organization subscribers,
    152:52C.
  Rejected risk policy, appeal from
    discriminatory premiums,
    152:65K.
Disease as personal injury, **152:1.**
Disfigurement, compensation,
  152:36.
Dismissal and nonsuit.
  Notice of claim after
    discontinuance of
    third-party action, **152:41.**
  Third person, discontinuance of
    action against, **152:15.**
Dispute.
  Controversy or dispute. See
    within this heading,
    "Controversy or dispute."
Dispute resolution division, **152:10
  et seq.**
  Attorney representation before,
    152:7C.
  Referral of claim, **152:10,
    152:10A.**
Distribution of losses among
  insurers, **152:65C.**
District employees.
  Public employees. See within
    this heading, "Public
    employees."
Dividends, classification or rate
  containing provisions,
  152:53A.

WORKERS' COMPENSATION
—Cont'd
Division and board of industrial
accidents, **152:1**
et seq.
  Advisory council, **23E:6,**
  23E:15-23E:17.
  Agents furnishing benefits to
  public employees,
  supervision, **152:75.**
  Agreement for compensation,
  filing with and approval of
  board, **152:6.**
  Appeal and review, **152:11,**
  152:11C.
  Atomic energy, studies and
  recommendations,
  6:91.
  Attorney general,
  representation, **152:11.**
  Cities and towns, payment of
  certain awards approved by
  division, **44:31.**
  Clerk of court to forward
  copy of judgment,
  152:11.
  Complaint against employers
  failing to provide
  compensation, **152:25C.**
  Confidential secretary,
  30:7.
  Contracts as to compensation,
  filing with and approval by
  board, **152:6.**
  Decisions of division or
  reviewing boards thereof.
  Enforcement, **152:16.**
  Not suspended by appeal,
  152:17.
  Presentation of certified copies
  of to courts for decree,
  152:11.
  Defined under workers'
  compensation law,
  152:1.
  Dependency, finding as to status,
  152:32.
  Depositions of medical
  witnesses, taking,
  152:5.
  Examinations, inspections, and
  investigations. See within
  this heading,
  "Examinations, inspections,
  and investigations."
  Fees, **152:13.**
  Hearings. See within this
  heading, "Hearings."
  Hospital and medical records,
  inspection, **152:20.**
  Information by insurance
  companies on request,
  152:63.

WORKERS' COMPENSATION
—Cont'd
Division and board of industrial
accidents —Cont'd
  Introduction in evidence in
  proceedings before
  industrial accident board of
  medical reports of
  incapacitated, disabled, or
  deceased physician who
  attended or examined the
  plaintiff, **152:20B.**
  Labor and workforce
  development department.
  Laser equipment, effect of
  health department's
  authority to regulate use,
  111:5I.
  Reports as to occupational
  diseases, department to
  furnish to division,
  149:11.
  Licensing of self-insurers,
  152:25A.
  Lien on lump sum settlement,
  division or single member to
  determine fair and
  reasonable amount for
  discharge, **152:46A.**
  Lump sums in lieu of weekly
  payments, approval,
  152:48.
  Medical bills of workers,
  payment by insurance,
  152:7.
  Medical examiner's report of
  death, **38:7.**
  Medical witnesses, taking
  depositions, **152:5.**
  Notice. See within this heading,
  "Notice."
  Occupational or industrial
  diseases, reports to division,
  149:11.
  Order of member.
  Hearing on failure to reach
  agreement regarding
  compensation, order
  resulting, **152:7.**
  Supreme judicial court's
  modification of order
  pending review,
  152:17.
  Party to review proceedings,
  board, **152:11.**
  Payment of compensation to
  certain state employees
  injured in state service,
  30:58.
  Physicians, report as to
  industrial diseases, **149:11.**
  Industrial diseases, report,
  149:11.

WORKERS' COMPENSATION
—Cont'd
Division and board of industrial
accidents —Cont'd
  Powers and duties, **152:2.**
  Promulgation of regulations
  concerning, **152:5.**
  Records and recording.
    Access, **152:5.**
    Copy of notice of insurance
    coverage, **152:22.**
    Findings and ruling of
    member holding hearing,
    152:8.
  Name and address of agents
  furnishing benefits to
  public employees,
  152:75.
  Reports. See within this
  heading, "Reports."
  Rehabilitation board. See within
  this heading, "Rehabilitation
  board."
  Rehabilitation commission for
  vocational training of
  handicapped persons, **6:76,**
  6:81.
  Reports. See within this
  heading, "Reports."
  Retired members, recalled for
  temporary service,
  32:91.
  Rules, authority, **152:5.**
  Secretary, **30:7.**
  Single member.
    Decisions of single member,
    presentation of certified
    copies to courts for decree,
    152:11.
    Hearings. See within this
    heading, "Hearings."
  Third parties, settlement by
  agreement of actions
  against, presiding judge to
  exercise powers of board,
  152:15.
Wages.
  See WAGES, SALARIES, AND
  COMPENSATION.
Witnesses. See within this
heading, "Witnesses."
Doctors.
  Physicians. See within this
  heading, "Physicians."
Domestic servants, **152:1.**
  Defenses in actions for
  injuries to part-time
  domestic servants,
  152:67.

WORKERS' COMPENSATION
—Cont'd
Double compensation for willful misconduct by employer, **152:28.**
Ears, loss of hearing, compensation, **152:36.**
Educational institutions, **152:1, 152:69.**
    See SCHOOLS AND EDUCATION.
Elderly persons, partial incapacity, **152:35E.**
Elder service corpsmen, exemption, **19A:13.**
Election.
    Employers.
        Classifications of employees, **152:1.**
        Non-negligence as defense, **152:67.**
        Insurer, optional deductibles offered, **152:25A.**
    Public employees' election as to pension or workers' compensation, **152:73.**
Electrical company or governmental unit furnishing aid to other such company or unit, reimbursement for workers' compensation expenses for employees, **152:74A.**
Electronic recording, taking evidence with aid, **152:8.**
Emotional or mental disability.
    Mental condition or capacity. See within this heading, "Mental condition or capacity."
Employee defined, **152:1.**
Employee leasing company defined, **152:14A.**
Employer defined, **152:1.**
Employers' Liability Act not applicable to employees, **152:68.**
Employment and training division in labor and workforce department, **152:1, 152:30I, 152:31.**
Employment security as affected, **151A:25.**
Enforcement.
    Decisions of division, **152:16.**
    Orders, **152:12, 152:12A, 152:17.**
    Provisions of law, designation, powers, and duties of agents to enforce, **152:75.**
Entry.
    Investigations, entry, **152:2.**

WORKERS' COMPENSATION
—Cont'd
Entry —Cont'd
    Safety rules, entry to enforce, **152:64.**
Evidence.
    Admissibility, **152:7B.**
    Board proceedings, **152:11B.**
    Cancellation of insurance, affidavit of sending notice, **149:34A.**
    Death of employee at place of employment as prima facie evidence of applicability of Act, **152:7A.**
    Hospital records, **152:20, 152:20A.**
    Industrial accident board, introduction in evidence of medical reports of incapacitated, disabled, or deceased physicians who attended or examined plaintiff, **152:20B.**
    Physician's report, **152:20A, 152:20B.**
    Presumptions and burden of proof. See within this heading, "Presumptions and burden of proof."
    Statements of employees, **152:7B.**
    Transcription, **152:8.**
    Witnesses. See within this heading, "Witnesses."
Examinations, inspections, and investigations, **152:2.**
    Administration division, **23E:3.**
    Division of industrial accidents, investigations by, **152:2.**
    Injured employee, examination.
        Discontinuance of compensation.
            For failure to report for examination, **152:29.**
            Report of examination in support, **152:29.**
        Furnishing copies of reports, **152:20A.**
        Impartial physicians.
            Appointment of additional physician in absence, **152:9A.**
        Insurer's physician, **152:45.**
        Procedure, **152:9A.**
        Public employee, **152:69B.**
        Refusal to submit to, **152:45.**
        Reimbursement for travel expense and loss of wages, **152:45.**
        Reports. See within this heading, "Reports."

WORKERS' COMPENSATION
—Cont'd
Examinations, inspections, and investigations —Cont'd
    Injured employee, examination —Cont'd
        Yearly physical examination for hospitalized employee, **152:30.**
    Insurer under rejected risk policy, inspection of risks, **152:65J.**
    Rating organizations, **152:52C.**
    Records, **152:5, 152:20, 152:25I.**
    Safety rules, inspectors for enforcement, **152:64.**
    Single member of division, investigations, **152:8.**
Excess recovery against third party, disposition, **152:15.**
Exclusion relative to sales person affiliated with real estate broker, **152:1.**
Execution.
    Exemption from attachment, execution, etc. See within this heading, "Exemption from attachment, execution, etc."
Executors and administrators.
    Appointment, payment of expenses, **152:39.**
    As employers, **152:1.**
    Death benefits, payment, **152:39.**
    Signing notice of claim for compensation, **152:42.**
Exemption from attachment, execution, etc., **152:1.**
    Compensation payments, **152:47.**
    Self-insurer, bonds deposited, **152:25A.**
Expenses.
    Briefs, expenses of printing, **152:11, 152:11A, 152:65.**
    Claims for deposit or reimbursement, payment or expense of defense, **152:65.**
    Costs of action. See within this heading, "Costs of action."
    Dispute procedures, **152:11B.**
    Fees. See within this heading, "Fees."
    Hospital expenses, **152:30.**
    Insurer, payment of expenses, **152:10.**
    Loss control standards for costs of compensation, **152:53A.**
    Medical, surgical hospital, and nursing expenses, **152:30.**
    Printing expenses on appeal or review, **152:11, 152:11A, 152:65.**

WORKERS' COMPENSATION
—Cont'd

Expenses —Cont'd
Self-insurance, **152:25I,
152:25M.**
Traveling expenses. See within
this heading, "Traveling
expenses."
Trust fund, representation,
152:65.
Vocational rehabilitation
procedures, **152:30H.**
Extraordinary losses, self-insurer's
reinsurance against,
152:25A.
Extraterritorial injuries.
Out-of-state employment,
injuries in. See within this
heading, "Out-of-state
employment, injuries."
Eyes.
Furnishing of artificial eyes,
152:30.
Injuries to, compensation,
152:36.
Farm laborers, **152:1.**
Federal employers' liability act, as
affecting, **152:25A.**
Fees.
Appeals to reviewing board,
152:11C.
Commission fees to agents or
brokers, **152:53A.**
Counsel fees. See within this
heading, "Counsel fees."
Depositions, fees, **152:5,
152:9A.**
Dispute procedures, **152:11B.**
Division and board of industrial
accidents, **152:13.**
Physicians. See within this
heading, "Physicians."
Rating organization license,
152:52C.
Self-insurance group, application
fees, **152:25G.**
Stenographic services in taking
depositions, **152:5.**
Witnesses, **152:5, 152:11B,
262:29.**
Feet, loss, **152:36.**
Fellow worker's activities, injuries,
**152:26, 152:26B, 152:27,
152:66, 152:67.**
Fiduciary.
Personal representatives. See
within this heading,
"Personal representatives."
Filing.
Records and recording. See
within this heading,
"Records and recording."

WORKERS' COMPENSATION
—Cont'd

Finality.
Res judicata. See within this
heading, "Res judicata."
Finances and funds.
Funds. See within this heading,
"Funds."
Findings of fact.
As conclusive on appeal, **152:11.**
Filing of findings in
single-member hearing,
152:8.
Finality of finding as to
termination of incapacity,
152:12.
Fines or imprisonment.
Attorney or expert witnesses,
concealment or failure to
disclose information, **152:14.**
Compensation, failure to
provide, **152:25C.**
Correctional institutions,
application, **152:74.**
Industrial accidents division,
failure to give notice of
injuries, **152:19.**
Insurance requirement,
violation, **149:34A.**
Insurers, violations of
requirements, **152:52E.**
Issuance of insurance policies
while in default with respect
to deposit with state
treasurer, **152:60C,
152:60D.**
Orders as to deposit with state
treasurer, failure to comply,
152:60C, 152:60D.
Rating organizations, violations,
152:52E.
Required reports as to injuries,
failure to make, **152:19.**
Self-insurance groups, **152:25C,
152:25S, 152:25T.**
Special revenue fund, fines paid
into, **152:6B.**
Weekly wages, failure to
withhold, **149:148B.**
Fingers, injury or loss, **152:36.**
Firemen.
Excluded, **152:69.**
Leave without loss of pay for
certain incapacitated
firefighters waiving
provisions, **41:111F.**
Foot, loss, **152:36.**
Foreign commerce.
Employment, **152:1.**
Return of deposits to certain
self-insurers, **152:25A.**

WORKERS' COMPENSATION
—Cont'd

Foreign insurance companies.
Bond, **152:61.**
Ceasing to do business,
requirements, **152:62.**
Licenses. See within this
heading, "Licenses."
Trustee for companies ceasing to
do business, **152:62.**
Foreign state.
Out-of-state employment. See
within this heading,
"Out-of-state employment,
injuries."
Former spouses, death benefits
payable to children, **152:31.**
Fraud and deceit.
Costs of actions, fraudulent
claims, **152:14.**
Self-insurance, **152:25M.**
Frivolous proceedings, costs,
152:14.
Frostbite, **152:26.**
Funds.
City or town, payment of
charges for insurance funds,
40:13A.
Reserves, **152:25Q, 175:12,
175:12A.**
Self-insurance groups, financial
condition statements,
152:25N.
Special fund. See within this
heading, "Special fund."
Funeral expenses, payment,
152:33.
General and special employers,
liability as between, **152:18.**
General Court.
Division and board of industrial
accidents. See within this
heading, "Division and
board of industrial
accidents."
General health services, review of
rates paid, **152:13.**
Governmental unit or electrical
company furnishing aid to
other such unit,
reimbursement for expenses of
compensation for employees,
152:74A.
Guardian.
Claiming rights of ward, **152:40.**
Expenses of appointment,
payment, **152:39.**
Handicapped persons.
Incapacity or disability as
prerequisite to payment of
compensation, **152:29.**

WORKERS' COMPENSATION
—Cont'd
Hand, loss, **152:39.**
Health care finance and policy
  division to establish rates of
  payment to hospitals for
  covered services, **152:13.**
Health insurance.
  Accident and sickness insurance.
    See within this heading,
    "Accident and sickness
    insurance."
Health, welfare, and retirement
  funds law, applicability,
  151D:7.
Hearing, impairment of,
  compensation, **152:36.**
Hearings.
  Administrative justice to
    arrange, **152:11.**
  Appeal and review. See within
    this heading, "Appeal and
    review."
  Death benefits, hearing in
    respect, **152:31.**
  Dispute resolution division,
    152:7C, 152:11.
  Evidence. See within this
    heading, "Evidence."
  Hazardous employment,
    hearings, **152:1.**
  Medical benefits, claim may be
    heard as conference, **152:13.**
  One member of division.
    Agreements for compensation,
      152:7.
    Disagreements as to
      compensation, **152:7.**
    Findings, filing, **152:8.**
    Order resulting from hearing
      on disagreements as to
      compensation, **152:7.**
  Place, **152:8.**
  Rating organizations, hearing on
    actions, **152:52C, 152:52D.**
  Revocation of license,
    152:52E.
  Rehearings as to incapacity,
    152:12.
  Release of employer from
    liability by employee's
    submission, **152:23.**
  Reviewing board. See within this
    heading, "Reviewing
    boards."
  Self-insurance groups, **152:25H,
    152:25O.**
  Time for filing decision, findings
    and rulings, **152:8.**
  Total and permanent incapacity,
    hearing as to discontinuance
    of payment under
    circumstances, **152:34A.**

WORKERS' COMPENSATION
—Cont'd
Heat exhaustion, **152:26.**
Heirs.
  Next of kin. See within this
    heading, "Next of kin."
Highways, injuries, **152:18.**
Hiring preferences for those losing
  jobs due to injuries, **152:75A.**
Home owner as employer, **152:1.**
Hospital expenses, **152:30.**
Hospital records, as evidence,
  152:20, 152:20A.
Hospitals and health care
  facilities, rates of payment
  and quality control systems,
  152:13.
Housing and redevelopment
  authorities, effect of payment
  of compensation benefits,
  32:28.
Husband and wife.
  Death. See within this heading,
    "Death."
Imprisonment.
  Fines or imprisonment. See
    within this heading, "Fines
    or imprisonment."
Incapacity or disability as
  prerequisite to payment of
  compensation, **152:29.**
Incompetency.
  Mental condition or capacity. See
    within this heading, "Mental
    condition or capacity."
Increased compensation, payment
  for subsequent injuries,
  152:35B.
Indemnity recoverable from other
  persons, **152:18.**
  Excess, disposition, **152:15.**
Independent arbitrators, dispute
  procedures, **152:10B.**
Independent contractors, liability,
  152:18.
  Exception of incidental contract,
    152:18.
Industrial accident rehabilitation
  board.
  Rehabilitation board. See within
    this heading, "Rehabilitation
    board."
Industrial accidents division.
  See INDUSTRIAL ACCIDENTS
  DIVISION.
Industrial accidents division and
  board.
  Division and board of industrial
    accidents. See within this
    heading, "Division and
    board of industrial
    accidents."

WORKERS' COMPENSATION
—Cont'd
Industrial diseases, physicians to
  report to labor and workforce
  development department,
  149:11.
Infectious disease as personal
  injury, **152:1.**
Information or information
  services, **23E:3, 152:6A,
  152:63.**
Injunction against insurance
  company refusing or
  neglecting to comply with
  provisions as to rejected risks,
  152:65L.
Insanity.
  Mental condition or capacity. See
    within this heading, "Mental
    condition or capacity."
Insurance agents.
  Agents. See within this heading,
    "Agents."
Insurance commissioner.
  Commissioner of insurance. See
    within this heading,
    "Commissioner of
    insurance."
Insurance rating organizations.
  Rating organizations. See within
    this heading, "Rating
    organizations."
Insured person, defined, **152:1.**
Insurer, **152:52B-152:65.**
  Appeal and review. See within
    this heading, "Appeal and
    review."
  Assessments against to balance
    special fund, **152:65.**
  Authorization to insure
    compensation, **175:93.**
  Companies insuring
    compensation,
    152:52B-152:65.
  Costs of action, insurer's
    liability, **152:10-152:14.**
  Defined under work, **152:1.**
  Double compensation paid as
    result of employer's willful
    misconduct, recovery from
    employer, **152:28.**
  Fines and penalties, **152:52E.**
  Foreign insurance companies.
    See within this heading,
    "Foreign insurance
    companies."
  Information to be supplied at
    request of industrial
    accidents division, **152:63.**
  Insolvent domestic insurance
    company, preference of
    compensation claims
    against, **175:46A.**

WORKERS' COMPENSATION
—Cont'd
Insurer —Cont'd
Interest charges, priority of insurer's claims, **152:52B.**
Interinsurance exchange, **152:1.**
Judgments paid by insured, insurer's liability, **152:25.**
Licenses. See within this heading, "Licenses."
Lien of insurer against award or lump-sum settlement paid insured under policy excluding insurer from obligation for which employer may be held liable, **152:46A.**
Payment of compensation. See within this heading, "Payment of compensation."
Qualification of insurer, certificate, **152:60C.**
Reciprocal insurance exchanges. See within this heading, "Reciprocal insurance exchanges."
Report to division as to compensation paid, **152:19.**
Reserves for claims, computation, **175:12, 175:12A.**
Respective liability of two or more insurers, **152:15A.**
Safety rules, insurers may prescribe, **152:64.**
Self-insurance. See within this heading, "Self-insurance."
Service of notice of claim for compensation, **152:43.**
Several companies, joint policy, **152:56.**
Intentional injury.
Willful misconduct. See within this heading, "Willful misconduct."
Interest on money.
Appeal cases, interest, **152:50.**
Awards, interest, **152:50.**
Bonds deposited with state treasurer, payment to employer, **152:25A.**
Priority of insurer's claims, **152:52B.**
Interinsurance exchange as insurer, **152:1.**
Interstate commerce.
Foreign commerce. See within this heading, "Foreign commerce."

WORKERS' COMPENSATION
—Cont'd
Investigations.
Examinations, inspections, and investigations. See within this heading, "Examinations, inspections, and investigations."
Joinder of employer after certificate of approval issued, self-insurance, **152:25K.**
Joint and several liability as to injury in concurrent service of two or more employers, **152:26B.**
Joint and several policies of insurance, **152:56.**
Joint enterprise as employer, **152:1.**
Judges or justices, **152:5, 152:9A, 152:11 et seq.**
Judgments, decrees, and orders.
Division and board of industrial accidents. See within this heading, "Division and board of industrial accidents."
Insured, insurer's liability for judgments paid, **152:25.**
Labor and workforce development department.
Industrial accidents division within.
Division and board of industrial accidents. See within this heading, "Division and board of industrial accidents."
Statistics and data on workers' compensation to be furnished to department, **152:19.**
Lead poisoning, records to be kept, **151B:4.**
Leave of absence.
Fire fighters and police officers waiving provisions of, leave without loss of pay, **41:111F.**
Sick leave by public employees, **7:28, 30:58, 152:69.**
Left arm, loss, **152:36.**
Legal expenses.
Counsel fees. See within this heading, "Counsel fees."
Leg, loss, **152:36.**
Artificial limbs, compensation, **152:30.**
Letters rogatory, **152:5.**

WORKERS' COMPENSATION
—Cont'd
Licenses.
Domestic insurance company, revocation of license for failing to comply with deposits with state treasurer, **152:60C.**
Foreign insurance company, **152:61.**
Revocation, **152:62, 152:65L.**
Insurer, revocation of license of, **152:52E, 152:60C.**
Rating organizations, **152:52C.**
Revocation, **152:52E.**
Rejected risks, revocation of insurer's license for violations, **152:65L.**
Revocation of insurer's license, **152:52E, 152:60C.**
Self-insurance. See within this heading, "Self-insurance."
Traveling amusements not domiciled in state, workers' compensation insurance prerequisite to licensing, **140:181.**
Liens, **152:46A.**
Limitation of actions.
Limitation of time. See within this heading, "Limitation of time."
Limitation of time.
Appeal, time, **152:8.**
Claim for compensation, **152:41.**
After action for third person is discontinued, **152:41.**
Failure or neglect, **152:49.**
Common-law rights, retention, **152:24.**
Death claim.
Death. See within this heading, "Death."
Filing decision, findings, and rulings, **152:8.**
Insurer's action against third party, **152:15.**
Mental or physical condition or capacity as affecting time limit for notice of claim, **152:41.**
Motor vehicles, **260:4, 260:4B.**
Rehearing on incapacity, petition, **152:12.**
Rejected risks.
Orders or rulings, filing petitions for review, **152:65M.**

WORKERS' COMPENSATION
—Cont'd
Limitation of time —Cont'd
Rejected risks —Cont'd
Policies, appeal on grounds of
unreasonable premium,
152:65K.
Report of injuries by employer,
152:19.
Third party, insurer's action
against, **152:15.**
Liquidation of self-insurance
groups, **152:25R.**
Lists.
Division and board of industrial
accidents. See within this
heading, "Division and
board of industrial
accidents."
Location.
Place. See within this heading,
"Place of injury."
Loss incurred, defined,
152:65G.
Lump sum.
Payment of compensation. See
within this heading,
"Payment of compensation."
Maintenance as affecting amount,
152:69.
Massachusetts Bay transportation
authority, **161A:36.**
Massachusetts Water Resources
Authority, election of workers'
compensation or pension,
152:73.
Masters of vessels, **152:1.**
Maximum benefits, **152:34,**
152:34A, 152:35,
152:35A.
Medical and physical examination.
Examinations, inspections, and
investigations. See within
this heading,
"Examinations, inspections,
and investigations."
Medical examiners, duties in case
of death, **38:6, 38:7.**
Medical reports of physicians.
Reports. See within this
heading, "Reports."
Medical service corporation not
liable for expenses chargeable
to workers' compensation,
176B:14.
Medical, surgical, hospital, and
nursing expenses, **152:30.**
Members and membership,
self-insurance groups,
152:25J-152:25M.

WORKERS' COMPENSATION
—Cont'd
Mental condition or capacity.
Coworker's mental condition due
to military service, injury
caused, **152:26.**
Guardian of incompetent.
Guardian. See within this
heading, "Guardian."
Limitation of time for notice of
claim as affected,
152:41.
Presumptions where employee
mentally unable to testify,
152:7A.
Suicide while insane, **152:26A.**
Waiting period, **152:29.**
Military service.
Assignment of veterans' benefit
proceeds to cover workers'
compensation benefits,
115:5.
Coworker whose physical or
mental condition due to,
injury, **152:26.**
Injuries to disabled veterans,
152:37A.
Lien on compensation paid to
veterans for benefits,
152:47.
Minors.
Death benefits payable to.
Death. See within this
heading, "Death."
Guardian. See within this
heading, "Guardian."
Lump sums in lieu of weekly
payments, **152:48.**
Parents, payment of balance of
compensation for specific
injuries, **152:36A.**
Willful misconduct in employing,
152:28.
Young employee, compensation,
152:51.
Misconduct.
Willful misconduct. See within
this heading, "Willful
misconduct."
Mistake, delay in filing claim,
152:49.
Modification of liability, **152:66,**
152:67.
Motor vehicles.
See MOTOR VEHICLES.
Municipal court of Boston, appeals
to.
Appeal and review. See within
this heading, "Appeal and
review."

WORKERS' COMPENSATION
—Cont'd
Municipal lighting and heating
plants.
Cadet engineers, **164:69E.**
Manager, **152:69.**
Municipal officers and employees.
Public employees. See within
this heading, "Public
employees."
Negligence as affecting recovery,
152:66, 152:67.
New jobs, co-operation by
department to make,
152:30I.
Next friend claiming rights,
152:40.
Next of kin.
As dependent, **152:1.**
Death benefits payable, **152:31.**
Non-stock pool, distribution of
losses, **152:65C.**
Nonsuit.
Dismissal and nonsuit. See
within this heading,
"Dismissal and nonsuit."
Notice.
Cancellation of policy, **149:34A,**
152:65B.
Claim for compensation,
152:41.
Form, **152:42.**
Lack of notice as bar to
proceedings, **152:44.**
Service, **152:43.**
Signing, **152:42.**
Time for giving, **152:41.**
To insurer, **152:41.**
Validity, **152:44.**
Contracts and agreements. See
within this heading,
"Contracts and agreements."
Coverage, notice to employees,
152:21, 152:22.
Termination of coverage,
152:22.
Disagreement as to agreed
compensation between
parties, **152:7.**
Division of industrial accidents.
Cancellation or termination of
policy, notice to division,
152:63.
Issuance or renewal of
insurance policy, notice to
division, **152:63.**
Evidence of notice of
cancellation of insurance,
affidavit, **149:34A.**

WORKERS' COMPENSATION
—Cont'd
Notice —Cont'd
Injury, **152:6.**
Inaccurate information as
affecting validity, **152:44.**
Presumption, **152:7A.**
To division, **152:19.**
Previous physical impairment,
employer's knowledge,
152:37.
Rejected risk policy, notice of
cancellation, **152:65B.**
Retention of right at common
law by employee, **152:24.**
Self-insurance groups, **152:25K.**
Termination of insurance
coverage, **152:22, 152:63.**
Nurses employed by state or its
subdivisions, compensation,
152:69.
Nursing expenses.
Medical, surgical, hospital, and
nursing expenses, **152:30.**
Oaths, administration, **152:5.**
Occupational diseases, physicians
to report to labor and
workforce development
department, **149:11.**
Offer to pay compensation, **152:10.**
Opinion of insurance commissioner
as to insurance policy, review,
152:55.
Optometric service corporations,
liability, **176F:14.**
Orders.
Division and board of industrial
accidents. See within this
heading, "Division and
board of industrial
accidents."
Judgments, decrees, and orders.
See within this heading,
"Judgments, decrees, and
orders."
Out-of-state employment, injuries.
Compensation, **152:26.**
Defenses not available to
uninsured employer, **152:66.**
Payment of compensation,
152:66.
Parents.
Minors. See within this heading,
"Minors."
Partial incapacity,
152:35-152:36A.
Maximum weekly benefits
payable, **152:35.**
Public employees, employment,
152:73A.
Partially dependent survivors,
death benefits payable,
152:31.

WORKERS' COMPENSATION
—Cont'd
Partnership.
As employer, **152:1.**
License for partnership to work
as workers' compensation
rating organization,
152:52C.
Part-time domestic servants.
Domestic servants. See within
this heading, "Domestic
servants."
Payment of compensation,
152:26-152:51.
Anticipation of settlement of
controversy as to which
insurer is liable, **152:15A.**
Apportionment. See within this
heading, "Apportionment."
Balance due for specific injuries,
152:36A.
Benefits determination under
law in effect on date of final
decision, **152:51A.**
Contest of claim, **152:7.**
Default or arrest warrant
outstanding, **152:7.**
Disabled war veterans, **152:37A.**
Discontinuance of payments. See
within this heading,
"Discontinuance of
payments."
Effect of filing actions against
third parties without
election, **152:15.**
Extension of payments, **152:8.**
Health care finance and policy
division to establish rates of
payment to hospitals,
152:13.
Hospitals and health care
facilities, **152:13.**
Increased compensation, for
subsequent injuries,
152:35B.
Independent contractors,
insurer's recovery of
compensation payments,
152:18.
Insurance of injured employee
not deductible, **152:38.**
Joint and several liability for
injury in concurrent service
of two or more employers,
152:26B.
Lump sum.
Fair and reasonable amount of
settlement used for
discharge of lien to be
determined by division of
industrial accidents where
employee and lienholder
unable to agree, **152:46A.**

WORKERS' COMPENSATION
—Cont'd
Payment of compensation —Cont'd
Lump sum —Cont'd
In lieu of weekly payments,
152:36, 152:48.
To dependents of deceased
employee, **152:36A.**
Maximum benefits, **152:34,
152:34A, 152:35, 152:35A.**
Medical, surgical, hospital, and
nursing expenses, **152:30.**
Modification or termination of
payments, **152:8.**
Offer to pay, effect on costs of
action, **152:10.**
Out-of-state employment
injuries, **152:66.**
Public employees. See within
this heading, "Public
employees."
Release of employer from
liability, **152:23.**
Savings of injured employee not
deductible, **152:38.**
Specific injuries, payments,
152:36-152:36B.
Subsequent injuries, **152:35B.**
Suspension, **152:45.**
Termination or modification of
payments, **152:8.**
Vouchers required, **152:69B,
152:70.**
Waiting period, **152:29.**
Weekly payments. See within
this heading, "Weekly
payments."
Young employees, payments,
152:51.
Payment of judgment by insured,
recovery, **152:25.**
Penalties.
Fines or imprisonment. See
within this heading, "Fines
or imprisonment."
Pension and retirement benefits as
affecting compensation to
public employees, **32:14,
152:73.**
Pensions.
Retirement systems and
pensions. See within this
heading, "Retirement
systems and pensions."
Performance reports,
self-insurance groups,
152:25N.
Permanent and total incapacity,
152:34, 152:34A, 152:34B.
Additional compensation for
dependents, **152:35A.**

WORKERS' COMPENSATION
—Cont'd
Permanent and total incapacity
—Cont'd
Discontinuance of payments,
proceedings, **152:34A.**
Hands or feet, **152:36.**
Legs or arms, **152:36.**
Lump sum payments, **152:36,
152:48.**
Personal injury, defined, **152:1.**
Personal representatives.
Executors and administrators.
See within this heading,
"Executors and
administrators."
Guardian. See within this
heading, "Guardian."
Physical activities of fellow
workers causing injury,
152:26, 152:66, 152:67.
Physicians.
Depositions.
Medical witness, deposition,
152:5.
On behalf of injured
employees, payment of
fees of physicians giving,
152:9A.
Division and board of industrial
accidents, report as to
industrial diseases, **149:11.**
Employee engaging own,
152:9A, 152:30.
Examination of injured
employee.
Examinations. See within this
heading, "Examinations,
inspections, and
investigations."
Expenses of care and treatment
by physicians.
Medical, surgical, hospital,
and nursing expenses,
152:30.
Fees, **152:9A, 152:11A, 152:13.**
Approval, **152:13.**
Depositions on behalf of
injured employees,
payment of fees of
physicians giving, **152:9A.**
Dispute resolution division,
152:11A.
For appearing at hearings to
determine total
incapacity, **152:34A.**
Payment, **152:9A.**
Reports. See within this
heading, "Reports."
Roster of, dispute resolution
division, **152:11A.**

WORKERS' COMPENSATION
—Cont'd
Physicians —Cont'd
Services, allowance for expense
of.
Medical, surgical, hospital,
and nursing expenses,
152:30.
Place of injury.
Hearing, **152:8.**
Statement in claim, **152:49.**
Policemen.
Cadets as covered employees,
147:21A.
Excluded, **152:69.**
Leave without loss of pay for
certain police officers
waiving provisions, **41:111F.**
Reserve or special officer
employed by contractor,
152:1.
Pooling of risks.
Assigned risk pool. See within
this heading, "Assigned risk
pool."
Poor persons.
See POOR PERSONS.
Posthumous children as
dependents, **152:32, 152:35A.**
Preferences and priority of claims,
152:52B, 175:46A.
Preliminary conference, purpose
and effect, **152:7C.**
Premiums.
Assigned rejected risks,
employer's appeal on
grounds of unreasonableness
of premiums, **152:65K.**
Definition of premiums written,
152:65C.
Health care services rates of
premiums, **152:13.**
Priority of claims, **152:52B.**
Regulation of authorized
carriers, **152:53A.**
Special rates prohibited,
175:182-175:184.
President of corporation liable for
failure to provide
compensation, **152:25C.**
Presumptions and burden of proof.
Cause of injury, presumptions,
152:7A.
Deceased employee,
presumptions in favor,
152:7.
Dependents of deceased
employee, **152:32, 152:35A.**
Employment, **152:26.**
Mentally or physically unable to
testify, presumptions in
event of employee being,
152:7.

WORKERS' COMPENSATION
—Cont'd
Presumptions and burden of proof
—Cont'd
Reserve or special police
employed by contractors,
152:1.
Simplifying procedure, **152:7A.**
Previous physical impairment,
reimbursement to employer or
insurer for payments for
injuries to employee having,
152:37.
Principal and agent.
Agents. See within this heading,
"Agents."
Printing expenses on appeal,
152:11, 152:11A, 152:65.
Priority of claims, **152:52B,
175:46A.**
Prisons.
See CORRECTIONAL
INSTITUTIONS.
Procedural nature of amendments
of law, **152:2A.**
Procedure, **152:5-152:25, 152:70.**
Process and service of process.
Insurance commissioner, service,
152:25G.
Notice of claim for
compensation, **152:43.**
Professional athletes, **152:1.**
Proposed workers' compensation
group, self-insurance,
152:25G.
Prosthetic appliances, furnishing,
152:30.
Public assistance to poor persons.
Welfare aid. See within this
heading, "Welfare aid."
Public contracts.
Contracts and agreements. See
within this heading,
"Contracts and agreements."
Public employees.
Agents to furnish benefits,
designation, **152:75.**
Application of law, **152:74.**
Appropriations by
municipalities, **40:5, 40:13A.**
Boards and commissions,
application of law to
employees, **152:74.**
Cadet engineers as municipal
employees, **164:69E.**
Civil service, employment of
partially disabled employees
within, **152:73A.**
Commonwealth exempted from
self-insurance provisions,
152:25B.

WORKERS' COMPENSATION
—Cont'd
Public employees —Cont'd
Commonwealth laborers and
mechanics, compensation as
exclusive remedy, **152:68.**
Compensation in lieu of
maintenance, amount,
152:69.
Conflicting jurisdiction or
powers of departments,
30:5.
District laborers or mechanics,
compensation as exclusive
remedy, **152:68.**
Division of industrial accidents,
payment by cities and towns
of certain awards approved,
44:31.
Elder service corpsmen as not
Commonwealth employees
for workers' compensation
purposes, **19A:13.**
Elected or appointed officers,
extension of coverage to
certain, **152:69.**
Election between compensation
and pension, **152:73.**
Examination and investigation
as to Commonwealth
employees, **152:69B.**
Exclusiveness of compensation
remedies, **152:68, 152:71.**
Extension of coverage to certain
elected or appointed officers,
152:69.
Firemen. See within this
heading, "Firemen."
Governmental duties, employees
engaged, **152:74.**
Industrial accidents board,
payment of compensation to
certain state employees
injured in state service,
30:58.
Insurance coverage of, **152:69.**
Laborers or mechanics for
towns, cities, and counties,
compensation as exclusive
remedy, **152:68.**
Leave of absence. See within
this heading, "Leave of
absence."
Maintenance as affecting
compensation, **152:69.**
Medical, surgical, hospital and
nursing expenses, **152:69B.**
Nurses employed by state,
workers' compensation,
152:69.

WORKERS' COMPENSATION
—Cont'd
Public employees —Cont'd
Other governmental unit,
reimbursement to unit
furnishing aid for expenses
incurred in providing
workers' compensation to
employees, **152:74A.**
Other remedies excluded,
152:71.
Overtime credit as affecting
compensation, **152:69.**
Partially disabled employee,
employment, **152:73A.**
Payment of compensation,
152:69.
Pension rights as affected,
32:14, 152:73.
Policemen. See within this
heading, "Policemen."
Procedure for payment of
compensation, **152:70.**
Proprietary functions, employees
engaged, **152:74.**
Recovery of compensation paid
to public employees, action,
152:73.
Regional school district
employees, **152:69.**
Retirement benefits, **32:14,
152:73.**
School personnel, **152:1, 152:69.**
See SCHOOLS AND
EDUCATION.
Self-insurance.
Exemption of counties, cities,
and towns, **152:25B.**
Reserves, establishment by
municipalities, **40:13C.**
Sick leave as affecting payment
of compensation, **7:28,
30:58, 152:69.**
Temporary replacement of
partially disabled
employees, **152:73A.**
Treasurer of city or town,
payment, **114:19, 114:25,
152:70.**
Tuberculosis hospital district
employees, payment of
compensation, **152:69.**
Vacation credit as affecting
compensation, **152:69.**
Vouchers required for payment
of compensation, **152:69B,
152:70.**
Waiver of common law rights,
152:72.
Welfare district employees,
benefits, **152:74.**

WORKERS' COMPENSATION
—Cont'd
Question of law, effect of
certification, **152:11.**
Quorum, meetings of workers'
compensation advisory council,
23E:15.
Rate of compensation.
Payment of compensation. See
within this heading,
"Payment of compensation."
Rating Bureau's Workers'
Compensation Trust Fund,
26:8E.
Rating organizations.
Appeal.
From orders and decisions of
commissioner, **152:52F.**
To commissioner from action,
152:52D.
Commissioner of Insurance. See
within this heading,
"Commissioner of
insurance."
Contracts between insurance
companies and agents not
affected by act, **152:52C.**
Co-operation authorized,
152:52C.
Discrimination against
subscribers, prohibition
against, **152:52C.**
Examination, **152:52C.**
Hearings. See within this
heading, "Hearings."
Licenses. See within this
heading, "Licenses."
Partial invalidity of law,
152:52G.
Payment of compensation, rate
provisions applicable to
insuring, **175A:4.**
Payment of dividends,
prohibition against
regulation, **152:52C.**
Penalty for violations, **152:52E.**
Public inspection of report on
examination, **152:52C.**
Rates, regulations, **152:52C.**
Reasonableness of rules and
regulations, hearings to
determine, **152:52C.**
Report on examination, **152:52C.**
Review of co-operative activities,
152:52C.
Real estate broker, employment
exclusion as to salesperson
affiliated, **152:1.**
Receivers.
As employers, **152:1.**
Deposit with state treasurer,
duties, **152:60.**

WORKERS' COMPENSATION
—Cont'd
Receivers —Cont'd
 Priority of workers'
  compensation claims,
  175:46A.
Reciprocal insurance exchanges.
 As insurer, **152:1.**
 Laws applicable, **175:94J,
  175:94M.**
 Prerequisites to doing business,
  175:94D, 175:94E.
Reclamation districts authorized to
 provide insurance coverage,
 252:6A.
Recording machine or device,
 admissibility in evidence of
 claimant's statement taken,
 152:7B.
Records and recording.
 Claim for benefits, **152:10.**
 Division and board of industrial
  accidents. See within this
  heading, "Division and
  board of industrial
  accidents."
 Examination, **152:5, 152:25I.**
 Fees, **152:7F.**
 Finding and ruling of member
  holding hearing, filing,
  152:8.
 Hospital records, **152:20,
  152:20A.**
 Injuries, employer's duty as to
  recording, **152:19.**
  Penalty for failure to make
   required reports, **152:19.**
 Insurance carriers, **152:53A.**
 Insurance commissioner's
  examination, **152:25I.**
 Lead poisoning, **151B:4.**
 Name and address of agents
  furnishing benefits to public
  employees, **152:75.**
 Notice of insurance coverage,
  filing copy, **152:22.**
 Physician examining injured
  employee, filing copy of
  report, **152:45.**
 Reports. See within this
  heading, "Reports."
 Rules and regulations, **152:5,
  152:7G.**
 Self-insurance group, **152:25I.**
 Statement of compensation
  payments made, filing,
  152:19.
  Penalty for failure to make
   required reports, **152:19.**
 Transcripts. See within this
  heading, "Transcripts."

WORKERS' COMPENSATION
—Cont'd
Recoupment of benefits by
 employer, **152:11D.**
Recovery of compensation paid.
 Double compensation based on
  employer's willful
  misconduct, insurer's
  recovery from employer,
  152:28.
 Public employee, action for
  recovery of compensation,
  152:73.
 Subcontractors, insurer's
  recovery, **152:18.**
Refunds.
 Self-insurance groups, **152:25P.**
 Sick leave credits, injured state
  employee having, **30:58.**
Regional school district employees,
 152:69.
Registered mail, service of notice
 of claim for compensation,
 152:43.
Rehabilitation board.
 Advisory council of
  rehabilitation commission,
  chairman as member, **6:76.**
Rehearings, **152:12, 152:16.**
Reimbursement.
 Defense, payment of expense,
  152:65.
 Governmental unit or electric
  company giving aid to other
  such unit or company for
  compensation payments,
  152:74A.
 Insurers' lien on awards,
  152:46A.
 Previously impaired employees,
  152:37.
 Public assistance to poor
  persons, assignment of
  benefit payments in
  reimbursement, **118:11.**
 Travel expenses and loss of
  wages in connection with
  examination, **152:45.**
Reinsurance.
 Minimum amount, **152:25A.**
 Pools for rejected risk policies,
  152:65C, 152:65O.
  Rules and regulations,
   152:65H.
 Self-insurers, **152:25A.**
Rejected risks, assigning and
 pooling, **152:65A-152:65M.**
 Appeal and review. See within
  this heading, "Appeal and
  review."
 Calculation of distribution of
  risk among insurers,
  152:65A.

WORKERS' COMPENSATION
—Cont'd
Rejected risks, assigning and
 pooling —Cont'd
 Cancellation of policy, **152:65B.**
 Distribution among insurers,
  152:65A.
 Injunction against domestic
  insurance company,
  152:65L.
 Inspection of risk by insurer,
  152:65J.
 Issuance by one insurer of policy
  to employer, assignment to
  another insurer, **152:65D.**
 Liability, **152:65I.**
 Limitation of time. See within
  this heading, "Limitation of
  time."
 Losses, distribution, **152:65C.**
 Loss incurred, defined, **152:65G.**
 Non-stock pool, distribution of
  losses, **152:65C.**
 Premiums written, defined,
  152:65C.
 Primary liability of insurer to
  pay compensation, **152:65I.**
 Refusal or neglect of insurer to
  comply with provisions,
  152:65L.
 Reinsurance. See within this
  heading, "Reinsurance."
 Review.
  Appeal and review. See within
   this heading, "Appeal and
   review."
 Revocation or suspension of
  license, **152:65L.**
 Rules and regulations of
  reinsurance pool, **152:65H.**
 Stock pool, distribution of losses,
  152:65C.
 Time, limitation of.
  Limitation of time. See within
   this heading, "Limitation
   of time."
Release.
 Acceptance of payment by
  employee as release of
  employer's liability, **152:23.**
 Injured persons in hospitals,
  271:44.
Religious institutions, **152:1.**
Renewal of policies, notification of
 industrial accidents board,
 152:63.
Reports.
 Administration division, **23E:3.**
 Earnings of employees receiving
  weekly compensation,
  152:11D.

WORKERS' COMPENSATION
—Cont'd
Reports —Cont'd
Employer's duty as to recording of injuries, **152:19.**
Penalty for failure to make required reports, **152:19.**
Examination of rating organizations, **152:52C.**
Inspection of risks by insurer, **152:65J.**
Insurer's report as to compensation paid, **152:19.**
Labor and workforce development department.
Occupational diseases, department to furnish industrial accidents division with reports, **149:11.**
Physicians to report, **149:11.**
Medical examiner's report of death to industrial accident's division, **38:7.**
Medical reports of physician's examination of injured employees.
Deceased physicians' reports, admissibility in evidence, **152:20B.**
Discontinuance of compensation, medical examination report in support, **152:29.**
Filing, **152:45.**
Furnishing employee with copies, **152:20A.**
Labor and workforce development department, request for reports, **149:11.**
Notice of injury, required reports, **152:6.**
Occupational or industrial diseases, reports to industrial accidents division, **149:11.**
Performance reports, self insurance groups, **152:25N.**
Statements. See within this heading, "Statements."
Time for filing decision, findings, and rulings, **152:8.**
Time requirements as to making, **152:19.**
Vocational rehabilitation services, **152:30F.**
Workers' compensation advisory council, **23E:17.**
Request for copy of written statement of employee, **152:7B.**

WORKERS' COMPENSATION
—Cont'd
Reserves, **40:13C, 175:12, 175:12A.**
Self-insurance group, **152:25Q.**
Res judicata.
Board orders, **152:16.**
Incapacity, finding, **152:12.**
Restructuring of administration division, **23E:3.**
Retirement systems and pensions, **32:14, 32:28, 152:73.**
Intragovernmental service fund, chargeback, **29:2Q.**
Reversal on appeal, **152:17.**
Review.
Appeal and review. See within this heading, "Appeal and review."
Reviewing boards.
Amending decision of member, **152:10.**
Decisions.
Division and board of industrial accidents. See within this heading, "Division and board of industrial accidents."
Defined, **152:1.**
Dispute resolution.
Appeal from reviewing board, **152:12, 152:12A.**
Appeal to reviewing board, **152:11C.**
Hearings, **152:10.**
Death benefits, hearing in respect to payment, **152:31.**
Total and permanent incapacity, hearing, **152:34A.**
Revocation of license.
Licenses. See within this heading, "Licenses."
Right arm, loss, **152:36.**
Rogatory letters, **152:5.**
Rules of procedure, **152:5.**
Safety rules and regulations by insurer, **152:64.**
Salesperson affiliated with real estate broker, employment exclusion, **152:1.**
Savings of injured employee not deductible from compensation, **152:38.**
School personnel, **152:1, 152:69.**
See SCHOOLS AND EDUCATION.
Seamen, **152:1.**
Self-employment earnings of employees receiving weekly compensation, **152:11D.**

WORKERS' COMPENSATION
—Cont'd
Self-insurance, **152:25A et seq.**
Addition of new members to board of trustees, **152:25K.**
Applications, **152:25G.**
Attorney, appointment of insurance commissioner, **152:25G.**
Bankruptcy or insolvency, **152:25K, 152:25R.**
Bonds, **152:25G.**
Cease and desist orders, **152:25T.**
Certificate of approval, **152:25E-152:25H, 152:25K, 152:25U.**
Classification and experience rating systems, **152:25O.**
Costs and expenses, **152:25I, 152:25M.**
Death, payment into special fund, **152:65.**
Definitions, **152:25E.**
Deposits with state treasurer. See within this heading, "Deposits with state treasurer."
Exceptions to application of law, **152:25A, 152:25B.**
Expenses of assessment, **152:25A.**
Fees, **152:25G.**
Financial condition, statement, **152:25N.**
Fraudulent solicitation of membership, **152:25M.**
Hearings, **152:25H, 152:25O.**
Insurance commissioner, **152:25G, 152:25I.**
Joinder of employer to propose group after certificate issued, **152:25K.**
Joint and several liability for injury in concurrent service of two or more employers, **152:26B.**
License, **152:25A.**
Revocation, **152:25A, 152:25D.**
Solicitation of membership by licensed agents, **152:25L.**
Liquidation for insufficient funds, **152:25R.**
Members and membership, **152:25J-152:25M.**
Minimum amount of reinsurance, **152:25A.**
Notice, **152:25K.**
Optional deductibles offered by insurer, **152:25A.**
Penalties, **152:25C, 152:25S, 152:25T.**

WORKERS' COMPENSATION
—Cont'd
Self-insurance —Cont'd
Performance report, **152:25N.**
Premium rates and
contributions, **152:25O,
152:25Q.**
Proposed workers' compensation
group, **152:25G.**
Public employees. See within
this heading, "Public
employees."
Records of proposed group,
examination by insurance
commissioner, **152:25I.**
Refunds, **152:25P.**
Reimbursement for payments for
injury to previously
impaired employee, **152:37.**
Reinsurance against
extraordinary losses,
152:25A.
Reserves, **152:25Q.**
Return of deposits to
self-insurers, **152:25A.**
Service companies, revocation of
license for engaging,
152:25D.
Service of process on insurance
commissioner, **152:25G.**
Solicitation of membership,
152:25L.
Termination, cancellation, or
revocation, **152:25H,
152:25K, 152:25U.**
Trustees, **152:25J, 152:25K.**
Service company engaged by self
insurer, revocation of license,
152:25D.
Settlements by agreements in
actions against third parties,
152:15.
Several employers, injury in
concurrent service, **152:26B.**
Shipmasters, **152:1.**
Sick leave by public employees,
7:28, 30:58, 152:69.
Sickness insurance.
Accident and sickness insurance.
See within this heading,
"Accident and sickness
insurance."
Signature on claim, **152:49.**
Single member of industrial
accident division.
Division and board of industrial
accidents. See within this
heading, "Division and
board of industrial
accidents."
Sisters of deceased employee,
payment of balance of
compensation, **152:36A.**

WORKERS' COMPENSATION
—Cont'd
Special employer and general
employer, liability for workers'
compensation as between,
152:18.
Special fund, **152:65.**
Appeals to supreme judicial
court, printing expenses,
152:11, 152:65.
Appropriations, **152:37A.**
Assessment of insurers and
self-insurers for amounts
required to balance fund,
152:65.
Compensation due employee
who dies without relatives
paid into, **152:36A.**
Custody, **152:65.**
Death, injuries resulting,
152:65.
Dependents, fund in absence,
152:36A.
Disabled war veterans, injuries,
152:37A.
Fines paid, **152:6B.**
Insurer's payment into, **152:65.**
Payment of expense of defense
or prosecution of certain
claims, **152:65.**
Specific injuries, payments,
152:36, 152:36A.
Speedy disposition of cases,
152:11.
Spouse, surviving.
Death. See within this heading,
"Death."
State employees.
Public employees. See within
this heading, "Public
employees."
Statements.
Compensation payments made,
filing of statement, **152:19.**
Reasons for discontinuing
payments, **152:29.**
State treasurer.
Deposits with state treasurer.
See within this heading,
"Deposits with state
treasurer."
Payment, **152:70.**
Payment for injury caused by
fellow employees, **152:26.**
Special fund, custody, **152:65.**
Stay on appeal, **152:17.**
Stenographic services for
depositions, fee, **152:5.**
Stock pool, distribution of losses,
152:65C.
Students of employees injured,
152:31, 152:35A.

WORKERS' COMPENSATION
—Cont'd
Subcontractor.
Incidental contract, exception,
152:18.
Insurer's recovery of
compensation payments,
152:18.
Subrogation, insurer's right,
152:15, 152:18.
Subsequent injuries, payments of
compensation, **152:35B,
152:37.**
Substantive nature of amendments
of law, **152:2A.**
Suffolk County.
Appeals to municipal court of
Boston in.
Appeal and review. See within
this heading, "Appeal and
review."
Special provision for public
employees of, regarding
compensation, **152:69.**
Suicide.
Dependents' right to recover as
affected, **152:26A.**
Insanity, suicide while in
condition, **152:26A.**
Presumption, **152:7A.**
Sunstroke, **152:26.**
Superior court.
Appeals to.
Appeal and review. See within
this heading, "Appeal and
review."
Jurisdiction, **149:34A, 152:11B.**
Supplemental benefits.
Partial incapacity, **152:35C.**
Total and permanent incapacity,
152:34B.
Supreme Judicial Court, appeals
to. See within this heading,
"Appeal and review."
Surety bonds of self-insurer,
152:25A.
Surgical expenses.
Medical, surgical, hospital and
nursing expenses, **152:30.**
Surviving spouse.
Death. See within this heading,
"Death."
Suspension of decision of board or
division pending appeal,
152:17.
Suspension of right to
compensation, **152:45.**
Termination.
Cancellation. See within this
heading, "Cancellation."
Termination of disability.
Employers' report, **152:19.**

WORKERS' COMPENSATION
—Cont'd

Termination of disability —Cont'd

Finding of termination of incapacity not final, **152:12.**

Third person.

Discontinuance of action against, on notice to insurer, **152:15.**

Election of employee to sue, **152:15.**

Employee's right or action against, **152:15.**

Insurer's action against, **152:15.**

Legal liability, **152:15.**

Payment of benefits, effect of filing third party action, **152:15.**

Settlement by agreement of action against, **152:15.**

Time.

Appeal, time for.

Appeal and review. See within this heading, "Appeal and review."

Cases to which the law in effect on date of decision applies, **152:51A.**

Common-law right of employees, notice of retention, **152:24.**

Conciliation period, **152:10.**

Decision of single member upon hearing, time for claim for review, **152:10.**

Filing claim and notice, **152:41.**

Hearing by single member of industrial accident division, time for holding, **152:7.**

Incapacitation, time of, **152:29.**

Injury, time of, statement in claim, **152:49.**

Limitation of time. See within this heading, "Limitation of time."

Mid-term notice of cancellation of policy, **152:55A.**

Notice of claim for compensation, time, **152:41.**

Partial incapacity, **152:35C, 152:35E.**

Reports. See within this heading, "Reports."

Temporary orders, dispute procedures, **152:10A.**

Weekly payments. See within this heading, "Weekly payments."

Toes, loss or injury, **152:36.**

Toll free information number maintained by administration division, **23E:3.**

WORKERS' COMPENSATION
—Cont'd

Total and permanent incapacity.

Permanent and total incapacity. See within this heading, "Permanent and total incapacity."

Town employees.

Public employees. See within this heading, "Public employees."

Transcripts.

Board proceedings, **152:11B.**

Evidence at hearings, transcript, **152:8.**

Recorded statement, transcript to be furnished to claimant, **152:7B.**

Transfer of cases to and from supreme judicial court, **211:4A.**

Transportation areas, rights of employees of private companies acquired, **161:147.**

Traveling amusements not domiciled in state, workers' compensation insurance as prerequisite to licensing, **140:181.**

Traveling expenses.

Medical examination, reimbursement for travel, **152:45.**

Witnesses, **152:5.**

Treasurer of city or town, payment, **114:19, 114:25, 152:70.**

Treasurer of corporation liable for failure to provide compensation, **152:25C.**

Treasurer of state.

State treasurer. See within this heading, "State treasurer."

Trial.

Hearing. See within this heading, "Hearings."

Preferences of cases, **152:11.**

Trustee.

Companies ceasing to do business, trustee, **152:62.**

Employee, **152:1.**

Employer, **152:1.**

Self-insurance, **152:25J, 152:25K.**

Transfer of deposit with state treasurer, **152:59.**

Trustee process.

Exemption from attachment, execution, etc. See within this heading, "Exemption from attachment, execution, etc."

WORKERS' COMPENSATION
—Cont'd

Tuberculosis hospital district employees.

Public employees. See within this heading, "Public employees."

Unemployment compensation as affected, **151A:25.**

Unsoundness of mind.

Mental condition or capacity. See within this heading, "Mental condition or capacity."

Value of outstanding claims, computation, **152:58.**

Veterans.

Military service. See within this heading, "Military service."

Victims of violent crime, **258C:10.**

Vocational rehabilitation, **23E:3, 152:30E-152:30I.**

Void contracts, **152:54A.**

Voting, meetings of advisory council, **23E:15.**

Waiting period before commencement of compensation, **152:29.**

Waiver, **152:24.**

Appeals to reviewing boards, **152:11C.**

Common law. See within this heading, "Common law."

Compensation, prohibition of waiver of right, **152:46.**

Dispute procedures, **152:11B.**

Leave without loss of pay for certain incapacitated firefighters or police officers, **41:111F.**

Weekly payments.

Changes, **152:12.**

Lump sum in lieu, **152:36, 152:48.**

Maximum payments, **152:34, 152:34A, 152:35.**

Notice, **152:7.**

Partial incapacity, **152:35.**

Total and permanent incapacity, **152:34, 152:34A.**

Wages.

Weekly wage. See within this heading, "Weekly wage."

Weekly wage.

Average, **152:1, 152:6.**

Failure to withhold, **149:148B.**

Welfare aid.

Assignment of benefit payments in reimbursement, **118:11.**

Liens on workers' compensation payments to extent, **152:46A.**

WORKERS' COMPENSATION
—Cont'd
Welfare aid —Cont'd
Medical assistance division,
118E:22.
Welfare district employees,
benefits, **152:74.**
Widows.
Death. See within this heading,
"Death."
Willful misconduct.
Employee.
Bar to compensation, **152:27.**
Presumptions, **152:7A.**
Employer, double compensation
in cases, **152:28.**
Witnesses.
Compelling attendance, **152:5.**
Fees for attending, **152:5,**
152:11B, 262:29.
Travel pay, **152:5.**
Wrist, severance of hand, **152:36.**
Young employee, compensation,
152:51.

**WORKERS' COMPENSATION
ADMINISTRATION
OFFICE.**
Establishment within human
resources division, **7:4A.**

WORKERS' MEMORIAL DAY.
Establishment, **6:15KKK.**

**WORKFORCE TRAINING
FUND, 29:2RR.**

WORKINGMEN'S TICKETS.
Carriers, **159:5, 159:18, 160:198,**
161:107.

WORK PRODUCT.
Attorneys, criminal rules, **Crim R
14.**
Criminal rules, **Crim R 14.**
Mediator's communications,
233:23C.
Medical peer review committees,
111:205.

**WORK RELEASE PROGRAMS.
See CORRECTIONAL
INSTITUTIONS.**

**WORKSHARING PROGRAM,
151A:25, 151A:29D.**

WORKSHOPS.
Defined, **6:77.**
House of correction, **126:8.**

**WORKS OF ART.
See ART AND ARTISTS.**

**WORK STOPPAGES.
See LABOR RELATIONS AND
DISPUTES.**

WORK-STUDY PROGRAM.
Board of higher education, **15A:16.**
Co-operative work-study program
by minor while attending
school as authorizing
employment without
educational certificate,
149:95A.

**WORK-TRAINING
PROGRAMS.**
Disadvantaged persons,
appointment to civil service
positions, **31:47A.**
Mental health, programs for
patient-trainees, **123:29.**

**WORLD ATHLETIC
COMPETITION.**
Commonwealth employees, leaves
of absence, **30:9G.**

**WORLD HEALTH
ORGANIZATION.**
Licensing of physicians graduating
from foreign medical schools
recognized, **112:2.**

WORLD WAR I.
Flags, **8:17A.**
Orange peace statue.
Official peace statue of
Commonwealth, **2:45.**
Veterans.
See VETERANS AND
VETERANS'
ORGANIZATIONS.

WORLD WAR II.
Flags, **8:17A.**
Memorial commission, **6:17,**
6:124A.
Pearl Harbor Day, observance,
6:12DD.
U.S.S. Massachusetts as memorial,
6:124A.
Veterans.
See VETERANS AND
VETERANS'
ORGANIZATIONS.

WORMS.
Canker worms, **132:11-132:27,**
266:119.
Municipal regulations as to taking,
130:52.
Webworms, suppression, **132:11.**

WORN RECORDS.
Preservation and copying, **66:9.**
Rerecording, **36:17.**

WORTHINGTON.
Congressional district, **57:1.**
Medical examiner district, **38:1.**
Senatorial district, **57:3.**

WORTHLESS CHECKS, 266:37.
Bad checks generally.
See CHECKS.

WORTHLESS DEBTS.
Bad debts.
See BAD DEBTS.

WRECKS AND WRECKAGE.
Salvage.
See SALVAGE.
Shipwrecks, **91:38-91:49.**
See SHIPWRECKS.

WRENTHAM.
Congressional district, **57:1.**
District court, **218:1.**
Medical examiner district, **38:1.**
Senatorial district, **57:3.**

WRESTLING.
Sunday sports, licensing, **136:4.**

WRINKLING.
Tanning facilities, **111:209.**

WRIST.
Workers' compensation for
severance of hand, **152:36.**

**WRITE-IN BALLOTS.
See ELECTIONS.**

WRONGFUL DEATH,
229:1-229:11.
Abortion or attempted abortion,
medical examiner's duties as
to death, **38:6.**
Administrators.
Executors and administrators.
See within this heading,
"Executors or
administrators."
Agents, liability for acts, **229:2,**
231:85.
Amendment of actions brought
under wrong section, **229:6D.**
Apportionment of damages, **229:1,**
229:6E.
Automobiles.
See MOTOR VEHICLES.
Breach of warranty, liability for
death resulting, **229:2.**
Burial expenses, **229:2.**
Care and assistance, damages for
loss, **229:2.**
Carriers.
See CARRIERS.
Charges, expenses, and costs,
damages recovered as subject,
229:6A.
Children causing, parents' liability,
231:85.
Conscious suffering, recovery of
damages, **229:6, 229:6C.**

WRONGFUL DEATH —Cont'd

Contributory negligence, amount of damages as affected, **231:85.**

Costs.

Expenses. See within this heading, "Expenses."

Counties.

Defective way, damages for death caused, **229:1.**

Limitation of time for bringing of action, **260:4.**

Criminal offense of causing death by reckless, etc., operation of motor vehicle, **90:24G.**

Custodian of injured person, presumption of negligence, **231:85.**

Damages.

Amount of damages, **229:2, 229:6E.**

Apportionment of damages, **229:1, 229:6E.**

Breach of warranty resulting in death, **229:2.**

Conscious suffering, recovery, **229:6, 229:6C.**

Contributory negligence, amount of damages as affected, **231:85.**

Defective way, damages for death resulting, **229:1.**

Degree of culpability of person liable, assessment of damages with reference, **229:6E.**

Distribution, **229:1.**

Employee, liability of employer for death, **229:2B.**

Expenses. See within this heading, "Expenses."

Interest on damages, **229:11.**

Negligence resulting in death, **229:2.**

New assets of estate, damages treated, **229:6B.**

Punitive damages, **229:2.**

Willful, wanton or reckless conduct resulting in death, **229:2.**

Decedent's estate.

Estate of deceased. See within this heading, "Estate of deceased."

Defective way, damages for death, **229:1.**

Distribution of damages, **229:1.**

Domestic servants, death caused by fellow employees, **229:2B.**

Due care on decedent's part, presumption, **231:85.**

WRONGFUL DEATH —Cont'd

Employers and employees.

Master and servant. See within this heading, "Master and servant."

Estate of deceased.

Conscious suffering, damages recovered to be held as assets of estate, **229:6.**

Damages recovered as subject to charges of administration and expenses, **229:6A.**

Executors or administrators. See within this heading, "Executors or administrators."

New assets of estate, damages, **229:6B.**

Executors or administrators.

Commencement of action, **229:1, 229:2.**

District and municipal court rules of civil procedure as applicable to substitution of executor or administrator in actions for wrongful death, **230:11.**

Enforcement of action for death against executor or administrator where tortfeasor dies first, **229:5A.**

Exemplary damages, **229:2.**

Expenses.

Estate of deceased, damages recovered as subject to charges and expenses, **229:6A.**

Funeral expenses recoverable, **229:2.**

Farm laborers, death caused by fellow employees, **229:2B.**

Fellow employees, death of employee caused, **229:2B.**

Funeral expenses, **229:2.**

Guidance, counsel, and advice, damages for loss, **229:2.**

Highways and streets, death resulting from defects, **229:1.**

Income, damages for loss, **229:2.**

Interest on damages, **229:11.**

Labor and employment.

Master and servant. See within this heading, "Master and servant."

Limitation of actions, **260:10.**

Counties, **260:4.**

Defective way, action for death resulting, **229:1.**

Employee, action for death, **229:6F.**

Negligence, action for death resulting, **229:2.**

WRONGFUL DEATH —Cont'd

Limitation of actions —Cont'd

Willful, wanton or reckless conduct, action for death resulting, **229:2.**

Master and servant.

Acts of servants, liability, **229:2.**

Conscious suffering of employee, recovery against employer, **229:6C.**

Fellow employee, death of employee caused, **229:2B.**

Limitation of action for employee's death, **229:2.**

Negligence of employer, liability of employer for death of employee resulting, **229:2B.**

Notice to employer, **229:6F.**

Medical examiner's duties as to death resulting from abortion or attempted abortion, **38:6.**

Medical reports of deceased physicians, admissibility in evidence in actions of tort for death, **233:79H.**

Minor children, parents' liability for death caused, **231:85.**

Motor carriers.

See CARRIERS.

Motor vehicles.

See MOTOR VEHICLES.

Negligence resulting in, **90:24G, 229:2, 229:2B.**

New assets of estate of deceased, damages recovered treated, **229:6B.**

Notice.

Defect in way, notice, **229:1.**

Time, place and cause of injury to employee, notice to employer, **229:6F.**

Pain and suffering, damages recoverable for conscious suffering, **229:6, 229:6C.**

Parents' liability for death caused by minor children, **231:85, 231:85G.**

Passengers of common carrier, liability for death, **229:2.**

Presumptions.

Due care on part of decedent, **231:85.**

Negligence by agent or custodian of injured person, **231:85.**

Prior death of tortfeasor, action for death in event, **229:5A.**

Punitive damages, **229:2.**

Railroad, liability of operator, **229:2.**

Reckless conduct resulting in death, **90:24G, 229:2.**

WRONGFUL DEATH —Cont'd
Servant.
Master and servant. See within this heading, "Master and servant."
Services, damages for loss, **229:2.**
Society and companionship, damages for loss, **229:2.**
Statute of limitations.
Limitation of actions. See within this heading, "Limitation of actions."
Street railway, liability of operator, **229:2.**
Substitution of executor or administrator in action, **230:11.**
Tortfeasor dying first, action for death in event, **229:5A.**
Trespassers on railroad property, liability for death, **229:2.**
Warranty, liability for death resulting from breach, **229:2.**
Willful, wanton or reckless conduct, **229:2.**

X

X CO-ORDINATE.
Surveying definitions, **97:10.**

XEROGRAPHY.
See PHOTOSTATIC COPIES.

X RAY MACHINES.
Sales of guns designed to elude x-ray machines and metal detectors, **140:131N.**

X RAYS.
Chiropractic examinations utilizing, **112:89.**
Dental hygienists as qualified to take dental x rays, **112:51.**
Fluoroscopic shoe-fitting machines, forbidden, **111:186A.**
Liability insurance may include expenses, **175:111C.**
Medical care and assistance programs, services for which financial assistance provided, **118E:6.**
Medical malpractice, instructions to jury, **231:60J.**
Medical x-ray technicians.
See MEDICAL X-RAY TECHNICIANS.
Motor vehicle insurance protection against costs, **90:34A.**
Municipal hospital technicians temporarily reemployed without make-up payments or credit in retirement system, **32:3.**

X RAYS —Cont'd
Ordinary disability retirement, authority to make X rays with respect, **32:6.**
Physical therapists not authorized to use, **112:23A.**
Physicians and surgeons.
Malpractice, instructions to jury, **231:60J.**
Membership on radiation protection advisory council, **111:4F.**
Shoe-fitting machines, supervision of operation, **111:186A.**
School employees to take periodic examinations, **71:55B.**
Shielding devices required in use, **111:5J.**
Shoe-fitting machines, operation, **111:186A.**
Technicians.
See MEDICAL X-RAY TECHNICIANS.

XYLENE.
Driving under influence, **90:21.**

Y

YACHTING CORPORATIONS.
Annual return, **180:26A.**
Boxing matches, forfeiture of charter for violations, **180:28.**
Bylaws, **180:7.**
Change of name, **180:11.**
Change of purpose, **180:10, 180:11.**
Directors, officers and agents, **180:7.**
Gaming laws, forfeiture of charter for violation, **180:27.**
Incorporation, **180:1-180:11.**
Investigation before incorporation, **180:5, 180:6.**
Liquor laws, forfeiture of charter for violation, **180:27.**
Organization, **180:3.**

YANKEE DIVISION VETERANS ASSOCIATION.
Insignia, unlawful use, **266:70.**
Patriotic holiday observances, municipal appropriations, **40:5.**
Quarters, **40:9.**
Uniform, unlawful use, **264:10A.**

YARDS.
House of correction, **126:8, 126:9.**
Railroads.
See RAILROADS.
Tenement house regulation definition, **144:2, 145:2.**

YARDS —Cont'd
Zoning and planning.
Public buildings, regulation, **40A:3.**
Single or two family residences as affected by subsequent enactments, **40A:6.**

YARMOUTH.
District court, **218:1.**
Medical examiner district, **38:1.**

Y CO-ORDINATE.
Surveying, definitions, **97:10.**

YEAR.
County finance.
See COUNTY FINANCE.
County treasurer.
See COUNTY TREASURERS.
Employment security.
Eligibility for benefits based on services performed during preceding benefit year, **151A:31.**
Erroneous payments of employment security benefits, recovery, **151A:42B.**
Income tax.
See INCOME TAX.
Recovery of erroneous employment security payments to claimant, **151A:42B.**
Schools.
See SCHOOLS AND EDUCATION.
Statute of frauds, contracts not to be performed within one year, **259:1.**
Statutory construction, **4:7.**
Taxable year for income tax purposes.
See INCOME TAX.
Unemployment compensation.
Employment security. See within this heading, "Employment security."
Year of service, defined, **149:184.**

YEARS, ESTATES FOR, 186:1 et seq.
See ESTATES FOR YEARS.

YEAS AND NAYS.
Mayor's veto, overriding, **39:4.**
When to be entered on journal, **US Const Art 1 Sec 5 cl 3.**
When vote must be taken by, **US Const Art 1 Sec 7 cl 2, 3.**

YELLOW DOG CONTRACTS.
Forbidden, **149:20, 149:20A.**
Penalty, **149:180.**

YELLOW PERCH.
Sale prohibited, **131:22.**

YIELD SIGNS.
Motor vehicles, regulating
operation, **89:9.**

YOUTH AUTHORITY ACT,
120:1 et seq.

YOUTH COMMISSION OF
CITY OR TOWN, 40:8E.

YOUTH CONSERVATION AND
SERVICE CORPS, 78A:1 et
seq.
Activities of corps, **78A:3.**
Annual report of corps, **78A:7.**
Conditions for provision of corps
services, **78A:4.**
Definitions, **78A:1.**
Funding decisions, **78A:4.**
Powers and objectives of corps,
78A:2.
Private employment of former
corps members, **78A:5.**
Requirements for operation of
corps, **78A:6.**

YOUTHFUL OFFENDERS.
See JUVENILE COURTS AND
DELINQUENT CHILDREN.

YOUTH HONOR DAY.
Observance, **6:15G.**

YOUTH IN GOVERNMENT
DAY.
Annual observances, **6:15WW.**

YOUTH ORGANIZATIONS.
Boxing matches at, age regulations
inapplicable, **147:39.**
Stocking private waters for
members, **131:4.**
Swimming pools, safety
requirements, **140:206.**

YOUTH SERVICES
DEPARTMENT AND
MASSACHUSETTS
TRAINING SCHOOLS,
18A:1 et seq., 120:1 et seq.
Accountings by superintendents of
industrial institutions, **35:45,**
120:8.
Administrative Procedure Act,
applicability, **30A:1B.**
Advisory committees.
Commissioner as member of
advisory committees to
other official bodies, **6:127,**
6:156, 6:168, 90A:1.
Department, advisory
committee, **18A:9.**
Education commissioner. See
within this heading,
"Education commissioner as
member of advisory groups."

YOUTH SERVICES
DEPARTMENT AND
MASSACHUSETTS
TRAINING SCHOOLS
—Cont'd
After-care, delinquency prevention
and community services
bureau.
Duties and responsibilities,
18A:6.
Establishment, **18A:4.**
Agents.
See AGENTS AND AGENCY.
Age of majority, discharge upon
attaining, **120:16.**
Agreements for separate care and
special treatment in
institutions, **120:10.**
Aiding escape from custody,
penalty, **120:26.**
Aid to persons given conditional
release or discharge, **120:11.**
Annual report to governor and
general court, **120:22.**
Anti-social tendencies, correction,
120:6A.
Appeals from commitments to
custody, **119:56.**
Arrest after escape or breach of
parole, **120:13.**
Assault and battery on department
employees, **265:13D.**
Assignment of counsel for inmates,
278:16.
Assistant commissioners, **18A:4.**
Bureau of after-care,
delinquency prevention and
community services, **18A:6.**
Bureau of educational services,
18A:7.
Bureau of institutional services,
18A:8.
Clinical services bureau, **18A:5.**
Birth of children to inmates,
subsequent care, **119:23A.**
Bond of superintendent, **120:8.**
Boston juvenile court's
administrative assistant to
coordinate activities, **218:58A.**
Breach of parole, arrest and
detention, **120:13.**
Building improvements,
expenditure of gifts, **120:24.**
Bureaus, **18A:4 et seq.**
Chaplains of industrial schools,
120:3.
Civil rights, discharge from
custody to result in full
restoration, **120:21.**
Civil service.
Appointment and removal of
employees as subject, **18A:1.**

YOUTH SERVICES
DEPARTMENT AND
MASSACHUSETTS
TRAINING SCHOOLS
—Cont'd
Civil service —Cont'd
Assistant commissioners as
subject, **18A:4.**
Commitment of child to care of
department not to disqualify
from future employment,
120:21.
Deputy commissioner as subject,
18A:3.
Claims for property damaged by
escaping inmates, **120:13A.**
Clinical services bureau, **18A:4.**
Duties, **18A:5.**
Commissioner of corrections.
Corrections commissioner. See
within this heading,
"Corrections commissioner."
Commissioner of probation.
Probation and parole. See within
this heading, "Probation and
parole."
Commissioner of youth services,
18A:1.
Agents employed for
investigation, **120:12.**
Agreements for separate care,
120:10.
Appointment of superintendents,
chaplains, etc., **120:3.**
Assistant commissioners. See
within this heading,
"Assistant commissioners."
Chaplains of institutions,
appointment, **120:3.**
Criminal history systems board,
member, **6:168.**
Criminal justice committee,
membership, **6:156.**
Criminal justice training council,
membership, **6:116.**
Department advisory committee,
membership, **18A:9.**
Deputy commissioner, **18A:3.**
Duties, **18A:2.**
Foster or detention homes,
transfer of children,
119:68B.
Health and welfare commission
advisory committee,
membership, **6:127.**
Highway safety committee,
membership, **90A:1.**
Inspections, **120:10.**
Law enforcement agencies,
120:10.
Places of detention and
diagnosis, powers, **120:11.**

**YOUTH SERVICES
DEPARTMENT AND
MASSACHUSETTS
TRAINING SCHOOLS**
—Cont'd
Commissioner of youth services
—Cont'd
Qualifications. See within this
heading, "Qualifications."
Rogers Fund, **120:9.**
Rules and regulations for
institutions and agencies,
duties, **120:4.**
State council on juvenile
behavior, membership,
6:159.
Superintendents. See within this
heading, "Superintendents
of schools and institutions."
Youth services coordinating
council, duty to convene,
120:10.
Commitments to custody, **119:58.**
Adjudication and proceedings
after adjudication, **119:58.**
Age as affecting, **119:58, 119:72,
119:72A, 119:74.**
Appeals, **119:56.**
Confinement of children, **120:6.**
Criminal proceedings, **119:84.**
Dangerous juveniles,
proceedings against
discharge, **120:17 et seq.**
Discharge of committed person.
See within this heading,
"Discharge of committed
person."
Disqualification for public
service, commitment of child
not to act, **120:21.**
Feeble-minded persons,
recommitment, **120:14.**
Foster homes, care of child in,
pending examination or
trial, **119:68.**
Information available to board,
119:69A.
Inspection of records, **120:21.**
Liberty under supervision,
120:6.
Motor vehicle laws, juvenile
violators, **119:58B.**
Pending examination or trial,
119:68.
Records of commitment.
Examination of children
committed, records, **120:5.**
Inadmissible in other
proceedings, **120:21.**
Inspection of, restricted,
120:21.

**YOUTH SERVICES
DEPARTMENT AND
MASSACHUSETTS
TRAINING SCHOOLS**
—Cont'd
Commitments to custody —Cont'd
Restoration of civil rights upon
discharge of one committed
for crime, **120:21.**
Study of children committed.
See within this heading,
"Study of children
committed."
Suspension of commitment,
279:2.
United States courts, children
committed, **120:25.**
Warrant of commitment, **119:84.**
Communication with prisoners,
penalty, **268:30.**
Compensation for property
damaged by escaping inmates
of institutions, **120:13A.**
Compensation of commissioner,
18A:1.
Conditional release or discharge,
aid to persons receiving,
120:11.
Confinement of committed persons,
120:6.
Contracts and agreements for
separate care and special
treatment in institutions,
120:10.
Control of industrial schools,
120:2.
Coordinating council for youth
services, **120:10.**
Corporate character, **120:1.**
Correctional institutions and
facilities.
Detention facilities. See within
this heading, "Detention
facilities."
Correction of socially harmful
tendencies, **120:6A.**
Corrections commissioner.
Advisory committee for youth
services department,
corrections commissioner as
member, **18A:9.**
Coordinating council, corrections
commissioner as member,
120:10.
Transfer of corrections
department prisoners to
youth services department,
120:15.
Costs.
Expenditures. See within this
heading, "Expenditures."

**YOUTH SERVICES
DEPARTMENT AND
MASSACHUSETTS
TRAINING SCHOOLS**
—Cont'd
Criminal history systems board,
youth services commissioner
as member, **6:168.**
Criminal justice committee, youth
services commissioner as
member, **6:156.**
Criminal justice training council,
youth services commissioner
as member, **6:116.**
Damage to property by escaping
inmates, claims, **120:13A.**
Dangerous juveniles, proceedings
against discharge, **120:17 et
seq.**
Delinquent children, services for,
120:1 et seq.
Dentists, employment, **120:2.**
Detention facilities.
Approval, **119:67.**
Authority to provide, **119:68,
119:68B.**
Establishment and operation,
120:11.
Use, **120:10.**
Diagnostic study, **119:68A,
119:68C.**
Places, **120:11.**
Discharge from employment of
superintendent or assistant
superintendent of training
school, just cause required,
35:51.
Discharge of committed person,
119:68, 120:6.
Age to be reached, **120:16.**
Conditional release or discharge,
aid to persons given, **120:11.**
Control as affected, **120:10.**
Dangerous juveniles,
proceedings against
discharge, **120:17 et seq.**
Delinquent children at age of
majority, **120:16.**
Failure to examine committed
child as ground, **120:5.**
Parole, release under.
Probation and parole. See
within this heading,
"Probation and parole."
Restoration of civil rights upon
discharge of one committed
for crime, **120:21.**
Dispensaries and clinics.
Clinical services bureau. See
within this heading,
"Clinical services bureau."

**YOUTH SERVICES
DEPARTMENT AND
MASSACHUSETTS
TRAINING SCHOOLS**
—Cont'd

District offices, establishment,
18A:1.

Disturbing, as criminal offense,
268:30.

Educational facilities and
institutions, **120:10.**

Educational services bureau in
education department.
Duties and responsibilities,
18A:7.

Establishment, **18A:4.**

Educational training and
activities, **120:6A.**

Education commissioner as
member of advisory groups.
Advisory committee, **18A:9.**
Coordinating council, **120:10.**

Education department.
See EDUCATION
DEPARTMENT.

Effectiveness of reformation
method, inquiry into, **120:22.**

Eligibility of commissioners.
Qualifications. See within this
heading, "Qualifications."

Employees, **18A:1, 120:2, 120:3,
120:12.**
Appointment and removal,
30:9B, 30:9D.
Civil service. See within this
heading, "Civil service."
Hours of labor and overtime pay
laws inapplicable, **149:30A,
149:30B.**
In-service training programs,
duty of educational services
bureau, **18A:7.**
Jury service, exemption, **234:1.**
Removal, suspension, transfer,
etc., **18A:1, 30:9B.**
Tenure of teacher, **30:9D.**
Vaccination of employees or
inmates, **111:182, 111:183.**
Working on holidays, **30:24A.**

Escape from custody, **120:13.**
Aiding in, penalty, **120:26.**
Arrest after, **120:13.**
Claims for property damaged in
course, **120:13A.**
Compensation for property
damaged by escaping
inmates of institutions,
120:13A.
Penalty, **120:26.**

Examination.
Records and examinations. See
within this heading,
"Records and examinations."

**YOUTH SERVICES
DEPARTMENT AND
MASSACHUSETTS
TRAINING SCHOOLS**
—Cont'd

Executive secretary for advisory
committee, **18A:9.**

Expenditures, **18A:1, 229:6A.**
Gifts, expenditure, **120:24.**

Experts, employment, **120:2.**

Federal courts, custody as to
commitments, **120:25.**

Federal funds, disposition, **18A:1.**

Feeble-minded persons,
recommitment, **120:14.**

Foreign states, authority to use
facilities, **120:10.**

Foster homes, provision, **119:68,
119:68B.**

Framingham correctional
institution, transfers, **120:15.**

General court, annual report,
120:22.

Gifts, expenditure, **120:24.**

Governor.
Annual report of youth services
commissioner, **120:22.**
Highway safety committee of
governor, youth services
commissioner as member,
90A:1.

Guardian of children, acting,
120:23.

Health and human services
executive office, agencies
within, **6A:16.**

Health and welfare commission
advisory committee,
membership, **6:127.**

Hearings in juvenile court,
attendance of agent, **119:55.**

Henry B. Rogers Fund, **120:9.**

Highway safety committee,
membership, **90A:1.**

Hours of labor and overtime pay
laws inapplicable to
employees, **149:30A, 149:30B.**

Industrial schools, **18A:8, 120:2 et
seq., 151A:30.**

Information to be furnished to,
after commitment, **119:69A.**

Insanity.
Mentally ill inmates. See within
this heading, "Mentally ill
inmates."

Inspection of public and private
institutions used, **40:36B,
111:20-111:22, 120:10.**

Institutional services bureau.
Duties and responsibilities,
18A:8.

**YOUTH SERVICES
DEPARTMENT AND
MASSACHUSETTS
TRAINING SCHOOLS**
—Cont'd

Institutional services bureau
—Cont'd
Establishment, **18A:4.**

Inventories of institutions under
supervision, **120:22.**

Jury and jury trial.
Exemption of employees from
jury service, **234:1.**

Juvenile courts, relation to,
119:69A.

Knowledge.
Notice or knowledge. See within
this heading, "Notice or
knowledge."

Law enforcement facilities, **120:10.**

Liberty under supervision for
committed persons, **120:6.**

Lyman school.
See LYMAN SCHOOL.

Majority age, discharge upon
attaining, **120:16.**

Medical care and treatment.
Clinical services bureau. See
within this heading,
"Clinical services bureau."
Provision, **120:6A.**
Use of medical facilities and
institutions, **120:10.**
Vaccination of inmates and
employees, **111:182,
111:183.**

Medical facilities and institutions,
120:10.

Mentally ill inmates.
Advisory committee,
membership of
commissioner of mental
health, **18A:9.**
Application for new commitment
to proper agency, **120:14.**
Coordinating council,
commissioner of mental
health as member, **120:10.**
Physicians, employment, **120:2.**
Psychiatric treatment, **120:6A.**
Recommitment, **120:14.**
Sexually dangerous persons,
120:14.

Missing children, report to central
register for missing children,
22A:7.

Modification of orders, **120:6.**

Motor vehicle violations,
commitments to board,
119:58B.

Norfolk correctional institution,
transfers, **120:15.**

YOUTH SERVICES DEPARTMENT AND MASSACHUSETTS TRAINING SCHOOLS
—Cont'd

Notice or knowledge.
Claims for damage by escaping inmates of institutions, notice, **120:13A.**
Furnishing information to board, **119:69A.**
Outside Commonwealth, authority to use facilities which are, **120:10.**
Pardon of child under 17 sentenced to death, custody after, **127:152.**
Parole.
Probation and parole. See within this heading, "Probation and parole."
Personnel of.
Employees. See within this heading, "Employees."
Physical education, **120:6A.**
Physicians, employment, **120:2, 120:3.**
Placement of children, **120:12.**
Places of detention and diagnosis, establishment and operation, **120:11.**
Potential psychotic in custody of, application for new commitment to appropriate agency, **120:14.**
Prevention of juvenile delinquency, program, **18A:2.**
Procedure and effect of sealing certain delinquency records files, **276:100B.**
Private institutions, powers, **120:10.**
Probation and parole.
Advisory committee, commissioner of probation as ex officio member, **18A:9.**
Commissioner of probation, department of youth services to supply information, **276:100.**
Cooperation of probation commissioners and officers, **120:22.**
Coordinating council, commissioner as member, **120:10.**
Inmate, parole, **120:12.**
Breach, **120:13.**
Officers.
Probation officers. See within this heading, "Probation officers."

YOUTH SERVICES DEPARTMENT AND MASSACHUSETTS TRAINING SCHOOLS
—Cont'd

Probation officers.
Co-operation, **120:22.**
Information to be furnished by department, **276:100.**
Interference with activities of department by probation officers prohibited, **276:97.**
Officers.
Probation officers. See within this heading, "Probation officers."
Youth services board furnishing information, **119:69A.**
Program for prevention of juvenile delinquency.
Prevention of juvenile delinquency. See within this heading, "Prevention of juvenile delinquency, program."
Psychiatrists, employment, **120:2.**
Psychologists, employment, **120:2.**
Public facilities and institutions, authority to use, **120:10.**
Public officers and employees.
Employees. See within this heading, "Employees."
Qualifications.
Assistant commissioners, **18A:5-18A:8.**
Commissioners of youth services, **18A:1.**
Deputy commissioner, **18A:3.**
Recommendations for legislation, **120:22.**
Reconfinement, order, **120:6.**
Records and examinations, **120:1, 120:5.**
Children committed, records of examinations, **120:5.**
Commitment, records of.
Commitment to custody. See within this heading, "Commitments to custody."
Failure of department to examine committed child as ground for release from custody, **120:5.**
Institutions used by department, examination or inspection, **120:10.**
Sealing of certain delinquency records, procedure and effect, **276:100B.**

YOUTH SERVICES DEPARTMENT AND MASSACHUSETTS TRAINING SCHOOLS
—Cont'd

Records and examinations
—Cont'd
Study of children committed. See within this heading, "Study of children committed."
Superintendents' books and documents, **35:45, 120:8.**
Release of inmate.
Discharge of committed person. See within this heading, "Discharge of committed person."
Religious belief, placement of children in accordance, **120:12.**
Revocation of orders, **120:6.**
Rogers Fund, **120:9.**
Rules and regulations for institutions and agencies, **120:4.**
Salary and compensation of commissioner, **18A:1.**
Sealing of certain juvenile delinquency records files, procedure and effect, **276:100B.**
Segregative facilities, **120:10.**
Sexually dangerous persons, recommitment, **120:14.**
Shirley industrial school.
See SHIRLEY INDUSTRIAL SCHOOL.
Socially harmful tendencies, correction, **120:6A.**
Social workers, employment, **120:2.**
Special care and treatment, agreements, **120:10.**
Special foster homes, provision, **119:68B.**
Statutes distributed to superintendents of training schools, **5:3.**
Study of children committed, **120:5.**
Diagnostic study. See within this heading, "Diagnostic study."
Succession to powers and duties of former trustees, **120:1.**
Superintendents of schools and institutions.
Accounts, **35:45, 120:8.**
Appointment by commissioner, **120:2, 120:3.**
Bond, **120:8.**

YOUTH SERVICES DEPARTMENT AND MASSACHUSETTS TRAINING SCHOOLS
—Cont'd
Superintendents of schools and institutions —Cont'd
Discharge from employment, just cause required, **35:51.**
Duties under direction of commissioner, **120:7.**
Powers, **120:7.**
Records, **35:45, 120:8.**
Statutes, delivery to superintendents of copies, **5:3.**
Supervisory facilities, **120:10.**
Suspension of commitment of child to custody, **279:2.**
Training required for employees, **41:96B.**
Transfer of inmates, **120:10, 120:15.**
Trespassing upon land of, penalty, **266:123.**
Trust funds for Massachusetts training schools, **10:15, 120:1.**
Unclaimed funds of wards, disposition, **120:23A.**
Vaccination of inmates and employees, **111:182, 111:183.**
Valuation of property of institutions, **58:13.**
Vocational training, **120:6A, 151A:30.**
Warrant for commitment of child, **119:84.**
Witnesses for inmates, **278:16.**
Youth services coordinating council, membership and duties, **120:10.**

Z

ZEPPELINS.
Insurance, **175:47, 175:93A, 175:93C, 175:117A.**

ZERO POWER COSTS.
Definitions, **164:94G.**

ZONE FARES.
Street railway transportation areas, **161:156.**

ZONE WATERS.
Environmental affairs executive office, duties and functions, **21A:2.**

ZONING AND PLANNING,
40A:1 et seq., 40B:1 et seq., 41:70-41:72, 41:81A et seq.
Abandonment as affecting nonconforming use status, **40A:6.**

ZONING AND PLANNING
—Cont'd
Accessory uses, special permits, **40A:5, 40A:9.**
Additions to ordinances and bylaws, **40A:5.**
Adjacent cities and towns to receive notice of adoption or change of ordinance or bylaw, **40A:5.**
Administrator, zoning, **40A:13.**
Defined, **40A:1A.**
Procedure for appeal of decisions, **40A:15.**
Zoning board of appeals hearing appeals from decisions, **40A:14.**
Adoption of improved method of planning, **41:81B.**
Adoption of ordinances and by-laws, **40A:1A, 40A:5.**
Adult entertainment clubs, **40A:6, 40A:9A.**
Advertising and advertisements.
Board of appeals, time and place of hearings, **40A:15, 41:81AA, 41:81T.**
Prior nonconforming uses, **40A:6.**
Subdivision control law, advertising notice of hearings, **41:81AA, 41:81T.**
Advice and advisory bodies.
Hazardous waste, advisory committee, **21C:3.**
Aggrieved persons, appeals to permit granting authority, **40A:8.**
Agriculture.
See AGRICULTURE.
Airport approaches, height limitations of structures within, **90:35A-90:35D, 90:40A et seq.**
See AIRPORTS AND LANDING FIELDS.
Aldermen and selectmen.
Selectmen or aldermen. See within this heading, "Selectmen or aldermen."
Alteration, amendment, or change.
City councils, changes or additions to official maps, **41:81F.**
Endangered species, alteration of significant habitat, **131A:4.**
Nonconforming use, **40A:6, 90:40D.**
Official maps, **41:81F, 41:81T.**

ZONING AND PLANNING
—Cont'd
Alteration, amendment, or change
—Cont'd
Ordinances and bylaws.
Amendment of ordinance or bylaw, **40:32B, 40A:5, 40A:6, 41:72, 121A:1.**
Reconsideration of proposed change, **40A:5, 40A:8, 40A:16.**
Streets.
Alteration, relocation or discontinuance of public ways and parks. See within this heading, "Alteration, relocation or discontinuance of public ways and parks."
Subdivision plans, **41:81O, 41:81U, 41:81W, 41:81X.**
Alteration, relocation or discontinuance of public ways and parks.
Approval of planning boards, **41:81G.**
Reference to planning boards, **41:81G, 41:81I.**
Showing on official maps, **41:81H.**
Amendment of ordinance or bylaw, **40A:5.**
Publication of notice of hearing as to amendment, **40A:5.**
Recorded subdivision plan as affected, **40A:6.**
Annual reports of planning boards, **41:71, 41:81C.**
Appeals, **40A:15.**
Administrator's actions, appeal, **40A:13.**
Board of appeals. See within this heading, "Board of appeals."
Judicial review, **40A:15, 40A:17.**
Land court. See within this heading, "Land court."
Lapse of special permit as affected, **40A:9.**
Low and moderate income housing, **40B:20-40B:23.**
Notice and hearing, **40A:15, 40A:17.**
Permit granting authority, appeals, **40A:8.**
Special permits and variances, **40A:9, 40A:11, 40A:15, 40A:17.**
Stay of termination of rights pending appeal, **40A:6.**
Subdivision control. See within this heading, "Subdivision control."

ZONING AND PLANNING
—Cont'd

Appeals —Cont'd

Superior court, **40A:17, 41:81BB.**

Appointment of counsel in action for review, **40A:17.**

Appropriations by cities and towns for planning and survey boards, **40:5, 40:44B, 41:72.**

Area requirements for single or two-family residences as affected by subsequent enactments, **40A:6.**

Art commission, **41:82-41:84.**

Assessors.

Certification of parties in interest, **40A:11.**

Plans of assessors as basis for district maps, **40A:4.**

Associate members of planning board designated as special permit granting authority, **40A:9.**

Attorney general, approval of zoning ordinance or bylaw, **40A:5.**

Attorneys at law, appointment of counsel in action for review of zoning provision, **40A:17.**

Billboards as prior nonconforming uses, **40A:6.**

Board of appeals, **40A:12 et seq., 41:81Z to 41:81CC.**

Administrator, appointment, **40A:13.**

Adoption of rules, **40A:5, 40A:12.**

Advertising place and time of hearings, **40A:15, 41:81AA, 41:81T.**

Appeals, **40A:15, 41:81BB.**

Change or adoption of ordinances and bylaws, powers and duties with respect, **40A:5.**

Establishment, **40A:12.**

Form of vote, **40A:15.**

Hearings, **40A:15, 40A:17.**

Meetings, **40A:15, 41:81AA.**

Ordinances or bylaws adopted or changed by amendment, **40A:5.**

Powers and duties, **40A:14.**

Procedure, **40A:15.**

Public hearing of, appeals, publication of date, **40A:15.**

Reconsideration of appeal, **40A:15, 40A:16.**

Records, **40A:15.**

Removal from office, **40A:12, 41:81A, 41:81Z.**

ZONING AND PLANNING
—Cont'd

Board of appeals —Cont'd

Representation of party interested in matter pending before, member prohibited, **40A:12, 41:81A.**

Reversal of orders, **40A:15.**

Rules, **40A:12, 40A:15.**

Special permits, **40A:11.**

Subdivision control. See within this heading, "Subdivision control."

Vacancies, **40A:12, 41:81A, 41:81Z.**

Bonds posted, **40A:17, 41:81BB, 41:81U.**

Boundaries.

See BOUNDARIES AND MARKERS.

Building commissioners, enforcement of ordinances and bylaws, **40A:7.**

Building inspectors.

Inspector of buildings. See within this heading, "Inspector of buildings."

Building permits.

Permits. See within this heading, "Permits."

Bulk of public buildings, regulation, **40A:3.**

Bylaws and ordinances, **40:32B, 40A:5, 40A:6, 41:72, 121A:1.**

Cemeteries at or near water supply, approval of plan, **114:35.**

Chairman of zoning board of appeals, **40A:12.**

Change.

Alteration, amendment, or change. See within this heading, "Alteration, amendment, or change."

Charter of city or town, questions as to adoption of plan F, **43:9B.**

Child care facilities, **40A:3, 40A:9C.**

City and town clerks.

Appeal to superior court, notice, **40A:17.**

Subdivision control. See within this heading, "Subdivision control."

Variance or special permit, recording notice, **40A:15.**

City councils.

Adoption of official map, **41:81E.**

Appeals, **40A:12, 40A:17.**

Changes or additions to official map, **41:81F.**

ZONING AND PLANNING
—Cont'd

City councils —Cont'd

Improved method of planning as affecting powers, **41:81G.**

Ordinances or bylaws adopted or changed by amendment, **40A:5.**

Rehearing required when final action delayed on amendments, **40A:5.**

Reports, **41:81C.**

Special permits, **40A:9.**

Terms of planning board members, city council to fix, **41:81A.**

City engineer, **40A:11, 41:73, 41:75.**

City planning boards, **41:70-41:72, 41:81A et seq.**

Clerks of city or town.

City and town clerks. See within this heading, "City and town clerks."

Clerks of zoning boards of appeals, **40A:12.**

Cluster development, **40A:9.**

Coal mine regulations as affecting, **21B:13.**

Community residence, disabled persons, **184:23D.**

Complaints in action for judicial review, **40A:17.**

Condominiums, applicability of subdivision control law, **183A:15.**

Conservation commission to review special permits, **40A:11.**

Constitution of Massachusetts, power of general court as to building zones in cities and towns, **MA Const Amend Art 60.**

Construction of regulations, petitions to obtain, **240:14A.**

Construction or laying out of public ways or parks.

Contractor's bond as security for construction of ways, planning board as requiring, **41:81U.**

Exterior lines of ways, establishment, **41:80, 41:81J.**

Reference to planning boards, **41:81G, 41:81I.**

Showing on official maps of establishment, **41:81H.**

Special permits, **40A:9.**

Subdivision control law, **41:81U, 41:81Y.**

ZONING AND PLANNING
—Cont'd

Costs.
See EXPENSES AND EXPENDITURES.
Counsel in actions for judicial review, **40A:17.**
County planning board, community affairs commissioner as member, **23B:1. (note)**
Coverage requirements of public buildings, **40A:3.**
Custodian of plans and records, **41:81A.**
Damages, liability of cities and towns, **41:81, 41:81B, 41:81F.**
Date.
Time or date. See within this heading, "Time or date."
Declaratory judgment action to test validity of ordinance or bylaw, **40A:5, 240:14A.**
Decrees.
Judgments and orders. See within this heading, "Judgments and orders."
Dedication for public use not to be required under subdivision control law, **41:81Q.**
Defects in adoption procedure as affecting validity of ordinance or bylaw, **40A:5.**
Definitions, **40A:1A.**
Adult paraphernalia store, **40A:9A.**
Adult video store, **40A:9A.**
Establishment which displays live nudity for its patrons, **40A:9A.**
Density of population, special permit for increase, **40A:9.**
Depth requirements for single or two-family residences as affected by subsequent enactments, **40A:6.**
Detrimental character or use.
Nonconforming uses as affected, **40A:6.**
Variances as affected, **40A:10.**
Disabled persons, community residence, **184:23D.**
Disapproval of subdivision plan as affecting land's exemption, **40A:6.**
Discontinuance of ways and parks.
Alteration, relocation or discontinuance. See within this heading, "Alteration, relocation or discontinuance of public ways and parks."

ZONING AND PLANNING
—Cont'd

Districts.
See DISTRICTS.
Drains.
Sewers and drains. See within this heading, "Sewers and drains."
Duties of planning boards, **41:70, 41:81B.**
Educational purposes, restrictions on regulation of land used, **40A:3.**
Effective date of ordinance, **40A:5.**
Elections.
Adoption of ordinance, **40A:5.**
Hearings prohibited on dates, **40A:11.**
Planning boards, election or appointment, **41:81A.**
Endangered species, alteration of significant habitat, **131A:4.**
Enforcement, **40A:7.**
Engineer of city or town, **40A:11, 41:73, 41:75.**
Entry upon lands, **41:79, 41:81B, 41:81CC.**
Environmental affairs executive office, duties and functions, **21A:2.**
Environmental code of state, effect on subdivisions, **111:127P.**
Environmental protection department, special permits, **40A:9.**
Establishment of planning boards, **41:70, 41:81A.**
Exceptions and exemptions.
Subsequent enactments, exemptions, **40A:6, 112:81R.**
Variance. See within this heading, "Variances."
Existing buildings, uses, etc.
Nonconforming use. See within this heading, "Nonconforming use."
Existing survey boards.
Survey boards. See within this heading, "Survey boards."
Expenses.
See EXPENSES AND EXPENDITURES.
Exterior lines of ways, establishment, **41:80, 41:81J.**
Family day care homes, exemption, **40A:3.**
Farming.
See AGRICULTURE.
Fee for recording special permit or variance, **40A:11.**

ZONING AND PLANNING
—Cont'd

Filing.
Records and recording. See within this heading, "Records and recording."
Financial hardship as ground for variance, **40A:10.**
Fines and penalties, **40A:7.**
Hospital in location prohibited by zoning ordinance, **111:75.**
Flood plain regulations, **40A:3.**
Floricultural use as requiring special permit, **40A:3.**
Former planning boards, superseding powers, **41:81B.**
Frontage requirements for single or two-family residences as affected by subsequent enactments, **40A:6.**
Governmental bodies as exempt, **40A:3.**
Growth and development policy committees, cities and towns, **40:4I.**
Hampden County housing court, judicial review, **40A:17.**
Hardship as ground for variance, **40A:10.**
Hazardous waste advisory committee, membership, **21C:3.**
Hazardous waste facilities, **40A:9.**
Health boards.
Powers, **111:143-111:154.**
Report as to approval or disapproval of subdivision plan, **41:81U.**
Special permits, review, **40A:11.**
Subdivision control law, approval of board, **41:81M, 41:81S, 41:81U.**
Hearing.
Notice and hearing. See within this heading, "Notice and hearing."
Height of public buildings, **40A:3.**
Highways and streets.
Ways and parks. See within this heading, "Ways and parks."
Horse or dog racing meetings as affected by regulations, **128A:3.**
Horticultural use as requiring special permit, **40A:3.**
Hospitals, location, **111:75.**
Housing.
Housing and urban renewal. See within this heading, "Housing and urban renewal."

ZONING AND PLANNING
—Cont'd
Housing —Cont'd
Master plan, **41:81D.**
Housing and community
development department,
23B:3, 40A:5.
Commissioner as member of
county planning board, **23:1.**
Copy of ordinance furnished,
40A:5.
Submission of completed plans
to community services
division, **41:71,
41:81C-41:81E.**
Housing and urban renewal.
Effect of zoning laws and
ordinances on low and
moderate income housing
projects, **40B:21, 121B:28.**
Operating agencies, application
of zoning ordinances,
121A:1, 121A:4, 121B:12.
Improved method of municipal
planning, **41:81A et seq.**
Indorsement of subdivision plans.
Subdivision control. See within
this heading, "Subdivision
control."
Injunction to restrain violations,
40A:7, 41:81B, 41:81Y.
Inspection of zoning maps for
proposed changes, **40A:5.**
Inspector of buildings.
Appeal of action, **40A:8.**
Enforcement of ordinances and
bylaws, **40A:7.**
Intensity of use, special permit for
increase, **40A:9.**
Interim zoning boards of appeals,
city councils or boards of
selectmen, **40A:12.**
Intervention in appeal to superior
court, **40A:17.**
Invalidity, procedure for
establishing, **40A:5, 240:14A.**
Judgments and orders.
Declaratory judgment as to
zoning law or regulation,
240:14A.
Subdivision plan's disapproval
as affecting land's zoning,
40A:6.
Judicial review.
Appeals. See within this
heading, "Appeals."
Jurisdiction.
Land court, **40A:17, 41:81BB,
41:81FF, 185:1.**
Superior court, **40A:7, 40A:17,
41:81B.**

ZONING AND PLANNING
—Cont'd
Land court.
Jurisdiction, **40A:17, 41:81BB,
41:81FF, 185:1.**
Subdivision control. See within
this heading, "Subdivision
control."
Landowners' requests for adoption
or change of ordinances or
bylaws, **40A:5.**
Land surveyors, exemption from
law, **112:81R.**
Lapse.
Special permit, **40A:9.**
Variance, **40A:10.**
Laying out public ways or parks.
Construction or laying out of
public ways or parks. See
within this heading,
"Construction or laying out
of public ways or parks."
Licenses.
Permits. See within this
heading, "Permits."
Limitation of actions, **40A:7.**
Subdivision control. See within
this heading, "Subdivision
control."
Limitations.
Building permits, **40A:14.**
Penalties for violations of
ordinances and bylaws,
40A:7.
Subdivision control, limitation
upon scope, **41:81DD.**
Subject of ordinances and
bylaws, **40A:3.**
Lots.
Dwelling, prohibiting more than
one on same lot, **41:81Q.**
Law governing, lots shown on
plans previously submitted
to planning board, **40A:6.**
Regulation of area of public
buildings, **40A:3.**
Subdivision control law,
definition, **41:81L.**
Low to moderate income housing,
special permits as predicated
upon providing, **40A:9.**
Mailing of notice as to adoption or
change of ordinance or bylaw,
40A:5.
Maps and plans, **40A:4.**
Inspection, **40A:5.**
Official maps. See within this
heading, "Official maps of
cities and towns."
Subdivision control. See within
this heading, "Subdivision
control."

ZONING AND PLANNING
—Cont'd
Maps and plans —Cont'd
Subsequent enactments as
affecting adoption and
approval of plans, **40A:6.**
Survey boards. See within this
heading, "Survey boards."
Markers.
See BOUNDARIES AND
MARKERS.
Master plan of municipal planning
boards as affecting, **41:81D.**
Mayors to appoint and remove
members of boards, **40A:12,
41:70, 41:81A.**
Meetings of zoning board, **40A:15,
41:81AA.**
Membership of planning board.
Improved method of municipal
planning, **41:81A.**
Special permit granting
authority, associate
members of board
designated, **40A:9.**
Mobile homes permissible as
residences for owners of
homes destroyed by natural
holocausts, **40A:3.**
Monuments.
See BOUNDARIES AND
MARKERS.
Moratoriums.
Consideration of ordinance or
bylaw after disapproval,
40A:5.
Favorable action following
adverse ruling, **40A:16.**
Subdivisions, **40A:6.**
Zoning administrator, appeals,
40A:13.
Motor vehicle junkyards, location,
140B:2.
Multi-family use in nonresidential
area, special permit, **40A:9.**
Municipal officers, appeal to
permit granting authority,
40A:8.
Municipal planning boards,
41:70-41:72, 41:81A et seq.
New or relocated public ways or
public parks to be shown on
official map, **41:81H.**
Newspapers, publication of notice
of hearing, **40A:5.**
Noisome or offensive trades or
businesses, regulation by
health boards,
111:143-111:154.

ZONING AND PLANNING
—Cont'd
Nonconforming use.
Airport approach regulations, permit for erection, replacement, or alteration of structures, etc., **90:40D.**
Alteration or change, **40A:6, 90:40D.**
Increase in area requirement as affecting, **40A:6.**
Public service corporations, **40A:3.**
Recorded subdivision plans, **40A:6.**
Uses preceding statute, **40A:6.**
Zoning as affecting, **40A:3, 40A:6.**
Nonresident property owners to receive notice of adoption or change of zoning ordinance, **40A:5.**
Nonuse as affecting nonconforming use status, **40A:6.**
Notice and hearing, **40A:11.**
Adoption or change of ordinances or bylaws, **40A:5.**
Amendment of ordinances or bylaws, publication of notice of hearing, **40A:5.**
Appeals, **40A:15, 40A:17.**
Board of appeals, time and place of learnings, **40A:15, 41:81AA, 41:81T.**
Buildings, zoning violations, proceedings, **40A:7.**
Change of regulations, **40A:5.**
Change or adoption of ordinance or bylaw, hearing, **40A:5.**
Decision of zoning board of appeals, requirements, **40A:15, 40A:17.**
Failure to construct ways or streets, **41:81U.**
Ocean sanctuaries, permit for waste disposal, **132A:16E.**
Official maps, hearings, **41:81F, 41:81T.**
Permit issued prior to, **40A:6.**
Prior nonconforming uses, **40A:6.**
Procedure for conducting hearing, **40A:15.**
Publication. See within this heading, "Publication."
Special permit, **40A:9, 40A:15.**
Subdivision control. See within this heading, "Subdivision control."
Superior court, notice of appeals, **40A:17.**

ZONING AND PLANNING
—Cont'd
Notice and hearing —Cont'd
Survey boards. See within this heading, "Survey boards."
Urban redevelopment corporations, planning board, **121A:6.**
Variance, **40A:10.**
Violations, proceedings, **40A:7.**
Number of dwellings on lot, **41:81Q.**
Nursery stock, **40A:3.**
Ocean sanctuaries, notice of application for variance to permit waste disposal, **132A:16E.**
Official maps of cities and towns, **41:81E-41:81H.**
Adoption, **41:81E.**
Alteration, relocation or discontinuance of public ways and parks in accordance, **41:81G, 41:81H.**
Changes or additions, **41:81F, 41:81T.**
Establishment of public ways or parks to be shown, **41:81H.**
Exterior lines of ways, **41:81J.**
Notice and hearing as to changes or additions, **41:81F, 41:81T.**
Subdivision control. See within this heading, "Subdivision control."
Town meetings. See within this heading, "Town meetings."
Open spaces.
Master plan, **41:81D.**
Public buildings, regulation of open space, **40A:3.**
Special permit as predicated upon providing, **40A:9.**
Orders.
Judgments and orders. See within this heading, "Judgments and orders."
Ordinances and bylaws, **40:32B, 40A:5, 40A:6, 41:72, 121A:1.**
Organization of planning boards, **41:81A.**
Outdoor advertising adjacent to interstate and primary highway systems in certain areas, control, **93D:2.**
Outer continental shelf, activities requiring on shore facilities, **131:40.**
Overhead wires and poles, determination as to prohibition of new construction or progressive removal, **166:22B.**

ZONING AND PLANNING
—Cont'd
Parking around public buildings, **40A:3.**
Parks.
Ways and parks. See within this heading, "Ways and parks."
Parties.
Appeals to superior court, **40A:17.**
Definition of parties in interest, **40A:11.**
Standing to appeal to permit, **40A:8.**
Pedestrian improvements, special permits as predicated, **40A:9.**
Penalties.
Fines and penalties. See within this heading, "Fines and penalties."
Permits.
Accessory uses, special permits, **40A:5, 40A:9.**
Appeal to granting authority, **40A:8, 40A:15.**
Certification of parties in interest, **40A:11.**
Definitions, **40A:1A.**
Limitations, **40A:14.**
Nonconforming uses, approval, **40A:6.**
Notice, applicability of zoning ordinances issued prior, **40A:6.**
Power of board to impose limitations, **40A:14.**
Procedure on appeal, **40A:15.**
Special permits. See within this heading, "Special permits."
Standing to appeal, **40A:8.**
Subdivision control law, **41:81AA, 41:81Y.**
Subsequent enactments as affecting, **40A:6.**
Variances. See within this heading, "Variances."
Withholding, **40A:7.**
Petitions for special permits, **40A:11.**
Physically handicapped, exemptions applicable to ramps, **40A:3.**
Planned unit development defined, **40A:9.**
Planning boards, **40A:5, 40A:6, 40A:11, 41:70-41:72, 41:81A et seq.**
Plans.
Maps and plans. See within this heading, "Maps and plans."
Playgrounds, acquisition, **45:14.**

ZONING AND PLANNING
—Cont'd

Pleading on appeals, **40A:17.**

Posting of notice of hearing on adoption or change of ordinance or bylaw, **40A:5.**

Powers and duties of planning boards, **41:81B.**

Preference of actions for judicial review, **40A:17.**

Presumptions.
License or authority, acting without, **143:60.**
Special permit, acquiescence in granting, **40A:11.**

Prior nonconforming uses.
Nonconforming use. See within this heading, "Nonconforming use."

Private ways.
Survey boards. See within this heading, "Survey boards."

Process, service of notice of superior court appeal, **40A:17.**

Publication.
Bylaws, manner of publication, **40:32, 40:32A.**
Notice and hearing. See within this heading, "Notice and hearing."

Public buildings as subject, **40A:3.**

Public inspection of proposed ordinance or bylaw, notice to indicate place, **40A:5.**

Public service corporations, regulation of use of lands, **40A:3.**

Public utilities.
See TELECOMMUNICATIONS AND ENERGY DEPARTMENT.

Recommendations of planning boards, **41:81C.**

Reconsideration of proposed change, **40A:5, 40A:8, 40A:16.**

Records and recording.
Custodian of plans and records, **41:81A.**
Filing of proceedings records, **40A:15.**
Metropolitan area planning council, duties, **40B:25.**
Municipal planning boards, master plan, **41:81D.**
Nonconforming uses, recorded subdivision plans, **40A:6.**
Proceedings before zoning boards of appeals, requirements, **40A:15.**
Reports. See within this heading, "Reports."

ZONING AND PLANNING
—Cont'd

Records and recording —Cont'd
Special permit or variance, **40A:9, 40A:11, 40A:15.**
Subdivision control. See within this heading, "Subdivision control."
Survey boards, plans, **41:78.**
Telecommunications and energy department, fees for filing applications or documents, **25:10B.**

Recreation, master plan, **41:81D.**

Redemption in part from tax sales under subdivision control law, **60:76A.**

Reference of certain matters to planning boards, **41:81G, 41:81I, 41:81Q.**

Regional and local planning.
Adoption or change of ordinance or bylaw, notice, **40A:5.**
Districts, **40B:1 et seq.**
See REGIONAL PLANNING DISTRICTS.
Environmental affairs executive office, duties and functions, **21A:2.**
Hazardous waste advisory committee, membership, **21C:3.**
Housing and community development department, powers and duties, **23B:3.**
Interstate compacts.
See INTERSTATE COMPACTS AND AGREEMENTS.
Permit granting authority, appeal, **40A:8.**
Request for adoption or change of ordinance or bylaw, **40A:5.**

Regional planning districts.
See REGIONAL PLANNING DISTRICTS.

Regional refuse disposal districts.
See REGIONAL REFUSE DISPOSAL DISTRICTS.

Regional school districts.
See REGIONAL SCHOOL DISTRICTS.

Register of deeds.
Subdivision control. See within this heading, "Subdivision control."

Rehearing on proposed zoning amendments, **40A:5.**

Religious purposes, restrictions on regulation of land used, **40A:3.**

ZONING AND PLANNING
—Cont'd

Relocation of ways and parks.
Alteration, relocation or discontinuance. See within this heading, "Alteration, relocation or discontinuance of public ways and parks."

Removal of members of board of appeals, **40A:12, 41:70, 41:81A, 41:81Z.**

Repeal of ordinances and bylaws, **40A:5.**

Reports, **41:71, 41:81C.**
Director of housing and community development, **40C:3.**
Health board or officer making report as to approval or disapproval of subdivision plan, **41:81U.**

Representation of party interested in matter before board, member prohibited, **40A:12, 41:81A.**

Request for adoption or change of zoning ordinance and bylaws, **40A:5.**

Residential zone, subdivision lots, **41:81S, 41:81U.**

Review.
Appeals. See within this heading, "Appeals."

Rules.
Issuance of special permits, **40A:9.**
Subdivision control. See within this heading, "Subdivision control."
Zoning boards of appeals to adopt, **40A:12.**

Scientific research and development, special permits, **40A:9.**

Security required under subdivision control law for completion of required ways and services, **41:81U.**

Selectmen or aldermen.
Acting as planning board, **41:81A.**
Adoption or change of ordinances or bylaws, **40A:5.**
Consent to reconsideration of appeal or petition for variance, **40A:16.**
Enforcement of ordinances and bylaws, **40A:7.**
Hearing on adoption or change of ordinances or bylaws, **40A:5.**

ZONING AND PLANNING
—Cont'd
Selectmen or aldermen —Cont'd
Improved municipal planning as affecting powers, **41:81G.**
Interim zoning boards of appeals, **40A:12.**
Metropolitan area planning council, appointment of members, **40B:24.**
Regional district planning commissions, **40B:4.**
Reports and recommendations, **41:81C.**
Subdivision control law, duties, **41:81DD, 41:81Z.**
Survey boards.
Acting as survey boards, **41:73.**
Effect of laws, **41:77.**
Withholding building or construction permits in violation of ordinances or bylaws, **40A:7.**
Zoning board of appeals, may act, **40A:12.**
Service of notice of superior court appeal, **40A:17.**
Setbacks for public buildings, **40A:3.**
Several dwellings on same lot, **41:81Q.**
Sewers and drains.
Effect of lack of survey board's approval, **41:77.**
Subdivision control law.
"Drainage" defined, **41:81L.**
Permit for construction of individual sewage system in absence of public or community sewer, **41:81U.**
Proposed subdivision's use of system, **41:81U.**
Shape of land as affecting granting of variance, **40A:10.**
Signs as prior nonconforming uses, **40A:6.**
Single family dwelling.
Limitation as to regulating interior area, **40A:3.**
Subsequent enactment as affecting, **40A:6.**
Snob zoning law, **40B:20 et seq.**
Soil conditions as affecting granting of variance, **40A:10.**
Solar energy.
Definitions, **40A:1A.**
Special permits, protection of access to sunlight, **40A:9, 40A:9B.**
Sunlight, protection of access, **40A:3.**

ZONING AND PLANNING
—Cont'd
Solid waste management, permission for construction or expansion on any locus zoned for industrial use, **40A:9.**
Special permits, **40A:9.**
Accessory uses, special permits, **40A:9.**
Adult bookstores and theaters, **40A:9A.**
Agricultural use, **40A:3.**
Appeals, **40A:9, 40A:11, 40A:15, 40A:17.**
Approval, **40A:9, 40A:15.**
Certificate of special permit, contents, **40A:11.**
Cluster development, **40A:9.**
Definitions, **40A:1A.**
Environmental protection department, **40A:9.**
Filing procedures, **40A:9, 40A:15.**
Nonconforming uses, approval, **40A:6.**
Petitions, submission, **40A:11.**
Recording notice, **40A:15.**
Review of application, **40A:11.**
Shared elderly housing, **40A:9.**
Solar energy, protection of access to sunlight, **40A:9, 40A:9B.**
Subsequent enactments as affecting, **40A:6.**
Withdrawal of application, **40A:16.**
Zoning board of appeal's powers, **40A:14.**
Speedy trial of appeals under subdivision control law, **41:81BB.**
Stables, **111:155-111:158.**
Standing to appeal to permit granting authority, **40A:8.**
State and state agencies as exempt, **40A:3.**
State building code as affecting, **40A:3.**
Statute of limitations.
Limitation of actions. See within this heading, "Limitation of actions."
Stay or supersedeas.
Disapproval of subdivision plan as affecting exemption of land from zoning law, **40:6.**
Termination of rights pending appeal of plans, stay, **40A:6.**
Studies of resources, **41:81C.**
Subdivision control, **41:81K to 41:81GG.**
Acceptance of law, **41:73, 41:81EE, 41:81N.**

ZONING AND PLANNING
—Cont'd
Subdivision control —Cont'd
Adoption of zoning laws as affecting recorded subdivision claim, **40A:6.**
Advertising, **41:81AA, 41:81T.**
Amendment or change of plans, **41:81O, 41:81U, 41:81W, 41:81X.**
Appeals.
Advertising of hearings by appeals board, **41:81AA, 41:81T.**
Approval, determination that plans require, **41:81P.**
Boards, **40A:17, 41:81Z to 41:81CC.**
Bonds posted, **40A:17, 41:81BB.**
Building permits may be issued by boards, **41:81AA, 41:81Y.**
Certificate as to approval of plan to superior court, **41:81X.**
Costs on appeal, **41:81BB.**
Hearing, **41:81AA.**
Land court jurisdiction, **40A:17, 41:81BB.**
Limitation of time, **41:81BB.**
Meetings, **41:81AA.**
Members, appointment, terms, removal, **41:81Z.**
Notice of hearings, **41:81AA.**
Right of judicial appeal, **40A:17, 41:81BB.**
Rules, **41:81AA.**
Speedy trial, **41:81BB.**
Superior court, **41:81BB.**
Applicant to bear expense of giving notice of hearings on plans, **41:81T.**
Appropriations by towns, expenditure, **40:5.**
Approval or disapproval of plans submitted, **40A:4, 41:81P, 41:81X.**
Building permits, **41:81AA, 41:81Y.**
Certain lapse as exempt from application of zoning laws, **40A:6.**
Certificates and certifications.
Conclusiveness of certificates on plans, **41:81X.**
Definitions, **41:81L.**
Rules and regulations of planning boards, **41:81N.**
Superior court, certificate as to approval of plan, **41:81X.**

ZONING AND PLANNING
—Cont'd
Subdivision control —Cont'd
City or town clerk.
Approval, notice as to plan
requiring, **41:81P.**
Certificate of action of
planning board filed,
41:81U.
Certificate on plan, **41:81X.**
Delivery of certificate to
person submitting plan,
41:81V.
Court approval of plan,
certificate, **41:81X.**
Custodian of planning board
records and plans,
41:81A.
Delivery of certificate to
person submitting plan,
41:81V.
Final approval of plan,
certificate, **41:81V.**
Notice.
Action taken on plan,
41:81S.
Approval, notice as to plan
requiring, **41:81P.**
Submission of plan, **41:81T.**
Plans submitted, **41:81S,
41:81U.**
Preliminary plans, notice of
approval or disapproval,
41:81S.
Recording plans, certificate,
41:81X.
Rules and regulations filed,
41:81Q.
Conclusiveness of indorsements
and certificates on plans,
41:81X.
Condominiums, applicability of
law, **183A:15.**
Construction of ways and
municipal services, alternate
security, **41:81U.**
Continuing powers of certain
boards, **41:81GG.**
Costs on appeal, **41:81BB.**
Court approval of plans on
appeal, indorsement,
41:81X.
Dedication for public use not to
be required, **41:81Q.**
Definitions under subdivision
control law, **41:81L.**
Definitive plans, date of
approval, **40A:6.**
Disabled persons, community
residence, **184:23D.**

ZONING AND PLANNING
—Cont'd
Subdivision control —Cont'd
Disapproval of plan as affecting
exemption of land from
applicability of subsequent
zoning law, **40A:6.**
Drains.
Sewers and drains. See within
this heading, "Sewers and
drains."
Entry upon land, **41:81CC.**
Environmental code of state,
111:127P.
Expense of applicant for notice
of hearings on plans,
41:81T.
Grantor's liability to grantee for
failure to comply, **41:81Y.**
Gravel, approval of right to
remove, **40:21.**
Health, approval of board,
41:81M, 41:81S, 41:81U.
Indorsements.
Approval not required under
subdivision control law,
indorsement, **41:81P.**
Approval of plan, indorsement,
41:81V.
Conclusiveness of indorsement
on plan, **41:81X.**
Definition of subdivision,
41:81L.
Injunction to restrain violations,
41:81Y.
Land court.
Acceptance of law, notice,
41:73, 41:81EE, 41:81N.
Change of plans, action,
41:81W.
Jurisdiction, **41:81BB,
41:81FF.**
Plans of land, acceptance,
41:81X.
Recording notices, **41:81X.**
Registration or confirmation
before effective date of
law, **41:81FF.**
Rules and regulations, filing,
41:81EE, 41:81Q.
Layout of public ways and
buildings within
subdivision, **41:81Y.**
Legislative statement of
purpose, **41:81M.**
Limitation of actions, **41:81Y.**
Appeal, **41:81BB.**
Limitation upon scope,
41:81DD.
Lot, defined, **41:81L.**
Maps or plans, **41:81S, 41:81U.**
Advertising of hearings,
41:81T.

ZONING AND PLANNING
—Cont'd
Subdivision control —Cont'd
Maps or plans —Cont'd
Approval by planning board,
**40A:6, 41:81O, 41:81U,
41:81V, 41:81W.**
Buyer of lot, submission,
41:81Y.
Certificates.
Delivery of plan and
certificate to person
submitting plan,
41:81V.
Failure of planning board to
file certificate of action
with clerk, **41:81U.**
Change or modification,
**41:81O, 41:81U, 41:81W,
41:81X.**
Custodian, **41:81A.**
Delivery of plan and certificate
to person submitting plan,
41:81V.
Expediting, **41:81U.**
Hearing, **41:81T.**
Land court's acceptance of
plans, **41:81X.**
Liability of persons executing
deeds where subdivision
made without required
plan, **41:81Y.**
Methods of submitting to
planning board, **41:81O.**
Modification of plans, **41:81O,
41:81U, 41:81W, 41:81X.**
Moratoriums on subdivision
plans, **40A:6.**
Notice, **41:81P, 41:81T.**
Official map in city or town,
41:81V.
Preliminary plans, **41:81L,
41:81S.**
Recording, **40A:4, 41:81P,
41:81X.**
Preliminary plans, **41:81S.**
Prior recording, registration,
or confirmation of
subdivision plans, law
as affecting land in
case, **41:81FF.**
Referral to other board or
person not to be required,
41:81Q.
Registers of deeds, duties,
41:81X.
Rescission of approval of
definitive plans, **41:81X.**
Submission of plan, **41:81T.**
Meetings of appeals boards,
41:81AA.

ZONING AND PLANNING
—Cont'd
Subdivision control —Cont'd
Monuments and marks,
41:81CC.
Moratoriums on subdivision
plans, 40A:6.
Nonacceptance of law,
transmittal of statement,
41:73.
Notices.
Action of board on plan,
41:81U.
Advertising notice of hearings,
41:81AA, 41:81T.
Appeals board, hearing,
41:81AA, 41:81T.
Applicant to bear expense of
giving notice of hearings
on plans, 41:81T.
Building permits, issuance by
appeals boards, 41:81AA.
Completion of required works
and services, 41:81U.
Expense of applicant as to
hearing on plans, 41:81T.
Hearings on proposed rules
and regulations, 41:81Q.
Recording, 41:73, 41:81EE,
41:81N, 41:81X.
Rules and regulations, notice
and hearing, 41:81Q.
Submission of plan, notice to
city or town clerk, 41:81T.
Time for giving notice as to
plan requiring approval,
41:81P.
Ordinance or bylaw applicable
on approval of plan, 40A:6.
Parks may be required, 41:81U.
Permits for building, 41:81AA,
41:81U, 41:81Y.
Playgrounds may be required,
41:81U.
Preliminary plans, 41:81S.
Prohibition of more than one
house on same lot, 41:81Q.
Public utilities, provisions as to
underground public utility
systems, 41:81M, 41:81Q.
Public ways, 41:81DD, 41:81Q,
41:81Y.
Purposes of law, 41:81M.
Real estate time-shares, 183B:9.
Recording.
Amendment or change of
plans, 41:81W.
Court approval of plans,
requirement of
indorsement, 41:81X.
Effective date of law, effect of
recording before, 41:81FF.

ZONING AND PLANNING
—Cont'd
Subdivision control —Cont'd
Recording —Cont'd
Notices, 41:73, 41:81EE,
41:81N, 41:81X.
Preliminary plans, 41:81S.
Rules and regulations,
41:81EE, 41:81Q.
Redemption in part from tax
sales, 60:76A.
Register of deeds.
Definitions, 41:81L.
Duties as to plans, 41:81X.
Transmitting statements,
41:73, 41:81EE.
Removal of appeals board
members, 41:81Z.
Reports by health boards or
officers as to plans,
furnishing copies, 41:81U.
Revocation of disapproval of
definitive plan and approval
of amended plan, 41:81U.
Rules and regulations, 41:81N,
41:81Q-41:81S.
Appeals board, 41:81AA.
Recording, 41:81EE, 41:81Q.
Waiver of strict compliance,
41:81R.
Security required prior to
approval of definitive plan,
41:81U.
Selectmen or aldermen, duties,
41:81DD, 41:81Z.
Sewers and drains. See within
this heading, "Sewers and
drains."
Short title of act, 41:81K.
Soil, approval of right to remove,
40:21.
Speedy trial of appeals,
41:81BB.
Subdivision defined, 41:81L.
Submission of plans to planning
board, 41:81O.
Subsequent enactments, 40A:6.
Superior court.
Appeals, 41:81BB.
Certificate as to approval of
plan, 41:81X.
Enforcement of law, 41:81Y.
Surveys, authorized, 41:81CC.
Territory where effective,
41:81N.
Town clerks, duties as to
certificates of court
approval of plans, 41:81X.
Unconstitutionality of part of
law, 41:81GG.
Tax lien certificates, recording
requirements, subdivision
plans, 60:23.

ZONING AND PLANNING
—Cont'd
Subdivision control —Cont'd
Tax sale under, partial
redemption, 60:76A.
Time or date.
Approval or disapproval of
plans, 40A:6, 41:81S.
Notice as to plan requiring
approval, time for giving,
41:81P.
Time-shares, 183B:9.
Town appropriations,
expenditure, 40:5.
Transmittal of statement as to
nonacceptance of subdivision
control law, 41:73.
Underground utility systems,
41:81M, 41:81Q.
Waiver of strict compliance with
rules, 41:81R.
Substantial extension or change of
use as affected by subsequent
enactment, 40A:6.
Substantial hardship as ground for
variance, 40A:10.
Superior court.
Appeal, 40A:17, 41:81BB.
Costs, 40A:17.
Jurisdiction, 40A:7, 40A:17,
41:81B.
Procedure, 40A:17.
Subdivision control. See within
this heading, "Subdivision
control."
Supersedeas.
Stay or supersedeas. See within
this heading, "Stay or
supersedeas."
Superseding powers of former
planning boards, 41:81B.
Survey boards, 41:73-41:81.
Aldermen.
Selectmen or aldermen. See
within this heading,
"Selectmen or aldermen."
Appointment and terms of
members, 41:73.
Appropriations by towns, 40:5.
Approval, plans not to be
recorded prior, 41:78.
City engineer, 40A:11, 41:73,
41:75.
Compensation, 41:73.
Construction of ways not in
accordance with plans
forbidden, 41:77.
Entry upon lands, right, 41:79.
Existing boards.
Continuance, 41:73, 41:81GG.
Superseding powers, 41:81B.

ZONING AND PLANNING
—Cont'd

Survey boards —Cont'd

Exterior lines, establishment, **41:80.**

Monuments and marks, entry upon lands for placing and maintaining, **41:79.**

Nonacceptance of subdivision control law, statement as to, transmittal to register of deeds and to land court, **41:73.**

Notice and hearing.

New plans, substitution, **41:76.**

Private ways, approval of plans, **41:74.**

Public ways, plans of boards, **41:75.**

Planning boards under improved method of municipal planning, effect of establishment, **41:81B.**

Plans.

Construction of ways not in accordance with, forbidden, **41:77.**

Preparation by boards, **41:75.**

Private persons, filing, **41:74.**

Public ways, notice and hearing regarding plans, **41:75.**

Recording, **41:78.**

Substitution of new plans, **41:76.**

Private ways open for public use.

Nonapproval by board, **41:77.**

Plans for, filing and approval, **41:74.**

Sewer and drains, effect of lack of approval, **41:77.**

Recording of plans, **41:78.**

Selectmen or aldermen. See within this heading, "Selectmen or aldermen."

Substitution of new plans, **41:76.**

Superseding powers of existing survey boards, **41:81B.**

Terms of office, **41:73.**

Ways and parks.

Public ways, plans, **41:75.**

Tax assessors.

Assessors. See within this heading, "Assessors."

Tax bills, notice provisions as to adoption or change of zoning ordinance or bylaw to be contained, **40A:5.**

Taxing of costs in action for judicial review, **40A:17.**

ZONING AND PLANNING
—Cont'd

Tax sale under subdivision control law, partial redemption, **60:76A.**

Ten thousand in population, cities and towns over, **41:70, 41:81A.**

Terms of office of planning or survey board members, **41:73, 41:81A.**

Time or date.

Effective date of ordinance, **40A:5.**

Lapse. See within this heading, "Lapse."

Laws applicable to plans as determined by date of approval by planning boards, **40A:6.**

Limitation of actions. See within this heading, "Limitation of actions."

Moratoriums. See within this heading, "Moratoriums."

Ordinance or bylaw, effective dates, **40A:5, 40A:6.**

Special permits, when to take effect, **40A:9.**

Subdivision control. See within this heading, "Subdivision control."

Terms of office of board members, **41:73, 41:81A.**

Title of act, **40A:1, 41:K.**

Topography as affecting granting of variance, **40A:10.**

Town clerks.

City and town clerks. See within this heading, "City and town clerks."

Town meetings.

Adoption of official map, **41:81E.**

Changes or additions to official maps, **41:81F.**

Election of members of planning board, **41:70, 41:81A.**

Reports, **41:81C.**

Traffic improvements, special permit as predicated, **40A:9.**

Trial.

Notice and hearing. See within this heading, "Notice and hearing."

Preference in action for judicial review, **40A:17.**

Two-family use as affected by subsequent enactment, **40A:6.**

Unfavorable action.

Annulment of favorable decision of board by court, **40A:16.**

ZONING AND PLANNING
—Cont'd

Unfavorable action —Cont'd

Reconsideration of proposed change after, **40A:5, 40A:16.**

Unhealthful or offensive trades or businesses, powers of health boards over location, **111:143-111:154.**

Uniformity of uses within districts, **40A:4.**

Urban renewal.

Housing and urban renewal. See within this heading, "Housing and urban renewal."

Vacancies, filling, **40A:12, 41:81A, 41:81Z, 41:106B.**

Validity of zoning laws and building restrictions, petitions to determine, **40A:7, 240:14A.**

Variances, **40A:10.**

Appeals, **40A:9, 40A:11, 40A:15, 40A:17.**

Certificate of variance, contents, **40A:11.**

Filing procedures, **40A:9, 40A:15.**

Hardship, **40A:10.**

Ocean sanctuaries, waste disposal, **132A:16E.**

Withdrawal of application, **40A:16.**

Zoning board of appeal's powers, **40A:14.**

Violations of ordinances and bylaws.

Appeals to permit granting authority, **40A:8.**

Fines and penalties. See within this heading, "Fines and penalties."

Injunctions against violations, **40A:7, 41:81E, 41:81Y.**

Limitations on penalties, **40A:7.**

Notice, **40A:7.**

Viticulture, exemptions, **40A:3.**

Voting.

Board of appeals, **40A:15.**

Elections. See within this heading, "Elections."

Issuance of special permit, **40A:9.**

Waiver.

Exemption provisions, manner of waiver, **40A:6.**

Notice of public hearing, **40A:11.**

Strict compliance with rules under subdivision control law, waiver, **41:81R.**

Water supply, approval of plan for cemeteries at or near, **114:35.**

ZONING AND PLANNING
—Cont'd
Ways and parks.
Acquisition of playgrounds,
45:14.
Adoption of official map, **41:81E.**
Advertising in unzoned
commercial areas adjacent
to interstate and primary
highway systems, control,
93D:2.
Alteration, relocation or
discontinuance. See within
this heading, "Alteration,
relocation or discontinuance
of public ways and parks."
Approval of planning board
required, **41:81G.**
Bond to secure construction of,
planning board's action to
enforce, **41:81U.**
Boundaries, planning board may
establish, **41:81J.**
Changes or additions to official
maps, **41:81F, 41:81T.**
City council's power as affected
by planning provisions,
41:81G.
Commissioners of parks, town
boards authorized to act,
41:72, 41:81C.
Construction or laying out. See
within this heading,
"Construction or laying out
of public ways or parks."
Establishment shown on official
maps, **41:81H.**
Failure to construct, planning
boards to give notice,
41:81U.
Master plan, **41:81D.**

ZONING AND PLANNING
—Cont'd
Ways and parks —Cont'd
Outdoor advertising adjacent to
interstate and primary
highway systems in certain
areas, control, **93D:2.**
Private ways.
Survey boards. See within this
heading, "Survey boards."
Selectmen's powers as affected
by planning board
provisions, **41:81G.**
Subdivision control law,
41:81DD, 41:81U, 41:81Y.
Survey boards. See within this
heading, "Survey boards."
Wetlands regulations as affecting,
40A:3.
Width requirements for single or
two-family residences as
affected by subsequent
enactments, **40A:6.**
Withholding of building permit,
40A:7.
Written protest against changes,
40A:5.
Yard requirements.
Public buildings, **40A:3.**
Single or two-family residences
as affected by subsequent
enactments, **40A:6.**
ZONING APPEALS ACT,
40B:20-40B:23.
ZOOBOW.
Unlawful possession, **269:10,**
269:12.
ZOOS.
Commonwealth zoological
corporation, **92B:1 et seq.**
Annual reports, **92B:6, 92B:12.**
Appropriations, **92B:2.**

ZOOS —Cont'd
Commonwealth zoological
corporation —Cont'd
Asset management and
maintenance, **92B:9.**
Audit of books and records,
92B:8.
Board of directors, **92B:2 et seq.**
Contracts and agreements,
92B:10.
Definitions, **92B:1.**
Employment practices, **92B:4.**
Franklin Park Zoo, **92B:11.**
Fund raising, **92B:6.**
Hiring of personnel, **92B:4.**
Inspection of books and records,
92B:2.
Internal Revenue Service, filing
with, **92B:6.**
Master plan for operation and
improvements, **92B:6.**
Police protection, **92B:5.**
Powers and duties of board,
92B:5, 92B:6.
President of board, **92B:3.**
Records and reports.
Annual report, **92B:6, 92B:12.**
Biennial audit, **92B:8.**
Inspection of books and
records by board
members, **92B:2.**
Tax deductions for contributions,
92B:6.
Walter D. Stone Memorial Zoo,
92B:11.
Exhibition of wild animals,
272:77B.
Fish and game licensing
requirements, exemptions,
131:29.
Franklin Park Zoo, **92B:11.**
Walter D. Stone Memorial Zoo,
92B:11.

Popular Names Table

P

POPULAR NAMES OF MASSACHUSETTS STATUTES.

Abandoned Property Act, **200A:1 et seq.**

Abortion Act, **272:19 et seq.**

Abortion Procedures Act, **112:12I et seq.**

Absentee Voters Act, **54:86 et seq.**

Abuse of Elderly Persons Act, **19A:14 et seq.**

Accountants' Registration Act, **112:87A et seq.**

Acknowledgments Act, **183:30 et seq., 183 Appx.**

Administrative Procedure Act, **30A:1 et seq.**

Adoption Act, **210:1 et seq.**

Adverse Party Act, **233:22.**

Affirmative action office.
Established within human resources division, **7:4A.**

Age Discrimination Act, **151B:4.**

Aid to Dependent Children Act, **118:1 et seq.**

Aircraft Financial Responsibility Act, **90:49B et seq.**

Airport Zoning Act, **90:40A et seq.**

Alcoholic Beverage Control Act, **138:1 et seq.**

Anatomical Gift Act, **113:8 et seq.**

Annualized Income Installment Act, **62B:13, 62B:14.**

Antenuptial Contract Act, **209:25.**

Anti-Anarchy Act, **264:11.**

Anti-Communism Act, **264:16 et seq.**

Anti-Contraceptive Act, **272:20, 272:21.**

Anti-Dilution Act, unfair competition, **110B:1 et seq.**

Anti-Discrimination Act.
Employment, **149:24A et seq., 151B:1 et seq.**
Housing, **151B:1 et seq.**
Schools, **76:5, 151C:1 et seq.**

Anti-Injunction Act, **214:6.**

Anti-Lapse Act.
Devisees and legatees, **191:22.**

Anti-Lobbying Act, **3:39 et seq.**

Anti-Monopoly Acts, **93:1 et seq.**

Anti-Snob Zoning Law, **40B:20 et seq.**

Anti-Stalking Act, **265:43.**

POPULAR NAMES OF MASSACHUSETTS STATUTES —Cont'd

Anti Subversive Control Act, **264:16 et seq.**

Anti-Trust Act, **93:1 et seq.**

Apple Grading Act, **94:101 et seq.**

Appliance Efficiency Standards Act, **25B:1 et seq.**

Apportionment Act.
Estate taxes, **65A:5.**

Arbitration Act, **251:1 et seq.**
Death taxes, **65B:1 et seq.**
Labor disputes, **150:1 et seq.**

Architects' Registration Act, **112:60A et seq.**

Arrests Act, **276:21 et seq.**

Arts and Humanities Council Act, **15:54 et seq.**

Asset Management Board Act, **7B:1 et seq.**

Assignment of Dower Act, **189:1 et seq.**

Assignment of Wages Act, **154:1 et seq.**

Atomic Energy Commission Act, **6:85 et seq.**

Attorney's Lien Act, **221:50 et seq.**

Auditors Act, **221:53 et seq.**

Automobile Club Services Act, **174B:1 et seq.**

Automobile Compulsory Insurance Act, **90:34A et seq., 175:113A et seq.**

Baby Wagner Act, **150A:1 et seq.**

Ballot Law Commission Act, **55B:1 et seq.**

Banking, **167:1 et seq.**
Deposits and collections, **106:4-101 et seq.**

Barbers Act, **112:87F et seq.**

Bartley-Fox Gun Control Law, **269:10.**

Bay State Skills Corporation Act, **40I:1 et seq.**

Beano Act, **271:22A.**

Benefit Rule Act.
Inheritance, **206:27B.**

Bid Act.
Public contracts, **149:44A et seq.**

Bilingual Education Act, **71A:1 et seq.**

Billboard Regulatory Act, **93:29 et seq.**

Bills of Lading Act, **108:42 et seq.**

POPULAR NAMES OF MASSACHUSETTS STATUTES —Cont'd

Birth Control Act, **272:21.**

Blasphemy Act, **272:36.**

Blue Laws, **136:1 et seq.**

Blue Sky Laws, **110A:101 et seq.**

Board of Survey Act, **41:73 et seq.**

Boiler Inspection Act, **146:5 et seq.**

Boston Public Health Act of 1995, **Spec L 70:1 et seq.**

Bottle Bill, **64H:6, 94:321 et seq.**

Boulevard Stop Act, **89:9.**

Building Code, **143:1 et seq.**

Bulk Sales, **106:1 et seq.**

Bulk Transfers, **106:6-101 et seq.**

Bungee Jumping Act, **22:11B, 149:129D.**

Business Certificate Act, **110:5.**

Business Corporation Act, **156:1 et seq., 156B:1 et seq.**

Business Names Registration Act, **110:5.**

Business Practice Regulation and Consumer Protection Act, **93A:1 et seq.**

Business Transacted with Broker-Controlled Insurer Act, **175:174F et seq.**

Buy Massachusetts Program Act, **23A:10A.**

Campaign Act Election, **55:1 et seq.**

Carjacking Act, **265:21A.**

Caseload increase mitigation fund, **29:2NN.**

Casualty and Surety Rate Regulatory Act, **175A:1 et seq.**

Cemetery Act, **114:1 et seq.**

Central Register for Missing Children, **22A:1 et seq.**

Certificate of Title Act, **90:1 et seq.**

Certification Act, **78:22 et seq.**

Channel Encroachment Act, **91:12A.**

Charitable Corporations Act, **180:1 et seq.**

Charitable Funds Solicitation Act, **68:18 et seq.**

Charitable Trust Act, **12:8 et seq.**

Charter schools, **71:89.**

Check Cashers Licensing Act, **169A:1 et seq.**

POPULAR NAMES OF MASSACHUSETTS STATUTES —Cont'd

Chemical Test for Intoxication of Drivers Act, **90:24.**

Child Care Affordability Scholarship Assistance Fund Act, **28A:5A.**

Child care fund, **29:2LL.**

Child care quality fund, **29:2JJ.**

Child Custody Jurisdiction Act, **209B:1 et seq.**

Child Labor Act, **149:56 et seq.**

Children's and seniors' health care assistance fund, **29:2FF, 211F:1 to 211F:6.**

Chiropody Act, **112:13 et seq.**

Chiropractic Act, **112:89 et seq.**

Cigarette Excise Act, **64C:1 et seq.**

Cigarette Excise Stamp Act, **64C:29 et seq.**

Civil Damage Act, **138:69 et seq.**

Civil Service Act, **31:1 et seq.**

Clean elections law, **55a:1 to 55a:18.**

Clean Waters Act, **21:26 et seq.**

Coal Mining Regulatory and Reclamation Act, **21B:1 et seq.**

Coastal Facilities Improvement, **21F:1 et seq.**

Collection Agencies Act, **93:24 et seq.**

Commercial Bribery Act, **271:39.**

Commercial Feed Act, **128:51 et seq.**

Commercial Motor Vehicles, Uniform Act, **90F:1 et seq.**

Commitment Act Mentally Ill, **123:5 et seq.**

Committee for Public Counsel Services, **211D:1 et seq.**

Common Day of Rest Act, **136:1 et seq.**

Common Disaster Act, **190A:1 et seq.**

Common Trust Fund Act, **203A:1 et seq.**

Communist Act, **264:16 et seq.**

Community Development Finance Corporation, **40F:1 et seq.**

Community Economic Development Assistance Corporation Act, **40H:1 et seq.**

Comparative Negligence Act, **231:85.**

Competency of Witnesses, **233:20.**

Competitive Bidding Act, **29:8A et seq.**

POPULAR NAMES OF MASSACHUSETTS STATUTES —Cont'd

Compulsory Insurance Act, **90:34A et seq., 175:113A.**

Compulsory School Attendance Act, **76:1 et seq.**

Compulsory Vaccination Act, **111:181 et seq.**

Conciliation Act Labor disputes, **150:1 et seq.**

Condemnation Act, **79:1 et seq.**

Condominium Act, **183A:1 et seq.**

Conflict of Interest Act, **268A:1 et seq.**

Conscious Suffering Act, **229:6 et seq.**

Consumer Credit Cost Disclosure Act, **140D:1 et seq.**

Consumer Protection and Regulation of Business Practice Act, **93A:1 et seq.**

Container Act.
Milk products, **110:21.**

Contingent Remainder Act, **184:2, 184:3.**

Continuity Act.
Dissolved corporations, **155:51.**

Contribution Among Tortfeasors Act, **231B:1 et seq.**

Contributory Retirement Act, **32:1 et seq.**

Controlled Substances Act, **94C:1 et seq.**

Controlled Substances Tax Act, **64K:1 et seq.**

Controlled Substances Therapeutic Research Act, **94D:1 et seq.**

Co-Operative Corporations Act, **157:1 et seq.**

Co-Operative Housing Corporations Act, **157B:1 et seq.**

Corporation Act, **156:1 et seq.**

Corporation Continuity Act, **155:51.**

Corporation Dissolution Act, **155:50 et seq.**

Corporation Excise Tax Act, **63:30 et seq.**

Correspondence Schools Act, **75C:1 et seq.**

Corrupt Practices Act, **55:1 et seq.**

County Charter Procedures Act, **34A:1 et seq.**

Cox-Phillips Act, **214:6.**

Credit Life Insurance and Credit Accident and Health Insurance Act of 1988, **175:110 et seq.**

Credit Regulation Act, **140D:1 et seq.**

POPULAR NAMES OF MASSACHUSETTS STATUTES —Cont'd

Credit Union Act, **171:1 et seq.**

Crime Victims Compensation Act, **12:11K, 258A:1 et seq., 258C:1 et seq.**

Criminal Extradition Act, **276:11 et seq.**

Criminal Interstate Rendition Act, **276:11 et seq.**

Criminal Offender Record Information System Act, **6:167 et seq.**

Criminal Pleadings Act, **277:1 et seq.**

Curfew Act, **40:37A et seq.**

Cy Pres Act, **214:3.**

Date rape drugs, **272:3.**

Daylight Saving Time Act, **4:10.**

Day of Rest Act, **136:1 et seq.**

Dead Man's Act, **233:65.**

Death Act, **229:1 et seq.**

Death Tax Act, **65B:1 et seq.**

Declaratory Judgments Act, **231A:1 et seq.**

Declaratory Procedure Act, **231A:1.**

Defamation by Radio Act, **231:91A.**

Delinquent Children Act, **119:52 et seq.**

Dentistry Act, **112:43 et seq.**

Department of Commerce Act, **23A:1 et seq.**

Department of Public Works Reorganization Act, **16:1 et seq.**

Dependent Children Aid Act, **118:1 et seq.**

Descent and Distribution Act, **190:1 et seq.**

Desertion and Nonsupport Act, **273:1 et seq.**

Disclosure Act.
Welfare funds, **151D:1 et seq.**

Discrimination Act, **149:24A et seq.**

Discrimination in Housing Act, **151B:1 et seq.**

Displaced Homemakers, **40I:7A et seq.**

Disposition of Unclaimed Property Act, **200A:1 et seq.**

Dispute resolution office.
Established within human resources division, **7:4A.**

Dissolution Act.
Corporations, **155:50 et seq.**

District Court Reorganization Act, **218:6.**

District Courts Remand Act, **231:102C.**

POPULAR NAMES OF MASSACHUSETTS STATUTES —Cont'd

Districting Act.
General Court, **57:1 et seq.**

Divorce Act, **208:1 et seq.**

Documents of Title, **106:7-101 et seq.**

Dog Act, **140:136A et seq.**

Dog Bite Act, **140:155.**

Dram Shop Act, **138:69.**

Due Care Statute, **231:85.**

Durable Power of Attorney, **201B:1 et seq.**

DWI Laws, **90:21 et seq.**

Early Childhood Intervention Services, **111F:1 et seq., 111G:1 et seq.**

Earned income tax credit.
Income tax, **62:6.**

Eavesdropping Act, **272:99.**

Educational Financing Authority Act, **15C:2.**

Eight Hour Act.
Public employees, **149:30 et seq.**

Election Act, **54:1 et seq.**

Election Campaign Act, **55:1 et seq.**

Electricians Act, **141:1 et seq.**

Emergency Labor Disputes Act, **150B:1 et seq.**

Eminent Domain Act, **79:1 et seq.**

Employee Cooperative Corporations Act, **157A:1 et seq.**

Employee relations office.
Established with human resources division, **7:4A.**

Employees' Welfare Fund Disclosure Act, **151D:1 et seq.**

Employers' Liability Act, **153:1 et seq.**

Employment Agency Act, **140:46A et seq.**

Employment Security Act, **151A:1 et seq.**

Endangered Species Act, **131A:1 et seq.**

Environmental Policy Act, **30:61, 30:62.**

Equal Pay Act, **149:105A et seq.**
Teachers, **71:40.**

Ernestina Commission Act, **6:182A et seq.**

Escheat Act, **200A:1 et seq.**

Estate Tax Act, **65A:1 et seq.**

Estate Tax Apportionment Act, **65A:5.**

Exemption from Taxation, **59:5.**

Exposition building maintenance fund, **128:38B.**

POPULAR NAMES OF MASSACHUSETTS STATUTES —Cont'd

Factors Act, **104:1 et seq.**

Fair Educational Practices Act, **151C:1 et seq.**

Fair Employment Practices Act, **151C:1 et seq.**

Fair Housing Act, **151B:1 et seq.**

Fair Information Practices Act, **66A:1 et seq.**

Fair Trade Act, **93:14E et seq.**

False Advertising Act, **266:91.**

Family and medical leave, **149:52D.**

Federal Facilities Reserve Fund Act, **29:2.**

Federal Safe Drinking Act Assessment, **21A:18A.**

Felony Murder Act, **265:1, 265:17, 265:18, 265:21.**

Fertilizer Act, **128:64 et seq.**

Fictitious Name Act, **110:5, 110:6.**

Fielding Act.
District Courts, **218:19, 223:2.**

Fifty Year Mortgage Foreclosure Act, **260:33.**

File and Use Act.
Insurance rates, **174A:1 et seq.**

Filled Milk Act, **94:17A.**

Finance Act.
Municipal, **44:1 et seq.**

Finance Reorganization Act, **7:2 et seq.**

Financial Responsibility Act.
Aircraft, **90:49B et seq.**
Motor vehicles, **90:34A et seq., 175:113A.**

Fire, Marine and Inland Marine Rate Regulatory Act, **174A:1 et seq.**

Firemen's Pension Act, **32:80 et seq.**

Fire Prevention Act, **148:1 et seq.**

Fire Safety Act, **143:3 et seq.**

Fireworks Act, **148:39.**

Fish and Game Law, **131:1 et seq.**

Flag Desecration Act, **264:1 et seq.**

Flag Salute Act, **71:69.**

Forced Share Act, **191:15.**

Foreign Corporations Act, **181:1 et seq.**

Foreign Executed Wills Act, **191:5.**

Foreign Money Judgments Recognition Act, **235:23A.**

Forestry Act, **132:1 et seq.**

Forty-Eight Hour Act.
Women and children, **149:56.**

Fraternal Benefit Societies Act, **176:1 et seq.**

POPULAR NAMES OF MASSACHUSETTS STATUTES —Cont'd

Fraudulent Transfer Act, **109A:1 et seq.**

Full Crew Act.
Railroads, **160:185.**

Furniture and Bedding Label Law, **94:270 et seq.**

Gaming Act, **271:1 et seq.**

Garnishment Act, **246:1 et seq.**

Gas and Electric Company Act, **164:1 et seq.**

Gasoline Tax Act, **64A:1 et seq.**

Ghost in the attic statute, **93:114.**

Gift Enterprise Act, **271:29.**

Gifts to Minors Act, **201A:1 et seq.**

Good Samaritan Act, **112:12B.**

Good Samaritan Law, **112:12B.**

Graham Act, **32:1 et seq.**

Great Ponds Act, **91:1 et seq.**

Group Insurance Act (municipal Employees), **32B:1 et seq.**

Group Insurance Act (state Employees), **32A:1 et seq.**

Group Libel Act, **272:98C.**

Gun Control Act, **140:121 to 140:131P.**

Habitual Criminal Act, **279:25.**

Hairdressers Act, **112:87T et seq.**

Hatch Act, **131:40.**

Hate Crimes Data Act, **22C:32 et seq.**

Hawkers and Peddler Act, **101:13 et seq.**

Hazardous Substances Labeling Act, **94B:1 et seq.**

Hazardous Waste Facility Siting Act, **21D:1 et seq.**

Hazardous Waste Management Act, **21C:1 et seq.**

Health and Educational Facilities Authority Act, **Spec L 53:1 et seq.**

Health and Welfare Act, **23:10D et seq., 151D:1 et seq.**

Health and Welfare Commission Act, **6:125 et seq.**

Health Care Proxies Act, **201D:1 et seq.**

Health Maintenance Organizations Act, **176G:1 et seq.**

Health Protection Fund Act, **29:2T.**

Health, Welfare and Retirement Funds Act, **151D:1 et seq.**

Hearsay Act, **233:65.**

Heart Act, **32:94.**

Heart Balm Act, **207:47A.**

Helmet Law, **90:7.**

Highway Act, **81:1 et seq.**

POPULAR NAMES OF MASSACHUSETTS STATUTES —Cont'd

Highway Defects Act, **84:15 et seq.**

Highway Safety Act, **90A:1 et seq.**

Historical Commission Act, **9:26 et seq.**

Historic District Act, **40C:1 et seq.**

Home and Family Advisory Council Act, **6:151 et seq.**

Home Invasion Act, **265:18C.**

Home Rule Procedure Act, **43B:1 et seq.**

Homestead Exemption Act, **188:1 et seq.**

Horace Mann charter schools, **71:89.**

Hospital Survey and Construction Planning Act, **111:55.**

Housing Authority Law, **121B:3 et seq.**

Humanities and Arts Council Act, **15:54 et seq.**

Human resources division. Establishment, **7:4A.**

Identity fraud, **266:37E.**

Impoundment Site Loan Act, **21:9A.**

Incinerator Bond Act, **92:9A.**

Income Tax Act, **62:1 et seq.** Corporations, **63C:1 et seq.**

Incoming teacher signing bonus program, **15A:19B.**

Indeterminate Sentence Act, **279:24.**

Industrial Development Financing Act, **40D:1 et seq.**

Industrial Homework Act, **149:143 et seq.**

Industrial Service Program Act, **23D:1 et seq.**

Industries Act, **149:1 et seq.**

Inheritance Tax Act, **65:1 et seq.**

Injunction Act, **214:1 et seq.**

Inland Wetlands Act, **131:40A.**

Insurance Act, **175:1 et seq.** Motor vehicles, **90:34A et seq., 175:113A.**

Insurers Insolvency Fund Act, **175D:1 et seq.**

International and Interstate Procedure Act, **223A:1 et seq.**

Interstate Co-Operation Commission Act, **9:21 et seq.**

Interstate Corrections Compact Act, **Spec L 138:1.**

Interstate Rendition Act, **276:11 et seq.**

Interstate Supervision of Probationers and Parolees Act, **127:151A et seq.**

POPULAR NAMES OF MASSACHUSETTS STATUTES —Cont'd

Intestacy Act, **190:1 et seq.**

Intoxicating Liquor Act, **138:1 et seq.**

Investigation Act. Labor disputes, **150:3.**

Investment Securities, **106:8-101 et seq.**

Iron Curtain Act, **206:27B.**

Jewelers' Lien Act, **255:31C.**

Joint Exercise of Powers Act, **40:4A.**

Joint Tortfeasors Contribution Act, **231B:1 et seq.**

Judgment Interest Act, **231:6B.**

Judicial Notice Act, **233:70.**

Juvenile Act, **119:1 et seq., 120:1 et seq.**

Juvenile Delinquency Act, **119:52 et seq.**

Juvenile Offender Act, **119:74 et seq.**

Keniston Act, **53:18.**

Killer Bar Law, **90:24J.**

Labor Act, **149:1 et seq.**

Labor Arbitration Act, **150C:1 et seq.**

Labor Disputes Act, **150B:1 et seq.**

Labor Disputes Conciliation Act, **150:1 et seq.**

Laborers' Pension Act, **32:77 et seq.**

Labor Injunction Act, **214:6.**

Labor Relations Act, **150A:1 et seq.**

Land Court Act, **185:1 et seq.**

Landlord and tenant. Rent control prohibition, **40P:1 to 40P:5.**

Land Title Registration Act, **185:1 et seq.**

Lapse Act. Legatees and devisees, **191:22.**

Legal Assistance Corporation Act, **221A:1 et seq.**

Legislative Agents Act, **3:39 et seq.**

Lemon Law, **90:7N et seq.**

Liability Insurance Act. Motor vehicles, **90:34A et seq.**

Librarians Certification Act, **78:22 et seq.**

Lien Act, **254:1 et seq.**

Limited Access Highway Act, **81:7A et seq.**

Limited Dividend Act, **121A:9.**

Limited Partnership Act, **109:1 et seq.**

POPULAR NAMES OF MASSACHUSETTS STATUTES —Cont'd

Line of duty death benefits. Public safety department, **32:100A.**

Line of Duty Presumption Act, **32:94.**

Liquidation Act, **175:180A et seq.**

Liquor Act, **138:1 et seq.**

Little League Bill, **231:85V.**

Little Norris-La Guardia Act. Labor injunctions, **214:6.**

Little Taft-Hartley Acts, **150A:1 et seq., 150B:1 et seq., 214:6A.**

Little Wagner Act, **150A:1 et seq.**

Living Wills, **201B:1 et seq.; 201D:1 et seq.**

Lobbying Act, **3:39 et seq.**

Local consumer inspection fund, **29:200.**

Lodging House Act, **140:22 et seq.**

Long Arm Service of Process Act, **223A:1 et seq.** Nonresident motorists, **90:3A et seq.**

Lord Campbell's Act, **229:1 et seq.**

Lord's Day Act, **136:1 et seq.**

Lottery Act, **10:22 et seq., 271:7 et seq.**

Low-Level Radioactive Waste Management Act, **111H:1 et seq.**

Malpractice Evidentiary Act, **233:79C.**

Managing General Agents Act, **175:177F et seq.**

Marketable Title Act, **184:26 et seq.**

Marriage Evasion Act, **207:10 et seq, 207:50.**

Married Women's Property Act, **209:1.**

Massachusetts Appliance Efficiency Standards Act, **25B:1 et seq.**

Massachusetts Child Custody Jurisdiction Act, **209B:1 et seq.**

Massachusetts Endangered Species Act, **131A:1 et seq.**

Massachusetts Hazardous Waste Facility Siting Act, **21D:1 et seq.**

Massachusetts Hazardous Waste Management Act, **21C:1 et seq.**

Massachusetts Industrial Service Program, **23D:1 et seq.**

Massachusetts Limited Liability Company Act, **156C:1 et seq.**

POPULAR NAMES OF MASSACHUSETTS STATUTES —Cont'd

Massachusetts Oil and Hazardous Material Release Prevention and Response Act, **21E:1 et seq.**

Massachusetts Product Development Corporation, **40K:1 et seq.**

Massachusetts Prudent Investor Act, **203C:1 to 203C:11.**

Massachusetts sentencing commission, **211E:1 to 211E:4.**

Massachusetts state exposition building maintenance fund, **128:38B.**

Massachusetts Tort Claims Act, **258:2.**

Massachusetts Water Management Act, **21G:1 et seq.**

Masshealth program, **118E:9A, 118E:9B.**

Master teacher corps program, **15A:19C.**

Maximum Hour Act, **149:30 et seq.**

Meat and Poultry Inspection Act, **94:146 et seq.**

Mechanics' Lien Act, **254:1 et seq.**

Medicaid False Claim Act, **118E:21A et seq.**

Medical Practice Act, **112:2 et seq.**

Mental Health Services Act, **19:17 et seq.**

Mercy Act, **265:2.**

Metropolitan District Incinerator Bond Act, **92:9A.**

Military Aid Acts, **115:1 et seq.**

Militia Act, **33:1 et seq.**

Milk Control Act, **94A:1 et seq.**

Milk Products Container Act, **110:21 et seq.**

Mill Act, **253:1 et seq.**

Minimum Fair Wage Act, **151:1 et seq.**

Misbranding Act, **94:186 et seq.**

Model Water and Sewer Reorganization Acts, **40N:2.**

Monopoly Act, **93:1 et seq.**

Mortgage Foreclosure Act, **26:33 et seq.**

Motorboat Act, **90B:1 et seq.**

Motor Carrier Act, **159B:1 et seq.**

Motor Fuel Sales Act, **94:295A et seq.**

Motorist Act (nonresident), **90:3, 90:3A.**

Motor Vehicle Act, **90:1 et seq.**

Motor Vehicle Certificate of Title Act, **90:1 et seq.**

POPULAR NAMES OF MASSACHUSETTS STATUTES —Cont'd

Motor Vehicle Compulsory Insurance Act, **90:34A et seq., 175:113A.**

Motor Vehicle Excise Act, **60A:1 et seq.**

Motor Vehicle Liability Insurance Act, **90:34A et seq.**

Motor Vehicle Sales Finance Act, **255B:1 et seq.**

Motor Vehicles Financial Responsibility Act, **90:34A et seq., 175:113A et seq.**

Motor Vehicles Registration Act, **90:1 et seq.**

Multiple Offender Act, **279:25.**

Municipal Employees Relations Act, **150E:1 et seq.**

Municipal Finance Act, **44:1 et seq.**

Municipal Planning Act, **41:70 et seq.**

Municipal Zoning Act, **40A:1 et seq.**

Negotiable instruments, **106:3-101 et seq., 106:3-201 et seq.**

Nine Hour Act, **149:56.**

No-Fault Motor Vehicle Insurance Act, **90:34M.**

Nonresident Motorist Act, **3A, 90:3.**

Northeast Interstate Dairy Compact, **Spec L 139:1 et seq.**

Nurses' Registration Act, **112:74 et seq.**

Nursing Home Administration Registration Act, **112:108 et seq.**

Obscene Literature Act, **272:28 et seq.**

Ocean Sanctuaries Act, **132A:12A et seq., 132A:18.**

Oil and Hazardous Material Release Prevention and Response Act, **21E:1 et seq.**

Old Age Assistance Act, **118A:1 et seq.**

Old Age Tax Abatement Act, **59:5.**

Oleomargarine Act, **94:49 et seq.**

Ombudsman Program, **19A:27 et seq.**

Omitted Child Statute, **191:20.**

Omnibus Privacy Act, **66A:1 et seq.**

One Day's Rest in Seven Law (labor), **149:47 et seq.**

Optional Forms of Municipal Administration Act, **43C:1 et seq.**

POPULAR NAMES OF MASSACHUSETTS STATUTES —Cont'd

Optometrists' Registration Act, **112:66 et seq.**

Optometry Act, **112:66 et seq.**

Organ Transplant Fund, **10:35E.**

Outdoor Advertising Act, **93:29 et seq.**

Out of State Probationer and Parolee Supervision Act, **127:151A et seq.**

Padlocking Act, **139:16A.**

Parole Act, **127:128 et seq.**

Parolee Supervision Act, **127:151A et seq.**

Partnership Act, **108A:1 et seq.**

Patients' Bill of Rights, **111:70E.**

Peaceful Persuasion Act, **149:24.**

Pension Act, **32:1 et seq.**
 Firemen, **32:80 et seq.**
 Laborers, **32:77 et seq.**
 Policemen, **32:83 et seq.**

Period in Gross.
 Perpetuities, **184A:3.**

Perpetuities Act, **184A:1 et seq.**

Perry Act.
 Suspension of employee, **30:59.**

Personal Property Exemption Act, **235:34.**

Personal Protection Insurance Law, **90:34M.**

Pesticide Control Act, **132B:1 et seq.**

Pharmacists' Registration Act, **112:24 et seq.**

Phillips-Cox Act, **214:6.**

Photographic Copies of Business and Public Records As Evidence Act, **233:79E.**

Physical Therapy Act, **112:23A et seq.**

Physician's Registration Act, **112:2 et seq.**

Planning Act, **41:70 et seq.**

Plant Closing Act, **151A:71A.**

Plant Pest Control Act, **128:16 et seq.**

Playgrounds Act, **45:14 et seq.**

Plumbing Act, **142:1 et seq.**

Podiatrists' Registration Act, **112:13 et seq.**

Policemen's Retirement and Pension Act, **32:83 et seq.**

Ponkapoag recreational fund, **29:2U.**

Poor Act, **117:1 et seq.**

Poultry Bonding Act, **94:152A et seq.**

Practice Act, **231:6 et seq.**

Presumption Statute (compensation), **152:7A.**

POPULAR NAMES OF MASSACHUSETTS STATUTES —Cont'd

Pretermitted Child Act, **191:20.**

Prevailing Wage Act, **149:26 et seq.**

Primary Election Act, **53:23 et seq.**

Printers' Ink Act, **266:91.**

Privacy Act, **66A:1 et seq.**

Probation Act, **276:83 et seq.**

Probationer and Parolee Supervision Act, **127:151A et seq.**

Professional Corporation Law, **156A:1 et seq.**

Professional Engineers Registration Act, **112:81D et seq.**

Proposition 2½, **59:21C.**

Prudent investor act, **203C:1 to 203C:11.**

Psychologists' Registration Act, **112:118 et seq.**

Psychopathic Personality Act, **123A:1 et seq.**

Public Accommodations Act, **272:98.**

Public Building Act (construction and Repair), **149:29.**

Public Employees Retirement Act, **32:1 et seq.**

Public Parks Act, **45:2 et seq.**

Public Utilities Seizure Act, **150B:1 et seq.**

Public Works Act, **149:44A et seq.**

Public Works Department Act, **16:1 et seq.**

Pure Food and Drugs Act, **94:186 et seq.**

Qualifying Income Interest for Life, **65A:5, 65A:5A.**

Quiet Title Act, **240:1 et seq.**

Quo Warranto Act, **249:6 et seq.**

Racial Imbalance Law, **15:1I et seq., 71:37C, 71:37D.**

Racing Act, **128A:1 et seq.**

Railroad Full Crew Act, **160:185.**

Rate Regulation.
  Casualty and surety insurance, **175A:1 et seq.**
  Fire, marine, and inland marine insurance, **174A:1 et seq.**

Real Estate Brokers' Act, **112:87PP et seq.**

Real Estate Time-Share Act, **183B:1 et seq.**

Reapportionment of Legislature, **57:4.**

Recording Acts.
  Real property, **183:4.**

POPULAR NAMES OF MASSACHUSETTS STATUTES —Cont'd

Regional Planning Law, **40B:1 et seq.**

Regional School District Act, **71:14 et seq.**

Regional Transportation Authority Act, **161B:1 et seq.**

Registered Physical Therapists Law, **112:23A et seq.**

Registration Act.
  Business names, **110:5.**
  Dentists, **112:43 et seq.**
  Land, **185:1 et seq.**
  Optometrists, **112:66 et seq.**
  Pharmacists, **112:24 et seq.**
  Physicians, **112:2 et seq.**
  Professional engineers, **112:81D et seq.**
  Veterinarians, **112:54 et seq.**

Regulation of Business Practice and Consumer Protection Act, **93A:1 et seq.**

Regulatory and Reclamation Act.
  Coal mining, **21B:1 et seq.**

Rehabilitation and Treatment Act.
  Alcoholism, **111B:1 et seq.**

Reinsurance Intermediary Act, **175:177M et seq.**

Religious Freedom Act, **119:33.**

Religious Protection Act, **210:5B.**

Remand Act.
  District Court, **231:102C.**

Rental Assistance Act, **121B:42 et seq.**

Rent Control Prohibition Act, **40O:1 et seq.**

Reorganization Act.
  District Court, **218:6.**

Representative Town Meeting Act, **43A:1 et seq.**

Resale of Tickets Act, **140:185A et seq.**

Resale Price Maintenance Act, **93:14E et seq.**

Retail Installment Sales and Services Act, **255D:1 et seq.**

Retirement Act, **32:1 et seq.**
  Firemen, **32:80 et seq.**
  Laborers, **32:77 et seq.**
  Policemen, **32:83 et seq.**

Retraction of Libel, **231:93, 260:32.**

Revised Uniform Limited Partnership Act, **109:1 et seq.**

Right to Bargain Act, **150A:3.**

Right to Know, **111F:1 et seq.**

Right to Organize Act, **150A:1 et seq.**

Room Occupancy Excise Tax Act, **64G:1 et seq.**

POPULAR NAMES OF MASSACHUSETTS STATUTES —Cont'd

Rule Against Perpetuities Act, **184A:1 et seq.**

Sabbath Act, **136:5, 136:6.**

Safe Driver Insurance Plan, **175:113P.**

Safe Roads Act, **90:23 et seq., 90C:2, 218:26, 258A:1.**

Safety Act.
  Fire in public buildings, **143:3 et seq.**

Sale of Securities Act, **110A:1 et seq.**

Sales, **106:2-101 et seq.**
  Commercial Code, **106:2-101 et seq.**
  Motor fuel, **94:295A et seq.**

Sales Tax Act, **64H:1 et seq.**

Savings Act.
  Statute of limitations, **260:32.**

School Attendance Act, **76:1 et seq.**

School Discrimination Law, **76:5, 151C:1 et seq.**

Secured Transactions, **106:9-101 et seq.**

Securities Act, **110A:101 et seq.**

Sedition Act, **264:11.**

Seed Act, **128:84 et seq.**

Seizure Act.
  Public utilities, **150B:1 et seq.**

Selective Regulations Act.
  Coastal wetlands, **130:105.**

Service At Cost Act.
  Street railways, **161:115 et seq.**

Sex Offenders Act, **123A:1 et seq.**

Sexually Dangerous Persons Act, **123A:1 et seq.**

Sexual Psychopaths Act, **123A:1 et seq.**

Shade Tree Act, **87:1 et seq.**

Shareholders Appraisal Act, **156:46.**

Shellfish Act, **130:37 et seq.**

Short Form of Deed Act, **183:8 et seq.**

Simulcast Wagering of Horse and Dog Racing Act, **128C:1 et seq.**

Simultaneous Death Act, **190A:1 et seq.**

Single Audit Act of 1984, **44:40.**

Six Percent Act, **107:3.**

Slamming.
  Local and long distance service providers.
    Unauthorized switching, **93:108 to 93:113.**

Slichter Acts, **150A:1 et seq., 150B:1 et seq.**

POPULAR NAMES OF MASSACHUSETTS STATUTES —Cont'd

Small Loan Act, **140:96 et seq.**

Small Value Cases Transfer Act, **231:102C.**

Snob Zoning Law, **40B:20 et seq.**

Social services program fund, **29:2MM.**

Social Workers' Licensing Act, **112:130 et seq.**

Soil Conservation Act, **128B:1 et seq.**

Solid Waste Disposal Act, **16:18 et seq.**

Special Fuel Tax Act, **64E:1 et seq.**

Special needs awareness day, **6:15BBBB.**

Speedy Trial Act, **231:59A et seq.**

Spinners' Lien Act, **255:31A, 255:31B.**

Spite Fence Act, **49:21 et seq.**

Stalking Act, **265:43.**

Stamp Tax Act, **64D:1 et seq.**

State Ballot Law Commission Act, **55B:1 et seq.**

State exposition building maintenance fund, **128:38B.**

State Labor Relations Act, **150A:1 et seq.**

State Lottery Law, **10:22 et seq.**

Statewide Emergency Telecommunications Board Act, **6A:18B et seq.**

Statute of Descent and Distribution, **190:1 et seq.**

Statute of Frauds, **259:1 et seq.**

Statute of Limitations.
 Civil, **260:1 et seq.**
 Criminal, **277:63.**
 Probate, **197:9.**

Stockholder Wage Liability Act, **156:35.**

Stop and Frisk Act, **41:98.**

Student Loan Authority Act, **15C:1 et seq.**

Subdivision Control Act, **41:81K et seq.**

Substituted Service Act, **181:4, 181:15.**

Subversive Activities Control Act, **264:16 et seq.**

Succession Tax Act, **65:1 et seq.**

Summary Process Act, **239:1 et seq.**

Sunday Act, **136:1 et seq.**

Superfund, **21E:1 et seq.**

Survival of Actions, **228:1.**

Tag Act.
 Vehicles, **90:20C.**

POPULAR NAMES OF MASSACHUSETTS STATUTES —Cont'd

Tagging Law.
 Graffiti, **126B, 266:126A.**

Tax Assessment Act, **59:11 et seq.**

Tax Exemption Act, **59:5.**

Tax Title Act, **60:64 et seq.**

Teacher quality endowment fund, **10:35S.**

Teachers' Equal Pay Act, **71:40.**

Technology Development Corporation Act, **40G:1 et seq.**

Technology 2000 Partnership Act, **23F:1 et seq.**

Tenement House Act, **144:2 et seq., 145:2 et seq.**

Testamentary Additions to Trusts Act, **203:3B.**

Testimonial Dinner Act, **268:9A.**

Three Day Marriage Act, **207:19 et seq.**

Three Judge Act.
 Labor disputes, **212:30.**

Time Share Act, **183B:1 et seq.**

Title Defects Act, **184:24.**

Tolling Act, **260:12.**

Tomorrow's teachers scholarship program, **15A:19D.**

Torrens Act, **185:1 et seq.**

Tort Claims Act, **258:2.**

Towing Act, **40:22D.**

Town and Country Planning Act, **41:81D.**

Toxic Substances Act, **111F:1 et seq.**

Toxics Use Reduction Act, **21I:1 et seq.**

Trademark Act, **110:1 et seq.**

Trademark Dilution Action, **110:1 et seq.**

Trade Secrets Act, **266:30.**

Trading Stamp Act, **93:14L et seq.**

Transfer Act.
 Small value cases, **231:102C.**

Transfer of Venue Act, **223:15.**

Transient Vendors Act, **101:1 et seq.**

Transitional aid to needy families fund, **29:2KK.**

True Name Act.
 Lodging registration, **140:27 et seq.**

Trust Company Act, **172:1 et seq.**

Truth in Lending Act, **140D:1 et seq.**

Truth-In-Savings Law, **140E:4.**

Turnpike authority, **81A:1 to 81A:31.**

Unauthorized Insurers Process Act, **175B:1 et seq.**

POPULAR NAMES OF MASSACHUSETTS STATUTES —Cont'd

Unclaimed Property Act, **200A:1 et seq.**

Underground Storage Tank Cleanup Fund Act, **21J:1 et seq.**

Unemployment Compensation Act, **151A:1 et seq.**

Unfair Competition Act, **93:1 et seq.**

Unfair Sales Act, **93:14E et seq.**

Unfair Sales Act for the Retail Sale of Motor Fuels, **94:295P et seq.**

Uniform Acknowledgment Act, **183:30, 183:31, 183:33, 183:41, 183:42.**

Uniform Act to Secure the Attendance of Witnesses from Without a State in Criminal Proceedings, **233:13A et seq.**

Uniform Aircraft Financial Responsibility Act, **90:49B et seq.**

Uniform Arbitration Act, **251:1 et seq.**

Uniform Bills of Lading Act, **108:42 et seq.**

Uniform Commercial Code, **106:1 et seq.**
 Bank deposits and collections, **106:4-101 et seq.**
 Bulk transfers, **106:6-101 et seq.**
 Documents of title, **106:7-101 et seq.**
 Investment securities, **106:8-101 et seq.**
 Leases, **106:2A-101 et seq.**
 Negotiable instruments, **106:3-101 et seq., 106:3-201 et seq.**
 Sales, **106:2-101 et seq.**
 Secured transactions, **106:9-101 et seq.**

Uniform Common Trust Fund Act, **203A:1 et seq.**

Uniform Contribution Among Tortfeasors Act, **231B:1 et seq.**

Uniform Criminal Extradition Act, **276:11 et seq.**

Uniform Criminal Interstate Rendition Act, **276:11 et seq.**

Uniform Custodial Trust Act, **203B:1 et seq.**

Uniform Declaratory Judgments Act, **231A:1 et seq.**

Uniform Desertion and Nonsupport Act, **273:1 et seq.**

POPULAR NAMES OF MASSACHUSETTS STATUTES —Cont'd

Uniform Durable Power of Attorney Act, **201B:1 et seq.**

Uniform Foreign Executed Wills Act, **191:5.**

Uniform Foreign Money Judgments Recognition Act, **235:23A.**

Uniform Fraudulent Transfer Act, **109A:1 et seq.**

Uniform Gifts to Minors Act, **201A:1 et seq.**

Uniform Insurers Liquidation Act, **175:180A et seq.**

Uniform Interstate and International Procedure Act, **223A:1 et seq.**

Uniform Interstate Family Support Act, **209D:1-101 et seq.**

Uniform Limited Partnership Act, **109:1 et seq.**

Uniform Management of Institutional Funds Act, **180A:1 et seq.**

Uniform Marriage Evasion Act, **207:10 et seq.**

Uniform Motor Vehicle Certificate of Title and Anti-Theft Act, **90D:1 et seq.**

Uniform Negotiable Instruments Act, **107:1 et seq.**

Uniform Operation of Commercial Motor Vehicles Act, **90F:1 et seq.**

Uniform Partnership Act, **108A:1 et seq.**

Uniform Photographic Copies of Business and Public Records As Evidence Act, **233:79E.**

Uniform Procurement Act, **30B:1 et seq.**

POPULAR NAMES OF MASSACHUSETTS STATUTES —Cont'd

Uniform Securities Act, **110A:101 et seq.**

Uniform Simultaneous Death Act, **190A:1 et seq.**

Uniform Statutory Will Act, **191B:1 et seq.**

Uniform transfer on death security registration act, **201E:101.**

Uniform Transfers to Minors Act, **201A:1 et seq.**

Uniform Warehouse Receipts Act, **105:55 et seq.**

Unlimited Time Act.
Real property, **184:23.**

Urban Redevelopment Corporation Act, **121A:1 et seq.**

Urban Renewal Act, **121B:45 et seq.**

Use Tax Act, **64I:1 et seq.**

Vaccination Act, **76:15, 111:181 et seq.**

Vagrancy Act, **272:66.**

Veterans Housing Act, **121B:34 et seq.**

Veterans' Preference Act, **31:3.**

Veterans' Retirement Act, **32:56 et seq.**

Veterans' Tenure Act, **30:9A, 31:21 et seq.**

Veterinarians' Registration Act, **112:54 et seq.**

Viatical settlement act, **175:212 to 175:223.**

Victim Assistance, **258B:9.**

Visual Tag Act, **90:20C.**

Voters' Registration Act, **51:1 et seq.**

Voting Time Act, **149:178.**

Wage Act, **151:1 et seq.**

Wage Assignment Act, **154:1 et seq.**

POPULAR NAMES OF MASSACHUSETTS STATUTES —Cont'd

Wage Payment Act, **149:148 et seq.**

Wait and See Act, **184A:1 et seq.**

Warehouse Receipts Act, **106:7-501 et seq.**

Warranty Act.
Insurance contract, **175:186.**

Water Lien Act, **40:42A et seq.**

Water Management Act, **21G:1 et seq.**

Water Pollution Abatement Projects Administration Fund Act, **21:27A, 29:2W.**

Water Pollution Control Act, **21:26 et seq.**

Weekly Wage Payment Act, **149:148 et seq.**

Weights and Measures Act, **98:1 et seq.**

Welfare Funds Disclosure Act, **151D:1 et seq.**

Wetlands Protection Act, **131:40, 131:40A.**

WIC Program Act, **111I:1 et seq.**

Wills Act, **191:1 et seq.**

Withholding of income tax, **62B:1 et seq.**

Witness Assistance, **258B:9.**

Women's, Infants' and Children's Program Act, **111I:1 et seq.**

Workmen's Compensation Act, **152:1 et seq.**

Worthless Check Act, **266:37.**

Wrongful Death Act, **229:1 et seq.**

Yellow Dog Contracts Act, **149:20A.**

Youth Authority Act, **120:1 et seq.**

Youth Conservation and Service Corps Act, **78A:1 et seq.**

Zoning Act, **40A:1 et seq.**

LEXIS Publishing™ solicits your help in making this index as complete, accurate and useful as possible. Please use these postage paid cards to advise us of any errors or omissions you may find, or to recommend any other improvements. You may also contact a member of our Indexing Staff by calling toll-free **1-800-897-7922**, by faxing toll-free **1-800-643-1280** or by Internet E-mail **llpindexing@lexis-nexis.com** to make suggestions or obtain assistance.

Name of Publication _____

(a) I had difficulty/was unable to locate the § pertaining to _____

_____

(b) §(§) _____ should be indexed under _____

_____

(c) The reference following the index entry _____

_____ on page _____ of Vol. _____ should read § _____

(d) Other suggestions: _____

_____

_____

Name _____ Phone _____

Firm _____ Address _____

City _____ State _____ Zip _____

Name of Publication _____

(a) I had difficulty/was unable to locate the § pertaining to _____

_____

(b) §(§) _____ should be indexed under _____

_____

(c) The reference following the index entry _____

_____ on page _____ of Vol. _____ should read § _____

(d) Other suggestions: _____

_____

_____

Name _____ Phone _____

Firm _____ Address _____

City _____ State _____ Zip _____

BUSINESS REPLY CARD

FIRST CLASS   PERMIT NO. 6   CHARLOTTESVILLE, VA

Postage will be paid by addressee

LEXIS Publishing™
Post Office Box 7587
Charlottesville VA   22906

BUSINESS REPLY CARD

FIRST CLASS   PERMIT NO. 6   CHARLOTTESVILLE, VA

Postage will be paid by addressee

LEXIS Publishing™
Post Office Box 7587
Charlottesville VA   22906